THE
PULPIT COMMENTARY

Edited by

H. D. M. Spence

and

Joseph S. Exell

Volume 3
DEUTERONOMY
JOSHUA and JUDGES

Wm. B. Eerdmans Publishing Company, Grand Rapids, Michigan

THE PULPIT COMMENTARY

Edited by

H. D. M. Spence *and* Joseph S. Exell

This large-type edition republished
from new plates by

WM. B. EERDMANS PUBLISHING COMPANY
Grand Rapids, Michigan

ISBN 0-8028-8060

Reprinted, September 1980

Photolithoprinted by Eerdmans Printing Company
GRAND RAPIDS, MICHIGAN, UNITED STATES OF AMERICA

DEUTERONOMY

EXPOSITION BY

W. L. ALEXANDER

HOMILETICS BY

C. CLEMANCE

HOMILIES BY VARIOUS AUTHORS

J. ORR R. M. EDGAR

D. DAVIES

THE
BOOK OF DEUTERONOMY

INTRODUCTION.

§ 1. Title and General Character.

This book, which ranks as the closing book of the Pentateuch, the Fifth of the Fifths of the Law (חֹמֶשׁ חוּמְשֵׁי תּוֹרָה), as the Jews designate it, is in the Hebrew canon named from its two initial words, 'Elleh Had-debhârîm (אֵלֶּה הַדְּבָרִים), or simply Debhârîm, according to an ancient usage with the Jews (Origen on Ps. i. ap. Huetii 'Origeniana,' tom. i. p. 47; Jerome, 'Prol. Gal.'). The name Deuteronomy it received from the Greek translators, whom the Vulgate follows (Δευτερονόμιον, Deuteronomium). Probably this was the name in use among the Hellenistic Jews, for this may be regarded as a fair rendering of the phrase, Mishneh Hat-torah (מִשְׁנֶה הַתּוֹרָה), "Iteration of the Law," by which some of the rabbins designate this book—a phrase taken from ch. xvi. 18, though there having a different sense (see note on the passage). The name "Deuteronomy" is thus somewhat misleading, as it is apt to suggest that there is in this book either a second code of laws or a recapitulation of laws already delivered, whereas it is rather a summary, in a hortatory manner, of what it most concerned the people to keep in mind, both of the Lord's doings on their behalf, and of what it was his will they should specially observe and do when settled in the promised land. Many parts of the Law, as already promulgated, are not so much as alluded to; very few new laws are enunciated; and in general it is the civil and social rather than the ceremonial institute, the personal and ethical rather than the political and official aspect of the Law, that is dwelt upon. This character of the book some of the rabbins have signalized by the title Sepher Tôkâhôth, "Book of Admonitions or Reproofs," with special reference to ch. xxviii. The unsuitableness of such a title to the book as "Deuteronomy," was long ago pointed out by Theodoret, who asserts ('Quæst. I. in Deut.') that it is not a second Law that Moses here gives, but that he only recalls to memory what had been already given.

The book is thus neither properly historical nor properly legislative, though in a measure it is both. It is historical, inasmuch as it records certain things said and done at a particular time in the history of Israel; and it is legislative, inasmuch as it enunciates certain statutes, ordinances, and rules which the people were bound to observe. But properly it is a hortatory book—a book of orations or discourses (דְּבָרִים), in which the subjectivity of the author is throughout prominent. In this respect it is markedly different from the earlier books of the Pentateuch, in which the objective element prevails. "In Deuteronomy it is the paraenetic element that is especially predominant; in place of the objective rigorous injunction, there is here the most impressive exhortation; in place of the letter, legally imperative and averse from development, which finds the ground of its highest necessity in itself, there prevails here reflection on the Law, and on this line the latter is brought nearer to the feelings. The book has thus a prophetic colouring, the germ of which we have already seen in the close of Leviticus, but which has here a wider compass and authoritative significance. The book is a foretype of the prophetic discourse; and from this peculiarity may be explained how, for instance, a later prophetism (Jeremiah and Ezekiel) connects itself with this type" (Hävernick, 'Einleit,' i. 522; cf. 'Introd. to the Pentateuch,' translated by Thomson, p. 338).

§ 2. CONTENTS OF THE BOOK.

The book consists chiefly of three lengthened addresses, delivered by Moses to the people on the eastern side of the Jordan, after they had obtained possession by conquest of the region stretching northwards from the borders of Moab towards those of Aram. After a brief notice of the circumstances of time and place when the addresses were uttered (ch. i. 1—5), the first address begins. Moses first of all recalls to the recollection of the people certain important particulars in their past history, with the view apparently of preparing them for the admonitions and injunctions he is about to lay upon them (ch. i. 6—iii. 29). This recapitulation is followed by a series of earnest exhortations to obedience to the Divine ordinances, and warnings against idolatry and the forsaking of Jehovah, the God of their fathers, and the only true God (ch. iv. 1—40). To this address is appended a short historical notice of the appointment of three cities of refuge on the east side of the Jordan (vers. 41—43).

The second address, which is also introduced by a brief notice of the circumstances under which it was delivered (ch. iv. 44—49), extends over twenty-one chapters (ch. v.—xxvi.). In it Moses goes over the leading ethical precepts of the Law which he, as the servant of God, had already declared to the people. He begins by reminding them how God had made a covenant with them in Horeb, and then, having repeated the "ten words" of the covenant—the ten commandments which Jehovah spake to the assembled multitude—and having uttered a general exhortation to obedience (ch. v. 1—33), he proceeds to admonish the people to love Jehovah the one God, to be obedient to his Law, to teach it diligently to their children, and to avoid all intercourse with the idolatrous nations of Canaan, on the possession of which they were about to enter. This admonition is enforced by threatening of judgments on idolaters; victory over the Canaanites is promised; the gradual but utter extinction of these idolatrous peoples is foretold; and a command is given to destroy all objects of idolatrous worship to be found in the land (ch. vi. 1—vii. 26). A cursory review of God's dealings with Israel in guiding them through the wilderness is then taken, as furnishing ground for enforcing obedience to the Law; the danger of self-confidence and forgetfulness of God is pointed out; cautions are given against self-righteousness and spiritual pride; and, to enforce these, the people are reminded of their sins and rebelliousness in the wilderness, of Moses' intercession for them, and of God's grace and goodness, especially as shown in his restoring the two tables after they had been broken, and writing on them anew the law of the ten commandments (ch. viii. 1—x. 5).

At this point a short notice of the journeyings of the Israelites in the region of Mount Hor is introduced, with notices of the death of Aaron, of the continuance of the priesthood in his family, and of the separation of the tribe of Levi to the service of the sanctuary (ch. x. 6—11). The address is then resumed, and the people are exhorted to fear, obey, and love the Lord; and this is enforced by reference to God's claims upon them, the blessings that would ensue if they yielded to these claims, and, on the other hand, the curse that disobedience would bring upon them. In connection with this the command is given that, when they should be come into the promised land, the blessing should be put upon Mount Gerizim and the curse upon Mount Ebal, the situation of which is indicated (ch. x. 12—xi. 32).

After this Moses enters on a more minute detail of the laws which the people were to observe when settled in Canaan. Directions are given as to the destruction of all monuments of idolatry, and they are enjoined to preserve the worship of Jehovah and to present the appointed offerings to him in the place which he should choose, where also the sacrificial meal was to be eaten (ch. xii. 1—28). All intercourse with idolaters and all curious inquiries concerning their rites are to be avoided; all who would seduce to idolatry are to be put to death, even though they pretended to be prophets and to speak under Divine sanction; even the nearest relations who act this part are not to be spared; and all idolatrous cities are to be destroyed (ch. xii. 29—xiii. 18). The people are cautioned against joining in or imitating the mourning customs of the heathen, and against eating the flesh of unclean animals or of animals that had died of themselves; they are directed as to the laying aside of tithes for sacrificial meals and for the poor; they are enjoined to observe the seventh year of release for poor debtors and of emancipation for the bondman; they are commanded to dedicate to the Lord the first-born of sheep and oxen; and they are instructed to observe the three great feasts of Passover, Pentecost, and Tabernacles (ch. xiv. 1—xvi. 17). From these religious regulations Moses passes on to others more of a civil and social character, giving directions as to the appointment of judges and magistrates, the trial of idolaters and criminals of various classes, the choice and duties of a king, and the rights of priests and Levites; the promise of a Great Prophet like unto Moses, whom they are to hear and obey, is given; and the proper test by which any one pretending to be a prophet is to be tried, is prescribed (ch. xvi. 18—xviii. 22). Following these come some regulations as to the appointment of cities of refuge for the manslayer, the maintenance of landmarks and boundaries, the number of witnesses required to establish a charge against any one, the punishment of false witnesses, the conduct of war, exemption from service in war, the treatment of enemies, the besieging of towns, the expiation of murder where the murderer is unknown, the treatment of women taken in war, the just exercise of paternal authority, and the burial of malefactors who had been executed (ch. xix. 1—xxi. 23). The address is concluded by a series of miscellaneous injunctions relating to rights of property, the relation of the sexes, regard for animal and human life, the avoidance of what would confound distinctions made by God in the natural world, the preservation of the sanctity of the marriage bond, and the observation of integrity and purity in all the relations of life, domestic and social. After appointing the eucharistic services on the presentation of the firstfruits and tenths of the products of the field, the address is wound up with a solemn admonition to attend to and observe what the Lord had commanded (ch. xxii. 1—xxvi. 19).

In his *third* address, after directing that the Law should be inscribed on two stone pillars to be set up on Mount Ebal, when the people should have obtained possession of Canaan, Moses proceeds to charge them to proclaim in the most solemn manner, after offering burnt offerings and sacrifices, the blessing and the curse by which the Law was sanctioned, the former on Mount Gerizim, the latter on Mount Ebal (ch. xxvii. 1—26). He then more fully sets forth the blessings that should come upon the people if they hearkened to the voice of the Lord, and the curses that would befall them if they neglected his word or refused to obey it (ch. xxviii. 1—68). Moses then recapitulates what the Lord had done for Israel, and, after again referring to the blessings and curses of the Law, adjures the people to accept the covenant which God was graciously pleased to make with them, to adhere to it constantly, and so, having blessing and curse, life and death, set before them, to choose the former for themselves and their posterity (ch. xxix. 1—xxx. 20).

These three addresses of Moses to the people are followed by an account of the closing scenes and acts of his life. A few words of encouragement addressed to the people introduce the appointment of Joshua to be his successor as the leader of Israel; the Law written out by Moses is handed over to the custody of the priests, with a command that it shall be read every seventh year to the people at the Feast of Tabernacles; Joshua is summoned with Moses into the presence of Jehovah, and receives from him his commission and authority; and Moses is commanded to write a song, and teach it to the people (ch. xxxi. 1—22). The active life of Moses was now drawing to its close. He puts the last hand on the writing of the Law; composes the song which God had commanded him to write; utters a few words of encouragement to Joshua; delivers the book of the Law to the priests that bore the ark of the covenant, with the injunction to them to put it in the side of the ark; and summons the elders of the tribes and their officers to hear from his lips, ere he left them, his solemn charge, and listen to the words of the song he had composed (vers. 23—29). Then follows the song itself; after which comes a short exhortation to the people by Moses, followed by the Divine intimation of the approaching decease of their great leader and lawgiver (ch. xxxii. 1—52). Next is inserted the blessing which Moses pronounced upon Israel in its separate tribes (ch. xxxiii. 1—29); and to this is appended an account of the death and burial of Moses, with his eulogium (ch. xxxiv. 1—12). With this the book terminates.

§ 3. Design of the Book.

From the survey of the contents of this book, it is apparent that it is not intended as a supplement to the other books of the Pentateuch, but rather is to be viewed as a closing appeal, on the part of the great leader of Israel, to those whom he had conducted and formed into a nation, directed towards inducing them to keep inviolate the covenant of the Lord, that it might be well with them and their children. With this in view, Moses selects those facts in the past history of the people the remembrance of which was most fitted to preserve them in their dependence upon and allegiance to Jehovah, and those parts of the legislation already enacted as bore most closely on the covenant relation of Jehovah to his people. It is in accordance with this design that laws of a general kind, or such as relate to official functionaries and acts, should be only briefly referred to or altogether passed over; and also that instructions as to the proper ordering of matters which could be attended to only after the settlement of the nation in Canaan, should form an important element among the farewell counsels of him who had brought them to the confines of that land, but was not himself to enter it with them.

§ 4. Author and Date of the Book.

This book presents in the general such a uniformity of representation and character, such sameness of style and method, that there can be no hesitation in accepting it as, in the main, the work of one author. Was that author Moses? That he was is the commonly received belief, handed down from a remote antiquity, and which was not seriously questioned till comparatively recent times. Many objections, however, have been advanced against it of late; and this renders it necessary that the evidence, both in support of the traditionary belief and against it, should be carefully collected and weighed.

I. In favour of the Mosaic authorship of the book there is—

1. The weight of traditional authority. In the Christian and in the Jewish Church, so far back as we can trace, this book has been reputed the work of Moses. As to this there can be no legitimate question; the fact is indubitable. The stream of testimony may be traced from the Christian Fathers of the second century after Christ, with hardly a break, up to the time of David (cf. 1 Kings ii. 3; viii. 53; 2 Kings xiv. 5, 6; xviii. 6, 12, with ch. xxix. 9; ix. 26; xxiv. 16; x. 20). Moses is thus, so to speak, in possession, with a title which has been admitted for more than three thousand years. On those, therefore, who would dislodge him lies the burden of proving that this title is false; and this can be done only by showing from internal evidence that the book *cannot* be the writing of Moses. It will be incumbent on them also to show how this title could have been acquired, if purely fictitious—how this universal belief could have arisen, if without foundation in fact.

2. The testimony of our Lord and his apostles, as recorded in the New Testament, gives special weight to this tradition. Our Lord quotes from this book as part of the sacred writings, using the formula, " It is written," by which is indicated that the passages quoted are from the sacred canon (comp. Matt. iv. 4; ix. 7, 10, with ch. viii. 8; vi. 16; vi. 13), and recognizing it as the "Law" given by God to Israel (Matt. xxii. 24 compared with ch. vi. 5; x. 12). He expressly refers to and cites this book as the work of Moses (comp. Matt. xix. 7, 8; Mark x. 3, 4; John v. 46, 47; possibly also John vii. 19); and he implicitly attests this by assenting to the assertion of it by others (comp. Mark xii. 19; Luke xx. 28). St. Peter, in his address to the people who were collected together after the healing of the lame man at the gate of the temple, cites a passage from this book as the saying of Moses (Acts iii. 22); St. Stephen does the same in his apology to the Sanhedrim (Acts vii. 37); St. Paul quotes from this book as from Moses, in the same way as he quotes from the Book of Isaiah as from Isaiah (Rom. x. 19, 20), and at other times prefaces his citation with the words, " It is written" (Rom. xii. 19; Gal. iii. 10); and the apostles generally freely refer to the Law, *i.e.* the Thorah, or Pentateuch, including, of course, the fifth book, as of Moses. Now, the testimony of our Lord and his apostles cannot be regarded as a mere link in the chain of tradition on this point. It *is* that, but it is more than that; it is an authoritative declaration, from which it is maintained there is no appeal. Jesus, " the faithful and true Witness," and himself " the Truth," could utter only what is true; and knowing that his words, even the most minute and least weighty, were to endure for ever (Matt. xxiv. 35), and to guide the judgments and opinions of men to the latest generations, he

would be careful to order his speech so as in every case to express only what was in accordance with truth and fact. But it may be asked, "Might not our Lord have cited a passage from one of the Pentateuchal books as a saying of Moses, merely because these books were commonly called by the name of Moses, without meaning to affirm that they were actually written by him; just as one who had adopted the Wolfian theory of the composition of the 'Iliad' and 'Odyssey' might nevertheless continue to cite from these as the works of Homer, though he doubted if Homer ever existed, and felt sure that no one man composed these poems as they are now extant?" But to this it may be replied that the cases are not parallel. When one quotes from the 'Iliad,' or the 'Odyssey,' or from any classic writing, it is for the sake of the sentiment or expression that the quotation is made, and it matters not how the source of the quotation is designated, provided the designation be such as shall direct the reader or hearer to where the passage quoted is to be found. In our Lord's citations from the book of the Law, however, the important thing is not the mere words of the passage or the mere sentiment of it, but the *authority* of the utterance, and as that was derived entirely from its being part of the Law given by Moses in whom the Jews trusted (John i. 17; v. 45; vii. 19), it was essential to the validity of his argument that it should be from Moses and none other that his citation was made. When, therefore, our Lord adduced a passage as a saying of Moses, he must have meant that the saying adduced was actually uttered by Moses—in other words, that it was found in a book which not only carried on it the name of Moses as a popular and convenient designation, but of which Moses was really the author.

3. The antiquity of the book favours the ascription of it to Moses as its author. That the book is of early date is shown partly by the allusions to it in books that come after it in the canon, partly by certain peculiarities of language by which it is marked, and partly by certain statements and references contained in it.

(1) In the Book of Jeremiah there are so many expressions, phrases, utterances, coincident with such in Deuteronomy, that there can be no doubt that the author of the one book must have had the other before his mind whilst composing his own. The only question that can be raised is whether Jeremiah cited from Deuteronomy or the author of Deuteronomy cited from Jeremiah, if indeed the same person were not the writer of both books. This point will come to be considered subsequently; at present it is sufficient to note that these coincidences afford certain evidence of the existence of the Book of Deuteronomy in the time of Jeremiah.

That it was known to Isaiah and used by him may be inferred from a comparison of the following passages:—Isa. i. 2 with ch. xxxii. 1; Isa. i. 10 with ch. xxxii. 32; Isa. i. 17 with ch. xxviii. 27; Isa. xxvii. 11 with ch. xxxii. 28; Isa. xli. 8 with ch. vii. 6 and xiv. 2; Isa. xli. 10 with ch. xxxi. 6; Isa. xlii. 2 with ch. xxxii. 15; Isa. xlvi. 8 with ch. xxxii. 7; Isa. l. 1 with ch. xxiv. 1; Isa. lviii. 14 with ch. xxxii. 13; Isa. lix. 10 and lxv. 21 with ch. xxviii. 29; Isa. lxii. 8, etc., with ch. xxviii. 31.

In Amos and Hosea there are allusions to passages in this book which prove that it was known in their day. Of these the following may be noted :—

Amos iv. 6—10 and v. 11 compared with ch. xxviii. 15, etc. In Deuteronomy certain judgments are announced as to come on Israel if apostate and impenitent; in Amos certain judgments are declared as having come on Israel because of their apostacy and impenitency; and the two are so closely identical that the prophet must be regarded as describing the fulfilment of a threatening predicted by the lawgiver. Famine, drought, blasting, and mildew, the ravages of the locust, pestilence, the diseases of Egypt, and the calamities of war are described by the prophet as what had come on Israel; and these are what are threatened in Deuteronomy in the same or equivalent words. Compare especially Amos iv. 6 with ch. xxviii. 17, 38—40; Amos iv. 7 with ch. xxviii. 23, 24; Amos iv. 9 with ch. xxviii. 22, 38, 42; Amos iv. 10 with ch. xxviii. 21, 27, 26; Amos v. 11 with ch. xxviii. 30, 39.

In Amos vi. 12 the prophet charges the people with having "turned judgment into gall (*rosh*), and the fruit of righteousness into hemlock (*la'anah*)." Compare ch. xxix. 18 [17], where the people are warned against apostasy, " Lest there should be among you a root that beareth gall and wormwood (*rosh we la'anah*)."

Amos viii. 14, " They that swear by the sin of Samaria, and say, Thy God, O Dan, liveth" (cf. 2 Kings xii. 28, 29). Ch. ix. 21, "And I took your sin, the calf which ye had made," etc.; ch. vi. 13, " Thou shalt fear Jehovah thy God, and serve him, and shalt swear by his Name."

Amos ix. 14, 15, " And I will turn (*weshabhti*) the captivity of my people of Israel, and they shall build the waste cities, and inhabit them; and they shall plant vineyards, and drink the wine thereof; they shall also make gardens, and eat the fruit of them. And I will plant them upon their land, and they shall no more be pulled up out of their land which I have given them, saith Jehovah thy God." Ch. xxx. 3, " Then Jehovah thy God shall turn (*weshabh*) thy captivity, and have compassion upon thee, and will return and gather thee from all the nations, whither Jehovah thy God hath scattered thee;" ver. 5, "And Jehovah thy God will bring thee into the land which thy fathers possessed;" ver. 9, " And Jehovah thy God will make thee plenteous in every work of thine hand, in the fruit of thy body, and in the fruit of thy cattle, and in the fruit of thy ground, for good," etc. "This passage forms the basis of all the passages in the Old Testament in which the very peculiar formula שָׁב שְׁבוּת occurs " (Hengstenberg).

Turning now to Hosea, the following correspondences with Deuteronomy may be noted :—

Hos. iv. 14, " They sacrifice with the *kedéshoth* " (women consecrated to prostitution in the service of a heathen deity). Ch. xxiii. 17, 18, " There shall be no *kedéshah* [consecrated harlot] of the daughters of Israel, . . .

thou shalt not bring the hire of a *kedéshah* . . . into the house of the Lord." Only in these passages and in Gen. xxxviii. 21, 22, is this word found.

Hos. v. 10, "The princes of Judah were like them that remove the bounds (*massígei gebúl*)." Ch. xix. 14, "Thou shalt not remove thy neighbour's landmark (*lo tassíg gebúl*);" ch. xxvii. 17, "Cursed be he that removeth his neighbour's landmark (*massíg gebúl*)." Hos. v. 14, "I will take away, and none shall rescue (*eyn matzíl*)." Ch. xxxii. 39, "And there is none that rescueth out of my hand (*eyn m'yádi matzíl*)." (Cf. also Hos. ii. 10 [Heb. 12].)

Hos. vi. 1, "Come, and let us return unto the Lord; for he hath torn, [cf. Hos. v. 14] and he will heal us; he hath smitten, and he will bind us up." Ch. xxxii. 39, "I kill, and I make alive; I wound, and I heal."

Hos. viii. 13, "They shall return (*yashubhu*) to Egypt." Ch. xxviii. 68, "The Lord shall bring thee (*heshibhka*) into Egypt again."

Hos. xii. 13, "By a prophet the Lord brought Israel out of Egypt, and by a prophet was he preserved." Ch. xviii. 18, "A Prophet . . . like unto thee." Only here is Moses described as a prophet.

Hos. xiii. 6, "According to their pasture, so were they filled; they were filled, and their heart was lifted up; therefore have they forgotten me." Ch. viii. 14, "Then thine heart be lifted up, and thou forget the Lord thy God," etc.

Hos. xiii. 9, "This (*shihethka*) hath corrupted [destroyed] thee, O Israel, that thou art against me [who am] in thy help." Ch. xxxii. 5, "A perverse nation hath become corrupt towards him (*shiheth lo*);" ch. xxxiii. 26, "Who rideth upon the heaven in thy help."

The coincidences thus noted are not, it must be confessed, all of equal weight and evidential value; but, on the other hand, none of them can be certainly declared to be accidental, and some are of such a character as almost to force the conclusion that the prophets Hosea and Amos had in their hands the Book of Deuteronomy, and freely cited from it. Assuming this, something more is proved than that this book was extant in the days of these prophets. As these were prophets, not of Judah, but of Israel, their references to Deuteronomy may indicate the reception of that book in Israel as a sacred book; and as it is not probable that any book would be so received in the kingdom of Samaria which had not been carried by the ten tribes with them when they broke off from Judah, it would follow that this book was known and reverenced at the time of the separation. But if it was thus accredited in the beginning of the reign of Rehoboam, the probability is that it was so in the reigns of his predecessors, Solomon and David; for it is incredible that it could have attained to universal acceptance at the moment of his accession to the throne, if it had not been by long usage already established. It may indeed be said that the better part of Israel was never wholly alienated from Judah religiously, but continued to regard the temple at Jerusalem as the national sanctuary. But that this would have led to the acceptance by the nation generally of a book pretending to be from God, which was unknown to their fathers, and which had come into existence in Judah after the separation of the tribes, cannot be believed; national enmity and sectarian jealousy, to say nothing of pious zeal for God, would have effectually prevented that, the more especially in respect of a book by which their whole religious position and system was condemned.

The conclusion above announced is corroborated by the references to Deuteronomy in the narrative of the Books of Kings.

Reference has been already made to passages in these books in which the Book of Deuteronomy is expressly referred to as the Law of Moses, and as written by Moses. What has now to be considered are allusions to things contained in that book, and apparent quotations from it.

1 Kings viii. 51, "For they are thy people . . . which thou broughtest forth out of Egypt, from the midst of the furnace of iron." Ch. iv. 20, "And the Lord hath taken you, and brought you forth from the furnace of iron, out of Egypt."

1 Kings xvii. 1. Here Elijah announces to Ahab that the judgment threatened in ch. xi. 16, 17, against idolatry in Israel, should now be inflicted, because of his having set up an altar to Baal, and placed beside it an Asherah for idol-worship.

1 Kings xviii. 40. In the order given by Elijah as to the treatment of the priests of Baal, the prophet follows the Divine injunction as given in ch. xiii. 15, 16, and xvii. 5; without which it is inconceivable that he should have ventured to enjoin on the king such extreme measures.

1 Kings xxi. 10. The appointment of *two* witnesses in order to convict Naboth of blasphemy points to the observance in Israel of the law recorded in ch. xvii. 6, 7; xix. 15.

1 Kings xxii. 11. "The symbolical act of the false prophet Zedekiah, here described, is an embodying of the figure in ch. xxxiii. 17. This illustrious promise, specially applicable to the posterity of Joseph, was the basis on which the pseudo-prophets built; only they overlooked the one thing, that the promise was conditional and the condition was not realized. . . . The reference to the Pentateuch here is the more important since Zedekiah was one of the prophets of the calves, and since the symbolical act could have been undertaken only on the presumption that its meaning, resting on the Pentateuch, was intelligible to those present, and especially to the kings " (Hengstenberg, i. 132).

2 Kings ii. 9. Elisha, as the firstborn of Elijah in a spiritual sense—his γνήσιον τέκνον, according to their common office as prophets—asks of Elijah that the portion legally due to the firstborn son might be his, that a double portion (פִּי שְׁנַיִם) of his father's possessions, his spirit, might be given to him. This points back to ch. xxi. 17, where the law relating to the right of the firstborn is enunciated. It is noticeable that in both passages the same peculiar phrase, פִּי שְׁנַיִם, a mouthful of two, occurs, and in this sense only in these two passages.

2 Kings vi. 28—30. The extreme horror of the king on hearing the woman's story, and his penetential observance in consequence, are best accounted for by a reference to ch. xxviii. 53, 57, 58. The king recognized in what the woman told him a fulfilment of the threatening denounced in this passage; and so, while the lesser calamities that had befallen his people in consequence of the siege of the city by the Syrians had failed to move him, this most terrible tale filled him with horror and drove him to penitence.

2 Kings xiv. 6. Here is an express quotation of a law which is found only in ch. xxiv. 16.

2 Kings xviii. 6, "For he clave to the Lord, and departed not from following him," etc. Ch. x. 20, "Thou shalt fear the Lord thy God; him shalt thou serve, and to him shalt thou cleave," etc.

Besides these references to Deuteronomy, there are many in the two Books of Kings to other parts of the Pentateuch, going to prove that that book in its entireness was known and accepted in the kingdom of Israel from the time of its first establishment. "Indeed," as has been remarked, "the entire action and operation of the prophets in the kingdom of Israel is an inexplicable riddle if we do not assume the public recognition of the Pentateuch in this kingdom as its basis. With all the annoyances which the prophets occasioned to the kings, and the priests who were in close alliance with them, there never came to be a systematic and thoroughgoing persecution of them so as to extirpate them. This suggests, unless we set aside all probability and all historical analogies, the possession by them of an external right whereby hatred against them was restrained, and the following out of extreme measures prevented. But on what could such an outward right be well based if not on the public acknowledgment of the Pentateuch, on which they grounded their censures, with which they connected their threatenings, and whose prophet-law they maintained against their opponents?" (Hengstenberg, i. 140).

Ascending to the earlier books, the following correspondences between them and Deuteronomy may be noted:—

2 Sam. vii. 6, "During all [the time] that I walked with all the children of Israel," etc. Ch. xxiii. 14, "For Jehovah thy God walketh in the midst of thy camp" (cf. Lev. xxvi. 12, "And I will walk amongst you"). Only in these three passages does this peculiar phraseology occur. 2 Sam. vii. 23, "And what one nation in the earth is like thy people, even like Israel, whom God went to redeem for a people to himself . . . thy people, which thou redeemedst to thee from Egypt, from the nations and their gods?" Ch. vii. 8, "The Lord hath redeemed you out of the house of bondmen, from the hand of Pharaoh king of Egypt" (cf. also ch. ix. 26; xiii. 5; xv. 15; xxi. 8; xxiv. 18). This expression may be said to be specially Deuteronomic.

1 Sam. ii. 2, "There is none holy as the Lord: for there is none beside thee: neither is there any rock like our God." Ch. iv. 35, "Know that the

Lord he is God; there is none else beside him;" ch. xxxii. 4, 15, 18, 31, "He is the Rock, his work is perfect . . . the Rock of his salvation . . . the Rock that begat thee . . . For their rock is not as our Rock," etc. 1 Sam. ii. 6, "The Lord killeth, and maketh alive : he bringeth down to the grave, and bringeth up." Ch. xxxii. 39, "See now that I, even I, am he, and there is no god with me : I kill, and I make alive; I wound, and I heal," etc. 1 Sam. ii. 29, "Wherefore kick ye at my sacrifice and at mine offering, which I have commanded?" Ch. xxxii. 15, "Jeshurun waxed fat, and kicked." The verb בָּעַט, to kick, occurs only in these two places.

1 Sam. viii. 1, "And it came to pass that Samuel when he was old made his sons judges over Israel." Ch. xvi. 18, "Judges and officers shalt thou make thee in all thy gates." In making his sons judges, Samuel was carrying into effect the law enunciated in Deuteronomy. As Samuel thus obeyed the Law, so his sons transgressed it, for they took bribes (*shohad*, 1 Sam. viii. 3), contrary to the injunction, "Thou shalt not respect persons, neither take a gift [bribe, *shohad*]," etc. (ch. xvi. 19). 1 Sam. viii. 5, "Now make us a king to judge us like all the nations." Ch. xvii. 14, "And shalt say, I will set a king over me, like as all the nations that are about me."

1 Sam. x. 1, "The Lord hath anointed thee to be captain over his inheritance." Ch. xxxii. 9, "The Lord's portion is his people; Jacob is the lot of his inheritance." 1 Sam. x. 25, "Then Samuel told the people the manner of the kingdom," etc. The manner (the law, the legitimate order, *mishpat*) of the kingdom was what had been prescribed; and it is only in Deuteronomy that this prescription is given (cf. ch. xvii. 14, etc.).

1 Sam. xv. 2, "Thus saith the Lord of hosts, I remember that which Amalek did to Israel, how he laid wait for him in the way, when he came up from Egypt." Ch. xxv. 17, "Remember what Amalek did unto thee by the way, when ye were come forth out of Egypt."

1 Sam. xxviii. 3, "Saul had put away those that had familiar spirits, and the wizards, out of the land." Ch. xviii. 10, 11, "There shall not be found in thee . . . a consulter with familiar spirits, or a wizard."

Judg. i. 20, "And they gave Hebron unto Caleb, as Moses said." Ch. i. 36, "Save Caleb the son of Jephunneh; he shall see it, and to him will I give the land that he hath trodden upon."

Judg. ii. 2, "I said . . . And ye shall make no league (*lo tikrethu berith*) with the inhabitants of this land; ye shall throw down their altars." etc. Ch. vii. 2, "Thou shalt . . . utterly destroy them; thou shalt make no covenant with them (*lo tikroth lahem berith*);" ch. xii. 3, "And ye shall overthrow [throw down] their altars." Judg. ii. 3, "And their gods shall be a snare unto you." Ch. vii. 16, "Neither shalt thou serve their gods; for that will be a snare unto thee." Judg. ii. 15, "The hand of the Lord was against them for evil, as the Lord had said, and as the Lord had sworn unto them." Ch. xxviii. 15, etc. Judg. ii. 18, "For it repented the Lord because of their groanings by reason of them that oppressed them and vexed them." Ch. xxxii. 36, "For the Lord shall judge his people, and repent himself for his servants, when he seeth that their power is gone."

Judg. iv. 14, "And Deborah said unto Barak, Up; for this is the day in which the Lord hath delivered Sisera into thine hand: is not the Lord gone out before thee?" Ch. ix. 3, "Understand therefore this day, that the Lord thy God is he which goeth over before thee."

Judg. v. 4, 5, "Lord, when thou wentest out of Seir, when thou marchedst out of the field of Edom, the earth trembled, and the heavens dropped, the clouds also dropped water. The mountains melted before the Lord, even that Sinai from before the Lord God of Israel." Ch. xxxiii. 2, "The Lord came from Sinai, and rose up from Seir unto them; he shined forth from mount Paran," etc. Judg. v. 8, "They chose new gods (*elohim hadáshim*)." Ch. xxxii. 17, "They sacrificed . . . to gods whom they knew not, to new (*hadáshim*) gods that came newly up," etc.

Judg. xi. 15, "Israel took not away the land of Moab, nor the land of the children of Ammon," etc. Ch. ii. 9, 19, "And the Lord said, Distress not the Moabites, neither contend with them in battle: for I will not give thee of their land for a possession . . . When thou comest nigh over against the children of Ammon, distress them not, nor meddle with them: for I will not give thee of the land of the children of Ammon any possession."

Judg. xiv. 3. The parents of Samson expostulate with him as to his intention to take a wife "of the uncircumcised Philistines." But there was no reason why he should not do this, if it so pleased him, except that it was expressly prohibited by the law of God as recorded in ch. vii. 3. It would thus appear that that law was known and recognized as binding on the people of God in the days of the judges.

Ruth iv. 2—12, "And he took ten men of the elders of the city," etc. The entire narrative in this context points to the law of the levirate in ch. xxv. 5—10. "The real relation of the *goel* [kinsman] in Ruth to the *yabam* [husband's brother] in the law is unquestionable. 'Each was bound to raise offspring to the dead from the wife of the dead. The reason in both cases was the same, that the name of the dead might not perish from Israel, nor from his family. In fine, in both cases, if the party refused to marry the wife of the deceased, this was attested by the taking off of the shoe' (Perizonius, 'Dissert.,' vii. p. 79). No less undeniable and still more decisive is the *verbal* reference to the law, which is equivalent to an actual citation of it. Compare only ch. xxv. 6, 'And the firstborn which she beareth יָקוּם עַל־שֵׁם אָחִיו הַמֵּת,' with Ruth iv. 5, 'Of Ruth the Moabitess, the wife of the dead, to raise up the name of the dead upon his inheritance (לְהָקִים שֵׁם־הַמֵּת עַל־נַחֲלָתוֹ).' The name of the dead could only be raised up, according to the law, by a son being ascribed to him. This kind service Boaz was prepared to render to him; the *goel* must either do what Boaz proffered, or he must transfer to him, as the next *goel*, the right of redemption. Still more complete is the reference to ch. xxv. 6 in Ruth iv. 10, 'I take to me Ruth as my wife, to raise up the name of the dead upon his inheritance, and that the name of the dead be not cut off from among his brethren, and from the gate of his place.' According to ch. xxv. 9, the transaction between the brother-in-law and the sister-in-law must take place in the presence of the elders; in Ruth iv. 2 it is said, 'He took ten men of the elders of the city.' In ch. xxv. 9 it is said, 'So shall it be done unto that man *who buildeth not up his brother's house;*' with which compare Ruth iv. 11, 'The Lord make the woman that is come into thine house like Rachel and like Leah, which two did build the house of Israel;' *i.e.* since thou, according to the prescription, hast builded up the house of thy brother, may the Lord make, etc. That Deuteronomy is older than the Book of Ruth is seen from this, that the author of the latter describes the symbolical act of pulling off the shoe as a usage that had descended to his time from former times, whilst in Deuteronomy it appears as then in common use, and of itself clear" (Hengstenberg, ii. 104). It may be added that it is by reference to the usage prescribed in Deuteronomy that the words of Naomi to her widowed daughters-in-law (Ruth i. 11) are to be understood.

It does not seem necessary to carry this investigation further; the instances adduced are sufficient to show that when the Books of Samuel, Judges, and Ruth were written, the Book of Deuteronomy was extant and commonly known; for the alternative hypothesis, that the author of Deuteronomy, writing at a time subsequent to the appearance of these books, carefully picked out of them a number of small particulars and adapted the statements of his own book to these, so as to give the appearance of an undesigned coincidence between his book and the others, is too violent to be entertained. It thus appears that all through the history of Israel, from the times immediately succeeding those of Moses and Joshua, this Book of Deuteronomy was known and in common use in Israel.

(2) The antiquity of this book is vouched for by the archaisms with which it abounds. " The use of הוּא in both genders, which occurs one hundred and ninety-five times in the Pentateuch, is found thirty-six times in Deuteronomy; while of the eleven places in which הִיא is written not one is in this book. In Deuteronomy, as in the other books, a maiden is called נַעַר; only in one passage (ch. xxii. 19) is נַעֲרָה used. The demonstrative pronoun הָאֵל, which is not found out of the Pentateuch except in 1 Chron. xx. 8 (cf. Ezra v. 15; Aramaic), is not only to be read in Gen. xix. 8, 25; xxvi. 3, 4; Lev. xviii. 27; but runs through Deuteronomy (cf. ch. iv. 42; vii. 22; xix. 11). So also the *He locale*, so rare in the later usage of the language, the old rare writing תִּמְצֶאןָ (Jahn in Bengel's 'Archiv.,' ii. 582) and the future ending וּן־ are common. The last of these, according to the investigation of König (Heft. ii. of his 'Alt-test. Studien'), is more frequent in the Pentateuch than in any other Old Testament book, and is found in Deuteronomy fifty-eight times, as also twice in the Pret. viii. 3, 16 יְדְעוּן, of which the Old Testament has only one other instance—Isa. xxvi. 16. Among these archaisms common to Deuteronomy with the other Pentateuchal books may be reckoned also the shortening of the Hiph. לְעַשֵׂר (ch. xxvi. 12), and often the use of קְרָא equi-

valent to קָרָה, to meet; the construction of the passive with the אֵת of the object
(*e.g.* ch. xx. 8); the changes of the common כֶּבֶשׂ into כֶּשֶׂב, lamb (ch. xiv. 4); the
use of זָכוּר equivalent to זָכָר, a word lost to the post-Pentateuchal language
(Dietrich, 'Abhandlungen,' s. 89), ch. xvi. 16; xx. 13; and many old
words, such as אָבִיב and יְקוּם, and among these such as are found only in
Joshua, as אֲשֵׁדוֹת, or in Ezekiel, whose language is framed on that of the
Pentateuch, like מִין. Also in hapaxlegomena, which in an old language
abound, Deuteronomy is not poor. Examples of these are חֶרְמֵשׁ (for the later
מַגָּל); the old Canaanitish עַשְׁתְּרוֹת הַצֹּאן, increase of the flock; יְשֻׁרוּן (as a name
of Israel, borrowed by Isaiah, xliv. 2); הִרְבִּית, to be silent; הֶעֱנִיק, to lay upon
the neck; הִתְעַמֵּר to take possession of, to lay hands on. To the antique and
genuinely Mosaic peculiarities of the Deuteronomist belongs also his love of
pictures: a root of hemlock and wormwood sprouts (ch. xxix. 18), head and
tail (ch. xxviii. 13, 44), the saturated with the thirsty (ch. xxix. 19); and comparisons: as a man beareth his son (ch. i. 31), as bees do (ch. i. 44), as a man
chasteneth his son (ch. viii. 5), as the eagle fluttereth (ch. xxviii. 49), as the
blind gropeth (ch. xxviii. 29). Of such comparisons I know only three in
the other books: 'As the ox licks up the grass of the field' (Numb. xxii. 4,
in the Balaam section); 'As a flock that hath no shepherd' (Numb. xxvii. 17);
'As the guardian bears the suckling' (Numb. xi. 12); both in the mouth of
Moses" (Delitzsch, 'Die Genesis,' Einleit, s. 27 f.). To these may be
added certain words and phrases found in the earlier books, but which
would seem to have become obsolete or to have been regarded as archaic in
the times subsequent to that of Samuel:—As for instance, שְׁעָרִים, gates, for
habitations generally; nineteen times in Deuteronomy; elsewhere once, in
Exod. xx. 10, in a document acknowledgedly Mosaic; and occasionally but
rarely in poetical pieces (Ps. lxxxvii. 2 [but see Hengstenberg *in loc.*];
Isa. iii. 26; lx. 18 (?); Jer. xiv. 2). שֹׁטְרִים, officers; seven times in Deuteronomy; elsewhere Exod. v. 6, 10, 14, 15, 19; Numb. xi. 16; Josh. i. 10;
iii. 2; viii. 33; xxiii. 2; xxiv. 1; Chron. six times. רֵיקָם, empty, in the
sense of without an offering; ch. xvi. 16; Exod. xxiii. 15; xxxiv. 20;
1 Sam. vi. 3; not elsewhere. עִנָּה אִשָּׁה, to humble a woman; ch. xxi. 14; xxii.
24, 29; Gen. xxxiv. 2; Judg. xx. 5; 2 Sam. xiii. 12, 14; Lam. v. 11;
Ezek. xxii. 10, 11. סוּר יָמִין וּשְׂמֹאל, to turn to the right hand or to the left, of
departures from God's Law; ch. v. 32; xvii. 28; xxviii. 14; Josh. i. 7;
xxiii. 6. הֶאֱרִיד יָמִים, to prolong days, to live long; eleven times in Deuteronomy; elsewhere only Exod. xx. 12; Josh. xxiv. 31; Judg. ii. 7; 1 Kings
iii. 14; Eccles. viii. 13; Isa. liii. 10. תְּמוּנָה, likeness, similitude; ch. iv. 12,
15, 16, 23, 25; v. 8; Exod. xx. 4; Numb. xii. 8; Job iv. 16 (image, form,
shape); Ps. xvii. 15. כֹּהֵן; this term is in Deuteronomy, as in the other Pentateuchal books, used only of persons exercising sacerdotal functions; in later
times it came to be used also of civil officers and counsellors of the sovereign
(cf. 2 Sam. viii. 18; xx. 26; 1 Kings iv. 2, 5; 1 Chron. xxvii. 5). אִשֶּׁה, fire

offering; ch. xviii. 1; often in the Pentateuch; once in Josh. xiii. 14; and once in 1 Sam. ii. 28. כִּלְאַיִם, two things heterogeneous; ch. xxii. 9; elsewhere only in Lev. xix. 19. גּוֹזָל, a young bird; ch. xxxii. 11; Gen xv. 9; not found elsewhere. זָכוּר, a male; ch. xvi. 19; xx. 13; elsewhere only Exod. xxiii. 17; xxxiv. 23. נְקֵבָה, female; ch. iv. 16; often in the Pentateuch; once in Jer. xxxi. 22. אָבִיב, the month Abib; ch. xvi. 1; Exod. ix. 31; xiii. 4; xxiii. 15; xxxiv. 18; Lev. ii. 14; nowhere else. שֶׁגֶר, young of a beast; ch. vii. 13, 28; iv. 18, 51; elsewhere only Exod. xiii. 12. יְקוּם, substance, living thing; ch. xi. 6; Gen. vii. 4, 23; nowhere else. סְנֶה, bush; ch. xxxiii. 16; elsewhere only in Exod. iii. 2, 3, 4.

(3) The antiquity of the book is further guaranteed by certain statements and references contained in it.

Ch. vii. 1, etc. Intercourse with the nations of Canaan is here strenuously forbidden to the Israelites. This was fitting before they took possession of that land; at a later period such a prohibition would have been superfluous, if not ridiculous.

Ch. xxv. 9. Reference is here made to the taking off of the shoe as a symbol of the transference of an inheritance, in a way which shows, as already observed, that the usage was then common. In the time of the judges this was regarded as a usage of "the former time" (Ruth iv. 7). The time of Deuteronomy, therefore, must have preceded that of the judges.

Ch. xxv. 17, etc. The Israelites are commanded to remember what Amalek did to them by the way, as they came out of Egypt, etc. Such an injunction it would have been absurd to publish in writing at a much later period in the history of Israel, long after the Amalekites had ceased to exist as a nation. So also of the Canaanites (ch. xx. 16—18).

Ch. xvii. 14, etc. It is here assumed that at some future time the people of Israel would propose to set a king over them, like all the nations about them, and directions are given as to the choice of a king in this case, and as to the conduct of the king when he should be chosen. The fair presumption from this is that the book in which these are recorded must have been written before the time of Samuel; for it is not credible that any writer would have introduced into his narrative any such statements posterior to the election of Saul to be King of Israel. Especially is it to be noted that one of the directions given is that the king is "not to multiply horses, nor cause the people to return to Egypt, to the end that he should multiply horses; forasmuch as the Lord hath said unto you, Ye shall henceforth return no more that way." Such a cautionary injunction was fitting at a time when there was some danger of the people being seduced into returning to Egypt; at a later period, long after they had been settled in the promised land, it would be simply preposterous. It has indeed been said, on the other hand, that, had this book been then extant, Samuel must have known this passage, and in that case would not have rebuked the people as he did for their sin in desiring a king. There would be some force in this did the passage in Deuteronomy contain an enactment that a king should be chosen or express approval of such an act. But this is not the case; rather is the contrary implied, for it is plain, from the manner in which the subject is introduced, that the anticipated act was not regarded by the speaker with approval, but was rather viewed by him as a wilful departure from an order instituted by God, prompted by a desire on the part of the people to be like to the nations around them; in fact, a species of apostacy from Jehovah, second only to a renunciation of him for other gods. When Samuel, therefore, rebuked the people, even whilst conceding their request, he spoke in the very spirit of this passage, and not improbably with this very passage in his mind.

It has also been urged that, as the appointment of a king was incompatible with the Theocracy, it is highly improbable that any such thing would have been contemplated and legislated for by Moses. It is to be observed, however, that the king whom it was supposed the people were to be allowed to set up was not to be an autocrat or one whose rule was to be independent; he was to be one whom God should choose, and who was to be under law to God, and so was really to be the vicegerent of Jehovah, the Great King. By the appointment of such a king, therefore, the Theocracy remained intact. The administration of government by means of a king whom God should choose no more superseded the supreme kingship of Jehovah, than the administration of law by judges interfered with his supremacy as Lawgiver and Judge.

. It is further asked—Had this passage been in existence and known, how could Solomon have dared to contravene it as he did by multiplying wives and sending to Egypt for horses? But Solomon, we know, dared to do many things which were contrary to law, both Divine and human. His having many wives and concubines was as much against the law of the Decalogue as against the law in ch. xvii. 14—17.

Ch. xxvii. 11—26. Directions are here given concerning blessing and cursing on Mount Gerizim and Mount Ebal. These, however, are of a very general character, details evidently being left to the discretion of the parties by whom the injunction was to be carried into effect. An author writing after the event would, it is presumed, have been more precise, and would have so framed his statement as to present to his readers a distinct and easily apprehensible representation of the whole transaction.

Ch. xix. 1—10. Here it is enacted that, on the establishment of the people in Canaan, the land is to be divided, and certain cities to be set apart as places of refuge for the manslayer. This is a law which could be obeyed only at the time of the entrance of the people on the possession of the land, and which, therefore, it would be absurd to prescribe in a book written long after that took place.

In several parts of the book allusion is made to the condition of the Israelites as then in the wilderness, and to their experiences there as then recent (cf. ch. i.—iii.; iv. 3, 4, 44—49; vii. 1; viii. 1; ix. 1;

xi. 8, etc., 30, 31 ; xiii. 12 ; xviii. 9 ; xix. 1 ; xxvii. 2). Unless, then, the book be put aside as a pure fiction, it must be accepted as of an age not later than the time of the arrival of the Israelites on the eastern side of the Jordan.

From these considerations the high antiquity of this book may be fairly inferred. This not only falls in with the supposition that it is in the main the writing of Moses, but lends support to that supposition; for Moses is the only person of whom we know anything who at that early period can be supposed to have composed such a book, and as the book professes to be his, the presumption is very strong that he and no other is the author of it.

4. The aspect and attitude of the writer, both retrospective and prospective, are those of one in the position of Moses at the time immediately before the entrance of the Israelites into Canaan. The book presents itself as Mosaic, and with this the entire costume and colouring of the book is in keeping. "There is nowhere even a single expression which is not suited to the position of Moses at that time; the standpoint throughout the whole book is the same; the situation is ever that of one on the borders of the promised land. To that which in later times was the centre of the popular life—to Jerusalem and its temple, to the kingdom of David—there is not a single reference such as would transgress historical limits. The occupation of the land is only in the general assumed as about to take place; nothing is said as to the special relations of Israel in the land when conquered. The principal foes are the Canaanites, who, from the beginning of the period of the judges, retire into the background, and, after Judg. v., nowhere play any notable part. (For exact acquaintance with the early relations of the peoples in the Mosaic times, see ch. ii.; in respect of the geography of the scene of the last wandering, ch. i. 1, etc.) Specially noticeable are the very vivid reminiscences of Egypt; the motives to kindness towards servants thence taken (ch. v. 15 ; xv. 15 ; xvi. 12 ; xxiv. 18); the references to diseases peculiar to Egypt in the threatening of punishments (ch. xxviii. 27, 35); the references to deliverance from thence in the promises (ch. vii. 15 ; xxviii. 60); the exaltation of Canaan by comparison with Egypt (ch. xi. 10); a highly graphic representation of the old Egyptian agriculture, to which the monuments bear witness." Besides these references to Egyptian usages, etc., may be mentioned the command to bear the words of the Law as an amulet on the hand and breast (ch. vi. 8, etc.; xi. 18; cf. Exod. xiii. 16), and to inscribe them on the door-posts of the house (ch. xi. 20); the command to write the Law on stones plastered with mortar (ch. xxvii. 18); the mode of punishment by the stick, the Egyptian bastinado (ch. xxv. 2, 3); the method of irrigation (ch. xi. 10); the function of the scribe in the military arrangements of the Egyptians (ch. xx. 5). There are also frequent retrospective glances in the book to the residence of the Israelites in Egypt as of recent occurrence (ch. vi. 21, etc.; vii. 8, 18 ; xi. 3). Such a statement also as the following is intelligible only on the supposition that it is the utterance of one addressing those who were contemporaneous with the

event referred to:—"Your eyes have seen what the Lord did because of Baal-peor: for all the men that followed Baal-peor, the Lord thy God hath destroyed them from among you. But ye that did cleave unto the Lord your God are alive every one of you this day" (ch. iv. 3, 4). The inference is irresistible: either these words were uttered at the time indicated by "this day" or the statement is a fiction. These allusions are so numerous and precise that it may with justice be said, "If Deuteronomy is not the work of Moses, there is here the most exquisite of literary frauds, and that in an age which had not as yet acquired the art of transporting itself into foreign individualities and situations" (Hengstenberg).

5. The passage just quoted suggests a weighty consideration in favour of the Mosaic authorship of this book. If the book is not by him, if it is the production of a later age, it must be regarded as a forgery. For beyond all question, the book not only contains discourses alleged to have been uttered by Moses, but also claims to have been written by him (cf. ch. i. 1; xxix. 1; xxxi. 1, 9—11, 24). Are we, then, to pronounce this book a forgery? If so, the book cannot be regarded as one of the ἱερὰ γράμματα, the sacred writings—as really belonging to the γραφή Θεόπνευστος, as being a book given by Divine inspiration. For the religious consciousness recoils from the thought that God would either originate or sanction a deliberate untruth. We may admire the genius of the man who could produce so consummately skilful a fiction; but we can never believe that it was by Divine direction and with help from above that he composed it, or that it was sent forth with the authorization of him "all whose words are true." Nor is it easy to conceive how what must have been known to be a fraud could have found acceptance and been reckoned among the sacred writings of the Jews. It has, indeed, been pleaded that there was no fraud in the case; that, as all knew that the book was not written by Moses, none were deceived by the ascription of it to him, any more than those who heard Herodotus read his history at the Olympic games were deceived by the ascription to his heroes of the speeches which he had himself composed. But on this supposition, how are we to account for the author of the book ascribing it to Moses at all? Herodotus made speeches for his characters and inserted them in his history, merely to give completeness to his story and as a display of literary skill. But no such motive could have induced the author of Deuteronomy, supposing him to be some prophet or scribe of a later age, to have ascribed his work as a whole to Moses. He could do this only in the hope of thereby investing it with greater authority, and procuring for it a more ready acceptance and deferential regard. But for this it was essential that the book should be *believed* to be by Moses; the moment it was known not to be by him, the author's design would be wholly frustrated. The author must, therefore, have *intended* it to be accepted as really the work of Moses; and if it was not so accepted, it must have been repudiated as a too manifest forgery to be endured. Its acceptance by the Jews and its place in the canon is thus utterly unaccountable on the

supposition that it is the production of a writer of an age later than that of Moses.

II. These considerations give strong support to the traditional belief that this book is what it professes to be—the work of Moses. It is possible, however, that other considerations, drawn from the book itself, may outweigh these, so as to make it uncertain whether Moses wrote this book or not, if they do not render it highly probable that it must be ascribed to some later writer. Such considerations, it is maintained, are to be found, and they have been strenuously urged by many critics of note as fatal to the claims of the book to be regarded as the genuine work of Moses. To these attention must now be directed.

1. It is alleged that not only is this book in style, phraseology, and manner of thought different from the other Pentateuchal books, but that its contents present so many discrepancies to the other books that it cannot be regarded as the product of the same author.

This consideration, it is obvious, is of force as against the genuineness of Deuteronomy only on the assumption that the other books of the Pentateuch are the writing of Moses. If this be denied or questioned, the objection becomes invalid. For in that case any alleged discrepancies would prove nothing more than that this book is not from the same hand as the other books; they would leave the claims of this book, which professes to be the work of Moses, unaffected.

It may also occur to the inquirer that, even on the assumption just referred to, the force of an argument of this sort is not great. For whilst it is quite conceivable that the style and phraseology and manner of thought of an author may differ at one period of his life from what they were at another, or may acquire a different character as they are used on different subjects or with a different purpose, and that in the course of forty years such changes may take place in the condition, circumstances, and relations of a community that an author writing near the end of that period may have much to narrate concerning them that is not in accordance with what he has narrated in books written long before; it is to be noted that such discrepancies are the very things a forger would be most careful to avoid. His aim would be to imitate the style and manner of thought of his author as closely as possible, and as he would have before him what that author had written, he would be careful to conform all his own statements to what he found set forth by him. If discrepancies, then, are found to exist between Deuteronomy and the other Mosaic writings, this would rather be in favour of the genuineness of the former than otherwise.

As respects style and method and manner of thought, such variations as may be detected in this book from the earlier books are sufficiently accounted for by the fact that, whilst the latter are purely narrative or didactic, this is hortatory and admonitory. The style and manner of a legislative code, or even of simple narration, must needs be departed from in a popular address, unless the speaker means to exhaust the patience of his audience and thereby frustrate his own effort.

"A good example of the fundamental difference in legal style between the Levitical Law and the Deuteronomic code is found in Numb. xxxv. compared with ch. xix." (Robertson Smith, p. 433). That differences of expression and phraseology are to be found in these two passages is manifest at a glance; but that they are "fundamental," or such as would disprove identity of authorship in the two writings, may be denied. For these differences are only such as may be found in the writings of any author who has occasion to repeat in substance what he had put forth more at large in an earlier writing. In Numbers the cities are called throughout "cities of refuge," in Deuteronomy they are described as cities to which the homicide may flee (for refuge, of course); in Numbers the man for whom a place of refuge was to be provided is described as one who had slain another "at unawares" (*bishgaga*, through error or mistake), in Deuteronomy he is described as one who killeth his neighbour "ignorantly" (*bibhli da'ath*, without knowledge, unintentionally), but also as one who had done it "unawares" (ch. iv. 42); in Numbers it is "any person" who is supposed to be killed, in Deuteronomy it is "his neighbour" whom the homicide is said to slay; in Numbers the murderer is described as one who "thrust him [his victim] of hatred" (*b'sin'ah*), in Deuteronomy it is said "if any man hate" (*sonay*)—in the one place the noun is used, in the other the cognate verb. Such differences surely cannot be regarded as "fundamental." Of more weight, apparently, is the difference in the description of what constitutes murder as distinguished from simple homicide, given in the two books respectively; the one book giving a detailed description, while the other furnishes only one exemplary illustration from actual experience of what is intended. But this is only such a difference as might be expected between a legal document and a popular address in reference to the same subject. Another difference alleged is that "the judges in the one are 'the congregation,' in the other 'the elders of the city.'" But there is a mistake here. In Deuteronomy nothing is said about "judges;" the function assigned to the elders is executive, not judicial; they are to apprehend the criminal and bring him to suffer the penalty to which he had been adjudged. "In addition," it is said, "there is a substantial difference in the laws themselves, inasmuch as Deuteronomy says nothing about remaining in the city of refuge till the death of the high priest." Had Deuteronomy said that the refugee was to remain till his own death in the city of refuge, or till the death of some other person than the high priest, there would have been a substantial difference between the two laws; as it is, Deuteronomy only omits what it was not needful for the speaker to state. When it is remembered that these differences are alleged as "fundamental," it will be seen of how little moment are the other differences in style and phraseology which may be adduced between Deuteronomy and the other Pentateuchal books.

Of the material discrepancies alleged, the following are the most important:—

Ch. i. 22, etc. Here the sending of the spies is said to have been at the suggestion of the people, whereas in Numb. xiii. 1, 3 it is by command from God that the spies are said to be sent. There is, however, no real discrepancy here; the passage in Deuteronomy simply contains an addition to the narrative in Numbers. The proposal originated with the people, but it was not until authorized by God that Moses carried it into effect. For the rest, the two narratives are in full accordance.

Ch. i. 37; iii. 26; iv. 21. In these passages Moses appears as casting the blame of his exclusion from the promised land on the people, whereas in Numb. xx. 12 it is in consequence of his own defective faith, and in Numb. xxvii. 14 as a punishment for his rebelliousness, that this is said to have come upon him. But that there is no discrepancy here is rendered certain by the fact that in ch. xxxii. 51 the same cause is assigned for his exclusion as in Numbers. The two statements are easily reconciled. The immediate reason of the exclusion was Moses' own sin; the ultimate reason was the rebelliousness of the people, which gave occasion to that sin (cf. note on ch. i. 37).

In Deuteronomy it is prescribed that sacrifices shall be offered only in *one* place, whereas the other books say nothing of this, and in one passage express mention is made of many places of worship (Exod. xx. 24). But (1) it is not true that no mention is made of this in the other books, for in Lev. xvii. 8, 9 the law regarding the offering of sacrifice only in the one place, viz. at the door of the tent of meeting, is announced even under more stringent conditions than in Deuteronomy; and (2) the declaration in Exod. xx. 24 was uttered shortly after the giving of the Law on Sinai, when the people had the prospect of moving from place to place, and of the sanctuary moving with them, and was intended to assure them that wherever that sanctuary was pitched there worship might be acceptably offered.

When Numb. xviii. 20—32 is compared with ch. xiv. 22—29, it is alleged that "it cannot escape any one who makes the comparison without prejudice, that the two laws differ from each other in respect both of content and character." In Numbers it is prescribed that the Levites shall not have any fixed possession among the sons of Israel, but shall receive, for the service in the sanctuary binding on them, all the tithes which properly belong to Jehovah, and from these they shall again pay a tenth part to Aaron the priest. In Deuteronomy, on the contrary, the Israelites are enjoined to bring before the sanctuary the tithe of all the produce of their fields and their cattle, either in kind or in money, and there, in honour of Jehovah, to eat it with their families in joy and festivity; only along with this it is enjoined that they are not to forsake the Levite who has no possession of his own, but each third year they must retain all the tithes of their income and bestow them as a beneficence on the Levite, the stranger, the widow, and the orphan in their gates. These two laws, it is alleged, differ so both in content and in character that it cannot be supposed that

Moses could have enacted both; and as the enactment in Numbers is undoubtedly the original, that in Deuteronomy must belong to a later age (Bleek). That these two laws differ from each other is indisputable, and the difference is such that, supposing them to relate to the same object, there is no possibility of harmonizing them; the one must exclude the other. But it is conceivable that Moses, after enacting the general law of tithes as a provision for the Levites, should, in the prospect of the people settling in a rich and fertile land where the produce of their possessions would be great, prescribe the giving of an additional tithe, to be devoted to sacred festivity and for the benefit of the poor and needy, in which benefit the Levite was to share. That such an additional tithe was actually made and rendered by the Israelites in Palestine, appears certain from the testimony of the Talmudists and Josephus; by the former of whom the מַעֲשֵׂר שֵׁנִי, or second tithe, is distinguished from the מַעֲשֵׂר רִאשׁוֹן, the first tithe—that for the Levites; and the latter of whom expressly says that, besides the two tithes which were to be levied yearly, one for the Levites and another for feasting, there was to be every third year a third tithe for distribution to the poor and needy ('Antiq.,' iv. 8, 22). In the Book of Tobit the second tithe (δεκάτη δεύτερα) is mentioned (i. 7), and the LXX. refer to the δεύτερον ἐπιδέκατον (ch. xxvi. 11). There seems no doubt, then, as to the existence of a second tithe among the Jews. What is called the "third tithe" (Josephus, l. c.; Tobit i. 8), was only "this second tithe converted into the poor tithe, to be given to and consumed by the poor at home" (Ginsburg, 'Kitto's Cyclopædia,' iii. 1012). This being the case, we are justified in regarding the law in Deuteronomy as not exclusive of that in Numbers, but rather as supplementary to it, as an additional prescription for the benefit of the Levites, who as a tribe were without possessions in the land, as well as the poor and destitute. As both laws were apparently in operation at a late period, the one obviously does not abrogate or exclude the other, and therefore there is no reason why both should not have been appointed by Moses.

Ch. xii. 17, 18. Here the people are enjoined to eat the firstlings of their herds before the Lord, in the place which he shall choose. But in Numb. xviii. 15—18 the flesh of the firstlings is said to belong to the priest: "The flesh of them shall be thine, as the wave breast and as the right shoulder are thine." How, then, it is asked, could the people eat the firstlings if they were to be given to the priest? There is here, it must be allowed, an apparent contradiction. It is, however, only apparent. The qualifying clause, "as the wave breast and as the right shoulder are thine," indicates that it was not the whole animal that was to be given to the priest; the distribution was to be according to the norm established in the case of the *shelamim*, or peace offerings (Lev. vii. 28, etc.), that is, after the fat had been burnt on the altar, the wave breast and the right shoulder were to be the portions of the priest. The rest of the animal, therefore, remained with the offerer, and might be eaten by him. There is thus between the two laws no real contradiction (see note in Exposition). "It is not said in Numbers that all the flesh of the firstlings belongs to the priests, nor in Deuteronomy that the people are to eat all of it" (Curtiss).

According to Exod. xxix. 27, 28, and Lev. vii. 28—34, the breast and the right shoulder of all thank offerings belonged to the priest; according to ch. xviii. 3, he was to receive the fore leg, the two cheeks, and the maw. This latter ordinance is said to be an alteration of the earlier law, which cannot be supposed to have proceeded from Moses. But what is prescribed in Deuteronomy as the priest's due is not said there to be *all* that he shall receive; it appears rather as an addition to what the earlier law assigned to him. This is "evident from the context, since the heave leg and the wave breast belonged to the firings of Jehovah mentioned in ver. 1, which the priests had received as an inheritance from the Lord; that is to say, to the *tenuphoth* of the children of Israel, which the priests might eat with their sons and daughters, though only with such members of their house as were Levitically clean (Numb. xviii. 11); and also from the words of the present command, viz. that the portions mentioned were to be a right of the priests on *the part of the people,* on the part of those who slaughtered slain offerings, *i.e.* to be paid to the priest as a right that was due to him on the part of the people" (Keil). Whether it was from animals offered in sacrifice alone that this portion was to be given to the priests, or whether the right of the priests extended also to animals slain for domestic use, has been made a matter of question. But this is immaterial as regards the relation of the law in Deuteronomy to the law in Exodus and Leviticus; for in either case the portions assigned to the priests were a gift from the people, distinct from and in addition to what the priest claimed as part of his inheritance from the Lord.

"In the other books the Levites appear always as servants of the sanctuary, in sharp distinction from the priests the sons of Aaron. In Deuteronomy the Levites appear as sustaining priestly functions, and the priests are called 'sons of Levi' or 'the priests the Levites,' as elsewhere only in the later books" (Bleek). That the priests should be described as "the sons of Aaron" is only what might be expected, inasmuch as the priesthood was restricted to the Aaronic family; and that they should be called " sons of Levi" and "Levites" is equally natural, seeing all the priests were descended from Levi, and belonged to that tribe. The only thing to be accounted for is that in the earlier books they should be described as "sons of Aaron" and never be called "Levites" or described as "sons of Levi," and that in Deuteronomy they should never be described as "sons of Aaron" but always as "Levites" or "sons of Levi." Is this a mere difference of phraseology, or does it imply such a difference in the actual constitution of the priestly order as to necessitate the conclusion that the Book of Deuteronomy belongs to a later age than that of Moses? In regard to this it may be observed: (1) The mere fact that an author uses expressions, names, or titles which are found elsewhere only in books of later date, affords no proof that his book itself is of later date than that traditionally assigned to it, because the expressions, names, or titles may have originated with him or come into use in his time. (2) The mere fact that certain phrases or names used by an author are not found in books confessedly written by him but older than the date assigned to this particular book, affords no proof that his book was written at a much later date, because the new words, names, or phrases may have come into use during his lifetime, but after his earlier writings were issued. (3) As a considerable time elapsed between the writing of Exodus and Leviticus and the writing of Deuteronomy, phraseology which was fitting at the earlier period may have become less fitting at the later, and consequently Moses may have felt it necessary to depart in his latest writing from phraseology which he used freely in his earlier writings. (4) The appointment of Aaron and his sons to the priesthood preceded the consecration of the tribe of Levi to the service of the sanctuary, and was an appointment wholly independent of that tribe. The priesthood was at first that of a family, not that of a tribe; it was purely Aaronic, not in any proper sense Levitical. At first, then, it was only as "sons of Aaron" that the priests could be designated; but after the consecration of the tribe to which that family belonged, such designations as "sons of Levi," "the priests the Levites," became fitting designations of the priests. The phrase "sons of Aaron" was thus the earlier, the phrase "sons of Levi" the later, formula of designation. It is not improbable that gradually the earlier designation fell into desuetude, and the later came to be that alone in use; and in this case Moses, writing near the end of his life, would naturally use the designation which by that time had come to be the proper designation of the priests.

As respects the discharge of priestly functions by the Levites, it may be observed: (1) In the general that, as the tribe of Levi included the priestly order, what was done by the priests may be popularly described as done by Levites; just as one might say that a certain act was the act of the Church, though properly it was the act of only certain officials in the Church. On this principle we may account for its being stated that the tribe of Levi was separated by Jehovah to bless in his Name (ch. x. 8), though this was the special function of the priests; just as in ch. x. 8 and xxxi. 25 it is said that it was the duty of the tribe of Levi to bear the ark of the covenant, whereas this belonged specially to the Kohathites, a family in that tribe. (2) As in a graduated hierarchy the higher office includes the lower, so the duties properly belonging to the lower functionary may, on occasions of special solemnity, be undertaken by the higher. Thus we may account for the priests on special occasions bearing the ark, which ordinarily it was the part of the Kohathites to do (cf. ch. xxxi. 9). (3) When those who are set apart as ministers to a superior functionary are called actually to assist him in his service, they may without offence partake of the privileges which belong properly to the superior. On this ground we may account for the statement in ch. xviii. 1, 8, that the Levite who might of his own choice attend upon the service of the sanctuary should have the privilege of partaking with the priest of the sacrifices offered there, though this, according to the Law, was the privilege of the priest only (cf. Lev. vi. 18, 29 ; vii. 6). As the Law allotted these to the priest, but did not prohibit the giving of a portion of them to the attendant Levite, the prescription that the Levite was to have a share with the priest is not a repeal of the older enactment, but only an addition to it.

"According to Numb. xxxv. 1—8, the Levites were to have cities assigned to them as their own, in all forty-eight, with fields attached for their cattle, and these were by lot given to them by Joshua (Josh. xxi.). Of any such relations, of special cities of the Levites, nothing is found in Deuteronomy ; here the same appear, at least for the most part, as homeless, living scattered among the rest of the Israelites in the different towns ; this is presumed, and legal prescriptions refer to it (cf. ch. xii. 12, 18, etc. ; xiv. 27—29 ; xvi. 11, 14 ; xviii. 6 ; xxvi. 12)" (Bleek). In these passages the Levite is represented as living within the gates of the people, and this is assumed to mean that he was there as a stranger who, having no home of his own, had to be dependent on the hospitality of others for a residence. But this does not seem to be the meaning of the phrase. The Levites had, in accordance with the law in Numbers, fields and towns assigned to them ; but they were not the sole occupants of these ; they were only a portion, in most cases only a minor portion, of the inhabitants. The town thus properly was not Levitical ; it was a town of Israel, in which the Levites had residences, with fields appertaining. Hence the description, " the Levite within thy gates ; " not that the Levite was homeless, but that his home was within the precincts of one of the cities of Israel (Keil, ' Comment. on Joshua,' p. 211 ; Kitto, ' Cyclopædia,' ii. 826). Even if the town had been occupied wholly by the Levites, they might still have been said to dwell within the gates of the people, inasmuch as the towns allotted to them were not in a region of their own as a tribe, but were taken from the portions of the other tribes throughout the country. It is further assumed in this objection that Deuteronomy makes the only source of maintenance for the Levites to be the share in the sacrificial feasts of the tithes which it assigns to them ; whereas the right of the Levites to partake of the tithes received from the nation is distinctly recognized in Deuteronomy, as in the earlier law (cf. ch. x. 9 ; xiv. 22 ; xviii. 2 ; xxvi. 12).

2. It is alleged that there are statements in the book which could not have been made by Moses, but betray the hand of a writer of a much later age.

Ch. i. 1. The expression, " beyond the Jordan (בְּעֵבֶר הַיַּרְדֵּן)," here and in ver. 5, is, it is alleged, plainly the writing of one whose position was on the west of that river, and therefore must have been written after the death of Moses. It must strike one, however, that it is very improbable that any one writing in the person of Moses, and wishing to be taken for Moses, would make a mistake of this sort, and on the very threshold of his work betray himself so foolishly. There is, however, no mistake in the case.

The phrase, "beyond the Jordan," was the established and current designation of the country to the east of the Jordan where Moses then was; nor is there any reason to believe that this came into vogue only after the Israelites had occupied Canaan. Moses, therefore, dating his book from the place where it was written, indicates that place by its proper name, the name by which alone it was known. So also in referring to localities within Palestine, he describes them by the names given to them by the inhabitants of the country, and by which they were properly known. Thus as the common name for "westward" was in Hebrew "seaward," and the name for "southward" was "towards the Negeb" (the usual appellation of the arid district to the south of Palestine), Moses uses these terms even when writing where the sea was not to the west or the Negeb to the south of the place where he was. This, indeed, has been urged as an argument against the Mosaic authorship of the Pentateuch. But without reason; for when designations are once given to localities, they become proper names, and are used without respect to their original or etymological signification. It is simply absurd to ask, "Would Moses, writing at Sinai, have spoken of the Negeb as to the south of him when it was really to the north?" Moses says nothing of the sort. Writing in Hebrew, and for Hebrews, he uses the expression, "towards the Negeb," because that is the Hebrew for "southward." Suppose a person, writing in Edinburgh, to say of a certain event that it took place in Norfolk, or of a locality that it is in Sutherland; what would be thought of a critic who should argue that neither statement could have been written in Edinburgh, because in relation to that city Norfolk (North-folk) lies to the south, and Sutherland (Southern-land) lies to the north? Or, suppose Cæsar, when on the north of the Alps, to have dated one of his Commentaries from Transalpine Gaul, would any one have held this to prove that that book was spurious, and must have been written by some one south of the Alps?

Ch. ii. 12. The remark, "As Israel did unto the land of his possession, which the Lord gave unto them," presupposes a time when the Israelites were already in possession of Canaan, and had expelled the peoples formerly dwelling there—a time, therefore, posterior to that of Moses. Here it is assumed that the land referred to is Canaan, and on this assumption it appears certain that the passage could not have been written by Moses. But is it Canaan that is here referred to? In ch. iii. similar phraseology is used of the district east of the Jordan, already captured by the Israelites, and assigned to the two and a half tribes; in ver. 18 it is described as the land which the Lord their God had given them "to possess," and in ver. 20 as their "possession" which had been assigned to them by Moses. As these tribes were part of Israel, the land of their possession might well be called "the land of the possession of Israel;" and it is to this, doubtless, and not to Canaan, that Moses here refers. This is rendered certain by the fact that it is for the purpose of encouraging the people to go on to the conquest of Canaan, that the reference to what had already been achieved by them is made. A later writer would never have committed the gross absurdity of representing Moses as encouraging the people to undertake the conquest of Canaan, by telling them that they had already conquered that land and were in possession of it.

Ch. xix. 14 and xx, 5, 6. Here, it is alleged, certain relations which imply a later period are assumed as present. But this overlooks the ideal standpoint of the Deuteronomic legislation, which is that of faith in the Divine promise that Israel should certainly possess and dwell in the land of Canaan. Hence the speaker throughout speaks as if the people were already settled there, and legislates accordingly. In the passages cited he simply assumes that certain relations, which were sure to exist after the people were settled in the land, already existed.

Ch. xxiii. 12, 13. This is adduced as in itself a very convincing proof of the unhistorical character of the whole narrative, because it involves the absurdity of enacting what was obviously impracticable (Colenso). But this assumes that the enactment has reference to the conduct of the people whilst encamped in the wilderness, whereas the precept has reference to a camp such as soldiers might form should they at any time march out against their enemies. It is to the preservation of the purity of a military camp in the time of war that the injunction has respect, and not to anything connected with the domestic encampment of the people, either in the wilderness or elsewhere. It would have been absurd had Moses given such an instruction as this to the whole camp of the Israelites during their wanderings, especially had he reserved it till the very close of their wanderings, just when instructions of this sort became unnecessary.

In ch. xxxii. and xxxiii. are passages which have been alleged as against the genuineness of the book. As these apply specially to that part of the book, and do not directly affect the book as a whole, the consideration of them may be deferred till the question of the integrity of the book comes under notice. (See § 6.)

3. As against the antiquity of the book, it is alleged that certain things forbidden or denounced in the book were done by individuals in times subsequent to those of Moses; and this, it is alleged, would not have been had the book been in existence at the time in which these persons lived. Thus in ch. xvi. 22 it is enjoined, "Neither shalt thou set up a *maççeba ;* which the Lord thy God hateth." A *maççeba* was a pillar, usually of rough, unhewn stone, and when set up beside an altar was there for idolatrous purposes; and this is what is forbidden here. Notwithstanding this, *maççebas* it is alleged, continued to be set up for worship even by men of eminent piety among the Israelites; in proof of which the following passages are referred to:—Josh. xxiv. 26 ; 1 Sam. vi. 14 ; vii. 12 ; 2 Sam. xx. 8 ; 1 Kings i. 9 ; vii. 21 ; Hos. iii. 4. "This detail is one of the clearest proofs," it is said, "that Deuteronomy was unknown till long after the days of Moses. How could Joshua, if he had known such a law, have erected a *maççeba*, or sacred pillar of unhewn stone, under the sacred tree

by the sanctuary at Shechem?"[1] But what proof is there that it *was* a *maççeba* which Joshua erected? The record simply says it was "a great stone," and the same is the expression used in the majority of the other passages, in some without the epithet "great;" in none but the last does the term *maççeba* occur. By what right, then, is it assumed that these stones were of the kind forbidden in Deuteronomy? All *maççebas*, it may be supposed, were stones, but all monumental stones were not *maççebas*. The word used in 1 Kings vii. 21 is "pillar" (*'ámúd*), and this certainly was not a *maççeba;* what Solomon set up by Divine direction "in the porch of the temple" were pillars, monumental as well as ornamental, but not in any way connected with worship except as they stood at the entrance to the place of worship.[2] As for the Hosea passage, it has no bearing on the point at issue; in declaring that Israel should be without worship of any kind, sacred or idolatrous, it only declares implicitly what the history attests explicitly, that idolatrous usages had been in Israel, not that these were ever regarded as lawful, or were practised by those who professed to be worshippers of Jehovah.

But "this law," it is added, "was unknown to Isaiah, who attacks idolatry, but recognizes *maççeba* and altar as the marks of the sanctuary of Jehovah," and in proof of this Isa. xix. 19 is adduced, "In that day there shall be an altar to Jehovah within the land of Egypt, and a pillar (*maççeba*) at the border thereof to Jehovah." But this passage asserts something very different from what it is adduced to prove; it asserts that the pillar was erected, not at the sanctuary of Jehovah, but at the border of the land of Egypt. It is not, therefore, a *maççeba* of the kind condemned in Deuteronomy that is here referred to, but a stone set up as a landmark or terminal index. The reference, consequently, is irrelevant to the present discussion.

4. Much weight is attached to the fact that, not only during the unsettled times of the judges, when "there was no king in Israel, but every man did that which was right in his own eyes," but on to a later period, even to the time of David, the law of a central sanctuary at which alone sacrifice was to be offered was disregarded, and even pious men, like Samuel and David, scrupled not to offer sacrifice at any place where they might chance to be at the time; conduct which, it is maintained, argues on their part a total ignorance of any such law as that in ch. xii. 6, 11, and by consequence the non-existence of that law, or of the book in which it is recorded, in their day, seeing, had the book existed, they could not have been ignorant of what it prescribes. This has been put forth as conclusive against the pretensions of the book to be of a date as

---

[1] 'The Old Testament in the Jewish Church,' p. 354.

[2] The significance of the pillars appears from their names. "They were the monumental witnesses that the God of the covenant had now taken for ever his abode in this sanctuary in the midst of his people, and would manifest thence his might and majesty for their help" (Riehm, 'Handwörterb. des Bibl. Altertums,' s. 653).

early as the time of Moses. On examination, however, it will be found not
to be by any means so conclusive as has been pretended.

(1) It is to be observed that the mere fact of the non-observance of a law,
even by good men, does not necessarily involve the assumption that the law
was not then known or did not then exist. This is only a *conjecture*, which the
critic puts forth as accounting for the fact, and which can be accepted only
as it appears probable. But on what does the alleged probability of this
conjecture rest? Only on the counter-improbability of good men acting as
Samuel and others did had the law been then in existence. That is to say,
it is probable they did not know the law because it is not probable that,
had they known it, they would have neglected it. To one accustomed to
weigh historical evidence, this cannot but appear anything but conclusive.
Good men often do very unexpected things; and unless we know all the
circumstances, it is impossible to determine beforehand what they will do
or will not do in any particular case. Even when all the circumstances
are known, the chances of any given course being followed are not such
that a prudent man will risk much on the anticipation.

(2) So far as the circumstances are known to us, they suggest another and
different reason for the conduct of the pious men of Samuel's time in the
matter referred to than that adduced by the objector; they make it highly
probable that the law of the central sanctuary was neglected, not because
it was unknown, but because the means of observing it were wanting. The
central sanctuary was where God chose to put his Name, and where was his
habitation (ch. xii. 5, 21), and this was where the ark of the covenant was.
There it was that God had engaged to meet his people, and there it was
that his Name was put (Exod. xxv. 22; 2 Sam. vi. 2). Now, during the
whole of Samuel's time and part of that of David, the ark was in abeyance,
nor was there any sanctuary in which it was placed. After the destruction
of the sanctuary at Shiloh, the ark was for a season a captive in the land of
the Philistines, and when at length it was restored, it was only to find
temporary accommodation in private houses and unconsecrated courts, until
it was brought up by David to Jerusalem. During all this time, therefore,
there was no central sanctuary to which the worshipper could bring his
offering, and consequently no one place more legitimately appropriate for
this act of worship than another. The alternative before the men of that
time was thus, either to omit the offering of sacrifice altogether or to offer
it at such places as were most convenient and suitable for such a service.
They chose the latter; and in so doing they obeyed the earlier and more
general law (Exod. xx. 24), while they neglected the later and more
special one—not because they were ignorant of the latter, but because they
had not the means of obeying it (comp. 1 Kings iii. 2).

(3) It is to be noted that the law in Deuteronomy appointing the one
place for sacrificial worship is not absolute and unconditioned. It is
expressly qualified by the condition of the Lord's giving them rest from all
their enemies round about (ch. xii. 10). Until this was done, then, the law

was in abeyance; so that, if circumstances required, other methods than that which it prescribed of observing the primary and absolutely imperative ordinance of sacrifice might be followed. We find, accordingly, that it was only as it was considered that the Lord had given them rest from their enemies that it was deemed fitting to fix upon a certain place to which the people might repair as to the dwelling-place of Jehovah, to present their worship and offerings. Thus, after the occupation of the land by the Israelites, it was not until the land was subdued before them, and the Lord had given them rest round about, that the congregation of the children of Israel assembled at Shiloh, and set up the tent of meeting there (Josh. xviii. 1; xxi. 44; xxii. 4). The rest, however, which was then given to them was not destined to be permanent. Times of unsettlement ensued, and at length the sanctuary at Shiloh was everted and the ark of the covenant carried away by hostile invaders; nor was it till the time of David that it could be said definitively that the Lord had given rest to his people from all their enemies, as he had promised. Then at length the occasion had arrived when a house might be built for the Lord to dwell in; and David, recognizing this, determined, seeing "the Lord had given him rest round about from all his enemies," to build a house unto the Name of the Lord; and though he was not permitted to carry this into effect, because of the wars in which he had been engaged in the earlier part of his reign, his purpose was approved of by God (2 Sam. vii. 1; 1 Kings viii. 18). The fact that in the usages of the nation there was this connecting of a time of rest from all enemies with the setting up of a fixed place for the sanctuary, is surely a strong indication that the law of Deuteronomy was all along known and respected by them; and, at the same time, we may see from this how it was that, pending the arrival of the promised rest, good men were found offering worship and sacrifices elsewhere than at a central sanctuary.

(4) That the law of Deuteronomy respecting the offering of sacrifice only at the place which the Lord should appoint was known and reverenced from the earliest times, is placed beyond doubt, not only by the constant references, in the early historical books, to the "house of the Lord" as the place where worship and sacrifice were to be offered, but especially by what is recorded in Josh. xxii. The indignation of the people against their brethren who had erected an altar on the border of Jordan before they crossed it to return to their own possession on the eastern side of that river; the earnestness with which the latter hastened to assure the people that they had erected the altar, not to establish an independent worship, but rather that it might stand as a permanent witness that they still adhered to and claimed to have part in Jehovah as their God; and the solemnity with which they disclaimed any intention to rebel against the Lord by building an altar for burnt offerings, for meat offerings, or for sacrifices besides the altar of the Lord that was before the tabernacle;—all incontestably show that this law was known and recognized as imperative at the time of the

settling of the people in the promised land. It was this law which they who had built the altar so earnestly disclaimed having broken; it was zeal for this law which stirred the other tribes to such wrath against their brethren when they supposed it had been violated by them.

5. Great stress has also been laid on the fact that non-priestly men, like Samuel, David, and Solomon, offered sacrifices, contrary to the express law which enacts that this shall be done only by the priest. This law appears only in the middle books of the Pentateuch (Lev. i. 9, etc.; v. 8, etc.); but it is assumed in Deuteronomy as existing, and the objection may therefore be considered here. In regard to it, it might be observed that, though the law constitutes the priest as the proper presenter of the sacrifice, it does not enact that no other but a priest shall at any time or under any circumstances present sacrifice. It was according to order that the priest should present the sacrifice; but order is not so imperatively binding that it may never under any circumstances be departed from. If laymen, then, on special occasions, assumed to themselves this priestly function, this does not prove that the law was unknown to them and did not exist in their day; it only shows that on such occasions the law might be suspended and neglected without offence. Especially was this allowable when, by a special mani-festation, God came to his servants, and so virtually consecrated the place where he appeared and authorized his servants, though not priests, to offer sacrifice and worship him; as in the case of the people at Bochim (Judg. ii. 1—5), of Gideon (Judg. vi. 20—22, 25), and Manoah (Judg. xiii. 16—23). In other cases it may be asked—Did these non-priestly men really themselves make sacrifices? It is said, "They sacrificed to the Lord," or "They offered sacrifices;" but does this mean that with their own hands they slew the victims and offered the blood upon the altar? Are not such statements to be understood according to the old juridical brocard, "Qui facit per alium facit per se"—as simply intimating that the persons named presented sacri-fice in the legal way by means of the priest? In the case of Solomon this *must* be the interpretation put upon the phrase; for as that monarch, at the dedication of the temple, "offered unto the Lord two and twenty thousand oxen, and a hundred and twenty thousand sheep" (1 Kings viii. 63), it would be monstrous to suppose that he killed all these animals himself and presented them with his own hand on the altar. Besides, be it observed that there was an offering and an offering; the man who brought the sacrificial victims offered, and the priest who presented to the Lord offered. This is evident from the very terms of the law in question (cf. Lev. i. 3, etc.; ii. 1; vi. 1, 4; ch. xii. 14 xviii.; 3, 4, etc.). We interpret fairly, then, when we understand the assertion that Samuel, David, and others offered sacrifice, as meaning nothing more than that they brought the victims which were offered in sacrifice according to the law.

From this survey it appears that there is nothing in the contents of this book or in the conduct of notable individuals in relation to its enactments that effectually militates against the conclusion, so strongly vouched for by the general character of the book as well as by particular statements in it, as to its being the writing of Moses.

§ 5. RELATION TO JEREMIAH.

It must strike every one who compares Deuteronomy with the writings ascribed to the prophet Jeremiah that the author of the one book must have been very familiar with the other. The resemblances between the two are numerous and marked. Words are used in both which are found nowhere else; passages in the one are identical with, or closely similar to, passages in the other; sentiments prominent in the one are prominent also in the other; and, in general tone and form of thought, the two remarkably resemble each other.

To account for these points of resemblance, it seems sufficient to suppose that the prophet, from much familiarity with the Book of Deuteronomy, had so transported into his own mind its phraseology and sentiments that these naturally flowed from his pen when he himself began to write. That Jeremiah would be well acquainted with Deuteronomy can be readily believed. As a priest, the study of the Law in all its parts must have been his occupation from his youth upward; and called as he was to act as a reprover and admonisher of the people in dark and disastrous times, Deuteronomy would be the part of the Pentateuch to which he would most frequently turn, both that he might feed his own mind with thoughts appropriate to his position, and that he might have suggested to him what it would be fitting to address to the people. In his time also the Book of the Law was discovered and drawn from its obscurity into prominent notice, and a fresh impulse given to the study of it both among the rulers and teachers of the nation and through the community at large. That book was probably the entire Pentateuch, possibly the original copy placed in charge of the priests by Moses, and which had been allowed for many years to fall out of sight; but the part which seems to have excited most interest and been most attended to was undoubtedly Deuteronomy (cf. 2 Kings xxii. 13, 16, 17 and xxii. 2—25 with ch. xxviii. and xxix.; xii. 2, 3; and xvi., xviii.). This book, therefore, must have been constantly before the mind of Jeremiah during his ministry in Judæa, and if so, it is no wonder that its words and phrases and sentiments should be found so frequently recurring in his writings.

To some it has appeared that more than this is to be inferred from the resemblances which the writings of Jeremiah bear to Deuteronomy; and they have advanced the opinion that this book itself is from the pen of the prophet of Anathoth. For this opinion, however, the support is of the slightest. A number of words common to both writings, a similarity of phraseology, an occasional identity of sentiment and mode of thought, can never be held to furnish adequate proof of an identity of authorship, for it is always open to the inquirer to account for these coincidences by a presumed acquaintance on the part of the later writer with the writings of the earlier. It would be otherwise were there a large number of words, phrases, and sentiments *peculiar* to both writings, *i.e.* found in both of them but nowhere else. This, however, is not the case with the writings of Jeremiah and Deuteronomy. On the contrary, a large number of words peculiar to the one are not found in the other, and in respect of sentiment also considerable diversity prevails. The discord between the two is thus greater than the agreement; so that if the question of authorship is to be determined by such considerations—and by these alone is it proposed to determine it—the only conclusion to which we can come is that the Book of Deuteronomy and the writings of Jeremiah are not from the same author nor are even of contemporary authorship.[1]

Before passing from this part of the subject, it is necessary to advert to the reproach which is cast upon the prophet by the supposition that he was the author of the Book of Deuteronomy. Whether he wrote this book of his own accord, or, as has been suggested, conspired with his relative Hilkiah to produce it and give it forth as the Book of the Law found in the temple, the prophet must be regarded as having deliberately lent himself to false-hood, to practise an imposition in the name of God upon the people. Can this be believed of one like Jeremiah, or indeed of any one who was a true prophet of Jehovah? It has indeed been said that, in that early age, " when notions of literary property were yet in their infancy, an action of this kind was not regarded as unlawful. Men used to perpetrate such fictions as these without any qualms of conscience." [2] This may be true of the later times of ancient literature, when the making of books had become a source of livelihood, and was practised by many who, not having power enough to write what would command attention of itself, used to send forth their productions under the veil of some great and venerable name; but of the early age of literature it is not true, nor was the practice at any time regarded as laudable,[3] and least of all is it true in respect of the sacred literature of the Hebrews. There is not the shadow of evidence that such practices were known among the Hebrews of the time of Jeremiah or any earlier time, and one can hardly conceive the possibility of such a thing being tolerated among them. Be this, however, as it may, the fact remains that if Jeremiah wrote this book and issued it as a writing of

---

[1] For the details bearing on this question, see König, 'Alt-test. Studien,' 2 Heft.; 'The Mosaic Origin of the Pentateuch, considered by a Layman of the Church of England,' pp. 179—189; 'Speaker's Commentary,' vol. i. pt. ii. p. 795.

[2] Kuenen, 'Religion of Israel,' ii. 18, 19.

[3] Galen, a very competent witness, says that it was not till the age of the Ptolemies, when kings were rivalling each other in the collecting of libraries, that the roguery (ῥαδιουργία) of forging writings and titles began; and this was done by those who hoped thereby to obtain money by presenting to the kings books pretending to be written by illustrious men (Galen, 'Comment. ii. in Hip. de Nat. Hom.'). It is plain from this that even when this practice was most common it was not regarded as lawful; but, on the contrary, was even among heathens denounced as a "roguery."

Moses, he was guilty of a forgery and a falsehood ; and thus not only is a shadow cast over his character as a man, but his reputation as a prophet is damaged. For if he could publish as from Moses what was not from Moses but from himself, what security is there that what he utters as a message from the Lord is not merely some invention of his own? To those who look upon the ancient Hebrew prophets as mere *litterateurs*, who exercised their craft as they best could, according to the measure of their own powers, this may seem a very small matter; but those who believe that the prophet of old was one chosen by God to be the medium of communication between God and man, one who was moved by the Holy Ghost to speak what he uttered, and who was bound under the most solemn sanctions to speak God's word faithfully to the people, will not so regard it. To them it will appear nothing less than an impeaching of the claims of one of the greatest of the prophets to be an ambassador from God and interpreter of his mind to men, and by consequence a detracting from the authorship of his writings as Divine, and not of his only, but by implication of all the prophetic Scriptures.

§ 6. INTEGRITY OF THE BOOK.

Whilst accepting the book as, on the whole, the writing of Moses, it may yet be fairly inquired whether every part of it as we now have it proceeded from his pen, or whether there may not be portions of it which are additions to the original writing, or interpolations introduced by some later writer. That there are such has been confidently affirmed.

The parts which have been thus stigmatized are chiefly these: the title and introduction (ch. i. 1—5; the ethnological notices (ch. ii. 10—12, 20—23); the account of the cities of refuge on the east of Jordan (ch. iv. 41—43); Moses' song (ch. xxxii. 1—43); the blessing of the tribes (ch. xxxiii. 1—29); the account of Moses' last journey, death, and burial (ch. xxxiv. 1—12).

Regarding the first of these, it may suffice to say that, though it is quite possible that the title and introduction may have been prefixed to the original work by a later hand, there is nothing to show that this is really the case; and whilst, on the one hand, there is no reason why this may not have been written by the author of the work himself, it is, on the other, probable that it was placed there by him, since without it his work commences so abruptly that it is inconceivable that any skilled writer should have allowed it to go forth in such condition.

The passages containing the ethnographical notices have, it must be confessed, very much the appearance of being interpolations, and may possibly be glosses that have been introduced by some editor of the work into the text. At the same time, it is not incredible that Moses may have inserted, parenthetically, the notices which these passages contain. The mention of the Moabites, to whom God had given a possession by expelling from the land its former occupants, not unnaturally leads to a description of the nations so expelled; and this it was of use for Moses to give, because it showed the Israelites that the right of the children of Lot to the undisturbed occupancy of their territory rested on the same grounds as rested the right of the Israelites to the lands they had taken from the Amorites, and as would rest their right to the occupancy of the land the Lord was about to give them in Canaan; and further, because it showed that, if the children of Lot could cast out nations so mighty and powerful as the Emim, and the children of Esau could dispossess the Horim, there was no reason to dread that Israel would be baffled in grappling with the Anakim, who then possessed Canaan and were of the same race as the Emim. There was thus a practical end to be gained by the insertion of such notices, if done by Moses; whereas if done by a later editor they would possess only a slight antiquarian interest, hardly sufficient to induce any one to take the trouble of writing them, certainly not sufficient to induce any judicious editor to incorporate them with the text. The presumption, therefore, is in favour of their having been inserted by Moses himself. A modern writer would have thrown them into a note; but as this method had not come into use in ancient times, it was only by way of parenthesis that Moses could introduce them. Whichever hypothesis be adopted, whether these passages be regarded as written by Moses or whether they be pronounced to be the insertions of a later writer, as they are manifestly excrescences, their excision would not in any way affect the integrity of the book.

The passage, ch. iv. 41—43, has been supposed to be an interpolation on the ground that it has no relevance either to what goes before or to what follows. But were this the case, why should the passage have been inserted at all? It could not drop into this place by accident; and he must be a bungling editor indeed who should gratuitously insert in the body of another man's work a passage which has no relation to the context in the midst of which it is thrust. If, however, Moses himself inserted this passage, we may see at once why he did so. He had just finished his first address, and was about to enter upon his second. An interval between the two thus ensued, and during this Moses, in obedience to the Divine injunction (Numb. xxxv. 6, 14), set apart cities of refuge in the district to the east of Jordan, recently conquered by the Israelites. Not improbably (as has been suggested) he chose this time for doing this, " not only to give the land on that side its full consecration and thoroughly confirm the possession of the two Amoritish kingdoms on the other side of the Jordan, but also to give the people, in this punctual observance of the duty devolving upon it, an example for their imitation in the conscientious observance of the commandments of the Lord, which he was now about to lay before the nation " (Keil). The passage is, therefore, not only in its proper place as part of the historical narrative, but it has a close, intimate relevancy to the main theme of Moses' admonitions in his addresses to the people.

The song or ode contained in ch. xxxii., though expressly declared to have been composed by Moses, uttered by him in the hearing of the people, and written by him to be preserved in Israel as a witness against them should they apostatize from Jehovah, has been adjudged by many critics to be the production of some unknown writer of a much later age. This judgment is grounded partly on the language and style of the ode, partly on certain statements in it which it is alleged contain allusions to events and circumstances in the later history of Israel.

1. It is alleged that the style and tone of this composition are so different from the style and tone of the preceding part of this book, that it cannot be regarded as proceeding from the same author. This, however, is really saying nothing more than that this is a poem, whereas the preceding part of the book is in prose. For in a poem the style of language and tone of thought are necessarily different from what characterizes prose compositions; to the poet belong "thoughts that breathe and words that burn," and he is no poet whose thoughts and words are not of this sort. When, therefore, an author passes from simple narrative or expository and hortatory discourse, to give utterance to feeling and sentiment in song, he of necessity adopts a style and mode of thought more or less differing from those of his other compositions, else his utterance ceases to be poetry. Now, this ode is poetry of a very high order; and to this its peculiarity of expression and sentiment is due, not to its being the production of another than the author of the other parts of this book.

It is further to be observed that, whilst this ode differs in diction and cast of sentiment from the preceding parts of this book, as poetry differs from prose, there is nothing in it alien from or contradictory of the sentiments and utterances of Moses in his addresses to the people, reported in the preceding parts of this book. On the contrary, there are not a few coincidences both in thought and expression which may well be regarded as *pro tanto* proofs of an identity of authorship in this and the other parts of this book (see Keil, 'Biblical Commentary,' vol. iii. p. 466).

Worthy of notice also are the coincidences between this ode and Ps. xc., a composition admittedly of great antiquity, and which is with much probability attributed to Moses as its author (see Ewald, 'Die Dichter des Alt. Bundes,' Bd. i. Th. ii. s. 31; Hengstenberg, 'Die Psalmen,' Bd. iii. s. 529; Bleek, 'Einleit in. d. A. T.,' s. 615, English translation, ii. p. 234). Both in mode of expression and in cast of sentiment the two odes resemble each other (comp. ch. xxxii. 7, 18, 4, 36, with Ps. xc. 1, 15, 13, 16), and thus favour the supposition that both have proceeded from one author.

2. It is urged that this song is so constructed that the Divine guidance of Israel (ver. 12, etc.) and their ingratitude (ver. 15, etc.) are referred to as things already past. But this ignores the *prophetic* character of the song, and mistakes the style of prophetic utterance. Moses was a prophet; and the prophets, or seers, not only looked to the future, but beheld it as present; and the energy of their perception of it stamped itself on their words so that they very frequently represent as actually before them or as already done what in reality was yet future. So familiar is this usage that gram-

marians have recognized "the prophetic perfect" as an idiom of the Hebrew. Nor is it in prophecy alone that this presentation of the future as actual is to be found; the poet also claims liberty to do the same, and exercises it freely. Even if Moses, then, be regarded as only an uninspired poet, the use of the preterite in the passages referred to may be accounted for without supposing that the song is the production of a later writer.

3. The occurrence of Aramaic words and forms in the song has been alleged as an evidence of its late composition. That a few such are to be found may be admitted, though there are fewer than has sometimes been insinuated; but be their number what it may, their presence proves nothing as to the lateness of composition, or it proves too much; for as the presence of Aramaisms in a book is a sign of either very early or very late composition (cf. König, 'Alt-test. Studien,' ii. 8), if the early date of this song be denied, these Aramaisms would go to show that it must have been written in the latest age of ancient Hebrew literature. This, however, no one will accept; the latest date supposed for it by any of those who refuse to regard it as Mosaic is the age immediately succeeding the revolt of Jeroboam. These Aramaisms, then, so far as they have any weight, point to an early age for the composition of this song; and so fall in with the supposition that it was written by Moses.

4. The song, it is alleged, contains allusions to a state of things which did not arise till the time of the kings after the revolt of Jeroboam; it dwells upon the falling away of Israel from allegiance to Jehovah, upon the evils of this, and upon the hope of a restoration to forfeited privileges when the Lord should remember his covenant with Israel and be "merciful to his land and to his people;" and such it is supposed could be the theme of a poet only after he had witnessed a state of religious degeneracy and political disorder such as emerged in Israel after the revolt of the ten tribes. It is to be observed, however, that the language of the song is in this respect quite general; there is no part of the description which indicates a reference to the condition of the people at any special time during the decline of the Israelitish kingdom; nor is the apostacy of the people, with its melancholy results, more pointedly alluded to here than it is in other parts of Deuteronomy, as for instance in ch. xxviii. The truth is, that the possibility of this and the dread of it pressed continually on the mind of Moses at this time, and breaks forth throughout his farewell addresses; and if here his language becomes more animated and his delineation more vivid, it is only because there is here the impassioned utterance of the poet, whilst in his addresses he restrains himself within limits befitting hortatory address.

But even supposing it could be shown that in this ode there are references to things which actually occurred in the history of the nation at a later period, it would not follow that the song could not have been written by Moses. For we must not ignore the prophetic character of the song. Moses was a prophet—a prophet of the highest order, the very type and paradigm of a prophet (ch. xviii. 18), and he here speaks as one on whom the prophetic afflatus had fallen, and whose mental eye had been opened so that he saw in vision scenes and events yet future as if they were actually present. The standpoint, therefore, of the poet is not his own time, but a time into which he is transported; and the people to whom he speaks are not his own contemporaries, but those whom he sees in vision—Israel in the after-time. This is characteristic of all prophetic utterances; the prophet speaks of what is yet future as if the whole were before his eyes at the time. The assertion, therefore, "that the entire ode moves within the epoch of the kings who lived many centuries after the time of Moses, rests upon a total misapprehension of the nature of prophecy, and a mistaken attempt to turn figurative language into prosaic history" (Keil).

It may, indeed, be affirmed that such a thing as a presentation to the inner sense of the prophet of things yet future is an impossibility; but this is a mere dogmatic assumption, which not only cannot be proved, but which is made in the face of facts that are incontestable. Now, if it was possible for Moses under the hand of the Lord to see the future, to have a vision of the nation falling away from the Lord and suffering under calamities which their apostacy had brought upon them, what more natural, what more fitting than that, ere he finally retired from the post he had so long occupied as their leader, teacher, and ruler, he should sound in their ears a loud note of warning such as this ode contains, and should leave the ode with them as a perpetual protest against their unfaithfulness, and an enduring witness for God amongst them?

The genuineness of ch. xxxiii., containing the blessing of the tribes, has been called in question on very much the same grounds as those on which the song of Moses, in the preceding chapter, has been assailed. It is needless to repeat what has been already advanced in reply to the arguments founded on peculiarity of style, diction, and general literary character in this composition as compared with the prosaic parts of this book. But this chapter has more the appearance of a mere appendix to the book than the song has; it is not said to have been written by Moses, as the song is said to have been written by him; and it appears with a heading which must be ascribed to the pen of another than Moses, for, by describing Moses as "the man of God," the author of this heading clearly distinguishes himself from Moses, and applies to him a phrase by which, apparently, it was customary at a later period to designate him (comp. Josh. xiv. 6; Ps. xc. 1). This makes it necessary that we should see whether in the contents of this poem there is, as alleged by many modern critics, anything incompatible with the supposition that it was composed and uttered by Moses.

1. The allusions to the localities of some of the tribes in Canaan indicate, it is said, an acquaintance with a state of things which did not exist till after the division of the land by Joshua, and a knowledge of the country such as Moses could not have possessed. Thus it is said of Zebulun, "They shall suck of the abundance of the seas, and of treasures hid in the sand" (ver. 19); of Naphtali, that they should "possess the west and the south"

(ver. 23); and of Asher, that he should "dip his foot in oil," and that his "shoes should be iron and brass" (vers. 24, 25). It must be allowed, however, that these descriptions are far from precise, and indicate nothing beyond a very general acquaintance with the form of the country as a whole, and the character of the district assigned to each of these tribes. Now, not to mention that Moses might have visited Canaan while a shepherd in the desert, it cannot be supposed that he would be so long on the confines of Canaan, and where he would come into intercourse with many who had explored that country from end to end, without making himself acquainted with it so far at least as the general topography of it was concerned, along with the natural peculiarities of its different districts. And as the division of the land and the location of the different tribes had been already arranged (Numb. xxxiv.), it required no great intelligence on the part of Moses to foretell to Zebulun that he should draw wealth from the sea on the borders of which he was to be located, or to assign to Naphtali that he should possess a district fanned by the sea-breeze and turned to the genial south, or to announce to Asher that his should be rich and fertile soil and that his dwelling should be strong and secure (see the notes on these passages in the Exposition). Even, then, if we look on Moses as simply a man of superior intelligence, and take no account of him as a prophet, there seems no reason in what these verses contain for our concluding that they could not have been uttered by him.

2. It is alleged that in ver. 5 there is reference to a monarchical form of government as existing when this poem was composed. But this rests on an entire misconception of what this verse states. The king there spoken of is not one of the kings of Judah or Israel, neither is he Moses himself, but Jehovah, the true King of Israel from the first (see note).

3. Ver. 7 is alleged to contain a reference to the division caused by the secession of the ten tribes, and an aspiration for a reunion of the whole under the sceptre of Judah. This, however, rests on what is a misinterpretation of the verse. There is nothing here about the divisions of Israel, or about the sorrow of Judah over these and Judah's desire that they might be healed. The verse simply expresses a wish that Judah may ever have a safe and jubilant return from conflict, that he may always have strength to defend himself, and may obtain help from Jehovah against all his enemies whoever they might be. Such a wish might be uttered at any time; it is, in fact, correlative to what Jacob predicted long before concerning Judah's leadership of his brethren and successes in war (Gen. xlix. 8, 9), and no more refers to the peculiar state of things in Israel at any subsequent period of its history than does the utterance of the patriarch. It is, besides, absurd to take the words, "bring him unto his people," as equivalent to "bring his people back to him."

4. "The contents of most of the utterances, and especially the conclusion of the whole ode (vers. 26—29), make it indubitable that it was composed at a time when the people of Israel, including the ten tribes, were on the whole

in a happy condition." " The original composition of this ode appears, as is most probable, to have been made in the period between the death of Solomon and the beginning of the Assyrian Exile, most probably in 800 B.C., when both kingdoms were governed by strong and powerful kings, Israel by Jeroboam II. and Judah by Uzziah." So Bleek (' Einleit,' s. 305), following here the leadership of Graf against his own earlier opinion that this ode is older than the blessing of Jacob. Ewald's view is that it was written about the time of Josiah; whilst Hoffmann and Maurer bring it down to the date of the Exile. It may suffice here to cite, in opposition to the view of these critics, the words of Knobel, who, no less than they, maintains the late origin of this poem: " There is no trace here of allusion to national misfortunes which befell the Hebrews in the Syrian, Assyrian, and Chaldean periods. The political no less than the religious condition of the people was satisfactory; at least, the author does not even remotely refer to any religious indecencies such as are so strongly denounced in ch. xxxiii.; rather does he commend Zebulun and Issachar for bringing 'sacrifices of righteousness' (ver. 19). All this forbids the placing of this ode in the time of the Exile (Hoffmann; Gesenius, ' De Pentat. Samar.,' p. 7), or in the time of Josiah (Ewald, ' Gesch. Isr.,' i. 171), or in that of the second Jeroboam (Graf), or indefinitely in the period of the two kingdoms (Von Lengerke, ' Kenaan,' i. s. cxix. f.); it belongs to a much earlier time, though it did not, as the older critics thought, originate in that of Moses; . . . it declares itself to be of the time when David was a fugitive from Saul" (' Erklärung,' s. 339). This opinion of Knobel is just as arbitrary as any of those which he condemns; for none of them does the text give any real authority. Knobel's " own arguments," as has been justly observed, " ought in consistency to have carried him further, and led him to place it much earlier. For it is impossible to explain how the disasters, apostacies, and confusion of the latter part of Saul's reign, and still more those of the times of the judges, could have happened at a date not long before that, in which the song was penned " (' Speaker's Commentary,' vol. i. pt. ii. p. 926). It may be added that the differences of these critics as to the probable date of this poem sufficiently show the insecurity of the data on which their conclusions rest; for unless the historical events and actual facts supposed to be alluded to in a poem are so described as not to be mistakable, it cannot be known that there are any such allusions in the piece at all.

There seems no substantial reason, then, for doubting or questioning the genuineness of this sacred poem. Whether Moses wrote it or not, he must be accredited with the authorship of it; and if he was the author of it, he probably also committed it to writing—else how could it have been preserved?

That the concluding chapter of the book is not from the pen of Moses, but is the production of a later age, is so evident from the contents of the chapter, that no one now thinks of disputing it. Philo, indeed (' De Vita Mosis,' iii. § 29), and Josephus (' Antiq.,' iv. 8, 48) do not hesitate to ascribe it to Moses, who they think was enabled to narrate his own death and burial by Divine inspiration; and in this they have been followed by not a few of a former age. In the Talmud, Joshua is said to be the author of this chapter, which he appended to the writing of Moses after his death ('Baba Bathra,' fol. 14, 2); and this also has been extensively accepted. The whole chapter, however, cannot have been written by Joshua, for the statement in ver. 6, "No man knoweth of his sepulchre unto this day," and the declaration in ver. 10, that "There arose not a prophet since in Israel like unto Moses," evidently proceed from a much later age than that of Joshua. The whole chapter may have been written and appended to the original writing of Moses by Ezra, who was "a ready scribe in the Law of Moses, which the Lord God of Israel had given" (Ezra vii. 6), and of whom Jewish tradition attests that "the Thorah was forgotten by the Israelites until Ezra went up from Babylon and re-established it" ('Succa,' 20 a).

As a whole, then, with one acknowledged and one or two possible but slight exceptions, this book may be pronounced the genuine production of the great leader and legislator of Israel.

§ 7. ANALYSIS OF THE BOOK.

TITLE AND INTRODUCTION. Ch. i. 1—5.

I. FIRST OR INTRODUCTORY ADDRESS. Ch. i. 6—iv. 40.
  The new beginning and review of the journeyings of Israel from Kadesh to the river Arnon, the frontier of the Amorites. Ch. ii. 1—23.
  First war of conquest. Ch. ii. 24—iii. 17.
  Conclusion of historical recapitulation. Ch. iii. 18—20.
  Joshua appointed Moses' successor. Ch. iii. 21—29.
  Admonitions and exhortations. Ch. iv. 1—40.
  Appointment of three cities of refuge beyond Jordan. Ch. iv. 41—43.

II. SECOND ADDRESS OF MOSES. Ch. iv. 44—xxvi. 19.
  Introduction. Ch. iv. 44—49.
  The Decalogue the basis of the covenant, the essence of the whole Law, and the condition of life and felicity. Ch. v. 1—33.
  First and great commandment. Ch. vi. 1—25.
  Entire separation from idolatry. Ch. vii. 1—26.
  Exhortations to obedience enforced by a review of God's dealings with Israel in the wilderness. Ch. viii. 1—20.
  Dissuasives from self-righteousness. Ch. ix. 1—29.
  Renewed exhortations to obedience. Ch. x. 1—xi. 33.
  Announcement of particular statutes and rights. Ch. xii. 1—xxvi. 19.

III. THIRD ADDRESS OF MOSES. Ch. xxvii. 1—xxviii. 68.
  The Law to be inscribed on stones, an altar to be built, and the blessing and curse to be uttered on Gerizim and on Ebal when Canaan was occupied by the Israelites. Ch. xxvii. 1—13.
  Curses and blessings pronounced, judgments threatened in case of disobedience. Ch. xxvii. 14—xxviii. 68.

IV. RENEWAL OF THE COVENANT IN THE PLAINS OF MOAB, AND EXHORTATION TO KEEP IT. Ch. xxix. 1—xxx. 20.

V. EXHORTATION TO THE PEOPLE AND TO JOSHUA; DELIVERY OF THE LAW TO THE PRIESTS; MOSES COMMANDED TO COMPOSE A SONG; CHARGE TO JOSHUA. Ch. xxxi. 1—30.

VI. SONG OF MOSES. Ch. xxxii. 1—43.
    Moses' last words. Ch. xxxii. 44—52.
VII. BENEDICTION OF MOSES. Ch. xxxiii. 1—29.
VIII. DEATH, BURIAL, AND ENCOMIUM OF MOSES. Ch. xxxiv. 1—21.

§ 8. LITERATURE.

HISTORICO-CRITICAL. Carpzov, 'Introductio ad Libros Canonicos, V. T. Omnes' (Lips., 1741); Eichhorn, 'Einleitung in das A. T.' (5 Bde., Göttingen, 1820—24); Jahn, 'Einleit. in die Göttlicher Bücher des Alt. Bundes' (Wiesn, 1803); Augusti 'Grundriss, Einer Hist.-Krit. Einleit. ins A. T.' (Leipzig, 1827); De Wette, 'Lehrbuch der Hist.-Krit. Einleit. in die Kanon. und Apokryph. Bücher des A. B.' (Leipzig, 1840); Hävernick, 'Handbuch der Hist.-Krit. Einleit. in das A. T.' (Erlangen, 1836); 'Introduction to the Pentateuch' (translated by Thomson, Edinburgh, 1850); Hengstenberg, 'Die Authentic des Pentateuches' (Berlin, 1836—39); 'Genuineness of the Pentateuch' (translated by Ryland, Edinburgh, 1847); Keil, 'Lehrbuch der Hist.-Krit. Einleit. in die Kanon. Schriften des A. T.' (Erlangen, 1853, translated by Douglas, 2 vols., Edinburgh, 1869); Bleek, 'Einleit. in d. A. T.' (Berlin, 1860; translated by Venables, 2 vols., London, 1875); Riehm, 'Die Gesetzgebung Mosis im Lande Moab' (1854); Davidson, 'Introduction to the Old Testament' (3 vols., London, 1862); Colenso, 'The Pentateuch and Book of Joshua critically examined' (1862); 'The Mosaic Origin of the Pentateuch considered' (by a Layman, London, 1864); Kuenen, 'Religion of Israel' (2 vols.); Vaihinger, Art. "Pentateuch" (in Herzog's 'Encyclopædia,' Bde. xi.); Curtiss, 'The Levitical Priests: A Contribution to the Criticism of the Pentateuch' (Edinburgh, 1877); Wellhausen, 'Geschichte Israels' (Bde. i., Berlin, 1878); Robertson Smith, 'The Old Testament in the Jewish Church' (Edinburgh, 1881); 'Deuteronomy the People's Book.'

EXPOSITORY. Besides the general commentaries, in all of which expositions of Deuteronomy are to be found, the following more special treatises may be enumerated:—Calvin, 'Commentarii in Quatuor Reliq. Mosis Libros in Formam Harmoniæ Digest.' ap. Opp. Omnia (tom. i. edit. Amsterdam, 1771); Gerhard, 'Comm. super Deuteronom.' (Jena, 1657); Ainsworth, 'Annotations on the Five Books of Moses, the Psalms, and the Song of Solomon' (fol., London, 1639, 2 vols. 8vo, Glasgow, 1843); Rosenmüller, 'Scholia in Pentateuchum in Compendium Redacta' (Lips., 1828); Baumgarten, 'Theologischer Commentar. zum Pentateuch' (Kiel, 1843, 1844); Schultz, 'Das Deuteronomium' (Berlin, 1859); Knobel, 'Die Bücher Numeri, Deuteronom. und Josua erklärt' (Leipzig, 1861); Vitringa, 'Commentarius in Carmen Mosis cum Prolegomenis' (Harlingen, 1734); Dathe, 'Dissertatio in Canticum Mosis in Opuscc. ad Crisin. et Interpretationem Vet. Test. Spectantia' (p. 197, Lips., 1796); Ewald, 'Das Grosse Lied' (in 'Jahrb. d. Bibl. Wissenschaft'), 1857; Kamphausen, 'Das Lied Mosis' (Leipzig, 1862); Hoffmann, 'Comment. in Mosis Benedictionem' (in Keil's 'Analekten' iv. 2, Jena, 1823); Graf, 'Der Segen Mosis' (Leipzig, 1857).

THE
BOOK OF DEUTERONOMY

—◆—

TITLE AND INTRODUCTION
CHAPTER I. 1—5.

EXPOSITION.

CHAPTER I.

Vers. 1—5.—In these verses we have the inscription and general introduction to the book, announcing the contents of the book, the author of it, the parties whom he addressed, and the time and place of his addresses.

Ver. 1.—**These be the words.** Some would render here "Such are the words," and understand the expression as referring to the preceding books. But it seems more natural to refer it to what follows—to the addresses in this book. The pronoun *these* (אֵלֶּה) may be used with a prospective reference, as well as with a retrospective (cf. *e.g.* Gen. ii. 4; vi. 9). The author does not by this connect this book with the preceding, but rather distinguishes it. The subscription to Numbers (xxxvi. 13) indicates that what precedes is occupied chiefly with what God spake to Moses; the inscription here intimates that what follows is what Moses spake to the people. This is the characteristic of Deuteronomy. **Unto all Israel.** It cannot be supposed that Moses spoke to the whole multitude of the people so as to be heard by them. Hence the Jewish interpreters say that he spoke to the elders of the people, who carried his words to the people at large. This is just; for what was thus mediately communicated to the people might be fairly described as spoken to them; and we find from other passages in the Pentateuch that the phrase, "the elders of Israel," in

the mind of the writer, was equivalent to "the congregation of Israel" (comp. *e.g.* Exod. xii. 3 with ver. 21; Lev. ix. 1 with ver. 5). But through whatever medium conveyed, it was to the people that these words were addressed; this is emphatically a book for the people. **On this side Jordan.** This should be *On the other side* or *beyond Jordan*, and so also in ver. 5, as in ch. iii. 20, 25. The word here used (עֵבֶר) means properly something beyond, over, or across, and indicates that which, to the speaker, lies on the *other* side of some line or limit. When coupled with "the Jordan," it usually indicates the region to the *east* of that river; only in one or two instances, where the speaker takes his standpoint on the east of the river, does it designate the regions to the west of Jordan (ch. iii. 25; xi. 30). The phrase "beyond Jordan" seems to have been the established designation of the region east of the Jordan (cf. Ezra iv. 10, and Canon Rawlinson's note there). It is this, unquestionably, which is here so designated, as what follows expressly shows. **The wilderness.** This term is used of any extensive district not occupied by inhabitants or subjected to culture; hence of vast prairies or pasture-lands, as well as of places properly desert and desolate. It here denotes the grassy plains or downs on the east and south-east of the Jordan, in the land of Moab (ver. 5). **In the plain;** in the 'Arâbah. This is properly the whole of that remarkable depression which stretches from the source of the Jordan on to Akâbah, or the Ailanitic Gulf; but here it is only that part of it which extends from the south end of the Dead Sea to Ailah (ch. ii. 8). This part still bears the name of the 'Arâbah, the northern part being known as the Ghôr (Smith's 'Dictionary,' vol. i. p. 87; Kitto's 'Cyclopædia,' vol. i. p. 178). **Over against the Red sea.** The name by which the Red Sea is elsewhere designated is *Yam-suph* (יַם־סוּף); here only the latter word occurs, and this has led some to doubt if the Red Sea be here intended. Patrick, Rosenmüller, and others suggest that *Suph* denotes some place in that region, probably Suphah (Numb. xxi. 14, margin, Authorized Version), so called because lying at its extremity, as the verb *suph*, from which it comes, means, to come to an end; but it is not certain that Suphah designates a place in Numb. xxi. 14. The Hebrew word סוּפָה means a tempest or whirlwind; and this meaning may be assumed here, as it is by Gesenius, Keil, and others: "Waheb [he conquered] in a storm." Knobel suggests that probably the pass now called Es Sufâh, on the north side of the Wady Murreh—the Maaleh-acrabbim (Scorpion-ascent) of Josh. xv. 3—is meant; others have suggested Zephath (Judg. i. 17; comp. Numb. xiv. 45), and others Zuph (1 Sam. ix. 5). It is probable, however, that *Suph* is here merely a breviloquence for *Yam-suph*, the Red Sea; and so all the ancient versions take it. The identification of the *Yam-suph* of the Old Testament with the ἐρυθρὰ θάλασσα of the Greeks, the *mare erythræum*, or *rubrum*, of the Latins, is due to the LXX., which other versions have followed. The identification is undoubtedly correct (cf. Numb. xxxiii. 10 and 1 Kings ix. 26). *Yam-suph*, indeed, means simply sea of weeds, and might be the name of any sea in which algæ are found; but these passages clearly prove that by this the Hebrews designated the Red Sea. At what part of this sea the Israelites crossed, and the hosts of Pharaoh were submerged, is and must remain uncertain, because we know not what was the condition of the Isthmus of Suez at the time of the Exodus. It is probable it was not at any part of what is now known as the Red Sea or Gulf of Suez. Brugsch Bey places it at that—

"Serbonian bog
Betwixt Damiata and mount Casius old,
Where armies whole have sunk."
(Milton, 'Paradise Lost,' Bk. ii. 592.)

But this has not been accepted by scholars generally (see *Edinburgh Review*, No. 307; Conder's 'Handbook to the Bible,' p. 247; *Quarterly Statement of the Palestine Exploration Fund*, July and October, 1880). It seems probable that originally only a marshy district lay between the Gulf of Suez and the Mediterranean; and somewhere in this probably the passage of the Israelites and the drowning of the Egyptians occurred. **Between Paran, and Tophel,** etc. This serves more fully and particularly to indicate the locality here intended; but the details present considerable difficulty. Taken in connection with the words "over against the Red sea," the names here given can only be regarded as intended more precisely to indicate the region in which the Israelites had been during the forty years of their wandering. *Pâran:* this is the name of the wilderness bordering on Idumea, where the Israelites encamped (Numb. x. 12; xii. 16); the place of their encampment being Kadesh, in the wilderness of Zin (Numb. xiii. 21, 26), which was the eastern part of the wilderness of Pâran, *hod.* Wady Murreh. The wilderness of Pâran corresponds in general outline with the desert of Et-Tîh. This is a vast plateau of irregular surface stretching from the Et-Tîh range northwards to the boundaries of the Holy Land, and from the Gulf of Akâbah and the Wady el 'Arâbah on the east to the Gulf of Suez and the Mediterranean on the west. It is described as "a chalky formation, the chalk being covered with coarse gravel, mixed with black flints and drifting sand;" not, however, wholly sterile: in many parts vegetation abounds, considerable portions are under cultivation, and there are evidences that at one time water was abundant there (Smith, ii. 767; Kitto, iii. 1077; Drew, 'Scripture Lands,' p. 80). It is not, however, to the wilderness of Pâran that the reference is in the text, but to some definite locality or spot in the region in which the Israelites then were, or which they had recently passed through. It has been suggested that the place now called Feirân, and where there are the ruins of a town, once of some importance in the early history of Christianity, is the Pâran of this passage, as it apparently is the Pâran of 1 Kings xi. 18. But this locality at the base of Jebel Serbail is much too far west to be the Pâran here referred to. More probable is the suggestion that it is the Faran mentioned by Eusebius and Jerome ('Onomast.,' *s.v.* Φαράν), a city to the east (north-east) of Ailah or Elath, about three days' journey (Reland, 'Palest.,' p. 556; Winer, 'Realwörterbuch,' *s.v.* Pharan). *Tophel:* this name occurs only here; it is supposed to be the place now called Tufailah or Tafyleh, a large village of six hundred inhabitants, between Bozrah and Kerak, on the eastern slope of the mountains of Edom (Burckhardt, 'Syria,' p. 402; Robinson, 'Bib. Res.,' ii. 570). As this is a place where the Syrian caravans are supplied with provisions, it has been conjectured that the Israelites, when at Oboth (Numb. xxi. 10, 11), may have resorted to it for a supply, and that it was here that they purchased meat and drink from the children of Esau (ch. ii. 29). **And Laban.** *Laban* is generally identified with Libnah, the second place of encampment of the Israelites on their return from Kâdesh (Numb. xxxiii. 20, 21). Knobel, however, thinks it is the place called by Ptolemy 'Aὔαρα, lying between Petra and Ailah; this name, from the Arabic حار (he was white), having the same meaning as the Hebrew לָבָן. **Hazeroth** is supposed to be the place mentioned in Numb. xi. 35; xii. 16, from which the Israelites entered the wilderness of Pâran; but as the other places here mentioned are on the east side of the 'Arâbah, it is not probable that this Hazeroth is the same as that of Numbers, which must have been not far from Sinai, in a northerly or north-westerly direction from that mountain, probably at or near to the fountain now called El Hudherah (Wilson, 'Lands of the Bible,' i. 235; Kitto, 'Cyclopædia,' ii. 243). There were probably several places bearing the name of *Hazeroth*, i.e. villages. **Dizahab.** This is generally identified with Dhahab, a place on a tongue of land in the Gulf of Akâbah. But it is extremely improbable that the Israelites ever were at this place, the approach to which is exceedingly difficult; and the mere resemblance of the names Dîzâhâb and Dhahab is not sufficient to prove the identity of the places. There were probably more places than one which were named from *zahab* (gold) in the region traversed by the Israelites. There is a Dhahab on the east of the Jordan near the Zerka or Jabbok, a double mound, which is said to derive its name from the yellowish colour of the sandstone rock of which it consists, and which is metalliferous. In the Arabic of the Polyglot, Dizahab appears as *Dhi-dhahab*, which signifies "*auro præditum* vel *ab auro dictum;* nam דו vel ד׳, apud Arabes in compositione nominum propr. idem est ac Heb. בעל" (J. H. Michaelis). There is a various reading here, *Di-waheb*, and this has been supposed to connect this place with the Waheb of Numb. xxi. 14. But, as above noted, it is by no means certain that Waheb is there the name of a place; it may, as Bishop Patrick suggests, be that of a man, some hero or chief, who was conquered in Sufah or in a storm. Waheb is a name among the Arabs. The maternal grandfather of Mohammed had this name (Abul-Pharaj, 'Hist. Dynast.,' p. 161, edit. Pococke, Oxon., 1663); and the sect of the Wahabees take their name from Abdul Wahab, a fanatic who ap-

peared about the beginning of last century. The words "between Paran and Tophel" have been taken to indicate the termini of the wanderings; at the commencement of these the people were at Pâran, and towards the close of them they were at Tophel. "Looking from the steppes of Moab over the ground that the Israelites had traversed, Sûph, where they first entered the desert of Arabia, would lie between Pârân where the congregation arrived at the borders of Canaan toward the west, and Tophel where they first ended their desert wanderings thirty-seven years later on the east" (Keil). But this assumes that Pâran here is the wilderness of Pâran.

Ver. 2.—**Horeb.** The name generally given to Sinai in Deuteronomy (see introduction, § 4). Sinai, however, occurs in ch. xxxiii. 2 of this book. **By the way of mount Seir,** *i.e.* by the way that leads to Mount Seir; just as in ch. ii. 1, "the way of the Red sea" is the way that leads to that sea (see also Numb. xiv. 25). *Mount* is here, as often elsewhere, for *mountain range*. The mountain range here referred to seems to have been, not that on the east of the 'Arâbah, but what is in vers. 6 and 19 called "the mountain of the Amorites," "the Seir by Hormah" of ver. 44, *i e.* the southern part of what was afterwards called the mountains of Judah. According to ver. 19, the Israelites, when they left Horeb, passed through the wilderness along the way that led to the mountains of the Amorites, and came to Kâdesh-barnea. Kâdesh must, therefore, be looked for, not on the eastern side of the 'Arâbah, but somewhere in the wilderness of Zin. It has been identified with the place now known as 'Ain Kûdes, near the northern extremity of Jebel Halal, and to the east of that hill; but this is far from being certain. Moses reminds the Israelites that the distance between Horeb and Kâdesh is eleven days—*i.e.* about one hundred and sixty-five miles, the day's journey being reckoned at fifteen miles—not to give them a piece of information, but rather to suggest to them how, in consequence of rebellion, a journey which might have been so easily accomplished, had been protracted through many wearisome years.

Vers. 3, 4.—Here is intimated the *time* when the following addresses were delivered to the people. It was on the first day of the eleventh month in the fortieth year; therefore near the end of their wanderings, and towards the close of the lawgiver's own career. He could thus speak to them according unto all that the Lord had given him in commandment unto them, *i.e.* in accordance with the legislative contents of the preceding books (comp. ch. iv. 5 23;

v. 28—33; vi. 1). It was also after the destruction of Sîhon and 'Og (Numb. xxi. 21—35). This also is significant. By the destruction of these kings, who sought to bar the access of the Israelites to the promised land, God had given proof that he would indeed fulfil his promise to his people, and had at once laid them under obligations to obedience, and given them encouragement to go forward on the course to which he had called them. The "he" here is Moses, who, at the command of God, had led the Israelites against Sîhon and 'Og. **Edrei,** *hod.* Draa (Numb. xxi. 33) was the second capital of 'Og; he "reigned in Ashtaroth and in Edrei" (Josh. xiii. 12). Here, however, it denotes the place where he was slain in battle, and the words "in Edrei" are to be referred to the verb "smote" and not to "dwelt" (cf. ch. iii. 1: Numb. xxi. 33).

Ver. 5.—The locality is again described **as beyond Jordan** (see on ver. 1), and **in the land of Moab.** This designates the region elsewhere called *Arboth Moab*—the Plains of Moab (Numb. xxii. 1; ch. xxxiv. 1, etc.), the region on the east of the Jordan, opposite to Jericho, now known as the region of Kerak (Burckhardt, 'Syria,' p. 377, etc.; Robinson, 'Bib. Res.," ii. 569).

Began; rather *set himself to.* The Hebrew word signifies to undertake, to betake one's self to, and so to begin. It is variously rendered in the Authorized Version (comp. Gen. xviii. 27, "taken it upon me;" Exod. ii. 21, "was content," had made up his mind; 1 Sam. xii. 22, "it pleased;" xvii. 39, "assayed," etc.). **To declare,** *i.e.* make clear, explain, expound (Hab. ii. 2, "make plain"). The Hebrew word here used (בָּאַר) signifies primarily to cut or dig, then to cut into, to grave, and then to cut or dig out so as to make evident, to declare, to make plain. What Moses set himself to do, then, was not to publish a new law, but to make plain to the people the Law already promulgated, to set forth clearly and pointedly what they were required by the Law to be and to do. This explains more fully the "spake" (דִּבֶּר) of ver. 3. This exposition of the Law was designed specially for the sake of those who, at the time the Law was first promulgated, either were not born or were incapable of understanding it (Grotius). The expression used by Moses plainly indicates that this book was not intended to furnish a second code of laws different from the former, but simply to explain and enforce what had before been enjoined.

PART I

INTRODUCTORY ADDRESS

CHAPTER I. 6—CHAPTER IV. 40.

Ver. 6.—With this verse begins Moses' first address to the people, which extends to the end of ch. iv. It is of an introductory character, and is occupied chiefly with a retrospective survey of the events that had occurred during the forty years of their wanderings. By this Moses reminded the people how God had fulfilled his promises to them, and at the same time, how they had by their rebellion drawn down on them his displeasure, which had caused their wanderings to be so much more protracted than they would otherwise have been.

Vers. 6—8.—The Lord's command to depart from Horeb, and his promise to the people.

Ver. 6.—**The Lord our God**—*Jehovah our God.* The use of this epithet implies the covenant union of Israel with Jehovah, and presupposes the existence of that covenant which was entered into at Sinai. **In Horeb.**

This was the starting-point, so to speak, of Israel's being as the special people of God —his *segullah* (סְגֻלָּה, Exod. xix. 5), his special treasure. There he made himself known to them as Jehovah, the Eternal and Unchangeable, and entered into covenant with them; and there they received that Law, on the keeping of which depended their retention of the privileges to which they had been elected. At Horeb the Israelites had remained for about a year (comp. Exod. xix. 1 and Numb. x. 11, 12), and as the purpose for which they had been brought thither was answered, they were enjoined to move, not indeed by express command, but by the rising of the cloud from over the tabernacle, which was the signal of their march (Numb. ix. 15, etc.; x. 11—13), preceded by the instructions they had received preparatory to their removal (Numb. i.–iv. 7). **Ye have dwelt long enough in this mount.** The Israelites remained at Sinai from the third month of the first year to the twentieth day of the second year after they came out of Egypt (cf. Exod. xix. 1 and Numb. x. 11).

Ver. 7.—**Go to the mount of the Amorites, and unto all that dwell thereon**; literally, *its dwellers* or *inhabitants* (יֹשְׁבָיו). The mountain range of the Amorites, afterwards called the hill country of Judah and Ephraim, was the object which would first strike the view of one advancing from the south; and so, it stands here for the whole land of Canaan, with which it is in this context identified. Those "that dwell thereon" are the inhabitants of the whole of Canaan. The Amorites (Hebrew *Emori*, so called from Amor, or Emor) oftener tl an once appear as standing for the Canaanites generally (cf. Gen. xv. 16; Deut. i. 20, 21, etc.). That all the inhabitants of Canaan are intended here is evident from the specification of the different districts of the land of Canaan which immediately follows. **In the plain**: the '*Arâbah* (see ver. 1). **In the hills**: the hill country of Judah (Numb. xiii. 17). **In the vale**: the *shephêlah*, or lowland, the country lying between the mountain range of Judah and the Mediterranean Sea, and stretching northwards from the parallel of Gaza to that of Carmel. **In the south**: the *negeb*, or southland (literally, *dryness*), the district which formed the transition from the desert to the cultivated land, extending from the south of the Dead Sea westwards to Gaza, a vast steppe or prairie, for the most part pasture-land. **The seashore**: the narrow strip of land on the coast of the Mediterranean from Joppa to Tyre (in the New Testament, "the coast of Tyre and Sidon," Luke vi. 17). **The land of the Canaanites**: the whole country of which these were the separate parts. **And unto Lebanon**: the *White Mountain*, so called, probably, from the snow which rests on its summit. **The great river, the river Euphrates**. The Phrath, or Euphrates, which has its sources in the mountains of Armenia, and in its course divides Armenia from Cappadocia, formed the eastern limit of the territory promised by God to Abraham. The epithet "great" seems to have been commonly applied to it. Callimachus calls it Ἀσσυριοῦ ποταμοῖο μέγας ῥόος ('In Apoll.,' 107), and Lucan has—

"Quaque caput rapido tollit cum Tigride
  magnus
Euphrates."

(' Phars.,' iii. 256.)

As by much the most considerable river of western Asia, the Euphrates was known as "the river" *par excellence* (cf. Exod. xxiii. 31; Isa. viii. 7; Jer. ii. 18; Ps. lxxii. 8). The mention of Lebanon and the Euphrates is not, as Keil suggests, "to be attributed to the rhetorical fulness of the style;" but is due to the fact that these were included in what God promised to Abraham and his seed (Gen. xv. 18; Exod. xxiii. 31; Deut. xi. 24).

Ver. 8.—**Behold, I have set the land before you**: literally, *have given the land before you*, i.e. have made it over to you, that you may go and take possession of it. The Lord had placed this land in the power of the Israelites, had given it up to them to possess and use it, according as he had sworn to their fathers, the patriarchs, to give it to them and their seed (comp. Gen. xii. 7; xiii. 15; xv. 18, etc.; xxii. 16). At Horeb, therefore, they received the charter of their inheritance, and might have gone on at once to take possession of the land. The delay that had occurred had arisen solely from their own waywardness and perversity, not from anything on the part of God.

Vers. 9—18.—Moses reminds them that he had done all that was required on his part to conduct the people to the enjoyment of what God had freely given to them. The people had so increased in number that Moses found himself unable to attend to all the matters that concerned them, or to adjudicate in all the differences that arose among them. God had brought to pass that which he had promised to Abraham (Gen. xv. 5), that his seed should be as the stars of heaven for multitude; in this Moses rejoiced, nay, he would even that their numbers were, with the Divine blessing, increased a thousandfold beyond what they were. But he found the burden, the weight of care and trouble, especially in connection with their strifes and suits thereby brought on him, too much for him; and, therefore, whilst they were still at Horeb, he had, following the advice of Jethro, his father-in-law, counselled them to select competent men from among themselves, who should relieve him by attending to those duties which he found it too burdensome for him to have to attend to (cf. Exod. xviii. 13, etc.). This appointment of captains was quite distinct from that of the elders whom God directed Moses to select that they might assist him in bearing the burden of the people (Numb. xi. 10, etc.). The occasion of the appointment was the same in both cases, viz. the complaint of Moses that the task was too onerous for him, but the time, the place, and the manner of the two transactions were different.

Ver. 9.—**I spake unto you at that time.** The somewhat indefinite phrase, "at that time" (comp. Gen. xxxviii. 1), does not refer to the time *after* the people departed from Horeb, but to the time generally when they were in that region (see Exod. xviii. 5, 13). "The imperfect (וַיֹּאמֶר, I spake), with *vaw rel.* expresses the order of thought and not of time" (Keil). It is not mentioned in Exodus that Moses spake to the people, as here stated, but what Jethro said to him to this effect is recorded; and as Moses proceeded to put in execution what his father-in-law advised, it is probable that in doing so he told the people what he proposed to do, with his reasons for so doing, and obtained their assent, as here mentioned.

Ver. 10.—Notwithstanding the cruel oppression to which they were subjected in Egypt, the Israelites had so increased in numbers that they went out of the house of their bondage a mighty host. **Ye are this day as the stars of heaven for multitude** (cf. Gen. xv. 5; xxii. 17). God had promised to Abraham that his seed should be as the stars of heaven for multitude; and Moses here reminds the people that this promise had been fulfilled. This is hardly to be regarded as the utterance of hyperbole. When God gave the promise to Abraham it was to the stars *as seen by the patriarch*, not as actually existing in the immensity of space, that reference was made; and as the number of stars which can be taken in with the naked eye does not exceed 3000, and as Israel at this time numbered more than 600,000, counting only the adult males (Numb. ii. 32),—it might be literally said of them that they had been multiplied as the stars of heaven. The comparison, however, imported nothing more than that their numbers were very great.

Ver. 11.—It was not the vast increase of the people in numbers that distressed Moses, rather was this to him a matter of rejoicing, and his desire was that their increase might become still greater, even a thousandfold. But he felt his own inability, as leader, ruler, and judge, alone to cope with so vast a multitude.

Ver. 12.—Moses appeals to the good sense of the people themselves: **How can I myself alone bear your cumbrance, and your burden, and your strife?** *Cumbrance:* this is a just rendering of the Hebrew word טֹרַח, from טָרַח, which, though it occurs only in the Hiphil in Hebrew, in the sense of to cast down (Job xvii. 11), probably was in use also in the Kal, in the sense of to lay upon, to encumber, which is the meaning of the cognate Arabic طرح followed by عَلَى. *Burden* (מַשָּׂא, from נָשָׂא, to lift up, to carry, to bear), something lifted up and carried, a load or burden. *Strife:* (רִיב) here, not mere contention, but litigation, suit-at-law. Some understand all these three, of troubles and burdens laid upon Moses, by his being called upon to compose differences, and adjust competing claims among the people. But other burdens besides these came upon him as the leader of the nation; and it seems best, therefore, to understand the first two of troubles and burdens generally.

Ver. 13.—**Take you**; literally, *give to you* or *for you*, i.e. *yourselves*. The selection was to be made by the people themselves. Jethro, in giving Moses the advice on which he thus acted, described the men who were to be selected as "such as fear God, men of truth, hating covetousness" (Exod. xviii. 21). Moses here describes them rather by qualities, indicating ability and fitness for such a post as that to which they were to be called; they were to be **wise** (which, indeed, may be regarded as comprehending all good moral qualities); **understanding** men, men of discernment and sagacity, as well as intelligence; **and known among their tribes**, men of good repute in the community ("quorum conversatio sit probata," Vulgate; comp. Acts vi. 3; 1 Tim. iii. 7). **And I will make them rulers over you**; literally, *will set them for your heads*, i.e. will appoint them to act as superintendents, managers, and judges over you.

Vers. 14, 15.—The people approved of the proposal, and acted upon it; and Moses accordingly appointed the persons selected to be chiefs **over thousands, and over hundreds, and over fifties, and over tens** (Exod. xviii. 21); he appointed men also to be **officers**, that is, persons who should preserve order in the tribes, keeping the registers, acting as scribes, to prescribe and to take account of work, and perhaps also attending to fiscal arrangements (שֹׁטְרִים, *shoterim*, a word of general application; cf. Exod. v. 6, 10, 14; Josh. iii. 2; 2 Chron. xxvi. 11, etc. LXX. γραμματεῖς and γραμματο-εισαγωγεῖς). In Exodus, Moses is said to have chosen these functionaries (xviii. 25); but what many do under the direction of one may be said to be done by him.

Vers. 16, 17.—In installing the judges, Moses solemnly charged them to deal impartially, fairly, and equitably with those who might come before them.

Ver. 16.—**Hear between your brethren**, *i.e.* hear impartially both parties, **and judge righteously between man and man**, whether both parties are Israelites, or one of the parties **a stranger**.

Ver. 17.—**Ye shall not respect persons**; literally, *look at* or *regard faces*, i.e. ye shall not deal partially, favouring the one party rather than the other (comp. Exod. xxiii. 2, 3; Lev. xix. 15); the small as well as the great were to be heard, and neither for favour nor from fear were they to pervert justice. **The judgment is God's;** *i.e.* appointed by God and administered in his name, the judge acting for God and by his authority, and being answerable to him (comp. 2 Chron. xix. 6). Hence the phrases, "to inquire of God," "to bring before God" (Exod. xviii. 15, 19; xxi. 6; xxii. 8, etc.)— phrases still in use among the Arabs for a summoning to judicial trial. In the case of a matter coming before the judges which they found it beyond their power to decide, they were to bring it before Moses as a superior authority (see Exod. xviii. 26). "Some think there were certain causes reserved to the cognizance of Moses; but the contrary appears by these words, that all manner of causes were brought before the judges; and they, not the people, brought such causes before Moses as they found too hard for them to determine. So that they, not the person whose cause it was, judged of the difficulty of the cause. See Selden, lib. i. 'De Synedriis, cap. xvi." (Bishop Patrick).

HOMILETICS.

Vers. 1—5.—*The Word of God full of hidden treasure.* We cannot get very far in these preliminary verses ere we are struck with a phrase which is a most suggestive one, and should not be lightly passed over, viz. "On this side Jordan, in the land of Moab, began Moses *to declare* this law," literally, to dig it, *i.e.* to go deeply into it, and to turn up again its contents, so that, to all the advantage of a generation of culture, the people might see that there was more meaning, and also more glory in the Law of God than they were able to discern in the first years of their national existence. Observe—

I. There is a mine of wealth in the Law of God. This is the case, even if we thereby intend the Mosaic Law alone. Its theology, its ethics, its directory of religious faith and worship, its civil and political code for the Hebrew commonwealth, are all so pure and elevated, that no account can be given of how any man at that age of the world could have propounded such a system, save that he was taught of God (cf. 2 Pet. i. 21). (See Homiletics, ch. v. 7—22.) If, moreover, we would see how the devout Hebrews estimated the Law, let us turn to Ps. xix.; ciii. 7, *et seq.* Our Saviour honoured the Law, and maintained it in all its integrity (cf. Matt. v. 17, 18). He removed the glosses by which it had in his time become disfigured, but he never depreciated it. We are by no means to confound "the Law" with the abstract idea of "law." See how sharply the Apostle Paul distinguishes between these two in Rom. iii., especially in ver. 21, "But now there has been manifested a righteousness of God *apart from law,* being witnessed by THE Law and the prophets." The Law given by Moses is based on the gospel (cf. Gal. iii.; see also Homiletics, ch. v. 6). If, however, to all that Moses gave, we add all "the grace and the truth" which came in by Jesus Christ, how unsearchably vast is the wealth stored up for us in the "Word of everlasting Truth!"

II. The effort of digging into this mine will be well repaid. How much difference there is between a man who knows only *what men say about* the Book, and one who knows the Book for himself! The one may be easily beguiled into the belief that it is so out of date that it is scarcely worth while to study it at all. The other will find it so far ahead of the actual attainments of the wisest and best of men, that he will pity those who dismiss it with but a glance from afar. The continuous, careful, thorough student of the Law of Moses, will be ever discovering a richness in it which will at once astonish and enrapture him. Its harmony with, its historical preparation for, the gospel, will be continually disclosing to him new proofs of its Divine original, that will be worth more *to him* than any merely "external evidence." And when the whole Word of God is made the constant study of one whose heart is open to the truth and loyal to God, such a one will find fuller and richer meaning in *single words,* such as *gōel,* "grace," "righteousness," etc., when these words are put to their highest use in Divine revelation, than in whole tomes of merely human lore!

III. The Word should be dug into, that we may appropriate its contents, by enlightened reason and lowly faith. These treasures are for the use of all, not merely to gratify them with the consciousness of ever making new discoveries, but to make them richer in the accumulating stores of holy thought. And if we, in the right spirit, explore these sacred pages, we shall ourselves become richer in knowledge, in gladness, in hope. If we cultivate a willingness to do God's will, and seek to know the truth for the purpose of doing the right, we shall find that much that is "hidden from the wise and prudent" is, by means of the Book, "revealed unto babes."

IV. THE MORE WE THUS DIG INTO THE BOOK OF THE LAW, THE MORE EXHAUST-LESS IT WILL SEEM. No one is there, who lovingly and prayerfully studies it, who will not come to say, with a feeling that becomes intenser year by year, "There remaineth very much land to be possessed." "High as the heaven is above the earth, so are" God's "ways higher than" our "ways, and" God's "thoughts than" our "thoughts"!

V. THE ACCUMULATING STORES OF HOLY THOUGHT SHOULD BE TRANSMUTED BY US INTO THE WEALTH OF HOLY LIFE. It is not for nought that our God has so enriched this world with thoughts from heaven. It is not merely that the intellect may be furnished or the taste for research gratified. Oh no; it is for our life. Heaven has poured forth its wealth upon earth, that earth may send up its love and loyalty to heaven. Precious are the riches of truth. The riches of holiness are more precious still. God gives us the first that we may yield him the second. God would win Israel's love by unveiling his own. So now, "God commendeth his love toward us, in that, while we were yet sinners, Christ died for us." How great will be our guilt, how severe our condemnation, if we let such priceless disclosures remain unnoticed and unused! It were better for us not to have known the way of righteousness than, after we have known it, to turn from the holy commandment delivered unto us. May we, through the Spirit, so use the truth of God as to find our joy and salvation in the God of the truth!

Vers. 1—8, together with Exod. xxiii. 20—33.—*The Hebrew right to Canaan.* Moses is reviewing the career of Israel, and is endeavouring to set before the people the patience and faithfulness of God, as well as their own waywardness. In the part of his review which is before us just now, he points to the time when their sojourn in Horeb was about to close. Laws and ordinances had been given. The nation was formed. Preparations for departure would have to be made. To this they are incited by a renewal of the Divine gift to them of the land of Canaan. The bare and brief recital in the verses referred to above may be advantageously compared with Exod. xxiii. 20—33. A subject is here brought before us of great importance, viz. *The right of the Hebrews to Canaan, and the purpose of the Divine Being in granting it to them.* We have here—

I. THE HEBREW RIGHT TO CANAAN DIVINELY CONFIRMED. A double use has been made of the command to dispossess the Canaanites: 1. By sceptics, to impugn the morality of the Old Testament. 2. By professing Christian men, to justify wars of aggression now. Now we might meet both these by one short and ready reply, viz. "If God *commanded* the Hebrews to exterminate the Canaanites, no defence is required; if God *did not* command them, no defence avails." But there is a more appropriate way of meeting the two cases. As to the first, we would say, "Before you pronounce it immoral, look at the entire bearings of the case, that you may see if the Israelites had an adequate warrant for the course they took." As to the second, "Before you regard this as a pattern, look at the entire bearings of the case, that you may see if there is any ground for adducing the wars of the Hebrews as a justification or palliation of aggressive war now." If men go to the Book to learn what the Israelites did, they must in all fairness go to the Book to see the grounds on which they did it. And the same teaching that will answer the one question, Were they justified? will also answer the other, Should we be justified in imitating them? Thirteen points present themselves for distinct and cumulative consideration. We can but name them. (1) God spake to Moses. (2) In speaking to Moses, God but confirmed the promise made to Abraham, Isaac, and Jacob. (3) God defines the bounds of the land to be possessed. (4) God makes the claim, "All the earth is mine;" consequently he has a right to give the land to whomsoever he will. (5) In choosing Israel, God would have a people for himself who should be his witnesses. (6) God foresaw the time for carrying out this plan (Gen. xv.). (7) The preparation of the land was of God (Exod. xxiii. 20). (8) The ground on which the Canaanites were dispossessed was their enormous wickedness (ch. ix. 4, 5). (9) Israel was consequently only the means in the Divine hand of carrying out an explicit Divine purpose. (10) To spare the Canaanites would have been to infect Israel with their abominations. (11) *God* would deliver the nations into Israel's hand. (12) On a land and among a people recognized as God's, the Most High would reassert in the world the well-nigh forgotten truth, "The Lord our God is holy." (13) Even *Israel's* continuance in the land would depend on their maintenance of the principles which had been entrusted to their keeping, and on their loyalty to the God who had chosen them for his own (ch. xxviii. 49). When we put all these principles together, the two questions suggested at the outset receive a direct and sufficient reply.

II. ACCESS TO CANAAN DIVINELY SECURED. "I will send an angel before thee" (Exod. xxiii. 14; xxxii. 34; Isa. lxiii. 9; Mal. iii. 1; Acts vii. 38, 53; John i. 51). It is only as we study the more advanced revelations of the New Testament as to the place of angels in the Divine administration, and the lordship of Jesus Christ over them, that all these texts of Scripture are seen to fit in together. Note the specific statements in Exod. xxiii. as to God clearing Israel's way.

III. DUTY IN REFERENCE TO CANAAN DIVINELY REGULATED. Negatively: they were neither to bow down to false gods nor to mix with the heathen. Positively: they were to serve and fear God and to practise the right.

IV. PROMISES CONCERNING PROSPERITY IN CANAAN DIVINELY GIVEN (Exod. xxiii. 25). Blessing on food, health, long life (cf. Matt. vi. 33; Ps. xci. 16). A separate homily might well be devoted to the temporal benefits naturally resulting from obedience to God.

The application of all this to us in these days is manifest. 1. What Israel was once in the world God expects his Church to be now (cf. Exod. xix. 5, 6 with 1 Pet. ii. 9). 2. In Jesus Christ we have a new covenant, a better ministry, greater promises (Heb. viii. 6). 3. We have a commission for the world. We have to co-operate with God in bringing about new heavens and a new earth, by working in accordance with his plan of redeeming and educating our race. We have no commission to destroy. The Lord hath given us a power for edification but none for destruction. Our commission runs, "Go, baptize and teach." We have not to supersede the occupation of territory held by a barbarous nation, through its enforced occupation by a civilized one, but to go and teach all nations that each nation may supersede its own barbarism by a civilization that is equally its own. 4. This commission is to be fulfilled by the Word of Truth, by the power of God. By spiritual weapons only can our victories be won. In the might of a love that has conquered us, and in that might alone, we are to go forth to make the conquest of the world.

> "These weapons of the holy war,
> Of what almighty force they are,
> To make our stubborn passions bow,
> And lay the proudest rebel low!"

Vers. 6—18.—*Rules to be observed in choosing rulers.* This paragraph may with advantage be compared with Exod. xviii., in which there is a fuller account of the circumstances under which the choice of judges and magistrates was proposed and made; this important step towards the order and consolidation of the national life was taken at the suggestion of Jethro, the father-in-law of Moses. Referring to the exposition of that chapter for the historic detail, we note here simply: 1. That the choice of rulers, etc., is put into the people's hands; they are to select, Moses is to ratify the selection. 2. They are to choose men of righteousness, who will fear God and do justice. 3. When the judges are chosen, Moses seeks solemnly to impress on them the high and holy responsibilities of their office. 4. The supreme reason for this care in judging rightly is found in the fact that the cause is God's, *i.e.* that they are rulers under God and for him—representing Divine laws in the earthly sphere. The state is sacredly to be governed by the laws of righteousness, and by such laws alone. Hence a subject is opened up to us which is of no small moment, viz. *Principles and facts to be borne in mind in choosing rulers of the people.* Observe—

I. THAT THE CHOOSING OF MEN TO TAKE PART IN MAKING OR ADMINISTERING A NATION'S LAWS IS A SOLEMN AND MOMENTOUS CONCERN. It matters comparatively little, so far as our present topic is concerned, what may be the peculiar form of government adopted, or what may be the mode of choosing men for office in the State. For 1. The position such men occupy is an exalted one. It is self-evident that when they have to take part in governing or carrying out the laws of the land, it is of the utmost moment that they should be men who are capable of perceiving what measures will tend to the people's good. A country may be perishing from the want of good laws, if its rulers are not competent, wise, and just. 2. The influence such men wield in private circles is largely increased from the fact of their public position. 3. Their representative character is another element of great moment. Great men and good will elevate common questions to their own level; while worthless men will fail to appreciate the importance of the greatest questions of the day. 4. The great matters which may—nay, must—come before the rulers of a nation, are such as may involve that nation's honour or discredit among the nations of the world; yea, more, they are such as will do much, according as they are decided, to bring upon a people the blessing or the wrath of Almighty God! Hence—

II. THE POSSESSION OF A POWER TO PUT MEN IN SUCH AN OFFICE OR OFFICES, IS A TRUST FOR THE USE OF WHICH THOSE WHO POSSESS THAT POWER ARE RESPONSIBLE TO THEIR COUNTRY AND THEIR GOD! The decisions of earthly judges ought to be the earthly expression of heavenly law. Hence to let whim, or caprice, or passion, or partizanship carry us away, when such concerns are at issue, and to forget the ever-lasting laws of righteousness, is to tamper with the public interest, and to betray a solemn trust. Therefore—

III. IN THE DISCHARGE OF THIS TRUST, STRICT REGARD MUST BE PAID TO PERSONAL CHARACTER. (See Exod. xviii. 21.) Even a pagan felt this. It was the priest of Midian who said, "Thou shalt provide out of all the people able men, such as fear God, men of truth, hating covetousness"—a fourfold qualification, so comprehensive that, where it is possessed, a man may be safely entrusted with any office. Such men will undertake their work as those who are responsible to God; they will ever be on the look out to perceive what the interests of their country may require at their hands; they will seek to qualify themselves to take part in the public questions which will come before them; without seeking their own honour, they will aim at judging as is wisest and best; and their supreme aim will be that the government they help to administer should be ever in harmony with righteousness and truth. If all its public men answer all these requirements, a country cannot go far wrong; but if a nation's leaders are themselves lacking in virtue, how can there be any security for that righteousness and truth which exalt a nation, when a country is at the mercy of men who know not the one neither regard the other?

IV. A CONSIDERATION WHICH GIVES INFINITE WEIGHT TO THE ABOVE PRINCIPLES IS THAT THE JUDGMENT OF EARTHLY RULERS IS INTENDED, IN ITS WAY, TO BE A COPY OF THE DIVINE. "The judgment is God's," says Moses. It is God's judgment, expressed through his own appointed officers (see Rom. xiii.). Secular judgments should have sacred principles underlying them. And we cannot divorce the secular from the sacred without great mischief accruing. But, finally: the judgment is God's in another sense. HE is the Supreme Judge; and whether men use *their* judgment well or ill, God will exercise his own. The principles of the Divine government of nations are developed by Isaiah, Jeremiah, Hosea, Amos, and others. No nation can escape from the sway of the Mighty One; if God's laws are set at nought, his judgments will follow, that, while they are abroad in the earth, the inhabitants thereof may learn righteousness.

HOMILIES BY VARIOUS AUTHORS.

Vers. 1—8.—*Divine covenant and human conduct—the two hemispheres of a complete life.* I. AN ELECT MAN, THE BEST OF THE AGE, BECOMES A MEDIUM OF REVELATION BETWEEN GOD AND MEN. As in nature, so in human life, there are numberless grades of office and of function. At Sinai, we have God, angels, Moses, priests. The trans-parent candour and fidelity of Moses, as a subaltern in God's great host, is a light to all future ages. As the uncreated light left an abiding impress on the face of Moses, so the known will of God shone out lustrously in Moses' life. *All* that Moses heard, he communicated by word, and temper, and influence, and deed.

II. MATERIAL PENURY A CONDITION FOR HEAVENLY ENRICHMENT. The scene for the revelation of God, is the wilderness. Stript of earthly luxuries, the mind opens its portals to heavenly visitation. This is not a necessity arising out of the nature of things, but it is a necessity for man in his present state. The son of Zacharias, though a priest, turned his back upon the temple, and chose the wilderness as the theatre most suitable for his ponderous undertaking. *This* the spirit of prophecy had foreseen. It was in the desert, Jesus fed the thousands by a creative word. In the desert, Paul was equipped for shaking the foundations of paganism. In Patmos, John passed through the portals of the spirit-world.

III. HUMAN POWER IS FORMAL—GOD'S POWER REAL. To the eye of mortal sense, the Hebrews, drilled and officered, fought victoriously with Amalek and Moab ; nevertheless, a clearer vision sees that it was God that slew Sihon, King of the Amorites, and Og, King of Bashan. Let us be sure that what *we* do, *God* does by us ! Be we the agents; God the principal! In righteous warfare, " He teacheth our fingers to fight." In us hourly let God be immanent. " God wills it," therefore let us will it also. " He worketh in us."

IV. MEDITATION AND ACTION INTEGRAL PARTS OF HEALTHFUL LIFE. " Ye have dwelt long enough in this mount." The body may be wrecked by surfeit, as well as by hunger. Knowledge is not entirely *ours*, until it is reduced to practice. Heavenly wisdom is essentially practical. All light is designed for service. The doctrines of religion are raw materials, which are to be put into the warp and woof of our daily life. Is " the Lamb the light of the heavenly place " ? The saints " follow the Lamb whithersoever he goeth." Meditation qualifies for action ; action demands new meditation. These are the two wings, without *both* of which the eagle cannot rise. " Come ye into the desert ; " " Go and preach ; "—these are the twin behests of Christ.

V. GOD'S ABSOLUTE PURPOSES LEAVE FULL SCOPE FOR MAN'S OBEDIENCE. How the two things are co-related, we cannot ascertain. The point of junction is among the incomprehensible—beneath the surface of things. There is now and again seeming discord ; but as we listen on there is a profounder harmony. The Lord sware unto the patriarchs to give them the land of Canaan. Yet the spies brought back an ill report ; and the people debated and murmured, vacillated and countermarched, as if they had been the umpires of their destiny.

VI. GOD'S PROVISION IS ALWAYS MORE AMPLE THAN MAN'S DESIRE. God's plan for Israel's territory extended from Mount Lebanon to the Euphrates; but Israel never rose to the full height of God's design. " Ask what I shall give thee " is still the message from heaven to every man. " Open thy mouth wide, and I will fill it." " We have not because we ask not." There is abundance of sea-room in God's plan for the largest human endeavour ; and every day the voice of the Great Proprietor reminds us, " There is yet very much land to be possessed." " All things are yours."—D.

Vers. 9—18.—*The blessing of good government.* I. A WISE MAN DISAVOWS ABSOLUTE MONARCHY. Legislation, the most difficult department of government, had been furnished for Israel by the Supreme Mind of the universe ; yet Moses found the task of administration too much for a single arm. The aim of every ruler ought to be, not personal power, but universal service—the greatest good of the greatest number. No wise man will expose himself to the tremendous temptation of personal aggrandisement. Beside, it is a boon to others to exercise the faculties of discrimination and judgment.

II. POPULAR CHOICE OF RULERS TO BE DETERMINED BY A SINGLE LAW, VIZ. PERSONAL MERIT. To lift the voice for an unqualified ruler is a crime against the State—an injury, and not a benefit, to the person elect. To allow personal qualification to dominate the choice, is to make God the umpire. This is, in civic affairs, " to do his will on earth as it is done in heaven."

III. THERE IS ROOM, BOTH IN THE CHURCH AND IN THE STATE, FOR VARIOUS OFFICES. If a man cannot rule five thousand, he may be able to rule fifty. Service in a subordinate station may qualify for higher dignity. Gradation of rank best conserves the interests of the nation. " Order is Heaven's first law."

IV. ALL HUMAN AUTHORITY IS IN THE STEAD OF GOD. " The judgment is God's."

Magistrates act in God's stead. Parents likewise. Every man is bound to act as God would act. He represents God always and everywhere. All talent is a trust. We are the stewards of God's estate.

V. HUMANITY IS FAR SUPERIOR TO NATIONALITY, CLASS, OR SECT. Every man, however poor or ignorant, is to be accounted a brother. In the commonwealth of Israel there are no strangers. Nationality is but a pasteboard separation. "God hath made of one blood all nations." The great divider is sin. A heaven-kindled eye penetrates through every crust of barbarism and vice, and sees a *man* beneath. Here is a kingly nature, though now enslaved.

VI. GROWTH OF NUMBERS IS A TOKEN OF DIVINE APPROBATION. In the ratio of material abundance and contentment, is increase of population. It was one of the presages of Messiah's kingdom, "they of the city shall flourish like grass of the earth." In heathen lands population is sparse. War and pestilence decimate the ranks. In proportion as sound Christianity prevails, the subjects of the state augment. Every additional man ought to be an increment of strength and usefulness.

VII. PRAYER HAS A RECOGNIZED PLACE IN GOD'S GOVERNMENT. Promise always waits on prayer, as harvest waits on the husbandman's toil. However abundant are the promises, yet for the fulfilment God will be inquired of to do it for us. When prayer has its root in God's specific promise, it must bear fruit in proportion as faith enlarges her boughs. This is wise building, for we found our expectations upon eternal rock.

VIII. GOOD MEN GREATLY DESIRE THEIR COUNTRY'S GOOD. Patriotism is a goodly virtue, though not the noblest. To fence ourselves round with selfish interests is despicable. We envy not that man's narrow soul who has no sympathy nor energy for his nation's weal. The best Christian will take some interest in everything—in municipal matters, international treaties, literature, science, commerce, art. In the broadest sense, he is a citizen of the *world*. He lives to bless others. This is Christ-like.—D.

Vers. 1—4.—*The Deuteronomic discourses.* I. THE SPEAKER. "Moses." Though an hundred and twenty years old, "his eye was not dim, nor his natural force abated" (ch. xxxiv. 7)—a statement borne out by the sustained eloquence of these addresses. He speaks with the authority of a prophet, the affection of a patriot, and the earnestness of a dying man.

II. THE HEARERS. "All Israel." A new generation had sprung up from that which had received the Law at Sinai. 1. All are concerned in hearing God's message. "It is your life" (ch. xxxii. 47). 2. New-comers need new teaching.

III. THE SITUATION. "In the wilderness"—still there at the end of forty years. The places named (ver. 1), suggestive of past wanderings and rebellions. Form a background to the discourses that follow, and point home their lessons. We learn: 1. The value of association as an aid in teaching. 2. Our past cannot be got rid of, but it may be utilized. 3. God's Word is to be pondered in the light of bygone experiences. 4. The comparison of our actual situation with what it might have been (ver. 2) is often a salutary exercise (cf. Luke xv. 17).

IV. THE SUBJECT. "All that the Lord had given him in commandment." We find that this does not refer to a new commandment, but to the old commandment which they had from the beginning (cf. 1 John ii. 8). 1. Men crave for novelty, but the function of the preacher is to remind them of the truths which do not change, and to give "line upon line, precept upon precept," until loyal and hearty obedience is rendered to the same. 2. Exhortation is most effective when it takes as its basis the sure Word of God. 3. God's Word is to be spoken in its entirety.

V. THE TIME. "In the fortieth year, in the eleventh month"—when the attack on the Canaanites was about to be renewed, and after signal tokens of Divine favour had already been granted (ver. 4). 1. God's mercies call for renewed dedication (Ps. cxvi. 12—14). 2. The recollections of wasted years should prove an incentive to obedience in the future (Rom. xiii. 11, 12; Eph. v. 15, 16; 1 Pet. iv. 3). 3. We need God's commandment in our memories and hearts when entering on work in which formidable opposition is to be encountered, and which will put our fidelity to a severe test.

VI. THE MOTIVE. 1. *The natural solicitude of old age.* It is characteristic of old age to fall back upon and reiterate previous counsels. Compare Peter in his second

Epistle (i. 16); the traditional stories of the old age of John; Paul in the pastoral Epistles, "urging and repeating and dilating upon truths which have been the food of his life" (Alford). 2. *The lawgiver's knowledge of the rebelliousness of the people's disposition* (ch. ix. 24). 3. *The Divine command* (ver. 3). This had respect to the altered circumstances of the new generation, and to the prospect of their entering the land promised to their fathers, continuance in which was conditional on obedience.—J. O.

Ver. 2.—*The might-have-beens of life.* In its present setting this brief geographical note was, doubtless, meant to suggest the lesson of the evil results of disobedience. "Eleven days' journey," yet the fortieth year still saw them in the wilderness. We learn: 1. Sin turns short ways into long ones. 2. Sin entails on the transgressor needless trouble and sorrow. 3. Sin fills life with fruitless regrets. 4. Sin delays fulfilment of God's promises.

The path of obedience is in the end the shortest, easiest, safest, and happiest.—J. O.

Vers. 6—9.—*A summons to advance.* Moses begins by reminding the Israelites how God had formerly summoned them to march upon Canaan. The summons came to them at Horeb, after a sojourn of eleven months. The verses may be applied to illustrate—

I. The Church's danger—to abide at the mount, to settle down into a state of apathy or simple receptivity. This is met by the call to action—" Ye have dwelt long enough in this mount: turn you, and take your journey" (vers. 6, 7). Notice: 1. *Israel's stay at the mount was good while it lasted.* There the nation enjoyed a season of rest, ratified its covenant with God, received the Law, constructed a sanctuary, and was otherwise equipped and organized. There must be times of getting, of learning, of consulting for one's own edification, else it will go hard with us in the work and battle of life. But 2. *There was a danger that Israel's stay at the mount might last too long.* So is it with the Church, when she concentrates her attention too exclusively on her own spiritual improvement, and forgets her mission to the world. We have to remember that we get and learn only that we may apply and act. There is the peril of religion becoming a species of enjoyment. We luxuriate in retired communion, in restful fellowship with God, in converse with fellow-believers, in Church ordinances; and we think how sweet it would be if this could always last. But we are wrong. It would not be good for us always to be in this state of simple receiving. Religion, divorced from active employment, must soon lose its robustness, and degenerate into a sickly religiosity. There are many, many Christians who have been long enough, and far too long, in the mount, and it would be well for themselves if they could hear this voice summoning them to go forward.

II. The Church's destiny—to possess the land. The type was the land of Canaan; the antitype, so far as it lies in time, is the world, which it is the Church's calling to conquer for Christ, and for her own possession. St. Paul gives this interpretation in Rom. iv. 13. Taking the passage in this light, and reading the wider truth into it, we get the idea of a land which is: 1. *Known to God* (ver. 7). Known thoroughly, in all its parts, peoples, districts, conformation, accessibilities, and inaccessibilities. In advancing to take possession of the world for Christ, we have the encouragement of thinking that he knows precisely to what kind of work he is sending us, and yet promises success. India, China, Africa, etc.,—he knows them all, yet he says, " Go in and possess." 2. *Gifted by God* (ver. 8). It is long since the oracle declared that God had given Christ the heathen for his inheritance, and the uttermost parts of the earth for his possession (Ps. ii. 8). The Church, as one with Christ, shares in his kingdom, and shall yet inherit the whole earth. 3. *The conquest of which is commanded by God.* Not, indeed, by carnal weapons, as the Israelites were commanded to conquer Canaan, nor yet by the destruction of those against whom we war; but by the nobler weapons of the truth, and by seeking men's salvation. This is a benigner method of conquest, and it will prove successful if we advance with faith and courage. Those who persist in hardening themselves must indeed be destroyed; but not by us. The Lord puts no weapon of a kind to injure any into our hands; but bids us leave vengeance with himself. Our means are the preaching of the gospel, prayer, holy living, organized and beneficent activity to reach the lost sheep of our great communities, and multiplied missionary agencies in foreign lands.

III. THE CHURCH'S DUTY—to obey her Lord, and go forward at once to this great work. 1. He gives no alternative. 2. The command is express. 3. The world sorely needs our work. 4. Every motive of gratitude and compassion should urge us to it. —J. O.

Vers. 10, 11.—*Israel's increase.* These verses embody the expression of a very natural state of feeling in contemplating the marvel of the Church's growth.

I. THE CHURCH'S INCREASE AN OBJECT OF DESIRE. " The Lord God of your fathers make you," etc. (ver. 11). Such increase is : 1. A token of Divine favour (Acts xi. 24). 2. A manifestation of Divine power (1 Cor. i. 18—30 ; Eph. i. 19 ; 1 Thess. i. 5). 3. A source of blessing to the world (Ps. lxvii.). 4. A fulfilment of the Divine counsels (Eph. i. 10). 5. Means the ascendancy of true religion.

II. THE CHURCH'S INCREASE AN OBJECT OF WONDER. (Ver. 10.) The rapid spread, the extraordinary victories, the prolonged empire, and the undecaying vitality of the Christian religion are the most wonderful things in history, and a proof of its Divine origin. As Israel increased by the Divine blessing at an unprecedented rate, and in spite of all Pharaoh's attempts to check the increase, so has the Church flourished and spread, proving herself in her unarmed strength more than a match for the deadliest powers which can be arrayed against her. The present century has witnessed a re-markable revival of this propagative energy of Christianity (comp. Numb. xxiii. 23).

III. THE CHURCH'S INCREASE A MATTER OF PROMISE. (Ver. 11.) The promise to Abraham of a countless seed embraced in its widest import the spiritual, not less than the natural, Israel—his seed in Christ (Rom. iv. 16 ; Gal. iii. 7—10, 14, 16, 26, 29). (Cf. the promises in Isa. liii. 10—12 ; liv. 1—3 ; lx. 1—12, with Dan. ii. 35, 44 ; Matt. viii. 11 ; Rev. vii. 9).—J. O.

Vers. 9—16.—*Division of labour.* (Cf. Exod. xviii. 13—27.) An instance of a good idea (1) suggested, (2) readily adopted, (3) generally approved of. Reminds us that division of labour is as important in Church work as in the arts.

I. THE NEGLECT OF DIVISION OF LABOUR LEADS TO SERIOUS EVILS. 1. The work is not overtaken. " Not able " (ver. 9). 2. Those who have to do it are greatly over-taxed. " Cumbrance," " burden " (ver. 12). 3. Energy is wasted on subordinate tasks which might be applied to better purpose.

II. THE ADOPTION OF DIVISION OF LABOUR SECURES OBVIOUS ADVANTAGES. 1. Re-lieves the responsible heads. 2. Expedites business and promotes order. 3. Secures that the work is better done. 4. Utilizes varieties of talent. But parties must be as willing to co-operate as they were here.

III. RIGHTLY TO SECURE THE ADVANTAGES OF DIVISION OF LABOUR THERE MUST BE EFFICIENT ORGANIZATION. When Moses took in hand the appointment of assistants, he did it thoroughly (ver. 15). The work which each is to do must not be left to haphazard, or to " understandings," or to the tastes and inclinations of individuals, but should be definitely marked out. There must be organization and distribu-tion of tasks on a general plan, which, while it affords room for all grades of talent, allots work with a view to the aptitudes which each is known to possess. It is characteristic of Moses' scheme : 1. That it took advantage of existing institutions. 2. That it rested on a broad, popular basis ; elective (ver. 13).—J. O.

Vers. 16, 17.—*Judging.* The rules here laid down, while primarily applicable in the administration of law, are, in their spirit and for the most part in their letter, equally fitted to guide our private judgments. A proneness to judge is condemned by Christ (Matt. vii. 1) ; but his rebuke of the censorious spirit is not to be read as for-bidding the framing of such judgments upon the character, actions, and pretensions of others as the circumstances of our position may render necessary. We are called every day of our lives to form, and frequently to express, judgments upon men, measures, causes, theories, disputes, proposals ; judgments as to true and false, right and wrong, wise and unwise, expedient and inexpedient. Matters are appealed to us as individuals, or as a part of the general community, on which judgment is expressly asked. We must judge that we may know how to act. All this involves the possi-bility of judging rashly ; of judging with bias and prejudice ; of judging so as to do wrong to individuals; of judging so as to injure truth and retard progress and improvement. The text teaches us, on the contrary—

I. THAT CAUSES, BEFORE BEING JUDGED, ARE TO BE FAIRLY HEARD. How many judgments are passed daily in utter ignorance of the real facts of the case, and without any attempt to ascertain them, perhaps without the means of ascertaining them! Such judgments are *ipso facto* unjust. It is only by the rarest chance they can be right, and their rightness being accidental does not justify them. Let judgments be reserved for cases in which we have an opportunity of full investigation. Hear both sides, and hear them (1) fully, (2) candidly, and (3) patiently.

II. THAT CAUSES, AFTER BEING HEARD, ARE TO HAVE JUDGMENT PASSED UPON THEM WITH STRICT IMPARTIALITY. "Judge not according to the appearance," said Jesus, "but judge righteous judgment"—an instance illustrating that wider view of judging which we are here taking (John vii. 24). Equal measure is to be meted out to all. We are to judge impartially as between brother and brother, fellow-citizen and foreigner, rich and poor, applying the same principles and standards to each case, and keeping in view the essential merits as the one thing to be regarded. This is the plain rule of justice, though we all feel how difficult it is to act up to it.

III. THAT JUDGMENT UPON CAUSES IS TO BE GIVEN FEARLESSLY. "Ye shall not be afraid of the face of man." (Cf. the Regent Morton's eulogy on Knox—"There lies he who never feared the face of man.") Even when just judgment is being pronounced internally, the fear of man, or the desire of man's favour, or the dread of temporal consequences, often leads to a time-serving tampering with conviction, to a saying and doing of the thing we do not at heart approve of. This is the worst kind of cowardice.

IV. THAT JUDGMENT UPON CAUSES IS TO BE GIVEN UNDER A DUE SENSE OF RESPONSIBILITY TO GOD. "The judgment is God's." Judges are his vicegerents, deriving their authority from him, expressing the judgment of his righteousness, anticipating his own final judgment, and themselves responsible to him for the manner in which they exercise their functions. Every biassed, untrue, and insincere judgment is a misrepresentation of that truth and rectitude which have their ground in God's own being.

V. THAT IN CAUSES ON WHICH WE ARE INCOMPETENT TO PRONOUNCE, JUDGMENT IS NOT TO BE ATTEMPTED. (Ver. 17.)—J. O.

Vers. 1—18.—*The impartiality of God to be reflected in the judges of his people.* In the following Homilies we adhere to the traditional view of the Mosaic authorship of the book, believing that no sufficient evidence has yet been adduced by the critics for departing from that view. Moses enters upon his addresses in the land of Moab by recapitulating the salient points of the Exodus. The first notable reference is to the appointment of the judges. The qualifications and directions here recorded are fitted to throw precious light upon the Divine character. Here let us notice—

I. There was to be NO RESPECT OF PERSONS IN JUDGMENT. And here we may quote a definition which will materially aid us in this subject: "By the word *person* the Scripture signifies not a man, but those things in a man which, being conspicuous to the eyes, usually conciliate favour, honour, and dignity, or attract hatred, contempt, and disgrace. Such are riches, wealth, power, nobility, magistracy, country, elegance of form, on the one hand; and on the other, poverty, necessity, ignoble birth, slovenliness, contempt, and the like." These Jewish judges, therefore, were directed to allow none of these personal accidents to influence their judgments in the cases committed to them, but to decide as matters of pure equity.

II. There was to be NO FEAR OF MAN in their judgments. The consequences to themselves were not to be regarded. They were to be fearless officers, representing the Most High.

III. We see here that WITH GOD THERE CAN BE NO RESPECT OF PERSONS AND NO FEAR OF MAN. The strict impartiality of God has been questioned, if representations of his procedure drawn from the Divine Word are accepted. Now, the whole plan of salvation by *grace* appears favouritism and partiality. What is the meaning of "grace"? Undoubtedly *free, unmerited favour.* If, then, salvation is by grace (Eph. ii. 8), must not God be liable to the charge of partiality? Such, at least, is the reasoning of some in the interests of certain systems.

But when the matter is looked into more closely, we find that salvation by free grace is the most conclusive evidence of God's *impartiality*. It is really saying to all men, "Unless you give up the notion of recommending yourselves to me; unless you surrender the idea of some special claim in your being or your life upon me; unless, in a word, you lay aside the fancy that you must be partially and exceptionally treated, which is the whole meaning of self-righteousness, I cannot save you." This is impartiality *par excellence ;* and this is exactly God's position in offering salvation to men.

All who refuse salvation are really refusing to be treated impartially, and are clamouring for exceptional consideration on the ground of some fancied merit. The rejected at the last will be found to be those who wanted favouritism, but put away free grace. The line of thought opened up here may be profitably carried on.—R. M. E.

EXPOSITION.

Vers. 19—28.—Here Moses passes from the judges to the people at large; from charging officials to judge righteously, to reminding the people that they also had received from him commandments which they had to obey. The "things" referred to are either the injunctions specified in Exod. xxi., etc., or simply the instructions mentioned in the preceding verses. God had called the Israelites out of Egypt that they should go up at once to Canaan, and he had by Moses done all that was needed for this. But they had been rebellious, and had opposed God's commands, the consequence of which was that they had been made to experience various trials, especially to wander nearly forty years in the wilderness, so that of those who came out of Egypt only two were privileged to see the promised land. The words of Moses in this section supplement and complete the narrative in Numb. xiii.; but the words are those, not of a compiler, but of one who had been himself a witness of all he narrates.

Vers. 19—26.—That great and terrible wilderness: the desert forming the western side of the Stony Arabia. It bears now the name of *Et-Tih*, i.e. The Wandering, a name "doubtless derived from the wanderings of the Israelites, the tradition of which has been handed down through a period of three thousand years. . . . It is a pastoral country; unfitted as a whole for cultivation, because of its scanty soil and scarcity of water" (Dr. Porter, in Kitto's 'Biblical Cyclopædia,' vol. iii. p. 1075). In the northern part especially the country is rugged and bare, with vast tracts of sand, over which the scorching simoom often sweeps (see on ver. 1). This wilderness they had seen, had known, and had experience of, and their experience had been such that the district through which they had been doomed to wander appeared to them dread-

ful. Passing by the way of the Amorites, as they had been commanded (ver. 7), they came to Kâdesh-barnea (see Numb. xii. 16). Their discontent broke out oftener than once, before they reached this place (see Numb. xi., xii.); but Moses, in this recapitulation, passes over these earlier instances of their rebelliousness, and hastens to remind them of the rebellion at Kâdesh (Numb. xiii., xiv.), because it was this which led to the nation being doomed to wander in the wilderness until the generation that came out of Egypt had died. It was through faith in God that Canaan was to be gained and occupied by Israel; but this faith they lacked, and so they came short of what God had summoned them to attain (Ps. lxxviii. 22; cvi. 24; Heb. iii. 18, 19; comp. 2 Chron. xx. 20; Isa. vii. 9). Hence, when they had come to the very borders of the promised land, and the hills of Canaan were before their eyes, and Moses said to them, in the name of God, **Go up, possess** ("asyndeton emphaticum," Michaelis), they hung back, and proposed that men should be sent out to survey the land and bring a report concerning it. This was approved of by Moses; but when the spies returned and gave their report, the people were discouraged, and refused to go up. They were thus rebellious against the commandment (literally, *the mouth*, the express will) of Jehovah their God; and not only so, but with signal ingratitude and impiety they murmured against him, and attributed their deliverance out of Egypt to God's hatred of them, that he might destroy them (see Numb. xiii. 1—33, to which the narrative here corresponds).

Ver. 27.—Ye murmured in your tents; an allusion to what is recorded in Numb. xiv. 1, etc. Moses addresses the people then with him as if they had been the parties who so rebelled and murmured at Kâdesh, though all that generation, except himself, Joshua, and Caleb, had perished. This he does, not merely because of the solidarity of the nation, but also that he might suggest to them the possibility that the same evil spirit might still lurk among them, and consequently the need of being on their guard against allowing it to get scope.

Ver. 28.—**Our brethren have discouraged our heart**; literally, *have melted* or *made to flow down our heart* (הֵמַסּוּ, Hiph. of מָסַס, to flow down or melt), *have made us faint-hearted*. **The cities are great and walled up to heaven**; literally, *are great and fortified in the heavens*. To their excited imagination, the walls and towers of the cities seemed as if they reached the very sky; so when men cease to have faith in God, difficulties appear insurmountable, and the power of the adversary is exaggerated until courage is paralyzed and despair banishes hope. **Sons of the Anakims**; elsewhere (Numb. xiii. 22; Josh. xv. 14; Judg. i. 20) *children or sons of the 'Anak*. 'Anak may originally have been the proper name of an individual, but it appears in the Bible rather as the designation of the tribe. It is the word for *neck*, and this race, which were strong and powerful men, or their progenitor, may have been remarkable for thickness of neck; this, at least, is more probable than that it was from length of neck (Gesenius) that they got the name, for a long neck is usually associated with weakness rather than strength. Some have supposed the Anakim to have been originally Cushites; but the origin of the tribe is involved in obscurity.

Vers. 29—40.—Moses endeavoured to rouse the drooping courage of the people, and persuade them to go up by reminding them that God, who was with them, would go before them, and fight for them as he had often done before; but without success, so that God was angry with them, and forbade their entrance into Canaan. This is not mentioned in Numbers, probably because Moses' appeal was unsuccessful. The whole of that generation was bound to fall in the wilderness, except Caleb and Joshua; only their children should enter the promised land.

Vers. 29, 30.—Moses exhorts the people not to be afraid, as if they had to encounter these terrible enemies solely in their own strength; for Jehovah their God was with them and would go before them, as he had gone before them hitherto, to protect them and strike down their enemies.

Ver. 31.—Not only at the Red Sea did God appear for the defence of his people and the discomfiture of their enemies, but also in the wilderness, which they had seen (as in ver. 19), where (אֲשֶׁר, elliptically for אֲשֶׁר בּוֹ) Jehovah their God bore them as a

man beareth his son, sustaining, tending, supporting, and carrying them over difficulties (comp. Numb. xi. 12, where a similar figure occurs; see also Isa. xlvi. 3, 4; lxiii. 9, etc.; Ps. xxiii.).

Vers. 32, 33.—**Yet in this thing ye did not believe the Lord your God**; literally, *With this thing* [or *With this word*] *ye were not believing in Jehovah your God*. The Hebrew דָּבָר, like the Greek ῥῆμα, signifies either thing or word. If the former rendering be adopted here, the meaning will be, Notwithstanding this fact of which you have had experience, viz. how God has interposed for your protection and deliverance, ye were still unbelieving in him. If the latter rendering be adopted, the meaning will be, Notwithstanding what I then said to you, ye remained unbelieving, etc. This latter seems the more probable meaning. In the Hebrew text there is a strong stop (*athnach*) after *this word*, as if a pause of astonishment followed this utterance—Notwithstanding this word, strange to say! ye were not believing, etc. The participle ("believing") is intended to indicate the *continuing* of this unbelief. So also in ver. 34, the participle form is used—"who was going in the way before you," to indicate that not once and again, but continually, the Lord went before them; and this made the sin of their unbelief all the more marked and aggravated. (For the fact here referred to, see Exod. xiii. 21, etc.; Numb. ix. 15, etc.; x. 33—36.)

Ver. 34.—**And the Lord heard the voice of your words, and he was wroth, and sware**, etc. (comp. Numb. xiv. 21—24).

Vers. 35, 36.—They were all, the whole generation of them, evil, and therefore not a man of them should see the good land which God had promised to their fathers, with the exception of Caleb, who had wholly followed the Lord—had remained steadfast and faithful whilst the others fell away. Joshua also was exempted from this doom; but before mentioning him, Moses refers to himself as having also come under the Divine displeasure.

Ver. 37.—**The Lord was angry with me also for your sakes, saying, Thou also shalt not go in thither.** This must be regarded as parenthetical, for what he here refers to in regard to himself occurred, not at the time of the rebellion at Kâdesh, but at the time of the second arrival of the people at that place, many years later. This parenthetical reference to himself was probably thrown in by Moses for the purpose of preparing for what he was about to say respecting Joshua, in whom the people were to find a leader after he himself was gone. It may be noted also that Moses distinguishes between the anger of the Lord against him, and the wrath which broke forth upon the people—a distinction which is aptly preserved in the Authorized Version by the words " was wroth " (קְצַף) and " was angry " (אָנַף). **For your sakes**; rather, *because of you, on account of you.* The Hebrew word (גָלַל) comes from a root meaning to roll, and signifies primarily a turn in events, a circumstance, an occasion or reason. Moses reminds the Israelites that the misconduct of the people was what led to God's being angry also with him (see Numb. xx. 7, etc.; comp. Ps. cvi. 32, 33).

Ver. 38.—Though the rebellious generation were to perish, and Moses was not to be permitted to enter Canaan, God would not depart from his promise, but would by another leader bring the people to the inheritance which he had sworn to their fathers to give them. (For the account of Joshua's appointment and installation, see Numb. xxvii. 15—23.) **Which standeth before thee**; *i.e.* to be thy minister or servant (Exod. xxiv. 13; xxxiii. 11; Numb. xi. 28; comp. for the meaning of the phrase ch. x. 8; xviii. 7; Dan. i. 5). **Encourage him**; literally, *strengthen him* (comp. ch. iii. 21, 22; xxxi. 7, 8). **Inherit it**; the "it" refers back to ver. 35, "that good land." In vers. 8 and 21, the land is spoken of as to be possessed by the Israelites; here it is spoken of as to be inherited by them. The former has reference to their having to wrest the land by force from the Canaanites (יָרַשׁ, to occupy by force, to dispossess; cf. ch. ii. 12, 21, 22, where the verb is, in the Authorized Version, rendered by " destroy"); the latter has reference to their receiving the land as a heritage (נָחַל) from God, who, when he divided to the nations their inheritance, assigned Canaan to the children of Israel (ch. xxxii. 8). " Joshua the executor of the inheritance " (Schroeder).

Ver. 39.—Only among the young of that generation should the inheritance be divided, as they had no part in the rebellion of their seniors. **Your little ones**; *i.e.* children beginning to walk (טַף, from טָפַף, to trip, to take short and quick steps). **And your children**—boys and girls—**which in that day had no knowledge between good and evil**; rather, *of whom* [ye said] *they know not to-day good and evil.* The Hebrews were wont to express totality or universality by specifying contradictory opposites, as, *e.g.* great and small (2 Chron. xxxiv. 30), master and scholar (Mal. ii. 20), free and bond (Rev. xiii. 16; xix. 18), shut up and left (ch. xxxii. 36, where see note; 1 Kings xiv. 10), etc. Accordingly, when *good* and *evil* are set over against each other, the notion of entireness or universality is expressed. Thus, when Laban and Bethuel said to

Abraham's servant, " We cannot speak unto thee bad or good " (Gen. xxiv. 50), the meaning is, We can say nothing at all. Absalom spake to Amnon " neither good nor bad " (2 Sam. xiii. 22); that is, he did not say anything to him. The woman of Tekoa said to David, " As an angel of God, so is my lord the king to discern good and bad " (2 Sam. xiv. 17); *i.e.* There is nothing the king does not know—his knowledge is universal. Hence to know good and evil came to mean to be intelligent, and not to know good and evil to be unintelligent, as is a babe. The children here referred to knew nothing, and consequently could not be held as morally responsible; comp. Isa. vii. 15; Homer, 'Odyssey,' xviii. 228—

" οἶδα ἔκαστα
ἐσθλά τε καὶ τὰ χέρεια· παρὸς δ' ἔτι νήπιος ἦα."

Ver. 40.—The command to go to the mount of the Amorites (ver. 7) is recalled, and they are ordered to turn into the wilderness and go by the way leading to the Red Sea (comp. Numb. xiv. 25).

Vers. 41—46.—The people, appalled at the prospect of another sojourn in the wilderness, yet still rebellious and disobedient to God's command, though professing penitence, determined, in spite of direct prohibition on the part of God by Moses, to go up and force their way into Canaan; but were punished for their presumption by being utterly defeated and put to flight by the Amorites (comp. Numb. xiv. 40—45).

Ver. 41.—**We have sinned**; in Numbers it is simply said that " the people mourned greatly" (bemoaned themselves, יִּתְאַבְּלוּ); but this is not incompatible with the statement here that they confessed their sins; the one would naturally accompany the other. Their confession, however, was in word only; their conduct showed that it was not sincere. In Numbers (xiv. 44) it is said, " They presumed to go up;" here it is said (ver. 41), **Ye were ready to go up**, rather, *Ye acted heedlessly with levity*, or *frivolously, to go up.* The verb here (וַתָּהִינוּ) occurs only in this place, and is of doubtful signification. The Rabbins compare it with the הִנֶּנּוּ, lo we! here we be! of the people in Numb. xiv. 40. It is the Hiph. of הוּן, which is supposed to be the same as the Arabic هٰان, to be light, easy; and from this the meaning, " ye went up heedlessly," is deduced. None of the ancient versions, however, give this meaning. The LXX. has συναθροισθέντες ἀνεβαίνετε εἰς τὸ ὄρος; the Vulgate, *instructi armis pergeretis in montem;* Onk., למסק ושריתון (and ye began to ascend); Syriac, ܠܡܣܩ ܢܦܩܘ (and ye incited yourselves to go up).

Ver. 42.—Moses, by the command of God, warned the people that, if they presumed to go up, they should go without his protection, and so would certainly fall before their enemies.

Ver. 43.—In vain were they thus warned. Moses spoke to them as God commanded, but they would not be persuaded. **Went presumptuously**; rather, *acted insolently and went up;* margin, Authorized Version, " Ye were presumptuous, and went up." The verb here (הֵזִיד, from זוּד, to boil) signifies tropically, to act proudly, haughtily, insolently (comp. Neh. xi. 29, Authorized Version, "dealt proudly ").

Ver. 44.—**The Amorites**, for the Canaanites generally; in Numbers, the Amalekites are specially mentioned as joining with the Amorites in chastising the Israelites. These tribes came down from the higher mountain range to the lower height which the Israelites had gained, and drove them with great slaughter as far as Hormah, in Seir, chasing them as bees do, which pursue with keen ferocity those who disturb them. Hormah (Ban-place), the earlier name of which was Zephath (Judg. i. 17), was a royal city of the Canaanites, taken by the Israelites towards the close of their wanderings, and placed by them under a ban (Numb. xxi. 1, etc.), which ban was fully executed only in the time of the Judges. It is here and elsewhere called Hormah by anticipation. The old name Zephath seems to have survived that given to it by the Israelites in the name Sebaita or Sepata, the Arabic form of Zephath, the name of a heap of ruins on the western slope of the rocky mountain-plateau Rakhmah, about two hours and a half south-west of Khalasa (Ritter, 'Geography of Palestine,' i. 431 ; Palmer, 'Desert of Et-Tîh,' p. 289, etc.). This is a more probable identification than that of Robinson ('Res.,' ii. 18), who finds Hormah in the rocky defile of Es-Sufâh, an unlikely place for a city of the importance of Zephath to be in.

Ver. 45.—**Ye returned**; *i.e.* either to Kâdesh, where Moses had remained, or from their rebellious and defiant attitude to one of apparent submission and contrition, or the whole phrase, " Ye returned and wept," may mean merely that they wept again, as in Numb. xi. 4, where the same words are used. **And wept.** They mourned their misfortune, and complained on account of it (comp. for the meaning of the phrase, Numb. xi. 4, 18, 20). **Before Jehovah**; *i.e.* before the tabernacle or sanctuary (comp. Judg. xx. 23, 26). Their mourning was not that of true repentance, and, therefore, the Lord would not listen to them or give heed to their wail (comp. Prov. i. 24, etc.).

Ver. 46.—It was unnecessary that Moses should tell the people the precise length of time they abode in Kâdesh after this, because that was well known to them; he, therefore, contents himself with saying that they remained there as long as they did remain (comp. for a similar expression, ch. ix. 25). How long they actually remained there cannot be determined, for the expression, many days, is wholly indefinite.

HOMILETICS.

Vers. 19—33.—*Sending the spies.* This paragraph contains a brief review of events which are recorded in Numb. xiii., xiv. Israel had left the wilderness of Sinai ; the cloud now rested in the wilderness of Paran. At this point they were not very many days' journey from the land of promise. But it would seem that they did not like to go in and take possession of the land without more information than they as yet possessed as to its accessibility and its fitness for their permanent home. So they proposed that spies should be sent ahead. We gather that, at the desire of the people, Moses asked advice of the Lord, and in consequence he was bidden to accede to their request. Twelve men were sent. Ten brought an evil report of the land; two only were full of heart and hope, strong in faith, giving glory to God. *Numbers* carried more weight than *worth.* The report of ten bore down that of two. The people would not believe the Lord. They said in their unbelief, " Let us make a captain, and return into Egypt," and even (Neh. ix. 17) "appointed a captain to return to their bondage." And a sad and sorrowful glance does Moses cast over the sin of that time. Let us glance at it too. We will endeavour to gather a true estimate of the course which Israel took, taking care, as we go on, to see how far the incidents recorded here convey instruction to many whose feelings are analogous to theirs. In estimating this case, let us look—

I. AT THE COURSE ISRAEL TOOK IN SENDING THE SPIES. 1. *It was unnecessary.* For they had been redeemed by a strong hand and by a stretched-out arm from the bondage and degradation of Egypt; their deliverance had been effected for them by the free love, spontaneous care, and watchful providence of God. Surely it should not have been hard to argue on this wise : "He who has shown us such wondrous mercy will not be wanting to us to the end." It was surely needless to send out any scouts to Canaan, to survey the land before them. A wiser and better care than theirs had done this for them, and there was no more need for them to send to spy out the land than to have sent pioneers to clear their way through the deep! But, in thus chiding Israel, are we not really rebuking ourselves? We have to bethink us of a rescue, before which that of Israel fades into nothingness. And how has our rescue in Christ been effected? By *our* power or skill? Nay, but by a wisdom, power, and love, which in blessed union did combine in the cross of Christ to save us. Is not, then, the inference more than warranted, "He that spared not," etc. But if so, why need we strain our eyes to pierce the gloom that hangs over our future course? We need not faithlessly forecast. 2. *It was undesirable*, and that on several grounds. (1) It was manifestly hindering their march. (2) They were confronted by the prospect of an accumulation of difficulties which would come only one at a time. (3) Israel therefore darkened the present by prying into the future. So it is now. "Sufficient unto the day is the evil thereof." Our daily course, with its mingled comforts and cares, may be so peaceful if we will calmly leave the future to him who knows and plans all; but if we, with our short foresight and our little strength, will foolishly set before us in one perplexing combination all the difficulties which will come only one by one; if we think and speak as if our God would leave us alone when they come,—we shall dishonour him, and shade the present by anticipating the future.

II. LET US LOOK AT THE CONCLUSION TO WHICH ISRAEL CAME ON THE REPORT OF THE SPIES. They resolved to go back and to return to Egypt, and appointed a captain to lead them. It was one-sided, forgetful, ungrateful, and ruinous. 1. *It was one-sided*. True, the sons of Anak were in the way. But who was above them all? See Caleb's putting of the case, in Numb. xiv. 6—9. 2. *It was forgetful*. For was not the fact of all these enemies being in the land explicitly named in one of the earliest promises (Exod. iii. 17); and had not God promised to drive them out? 3. *It was ungrateful*. After all the love which had been shown them, how could they so requite it? 4. *It was ruinous* (see Numb. iv. 33—38; ch. i. 32—39). But are there not some now who start fairly in the Christian race, or seem to do so, and yet who, when some difficulty meets or threatens them, turn back and go away (cf. Matt. xiii. 20, 21)? Nor can we safely neglect the warning consequent on this incident given in Heb. iii. 4. To quit the leadership of Christ because of present or impending difficulties will be much more grievously sinful than it was for Israel to propose to quit the leadership of Moses. The four points named above will apply also here. It will be: 1. *One-sided*. For supposing, as we try to peer into the future, possible or even certain difficulties do present themselves, ought we not to remember that with the demand on the strength there will be given strength to meet the demand? Why look at one without looking at the other? 2. *It will be forgetful*. For what are the words of Holy Writ? What are we bidden to expect? Have we ever been told that we are to have a smooth path through life? Have we never read that "through much tribulation we *must* enter the kingdom"? Have we not read that we must expect to be "partakers" of Christ's sufferings? 3. *It will be ungrateful*. Did not our Saviour tread a thorny path for us; and have we no return to make in treading a thorny path for him? Do we thus intend to repay the sorrow and blood of Calvary? 4. *It will be ruinous* if we turn back. Difficulties we seek to shun will be multiplied a hundred-fold. The ease we would fain secure will not be ours. While, instead of having to conquer the sons of Anak, we shall have to encounter the condemnation of our Saviour and Lord. Let us press onward still to the rest which remaineth. On! for *honour* demands it. On! for *gratitude* requires it. On! for love, infinite love, expects it. On! only a step at a time, and if the giant Anakim appear, the Lord will fight for us. On! and if we come to Jericho's walls, faith's trumpet blast shall bring them to the ground. On! and you will have many a cluster of grapes sent to you by the Lord of the land, to show you its richness, and that you may taste of its fruits ere you enter there! Trust your God, ye people, follow the Lord fully, and not all the powers of earth or hell shall keep you from the promised rest!

Vers. 32—35.—*The grievous consequences of unbelief.* Moses rehearses in the hearing of Israel the strange story of "their manners in the wilderness," and reminds them how their unbelief had provoked the Lord to anger, and had deprived vast numbers of them of the rest they had hoped to enjoy. We ought to be at no loss how to apply this to present day uses. The Holy Ghost, by the mouth of David, renews the warning voice. The writer of the Epistle to the Hebrews, both by argument and exhortation, repeatedly says, Take heed lest a like evil befall you (Heb. iii. 7—19; iv. 1—11). Whence observe—

I. HERE IS A REMARKABLE FACT TO BE NOTED: viz. Divine arrangements apparently failing of their end through the misconduct of man. 1. God had made provision for securing the entrance of Israel into their land. Early had the promise been made. Long and patiently did the patriarchs await its fulfilment (Heb. xi. 13). God had watched over his people's wanderings. He beheld them in Egypt. When the time for liberating them was come, Moses was at hand. Israel had but to stand still, and see the salvation of the Lord, again and again. The Law was given from Sinai. Manna descended from heaven. Water gushed from the rock. The pillar of fire and of cloud was their guard, light, or shade. They knew what God intended to do for them. The promise was clear; the conditions were plain; the warnings were solemn; the threatenings were terrible. No excuse of ignorance could be pleaded by the people. Yet: 2. All were insufficient to prevent their defection of heart from God. They were perpetually doubting God. " Ten times " [1] (Numb. xiv. 22). Unbelief led to the breaking forth of lust. They forfeited the promise; and of the many thousands who started for Egypt only two survived to enter Canaan. "So we see that they could not enter in because of unbelief."

II. THERE IS GREAT DANGER LEST THE PARALLEL BETWEEN OURSELVES AND ISRAEL, ALREADY SEEN IN GREATER MERCY, SHOULD BE SEEN AGAIN IN A GREATER RUIN. There is already a parallel in mercy. 1. There is a complete arrangement for meeting all our wants on the way to a nobler rest. 2. In treading the way, we have a far better Leader than Moses. 3. We have far clearer light than Israel had. 4. We have fuller and richer promises. 5. We have a far higher rest in view. 6. Throughout the way there will be demands on our faith. 7. There is a danger *from within*, lest we should distrust God. Are we not conscious of such a danger? Our hearts are sinful, and predisposed to doubt. We *have* doubted God very much, and thus wronged him in times gone by. Such unbelief may take or may have taken the form of presumption or of despair. For an illustration of the former, see next Homily. The latter kind of unbelief may be almost indefinitely varied. Men may doubt (1) the power of God to bring them to the rest; or (2) the willingness of God to do it; or (3) the readiness of God to bring *them* to the rest, without questioning his care for others; or they may even go so far as to doubt (4) whether the promises of the rest be Divine; (5) whether there is any such rest as the one promised; and even (6) whether there is any God of promise. Whichever of these forms a despairing unbelief may assume, the evil of it is sufficiently manifest. It is the greatest dishonour which we can cast on God, to allow the thought to gain the mastery, that we are flung down hither without any sure destiny of blessedness being disclosed, or without any certainty of reaching it being made known. Besides, doubt prevents work; it paralyzes. Doubting God gives the rein to every lust. 8. And unless we "take heed," if we suffer doubt to get the mastery, as Israel lost their rest, we shall lose ours. What present rest can we have while unbelief has the upper hand? Doubt is essentially unrest. How can we enjoy any future rest? What sympathy with God can we have? Besides, God declares, "They *shall not enter* into my rest." In that heavenly rest none can or will share who do not implicitly believe the promise and loyally obey the precept. 9. And how much more serious it will be to trifle with Christ, than to slight Moses (Heb. x. 28—31)!

But there is a very bright side to this subject. While unbelief will shut us out of heaven, *nothing else will!* Nothing can shut us out of heaven but doubting God! Poverty cannot. Persecution cannot. Reproach cannot. Obscurity cannot. No one

[1] Ten times: Exod. v. 20, 21; xiv. 11, 12; xv. 22—27; xvi. 2, 3, 20, 27; xvii. 1—7; xxxii.; Numb. xi. 1—3, 4—35; xiv.

shall ever sink who trusts his God. See that young and weak believer who has turned
his back on the world, and set his face heavenward. A thousand difficulties bristle up
in all directions. But he meets them all, saying, " God called me, God will help me,
God will lead me, God will guard me."

> " A feeble saint shall win the day,
> Though death and hell obstruct the way ! "

Yea, even so ! " Them that honour me," saith God, " I will honour." But, must we
not look to him who awakened our faith, to sustain it ? 'Tis even so. Ever have we
to say, " Give what thou commandest, and then command what thou wilt." " Lord,
we believe ; help thou our unbelief." And is there not enough revealed of God
and of his wondrous love in Christ to put every doubt to flight, when all that God
is to us is laid home to our hearts by the Holy Ghost ? Here, indeed, is a quickening,
inspiring, sustaining force, of which Israel knew little or nothing. " Greater is he that is
for us than all they which be against us." " He that spared not his own Son, but gave
him up for us all, how shall he not with him also freely give us all things ? " Let us
doubt ourselves as much as we will, but our God and Saviour—never. He hath said,
" I will never leave thee nor forsake thee." " Hath he said, and shall he not do it ?
Hath he spoken, and shall he not make it good ? "

Vers. 41—46.—*Forced back !* In the preceding paragraph we had an illustration of
unbelief in doubting the promise of God, and of the effect of that unbelief in excluding from the promised rest. Here we have an illustration of a like unbelief working
in precisely the opposite direction ; as Israel feared to go up notwithstanding the
promise of God, so now we find them resolving to go up in spite of the prohibition
of God, " acting," as an expositor remarks, " in contempt of the threatening, as they
had before acted in contempt of the promise, as if governed by a spirit of contradiction." The points in the history which should be noted are these. 1. As the men of
that generation (two only excepted) were debarred from entering Canaan, they have to
wander in the desert for forty years. 2. They rebel against this Divine arrangement,
though we, who at this distance of time " see the end of the Lord," can perceive how
much mercy there was in it. 3. There was a short way to Canaan, through a hill
country, which to human judgment would seem preferable to a "march far wandering
round." 4. In this route enemies would surely assail—Amorites, Amalekites, etc.
5. Israel made light of these difficulties. 6. God forbade their going up. Moses forbade
them. The ark was not moved from its place in the camp. 7. The people were
resolved to go up, defiantly, *insolently* (Gesenius, *sub verb.*). 8. They paid dearly for
their presumption. They were forced back. 9. They grieved and wept over their
disappointment. 10. Such weeping God does not regard. "Tears of discontent must
be wept over again." As they had before found out the folly of distrusting God's
strength, so now they had to bewail the uselessness of presuming on their own ! We
cannot be wrong in continuing to follow the apostolic teaching in regarding the Canaan
of Israel's hope *as a type of the higher "rest"* which "remaineth for the people *of
God"* (cf. Heb. iv. 1).

I. THE LAW OF OLD IS IN FORCE STILL, THAT THE UNBELIEVING SHALL NOT ENTER INTO
REST. This is the teaching, under varied forms, of no small part of the Old Testament
and of the New. We may inquire, if we will, into the philosophy of this ; and in
doing so, we shall find but little difficulty in seeing the essential impossibility of one
who doubts God finding rest anywhere. Doubt *is* unrest. But whether or no one can
discern the deep reason of it, there stands the word, with its awful bar, " He that
believeth not is condemned already."

II. IT IS A DREARY OUTLOOK FOR THE UNBELIEVER. To wander on, and to be moving
towards some destiny or other, but yet to have no prospect of rest at the end of the
journey, is it not dreary ? We do not deny that men may, as they say, resign themselves to the inevitable. And we even admit that men may so far control themselves,
as, with stoical unfeelingness, to take "a leap in the dark." But not all this can blind
us to the misery of those who move on under the ban, " The unbeliever shall not see
rest."

III. THE SAME UNBELIEF WHICH DOUBTS THE PROMISE ALSO DESPISES THE THREATEN-

ING. Both promise and threatening come from one and the same God; hence whoever doubts *him* will be as likely to question one as the other. And it is very, very easy for unbelief to urge plausible arguments or questionings concerning the threatenings; *e.g.* "Has *God* said *that?*" "God will not be so severe;" "God cannot mean *me;*" "Who can tell whether the judgment day will ever come?" etc.

IV. THIS UNBELIEF MAY MAKE A DESPERATE EFFORT TO PROVE THE THREATENING NULL AND VOID. "We WILL go up!" How much does this remind us of what our Saviour says in his Sermon on the Mount (cf. Matt. vii. 22)! As if unbelief would carry its daring up to the very judgment seat (see also Matt. xxv. 10—12; Luke xiii. 24—26).

V. AN ATTEMPT TO ENTER THE REST IN A WAY CONTRARY TO GOD'S WORD, WILL BE FORCED HELPLESSLY BACK. Israel was disastrously repulsed, and found it "hard to kick against the pricks." "Woe unto him that striveth with his Maker!" "Hath any hardened himself against God, and prospered?" (see continuation of New Testament passages referred to above). Man can do many wonderful things, but there are five things he never can do: He cannot *evade* the sentence of God; he cannot *postpone* it; he cannot *nullify* it; he cannot *modify* it; he cannot *impeach* it. "We are sure that the (δικαίωμα) sentence of God is according to truth."

VI. THE WEEPING OF DISAPPOINTMENT WILL BE UNAVAILING. "Ye returned and wept before the Lord; but the Lord would not hearken to your voice, nor give ear unto you." It will be of no use whatever trying to enter Canaan if the sentence has finally gone forth against us, "Ye shall not see my rest;" nor will it avail to try to enter by any other than God's own appointed way; nor will the murmuring, or wailing, or gnashing of teeth at all alter the matter. There may be as much unbelief in tears as in trifling. By no other means than implicit faith in and unswerving loyalty to God in Christ, can we find rest for our souls either here or hereafter. Oh that sinful men would "hear the voice of Jesus say," "Come unto me, all ye that labour and are heavy laden, and I will give you rest"! Apart from Christ, our souls must wander in dry places, seeking rest and finding none.

HOMILIES BY VARIOUS AUTHORS.

Vers. 19—46.—*Irrecoverableness of wasted opportunity.* I. THE CULMINATION OF OPPORTUNITY OFTEN FINDS A MAN UNPREPARED TO OCCUPY IT. The point of time referred to here was *the supreme moment* in Israel's history. They had relinquished Egypt, endured privation, performed a toilsome journey, for one object, viz. to possess Canaan; yet, when they touched the threshold of the inheritance, they failed to rise to the conception of their privilege. They hesitated, dawdled, feared—and failed. Men play with opportunity as a toy, and when their eyes open to see its value, lo! it has vanished. Possibly, there is a supreme moment in every man's history; yet often he is too indolent to improve it. Every morning is not a May-day. Many reach the margin of a glorious destiny, and then turn back to the desert, The path of duty is very plain; but self-indulgence makes us blind as a mole.

II. THE DISHONESTY OF PRUDENTIAL PLEAS. These Hebrew men thought themselves very sagacious to suggest the experiment of the spies; and God endured their whim. Yet there was no reason for this precaution. With God as a Pioneer and Protector, they might have known that it was safer to follow the fiery pillar than to remain at ease in their tents. The command was plain—"Go up and possess." Therefore all delay, and all reconnoitring, was sin. If we were to deal honestly with inclination, if every whisper of conscience were obeyed, we should often see through the thin guise of our own pretences; we should strip the veneer of insincerity from our deeds. In some dark cavern of our hearts we may find, by honest search, some wish that we are ashamed to avow. There is often a conspiracy in the man against himself. We hunt for excuses to cover disobedience.

III. UNBELIEF DEVELOPS, THROUGH MANY STAGES, INTO RANK REBELLION. The report of the spies confirmed the word of God. *This* always accords with external fact, and with human experience. God had *not* said that the Canaanites were few or weak. What mattered it how tall and brawny they were, if so be God were on their side, and fought for them? Old Unbelief is a fool, and ought to be decorated with cap and bells. Unbelief is poison, and saps the basis of our strength, enervates our courage, and melts our iron into flux. Unbelief develops into falsehood, and perverts the truth of God into lying. Unbelief maligns and traduces God—charges him with the basest crime. It calls evil good; purest love it styles blackest hate. It is the essence of blasphemy. It is the crime of crimes—the seed of misery—the germ of hell.

IV. THE RETRIBUTIONS OF GOD ARE SEVERE AND EQUITABLE. Much that human judgment deems to be retribution is not penalty. Bodily suffering is usually corrective, not destructive. The retributions of God are co-related to the sin. Men pamper the passion for drink: inappeasable thirst shall be their doom. Men say to God, "Depart from me!" God responds, "Depart from me!" The Hebrews would not march into possession of Canaan: therefore they shall dwell and die in the desert. Retribution is related to sin as fruit to blossom—as wages to work. There comes a point where return is impossible. God swears that it shall be so. The oath is an oath of righteousness. Nevertheless, out of the crowds of the nameless ungodly, individual liegemen shall be honoured, even Caleb and Joshua. These are elect spirits—choice natures. In the day of overwhelming calamity, God does not overlook the solitary righteous. "He hideth him in the hollow of his hand." The proofs of inviolable equity are written in gigantic capitals on the heavens and on the earth.

V. THE FORECASTS OF FEAR ARE OFTEN THE REVERSE OF REALITY. Cowardly and disobedient Hebrews pretended a far-reaching concern for their children. "If we are slain in this invasion of Canaan, what will become of our little ones?"—thus argued these malcontents. "Can we endure to think that they shall become a prey to these human wolves?" They were frightened at a mirage—terrified at the shadow of their own folly. *Facts* were the very reverse of their fears. These "little ones" God would take into training—drill them by the hardy discipline of the wilderness, and qualify them for warfare and for conquest.

VI. REPENTANCE HAS MANY COUNTERFEITS. There is often confession of our folly, and yet no repentance; promise of amendment, yet no repentance. There may be poignant regret for the past, bitter shame, sharp remorse, deep compunction, severe self-judgment, yet no repentance. For repentance is soul-submission unto God. It brings our feeling, desire, will, into harmony with God's feeling and will. Repentance has not thoroughly penetrated the soul until we love what God loves, and hate what God hates. True repentance works for righteousness. Deceit may so worm itself in the heart as to intertwine itself round every fibre of our being. We may ultimately become so blind as not to discern between truth and falsehood. The repentance of these Jews was a carnal sorrow that produced fruits of death.

VII. PRESUMPTION IS AS CRIMINAL AS PUSILLANIMITY. We dishonour God as much by going beyond the line of duty, as by falling short of it. Each alike is an act of disobedience. We cannot atone for cowardice yesterday by an excess of rashness to-day. The essence of obedience is promptitude. It is *not* the same whether we observe the command to-day, or to-morrow. Between the two there may be a gulf deep as hell itself. The prohibitions of God are as sacred as his positive commands. What is a duty to-day may be a sin to-morrow, because the precept may be withdrawn. Some commands are eternally permanent; some have only temporary prevalence.

VIII. REPENTANCE OFTEN COMES TOO LATE. During life-time, repentance has moral productiveness. We may not attain the precise object, which by repentance we hoped to gain; nevertheless, real repentance brings relief and gladness to the soul! Esau was afterwards a better man for his repentance, though he could not recover his birth-right. To these Hebrews, repentance came too late for them ever to possess the earthly Canaan: let us hope it availed to gain them the heavenly. It is possible for repentance, long-delayed, to be unavailing. "Because," says God, "I have called, and ye refused . . . I also will laugh at your calamity. . . . Then shall they call upon me, but I will not answer." "He sware in his wrath, They shall not enter into my rest." When all gracious remedies are exhausted, "it is impossible to renew men unto repentance." It is a perilous thing to tamper with conscience, or to trifle with God.—D.

Ver. 19.—"*That great and terrible wilderness.*" An emblem of the rough and afflictive way by which God leads his people to the higher rest.

I. THE FACT OF THIS WILDERNESS DISCIPLINE. We need not exaggerate. We admit all that can be said of the world as a fair and delightful residence, in which we have much to make us happy. But it cannot be denied that the picture has a darker side. The man who has drunk deepest of the world's pleasures is he who can tell best how unsatisfying it is as a portion for the spirit. There are more sad and weary hearts in this same world than a glance at the surface of society would lead us to suspect. There are numbers to whom life is one hard, dreary, terrible, hopeless struggle with adverse conditions. The joy of a life is often blighted by a solitary stroke; and in how many cases does some secret grief embitter what seems from the outside a prosperous existence! The believer is no more exempt than others from these ordinary griefs of life— from poverty, trial, pain, bereavement. But he has thoughts and feelings of his own, which add to the pain of his situation. He is a Christian, and contact with the world's evil tries and grieves him as it will not do a worldly man. His hope is beyond, and this makes earth, with its imperfect conditions, its broken ideals, its unsatisfied yearnings, seem drearier to him. Like his Master, his ear is quicker to catch the strain of human woe—"the still sad music of humanity"—than the strain of noisier mirth. All this compels him to look at life prevailingly under an aspect of privation, discipline, and trial, and it is in no unreal sense that he speaks of it as the "wilderness." When troubles crowd on him, it is literally, as to others, "waste and howling," a "great and terrible" desert.

II. THE ENDS OF THIS WILDERNESS DISCIPLINE. These are numerous. 1. In part *the discipline is inevitable*—bound up with the conditions of existence in a world "made subject to vanity." But: 2. *The discipline is useful.* (1) It tries and proves the heart (ch. viii. 2). (2) It inures to hardship. (3) It develops the nobler qualities of character —faith, patience, resignation, etc. (Rom. v. 3). (4) It makes the rest sweeter when it comes (Rev. vii. 14; xiv. 13).—J. O.

Ver. 21.—*Courage.* "Fear not, neither be discouraged" (cf. Josh. i. 7, 9).

I. GOD'S WORK NEEDS COURAGE. 1. The enemies are *many*. 2. The enemies are *strong*. 3. Humanly speaking, *we are feeble in comparison with them.* Distinguishing between real and nominal Christianity, it might be plausibly held that there is to-day greater talent, intellectual power, wealth, rank, and social influence enlisted on the side of unbelief than on the side of faith. But the true citadel of unbelief is the evil heart; and what powers of our own are sufficient to storm that?

II. IN GOD'S WORK THERE IS EVERY REASON FOR COURAGE. 1. God is with us. Our cause is his cause. 2. He has promised victory, and he is able to keep his promise. 3. The past should encourage us. The Church can never come through greater conflicts than those in which she has already proved herself victorious.—J. O.

Vers. 22—32.—*The mission of the spies.* We see from two instances in this chapter how God's plans leave wide room for the independent action of the human mind. Moses got the suggestion of appointing judges from Jethro; the idea of sending spies to reconnoitre the Holy Land originated with the people. The source from which it came made the motive of it doubtful, but as in itself a measure of prudence, Moses was well pleased with it, and, with God's permission, adopted it. We have here—

I. A POLICY OF CAUTION. Caution is in itself a virtue. It is never wise to rush into undertakings without well-planned measures. The more knowledge we have to guide us in entering upon difficult duty the better. The sending out of these spies was fitted to procure for the Israelites valuable information as to the nature of the land, the best mode of attack, the state of feeling among the inhabitants, etc. The Church would do well to improve upon the hint thus given, and have men out on the field, to keep a sharp watch on the fortifications and movements of the enemy, and bring back intelligence which may encourage, guide, or otherwise help those whose time and thought are devoted to the actual warfare.

II. AN UNEXPECTED RESULT OF THAT POLICY. The spies, with two exceptions, brought back a most disheartening and ill-advised report. We see here the danger of a policy of caution, when that springs from over-fearfulness or an original indisposition to advance. When caution is divorced from courage, and gets the upper hand, its natural tendency is to neutralize enthusiasm, to concentrate attention on difficulties, to play into the hands of those who don't want to do anything, and to furnish them with excuses and arguments for delay. It was so here. The real secret of the desire of the people to have spies sent out was their lurking disbelief and fear. The spies themselves shared in this fear. With the exception of Caleb and Joshua, they seem to have had an eye for little else than difficulties. They admitted the goodliness of the land, and brought with them a splendid sample of its fruit (ver. 25). But in every other respect their report was calculated to dispirit. It is a sad thing for the Church when those who ought to animate and encourage her begin themselves to show the craven spirit. Yet over-cautious people are apt, often unwittingly, to do the very work of these spies, by magnifying difficulties, looking only to discouragements, and standing in the way of plans and efforts which would do great good.

III. A REBELLION OF THE PEOPLE. That rebellion was the result of downright unbelief (ver. 32), and illustrates its work (cf. Heb. iii. 19). We see in it how unbelief: 1. *Looks only to the seen.* They thought only of the size of the people and the strength of the cities (ver. 28). The help of their invisible King was to them as if it were not. They had not the slightest hold upon the reality of it. 2. *Sees only the discouragements of duty.* There was a bright side as well as a dark one to the report brought to them, but nothing would make them look at the bright one. The same two sides—a bright and hopeful side, and a side of difficulty—exist in every situation, and it is a test of character which we are most given to dwell upon. 3. *Misreads the providence of God.* What greater perversion of God's kind dealings could human nature be guilty of than that in ver. 27? 4. *Is blind to the lessons of the past.* They had just been delivered from Egypt, had seen mighty miracles, had been brought across the Red Sea, had been strengthened to conquer the Amalekites, etc.; but all is already forgotten. 5. *Issues in flat refusal to do God's will.* That is the upshot of unbelief, wherever it exists.

The report of the spies, confirmed by the grapes of Eschol, suggests that there is very much in the world which makes it worth conquering for Christ (genius, art, beautiful natural characteristics, etc.).—J. O.

Vers. 31—33.—*Love in the wilderness.* A beautiful passage, laden with God's compassions. We have in it—

I. TENDER LOVE. The love is likened to that of the best of fathers to a son (cf. Ps. ciii. 13). The New Testament goes further. It not only *likens* God to a father, but tells us he *is* one. He is "our Father in heaven," "the God and Father of Jesus Christ our Lord." This full revelation of Fatherhood only a Son could have given; and as given in the gospel it is the believer's daily comfort (Matt. vi. 25—34).

II. CONSTANT CARE. This arises out of the relation and the love. It is a care: 1. *Unceasing.* "All the way." 2. *Provident.* "Who went in the way before you, to search you out a place to pitch your tents in." 3. *Comprehensive;* embracing every want of our lives. God "bare" Israel, *i.e.* took the entire charge of the nation upon himself; the whole responsibility of seeing them fed, led, clothed, kept, and brought safely to their final destination. So does he provide for his children in Christ. 4. *Tenderly sympathetic.* "As a man doth bear his son." And God has to bear with, as well as bear us.

III. SPECIAL GUIDANCE. This is included in the care, but is more prominent as a peculiar manifestation of it (ver. 33). Guidance is never wanting to those who need it. It is from day to day—just sufficient to show us present duty. It is given in the Bible, in the indications of providence, and in that inward illumination which enables us to discern the Lord's will in both. It was furnished to the Israelites through the pillar of cloud and fire—the symbol: 1. Of fiery guardianship with grateful shade. 2. Of guiding light with attendant mystery. 3. Of light shining to us in the midst of dark providences. 4. Of the adaptation of God's guidance to our needs—by day the cloud, by night the fire.—J. O.

Vers. 34—40.—*The excluded and the admitted.* I. THE EXCLUDED. 1. *That whole unbelieving generation,* with two exceptions (ver. 35). Note: (1) Their unbelief and disobedience did not frustrate God's purpose of the occupation of the land. Canaan was occupied after all. So heaven will be peopled, the world conquered, and God's work done, though we in our folly and sin rebel and stand aloof (Matt. iii. 9). "It remaineth that some must enter in" (Heb. iv. 6). (2) Their unbelief and disobedience effectually excluded themselves. God sware it in his wrath, and the sentence admitted of no reversal. A foreshadowing of the final exclusion from heaven of those who persistently disobey (Matt. vii. 21—24; Luke xiii. 24—29; Heb. iv. 11; Rev. xxii. 11—16). 2. *The holy Moses* (ver. 37; cf. on ch. iii. 26; iv. 21; xxxiv. 4). The exclusion of Moses will be more fully considered afterwards, but we learn from it here that God's apparent severity is often greatest to his own people (Amos iii. 2), and that the share which others have had in leading us into sin does not abate our own responsibility in the commission of it. This greater apparent severity (1) repels the charge of favouritism; (2) gives a peculiarly impressive demonstration of the evil of sin; (3) reminds us that sin in God's people is more dishonouring to him than it is in others; (4) warns the wicked. For if judgment begin at the righteous, "what shall the end be of them that obey not the gospel of God? And if the righteous scarcely be saved, where shall the ungodly and the sinner appear?" (1 Pet. iv. 17, 18).

II. THE ADMITTED. These were to be: 1. *The faithful two*—Caleb and Joshua (vers. 36, 38). The former is signalized as having "wholly followed the Lord," and Joshua was a man of like faith and staunchness in a time of general defection. Such persons God will singularly preserve and honour. Their place in heaven will be a high one. "We must, in a course of obedience to God's will and of service to his honour, follow him *universally*, without dividing; *uprightly*, without dissembling; *cheerfully*, without disputing; and *constantly*, without declining; and this is following the Lord fully" (Matthew Henry, on Numb. xiv. 24). 2. *The younger generation* (ver. 39). Instead of the fathers, God would take the children. What a rebuke!—(1) of their *groundless fears.* "Your little ones, which ye said should be a prey." (2) Of their *unmanly cowardice.* Their little children, types of all that was humanly feeble, would do the work they were afraid to attempt. (3) Of their *inconsiderate selfishness.* They were not ashamed to hand down to these children their own abandoned life-tasks, with all the work and peril, if also with all the reward and honour, attending their accomplishment. Was not this to make themselves objects of contempt to their own offspring? "Let no man take thy crown," least of all thine own child.—J. O.

Vers. 40—46.—*Tardy repentance.* In the conduct of these Israelites we have a typical exhibition of human nature. In its folly, its fickleness, its unreasonableness, and its obstinacy. Forbidden to enter Canaan, they change their mood, and nothing will serve them but to "go up" and do the thing they had formerly said they would not do. They are vociferous in their professions of repentance, and will not be reasoned out of their self-willed purpose, but persist in following it up to their own after discomfiture. We have here to notice—

I. HOW UNCHANGED CHARACTER MAY COEXIST WITH A CHANGED FORM OF MANIFESTATION. Underneath these loud professions of repentance, "We have sinned" (ver. 41), it is not difficult to detect: 1. The old *unbelief.* They disbelieve God's threatening, as before they refused to believe his promise. 2. The old *self-will.* It is not what God wills, but what they will themselves, that is to be done. They do not ask, "Will God permit us to do this?" but they take the law into their own hands, and ignore God's wishes altogether. 3. The old *contumacy.* Their wills are wholly unsubmissive. In revolt yesterday against their duty, and to-day against their punishment. They will not hear warning (ver. 43), but pursue their own way. All this stamps their repentance as not only tardy, but insincere. Analogous to much of the repentance caused by fear of punishment, fear of exposure, fear of death; and points to the defects in superficial repentance generally.

II. HOW INSINCERE REPENTANCE NATURALLY PASSES OVER INTO PRESUMPTUOUS SIN. It does this inasmuch as there was never in it the element of real submission. The undertaking of the Israelites was typical of many more. It was: 1. Presumptuously *conceived.* 2. Presumptuously *prepared for.* 3. Presumptuously *persevered in.* It is, therefore, the type of all undertakings set on foot and carried out (1) in defiance of God's will; (2) without God's assistance; (3) in face of God's expressed displeasure. It is a case, in short, of flying in the face of God; of defying him, and entering into direct contest with him; as every one does whose schemes are in opposition even to natural and economical, and still more if they are in opposition to moral and spiritual, laws; or in any way contrary to what we know to be God's will. Presumption may show itself in refusal to be saved, except in ways or on terms of our own dictation.

III. How GODLESS ENDEAVOUR RECOILS IN DISASTER ON THOSE WHO PERSIST IN IT. (Ver 44.) So must it be with all schemes that have God's frown upon them.

Note—1. Repentance may come too late (ver. 45; Matt. xxv. 11; Luke xiii. 25). 2. Disobedience may cloak itself in the guise of obedience (ver. 41). 3. The test of obedience is willingness to do what God requires *at the time he requires it*, and not at some time of our own.—J. O.

Vers. 19—33.—*The unbelief in sending and in hearkening to the spies.* Moses reminds his audience of the conduct of their fathers at Kadesh-barnea, when exhorted to go up and possess the land. Duty was clear. They had been brought up out of Egypt for the very purpose of entering into and possessing the land of Canaan. But instead of courageously following the path of duty, they resolved to send over spies. The result was an evil report and an evil resolution on the people's part not to attempt invasion. The bitter end was death in the wilderness and exclusion from the land of promise.

I. GOD OFFERED CANAAN TO HIS PEOPLE AS A SUITABLE INHERITANCE. It was the promise of this land which led to the exodus. The sojourn at Horeb was to organize the nation and give it laws. All was ready for an entrance into the land. Its suitability was guaranteed in the Divine promise; and if the people had been willing to walk by *faith*, then the invasion would have been immediate and successful. (On the suitability of the land, cf. Moorhouse's 'Hulsean Lectures,' the last sermon in the volume, on 'The Land and the People.' In Kinglake's 'Invasion of the Crimea,' we have a similar instance in the allies not taking Sebastopol by assault immediately after Alma.)

II. THE SUGGESTION ABOUT SPIES WAS REALLY A RESOLVE TO WALK BY SIGHT AND NOT BY FAITH. Moses at first approved of it, although it never came from him. He thought that anything the spies *saw* would only confirm them in the resolution to invade the land. But in principle it was unbelief in God. It was virtually resolving not to follow his advice unless it *seemed* the best. It was putting clear duty to the trial of prudence. It was a resolve to walk by appearances and not by faith. And this is the universal tendency of the human heart. Prudence often conflicts with faith and hinders wholesome action. Prudence has no voice in the matter after God has spoken. He may lead us through over-prudence, in absence of express commandment; but when the command is clear, prudence should hide its head and allow *faith* to obey.

III. IT WAS STILL WORSE TO HEARKEN TO THE SPIES WHOSE COUNSEL CONFLICTED WITH THE COMMAND OF GOD. Having embarked on prudential considerations, they must needs follow them out to their unbelieving end. The spies returned, and could not but acknowledge that the land was good. From Eshcol they carried on a staff a bunch of grapes sufficient of itself to vindicate the Divine choice of the land. "But the inhabitants," said ten of the spies, "are gigantic, and the cities walled up to heaven; and there is no use in thinking of successfully invading it." In vain did Caleb and Joshua counsel courage instead of cowardice, faith instead of fear. The people resolved to take counsel of their fears and unbelief. They *would not* enter the land of promise.

So is it often in the lives of men. God offers salvation and a good land to all who will believe upon him. But men fear the giants and their castles. They imagine that the difficulties of the life of faith are beyond their powers, and so shirk them.

But when God points out a path of difficulty, it is not that we may encounter its perils in our own strength, but in his. Faith will carry us through, while sense and sight are sure to fail us.—R. M. E.

Vers. 34—46.—*The heirs of promise.* We have in this passage the result of unbelief. The dread of the people was lest their little ones should become a prey to their gigantic foes in Canaan. The Lord now declares that these little ones shall be the possessors of the land, while they themselves shall be denied an entrance, since they refused it when offered to them. The only exceptions are to be Joshua and Caleb, who made the good report and gave the good counsel. Even Moses is included in the doom of exclusion. The subsequent attempt and the subsequent tears had no effect in reversing the deserved sentence. We learn from this passage such practical lessons as these :—

I. GOD'S GRACIOUS OFFERS ARE NOT TO BE TRIFLED WITH. The promised land lay open to the Israelites, who had been mercifully guided to its gates. The all-important "Now," the time for decisive action had come, and it remained with them to determine whether they would go in and receive the blessing, or remain without. They preferred to delay, to trifle with the offer, and so the time went past.

So sinners are offered pardon and acceptance as an immediate boon (2 Cor. vi. 2), but when the offer is despised and trifled with, it may be withdrawn (Prov. i. 24—33).

II. PRESUMPTION IS A POOR SUBSTITUTE FOR FAITH. When the people saw the mistake they had made, they would go up and fight in a spirit of presumptuous chagrin. They now fought *without commissions*. The result was disastrous defeat, and a hurling of them back from the gates of Palestine to the great and terrible wilderness. God was not with them in their presumption, since they would not follow him in humble faith.

So may it be with sinners. Despised mercy may be succeeded by deserved defeat. The wild and proud efforts of presumption are in striking contrast to the quiet courage of faith. Toil and tears may be insufficient to retrieve disaster when once courted by unbelief.

III. JOSHUA AND CALEB'S GOOD FORTUNE SHOWED WHAT WAS POSSIBLE TO WHOLE-HEARTED FAITH. These two spies, in wholly following the Lord and in counselling courage, showed an humble faith. They stood alone faithful in face of an unbelieving majority, and God gave them a corresponding assurance that they should enter into the land. They were greatly honoured in being allowed to do so.

And they are surely encouragements to believing souls throughout all time.

IV. THE ASSURANCE OF THE CHILDREN THAT THEY SHOULD BE HEIRS OF THE LAND VINDICATED GOD'S PROCEDURE AND FAITHFULNESS. The little ones, for whom they feared, are selected as the heirs of promise. But they are to get the land after discipline and sorrow in the wilderness. God's ways are not ours. Yet wisdom regulates them all.

And the Divine grace was magnified in this arrangement. The Israelites, as they died in the wilderness, would be *cheered* by the thought that, though they were justly excluded from the land because of their unbelief, their children would receive the inheritance in the exercise of faith. The judgment on the fathers would be sanctified, like the sickness of Hymenæus and Alexander (1 Tim. i. 20), and their spirits, let us hope, saved in the day of the Lord Jesus (1 Cor. v. 5).—R. M. E.

EXPOSITION.

CHAPTER II.

Vers. 1—23.—THE NEW BEGINNING AND REVIEW OF THE JOURNEYINGS OF ISRAEL FROM KADESH TO THE RIVER ARNON, THE FRONTIER OF THE AMORITES. At this point the language of address is exchanged for that of narrative. The change of subject from "*ye* abode" to "*we* turned," became necessary when Moses passed from exhorting and warning the people to narrating what happened after they resumed their journeyings; and gives no support to the notion of some recent German critics, that Moses left Kâdesh with only a portion of the people, while the rest remained there, so that no entire departure of Israel from Kâdesh ever took place—a notion which the whole tenor of the subsequent narrative contradicts. In obedience to the Divine command (ch. i. 40), the people, after tarrying for a while at Kâdesh, took their departure and marched in the direction of the Yam-suph (Numb. xiv. 25).

Ver. 1.—**And we compassed mount Seir many days.** These "many days" are the thirty-eight years during which the people wandered in the wilderness before they camped the second time at Kâdesh; their going round Mount Seir, which was in Edom (Gen. xxxvi. 8, 9, 20), is descriptive of their nomadic wanderings in various directions, west, south, and south-east of that mountain (Numb. xxi. 4). "Crossing the long, lofty mountain chain to the eastward of Ezion-geber (Numb. xxi. 4, 5), the Israelites issued into the great and elevated plains which are still traversed by the Syrian pilgrims on their way to Mecca; and appear to have followed *northward* nearly the same route which is now taken by the Syrian Hadgi along the western skirts of this great desert near the mountains of Edom" (Robinson, 'Bib. Res.,' i. 253, 559). Mount Seir is now *Jebâl* and *esh-Sherah*. This mountain range is a continuation of that which sur-rounds the eastern side of the Dead Sea. The details of this protracted wandering are passed over by Moses as not required by his purpose here.

Vers. 2, 3.—When Israel, after their long and disheartening wandering, were at the south-eastern end of the 'Arâbah, God gave them the word to turn their march north-ward towards Canaan. The route they pursued was along the eastern boundary of Edom (comp. Numb. xxi. 10, etc.).

Ver. 4.—It would appear that the Edom-ites made preparations to resist the pas-sage of the Israelites through their territory (Numb. xx. 18—20). As the Israelites, how-ever, kept on the outskirts of their country, and did not attempt to penetrate into the interior, the Edomites did not attack them or seek to hinder their progress. The Israelites, on the other hand, were strictly forbidden to invade that country in a hostile manner; they were to watch over them-selves, so as not to be tempted to make war on the Edomites, who were their brethren; as God would not give them any part, not so much as a foot-breadth, of that land, for he had given Esau (*i.e.* the race descended from Esau, the Edomites—LXX., τοῖς υἱοῖς Ἠσαῦ) Mount Seir for a possession. **They shall be afraid of you** (see Exod. xv. 15).

Ver. 5.—**Meddle not with them**; literally, *Excite not yourself against them*, i.e. so as to strive in battle with them; comp. the use of the verb in Jer. l. 24, "hast striven" (Authorized Version); Dan. xi. 25 (where מִלְחָמָה, war, is added), "shall be stirred up to battle" (Authorized Version). Accord-ingly, they were enjoined to buy from them for money food and water as they required. Two different words in the Hebrew are rendered here by "buy" in the Authorized Version; the former, שָׁבַר, a denominative from שֶׁבֶר, grain, properly means to deal in grain, whether as buyer or seller, and so to buy food; the latter, כָּרָה, means primarily to dig (a well, *e.g.* Gen. xxvi. 25), and, as used here, probably conveys the idea that the Israelites were to pay for permission to dig wells in the country of the Edomites to supply themselves with water as they passed along; this, however, does not necessarily follow from the use of this word, for it has also the meaning to buy (comp. Hos. iii. 2, and the corresponding Arabic verb, *karâ*, which in certain conjugations has the mean-ing to borrow or hire).

Ver. 7.—They were enabled to buy what they required—**For the Lord thy God hath blessed thee in all the works of thy hand;** their flocks and herds had increased during their wanderings (Numb. xxxii. 1); and they may have gained wealth by cultivating the soil at places where they had made a lengthened sojourn, or by traffic with the tribes of the desert with whom they came in contact. Jehovah their God had **known**—had noted, observed, had regard to, had cared for (comp. Gen. xxxix. 6; Ps. i. 6; Prov. xxvii. 23) – **their** walking—their pere-grinations—**through this great wilderness;** he had been their Leader, had chosen for them places to rest in, had provided food for them, and had been their Protector and Guardian all through the forty years of their pilgrimage, so that they had wanted for nothing (ch. i. 33; viii. 2, 3, 15, 16; comp. Ps. xxiii. 1—6). "He sufficiently supplied what was needful for thee when thou walkedst through this great wilderness; for these forty years the Word of Jah thy God hath sustained thee; nor hath anything been wanting to thee" (Chaldee Para-phrase). **Forty years** (Numb. xiv. 33). "From the fifteenth day of the first month in which their fathers came out of Egypt (Numb. xxxiii. 3), to the tenth day of the same month in which they went over Jordan into Canaan (Josh. iv. 19), there were but *five* days wanting of complete forty years" (Patrick).

Ver. 8.—**And when we passed by from our brethren the children of Esau, which dwelt in Seir, through the way of the plain from Elath, and from Ezion-gaber, we,** etc. Rather, *And we passed by from* (away from) *our brethren the sons of Esau, who dwelt in Seir, from* (off from, *i.e.* alongside, but at some distance from) *the way of the 'Arâbah, from* (off from) *Elath and from Ezion-geber.* And so, in obedience to the Divine command, the Israelites passed from the territory of the Edomites without entering it, and went by their border on the east side of the 'Arâbah, and from beside Elath and Ezion-geber, both ports at the northern extremity of the Elanitic Gulf of the Red Sea (Numb. xxxiii. 35). Thus they came to where they were then encamped, in the steppes of Moab. "Probably they followed the still used caravan route to Damascus, between the east side of the cultivated land, and the west side of Arabia Deserta" (Schroeder).

Elath or *Eloth* (אֵילַת, אֵילוֹת, palmgrove)—the Αἰλὰθ of Josephus, 'Antiq.,' ix. 12; the Ἔλανα of Ptolemy (v. 17)—was a city of Idumea, situated on the eastern gulf of the Red Sea. Its ruins are still traceable near the modern fortress of Akâbah, on the northwest (Burckhardt, p. 509; Robinson, i. 241). Ezion-geber (עֶצְיוֹן גֶּבֶר, backbone of a man, so called probably from the rugged and jagged rocks in its vicinity), a seaport near to Elath (cf. 1 Kings ix. 26; 2 Chron. xx. 36).

Ver. 9.—The Moabites, being the descendants of Lot, and so allied by race to the Israelites, the latter were commanded to pass through their country without offering them any injury or assault. **Ar**, a border-town of Moab (Numb. xxi. 15), here put for the country itself. It is the Areopolis of the Greeks, and was, as Jerome tells us, destroyed in a single night by an earthquake. A hill, with ruins a short distance southwest from Ara'ir, is supposed to be its site.

Vers. 10—12.—The mention of the Moabites gives occasion to the author to introduce some notices of the ancient inhabitants of Edom and Moab. In Moab dwelt, in the earlier times, the Emim, a giant race, potent and numerous, like the 'Anâkim. They were also, like the 'Anâkim reckoned among the Rephâim, but were by the Moabites called Emim. The word **Emim** means frightful, and was given to these men probably because of their huge stature and fierce aspect. **Anakims** (see ch. i. 28). *Rephâim* seems to have been a generic name of these gigantic Canaanitish tribes (see Gen. xiv. 5; xv. 20). **The Horim** appear from the name (from חוֹר, a cave) to have been a Troglodyte race, inhabiting the caves which abound in the Edomite range, and with whom, perhaps, originated the conception which was at a later period carried out in the marvellous rock city of Petra. Of their own origin nothing is known. **As Israel did** [or *has done*] **unto the land of his possession.** This cannot be regarded as uttered proleptically; it must either be the insertion of a later age, or it must refer to the conquest which had actually been made before this by the Israelites of the land to the east of the Jordan, and which is, in ch. iii. 20, described as the possession which the Lord had given to the two tribes and a half to whom it had been assigned. The latter is the preferable supposition.

Vers. 13—15.—Ver. 13 connects with ver. 9, the intermediate verses being a parenthesis, introduced for the purpose of reminding the Israelites that the Edomites and Moabites had received their territory by gift from God, the earlier inhabitants

having been cast out by him that they might take their lands (see vers. 21—23). There is no need, therefore, for the insertion "I said," in ver. 13; the words are those of Jehovah, not of Moses.

Ver. 13.—**The brook Zered;** either the stream of the Wady el Ahsy (Robinson, ii. 157; Ritter, iii. 78), or that of the Wady Kerab (Keil, Kurz, etc.); see Numb. xxi. 11, and Smith's 'Dictionary,' iii. 1842. This brook formed the boundary line between Edom and Moab, and was the limit of Israel's wanderings in the wilderness. They crossed it thirty-eight years after the doom had been pronounced upon them at Kâdesh, and during that period the entire generation of those who had rebelled had died out.

Ver. 14.—**Men of war;** those of age sufficient to go forth to war, viz. twenty years old and upwards (Numb. i. 3; xiv. 29). These, as the responsible transgressors, all perished; the whole generation passed away, and was consumed (תַּם; cf. ch. v. 15; Ps. lxxiii. 19), as God had sworn (Numb. xiv. 28, 29).

Ver. 15.—**For indeed;** rather, *And also;* not by natural causes alone, but by the hand of God, *i.e.* by special penal judgments also, were they troubled and destroyed (cf. Numb. xvi. 31, etc.; xvii. 12, 13; xxi. 6; xxv. 1—9).

Vers. 16—19.—The generation that sinned having quite died out, the people were now to cross the border of Moab and advance to the conquest of the promised land. To the east of Moab was the country of the Ammonites; these, also, the Israelites were to leave unassailed, for the Lord had given to them their land for a possession (cf. ver. 9).

Ver. 18.—**Coast of Moab;** the boundary of Moab, which was the river Arnon, *hod.* Mujeb (Numb. xxi. 13—15; xxii. 36).

Ver. 19.—**Over against the children of Ammon.** As the Israelites were passing eastward of Moab; when they crossed the Arnon, the Ammonites, whose dwelling was in the wilderness east of the Jordan, would be almost in front of them. The Israelites came over against them after they conquered Sihon (cf. Numb. xxi. 24).

Vers. 20—23.—Another parenthetical insertion, containing some ethnographical notices, intended, probably, to confirm the assertion that to the children of Ammon God had given their land for a possession. There is no sufficient reason for supposing that this paragraph is an interpolation, or gloss, inserted by some later writer. It lay as much in the way of Moses to introduce such ethnographical notices as in that of any writer of a later age.

Ver. 20.—Before the Ammonites, the land was occupied by a gigantic race, called by them, **Zamzummim** (probably *noisy ones*, from זָמַם to hum, mutter; or, as the verb also signifies, to muse or meditate, perhaps *moody ones;* whether the same as the Zuzim of Gen. xiv. 5—LXX., ἔθνη ἰσχυρά, as if from זוז, to overflow, to abound—is uncertain). The colossal stone monuments, resembling what in Europe are known by the Celtic names of *dolmen, menhir,* and *cromlech,* still to be found in the land of Moab, are supposed to be the work of these aboriginal inhabitants of the country, the gigantic Emim and Zamzummim. This giant tribe the Lord had destroyed before the Ammonites, just as he had destroyed the Horim before the children of Esau in Seir.

Ver. 23.—So also the Caphtorim, who came from Caphtor (Gen. x. 14), probably the island of Crete (Ritter, iii. 262), drove out the Avim, a Canaanitish race, who dwelt in villages (*Hazêrim,* חֲצֵרִים) as far as Gaza (Azzah), and took possession of their land; though it would appear some of them still remained among the Philistines (who were Caphtorites, Amos ix. 7; Jer. xlvii. 4), and were among the tribes not subdued by the Israelites under Joshua (Josh. xiii. 3). These Caphtorim were, like the Israelites, immigrants, who drove out the original occupants of the country; and on this account, probably, are referred to by Moses here. "This is so often repeated, to possess the minds of the Israelites with a sense of God's providence, which rules everywhere; displacing one people, and settling another in their stead, and fixing their bounds, also, which they shall not pass without leave" (Patrick).

Vers. 24—37.—CONQUEST OF THE KING-DOM OF SIHON. Sihon and his people were Amorites, who had settled on the east of the Jordan in Gilead. But though not included in the original promise to Abraham, God had assigned this territory to the Israelites; and, therefore, he commanded the people under Moses to cross the Arnon, and take the first step towards possessing the promised land, by assailing Sihon, King of Heshbon, assuring them that from that day he would "put the dread and fear of them upon all nations under the whole heaven," that is, all nations, wherever placed, to whom the fame of the Israelites should come (comp. Exod. xxiii. 27; ch. xi. 16), so that on hearing thereof, they should tremble and

writhe as in pain (וְחָלוּ, comp. Isa. xiii. 8). Moses, however, in the first instance, sent a message of peace to Sihon, proposing to pass through his territory on the same terms as he had made with the Moabites and Edomites, travelling by the highway, and paying for such provisions as his followers required. But this Sihon refused, and came out against Israel, with all his people, to battle. The issue was that he was utterly discomfited; all his towns were captured, he and all his people utterly destroyed, and the cattle and spoil of the whole country taken for booty. Israel thus became possessed of that entire territory, though it did not lie within the bounds of the land promised by God to Abraham, which was the reason, probably, why Moses made overtures of peace to Sihon, and would have passed through his country amicably, had he been permitted; but comp. ch. xx. 10.

Ver. 26.—**The wilderness of Kedemoth** (comp. Numb. xxi. 13); so named from the town of Kedêmoth, an old Amorite town, on the right bank of the Upper Arnon; at a later period, a Levitical city in the tribe of Reuben (Josh. xiii. 18; xxi. 37; 1 Chron. vi. 79). The name (from קֶדֶם, the east), signifying eastern parts, indicates that it was situated on the eastern boundary of the Amorite region, so that the desert named from it must have bordered on the great Arabian desert; it may have been on what is now the Derb el Haj, or Pilgrims' Road, probably, at Kal'at Balûa.

Ver. 27.—**Along by the high way;** literally, *by the way, by the way,* i.e. always, continuously by the way, the public road, called in Numb. xx. 17 and xxi. 22, "the king's way," probably because made and kept up by the king.

Ver. 29.—**As the . . . did unto me.** This refers expressly to the fact that the Edomites and Moabites did not *hinder* the Israelites from passing through their country, though they were far from friendly, and dealt in an unbrotherly way with them, for which the Moabites were afterwards placed under a ban (Deut. xxiii. 3).

Ver. 30.—**Heshbon,** the chief city of the Amorite king, Sihon. Some ruins on a hill east of the upper end of the Dead Sea, and bearing the name Chesbân, mark the site of this once large and important city. Sihon rejected Moses' overtures of peace, because God had **hardened his spirit, and made his heart obstinate;** literally, *had sharpened his heart,* had made his determination keen. It is not to be supposed that any influence was *directly* exerted on him, to make him obdurate and persistent in his hostility to the people of God; the expression " he would not " indicates that it was of his own will that Sihon acted; but it was the will and purpose of God that Sihon should be destroyed, and his country taken by the Israelites, and so he was placed in circumstances by which, " given over to a reprobate mind," he was confirmed and strengthened in his determination to pursue a course which led to his destruction; like Pharaoh, by the circumstances in which God placed him, he found scope for the display and for the confirmation of a stubborn, pertinacious pride of spirit, which led ultimately to his ruin. Nothing so hardens the heart as resistance to God's overtures of peace. **As** appeareth **this day;** i.e. as present experience shows; in Sihon's refusing to let them pass, there was already an actual beginning of the fulfilment of God's purpose to deliver him into the hand of the Israelites.

Vers. 31—37.—God had determined to give Sihon and his land to the Israelites, and so certainly should this be done, that Moses is exhorted already to begin to seize, in order to possess the land. Sihon initiated hostilities by coming out with all his host to fight against Moses and the Israelites. The battle took place at Jahaz (or Jahazah, or Jahza), a town between Medeba and Dibon (Euseb.; cf. Numb. xxxiii. 45), afterwards belonging to the tribe of Reuben (Josh. xiii. 18), and assigned to the Levites of the line of Merari (Josh. xxi. 36; 1 Chron. vi. 78). The war was one of extermination, in which all the people of Sihon were destroyed, from one end of his dominion to the other; all his cities were devoted irredeemably (comp. Lev. xxvii. 29), and only the cattle and the material property were preserved as booty by the conquerors (Numb. xxi. 23—26).

Ver. 32 (cf. Numb. xxi. 23).—**Jahaz** (יָהַץ, downtrodden), elsewhere Jahazah (יַהְצָה), a city of Moab, afterwards assigned to the tribe of Reuben, and allotted to the priests (Josh. xiii. 18; xxi. 36; 1 Chron. vi. 63; Isa. xv. 4; Jer. xlviii. 34).

Vers. 33, 34 (cf. Numb. xxii. 24, 25; xxxii. 34, 35, etc.).—**And utterly destroyed the men, and the women, and the little ones, . . . we left none to remain.** As the Amorites came out of Canaan, they belonged to the race which God had doomed to destruction. The Israelites, therefore, had a commission to extirpate them. *Utterly destroyed;* literally, *devoted* or *placed under a ban,* which

of course implied utter destruction. *The men, and the women, and the little ones, of every city;* literally, *every city of men and women and little children.* The phrase " city of men " can hardly mean, as Rosenmüller affirms, " men of a city; " the hypallage here would be too violent. It rather means " a peopled city," " a city inhabited by men." The word rendered " men " (מְתִים) does not designate males as opposed to females, but is a designation of human beings in general (cf. Job xi. 3; xxiv. 12 [Heb. xx. 48]; xxxi. 31; Ps. xxvi. 4, " vain persons," Authorized Version, literally, *men of emptiness* or *of falsehood,* etc.). The passage might be rendered, *every inhabited city, even the women and the little children.*

Ver. 36.—**Aroer,** one of the Amorite cities, on the right bank of the river Arnon (cf. Josh. xii. 2; xiii. 16). On the Moabite Stone, King Mesha says, " I built Aroer; " but this can only mean that, after some temporary condition of decay or ruin, he rebuilt it. On the borders of the northern side of the Wady Mojeb, there are heaps of ruins bearing the name of Ara'ir, which probably mark the site of this ancient town. There was another Aroer, belonging at a later period to the tribe of Gad, and opposite to Rabba, the chief city of the Ammonites (Josh. xiii. 25; 2 Sam. xxiv. 5); and still another in the south of Judah (1 Sam. xxx. 28), probably in what is now known as the Wady A'rârah. **The city that is by the river;** properly, *in the river* or *wady;* i.e. Ar, the capital of Moab, which was in the valley of the Arnon, and which is mentioned here as marking the exclusive limit of the country that was captured. The word rendered " river " (נַחַל) is used of the valley or ravine (Arabic, *wâdy*) through which a stream flows, as well as of the stream itself (cf. Gen. xxvi. 19; Numb. xxiv. 6, etc.). Ar is elsewhere called Ar of Moab (Isa. xv. 1). **Even unto Gilead,** i.e. Mount Gilead, which rises to the north of the Jabbok (*hod.* Zerka).

Ver. 37.—In obedience to the Divine injunction, the Israelites left untouched the country of the Ammonites, situated on the eastern side of the Upper Jabbok. **Cities in the mountains;** the towns in the Ammonitish highlands. In Josh. xiii. 25, half of the land of the Ammonites is said to be assigned to the tribe of Gad; but that refers to the part of the land between the Arnon and the Jabbok, which had been taken from the Ammonites by the Amorites, and was in the possession of the latter at the time of the Israelitish invasion (Judg. xi. 13, etc.). **Whatsoever the Lord our God forbad us:** literally, *all that Jehovah our God commanded us,* sc. *not to come into.*

HOMILETICS.

Vers. 1—23 (specially ver. 7).—*God's knowledge of our pilgrimage.* (For the historical and geographical details connected with this section, see the Exposition.) Moses here reviews the career of Israel during the wanderings, with reference to their treatment of the nations through whose territory they required to pass on their way. They, though the favoured people of Jehovah, were not allowed to transgress the common laws of righteousness, by levying any demands on the nations through whose country they passed, nor to "distress" in any way those peoples whom the Lord had not delivered into their hands. They were to labour for their own sustenance, and to purchase, at a fair rate, meat or drink. And so far as this precept was concerned, they seem to have been (notwithstanding their waywardness in other respects) loyal to the Lord their God. These directions against transgressing the rules of right in national intercourse, were a most important part of the education of a people, where God was forming a commonwealth with this (then) unique feature, that *its corner-stone was righteousness.* (For an admirable survey of the fundamental principles of the Hebrew polity, home and foreign, see Wines's 'Commentaries on the Laws of Moses.') And as Moses is now reviewing the stages in their experience when they passed through an alien's land, he reminds them how faithful God had been to them; that they had had no need to depart from the Divine injunctions, for their good and gracious God had taken all their need into account. "*He knoweth thy walking through this great wilderness.*" This clause contains a world of meaning in itself, and opens up a most fruitful theme for the Christian's meditation and for pulpit exposition, viz. *God's knowledge of our pilgrimage in life.* Three inquiries invite our notice—

I. WHAT IS IT THAT GOD IS HERE SAID TO KNOW? "Thy walking." We understand Moses as here referring to the walking, viewed objectively, not subjectively. The sentence would be true in both respects; but, nevertheless, the reference does not seem to be to the manner of Israel's walking, but to the pilgrimage itself. What was true of them is also true of us. He knoweth *our* walking, etc. 1. The *meaning* of our pilgrimage is known to him—as being that of moral and responsible beings, made in the image of God, and as having for its purpose the education of character for eternity. 2. He knows the *difficulties* of the pilgrimage—the obstructions with which we are continually meeting, thwarting, perhaps, our fondest plans and wishes. 3. He knows the *trials* of the way. Not only the trials which are "common to man" in general, but also those indefinable, *felt* peculiarities, which are ours and ours only, which we cannot unfold to a single soul on earth. 4. He knows the *enemies* which beset us: their strength, number, malice, and craft. 5. He knows the appointed *goal* at the end of the pilgrimage, and all the glorious possibilities which may be unfolded in the realization of our destiny. 6. He knows the *wants* of each and of all, temporal and spiritual; that we are helpless to the attainment of life's end, without constant supplies from him.

II. WHAT IS HERE MEANT BY GOD'S KNOWING ALL? 1. Obviously, his perfect, full, entire *acquaintance*, not only with the pilgrimage in general, not only with such particulars of it as those we have just named, but also with *every detail* of each particular. He seeth the whole of everything. 2. But it is not a *bare* seeing; the knowledge is attended with a *fatherly interest* in all that concerns the welfare of his children. He "taketh pleasure in them that fear him." "He careth for" us. The training of his children for a home by means of a pilgrimage thither, is one of the most kind and loving designs of the heart of infinite love! 3. The knowing includes the *actually taking into account* all the need of our pilgrimage, in his words, works, and ways. (1) In the *promises* he makes, all things are taken into account. These promises are not merely applicable in part, or at times, but wholly and always. (2) His *precepts* too are framed according to the same perfect knowledge. (3) His *providential mercies*, general and special, meet the wants of to-day and prepare for those of to-morrow. He works for our future, that we may live by the day. (4) In his *great redemptive provision* for our spiritual training, there is the same forethoughtfulness. (5) In his *distinctively personal and individual care* over each one, the whole of our pilgrimage is taken into account. No one is confused with any one else. The Great Father's family is not so large as to tax him. He can care as lovingly for each as if each one were all!

III. WHAT IS THE PRACTICAL VALUE TO US OF SUCH KNOWLEDGE? The value of it is *infinite*. On three main points, however, the preacher may dwell, and revel in the luxury they afford. 1. If life's pilgrimage is just beginning, this Divine knowledge, so applied, may yield us *guidance* in treading the way. For if God has so mercifully taken all things into account in promise and precept, then we never need to depart a hair's breadth from the right path, for the sake of securing any apparent advantage whatever. This is specially suggested by the way in which Moses uses the words. 2. If we are just in the mid part of the pilgrimage, we may find *immeasurable comfort* under the difficulties of the way. All our responsibilities are accurately estimated, all wants perfectly considered, all supplies certainly ensured. What more could we desire? 3. If we make use of the Divine knowledge in the ways we have specified, we shall find that it will also give us a *song of thankfulness* when near the end of the way. At the point of time referred to in the text, Israel was near the verge of Canaan. And the words are retrospective. They are a testimony to Divine faithfulness and care; "These forty years the Lord thy God hath been with thee; thou hast lacked nothing." So may the believer say and sing as he closes stage after stage of life; so *will* he sing when he closes the last stage of all :—"Not one thing hath failed of all that the Lord hath spoken." The more life unfolds to him of his own weakness, the louder and sweeter will be his song over Divine care; yea, he will go singing to the heavenly rest!

HOMILIES BY VARIOUS AUTHORS.

Vers. 1—23.—*International relationships.* The wilderness state is the most salutary for men. Prematurely to enter into the land of rest would prove an endless calamity. Theoretically, it is possible to gain heaven too soon. Even "the Captain of our salvation was made perfect through suffering." That heaven may be to us a perfect paradise, there must be complete harmony between the soul and its environment.

I. GOD BRINGS NATIONS INTO CONTACT FOR RECIPROCAL MINISTRATION. So long as the conviction prevails that distinct nations are natural foes, it is best for them to remain apart. Mountains and seas and languages are God's bulwarks of peace. Yet this is but a temporary arrangement. Nationality has its use, but is liable to great abuse. God has given a monopoly of blessing to no one nation, that all may feel mutual interdependence. The products of nature are the property of all; yet personal interests are to be respected. The life-long enjoyment of Divine bounty should make us grateful, modest, and benevolent.

II. COMMERCE WITH OTHERS AN OCCASION FOR SELF-CONTROL. We are often ignorant of the selfishness and arrogance of our own hearts, until our material interests come into seeming conflict with the interests of others. In the presence of a stalwart foe, our courage or our cowardice is made manifest. We know not whether good seed or bad lies in our fields, until the summer sun makes them spring. On the wheel of the lapidary the qualities of the jewel are revealed. Such occasions for knowing ourselves —testing ourselves—disciplining and controlling ourselves, must be highly prized. The ruler of his own nature, especially under sore provocation, is a genuine victor.

III. OUR SUPERIOR STRENGTH AFFORDS NO WARRANT FOR VIOLENT INVASIONS. *Might* has a terrible proneness to warp our sense of *right*. Unless might is penetrated through and through with a spirit of righteousness, it is a body without a soul; it soon becomes a despicable corpse. Mere strength gives to no man, and to no body of men, warrantable authority to rule. It is base and self-degrading for strength to trample on weakness. Real strength displays its latent reserves when it stoops to protect—when it endures rather than contends. Violence is essential weakness, the scarecrow of power.

IV. OUR NATURAL RELATIONSHIPS HAVE A CLAIM UPON OUR REGARDS. What God hath constructed, man may not wantonly destroy. We are to "honour all men," but to "*love* the brotherhood." We may send our portions of sympathy to the uttermost circumference of the human circle, but we are to reserve a double portion for kindred.

Spiritual ties are superior to all the bonds of nature, but they need not be separate and distinct. The *natural* may, yea *ought*, to be the foundation on which the *spiritual* relationship is built. *He* who affirmed that "all who did the will of his Father were his mother, sisters, brothers," said also as he commended his human mother to his disciple's care, "Behold thy mother!"

V. A SENSE OF GOD'S PRESENCE FOSTERS SELF-ABNEGATION. Because we have so many proofs that God is about us, safeguarding our interests, we shall not be so anxious to extort our fancied rights. "He is at my right hand: I shall not be moved." "Let your moderation be known unto all men: the Lord is at hand." We have an all-wise, all-mighty, and omnipresent Defender; therefore we will not fear. We will not avenge seeming injuries: the Lord doth fight for us. "Vengeance is his."

VI. THE DISPLACEMENT OF SUCCESSIVE HUMAN RACES IS AN ORDINANCE OF GOD. Throughout the entire plan of God's providence the same law is manifest. In the formation of the earth's crust we see that one order of life passed away—another order appeared. This phrase of God's procedure science has labelled "the survival of the fittest." Is man the final link in this magnificent series? All oracles are dumb. Yet this law of successive development is apparent everywhere. History and ethnology record the facts; the Bible ascribes them to the personal God. Whatever were the motives or the passions which prompted Esau to evict the Horims, or Moab to displace the Emims, or the Caphtorims to dislodge the Avims, *this much* is plain—that the hand of the Lord wrought behind the human machinery. *Bad* as some of these races seem to have been, they were, without doubt, an improvement on the preceding. "First that which is natural; afterward that which is spiritual." The world's amelioration may be waiting for our removal.

VII. THE DEATH OF UNITS PROMOTES THE WELFARE OF THE NATION. The patience of Jehovah is conspicuous in that he did not destroy the murmurers and recusants in Israel with a stroke. He used them still as the natural protectors of the younger members, and when *these* reached maturity of courageous faith, the older portion fell away, like useless husk and chaff. As in the human body, so long as cellular tissue dies and is replaced by fresh development, there is health; so in the race, the removal of effete elements secures the advancement of the whole. Yet it is not *inevitable* that the separate units of mankind should absolutely perish. The same law of development may prevail in each separate person. The inferior parts of our being may minister to the growth of the higher. The outward man, like the husk, may perish, while, withal, the inner man may be renewed daily, and be fitted for a higher plane of existence. Death is the gate of life.

VIII. GOD EXTENDS A WATCHFUL SUPERINTENDENCE OVER ALL THE NATIONS OF THE EARTH. The children of Ammon rose in arms against the Zamzummims, and defeated them, yet (though they knew it not) it was Jehovah who destroyed their foes. God has a thousand various methods for ruling a nation's career and destiny. Because Britain has come into a larger heritage of blessing than other empires, or because many of the British people consciously recognize the sceptre of Jehovah, we may not conclude that the Zulus or Papuans are not equally overruled by him. "His kingdom ruleth over all." Respecting Cyrus, King of the Medes, God said, "I girded thee, though thou hast not known me." There is an unseen and an unrecognized sceptre directing all the movements of the world, controlling and restraining even wickedness itself! The errors of the heathen are, after all, partial truths, and God is leading their minds onward from obscurer to clearer light. Sometimes, we must admit, there is a temporary submergence—the advancing light is for a time eclipsed by a wave of darkness. Nevertheless, through long periods of human history, we can for the most part discover progress. *Eternity* is God's abode, and we discern but fragments of his work.—D.

Vers. 24—37.—*Warrantable warfare.* Sihon, King of Heshbon, opposed with physical force the fulfilment of Israel's destiny; and, having provoked war, provokes it to his own destruction.

I. THE NECESSITY FOR WAR. The question whether war is ever just and legitimate must be answered in the affirmative. Still, this does not justify all war. The majority of wars are indefensible. War is a barbarous instrument; and, as intelligence advances, can be replaced by better methods of conquest. But it sometimes becomes the last and desperate alternative. If war has been tolerated in heaven, it may be *tolerated* on earth. Even a war of extermination may be, under some *conceivable* circumstances, a necessity. In this case we may look : 1. *At the human side of the war.* (1) *There was an arrogant rejection of equitable demands.* No man, and no State, holds an absolute and irresponsible right to the surface of the globe. "The earth is the Lord's." We may acquire, by inheritance, or purchase, or culture, personal interests in the land, which others are bound to respect. Yet personal interests are to be subservient to a nation's good. The lesser must yield to the greater. Israel justly demanded a right of way to his own possessions. The terms proposed by the Hebrews were fair and equitable, and the onus of war fell on him who rejected them. (2) *Israel could point to his pacific and honourable conduct in passing through the territories of Ammon and Esau.* A reputation for trustworthiness in observing a treaty had been already established. (3) *The rejection of Israel's proposal involved a deprivation of Israel's natural rights.* The patriarch Jacob had acquired by purchase and by culture much land in Canaan ; and now, released from prolonged captivity, the people claim their ancestral estates. If we leave out of view the commands of Jehovah, there was ample reason, founded in common justice, why the Hebrews should demand a passage into Canaan. 2. *Let us contemplate the matter on the Divine side.* This invasion was a plain intimation of Jehovah's will. (1) *It is not man's place to sit in judgment on his God.* We are largely ignorant of all the factors in this case. There are vaster considerations than we can reach—problems which we cannot solve. Our moral judgments are often warped by weak and morbid sentiments. Righteousness, in its very nature, is superior to pleasure. "Shall not the Judge of all the earth do right?" (2) *We are assured that the guilt of the Amorites was great.* What forms this guilt assumed we are not fully told, but certain it is that most flagrant corruptions flourished among them. He who uses elemental forces and angelic agents to execute his judicial verdicts, is equally at liberty to employ men as the officers of his vengeance. (3) *Very probably this was a signal act of retributive justice.* Possibly they had acquired the territory by violence and bloodshed, and had now to yield it again to the arbiter of war. "They that take the sword shall perish with the sword." (4) *Certainly this calamity was in the line of the world's progress.* Mankind has been benefited by the overthrow of corrupt empires. This was the rough pathway along which Israel fulfilled its beneficent destiny.

II. THE PRECISE OCCASION FOR THIS WAR. This is attributed to the stolid perverseness of one man—Sihon, King of Heshbon. Is it to be tolerated that the march of a nation's destiny is to be baffled by the ignorance, or lust, or stupidity of *one* man? 1. *This obstinacy of the royal will must be attributed to natural causes.* God never compels a man to be bad. Human nature was the same in Sihon's day as in ours. Insolent arrogance is a growth. Sihon had for many years repressed nobler instincts, stifled generous feeling, pampered selfishness and pride ; hence blind obstinacy became in him despotic. Corrupt principles spring from tiny seeds. 2. There are stages in a man's career when his *choice* becomes his *fate.* By the operation of God's unseen laws and mysterious forces, habits become as fixed as granite. The hardening process becomes irreversible, and truly it is said that *God* does it. We can choose whether or not to prepare our artillery, manufacture our explosives, or light the fusee, but at that point human control ends ; the cannon-ball wings its way by laws imposed by God, and it is now entirely at his disposal. So in the moral sphere, there is a point at which human choice ends, and in his judicial capacity God steps in and fixes irreversibly the matter. "He that is filthy, let him be filthy still." We slowly and imperceptibly harden our sentient natures ; then God fixes them with his judicial act, and we are held in the iron manacles of doom.

III. THE SECRET OF SUCCESS IN WAR. 1. *God's promise of success does not exclude human exertion.* His promise always presupposes man's wise activity. His pledge of help is intended to stimulate, not supplant, brave endeavour. We can only move successfully in the line of God's promise. 2. *God's initial processes should be closely followed by our activity.* "I have begun," said God (ver. 31), therefore "begin to possess." We should follow *hard* upon God's path, then his right hand will uphold us. If tardiness enchain our feet, we may soon lose the trace of his footprints. 3. *One brave deed is the forerunner of many successes.* The report of Israel's martial prowess flew as on the wings of the wind, and the widespread fear it induced made further conquests easy. The fruits of good or evil deeds may reproduce themselves through all time. The first step in a new course is pregnant with importance. 4. *Strict obedience is the highway to large success.* When the command of God is plain, there is no place for hesitation. Bravery grows and flourishes in an atmosphere of loyalty. During the last thirty-eight years of wilderness life, the faith and love of the young Hebrews had immeasurably grown, and their prompt obedience was the early firstfruit. They were wedded in faithful love to God. Speaking of this period at a later date, God says by his prophet, "I remember thee, . . . the love of thine espousals, when thou wentest after me in the wilderness." In keeping all the "commandments" of God, they found a large reward.—D.

Vers. 4—10, 17—20.—*Edom, Moab, Ammon.* The Israelites are strictly enjoined not to molest these three peoples, or to attempt to rob them of any portion of their territory. The ground of this injunction is that God had given them the territory they possessed, and had *not* given it to the Israelites. Additional reasons why Israel was not to molest them lay in the facts that they were kinsmen (ver. 4) and that Israel was amply provided for already (ver. 7). God's people have little need to covet the possessions of the worldly. Apart from questions of their rights, kinsmen are entitled to be treated with special kindness and forbearance. We learn from this passage—

I. THAT THE PROVIDENCE OF GOD IS MINUTELY CONCERNED IN THE SETTLEMENT OF NATIONS. (Vers. 5, 9, 19.) It is not by accident that they are where they are. God marks out for them the bounds of their habitation. This is a fundamental idea in Scripture (Gen. x.; Deut. xxxii. 8; Acts xvii. 26). In the verses before us the territories of Edom, of Moab, and of Ammon are spoken of as being a gift to them from God, as directly as Canaan was a gift to the Israelites. It does not alter this fact, though it renders the comprehension of it more difficult, that men's own violent and aggressive dispositions are often the means by which these secret purposes of God are fulfilled (vers. 12, 22, 23). The barbarian incursions which overthrew the Roman empire were prompted by mere love of conquest, with the hope of enrichment by slaughter and pillage; but we may trace the providence of God working through them for the formation of modern Europe. Our own acquisition of India was not without blame; but we may see in our present possession of it a gift of God which, with our other territories in different parts of the globe, we are bound to use for his glory. This is the highest view we can take of the possession of territory, and one which, so far from justifying unlawful aggression, leads us to refrain from it. It is to be remarked, however, that the possessions which God gives to nations are not irrevocable—not for ever. Instances of dispossession occur in these verses, and Edom, Moab, and Ammon themselves have long since been dispossessed. "Be not highminded, but fear" (Rom. xi. 20).

II. THAT THE RIGHTS OF NATIONS ARE TO BE SACREDLY RESPECTED. These verses teach lessons which might be pondered with advantage by the most advanced modern nations. They teach: 1. *Scrupulous respect for international rights.* It can never be our duty wantonly to invade the territories of those at peace with us, or, from motives of ambition, to seek pretexts of war with them. They are as entitled to the peaceable possession of what they have, as we are to the peaceable possession of the lands belonging to us. The right of the stronger is not to rule our policy. 2. *Scrupulous justice in international transactions.* The Israelites might have used force, but they were to deal justly, and honestly to pay for everything they received (vers. 6, 29). 3. *Scrupulous self-restraint under circumstances of provocation.* The Edomites had refused the Israelites a passage through their mountains, and had entailed on them a long, painful, and circuitous journey; Moab had employed Balaam to curse them, and had, with Midian, done them yet worse evil (Numb. xxv. 1); but not even these provocations were to tempt them to retaliation. How many modern nations would have made a *casus belli* of far less? Forgiveness of injuries should have a place in our international as in our private dealings, and it is strange if we have to be sent back to the Jews of Canaan-conquering notoriety to learn it. It is to be added—

III. THESE INSTRUCTIONS WERE A VALUABLE DISCIPLINE TO THE JEWS THEMSELVES. 1. *It taught them to recognize the Divine gift as the ground of their own tenure of Canaan.* If the Divine providence so guarded these neighbouring peoples, and would not allow one foot of their land to be taken from them against his will, how much more might the Jews, if obedient to the covenant, depend on being preserved in theirs! If God gave, who could take away ? 2. *It taught them to distinguish their commission to destroy the Canaanites from one of rude conquest.* It teaches *us* also to take a just estimate of those acts of the Israelites in destroying the Canaanitish nations on which so much indignation has been expended. Their conduct here shows how far they were from being actuated by the motives often ascribed to them. This high sense of honour, this scrupulous justice, this exemplary self-restraint prove that it was in no bloodthirsty, slaughter-loving spirit they were proceeding to their work; and show how at every step they were guided by God's will, fell in with the lines of his providence, and wrought out his wishes and purposes. They help us to conceive of the destruction of the Canaanites, not as a barbarous massacre, but as the execution of a long-delayed, deliberately pronounced, and most justly deserved sentence of Heaven.—J. O.

Vers. 10—13, 20—24.—*The Emims, Horims, Zamzummins, etc.* If these verses are part of the context of the original speech, and not a later insertion, they must be viewed as scraps of history introduced to encourage the Israelites in their work of conquest, and to dispel their apprehensions by showing what had been done by others. They suggest—

I. THAT THE PRESENT MAY LEARN FROM THE PAST. History, sacred and secular, is a powerful influence in forming the characters of the living race. The brave deeds, the conquests, the self-sacrificing endurances of those who have lived before us, are of use to rouse from apathy, and to inspire with courage and enthusiasm. The early conquests of the gospel help us to believe in its power to overcome existing oppositions.

II. THAT THE CHURCH MAY LEARN FROM THE WORLD. The holy nation is here incited by pointing to what other peoples have done in pursuit of their secular ambitions. If the Moabites could drive out the Emims, "a people great, and many, and tall, as the Anakims" (ver. 10), and if the Edomites and Ammonites could do the like in their respective districts, why should Israel fear the enemies to be encountered in his? We may learn much from men of the world—from the boldness of their plans, their ingenuity in surmounting difficulties, their admirable perseverance, their self-denial in working out their ends, etc. Were the Church half as diligent, wise, and determined in the prosecution of her work, as they are in making the schemes which they adopt succeed, it would be the inauguration of a day of splendid spiritual successes.

III. THAT THE DESPONDING MAY LEARN FROM THE SUCCESSFUL. It is something to feel that we are not the first who have had to face giants. What has been done once can be done again, and it is a great matter to be able to point to cases in which the very difficulties we are contending with have been successfully surmounted.—J. O.

Vers. 14, 15.—*Dying out.* These thirty-eight years form a mélancholy parenthesis in the history of Israel. A death-silence reigns in the narrative in regard to them. The ninetieth Psalm is apparently a memorial of them—the dirge of Moses over the fallen. One or two incidents, and a few laws in Numbers may belong to this period; otherwise we have only these brief epitaph verses. As here described, they form a fitting image of godless existence generally—

I. IN ITS WANT OF HISTORY. History is meant to preserve that which is of permanent worth. The unessential, the evanescent, are not held deserving of its record. But from the spiritual standpoint there is no life of permanent worth but that which is lived in God and for his glory. Relatively to this world, the godless man may have a history; but relatively to eternity, he has lived to no end which ensures his being held in remembrance. He will be forgotten, and his life be a blank in the records which alone will interest a heavenly society.

II. IN ITS ESSENTIAL UNPROFITABLENESS. 1. It is without proper *purpose.* That thirty-eight years was one of purposeless existence. It had no right end. Men might engage in various pursuits, but their existence as a whole had lost its value. They were there but to draw out their profitless days till death came to end the scene. The godless man is in the same position—his existence as a whole has no proper end, and he is made to feel this the more keenly the longer he lives. 2. It is without proper *joy*. There could be no true joy in men's hearts during that wretched time of waiting for the grave. Is there any in the life of the worldling, or of any ungodly man? Ask Byron, Goethe, Rousseau, or whoever else has given confessions on the subject, and we will need no other witness. 3. It is without *hope*. For what is there to give it?

III. IN ITS BEING SPENT UNDER GOD'S WRATH. The feeling that it is so darkens life, troubles conscience, makes death terrible, and awakens fearful and well-founded presentiments of future evil.—J. O.

Vers. 24, 25 —*The effects of Israel's conquests.* Would induce widespread dread and anguish. Apply to the Church.

I. GREAT VICTORIES OF THE CHURCH WOULD SPEEDILY GET NOISED ABROAD. The world has too much lurking fear of the truth of Christianity not to be sensitive to such reports. They would soon spread. They would find their way into circles little thought of.

II. GREAT VICTORIES OF THE CHURCH WOULD BE THE SUREST TOKEN THAT GOD WAS WITH HER. Were there a return of Pentecostal days, and conversions by thousands at a time; or were there such revivals as the Church has sometimes seen at special times and places;—were these becoming general, and multitudes were filled with the power of God's Spirit as the result—it would have a marvellous effect in producing widespread conviction that the religion of Christ was true, and that God's might was being exerted through it. It would be the best "evidence" of Christianity. Why should not the Church work, pray, and hope for such glorious successes? They are possible; they are promised; they will yet come.

III. GREAT VICTORIES OF THE CHURCH WOULD INSPIRE WIDESPREAD FEAR. Anything does that which brings the Divine sensibly near to human beings (Luke v. 8). But sinners in particular fear any near manifestation of God. They know, like the devils who besought Christ to let them alone, what that means for them. One result of the conquests of the early Church was that "fear" fell on those who witnessed them (Acts ii. 43). The Church is never so safe as when she is bold, aggressive, and successful.—J. O.

Vers. 26—37.—*The conquest of Sihon.* Sihon, though an Amorite, was not to be unconditionally destroyed. He had, like Pharaoh, an opportunity given him of averting ruin by acceding to a most courteous and reasonable request; but, like Pharaoh in this respect also, he hardened his heart, and took the course which made his destruction inevitable. We are led to consider—

I. SIHON'S OPPORTUNITY. (Vers. 26—30.) It was not given him in the hope that he would avail himself of it; for it was foreseen that he would refuse it and be hardened by it. But the sinner's hardness of heart is not a reason why the opportunity of securing his salvation should be withheld from him, or why every gracious means should not be employed to overcome his hardness. It is, indeed, necessary that this should be done, in order that the responsibility of his ruin may rest entirely on himself. It lay in the counsel of God that this king's territory should be given to the Israelites, but only on condition of his refusal of the request made to him. It was otherwise with the gift of Canaan, which was absolute, and permitted of no overtures of peace being made to the inhabitants. Their day of grace was past: to Sihon there still remained this last momentous and decisive opportunity. The last opportunity will come some day to all who harden themselves in sin (cf. Matt. xxiv. 37, 38; Luke xix. 42). This message of Moses to Sihon was: 1. *Peaceable* (ver. 26). Peaceful means should be exhausted in a cause before resorting to force. They should be exhausted even with those who are not likely to be influenced by them. This is due to the cause, due to ourselves, and due to the person approached. Men must at least have the opportunity given them of acting reasonably and generously. 2. *Courteous* (vers. 27, 28). No message could have been couched in more modest or conciliatory terms. A courteous tone is to be adopted towards men, even when we foresee that they will not reciprocate it. 3. *Perfectly sincere.* This was proved by the justness of Moses' dealings with Edom and Moab, to which he makes reference (ver. 29). 4. *Justified by necessity.* Only thus could they reach the land which God had given them (ver. 29).

II. Sihon's obstinacy. "The Lord thy God hardened his spirit, and made his heart obstinate" (ver. 30); not, indeed, by any evil influence exerted on his soul, but by giving him up to his naturally obdurate disposition, and by placing him in circumstances which he knew would have a hardening effect, though in themselves of a character fitted rather to soften. 1. The hardening of the heart, so far as it is a result of evil courses, is *a work of God operating in the laws of our mental and moral nature.* Sin naturally operates to blind the mind, sear the conscience, destroy the generous affections, etc. But these effects are as truly a judicial operation of God in the soul, of a punitive nature, as was the Flood, the destruction of the cities of the plain, or any other outward expression of his wrath. 2. The hardening of the heart, so far as it is the result of acts of providence, is *a work of God operating in the moral government of the world.* Both mercies and judgments have a hardening effect on those who refuse to be taught by them. This result, foreseen by God, may be also *willed,* as a just punishment for voluntary transgression (Isa. vi. 9, 10); while, as a foreseen fact, a sinner's hardness of heart may be taken up as a link in the further development of God's purposes. 3. The hardening of the heart, as flowing from influences which ought rather to have melted and subdued it, *is a result for which the sinner himself is justly held responsible.* God wills not the death of any. The mingled goodness and severity of his dealings with men are meant to lead them to repentance. But the very things which are designed to produce a softening and converting effect on souls, are those which frequently harden and sear them—the discipline of sorrow, the preaching of the gospel, warnings and expostulations, etc. Hardness induced by such causes is the most invincible of all, and brands the obdurate transgressor as ripe for God's judgments (Prov. xxix. 1).

III. Sihon's destruction. (Vers. 32—37.) 1. It was *self-sought.* "Then Sihon came out," etc. (ver. 32). The sinner's destruction is of his own seeking. 2. It was *achieved by Divine aid.* "The Lord our God delivered him before us" (ver. 33). So are all spiritual victories. It is the Church's comfort in her conflicts to know that she has this power to depend on. 3. It was *total.* "Utterly destroyed" (ver. 34). A type of the utter destruction awaiting all who resist and oppose the Divine will; said of the Church, "The nation and kingdom that will not serve thee shall perish" (Isa. lx. 12); of Christ, "Every soul which will not hear that prophet shall be destroyed from among the people" (Acts iii. 23; cf. 2 Thess. i. 9, 10).—J. O.

Vers. 1—23.—*God's faithfulness in dealing with nations outside the covenant.* We have here strict injunctions given to the pilgrims not to disturb the children of Edom, nor the Moabites, nor the children of Ammon, because they were occupying the district assigned them. These tribes, though related to Israel, were not in the covenant. Still God had guaranteed to them certain temporal blessings, and he shows himself faithful in his dealings with them.

I. God is a righteous Governor among the nations. It is in equity that he rules. His judgment is always according to truth. Having written the law of conscience upon every human heart, he can justly judge men thereby. They are laws unto themselves, and so will be held accountable for their relation to their law, or, as we might call it, inward light (cf. Rom. ii. 14, 15).

II. Temporal advantages are gifts of God. The laws which regulate nature are, we believe, the ordinances of God. Hence the benefits irreligious nations receive through the laws of nature are really the gifts of his bounteous hand. Though the nations may not so regard them, the people of God can form no other notion of them.

As gifts, they are *undeserved.* Hence it is part of God's scheme of mercy so generously to treat the race of men. We must look to Christ's atonement for an explanation on the ground of justice of this merciful treatment of mankind. The death of Jesus purchased temporal as well as spiritual blessings, and its vast application should be recognized and known. In this sense he did "die for every man."

III. The constancy of the laws of nature is to be traced to the faithfulness of God. No other hypothesis can be offered so consistent with the facts. The promises treasured up in nature are promises of God, and the laws which secure their fulfilment are the ministers of his faithfulness.

IV. The faithfulness of God in the cases referred to was not recognized by

THE TRIBES PROFITING BY IT. In seizing the places allotted to them by God, the Edomites, Moabites, and Ammonites fought each for his hand and in no religious spirit. They overcame and exterminated races of giants who formerly possessed the land. All the while, God's plan and faithfulness were receiving illustration and fulfilment. The exercise of human freedom did not militate against, but secured the Divine pleasure.

V. GOD'S BOUNTY TO NATIONS OUTSIDE THE COVENANT IS INTENDED TO ENCOURAGE HIS OWN PEOPLE. The Israelites would be the better prepared to meet and master the giants in Canaan after seeing the Edomites, Moabites, and Ammonites snugly dwelling in the inheritances of gigantic predecessors. If these tribes, without any sense of dependence upon the Almighty, overcame the giants opposing them, what will not be possible to *faith* ?

And the whole government of the world is really intended to foster confidence in God's covenant faithfulness and to forbid all despair.—R. M. E.

Vers. 14—18.—*The wasting of the warriors.* There was evidently a considerable knowledge of "the art of war" in the Israelitish host on leaving Egypt. Moses was versed in it, as in so much more, and the mixed multitude which accompanied the exodus would also contain men skilled in arms. And experience of opposition on the part of Amalek, etc., would elicit a martial spirit throughout the host.

Moreover, the presence of seasoned men, or "veterans," gives confidence to young troops in actual conflict. The world would say, "By all means retain the veterans for the purpose of invasion." Yet, strange to say, God kept the host wandering till the warriors were all weeded out, and buried in the wilderness. The invasion is to be made by the rising generation, which had never seen the military art or reviews in Egypt. From this we learn—

I. THAT GOD'S WAYS ARE NOT OUR WAYS, NOR HIS THOUGHTS OUR THOUGHTS. In fact, his plans are often constructed so as to baffle worldly wisdom. We see this in this invasion of Canaan; we see it in his way of salvation by Jesus Christ; we see it in his providential dealings.

II. THE ART OF WAR IS NOT SO IMPORTANT AS THE ART OF FAITH. The experience of the veterans was as nothing in comparison with the courageous faith in God. This made heroes of the children who would, they thought, be a prey. All wisdom of man becomes vain when unsustained by confidence in God.

III. SOLDIERS' GRAVES HAVE OFTENTIMES BEEN THE MELANCHOLY CONDITION OF SUCCESS. It was really after sacrifice, the sacrifice of the whole fighting army of Israel, that success came. There grew out of their graves warning and inspiration. And it has been over the graves of soldiers that almost every progress of the world has been made. Multitudes had to be buried on the battle-fields before the promised land of peace could be entered. The buried warriors constituted the holocaust which was presented before the blessing came.

IV. THE DESTRUCTION OF FALSE TRUSTS IS OFTEN THE PREPARATION FOR TRUE ONES. The temptation to trust in the veterans and their military ideas is taken away by the death of the warriors. So is it that God removes from us every false refuge. Thus we learn to trust in the living God, and to fight his battles in his own way. Providence is oftentimes just the removal of the warriors who were so wise in their own eyes and so able to take the best course, that the people may follow the Lord only.

Happy for each soul it is to be deprived of every false support, and to be led to trust Christ alone! Into real rest the soul enters by faith—the promised land lies open to the trustful soul, while its gates are closed against the self-confident ones.—R. M. E.

Vers. 24—37.—*The destruction of Sihon, King of the Amorites.* Moses here recalls the first stage in the conquest. By Divine direction, the pilgrims are to advance upon the land of the Amorites, and they are promised an important victory over them. And here we have to notice—

I. THE REASONABLE PROPOSAL MADE TO SIHON THE KING. (Vers. 26—29.) This was for permission to pass through his land to Canaan, undertaking to disturb nothing and to pay for all supplies. Nothing could be more reasonable. The onus was thus thrown on Sihon of determining whether he would befriend God's people or oppose them.

And this reminds us of the most reasonable offers God, in his gospel, makes to men. He acts the friendly part, and if men take it in good faith, all is well.

II. THE REFUSAL OF THE HARD-HEARTED KING. (Ver. 30.) Sihon quite needlessly resolves to oppose their passage to Canaan. He likely had heard of or remembered the former unsuccessful attempt thirty-eight years before at Kadesh, and so he imagines that a little opposition will deter them and turn them from their purpose. The hardening of heart, here attributed to God, means simply that the providences, instead of softening Sihon's nature, had through his own self-will an entirely opposite effect. The heart gets hardened through the corruption of the will.

It is similarly with those who reject the offer of salvation.

III. BATTLE IS THUS FORCED UPON THE PILGRIMS. (Vers. 31, 32.) This battle of Jahaz was a decisive one. The pilgrims were so numerous that Sihon had to bring out *all* his host. Into it the Israelites entered with the assurance of victory, and this largely secured it.

It is so in the spiritual warfare. The enemies of God's people are met by a host confident in success, because promised by God. This of itself is half the battle.

IV. THE PENALTY OF OPPOSITION TO GOD'S PLANS IS EXTERMINATION. (Vers. 33, 34.) If men will oppose God, they must take the consequences. God must be supreme. He can allow no victorious opposition. His enemies must lick the dust. It is a mortal combat into which they must enter who fight against him.

The propriety of the extermination rests in the Divine command. God has the right to dispose as he sees fit of his creatures. If they oppose his will, which is always right, they may justly be taken away with a stroke, and that without remedy.

V. THE LIMITATIONS SET BEFORE THE CONQUERORS. (Vers. 35—37.) They took the cattle and a certain portion of the land, but they did not overrun the whole country. The land of the children of Ammon was exempt from the invasion. It was forbidden ground.

So is it always. God sets limits to success. It is well he does. Ambition must abide by his decree, and not overstep due bounds. When his will is thus respected, and self-repression and self-discipline rigidly enforced, all is well. The dangers of success are thus avoided, and real elevation of spirit is experienced.—R. M. E.

EXPOSITION.

CHAPTER III.

Vers. 1—11.—CONQUEST OF OG, KING OF BASHAN. The Amorites had wrested from Moab a portion of the territory taken by the Moabites and the Edomites from the giant aborigines; and Og, who was of the same giant race, ruled over the northern half of the region of Gilead and over all Bashan. This district also God purposed Israel to possess; and therefore, before crossing the Jordan, a diversion was made northwards by the Israelites, for the purpose of attacking this powerful chief. Og encountered them with all his host, but was signally defeated, and he and all his people were exterminated. Not fewer than three score fortified cities, besides villages, were captured by the Israelites, the whole country was subjugated, and all the cattle and material property taken as booty (cf. Numb. xxi. 33—35).

Ver. 1.—(Cf. Numb. xxi. 33.) **We turned**

—*i.e.* took a new route—**and went up** (וַנַּעַל, and we ascended). As Bashan was an upland region, they are very properly said to have gone up. **Edrei**, *hod.* Draa, with Roman and Arabian ruins, nearly three miles in circumference, but without inhabitants; not the same as the Edrei of ver. 10.

Ver. 2.—(Cf. Numb. xxi. 31, etc.)

Ver. 4.—**Threescore cities**; probably the same as the Bashan-havoth jair, afterwards mentioned (ver. 14). **The region of Argob, the kingdom of Og in Bashan.** The region of Argob comprised the kingdom of Og, and Bashan was another name for the same country; extending from the Jabbok to Hermon, and embracing both the northern part of Gilead, and what was afterwards in a stricter sense Bashan, viz. the land north of the Wady Zerka (*hod.* Jebel Ajlûn) to Hermon. The name *Argob* is supposed by some to be given to the district from a town of that name, fifteen Roman miles eastward from Gerasa, a city of Arabia (Eusebius); but more probably it is derived from the character of the district, either as *deep-soiled* (from רֶגֶב, a clod), or as *rugged* and *uneven* (רֶגוֹב, from רֶגֶב, akin to רָגַם, **to** heap up), just as the neighbouring district to the east and north-east received the name *Trachonitis* (from τραχών, rough, rugged); in the Targum, indeed, *Trachona* (טרכונא) is the name given here for Argob. This district is now known as the province of *El-Lejah* (The Retreat). It is described as oval in form, about twenty-two miles long by fourteen wide; a plateau elevated about thirty feet above the surrounding plain. Its features are most remarkable. It is composed of a thick stratum of black basalt, which seems to have been emitted in a liquid state from pores in the earth, and to have flowed out on all sides till the whole surface was covered. It is rent and shattered as if by internal convulsion. The cup-like cavities from which the liquid mass was projected are still seen, and also the wavy surface such as a thick liquid generally assumes which cools as it is flowing. There are deep fissures and yawning gulfs with rugged, broken edges; and there are jagged mounds that seem not to have been sufficiently heated to flow, but which were forced up by some mighty agency, and then rent and shattered to their centres. The rock is filled with air-bubbles, and is almost as hard as iron. (Dr. Porter, in Kitto, 'Biblical Cyclopædia,' iii. 1032; see also the same author's 'Five Years in Damascus,' ii. 240, etc.; and 'The Giant Cities of Bashan'; Burckhardt, 'Travels in Syria,' p. 110, etc.; Wetstein, 'Reisebericht üb. Hauran,' p. 82, etc.; a paper by Mr. Cyrill Graham in the *Cambridge Essays* for 1858; and Smith's 'Dictionary,' art. 'Trachonitis.') The entire trans-Jordanic region was thus captured by the Israelites.

Ver. 5.—**All these cities were fenced with high walls, gates, and bars**; literally, *double gates and a bar*. These cities, with their marvellous erections, are believed to be still existing in the Hauran. Over that district are strewn a multitude of towns of various sizes, all constructed after the same remarkable fashion. "The streets are perfect, the walls perfect, and, what seems more astonishing, the stone doors are still hanging on their hinges, so little impression has been made during these many centuries on the hard and durable stone of which they are built" (Graham, *Cambridge Essays*, p. 160). These doors are "formed of slabs of stone, opening on pivots which are projecting parts of the stone itself, and working in sockets in the lintel and threshold." Some of these gates are large enough to admit of a camel passing through them, and the doors are of proportionate dimensions, some of the stones of which they are formed being eighteen inches in thickness. The roofs also are formed of huge stone slabs resting on the massive walls. All betoken the workmanship of a race endowed with powers far exceeding those of ordinary men; and give credibility to the supposition that we have in them the dwellings of the giant race that occupied that district before it was invaded by the Israelites. "We could not help," says Mr. Graham, "being impressed with the belief that had we never known anything of the early portion of Scripture history before visiting this country, we should have been forced to the conclusion that its original inhabitants, the people who had constructed those cities, were not only a powerful and mighty nation, but individuals of greater strength than ourselves."

Ver. 6.—(See ch. ii. 34.)

Ver. 8.—**Hermon** (חֶרְמוֹן), probably from חָרַם, to be high, "the lofty peak," conspicuous on all sides. By some the name is supposed to be connected with חֵרֶם, a devoted thing, because this mountain marked the limit of the country devoted or placed under a ban; and it is certainly remarkable that, at the extreme north-east and the extreme south-west of the land conquered by the Israelites, names derived from *Herem*, viz. *Hermon* and *Hormah* (ch. i. 44), should be found; as if to indicate that all between was devoted. Hermon is the southernmost spur of the Antilibanus range. It is "the second mountain in Syria, ranking next to the highest peak of Lebanon behind the cedars. The elevation of Hermon may be estimated at about 10,000 feet. The whole body of the mountain is limestone, similar to that which composes the main ridge of Lebanon, the central peak rises up an obtuse truncated cone, from 2000 to 3000 feet above the ridges that radiate from it, thus giving it a more commanding aspect than any other mountain in Syria. This cone is entirely naked, destitute alike of trees and vegetation. The snow never disappears from its summit" (Porter, 'Handbook, Syria and Palestine,' p. 431). At the present day it is known as *Jebel esh-Sheikh* (The Chief Mountain), also *Jebel eth Thelj* (The Snow Mountain). Anciently also it had various names. By the Hebrews it was known also as *Sion* (שִׂיאֹן, the high, ch. iv. 48); by the Sidonians it was called *Sirion* (שְׂרִיֹן=שִׂרְיֹן, a cuirass or coat of mail), probably from its shining appearance, especially when covered with snow; and by the Amorites it was called *Senir*, a word probably of the same meaning. These names continued in use to a late period (cf. Ps. xcix. 6; Ezek. xxvii. 4; Cant. iv. 8; 1 Chron. v. 23).

Ver. 10.—The different portions of the conquered territory are here mentioned. 1. **The plain** (הַמִּישֹׁר, the level country); the table-land south of Mount Gilead, as far as the Arnon. 2. The whole of **Gilead**; the hilly country north of the Jabbok, between Heshbon and Bashan, between the northern and southern table-land. 3. **All Bashan**, as far eastward as Salchah, the modern Szalkhat or Szarkhad, about seven hours to the east of Busra, and northwards to Edrei, *hod.* Edra, Ezra or Edhra', an extensive ruin to the west of Busra, still partially inhabited.

Ver. 11.—Bashan was of old possessed by a giant race, the Rephâim (Gen. xiv. 5); but of these Og, King of Bashan, was, at the time of the Israelitish invasion, the sole remnant. His vast size is indicated by the size of his bedstead, which was preserved in Rabbath-Ammon, perhaps as a trophy of some victory obtained by the Ammonites over their gigantic foe. This measured nine cubits in length, and four in breadth, " after the cubit of a man," *i.e.* according to the cubit in common use. Taking the cubit as equal to eighteen inches, the measure of the bedstead would be thirteen feet and a half by six feet. That Og even approximated to this height is incredible; if he reached nine or ten feet his height would exceed that of any one on record. It is probable, however, that he may have had his bed made vastly larger than himself, partly from ostentation, partly that he might leave a memorial that should impress upon posterity a sense of his gigantic size and resistless might; just as Alexander the Great is said (Diod. Sic., xvii. 95) to have, on his march to India, caused couches to be made for his soldiers in their tents, each five cubits long, in order to impress the natives with an overwhelming sense of the greatness of his host. It has been suggested that it is not a bed that is here referred to, but a sarcophagus of basalt or ironstone in which, it is supposed, the corpse of Og was placed, and which was afterwards carried to Rabbath, and there deposited (J. D. Michaelis, Winer, Knobel, etc.). This implies that the passage is a later insertion, and not part of the original narrative as given by Moses. But with what view could such an insertion be introduced? Not to establish the credibility of the story of the victory of the Israelites over Og, for the existence of a sarcophagus in which a corpse had been placed would only attest the fact that such a one once lived and died, but would prove nothing as to how or when or where he came by his death. Not to show the vast size of

the man, for a sarcophagus affords no measure whatever of the size of the person whose remains are placed in it, being an honorary monument, the size of which is proportioned to the real or supposed dignity of the person for whose honour it is made. A bed, on the contrary, which a man had used, or at least had caused to be made for himself, would afford some evidence of his size; and there is an obvious reason for Moses referring to this here, inasmuch as thereby he recalled ·to the Israelites the remembrance, on the one hand, of what occasioned the fear with which they anticipated the approach of this terrible foe, and, on the other, of the grace of God to them in that he had delivered Og and all his people into their hand. It is idle to inquire how Moses could know of the existence of this bed at Rabbath; for we may be well assured that from all the peoples through whose territories he had passed reports of the strength and prowess and doings of this giant warrior would be poured into his ear.

Vers. 12—17.—*Distribution of the conquered land.* The countries thus conquered by the Israelites were assigned by Moses to the tribes of Reuben and Gad and the half tribe of Manasseh. The southern portion, from Aroer, in the valley of the Arnon, to the Jabbok, with its towns (see Josh. xii. 15—20, 24—28), was assigned to the Reubenites and the Gadites; and the northern portion, from the Jabbok, comprehending, with Gilead, the whole of Bashan, or Argob, to the half tribe of Manasseh.

Ver. 13.—The last part of this verse is differently construed and rendered by different translators. By some the clause **all the region of Argob** is connected with what precedes, while others regard this clause as in apposition with what follows. Targum: "All the region of Trachona, and all that province was called the land of giants;" LXX.: "And all the region of Argob, all that Bashan: the land of the Rephaim it was reckoned;" Vulgate: "The whole region of Argob, and all Bashan is called the land of giants." Modern interpreters for the most part adopt the order of the Targum. The clause may be rendered thus: *The whole region of Argob as respects all Bashan* [i.e. in so far as it formed part of the kingdom of Bashan under Og] *was reputed the land of the Rephaim.*

Ver. 14.—Jair, a descendant of Manasseh

by the mother's side (his father was of the tribe of Judah, 1 Chron. ii. 22), obtained the Argob region unto—*i.e.* inclusive of (see Josh. xiii. 13)—the territory of the Geshuri and Maachathi. These were small Syrian tribes located to the east of Hermon. As *Geshur* signifies a bridge, it has been conjectured that the Geshurites were located near some well-known bridge across the Jordan, of which, perhaps, they were the keepers, and from this took their name. Maachah is called Aram- (Syria-) Maachah in 1 Chron. xix. 6. According to the ' Onomasticon,' it was " a city of the Amorites, by the Jordan, near Mount Hermon " (*s.v.* Μαχαθί). It had in later times a king, who allied himself with the Ammonites against David (1 Chron. xix. 7). These tribes were subdued, but not destroyed, by the Israelites; and at a later period seem to have regained their independence, and to have formed one kingdom (comp. 2 Sam. iii. 3; x. 6; xiii. 37; xv. 8; 1 Chron. iii. 2). And called them after his own name, Bashan-havoth-jair. The word *havoth* (properly *chavvoth*, חַוֹּת) is the plural of a word meaning life, and *Chavvoth-Jair* probably signifies Jair's livings, not Jair's villages, for these were apparently fortified cities (vers. 4, 5; Josh. xiii. 30; 1 Kings iv. 13). These were recaptured by the Geshurites, aided by the Arameans (1 Chron. ii. 23, "And Geshur and Aram took Chavvoth-Jair from them," etc.); at what time is unknown. From Numb. xxxii. 42, it appears that Nobah, also a family descended from Machir, took certain towns, viz. "Kenath and her daughters" in this district; these, with the twenty-three Havvoth-Jair, made up the sixty towns which "belonged to the sons of Machir the father of Gilead " (1 Chron. ii. 23). Nobah was probably in some way subordinate to Jair, and so in this rhetorical discourse, where it is not the purpose of the author to enter on minute details, the whole of these cities are included under the name Havvoth-Jair. Unto this day. "This does not necessarily imply a long time; and Moses himself may have used this expression, though only shortly after the event, in order to give prominence to the capture of the fortified cities of the giant king Og, by the Manassites for the encouragement of the Israelites" (Herzheimer).

Ver. 15.—(Cf. Numb. xxxii. 40; 1 Chron. ii. 22.)

Vers. 16, 17.—The possession of the tribes of Reuben and Gad is here more exactly defined. Its southern boundary was the middle of the valley (the wady) of the Arnon; half the valley, and the border, *i.e.* the middle of the ravine (or wady) and its edge; a more precise definition of the river Arnon; the brook which flowed through the middle of the ravine was to be their boundary line to the south. On the northeast the Upper Jabbok (*Nahr Ammân*) was to be their boundary; this separated them from Ammonitis, the region of the children of Ammon (Numb. xxi. 24). On the west the 'Arâbah (*Ghôr*), and the Jordan and its border (its east bank), from Chinnereth (Kinnereth), a fenced city by the sea of Galilee, thence called "the sea of Chinnereth" (Numb. xxxiv. 11; Josh. xii. 3; xix. 35),'to the sea of the 'Arâbah, the salt sea, under Ashdoth-pisgah—the slopes (literally, *the outpourings*, the place where the mountain torrents flow out, hence the base of the hill) of Pisgah (Numb. xxi. 15; xxvii. 12)— eastward; *i.e.* simply the east side of the 'Arâbah and the Jordan.

CONCLUSION OF HISTORICAL RECAPITULATION. Vers. 18—29.

Vers. 18—20.—Moses reminds the two and a half tribes of the conditions on which they had received the possessions they had desired beyond Jordan (see Numb. xxxii. 20—32). All that are meet for the war; literally, *all the sons of might* (בְּנֵי חַיִל), *i.e.* not all who were men of war or of age to go to war, but men specially powerful and fitted for warlike enterprise. Until the Lord hath given rest unto your brethren (comp. Exod. xxxiii. 14).

Vers. 21, 22.—*Joshua appointed as Moses' successor in the leadership.*

Ver. 21.—At that time, *i.e.* after the conquest of the land on the east of the Jordan (see Numb. xxvii. 12, etc.). Thine eyes have seen, etc. Joshua was directed to what he had himself witnessed, what his own eyes had seen, in the destruction of Sihon and Og and their hosts, that he might be encouraged to go forward in the course to which he had been called; and the people are reminded of this, that they may keep in mind what God had done for Israel, and may without fear follow Joshua as their leader to the conquest of Canaan (comp. ch. xxxi. 23).

Ver. 22.—The "he" here is emphatic; as God himself would fight for them, why should they be afraid?

Vers. 23—29.—*Prayer of Moses.* Moses knew that he was not to enter the promised land with the people; but, reluctant to relinquish the enterprise which he had so far conducted until he should see it successfully finished, he besought the Lord that at least he might be permitted to cross the Jordan, and see the goodly land. This prayer was presented probably just before Moses asked God to set a man over the congregation to be their leader to the promised land (Numb. xxvii. 15—17); for the command to give a charge to Joshua, in that office, follows immediately, as part of God's answer to Moses' request (ver. 28), and the expression "at that time" (ver. 23) points back to the charge of Moses to Joshua, as contemporaneous with the offering of his prayer. In this prayer Moses appeals to what he had already experienced of God's favour to him, in that he had begun to show him his greatness and his mighty power. The reference is to the victories already achieved over the Amorites; these were tokens of the Divine power graciously manifested to Israel, and Moses appeals to them as strengthening his plea for further favours (comp. the pleading, Exod. xxxiii. 12, etc.).

Ver. 24.—**O Lord God**: *O Lord Jehovah.* **For what God**, etc. (comp. Exod. xv. 11; Ps. lxxxvi. 8; lxxxix. 6; cxiii. 5, etc.). "The contrast drawn between Jehovah and other gods does not involve the reality of heathen deities, but simply presupposes a belief in the existence of other gods, without deciding as to the truth of that belief" (Keil).

Ver. 25.—**That goodly mountain**; not any mountain specially, but the whole mountain elevation of Canaan, culminating in the distant Lebanon, as it appeared to the eye of Moses from the lower level of the 'Arâbah. This was "goodly," especially in contrast with the arid and sunburnt desert through which the Israelites had passed; the hills gave promise of streams that should cool the air and refresh and fertilize the land (see ch. viii. 7, etc.). Moses longed to go over if but to see this land, and to plant his foot on it; but his request was not granted.

Ver. 26.—**The Lord was wroth**, etc. (cf. ch. i. 37; Numb. xx. 12; xxvii. 13, 14). **Let it suffice thee**; literally, *Enough for thee!* i.e. either Thou hast said enough; say no more, or Be content; let what I have done, and the grace I have given, be enough for thee (comp. the use of this formula in Gen. xlv. 28; Numb. xvi. 3; ch. i. 6; ii. 3). Keil and others refer to 2 Cor. xii. 8, as "substantially equivalent," but the expression there seems to have quite a different meaning and reference from that used here.

Ver. 27.—Comp. Numb. xxvii. 12, of which this is a rhetorical amplification. There the mountains of Abarim are mentioned; here Pisgah, the northern portion of that range, is specified. **The top of Pisgah**; *i.e.* Mount Nebo (ch. xxxiv. 1). **Westward**; literally, *seaward*, i.e. towards the Mediterranean; **northward** (צָפוֹן, hidden or dark place, where darkness gathers, as opposed to the bright and sunny south); **southward**, towards the right-hand quarter (תֵּימָן, from יָמִין, the right hand; cf. Exod. xxvi. 18, "to the south towards the right hand"); **eastward**, towards the dawn or sunrising; cf. ch. iv. 47 (מִזְרָח, from זָרַח to shine forth).

Ver. 28.— (Comp. ch. i. 38; iii. 21; xxxi. 7; Numb. xxvii. 23.)

Ver. 29.—**In the valley over against Bethpeor**; *i.e.* in the plains of Moab (Arboth Moab, Numb. xxii. 1; cf. ch. iv. 46; xxxiv. 6). Beth-pe'or, *i.e.* the house or temple of Pe'or, the Moabitish Baal. There was a hill Pe'or, in the Abarim range, near to which this town was; it was opposite to Jericho, six Roman miles north of Libias (Eusebius); it was given to the tribe of Reuben (Josh. xiii. 20). In passing from the historical recapitulation, Moses indicates precisely the locality in which they were when this address was delivered.

HOMILETICS.

Ch. ii. 24—iii. 11.—*The last of the giants.* Though Israel was not allowed to plunder or in any way to behave uncourteously to peoples who permitted them to pass through their territory without obstruction, yet, if they were obstinately opposed, they were to maintain their ground, and to force a passage through. There are recorded here two conflicts of this kind, which were memorable in after-days, and which gave a colouring to the sanctuary songs (cf. Ps. cxxxvi.). Sihon, King of the Amorites, and Og, the King of Bashan, fought against the people of God, were utterly vanquished, and their land was taken possession of by those whose course they obstructed. We may find in this apparently unpromising theme a topic for pulpit teaching, which may furnish instruction in the ways of God, of which we cannot afford to lose sight. Either of the two cases before us will equally avail for this purpose. We propose to study the overthrow of *Og, and the passing away of the last of the giants.* Observe—

I. THERE IS SOMETHING OF MYSTERY ABOUT THIS PASSAGE, WHICH WE PROPOSE TO CLEAR UP. There are three points respecting Og which, *at first sight*, have an aspect of romance about them: 1. The account of the king and his bedstead. 2. The race of giants. 3. The sixty great cities and unwalled towns—a great many, and that within a space less than that covered by some of our English counties. We can quite imagine a superficial reader, specially if he be one who has a keen appreciation of the liberty of doubting, and who restlessly chafes against the Old Book, saying, "There, it is absurd upon the face of it, just like the legends of other peoples—a piece of mythology." That is the rough-and-ready way in which Moses is dealt with now by many who ought to know better. We are prepared to contest these sceptics at every point, and, what is more, to affirm that a careful study of the latest researches will confirm Moses' statements, and not overthrow them (see the Exposition on this passage; also Dr. Kitto's 'Daily Bible Readings,' *in loc.*; specially Rev. J. L. Porter's 'Giant Cities of Bashan'). When we sufficiently avail ourselves of the light which modern travel and research have thrown upon the Bible, we find that what seemed romantic and almost legendary before, appears to be exact, literal, sober truth. This is an age of scepticism as regards the old *Word*, and of resurrections as regards the old *world*; the latter at every step are putting the former to shame. Every word of God is pure, and, however some may load it with reproach, it shall be more than vindicated, and shall abide when the last of the sceptics, like the last of the giants, shall have passed away!

II. THERE IS HERE VERY MUCH INSTRUCTION SUGGESTED IN THE WAYS OF GOD, TO WHICH IT BEHOVES US TO TAKE HEED: as we are presented with this topic for meditation—*The passing away of nations and the incoming of others.* 1. *What a retrospect does the history of the rise, progress, and abandonment of these giant cities, and the dwindling away of a stalwart race, call up before our imagination!* Sixty strong cities. More than forty unwalled towns, of which the remains *may even now be seen!* What a hum of busy life must there have been at one time! and what a degree of civilization at that remote period! "When Israel was a child," a world of strong, skilled life had reached its prime; of some arts a knowledge was then possessed which, somehow or other, we have lost and cannot regain. We can gather, to some extent, what they were, from silent, monumental speech; but while the cities remain, the nation which reared and owned them has quite passed away! Strange spectacle! Huge mystery! That pillars and monuments and records (even on papyrus) should survive the wreck of ages, while the *men* who originated all have mouldered long in dust! 2. *How humiliating to see the powerlessness of a nation to guard itself, even when it erects buildings which for ages will survive itself!* Those stout walls of Bashan have defied the tempests of three thousand years! But of the men whose wit devised and whose hands wrought them not a trace is left. Is it so? Can a nation fashion that which shall resist the wear and tear of millenniums, and yet do nothing to arrest its own decay? How insignificant does this make a nation seem (cf. Isa. xl. 17)! 3. *How unimportant is it to the world at large whether one nation or another is uppermost!* Bashan's people are gone, and not for thousands of years has there been a lament that that race has ceased to be! We *ought* to learn this lesson: A nation that seems great at one moment, may disappear from the scene of busy life, and, after a temporary shock, a short inconvenience, perhaps, the world would soon adjust itself to the change, and would go on as before! 4. *Nevertheless, no nation passes away without some advance in the unrolling of the great map of God's providence.* God may make much of that of which men make nothing. It was not for nought that Og and his people were dispossessed. Great strength was combined with ghastly wickedness. This is the reason why they were swept away. The wheels of providence are "full of eyes." Unless a nation is accomplishing God's purposes, it will not be spared to fulfil its own! God will rid the world of plague-spots. 5. *By sweeping away Og and his people, the way was cleared for planting in their territory a people who should have a nobler faith, even a faith in the One living and true God, and who should also set up a higher standard for national life and personal character.* The corner-stone of Israel's polity was righteousness. Hence we should be prepared to sing right joyously the old Hebrew song in Ps. cxxxvi., and to see in the dispossession of Og a proof of the Divine mercy to the world! Hence: 6. *We who know God's Name can look with calm serenity on national catastrophes.* Nations have been, and may yet be, swept off; but in all the transitions of power from one people to another, we see the onward march of One who is but putting down that which is ill, that he may ultimately reset the world in goodness, truth, and love. We can join anticipatively in the song in Rev. xv. Note, in conclusion: (1) Whether a nation is likely to continue in being or no depends on the degree to which it is fulfilling *God's* designs, and not at all on the measure with which it is carrying out its own. (2) Whether it is best for the world that a nation should continue in being depends on the virtue, purity, and piety of the people who compose it. (3) If virtue be a-wanting, no number of cities and towns, nor any strength and hardness in the race, will ever shield a nation from absolute extinction. God can raise up better peoples. He is able "of these stones" to raise up children to Abraham. (4) God deals with *nations* in *this life*; with *individuals*, in the next also. "Whatsoever a man soweth, that shall he also reap."

Vers. 23—27.—(See Homiletics, ch. xxxii. 41—52, and ch. xxxiv.)

HOMILIES BY VARIOUS AUTHORS.

Vers. 1—20.—*Self-propagating conquest.* There is solid truth in the French proverb: "It is the first step that costs." An untried course makes large demands on a man's thought, self-watchfulness, and energy; but when habit is acquired, the machinery of the soul works with smooth facility. Enterprises which are most arduous at the first, become by repetition as simple as a natural instinct.

I. CONQUEST INDUCES NEW ENERGY. The joy of conquest is a spur to fresh endeavour. The appetite for adventure and exertion is whetted, and is not easily controlled. Herein lies the secret cause of Alexander's tears, that there were no further worlds to be conquered. The selfsame law of inertia, which hinders senseless matter from originating motion, operates to keep it in incessant motion when it has once begun.

II. CONQUEST GENERATES LARGER AND MORE COURAGEOUS FAITH. The man who (conscious of Divine assistance) has gained a triumph, listens with docility to every fresh whisper from the lips of Jehovah. So David, after many conquests over the Philistines, asks again with child-like simplicity, "Shall I go up against them? Wilt thou deliver them into my hands?" The successful efforts of robust faith will lead a man to keep very close to God. They do not puff up with pride; they humble us by a sense of the Divine goodness. In the spiritual world as in the material, there operates the law of action and reaction. Faith promotes success, and success invigorates faith.

III. ONE TRIUMPH MAKES ALL TRIUMPH POSSIBLE. An atom is a type of the world. An organic cell is a type of the animal. A leaf is a type of the tree. So *one* triumph is the pattern and pledge of all triumph. We become, in holy warfare, "more than conquerors;" for we have qualified ourselves for further warfare and for easier conquests. Og, King of Bashan, may have been a more formidable foe than Sihon, King of Heshbon; the walls and gates of Bashan may have been tenfold more impregnable than those of Heshbon; nevertheless, the Divine succour which had been afforded to the Hebrews was competent for every exigency, and if only faith could rise to the height of its resources, no opposition could withstand it. What though Og be a stalwart giant—the last of his race—the God that made him can destroy him! The God who is at our back can give us victory over every foe. Conscious of the power and skill of our heavenly Ally, we can say, "God is with me, therefore I must prevail."

IV. THE TRIUMPH OF THE WHOLE CHURCH DEPENDS ON THE BRAVE EXERTION OF INDIVIDUALS. In every community we shall find a variety of temperaments—some sluggish and some sanguine. The faith of a few will reproduce itself in others. The glowing zeal of one will be contagious. Among the enormous host of the Hebrews two names are singled out for honour—Jair and Machir. In all warfare, much depends on the heroic examples of a few leaders. The tone of feeling and courage percolates through all the ranks of the army, and braces every man to fulfil his part. Every member of the Church helps or hinders the Church's conquests. The son of Jesse infused a spirit of bravery into *all* the tribes of Israel, and knit them into organic unity.

V. REAL CONQUEST BRINGS ABIDING RESULTS. This triumph of the Israelites put them into permanent possession of lands and cities and palaces. Better still, it developed the qualities of faith and courage—brought into play generous and self-abnegating sentiments. Such principles as these made secure to them the possessions they had won. As a few seeds will bring a large harvest, so a complete mastery over any real foe bears rich and remote advantages. We do well to *discover* our foes, fasten attention on them, and give no quarter until they are destroyed. So ingrained was idolatry in these Amorites, that the moral pollution could only be removed by the destruction of the people.

VI. THE EFFECT UPON OURSELVES OF CONQUEST SHOULD BE TO DEVELOP OUR BROTHERLY SYMPATHY. Those who have fought at our side, and been mutually helpful, deserve a place in memory and affection. If by their co-operation we have gained a conquest, gratitude impels us to continue the alliance until they obtain their possessions also. It is noble to sacrifice ease and material advantage for the purpose of serving our brethren. Self-conquest will prompt us to empty self, if only we can enrich others. This is to follow the highest example—to be as God. The glory and excellence of spiritual possessions is *this*—they are not diminished by communication. We give, and still have.

VII. CONQUEST SHOULD DEEPEN OUR SENSE OF OBLIGATION TO THE SUPREME GOD. There is a strong tendency in all success to foster pride and self-esteem. Crowds of successful men bow down to their own net, and burn incense to their drag. They recognize the visible instrument, rather than the invisible Cause. Moses had to withstand the current of popular feeling, when, in the flush of triumph, he reminds them emphatically, " The Lord your God hath given you this land." Poverty often drives us to God : fulness ofttimes keeps us from him. Yet every factor in the achievement of victory was of God, and to him was all praise due. " His right hand, and his holy arm, gain for us the victory."—D.

Vers. 21—29.—*Prospect of death.* In the full career of triumph, Moses has inward presentiment, and external announcement, that his end was near. Nature has a greater repugnance to death when we are enveloped in the bright sunshine of prosperity. The contrast is more marked. Decay and disease are natural forerunners of dissolution ; but in Moses these were wanting. With him, the gravamen of the trial was that his life-work was incomplete. The closer we approach to the final stroke of an undertaking, the deeper becomes our anxiety for a successful issue. " How am I straitened till it be accomplished ! "

I. WE HAVE HERE SAGACIOUS PROVISION TO CONSUMMATE HIS WORK. In the judgment of a good man, the perpetuation of his work by others is vastly more important than the continuance of his own life. Individuals pass away, but the progress of the race continues. Up to this point in Israel's pilgrimage, Moses had been unequalled as a leader; no one among the tribes could have filled his place. But now, a military general, rather than a legislator, is needed, and Joshua has been gradually moulded by a Divine hand for this work. We may safely trust human interests with God. 1. *The experience of age conveys its lessons to youth.* Joshua was scarcely a young man, as *we* reckon years; yet, compared with Moses, he was juvenile and inexperienced in governing men. Age is a relative quality. The lesson was directly to the point—straight at the bull's-eye of the target. " Fear not." *Courage*, just then, was the " one thing needful." 2. *The command was founded on the most solid reasons*, viz. the irresistible might of Jehovah, and the unchangeableness of his purposes. What he *had* done, he could yet do. What he *had* done was a revelation of what he designed to do. *Observation* of God's deeds and methods fosters valorous faith. " Whoso is wise, and will observe these things, even he shall understand the loving-kindness of the Lord."

II. PRAYER THAT LIFE MAY YET BE PROLONGED. It savours of submissive meekness to the Divine will that Moses first provided for the nation's welfare, in view of the contingency of death, and then prays that the stroke may be delayed. The latter is secondary. 1. *The prayer was earnest.* " I besought the Lord." There is indication that it was oft repeated and long continued. 2. *The prayer was inspired by noble motive.* An unusual display of God's greatness had been made in the defeat of the two kings, and Moses longed to see further unfoldings of God's might. Still, his prayer was, " I pray thee show me thy glory ! " God had only *begun* to act; Moses yearned to see the final consummation. 3. *Yet this prayer was refused.* Unerring wisdom perceived that it was best to refuse—*best*, perhaps, for Moses himself—and best for Israel. It is better for a man to present an unsuccessful prayer, than not to pray at all. *Some* blessing is the fruit. 4. *The denial was a vicarious chastisement.* We have, in God's kingdom, vicarious blessing and vicarious suffering. For Joseph's sake, the house of Potiphar was blessed. For David's sake, Solomon finished his reign in peace. For Paul's sake, the crew of the doomed vessel escaped. On the other side, God was wroth with Moses for the Hebrews' sake. Present chastisement better far than final banishment. 5. *Divine tenderness is displayed even in refusal.* The refusal was not wholly from anger; there was a large admixture of kindness. Anger for the sin; kindness for the man. It is as if God had said, "It pains me sore to impose this chastisement; nevertheless, it must be done, and you will add to my pain by seeking an escape." God beseeches him to urge no further. Up to this point, prayer was fitting; *beyond* this, prayer would have been fresh guilt. 6. *Yet compensation for the loss is granted.* Prayer is never wholly unsuccessful. A gracious concession is made. Moses had asked to *see* the land; he shall *see* it, although his foot shall not tread it. The eye and the heart of the man of God shall be gladdened. Without doubt, Moses' natural eyesight had been preserved for this selfsame occasion, and special power of vision also was vouchsafed in that eventful hour, when Moses stood on Pisgah's peak. He shall *see* it without the toil of travel, without the peril of the conflict. 7. *A crowning kindness is shown in confirming the succession to Joshua.* Though the workman is to be removed, the work shall advance. It was a sweet solace to the mind of Moses that Joshua should have been accepted in his stead. His cherished purpose shall be accomplished, although by other hands. The spirit of Moses would survive in Joshua. "Being dead," Moses would still speak and act. The body may dissolve, but the moral courage and heroic valour are transmitted to another.

Rest is the reward of toil, and the cradle of new exertion. "So we abode in the valley." The valley of Beth-peor was the preparation for Pisgah's peak. Humiliation before exaltation.—D.

Vers. 1—12.—*The conquest of Og.* Og, King of Bashan, was a yet more formidable adversary than Sihon. We read with wonder of that extraordinary territory over which he ruled, the region of Argob, with its sixty cities built of black stone, hard as iron, and perched amidst the masses of basaltic rock, which are the characteristic feature of the district, and which formed an apparently impregnable barrier against assault. The suddenness, completeness, and decisiveness of the conquest of this region, naturally so strong, so thickly peopled, so powerfully defended, and ruled by a king of the race of giants, is in any view of it, an astonishing fact, and would naturally raise the courage of the Israelites to the highest pitch of confidence, while striking dismay into surrounding nations (ch. ii. 25). We consider—

I. Og's CONFIDENT ATTACK. Like Sihon, he came out against the Israelites, "he and all his people" (ver. 1), and doubtless with great hopes of success. Had he been less confident, he would probably have remained within his fortifications. Though Joshua speaks (xxiv. 12) of him being driven forth by the hornet, the spirit of the attack reminds us of Goliath's boastful advance against the armies of Saul (1 Sam. xvii. 4—12). His assault symbolizes the giant-power of the world in its hostile relations to the Church: pagan—papal—infidel; science—learning—philosophy; powerful in itself, strongly entrenched, boastful in spirit. Voltaire boasted that it took twelve men to set up Christianity, but he would show that one man was sufficient to overthrow it. Christianity lasts still, but Voltaire——?

II. HIS COMPLETE ROUT (vers. 3—8). Moses dwells on the details of this astonishing victory with lively gratitude and wonder. The victory was, as in Sihon's case, complete, only here more remarkable from the strength of the cities and towns. And again all the people were devoted to destruction (ver. 6). Somewhat analogous to this rout have been many of the victories of Christianity. We think of the downfall of ancient paganism, so strongly entrenched, but now swept so entirely from the earth; of the collapse of eighteenth-century deism; of the mighty men of their own days, boastful of their power to destroy the Church's faith, who are now, like Og, only remembered by their coffins. The tomes of Voltaire, Bolingbroke, Shaftesbury, and a host of others lie unread on dusty shelves, while the Bible is multiplying its circulation every year. New, and it may be even mightier, foes are springing up in our modern agnostic and positivist and pantheistic schools, but to the serious student of history there can be no real doubt as to the issue of the conflict.

III. THE OCCUPATION OF HIS LAND (vers. 9—12). The land and the cities thus conquered were taken possession of by the conquerors, and as speedily as possible occupied. The enemy was dispossessed and spoiled. So did the Church in the early centuries first conquer, and then possess the ground previously held by paganism. "We are of yesterday, and yet we have filled every place belonging to you—cities, islands, castles, towns, assemblies, your very camp, companies, palace, senate, forum. We leave you your temples only" (Tertullian). The same thing takes place as often as the treasures of unbelieving science, learning, and philosophy, in their varied forms and applications (inventions, arts, etc.), fall into the hands of the Church, and are made to subserve her ends. The unbelieving criticism of the Bible, e.g., has furnished a vast amount of material available for the purposes of faith. So the discoveries of science, which were dreaded as hostile, prove at last to be confirmatory and helpful, and are appropriated by belief. Every victory of Christianity in the outward world, or in the regions of thought, enlarges its possessions and extends its influence.—J. O.

Ver. 6.—*The destruction of the populations.* The difficulty is often urged of the numerous cases of the destruction of entire populations recorded in Scripture, and said to be commanded by God. It is a difficulty which all have felt, and which deserves remark. It is not questioned that, as a matter of *policy*, it was wise to root out these populations from the lands in which they dwelt; but the justice and humanity of the measure are thought to be more doubtful. The believer, on the other hand, cannot take a condemnatory view of these transactions (so far as covered by express command); but must treat them as he would treat similar difficulties in the ordinary providence of God, as matters which *appear* to conflict with the Divine goodness and justice, while doubtless admitting of a perfect reconciliation with both. But it may be suggested—

I. THAT THE FINER METHODS OF MODERN WARFARE CANNOT REASONABLY BE LOOKED FOR IN RUDER AGES. War in any case is an evil of terrible magnitude. The sufferings it inflicts, even when conducted most humanely, are incalculable. It is not the men in arms alone who suffer, but the populations whose villages are burned, whose fields are devastated, whose aged and sickly are driven out to perish, whose wives and mothers mourn their dead thousands. Modern warfare has, however, its alleviations, the result of centuries of civilization and of the growth of Christian feeling. These did not, and could not, exist at the time of the conquest. It is not in analogy with God's method of operation to suppose that he should have miraculously anticipated the work of long ages of development, and grafted on these wars the military science of the nineteenth century—a science equally unsuited to the intelligence of the invader and to the tactics of the enemy. It would be as reasonable to allege that God should have anticipated the discoveries and methods of modern surgery, or armed the Israelites with nineteenth-century weapons. What may reasonably be expected is that, adopting as a basis the methods of warfare then customary, the evils of these should as far as possible be mitigated, and any improvements be introduced which the rudeness of the times admitted of. How far this was accomplished will appear to any one who studies the accounts of ancient warfare, with their shocking barbarities, mutilations, tortures; scarcely a trace of which is to be found in the wars of the Israelites, and none in the Law.

II. THAT THE EXTERMINATION OF WHOLE POPULATIONS WAS NOT THE RULE OF JEWISH WARFARE, BUT WAS INVARIABLY A PUNISHMENT INFLICTED FOR SIN. The proof of the former of these propositions will be found in ch. xx. 10—16; and examination of the special cases will show the correctness of the latter. The destruction of the Canaanitish nations, in particular, is put expressly on the ground of their horrible and nameless iniquities (Lev. xviii. 24, 25). It was the execution of a long-delayed and richly deserved judicial sentence. The Midianites and Amalekites incurred this doom through sins against Israel (Numb. xxxii. 16; Exod. xvii. 16); as also to some extent did Sihon and Og. But while we cannot speak absolutely as to the moral state of the nations under these kings, it may be inferred that the cup of their iniquity had, in the Divine estimation, become full like the others. Do we condemn the sentence as too severe? Or must we not leave the judgment on a point like that to the Judge of all the earth? The essential difficulty is not greater than in the judgments of the Deluge or the destruction of Sodom and Gomorrah, in which God claimed a like right to dispose of human life, and to vindicate his justice by the destruction of it. We ought rather to read in the severity of these punishments the awful lesson of sin's evil and enormity, and of the abhorrence in which it is held by the holy Lawgiver. The emphasizing of guilt and its deserts was a necessary preliminary to the introduction of the gospel.

III. THAT GOD IS AS SEVERE IN HIS DEALINGS WITH SIN IN HIS OWN PEOPLE AS IN HIS ENEMIES. This is a point which is surely of great moment. If severe in punishing these wicked nations, God is not less sparing of Israel when it follows in their ways, and does what is wrong. We think here of the destruction of thousands of their number for the sin of the golden calf (Exod. xxxii. 28), and for the sin of Baal-peor (Numb. xxiii. 5); of the plagues, fiery serpents, etc., which chastised them for disobedience; of their defeat at Ai (Josh. vii. 4), and of the threatenings recorded against them in this book (ch. xxviii.). We think of Moses himself excluded from the land of promise. Nor is sin made less of in the New Testament than in the Old. In the cross of Jesus, where the Holy One is made a curse for sinners, a far more affecting demonstration is given of the judicial sternness of God, than in the destruction of the nations of his foes. There is with God no respect of persons; and if one can believe in his love to Israel notwithstanding these inflictions, he may believe in his love and justice notwithstanding the punishments inflicted on the sinful nations around. As regards the Canaanitish nations, their rooting out, so just otherwise, was plainly necessary for the preservation of Israel's purity (ch. vii. 1—6).—J. O.

Vers. 12—20.—*Distribution of territory.* I. CONQUERED TERRITORY IS NOT TO BE LEFT UNOCCUPIED. This is a sound principle. Has a vice been conquered?—replace it by a contrary virtue. Has a soul been converted?—set it to Christian work. Has a new district or a portion of heathenism been won for Christ?—plant it with Christian agencies, industries, and institutions. Replace bad books by good ones; sinful amusements by such as are healthful; pernicious customs by pure forms of social life. Unoccupied territory will soon fall back into the hands of the enemy.

II. CONQUERED TERRITORY IS TO BE WISELY DISTRIBUTED. The distribution of the conquered districts suggests to us how, in the occupation of the fields of service which God gives her, the Church should study order, peace, and the attainment of the higher ends of possession, by wise arrangements. There should be no clashing or confusion of spheres in the kingdom of Christ. We have illustrations of the violation of this rule in the occupation of limited districts by a great number of rival Churches, often working in antagonism to each other; in the appointment of individuals to posts for which they are unsuited; in the confusion arising from workers not knowing their own departments of service, or not keeping to it when known. Whereas here: 1. Each had his portion *carefully defined.* 2. Respect was had to *the talents and callings* of those who were to occupy. "A place for cattle," "much cattle" (Numb. xxxii. 1; cf. ver. 19). 3. Individuals *had their own conquests secured to them* (ver. 14). A man's spiritual conquests are always secured to himself—his conquests *over* himself; and they are his greatest possessions. True also of conquests for Christ in conversions (1 Thess. ii. 19). Should be a principle recognized in the work of the Church.

III. CONQUERED TERRITORY IS HELD ON CONDITION OF ASSISTANCE TO OTHERS. (Vers. 18—21.) 1. Each branch of the Church is to assist the others. 2. It holds its privileges on this condition. 3. The rest of all is needful to the perfect rest of any (Heb. xi. 40).—J. O.

Vers. 21, 22.—*Encouragement.* We notice: 1. Past mercies are a pledge of future ones. "Thine eyes have seen," etc. 2. The past victories of the Church mirror her future conquests. "So shall the Lord do," etc. 3. The conditions of success in spiritual conflict are (1) fearlessness, (2) dependence on Divine aid. "Fear not," etc.—J. O.

Vers. 23—29.—*God's refusal of man's wishes.* We have in this singularly pathetic passage of the private history of Moses—

I. An AFFECTING ENTREATY. "I pray thee, let me go over, and see the good land," etc. (vers. 24, 25). In this speaks: 1. The *man*. How hard to flesh and blood to be cut off just then! To see the goodly land (ver. 27), but not to enter it. Yet not an uncommon experience. Few things are more painful than to be removed when just on the verge of some great success; when the hopes of a lifetime seem just about to be realized; when some great cause with which we are identified is on the eve of final victory. 2. The *patriot*. There never beat in human breast a more patriotic heart than that of Moses, and it was supremely hard to step aside and commit the leadership into other hands, when all his wishes for his nation were so nearly fulfilled. It was Israel's triumph, not his own, he wished to celebrate. 3. The *saint*. For Moses' deepest longing in the matter after all was to see God glorified—to witness his greatness and his mighty hand (ver. 24). No man had ever seen as much of God's greatness and glory as he had, but what he had seen only whetted his desire to see more. It is always thus with saintly natures. The thirst for the manifestation of God increases with the gratification of it (Ps. lxiii. 1—6; cf. Exod. xxxiii. 18—20). "Father, glorify thy name" (John xii. 28).

II. A DECISIVE REFUSAL. 1. The *cause* of it. "Wroth with me for your sakes" (ver. 26). How painful to feel that misconduct of ours has involved any (1) in sin, (2) in penalty, (3) in disappointment! 2. The *severity* of it. It seems a great punishment for a not very great offence. Yet how often do we find that one false step, "one pause in self-control," entails on the individual irretrievable loss! God could not allow the sin of one who stood in so close and personal relation to him to pass without putting on it the stamp of his severe displeasure. 3. The *irreversibility* of it. He who had succeeded so often in saving Israel by his powerful intercession, fails in his intercession for himself. "Let it suffice thee; speak no more unto me of this matter" (ver. 26). Moses, the mediator and representative of the Law, must, when he sins, undergo its severity. In a case so typical, a reversal of the sentence would have shaken faith in all God's threatenings. He interceded for others, but there was no second Moses to intercede for him. Those who live nearest to God, and are most honoured by him, must expect to be treated with exceptional strictness for their faults; as a father is more particular about the morals of his own son than about those of servants and aliens.

III. A PARTIAL COMPENSATION. It was given him: 1. *To see the goodly land* (ver. 27). Even this he must have felt to be a great boon, and how his eyes, supernaturally strengthened, must have drunk in the precious vision! How many toilers have to leave the world in this frame of mind—getting glimpses of a future they do not live to inherit! 2. *To know that his successor was ready* (ver. 28). There are few sights more suggestive of magnanimity than Moses meekly surrendering his own dearest wishes, and helping to prepare Joshua for the work which he coveted so much to do himself. It may be felt by us that there was kindness as well as severity in the arrangement which gave Israel a new leader. "The conquest of Canaan—a most colossal work—demanded fresh, youthful powers" (Oosterzee). The work of Moses was indeed done on earth, and he had to pass away to make room for instruments better fitted to do the work of the new age.

CONCLUSION. In this refusal see (1) God's severity, (2) God's kindness. For in addition to the point just mentioned, we can see how, from his temporal loss, Moses reaped a great spiritual gain—the perfecting of his will in its choice of God as its exclusive portion, and in entire acquiescence in Divine arrangements. This great renunciation was the last sacrifice asked of him, and he rose to the heroic height of making it.—J. O.

Vers. 1—17.—*The destruction of Og, King of Bashan.* We have here an account of another conquest, for which the victory over Sihon, King of the Amorites, prepared the people. Bashan was "called the land of the giants" (ver. 13), and Og, the king, was manifestly the greatest of the giants—hence the particulars about his bedstead, as being nine cubits long and four broad (ver. 11). In a rude age and country, *force* was the recognized ruler, and the biggest man in consequence was chosen chief. It was living and reigning by *sense* and *sight*—the world's regular way. Here, then, let us observe that—

I. The victory over Sihon, King of the Amorites, was a needful preparation for the more serious enterprise of the conquest of Bashan. The Lord leads his people, even in *war*, "from strength to strength." They try their swords upon the Amorites successfully before attempting to subdue the giants. They get a taste of successful war before they are asked to undertake the greater and more serious task of exterminating the giants of Bashan.

And so it is in fighting the good fight of faith. One little victory over an easily besetting sin gives nerve for a greater task. The muscles of the soul grow strong through exercise, and greater victories are gained. Faithfulness in the little conducts to faithfulness in that which is much (Luke xvi. 10).

II. The giants by their unwalled towns proved their intense feeling of security. They had their strongholds, no doubt, as "the giant cities of Bashan" still attest. But they had "unwalled towns a great many" (ver. 5). It is evident from this that their sense of personal security was intense. They confided in their size and powers. They imagined no one would have the temerity to attack them. It was the contrast to "assurance of faith"—what we might call "the assurance of sense."

And this characterizes the enemies of God's people more or less always. Self-confidence is the source of their power and of their misfortune in the end. It is an easy victory eventually which the Lord's people, who have learned to have "no confidence in the flesh" (Phil. iii. 3), obtain over their self-confident foes.

III. The victory over the giants was complete, amounting to an extermination. "And we utterly destroyed them, as we did unto Sihon, King of Heshbon, utterly destroying the men, women, and children, of every city" (ver. 6). This was absolutely necessary, as well as by the giants deserved. Had such foes been spared in the rear of the invasion, the Israelites would have had no sense of security. It was impossible to "mask these fortresses," as great armies can sometimes afford to do in modern warfare. It was better to exterminate these foes. They did so as the servants of God. His command was their warrant, and made their act defensible on moral as well as strategic grounds.

And the victory God gives his people over their sins and foes is at last complete.

IV. The allotment of Bashan and the lands on this side Jordan gave the invaders of Canaan an important base of operations. No longer would they be, like Sherman in his advance through Savannah, marching on without a base. God gave them in Bashan the leverage they needed. Here they quartered the non-combatants till the land over Jordan was won.

And so is it in the spiritual life. Out of one conquest future conquests are organized. We go forward in God's guidance along a safe path to perfect victory.—R. M. E.

Vers. 18—20.—*The pioneers of the invasion of Palestine.* Here the Reubenites, Gadites, and Manassites are directed to "intern" their wives, little ones, and cattle in the cities of Bashan, which were now literally free from the race of the giants, and then to go armed across the Jordan before their fellows, the van of the invading host. These pioneers become thus the least encumbered of the invaders. Their non-combatants are safe in the cities of Bashan, their cattle are in good pastures, they may go with easy minds and light hearts to the war. Their purpose in the invasion is not selfish, but perfectly disinterested. They go to fight for their brethren, and to carve out homes for them beyond the river.

We have here a Divine law, as it seems to us, of very practical application. To sketch this let us notice—

I. God gives rest and inheritance to individuals that they may interest themselves in securing similar blessings for others. Beginning with the lowest inheritance, we would observe that, when God gives individuals *riches*, it is not that they may be *excused* from public work, but *enabled* for it. A servant of God who finds himself wealthy is not superannuated, but supported for public ends. He is bound to do all he can with and by his means.

But this law has a still happier spiritual side. When God blesses us with assurance of salvation, it is that his way may be known on earth, and his saving health among all nations (Ps. lxvii. 1, 2). He makes us peaceful and happy in Christ that we may, with unburdened spirits, seek the salvation of those around us.

II. Assurance of salvation should therefore be sought by each of us on public grounds. It is not a personal matter only, but a public interest as well. The world will be less benefited by us if we are constantly in doubt about personal salvation. We are in such a case marching without a base. It is a risky kind of warfare.

Let us seek from God, on *public* grounds, the priceless blessing of assurance, and then we shall be able to lose sight of self in seeking the common weal.

III. Disinterestedness is the secret of successful warfare. The Reubenites and their fellows in the van must have commanded the respect not only of those behind them, but of the Canaanites with whom they had to contend. It was the first time, since Abraham's rescue of Lot, that warriors had appeared from purely disinterested motives in the field of battle.

And in matters spiritual it is the same. The ministry of Christ is, speaking generally, an ill-paid profession. There is the less chance, then, of men entering this service for a piece of bread. Disinterestedness is more likely to be the rule. With other Christians it is the same. When people are compelled to recognize disinterestedness, the chief part of the battle is won.

IV. The thought of having helped others to rest in the Lord enhances our own rest in him. The Reubenites, etc., must have come back to their homes in Bashan with great satisfaction. They felt that they had done a good, unselfish work in the campaign. They were not fighting for their own hand, but for the welfare of others. So in the spiritual warfare, when we become instruments in God's hand in leading others to rest in him, we find our rest deepened and made more glorious. May it be the joy of many !—R. M. E.

Vers. 21—29.—*Moses' longing to enter the promised land refused.* The two conquests over Sihon and over Og had filled Moses with a sense of God's matchless power. With a warrior's instinct—for he had had a warrior's training, it is believed, in Egypt, in his youth—he saw in this first portion of the fight the assurance of a glorious invasion. He longed to be at its head, and to see the land which God had promised actually won. Will he not get complete the work he has been instrumental in beginning? He pleaded with God for it, but all he gets is a Pisgah-view; he is denied an entrance into the land.

I. It was natural for Moses to long for the completion of his work. The Exodus was his special work. All else in his life was preparatory to this. But the Exodus was to be finished in the invasion of Canaan and the settlement of the people there. Moses is now so interested in the work which he has had on hand for forty years that he is loth to leave it.

So with God's servants often. They form plans, plans manifestly Divine, and they long to complete them. But God does not respond always to these very natural desires. Public work is attempted—literary work—but the sowing and the reaping are often separated. One soweth, another reapeth.

II. It is a great privilege to be allowed to encourage those coming after us. Moses is directed to encourage Joshua. This is something done towards successful invasion. An encouraged Joshua may do better than an ever-present Moses. And the privilege of encouragement is greatly prized. Joshua receives all from Moses that son could receive from father, that a leader could receive from his superior and guide (vers. 21, 22).

And our successors should be encouraged by us all we can, as one of life's last and best privileges.

III. A Pisgah-view is fitting compensation, backed up as it was by special care. Moses saw the land at last, and died with God, reserved by the All-wise for an entrance into Canaan at the transfiguration of Christ. The view from Pisgah was grand, but the view on Hermon was grander. His entrance of the land with Elijah in glory was grander than an entrance at the head of the hosts of Israel.

And these views from Pisgah may still be ours if we seek the appointed mountain-top of God. He calls us to mountain-tops of prayer and meditation, and shows us wondrous glimpses of his glory and his promises. To be with him there is compensation for much disappointment.

IV. A faithful son may experience a father's deserved wrath. Moses admits that God was wroth with him, and states the reason. It is well to recognize that deserved wrath and chastisement may coexist with profound and tender love. Moses was well beloved, even though excluded from the land of promise. God gave him paradise instead of Canaan.—R. M. E.

EXPOSITION.

CHAPTER IV.

Vers. 1—40.—ADMONITIONS AND EXHORTATIONS. Moses, having presented to the people certain facts in their recent history which had in them a specially animating and encouraging tendency, proceeds to direct his discourse to the inculcation of duties and exhortations to obedience to the Divine enactments. This portion also of his address is of an introductory character as well as what precedes.

Vers. 1—8.—_Exhortation to the observance of the Law generally._ The Law was to be kept as a complete whole; nothing was to be taken from it or added to it; it comprised the commandments of Jehovah, and therefore they were not only to do it as what Moses, their leader and lawgiver, had enjoined, but to keep it as a sacred deposit, not to be altered or tampered with, and to observe it as what God their Sovereign had enacted for them. The dignity and worth of the Law are here asserted, and also its completeness as given by Moses. Any addition to it, no less than any subtraction from it, would mar its integrity and affect its perfection. Altered circumstances in process of time might, indeed, lead to the desuetude of some parts of the Mosaic enactments, and new institutions or laws might be required to meet a new condition of things, or even in that new condition to fence and sustain the primitive code; but that code was to remain intact in the Statute-Book, and no alterations were to be made upon it that should affect its substance or nullify any of its principles. New laws and institutions appointed by God would, of course, have the same authority as those originally ordained by Moses; and such, it can hardly be doubted, were in point of fact under the Hebrew monarchy introduced by the prophets speaking in the name of God. The Law, nevertheless, was kept substantially entire. Even under the new

dispensation, the Law has not been abolished. Christ, as he himself declared, came not to destroy the Law and the prophets, but to fulfil them (Matt. v. 17). The sin of the Pharisees, for which they were censured by our Lord, lay in this, that they taught for doctrines the commandments of men (Matt. xv. 9), and had "made the commandments of God of none effect by their traditions" (Matt. xv. 6).

Vers. 1, 2.—Now therefore; rather _And now._ With this Moses passes from referring to what God had done for Israel to admonish Israel as to what they had to do as the subjects of God and the recipients of his favour. They were to give heed to all the statutes and judgments which Moses, as the servant of God, had taught them, in order that they might do them. **Statutes** (חֻקִּים), the things prescribed or enacted by law, whether moral, ritual, or civil; **judgments** (מִשְׁפָּטִים), _rights_, whether public or private, all that each could claim as his due, and all he was bound to render to God or to his fellow-men as their due. These two comprehend the whole Law as binding on Israel. On the doing of these by the people depended _life;_ these had been made known to them, not merely for their information, but specifically that they might do them, and thereby have life; not long life in the promised land alone, though this also is included (ver. 40; ch. v. 33; vi. 2, etc.), but that higher life, that life which man lives "by every word that proceedeth out of the mouth of the Lord" (ch. viii. 3; cf. Lev. xviii. 5; Ezek. xx. 11; Matt. iv. 4), that spiritual life which is in God's favour (Ps. xxx. 5). Enjoying this life as the fruit of obedience, they should also possess as their inheritance the land promised to their fathers.

Vers. 3, 4.—The people had had personal experience of the danger, on the one hand, of transgressing, and the benefit, on the other, of keeping God's Law; they had seen how those who sinned in worshipping Baal-peor were destroyed (Numb. xxv. 3, 9), whilst those who remained faithful to the Lord were kept alive. This experience the people had had only lately before, so that a reference to it would be all the more impressive. **Baal-peor,** the idol whose _cultus_ was observed at Peor. Baal (*Bal, Be'el, Bel,* Lord) was the common name of the supreme deity among the northern of the Semitic-speaking people, the Canaanites, the Phœnicians, the Aramæans, and the Assyrians. There were thus many Baals. Followed: *walked after;* a common Biblical expression for religious adherence and service (cf. Jer. viii. 2; ix. 14; and with a different formula, Numb. xxxii. 12; Deut. i. 36; Josh. xiv. 8; Judg. ii. 12, etc.). **Ye that did cleave unto Jehovah your God.** "To cleave unto one" is expressive of the closest, most intimate attachment and communion (cf. Gen. ii. 24; Isa. xiv. 1). The phrase is frequently used of devotion to the service and worship of the true God (cf. Deut. x. 20; Josh. xxii. 5; xxiii. 8; Acts ii. 23, etc.); here it expresses the contrast between the conduct of those who remained faithful to Jehovah and those who forsook him to worship Baal. **Are alive every one of you this day.** "Thus they that keep themselves pure in general defections, are saved from the common destruction (Ezek. ix. 4—6; 2 Tim. ii. 19; Rev. xx. 4)" (Ainsworth).

Vers. 5, 6.—The institutes of Moses were the commandments of Jehovah, and therefore obedience to them was imperative. By this was conditioned the enjoyment by Israel of the promised land; and this would be their **wisdom and understanding in the sight of the nations;** to themselves it would be life, and to the nations it would convey an impression of their being the depositories of true wisdom and knowledge, so that they should be constrained to say, **Surely a wise and understanding people is this great nation.** "The fruit of the righteous is a tree of life; and he that is wise winneth souls" (Prov. xi. 30). God's statutes make wise the simple (Ps. xix. 8; cxix. 98, 99); and they who are thus made wise attract the attention of others by the fame of their wisdom. Thus the Queen of Sheba heard in her distant country of the wisdom of Solomon, and came to him to commune with him of all that was in her heart (1 Kings x. 1, etc.); and many throughout the ages who were seeking after truth among the heathen, were drawn to Israel by seeing how with them was the true knowledge of God. Israel was thus exalted because God was nigh to them, ready to hear their cry and to give them what they needed; which none of the gods of the nations were or could be to their votaries; and because, in the Law which God had given them, they had such instruction and direction as no heathen nation possessed.

Vers. 7, 8.—Translate, *For what great nation is there that hath gods that draw near to it, as Jehovah our God whenever we call upon him? And what great nation is there that hath righteous statutes and ordinances like this whole Law which I am giving before you this day?* (comp. ch. xxxiii. 29; Ps. xxxiv. 17—20; cxlv. 18; 1 Sam. xiv. 36; 1 Kings xviii. 26—29, 37; Jas. iv. 8). "True right has its roots in God; and with the obscuration of the knowledge of God, law and right, with their divinely established foundations, are also shaken and obscured (cf. Rom. i. 26—32)" (Keil).

Vers. 9—14.—The possession of the oracles of God by Israel was a benefit to them only as these were kept in mind and reverently obeyed. Therefore they were to take heed and diligently beware of forgetting the circumstances under which the Law had been received at Horeb. God had then commanded the people to be gathered together, so that they stood before the Lord, were in his manifested presence, and were made to hear his voice speaking to them from amidst the fire and the clouds that covered the mount. They had thus actual evidence and guarantee that the Law they had received was Divine; and this they were to keep in mind as long as they lived, and to communicate to their children in all coming time, that so they might fear the Lord; for on this rested that covenant which God had made with Israel, and which they were to keep as the condition of their continuing to enjoy privilege and life.

Ver. 9.—**Keep thy soul diligently;** *i.e.* Be very careful to preserve thy life (cf. Job ii. 6; Prov. xiii. 3; xvi. 17; xix. 16; in all which passages the same formula is used as here). The Hebrew (נֶפֶשׁ) means primarily breath, then vital principle, natural life (*ánima*), then soul life, the soul or mind (*animus*). The forgetting of the wonders they had seen would lead to their forgetting God, and so to their departing from him, and this would mar and ultimately destroy their life (cf. Josh. xxiii. 11—16). **The things which thine eyes have seen** (see Exod. xix. 10, etc.).

Ver. 10.—Specially **the day.** The word "specially," introduced by the translators into the Authorized Version, is a needless interpolation. With this verse begins a new sentence, which is continued in ver. 11 on to the end of ver. 13. Render, *On the day* [i.e. at the time, the יוֹם is an adverbial accusative] *when ye stood before Jehovah your God in Horeb, . . . when ye came near and stood, . . . then Jehovah spake to you,* etc.

Ver. 11.—**The mountain burned with fire unto the midst** [unto the heart] **of heaven;** *i.e.* up to the very skies; a rhetorical description of the mighty pillar of fire that blazed on Sinai, and betokened the presence of him whose symbol is fire. **With darkness, clouds [cloud], and thick darkness**; underneath the fire was a cloud of deep darkness, out of which it blazed, the "thick cloud" of Exod. xix. 9, 16, and the "smoke" out of which the lightnings flashed, and over which the glory of the Lord, like devouring fire, rested on the top of the mountain (Exod. xix. 18; xx. 18; xxiv. 16, 17).

Ver. 12.—On this occasion the people **heard the voice of the words, but saw no similitude**; there was no form or shape apparent to the eye. No man can see God's face (Exod. xxxiii. 20, 23); "no man hath seen God at any time" (John i. 18); and though the nobles or elders of Israel who went up with Moses into the mount are said to have seen God, it is evident that what they saw was only some luminous manifestation of his glory, and not a form or shape of which a similitude could be made (Exod. xxiv. 9—17). Even Moses, with whom God said that he would speak mouth to mouth, and who should behold the similitude of God (Numb. xii. 8), was told that he could not see his face, his essential personality, but only his back, the reflection of his glory (Exod. xxxiii. 18—23).

Ver. 13.—**His covenant**; God's gracious engagement with Israel for their good, and by which they were bound to observe all his commandments. God declared this at Sinai when he uttered the ten commandments (words, דְּבָרִים), "the words of the covenant, the ten words" (Exod. xxxiv. 28), which he afterwards gave to Moses on two tables of stone, written with the finger of God (Exod. xxiv. 12; xxxi. 18). Besides these, there were other statutes and ordinances which Moses was commanded to teach the people, and which, with them, comprised the Law given at Sinai (see Exod. xxi. and following chapters).

Vers. 15—20.—As the people had seen no form or figure when God spake to them, so they were to beware for their very lives (cf. ver. 9) of acting corruptly by making any kind of image, whether of man or of beast, for the purpose of worshipping God as represented by it; they were also to beware of being so attracted by the splendour of the heavenly bodies as to be forcibly seduced to worship them and offer them religious service. They were not in this respect to imitate the heathen; for God, who had delivered them out of the furnace of Egyptian bondage, had taken them for himself to be his special possession; and therefore they were to take heed not to forget the covenant

of Jehovah their God, nor to offend him by making any image or representation of him as the object of worship. Among the heathen, and especially in Egypt, images were the very pillar and support of religion; but in Israel, as God had revealed himself to them without form, it was as a spirit he was to be worshipped, and not under any outward representation.

Ver. 16.—**Graven image** (פֶּסֶל), carved work or sculpture, whether of wood, or metal, or stone—**the similitude of any figure** —the form of any idol (סֶמֶל, form, statue, idol)—**the likeness**—figure (תַּבְנִית, a building, a model, a form, or figure)—**of male or female**—in apposition to *graven image*, and illustrative of it.

Vers. 17, 18.—**The likeness**—the figure— **of any beast**, etc. A warning against the animal-worship of Egypt.

Ver. 19.—**Lest thou lift up thine eyes unto heaven**, etc. The worship of the heavenly bodies, especially star-worship, prevailed among the Canaanites and many of the Semitic tribes, but was not confined to them; the Egyptians also reverenced the sun as Ra, the moon as Isis, and the stars as the symbols of deities. The Israelites were thus, both from past associations and from what they might encounter in Canaan, exposed to the danger of being seduced into idolatry. **Shouldest be driven**: *shouldest be urged on, drawn*, or *constrained* (cf. ch. xiii. 13). **Which the Lord thy God hath divided unto all nations under the whole heaven**, God had allotted (חָלַק) to all mankind the heavenly bodies for their advantage (Gen. i. 14—18; Ps. civ. 19; Jer. xxxi. 35); it was, therefore, not competent for any one nation to seek to appropriate them as specially theirs, and it was absurd for any to offer religious service to objects intended for the service of man. Targum: *Which the Lord thy God prepared for all peoples under heaven;* Vulgate: *Quæ creavit Dominus Deus tuus in ministerium cunctis gentibus.* This seems better than the interpretation that God had "allotted them for worship, *i.e.* had permitted them [the nations] to choose them as the objects of their worship" (Keil, etc.); for: 1. There is no distinction here between the Hebrews and the other nations of the earth; "all nations" includes them as well as the heathen. 2. Though God permitted the heathen to worship the heavenly bodies, he never allotted these to men in order that they might worship them. "It noteth God's bounty in giving all people the use of those creatures, and the base mind of man to worship such things as are given for servants unto men" (Ainsworth).

Ver. 20.—**Iron furnace**—furnace for smelting iron: "figure of burning torment in Egypt" (Herxheimer). This reference to the smelting of iron shows that, though the implements of the ancient Egyptians were mostly of copper, iron must also have been in extensive use among them. Other references to the use of iron are to be found in the Pentateuch; see Gen. iv. 22; Lev. xxvi. 19; Numb. xxxv. 16; ch. iii. 11; viii. 9; xix. 5; xxvii. 5 (Goguet, 'Origine des Lois,' i. 172; Wilkinson, 'Ancient Egypt,' i. 169; ii. 155). **To be unto him a people**, etc. (cf. Exod. xix. 4—6; ch. vii. 6).

Vers. 21—24.—Moses, after again referring to his being not permitted to enter Canaan, takes occasion anew to warn the people against forgetting the covenant of Jehovah and making any image of God, seeing he is a jealous God, and a consuming fire.

Ver. 21.—**The Lord was angry with me . . . and sware**, etc. Neither in Numb. xx. 12, nor in Numb. xxvii. 12—14, is there any mention of God's having *sworn* that Moses should not enter Canaan with the people; but it is absurd to suppose, as some have done, that the writer here has confounded this with what is recorded in Numb. xiv. 21, 28,—that is inconceivable; and it certainly does not follow, because no mention is made in Numbers of God's having sworn, that he did not swear on this occasion; if he confirmed with an oath his decree that the generation that rebelled at Kâdesh should not enter Canaan, the probability surely is that he would do the same when he announced to Moses the decree that he should not conduct Israel into the promised land. "It is perfectly obvious, from ch. iii. 23, *sqq.*, that all the details are not given in the historical account of the event referred to" (Keil).

Ver. 23.—**A graven image, or the likeness of any** thing, etc.—literally, *a graven* (sculptured) *image of a form of all that Jehovah thy God hath commanded thee*; *s.c.* not to make (cf. ch. 16—18 and ii. 37).

Ver. 24.—**A consuming fire.** When God spoke to Israel at Sinai, his glory appeared "like devouring (consuming) fire on the top of the mount" (Exod. xxiv. 17); and in allusion to this Moses here calls God "a consuming fire." He is so to all his enemies, and to all who disobey him; by severe inflictions he will punish, and, if they persist in their hostility and rebellion, will ultimately destroy them (comp. ch. ix. 3; Isa. x. 16—18; Amos v. 6; Zeph. i. 18; Heb. xii. 29). **A jealous God**; LXX., Θεὸς ζηλωτής· God has a burning zeal for his own glory; he guards it with jealous care; and he will not spare those who do him dishonour, especially those who are guilty of idolatry, whereby they "change the truth of God into a lie" (Rom. i. 25; cf. Exod. xx. 5; ch. vi. 14, 15; xxxii. 16, etc.; Ps. lxxviii. 58, etc.; Nah. i. 2). He is jealous also over his people, because he loves them, and will not endure any rival in their affection and devotion.

HOMILETICS.

Vers. 1—4.—*Life and prosperity dependent on obedience to God.* In this paragraph Moses indicates, by the word "therefore," the purpose he has had in the review in which he had been indulging. It was not for the mere rehearsal's sake that the varied incidents in Israel's career were thus recalled to memory, but to stimulate the people anew to obedience, by reminding them how strong was the reason for it, and how great would be the blessedness of it. It was then, as it is now, "godliness is profitable for all things;" and though that would be a low standard of virtue attained by a man who served God merely for what he could get by it, yet, on the other hand, *if no good came of it*, the reason for it would certainly be seriously affected in the influence it had on a man. There is a mean and selfish form of utilitarianism. But if, when a man contends for utility as the foundation of virtue, he means by utility "a tendency to promote the highest good, on the largest scale, for the longest period," there is nothing selfish or mean about the theory *then*, whether we accept it as sound philosophy or no. And it is certain that our Lord Jesus Christ meant considerations of profit to weigh with men (see Matt. xvi. 25, 26). Observe—

I. GOD'S STATUTES AND JUDGMENTS ARE THE BEST MORAL AND SPIRITUAL FURNITURE WITH WHICH A PEOPLE CAN BE ENRICHED. The word "statutes" includes "the moral commandments and statutory covenant laws." "Judgments" are precepts enjoining what is due from men to man or to God. Sometimes we get the word "commandments," including both the former; at other times we have the word "testimonies," in which duty is looked at as that concerning which God bears testimony to man

Now, men will rise or fall according as the moral nature is cultured or neglected. And it is because the Divine precepts constitute a directory for our highest selves, that they are so invaluable to us. Doubtless, to some extent, the Law of God is still graven in the hearts and consciences of men ; and if men were perfect, the Law written on the heart would be clear enough. But as men neglect God's Law, they come to fail in discerning it. The characters written inwardly are more and more faint, and, lest it should cease from among men, our God has had his will graciously recorded in a Book, our constant standard of appeal, our unvarying directory of right !

II. THESE STATUTES AND JUDGMENTS ARE TO BE PRESERVED INTACT. "Ye shall not add unto the word which I command you, neither shall ye diminish ought from it." The manifestation of the tendency of men to do one or the other, yea both, is one of the saddest chapters in human history (see Homily on ch. xii. 32). (Cf. Jer. xxvi. 2; Prov. xxx. 6; Rev. xxii. 18, 19; Matt. v. 19; xv. 1—13.) Scepticism violates God's Law by subtracting from it ; superstition, by adding to it. Our appeal must ever be "to the Law and to the testimony," and the appeal will only be valid, nay, will only be possible, as both are preserved intact and kept free from the tampering of men.

III. THEY ARE TO BE PRESERVED IN THEIR ENTIRETY, IN ORDER THAT THEY MAY BE OBEYED IN THEIR ENTIRETY. Hearken, for to do them (see John xiii. 17; Jas. i. 22). A mere reverence for the letter, without obedience to the spirit, is displeasing to God. Jesus Christ complained of this among the Jews (John v. 38—40). A written law, honoured as to its preservation, but yet neglected in life, is a silent witness against us (John v. 45). Men may rest in *having* the oracles of God, and may cherish even up to the last, vain hopes of acceptance on the ground of privilege, but they will be undeceived (Matt. vii. 21—27). Obedience to the Law of God includes the two great duties of trust in a great salvation and loyalty to moral precepts. No man was allowed to trifle with the sacrificial code any more than with the ethical : both formed parts of the Law; both were to be observed with equal exactitude.

IV. OBEDIENCE TO THE LAW WOULD BE FOR ISRAEL'S WEAL, AND WAS THE CONDITION OF THEIR CONTINUANCE IN THE LAND. Ver. 1, "That ye may live," etc. The word "life" is very far from being a mere synonym for "existence." It is equivalent to "*healthful existence*," a state of being in which all his powers and functions are in harmonious exercise, and directed to their proper objects and ends. Nor can any one doubt that obedience to the laws of God has a tendency to promote true comfort and success in this life, while it is certainly the truest, yea, the only, preparation for the next. Besides, the blessing of God is promised to the obedient. If a man's life *accords with* the laws of God, he will find out how conducive obedience is to good. But if he "strives with his Maker," his life-course will bristle up with prickles everywhere.

V. AS WE LOOK ROUND, WE MAY SEE SAD EXAMPLES OF THE REVERSE, FROM WHICH WE MAY TAKE WARNING. (See the sad history of Baal-peor, referred to in ver. 3.) Surely we should take warning from that, and from too many similar instances. The prevalence of lust will be destructive of life's beauty, peace, power, and hope.

VI. THE EXPERIENCE OF THE PEACE AND JOY, ATTENDANT UPON A LIFE OF LOYALTY TO GOD, IS A STRONG ARGUMENT FOR CONTINUANCE THEREIN. Ver. 4, "Ye that did cleave unto the Lord your God are alive every one of you this day." What would the victims of lust and greed and passion give if they could but have the calm peacefulness of one who follows the Lord fully ! But that cannot be. The test of a life for God is God's own seal to its worth in his eye (cf. Ps. xci.); while (*cœt. par.*) long life is ensured by the healthy state of body which a righteous life induces. And the hope— the good hope *through grace*—which gilds the outlook, oh, the unutterable joy of that !

IN CONCLUSION. 1. It is just as imperative, in a Christian point of view, for us to combine obedience to the sacrificial and ethical law of the gospel, as it was for the Hebrews to obey both parts of their Law. No outside virtues performed in a legal, self-righteous spirit will save us. Nor will any trust in the sacrifice of Christ, apart from holiness, be accepted. Both faith in Christ and holy living, form inseparable parts of a true obedience to God. 2. The rich fulness of peace which those enjoy who trust, love, and obey, is far greater under the gospel than it could have been under the Law of Moses, because, in Christ, the revelation of Divine love is so much clearer, and the "blessed hope" is so much brighter. Christ gives us a rest in himself, and the life he quickens and sustains in believers is a restful life (see Rom. v. 1—11; Phil. iv. 4—7). "Though now we see him not, yet believing, we rejoice with joy unspeakable and full of glory." This is life indeed!

Vers. 5—9.—*National greatness dependent on obedience to God.* In these verses we have a continuation of the address of Moses to the people. He had previously reminded them of incidents which had occurred. He here points out to them the advantageous position they are privileged to occupy, and shows them how to maintain and perpetuate it. He reminds them of the following points:—1. That theirs was the very special privilege of having God nigh unto them as the Lord their God (see also vers. 32—34). 2. That they would occupy a prominent place among the nations round about (cf. Exod. ix. 16; xv. 14; Numb. xiv. 13—21; ch. xxviii. 10). 3. That the corner-stone of their national life and honour was the worship of God and the practice of righteousness. Their "statutes and judgments" were characterized by this special mark—they were *righteous* above those of any other nation[1] (ver. 8). 4. That the carrying out into action of these precepts was their only wise course (ver. 6). 5. That such wisdom would be their true greatness, and such greatness would win them regard and honour from surrounding peoples (ver. 6). [This was actually the case to a very large extent. Our space will not allow us even to touch on the matter here; but careful research will show the student how Israel's greatness has manifested itself in the influence exerted by them in modifying the religion, philosophy, literature, politics, institutions, and moral judgments of the world. First, among the Egyptians, Canaanites, and Phœnicians; and then among the Assyrians, Persians, Greeks, and Romans. See Wines, Gale, Stillingfleet, and others.] 6. That it behoves them to "keep and do" these precepts, to retain them in their heart, to hand them down to their children, and to take constant care of themselves. In turning all this to pulpit use for modern times, observe—

I. THERE ARE CERTAIN PRINCIPLES, THE APPLICATION OF WHICH WILL SECURE THE TRUE GREATNESS OF A PEOPLE. It is becoming to a true patriot to think of his country as being renowned among the nations of the earth. Jehovah evidently meant the people to be moved by such an ambition. It is far more healthful to direct natural desires into a right channel than to try to suppress them. Let a man cherish the most fervent wish to see his country unsurpassed among the people. God promises this as the result of his blessing. Thou shalt be "the head, and not the tail." But observe: *No conspicuousness is so much to be desired as that arising from wisdom and understanding.* The prominence which arises from moral influence is that alone which is worth striving after. Any influence by which we help to lift up other nations in virtue and power, is worth infinitely more than that which comes of martial valour, or diplomatic tactics, or such supremacy over a people as shall simply make them stand amazed at the length of our purse, or the precision and deadly fire of our arms. To be known as the wisest people, so that others seek in friendly emulation to learn from us—this is an eminence any patriot well may desire for the land he loves. But observe: *This will depend on the amount of moral culture in a people,* i.e. on the degree of clearness with which a people see what is right, on the measure of force they put forth in the pursuit of it, and on the firmness with which they insist on the right being paramount to any considerations of power, expediency, or gain. "The throne shall be established in righteousness." "Righteousness exalteth a nation; but sin is a reproach to any people." Not only in the individual, the family, and the social life must righteousness be the chief corner-stone of a common weal, but in those acts in which a man has to play the part of a citizen, and in which a nation has to do with other nations. Righteousness may not be eliminated from politics, nor may it play a subordinate part. Universal, eternal, unchangeable, are the laws of righteousness, and by whomsoever they are violated—by individuals, families, Churches, or nations—such violation will surely be followed by remorse and shame. *The truest form of moral culture is loyalty to the Divine Being and his commands.* No nation ever has or ever can thrive without the recognition of a Great Supreme. It is only the fool, the "*nabal*," the withered one, who

---

[1] Should the difficulty here suggest itself, whether the command to exterminate the Canaanites was right, see the suggestions in Homily on ch. i. 1—8, by way of reply.

says there is no God. And no nation which ignores the duty of loyalty to God will ever be great. But then in the Book, as the world's grandest moral text-book, there are statutes, precepts, testimonies, judgments, for the regulation of life, both individually and collectively. The appeal of ver. 8 is still valid, " What nation is there . . . that hath statutes and judgments *so righteous* as all this Law, which I set before you this day ? " We know how the Law may be summed up : " All the Law is fulfilled in one word, even in this : Thou shalt love thy neighbour as thyself. Love worketh no ill to his neighbour ; therefore love is the fulfilling of the Law." *And this principle of love to all, carried out in loyalty to God, will ensure that greatness which is most worth having.* The Egyptians were at one time renowned for learning, the Phœnicians for their commerce ; the men of Bashan for their giant strength ; Greece for its philosophy ; Rome for her " imperium et libertas." Their sway has gone. But the Hebrew race, by whom first and alone this law of love was proclaimed as the one guiding principle of a nation's life, is living in its literature the grandest of all lives, and swaying, with the sceptre of its *one Perfect Man*, men of different nations, tribes, and tongues in every quarter of the globe. Yes, this one law of love has given to the Hebrew race a greatness it will never lose. The brightest streaks of light on the globe now are to be discerned only where the law of love is known and obeyed ; that law given by Moses, brought in by Jesus Christ. And in proportion as nations follow and act out this law, will they attain to the only greatness on which heaven smiles. " The world passeth away and the lusts thereof ; but he that doeth the will of God abideth for ever." This righteousness is in itself an armour of light—a nation's best defence. For on " the righteous nation which keepeth the truth " will God's blessing rest, and, next to the Divine blessing, the good will of the nations is our surest and happiest guard.

II. HERE IS AN APPEAL TO THE PEOPLE AS INDIVIDUALS TO TAKE HEED TO THESE PRINCIPLES. The appeal is fourfold in this paragraph. 1. " *Keep therefore and do them.*" There is as much obedience to God in the nation as is rendered to him by individual souls, *and no more*. Hence it is the part of the true patriot who desires his nation's greatness to see that he is living the life which will help to make the nation great. 2. This is not to be superficial work, but the Law is to be *in the heart*. Not an accidental, surface life, but an intelligent and designed direction of the inner and outer life according to God's ways and Word. 3. This law of righteousness, truth, and love *is to be handed down* from sire to son, and so on to generation after generation. The parent is to be the true depositor, conservator, teacher, and transmitter of God's Law. He is to live after he has gone in the truth he has taught, and, when he is dead, his speech is to be moulding the young hearts of a nation. 4. Each one is to put a careful guard around himself, lest any of the baneful influences around him should destroy or weaken his loyalty to God and the right. " Take care of thyself ; "—such is the meaning of the phrase in ver. 9 (cf. Prov. iv. 23, " Keep thy heart with all diligence ; for out of it are the issues of life "). It is easy to gather from the Book of Deuteronomy against what influences the ancient Hebrews would have to guard. These influences, hostile to unswerving loyalty, vary with each land and race and age. A careful observation and knowledge of the times will show us against what foes we have at all points to be armed. Let us take the whole armour of God. Let us save ourselves from this untoward generation. Let us play the man and the citizen, with hearts loyal to our Saviour, jealous for the right and the true, fearing God, but having no fear beside!

Vers. 11—20.—*Israel's peculiar relation to God.* This paragraph sets forth in earnest appeal the peculiar and distinctive relation to God in which Israel was placed. (For the precise details of the point in their history here referred to, see Exod. xix. ; and for the application of several of the expressions used both here and there to believers in Christ under the Christian dispensation, see 1 Pet. ii. 9.) Here is a noble theme for the preacher—*Israel's special relation to God, typical of and fulfilled in the present relation of Christian people to him.*

I. LET US STUDY THE PECULIAR RELATION OF ISRAEL TO GOD. " The Lord hath taken you, and brought you forth out of the iron furnace, . . . to be unto him *a people of inheritance,*" *i.e.* a purchased or acquired people. So in Exod. xix. 5, 6. The Lord had called Abraham, had made promises to him and to his seed. These promises ran down through Isaac and Jacob and the twelve patriarchs. Now *their* descendants had become numerous enough to form a nation; as such they had been duly constituted, with this peculiar feature—they were to be God's nation. They had been freed by him, they were consecrated to him, and were being trained by and for him. Hence, as Kalisch remarks, every subject is as it were a priest, and every civil action assumes the sanctity of a religious function: idolatry was an offence against his sovereignty, and therefore punishable with death; so blasphemy, false prophecy, sabbath-breaking, were visited with the like punishment. Disrespect to elders, disobedience to parents (they being the representatives of God), were visited with sore penalties. Hence, too, the whole land belonged to God. The people were but tenants, and in the year of jubilee land reverted to its former owner or his heirs. The Israelites were the subjects and servants of God alone. Slavery, therefore, though not peremptorily put down, was so regulated that the slave went out free in the seventh year; and if he did not desire the freedom, he was branded with an ignominious mark because he refused the immediate sovereignty of God.[1] Now, this expression, "God's nation," is the key wherewith to interpret many of the enactments which seem to us unintelligible, and many of the punishments which seem unusually severe. This truth, that Israel is the Lord's people, runs through the Old Testament Scriptures, as will be seen if we note the varied names by which they are distinguished. 1. God's son, his firstborn (Exod. iv. 22, 23; Jer. iii. 4, 9; Hos. xi. 1). 2. Firstfruits (Jer. ii. 3). 3. *The* people of God (Ps. lxxxi. 8—11; 2 Sam. vii. 23, 24). 4. God's inheritance (ch. xxxii. 9). 5. *The* people (ch. xxxiii. 29). 6. The chosen ones (Ps. xxxiii. 12; ch. vii. 6). 7. His flock (Jer. xiii. 17; Ps. c. 3). 8. The holy people (ch. vii. 6; Jer. vii. 44). 9. The righteous people (Numb. xxiii. 10; Exod. xix. 6). 10. The house or the family of God (Isa. i. 2). 11. A kingdom (Ps. lxxxix. 18). Thus all Israelites were subjects of the same eternal, perfect King, all equal in dignity, rights, and duties. There was among them no institution resembling caste. All were equal in Heaven's eye; all enjoyed scope for the development of their spiritual nature. The poorest herdsman might become a prophet, if filled with the Spirit of God. And the intended differential feature of the whole nation was given to it by the revealed character of its King, "Be ye holy; for I am holy." It is no wonder that a people, selected thus for such a close relationship to God, should be called in the text, "a people of inheritance." Not, indeed, in Israel alone, was there a theocratic form of government. The kings of Egypt, the monarchs of Persia and Thibet, pretended to rule as the representatives of the gods. Minos among the Cretans, Lycurgus the Lacedæmonian, Numa of Rome, and Mohammed, all pretended to have in some sort Divine authority; but these were only the mimicry of the true, and were all lacking in *the supreme point* to and for which Jehovah was educating Israel, even for "righteousness and true holiness." It is easy enough to win converts by a certain mimicry of the Divine. The early history of many a nation is laden with mythology, but the early history of Israel stands out in clear and startling distinction from that of other peoples, in the clearness with which they witness for the one living and true God, the accordance of their early records with known life and manners, and the clear and striking demand in their precepts for love and goodness, holiness and truth. This was at the time, and ever will be in the history of that age, the one bright spot amid the surrounding gloom. The people were "a peculiar treasure to God above all people."

II. What Israel was designed to be among the nations, Christian people are to be wherever they are: a holy people unto the Lord their God. The Apostle Peter intimates this in the verse to which we referred at the outset (see also Titus ii. 14; Eph. ii. 10; 1 Pet. i. 15, 16). There are many more passages in which believers are spoken of not only individually but collectively, as making up a family, a household, a city, a commonwealth (Eph. ii. 12, 19; Phil. iii. 20, Greek). And there are four features which mark this new commonwealth, which correspond to those which marked that of the Hebrews. 1. *The members of this Christian commonwealth are redeemed* (cf. 1 Pet. i. 18, 19). From the curse of the Law, from the bondage of sin, believers have been redeemed by an offering of unspeakable value, even the precious blood of Christ. 2. *Thus redeemed, they come to have such a knowledge of God as their God as the world has not and cannot have* (Rom. viii. 15; Gal. iv. 5—7). They are

[1] See Kalisch, *in loc.*, to whom we are indebted for much light on this theme.

redeemed out of a state of servitude into a state of sonship (cf. John viii. 34—36). 3. *They are redeemed to a life of close fellowship with God* (cf. ch. iv. 7; 1 John i. 1—3). They are at home in God. 4. *They are redeemed to this close fellowship with God, that thereby they may become pure;* and that in this life of purity they may " show forth the praises of him who hath called them out of darkness into his marvellous light." Not one of these four stages must be lost sight of; redeemed *out of* sin and servitude, *into* sonship, *to* fellowship, *for* holiness. Not one of these features must be left out; nor can the order in which we have put them be reversed or even transposed. The only mark by which the world can know God's people is—*their holiness* (Heb. xii. 14). It is not for nought that Scripture speaks of a great redemption. And no preacher preaches the gospel fully, who does not insist on its side of ethics as well as on its side of grace. And no professing Christian is worthy of the name he bears, who loses sight of holiness as the end to be attained, any more than he would be if he were to lose sight of the grace of God as that by which alone he can attain the end. How many of the controversies in the Church of God have arisen from an unequal perception of the varied truths of God's holy gospel! Out of an inadequate view of the evil of sin and of its affront to God's honour and government, many have felt but feebly the need of the Great Atoning Sacrifice, whereby the injured honour of the Law was vindicated and a redemption for man made possible! And then, on the other hand, through dwelling all but exclusively on the evil *from* which man is rescued, others have failed to insist sufficiently on *the holiness* for the sake of enabling him to attain which his rescue was effected at such a cost. Perhaps few preachers present in perfection an *exactly balanced* gospel. It is a doctrine according to godliness. Some decry doctrine because they see around them such a lack of godliness. But if we would have the godliness which is to illustrate the doctrine, we shall never secure the end by weakening the exhibition of the doctrine which, rightly used, will certainly lead to it. And not only do preachers need to take heed to both doctrine and practice, but private professors also. If we want the world to understand the value of the Christian religion as an object of revelation, we must show its power in a holy, personal life. If we want others to believe its doctrines to be superior to any other doctrines, we must show that the life it secures is superior to any other life. Thus must we be, like Israel, a peculiar people; showing to others that we have not been redeemed in vain. Be it ours to let our light so shine before men, that they may see our good works, and glorify our Father which is in heaven. Thus shall we show we are his people indeed.

Vers. 21—24.—*God a consuming fire.* "The Lord thy God is a consuming fire, even a jealous God." This is no obsolete sentence. The writer of the Epistle to the Hebrews quotes it, and urges the truth it expresses as a reason for serving God "with reverence and godly fear: for," he adds, even " *our* God is a consuming fire." Perhaps the first impression which these words would convey to the earnest and thoughtful mind would be that of terror. Perhaps, too, some may even almost shudder at such a representation of God, and may at once declare that it belongs to a past age, and to a decaying order of ideas. But others who are more cautious would be likely to say, " We must be quite sure that we understand the phrase before we say that." Doubtless we say with pleasure, "God is light," "God is love," but who can delight in saying, "God is fire"? Is it possible that any one can go even further, and delight in saying, " *Our* God—the God who is in covenant relation to us—is a consuming fire"? Does not the phrase act as a repellent force, and inspire one with dread? No doubt it may have that effect in many cases, specially if men have carelessly fastened on one aspect of things, or where they have been misled by a popular misquotation, "God *out of Christ* is a consuming fire." For whatever the phrase means, it is just as true that God in Christ is a consuming fire, as that God out of Christ is so. The phrase is one which should be thoughtfully and devoutly studied in the general light of Scripture teaching, in order that in God's light we may see light. It may be, if thus we try to feel our way to its meaning, that it opens up views of God with which we would not willingly part.

I. WHAT IS THE MEANING OF THE PHRASE IN THE TEXT? It must have often struck an attentive reader of the Bible how frequently the figure of " fire " is found therein, both in connection with man's offerings to God, and with God's manifestations of himself to man (cf. Gen. iii. 24; viii. 20; xv. 17; Exod. iii.; xix.; Isa. iv.; xxxi. 9). Now, whatever may be the attribute of God here set forth under the figure of fire, it, like all God's attributes, must be twofold in its action *in a sinful world.* The action of fire is according to the object on which it acts. 1. *There is a terrific action of fire.* It tries what is bad (1 Cor. iii. 13). It consumes (Lev. x. 2). It appals (Numb. xi. 1—3; Isa. xxxiii. 14). It destroys (2 Kings i. 12; Luke iii. 17; John xv. 6; Ps. xcviii. 3; Heb. vi. 8). 2. *There is a kindly action of flame.* It enkindles (Lev. ix. 24). It tries (1 Pet. i. 7; Isa. xlviii. 10). It purifies (Ps. xii. 6). It guards (Zech. ii. 5; 2 Kings vi. 17; ch. ix. 3). It escorts (2 Kings ii. 11). It guides (Exod. xl. 38). It enlightens (Ps. lxxviii. 14). It is as a pavilion of glory (Exod. iii. 2; Isa. xxxiii. 14—17). Now, widely different as is the action or the meaning of flaming fire from heaven in all these cases, the difference is not in the flame, but in the material on which it acts. The same fire that melts the wax will bake the clay. So the very same attribute of God in which the righteous may glory will be a terror to his enemies. 3. *Fire, when spoken of in reference to God,* is an emblem of: (1) *Purity.* In Exod. iii. 2—5, God would signify that in his redeeming love he, the holy God, would dwell with men, and that men might dwell in the midst of his blazing holiness, and yet be perfectly at home. (2) *Power* (ch. ix. 3; vii. 8). Power exerting itself on behalf of those who love him. (3) *Jealousy* (ch. iv. 23, 24). (4) *Anger* (ch. vi. 15). Thus there are these four conceptions to be attached to the use of the phrase "a consuming fire," viz. a pavilion of purity in which Israel might dwell unharmed; a jealousy which could brook no rival; an anger which would go forth against sin; a power which would guard its own as with tongues, yea, with walls of flame. 4. *But we may take another step, and reduce this fourfold conception to a twofold one.* There is anger against sin *because* of spotless purity. There is jealousy which will brook no rival, and a power that will guard its own *because* of intensest love. Thus the consuming fire is purity, in which righteousness may dwell, and in which sin is consumed; and love, which is mighty in its active care, and jealous of any rival in the human heart. 5. *We may simplify yet again, and reduce the twofold conception to a unity,* and say that God is a consuming fire, inasmuch as he is perfect love—pure love, active love, jealous love; so that our text is but another way of saying, "God is light," "God is love." Let us now—

II. LOOK AT THESE THREE FORMS OF THE EXPRESSION "PERFECT LOVE," AND SEE WHAT THEY INVOLVE. 1. *Pure love.* God is a flaming fire of infinite purity, and yet a burning flame of tenderest love. He receives the sinner on a basis of righteousness. He makes men who are in covenant relation to him perfectly pure. They are to be tried and purified and made white, till they are without fault before the throne of God. Would we have it otherwise? God's love without its purity would be worthless to us! 2. *Active love.* God castles his saints in a wall of fire (Isa. iv. 6), while he also destroys their foes as with a tongue of fire. 3. *Jealous love.* There is a hateful jealousy. There is a rightful one. The first it would be unworthy of a man to possess; the second, a man would be unworthy of himself if he did not. A father would be worth little if he were not jealous for the purity of his child; so would a husband if not jealous for the honour of his wife; or an Englishman, if not jealous for the honour of his queen! Even so, it would be unworthy of God if he were not jealous, in the scriptural sense. Note: (1) God's love is jealous for the first place in our hearts. (2) God is jealous for his own purity, holiness, and truth. (3) He is jealous for the honour of his Son. He will not let one be lost who receives him, nor will he let one be saved who trifles with him. To go against Christ is to rush into the consuming flame!

III. WHAT ARE THE PRACTICAL USES TO BE MADE OF THIS SUBLIME ATTRIBUTE OF GOD? (See the use made of it in the Epistle to the Hebrews, ch. xii., the last three or four verses.) 1. Is God thus a consuming fire? Then let us never attempt to draw nigh unto him without a recognition both of his purity and of our sinfulness. No service is accepted before God which does not take account of sin, and in connection with which there is not "reverence and godly fear." 2. Do not let us think of any mode of recognition of sin which ignores God's own way, viz. that of an atoning sacrifice. God will jealously guard the honour of his dear Son. "If they escaped not who refused him that spake on earth, much more shall not we escape, if we turn away from him that speaketh from heaven." 3. If thus we are penitently making use of the atoning sacrifice of Christ as our only means of approach to and ground of hope in God, then let us glory in this holy, jealous love, which guards us as with a wall of fire, and is our everlasting guarantee that we shall not be put to shame. 4. Let us remember that it depends on ourselves whether the "consuming fire" is a flame at which we tremble, or a pavilion in which we can hide. God cannot deny himself. He will not deal with the sinner on any principle which ignores the great atonement which his Son has effected, or which admits of his accepting the service of a divided heart. It is for us to say whether the great redeeming work of Jesus shall be the means by which we are raised to fellowship in infinite holiness, or whether it shall be to us the savour of death unto death. It must be one or the other. If we receive it, it will bring us to eternal rest in God; if we reject it, it will deepen our condemnation more terribly than if no Saviour had been provided! *Our* God is a consuming fire. If, in Jesus, we draw near to him, that burning, blazing holiness shall be the secret place of his tabernacle in which we are safely hidden. If we neglect this great salvation, as men unpardoned and unsaved, we shall remain, and at the flame of Jehovah's purity we shall tremble for ever! Sinner, say, oh say, shall this fire of God's perfect love surround you ever as a wall of protection, or shall it terrify and consume you as devouring flame?

HOMILIES BY VARIOUS AUTHORS.

Vers. 1—13.—*The sacredness of the Divine Law.* Law, being the utterance of righteousness, is unalterable as righteousness itself, *permanent* amid all the mutations of human affairs. Its requirements are statutes, stable as the everlasting hills.

I. LAW IS THE VERITABLE VOICE OF GOD; the manifestation of his thought; the mirror of his mind. "The Lord *spake* unto you." "Out of the midst of the fire"— the flame of holiness and zeal—issues every command. If man's moral nature has an open ear, it may often detect the imperial voice of Heaven. 'Tis not to *sight* God reveals himself, but to the ear. His messengers are emphatically "a voice." "Faith comes by hearing."

II. LAW, IN ITS SPHERE, IS PERFECT. Over every work of his hands God pronounces the verdict "Very good;" and Law, being the instrument with which he works, is "holy, just, and good." For *unrighteous* man there may be something more precious than Law; but when restored to God, Law is his delight. In the domain of belief we cannot augment or diminish God's Law without self-injury. Perfection cannot be improved upon. In the sphere of practice, to halt short of the line of duty, or to go beyond the line, is alike an offence. Self-mutilation, or blemish, is the effect.

III. THE VERACITY OF LAW ATTESTED BY ACTUAL EXPERIENCE. Every honest-minded man may discover whether or not the written Word embodies a Divine Law. If a genuine Law, its authority is ratified by an honest conscience; as sanctions, whether of commendation or curse, are witnessed by every clear-sighted eye. Every truthful man is a witness that God's laws (whether written in external nature, in man's constitution, or in Scripture) bring life to the obedient, death to the transgressor. Not a Law is revealed in the Scriptures, but it tends to righteousness, happiness, life!

IV. DIVINE LAW ASSERTS ITS AUTHORITY OVER THE WHOLE MAN. 1. Over the intellect, for it demands attention, investigation, comparison, and discrimination. 2. Authority over the affections, for it demands reverence, esteem, choice, and love. 3. Authority over the moral faculty; for it demands assent, response, and loyalty. 4. Over the active powers, for it requires watchfulness, self-restraint, uninterrupted deference, and uncompromising service.

V. LAW IS THE PATHWAY TO TRUE EMINENCE. Every successful application of science to practical life is simply a treading of the pathway of law. So long as man finds the footprints of God's Law, he moves onward. There is no real progress in any department of human life, except along the line of God's Law. To find *that,* and to follow it, is success. This is equally true in the spiritual province. This is the quintessence of wisdom—the stepping-stone to eminence! What men—what nation— have ever reached to permanent greatness, save they who have trodden the path of Divine Law?

VI. LOYALTY TO GOD'S LAW BRINGS US NEAR TO GOD. As when we follow up the footprints of a man rapidly enough, we at length come up with the man himself; so, as we pursue the pathway of Law, we come soon without the hallowed precincts of God's presence. We see the working of the heavenly machinery, the movements of God's thought and purpose. We move with it, and ever come nearer to the central light and love. It is a *narrow* path, and few they are who find it.

VII. A SPIRIT OF OBEDIENCE IS SELF-PROPAGATING. Like plants in the garden, every righteous man bears seed after his own kind. Without formal teaching, the beauty of his life will be a living lesson—the fragrance of his deeds will be contagious. They who love God's Law will be zealous to teach God's Law, and to commend it to others. A fine trait in Abraham's character comes into view when God said, "I know Abraham, that he will command his children and his household after him." Every man bequeaths to posterity a large legacy of blessing or of bane.

VIII. THE LAW OF GOD IS DESTINED TO HAVE PERMANENCE IN HUMAN LIFE. There was high significance in the fact that the Decalogue was written, not in rays of light upon the sapphire firmament, nor in legible characters upon parchment, but *on stone*. The stone of Sinai is said to belong to one of the oldest formations—the granite period. The forms and modes of law may undergo change to meet the growing necessities of men; but the inner sense—the kernel—of every law still abides. "Heaven and earth may pass away," all material stricture may undergo radical change—but the words of God can undergo no change. What is *true* once is *true always!* What was *right* a myriad of ages since, retains all its authority to-day, and will be obligatory world without end. The sum and substance of moral law is writ by the finger of God, and graven on the solid rock!—D.

Vers. 1—28.—*The curse of idolatry.* Idolatry is the general bias of fallen humanity, the perversion of an innate principle, the misgrowth of the religious instinct. Men everywhere "feel after God, if haply they may find him." Absolute atheism cannot long endure anywhere. If men reject a personal Deity, they invent an inferior God, and practically worship that. The wildest atheist which the world has seen, must admit that there is some power or force in the world superior to himself. There is no resting-place for reason, short of a spiritual God.

I. IDOLATRY WAS THE PREVALENT DANGER OF THE PATRIARCHAL AGE. During the childhood of men, they are under the domination of the bodily senses. They demand a god whom they can see and handle and hear. The kindred of Abraham were addicted to idolatry. The wife of Jacob furtively abstracted the teraphim of her father, and held them in a measure of reverence. Even Moses yearned for a visible Deity. "I beseech thee, show me thy glory!" The absence of Moses from the camp for forty days sufficed for the people to relapse into idolatry. Throughout their history, every decline in religious feeling showed itself in a fresh lapse towards idolatry.

II. IDOLATRY GROSSLY CORRUPTS ITS VOTARIES. The object which is at first selected to be a *symbol* of the Deity, soon detains on itself the homage of the worshipper, and becomes his Deity. Matter is at the antipodes from spirit. The laws and forces working in material nature may help us to understand the Divine Being, but matter itself *never*. Apart from a written revelation, we best rise to the knowledge of God through the contemplation of our own minds and consciences. The object of our worship moulds us after itself. The worshipper of beasts becomes bestial. "They that make them become like unto them." This is God's law.

III. MATERIAL IMAGES DEGRADE THE GODHEAD. For God is a Spirit, and cannot be represented by material images. For matter can convey no impressions of omnipresence, or of eternity, or of moral qualities, or of emotions, affections, or joys! Representation by material images strips our God of all that is noblest in his nature, of all that is distinctive in the Godhead. It cloaks his perfections and eclipses his glory.

IV. IDOLATRY ANNULLED THE COVENANT BETWEEN GOD AND ISRAEL. That gracious compact required upon the part of the Israelites the honest recognition and worship of the One Jehovah. Unfaithfulness on this vital point invalidated the entire covenant; God had pledged himself specially to be their God, on condition that they were his loyal people. All the resources of God's kingdom were pledged to Israel in that covenant. It was an act of mercy that God should bind himself in any form to his creatures, and this superabundant grace ought to have held their homage by closest and tenderest ties. *His* part of the covenant, God had conspicuously observed in the release of his people from the "iron furnace." Was not every sign and wonder wrought in Egypt a fresh seal upon the heavenly bond? This covenant, between a gracious God and undeserving men, idolatry destroyed.

V. OUR KNOWLEDGE OF GOD IS DESIGNED AS A REGULATIVE FORCE. There are limitations to our knowledge of God imposed by our constitution, and further limitations imposed by our sin. *These latter* can be removed at once by the redemptive power of Christ; and the first named shall gradually be relaxed in the resurrection state. *Fire* does not represent God, except so far as it *consumes*, and this illustration is meant to check our presumption; 'tis not for the satisfaction of a curious intellect, but to restrain a wayward life. Knowledge of God, which is honestly reduced to practice, becomes larger and clearer knowledge. "Then shall we know if we follow on to know the Lord."

VI. INIQUITY BECOMES ITS OWN PUNISHMENT. Throughout the Scriptures this doctrine is taught, that sin ripens and culminates in punishment. The penalty threatened upon the idolatry of the Jews was *this,* that they should be driven into a heathen land, and be compelled to serve the senseless blocks of wood and stone. The punishment of avarice is *this,* that the sensibilities become as hard as gold. The penalty of drunkenness is *this,* that the morbid appetite grows into an uncontrollable passion! The voice of doom says, "He that is filthy, let him be filthy still."

VII. PRESENT PUNISHMENTS ARE THE TYPE OF FUTURE PUNISHMENTS. The penalty to be imposed on the Jews for disloyalty, was banishment from Canaan—defeat, scattering, death. So the final penalties revealed for reprobate men are exclusion from the heavenly Canaan; banishment to the darkness they have preferred; utter destruction. Each man "goes to his own place."

VIII. SUFFERING FOR OTHERS, A PATHWAY TO HUMAN HEARTS. In connection with these fatherly counsels, Moses again reminds the people of his privation on account of their sins. The blame of his exclusion from Canaan he attributes to them. He who aforetime had prayed that, for the sake of Israel, his own name might be blotted out of God's book, now submits to this chastisement for the people's good. But Moses would not throw away the advantage which this fact might bring. In his desire for the people's good, he converts it into a persuasive argument, by which to confirm their loyalty to God. As if, should every other appeal fail, this appeal to their sensibility might succeed. It is as if he had said, "Remember what I am called to endure for *you!* Let your requital be unswerving obedience to my God." Here he serves as a feeble type of Jesus.—D.

Vers. 1, 2.—*Acceptable obedience.* I. ITS BASIS—the Divine command. "Statutes and judgments." Action originating in self-will, however correct in moral form, is not obedience.∵ It is God's command which is the rule and starting-point. Recognition of his authority is essential. Kant distinguishes religion from morality thus— "Religion is the doing of all duties as if they were Divine commandments." The objective rule is found in the inspired Scriptures.

II. ITS CHARACTER. It must be: 1. *Entire,* not partial. Having respect to all that God reveals. 2. *Honest,* neither altering, mutilating, adding to, nor subtracting from (cf. Matt. v. 19; xv. 6, 9). 3. *Persevering.*

III. ITS REWARD. "Life," possession of blessings. This reward not legal, but of grace through Christ, as on the legal basis no one can attain to it (Rom. iii. 20). But though, as sinful, we cannot have life *through* obedience, we still have it *in* obedience. "Not every one that saith unto me, Lord, Lord, shall enter into the kingdom of heaven; but he that doeth the will of my Father which is in heaven" (Matt. vii. 21; Rom. ii. 7).—J. O.

Vers. 6—10.—*A nation's glory.* I. A NATION POSSESSING GOD'S WORD IS SUPREMELY FAVOURED. (Ver. 8.) Even to *have* such a Law as Israel possessed exalted her to a position of unique greatness. The knowledge of the true God—light on the great principles of conduct—equitable statutes—institutions adapted to promote material, moral, and spiritual well-being. Our own nation is exceptionally favoured in the plentiful enjoyment of religious privileges—Bibles, churches, sabbath schools, evangelistic agencies, Christian literature, etc., bringing the highest knowledge within the reach of the humblest; while the laws, institutions, etc., under which we live, as the fruit of a Christian civilization, are not surpassed by any on the earth. God has indeed, favoured us to an unexampled degree in every religious respect.

II. A NATION ENLIGHTENED BY GOD'S WORD IS SUPREMELY WISE. To have is much, but to be truly "a wise and understanding people," we must "keep and do" (ver. 6). It is not in knowing, but in adopting, the wise course that we show ourselves truly wise. Wisdom is the course that conduces to the formation of a brave, noble, resolute, happy, and contented people; and the nation that loves God's Word, fears God himself, and applies the teaching he has given it in the various spheres of domestic, social, commercial, and political existence, is indubitably in possession of that wisdom. It is to be regretted that the nations most peculiarly privileged do not always set that store upon their privileges which they should do, or make a good use of them. The amount of irreligion, infidelity, and general indifference to the Word of God in our own land is a startling omen for the future. Britain's greatness will soon wane if she abandons her respect for the Bible, the sabbath, and the guiding principles of revelation.

III. A NATION ORDERING ITSELF BY GOD'S WORD IS SUPREMELY EMINENT. (Ver. 7.) Its prosperity: 1. Rests on a solid foundation. 2. Is built up under 'conditions that ensure its permanence. 3. Is secured by a special blessing of God. And this is a matter admitting of ample historical verification. Compare: 1. Pagan nations with Christian. 2. Unbelieving nations with believing (France: Britain). 3. Roman Catholic nations with Protestant (see Laveleye on 'Protestantism and Catholicism in their bearing upon the Liberty and Prosperity of Nations'). 4. Sabbath-desecrating nations with sabbath-keeping. It will be found that the Bible-loving, Bible-obeying, sabbath-keeping nations exhibit: (1) an intellectual superiority; (2) an ethical superiority; (3) a superiority in political institutions; (4) a superiority in material respects (trade, commerce, wealth, etc.).

IV. A NATION OBEYING GOD'S WORD WILL HAVE THE SOURCE OF ITS GREATNESS ACKNOWLEDGED BY OTHERS. (Ver. 6.) They will not only own to its eminence, but they will discern its true cause, and acknowledge that it springs from its religious faithfulness. Numerous testimonies of this kind exist to the source of the national greatness of our own country.

Lessons—1. Value our religious privileges. 2. Seek the furtherance of religion in the community. 3. Be diligent in the training of our children (ver. 9). 4. Extend our blessings to others.—J. O.

Ver. 9.—*The religious education of children.* 1. God's way of handing down the fruits of present privilege. 2. God's way of maintaining his witness in the world. 3. God's way of extending his Church. The natural law of the increase of population leads, where parents are faithful, to a constant increase in the number of the godly.—J. O.

Vers. 10—14.—*The revelation at Horeb.* A revelation—

I. OF THE SPIRITUALITY OF GOD'S NATURE. "Ye saw no similitude" (ver. 12). A wonderful truth to be impressed on the minds of a people fresh from contact with the debasing idolatries of Egypt. A truth: 1. Difficult to grasp. 2. Elevating in its influence. 3. The apprehension of which is necessary for spiritual worship (John iv. 24).

II. OF THE HOLINESS OF GOD'S CHARACTER. The lightnings that played about the mountain, the fire burning in the midst of it (ver. 11), the fiery law that was given,—all bespoke the awful and terrible holiness of him whose voice was uttering words of dreadful import to transgressors.

III. OF THE VERITIES OF GOD'S LAW. Then were spoken the ten commandments (vers. 10, 12)—the sum and substance of moral duty—the rule of life to believers—the Law which condemns and slays transgressors. Christ is "the end of the Law of righteousness to every one that believeth," and only in him can we escape from its condemning power (Rom. viii, 1; x. 4).

IV. OF THE TERRORS OF GOD'S MAJESTY. God surrounded himself with these signs of his greatness, power, wrath, and holiness: **1.** That we may reverence and fear him. **2.** That we may be kept from presumption in our approaches to him. **3.** That we may feel the awfulness of his Word. Recalling this scene, the Israelites should have been preserved from ever trifling with it. God's Word should be handled and read with a deep feeling of reverence. **4.** These terrors suggested that the Law, in itself considered, is not a saving, but a destroying power. The whole manifestation was overcast with threatening.—J. O.

Vers. 15—20.—*Warning against heathenish idolatry.* I. THE ORIGIN OF HEATHEN IDOLATRY. The result of a "corruption" (ver. 16). Not a stage in the advance upwards from fetichism, etc.; but, as inquiries are tending more and more to show, the consequence: **1.** Of a depravation of the idea of God. **2.** Of a corruption of the worship of God. **3.** Arising in turn from the substitution of the creature for God in the affections (cf. Rom. i. 20—26). II. THE FORMS OF HEATHEN IDOLATRY. **1.** Hero-worship (ver. 16). **2.** Animal-worship (vers. 17, 18). **3.** Nature-worship (ver. 19). Greek idolatry furnishes conspicuous instances of the first; Egypt was notorious for the second, so Hinduism; while Parseeism, and the early Vedic worship illustrates the third (cf. Job xxxi. 21). III. THE FRUITS OF HEATHEN IDOLATRY. **1.** A degraded intellect. **2.** Degraded affections. **3.** Degraded morals (Rom. i.). Therefore Israel must not "corrupt" themselves.—J. O.

Ver. 20.—*The iron furnace.* God had passed his people through a hot furnace in the terrible sufferings they endured in Egypt, but with the gracious purpose of ultimately delivering them, and giving them an inheritance in Canaan. We learn— I. THAT GOD'S PEOPLE ARE SOMETIMES SUBJECTED TO SUFFERINGS OF INCREDIBLE SEVERITY. The expression an 'iron furnace," *i.e.* a furnace for smelting iron, conveys no weaker an idea. We know that in fact it sometimes is so. Bodily anguish—mental anguish—stroke after stroke of heaviest trial. An instance in the history of Job. Shakes faith to its foundations—seems to argue that God has utterly forsaken them. II. THAT THESE SUFFERINGS ARE APPOINTED, AND SERVE DISCIPLINARY ENDS. The use of the figure of a furnace implies a purpose in the sufferings. Iron is put into the furnace deliberately, and with a design. Trials, difficult enough to bear in the faith that God sends them, would ofttimes be absolutely intolerable without that faith. The furnace acts on the tough, hard, impure iron to separate it from dross, and make it soft and workable. The severe sufferings through which God passes believers: **1.** Purify character. **2.** Make the nature plastic to God's will, and subdue it to meekness. **3.** Fit the man thus sanctified for new and higher uses. III. GOD HAS AN INHERITANCE IN STORE FOR THOSE WHO ENDURE THE FURNACE SUCCESSFULLY. **1.** Their sufferings fit them *to be* God's inheritance. "To be unto him a people of inheritance." He has to melt, mould, and spiritually prepare for his own indwelling those whom he chooses. **2.** Their sufferings fit them for the inheritance which God gives them (1 Pet. i. 3—10). By creating a pure, chastened, heavenly disposition. By strengthening faith, brightening hope, and increasing love. By subduing pride, rebellion, and impatience; and making the will absolutely pliant in the hands of the Divine.—J. O.

Vers. 1—14.—*Obedience the secret of success.* Moses here reminds Israel of the privilege it possesses as a nation in having the oracles of God committed unto it (Rom. iii. 2). He urges obedience upon them as the one purpose for which they are to be introduced into the promised land. National prosperity depends upon this. And here we have to notice— I. DISOBEDIENCE HAS ALREADY PROVED FATAL. He recalls the terrible experience in connection with Baal-peor—how the people in large numbers became lewd idolaters with the Israelites (Numb. xxv.), and how fierce anger from the Lord visited the people. In Canaan they shall be exposed to similar temptations, but the chastisement at Baal-peor must not be lost upon them. Past judgments are to secure more complete obedience.

II. GOD'S NEARNESS TO THEM SHOULD PROVE A HALLOWING PRIVILEGE. How gracious is God to dwell among them, always near at hand to be inquired of, a most serviceable King! He dwelt in their midst as a Pilgrim with his people. Upon his accessibility and wisdom they could always calculate. This distinguished Israel from the other nations.

Such a privilege should of itself hallow them, and make them to abide under his shadow. Equally near is God still to all of us who seek him.

III. HIS LAW IS WISER THAN ALL MAN'S DEVELOPED LEGISLATION. The surrounding nations had their laws and customs, but the superiority of the Mosaic code was admitted by all acquainted with it. It was an immense moral advance for Israel, as great an advance as in that rude age they could take in.

Similarly, the morality of the gospel is ahead of all jurisprudence. Indeed, enlightened legislation and reform tend towards the scriptural ideal. God is wiser than man, and the Bible better than all acts of parliament.

IV. THE LAW WAS GIVEN AS A RULE OF LIFE FOR A COVENANT PEOPLE. They were redeemed from bondage, and then received the Law at Sinai to guide their redeemed lives. Obedience should be a matter of gratitude for deliverance, and would prove the secret of success.

It is so still. "Christ redeems us from the curse of the Law, being made a curse for us." But as grateful and saved people, we feel that we are "under the Law to Christ" (1 Cor. ix. 21).

And this grateful obedience proves the secret of comfort and success. It is the meat of life to do the will of him who hath sent us, and to finish his work (John iv. 34). Palestine becomes "paradise regained" to the grateful and obedient souls. We find a promised land where God's precepts are gratefully observed by redeemed souls. It is the attitude within, rather than the circumstances without, which constitutes life a blessed country and an antepast of heaven.—R. M. E.

Vers. 15—24.—*The Divine jealousy of graven images.* The great temptation of Israel was to idolatry. Images were worshipped by all those nations among whom they came, and they were in constant danger of conforming to the sinful practice. Hence this warning and statement about the Divine jealousy. Let us observe—

I. THAT JEALOUSY PRESUPPOSES LOVE. Love must be strong as death, else jealousy will not be cruel as the grave; nor will its coals prove coals of fire, having a most vehement flame (Song of Solomon viii. 6). The God who proves so jealous is he whose essence is *love*. If God did not love men so much, he would not be so jealous when they turn away from him. He knows that, as a wife cannot be happy separated from her loving husband, no more can the human spirit be, away from him.

Israel then and we now have to deal with a God of love.

II. GOD IS JEALOUS WHEN MEN GIVE HIM VISIBILITY. Idolatry is trying to help worship through the aid of the senses. The image is not regarded as the god, but his likeness. Man embodies his ideas of God in outward forms.

But imagination is not *creative;* it combines in new relations what has already been given to it. Hence idolatry has never done more than place the creatures, whether beast, or bird, or fish, or reptile, or the heavenly bodies, in new relations to the invisible Divinity.

God resents this visibility as degradation. He knows that man becomes degraded by such associations. Hence his deserved wrath against idolatry.

III. IF GOD BE NOT OUR KINDLING FLAME, HE WILL IN JEALOUSY BE OUR CONSUMING FIRE. It is at the torch of the Divine that the human soul becomes enkindled. The flaming fires of Pentecost sublimate the soul and fit it for primeval powers. It is this warning, elevating influence that is love's natural action.

But when rebellious man turns the grace of God into lasciviousness; when love is ignored instead of returned, and the soul seeks in the things of sense what God only can give,—then love begins to burn as jealousy with a vehement, consuming flame.

IV. IT BECOMES US CONSEQUENTLY TO WORSHIP GOD IN THE SPIRIT. We must keep upon the serene heights of faith, and not fall into the degradation of superstition. We are made for better things than weakly to associate in our minds the invisible and eternal God with the creatures of sense. Let us give faith proper scope, and the worship of God will prove both possible and delightful.

But the worship of God through images makes stocks and stones of men. "They that make them are like unto them; so is every one that trusteth in them" (Ps. cxv. 8). May our worship raise us and not degrade us! Superstition degrades, but worship of the invisible God in the Spirit elevates and ennobles our souls.—R. M. E.

EXPOSITION.

Vers. 25—31.—Moses enforces the warning against idolatry, by predicting the evil that should come upon the nation through the apostacy of those who should in after times turn from Jehovah to strange gods. When they should have begotten children and children's children, and had been long in the land, i.e. when in after years a generation should arise that had not known the things they had seen, or had forgotten them (ver. 9), and the nation should then become wanton and corrupt, and fall into idolatry (cf. ch. vi. 10, etc.; viii. 7, etc.; xxxi. 20, 21; xxxii. 15, etc.; Hos. xiii. 6); then should they utterly perish from off the land of which they were now about to take possession.

Ver. 25.—Have remained long in the land; literally, have become old, an ancient nation, etc. To provoke him to anger; i.e. so as that he should be displeased and grieved, and roused to punish.

Ver. 26.—I call heaven and earth to witness. Moses speaks in the name of the Lord of all, and so calls to witness the whole created universe to attest his words; the heavens and earth are witnesses for God, and when evil comes on those who transgress his Law, they declare his righteousness (Ps. l. 4, 6), in that what has befallen the sinner is only what was announced beforehand as the penalty of transgression. Soon; hastily (מַהֵר), without delay (cf. ch. vii. 4, 22 ["at once," Authorized Vers.]; ix. 3 ["quickly"], 12, 16). Prolong days; usually equal to have a long life (cf. ch. v. 16; vi. 2; xi. 9; xvii. 20, etc.); here it means "continue long to occupy." Only as they continued faithful to Jehovah could they continue as a people to possess the land; severed from him, they lost their title to occupy Canaan, and ceased to be his special people; as a nation they would be destroyed by being scattered among other nations. From Lev. xxvi. 33, etc., and ch. xxviii. 64, it is evident that the author had in view "all the dispersions which would come upon the rebellious nation in future times, even down to the dispersion under the Romans, which continues still; so that Moses contemplated the punishment in its fullest extent" (Keil).

Ver. 27.—Few in number; literally, men of number, i.e. that may be counted; few as compared with the heathen among whom they should be dispersed (Gen. xxxiv. 30). Shall lead you. The verb here (נָהַג, Piel of נָהַג) is frequently used in the sense of conducting gently and kindly (Isa. xlix. 10; lxiii. 14; Ps. xlviii. 14; lxxviii. 52); but it also means to drive, to carry off, to convey forcibly (Exod. xiv. 25; Gen. xxxi. 26; Exod. x. 13; Ps. lxxviii. 26); the connection shows that it is in the latter sense it is to be taken here. Dispersed among the heathen, they, who had dishonoured God by making an image to represent him, should be compelled to do service to mere dead idols, the work of men's hands, which not only could not hear or see, as God can, but also could not perform even such animal functions as eating and smelling (Ps. cxv. 4—7; Jer. x. 3—9). These idols are called "gods" by Moses, because they were so counted by those who worshipped them; elsewhere he stigmatizes them as "abominations," things to be loathed and abhorred (שִׁקּוּצִים, ch. xxvii. 15; xxix. 17). As had been their sin, so should be their punishment; as they had dishonoured God, so should they be themselves dishonoured; as they had worshipped by an image him who is spirit and without form, they should be made to sink down to an utterly materialized worship, that of mere idols, the work of men's hands; as they had apostatized from the one holy and true God, they should be degraded to become the servants of abominations, objects of loathing and abhorrence (Jer. xvi. 13; Acts vii. 42). God, however, would not utterly cast them off: if, in their misery and degradation, they should repent and turn again to him and seek him sincerely and earnestly, they should find him; for he is a merciful God, and mindful of the covenant which he sware unto their fathers (cf. Lev. xxvi. 39, etc.).

Ver. 29.—With all thy heart and with all thy soul. As true religion consists in loving the Lord with all the heart and soul, the whole inner nature (ch. vi. 5; x. 12), so true repentance consists in a turning from sin and all ungodliness to God, in a coming from a state of enmity to him, or of indifference to his claims, to honour, reverence, and serve him intelligently and sincerely, thinking of him aright, adoring his perfections, delighting in him as the alone good, giving to him that honour which is his due, and doing his will from the heart (cf. 2 Chron. xv. 15). When men have apostatized from God, it is often by means of "tribulation" that they are brought to a right state of mind towards him, and to a true repentance "not to be repented of;" and to effect this is the design of all the chastisements which God sends on his own people (Heb. xii. 5—11; cf. Jer. xxiv. 7; xxix. 10—13; l. 4, etc.; Ezek. vi. 11, etc.).

Ver. 30.—In the latter days; *in the afterward of days* (בְּאַחֲרִית הַיָּמִים; "end," ch. xi. 12)—a phrase used sometimes to designate the times of the Messiah (Isa. ii. 2; Hos. iii. 5; comp. Acts ii. 17; 1 Pet. i. 20; Heb. i. 1; 1 John ii. 18); but here, as generally, it simply indicates futurity, the time to come (cf. Gen. xlix. 1; Numb. xxiv. 14; ch. xxxi. 29, etc.). This, however, may include the far distant future, and so points to the time when Israel shall finally return to the Lord and be saved, through the acknowledgment of him whom they despised and rejected when he came as the Messiah promised to the fathers. As St. Paul grounds the assurance of the final redemption of Israel, as a whole, on their calling of God (Rom. xi. 26—29), so Moses here sees in God's covenant the ground of the ever-watchful care and grace of God to Israel, and the security of their final restoration as a nation.

Ver. 31.—Will not forsake thee; literally, *will not let thee loose*, will not lose hold of thee, will not cast thee off (cf. Rom. xi. 1, etc.). "Israel will return and find God, because he loses not hold of it" (Herxheimer). "The sinner will incline to seek God only when he apprehends him as gracious and ready to hear" (Calvin).

Vers. 32—40.—Still more to enforce his warning against apostasy, and urge to obedience and faithful adherence to the service of Jehovah, Moses appeals to what they had already experienced of God's grace in the choosing of them to be his people, in his speaking to them to instruct them, and in the miracles which he had wrought for their deliverance and guidance; grace such as had never been showed before to any nation, or heard of since the creation of the world, and by which those who had experienced it were laid under the deepest obligations of gratitude and duty, to love and serve him by whom it had been showed. With this appeal he closes his first address.

Ver. 32.—For. This connects the statement that follows with that which precedes as its cause; it is *because* Jehovah is a merciful God, that the unparalleled grace showed to Israel had been displayed. The days that are past, etc., *i.e.* inquire from the earliest time of man's abode on the earth. From the one side of heaven unto the other; search the records of all times and places, whether any so great a thing has ever happened or been heard of.

Ver. 33.—(Cf. ver. 12; v. 22—26; Gen. xvi. 13.)

Ver. 34.—Hath God assayed, etc.; hath he ever made the attempt to come on the earth and take a nation from the midst of a nation, as he took the Hebrew people from among the Egyptians? By temptations (מַסֹּת, plu. of מַסָּה, a testing, a trial)—*i.e.* by the plagues inflicted on Pharaoh and his people, whereby they were tested and tried—by signs and by wonders. "The *wonder* (מוֹפֵת) differs from the *sign* (אוֹת) in this, that the former denotes the properly marvellous, the extraordinary, the uncommon, consequently the subjective apprehension of the miraculous event; the latter the significant element in the miracle, the reference to the higher, Divine design, the purpose of God in it, consequently to the objective side of the miracle (comp. ch. xiii. 2)" (Hävernick, 'Comment. üb. Ezech.,' p. 161). By war (cf. Exod. xiv. 14; xv. 3—10); by a mighty hand, and by a stretched out arm (Exod. vi. 6; xiv. 8; ch. v. 15); and by great terrors (Exod. xii. 30—36), the effect on the Egyptians of the Divine inflictions (cf. Ps. cv. 27—38; cvi. 21, 22).

Ver. 35.—All this Israel was made to see, in order that they might know that Jehovah is alone God, and beside him is no other. God (הָאֱלֹהִים, the God), the one living and true God.

Ver. 36.—(Cf. Exod. xx. 18—22.) To indicate still further the pre-eminence of Israel, Moses emphasizes the supernatural character of the revelation God had given to them, and the awful manner of its delivery; God spake to them with audible voice, out of heaven, amidst fire, and they heard his words out of the fire. To instruct thee. The verb here used (יָסַד) means primarily to bind and thence to correct, to chasten, which meaning some interpreters would give here. But the word means also to correct by instruction, to instruct or persuade (cf. Isa. viii. 11; xxviii. 26; Ps. xvi. 7); and the connection, both with what precedes and with what follows, requires this meaning here.

Vers. 37.—And because he loved thy fathers (cf. Gen. xv. 5—7; Exod. xiii. 15—17, etc.). Inasmuch as God had loved their fathers, the patriarchs, and had chosen them their descendants to be his people, and had delivered them out of Egypt, that he might establish them in the promised land, having driven out thence nations mightier than they, therefore were they to consider in their heart and acknowledge that Jehovah alone is God, and that in the wide universe there is no other. The apodosis in this sentence begins at ver. 39, and not, as in the Authorized Version, at "he chose," in ver. 37, nor at "brought thee," as some suggest. **Because he loved thy fathers, and chose his** [*i.e.* Abraham's] **seed after him, and brought thee, etc.,**—for all this *thou shalt keep his statutes*, etc. **In his sight**; literally, *in his face*, i.e. in his presence, by himself present with them; with special reference to Exod. xxxiii. 14, where the same word is used as here. Onkelos has here "by his Word," and the rabbins explain it of "the angel of his presence, as it is said, Isa. lxiii. 9" (Bechai, fol. 194 b).

Ver. 38.—**As it is this day**; as this day has shown, or as it has come to pass this day, in the overthrow, namely, of Sihon and Og.

Ver. 39.—**Know therefore this day, and consider it in thine heart**, etc.; literally, *bring back into thy heart.* "Because we cannot lay hold of spiritual things in thought instantly in a moment, God commands *to make them to revert*, i.e. again and again to recall them to the mind" (Bechai, fol. 194 b).

Ver. 40.—**Upon the earth,**—rather *upon the land* (הָאֲדָמָה)—**which the Lord thy God giveth thee for ever.** The comma after "thee" in the Authorized Version should be deleted. "The sum of this whole exhortation is (1) to acknowledge and lay to heart that God is the alone God of the universe, in heaven and on earth; hence (2) to be obedient to his laws; and so (3) to have, as a recompense, a happy continuance in the beloved land" (Herxheimer). The conclusion of the exhortation reverts to its beginning (comp. ch. v. 40; ver. 1).

Vers. 41—43.—APPOINTMENT OF THREE CITIES OF REFUGE BEYOND JORDAN. A short historical notice is here inserted, probably because it was during the interval between the first and second addresses of Moses that he carried into effect the Divine command to appoint cities of refuge for the manslayer (Numb. xxxv. 9, etc.; cf. Exod. xxi. 13). This notice, therefore, is here in its proper place in the order of the narrative. That Moses should, just at this stage, have made this appointment was fitting and proper, seeing he had been urging on the people obedience to the Divine statutes

and commandments, and had represented their conquest of the territory of Sihon and Og as an earnest of their ultimate possession of the whole land of the Amorites. By appointing these cities, Moses gave an example of obedience to God's injunction, and, at the same time, not only asserted on the part of Israel a right of proprietorship in this trans-Jordanic territory, but assumed as certain that, on the other side of Jordan also, the same right of proprietorship should be possessed and exercised by Israel in the fulfilling of the whole law concerning cities of refuge (cf. ch. xix. 1, etc.). That this section belongs properly to Numb. xxxv., xxxvi., and has been interpolated here by some later hand, is a pure assumption, for which there is no ground.

Ver. 41.—**On this side Jordan**; beyond Jordan, more expressly defined as **toward the sun rising**, viz. on the east of that river.

Ver. 42.—**Unawares**; literally, *in lack* or *want of knowing* (בִּבְלִי־דַעַת), *i.e.* unconsciously, unintentionally; in Numb. xxxv. 31, 15, another word (בִּשְׁגָגָה, by mistake) is used, rendered in the Authorized Version by "unwittingly;" in Josh. xx. 3, both words are used. **In times past**; literally, *yesterday, three days since,* i.e. formerly, heretofore (cf. Gen. xxxi. 2; Exod. v. 8).

Ver. 43.—Names of the cities set apart. **Bezer**; LXX. βοσόρ; one of the cities of the plain or table-land of the Amorites, on the east of Jordan (ch. iii. 10; Josh. xx. 8), afterwards a Levitical city in the tribe of Reuben (Josh. xxi. 36). It is probably the Bosor of 1 Macc. v. 36; it has not been identified with any existing locality, but the ruined heaps of Burazin to the east of Hesbân, or those of Berza in the same district, may mark its site. **Ramoth in Gilead**; probably the same as Ramoth-mizpeh (Josh. xiii. 26); it lay to the north-west of Philadelphia (Rabba or Rabbath-Ammon, *hod.* Ammân), on the Jabbok ('Onom.,' *s.v.* "Rammoth" and "Remmoth"); a Levitical city in the tribe of Gad (Josh. xxi. 38), *hod.* Es Salt, six hours from Ammân (Von Raumer, Porter). **Golan in Bashan.** Eusebius identifies this with Gaulon, a very large village in Batanæa, from which the surrounding region had its name, viz. Gaulonitis, *hod.* Jolan ('Onom.,' *s.v.* "Gaulon"); it was a Levitical city in the tribe of Manasseh (Josh. xxi. 27; 1 Chron. vi. 71); it has not been identified.

PART II

SECOND ADDRESS OF MOSES.

CHAPTER IV. 44—CHAPTER XXVI. 19.

THIS address is introduced by a general notice of what is to form the subject of it, viz. the Law, with a more especial description of that in its different parts, as consisting of ordinances, statutes, and rights; together with a reference to the place and time when this address was delivered.

Ver. 44.—**This is the Law**—the Tôrah—**which Moses set before the children of Israel.** " He meaneth that which hereafter followeth; so this belongeth to the next chapter, where the repetition of the laws begins" (Ainsworth); cf. ch. ver. 1; vi. 1; Lev. vi. 9; vii. 1, etc.

Ver. 45.—**Testimonies**; ordinances attested and confirmed by God; the word used here (עֵדֹת, plu. of עֵדָה) occurs only in Deuteronomy (here and ch. vi. 17, 20) and in the Psalms. **Statutes and judgments** (cf. ch. iv. 1). **After they came forth out of Egypt;** " i.e. not immediately after their exit, but, as ver. 46 shows, when they were already beyond Jordan" (Herxheimer); literally, *in their coming out;* i.e. during the process of their passing from Egypt to Canaan; more exactly defined by what follows.

Ver. 46.—**In the valley** (cf. ch. iii. 29). **In the land of Sihon;** on ground already captured and possessed by Israel (cf. ch. ii. 32—36; iii. 1—17; ver. 48; cf. ch. iii. 9, 12—17).

HOMILETICS.

Vers. 25—28.—*Penalties of disobedience and apostacy.* (See Homiletics, ch. xxviii.)

Vers. 29—31.—*Punishment not rejection.* (See Homiletics, ch. xxx. 1—5.)

Vers. 32—36.—*Israel's peculiar greatness.* (See Homiletics, ch. iv. 11—20; v. 6; xxxiii. 29.)

Vers. 37, 38.—*The dispossession of the Canaanites.* (See Homiletics, ch. i. 1—8.)

Vers. 39, 40.—*Loyalty to God the basis of national prosperity and of family happiness.* (See Homiletics, ch. iv. 1—4 and 5—9.)

Vers. 41—43.—*The cities of refuge.* (See Homiletics, ch. xix.)

Vers. 44, 45.—*The Law : its value.* (See Homiletics, ch. v. 22—33.)

Vers. 44—49.—*The territory of Sihon and Og occupied by others.* (See Homiletics, ch. ii. 24—iii. 1—11.)

HOMILIES BY VARIOUS AUTHORS.

Vers. 23—32.—*National backsliding.* The history of the Jews is an unanswerable argument in favour of the truth of prophecy and the reality of Divine revelation. The singularity of that history is such as can only be fully accounted for on the idea of a supernatural Providence interesting itself in their fortunes; but the strangest fact is in that, their own sacred books, this wonderful history is predicted with minute precision. The Book of Deuteronomy furnishes a series of these predictions, the extraordinary character of which is not removed by any date to which the book may be assigned. We may read this passage first as a prophecy, then as a warning.

I. A PROPHECY. It does not, as several later passages do, put the backsliding of the Jews hypothetically, but states the fact plainly that they will backslide—takes it for granted (ver. 25). There is a prediction: 1. Of national *apostacy*. The whole history of Israel, beginning with the time of the judges (Judg. ii. 19), is a commentary on this statement. 2. Of national *rejection* (vers. 26—29). How remarkably has this testimony been fulfilled in the rooting out of both Judah and Israel from their own land; in their scattering throughout the nations, in every region and country under heaven; in their preservation amidst all vicissitudes as a distinct people; in the conformity to alien worships, customs, and beliefs, to which they have so often been compelled; in the miseries and indignities which they have endured! Surely we are entitled to ask from the unbeliever that he should give us, when rejecting revelation, some satisfactory explanation of these coincidences. 3. Of *national repentance* (vers. 29—32; cf. ch. xxx.). Though yet unfulfilled, there can be little doubt in the minds of any who study past fulfilments, that this prophecy of the repentance of Israel will in God's good time receive its accomplishment also (Zech. xii. 10; Rom. xi. 26).

II. A WARNING. We learn the truths: 1. That backsliding is possible from a state of high attainment. 2. That backsliding is commonly of gradual development (ver. 25). 3. That backsliding may assume very aggravated forms. 4. That backsliding exposes to severe punishment from God. But, finally, and for our encouragement: 5. That backsliding, if repented of, will be graciously forgiven.—J. O.

Vers. 32—41.—*The wonderfulness of Israel's history.* I. THE WONDERFULNESS OF REVELATION AT ALL. (Ver. 33.) It may be argued with great propriety that man needs a revelation; that if there is a God, it is probable he will give one; that the absence of all special revelation would be a greater wonder than the fact of a revelation being given. Yet, when the mind dwells on it, the sense of wonder grows at the thought of the Eternal thus stooping to hold converse with finite, sinful, dying men on earth. Whatever enhances our conceptions of God's greatness, intensifies in the same measure our wonder at the condescension, grace, and love implied in special revelation (Ps. viii.).

II. THE WONDERFULNESS OF GOD'S REVELATION OF HIMSELF IN ISRAEL'S HISTORY. (Vers. 34—39.) God revealed himself *to* Israel; but, inasmuch as the calling, deliverance, and whole history of the nation was full of the supernatural, he was revealed also *in* Israel—in its history. The miraculous element in the history of Israel is urged as a reason for rejecting it. But remark: 1. *It claims to stand out as something absolutely unique in time.* This is no case of the vulgar supernatural, begotten of a childish, miracle-loving age. Moses is as conscious of the marvel, of the exceptional character of the occurrences he narrates, as any of his critics; probably more so. He rises to the grandeur of the subject he speaks of, and puts it on the express ground that nothing like it was ever known, or rumoured, in history. 2. *An adequate reason existed for these wonders.* The interposition of God, as narrated in these verses, the whole revelation, with its terrors, its signs and wonders, its fire, its lawgiving,—is abundantly worthy of the Being who is said to have revealed himself, and of the ends for which that discovery of himself was made. On the other hand, it rises high above what man would naturally have imagined God to do, had he set himself to invent a story of the kind. 3. *The wonders are well attested.* Moses appealed to a generation, the older part of which had witnessed them. Critics dispute the Mosaic authorship of the address; but apart from this, it is to be said that the whole after-history of the nation rests on their reality. There is, however, an inherent sublimity, fitness, vividness, sense of reality in the narratives, and in this appeal to eye-witnesses, which speaks of itself for the truthfulness of the history. When narratives of the same kind, presenting the same marvellous characteristics, can be produced from other literatures, and laid alongside of these, we will be able to believe in their legendary or invented character. 4. *These wonders established a unique claim on Israel for obedience and fidelity* (vers. 39, 40).

III. THE WONDERFULNESS OF GOD'S REVELATION OF HIMSELF IN ISRAEL IS SURPASSED BY HIS REVELATION OF HIMSELF IN CHRIST. These wonders in Israel were but the earlier acts in a great drama, of which the later belong to the dispensation of the gospel. While Moses appeals to the *limited* character of the former revelation as enhancing its wonder (ver. 34), it is the greater marvel of the revelation in Christ, that it is *universal* in its scope, and brings in a redemption which all can share. We think here of the incarnation, the miracles of Christ, the resurrection, the outpouring of the Spirit, the miraculous spread of the gospel, subsequent reformations and revivals, conversions, the supernatural power exhibited in the renewal and sanctification of souls, the successes of missions, etc. (cf. Heb. ii. 1—5). The appeals of Moses, and his exhortations to wonder and obey, come down to ourselves, accordingly, with enormously enhanced force. —J. O.

Ver. 37.—*Beloved for the fathers' sake.* We learn, taking this verse with the context—

I. THAT THE PIETY OF ANCESTORS IS REMEMBERED BY GOD IN HIS DEALINGS WITH THEIR DESCENDANTS. He remembers: 1. Their piety. 2. The love he bore them. 3. His promises. 4. Their prayers.

II. THAT THE PIETY OF ANCESTORS IS A FREQUENT GROUND OF LONG-SUFFERING AND FORBEARANCE. It was so with Israel (ch. ix. 5); Solomon (1 Kings xii. 12), etc.

III. YET THAT THE PIETY OF ANCESTORS WILL NOT OF ITSELF SECURE SALVATION. The Jews were not to be exempted from chastisement for personal transgressions. If " they abide still in unbelief" (Rom. xi. 23), they cannot be saved. There cannot be salvation without personal faith and obedience.—J. O.

Vers. 29—40.—*The mercy of God.* The knowledge of his own deceitful heart, and his observation of others' waywardness, convinced Moses that, in spite of all warning and appeal, the people might yet wander into evil ways. But Moses had also such a comprehensive vision of God's mercy, that he foresaw that there would be room for repentance even in the land of exile, and that Divine mercy would be available in every extremity of distress. Since God had designed to show mercy unto Israel, Moses felt assured that he would not allow his gracious designs to be frustrated.

I. AFFLICTION OFTEN REVEALS TO OUR MINDS OUR NEED OF MERCY. Amid the joyous excitements induced by earthly prosperity, men forget the deeper needs of the soul. They spend life as if they had no soul, as if this earth were their all. But the deep gashes, which suffering makes, become mouths through which the imprisoned soul makes herself heard. When events defeat our selfish plans, or when health is interrupted, we are made to feel that there is a higher Power than ourselves, who reigns upon the throne, and often, in sheer despair of other help, we appeal to him for mercy; like Manasseh, who had long hardened his heart against God, yet, when he was in sore affliction, sought Jehovah's face. When brought to the lowest ebb, the prodigal son bent his steps homeward. Affliction often serves as the shepherd's crook.

II. EARNEST APPEAL FOR GOD'S MERCY IS NEVER UNSUCCESSFUL ON EARTH. From the furthest limit of apostacy the cry for help is heard. There is no spot on earth from which lines of connection with heaven will not be found. Our God is not wont to hide himself in secret places, where the eye of faith cannot find him. If only the bow be well bent by the arm of spiritual earnestness, and the arrow be feathered with faith, and aimed by heavenly wisdom, it must penetrate the skies. Without gracious influences from above, men will not pray; but whensoever they do pray, they shall be heard. The prayer of the rich man in his torments was unheard, because it was a godless and a selfish prayer, and because we have no ground for expecting mercy when life has closed; in his case there was no appeal for mercy.

III. GOD'S MERCY IS THE MOST ATTRACTIVE REVELATION OF HIMSELF FOR SINNERS. So far as we know, this revelation of his merciful character was reserved for guilty men. In the construction of this material universe, we see chiefly a forth-putting of amazing *power.* In the creation of sentient beings, capable of deriving pleasure from the processes of natural law, we see in active exercise the qualities of wisdom and benevolence. In the Divine treatment of apostate angels, we discover brilliant coruscations from the flames of justice. In the provision of pardon and hope for human transgressors, we see in God's nature the fascinating quality of mercy. This mercy manifests itself in a thousand ways, and is a prolific parent of blessing. It restrains from flagrant sin. It envelops the sinner in a network of heavenly influence. It holds back the hand of justice from summary destruction of the culprit. Though men forsake God, he does not forthwith forsake them. Retaliation finds no place in the Eternal Mind. It is negative and positive good.

IV. This mercy is secured to men by covenant. A covenant is a compact or treaty made between two persons, and which is intended for the advantage of all parties interested. But it is a pure act of condescension, when God undertakes to bind himself in solemn engagements with his feeble and fallen creatures. This gracious procedure is taken in order to encourage our trust, and to pierce unbelief through and through with a two-edged sword. *Now* that God has made a covenant with men, and repeated it age after age, his truth and faithfulness and integrity are pledged for our salvation. He made a covenant with Christ, by which he secured to him an ample recompense of redeemed men, and our Lord pleads in prayer for the fulfilment of his Father's covenant. So gracious is the covenant that God makes with us—the new covenant—that he writes it on the tablet of our minds, yea, deeply engraves it upon the soft affections of our hearts.

V. This mercy is made conspicuous by the mighty deeds of God. Moses reminds the Hebrews of the splendid tokens of God's goodness they had seen; for every one of these was a pledge of unchanging love. God's signal emancipation of the people from the iron bondage of Egypt; his care over them throughout the desert pilgrimage; his unprecedented revelation of himself on Horeb, in fire and cloud and voice;—*all these things* were tantamount to fresh covenants—earnests of yet larger blessing. In deeds, more eloquent than words, he assured them that all his resources were available for them. And we, in New Testament times, can make this argument stronger still. Calvary serves as a platform, on which we may erect a magnificent structure of expectation. If God had meant to desert us, would he have shown to us such kindnesses as these?

VI. God distributes his mercy in various measures. He did for the Hebrews what he did not do for other nations of that period. In the way of providence, and in the way of revelation, he deals differently with separate nations, and with individuals. We cannot understand all the rules and methods by which he is pleased to work, but we can leave it to himself to justify his ways. Because mercy snatched the crucified thief from the jaws of perdition at the last moment of life, it is criminal presumption for any other man to expect mercy in his last hour.

VII. Mercy flows to men through a vicarious channel. God assured *that* generation of the Jews, that *they* were blessed for *their fathers'* sake. Not on the ground of personal merit, nor on the ground of personal claim, did God show them his distinguishing favour, but because he had loved Abraham their father, and for *his* sake loved his seed. Learn here how greatly God loves a good man! Abraham was not destitute of fault; yet so conspicuous was his practical faith, that God could not do enough for him during an earthly life-time. The benediction of God overflowed (like the oil on Aaron's head), and descended to the skirts of his posterity. So, and much more, the love which God bears his only Son flows to us for his Son's sake. The same rich quality of love God cherishes for his Son, he cherishes for us. The gift of salvation can flow to us in no other way than through this channel of vicarious merit. "God, in Christ, reconciles the world unto himself."

VIII. God's mercy a potent inducement for loyal obedience. When all other methods have failed to elicit a man's loyalty, the unexpected display of mercy has often succeeded. Justice, and honour, and all sense of obligation in man have been appealed to over and over again, and always in vain. No appeal moves his callous nature, except the plaintive voice of love. We may tell him of the measureless power of Jehovah, of his inflexible justice, of his inviolable truth, of his fixed determination to root out sin from his kingdom; he hears it all unmoved. But tell him of Jehovah's overflowing mercy, of his tender love for the chief of sinners, of the costly provision of salvation; and by the gracious application of this by the Divine Spirit, man's nature relents, becomes docile, and enshrines the Law of God in its inmost centre. "Man!" says the silvery voice of mercy, "thy sins are forgiven thee." And the swift response is, "Lord, *what* wilt thou have me to do?"—D.

Vers. 41—43.—*The cities of refuge.* Regard for human life is more important than regard for private property. With legislative prescience, Moses secured three cities on the east of Jordan as sanctuaries for fugitives, before the land was allocated to their several families. Still further security for the unwary manslayer was obtained by the decree that these cities should be occupied by families of the Levites.

I. God's HIGH REGARD FOR HUMAN LIFE. This Divine thoughtfulness for men is impressive. Not a life was to be wantonly wasted. Human life, it is plain, was counted inferior in value to the interests of public justice; but it was to be sacredly protected against private revenge. This humane provision was all the more required at that time when Israel had been commanded to slay such vast numbers of Canaanites. Inevitably, human sensibility would be blunted, and a grave peril arose that human life would be cheaply rated. The entire land, purchased at such great cost, was a *temple*—a sacred enclosure—which God had chosen for his abode, and the shedding of innocent blood would degrade and desecrate the hallowed soil. Human life, sustained by God with exquisite pains—capable of eminent usefulness—is appraised by God as of great value.

II. THE JUDICIOUS ADJUSTMENT OF RIGHTEOUSNESS AND PITY. Both these are sentiments implanted in the breast by a Divine hand; both serve the interests of humanity; and both have a fitting sphere in which to move. For the nation's good, the conscience of every man should be kept in healthful activity. It needs illumination, discipline, vigour. The moral sense is as liable to injury, disease, and decay, as any other faculty of mind. It may be deficient in wisdom; it may be overburdened with sensitiveness; it may magnify molehills into mountains; it may act with precipitate haste. Side by side with unrelenting hostility for sin, should dwell honest pity for the sinner. This provision of "sanctuaries" in Israel was in no wise an interference with the proper procedure of justice. By the decision of competent magistrates the fugitive might yet be handed over to the executioner. It gave full opportunity for investigation. It safeguarded a suspected man, if he were innocent of the greater 'crime. It taught men to draw a deep line between unintentional injury and premeditated murder. It shielded from needless death many a useful life.

III. PROMPT AND SEVERE EXERTION WAS THE CONDITION OF ESCAPE. When a man was killed, his next of kin was expected to avenge his blood. This rough ministry of justice was needful in those early days. It strengthened family ties. It fostered a spirit of brotherhood. It was a shield for the weak and defenceless. If one man had slain another, the presumption was that it had been maliciously done, and prompt vengeance was preparing for him. He had placed himself (inadvertently, it may be) in a serious plight. He was exposed to a sudden reprisal. Before an hour his own life might be forfeited. If his conscience told him that he was innocent, there was a possibility of escape. But he must promptly flee. He must bid a hasty adieu, or none at all, to wife and children, and run at highest speed for the refuge city, for vengeance is swift-footed as an antelope. Every muscle must be strained to the utmost; his eye must be on every bush and rock, lest the foe should be lurking in ambush; his last resource of strength must be expended upon his flight; he must go direct as an arrow for the provided sanctuary. So for every guilty son of Adam there is a refuge provided on the hill called "Calvary;" and because Death rides apace upon our heels, we are charged to flee—to flee for very life—to this capacious Refuge. *So run*, that ye may be safe!—D.

Vers. 25—31.—*Judgment leading to mercy*. After stating the fact of God's jealousy in the matter of graven images, Moses goes on as a prophet to declare that, if they corrupt themselves in this way in Canaan, the result will be their destruction and dispersion. But in dispersion, if they turn with all their hearts to God (ver. 29), they shall find him and be restored. God is merciful as well as jealous (ver. 31). The following thoughts are hereby suggested :—

I. JUDGMENT IS WITH A VIEW TO AMENDMENT. Of course, the *incorrigible* stage may eventually be reached. But until this spirit is manifested, judgment is remedial. The dealings of God with Israel, as we know from the history, were in hope of national amendment. Defeat at the hand of their enemies, exile in Babylon, and all the severe dispensations were to bring them to their senses and lead them to return to God. Judgment, in fact, is first the servant of mercy.

II. TRIBULATION SHOULD AT ONCE LEAD US TO HEART-SEARCHING. It is not an infallible sign of special sin, as the case of Job proves. But the probabilities are in favour of supposing that some special sin has called for special sorrow. Let self-examination, then, be the rule in the midst of all our tribulations. God is calling us in trumpet-tones to return to his embrace.

III. MERCY FINDS IN TROUBLE A SPLENDID SPHERE. The riches of God's grace and mercy can be displayed only in the permitted extremities of human experience. Tribulation, exile, the bitterness which no earthly intermeddling can relieve, are so many worlds into which mercy enters to assert its power and to reign.

The permission of evil has here the only explanation which the present life allows. We shall learn more afterwards, but meanwhile this is all we can learn here.

IV. THE MERCIFUL ONE COUNSELS SOULS TO RETURN AT ONCE TO COVENANT RELATIONS. A loving God is jealous of the defections of his people—hence the judgment and the tribulation. But in mercy he counsels return, and promises to receive them into covenant relationship again. Here alone can we have peace and satisfaction of a permanent character.

Outside the covenant there can be no real comfort or joy. In covenant relations with God, there is a charmed circle, and peace passing all understanding. As Israel returned after the exile, may we return from our backslidings to the consolations of the covenant again!—R. M. E.

Vers. 32—40.—*The deliverance of the Lord's people unparalleled.* Moses would have the Israelites to regard God's deliverance of them from Egypt as a matter for the most grateful admiration. There had been nothing like it since the beginning of the world. There was direct and immediate communion with God; there was deliverance of the people from Egypt by unexampled judgments; and all was to show his character as a sovereign and loving God. The effect of such a discipline should be *filial* obedience. It suggests the following lessons :—

I. THE LORD'S PEOPLE SHOULD GRATEFULLY STUDY THEIR DELIVERANCE. The marvellous Exodus from Egypt and communion at Sinai were deserving of the most faithful study. No people had ever been so favoured before.

But our personal deliverance from the bondage of sin, our march through the wilderness of life, our fellowship with God from the mountain-top of ordinances, the entire experience of a spiritual soul, combine to eclipse even the discipline of Israel. Each one is prepared, who understands his state, to say, " Come and hear, all ye that fear God, and I will declare what he hath done for my soul " (Ps. lxvi. 16).

II. UNPARALLELED EXPERIENCE FROM GOD ARGUES AN UNPARALLELED GOD. For it is a revelation of his powers and character he makes in these matters, and we are expected to reason from our experience up to himself. " Unto thee it was showed," said Moses, " that thou mightest know that the Lord he is God; there is none else beside him." He moves in an unparalleled fashion, that we may recognize in him the unparalleled One.

The use of personal experience is, therefore, to reach the Divine side of it, and see what reflection of Deity it presents.

III. IT WAS GOD'S LOVE WHICH HE ILLUSTRATED IN BRINGING ISRAEL FROM EGYPT TO CANAAN. The casting out of the Canaanites, the extermination of the idolaters, was judgment justly exercised upon them; but it was love towards Israel. Hence one of the psalmists makes these conquests a proof that " his mercy endureth for ever " (Ps. cxxxvi. 17—22).

And God's dealings with his people always are to illustrate his love. They find how all things work together for good unto them (Rom. viii. 28).

IV. IT IS FILIAL OBEDIENCE HIS PEOPLE SHOULD RENDER. The similarity between ver. 40 and the fifth commandment of the Decalogue is certainly remarkable. The idea of God's fatherhood is as certainly in the mind of Moses and of the filial obedience of Israel. Long life is attached to their filial obedience to God, as it is attached in that commandment to the filial obedience we render to man.

And indeed this " fatherhood of God," with its correlative " sonship of man," constitutes the crowning relation into which God and man come. How glorious it is! Earth becomes the school of God's children; the promise of the life that now is cheers them on, and heaven contracts the kindly light of home.

We should never rest contented till our study of God's dealings leads us into assurances and hopes like these. The Israelites were to be obedient, and in consequence successful children; and the same blessed conditions become ours by faith!—R. M. E.

Vers. 41—43.—*The cities of refuge beyond the Jordan.* After the discourse contained in the preceding portion of this book, Moses seems to have taken a breathing time, during which he designated Bezer in the wilderness, Ramoth in Gilead, and Golan in Bashan, as cities of refuge. To these the menslayers were directed to flee, when they had been guilty, not of murder, but of manslaughter. In this way a distinction was introduced in the Mosaic code between manslaughter and murder, which did not obtain in the code of revenge among the other nations.

And here let us observe—

I. RETALIATION CONSTITUTED THE RUDE JUSTICE OF THIS EARLY AGE. Vengeance seems dreadful to many because we live under an organized system of public justice. But if we were translated to some uncivilized country, where each one is forced to fight for his own hand, we should regard it less painfully. We should recognize it, in fact, as a necessary assertion of justice.

" Vengeance is mine ; I will repay, saith the Lord," seems dreadful only to those who have not appreciated the need of a perfect public justice. The Divine vengeance will be public and perfect, from which there will and can be no appeal.

II. RETALIATION, SUCH AS THE MOSAIC CODE PRESCRIBED, DEMANDED COURAGE AND SELF-DENIAL. The kinsman was directed to pursue the manslayer, and to seek the payment of life for life. It was not one of those feats which would be lightly undertaken. In fact, it was one of those dangerous duties, which a person would shirk if he could. The command reinforced the courage and sustained the self-denial of the people (cf. Mozley's ' Ruling Ideas in Early Ages,' pp. 180—221).

And in the Divine vengeance—with reverence would we say it—there is needed courage and self-denial. The infliction of it is *forced* upon him.

III. THE CITIES OF REFUGE AFFORDED PROTECTION TO THE MANSLAYER WHO DID NOT DELIBERATELY TAKE AWAY LIFE. Here the manslayer lived in lonely exile till the death of the high priest. This milder sentence, however, was preferable to a violent death. The opportunity was afforded of examining himself and of being penitent for his sins.

The sojourn in the city of refuge corresponds to the spiritual experience of those who have betaken themselves to Jesus under a sense of their sin and bloodguiltiness, to find under his wings freedom from condemnation (Rom. viii. 1), and the necessity of great watchfulness and circumspection. If the manslayer had left the city of refuge, he would still have been liable to the avenger.

IV. BUT WHEN THE HIGH PRIEST DIED THE MANSLAYER REGAINED LIBERTY AS WELL AS LIFE. " Life in Christ " is indicated by the sojourn in the city of refuge. But liberty through the death of Christ is indicated by the release at the death of the high priest.

It takes many relations to bring out the truth as it is in Jesus. He is our *Goel*, or Avenger, as we have seen where he says, " Vengeance is mine." He is our City of Refuge ; he is our High Priest, whose death secures the return of the exile. May Jesus be all in all to us !—R. M. E.

Vers. 44—49.—*The circumstances under which the Law was reiterated.* These verses are manifestly introductory to the discourse of the succeeding chapters. Moses is about to declare the " testimonies " (הָעֵדֹת), what comes forth from God to indicate his will ; and the " statutes " (הַחֻקִּים), the defined duties of moral obligation ; and the " judgments " (הַמִּשְׁפָּטִים), or mutual rights of men. The conditions of his speech are here detailed.

I. THE ISRAELITES HAD RECEIVED AN EARNEST OF THE PROMISED INHERITANCE. They had got, as we have seen, the land of the Amorites. The kingdoms of Og and of Sihon were already in the hands of the two and a half tribes. Moses had a vantage-ground, therefore, from which to plead the claims of God.

And so, when we get an earnest of the promised inheritance in the gift of the Spirit, we are more likely to yield ourselves to the Divine demands (Eph. i. 14). We have an inheritance on this side the Jordan of death, more important than the pastures of Bashan, and God, having given us this, may well make demands upon us.

II. THE EXPERIENCE THROUGH WHICH THEY HAD PASSED WAS ALSO MOST IMPORTANT. For the temporal inheritance in Moab and Bashan was a minor part of their gifts from

God. Their fellowship at Sinai, their wanderings through the wilderness, the chequered experience of judgment and of mercy, all combined to make the Israelites in Moab a favoured people. No other nation had had such an experience and history.

III. THE REITERATION OF THE LAW WAS IN THE MIDST OF HAPPIER CONDITIONS. At Sinai their fathers and themselves had witnessed awe-inspiring wonders. The mount was the centre of quaking and fear. Even Moses had to yield to the panorama of terror, and to say, "I exceedingly fear and quake." But now in Moab all around them is bright and hopeful. Mercy encompassed them, and so they were more likely to enter into the spirit of the Law, which Moses makes out to be *love* (ch. vi. 1—5).

IV. WE LEARN FROM THIS THAT GOD FIRST GIVES BLESSINGS AND THEN ASKS OBEDIENCE. It is here that we see plainly the essence of the gospel. The glad tidings consist of the offer of a full and free salvation to the sinner, on the ground that he is a sinner and cannot save himself. The salvation is saddled with *no* condition. This is the trouble—it is too good news to be true, in the sinner's sight. He can hardly credit such free gift—he would rather pay something for it. But God is firm, and will make no half bargains.

But when the sinner has been redeemed from Egypt and brought to God, he is expected in gratitude to obey God's Law. It is his rule of life, and he renders obedience to it willingly.

People "put the cart before the horse," and fancy God will take something in part payment, and could not think of refusing them! Nothing is so important just now as clear views about the plan of salvation.—R. M. E.

EXPOSITION.

CHAPTER V.

THE DECALOGUE THE BASIS OF THE COVENANT, THE ESSENCE OF THE WHOLE LAW, AND THE CONDITION OF LIFE AND FELICITY.

Vers. 1—33.

Vers. 1—5.—Moses reminds them of the making of the covenant at Horeb, and of the revelation of the fundamental law of the covenant there. As he was about to recapitulate the laws which God their King had enacted, it was fitting that he should refer at the outset to that covenant relation between Jehovah and Israel on which all the injunctions of the Law rested.

Ver. 1.—And Moses called all Israel [called to all Israel], and said. "The calling refers not to the publicity of the address, but to the clear voice which, breaking forth from the inmost heart of Moses, aimed at penetrating, as far as possible, to all (Gen. xlix. 1; John vii. 37)" (Schroeder). (Cf. also Prov. viii. 4.)

Vers. 2, 3.—Not with our fathers, the patriarchs (cf. ch. iv. 37.) The covenant to which Moses refers is not that made with Abraham, but that made at Sinai, with Israel as a people; and though the individuals who were then present had all perished with the exception of Moses, Joshua, and Caleb, the nation survived, and as it was with the nation as an organic whole

that the covenant had been made, it might be with propriety said that it was made with those whom Moses addressed at this time, inasmuch as they constituted the nation.

Vers. 4, 5.—The Lord talked with you face to face. God spoke to them immediately, in their presence and to their face, from the mount, as one person might to another. There is a slight difference in form between the phrase here and that in Exod. xxxiii. 11 and ch. xxxiv. 10, where it is used in reference to Moses, but it is so slight (בְּפָנִים instead of אֶל־פָּנִים) that no difference of meaning can be elicited. God spake directly to the people, as he did to Moses, only Moses was admitted to closer communion with him than the people were. This difference is sufficiently indicated in ver. 5, where the mediatory function of Moses, in the promulgation of the Law and the making of the covenant, is described as necessitated by the fear of the people, and their not going up into the mount (cf. Exod. xix. 19, etc.). This is referred to more fully afterwards (ver. 23, etc.). I stood between the Lord and you; *i.e.* acted as mediator; LXX., εἰστήκειν ἀνὰ μέσον (cf. Gal. iii. 19).

Ver. 6.—I am Jehovah thy God. "The Law, the establishing rule for men, can proceed only from him who alone and over all stands fast; *i.e.* from God, specially as Jehovah. The eternal, unchangeable One, since he demands the obedience of faith (is not merely the moral imperative), must not only reveal himself, but in revealing himself must claim Israel as loyal and faithful; *thy God*" (Schroeder).

Vers. 7—21.—*Repetition of the ten commandments.* On these, as the basis of the covenant, the whole legislation rests, and therefore a rehearsal of them is a fitting introduction to a repetition and enforcement of the laws of the theocracy. Some differences appear between the statement of the "ten words," as given here and as given in Exod. **xx.** It is chiefly in the fourth commandment that these are to be found. It begins here with "remember" for "keep;" reference is made to the command of God as sanctioning the sabbath (ver. 12), which is omitted in Exodus; a fuller description of the animals to be exempted from work on that day is given (ver. 14); the words, "that thy manservant and thy maidservant may rest as well as thou," are added (ver. 14); and in place of a reference to the resting of God after the Creation as the ground of the sabbath institute, as in Exodus, there is here a reference to the deliverance of the Israelites out of bondage in Egypt as a reason why the Lord commanded them to keep the sabbath day (ver. 15). In the fifth commandment there are two additions here—the one of the words, " as Jehovah thy God hath commanded thee," and the other of the words, " that it may go well with thee " (ver. 16). In the tenth commandment, the first two clauses are transposed, " desire " appears in place of " covet " in relation to " wife," and " field " is added to the specification of objects (ver. 21). These differences are of little moment. The only one demanding notice is that in the fourth commandment, where different reasons are assigned for the ordinance of the sabbath. The two reasons assigned, however, are perfectly compatible; the one is fundamental and universally applicable, the other is subsidiary and special in its application; the one is a reason why the sabbath was originally instituted and is for all men, the other is a reason why it was specially and formally instituted in Israel and was especially memorable to that people. In a popular address to them it seems fitting that the latter rather than the former should be the one adduced. As a memorial of their deliverance from Egypt, the sabbath was all important to them, for by it they were con-

stantly reminded that "they were thereby freed from the dominion of the world to be a peculiar possession of Jehovah, and so amid the toil and trouble of the world had part in the holy rest of their God" (Baumgarten). It was also fitting in a recapitulatory address that special emphasis should be laid on the fact that what the Law enunciated was what " the Lord had commanded." The addition of " field " in the tenth commandment is probably due to the fact that now, the occupation and division of the land having begun, the people were about to have, what they had not before—each his own property in land. In the tenth commandment, also, there is a difference in the two accounts worthy of notice. In Deuteronomy, " field " is added to the enumeration of objects not to be coveted, and the " wife " is put first and apart, while in Exodus the " house " precedes the " wife " and the latter ranks with the rest. In Deuteronomy also this separation of the wife is emphasized by a change of the verb: " *Neither shalt thou* desire (תחמד) *thy neighbour's wife, neither shalt thou* covet (תתאוה) *thy neighbour's house,*" etc.

Vers. 7—16.—FIRST TABLE OF THE LAW · *præcepta pietatis.*

Ver. 7.--In this, the first commandment, the great principle and basis of all true religion is asserted—monotheism, as opposed to polytheism or pantheism There is but one God, and that God is Jehovah, the self-existent and eternal, who yet has personal relations with men.

Vers. 8—10.—Here the spirituality of God is asserted, and, in the prohibition of the use of images in the worship of the Deity, all idolatry is denounced, and all deification of the powers of nature in any sense is prohibited. By the Jews, this commandment was not always regarded, for they were not unfrequently seduced into following the idolatrous usages of the nations around them. It does not appear, however, that, though they set up images of the idol-gods whom they were thus led to worship, they ever attempted to represent by image or picture the great God whom their fathers worshipped—Jehovah—by whom this command was given; and at a later period, when they had long renounced all idolatry, they became noted as the one nation that adored the Deity as a spirit, without any sensible representation of him: " Judæi mente sola unumque Numen intelligunt . . . igitur nulla simulacra urbibus suis, nedum templis sinunt" (Tacit., 'Hist.,' v. 5). It appears that, by many of them at least, the commandment was regarded as prohibiting absolutely the graphic and plastic arts (Philo, 'Quis Rer. Div. Hær. sit.,' p. 496, edit. Mangey; 'De Ebriet.,' p. 374; 'De Gigant.,' p. 270). This may account for the low state of these arts among the Jews, and for the fact that they alone of the civilized nations of antiquity have left no monuments of art for the instruction or admiration of posterity. Thou shalt not bow down thyself unto them, nor serve them; LXX., Οὐ προσκυνήσεις αὐτοῖς, οὐδὲ μή λατρεύσῃς αὐτοῖς. Every kind of worship of images is forbidden, alike that of *proskunesis* and that of *latria*. And shewing mercy unto thousands; *i.e.* to the thousandth generation (cf. ch. vii. 9).

Ver. 11.—Thou shalt not take the name of the Lord thy God in vain; literally, *Thou shalt not take* [or *lift*] *up the Name of Jehovah thy God to vanity*. This commandment forbids not only all false swearing by the Name of God, but all profanation of that Name by an irreverent or light use of it (Lev. xix. 12).

Vers. 12—14.—Keep the sabbath day to sanctify it, as the Lord thy God hath commanded thee. This phraseology implies that the sabbath institute was already well known to the people of Israel; so that this commandment was intended, not to enact a new observance, but to enforce the continuance of an observance which had come down to them from earlier times. The sabbath was to be kept by being *sanctified*. This means that it was to be consecrated to God to be used as he had appointed. The sanctification of any object "always goes back to an act of the Divine will, to Divine election and institution. In other words, it is always a state in which the creature [or institute] is bound to God by the appointment of God himself, which is expressed by קְדֹשׁ שׁ, קְדֹשׁ, הִקְדִּישׁ, קְדַשׁ" (Oehler, 'Theology of the Old Testament,' vol. i. p. 155). The sanctification of the sabbath, accordingly, was the consecration of that day to the Lord, to be observed as he had enjoined, that is, as a day of rest from all servile work and ordinary occupations. Among the Jews, those who were careful to keep this law "rested the sabbath day according to the commandment" (Luke xxiii. 56). Not, however, in mere indolence and idle vacancy, unworthy of a man. Not thus could the day be sanctified to the Lord. Man had to "release his soul and body from all their burdens, with all the professions and pursuits of ordinary life, only in order to gather himself together again in God with greater purity and fewer disturbing elements, and renew in him the might of his own better powers"

(Ewald, 'Antiquities of Israel,' p. 102). In the sabbath institute, therefore, lies the basis of spiritual worship and pious service in Israel.

Ver. 16.—The germ of society is the family, and the family is sustained only as the authority and rule of the heads of the house are upheld and respected. The command, then, to honour parents may be justly regarded as asserting the foundation of all social ordinances and arrangements. Where parents are not honoured, a flaw lies at the basis, and the stability of the entire social fabric is endangered.

Vers. 17—21.—SECOND TABLE OF THE LAW: *præcepta probitatis*.

In the enactments of the second table there is a progression from the outward to the inward. First, sins of *deed* are prohibited, such as murder, adultery, and theft; then sins of *word*, such as injury of a neighbour's good name by false testimony; and finally, sins of *the heart*, which do not come into open manifestation, such as covetousness and evil desire. The "commandment" is thus seen to be "exceeding broad" (Ps. cxix. 96). So that only the man "who hath clean hands and a pure heart, and who hath not lifted up his soul to vanity, nor sworn deceitfully," shall "ascend into the hill of the Lord, or stand in his holy place" (Ps. xxiv. 3, 4).

Vers. 22—27.—Here is an expanded citation of Exod. xx. 15—18, addressed by Moses to prepare the way for the solemn admonition to observe and do all that the Lord had commanded them, with which he passes on to the enunciation of the various statutes and ordinances he had been enjoined by God to lay upon them.

Ver. 22.—And he added no more. "Only these ten words did God speak immediately to you; all the rest he spoke afterwards by me" (Herxheimer); cf. Numb. xi. 25, where the same formula occurs, "and they added not," *i.e.* they prophesied only when the Spirit of God came on them, but this was not continuous. And he wrote them in two tables of stone. This anticipates what is recorded in its proper historical connection in ch. ix. 10, 11.

Vers. 23—27.—In a purely historical narrative such as that in Exodus, a condensed statement of what took place on this occasion was sufficient; but in an address to the people, it was fitting that Moses should give it in fuller detail, especially in view of what follows.

Vers. 28, 29.—The words of God in reply to those of the people are not given in Exodus; here they are fittingly inserted God approved of their words because they expressed a proper reverence and a due sense on their part of the unworthiness of sinful men to come into the presence of the great and holy God; but knowing their fickleness, and proneness to forget and depart from him, he added, **Oh that there were such an heart in them that they would fear me and keep all my commandments always!** God looks upon the heart, and will accept no service or worship that is not rendered from the heart. Only they who do his will from the heart (Eph. vi. 6) really fear and keep his commandments. The tongue may sometimes promise what the heart does not guarantee; and so when the occasion that provoked the utterance has passed, the whole may be forgotten, and the promise never be fulfilled.

Vers. 30, 31.—The people were commanded to return to their tents, and Moses was appointed to act as mediator between God and them, receiving from him his commandments and communicating them to the people.

Vers. 32, 33.—Moses winds up this part of his discourse by exhorting them to observe and do all God's commandments, not in any way departing from that course of action to which he had called them, that they might live, and it should be well with them in the land they were about to possess.

Ver. 32.—**To the right hand or to the left.** "This signifieth an exact care to walk in God's Law, as in the highway, from which men may not turn aside, as in Deut. ii. 27 " (Ainsworth); cf. ch. xvii. 11, 20; xxviii. 14; Josh. i. 7; Prov. iv. 27; Isa. xxx. 21. "To receive what God enjoins is only half obedience; it belongs thereto also that nothing be required beyond this. We must not desire to be more righteous than as we are taught by the Law" (Calvin).

HOMILETICS.

Ver. 6.—*The Divine Law based on a divinely revealed relationship.* "I am the Lord *thy* God," etc. This little word *thy*, in this connection, gives us the basis on which the Law was set. Of the event called "the giving of the Law," we feel the thrill even now. That Law has in it four features, corresponding to one or other of the aspects in which the people to whom it was first given may be regarded. They were (1) members of the great human family, moral, responsible beings, amenable to the government of God. They were (2) a Church in the wilderness, with their own institutions, which embodied the worship appropriate to the religion enjoined upon them. They were (3) a people rescued from bondage, about to have a commonwealth of their own, for which sundry civil and political regulations had to be provided. They were (4) a nation which for years was to be in a wandering state, yet destined in the long run to find a home in Palestine. Adapted to them in this last-named aspect, they had sanitary laws; for them in the third aspect there were civil and political laws; for them in the second aspect there were religious institutions; and for them in the first aspect there was the great moral law. The set of rules having reference to health would be binding only so far as the laws of climate and modes of life necessitated their continued observance. The civil law would be but temporary so far as it received its complexion from the idolatrous surroundings of the people. The ceremonial law would pass away *in form,* but the underlying principles of it are permanent. The moral law is unchanging as man's nature, and enduring as his relation to God. It is given in the ten commandments, of which the *first* enjoins supreme love to the Divine Being: the second, recognition of the spirituality of the Divine nature: the third, reverence for the Divine Name: the fourth, care for Divine worship: the fifth inculcates religion in the home: the sixth, the religion of the temper: the seventh, the religion of the body: the eighth, the religion of the hand: the ninth, the religion of the tongue: the tenth, the religion of the heart. But antecedently to the Law in any of its aspects, there is a question of deep interest and importance, viz. From whom came it? The reasons for obedience to it come very largely out of the answer to be given to that question. Now, the words in ch. v. 6, which precede the Law itself, are not merely a preface *to* it, they are at once the basis of it and the reason for obedience to it. And these words should be opened up clearly in every case where the Decalogue is about to be expounded. *The* Law is not set on *law,* but on *grace!* For observe—

I. HERE IS A SPECIAL VIEW OF GOD PRESENTED TO THE PEOPLE TO DRAW FORTH THEIR ATTENTION AND WIN THEIR ALLEGIANCE. "*Thy* God." The Hebrews were never expected to believe in, obey, or love an absolutely unrelated Being. THERE IS

NO SUCH BEING! God is related to all the creatures he has made. Hence our knowledge of him is not unreal, because it is relative; but real, because in knowing God's relations to us, we, so far, know him as he is. God was Israel's Redeemer. He had redeemed them that they might be his. He would have the entire life of his redeemed ones spent in covenant relationship with him. Hence he sets his own Law on the basis of those relations. And so it is now. We are not expected to love a Being whose relations to us are doubtful or obscure, or whose mind and will towards us are unknown. We love *because* he first loved us.

II. THE VARIED ASPECTS OF CHRISTIAN TRUTH ARE SET UPON A LIKE BASIS, AND HAVE IN IT THEIR REASON AND POWER. The following suggestions may be developed largely with great advantage. 1. The conception of law is materially changed when we know that it comes from One who loves us infinitely, and cares for us with a tender care. This gives sweetness to the command. We are "under law to Christ." 2. "The Lord *thy* God;" that gives the worship of God its charm. 3. This is the truth which is objectively disclosed by the Incarnation. 4. It is the truth which the Holy Ghost graves on the hearts of the saints (Rom. viii. 15). 5. This truth shows us that real religion is love responding to love (1 John iv. 19). 6. It gives a manifest ground for trust. We *know* whom we have believed. 7. It gives a charm to every precept. 8. It gives meaning to every trial (ch. viii. 5). 9. It is in the light of this truth that prayer becomes possible, and is seen to be reasonable. 10. This gives a solemn aspect to our responsibility (Ps. lxxxi. 10; Amos iv. 12; Heb. iv. 13). 11. The fuller understanding of the words, "My God," will be the result of ripeness in grace (Zech. xiii. 9; Isa. xli. 10—20). 12. This is pre-eminently the truth which gives its certainty and its glow to the hope of future glory (Mark xii. 26; Heb. xi. 16; Rev. xxi. 3, 7).

III. SEEING THE WIDE BEARING AND VAST IMPORTANCE OF THE TRUTH IN THE TEXT, WHAT SHOULD BE WITH US ITS PRACTICAL OUTCOME? 1. Seeing the fearful havoc agnosticism would make, if it should ever come to govern human thinking,[1] let us show men: (1) That a God *out of relation* to us does *not* exist. (2) That the one God *is* related to us as Creator, etc. (3) That his varied relations are explicitly revealed, specially through the Son and through the Holy Ghost. (4) That these relations are to be apprehended by our moral and spiritual nature, and not by the intellect alone. It should never make us stagger that, after getting to the very outer rim of natural knowledge, men should look out on an awful blank, and call it "the great unknown." It shows us only that they cannot find God *in that way*—not that there is no way of finding God, still less that God cannot find us or make his communications intelligible to us. Do not let us suffer men to think that God cannot be found because no one can find him out to perfection! He is *our* God. 2. Since God is *our* God, let us cultivate fellowship with him. It is for this purpose he hath revealed himself, that we may come to him (1 John i. 1—3; Heb. x. 19—22). 3. Let us seek to realize the blessedness of a known and happy relationship to God, enjoyed through Christ, by the Spirit, in a life of penitence, faith, devotion, and love (Isa. lxi. 10; 1 Chron. xii. 18; Ps. lxviii. 28; xlvi. 1; xviii. 29; cxlvi. 5). 4. Let faith in the love of *our* God fill up our duties with glorious meaning, and make the discharge of them a delight (ch. vi. 5; xxviii. 58; Lev. xxv. 38; xi. 45; Isa. xli. 10; Jer. iii. 13; Micah vi. 8; Rom. xii. 1). 5. Let the fact that God is *our* God create, confirm, and perpetuate our assurance of immortal blessedness. See the wonderful words in Matt. xxii. 31, 32; Heb. xi. 16. As if God would be ashamed to be called *our* God, if he did not mean to do something worthy of the name! Wondrous grace! How perfect the reconciliation effected by Christ, to bring together the holy God and sinful men in blest accord and union for ever!

Ver. 7.—*The first commandment. God the sole object of worship.* "Thou shalt have none other gods before me." So runs the first of the ten commandments. (For the specific direction of each, see enumeration in Homily on ver. 6; for the completeness of the whole, see Homily on vers. 22—33.) It has been well observed, in reference to the delivery of the ten commandments, that "this is the only authentic case in the history of the

---

[1] See this vividly illustrated in a poem by Mr. Buchanan, entitled, 'Justinian,' *Contemporary Review*, January, 1880.

world of a newly formed nation receiving at once, and from one legislator, a complete code of laws for the direction of their whole future life." They are, in outline, the Old Testament revelation of God's will. If any one would wish a clear statement of Old Testament morality, he should be referred to these sayings, or to our Saviour's brief epitome of them. We should do very wrongly if we expounded the Decalogue *merely* as the Hebrews might have done at the time it first was given. Comparison of corresponding or parallel passages in the New Testament will help us in the exposition and enforcement of these ten words. A reference to Matt. v. 17—20; xv. 1—9; xix. 16—19; xxii. 36—40; Luke x. 25—28; xvi. 31; John v. 46, 47, will help 'to show what regard our Lord paid to the Mosaic Law. Bearing this in mind, we will endeavour now to sketch in outline an exposition of the first commandment, using the clearer teaching of the gospel to give us any additional light and force in so doing. Thus saith the Lord, "Thou shalt have none other gods before me."

I. THIS COMMAND AT ONCE SETS ASIDE THE CLAIMS OF ANY OTHER SUPPOSED GODS. (Cf. ch. iv. 19; Exod. xxiii. 24, 25.) "None other gods before me," *i.e.* "over against me. I will suffer no rival deity; you must worship no other god," etc. Does, then, the command permit Israel to suppose that there *is* any other god whom they could possibly worship? Not by any means. It recognizes the fact of the existence of idolatry round about them. According to the heathen conception, there were gods many and lords many. Israel was not to regard one of all the gods adored by the heathen. This is the very gracious way in which our Father in heaven would help his children in those young days to higher thoughts about himself. Is it not always the case with young children now? They have to be told what they may or may not do, and as they get older they will discover the *reason.* *Indoctrinate into dogma by means of precept.* This was the way God taught Israel "when he was a child," by putting *this* precept in the front. Had Moses discoursed to the people on the philosophic excellence of monotheism, and so on, he would have been virtually speaking in an unknown tongue. They would not have caught a glimpse of his meaning; but they could understand *this.* And the faithful obedience to this precept would be for them the very surest way of learning the doctrine which lay beneath it. By serving *only* one God, they would best come to learn that there was no god but *the One.* But further. This commandment is much more than a mere prohibition of what we usually call idolatry. It is a declaration of the Divine intolerance of any rival in the heart. Though we acknowledge that there is but one God, yet that is practically the idol of our hearts which engrosses our dearest affections, and with a view to which we shape our lives. God wants the innermost sanctuary of our hearts to be sacredly reserved for him.

II. THE PEOPLE WERE TO DRAW OFF THEIR REGARD FROM OTHER GODS, THAT ALL THE POWERS OF THEIR SOULS MIGHT BE CONCENTRATED ON GOD. (See ch. vi. 5.) In our text, the form is negative; the intent is positive. They are to know *none but* God, that they may concentrate all their strength *on* God. In fact, the command is equivalent to this: "Let all your personal, family, social, national life be regulated completely by the commandments of your God. And let this be done from love." Is it asked, "Is this practicable? Can a man put forth all his strength for God when his energy is absorbed in trade?" We answer, "Yes; by regulating his business rightly, as God wills." "Can a mother put forth all her strength on loving God, when the care of her family is taxing and even straining all her powers?" We answer, "Yes; by training her children for God." And so on in each one of life's tasks.

III. THIS IS SET ON GROUNDS OF TENDER APPEAL. (See the preceding Homily.) God does not say, "When you love me supremely I will redeem you from Egypt;" but "I *have* redeemed you, therefore yield me your all." The religions of man go out to an unrevealed Being, if perchance he may be propitiated. Scriptural religion is the response of the heart of man to the revealed love of the Infinite One. Hence the gospel claim is, in substance, like the Mosaic, although its form is new, and the view we get of Divine love is larger (see Rom. xii. 1). In both, duty is the same : the whole heart of man is demanded for God. But note the advance in light, tenderness, and strength in (1) the mercies of God; (2) the "beseeching" tone; (3) the "consecration of a living sacrifice" asked; (4) the reason given, "Your reasonable service." Here is the difference in the method of the gospel.

IV. THIS PRECEPT IS HERE SET IN THE FOREFRONT OF ISRAEL'S NATIONAL LAWS.

It was the law for each one's life. It was the rule for all. In their legislation, the supreme feature was to be the national recognition of God. And even now, yea, ever, so far as the legislation of any people is based on righteousness, so far as that legislation recognizes the rights of the Great Supreme, so far as a people are loyal to God, to that extent will there be the surest guarantee for individual, family, social, and national prosperity. If ever a nation *as such* should "break his bands asunder," and inaugurate an age of reason *versus* faith, instead of a reasonable faith, the reign of terror would not be far off. And it is owing to the supreme importance of thus launching into the world a nation with God for its Lord, and righteousness for its law, that the open transgression of this first commandment was so severely punished, as being a crime against the State as well as a sin against God (ch. xiii. 7—12, 13—18; xvii. 2—7). (The frequent phrase "cut off" does not refer to punishment in another life, but to a man's being "cut off" from the congregation.) And even now fidelity to God is the supreme condition of a nation's well-being; and that man is playing foully with the highest interests of a people, who is seeking to undermine its allegiance to heaven.

V. Is this the Law? Then let us make three uses of it. 1. As a *touchstone*. It reveals guilt. The *need* of any such command is a very humiliating fact. "The law is not made for a righteous man." "By law is the knowledge of sin." This precept (1) discloses the world's sin. (2) It shows the deep root that sin had in the natures even of the freed people, that they should need such legislation to grave this precept on their hearts. (3) It shows *our* sin, that we should need the written Law. If we were what we ought to be, we should do God's will spontaneously without needing a written law at all! 2. As a *judge*. This being the Law, we see how it is that as by law we stand convicted, so by it we stand condemned, "subject to the sentence of God," for failures innumerable; and our guilt is the greater, since he who asks our heart reveals his own love that he may call forth ours. This Law is a perpetual, silent accuser (see John v. 45). 3. *As a child-guide to Christ* (see Gal. iii. 24, Greek). God only is greater than law. And he alone can restore those who, having broken law, must needs, in the ordinary course of things, be regarded and dealt with as lawbreakers. For restoration, three things are required: (1) Forgiveness; (2) justification; (3) re-creation. Bare Law does not provide for either of these, but God in his Law has witnessed concerning this great restorative scheme. So says Paul in Rom. iii. 21, "But now there has been manifested a righteousness of God apart from law, being witnessed by the Law and the prophets," etc. So in Rom. i. 16, 17, "I am not ashamed of the gospel of Christ, . . . for therein there is revealed a righteousness of God by faith, with a view to [the production of] faith." By believing in Christ, forgiveness is sure to the penitent, and grace re-creates the man, writing the Law on the heart, so that we obey and love God, not because God says we must, but because we are remade so that we can do nothing else. And what we need is to have our whole nature so reset by Divine grace, that we shall instinctively see God's will and do it, without needing any precept at all. As by the regenerative efficacy of the Holy Ghost we attain to this, shall we understand what it is to do the will of God on earth, "even as it is done in heaven."

Vers. 8—10.—*The second commandment. The spirituality of Divine worship.* It is sometimes said that there is a reason attached to this second commandment. It is scarcely accurate to affirm that. There is a double *sanction* attached to it to enforce it, but there is no mention made here of a *reason*, strictly so called. We will, however, incorporate in this Homily the true reason which underlies this precept. But we shall have to go to the New Testament for the clearest statement of that. Let us then, in connection with the above, ask the reader to turn to John iv. 24, in which he will find a deep reason for the second commandment. We will first of all, as briefly as we can consistently with clearness, open up the contents of this command, and will then endeavour to unfold the double sanction by which it is guarded.

I. Its contents. The *first* commandment claims for Jehovah alone the love and worship of the people. The *second* warns off from any mode of worship which would bear a resemblance to or which would be a compromise with idolatry. While Israel was in Egypt, there had been a general worship on the part of the Egyptians, of bird, beast, and reptile, not for their own sake, but as representing some attribute of the invisible God.

The forms of Egyptian worship, the names of Pasht, Osiris, etc., must be done away with. *No representation* of the object of worship was to be allowed. However much men might have pleaded that sense was an aid to faith, the stern "Thou shalt not" peremptorily barred the way. We know the reason *why,* as they in their childhood did not. God is spirit. Being spirit, it is only by spirit that he can be approached. No *merely* bodily act can possibly be worship. Further, neither God nor any one of his attributes can be represented by any physical form. Whatever idea of Jehovah may be gained or retained through impressions derived from beholding a sensible object with the bodily eye, will be an idea representing *it,* not *him.* It will be a thought of God formed by the image and limited by it—not the true thought given by revelation. Obviously, however, this command did not forbid decorative designs in the tabernacle or the temple (cf. Exod. xxv. 18, 20, 34; xxvi. 32; Numb. xxi. 8, 9; 1 Kings vii. 25; x. 20). But never were any creature-forms allowed, either as objects of worship or as aids to it. Nor can we read through Hebrew history without seeing how much need there was of such a command. Ere long, the people were dancing round the golden calf! And in the days of Jeroboam two calves were set up—one in Bethel, another in Dan. But surely the history of Christendom is even a sadder one than that of the Hebrews. Ere four centuries of the Christian era had passed away, how did the Christian Church lapse into repeated breaches of this law! "An enormous train of different superstitions was gradually substituted in the place of true religion and genuine piety. . . . Images were not as yet very common. But it is certain that the worship of the martyrs was modelled by degrees according to the religious services that were paid to the gods before the coming of Christ."[1] It is true, indeed, that in 726 A.D. Leo III. issued an ordinance forbidding the use of images in churches, as heathenish and heretical, and a Council of Constantinople, in 754 A.D., sanctioned that condemnation. Another Council, which met at Nice in 789 A.D., declared the previous Council heretical, and ordained the worship of pictures in churches. The decisions of this Council were rejected at a Council in Frankfort, in 794 A.D. Also at another in Constantinople, in 815 A.D., all worshipping of pictures and images was forbidden. In 869 A.D. the iconoclasts were condemned. Thomas Aquinas, in the thirteenth century, affirmed a threefold use of images, and declared that like homage is due to the image of Christ as to Christ himself! And we know but too well what the later history of Rome has been, how pagan rites have become more and more mingled with Christian service. The Saviour is approached through the crucifix, and fed upon through the bread; and, as if blind to the warnings of history, ritualism openly proclaims that the best exposition of doctrine is that which meets the eye rather than the ear. Perhaps it is not to be wondered at, that in Roman Catholic catechisms the second commandment *is left out;* and not even Luther was sufficient of a reformer to restore the missing law in his catechism—an easy way, indeed, of blinding the people to the evil of a mistaken ritual, to *leave out* the authoritative command, obedience to which would render such evil impossible!

II. THE DOUBLE SANCTION ATTACHED TO THIS LAW. The first is drawn from the Divine nature, the second from the Divine administration. 1. *From the Divine nature.* "I the Lord thy God am a jealous God." "They that worship him *must* worship him in spirit and in truth." God is jealous: (1) For *truth* in his worship. He would have us *think* of him as glorious in power, wisdom, righteousness, holiness, and love. Our thoughts of God can be but limited at the best. They need not be untrue. But untrue and dishonouring to him they certainly will be if we come at them through the means of any graven image. We do not even except the crucifix. It represents the bodily form of Christ. It may represent the nails, the wounds, the spear, the crown of thorns, the pain-crushed brow; and we confess it may be possible, by looking at these physical marks, to receive so vivid an impression of the physical suffering that we may be wrought up to agony in thinking of it! But even then this is only knowing Christ after the flesh; it is making an idol of his humanity; and in sympathy with the anguish of his bodily woes, we may altogether miss the acting of faith in that atoning sacrifice which lay among the things unseen and eternal! (2) For *spirit* in his worship. The worship paid to a spiritual Being is nothing if it be not spiritual worship. But in the endless bowings and prostrations, genuflexions, cross-

---

[1] Mosheim, vol. i. p. 366.

markings, and waving of the body at the word " Jesus," there is, at least in appearance, a taking for granted that bodily postures are spiritual attitudes. (3) God would have man lifted up to a higher level by the worship of him. But the sorry record in history of the breaches of the second law shows us four transitions: (a) An object which at first represents the Being who is worshipped, comes at length to be worshipped.[1] (b) Worship paid through the body will sink to merely bodily worship. (c) When the lofty platform of spiritual worship is quitted, religious service will inevitably lose its meaning. Sense first comes as " an aid to faith," and then is put in the place of it! (d) When this is the case, the vitalizing force of religion is gone, and man, sinking in religious vitality, sinks also in morality (see Jer. vii. for an illustration of this in the Hebrew people; see Rom. i. for illustrations of it in the Gentile world). 2. *From the Divine administration.* " Visiting the iniquities," etc. It would not have seemed wonderful to have found this second sanction appended to such sins as murder, adultery, etc.; but how is it that it follows on so apparently slight an offence as the use of graven images? *Because of the sure and inevitable quadruple transition already referred to.* He who comes to lose the life of religion will, so far, be undermining the foundations of morality, not only for himself, but for those who come after him. (1) What a man is, and what his family are or may be, are regarded as bound up together by an unalterable law of God. (2) Evil follows on from generation to generation. A ghastly inheritance to hand down—formalism and idolatry! (3) But if a man maintains the true spiritual worship of God in his family, that too will be handed down to those who follow him as a priceless heritage; not only to those who come in the physical line: our Lord's words in John viii. should teach us to look beyond that. (4) In the mercy of God the influence of a man's *good* is more lasting than the influence of his evil. Evil—to third or fourth generation. Good—to thousands [of generations]. The influence of Paul, *e.g.* at this moment, is prodigious; that of Nero is *nil.* *Learn, in conclusion:* 1. We receive an influence from the generations which preceded us; we shall transmit one to the generations that will follow. (We do not think this latter consideration is sufficiently pressed on the people, either on its physiological or on its spiritual side.) 2 Whoever wishes to ensure a prolonged influence that shall blessedly affect generations to come, let him bend all his force to the upholding of the worship of God in purity, in spirit, in truth. So much depends on this. The weal of the land in which we dwell is dependent thereon. Oh! for our own sakes, for our country's sake, for our children's sakes, let us contend earnestly for the maintenance of the worship of God in simplicity and in truth!

Ver. 11.—*The third commandment. Reverent regard for the Divine Name.* The " Name" of God is the form of speech for God himself. " To take" the Name of God means " to take it up"—to use it in any way, which may be done either by speaking *to* him, *of* him, *for* him, or *against* him. " To take up this Name in vain" means to take it up falsely or vainly. And inasmuch as it has been so grievously common to use the Name of God profanely in oaths, this third commandment has come to be regarded chiefly as a prohibition against swearing. It is *that,* but it is a great deal more. This commandment is " exceeding broad." It may be wronged, not only by an undue limitation of it, but also by a too slavish adherence to the letter of it ; *e.g.* according to the teaching of the rabbis, certain oaths were harmless if the Name of God was not specifically mentioned in them (cf. Matt. xxiii. 16—22). Further, the expression " in vain" was interpreted as meaning " if you take an oath you must fulfil it ; " take as many oaths as you please, so long as you do not break them, and thus turn them into falsehood. The effect of this cold and superficial teaching of the rabbis was twofold. It created artificial distinctions which our Saviour did not recognize, and it obliterated such as were of great importance in his eye. It is needful for us, then, to be guided by the spirit of our Lord's teaching, if we would rightly develop this third law. Since our Saviour in his Sermon on the Mount removed the glosses with which the rabbis had overlain the Law and restored it to its pristine clearness and purity.

I. WHAT IS FORBIDDEN BY THIS THIRD COMMANDMENT ? We are all aware that some have regarded our Saviour's words, " Swear not at all," as prohibitive of solemn oath-

---

[1] See Dr. R. W. Dale's book, 'The Ten Commandments,' pp. 48, 49.

taking in a court of justice. We cherish all respect for those who so regard them, but we cannot view them in this light, for the following reasons: (1) The occasion on which our Lord uses the words seems to refer rather to habits in private life. (2) Christ and his apostles solemnly appealed to Heaven. (3) In Heb. vi. the oath of God is spoken of by the sacred writer, and we cannot suppose this would have been if *all* oath-taking were wrong. We cannot think that, even by way of accommodation, the Most High would represent himself as doing that which it would be always wrong for his creatures to do. (4) In prophetic language there is predicted a swearing by the Name of God, which is regarded as obviously right (Isa. xlv. 23; see also ch. vi. 14). These reasons seem to us to set the matter entirely at rest. And the view that Christ was referring to men's ordinary conversation when he said, "Swear not at all," is confirmed by Matt. v. 37; the meaning of which evidently is: "If it is needful for you to interlard your conversation with sundry adjurations, you are the victims of a spirit of falsehood which has 'the evil one' for its father!" Further, this precept covers a far wider range than that of swearing. It forbids any "taking up" of the Divine Name which is not true as to loyalty of purpose, actual fact, and after-fulfilment. This precept manifestly prohibits: 1. *All scoffing at sacred things;* not merely at the *word* "God," or at the doctrine of the Divine existence, but ridiculing the Bible as the Book of God, the sabbath as the day of God, Christians as the people of God, and religion as obedience to God. The mild and supercilious scorn of modern scepticism is equally a violation of this precept—it tramples under foot the Son of God. 2. *Perjury is another form of violation of this command.* The idea of swearing is that of calling God to witness; and to invoke that great and awful Name to witness a lie is one of the most grievous breaches of this law. 3. *Profanity also is here forbidden,* i.e. taking the Name of God on the lips on every trifling occasion. This is now thought, as indeed it is, ungentlemanly, to a far greater extent than was the case fifty years ago. So far well. Only let us take care that for a custom to be *out of fashion,* does not act with us more powerfully than its offensiveness to God, in inducing us to give it up! Some are more concerned at a hole in their manners than at a breach of morals. These things ought not so to be. 4. *Frivolity in reference to Divine things is a transgression of this command.* This is by no means to be confounded either with scoffing or with profanity. It may be found where there is great reverence for God, great kindness of heart, combined with an excessive fondness for raising a laugh. And where this is the case, even sacred things are but too seldom exempt from frivolous treatment. We recall some acquaintance whose chief, yea, whose only apparent fault, was the extreme tendency to turn everything into a joke, even things most sacred. Many were ready to excuse the frivolity for the sake of the talent it revealed. But they are "nowhere" now. Their levity was their ruin. Wit and humour have indeed a place of no mean value in social life. Social evils are often exposed more effectively in scorn and satire than in graver speeches. But there is no tendency of any man which needs to be more wisely cultured, more carefully and prayerfully guarded, and more conscientiously directed, than that to which we are now referring. Apart from this, there is exceedingly great danger of its leading to the "taking the Name of God in vain." 5. There may be a breach of this commandment without frivolity (as usually understood), even where there is no sense of humour and no talent for witticisms, in the indulgence of a vicious habit, much more easily formed than broken off, of *interlarding the conversation with certain well-known epithets.* We know what these were in Christ's time (see Matt. xxiii. 16—22; v. 33—36). This is conceited talk, and it is sinful talk. 6. *False teaching for God breaks this law* (see Jer. xxiii. 21—24, 31). There are several ways by which, in teaching others, the Name of God may be taken falsely. Either (1) by declaring as God's what he has *not* said; or by (2) denying what he *has* said; or (3) by calling in question the truth of what he has spoken. The first was common in the days of Jeremiah; the second and third are at once more ancient and more modern. *Whenever any ambassador for God gives his own thoughts as if they were God's message,* he is taking the Name of God in vain. Or if a man, while professing to speak for God, is speaking with the desire to exalt himself, he is guilty of the same sin. 7. *Hollowness and formality in the professed worship of God are breaches of the third commandment.* We take God's Name in vain if we sing "the songs of Zion" with a vacant heart, or outwardly join in the prayers of the sanctuary without devotion in the soul (Ezek. xxxiii. 30, 31; Isa. xxix. 13). Oh, the number of times we have been on our knees and have used the Name of God in "indolent vacuity of thought"! "Who is able to stand before this holy Lord God?" 8. *We may break this commandment by vowing unto God, and then not fulfilling the vow.* When at the Lord's table, we take the sacramental oath of obedience to our Great Commander, and if we are not true to that, we add sin to sin by "taking the Name of God in vain."

II. How is this precept guarded? "The Lord will not hold him guiltless," etc. God may or may not mark this sin by visitations of temporal judgment; there are many cases in which levity has been the ruin of a man, even temporally. But the probability is that the more occult and deceptive forms of this sin will leave no appreciable mark on a man's earthly career. The marking of the guilt will be between God and a man's own soul. Hollow prayers bring no blessing; empty worship no growth in grace. Violated vows will bring down the displeasure of God. If God were to visit upon us all the sins of unreality and formalism, of mechanical routine, and of heartless work in his service, we should be lost men! "God often sees more in our prayers to disgust him than to please him," says Charnock. The Lord pardon the iniquity of our holy things!

III. How should this precept be used? 1. *As a probe.* Possibly, when a preacher takes this text, some may say, "We don't need that. We never break God's law so!" Possibly not, in the conventional sense in which the text is often used now. But what about that conversation laden with frivolity? What about that lesson which had more of self than of God in it? What about the songs of the sanctuary, enjoyed for the sake of the music, without a thought of the words? What about the forgotten vows? Surely we can all recall so many breaches of this third commandment that, if we had not a pardoning God, we should be shut up in despair! 2. *To quicken to penitence.* By so much as our conviction is deep that we have broken this commandment a thousand times, by so much should our penitence be deep *and definite* before God. 3. *To lead us to earnest entreaties for forgiveness.* If we were not permitted to ask this, it would be all over with us, even if the third commandment were the whole of the Law. 4. *To lead to fervent prayer for daily heart-renewal.* "Out of the abundance of the heart the mouth speaketh." If the heart is right the tongue will be right. "If a man offend not in word, the same is a perfect man." Well may we pray that every word we speak may be conformed *to truth (for in each of the eight ways named above there is a violation of truth).* When our heart, thoughts, words, and deeds are in harmony with God's nature and will, then shall we be true to the duty implied, and free from the sin forbidden, in the third commandment.

Vers. 12—15.—*The sabbath, or a rest-day for man.* (For a notice of the variations between the wording of this command in Exod. xx. and in this chapter, see Exposition.) No Christian preacher could wisely deal homiletically with the question of the Divine intent in the appointment of a seventh-day rest, without noting, in connection with our text, the teaching of our Lord and his apostles thereon. In developing the true doctrine and use of our rest day, let us—

I. Indicate several principles from which our conception of the Hebrew sabbath must start. The Hebrew sabbath has a far-back look. "The seventh day is the sabbath of the Lord thy God." What spaces of time the "six days" represent we may perhaps never know in this life. One thing is clear—a "day" of Divine action *must* be indefinitely longer than one of man's days. This far-back look, moreover, reveals to us a method of Divine work, after which ours is to be modelled. As man's nature is made in God's image, so our time is to be portioned out after God's order. Further, the basis of the right observance of the day is that of "*rest.*" The word "sabbath" means that; whatever else may have been connected with the day, the notion of *rest* lay beneath all. While the Hebrews were to regard the observance of the day as a part of their covenanted duty as a nation, yet the rest was not for them as Hebrews only, but as *men.* The sabbath was made *for man.* Work was to be laid aside, that man might give himself up to *a holy and happy day of rest and worship.* With a view, moreover, to securing all this, the work of the six other days was to be arranged.

II. The subsequent precepts are all in the same direction. Never is there anything out of harmony with this benign command to rest (see Exod. xvi. 29 ; xxiii. 9—13 ; xxxi. 13 ; xxxiv. 21 ; xxxv. 1—3 ; Lev. xix. 3, 30 ; xxxiii. 3 ; xxvi. 2 ; Numb. xv. 32—36). Of such importance to the good of the people was their rest day, that if a man attempted to turn it into a day of common work, he was to be stoned ! Severity to the one was a guard of mercy round all ! If the people could not or would not guard their rest day for themselves, the great Lord who gave it would shield it for them all ! In course of time these precepts were grievously disobeyed, either by an entire neglect of the day, or by a merely *formal* observance of it (2 Chron. xxxvi. 21 ; Neh. ix. 14 ; x. 31 ; xiii. 15, 16 ; Isa. i. 13 ; lvi. 2 ; lviii. 13 ; Jer. xvii. 19—27 ; Ezek. xx. 12, 13 ; xxii. 8, 26). Later on, when Jesus Christ came, many had lost the spirit of the day in the letter ; so that the day which was given to man as a boon of mercy had come to be a chafing yoke and a grievous burden. Consequently, *not even Jesus Christ was a sufficiently strict sabbath-keeper for the Pharisees* (Matt. xii. 1—8 ; Mark ii. 23—28 ; iii. 1—5 ; Luke xiii. 10—17 ; John v. 1—16 ; vii. 23, 24). Hence, Jesus in his teaching respecting the sabbath, did not *divert it from,* but *restored it to,* its original intent. The sabbath *as God made it,* was restful, beautiful, and *free.* As rabbinical teaching had *perverted* it, it was rigid and burdensome. Men came to be on the sabbath under a hard yoke ; but it was *man's* yoke, not God's (see in Dr. Geikie's ' Life of Christ ' abundant illustrations of this).

III. NEW TESTAMENT INDICATIONS VARY IN FORM BUT ACCORD IN SPIRIT. We find in the New Testament some passages which indicate some observance of the *first* day of the week (John xx. 19—26 ; Acts xx. 7 ; 1 Cor. xvi. 2 ; Rev. i. 10). It is remarkable how few there are of such. We have no specific precept to direct us with regard to a Christian sabbath. There is nothing *very* clear on the matter, either in the Gospels or the Epistles. Judaism is waning ; what is *peculiar to it* dies away ; what is world-wide and for humanity, lives. We seem to see the seventh day receding from our gaze, its lustre fades and is lost in the brightness of the first day. There is a dissolving view. Winter is succeeded by spring. Here is something which has Christ's sanction and apostolic warrant, viz. meeting on the first day. *It* is the day of religious assembling, the day of " breaking bread." The God of Sinai has invested the Son of man with all power in heaven and in earth. He is the Lord of the sabbath. Memories of the great deliverance wrought by him eclipse those of the deliverance from Egypt. Wherefore, ever after, rest-day becomes " *the Lord's* day." Ignatius says, " Let every friend of Christ celebrate the Lord's day." Justin Martyr, " On the Lord's day, all Christians in the city and in the country assemble together, because that is the day of the Lord's resurrection." Tertullian, " The Lord's day is the holy day of the Christian Church. So gradually, however, did the seventh-day sabbath change into the first-day rest, that we find for a while *both* days observed. Accordingly we find, in ' The Apostolic Constitution,' both days named as days for the assembling of the Church ; that on the sabbath *and* on the Sunday the slaves should rest from their labours, and attend church with the rest to hear the sermon. But as the new skin is forming under the surface, the old is getting looser and looser. Yet for a time, *there are two coverings.* Soon, however, the old is shuffled off, and only the new is seen. The sabbath is lost, but rest-day reappears as *the Lord's day* !

IV. HOW STANDS THE REST-DAY NOW ? The fourth commandment had a natural basis and a religious one. It gave a day of rest for man *as man,* and, as such, has never been repealed. God has never taken away the world's rest-day. It is ours still—a priceless heritage. The *religious* side of the Hebrew sabbath, though abolished *so far as the observance of Jewish rites is concerned,* was at once taken up by the Christian Church, and Christians have, as we well know, by meeting for worship on the first day, recognized the principle of a *world's rest-day,* and have used it for the higher purposes of the kingdom of heaven. And now to us the Lord's day is (1) our day of rest from earthly toil ; (2) the day of hallowed calm ; (3) of richest memory ; (4) of united worship ; (5) of mutual recognition of our common relationship to one God and Saviour ; (6) of spiritual training ; (7) of holiest service for the Master ; (8) of noblest outlook (see Dr. R. W. Hamilton's ' Horæ Sabbaticæ ').

V. WHAT IS OUR DUTY WITH REGARD TO OUR REST-DAY ? 1. As men, let us regard it as an inestimable boon for the right use of which we are responsible to God. We are so made, as to our physical constitution, that we *require* one day's rest in seven. Then let us *take* the rest gratefully. 2. As citizens, we have a trust to guard for our fellow-countrymen. Legislation can never direct a man how to spend his rest-day, but it may do something to guard it for him. While we use the rest wisely, so that it makes us not only brisker animals, but holier men, let us also give others the rest. 3. As Christians, we have a sacred day for sanctuary worship, and for home and school instruction. We should do everything to show the young that the Sunday is a bright, light, cheery day, remembering that whatever helps best to *health, rest, worship, and holiness is*, and *always has been*, lawful on the sabbath day. 4. As workers for God, the rest day is our glorious day of special service for Christ and for souls, in the very fatigue of which the spirit finds refreshment. Then surely we enter into the Master's spirit. Our meat is to do the will of him who hath sent us, and to finish his work.

Ver. 16.—*The fifth commandment. Honour due to parents; or, the religion of home life.* Many are the passages in the Word of God which speak of or refer to the duty of children to their parents; *e.g.* Exod. xxi. 15, 17; Lev. xix. 3; xx. 9; ch. xxi. 18—21; xxvii. 16; Ps. lxxviii. 5—8; Prov. x. 1; xiii. 1; xx. 20; xxiii. 22; xxx. 17; Jer. xxxv. 18; Ezek. xxii. 7; Matt. xv. 4—9; Col. iii. 20. It is worthy of careful noting, that when God would launch forth into the world a new national life, he lays great stress on the recognition of and regard to *family sacredness.* At the outset of the redemption from Egypt, family life was specially hallowed (cf. Exod. xii. 24—27; xiii. 8, 9). The covenant of circumcision handed down from Abraham was to be observed. Children were to be sealed as the Lord's, and brought up in his fear. That is here assumed. It was the understood law. And now, when a moral code for the nation and for the world for all time is to be laid down, the very next precept to those relating immediately to the honour due to God himself, is this—"Honour thy father and thy mother." Not, indeed, that they were to render them a blind obedience, for see Ezek. xx. 18, 19. If the parents were bad, the best honour the children can render them is to become better than they were. So that we may note, once for all, in passing, that the commandment recognizes it as incumbent on parents to see that their lives and rules are such as their children *can* honour, and that *their* precepts accord with those of the Father of spirits. Throughout our homiletic application of this fifth commandment, we shall assume this to be the case. It is, indeed, understood by many, that this command is to be regarded not only as requiring obedience in the family, but "as requiring the preserving the honour and performing the duties belonging to every one, in their several places and relations, as superiors, inferiors, or equals;" and as forbidding "the neglecting of or doing anything against the honour and duty which belongeth to every one, in their several places and relations." Doubtless this is so. But there is quite as much as we can compass in the brief space afforded us, in the specific duty named in the text. Let us—

I. INQUIRE IN WHAT WAYS THIS PRECEPT MAY BE FULFILLED. 1. During the earlier stages of life, while needing the fostering care and sheltering love of the home, *implicit obedience* is a child's first duty. We not only say that it is next to his duty to God, but that it is a *part of it.* The parent's precepts may be distasteful, even rigid, but if they are right, it is the child's part implicitly to obey. 2. *Honouring* parents is the form which obedience will take when the child is growing up towards manhood. No wise parent would think of directing a lad of sixteen as closely as he would a child of six years; at the same time, though the father may give him more liberty, it may not be either wise or right on the son's part to *take* all the liberty which is given. At that age his own sense of honour and right ought to be sufficiently strong to guide him; and respect and reverence for his parents will create a loyal regard to their wishes when once they are known, and will lead him to deny himself a great deal that might be gratifying to him, rather than cause pain to or cross the wishes of those to whom he owes his life. Rude words to a parent, "answering again," disputing his rule in the house, will be utterly out of the question where a youth wishes to live in the fear of God. 3. Supporting them may become a duty. There will come a time, if the parents are spared to see their children grow up in life, when they will lean on the children, rather than the children on them. If the children are worthy, they will *let* their parents lean on them, and will show them that they can be as faithful to their parents in their weakness, as the parents when in their strength were to them. 4. Becoming an honour to them is another way of honouring them, *i.e.* by living so that they can feel proud of what their children *are*, quite apart from what they do. If a father can say, "My son never gave me an uneasy thought about him," that is such a testimony as a son might well wish him to be able to bear. 5. By guarding very jealously the sacredness and purity of England's family life, the commandment may be obeyed. We may honour our parents by honouring that holy marriage tie which made them what they were to us. 6. By guarding and handing down to others the holy faith in which they have trained us (Ps. lxxviii. 1—8 ; 1 Chron. xxviii. 9). We may well desire to honour them by taking on our lips that dear Name which gladdened them in life and sustained them in death. 7. There is another way of honouring parents which we would there were no occasion to name. But there is a drift clearly to be discerned in some directions of English life, which makes a warning imperative (see Matt. xv. 1—9). The Jewish rabbis put their Church and their rabbinical rules between a child and his parents. Modern (so-called) priests are doing the same now. Hence this rule : Honour your parents by refusing to let any priest edge his way in between you and them. In Divine institutions, the priest is *nowhere* compared with the parent. And under the Christian economy he has no right to be. He is humanity's pest and plague. "Honour thy father and thy mother," and never allow a priest to tamper with the sacredness of home !

II. BY WHAT SPECIAL ARGUMENTS MAY A CHRISTIAN TEACHER ENFORCE THIS DUTY ? 1. Here let us set in the front a reason given by Paul in Eph. vi. 1, "It is right (δικαιον)." There is another word which is usually translated "right," viz. ευθυς, which is the equivalent of "straightforward." But the word here used is "just." Obedience to parents is simply a piece of bare justice. For, consider how much we owe them. When we first came into being their care and watchfulness guarded and supplied us long ere we knew aught. They thought us, perhaps, something *wonderful*, when no one else thought anything of the kind, save in the reverse sense. Ought not all this to be repaid ? 2. It is well-pleasing to the Lord. He has in this " set us an example, that we should follow his steps." 3. There is a specific promise made to the obedient and loyal, *as such*, " That it may go well with thee," etc. In the culture of home obedience will be found a strong safeguard of character. Vicious excesses will not exhaust. Insubordination and recklessness will not blight life's prospects. Hence *cæt. par.* such a life, being the purest and happiest, will also be the longest. 4. Such home virtue is a contribution of no mean value to the stability of a state. The reference of Moses is to the weal of the nation as well as to that of the home. The downfall of Israel's glory is attributed to two evils: neglect of sabbaths, and making light of father and mother. No nation can prosper without purity in the home. 5. Such virtue brings great joy. "A wise son maketh a glad father." There is joyousness on both sides. This is the beauty with which God's blessing makes the plants of virtue to bloom. It is like the fragrance exhaling from a bed of violets quietly blossoming in a shady lane. 6. The neglect of this will ensure many unavailing regrets on both sides in after life. "A foolish son is the heaviness of his mother." Many an undutiful son, when laying his parents' remains in the grave, would give all he has if he could but call them back, if he could atone for his sin, or could cancel the past ! Disobedience treasures up sorrow. God may and will forgive the sin, when repented of, but the penitent will never forgive himself; he will often moan out, "Thou makest me to possess the iniquities of my youth!" 7. The curse of God will rest on those who are loose and disloyal at home. Richard Knill so regarded this fifth commandment, that he would not even go out as a missionary without his mother's consent. He said, " *I know that God never smiles on a boy that breaks his mother's heart.*" (See Prov. xxx. 17.) And who does not know how often it is proved true, "With what measure ye mete it shall be measured to you again "? Jacob deceived his father, and his sons deceived him. Can any observant man reach middle life without having had oft to make such notes as these : " A " honoured his parents, and honour has attended him. "B" *dis*honoured his parents, and his lamp has gone out in darkness? Though *the* judgment has not yet come, yet there is a judging process of God's providence continually at work. 8. The observance of this rule is the best possible preparation for serving our generation according to the will of God. He who is a blessing in the home will never be a curse out of it ! The habits of self-restraint, of courtesy, of respect to superiors, well learnt and practised at home, will not be thrown off when outside its walls. Men learn to command well by first obeying well. Even Christ's own preparation for active service was found in filial obedience at home; and he is not only our perfect example, who shows us what to do, he is also our omnipotent Saviour, who will give us strength to do it. Be it ours to repent not only of sin in general, but of *the* sin of disobedience to parents. Let us ask his forgiveness as well as theirs, if the latter is yet possible. Let us implore his renewing grace that we may henceforth keep this and every command, not only because it is written in the Book, but because the love of it is graven on our hearts. It will be no small addition to the joy of retrospect, if, as we afterwards look back on our home life, we can think of it as one of filial loyalty on one side and of parental delight on the other!

Ver. 17.— *The sixth commandment. The religion of the temper.* If a preacher were to announce this as a text in one of our Christian congregations, some of his hearers might be disposed to say, "Such a text might be appropriate enough if the preacher were expounding the Word of God to Zulus, but for us civilized, not to say Christianized, people, it is out of place!" Obviously such a remark would be based on an acknowledged fact, that *murder* is one of those sins against God which are also a crime against human law, and that no one in a congregation of ordinary character would be likely to dream of committing it. That is so. But we are apt to forget that even among Christian congregations it was not always so. When Peter is writing to believers, he deems it needful to say, "Let none of you suffer as a *murderer*," etc. And even now, in heathen lands, in many an audience of men just reclaimed from barbarism, it might be necessary for a missionary to preach from this text, adhering to it simply in the negative form, " *Thou shalt not kill.*" In endeavouring now to "open it up" for pulpit use, we would recall to the reader some elementary principles concerning the law already named. 1. That the Law was first given in infantine form. God laid down precepts rather than assigned reasons. 2. That the form in which the Divine Being could put the most effective guard around human life was by a stern and strong prohibition like this, proclaimed amid thunder and lightning, terror and flame. 3. That though the form of the precept is negative, yet it has a positive significance, of such depth and breadth that, even though we may shrink with horror from transgressing the former, it is by no means an elementary stage of Christian character which any one has reached if he attains to the latter. So far were the Jewish rabbis from catching the spirit of this command, that they dealt with it as if the negative prohibitions of the act of murder were the whole of its meaning. Our Lord, in his Sermon on the Mount, shows us how much deeper than this the precept goes (see Matt. v. 21—26). And the Apostle Paul, in Rom. xiii. 9, 10, indicates what positive virtue must be cultivated, the maintenance of which will make it impossible to transgress the sixth commandment. If we include in our Homily a notice of these later teachings, it may appear that, even with all our advances, there is something here for us to study, some holy practice for us yet to strive after, urged upon us by weighty reasons, which, though not presented in the world's childhood, are set in full force in "these last days." Let us, then—

I. LOOK AT THE MEANING OF THIS COMMAND. It is sixfold. 1. It forbids the taking of human life from passionate vindictiveness. The Hebrews had, as we have, two verbs with the distinctive meanings of "to kill" and "to murder." We see in the quotation in Matt. xix. 18, and from the reference in Matt. v. 21, that the Saviour regards the command as a prohibition of passionate lawlessness. But even had we not that light from Christ's teaching, the legislation of Moses himself would shut us up to the same conclusion. For in the administration of justice and in necessary war, the taking of life was commanded (see Numb. xv. 35; xxxv. 31; Exod. xxi. 12—14). So that, unless we regard the lawgiver as setting enactment against enactment, there is in this commandment a prohibition of passionate outbreaks, but neither of capital punishment nor necessary war. 2. It forbids any carelessness by which the life or weal of our neighbour would be risked (Exod. xxi. 28, 29). Wherever human life is risked by insufficient precaution, there is a breach of the sixth commandment. 3. It forbids that anger which takes the form of a revengeful spirit. So Christ teaches. This precept strikes at the thoughts and intents of the heart. Every time a schoolboy angrily lifts a hand to hurt his school-fellow, he is breaking in spirit this commandment. 4. It forbids that indifference in our life to the power of example which would put a stumbling-block or an occasion to fall in a brother's way (see Matt. xviii. 1—3 ; Rom. xiv. 5). If by careless living we "destroy" him for whom Christ died, we are breakers of this law. 5. It forbids dislike and hatred to our brother, and also a selfish isolation and neglect of him (1 John ii. 9—11; iii. 14, 15). If we are merely pursuing our own ends in life, and are not caring whether our brother is saved or lost, this law condemns us. If we even refrain from helping our brother in difficulty or trial, we are guilty (Prov. xxiv. 11, 12 ; Isa. lviii. 6, 7). We may "kill" by withholding the help which might save! 6. It requires, therefore, the cultivation of that kindly spirit of genial benevolence, which would seek in every way to promote the gladness and safety of the society in which we move, and of men at large. Negative in form, the sixth commandment is positive in intent. "Thou shalt not kill" is but the elementary form in which God asserts the great law of mutual dependence and interdependence. "Love worketh no ill to his neighbour. Therefore love is the fulfilling of the Law." Would we keep the commandment, "Thou shalt not kill"? Let us read it in the New Testament light, "Thou shalt *help* thy neighbour." "He that loveth another hath fulfilled the Law."

II. WE WOULD THROW OUT A FEW HINTS AS TO THE GROUND ON WHICH THIS PRECEPT IS OR MAY BE ENFORCED. 1. The preciousness of man in God's sight. He who killed a beast had to make it good; but no satisfaction might be taken for the life of a murderer (see Gen. ix. 6). 2. The spiritual nature of man. 3. The high and holy destiny designed for man forbids any tampering on our part with him or with it.

III. WE HAVE, MOREOVER, IN THE NEW TESTAMENT, A NEW SPRING OF ACTION DISCLOSED. This should actuate us in refraining from violating, and in seeking to fulfil, the law of love. 1. The incarnation of the Son of God is so touching a revelation of the greatness of man, and does of itself so elevate him, that no one realizing it can trifle with man. 2. The atoning sacrifice gives new views of man. After the Apostle Paul has been referring to the death of Christ, he says, "Wherefore henceforth know we no man after the flesh." Christ's death for every man has shown us a halo of glory around every man. We look at him no more according to the accidents of birth, position, colour, clime; we judge all men thus : "*Christ died for them.*" Oh! it is this cross which teaches us that reverence for human nature, which else we had lost altogether. 3. The incarnation and the atoning sacrifice of the Son of God not only give us the moving spring whereby to rise to a proper view of the greatness of man, but also the supreme reason for devoted love to him, for Christ's sake (1 John iv. 11, 20; see Eph. iv. 31; v. 1, 2). With what immeasurable strength does the gospel bind us to fulfil " the royal law," " Thou shalt love thy neighbour as thyself " !

IV. THIS NEWLY ILLUMED PRINCIPLE OF LOVE WILL ENSURE THE FULFILMENT OF THE SIXTH COMMANDMENT, AND WILL EVEN MAKE A BREACH OF IT IMPOSSIBLE. God would have us lifted up by his love to so high a level, that we shall learn to love like him, even with a love (1) of good will, (2) of compassion, (3) of forgiveness, (4) of actual service, (5) of self-denying sympathy and devotion. This is the love which "is born of God." This is the Divine philosophy of obedience to law. Learn, in conclusion : 1. *It is to revelation alone that we owe the clearest view of human dignity.* It is not from philosophy, nor from natural science that we learn to appreciate man. Whatever science may have to say as to his physical organism (and what it can say must depend on its own appropriate evidence), it is the "image of God" which he bears, that is his true dignity, and around it is the Divine guard so stringently placed. 2. *From God's revelation to man we learn respect for man as man.* Human life is held very cheaply in lands where the gospel is unknown, and even in lands where it is known by men who reject it. There are some, indeed, who reject gospel light, yet borrow gospel morality, and call it theirs, while others who treat it as "a strange thing" are already darkly suggesting a "morality" gross as that of pagan days. 3. *From God's revelation we gather the only guarantee for human security and peace.* It is by the cross and by the cross alone that the unity of man in a world wide brotherhood of love will ever be secured. 4. *It is only by the new life bestowed by the Spirit of God that we come to possess and practise this love to which the cross constrains.* We may all of us have refrained from an open breach of the letter of the sixth commandment. Not one of us can stand its searching test in the light of God's pure Word! Ah! "*this commandment fit for Zulus*"? There is not a man amongst us who in the presence of its all-searching light, is not utterly condemned! (Jas. ii. 10.) "Lord, have mercy upon us, and incline our hearts to keep this law!"

Ver. 18.—*The seventh commandment. The religion of the body.* In the second part of the Decalogue there are stern prohibitions against sin, without any positive indication of the opposite virtue. Nor is there a hint of how to attain such a life as shall make an offence against the commandments impossible, so that unless we recognize the educatory purpose of the Law, we shall at once underrate it and yet overrate it. We shall underrate it if we forget that it was just what was wanted, and all that could be serviceable at the time of its promulgation; we shall overrate it if we think that the mere prohibitory letter of this precept expresses the whole will of God in the matter to which it refers. We will, therefore, set side by side therewith, New Testament teachings. First, let us look at Matt. v. 27—29. Just as in referring to rabbinical teaching on the sixth commandment, Jesus Christ tells us that it is not only the open act of murder which is forbidden, but even the spirit of anger and revenge which might lead to it; so here, it is not merely the open act of physical degradation which is forbidden, but even the spirit of unhallowed passion which, if unbridled, might lead to *it*. Nor must we stop here. The New Testament opens up to us the Divine will in the positive direction (1 Thess. iv. 3—5). We are told also what is the true secret of attaining a life which conforms to that will (Gal. v. 16). If we cultivate the life of God in the spirit, the lower life will be in due subjection. Reasons, moreover, which were not given in Israel's childhood are given now (1 Cor. vi. 19, 20); while the issues of a life in which these are lost sight of, are put before us in dread array (1 Cor. ix. 27). Hence a homiletic treatment of this seventh commandment can only be effective as it deals with it as but one branch of a subject, wide, deep, and high, viz. " *The religion of the body.*" Observe—

I. GOD CLAIMS THE GOVERNMENT OF OUR WHOLE NATURE. We regard man's nature as triple—body, soul, and spirit. As an acute and learned divine remarks, "The body is the link between the soul and the world, the soul is the link between the body and the spirit; the spirit is the link between the soul and God." It is in reference to our spirit-nature that we are made in the image of God. *He* is "the Father of spirits." The same Book which reveals God to us, reveals us to ourselves. Any one who understands the structure of his own nature, will perceive which part thereof was meant to rule the rest. The body is to be at the service of the soul, the soul is to be regulated by the spirit, and God is to govern all. But it is by the great work of redemption that the stamp of true dignity has been most clearly impressed on man. The Apostle Paul tells us that it was through the cross that he learned truly to estimate human nature (2 Cor. v. 16). And elsewhere he argues, "Ye are bought with a price; *therefore* glorify God in your body." Christ is "the Saviour *of the body*." If we are the Lord's, *our body* is the temple of the Holy Ghost. No part of the body is base unless basely used. All its functions are to be discharged "in sanctification and honour."

II. THIS SACREDNESS OF OUR WHOLE NATURE, AS REDEEMED BY CHRIST, SHOULD LEAD TO A "RELIGION OF THE BODY" ON THE PART OF THOSE WHO HAVE NOT ENTERED ON THE MARRIED STATE. This seventh command is far broader in spirit than the mere letter would indicate. It condemns all impurity of every kind, it forbids us to let the lower self run off with the higher, and, like the preceding commands, though negative in form, it is positive in substance. It bids us: 1. Let our own nature be duly honoured, and self-respect be diligently cultivated. 2. Observe towards others that self-same respect which we owe to ourselves, on the same ground, and for the Lord Jesus Christ's sake. The art of " bridling the whole body " is one of the most important in a life of godliness.

III. A DUE REVERENCE FOR THE SACREDNESS OF HUMAN NATURE WILL IMPART SANCTITY TO THE MARRIAGE TIE. Marriage is God's holy ordinance. It is not a sacrament, in the same sense in which Baptism and the Lord's Supper are. Neither is it *merely* a civil contract, as is sometimes shockingly said. It is a union of two in the closest ties of nature, based on an affinity of spirit which leads each to see in the other what each most admires. It is a union of spirit in the Lord (if it be all that it should be); each one of the two ceases to live in and for himself or herself, and begins practically to unlearn selfishness by living for the other, and thus the reciprocal outgoing of affection is a formative action of spirit, and tends to the very noblest culture of life. And where the Divine idea of marriage is carried out, the purely natural side of it will be by no means the only one or even the highest (see Matthew Henry's touching words on the creation of woman, and also Kalisch's most admirable remarks in his commentary on Exod. xx. 14, on the position of woman under the Hebrew economy). There are spheres of duty which are most appropriately filled by men, e.g. those in professional and commercial life; there are other spheres which are most appropriately filled by women, e.g. those in the quiet of the home. And the work of one is the supplement and complement of the work of the other. Hence each one looks to the other for the discharge of special service. Thus there is a mutual leaning on one another. And if the crowning joy of married life be present in both being one in the Lord, in their spiritual fellowship they fan each other's love to him who died for them. Each will supply what the other lacks. Perhaps the strength of the man may lie chiefly in intellectual power. That of the woman will lie in tenderness, and also in far keener and surer perceptions and more swiftly acting intuitions. Thus, through one being the fitting complement of the other, they become mutual helpers in all that is right and wise and true; and as even before they were made one, each one knew how to possess his vessel in sanctification and honour, so, when they are one, each honours the other, by making the sacred union subservient to virtue and to the honour of God. Thus rolling years do but deepen the fondness and sweetness of their love, and if it becomes calmer and less demonstrative, it is because it has become fuller, richer, and stronger. When youthful ardour dies down, the holy tie is holier than ever; their very souls become knit together in one. The care of one is the care of both; the joy of one is the joy of both; and any unkindness that stings one wounds both. As two trees side by side in a grove, their arms interlace and interlock, yet each has its separate root. So husband and wife, as trees of the Lord's own right hand planting, do through the whole of this earthly life become interlocked with growing firmness, while their one Saviour in whom they live is the common joy of their spirits, their one hope for eternity! That there are innumerable cases in which a noble type of Christian excellence is reached by the unmarried, we all know. While marriage opens up those claims in the discharge of which the most symmetrical character is usually formed, yet Divine grace can so sway the spirit as to culture it nobly for eternity, irrespectively of these sacred ties. There are fathers and mothers in Israel who are so by spiritual relationship. Thus, when our nature is duly honoured in ourselves and others, by its uppermost part being kept uppermost, out of loyalty to Christ, it is possible for both the married and unmarried to glorify God *in their body* as well as in their spirit.

IV. It is obvious that if through the redeeming grace of God we have our whole being thus lifted up into a higher region, the stern "thou shalt not" of Sinai will be needed no more. We shall have risen to a sphere in which the transgression of the seventh commandment will be impossible (see 1 John iii. 9; Gal. v. 16, 24). The sure guarantee of our keeping this law, in the spirit as well as in the letter, is for us to be so re-created by God's Spirit, that it shall be impossible for us to break it. "The law is not made for a righteous man."

V. We should not fail to note the imperativeness of the law. If there are those who are not in the region of a higher life, as indicated above, they should be reminded that this law, in its wide sweep and searching depth, condemns all impurity of every kind; it discerns "the thoughts and intents of the heart." Hence the words in Matt. v. 28; hence the warnings in Mark ix. 43, 45, 47. *One indulged sin will drag the whole man after it.* "Science," says Dr. Farrar, "confirms by decisive evidence that the Lord avenges the sins of the flesh. It tells us that men must possess in manhood the sins of their youth; that if they sow to the flesh, they will of the flesh reap corruption; that the punishment of sensuality, working not by special interventions, but by general laws, bears a fearful resemblance to the sin itself; that the Nemesis of a desecrated body is an enfeebled understanding, a tormented and darkened soul;" and—the writer might have added—a face from which the lustre of the Divine has departed, and in which the lines of a true manhood are manifestly vitiated and defaced, and even exchanged for lines of sin and of shameless vice. Let all take heed and remember: 1. That where each one's weak point is, a sentinel should be kept on watch. 2. We are not safe till the very thoughts are under control. 3. Only the Spirit of God can give us power equal to this. 4. Unless we keep ourselves in subjection we shall be cast away.

Ver. 19.—*The eighth commandment. The religion of the hand.* There is much to be said in favour of the proposition that utility is the foundation of virtue; and provided that the sentence be well cleared up and guarded from abuse, and provided also that the word "utility" be lifted up to its highest, and spread over its broadest significance, the maxim is less objectionable than it would otherwise appear. While it, however, has been and will be discussed in the philosopher's class-room, for ages, we may safely go so far as to say, "That is right which renders the highest service to mankind, and by its having this tendency, we know it to be right." Now, among serviceable institutions is that of property, which, as men are constituted, is a necessity of social weal. If rightness consists in recognizing the rights of each, the necessity of property comes out of the equality of natural rights. If a man is alone in the world, he may call it all his own. If there is a brother man with him, they must divide it between them. Apart from the institution of property, one incentive to labour would be gone. Who would be likely to toil day by day for that from which he would obtain nought when the work was over? Now, it is the social law of the institution of property, Divine yet natural, yea, natural *because* Divine, the existence of which is here assumed, and the recognition of which is here enjoined: in the barest and most elementary form, it is true, yet in the very form best according with the circumstances under which it was given; in a negative form, too, like the other commands, but yet with a positive intent. Perhaps there is no one of the commandments which is more extensively commented on, and repeated in so many forms in the Old Testament, nor one the violation of which is so variously prohibited. Our simplest mode of treating it homiletically seems to be to point out in turn the negative prohibition, and the positive duty which is to be set over against it.

I. Let us indicate the numerous forms into which this precept is thrown in Scripture. If we regard *the spirit* of it, and read it by the light of Old Testament teaching, we shall find it set in great variety of ways. 1. It forbids our depriving any man of any right whatever (Lam. iii. 35, 36). 2. It is forbidden to gain an undue advantage at another's expense (Exod. xxiii. 3, 6, 8, 9; Lev. xix. 15; ch. xvi. 19, 20). 3. It is forbidden to accumulate wealth by unlawful practices (Prov. x. 2; xv. 6). 4. It is forbidden to take long credit (Prov. iii. 28; Lev. xix. 13). 5. It is forbidden to oppress a poor man in his cause (Exod. xxii. 26, 27; ch. xv. 7, 10—13, 17, 18; Prov. xxii. 22, 23; Micah ii. 1—3; iii. 1—4). 6. It is forbidden to pay insufficient wages (ch. xxv. 4; xxiv. 14, 15). 7. To lend money in any oppressive or exacting form (Exod. xxii. 25; Lev. xxv. 35—38; ch. xxiii. 19). "The name 'usurer'—*neshec*—which is derived from biting, sounded badly, since no one chose to be likened to a hungry dog, who fed himself by biting others" (Calvin). 8. To take advantage of the stranger, the widow, and the fatherless (Exod. xxii. 21—24; ch. x. 17—19; Lev. xix. 33, 34). 9. Unfair trading (Lev. xix. 35, 36; ch. xxv. 13—16; Prov. xi. 1; xvi. 11; xx. 10, 23; Micah vi. 10—12). 10. Imperilling another's property (Exod. xxi. 33—36). 11. Life-long slavery (Exod. xxi. 2; ch. xv. 12—18). 12. Connivance at wrong (Prov. xxix. 24). 13. Respect of persons (Exod. xxiii. 1—3). 14. Revengeful mischief even in war-time (ch. xx. 19, 20). 15. Removing a neighbour's landmark (ch. xix. 14). 16. Withholding from the service of God (Mal. iii. 8, 9). Whenever we withhold what is due to God, or keep back what we owe to man,—if the master is unjust to his servant, or the servant wastes the time or the goods of his master; if a man is guilty of trickery in trade, by adulteration of goods, or scant weight, or short measure; if a man is in any way deprived of his own right or freedom; if we take undue advantage of any one for our own benefit, we are guilty of breaking the command "Thou shalt not steal."

II. Let us indicate the preceptive words which are set over against these prohibitive ones. In the fuller teaching of Moses there was not wanting an indication of an opposite duty, the cultivation of which would make a breach of the eighth commandment altogether out of the question. The people were to aim at cherishing a kindly feeling for each other, and instead of wishing to enrich themselves at another's expense, they were to seek to enrich others, and to find their joy in helping the needy (Exod. xxiii. 4; Lev. xxv. 35; ch. xv. 7—10; xxii. 1—3; xxiii. 19; xxiv. 19). While in Proverbs, the contrast between sloth and industry is said to be one mark of difference between the righteous and the wicked.

III. The teaching of the New Testament is still more explicit. (See Acts xx. 35; 1 Cor. x. 24; Phil. ii. 4, 5; and *specially* Eph. iv. 28.) The *words* of our blessed Lord lingered in the apostles' ears as the strains of a lovely song. His *life* too seemed to say, "Be ever ready to give up what is your own, if thereby you can help another." So that not only is there to be such respect for the rights of others, that we do not infringe on them by abstracting from his property; but over and above the institution of property, which is recognized and guarded, there is the institution of labour, which is to be looked at, utilized, sanctified, so as to subserve the enrichment of others. So that we come at this specific rule: *Labour, and sanctify your labour for others; then you will be in no danger of depriving them of the fruits of their labour!* The political economist says, "Regulate labour so as best to subserve the production of wealth." So far, good. But Christian maxims go higher, and say, "Pursue and regulate labour with a view of promoting each other's well-being." Now, in this sanctification of labour there are four rules to be observed. 1. *Labour as servants of Christ.* This is a specific direction both for employer and employed. Both are amenable to him who is the Head and Lord of the human race. In his eye the interests of the human family are the supreme concern on this globe. Material wealth is to him as nothing. Men are his purchased possession; and if by labour we increased the material wealth of this country a thousand-fold, if thereby one soul were destroyed, his curse would rest upon such labour. 2. *Labour with an eye to the glory of God:* not only as his servants, but so that all our labour may promote that great end for which he lived and died; and just in proportion as this is the case, will Christ approve our toil. 3. *Labour in accordance with and for the promotion of another's good.* We are to let all our labours be in harmony with another's well-being. We may not make ourselves rich at the expense of others; but only as our weal accords with theirs. All this, of course, applies nationally as well as individually. It is as clearly wrong for a nation to steal a continent as for a man to steal a shilling! And if we so labour as to ignore the good of another, we shall find that "there is a God that judgeth in the earth!" 4. But it is not enough that there should be an absence of spoliation or greed, nor that labour should *merely accord* with human good; it is required of us that *one direct object and aim of our labour should be the increase of our wealth that we may have the wherewith to give.* As between man and man, the great God upholds our right to the produce of our labour. As between ourselves and *him,* he says, "Use for your brother's good, the wealth you get. You are but a steward. Nothing is yours absolutely. What hast thou that thou hast not received? Work, that you may get. Get, that you may have to give." "The poor shall never cease out of the land." If, by any sudden spurt, wealth could be equalized to-day, it would be unequal in twenty-four hours, and in twelve months scarcely a trace would be left of the readjustment. Some would be workers and some idlers; some spendthrifts and some misers; and any rectification of property, apart from the right-setting of men, would be of no avail. And, at any rate, so long as there are claims upon our sympathy, so long our labour is to have this stamp upon it: *Labour, to gain the power of giving;* and this is the antidote for any danger of breaking the eighth commandment. Yet, strange to say, there are not wanting those who object, on grounds of "political economy," to the withdrawal of a man's gains for the purposes of benevolence (see Mr. Herbert Spencer, *Contemporary Review,* xix. 556). Now, no one would question that there is a large amount of unwise charity; but the proportion is insignificant between that and the vast amount of ill-gotten and ill-used wealth in our cities and towns. The former is not worth naming by the side of the latter. And the hearts of men are not so over-generous that they need to be dissuaded from giving, by arguments which could hold only if men were nought else but wage-getting animals! But whoever fulfils his labour in a spirit of loyalty to Christ and of kindliness to his brother, will find in labour so discharged, a holy and blessed discipline of character. Shall *we* live under the low, selfish calculations of earth, or under the higher regulations of heaven? There *is* a wealth—a wealth most to be coveted—which comes not as a heritage of birth, but as the reward of giving to others according as they have need. Acting on worldly maxims, a man might live for a thousand years and he will never have it. Acting on Christ's rule, he will reap it as sheaves of golden grain. It is this: "The blessing of him that was ready to perish came upon me: and I caused the widow's heart to sing for joy!"

Ver. 20.—*The ninth commandment. The religion of the tongue.* This command gives us a precept touching our words. Inasmuch, however, as it is here given to us in barest, briefest, most elementary form, it would not be well if in the homiletic treatment of it we did not place side by side therewith the varied Scriptures which set before us the duty of regulating our speech. We will ask, and endeavour to answer, five questions concerning this commandment.

I. WHAT IS HERE PROHIBITED? Just as the sixth commandment throws a guard around human life, the seventh around purity, the eighth around the rights of property and labour, so this ninth throws a shield over every man's reputation. A stern "Thou shalt not injure thy neighbour's fair name" is one of the mandates of Sinai, issued amidst thunder and fire! The *immediate* reference would seem to be to bearing testimony in a court of justice. A part of the judicial code of Moses had reference to this (ch. xix. 16—19). But the precept goes further than this in its spirit. We read in Exod. xxiii. 1, "Thou shalt not raise (or receive) a false report;" literally, "Thou shalt not bear it;" *i.e.* you are to have nothing to do, either in making or taking it. Further (Lev. xix. 16), we are not to give way to gossip and scandal (see Ps. xv. 3). Nor are we to make any statement that is prejudicial to the interests of another, unless we are sure of its accuracy, and unless also the good of society requires us to make it. Further (Ps. xxxiv. 13), our lips are to speak no deceit nor guile of any kind, either in what is said or in the manner of saying it. If we needlessly tell of another's wrong act, instead of seeking to cover it, under the appearance of virtue in denouncing it, God may see a spirit of malice or revenge in naming it; and any act of another's mentioned in such a spirit is sure not to be construed by us in perfect fairness, and therefore it will certainly become, so far as it is unfair, a false report, whatever foundation of fact there may be in it. The precept, moreover, forbids sitting in judgment on individuals, so as to denounce *them* when we are contending against what we consider to be unsound in their faith, or unright in their practice. But further still does the precept reach. It forbids any *thoughtless* word which might unwillingly injure another (see Matt. xii. 33—37). How true is Heb. iv. 12! Every uncharitable thought of another, which might prompt an uncharitable word respecting him, is condemned by the holy Law of God!

II. WHAT IS THE POSITIVE DUTY TO BE OBSERVED? We have only to look at gospel law, as brought out by the Apostle Paul in Eph. iv. 25—32, to see this. 1. *Truth* is ever to mark our speech. The true in thought is to be aimed at, in order that there may be truth, absolute truth, on the tongue. No "pious frauds" are allowable. 2. *Love* is to rule. While a supreme regard to truth will guard us from violating it consciously, a due cultivation of the spirit of love will guard us from forming those harsh judgments of others which might lead us to violate truth unconsciously by misjudging their actions. 3. Where truth and love reign, there will be *self-restraint*. A check will be put on unkind feeling of every sort. "Love beareth all things, believeth all things, hopeth all things, endureth all things." Note further. In this ninth command the relations between men are supposed to be reciprocal. "Thy neighbour." If any ask, Who is my neighbour? let Christ give the answer, "*You may make yourself neighbour to any man by cherishing a readiness of disposition to do him a kindness*" (see Luke x. 29—37). No distinction of race, colour, or clime is to be allowed to stand in the way of our being true neighbours to men, the wide world over.

III. BY WHAT RULE, STANDARD, OR MODEL, SHOULD WE BE GUIDED? 1. "Thou shalt love thy neighbour *as thyself*." That, applied to this command, would mean, "Be as careful of another's reputation as you are of your own." There is another rule. 2. *Be imitators of God.* "Let all evil-speaking . . . be put away from you . . . and be kind to one another . . . even as God in Christ hath forgiven you." The world's rule is: exalt yourself at the expense of others. Christ's rule is: exalt others at the sacrifice of yourself.

IV. WHAT REASONS SHOULD WEIGH ON US IN LEADING US TO RESTRAIN THE TONGUE IN THE INTERESTS OF OTHERS? 1. The fact urged by Paul, that "we are members one of another." In social life we are dependent on each other for the enjoyments which sweeten it, the luxuries which enrich it, the comforts which gladden it, and for the necessaries which make it possible; and, excepting so far as truth governs words and acts, the very props of social life are wanting, and its cohesive force is gone. If the eye refused to be true to the brain, or if the ear, the hand, or the foot resolved to be at variance with the decisions of the will, life would soon be intolerable, and must ere long come to an end. Even so, we cannot tamper with the law of truth in speech without doing our part towards poisoning the currents of thought, feeling, and action which flow through society, and so far as we bear false witness of any kind with the view of gaining advantage at another's cost, we are aiding the infernal work of setting men at variance with each other, by loosening the bonds of mutual confidence which should unite them all! 2. *If the tongue is duly bridled, the whole body will be under command.* So the Apostle James declares (Jas. iii. 2). Our whole being is to be in subjection to God, body, soul, and spirit. And that means that we are to guard our lips. If we are successful here, that indicates so far a mastery over ourselves. We can bridle the whole body if we can but curb the tongue. "Let every man be swift to hear, slow to speak." A man may do very much to make or mar himself according as he has learned the right government of the tongue. 3. *If the tongue is not bridled, we have no religion at all!* So the same apostle (Jas. i. 26). Let us lay that word to heart. Whatever may be the outside profession, if we do not govern our tongue for God, if we use it for gossip, trifling, scandal, slander, our very profession of Christ's name is a cheat and a lie. 4. The thought of *the coming judgment* should lead us to govern our tongue (Matt. xii. 37). One would think that such words as these would make men more careful how they use the tongue! Are we so governing our words that we should confront without shame all those that we have ever spoken, when set in array before us? "We *must* all stand before the judgment seat of Christ." How will backbiters, slanderers, and retailers of gossip meet the eye of the Great Judge of all?

V. HOW ARE WE TO LEARN OBEDIENCE TO THE PRECEPT OF THE TEXT? 1. Let us awake to the importance, as before God, of remembering his perfect knowledge of our words (Ps. cxxxix. 4). Let us cultivate the impression such a thought is calculated to produce. 2. Let us resolve and act (see Ps. xxxix. 1). So said David. Let such a resolution be formed and carried out. 3. Much may be done by auxiliary means, in the way of lessening the temptation to offend with the tongue. Very much of the habit of idle gossip results from unintelligence. Some have nothing to talk about, and for want of a well-stored mind, they fall a-slandering their neighbours. Over and above other means which are more directly religious of reducing the evil of an unbridled tongue, there is this serviceable one: furnish the mind with so much valuable knowledge, that you will be so occupied with useful talk that you have no time for idle words. 4. Let there also be devout attention to the more spiritual aspects of the case. Let the earnest prayer go up (Ps. cxli. 3), and, remembering the Saviour's words, "Out of the abundance of the heart the mouth speaketh," let us earnestly plead with God for daily renewal in the spirit of our mind, since, when the heart is right, the words cannot be wrong. Maybe some of us used to think concerning the ten commandments, "All these have I kept from my youth up." But, alas, so far from that, unless we are converted and renewed, we shall never keep even this one. Under its severe tests we have broken down thousands of times, and have abundant reason to cry, "God be merciful to me the sinner!" A tree is known by its fruit. The righteousness of the Law never will be fulfilled in us as it must be if we are to enter heaven, unless our hearts are so sanctified, and so imbued with the spirit of love, that by never violating charity in the thoughts we think, we never violate it in the words we speak. May God thus sanctify us! "Lord, have mercy upon us, and incline our hearts to keep this law."

Ver. 21.—*The tenth commandment. The religion of the heart.* This commandment is in some respects the most manifestly sweeping and searching of all. It even more fully than the others illustrates Heb. iv. 12. If any reader has thought that in making such heart-work of the preceding, we have gone beyond the scope of the Decalogue, this verse should serve to correct such an impression, for it deals *verbally* with the unexpressed wishes of the soul, and lays a restraint upon them. We will first of all—

I. INQUIRE INTO THE GROUND WHICH THIS PRECEPT COVERS. Recognizing the neighbourly relation between man and man, and people and people, and implying the duty of each individual and of each nation cherishing a kindly feeling for another, it not only forbids the violation of neighbourliness by any outward act of unkindness and wrong, but even the *desire* out of which such unneighbourly acts might arise. "Thou shalt not covet." "As it was given," said an earnest preacher, in the winter of 1870, "in the first instance to a nation, it is natural to consider some of the ways in which a nation may violate it. The history of the world is stained and darkened by the crimes to which nations have been driven by the spirit of covetousness. A great and prosperous people cannot endure that the corn-fields and vineyards and the noble river which can be seen from its frontiers should belong to a neighbouring power." "Sooner or later it is almost certain that this national covetousness will end in a war of aggression or conquest. Some pretext will be found for a quarrel . . . by some means or other there will be a justification discovered, or created, or alleged, for seizing by force of arms what the heart of the nation longed for" (R. W. Dale). But since the command forbids even the covetous *desire*, the justification alleged may be as wicked as the war itself; it may be but a cloak to hide from the undiscerning that covetousness which not the thickest veil of night can hide from him whose eyes are as a flame of fire. It is, however, chiefly with the application of this command to the individual that we have now to do. It forbids: 1. Desire after lower good to the neglect of the higher. 2. Desire after improper objects. 3. Desire after lawful objects carried to an improper degree. 4. Desire to gain any object in an improper manner. 5. Any desire after what belongs to another, which is inconsistent with the rule, "Thou shalt love thy neighbour as thyself." It forbids too: 6. Discontent with the allotments of Divine providence. A discontented spirit is but one form of covetousness, albeit it is a very unamiable one. We are not to be envious of another's possessions, nor for a moment to allow the wish, if our neighbour is rich and we are poor, that his wealth and our poverty should change hands. On the other hand, there is to be a thankful content with the mercies we possess, and a joy in our neighbour's joy if he has more than we have. So far from wishing to gain advantage at another's cost, we are to rejoice in another's good as really as if it were our own. So runs the precept (Rom. xii. 15). It is much easier to "weep with them that weep," than it is to "rejoice with them that do rejoice." When we do the former, we may have the secret thankfulness that we are spared the sorrow of others; but when the latter, our joy is apt to be checked by the secret wish that we were possessors of their cause of joy. Our obedience to this precept is not complete till we can "weep" or "rejoice" with others with *equal* readiness. In a word, the tenth commandment requires *entire unselfishness*. "Love is the fulfilling of the Law."

II. This command makes very remarkable revelations. Sin is defined by the Apostle John as "the transgression of Law." Consequently, wheresoever the Law reaches, there would the transgression of it come under that term, "sin." Hence, by the Law is the knowledge of sin. We find accordingly that one of the most noted characters in New Testament history gained, not only from the Decalogue, but from this particular precept, his first deep convictions of sin (see Rom. vii.). Making a like use of it, we see: 1. That this law reveals that to be sin which else would not have been suspected as such. If we were asked by some to point out the marks of sin in the world, they would refer us to war, oppression, tyranny, etc. But God's Word strikes at the *lusts* out of which these evils come (Jas. iv. 1). 2. This law reveals to us how deeply sin has struck its roots in our nature, that it has permeated and saturated our very *thoughts*, and made them selfish. 3. We see too by the same light that many an apparently good act before men has been rotten by reason of the "lust" in which it had its root. 4. So that we also learn that a man may be altogether blameless in the sight of his fellows, and yet be condemned in the sight of God. God judges acts by motives. Have *all* our *motives* been pure? 5. Thus we see that there is quite enough in heart sins to shut us out from the kingdom of heaven. 6. Thus, by this commandment, and *a fortiori* by all the commandments together, there is revealed to us the impossibility of any one who starts with a burden of accumulated guilt, attaining to the righteousness which is of the Law (Rom. vii. 9, 10). Thus the Law reveals a mischief which it is not its province to cure.

III. While Law reveals mischief, the Gospel reveals a remedy for it. 1. It shows us how grace would cut up covetousness by the root. (1) Our Lord shows us by his teaching that our true wealth consists in what we *are* rather than in what we have (Luke xii. 13—20). (2) When penitent, he forgives the past. (3) He re-creates the soul, and lifts us up *by promises* to a higher level (2 Pet. i. 3, 4 ; Matt. vi. 33 ; Luke

xii. 29; Heb. xiii. 5). (4) Nor is the element of holy warning wanting (1 Cor. x. 1—6, 12). 2. It shows us a sphere in which the natural ambition may have legitimate play without degenerating into lust. For, it may be urged, "If we had no desire after the improvement of our condition, we should do away with enterprise? Ought not a young man to be anxious to rise in the world?" Certainly. *But not at the expense of others.* In a right direction a man not only may, but should, make the very utmost of himself for which his power capacitates him (1 Tim. iv. 8 ; Prov. xxx. 5—9). Another may say, "I have the organ of acquisitiveness very strongly developed. I am so made that I must get, so that if I am anxious to have more, I am only acting out that which is imbedded in the structure of my physical frame." *Acquisitiveness!* an excellent organ to have, and one which makes it specially desirable to decide of what its possessor shall be acquisitive. If it is a necessity of any one's nature to be ever getting, the greater the need that he should be rightly getting the right. Now, while God's Law condemns acquisitiveness in the wrong direction, yet God's grace and gospel open up the grandest possible field for its exercise. By all means let any one develop that noble capacity (Prov. iii. 16; iv, 5—7; 1 Cor. xii. 31). The surest way of guarding against covetousness of ill will be so to develop this eagerness after good that the other cannot coexist (1 John ii. 15). There is no faculty of our nature which can be developed to finer issues than this desire of having, if it be reset by Divine grace, and guided by the Spirit of God. No function of the soul is common or unclean, unless we make it so. Here is the right sort of covetousness (Phil. iii. 8), "*That I may win Christ.*" Let all our power of coveting go out after him. He will bring with him durable riches and righteousness. The wealth we have *in* him will be vastly more than aught we can have from him, and by "the expulsive power of a new affection" he will wean us from the false craving for earth, and ever satisfy us with himself!

Vers. 22—33.—*The Law as a whole, and its effect upon the people.* In the account of the reception of the Law which we have in the Book of the Exodus, it would seem probable that we have a record which was penned at or near the time of the occurrence. The one before us is declared to be some thirty-nine years after. Moses was then verging towards the end of his career. He indulges in a retrospect of the eventful scenes, and rehearses them in the ears of the people. As we have seen in the first Homily, he "dug" into the Law, and dug up its contents. With this passage as our guide, as we have looked at each command in the Decalogue separately, let us survey it in its entirety.

I. THE LAW IS TO BE REGARDED AS A UNITY. It is not made up of isolated precepts. Our Saviour declares that it is summed up in two commandments. And the apostle reminds us that "Love is the fulfilling of the Law :" love to God the root, and love to man the fruit. Taking them in order, the first four require of us a love that shall worship God alone, honouring his nature, revering his name, and guarding his rest day for his special service. The six later ones enjoin love to man, requiring loyalty in the home, restraint in the temper, purity of the body, fidelity of the hand, government of the tongue, unselfishness in the heart. What a space of ground all that covers! What part or power of our being is there that is not held in its comprehensive grasp? And how deeply it strikes! It is a "critic" of the thoughts and intents of the heart. No superficial obedience can meet its claims. It is not difficult to see the purpose which it was designed to serve. It was the basis of Israel's national life and legislation. It was for the instruction of the nations round about (ch. iv. 6). And though it was set on a basis of redeeming mercy, it was designed to awaken the conscience to a sense of sin, to take the people to school, and thus to become their child-guide unto Christ. As compared with the simpler patriarchal dispensation, it was an apparent retrogression for the purpose of a spiritual education. It was a form, written, of that high, that holy, that eternal law of righteousness which is the same for all times, all places, and all peoples, yea, of that Law of perfect love which the Divine Being fulfils in absolute perfection, and after which he would have his creatures conformed.

II. THIS LAW CONTAINS WITHIN ITSELF THE EVIDENCE OF ITS DIVINE ORIGIN. An able American commentator on the Laws of Moses (Dr. Wines), tell us of a distinguished lawyer who had been sceptical on the subject of Divine revelation, and who undertook the study of the Old Testament with a view of satisfying himself as to the validity of its claims to be an inspired writing. When he came to the Decalogue, and had given it an attentive perusal, lost in admiration of its superhuman perfection, he exclaimed, " *Where did Moses get that Law?* " He applied himself to the study of the question, and the result was the removal of every sceptical doubt, and the attainment of a clear and earnest conviction of the Divine original of the Law. Nor is it surprising that a legal mind, accustomed to weigh evidence, should come to such a conclusion; for when we know how early in the world's history this Law was promulgated, it is very marvellous to find that an infant nation should, at starting, have a code of moral law so complete; yea, so elevated, that no other nation at that time presented anything like it, and that even now, 3300 years afterwards, not the wisest man in the world can suggest anything loftier! The kingdoms of Babylon, Assyria, Egypt, have furnished us with nought like this, to say nothing of the Roman, Grecian, and Persian empires, the earliest of which was not founded for centuries after. And if, leaving the merely civil and political side of legislation, we ask for an embodiment of a moral and religious code on which legislation could safely be based, we do not find aught to be compared with this. Nor, if we look at the record of the national life of the very people to whom this Law was first given, do we find that even they approximated to conformity to it. In fact, nothing is more marked in their subsequent literature than their grievous departure from their own standards. When man makes any code of laws, those laws reflect himself and his own standard of attainment. But here is a code far beyond the attainment of any yet recorded nation. It is not necessary, however, to go to ancient nations to show that this Law betokens a higher than human origin. Look at legislation now. Look at the moral sentiment of peoples now. What is the cry? Love thy neighbour as thyself? Emphatically *no!* But " take care of your own interests, and let your neighbours look after themselves!" " Remove your neighbour's landmark as you think well!" Why, if no nation in the world is good enough to adopt the standard of the Decalogue, could it have *created it*, without ever having had any of its educating influence? And if no nation now could do it, how could they who were just liberated from centuries of slavery? But more than this. This Law is high above the attainment of well-trained Christian congregations. Let a minister proclaim the mercy of God in forgiving sin, and his preaching may charm. Let him insist on the demands of God's righteousness, and while some earnest holy souls will lay it to heart, and humble themselves before God, many will be offended at the enforcement of righteousness; and even now many a minister is persecuted for righteousness' sake. *This Law from man? No!* it is too good for that. When man is brought face to face with its holy heart-searchingness he *hates* it! But again. Take the most advanced and holiest Christian you can find. Let him stand in full front of this holy Law—and soon he will be crying out, in agony, " God be merciful to me the sinner!" " But," it may be said, "are not Christians always preaching up to a higher level than that of their attainments?" Certainly; but why? Because they feel and know that here is a Law which they certainly did not originate, which is infinitely above them, and which, by being so, proclaims its intrinsic authority, and proves itself Divine. When such a Law is given, conscience can look at it and say, " *That's right.*" But to *create* a code above itself, is what no nation ever was able to do. This Law shines by its own light, and is " a lamp unto our feet and a light to our path."

III. WHEN PERCEIVED IN ALL ITS GRANDEUR, THIS HOLY LAW FILLS WITH AWE AND TERROR. The thunder, lightning, flame, etc., revealed a majesty that Israel could not endure (vers. 25, 26; cf. Heb. xii, 18—21). But all this terror was nothing compared with the dread that comes over a man when his inmost self is confronted with the Law in its deep heart-searchingness (cf. Rom. vii. 9).

IV. GOD TREATS THE TERROR VERY GRACIOUSLY. 1. Israel was called near to the mount to meet with God, that they might learn a solemn awe, and then sent back to their tents, to wonder and to do. 2. God hearkens to their voice, and appoints a mediator—even Moses (Gal. iii. 19, 20). *We* are come to Jesus, the Mediator of the new covenant (Heb. xii. 24). 3. Israel is reminded that what is needed on their part is, not emotion, but devotion (ver. 29). God wants of us a heart to love and obey. Of itself, the Law does but shut us up to see the necessity of a power for righteousness which it cannot give (Gal. iii. 21). God has made with us a new covenant. The old covenant says, " Do this, and you will live." The new one says, " Live, and you will do this " (cf. Jer. xxx. 31; Heb. viii. 6—13). 4. The people are assured that faithful obedience to the Law of God will ensure the well-being of the nation, its long continuance in the land, and the comfort and peace of the family as well as of the individual. Even so. We have in the Law of God a rule of life absolutely perfect. What is wanted is but obedience to it. This is the one thing to be desired (Jas, i. 22). It is bitterly to be lamented when this obedience is not given (Ps, lxxx. 8—16). When this is the case, the Law becomes a silent accuser (see John v. 45). It is this unwillingness to keep God's Law which is charged against men as sin. It is of this sin of disloyalty that men are called on to repent (Rom. ii. 1—16; Ezek. xviii. 30; Matt. iii. 2; Luke xiii. 3; Acts xx. 21). God in his great love offers to law-breakers, when penitent, the privilege of starting afresh (Acts ii. 38). God forgives the penitent, and imparts new life and strength through the power of the Holy Ghost, to re-set and restore the nature disorganized by sin. Then the righteousness of the Law is fulfilled as men walk not after the flesh, but after the Spirit. Then life has found its true support, is tending to its right issue, is realizing its highest ideal, and has its noblest outlook. Let us all, then, conscious of innumerable failures in obedience, penitently throw ourselves on Divine grace and love, and seek for energy Divine to work in us, cancelling the guilt of the past, creating the life of God within; so will it be well with us for ever and ever !

HOMILIES BY VARIOUS AUTHORS.

Vers. 1—5.—*The Abrahamic covenant renewed.* So solicitous was God for the well-being of Israel that, on critical epochs in their history, he reminds them of their privileged condition. Three main thoughts arrest our attention—

I. COVENANTED BLESSING SECURED. God has not stood out for the maintenance of his rights; he has stooped to fetter his liberty—to bind himself to generous deeds. 1. *He allows us to hold proprietorship in him.* We can claim him to be *" our God."* The Proprietor of all worlds permits fallen men to assert proprietorship in him! Herein is love ! We can call upon him, in justice, to fulfil his self-imposed obligations. 2. *A covenant implies reciprocal engagements.* It is a deed of grace. God binds himself as a Friend and Defender to us, on condition that we bind ourselves in obedient loyalty to him. Failure on one side releases the other party from his pledge. 3. *A covenant includes mutual consent.* No covenant is really valid, is not complete, until both parties have sworn to observe it. There may be command, law, decree, proceeding from God to man; but no covenant is really in force until we personally have accepted its terms, and bound ourselves by willing act to observe it. *Then,* our whole being— property, talent, blood, life, are pledged.

II. MEDIATION PROVIDED. This is a further mark of condescending grace. When two parties are alienated, it is always deemed an advantage to one party to have a mediator chosen from its ranks. God allows a man to mediate between Israel and himself. " I stood between the Lord and you." 1. *Such mediation was needful, because of mutual disparity.* Man is finite; God infinite. Man is for self; God is self-oblivious. Man is earthly minded; God is purely spiritual. That the two may coalesce in senti-ment, purpose, life, mediation of some sort is required. 2. *Mediation is needful, because of man's selfish fear.* The people were " afraid, by reason of the fire "—afraid for their own interests and pleasures. Were men impelled by wisdom, they would count it the highest privilege possible to approach God. What, though we have sinned;—inas-much as God has revealed himself as the Source of mercy, and has deigned to visit us, should we not gladly respond to his proposal, and draw nigh? What, though he is dressed in garments of flame;—if we are penitent, the consuming flame will consume *only* our sin; it will benefit and burnish *us.* This is our honour and our joy—to come very near to God, and to gain larger acquaintance with him. If renewed, our former aversion is turned into longing desire. 3. *This mediation was very imperfect.* It served a present purpose, viz. a mediation for communicating truth, a mediation for obtaining favour. It speaks a volume for the character and faith of Moses, that he was not afraid to draw near. Imperfect though he was, he displayed a rare spirit of self-sacrifice. "Pardon, I pray thee, this people! or else, blot out my name from thy book!" Here was a vivid type of Jesus.

III. HUMAN OBLIGATION INCREASED. In the very nature of things, kindness on the one side begets obligation on the other. 1. *This obligation is personal.* "The Lord hath not made *this* covenant with our fathers, but with *us.*" God's covenant with men is renewed age after age. It is a covenant with *us*, if we will accept the terms. Are we willing to be *his—wholly his?* Then the covenant is settled, "ordered in all things and sure." 2. *This obligation is all-embracing and complete.* It includes every part of our nature, every moment in our history, every interest we have in life. Attention is demanded. The ear must be reserved for God. Intellect is pledged. We must "*learn* the statutes and judgments." Active and dutiful service is due. Like the true Son, our intention must be, "I do always the things that please" the Father!—D.

Vers. 6—21.—*The Divine plan for the conduct of our life on earth.* Had we been left in ignorance what the Divine intention in human life was, it had been a calamity indeed. Waste and failure must have been the disastrous result. For every honest-minded man, ample direction from the Supreme Source of authority is supplied. The most cogent argument is not always the most convincing. God might *here* have prefaced his ten words with a proper assertion of his indisputable sovereignty. But he prefers to appeal to his recent interposition—his emancipation of the people from Egyptian bondage. As if he had said, "*I,* who released you from grinding misery—*I,* who created your liberty, and founded your nation, *now* command your loyalty. Let the lives which *I* have ransomed be spent as I now direct."

I. How HUMAN LIFE IS TO BE DIRECTED GOD-WARD. 1. *That God must be supreme in our regard and affection.* "Thou shalt have none other gods before *me.*" This claim is founded in absolute right. The Proprietor has complete dominion over the work of his hands. If his workmanship does not please him, he is at liberty to destroy it. His claim is further pressed on the ground of his transcendent excellence. Essential and unapproachable goodness is *he;* hence his claims on worship rest upon his intrinsic worth. And his claim to reverent regard proceeds likewise on human benefit. God's glory and man's advantage are only different aspects of the same eternal truth. To give him *all* is to enrich ourselves. 2. *That God must be supreme in our acts of worship.* To picture him forth by material images is an impossibility. The plausible plea of human nature has always been that material forms serve as *aids* to worship the Unseen. But the facts of human experience have uniformly disproved this hypothesis. It may cost us severe exertion of mind to lift our souls up to the worship of the true God; yet this very exertion is an unspeakable advantage. God has no pleasure in imposing on us hard tasks *for their own sake;* yet, for the high gain to his servants, he does impose them. Throughout the Scriptures, idolatry is represented as spiritual adultery; hence, condescending to human modes of speech, the displeasure of God is described as *jealousy.* Jealousy is quick-sighted, deep-seated, swift-footed. All revelation of God is an accommodation to human ignorance and feebleness. The visitation of punishment upon the children, and upon the children's children, is not to be construed as excessively severe, much less as unrighteous. The thrice-holy God can *never* be unjust. The idolatrous spirit would be entailed to children by natural law; hence punishment would culminate in final disaster. The *menace* was gracious, because, if parents will not abstain from sin for their own sakes, they sometimes will for the sake of their children. The mercy shall be far more ample than the wrath. The anger may be entailed on a few, and that in proportion always to the sin; the mercy shall flow, like a mighty river, to "thousands." True worship fosters love, and stimulates practical obedience. 3. *God's authority is supreme over our speech.* The faculty of speech is a noble endowment, and differentiates man from the inferior races. The tongue is a mighty instrument, either for evil or for good. (1) We take God's Name in vain when we make an insincere or superficial profession of attachment. We wear his Name lightly and frivolously if our service is formal and nominal. (2) We take his Name in vain when we are unfaithful in the performance of our vows. Men pledge themselves to be his in moments of peril, and forget their pledges when safety comes. (3) We take God's Name in vain when we use it to give force and emphasis to a falsehood. Whether in private converse, or in a court of justice, we use God's Name to produce a stronger persuasion in others' minds, we contract fearful guilt if we use that sacred Name to bolster up a lie. (4) We take God's Name in vain whenever we use it needlessly, flippantly, or in jest. The moral effect upon men is pernicious, corrupting, deadly. The penalty is set forth in negative language, but it is intended to convey deep impression. Others may hold it as a venial sin; not so God. 4. *God's authority over the employment of our time.* All time belongs to God. He hath created it. Every successive breath we inspire is by his sustaining power. Since we are completely *his*, his claim must be recognized through every passing minute. But just as he allows to men the productions of the soil, but requires the firstfruits to be presented to him—the earnest of the whole; so also the firstfruits of our time he claims for special acts of worship. One day in seven he requires to be thus consecrated; but whether the first or the seventh depends wholly on the mode of human calculation. The grounds on which the institution rests are many. Even God felt it to be good to "rest" from his acts of creation. In some sense, he ceased for a time to work. Review and contemplation formed his sabbath. His claims to have *his* day observed are myriad-fold. If sabbath observance was beneficial for Jews, is it not for Gentiles? If it was a blessing to man in the early ages, has it now become a curse? Even the inferior creation was to share in the boon. Strangers and foreigners would learn to admire the gracious arrangement, and learn the considerate kindness of the Hebrews' God.

II. WE LEARN HOW OUR LIFE IS TO BE CONDUCTED MAN-WARD. 1. *In accordance with the degree of kinship.* A parent has claims beyond all other men upon our love, obedience, and service. Parents are deserving our heartfelt honour. They claim this on the ground of position and relationship, irrespective of personal merit. Parents stand towards their children, through all the years of infancy, in the stead of God. For years the human babe is wholly dependent upon its parent; and this serves as schooling and discipline, whereby it learns its dependence upon a higher Parent yet. The disposition and conduct required in us towards our parents is the same in kind as that required towards God. Filial reverence is the first germ of true religion. Hence the promises of reward are akin. The family institution is the foundation of the political fabric. The health and well-being of home is the fount of national prosperity. If parents are honoured, "it shall be well with thee." *This*, a law for individuals, a law for society, and a law for nations. 2. *Our duty towards all men.* We are to respect their *persons.* Their life and health are to be as dear to us as our own. We are to respect their *virtue.* The lower passions are to be held in restraint. Occasions for lust must be avoided. A bridle must be put upon the glances of the eye. We are to respect their *property.* This duty has extensive scope. It means that we should deal with others as if they were ourselves. All dishonest dealing, false representations in commerce, overreaching in bargains, fraudulent marks, are condemned. We are to have respect to their *reputation.* It ought to please us as much to see a conspicuous virtue, a generous quality, in another, as if it shone in ourselves. Idle tale-bearing is forbidden, as also detraction, slander, unfavourable interpretation of others' deeds, and suspicion of their motives. We are charged, as the servants of God, to "love our neighbours even as ourselves." 3. *This Divine Law carries its sanctions into our interior life.* "Thou shalt not covet." Improper and irregular desires are to be repressed. Like a wise Ruler, God proceeds to the very root of sin—to the very core of evil. 'Tis easiest to strangle the serpent at its birth. If only this fountain were pure, all its streams would be likewise pure. Let the salt of purification be applied here! There *is* scope for coveting—a direction in which it may lawfully run. It may run Godward. It may fix its eyes and its hands on heavenly treasures. For in securing these we defraud no one else. Therefore, we may with advantage all round "covet earnestly the best gifts." Desire after heavenly gifts and riches is never untimely or excessive, never irregular or inordinate. Hence, as an antidote to a covetous disposition, we may well nourish heavenly hope. "Delight in God" will bring a most satisfying fruition of desire. Sowing in this fertile field yields a prolific harvest. The Decalogue is complete. God "added no more." Authority centres here.—D.

Vers. 21—33.—*Character determines environment.* I. THE STORMY ELEMENTS OF

NATURE SERVE AT TIMES AS THE FITTING ROBES OF DEITY. All natural objects are the projections in space of his creative voice. He spake and they appeared. *He* is still behind all phenomena—the only real substance. Since he is all-wise, the sole fount of knowledge, the true Revealer of secrets, he is properly said to be apparelled with *light*. The rainbow is his diadem, the morning sun is his radiant face, the thundercloud his chariot. To human eyes, he can only be visible in such forms as these. His holiness can be visibly expressed in no other form than fire. The profound inscrutableness of his will is best made manifest by the "thick darkness." His insufferable glory is attempered by a cloud. His kingly power is betokened by a "great voice." Such is his fitting environment.

II. THE NEAR APPROACH OF GOD IS INTOLERABLE TO SINFUL MEN. The unrenewed man shrinks from contact with absolute purity. He is in an uncongenial atmosphere —like a fish out of its native element. What tremendous losses foolish man submits to rather than abandon sin—losses of privilege, friendship, joy! So Peter prayed, when the vision of Christ's wondrous power dawned on him, "Depart from me, for I am a sinful man, O Lord." But the renewed man yearns and pants for a nearer, and yet nearer, approach to God. "I pray thee, show me thy glory!" *This* is his joy—to be near God, to grow like him. And yet, how often do we shrink from the passage of death, the passage by which we penetrate into the inner palace of Deity! Whatever brings us into nearer fellowship with God ought to be welcomed.

III. A SIGHT OF GOD KILLS EITHER THE SIN OR THE SINNER. There is no question that God intends the former, but if the guilty man will not part with his sin—identifies *himself* with *it*—then he too dies. To *know* God, and his redeeming Son, is tantamount to eternal life. But to know God only in his judicial character, to have defective acquaintance with him, alarms and kills. The love of sin perverts the judgment, and destroys good logic. These Hebrews said, "We have seen this day that God doth talk with man, and he liveth;" and then they inconsistently add, "Therefore why should we die?" In presence of that mystic flame, they promise loyal obedience. If only life may be spared, and God's commands be conveyed in a less alarming manner, they pledge themselves to be his liege servants. Alas! men little know their own weaknesses! So men still say that if they had such a revelation as they wished—such in *degree*, and such in *kind*—they would yield compliance! Yet the real difficulty arises not from defects in the external revelation, but from the internal disposition.

IV. GOD'S APPORTIONMENT OF HONOUR AND DISHONOUR APPROVED BY MEN. How different his language to different persons! To some, "Go, get you into your tents again;" to another, "Stand thou here by *me*." To dwell near to God, and to enjoy his revelations of light and love—this is really man's crowning privilege, *this* his heaven. Yet the bulk of men are blind to their own good, dead to noblest joy. To possess any pleasure, their environment must be suited to their character; the external must correspond with the internal. "Depart from me!" says man to his Maker. "Depart from *me*!" responds our God. "Out of our own mouths we are judged."

V. OBSERVE GOD'S INTENSE LONGING FOR MAN'S GOOD. How pathetic are such ejaculations as these, "Oh that there were such a heart in them, to fear *me* always!" 1. Religion must be a matter of the heart. 2. Religion is not a compulsory, but voluntary, service. 3. Religion commands the allegiance of the whole man—his reverence, submission, and practical service; and *that* not spasmodic, but continuous. 4. Religion brings largest benefit to ourselves and to our children. Even bad men have, *at times*, desires after a better life—fitful moods of regret and aspiration. God, in his wondrous patience, smiles on these—approves a passing thought or a transient feeling—and says, in his paternal love, "Would that this frame of feeling continued!" These are the openings of opportunity's golden door.

VI. THE WORLD'S OBEDIENCE IS DEPENDENT ON HUMAN MINISTRIES. The majority of men will not listen to God unless he speak to them through human agencies. Men will only read God's Word as it is written, in large capitals, in saintly lives. Thus God commanded Moses: "*I* will speak unto *thee*: ... *thou* shalt teach *them*, that they may do." The pardoned man becomes God's interpreter to the world. "Speak *thou* to us," they say, "and we will hear." "As Christ was, so we are to be in the world"—

light-bearers. The heathen nations learn only *through the Church* the redeeming work of God.—D.

Vers. 1—33.—*Reminiscences of Horeb.* I. THE COVENANT. (Vers. 2, 3.) 1. Proposed by God (Exod. xix. 3—7). 2. Accepted by the people (Exod. xxiv. 7). 3. Entailed obligations on subsequent generations (cf. ch. vi. 2). In this covenant, formally ratified by sacrifice (Exod. xxiv. 6, 7), Israel (1) accepted Jehovah to be its spiritual and temporal Sovereign. (2) Pledged itself to observe his Law. (3) Was adopted by him as his peculiar people. (4) Had every blessing secured to it on condition of obedience (Exod. xxiii. 22—27). The new covenant in Christ, while in many respects different from, and superior to, that of Horeb, yet resembles it in several of these particulars.

II. THE LAW. (Vers. 6—22.) 1. Holy in its nature. 2. Internally complete as a summary of duty. "He added no more" (ver. 22). 3. Explicative of the character of God. The *absoluteness* and *unity* of God, *e.g.* taught in first commandment; his *spirituality, jealousy* of his *honour, sovereignty, love,* and *mercy,* in second commandment; his *holiness,* in third commandment; his *searching of hearts,* in tenth commandment; while in all he appears as the Source of moral obligation, and the Guardian of rights. 4. To be kept from the motive of love (ver. 10). This Law is not abolished, but fulfilled in Christ, by whose Spirit its precepts are written in the minds and hearts of believers (2 Cor. iii. 3; Heb. viii. 10).

III. THE MEDIATOR. (Vers. 5, 22—33.) The mediation of Moses was: 1. *Craved by the people* (vers. 23—28). The manifestation of God's holiness overwhelms sinful men (cf. Isa. vi. 3—6). Moses not only *endured* this manifestation, but went up alone into the thick darkness where God was. How exceptionally great he appears in this! 2. *Acquiesced in by God* (vers. 28—32). This transacting through a mediator was in harmony with the principle of his dealings with them from the first. A figure of the mediation of Christ. 3. *Suitable in itself.* As tending to enhance in their minds the impression of God's holiness and the feeling of their own sinfulness.—J. O.

Vers. 2, 3.—*The covenant at Horeb.* Here spoken of as distinct from the older covenant made with the patriarchs (Gen xv., xvii.).

I. ITS RELATIONS TO THE COVENANT MADE WITH THE FATHERS. It was not a new thing absolutely. It rested on that older covenant, and on the series of revelations which sprang out of it. It could not disannul that older covenant (Gal. iii. 17). It could not run counter to it (Gal. iii. 21). It must, though "superadded," be in subserviency to it (Gal. iii. 15—26). But that covenant made with the fathers was: 1. Of promise (Gal. iii. 18). 2. Couched in absolute terms. God pledged his perfections that the promise conveyed in it would be ultimately realized (Rom. iii. 3). 3. In which an interest was obtained by faith (Gen. xv. 6; Rom. iv. 3—23). 4. While yet it bound the person received into covenant to a holy life (Gen. xvii. 1). The new covenant could "make void" the older one in none of these particulars.

II. ITS DISTINCTION FROM THE COVENANT MADE WITH THE FATHERS. 1. It was a *national* covenant, having reference primarily to national existence and prosperity. 2. It was a covenant of *Law.* It was (1) connected with a promulgation of Law, and (2) required obedience to the prescribed Law as the condition of acceptance. Does this look like a retrograde step in the Divine procedure, a contradiction of the covenant with Abraham? Seemingly it was so, but the backward step was really a forward one, bringing to light demands of the Divine holiness which it was absolutely essential man should become acquainted with. Two points have to be noticed : (*a*) that obedience was not made the *ground of admission* to the covenant, or aught else than the condition of *continuance* in privileges freely conferred ; and (*b*) that the requirement of obedience did not stand alone, but was connected with provisions for the removal of the guilt contracted by transgression and shortcoming. This brings into view the peculiar feature in the covenant of Horeb—the hidden grace of it. In form and letter it was a strictly legal covenant. Obedience to the Law in all its parts, and without failure, was the technical condition of the fulfilment of promise, and of continuance in covenant privilege (cf. Matt. xix. 17; Rom. x. 5; Gal. iii. 10). The fact that atonements were provided to remove the guilt which otherwise would have broken up the covenant, is proof that such was its constitution. The same fact shows that in the structure of the covenant it was recognized that sin and shortcoming would mark the history of Israel; that, on the strictly legal basis, standing in the state of acceptance was impossible. A theoretically perfect obedience no Jew ever rendered. His standing in no case was in virtue of a perfectly fulfilled Law, but was *due to forgiving mercy, which daily pardoned his shortcomings, and gave him an acceptance which these shortcomings were as constantly forfeiting.* It was faith, not works, which justified him; while yet, in harmony with the unalterable law of moral life, it was his duty to aim at the realization of the ideal of righteousness which the Law presented. Just as with Abraham, the faith which justified him, and did so before a single work had issued from it (Gen. xv. 6; Jas. ii. 23), was a faith which "wrought with works," and "by works was faith made perfect" (Jas. ii. 22). It follows from these peculiarities, and from the statements of Scripture, that it was: 3. A *preparatory* and *temporary* covenant. Its leading design was to develop the consciousness of sin, to awaken a feeling of the need of redemption, to evince the powerlessness of mere Law as a source of moral strength, to drive men back from legal efforts to faith, and so, finally, to prepare the way for Christ (Rom. iii. 20; Gal. iii. 23, 24, etc.). In this we discern the reason of the severe and threatening form in which it was couched, and of the terrors which attended its promulgation. It was a covenant which could not of itself save or do aught but kill (2 Cor. iii. 6—12).—J. O.

Ver. 5.—*Mediation.* I. MEDIATION IN GENERAL. Mediation has a God-ward side and a man-ward side. The requirements of God's holiness—the needs of man's heart. 1. *On God's side,* communion with sinners can only be maintained on terms which uphold righteousness and law, and do not derogate from the sanctity of the Divine character. 2. *On man's side,* there is (1) the feeling of *weakness and finitude,* awakening terror in presence of the Infinite (vers. 25—27). (2) The feeling of *sin,* giving rise to the craving for a holier one to stand between him and God. (3) The feeling of *need*—the soul's longing for fellowship with God; giving rise to the desire for one to mediate in the sense of making peace, of bringing about reconciliation (Job xvi. 21). II. THE MEDIATION OF MOSES A TYPE OF THAT OF CHRIST. We trace the resemblance: 1. *In his willingness to mediate.* So did Jesus most willingly undertake to stand between God and sinners (Heb. x. 5—10). 2. *In his acceptance as mediator* (ver. 28). So was Christ called to this office by the Father, invested with all the powers necessary for the right discharge of its duties, and accepted in the discharge of them (Isa. xlix. 8; Matt. iii. 17; xvii. 5; Heb. v. 4—11). 3. *In the work he did.* (1) Conveying God's words to the people (cf. John xvii. 6—9). (2) Conveying the people's words to God (ver. 27). Jesus is in like manner the medium through whom prayer, worship, etc., ascend to the Father (Eph. iii. 18; Heb. iv. 14—16). (3) Frequently interceding for them, and obtaining pardon for their sins (Exod. xxxii. 11—15; Numb. xiv. 13—21, etc.). So does Jesus ever live to intercede for us, and advocate our cause (Rom. viii. 34; 1 John ii. 1). (4) Even, on one notable occasion, offering himself as a sacrifice for their sin (Exod. xxxii. 32). What Moses *would* have done, had it been possible so to save the people from destruction, Christ did (Gal. iii. 13, etc.).—J. O.

Ver. 8.—*The iniquity of the fathers visited on the children.* I. A FACT AMPLY ATTESTED. Borne out 1. *By Scripture instances* (Josh. vii. 24; 2 Sam. xii. 14; 1 Kings xxi. 21, 29, etc.). 2. By *observation and experience.* The case of children suffering in mind, body, character, and fortune, as the result of the sins of parents, is one of the commonest and saddest things in life. 3. *Science.* The law of heredity. (For illustrations, see Rev. Joseph Cook's 'Lectures.') 4. *Literature.* Especially do the Greek tragedies give expression to, and strikingly work out, this thought. II. A FACT MYSTERIOUS, YET TO BE VIEWED IN THE LIGHT OF VARIOUS RELIEVING CONSIDERATIONS. The difficulty is one of natural, quite as much as of revealed, religion. The following considerations relieve it only in part: 1. Every original disadvantage will be taken into account by the Searcher of hearts in estimating personal responsibility (Luke xiii. 48). 2. The final judgment on a man's character will turn, not on inherited tendencies, but on what he has made himself by his own moral determinations (Ezek. xviii.). 3. The less favourable conditions in which the sins of parents have placed the individual cannot turn to his ultimate disadvantage if he struggle well and persevere to the end (see 'Speaker's Commentary' on Exod. xx. 5). 4. It is open to the evil-doer to cut off the entail of punishment by choosing for himself the way of righteousness (Ezek. xviii. 15—18). God is reluctant to contemplate the heritage of evil descending further than the third or fourth generation, while thousands of generations are spoken of in connection with the blessing. 5. Experience of the effects of a parent's evil-doing is designed to act as a deterrent from like sins. The child is less likely to imitate the parents' vices, suffering these results, than if entirely exempt. 6. The Law is the consequence of a constitution of society originally intended for the conveyance, not of evils, but of blessings. This is a consideration of importance as throwing light on the equity, as well as on the goodness, of Divine providence. The design of the organic constitution of society is obviously to hand down to succeeding generations the moral gains of those which precede. It is sin which has wrought the mischief, reversing the operation of a constitution in itself beneficent, and making that which is good work death to so many.

Lesson—The tremendous responsibility of parents, and of all who have it in their power to influence the destinies of posterity.—J. O.

Vers. 12—15.—*The sabbath.* I. WHAT? The essential point in the institution is the sanctification to God of a seventh part of our time, of one day in seven. Which day of the seven is observed is indifferent, not in the sense of being left to individual choice, but in respect of any inherent sanctity in one day above another (Rom. xiv. 5). The day is made holy by the Divine appointment, and by the uses we put it to. We sanctify the sabbath: 1. *By observing it as a day of rest from secular toil.* The need of a rest day in the week is universally acknowledged. Every effort should be made to extend the boon as widely as possible, and to avoid infraction of the rights of others in connection with it. Our aim should be to lessen Sunday work, not to increase it. Apply to railways, steamboats, post-office work, museums, etc. 2. *By devoting it principally to religious uses.* It is only by conserving the sabbath as a day sacred to religion that we can hope to preserve it as a day free from toil. We need, for spiritual purposes, all the opportunities it gives us.

II. FOR WHOM? The answer is—for man. This is shown: 1. From *its primeval origin.* That the sabbath dates from creation is implied in the narrative in Genesis (ii. 3), in the terms of the command (Exod. xx. 8—11), in Christ's words (Mark ii. 27), in the argument in Hebrews (iv. 3, 4), and in the recently deciphered Chaldean traditions. While it may be argued, that if designed to commemorate creation, this is a matter which concerns all men equally with the Jews. 2. From *its place in the moral law.* It is certainly remarkable, if the sabbath is a purely Jewish institution, that it should be found embodied in the first of those two tables which by their contents, as well as by the manner of their promulgation, are shown to be of a distinctly moral nature. 3. *From the respect paid to it by the prophets* (see Isa. lviii. 13, 14). The language here employed is very different from that which prophets were accustomed to use of purely ceremonial institutions. 4. From *Christ's defence of it.* It is noticeable, and supports our view, that while frequently charged with breaking the sabbath law, the Saviour never once admits the charge. He carefully defends himself against it. He unceremoniously clears away the rubbish which the Pharisees had heaped upon the institution; but the sabbath itself he never speaks of as a thing to be abolished. He sets it in its true light, and shows high respect for it. 5. From *its reappearance in the new dispensation in a form adapted to the genius and wants of Christianity.* The *name* sabbath is not found in the New Testament, applied to the first day of the week, but the *thing* appears in that weekly festival of the Apostolic Church—the Lord's day. 6. From *the proved adaptation of the sabbath to the constitution of man's nature.* The seventh-day rest is found by experience to be essential to man's welfare. It ministers to physical health, mental vigour, moral purity, and religious earnestness. The sabbath-keeping nations are by far the happiest, most moral, and most prosperous. These reasons combine to show that this institution is one intended and adapted for the whole human family.

III. WHY? The institution, as seen above, is grounded in deep necessities of man's nature. It is, moreover, a suitable recognition of the Creator's right to our worship and service. But further, it is: 1. *Commemorative* (1) of creation, (2) of redemption—in the case of Israel, of redemption from Egypt (ver. 15); in the case of the Christian, of redemption through Christ. 2. *Prefigurative*—of the rest of heaven (Heb. iv. 9).—J. O.

Ver. 16.—*Honour to parents.* We prefer the arrangement which regards the fifth commandment as the last of the first table—honour to parents being viewed as honour to God in his human representatives.

I. PARENTS STAND TO THEIR CHILDREN IN THE RELATION OF REPRESENTATIVES OF THE DIVINE. They represent God as the source of their offspring's life; they have a share of God's authority, and ought to exercise it; but much more ought they to represent God to their children in his unwearied beneficence, his tender care, his exalted rectitude, his forgiving love. With what intelligence or comfort can a child be taught to think of a Father in heaven, if its earthly parent is wanting in dignity, kindness, truthfulness, or integrity? How many fathers are thus spoiling for their children their whole conceptions of God! And with what anxiety and care should earthly parents study to leave such an impression on their children's minds as will make the idea of God delightful and consolatory to them, while inspiring them towards him with proper feelings of reverence!

II. PARENTS ON THIS ACCOUNT ARE TO BE HONOURED BY THEIR CHILDREN. They are to be regarded with affection, treated with respect and deference, promptly and cheerfully obeyed, and, where needful, liberally supported (Matt. xv. 4—7; 1 Tim. v. 8). Even the failure of parents to do all their duty to their children does not exonerate the children from the obligation of treating them with respect. Young people need to be reminded that failure in this duty is peculiarly offensive to God. We are told that when Tiyo Soga visited this country, a particular thing which astonished him was the deficiency in respect for parents compared with the obedience which prevailed in the wilds of Kaffraria.

III. THE HONOURING OF PARENTS HAS ATTACHED TO IT A PECULIAR PROMISE. Length of days and prosperity. The promise is primarily national, but it has fulfilments in individuals. 1. A *special blessing* rests on the man who shows his parents due respect. That has often been remarked. 2. There is also a *natural connection* between the virtue and the promise. Respect for parents is the root at once of reverence for God and of respect for the rights of others. Hence the place of the commandment in the Decalogue. It engenders self-respect, and forms the will to habits of obedience. It is favourable to the stability, good order, and general morals of society. It therefore conduces to health, longevity, and a diffusion of the comforts of life, furnishing alike the outward and the inward conditions necessary for success.—J. O.

Ver. 22.—*Moral Law.* I. THE TEN COMMANDMENTS A DISTINCT PART OF GOD'S REVELATION. 1. They were spoken by God's own voice from the midst of the fire (ver. 24). 2. They only were thus promulgated; "he added no more." 3. They were written on tables of stone. 4. They were deposited in the ark of the covenant (Exod. xxv. 16). These facts show that they held a distinct place in the Law-giving at Sinai, and that they are not to be confounded with the ceremonial and judicial statutes, subsequently given.

II. THE GROUNDS OF THIS DISTINCTION. The Decalogue was: 1. An epitome of universal moral truth. 2. Internally complete as such—the first table laying down our duties to God, as respects his being, his worship, his Name, his day, his human representatives; the second forbidding all injury to our fellow-men (injuries to life, property, chastity, character), while requiring by implication the fulfilment of all positive duties, and the regulation even of our secret thoughts. 3. The basis of the covenant with Israel. The foundation on which all subsequent legislation was reared.—J. O.

Vers. 23—28.—*The element of terror in religion.* I. THE FACT OF TERROR. It is not unnatural that man should tremble in presence of any near manifestation of the Divine. The chief cause of this terror is the consciousness of sin. Guilty man fears his Judge. The text is an instance of this terror, but the same thing has often been witnessed. 1. *In presence of unusual appearances of nature.* Comets, eclipses, unusual darkness, thunderstorms, earthquakes, etc. 2. *Under the powerful preaching of judg-*

ment. Felix under the preaching of Paul (Acts xxiv. 25). Massillon bringing the French court to their feet in terror, as he described the Lord's coming. Whitfield's oratory and its effects. 3. *In prospect of death.* There are few in whom the approach of death does not awaken serious alarms. The effect is most conspicuous in times of sudden danger, as in shipwrecks, etc.

II. THE INFLUENCE OF TERROR. Usually, as here : 1. *It extorts confession of the truth.* The Israelites spoke of God in juster terms than ever they had done before, or perhaps ever did again. Terror draws from the soul strange acknowledgments. The white face of the scoffer shows how little, in his heart, he disbelieves in the God he would fain have disavowed. The self-righteous man is made suddenly aware of his sins. The blasphemer stops his oaths, and begins to pray. The liar for once finds himself speaking the truth. 2. *It awakens the cry for a mediator.* Thus we see it leading men to send for ministers or lay Christians to pray for them, or crying for mercy to the Saviour or to saints. 3. *It prompts to vows and promises.* In their terrified moods, men are willing to promise anything—whatever they think will please or propitiate God (ver. 27). They will repent, will pray, will go to church, will make restitution for wrongs, will abandon vices, etc.

III. THE INEFFICACY OF TERROR AS AN INSTRUMENT OF CONVERSION. Terror, when excited by just views of sin, has its uses. It breaks up the hardened crust of indifference, ploughs into the nature, and prepares it for the reception of better teaching. But terror of itself cannot change the heart. It is the message of love which alone can exalt, renovate, and truly convert. Not the Law, but the cross. The Law is only useful when employed as a schoolmaster to bring to Christ. These Israelites soon forgot their terrors, and in less than forty days had made for themselves a golden calf. The jailor's terrors (Acts xvi. 27) would have wrought death, but the words, " Believe on the Lord Jesus Christ," etc. (ver. 31), made him live anew.—J. O.

Vers. 28, 29.—*God's desires for man's good.* A gleam, from amidst the terrors, of the Divine loving-kindness and tenderness.

I. GOD WELCOMES IN MAN THE FAINTEST TRACES OF A DISPOSITION TO RETURN TO HIM. (Ver. 27.) This trait in the Divine character is scarcely recognized by us as it should be. We are apt to take for granted that till conversion is absolutely complete— till it is in every respect sincere and thorough, it can obtain no favour in the eyes of Heaven. Scripture teaches, on the contrary, that God wills to recognize in man any signs of turning towards himself, and would fain, by holding out encouragements, ripen these into thorough conversion (1 Kings xxi. 27—29 ; Ps. lxxviii. 34—40; Jonah iii. 10).

II. GOD IS NEVERTHELESS AWARE OF ALL THAT IS LACKING IN HEARTS NOT COMPLETELY SURRENDERED TO HIM. The professions of the Israelites did not deceive him. He knew the superficiality of their states of feeling. They lacked yet " one thing " (Mark xi. 21)—the entire surrender of their hearts to him. We have the same discernment in the New Testament (John ii. 25 ; Acts viii. 21 ; Rev. iii. 1; cf. 1 Kings xv. 3; Matt. xiii. 20, 21).

III. GOD DESIRES IN MAN THAT THOROUGHNESS OF CONVERSION WHICH ALONE CAN SECURE OBEDIENCE, HAPPINESS, AND PERSEVERANCE. What God desires in man is heart-religion ; this has : 1. Its seat in the heart. 2. Its principle in the fear of God. 3. Its outcome in obedience. 4. Its test in perseverance. 5. Its reward in blessedness. It is God's love which here speaks, but also his righteousness, which is necessarily averse from whatever is unreal, and desires to see goodness triumphant.—J. O.

Vers. 1—21.—*The Decalogue.* Moses here recalls the Sinaitic covenant, and wishes the Israelites to remember that, though given to their fathers primarily, it was also applicable to them. They were in many cases present as children then, and they were represented by their parents. Moses speaks with authority as having been mediator (ver. 5) on the occasion.

There are the following lessons to be learned from the Decalogue as here given :—

I. THE COVENANT IS BASED UPON A MERCIFUL DELIVERANCE. God gives his Law to his people after their deliverance from Egyptian bondage. It is intended to be a rule of life for those already redeemed. The gospel precedes the Law—Moses the deliverer precedes Moses the lawgiver; the Lord was first known as the fountain of freedom, and then as the fountain of that Law within whose bounds freedom is to be realized.

II. THIS LAW COVERS OUR RELATIONS BOTH TO GOD AND MAN. 1. The Laws relating to *God*. These embrace the four which come first, *i.e.* (1) the law against *polytheism* or *atheism*. This law is broken when we live " without God in the world," ascribing to luck, chance, or fortune what is due to God's providence. It is broken when we worship *self*, or *fame*, or *ambition* (cf. ' The Life and Letters of J. H. Thornwell, D.D., LL.D.,' p. 142 ; also Dale's ' Ten Commandments; ' Washburn's ' Social Law of God ;' and Crosby's ' Thoughts on the Decalogue '). (2) The law against *sensuous worship*. For the second commandment is broken in so far as our worship is not " in spirit and in truth." (3) The law of *reverence*. Any spirit of undue familiarity which leads to the least trifling before God is a breach of this third commandment. (4) The law of *consecrated time*. This fourth commandment is an acknowledgment that *all* time is God's by right, and the seventh portion *should be* by special obligation. In Deuteronomy the sabbath is based, not on creation, as in Exodus, but on the deliverance from Egypt. Each great providence increases our obligation thus to acknowledge God. Hence the Lord's day is made commemorative of our Lord's resurrection.

2. The laws relating to *man*. These embrace the succeeding *six*, thus : (1) The law of the *family*. This is the first commandment with promise (Eph. vi. 2). (2) The law of *social love*. For we are to avoid not only murder, but the unholy anger of which it is the manifestation (Matt. v. 22). (3) The law of *social purity*. We must be pure in thought, as well as in act, as our Lord has shown us (Matt. v. 28; also Mark vii. 21—23). (4) The law of *honesty*. This must be in God's sight and in man's (2 Cor. viii. 21). (5) The law of *veracity*. Restraining the turbulent tongue (Jas. iii. 6, 9). (6) The law of *contentment*. The curbing of covetousness, which is idolatry (Col. iii. 5).—R. M. E.

Vers. 22—33.—*How Moses became mediator*. The ten commandments were a *direct* communication from God to Israel. But it was too much for their sinful, terrified souls to stand, and so Moses is entreated to stand between God and them, and be the medium of communication between them. The Lord approved of the arrangement, and installed Moses into the office (cf. Exod. xx. 18—21). This suggests—

I. THE CRY FOR A MEDIATOR AROSE OUT OF THE FEARS OF MEN. The surpassing glory of God makes such a terrific impression on the hearts of sinners that they cry instinctively for mediation. It is a need of mankind when aroused to a true sense of the majesty and purity of God.

Those who question the necessity of mediation are really wanting in the due sense of God's exceeding majesty and glory.

II. THE OFFICE OF A MEDIATOR NECESSITATED MUCH PERSONAL SELF-DENIAL. It was doubtless a great honour conferred on Moses ; but it was also a great burden. Thus he declared his own fears in the circumstances. " I exceedingly fear and quake " was his testimony about the experience on the mount. Besides, the forty days' seclusion and fast and all the attendant anxieties and troubles showed that it was most assuredly *no* sinecure.

And these trials of Moses only faintly typify the severe strain and trial borne by Christ, the one Mediator between God and man.

III. THE MEDIATION WAS LAW-GIVING. Moses was to convey " the commandments, and the statutes, and the judgments " of God unto the people. It was didactic—its purpose was the conveyance of truth. It was a *prophetic* office, consequently, which Moses in this instance received. The *priestly* was made over to Aaron, on the principle of a " division of labour."

And so Christ is the great mediating Prophet. He came forth from the secret place of God to convey to us what God is. He came down from heaven. He testified about heavenly things (John iii. 11—13). And in the perfection of mediation, he embodied the truth, and was able to say, " I am the truth " (John xiv. 6). Jesus was a living Law.

IV. OBEDIENCE SHOULD RESULT FROM THE MEDIATION. The whole Law was a " commandment with promise." This is shown in ver. 33. The children of Israel were to conduct themselves obediently as the children of God, and they would realize in all its breadth the promise of the fifth commandment. The Law was a Law of well-being (ver. 29). Obedience was the condition of continued prosperity in the land.

And the same arrangements continue. Obedience to God's Law still secures the promise of the life that now is, as well as of that which is to come. Not, of course, that the saints are always prosperous in this world; were this the case, saintship would be a very mercenary business. But other things being equal, the tendency of obedience is to present as well as future well-being. God makes no promise, but threatening, to the disobedient.—R. M. E.

EXPOSITION.

CHAPTER VI.

Vers. 1—3.—Some connect this with what goes before, and take it as a sort of epilogue to the preceding discourse; but it is rather to be regarded as introductory to what follows. Being about to enjoin upon the people the commandments they were to obey in the land on which they were about to enter, Moses prefaces this with a general announcement of what he was about to deliver, and with a statement of the reason for such deliverance, and of the benefits that would flow from the observance of what should be enjoined.

Ver. 1.—These are the commandments. In the Hebrew it is, *This is the commandment,* i.e. the sum and substance of the Divine enactment; equivalent to "the Law" (ch. iv. 44). "The statutes and judgments" (rights) are in apposition to "the commandment," and explain it.

Ver. 2.—The reason for this announcement of the Law was that the people might fear the Lord, so as to keep all that he enjoined, they and their children, from generation to generation, and that they might thereby continue long in life, and in the enjoyment of the advantages accruing from the land of which they were about to take possession.

Ver. 3.—God had promised from the first to the patriarchs that he would make of their posterity a great nation (Gen. xii. 1; xvii. 6; xviii. 18). But the fulfilment of this promise was conditioned by their continuing as a people in the fear of God, and in obedience to his Law. Everything, then, depended on their hearing what Moses had been commanded to teach them, and observing to do it (cf. Lev. xxvi. 9, etc.). **In the land,** etc. This is to be connected with the clause, "that it may be well with thee, and that ye may increase mightily;" the land was to be the scene and sphere of their prosperity and increase. Some would render thus: "As the Lord God of thy fathers hath promised thee a land," etc., i.e. a place in which thou mayest prosper and increase; the other, however, is the more natural construction and rendering. There is, indeed, no preposition before "the land" in the Hebrew; but nothing is more common in that language than for the accusative of a noun to be used adverbially to describe the place where anything is done. **Milk and honey;** emblem of fruitfulness and sweetness (Song of Solomon iv. 11); proverbially descriptive of Canaan, as rich in pasturage for flocks, and abounding in flowers whence the bees could extract honey (cf. Exod. iii. 8, 17).

Vers. 4—25.—THE FIRST AND GREAT COMMANDMENT. "In the fear of Jehovah all true obedience is rooted (vers. 2, 3); for this is the first and most intimate fact in the relation of Israel and Jehovah (ch. v. 26). But where the supreme fear of Jehovah hinders men from allowing self to preponderate in opposition to God, there will be no stopping at this renunciation of self-will, though this comes first as the negative form of the ten commandments also shows, but there will come to be a coalescence of the human with the Divine will; and this is love, which is the proper condition of obedience, as the ten commandments also indicate (ch. v. 10)" (Baumgarten).

Ver. 4.—Hear, O Israel: The Lord our God is one Lord. This is an affirmation not so much of the *moneity* as of the *unity* and *simplicity* of Jehovah, the alone God. Though Elohim (plu.), he is one. The speaker does not say, "Jehovah is alone God," but "Jehovah our Elohim is one Jehovah" (comp. for the force of אֶחָד, Exod. xxvi. 6, 11; Ezek. xxxvii. 16—19). Among the heathen there were many Baals and many Jupiters; and it was believed that the deity might be divided and communicated to many. But the God of Israel, Jehovah, is one, indivisible and incommunicable. He is the Absolute and the

Infinite One, who alone is to be worshipped, on whom all depend, and to whose command all must yield obedience (cf. Zech. xiv. 9). Not only to polytheism, but to pantheism, and to the conception of a localized or national deity, is this declaration of the unity of Jehovah opposed. With these words the Jews begin their daily liturgy, morning and evening; the sentence expresses the essence of their religious belief; and so familiar is it to their thought and speech that, it is said, they were often, during the persecution in Spain, betrayed to their enemies by the involuntary utterance of it.

Ver. 5.—To the one indivisible Jehovah undivided devotion and love are due. Hence the injunction, **Thou shalt love Jehovah thy God with all thine heart, and with all thy soul, and with all thy might.** The "heart" is the inner nature of the man, including his intellectual, emotional, and conative faculties; the "soul" is the personality, the entire self-consciousness; and the "might" is the sum of the energies, bodily and mental. Not by profession merely is Jehovah to be loved; the whole man, body, soul, and spirit, is to be yielded to him in holy and devout affection (cf. Matt. xxii. 37; Mark xii. 33; Luke x. 27; Rom. xii. 1). The last letter of the first word, and the last letter of the last word in this verse are larger than the ordinary size (*majuscula*), and as these two form the word for witness (עד), the Jews say that they are written thus "that every one may know, when he professes the unity of God, that his heart ought to be intent and devoid of every other thought, because God is a *witness*, and knoweth everything" (R. Bechai, fol. 195, quoted by Michaelis, 'Bib. Heb.,' *in loc.*).

Vers. 6, 7.—Where true love to God exists in the heart, it will manifest itself in a regard to his will, and in the diligent keeping of his commandments. Hence his words were to be not only in the memory of the people, but laid upon their heart (cf. **ch. xi.** 18), that they might be ever present to the thought and will. They were also to be inculcated upon their children, and to be the subject of conversation on all fitting occasions between them, the members of their household, and even their casual associates. **Thou shalt teach them diligently unto thy children;** literally, *Thou shalt sharpen them to thy children,* impress them upon them, send them into them like a sharp weapon.

Ver. 8.—The words of God were to be bound for **a sign** [a memorial or directory] **upon thine hand,** the instrument of acting, and to be as **frontlets** [fillets or bands] **between thine eyes,** the organs of direction in walking or moving, and so on the forehead, the chamber of thought and purpose; and they were to inscribe them on the posts of their houses, and on their gates. The purport of this is that they were constantly and everywhere to have these commandments of the Lord in view and in mind, so as to undeviatingly observe them. It seems, however, to have been a custom widely prevalent among the ancient Eastern peoples to carry about their persons slips of parchment or some other material, on which were written sentences of moral or religious import; and such sentences they were also wont to inscribe on conspicuous places of their dwellings; usages still to be found among the Moslems (see Wilkinson, 'Ancient Egyptians,' iii. 364; Lane, 'Modern Egypt,' i. 338; Russell, 'Nat. Hist. of Aleppo;' Thomson, 'Land and the Book,' i. 216), and the latter of which was not altogether unknown among Western nations (cf. Virgil, 'Georg.' iii. 26, etc.), of which traces may still be seen in Switzerland, Germany, and on old houses in both England and Scotland. This custom originated, probably, in a desire to have the sentiments inscribed always in mind; but for the most part these inscriptions came to be regarded as amulets or charms, the presence of which on the person or the house was a safeguard against evil influences, especially such as were supernatural. By the Jews this custom was followed; and they regarded it as authorized by the injunction of Moses in this passage. Taking his words literally, they had their tôtâphoth and their mezuzah, the former of which—the phylacteries of the New Testament—were strips of parchment, on which passages of the Law (Exod. xiii. 2—10, 11—17; ch. vi. 4—10, 13—22) were written, and these, enclosed in a box, were bound on the forehead and left wrist, and worn at prayers by the worshippers; the latter a slip of parchment, on which were written certain passages of Scripture (vers. 4—9; ch. xi. 13—21), and which, enclosed in a reed or cylinder, was fixed on the right-hand doorpost of every room in the house (see arts. 'Mezuzah' and 'Phylacteries' in Kitto's 'Biblical Cyclopædia,' 3rd edit.).

Vers. 10—12.—As the Israelites were about to enter upon the possession of a rich and fertile land, where everything for their accommodation and comfort was already provided for them, there was a danger of their being so engrossed with their new possessions as to forget the Lord and his gracious dealings with them. They are, therefore, here warned against the danger to which they would be thus exposed. **House of bondage** (Exod. xiii. 3).

Vers. 13—18.—**Thou shalt fear the Lord thy God.** The fear of the Lord—that reverent awe which is akin to love—is the beginning of wisdom and the foundation of piety; where it is in the heart it will lead to serving of the Lord in holy obedience; and they in whom it dwells will swear by his Name, recognizing his presence and omniscience, and not daring to asseverate anything but what they know to be true. Thus, really believing in God and reverently worshipping him, the Israelites would be careful not to go after other gods, or to give to any object that homage which is due unto Jehovah alone, knowing that this he will not endure or suffer with impunity; for he is a jealous God, and them that thus dishonour him he will destroy (Exod. xx. 5; ch. iv. 24, etc.). Thus also they should be kept from murmuring against God, and thereby tempting him—putting him, as it were, to the proof, and calling in question his presence and his power, as they had done at Massah (Exod. xvii. 1—7). Without this genuine religious principle there will be no sincere worship, no true reverence, no real obedience, rendered unto God. But where this dwells in the heart it will influence the whole life, so that the commandments of God shall be diligently kept, and that which is good and right in his sight shall be done.

Ver. 19.—**To cast out**, etc.; rather, *to the casting out of*, etc. The infin. here expresses the carrying out of the action intimated in the words, "that it may be well with thee" (cf. Exod. xxiii. 27, etc.; xxxiv. 11).

Vers. 20—25.—The injunction to teach the words of the Lord to the children (ver. 7) is here more largely explained. When asked by their sons the meaning and reason of the commandments and institutes which they observed, they were to show them what the Lord had done for his people in bringing them out of Egypt and establishing them in Canaan, and how he had enjoined on them all these statutes that they might fear Jehovah their God for their good always, and for their preservation and safety.

Ver. 22.—**Signs and wonders** (cf. ch. iv. 34).

Ver. 25.—**And it shall be our righteousness**; literally, *And righteousness shall be to us*, i.e. we shall be held righteous by God if we observe to do all that he has enjoined (comp. Rom. x. 5; vi. 16; Phil. iii. 6). **Before the Lord**, i.e. not only in his sight, but according to his judgment, so as to be approved of him (cf. Ps. lvi. 13; cxvi. 9).

HOMILETICS.

Vers. 1—3.—*Obedience to God conducive to the highest good.* The Lord God had launched forth into the world a new nation, the basis of whose constitution was specifically religious. The worship, fear, and service of the one living and true God were the prime duties enjoined on the people, without which no bare morality as between man and man was accepted before him. In this paragraph, however, we get no indications of duty which have not previously been included in the ten commandments. How can we? The whole ground of duty was covered by them. Still, the same truths are ever being thrown into forms fresh and new. The primal laws of duty are not many; they may soon be recounted. But we need "line upon line, precept upon precept," that the very precepts which perhaps we deem commonplace may be graven on our hearts, and there become living powers! In the three verses before us the enjoined duties are summed up in the one phrase, "the commandment" (ver. 1: the word is singular, and includes in its meaning both statutes and judgments). Four expressions show how "the commandment" is to be kept. 1. There is to be a fear of the Lord; a fear based on trust, not on distrust. 2. The Divine appointments are to be the rule of life. 3. The nurture and training of the family are to be in entire harmony therewith. 4. This family loyalty to God is to be continuous and unswerving—"all the days of thy life." And in wealth and variety of diction the Legislator points out that in this loyalty of being Israel would find its *well*-being. Whence we get the topic for our present Homily: *That our highest interests are ensured by the fulfilment of the Divine commands.* Observe—

I. IT IS SUPPOSED THAT MEN WILL NOT BE INSENSIBLE TO THE QUESTION—"WHAT WILL BE MOST PROFITABLE TO US?" As a matter of fact, they *do* regard the measure of profit likely to accrue, as something which regulates their movements. Nor is there anywhere in the Word of God any censure passed on this. In fact, even our Saviour himself appeals to considerations of profit in Matt. xvi. 25, 26. So also does the Apostle Paul in 1 Tim. iv. 8. The working of self-love is recognized without rebuke in the Law, "Thou shalt love thy neighbour *as* thyself;" and it is even remotely enjoined in the words, "Do thyself no harm." The distinction between self-love and selfishness is very decided, yet is far too little noticed. Selfishness is having regard to our own interests *in distinction from* those of others; self-love has regard to our own interests *in harmony with* those of others. The first is sinful; the second is lawful; yea, more, to fight against our highest interests would be wrong. We may demur to the maxim that "utility is the foundation of virtue," and rightly so, if "utility" be taken in the selfish aspect thereof. But if by "utility" we mean "the tendency to promote the highest good over the widest sphere, for all time," then the maxim is lifted up to a higher level, and becomes at least practically wholesome, even if it may be objected to on philosophical grounds. If, then, we do but entertain a right and scriptural view of what our highest interests are, it is lawful for us, and even binding on us, to have a regard to them; and it is to the desire in that direction that the passage before us makes its appeal.

II. It is shown here that there is a course of life which is appointed for us by God. The appointments of God for us are specified here. We are to "fear the Lord." Evidently this is to be a fear, not of dread, but of love; for see ver. 5. In Ps. cxxx. 4 we read, "But there is forgiveness with thee, that thou mayest be feared." God forgives, and so takes away the fear of the offender, that the fear of offending may take its place. There is to be dread of sin, but not of God. The fear is to be suffused with tenderness and brightened with joy (Ps. xxxiii. 1). See the phrases in this section, even touching in their pathos—"God," "thy God," "the God of thy fathers." Yea, it is our own God who lays down our life-rules, and by all the force of his tender love would he win us to obedience.

III. In following God's appointed way we ensure our own highest good. (Vers. 2, 3.) The *elements* of good which obedience ensures are: 1. Peace. We remarked above that the fear of God, which we are called on to cherish, is one based on trust. The Christian form of this is reliance on the Lord Jesus Christ in all the aspects in which he is revealed to us as ours. The effect of this is named in Rom. v. 1. Then there will be peace of conscience (see Isa. xxxii. 17; Phil. iv. 6, 7; Matt. xi. 29). 2. Harmony. Our nature will be in self-accord when what we are and do corresponds to what we ought to be and do. There will be no schism between the judgment and the affections. 3. Health. Other things being equal, the man who is most obedient to God's laws will have the soundest health in body, soul, and spirit. The gladsomeness and ease of a sound and well-balanced constitution will be his. Hence: 4. Continuance will be a part of the reward—"that thy days may be prolonged" (see Ps. xci. 16; cf. Eph. vi. 3; Ps. xxxvi. 9, 28, 34). The *forms* in which the rewards of loyalty to God will show themselves are very varied. The *individual* will find that godliness has "promise of the life that now is, and of that which is to come." The *family* will find that "he blesseth the habitation of the just." The *city* will find that the keeping of God's commandments is among the things "which belong unto its peace." And "the righteous nation which keepeth the truth" will find that "salvation doth God appoint for walls and bulwarks" (see Isa. xxvi. 1, 2; xlviii. 17). It is a remarkable instance of the Divine condescension to our ways of thinking, feeling, and acting, that our God should stoop to teach us what is profitable to ourselves, and that he should deign in mercy to reward with honour and peace those who fear him (Ps. lxii. 12). Mercifully meeting us on the low ground on which we too frequently stand in looking out for profit, God would raise us up to the higher platform of a pure, self-abandoning self-forgetfulness and love, in which we are content to be nothing, that God may be all in all. For observe—

IV. Apparent exceptions to this rule are exceptions only in appearance. Sometimes obedience to God may be attended with a most unusual amount of affliction or of persecution. Take, *e.g.* the roll of worthies referred to in Heb. xi. 32—39. Can we say it was for their "profit" to serve God? Most certainly we can. For: 1. By their endurance they became witnesses for God, and served their generation in the very way they would most have desired could they have seen as God sees. 2. Their afflictions were the means of purifying their characters, strengthening their principles, and ripening their virtues. 3. In the midst of all, God was himself to them "their exceeding joy;" and what they had *in* him was, even on earth, an ample recompense for all that they had suffered *for* him. 4. They had respect to the recompense of reward (Heb. xi. 10, 16, 26). 5. Their sufferings are long ago forgotten in the rest of the unseen state where they are "inheriting the promises" (Heb. vi. 12). They had faith to believe them and patience to wait for them, and now they have entered into "the rest." Who need wish to change their lot for the smoothest and most prosperous career of a man "without God in the world"? Virtue may for a while seem "to have the worst of it," but "they that are losers for God shall never be losers by him in the end."

V. OBEDIENCE IS EXPECTED TO BE THE RESULT OF AN INTELLIGENT AND CULTURED FAITH, AND NOT OF A BLIND ONE. Ver. 1, "The Lord your God commanded to teach you." Nowhere has the adage, "Ignorance is the mother of devotion," less warrant than in the Word of God. The priests of a spurious or alien faith may inculcate blind submission. Not so any of the inspired writers, whether legislators, prophets, or apostles. Men were to be taught not only what God required, but why he required it, that they might render him the homage of a heart quickened to love through the truth which reached the understanding and "commended itself to every man's conscience." God appeals to reason (Isa. i. 18).

Vers. 4—9.—*Truth and godliness to be perpetuated by means of home training.* In this paragraph, the aged lawgiver rehearses the sum and substance of the Law he had delivered, and is showing what provision God had made in the structure of society for the maintenance and perpetuation of truth and godliness. It is easy to see how very incomplete his work would have been, had he not been guided to make provision for its perpetuation after his death. Doubtless God designs to use various kinds of workers in his field. Some may, like Whitefield, make a great impression while their oratory is swaying its thousands and tens of thousands. Others may be like Wesley, who not only moved the people for a generation by his pulpit power, but also prepared the way by his organizing skill for a great institution which should last for ages. Now, it is not for us to disparage one man because he does not do the work of another, but certain it is that, other things being equal, there is no comparison between the power of a man whose felt influence passes away with his life, and that of one whose works follow him, in the productions of his pen or the creations of his up-building skill. Now, it was not by one like Aaron, eloquent though he was, that the continuance of the Hebrew faith and life was to be secured. He gives us no proof of stability or of that kind of power which ensures its own reproduction. *That* was found in Moses, a man naturally slow of speech, who, in spite of his occasional outbreaks of vehemence, was yet a patient, wise, faithful leader, by whose practical genius provision was made for the permanence of Israel's religious ordinances and life. Moved by the Holy Ghost, he called into existence those great institutions of worship and teaching, by means of which even we down to this day are feeling the impulses which started from Mount Sinai. In the six verses before us, we have what may be called a threefold appointment of God, which in all its essential features is as much in force now as ever. We propose to study it, not so much in its historical and local aspect, as in its bearing on us and on all men for all time.

I. HERE, AT THE BACK OF NATIONAL LIFE, IS SET THE EXPRESSION OF A CONDENSED THEOLOGY. "The Lord our God is one Lord." Time was when this verse was quoted in the Socinian controversy in proof of the unity of God, as against the Trinitarians, though it has in fact no bearing on the matter at all. It refers, not to the nature of the Divine Being *in himself*, but is rather set over against the faiths with which Israel had been surrounded, of "lords many and gods many." In contrast from polytheism, it declares that there is but one Great Supreme, who is the Lord of heaven and earth. And this is not the basis of Israel's faith alone, but of ours likewise. We know more of God than the Hebrews did, but what they knew we retain. In atheism, the highest intellectual natures never can rest. Deism chills. Pantheism ignores personality. The God of the Bible, as revealed to us, satisfies the cravings of intellect and heart. In Jesus Christ, God is "manifest" as nowhere else. Nor should we leave out the touching word, "the Lord *our* God." We have one God and Father of all, to whom the vast and the minute are equally distinct, and by whose hand both are moved with equal ease; who, while he rolls the stars along, can take under his special sheltering love the widow and the fatherless; who hears the orphan's moan and dries the falling tear. It is our inestimable privilege to know that infinitely above us, combined with an arm of mighty power, there is a heart of tenderest love, whose great concern it is to heal the wounds, to dry the tears, and obliterate the sins of a bleeding, weeping, guilt-stained world! What a revelation is this to our race! Well might Moses bid Israel "hearken"! For surely this one message to man, that there is a redeeming God whom he may call his own, is our gospel, our life, our joy, our crown!

II. FRONT OF THE CONDENSED THEOLOGY, WE HAVE HERE CONDENSED RELIGION. (Ver. 5.) The fundamental truth of theology is to be fruitful in practical godliness. God's revelation of himself *to* man is meant to be a redemptive power *in* man. Man has heart, soul, strength, understanding, emotion, will, energy. God would have no schism in our being. Our varied parts and powers are to be in tune. There is no need for us to present the sad spectacle of the heart going one way, while duty and conscience point another. Apart from the dissipation of force which that involves, what reproach and self-loathing such inward discord must ensure! Now, we have one inner faculty, even that of *love*, which is meant to rule, and does in fact rule, the man. According to the love, so intellect thinks, emotion feels, will decides, life moves. Our text says, let love be *all* concentrated on one grand object—God! Let him have all (see chs. x. 12; xi. 1, 13, 22; xix. 9; xxx. 16). Not even in the New Testament have we a greater commandment than this (Matt. xxii. 37—40). "The love of God which the gospel demands is more intensive and cordial than that which the Law of Moses demands of the Israelites, according to the gradual unfolding of the love of God himself, which was displayed in a much grander and more glorious form in the gift of his only begotten Son for our redemption than in the redemption of Israel out of the bondage in Egypt" (Keil). Thus closely related are theology and religion—God as revealed to us in Christ —that is theology; our love responding to God's—that is religion. Without the first, in what could the religious faculty find a proper object? Without the second, infinite love is defrauded of its rights! Still, a third question naturally follows: granted that in this interlacing of theology and religion we have both interpreted in meaning and both realizing their aims, what means can be devised to ensure the preservation of both through generation after generation?

III. HERE IS A SPECIAL ARRANGEMENT DIVINELY APPOINTED, TO CONSERVE AND PER-PETUATE BOTH. 1. The home is here supposed to be a centre in which the conserving forces of truth and godliness are to be themselves conserved. What a profound principle Moses here indicates, viz. that a nation will be good or bad according to its home life! Wonderful! that an infant nation should, at starting, have this truth deep graven in its statutes;—our land will be as our homes are! 2. In the home, our God looks to the parent to give it its character, tone, and influence. A child's religious faith is, in a high and holy sense, to be chosen for him by anticipation, by those who were "in Christ before" him. 3. The truths mentioned in sections 1 and 2 are to be in the parents' heart, that they may be poured out anew from thence as rivers of living water. Hence the word in ver. 7, "Thou shalt sharpen them;" coming fresh out of the sanctuary of a living soul, they are to be pointed, quick, and breathing truths. 4. By a variety of ways, the parent is to see his child's spirit early saturated with the truths of God. (1) By talking of them, in the house and out of it (ver. 7). (2) By exhibiting them, not only in the literal sense (see art. 'Phylacteries'[1]), but in a higher spiritual one. (3) By writing them (ver. 9; see art. 'Mezuzah'[2]). Thus the child is *from the first* to be regarded as God's child, to be trained for him. He is to receive God's Word through the avenues of eye, ear, intellect, heart. Divine truth is to be ever before him, night and day, indoors and out. Those who gave him birth and who love him best, are to mould his young life for God; he is to grow up as the Lord's rightful possession, with the view of his afterwards saying, in the spirit of devout surrender, "I am the Lord's!" (Isa. xliv. 5).

Note—Whatever was essential in the days of Moses, in the training of children for God as the means of guarding a nation, is not less needful now (Eph. vi. 4). The wider the range of human learning becomes, the more needful it should be rightly directed; otherwise the greater the attainment, the greater the peril!

Vers. 10—19.—"*Dangers ahead! Beware!*" The forecast of Moses is here directed to a period when Israel would have taken possession of the promised land (ver. 10),

[1] In Dr. Alexander's edition of Kitto's 'Biblical Cyclopædia.'   [2] Ibid.

There, their deliverance would be entire and complete. No longer would they be wanderers hither and thither, but would be occupants of a land that they would call their own. Neither from the nation to which they were once in bondage, nor from those which they were called on to supplant, would they fear aught any longer! And yet there is throughout this paragraph a voice of warning, as if danger would attend them still! It would be so. But the danger would be from within rather than from without: " When thou shalt have eaten and be full; then beware lest thou forget the Lord," etc. Whence, observe—

I. NO AMOUNT OF OUTWARD PROSPERITY CAN DELIVER A MAN FROM HIMSELF! By the time the state of calm was attained, which is here indicated, there would cease to be danger from hostile foes, at least for a while; but there would be perils of another kind, which would attend them even in the promised land. If Israel could have left themselves behind, it had been otherwise; but alas! go where they might, they must perforce take themselves with them, with all their liability to err, all the proneness to sin, and all the temptation to doubt or to pride. And not all the spears and slings of warriors could put the people in such peril as the corruptions of their own hearts! And so it is with us now and ever. We carry ourselves about with us everywhere; we cannot escape. There is within each one's heart a "root of bitterness," "a root that beareth gall and wormwood;" and let earthly circumstances be as fair, as easy, and as pleasant as they may, yet, unless we heed the danger within, they can do but very little to ensure our peace. And herein lies the great mistake of monasticism, as even Augustine reminded his hearers. He told them that it was vain for them to attempt to flee out of the world in order to escape corruption, for wherever they might be they would carry the evil within them. Never let us look to outer circumstances alone to ensure our entire rest. Not even a perfect world could bring us that, unless we were first made perfect.

II. THERE ARE THREE PERILS SPECIFIED HERE TO WHICH PROSPERITY MAY EXPOSE US. 1. The first is that of "forgetting the Lord" (ver. 12). When fields and vineyards and oliveyards increase, and our cup is overflowing, then we are apt to lose sight of him to whom we owe all; and this not only in the receiving but in the using thereof (cf. Hos. x. 1). Too apt are we to say in our pride, "My river is my own; I have made it for myself." So also are we apt to let our enjoyments conceal our God from view, and to think only of the mercies, while we forget to glorify God in the use of them. Nor is it any uncommon evil for men to be so set upon the enjoyment of this world's comforts, as to forget almost or altogether that higher world for which they are bound to live, and that future life on which all soon must enter. 2. Another danger indicated is that of undue tolerance of the idolatries which were round about them (ver. 14). One effect of prosperity is easy-goingness; and that, unless checked and guarded, will degenerate into a looseness of principle, whereby, under cover of suavity and amiability, respect for the convictions of others may come to be substituted by our having no very strong ones of our own. Nothing is more common than to see worldly aggrandizement attended by deterioration of moral sensibility. 3. A third danger specified is that of "tempting the Lord" when prosperity meets with a check. This seems to be the danger indicated in ver. 16, by a reference to "Massah" (see Exod. xvii. 2—7). At this place of sojourn there was a lack of water. The people murmured. They tempted the Lord and said, "Is the Lord among us or not?" As if they ceased to believe in God's presence with them, the moment he made them thus feel their dependence upon him! Strange perversity! Yet how like ourselves! The course of worldly prosperity scarcely ever runs with absolute smoothness for many years together. And the self-will engendered and strengthened in times of ease leads men to repine and complain bitterly the moment that ease receives a check. In times of prosperity men forget God, and then when adversity comes they often complain as if God had forgotten them. How much does God see, even in the people he takes for his own special care, to tax his patience, and to try his long-suffering love!

III. BY WAY OF GUARDING THEM BEFOREHAND AGAINST THESE PERILS, MOSES SHOWS ISRAEL THE DUTIES WHICH THEY ARE DILIGENTLY TO OBSERVE. 1. They are to fear the Lord only (ver. 13). 2. They are to swear by him only (see LXX. and Matt. iv. 10), i.e. to cherish a profound reverence for him as the Author of all mercies, and as the sole Regulator of their lives. The honour of his Name is to be supreme. 3. They are to give the supreme affection of the heart to God, so that they may not provoke his jealousy (ver. 15). 4. They are to serve him by constant obedience (ver. 18). By the constant recognition of these four duties, they will do much to guard themselves from yielding to the perils attendant on their growing wealth and ease. (This may be compared with the apostolic maxim, "Walk in the Spirit, and ye shall not fulfil the lusts of the flesh.") Evil is most successfully counteracted by the positive and earnest pursuit of the opposite good.

IV. IF THESE DUTIES WERE LOYALLY DISCHARGED, EARTHLY PROSPERITY AND SPIRITUAL WEAL WOULD GO TOGETHER. Ver. 18, "That it may be well with thee," etc. Whether our earthly circumstances are helps or hindrances to us Godward, will depend much more on what we bring to them than on what they bring to us. And however, on the side of this life, things may favour us and circumstances befriend, it is only as they help us to serve God better that they are really blessings to us: it is "well" with us only when God is well pleased with us. So much stress did Moses attach to the maintenance of unswerving loyalty to God, that he intimates that the possession of the land is secured to them only so far as they are true to their Great Deliverer (vers. 18, 19).

V. SINCE THE TIME OF MOSES, THIS PARAGRAPH HAS BECOME FAR MORE SACRED TO US, BY THE USE WHICH OUR SAVIOUR MADE OF IT IN A TIME OF SORE TEMPTATION. It is never to be forgotten, that our Lord repelled the tempter by the words, "It is written," etc. Of the three passages used as weapons for the discomfiture of the evil one, two are taken from this very paragraph (see Matt. iv. 7, 10). So that we are warranted in using it as our armoury from whence we may fetch the darts which shall make the tempter flee. These precepts cannot be needed by us less than they were by the Son of man. From him let us learn a use of the Divine Word that may serve us in a thousand assaults of the destroyer. For not until we do this can we discover the varied uses to which we may put the Word of God in the actual struggle of life. We, like our Master, have to be made perfect through suffering. Now we may suffer from want, hunger, and privation; and at another time all the kingdoms of the world, in a moment of time, may be set before us, to dazzle by their glare. We need to take to us the whole armour of God, that we may be able to stand in the evil day, and having done all, to stand. Go wheresoever we may, let our surroundings be easy and prosperous as they may, dangers will attend us everywhere, till we cross the pearly gate across whose threshold sin never comes. At one time it may be that adversity makes us fretful and apt to tempt the Lord, and then at another prosperity may make us slothful, and a sinful indifference may lull us to sleep. Our chief dangers are from within. But here in this holy Book are promises to cheer us when drooping, and warnings to quicken us when sluggish. Here is an arsenal from whence we may fetch our weapons, and a storehouse whence we may draw our supplies. Yea, in this wondrous quiver there are arrows which will be sharp in the hearts of the King's enemies, which shall pierce them to their fall!

Vers. 20—25.—*The value of history in parental teaching.* The Bible is pre-eminently a family Book. Israel's national life was supposed to find its centres of strength and permanence in godly homes. It would not be easy to find words which should overrate the importance of such a principle as this. That a young nation should at the outset of its existence have this laid down as a first law of its life: "The land will be as its homes are;" is an indication of the Divine guidance which was vouchsafed to him on whom, under God, the foundation of its national life depended. In the paragraph before us there are seven lines of thought suggested.

I. AS YOUNG LIFE COMES NEWLY INTO BEING, IT FINDS ARRANGEMENTS IN LAW AND PRECEPT READY TO HAND. Parental life holds a great trust in charge, to be committed to those who shall come after; that though one generation passeth away and another cometh, there may be no break in the continuity of holy thinking and living, from age to age. The Hebrews had their Law, which, as a revelation from God, was in advance of aught possessed by the rest of the world, and in which was couched the germ of larger truth that was to follow. There might be more light thrown upon it; there was never to be a forfeiture of it. Hence there were special reasons why parents should guard it intact for all the ages that were to follow.

II. YOUNG LIFE IS SUPPOSED TO BE AN INQUIRING LIFE. (Ver. 20.) It is not supposed that the children will lend themselves to either of two extremes: they will neither wildly tear up and obliterate "the old paths," nor will they walk in them heedlessly and without inquiry. The course here indicated is that which any sensible, well-disposed youth would naturally follow. He would ask, "What mean," etc. However a spurious priesthood may demand a blind and uninquiring faith, the Word of God never does anything of the kind. Reason is made for reverent inquiry, but it may be neither deified nor stultified. And what can be more charming than the honest, eager inquisitiveness of the young, asking for the reasons which govern the faith and worship that they find at work before their eyes? Specially delightful is such inquiry, when the parent is well able to give his answer.

III. THERE IS AWAITING THE YOUNG INQUIRER THE STORY OF A GREAT DELIVERANCE. (Vers. 21, 22.) The rescue from Egypt always formed the grand historic background of Israel's life (see Ps. lxxviii.; xcix.; cv.; cvi.; ciii. 7). Here was a disclosure of Divine love and care, the like of which had never been known. The great institution of sacrifice revealed provision for pardoning love. The precepts for the individual, the family, the nation, told what sort of a people God would have them be; while the oft-recurring strains, "I gave Egypt for thy ransom," "I brought thee up out of the land of bondage," would evoke all their national ardour, and create and foster an historic pride. The life-histories, too, of their fathers, Abraham, Isaac, and Jacob, would tell of the blessedness of having God as their God: and these, instilled into the heart with all the sweetness of fond parental love, would lead the young Israelite, when the teaching was sanctified by God's grace, to say right joyously, "This God shall be my God for ever and ever!" Yes! the young life ever coming on earth is not to be left to grope its way. The light from the past is to be handed down for the ages to come, that sire and son and son's son may rejoice in the same God, and ensure a blessed continuity of holy faith and consecrated life.

IV. THE GREAT DELIVERANCE WAS EFFECTED THAT THE RESCUED PEOPLE MIGHT BE A NEW NATION WORTHY OF GOD. Ver. 23, "That he might bring us in, to give us the land which he sware unto our fathers." And in this new relation they were to be witnesses for God (Isa. xliii. 10). They were to be a distinct, compact people, with faith, laws, and polity, higher than the rest of the world, holding in trust for mankind, till the fulness of times, much precious truth which was to find its outcome in a great, world-wide deliverance which should overshadow all; while the Israel of God was to merge into a spiritual Israel, made up of all who are Christ's, known as a "peculiar people, zealous of good works."

V. IN THIS CONTINUED LIFE, WORTHY OF GOD, WOULD THE JUSTIFICATION OF ISRAEL'S FAITH AND OBSERVANCES BE FOUND. "It shall be our righteousness," etc. (ver. 25). It is scarcely possible to regard these words as having reference to any doctrine of justification by faith; for though, even as far back as Abraham's days, that *was* a doctrine, yet it was not formulated till the times of the gospel, by Paul. The meaning of the phrase seems to be: "This will be our justification of our position and claims; we claim to be a people of God, above all the nations that are on the face of the earth, and we shall vindicate that claim, not by words only, but by being what we profess to be." Thus would the parent quicken his child, and stimulate and inspire him to be *all* that his glorious faith bade him be—"holy unto the Lord his God!"

VI. IN THIS ARRANGEMENT, THE DIVINE BENEVOLENCE WAS AS MANIFEST AS GOD'S REGARD FOR HIS OWN HONOUR. Ver. 24, "To fear the Lord our God, for our good always." The glory of God and the good of man are in harmony. So has God constructed the universe, so doth he carry on his government, as to ensure that "they that honour him, he will honour." "All things work together for good to them that love God." "Great peace have they which love God's Law; and nothing shall offend them." "Godliness is profitable unto all things." "Seek ye first the kingdom of God, and his righteousness; and all these things shall be added unto you."

VII. NOT ONLY WOULD ISRAEL, BY OBEDIENCE, ENSURE ITS OWN GOOD, BUT ALSO ITS CONTINUANCE IN THE LAND. Ver. 24, "That he might preserve us alive." Repeatedly do we read that the prolongation of Israel's days in the land depended on their loyalty to God. The land was given them, not for their own sakes merely, but for God's. If they continued there, faithfully witnessing for him, the land would be continued to them ; if not, they would have to quit, and give up the possession thereof to strangers. This is precisely the principle on which God governs the nations now. No nation can preserve itself in being by any other policy than that of obedience to God. Disloyalty to God and the right is the surest possible policy of decomposition. Even attempts at self-preservation which violate God's laws will fail of their end. And is it not of vast significance that these are the principles by which the young life of a nation is to be moulded ? Whatever allowance must be made for changing circumstances, however true it may be that no nation now holds exactly the same place in the world that Israel did, yet it is also true that all the more substantial part of the seven lines of thought here indicated is unchanged and unchangeable. Christian parents are inheritors of the truth of God : they hold it in trust for their children : they, as they grow up, will inquire concerning it : its historic basis is the great deliverance effected by the Lord Jesus : Christians are now God's peculiar people : they are redeemed that they may be holy, and that in holiness they may train succeeding generations : and just in proportion as through them loyalty to the truth and to God is leavening their posterity, are they bringing honour to the cause they espouse. Hebrews were to be conservative. Christians are to be also aggressive. We are to be "the light of the world," and "the salt of the earth." By the light of God's love we are to scatter men's darkness, and by the salt of God's truth are we to stay its corruption. And just so far as our nation is imbued with righteousness and truth, will it have within it the guarantee of its own perpetuation. The best defence is the armour of light. Without righteousness and the fear of God, not all the pretence and brag—not all the fleets or armies at command, can ever guard a nation from decay. "If the salt have lost his savour, . . . it is thenceforth good for nothing but to be cast out, and to be trodden under foot of men."

HOMILIES BY VARIOUS AUTHORS.

Vers. 1—3.—" *Obedience the end of Law.*" All the machinery of law is abortive, unless obedience be the result. As a mother teaches her children, giving them "line upon line," frequent repetition and variation, so Moses patiently taught Israel. He was "faithful in all his house."

I. See the internal excellence of God's Law. It has so many qualities of merit, that no one word in human language can express them all. They are "commandments," which word indicates the just authority from which they emanate. They are "statutes," implying their fixed and permanent character. They are "judgments," a description which denotes thoughtful deliberation, patient forethought, and sagacious decision. No greater benefactor can men have than a wise legislator. These Laws, if reverently observed, would have been "health to the marrow," and life to the nation.

II. The design of God's covenant was hearty and complete obedience. It was unprofitable for God to command, or for Moses to teach, unless the people obeyed ; just as it is futile for the husbandman to plough his land, pulverize the clods, sow the seed, water his crops, if no harvest ensue. The end which God had clearly in view— the only end worthy of him, was not Israel's possession of Canaan, nor prosperity there ; the *final end* was obedience. The land was selected to be a theatre for practical righteousness. The land would be forfeited if righteous obedience did not abound. And obedience, to be acceptable, must be real. External conformity to law would not suffice. The whole soul must yield compliance. There must be harmony between man's will and God's. Obedience would foster reverence, and reverence would strengthen love. There is action and reaction amid the forces of the soul.

III. Pious obedience is entailed. It is a moral inheritance passing from father to son. Formal and superficial obedience will not reproduce itself in others, will not bear seed of the true kind. But genuine, vital piety is contagious. If bad qualities are communicated, surely good qualities are also. Else truth would be feebler than error, virtue feebler than vice. Thorough, straightforw^rd, transparent, cheerful piety is the greatest power in the world. For our children's sake, and for our children's children, let reverent obedience brighten and beautify our life !

IV. Pious obedience produces present fruits. Its rewards are not wholly reserved

for the future. On earth some advantages are reaped. 1. *Length of days is a result.*
"Thy days may be prolonged." A green old age is a beautiful thing. "The wicked
shall not live out half their days." 2. *Numerous progeny is a result.* "Ye may
increase mightily." A growing population is universally regarded as a token of
material prosperity. "They of the city shall flourish as grass of the earth."
Success in all enterprise is announced as an effect. "It shall be well with thee."
3. Robust health, domestic comfort, national peace, prolific harvests, security, contentment, honour,—*these* are among the fruits to be anticipated. Obedience is an investment of moral capital, which brings largest and safest results.—D.

Vers. 4—9.—*Love, the root-principle of obedience.* Attention is summoned for the
reception of central truth, viz. the unity of the Godhead. At that period, this doctrine
was in great peril. All the Orientals believed in "lords many and gods many."
Science here confirms Scripture. The unity of design, running through all natural
law and force, indicates clearly unity of the Creator. To know the true God is, for
honest minds, to love him. But rebellion of heart has engendered repugnance towards
God—dislike, hatred, enmity.

I. THE SOURCE OF ALL AUTHORITY IS A BEING OF ESSENTIAL GOODNESS. 1. *He is
sole Monarch, incomparable and unapproachable.* He dwells alone, higher than the
highest creature. The disparity between him and an archangel is immeasurable.
2. *He is absolutely perfect.* Every attribute and quality that is essential to perfection is
found in him. "He is light," having no dark shade anywhere. 3. *He is the Source of
life:* Jehovah—the Living—the Life-giving. All we have, and are, and hope to be,
is derived from him. 4. *He has deigned to come into intimate relation with us.* He
has made a voluntary compact with us. He calls us his people. He allows us to call
him *our God.* We have a proprietorship in him.

II. THIS GOD DESERVES THE CENTRAL PLACE IN OUR HEARTS. Because of the moral
beauty and essential goodness of our God, he is incomparably most worthy of human
love. To give to any other a higher place in our affection than we give to God, would
be an outrage against righteousness, fitness, and self-interest. For all these faculties
and susceptibilities of the human heart have been fashioned by God himself, and have
been fashioned for *this very* purpose, viz. that we should bestow our worthiest love on
him. If this eternal design be frustrated, there is violence, disharmony, misery within.
Such love is commanded. It is a duty as well as a privilege. Though we cannot
instantly and summarily command our love, we can *indirectly.* We can fix our
thought on the worthiest object of love. We can contemplate his charms. We can
appreciate his goodness. We can assure ourselves of his love. It is to be an intelligent, reasonable, practical love.

III. THE LOVE OF THE LAWGIVER PRODUCES LOVE TO HIS LAW. Law is a projection of God's thought, a mirror of his mind, an overt act of love. The true child
will highly esteem every known wish of its father. To have practical direction from
an unseen father will be treasured as a choice token of that father's regard. If children,
we shall hide every word of our father in our memory and in our love. Every wish of
his heart will be a visible feature in *our* life. It may be painful to the flesh, but it
will be pleasant to the soul. To the dutiful child, obedience is a luxury, a banquet of
joy. "Oh! how I love thy Law!" exclaims the pious Psalmist. "Thy Law is within
my heart." Thy Word is to me as honey, as the droppings of the honeycomb.

IV. LOVE IS THE MOTIVE-POWER OF SPEECH. The tongue is the servant of the
heart. We speak freely and fluently of that which is dear to our hearts. The child
will speak freely of its toys and games, the farmer of his crops, the artist of his works.
If men esteemed and valued God's Word, they would spontaneously converse of it,
morning, noon, and night. It would be a painful restraint upon our desire if we withheld our speech. This precept of Moses need not be an external law imposed upon us
from without; it may become the living law within, "the law of the Spirit of life."

V. LOVE CONSTRUCTS ITS WHOLE LIFE ON THE MODEL OF GOD'S LAW. The *hand*
will become the instrument of righteousness. On *it* will be written God's Word, viz.
industry, honesty, restraint, generous kindness, helpfulness. God's Word will be our
ornament. Instead of gold and jewels upon the forehead, "our adornment will be"
modesty, chastity, cheerfulness, moral beauty. God's Name will be indelibly inscribed

upon our foreheads. Our domestic affairs will be ordered by the Divine will. We shall write his Word on the posts of our houses. Every home in which love dwells will be a temple. Order, active piety, frugality, peace, mutual service, will be the principles conspicuous in godly homes. And our municipal and political life will be conducted on the same line of obedience. Legislation, justice, taxation, commerce, literature, art, will all be consecrated to God's glory. As the flowers of earth send their fragrance heavenward, so from every act of ours a fragrance of homage should ascend to God.—D.

Vers. 10—19.—*The peril of prosperity.* Secular prosperity is hazardous. Unless the ship have ample ballast in the hold, a strong gale, however favourable, will be likely to capsize the ship and bury her in the caverns of the sea. The greater our earthly abundance, the greater our need of religious principle.

I. WISE MEN INHERIT THE FRUIT OF OTHERS' LABOURS. Under the leadership of God, the Hebrews inherited cities which the Canaanites had built, and vineyards which the Amorites had planted. If we knew *all* the facts of the case, we should admire this as an act of righteous wisdom. We *do* know that the iniquity of the Amorites was a cup full to the brim. The Hebrews, with all their faults, were a superior race. Similar displacements have gone on in all the lands of the world. It is an instance of the "survival of the fittest." Redeemed men are destined to be the lords of the earth. The Church shall possess and rule the world. "*All* things are ours." This inheritance of Canaan, with its cities and cattle and wealth, ought to have produced a deep sense of gratitude. All the Hebrews enjoyed they owed to the bountiful hand of God.

II. SUDDEN PROSPERITY IS A SEVERE STRAIN ON PIETY. The sense of daily and hourly dependence upon God for material food is an advantage; it is a constant incentive to gratitude and faith. Poor human nature cannot bear much indulgence. Poverty is more conducive to piety than wealth has ever been. Hence our Lord chose a state of poverty as most suited to his mission. "How hardly shall they that have riches enter into the kingdom of heaven!" So long as men continue in the flesh, they prefer a *visible* God to an invisible. So they say to gold, "Thou art my god." To be singular in religious belief and practice is always an arduous effort. The example of others has always been a sore temptation. Unless we can persuade *them* by the force of our superior faith, they are sure to bias us injuriously. Our safety lies in a stalwart and fearless piety.

III. TO FALL FROM THE FAVOUR TO THE FROWN OF GOD IS IMMEASURABLE AND COMPLETE. It would have been better for their peace and their reputation not to have inherited the land, than to be ejected from it again. It is a tremendous calamity, having been lifted high, to be thrown down. The effect of disloyalty among the Hebrews would not simply be a replacement in their former state; it would be destruction from the face of the earth. In the realm of morals, we cannot descend to a station we had occupied aforetime. If there is declension, retrogression, fall, it must be to a lower level than *that* we formerly held. The penalties imposed by righteousness are complete and remediless. We may well "stand in awe and sin not." It is perilous in the extreme to "try" God's patience—to make experiments on the long-suffering of God. *Suddenly*, he "whets his glittering sword, and his hand takes hold on judgment."

IV. HOPE IS AN INSPIRATION OF STRENGTH. Although Moses has addressed to them these cautions, and pointed out these perils, he will not think so meanly of them as to forecast their fall. He will cherish in his own breast the bright hope of their loyalty. He will call into exercise their own best principles and aspirations. He confidently predicts their wise and upward course, and sketches before their eyes their future greatness and security. Herein is wise generalship. If hope kindles her lamp in the human breast, all is not lost. This is Heaven's cordial for a fainting soul.—D.

Vers. 20—25.—*The parental office.* In the Mosaic economy, the parental office is made prominent, and parental influence is pressed into service. All God's arrangements for training mankind dovetail into one another.

I. THE DUTY OF A PARENT TO PROVOKE RELIGIOUS INQUIRY. No greater folly can be perpetrated than the attempt to repress inquiry. Inquiry is the king's highway to wisdom, and who dare block it up? God loves to hear honest inquiry. To afford instruction is the delight of the Divine Spirit, but what instruction will be valued if no spirit of inquiry is awake? Some questions which we ask can never be solved; they are beyond the range of the human mind. Some questions God *will* not answer, because they are vain and useless. But honest questions, with a view to practical obedience, God delights to hear. You can do the young no better service than encourage their minds to inquire after religious facts. "What mean these things?"

II. THE DUTY OF A PARENT TO ANSWER FULLY CHILDREN'S QUESTIONS. It is childish folly to attempt to conceal our lowly origin. There is no real disgrace in an obscure parentage. To have been formerly enslaved, or imprisoned, or oppressed, through man's injustice, is an honour, not a stigma of reproach. There is no real shame, except such as proceeds from wrong-doing. It will do *us* good, it will do our children good, to see the "rock whence we were hewn, the hole of the pit from which we were digged." It will foster humility, gratitude, contentment, trust. It will lead us afresh to adore the Divine goodness, and to count ourselves and our children the servants of this mighty God. Never let true Israelites forget that all they have they owe to God! Unto this state of happy privilege a Divine hand has brought us.

III. THE DUTY OF A PARENT TO OPEN UP GOD'S BENEFICENT INTENTION. If any man is too indolent to investigate truth for his own sake, he may be provoked to do it for his children's sake. We should have such a firm conviction that every arrangement and command of God was "for our good always," that we can demonstrate it to our children. Our knowledge of God and of his practical dealings should be so broad and clear that we might see and feel that his care for our good was paramount. This is the first and loftiest end he seeks—not our enjoyment, but *our good*. Not to demonstrate his power, or his consistency, or his determination to conquer,—these are not his foremost aims, but "our good always." His costliest deed of condescension was the yielding of his Son to death. And where shall we seek the moving principle? In his own future glory merely? No! In his love for the world! Yet his glory, and man's real good, are but the separate threads that make one cord.

IV. THE DUTY OF A PARENT TO PROMOTE HIS CHILDREN'S RIGHTEOUSNESS. "It shall be our righteousness, if we observe to do all these commandments." No more conclusive argument can parents use; no loftier end can they contemplate. *To become righteous—* this is to be the lofty ideal we set before our children. But commensurate with the grand acquisition must be the care that we promote it by proper and practicable methods. It is impossible for guilty men to regain righteousness by their own efforts or merits. But real righteousness is provided for us by the bounty of God, and is offered to us in Christ as a free gift. "He hath brought in everlasting righteousness, which is for all and upon all that believe." Our ambition for our children must be the highest—not that they be richly dowered, or learned, or placed in earthly rank, but that they may be internally and thoroughly righteous.—D.

Ver. 2.—*Descending obligations.* I. CHILDREN WITH THEIR PARENTS ARE INCLUDED IN THE COVENANT. This has been a general principle in God's dealings with his servants. We have it affirmed, both in the covenant with Abraham (Gen. xvii. 7—15) and in the later covenant with Israel (ch. xxix. 10—12). It was signified in the rite of circumcision. The Israelitish child was regarded as within the covenant, a genuine member of the theocracy, till by a personal act of apostasy—if unfortunately it should be so—he severed himself from its blessings. Similar language is used of the children of Christian believers (Acts ii. 39; 1 Cor. viii. 14). Received into the Church by baptism, they are recognized with their parents as interested in the promise; they are expected, on coming to years of discretion, freely to appropriate the obligations of the Christian life; and they are, in case of refusal, justly regarded as apostates from Christ.

II. THE STANDING OF CHILDREN IN THE COVENANT ENTAILS SERIOUS OBLIGATIONS ON THE PARENTS. 1. Religious *instruction* (vers. 6, 7, 20; Exod. xiii. 8, 14, etc.). The children had not been personally at Horeb. They had not seen the mighty works of God in Egypt and the desert. It was the duty of parents to acquaint them with the history, and to instruct them in their duties. 2. Religious *training*, which is education in act, as instruction is education in word (Gen. xviii. 19; ch. xxi. 18; Prov. xxix. 15, etc.). 3. Religious *example*. The parent is to be one who loves the Lord for himself (ver. 5). The Word is to be in his own heart (ver. 6). Only thus will he teach with effect. All this has its counterpart in the duties of Christian parents (Eph iv. 4; 1 Tim. iii. 4; 2 Tim. iii. 15, etc.).

III. THE STANDING OF CHILDREN IN THE COVENANT ENTAILS SERIOUS OBLIGATIONS ON THE CHILDREN. Where parental duties had been fulfilled, the Israelitish child was under the most sacred obligations to choose and adhere to the God of his fathers, and to serve him in the way prescribed. There was in this no interference with freedom, for when God proposes covenant relations to a human being, while it is his privilege, it can never be aught else than his duty to accept them. In the Christian Church, a like obligation rests on the children of believers. The baptized child is bound to serve God, and, if properly instructed (Matt. xxviii. 19), it cannot evade the responsibilities thus laid upon it. Great is the guilt of a child brought up in a Christian home. if wantonly it apostatizes.—J. O.

Vers. 4, 5.—*The great commandment.* I. THE GROUND OF IT. A just view of God. The view given in ver. 4 is as comprehensive as it is sublime. It embraces two parts mutually complementary. 1. *God's absoluteness and unity*—" Jehovah one." 2. *God's personal relation to Israel*—" Your God." The two are combined: 3. In *the covenant name*—" Jehovah." This, on the one hand, denotes God as the Eternal—the ever-living, the self-*existent*, and therefore self-*consistent* One. On the other, it gathers into its rich significance the love, and truth, and faithfulness of centuries of gracious revelation. It will not awaken love to God to think of him merely as absolute Deity. It is the discovery of what else is contained in the Divine essence; above all, the revelation of his love, grace, and covenant-keeping faithfulness, which attracts affection. While, *without* the revelation of God as one and absolute—exclusive, self-subsisting Deity—it would be impossible to raise the demand for love to the requisite moral height. In Jesus Christ the revelation of God reaches its highest point. Only the Son could reveal him in the fulness of his glory and love.

II. THE HEIGHT OF IT. It requires not merely that God should be loved, but loved with all the powers of our being, and with all the energy of these powers. 1. *With clear intelligence*—" mind " (Matt. xxii. 37; Mark xii. 33). 2. *With undivided affection*—" heart." 3. *With entire self-surrender*—" soul." 4. *With strenuous energy*—" might." The right view of God is obviously presupposed in the command to love him. The command would be unmeaning as addressed to a polytheist, a pantheist, an agnostic, or even to a deist disbelieving in revelation. But this view of God being given, the demand, as obviously, could not be placed lower. God as Creator and Saviour cannot accept a place in our affections lower than the supreme one. He will have this or none. It is due to our morally perverted state that this demand should ever be felt by us to be unreasonable. Pure beings would not feel it to be so. They would delight in the exercise of love to God, and find it natural and easy. The angels, Christ, the just made perfect, love the Father thus. Nor ought the height of this demand unduly to discourage us. Love to God is truly begotten, though not yet perfected, in every heart which has made choice of God as its supreme Portion, and cleaves to him with constancy. God has the ruling place in such a heart, and it needs but growth to raise our love to its required purity and vigour. What is left unattained on earth will be attained in heaven.—J. O.

Vers. 6—9, 20—25.—*The religious education of children.* A matter much insisted on in these addresses (cf. ch. xi. 18—22). We learn—

I. THAT THE RELIGIOUS EDUCATION OF CHILDREN IS GOD'S WAY OF PERPETUATING VITAL RELIGION. Without this, religion would soon die out; with it, a holy seed will be kept up in times of greatest declension.

II. THAT THE RELIGIOUS EDUCATION OF CHILDREN DEVOLVES PRIMARILY ON THE PARENT. The Church, Sunday schools, etc., may assist, but nothing can relieve the parent from this duty, or compensate for his neglect of it (Eph. vi. 4; 2 Tim. i. 5).

III. THAT THE RELIGIOUS EDUCATION OF CHILDREN IS TO BE CONDUCTED WITH GREAT CARE AND FAITHFULNESS. 1. Very *diligently* (ver. 7). It is to be gone about most painstakingly and systematically. " In thine house, and when thou walkest by the way, and when thou liest down, and when thou risest up." There is need for specific teaching at regular times, but the text indicates a broader view of this part of parental duty. An element pervading the whole life, blending with all occupation, insinuating its pleasant influence in all our intercourse with our children. 2. Very *particularly* (vers. 21—25). A specimen is given of the careful instruction parents are to study to impart. 3. *Taking advantage of a child's natural curiosity* (ver. 21). The principle of curiosity is strong in children. It early manifests itself in reference to religion. The Bible, with its delightful variety of story, parable, proverb, etc., is peculiarly adapted for the instruction of the young.—J. O.

Vers. 8, 9.—*God's words to be valued.* The usages to which allusion is made suggest—
I. THE DUTY OF A HIGH VALUATION OF GOD'S COMMANDS. Only precepts highly valued would be treated as described.
II. THE NECESSITY OF TAKING MEANS TO SECURE THE KEEPING OF GOD'S COMMANDMENTS IN REMEMBRANCE. We may keep the injunction in spirit: 1. By frequent reading of Scripture (Ps. i. 2; cxix. 11—16). 2. By frequent converse with others (Mal. iii. 16). 3. By frequent recalling of God's words to our thoughts (Heb. ii. 3). 4. By the use of such expedients as experience suggests—a privately marked Bible, etc.
III. THE IMPORTANCE OF CARRYING GOD'S COMMANDMENTS INTO EVERY DETAIL OF LIFE. Hands, eyes, doorposts, etc.—our working, seeing, home occupations, etc.—J. O.

Vers. 10—16.—*The creature displacing the Creator.* I. THE PRONENESS OF THE HEART TO ADMIT THE WORLD INTO GOD'S PLACE. (Ver. 12.) The tendency is universal. A result of the Fall, in subverting the original constitution of man's nature. That result twofold: 1. In giving to the worldly and sensuous principles in the soul an undue predominance; while: 2. Destroying that love of God, and sense of dependence on him, which would counteract their operation. There may be no "going after other gods" in the sense of ver. 14, yet the first commandment may be broken by making the world itself our god—giving it the place of the true God in our affections. The principle of worldliness usually operates secretly. The heart is "secretly enticed," does not perceive the progress of its declensions (Hos. vii. 9), fights against the admission of it (Rev. iii. 17).
II. THE PECULIAR CONNECTION OF THIS TEMPTATION WITH PROSPERITY. (Vers. 10, 11.) Not, indeed, so peculiarly connected with it, but that the poor man may fall into the same snare. But riches unquestionably constitute a temptation which few succeed in resisting (cf. ch. viii. 11—19; Prov. xxx. 8, 9; Matt. xix. 22—27; 1 Tim. vi. 9, 10, 17, etc.). The temptation is the greater: 1. If worldly possessions *are very abundant* (ver. 11). 2. If the prosperity *is sudden* (vers. 10, 11). 3. If it *is freely enjoyed* (ver. 11)—"hast eaten, and art full" (ch. viii. 10).
III. THE SAFEGUARDS AGAINST THIS TEMPTATION. There *are* safeguards. Bible examples show that riches *may* be used with glory to God, happiness to self, and good to mankind (Abraham, Joseph, Job, Daniel, etc.). Among the foremost we would place the cultivation of a thankful spirit (cf. ch. viii. 10)—the remembrance of God as the Giver of what we have; also the remembrance of God's past mercies to us (vers. 12, 13). Other safeguards are: 1. *Serving God with our possessions* (ver. 13). The serving will include serving with our wealth, using what he has given for his glory, as good stewards, and not luxuriously and wastefully spending all on self (Luke xii. 15—21). 2. *Making public acknowledgment of God* (ver. 13). The spirit of this command is kept by being willing, on all proper occasions, boldly and without shame to avow God to be our God. The man of wealth who will do this is carried at one stroke above half the dangers of his position. 3. *Non-conformity to the world's ways* (ver. 14). It is not easy to avoid being led away by fashion, love of appearance, social custom, etc. The good man will beware of the snare, and keep aloof (Rom. xii. 2).
IV. THE PENALTY OF YIELDING TO THE TEMPTATION. (Ver. 15.) God's wrath is kindled and destroys the transgressor. 1. He is destroyed *spiritually.* 2. He may be *temporally* (Ps. xxxvii. 35; lxxiii. 18, 19). 3. He will be *eternally.*—J. O.

Ver. 16.—*Tempting God.*—Wealth has its temptations; so has poverty. It incites to unbelieving murmurs, and to a spirit called here "tempting the Lord."

I. THE NATURE OF THIS SIN. The peculiarity of it deserves to be carefully studied. It is apt to be taken for granted that "tempting God" means simply provoking him to anger. This, however, is a sense of tempting scarcely applicable to the Divine. God can be provoked to wrath, but he is not "tempted" thereby (Jas. i. 13). "Tempting," in the sense of the text, means "putting to the proof," "imposing tests." Professor Tyndall's famous proposal of a prayer test would have fallen under this description. That this is the right view of the sin is plain from the narrative, and from allusions in the Psalms. "They tempted the Lord, saying, Is the Lord among us or not?" (Exod. xvii. 7). "They tempted God in their hearts . . . they said, Can God furnish a table in the wilderness?" (Ps. lxxviii. 18—20). In this view of it the appositeness of the Saviour's quotation of the passage becomes more obvious (Matt. iv. 7).

II. THE OCCASION OF THE SIN. A result of the want of food and water. Poverty suggests this class of doubts, and inspires the thought of putting God to some test of his faithfulness. But the temptation may originate in other causes—in intellectual doubt, in a sign-seeking spirit (Matt. xvi. 1), in downright presumptuousness.

III. THE EVIL OF THIS SIN. 1. *Its root of unbelief.* It is a "limiting of the Holy One of Israel" (Ps. lxxviii. 41). 2. *Its querulous impatience.* Instead of trusting God, waiting upon him, and seeking light and help in a proper spirit, it flies in God's face, accuses him of unkindness, and complains of his injustice. 3. *Its daring presumption* in presuming to lay down rules to the Almighty, to which he is required to conform. God brings us into situations of trial, not that we may apply tests to *him*, but that he may test *us*—test our faith, our patience, our humility. For those who come successfully through the trial there is the great reward of having dark things at length cleared up, and of being purified and strengthened by the struggle. Failure, on the other hand, exposes to severe chastisements.—J. O.

Ver. 25.—*Our righteousness.* As contrasted with Pauline sayings, the text is an illustration of the maxim, "On the outside of things look for differences, on the inside for likenesses" (Hare). The form is that of the Law, the spirit is that of Christ, whose gospel is the key to the Law's utterances.

I. A REQUIREMENT WHICH ONE ONLY, VIZ. CHRIST, HAS PERFECTLY FULFILLED. "This is the name whereby he shall be called, the Lord our Righteousness" (Jer. xxiii. 6). He "is the end of the Law for righteousness to every one that believeth" (Rom. x. 4). How? In the strictly legal, as in the strict ideal sense, righteousness requires an absolutely perfect fulfilment of every one of God's commandments. The Jewish covenant required no less. The Jews were to live in their righteousness, *i.e.* in perfect keeping of the whole Law. But in point of fact, no Jew ever rendered perfect obedience. In many things, like others, he offended, and the covenant footing was only maintained through daily pardon of daily offences. Christ is our Redeemer from the curse thus entailed by transgression (Gal. iii. 13). As the Lord's righteous Servant, and Fulfiller of the Law, he has implemented the condition of acceptance in such a way that his obedience carries with it results to others as well as to himself (Rom. v. 17—21). In him the believer is justified. He claims him as the Lord *his* Righteousness. Christ has for him at once fulfilled the Law's precept, and abolished its penalty. Sinful in himself, in Christ his sins are covered, and justification is obtained (Rom. iii. 22—27; viii. 1—4; 1 Cor. i. 30; 2 Cor. v. 21).

II. A REQUIREMENT WHICH BELIEVERS IN CHRIST ARE ENABLED TO FULFIL, THOUGH IMPERFECTLY, YET ACCEPTABLY. The utmost that the Jew could render was that imperfect but sincere obedience which is still the mark of the true believer. The believer's *duty* is to render a perfect obedience; his *privilege* is that, falling short of this, his sincere though faulty obedience will be graciously accepted for the sake of Christ. In harmony with his calling, it was to be the Jew's aim to realize the righteousness which the Law set before him. But in his inability to do this the weakness of the Law revealed itself, and in contrast with this weakness (Rom. viii. 3) is the power of the gospel, enabling the believer to triumph, and to bring forth fruit unto holiness, the end of which is everlasting life (Rom. vi. 22). This also is a "righteousness of faith," as springing from faith, and rendered possible through it. It is *his* righteousness, yet in a deeper sense not his, but Christ's, for it is the work of Christ living in him (Gal. ii. 20). It is not the ground of acceptance, but a result of it;

not a title to heaven, but meetness for it. It is itself a gift of grace, part of Christ's salvation (Matt. v. 6; Eph. v. 9, 10; Phil. ii. 12, 13; 1 Pet. ii. 24; 1 John iii. 7—10; with Rom. vi., vii., viii.).—J. O.

Vers. 1—5.—*The essence of the Decalogue is love.* Moses here applies the Decalogue to their present circumstances. He wishes them to enter Canaan in an obedient spirit. He knows that the well-being of the commonwealth depends upon it. To assist them in the understanding of the Law, he sums it up in one all-embracing principle of love. God as the supreme object is to receive the homage of the entire nature of man.

I. MOSES INSISTS ON THE UNITY AND ABSOLUTE CHARACTER OF GOD. This would distinguish Israel from the polytheists around them. "Jehovah our Mighty One is one Jehovah"—the uncaused, self-existent One in his absolute unity and strength. All perfection is thus briefly attributed to him.

II. GOD CAN BE THE OBJECT OF LOVE. His unity is not an unsocial thing. Within his being there are social qualities demanding, and from all eternity receiving, satisfaction. Hence we believe in what Jon. Edwards called a "social Trinity." Our social nature is the reflection of God, since we were made in his image. His unity does *not* imply that in the by-past eternity, before anything was made, he was alone. It was the fellowship of "Father, Son, and Holy Spirit"—three Persons in the one Godhead.

The Trinity makes God lovable, for it is the condition of the satisfaction from all eternity of his social qualities.

III. GOD DESERVES THE LOVE OF OUR WHOLE BEING. Heart, soul, and might are to be enlisted in this service. Our love to him should be intellectual and also emotional; it should be passionate and strong; an all-embracing energy of our nature.

All our faculties are appealed to by the Divine nature. 1. Our *understanding* is enlisted by God as the *Infinite Mind*. All our intellectuality finds its counterpart and culmination in the infinite intellectual powers which God possesses and exercises. We rest upon his superior intellectual power. 2. Our *affections* are enlisted by God as the *Fountain of affection*. God is a Heart of unspeakable tenderness as well as a Mind of infinite grasp. And so he elicits the love of the heart as well as of the mind. 3. Our *will* is swayed into passionate devotion by God as the *Infinite Will*. If the spectacle of will in resistless benevolence commands the homage of our powers, then God entrances our whole will-power into passionate devotion. 4. Our *strength* is enlisted by God as the embodiment of vital energies and powers in their highest form. So that as a matter of fact, God fits into every fold of human nature and elicits its loving and adoring homage.

IV. LOVE MAKES LAWKEEPING DELIGHTFUL. The Law is not a pain to any who love the Lawgiver. Love is the essence of true loyalty. It makes service freedom. It is this which we must cultivate daily, and then life becomes delightful.—R. M. E.

Vers. 6—25.—*Family training is to propagate the Law.* The Law has as its essence love. In the family, love's home and circle, this Law is to be propagated. And here we are to notice—

I. PARENTS ARE TO IDENTIFY THEMSELVES WITH GOD'S CAUSE. The Jews were directed to wear portions of the Law upon their persons. This is the sign of identification with it in a rude age. The idea is *parental profession*, a glad identification of themselves with the Lord's cause.

II. THE HOME IS ALSO TO BE CONSECRATED AS A GODLY HOME. God's Law was to be written on the posts of the house and on their gates. This, like the last, meant the identification of the house with God's cause.

Now, there is as much difference between an ungodly home and a godly one as between an unconverted person and a converted one (cf. Pressensé's 'La Famille Chrétienne,' a most admirable course of sermons).

III. THE CHILDREN ARE MANIFESTLY MEANT TO BE THE COMPANIONS OF THE PARENTS. The little ones are to have their parents' society at home and abroad, at morning and at night (ver. 7).

The mistake made by many parents is not making themselves sufficiently companionable. It is companionship that after all determines the bent of children.

IV. THE HOME TRAINING IS TO BE RELIGIOUS. God's Law is to be brought in, morning, noon, and night, as the great interest. Of course, if parents are to do this as God intends, his Law must be a great personal interest to themselves. They must delight in it and love it, and make it a matter of study continually.

V. AMID THE SECULARITIES OF EDUCATION THE HOME MUST BE THE MAINSTAY OF RELIGION. With the parent the responsibility of training and interesting the children in religion eventually rests. To the well-ordering of Christian homes, Church and State must alike look as the last refuge.

The adjustment of rival interests in education is well-nigh impossible, and so it becomes all the more needful that the home should be made to supply the religious element, whatever course educational arrangements and legislation may take.

VI. PROSPERITY MUST NOT ENGENDER ATHEISM. This is the warning here given to Israel. God might be forgotten amid the success and prosperity of Canaan. For it is prosperity, not adversity, which as a rule engenders atheism. The prosperity of the prodigal led him away to the far-off land of forgetfulness of God, while his adversity brought him back (Luke xv. 11—32).—R. M. E.

EXPOSITION.

CHAPTER VII.

ENTIRE SEPARATION FROM IDOLATROUS NATIONS ENJOINED.

Vers. 1—4.—The Israelites were about to enter on a country occupied by idolaters, and they are commanded not to spare them or to allow them to continue in their proximity, or to have any friendly relations with them (cf. Lev. xxvii. 28). The Lord would cast out these nations, and deliver them, though greater and mightier than they, into their hands; and they were to smite them and place them under the ban; they were to make no covenant with them nor form any alliances with them (cf. Exod. xxiii. 32; xxxiv. 12—16), lest they should thus be drawn into idolatry, and so the anger of the Lord be kindled against them, and his vengeance brought upon them.

Ver. 1.—(Cf. Gen. xv. 19—21.) Of the ten nations named by God in his promise to Abraham, only six are mentioned here, those omitted being the Kenites, the Kennizites, the Kadmonites, and the Rephaim. The Rephaim were by this time extinct as a tribe, Og, "the last of the Rephaim," having been conquered, and he and his people destroyed by the Israelites. The three other tribes lay probably beyond the confines of Canaan, in that region promised to Abraham, but which was not included in the territory conquered by the people under Joshua. This may account for their not being mentioned here. One nation, the Hivites, appears here which is not in the enumeration in Genesis. This name seems to have been borne by more tribes than one, or by a tribe existing in divisions widely scattered, for we find the Hivite in the centre of Palestine (Gen. xxxiv. 2), in the Shephelah (Josh. ix. 7; xi. 19), in the land of Mizpeh under Hermon (Josh. xi. 3), "in Lebanon, from mount Baal-hermon to the entering in of Hamath" (Judg. iii. 3), and among tribes in the north of Canaan (Gen. x. 17; 1 Chron. i. 15). Their principal settlement was probably in that part of the country where the Antilibanus range terminates in Mount Hermon.

Ver. 3.—**Neither shalt thou make marriages with them.** Brought into intimate relations with idolaters, they might be seduced into idolatry; and where marriage was contracted with an idolater, the children might be brought up in idolatry. Such unions were forbidden.

Ver. 4.—**From following me;** literally, *from after me,* i.e. from being my servant and worshipper. **Suddenly;** rather, *speedily* (מַהֵר, infin. of מָהַר, to be quick, to hasten, used as an adverb).

Vers. 5—8.—They were not only to have no fellowship with the idolaters, but they were to root out their idolatry, everting their altars and destroying their idols; and this because they were a holy people, graciously chosen of God to be his special possession —a high privilege and honour which they were to be careful not to cast away.

Ver. 5.—**Cut down their groves;** rather, *cut* or *hew in pieces their ashērahs.* These were, apparently, wooden pillars of considerable height, which were firmly planted in the ground (comp. Judg. vi. 25—27; ch. xvi. 21), and were consecrated to the worship of a female deity, the companion of Baal; probably the same as that afterwards known as Astarte, the Venus of the Syrians (see note on ch. xvi. 21).

Ver. 6.—**An holy people**; a people consecrated to God, to be holy as he is holy (cf. Lev. xi. 43—45; xix. 2; xx. 26; xxi. 6; ch. xxiii. 14). **A special people unto himself**; literally, *to be to him for a people of property* (סְגֻלָּה), a people his own, his peculiar property (cf. Exod. xix. 5; ch. xiv. 2; xxvi. 18; and, for the meaning of the word, 1 Chron. xxix. 3, "mine own proper good;" Eccles. ii. 8, "peculiar treasure of kings"); LXX., λαὸς περιούσιος, applied by St. Paul to Christians as the chosen and special property of Christ (Titus ii. 14). **Above all people**; rather, *out of* or *from among all the peoples*.

Ver. 7.—**Set his love upon you.** The Hebrew verb meaning primarily to cleave to, to be attached to, is used to express ardent and loving affection (cf. Gen. xxxiv. 8; ch. x. 15; Isa. xxxviii. 17). **The fewest of all people.** It might have been supposed that, in choosing a people to be his special treasure, the Almighty would have selected some one of the great nations of the world; but, instead of that, he had chosen one of the smallest. They had, indeed, grown till now they were as the stars for multitude; but it was not in prospect of this that they were chosen. The election of Israel was purely of grace.

Ver. 8.—**Because the Lord loved you.** Targum Onkelos, "Because he had complacency in you;" Vulgate, *quia vobis junctus est.* "Instead of saying, He hath chosen you out of love to your fathers, as in ch. iv. 37, Moses brings out in this place love to the people of Israel as the Divine motive, not for choosing Israel, but for leading it out and delivering it from the slave-house of Egypt, by which God had practically carried out the election of the people, that he might thereby allure the Israelites to a reciprocity of love" (Keil).

Ver. 9.—**To a thousand generations**; rather, *to the thousandth generation.* As God is faithful to his covenant, and will show mercy and do good to those that love him, whilst on those who hate him he will bring terrible retribution, the people are warned by this to take heed against rebellion and apostacy from him (comp. Exod. xx. 5).

Ver. 10.—**And repayeth them that hate him to their face.** The phrase, "to their face" (אֶל פָּנָיו, to their faces), has been variously explained. It has been taken as meaning, instantly, *statim, haud cunctanter* (Vulgate, Gesenius); openly, manifestly, *palam* (Grotius, Calvin, Michaelis); during life, *in hac vita* (Targum, Vatab.); in their presence, in their own sight (LXX., κατὰ πρόσωπον: Rosenmüller). The last seems the best. פָּנֶה signifies properly, front, and

אֶל פָּנָים, to the front, before, in presence (cf. Lev. ix. 5; Exod. xxiii. 17). The hater of God should be repaid, so that the man should himself see and feel that he had been smitten of God (cf. Isa. lxv. 6; Job xxxiv. 11; Ps. lxii. 13). And this retribution should come speedily: **He will not be slack to him that hateth him**; *i.e.* he will not delay to repay him.

Ver. 11.—As God would thus summarily avenge himself of his adversaries, the people are exhorted to keep all his commandments, statutes, and rights.

Ver. 12.—On the other hand, obedience would bring blessing. **Wherefore it shall come to pass, if ye hearken.** The Hebrew conveys the idea of a reward as consequent on their hearkening; as there would be retribution for transgression, so would there be recompense for obedience. The Hebrew word represented by "wherefore" in the Authorized Version (עֵקֶב, from עָקֵב, the heel) denotes that which comes after, the end or last of anything (Ps. cxix. 33, 112), hence recompense, reward, wages, as the end or result of acting (Ps. xix. 11; xl. 15; Isa. v. 23, etc.). The clause might, therefore, be translated, *As a consequence* or *recompense of hearkening, . . . it shall be that,* &c. **Judgments**, *i.e.* rights, rightful claims (מִשְׁפָּטִים). God, as the Great King, has his rights, and these are to be rendered to him by his subjects and servants. **The mercy,** *i.e.* the kindness, the favour (חֶסֶד), showed in the promises which God gave to their fathers, and engaged by covenant to fulfil.

Ver. 13.—This favour would take effect in a blessing on the fruit of the womb, the produce of the field, and the increase of their flocks and herds (comp. Exod. xxiii. 25—27). **Thy corn, and thy wine, and thine oil.** These comprise the fruitful products of the soil, and in their combination express general fertility and abundance. By *corn* (דָּגָן) is undoubtedly to be understood the cereal products generally used for food. It may be doubted if *tirosh* (תִּירוֹשׁ) properly means wine. The word is often rendered in the Authorized Version by new wine, and this is the meaning generally given in the lexicons. As, however, it is almost constantly joined with corn and oil, the immediate products of the soil—at least as unchanged by any process or manufacture—it is rather to be regarded as designating ripe grapes than wine. That, moreover, which was to be *gathered* (ch. xi. 14), which might be *tithed* (ch. xii. 17; xiv. 23), which might be described as *fruit* (2 Chron. xxxi. 5), as *being in the cluster* (Isa. lxv. 8), and as capable of being *dried up* or *parched* (Joel i. 10), and *trodden* (Micah vii. 15), could not be a fluid like fermented wine. As the grape juice, however, was that from which wine was elicited, *tirosh* is sometimes used tropically for wine (Isa. lxii. 8; Hos. iv. 11), just as *corn* is used for bread (Lam. ii. 12; Hos. vii. 14). The *oil* here mentioned, and elsewhere joined with *dagan* and *tirosh*, is the pure fresh olive oil (יִצְהָר, from צָהַר, to shine), obtained by pressure from the berries of the olive, and used for food as well as for other purposes by the Jews (see notes on ch. viii. 8). **Flocks of thy sheep.** The Hebrew is very peculiar here; the same expression occurs only in this book (ch. xxviii. 4, 18, 51). Literally rendered, it is *the Astartes* (Ashtaroth) *of thy sheep.* Kimchi says it means "the females of the sheep" (נקבות הצאן), and this Gesenius adopts, rendering the phrase by "ewes." Astarte ('Ashtoreth, plu. 'Ashtaroth) was the Phœnician Venus, and it is supposed that the females of the flock were called Astartes or Venuses, as propagating the flock. There is, however, another way of explaining the word as here used, by referring it to a root *'ashar* (עָשַׁר), signifying to be multiplied, to be rich; whence the name given to the females as the multipliers of the flock, without any reference to Astarte.

Ver. 15.—The mercy of God should be showed to them also in preserving them from sickness, especially of a virulent and dangerous kind, such as they had seen in Egypt, where disease has in all ages readily assumed a malignant character ('Encyc. Brit.,' art. 'Egypt'), and where especially cutaneous diseases of the worst kind prevail (comp. ch. xxxviii. 27). Such diseases the Lord would rather cause to fall on their enemies.

Vers. 16—26.—The heathen they were utterly to extirpate from the land which God was about to give them; mighty as these nations were, they were not to be afraid of them, for God would be with his people, and would deliver these nations, with their kings, into their hands. Not all at once, however, should the former occupants of the country be driven out; this should be done by degrees, lest, the land being suddenly depopulated, the wild animals would increase too much, so as to be a source of

danger and trouble to the settlers; but ultimately they should be utterly destroyed, and with them all the objects and implements of their idolatrous worship.

Ver. 16.—**And thou shalt consume**; literally, *eat, devour* (וְאָכַלְתָּ). Unless they consumed them as one consumes food, they would be a snare to them, by tempting them to join in their idolatry.

Vers. 17, 18.—**If thou shalt say in thine heart.** The thought might rise in their minds, How can we ever compete with nations so much more powerful than we? But such thoughts they must repress, remembering what God had done for them to Pharaoh and the Egyptians, and resting assured that the same would he do to the Canaanites.

Ver. 19.—**Temptations**, etc. (cf. ch. iv. 34; vi. 22).

Ver. 20.—**Hornet** (cf. Exod. xxiii. 28). Instances are on record of armies being obliged to give way before swarms of insects by which they were attacked (as in the case of Julian, who was compelled by a host of flies and gnats to change his route in retreating from Parthia; Amm. Marcell., 24, 8); but it may be doubted if the statement here is to be understood literally, and not rather figuratively, as expressive of many and varied evils with which the fugitive Canaanites were to be visited until they were extirpated (cf. Josh. xxiv. 12, compared with x. 22—27).

Ver. 22.—(Cf. Exod. xxiii. 30.)

Ver. 24.—The kings also of these nations should they utterly destroy, so that their memory should perish from the earth.

Vers. 25, 26.—The idols of the Canaanites they were utterly to destroy by fire, not saving even the silver or gold with which the images were overlaid, lest, if that were coveted and retained, it might bring them under the ban which fell on all things connected with idolatry; as happened in the case of Achan (Josh. vii.).

Ver. 26.—**Cursed thing**; *a thing devoted* (חֵרֶם), either, as in this case, to destruction (comp. also 1 Kings xx. 42; Zech. xiv. 11; Mal. iii. 24; [iv. 6]) or, as elsewhere, to God (Lev. xxvii. 21; Numb. xviii. 14).

HOMILETICS.

Vers. 1—11.—*A holy people's policy of self-preservation.* We have in this paragraph a glance onward to the time when Israel's march through the wilderness would be completed, and when the people to whom God had given the land should be confronted with those who had it previously in possession. In our Homily on it let us observe—

I. WE HAVE HERE POINTED OUT THE CONDITIONS UNDER WHICH ISRAEL WOULD TAKE

POSSESSION OF THE LAND. 1. There was a great covenant promise which had been handed down to them from preceding generations, and which involved results which would be far-reaching both as to time and place, touching every family of man, through every age of time. In a word, it was nothing less than the Divine covenant of human redemption, in the fulfilling of which a Great Mediator should come, while *in* Israel the purity of the line of his descent was to be guarded, and by and for it there was to be held in possession a tract of land on which the great work of the Mediator should have its earthly basis and historic ground. 2. With this far outlook in view, Israel was to be a people "unto the Lord their God." It was to hold a place among the nations which was unique. One of the smallest as to territory and numbers, it was to strike the deepest as to its worth and power! 3. Hence Israel was to be a *holy* people (ver. 6). It was to bear a specific character *religiously*, as it was to take a peculiar place *historically*. Hence its moral and spiritual elevation is the first thing to be secured. The revelation of God which the people possessed had no mean uplifting power. The eternal God was Israel's refuge, and underneath were the everlasting arms. The institutions of mediation, priesthood, sacrifice, were deep and solemn lessons in the evil of sin and the righteousness of God. And the moral law which Israel possessed was so pure, so complete, even in the infancy of the people, that to this day not the wisest men of the world can find a defect therein, nor can they suggest aught to supplement it. 4. Israel would, nevertheless, be in great danger (ver. 4). The land of Canaan, though beautiful, fruitful, and gay, was a nest of impurity. The foulest pollutions were debasing the people, and, apart from some special guard, they were far more likely to infect Israel with the *virus* of their idolatry than Israel was to cleanse them by the strength of counteracting virtue. And when we come to think of what vast importance to the world was the choice of one people who should serve as leverage for the rest, we discern the reason for the imperative injunctions which follow as to the policy which Israel was to pursue with reference to the peoples of Canaan.

II. HERE IS A THREEFOLD LINE OF POLICY ENJOINED. 1. A policy of separation (ver. 3, "Neither shalt thou make marriages with them"). Thus does the Most High, in the early training of a people for himself, let them see how completely they are to be the Lord's; and that marriage, which from the worldling's point of view is so apt to sink into a mere union of bodies, is, from the point of view of one who would be holy to the Lord, to be at once regulated by God and elevated for him. Who cannot see the impossibility of married life being as blessed as it may be if husband and wife are dissevered on the very matter on which joint sympathies should be fondest and strongest? The principle here enjoined is carried over into the New Testament, in such words as these: "Be not unequally yoked together with unbelievers." In this stern interdiction of mixed marriages under the Law, our God would teach us for all time that life's dearest bond is to be formed only in subjection to his will whose we are, and whom we should serve. 2. A policy of religious intolerance (ver. 5). As Israel was to possess the land for God, so it was to suffer his worship alone to be observed. Whatever was contrary thereto was to be taken out of the way. An external religion is virtually destroyed when its external observance is made impossible. 3. A policy of extermination in war. The Canaanites had had their day of grace (Gen. xv. 16). And now, lest they continue to pollute the land, they are to be swept away "with the besom of destruction" (see Homily on ch. i. 1—8). If Israel had no Divine command to this effect, no one would pretend to justify this part of their policy. If they had, it needed no justification. God may sentence a people to ruin in any way he pleases. And when a nation has given way to such nameless and shameless wickedness that its land groans beneath the burden of its crimes, it is mercy to the world when the evil is "stamped out." And though such exterminative policy on the part of any nation can be justified only on the ground of a Divine warrant, yet the warrant having been given in this case, that policy does but illustrate a truth which the Most High has again and again declared, that no nation has any absolute right in itself or its land. It holds its existence subject to God's will, and to that will alone; and if it is good for the world that it should give place to others, he will cause it to pass away, and will bring another people on the soil.

III. ISRAEL'S POSITION AND POLICY, SO REGARDED, FURNISH US WITH PRINCIPLES OF ETERNAL AND UNIVERSAL APPLICATION. They are these: 1. The actual value of any nation or people in the world depends on the degree to which they subserve God's purpose, and not on the extent to which they fulfil their own. Nations have but a passing loan of power from the Great Supreme, held in trust for his honour and the world's good; and when they lose sight of that, they are grievously forgetting the things which belong unto their peace. 2. If a nation is to preserve itself for God, corrupting influences are to be put away. We have seen (Homily on ch. ii. 24) how much importance is attached by God to the training of the family. We see in this paragraph how much importance is also attached to those influences *which go beforehand* to *make* the family. How does the Most High set himself against all those corruptions that poison the social fabric and break up the sacredness of the home! And how jealously does he guard his own worship from the defiling additions and commandments of men! 3. When a nation is loyal to its God, by putting away sin and nurturing righteousness, it will ensure the Divine blessing and its own permanence (ver. 9). God reserves the entry through the gates of honour to "the righteous nation which keepeth the truth." 4. The elevation ensured and given to nations which promote righteousness is the one which, if we see as God sees, we shall value most. Godless men may covet an ascendency backed by guns and swords, armies and fleets. The believer in God covets only an uplifting that comes of the Divine blessing on "a wise and understanding people." 5. If loyalty to God and truth is wanting, a nation ensures its own downfall (ver. 10; see Ezek. xvii.; xxvii. 3; xxviii. 2—10; Amos ii. 9; Obad. 3, 4). 6. What Israel was designed to be among the nations, regenerated men are in their own nation— "a holy people unto the Lord their God." They are "the light of the world," "the salt of the earth." The earth is full of corruption, and is and must be rapidly decomposing unless some salt be thrown into it to check the decomposition. Christians are the "salt" of the earth. Their value is in their "savour," not in their name. And if they let the "savour" die out, no name of discipleship will be of any use to them. (On savourless salt, see Thomson's 'Land and the Book,' p. 382.) Christians may not separate their Christianity from their citizenship. They are to be Christian citizens; and do we not learn by abundant teachings in the Old and New Testament that God spares many a guilty city for the sake of the righteous that are therein? (See the history of Abraham's intercession for Sodom.) And can we forget the teaching of the prophet Ezekiel, that nations may become so corrupt that even the righteous element therein avails not to stay the ruin (Ezek. xiv. 12—21)? 7. Hence the principles involved in this paragraph should convey, and should be made the basis of, an earnest warning and appeal to men to remember that the day of grace for the nation, as well as for themselves, has its limit. God is long-suffering. He bears long, but he will not bear always (cf. Isa. v. 3—7; i. 5—24; Luke xix. 41—44; xiii. 6—9; Matt. xxi. 33—44; Rev. ii. 21—23). Oh, how earnestly should men turn to God while yet there is hope! For their own sakes, that they may be saved, and for the sake of others too, that they may become co-operators with God in purifying and saving men!

Vers. 12—15.—*Temporal prosperity a result of obedience to Divine Law.* The aged lawgiver in this paragraph shows the people how largely their well-being depends on obedience to God, and also to what an extent that well-being would be manifest even in temporal matters; in the healthfulness of body which would be enjoyed by them, and in the success with which they should tend their flocks and herds. They should be free from the sicknesses and diseases with which Egypt abounded; and should, in the enjoyment of such immunity, have the sign and token of the blessing of Heaven on an obedient people. Now, it has long been regarded as one mark of the old covenant, that, in condescension to the people, God spake so much of temporal blessings as the reward of obedience in the early messages which were delivered to our fathers. It is also looked on as one specific mark of New Testament teaching, that the promises of God now lie mainly in the direction of spiritual good; and so much has this aspect of things come in our days to be looked at, that it is by no means unlikely that we may be in danger of carrying our views thereon to such an extreme as to regard temporal comforts as *no mark at all* of Divine approval. It is well worth our while, therefore, to look into this matter, to see if we can so formulate the teaching of God's Word thereon as to show the harmony between it and the actual facts of life on this question: How far may abundance of temporal good and freedom from sickness be looked at as a proof of

Divine favour? We shall regard the actual history before our eye as at once a basis for, and an illustration of, our remarks.

I. GOD HAD IN GREAT MERCY REMOVED ISRAEL FROM EGYPT, WHICH WAS NOT ONLY THE SEAT OF POLITICAL OPPRESSION, AND A REGION OF FOUL IDOLATRY, BUT ALSO A LOCUS AND FOCUS OF MANY PESTILENTIAL DISEASES. (See Mr. Lane's 'Modern Egyptians;' the art. 'Egypt' in 'Encyc. Brit.;' and in Smith and Kitto's Dictionaries of the Bible.) Probably the land of Goshen might be a healthier district than the region of the city itself; still it is extremely questionable whether such a race as Israel was designed to be, could, even physically, have been with any certainty developed in Egypt itself. It is no mean mercy to have our earthly lot cast in a healthy locality. It is not possible, indeed, to escape temptations from without or from within, go where we may, but it is certain that (cæt. par.) it is much easier to resist evil and to cultivate virtue where climate and atmosphere tend to promote bodily vigour. The history of the world affords proof enough that climatic influences will not do everything for man; but that is no reason for underrating their value, nor for losing sight of the mercy where "the lines are fallen to us in" healthful and health-giving places.

II. THOUGH FREE FROM LIABILITY TO EGYPTIAN DISEASE, ISRAEL'S HEALTHFULNESS AND WEAL WOULD DEPEND ON OBEDIENCE TO GOD'S LAW. No land can give us any immunity from the consequences of breaking law, however life-giving its breezes. God's physical and moral laws are interlaced and intertwined. Obedience or disobedience to either may have its full effect in its own direction. Obedience or disobedience to both will have its complicated effects in both directions. Many speak of law as if it acted without God; and, maybe, some think of God as if he acted without law. We need not commit either mistake. Let us carefully avoid both. Let us reverence every law of God, physical or moral, because it is his; and let it be our study to understand them in every department in which they are presented to us. Mr. Binney once made the startling statement, that, "barring accidents, a man can live pretty much as long as he pleases!" By which he meant, of course, that there are certain Divine laws and rules, obedience to which tends to the preservation of health, and consequently to the prolongation of life. And, if these laws are neglected, we may create disease, affliction, and trouble for ourselves, and breed even death, however healthful the locality in which we dwell. Hence it is not surprising to find in this paragraph another principle indicated.

III. SUPPOSING THE PEOPLE TO BE OBEDIENT TO GOD'S LAW, HEALTH AND WEAL WOULD FOLLOW BY WAY OF NATURAL CONSEQUENCE. The original (ver. 12), by a peculiar Hebrew idiom, shows this. "And (it) shall be (the) heel," i.e. the end, and so the consequence. Whatever may be the kind of weal desired, the laws of God in that direction should be studied, understood, and followed. Whether in the regulation of the production or sustentation of life; in agricultural pursuits; in the spheres of capital and labour, and their mutual relations; in the creation, distribution, increase, and expenditure of wealth; in the higher region of the cultivation of the national and social virtues of truth and goodness; in the still higher region of family piety; or in the highest region of all, even that of personal love and devotion to God, the old words will be proved true; "Them that honour me, I will honour." No doubt we are often meeting with cases which seem anomalous; they accord with no known rule whatever. But we shall find that we do not know the whole of such cases, nor even enough of them to enable us to judge concerning them. Till we know more we must suspend judgment. No perplexities of this sort give any warrant for disturbing first principles. In any region in which God has laws we may have duties; and it is a very partial and unhealthy piety which would underrate intelligent action in any department. In whatever department there is neglect, in such we may expect failure. And where there is obedience, there will be the reward.

IV. THOUGH THE REWARD MAY COME IN THE WAY OF NATURAL CONSEQUENCE, YET NONE THE LESS IS IT GOD'S BLESSING. The result is from him, because the Law is from him. Nor is it one whit the less from God, if we are able to trace every step of the coming of a blessing. A man's work is not less his because he does it somehow. Nor is it attributed the less to him because it is known how he did it. Why should men be less reasonable in recognizing God's work, when the laws of the working are manifest to us? "The hand of the diligent maketh rich," is one truth; "the blessing of the Lord, it maketh rich," is another. We may ignore neither, but should reverently admit and act on both.

V. ON WHAT A FRAIL CONDITION, HOWEVER, WAS ISRAEL'S NATIONAL WEAL SUSPENDED! "If ye hearken to these judgments," etc. The laws were right, kind, benevolent. The land was beautiful, fertile, healthful. All that was wanted was obedient people. Israel needed as much to be delivered from themselves as to be rescued from the Egyptians. And, in fact, there was among them a redeeming and sanctifying work, carried on through God's Spirit, though it is not named in this paragraph; nor was it as fully revealed as now, how, in his infinite grace, our God created in his people the obedience which, in his Law, he commands. "The righteousness of the Law is fulfilled in those who walk not after the flesh, but after the Spirit." The Law given to Israel was a child-guide with a view to Christ. The first covenant proved brittle in their hands, and so they learned the need of another, which should be for ever safe in God's hands. The first says, "Do this, and live." The second, "Live, and you will do this." And even now, putting the matter generally, we may say God governs. nations, as nations, by the first covenant. He governs his own believing people by the second. Hence, in dealing with men and nations, the Christian preacher has ever to expound and enforce the everlasting laws of righteousness, and by revealing men's failure therein to convict of sin; while in building up the Church he has to show the glory of the Holy Ghost as the Creator and Sustainer of spiritual power.

Vers. 17—25.—*An anxious question, or dreading difficulties.* In this paragraph there are some verses which are in the main a repetition of the enforcement of the policy of separation and extrusion which Israel was to adopt towards the Canaanites. But there is one distinctive feature in it which presents several points altogether new, the historical side of which we may first look at, that we may there see how peculiarly full this passage is of bright and gladsome teaching for us.

Here is a question (ver. 18) which Israel would not be unlikely to ask, at least occasionally. Doubtless, just at the time when they were in the flush of joy at the destruction of Pharaoh and his hosts, or when they had experienced some great deliverance from pressing want, their hearts would be brave and strong. But, like some others since have been, they were largely the creatures of circumstance. Now up, now down. Now so elated that they think they can get through anything, now so depressed that they dread everything. The time would come when in view of the possible struggles which the possession of Canaan might involve, many an Israelite would say, "These nations are mightier than I; how can I dispossess them?" and they must have been more than human if the heart did not now and then give way. For there were seven nations to supplant; and over and above the numerical force against which Israel would have to contend, there would be the fact that they were strangers to the land; they had been kept in serfdom; they were unskilled in the art and practice of war; so that, on the human side, the advantage was very greatly with the Canaanites, while Israel incurred a very serious risk. Now, though Jehovah was very wroth with the people when in their guilty unbelief they proposed to turn back at the evil report of the spies, he sees a great difference between a deeply rooted distrust, and an occasional cloud that may shade the spirit; and while in his holy wrath he condemns the first, in his tender compassion he anticipates and guards against the second. Hence, from vers. 18 to 24, we have the cheering voice of the great lawgiver, grandly uttering, in his hundred and twentieth year, words to empower the heart, and showing Israel, in the Name of the Lord of hosts, how much more there is to animate them than there can possibly be to discourage and depress. He (1) reminds them no fewer than eight times of the Name of the Lord their God; (2) bids them look back to past miracles and wonders, and to see in them pledges of future help; (3) shows them how the providential action of God, which' was *for* them, would be against their foes; (4) assures them that God would be among them as an ever-present Helper and Friend; and (5) points out that, though the process of driving out the Canaanites might be slow, yet if it were done more rapidly, it would be attended with great peril from other and unexpected quarters; that both tribes of men and herds of beasts would be kept in abeyance for their sakes; so that though they were led by a tedious route, it would be the safest way! Now, surely we ought not to pass over a passage so full of interest and instruction for our everyday life as this, presenting to us, as it does, two distinct lines of thought.

I. THE DIFFICULTIES OF LIFE AS ANXIOUSLY DREADED BY US. "These nations are more than I; how can I dispossess them?" These Israelites were not the only people who have cast glances ahead, and who, foreseeing, as they thought, difficulties in the distance, have exclaimed, "How shall we get through them?" We do not refer now to such as have no living faith in God, and who are perpetually giving way to dark and sinful unbelief; nor have we mainly in view those who have never yet been led out of "the house of bondage." But, keeping as closely as we can to the cases suggested by the paragraph, we refer to those who, through mercy, know what a great deliverance has been wrought for man in Christ; to whom that redemption has become a living power through the energy of the Holy Ghost; and who yet, notwithstanding all, have their moments of despondency, when looking or trying to look far ahead,—they see innumerable obstructions confronting them, and ask in anxious sadness, "How can we meet them all?" This main inquiry may take one or more of the following forms: 1. The special ends and aims even of my earthly life; how can I accomplish them? 2. The difficulties in the way of my much-loved work for Christ; how can I overcome them? 3. The hardships to be met in running the Christian race; how can I encounter them? 4. The many hindrances which oppose themselves to the advance of the cause of God; how can the Church overcome them? 5. All the foes, without and within, which threaten the possession of Canaan; how can we vanquish them? Say, is there to be found any believer in whose spirit such questions as these do not now and then arise, and who does not occasionally shiver from the chill of a doubting forecast? Therefore let us see in this passage—

II. THE DIFFICULTIES OF LIFE GRACIOUSLY ANTICIPATED AND PROVIDED FOR BY GOD. The following points will be found, explicitly or implicitly, in the paragraph: 1. "The Lord *thy* God." That Name is a guarantee of all you want by the way. "Greater is he that is for you than all they which can be against you." There is more meaning in that one Name than in all other names besides. "If God be for us, who can be against us?" 2. God will go before you to clear the way (ver. 20). All nature waits on him. Fire, thunder, lightning, hail; flies, worms, locusts, hornets; ay, men, devils, angels, must do his work when he calls. 3. God will be with you, to empower you in the way (ver. 21). If God is not on our side, there is but weakness, whatever the seeming power. If God is on our side, there is power, whatever the seeming weakness. 4. God will choose his own best methods of helping you in the way (ver. 22). "Little by little." A more rapid clearance would have brought other dangers. God "gently clears our way." 5. God's past deliverances are pledges that he will not forsake you by the way (vers. 18, 19; see Ps. lxiii. 7; Rom. viii. 32; v. 10). 6. It is one of "the secrets of the Lord," to cause us to meet and grapple with things and beings mightier than we are, that we may cease to rely on ourselves, and be flung upon him, the Almighty One, for strength. The tendency to self-trust and self-laudation is very strong (see ch. viii. 17, 18). Study the history of Gideon, and his band of three hundred men. This education in trust is also an education in holiness. We have, by meeting difficulties which are beyond us, to learn how much we want God. And yet God will not be with us except as we are loyal to him (see Josh. vii.). Ah! it is by these difficulties in life, by our manner of meeting them, and by God's dealing with us under them, that we are to be *educated for eternity!* Oh! if all were smooth, if we had no complications to meet, no trials to bear, how might we go on drifting down the stream, slumberously calm, dangerously secure, till we awoke, perhaps, too late, to find ourselves a wreck and a ruin! It is by these breaks in our peace, by these cares and hard struggles, which fling us on our God, that we are taught how much we want him, and how ill we could do without him! On the journey of life we have all entered, and the supreme question for us is not, "Will it be smooth or rough?" but "How will it end?"

HOMILIES BY VARIOUS AUTHORS.

Vers. 1—11.—*Israel's iconoclastic mission.* Material idolatry is the great peril of humanity. To what corruption and misery such idolatry leads, *we* in Christianized

England can scarcely conceive. What the history of our world would have been if that hotbed of Canaanite corruption had continued, it would be difficult to imagine. Many methods were open to God by which he might arrest that plague of vice; out of them all, his wisdom selected *this*, viz. to employ the Hebrews as his ministers of destruction.

I. CONSIDER MEN AS ELECTED BY GOD TO OFFICE AND TO SERVICE. We may safely suppose that every nation fulfils some purpose foreseen by God—perhaps appointed thereto by him. Possibly every man, though he may not rise to the realization of God's highest ideal, yet may fulfil some inferior purpose of God. The Hebrews had a very special honour conferred on them. They were chosen unto holiness, chosen to be the ministers of God's righteousness. The glory was eminent, and the Jews failed to reach it. The Most High God condescended to enter into closest alliance with Israel, deigned to be called their God, and took their interests into his care. So long as they kept his commandments, he kept his covenant. His faithfulness was an infinite quantity, but it was conditioned by Israel's obedience. No evidence was lacking to Israel touching the friendly protection and help of Jehovah. Their loyalty as *subjects* was met cordially by his favour as *Sovereign*. Their admitted weakness was met by the Divine strength. Their poor, shallow love was met and recompensed by his rich affection.

II. THE GROUNDS OF GOD'S CHOICE. 1. *This is declared negatively.* It was not on the ground of their numbers or their strength. *That* strength and magnitude of the nation were the effect of God's choice, not its cause. They were not chosen because of superior holiness, but with a view to make them holy. Some reason there is for God's choice, but that reason is not often revealed. Possibly it is too recondite for man's understanding, or the further pursuit of the inquiry might divert him from practical obedience. 2. *It is stated positively that this choice was the outcome of love.* There must have been the potency, perhaps the promise, of good in the Hebrews, in order to attract the love of God. If there was no positive wickedness, God would delight in them as the product of his own skill. His gracious dealings hitherto had been *in respect of the oath made to their fathers.* God's great love to Abraham had perpetuated itself in his seed. Who can measure what a life of blessing each one of us may communicate to generations yet unborn? Divine grace in us is not terminal.

III. THE DESIGN OF GOD'S CHOICE—GENERAL AND SPECIAL. *The general design was holy character.* Choice to office and to honour depended on attainment of character. *Holiness* is the highest perfection of man, therefore the highest design of God. Holiness is a far higher acquisition than wisdom or strength. The seven nations of Canaan were greater and mightier than Israel, yet those nations fell before the holy people. Purity shall eventually displace power. Right *is* genuine might. *Holiness* has, by Divine appointment, an everlasting tenure. *The design of God's choice of Israel was also special*, viz. *to overturn idolatry.* The *general* vocation included the *special.* To be holy would necessitate conflict with sin. Light must contend with darkness. Opposite principles must contend for the mastery. The holier we become, the more resolute will be our battle with idolatry. We shall feel towards it, and act towards it, as God does. For us to *live* (if we be God's consecrated sons), and for us to *oppose idolatry*, is identical. " No peace with sin " is our loyal motto.

IV. THE REALIZED RESULTS OF THE DIVINE CHOICE. Already the Hebrews had obtained a signal triumph over the Egyptians, as the proof of God's gracious intentions towards them. *That* triumph was singular, surprising, and complete. *He*, who could secure such a triumph for Israel, could give them easy conquest over any adversary. They knew how to touch the secret springs of success. The pathway to renown was open. There was scarcely room for a doubtful issue, for from a greater foe God had already delivered them.

V. THE HONOUR CONVEYED IN THIS CHOICE, VIZ. TO BE CO-WORKERS WITH GOD. God would cast out the seven nations of Canaanites, therefore the Hebrews must smite them. God would deliver them up, therefore Israel was to destroy them. In every step they were to be coadjutors with God. We are not to suppose that the Canaanites were passively slaughtered. In every case they provoked severity of treatment. So completely had the idolaters identified themselves with idolatry, that, to destroy the latter, Israel had to destroy the former. When God, the Great Proprietor of all, imposes a command upon us, however repulsive to our own feeling, it would be flagrant disloyalty on our part, yea, gross sin, to disobey. Punishment by the sword cannot be a more unrighteous act than punishment by cholera or by plague; and if men admit the justice of the one, they should also of the other. Human pity must sometimes be kept in abeyance.

VI. GOD'S DESIGNS, IF NOT FOLLOWED, VISIT MEN WITH DESTRUCTION. The alternative of not executing God's high commission was appalling. If any false sentiments of pity diverted them from the plain path of duty, the Hebrews would have become partakers of idolaters' sins. Any concession or compromise with the Canaanites would be (and in fact *was*) fatal to themselves. Can one touch pitch and not be defiled? The slightest connivance with the abomination would be a moral poison. They too would be accursed. For God will not endure to be trifled with. To his friends he is infinitely gracious, and blesses, for their sakes, their posterity; but his foes he repayeth to their face. We have to make our choice between complete devotement to God's cause and complete destruction.—D.

Vers. 12—26.—*Reward in proportion to arduous service.* The enterprise upon which the Jews were entering was one of prodigious difficulty. They had to contend at the same time with stalwart human foes, and with the internal foes of evil lust. Here was a splendid field for eternal renown. In proportion to the difficulty of the enterprise would be the glory of success.

I. OBSERVE THE DISCOURAGING ASPECTS OF THE UNDERTAKING. 1. *Their adversaries were more numerous than they.* The adhesion of numbers to a particular side naturally excites enthusiasm. Yet, in war, unless order and discipline be maintained, mere numbers have contributed to defeat. 2. *The Canaanites were actually in possession.* They could, therefore, choose their military positions, and felt that they were fighting for their altars and their homes. 3. *The Hebrews were the subjects of internal fears.* Their fathers had actually refused to fight with the giant races of Canaan, and had turned back again into the desert. The habit of fearless courage was not suddenly engendered: it was a growth. 4. *The Hebrews had also a lingering lust for the costly things devoted to idolatry.* To suppress their own concupiscence was as arduous as to withstand the Amorites. Hence, on many occasions, their hearts counselled compromise and alliance. 5. *They could anticipate only tardy results.* If there had been the prospect of swift progress of triumph—the rapid march from victory to victory—they could have braced themselves up for a brief campaign. But they knew that slow processes of siege, with its privations and exposures, were essential. God had forewarned them that he would not drive out the heathen suddenly, lest other evils should ensue. They had to contend with their own impatience. 6. *The necessity for extermination added to the difficulty of the war.* If, when the Canaanites had suffered defeat in two or three pitched battles, the Hebrews had been permitted to accept a surrender and make them tributaries, their task had been comparatively easy. But the command of Jehovah was unmistakable: Israel was bound to destroy their foes, "with a mighty destruction," till they were consumed. So neither can we have peace until every sin within us is completely annihilated.

II. OBSERVE THE ENCOURAGING ASPECTS OF THEIR WORK. 1. *God's immeasurable might.* The *visible* features of the undertaking were depressing enough; but faith could discover an invisible Ally, who was more than a match for all opposition. If we can only realize that God is on our side, we shall be confident of victory. 2. *God's past deliverances should assure us for the future.* What an unchanging God has done for us, he *can* and *will* do again. Omnipotence is never exhausted. It is impossible for God to be inconsistent with himself. 3. *God's plain promises of help.* If we can only be absolutely sure of a promise from God, we may set at defiance every fear, and calmly face every foe. "He is not a man, that he should lie." 4. *Proofs that God is even now present.* "The Lord thy God is among you." If we would only rub off from our eyes the drowsiness of unbelief, we might see the tokens of God's presence on every side—the footprints of his feet, as he leads our way. The Good Shepherd always goes before his sheep. 5. *In God's service the meaner forms of life often become efficient allies.* The locusts have been commissioned to do service for God. In Egypt, flies and lice formed a brigade in his army. So *now* also wasps and hornets were sent out as sappers and miners to prepare Jehovah's way. Let no insignificant helper be despised!

III. THE LARGE REWARDS OF FAITHFUL SERVICE. 1. *The rewards were based on Divine equity.* If *we* keep his precepts, *he* will *keep* his covenant. A singular thread of equity runs through all God's dealings. History supplies a thousand examples. We may find fresh ones daily in our own observation. 2. *The rewards are various and ample. They embrace the present and the future.* To be the conscious object of God's love is a rich reward; and the smile of God will make all our ways to prosper. Large and rapid increase has been, from the Creation, a mark of Jehovah's favour. " Be fruitful, and multiply, and replenish the earth." 3. *The rewards are distinctive.* Not only do they impart a large measure of personal enjoyment, but they are known and recognized by others as the rewards conferred by God. They make men conspicuous among their fellows. " A thousand shall fall at thy side, and ten thousand at thy right hand; but it shall not come nigh thee." As our work and warfare are spiritual, so are our rewards spiritual also. Our reward, as conquerors over sin, is manifold, generous, enduring, satisfying. God will surely distinguish between the righteous and the wicked—between him that serveth him well, and him that serveth him not. In honour, they shall be as the antipodes asunder.—D.

Vers. 1—6.—*Judgment without mercy.* This decree is to be viewed—

I. AS A JUST JUDGMENT ON PEOPLES WHOSE INIQUITIES CRIED FOR VENGEANCE. The doomed nations had been long borne with (Gen. xv. 16). Their iniquities were of a kind and degree of enormity which imperatively called for a Divine interposition (Lev. xviii. 27, 28; ch. ix. 4). This was the true ground of God's dealings with them, and furnishes a sufficient answer to all cavils. The destruction of the comparatively innocent with the guilty may be explained in part by the existence in the offspring of the hereditary evil of their race. How often, under the Divine government, do we see illustrations of the same principle—the temporal consequences of transgression overflowing on those related to the transgressor! The lesson taught is God's inflexible determination to punish evil. There can be no ultimate toleration of sin in God's universe. It must be judged, rooted out, and the sinner who identifies himself with it destroyed.

II. AS A CLEARING FROM IDOLATRY OF THE LAND OF GOD'S ABODE. Not only could the practice of idolatry not be endured, but even its unhallowed monuments must not be permitted to remain, polluting with their presence the land of God's habitation—the peculiar seat of his majesty, the place of his holiness. Every trace of these impure worships must be swept away (ver. 5). The lesson taught is God's hatred of idolatry. It is a secondary matter that the gods are of wood and stone, and the worship one of altars, groves, and pillars. There is the formal idolatry of heathenism, and there is the less-avowed, but not less real, idolatry of hearts which have set up rival objects to God in their secret places—which have substituted the creature, in some form of it, for the Creator. The forms are as numerous as ever were the idols of heathen temples. A man may be an idolater of reason; he may worship art; he may bow at the shrine of mammon (Matt. vi. 24; Eph. v. 5); his god may be the praise of men; he may fling himself to be crushed before the worse than Juggernaut car of fashion; he may be a votary of lewdness. The worship may be avowed, or hidden away in secret desires and imaginings. It may be rendered in the most diverse places—in the laboratory, at the desk, in the art studio, in home circles, on the broad stage of public affairs, in the saloons of gay society. The real point of importance is that it is of the nature of idolatry, and that God abhors it and declares it to be incompatible with his residence in the heart. " The idols he shall utterly abolish " (Isa. ii. 18).

III. AS A PROTECTION TO THE ISRAELITES THEMSELVES. The tolerated presence of idolatry in Canaan would have been to the Israelites an irresistible temptation (ver. 4). We are taught: 1. To seek our friendships and alliances elsewhere than among the ungodly. 2. That it is our duty, not only to avoid occasions of sin, and to keep as far out of harm's way as possible, but to labour for the entire removal from our midst of what experience shows to be a deadly snare (Isa. lvii. 14).

Finally, severe as these commands are, we see reflected in them the three principles which, under widely different forms of manifestation, are to this hour to regulate the relation of God's servants to the evil of the world. 1. No toleration of it (Matt. v. 29, 30). 2. No communion with it (2 Cor. vi. 14—18). 3. Unceasing war against it (2 Cor. x. 4; Col. iii. 5).—J. O.

Vers. 3, 4.—*Marriage in the Lord.* This law, forbidding marriages with the ungodly, is one for all time. The apostle revives it in 1 Cor. vii. 39. That marriage should be only in the Lord is evident—

I. FROM THE TRUE IDEA OF MARRIAGE. Two individuals unite their lives, and enter into a fellowship the most intimate possible—to what end? Surely that their natures may be raised to greater perfection, and that they may be better enabled to attain the ends of their existence. This implies a certain harmony of disposition, an essential accordance in the views taken of life and its duties. It is a union, as one has said, not merely between two creatures, but also between two spirits. But what communion, it may be asked, can exist in spiritual respects between two persons severed from each other in the deepest principles of their lives?

II. FROM A REGARD TO THE DIVINE BLESSING. Where one partner is irreligious, the blessing cannot rest upon the home in the same degree as where both are "heirs together of the grace of life" (1 Pet. iii. 7). Believers are to "agree" as touching what things they shall ask (Matt. xviii. 19). Variances even in godly households result in prayers being "hindered" (1 Pet. iii. 7). How much sadder the case of a home, so-called, where husband and wife stand so far apart that they cannot unite in prayer at all! And who that values God's blessing would willingly enter into a relation which inevitably stints and limits it?

III. FROM THE DANGER ACCRUING TO SPIRITUAL LIFE. The danger is not imaginary (1 Kings xi. 3). Where spiritual life is not destroyed, as we may hope that often it is not, yet nothing but harm can come from an association in every respect adverse to it. How intolerable to a spiritual mind to endure "the blight of all sympathy, to be dragged down to earth, and forced to become frivolous and commonplace; to lose all zest and earnestness in life; to have heart and life degraded by mean and perpetually recurring sources of disagreement" (F. W. Robertson)! This is the species of living death to which unequal yoking not unfrequently leads. The effects on offspring are also to be considered. Yet such marriages are rushed into, and, in the prevalent anxiety to make marriage the stepping-stone to wealth and social position, seem likely to become increasingly numerous. Would that men were wise, that they understood these things!—J. O.

Vers. 6—9.—*Reasons for non-conformity to the world, and for aggression on its evil.*
I. THE HOLINESS OF OUR CALLING. (Ver. 6.) The believer stands to God in the relation described in this verse. He is one chosen from the unholy mass to be peculiarly God's property. He belongs to God in body, soul, and spirit. He is a vessel for the Master's use. His every power is to be consecrated. What higher dignity could a human being sustain than that? But the obligations are coextensive with the honour. This man is, in virtue of his holiness, summoned to take up an attitude of non-conformity to the world (Rom. xii. 2). In virtue of the same holiness, he is bound to unite with others in a sacred crusade against its evil.

II. THE GRACE OF OUR ELECTION. (Ver. 7.) This puts another powerful weight into the scale. Standing in so close and honourable a relation to God, the believer is bid look to the rock whence he is hewn, and the hole of the pit whence he is digged. Who made him to differ? Whence this mercy shown peculiarly to him? We need not press texts on election in favour of any special theory. Sufficient that every believer is willing to confess, as regards his own salvation, that "it is not of him that willeth, nor of him that runneth, but of God that showeth mercy" (Rom. ix. 16). An elective purpose comes to light in his spiritual history (Eph. i. 4, 5). When tracing his salvation to its source, he is constrained to say, "God, who is rich in mercy, for his great love wherewith he loved us, even when we were dead in sins, hath quickened us together with Christ" (Eph. ii. 4, 5). All this implies special obligation to God's service.

III. THE MIGHT OF OUR REDEMPTION. (Ver. 8.) The redemption from Egypt, with its tragic accompaniments and mighty signs and wonders, was but a faint type of the greater deliverance which God has now wrought for his Israel in Christ. We are entitled to put the greater for the less, and to plead the stronger claims which the redemption from sin and wrath establishes on the redeemed soul. The cost of our salvation is Christ's blood. What return can we conceivably make exhaustive of our obligations to Father and Son for so great a sacrifice?—J. O.

Vers. 9, 10.—*Lessons from history.* I. A LESSON IN GOD'S GOODNESS. In putting Israel into possession of the land of promise after so long a period of waiting, and at the cost of so much miracle, God gave the nation an irrefragable proof of his covenant-keeping faithfulness. How many difficulties, to the human eye, stood in the way of the fulfilment of that promise! And by what nice adjustments of providence, and what a subtly linked succession of events, was the fulfilment at length brought about! Israel had to be taken down to Egypt, there preserved till it grew and multiplied, passed through the iron furnace of affliction, brought up again with a mighty hand and a stretched-out arm, conducted and provided for in the wilderness, legislated for and organized, strengthened to overcome its enemies. At what an expenditure of wisdom and power was all this accomplished! And how much forbearance and tenderness had to be shown to the people themselves in the course of their rebellious history! Faithfulness was thus emblazoned on every part of God's dealings with them. Another and greater promise, which hung still longer in suspension, has been fulfilled in the coming of that "Seed" in whom already all families of the earth are beginning to be blessed (Gen. xxii. 18; Gal. iii. 16). This fulfilment, above all, demonstrates that Jehovah, he is God, the faithful God, keeping covenant with them that love him.

II. A LESSON IN GOD'S SEVERITY. (Ver. 10.) That had been taught to Israel by many passages in their own history. They had seen God's judgments upon Pharaoh. They had experienced his severity in the plagues, etc., which had swept their own camp in punishment of disobedience. They had witnessed a whole generation turned back to perish in the wilderness. The lesson was now to be taught them by the destruction of these wicked nations. And as if to burn it more deeply, and for ever, into their minds and consciences, the sword of execution was put into their own hands. The two lessons need to be read together. God's severity, divorced from the discoveries of his grace, might appear to the on-looker harsh and cruel, whereas, as Bible history shows, judgment is "his strange work" (Isa. xxviii. 21). On the other hand, the remembrance of his severity is needed to prevent the abuse of his goodness (Rom. xi. 22).—J. O.

Vers. 12—16.—*The rewards of obedience.* If Israel fulfilled its vocation, in keeping itself separate from the idolatries of the heathen, and in destroying them from the land; if further, in possession of the land, it adhered to God's commands, God would make his blessing rest on it in every sphere and department of existence.

I. TEMPORAL PROSPERITY IS A LEGITIMATE OBJECT OF DESIRE. Otherwise it could not be named as part of the blessing, nor could the hope of it be held out as an encouragement to the obedient. We naturally desire to see our affairs prospering. We justly rejoice in the prosperity of our nation. We are glad when trade is brisk, wages good, the comforts of life diffused through the different orders of society. But: 1. Prosperity is to be desired only in subordination to higher ends (Matt. v. 33). 2. Only in so far as it is good for us (3 John 2). 3. Not in excess (Prov. xxx. 8, 9). If God, in the exercise of his higher wisdom, withhold prosperity from us, the loss will be compensated by better blessings (Mark x. 29, 30).

II. TEMPORAL PROSPERITY, IN SUCH MODES AND DEGREES AS GOD SEES BEST, IS AN EFFECT OF THE DIVINE BLESSING. Godliness has promise of the life that now is and of that which is to come (1 Tim. iv. 10). It naturally tends to prosperity. Religion teaches men to be sober, righteous, and godly (Titus ii. 12). It condemns idleness, waste, dishonesty, and the whole series of vices which wreck health, squander property, and destroy confidence. Where religion prevails, men will be industrious, conscientious, orderly, and reliable. But, in addition to this natural tendency of religion to prosperity, there rests on the good man's lot what is distinctively spoken of as the Divine blessing. This will mingle itself with all he has and with all he does. It gives him favour in the eyes of men (Gen. xxxix. 21). It opens up his way for him (Ps. xxxvii. 5). It protects him from injury (Ps. xxxvii. 33, 39). It overrules all events and influences, so that they work for his good. This is forcibly illustrated in the text, where blessing is represented as descending on the home, on the products of the land, on flocks and herds, on the bodily life, etc. The counterpart of the blessing is the curse (ver. 15). The wicked often prosper, but it is prosperity unblessed and unenduring.—J. O.

Vers. 17—25.—*God for us.* The numbers, strength, and fortified security of the seven nations made the conquest of Palestine a task of difficulty, and might naturally produce a disheartening effect on the invaders.

I. A NATURAL FEAR. (Ver. 17.) Like disheartening feelings may assail ourselves in presence of the strong spiritual opposition to be encountered in seeking to win the world for Christ. Our enemies are neither weak nor few; we will do well not to underrate them. The larger part of the globe is yet unoccupied by Christianity. Heathen systems are in possession, supported by the combined influences of tradition, custom, prejudice, and superstition, and presenting an apparently impregnable front to the thin ranks of their assailants. At home, how much of the Christianity is merely nominal! and how much of it is corrupted! We live in days of intense worldliness. The sceptical spirit, likewise, is pronounced and active. Brain and pen power of the highest order is enlisted in its service. Unbelieving science, infidel philosophy, rationalism in the Church. The press is a tower of strength to anti-Christian views of life and duty. While, at the other end of the social scale, the multitudes are sunk in indifference and vice. How are all these enemies to be overcome? May we not fear that, work as we will, we cannot succeed? The fears are groundless; but they are not without their use, if they make us feel that the conquest of the world is not to be achieved without much hard fighting.

II. A GROUND OF ENCOURAGEMENT. (Vers. 18—22.) This encouragement resolves itself into the simple truth that God is for us. He is mightier than our enemies, and will work on our behalf to secure their overthrow. 1. *With supernatural power.* In the past he had shown "signs and wonders," and had brought forth his people with a mighty hand (vers. 18, 19). The same power would help them still. It is encouraging to recall the supernatural strength for conquest which the gospel has already displayed. Think of our own land penetrated by a faith which sprang up 1800 years ago in remote, despised Judæa, with churches for Christ's worship dotting almost every street of every city, town, village, hamlet, throughout its length and breadth! How Utopian would such a work of conquest have seemed at the beginning—a dream of insanity! And this Divine energy for conquest inheres in the gospel to-day as truly as it did of old. 2. *With providential aids* (ver. 20). "Hornets"—types of secret, providential allies working under God's direction. The forces of providence are on the side of those who are working for the advancement of his kingdom. There are such secret allies in men's own hearts. We may compare to the hornets the secret thoughts and feelings—the stings of conscience, guilty fears, feelings of dissatisfaction, etc.—which, operating within, drive men out to join issue with the Spirit in his truth. God has his "hornets" also for arousing his own children out of their sloth and self-indulgence and forgetfulness of duty—sharp trials, vexations, griefs, etc.

III. A METHOD OF CONQUEST. "Little by little" (ver. 22). A law of providence and grace. Little by little God gives a man conquest over the evil in self, and his nature is sanctified. Little by little the world is conquered for Christ. The reason of the law is obvious. There is no advantage in having more than can be rightly used; *e.g.* a man who has more money than he can turn to good account, who has a larger estate than he can manage, who reads more books than he can mentally digest. The best method is "little by little"—mastering, consolidating, using what we have, before hasting to get more.—J. O.

Vers. 25, 26.—*The cursed thing.* The Israelites were not to desire the silver and gold on the graven images. They were not to take it. They were not to bring it into God's house. They were to detest and abhor it, to count it an abomination, a cursed thing, and to beware lest, by lusting after it, they became accursed like unto it. We are taught a lesson—

1. OF DISINTERESTEDNESS IN GOD'S SERVICE. No motive of gain was to be allowed to

mingle with their work. Their service was to be disinterested. Under the cloak of religious zeal there was to be no gratification of covetousness.

II. OF AVOIDING OCCASIONS OF SIN. The gold and silver of the idols tended to ensnare. There would be a temptation to a superstitious and idolatrous use of it (Judg. viii. 27).

III. OF REFUSING GAIN DERIVED FROM IMMORAL SOURCES. The Church is not profited by an influx of the money of the worldling. Still less are the gains of sin to be coveted by her: money derived from gambling, immoral speculation, bubble companies, gin-palaces, sale of irreligious and immoral books, etc.

IV. OF HEARTY DETESTATION OF EVIL. The gildings of vice have an attraction for many who dislike the thing itself. But vice is to be abhorred in its gilded forms, as in every other. "Looking begets liking."—J. O.

Vers. 1—5.—*Extermination with a moral purpose.* When the Israelites were to cross into Canaan, they were directed to *exterminate* the seven nations they would find there. This is their commission. The invasion is to be conducted upon this principle. And here let us notice—

I. NATIONS, LIKE INDIVIDUALS, MAY BECOME INCORRIGIBLE. There can be no doubt that sin tends to a final and incorrigible condition if the Divine mercy is not accepted and allowed to exercise its undermining power. These nations of Canaan were manifestly in this hopeless, utterly ruined state. God regarded them as beyond redemption, and their continuance would only prove pestilential.

It is well for individuals, as well as nations, to realize this sad possibility.

II. GOD HAS EVERY RIGHT TO REMOVE INCORRIGIBLES FROM THE EARTH. As Creator, he has given them every advantage and chance. But the deceitful heart has spurned admonition and mercy. The result is that there is nothing left for them but to be cut off righteously, and that without remedy.

But the propriety of extermination should be determined by the Lord himself (cf. Dr. Mozley's 'Old Testament Lectures,' No. IV., on 'Exterminating Wars').

III. THE ISRAELITES WERE SENT INTO CANAAN TO ESTABLISH THE TRUE WORSHIP OF GOD. They were not to be ashamed of their religion, but to establish it, and to allow nothing to interfere with it. As Abraham had entered Canaan centuries before as the promulgator of a new religion, so his descendants were to enter into the promised land with the view of establishing the religion of Abraham in spite of all possible opposition. They were not ordinary but *religious* emigrants.

IV. THE SPARING OF THE CANAANITES WOULD ONLY ENDANGER THEIR RELIGIOUS FAITH. Some people think they may associate with irreligious people, and even marry them, in the hope of bringing them to a better way of thinking. The plea is generally one got up in the interests of self-pleasing instead of duty. But such hopes are generally disappointed; and the Apostle Paul warns us distinctly against the temptation (2 Cor. vi. 14).

Now, the Israelites were warned against making any covenant with the Canaanites or showing any mercy towards them. Association would only lead to apostacy on the part of Israel. It would be allowing the pestilence to propagate itself. The alternative for Israel was "Exterminate these incorrigible sinners, or by their seductions they will lead you on to your destruction at the hands of a just God" (ver. 4).

V. EXTERMINATION MAY CONSEQUENTLY, IN SOME CASES, BE THE ONLY COURSE CONSISTENT WITH THE DIVINE HONOUR AND THE INTERESTS OF HIS KINGDOM. If people have a right to preserve themselves from a physical pestilence, have they not an equal right in the case of moral pollutions? Besides, the clear direction of God vindicates the whole procedure as right as well as wise (cf. Jellett's 'Moral Difficulties of the Old Testament,' p. 38; also Dr. Arnold's 'Sermons on Interpretation of Scripture,' p. 31). —R. M. E.

Vers. 6—8.—*On the election of nations.* We are here introduced to remarkable words touching the election of, or we might say, *selection* of the Jews. The leading principles of the Divine administration are here set before us. The following points may be noticed:—

I. THE JEWS WERE SELECTED NOT ON ACCOUNT OF ANY NATIONAL SUPERIORITY.

Moses tells them that, numerically, they were the fewest of all people. It was not numerical strength, nor national advantages of any kind, which induced God to select them.

II. THEY WERE SELECTED BECAUSE GOD CHOSE TO SET HIS LOVE UPON THEM. "The Lord did not set his love upon you, nor choose you, because ye were more in number than any people; . . . but because the Lord loved you." It was sovereign love which is its own reason. And, in the last resort, it is to this we must come. We can give no better account of the matter than that God chose to do it.

III. THE DELIVERANCE FROM EGYPT WAS THE PROOF OF HIS SOVEREIGN LOVE. Hereby he kept his promise made to their fathers, and fulfilled his own gracious purpose. The series of judgments, the outcome of his mighty hand, which proved how infinitely stronger it was than the hand of Pharaoh, while severe to Egypt, were love-tokens to Israel.

IV. THE CHOICE OF ISRAEL WAS WITH A VIEW TO THEIR BEING A HOLY PEOPLE AND A SPECIAL PEOPLE UNTO THE LORD. Electing love extended to a nation or a people is really a Divine *investment*. The result is the holiness and consecration of the people. It is this holiness, this sense of consecration, which proves the electing love of God. And this is all the more intense when it is seen clearly that God's love is manifested, not on the ground of national or personal merit, but as a matter of free grace.

And, doubtless, the Jews proved themselves a special people, although far from a perfect people. They were the custodians of the holy oracles for ages. They showed, and they still show, wonderful linguistic and other qualifications. All this, let us believe, is due to that grace and Divine development through which, as a nation, they were permitted to pass.

The practical application of this subject is surely this: 1. To receive God's mercy under an abiding sense that it is undeserved. 2. To cultivate the sense of obligation to God for his undeserved mercy, which it is intended to foster. 3. And to realize the consecration of spirit through which all that is noble in human life comes. God saves us that we may serve him. He shows us his loving-kindness that we may become through it "a peculiar people, zealous of good works."—R. M. E.

Vers. 9—16.—*The Divine veracity.* Moses here speaks of the Divine faithfulness to those that *love* him, and also to those that *hate* him. Those who love him will have his mercy unto a thousand generations; those who hate him will have their hatred returned. He will repay such to their face.

Let us look at the Divine veracity in the two aspects of blessing and of judgment.

I. GOD'S GRATITUDE FOR MAN'S LOVE. God has a love of sovereignty, as we have just seen, which has no reason but itself; and he has also a love of *gratitude* for love shown to him. It is of this Moses here speaks. It is thus expressed elsewhere: "I love them that love me." And here notice—

1. *When we love God we try to keep his commandments.* This is exactly what Christ, incarnate Love, claimed. "If ye love me, keep my commandments." Love is the spirit in which Law should be kept, and through which Law becomes blessedness.

2. *Obedience secures blessing.* God promised Israel certain temporal blessings: increase of the nation and fertility of soil and increase of their flocks and herds. And, in the rude age in which they lived, it was needful to encourage them by such very sensible signs.

This is not so needful now. The blessing comes now in more *spiritual* ways, but still it comes in the wake of obedience. Answers to prayer are still doubted by men who doubt God's existence and reign, but they are most thoroughly believed in by believers. The blessing comes to those who look for it.

3. *It is expected to characterize generations.* For this is the greatest blessing of all when the succeeding generation grows up true to God. It is this form of the Divine faithfulness which is most sought—that even to a "thousand generations" they may remain true to him.

II. GOD'S RIGHTEOUS WRATH AT MAN'S HATRED. Under a righteous government, hatred should have its retribution just as well as love its reward. So is it with God. Men may hate him, and when he repays them to their face they are getting only their due.

God is as faithful in his threatenings as in his promises. Why should he not be so? And his hatred can have but one issue—destruction! How needful, then, to lay down the arms of our rebellion! If our hard hearts cherish any hatred towards him, the sooner we repent of this the better, and take refuge in his love. He waits to be gracious; but, should we despise his mercy and still do him the injustice to hate him, we must prepare for encountering his righteous wrath.—R. M. E.

Vers. 17—26.—*Canaan gradually won.* The winning of the whole land seemed a great task—too great for sense and sight. But the Divine programmes, though comprehensive, are taken in detail. The Israelites are to win the country little by little, and remove the people gradually. In this patient work they may expect the co-operation of God.

I. THE WORK BEFORE US SEEMS OF OVERPOWERING DIMENSIONS. Must we win a victory over all the evil within us? and then contemplate a victory over all the evil around us? Both problems are vast. The more we know our own hearts, the greater seems the extent to be won. The more we know of the world around us, the more appalling seems the proposal of God. It is a great work we are asked to do certainly.

II. BUT BY-PAST DELIVERANCES OF GOD ARE INTENDED TO REINFORCE OUR FAITH. Just as the mighty deliverance from Egypt was set before the Israelites to encourage them in their invasion, so our individual conversion should reinforce our faith in the power of God. The God who can conquer such hearts as ours can surely help us in further conquests. We hope for victory because of victory already won.

III. VICTORY IN DETAIL IS BETTER THAN VICTORY WHOLESALE. We imagine that victory at once over all internal and external enemies would be better than victory covering long years and entering into vast details. But, if Israel had been able to smite all the Canaanites dead at a blow, the beasts of the field would have so overrun the land that it would have been reduced to wilderness, instead of being a land of promise. It is better, therefore, to overcome the Canaanites gradually. They will protect the inheritance from the wild beasts till the heirs arrive.

In like manner, it is better—

1. *To beat our sins in detail.* We are better acquainted with our own nature and God's grace when we have to deal with our sins in detail. We get gradually better and purer and more humble. This is better than a leap into perfection out of sin.

2. *It is better to win the world in detail.* God is not going to give the earth to his people some fine morning, and save us the trouble of winning it. It is better for us to plod on, winning country after country, and individual after individual, and the whole world at last.

3. *The promised land is to be made a holy land.* The Israelites were to remove the Canaanites and their abominable modes of life and worship, to make of Palestine a holy land. Jerusalem—Elkoods—the holy city, is to be the expression of the Divine idea.

Let us conform our hopes to God's magnificent designs, believing that the gradual is generally the best, the microscopic work the most beautiful in the end.—R. M. E.

EXPOSITION.

CHAPTER VIII.

FURTHER EXHORTATION TO OBEDIENCE, ENFORCED BY A REVIEW OF GOD'S DEALINGS WITH ISRAEL IN THE WILDERNESS.

Vers. 1—6.—That they might be induced the more faithfully to observe all the commandments which had been enjoined upon them so as to go on and prosper, they are called to remember the experiences of the forty years in the wilderness, when God guided them and disciplined them for their good. He humbled them that he might test the state of their heart and affections towards him, using the distress and privations to which they were subjected as means of bringing out what was in them, and of leading them to feel their entire dependence on him for help, sustenance, and guidance. Not only by commands difficult to be obeyed laid on men, and by mighty works done in their view, does God prove men (cf. Gen. xxii. 1, etc.; Exod. xv. 25; xx. 20); but also by afflictions and calamities (Judg. ii. 22;

iii. 4; Ps. xvii. 3; lxxxi. 7, etc.), as well as by benefits (Exod. xvi. 4). Humbled so as to see his own weakness, chastised out of all self-conceit by affliction, man is brought to submit to God, to hear and obey him; and along with this the experience of God's goodness tends to draw men, in grateful acknowledgment of his mercy and bounty, to yield themselves to him and sincerely and lovingly to serve him (cf. Rom. ii. 4).

Vers. 1, 2.—God's dealings with the Israelites were disciplinary. Both by the afflictions and privations to which they were subjected, and by the provision they received and the protection afforded to them, God sought to bring them into and keep them in a right state of mind towards him—a state of humble dependence, submissive obedience, and hopeful trust. But that this effect should be produced, it was needful that they should mark and remember all his ways towards them.

Ver. 3.—God humbled the Israelites by leaving them to suffer hunger from the want of food, and then supplying them with food in a miraculous manner. They were thus taught that their life depended wholly on God, who could, by his own creative power, without any of the ordinary means, provide for the sustaining of their life. And fed thee with manna (cf. Exod. xvi. 15). It is in vain to seek to identify this with any natural product. It was something entirely new to the Israelites—a thing which neither they nor their fathers knew; truly bread from heaven, and which got from them the name of *manna* or *man*, because, in their wondering ignorance, they knew not what to call it, and so they said one to another, *Mân hoo?* (מָן הוּא), *What is it?* and thenceforward called it *man.* That he might make thee know, etc. "Bread," which the Jews regarded as "the staff of life," stands here, as in other places, for food generally; and the lesson taught the Israelites was that not in one way or by one kind of means alone could life be sustained, but in the absence of these God could, by his own fiat, provide for the sustenance of his children. Every word—literally, *all,* everything whatever—that proceedeth out of the mouth of the Lord, *i e.* all means which God has by his word provided, or by his word can provide, for the sustenance of life. So our Lord cites this passage in replying to the tempter, who had suggested that if he was the Son of God he might relieve himself from the pangs of hunger by commanding the stones which lay around to become bread. Our Lord's reply to this is virtually, "I have this power, and could use it, but I will not; for this would imply impatience and distrust of God, who has engaged to sustain the life of his servants, and who can, by the mere word of his mouth, by his creative will, provide in an extraordinary way for the sustenance of life when the ordinary means of life are wanting." "Jesus means to say, 'I leave it with God to care for the sustaining of my life, and I will not arbitrarily and for selfish ends help myself by a miracle'" (De Wette, note on Matt. iv. 4; see also Meyer on the place).

Ver. 4.—As the manna furnished by God's creative power saved them from hunger, so by God's providence and care their raiment was marvellously kept from decay, and they had not to go barefoot from their sandals being worn out. Waxed not old upon thee; literally, *did not fall away, waste away from upon thee.* This cannot mean that such was the abundant supply of raiment to the Israelites in the Arabian desert, that there was no need for them to wear garments rent and tattered from long use, as they had large flocks and herds whence a sufficient supply of wool and leather could be obtained, and there were among them skilled artificers, by whom these could be made into articles of clothing (Rosenmüller, J. D. Michaelis, etc.). For, as Knobel observes, "This were something too insignificant beside the miraculous manna; and besides, this does not lie in the expression, which rather intimates that the clothes upon them were not worn out nor fell from them in rags, because God gave them a marvellous durability." At the same time, there is no reason to suppose that the Israelites did not make use of such supplies as were within their reach for purposes of clothing, any more than that they lived only on manna during the forty years of their wandering. Still less need we resort to such fanciful suppositions as that the garments of the Israelitish children expanded as they grew up, like the shells of snails—which is the notion of some of the Jewish rabbins, and adopted by some of the Christian Fathers (see Deyling, 'Obss. Sacc.,' II. xvii. p. 247). Neither did thy foot swell. The verb here is found in only one other passage (Neh. ix. 21), where this passage is repeated; and the meaning is doubtful. The LXX. render here by ἐτυλώθησαν, *became callous;* but in Neh. the rendering they give is διερράγησαν, *were torn,* the object torn being, according to the Cod. Vat., πόδες αὐτῶν, *their feet,* according to the Cod. Alex., τὰ ὑποδήματα αὐτῶν, *their sandals.* In ch. xxix. 5, the shoe or sandal is specially mentioned in the same connection as here. The verb, however, cannot mean tear or torn, neither does it mean swell; the idea involved is rather that of softening, or melting, or flowing; and the meaning here seems to be, "Thy foot did not get into a bruised and wounded state"—which would have been the case had their sandals not been preserved from breaking or being worn out.

Ver. 5.—Thus God educated, disciplined, and trained his people as a father does his child. **Chasteneth**. The idea is not so much that of *punishment* or *chastisement*, properly so called, as that of *severe discipline* and *training*. God made them feel his hand upon them, but ever for their good; the end of the discipline to which they were subjected was that they might keep his commandments and walk in his ways, so as to enjoy his favour (cf. Heb. xii. 5, etc.).

Vers. 7—20.—The land on which they were about to enter is described as a good land, fertile and well watered, and yielding abundant produce to its cultivators; and they are cautioned against forgetting, in their enjoyment of the gift, the bounty of the Giver, or congratulating themselves on having achieved the conquest of such a land, instead of gratefully acknowledging the grace which had sustained them during their protracted wandering in the wilderness, and by which alone they had been enabled to take possession of that favoured land.

Vers. 7, 8.—**Brooks of water**, running streams, mountain torrents, and watercourses in the narrow valleys or wadys; **fountains**, perennial springs; **depths**, "the fathomless pools from which such streams as the Abana (now Barada), near Damascus, spring up full-grown rivers, almost as broad at their sources as at their mouths" (Conder, 'Handbook to the Bible,' p. 214), or this may include also the inland seas or lakes, such as the sea of Galilee and Lake Hûleh. Palestine is in the present day, on the whole, well supplied with water, though the distribution is very unequal, many parts being almost wholly destitute of supply, except from what may be collected from rain in tanks or cisterns; and there is no reason to suppose it was different in the ancient times. As compared, however, with the desert to which the Israelites had been so long accustomed, and even with Egypt from which they had escaped, the country on which they were about to enter was well watered.

Ver. 8.—"Palestine has been celebrated in all ages for three products: corn, wine, and oil, which still continue to be its most valuable crops" (Ibid., p. 189). The principal corn crops were wheat and barley. The vine was largely and carefully culti-

vated; the olive required little cultivation, being almost a spontaneous growth, and forming one of the most valuable productions of the country; the fig was also indigenous in Palestine, and still grows there, both wild and cultivated, in abundance; that the pomegranate (*rimmon*) also was very abundant may be inferred from the number of places named from this (cf. Josh. xv. 32; xix. 7, 13; Judg. xx. 45, 47; xxi. 13; 1 Chron. iv. 32, etc.). **Honey.** The word so rendered (*d'bash*) is used both of the honey of bees (Lev. ii. 11; ch. xxxii. 11; 1 Sam. xiv. 26, etc.; Ps. lxxxi. 17; Prov. xvi. 24, etc.), and of the honey of grapes, a syrup obtained by boiling down the newly expressed juice of the grape to a half or third part of its bulk, and still known among the Arabs by the name of *dibs* (Robinson, 'Bib. Res.,' ii. p. 442; Smith, 'Bib. Dict.,' *s.v.* 'Honey'). In the wilderness, the people had murmured that they had been brought into an evil place, no place of figs, or of vines, or of pomegranates; and where there was no water to drink (Numb. xx. 5). Moses here tells them that the land they were about to occupy was not such a place, but one abounding in all those things of which they had found the wilderness so destitute.

Ver. 9.—**A land whose stones are iron.** Minerals do not abound in Palestine; the hills are for the most part calcareous; but by the side of the limestone in the north of Canaan ferruginous basalt appears in large masses, and on Lebanon ironstone abounds. Near Tiberias are springs largely impregnated with iron, as are also those at Hasbeija, on the Hermon range, as well as the soil around that place. Traces of extinct copper works are also to be found on Lebanon (cf. art. 'Metals,' in Kitto and Smith; Ritter, 'Geography of Palestine,' i. 248). The Israelites, however, do not seem to have carried on mining operations themselves, but to have been content to obtain supplies of the useful metals from their neighbours (2 Sam. viii. 8; 1 Chron. xviii. 8; xxii. 3, 14).

Ver. 10.—**When thou hast eaten and art full, then thou shalt bless the Lord thy God.** "From this place the Jews have made it a general rule, or, as they call it, an affirmative precept, that every one bless God at their meals, that is, give him thanks for his benefits; for he blesses us when he bestows good things on us, and we bless him when we thankfully acknowledge his goodness therein" (Patrick).

Vers. 11—14.—Wealth is apt to engender in the possessor of it a spirit of self-gratulation and pride, and abundance of good things to induce men to be luxurious, "to trust in uncertain riches," and to be forgetful of the bounteous hand from which all that they enjoy has come. Against this the people are here cautioned and warned.

Ver. 15.—**Who led thee through that great and terrible wilderness, wherein were fiery serpents**, etc. "The fiery serpent" and "the scorpion" (sing.) are in apposition to the "wilderness," and illustrate its terribleness. *Fiery serpents*—ὄφεις τοὺς θανατοῦντας, LXX.—or burning serpents, so called from the burning pain caused by their bite; probably the cerastes, or one of the naja species (cf. Numb. xxi. 6).

Ver. 16.—The grand end of all God's dealings with the Israelites in the desert, both the trials to which they were subjected and the benefits they received, was that he might do them good ultimately. **Thy latter end**; not the end of life, as in Numb. xxiii. 10, but the state ensuing on the termination of their period of discipline and probation in the desert (cf. Job viii. 7; xlii. 12; 2 Pet. ii. 20). God thus dealt with the Israelites as he still deals with his people; he afflicts them not for his pleasure but for their profit (Heb. xi. 12); he subjects them to trial and varied discipline that he may fit them for the rest and joy that in the end are to be theirs.

Vers. 17, 18.—The blessing in store for them was God's free gift to them; and when they came to enjoy it they were not to allow themselves to say in their heart, *i.e.* to think or imagine, that the prosperous condition in which they were placed was the result of their own exertions; they were to ascribe all to God's gracious bounty, for from him had come the power by which prosperity had been gained, and this he had given, not on account of any merit in them, but that he might fulfil his covenant engagements to their fathers. **Get wealth** עָשָׂה חַיִל, to make strength, to gather substance (Gen. xii. 5), to procure wealth (Ruth iv. 11, margin; Ezek. xxviii. 4). **As it is this day.** "As was quite evident then, when the establishment of the covenant had already commenced, and Israel had come through the desert to the border of Canaan (see ch. iv. 20)" (Keil).

Vers. 19, 20.—Moses enforces his counsel by reminding them again that only destruction awaited them should they forget the Lord their God and apostatize from him (cf. ch. iv. 25, etc.; vi. 14).

HOMILETICS.

Vers. 1—6.—*Life's meaning discerned by the retrospect of it.* The remark has not unfrequently been made that incidents closely connected cannot be rightly understood till the time has come for them to be reviewed in their entirety as matters of history. What is true of events generally, applies in all its force to the wonders included in the rescue and wanderings of the people of Israel. And that which may be said of them, holds good, in this respect, of the life-story of God's children now. Two words would sum up the pith of their experience—"redemption," "training." Redeemed first, trained afterwards. Redeemed, that they might be trained; trained, that they might become worthy of the redemption. Both the redemption and the training had in Israel's case a depth of meaning of which the people knew little at the time, but which Israel's God intended from the first. Afterwards, their varied experiences, when reviewed as a piece of history, became matter for grateful record and adoring praise. The paragraph before us now is "*the aged lawgiver reviewing the experiences of Israel in their wanderings.*" Four lines of meditation open up—

I. THERE ARE MANY LESSONS WHICH GOD'S CHILDREN NEED TO LEARN. 1. "To humble thee" (ver. 2), *i.e.* to bring them to feel their dependence on God. This, indeed, seems such an obvious truth, that men ought not to need to be taught it. But we must remember that, before we are redeemed, our training for eternity has never begun at all, and that when redemption is with us a realized fact, we then present ourselves to God only in the rough, relying on his love to make us what we should be. And one of the lessons we have thoroughly to learn is that "without Christ we can do nothing." 2. "To prove thee" (ver. 2). A double proof is indicated. (1) What they were: "To know what was in thine heart." (2) What they would do: "Whether thou wouldest keep his commandments, or no." There is no subject on which the young convert is so ignorant as—himself; and he never can become what a Christian should be till he sees his own conceit. He must become a sadder man ere he can be a wiser one. 3. "That he might make thee know that man doth not live by bread alone." It has been remarked that, as Moses in this clause refers to the manna, the meaning is : (1) That it is not from nature but from nature's God that supplies come. (2) That God is free to adopt any course he pleases in providing food. Doubtless this is true. But it is not the whole truth, nor do we deem it *the* truth here intended. We know that with these words our Saviour repelled one assault of the tempter. This being so, we are set somewhat on a different track for their interpretation (cf. Matt. iv. 3, 4). Our Saviour's reply is, in effect, " Man has a double life, not only that of the body, but also that of the spirit; you ask me to nourish the lower at the expense of the higher—to get food for the body by a negation of the self-sacrifice for which I came. It is not bread alone which sustains the man. He has a higher self, which lives on higher food, and I cannot pamper the lower at the cost of the prostration of the higher." Now, with such light thrown on the passage by our Lord, we are led to regard the words of Moses as referring not only to the supply of food, but rather to the entire discipline in the wilderness, as intended by God to bring out to the people the reality and worth of the nobler part of man. Our God cares more for growth of soul than for comfort of body. His aim is not only to find us food, but to train us for himself. Nor was it that they only might learn these lessons, but that others in after time might see on what rough and raw material the Great Educator will condescend to work, and with what care he will work upon it.

II. God adopts varied methods of teaching these needed lessons. The clauses in the paragraph indicate these. 1. There was " the way " by which they were led. It was not given to Israel to choose it. It was not the shortest way. It was " the right " way, appointed by God. 2. The method of sending supplies : " Day by day the manna fell." They were thus taught to live by the day. 3. The disappointments they met : " These forty years." If they had been told, when they set out from Egypt, that so long a period intervened between them and Canaan, they would scarcely have set out. And if God were to unveil to us the incidents of coming years, we could not bear the sight. 4. The wants they felt : " He suffered thee to hunger." God sometimes lets his people feel how completely they are shut up to him. 5. Yet there were constant proofs of thoughtful care (ver. 4). We do not understand any miracle involved here, still less so odd a one as the rabbis suggested, that the children's clothes grew upon their backs. The meaning of Moses surely is, " God so provided for their wants that they needed not to wear tattered garments, nor to injure their feet by walking without shoes or sandals." 6. There was also chastening (ver. 5). This word includes not only correction but all that belongs to the training of a child (cf. Heb. xii. 7; 2 Sam. vii. 14 ; Ps. lxxxix. 32 ; Job vii. 17, 18 ; Prov. iii. 11, 12 ; Rev. iii. 19).

III. There is a reason indicated here why God takes so much pains to teach these lessons. Ver. 5, " As a man chasteneth his son." We might well ask, Why should the Great Supreme do so much to educate into shape such raw and rough natures as ours ? That he should do so at all is, *per se,* far harder to believe than any apparent variation of the ordinary course of physical nature. The reason is found in the words, " Ye are sons." Israel was God's son, even his firstborn. Believers are the adopted children of God ; hence the greatness of their destiny, and the earnestness of their Leader in training them for it. It may be said, indeed, by an unbeliever, " *I have all these changes in life, but they are not training me,*" etc. No, because the one condition is wanting under which all these come to be a training—sonship. This order is never reversed—rescued, *then* educated. If men have not known the first, they cannot understand the second.

IV. If God cares so much to train, we should carefully consider what his training means. (Vers. 2, 5.) Let us understand what a high moral and spiritual aim God has in the culture of this life of ours ! *The life of a man* is not a mere material something, on a physical basis; it is the expression of a plan of God. Then let us be as anxious to be rightly educated for eternity, as God is so to educate us. Never let us allow the lower ends of life to master the higher (ver. 6). Ever let us keep the end of life in view. For eternity we are meant, and for eternity we should live. *Some have life largely in retrospect, even now.* Do they not see that the past is explained by the present ? Even so the present will be explained by the future (John xiii. 7). Let them rejoice that they have a Father who guides by the way which he sees to be right, and not " according to their mind." *Some have life before them.* 1. Let it be the supreme desire to let life become what God wants it to be—a continuous advance in preparation for heaven. This is of more consequence than all the ease and comfort in the world. 2. Recognize and praise the kindness of God in giving men these chequered experiences of life, if they do but educate for higher service. Don't let us wonder if we cannot understand God's ways at the time. We shall in the end. 3. If we want God to train us for glory—first, we must come out of Egypt. The education cannot begin in the land of bondage,—we must first be the Lord's free men ; then, let us leave the way and method of the culture entirely to God. If he were to let us choose the way, what mistakes we should make ! Our faith in God even in youth should be such as to lead us to say, " Father, my supreme desire is to grow like thee, and to live with thee. I know not by what paths I need to be led, nor through what discipline I need to be brought, to bring about this end. I leave all in thy gracious hands, desiring that thine infinite wisdom and love should order all things for me. Here I am. Take me as I am, all guilty and defiled. Make me what I should be ; and if by thy grace I am ripened for and led to Canaan, then will I sing, ' Blessing, and honour, and glory, and power, to him which sitteth upon the throne, and to the Lamb, for ever and ever ! ' "

Vers. 7—10.—*The duty of thankfulness for the bounty of God in nature.* The people of Israel were being led by the Lord their God to a land beautiful, luxuriant, fruitful. (For an account of the productions of Palestine, of the fertility of its soil, and of the treasures hidden in its hills, see works by Kitto, Stanley, Wilson, Thomson, and others; as well as Bible dictionaries and cyclopædias, under the several headings.) Evidently, at the time Moses uttered the words before us, the people had not reached that land ; though they were expecting shortly to do so. In view thereof, Moses bids them (ver. 10) bless the Lord their God for the good land he had given them. Hence our subject : " the duty of recognizing the hand of God in the bounties of nature, and of thankfulness for the use of them."

I. THERE IS A MARVELLOUS ADAPTATION IN EXTERNAL NATURE TO THE CONSTITUTION AND WANTS OF MAN. (Each of the varied terms used in vers. 7—9 will afford vast scope for the expansion of this thought. And the wider the range of knowledge, the greater delight will such expansion afford to one who longs to make others see the variety of the Divine goodness.) What a vast and prolonged preparation must there have been to fit this world for the use of those who should hereafter dwell upon it ! And then, when all is ready, man, the crown of God's earthly creation, comes last upon the scene, with " all things put under his feet."

II. ALL THE WEALTH OF EARTH IS A GIFT TO MAN. " The good land which he hath given thee " (ver. 10). It is but reasonable that we look at the profusion of riches upon and within the earth as a " gift." " What have we that we have not received ? " Where were we when " the foundations of the earth " were laid ? Yet some would have us adopt a " religion of humanity," as if humanity were to be praised for the physical basis of its own existence ! A Power not in man nor of man hath given us all.

III. THE GIFT COMETH FROM A PERSONAL BEING. " The Lord thy God for the good land which *he* hath given thee." The Power from which nature's wealth cometh, is not a blind non-intelligent force. For man's own intelligence has to be accounted for ; and even if impersonal forces could have wrought out matter, it is axiomatically certain that impersonality could not produce personality. So far natural religion can go. But our text takes us further.

IV. NATURE'S WEALTH COMETH FROM THE LORD OUR GOD. " *Our* God." He is not an " Unknown." We may not set up an altar, 'Αγνώστῳ Θεῷ. We know him as a redeeming God, as One who delights to exercise loving-kindness, righteousness, and judgment in the earth. And since God is revealed to us in Christ, we learn thereby that the long preparations of earth have been going on with a view of setting up on it the new creations of redeeming grace. This is " the hidden wisdom, which God ordained before the world, unto our glory." Oh, the boundless meaning of the expression, " The Lamb slain from the foundation of the world " !

V. ALL THIS SHOULD CALL FORTH SPECIAL THANKFULNESS FROM OUR HEARTS AND LIPS. " Thou shalt bless," etc. We may go very far beyond the merely personal consideration which Moses suggests here. We know more clearly, therefore we should praise more intelligently, devoutly, and warmly. Israel might include some, *we* should take in all, the following considerations, to stimulate to intense thankfulness. 1. We were nothing, had nothing, and yet we have all given to us "richly to enjoy." 2. We are sinful, and have forfeited thereby even our natural claim. Yet all is continued to us, in unwearying kindness and unabated faithfulness. 3. We have not only the actual possessions of earth's wealth, but are put in possession of the mind and purpose of the Great Framer of all, that ours may be the praise of understanding hearts. 4. We read that God wills to have on this globe a ransomed people, ours, therefore, may well be the jubilant praise of redeemed men. 5. We are not here merely to enjoy this world and then to know no other, but to enjoy this world as a stepping-stone to another. Hence ours should be the triumphant shout of men with a glorious destiny ahead, and of those who use this world so as to help them to a better. Finally: 6. The present form of earth is destined to fall away. God will "make all things new" (Ps. cii. 26 ; Heb. i. 12 ; 2 Pet. iii. 13). We for whom this world was made, will then be rejoicing in God, and will be enraptured to see what ever-advancing forms of beauty "he hath prepared for them that love him." Thus ours should be the praise of men on whom even the too oft-repeated dirge, "passing away," leaves no trace of gloom or of regret. If we are the redeemed of the Lord, our life may be a song of thanksgiving, and our death a shout of victory!

Vers. 11—18.—(See Homiletics : ch. vi. 10—19.)

Ver. 16.—(See Homiletics : ch. viii. 1—6.)

Vers. 17, 18.—*Danger of self-glorification.* The enjoyment of God's mercies, which should be so provocative of thankfulness, may become a snare, if we are not careful to guard against their misuse. Several of the dangers to which prosperity makes us liable are dealt with in the Homily referred to above. Here, there is one specially named, which is perhaps the most common of all, viz. that of attributing success in life to one's own skill, or wisdom, or might : "And thou say in thine heart, My power and the might of mine hand hath gotten me this wealth" (see Ezek. xxviii. 4, 5 ; xxix. 3 ; Ps. xii. 3 ; Judg. vii. 2). So strong is the tendency to accredit ourselves with any gains which may be ours, in a vain, self-glorifying spirit, that we cannot be too anxious to guard against it, by exposing the sin and evil of it.

I. IT IS UNTRUE. However much care we may have taken to ensure success, whether we gain our end or no, has been dependent at every moment on a conjunction of circumstances, which we were as powerless to bring about or to avoid, as to create the tides or arrest the moon. And even the ability to take care, and to put forth effort, has been a gift. We are violating the first rudiments of most certain truth, when we take the credit of success in life to ourselves.

II. IT IS DISLOYAL. For it is God who gives us the power to get wealth. We owe all we have to his bounty, and even the very breath we draw, to his unceasing care. The laws on which we have relied to bring prosperity have been of God's creation. And for a creature to plume himself on the gifts of the Creator, who can adequately set forth *such* injustice to high Heaven?

III. IT IS UNGRATEFUL. For, as if it were not enough that the Most High should have all our faults to bear with unceasingly—is it not marvellously ungrateful that creatures who would have long ago been cut down except for the long-suffering of God, should pride themselves on the abilities which have been in such forbearance continued to them?

IV. IT IS MOST MISCHIEVOUS IN ITS EFFECTS. For it nurses pride, instead of fostering thankfulness. It genders selfishness, it freezes benevolence, and will surely breed a covetous, tyrannous, haughty disposition, if not fought against and overcome.

V. IT IS OFFENSIVE IN GOD'S SIGHT. (Prov. vi. 16, 17 ; Jas. iv. 6 ; 1 Pet. v. 5.) God sets himself in array against pride of heart. How can it be otherwise? "What communion hath light with darkness?" God will dwell with the contrite and humble spirit, but "the proud he knoweth afar off."

VI. IT IS THE REVERSE OF THAT WHICH GOD'S DESIGNS. (Ver. 16.) For the varied experiences of life are an appeal of God to men as moral beings, "to humble them and prove them;" and if, in spite of all, any take the credit to themselves of their own prosperity, God's own intent in their life-history is being reversed.

VII. IT WILL SOONER OR LATER BRING HUMILIATION AND SUFFERING. (Prov. xxix. 23.) Again and again does our Saviour also lay down this principle, that pride exposes to much shame (Matt. xxiii. 12; Luke xiv. 11; xviii. 14). It is not for us to say, in any individual case, in what form the debasement or disappointment will come. But come it will. It may be in one or more of the following ways: 1. By the removal of the wealth which was gained, and a sudden plunge from prosperity to adversity. It is sad when men have to part with all before they will learn that God gave all! 2. By depriving men of any further power to attend to worldly concerns, they may have to see their utter helplessness without God. 3. By a searching dealing with the spirit in the furnace of tribulation, God may graciously burn up the pride, and purge away corruption. But the process is a terrific one, even here. It is being saved, "yet so as by fire." Still, it is better to be saved, even thus, cost what it may (1 Cor iii. 18). It is only when God succeeds in "humbling" us, that he can do us good "at the latter end." 4. If, after all warnings, teachings, and strivings, God's voice is still unheard, and pride still rears itself up against him, he will reckon the proud one as "the chaff which the wind driveth away." And oh, how will this self-elation shrivel up then (see Isa. ii. 10—22)! God will not give his glory to another (1 Sam. ii. 30; Mal. iv. 1). What reversals of position will that day witness! That which the world reckoned as "great wealth" will come to nought, and the "wealthy" one will be bankrupt for eternity; while those who in lowliness of spirit have received thankfully the least of God's gifts, shall have *him* as their "exceeding great Reward." To such he will say, "Friend, come up higher!"

Vers. 19, 20.—(See Homiletics: ch. xxviii.)

HOMILIES BY VARIOUS AUTHORS.

' Vers. 1—6.—*The moral uses of memory.* The memory of man exerts a mighty influence over his history and his destiny. Minus memory, man would be altogether another being. Remembrance of the past is a guide-post, or a beacon, for the future. The key-word of this passage is "all:" "all the way;" "every word;" "all the commandments."

I. THE SCOPE OF MEMORY. "All the way which the Lord thy God hath led thee." 1. *Remember thy needs*—how many, how various, how urgent. Our hourly dependence upon material substance for food, and upon a Power beyond and above ourselves, ought to make us profoundly humble. Is there an occupant of this globe so full of need of many sorts as man? 2. *Remember thy special perils.* Every man has his particular dangers, as the Hebrews had in the desert—perils arising from outward circumstance, moral temptations, evil powers, personal defects and infirmities, distinctive vocation. 3. *Remember God's suitable supplies.* Their needs in the desert were *unique* and *unprecedented;* yet God was prepared for every emergency. It was open to him either to diminish the need, or else to institute new methods of supply. What if the sandy soil refused to yield a harvest! *He* can distil a harvest from the dewy air. What if flax be wanting as a material from which to fabricate raiment! *He* can stay, by a volition, the progress of decay and wear. What though the journeys tend to injure and blister the feet! *He* can make the skin durable as iron and brass. There shall be special blessing for special need. Every man's history is more or less *special*. Every point of *our* past history teems with footprints of God. Placed under the microscope of pious memory, every atom yields surprising lessons, sparkling truths.

II. THE MORAL USES OF MEMORY. They may be summed up under one head, viz. to perceive that God was in every event—that every word of God is a force for giving life. 1. *A calm review of the past discovers the moral purpose God has kept in view.* As when a man stands in the midst of complicated machinery, he is deafened by the roar, and bewildered by the manifold movements, that he cannot detect the definite end which that machine serves. To gain that knowledge, he must move away, and take in by one glance the effect of the whole. So, amid the whirl and excitement of passing events, we do not discern the definite purpose God has in view. We must get a bird's-eye view from a new elevation. To reduce the pride of man's heart, to persuade him that God rules, are laudable purposes of Divine leadings. 2. *The remembrance of the past exhibits the fatherly disciplines of God.* Mingled tenderness and severity is conspicuous in God's dealings. We can see *now* that we had the sunshine of his favour when we kept the pathway of obedience, and that as often as we became wayward, the rod of his indignation fell. We can see *now* the likeness between God's treatment of us, and our fatherly treatment of our children. Faithful discipline is better every way than foolish fondness. 3. *Memory revealed to them the fact that God was making in their life a great experiment.* The vicissitudes and hardships and surprising deliverances in the wilderness were now seen to be tests, by which God would discover whether the people were worthy of Canaan, competent to be the depository of his truth. The object was to *prove* them, whether they could be entrusted with this Divine mission. So, every man's life is God's experiment. The question to be solved in each of our lives is this, " Are we worthy a place in God's eternal kingdom ? " Every effort is made by God to make this experiment successful. 4. *A review of the past serves to show that man has a nobler life than that of the body.* The main purpose why the Hebrews had been fed for forty years on manna was *this*, viz. to demonstrate that our well-being is not dependent on material things. Man lives not by bread, but by the Divine word. Even bread itself is a product of God's word. All the processes of mastication, digestion, assimilation, are the effects of Divine command. Our entire life is nourished by the word of God. Practical obedience is to the soul's life what digestion is to the life of the body. "My meat and drink is to do the will of my Father in heaven."

III. THE BENEFICENT EFFECTS OF A MEMORY DEVOUTLY EXERCISED. If we remember "all the way"—its subtle and intricate windings, and the faithful leadership of our Guide; if we appreciate the vital value of "every word" of Jehovah; we shall resolve henceforth to keep "all his commandments." 1. *Remembrance will excite gratitude.* Our gratitude is largely deficient, because we do not consider and reflect. If memory will fulfil her office well in supplying fuel for the altar of the heart, the flame of love will burn with a more constant glow. 2. *Remembrance of Divine favours will convince us that God's interests and ours are identical.* It is the natural effect of sin to persuade us that God is our enemy. We say, "Depart from us." But, when with ʟunbiased mind we ponder the proofs of God's kindness, we yield to the evidence that he is a true Friend. Experience teaches us that it is our interest to obey. 3. *Remembrance of past favours aids the operations of conscience.* The conscience becomes hard before it becomes blind. Whatever keeps alive *feeling* in the conscience benefits the whole man. If there be light and life in a man's conscience, he will resolutely say, "I must not sin. I will fear God and keep his commandments." 4. *Vivid remembrance of God's past goodness is a vigorous incentive to obedience.* A sense of obligation for the past cannot fully express itself, except in acts of hearty obedience. When we realize fully that our every step has been under God's guidance, that every good thing has come from our Father's hand, and that every *word* of his is empowered to give us joyous life,—then are we constrained to say, "All that the Lord commandeth us will we do."—D.

Vers. 7—20.— *Wealth perilous to piety.* God's policy in the government of men is to win by prodigal kindness. A churlish parsimony has never been found with him ;— the very opposite. An open eye discovers widespread munificence—a royal banquet. The present is only a sample of the future. The full inheritance is always the object of hope. The children of a king have large expectations. This passage contains—

I. A NOTABLE INSTANCE OF DIVINE MUNIFICENCE. 1. *The heritage of Israel was a " good land."* Both climate and soil were suited to every variety of natural production. The fruits of the North, and the fruits of the Tropics, might alike find a home there. Untold ages had passed, during which God had been slowly preparing that land for Israel, and storing it with elements of fertility, and wealth of minerals. 2. *Others had been employed to bring the virgin soil under culture.* The harder and more unprofitable toil had been accomplished. The house of Israel was already well furnished, as when a bridegroom brings home his bride. 3. *There was every variety of provision.* This betokened thoughtful foresight and tender affection. No needed good had been overlooked. The beneficent Creator had furnished, not only the necessaries of life, but every luxury. Whatever could please the palate, or gratify a taste, or invigorate the health, was there. These were pictures of heavenly good ; for as yet the people could not appreciate the imperishable treasures of the spirit-land. 4. *This inheritance was unpurchased and unreserved.* It made them, body and soul, debtors to God. Had they preferred to purchase it with money, they had nought of their own ; they could not create the medium of barter. They had not obtained it by the merit of obedience. They were the recipients of distinguished favour—pensioners on the Divine bounty. If it be said that they obtained the land by right of conquest, it must be counter-said that the Lord had given them victory. The battle was the Lord's. Herein God designed to conquer their proud spirits by the generosity of his love. 5. *This inheritance was not the final end.* God had ulterior purposes of good yet beyond, towards the realization of which this was a stepping-stone. His next design was to "establish his covenant with them." At present, they were reaping the fruit of their fathers' faith. This was a reward for Abraham's piety. If they should prove faithful, they too should be promoted to higher things. Canaan was not a home, but a school-house.

II. THE PASSAGE CONTAINS VALUABLE COUNSEL. The counsels of clear-eyed, venerable wisdom are more precious than pearls. 1. *The counsel prescribes grateful recollection.* Having received such measureless kindness, it would be the rankest villany to forget the Giver. Over the sunken rock of ingratitude a triple beacon stands : "Beware!" Give this murderous reef ample sea-room. *Here* many a gallant ship has gone to pieces. 2. *The counsel directs suitable requital.* "Thou shalt *bless* the Lord thy God!" But can man confer any blessing on his Maker? Can we add to God's wealth or enjoyment ? In a sense we can. Dispositions are accepted as deeds. If we are not willing to give to God *all we have,* our hearts are base. We can bring him the wealth of our love. We can bring him the music of our praise. We can bring him the devotion of our lives. Does his voice whisper to us from heaven, "It is well that it is in thine heart"? Does he smell the sweet savour of our sacrifice? 3. *The counsel includes practical obedience.* Obedience, if genuine, will be complete. It will embrace every known command. If we observe some commandments, and consciously neglect others, *this is not obedience ;* we are merely doing our own will. Whether we perceive the reason of the command or not, we shall honour it as our Lord's will—as our Lord himself. No matter what compliance costs, we will give it. Ours not to reason why. True obedience is hearty, complete, perpetual.

III. THIS PASSAGE INDICATES IMMINENT PERILS. 1. *Wealth often leads to fleshly indulgence.* With abundance in our possession, it is easier to indulge the appetites than to deny them. Yet the higher life can only be developed at the expense of the lower. "Flesh and blood cannot inherit the kingdom." 2. *Wealth breeds self-sufficient pride.* It serves to weaken our sense of dependence upon God. When from our visible stores every felt need can be supplied, we are prone to forget the unseen Giver. Most men may well thank God that the temptations of wealth dwell not under their roofs. "How hardly shall they that have riches enter into the kingdom of God!" In the hot-bed of riches, the flower of sweet humility does not thrive. 3. *Wealth loses sight of its own origin.* It has a short memory for obligations. The millionaire soon forgets the days of poverty and struggle—forgets the Friend who succoured him in his extremity—kicks away the ladder by which he rose. Riches naturally encumber and stifle the flame of religious feeling. 4. *Riches beget in us false confidence.* Like Nebuchadnezzar, we say, "Is not this great Babylon, that *I* have built?" We find a delicious pleasure in hearing our own skill and sagacity praised. The tide of natural feeling sets strongly towards self-trust. 5. *Riches tend towards idolatry.* In the days of poverty we did not object to be accounted singular ; but in the time of wealth we aspire to do as others do. It is arduous to have to think for one's self, to rely upon one's own judgments, to pursue a course which men will ridicule. If others bow down to their own net, or rear a popular idol, we too must bow down and worship it. Wealth has given us prominence, set us on high, and we must not risk our new reputation. It is easier to drift with the stream than to stem it. 6. *Justice, with her balances and sword, is always nigh.* No man can defraud God. If the Amorites were thrust out from the land because they had become flagrant idolaters, so also shall the Israelites if they become votaries of idols. As the Hebrews conquered the Canaanites, so did the Assyrians vanquish the Hebrews. One law shall prevail for all. If we have not been overwhelmed in one disaster, we may be overtaken suddenly by another minister of justice. Sin shall bear its own proper fruit. Every nation and every individual shall " go to his own place." From the summit of earthly magnificence to the lowest pit of misery, there is often a single step. " I saw," says Bunyan, " that there was a way to hell, even from the gate of the celestial city." " Be not highminded, but fear." Riches make a slippery descent to ruin.—D.

Vers. 2—6.—*The uses of adversity.* It is a great matter when in any experience of life we can read the Divine purpose in bringing us through it. The speaker in these verses unfolds the design and lessons of the wilderness discipline. Our Lord, in the temptation, found an application to himself (Matt. iv. 4). Every believer will find the same in seasons of adversity.

I. ADVERSITY A DIVINE ORDINANCE. (Ver. 2.) 1. *Divinely sent.* " The Lord thy God led thee" (cf. Matt. iv. 1). Jesus led of the Spirit into the wilderness. Adversity may come through natural laws, as the necessary result of sin or folly; even so it is of God's ordinance—the punitive expression of his will. But adversity is not necessarily punitive. The best man living may be led into straits of affliction, of which his own actions are not in the least the causes (Job i., ii.). It is God who has " led " him thither for some purpose of his own. 2. *The duration of which is divinely determined* : " these forty years." God marks for us the term of our probations. Jesus was " forty days " without bread (Matt. iv. 2).

II. THE GRACIOUS USES OF ADVERSITY. That of the Israelites was designed: 1. *To humble them.* It aimed at destroying the spirit of self-dependence, out of which comes pride and haughtiness (vers. 17, 18). It made them feel how absolutely they depended for everything upon God—taught them how at every step they hung upon his will. 2. *To teach them reliance.* Faith is reliance on a Divine Power working for us and in us. " What shall we eat? What shall we drink? Wherewithal shall we be clothed?" Faith cannot tell, but it waits God's time and God's way of providing, confident that in his own way he *will* provide. This was Christ's attitude in the wilderness (Matt. iv. 4). 3. *To test obedience.* Adversity acts as a test of the disposition. The end of God's discipline is to bring to light hidden lines of character, and to advance life to a crisis. It forces us to moral determination. Will we obey God or will we not? The younger generation of Israel, whatever their faults, showed by their conduct then and thereafter (Josh. xxiv. 31) that the discipline of the wilderness had not been without good results.

III. GOD IS WITH US IN ADVERSITY. Though bread failed, God fed them with manna (ver. 3). Their every want was supplied. Jesus teaches us to trust the Father for the supply of all our needs (Matt. iii. 25, 34). His own trust, vindicated in the refusal to make stones into bread, was rewarded by angels ministering unto him (Matt. iv. 11). He " ate angels' food " (Ps. lxxviii. 25). *Our* wants are not supplied by miracle, but by providence, which is all-sufficient to provide for us in every ordinary case.—J. O.

Ver. 3.—*Not bread, but God's Word.* The lesson of the manna gathered up into one concise sentence. It teaches us—

I. TO SEE GOD IN SECONDARY CAUSES. The Word of God is as truly the creative and nourishing principle in ordinary bread as it was in the *extraordinary* supply of manna. It is not bread, as something subsisting independently, but bread as the product of Divine power, and as possessing properties which the Word of God imparts to it and upholds in it, which is the staff of life and the object of our prayers (Matt. vi. 11).

II. TO BELIEVE IN GOD ACTING ABOVE NATURE AS WELL AS IN IT. If God wills life to be sustained, he can sustain it in other ways than by bread. He is not tied up to one set of means. He can act, if it pleases him, independently of means altogether, the creative word being sufficient to sustain. This is the direct meaning of the text, and a part of the significance of Christ's answer to the tempter (Matt. iv. 4).

III. TO RECOGNIZE IN MAN THE EXISTENCE OF A HIGHER LIFE THAN THE PHYSICAL.

The physical is not the highest in us. We do not live by bread alone. A higher life is found in depending on God's Word, in obeying it, and in abiding by it, whatever the immediate consequences. The lower life may need to be given up that the higher may be saved (Matt. xvi. 25).—J. O.

Ver. 5.—*God the Chastener.* I. CHASTISEMENT IS A NECESSITY OF OUR MORAL NATURE. He is no wise parent who spares the rod when the good of the child requires that chastisement be administered. Gentler methods failing, the undutiful son *ought* to be chastised. He *deserves* it. He *needs* the discipline. It acts wholesomely upon him, awakening conscience, begetting respect for paternal authority, deterring from evil, leading probably to penitence and submission.

II. CHASTISEMENT IS AN ESSENTIAL PART OF GOD'S TREATMENT OF HIS CHILDREN. His chastisements proceed from love (Heb. xii. 6). They are wisely meted out, and are always for our profit (Heb. xii. 10). God can *bear* to punish. He will not allow our faults to slip. He will make us feel when we do wrong, hedging up our way, and laying stripes upon us. God's children have the comfort of knowing that they are thus in a Father's hand, and that in all they suffer they are being chastened by unerring love and wisdom.

III. CHASTISEMENT IS A PART OF GOD'S DISCIPLINE OF US FOR WHICH WE SHOULD BE GRATEFUL. Not murmuring, but submitting to it. Without this chastisement: 1. How forgetful of God would we soon become! 2. How haughty and self-willed! 3. How dilatory in duty!—J. O.

Vers. 7—10.—*The good land.* I. A LAND OF GREAT NATURAL ADVANTAGES—*a wealthy possession.* Wood, water, metals, a fertile soil, good pasturage, honey in the clefts of the rocks, etc. (ch. xi. 11, 12; xxxiii. 13—16, 19, 25). Dr. Dykes remarks on it as uniting, as no other does, the two indispensable conditions of central position and yet of isolation, and points out that few regions offer so few temptations to corrupt the simplicity of their inhabitants, or better facilities for the defence of their liberties ('Abraham,' ch. iii.). A yet richer inheritance awaits the Christian, who is brought through the fire and water of tribulation to "a wealthy place" (Ps. lxvi. 12; 2. Cor. iv. 17, 18; Heb. xi. 16; 1 Pet. i. 4).

II. A LAND OF GREAT OUTWARD PLEASANTNESS—*a beautiful possession.* The speaker dwells in captivating detail on the features of its beauty—its hills and valleys, gushing with springs and cleft with innumerable water-courses; picturesque in its scenery, richly cultivated, diversified in its natural productions; blending with its agricultural and pastoral beauties the graces of the vine-clad slope, of the olive garden, of orchards of luscious fruits. A type of the fairer land beyond—the Canaan of the skies.

III. A LAND OF EXHAUSTLESS PLENTY—*a satisfying possession.* "Eat bread without scarceness," etc. (ver. 9). God was not ashamed to be called their God, having provided for them so rich a possession. Yet how poor were its satisfactions as compared with those which await believers (Rev. xxi. 4)!

The land was given them in fulfilment of promise; for the possession of it God had been preparing them in the wilderness; and the sharpness of the desert experience made the rest and delights of it sweeter when they came. "Trials make the promise sweet," etc.—J. O.

Vers. 10—19.—*The dangers of wealth.* I. WEALTH IS DANGEROUS WITHOUT THE PREVIOUS TRAINING OF ADVERSITY. Those who, cradled in the lap of luxury, have never known struggle and difficulty are rarely persons of meek, humble, chastened dispositions. As rarely are those whose schemes have been so uniformly prosperous as to give colour to the thought, "My power and the might of mine hand hath gotten me this wealth." The former class lack moral fibre, are seldom competent to grapple with the problems of earnest life, shrink from action, and consequently fall an easy prey to the temptations of their wealth. The others are bold, daring, self-sufficient, and superior to religious considerations. They waive God aside from their plans and schemes—"I do not need that hypothesis"—and refuse to worship, honour, pray to, or serve him. Adversity, to a certain extent, tends to correct these faults. It teaches humility and dependence, proves the heart, and forms it to habits which enable it to use wealth rightly.

II. WEALTH IS DANGEROUS, EVEN WITH THE TRAINING OF ADVERSITY, UNLESS THE LESSONS OF ADVERSITY HAVE BEEN IMPROVED. Adversity, unhappily, does not always produce in men's hearts the salutary effects which philosophy assigns to it. It may harden instead of softening and subduing. Multitudes pass through it and are none the better. They are unyielding, unsubmissive, impenitent. They grow bitter in spirit, and accuse the God of heaven. In such a case the return of prosperity, or the gift of it, is no blessing. The heart gets haughtier than ever, and God is defied (Obad. 3, 4). It is a serious question for a *nation* to put to itself, after passing through a period of adversity, Is it morally the better for its sufferings? For, if not, the revival of prosperity will mean but the revival of the old follies, extravagances, and inflations—the very things which formerly led God to turn his frown upon it.

III. THERE IS A DANGER, WHEN WEALTH COMES, OF THE LESSONS LEARNED IN ADVERSITY BEING AGAIN FORGOTTEN. This is the peculiar danger apprehended in the text. Wealth has so subtle and ensnaring an influence, it draws the affections so stealthily away from God, that no temptation is to be compared with it in point of insidiousness. A threefold danger: 1, Undue elation of heart. 2. Forgetfulness of God. 3. A spirit of self-sufficiency and self-glorification. The preventive lies in the cultivation of a thankful spirit (ver. 10), and in the recollection that the power to get wealth is not of ourselves, but from God (ver. 18). This is the root-error in the matter—stopping at second causes, putting nature and nature's laws, or our own wisdom, energy, and forethought, in place of him without whom we could not think a thought, move a muscle, or carry through to completion one of our purposes. Best preventive of all is the laying up of treasure in heaven; for, "where your treasure is, there will your heart be also" (Matt. vi. 19—22).—J. O.

Ver. 10.—*The blessing of a thankful spirit.* I. A THANKFUL SPIRIT CONSERVES THE BLESSINGS OF THE PAST. It goes back on God's dealings with it. It keeps alive the memory of his goodness. It delights in counting over the blessings it has received (Ps. xl. 5). In it the fountain of gratitude can never get frozen up, for the springs are daily flowing from a warm heart (Ps. ciii. 1—4).

II. A THANKFUL SPIRIT ENABLES US TO USE ARIGHT THE BLESSINGS OF THE PRESENT. It guards against sinful elation, against proud self-sufficiency. It keeps us from forgetting whence our blessings flow. By a sense of God's goodness daily renewing itself, it makes the heart kind and sympathetic, sensitive to the wants and woes of others. The spirit is softened and sweetened. Under adversity, it conduces to resignation and cheerfulness.

III. A THANKFUL SPIRIT HELPS US TO PRAY FOR BLESSINGS IN THE FUTURE. Hence the rule that prayer is to be accompanied with thanksgivings (Eph. v. 20; Col. iii. 15; Phil. iv. 6). Thanksgiving strengthens faith, gives encouragement, enables us to pray with due submission to God's will, prepares us for the reception of the blessings that we seek. Without thankfulness for past mercies, it is impossible to pray aright for future ones.—J. O.

Ver. 16.—*Good at the latter end.* I. GOD'S DISCIPLINE OF US IS NOT WITHOUT ITS END. No man even, whose action has any meaning in it, but has an end in what he does. It may be alleged that God's action has regard to men only in the mass; that in that view of it his action has an end; but that a special purpose is not traceable in his dealings with individuals. The truer philosophy sees purpose everywhere. The individual soul is of interest to God. He deems it worthy of being an end in itself. Though subordinately to the general good, he shapes his providence with a view to its individual well-being (Matt. x. 29—31). For—

II. GOD'S DISCIPLINE OF US IS MEANT TO TURN TO OUR ULTIMATE ADVANTAGE. "To do thee *good* at thy latter end." The *immediate* object of God's discipline is to form character; to create and develop love, trust, and obedience; to uproot evil dispositions; to break down self-will and self-dependence. The *ultimate* end of it is the service and blessedness of heaven. There may be some service which God is preparing us for on earth, some possession he wishes to give us, some trust he is about to repose in us.

But heaven is the goal of all (2 Cor. iv. 17; 1 Pet. i. 7; Rev. iii. 10—13; vii. 13—17).

III. THE END OF GOD'S DISCIPLINE OF US WILL NOT BE FULLY SEEN TILL THE GOAL IS REACHED. Till then our duty is to do present work, and improve by present training.—J. O.

Vers. 1—6.—*The lessons of the wilderness.* Moses here recalls the leadings of God in the wilderness, for the warning and instruction of the Israelites. And we are taught, surely, such lessons as these—

I. THE WAY OF SALVATION IS ONE ALSO OF HUMILIATION. This is, indeed, God's plan, "to hide pride from us." The way of salvation through Christ is *humiliating.* We are proved by it and made to see what is in our heart.

II. AT THE SAME TIME, IT IS A WAY OF MARVELLOUS MERCY. For God supplies our wants and sustains us in a truly marvellous way, like the Israelites in the wilderness. Thus—

1. *The manna was to teach them dependence on his word.* It was given when they were hungry and despairing; it was given daily; its only guarantee of continuance was God's promise;—all was, therefore, to keep them depending upon his sure word.

And life's discipline brings us to the same persuasion that man must live upon the promise proceeding out of the mouth of God (cf. Matt. iv. 4). Our Saviour vanquished Satan's insinuation that he must use his miraculous power or perish, by resolving to continue trusting in God.

2. *The raiment did not wax old, to strengthen still further their trust.* It was a wonderful arrangement which allowed them forty years' wear in the wilderness out of the same garments. It must have been good clothing from Egyptian looms. But after starting there it remained, resisting the tooth of time. Each Israelite had evidence on his person of a particular providence.

3. *Neither did the pilgrims become footsore.* Their feet did not swell. They were made equal to their journey. The wilderness was not *too* rough for them. Their freedom from bodily inconvenience must have been a great source of satisfaction and comfort to them.

In a similar way does God supply all our need and fit us for our pilgrimage.

III. GOD'S CHASTISEMENTS ARE PATERNAL. So was it with Israel in the wilderness. They suffered at the hands of God, but it was what wayward children might expect from a faithful parent.

So is it with ourselves (cf. Ps. ciii. 13; Heb. xii. 1—14). Pain becomes blessed when we know that love sent it for a gracious purpose. We are all in the hands of a Father in heaven. He deals with us according to his infinite wisdom and love. Let us make more of the lessons of this wilderness journey than ever, and go on in the strength of God towards the everlasting home, profiting by his chastisements on the way.—R. M. E.

Vers. 7—20.—*God forgotten amid second causes.* The support of the wilderness was manifestly miraculous. They could not doubt their dependence there upon God. They might murmur even amid daily miracle, but they could not doubt it. It would be different in Canaan, and it is in view of this Moses warns them. There they would get sustenance in ordinary ways; and they might say that their own power, and not God's blessing, made them wealthy.

I. THERE IS A VERY GREAT TENDENCY TO FORGET GOD AMID THE ORDER OF NATURE. It is supposed God has nothing to do, because we get our supplies through steady "second causes." But God claims recognition when he blesses us through ordinary channels as well as when he blesses us through extraordinary. The natural order is either due to God or arranged itself. We have not credulity sufficient for the latter hypothesis, and must accept the former.

II. WHEN GOD ASKS US TO BE FELLOW-WORKERS WITH HIM, IT IS NOT TO BE ENGROSSED WITH OUR WORK AND TO IGNORE HIS. In the wilderness God fed them out of his own hand, so to speak. But in Canaan he directed them to work for their daily bread. They were raised from being "spoon-fed" to be "fellow-workers." The temptation in Canaan was to think that their own hand and power had produced the wealth.

It is the same still. From being fellow-workers with God, men, by mere forgetfulness, pass into the delusion of being sole workers. Life is workable, they think, without God. Atheism is the principle underlying such a life.

III. This unholy independence of spirit is the sure prelude of national decay. It is not national "self-reliance" which serves a state, but national reliance upon God in the use of the means he has appointed. Nations that think they can get on alone are left at length to do so, and God-deserted they perish.

The Canaanites were illustrating this in their own case. They should be a warning to Israel. Living without God in the world, depending on themselves, they were about to be removed violently from their ancestral seats. It was so afterwards with Israel. They were as a nation effaced from the land where they had been placed in probation. The captivity of the ten tribes was terrible, and so was that of Judah and Benjamin.

It is this which nations must still guard against. God will not be ignored. If nations attempt it, they only efface themselves. Dying dynasties and scattered nations proclaim the existence and retribution of God.

IV. How needful, then, to recognize God's hand in all things! The procession of nature—all that is beautiful in second causes, has come from him. The " First Cause " may surely be allowed to work through " second causes " without forfeiting his right to recognition and thanksgiving. Our times are largely atheistic, because our little knowledge of second causes affords such fussy occupation to us, that we have not taste or time to see the First Cause behind all and using all for his glory.—R. M. E.

EXPOSITION.

CHAPTER IX.

Dissuasives from Self-righteousness.

Vers. 1—6.—Israel might acknowledge that it was of God's free gift that they possessed the land of Canaan, and yet might flatter themselves by thinking it was because of their righteousness and goodness that the gift was bestowed. To guard against this, Moses tells them that not because of their righteousness would God go before them and drive out the mighty peoples that then occupied the land, but because of the wickedness of these peoples themselves were they to be extirpated (vers. 1—6). He further reminds them of their transgressions in the past, and how they thereby came under the Divine displeasure, and were saved from destruction only through his earnest intercession (vers. 7—24).

Ver. 1.—This day; at this time, very soon. Nations, etc. (cf. ch. vii. 1). Cities (cf. ch. i. 28).

Ver. 2.—Anakim (cf. ch. i. 28). It was a common saying, Who can stand before the sons of Anak! But even these gigantic foes should be unable to stand before Israel (cf. ch. vii. 24).

Ver. 3.—Understand therefore this day; rather, And thou knowest to-day or now. The expression corresponds to ver. 1, " Thou art to pass . . . and thou knowest." In the victory they had obtained over Sihon and Og, they had already had experience of the Lord's going before them, and leading them

on in triumph. The repetition of the He in this verse is very emphatic. Consuming fire (cf. ch. iv. 24). Quickly, or suddenly. There is no contradiction here of what is said in ch. vii. 22; for there the reference is to the possession of the land by Israel, here it is to the destruction which was to come on the Canaanites—the former was to be by degrees, the latter was to come suddenly and overwhelmingly. As Jehovah hath said unto thee (cf. Exod. xxiii. 23, 27, etc.; ch. ii. 24, etc.).

Vers. 4, 5.—Speak not thou in thine heart (cf. viii. 17). The distinction between righteousness and uprightness (straightness) of heart, is that the former (צֶדֶק) has reference to rectitude of conduct, the latter (יֹשֶׁר) to rectitude of motive and purpose. " By naming justice [righteousness], he excludeth all merit of works, and by righteousness [uprightness] of heart, all inward affections and purposes, which men might plead, notwithstanding that they fail in action. Yet these two are the chief things which God respecteth in men (Ps. xv. 1, 2; 1 Chron. xxix. 17) " (Ainsworth).

Ver. 6.—Stiffnecked, hard of neck; stubborn, obstinate, rebellious.

Vers. 7—25.—Moses reminds them of many instances of their rebelliousness by which they had provoked the Lord, from the time of their escape out of Egypt until their arrival in the plains of Moab. Their rebellion began even before they had wholly escaped from their oppressors, before they had passed through the Red Sea (Exod.

xiv. 11). Even at Horeb, where, amid the most affecting manifestations alike of the Divine majesty and the Divine grace, just after the Lord had spoken to them directly out of the fire, and whilst Moses had gone up to receive the tables of the Law, on which the covenant of God with Israel was based, and whilst that covenant was being struck, they had sinned so grievously as to make to themselves a molten image, which they worshipped with idolatrous rites (Exod. xxxi. 18—xxxii, 6; cf. ch. xxiv. 12, etc.).

Ver. 9.—The clause, **Then I abode . . . water**, is a parenthesis; the sentence runs on from **When I was gone**, etc., to **Then** [not *And*] **the Lord delivered unto me**, etc.

Ver. 10.—**The day of the assembly**; the day when the people, called out by Moses, were gathered together in the plain at the foot of Mount Sinai (Exod. xix. 17).

Vers. 12—14.—(Cf. Exod. xxxii. 7—10.) **Let me alone**; literally, *Desist from me*, i.e. Do not by pleadings and entreaties attempt to prevent me; in Exod. xxxii. 10 the expression used is, "Let me rest; leave me in quiet (הַנִּיחָה לִּי); cease to urge me."

Ver. 17.—Moses cast from him the two tables of stone on which God had inscribed the words of the Law, and broke them in pieces in the view of the people, when he came down from the mount and saw how they had turned aside from the right way, and were become idolaters. This was not the effect of a burst of indignation on his part; it was a solemn declaration that the covenant of God with his people had been nullified and broken by their sinful apostasy.

Vers. 18—20.—Moses interceded with God for the people before he came down from the mount (Exod. xxii. 11, etc.); but this he passes over here, merely referring to it in the words, "as at the first," and makes special mention only of a subsequent intercession, that mentioned in Exod. xxxiv. 28. In the account in Exodus nothing is said of Moses interceding for Aaron specially, as well as for the people generally; but prominence is given to this here, "not only that he might make the people thoroughly aware that at that time Israel could not boast even of the righteousness of its eminent men (cf. Isa. xliii. 27), but also to bring out the fact, which is described still more fully in ch. x. 6, *sqq.*, that Aaron's investiture with the priesthood and the maintenance of this institution was purely a work of Divine grace" (Keil). That Aaron, however, was regarded as especially to be blamed in this matter is clearly intimated in Exod. xxxii. 21, 22.

Vers. 22—24.—Not only at Horeb, but at other places and on other occasions, had Israel provoked the Lord to wrath by their contumacy. **At Taberah**, by their complaining and discontent (Numb. xi. 1—3); **at Massah**, by their murmuring because of the want of water (Exod. xvii. 1, etc.); **at Kibroth-hattaavah**, by despising the manna, and lusting for flesh to eat (Numb. xi. 4, etc.); and at **Kadesh-barnea**, when on the confines of the promised land, they distrusted God, reproached him for having brought them there to be destroyed, and sought to return to Egypt (Numb. xiv. 1, etc.; ch. i. 26). "The list is not arranged chronologically, but advances from the smaller to the more serious forms of guilt. For Moses was seeking to sharpen the consciences of the people, and to impress upon them the fact that they had been rebellious against the Lord (see at ver. 7) from the very beginning, 'from the day that I knew you'" (Keil).

Ver. 25—29.—Having enumerated these instances of the rebelliousness of the people, Moses reverts to the apostasy at Sinai, in order still more to impress on the minds of the people the conviction that not for any righteousness or merit of theirs, but solely of his own grace, was God fulfilling to them his covenant with their fathers.

Ver. 25.—**Thus I fell down before the Lord forty days and forty nights, as I fell down at the first**; rather, *the forty days and forty nights in which I fell down*. The reference is to the intercession before Moses came down from the mount, described in Exod. xxxii. 11—13. (For the form of the expression, cf. ch. i. 46.)

Vers. 26—29.—In these verses the substance of Moses' intercession is given, and it is substantially in agreement with the account in Exodus. Moses pleaded with God not to destroy that people which was his own, which he had redeemed for himself and brought out of Egypt; besought him to remember their pious ancestors, and not to look on the stubbornness and sin of the people; and urged that the Divine honour was concerned in their being conducted to Canaan, and not let perish in the wilderness.

Ver. 28.—**The land**, that is, the people of the land, as in Gen. xli. 36—the Egyptians; the verb, accordingly, is in the plural. Were the Israelites to perish in the wilderness, the Egyptians might say that God had destroyed them, either because he was unable to obtain for them the land he had promised them, or because he had ceased to regard them with favour, and had become their enemy. Neither of these could be, for were they not the people of his inheritance, and had he not showed his power already in delivering them out of Egypt?

"As Moses in this chapter recalls to the remembrance of Israel this and that *place*, *time*, and *occasion* of their sinning, so should each one often seriously reflect on his past life. This conduces to humility, to watchfulness, and to effort at improvement" (Herxheimer).

HOMILETICS.

Vers. 1—3.—(See Homily on ch. iv. 23, 24.)

Vers. 4, 5.—(See Homilies on ch. iii. 11; vii. 1—11.)

Vers. 6—12.—*A six-weeks' religion; or, emotional religiousness not vital godliness.* The homiletic treatment of the incidents referred to in ch. ix. 1—x. 5, will require a careful comparison of these chapters with the fuller account in Exod. xxxii.—xxxiv. The special object, however, which Moses has here in view, is to show how entirely God's mercy to Israel was a self-moved one, and that it was not due to any virtue on the part of the people. So far from that, they had been wayward from the first. Even in Horeb (for such is rather the force of the particle rendered "also" in ver. 8), "Even in Horeb, ye provoked the Lord to wrath." Here is suggested our first study of this sad incident in Israel's history. Its occurrence was on this wise—

About fifty days after leaving Egypt, they were gathered beneath Mount Sinai, to receive the Law from the Great Supreme. They reverently watched when Moses went up; they saw the bounds put, beyond which they must not pass; they trembled at the majesty which was before and above them, and awaited the words which should be spoken. The words of the vow went up from their lips, "All that the Lord hath spoken we will do." Having received the Law, Moses went down and rehearsed it to them. A *second* time they responded, "All that," etc. This was not enough. The Law was to be written, and read over to them, that their vow might be neither blind nor rash. And a *third* time the same response was returned. Whereupon the covenant was ratified with blood, which was sprinkled on the book and all the people, saying, "This is the blood of the covenant," etc. (see Exod. xxiv. 3—8). It seemed as if a fair start had been made. Egypt had been conquered, the people had thankfully accepted the new state of things on which they had entered, and nothing was wanting but the carrying out of that allegiance they had so repeatedly vowed. Moses, however, has yet to be a while in solitude with God, to receive further instructions; hence, having made arrangements for the conduct of affairs in his absence, he again ascends the mount, and is there for forty days. Unable to understand the reasons for so long a delay, the people think that Moses has disappointed them, or that he is lost on the mountain, or has perished in the flame! The thought, once conceived, gathers strength, and the very people who a few weeks before had seemed so impressible for good, are now as inflammable for evil! They rush upon Aaron, saying, "Up," etc. They wish for something to strike the senses. The pure conception of an unseen God they were not cultured enough to retain. Aaron was far too easily wrought upon by them. If it be thought that he expected the people's love of finery to be stronger than their idolatrous propensity, and that they would withdraw *their* demand when he made his for their ear-rings, etc., we save Aaron's principle, but at the expense of his judgment. Anyway, the calf is made. It is not the calf, however, that they worship, for they proclaim a feast *to Jehovah*; it is the second commandment they are breaking, not the first. Alas! alas! their triple vow, ratified with blood, they break, and in less than six weeks they are openly and riotously setting at nought the very Law they had sworn to obey! How can such a fearfully rapid retrogression be accounted for? If we regard it as a mere piece of history, with which we have no concern, we shall miss the intent of the writer (for see 1 Cor. x. 1—12). Here are men who at one moment bid so fair, yet so shortly after upsetting all! The theme thus opened up to the preacher is surely this—"*Emotional religiousness not vital godliness.*" No one with much knowledge of human nature, and certainly few pastors of any lengthened experience, can have failed to observe cases far too nearly resembling that before us, of a merely transient emotion in religion, raising the hopes of anxious observers one day, only to disappoint them ere many days are over, and compelling the plaintive words, "Your goodness is like the morning cloud and the early dew, it goeth away!" And, maybe, the change is as inexplicable to themselves as it is disheartening to others. It may be helpful if we try to remove the perplexity by a study of several inquiries which such cases suggest.

I. How far does this emotional religiousness go? There may be a "receiving the Word with joy;" giving to it, not only a respectful attention, but even mental credence, gladsome admiration, and a profound conviction that the gospel message exactly meets the need of guilty, sinful man. And when the beauty, purity, and triumphant issue of a genuine Christian life are set forth, there may be an eager desire awakened to know its blessedness, and an inward resolution formed to serve the Lord. The young inquirer seems, perhaps, at such a stage to have been wafted, as by a Divine breath, to a region of halcyon calm, and with the sincerity and dash of a Peter says, "Now I am saved; though all men should deny Christ, yet I never will!" And such a case is looked at with tender, glad, yet anxious hopefulness, by some that are watching for souls more than they that watch for the morning. And yet, notwithstanding all, there is a grievous defect, not yet apparent to human eye, but destined ere long to reveal itself to the bitter disappointment of many a thoughtful friend!

II. What is there defective in this case? There is: 1. Defective knowledge of self. 2. Defective knowledge of what the Christian life is, as one of "patient continuance in well-doing." 3. Defective knowledge of the truth as it is in Jesus. 4. A non-apprehension of the Lord Jesus Christ as the sole Source of life, energy, and power. 5. Emotion is mistaken for principle, and feelings about religion for a real surrender of heart and life to God.

III. Severe tests await such a one. (Cf. Matt. xiii, 20, 21; Luke xiv. 27, 28.) Days in which all things run smoothly are not those which test of what stuff men are made. No one's life, however, is made up of smooth days only. There are occasions which put every part of a man on the rack. And there are testing times in store for the young emotionalist. 1. Affliction for the Word's sake will come. 2. Persecution may come. 3. Scepticism, or cross-currents of public sentiment may disturb. 4. Or abounding worldliness may bring a chill or even a blight. Some trial or other will surely come to test each and all. It may come suddenly as a storm of wind on a lake, or may act slowly yet surely as the waters wear away the stones. Somehow or other, come it will; and where there is profession without possession, sad will be the end, for—

IV. Such tests will be fatal. Only forty days after their vow, Israel broke down. The terrors of Sinai could not maintain Israel's loyalty. Nor will even the pathos of Calvary, of itself, avail now. The following results will follow, sooner or later, if beneath the outward vow there has been no surrender of heart and life to God. 1. Emotion will die out. Men cannot live at fever heat; it is not desirable that they should. If beneath the emotion there is living principle, though the emotion lessen, that will strengthen. But if there is no such living principle, the emotion will leave nought behind it but sadder lack of it than ever. 2. External membership will come to be rested in, as if it "covered a multitude of sins." 3. There will be a growing indifference to the higher and more spiritual work of the Christian life—both in private, social, and Church duties. 4. There may even be a collapse into a state of more thorough worldliness than before any profession whatever was made; and "the last state of that man is worse than the first." Of all the members of Christian congregations, those are the hardest to move who made a profession in a swell of emotion, without quickening of conscience or the renewal of the heart!

V. What is needed in such cases? 1. Deep and genuine conviction of sin and repentance before God; a quickening unto righteousness, which is born of the Spirit. 2. Heart-surrender to God; this cannot be brought about through being borne along in a crowd as on a wave of religious ecstasy, any more than the patients in a hospital can be cured en masse. 3. New life towards God, created, sustained, perpetually increased by the supply of the Spirit of Jesus Christ, renewed by faith, and aided by communion with God.

In conclusion. Let all beware of trusting to "frames and feelings." Emotion is not devotion. And on the other hand, let us take care not to fall into the opposite error. "Ah," say some, "see what comes of religious excitement. It is time there was a protest against it!" But we make no protest whatever against excitement, but against *mere* excitement, which is a very different thing. Because a blaze cannot be kept up without fuel, that is no reason why, with plenty of fuel constantly supplied, a fire should not be kept ablaze! It is true that if there is nought but emotion, it must die out and be followed by a collapse; but that is no reason for letting real life be attended with so little emotion, that others see scarcely any signs of the life at all. Ah! what we all want, and always want (and, thank God, what we may always have), is a fulness of life, direct from him, which only *he* can give, and which, through the cross, and by the power of the Spirit, can alone be maintained, perfected, and glorified!

Vers. 13—21, 25—29.—*True greatness manifested in a great emergency, by self-sacrifice and intercession.* As were marked in the previous Homily, these incidents can only be rightly arranged by a preacher, for the purpose of preaching thereon, so far as the entire narrative is before his view. Hence a junction of this paragraph with Exod. xxxii. is imperative, and will here be taken for granted. There would seem to have been a compilation of several documents. It is not easy to gather therefrom, *with exact precision*, the order of events, though there is no difficulty in setting the whole with sufficient consecutiveness for all the purposes of practical teaching. Note—

I. HERE IS A GREAT CRISIS. Israel was making a feast unto Jehovah, letting the calf represent to them the God who had brought them out of Egypt. The people were observing the customs of the very nation from which they had been redeemed—dancing before the idol, polluting themselves with unclean and unhallowed rites, and making the hills to re-echo with their boisterous revelry and song! And all this beneath that very mount where they had sworn, "All that the Lord hath spoken we will do!" 1. In the first instance, the lamentable defection of the people was made known to Moses, either by a silent suggestion from the Great Invisible, with whom he was in adoring fellowship, or by one of the angel bands with whom he was surrounded (Exod. xxxii. 7, 8). 2. God bids Moses "go down"—not merely, as might at first seem, "go down and see," but "Continue the fellowship no more; leave me alone; I will make of thee a great nation. Let my wrath wax hot against them, that I may consume them!" Awful words (vers. 13, 14)! 'Tis a terrible crisis in the great leader's experience. With agonizing heart, he comes down to see—not without pleading with God for Israel (see below)—and he reaches Joshua, where, though even yet too far off to see, he is near enough to hear the shouts wildly ringing through the air. 3. At length Moses gets near enough to see (ver. 16). *There they are!*—the calf, the dancing, the impure orgies as of a heathen feast! Oh, how bitter must have been the anguish of Moses at such a sight! 4. And what an alarming possibility he had to face—even that of the entire rupture of the whole covenant between the people and Jehovah! Hear how the Voice on the mount spake, "Thy people have broken the covenant; let me alone," etc. In what stronger way, ah! in what other way, could the people at such a time have been taught that, as they were now actually breaking the very covenant God was confirming with Moses for them, if God now dealt with them after their sins, he would have cast them off completely? *They* were not necessary to the fulfilment of the covenant made with their fathers. Moses was of Abraham's seed, and God might have begun afresh with him, and have made of him a nation greater, mightier, more loyal than they! Was there ever such a crisis? With all the responsibility Moses had resting on him, he must have been crushed had he not been divinely sustained. But great crises bring out the greatness of great men. Moses was a man "slow of speech," and probably slow to act, but he had strong convictions of truth and duty, and when wrought up to a white heat, he would show the true nobility of his character.

II. THE GREATNESS OF THE CRISIS OCCASIONS A REMARKABLE SERIES OF ACTS ON THE PART OF MOSES. 1. He is angry (Exod. xxxii. 19). This was a holy anger; the sight roused the meekest of men, and well it might. It would have been wicked in Moses if he had not been angry! There is a wide difference between a passionate feeling of personal resentment, and indignation at witnessing an outrage on right. The

holier a man is, the more will he suppress the one, the more will he develop the other!
2. He breaks the tables (ver. 18). This is a symbolic act, reminding the people that
by their apostacy they had violated their covenant vows. 3. He grinds the calf to
powder, etc. (ver. 21). Another symbolic act, meaning, "This sin will come back to
them again; it will mar their joy for long to come." 4. He calls Aaron to account
(Exod. xxxii. 21—24). "There came out this calf." Aaron! you, the eloquent man,
making a silly speech like that! Oh, the wonderful touches of nature in the Old
Book! Moses, the truly brave man, though slow of speech, can speak to purpose at
such a time as this; but Aaron, eloquent as he is, when his conscience is ill at ease,
makes the lamest and tamest excuse. 5. He ascertains how far the contagion has
spread (Exod. xxxii. 25—29). Was it a revolt of all the people, or had many been
drawn away at suggestion of the few? "Who is on the Lord's side?" 'Tis not enough
for people *to be* on the Lord's side, specially in days of abounding iniquity; they must
say on which side they are. The sons of Levi come forward, and are entrusted with
the awful task of stamping out the evil. Better for 3000 to die than for 2,000,000 to
be infected with a mortal poison! That was a holy defensive war. And it speaks
volumes for the grandeur of the moral power of Moses, that he could so inspire the men
of his own tribe to chastise the revolt and save the people. 6. But the most striking
feature of the spiritual heroism of Israel's leader is, that he pleads with God. In
this he reveals a force of character and an unselfishness of spirit which are far too rare
even in these "advanced" times. Let us watch this pleader. (1) He acknowledges
the greatness of the sin. At first, before he was near enough to see, he asks, "Lord, why
doth thy wrath?" etc. But afterwards, he puts no such question. "Oh! this people
have sinned a great sin." He cannot palliate it. (2) He entreats the Lord not to consume them, but to turn from his fierce wrath, and to bring them yet into the promised
land. (3) He uses arguments in prayer. (*a*) The honour of God's Name among the
nations. Joshua, David, Jeremiah, did the same. (*b*) He pleads the Divine acts
already put forth on behalf of the people, as if he would say, "Didst thou not know
from the first what they were?" (*c*) He pleads the Divine promises; "remember
Abraham," etc. (4) Moses prays for Aaron (ver. 20)! Aaron "can speak well," but he
acted ill. He broke down when put in charge. Though appointed by God as special
helper to Moses, he proved himself unreliable. Yet not a word of complaint appears to
have been uttered to him, only a prayer offered *for* him by the very brother who had
relied on him in vain! (5) There is a more wonderful feature still in his prayer, viz.
this: a conception which to self-seekers would have been most captivating, has for
him no charm whatever—"I will make of thee a great nation;" "let me alone, that I
may destroy them," and I will begin afresh with you, and make you the head of a
less unworthy race! Would not that have fired his ambition, if he had had any?
But no! see the lot which he preferred (Exod. xxxii. 32, 33): "No! I cannot accept
any position, however elevated, if they perish! Oh, forgive them! If not, *let us all
perish together.*" Noble captain he! if the ship sinks, he will go down with it. He would
rather not live if vessel and passengers are beneath the waves! (Cf. Rom. ix. 2, 3, with
which passionate fervour the prayer of Moses may well be compared.) (6) This intercession was long continued (ver. 25): "forty days and forty nights!" All this while
the cry was ever and anon going up from his heart,"Forgive them! forgive! forgive!"
    Have we not here, in Moses, a model of intercessory prayer? Men who can thus
plead with God are the greatest heroes of the Church. We can imagine that some may
object, and may seek to turn the edge of the truth, so that it makes no impression, by
saying, "Ah! but see what a great occasion that was! give us an occasion like that,
and maybe we should pray like that! It is folly to bring the acts of a man at a
period of such intense excitement, and tell us that we ought to pray like that. We
are told that we cannot live at boiling point; then, why adduce Moses, on such an
occasion, as a sample of what we should do on ordinary occasions?" No, we do not
always want boiling water, but what sort of water would that be which no amount of
heat ever could get to boil? We do not and cannot expect to be always in the midst
of violent crises. But who are the men who are to be relied on when the crises come?
Where was Aaron now? What of him? There is no indication that he ever caught
a glimpse of the tremendous crisis he had helped to bring about! "*There came out
this calf!*" How Moses could restrain himself at such words, we cannot imagine.

But even if Aaron had not shown such utter inability to perceive the seriousness of the moment, how could he now take any active part in vindicating the injured rights of God before the people, or in craving mercy for the people from God? Complicity with evil means paralysis of power in speeding the right. If Aaron had not had a brother to plead for him with God, he would have been swept away with the besom of destruction! He can talk well rather than stand firm. There is a similar contrast here between Moses and Aaron, to that between Abraham and Lot. Abraham pleaded for the doomed city. Lot's aims in life had been too selfish for him to be a pleader. And we fear there are some who, if their own dear land were brought to a mighty crisis, would just read the daily papers to gratify curiosity, or to give them something to talk about, but as for taking the case of a nation on their hearts before God, they could do nothing of the kind! If they are succumbing to the evils of the day, they can have no strength in intercessory prayer, nor can they be of any use in national struggles. The Moses of Exod. xxxii. is the same self-forgetful Moses of Exod. ii. If men want to be the heroes of their age, let them try the power of intercessory prayer. Such heroism is of a kind the world cannot appreciate, but is recorded in God's book of remembrance; "And they shall be mine, saith the Lord of hosts, in that day when I make up my jewels."

Vers. 22, 23.—Taberah (see Homily on Numb. xi.). Massah (see Homily on Exod. xvii.). Kibroth-hattaavah (see Homily on Numb. xi.). Kadesh-barnea (see Homily on ch. i. 19—40).

HOMILIES BY VARIOUS AUTHORS.

Vers. 4—7.—*Self-righteousness.* Strange capacity of human nature for self-delusion! It was an extraordinary error to fall into, when the Jew began to fancy that by his own power and might he had conquered Palestine (ch. viii. 17). Yet more extraordinary was the delusion that he had been brought into the land on account of righteousness. The two errors sprang from the same root. The worldly mind, which spurns at the acknowledgment of God's bestowal of what it has, has its counterpart in the self-righteous mind, which attributes God's dealings with it to its superior sanctity. Self-exaltation, pride, in both. In the one case, "*my* power," etc., in the other, "*my* righteousness." I. THE NATURE OF THE ERROR. A magnified opinion of one's righteousness. The idea that it is *our* righteousness which is the meritorious ground of the bestowal of blessing. The Jews might not suppose that they were absolutely righteous—though some of the later Pharisees seem almost to have got this length (Luke xviii. 11). But they thought that they were *so* far righteous as to have established a claim on God's justice for what they had. This is a state of mind into which men glide half unconsciously. We often say it "in our hearts," when we would be ashamed to avow it with our lips. The self-complacency, *e.g.* which accepts prosperity as the reward of superior virtue; the self-satisfaction which esteems such reward due to it; the complaint of injustice which is raised when blessings are removed,—betray its presence. In the spiritual sphere, the tendency is evidenced in the denial of the need of salvation; in the self-justifying spirit which refuses to accept the position of one condemned, and justly exposed to wrath; in the reassertion in subtler or coarser forms of the principle of salvation by works. In whatever degree a man thinks himself *entitled* to acceptance with God, and to spiritual blessings, whether on the ground of obedience to prescribed rules, or on the ground of internal characteristics (faith, holiness, etc.), he is permitting himself to fall into this error. II. THE SOURCE OF THE ERROR. The Israelites might fall into it: 1. *By emphasizing their acts of obedience and forgetting their rebellions.* This, as Moses shows, is practically what they did. It is not an uncommon fault. We forget our sins, and, thinking only of obediences, slide by easy stages into a self-satisfied and pleased view of ourselves. 2. *By comparing themselves with the former generation.* They had not been, as their fathers were, absolutely disobedient and recalcitrant. They were going up to possess the land. This comparing of ourselves with others is not wise. If a little in advance of our neighbours, it is extremely apt to inflate our consciousness of integrity (2 Cor. x. 12). 3. *By arguing from the fulfilment of promise.* God had promised victory and possession on condition of obedience. Having got the blessings, they might argue that, in God's judgment, they must have been obedient. We, in like manner, may argue from God's kindness to us that we must have been peculiarly, pleasing to him. Hence that we are *deserving* of what we have received. The spring of all is the natural egoism of the heart. It is its own centre. It wishes to exalt and glorify itself. It has no idea of glorying only in God. It is self-exalting, not God-exalting (1 Cor. i. 29—31; Gal. vi. 14; Phil. iii. 7—10).

III. THE REFUTATION OF THE ERROR. Even perfect righteousness would not justify self-righteousness. The very indulgence of the self-glorying spirit refutes the contention of righteousness. Whoever is the righteous man, it is not he who boasts of righteousness!

> "For merit lives from man to man,
> And not from man, O Lord, to thee."

But: 1. *We are not righteous.* The only justifying righteousness is a perfect one, and that no man can plead. The legal ground is destroyed when we admit failure in even one point (Jas. ii. 10). 2. *We are, in many ways, disobedient and rebellious.* Past acts testify against us. Our daily life testifies against us. He knows little of self who does not read, in his disinclinations to duty, in his reluctant performances, in his rebellions at difficulties, in his secret impatience, in his frequent inclining to things forbidden, the signs of a wayward and rebellious disposition.

The true ground on which blessing is bestowed is wrapped up in that old oath sworn to the fathers (ver. 5), in the seed of Christ, in whom only we have acceptance.—J. O.

Vers. 8—22.—*The sin at Horeb.* Moses dwells on this sin, alike as memorable in itself, and as illustrating the proposition that the people had again and again forfeited their covenant standing by their acts of disobedience.

I. THE ENORMITY OF THIS SIN. 1. It was a sin *committed immediately after solemn covenant with God* (ver. 9). The transactions recorded in Exod. xxiv. 3—9 were not yet forty days old. The people had literally heard God speaking to them. They had acknowledged the solemnity of the situation by entreating Moses to act as mediator. They had formally, and under awful impressions of God's majesty, pledged themselves to life-long obedience. Yet within that brief space of time they broke through all restraints, and violated the main stipulation of their agreement, by setting up and worshipping the golden calf. A transgression showing greater levity, temerity, deadness to spiritual feeling, and perversity of disposition, it would be difficult to conceive. Perhaps the case is not a solitary one. Can none remember instances of solemn vows, of sacred engagements, of deep impressions, almost as soon forgotten, almost as recklesly followed up by acts of flagrant transgression? 2. It was a sin *committed while Moses was in the mount, transacting for them* (vers. 9—12). Moses, for an obvious reason, rehearses the circumstances of his stay in the mount, and of his interview with God. He had gone to receive the tables of the Law. He recalls, as in striking contrast with the levity of the multitudes below, his rapt communion of forty days and nights. Sin needs a background to bring it out in its full enormity. That background is furnished in these details. The people are pointed to the tables as the rule of the obedience they had pledged themselves to render. They are reminded that their sin was perpetrated at a time when God was yet transacting with them, and when their minds ought to have been filled with very different thoughts. Do we reflect on the aggravation given to our own sins by the presence of our Mediator in the heavenly mount, and by the ceaseless and holy work he is there conducting on our behalf? 3. It was a sin of *daring enormity in itself.* The making of the golden calf, after what had happened, can only be characterized as an act of shocking impiety. The worship was doubtless accompanied by profane and lewd revellings. This under the eye of their God and King.

II. THE CONSEQUENCES OF THE SIN. 1. *It involved the forfeiture of covenant privilege,* signified by the breaking of the tables of the Law (ver. 17). This was the first light in which the Israelites had to view it. It refuted their idea that they got the land in virtue of their righteousness. True, the sin had been committed by the preceding generation, but the covenant being national, and laying obligations on all, involved them as well as their parents in the consequences of disobedience. If they stood still in covenant relation, it was of God's mercy which had restored them. For a time that covenant was actually broken. Nor, if that argument was necessary, had they failed in their own persons to renew the deed of apostacy (ver. 22). Every believer feels that his standing before God is likewise of pure grace. Were sins imputed to him to his condemnation, he could not stand a single hour. 2. *It provoked God to hot displeasure* (vers. 19, 20). As all daring and presumptuous sin does. 3. *But for Moses' intercession, it would have involved them in destruction* (vers. 14, 19, 20). This was no mere drama *acted* between God and Moses, but a most real wrath, averted by the real and earnest intercession of a godly man. Had Moses not interceded, the people would have been destroyed. Not that we are to conceive God as swayed by human passions, or as requiring to be soothed down by human entreaty. But sin does awaken his displeasure. There burns in his nature a holy wrath against it, which, when he decrees to consume his adversaries, is not to be laid aside save on such ground as we have here. It is the existence of wrath in God which gives reality to propitiation and meaning to his mercy. Learn: (1) How evil sin is in the sight of God. (2) How fearful in its results to the transgressor. (3) How mighty intercession is in procuring pardon.—J. O.

Vers. 24—29.—*Moses' intercession.* I. IN THE SPIRIT OF IT: 1. How absolutely *disinterested* (ver. 14)! He sets aside, without even taking notice of it, the most glorious offer ever made to mortal man—"I will make of thee a nation," etc. 2. How intensely *earnest* (ver. 18)! Moses feared greatly. He had a most overwhelming sense of the reality of the wrath he sought to avert. But his heart was agonizing to save his nation, and he seemed to clasp the feet of God in the spirit of one who would not, could not leave, till he obtained what he sought. A lesson in prayer. 3. How perseveringly *prolonged* (ver. 25)! He prayed by his silence as well as by his speech. The whole scene is a striking illustration of the intercession of the Saviour.

II. IN THE MATTER OF IT. It is not much, as M. Henry remarks, that he can say for them. He appeals, however, to three principles in the Divine character which really govern the Divine action. 1. To God's *regard for his own work* (ver. 26). The finishing of work he had begun (Phil. i. 6). 2. To God's *regard for his own servants* (ver. 27). The love he bears to the fathers (ch. iv. 31; x. 15). 3. To God's *regard for his own honour* (ver. 28). He cannot bear to think of God's action being misconstrued—of God's honour being compromised. Points in God's heart on which all intercession may lay hold.—J. O.

Vers. 1—6.—*Against self-righteous conceit.* Sanguine expectation of success in war is a potential force of immeasurable value. If the expectation be ill-founded, it is worse than none. It will not stand as substitute for other equipment, but it serves as a final edge upon the well-tempered blade. Like the figure "nought," which increases the sign of value only when added to other figures, so sanguine anticipation of triumph is only forceful when based on solid qualities.

I. OBSERVE THE FORMIDABLE CONTEST. God has never encouraged his servants to underrate difficulties. Jesus Christ did not overcolour the advantages of his service. 1. *The Amorites were superior in stature.* This might, in itself, become an instrument of strength; it might prove a source of weakness. The larger the machinery, the greater motive power is demanded. 2. *The Amorites excelled in martial courage.* "They were mightier." The land had become divided into petty kingdoms, and it is evident that deadly wars between the tribes were frequent. Such practice had developed warlike skill. 3. *They fought behind well-built ramparts.* Their cities were fortresses, while the Hebrews, unskilled in war, had to fight in the open field. Defenders of bastioned homes have great advantage over foreign assailants. 4. *The Amorites possessed a wide reputation.* This would serve to brace to the highest pitch the courage of the inhabitants, while it would serve to dismay the besieging army. Every visible and material advantage was on the side of the Canaanites.

II. LEARN THE SECRET OF ISRAEL'S TRIUMPH. 1. *God's alliance outmatches all martial opposition.* The *unseen* power is always greater than the *seen.* God's arrows find their way through the best-jointed harness. The simple breath of Omnipotence withers all opposition. Whatever we omit to take to the battle-field, let us not omit to take God. 2. *Occult forces often lead the van.* In advance, even of their vanguard, unseen pioneers would sap the foeman's strength. As fire devours the stubble, so would the Canaanites' strength become as rottenness. Hornets, pestilence, lightning, hail—a thousand agencies God employs as the real army in advance of the human host. 3. *God's work and man's reciprocally interlace:* God will never do our part; we can never do God's part. ¦There is scope everywhere for human agency, but it must never invade the Divine province. We are to work because God works *with* us—*in* us. God promised that he "would bring down the enemy;" Israel was "to drive them out."

III. MARK THE GROUNDS OF GOD'S AWARD. He fought on the side of Israel, and against the Canaanites, *for specific reasons.* Some of these are mentioned for the instruction of men. Strong inducements disposed the Hebrews to regard themselves as the favourites of Heaven, on the ground of their superior goodness. This was corrupt fruit from an evil tree. These were false flatteries, forged by Satan. Against these fortresses of self-righteousness Moses was directed to hurl the battering-ram of reproof. 1. *Human righteousness not meritorious.* It is not meritorious, because it is deficient. All true righteousness has some merit; but if the unrighteousness in a man's life exceed the righteousness, then blame must exceed approval. The Canaanites were evicted because of moral rottenness, the fruit of gross idolatry. Loyalty to God alone could entitle the Hebrews to replace them. In *this* they had been signally wanting. 2. *Material possessions have often a vicarious origin.* They are given to one for the sake of another. The faith of Abraham had borne a long succession of fruits. There is a principle of moral solidarity in the human race. We are not distinct units, but component parts—members one of another. 3. *We see the inviolability of God's promise.* To our purblind eyes that promise often seems to fail; yet failure is absolutely impossible. *His* time and *man's* time do not always correspond. God's words must be taken as expressive of God's conceptions. *His* words are expansive enough to contain an infinitude of meaning.—D.

Vers. 7—17.—*Human memory a repository of guilt.* The memory of man is a book of God; and, though the entries may be temporarily obscured, yet the light of eternity will make them all legible. The present tendency of sin is to weaken memory; its effect, to obliterate recollection. Our profoundest gratitude is due to the man that reminds us of our falls.

I. REMEMBER SIN IN THE LIGHT OF ITS OBJECT, VIZ. OF GOD. Discourtesy to a king is a graver offence than discourtesy to an equal. Sacrilege is worse than common theft. 1. *This was sin against a known God.* The evidence of his existence had been made as clear to them as noonday. The main attributes of his character had been plainly revealed, especially power and justice and goodness. They could not wear a mask of pretended ignorance. 2. *He had been to them a most generous God.* For their release signal power had been displayed. The course of nature had apparently been interrupted. To deliver them hosts had been destroyed, and the majestic hand of God had supplied their daily meal. 3. *He had been a much-suffering God.* They had been like petulant, discontented children; and he had been to them a pitiful and indulgent Father. In the midst of needful supply they had been basely unthankful. They had wounded him in the tenderest parts of his nature, insulted his majesty, spurned his laws, and covered him with contempt. Yet he had spared them. He had imposed on himself strong restraints, so that righteous anger should not break forth. The noblest features of human love are but feeble reflections of his patient compassion; and against such a God their sin was hurled. 4. *He had been a God in covenant with them—their God.*

II. REMEMBER SIN IN THE LIGHT OF RIGHTEOUSNESS. We perceive things best when placed in absolute contrast. 1. *There was the sin of inattention.* God had deigned to speak, but they "would not hear." The ear had been fashioned for this special end that they might hear God's voice; they had abused and injured the delicate faculty. They that *will* not hear *shall* not hear. 2. *There was the sin of ingratitude.* We can conceive of no baser sin than this. 'Tis a double crime—a violation of heart and conscience.

3. *There was the sin of disbelief.* The God of truth had promised, but they had treated his word as a lie. They had enjoyed ocular demonstration of his faithfulness, yet they trusted their own fears and fancies rather than their God. 4. *There was the sin of overt rebellion.* They professed to regard God as their Leader and King; yet, as soon as service was irksome to flesh and blood, they resented his authority. Once and again they chose human leaders in opposition to the Supreme King. 5. *There was the sin of self-will.* Their characteristic sin was "stiff-neckedness." "Our wills are our own," said they in substance; "who is Lord over us?"

III. REMEMBER SIN IN THE LIGHT OF SPECIAL PRIVILEGE. 1. *Theirs was sin against the light.* While others had only the light that comes through nature, they had possessed the light of special revelation. They had not appreciated the light. In various measures they had preferred the darkness. 2. *It was sin against the inner light of conscience*—sin against personal convictions of duty. They had trifled with the regal voice of conscience, and bribed it to be silent. They had encouraged appetite and passion to speak, and their clamorous voices had prevailed. 3. *Theirs was sin against faithful warning.* The penalties of contumacy had been prominently set before them. The hints of nature and the dark presages of conscience had been supplemented by the clear announcements of Divine warning. For the fascinating fruit of present pleasure they risked expulsion from the garden—loss of the great inheritance. 4. *It was sin against covenant engagements.* They had made an overt treaty with God to serve him. When the Voice from heaven had spoken at Sinai, they had quaked and said, "All that the Lord our God shall speak unto us will we do." Every step in their deliverance had been taken on the understanding that they would be loyal servants of the heavenly King. Thus every element of wickedness was mingled in their conduct. And is it not in ours also? 5. *It was sin in the very presence of God—sin at Sinai.*

IV. REMEMBER SIN IN THE LIGHT OF EXPERIENCE. 1. *They had seen the direful effects of disobedience in others.* Their eyes had beheld what God did to the Egyptians for their impious arrogance. They had seen their own comrades die for their petulant murmurings. They had seen a host of people slain for idolatry. Poisonous serpents had slain a myriad. The earth had opened and swallowed the sons of Korah. Their own memories contained abundant records that the fruit of transgression was death. Yet they sinned still. 2. *They had seen the rewards of obedience among themselves.* So long as they had followed the precepts of Jehovah they had prospered. They had sprinkled their doorposts with the Paschal blood, and the angel of destruction had spared their firstborn. They had crossed the Red Sea by a perilous path, and had gained a mighty triumph. They had followed Moses into the wilderness, and had been daily fed by a miraculous hand. It was obvious that obedience secured blessing. They had seen Moses exalted to regal power by virtue of his unwavering faith in God. 3. *They had felt the scourge of Divine anger for their own follies.* For eight and thirty years they had sojourned in the wilderness beyond what was needful, because they would not believe God's promise. A thousand ills had afflicted them, every one of which was a chastisement for sin. Yet they dallied and coquetted with the accursed thing, as if it were a pleasant toy. And are we any better than they? If unpardoned, memory is preparing a scourge of scorpions with which to chastise us. "Son, remember!"—D.

Vers. 18—29.—*The place of human mediation.* The best men have always desired to intercede for the bad. True holiness is benevolent.

I. MEDIATION CONCERNS ITSELF WITH THE INTERESTS OF BOTH PARTIES. Moses had at heart the honour of God—the maintenance of his just rule, while he also identified himself with the well-being of the Hebrews. If there be, on the part of the mediator, a leaning to the interests of the one party rather than the other, his office will fail. One party or both will reject him. His mission proceeds on the ground that there is an advantage common to both to be obtained by reconciliation. There is a point where God's interests and man's touch and blend. The business is to find that point, and to persuade both parties there to meet.

II. MEDIATION IS ITSELF A FRUIT OF DIVINE MERCY. The disposition in the heart of Moses to intercede was a disposition implanted by God, and all the energy with which he pursued this mission was energy sustained from heaven. Further, the willingness, on the part of God, to allow any suit on behalf of rebels, was an act of pure mercy. It is no less absurd than profane to speak of man, the mediator, as showing more benevolence than God. The whole arrangement is one of purest kindness, and Moses was richly blest in his generous undertaking.

III. MEDIATION REQUIRES THE MOST COMPLETE SELF-SACRIFICE. For forty days and forty nights Moses was prostrate before the Lord. Personal needs, personal interests, personal honour, were all forgotten. Here was the completest devotion of himself to this cause. There is a profound mystery in this number of *forty*. It is not a natural cycle. Like the number seven, it is sacred to religion. For forty days and nights Moses waited before God, undergoing spiritual receptiveness for the revelation of his will. For forty years the Hebrews dwelt in the wilderness. For forty days Elijah tarried in Horeb. For forty days Jesus endured the temptations of the desert. For forty days he abode with men subsequent to his resurrection. All that human nature could endure, Moses endured to obtain pardon for Israel. For if pardon be too cheaply bought, it is not valued. Only in the lurid light of sin's curse do we see the glory of forgiveness.

IV. MEDIATION ACKNOWLEDGES SIN TO THE FULL. There is no extenuation of the deed, no paring down its dimensions, no cloaking any part of its baseness, no endeavours to put other colours on it than its own. It is because sin is so malignant and so ruinous that it is so desirable to rescue the sinner from its awful spell. It is because it is so dishonouring to God that it is worth while, at any price, to remove it from his universe. The anger of Jehovah is no mere passing or capricious feeling. It is sentiment arising out of the most righteous principle. Such anger against sin is essential to the Godhead. We need not be afraid of the introduction of anthropomorphic conceptions. The longer Moses remained prostrate before God, the clearer came into view Israel's sin in the light of the Divine purity.

V. MEDIATION INCLUDES THE LARGEST REPARATION. The mission of Moses as mediator had a part manward as well as Godward. The whole work was not done upon his knees. With both his hands he brake and burnt the graven image, dishonoured the deity they had fashioned, reduced it to powdered dust. This would expose the impotence of the idol, the vanity of the idol system, and the insane folly of presenting to such a molten image Divine honours. Nor was this all. The fine dust that remained after the burning was cast into the brook, so that they were compelled to drink it in the exigency of their thirst. St. Paul tells us that the rock from which this stream flowed symbolized Christ; hence we see, in a figure, how the living stream from him, the Fount, bears away our sin into oblivion. Repentance upon our part is not thorough, nor sincere, unless we make whatever reparation is within our reach.

VI. MEDIATION EMBRACES VERBAL INTERCESSION. The final outcome of mediation is prayer. "Father, forgive them!" said the dying Saviour. "He ever liveth to intercede." 1. *Moses pleads God's proprietorship in this recreant people.* "They are thine inheritance." "The Lord's portion is his people." From them he shall obtain more satisfaction than from planets and stars and suns. 2. *God's self-consistency is an argument in prayer.* He had already redeemed them from Egyptian bondage. He had taken great pains with them hitherto, and had expended great power on their behalf. And he had not done this in ignorance. The latent evil in their hearts he had perceived. The future of their lives he had foreseen. Hence it would be consistent with his past favours to dispense fresh mercy. 3. *God's covenant and promises are proper arguments in prayer.* He loves to be reminded of his engagements, because this remembrance deepens our sense of his faithfulness. He had engaged to bring this people to the land of promise, not for their sakes, however obedient they might be, but for their fathers' sakes. Hence their rebelliousness did not vitiate the original engagement; and although individuals might justly be destroyed—yea, that whole generation —still the posterity of Abraham must eventually enter the land. 4. *The reputation and credit of God form also staple arguments in prayer for others.* The natural effect produced on men's minds by God's dealings must be taken into account. Our God is not indifferent to the homage and praise of men. It is to him a great delight to receive the incense of heartfelt love. His reputation in his universe is a very precious thing, and it becomes us on all occasions to guard it well. He has formed us into a people for this very purpose, " that we should show forth his praise."

VII. HUMAN MEDIATION, IF EARNEST AND PERSEVERING, SUCCEEDS. " The Lord hearkened unto me at that time also." Here is great encouragement for our intercession now ! Abraham did not cease to gain successes for Sodom until he ceased to pray ; and had he continued, possibly the city might have been spared. What genuine and honest intercession has ever failed ? " The fervent prayer of a righteous man availeth much." Every instance of successful intercession recorded in history is a cordial to revive our drooping faith. Is not God even now waiting to hear human intercession, that he may do great things for his Church ? " Give him no rest, till he make Jerusalem a praise in the earth."—D.

Vers. 1—6.—*The policy of reprobation.* Moses here indicates very clearly what lay at the foundation of the invasion. It is to be carried on successfully as a judgment upon Canaanitish sin. It is no merit in the victors, but the demerit of the vanquished, which determines the Divine dealings. In one word, it is a policy of *reprobation.* And here let us observe—

I. THAT REPROBATION IS THE OPPOSITE OF APPROBATION. Great confusion of thought exists upon this subject through losing sight of this. The conduct of the Canaanites had been going on from bad to worse, and it was impossible for God to approve of it. He had no alternative but to loathe them for their iniquities, and to arrange their fate accordingly. Reprobation in the last resort, in the case of those finally impenitent, is a necessity with God; he cannot but loathe those guilty of such conduct (cf. Robert Hall's ' Help to Zion's Travellers,' p. 45).

II. A VICTORY IS AT ALL EVENTS A JUDGMENT ON THE VANQUISHED. It has indeed been said that the next worst thing to a defeat is a victory, by which it is indicated that both sides suffer, but the vanquished more than the victors. In the invasion of Palestine, the Canaanites were to be vanquished because of their disobedience. It was judgment to them—God's judgment, and thoroughly deserved.

III. IT MATTERS NOT TO GOD, AND SHOULD NOT TO HIS SERVANTS, HOW GREAT HIS ENEMIES MAY BE. The Canaanites were men of gigantic size, with great cities, fenced up to heaven. They were outwardly much more than a match for Israel. And this was doubtless to try the faith of Israel, and to see if they would live by sight in this matter, or trust in their Almighty King. It is for the Lord's people to remember that " greater is he that is for them than all that be against them," and that with God they are sure of ultimate victory.

IV. SUCCESS IS INTENDED TO TEST THE PEOPLE OF THE LORD. Israel is told expressly that they are a stiffnecked people. The conquest is not to be on account of any merit of theirs. But it will test their loyalty to God. It has been observed that conquest has generally exercised a retributive influence upon the conquerors (Goldwin Smith, in *Fortnightly Review* for July, 1877). It was for Israel to determine whether their stiff-neckedness would continue or would succumb. If they interpreted their triumph properly, as the gift of free grace, they would settle down after it to grateful obedience.

V. THE INVASION IS A TYPE OF DIVINE GRACE MANIFESTED STILL. Sinners are like the Israelites, with nothing in the way of merit to recommend them. But God comes in his gospel and offers them a complete victory over sin, Satan, and the world, as a free gift.

These enemies seem gigantic like the Canaanites. We could not overcome them in our own strength ; but greater is he that is for us than all that be against us. We find ourselves coming off more than conquerors through him that loved us.

And every spiritual victory is meant to test and strengthen us. It should increase our gratitude and ensure increased obedience.

It is well, moreover, to remember that the triumphs now are granted as free gifts, not as rewards of merit. After we have as disciples done our very best, we should be ready to acknowledge that we are only unprofitable servants, we have only done what it was our duty to do.

God is able to give us the victory over our greatest enemies, but he will do so in such a way as to secure the heartfelt gratitude and homage of his believing people. He is a faithful Promiser ; having made the promise to Abraham, Isaac, and Jacob, he will not forsake their seed, but give the victory in his own time and way to all who trust him.—R. M. E.

Vers. 7—29.—*Humiliating memories.* Following up the idea of their waywardness, Moses proceeds to recall instances of it. The remembrance of sin is salutary, if it induces humiliation; but detrimental, if it induces a repetition of the sin. When assured of its forgiveness, we should forget it, so far as the remembrance would provoke repetition. Moses here recalls sin, that it may be salutary in the remembrance.

I. THEIR REBELLION HAD BEEN CONTINUAL. (Vers. 7, 24.) It would seem that the pilgrimage of the people had been one long rebellion—God manifesting his mercy, man manifesting his ingratitude. And may this not be said of all the Lord's people? They have been rebellious in the midst of manifold mercy.

II. THE SIN AT HOREB WAS A SPECIAL PROVOCATION. (Vers. 8—12.) So grievous had it been that God threatened them with destruction. It took place while the mediator was, through fasting and prayer, receiving the Law. The circumstances made it more aggravated.

And it is well to remember our special provocations of God, if we are thereby strengthened against a repetition of them.

III. THE DANGER INCURRED BY ISRAEL WAS VERY GREAT. (Vers. 13, 14.) God proposed to consume them in a moment, and to make of Moses a nation greater and mightier than they. It was at once a testimony to the enormity of their sin and a test of the magnanimity of Moses. Instead of accepting the great opportunity, he set himself to intercede for the pardon of their sin.

IV. IT INVOLVED THE BREAKING OFF OF COVENANT RELATIONS. (Vers. 15—17.) The two stone tables were the sign of the covenant existing between God and them. Moses had just been negotiating the settlement. But now one party had proved unfaithful, and so he had them broken before their eyes. Their idolatry had broken the commandments, and so the relations between God and them were meanwhile at an end.

V. THE INTERCESSION WAS PROLONGED AND SUCCESSFUL. (Vers. 18—21, 25—29.) The intercession of Moses was even more severe than the previous mediation. The second period of forty days and nights was a most severe ordeal through which to pass. It shows that intercession is most laborious duty, if adequately discharged. It shows, moreover, that the intercession of Christ, of which that of Moses was typical, is a most serious and severe service. It has been very properly called the prolongation of the atonement; just as the atonement is a most magnificent intercession (cf. Dr. Hugh Martin on 'The Atonement,' pp. 104—168). The two are complementary. The agony of Moses on the mount must have been most severe and trying—death under ordinary conditions is nothing to it.

VI. OTHER REBELLIONS OF A MINOR CHARACTER MUST ALSO BE NOTICED. (Vers. 22, 23.) Taberah, Massah, Kibroth-hattaavah, and Kadesh were all scenes of rebellion against the Lord. The history was a sad one, but the remembrance of it would humble them, and fit them for that complete reliance upon the Lord on which their triumph must rest.

"Humble yourselves under the mighty hand of God, and he will exalt you in due time." "He that humbleth himself shall be exalted." This is the law for nations as well as for individuals. Salvation and victory are through paths of humiliation, which make all the sweeter the blessing when it comes. Sin is thus *sanctified* in the remembrance when it leads to humiliation and victory beyond it.—R. M. E.

EXPOSITION.

CHAPTER X.

RENEWED EXHORTATIONS TO OBEDIENCE.

Vers. 1—11.—*Moses' intercession and its results.*

Ver. 1.—**At that time.** When Moses thus interceded, God commanded him to prepare two new tables of stone, and to construct an ark in which to keep them (cf. Exod. xxxiv. 1, etc.). Directions had been given for the construction of the ark before the apostacy of the people, and it was not made till after the tabernacle had been erected, nor were the tables placed in it till the tabernacle had been consecrated (cf. Exod. xxv. 10, etc.; xl. 20). But as the things themselves were closely connected, Moses mentions them here together, without regard to chronological order.

Vers. 6, 7.—Not only did God, of his grace and in response to the intercession of Moses, give to the people, notwithstanding their apostacy, the ark of the covenant with the new tables of the Law, but he followed this up by instituting the high priesthood; and, when Aaron died, caused it to be continued to his son Eleazar. This Moses reminds the people of by referring to a fact in their past history, viz. their arrival at Mosera, where Aaron died, and Eleazar succeeded him in his office. Beeroth of the children of Jaakan (wells of the sons of Jaakan); the same place as Bene-jaakan (Numb. xxxiii. 31), probably the Horite tribe, called 'Akan (Gen. xxxvi. 27), for which, apparently, should be read Jakan, as in 1 Chron. i. 42. Mosera; Moseroth, plu. of Mosera (Numb. xxxiii. 30). As Aaron died there, Mosera must have been in the vicinity of Mount Hor. Gudgodah, Hor-hagidgad (Numb. xxxiii. 32); cave of Gidgad, a place of caves. Jotbath, Jotbathah (Numb. xxxiii. 33), a district abounding in streams, whence probably its name, Jotbathah, pleasantness, from יָטַב, to be good, to please. None of these places have been identified. Robinson mentions a Wady el Ghadaghidh, a broad sandy valley diverging from the Wady es Jerâfeh, in the desert of Et-Tîh, and this has been supposed to indicate the site of Gudgodah; but the difference of the consonants in the two words is such as to render this identification more than doubtful. In the Arabic of the London Polyglott, גדגדה is represented by جلاجل (Judjuda), which is totally different from Ghadaghidh. All the places, however, must have been in the 'Arâbah, and in the region of Mount Hor, or not far distant. That the places mentioned here are the same as those in Numbers cannot be doubted. The two passages, however, relate to different journeys; that in Numbers to the journeying of the Israelites from the wilderness of Sinai to Kâdesh, that in Deuteronomy to the march in the fortieth year, when they went from Kâdesh to Mount Hor.

Vers. 8, 9.—Moses, here resuming the form of address, refers to the separation of the tribe of Levi to the holy service.

Ver. 8.—At that time; the time when the covenant was restored at Sinai, not the time when Aaron died. The appointment of the tribe of Levi for service took place in connection with that of Aaron and his sons to the priesthood (Numb. iii. 4). The service to which the tribe of Levi was chosen appertained to the tribe as such, including the priests as well as the non-priestly Levites, though parts of it specially belonged to the one class rather than the other. Thus the bearing of the ark was the special duty of non-priestly Levites, the Kohathites (Numb. iv. 4, etc.; 1 Chron. xv. 15); but was also, on peculiarly solemn occasions, discharged by the priests (Josh. iii. 6, etc.; vi. 6; viii. 33; 1 Kings viii. 3, 6, etc.). To stand before the Lord to minister unto him was the special function of the priests (ch. xvii. 12; xxi. 5; Ezra xl. 46; xliv. 15, 16); but as the service of the Levites was also a sacred service, they too are said to stand to minister before the Lord (ch. xviii. 7; 1 Chron. xv. 2; 2 Chron. xxiii. 6; xxix. 4, 5, 11, 12). To bless in his name does not mean, as some propose, to invoke the Name of God, or to praise his Name, but to pronounce a benediction or invoke a blessing on the people in his Name (cf. 2 Sam. vi. 18; 1 Chron. xvi. 2). This was the special duty of the priests (cf. Numb. vi. 22—27; ch. xxi. 5; 1 Chron. xxiii. 13), but might also be done by others (as by David), and in this benediction the Levites might join (2 Chron. xxv. 27).

Ver. 9.—(Cf. Numb. xviii. 20—24.)

Vers. 10, 11.—Moses here sums up the general result of his intercession. As at the first, he was on the mount the second time forty days and forty nights; and in response to his pleading, the Lord willed not to destroy Israel, and commanded him to resume his place as leader of the people, and conduct them to the promised land. "This commandment and promise was a testimony that God now was reconciled unto them by the intercession of Moses" (Ainsworth).

Vers. 12, 13.—God had showed great favour to Israel; what return did he require? Only what, without any prescription, they were bound to render—fear, love, and obedience (comp. Micah vi. 8). To fear the Lord thy God (cf. ch. vi. 2, 13). To walk in all his ways; to receive his truth, accept his law, and follow the course of conduct which he prescribes (cf. Gen. xviii. 19; Ps. xxv. 4, 5; lxvii. 2; Acts xviii. 25, 26). To love him (cf. Exod. xx. 6). "Fear with love! Love without fear relaxes; fear without love enslaves, and leads to despair" (J. Gerhard). There is a fear with which love cannot coexist—a fear which hath torment, and which love casts out as its antagonist (1 John iv. 18); but the fear of God which he requires is that pious reverence which not only can coexist with love to him, but is not where love is not. And to serve the

Lord thy God with all thy heart and with all thy soul. Love prompts to service. Where-ever love fills the heart, it seeks expression in acts of service to its object; and where no such expression comes forth, the evidence is wanting of the existence of the emotion in the bosom (cf. John xiv. 15, 23; Gal. v. 13; 1 John iii. 18). For thy good (cf. ch. v. 29; vi. 24). "In serving the Lord the glory redoundeth unto him, the benefit to ourselves; for them that honour him he will honour (1 Sam. ii. 30), and 'godliness hath the promise of the life that now is, and of that which is to come' (1 Tim. iv. 8)" (Ainsworth).

Vers. 14, 15.—To love and serve the Lord, Israel was specially bound, because of God's love to them and choice of them to be his people. He, the Lord and Proprietor of the universe, was free to choose any of the nations he pleased, and needed not the service of any, but of his free grace he chose Israel, in whose fathers he had delight, to love them (cf. Exod. xix. 5). The heaven and the heaven of heavens; the highest heavens, all that may be called heaven, with all that it contains. Delight ("set his love upon," ch. vii. 7); literally, *cleaved to, was attached to.* "Affection, love, choice, the three momenta prompting from the innermost impulses to the historical act" (Lange).

Ver. 16.—They were, therefore, to lay aside all insensibility of heart and all ob-duracy, to acknowledge God's supremacy, to imitate his beneficence, and to fear and worship him. Circumcise therefore the fore-skin of your heart. As circumcision was the symbol of purification and sign of con-secration to God, so the Israelites are en-joined to realize in fact what that rite symbolized, viz. purity of heart and recep-tivity for the things of God. This is en-forced by the consideration that Jehovah the alone God, the Almighty, is mighty and terrible without respect to persons, and at the same time is a righteous Judge, and the Protector of the helpless and destitute.

Ver. 17.—God of gods (Ps. cxxxvi. 2). Not only supreme over all that are called god, but the complex and sum of all that is Divine; the Great Reality, of which the "gods many" of the nations were at the best but the symbols of particular attributes or qualities. Which regardeth not persons; is not partial, as a judge who has respect to the condition and circumstances of parties rather than to the merits of the case (cf. Lev. xix. 15; Acts x. 34; Eph. vi. 9; Jude 16). Nor taketh reward; doth not accept presents as bribes (cf. ch. xvi. 19; 2 Chron. xix. 7; Job xxxiv. 19; Micah iii. 11).

Vers. 18, 19.—As the impartial and in-corruptible Judge, God executes the judg-ment of the fatherless and widow, vindicates the right of the defenceless (Ps. lxviii. 6; cxlvi. 9); and as the God of the whole earth, he loveth the stranger, helpless, and it may be oppressed, and giveth him food and raiment. Following him, Israel, as his people, were to be benevolent to the stranger, inasmuch as they themselves had been strangers in Egypt, and knew by experience what it was to be a stranger (cf. Exod. xxii. 20; Lev. xix. 33, 34). They were to love the stranger as God loves him, by relieving his necessities (cf. Jas. ii. 15, 16).

Ver. 20.—Reverting to his main theme, Moses anew exhorts Israel to fear Jehovah their God, and to show true reverence to him by serving him, by cleaving to him, and by swearing in his Name (cf. ch. iv. 4; vi. 13; Acts xi. 23). Such reverence was due from Israel to God, because of the great things he had done for them, and those terrible acts by which his mighty power had been displayed on their behalf.

Ver. 21.—He is thy praise, *i.e.* the Object of thy praise; the Being who had given them abundant cause to praise him, and whom they were bound continually to praise (cf. Ps. xxii. 3; cix. 1; Jer. xvii. 14). Terrible things; acts which by their greatness and awful effects inspired fear and dread into those by whom they were witnessed. For thee; literally, *with thee,* i.e. either in thy view or towards thee, for thy behoof (comp. ch. i. 30; 1 Sam. xii. 7; Zech. vii. 9; and such an expression as "deal kindly [lite-rally, *do kindness*] with," Gen. xxiv. 49, etc.).

Ver. 22.—Among other marvellous acts toward Israel, was one done in Israel itself; they, whose fathers went down to Egypt only seventy in number (Gen. xlvi. 26, 27), had, notwithstanding the cruel oppression to which they were subjected there, grown to a nation numberless as the stars (cf. Gen. xxii. 17; ch. i. 10; Neh. ix. 23).

HOMILETICS.

Vers. 1—5, 10, 11.—*The results of the intercessory prayer of Moses.* In these verses we have a very brief statement of the results of the pleading of Moses for Israel with God, which can only be duly appreciated when set side by side with the fuller account in Exod. xxxiii., xxxiv. It is clear, even from the few words here given us, that the Lord's wrath was turned away, that the covenant and the covenant promise were again renewed. But we must at least indicate the points of detail ere we can gather up the sublime teachings of the whole.

I. THE RESULTS OF THE INTERCESSION OF MOSES. 1. *Generally.* "The Lord repented," etc. (Exod. xxxii. 14). The passage in Numb. xxiii. 19 is by no means contrary to this. It means that there is no fickleness nor falseness in the Divine promises, and that the fulfilment of them is not subject to human caprice; which is gloriously true, and in perfect harmony with the before-named words. These do not denote a change in the mind of God, but rather a change in the Divine acts. God's promises are, in an important sense, conditional, and his threatenings too. If we reject the promise and fail to rely upon it, it will not be fulfilled in our case; so, if we repent and turn from sin, the threatenings will cease to apply to us. The virtual withdrawal of promise or threatening is called "repenting," not because God changes his will, but because he varies his action. God may plan and effect a change without ever changing a plan. 2. *In detail.* (1) There were two manifest tokens of the Divine displeasure. (*a*) Exod. xxxiii. 7; the tabernacle of Moses, where he would hear the causes of the people, and maintain the mediatorship, was removed from within the camp to the outside of it. Still, mercy and judgment were blended, for the pillar of cloud did not forsake them. (*b*) Exod. xxxii. 34, 35; this is very obscure; but it at least means that, though they were forgiven, yet they were chastised. In after times, the Jews were wont to say that never any trouble came upon them without an ounce of the dust of the golden calf in it. The intercession of Moses, though it secured inestimable blessings, yet did not avail to remove all reminders of their sin, or to make things as though it had not been. (2) Dire threatenings were removed one by one. (*a*) They should not be consumed, still, only an angel should go with them (Exod. xxxiii. 2, 3). (*b*) The Divine presence *should* go with them (vers. 12—14). (3) Abounding mercy is vouchsafed. The mercy is gradually brought out more and more fully, as Moses pleads more and more persistently. (*a*) Though the tabernacle is out of the camp, yet communication with Jehovah is still maintained (Exod. xxxiii. 9). (*b*) The old promise is renewed (Exod. xxxiii. 12—14). "Rest!" Rest in God. What less, what more, could they desire? (*c*) There was a formal renewal of the covenant (ch. x. 1—5). (*d*) Jehovah grants a new disclosure of his glory. The recent exhibition of the frailty of man might well have crushed Moses if he had not been sustained by a new vision of God. And what a vision! What a declaration! Nowhere else on earth had a Name so glorious then been proclaimed (Exod. xxxiv. 6—9). (*e*) The long-continued communion with God illumed the face of Moses (Exod. xxxiv. 29—35). Was this supernatural or miraculous? Supernatural? Yes. Miraculous? No. We believe intensely in *the religion of the face* (see Acts vi. 15; *vide* a lecture by Joseph Cook, of Boston, on 'The Solar Light'). Moses was full of the Holy Ghost. The lustre without was but the index of the light within. He had gone in unto God to plead for others, and he was rewarded openly, by bringing down from the mount a radiance that told with whom he had been! If our faces were oftener directed towards God in intercessory prayer, they would certainly beam with new light, and men would take knowledge of us that we had been with Jesus. (We have passed very rapidly over these details, as they have been dealt with separately in the Book of the Exodus, for the purpose of devoting somewhat more space to gathering up the lessons taught us thereby.)

II. THE LESSONS TAUGHT BY THIS NARRATIVE. 1. We see here the abounding mercy of God—how slow he is to anger, how ready to forgive. We can imagine, indeed, an objector interposing here, and saying, "Precisely the reverse. The fact of the severity of God's judgments being abated, removed, and even exchanged for mercy, just in response to the intercession of Moses, seems to make Moses appear more merciful than God." Perhaps it seems so at first, but it only seems. And even the seeming ceases when we look all round. For was it not the same God whom Israel had offended, who had given them Moses, who taught him to pray, and who sustained his pleading power? So that the lines of judgment and of mercy have a common meeting-point in the same hand. Besides, we must never forget that the Great Father adapts himself in the methods of his teaching to the capacities of the child in learning. And even the severity of the judicial sentence comes out of mercy. When will men learn the profound truth in Ps. lxii. 12? The greatest mercy which can be shown to a people is to educate them in righteousness. How constantly are men making the mistake of regarding suffering as the grievance rather than sin! as if it were not the sin which is the people's bane, and the suffering consequent on it which is really their guard, that they may learn to dread the sin which brings such sorrow with it. And if the Great Lord, over and above the merciful threatenings which show the evil of sin in his sight, provides Israel with such an intercessor as Moses, and if by virtue of his pleas will withhold the dreaded stroke, and for the uplifted arm of justice will show the directing and sheltering hand,—both the one act and the other are joint illustrations of that glorious Name, the Lord *thy* God! There is no schism in the manifestation of that Name. The terror and the kindness perfectly accord, and it is only our defective sight which makes them appear inharmonious in hue. The very God who guards Law by the holiest sanctions, has provided also in his government for the efficacy of interceding prayer! "He retaineth not his anger for ever, because he delighteth in mercy." 2. This mediatorship of Moses is but one illustration of the working of a permanent law, that God wills to be approached by his saints in prayer on behalf of others. It were well if some were to collate the intercessory prayers in the Bible, and the passages which bear on the theme of pleading for others. The Apostle Paul understood the blessedness of intercessory prayer. He himself rose to a glorious height in this sublime act, and yet he declares his own dependence on and appreciation of the prayers of the saints. Nor do we at all understand *the priesthood of believers*, till we regard this as one of its special privileges, functions, and duties. Let those who "profess and call themselves Christians" see to this. Let them rise to this high and holy service. Let them enter into their closets, fall on their knees, and pour out before God petitions for all. We sometimes ask whether the yearning spirit of intercession is dying out amongst us (Joel ii. 16—18). 3. This Divine law, of the power of intercession, has its supreme illustration in a greater than Moses (Heb. vii. 25), even in him, of whom in so many respects Moses was a type. Human mediation may achieve much, but ah! even the men who plead most with God for others do feel most *their* need of One to plead for them! There, there, at the Father's throne, is One who, having given himself a ransom for many, does present his own work as the ground on which the coming sinner may be forgiven, accepted, and saved. 4. There are three things which no intercession, either of saints on earth or of a Saviour in heaven, can secure. Why? Because in the nature of things they are impossible, and therefore for them no holy one can intercede. (1) No intercession can secure men against either the inward smart or physical consequence of committed sin, even though it may have been repented of and forgiven. There is nothing in the freeness of Divine grace to afford the slightest encouragement to men in playing or parleying with sin. "In the day when I visit, I will visit their sin upon them," is as irrevocable a law as any other. It is quite true that if the worldling, or the drunkard, or the fornicator, repents, he will obtain mercy; quite true that he will be a child of God, and will be trained for the Father's house. But—the enfeebled will, the sapped strength, the deteriorated judgment, the haunted and haunting memory of evil, will abide with him, and will cast their shade over all his remaining days. The bitter taste of committed sin will come up into the soul a thousand times; and though it is true that even *that* will be sanctified, and will prompt new prayers for restraining and renewing grace, yet, oh, how far more peaceful would life be, if such nausea had not been made an enforced part of its experience! While no penitent need despair of mercy, yet, for all that, he may well dread the sins which, even after forgiveness, will "bite like a serpent, and sting like an adder"! (2) No intercession can secure pardon for sin which is not repented of and forsaken. Hence, whoever there may be who is valuing the prayers of others on his own behalf (and few, surely, would be *so* indifferent as to set *no* value on a father's, mother's, brother's, sister's prayers), let us remind such a one that, unless he repents of sin, those petitions will avert no sorrow, no judgment, no ruin. No; not even the atonement of Christ was ever intended to save people *in* sin, but *from* it. "God commandeth all men everywhere to repent." (3) If repentance be delayed, there may come a point beyond which no intercession will avail, because the "day of visitation" is past (see Jer. vii. 16). There is a limit beyond which not even the vine-dresser dares to ask for further postponement of the sentence (Luke xiii. 9 ; see Luke xix. 41—44; Rev. ii. 21). "Now is the accepted time; now is the day of salvation" (cf. Isa. v. 3—6). And if after all the blended judgment and mercy in the way of providence; if after all the teachings, prayers, and intercessions as means of grace; if after all the striving of God's Spirit with men, there is a steady, stout, obstinate resistance to all,—then, such is the view of the holy ones on earth and in heaven, such the view of our Great Intercessor, of the evil of sin and the honour of God, that not from one pleader, however powerful or however tender, can there come even one more request for any further arrest or delay of the judgments of God. In the treatment of every sinner, love, justice, mercy, forbearance, will all have played their part, and if, after all the patience of a God and the entreaties of man, impenitent he still remains, all heaven will acquiesce in the justice of the verdict—his blood shall be upon his own head!

Vers. 12—16.—*Israel's duty summed up and touchingly enforced.* The rehearsal and review of Israel's waywardness, in which the great lawgiver had been reminding the people how much God had had to bear with from them, must have been extremely painful to him, as it was reproachful for them. That part of the review closes with the eleventh verse. And then follows thereon one of the most tender and touching appeals to which the old man could give vent. The two first words of the twelfth verse, "And now," convey a world of meaning. We think we see the lips of Moses quiver, we hear his voice falter, we note the tear standing in his eye, as, with intensely deep pathos and loving solicitude, he shows Israel how past waywardness on their part, and forbearance and forgiveness on God's part, gave them an urgent reason why they should seek henceforth to love, not in word only, but in deed and of a truth. There are two lines of thought suggested by this paragraph.

I. HERE IS THE SUM OF ISRAEL'S LIFE-DUTY NEWLY ENJOINED. This may be set under six heads, which will be but enumerated here. 1. They must cease their rebellious spirit: "be no more stiffnecked." 2. They must fear the Lord their God. 3. With fear they must blend love. 4. To love and fear they must add loyalty of action, by walking in God's ways. 5. They must observe alike the commandments or moral precepts, and the statutes or several appointments. 6. And finally, they must guard against all merely surface work: "Circumcise the foreskin of your heart." Though there were many more rites in Judaism than there are under Christianity, yet a merely ritual service was no more acceptable then than now. This summing up of life's duty should be compared with that in Micah vi. 8.

II. HERE IS A GREAT REASON FOR DISCHARGING THAT DUTY ENFORCED BY TENDER APPEAL. In this appeal, as we venture to call it, there are but few words. But how full of meaning they are! The word "now"—*nunc*, at this time; and as put here it may suggest six queries, each of which contains a most tender reason for future loyalty, which the preacher may well urge with all possible force. We will name the queries one by one. 1. *And now, Israel,* have you not been thus wayward long enough? Is it not time that you reconsidered the position in which you stand with reference to Jehovah? Look! See where you are! Think how long you have been trying God's patience and long-suffering! 2. *And now, Israel,* since God has continued to spare you, since he has forgiven you and not cast you off, since he has consented to bear with you still,—will you not renew your vows, with less, indeed, of self-confidence, but with more of penitential loyalty? 3. *And now, Israel,* think again, "what doth the Lord thy God require of thee?" Is it more than what is reasonable and right? Could he ask less consistently with his righteousness and honour? Are not all his commands wise and right? Is it not an easy yoke to love a God so kind, to fear a God so holy, to obey a God so faithful and true? 4. *And now, Israel,* look at the fact that all God's commands are for your good (ver. 13)! A perfect obedience would ensure perfect content. All the while you have been rebellious against the Lord, you have been fighting against your own highest interests. God's honour and your happiness require precisely the same course of life. 5. *And now, Israel, do* remember this, for consider how great is the Divine condescension in caring for you at all (ver. 14): "Lo! the heaven and the heaven of heavens is the Lord's thy God, the earth also, with all that therein is." And what, what but infinite love should lead him thus to stoop from his high throne to care for you? It is not for your righteousness, for you are a stiffnecked people. No account can be given of why God should care for you so, save that he loves to do it. Then surely the reason is overwhelmingly strong for your gratitude, loyalty, and love. 6. *And now, Israel,* seeing these things are so, could you do less for such a God than he asks of you, even if he did not ask it? So rich should be your joy in him, so reverent your fear, so devout your love, that you would with ready mind *give* God all, even if he did not require all. *What he is to you should lead you to be to him* all that he would have you be. Such seems to us to be a true expansion of the pathetic plea which this passage contains, which the connection in which it stands necessarily suggests. How much stronger every one of the six points may be made from the evangelic standpoint, the Christian preacher will in a moment see. By as much as the love of God in the great redemption in Christ Jesus is a grander disclosure than his love as revealed in the deliverance from Egypt, by so much should each argument be the more tender and strong. When we read, "God commendeth his love toward us, in that, while we were yet sinners, Christ died for us," what *can* the proper response for our hearts be but this, "We love him, because he first loved us"? Such love should constrain us to obey, even if we had no written Law by which obedience was required.

Ver. 17—xi. 1.—*God no respecter of persons.* Having reminded the people of their duty towards God, the aged lawgiver next shows the people what their God is to them, and draws from thence a new argument for obedience and love towards him. In doing this, however, while there is much which we treat of in other Homilies, there is one special sentence, peculiar to this passage, which is yet made so much use of in the teachings of other parts of the Word of God, that we feel called on to note it as the centre point of this paragraph, to show what the truth is which is indicated therein, and the bearing of that truth on the various phases of life and duty. We have in the Word of God no fewer than ten or twelve quotations or uses of this text, each one setting it in some special aspect as a point of doctrine, or drawing therefrom some special inference on a matter of duty. These several allusions, direct or indirect, will suggest the plan of this Homily. The verse thus frequently referred to is the seventeenth. "For the Lord your God . . . regardeth not persons, nor taketh reward."

I. What do such words mean, as a statement of truth? We might not have seen much in them, if the Holy Ghost had not inspired the sacred writers to quote them so frequently in new and varied lights. Being thus quoted, however, we ought to show by reference to the several quotations, the varied phases of their meaning. 1. *God knows no distinctions in his moral government of the nations.* This is suggested by the words in this passage. Moses says, in effect, to Israel, "You have been chosen, out of all the nations, to receive a special revelation, and to be made the bearers of a special mission to the world; but do not think that because of that you are at liberty to trifle with the rules of the Divine Law: God will not tolerate sin in you any more than he will in other nations. Think not that he frowns on iniquity on Canaan and regards it more mildly with you. 'He regardeth not persons.' And only as you are loyal to him, and faithful in doing the right, will he smile upon you." 2. *God makes no distinction in the basis on which men are accepted in his sight.* The Apostle Peter throws quite an unexpected (and we fear to a large extent an unperceived) light on these words in Acts x. 34. He is preaching to Cornelius; he is opening the kingdom of heaven to the Gentile. To induce him to do this, he needed the vision of the great sheet let down from heaven. That gave him a new revelation. God's grace was larger than he had thought for. He had never seen till then the deep meaning of the words in his old legislator's code. He saw them *then,* and they shone with glory— "Of a truth . . . but *in every nation."* As if he had said, "I used to think that because our nation was favoured with more light, therefore it stood on another basis for acceptance and safety. And now I find that the great plan of God's grace so covers the globe, that *in every nation,* he who fears God and follows the light is accepted with him!" Men are saved, not according to the measure of light which they have received, but according to the use they have made of the light which God has given them. 3. *God is exercising over every man a present judgment according to perfect impartiality.* The truth just now referred to made so deep an impression upon the Apostle Peter, that he refers to it again in 1 Pet. i. 17, and would have the thought of the absolute impartiality of God act as a perpetual influence on believers, generating and maintaining a holy fear. There is no favouritism with God. He regards not the person, but the deed; "judging according to every man's *work."* 4. *God revealed*

this attribute of his in the Lord Jesus Christ. For this side-light on the truth,
we are indebted to a scribe, an uninspired man, who, possibly indeed in flattery,
but we rather think otherwise, intimates that this attribute of impartial equity,
which his lawgiver attributed to the Divine Being, was manifest conspicuously
in the Lord Jesus Christ (see Mark xii. 14). However he may have meant it, he
certainly uttered a profound and glorious truth. For who, on earth, ever so clearly
showed himself no respecter of persons, as our Divine Lord and Master? 5. *Precisely the
same feature of God's government will mark the final judgment* (Rom. ii. 11, 16).
There will be one rule of righteousness, which will be inflexibly adhered to then, and
which not even the glorious grace manifested in the gospel will deflect or obscure.
Not from the most hidden souls, nor from the most prominent, will any impeachment
of the Divine righteousness ever rise up. The great system of mediatorial administration may then reveal a plan of larger grace than ever entered into the heart of
man to conceive, but most assuredly there will be no flaw in its equitable impartiality, for " there is no respect of persons with God." That very impartiality will
bring about many startling changes, for " many that are first shall be last, and the last
first."

II. To whom are these words applied in Scripture, as a directory of duty?
1. *They are applied to the querulous.* This absolute righteousness being revealed as an
attribute of God, should teach men to be cautious, who are too ready to pass judgment
on the ways of God when they are past finding out. Such is the use to which Elihu
applies the doctrine. He did not understand Job's case, perhaps, any better than
Eliphaz, Bildad, or Zophar; but in this point he is undoubtedly correct. We *know*
God *is* righteous, therefore we must not impeach what he *does.* 2. *They are applied to
magistrates and judges* (see 2 Chron. xix. 6, 7). The like equity to that which marks
the Supreme Judge should characterize all who have to administer justice in any
nation. 3. *They are applied by Paul as a guide in religious controversy* (Gal. ii. 6).
" God accepteth no man's person, therefore," says Paul, "neither might I. Truth
with me must be supreme, and even if James, Cephas, or John, who seemed to be
pillars, were to utter aught inconsistent with the gospel or grace of God, whosoever
they are, it matters not." The truth, not the person, commands our homage. Well
would it have been if in all ages this had been a guiding principle in the controversies
of the Church. Well would it be, if it were men's guide now. 4. *The words are
applied to individual treatment and judgment of others in the varied relations of private
life* (Col. iii. 25). A man, however lordly, or however lowly, will receive from God a
reward or penalty according to *what he hath done,* and not according to his station in
life. And we, like God, must apply like moral rules all round, and never justify a bad
act because done by a rich man, nor depreciate a good act because done by a poor one.
5. *They are applied to masters with regard to their treatment of servants* (Eph. vi. 9).
We must not forget that the " servants " here referred to were " slaves." Neither Jesus
Christ nor his apostles, any more than Moses had done, made any open attack on
slavery. But by teaching this principle of the equality of men in God's sight, they
dropped a truth which, when it had time to grow, would cause slavery to fall, by
uplifting the people to so high a standard of moral virtue that it would no longer be
tolerated by them. And even now there is need for the continued reiteration of the same
truth, that masters on the one hand may feel their responsibility to God for dealing justly
with their servants, and that servants may feel their responsibility for doing justice
to their masters. 6. *They are applied to Church members, in reference to their treatment
of the poorer members* (see Jas. ii. 1—9). Church life is social life gathered round the
cross. " Life's poor distinctions vanish here." " The rich and the poor meet together,
and the Lord is the Maker of them all." Each one is at liberty to form his own private
circle of friendship, according to taste, culture, etc. But in Church life, work, and
worship, all ranks meet on one common platform, acknowledging " one Lord, one faith,
one baptism," and recounting in song one common salvation. The artificial distinctions
set up by men are nothing in the eye of God. To reproduce them in the Church is an
offence in his sight. If here we have respect of persons, we commit sin, and are convicted of the Law as transgressors. 7. *The principle implied in the words is taught by
the evangelist in its most impressive form in the cross of Christ.* Such, surely, is the
conclusion to be drawn from the weighty words of the Apostle Paul, " Wherefore,

henceforth know we no man after the flesh " (2 Cor. v. 16). " Wherefore; " because Christ died *for all*. " Henceforth; ". from the time that we understand the world-embracing purpose of his death, do we know no man after the flesh. The little distinctions men make so much of here, all vanish in the light of the cross. We ask not whether men are rich or poor; we ask not their name, nationality, or rank. " Christ died for all." That stamps on every man's brow the inscription, " Dear to Christ." Wherefore he will be dear to us for Christ's sake, the wide world over, whatever his caste, country, colour, or clime. If Christ died for all, we preach to all. So that the very principle which under the old covenant is enforced by Law, is under the new created by love. That selfsame impartiality disclosed from Horeb in the methods of Law, is again revealed from Calvary in the methods of God's grace. And thus, through Old and New Testaments the appeal is the same, though made first through thunder, and afterwards through tears. " Be ye imitators of God." Plant your feet firmly on the revealed doctrine of the impartial equity of God. Accepting that, acquiesce with loving submission in the mysteries of his ways, even when they are in the deep waters, and when his footsteps are not known. Then seek in your sphere to follow God in his. Let the judge and magistrate in his decisions, the disputant in his arguments, the private individual in his home sphere, the master in ruling, the servant in obeying, the Church member in his worship and fellowship with his brethren, the evangelist in evangelizing,—all remember that as there is no respect of persons with God, there must be none with them. And let all strive to be like God, who in his Law encircles all men with one bond of duty, while in his gospel he holds them all under one dispensation of grace !

HOMILIES BY VARIOUS AUTHORS.

Vers. 1—12.—*Tokens of mercy*. Various pledges of his forgiveness were given by God to the people.

I. THE RENEWAL OF THE TABLES. (Vers. 1—5.) 1. *Reconciliation to God is only possible through return to obedience*. God cannot but require that we accept his commands, and make them the rule of our life (Matt. v. 19, 20; Rom. vi. 13—23). Such return to obedience is involved in gospel faith (Rom. vii. 4). " Repent ye " (Mark i. 15). 2. *The Law is one and unalterable* (ver. 4). We must change; God cannot. 3. *The Law underlies the mercy-seat* (ver. 2). A testimony against sins, yet the foundation of the covenant. In redemption, the covenant obligation is not annulled, but fulfilled representatively in the spiritual Head—Christ. In receiving Christ, the Law's Fulfiller, we bind ourselves to be fulfillers of it also, as no longer servants of sin, but of righteousness (Rom. vi.). Our justification is in him; his Spirit of life is in us (Rom. viii. 1, 2; Heb. x. 16).

II. THE SETTLEMENT OF THE MINISTRY OF RELIGION. (Vers. 6—10.) The renewal of the high priesthood in the person of Eleazar (ver. 6); the separation of the tribe of Levi for the service of the sanctuary (vers. 8, 9). The existence of ordinances is a proof of continued mercy. God punishes unfaithfulness by removing the candlestick out of its place (Rev. ii. 5). The gospel ministry is Christ's gift to his Church (Eph. iv. 11). *Means* of grace end with the close of the *day* of grace (Matt. xxviii. 20; 2 Cor. vi. 1, 2), and the removal of the individual from their midst ends the day of grace to him (Heb. ix. 27).

III. THE COMMANDMENT TO GO FORWARD. (Vers. 7, 11.) We also are commanded to go forward—to advance to the conquest of the world—to press to heaven. So long as that command stands unrepealed, so long may sinners be assured that the day of grace lasts, and that they are warranted in believing in the mercy of God towards them.—J. O.

Vers. 12, 13.—*The supreme requirement*. With this Moses began (ch. vi. 4), and with this he ends. The sum of the Law, and the sum of all his exhortations. It all and always comes back to this (Eccles. xii. 13) : " What doth the Lord require of thee?" etc. We have here: 1. The *central* requirement. 2. The *all-embracing* requirement. 3. The *indispensable* requirement; that for which nothing else can be accepted as a substitute. 4. The requirement of *kindness*—"for thy good." 5. A *reasonable* requirement. This love and obedience were due from Israel for God's mercies to them. As in the gospel, grace precedes, obedience follows. Saved by grace, we are to make such return as is possible by loving and fearing God, and diligently keeping his commands (Luke vii. 47; Rom. vi. 13; vii. 6; Eph. ii. 8—11).—J. O.

Vers. 14—22.—*The supreme persuasive.* The revelation of God's character in its double aspect of exalted might and of condescending grace.

I. GOD EXALTED, YET STOOPING. (Vers. 14—16.) The wonder of revelation: 1. *That One so exalted should stoop at all.* The wonder is not abated by reflecting that infinite perfection must include infinite mercy with every other attribute. It fills us with amazement to think of the Possessor of heaven and earth stooping to hold friendly converse with his creature, man. The Bible dwells on the thought with astonishment (1 Kings viii. 27; Ps. viii. 3, 4; cxlvii. 3—6; Isa. lvii. 15). Modern science indirectly testifies to the wonder in objecting that, with our enlarged conceptions of the universe, it is impossible to believe that God should feel the special interest in man which the Bible says he does. 2. *That One so exalted should stoop so far.* God's depth of condescension seen peculiarly in the gospel. (1) In sending the Son. (2) In surrendering him to death. (3) This for enemies. (4) In dwelling by the Spirit in imperfectly sanctified hearts (John iii. 16; Rom. v. 6—10; viii. 32; 2 Cor. vi. 16—18; Gal. v. 17). The persuasiveness of the revelation lies in its *blending* of majesty with grace.

II. GOD MIGHTY AND EQUITABLE, YET TENDERLY SYMPATHETIC. (Vers. 17—20.) Another aspect of the Divine greatness, blending with lowliness, which attracts the heart. The combination of great strength with great gentleness; of judicial sternness with humane consideration of those in distress, are sufficiently rare to be always striking. We marvel when, in the hero of a hundred battles, we discover a heart of woman's tenderness; when in the judge whose strictness on the bench every one remarks, we light on a spring of deep and genuine compassionateness. It is this combination we see in God. A God of gods, a Lord of lords; great, mighty, terrible, sternly just; yet, what might seem incompatible with this, tenderly and touchingly compassionate. His might and equity, so terrible to evil-doers, he throws as a shield around the fatherless, the widow, and the stranger. He executes their judgment. They are his peculiar care. Them, above all others, will he not allow to be wronged (Ps. lxviii. 5).

III. GOD OMNIPOTENT, YET HIS OMNIPOTENCE EXERTED IN DEFENDING AND BLESSING HIS CHURCH. (Vers. 21, 22.) Power in itself awakens fear; power known to be engaged in our protection and for our good inspires the highest confidence. Moses recalls to the Israelites, as a reason for fearing and loving God, his acts of power on their behalf, especially his power as exerted in their extraordinary increase. God's power may be viewed as displayed: 1. In the Church's *redemption* (Col. i. 13). 2. In the Church's *increase* (Acts v. 38, 39). 3. In the Church's *protection from her foes* (Matt. xvi. 18; Acts iv. 24, 31). The individual Christian will have reason to rejoice in the same power as exerted in his conversion (Eph. i. 19), in his upholding (Jude 24), in his protection (Rom. viii. 35—39), in his ultimate salvation (1 Pet. i. 5).—J. O.

Ver. 16.—*Heart circumcision.* I. HEART CIRCUMCISION IN ITS IMPORT. 1. *Betokens the existence of natural impurity.* The rite of circumcision, as the initiatory rite of the covenant, taught that man, in his natural, unpurified state, is unfit for fellowship with God. "In us, that is, in our flesh, dwells no good thing" (John iii. 6; Rom. vii. 18). It was a symbol of the putting away of "the filth of the flesh"—a truth now signified in baptism (Col. ii. 11; 1 Pet. iii. 21). 2. *Illustrates the painful nature of the renunciation of fleshly lusts.* The operation was sharp, painful, bloody. It vividly set forth at once the necessity of renouncing the lusts of the flesh, and the pain attendant on the act. We are called on to *mortify* our members which are upon the earth (Col. iii. 5). The process is described as a *crucifying* of the flesh, with its affections and lusts (Gal. v. 24). The deepest form which this renunciation can assume is the renunciation of the principle of self-will in its entirety, the sharp excision of evil in its root. 3. *Implies the grace of the covenant.* The reception of God's grace as exhibited in the covenant is the condition of the possibility of this renunciation. We achieve it, not in our own strength, but through the impartation of a new principle of life. Paul makes it a result of faith in the risen Christ (Col. ii. 12). The circumcised heart marks the accepted and restored recipient of the grace of God—a child of the spiritual covenant, one born again.

II. HEART CIRCUMCISION IN ITS NECESSITY. 1. *As distinguished from outward circumcision.* The latter was valueless without the former. Being but a symbol, its sole worth lay in that which it represented. The true Jew was he who was one inwardly, whose circumcision was "that of the heart, in the spirit, and not in the letter" (Rom. ii. 28, 29). The remark applies to baptism. It also is but a symbol, and without the grace which it exhibits, and the inward renewal which it betokens, it is a dead work, a valueless rite, leaving its subject as little a Christian as at first. So with all ceremonies. 2. *As a positive qualification for God's service.* Pure obedience can flow only from a pure heart, a renewed will. It is not a fruit of the flesh. The flesh must be renounced, and a new and spiritual nature begotten in us before we can render it. What is needed is not *reformation*, but *regeneration*—a new birth, a new creation, a new heart (John iii. 3; Rom. vii. 18—25; viii. 7; 2 Cor. v. 17; Gal. v. 16—25).—J. O.

Ver. 19.—*Love the stranger.* The precept has numerous applications—

I. To LITERAL STRANGERS. Persons from foreign countries, or from distant parts of our own country, settling in our midst. Why should these be treated so often as intruders, "incomers," persons to be jealously watched and suspected, instead of being taken by the hand and welcomed?

II. To THE UNFRIENDED AND HELPLESS. To all whose hearts are lonely, and their lives destitute of the cheer given by the love and sympathy of friends. To the fatherless and the widow—strangers in a very true sense in a world where selfish interests so hugely predominate.

III. To YOUNG MEN IN GREAT CITIES. Often lost for lack of some one to take a kindly interest in them.

IV. To STRANGERS TURNING UP IN CHURCHES. Coldness here repels many who might otherwise be won to interest in religion, and secured for Christ. Brotherly and friendly attention, a kind word, the warm shake of a hand, the courteous offer of a pew,—how far will they often go? They are, like "good words," worth much, and cost little.

Show kindness to strangers: 1. *Because they peculiarly need it.* "The heart of a stranger." 2. *Because God loves them.* He will avenge their wrongs. He will reward kindness shown to them (Matt. xxv. 35). 3. *We may be placed in similar circumstances.* Changes in fortune (Ruth i. 19—22).—J. O.

Ver. 20.—*Religion in brief.* A text made illustrious by our Saviour's use of it. Like ver. 12, a summary of duty, but in a form giving prominence to the truth that fear of God works from within outwards. This central religious principle particularizes itself into—

I. SERVING HIM—or religion in deed. In resistance of all seductions to a counter-service (Matt. iv. 10). In the faithful and diligent discharge of all duties.

II. CLEAVING TO HIM—or religion in heart. Fear and love, rooted in faith, here reveal themselves as an energy of trust and adherence. They dread separation from God as the worst evil. They hold by him for support, for keeping, for strength, for direction.

III. SWEARING BY HIS NAME—or religion in word. This includes religious oaths, but denotes also willingness at any time to make public confession of God.

IV. REJOICING IN HIM. "He is thy praise" (cf. Phil. iv. 4).—J. O.

Vers. 1—5.—*The Law deposited in the ark.* The first attempt to convey God's Law to man in a written form had proved a failure. The human links in the system had snapped. Moses had overrated the people's loyalty. The people had overrated their own strength of purpose. So far, the Law had been to them a ministration of death. But knowledge grew out of experience.

I. WE SEE THE HUMAN FACTOR IN DIVINE REVELATION. The conceptions that dwell in God's mind are incomprehensible until they are put into human mould. This introduction of a human element implies limitation, but does not imply error. The prophet becomes the channel through which Divine communications flow; but the prophet needs great subjective preparation to receive the message. He must leave the throng and bustle of men, ascend above the low cares of earth, and spend forty days in communion with heavenly realities, before he is competent to receive the gift of Divine Law. Such absorption of mind in Divine fellowship will make us also susceptible of larger revelation. Obedience likewise to Divine command fits us for this fellowship.

II. WE SEE THE PERMANENCY OF GOD'S LAW. 1. *The words that were written on these second tablets were the same as were written on the first—were the same as were spoken in the flame.* Though man may violate and break his Law, God does not modify nor reduce his claims. 2. *They were recorded on stone,* on the granite stone of Sinai. There is significance to be found in the material chosen. In many respects stone tablets would involve inconvenience, but the impression to be made on men's minds was of the first importance, and God does nothing without reason. 3. *They were to be preserved in a chest.* Thus they would be handed down from age to age as the unchanging will of God.

III. WE SEE THE SUCCINCTNESS OF GOD'S COMMANDS. These cardinal precepts were but ten, which might easily be laid up in memory, and recited by aid of the fingers. In the absence of writings, this natural aid to memory would be in common use. Yet, though few in number, these ten words were pregnant with meaning—were living seeds of truth, which, planted in the soul, would yield a copious harvest. The two stone tablets may have been ordered to correspond with the two hands, or to embrace man's twofold relationship—Godward and manward.

IV. THE CONSERVATION OF THE LAW IN THE ARK IS HIGHLY SUGGESTIVE. 1. *It is suggestive of mystery.* Since the human mind cannot measure the universe, mystery is necessary—mystery is wholesome discipline. 2. *It is suggestive of protection.* The stony tablets needed protection against the ebullitions of Moses' anger. They needed to be hid to prevent their becoming an object of idolatry. 3. *It is suggestive of value.* They had both an extrinsic and an intrinsic worth. They would be valued as rare and unique. They ought to have been valued more highly still as the records of God's will. 4. *It is suggestive of the use men should make of them.* This hidden deposit is symbolical. As the material temple is the symbol of the human soul, in which God most of all prefers to reside, so the word of God is required to be enshrined within. "Thy word have I hid in mine heart." The word is the true forerunner, which prepares the way for the entrance of the Living God.—D.

Vers. 6—11.—*Progress.* Progress is the law of human life. Perfection is reached only by steady advancement.

I. PROGRESS IS MARKED BY DISTINCT STAGES. There are times for action, and times for rest. Neither body nor mind can, in our present state, bear the strain of continuous exertion. There is an advantage in an occasional halt, by which we can review the past, measure our progress, examine our resources, and reconnoitre the future. The soul is many-sided, and advance in knowledge, devout feeling, practical exertion, self-denial, cannot be made at one and the same time. To-day we gain clearer perception of heavenly truths; to-morrow we exercise our best affections on abject sufferers; the day following we fight with the enemy with sword and buckler.

> "Each morning sees some task begun,
> Each evening sees its close."

II. PROGRESS IS ACCOMPANIED BY CHANGEFUL INCIDENT, PAINFUL AND PLEASANT. At one halting-place Aaron died, and the camp was plunged into bitter mourning; at another halt they came upon streams of refreshing water. Yet all events may minister to the soul's progress. There are no absolute impediments to the highest progress. "Out of the eater comes forth meat." "All things work together for good." The *order* of experience usually happens, as in this case, viz. first the bitter, then the sweet; first loss, then gain. The evening and the morning make one day. "Blessed are they that mourn: for they shall be comforted."

III. THERE IS PROGRESS TOO IN THE DEVELOPMENT OF GOD'S PLANS. At another stage of their pilgrimage, God chose the tribe of Levi to minister unto him in sacred things. Heretofore, the firstborn in each family was claimed by God as his special minister; now a particular tribe is selected on the ground of its zealous exertions in God's cause. Character, not the accident of birth, is the basis of God's approval. In God's kingdom, *he* bears the palm who merits it. Higher service is to be accounted the most honourable reward. Promotion to a nearer fellowship with God—this ought to be our richest joy.

IV. THERE IS PROGRESS SHOWN ALSO IN THE NATURE OF DIVINE AWARDS. It had been considered hitherto that the supreme mark of Jehovah's favour was the gift of Canaan. *Now* the people are gradually led to perceive that there is something better than *that*. One tribe, and *that* the most signally separated by God for favour, is deprived of participation in the promised land. The Levites, like Abraham, though dwelling in the land, shall possess no personal property in fields or vineyards. Their advantage it shall be, to be exempt from the cares and ambitions and jealousies pertaining to landed estate. An inheritance shall be theirs, boundless in extent; satisfying in its nature; inalienable in its tenure; uncorrupting, yea, ennobling, in its effect upon the possessor; uncreated, and therefore undecaying. Their inheritance was *God himself*. He who has God, has all things. The universe is his.

V. TRUE PROGRESS IS THE RESULT OF COMBINED CONTEMPLATION AND ACTION. In the busy life of our Lord, communion with God and intense activity sweetly blended. To be always on the mount would make us pietists and recluses and mystics—hot-house plants. To be always on the field of action will make us narrow, hard, arrogant, self-reliant. Both sides of our nature must grow in ratio, if we are to be full-orbed, attractive Christians. The ferry-boat of the gospel, which is to carry men to the other side, must be rowed with two oars—prayer and labour.

VI. THE PROGRESS OF ONE IS THE PROGRESS OF MANY. A useful principle of emulation appears in human nature. It is painful to be left behind in the race. If we cannot be in the front, we wish to be near it. Every man has a following. We cannot go to heaven or to hell alone. With more or less of persuasiveness, every man is saying, "Come with me!" Is *my* influence beneficial or baneful?—D.

Vers. 12—22.—*Knowledge of God the parent of obedient faith.* Every honest view we take of God's service brings to light fresh features of attractiveness. It is the only right course. It satisfies conscience, reason, affection, desire. Having right dispositions and purposes in life, all larger knowledge of God makes service pleasant; yea, true service ministers to our best life.

I. THE REASONABLENESS OF GOD'S SERVICE MAY BE DEDUCED FROM THE PERFECTION OF HIS CHARACTER. 1. *His supremacy.* He is "God of gods." He stands alone, the sole Creator, but himself uncreated. His claims upon his creatures are absolute, unlimited, and unconditioned. 2. *His equity.* If, at any time, men suspect any unrighteousness in God, it is because of some obliqueness of vision, or some defect in their mental instrument, or some deficiency of knowledge. No shadow of partiality has ever once been found in him. The favourites of God have been the most chastised. 3. *His immense power.* He is "mighty and terrible." A breath of God can create; a breath can destroy. "With the breath of his mouth he will slay the wicked." 4. *His goodness and pity.* His goodness is profuse, is distributed with royal generosity, without stint. But his special care is reserved for the helpless. Widows and orphans have exceptional protection and defence. He makes *their* case his own, and becomes their unseen Patron. Human monarchs lavish their favours upon those who can do them most service; God lavishes his kindness upon the most needy. Want is the passport to his storehouse. Infinite worth belongs to him.

II. THIS REASONABLENESS OF SERVING GOD IS SEEN IN HIS GRACIOUS TREATMENT OF MEN. 1. *There was no need, so far as we can discover, that God should be served by men.* The heaven was *his*, and all previous orders of intelligent beings. The earth also was *his*, and all its various contents. Here was large scope for the display of his perfections. If men were rebellious, he could readily crush the race, and sweep it from the face of the earth. And no other motive for his kindness to men can we discover, than that of generous and irrepressible love. 2. *He has made covenant engagements with them.*

Moses never fails to remind Israel that the God of heaven was *their God*. With condescending grace, that excites our perpetual surprise, God had chosen them to be recipients of special blessing. He had found "delight in their fathers;" and for the fathers' sakes had loved the children. *We*, too, who believe in Christ, "are Abraham's seed, and heirs according to the promise." God regards renewed men as his treasure, his portion, his jewels. They are dear to him as "the apple of his eye." There is no service he will not render for them, "no gift will he withhold." He has redeemed them with life-blood, and esteems them as unspeakably precious. They are destined to share his society, his possessions, his throne, his image. God has bound himself to us by most solemn compacts, and all his vast resources are pledged to us. It is a covenant made in heaven, and "is ordered in all things and sure."

III. This reasonableness is seen in the self-advantage of serving God. 1. *It is "for our good."* Every command may not be pleasant to flesh and blood, nor always to appetite and inclination; but obedience is salutary to all the better parts of man's nature. "In keeping his commandments we have great reward." There is large *present* benefit, and there is larger *prospective* good. 2. *It is a credit to us to serve such a God.* "He is our praise." The statesmen and ambassadors and generals of England count it high honour to serve Britain's queen. How vastly greater the honour to serve the King of kings! We may suffer passing reproach from our attachment to Christ, but reproach is like the early hoar-frost, which the ascending sun will scatter. If men do not perceive the honour, it is because they are blind. "My soul shall make her boast in the Lord." 3. *God's past goodness excites our largest hope.* God had already done great things for Israel. He had multiplied them in Egypt a thousandfold. Nor had he reached the end of his power nor the end of his intentions. What he had done was only a sample of what he yet meant to do. A world of good is yet in store for each believer. We shall never touch the furthest limits of God's beneficence. "Eye hath not seen it." To his faithful servants the invitation is repeated a thousand times over, "Come up higher."

IV. This reasonableness is seen in the kind of service required. Nothing more is demanded than our thoughtful reason and enlightened conscience approve. 1. *Reverence.* We have only to know God in order to yield him the reverence of our souls. If we could perceive his inherent majesty, his real excellence, and his unsullied purity, we should (if feeling were right) instinctively yield to him the profoundest reverence of our hearts. Were it not for the corrupting effects of sin, this would be natural. 2. *Submission to his superior will.* By virtue of his wisdom, he has a right to counsel. By virtue of his relation as Monarch, he has a right to command. By virtue of his supremacy as Creator, he has claims on every part of our nature and on every moment of our time. His will is excellent, benevolent, unerring. To take his will, not ours, for chart and compass is simplest duty, ay, is largest privilege. "Be no more stiffnecked." A pliable will alone makes a dutiful child. 3. *Hearty love.* That we can love at all is due to him. The power to cherish love, to receive love, is his gift. Hence, if we love at all, our love belongs to him. If we love in proportion to benefits received, or in proportion to the worth of the object, or in proportion to the love expended on us, then all our love will centre in God. 4. *Practical service.* Genuine love will always seek some channel for its outflow, and service for love's object is a delight, and is only love in active exercise. It would be a restraint and a pain for love to be silent. She would justly count it bondage to be caged up within the heart. Having feet, it would be a restraint not to walk; how great the honour to be able to walk in God's paths, in the highways he himself doth take! True service for God is freedom, life, joy, heaven. If we love we must obey. 5. *Such service makes us Godlike.* God counts it a joy to serve us, though he is under no obligation of law or right so to do. To serve him means that we grow like him. We imitate him first in actions, then in disposition, then in purposes, then in character. Said Moses significantly to Israel, "God loveth the stranger. . . . Love ye therefore the stranger." Through every hour of every day we may be climbing heavenwards, becoming Godlike. Every duty may become to us an instrument actively moulding us into the image of perfection. The obedience that springs from love is a pathway of flowery pleasantness, ascending gradually to the hills of frankincense, and to the presence of God.—D.

Vers. 1—5.—*The covenant renewed.* The severe intercession of Moses succeeds at last, and he is directed to get two tables like unto the first, and to bring them up to God for his inscription upon them. He was also directed to make an ark for their reception. There was thus provided the tables of the testimony, and a place in which to keep them.

And here we have to notice—

I. MAN IS ASKED TO PROVIDE THE TABLES. God loves the co-operation of his people as far as possible. "Fellow-workers with God" is our highest honour. Just as when Christ was raising Lazarus he allowed men to roll away the stone (John xi. 39—41), so when he would write the Decalogue anew, he directs Moses to provide the tables. This is better than to encourage man's indolence by God doing all.

In the very same way it is upon "the fleshy tables of the heart" God writes his Law (2 Cor. iii. 3). Man, so to speak, provides the material, offers his heart for the sacred inscription, and thus becomes a living epistle, known and read of all men.

II. GOD'S WILL IS UNCHANGING. The two new tables received the same words as the first which were broken. The second edition of the Decalogue was identical with the first. God's will may be stereotyped, it is so perfect and changeless.

Man may be wayward; but God will not alter his standard to suit man's low ideal. The Divine plan is to keep before man the unchanging Law, and bring him by easy stages up to it. There is no depreciation of the Divine requirements.

III. THE ARK WAS PRIMARILY INTENDED AS A DEPOSITORY OF THE LAW. This chest of shittim wood, made strong and beautiful, was evidently meant as a "safe," where this precious deposit, this oracle of God, should be placed. There was nothing so precious in the keeping of Israel. It was their great riches. What advantage had the Jew? "Much every way: chiefly, because that unto them were committed the oracles of God."

And this ark not only typified the care taken of the canon, but also it would seem Christ himself, who, as the Ark, kept the Law in its entirety; it was the expression of his own will, and it was the deposit within him. "Think not that I am come. to destroy the Law, or the prophets: I am not come to destroy, but to fulfil" (Matt. v. 17).

IV. SANCTIFIED MEN ARE SIMILARLY TO BE DEPOSITORIES OF GOD'S HOLY WILL. Those who are regenerated hide God's Law in their hearts, as Christ says prophetically he did (Ps. xl. 8). The preservation of the sacred books has been wonderful—but better is it to have truth settled in the soul and manifested through the life. The blessedness of him who makes God's Law his meditation day and night is great indeed (Ps. i. 2). "This is the covenant that I will make with them after those days, saith the Lord, I will put my laws into their hearts, and in their minds will I write them, and their sins and iniquities will I remember no more" (Heb. x. 16, 17).

When God's word and will are so deposited; when human hearts receive, like Lydia's, the truth,—then is it carried not only through the wilderness of life, but out into "the undiscovered lands." The ark of shittim wood, so strong and precious, only faintly images the more precious receptacle of the human heart, rendered by Divine grace strong and true, which accepts of God's word of promise, and becomes thereby partaker of the Divine nature and escapes the corruption of the world (2 Pet. i. 4).—R. M. E.

Vers. 6—9.—*The separation of the sons of Levi.* The tables of stone in the ark had to be committed to special officers. These were the sons of Levi. God called them to this, a high and glorious honour surely. They were also to minister unto him and to bless in his Name. To this order of men no mere temporal inheritance was given; God was their inheritance.

I. IT IS SURELY DESIRABLE THAT A SPECIAL ORDER OF MEN SHOULD BE SET APART FOR THE CUSTODY OF THE DIVINE WORD. This was the primary office of the sons of Levi, custodians of the ark of the covenant. In this respect they resemble the Christian ministry, whose great office is to keep and to propagate the Divine Word. In the "division of labour" to which human wisdom brings us, it is surely important that a special class should be charged with the sacred deposit of the Divine Word. Men secularized by business cannot be expected to handle the Word of God with the wisdom and power of those who are set apart for this special purpose.

II. THE SONS OF LEVI WERE ALSO TO BE MINISTERS UNTO GOD. They were directed to stand and officiate. They were the ministers of *God*. They were *his* servants, not man's. We do not now refer to the *priestly* rites, through which they passed according to the Mosaic Law. These were special and temporary. They typified the priestly office fulfilled by Christ, and, when fulfilled, no longer needed. But the general idea of ministration in God's presence and for the Lord is surely the very essence of the ministerial office.

III. THE SONS OF LEVI WERE ALSO TO BLESS IN THE NAME OF THE LORD. They were charged to pronounce certain benedictions in God's Name. And this right is manifestly continued in the Christian Church. The pronouncing of the benediction is surely something more than a mere prayer breathed to heaven for the blessings specialized. Is it not the assurance on the part of God's officer that the blessings are conveyed to those waiting to receive them (cf. Numb. vi. 24 and 2 Cor. xiii. 14)?

IV. IT WAS ARRANGED THAT THE LEVITES SHOULD NOT BE SECULARIZED, BUT SHOULD LIVE AT THE ALTAR OF GOD. "Wherefore Levi hath no part nor inheritance with his brethren; the Lord is his inheritance, according as the Lord thy God hath promised him." This means that this tribe was not to be secularized by worldly anxieties and common cares. The Lord guaranteed their support by arrangements at his altar.

And "ministerial support" should mean no more! It is a Divine expedient to secure a class of men for his service, emancipated from secular cares and troubles. The privilege of studying and enforcing God's Word is great and glorious. We only ask such support as ministers as will preserve us from corroding cares, and enable us with free spirits to give ourselves to this high business.

It is this only we ask for, the freedom from the secularity which the world demands even when one is most watchful, in business struggles, against it. It is when a believing Church gives the ministry of Christ such emancipation all round that they may expect the ministerial office to be fulfilled with superior power and to command the ablest men.—R. M. E.

Vers. 10—22.—*New obedience.* Moses, having detailed the success of his intercession in Horeb, and that the threatened doom was averted and the pilgrimage proceeded with, goes on in this passage to analyze the obedience to be rendered. It is all summed up in fearing the Lord, walking in his ways, loving him, serving him with heart and soul, and keeping his commandments. Let us try to grasp the description of *new obedience* here presented.

I. ISRAEL WAS TO BE A GOD-FEARING PEOPLE. A fine word this, "the fear of God"— not indicative of slavish consternation, but of reverential awe. It is the fear which springs from a fitting sense of God's greatness and majesty. He is too great and too glorious (ver. 17) for any of his people to trifle with or to presume upon him, as in the familiarities of ordinary intercourse.

II. AND CONSEQUENTLY ISRAEL WILL SERVE GOD WITH HEART AND SOUL. For when in faith we fear God, we find that "faith worketh by love," and so we throw ourselves "heart and soul" into his service. We adore his excellencies, and then are "proud to serve him." His commandments become our *songs* in the house of our pilgrimage, and we find in keeping them a great reward (Ps. cxix. 54; xix. 11).

III. THE NEED OF SPIRITUAL CIRCUMCISION WILL THEN BE FELT. "The circumcision of the foreskin of the heart" can only mean the use of all lawful means to restrain the wilfulness and waywardness of the heart. The lusts must be subdued, of which self is the centre and selfishness the essence. God has become central and supreme, and so all that interferes in any way with his rights must be "cut off," no matter how painful the process be. This is the cure for "stiffneckedness."

IV. THE CARE OF THE FATHERLESS, WIDOW, AND STRANGER, IS FELT TO BE DIVINEST DUTY. God is impartial, he respects not persons. He is just in all his reign. But he is also compassionate, and makes the defenceless and the helpless his special care (vers. 17, 18).

And in this we feel it our privilege as well as duty to follow him. This is manifested in—

1. *Orphan societies.* Where the widow is considered with the fatherless, and as much of the wrecked home as can be kept together is tried by loving care to be pre-

served. We are finding more considerate ways every day of ministering to the lonely and the desolate.

2. *Hospitality.* This means *love* manifested to a stranger because he is a stranger. There is a speculative hospitality that is poor and mean; and there is a Divine hospitality that asks those who cannot repay the attention, and asks them for the good Lord's sake.

For if we are redeemed of God, like Israel, we must feel that it is due to God's kindness to strangers. We were naturally "aliens," but his love made us friends, and we have entered into his fellowship and joy. It is this felt obligation which sustains the attention to "strangers" which the Lord enjoined.

It is evident that the Jewish religion was intended to be a lovely thing because a thing of love; a matter of broad and genial sympathies and of noble efforts after divinest duties.—R. M. E.

EXPOSITION.

CHAPTER XI.

Moses here renews his exhortation to obedience, enforced by regard to their experience of God's dealings with them in Egypt and in the wilderness, and by consideration of God's promises and threatenings. The blessing and the curse are set before them consequent on the keeping or the transgressing of the Law.

Vers. 1—12.—Israel was to love the Lord, and manifest this by the steadfast observance of all that he had enjoined upon them.

Ver. 1.—**His charge**; what he has appointed to be observed and done (cf. Lev. viii. 35; Numb. i. 53); more fully explained by **his statutes, and his judgments, and his commandments.**

Ver. 2.—**Know ye**; take note of, ponder, lay to heart. The words that follow, **for . . . seen**, are a parenthesis thrown in by the speaker to attract the attention especially of the older generation, who had witnessed the acts of the Lord. The words, *the chastisement*, etc., are to be connected with *know ye*, as the object of the knowing, **And know ye this day the chastisement**, etc. **Which have not known, and which have not seen**; *supp.* "what ye have known and seen." **Your children**; those born during the wandering in the wilderness. **Chastisement**; not punishment, but discipline, education, training (LXX., παιδεία), including both correction and instruction (cf. the use of the Hebrew word מוּסָר in Prov. i. 2; v. 12; vi. 23, etc.). **His greatness . . . stretched out arm** (cf. ch. iii. 24; iv. 34).

Vers. 3, 4.—(Cf. ch. iv. 34; vi. 22; Exod. xiv.)

Ver. 5.—**What he did unto you in the wilderness.** The doings of God to the people in the wilderness comprehend the manifestations of his omnipotence, both in their guidance and protection, and in the punishment of those who transgressed. One instance of the latter is expressly referred to—the destruction of those who joined in the insurrection of Korah (cf. Numb. xvi. 31—33). Moses does not mention Korah himself here, but only his accomplices Dathan and Abiram, probably, as Keil suggests, "from regard to his sons, who were not swallowed up by the earth along with their father, but had lived to perpetuate the family of Korah;" perhaps also because, though Korah was at the head of the insurrection, Dathan and Abiram were the more determined, audacious, and obdurate in their rebellion (cf. Numb. xvi. 12—15, 25, 26), so that it came to be named from them.

Ver. 6.—**All the substance that was in their possession**; literally, *every living thing* (Gen. vii. 4, 23) *that was at their feet*, i.e. all their followers (cf. "all the people that follow thee," Exod. xi. 8; "all the men that appertained unto Korah," Numb. xvi. 32).

Vers. 7—9.—Thus from what they themselves had witnessed does Moses admonish the elder members of the congregation, summoning them to recognize in that the purpose of God to discipline and train them, that so they might keep his commandments and be strengthened in soul and purpose to go in and possess the land, and to live long therein (ch. i. 38; iv. 26; vi. 3).

Ver. 7.—For *but*, read *yea*: **Yea, your eyes have seen**, etc.

Vers. 10, 11.—An additional motive to fidelity and obedience is here adduced, drawn from the peculiar excellence and advantages of the land. Canaan was not like Egypt, a country that depended for its fertility on being irrigated by man's labour or by artificial processes, but was a land where the supply and distribution of water was provided for in natural reservoirs and channels, by means of which the rain which God, who cared for the land, sent plentifully on it, was made available for useful purposes. In Egypt there is little or no rain, and the people are dependent on the annual overflowing of the Nile for the proper irrigation of their fields; and as this lasts only for a short period, the water has to be stored and redistributed by artificial means, often of a very laborious kind. **Wateredst it with thy foot.** " The reference, perhaps, is to the manner of conducting the water about from plant to plant and from furrow to furrow. I have often watched the gardener at this fatiguing and unhealthy work. When one place is sufficiently saturated, he pushes aside the sandy soil between it and the next furrow with his foot, and thus continues to do until all are watered. He is thus knee-deep in mud, and many are the diseases generated by this slavish work. Or the reference may be to certain kinds of hydraulic machines which were turned by the feet. I have seen small water-wheels, on the plain of Acre and elsewhere, which were thus worked; and it appeared to me to be very tedious and toilsome, and, if the whole country had to be irrigated by such a process, it would require a nation of slaves like the Hebrews, and taskmasters like the Egyptians, to make it succeed. Whatever may have been the meaning of Moses, the Hebrews no doubt had learned by bitter experience what it was *to water with the foot*; and this would add great force to the allusion, and render doubly precious the goodly land which drank of the rain of heaven, and required no such drudgery to make it fruitful " (Thomson, ' The Land and the Book,' ii. 279; edit. Lond. 1859). Philo describes a machine of this sort as in use in Egypt ('De Confus. Linguar.,' Opp. i. 410, edit. Mangey); and in that country, " a garden of herbs " is still generally watered by means of a machine of simple construction, consisting of a wheel, round which revolves an endless rope to which buckets are attached; this is worked by the feet of a man seated on a piece of wood fastened by the side of the machine, labour at once monotonous and severe (Niebuhr, ' Voyage en Arabie,' i. 121, 4to, Amst. 1776; ' Description de l'Arabie,' i. 219, 4to, Paris, 1779; Robinson, ' Bib. Res.,' i. 542; ii. 21).

Ver. 12.—**Careth for**; literally, *searcheth or inquireth after*, i.e. thinks about and cares for (LXX., ἐπισκοπεῖται, *oversees*; cf. Job iii. 4; Ps. cxlii. 4; Jer. xxx. 17; Ezek. xxxiv. 8; Isa. lxii. 12). **The eyes of the Lord thy God;** *i.e.* his special watchful providence (cf. Ps. xxxiii. 18; xxxiv. 15; Ezek. iv. 5). It was a land on which Jehovah's regard was continually fixed, over which he watched with unceasing care, and which was sustained by his bounty; a land, therefore, wholly dependent on him, and so a fitting

place for a people also wholly dependent on him, who owed to his grace all that they were and had.

Ver. 13.—Being thus wholly dependent on God, it behoved them to be careful to attend to his commandments and to obey them, that so his blessing might be continued to them and to the land. If they would love and serve the Lord as they were bound to do, he would give them the rain of their land, *i.e.* rain for their land, such as it required (cf. " rain of thy seed," Ps. xxx. 2, 3), in the proper season, the early and the latter rain, so that they should fully enjoy the benefits of the land.

Ver. 14.—**The first rain;** the rain which falls from the middle of October to the end of December, which prepares the soil for the seed, and keeps it moist after the seed is sown. **The latter rain;** that which falls in March and April, about the time when the grain is ripening for harvest; during the time of harvest no rain falls in Palestine. But if they allowed themselves to be deceived and misled, so as to apostatize from the Lord and serve other gods and worship them, the Divine displeasure would be shown in the withholding from them of the blessing, so that they should miserably perish.

Ver. 16.—**That your heart be not deceived;** literally, *lest your heart be enticed* or *seduced* (יִפְתֶּה). The verb means primarily to be open, and as a mind open to impressions from without is easily persuaded, moved either to good or evil, the word came to signify to induce in a good sense, or to seduce in a bad sense. Here the people are cautioned against allowing themselves to be enticed so as to be led astray by seductive representations (cf. Job xxxi. 27; Prov. xx. 19 [" flattereth "]; Job v. 2 [" silly one "]; Hos. vii. 11).

Ver. 17.—**He shut up the heaven.** " The heaven conceived as a womb " (Schulz); cf. Gen. xvi. 2. The want of rain was regarded as a sign of the Divine displeasure and as a curse (1 Kings viii. 35; Zech. xiv. 17; Rev. xi. 6).

Vers. 18—20.—(Cf. ch. vi. 7—9.)

Ver. 21.—(Cf. ch. iv. 40; vi. 2.) **As the days of heaven upon the earth;** as long as the heavens continue stretched over the earth, *i.e.* to the end of time, for ever (cf. Job xiv. 12; Ps. lxxxix. 29; Gen. viii. 22).

Vers. 22—25.—If they were sedulous to keep God's commandments, and faithfully adhered to him, loving him and walking in all his ways, he would drive out before them the nations of the Canaanites, and cause them to possess the territory of nations greater and mightier than themselves. Every place on which the soles of their feet should tread should be theirs, *i.e.* they had but to enter the land to become possessors of it. This is more exactly defined as restricted to the land the boundaries of which are given—from the Arabian desert on the south to Lebanon on the north, and from the river Euphrates on the east to the Mediterranean on the west (ch. i. 7). **From the wilderness and Lebanon**; read, *even unto Lebanon*; הַלְּבָנוֹן is for עַד־הַלְּבָנוֹן (cf. עַד הַיָּם in the end of the verse). **The uttermost sea**; rather, *the hinder sea* (Numb. xxxiv. 6), the sea that lay behind one looking to the east (ver. 26; cf. ch. vii. 24; ii. 25; Exod. xxiii. 27).

Vers. 26—32.—Moses, in conclusion, refers to the blessing and the curse consequent on the observance or the transgression of the Law, and prescribes that when they had entered on possession of the land the blessing should be proclaimed from Mount Gerizim, and the curse from Mount Ebal.

Ver. 26.—**Behold, I set before you**; place for your consideration (ch. iv. 8; xxx. 15), so that you may see whither tends obedience on the one hand, and disobedience on the other.

Ver. 28.—**Other gods, which ye have not known**; in contradistinction to Jehovah, the revealed God, made known to them by word and deed.

Vers. 29, 30.—(Cf. ch. xxvii. 11.) **Thou shalt put the blessing**; thou shalt give (נָתַתָּה), *i.e.* give forth, utter, announce, proclaim (cf. Gen. xlix. 21; Job i. 22 [gave, *i.e.* uttered impiety to God]; Ps. l. 20 [gavest, didst utter, slander]). The two mountains named stand opposite to each other, with a valley between, about two hundred yards broad at the widest part, in which stood the town of Shechem, now Nablûs. They were selected for the purpose mentioned, doubtless, because of their relative position, and probably also because they stand in the centre of the land both from north to south, and from east to west. It has been suggested that Ebal was appointed for the uttering of the curse, and Gerizim for the uttering of the blessing, because the former was barren and rugged, the latter fertile and smooth; but this is not borne out by the actual appearance of the two hills, both being equally barren-looking, though neither is wholly destitute of culture and vegetation. That Gerizim was selected for the blessing because of its position on the south side of the valley "towards the region of light," while Ebal was appointed for the curse because it was on the north side, can be regarded only as an ingenious fancy. In ver. 30, the position of the two mountains is defined as **on the other side of Jordan**, *i.e.* on the side opposite to where the Israelites then were, the western side; **and as by the way**—rather, *behind the way*—**where the sun goeth down**; *i.e.* the road of the west, the great road which passed through the west-Jordan country, and which is still the main route from south to north in Palestine (Ritter, iv. 293, etc.; Robinson, iii. 127), passing Nablûs and the two mountains on the east, so that they are *behind* it. **Which dwell in the champaign**; in the 'Arâbah (see ch. i. 1), "mentioned here as that portion of the land on the west of the Jordan which lay stretched out before the eyes of the Israelites, who were encamped in the steppes of Moab" (Keil). **Over against Gilgal**; *i.e.* not the Gilgal mentioned in Josh. iv. 19, which was east of Jericho (*hod.* Jiljûlia), nor the Gilgal of Josh. xii. 23 (probably the modern Jiljulieh, in the plain of Sharon), but the Gilgal of Josh. ix. 6; x. 6; and 2 Kings ii. 1 (*hod.* Jiljilia), to the north of Bethel, from which there is "a very extensive prospect over the great lower plain, and also over the sea" (Robinson, 'Bib. Res.,' iii. 138); so that the mountains by Nablûs may be very well described as "over against it." **Beside the plains of Moreh**; for "plains" read *oaks* (cf. Gen. xii. 6; xxxv. 4).

Vers. 31, 32.—The assurance that they should pass over Jordan and possess the land of Canaan, is assigned as a reason and motive why they should **observe to do all** that God had commanded them.

HOMILETICS.

Vers. 2—9.—*The voice of God in passing events to be heeded, interpreted, and obeyed.* As in former paragraphs, we have here much repetition of the same teachings which had been already given. We therefore select for homiletic treatment the one distinctive feature which marks it. The people of God are now on the verge of Canaan. Multitudes of them had been born since the march through the wilderness had begun forty years before. They could not have seen the wonders in Egypt, nor could they know, except by report, of the manifestations of the Divine displeasure at the rebellious spirit manifested by the people during the first years of their course. But there are still some seniors left who had seen all. To these Moses makes his appeal, ere the discourse in which he exhorts to obedience is brought to a close. And he urges them anew, from a consideration of the deep meaning of the events which their own eyes have seen, to learn to be faithful and obedient. We by no means understand Moses as intending to say that the children are not before him to hear his words, but rather that the argument he is now using is specially for the sires rather than the sons. It is in effect this: "You, the seniors among the people now, *have seen* all these things. God has spoken in them directly to you: therefore, it is incumbent upon you to assign to these events their true meaning, and to give them their rightful power over you." Whence we get the topic named above for our Homily: "*The voice of God in passing events to be heeded, understood, and obeyed.*"

I. HERE ARE STIRRING EVENTS WHICH HAD OCCURRED UNDER ISRAEL'S OWN EYES. Three of them are specially named. 1. The plagues brought on Pharaoh and the land of Egypt. 2. The overthrow of the Egyptians in the Red Sea. 3. The overthrow of Korah, Dathan, and Abiram. (For remarks on these, see Exposition, and Homilies *in loc.* For much light on the second, see Brugsch's 'Egypt.')

II. HERE IS A SPECIFIC MEANING GIVEN TO THESE EVENTS. They are all called "*chastisement*" (ver. 2). They are not only referred to as works of greatness, deeds of power and of terror, but their moral meaning (which is infinitely more important) is given in the word "chastisement." It is of very much more consequence to understand the *meaning* of an event, than to merely have the event stored up in memory as a piece of history. In fact, it may fairly be questioned whether the latter is of any value at all. Of what value is it to a student to know that King John signed Magna Charta, unless he knows the meaning thereof, as related to the rise and growth of the British Constitution? Even so it is not of the slightest service to know of Red Sea wonders, nor of the plagues in Egypt, unless their place and meaning in history are known. This is the case likewise with events of much greater moment. Not even the wonders of Gethsemane and Calvary are exempted. If regarded only as incidents in history, apart from their spiritual, redemptive meaning, they will serve us nothing. "As the body without the spirit is dead," so facts without their significance are dead also. Hence it is that the attention of Israel is recalled to these olden wonders as "chastisements" from the Lord their God.

III. THESE EVENTS MAY BE DIVIDED INTO TWO CLASSES; in each class a like principle is illustrated, though in a different form. 1. The first two were the chastisement of Egypt on behalf of God's oppressed people, showing them the strength of his arm and the value of his covenant love. 2. The third was the chastisement of the chosen people themselves, when they rebelled against the divinely appointed order with reference to the priesthood. In the former cases, God's jealous love on behalf of his people was proven; in the latter case, God's jealousy for his own honour, in maintaining his appointed order and ordinances unimpaired. In the former, that jealousy chastised Egypt for Israel's sake; in the latter, Israel for Jehovah's sake. Thus Israel would have before them the lesson that, as God in his love would snap the fetters that bound them, so in his purity he would remove the stains that disfigured them; that as they rejoiced in the love of God which was round them as a mighty guard, so they might also cherish a holy fear of that purity which would mark its displeasure at their wayward-ness and sins.

IV. SUCH EVENTS, SO FULL OF MEANING, SHOULD HAVE A CONSTANT EFFECT IN IMPELLING TO OBEDIENCE, AND IN QUICKENING AND SUSTAINING A REVERENT FEAR AND LOVE. God meant much in bringing them to pass, and they should mean much in the use they made of them (vers. 8, 9). If they laid them to heart, and acted out the lessons they were designed to teach, they would continue in the land which God had assigned to them. The reference in the phrase, "that ye may prolong your days in the land," is rather to Israel's continuance as a nation, than to the long life of the individual. *National continuance dependent on national obedience*, is the one truth most frequently named in the exhortations of Israel's lawgiver.

V. ALL THIS HAS A PRESENT-DAY APPLICATION TO THE PEOPLE OF GOD NOW. Forms change; but principles never. There are few passages, even in the grand old Book, that open up a wider scope or a sublimer field for the preacher's efforts than the one before us. The following enumeration of the successive links of thought may be helpful. Our pages give no space for more. 1. At the background of the Christian dispensa-tion there are solid and substantial historical facts on which we can ever fall back.

2. Though the facts, comprised in the birth, cross-bearing, resurrection, and ascension of our Lord Jesus Christ, did not occur in our times, yet the evidence thereof has come down to us in unbroken line, and with unimpaired force. **3.** The meaning of these facts is even better known now than it was at the moment of their occurrence; for their significance has been recorded for us in books which have survived fire and flood, and have reached us in all their integrity. **4.** There are other sets of facts connected therewith of which we are witnesses, viz. that the gospel of Christ has been the power of God unto salvation to those who believe it, and that believers therein are the guardians of it, holding it in trust for others. **5.** Those thus guarding the faith of Christ are the present " commonwealth of Israel; " taking the place in this economy of the Israel of old. They are not indeed visibly one now as in ancient days. But they form a host a hundredfold more numerous, ranged under differing names, yet guarding the ancient faith. **6.** Those Churches which are faithful to their acknowledged mission, prolong their days in the land; while those which, either in faith or life, are less loyal and true to their God, die out, and " the candlestick is removed out of its place." **7.** This law of Church life is a perpetual declaration of God's jealousy for his honour. " In proportion to their faithfulness or unfaithfulness," says a modern writer, " particular Churches overcome the world, or are overcome by the world." Thus God shows his care for these supreme facts of our faith, by saying to Churches, " If you guard them, you live ; if you guard them not, you die." In the great redemption which is in Christ Jesus, God has broken the fetters which bound man. In his watchful jealousy, he will bring honour to the Church which holds forth and acts out his redemption, and will bring shame to one which represses it, weakens it, or turns the grace of God into lasciviousness. Just as our God cared not for Israel to remain a nation unless they preserved his honour unimpaired, so he cares not for the continued existence of any Church, unless it is " earnestly contending for the faith once delivered to the saints." **8.** While, however, the claim and demand of God upon the fidelity of his Israel now is as strong as ever, yea stronger, the mode in which that claim is presented is vastly more tender than in ancient days. In the Epistles to the seven Churches we have a kind of appeal to the Christian Israel, analogous to this of Moses to the Hebrew Israel. But, in lieu of the thunder, trembling, and flame of Sinai, we have the pathos and love of Gethsemane and Calvary. Can we resist such appeals as those which Christ presents? Can we consent to keep back from man the cross, with all its fulness of meaning ; or fail to respond to it by intensest love and closest obedience? May our once suffering and now glorified Lord make us faithful, and keep us so till death!

Vers. 10—17.—*The order of nature subservient to moral purposes.* (For information concerning methods of irrigation in Egypt, see the Exposition, and works on the subject.) Moses here reminds the people : **1.** That the land of Canaan would not require artificial irrigation, as that of Egypt had done ; that it was a land specially cared for by God, who gave it the early rain after the sowing, and the latter rain before the harvest ; so that there would be no occasion for them to put forth the same kind of labour that had been performed in the land of their bondage. **2.** That if they were obedient and true to their vows, the fruitfulness of Canaan would be ensured through the continuance of the early and the latter rain. **3.** But that if they allowed themselves to be seduced to the service of other gods, the Lord's wrath would be kindled, the heaven would be shut up, the rain would be withheld, and so from want of sustenance the people would perish. Now, it is evident that this is one of those passages with which what is called " modern thought " ventures specially to come in conflict. We do not now concern ourselves with any physical theory of the working of nature which the Hebrews may have had. Moses did not give them any. It was not his province, which was simply to teach them the moral and spiritual laws under which they were placed ; to show them that these were such as to subserve their training in righteousness, and that nature itself was so regulated by Jehovah, as to be a most important factor in the educational forces which were at work on their behalf. The series of thoughts here given opens up a most important theme for pulpit teaching; viz. *The order of nature subservient to moral purposes.*
I. LET US INDICATE THE MAIN THOUGHTS WHICH ARE CONTAINED IN THIS PASSAGE. **1.** The sending of rain from heaven is an act of God (Jer. xiv. 22). This is a truth

taught by natural religion, and recognized in the whole of Scripture. 2. The sending of the rain from heaven is an act of, and to us a proof of, the Divine benevolence (Matt. v. 45). 3. There was manifest kindness to Israel, in leading them to a land so spontaneously and richly fruitful as Palestine. In Egypt, where rain falls so seldom, God had taught man to water it by artificial means, and compensated for the want of rain by the periodical rise of the Nile. But whereas in Palestine there was no such phenomenon, and as the people would have perished therein from want, had artificial means of watering it been required ere these irrigating measures could have been carried out, it was no mean mercy that they were led to a land which did not need them. They lose very much who do not see proofs of Divine care in these natural counterpoises and compensations. Moreover, had the fruitfulness of Canaan been dependent on Israel's " watering it with the foot " they might, in their ignorance, have attributed its fertility to their own wit or wisdom ; but no *such* self-laudation could well arise where all had been secured for them by a Power not their own. 4. Nevertheless, however richly Canaan might be blessed with the rain of heaven, that gift of God was by no means absolute or irrevocable, but would be so bestowed as to serve the purpose of a moral training. In ' Footnotes from the Page of Nature,' Dr. Macmillan clearly shows that there is a law of nature, by virtue of which each order of life exists for the sake of that which is above it. We have but to widen and generalize this principle, and we get exactly the same truth in the Word which is revealed in the world, viz. that the physical exists for the moral, and is so regulated as to be subservient thereto. All things are for man. "He giveth us rain from heaven, and fruitful seasons, filling our hearts with food and gladness." And if thus God cares for the bodily wants, how should he but care the more for the moral growth of the creature— man? 5. From this general principle, two details naturally follow. (1) That rain will be continued if the people are obedient. (2) That if they disobey, and serve other gods, rainlessness and dearth will be the sad reminders of their sin (see ch. xxviii. 23, 24; 1 Kings viii. 35; xvii. 1; 2 Chron. vi. 26, 27; vii. 12—14; Jer. xiv. 1—7, 17— 22; Amos iv. 6—8; Hag. i. 7—11; Hos. i. 8, 9). It is no valid objection to say that there is no *nexus* between the obedience or disobedience of a man, and the fall of rain. For, first of all, in such a statement there is a gross *petitio principii*. The whole thing in question is assumed ; and secondly, according to the fourth principle named above, the Scripture theory is, not only that there is a *nexus*, but that it is a known and intelligible and a reasonable one : viz. God gives or withholds rain. He values his people's comfort, but their virtue more. *He* varies the course of nature so as to subserve the latter end. Hence there is a connection between human obedience to God, and a shower of rain. The obedience is *to* God, the rain is *from* him. But let us now pass on—

II. To show how these thinkings should guide us in reference to some of the present perplexities of human thought. And perhaps we may meet these, and clear up the passage before us, most effectually, by at once putting the question, " *Is it right to pray for rain ?* " We must again divide this question into two ; and must first ask, " What do we mean by praying for rain ? " or " What *is* that praying for rain for which alone any devout and intelligent believer would argue ? " 1. It is not meant that those who never pray at all should pray *but* for rain, and selfishly beg a gift from a Being to whom, except when they are in trouble, they do not care to speak. 2. It is not meant that men should ask distrustfully, as if they thought their words would move the Most High to pity. 3. It is not meant that any request for rain should be absolute, or sent up in a spirit of querulousness or dictation. 4. It is not thought that any law of nature needs to be interfered with, or altered, or modified, in order to bring an answer to such a request. But: (1) It is known and believed that all nature is perfectly plastic in the Creator's hands. (2) It is contended that God can modify the *course* of nature without varying a *law*. Why, even man can do this: he can drain a morass, or carry off a lake, and change the climate and vegetation of a district for ever afterwards ; and if man can do this in part, surely God can do it infinitely. (3) It is urged that those who in *every* thing by prayer and supplication make their requests known unto God, need not alter their course because the present trouble is a want of rain ; but that they may lay this, in common with all other things, before God in prayer : reverently acknowledging his greatness, humbly acknowledging that their sins deserve his rebuke, and submitting thereto with lowliness and contrition of heart. (4) It is asserted that any such devout souls, in any distress whatever, can, may, ought to entreat the Lord their God that he would have mercy upon them, remove his stroke, and grant them their request. This is that for which alone we contend. Now, there are reasons for taking up such a position, which cannot be set aside, and when put together in cumulative force, they seem to us to leave no special difficulty on this point remaining. (1) There is a God and Father of all. (2) He loves to be approached in prayer (Ps. l. 15). (3) Whatever is a care on his children's heart is a care on his (Isa. lxiii. 9; 1 Pet. v. 7). (4) God's great concern for the people is their moral training (ch. viii. 2—5). He so distributes physical good that the higher end may be subserved. (5) We are taught by our Lord himself to pray, "Give us day by day our daily bread;" and if so, it follows that we may pray for the continuance of the means on which the supply of daily bread depends. As rain is one of the very chief of these means, it follows that the children of God *may* pray for rain. But it may be objected, 1: The laws of nature are fixed. Be it so. The *course* of nature is not (see remarks above). God may modify an order without altering a law. What man can do in limited measure, God can do in unlimited degree. Objection 2: Prayer cannot change the mind of God. True. We neither seek nor desire to do this. We do not know what *is* the mind of God until he tells us. He has said, " Ask, and ye shall receive." If then it is the mind of God that his creatures should ask before receiving, it is of no use to think that the mind of God will change, and that they will receive without asking. Objection 3: If, as is affirmed, sin is the reason for drought, then the only thing which meets such a case is putting away the sin, and not *prayer !* We reply, the Scriptural teaching is that there must be confession, repentance, and prayer (see 1 Kings viii. 35). Not one alone, but all combined. Thus all the objections fail. Finally, we would conclude with one earnest inquiry, the working out of which would demand a long discourse. We can but put it, and let it drop as a seed into some hearts. Given, man as a moral being, with indefinite possibilities of development for holiness or sin, which theory of the constitution of nature most accords with the constitution of man? That which represents physical force as controlled for the purposes of his moral culture, or that which represents the nobler aspirations as hopelessly baffled by a non-moral, bare physical force? Reader, " Consider what we say; and the Lord give thee understanding in all things."

Vers. 18—21.—(See Homily on ch. vi. 4—9.)

Vers. 22—25.—*The moral power of national righteousness.* There was a definite territory assigned by God to Israel. They were promised *it*, but the prohibition against going beyond what God had allotted them, was as remarkable and strong as the assurance of their possessing such allotment. The bounds here specified are stated afresh in Josh. i. 3, 4. In the days of Solomon these boundaries were actually theirs. But, as is well known, they were a people untrained for war; in regard to military skill and warlike appliances, other nations were vastly more than a match for them, leaving out of the question Israel's paucity in numbers. But (and it is not the least striking feature in the Mosaic legislation) they were to have power of another kind, even that which was moral, a power arising from their righteousness, and also dependent upon it. And in this passage: 1. Moses afresh reminds the people of their duty—to keep the commandments of the Lord their God. 2. He points out that their loyalty to God and assurance of his protection would give them irresistible strength. 3. The knowledge of this higher order of moral life, and of the promised guard of their covenant God, would so influence the other nations that they would be inspired with dread (see Josh. ii. 9, 10, 11). 4. This dread of Israel which the nations round about would feel would clear their way, would ensure their conquest, and would be a security for them in retaining their possessions. From all this we get one of the most important lessons suggested which can possibly be taught on national affairs, viz. *That the kind of power over other nations, which a people may well desire the most, is that which comes from the influence of its own righteousness.*

I. NATIONAL POWER IS UNIVERSALLY COVETED. Nor, provided sundry conditions are fulfilled which will be presently named, is this wrong. No nation ought to consent to be a cipher among nations. Just as really as a man may well wish to be something amongst his fellows, so should a people wish to be something in the regard of neighbouring states.

II. It is most important that the power of a nation over others should be that of the highest kind. One nation may be chiefly great in its commercial enterprise, another in its culture of art, a third in the renown of its orators or poets, a fourth in its philosophic wisdom, a fifth in its military or naval fame; but there is a power, unlike all these, after which Israel was bidden to aspire.

III. That is the power most to be desired which would make it worth while to perpetuate the nation possessing it, for the sake of the world's good. Moses, under Divine direction, is continually recognizing this, by putting Israel's continuance in the land as conditioned on their loyalty to Jehovah and his laws.

IV. The only power which is absolutely necessary to the world's good is that of righteousness. This unites a people. This gives clear heads, strong frames, valiant hearts. A nation whose heart is soundly righteous will not fight unless it must; but if it must, it will fight grandly and for a righteous aim.

V. This power of righteousness will have a manifold effect with regard to other nations. 1. As a rule, it will ensure their good-will. 2. Appealing as it does to man's sense of justice, it will help to ward off attacks from without. 3. Where it fails to do this, and where an attack has to be resisted, if in the hour of their need they cry unto God, they will find that he shields them in the day of battle (see 2 Chron. xx. 1—29).

VI. This power may even be developed and strengthened by repeated and arduous conflict. (See 2 Chron. xx. 29.) When a people are with one heart loyal to God, and do with one voice cry unto him, they will find out that Jehovah hears, and that God speeds the right. And may we not appeal fearlessly to every one of our readers, and say, Is not this power of righteousness pre-eminently that which the world wants? This being so, we may bring this series of remarks to a close by observing—

VII. That the great God of nations will set his seal of approval on peoples that so cleave to the right, by giving again and again the victory to that which, humanly speaking, is the weaker side. Scripture cases of this abound: Israel and Pharaoh; Gideon and the Midianites; Hezekiah and Sennacherib; Jehoshaphat and the Ammonites; and (in another sense) Elijah and the priests and prophets of Baal. The Word of God is continually showing us that power is not always where it seems to be, but very often where it seems not to be: Joseph, Daniel, Peter, etc. From all these considerations, there may be drawn out an earnest appeal to men, even if they aim at nought higher than to be the true lovers and guardians of their country and nation, to seek for the sake of their own dear land, to love and to practise righteousness. Nor let it be supposed that this statement is at all affected by the fact that we are "not under the Law but under grace." Grace reigns through righteousness, and only through righteousness. Infinite grace has offered a Sacrifice which has done away with the need of continuing the sacrifices of the ceremonial law. But grace never has and never will abate one jot or tittle of the demands for righteousness which mark the moral law. Never! And if we are rescued from condemnation, if we are made sons of God, it is not that we may be absolved from the obligation to right-eousness; but that "the righteousness of the Law may be fulfilled in us" from the spontaneity of personal choice, without the need of any command to enforce or pressure to constrain. And inasmuch as only in a perfectly righteous people can there be an absolute guarantee of permanence, it follows that only the people in the commonwealth of Israel will constitute "the eternal city." For there "the people shall be all righteous," and then "they shall inherit the land for ever." Right-eousness and permanence are thus linked together in the prophetic outlook of Isaiah, as really as in the legislation of Moses (see Isa. lxi. 21). In this new and nobler world, righteousness will come into being, not as a response to a Divine command, but as the product of a Divine creation. And then around it there shall be an eternal guard. No enemy from without shall dare to attack; no foe from within shall weaken. "Salvation will God appoint for walls and bulwarks."

Vers. 26—28.—*The dread alternative before every man.* Perhaps, strictly speak-ing, the final paragraph of this chapter includes vers. 26—32. The reader thereof will, however, observe that, while in its entirety it deals with the blessing and curse, yet the first three verses deal with them as resting *on the* people, the remaining verses regard them as pronounced *by* the people. The theme indicated by the latter half is treated on at ch. xxvii. We therefore confine our remarks to the former section of these words. They present to us the dread alternative which is before every man, as our theme for consideration. Lest any should seek to blunt the edge of our words by saying, " We don't like the word ' curse ; ' it belongs to an older dispensation," we would observe at the outset that the same alternative is presented to us, though it may be in other words, by the Lord Jesus Christ, in John iii. 18—21. We do not say that there is no difference in meaning beyond the varied phraseology, but simply point out just now, that, under Christ, as under Moses, there is set forth the sharp contrast, in one case of blessing and curse, in the other case of acceptance and condemnation. One or other of these belongs to every man. Here is a mighty theme, in which the preacher has " by manifestation of the truth to commend himself to every man's conscience in the sight of God."

I. MAN HAS A MORAL NATURE. The denial of this by some, and the baseness of the lives of others, no more interfere with the general truth of this, than cases which are abnormal in the physical world do with well-ascertained truth in the physical departments. Man has a συνείδησις, a power of discerning moral distinctions. If he fails to give proof of that, he is a perishing man.

II. THE POSSESSION OF A MORAL NATURE INDICATES THE EXISTENCE OF MORAL LAW. This is, in fact, the objectivity which is before the moral sense, and perceived by it.

III. THE EXISTENCE OF A LAW IMPLIES THAT OF A LAWGIVER; the existence of a moral law, that of a moral Lawgiver, who is himself the Lord of right, the God, " with whom is our account." The moral sense of man postulates this ; the all but universal conviction of mankind affirms it ; the sense of sin is its constant demonstration. The experience of men like Enoch, who in the olden time " walked with God," is proof that at any rate some human spirits lean on the Eternal One, as really as the body depends on air and food.

IV. THE MORAL LAWGIVER REVEALS HIMSELF. Not only do previously mentioned facts show *that* he is, but we know also *what* he is. The Law given by Moses, and the proclamation of Jehovah's Name to him, disclose the greatness of the Divine being ; the fuller word of prophet and psalmist likewise. The Incarnate Son revealed him. The Holy Ghost unveils him to the watchful eye and yearning heart. " The Lord *your* God."

V. THE GREAT LAWGIVER HAS GIVEN DEFINITE COMMANDS. Chiefly, *as* Lawgiver, in the Law. Chiefly, as also a great Benefactor, in the gospel. In the one aspect his Law is " do ; " in the other his Law is " receive." In the former a course of life is marked out in detail ; in the latter, a redemption by infinite grace is made known for " the obedience of faith." So that, as it speaks to us, Law says (for we are under Law to Christ), " Receive in loving faith the redemption, even the forgiveness of sins, and then, by the renewed energies of a God-inspired life, walk not after the flesh but after the spirit."

VI. THE DIVINE LAWGIVER REGARDS MEN ACCORDING TO THEIR MEASURE OF LOYALTY TO THE RIGHT AND THE TRUE, *i.e.* as far as they have the opportunity of knowing what is right and true ; for some nations may even as yet not have any written law. In such case Peter's words apply (Acts x. 34, 35). We can suppose others who have the Law only. *We* have the revelation of God both in Law and in gospel ; to us is the word of salvation sent (cf. John vi. 29). According as we receive it or no, God approves or disapproves, accepts or disowns. Is it possible to suppose it otherwise ? Can any one think that a holy Lawgiver should give forth a perfect Law, and then be unconcerned as to whether men obey it ? Can it be imagined that he should send his only begotten Son into the world, and then leave it optional with men as to how they should treat him to whom is given all power in heaven and on earth ? There is indeed (see Homily on ch. x. 17—xi. 1) no respect of persons as to rank, or caste, or colour, or clime. The wide world over, right and equity are the Divine delight ; but since right is right, and God is God, there must eternally remain the great gulf fixed between the loyalty of heart which he approves, and the disloyalty of soul which the Most High cannot but condemn. The throne of the Eternal is established in righteousness.

VII. THIS APPROVAL OR DISAPPROVAL OF GOD IS THE BLESSING OR CURSE. (Cf. Ps. i. 6.)

And it would be well could it be impressed on every conscience that, even if there were no certainty of any visitation or punishment from God in token of his displeasure, yet that displeasure itself is so awful a curse, that to be conscious of it is the germ of hell; while, quite apart from aught that he may send to us, the consciousness of having his approval is a sufficient, a heavenly, an " exceeding great " reward! The light in which God views us is of infinitely more moment than the gifts he sends or the chastisements he inflicts. Take an illustration from a lower sphere. Let it be supposed that a man whose life and writings are corrupting the morals and helping to blight the faith of his countrymen, is admitted, in course of events, to the assembly of British senators. He is there as one of its members. But he knows that the grandest, purest, most philanthropic and self-sacrificing of human-kind regard him and his views with unutterable loathing, not because of any vindictive feeling against him, but because of the solemn interests which in his hands are imperilled and shamed. Nothing is done to him; but he knows that this is how he and his views are regarded by those whose esteem is most worth having. Would not such a state of things be intolerable torture to him? Or supposing him "past feeling," would his case be the less pitiable? Or supposing him so puffed up with pride and conceit as to regard the rest of his fellows as kept virtuous by a superstition whose elevating power he does not desire to know, would not the disapproval of the mass of the people—too deep for any words to express—be as a blighting curse upon him, even though no other penalty were imposed; and would not that disownment be a heavier penalty than any outward punishment could be? But oh! what, what is the disapproval of man, or of men, compared with the frown of God?

VIII. THIS APPROVAL OR DISAPPROVAL WILL, SOONER OR LATER, BE MANIFEST. It is true, in more senses than one, "Thou art a God that hidest thyself" (cf. Ps. l. 21). But "though hand join in hand, the wicked shall not go unpunished." The curse will show itself in nations, by their humiliation and destruction. So Egypt, Tyre, Chaldea, Jerusalem, etc. It will reveal itself in families by a "sword in the house" for many a long year (1 Sam. iii. 13, 14; 2 Sam. vii. 14). It will be manifest in the individual. This κρίμα—yea, κατακρίμα—of God has three stages. 1. A present, though it may be a comparatively silent one, either in a stinging conscience, or one "seared as with a hot iron." 2. A further one, on the exchange of worlds, when earth and sense are thrown off, and the Great Invisible is near. "Now, Mr. T——," said a departing sinner to the missionary who was by his bedside, "my judgment has just begun!" 3. A future one, at the day of judgment, when God shall judge the secrets of men (cf. Matt. xxv. 31—46). Disobedient hearts are but treasuring up to themselves wrath against the day of wrath and revelation of the righteous judgment of God, to be disapproved, finally, by him from whose sentence there can be no appeal. Is not a heavy curse, indeed, involved in all that?

IX. HERE IS GROUND ENOUGH FOR SOLEMN APPEAL TO MEN. "I set before you this day a blessing and a curse." Oh! if men would but take the pains to quit a while in thought this busy scene in which they live and move almost in perpetual whirl; if they would but anticipate by earnest reflection that usherment into the presence of God which their departure hence must bring; if they would but set the judgment scene, as sketched by Christ, before their view, methinks they would see the deep and solemn reason why the preacher now—even now—says, "Flee from the wrath to come." For the wrath will come, i.e. it will manifest itself. It exists now. The eternal antagonism of a holy God to ill of every kind necessitates it. And as surely as God is ever on the side of right, so surely will he have it shown, ere long, that such is the case. Then let the sinner, condemned even now by his own conscience—how much more by God!—flee for refuge from the coming storm. There is a refuge; it is ours the moment that we flee to it. But if when the storm comes we are not found there, we must perish—perish with the double disapproval of Heaven on our heads: disapproved as breakers of law; disapproved as neglecters of grace.

HOMILIES BY VARIOUS AUTHORS.

Vers. 2—10, 18—22.—*Obligations arising from personal experience.* "Chastisement" (ver. 2) in its wide sense of discipline. The educative process by which God converted, or aimed at converting, the hordes who left Egypt into a nation of brave, free, God-fearing, self-respecting, obedient men and women. This education blended deliverance with judgment on their enemies; loving-kindness in the bestowal of mercies, with severe chastisements in cases of rebellion; attention to their necessities, with frequent exposure to adversity, and consequent trial of their faith and patience. They had been put to school with the Almighty as their Teacher; their lesson-book was the whole extraordinary series of occurrences in Egypt and the desert; the end of the training was to form them to obedience.

I. THREE PHASES OF GOD'S INSTRUCTION OF HIS CHURCH. 1. *The shattering of worldly power hostile to the Church* (vers. 3, 4). Pharaoh, in his pride and obstinacy, is a type of world-power universally, in its opposition to God's kingdom (Rom. ix. 17). But though again and again the waves have thus roared, and the floods have lifted up their voice (Ps. xciii, 3, 4), the Lord on high has shown himself mightier than the noise of many waters, yea, than the mighty waves of the sea (cf. Ps. lxxxiii.; Isa. xxxvii.; 1 Macc. iv.; Acts iv. 23—34; Rev. xix. 19; xx. 8, 9). 2. *The preservation and guidance of the Church itself* (ver. 5). In securing the perpetuation of a godly remnant in times of greatest apostasy (1 Kings xix. 18; Rom. xi. 5; Rev. iii. 5; xi. 3; xii. 17); in providing her with a succession of godly teachers (Matt. xxviii. 20; Eph. iv. 11—14); in supplying her necessities, spiritual (John vi. 32, 33; 1 Cor. x. 4; xii. 13; Eph. iii. 16; Phil. iv. 19) and temporal (Matt. x. 9, 10; Acts iv. 34; 1 Cor. ix. 14; Phil. iv. 15, 16); in opening up the path of duty (Acts xvi. 10; Rom. xv. 30, 31; 2 Cor. x. 12—17), in conducting her from one stage of attainment to another (Eph. iv. 12, 13). 3. *The overthrow of antichristian rebellion within the Church* (ver. 6). The insurrection of Korah and his company may be taken as representative of antichristian movements generally. These are bound to arise, but will infallibly be crushed (2 Thess. ii. 3—13; 1 John ii. 18; Rev. xvii.).

II. OBLIGATIONS ARISING FROM EXPERIENCE OF GOD'S WONDERFUL WORKS. The older portion of that generation had personally witnessed the wonderful works referred to. This gave them a certain advantage, and made disobedience doubly culpable. These works of God had been: (1) in origin, supernatural; (2) in kind, of stupendous magnitude; and (3) had extended over a long period of time. Those who have lived through any period signalized by remarkable workings of God on behalf of his Church, or whose individual experiences have been remarkable, may learn a lesson. Apply to reformation times, times of religious revival, of deliverance from persecutions, of the forth-putting of God's power in missions, etc. (2 Chron. xxxi. 25, 26; Ezra iii. 10—13; vi. 22; Esth. ix. 27; Ps. xl. 10; cxvi. 6—9; Acts xv. 12). Such experiences: 1. *Furnish peculiar evidences of God's grace and power, of the reality of his working in salvation and judgment.* These evidences, while not losing their value to later generations, are necessarily of greatest force to those who witness the events. 2. *Create impressions of God's character and attributes not so readily created by report.* It is much to hear of the wonderful works of God from credible witnesses, but hearing with the ear cannot equal, in impressiveness and force, seeing with the eye (Job xlii. 5). 3. *Imply a personal discipline which others have not had the benefit of.* The lessons of our experiences may be conveyed to posterity, but the results of them in personal character remain with ourselves. All this lays on those who have had such experiences very special responsibilities. These relate (1) to personal obedience (ver. 8); and (2) to the education of children (vers. 18—21). How are our children to know of God's mighty works in former days, or get the benefit of our own experiences; how are they to be convinced, moved, or instructed by these things, save as the result of diligent parental teaching? —J. O.

Vers. 10—18.—*Canaan and Egypt.* I. ITS CONTRAST WITH EGYPT. (Vers. 10, 11.) Not, like Egypt, a land rainless and artificially watered. It had no Nile. It drank in water from the rains of heaven. It was thus in a peculiar way a land dependent upon God. Egypt's fertility depended on God also, but less directly. Its contrivances for irrigation gave it, or might seem to give it, a semi-independence. Palestine was a land, on the contrary, whose peculiar conditions made it dependent for fruitfulness on the direct gift to it of rains from heaven. It was a land requiring a providential adjustment of conditions—a daily care—to make it yield the utmost it was capable of (ver. 12).

The truth here figured is that God wills the believer to put his life day by day under his immediate care. The worldly man may desire, and in a measure may be allowed to attain, a position of relative independence of God : he may get (within limits) the order-ing of his own plans and ways, and by ingenious contrivances and manipulations of laws of nature, he may think to put himself beyond the power of God's interference with him. But the godly man will neither desire this nor be content with it. He wishes God's eyes to be upon his lot day by day, " from the beginning of the year even unto the end of the year." There is, within the ordinary providence of God, a *special* providence to be recognized over God's people, over Christ's Church, and over nations that adhere to God's ways.

II. THE RESULTS OF THIS CONTRAST TO THE INHABITANTS. (Vers. 13—18.) The directness of the dependence of Canaan on God's care made it, to a greater degree than Egypt could have been, suitable for the operation of a system so intimately bound up with temporal rewards and punishments. Should the people prove obedient, God engages to bless them with rains, and make the land fruitful (vers. 13—16). But should they disobey, the peculiar conditions of the land put it in his power to scourge them, as he so often did, with drought and famine (1 Kings xvii. 1; Joel i.; Hag. i. 10, 11). So he threatens (vers. 16, 17). It is a blessed but a perilous position which God's people are called to occupy. It secures to them unwonted favours, but it exposes them also, if disobedient, to chastisements and punishments of a peculiarly direct and severe kind. The higher the position of nearness to God, the greater the responsibility which that position entails upon who enjoy it.—J. O.

Vers. 26—29.—*The great alternative.* I. GOD SUMMONS US TO DECISION. 1. His revelations *lay the ground for it.* " Light is come into the world " (John iii. 19). 2. They *demand it.* Men would trifle, but God says, " Now" (2 Cor. vi. 2). Men would put off, but God urges to decision (Josh. xxiv. 15). 3. They *shut men up to it.* When light comes, decision is inevitable. We must settle what our attitude towards it will be. In decreeing *not* to choose, we in reality *do* choose.

II. THE DECISION TO WHICH GOD SUMMONS US TURNS ON A SINGLE POINT. The point is obedience. Will we obey or will we not (ver. 27)? It was so under the Law, and it is so under the gospel. What the gospel asks from us is " the obedience of faith" (Rom. xvi. 26). This tests our disposition thoroughly. True faith carries with it the surrender of the will to God and Christ. It is the root and principle of all holy obedience. Men will not come to Christ ; why? The reason is that they cannot bring themselves to yield up their wills to him as he requires. They " love the darkness rather than the light " (John iii. 19—22). Refusal to decide for Christ is equivalent, for the time being, to deciding *against* him (Matt. xii. 30).

III. THE DECISION TO WHICH GOD SUMMONS US INVOLVES THE ALTERNATIVE OF A BLESSING AND A CURSE. That was what it came to then, and it is the same still. Blessing or curse ; life or death. Whether God is to be our God, blessing us, renew-ing our inward life, enriching us with his Spirit, bestowing on us grace here and glory hereafter ; or whether we are to live beneath his frown, withering up under it in body and soul, and vanishing at last into outer darkness. It is an old question whether a man can voluntarily choose what is for his hurt. Possibly he cannot without first listening to the tempter who bids him believe that the course he pursues will *not* be for his hurt. But none the less is every sinner taking the path which ends in destruc-tion (Matt. vii. 13). His interest, did he but see it, or would he but believe it, is entirely in the line which God wishes him to follow. The terminus of the one road is death (Rom. vi. 21), of the other life everlasting (Rom. xi. 22).—J. O.

Vers. 22—26.—*Vastness of promise.* An inspiring statement of what God would do for the obedient nation. Shining through it we see the promise to the Church. God promises—

I. VICTORY OVER ALL ENEMIES. (Ver. 23.) The strongest spiritual foes will go down if we cleave to God. Though greater and mightier than we, they shall be overthrown.

II. ENLARGEMENT OF BOUNDS. (Ver. 23.) They would grow numerous, fill the land, and spread beyond it. A wider prospect is held out to the Church. Her possession is the earth. If faithful, she has the means within herself to spread abroad her conquests, and occupy from sea to sea.

III. MORAL SUPREMACY. (Ver. 25.) Israel's power would be acknowledged—her influence felt. Men would dread her hostility. The felt presence of God in a man, or in a Church, has a power to inspire fear. Its awing effect is felt often where it is not acknowledged.—J. O.

Vers. 29, 30.—*Gerizim and Ebal* (cf. ch. xxvii.). This putting of the blessing and the curse on Gerizim and Ebal had significance—

I. AS A SOLEMN TRANSFERENCE OF THE BLESSING AND THE CURSE TO THE LAND OF POSSESSION. Blessing and curse, representing the award of eternal righteousness, must follow us so long as disobedience is possible. "If ye live after the flesh, ye shall die" (Rom. viii. 13). "That which beareth thorns and briers is rejected, and is nigh unto cursing; whose end is to be burned" (Heb. vi. 8). In heaven there is "no more curse" (Rev. xxii. 3), but only because, confirmed in holiness, God's servants can no more fall away.

II. AS A SOLEMN REMINDER OF THE TENURE ON WHICH THE LAND WAS HELD. We cannot render perfect obedience, but our duty is to aim at it. The condition of inheritance is that we are doers of the Father's will (Matt. vii. 21).

III. AS CONNECTED WITH A SOLEMN RENEWAL OF VOWS. Fitting on such occasions that both blessing and curse should be remembered.—J. O.

Vers. 1—7.—*Ocular demonstrations of God's nearness increase human responsibility.* Men disposed to scepticism often ask for clearer proof of the existence of God. But they deceive themselves. If they used well such evidence as they have, they would find it ample. We should not overlook the fact that the Hebrews, under Moses, and that the Jews in the days of Christ, had clearest demonstrations of God's presence. Yet they believed not; they were conspicuous examples of unbelief.

I. EXTERNAL EVIDENCES OF RELIGION HAVE BEEN SUPPLIED TO SOME PERSONS ABUNDANTLY. 1. *The Hebrews had every possible demonstration of God's existence.* The Most High deigned to reveal himself to the eye and to the ear, in forms adapted to produce complete conviction, and to overthrow all doubt. The people were more than content. They asked that such overpowering displays of the Godhead might be withdrawn. 2. *They were convinced of the regal power of Jehovah.* To resist *him* they plainly saw was an impossibility. Pharaoh was the personation of worldly power; yet Pharaoh and his captains and astrologers and host had been completely swept away by the breath of Jehovah's power. The irresistible might of Jehovah was as evident as their own existence. 3. *They saw that the Omnipotent God was the Friend of men.* That all the resources of Jehovah were employed on behalf of his friends, not one in the Hebrew camp could question. God had used every plan to persuade Pharaoh to yield compliance, and it was only after long waiting and repeated warning that vengeance was decreed. 4. *They had plainest proof of the judicial faithfulness of God.* For they had themselves suffered his chastisements. Resistance of Divine authority had been followed by judgment among the Hebrews, as among the Egyptians. Favouritism, exceptional treatment, escape from magisterial detection,—these things were out of question. The inviolable rectitude of God's administration was clear as noon-day.

II. EXTERNAL EVIDENCES SERVE AS A MEASURE OF RESPONSIBILITY. 1. *They satisfy all the requirements of intellect.* Responsibility depends on two things, viz. (1) sufficient information; (2) ability to obey. If between opposing probabilities there is the smallest preponderance in favour of belief in God, such balance of probability must determine our conduct. Hereafter, hesitation is criminal. Every piece of additional evidence is additional responsibility. It relieves us from the weakness of recurring doubt. God makes due allowance for deficient knowledge. "The times of human ignorance God winked at," *i.e.* overlooked. 2. *External demonstration does not ensure spiritual impression.* The diligent inquirer will find a thousand evidences of duty where an indolent man will see none. So where within a man feeling is susceptible, a tithe of existing knowledge will suffice to produce glad obedience. It is incumbent on men to *weigh well* all the evidence of religion they possess, and to respond, in feeling and affection and active effort, to every claim which conscience recognizes. 3. *It is a duty to ascertain our personal responsibility.* We may find benefit in comparing our privileged position with the position of others. If, with the measure of knowledge we possess, we are still rebellious, what is likely to be the conduct of those less privileged? If *we*, to whom special revelation has been made, waste the possession, will not our own children pronounce our condemnation, because we have denied to them the help of our testimony?

III. EXTERNAL EVIDENCES MAY ONLY INJURE OUR SOULS. 1. *Misuse of superior knowledge is a crime.* If God has condescended to give us instruction respecting himself and his purposes of mercy, it is sheer ingratitude on our part to neglect it. Blindness has deprived us of the highest good. 2. *Resistance of conscience does permanent injury to the soul.* The abuse of any material instrument is an injury. The conscience is an instrument of the soul's life. To neglect its magisterial voice is to make ourselves deaf. To resist its instincts is to strangle them. Not to act according to our enlightened reason, is to injure reason as an instrument. If we recklessly nip the first buds of affection, we necessarily destroy its proper fruit. In thoughtless resistance of truth, men are preparing the elements of a direful doom. While obedience to God makes a man strong, rebellion effeminates all the nobler powers of the soul. It enervates, corrupts, destroys. 3. *Unfaithfulness to convictions will necessitate severest retribution.* It is an ascertained fact that punishment will be in proportion to desert. The servant ignorant of his Lord's special requirements is counted worthy of some stripes; but he who knew his Lord's will, and flagrantly neglected it, is awarded "many stripes."

The mere possibility of Israel's unfaithfulness kindled the earnest anxiety of Moses.—D.

Vers. 8, 9.—*Obedience leads to prolonged possession.* We may learn here—

I. THAT COMMANDS MAY CARRY A SUPREME OBLIGATION, THOUGH SPOKEN BY MAN.

II. THAT OBEDIENCE IS VAIN, UNLESS IT COVERS THE WHOLE AREA OF DUTY.

III. THAT COMPLETE OBEDIENCE IMPARTS STRENGTH TO THE WHOLE MAN.

IV. THAT SUCH STRENGTH PRESSES INTO THE POSSESSION OF NEW KINGDOMS.

V. THAT THE OATH OF GOD, AND THE DEVOUT ACTIVITY OF MAN, CO-OPERATE FOR THE HIGHEST ACQUISITIONS.—D.

Vers. 10—17.—*Valuable possessions reserved for the righteous.* The land of Palestine has always been a coveted prize by the surrounding nations. Compared with the territory south and east, it possesses qualities of excellence and beauty. But its fertility depends upon the rain supply, and rain supply was suspended on righteous loyalty.

I. A MORAL PURPOSE UNDERLIES THE GEOLOGICAL CONFIGURATION OF OUR GLOBE. God can never experience surprise in the beneficial coincidences of events. "Known unto God are all his works from the beginning of the world." If heaven has been undergoing a process of preparation from a period anterior to the formation of our globe, we need feel no surprise that, in arranging the strata of the earth, God should have been animated with motives of righteous benevolence towards men. And if the structure of hill and valley is the visible projection of a generous moral purpose—a part of the plan for the religious education of men—we may conclude that all the forces and phenomena of nature have vital connection with the religious development of our race. Israel was sent into Canaan because amongst its hills and valleys its history and fortunes could best be unfolded.

II. GOD'S PATERNAL CARE OF MEN EXTENDS TO THE WHOLE OF THEIR ENVIRONMENT. The sagacious love of God condescends to every minutiæ of human life. Our God has infinite leisure for everything. His eyes are daily upon our farms and shops. He is our Bulwark and defends our coasts. He knoweth what we have need of.

III. THE RICHEST EARTHLY POSSESSION LEAVES MEN WHOLLY DEPENDENT ON GOD. Instead of our possessions liberating us from dependence on God, they increase our dependence; for *now* we need his protection for our property as well as for ourselves. Possessions (so called) are only channels through which true blessing flows, and our great business is to keep the channel clear. The hills of Canaan obtained their irrigation from the springs of heaven, and only obedient faith can unlock these springs.

IV. FILIAL OBEDIENCE SECURES MATERIAL PROSPERITY. Such prosperity is the picture and symbol of spiritual good. But material benefits were the only rewards which these Hebrews could appreciate. "Godliness is" still "profitable for *all* things." The source of all real prosperity is in heaven.

V. EVEN SECRET SIN SETS IN MOTION A SERIES OF GIGANTIC EVILS. The heart is easily taken by semblances and promises of good. The falsehoods of Satan are very plausible. A sentinel needs to be placed at every portal of the soul. Self-deception ends in total destruction. We do not sin alone, nor suffer alone.—D.

Vers. 18—21.—*God's Word potent to dominate the whole life.* The Word of God, like light, is diffusive. It propagates itself. So long as its proper field of activity is unoccupied, it must spread. It radiates its magnetic influence on every side.

I. TRUTH, POSSESSING THE HEART, BECOMES THE FOUNT OF ALL RIGHTEOUS PRINCIPLE. As the pulverized soil is the proper home of seed; as the housewife's dough is the proper home of leaven; so the heart of man is the proper abode of truth. On stony tablets, in books, or in speech, it is only in transit towards its proper destination. Received and welcomed into the soul, it begins a process of blessed activity; it vitalizes, ennobles, beautifies every part of human nature. It is the seed of all virtue and goodness—the root of immortal blessedness.

II. RIGHTEOUS PRINCIPLE DOMINATES ALL OUR ACTIVE POWERS. The hand is the servant of the heart. What the mind plans, the hand executes. To bind God's precepts upon our hands is to remind ourselves that the hand, as the representative of active faculty, belongs to God. Embargo is laid upon it to do no violence to others' persons or to others' property. It must not strike nor steal, for it has become an instrument sacred to God. Nor must it be defiled with idleness, for it is the property of him who incessantly works, nor may the eye wantonly wander after forbidden objects. The eye led Eve into transgression. "Let thine eye look straight before thee." "Look not upon the wine when it sparkles in the cup." The eye is a potent instrument for evil or for good.

III. RIGHTEOUS PRINCIPLE, SPRINGING OUT OF LOVE OF TRUTH, MAKES US WITNESSES FOR GOD. As on the high priest's forehead there was inscribed the motto, "Holiness unto the Lord;" so, in substance, the same truth is written on every servant of God. He is a consecrated man. His finely arched brow is his glory, and his glory is devoted to God. In every circumstance he desires to magnify his God. His house is God's house; hence on gate and lintel the precepts of God are conspicuous. Hospitality and contentment, peace and kindness, dwell there, for it is the home of God.

IV. RIGHTEOUS PRINCIPLE MOULDS POSTERITY. What we are, in great measure our children will be. Moral qualities are entailed. In their tender years, their young nature is plastic and impressible. If our hearts are full of God's truth, it will rise and overflow our lips as water from a well. Far from being an irksome task to speak God's truth, it will be a pleasurable instinct. All time, from early morn till evening repose, will be too short to utter all God's truth. "Living epistles" describe the office of the godly.

V. RIGHTEOUS PRINCIPLE SECURES PERMANENT ENJOYMENT. Truth in the heart is translated into righteousness in the life, and righteousness makes heaven. No enjoyment can be perfect in which our children do not share; and in sharing our joys with our children, we multiply our joys beyond all arithmetical measure. Such days of consecrated service will be "days of heaven upon earth."—D.

Vers. 22—25.—*He who best serves is most fit to rule.* Golden links of life unite our pious love with universal conquest. "All things become ours, if we are Christ's."

I. LOYAL OBEDIENCE GENERATES LOVE. It is quite true that love is the mother of obedience; it is also true that obedience fosters and intensifies love. The earth receives heat from the sun, but it gives out heat likewise. The sentiment of love in the breast will dwindle and die unless it have practical exercise. Diligent and thoughtful service will bring us nearer God, make God more precious to us, and bind us to him in tenderer bonds. There is an interlacement of affection. Our desires send deep their roots in God, and an indissoluble alliance is the result.

II. UNION WITH GOD SECURES HIS PRACTICAL AID. We are required "to cleave to him." The effect is that he will cleave to us, and prove a real Ally, an almighty Helper. He will drive out all our foes for us, however great and mighty they be. Our foes become his foes. He identifies himself with our cause; or, what is the same thing, we identify ourselves with *his*.

III. DIVINE ASSISTANCE MAKES US ALL-CONQUERING. " No man shall be able to stand before us." Good men will be drawn to us in sacred friendship; bad men will be held fast in the mysterious spell of awe. We shall be known as the friends and allies of God; and, in proportion as we are like him, men will feel for us the dread they feel for God.

IV. SUCH VALIANT STRENGTH WILL INTRODUCE US TO UNIVERSAL INHERITANCE. " Every place whereon the soles of our feet shall tread shall be ours." In such covenant alliance with God, we shall walk through his universe as " *his 'heirs.*" Every element of material substance, every event in time, every circumstance and experience, shall conduce to our profit. The world shall be laid under tribute to our best life. We shall extract advantage and joy from adversity itself.—D.

Vers. 26—32.—*Startling alternatives.* Our life is hourly a choice of alternatives. We can go to the right or to the left. Choice is incessantly demanded, and the issues of our choice are momentous.

I. THE REVELATION OF GOD'S WILL MAY BE A SOURCE OF ABSOLUTE BLESSING. Such revelation is the disclosure of man's true paradise. It is the opening of the door of God's own palace; and, unworthy though we are, we may enter and find rest. To do God's will is to be Christ-like—is to be a true son, and to possess a son's joy. Every step we take along that way of obedience is a step nearer God, from whose smile we obtain exquisite pleasure, and in whose society we find our heaven.

II. WE CANNOT REMAIN THE SAME, AFTER OBTAINING THE KNOWLEDGE OF GOD'S WILL AS WE WERE BEFORE. Necessity requires that we should be either better or worse. You cannot dwell for an hour in the society of a good man, and continue in the former state of feeling. The fire that does not melt, hardens. To know God's will, and not to do it, inflicts unspeakable mischief upon the soul. Resistance of inward convictions begets callosity of heart, and blasts the budding life of conscience. Wanton treason against God is incipient hell. It is the darkening of the understanding, and the en-slavement of the will. No blacker curse can enwrap a man than this.

III. MATERIAL NATURE FORECASTS THE ALTERNATIVES OF BLESSING OR WOE. The visible universe is a projection of God's thought, and all the forces of nature are the agents of God. We find upon this globe elements that minister to our development and strength and joy. We find also elements that are repulsive, menacing, and destructive. The cloud-capped peaks may draw around us the lightnings of vengeance, or may melt the laden cloud and distil showers of blessing. The twin mountains of Ebal and Gerizim were baptized as perpetual preachers of life and death. We may find " sermons in stones," lessons in leaves, counsels in running brooks.

IV. MATERIAL POSSESSIONS ARE NOT ABSOLUTE BLESSINGS. God here distinctly assures the Hebrews that they shall enter Canaan; but whether they should dwell under the frowning peaks of Ebal, or on the sunny slopes of Gerizim, was suspended on their loyal obedience. Even to the possessors of the promised land, there stood the dark possibility of the curse. Neither money nor learning makes a man; it is the power to use it.—D.

Vers. 1—9.—*Divine judgments upon others, to ensure obedience in us.* Moses wishes to bring all possible motive to bear upon the people to secure their obedience in Canaan. He has just been speaking of their national development from a family of seventy to a multitude as numerous as the stars. Such a blessing should encourage them to love the Lord their God, and to ." keep his charge, and his statutes, and his judgments, and his commandments, alway." Obedience is thus founded upon *gratitude*, which is God's invariable p'an.

But in these verses before us, Moses takes what we may call the *converse* method. He calls up in succession the judgments with which God visited both the Egyptians and their own forefathers on account of disobedience. He calls upon them to recognize (וַיִּדְעֶם) the "chastisement" (מוּסַר) with which God had signalized the disobedience of the Egyptians and of the Israelites. The following lessons are in these verses suggested.

I. GRATITUDE IS THE FOUNDATION OF NEW OBEDIENCE. This is God's plan. He does not say, "Obey, and I will save you for your obedience," but "Take salvation as a free gift, and then obey me as a matter of gratitude." "If ye love me, keep my commandments." He secures the love by sovereign mercy, and receives obedience as his return upon his investment. Obedience is God's dividend upon his investment of love.

Those who would make "good works" the *root* of salvation instead of the *fruit* of salvation, are reversing the whole procedure of God.

II. GRATITUDE MAY BE REINFORCED BY A STUDY OF THE CONSEQUENCES OF INGRATITUDE IN OTHERS. For what God strikes at is ingratitude. The Egyptians were ungrateful. They should have recognized God's *mercy* in their fertile land, in their civilization and advancement, in the mission of Moses, and in the character of the earlier plagues. God had visited Egypt with his love—love which was undeserved, love which remained unrequited. When he revealed "his greatness, his mighty hand, and his stretched out arm," it was against Egypt's ingratitude and consequent disobedience. The *dénouement* at the Red Sea was judgment upon ingratitude and persevering impiety.

Now, the study of all this, here recommended by Moses, was well fitted to foster gratitude in the hearts of the Israelites. Here was unrequited love receiving its vindication in the series of disasters which culminated in the Red Sea. "We must be thankful," they might well say, "that our ingratitude in past years has not been similarly treated, and for the coming time we must cultivate gratitude and the obedience it secures."

III. GRATITUDE MAY ALSO BE REINFORCED BY A STUDY OF THE CONSEQUENCES OF SELF-CONFIDENCE. For this seems to be the idea of Moses in bringing forward the case of Dathan and Abiram. As descendants of Reuben, the firstborn of Jacob, they imagined that they had the right to the *primacy* in Israel. Hence they disputed the rights of Moses and of the priestly line of Aaron. They insisted on their right of *primogeniture* as valid in the government of God.

But God recognizes no such personal claims, and he visited the presumption with swift destruction. The study of this "chastisement" would deliver Israel from all confidence in themselves. They would recognize that personal claims are not accepted by a sovereign God; that in consequence they must in humility approach him, thankful for spared lives and continued mercy, and anxious to testify by obedience to their genuine thankfulness.

IV. OBEDIENCE WILL BE FOUND TO BE THE SECRET OF STRENGTH AND SUCCESS IN THE INVASION. For while obedience rests on gratitude, it elicits gratitude from God. If God expects us to be grateful for his love, he shows us the example in being grateful for ours. "I love them that love me," he says (Prov. viii. 17); and again, "He that hath my commandments, and keepeth them, he it is that loveth me: and he that loveth me shall be loved of my Father, and I will love him, and will manifest myself to him" (John xiv. 21; see also ver. 23). Now, this is what we do not hesitate to call *Divine gratitude.*

Hence Israel found that obedience rendered thankfully to God received a grateful reward from him in strength to invade and conquer the land of Canaan, and, secondly, in strength to prolong their days in it. A similar experience is realized by God's servants still. Obedience is rewarded graciously and gratefully. Strength is found equal to our day, as we make our pilgrimage to God. How important, then, to obey from a proper motive, and at the same time to receive with proper delight the gracious return which a grateful God bestows!—R. M. E.

Vers. 10—17.— *The land of promise.* Moses now proceeds to indicate the characteristics of Canaan, and to contrast it with Egypt, which they had left. Egypt is not dependent upon the rains of heaven as Canaan is. The overflowing Nile has only to be guided along the water-courses in the proper season, and the fertility of the Nile valley is secured. The work of irrigation, the watering with the foot (ver. 10), is the one thing needful in Egypt. But Canaan depends upon the continual care of God, his eyes being on it from the beginning to the end of the year, dispensing "the first rain and the latter rain," in order to the harvest. In Egypt, the blessing is given "wholesale"—the Nile brings down from the interior the water the valley needs. In Canaan, the mountain ridge between the Nile valley and the valley of the Euphrates, there is constant dependence experienced upon the bounties of heaven. This suggests— •

I. THAT CANAAN WAS A SPLENDID LAND IN WHICH TO TRAIN UP A SPIRITUAL PEOPLE. It was not naturally so fertile as either the valley of the Nile or the valley of the Euphrates. Hence famine touched it more quickly than either Egypt or Assyria. But it was fitted to foster dependence upon God and hope in him. If the inhabitants were obedient, then the land might flow with milk and honey; if disobedient, it might become brown and bare through the withholding of the rain.

Hence we find, in Egypt and in Assyria, a turning of the people to the worship of the *inorganic* and the *organic* forces of nature respectively. The valleys, being in some measure more independent of the changing seasons, seem to have nurtured independence of God; while the hills of Syria, like the Highlands of Scotland and of Switzerland, fostered more faith in the Supreme. "Those Syrian hills," says a living writer, "are the Spirit's throne, where, lifted above the deserts of earth, it sits nearest to heaven, while spread beneath it on either hand, resting on the desert's level as their home, are nature's twin provinces of matter and life, rich and green with the beauty and greenness of time, always imposing and often victorious in the region of sense; but doomed, like all things visible and temporal, to fall before the power which shall yet clothe itself with their glory, and which is itself unseen and eternal."

II. THE BLESSINGS WERE GUARANTEED ON CONDITION OF MAN LOYALLY CO-OPERATING WITH GOD. Canaan was no land for indolent lotus-eaters; it was not—

"A land where all things always seem'd the same!"

It was a land where man must co-operate with God in order to the blessing—a land where man realized the dignity of being a "fellow-worker with God." It would be a land of promise and of real blessing on no other condition.

If man were asked for no effort, if everything grew to please his taste and palate spontaneously, if daily bread came without even the trouble of asking, it would be a land of danger and of moral death. Better was it for Israel to have themselves bound by a wholesome destiny to dependence on God and co-operation with him, than if the land bore spontaneously all man's needs.

III. WE NEED LOOK FOR NO OTHER LAND OF PROMISE IN THIS WORLD OR THE NEXT. The idea of "independence" is the great danger of the human heart. We would be indebted to nobody, not even God, if we could. Alas, for our pride! Now, it so happens that we cannot become independent of God's bounty, no matter how hard we try. And it is best so. The land of promise is the land where we depend *humbly* upon God, and are thus most independent of persons and things around us.[1] The land of promise is where we do our honest share of public work, and get our share of the fruits of industry.

And in the life beyond death we need not desire an inglorious idleness, which is some folk's notion of "everlasting rest," but we shall have there the privilege of serving God "day and night in his temple." A life of consecration is the true "land of promise." It is the only deep enjoyment, it is the only worthy inheritance.

Let us then resolve (1) to trust God so lovingly as never to harbour even in thought the hope of independence of him; and (2) to co-operate with him as life's highest privilege and honour. We have entered "the land of promise" when we have learned to trust God; and we are enjoying it when we have learned to be "fellow-workers with him."—R. M. E.

Vers. 18—25.—*Family training an element of success.* As in ch. vi. 6—25, Moses again insists on the words of God being preserved among the people by faithful family instruction. The "home school" is, in fact, the great factor in national success. Education must give due prominence to the family institution, as the providential unit of mankind. And here let us notice—

I. GOD'S WORDS ARE TO BE RECEIVED FIRST OF ALL INTO THE HEART. It is when individuals, and especially parents, receive God's testimony into the heart, as Lydia did

---

[1] Cf. Sir Henry Taylor's 'Notes from Life,' Essay ii., 'Humility and Independence.'

(Acts xvi. 14), that it is likely to bloom out in a fitting public profession. It is "with the heart man believeth unto righteousness," and then "with the mouth confession is made unto salvation" (Rom. x. 10). As the ark received the tables of the Law, so the heart of man is to be the depository of the Divine commandments.

II. GOD'S WORDS ARE TO BE KEPT BEFORE OUR OWN EYES AND THE EYES OF OTHERS. This seems to be the idea about the frontlets between the eyes—in this way others had the words displayed for their benefit; whereas the placing them upon the hand was for the individual's own memorial (cf. Isa. xlix. 16). So the person heartily interested in God's Word will make arrangements to remind himself continually of it, and also to keep it before the minds of others. Religion thus becomes not only a constant personal experience, but a constant public profession.

III. GOD'S WORDS ARE TO BE THE STAPLE OF HOME TRAINING. The children are to be taught them at home, when the "home school" is gathered together. God's words are also to be the staple of conversation when parents and children are enjoying their saunters together. And the first thought of the morning and the last at night should be of God's commandments. In this way the indoctrination of the rising generation is to be secured. Well would it be for us still if these old Jewish rules were practised.

IV. THE HOUSEHOLD IS TO MAKE PUBLIC PROFESSION OF RELIGION AS WELL AS THE INDIVIDUAL. Some individuals content themselves with a personal concern in religion, and are willing to be members of a household which does not collectively identify itself with God. But the Jew was to write God's commandments on the doorposts and on the gates of his house. The household was thus to be God's. The fact is that households need conversion just as individuals do. There is as much difference between a religious household and a worldly one as there is between a converted and an unconverted individual. The direction given consequently to the Jews covered the household as well as the person, and was thus perfect.

V. THE RESULT OF SUCH FAITHFULNESS WILL BE COMPLETE SUCCESS. The Lord engages to drive out the nations from before them, even though they be greater and mightier than Israel. He will make the obedient ones resistless. He will make the fear of them to fall like a nightmare on their enemies, and not one of them will be able to stand before them.

And surely all this is but a type of the *success* which still waits upon God's obedient people. Not, of course, that temporal success is the form of success desired or granted now. Many of God's people continue poor, but they succeed in life nevertheless. When they have grace to show a contented spirit amid their limited resources, they succeed in demonstrating that God is all-sufficient, and are the best testimony to the reality of religion before men. When the saints can sing with Habakkuk, "Although the fig tree shall not blossom," etc., "yet I will rejoice in the Lord, I will joy in the God of my salvation" (Hab. iii. 17, 18), they have really prospered in all life's essentials. It is thus in various ways the Lord fulfils his covenant engagements, and makes all that his people do to prosper (Ps. i. 3).

Obedience is consequently the charter of success. But we leave to our loving Father to determine what our success will be. We do not insist on its assuming the form of gold and silver, venison and champagne. The success of self-conquest, the success of being public benefactors, the success of serving our generation by the will of God ere we fall on sleep,—this is better far than the success of invading hosts with the laurels dipped in gore.

> "Not fruitless is thy toil
> If thou my cross wouldst bear;
> I do but ask thy willing heart,
> To grave my image there.

> "For each net vainly cast,
> Stronger thine arm will prove;
> The trial of thy patient hope
> Is witness of thy love.

"The time, the place, the way,
　　Are open to mine eye;
　I sent them—not to gather spoil—
　　To labour patiently." [1]

R. M. E.

Vers. 26—32.—*Life's solemn alternative.* Moses here sums up his exhortation with the alternative of a blessing or a curse. Obedience secures the blessing; disobedience the curse. He also directs them to go through a solemn service when they reach Mounts Gerizim and Ebal, by pronouncing the blessings and the curses from these mountains respectively. By the law of association, the very landscape was to witness to the truth of God. We are here reminded of such lessons as these—

I. God's MINISTERS, LIKE MOSES, ARE CONSTANTLY TO SET BEFORE THE PEOPLE THE SOLEMN ALTERNATIVE OF A BLESSING OR A CURSE. The gospel is the offer of a blessing to those who are willing to trust God as he asks them to do; while, on the other hand, it is of necessity backed up by a threatened curse, if men refuse to trust him, and will not humble themselves before him. Each one chooses for himself either the blessing or the curse, and there is no use in laying the blame on others.

II. THE REJECTION OF THE GOSPEL IS AFTER ALL A PREFERENCE OF OTHER GODS TO THE ONLY LIVING AND TRUE GOD. The idolatry which was the danger and temptation of Israel is reproduced in all who reject the mercy manifested in Christ. Some other object of worship has really been selected; the ·world, or wealth, or self, or power is expected to do for the unbelieving soul what God alone can. His attributes are made over to these creatures, and a false confidence takes the place which the true should occupy. Unbelief is really idolatry at bottom.

III. THE SOCIAL STUDY OF GOD'S PROMISES AND THREATENINGS IS MOST IMPORTANT. Moses, to impress the people more, directs them to assemble at Gerizim and Ebal, and there, dividing into two congregations, to go through the blessings and the curses publicly. The solemnities of that occasion would doubtless be greatly sanctified. In the very same way, the private study of God's Word is not sufficient. "The Lord loveth the gates of Zion more than all the dwellings of Jacob" (Ps. lxxxvii. 2). The solemn and leisurely study of God's Word in public is owned more than any private study of the Word can be. Both are needful, but our expectation should be highest in connection with the public preaching of God's Word. When a minister takes the people in an interesting manner through the truth contained in a paragraph, or even in a verse, there is much more realized than in the more hurried private reading. The sanctions of social worship are most important, and he is not in a safe way who despises them.

IV. NATURAL ASSOCIATIONS MAY OFTEN BE HELPFUL TO THE CAUSE OF TRUTH. Scenes of great historic deeds become in a measure sanctified. They are "holy places" to the human race. Battle-fields, birthplaces, senates, forums, as well as churches, become hallowed to the historic mind. The laws of association secure a perennial influence. The soul must be dead indeed who can visit such scenes unmoved.

It was this law of association which Moses brought into play in connection with Gerizim and Ebal. Never afterwards would they be visited by the descendants of these Israelites without a solemn feeling, and a recall of some at least of the blessings and the curses uttered there. Without any sympathy, therefore, with the "consecration" of places as generally understood, which may savour largely of superstition, we cannot but admit that natural associations should not be disregarded. Indeed, it is in this way the world is becoming richer with the years. Places are becoming every year associated with noble deeds—*Gerizims* are being multiplied as scenes of blessing; on the other hand, *Ebals* are also increasing, like beacons, on the dangerous places of human experience; but both undoubtedly meant by Providence to influence for good, and, through the law of association, our race. And some souls have "the place of mercy" marked clearly in their experience, and can sing—

"Oh, sacred hour! oh, hallowed spot,
　Where love Divine first found me!

[1] 'The Shadow of the Rock, and other Religious Poems,' p. 132.

Wherever falls my distant lot,
My heart will linger round thee.
And when from earth I rise to soar
Up to my home in heaven,
Down will I cast my eyes once more
Where I was first forgiven." [1]

R. M. E.

EXPOSITION.

ANNOUNCEMENT OF PARTICULAR LAWS.

CHAPTER XII.—CHAPTER XXVI.

Moses, having in his first address cast a glance at the events which had transpired between Sinai and the plains of Moab, and in his second recapitulated what had happened at Sinai, repeated the Decalogue, and urgently counselled the people to be obedient to the Divine commandment, and steadfast in their adherence to Jehovah as their God and King; proceeds now to set forth certain laws which it specially behoved them to observe. These are for the most part the same as those already recorded in the previous books; but a few are new, and are to be found only here. No special order or plan of exposition is here observed; the speaker uses that freedom of discourse which was fitting in a popular address. One or two historical narratives are interpolated; but the address as a whole is hortatory, and is designed to direct to the proper regulation of the ecclesiastical, social, and domestic life of the Israelites when they should be settled in Canaan.

CHAPTER XII.

PLACES AND MONUMENTS OF IDOLATRY TO BE DESTROYED; JEHOVAH TO BE WORSHIPPED IN THE ONE PLACE WHICH HE SHALL CHOOSE; INSTRUCTIONS AS TO THE USE OF FLESH FOR FOOD; AND CAUTIONS AGAINST BEING ENSNARED INTO FOLLOWING THE HEATHEN IN THEIR MANNER OF SERVICE.

Ver. 1.—**These are the statutes and judgments** (cf. ch. iv. 1; vi. 1). Moses, as the servant of God, had taught Israel statutes and rights, as God had commanded him (ch. iv. 5); and now he recapitulates the principal of these for their guidance in the way of obedience. These they were to observe all the days of their life upon the land that was to be given them; the land was the Lord's, and there, as long as they possessed it, the Law of the Lord was to be paramount.

Vers. 2, 3.—In order to this, Israel was, as soon as the land was possessed, to destroy all the objects and means of idolatrous worship in the land. **Upon the high mountains, and upon the hills, and under every green tree** (cf. Isa. lvii. 7; Jer. ii. 20; iii. 6; xvii. 2; Hos. iv. 13; 2 Kings xvi. 4; xvii. 10). The heathen had their places of worship on lofty elevations, probably because they imagined they were thus nearer to the object of their worship; and they sought also the shade of woods or thick-foliaged trees (Ezek. vi. 13), under which to perform their rites, as tending to inspire awe, and as in keeping with the mysterious character of their rites. These places of heathen worship in Canaan the Israelites were utterly to destroy, along with the images of their deities and other objects of idolatrous worship. **Burn their groves;** *their asherahs,* idol-pillars of wood (cf. ch. vii. 5).

Vers. 4—6.—The heathen placed their altars and offered their worship wherever they thought fit, according to their notions of the deity and his service; but Israel was not to do so unto Jehovah their God: he himself would choose the places where he was to be worshipped, and there alone might they come with offering and service. As the revealed God—the God whose being and perfections had been made known, not by a vague revelation of him in nature merely, but expressly by his putting or recording his Name historically and locally among men (cf. Exod. xx. 24)—so should there be a definite place chosen and appointed by him where he would come to receive the worship of his people, where he would record his Name, and where he would be known for a Refuge and a Helper to all who put their trust in him (Ps. xlviii. 3; lxxvi. 1, etc.; Dan. ix. 18). The Name of God is God himself as revealed; and he puts his Name on any place where he specially manifests himself as present (cf.

[1] From Randolph's selections, entitled 'Unto the Desired Haven,' p. 119.

1 Kings viii. 29), and which is consequently to be regarded as his habitation or dwelling-place. Hence the temple at Jerusalem was in later times known as the place of the Name of Jehovah (Isa. xviii. 7), the dwelling-place of his glory (Ps. xxvi. 8). But he is the God of the whole earth, and therefore, wherever he is pleased to reveal himself, in whatever place he makes his Name to be known, there he is to be worshipped. There is no reference in this passage to the temple at Jerusalem specially, as some have supposed; what is here enjoined is only a practical application of the Divine promise, that in *all* places where God would record his Name, there he would come to bless his people (Exod. xx. 24). The reference here, therefore, is quite general, and applies to any place where, by the Divine appointment, the tabernacle might be set up and the worship of Jehovah instituted. **Unto his habitation shall ye seek.** To seek to any place means, primarily, to resort to it, to frequent it (cf. 2 Chron. i. 5), but with the implied purpose of inquiring there for something, as for responses or oracles, when the place resorted to was that in which God had put his Name.

Ver. 6.—To the appointed place all their sacrificial gifts and offerings were to be brought, and there they were to keep their holy feasts. The gifts are classified in groups. 1. **Burnt offerings and sacrifices,** the two principal kinds of altar offerings, with which meal offerings and drink offerings were united (Numb. xv. 4, etc.). 2. **Tithes and heave offerings** (cf. Lev. xxvii. 30—33; Numb. xviii. 21—24). The heave offerings are described as **of your hand,** either because offered by the offerer's own hand, or to indicate such gifts as were made off-hand (so to speak), voluntary offerings made in addition to the legal offerings from an immediate impulse of grateful emotion. 3. **Vows and freewill offerings,** sacrifices which were offered in consequence of vows or of spontaneous impulse (cf. Lev. vii. 16; xxii. 21; xxiii. 38; Numb. xv. 3; xxix. 39). 4. **Firstlings of their herds and of their flocks** (cf. Exod. xiii. 2, 12, etc.; Numb. xviii. 15, etc.).

Ver. 7.—**And there ye shall eat before the Lord.** The injunction here and in ver. 17, respecting the eating by the offerer of the firstlings of his flocks and herds, appears to be inconsistent with the injunction in Numb. xviii. 18. There it seems as if the *whole* of the flesh was to be given to the priest. "And the flesh of them shall be thine [the priest's], as the wave breast and as the right shoulder are thine." This may be taken to mean that just as the wave breast and the right shoulder are the perquisites of the priests in the case of other offerings, as *e.g.* the peace offering, so in the case of the firstling offering the whole flesh shall be the priest's; and thus taken, the passage presents an unquestionable discrepancy to that in Deuteronomy. But probably the passage is not to be so taken. The particle translated "as" (כְּ) not unfrequently occurs in the sense of "according to, after the manner of," implying conformity to some rule or model (Gen. xliv. 2; Exod. xxi. 9; xxxix. 8; Lev. v. 10; Numb. viii. 4; ix. 3; xxix. 18; Ps. vii. 18; Zech. ii. 10 [6], etc.). The passage, therefore, may be rendered thus: *And the flesh of them shalt thou take after the manner (or according to the rule)*, of the wave breast, etc., *i.e.* not the whole of it, but only these parts. So the LXX. seem to have taken the passage: καὶ τὰ κρέα ἔσται σοι, καθὰ καὶ τὸ στηθύνιον τοῦ ἐπιθέματος· καὶ κατὰ τὸν βραχίονα τὸν δεξιὸν σοι ἔσται. Of some of the offerings the whole was received by the priest, as in the case of the sin offering and trespass offering (Lev. vi. 25, etc.; vii. 1, etc.); while of others only certain portions, viz. the wave breast and the heave shoulder, were given to him, as in the case of the peace offering (Lev. vii. 28, etc.). The purport of the law in Numb. xviii. 18 is that, in respect of the firstling offering, the allotment to the priest shall be after the same manner as in the peace offering. There is thus no discrepancy between the two passages. The animal belonged originally to the offerer; when he brought it before the Lord part of it was consumed on the altar, part of it was assigned to the priest, and the rest, as a matter of course, remained with himself. The law in Numbers, addressed to the priest, intimates what *he* might claim as his portion; the law in Deuteronomy, where the people are addressed, directs them how to use the portion that remained with *them*. It may be added that, even supposing that all the flesh was given to the priest, yet, as it had to be consumed on the day in which the sacrifice was offered, and as every clean person in the house might partake of it, it is almost certain that the offerer would, as a matter of course, share in the meal, as was usual in the case of sacrificial meals. **Rejoice in all that ye put your hand unto;** enjoy whatever your hand may gain, whatever you may earn, all the good which the Lord may give you (cf. ver. 18; xv. 10; xxiii. 20; xxviii. 8, 20). The phrase is peculiar to Deuteronomy; but comp. Gen. iii. 22; Isa. xi. 14.

Vers. 8—10.—In the wilderness, while leading a nomadic life, no certain place could be appointed to them for the observance of sacred rites; each man did in that matter as suited his own convenience. But after they were settled in Canaan it should no longer be so; a certain order and fixed locality should be determined for their worship and service; when they had passed over Jordan the Lord would give them rest from all their enemies, and then all irrregularity and arbitrariness in the matter of worship must cease, and all their gifts and offerings must be brought to the place which Jehovah their God should choose. Ye dwell in safety; rather, *dwell securely*, not only safe from assault, but without fear or anxiety (cf. Judg. vii. 11; xviii. 7).

Ver. 11.—All your choice vows; *i.e.* all the vows of your choice, all that ye choose to make; the vow was purely voluntary; it became obligatory only after it was made.

Ver. 12.—Of their offerings they should make a festive meal for themselves and their household; and of this the Levite who might happen at the time to be resident among them was to partake. Rejoice before the Lord. This phrase occurs frequently in this book (ch. xiv. 26; xvi. 11, 14; xxvi. 11; xxvii. 7); elsewhere it appears only once—Lev. xxiii. 40, where it is used with reference to the Feast of Tabernacles. Moses now enjoins this festivity to be observed in connection with all the sacrificial meals. The Levite that is within your gates. The Levites had no share in the land as the property of their tribe; but they had towns allotted to them among the different tribes (Numb. xxxv.), so that in this way they were dispersed through the nation. Hence, perhaps, they are described as "within the gates" of the rest of the people. Or, as the Levites seem to have itinerated in the discharge of various offices among the people, the phrase may designate them as on this account occasionally resident among others in their community; just as "the stranger that is within thy gates" means the person of some other nation who for the time being was resident in any of the towns of Israel.

Vers. 13—16.—They were to beware of offering sacrifice in any place that might seem to them best; their offerings were to be presented only in that place which God should choose. But this did not imply that they were not to kill and eat in their own abodes whatever they desired for food, according to the blessing of Jehovah their God. Only they were to abstain from eating of blood (cf. Gen. ix. 4; Lev. vii. 26); that they were to pour on the earth as if it were water. Burnt offering; this is named *instar omnium*, as the principal offering. Whatsoever thy soul lusteth after. To "lust," in old English, means simply to will, choose, desire; it is the same word as "list," or, as it is sometimes spelt, "lest," and does not, as now, imply anything evil. As of the roebuck, and as of the hart; probably the gazelle and fallow deer. As these

were animals that could not be offered in sacrifice, the distinction between clean and unclean, on the part of the eaters, did not come into consideration.

Vers. 17—19.—(Cf. vers. 6, 7, 12.) Thou mayest not eat; literally, *thou art not able to eat;* i.e. there is a legal inability to this. So the verb to be able (יָכֹל) is frequently used (cf. Gen. xliii.; Numb. ix. 6; ch. xvi. 5; xvii. 15, etc.).

Ver. 20.—When the Lord thy God shall enlarge thy border. These laws were to continue in force even when God should, according to his promise (Gen. xv. 18; Exod. xxiii. 27—31), extend the boundaries of their land.

Vers. 21—23.—If the place ... be too far from thee; this supplies the reason for the alteration of the law in Lev. xvii. 3. Only be sure; literally, *only be strong;* i.e. be firm and resolute, steadfastly resisting the temptation to eat it. The blood is the life (cf. Gen. ix. 4; Lev. xi. 1; xvii. 11). The word used is *nephesh* (נֶפֶשׁ). By this word the Hebrews designated the animal life-principle in men and in beasts; and as without this the body was a mere inert mass, the word came to be used for "life" generally. Of this life the blood was believed to be the seat, and was regarded as the symbol, so that to shed blood was tantamount to the taking away of life. As the blood, moreover, was the life, in it was supposed to lie the propitiatory power—the power, when shed, of atoning for sin, as the giving of life for life. The prohibition of eating it doubtless had respect to this. It was not merely to prevent ferocity in men towards the lower animals (as Rosenmüller suggests) that the eating of blood was interdicted, but specially because there was in this a sort of profanation, a putting to a common use of what appertained to a sacred rite.

Vers. 26, 27.—The holy things; *i.e.* the offerings prescribed by the Law; "hallowed things" (Numb. xviii. 8; cf. Lev. xxi. 22). Which thou hast; literally, *which are to thee;* i.e. which are binding on thee. Thy burnt offerings, the flesh and the blood; *i.e.* the flesh and the blood of the burnt offerings which were to be laid upon the altar (Lev. i. 5—9). The blood of thy sacrifices (*zebachim*) shall be poured out upon the altar. This refers to the ritual of the *shelamim*, or peace offering (Lev. iii. 2, 8, 13). The word *zebach* (זֶבַח) is never used in the Pentateuch of an atoning sacrifice (Oehler, 'Theology of the Old Testament,' ii. 2); it is used only of such offerings as furnished a sacrificial meal; hence it is added here, and thou shalt eat the flesh.

Vers. 29, 30.—Here the speaker reverts

to the admonition with which he began this part of his address (ver. 2); and warns the people against having any intercourse with the Canaanites in their idolatrous practices. **That thou enquire not after their gods.** It was a general belief among the heathen that to ignore or neglect the deities of a country was sure to bring calamity (cf. 2 Kings xvii. 26); hence the need of cautioning the Israelites against *inquiring* after the gods of the Canaanites when they should be settled in their land.

Ver. 31.—**For even their sons and their daughters have they burnt in the fire to their gods.** Elsewhere the phrase used is "make to pass through the fire " (ch. xviii. 10), or simply " make to pass through to Molech" (Lev. xviii. 21; Jer. xxxii. 35).

This has led some to maintain that the ceremony described was merely a februation, a lustration by fire, and not an actual burning alive of these victims; but there can be no doubt that both among the Ammonites and the Phœnicians, and indeed wherever the worship of Baal or Molech was followed, the offering of children in sacrifice by burning prevailed (Münter, 'Religion der Karthager,' p. 18, 2nd edit.; Selden, 'De Diis Syris Syntag,' i. c. 6, pp. 93, 257, edit. Beyer, Amst., 1680).

Ver. 32.—The admonition in this verse is best regarded as forming an intermediate link between this chapter and the following, " closing what goes before and introductory to what follows" (Keil).

HOMILETICS.

Vers. 1—32.—*Regulations for Divine worship: specific rules embodying permanent principles.* With this twelfth chapter an entirely new set of instructions begins. Up to this point the exhortations have been for the most part moral: now they are positive. Hitherto the precepts have been, speaking generally, concerning duties which God commanded because they were right; but from this point they concern duties which became right because God had commanded them. Of all specific directions which Moses gave to Israel, none could possibly be more important than those which had to do with the Divine worship. A true, wise, spiritual worship, established and maintained, would do very much to ensure Israel's weal in every other respect; while if corruption was admitted and tolerated here, its ill effects would soon be seen through the length and breadth of their land. In dealing homiletically with this chapter, we must take it as a whole. To sever it into paragraphs would be to conceal its unity; taking it, however, as one, we shall see how very far more than is generally supposed, the observance of God's worship among the Hebrews was based on everlasting principles both as to its matter and its manner; and that while there was much ritual in external forms, yet Judaism was not ritualistic in any sense which would imply the efficacy of ritual by itself to bring about spiritual results. Let us enumerate the principles which here are embodied in the directions for the worship of God. The forms in which the principles are expressed may change; the principles themselves, *never!*

I. HEBREW WORSHIP WAS TO BE IN ALL RESPECTS A PROTEST AGAINST SURROUNDING IDOLATRY. (Vers. 2, 3, 29—31.) They were not only to carry out a policy of destruction, in sweeping from the land every vestige of ancient heathen worship (see Homily on ch. vii. 1—11), but were to avoid everything like imitation of it. Theirs was a new nationality, a new deliverance, a new faith, and it must be a new kind of worship, corresponding in its purity to the holiness of Jehovah, and in its intelligence to that knowledge of him which they were expected to cultivate in themselves and hand down to others. And so now, if there are corrupt forms of worship, such as Rome's pagan ceremonies baptized with the Christian name, the worship of God's true Church must needs be a protest against it, and a contention for " the simplicity which is in Christ."

II. IT WAS TO BE ACCORDING TO DIVINE DIRECTION. They might not consult their own religious sentiments, as the heathen did, in choosing *e.g.* the tops of the hills for worship, because they thought so to get nearer God. Israel must consult revelation, and follow it. So with the Church of God now. True, we have not such minute rites enjoined as Israel had, for we need them not now. But in our New Testament writings all needful instructions are given for those who would worship the Father in spirit and in truth.

III. THE DIVINE RULES WERE TO BE PRECISELY ADHERED TO. They might not be swerved from, either by addition or diminution (ver. 32). This is indeed but an extension of principle No. 2; but it requires in our day to be noticed separately; since many will admit, generally, that worship must be according to Scripture, who nevertheless also maintain that the Church may direct as to forms of worship. But we cannot forget two facts: one, that at the close of the New Testament there is a like caution and prohibition to that given here; another, that the entire course of Church history shows us that men know not where to stop when they once diverge from "the Book," and that departures therefrom little by little, even under Church authority, do ultimately land men in the complicated and superstitious ceremonial of the Church of Rome.

IV. THERE WAS TO BE (after they were settled in Palestine) ONE PLACE WHICH GOD CHOOSE TO PUT HIS NAME THERE. And this place where God would meet with his people is called, in the beautiful Hebrew phrase, God's *rest* (ver. 5), " his habitation " (cf. Ps. cxxxii. 13, 14). Thus would God, in his condescending love, launch a new thought into the world, in a form in which the people could understand it; viz. that God's home is with his believing worshippers. It was necessary, for a while, to associate that truth with one special *place*, until " the fulness of times " should come, when One should say—John iv. 20—24; Matt. xviii. 20; and when Christians should learn that *they* are the home of God (1 Cor. iii. 16; Eph. ii. 22).

V. TO THIS PLACE THE TRIBES WERE TO COME AND WORSHIP TOGETHER. Thus the unity of God's redeemed people in him, would be continually before their eyes. Though the times in the year were not many when the people were thus to meet as one nation and commonwealth, yet they were frequent enough to ensure their thoughts turning thereto, either by retrospection or anticipation, from one year's end to another. Here is the germ seed of the doctrine of the unity of God's Church. Many tribes, one redeemed people. And is it not precisely this principle which is brought out in the New Testament, only in far grander form? (see Rev. vii.; Eph. ii.; John xvii.; Rom. xii.). Is not the Christian unity a union of many tribes and tongues in one deliverance, and one Deliverer?

VI. THE FORMS OF ISRAEL'S WORSHIP WERE TO BE SUFFICIENTLY VARIED TO REFLECT THE CHANGING ASPECTS AND CIRCUMSTANCES OF LIFE. These forms are sevenfold. In each case, however, an offering was brought to God. It might be typical, symbolic, eucharistic, dedicatory, or votive. (For specific treatment of each kind, see Kurtz, and Kalisch, *in loc.*) There were: 1. Burnt offering. 2. Sacrifices. 3. Tithes (ch. xxvi. 12). 4. Heave offerings. "Quæ sponte dabatur Deo " (Buxtorf). 5. Vows (Ps. lxxvi. 11). 6. Free-will offerings (1 Chron. xxix. 17; ch. xvi. 10). 7. Firstlings of herds and flocks (Exod. xiii. 12; Neh. x. 35—37; Prov. iii. 9; Ps. lxvi. 13—16). How varied! There were sacrifices of atonement and of consecration; offerings of consecration and thanksgiving. Each changing scene of life was to call forth its act of devotion to God.

VII. IT WAS TO BE A FAMILY AND HOUSEHOLD WORSHIP. (Ver. 18.) Not the head of the house only, but the children, yea, even the little ones had their recognized place in the house of God (ver. 12). And the slaves too! The stranger and the sojourner might also come. *The religion of the family was a keystone of Israel's national life;* and it will be a very serious thing for any nation, if family religion comes to be slighted or ignored. Never let us rob the children of their rightful place in Christian ordinances and in the house of God.

VIII. IT WAS TO BE A JOYFUL WORSHIP. Ver. 12, "Ye shall rejoice before the Lord your God." The pagan worship never was or could be a glad one. The heathens feared their gods, dreaded them, sought to propitiate them, but as for being glad in them because of any loving care on the part of their gods towards them, they knew nothing at all about any such blessing. But Israel did. They worshipped Jehovah, a redeeming God, who had manifested his Name to them. Hence such psalms as the twenty-third and the one hundred and third, could be prepared for their gladsome worship and song. Much more may we " Rejoice in the Lord."

IX. ISRAEL'S WORSHIP WAS TO BE SUPPORTED BY THE CONTRIBUTIONS OF THE PEOPLE. (Ver. 19; and see ch. xviii. 1—8.) Thus were the people at large from the first to be educated "in giving to God," and in maintaining, at their own cost, the worship and ordinances of God, so as to hand them down intact and untainted to their children and their children's children. How clearly is this principle reproduced in the New Testament! (see 1 Cor. ix. 9—14). Though there is far less detail, yet it is not supposed that less will be done, but rather more; such verses as 2 Cor. viii. 7—9, how much they imply and suppose! Surely it would be well if our Churches everywhere recognized the nine principles of Divine worship which we find laid down by Moses. It may fairly be made a question whether even the purest Church is found recognizing them all; and yet, which one of the nine is repealed or even modified under the gospel? Of necessity, forms have changed. But so long as we need the ordinances of Christian worship at all, so long must we assert and maintain all that we find inculcated here: simplicity *versus* false ceremonialism; exact loyalty to Divine direction; recognizing the Church as "the rest" of God, where the tribes are many, but the commonwealth one; letting the worship reflect life's varied moods; letting it be a joyous family worship, maintained and supported by our contributions and our prayers.

HOMILIES BY VARIOUS AUTHORS.

Vers. 1—5.—*Destruction of monuments of idolatry.* Israel's entrance into Canaan was the entrance of true knowledge, of pure forms of religion, of cleansed morals. The worship of Jehovah was the very antithesis of that of which these altars, pillars, and graven images, were the polluted memorials. "What did the grove conceal? Lust—blood—imposture. What sounds shook the fane? Alternate screams of anguish and the laughter of mad votaries. What was the priest? The teacher of every vice of which his god was the patron and example. What were the worshippers? The victims of every woe which superstition and sensuality can gender, and which cruelty can cherish" (Isaac Taylor). Why should the last trace of these hateful worships not be removed from the land of God's abode? (see on ch. vii. 1—6). These commands had—

I. A GROUND IN RELIGIOUS FEELING. Even the dumb memorials of iniquity will excite in pure minds feelings of horror and revulsion. It is positive pain to look upon them. The only sentiments which these monuments of a dark polytheism—suggestive of every species of wickedness, and steeped in foulness through the cruel and lustful rites once associated with them—could awaken in the minds of devout worshippers of Jehovah were those of inexpressible abhorrence. The sooner they were swept away the better. Healthy moral instincts will lead us to hate "even the garment spotted by the flesh" (Jude 23).

II. A GROUND IN PRUDENCE. It removed from Israel's midst what would obviously have proved a snare. Prone of their own motion to idolatry, how certainly would the people have been drawn into it had idol sanctuaries, idol altars, idol groves stood to tempt them at every corner, met their gaze on every hill-summit. A wise legislation will aim at the removal of temptations. The business of legislation, as has been well said, is to make it as easy as possible for the people to choose virtue, and as difficult as possible to choose vice.

III. A GROUND IN POLICY. The design of Moses, to gather the life and religion of the people round a central sanctuary, would plainly have been frustrated had innumerable sacred places of repute, associated with the old idolatry, been allowed to remain unshorn of their honours. On the same principle, missionaries, in order to prevent relapses into idolatry, have often found it needful to get their converts to collect their idols, and unitedly to destroy them—burning them, it may be, or flinging them into some river.—J. O.

Vers. 6—29.—*The central sanctuary.* There are difficulties connected with this law from which conclusions have been drawn adverse to the Mosaic authorship of Deuteronomy. These arise: 1. From the lack of evidence that the law was in force in the days of the judges and earlier kings. 2. From the practice of judges, kings, prophets, and other good men in offering sacrifices elsewhere than at the prescribed centre. 3. From the mention of other sanctuaries in the history (*e.g.* Josh. xxiv. 26; 1 Sam. vii. 26, LXX.). But: 1. Ver. 10 shows that it was not *contemplated* that the law should come into perfect operation till the land was settled, and till a place for a fixed centre had been definitely chosen. In point of fact, the unsettled state of matters lasted till the reign of David (2 Sam. vii. 1). Accordingly, in 1 Kings iii. 2, it is not urged that the law did not exist, or that it was not known, but the excuse is advanced for irregularities that "there was no house built unto the Name of the Lord until those days" (cf. 1 Kings viii. 29; ix. 9; 2 Chron. vi. 5, 6). 2. While the law lays down the general rule, it is not denied that circumstances might arise, in which under proper Divine authority, exceptional sacrifices might be offered. This fully explains the cases of Gideon (Judg. vi. 18, 26), of Manoah (Judg. xiii. 16), of David (2 Sam. xxiv. 18), of Solomon (1 Kings iii. 4, 5), of Elijah (1 Kings xviii. 31). 3. Even while the tabernacle was at Shiloh, the ark, for reasons unknown to us, was moved from place to place—a circumstance which accounts for sacrifices being offered at the spots where, for the time being, it was located (Judg. xxi. 2). We may infer the presence of the ark in Judg. xx. 26 and on various other occasions. 4. It is not fair to plead, as contradictory of the law, the falling back on local sanctuaries in periods of great national and religious disorganization, as when the land was possessed by enemies (Judg. vi. 1—7), or when the ark was in captivity (1 Sam. vi. 1) or separated from the tabernacle (2 Sam. vi. 11); much less the prevailing neglect of this law in times of acknowledged backsliding and declension. In particular, the period following the rejection of Eli and his sons (1 Sam. ii. 30—35) was one of unusual complications, during which, indeed, Samuel's own person would seem to have been the chief religious centre of the nation. 5. It may further be remarked that the worship at local sanctuaries, having once taken root, justified perhaps by the exigencies of the time, it would be no easy matter to uproot it again, and a modified toleration would have to be accorded. Whatever difficulties inhere in the view of the early existence of this law, it will be found, we believe, that equal or greater difficulties emerge on any other reading of the history. This law was—

I. AN ASSERTION OF THE PRINCIPLE THAT GOD'S WORSHIP MUST BE ASSOCIATED WITH HIS PRÉSENCE. (Vers. 5—11.) The sanctuary was constituted by God having "put his Name" there. Under the New Testament the worship of the Father "in spirit and in truth" is liberated from special sacred places (John iv. 24), but the principle holds good that his being "in the midst" of his people is essential to worship being acceptable (Matt. xviii. 20).

II. AN IMPORTANT MEANS OF KEEPING ALIVE THE SENSE OF NATIONAL UNITY. The union of the tribes was far from being close. Tribe feeling was often stronger than national feeling. A powerful counteractive to the local interests, and to the jealousies, rivalries, and feuds which tended to divide the nation, was found in the central sanctuary, and in the festivals therewith connected. Like the Olympic games in Greece, the sanctuary festivals formed a bond of unity for the entire people, helped them to realize their national distinctness, and awakened in them lofty and patriotic aspirations. In the Christian Church, everything is valuable which helps to develop the sense of catholicity.

III. A MEANS, FURTHER, OF INFUSING WARMTH AND VITALITY INTO RELIGIOUS SERVICES. In religion, as in other matters, we need to avail ourselves of social influences. We need public as well as private worship. The self-wrapt man grows cold. There is a time for outward demonstration, not less than for internal meditation. Sharing our gladness with others, it is multiplied to ourselves a hundred-fold. The importance, in this view of them, of the sanctuary festivals, was very great. They were, from the nature of the case, "events," matters to be looked forward to with interest, and long to be remembered after they had taken place. They involved preparations, and often long journeys. Everything about them—the journey in company with neighbours, the season of the year, the friendly greetings, the exhilaration of the scene as they neared the sanctuary, the varied and solemn services at the sanctuary itself—was fitted in a singular degree to exalt, awe, quicken, and impress their minds. Such influences, even in gospel times, are not to be despised.

IV. A COUNTERACTIVE TO IDOLATRY. It put something in place of that which was taken away. It provided counter-attractions. Negation is not an effective instrument of reform. If we remove with one hand, we must give with the other. Our methods must be positive.—J. O.

Vers. 5—9.—*Public worship*. A necessity of our spiritual life. Prompted by a community of privileges, interests, feelings, hopes, duties, temptations, aspirations; "One Lord, one faith, one baptism" (Eph. iv. 3—7). It is required in it—

I. THAT GOD BE PRESENT WITH HIS PEOPLE. We meet in his Name. His presence is promised (Matt. xviii. 20). Without that presence sought and obtained, worship is in vain.

II. THAT IT BE PURE AND SCRIPTURAL. Not "will-worship" (Col. ii. 23); not corrupted by the ingrafting upon it of heathen superstitions. Christianity has often been thus corrupted. The papal mariolatry and worship of images, with the whole-sale importation into Christianity of rites and ceremonies drawn from paganism, is a glaring instance. God forbids any mixture of the old worship with the new. The very names of the gods of the Canaanites were to be destroyed (ver. 3). Worldliness, not less than superstition, may intrude itself into worship, and destroy its purity (John ii. 13—17; Jas. ii. 2, 3).

III. THAT IT BE ORDERLY. (Ver. 8.) Paul pleads for order in the Christian Church (1 Cor. xi., xii.).

IV. THAT IT GIVE EXPRESSION TO THE VARIED WANTS OF THE RELIGIOUS NATURE. (Vers. 6, 7.) The prescribed sacrifices constituted a complex medium for the expression of the complex life and aspirations of the nation. It is to be noted that, save on days specially devoted to the remembrance of sins, a predominatingly joyful tone pervaded the services. This tone of joy should characterize yet more decidedly the services of Christians, coming before the Lord, as they are commanded to do, "to offer up spiritual sacrifices" (Phil. iv. 4; Col. iii. 16'; 1 Pet. ii. 5).

V. THAT IT BE ASSOCIATED WITH REMEMBRANCE OF THE POOR. (Vers. 7, 12, 18; ch. xvi. 11, 14.) One of the first effects of Christ's love in a heart should be to open it up in sympathy and kindness to all in need (Acts ii. 45; iv. 34, 35; Rom. xv. 25; 1 Cor. xii. 26; 2 Cor. viii., ix.).—J. O.

Vers. 15, 16, 20—26.—*The Divine regulation of food.* All animals for food had formerly to be killed at the door of the tabernacle (Lev. xvi. 1—8). Probably the rule was not strictly observed (ver. 8), but in view of the occupation of the land, the prohibition is relaxed. Note—

I. OUR RIGHTS IN THE USE OF FOOD TAKE THEIR ORIGIN FROM GOD. This is taught in the account of creation (Gen. i. 29, 30), in the grant of flesh to Noah (Gen. ix. 3, 4), in the Levitical restrictions on animal food (Lev. xi.), and in passages like the present.

II. OUR MANNER OF THE USE OF FOOD OUGHT TO BE GLORIFYING TO GOD. "Eating and drinking" is to be to God's glory (1 Cor. x. 31). 1. God's gift to be recognized in food. A motive for thankfulness. 2. God's blessing to be sought upon it. The example of Christ in this respect is noteworthy (Matt. xiv. 19, etc.). 3. Self-restraint is to be exercised in the partaking of it. The blood was not to be eaten.—J. O.

Ver. 19.—*The Levite.* The dues of the Levites consisted mainly of the tithes. The value of this legal provision has been frequently exaggerated. The mistake has lain in comparing it with the average of income over the whole nation, instead of with the incomes of the wealthier and middle classes. Comparing it with these, it will be found to have been liberal, but not excessive, even supposing it to have been conscientiously paid. This, however, it would seldom be. No tribunal existed to enforce payment. All depended on the conscientiousness of the individual tithe-payer. It is easy to see that an income of this sort was in the highest degree precarious, and that in times of religious declension, the body of the Levites would be reduced to great straits. These facts sufficiently account for the reiterated injunctions not to forsake the Levite, but to include him in every festive gathering. Three reasons for his liberal support: 1. His calling deprived him of the usual means of livelihood. 2. His office was one of service for the people. 3. His relation to the altar made neglect shown to him a dishonour done to God. Paul applies, in 1 Cor. ix. 13, 14, to the gospel ministry.—J. O.

Vers. 29—32.—*Unworthy inquiries.* We have here—

I. BALEFUL SUPERSTITION. The ground of these inquiries about the gods of the place was a lurking belief in their reality. There was a superstitious feeling that the woods, hills, streams, etc., must have their deities, whom it would be well to propitiate and worship. The country as a whole, and special districts of it, had gods, and, Jehovah notwithstanding, the superstitious part of the community stood in dread of them. Superstitions are hard to eradicate. We have examples in the survival of the belief in witches, fairies, charms, omens, lucky and unlucky days, etc., among ourselves. Till a recent period, it was the custom in parts of the Scottish Highlands to sacrifice bulls to local saints. And the practice of burying a live cock for the cure of epilepsy is said to survive till the present hour. Born of ignorance, and acting as a check on all enlightenment and progress, superstition is the parent of innumerable evils, besides debasing and enslaving mind and conscience. Its influence should be combated by every legitimate means.

II. PRURIENT CURIOSITY. The superstitious motive did not act alone. This itching desire to hear about the gods of the place, and how the nations served them, was symptomatic of a prurient disposition. There was, unfortunately, too much in the way in which these nations had "served their gods" to excite and interest the passions of the dissolute. It is a dangerous token when those who ought to know better begin to manifest a prurient curiosity about what is evil. It leads to prying into matters which had better remain hidden, to inquiries at persons whose very society is dangerous, to the reading of obscene books, the visiting of bad places, the keeping of immoral company, etc. At the bottom of such inquiries there is invariably a secret sympathy, which is bound, as time advances, to yield fruit in evil practices.

III. SERVILE IMITATION. The idolatry of the Israelites was signalized by a strange want of originality. They invented no gods of their own. They were content to be imitators. The nations before them had gods. The nations around them had gods. They wanted to be like the rest, and have gods too—hence their inquiries. A curious illustration of the force of the principle of imitation. It is one of the ruling principles in human nature. Imitation is easier than invention. The tendency invariably is to "follow the crowd." It matters nothing that it is "to do evil." The fashion of the time and place must be observed. There are people who would almost rather die than be out of the fashion. Yet what a weakness is this, and how opposed to all true and right manhood! "Be not conformed to the world" (Rom. xii. 2).—J. O.

Vers. 1—3.—*The invasion a religious one.* The Israelites were instructed to exterminate the Canaanites in consequence of their sins, as we have already seen; but in this passage we have strict injunctions given to destroy the places of worship which the Canaanites had used, "upon the high mountains, and upon the hills, and under every green tree," etc. They were, in fact, to be *iconoclasts*, and they were to leave no vestige remaining of the Canaanitish worship.

I. IT WAS THUS MADE EVIDENT THAT THE INVASION WAS RELIGIOUS IN ITS CHARACTER. Palestine, as we have already seen, was not a country of exceptional *natural* advantages. It was a good training school for a spiritual people. When the Lord, then, sent his emancipated people in to carry out such a programme as the destruction of the Canaanitish worship, it was evident to all that religion lay at the basis of the invasion. It was no tribal feud, but a contest for religious supremacy. As Abraham, their forefather, came to Canaan to be the exponent and founder of a new religion, so the descendants are required to expound the religion still more forcibly by putting down all traces of the heathen worship.

II. THE MULTIPLICITY OF CANAANITISH PLACES OF WORSHIP REALLY EXPRESSED THE POLYTHEISM OF THE PEOPLE. The Canaanites believed in the "gods of the hills," and "gods of the valleys," and "gods of the grove." Hence they erected altars with melancholy frequency over the land. It was not a sense of the omnipresence of a Supreme Being, but a belief in a multiplicity of gods, which led to such multiplicity of places of worship. The land was polluted with idols. Every green tree was supposed to overshadow a god. Altars, pillars, and groves sheltered and surrounded graven images. The *desecration* was all-prevailing.

III. THE POWER OF ASSOCIATION NECESSITATED THE COMPLETE DESTRUCTION OF THESE SIGNS OF IDOLATRY. If polytheism expressed itself so universally, then association would assert in the Israelitish mind a corresponding power, and lead weak minds to the idea that an idol was surely something in the world, when it secured such recognition. No wise leader could allow such temptations to remain before his people. Hence the Israelites are instructed to spare no trace of the old worship. Intolerance may be a duty in pure self-defence. It was a duty in this case divinely ordained.

IV. CURIOSITY IS NOT TO BE LEFT ANYTHING TO FEED UPON. For there is a prurient curiosity which only leads to sin. All humouring of this is evil. When a soul insists on tasting the fruit of forbidden trees, as a matter of curiosity, he only repeats the act of our first parents in Eden. No possible good can come of it. Much curiosity is indulged only to the deterioration of soul and body. Now, this would have been a danger with the Israelites. The worship of the Canaanites was so sensual and horrible, that the less known about it the better. Hence the command to destroy every vestige of it. It would be well for Christians more frequently to restrain their curiosity than they do. In many cases it would be well if every vestige of sinful practices were destroyed, instead of being preserved to satisfy an "idle curiosity."

V. THE WHOLESALE DESTRUCTION OF THE PARAPHERNALIA OF IDOLATRY WOULD BE THE BEST OF ALL DEMONSTRATIONS OF THE NOTHINGNESS OF THE IDOLS. For if these gods of Canaan had any power, they might be expected to vindicate their majesty against these spoilers. But Israel never suffered anything from the destruction of the idolatry. The only danger arose from the destruction not being as complete in some cases as God intended it should be. And it is important to have the impotence of God's foes made matter of demonstration. Sooner or later this is the case.

VI. THE GOSPEL OF JESUS CHRIST HAS ALSO ITS INTOLERANT, AS WELL AS ITS TOLERANT, SIDE. In a sermon on Matt. xii. 30, "He that is not with me is against me," Vinet, the greatest of the moral analysts, has expounded *L'intolérance de l'Évangile*, just as in a companion sermon on Luke ix. 50, "He that is not against us is for us," he expounds *La tolérance.*[1] It is well to realize that religion is not an easy-going matter, making things pleasant all round, but something requiring stern and uncompromising conduct oftentimes. We may suffer as much by an unenlightened latitudinarianism as by an unenlightened attachment to non-essentials in use and wont.—R. M. E.

Vers. 4—14.—*Centralization in worship.* It is quite unnecessary that we should here enter upon the criticism which has been raging upon this important passage, as indicating something post-Mosaic. The directions in Exodus do not necessarily imply a multiplicity of altars at the same time, but rather successive alterations of locality in conformity with the requirements of the pilgrimage. Besides, the genius of the Jewish worship implied the centralization of it in contrast to the multiplicity of places arising out of polytheism. The idea of a central altar is implied in the erection of the tabernacle at Sinai, and all the legislation which gathers round it. We believe, therefore, that Moses, in here formulating the centralization in worship, was merely making plainer what had already been implied.

I. CENTRALIZATION IN WORSHIP SEEMS A CONVENIENT STEPPING-STONE FROM THE DANGERS OF POLYTHEISM TO UNIVERSAL SPIRITUAL WORSHIP. Abraham, in setting up the new worship in Canaan, had erected altars at the different places where God appeared unto him. His fine intellect realized that it was the One God he worshipped at the different places. His descendants also, in their pilgrimage to Palestine, realized that it was the One God who called upon them out of the cloudy pillar to halt from time to time, and to erect his altar, and whom they there worshipped; and they would also feel that this direction about a single central altar was but the necessary corollary to the entire legislation. The ideal of worship, to which the Old Testament dispensation pointed, was, "when the true worshippers shall worship the Father in spirit and in truth: for the Father seeketh such to worship him" (John iv. 23); meanwhile it was most important to have the Divine unity publicly recognized and expressed by a central altar. At this they were to aim when settled beyond the Jordan.

II. THE CENTRAL ALTAR IS TO GATHER ROUND IT JOYFUL WORSHIPPERS. (Vers. 6, 7.) Burnt offering, sacrifice, heave offering, etc., were to reach their climax in the eating before the Lord the peace offering, and in the *joy* which springs from fellowship. This is the purpose of all worship. If joy be not reached, then the worshippers are living below their privileges.

III. ALLOWANCE IS MADE FOR THE EXIGENCIES OF THE MARCH AND OF WAR. Means of grace have to be extemporized often in times of battle and marches, and men

[1] 'Discours sur Quelques sujets Religieux,' pp. 214—237.

must do what is right in their own eyes, in a way that would not be lawful in times of settled avocations and of peace. Moses is instructed, therefore, to remind them of the freedom they necessarily practise in the unsettled condition, which must be relinquished when they settle down beyond the Jordan (vers. 8, 9).

IV. GOD RESERVES THE RIGHT OF CHOOSING THE CENTRAL PLACE OF WORSHIP. (Vers. 10—14.) This prevents all licence in such an important matter. It is not what they think advisable, but what God directs, that they are in the locality of worship to follow. This reservation is surely most significant. It indicates that in worship, which is the payment of due homage unto God, his will and wisdom are to be regarded as supreme. The right God holds in his hand of indicating whether he is to be worshipped in one place or everywhere.

V. GOD REVEALED THE CENTRAL PLACE IN DUE SEASON. A good deal of the current criticism seems to overlook the distinction between the *principle* of centralization in worship and the *place* where it was to be observed. The principle was stated long before the place was indicated. It was centuries before Jerusalem became the recognized centre of the Jewish religion. Had the name been indicated earlier, it would have prevented the natural development of the ritual in Canaan. It is not necessary to suppose that Moses had any definite idea of the central place when he uttered on the banks of the Jordan the will of God. God can express his will through historical developments, just as he can through natural developments. "The nature of things" may be justly regarded as the expression of the Divine mind; and so may a historical procession.

Meanwhile, it is well for us to rejoice in the freedom and universality of spiritual worship to which we have come. Now the true worshippers, emancipated from the cumbrous ritual through its fulfilment in Christ, can "worship the Father in spirit and in truth" in every place.—R. M. E.

Vers. 15—19.—*Private worship not the substitute for public.* While the central altar was ordained for the reception of the sacrifices and the place for the love-feasts of God's people, they were also allowed to slay and eat flesh meat at home. It must, of course, consist of the flesh of clean animals, and the blood must be carefully poured out unto the Lord; but, after these precautions, it was perfectly possible for the Jew to live luxuriously at home. In these circumstances he might say that the flesh killed carefully at home tasted as sweet as any peace offering enjoyed at the tabernacle, and that he would not trouble himself about the journey to the central altar. Such a conclusion the Lord expressly forbids. How, in such circumstances, will the Levites be sustained? Such private luxury must not be substituted for the public peace offering and the Levitical support connected with the ritual.

I. THERE IS A GREAT TEMPTATION WITH LUKEWARM PEOPLE TO MAKE PRIVATE WORSHIP DO DUTY FOR PUBLIC. It is insinuated that the Bible can be as well studied, and prayer as faithfully observed, and praise as joyfully rendered, amid the sanctities of home as in any congregation. But the fact is that the private worship is a sorry substitute for the public. Not to speak of the promise, "The Lord loveth the gates of Zion better than all the dwellings of Jacob," there is in the public congregation a power of sympathy, solemnity, and attention which is missed elsewhere. The private services, when separated from the public, fail to reach the professed ideal, and religious feebleness is the usual result.

II. PRIVATE CELEBRATIONS OF PUBLIC SOLEMNITIES ARE MOST PROPERLY FORBIDDEN. The Jew might have excused himself from journeying to the central altar by resolving on the solemnities at home. "I can share the tithes, and firstlings, and vows, and free-will offerings, and heave offerings with my neighbours, and not bother taking them to the tabernacle." And so men can still abstain from membership in Church organizations under the plea of private baptisms and private "tables;" but all this presumption is an abomination unto the Lord.

III. IT DENIES TO THE PUBLIC MINISTERS OF GOD THEIR DUE RIGHTS. For Levitical support, so carefully guarded in the commandment here, is surely equivalent to "ministerial support" still. The ministry of the Word means an order of men set apart from the secularities of life to give themselves unto prayer and to the ministry of the Word (Acts vi. 4). If it is highly expedient, as well as divinely ordained, that such an order should exist, then it is a serious responsibility on the part of any private person to refuse to acknowledge this Divine ordinance and its attendant rights. The pitifulness of the excuse, moreover, in refusing ministerial support because of private scruples, must strike the most superficial judge.

IV. THE LORD LEAVES THE LEVITE AS A CHARGE UPON THE GENEROSITY OF THE PEOPLE. The Levite was to be as a guest within the gates of the Jew (ver. 18). All the rights of hospitality, so to speak, were to be his. Moreover, it was to be an unending charge. "Take heed to thyself that thou forsake not the Levite as long as thou livest upon the earth." Thus an order of men are left upon the generosity of the people, to have their share as long as the world lasts. So is it with the Christian ministry. Public services, the public organizations of the Church, are all to be continued till the end of time, and hence the ministry will continue. Nor will its support severely tax the loyal Christian people.

We see how intimately the interests of God's servants are bound up with proper views about private and public worship. If these are judiciously disseminated, there is no fear of the Lord's servants being neglected. God's rights in the ordering of his worship must be first vindicated and recognized, and then- his servants' rights will follow.—R. M. E.

Vers. 20—28.—*The sanctity of blood.* The central altar was for the reception of the blood. And while the Jews remained in pilgrimage, every time they killed an animal out of their flocks or herds for family use they carried the blood to the tabernacle, that it might be duly disposed of by the priest. In case of the roebucks and harts, their blood was not sacrificial; it was therefore ordained that it should be poured out on the earth, and carefully and solemnly covered up. When they were settled in the land of Canaan, they were too far from the central altar to carry the blood of every animal out of the herd or flock which was slain to the appointed place. Hence they were allowed to deal with the domestic animals as with the products of the chase (ver. 22). It is to this fact of the sanctity of blood that we would now direct attention.

I. THE HEATHEN NATIONS WERE ACCUSTOMED TO MAKE DRINK OFFERINGS OF BLOOD. David refers to the fact when he says, "Their sorrows shall be multiplied that hasten after another god: their drink offerings of blood will I not offer, nor take up their names into my lips" (Ps. xvi. 4). These drink offerings of blood arose, doubtless, out of the *bloodthirstiness* of the heathen themselves. Men of blood thought their god delighted in bloodshedding as they did. It was human passion projected into the religious domain.

II. GOD SO DIRECTED HIS WORSHIPPERS ABOUT THE DISPOSAL OF THE BLOOD THAT THEY COULD NOT REGARD IT IN ANY OTHER LIGHT THAN AS A MOST SACRED THING. It was to be carefully carried to his altar and disposed of by the officiating priests, or, if this was not possible, it was solemnly poured into the earth, and covered carefully from all profane uses. On no account was it to be eaten: this would have profaned it.

III. THE REASON ASSIGNED WAS THAT THE LIFE WAS IN THE BLOOD. "Life" is the gift of God, the mysterious something which escapes our observation in analysis, which baffles our productive powers, and which works such wonders in the world of nature. As God's gift, it is to be holy in our eyes, and disposed of as he sees best.

IV. THE VICARIOUSNESS OF SUFFERING GAVE IT ADDITIONAL SANCTITY. For shed blood meant life sacrificed to sustain other life. Our bodies depend upon vicarious suffering for their sustenance. Sacrifice underlies the constitution of the world. It was meet, then, that this principle should be recognized and sanctified in the sight of men.

V. BLOOD HAD ITS RELIGIOUS FUNCTION, NOT A PHYSICAL FUNCTION, TO DISCHARGE IN THE MOSAIC ECONOMY. The God of Israel did not delight in blood, as the gods of the heathen were supposed to do. He singled it out for a religious use. It was to be the material of a holy act, wherever shed. This was undoubtedly to keep it so out of the sphere of physical elements that it could symbolize fully "the blood of Jesus Christ," by which the world is to be saved.—R. M. E.

Vers. 1—4.—*The doom of idolatry.* The reverse side of blessing is a curse. The abuse of the best things is the worst. In the ratio in which any institution has capacity to benefit, has it capacity to injure. The sun can quicken life or kill. The temple is a stepping-stone to heaven or a snare of hell.

I. BOTH NATURE AND ART HAVE BEEN PROSTITUTED TO BASEST USES. If men cannot find God in themselves, they cannot find him in material nature. Some "look through nature up to nature's God." Some look through nature to darkness, sensuality, and despair.

II. THE BEAUTIFUL MUST BE SACRIFICED TO MORAL NECESSITIES. Æsthetics must yield to ethics. Our moral exigencies are paramount. The voice of taste is the voice of a charmer. The voice of conscience is the voice of a king. If the creations of art are inimical to the interests of righteousness, they must be destroyed. Eternal life is beyond all price. Whatever keeps man from the living God is doomed.

III. TRUE LIFE HAS A DESTRUCTIVE SIDE. The growth of a plant involves the death of the seed. The life of the body is sustained by manifold death. Eternal life comes by the death of the Son of God. The inner life of piety is quickened by the death of self. True love to God is the hatred of his foes. Jesus Christ "came to destroy the works of the devil."—D.

Vers. 5—28.—*Characteristic signs of Jehovah's worship.* All the religious institutions of Moses were bulwarks against the idolatry of the period, and were admirably suited to the intellectual and moral condition of the people. The worship of the true God was characterized by—

I. A SINGLE, GOD-SELECTED SHRINE. As the heathen had gods many, they had plurality of temples, altars, and shrines. The single, central temple of Jehovah promoted at least two worthy objects. 1. *It kept alive in the people's memory the unity of God.* In that age, so addicted to idolatry, this was of the first importance. Intellectual belief in the one God would not, *in itself*, go for much; yet it would be the foundation for reverence, love, and loyalty. 2. *It promoted most vitally the unity of the nation.* In the absence of representative institutions and periodic literature, the common worship of the people at a central shrine was the most active factor in national unity. On this largely, as an instrument, the strength and safety of the nation depended. In the absence of this cementing element, the tribes would speedily have become factions—distinct entities—like the Canaanites who had preceded them.

II. GOD'S WORSHIP WAS CHARACTERIZED BY PROFUSE AND VARIOUS OFFERINGS. Every event in the life of the Hebrews to be connected with God, and to be associated with religion. Earth was to be joined to heaven by vital arteries of intercommunication. Thus the favour and benediction of God would be enjoyed in every circumstance of daily existence, and a joyous sense of God's fatherhood be kept alive. The arrangement would check avarice and earthly-mindedness. It would make conscience tenderly alive to sin, and promote in a thousand ways practical righteousness.

III. GOD'S WORSHIP WAS A DELIGHTFUL OCCUPATION. "Ye shall eat before the Lord . . . and shall rejoice." In observing the rites of idolatry, the Canaanites practised wanton self-mutilations. They stained the altars with their own blood. They made their children to pass through the fire. This was the invention of the diabolic spirit. But in God's temple is the sunshine of joy, the light of his face. For man's hunger he prepares a "feast of fat things," fat things "full of marrow," "wines on the lees well refined." At prodigious cost to himself, he has supplied the "bread of life," and living water from deep wells of salvation. And his gracious voice greets every comer *thus,* "Eat, O friends; . . . yea, drink abundantly."

IV. GOD'S WORSHIP HALLOWS ALL RELATIONSHIPS AND BRIGHTENS ALL PURSUITS. In the temple, men became conscious of a Divine presence, and felt within the stirrings of a new life. Religion developed their better nature. It made them acquainted with new relationships, and opened their eyes to the value of old ones. It created new and more generous emotions. Fountains of kindly feeling were unsealed within them, and sweet waters of practical kindness flowed out to the poor and the stranger. A new light beautified all toil, and they rejoiced in all they put their hand unto. Those who had been the ministrants of this fresh life and joy—the Levites—were to have a special place in their sympathy and regard. Sacred ties of generous affection were to knit them in one brotherhood.

V. THE WORSHIP OF GOD SANCTIFIES THE COMMON MEAL. The recognition of God and his claims allows us to enjoy all the provision of God with thankfulness and content. Every meal reminds us of God, and leads to fellowship with him. Each meal becomes a minor sacrament, and all food is consecrated to highest use. In this state of mind, excess of every kind becomes impossible, and the amplest enjoyment is not incompatible with vigorous piety.

VI. THE WORSHIP OF GOD TEACHES THE SUPERIOR WORTH OF HUMAN LIFE. All the requirements of the Levitical Law set forth the sacredness of life. Highest sanctions surrounded all life. The lives of inferior animals were generously cared for. But when the life of men was to be sustained, and sustained in richest vigour, the lives of animals were to be sacrificed. Yet even while this was done, the minds of men were to be impressed with a sense of the value of life; hence the blood of victims was to be poured upon the earth. As in redemption, so in daily sustentation, we are taught the costly price at which our life is procured. So high a value has God set upon man, that large sacrifices of herds and flocks are daily made for his behoof.

VII. CEREMONIAL LAWS POSSESSED AN ELASTICITY TO SUIT MEN'S ACTUAL NEEDS. Every moral law had an innate power and value, which never allowed a concession. To infringe a moral law, even the least, became a personal loss. But ritual law possessed a value only as the type and memorial of better things. Righteousness is of higher value than human convenience, but ritual is the servant of expediency. The shewbread was for the priests; yet David, in his hunger, might eat thereof and not sin. During the exigencies of desert life, circumcision was often deferred, the Passovers were irregularly observed, and to a large extent the Hebrews became "a law unto themselves." "If the Law of the Spirit of life" be within us, we shall discern when ritual may be profitably used and when it may be suspended.

VIII. THE WORSHIP OF GOD WAS FRUITFUL IN BLESSING. The design of God in every particular was solely the good of families, that "it may be well with thee, and with thy children." We do well to write this with a diamond pen on memory and heart, that God's claims and man's advantage are identical. The plan of human life is laid on the lines of righteousness, and along these lines alone is the road to immortal bliss. We cannot add to or take from the commands of God, without injury to ourselves and dishonour to him.—D.

Vers. 29—32.—*The subtle ensnarements of idolatry.* A spirit of vain curiosity is to be repressed at its beginning. So weak is human nature, and so subtle is the working of sin, that prying curiosity into evil customs works practical mischief. Human life, to be a success, must be a perpetual battle with moral evil. We cannot afford to parley with the enemy nor give him a single advantage. Incessant watchfulness is our safety.

I. IDOLATRY HAS GREAT FASCINATIONS FOR MAN'S SENSUOUS NATURE. There is in all men a yearning for *visible* signs of God. "Show us some sign!" is the natural demand of the human mind. Even Moses had passionately asked, "I beseech thee, show me thy glory." Satan employs a thousand wily artifices to corrupt the spiritual impulses of the heart. Speciously, idolatry asks to be tolerated as a *symbol,* and then detains our faith as if it were the *substantial object.*

II. IDOLATRY IS THE FRUITFUL PARENT OF VICE AND CRUELTY. We can never deal with forms of idolatry as if they were mere intellectual vagaries. The worship of material images has always been associated with sensuality, obscenity, and vice. It deteriorates human nature, hardens sensibility, and clips the wing of aspiration. When the seed has grown to the mature tree, human victims are demanded as oblations. "The children were compelled to pass through the fire." Atrocious cruelty is the last effect.

III. IDOLATRY IS HATEFUL IN GOD'S ESTEEM. It is impossible for us to err if we make the supreme God our model. To the extent that we know God, we must endeavour to assimilate our tastes to his, to love what he loves and to hate what he hates. Idolatry, in any form (whether of graven image, or material wealth, or human friend) is overt treason against God. If *we* cannot see the inherent wickedness of idolatry, it should be enough for us to know that it is an abomination before God, "a smoke in his eyes; a stench in his nostrils."

IV. IDOLATRY IS A SOURCE OF NATIONAL AND INDIVIDUAL RUIN. In that early period of human history, the spirit of idolatry must have been rampant. It was the curse of the age. Although the Hebrews had seen the practical effects of idolatry in Egypt; although they had themselves been the executors of God's vengeance against idolatry in Canaan; nevertheless the tendencies to idolatry were, humanly speaking, irresistible. It had been the source of Pharaoh's overthrow. It had been the occasion of a great slaughter among the Hebrews under the peaks of Sinai. It was the parent of the vices and crimes that prevailed among the Amorites. Idolatry is doomed by an eternal decree, and if men persist in identifying themselves with it, *they* are doomed also. Let us be well guarded against so insidious an evil!—D.

EXPOSITION.

CHAPTER XIII.

IDOLATERS AND ENTICERS TO IDOLATRY TO BE PUT TO DEATH.

Vers. 1—5.—The case supposed here is that of one professing to have supernatural intelligence, who should, by giving a sign or a wonder, endeavour to draw away the people to idolatry. Such a one was to be put to death.

Ver. 1.—A prophet (*nabhi*, נָבִיא); one who speaks from God, an interpreter to men of what God reveals or suggests to him (cf. for the meaning of the word, Exod. vii. 1 with iv. 16; also Jer. xv. 19). Dreamer of dreams. Not by visions or immediate suggestion only, but also by means of dreams, did God communicate with men (cf. Numb. xii. 6). The case supposed here, then, is that of one pretending to have had revelations from God through those media by which God was pleased to convey his will to men (cf. Hom., 'Iliad,' i. 62—

"'Αλλ' ἄγε δή τινα μάντιν ἐρείομεν. . . .
ἢ καὶ ὀνειροπόλον, καὶ γάρ τ' ὄναρ ἔκ Διός
ἐστιν.")

Sign or a wonder. A *sign* was some event foretold by the prophet, and the occurrence of which was a token that something else which he announced would happen or should be done (cf. 1 Sam. ii. 34; x. 7—9; 2 Kings xix. 29; Isa. vii. 11—14; xxxviii. 7; Mark xiii. 4, etc.). A *wonder* was a miracle, the performance of which gave proof of a Divine commission (cf. ch. iv. 24). These signs, it is assumed, should come to pass; nevertheless, the people were not to listen to the man who gave them to go after other gods. The mere fact that he sought to persuade them to forsake the worship of Jehovah was sufficient to prove him an impostor; for how could one who sought to seduce the people from God be sent by God? The sign which was given to authenticate such a message could only be one of those "lying signs and wonders after the working of Satan," by which his emis-

saries try to deceive and mislead; and was permitted by God only that their fidelity to him might be tested and proved. They had already received God's message; they had his word; and no teaching which contravened that, however apparently authenticated, could be from him, or was to be accepted by them (cf. Jer. xxix. 8; Gal. i. 8, 9; 1 John iii. 1, etc.). Come what might, they were to **walk after Jehovah their God, and keep his commandments, and obey his voice, and serve him, and cleave unto him.** The false prophet, as a public enemy and a suborner of treason against the King of Israel, was to be put to death; and so the evil would be put away from among them.

Vers. 6—11.—A second case supposed is that of temptation to apostacy proceeding from some near relative or intimate friend. Not only was this to be resisted, but no consideration of affection or bond of friendship was to be allowed to interfere with the stern sentence which doomed the tempter to death; on the contrary, the person tempted was to be the first to lay hands on the tempter and put him to death. This was to be done by stoning, and the person he had tried to seduce was to cast the first stone.

Ver. 6.—**Thy brother, the son of thy mother**; thy full brother, allied to thee by the closest fraternal tie. **The wife of thy bosom**; the object of thy tenderest affection, whom it is thine to protect and cherish (cf. ch. xxviii. 54, 56; Micah vii. 5). **Thy friend, which is as thine own soul**; *i.e.* whom thou lovest as thyself. The word translated "friend" (רֵעַ, for רֵעֶה) is from a verb which signifies to delight in, and conveys primarily the idea not merely of a companion, but of a friend in whom one delights; and the definition of true friendship is the loving another as one's self (Aristot., 'Eth. Nic.,' ix. 5). As commonly used, however, the word designates any one with whom one has any dealing or intercourse; and so our Lord expounds it (Luke x. 29, etc.). **Secretly.**

If the temptation was in private, and so known only to thyself.

Ver. 8.—**Pity, spare, conceal.** The accumulation of terms serves to make the injunction more solemn and impressive.

Ver. 11.—The penalty publicly inflicted, and therefore generally known, would have a deterrent effect on the community, so as to prevent the recurrence of such evil.

Vers. 12—18.—A third case supposed is that of the inhabitants of a city being seduced by wicked men into idolatry. In this case inquiry was to be made as to the fact; and if it was found to be so, the inhabitants of that city were to be put to the sword, all their property was to be burnt, and the city itself reduced to a heap; so should the anger of the Lord be averted from Israel, and he would do them good.

Ver. 12.—**Hear in one of thy cities.** The Hebrew phrase, "to hear in" (שְׁמַע בְּ) has sometimes the meaning of to overhear, as in Gen. xxvii. 5; 1 Sam. xvii. 28; Job. xv. 8; sometimes it means simply to hear, as in 2 Sam. xix. 36 [35]; in Job xxvi. 14, it has the force of to hear of or concerning, though some think this questionable. This latter is apparently the meaning here: *If thou hear concerning any of thy cities,* etc. **Saying.** This introduces what is heard.

Ver. 13.—**Men, the children of Belial;** *the sons of worthlessness,* utterly worthless persons. *Beli ya'al* (a compound of בְּלִי, not, and עָלָה, to ascend, to have worth, to profit) means primarily that which is low, hence worthlessness, naughtiness, wickedness. In ch. xv. 9, Belial is rendered in the Authorized Version as an adjective, "wicked," and also in Neh. i. 11. In Ps. xviii. 4, it is

rendered by "ungodly men." Most commonly it is treated as a proper name. But in all places the proper meaning of the word might be retained. The Hebrews described an object, of which any quality was predominantly characteristic, as the son of that quality. **Are gone out from among you;** have gone forth from the midst of you, *i.e.* have risen up among yourselves. **Withdraw.** The verb here is the same as that rendered by "thrust," in vers. 5 and 10. It conveys the idea of drawing away with some degree of force, not mere easy seduction, but impulsion by strong persuasion.

Vers. 14, 15.—After due inquiry, if it was found that such a thing had really been done in any of their cities, the extreme penalty was to be inflicted on the city and all its inhabitants—all were to be destroyed. **Smite . . . with the edge of the sword;** literally, *with the mouth of the sword,* as biting and devouring like a ravenous beast—a phrase for utter destruction.

Ver. 16.—**All the spoil thereof every whit, for the Lord thy God;** rather, *all the spoil* [booty] *thereof as a whole offering unto Jehovah thy God;* it was to be wholly devoted to God, and as such to be consumed by fire. "It was a destruction, and not properly an offering. Hence the author selects neither עוֹלָה nor חַטָּאת, but כָּלִיל, whole, whole offering (ch. xxxiii. 10; Lev. vi. 15 [22]), which word, in the law concerning offering, is no technical designation of any particular kind of offering. The rendering *omnino* is untenable" (Knobel). The city was to be made a ruin, never to be rebuilt; and thus was to be treated the same as a heathen, idolatrous city might be (cf. Numb. xxi. 3).

HOMILETICS.

Vers. 1—18.—*Temptations to depart from God to be resisted at all costs.* In the preceding chapter we had directions with regard to the worship of the true God. Here Israel is told what to do in case of temptation arising to worship false gods. The chapter in its entirety deals with this one topic. From it we might open up two main homiletic themes: (1) the treatment of error; (2) the test of truth. The second, however, we reserve till we come to ch. xviii. 21. The first, therefore, only, we deal with now. In doing this we must remember that Moses is not only the expounder of religious duty, but also of a judicial polity. He is not only the prophet, but the legislator. Israel's constitution as a nation was that of a *Theocratic Church-State.* It is supposed, in this chapter, that temptations to depart from God may come (1) from a professed prophet or wonder-worker, or (2) they may arise from the nearest relative or bosom friend, or (3) they may come from a town or city. In either case, the infection is to be "stamped out" at once. Any enticement to idolatry, come whence it may, is not to be tolerated for a moment. The wonder-worker is to be put to death; the friend is to be slain; the city is to be destroyed. All this may seem harsh. Perhaps it is not so harsh as it seems. There may be occasions when severity is the greatest kindness, and when tolerance would be the greatest unkindness. In the early Christian

Church, the sudden death of Ananias and Sapphira seemed severe. But the instantaneous cutting out of the canker of hypocrisy was, as it were, the surgical operation which only would save the Church. So here. There are three principles which were at stake in such cases as those here supposed. 1. The supremacy of Jehovah was the key-stone of their national constitution. Consequently, the attempt to draw Israel away after other gods was treason to the State, and must be dealt with accordingly. 2. The aim of Jehovah in choosing Israel was to separate to himself a people for his Name. Hence if they did not forcibly repress idolatrous worship, the very reason of their separate existence as a people would cease. 3. Since the very continuance of Israel depended on the continuance of their *raison d'être*, for them not to stamp out idolatry would be to blot out themselves. It is a commonplace saying with reference to legislation, that it is to be tested—not by the query, "What is abstractly the best?" but by another, "What will be the best for such and such a people?" Now, looking at all the circumstances of Israel, it would be very hard to say that any better, or even any other mode of securing the desired end could have been adopted. Here, as throughout the legislation, the people are supposed to be in full sympathy with Jehovah, and are themselves to co-operate in carrying out his Law (see Homily on ch. xxvii.). We have no warrant to apply the rules here given in detail, anywhere, because we have nowhere existing any people that, on the earthly side of its life, occupies a like position to Israel. Therefore no argument for a like extirpation of heresy can now be rightly maintained, because no parallel can now be shown of a nation with like constitution. But nevertheless, as in the preceding chapter we had permanent principles embodied under specific rules, so it is in this.

I. WE HAVE TRUTHS OF SUPREME MOMENT INDICATED HERE, WHICH ARE CAPABLE OF APPLICATION TO THE GOVERNMENT OF THE CHURCH OF GOD.[1] It is not possible to do more than briefly indicate the line of thought which such an application of the principles here laid down would involve. 1. Israel's place in the world is now filled by the Church of God, which is "the commonwealth of Israel," into which all enter who believe through grace. 2. The Church is set for the maintenance and defence in the world of the great truths of our most holy faith, and she is "earnestly to contend for the faith once (for all) delivered to the saints." 3. This Church is to be a self-governing body, having within itself all the powers and authorities for self-regulation and discipline. The Epistles to the seven Churches show this abundantly. 4. The Church is to be very jealous in guarding the glorious gospel of the blessed God. Amid all changes of public sentiment and opinion on minor points, she is to hold fast the cardinal truth, that no advance of public thought can warrant her in surrendering the one vital truth on which her existence depends, without which she would have had no existence, nor could show any reason why she should continue to exist. 5. This one truth, which she is to conserve intact age after age, is analogous to the one which Israel was so sacredly to guard. Israel was to keep watch over the truth—Jehovah, he is the Lord. The Church has now to guard the doctrine that Jesus is the Christ, the Son of the living God (see 1 John iv. 1—4). The Church might as well cease to be as let that truth go. It is "the doctrine which is according to godliness." She is to guard the doctrine which tends to godliness, and to maintain the godliness which is to illustrate the doctrine. 6. She has within herself means and powers for the defence of the faith, and for visiting with monition, censure, suspension, or excommunication, those who deny it or disgrace it (1 Cor. v.; Matt. xviii. 17—20; Titus iii. 10, 11, etc.). 7. Her weapons are not carnal. She has no power to use the sword (Matt. xxvi. 52; 2 Cor. x. 3—8). 8. Nor has the Church any power towards those that are not within her pale (1 Cor. v. 12, 13), *i.e.* she has no power of judging. She has to be a witness for God to the outlying world, and that she may be this she is to keep herself pure.

II. THE PRINCIPLES OF THE CHAPTER HAVE A CONSTANT APPLICATION TO THE

---

[1] Bishop Wordsworth has a very long and elaborate note on this chapter, which is well worthy of perusal, in spite of the fallacy which—doubtless from oversight—runs through it. The author says that it was on the principles here laid down that the Jews condemned our Lord to death. Surely not. True, our Lord wrought miracles. But he never wrought them to confirm any message about going and serving other gods. The most perfect loyalty to the great invisible Father marked the "only begotten Son." This chapter does not seem to apply to him in any such way.

INDIVIDUAL LIFE. "Ye shall walk after the Lord" embodies New Testament teaching as well as Old. On the basis of the chapter before us, the following outline of thought may well be filled up. 1. Absolute loyalty to Christ should be the governing principle of life. The Jehovah of the Old Testament is the Christ of the New. He is the Mediator of the new covenant. He is a Legislator of more glory than Moses (Heb. iii.). He appeals to us by righteousness, love, hope, fear. 2. Temptations to desert Christ's standard may pour in upon us from various quarters. The chapter suggests three. (1) A prophet. There may arise some new claimant for man's homage, or some philosopher who thinks to disprove the claims of Jesus by showing his own wondrous intellectual stature, etc. (2) The family. Seductions either to the false in faith or the corrupt in practice may come from those near and dear to us. (3) The city. A strong current of public sentiment, adverse to "the truth as it is in Jesus," may set in, and may threaten to carry us away. 3. These temptations are to be withstood at all costs. No "sign," no "wonder," is ever to be allowed to dazzle us for a moment. Christ's claims are so convincing to the conscience and heart, they are sustained by such overwhelming evidence, that nothing in any age can set them aside. The sovereignty of Christ is the fundamental law of our life. He will allow no rival whatsoever. Even if men should work miracles to lead us away from Christ, we are to follow Christ, and let miracles go for nought. Even under the Mosaic Law, miracles were not a *sufficient* test of truth. The doctrine they were intended to confirm must be put alongside therewith, and if this doctrine contravened the supreme canon of moral life, "Loyalty to God," it was to be set aside. So now. No physical wonder can ever justify us in ignoring supreme moral law. The Lordship of Jesus is our highest moral law. He is to us the embodiment of righteousness, truth, and love; yea, he is our incarnate God. 4. Though we may not visit our enticers with pains and penalties, yet, even now, the most sacred claims and relationships of our earthly life are to be renounced if they come into collision with our loyalty to Jesus (see Luke xiv. 26—33). Even though the temptations should come from all quarters at once, our loyalty to our Saviour is to remain unmoved. We may not halt, nor waver, nor seek a feigned neutrality (Matt. xii. 30). It will be a very far more serious thing for us if we let ourselves be seduced from loyalty to God as revealed in Christ, than it would have been for Israel if they proved fickle under the legislation of Moses (Heb. ii. 1—4; x. 28—31). How earnestly should we pray that we may be kept faithful to our dear Lord in heaven! How lovingly should we warn others, lest they swerve from their fealty to him (2 Pet. iii. 17, 18; Jude 17—25; Rev. ii. 10, 11; Matt. xxiv. 11—13)!

HOMILIES BY VARIOUS AUTHORS.

Vers. 1—6.—*False prophets.* In viewing the bearings of this passage on the credentials of revelation, two points should be observed. 1. The case supposed is one in which the prophet contradicts a revelation already received. 2. The prophet does not dispute the evidence of that earlier revelation. On the contrary, he admits it. He stands within the lines of it. He professes to speak under its authority. Yet he asks the people to violate its fundamental laws. This of itself was sufficient to convict him. His pretensions are disposed of by the simple fact that, professing to speak in the Name of God, he gives the people a message contradictory of what he admits God to have previously revealed. No sign and wonder can accredit contradictions. The prophet is inconsistent with himself, and is not to be listened to. Nay, his message had been anticipated, and the thing he bids the people do, expressly forbidden. Notice, then—

I. EXTERNAL MIRACLES DO NOT OF THEMSELVES ACCREDIT A REVELATION AS FROM GOD. (Vers. 1—3.) This prophet gives a sign or wonder—presumably a predictive word—and it actually comes to pass. The failure of his sign, according to ch. xviii. 21, 22, would have been a proof of falsity. The converse of this, however, that he speaks God's word because his sign has *not* failed, is not immediately to be admitted. There are other tests to be applied. In this case, the prophet's message is condemned because contradictory of what he himself allows to have been a true revelation. This raises the question of the value of miracles as credentials of revelation. That they have a value is not disputed, but not as mere signs and wonders. This will be best seen by contrasting the sign or wonder given by this prophet with the evidence of the earlier revelation. If we take the Scripture account of the founding of the Mosaic dispensation, it is impossible to question the magnificence and convincingness of the displays of Divine power and holiness therein contained. In founding his dispensations (Mosaic and Christian), God has not only given evidence, but an *amount* and *kind* of evidence which put the source of the revelation—admitting the facts to be as stated—beyond all cavil. For here, it is not merely the fact of miracle which is to be regarded, but the number, nature, magnitude, variety, spiritual quality of the supernatural events, in connection with the self-evidencing divineness of the revelation itself. The difficulty as to whether the miracle proves the doctrine, or the doctrine the miracle, or in what proportions the two factors combine, has little place in the actual evidences of revelation. The two cannot be separated, either in thought or in fact. Grant the authenticity of the miracles of the Gospels or of the Pentateuch, and it will not be disputed that they originated with God, not with Beelzebub. To this mass of evidence, overwhelming in its sublimity and convincingness—evidence embracing the wonders of Egypt, the displays of God's power, love, and grace in the events of the Exodus, the miracles of the desert, the stupendous revelations of Sinai, etc.—the prophet opposes a few stray signs and wonders. Which were the people to believe? Plainly, no sign or wonder would have justified an Israelite in believing a prophet whose teaching contradicted the first principles of *his* revelation; as no sign or wonder would justify us in believing teachings contradictory of the first principles of *ours*.

II. THE RISE OF FALSE PROPHETS IS TO BE ANTICIPATED. (Ver. 1.) The passage takes it for granted that they will arise. They did arise in Old Testament times, and they will do so again. Their appearance is predicted in connection with "the last days" (Matt. xxiv. 11; 1 Tim. iv. 1; 2 Pet. ii. 1). "Signs and wonders" will not be wanting (Matt. xxiv. 24; 2 Thess. ii. 9, 10). False teachers are included under the category of false prophets (Matt. vii. 15; 2 Pet. ii. 1). They assert as the truth of God principles and doctrines subversive of the revelation God has given. The readiness of people to believe them arises from want of knowledge (Eph. iv. 14); from the itch for novelties (2 Tim. iv. 3); from a diseased craving for the marvellous—witness the credulity displayed in connection with spiritualism (2 Thess. ii. 9—13); above all, from the adaptation of their teachings to the inclinations of depraved hearts (2 Tim. iii. 1—8).

III. THE RISE OF FALSE PROPHETS IS PERMITTED FOR THE SIFTING OF THE CHURCH. (Ver. 3.) God has thus much to do with their appearance that he permits it as a means of proving and sifting the Church. The trial is a searching and real one. The plausibility of their errors may occasion, even to believers, much mental conflict. But out of this conflict they come forth strengthened and purified, with firmer hold upon the truth, and clearer insight into Scripture. Those willing to be deceived are, on the other hand, led by the spirit of delusion. False prophets shake all but "the very elect" (Matt. xxiv. 24). The heresies, schisms, controversies, etc., which have agitated the Church, with the teachings of antichristian philosophy and science outside of it, have always had this effect of sifting, while in the end they have subserved the progress of the truth.

IV. THE TEACHING OF FALSE PROPHETS IS TO BE REJECTED. 1. Their doctrine is to be tried by its conformity with the rule of faith (Isa. viii. 20). John bids us "try the spirits," giving as the reason that "many false prophets are gone out into the world" (1 John iv. 1). 2. Their doctrine, if found contradictory of Scripture, is to be unhesitatingly rejected. 3. Of old, the prophet whose teachings struck at the foundations of the theocracy was to be put to death (ver. 5). This rule no longer applies. But it is the duty of the Church, in the exercise of her judicial functions, to deprive such a teacher of office and status in her ministry (see also 2 John 10, 11).—J. O.

Vers. 6—12.—*God or our brother.* Terribly stern is the duty here laid on the person enticed to idolatry. The law is adapted to an age of stern deeds, and to a people living under a stern dispensation. Yet, reflecting on the nature of the crime, on the constitution of the Jewish state, and on the issues to mankind which hung on the slender thread of this one nation's fidelity, it is difficult to see how it could well have been less stern than it is. Its severity was perhaps its mercy. Note, too, that the criminal could be executed only after formal impeachment, fair trial, and conclusively established guilt (cf. ver. 14; ch. xvii. 2—8; xix. 15—21).

I. GOD ALLOWS NO CLAIM OF NATURAL AFFECTION TO INTERFERE WITH HIGHER DUTY TO HIMSELF. It is the same stern voice which we hear even in the Gospels (Matt. viii. 21, 22; x. 37; Luke xiv. 26). The demands of God on his people's supreme and undivided allegiance are not now a whit less rigorous than they were of old.

II. GOD WOULD HAVE US REGARD THOSE WHO DELIBERATELY ATTEMPT TO SEDUCE US FROM HIM AS OUR WORST FOES. They really are so, whether they think it or not. No language is strong enough to paint the crime of seeking to seduce a soul from its allegiance to its God. The guilt of the man who deliberately sets himself to counter-work a child's affection for its parent, and to produce alienation of heart between them, is trivial in comparison with it. The crime is that of soul-murder. For in fidelity to God lies the happiness of life here, and salvation in the world to come. We are not, therefore, to allow any private affection to blind us to the enormity of this crime. Those whom we cherish as dearest are only the more guilty if they take advantage of our affection to betray us into deadly sin.

III. GOD REQUIRES THAT WE DO NOT SPARE THOSE WHO ARE GUILTY OF THIS CRIME. We are no longer called upon—and we may be thankful for it—to impeach our seducers, and lead them out to death. Our religion requires that we return good for evil, that we pray for those who injure us, that we seek their conversion and salvation. But it does not require of us that we do not abhor their conduct, and severely reprobate and denounce it. We fail in duty if there is not placed on all attempts at spiritual seduction the immediate brand of our strongest condemnation.—J. O.

Vers. 12—18.—*A city under ban.* The case here supposed is even more appalling than the former one, for it is the inhabitants of a whole city who, with all that they have, are to be destroyed. Yet, as it is certain that godly persons, dreading the execution of this sentence, would leave this city as soon as they found out what was going on—being very possibly the bearers of the tidings to others—the curse would practically take effect only on those who were in league with the idolaters. Searching investigation was to precede the infliction of doom (ver. 14).

I. EVIL-DISPOSED PERSONS CAN DO MUCH HARM. A few men—"children of Belial"—perhaps, at first, but one or two, succeed in seducing, and ultimately in destroying, a whole city. Their cancerous influence speedily infected the mass. Like fire breaking out in a little corner of a building, it soon involved the whole place in ruin. "One sinner destroyeth much good" (Eccles. ix. 18). "Evil communications corrupt good manners" (1 Cor. xv. 33). Evil is not to be thought lightly of, because at first confined to a few individuals, and circumscribed in its range of operations. It will spread faster than good.

II. THE SPIRITUAL CONDITION OF EACH CITY IS OF INTEREST TO THE WHOLE COMMUNITY. Disease in one part of the social organism will speedily communicate itself to the other parts.

III. IMMEDIATE ACTION SHOULD BE TAKEN TO REDUCE EVIL IN ITS CHOSEN SEATS. No longer, indeed, with carnal weapons. We have no warrant to proceed by fire and sword. A better way is open to us of reducing evil than by judicial slaughter. The wickedness of a city is doubtless a token of God's wrath resting upon it. If it repent not, his judgments will fall upon it with all the old severity. But it does not lie with us to give effect to these judgments; God keeps them in his own hand. Our work, meanwhile, is the happier one of seeking the reduction of evil by spiritual means—by reasoning, by persuasion, by preaching of the truth, by substituting good influences for bad ones. These weapons are adequate to the work for which they are given, and ought to be plied to the utmost. Places differ in spiritual character. There are those of which it may be said—as of Pergamos, "where Satan's seat is" (Rev. ii. 13)—that in them evil has a kind of stronghold. Against these, by preference, the assaults of God's servants should be directed. The apostles chose for their attacks the leading centres of pagan influence. One stronghold gained is worth a dozen outposts.—J. O.

Vers. 1—18.—*Idolatry to be treated as a capital crime.* This chapter relates to the Israelites themselves. As the government was a theocracy, idolatry in any form was *treason* against the Divine King, and justly punishable with death. The previous chapter (vers. 29—32) affords timely warning against sinful curiosity about heathen practices; and in this chapter the people are warned against all who would tempt them towards idolatry. The three cases mentioned are worthy of separate study.

I. THE FALSE PROPHET, WITH HIS SIGNS AND WONDERS. Moses admits the possibility of signs and wonders in the interests of idolatry. This raises the whole question of *miracles.* These may be "helps to faith," or they may be "a trial of faith."[1] It is evidently in the latter light that they are to be regarded when the wonder-worker wishes to lead them to idolatry. The horror of idolatry is really to fortify them against the miracle, so that, though it may try their faith, it will not overcome it. A miracle in itself, consequently, is not decisive, but must be taken along with the doctrine it proposes to support. God allows the miracle to be wrought by the false prophet to prove his people, " to know whether they love the Lord their God with all their heart and with all their soul " (ver. 3).

The false prophet is to be taken, as a criminal convicted of a capital offence, and put to death. He has acted a traitor's part among God's subjects, and must suffer a traitor's doom. By this terrible judgment does God stamp out all tendency to idolatry.

II. THE NEAR RELATIVE AS A SEDUCER TO IDOLATRY. The false prophet might fail, and a near relative succeed. The public miracle, with its meretricious ostentation, might be withstood, while the unostentatious and secret insinuation of a near relative might prevail. Hence the instruction in these verses, 6—11, as to how the idol-loving relative is to be treated. Not only is the insinuation to be put away, but the person making it, no matter how nearly related, is to be treated as a public criminal, and put to death. All the sympathy which blood relationship ensures is to be set aside before this crime of appalling magnitude, and the relative is to cast the first stone at the apostate, the execution being completed by " the hand of all the people."

III. THE APOSTACY OF A CITY. In this collective case, after a careful investigation, the utter destruction of the city is to be carried out, the idolatrous inhabitants are to be put to death, with all their cattle, their property burnt with fire, and the city to be never afterwards rebuilt (vers. 12—18). The idolatry, in propagating itself, must be stamped out even more carefully than in the individual cases of apostasy already mentioned. The sin must not be tolerated in the theocracy.

IV. WE SHOULD SURELY LEARN FROM THIS HOW HEINOUS EVERY KIND OF IDOLATRY IS TO THE MOST HIGH. We may be idolaters through covetousness (Col. iii. 5), through ambition, through any disposition to look for succour to things or persons instead of to God. It may be as needful for us to be exhorted against this sin, as it was for those to whom John in his Epistle wrote, " Little children, keep yourselves from idols " (1 John v. 21). The temptation is strong to live by sense and sight instead of by faith.

It will help us in withstanding temptation to remember how heinous the sin is! It is not less a sin because now idolaters are not taken out to a public place and executed. We deserve execution, though we do not receive it. For idolatry is high treason against God. When we trust, *e.g.* in money or in men, so as to attribute to them the powers belonging really to God, we rob him of his rights and bestow them upon others. If this was a capital offence in the Mosaic times, it is no less offensive to the Lord now. He is changeless in his judgments, and so must regard the iniquity as in the same serious light as ever. In such circumstances it surely becomes us—

1. *To humble ourselves most penitently before God because of our idolatries.* We have been guilty of greater crimes than we suspected, and consequently should entertain the deepest possible penitence.

2. *We should carefully abstain from all tendencies to an idolatrous spirit.* "Keep yourselves from idols," says John. It shows how much is in our own power. We can abstain from much idolatry, if we are only watchful. In loyalty to God, out of respect for his honour and glory, we ought to keep ourselves in a trustful, humble attitude

---

[1] Cf. Canon Mozley, ' On Miracles,' 2nd edit., p. 26; also Taylor's ' The Miracles: Helps to Faith, not Hindrances.'

towards him, and reject every temptation to transfer our allegiance. We shall thus find ourselves going forward steadily in the exercise of spiritual purity and power.— R. M. E.

Vers. 1—18.—*God's executioners upon idolaters.* No respecter of persons is God. The sin of all sins is idolatry, and such overt rebels against the supreme God shall be summarily punished, whether they be Amorites or Hebrews. As a rule, complete retribution is reserved for the future state; the full effect of evil ways is not seen in this life. Yet there are sins so flagrant—so mischievous in their present influence, that God employs his agents, personal or impersonal, to execute his verdicts promptly and manifestly. It is not that infinite justice is not content to wait; it is that God is so solicitous for the good of the human race, that he puts forth his hand to arrest the moral pestilence. In this chapter we learn—

I. That God had assured Israel of his unity, supremacy, and goodness. In that early age men had not indulged in intellectual speculation touching the existence of a God. Mind had not yet formulated its proofs, nor its disproofs. The tendency of depraved tastes and instincts was practically to ignore a spiritual Deity, and to put a rash confidence in inferior beings or in intermediate agents. The demonstrations which God gave of his supremacy, to Israel in Egypt, were demonstrations addressed to their practical experience. They had been bondmen. They had long endured a crushing oppression. They were reduced to a condition of abject and dependent weakness. By *whom* had they been rescued from Pharaoh's giant grasp? By whom? Not by any angelic champion, nor by any of the idols of the earth! Obviously, and without question, they had been recovered to freedom and to national life by the arm of Jehovah and by none other! Their new condition was the manifest proof that *God* reigned, and that he had gloriously triumphed. The unity and supremacy of the true God was established upon a solid basis. This cardinal truth shone upon the nation with the clear radiance of noon day. If anything was known *this* was known, that Jehovah was absolute Monarch—God of gods and Lord of lords. Of this grand truth Israel was a witness to all the nations of the earth.

II. That Israel's faith in God was sometimes put to severe tests by the pretexts of diviners. The dream of fanatics would *at times* be verified. The arts of necromancers would *sometimes* succeed. Base motives of gain and renown would keep these pursuits alive. The specious successes *may* have been fortunate coincidences. They *may* have been specially permitted by God for wise and practical purposes. They served as a test for the faith of Israel. Faith never put to the proof would soon lose its tone and fibre. Granted that the prediction of a soothsayer found fulfilment, was this sufficient ground for sundering their loyalty to Jehovah?—any ground for recognizing the power of an idol-god? Granted that something might be said on behalf of intermediate intelligencies—agents and servants of the Most High— did this warrant their offering to *such,* honours which were the prerogative of Jehovah alone? Had not Jehovah *alone* redeemed them from Egyptian misery, and led them through the wilderness? And did not every impulse of gratitude, and every principle of reason, require that Jehovah alone should be worshipped? These artifices of soothsayers would serve to test their faith, and (if faith was sound) to brace and strengthen it. For this they should have rejoiced greatly, that the "trial of their faith, more precious far than gold, though it were tried by fire, might appear unto praise and honour and glory."

III. That God had appointed Israel to be his executioner of all idolaters. The only reasonable ground on which the Hebrews could vindicate their possession of Canaan was, that the foul idolatries of the Canaanites had made them a pest and a curse upon the globe. And if now the conquerors should yield to the habits and vices of the conquered, reason and right would require that they likewise should be displaced. The Nemesis of extermination had fallen upon the dwellers in Canaan, not because they were Canaanites, but because they were *idolaters.* Abraham had been called out of Charran, and received the promise of Canaan, that he might be a living and loyal witness for God. And the special mission of Abraham's posterity was to stamp out idolatry, and to lift high the banner of Jehovah. To do this effectually, no connivance with the cursed thing must be tolerated. If the luminous agent employed to shed light makes alliance with the element of darkness, its mission is terminated: it is good for nothing. Hence, in order that the Hebrews might keep alive the lamp of heavenly truth, they must burn pure oil. The evil growth must be nipped in the bud. The dread disease must be checked at its very first symptom. If they are to continue "the sacramental host of God's elect," no secret foe must be concealed in the camp. The decree had gone forth, "Idolatry shall cease!" and Israel had been commissioned to execute that decree.

IV. That Israel's loyalty to God required the subordination of all other ties and claims. The ligaments of blood relationship are strong—dear as very life. The ties of friendship and of conjugal love are tender and sacred. No language can adequately set them forth. Yet God has a prior claim. His will forestalls every other obligation. The love which is due to him overleaps every boundary—absorbs every other affection. "With *all* the heart, and soul, and mind, and strength," *that* love to him, if adequate, must be. And this superior and incomparable obligation of love will sometimes necessitate most painful self-denial—the amputation of a right hand, the sacrifice of a right eye. The demand made upon the Jews, to slay a wife or child, if addicted to idolatry, was a demand replete with awful severity; yet no one can question its righteousness. And if so be the will of God is clearly understood, natural inclination must yield to dutiful obedience. Said the immaculate Son, "I do always the things that please *him*."

V. That the habit of idolatry must be rooted out, though it may require the most drastic measures. 1. *Searching investigation was first required* (ver. 14). They were to inquire—to inquire "*diligently*"—to search into the very heart of the matter. It would be a crime—yea, a murder—if they should act judicially on mere rumour or through any evil bias. The very utmost endeavours to reach the facts were required in the interests of truth and humanity. Certainty of the fact must precede any sentence of destruction. 2. *The perilous effects of evil influence* (ver. 13). Certain men of Belial can draw away into rebellion the inhabitants of a whole city. Some men of strong will and clever ingenuity are well adapted to lead their fellows; and men of weak judgment readily follow. Both classes err. Men of superior parts are highly responsible to use their powers as God-entrusted talents; and those possessing lesser capacity are bound to examine for themselves, and to suspend action until judgment is convinced. 3. *Where idolatry was clearly proved, the most complete punishment was exacted.* The whole Hebrew nation were at once converted into soldiers, and were summoned to assail that miscreant city. The body politic was to gather up into a point all its righteous strength, and expel that foreign evil from its midst. No mercy was to be shown; no life was to be spared. Not a lamb in the flock was to escape; not an ounce of spoil was to be gathered. The executors of God's vengeance must be above all suspicion of selfish and sordid interest. No material gain must accrue to them. The charred and blackened ruins of *that* city were to be a monument for ever of the righteous severity of Jehovah.

VI. That the design of punishment is the moral good of survivors. (Vers. 5, 11, 17.) The effect anticipated was *this*, "All Israel shall hear, and fear, and do no more any such wickedness." On God's side the result would be that he would "turn and show them mercy, and multiply" their numbers. Very clearly was it announced that this judicial action was the action of God—that righteous and obedient Hebrews were the officers of Jehovah. In view of the magnificent results upon the whole nation, yea, upon the world, this grave disaster might be patiently endured. To spare the lives of these rebels, and yet to retain the favour of Jehovah, was a sheer impossibility. A severe choice was demanded. The remedy was painful, but the effect anticipated was precious. The smile of God, and the moral elevation of the nation, were the practical fruits. In these benign results, the survivors would have great occasion for grateful joy. The destruction of sinners is a beacon-light, to which *we* also should take heed.—D.

EXPOSITION.

CHAPTER XIV.

HEATHEN CUSTOMS OF MOURNING TO BE AVOIDED. NO ABOMINABLE THING TO BE EATEN. MEATS CLEAN AND UNCLEAN. TITHES.

Vers. 1—21.—Israel, as the people of God, chosen by him to be his children by adoption, must not only abstain from idolatry, but also avoid all heathenish usages and practices, such as those connected with mourning for the dead, and those pertaining to the use of food.

Ver. 1.—**Ye are the children of Jehovah your God** (cf. Exod. iv. 22, etc.). As his children, it behoved them to avoid all that would be offensive to him or indicate distrust in him. **Ye shall not cut yourselves,** etc. (cf. Lev. xix. 28; xxi. 5; Jer. xvi. 6; xlviii. 36, 37; Ezek. vii. 18; xxvii. 31). ("Ex hac opinione sunt illa varia et detestabilia genera lugendi, pædores, muliebres lacerationes genarum, pectoris, feminum, capitis percussiones." Cicero, 'Tusc. Quæst.,' iii. 26; see also 'De Legibus,' ii. 25.)

Ver. 2.—(Cf. ch. vii. 6.) The reason assigned here is an emphatic expansion of the statement in ver. 1.

Ver. 3.—**Any abominable thing.** Any abomination, i.e. anything which is an abomination to the Lord, having been by him pronounced unclean and forbidden; "anything which I have put far away from you (i.e. made to be abominable to you)" (Targum Jonath.). "Every creature of God is good," and "there is nothing unclean of itself" (1 Tim. iv. 4; Rom. xiv. 14); "but by the ordinance of God, certain creatures, meats, and drinks were made unclean to the Jews, . . . and this taught them holiness in abstaining from the impure communion with the wicked" (Ainsworth).

Vers. 4—20.—The regulations here concerning food, and the animals the use of which is forbidden, are substantially the same as in Lev. ii. There are, however, some differences between the two accounts which may be noticed. 1. In Deuteronomy, the mammals which may be used for food are severally specified as well as described by the general characteristic of the class; in Leviticus, only the latter description is given. 2. In the list of fowls which may not be eaten, the ra'ah (glede) is mentioned in Deuteronomy, but not in Leviticus; and the bird which in the one is called da'ah, is in the other called dayyah (vulture). 3. The class of reptiles which is carefully described

in Leviticus is wholly omitted in Deuteronomy. 4. Winged insects are forbidden without exception in Deuteronomy; in Leviticus, the locust and certain other insects of the same kind are excepted. 5. Some slight differences in the order of enumeration appear.

Ver. 5.—**The hart;** ayyál (אַיָּל), probably the fallow deer, or deer generally. **The roebuck;** tsebi (צְבִי), the gazelle (Gazella Arabica). **The fallow deer;** yachmúr (יַחְמוּר), the roebuck. **The wild goat;** akko (אַקּוֹ), the ibex. **The pygarg;** dishôn (דִּישׁוֹן), some kind of antelope, probably the Gazella Dorcas. **The wild ox;** the'o (תְאוֹ), probably the bubale, or wild cow of the Arabs (Alcephalus bubalis), a species of antelope. **The chamois;** zamer (זֶמֶר), probably the wild sheep (Ovis Tragelaphus.

Ver. 13.—**The glede;** ra'ah (רָאָה). This word occurs only here, and it is supposed by some that, by an error of the copyist, substituting ר for ד, it has come instead of דָּאָה, as used in Lev. xi. 14. But it is more probable, as above suggested, that the da'ah of Leviticus is represented by the dayyah of Deuteronomy, and that consequently the reading ra'ah should be retained. This word, derived from רָאָה, to see, to look, would appropriately designate a bird of keen sight, one of the hawk species. The bird intended may be a buzzard, of which there are now several kinds in Palestine.

Ver. 21.—(Cf. Lev. xvii. 15; Exod. xxiii. 19; xxxiv. 26.) **The stranger that is in thy gates.** "The uncircumcised stranger that is in thy cities" (Targum), i.e. "a heathen who takes upon him that he will serve no idol, with the residue of the commandments which were commanded to the sons of Noah, but is not circumcised nor baptized (Maimonides, 'Issure Biah,' ch. xiv. § 7)" (Ainsworth). **Alien;** a foreigner, one not resident in the land of Israel.

Vers. 22—29.—A tithing of each year's produce of the cultivated ground was to be made; and this tithe was to be brought to the place which the Lord should choose, as also the firstling of the herds and flocks; and there a sacrificial meal was to be partaken of, that Israel might learn to fear Jehovah their God always, reverencing him as their Ruler, and rejoicing in him as the Giver of all good.

Ver. 22.—**Thy seed.** "Seed" here refers

to plants as well as what is raised from seed (cf. Jer. ii. 21; Ezek. xvii. 5, 6). The reference is to the second or festival tithe which was exclusively of vegetables.

Ver. 24.—In the land of Canaan, as the people would be dispersed over a wide tract, it might happen that the place which the Lord should choose was at such a distance from the usual residence of many that to observe this injunction would be to them very difficult, if not impossible. To meet this, therefore, it was enacted that the tithe might be commuted into money, and with this the things required for the sacrificial meals at the sanctuary might be purchased.

Ver. 26. — **Strong drink;** *shêcar* (שֵׁכָר). "Any drink which can inebriate, whether that is made from grain, or the juice of apples, or when honey is boiled into a sweet and barbarous potion, or the fruit of the palm [dates], is expressed into liquor, and the duller water is coloured by the prepared fruits" (Jerome, ' De Vit. Cler.').

Vers. 28, 29.—Every third year the whole tithe of the year's produce was to be set apart, not to be brought to the sanctuary to be eaten before the Lord, but as a portion in their towns for the Levite, the stranger, the widow, and the fatherless. **The end of three years;** *i.e.* as the third year expired, consequently, in the last year of the triennium (ch. xxvi. 12); just as " the end of seven years" means each seventh year (ch. xv. 1; xxxi. 10; Jer. xxxiv. 14). This was not an additional tithe, but the former differently applied; the tithe of the first and second years was to be eaten before the Lord at the sanctuary; the tithe of the third year was for the poor and needy.

HOMILETICS.

Vers. 1, 2.—*The people of God when death is in the home.* If God chose out a people for himself, with the view of planting in the world a new and nobler faith, it is no wonder if he would have the people superadd to that a new and higher life. But if the life is to be higher in any sense which could be acceptable to Jehovah, it must be one based on the new faith and manifesting itself to others in a new deportment, *i.e.* it must be both an outer and inner life. But if the people are just emerging from a semi-barbaric condition, it is not at all improbable that they may need to be dealt with as we deal with children. We give them technical rules first, and they have to learn reasons afterwards. Possibly, as the child grows up and gets beyond the rules which bound him once, he may smile at them, or rather at the childishness which needed them in earlier years; while at the same time he would, or at any rate he should, feel thankful to those who stooped to teach him *so that he could understand them.*

In this chapter, we have several illustrations of God's thus dealing with Israel. We now take the one in the first two verses. It is well known that heathen nations were very violent in their shows of grief over their dead, tearing the hair, cutting the face, beating the breast, etc., while the cutting of the flesh was likewise submitted to in honour of their gods (see Exposition, *in loc.*). Now, it was of vast importance to give Israel to understand how *entirely* they were to be the Lord's, how fully he was theirs, and how the blest mutual relation changed the very aspect of that frequent and certain family sorrow—death. We have not here any full opening up of that, but there is scarcely any room to doubt that it formed a very important part of Hebrew teaching; for the fact that all these heathen rites and orgies over the dead were entirely forbidden would be sure to lead many, especially of the young, to ask for the reason of such prohibition. And when we remember how careful was the preparation for meeting the inquisitiveness of childhood in other matters, we cannot imagine that this was an exception to the general rule. The prohibition of old customs would clear the way for teaching a new doctrine. And, as applied to Israel of old, the following six positions may be asserted and maintained. 1. They were to be a separate people to the Lord their God, not only in all the varied relations of life, but also in the presence of death. 2. Old customs of surrounding nations, at the death of their friends, were to be done away, as a sign of the different meaning and aspect of death, to the people of the Lord. 3. This changed aspect of death followed from their blessed relationship to God, and from God's blessed relationship to them. 4. This relationship involved and assured Israel of the continued life of their holy dead in God. Surely it was scarcely possible for them to think of Enoch, Noah, Abraham, as extinct. True, the light on the unseen life in the grave was dim, and the gloom of the grave was deep. But still, it was very far from having about it the hopelessness which marked the heathen world. 5. For, stretching far away in the future, there was the hope of a resurrection at the last day. This was involved in God's words to Moses, "I am the God of Abraham," etc. Many, perhaps the mass, of the people might not see that. But our Lord assures us that the doctrine is wrapped up there. 6. Consequently, there was no reason to justify a hapless, hopeless wail in the presence of death. Whence our subject for meditation is suggested to us—

THERE OUGHT TO BE A GREAT DIFFERENCE BETWEEN GOD'S PEOPLE AND OTHERS IN THE PRESENCE OF DEATH. In one sense, indeed, there is none; or, at least, none which can be discerned. One event cometh alike to all, even to the righteous and the wicked, and the house of the good man may be as frequently darkened by "the shadow of death" as that of another who fears not God. But still, when death does come, there may well be a very wide difference between those who are the children of God and those who are not, especially when the departed one is a member of "the whole family in heaven and on earth" (and such cases only do we note in this Homily). When the Christian expositor is opening up the principle contained in these verses, he can do so from much higher vantage-ground than one who confines himself to the Old Testament teaching. Some such main lines of thought as the following will be the Christian unfolding of the principles so long ago laid down. 1. There is a blessed relationship between God and his people. It is initiated in the new birth by the Holy Ghost. Those thus born anew are children of God—not merely under a national covenant, as sharing a common privilege, but as brought into a personal covenant through the impartation of a new life. The mark of this new birth is the saving reception of Christ by faith, and the effect of it is to transfer men from the region of darkness to that of light, "from the power of Satan unto God," and from being subjects of a kingdom, to their being citizens in God's city and sons in God's family—"fellow-citizens of the saints and of the household of God." 2. This blessed relationship is sealed and made sure by "the blood of the everlasting covenant." They are redeemed with the "precious blood of Christ." 3. It is ratified by the resurrection of Jesus Christ. He is the First-born out of the dead, and has "opened the kingdom of heaven to all believers." 4. This blessed relation continues undisturbed by the accident of death. "Christ died for us, that whether we wake or sleep we should live together with him;" "whether we live or die, we are the Lord's;" "Christ both died, and rose, and revived, that he might be Lord of the dead and of the living." 5. The resurrection of Christ's own will as surely follow his as the harvest follows the firstfruits. "Now is Christ risen from the dead, and become the Firstfruits of them that slept." 6. The distinctive features of the resurrection of the body are laid down for us by the Apostle Paul in 1 Cor. xv. Of these there are four. (1) That the body, as the seed, *must* be buried before it can rise again. (2) That the body sown is *not* the body that shall be. (3) That to every seed there is its own body. (4) That the precise relation or connection between the body that is sown and the body that will be raised is a secret in the mind of God. "God giveth it a body as it hath pleased him." These things we know: we know no more. If we let our affirmations go beyond the statements of Scripture, we shall plunge ourselves into inextricable difficulties, and we shall be even risking the credit of Scripture, since many will think that, in disposing of *our* affirmations, they demolish the teaching of the Book. In confining ourselves to the four points named by Paul in his great argument, we shall be remaining on ground that will ever be firm, and that can never be invaded. No physical science can affirm or deny either one or the other. There never lived, there never will live, the man who on scientific grounds can weaken either of them. Our holy and glorious faith is beyond such reach. 7. Therefore the reason for avoiding the hopeless sorrow of the pagan world is even vastly deeper and stronger than it was under Moses. If Israel might not sorrow as those without hope when they had the assurance, "I am the God of Abraham, the God of Isaac, and the God of Jacob," how much less should we, when earth has seen the Firstfruits of the great resurrection from the dead! How much light is thrown by Christ's grace and love into the portals of the grave, and what a hallowed and hallowing calm may pervade the chamber of death if our Lord is with us there! Yea, there is no real death to the believer. "Our Saviour Jesus Christ hath abolished death." He hath said, "If a man keep my sayings, he shall never taste of death." Then we may well bless our God that, amid the changing scenes of earth, we stand on ground which can never be shaken. There ariseth light in the darkness.

> " With joy we tell the scoffing age,
>   He that was dead has left his tomb;
> He lives above their utmost rage,
>   And we are waiting till he come."

Vers. 3—20.—*The people of God at their own table.* However far these minute regulations may seem at first from being appropriate themes for homiletic teaching, a closer study of them may show that they contain an amount of instruction which we could ill afford to lose. There are two principles, not unfrequently noted, that should be brought to bear on this and other chapters which contain regulations that may be entirely unneeded now. One is, that associations of evil may make a custom prejudicial which is in itself harmless; another, that great reasons underlying small actions may lift up action to the height of the reason which prompted it. If, indeed, there should be some of these minute instructions for which we *now* see no reason, it would be no great tax on one's understanding, were we asked to give credit to so great a legislator as Moses for having had a good reason for them, although it may not be in force at the present time. Still, we are not altogether in the dark as to some reasons which might then be of great weight for the observance of the distinction between clean and unclean meats. Trapp suggests as reasons: (1) that they might recognize God's hand in the supply, and God's law in the use, of their meats; (2) that there might be a distinction between them and other peoples: (3) that they might be taught to study purity. Dr. Jameson suggests also sanitary reasons. We would venture to include these, with others, under seven heads. 1. The Israelites were the children of the Lord their God, and that special relationship was to show itself in the sober, pure, and devout regulation of the several customs at the family table. 2. There was to be a separation between them and other nations; and a more effective barrier to intercourse could scarcely be found than one which made association at the same table all but impossible. 3. They were to learn that even the common business of eating was to be governed by holy laws. 4. Thus, by minute obedience to precept, they were to be indoctrinated into the principles of holiness. 5. Their social board was to be a standing protest against idolatrous customs; and also, 6. A perpetual rebuke of impurity and of any infringement of sanitary law. Let no one, then, think of this distinction between clean and unclean meats as a trifling one. *Nothing is trifling which helps on the education of souls for God.* 7. When, moreover, we glance at the tenth chapter of the Acts of the Apostles, we cannot but regard these regulations as also symbolic. This distinction in the lower orders of creation between clean and unclean, symbolized the difference between Israel and the nations from whom they were to dissociate themselves. The mass of the people may not have comprehended this. They were gradually led to understand doctrine by way of obedience to precept.

But, it may be asked, "What has all this to do with Christians now?" We reply, "Little, or nothing, so far as these special details are concerned, but much every way, so far as we have to do with the principles which underlie these details." That so far as details go, the Law is done away, is understood. The symbolic meaning is no longer in force, hence the symbol is needed no longer. From the yoke of these forms we are emancipated (cf. Acts x.; 1 Cor. x. 24—31; Rom. xiv.; 1 Tim. iv. 3—5). But still, there is an analogy, of which it would ill become us to lose sight, between the position of Israel then, and the duty of God's Israel now. Supposing now we were asked, "In what way does the gospel teach us the duty of God's people at their own family table?" we might suggest six or seven consecutive lines of thought.

I. The Christian is to be, in spirit, as distinct from the world as Israel was from the nations round about. It is not intended by this that, in the ordinary walks of life, a Christian may not act with ungodly men; for in such a case, as Paul teaches, he must needs go out of the world to be free from them (cf. 1 Cor. v.). But in his own voluntary association, he is not to be "unequally yoked together with unbelievers;" the gospel mandate is, "Come out from among them, and be ye separate, and touch not the unclean thing."

II. The Christian, being a redeemed man, by the fact of that redemption is claimed for Christ alone. " Ye are bought with a price; therefore glorify God in your body and your spirit, which are God's." "We are the Lord's." Our body, soul, and spirit are entirely his. The claim of Jesus Christ over us is that he shall govern the whole of us, always and everywhere.

III. Hence, loyalty to Christ, and the conservation of our whole life for him, is to regulate every detail of our life, work, walk, and conversation. So the apostle shows in Rom. xiv. that, *e.g.* in the tiny matter of "eating herbs," the Lordship of Christ is to be the supreme regulator of religious conviction.

IV. Nowhere is this scrupulousness in loyalty to be more exact than in the regulation of our own table. It is at their own board that some strive to make the greatest display, or to pamper their bodies with a superabundance of luxuries. But both "the lust of the flesh" and "the pride of life" are declared to be "not of the Father, but of the world." Hence they can have no place in a consistent believer's home life.

V. A Christian man is bound, not only for Christ's sake, but for his family's sake, to cultivate only such associations as will help to make or maintain the purity, piety, and Christian elevation of his home. If he seeks the associations of the wealthy or great, regardless of their religious views or habits, he is exposing his own consistency and his children's weal to very serious risk.

VI. The entire concern of eating and drinking is to be regulated by Christian principle. No doubt with many, without thinking on the matter, sound feeling and common sense keep them from going very far wrong, and perhaps even from going wrong at all. Still, the surest way of keeping right in little things is to recognize fully and clearly the true and proper motive which should impel, even in the trivialities of life.

VII. So also it may be that high and holy principle may lead a believer, without laying down a hard-and-fast line for all, to practise abstinence from this or that, out of regard to the well-being of others, or to practise seasons of occasional fasting when preparing for special service (cf. Matt. xvii. 21; Rom. xiv. 21; 1 Cor. viii. 13).

VIII. There is one grand rule given by the Apostle Paul, covering the whole ground, appropriate to all occasions (1 Cor. x. 31). On referring to that verse, its force will be seen to be this: "You will find many occasions in your walks through life in which it may not at first be clearly manifest to you what course you should adopt. I cannot lay down separate rules for every possible case. Take this as a comprehensive, sufficient rule, at all times, and everywhere, ' Whatever ye do, do all to the glory of God.' " And if we resolve to do only that which will most honour God, and seek grace from above to carry out our resolve, we cannot go far wrong. We shall not be unwise, but shall " prove what the will of the Lord is." We shall be " sincere and without offence till the day of Christ," to the glory of our Lord and Saviour.

Vers. 22—29.—*A threefold cord; or, the triple use of property.* These details which so frequently occur respecting the use of property, specially of that which is possessed or gained in the form of produce, may seem burdensome. Probably, to us, they would be so, but it is nevertheless a topic of perpetual interest for our day, to see how tenderly and lovingly the Great Father trained his people, by such minute regulations as were needful for them, to the practice and perception of principles which were to be ultimately the possession of the world—principles which would be a perpetual spring of holy and benevolent gladness. We say, advisedly, "practice and perception of principles," rather than "perception and practice." For though it may seem as if perception must come first, yea, though indeed it is logically prior to practice, yet when a race tainted with heathen customs and tendencies has to be educated out of them, the sure mode of effecting this is by giving them rules to be put into practice, as a leverage to raise them to value the principles which were the basis of those rules. Now in the paragraph before us we have "a threefold cord" of duty with regard to the religious use of the produce of the field. The question (with which the Exposition has dealt) whether the third-named tithe was actually such, or simply a special application of the second, does not affect the homiletic treatment of the paragraph before us. There is here indicated to us a triple use which was to be made of the produce of the land. The enactment, however, is so framed as to be an appeal to the religion and devotion of the people; it is not a mere civil statute, enjoining that, if such devotement is not made, it is to be recoverable under pains and penalties. If a man failed in his duty in these respects, there was no compulsory enforcement thereof. It was a sin before the Lord.

I. THE FIRST APPLICATION OF PRODUCE WAS FOR GOD'S SERVICE. It is taken for granted here that this was well understood (cf. Lev. xxvii. 30). Hence we find the general precept in Prov. iii., "Honour the Lord with thy substance, and with the first-fruits of all thine increase." There was to be a thankful recognition of God as the Author of all their mercies, without whose care and bounty no land would yield its supply; while there was also to be a recognition of themselves as devoted to the Lord, and that so completely and entirely, that the maintenance of his Name, honour, worship, and ordinances among them, was to be their first and chief concern. This two-fold recognition was to find corresponding practice in the offering of the first tenth of their produce for God. Now we have, under the New Testament, no such detailed precepts. The appeal of apostles there is rather to honour, gratitude, love; while for the most part they take for granted that these emotions will prompt to a worthy course. Take, e.g. such an exhortation as this, "See that ye abound in this grace also, . . . for ye know the grace of our Lord Jesus Christ," etc. If love to Christ is maintained in due fervour, it will prompt to corresponding devotion; and if by such constraining devotion, offerings to and for God are regulated, there will be no need, as indeed no one now has the right, to tell any man how much he ought to give to God. When a man carries out in all respects the precept, "Seek ye first the kingdom of God and his righteousness," that will certainly include and ensure his honouring the Lord with his substance. The faith was "once delivered to the saints," i.e. once for all, that they might guard and honour it, and also diffuse it through the world, and, without much detailed injunction, it is assumed that believers will be ready to devote themselves, heart and soul, to the spread of their Master's honour.

II. A SECOND RELIGIOUS APPLICATION THEREOF WAS TO FAMILY AND HOUSEHOLD USE. (Vers. 22—27.) When Israel should go up to the place the Lord their God should choose, they would go up to religious sacrifice and service. Hence all their family meals, then and there, would be baptized with the religious spirit. So all-pervading would be the presence of, and so sure the fellowship with, the Lord their God, that their family feasts on such occasions would be regarded as "eating before the Lord their God." And by thus eating before the Lord on these special occasions, they would learn to hallow home joys on every occasion. So ver. 23 intimates: "that thou mayest learn to fear the Lord thy God always." Considerable latitude was allowed them according to their distance from the place of meeting, etc.; they might first turn the produce into money, and then the money into provision, and so on. And they might purchase what they desired. For they were not slaves, but free men. They were the loved and happy people of the Lord, and as such were to rejoice before him in their family feasts, at their sacred festivals, that from the impulses of joy and gladness so sanctified then, they might come to realize how near God was to them, and how he would have them glory in him as theirs all the year round. It is not possible to overrate the value of this, even now. By a truly religious and devout man all the minor affairs of life are lifted up into the religious region. And he is not only at liberty to enjoy his possessions, when he has sanctified the firstfruits for God, but he ought so to enjoy them. God "hath given us all things richly to enjoy." And when a godly man gathers his family around him at his table, with the table abounding in ample provision, he may then joyfully "eat before the Lord his God," in the full assurance that such enjoyment is a part of the Divine intent, and that the love and care of God may and do put their own seal of hallowed and hallowing mirth upon the use of common things.

III. A THIRD RELIGIOUS APPLICATION OF PRODUCE WAS FOR THE USE AND ENJOYMENT OF OTHERS. (Vers. 28, 29.) Whether this special use which was enjoined for every third year involved the setting apart a third tithe, or whether it was a triennial application of the second, is a point the discussion of which belongs to others. But either way, the principle, we conceive, is the same, which we understand to be this, "Let a man be a man all round." God first, then home, then his neighbours. Such is to be the order of his action. A special care was to be taken of the Levite (who, by the way, was to be thought of every year), as having charge of religious arrangements, but, besides these, how wide a scope is here opened up to a man's kindness and generosity! "The stranger, and the fatherless, and the widow, . . . shall come, and shall eat and be satisfied." Is this an instance of *the hardness of Judaism?* They do not understand it who speak thus of it. Its spirit was kindness itself; for here the showing of goodness and benevolence to the poor and the needy is made a part of their religion. Need we ask the question whether Christianity has dropped this out? Details may change; principles, never! The Apostle James tells that the New Testament ritual is, "To visit the fatherless and widows in their affliction, and to keep himself unspotted from the world." Let us ask, in conclusion, *Which part of this threefold cord could be broken without serious injury?* For we see here that Judaism, in this triple direction of duty, does but recognize the triple relations of human life. We are related first and foremost to our God, to whom our supreme allegiance is due. We are related next to our home, to our families and households, whose interests and happiness it is our first earthly business to promote; and then to our fellow-citizens, to whom we are bound to do good, where we can and when we can. Finally, by way of ensuring the right discharge of other duties, special care is taken to guide Israel in regard to the right use of property. There is singular, yea, superhuman wisdom in this. Where a man's getting and giving are right, he is not likely to be far wrong in anything. Wisdom in adding to, and giving from, the contents of the purse, is a fair guarantee of wisdom in other directions. "The love of money is a root of all evil," and by so much as love of money tends to deteriorate character, by so much will its right use tend to elevate it. And the lifting up of character is the surest sign of the blessing promised (ver. 29).

HOMILIES BY VARIOUS AUTHORS.

Vers. 1—3.—*Self-respect in mourning.* Mourning customs have significance, as testifying to the ideas of God, of human worth, and of immortality, held by those who practise them. Those here forbidden were degrading in their own nature, and embodied the false idea that God is pleased with the self-inflicted miseries of his creatures. They are condemned—

I. As DISHONOURING TO THE CREATOR. God, the Creator of the body, cannot take delight in seeing it abused. This proposition seems self-evident. The idea above referred to, and which lies at the root of so many false religions, viz. that it is pleasing to the Deity to see his creatures torturing and defacing themselves, is a libel on the Divine character. The body is rather to be reverenced as one of the noblest of God's works. It is to be studiously preserved and cared for. Religion, with reason, enjoins, "Do thyself no harm" (Acts xvi. 28).

II. As INCONSISTENT WITH SELF-RESPECT. There is a propriety and decorum becoming in beings who possess reason. Wild and excessive grief, indicating the absence of power of self-control, lowers us beneath the dignity of rational existences. Neglect of the person, and, still more, wanton self-injury, in grief, betokens a like absence of proper self-respect. Least of all is such conduct excusable in those who claim the dignity of being God's children. They, of all others, ought to set an example of propriety and seemliness in behaviour. They are "an holy people," and must study to deport themselves worthily of their high calling. The priests of Baal (1 Kings xviii. 28) behaved like maniacs. David and Job behaved like religious men (2 Sam. xii. 20; Job i. 20, 21).

III. As IMPLYING THE ABSENCE OF RELIGIOUS CONSOLATIONS. The early Jews were not without these (Heb. xi. 13, 14). We in the Christian age have them still more abundantly. Therefore must we not sorrow "as those which have no hope" (1 Thess. iv. 13).—J. O.

Vers. 3—21.—*Clean and unclean.* The distinction of clean and unclean appears to have rested—

I. ON NATURAL GROUNDS. It is based to some extent on natural preferences and repugnances—an index, often, to deeper correlations. We instinctively recognize certain creatures to be unfit for food. The Law of Moses drew the line practically where men's unguided instincts have always drawn it. A lesson of *respect for natural order*. In diet, as in higher matters, we do well to follow Nature's guidance, avoiding violations of her laws, and refraining from obliterating her distinctions.

II. ON CEREMONIAL GROUNDS. The prohibition against eating of blood had consequences in the region of cleanness and uncleanness of food. All flesh-eating and blood-eating animals—all beasts and birds of prey—were of necessity excluded. Ceremonially unclean themselves, they could not be clean to those eating them.

III. ON SYMBOLIC GROUNDS. The symbolic traits observable in certain animals may have had to do with their rejection. We can see reason in the exclusion of creatures of cruel and rapacious habits, of those also in whose dispositions we trace a reflection of the human vices. It may be pushing the principle too far to seek recondite meanings in the chewing of the cud (meditation) and the dividing of the hoof (separation of walk), or in the possession of fins and scales in fishes (organs of advance and resistance). But a Law impregnated with symbolism could scarcely reckon as clean a filthy and repulsive creature like the sow. The accursed serpent, the treacherous fox, the ravenous jackal, even had they been suitable for food in other respects, could scarcely on this principle have been admitted. The reptile tribes generally, and all tribes of vermin, were similarly unclean by a kind of natural brand. A lesson of *seeing in the natural a symbol of the moral*. Nature is a symbolic lesson-book, daily open to our inspection.

The distinction once ordained, and invested with religious significance, observance of it became to the Jews a sign and test of holiness. The general lesson taught is that of *sanctification in the use of food*. Holiness, indeed, is to be carried into every sphere and act of life. Eating, however, is an act which, though on its animal side related to the grossest part of us, is yet, on its spiritual side, of serious religious import. It is the act by which we supply oil to the flame of life. It has to do with the maintenance of those vital functions by which we are enabled to glorify God in the body. There is thus a natural sacredness about food, and it is to be received and used in a sacred fashion. That it may be "clean" to us, it is to be "sanctified by the Word of God and prayer," being "received with thanksgiving of them which believe and know the truth" (1 Tim. iv. 3—5). It is to be remembered, too, that in the sphere of the higher life, if not in the lower, clean and unclean are distinctions of abiding validity. Intellect, heart, spirit, etc.—the books we read, the company we keep, the principles we imbibe.—J. O.

Ver. 21.—*Seething a kid in its mother's milk*. This precept, several times repeated in the Law (Exod. xxiii. 16; xxxiv. 25), may be connected with magical superstitions, but it is equally probable that the act was condemned as an outrage on the connection naturally subsisting between parent and offspring. It is thus related to the commands forbidding the killing of a cow and a calf on the same day (Lev. xxii. 28), or the taking a bird with its young (ch. xxii. 6), and to the precepts enjoining a scrupulous regard for natural distinctions—not sowing a field with mingled seed, etc. (Lev. xix. 19). It suggests—

I. THE DUTY OF CHERISHING THE FINER INSTINCTS OF OUR NATURE. The act here forbidden could hardly be called cruelty, the kid being dead, but it was unnatural. It argued a blunted state of the sympathies. A finer instinct, alive to the tenderness of the relation between parent and offspring, would have disallowed it. It is beautiful to see the ancient Law inculcating this rare and delicate fineness of feeling—this considerateness and sympathy even for dead animals. The lesson is that everything is to be avoided which would tend to blunt our moral sensibilities. The act has its analogue in higher relations. Not unfrequently has the affection of a parent been used by the ingenuity of cruelty to inflict keener tortures on a child; or, conversely, a child has been betrayed into disclosures afterwards used to injure the parent.

II. THE DUTY OF CONSIDERATION IN DEALING WITH IRRATIONAL CREATURES. 1. It is right that irrational creatures should be treated kindly. And if the Law required that this delicate consideration should be shown towards dead animals, how much more does it require of us kindly treatment of them while living! 2. Our behaviour towards irrational creatures, as seen above, reacts upon ourselves. In certain cases, this is readily perceived. Most people would shrink from the wanton mutilation of a dead animal, even in sport, and would admit the reactive effect of such an action in deadening humane instincts in him who did it. But it is the same with all cruelty and unfeelingness. Any action which, in human relationships, would be condemned as unsympathetic, will be found, if performed to animals, to have a blunting effect on the sensibilities of the agent. A man's dog is more to him than a brute. He is a friend. We can carry into our behaviour towards the irrational creatures many of the feelings which actuate us in our personal relations, and the more we do it, the better for ourselves.—J. O.

Vers. 22—29.—*The second tithe.* We adopt the usual view, that the lawgiver is here regulating the disposal of what, in later times, was called " the second tithe." The hypothesis that the book was written at a late date, when the gift of tithes to the Levites, prescribed in Numb. xviii., had fallen into disuse, is unsupported by evidence. The provision in Deuteronomy would have furnished no support worth speaking of to the enormous Levitical establishments of the post-Davidic period (1 Chron. xxiii.—xxvii.; 2 Chron. xxix.); nor are we prepared to concede, what is often so conveniently assumed, the non-authenticity of these sections of the chronicler. We learn—

I. THAT PIETY AND CHARITY ARE TO BE LIBERALLY PROVIDED FOR IN THE APPORTIONMENT OF INCOME. The tithes were to be faithfully and punctually set apart as a first charge upon the Jew's income. The second or vegetable tithe was appointed to be consumed in feasts at the sanctuary, or, in the third year, at home. A lesson is taught here as to the duty of liberal, systematic, and conscientious giving for religious and charitable purposes. Christians, it is true, are not under Law, but under grace. But it will scarcely be pleaded that on this account they are less bound to liberality than Jews were. The argument is all the other way : if this was done under Law, how much more ought to be done under the impulse of love to Christ ! Unfortunately, the duty of systematic and proportionate giving is but little recognized. It would put many a Christian to the blush if he would sit down at the year's end, and (1) reckon up the sum of his year's givings to Christ, and (2) calculate its proportion to what he has thought himself at liberty to expend upon his own comforts and pleasures. Nor will there be improvement in this matter till giving for religious and charitable objects is made a point in conscience, and till a suitable proportion of income is set apart for this purpose in advance. That proportion is to be determined by the degree to which God has prospered us (1 Cor. xvi. 2). The ever-widening operations of the Church at home and abroad, the constantly multiplying claims of a wise Christian philanthropy, render liberal givings increasingly necessary.

II. THAT OBEDIENCE TO THE SPIRIT OF A LAW IS OF GREATER IMPORTANCE THAN OBEDIENCE TO ITS LETTER. (Vers. 24—26.) God is not a hard master—reaping where he has not sown, and gathering where he has not strawed (Matt. xxv. 4). He is tenderly considerate of the circumstances of his people. He asks no more from them than they are able to render. Where laws could not be kept in the letter, modifications were introduced which made obedience practicable. This is seen in the accommodation of the laws of sacrifice to the circumstances of the poor (Lev. v. 7, etc.), in the rules for commutation (Lev. xxvii.), in the relaxation of the law about eating flesh (ch. xii. 21), in this law of tithes. Gleaming through these changes, it is easy to detect the principle that the letter of an ordinance is in all cases subordinate to the spirit of obedience which manifests itself through it; and that, while obedience to the letter is required where possible, the will, in circumstances where it cannot be observed, will readily be accepted by Jehovah for the deed.

III. THAT PROVIDED RELIGIOUS MOTIVES PREDOMINATE, AND OTHER DUTIES ARE NOT NEGLECTED, THE ENJOYMENT OF WHAT WE HAVE IS PLEASING TO GOD. (Vers. 25, 26.) True religion is not ascetic. It does not frown our joy. It regulates, but does not seek to banish, the pleasures of the festive board, and the flow of the soul connected therewith (John ii. 1—12; 1 Cor. x. 27; 1 Tim. vi. 18). The sanctuary services were associated with feasts, in which, of course, religious motives were expected to predominate. The eating was " before the Lord," and the guests were invariably to include the Levite, the stranger, the fatherless, and the widow. This would give a high-toned character to the feast, and would preclude coarse debauchery. Festivities should be so conducted that God's presence can be invoked, and his blessing asked on all that is said and done.

IV. THAT THE ENJOYMENT OF WHAT WE HAVE IS ENHANCED BY SHARING IT WITH OTHERS. (Ver. 29.) This is a truth recognized in all festivity. But the Law gave the truth a peculiar turn when it bade the Jew seek his guests among the classes who were most in need. The Saviour would have us recall our feasting to the like pattern (Luke xiv. 12—14). Each feast of the kind prescribed would be an invaluable education of the disinterested affections in their purest exercise. How far we have departed from this idea may be seen in the stiff, exclusive, and ceremonious, if often superb and stately, dinner-parties and public feasts of modern society. Which type of feast contributes most to happiness? And is it not in fulfilling the duties of a warm-hearted love that we are most entitled to expect blessing from our Maker (ver. 29)? When Jesus made *his* great supper, he acted on his own principle, and invited the "poor, and the maimed, and the halt, and the blind," to come and sit down at it (Luke xiv. 21).—J. O.

Vers. 1, 2.—*Sorrow is to be in holy hopefulness.* After guarding them so carefully from all idolatry, Moses next charges the Israelites not to imitate the heathen nations by mutilating themselves or making themselves bald for the dead. The reason assigned is their consecration unto the Lord. There must have been, therefore, in these heathen practices something unholy expressed. Let us first consider what this was, and then proceed to the lessons in the prohibition.

I. WHAT WAS MEANT BY CUTTING ONE'S SELF AND MAKING ONE'S SELF BALD FOR THE DEAD ? It implied manifestly some *post-mortem* merit and service. It was akin to the *sacrifices* which often have been presented in connection with death. It was the sacrifice of something short of life, but yet valuable. It was the sacrifice of sightliness, if not of beauty, in the interests of the dead. It implied that something could be done for the departed by those who remained, and which self-denying love gladly undertook.

Hence these practices brought out the hopelessness of sorrow as it exists in the heathen world, and the desire to propitiate offended Deity by sympathetic suffering and sacrifice.

II. THE PROHIBITION SUMMONED THE JEWS TO HOPEFUL SORROW. The dead were to be regarded as in the hands of God, and he was to be trusted with them absolutely. No *post-mortem* sacrifices were to be attempted, but the cases left with implicit confidence to the ever-living and gracious Father. "Prayers for the dead" and "Masses for the dead" but express the pitifulness of human hope, and the dread and doubt with which the dead are left in the hands of God. Israel was prohibited from any such infirmity.

III. THEY WERE EVEN TO REGARD THEMSELVES AS CONSECRATED TO THE LIVING GOD, AND CONSEQUENTLY NOT TO BE DESECRATED THROUGH MUTILATION FOR THE DEAD. The danger sometimes is for people to forget their dedication to God amid all the loneliness of their sorrow. The dead absorb attention. God has been removing "idols," but the idols have become, through death, more and more to them. Too much cannot be made of the dead, they think, and so they would make a perpetual dedication of themselves to the dead, forgetful of their relations to the living God above. Now, it is this everlasting relation which God insists upon. Nothing can be better, surely, than in sorrow to be reminded, "Thou art an holy people unto the Lord thy God, and the Lord thy God hath chosen thee to be a peculiar people unto himself, above all the nations that are upon the earth." It is just this which bereavement is intended to make emphatic. God claims us as his own : let not the dead make perpetual marks upon your persons, as if they had the right to your life-long service. This is *desecration* instead of *consecration*. Unreasonable attachment to the dead may be the denial of due consecration to the living God.

IV. UNCOMMON CONSECRATION TO GOD SHOULD BE OUR IDEAL. Israel was to be a peculiar people unto God "above all the nations that are upon the earth." All nations glorify God in some degree, even in spite of themselves. But his own people are wise in aiming at special consecration. There is nothing so important as the highest possible ideal. Devoted to this, we attain to something higher and nobler than is possible otherwise.

"Lord, we can trust thee for our holy dead,
    They, underneath the shadow of thy tomb,
Have entered into peace ; with bended head
    We thank thee for their rest, and for our lightened gloom."

R. M. E.

Vers. 3—11.—*A holy people will eat sanctified things.* The regulation of the diet of the children of Israel was most important in view of their remaining a "peculiar people" unto God. In no way half so effectual could they, as a nation, be kept distinct from other nations, with whom it was undesirable on religious grounds that they should associate. By interdicting some of the animals used by surrounding and heathen nations, the Lord, as far as possible, prevented Israel's association with them. To this they had been accustomed in Egypt ; for some of the animals they, as Israelites, would eat were regarded as sacred by the Egyptians, and on no account would be slain or eaten by them. Hence the slaves had never commingled with their taskmasters. The two rivers would not coalesce. The Canaanites and Phœnicians, again, ate freely of flesh that the Hebrew dare not touch ; and even the Arab would eat such animals as the camel, the hare, and the *jerboa,* all of which—the latter translated "mouse"—were forbidden to the children of Israel.

I. The regulation of meats is the most important way of separating one nation from all other nations. For if association at table is an impossibility, all other association will be very superficial and comparatively harmless. "Nothing more effectual," says Dr. Kitto, "could be devised to keep one people distinct from another. It causes the difference between them to be ever present to the mind, touching, as it does, upon so many points of social and everyday contact ; and it is therefore far more efficient in its results, as a rule of distinction, than any difference in doctrine, worship, or morals which men could entertain. . . . It is a mutual repulsion continually operating ; and its effect may be estimated from the fact that no nation in which a distinction of meats was rigidly enforced as a part of a religious system, has ever changed its religion."[1] And we are surely taught the wisdom of *expedients* to keep up the desirable separation between the Church and the world. If every religious *custom* were abandoned, and the conduct of religious people were conformed in all particulars to that of their worldly neighbours, religion would soon become a name, and nothing more. "Be not conformed to this world, but be ye transformed by the renewing of your mind" (Rom. xii. 2).

II. The distinction between the animals symbolized the distinction which should exist between God's people and the world. An excellent writer has suggested that in *individual* development we pass through the stages attributed to the organic world as a whole ; children, for example, passing through the "parrot" or the "monkey" stage.[2] "Animated nature" seems designed to mirror "human nature," whether in its evil or in its good propensities. Man finds himself in the image of the lower animals as well as, on his higher side, in the image of God. In conformity with this arrangement, then, the Jew was trained to regard certain animals as clean and edible, while others were unclean and forbidden. Towards the one class he was drawn, from the other he was repelled. Now, in the clean animals may be discovered certain good qualities, which make them fit illustrations of the moralities expected from an Israelite. For example, the characteristic of *rumination,* which belonged to the clean animals, was a fit type of that *thoughtfulness* and quiet *meditation* which should characterize the people of God. Again, *sure-footedness* characterizes the animals with the cloven hoof, which symbolizes the *steadfastness* of religious character. Speed and cleanliness also characterize the fishes that were accounted clean.

On the other hand, the unclean beasts, birds, and fish illustrate most powerfully the lustful, selfish, and impure spirit which characterizes unregenerate man. Not only, therefore, did the distinction among the animals secure the desired national separation, but also that poetic outlook upon nature which discovers in it a great parable for the soul.[3] Thus Emerson says, "Every rational creature has all nature for his dowry and

---

[1] 'The Pictorial Bible,' on Lev. xi.   [2] Cf. Secretan's 'Discours Laïques,' p. 74.
[3] Cf. Kurtz's 'Sacrificial Worship,' pp. 22, 23 ; also Principal Shairp's 'Poetic Interpretation of Nature ; ' Emerson's 'Miscellanies,' etc.

estate. It is his, if he will. He may divest himself of it; he may creep into a corner and abdicate his kingdom, as most men do, but he is entitled to the world by his constitution. In proportion to the energy of his thought and will, he takes up the world unto himself." What a richness of thought is thus afforded to the thoughtful soul!

III. THAT WHICH DIED OF ITSELF WAS ALSO EXCLUDED FROM THE DIET OF ISRAEL. In such a case there was no guarantee that the blood had been properly drained from the carcase, and that the atoning element had been solemnly eliminated from it. In fact, in such cases there is not the sacrifice of life which we have seen to obtain in the normal sustenance of the world. God's people consequently must avoid all contact with death, and keep themselves pure unto him. And this arrangement surely symbolized that watchfulness over our contact with the world, which should characterize all professors of religion. We must " keep our garments unspotted from the world," we must even in certain critical times " let the dead bury their dead," and deny ourselves that intercourse with the spiritually dead which otherwise might be most proper.

IV. A KID WAS NOT TO BE SEETHED IN HIS MOTHER'S MILK. A quotation from an old writer will best improve this commandment. " This is not the meaning of the command, Content yourselves to eat the kid, but take heed that ye eat not the dam also; neither is this the meaning of it, Ye shall not eat flesh with milk, as the Chaldee paraphrast paraphraseth it; neither is this the meaning of it, Take heed that ye seethe not the kid in the mother's milk, as the superstitious Jews expound it at this day; they will not seethe flesh and milk in one pot, neither will they cut both flesh and cheese with one knife; and amongst the precepts which they have written of things lawful to be eaten, they forbid the eating of flesh and milk together; but the meaning of the place seemeth to be this, Ye shall not eat of a kid as of a lamb (for so the LXX. translate it) so long as it sucketh the dam, for all this time it is as it were but milk; they might sacrifice it when it was but eight days old, but not to eat of it so long as it was sucking (1 Sam. vii. 9). 'Samuel took a sucking lamb and offered.'"[1] This would consequently form a ceremonial appendix to the *sixth* commandment, and would teach that abstinence from the semblance of cruelty which should characterize the people of the Lord. In accepting of God's bounty in the matter of flesh, care should be taken that no unnatural cruelty should be practised or encouraged.

The sanctified ones are thus taught to keep themselves separate from the world, to regard nature as a great parable for the soul, and to conduct themselves in that considerate spirit which should characterize the disciples of Jesus.—R. M. E.

Vers. 22—29.—*Systematic provision for fellowship with God.* From the arrangements about ordinary diet, we pass now to the minute directions about " eating before God." A tithe of the corn, the wine, and the oil, together with the firstlings of their flocks and herds, must be devoted to the purposes of fellowship. It is clear from this, then, that God designed a systematic storing of the tenth part of the Jewish income for the purposes of religion. If the Jew resided far from the tabernacle, then he was to sell the tithe, and turning it into money, he was to go up with this to the central altar, and there invest in whatever his soul desired, and partake of it all before God. In this the Levite was to have his share. Over and above all this, every third year there was to be a *second* tithe devoted to the delectation of the poor. Now, we learn from these arrangements—

I. THAT FELLOWSHIP WITH GOD IS THE CROWN OF TRUE RELIGION. A feast with God, he taking the best portions, his priests the next best, and the offerer joyful over the remainder of the sacrifice, constituted the glory of the Jewish ritual. All the sin offerings, burnt offerings, and meat offerings were valueless if not crowned by the peace offering and its feast of fellowship. No wonder our Lord makes out fellowship to be the substance of eternal life, when in his prayer he says, " And this is life eternal, to know thee, the only true God, and Jesus Christ, whom thou hast sent " (John xvii. 3). If we are not led up into this acquaintanceship, our religion is a name and not a reality.

II. THE FELLOWSHIP IS WELL WORTH ANY EXPENSE IT MAY INVOLVE. While it is, of course, true that God's blessings are gratuitous, " without money and without price," it is also true that a niggardly soul will fall out of fellowship. In fact, fellowship with God will seem so precious as to be worth infinitely more than all our possessions, and any proportion of these required by God for the maintenance of fellowship will seem a small price. Our conviction will be that of the psalmist, "The Law of thy mouth is better unto me than thousands of gold and silver."

Now, while God's favour is given freely, there must evidently be something about which he and we can have fellowship. In other words, fellowship requires a medium. Fellowship means having something in common. When we analyze all we have, we find that it is all "the gift of God." Jesus is his gift; the Holy Spirit is his gift; money is his gift; every good thing is his gift (Jas. i. 17). He has surely every right, then, to say to his people, "You must dedicate a proportion of my gifts to you, for the purposes of fellowship; let us have a tithe in common; let us rejoice mutually over it as *ours*." This was the principle underlying Jewish tithing—it is the principle underlying all genuine beneficence. We are only returning to God such a proportion of what he gives as shall be the medium of fellowship.

A peace offering at the tabernacle was a most precious commodity. It was an animal regarding which the worshipper and God agreed to say, "It is *ours*," and each to feast upon it. It was the organ and means of fellowship. It was a delight to God and to man. Who would not pay anything required for such a privilege? Man is honoured most highly in being allowed such a partnership with God.

III. THE SENSE OF FELLOWSHIP WITH GOD IN THE FEAST IS THE REAL PRESERVATION OF MAN FROM UNDUE INDULGENCE. It is noticeable that "wine" and "strong drink" (שֵׁכָר) might be included in the feast before God. The safety of the partaker lay in the sense of fellowship and its consequent consecration. Just as Paul afterwards maintained that "every creature of God is good, and nothing to be refused, if it be received with thanksgiving; for it is sanctified by the Word of God and prayer" (1 Tim. iv. 4, 5). It is the unhallowed use of God's gifts which is the danger. The temperance reformation will do well to keep in view this Divine side of the question, where in the last resort the stress must be laid.

IV. THE FELLOWSHIP WITH GOD IMPLIES THE INVITATION OF OTHERS TO SHARE THE BLESSING WITH US. Our households and the Levite are to be partakers with us of our sacred feasts. For God does not encourage *lonely* satisfactions; but as he calls us into his fellowship, it is on the understanding that we shall invite others, and make the fellowship a family thing. Now, the support of the Levites was to be a matter of cheerfulness and religious privilege. It was to be a joy embraced rather than a mere debt moodily discharged. It is surely here that "ministerial support" must be pleaded and advanced. It is not to be something doled out, but a feast of fellowship, the call of God's minister to share in our good fortune and success.

V. THE CARE OF THE POOR MUST ALSO BE PUT UPON THE BASIS OF FELLOWSHIP. It has been made a matter of law. And doubtless there is a noble element in the fact that a nation, passing beyond what old moralists called *duties of debt*, has entered upon *duties of merit*. Still, the national obligation embodied in the "poor rates" is apt to sap a certain amount of individual sympathy. The care of the poor is not the feast of joy and fellowship God meant it to be.[1] The three years' system brought under our notice in this passage was an effort, apparently, to bring the lonely and needy classes up to the standard of fellowship and of joy that the religious Jew himself had attained. It was the systematic effort to make the needy ones *glad before God*. And it is here that we find the goal of our exertions, whether to support a minister, to comfort a stranger, or a fatherless child, or a widow. Let all be guests of our love, and lifted, if possible, into our light and fellowship with God. For this we should strive evermore.

VI. THOSE WHO THUS HONOUR GOD WILL BE BLESSED AND HONOURED BY HIM. Not, of course, that systematic beneficence should be in any sense a speculation. It is not beneficence if it is a selfish investment. But at the same time, God blesses the system which recognizes obligation to him and tries to discharge it. The accurate survey of circumstances which systematic giving implies tends to financial success. There is no reason why religious men should not be "successful merchants." Were systematic

---

[1] Cf. 'The Philosophy of the Poor Laws,' in Miss Cobbe's 'Studies Ethical and Social.'

beneficence more general, there would be less failure and heart-burning in the walks of business.—R. M. E.

Vers. 1, 2.—*Against conformity with heathen customs.* Israel had been called to honourable privilege; therefore it was fitting there should be seemly conduct. Royal children should be royal in all their acts.

I. ISRAEL'S SPECIAL PRIVILEGE. They enjoyed a position superior to all the nations of the earth. 1. *They were the objects of God's choice.* Out of all the peoples and tribes which dwelt on this round globe, Israel had been selected for a noble purpose. We may not be able to divine the reason, for our knowledge is exceedingly small. Yet God, who does nothing unwisely, did in this matter the wisest thing. 2. *They had been chosen to sonship.* God had revealed himself to these Hebrews in a special and endearing character. Had he not informed them of his dispositions towards them and his loving interest in them, they would not have dared to call him Father. In special condescension he informed them that he would treat them, in all substantial respects, as a father doth his children. 3. *They had been chosen to righteous character.* By virtue of this choice, they were on the high road to perfection. Their destiny was not secured irrespective of their own will and choice. They were now consecrated to the Divine service of Jehovah, and must perform holy actions, foster holy habits, so as to acquire a holy character. This is man's highest reward—a heaven within.

II. A SPECIFIC PROHIBITION. A prohibition against self-mutilation. There were natural outlets for abundant grief—tears, sighs, and moans; these self-mutilations were unnatural and irrational. 1. *Because inordinate sorrow for the death of friends is sinful.* Moderate grief is allowable: it is the necessary concomitant of strong affection. But as we should enjoy every friend as a gift of God, so our sorrow at separation should be accompanied by filial submission. 2. *Because such symbols of mourning were often pretences.* Frequently, if not usually, this manifest sorrow was assumed. 'Twas mere trickery and falsehood. Such actions injured and deteriorated character. 3. *Because even the body is the property of God.* There is no part of his nature which the true Israelite does not recognize as belonging to God. Throughout, he is Jehovah's temple. Every faculty of body, every organ and member, is to be utilized for God, is to be preserved in health and vigour to do credit to Jehovah. "His Name is to be upon our foreheads." 4. *Because this self-mutilation would be conformity with heathen customs.* The practices connected with idol-worship were dictated by a spirit of cruelty—by the genius of Satan. Far as the east is from the west, or north pole from the south, were the followers of God to· withdraw from heathen practices. As sane men flee from pestilence, so should pious men avoid the neighbourhood of sin.—D.

Vers. 3—21.—*Discrimination in meats.* The prohibition of some kinds of food proceeds upon the principle that it is not wise to gratify every appetite. There must be denial somewhere. If every desire and lust of the body be indulged, injury will ensue to the nobler capacities of the soul. Pruning of the wild growths of carnal desire is essential to real fruitfulness. Divine restraints are acts of genuine kindness. Discrimination in animal food was based on true wisdom.

I. BECAUSE IT WAS A SANITARY BENEFIT. In that early age, the sciences of physiology and health were unknown, and even now they are in their earliest infancy. We are, however, now aware of the fact that some (at least) of the flesh prohibited to the Hebrews is more or less unwholesome. Nor is it improbable that in that Eastern climate some flesh is more unwholesome for food than in our own land. As a father cares for the health of his child, so God cared for every part of Israel's well-being. Nothing escapes God's attention. "The Lord is for the body." With infinite tenderness, God legislated for the meals of the Hebrews, and gave them the advantage of his unerring judgment.

II. BECAUSE PARTIAL ABSTINENCE WAS SALUTARY FOR THE SOUL. 1. *It taught them that fleshly appetite was not to be gratified for its own sake—not for mere pleasure.* To strengthen and broaden the desires of the mind is an advantage in itself; but, excessive strength of bodily appetite is an evil, an injury to the real man. The lesson requires to be early learnt, that our nature requires government, that our highest good can be reached only by self-restraint and self-mortification. Bodily desires and inclinations are designed to be servants, not masters. 2. *It exercised them in practical self-denial.* The noblest qualities of human character are acquired only by personal discipline. Some parts of our nature have to be repressed; some have to be stimulated. The fleshly propensities have always been unfriendly to the spirit's life. It is a lesson hard to be learnt, to forego lesser enjoyments for remote advantages. The favour and society of God amply recompense for all minor pains. 3. *The general rule of action was typical of higher truths.* All such animals might be eaten as " parted the hoof, and chewed the cud." There was, doubtless, a reason for this permission arising out of the constituent nature of the flesh. But spiritual lessons also were suggested, viz. that to be acceptable for God's service there must be with us mental digestion of his truth, and there must also be practical circumspection—in our daily walk a separation from worldly contamination.

III. BECAUSE THIS DISCRIMINATION IN MEATS WOULD CONSTITUTE A VISIBLE PARTITION FROM THE HEATHEN. To bring to a successful issue the Divine purposes in the Hebrew race, it was incumbent to maintain broad distinctions between them and the heathen round about. They lived a coarser and more animal life. Animal passions were fostered by the glutting of the appetites. Some of the animals denied as food to the Jews were used by the heathen for divination; therefore it was safest to label such animals and birds as an abomination. A wise captain will give to a sunken reef a wide berth. Further, these differences in social customs and domestic habits would serve as perpetual barriers against intermarriages with neighbouring tribes. This might appear unsocial and exclusive. But lesser good has to be sacrificed for loftier and eternal blessing. To every quibble of human reason it is surely enough to reply, " God knows best." This proscription of some kinds of food applied to the Jews only. They might supply to strangers among them food which they were forbidden to eat themselves. Thus a practical lesson was taught them that they were to be pre-eminently holy. The moral attainments of others were not to be the standards by which they should measure conduct. More plainly than speech did such prohibition say, " Be not conformed to the world." What it is allowable for others to do, may be sin for me to practise.

IV. BECAUSE THIS ARRANGEMENT SERVED FOR THE DAILY DISCIPLINE 'OF FAITH. Of the first importance was it that the faith of the Hebrews should be maintained, and that their faith should be practically displayed. Very clearly God had assured them that this was his will concerning them; and, whether any reason appeared for the demand or not, as his acknowledged servants they were bound to obey. Such a requirement had some correspondence with the test imposed on our first parents. The act forbidden might be in itself indifferent—having no moral character. Apart from the command, they might have eaten, or abstained from eating, without any violation of conscience. This would make the matter a better test of obedience. In abstaining from such and such meat, they did no one wrong; they violated no law of nature, no law of God : they did themselves no injury. They still had enough to meet all the necessities of hunger. Here, then, was [a true test whether men would simply obey God's word, even though obedience should mean privation. This was the discipline of faith.—D.

Vers. 22—29.—*God's claim upon our money gains.* In every province of human life God requires his proprietorship to be recognized. The seventh part of our time is hallowed for his service. The firstfruits of corn were to be devoted to religious uses. The firstborn in the household belonged to God, and was to be redeemed by substitution. And now, of all their yearly gains, one-tenth was claimed by God.

I. THE GROUND OF GOD'S CLAIM. His claim proceeds from his proprietorship. Towards the Hebrews he was obviously and directly landlord. He had put them into possession of their estates, and rightfully could exact from them a rent. And with respect to all national substance, God is absolute Proprietor. He has an original and indefeasible right as Creator; and it is his supreme power that maintains in existence the treasures of the earth. Even the power we have to accumulate wealth is desirved from the same beneficent Source. It is his *gift*, not that he has conveyed to us the irresponsible right in it, but simply in the sense that we had nothing with which to purchase it. " The earth is the Lord's, and the fulness thereof."

II. A DEFINITE PROPORTION DEMANDED. It was competent for God to make such terms as he pleased with men. He might justly have permitted for our own use a bare existence, and required us to devote to him the residue of our gains. Or he might very properly have exacted as his tribute one-half. Whatever had been his will in the matter, it would become us meekly to acquiesce. He *did* make known his will very clearly to the Jews, and his terms were very generous. So small a portion as one-tenth he condescended to take, and even this was expended in advantage for the nation. Many significant hints have we that, in unwritten form, this part of his will was made known to other nations. Among heathen tribes we find the custom prevails of con- secrating one-tenth of their harvests unto idol gods; and when Abraham returned from the conquest of the invaders, he gave to Melchizedek the tithe of all his spoils. Hence we may regard the law, not as exclusively Jewish, but as intended for all peoples.

III. THE METHOD OF ASSESSMENT. No official assessor was appointed. The cost of collection was *nil*. Each man was to act as his own assessor, and to separate, at harvest- time, God's share of corn and wine and oil. It was a transaction between each man and his God. It was Israel's privilege to live under the shield of Jehovah's arm, and therefore "ever in his Great Taskmaster's eye." The penalty for dishonesty was not immediate, nor visible. Every plan was devised to suit the convenience of the debtor. He might bring his tithe to the temple, either in kind or in coin. Jehovah was no hard Taskmaster, but a considerate and generous King. Giving to him was only another form of receiving. The absence of intermediary officers was a spiritual advantage. It brought each man into direct contact with God, and taught him to act with integrity towards the "Searcher of hearts."

IV. THE EMPLOYMENT OF GOD'S TITHE. The tithe here spoken of is not the tithe of all profits, which was due to the Levite, but a second tithe. The first tithe was regarded as an equivalent to the tribe of Levi, for Levi's share in the allotted posses- sions. Each man in the twelve tribes received, in the original distribution of land, one- twelfth more than his due, from the fact that Levi did not participate. In return for this increment of property, each proprietor paid to the tribe of Levi yearly one-tenth of the produce of the land. This was due as a legal right, and as a just equivalent for non- participation in the territory. But this second tithe was peculiarly the Lord's. Never- theless, it was returned, with added blessing, into their own bosoms. Its first use was to afford a banquet for the offerers themselves. The temple was to be the scene of sacred feasting. The guests might select such viands as pleased their taste. The over- shadowing presence of Jehovah would serve as a sufficient check against excess. To this banquet, in which the entire household shared, they were to invite the Levite, the stranger, the widow, and the orphan. The essential idea thus embodied was philan- thropy. The institution was intended to foster a spirit of benevolence and charity. The presence of the poor in their midst was to be accounted a benefit. It offered scope for the exercise of noblest dispositions. There was to be no niggardly stint in this provision, for it was at Jehovah's cost, and the occasion was to be characterized by unrestrained joy.

V. THE MORAL ADVANTAGES WHICH ENSUED. 1. *It served as a practical reminder of God's proprietorship in them and in their possessions.* Nothing is more easy than to forget our obligations; and such forgetfulness is an immeasurable loss. Not an item was there in their persons, property, or enjoyments, but came from the hand of a generous God. 2. *It was a potent check upon their worldly-mindedness.* The propen- sity for selfish avarice is indigenous in human nature. Every wise man will welcome any breakwater that will withstand this mischievous tide of cupidity. Thus God, with wondrous forethought, provided a safeguard against the abuse of prosperity. He designs to make even worldly gain serve as a stepping-stone to piety. Money is nothing more than means to an end. Reconciliation with God, and personal holiness,—these are to be the aims of human life. 3. *It fostered kindly dispositions among all classes of the people.* Though, as the children of Abraham, they enjoyed great external privileges, they were not to despise the stranger. Yea, he too might be admitted to a full share in their blessings. Brotherly love is a reciprocal boon: both parties are blessed. The fountain of love is replenished in the very act of giving. The *helped* to-day may become the *helper* to-morrow. We are only stewards of God's possessions.—D.

EXPOSITION.

CHAPTER XV.

THE YEAR OF RELEASE FOR THE BENEFIT OF DEBTORS AND THE EMANCIPATION OF HEBREW SLAVES. THE SANCTIFICATION OF THE FIRSTBORN OF CATTLE.

Vers. 1—6.—To the prescription of a tithe for the needy there is added a regulation for the behoof of debtors. The Israelites were not only to help the poor, but they were to refrain from what would be a hardship and oppression to them. Debtors, consequently, were not to be deprived of the benefit of the sabbatical year, for at the close of each seventh year there was to be a release. This does not imply that the debt was to be remitted, but only that the debtor was not then to be pressed for payment. As during the sabbatical year the land lay uncultivated, and the debtor consequently would earn nothing, it was reasonable that he should not then be pressed for payment. A law that every seventh year debts should be remitted, would have frustrated itself, for on such conditions no one would lend, and so there would be no debtors. This is an addition to the law of the sabbath-year (Exod. xxiii. 10, etc.; Lev. xxv. 2—7).

Ver. 1.—Release. The word thus rendered (שְׁמִטָּה, from שָׁמַט, to leave, to let lie fallow) occurs only here and in ver. 2; in Exod. xxxiii. 11 the cognate verb is used, and from this the word is best explained. The debt was to be *left* in the hands of the debtor, as the land was to be let lie or left untilled for that year.

Ver. 2.—Creditor; literally, *master of the loan of his hand*, equivalent to owner of what his hand has lent to another. Comp. the expression, "what was laid in his hand" (Lev. v. 21; Authorized Version, "in fellowship," Lev. vi. 2); and Neh. x. 32, "the debt of every hand" (Authorized Version, "the exaction of every debt"). Neighbour; here, *fellow-Israelite*. Exact it of his neighbour; literally, *press or urge his neighbour*, i.e. to pay. It is called the Lord's release; rather, *a release for Jehovah is proclaimed*; the sabbatical year, like the year of jubilee, was proclaimed, and it was for Jehovah, in his honour, and in accordance with his ordinance.

Ver. 3.—A foreigner; a stranger of another nation, having no internal social relation to Israel (נָכְרִי), as distinguished from the

stranger who lived among them and had claims on their benevolence (גֵּר). Of such they might exact a debt, without regard to the year of release. "This rule breathes no hatred of foreigners, but simply allows the Israelites the right of every creditor to demand his debts and enforce the demand upon foreigners, even in the sabbatical year. There was no severity in this, because foreigners could get their ordinary income in the seventh year as well as in any other" (Keil).

Ver. 4.—Save when there shall be no poor among you; rather, *only that there shall be no poor among you*; q.d., this ordinance is not intended to prevent creditors seeking the payment of their just debts, but only to prevent there being poor in the land. The reason assigned is that the Lord would greatly bless them in the land which he had given them, so that the creditor would be no loser by refraining from exacting his debt from his brother in the seventh year.

Vers. 5, 6.—This blessing, though promised and certified, should come only if they were careful to observe and do all that God commanded them. The for at the beginning of ver. 6 connects this with ver. 4. Thou shalt lend. The verb in Kal signifies to borrow on a pledge; in Hiph. to lend on a pledge, as here; it is a denominative from the Hebrew noun signifying *pledge*.

Vers. 7—11.—The reference to the release leads to a prescription regarding readiness to lend to the poor. They were not to harden their hearts against their poorer brethren, nor were they, in the prospect of the year of release, to refuse to lend them what was necessary for their uses, but, on the contrary, were to open their heart and their hand to them according to their need, lest the poor should appeal against them to God, and sin should lie upon them.

Ver. 7.—Harden thine heart; literally, *make strong*, so as to suppress natural compassion and sympathy.

Ver. 8.—Sufficient for his need, in that which he wanteth; literally, *the sufficiency of his need which he needeth*, i.e. whatever he might need to meet his requirements.

Ver. 9.—A thought in thy wicked heart; literally, *a thing in thy heart worthlessness*, i.e. a thing which is worthless and unworthy. The word used is *belial* (בְּלִיַּעַל), which does not denote that which is wicked so much as that which is worthless. Thus, "a man of Belial" is a worthless fellow—

not necessarily a wicked man (cf. ch. xiii. 13). **And it be sin unto thee;** *i.e.* entail guilt upon thee, and so expose thee to the Divine displeasure.

Ver. 10.—**Shall not be grieved;** literally, *shall not become evil,* i.e. shall not entertain a grudge. They were to give, not grudgingly or of necessity, merely through dread of God's displeasure, but cheerfully and spontaneously (cf. 2 Cor. ix. 7). For this God would bless them in all their works, so that they should not only be no losers, but should be gainers, by their generosity.

Ver. 11.—They were to open their hand wide to their poorer brethren, for there should always be such in the land. This statement is not inconsistent with that in ver. 4, for there it is the prevention of poverty by not dealing harshly with the poor that is spoken of; here it is the continuance of occasion for the relief of the poor that is referred to.

Vers. 12—18.—From injunctions regarding the treatment of the poor and of debtors the transition is easy to the law concerning slaves, inasmuch as it was through the stress of poverty that any became such from among their brethren. The law, as here laid down, is the same as that in Exod. xxi. 2—6, somewhat expanded; the most important addition being that the slave is not only to go free after six years of service, but is to be furnished by his master with the means of setting up a home for himself. The six years here specified are not to be confounded with the years ending at the sabbatical year; they are *any* six years during which the individual has been in bondage.

Ver. 14.—**Thou shalt furnish him liberally;** literally, *shalt lay on his neck,* i.e. thou shalt load him. The meaning is well expressed in the Authorized Version. This is the new prescription added to the earlier law.

Ver. 15.—Compliance is enforced by the consideration that the Israelites had been themselves bondmen in Egypt, and had been redeemed out of that bondage by God (cf. ch. v. 15; x. 19; xvi. 12; xxiv. 18, 22;

Exod. xxii. 20; xxiii. 9; Lev. xix. 34). As God had dealt by them, so it behoved them to deal by others in like condition and need.

Vers. 16, 17.—It might happen, however, that the slave chose rather to remain with his master than to be manumitted, and in that case he was not to be forced to go free, which would be a hardship to him, but was to be, by a formal process of nailing his ear to the door of his master's house, constituted his slave for life (cf. Exod. xxi. 5). This was not a painful operation, especially as the servant's ear was probably already pierced for a ring; nor does any infamy appear to have been attached to the bearing of this badge of perpetual servitude. There is no mention here, as in Exodus, of the matter being referred to the judges; and this has led some to suppose that, by the time this later prescription was given, the earlier usage had passed away; but it is more natural to suppose that this usage was so regular and well known that it was needless formally to announce it.

Ver. 18.—Where a slave determined to have his freedom, the master was to set him free without grudge; **for he hath been worth a double hired servant** to thee, **in serving thee six years;** literally, *double the hire of a hireling he hath served thee six years,* i.e. he hath saved to thee as much again as it would have cost thee to pay a hired labourer to do the same amount of work.

Vers. 19—23.—In ch. xii. 6, 17 and in ch. xiv. 23, reference is made to sacrificial meals, and to the appropriation of the firstlings of the herds and flocks thereto; Moses here reverts to this, and gives a fuller exposition of it. It is enjoined that, as all the firstborn were to be sanctified to the Lord (Exod. xiii. 2—13), they were not to work with the firstborn of their cattle, either by yoking the bullock to the plough or waggon or by shearing the sheep: these belonged to God, and were not to be put to any vulgar uses of men; year by year they were to be brought to the sanctuary, offered as sacrifices, and eaten before the Lord. If any of the firstborn animals were blind, or lame, or in any way blemished, such was not to be offered to the Lord, but might be used as food in their ordinary places of residence (cf. Lev. xxii. 19, etc.).

HOMILETICS.

Vers. 1—6.—*Divine checks on human greed.* In this paragraph the institution of the sabbatical year is presupposed (cf. Exod. xxiii. 9—13; Lev. xxv. 2—7). During this year the land was to rest, and it would doubtless be conducive to after-fruitfulness to give the soil this respite, by letting it lie fallow every seventh year, for at this time the effect of the rotation of crops was unknown.[1] We by no means affirm that such was the only reason for the appointment; yet nothing hinders us from regarding it as *a* reason. In that year there was to be a general remission of debts. To all appearance, there would, however, be one social danger arising from so peculiar an arrangement. Human nature, as regards capacity, aptitude, tact, kindness, hardness, etc., would differ as greatly among Hebrews as among any other peoples. There would be the wise manager, and the man who knew not how to manage at all. There would be some easily " taken in," and others watching for an opportunity of enriching themselves at another's expense. And among the harder men, the thought would naturally arise, " Well, if I must not work to increase my gains that year, I will at least secure all that I ought to have, by collecting all debts due to me, and this I will do with rigour." Now, here comes in this law mercifully guarding the weak against the rapacity of the strong, compelling men, at least outwardly, to show some regard for those who are somewhat behindhand in the race for life, and preventing the more successful ones from so exacting from poorer men as to reduce them to helpless dependence upon others. The following points may be noted. 1. The sabbatical year is here assumed, *ut supra*. 2. This year debts were to be remitted,—not cancelled, but pressure for payment was to be postponed. 3. Thus there was to be an enforced pause in the accumulation of wealth. 4. The sentiment of kindliness and forbearance as well as of justice in business life, was thus taught. 5. At the same time, there is a safeguard against the Hebrews being trifled with by foreigners by a misuse of this law. A foreigner (one who was so in all respects) might incur a debt in the sixth year, thinking that, as a Hebrew could not press for it the next year, he should have a long respite; while, as *he* was not bound by the Hebrews' Law, he could press for debts due to him! This would have been unequal. Hence God guards Israel against such inequality, and says, as a foreigner is not under this law so far as debts due to him are concerned, so neither is he included in it with regard to debts incurred by him; and the release is not intended to operate where its operation cannot be equal all round. 6. Moreover, there is in this law no encouragement to mendicancy, but rather such a check on pressure by the rich, and such an inculcation of regard for the poor, that beggary may be a thing unknown among them. The word " beggar " does not occur once in the Mosaic institutes (cf. Michaelis's ' Commentary on the Laws of Moses,' art. 142). Surely in all this there is abundance of material for homiletic teaching from a Christian point of view. The formal institution here referred to has passed away. But, if we follow out the formula already laid down, that *forms change, but principles never*,—we cannot be at a loss for an exposition of the ethical teaching which this paragraph suggests for all time. For, as is well remarked by Mr. Garden, " The spirit of this law is the same as that of the weekly sabbath. Both have a beneficent tendency, limiting the rights and checking the sense of property; the one puts in God's claims on time, the other on the land. The land shall keep a sabbath unto the Lord." " The land is mine." Let us, then, study *the Divine checks on human greed, as they are shown to us in the teaching of the New Testament.*

I. WE HAVE THE DISTINCT DECLARATION, " YE ARE NOT YOUR OWN." This is far wider and deeper than any analogous statement of Moses. For while Israel had been redeemed out of Egypt, so that God said, " I gave Egypt for thy ransom, Ethiopia and Seba for thee," we must all feel how infinitely short that comes of the tender pathos in 1 Cor. vi. 19, 20; 1 Pet. i. 18, 19. The phrase, " *Ye* are not your own," must needs cover the whole ground of all that we are and have. As "redemption" was the appeal at the basis of Israel's life, so is it in the case of God's people now.

II. WE ARE REDEEMED THAT WE MIGHT LIVE FOR GOD BY LIVING FOR OTHERS. We are expected to have " the same mind " which was also in Christ Jesus (Phil. ii. 1—8). Note the argument involved in 2 Cor. viii. 7, 9; also that in Rom. xiv. 7, *et seq.* See the purpose of Christ's redeeming work, as stated in Titus ii. 14; and also the law of the Christian life in Gal. vi. 1—10. In these passages there is so much of duty indicated with regard to others, that though little of minute detail is now specified, yet Christian men cannot go far wrong if their lives are regulated thereby (1 Cor. x. 24).

　　　[1] See art. ' Sabbatical Year,' in Smith's ' Bibl. Dict.'

III. THE PROHIBITION OF OUR LORD AGAINST COVETOUSNESS IS VERY STERN AND STRONG. (See Luke xii. 13—21.) At every stage of that paragraph there is some new and startling light in which the evil of covetousness is seen. 1. It cherishes a totally mistaken view of life (Luke xii. 15). 2. It is perilous (Luke xii. 20). Hence: 3. It is foolish (Luke xii. 20, 21). Strong checks these! Far stronger than Israel's.

IV. THERE IS A DIVINE STIGMA UPON COVETOUSNESS. (See Eph. v. 5; Col. iii. 5.) It is idolatry. It is giving to creature objects the regard which is due only to God. He would have us "in his light see light," and regard the greed of gain as an abominable thing.

V. THERE IS A DIVINE RULE FOR LABOUR. It is given us in Eph. iv. 28. The observance of this precept would prevent the social evil arising from covetousness on the one hand, and would create the good accruing from benevolence on the other. "Let him labour *in order that* he may have the wherewith to give!" How truly sublime! It is like the benevolence of God.

VI. THE CHRISTIAN TEACHER HAS SPECIAL INJUNCTIONS FOR THE RICH, with the giving of which he is charged. (1 Tim. vi. 17—19.) Thus the Christian code is by no means less comprehensive than the Mosaic. On the contrary, it is far more so. It is equally stringent in allowing no one to think of his property as his own.

VII. OUR GOD WOULD WIN AS WELL AS WARN. See Heb. xiii. 5, "Let your turn of mind be free from the love of money (ἀφιλάργυρος)." Why? "Because himself hath said, I will in no wise fail thee, neither will I in any wise forsake thee" (see also 2 Pet. i. 4). We are permitted, in Christ, to call God "ours," to find in his love our joy, in his wisdom and strength our stay, in his wealth our supply. Hence we ought to be lifted up above any consuming racking care, and to be loyally obedient to God's will in the sanctified use of all that we have (Matt. vi. 33).

Let any one set side by side the Mosaic regulations in the paragraph we have just been considering, with the seven considerations adduced from New Testament teaching. Let him compare them with one another. And, if we mistake not, he will find more than ample material for other Homilies on the height, the breadth, the depth, and the length of Christian ethics, as covering the entire ground of the relations of man to man and of man to God, and as requiring no less exactitude in detail through less detail being specified. It is said (and we fear it is said truly) that the great hindrance to God's work in the world is that the Christian name does not carry with it Christian morality. Ah! if it did, how luminous would such morality appear! Let but the above considerations be universally acted out, *on all sides*, and no more strifes between capital and labour would ever be known. The rich would neither oppress, nor despise, nor neglect the poor; the poor would no longer be jealous of the rich. Both would recognize their mutual relation to and need of each other. While, with universal righteousness and kindness, mendicancy would be a thing unknown. And never, never, till there is a new principle of love infused through the various classes of society, will such a consummation be attained! Still, however sad our hearts may be as we consider how far we are off from the mutual regard between owner and labourer which even Moses enjoined, let each of us feel his personal responsibility for fidelity to the Divine Law. Only as this is felt and discharged by each, can it be felt and discharged by all. The Lord make us and all men to abound in good will, and may the supreme benevolence which has its source in heaven flow o'er the world as a pure river of water of life!

Vers. 7—11.—*The duty of kindness to the poor.* There seems to be at first sight a discrepancy between the phrase in ver. 4 and that in ver. 11. The former is, "Save when there shall be no poor among you;" the latter, "The poor shall never cease out of the land." The first phrase is, however, a reason assigned for the injunction which had been given: it is equivalent to, "Simply, that there be no poor among you," *i.e.* this or that was an appointment in Israel, in order that the number of the poor might be reduced to a minimum, and that those who were poor might not become abjectly so. But no such external law could ever prevent some from falling back in the race. As long as men's constitutions, capacities, and characters were widely different, so would their measure of success be. A levelling of circumstances could be brought about only through a levelling of men, after all had been brought to a uniform starting-point.

Such genial enactments as the one in vers. 1—6 might prevent beggary, but would not do away with poverty. " The poor shall never cease out of the land." This phrase is not to be regarded as indicating a Divine appointment that it should be so, but as a Divine declaration that it would be so. As long as men are what they are, and the varied features of temperament and ability continue as they are, so long will there be abundant scope for the exercise of sympathy and of kindly help. The points noticeable in this paragraph are five. 1. Year after year fresh claims on the kindly help of the prosperous would be presented by their poorer brethren (ver. 11). 2. These claims were to be generously and even gladly met, as if it were a delight. We need not charge the writer with ministering to idleness and beggary (see reference to Michaelis, in previous Homily). The word for, yea, even the conception of, a beggar, as we now understand it, is entirely absent from the Mosaic statutes. Honest and diligent work is supposed to be universal; though it might not be uniformly skilful or successful. 3. The desire to evade any obligation thus presented, was a wicked violation of the spirit of the Law (ver. 9). 4. The cry of the neglected or oppressed poor would rise up to God, and be heard. 5. The Lord would remember the sin of cruel neglect and unkindness, or of haughty coldness.

Now, this chapter generally, and therefore this paragraph as a part of it, may be viewed in one of two aspects: either as a section of the Mosaic code of jurisprudence, or as an inculcation of social duty. It would be obviously beyond or beside our province to deal with it in the former aspect; we are concerned solely with the latter. We need not ask whether, in our New Testament standard, kindness to the poor is enjoined? That is understood. Our one query is this—

Now that we are under Christ, as our Leader, how is the duty of kindness to the poor put and enforced? 1. That duty which Moses enjoined as the leader and legislator of Jehovah's people, our Lord Jesus Christ set on the ground of his own sovereign right, and enforced by his own example. In that wondrous chapter of John's Gospel, the thirteenth, we are told that, when our Saviour had washed his disciples' feet, he told them that he had given them an example that they should do as he had done to them, and also said, " Ye call me Master and Lord: and ye say well; for so I am. If I then, your Lord and Master," etc. We cannot suppose that this one act of kindness and condescension was merely meant to be literally followed. It must have been a kind of representative deed, in which our Lord virtually said, " In whatever way you may comfort or soothe a worn and weary brother by ministering to his wants, do not shrink from doing it, even though it may involve many a lowly, self-sacrificing act." Surely this covers the ground indicated in this paragraph, and includes the duty of giving to the poor and helping the needy, whatsoever their need may be. 2. Our Lord regards the poor and needy as *his* poor: all, generally, because he died *for* them; some, especially, because he lives *in* them. Hence, whoever would act towards them so as to show them the power and glory of a living Saviour's sympathy, must let the poor feel through him the warm touch of a tender Saviour's love. Our Lord said in his intercessory prayer, " As thou hast sent me into the world, even so have I also sent them into the world." Thus believers are to act in the world in the name and on the behalf of our Lord Jesus Christ, as the friends and benefactors of men. 3. Our Lord reckons a kindness shown to men for his sake, as if it were done to him. Even in the Old Testament we get a thought akin to this (Isa. lxiii. 9). But in the New Testament the truth is more clearly defined (cf. Acts ix. 4, where it is presented to us in connection with the reverse of kindness). In Matt. xxv. 31—46 it is shown us more strikingly still. Christ and his people are one; and a kindness done to men, out of love to him, is done to him. Is there not a wondrous touch of nature here? Would not a mother feel a kindness shown to her son, for her sake, as if it were shown to her? If the mother were in England and the son in New Zealand, she would feel the same. And if the son were even base and unworthy, and love did cling to him for the mother's sake, she could not feel the kindness the less. And we are permitted to take this thought up into the heavenly region, and to read the amazing words, " Inasmuch as ye have done it unto one of the least of these, . . . ye have done it unto me." 4. Of so much importance is this kindness to the poor for Christ's sake to be reckoned by us, that we are to watch for and seize opportunities of doing " good unto all men, specially to them that are of the household of faith ; " yea, so labouring, we are even to support the weak, recalling those priceless words which an apostle was mercifully led to save from the peril of unrecorded sayings, " It is more blessed to give than to receive." Whenever and wherever there is presented to us a case of genuine need, there is an opportunity for honouring our Saviour which we must not suffer to pass by unimproved.   5. There are New Testament warnings against the neglect of the poor, which are not only not less severe than any in the Old Testament—they are even more so.   We may arrange them in three classes, giving one specimen under each.   (1) 1 John iii. 17 : If a man can knowingly neglect the poor, God's love is not in his heart.   Where love dwells in the heart, there will be corresponding words on the tongue, and corresponding blessings in the hand. (2) Jas. ii. 5—9 ; v. 1—4 : The Apostle James declares that to neglect or despise the poor is sin against God ; and that the cries of oppressed poverty will be heard in heaven.   (3) Matt. xxv. 31—46 : Our Lord has explicitly told us that in the day of judgment, the one test which will be applied to men, and by which their destiny will be decided, will be that of kindness to the poor for his sake !   Where that has been, penitence and faith have wrought out in love.   Where that has not been, there has been no love, and, consequently, neither faith nor penitent obedience.   It is not necessary to be openly wicked and profane, in order to incur rejection by the Great Judge at last.   There may have been not a single vice which shocked society or violated outward propriety.   Be it so.   Even then the absence of the activities of love will be a man's ruin.   He who has not lived to save his brother will not himself be saved.   A piety that is known only by negatives will be disowned by our sovereign Lord ; while genuine, active, unselfish love, though it may have had but a limited sphere for service, oft shedding a tear that it could do no more, will meet with the holy Master's loving recognition, and will receive his gracious reward !

Vers. 12—18.—*The rights of the slaves.*   By some who are but slightly acquainted with the subject, and who have too strong an *animus* against the Old Book to deal fairly with it, it has been made a matter of complaint against our Lord and his apostles that they did not put down slavery with a strong hand.   The same may be said of Moses. If, however, without prejudging the case, we reverently ask, Why was it that he, as a divinely commissioned legislator, tolerated the institution of slavery ? we are but proposing a question which opens up a field for thoughtful study, and we shall not be left without a satisfactory answer.   And in the answer which the facts will supply there will be contained a world of instructive teaching to the devout and thoughtful mind.   (The student would do well to examine the articles of Michaelis on this subject.) Putting the case generally, so as to prepare the reader for the details which follow, we would say—Moses found slavery existing ; he permitted its continuance, but he placed the slave-holder under such restrictions that the slaves would become conscious of their rights as men and as brethren ; he so limited slavery itself, that no Hebrew could be a slave for life, except of his own voluntary will ; and in his elevated ethical code, he repeatedly insisted on the equality of men before God ; thus dropping in men's minds such seeds of truth that, when they germinated and brought fruit, the institution of slavery would cease, because the peoples would come to be *educated out of it !*

If now we briefly enumerate the several provisions connected with slaves and slave-holding, we shall see, in detail, the proof of the above general remark.   1. The Hebrew slave might be held for six years only ; in the seventh he was to be permitted his freedom : excepting as provided in the eleventh detail.   2. There were other provisions, *e.g.* those connected with the year of jubilee, for ensuring the freedom of the slave, given in Lev. xxv.   3. Rigorous exaction and harshness were distinctly and sternly forbidden (Lev. xxv. 39—43).   If these injunctions and the reasons for them are considered, it will be seen that Hebrew slavery was unlike any other that the world has known.   4. If a master by revengeful treatment inflicted serious bodily injury on the slave, such slave was to have his freedom (Exod. xxi. 26).   5. Undue punishment was avenged by the judges (Exod. xxi. 20, 21).   6. The slave might acquire property of his own, and might even amass enough to buy his own freedom (Lev. xxv.). 7. There were special decrees for the benefit of the slave.   They were to be free from all manner of work on the sabbath day.   They had a right to fruit which grew spontaneously during the sabbatical year.   They were to have their share of the feasts at the great national festivals. 8. If they accepted freedom at the end of the sixth year, they were not to be sent away empty, but were to be furnished by their master, liberally and gladly, with a sufficiency wherewith to " start on their own account." 9. The idea of freedom was ever kept before them. They might not sell themselves for life to any one. They were the Lord's freemen, and they were not to pervert the Divine thought by becoming life-long bondmen (Lev. xxv. 42). 10. As the nation rose in intelligence, their laws became more and more liberal. Provisions which were intended at first only for the menservants, were extended, even in the lifetime of Moses, to the maidservants likewise (cf. Exod. xxi. 7 and ch. xv. 17). 11. If a slave did not accept his freedom when he might have it, he was to have his ears bored, that so he might bear about with him the brand that he had chosen servitude for life (vers. 16, 17). Surely the object of this apparently strange enactment was to create among the people a disrespect for self-chosen servitude, and so, silently yet powerfully, to lift them above it. And yet one more feature should be noted, viz. : 12. When a foreign slave escaped from his master, the moment he touched the Hebrews' soil he was a free man ! (ch. xxiii. 16). Surely no one can study all these details without seeing that the entire tendency of the Mosaic Law was to lift up the people, to advance their happiness, their freedom, their intelligence, and their mutual regard !

If now for a little we pass to the New Testament, to see how the apostles of Jesus Christ regarded and dealt with slaves and slavery, and what their teachings were on this subject, we find that very little is said. There is no denunciation of the institution, notwithstanding the very wide difference between slavery under the Hebrews and under the Greeks and Romans. But we find : 1. Rules for masters, demanding that they render unto their slaves that which is just and equal, since even they, with all their power, are not irresponsible, but have themselves a Master in heaven, to whom the slave is as precious as his owner. 2. They taught at the same time loyalty and obedience on the part of the slave, and urged on him the duty of so serving an earthly master that, in the very act thereof, he should serve a heavenly one. 3. That both master and slave would receive from their common Lord a reward according to their measure of fidelity ; " knowing that whatsoever good thing any man doeth, the same shall he receive of the Lord, *whether he be bond or free*." 4. They laid down afresh, in the name of the Lord Jesus, the old Mosaic law, that " there is no respect of persons with God ; " thus teaching the equality of all men in the eye of him " who judgeth according to every man's work."

Now, comparing the Old and New Testament treatment of slavery, what do we see? In the Old Testament a number of details which would work in the direction of freedom, and thoughts dropped which would bring slavery to an end. In the New Testament the details are not repeated. 1. Because, having been given once, repetition would have been of little service. 2. Because the apostles were not laying down laws for a commonwealth *in the same sense* that Moses was. But, though we have no repetition of details, we have (1) such an inculcation of kindness on one side and of loyalty on the other, as, when mutually heeded, would make slavery cease *to be* slavery in all save the name ; and (2) such a clear enunciation of the truth, that in Christ there is neither bond nor free, that, when the power of this Divine impartiality was felt, slavery would ultimately cease both in fact and in name the wide world over !

Thus we see that the Divine Being in his infinite wisdom has seen fit to adopt a similar process under both the Jewish and Christian dispensations, viz. that of educating men by the power of truth and goodness up to such a level, that they voluntarily put down this or that social wrong, instead of thrusting it out at once by a violent hand. Had *e.g.* this wrong of slavery been forcibly put down, the spirit of enslaving would have still existed on one side, and an opening for unbridled lawlessness might have been created on the other. But by the Divine process, slower though it be, the master is lifted up above the level of the tyrant, the slave comes to be regarded as a man and a brother, and ultimately the last fetter shall be snapped, and men brought unto the glorious liberty of the children of God !

Nor can we do justice to our theme unless we point out, for practical use and fervent exhortation, the spiritual significance of the whole.

I. THE EQUALITY OF MEN BEFORE GOD. The Divine love and regard embrace all. The overshadowing wing of mercy covers all, and the free offers of mercy are made to all (Isa. lv. 1—7).

II. BECAUSE OF THE VALUE GOD SETS ON EVERY MAN, HE FORBIDS ANY MAN TO TAKE ANOTHER CAPTIVE, AND FORBIDS MAN SELLING HIMSELF INTO CAPTIVITY OF ANY KIND. " Ye are bought with a price; be ye not the slaves of men."

III. WE ARE FREE FROM HUMAN FETTERS THAT WE MAY BE ABSOLUTELY FREE TO SERVE GOD. " As free, but not using your liberty for a cloak of maliciousness; but as the servants of God."

IV. ABSOLUTE LOYALTY TO GOD IS THE SUREST AND BEST GUARANTEE OF FIDELITY TOWARDS MEN. Nothing would be wanting between master and servant now, if both were purely loyal to the Great Supreme. He who is bound by the vow of a holy consecration to serve a holy God, may be trusted with any department of human service.

V. TO THIS OUR GOD WOULD WIN AND LEAD US, BY PATIENT TEACHING AND GRACIOUS TRAINING. It takes long to perfect a world or even a class.

Ver. 21.—*Sacrifices to be without blemish.* A reference to passages in the Books of Exodus, Leviticus, and Numbers, will show the frequency with which the injunction here contained was insisted upon, and the importance attached to it. Sacrifices offered to God must be without blemish. The entire Mosaic system of sacrifice was symbolic in relation to the Church that then was, and typical in relation to the Church of the future. We can scarcely miss the teaching of the enactment before us, if only we seek to interpret it with reverent and loyal hearts. Surely it taught two things in the region of law, and also two things in the sphere of grace. The former were: 1. That in the eye of the All-pure One, every moral flaw or defect was an offence, and therefore could not be accepted by him. 2. That as man was guilty before God, he could not, on the reckoning of bare law, be well-pleasing in the eyes of a righteous Being, to whom all evil was an abomination. The latter were: 1. That a flawless sacrifice was to be selected and offered to God by, and in the name, and on the behalf of, the guilty one. 2. That such flawless sacrifice, if offered in sincerity and penitence of spirit, would be accepted on his behalf. Now, we are not left to interpret the type as best we may, nor are we called on to offer the symbolic sacrifice. The antitype has come. The reality is ours. And an inspired interpretation of ancient rites is given us by apostles and prophets of our Lord and Saviour (cf. Heb. ix. 14; 1 Pet. i. 19; Eph. v. 27; 2 Pet. iii. 14; Jude 24; Rev. xiv. 5). With such teaching before us, we can see a sixfold significance in our text.

I. HERE IS A DIVINE APPEAL TO THE CONSCIENCE. It says, in language which ought never to be mistaken, " the least speck of sin is an offence to God ; " and guilty man cannot, on the ground of his own right, have any standing-ground for an instant before him. It is said that in the later days of the Jewish economy, when the offerer brought his sacrifice, the slaughterer (who was other than the priest) took a two-edged knife and ran it from the nape of the neck down the spine, laying it bare. Not unfrequently this would disclose a dark spot: this was a blemish ; the animal was unfit for sacrifice, and had to be cast away. Hence the allusion in Heb. iv. 12, which, so understood, has in it marvellous power. For this blemish did not appear on the surface, it came not out to the light till the spinal marrow was exposed to view. Hence, see Heb. iv. 13, specially the marvellous phrase, "πάντα δὲ γυμνὰ καὶ τετραχηλισμένα," κ.τ.λ. Every creature is " opened " unto the eyes of him with whom is our account. And though exterior conduct may be such as to commend itself to the eye of man, yet in the " marrow " of one's being there may be a sin which is an offence to God. May be? There *is.* There are sins upon sins, and there is sinfulness, which is the root and ground of all. And hence it must be the case that *sinful man has no right, on the ground of his own merits, to expect acceptance before God.* This is the very ground-work of evangelical theology. It is said, " Pectus facit theologum," but we would say rather (as has been remarked to us), " Conscientia facit theologum ; " for only as this appeal to the conscience is felt, will the after-appeals properly tell.

II. HERE IS A DIVINE INVITATION TO FAITH. There was to be a sacrifice chosen, without blemish, which was to be presented by and on behalf of the offerer (John i. 29). God has provided a Lamb for a burnt offering, and for a sin offering too (Isa. liii. 6 ; 2 Cor. v. 21). (For a discussion of the grounds on which the offering of the Body of Jesus Christ once for all could be valid for the race, see Dale on the Atonement, sect. x.) Suffice it here to say that this offering had the dignity of a Divine Sacrifice, the appropriateness of a human one, and the "sweet-smelling savour" of a perfectly pure one. Besides which it had all the spontaneity of a voluntary offering, and all the generosity of a noble self-surrender for the sake of others; in making which the Redeemer was satisfied. And this offering which infinite love has made, loving faith may take and call its own; and abandoning all pretence to a standing-ground in native right, it may find an everlastingly firm one in sovereign grace!

III. HERE IS A DIVINE CALL TO PENITENCE. The sacrifice was to be offered with confession of sin (see Lev. xvi. 21). All the several ordinances which were spread over different sacrificial services in Israel, find their varied significances grouped in one, in the attitude of the sinner before the cross of his Saviour. Well might Watts write, "My faith would lay her hand," etc. While we accept the Divine Sacrifice for sin, penitential confession over sin should ever mark us (see Ps. li.).

IV. HERE IS A DIVINE DEMAND FOR RECTITUDE OF HEART. When we bring our offerings to the Lord, no defect should be knowingly tolerated by us. Grace gives no warrant to laxity, and true penitence will be scrupulously intolerant of it (Ps. lxvi. 18). The freeness of pardon to the penitent involves no modification of ethical stringency, for the fact is, wherever there is any known tolerance of ill, to that extent penitence does not exist. God puts away sin by forgiving it, only as we put it away by repenting of it and casting it off.

V. HERE IS A DIVINE SUMMONS TO DEVOTION. Jesus died, the just for the unjust, that he might bring us to God. And where a man, sorry for sin, intolerant of the evil in his nature, struggling against it, and pleading with God to uproot it, casts himself before God in this genuine uprightness of soul, none of the imperfections over which he mourns shall prevent the Divine acceptance of such an offering, presented, as it will be, in the name of the spotless Son of God. The virtue of his spotless sacrifice ensures the acceptance of ours. Every true and sincere penitent is, on this ground of free grace and dying love, as well-pleasing to God and as near to his heart as the purest angel before the eternal throne. The offering to God of a broken and a contrite heart is one which he cannot and will not despise (see also Heb. xiii. 15, 16).

VI. HERE IS A DIVINE PROPHECY, TO INSPIRE HOPE. These sacrifices of ours, offered in penitence, faith, and love, are still but imperfect. And the holiest souls are most alive to such imperfection, and most sorrowful over it. Hence it should be no small joy to find in the Word of God precisely the same expressions used to express the future purity of believers that are employed to indicate the perfection of the Redeemer's sacrifice. As the one Great Sacrifice was "without blemish and without spot," so all those who are themselves living sacrifices to God, shall be "without spot or wrinkle, or any such thing." He who received them at first on the ground of his own purity, shall create in them a spotlessness like his own. They shall be "without fault" before the throne of God. And he who died for them shall then present them as his own!

Have we not here (in conclusion) a remarkable illustration of what the Apostle Paul so often speaks of as "the righteousness of God"? Each one of these six steps is a fresh aspect of it. The first shows the righteousness of God in taking cognizance of sin; the second, the righteousness of God in offering a spotless sacrifice for sin; the third, the righteousness of God in requiring penitential acknowledgment of sin; the fourth, the righteousness of God in demanding intolerance of sin; the fifth, the righteousness of God in accepting our consecration in the name of a Sinless One, only when we penitently put away sin; the sixth, the righteousness of God in ensuring that those who are living sacrifices to him shall ultimately be perfectly freed from all sin! Thus from beginning to end "grace reigns through righteousness, unto eternal life, by Jesus Christ our Lord." "Now unto him that is able to keep us from falling, and to present us *faultless* before the presence of his glory with exceeding joy, to the only wise God our Saviour, be glory and majesty, dominion and power, both now and ever. Amen."

HOMILIES BY VARIOUS AUTHORS.

Vers. 1—12.—" *The Lord's release.*" The sabbatic year was in many respects a year of mercy to the poor. The beautiful name given to it here—" the Lord's release "—suggests gospel ideas. It finds its higher counterpart in that "acceptable year of the Lord" (Luke iv. 19), which is the true "Lord's release." Christ came "to preach the gospel to the poor," and "to preach deliverance to the captives" (Luke iv. 18). This "accepted time" is the period of God's forbearance with our sins (2 Cor. v. 19; vi. 2). It is the time also of forgiveness of sins to those who believe—a "Lord's release" indeed, not from money debts, but from spiritual ones (Matt. vi. 12), not temporary, but eternal. It is the time of the setting free of bondsmen—Satan's captives—those held in thrall by evil (Rom. vi. 18; 2 Tim. ii. 26). We are taught by this law—

I. THAT THE POOR HAVE A CLAIM ON THE FORBEARANCE OF THE RICH. (Vers. 1—5.) Such a claim will willingly be recognized by the loving heart. It will shrink from pushing hard on any one. It will put itself in the debtor's place, and bear with him as long as possible. This was the lesson enforced by the law of "the release." It secured for the poor debtor a whole year of grace. It interposed a check upon the creditor's selfishness, and rebuked him if disposed to press hard upon his brother. It did more, testifying by its very existence to God's sympathy with the poor, and to his desire that they should be mercifully treated. The harshly exacting spirit, however common, is not God's or Christ's (Matt. xviii. 23—35). It is assumed, of course, that the case of poverty is genuine. There is no evidence that, even during the sabbatic year, the creditor was not entitled to recover his debt from a man well able to pay it.

II. THAT THE POOR HAVE A CLAIM ON THE ASSISTANCE OF THE RICH. (Vers. 7—12.) Assistance goes beyond forbearance. The Law requires, not simply that lenders of money should not be harsh and unforbearing in exacting its repayment, but that, where need exists, they should be willing, nay forward, to render such assistance as is in their power. Honest poverty—for such only is in contemplation—creates a claim which those "having this world's good" (1 John iii. 17) are not at liberty to disregard. Heart and hand are to be alike open to the cry of distress. The giving is to be : (1) liberal; (2) ungrudging; (3) disinterested (cf. Matt. v. 42). Note: 1. Liberal assist-ance in a time of need is worth many doles spread over a longer period. 2. Assistance, where practicable, should be given in the form of loans. This is the idea of the law, and it is in harmony with the best modern opinion. Loans are preferable to simple charity; they do not pauperize; they develop the principle of self-help, encourage diligence and thrift, and foster the spirit of honest independence. Those who cannot be helped save by gratuities must, of course, be helped cheerfully.

III. THAT LIBERALITY TO THOSE IN NEED TENDS TO OUR OWN ENRICHMENT. (Vers. 4—7, 10.) No truly liberal man will make this the motive of his liberality. But as a secondary encouragement to liberal giving, and as removing fears of the possible results to one's own fortunes, it deserves to be considered. The liberal soul is usually not the loser, but the gainer, by its liberality. Selfishness defeats itself. Subtle spiritual laws operate to produce this result. 1. Liberality reacts upon the soul itself to ennoble and expand its powers. This tends in the direction of enrichment. 2. The liberal man is loved and trusted. He gets kindness shown him for his kindness to others (Luke vi. 30—39). He is one whom neighbours and friends are always willing to serve, and to speak a good word for. 3. God's blessing is upon him (vers. 4, 10). Through that blessing he is prospered. He divides and conquers. By opening his hand liberally, he gets more than he parts with. "There is that scattereth and yet increaseth," etc. (Prov. xi. 24, 25).—J. O.

Ver. 11.—*The poor in the land.* The meaning is that there will always be greater or less scope for the exercise of the virtues of kindness and liberality,—that it is vain to hope for a Utopian condition of society in which there shall be absolutely no poor.

I. THIS DOES NOT IMPLY : 1. That many existing causes of poverty cannot be per-manently removed. 2. That every attempt ought not to be made to reduce poverty within its narrowest limits. The saying, "Ye have the poor always with you" (Matt. xxvi. 11), is no utterance of fatalism. Much can be done to reduce poverty. With the growth of society, still more as a result of the spread of Christian principles, numbers of the causes of poverty now existing may be expected to disappear (idleness, intem-perance, bad laws, merciless competition, class antagonisms, unfavourable sanatory conditions, etc.).

II. IT DOES IMPLY : 1. That under the most favourable conditions of existence on earth a residuum of poverty is still to be looked for. (1) There are *diversities of talents.* There will always be those whose abilities only fit them for the humblest positions in society. And these may be left friendless, or health may fail them, or they may live to old age, and become dependent. (2) There are *vicissitudes of fortune.* These come to the most fortunate of men, reducing them oftentimes to great straits. And it is too much to expect that, even under millennial conditions, the causes of such vicissitudes will altogether cease to operate. 2. That while poverty lasts, it is our duty to help to bear its burden. Poverty, in a state of society such as we anticipate as the goal of history, need never be the painful thing it is now. With loving hearts, and hands ready to help, its sting will be taken away.—J. O.

Vers. 12—19.—*Bondmen.* No argument in favour of modern slave-holding can be drawn from Hebrew bond-service. The Hebrew bondmen, unlike modern slaves, were incorporated as part of the nation; had legal rights; took part in the religious feasts; if mutilated or injured, thereby obtained their freedom. On the sabbatic year the Hebrew bondman regained his freedom, going out, not simply free, but loaded with presents. We learn—
I. THE NATURAL RIGHT OF MAN TO HIS FREEDOM. (Vers. 12, 13.) Freedom is man's birthright. It cannot be bartered. He must not be robbed of it by violence. If from temporary causes the use of it is lost, the right itself is not destroyed. So the Jews were taught by the return of every Hebrew to his freedom in the seventh year. It is a primary and unalienable right of man, which here, like underlying rock, juts to the surface.
II. THE RIGHT OF SERVANTS TO EQUITABLE AND GENEROUS TREATMENT. (Vers. 13—16.) Bondmen were not to be regarded as mere "hands," still less as chattels. They were to be kindly treated, and dismissed with presents. It is a principle of equity which comes to light in ver. 18. We may apply it to modern times by saying that if servants are worth more to us than their wages, it is but fair that they should participate in profits. The principle is already being recognized, and has in it the germ of the solution of many difficult problems in political economy.
III. THAT LOVE IS THE TRUE RECONCILER OF SERVICE AND FREEDOM. (Vers. 17, 18.) It made the service no service—no real bond-service. Compare Jacob's service for Rachel (Gen. xxix. 20). Were the law of love to rule more than it does in the relations of servants and masters, of employers and employed, it would greatly sweeten trade, commerce, manufactures, and domestic life. There are doubtless faults on the side of servants as well as of masters—but how seldom is any earnest attempt made to break down feelings of antagonism, and to bring in healthier relations! The law of Christ is the true cure for strikes, lock-outs, combinations, etc. Apply to the service of God in Christ. Law here, but also love, and through the love freedom in obedience. The highest freedom is in obedience to the law of holiness.—J. O.

Vers. 19—23.—*The firstlings.* The solution of the apparent discrepancy between this passage and Numb. xviii. 18 seems to lie in the custom of inviting the worshippers to share in the feasts provided by their offerings. View the sanctification of the firstlings as symbolical. 1. *Of God's claim on the first and choicest of what we have for his own service.* (1) Of our property. (2) Of our affections. (3) Of our powers of body and mind. 2. *Of God's right to redeemed life.* The firstlings were redeemed by God for himself on the memorable night of the deliverance from Egypt (Exod. xiii. 12). God claims redeemed life as peculiarly his own (Isa. xliii. 1—4; 1 Cor. vi. 20). 3. *Of God's right to young life.* A symbol of early consecration. 4. *Of happy fellowship with God.* The fellowship was a fruit of the dedication of the best.—J. O.

Vers. 1—6.—*The year of forgiveness.* We have here what we may call the "poor law" of Palestine. The poor were to be regarded as "brethren," they were to be treated as neighbours, as members of the one society. Money was to be lent them to give them a start in life (vers. 7—11), and if they were unable to repay it by the seventh or sabbatic year, they were to be forgiven the debt, "to the end that there be no poor among you" (ver. 4, margin). Usury was thus discouraged between brethren. Loans were to be acts of generosity, and the idea was distinctly to be kept in view that a person should sometimes lend, "expecting nothing again." With foreigners, that is, those not of "the household of faith," it might be different; the debt need not in this case be cancelled; the year of release was a Divine institution for the people of God. The Jews were intended, if obedient, to be creditors of the world, and debtors to none; and the poor brother was to have the joy in the sabbatic year of being forgiven.

I. THE DUTY OF FORGIVENESS WAS PRESCRIBED TO ALL THE BRETHREN. In fact, this poor law was the proclamation of the "brotherhood" of believers in the one God. Upon this forgiveness of debt was based. The creditor was to realize how much more blessed it is to give than to receive (Acts xx. 35); how blessed it is to be able to help a brother! Had the Jews been faithful, the parable of the good Samaritan would not have been such a wonder. It was just the spirit fostered by this institution of the year of release.

Now, this duty of forgiveness of the debts of brethren arises out of the forgiving character of God. As the common Father of these brethren in the faith, he inculcates forgiveness because he practises it. The experience of Israel in the wilderness was of a series of Divine forgivenesses, even though in forgiving them he took vengeance on their inventions (Ps. xcix. 8). And the beautiful parable about the two debtors (Matt. xviii. 23—35) is really meant to bring out the truth that *unforgivingness* is a violation of the family spirit encouraged by the king, and is the unpardonable sin.

II. THE IDEAL SET BEFORE THEM WAS TO BE THE EXTIRPATION OF POVERTY IN THE FAMILY OF GOD. It would most probably never be reached, but it is well to be aiming at the high and the noble, even though it may not be all attained. The marginal reading in ver. 4, which has received the *imprimatur* of Jonathan Edwards ('Works,' Tegg's edition of 1860, vol. ii. p. 164), brings out the beautiful aim thus set before Israel. The effort was to be to make Jewish poverty impossible. The same idea seized on the mind of the Church after Pentecost, leading to the trial of a *Christian commune*, wherein for a time it could be said, "Neither was there any among them that lacked" (Acts iv. 34). Poverty was for a time at least banished from the Christian Church. These strivings after an ideal shall be crowned at last with success when under the new *régime*, "They shall hunger no more, neither thirst any more; neither shall the sun light on them, nor any heat" (Rev. vii. 16).

III. THE OBEDIENT ARE INTENDED TO MAKE ALL MEN THEIR DEBTORS. The Lord promises his people, if they are only obedient, that they shall lend to many nations, but shall not borrow (ver. 6). It is sometimes thought to be a special benefit when a person can contract debt from all and sundry, his credit being so good. But it surely is a higher benefit to be in a position to *oblige everybody*. This is what God meant his people to be. Surrounding nations were to borrow from them, and own their indebtedness. And has not this a moral and spiritual side? The religious spirit is the *obliging* spirit, the spirit which hails with delight the opportunity of "doing good unto all men, especially unto such as are of the household of faith."

IV. IT IS THE SECRET OF SOVEREIGNTY TO BE ABLE TO OBLIGE OTHERS. For it is significant surely that the Israelites are told, immediately after the promise of being able to lend unto many nations, "and thou shalt reign over many nations, but they shall not reign over thee" (ver. 6). Rule arises out of obligation. Influence is acquired when we are able to befriend others. Doubtless many of the conquests of Israel were by *force* rather than by *finance*; but it is the peaceful acquisition of power that a Divine promise contemplates, and we begin to rule as "kings and priests unto God" when we become thoroughly obliging. It is thus love and loyalty are secured among men.

Thus we have in this arrangement of the year of release principles laid down that God has illustrated himself in his considerate and forgiving conduct towards us, and in which we are to try to follow him.—R. M. E.

Vers. 7—11.—*Open-handedness.* Having inculcated the forgiveness of a brother's debts during the sabbatic year, Moses now proceeds to speak of the open-handedness which should precede that year. It might be made a pretext for refusing a poor brother a helping hand that the year was almost on when the debt would be cancelled legally; but to make this a pretext for niggardliness would only betray wickedness of heart. The most beautiful consideration is thus inculcated for the poor; and as "the poor shall never cease out of the land," there will be the call evermore for this open-handed-ness. Now this poor-law regulation is a most beautiful illustration of what God does for us; and something like it will yet supersede the hard-heartedness of our national systems.

I. GENEROSITY SHOULD NOT BE TOO CALCULATING IN ITS TURN. Doubtless, often-times it receives a noble return, but this should not be too much regarded, lest the speculative spirit mar the motive altogether. Nor again should we harden our hearts under the persuasion that our generosity is misspent, and that we shall never be repaid in any way. God has himself shown us true generosity in making his sun to shine on the evil as well as on the good, and in sending his rain upon the unjust as well as the just. And hence we are exhorted to " lend, hoping for nothing again; and your reward shall be great, and ye shall be the children of the Highest: for he is kind unto the unthankful and to the evil " (Luke vi. 35). There is something noble in an uncalcu-lating generosity.

II. IT IS THE NEED OF THE POOR BROTHER WHICH WE ARE BOUND TO SUPPLY. That is, we are asked to supply him not with the luxuries or comforts of life, as if to these he had a right; but with his needs. The open-handedness will be considerate so far as not to encourage unworthy dependence. The brother will be helped in a brotherly way—enabled to help himself, and having his needs only supplied. This prin-ciple has been urged in connection with our national poor-law system. If it is lost sight of, then a premium is paid to idleness, and the " ne'er-do-wells " become the favourites of fortune.[1] Our Father in heaven acts in the same wholesome fashion. " He supplies all our *need* according to his riches in glory by Christ Jesus." He supplies us with salva-tion because we cannot save ourselves; he supplies us with what enables us to help ourselves. He could keep the whole world in idleness, " ladies and gentlemen at large," but he prefers to keep the whole world in work. Our reliance on God is for our need.

III. OPEN-HANDEDNESS FOR GOD'S SAKE IS SURE OF ITS REWARD. " The liberal soul shall be made fat." " He that watereth others shall be watered also himself." " There is that scattereth and yet increaseth." In this way the Lord showeth in both dispensations how " he loveth a cheerful giver." When a religious man, acting on principle, lives an open-handed life, he has the finest business stimulus. He works that he may have the more to give, and thus be the more God-like. There is nothing so hallows business in all its ramifications as this desire to be able to help those in need.

IV. IT IS A SOLEMN THOUGHT THAT THE POOR ARE NEVER TO CEASE OUT OF THE LAND IN THE PRESENT DISPENSATION. The unequal distribution of wealth, the im-provident habits of many, and the pressure of population upon subsistence seem destined to keep the poor always with us. And in consequence our Saviour stepped out of his rich condition in the bosom and home of the Father and became poor, that he might call every poor man a brother, and leave the poor his legatees after his departure. We need the spectacle of poverty to move our hard hearts to the generosity required. Were abundance the rule, and no human being wanted bread, the selfishness of the race would know no bounds. But the poor ones call for the sympathy which Jesus so abundantly deserves, and we can now sell our spikenard and give to them with all the careful calculation which a Judas once desired (John xii. 1—8).

Let our help to others be systematic, because conscientious, and then shall it prove a perennial rill, benefiting the lives of many as it wends its way down the vale of years to the ocean that engulfs us all.—R. M. E.

Vers. 12—18.—*The freedom of the slave.* The seventh year was the year of *personal* release as well as release from debt. Slavery among the Jews was utterly unlike the slavery of modern times. It arose when a Jew became bankrupt; he might then sell his services to his creditor, and pay off his debt by honest work. But beyond *six* years his service need not continue. As soon as the sabbatic year came round he could claim his liberty. In such a case, his master is counselled to be generous when he goes,

---

[1] Cf. J. S. Mill's 'Political Economy,' bk. V. ch. xi. § 13; also 'The Letters and other Writings of the Late Edward Denison, M.P.,' p. 63, etc.

that he may have something with which to begin the world again. "Thou shalt furnish him liberally out of thy flock, and out of thy floor, and out of thy winepress: of that wherewith the Lord thy God hath blessed thee thou shalt give unto him." On the other hand, if the service was so delightful to him that he would rather not leave, it was allowable to bore his ear through with an awl, that he might be recognized as a servant for ever.

I. LIBERTY IS RECOGNIZED IN GOD'S LAW AS EACH MAN'S RIGHT. It may be conditioned upon certain services, just as the liberty of Israel was conditioned upon God's redemption of them from Egypt; but come at last it will. No property in *persons* is recognized, merely in *services* for a certain definite period. Man-stealing, as we know from Exod. xxi. 16, was a capital crime, punishable with death, so that there is really no warrant in the Jewish institution for modern slavery.[1] Under Jewish law no involuntary servitude was allowed; and there was always the right to freedom in the sabbatic year.

And is there not underlying this arrangement for each man's liberty an under-tone of gospel truth? What is the gospel but a great provision for conferring spiritual liberty upon those who have sold themselves to sin, and are in bondage? The present dispensation is, in fact, the sabbatic year, wherein liberty is preached to the captives (Isa. lxi. 1, 2; Luke iv. 17, 18).

II. FREEDOM WAS TO BE CONFERRED IN A SPIRIT OF GENEROUS JOY. The ransomed one was not to be sent out empty-handed, but furnished liberally. Emancipation was not to be given with a grudge, but to be granted with joy and love-tokens besides. It was not to be something in which the master reluctantly acquiesced, but in which he gladly co-operated. In fact, God's joy in emancipating Israel from Egypt was to be the type of the joy of the Jewish master in liberating the slave.

And here again we have the type of the spiritual joy which the emancipation of souls should ensure in all who help therein. "There is joy in the presence of the angels of God over one sinner that repenteth." When he "drew nigh to the house, he heard music and dancing" (Luke xv. 10—25). No joy should be so deep as this of helping the slaves of sin to spiritual freedom.

III. LOVE ALONE COULD MAKE SERVICE PERPETUAL. For it is supposable that sometimes a slave found himself so happy with his master, especially if the master had made him his son-in-law (Exod. xxi. 4, 5), that he preferred slavery with love to liberty with separation. In such a case it was allowed him to have his ear bored and to become a perpetual slave, because a son. Such a service was indeed perfect freedom, because its spirit and motive were devotedness and love.

And it is this which is taken in Ps. xl. 6 as the prophetic type of the relation of Jesus Christ to his Father. He became by voluntary and loving contract the Father's Servant or Slave for ever. He found his service such a delight that liberty and independence could not be thought of.

And in this we surely follow in his steps. We are the Lord's slaves after having become the Lord's freemen. He delivers us from the slavery of sin, and then he introduces us to his service; and lo, we find it so blessed that we insist on our ears being bored, and our being made his slaves for ever. Now obedience is the slavery of love. When Law is delighted in, it is a "law of liberty," and the soul feels freedom perfect "under Law."

"Anywhere with Jesus, says the Christian heart;
Let him take me where he will, so we do not part;
Always sitting at his feet, there's no cause for fears;—
Anywhere with Jesus in this vale of tears.

"Anywhere with Jesus, though he leadeth me
Where the path is rough and long, where the dangers be;
Though he taketh from me all I love below,
Anywhere with Jesus will I gladly go.

*   *   *   *   *

[1] For a specious defence of slavery, cf. Thornwell's 'Collected Writings,' vol. iv. pp. 379—436; for the other side of the question, see Cheever's 'God Against Slavery,' especially ch. xiv., xv., xvi., xvii.

"Anywhere with Jesus, for it cannot be
Dreary, dark, or desolate where he is with me;
He will love me always, every need supply;—
Anywhere with Jesus, should I live or die."

R. M. E.

Vers. 19—23.—*The firstlings for God.* The firstlings which were males were not to be reared for work, but kept for communion. They were to constitute, if perfect, a peace offering before God; if imperfect, they were to be eaten at home, imperfect fellowship between imperfect persons. Just as in the firstfruits God claimed the first share; so in the case of the firstlings of the herd or flock, and the firstborn among men.

I. THE BEGINNINGS OF LIFE SHOULD BE RECOGNIZED AS GIFTS OF GOD, AND DEDICATED GRATEFULLY TO HIM. He is the Source of life; hence the firstlings should be the cause of quiet meditation and acknowledgment. Such increase should be the occasion of special fellowship with God, enlarging gratitude and dictating devotion.

II. IMPERFECTIONS IN GOD'S GIFTS SHOULD BE ACCEPTED BY MEN AS MORE THAN THEY DESERVE. The imperfect firstling, in being made a feast for men only, and not a sacrifice for God as well, seemed to say that, however imperfect God's gift may be sometimes, it should be gratefully accepted as beyond our desert. The blemished, the lame, the blind, when God sends them in his providence, we should not despise, but rather hail them as beyond our desert.

And if this was to be the case in the use of beasts, does it not throw clear light upon our conduct in the case of imperfect men? When children come into this world with any defect, let us not rebel against his will, but cherish the defective gift as reminding us how little we deserve, and by our love give such children compensation.

III. THE DEDICATION OF THE PERFECT FIRSTLING POINTED TO THE CONSECRATED FIRSTBORN, JESUS CHRIST. He is indeed the Firstborn of every creature. To him the firstlings and firstborn pointed. He was dedicated in life and death to the Father. He became the great Peace Offering which makes God and man one. And this suggests—

1. *The Father's delight in Jesus.* How it burst forth from time to time in "This is my beloved Son, in whom I am well pleased"! What delight in our Lord's life! what satisfaction in his obedience unto death! God well pleased!

2. *Our delight in Jesus.* Jesus becomes the medium of communion. We have him in common with God. "Our fellowship is with the Father, and with his Son Jesus Christ" (1 John i. 3). The more we meditate upon him, the deeper must be our delight.—R. M. E.

Vers. 1—11.—*A bulwark against cupidity.* Material prosperity was the only form of blessing that had attractive charm for the Hebrews. Neither mind nor conscience was yet sufficiently developed to value higher good. God had to raise them by slow and successive steps. Material prosperity had its dangerous side. It might foster pride, self-sufficiency, a sense of overweening superiority, and might lead to tyrannous treatment of others. Or, used in devout recognition of God, it might give scope for generous impulses, furnish leisure for intellectual pursuits, aid the culture of the æsthetic arts, diffuse religious knowledge, and practically relieve human distress. The institution of the year of release was designed to serve as a flood-gate, by which the tide of material wealth might be turned into the fittest channel.

I. MATERIAL WEALTH, WITH ITS CONCURRENT POWER, WAS A FRUIT OF RELIGIOUS OBEDIENCE. (Vers. 4, 5.) The acquisition of wealth is the effect of law. It does not follow an erratic course. If we can see the operation of fixed law in nature and in human life, we are constrained to believe that law (whether discovered or undiscovered) operates in getting wealth. In the case of the Hebrews, the law of earthly success was clearly revealed. In return for loyal obedience to Divine command, the soil should be fertile; early and latter rain should descend; a salutary awe should restrain the neighbouring tribes from predatory raids; the seasons should be auspicious; there should be plenty for man and for cattle. Still it is true that the "hand of the diligent maketh rich;" "them that honour me I will honour;" "godliness is profitable unto all things." Yet earthly prosperity is not the badge of piety. Many of God's saints are in the ranks of the poor. Imprudent courses, though pursued by the righteous, end in disaster. Prudent courses in business, assiduously pursued, even by the profane, terminate in worldly success.

II. MATERIAL WEALTH IS VERY UNEVENLY DISTRIBUTED AMONG MEN. Some men are creditors; some are debtors. Some begin life in affluence; some begin in poverty. Such varieties of human circumstance are best. They teach that the same hand that has fashioned material nature has moulded the externals of human life. Such a plan affords variety of occupation and pursuit. The poor are benefited by the "learned leisure" of the rich; the rich are benefited by the industry of the poor. Men require quiet freedom from bodily toil to investigate and to invent; men require the stimulus of hunger to perform arduous labour. It is a mutual benefit; the rich are as much indebted to the poor, as the poor to the rich. We learn also that material wealth is not the highest good that God has to bestow, or he would put it within every man's reach. It is but a visible symbol of invisible treasure.

III. MATERIAL WEALTH IS INTENDED FOR MUTUAL HELPFULNESS. It was never intended to be hoarded in caves or coffers. The possession of wealth carries an obligation to render high service to humanity. This very obligation to do good prevents an indiscriminate scattering of wealth. Simple communism would be an immeasurable curse. The industry and self-restraint which enable one nation to lend to another nation, give to the former immense influence and wholesome power. We are to distinguish between the objects of our help. We are not to treat brothers and fellow-citizens as we may aliens and strangers. We may exact from foreigners what, for a time, we have lent; but towards a fellow-citizen we should be lenient and indulgent, remembering that all wealth belongs absolutely to God. There is a volume of instruction in the fact that the Hebrews were restrained from parsimony by a Divine Law. Thus were they taught that "it is more blessed to give than to receive." Generosity strengthens the sense of brotherhood.

IV. THE WEALTH THAT CLOSES THE HEART AGAINST CHARITY BECOMES AN ACTIVE CURSE. (Ver. 9.) It is possible to abuse the most beneficent law of God or man. This very provision of God that, at the end of the septennial period, release should be afforded to all debtors, might become very prejudicial to the interests of the poor. The approach of the sabbatic year might make the Hebrew capitalists parsimonious and close-fisted. "Beware of this!" saith God. "Such an act will.be an act of unfaithfulness to me." Jehovah has constituted himself the Guardian of the poor. His eye is upon their straits; his ear is open to their cry. And if his stewards fail to fulfil their mission, to them it will be accounted sin. Thus we are taught to take large and extended views of human life. We are integral parts of a great system. Our conceptions of life must stretch beyond the narrow confines of time. We should aspire to think and feel and act as God does. *This* is God's great ambition, and for *this* he is now training us.—D.

Vers. 12—18.—*Slaves to be regarded as brethren.* Quiet revolutions are the most permanent and the most successful. Sudden and violent assaults upon social institutions are sure to provoke reaction. All great changes must commence in the thought and feeling of the people.

I. SOCIAL USAGES, THOUGH EVIL, MUST BE TEMPORARILY TOLERATED. It is difficult to realize the conditions of human life in the earlier ages of the world. Many found a livelihood, by the use of the sword and by violent plunder. The honest poor found very precarious opportunities for labour. Coin was almost unknown, and therefore wages must be paid in the form of food and raiment. Amid these circumstances, personal servitude became almost a necessity. It was a social usage liable to great abuse, and gradually degenerated into a system of evil oppression. Yet, as God patiently tolerates on his earth so many forms of evil, and quietly provides his remedy, so we should learn, not to connive at evil, but patiently to endure it, until a real remedy can be set in motion.

II. JEWISH SLAVERY WAS CURTAILED BY LIMITS OF TIME. In this way the back of the burden was broken. The bondage, which must terminate within a fixed period, was endurable. It inspired the oppressed with hope. It checked the violence of the oppressor. The slave-holder, if severely exacting, would earn an unenviable reputation, and every device would be resorted to by the emancipated to avoid that man's service. His lands might remain untilled, his flocks neglected, his vineyards unpruned, because of his oppressive treatment of former slaves. Divine wisdom had fixed this short term of service as a barrier against human cruelty.

III. Jewish slavery was further relieved by a spirit of generosity. It is possible to show a spirit of kindness everywhere. If we have an unpleasant duty to perform, firmness may be always tempered with kindness. God would not allow the Hebrews to deal with their bondmen on terms of mere justice. They were not permitted to extort all that was in the bond. To make the largest possible gain out of human flesh and blood was strictly prohibited. They might continue the usage of slavery for a time, but the system should be relieved and penetrated and embellished by acts of kindness. The day of release was not to be a day of mourning for the masters. They were to share in the gladness of the emancipated, to send them away laden with flocks and with fruit. In proportion as had been the industry and fidelity of the bondman, would be (unless his master were a brute) the bountiful reward. This new spirit of fraternal benevolence would speedily undermine and overthrow the old usage of slavery. Such is God's process of change.

IV. Generous kindness might secure the lifelong service of the slave. There was no necessity that the condition of the bondman should be one of hardship. Love might surmount all custom, rise above law, and transcend all considerations of gain. The spirit of religion can find its way down to the root of all wrong, eradicate all the evils that curse society, and make human life beautiful as heaven. In the very midst of slavery, it is possible for love to operate, to soften asperities, and lighten burdens. To this practical affection the hearts of slaves would soon respond. Their service would rise in quality, and would increase in indefinite measure. Kindness is a most remunerative investment. And at the close of the term of service, many a bondman would decline his freedom, and prefer the service of such a master for the possible drawbacks and risks of liberty.

V. Remembrance of our own obligation should make us indulgent to others. (Ver. 15.) If adversity has not made us tender-hearted, it has been wasted upon us. God has redeemed us from the bondage of sin, and redeemed us at costly price, and it is plain that we do not prize our redemption if we oppress others. The love of our heart, which God rightly claims for himself, he commands us to express in the form of practical kindness. God has identified his interests with the interests of humanity, so that we either promote both or neither.—D.

Vers. 19—23.—*The first for God.* As God is supreme, so his claim to recognition and obedience must have consideration prior to all other claims. Such priority is his indefeasible right; such priority best subserves the interests of men. The first day of the week he claims and hallows; the firstfruits of the soil he claims for religious offering; the first place in our affections he asks as his due; the firstborn, both of man and of beast, he marks as his own. This is his royalty.

I. The reproductions of life a continuous creation of God. It is acknowledged on every side that life can only spring from life. No arrangements of material atoms—no processes of chemical change with which men are acquainted—can produce life. It is a force unique in itself, and can only rationally be traced to the creative power of a personal God. The potency to reproduce life, which God has placed in all the species, is as clearly a demonstration of his creative energy as if he manifestly and alone created each individual being. We cannot escape from the conclusion that he is sole Life-giver. "I kill," saith God, "and I make alive."

II. The claim on the firstborn alone is a concession of the fullest rights of God. He has a rightful proprietorship in all life. But he allows to man, as his liege vassal, dominion over the inferior races of his creatures. Acknowledgment of man's subjection must, however, be made; tribute must be paid to the Heavenly King. This arrangement is an act of combined justice and kindness. For man's highest good, he must be kept in perpetual remembrance of his dependence and his obligation. If the springs of gratitude in man's nature should dry up, his loss would be immeasurable. Every memorial we have of God is a gospel.

III. GOD'S CLAIM AND MAN'S ENJOYMENT ARE IDENTICAL. This devotement of the firstlings to God was no real loss: it was every way a blessing. It cherished in them a feeling of filial dependence. It took them up to the temple, year by year, and so brought them into close contact with eternal things. It served to link religion with the commonest affairs of daily life. It taught them that God found a pleasure in their enjoyments, and that his commandments were promotive of real delight. Thus the acts of Jehovah's worship were not identified with fasting and austerity, but with eating and drinking in the sacred temple. The pleasure was all the greater because it was social. In the banquet and festivity the whole household partook.

IV. IMPERFECT SACRIFICES PROHIBITED. Very evident is it that this demand of the firstborn was designed for spiritual instruction. However great God's care for our bodily life appears, his desire for our souls' well-being is immeasurably greater. By such visible and impressive methods God sought to teach the Jews that perfection of nature was God's design, and that such perfection would alone find a place in his heavenly temple. The best feelings and aspirations of our nature yearn after perfection. Nothing less will satisfy the mind of God; nothing less will satisfy us. "Then shall I be satisfied, when I awake with thy likeness."

V. YET BLEMISHED LIFE IS BETTER THAN BARRENNESS. A lame or a blemished lamb—a firstborn—was not utterly useless. It served as food for man, it sustained human life. But it was deprived of the honour of being devoted to God. Imperfect service is not altogether useless in the world. If we do a kindness to a neighbour, though no love to God prompt the deed, some good will result. Continuance in good deeds will gradually lead to better feelings and to nobler purposes. He who serves well his fellow-men now, will ere long learn to serve God. Let us ever follow the best sentiments which arise within, though yet very imperfect.—D.

EXPOSITION.

CHAPTER XVI.

CELEBRATION OF THE PASSOVER FESTIVAL, THE FEAST OF PENTECOST AND OF TABERNACLES. APPOINTMENT OF OFFICERS FOR THE ADMINISTRATION OF JUSTICE AND PREVENTION OF IDOLATRY.

Vers. 1—17.—(Comp. Exod. xxiii. 14—19; xxxiv. 18, 22—26; Lev. xxiii. On the Passover, see Exod. xii.; xiii. 3—10.) The other great festivals of the Israelites, the Feast of Trumpets and the Day of Atonement, are not here referred to, because on these no assembling of the whole people at the sanctuary was required, and such assembling is the point of view under which the feasts are mainly regarded here.

Vers. 1—7.—The Feast of the Passover.

Vers. 1, 2.—The month of Abib (cf. Exod. xii. 2; xxiii. 15). The time is referred to as a date well known to the people. Keep the passover; make (עָשִׂיתָ) or prepare the passover. This injunction refers primarily to the preparation of the Paschal lamb for a festal meal (Numb. ix. 5); but here it is used in a wider sense as referring to the whole Paschal observance, which lasted for seven days. Hence the mention of sheep (צֹאן) and oxen (בָקָר) in ver. 2, and the

reference to the eating of unleavened bread for seven days "therewith," i.e. with the Passover. The animal for the Paschal supper was expressly prescribed to be a yearling of the sheep or of the goats (שֶׂה), and this was to be consumed at one meal; but on the other days of the festival the flesh of other animals offered in sacrifice might be eaten. The term "Passover" here, accordingly, embraces the whole of the festive meals connected with the Passover proper—what the rabbins call chagigah (Maimon., in 'Korban Pesach,' c. x. § 12; cf. 2 Chron. xxxv. 7, etc.).

Ver. 3.—Bread of affliction; bread such as is prepared in circumstances of trial and pressure, when there is no time or opportunity for the application of all the means required for the preparation of bread of the better sort. The Israelites had in haste and amid anxiety to prepare the Passover meal on the evening of their flight from Egypt, and so had to omit the leavening of their bread; and this usage they had to observe during the seven days of the festival in subsequent times, to remind them of the oppression the nation had suffered in Egypt, and the circumstances of difficulty and peril amidst which their deliverance had been effected.

Ver. 4.—No leavened bread; properly, no leaven (שְׂאֹר) (cf. Exod. xii. 15). Not only was no leavened bread (מַצָּה) or dough

(חָמֵץ) to be used by them, leaven itself was not to be in the house (cf. 1 Cor. v. 7; see Kitto's 'Cyclop. of Bibl. Lit.,' vol. iii. p. 429).

Vers. 5, 6.—Not in their own houses or places of abode might the Paschal lamb be slain and eaten, but only at the place which the Lord should choose to place his Name there. On the first occasion, while the people were still in Egypt and had no sanctuary or specially holy place where Jehovah's Name was set, the Passover was eaten in their own houses; but when God should choose a place as his sanctuary, only there could the ordinance be observed.

Ver. 7.—**Thou shalt roast.** The verb here primarily signifies to be matured by heat for eating; hence to be ripened as by the sun's heat (Gen. xl. 10; Joel iii. 13; Heb. iv. 13); and to be cooked, whether by boiling, seething, or roasting. Here it is properly rendered by *roast*, as it was thus only that the Paschal lamb could be cooked. **And go unto thy tents**; return to thy place of abode; not necessarily to thy proper home (which might be far distant), but to the place where for the time thou hast thy lodging. The phrase, "thy tents," which originally came into use while as yet Israel had no settled abodes in Canaan, came afterwards to be used as a general designation of a man's home or usual place of abode (cf. 1 Sam. xiii. 2; 2 Sam. xx. 1; 1 Kings viii. 66, etc.).

Ver. 8.—**On the seventh day** shall be a **solemn assembly.** This is not placed in antithesis to the injunction, **six days thou shalt eat unleavened bread**, as if the Feast of Unleavened Bread (*mazzoth*) lasted only for six days and the seventh was to be devoted to a service of a different kind; it simply prescribes that the seventh day of the festival was to be celebrated by an assembling of the whole of those who had come to the feast; the festival was to be wound up with a day of holy convocation, in which no work was to be done (Lev. xxiii. 36). On all the days unleavened bread was to be eaten, and on the seventh there was besides to be a *solemn assembly to the Lord* (עֲצֶרֶת לַיחֹוָה), called in Lev. xxiii. 36, "a holy convocation" (מִקְרָא קֹדֶשׁ).

Vers. 9—12.—*The Feast of Weeks* (cf. Exod. xxiii. 16).

Ver. 9.—From such time as **thou beginnest** to put **the sickle to the corn**; *i.e.* from the commencement of the corn harvest. The seven weeks were to be counted from this terminus; and as the corn harvest began by the presentation of the sheaf of the firstfruits on the second day of the Passover, this regulation as to time coincides with that in Lev. xxiii. 15.

Ver. 10.—This feast was to be kept with sacrificial gifts according to the measure of the free-will offerings of their hand, *i.e.* voluntary offerings which they gave as the Lord had blessed them; nothing was specially prescribed, each was to give of his own free-will as the Lord had prospered him. The word translated "tribute" in the Authorized Version (מִסַּת) occurs only here, and is of doubtful signification. The LXX. render it by καθὼς, as, according to; it is identical with the Aramaic מסת, ܡܣܬܐ sufficiency, enough, and may be understood here of the full measure according to which their offerings were to be presented. The **freewill offering of thine hand**, here referred to, belonged to the gifts of burnt offerings, meat offerings, drink offerings, and thank offerings which might be offered at every feast along with the sacrifices prescribed (cf. Lev. xxiii. 38; Numb. xxix. 39). Of the latter no mention is made here, as the law regarding them was already sufficiently proclaimed (Numb. xxviii. and xxix.); and in a popular address it was rather to what depended on the will of the people than to what was imperative by law, that attention had to be directed.

Ver. 11.—**Rejoice before the Lord.** "The expression, *to rejoice before the Lord*, denotes here nothing else than to honour him by sacred songs; comp. Spencer, 'De Legg. Heb. Ritual.,' p. 881, edit. 3" (Hävernick, 'Introd.,' p. 157). **In the place which the Lord thy God hath chosen to place his name there**; rather, *shall choose*, as in ver. 15.

Vers. 13—15.—*The Feast of Tabernacles*, properly, *Booths* (cf. Lev. xxiii. 33—44; Numb. xxix. 12—38). This feast was to be observed at the end of harvest, after the corn had been gathered into granaries, and the produce of the vineyard had been put through the press. Nothing is added here to the instructions already given respecting this festival; only the observance of it at the appointed sanctuary is enforced, and stress is laid on their making not only their sons and daughters and domestics, but also the Levite, the fatherless, the widow, and the stranger participators in their rejoicings. **Thou shalt surely rejoice**; rather, *thou shalt be wholly joyous*; literally, *rejoicing only*; Rosenm., "*admodum lætus.*"

Vers. 16, 17.—(Cf. Exod. xxiii. 17; xxxiv. 23.) The law is repeated here with the additional clause, "at the place which the Lord shall choose;" and the words, "not empty," are explained to mean with gifts according to the gift of their hands, according to the blessing of Jehovah their God, which he had given them.

Vers. 18—20.—Moses had at an earlier

period appointed judges to settle disputes among the people, and had given instructions to them for the discharge of their duty (Exod. xviii.; Deut. i. 12—18). Whilst the people were in the wilderness, united as one body and under the leadership of Moses, this arrangement was sufficient; but a more extended arrangement would be required when they came to be settled in Canaan and dispersed in towns and villages over the whole land. In prospect of this, Moses here enacts that judges and officers were to be appointed by the people in all their gates, in all their places of residence, which the Lord should give them.

Ver. 18.—**Judges and officers.** The "officers" (*shoterim*, writers) associated with the judges both in the earlier arrangements and in that which was to succeed were secretaries and clerks of court, and acted also as assessors and advisers of the judges. No instruction is given as to the number of judges and officers, or as to the mode of appointing them; nor was this necessary. The former would be determined by the size and population of the place where they were appointed, and the latter would, as a matter of course, follow the method instituted by Moses in the earlier arrangement (see ch. i. 13—15; Exod. xviii. 21—26).

Ver. 19.—(Cf. Exod. xxiii. 6, 8.) **Respect persons** (cf. ch. i. 17). **Pervert the words** [margin, *matters*] **of the righteous;** rather, *the case* or *the cause of the righteous*.

Ver. 20.—**That which is altogether just;** literally, *justice, justice.* The repetition of the word is for the sake of emphasis, as in Gen. xiv. 10, "pits, pits," equal to full of pits.

Vers. 21, 22.—In all states, the highest crime of which the judge has to take note is that of treason against the supreme power; and, under the theocracy, the act most distinctly treasonable was idolatry. In proceeding, therefore, to give some practical admonitions as to the things to be observed in the administration of justice, Moses begins by denouncing and forbidding this most flagrant form of iniquity.

Ver. 21.—**Thou shalt not plant thee a grove of any trees;** *thou shalt not plant*, i.e. place or set up, *an ashêrah of any wood.* The ashêrah was an idol of wood in the form of a pillar, usually placed by the side of the altars of Baal. It was the symbol of Astarte, the great Canaanitish goddess, the companion and revealer of Baal. The two are usually associated in the Old Testament (cf. Judg. ii. 13; vi. 28; 1 Kings xviii. 19; 2 Kings xxiii. 4). The rendering "grove" has been taken from the LXX. and the Vulgate; but that it is an error is evident from 1 Kings xiv. 23; 2 Kings xvii. 10; and Jer. xvii. 2; where the ashêrah is said to be *under* a green tree; and from the use of such words as *make, set up, cause to stand, build,* to denote the action of producing an ashêrah (cf. 1 Kings xiv. 15; xvi. 33; 2 Kings xvii. 16; xvii. 10; 2 Chron. xxxiii. 19; 1 Kings xiv. 23), none of which are appropriate to the planting of a grove. Here, indeed, the word "plant" is used, but this is only because, as the ashêrah was sunk in the earth that it might stand firm, it might be figuratively said to be planted, just as nails driven in are said to be planted (Eccles. xii. 11, where the same verb is used; comp. also Isa. li. 16; Amos ix. 15; Dan. xi. 25).

Ver. 22.—**Any image;** *any pillar*, etc. The Hebrew word (מַצֵּבָה, *mazzebah*) denotes generally any pillar or stone that is set up, whether as a memorial (Gen. xxviii. 18), or as a sign (Exod. xxiv. 4; Isa. xix. 19), or for purposes of utility or ornament (Jer. xliii. 13). Here, as in other passages, it is a pillar or statue set up as an object of worship (cf. 2 Kings iii. 2; x. 26; Hos. x. 1; Micah v. 12).

HOMILETICS.

Vers. 1—8.—*The Feast of the Passover.* (For a reference to the minute points of difference, necessitated by different circumstances, between the first passover and subsequent ones, see art. 'Passover,' in Smith's 'Bibl. Dict.;' see also the Exposition for its historical significance.) We now take for granted that all this is well understood by, and perfectly familiar to, the reader. Our purpose now is to "open up," not its historical meaning, nor even its symbolism for Israel, but its typical intent as foreshadowing gospel truths, showing how in Christ our Passover, and in the ordinance of the Lord's Supper as our Passover feast, the far-reaching significance of the offering of the Paschal lamb is most clearly seen.

I. ISRAEL'S PASSOVER HAS ITS ANTITYPE IN CHRIST. So argues the apostle, in 1 Cor. v. 7, "Christ our Passover is sacrificed for us." We cannot but feel here the wondrous condescension of our God in permitting us to look at aught so sublime as the sacrifice of his dear Son, through the means of aught so humble as the Paschal lamb. Yet it is an infinite mercy that, whatever might so help the conceptions of his children then, and whatever may so aid them now, the Great Father does not disdain to use. 1. The Lord Jesus Christ is our Sacrificial Lamb; so John i. 29; 1 Pet. i. 18, 19. He is spoken of as "the Lamb slain from the foundation of the world," and is beheld, in the Apocalypse, "a Lamb as it had been slain." He, too, is "without blemish." He was "without sin." In him alone is the ideal of a perfect sacrifice found. 2. The Passover was to be killed without breaking a bone thereof. This was fulfilled in Christ, that men might be aided in seeing the fulfilment of the type, through the close analogy of the treatment; and because "God would permit no dishonour to be done to the body of Christ, after the atoning act was complete" (Halley). 3. The blood of the first Paschal lamb was to be sprinkled on the posts of the doors, signifying that there must be the actual acceptance and application of the atoning blood, and that through the atoning blood so applied we are saved. 4. In the first instance, the lamb was offered without the intervention of a priest. So that, though priesthood was afterwards instituted for a time for educational purposes (Gal. iii.), yet the priest was in no wise necessary to ensure men's acceptance with God. 5. The flesh was to be eaten, in token of fellowship. It was thus "the most perfect of peace offerings," symbolizing and typifying communion with God on the ground of the atoning blood. In all these respects, how very far does the Christian Antitype surpass the Jewish type? Devout hearts may and do love to linger long in meditation on a theme so touching and Divine!

II. CHRISTIANS HAVE THEIR PASSOVER FEAST. 1. *Where?* Here we may be permitted to point out a distinction, which, though obvious enough at first mention thereof, yet is so far lost sight of in some directions, as to lead to serious error. In later times, though the lamb was slain at an altar, yet the feast thereon was at a table. So in heathen sacrifices too, the victim was slain at an altar, the sacrificial feast was at a table. Hence, analogy suggests that the spot where the Victim is slain should be called the altar, but that the sacrificial feast should be at a table. The writer of the Epistle to the Hebrews says, "We have an altar, whereof they have no right to eat which serve the tabernacle." The altar here meant is the cross on which the Saviour died. Besides, it is only on the theory that the sacrifice is actually *repeated* at Holy Communion, that there can be any possible warrant for calling the Lord's table an altar. But this theory is absolutely negatived by the statements in Heb. x. 10—14. The Victim was offered once for all on an altar, even the cross; but we partake at the Lord's *table*, of the sacrificial feast. 2. *What is the meaning of the feast?* (1) It is a standing historical declaration of the offering of God's one Great Sacrifice for the sins of the whole world. "Ye do show the Lord's death." It is declaration of the historic fact on the part of those to whom that fact is full of richest and most wondrous meaning. For it is the divinest expression of righteousness and of love that the world has ever known. (2) This sacrificial feast is the expression also of a sublime fact on the earthward side, viz. that by virtue of the redeeming efficacy thus continuously proclaimed, there has been formed a new commonwealth of Israel, to which belongs the freedom, immunity, and honour of a kingdom of God (see Eph. ii.). (3) It also seals a fellowship—a fellowship of redeemed souls, who have been bought with a price, and transferred from the kingdom of Satan to that of God's dear Son; in which they are raised up together and made to sit together in heavenly places in Christ Jesus, having here below a union of hearts which will be perfected in an unseen state. This fellowship is openly sealed by their taking of one bread and drinking one cup. (4) It is a joint pledge of loyalty to the Church's Head and Lord; in renewing their remembrance of his love to them, they seal afresh their pledge of love and allegiance to him. Hence the Lord's Supper came to be called *sacramentum*, the Church's military oath of obedience to her Great Commander. (5) It is a service of thanksgiving. Hence it came to be called *the Eucharist*. The Passover feast was a grateful recall of a mighty deliverance. So is the Christian feast. (6) It is a declaration of hope and expectancy. "Ye do show the Lord's death *till he come.*" Believers in Israel were expecting Canaan. We are waiting for the Son of God from heaven to bring us to our heavenly rest (Heb. iv.). 3. *How should the Christian feast be kept?* i.e. in what spirit? (cf. 1 Cor. v. 7, 8). Three or four suggestions will embody the chief hints hereon thrown out in the written Word. (1) The Passover was to be eaten with unleavened bread. All leaven was to be put away. So are believers to keep the feast with the unleavened bread of sincerity and of truth. They are " to examine themselves," and so to eat of that bread and drink of that cup. " As the scrupulous Israelites searched with lighted candles every hidden corner and dark recess of their houses for any latent particle of leaven, so let our language be, 'Search me, O God, and know my heart,' etc." (Bush). (2) It was to be eaten with bitter herbs, partly as in remembrance of the hard bondage and bitter sorrows of Egypt, and partly as shadowing forth the need of penitence for sin. We should mingle with our thanksgiving " penitential tears "—

> " And with our joy for pardoned guilt,
> Mourn that we pierced the Lord."

(3) It was to be eaten in a standing posture, as if ready to depart at a moment's warning. Even so we, as we gather round the sacramental board, are but on pilgrimage. We halt awhile to refresh us by the way, but we have, soon as our celebration-day is over, to renew our march in the desert, and to resume the toil and fight. We have not yet come to the rest and inheritance the Lord hath promised to give us. (4) The Apostle Paul says, " Let us keep the feast, not with the leaven of *malice*," etc., *i.e.* not with any ill feeling harboured in the soul, nor with ill actions practised in the life. For it is not only as so much evil in the individual that Paul there regards the κακία and πονηρία, but as so much pervasive leaven in the Church, that, if not cast out, will be its bane, yea, even its ruin (see 1 Cor. x. 16, 17). We should therefore cultivate always, and specially bring to the table of the Lord, a spirit of loving fellowship. So strongly did the early Christians feel this, that they were wont to ask of each other the mutual forgiveness of injuries before observing the sacred feast. And that same spirit of love, so specially incumbent then, should be the prevailing habit of soul with believers towards each other. For are not all redeemed by the same precious blood? Are not all members of one family? If our God loves us so much, in spite of our sins, as to own us as his, should not that shame us into a loving regard for each other in spite of our faults? With one Saviour, one salvation, one faith, one baptism, one hope, one home, well may we strive to keep the unity of the Spirit in the bond of peace, and to cultivate, in the fellowship of believers at the table of the Lord, the same spirit which alone will pervade the higher fellowship of heaven.

Vers. 9—12.—*The Feast of Weeks, or of Harvest.* (For the varied names given to this Feast of Weeks, see Kurtz, 'Sacrificial Worship of the Old Testament,' pp. 376, *et seq.* For an interesting statement as to the value to Israel of these national gatherings, see Wine's 'Commentaries on the Laws of Moses,' bk. ii. ch. i.) This Feast of Weeks was not commemorative in the same sense as that of the Passover; it was connected, not with a great national epoch, but with the seasons of the year and the times of harvest. The method in which it was to be observed is stated in Lev. xxiii. 10, *et seq.* We find there, and in the various Scripture references to this festival, the following principles indicated. 1. That the Hebrews were to regard the produce of the soil as given to them by the bounty of God. 2. That they were to honour Jehovah by a public thanksgiving for his goodness. 3. That they were to yield the firstfruits to him. 4. That they were to rejoice and be glad before him, for what he was and for what he gave. 5. That they were to recognize the equality before God of master and servant. National festivals were holidays for the labourer, and times when good will and kindliness towards the " stranger, the fatherless, and widow " were to be specially manifested. 6. They were thus to recognize their national unity by showing their joint thankfulness for a common mercy. These festivals would strengthen Israel's feeling of kinship, and these united gatherings before the Lord their God would proclaim, as often as they were held, their separation unto him. 7. Though this was a harvest festival, and as such chiefly expressive of thankfulness for the bounty of God as seen in nature, yet it was not to be observed without the sin offering, the burnt offering, and the meat offering (cf. Lev. xxiii. 18— 20). Other offerings were to be presented along with the offering for sin. Natural blessings are given to sinful men only under a dispensation of mercy which comes through a bleeding sacrifice.

Now all these forms have passed away. But the principles which underlay them are of eternal obligation. We trust we can see, by means of these signs, the everlasting truths signified by them. In each of the particulars named above some permanent principle is enclosed.

I. THE FRUITS OF THE EARTH ARE TO BE RECEIVED BY US AS GRANTED TO US BY THE BOUNTY OF A GRACIOUS GOD. So commonplace, or rather so well-known, a truth is this, that it is not easy for us to picture to ourselves a time when a nation needed to have it engraven on its heart and conscience by such means as these divinely appointed festivals. Still, we cannot be unconscious of forces around us being at work which, if we succumbed to them, would lead us to think of the ordinary products of the harvest-field as coming simply in due course of law, and to regard the Supreme Being as so remotely concerned in earth's fruitfulness, that it would be but a slight step to take to think of him as not concerned therein at all ! But in no part of the sacred records is any such thinking warranted. Reason itself would lead us to suppose that, if one order of creation is higher than another, the lower was made to serve it ; and consequently, that if man be the highest of all, that the rest is ordered to serve him. The Psalmist expressed this when he sang, "Thou hast put all things under his feet." Our Lord Jesus Christ points us to the most common blessings, even to the sun and the rain, in proof of the good will of a heavenly Father. And this is at once the philosophy and the faith of a Christian. It is the conclusion of sober sense ; it is the dictum of devoutness, piety, and love. "Whoso is wise and will observe these things, even they shall understand the loving-kindness of the Lord."

II. THE FRUITS OF THE EARTH SHOULD THEREFORE BE RECEIVED WITH THANKSGIVING. The doctrine that God is the benevolent Author of all our mercies is not to be a barren and unfruitful dogma. It is meant to call forth thankfulness. It is said of the heathen, "*neither* were they thankful." They did not know enough of God to understand what true thankfulness meant. But we do. He is revealed in Scripture as having such watchful concern for our good, that we may well feel an exuberance of thankful delight that our daily joys come to us from a fountain of love. And it behoves us to pay our God the homage of grateful hearts.

III. THIS THANKFULNESS SHOULD BE EXPRESSED PRACTICALLY. The truly loyal heart will need no reminder of this. *Cela va sans dire.* Jacob needed no precept to lead him to say, "Of all that thou givest me, I will surely give the tenth unto thee." Nor, if our hearts are as sensitive as they should be to our own unworthiness and to God's loving-kindness, shall we fail to "honour the Lord with our substance, and with the first-fruits of all our increase."

IV. OUR GRATITUDE TO GOD SHOULD TAKE THE FORM OF UNITED WORSHIP AND SONG. We may set apart special seasons for harvest festivals, or no, as circumstances dictate ; but certainly the Divine provision for the temporal wants of man should find gladsome acknowledgment in the social worship of a thankful people.

V. A UNITED ACKNOWLEDGMENT OF GOD'S KINDNESS TO US ALL SHOULD HAVE THE EFFECT OF PROMOTING KINDLINESS AMONG EACH OTHER. If God makes us glad with his loving goodness, we should make others glad with our radiant kindness (1 John iii. 17 ; iv. 11). The love streaming from heaven is revealed for the purpose of creating benevolence upon earth. The blessings that come to us, unworthy as we are, from the pure benevolence of God, should make us eager, as much as in us is, to emulate the goodness of heaven !

VI. For, lastly, NOT EVEN IN THANKFULNESS TO GOD FOR COMMON MERCIES MAY WE FORGET THEIR RELATION TO THAT DIVINE REDEMPTIVE PLAN WROUGHT OUT BY THE GREAT SON OF GOD. Israel's rejoicing was to be sanctified by a sin offering ; by which we see (1) that it is only because of God's mighty redeeming work that even the natural blessings of this earthly life are ensured to us. And (2) that it is only through the sin offering that our thank offerings are accepted before God. All our thanksgiving services *must* take the form and hue thrown on them by the fact that we are guilty men, living on the mercy of a forgiving and redeeming God. God expects the acknowledgment of this on our part. It would be unrighteous of him not to ask it, and unjust and ungrateful of us not to give it. Sin *is* in the world ; and *our* sin has helped to make the world what it is, as to the infusion of bitterness into it; it is only through the Divine redeeming energy of love which through and by our Lord Jesus Christ is being put forth, that the world still yields its treasures to the rebellious and ungrateful sons of men. So that with the praises for mercies so undeserved there should be a confession of sin, a turning anew unto the Lord, and a reconsecration of heart and life to him. For when we think how soon a slightly adverse action of God towards us might crush us; yea, that even the bare withholding of mercy would consume us; and when we add to that the thought of our innumerable provocations of One who cannot bear that which is evil, surely we must needs confess that there are no greater wonders than the patience, the love, the bounty of God!

Vers. 13—17.—*The Feast of Tabernacles, or of Ingathering.* "The festival of tabernacles, as originally instituted, presents but little symbolism. Its primary design was to give expression to joy and gratitude in view of the products of the earth, every kind of which had now been gathered; and it was therefore also called the Festival of Ingathering." As the Passover commemorated the first deliverance, so the Feast of Booths would recall the wilderness life. And "nothing was more natural than to associate in thought the richness of their inheritance with the probationary trials by means of which the nation had been prepared to possess it" (Atwater's 'History and Significance of the Sacred Tabernacle of the Hebrews,' Dodd and Co., New York, 1877). It is scarcely necessary here to do more than suggest the underlying principles which are presented here. They must needs have some similarity with those in the preceding Homily. Israel is taught the following truths: 1. After the corn and wine have been gathered in, and the anxieties of the year are so far over, they are then expected to look up gratefully to God as the Author of all. 2. God's mercies are to be enjoyed, in grateful and delightful repose. 3. With the gladsome rest there is to be associated a thankful memory of past guidance and help in the wilderness life. 4. In this rejoicing and thankfulness, master and servant are alike to share, as both equal in the sight of God. 5. By Israel's gladness, the sorrows of the poor, the sad, the lonely, are to be relieved, and the solitary ones are to be made conscious of a kindly care encompassing them. 6. The recognition of a reception of mercy is to be accompanied with a loving offering to God in return (vers. 16, 17). According to the blessing, so is to be the tribute. 7. Thus Israel's nationality is to be thrice sealed every year, as a specifically religious one, in holy and joyful covenant with the Lord their God. Manifestly on each of these points, Israel's temporary and local forms illustrated permanent and worldwide principles, in the exposition of which the Christian teacher may well delight.

Vers. 18—20.—(See Homily, ch. x. 17—xi. 1, "God no respecter of persons.")

Vers. 21, 22.—(See Homily, ch. v. 8—10, on "The second commandment," and also Homily, ch. xiii., on "Temptations to idolatry to be resisted.")

HOMILIES BY VARIOUS AUTHORS.

Vers. 1—9.—*The Passover.* The Passover was a sacrifice (Exod. xii. 2), and was connected with sacrifices (Lev. xxiii. 5—8; Numb. xxviii. 15—26); hence "flock and herd" (ver. 2) covering the sacrifices of the seven days' feast. It was the sacrifice which mediated the new relationship established between Jehovah and the people on the night of the Exodus. There was a fitness, at so solemn a crisis in the history of the chosen nation, in the line of demarcation between them and the Egyptians being drawn so strongly in atoning blood. Not for any righteousness of theirs, but through God's mercy, under cover of blood of atonement, was Israel—collectively a part of Egypt, and individually partakers of its guilt and corruptions—spared the stroke of judgment. The sacrifice then offered was: 1. *Pacificatory.* In their blood-sheltered dwellings, the Israelites enjoyed the presence of God, communion with God, peace with God. A feast of peace was held upon the flesh, as in the later peace offerings.

2. *Purificatory.* It sanctified the people in view of their departure from Egypt; and separation as a peculiar people to Jehovah—in view also of his peculiarly near approach to them in their deliverance. 3. *Protective.* As warding off the stroke of the destroying angel. Later Passovers, as the yearly presentation of the blood implied, were not only *commemorations*, but in some sense also *perpetuations* of the original one. The Passover, as observed from year to year, was—

I. A MEMORIAL. It stood as an historical monument, testifying to the reality of the events of the Exodus. In this view of it, it is of great value. No criticism of documents can impair its witness. It is a Bible outside of the Bible, confirmatory of the Bible narratives. No one has yet succeeded in showing how a festival like the Passover could have been introduced at any period later than that to which it historically refers. It has, so far as we can make out anything in history, been observed by the Jews from the very beginning of their national existence. Note to what it testifies—1. To the fact of the Exodus. 2. That the Exodus was accomplished without warlike resistance from the Egyptians. 3. That it was looked forward to, prepared for, sacrifice offered, and a sacrificial meal eaten, in anticipation of it. 4. That the preparations for departure were hurried, yet orderly. 5. That on the night in question a judgment fell on Egypt, from which the Israelites were exempted—a circumstance which gives to the feast its name, the Passover. The festival has thus all the value of a contemporary witness, and fully corroborates the Scripture history. The Lord's Supper, in like manner, is an historical witness, not to be got rid of, testifying to acts and words of our Lord on the night of his betrayal, and furnishing clear evidence as to the light in which his death was regarded by himself.

II. A TYPE. The typological features have often been dwelt on. 1. The *lamb*—select, unblemished, of full age, subjected to fire, unmutilated (John xix. 36), fitness of the victim to represent Christ (Isa. liii. 7). 2. The *blood*—atoning, need of personal application, sole shelter from death, under its shelter inviolable security (Rom. viii. 1). 3. The *feast*—the slain lamb the food of a new life (John vi. 51—57); a feast of reconciliation and peace, with fellow-believers, with bitter herbs (affliction, repentance), and without leaven—memorial of haste (ver. 3), but also emblematic of spiritual incorruption, of the purity which is to characterize the new life (1 Cor. v. 7—9); no part of the flesh to remain till morning (ver. 4), for same reason, to avoid corruption; the feast to last seven days—a week, an entire circle of time, symbolical of life-long consecration to holiness of walk. 4. The *redemption*—great, once for all, a redemption by blood and by power, from wrath, from bondage. All these types are conspicuously fulfilled in Christ.

III. AN ORDINANCE. 1. The first and chief of the feasts (ver. 1). 2. To be observed regularly (ver. 1). So now the Lord's Supper (1 Cor. xi. 25). 3. At the central sanctuary (vers. 2, 5, 6). Christians should seek to realize their unity with all saints at the Lord's table. 4. With due seriousness and solemnity (vers. 2, 6).—J. O.

Vers. 9—13.—*Pentecost.* I. A SACRED RECKONING. "Seven weeks shalt thou number," etc. (ver. 9). A week of weeks, seven times seven, hence the name, "Feast of Weeks" (ver. 10). The count began with the offering of the sheaf of firstfruits on Nisan 16, the second day of the Feast of Unleavened Bread (Lev. xxiii. 11). Till that sheaf was offered, no Israelite was permitted to eat of the new corn (ver. 14). With the arrival of the fiftieth day, inclusive of the second of Unleavened Bread, the labours of the harvest were presumed to be ended, and this festival ensued, at which baken loaves were presented to Jehovah (Lev. xxiii. 17), in token of consecration to him of the fruits of the harvest, and of dedication of the life which bread sustained. There is, intended or unintended, a beautiful symbolism in this sacred count, the divinely allotted period for the labours of the harvest, its days reckoned by heaven's calendar, the end, an "appearing before God" in the sanctuary. The harvest began with consecration (in the Passover sheaf), it ended with it (in the presentation of the wave loaves). So has the Christian his allotted work-time in the world, a sacred cycle of weeks, rounded off in God's wisdom for the work he means to be accomplished (John ix. 4); work in the Christian harvest-field, a work beginning in consecration, carried on in the spirit of consecration, and the termination of which is "entrance into the joy of the Lord."

II. A HARVEST THANKSGIVING. This was distinctly the idea of the Pentecostal festival. It was characterized: 1. By a devout recognition of the Divine bounty in the fruits of the earth. 2. By a voluntary dedication to God of part of what he had given. There was the public ceremony of the two wave loaves. But the Israelite was required in addition to keep the feast with "a tribute of a free-will offering of his hand" (ver. 10). The offering was to be voluntary, yet not without rule, but "according as the Lord thy God hath blessed thee." 3. By a willing sharing of God's bounty with the needy (ver. 11). The stranger, the fatherless, the widow, were, as usual, not to be neglected. The remembrance of former bondage in Egypt was to furnish the "touch of nature" which would make this duty easy (ver. 12). Note: (1) Our gifts to God are worthless, save as they are the expression of a willing mind (2 Cor. viii. 7—16; ix. 6—14). (2) Our gifts to God ought to be proportionate to our prosperity (1 Cor. xvi. 2). (3) God's goodness to us (in harvests, in trade, in business generally) ought to be acknowledged by liberal gifts for his service. (4) God's goodness to us (in deliverances, etc.) should open our hearts in sympathy for others.

III. A GOSPEL TYPE. The figure of the firstfruits finds an abundance of applications in the New Testament. It is employed of the Jews (Rom. xi. 16), sanctified in their covenant heads; of Christ, the "Firstfruits" of them that sleep (1 Cor. xv. 20—23); of first converts in a particular district (1 Cor. xvi. 15); of believers generally, as "a kind of firstfruits" of the redeemed creation (Jas. i. 18); of the 144,000 of the Apocalypse (Rev. xiv. 4), possibly "all the Church of Christ at any time on the earth; a limited company at any one time, capable of being numbered" (Rev. vii. 1—9). A more direct relation must be traced between the presentation of the firstfruits at Pentecost and the events consequent upon the Pentecostal effusion of the Spirit (Acts ii.). It is surely not to be ascribed to accident that, as our Lord died on the Friday of the Passover—probably on the 14th of Nisan—so the disciples were kept waiting for the promised effusion of the Spirit till "the day of Pentecost was fully come;" and that on this day the great ingathering of three thousand took place, embracing representatives from "every nation under heaven"—a truly glorious offering of "firstfruits." May we pursue the coincidence further, and see in Christ, the solitary sheaf, raised from the dead on the same day that the first-cut sheaf was presented in the sanctuary (Nisan 16), the firstfruits of the harvest in prospect; while in the Church constituted and consecrated at Pentecost, the day of the offering of the wave loaves, we have the firstfruits of the harvest as realized. The wave loaves correspond in significance to the meat offering, and still more nearly to the shewbread. Bread, as the staff of life, the nourishing principle, stands for the presentation to God of the life so nourished, involving the recognition of him as the Nourisher of it. In the possession of the believing heart by the Spirit of God, as the indwelling and abiding principle of spiritual life, we have the full realization of this thought, the fulfilment of the types of meat offering. The passage, Jas. i. 18, suggests the deeper idea that the Church constituted at Pentecost is itself only a kind of firstfruits of redemption. It is so in relation: 1. To the latter-day effusion of the Spirit (Acts ii. 17—20). 2. To creation as a whole (Rom. viii. 19—24). Other two points may be noted: 1. If our dates be correct, Pentecost, like the Resurrection, fell on the first day of the week—the Spirit was given on the Lord's day. 2. As Pentecost was held by the Jews in commemoration of the giving of the Law, so God signalized it as the day of the giving of the Spirit, thus superseding the old dispensation by the new.—J. O.

Vers. 13—16.—*The Feast of Tabernacles.* I. A FEAST OF THE INGATHERING. (Ver. 13.) Held in the seventh month, when all the fruits of the earth had been gathered in. Thus: 1. Every stage of labour was sanctified by the recognition of God. At the Passover, when the sickle was thrust into the virgin grain; at Pentecost, when the cereal crops were harvested; and now, at the close of the agricultural year, when the season's labours had yielded to the husbandman their full results. 2. The fruits of labour were sanctified by dedication to God. The usual feasts were held, and shared with the needy (ver. 14), and free-will offerings (vers. 16, 17) were presented to God. Bountiful giving is the appropriate return for bountiful receiving.

II. A MEMORIAL OF PAST WANDERINGS. (Lev. xxiii. 43.) During the seven days of the festival, the Israelites were to live in booths. This symbolized, and served to remind them of, the wandering, unsettled life of the desert. Booths were erections of simpler construction, and more in keeping with an agricultural festival, especially after the settlement in Canaan, than tents would have been. But there may have been an allusion also to actual circumstances of the journeyings, *e.g.* the first halt at Succoth, *i.e.* booths (Exod. xii. 3 ; see Stanley). This memorial was instituted : 1. That in the midst of their prosperity they might not forget the days of their adversity (ch. viii. 12—18). 2. That they might be reminded of God's gracious care of them. Booths or huts may, as Keil thinks, have been used instead of tents with reference to this idea. The booth was a shelter, a protection. So God promises to be to his Church, as he had been in the past, "a booth for a shadow in the daytime from the heat, and for a place of refuge, and for a covert from the storm and rain" (Isa. iv. 6). 3. That their enjoyment of the goodness of the land might be enhanced by feelings of warm gratitude, awakened by the sense of contrast.

III. An image of present pilgrimage. Though settled in Canaan, the Israelites were not to regard themselves as in possession of the final rest (Heb. iv. 7, 8). The pilgrim state continued (Ps. xxxix. 12). It does so still. We still inhabit tabernacles (2 Cor. v. 1). Spiritual rest, the inward side of the Canaan type, is attained in Christ; but the full realization of the rest of God lies in eternity. Till heaven is reached, our state is that of pilgrims—wilderness wanderers. "The admission of this festival into Zechariah's prophecy of Messianic times (Zech. xiv. 18) is undoubtedly founded on the thought that the keeping of the Feast of Tabernacles is an expression on the part of the nations of their thankfulness for the termination of their wanderings by their reception into the peaceful kingdom of Messiah" (Oehler).—J. O.

Vers. 18—21.—*Model judges.* I. Judges occupy a high and responsible position. 1. They are necessary. They require to be set up "in all thy gates . . . throughout thy tribes." 2. They represent God (ch. i. 17). They are called "gods" (Ps. lxxxii. 1). They are clothed with a portion of God's authority (Rom. xiii. 1). 3. They are set to uphold the sacred interests of justice. 4. They may, by wresting judgment, or by hasty and wrong decisions, inflict irremediable injury on the innocent. 5. The right discharge of their functions conduces in the highest degree to the stability, happiness, and material prosperity of society.

II. Judges are required to execute just judgment. 1. They are not to be swayed by private partialities—political, social, ecclesiastical. 2. They are not to make distinctions between rich and poor, *i.e.* "respect persons." 3. They are not to accept bribes. 4. They are, as administrators of a justice which is impersonal, to judge in every case according to absolute right.—J. O.

Vers. 1—8.—*The Passover, a memorial of deliverance.* The institution of the Passover (Exod. xii.) was preliminary to their deliverance from Egypt, just as the Lord's Supper was preliminary to the death of Jesus Christ, which it was designed subsequently to commemorate. On the first occasion it was a sacrifice presented *at home*, as was most proper. But when the central altar was set up in Palestine, it became the centre of the Passover festival, and to it the Jews in their multitudes repaired. This secured a national assembly under very solemn circumstances, and was an important element in sustaining the national spirit.

I. The deliverance of the soul from the bondage of sin should be held in perpetual remembrance. The Passover was the yearly celebration of national redemption. By it the Jews were annually reminded that they were a redeemed people. Gratitude to God would be elicited, and that self-denial and abstinence from evil which the unleavened bread typified. And it is evident that a similar memorial is contemplated in the New Testament dispensation. The Lord's Supper coming regularly round is intended to recall the deliverance from sin and guilt which we believe God has wrought for us, and to foster that holiness of walk which should characterize the redeemed of the Lord.

II. The deliverance of the soul has been through sacrifice. The Passover taught this, if it taught anything. Egypt had to part with her firstborn before God's firstborn, Israel, could be redeemed (Exod. xiii. 15). This was evidently the idea—the firstborn of Egypt must die to ensure the liberty of the firstborn of God (Exod. iv. 22,

23). This was the spirit of the Mosaic commission, "Thus saith the Lord, Israel is my son, even my firstborn: and I say unto thee, Let my son go, that he may serve me: and if thou refuse to let him go, behold, I will slay thy son, even thy firstborn."

But if the involuntary sacrifice of the Egyptian firstborn be primarily referred to in the Passover, it unquestionably refers secondarily and typically to the great voluntary sacrifice of Jesus Christ, through which our souls are redeemed. Hence Paul speaks of "Christ our Passover being sacrificed for us" (1 Cor. v. 7). Just as the blood was sprinkled on the doorposts and lintel that the destroying angel might spare the inmates, so the blood of Christ is sprinkled on our hearts and consciences, and our safety from condemnation becomes assured.

III. THE UNITY OF THE SACRIFICE THAT REDEEMS US WAS STRIKINGLY ILLUS-TRATED AT THE PASSOVER. None of the flesh was to remain until the morning, all was to be eaten or burnt with fire. The sacrifice was to be a finished unity, not a protracted feast, which might through delay become corrupt. So with the sacrifice of which it is the type. Jesus Christ was *once* offered to bear the sins of many (Heb. ix. 28). He was not allowed to see any corruption (Acts xiii. 37). The unity of the sacrifice —the once for all—was thus strikingly brought out.

Upon this our assurance of acceptance rests. We have now no doubt that the satisfaction is complete. "It is finished," said Jesus triumphantly on the tree. It is surely a matter of great moment and thankfulness to have our case disposed of at once, without uncertain delays, without any possible appeals. God is satisfied, and we are justified and free.

IV. SALVATION BY SACRIFICE IS WITH A VIEW TO HOLY LIVING. The Feast of Unleavened Bread *followed* the Passover. Leaven was the type of self-indulgence and sin. The unleavened bread indicated how hastily they had to flee out of Egypt, and how little consideration for self there could be in their flight. Paul interprets the reference for us when he says, "Therefore let us keep the feast, not with old leaven, neither with the leaven of malice and wickedness; but with the unleavened bread of sincerity and truth" (1 Cor. v. 8). The feast of unleavened bread symbolized, therefore, the life of holy living which succeeds our salvation. Self-righteousness reverses this Divine order. It insists on the holy living meriting the salvation; but God gives the salvation gratuitously, and respects the holy living as a matter of gratitude. We should not make the way more difficult than God has done.—R. M. E.

Vers. 9—12.—*Pentecost, the Feast of Firstfruits.* Fifty days after the Passover, or a week of weeks, came the second great national festival, when offerings were presented unto God of the firstfruits of the harvest, and a people already blessed recorded their thankfulness. It was also made a celebration of the giving of the Law from Sinai, which took place, according to calculation, exactly fifty days after the Passover. In consequence of this twofold reference to the harvest and to the giving of the Law, this Pentecostal festival acquired more popularity than was to be expected. In fact, from Acts ii., it seems to have drawn Jews and proselytes from all lands. These two references suggest a *moral* and a *typical* lesson respectively from the feast.

I. IT WAS THE EXPRESSION OF HARVEST THANKSGIVING. Here we have its moral meaning. It was an acknowledgment that God is the Author of the harvest, and should have the firstfruits. We never shall prosper unless we are grateful to the bountiful Giver. And the joy of harvest will be all the deeper when it is entertained before God. In harvest homes there should be the religious element continually. If God be forgotten, it is sheer and base ingratitude.

II. IT WAS TYPICAL OF THE PENTECOST OF THE CHRISTIAN CHURCH. The Jews celebrated on this festival the giving of the Law, and the blessings attending it. An interesting parallel may be traced between the Pentecost at Sinai and the Pentecost at Jerusalem.

1. The Jews celebrated the giving of the *Law*, while we celebrate the proclamation at Pentecost of the *gospel*. We have here a parallel and also a contrast. The gospel is the Law magnified and delivered as love.

2. The Jews received the Law as the rule of life after their deliverance through the *Paschal sacrifice*, as we receive the message of love on the foundation of *Christ our Passover* sacrificed fifty days before.

3. There were *wonderful works* attending both the Pentecosts: the fearful thunderings and lightnings at Sinai, and the rushing mighty wind and fire in the upper room at Jerusalem; the sound of the trumpet at Sinai, the sound of the gospel in many languages at Jerusalem.

4. There were *important effects* following both Pentecosts: thus the fear of the Israelites at Sinai, and the conviction of sin at Jerusalem; the separation and ceremonial at Sinai, Moses being constituted mediator, and the fellowship resulting at Jerusalem, when the three thousand were added unto the Church.

III. SYSTEMATIC BENEFICENCE WAS FOSTERED BY THE FESTIVAL. In giving to God "according as the Lord thy God hath blessed thee," servants, Levites, strangers, and the widow and fatherless are sure to be considered. This was the case too after Pentecost. The *Christian commune* was tried, which was a mighty though unsuccessful effort of beneficence. This law of beneficence must be obeyed by all Christian men.—R. M. E.

Vers. 13—17.—*The Feast of Tabernacles—life a tented state.* This was the third great festival, and it was after all the harvest and vintage had been gathered home. It was celebrated in the seventh month, from the fifteenth day to the twenty-second. It is also noticeable that it began five days after the great Day of Atonement, which was on the tenth day of this same seventh month. Sin pardoned, and the harvest saved, these were surely twin blessings at which poor sinners might well rejoice.

I. THE FESTIVAL WAS TO REMIND THE ISRAELITES OF THE PILGRIMAGE IN THE WILDERNESS. Their settling in Canaan was not to blot out the memory of their previous pilgrimage, and how they dwelt with God in tents. The same danger threatens God's children still. This world gets so settled and *home-like* that we forget the pilgrimage which life is meant by God to be. We need the exhortation of Peter, "Dearly beloved, I beseech you as strangers and pilgrims, abstain from fleshly lusts, which war against the soul" (1 Pet. ii. 11).

II. THE FESTIVAL WAS TO BE A JOYOUS ONE. It would be joyous on three accounts: (1) because of the ingathered harvest; (2) because of the complete atonement so recently past; (3) because of the time of year, the glorious October of Palestine. Hence the festival would be virtually a tenting out in the pleasantest time of the year, with minds delivered from all anxiety and fear.

And this is to indicate the high-water mark of Christian experience. We are living below our privileges if we are not rejoicing in God's providential goodness, and in his atoning grace, and in his beautiful world. "Rejoice in the Lord alway: and again I say, Rejoice" (Phil. iv. 4).

III. THE FESTIVAL FOSTERED HOPE. For if life as it now is should be regarded as a pilgrimage, an unsettled state, then each time we are reminded of this we learn to look for a better condition and more permanent abode. If I am reminded that I dwell in a tent of flesh, easily taken down, I learn to hope for the building of God, the "house not made with hands, eternal in the heavens" (2 Cor. v. 1).

> "A while on earth we roam
> In these frail houses which are not our home,
> Journeying towards a refuge that is sure,—
> A rest secure.
>
> *   *   *   *   *
>
> "For in our Father's house
> A mansion fair he has prepared for us;
> And only till his voice shall call us hence
> We dwell in tents."

IV. THE FESTIVAL FOSTERED FORETHOUGHT AND THRIFT. It had all the wholesome effect on them which an annual picnic has upon working people. They look forward to it and make preparation for it. Now, these festivals at the centre of the national worship were to be joyful and liberal times. They were not to appear empty-handed before the Lord. They were to be able to give at his altar and be hospitable as they had opportunity. Hence the festival cultivated thrifty habits in order to be openhanded when the glad day came. So should religion make us all!—R. M. E.

Vers. 18—20.—*Impartial judges.* We have here the election of judges or magistrates laid down as a duty. In the election they are to secure impartial and incorruptible men. A bribe is not to be thought of by the judges—nor are they to respect persons. And here let us notice—

I. THAT ALL JUDGMENT AMONG MEN IS THE FORESHADOWING OF A DIVINE JUDGMENT AT THE LAST. We live under a moral Governor who has not yet delivered final judgment upon his creatures. That final review of life is naturally expected from the imperfect justice of the world. Men in their judgments can at best only approximate to what will be the Divine decision.

II. GOD DEMANDS IMPARTIAL JUDGES FROM HIS PEOPLE BECAUSE HE IS THE IMPARTIAL JUDGE HIMSELF. The impartiality of God's administration will be vindicated at last. All seeming violations of the principle will be exhibited in their true light. For instance, God's plan of salvation is the very essence of impartiality, since it proposes to save men without regard to any personal consideration, as a matter of free grace alone. Whosoever takes exception to this is taking exception to the Divine impartiality.

Again, in providence we shall doubtless find that, by a series of compensations and of drawbacks, each person's lot in life is impartially and graciously ordered. The "favourites of fortune" find some drop of bitterness in their cup, and the sweetness is more apparent than real.

III. MEN NEED NOT TRY TO BRIBE GOD, HOWEVER THEY MAY SUCCEED WITH MEN. For although this may seem a strong way of putting it, it is nevertheless the attempt that sinners thoughtlessly make. For instance, when an anxious soul thinks that a certain amount of conviction of sin, a certain amount of penitence, a certain amount of frames and feelings, will secure acceptance and peace, he is proposing to bribe God. It is as if an insane person tried to corrupt a judge on the bench by the present of a bundle of rags—"all our righteousnesses are as filthy rags." God will take no bribe. He will accept no man's person. Unless we give up the idea of personal claim and personal fitness for his reception of us, we cannot be accepted.

IV. WE MAY EXPECT AN IMPARTIAL JUDGMENT AT THE LAST. It is Jesus who is to sit on the throne when the appeal cases from the injustice of earth to the justice of heaven are heard. He knows our cases so thoroughly that he cannot, as he would not, err. All wrongs shall then be righted; all unfair advantage taken shall then be condemned. "Behold, the judge standeth at the door." Let us see to it that we learn of him impartiality, and men shall regard us as truly Godlike in our dealings with them!—R. M. E.

Vers. 1—8.—*The Passover a memorial and a prophecy.* In a singular and a miraculous manner, the national existence of the Hebrews had commenced. God had signally interposed as their Champion, in a way altogether unparalleled. Without question, it was an event pregnant with vast issues to the history of mankind. Every opportunity was afforded Pharaoh to escape from destruction. The host of God, composed of natural forces and invisible powers, enclosed him gradually within narrower and narrower bounds, until the king himself was captured and destroyed. This was a conspicuous step in the development of the redemptive scheme. In that night of destruction the elect nation was born.

I. EMANCIPATION OF NATIONAL LIFE FROM BONDAGE IS A FIT SUBJECT FOR YEARLY COMMEMORATION. It is God's will that such commemoration should be observed, and be observed in a most religious spirit. The effect of such commemoration upon the minds of the people would be most beneficial. The nation is but a collection of units; and as every unit had shared in the boon, so every unit should partake in the acknowledgment. It is a sin when we forget our participation in national blessings. Our pious example will be a benign stimulus to others.

II. GRATEFUL COMMEMORATION SHOULD PERPETUATE ALL THE METHODS AND INCIDENTS OF THE DIVINE DELIVERANCE. 1. *Life had to be sacrificed in order to obtain that redemption.* It was, in the most proper sense, a *redemption.* They had belonged to God; a usurper had despoiled God of his right; hence, the people had to be "bought back." Natural agencies had been employed to soften Pharaoh's heart; but in vain. Nothing short of the death of the firstborn sufficed to procure deliverance. Therefore the commemoration of the event fitly included the sacrifice of the lamb.

2. *The release had been with haste.* *This* incident was deserving of commemoration. So urgent was Pharaoh's desire that they should depart, that they had not time to bake their daily ration of bread; hence the yearly commemoration was to be with "bread unleavened." Bodily appetites must be forgotten when the golden moment of emancipation dawns. 3. *The sense of obligation should be deep and abiding.* On this account, the commemoration was appointed to extend over seven days. Gladness was to be tempered with self-denial and pain.

III. Grateful commemoration takes the form of deeds and self-sacrifices. The gratitude that contents itself with words is cheap and shallow. God delights to hear the language of deeds. This is the real language of the heart. It feels the pain of restraint and disappointment, if it may not bring some visible expression of its love or perform some service for its friend. In the case of the Hebrews, long journeys had to be undertaken, lambs had to be slain, much time had to be devoted to the sacred festival. Yet all this was performed with radiant gladness.

IV. The commemoration of the Passover was to be observed under the solemn sanctions of religion. Under the theocratic government, every public act was baptized at the fountain of religion. Religion was not simply a particular department of the State: it was a spirit of heaven that ennobled and beautified every public deed. The Paschal lamb might not be slain anywhere, it must be slain at the temple gate. It was an offering made to God, and God at once returned it, with added blessing to the offerer. Thus, year by year, they professed that their emancipation was a gift from God, that national life and earthly home and prospective hope came from the goodness of God.

V. National emancipation was a prophecy of the world's redemption. A man is a type of a nation; a nation is a type of the world. What God *has* done for a nation, he is prepared to do (if need be) for the race. We too are under bondage, in the grasp of a mightier tyrant than Pharaoh. "Christ our Passover is for us slain." From all on whom is the effectual mark of Messiah's blood, doom is removed. "They shall never perish." Their destiny is the heavenly Canaan—the new Jerusalem. We too have our Paschal feast—the Eucharist. As the deliverance of the earthly Israel was complete, "not a hoof was left behind," so Christ Jesus shall eventually be Victor over all his foes. Redemption of the true Israel is in progress.—D.

Vers. 9—17.—*The Feasts of Weeks and of Tabernacles.* For the moral improvement of the Hebrews, it was desirable to keep alive among them the recollection of their early history. Prior to the invention of printing, and when written records would be scarce, memory and affection and conscience were impressed by the annual festivals. The Passover commemorated the national birth; the Feast of Tabernacles commemorated the tent life of the desert. The joys of harvest and of vintage were things unknown in the wilderness.

I. Material blessings afford pregnant reasons for religious joy. A frequent effect upon the mind of some large influx of wealth is to produce a sense of independence and self-sufficiency. The very event which ought, most of all, to lead men's thoughts up to God, leads to self-gratulation and self-trust. Now present need is met. We have stores of abundance. We can say to ourselves, "Soul, thou hast much goods laid up for many years." Therefore we must counteract this tendency. In very kindness to men's souls, God ordained this festival. He would have us to look from the gift to the Giver. It is his will that we should rejoice abundantly, but that our joy should be religious joy—a joy consecrated at the temple gate.

II. The festive seasons are fixed according to a religious measurement. (Ver. 9.) The year is a measurement of time fixed by a natural cycle. So also is the month, so also the day. But there is nothing in nature that marks the commencement and the close of the week. This is a measurement specially ordained of God. The visible universe is not the whole of existence. Another voice breaks upon the ear, softer than the music of nature, and more full of authority than the voice of Cæsar— a voice which makes a new boundary in time, and bids us to count our days by sevens.

III. Receiving should prompt us to a proportionate giving. (Ver. 10.) The gift to be brought to the temple is not specified. It might be a gift of corn, or of fruit, or of wine, or of money. The form of the gift was left to the option of the husbandman ; but *some* tribute was required, and the amount must be proportionate to the abundance of his crops. If plain and imperative law could make the Jews generous-hearted, God did his utmost to cultivate in them this excellence. Avarice was scouted by Divine Law.

IV. RELIGIOUS JOY SHOULD BE DIFFUSIVE. This giving to God was to be an act of gladness. It was not allowed to be with grudging or with gloom (ver. 11). God had no personal need for these material presents. They were expended at once in new blessing and joy. Not only was the household to share in the festive gladness, in the banquet and the song ; but the servant, the stranger, the poor Levite, the widow, and the orphan also. God's copious goodness in the harvest was designed to enlarge all narrow affections, and to thaw, in streams of kindness, all frozen sympathies. At such a season, they were reminded that they were not proprietors of anything, but put in offices of trust as the stewards of God.

V. A SENSE OF OBLIGATION SHOULD INSPIRE OBEDIENCE. (Ver. 12.) The hour of prosperity is the hour of reflection. By the law of associated ideas, the contrast is suggested. The mind, free from the pressure of care, retraces the past. We think of the "rock whence we were hewn, the hole of the pit whence we were digged." The recollection of our lowly origin—the dust of the ground—ought to affect us tenderly ; and our sense of devout obligation should stimulate new and larger obedience. If I owe so much to God, what can I otherwise do than keep his commandments with mind and heart and soul ? *Complete* obedience is a dictate of earliest intelligence.—D.

Vers. 18—22.—*The administration of justice.* True religion is related to true morality as the parent is related to the child. God cares as much that right disposi-tions should prevail between man and man as between man and God. By an eternal decree, religion and morality have been cojoined, and no man can put them asunder. He that loves God will love his brother also.

I. THE ADMINISTRATION OF SOCIAL JUSTICE IS ENTRUSTED TO IMPERFECT MEN. The laws of the Jews were framed in heaven, and were conveyed to men by the mediation of angels, but the administration and execution of these laws were imposed on men selected from among themselves. What men cannot do, God will do for them ; what men can do for themselves, God requires them to accomplish. This administration of Divine Law by men was a magnificent training for higher office. In the best sense, God desires that men "should be as gods." By handling the affairs of justice, they would best grow in the understanding of the Divine government.

II. EVERY TOWN WAS A TYPE OF THE WHOLE KINGDOM. Magistrates were to be appointed in every community, who should be kings in their sphere of jurisdiction. Such magistrates were the people's choice, and thus they were initiated into the art of self-government. Justice well administered in every town would secure the order and well-being of the nation. The burden of governing the whole nation would thus be reduced to a thousand infinitesimal burdens—each one easily to be borne. Duty well done in every individual sphere would make the world happy and prosperous.

III. THE SACRED INTERESTS OF JUSTICE OUTWEIGH ALL PERSONAL CONSIDERATIONS. Gifts from friends are not to be despised ; but if they have the feeblest tendency to weaken our sense of right or to bring discredit on public justice, they must be declined. If a man accepts the office of a ruler, he must be prepared to forego many private advantages and pleasures. He is the steward of public interests—the servant of justice. He is no longer his own master. Personal friendships must be forgotten in the judicial court. No regard must be had to any other interest save the interest of righteousness. *One* thing the magistrate must do, and *one* only ; he must be the mouthpiece of eternal righteousness. He may err, but he *must be honest.* Simple in-tegrity of purpose is the chief qualification to rule. He who candidly desires to do right will be guided by an unerring hand.

IV. THE CAUSE OF PUBLIC JUSTICE IS SERVED BY PUBLICITY. The administration of justice was to be in the gate—in the place of public concourse. From the free conflict of public opinion sparks of truth will be elicited. So weak and vacillating is ofttimes human purpose, that the blaze of mortal eyes is needed to keep that purpose steadfast. This mode of administering justice had also a deterrent influence on the immature and the vile ; it educated the public conscience.

V. JUSTICE HONESTLY ADMINISTERED SECURES NATIONAL PROSPERITY. It is the lesson of universal history that official injustice loosens all the bonds of society, and brings a kingdom into utter ruin. Men will patiently tolerate many abuses of power, but the public abuse of justice quickly brings deadly retribution. On the other hand, an honest and prompt administration of righteous law is the seed of order, content, and mutual confidence. It gives a sense of security; it fosters patriotism; it develops courage; it brings the smile and benediction of God.—D.

Vers. 21, 22.—*The pathways to temptation to be shunned.* A rash and hare-brained pilot may venture as near as he can to a sunken reef, but a wise captain will prefer plenty of sea-room. It is no proof of wisdom to tamper with temptation. One cannot handle pitch without being defiled.

I. GOD WISHES TO IMPART TO MEN HIS OWN FEELING TOWARDS IDOLATRY. (Ver. 22.) To be like God is the summit of every good man's ambition. This is God's intention also. But the attainment can only gradually be made. We must have God's thoughts rooted in us; we must cultivate similar feelings; we must cherish similar purposes or we cannot be like him in character. Idolatry corrupts the soul and generates death. To know and worship God leads up to richest life.

II. EXTERNAL AIDS TO IDOLATRY MUST BE CAREFULLY AVOIDED. A stone which is a stumbling-block to a child has no peril for a strong man; for the sake of the young and the weak, the stone should be taken out of the way. It is wise and noble to abstain from self-indulgences which will imperil the piety of others. A shady grove would be pleasant enough for worshippers in the scorching climate of the East; nevertheless, if it shall tend in the least measure to lure the ignorant into idolatry, we will forego the pleasure. This is Godlike, to deny self in order to bless others. If umbrageous groves make my weak brother to offend, I will endure the noontide heat so long as life shall last. Our mental tastes, our love of the beautiful, our desire for pleasure,—all must give way to honest endeavour for the moral elevation of the race.

III. GOD'S FATHERLY KINDNESS IS EXPRESSED IN THESE PLAIN PRECEPTS. We might reach these wise maxims as reasonable deductions from moral principles; yet they come to us clothed with irresistible authority, when they appear as the revealed will of God. A twofold light blends to point out the path of human conduct, viz. the light of conscience and the light of Scripture; yet these twin rays emanate from the selfsame sun. –D.

EXPOSITION.

CHAPTER XVII.

SACRIFICES TO BE OF ANIMALS UNBLEMISHED. IDOLATERS TO BE SOUGHT OUT, CONVICTED, AND PUT TO DEATH. THE HIGHER JUDICIAL COURT AT THE SANCTUARY. ELECTION AND DUTY OF A KING.

Ver. 1.—Not only was the setting up of idols an offence to be punished by the judge, but also all profanation of the service of Jehovah, such as the offering in sacrifice of any animal, bullock or sheep, that had any blemish or defect (cf. Lev. xxii. 19—24). **Evilfavouredness;** literally, *any evil thing,* i.e. any vice or maim (cf. Lev. xxii. 22, etc.).

Ver. 2.—In ch. xiii., Moses enacts what is to be done to those who seduce into idolatry. Here he declares what is to be done to those who are so seduced. **Done wickedness;** literally, *done the evil.* The definite article is prefixed; it is not any kind of wickedness that is here denounced, but the special sin

of idolatry, *the* wickedness κατ᾿ ἐξόχην. All idolatry was to be strictly suppressed—those convicted of it to be put to death by stoning.

Ver. 3.—(Cf. ch. iv. 19.) **Which I have not commanded;** *i.e. have forbidden,* a meiosis, as in Jer. vii. 31.

Ver. 5.—**Unto thy gates;** judicial proceedings were conducted at the gates of the city, and in some place outside the walls the sentence was executed on the condemned criminal (Neh. viii. 1, 3; Job. xxix. 7; ch. xxii. 24; Acts vii. 58; Heb. xiii. 12), just as, during the journey through the wilderness, it had been outside the camp that transgressors were punished (Lev. xxiv. 14; Numb. xv. 36).

Vers. 6, 7.—Only on the testimony of more than one witness could the accused be condemned (cf. Numb. xxxv. 30); and the hand of the witnesses was to be first against him to put him to death—a rule which would tend to prevent accusations being lightly adduced, as none would venture to witness against any one unless so deeply convinced of his guilt that they were willing to assume the responsibility of inflicting on him the last penalty with their own hands. **Worthy of death be put to death**; *i.e. adjudged* or *appointed to death;* literally, *the dead man shall die.* מֵת, the part. of מוּת, to die, is here equivalent to בֶּן מָוֶת, son of death (1 Sam. xx. 31), or אִישׁ מָוֶת, a man of death (1 Kings ii. 26), *i.e.* one assigned to death, already the property of death, and so as good as dead. **Put the evil away**; literally, *consume* or *sweep away the evil.* The verb בָּעַר means primarily to consume by burning.

Vers. 8—13.—So long as Moses was with the people, they had in him one to whom, in the last resort, cases might be brought for decision which were found too difficult for the ordinary judges (Exod. xviii. 19—26). But, as he was not to be always with them, it was needful to provide a supreme court, to which such cases might be carried when they could no longer be decided by him; and such a court is here appointed to be held at the sanctuary.

Ver. 8.—**A matter too hard for thee;** literally, *too marvellous;* something extra-ordinary, and which could not be decided by the ordinary rules of the judicature. **Between blood and blood, between plea and plea, and between stroke and stroke;** *i.e.* in cases where blood had been shed and death had ensued, either accidentally or from murderous intent (cf. Exod. xxi. 13, etc.; Numb. xxxv. 9, etc.); in cases of disputed rights and claims (cf. 2 Chron. xix. 10); and in cases where corporeal injury had been suffered, whether in strife or from assault (Exod. xxi. 18, etc.); and, in general, wherever matters of controversy—disputes as to what was lawful and right, might arise in their towns and villages. In all such cases recourse was to be had to the court at the sanctuary—"to the priests the Levites," *i.e.* the priests who were of the tribe of Levi, and to the judge presiding there—the lay judge associated with the high priest as president (see Oehler, in Herzog's 'Encyclop.,' vol. v. p. 58). It is not intended by this that an appeal was to lie from the lower court to the higher, or that the parties in a suit might carry it at once to the supreme judge; the meaning rather is that, when the ordinary judges found a case too difficult for them to deal with, they were themselves to transmit it to the supreme court for decision.

Ver. 9.—**Enquire;** what, namely, is "the sentence of judgment;" and this the judge

should declare. **Sentence of judgment;** literally, *word of right, verbum juris,* declaration of what was legally right.

Vers. 10—12.—This sentence, being founded on the Law, the suitors were to accept and implicitly obey. If any through pride or arrogance should refuse to accept the interpretation of the Law given by the priests, or to submit to the sentence pronounced by the judge, he was to be regarded as a rebel against God, and to be put to death, that others might be deterred from the like presumption (ch. xiii. 11). **The sentence, which they of that place which the Lord shall choose shall shew thee;** rather, *which they shall declare to thee from that place which the Lord shall choose.* **According to the sentence of the law;** literally, *according to the mouth of the Law;* i.e. according as the Law prescribes, according to the purport of the statute.

Vers. 14—20.—Israel, being under a theocracy, did not *need* an earthly king; but neither was this thereby precluded, provided the king chosen by the people were one whom Jehovah would approve as his vice-gerent. In case, then, of their coming to desire to have a king over them like the nations around them, Moses gives instructions here as to the choice of a king, and as to the duties and obligations resting upon those who might be elevated to that office. The form in which these are conveyed clearly indicates that, at the time this was uttered, the existence of a king in Israel was contemplated as only a distant possibility.

Ver. 14.—**When thou art come unto the land,** etc. This phraseology, which is common to the laws which respect the affairs of the Hebrews after they should be settled in Canaan, implies that this law was given whilst they were yet outside the promised land. It is plain also, from the tenor of the whole statement in this verse, that the legislator in this case is providing for what he supposes may happen, is likely to happen, but which he by no means desires should happen. Moses foresaw that the people would wish to be as the nations around them—governed by a king—and he legislates accordingly, without approving of that wish.

Ver. 15.—The prohibition to choose a foreigner indicates that the people had the right of election. In what way this was to be exercised, and how it was subject to the Divine choice, is not declared. Judging from what actually happened in subsequent history, it would appear that only on special occasions, such as the election of the first king or a change of dynasty, did God take the initiative, and through a prophet direct the choice of the people; ultimately the monarchy became hereditary, and it was understood that the prince who succeeded to the throne did so with the Divine approval, unless the opposite was expressly intimated by a message from God.

Vers. 16, 17.—Certain rules are prescribed for the king. It is forbidden to him to multiply horses, to multiply wives, and to amass large treasures of silver and gold, and he must have a copy of the Law written out for him from that kept by the priests, that he might have it by him, and read it all the days of his life. The multiplying of horses is prohibited, because this would bring Israel into intercourse and friendly relations with Egypt, and might tend to their going back to that country from which they had been so marvellously delivered ; a prohibition which could only have been given at an early stage in the history of the people, for at a later period, after they had been well established in Canaan, such a prohibition for such a reason would have been simply ridiculous. The prohibition to multiply wives and to amass large treasures has respect to the usage common from the earliest period with Oriental monarchs to have vast harems and huge accumulations of the precious metals, as much for ostentation as for either luxury or use ; and as there was no small danger of the King of Israel being seduced to follow this usage, and so to have his heart turned away from the Lord, it was fitting that such a prohibition should be prospectively enacted for his guidance. Both these prohibitions were neglected by Solomon, and probably by others of the Jewish kings; but this only in-

dicates that the law was so ancient that it had come in their time to be regarded as obsolete. The rule that the king was to write him a copy of the Law for his own constant use does not necessarily imply that he was to write this with his own hand ; he might cause it to be written by some qualified scribe for him.

Ver. 18.—A copy of this law; literally, a double of this Law, i.e. not, as the LXX. have it, "This reiteration of the Law" (τὸ δευτερονόμιον τοῦτο), but a duplicate or copy of the Pentateuchal Law. The Jews understand by "double" that two copies of the Law were to be made by the king (Maimon., 'De Regibus,' c. iii. § 1) ; but this is unnecessary : every copy of a law is a double of it. Out of that which is before the priests. The priests were the custodians of the written Law (ch. xxxi. 26) ; and from the text of their codex was the king's copy to be written.

Ver. 19.—And it shall be with him, etc. It was to be carefully kept by him, but not as a mere sacred deposit or palladium ; it was to be constantly with him wherever he was, was to be the object of his continual study, and was to be the directory and guide of his daily life (cf. Josh. i. 8; Ps. i. 2; cxix. 15, 16, 24, 97—99, etc.).

Ver. 20.—That his heart be not lifted up above his brethren. "Not imagining himself to be above all laws, nor slighting his subjects, as unworthy of his notice, but taking a due care to promote their happiness" (Patrick). He, and his children; properly, his sons (בָּנָיו). The legislator anticipated not an elective monarchy, but one hereditary in the same family (cf. Michaelis, 'Laws of Moses,' pt. i. § 54).

HOMILETICS.

Ver. 1.—(See Homily, ch. xv. 21, on "Sacrifices to be without blemish.")

Vers. 2—7.—*The sacredness of personal reputation seen in the regulations concerning human testimony.* So far as this passage presents to us the doctrine that idolatry, being apostacy from God, was treason to the Hebrew commonwealth, and was to be punished with death, the matter is dealt with in the Homily on the thirteenth chapter. An inquiry of great importance would sooner or later arise, and would, therefore, need to be provided for in the Mosaic institutes, viz. : "On what evidence shall any one be adjudged guilty of such a crime?" It will be seen here that, while God so guarded his own honour that it might not be sullied with impunity, so he guarded the reputation of the people that it might not be assailed or impeached on any frivolous pretext or any unproven report. The exactitude in the order of expression in the fourth verse is very noticeable : If it be so—and it be told thee—and thou hast inquired—diligently—and, behold, it is true—and the thing certain—then, and not till then, may the penalty be inflicted. Observe : 1. Every one was held to be innocent till he was proved otherwise. 2. No one's character was put at the mercy of any one unattested witness. 3. He who reported with his tongue should be the one to smite with his hand! (ver. 7).[1] A mighty stroke of policy this, to guard personal honour from assailment! It might sometimes make crime more difficult of proof, but it gave the innocent a wondrous guard against unjust accusation. Many would be ready to backbite who would shrink from stoning another. Men by thousands may be found who would not break bones, but who think nothing of breaking hearts. 4. The people were to co-operate in putting away the evil when once it was proved to exist. "Slow to suspect, but quick to put down evil," was to be the moral rule of their conduct in such cases. Now, of course, it is not our province to deal with all this from the purely legal point of view, as a matter of jurisprudence; but we cannot fail to indicate the moral principles which are here involved; and which a Christian teacher would do well to set in the light of Matt. vii. 1, 2. Observe—

I. OUR GOD WOULD ENLIST THE SYMPATHIES OF HIS PEOPLE IN PUTTING DOWN EVIL. We are to be workers together with him. He has redeemed us that we may be zealous of good works.

II. HE WOULD HAVE US VERY SENSITIVE to the honour of *his* Name, but also very sensitive to the spotlessness of *each other's* name and fame. This passage is quite as remarkable for the guard it throws around man, as it is for the concern it would evoke for the honour of God (see Ps. xv. 1—3; Lev. xix. 16; Ps. xxxiv. 13; 1 Pet. iii. 10).

III. WE MAY NOT REGARD ANOTHER AS GUILTY ON THE BARE EVIDENCE OF RUMOUR. Each one's reputation is too sacred in God's eye and ought to be too precious in ours for this. It is humiliating to think such precepts as these should be needed. "The Law is not made for a righteous man," and it is a sad proof of how much unrighteousness there is in the world that such a law should be needed still. Every one is to be regarded as innocent till he is proved guilty.

IV. IF THE PUBLIC GOOD REQUIRES IT, ILL REPORTS SHOULD BE EXAMINED. It may be painful work, but it has to be done sometimes. But we are tempted to think it would be a mighty safeguard against ill reports being raised on any light or frivolous pretext, if he who first moved secretly with his tongue were always required to be the first to smite openly with the hand!

V. SUCH REPORTS ARE TO BE PROVEN TRUE ERE ACTION IS TAKEN THEREON. No man's repute is to be smitten at a venture. To all men it is precious as life. The best men value it more than life. They would rather give up their breath than part with their honour. And the legislation of high heaven upholds them!

VI. PROVEN EVIL IS TO BE PUT AWAY. We are to be very slow to believe ill of another; "slow to speak." But when such ill is proved beyond doubt, then it behoves us to censure, to expose, to condemn it, and to put it away. We are to stand by a brother till he is shown to be guilty, but that once done, regard both for God and man requires us to disavow all sympathy with wrong, and to co-operate with the Great Supreme in the extirpation of ill.

Vers. 8—13.—*Religion the guard of justice.* In the preceding chapter, vers. 18—20, judges and officers are specified as appointed by God to be the guardians of justice and right. The Hebrew is very emphatic in ver. 20, "Justice, justice, shalt thou follow," etc. Manifold complications, however, would be sure to arise as the nation advanced, and as the primitive simplicity of their first settlement passed into more fixed arrangements as to property, etc. In such difficult cases, it might not be easy, and perhaps it would not always be possible, for the judges and *shoterim* to determine what *was* just. The legislator is here bidden, therefore, to make provision in case such perplexities should arise. When the people should come to the land which the Lord their God gave them, there would be one place which the Lord would choose to put his Name there. There should "thrones of judgment" sit. The priests, who would have to offer sacrifices and to intercede for the people before God, would also be expected to be so versed in the Law of God, that they could appropriately be regarded as the highest court of appeal, by whose decision the highest sanctions of religion would be brought to declare and enforce "justice, justice." Their decision was held to be given

---

[1] See in Keil on 'Pentateuch,' vol. iii. p. 381 (footnote), quotation from Calvin.

them by light from on high.[1] And when such decision was in accordance with the
Divine will, the people were bound by it. To resist it was "a presumptuous sin;"
and, withal, it was one of so deep a dye, that it was not safe for Israel that any man
should continue among them, who spurned the highest decisions which could possibly
be given. At the same time, there were sundry checks and counter-checks against the
abuse of this law. The authority of this highest court was relative or conditional, not
absolute. If priests became unfaithful, and their judgments unjust, then the sin
of presumption was chargeable upon them (cf. ch. xviii. 20; see also Jeremiah's,
Ezekiel's, and Malachi's charges against such unfaithful expounders). Note, further,
that as early as the time of the Judges, when the priests profaned their office, God set
them aside, and wrought and taught by means of the prophet Samuel. So that the
supreme court bound the people only so far as it was what it was designed to be, even
God's appointment for securing justice, by investing it with the sublime sanctions of
religion. But when it was that, and so far as it answered its end, its utterances were
to the people as the voice of God.

Now, we all know that, as a formal institution, this court of appeal has long since
passed away. But we greatly mistake if there are not couched here sundry momentous
principles, of which no age, country, or race can afford to lose sight. These principles
are—

I. THAT RELIGION IS THE TRUE GUARANTEE OF JUSTICE BETWEEN MAN AND MAN.
That in the course of time the essence of religion may have so evaporated, and its place
be so taken up by forms and ceremonies, that the connection between religion and justice
may seem to be lost, must be admitted to be a possibility, but it does not alter the
principle here enunciated. The guarantee of justice between man and man is found
in a power of appeal on both sides to a law of immutable right mutually acknowledged.
To such a law conscience, the regulative faculty, points with steady finger. Such law
obeyed, she approves the obedience, and when disobeyed, she condemns the disobedience. Both the approval and the condemnation of the voice within are witnesses to
the existence and government of a Great Judge of all, who, seated on the throne of
universal empire, issues his mandates to the world! And in the appeal from human
acts to the judgment of the Great Supreme, lies the safeguard of justice between man
and man.[2] In a word, religion is the sole adequate guarantee of morality. Both are
comprehended under the one word, "righteousness." Religion is righteousness towards
God; morality is righteousness towards man. If man ever comes to regard himself
as the supreme existence, empowered to *make* right right, and wrong wrong, instead of
regarding himself as subject to the everlasting laws of right, the best and dearest
privileges of the human family will be in imminent peril, and at best can endure but
for a while!

II. RELIGIOUS SANCTIONS FIND THEIR EXPRESSION IN THE LAW OF GOD. See Ps.
xix., in which the Psalmist extols the pure and holy Law of Jehovah, as being
the written expression of perfect right. In the ten commandments the various phases
of the right in act or thought are set forth. And according to the ordinance alluded
to in this paragraph, when a case arose which was too difficult to be solved by the
lower authorities, it might be taken up to a higher court, that the will of the Lord might
thereby be discovered by the most trustworthy exposition of the bearings of God's
Law on each particular case.

III. GOD'S HOUSE IS TO BE THE SEAT AND CENTRE WHERE RIGHTEOUSNESS IS EN-
THRONED, EXPOUNDED, AND ENFORCED. If in Israel a poor man could not get justice
elsewhere, he was to be sure of it in God's house. It was a pious Hebrew's delight to
inquire in God's temple. And we do not think adequately of the temple service if we
merely regard it as consisting of sacrifice and mediation; the holy house was also a
place where men could learn the mind and will of God in their bearing on the life of
man both in general and in specific cases. And one of the delights of the Psalmist's

---

[1] See Biblical Dictionaries on ' Urim and Thummim;' and also a suggestive chapter on
the same topic in Hengstenberg's ' Egypt and the Books of Moses,' p. 149, *et seq.*

[2] See a sermon entitled, 'The House of Commons and Atheism,' by R. W. Dale; and
also an article, 'Religion and Morality,' by Rev. Stanley Leathes, in *British Quarterly
Review*, July, 1880.

heart was this: "there are set thrones of judgment." And so now, in God's house, not only are we bidden to "behold the Lamb of God," but "to live soberly, righteously, and godly in this present world."

IV. GOD'S MINISTERS ARE TO BE THE EXPOUNDERS OF RIGHTEOUSNESS. There are no priests now, as of yore. But the Church of God has a ministry, and by this ministry the truth of God is to be "opened up" and "commended to every man's conscience as in the sight of God."

V. WHEN GOD'S HOLY AND RIGHTEOUS LAW IS EXPOUNDED TO THE PEOPLE, THEY ARE LOYALLY TO ACCEPT IT, SUBMIT TO IT, AND OBEY IT. And this, not because of him whose voice speaks, but because of him in whose behalf the preacher speaks. Men are to receive the truth, not as the word of man, but as the Word of God (cf. 2 Cor. x. 5).

VI. REFUSAL TO OBEY THE WILL OF GOD, WHEN CLEARLY EXPOUNDED, IS A PRE-SUMPTUOUS SIN. (See passages where same Hebrew word is used which is here rendered "presumptuous," specially Ps. xix. 13.) The epithet indicates the greatness of the sin. It is one which Jehovah specially hates, severely rebukes, and utterly condemns. He "resisteth the proud." He hides things from the wise and prudent. He scorneth the scorners. He taketh the wise in their own craftiness. First pride, then shame. "What shall the end be of them that obey not the gospel of God?"

Vers. 14—20.—*Kings subject to the King of kings.* In this paragraph we have directions to be attended to in case Israel should, in the course of time, desire a king. As things were, the Lord God was their King; and it would be a sinful discontent with the Divine arrangements if they wished any change in that respect in their national constitution. It would show an envious desire to be like unto the nations round about, and a craving after the pomp and display of the heathen world. Still, if such a wish should spring up, they are not to be violently coerced into the maintenance of the theocracy. They are to have their way. A dangerous permission this, but maybe it is a necessary one, to educate the people out of their perversity. The permission, however, is not left without its restrictions. Here are rules for the people, and also rules for their king whenever they should have one. The people are told that they must defer to the will of the Lord their God as to who should be their king; and also that they might not set one over them of an alien nation (ver. 15). And as for the king who should be chosen, for him there are four prohibitions and four commands. The prohibitions are these: (1) the king is not to take them back to Egypt; (2) nor to multiply cavalry; (3) nor to amass wealth; (4) nor to multiply wives to himself. The commands are these: (1) The Law of God is to be written, (2) retained, (3) read, (4) obeyed by him; and only as this is the case is there any promise of the stability of his throne. (For a grand commentary on all this, read 1 Sam. xii.) The history of the Hebrew nation continuously discloses the folly and danger of people and kings departing from the Law of God. Hence we have a fine homiletic theme for the preacher, when called on to preach a sermon on national affairs.[1] It is this: *Obedience to the Law of God the only stability of thrones.*

I. IT IS BY RIGHTEOUSNESS THAT THRONES ARE FIRM. Righteousness—according to the root of the word—is acting according to relation. Such is the significance of δικὴ. It is acting in harmony with the relations between man and man, and between man and God. When a sceptre is swayed rightly, the throne is established. 1. God has created man with power to perceive a distinction between right and wrong, and with a faculty which approves one and condemns the other. 2. When the right is manifestly done, the people are content. 3. Content of the people gives cohesion to the nation and support to the throne. 4. God's blessing is promised to the righteous. The signs of that blessing are seen in continuance and prosperity.

II. THE ONLY AUTHORITATIVE EXPOSITION OF RIGHT FOR THE WORLD IS IN THE WRITTEN LAW OF GOD. (See preceding Homily, Div. II.) Dr. Matthew Arnold speaks of the force pervading the Old Testament as "a power, not ourselves, that makes for righteousness." This is the peculiarity of Hebrew literature. Their kings are always estimated according to whether they did right "in the sight of the Lord."

---

[1] Dr. Jameson's 'Commentary' has several helpful illustrative references. The student may also, with advantage, consult Wine's 'Commentaries on the Laws of Moses.'

III. CONSEQUENTLY, IT IS BY OBEDIENCE TO GOD'S WRITTEN LAW THAT THRONES ARE MADE SECURE. This grand old Book is the charter of the people's liberties, because it demands that kings rule righteously. It is the monarch's best safeguard, because it insists on a method of government which will ensure the loyalty of a grateful people, and the blessing of the monarch's God! With regard to kings and nations, it is true, "Great peace have they which love thy Law, and nothing shall offend them." Earthly kings will ever find it true, "Them that honour me, I will honour."

Ver. 16.—"*No retreat!*" or "*The gate behind us closed.*" "Ye shall henceforth return no more that way." In these words, Moses reminds the people that Egypt once quitted was quitted for ever. If they should come in the course of time to desire and to choose a king, he must by no means take them back to Egypt; their dark experience of Egyptian bondage was never to be repeated. They should return that way no more. The only course open to them was to go onward to the realization of their destiny as a free people, for the gate behind them was closed, never to be opened again. The text may naturally be regarded as God's voice to his emancipated host, saying, "*No retreat!*" We shall apply this to the life of believers. It is true in two spheres.

I. IT IS TRUE IN THE SPHERE OF BEING. With regard to the old state of sin, out of which the children of God have been brought by the redemption which is in Christ Jesus and by the power of the Holy Ghost, it is true, "ye shall henceforth return no more that way." 1. *They may not if they would.* They have quitted the broad road which leadeth to destruction, and, through the gateway of repentance, have entered on "the King's highway of holiness." Having once come over from Satan to Christ, it is altogether forbidden them to dream of a return. Whosoever he be who has avowedly quitted the service of sin for that of the living God, never must he think of returning to the world he has left. Back to his old life of sin? Never! He is to reckon himself henceforth as "dead indeed unto sin, but alive unto God," and, whether living or dying, he is to be the Lord's. 2. *They would not if they might.* Not only is it the Law of God that they must not retreat, but the law of the Spirit of life in Christ Jesus leads them to say, "We will not, by the help of God." And herein is the blessed freedom of the new creature in Christ Jesus. What God wills, he wills. He has voluntarily left the world, and voluntarily he remains out of its camp. The very thought of "returning any more that way" is anguish to him. He has said to earth, once for all, farewell; to sinful pleasures, farewell; to the pride of life, farewell. He has cast in his lot with Christ, and he esteems reproach for him greater riches than the treasures in Egypt. He would not move a step that is not towards God and heaven. He has done with the vanities of earth, and can return no more that way!

II. IT IS TRUE IN THE SPHERE OF TIME. We can neither retrace the steps we have already trodden, nor recall nor reproduce the circumstances of bygone days or years. 1. *We cannot recall, or change, or obliterate the past, even if we would.* The trials and cares of bygone years are gone, never to be repeated. The actions of past years are done, and however we may desire it, they cannot be undone. There is no such thing as recalling a single moment, to correct what has been amiss, nor erasing a single word or deed so as to prevent its issues travelling on to eternity! We may do something now to shape future years, but—to alter past years—nothing. For good or ill they have left their mark. We can alter nothing. We can "return no more that way." 2. *The pilgrim, Zionward, would not retreat if he could.* The child of God who has been, however imperfectly, endeavouring in Divine strength to serve and please his Father in heaven, reviewing his years with their trials, afflictions, and cares, feels it to be a great joy to him that he can return no more that way. He would not linger here. He wants to speed him onward. He ofttimes sings at eventide, with thankful heart, "a day's march nearer home." The goal of his being is ahead. To serve God here is blissful. But he longs, not to repeat past imperfections, but to "go on unto perfection," to press forward towards the higher service of the heavenly world. He feels and knows that all the Divine arrangements for him are mercy and truth. He would not change them. Mercy shuts off the past beyond recall. Mercy opens the future.

> "Then, welcome, each declining day,
> Welcome, each closing year!"

HOMILIES BY VARIOUS AUTHORS.

Ver. 1.—*The blemished.* I. THE PRINCIPLE INVOLVED. God is to be served with our best. He rejects the blemished for his service. 1. He is *entitled* to our best. 2. He *requires* it of us. 3. Withholding it *argues unworthy views of God* and of what is due to him. It usually implies contempt of God and hypocrisy in his service (Mal. i. 12, 13).

II. APPLICATIONS OF THE PRINCIPLE. God is to receive from us: 1. The best of our *time*—when the head is clearest, the energies most vigorous, the capacity for service greatest, and when there is least distraction. We offer the blemished when we engross these portions of our time for self, and give to God only our late hours, or hurried snatches of a day crowded with unspiritual and exhausting occupations. 2. The best of our *age*—youth, the prime of manhood and womanhood, with all the service these can render. We offer the blemished when we conceive the purpose of dedicating to God, in old age, powers already worn out in the service of the world. 3. The heartiest of our *service*. Service performed half-heartedly and grudgingly falls under the category of blemished sacrifices. Work done in this spirit will never be well done. Services of devotion will be huddled through, sermons will be ill prepared, the class in the Sunday school will be badly taught, visitation duties will be inefficiently and unpunctually performed. It is the presentation to God of the torn, lame, and halt. 4. The first of our *givings.* Givings should be hearty, liberal, of our first and best, and in a spirit of consecration. To give what " will never be missed" is a poor form of service. It is little to give to God what costs us nothing. Still more conspicuously do we offer the blemished when we devote to God but the parings of a lavish worldly expenditure, or give for his service far below our ability.—J. O.

Vers. 2, 3.—*Sabæism.* The crime here ordained to be punished by death was sabæism, or the worship of the heavenly bodies. Though this was in some respects the noblest, as it seems to have been the most ancient, form of idolatry—the purest in its ritual, the most elevating in its influence, the least associated with vice, it was not to be tolerated in Israel. Its apparent sublimity made it only the more seductive and dangerous. It was a departure, though at first a very subtle and scarcely recognizable one, from pure monotheism—the beginning of a course of declension which speedily led in Egypt, Phœnicia, Babylonia, India, and most other nations to the grossest abominations. That the seductive influence of sun and star worship was powerfully felt by the ancients appears from Job xxxi. 26, 27. In Egypt, according to M. de Rouge (quoted by Renouf, 'Hibbert Lecture'), "the pure monotheistic religion passed through the phase of sabæism; the sun, instead of being considered as the symbol of life, was taken as the manifestation of God himself." Max Müller tells us ('Hibbert Lecture,' p. 13) that the "oldest prayer in the world" (?) is one in the Rig-Veda, addressed to the sun. The term for God, which is common to the Indo-Germanic races (deva, dæva, theos, deus, etc.), proves that the conception of the Divine among them was formed from that of light, and that the objects of their religious worship were the effects and appearances of light. All ancient mythologies turn, as their principal subject, on the sunrise and sunset, the battle between light and darkness, etc.

We learn: 1. It is the beginnings of evil which need most jealously to be guarded against. 2. Evil is not the less, but the more to be feared, that its first forms are usually pleasing and seductive. 3. It does not excuse evil that in its earlier forms it is still able to associate itself with worthy and noble ideas. 4. The workings of evil, however deceptive its first appearances, invariably end by revealing its true iniquity and hideousness. How astonishing the descent from the first enticing of the heart to worship sun or moon, and so to deny the God that is above, to the abominations and cruelties of Baal and Moloch worship! Yet the later excesses were present in germ from the beginning, and the descent was as natural and logical as history shows it to have been inevitable.—J. O.

Vers. 4—8.—*Criminal procedure.*   I. THE RIGHT OF THE CRIMINAL TO A FAIR AND FULL TRIAL.   The right is asserted in the Law of Moses as strenuously as it could be anywhere.   However abhorrent his crime, the criminal had every protection against unjust treatment which the Law could afford him.   He must be formally impeached, tried before judges, and legally convicted under stringent conditions of proof.   The evidence of one witness, however apparently conclusive, was not to be accepted as sufficient.   A second must confirm it.   The principle is a plain dictate of justice. Suspicion, rumour, dislike of the individual, or even moral certainty of his guilt, form no sufficient ground for condemnation.   He is entitled to demand that his crime be *proved* under legal forms.   A person really guilty may thus occasionally escape, but better this should happen than that the innocent should suffer.   Lessons: 1. The rule of criminal jurisprudence should be the rule of our private thoughts, and of our expressed opinions about others.   We are entitled to hold no man guilty of deeds for which we have not explicit proof.   2. While moral certainty of guilt may be created by proof which would not warrant judicial condemnation, we should beware of admitting as proof that which at the most only *seems* to tell against the person under suspicion.   3. Where no better ground exists for unfavourable judgment than vague, unsifted rumour, or the dislikes and prejudices with which a person is regarded, it is the grossest unfairness, and often great cruelty to the person concerned, to entertain evil reports, or even to allow them in the slightest degree to influence us.   4. Where opportunity for investigating reports to the discredit of another does not exist, or where we have no call to undertake such investigation, our duty is not to judge at all (Matt. vii. 1).   The utmost we should do is to exercise caution.

II. THE GRAVE RESPONSIBILITY WHICH RESTS ON WITNESSES.   This was well brought out by requiring that the hands of the witnesses should be first upon the condemned person to put him to death.   We may note: 1. That those who prefer serious accusations against others, ought to be prepared publicly to substantiate them.   Were this more insisted on than it is, it would quash in the birth not a few malicious accusations. 2. That blood-guiltiness rests on those who, by false testimony, whether borne publicly or in private, effect another's ruin.—J. O.

Vers. 8—13.—*The priest and the judge.*   The priests, in association with a judge or judges (ch. xix. 17), constituted a supreme tribunal to which difficult causes were carried, and whose judgment was to be final.   The priest had naturally a place in this supreme court: 1. As representing God in the theocracy.   2. As a member of the distinctively learned class of the nation.   3. As one whose special office it was to teach and interpret the Law of God (Lev. x. 11; ch. xxxiii. 10; Ezek. xliv. 24; Mal. ii. 7).   The differentiation of functions in society has long since taken learning in the law out of the hands of the clergy, but we may remark—

I. THAT SPIRITUAL AND CIVIL FUNCTIONARIES MAY RENDER EACH OTHER IMPORTANT ASSISTANCE.   The spheres of civil and spiritual jurisdiction are indeed distinct. Yet as the lawyer and judge, with their legal expertness, their knowledge of forms, and their experience in sifting evidence, are often of the greatest service in processes purely ecclesiastical, so, on the other hand, the best of them stand in need of that higher direction and enlightenment of the conscience from God's Word, which it is the business of a body of spiritual teachers to supply.   The ministers of religion have a function: 1. In upholding the Law of God as the supreme standard of right.   2. In furnishing general enlightenment to the conscience.   3. In reminding judges, the highest of them, of their duties and responsibilities before God as set "for the punishment of evildoers, and for the praise of them that do well" (1 Pet. ii. 14).

II. THAT LAWS BASED ON GOD'S WORD HAVE ATTACHING TO THEM A DIVINE AS WELL AS A HUMAN AUTHORITY.   The duty of the priest was not to invent laws, but to interpret the existing Law of God.   To it all cases of right had ultimately to be appealed.   God's Law, as exhibiting the unalterable principles of right, underlies human law and gives to it authority.   Whatever may happen in courts on earth, no decision will stand in the court of heaven which that Law is found to condemn.   Laws *e.g.* which invade rights of conscience, which (as in slave-holding countries) place the life of one man at the mercy of another, which are favourable to illicit relations of the sexes, which make light of divorce, which bear unequally on different classes of the community, which prop up abuses, etc., may be submitted to, but cannot be justified. Where, on the contrary, the law of a land is in essential harmony with the principles of righteousness, obedience to it becomes a duty of religion. He who sets it at nought strives with God not less than with man, is "as they which strive with the priest," and does "presumptuously" (cf. Hos. iv. 4).—J. O.

Vers. 14—20.—*The king in Israel.* We have here—

I. THE DESIRE OF A KING ANTICIPATED. (Ver. 14.) Moses anticipates that, when settled in the land, the people would desire a king, that they might be like other nations. This was: 1. A desire *springing from a wrong motive.* (1) As involving a low estimate of their privilege in being ruled directly by Jehovah. It was the glory and distinction of their nation that they had God so nigh them, and were under his immediate care and sovereignty. But they could not rise to the sublimity of this thought. They deemed it a grander thing to have a mortal as their king, to be like other nations, and be led, judged, and ruled by a visible monarch. Their demand was a substantial rejection of God, that he should not reign over them (1 Sam. viii. 7). (2) As involving the idea of a king modelled on the pattern of the kings around them. The king they wished for was one who would embody for them their own ideas of splendour and prowess, and these were of a purely carnal type. Saul, their first king, had many of the qualities which answered to *their* notion of a king, while David, ruling in humble subordination to the will and authority of Heaven, answered to the *Divine* idea. Piety and submission at every point to the will of God are not elements that bulk largely in the common conception of a monarch. (3) As involving self-willedness. The people did not humbly present their case to God, and entreat him for a king. They took the law into their own hands, and demanded one, or rather they declared their intention of setting one over them, irrespective of whether God wished it or not. 2. A desire *in some respects natural.* The spiritual government of an invisible Ruler was an idea difficult to grasp. The mind craved for some concrete and visible embodiment of that authority under which they lived. It probably lay in God's purpose ultimately to give them a king, but it was necessary that they should be made first distinctly to feel their need of it. The need in human nature to which this points is adequately supplied in the Messianic King, Christ Jesus. The central idea of the Kingship of Christ is the personal indwelling of the Divine in the human. In Christ, moreover, is realized the three things which ancient nations sought for in their kings. (1) An ideal of personal excellence. "Heroic kingship depended partly on divinely given prerogative, and partly on the possession of supereminent strength, courage, and wisdom" (Maine). (2) A leader inspiring them with personal devotion. (3) A bond of unity in the State, the monarch representing, as he does still, the whole system of law and authority which is centralized and embodied in his person. "The king is the dot on the *i*" (Hegel). The kingship in Israel typified that of Christ.

II. THE ELECTION OF A KING PROVIDED FOR. (Ver. 15.) The position of king in Israel was essentially different from that of the monarch of any other nation. While discharging the same general functions as other kings (ruling, judging, leading in battle), his authority was checked and limited in ways that theirs was not. He was no irresponsible despot, whose will was law and who governed as he listed. He filled the throne, not as absolute and independent sovereign, but only as the deputy of Jehovah, and ruled simply in the name and in subordination to the will of God—in this respect affording another marked type of God's true king, whom he has set on his holy hill of Zion (Ps. ii.). This fact gave rise to a second peculiarity, that he had no authority to make laws, but only to administer the Law already given. The manner of his election corresponded to these peculiarities of his position. 1. He was chosen under Divine guidance (cf. 1 Sam. x. 20, 21). 2. The Divine choice was ratified by the free election of the people (1 Sam. x. 24). From which we learn (1) that the throne is strong only when it rests on the free choice, and on the loyal affection of the body of the people. (2) That kingly, like all other authority, is derived from God. This is a truth of general application, though it was in a peculiar sense true of Israel. The Scripture gives no sanction to the "right Divine of kings to govern wrong." But popular sentiment has always recognized that a certain "divinity doth hedge a king." Ancient nations (Egypt, etc.) held him to be the representative of God on earth. The state and style with which a monarch is surrounded, and the homage paid to him, are expressions of the same idea. He embodies the functions of government, and has honour, majesty, and high-sounding titles bestowed on him on that ground. But this is simply to say that in certain respects he represents Deity. To constitute perfect " Divine right," it would be necessary : (*a*) That a monarch should occupy the throne with perfect Divine sanction. Most rulers, on ascending the throne, try to make out, however weakly, some shadow of right to it. (*b*) That he should govern in perfect accordance with the Divine will. The only perfect case of ruling by Divine right is the reign of Christ.

III. THE CHARACTER OF THE KING DELINEATED. (Vers. 15—20.) He was to be an Israelite—one of themselves. Then: 1. He was *not to multiply horses to himself;* that is : (1) He was not to be ambitious of military distinction. (2) He was not to place his main reliance for the defence of the nation on extravagant military preparations. (3) He was not, for the sake of supposed material advantage, to lead the people into ensnaring alliances. 2. He was *not to multiply wives to himself.* That is : (1) He was to avoid enervating luxury. (2) His court was to be chaste and pure. Cf. Tennyson, 'To the Queen:' "Her court was pure; her life serene," etc.; and ' Dedication' to the Idyls—

> " Who reverenced his conscience as his king ;
> Whose glory was, redressing human wrong ;
> Who spake no slander, no, nor listened to it ;
> *Who loved one only*, and who clave to her," etc.

3. He was *not to multiply to himself silver and gold ;* that is, he was not to affect the dazzle of imperial splendour, but to be simple and unostentatious in his manner of life. But : 4. He *was to be a diligent student of the Word of God.* (1) He was to write out with his own hand a copy of the Law. (2) He was to read in it diligently all the days of his life ; the result of which would be : (*a*) That he would be kept in the way of obedience; (*b*) that his heart would be preserved humble towards God and his brethren ; and (*c*) he and his seed would enjoy prosperity on the throne. What a noble sketch of the model king, yet how contrary to current ideas of royal greatness ! We have happily been taught in our own country to appreciate the advantages of a pure court, and to feel its wholesome influence on the general tone of morals, and we are able to understand, also, the beneficial effect of uprightness and piety in a sovereign in adding to the love, esteem, and reverence with which the sovereign is regarded ; but how far are we from dissociating the greatness of a reign from its external splendour, its military conquests, the wealth and luxury of its aristocracy, the figure it displays in the eyes of other nations, and the terror with which it can inspire them ! Nor do we look in sovereigns generally for all the virtues which we find in our own, but are apt to condone want of piety, and even acts of great iniquity, if they but prove themselves to be bold, energetic, and enterprising rulers. The character of the sovereign is in some respects of less moment than it once was, but its influence for good or evil is still very great, and the evil fruits reaped from the court life, say of a Charles II. or a George IV., are not exhausted in one or a few generations. Piety upon the throne will lead to piety in the court and throughout the nation, and will give an impulse to everything else that is good. Whereas an evil and corrupting example sows seeds of mischief, which may involve the nation in the greatest losses and disasters (see Massillon's sermon, ' Des Exemples des Grands ').—J. O.

Vers. 1—7.—*Idolatry a capital crime.* The closing verses of last chapter prohibiting groves near God's altar may be taken in connection with the verses now before us as constituting the solemn prohibition of idolatry. God will not have any rival, either sun, moon, or any of the host of heaven, not to speak of the more miserable idolatries of things on earth ; he makes idolatry a capital crime, and decrees death as its penalty. This brings out the enormity of the sin in the eyes of God; and it does not follow, because idolatry is not still visited with death, that it has become a lighter matter in the eyes of " the Judge of all the earth."

I. THE TEMPTATION TO NATURE-WORSHIP. When men are not watchful, they live by sight and forget the life of faith. Others make the senses the only organs of know-ledge, and base their so-called philosophy upon sensation. It is not to be wondered at, in such circumstances, that nature-worship prevailed in olden times and prevails still. A great deal of the antitheistic science of the present time is, when analyzed, just nature-worship. When men in their headstrong self-confidence attribute independent powers to nature; when they maintain—on what grounds they do not tell us, for it is a matter of *faith*, not of sight—that the "reign of law" is workable without God, then they are really *idolizing* nature. It seems a light thing to men to eliminate God from his works, but the sin will have to be answered for before the Judge.

Besides, it was more excusable in the old Israelite than in the modern philosopher. The heavenly bodies in these Eastern countries are so magnificent that the impression produced upon the gazer is akin to worship. It was little wonder if in an unwatchful moment he "beheld the sun when it shined, or the moon walking in brightness; and the heart was secretly enticed, or his mouth kissed his hand" (Job xxxi. 26, 27). The temptation to worship the heavenly bodies was strong and natural.

II. IN GOD'S SIGHT THE WORSHIP OF NATURE IS A CAPITAL CRIME. It is worthy of a violent death. Directions are given for the solemn execution. The witnesses, of whom there must be a plurality at least, are first to lay their hands upon the head of the idolater, then the whole people, doubtless through their representative elders, showing their acquiescence in the severe sentence; and then he is to be stoned to death. The idea is manifestly that he is unworthy of living longer when he has so far forgotten and ignored the claims of God.

And assuredly our scientific nature-worshippers are equally guilty, nay, more guilty, in God's sight. If they are not put to death by public law, it is not because their sin is changed in its heinousness, but because God has made their case a reserved one for himself. "Vengeance is mine; I will repay, saith the Lord."

III. IN THESE CIRCUMSTANCES WE ARE LEFT ONE WAY OF GETTING RID OF THE EVIL, AND THAT IS BY GOOD. God having withdrawn the prerogative of vengeance from men for sins against himself, and reserved the case for his own dealing with it, he has given us our direction in the words, "Be not overcome of evil, but overcome evil with good" (Rom. xii. 21). The Israelites in their rude time were directed to remove the idolater by *force;* we are to get rid of him by loving persuasion. The former was the easier remedy. To heap coals of fire on the head of our opponent and enemy is not so easy an operation. But it can be done. God shows us the example himself. While reserv-ing the prerogative of vengeance, he meanwhile manifests himself in Jesus Christ as the God of love. Though provoked by man's idolatries, he subjects him to the treat-ment of his love, and goes forth in converting power to meet his enemies. Of course the love is sometimes lost upon them, as we are accustomed to say. The appeal is rejected, but they have got the opportunity, and must account at last for despising it.

In his loving footsteps let us follow. The nature-worship and manifold idolatries are amenable to the treatment of enlightened love. Let us study candidly and care-fully the case, and administer with all tenderness the remedy. It may be that in some cases the old picture may be reversed. Instead of the imposition of hands in order to destruction, it may be an imposition of hands in ordaining to Divine work those who formerly ignored God altogether. However this may be, our duty is clear to try to overcome this particular evil by good.—R. M. E.

Vers. 8—13.—*The ruling power of the priests in the Jewish Church.* The govern-ment among the Israelites was first by an eldership elected on the representative principle. Thus in Gen. l. 7 we find at the funeral of Jacob "all the elders of the land of Egypt." Again, when Moses came from Midian to emancipate his brethren, he was directed to consult "the elders of Israel," who were to go in with him before Pharaoh (Exod. iii. 16, 18). After the Exodus, the priests were appointed as the ministers of religion; and with these were associated the elders selected to the number of seventy from those already in office, and to whom God gave his Spirit (Numb. xi. 16, etc.). When the people settled in Canaan, they were directed to elect judges for judgment. This was the distribution and development of the eldership. And in case of any special difficulty, the aggrieved parties were to repair to the place of the central altar, and there lay the matter before the priests and the judge. It follows that the priests had co-ordinate ruling power with the elders or judges, that they were *rulers* and officiating ministers besides. And here we have to notice—

I. THESE CHURCH OFFICERS EXERCISED THEIR AUTHORITY UNDER GOD AS KING. The Church was a theocracy, and God was regarded as ever present with his officers and people. The same is true in the Church still. It is a theocracy; an ever-present Jesus still presides even where two or three are met together for the purposes of Church government (Matt. xviii. 20).

II. THE PRIESTS AND THE JUDGE ARE TO SHOW THE PARTIES THE DIVINE LAW ON THE SUBJECT. The decision is to be expository of existing law, not a decision on the ground of expediency. Now this necessarily follows from the Kingship of God. His will must be paramount. His officers simply try to find out his will. A national parliament may manufacture laws; but Church officers take their laws from the inspired Statute-book. It is exposition of Divine Law that the ruler in God's Church is really concerned with.

III. THE CHURCH OFFICERS REQUIRED IMPLICIT OBEDIENCE FROM THE PEOPLE TO THEIR INTERPRETATION OF GOD'S WILL. In a rude age this was needful, implicit obedience such as we require from children. But when we reach the corresponding part of the New Testament economy, the exhortation is, " Prove all things, hold fast that which is good " (1 Thess. v. 21). The right of private judgment is admitted, and regulates the obedience. Just as when children grow to manhood, the implicit obedience demanded gives place to persuasion and the appeal to conscience.

IV. PRESUMPTUOUS DISREGARD OF GOD'S WILL EXPRESSED BY THE PRIEST AND JUDGE WAS PUNISHED WITH DEATH. This was disobedience in its generic form, and came under the penalty of death, just as in Eden. The aggrieved parties had appealed for light to God's officer; he was to be their Arbitrator, and they contracted to abide by his decision. Disobedience under such circumstances would overthrow the order both of Church and State. Hence the death penalty.

Presumptuous disregard of Divine commandments is not now less heinous than it was then, though it may escape for the time being such a terrible penalty. The judgment of God is only postponed. Should the presumption continue, the penalty will come at last with compound interest.

V. THE PATIENT STUDY OF GOD'S WORD IS SURELY A DUTY WHEN PRESUMPTUOUS DISREGARD OF GOD'S WILL IS SO HEINOUS A SIN. It should be our supreme desire to know what God would have us to do. This can only be known through systematic and patient study of the holy oracles. The priest with the Urim and Thummim is not now available. We must content ourselves with a quieter way. The Book is given instead of the oracle, and we are directed to consult it for ourselves. Approaching it in a patient, obedient spirit, we shall find it unlocking many a mystery to us, and affording us the light we need.—R. M. E.

Vers. 14—20.—*The limitations of monarchy.* We have here provision made for the probable demand of the people for a *visible* king like the other nations. The *unseen* King did not make the same sensation in their view, and hence Moses is inspired to anticipate the unbelieving demand. And here notice—

I. THE UNSEEN KING MUST HAVE THE SELECTION OF THE VISIBLE ONE. It is in this way that the monarchy, when it came, was kept under the control of God. The theocracy was still the fountain head of power. The people were not to choose their king. He was to have *Divine right.*

It is noticeable that, in giving them Saul, the Lord made emphatic the *sensationalism* that lay under the demand, for the visible king was head and shoulders above his brethren. David was also a big man, else Saul would never have offered him his armour, when proposing to fight the giant. And it is noticeable how the sensationalism is rebuked in the enemies of Israel producing Goliath as a champion, before whom it is evident that the big Saul feared and quaked.

II. THEY ARE NOT TO EXPECT OR TO THINK OF A STRANGER KING. Thus the patriotism of the people is fostered. It is one of themselves that is to have the kingship when it comes. It is interesting to notice this deliverance after the reservation already noticed. God's choice is thus guaranteed to Israel. He will stand to the nation, if the nation will be faithful to him.

III. THE KING IS NOT TO RELY UPON THE CAVALRY ARM. Palestine, being mountainous, did not require cavalry. Infantry would be more effective. Cavalry, if raised and relied on, would necessitate an alliance with a cattle-breeding country like Egypt, and would be the precursor of a "spirited foreign policy," such as proves ruinous to a pastoral people such as Israel was meant to be. There was thus a wise restraint laid upon the foreign policy of the nation; as God desired their separation from surrounding nations, and their religious stability upon the mountain ridges of Palestine, he warns them against this danger. Besides, the cavalry arm until recently was the most powerful in the service, and the charge of cavalry is something to be proud of or to fear. Now, of course, artillery has put cavalry out of its vaunted position. The temptation was to "trust in horses and in chariots," and not in the Lord. Hence the warning.

IV. THE KING IS NOT TO HAVE A SERAGLIO. For through the wives he will surely be unmanned and have his heart turned away from God. It is the *spiritual* disasters of polygamy which are here insisted upon. A divided heart socially must entail a divided heart spiritually. No wonder the Psalmist prayed, "Unite my heart to fear thy Name."

V. NOR IS THE KING TO AIM AT GREAT RICHES. For wealth is a great snare, and it competes with God for the heart. Money, like cavalry, is a most natural foundation of trust. A too wealthy monarch is likely to be worldly minded and unspiritual.

VI. THE KING IS TO MAKE A SPECIAL STUDY OF THE DIVINE LAW. He is to get a copy for himself—he is to have it daily read to him—and he is to allow its humiliating influence to be exercised over him so as to be obedient always. And if obedient, he is promised an hereditary interest in the throne. He was thus to be kept in subjection to the unseen King.

And though *we* may not aspire to kingships, we can profit by the warnings here prophetically addressed to the coming kings of Israel. For it is surely for us to *allow nothing seen and temporal to threaten our faith in God.* It may not be horses and chariots; it may not be money; it may be men in whom we are tempted to trust. Whatever it be, whether persons or things, that tempts us from our trust in God, it must be avoided. Better is it to be friendless, to be poor, to be solitary, than to be sceptical. Wordly success is where scepticism is born. The idols multiply as wealth and luxuries increase. There is something, we think, to hold by in the strain of life.

And whatever our position in this world, let us feel always not only our trust in God, but our subordination in all things to him. If he is King of kings, he is certainly Lord over us. Let us live under the theocracy, and serve him with our whole hearts.—R. M. E.

Ver. 1.—*The prevention of religious fraud.* Men who pride themselves on honesty towards their fellows are often dishonest in dealing with God. They are punctual in observing appointments with men; they are unpunctual in reaching the house of God. When the principle of piety in a man is weakened, he will stoop to many artifices to deprive God of his due.

I. AN IMPERFECT SACRIFICE SPRINGS FROM BLIND PARSIMONY. When piety declines, a man becomes the slave of his senses. He is moved or terrified only by what is visible. He is afraid of a human frown; he is impervious to the Divine displeasure. The lamb which is unfit for barter, and which is scarce fit for food, will be deemed good enough for sacrifice. Yet how mentally blind is the man! What thick scales he has manufactured for his eyes! Yet, "he that formed the eye, shall he not see?" And cannot God, with a breath, blast that man's prosperity, and cage his soul in bondage? He had thought to snatch from God a dollar, and lo! he loses everything!

II. AN IMPERFECT SACRIFICE VITIATES ITS SYMBOLIC EFFICACY. These animal sacrifices had many moral uses. They developed the sentiment of gratitude for gifts bestowed. They expressed the penitence of the offerer, who thereby confessed that for his sins he had deserved to die. And inasmuch as a lamb or a heifer was immeasurably inferior to man, the sacrifice betokened the offering of a better Sacrifice, which should be a real atonement. Now, if men were permitted to bring a blemished victim, it would no longer prefigure him who is the "Lamb without blemish and without spot." In such a case, the faith of the offerer was dead.

III. Such religious fraud was incipient atheism. Here was the budding of blackest sin—the first step on a slippery decline, which would land one in death. If I can set aside God's plain commands, as my selfishness desires; if I can treat God as my equal or my inferior, and devote to him only what is useless for myself;—I am on the very borders of utter atheism, and to-morrow shall be ready to say, "There is no God." Rankest unbelief often springs from practical disobedience. There is no neglect of God without self-injury.—D.

Vers. 2—7.—*Idolatry a crime against society.* Whether the fact be obvious to all men or not, *it is* fact that sin against God is also sin against human society. The relation of the Hebrew nation to God, is a type of the relation which God sustains to every nation. He is the Creator of individual life and of individual endowments. He is the Source of all the moral forces which bind men together in civil society. He has appointed to each nation its habitation, and has enriched it with more or less of material good. Hence every nation is under obligation to acknowledge and honour the one creating and reigning God.

I. The crime. The crime consisted in esteeming the creature above the Creator. This was a direct breach of treaty between God and the nation. On God's side the engagement was to bring them into the land of Canaan, and secure them against foes. On Israel's side the engagement was to worship no other Deity but Jehovah. Hence the violation of a covenant so openly made and frequently ratified was a flagrant sin. Yet with every nation such a covenant is made *by implication.* If life is obtained from the invisible God, it is held on conditions imposed by him, and every item of conduct which is contrary to his known will is an act of rebellion. If rebellion against an earthly king is counted highest crime, incomparably greater is a deed of open rebellion against the King of kings. Idolatry is the root-stem of grossest immorality.

II. The detection and proof of this crime. In proportion to the greatness of the crime must be the carefulness of investigation. No punishment is to be inflicted on the ground of suspicion or prejudice. Human life is to be accounted precious, but the interests of righteousness are more precious still. On both these grounds, the scrutiny must be *thorough.* To prevent any injury to the sacred cause of justice, through error, or incompetence, or malice, one witness must be incompetent to obtain a verdict. Security against injustice comes from corroborated testimony and from independent witnesses. While every man is bound, in his sphere, to think and act righteously towards his neighbours, he must safeguard himself against hasty judgments and against the whispers of slanderers. In many positions in life we are called to act in the place of God.

III. The punishment decreed. It was death by stoning. In that early age, and especially in the desert, there were no mechanical contrivances for suddenly extinguishing life. They were largely the children of nature, and possessed but few inventions of civilized life. The sagacity of Supreme Wisdom had placed frail man among natural forces, which might easily be employed in terminating bodily life. This arrangement impresses men with a sense of dependence. His bodily life succumbs to a stone. The unit must be sacrificed to the well-being of the community. "No man lives for himself."

IV. The instruments of the execution. The chief witness against an offender, became, by God's appointment, executor of the judicial sentence. This secured economy in the administration of law. It secured, to a large extent, veracity among witnesses, and moral certainty of the rightness of the verdict. Yet, that obloquy might not attach itself to one man alone, the whole community were charged to take part in the execution of the sentence. The deed would thus be the common deed of all. This practice would foster oneness of sentiment, oneness of purpose, and would promote harmonious national life.—D.

Vers. 8—13.—*High court of appeal.* We can imagine a condition of human society in which wrong-doing would at once declare itself by some visible pain or sign. We can imagine a condition of society in which God would himself step forth and punish every offence against truth or virtue. But then, men would lose the benefits of moral training which the present system ensures. This necessity for men to take part in the administration of justice brings large advantage.

I. HUMAN INTERESTS OFTEN BECOME VERY COMPLICATED. The interests men have in property, liberty, reputation, often become very involved. This arises largely from the operation of *selfishness*. Every item which will add to a man's self-importance he will sue for by every process of law. This comes from the neglect of the comprehensive precept, "Thou shalt love thy neighbour as thyself." Another great difficulty in the administration of justice arises from men's untruthfulness. The day will dawn when a stigma of shame will brand the man who withholds or violates the truth. If now, in every judicial inquiry, the whole truth, pure and simple, were forthcoming, decision and verdict would be a simple result.

II. THE MOST HOLY WILL BE, CÆTERIS PARIBUS, THE MOST SAGACIOUS. The man who lives nearest to God will obtain the most of God's wisdom. He will be free from base and selfish motive. He will be the most trusted by his fellows. He will have fullest access to God when intricate questions have to be solved. "If any man lack wisdom, let him ask of God." "Unto the upright there ariseth light in the darkness." But pretended piety will serve no practical good.

III. EVERY JUDGE AMONG MEN ACTS SPECIALLY IN THE STEAD OF GOD. To be the administrator of justice, to adjudicate between right and wrong, is the highest office which men can fill. No position is more responsible ; none more honourable. For all practical purposes, *his* decision must be regarded as the decision of God. Otherwise, there will be no termination to litigation and strife. From the verdict of the highest human judge, there is but one court of appeal, viz. the court of heaven. Without doubt, many judicial decisions on earth will be reversed by the Great Judge of all. This is sweet solace to the injured now. Yet it is nobler to suffer wrong at the hands of men than to resist by violence. For the present, we are to accept the sentence of the judge as absolute and obligatory. Our feet must diverge neither to the right hand nor to the left.

IV. CONTUMACY IS CRIME, PUNISHABLE BY DEATH. To despise the verdict of the judge is to weaken the authority of the State—is to sow the seeds of anarchy and ruin. Defective administration of law is better than none. "Rebellion is as the sin of witchcraft, and stubbornness is as idolatry." Yet, if contempt of human authority be accounted a capital crime, how much more criminal must be contumacy against God!

V. CAPITAL PUNISHMENT HAS FOR ITS END THE GOOD OF THE COMMUNITY. It is an advantage to remove from the circle of human society a pest—a firebrand. The authority of law, the sacredness of justice, are set on high in flaming characters, and on all classes of the community the impression is salutary. Reverence for constituted authority is strengthened, and unbiased minds learn the heinous wickedness of disobedience. The effect is virtue, order, peace.—D.

Vers. 14—20.—*Limitations round about a king.* A king is the creation of a nation's will. The nation does not exist for the king, but the king exists for the nation. His proper aim is not personal glory, but the widest public good.

I. KINGS ARE THE PRODUCT OF A DEGENERATE AGE. Since the King of heaven is willing to give his counsel and aid to men, it is for our honour and advantage to live under the direct administration of God; and it is only when piety and faith decline that men clamour for a human king. The conquests of Canaan by Israel had been most complete when Israel most carefully followed the commands of God. To sensitive minds, it would have been a dagger-thrust to imitate the practices of the degenerate heathen.

II. DIVINE LIMITATIONS ABOUT THE CHOICE OF A KING. In condescension to human infirmity, God will allow the elevation of a man to the throne. Through our own caprices, God ofttimes punishes us. Yet God kindly sets barriers about our capricious wills. For martial purposes, foolish men would often choose a stalwart giant, some Goliath, to be their king, though he be of foreign birth ; or some successful warrior to lead them forth to battle. This is prohibited. The nation is to be self-contained. All the elements of prosperity may be found within its own borders. The will of God must be respected. God himself will select the man, point him out by unmistakable methods, and the nation can do no more than gratefully accept God's wise decision. *He* will choose ; *they* must anoint.

III. DIVINE LIMITATIONS ABOUT THE CONDUCT OF A KING. To him does not belong the privilege to gratify every taste and temper. The very contrary. He is under greater obligations than any other man to restrain himself. Temptation will surround him on every side ; but he must meet temptation with vigilance, patience, firmness. To be a true king, he must first conquer himself. He must restrain carnal ambition. He must restrain love of display. He must restrain the passion for conquest. He must restrain sensual pleasure. He must restrain his avarice. His real distinction is not to have many horses, many wives, or great riches. His distinction is to be wise administrator of righteousness, the protector of public liberty and peace. To fulfil faithfully the functions of a king, he must walk circumspectly in the narrow way—be a loyal subject to the King of heaven.

IV. LIMITATIONS ABOUT THE PRIVATE LIFE OF A KING. His first concern must be respecting his personal fitness for such responsible office. No pains must he spare to obtain complete equipment. He must count no labour severe or menial by which he may qualify himself for kingly duties. His first duty is to obtain completest acquaintance with the will of God. To this end he must possess a copy of God's written Law, and in this Law he must meditate day and night. The spirit of this Law must animate his being and breathe in all his speech. God's Word must be his *vade mecum*, his daily compass and chart. He must move among his courtiers and governors as a visible embodiment of truth and purity, a living transcript of the Divine will. This is a true pattern of a king—a man who excels in wisdom, having learnt of God ; a man who is eminent for pious obedience, and writes in largest characters the model of a noble life. Such a man shall live. "Though he die, his influence and rule shall live."—D.

EXPOSITION.

CHAPTER XVIII.

RIGHTS OF THE PRIESTS AND THE LEVITES. THE ARTS OF DIVINATION OF THE HEATHEN TO BE AVOIDED. PROPHETS PROMISED WHOM ISRAEL MUST HEAR. THE FALSE AND PRESUMPTUOUS PROPHET TO BE PUT TO DEATH.

Vers. 1—8.—After the ruling powers, the judges and the king, come the priests and the Levites. In regard to them Moses repeats here the law as before laid down (cf. Numb. xviii. 20, 23, 24).

Ver. 1.—**The priests the Levites, the whole tribe of Levi**; *i.e.* the whole tribe of Levi, including both the priests and the general body of the Levites. **They shall eat the offerings of the Lord made by fire.** "The offerings of the Lord made by fire" (literally, *the fires* or *firings of Jehovah*, here referred to, were the meal offering, the sin offering, and the trespass offering (cf. Numb. xviii. 9). **And his inheritance**; *i.e.* of Jehovah, what was appropriated to him, and from him to the tribe of Levi, such as tithes, firstlings, and firstfruits.

Vers. 2, 3.—**As he hath said unto them** (cf. Numb. xviii. 20). **The shoulder, and the two cheeks, and the maw**; *i.e.* the front leg, the two jaw-bones, and the rough stomach of ruminants, in which the digestion is completed. These were regarded as the choice parts of the animal, and were to be given to the priests in addition to the wave breast and heave leg of the peace offerings (Lev. vii. 32, etc.; Numb. xviii. 11), which belonged to the firings of Jehovah, mentioned in ver. 1. To these the priest had a rightful claim ; they were his due (מִשְׁפָּט, *mishpat*, right). "This right was probably accorded to the priests as a compensation for the falling off which would take place in their incomes in consequence of the repeal of the law that every animal was to be slaughtered at the sanctuary as a sacrifice (Lev. xvii.; *vide* ch. xii. 15, *sqq.*)" (Keil). According to Josephus ('Antiq,' iv. 4, 4), Philo ('De Præmiis. Sacerdot.,' p. 832, Opp., tom. ii. p. 235, edit. Mangey), the Talmud, etc., this injunction relates to the slaying of animals at home for private use, and not such as were killed for sacrifice. But the use here of the sacrificial phraseology, **who offer a sacrifice** (זֹבְחֵי הַזֶּבַח, who slay victims for sacrifice—a phrase nowhere found except in connection with sacrificial rites) is adverse to this; and besides, how could such an enactment be carried out ? how could people, residing at a distance, convey to the priests the portions due to them every time they slaughtered an animal for domestic use? At the same time, the sacrifices here referred to do not seem to be included in the offerings by fire above mentioned; and these gifts to the priest seem to have been something over and above his ordinary dues. There is probability, therefore, in the suggestion that "the reference is to the slaughtering of oxen, sheep, or goats, which were not intended for *shelamim* in the more limited sense, *i.e.* for one of the three species of peace offerings (Lev. vii. 15, 16), but for festal meals in the broader sense, which were held in connection with the sacrificial meals prepared from the *shelamim*" (Keil).

Ver. 4.—In addition to the firstfruits already prescribed by the Law to be given to the priests (Numb. xviii. 12, 13), Moses here enacts that the first fleece of the sheep shall be given. All these, though legally prescribed, were free gifts on the part of the people; the neglect of the prescription incurred only moral blame, not judicial penalty.

Ver. 5.—The reason assigned for the enactment is that God had chosen the priest to stand and minister in the Name of Jehovah, *i.e.* not only by his appointment and authority, but with full power to act as mediator between the people and God. Him and his sons for ever; referring to the establishment of the priesthood in the family of Aaron.

Vers. 6—8.—Only a portion of the Levites were engaged in the service of the sanctuary; the rest lived in their towns throughout the country. It might happen, however, that a Levite, moved by pious feeling, would come to the place of the sanctuary to worship there; and it is prescribed that such a one should fare as his brethren the Levites engaged in the service of the sanctuary fared; he should minister along with them, and share with them in the gifts of the worshippers; and this in addition to any private means he might have from the sale of his patrimony. Where he sojourned. The Levite, though not homeless, was regarded as only a sojourner in the land, inasmuch as the tribe had no inheritance (נַחֲלָה) there. They shall have like portions to eat; literally, *they shall eat portion as portion,* i.e. share and share alike. That which cometh of the sale of his patrimony; literally, *his price upon* [the house] *of* [his] *fathers,* i.e. the produce of the sale effected on the house he inherited from his ancestry (cf. Lev. xxv. 33).

Vers. 9—22.—Moses was not only the leader and ruler of the people, he was also the medium through which God communicated with the people, gave them his laws,

and conveyed to them his word and will. In this respect his place could be supplied neither by priest nor by king. In the prospect of his demise, therefore, there required to be instituted another office, that of a prophet, one who should be between God and the people, as the channel through which Divine communications might pass to them. This office Moses here announces that God would establish among them when they had entered the promised land.

Ver. 9.—The abominations of those nations; *i.e.* certain forms of superstitious usage by which the heathen sought to procure the favour of their deities, to obtain from them direction and counsel, and to penetrate into the hidden future of events. Moses charges the people to avoid all such usages, and not even to learn to do after such abominations (cf. Lev. xviii. 21; Numb. xxiii. 23; Lev. xix. 26, 31).

Vers. 10, 11.—Maketh his son or daughter to pass through the fire (see note on ch. xii. 31). That useth divination (cf. Ezek. xxi. 21, where the different methods of divination are enumerated). An observer of times. This is according to the Targum, *observans horas*; the LXX. have κληδονιζόμενος, "one who augurs what is to happen;" Vulgate, *qui observat somnia atque auguria.* The word (מְעוֹנֵן) is part of a verb which signifies to cover, to use covert arts, to practise sorcery; though some derive it from the noun עָנָן, a thick cloud, and explain it as "interpreter of clouds;" while others trace it to עַיִן, the eye, and explain it as "one who cheats by optical fascinations" (so the Syriac, *fascinans oculis*), or "one who divines by inspection—an augur." An enchanter; one who practises magic, or divines by signs (cf. Gen. xliv. 5; Numb. xxiv. 1). It is sometimes said that the verb of which this word is a part (נָחַשׁ) is a denominative from נָחָשׁ, a serpent; whence it is inferred that the species of divination indicated by this word is *ophiomancy,* or divination by serpents, but this is not generally accepted by scholars. A witch (מְכַשֵּׁף; LXX., φαρμακός: Vulgate, *maleficus*); probably one who pretended to cure diseases, or procure some desired result, by means of nostrums and philtres. In the enumeration of the wise men of Babylon (Dan. ii. 2), the Mecashephim have a place beside the Hartummim, and in Gen. xli. 8 and Exod. vii. 11, they are joined with the Hachamim or Magi of Egypt; and this favours the conclusion that their sorcery had a quasi-scientific basis. The English word "witch" is now not restricted to the *female* practiser of unlawful arts; formerly it was applied to *males* as well, if not chiefly (Trench, 'Select Glossary,' p. 306). **A charmer** (חֹבֵר חָבֶר); a dealer in spells, one who by means of spells or charms pretends to achieve some desired result. The verb here used primarily means to bind, and the species of magic indicated is probably that practised by binding certain knots, whereby it was supposed that the curse or blessing, as the case might be, was bound on its object; this was accompanied apparently with incantation (Ps. lviii. 5). Comp. English *spell-bound*, and the phrase, "to rivet charms" (Jonson, 'Sad Shepherd,' ii. 2). A species of incantation known to the Romans consisted in tying knots with threads of different colours, three in number, which were supposed to become a *bond* to secure an object (cf. Virg., 'Eclog.' viii. 76, 77). **A consulter with familiar spirits.** This phrase conveys something different from what is expressed, in the Hebrew. שֹׁאֵל אוֹב is one who asks or inquires of an Ob, that is, a Python, or divining spirit. This spirit was supposed to be in the person of the conjurer, and to be able to reveal to him what was secret or hidden in the future (Lev. xx. 27; 1 Sam. xxviii. 7, 8; Acts xvi. 16). The notion of "a familiar spirit," *i.e.* a spirit not dwelling in the person, but with which he is intimate—generally the spirit of one who formerly lived on earth—is a modern notion not known to Scripture. The persons here referred to were probably ventriloquists (LXX., ἐγγαστρίμυθοι), and used their faculty in this respect for purposes of magic, pretending that they had within them a spirit which they could consult, and by which they could predict what would happen or reveal what was hid. **Wizard.** The English word "wizard" did not originally convey the idea of anything evil in the person of whom it was used; Milton applies it to the Magi who came to worship at Bethlehem ('Ode on the Nativity,' iv.); it meant merely "the wise one," or "the knowing one;" and thus is an exact equivalent for the Hebrew word here used (יִדְּעֹנִי, knowing, wise, from יָדַע, to know). **A necromancer**; one who professed to call up the dead, and from them to learn the secrets of futurity (cf. 1 Sam. xxviii. 7). (See on all these names the learned and copious dissertation of Dr. Holmes, art. 'Divination,' in Kitto's 'Bibl. Cyclop.,' 3rd. edit., i. 682.)

Ver. 12.—**All who practised such arts were an abomination unto the Lord,** and his people are forbidden to have anything to do with them. They are connected here with the Moloch-worship, because of the intimate relation between idolatry and the use of magical arts; and Moloch-worship is specially mentioned, probably because it was the form of idolatry with which the Israelites were most likely to come in contact, both where they then were and also in Canaan; not, as Keil suggests, because that form "was more intimately connected with soothsaying and magic than any other description of idolatry"—an assertion for which there is no evidence.

Ver. 13.—**Thou shalt be perfect with the Lord thy God.** The word translated "perfect" properly means *entire, whole,* answering to the Latin *integer;* it is used only in a moral sense, and is best rendered by "upright;" the Israelites were to be upright and sincere with, *i.e.* in relation with, Jehovah their God.

Ver. 14.—Though the heathen whose land they were to possess sought to diviners and enchanters, Israel was not to do so; as for them (the אַתָּה at the beginning of the clause is an emphatic nominative), Jehovah their God had not suffered (נָתַן, given, granted, allowed) them to do such things.

Vers. 15—22.—There should be no need for Israel to turn to heathen soothsayers, or diviners, or such like, because from amongst themselves, of their own brethren, would God raise up prophets like unto Moses, who, as occasion required, would reveal to them what God willed them to know.

Ver. 15.—**A Prophet.** The Hebrew word so rendered (נָבִיא) is a derivative from a verb (נָבָא), which signifies to tell, to announce; hence the primary concept of the word is that of announcer, or forth-speaker; and to this the word "prophet" (Greek προφήτης, from πρόφημι, I speak before or in place of) closely corresponds; the prophet is one who speaks in the place of God, who conveys God's word to men, who is an interpreter of God to men. (As illustrative of the meaning of the word, cf. Exod. vii. 1; iv. 16.) Hence Abraham is called a prophet (Gen. xx. 7), and the term is applied to the patriarchs generally (Ps. cv. 15); God conveyed his mind to them, and they spoke it forth to others (cf. Amos iii. 7). **Like unto me.** When the people heard the voice of God speaking to them at Sinai, and from the midst of the fire uttering to them the Ten Words, they were struck with terror, and besought that they might not again hear that awful voice, but that Moses might act as mediator between God and them—might hear what God should say, and speak it unto them (ch. v. 22—27). Moses thus became God's prophet to the people; and of this he reminds them here, as well as of the circumstances amid which he entered specially on this office (cf. vers. 16, 17). The phrase, "like unto me," does not necessarily imply that the prophet who was to come after Moses was to be in every respect the same as he; all that is indicated is that he would act as Moses had acted as a mediator between God and the people in the way of conveying his will to them.

Ver. 16.—**In the day of the assembly** (cf. ch. ix. 14; x. 4).

Ver. 18.—**And will put my words in his mouth**; will so reveal to him my mind, and so inspire him to utter it, that the words he speaks shall be really my words. The question has been raised whether, by the Prophet like unto Moses, here promised to the people of Israel, is to be understood some eminent individual, or whether this refers to the prophetic διαδοχή, or succession, that was to continue under the theocracy. For the latter the context strongly speaks, for (1) the contrast between what God here forbids the Israelites to do, viz. to resort to diviners and soothsayers, and the provision he would make for them so as to render this needless, point to a succession of prophets rather than to one individual; (2) the reference in what follows to the discrimination of false prophets from true prophets, shows that a multiplicity and a succession of prophets was in the view of the speaker, not a single individual; and (3) as a succession of priests, of judges, and of kings was contemplated in this part of the Mosaic legislation, the presumption is that a succession also of prophets was contemplated. At the same time, the use of the singular here is remarkable, for nowhere else is the singular, *nabhi*, employed to designate more than one individual; and this suggests that the reference here may be to some individual in whom not only was the succession to culminate as in its crown and eminence, but whose spirit was to pervade the whole succession,—that each member of it should exercise his functions only as that Spirit which was in them did signify (1 Pet. i. 11). It is possible also, as O. von Gerlach has suggested, that "Prophet" here may be used as "seed" is in Gen. iii. 15, and that this is a prediction of Christ as the True Prophet, just as the assurance to Eve was a prediction of the Messiah, who, as the Head and Crown of the "godly seed," should end the conflict with the serpent and his seed by a crushing victory. It is to be considered also that, whilst the words "like unto me" do not necessarily imply a resemblance in *all* respects between Moses and the Prophet here promised, and whilst they may be well applied to One superior in many respects to Moses, it would be taking

them at much below their real worth were we to understand them of one greatly inferior to Moses, as all the prophets who succeeded him in Israel were until the Chief came (ch. xxxiv. 10; Heb. iii. 1—6). Finally, there can be no doubt that the Jews expected that the Messiah would appear as the Prophet by pre-eminence, and that they founded that expectation on the promise here recorded (cf. John i. 21; vi. 14; Acts iii. 22—26; vii. 37). It may be added that our Lord seems to apply this to himself, when he says to the Jews, "There is one that accuseth you, even Moses, in whom ye trust. For had ye believed Moses, ye would have believed me: for he wrote of me" (John v. 45, 46; cf. also xi. 48—50). How early and how widespread was the expectation that the Messiah would come as a prophet, may be inferred from the existence of this among the Samaritans (John iv. 25). It is to be concluded, then, that this promise has reference ultimately to the Messiah, the Great Revealer of God, between whom and Moses there should be a long succession of prophets, so that there should always be a medium of Divine communication between Jehovah and his people.

Vers. 19—22.—To the Prophet who should thus speak to the people all that God should command him, they were to pay the utmost deference, and to his words they were to render implicit obedience.

Ver. 19.—**I will require** it **of him**; I will judge him and punish his disobedience (cf. Gen. xlii. 22; 2 Sam. iv. 11; Ps. x. 13, etc.).

Ver. 20.—If, however, a prophet should presume to speak in the Name of the Lord what the Lord had not commanded him to speak, or if he should speak in the name of other gods, not only was no regard to be paid to his words, but he was himself to be treated as a blasphemer, and to be put to death.

Vers. 21, 22.—The test by which it was to be discovered which was the true prophet and which the false, was the fulfilment or non-fulfilment of his prediction. The reference here is to the prediction of proximate events—events that were to happen within a limited period, but which were not such as one not divinely instructed could foresee. When such came to pass, the pretensions of the prophet were thereby substantiated, and his authority established (cf. 1 Sam. iii. 19; John ii. 18, etc.). This was a more certain test than such as was offered by signs and wonders (ch. xiii. 2, etc.).

HOMILETICS.

Vers. 1—8.—*The support of the ministry the duty of God's people.* In a note on a corresponding passage in Numb. xviii. 21, 22, Dr. Jameson remarks, "Neither the priests nor the Levites were to possess any allotments of land, but to depend entirely upon him who liberally provided for them out of his own portion; and this law was subservient to many important purposes, such as that, being exempted from the cares and labours of worldly business, they might be exclusively devoted to his service; that a bond of mutual love and attachment might be formed between the people and the Levites, who, as performing religious services for the people, derived their subsistence from them; and further, that, being the more easily dispersed among the different tribes, they might be more useful in instructing and directing the people." This suggestive note seems to us to contain the pith of the Mosaic instructions concerning the maintenance of the Levites. (For the several details, see Exposition.) We can scarcely fail to see in this passage principles far wider in their application than to the Jewish people alone, and reaching much further onward than the times of the old covenant. And though, as it falls to the lot of the preacher to expound these principles, it may not quite fall within his preference to do so, if he is, like the Levites, supported by the contributions of the people, yet, when he is continuously expounding the Word of God, he may not omit to teach the people that " he that is taught in the Word should communicate unto him that teacheth in all good things." This is part of the "counsel of God," and should not be withheld, since it is not for his own sake, but for the sake of the entire ministry of the Lord Jesus, for which, if he is faithful, he will plead. The principles which may be expounded by the ministers of the New Testament are these—

I. A GODLY, ABLE MINISTRY IS THE WANT OF THE PEOPLE. True, there are now no sacrifices to be offered, nor is there any complicated ritual of service to be performed; but there is a mighty work to be done in heralding the gospel " to every creature," and in "building up the body of Christ." And so long as sin and ignorance prevail, so long will the people need those who will lead the way in seeking their expulsion and extinction. For this end our Lord has instituted a New Testament ministry. The work now to be fulfilled is that of teaching and preaching Jesus Christ (Eph. iv. 1—16; 1 Cor. ix.). "Faithful men, able to teach," are to be appointed. These are the qualifications. The Church needs no priesthood in it. It is itself the priesthood for the world. Ministers do not come now in a family, a tribe, or line. The figment of apostolical succession is "less than nothing, and vanity." It is not by the law of " a carnal commandment " that any ministry is valid now. But wherever God's Spirit fills a man with holy yearning for this work, where the needful gifts are imparted, where God's providence leads and clears the way, and the divinely inspired voice of a free Christian people says to him, " Come and be our teacher and guide in the ways of the Lord," there are calls to a ministry such as cannot be mistaken, and such as ought not to be ignored. And when, on such a ministry, the seals of Divine approval are set, when the minister can see the law of Christ which is promulgated by his lips, reproduced in men's hearts and lives, when he can see many a wanderer reclaimed through his pleading and prayers,—then can his ministry show a like validity even with that of Paul, for he, like him, can point to one and another and say, " If I be not an apostle unto others, yet doubtless I am to you, for the seal of mine apostleship are ye in the Lord."

II. THE MINISTRY OF THE WORD DEMANDS THE DEVOTION OF THE ENTIRE LIFE. We by no means intend here that none should teach or preach but those who can give their whole time thereto. But that, as a part of the application of the " division of labour " in the Church, the demands on those who make the ministry of the Word their care are such, that only the entire consecration of their life to it will enable them fittingly to meet them. To take the oversight of the flock of God: to give unto each one their portion of meat in due season: to visit the fatherless and widow, the poor and the sick: to observe the signs of the times: to know what Israel ought to do, and to direct them in doing it: to keep abreast of the thinking of the day, whether helpful or adverse: and so to declare the whole counsel of God, as by manifestation of the truth to commend himself to every conscience:—all these things go to make up a work so varied, so momentous, so exhausting, that nothing less than "giving himself wholly" to it can enable any man even approximately to discharge it.

III. THIS BEING THE CASE, IT IS IMPERATIVE THAT THE MINISTER SHOULD NOT BE ENTANGLED IN IMPEDING CARES. The Levites were not to have great estates that might draw off their interest from the duties of their office, nor were they to be left at an uncertainty respecting the supply of their temporal need. Even so now. It will greatly fetter and hamper a minister if he is entangled with the affairs of his life, whether by having so much on his hands that his time is absorbed in secular, which ought to be devoted to sacred, things; or by having so little on which he can rely, that the anxiety about feeding the people with living bread, is diverted from its proper channel, by anxiety about having the "bread that perisheth" for himself and his.

IV. CONSEQUENTLY IT IS AN ORDINANCE OF GOD THAT THE MINISTRY, WHICH IS FOR THE PEOPLE, SHOULD BE THE CARE OF THE PEOPLE. This may be set on several grounds. 1. It is manifestly *right*. If a man gives up all ways of securing temporal comforts for the sake of serving the people, they are bound to secure him the temporal comforts in some other way. 2. The Apostle Paul distinctly lays it down as an appointment by the Lord Jesus (1 Cor. ix. 14). (Paul waived this right, rather than hinder the gospel by pressing it, as is now done under like circumstances; but it was a right, nevertheless, and a Divine appointment.) 3. Wherever a people cause a minister to be embarrassed in temporalities, they will suffer for it. The minister's work, teaching, and preaching will all bear the traces of such embarrassment, and will be the weaker for it. 4. This Divine ordinance helps to promote the mutual care of minister and people for each other. They reap his spiritual things; he reaps their carnal things. 5. There is also thus a high and holy spiritual education of the people, in calling out their own kindly and just activities to uphold that ministry by which they themselves are upheld. The ministry is not to be found for them, but to be maintained by them. Thus there is seen to be a guard against abuse of position on either side.

V. ISRAEL WAS TO GUARD ITS OWN PRIESTHOOD AS BEING ITSELF A PRIESTHOOD FOR THE WORLD. So Churches are to guard the honour of their own ministry, because they have a ministry for the world. It is not for the ministers' own sakes that they are to be thus cared for, but on account of the high and holy cause which they represent, and which they seek, however imperfectly, to maintain. They are to be esteemed very highly in love *for their work's sake*; for the work which they fulfil is that which is purifying and saving the world. It is, in fact, by thus supporting a ministry that the Church is fulfilling its commission, "to preach the gospel to every creature." Of course, it follows from all this, that a ministry can claim such and such support, only so far as it is carrying out the Divine intent, or seeking in all fidelity to do so. It is not that God has put clergy as a kind of official police over the people; but that those who love righteousness are to show it by upholding the preaching of righteousness, and that those who love their Saviour's Name are to sustain the heralds of that Name, both at home and abroad.

Vers. 9—14.—"*Spiritualism*" *condemned.* In the verses forming this paragraph, there are nine terms or phrases, each with its own special meaning,[1] pointing to some pagan superstition, against which Moses is warning the people. The variety and number of such terms show us how great a hold a spurious "spiritualism" had upon the people. The phenomena connected therewith, however, present to us an aspect of history that is worthy of careful study. In some sort, the pagan customs of olden times connected with divination may seem so completely out of date, that it may be thought useless for the preacher to allude to them now. But though some details connected therewith may vary, yet the two purposes for which men "divined" of old, are still

---

[1] The student may with advantage consult Gesenius for the elucidation of each term; pp. 603, 736, 644, 544, 418, 258, 18, 335, 209 (Bagster's edit.), contain the explanation required. The following works may be consulted:—Wallace on 'Miracles and Spiritualism;' Crook on 'The Phenomena of Spiritualism;' Asa Mahan on 'Spiritualism.'

sought to be accomplished, viz. : (1) the ascertainment of destiny ; and (2) a peep into the invisible realm of the departed. And not only so ; but the methods of a modern so-called " spiritualism " are so nearly analogous to those of ancient times, that it is as needful for the preacher now to warn the people against them, as it was for Moses to warn the Hebrews. Even among them, the roothold of this superstition was so strong, that Isaiah had to caution the men of his time against it, and to remind them of the more excellent way (see Isa. viii. 19, 20). But it is very remarkable that neither Moses nor Isaiah closes up the matter at once by saying, " You may as well give up all that, for you cannot possibly hold any communication with the departed." Neither of them suggests that the invisible world is absolutely closed against all possible access. Various reasons for this may be surmised. It may be that the question of the abstract possibility or otherwise of communications with the departed, formed no part of God's revelation to Moses ; or that God has not seen fit at any time to inform us thereon, deeming an education on the moral bearings of the question, of far greater moment than intelligence on its physical or metaphysical aspects. Any way, certain it is, that we are *not* called on to ask, *Can* we converse with the dead ? But we are rather forbidden to attempt it. Five reasons are suggested as we compare and unite the teachings of Isaiah and Moses.

I. It is unreasonable. "Should not a people seek unto their God ? " If they wish to commune with spirit, there is one Great Infinite Spirit with whom they can hold fellowship, who has said, " Call on me in the day of trouble." From him we may get at any time all needful light on the daily path, and all needful intercourse with the spiritual world. We may hear a voice behind us, saying, " This is the way, walk ye in it." And if we may consult the Great Supreme, why leave the highest authority, for the sake of consulting any others ?

II. It is unnecessary. For what is that we really need ? Light *for* the future, but not light *on* it ; and light *concerning* the invisible world, but not light *into* it. And these are given to us in the revelation of the Divine Word (see next Homily). The connection between this paragraph and the next should not be lost sight of. Moses says, " The Lord thy God will raise up unto thee a Prophet," etc. (ver. 15), *i.e.* not only one Prophet in the fulness of time, but also from time to time as may be needed, prophet after prophet shall be sent you to direct you in the truth, so that you will have no excuse whatever for seeking light elsewhere, or in any forbidden ways. If that was true of Israel, how far more is it true of us ! What a fulness of light and truth have we in Christ ! And now that we have an unction from the Holy One to teach us the deep things of God, it is a wildly foolish and needless step to go knocking at the gates of the invisible world !

III. It is useless. It might very fairly be asked, "If you get an answer, how are you to verify its worth ? " But Isaiah practically impales the " spiritualists " on the horns of a dilemma. " To the Law and to the testimony : if they speak not according to this word, it is because there is no light in them ; " *i.e.* supposing you consult the dead, and get an answer from them, that answer will either accord with " the Law and the testimony," or it will not. If it does, you are no better off than you were before, for you had it in the Book before you inquired. If it does not, still you are no better off, for " it is because there is no light in them," and if they have no light, they certainly cannot give any to you ! So that either way the inquiry after the dead is utterly useless. And besides, who ever heard of anything alleged to be communicated by " the spirits " which contained aught that was not previously known ? We have an infinitely more sure " word of prophecy," and we shall be guilty of the veriest folly if we forsake it for the random guessings of " spiritualism." Hence—

IV. It is sinful. The preacher may press this on the following grounds. 1. It is a wayward effort to force an opening into a region which God as yet sees fit to conceal from view. 2. It comes of a wish to get light on future issues rather than on present duty. Duty is ours, events are God's. 3. It involves the neglect of a rule which God has given, and a search after one which he has not. 4. It is a waste of time. 5. It puts a prying curiosity in the place of a lowly, loyal obedience. 6. It springs out of a guilty unbelief or from dissatisfaction with the ways of God. Why, even among the heathen who knew not God, it was regarded by him as an "abomination ; " how much more must he so regard it among a people to whom he has revealed himself in deepest, tenderest love? Have men not yet learnt that it is mercy which hides the future, and shrouds in veil the realm of the dead? Who of us could bear to háve either curtain drawn aside? Oh! it is no wonder that this spirit of false inquiry should be forbidden by God. We should frown on it in others, sternly and constantly, and it should not be so much as named among us as becometh saints.

V. THERE IS ANOTHER AND A BETTER WAY OF GETTING ALL THE LIGHT WE NEED. "The Law and the testimony." Here are the words of God which are to direct us. Here we may ",inquire of God," and to the lowly, childlike heart the Book will be full of divinest, holiest teaching. It will give us light on the daily path, and guide us to a course which has "promise of the life that now is, and of that which is to come." It abounds with promises that will cheer life's gloom, and chase away the darkness even from the grave. It opens up immortality and life. By its light we know that our departed ones in Christ, though absent from the body, are present with the Lord. Cheered by its words of hope, we can sing, "Thou shalt guide me with thy counsel, and afterwards receive me to glory!" We are not treading uncertainly. We walk not at random. We are not helplessly drifting down a current. We are "firm on the rock." We are surrounded with light from him who is "the Light of the world;" and with all this, cannot we wait a while, and let him who is redeeming us reveal the mysteries of the spirit world to us in his own good time rather than our own? Hush! these longings to know beforehand. Let us keep to the written Word. It tells us quite as much as we can bear to know while in these tabernacles of clay. Be it ours to study the Book of God: to take it not only as *a* guide, but as *the* guide; *not* simply as the only guide, but as the *all-sufficient* one, "until the day break, and the shadows flee away."

Vers. 15—22.—*God speaking to man through man.* The Exposition, as well as the Commentaries of Jameson and Keil, may, with great advantage, be consulted on this passage, and also Hengstenberg's 'Christology,' vol. i. pp. 96—107. Our brief homiletic sketches assume that the student has already mastered the exegesis, and comprehended the intent of the passage. Its connection with the preceding paragraph is obvious. The people had been warned against having recourse to familiar spirits, etc., on the ground that such practices were an abomination unto the Lord their God. But Moses would not only warn the people off the wrong ground, he would direct them to the right, by showing them the completeness of the Divine arrangements for supplying them from time to time with all the religious teaching they would require, in a way far more adapted to their condition and circumstances than by any unveiling of the secrets of the invisible world. They are reminded that when God came in grandeur to speak to them at Mount Sinai, they could not bear the sight nor the sound. They begged that Moses would speak to them, and not Jehovah; "lest we die," were their own words. So that it was clear they would be entirely unable to bear anything approximating to a full disclosure of the Divine. It must be toned and tempered within the limits of their capacities of reception and of their powers of endurance. Otherwise, it would fail of its end, by crushing those whom it was meant to train. Hence he who "knoweth our frame" graciously promises to speak hereafter to the people in their own dialect, as it were, and on their own level, by "raising them up a Prophet, from the midst of them, of their brethren, like unto Moses;" and thus would the needful messages from God be kept up, making it quite unnecessary for them to make use of unauthorized means of getting supernatural light. There would be, from time to time, one prophet raised up after another, culminating in *him* to whom they all gave witness. Thus our theme is, "*God speaking to man through man.*"

I. UNLESS A DIVINE REVELATION WERE ATTEMPERED TO OUR WEAKNESS, WE COULD NOT BEAR IT. The cry of Israel at Sinai, "Let not God speak with us, lest we die," is a "touch of nature." No man could bear the full blaze of God's glory. Unless there were a "hiding of God's power," we should be crushed by the revelation of it. We could no more endure the full disclosure of the Divine than our eyes could bear to gaze on the splendours of a noonday sun. Hence God, "who knows our frame," and who, therefore, knows what we can bear, meets our weakness by his tender mercy.

II. IN ORDER THAT THE REVELATION MAY BE SUCH AS WE CAN RECEIVE, GOD HAS SPOKEN TO MEN THROUGH MAN. As Sinai's terror, with the voice of Jehovah, was too much for Israel, Moses says, "The Lord thy God will raise up unto thee a Prophet from the midst of thee, of thy brethren, like unto me." Each of these phrases is emphatic, and is intended as the antithesis to the notion of overwhelming force. The meaning of Moses is twofold. 1. There shall be from time to time a prophet sent to you, through whom you may hear the voice of God. 2. There shall be hereafter a great Prophet, who shall be to you as the living Voice of God ; but he shall be also "of your brethren, like unto me." We know how true both are. There was from time to time a line of prophets who spake for God. There has come to earth a Prophet greater than all beside. *They* always pointed onward to another ; *he*, never, save as a heavenly gift from him was by him held in reserve, even the gift of the Holy Ghost. Thus God has come into communion with our race, to reveal his mind and will.

III. NEW MESSAGES, COMING IN A WAY SO SUITED TO US, FROM SO CONDESCENDING A GOD, BRING THEIR OWN AUTHORITY WITH THEM. (Ver. 19.) The message is not to be set at nought because the voice which speaks it is but human. If a prophet speaks only what the Lord hath spoken, though he may be a weak and frail instrument, though the burden of his message may be almost more than he can bear, yet, being borne along by the Holy Ghost to utter such words, they come with Divine authority. "The treasure is put into earthen vessels ; " but though the vessel is earthy, the treasure is Divine.

IV. THIS AUTHORITY REACHES ITS CLIMAX IN THE MINISTRY OF THE LORD JESUS CHRIST. Such, surely, is the import of the scene known as "the Transfiguration" (Matt. xvii.). Moses and Elias are there—the representatives of the Law and the prophets. They speak of the decease which Christ should accomplish at Jerusalem. Presently they vanish from the spot, and no one is left with the disciples save " Jesus only." Then a voice out of the cloud said, " *Hear him.*" In Acts iii. 20—26, we have the Apostle Peter's application of the very passage before us to the Lord Jesus Christ as *the* Prophet to whom all the rest did point. (See also Heb. i. 1—31; and for New Testament teaching as to the authority of Christ, and the importance of hearing and obeying him, see Heb. ii., ix., x.) So full is the revelation of God by Christ, that it is not only a revelation through him, but in him (John i. 1—18).

From these four principles involved in the paragraph, there are four inferences which may be safely and profitably drawn. 1. If the voice of God speaks to us suitably and adequately through the medium of human voices, then it is utterly needless for us to seek information and light by any forced attempts at gaining messages from the invisible world (see preceding Homily). 2. We are here furnished with a test as to what is truly a Divine message or no. There is, in fact, a twofold test. It is partly moral and partly physical. (1) Partly moral (ver. 22, " When," etc.). It is as if Moses said, " You only require a guide in case a ' prophet speaketh in the Name of the Lord,' for if he does not, you know what to do (cf. ch. xiii.). If he speaks in the name of other gods, you must reject him at once." Note : Any supposed message from God which violates the dictates of enlightened reason and conscience, must be set aside. (2) Partly physical. If a prophet speaks in the Name of the Lord, they are then to watch and see if the thing comes to pass ; and if not, then they may be sure that the prophet is a mere pretender; " he hath spoken presumptuously." 3. Here is an antidote to fear. " Thou shalt not be afraid of him." What is the connection between this and the preceding? Is it not this? Suppose that the " prophet" declares that this or that is about to happen, do not give way to excitement and alarm. Follow the voice of God, of which you are sure, and obey that, and come what will, all is well with you. You can afford to do this; " Study to be quiet, and to do your own business," and whether what the prophet declares come to pass or no, you are sure to be safe, if you have maintained unswerving loyalty to God. Nothing can harm you. So with us under the New Testament dispensation. Many affix dates to this or that. We heed them not. We have but to " wait for the Son of God from heaven." 4. The reception of the Divine message is a part of that obedience which every man owes to high Heaven. Its acceptance is not merely the adoption of a number of opinions. Oh no! Opinions are one thing, convictions are another. A man "holds" opinions, but convictions " hold " a man. His conscience is held fast in their grip. Even so it is with those who receive the words of the living God as their guide through life to immortality. Their whole being is held firmly in their strong yet loving and tender hold. A sceptic once said to the writer, " I tell you candidly, that if I wanted to point out the best specimens of humanity, I should point to some of *your way of thinking*."

So he put it, " of your way of thinking." How little does the outsider or unbeliever dream of the hold the Father's words have on us! Our whole being takes shape and outlook from them. Our fealty to him whom we know and love supremely, makes " the law of his mouth to be better to us than thousands of gold and silver."

HOMILIES BY VARIOUS AUTHORS.

Vers. 1—8.—*God's provision for the priests and Levites.* From the limitations of the monarchy, Moses next turns to the provision for the " priests the Levites, and all the tribe of Levi." They were not to receive any estate in Canaan beyond the suburbs of certain cities. They were to take " the Lord as their inheritance." We have already seen that Palestine was a good land for training up a *spiritual* people ; it was a land where *dependence* upon God was constantly enforced. But among this people, thus invited to depend upon God, there was a tribe whose dependence upon God was to be further stimulated by the absence of any tangible inheritance. Their life was thus to be a life of *trust* in God's continual care. In these circumstances the Lord made certain laws about the priests' due. He took good care of the tribe that trusted him. It has been supposed that the animals, of which the priests were to have a definite part, were not merely sacrifices, but also those privately slaughtered, and the words (וְבְחֵי הַזֶּבַח) translated " them that offer a sacrifice " will bear the rendering " those who slaughter animals." Still, it seems more probable that it was by the central altar that the priests and Levites were to live. Assuming this, then, the following lessons are here taught.

I. THOSE WHO TRUST GOD SHALL NEVER BE DISAPPOINTED IN THEIR ALLOTTED PORTION. For as a matter of fact, " the shoulder, the two cheeks, and the maw " were deemed dainty portions of the animal. The best portions ascended to God in the altar fire, and then the second best were assigned to the priests and Levites, while the offerer was content with what was left. God and his ministers were regarded as the *guests* of the Jewish worshippers, and, as the guests enjoy the best which we can offer in the exercise of our hospitality, the support of the priests and Levites was amply secured. These dues of the priests and Levites seem to have been regularly paid while the people remained true to God ; of course, their support would suffer in sinful and idolatrous times, yet, even when they suffered with the neglect of God's altar, it was suffering with God.

And as a rule those who trust God are not disappointed with his provision. Even when it is limited in amount, he is sure to give sublime compensations. Though ministerial support is not what it ought to be, there is no class of men who enjoy life so much as God's servants.

II. THOSE WHO ARE THE LORD'S CHOSEN SERVANTS ARE CALLED PRE-EMINENTLY TO THE LIFE OF TRUST. There is a great temptation to encircle ourselves with so much worldly possession as that trust in God will be difficult and seem superfluous. In other words, there is an effort to be able to live by sight rather than by faith. But the Master whom we serve is realized by faith, and his kingdom must be propagated by faith. Hence he so arranges the lot of his servants that a loud call for faith is always ringing in their ears, and they should never neglect that call. The priests and Levites were at liberty to purchase land and leave it to their children, and doubtless many of them so far " made assurance doubly sure, and took a bond of fate." Yet the life of faith, the dependence upon God's altar, was better and wholesomer than the life of sight.

III. THE PEOPLE HAD NO RIGHT TO WITHHOLD THE PRIESTS' AND LEVITES' DUE BECAUSE OF ANY PRIVATE PATRIMONY INDIVIDUALS MIGHT POSSESS. A good deal of deficient ministerial support is due to the people very unfairly discounting private incomes and often exaggerating them, so as to save themselves. Ministers may inherit means through the kindly consideration of parents and friends ; but this is no reason why people should hold their hand in the matter of ministerial support. The Lord specially provided that the Levite (ver. 8) should have like portions to eat, beside that which cometh of the sale of his patrimony. The truth is that private means invariably go to make a public ministry more effective, if the ministry is true at all. They are not selfishly utilized, but used as a matter of stewardship. In such circumstances, instead of being a hindrance to liberality, these private possessions should be a stimulus, as they are so much more in the line of things devoted to the Lord.

IV. Due respect should be shown to a devoted spirit. The case of the Levite here referred to corresponds to a minister who has responded to a Divine call, against what one might call the dictates of worldly prudence. He has followed the inward impulse (ver. 6), and come to aid the priests at the central altar from his snug patrimony at home. Such devotion is to be considered and rewarded. The Levite, who was so interested as to relinquish his country life and patrimony, deserved the payment of the dues at the altar. So with the generous devotion of the ministers of God. When men relinquish good worldly prospects for the Church, their doing so should be considered.—R. M. E.

Vers. 9—14.—*Divination forbidden.* The process of divination, in its different forms here referred to—" divination," " observing the heavenly bodies," " enchantment," " witchcraft," " charming," " consultation of spirits," " sorcery," and " necromancy "— was an effort to discover secrets by unwarrantable methods. It was man's longing for revelation undergoing degradation through the imaginations of men. It had been practised by the predecessors in Canaan, and in consequence they were being cast out. The Israelites were to deem it abomination, and unworthy of the people of God. From the succeeding verses, it is evident that it is to be contrasted with the Divine order of prophetical inspiration, and in consequence rejected with detestation.

I. Our ideas of revelation should be worthy of God. We have no right to expect God to degrade himself in the methods of revelation. Our own instincts should lead us to abhor such processes as have been adopted to secure the secrets of the Most High. All the mean and abominable ways which are here enumerated ought to have been renounced by thinking men instead of adopted. They are all unworthy channels for God's messages. Astrology, enchantment, necromancy,—all are miserable makeshifts for a decent mode of revelation.

God has in " divers manners " certainly made known his will to men (Heb. i. 1). He has used dreams (Gen. xxxvii. 8; Job xxxiii. 15), revealing to the soul, whose avenues of sensation are temporarily closed, the information it needed. The dream was the condition of the communication (Gen. xxviii. 12—22). God spoke when he had got man's ear shut to other things. And we can see this to be a most worthy way! Then by *angelic* visits he oftentimes revealed his will, instances of which are many in the Bible. This also was worthy. Last of all, by *inspiring men,* that is, through human nature, which is also eminently worthy of God. But the divination process is and should have been regarded as mean and contemptible.

II. It is evidence of the great credulity of men that divination has imposed upon them. In connection with " spiritualism," for example, we have examples of credulity now corresponding exactly to the divination of the earlier times. As if such mean methods would be adopted by the Infinite Majesty, who has spoken in these last days by his Son! The power of belief is incalculable. Credulity is the believing power exercised on false objects and on insufficient evidence. We have ample faith in the world, if we could only get it rightly directed. And sometimes we find men who are most sceptical about religious matters, most credulous about the novelties of spiritualism. They yield to phenomena a credence that they deny to the well-authenticated Word.

III. God's presence is to determine our conduct. When Moses says, " Thou shalt be perfect with (עִם) the Lord thy God " (ver. 13), the idea seems to be that the overshadowing Presence is to determine our conduct before him. We will strive to be perfect as he is, and not look for mean methods from him.—R. M. E.

Vers. 15—22.—*The promised Prophet.* From speaking of the paltry expectations about divination, Moses goes on to speak of the general plan of Divine revelation. The people had had the splendid chance of *direct* communion with God, without any mediation. God spoke to them from heaven at Sinai; but so afraid were they of *immediate* revelation that they implored Moses to mediate the message for them. He became consequently, with God's full approval, the human medium through which the Divine will was conveyed, which means God's *prophet*. They had had no difficulty in accepting the Divine messages through him. Now, Moses assures them that this method of mediation through human beings will continue. He puts the promise in comprehensive form, and says that through a Prophet like to himself will God continue to speak to them after he has gone, and his message they will reject at their peril.

I. LET US OBSERVE THE APPROPRIATENESS OF GOD REVEALING HIMSELF THROUGH A HUMAN BEING. For man is in the Divine image; if this be not the case, we can have no knowledge whatever of God. Man is the image of God; and hence God reveals himself to men through a man. The office of *prophet* is the most appropriate way of revealing God's will. And when we carry on this line of thought, we are landed in the idea that an *incarnation of God* alone could adequately convey to man the mind and nature of God. If any one wishes to follow out this line, he will get splendid help in Mr. R. H. Hutton's admirable essay on 'The Incarnation and Principles of Evidence.'[1]

II. IT SEEMS CLEAR FROM THE PROMISE THAT A SINGLE PROPHET AFTER THE SIMILITUDE OF MOSES IS TO BE THE MEDIATOR FOR THE AGES. Now, only one Person answers this description, and this is Jesus Christ. He was and is incarnate God. His Spirit he alone could take, and through its gift to men in the different ages make them the channel of God's revelation. As a matter of fact, "the testimony of Jesus is the spirit of prophecy;" and the prophets were his instruments in the history of the Church. God has spoken in the last days by his Son; and the prophets between Moses and Christ were really the inspired messengers of the one Great Prophet of God. This is the idea of Peter that the Spirit of Christ spoke in the prophets.[2] We thus see one Person embracing the mediating work of the different ages, and accomplishing it through holy men.

III. THE LIFE AND DEATH OF JESUS, THEREFORE, BECOME THE CLIMAX OF DIVINE REVELATION. The previous revelations were but foreshadowings of this perfect manifestation of God. A human history became the embodiment of Divine thoughts, mercies, self-denials, and self-sacrifice. The blaze of divinity that was intolerable at Sinai becomes not only bearable but entrancing in the face of Jesus Christ. The blinding brilliance has been so toned down that man can rejoice in Jesus as "God manifest in the flesh." "We beheld his glory"—it did not blind or scare men as at the holy mount.

IV. THE DISREGARD OF THE WORDS OF JESUS IS PUNISHABLE BY DEATH. This is the penalty pronounced. We see it in another form in the Epistle of Paul to the Corinthians, "If any man love not the Lord Jesus Christ, let him be Anathema Maran-atha." If disobedience to Moses was visited in many cases by death, how much more disobedience and disloyalty to Christ! (cf. Heb. x. 28—31). The gospel has penalties of the severest kind for its rejection, as well as bliss beyond compare for its reception. The alternative is thus clearly set before us.

V. THE PROPHETS SENT OF GOD SUBMIT TO THE TEST OF FULFILMENT, WHILE FALSE PROPHETS ARE TO BE DETECTED BY THEIR FAILURE. God's method being a human mediation, is liable to be imitated, and men from time to time will profess to be prophets, when they have no real commission. Now, God has such a control of the future that no unassisted, uninspired man can forecast it successfully. Sooner or later he is found out. Happy guesses soon run out, and the person is discredited. Hence it was the duty of Israel to weigh well the communication of the professed prophets, and to see wherein they were confirmed by subsequent events. The true prophets had their word fulfilled, and were Christ's messengers; the false prophets had their word discredited, and were acting presumptuously.

Let us hear the Great Prophet, and give him credit for all the predictions of the minor and but human prophets.—R. M. E.

Vers. 1, 2.—*The Lord our inheritance.* True of the priests and Levites, it is true also of each believer, that "the Lord is his inheritance" (Ps. xvi. 5, 6). He is in this respect a "priest unto God" (1 Pet. ii. 9; Rev. i. 6).

[1] 'Essays,' vol. i. pp. 227—284.
[2] 1 Pet. i. 11; also Hengstenberg's 'Christology of the Old Testament,' vol. i. pp. 104—115.

I. The meaning of the expression. Inheritance—equal to lot, part, share. Inheritance in families—the share which each receives of the patrimony. In the partition of Canaan, each tribe had its lot, its portion, its share. God's portion or inheritance was the tithes, with the prescribed parts of the sacrifices, the firstfruits, etc. Levi had as his portion God himself, involving a share of the provision from God's table (ver. 1).

II. The grandeur of the truth. 1. *The believer possesses God.* God is a better possession for the soul than any of his gifts. "It is a thought which lies at the foundation of all true religion, that God himself is the Supreme Good, the true and real portion of the soul. . . . More intimately than light becomes the possession of the eye on which it streams, or air of the organs of breathing which inhale it, or the food we eat, assimilated and diffused through the physical system, incorporates itself with the nature of him who partakes of it, does he, that Infinite One, the Light of all our seeing, the Bread of Life, the nutriment of our highest being, become the deep inward portion of each soul that loves him" (Caird, sermon on 'The Christian's Heritage'). 2. *In possessing God, the believer possesses all things.* And this, though in an outward sense he has nothing (2 Cor. vi. 10; cf. 1 Cor. iii. 21—23). (1) God provides for him out of the fulness at his command. Possessing God, the Possessor of all, he knows that he will want "no good thing" (Ps. lxxxiv. 11). Temporally and spiritually, he will be provided for, kept, saved, delivered (Ps. xxxvii. 3, 9, 11, 25, 34; cxxi.; Isa. xxxiii. 16; Matt. vi. 33; Eph. i. 3). (2) All things work together for his good (Rom. viii. 28). (3) He perceives and enjoys God in all things, as none else can (Ps. civ.). (4) He is one of the "heirs of God" in "the times of the restitution of all things" (Acts iii. 24), when the redeemed enter on their glory (Matt. xxv. 34). Let the saint reflect on his inheritance in God. (1) How surpassingly rich it is! (2) How delightsome it is! (Ps. xvi. 6). (3) How enduring it is—eternal! (2 Cor. iv. 17, 18). (4) How all-satisfying it is! (Ps. lxxiii. 26).—J. O.

Ver. 5.—*The priesthood.* Israel, as a holy nation, consecrated to God's service, was "a kingdom of priests" (Exod. xix. 6). This priestly character of the nation was represented formally in the tribe of Levi. The distinctive duties of the priesthood were discharged by the sons of Aaron, who were thus the priests strictly so called.

I. The priesthood in itself. 1. Chosen and set apart by God. "Chosen him out of all thy tribes." 2. Holy, indicated by bodily perfection (Lev. xxi. 16—24), holy garments (Exod. xxxix.), rites of dedication (Lev. viii.), ceremonial regulations and restrictions (Lev. xxi., etc.). 3. Represented the people before God (Exod. xxviii. 12). 4. Made propitiation for sins (Heb. v. 1). 5. Gave forth oracles (Numb. xxvii. 21). 6. Had for these purposes the right of approach to God.

II. The priesthood as typical. 1. Of *Christ.* The high priest, in particular, was typical of Christ as (1) the One Medium of approach to God (John xiv. 6; 1 Tim. ii. 5). (2) Inherently holy, absolutely without sin (2 Cor. v. 21). (3) Representing the Church before God in his person, work, and intercession (Heb. iv. 14). (4) In his having made reconciliation for the sins of the people—himself both Priest and Sacrifice (Heb. ii. 17; x. 12). (5) In being the organ of Divine revelations (Matt. xi. 27). (6) For this priestly work—to which he was divinely ordained (Heb. v. 5)—Christ has free and immediate access to the holiest of all, and has gained admission to the same for his people (Heb. ix. 12; x. 19). 2. Of *believers.* (1) Chosen (Ps. lxv. 4). (2) Consecrated (1 Cor. i. 2). (3) Having freedom of approach to God (Heb. x. 19). (4) Offering spiritual sacrifices (1 Pet. ii. 5). (5) Interceding for the world.—J. O.

Vers. 6—8.—*Love to the sanctuary.* God loves those who love the sanctuary.

I. Love to the sanctuary seen. 1. In desire for it (ver. 6). 2. In pain at being deprived of its ordinances (Ps. xlii. 1—7; lxiii.; lxxxiv.). 3. In overstepping the bounds of bare duty in attendance on it (ver. 6).

II. Love to the sanctuary rewarded. 1. By acceptance of those repairing to it. 2. By provision made for them (Ps. lxiii. 5).—J. O.

Vers. 9—14.—*Magic.* I. A stern prohibition of Canaanitish practices. The practice of magic is known to have been extensively developed in ancient Egypt and Chaldea. Numerous indications occur of its existence among the Canaanites (*e.g.* 1 Sam. xxviii. 7—10). The lower kinds of magic are of rank growth in all barbarous and semi-civilized communities. The priests combine the functions of diviners, prophets, exorcists, thaumaturgists, physicians, and makers of idols and amulets. The magic of the ancients was distinguished as good or bad, according as it was exercised to conjure diseases and to combat demoniacal influences, or was abused to work harm. This last, which was avowedly diabolical in its character, was what was properly called " sorcery," and was universally regarded with horror. The noteworthy fact, however, is that the books of Moses make no distinction as to kind, but forbid absolutely the practice of every species of magical art. Moses recognizes no magic that is good; he classes all under the same category of " abominations." The text is in principle a prohibition of the use of all such arts, whether the pretender to magical power believes in its efficacy or not. It prohibits, further, resort to such as profess these arts. The " spiritualistic " delusions of our time in all their varieties (spirit mediums, rappings, planchettes, etc.), with " fortune-telling," and superstitious practices supposed to bring good or to avert evil " luck," are condemned by the passage.

II. A REASON FOR THIS PROHIBITION. 1. The nature of the practices as " abominations." They were: (1) Irrational. (2) Evil. Moses, as noticed above, recognizes no " good " magic. It is viewed either as imposture or, assuming its reality, as demonish (Satanic). It was connected with foolish and wicked rites. 2. The character of the people as " perfect " (ver. 13). There could not be perfect love to God and communion with him, and trafficking with the devil at the same time. Love to God, faith in him, and entirety of devotion to him should preclude these superstitions. What he wills his people to know he will teach them by proper means; what he conceals they have no right to seek by means that are improper (Isa. viii. 19).—J. O.

Vers. 15—20.—*Prophecy.* The term " Prophet " covers the whole series of Old Testament prophets, culminating in Christ, the Prophet like unto Moses *par excellence* (see *infra*).

I. PROPHECY IN GENERAL. The prophet—what? Etymologically, one " boiling or bubbling over " with the Divine inspiration. No mere religious genius, but one truly and supernaturally inspired. A revealer and declarer of the will of God. Future events were foretold: 1. As signs. 2. In warnings and appeals. 3. In denouncing God's judgments. 4. In administering comfort. 5. In unfolding the Messianic hope. 6. In unfolding the Divine purpose underlying providential developments. Prediction is thus a true and vital element in prophecy, but it is far from being of the essence of it. It is the function of the prophet either to declare new truth—truth gained by direct revelation, and given forth with the authority of Heaven as a " word of the Lord," or, taking up truth already revealed, to revive and enforce it with supernatural power and fervour, applying it to the circumstances, exigencies, and evils of his particular time. " The *prophets* were men who, when facing the people, stood as it were *before God*, and thus spoke *fore* and *for* him " (Morison).

II. PROPHECY AND MOSAISM. It is noteworthy that Mosaism contemplated the rise of prophecy from the first, and left room for it in the arrangements of the economy. It even required it for the carrying forward of its objects to completion. The dispensation was not a final one. The kingdom of God had a future which it was the task of prophecy gradually to disclose. The Law enclosed innumerable spiritual germs, which it was the function of prophecy to expand and develop. It had, moreover, underlying its ceremonialism, a spiritual basis, which it was the business of the prophets to bring to light, and to recall to people's minds when they appeared in danger of forgetting it. Prophecy was thus a standing witness to the life, freshness, and power which lay in the heart of a religion largely wrapped up in legal forms. Then there was the necessity for new light and guidance under the conditions of advancing national life, and in times of national emergency. The Law left not a little scope for extended applications of its fundamental principles, and it lay with the prophets to furnish the direction required. All this, in addition to their more general function of rebuking, warning, and testifying, in times of declension, which, with the carrying forward the development of revelation in its relation to Christ and his kingdom, may be regarded as the chief part of their work.

III. PROPHECY AND HEATHEN MANTICISM. The connection shows that prophecy is given in lieu of the heathenish practices that are forbidden. If God forbids divination, necromancy, consultation of familiar spirits, etc., he gives something better—something that will lawfully supply the craving which these superstitions unlawfully sought to gratify. The soul: 1. Craves for a knowledge of God's will. 2. Desires guidance in critical times of life. 3. Ponders anxiously its relations to the invisible world and to the future. 4. Feels its personal unfitness for intercourse with God. These cravings were the strength of heathen sorcery, etc., and they were provided for in prophecy. This, it may be noticed, is throughout a characteristic of revelation—it does not simply remove the bad, but provides for the supply of the cravings to which the bad appeals. —J. O.

Vers. 15—19.—*The Prophet like unto Moses.* These chapters bring before us prophet. priest, and king—offices pointing forward to and culminating in Christ. Christ is distinctively, and in the complete sense, the Prophet like unto Moses (Acts iii. 22), Christ and Moses were alike—

I. As FOUNDERS OF DISPENSATIONS. It was the greatness of Moses that he was employed by God in inaugurating a new era in the history of his kingdom—in introducing a new order of things—in settling the foundations of a new economy. In this respect he stood at the head of the Old Testament line of prophets, and in a sense stood apart from them. "The Law was given by Moses" (John i. 17). He had the ordering and settling of the "house" of God in the form in which it was to last till Christ came, who, "as a Son over his own house," would revise its arrangements and reconstitute it on a new and better basis (Heb. iii. 2—7). Prophets subsequent to Moses stood within the lines of the economy already established. They could enforce and maintain, but while predicting the advent of a new age in which great changes would be wrought, they had no authority of themselves to introduce such changes. It was reserved for Christ to "change times and seasons," and so to alter and remodel Mosaic institutions, or supersede them by new ones, or abolish them by giving the substance for the shadow, as to place the Church upon a permanent and moveless basis, and adapt it for the reception of the Gentile nations.

II. IN THE FREEDOM OF INTERCOURSE WHICH THEY ENJOYED WITH GOD. Moses enjoyed, as was necessary, the freest intercourse with heaven. God spake with him, not in a vision, or dream, or in dark speeches, but "mouth to mouth" (Numb. xii. 6—9), "face to face" (ch. xxxiv. 10). This is made, in the passage last quoted, a feature of distinction between Moses and later prophets in Israel. In Christ, this peculiarity of the relation of Moses to God reappears in higher form. Intercourse with the Father reaches the highest degree of closeness and intimacy, the Son being in the Father, and the Father in the Son (John xiv. 10). Christ's insight into his Father's will was perfect (John v. 20, 21). His communion with the Father was habitual and uninterrupted. The New Testament apostles, in an inferior degree, shared in this higher footing, were habitually possessed by the Spirit, and spoke and wrote under his calm and abiding influence.

III. As MEDIATING BETWEEN THE PEOPLE AND GOD. (Vers. 16—18.) It was when the people were deeply conscious of their need of a mediator that this promise was vouchsafed. It had only, as regards mediation, a very inferior application to the Old Testament prophets. The fulness of its meaning comes to view in Christ.

These points involve others, as *e.g.* the resemblance between Christ and Moses: 1. In the degree of authority with which they were clothed, and in the mighty signs and wonders which authenticated their mission (ch. xxxiv. 11). 2. In the fulness and grandeur of the revelations made through them. 3. In the severe penalties attaching to disobedience to their words (ver. 19; Acts iii. 23; Heb. ii. 1—5; x. 28, 29).—J. O.

Vers. 20—22.—*The false prophet.* The failure of the word of a prophet was decisive proof that he had not spoken by Divine inspiration. Had his word not failed, it would not have followed that he was a true prophet, but it showed conclusively that he was a false one when his word *did* fail.

I. CERTAINTY OF FULFILMENT IS A CHARACTERISTIC OF GOD'S WORDS. If *e.g.* the prophecies of the Scriptures could be shown to have been falsified by events, it would, by the rule laid down in this fundamental prophetic charter, conclusively disprove their claims to inspiration. It is vain to think of defending the inspiration of the prophets, while conceding, with rationalistic writers, occasional failures in their predictions. The prophets themselves do not shrink from this test, but confidently appeal to it (Isa. xxxiv. 16). This shows how different their inspiration was from the ordinary inspiration of genius, both in their estimation of it and in fact. No man of genius, however wide his range of vision, be he a Bacon, a Shakespeare, a Goethe, or a Carlyle, would like to rest his reputation on the absolute unfailingness of his words. While prophecy affords conspicuous instances of the certainty of fulfilment characteristic of God's words, it is to be remembered that this certainty inheres in all God's words alike. No word of God or of Christ will fall to the ground unfulfilled (Matt. xxiv. 35). The thought should comfort God's people, and make his enemies tremble. Applies to promises and threatenings equally with predictions and doctrines.

II. THE PREDICTIONS OF SCRIPTURE ABIDE THIS TEST OF TRUE PROPHECY. The force of the evidence from prophecy can only be properly felt by those who have been at pains to examine the Bible predictions in detail. But it does not need more than an examination of the principal instances to convince us that here we have no chance guess-work, no mere forecasting of natural sagacity. We might point to the predictions in Deuteronomy respecting the future of the Jewish nation, and the punishment which would overtake them for their sins (ch. iv. 25—29; xxviii. 45—68); or to the Messianic prophecies (e.g. Isa. liii.); or to particular predictions delivered long before the events predicted occurred, or could have been foreseen, as when Amos (B.C. 787) predicts of Israel at a time when the king and nobles were lying on beds of ivory, and indulging in every species of dissipation and amusement—"Therefore will I cause you to go into captivity beyond Damascus, saith the Lord, whose Name is The God of hosts" (Amos v. 27), or when Micah (B.C. 710), a hundred years before the Captivity, foretells of Judah, "Zion for your sake shall be plowed as a field, and Jerusalem shall become heaps" (Micah iii. 12); "Be in pain, and labour to bring forth, O daughter of Zion, like a woman in travail: for now shalt thou go forth out of the city, and thou shalt dwell in the field, and thou shalt go even to Babylon; there shalt thou be delivered; there shall the Lord redeem thee from the hand of thine enemies" (Micah iv. 10). Discovery has not tended to discredit, but in several striking instances has confirmed the truth of prophecy, as in regard to Ezekiel's prediction of the conquest of Egypt by Nebuchadnezzar (ch. xxix. 8—16), a prediction pronounced by Kueuen and sceptical critics to be a mere guess, falsified by the event, but now strikingly confirmed from a contemporary hieroglyphic inscription (see Expositor, vol. x.). And while it is true that an isolated sign and wonder is not proof sufficient of Divine inspiration (ch. xiii.), it is certain that, taking into account the character of the prophets, the kind and number of their predictions, the holiness of their message, and the coherence of what they taught with earlier revelations, the evidence of their Divine commission is as strong as could be wished—is, in fact, decisive.—J. O.

Vers. 1—8.—*The true priest is the highest type of man.* God here lays down the lines along which men may rise to the dignity of the true priesthood. The ordinance did not secure the ideal reality. "The Law was weak through the flesh." Human choice and endeavour were requisite to attain to God's ideal priest. It is his privilege to receive from God, and to reveal to men.

I. DIVINE CHOICE AND HUMAN DESIRE MUST COMBINE TO MAKE A REAL PRIEST. The man, though born a Levite, must "come with all the desire of his mind unto the place which the Lord shall choose" (ver. 6). The human will must co-operate with God's will. This is the product of the second birth. In this ancient arrangement, we see the forecast of the Christian life—the true priesthood.

II. THE PRIEST'S OFFICE IS, NOT FOR HONOUR, BUT FOR SERVICE. "He shall minister in the Name of the Lord his God." In other words, he shall serve in the stead of God, and by his authority. This is the hardest work, yet the most honourable. No toil or self-sacrifice can he decline while appearing in the stead of God, for he serves the noblest part of man. In God's kingdom there is no honour apart from character; and character is attained by service.

III. THE PRIEST'S EARTHLY NEEDS SHALL BE MET WITHOUT ANXIETY ON HIS PART. "They that minister at the altar shall partake of the altar" (vers. 3, 4, 8). While we are employed on the King's errands, the King will provide our rations. We have a

Divine guarantee that bodily wants shall be supplied, for God himself is our inheritance. It is surely better to trust the Fount rather than the stream, the First Cause rather than the intermediate channel, the Creator rather than the creature. The priest shall be supplied before other men, for the firstfruits of corn and wine and oil are his. They that serve God without stint shall never be forgotten.

IV. THE TRUE PRIEST OCCUPIES THE APEX OF THE SOCIAL PYRAMID. The true priest really rules. For him all other orders of men toil. For the priest to possess any earthly inheritance would be a burden, a care, an injury. *Others* till the ground *for him*, thresh his corn, and winnow his grain. As a god, he receives. For other men the inferior creation toils and groans. The unreasoning animals bear his burdens and do his will. Yet *these* men, served well by the subordinate orders of life, wait upon the priest, and minister to his human [wants. And in return, the real priest ministers to the hunger of the soul, and supplies light and guidance and hope. The real priest is the greatest benefactor to the human race; the counterfeit priest is a *pest.*—D.

Vers. 9—14.—*Gross superstition the alternative of true religion.* The popular superstitions of every age are very seductive. Our only safeguard against them is complete loyalty to the living God. The indwelling Spirit is a Guide and a Defence.

I. MAN GENERICALLY CRAVES TO UNRAVEL THE FUTURE. In every sane mind the inquiry arises, "What is beyond phenomena? What is to happen to-morrow?" The present enjoyment may satisfy animals; it does not satisfy man. He has a faculty that lives in the future. He is ever forecasting life. This inquisitiveness, if repressed, becomes a passion—an insatiable fire. If there is no true oracle that will give reply to his queries, he will betake himself to false ones. If no reply is forthcoming, he is driven hither and thither by the demon of unrest.

II. THIS CRAVING FOR REVELATION LEADS TO CHILDISH SUPERSTITIONS. This conscious want of the soul clearly indicates that some provision has been made by God; but, lacking *this*, men betake themselves to a thousand subterfuges. The more shrewd and avaricious among them trade upon this prying curiosity, and invent a thousand frauds for self-enrichment. In olden times, every village had its self-anointed oracle; every nation has had its modes of divination. No price has been too great to pay for this envied knowledge. Parental feeling has been freely sacrificed at this blood-stained altar. Fathers have made their loved ones to pass through the fire, in order to avert supposed disaster. Without doubt, the devil has been the moving genius in these systems of enchantment.

III. CRUEL SUPERSTITIONS HAVE LED TO HEAVIEST DISASTERS. So deeply rooted had these systems of diabolic divinations become in the land of Canaan, that to extirpate them it was necessary to extirpate the people also. We are not at liberty to suppose that the Amorites were destroyed because of aberrations in intellectual belief. But the fruit of superstitious belief is soon experienced in sensuality, bestial excess, witchcraft, murder, war. Under such influences society is rent in pieces; every man's hand is red with rapine and blood. At length it becomes an act of necessity to remove such a people from the face of the earth. The deeds of the Canaanites had become a stench in Jehovah's nostrils—a detestation that could no longer be endured. Hence their extermination.

IV. OUR ONLY SAFETY IS IN LOYAL OBEDIENCE TO GOD. No resting-place can be found for intellect or heart of man between degrading superstition and religious faith. Who can solve mysteries but God alone? If God reveal to us our line of duty just to the extent that we really need it; and if, in addition, he give us the assurance that the soul's need shall be met as fast as that need arises;—*this* will satisfy every reasonable request. Men can and must trust the true God. As a child walks along the darkest road quite contentedly so long as its hand is in its father's hand, *so* with equal confidence may we confide in the safe and unerring guidance of our Almighty Parent. We have in God a perfect Friend; all that is needed for well-being is complete submission. "Thou shalt be perfect with the Lord thy God." To have recourse to witchcraft or divination is practical treason!—D.

Vers. 15—22.—*Presages of the true Prophet.* Captious men of the present day complain that they cannot see God—cannot hear his voice. In their heart they do not wish to see him. He will not reveal himself, as an object of curiosity, to the eye of speculation. He reveals himself to the conscience and to the loyal heart. But men do not wish to see him as the embodiment of righteousness. They shudder and flee away. Yet in no other way *can* they see him than as he truly is. In this circumstance of mutual estrangement there is need of a mediator—prophet.

I. GUILTY MEN DEBAR THEMSELVES FROM PERSONAL FELLOWSHIP WITH GOD. There is nothing in common between unrighteous men and a righteous God. They are mutually repellent. The heart-language of such men is *this*, "Let us not hear again the voice of the Lord our God; neither let us see this great fire any more." To *them*, his voice is the thunder of war; to *them*, his presence is a consuming fire. They have no eye except to see his burning anger. Hence they flee to hide themselves. Their wish projects itself into reality; he removes himself.

II. MEN'S DESIRE TO HOLD COMMUNICATION WITH GOD THROUGH A MEDIATOR CONCEDED. The gracious disposition of God towards men yields to his creatures' necessity. Ask what they will, if righteousness be not dishonoured, it shall be done. The all-wise God candidly admits that the Jews had, in this matter, spoken well. But the mediator must be a prophet. He must convey the thoughts and dispositions and will of God to men. Human obedience, to have any worth, must be intelligent—the fruit of choice and purpose.

III. THE PERFECT PROPHET IS INTRODUCED BY SUCCESSIVE STAGES. Our moral instincts often outrun our clear intelligence. The Jews desired an intermediate agent, who should convey God's will to them; but they scarcely knew what it was they asked for. Could any mortal man clearly reveal the mind of the Eternal? Would not the pure stream be defiled by the impure channel? Nevertheless, God will do the best for them in their present condition. As yet the perfect Prophet will not be understood nor appreciated. Knowledge of God's character and purpose sufficient for the present shall be revealed by imperfect men—types of the coming perfect Mediator. By easy gradations, the human family must be divinely educated.

IV. THE TRUE PROPHET IS A PERFECT VEHICLE OF GOD'S THOUGHTS. "I will put my words in his mouth." Unless the prophet be a mere mechanical automaton, his words must be the result of his thoughts. If God shall use a human person to reveal himself to men, he must use his mind, heart, and will: yea, his entire being. This has been realized only in the person of Jesus Christ our Lord. Hence he could say, "The words that I speak, I speak not of myself: but that Father that dwelleth in me, he doeth the works." Hence, again, "He that hath seen me hath seen the Father also." For the advent of this real Prophet, humanity stood for centuries on the outlook, on the watch-tower of hope.

V. CONTUMACY OF THE TRUE PROPHET IS CONTUMACY AGAINST GOD. Such is the value of this Divine gift, that to treat it with indifference is heinous crime. No human penalty may be annexed, but God himself undertook to punish the deed. Hunger is God's voice within the body, and he who disregards that voice shall surely die. Pain is God's voice in human nerves, and he who neglects that summons shall die. Truth is everywhere the voice of God, and to turn deaf ears to truth is to deprive one's self of life. And, by parity of reasoning, the voice of God is heard more clearly and more authoritatively yet, in the person of his dear Son: it is his prerogative to give to men eternal life. Hence, to turn a deaf ear to him is folly, contumacy, despair, ruin. God will exact a most fitting retribution.

VI. GOD SUPPLIES A TEST BETWEEN THE FALSE PROPHET AND THE TRUE. The eagerness of men to discover the Prophet of Jehovah, led many to impersonate him for the purpose of personal reputation and gain. Every true prophet of God came with sufficient credential, so that no candid mind need have been deceived. They had the power to read the near future: this was a token of their heavenly commission. But better still, their message commended itself to the conscience of the hearers; and *thus* might every hearer find in an honest conscience that the herald was from God. If the prophet summoned men to repentance and assured them of a share in the mercy of God, they could readily ascertain for themselves whether relief came to their burdened consciences—whether better feelings arose in the heart. The truth is never very far distant if we really wish to find it.—D.

EXPOSITION.

CHAPTER XIX.

Laws concerning Cities of Refuge. Landmarks not to be removed. Laws concerning Witnesses.

Vers. 1—13.—Moses had before this enunciated the law concerning cities of refuge for manslayers, and had already pointed out the cities on the east of the Jordan that were to be set apart for this (Numb. xxxv. 11, etc.; ch. iv. 41, etc.). He here repeats the law with special reference to the appointment of such cities "in the midst of the land," on the west of the Jordan, in Canaan itself; and he supplements the instructions formerly given with directions as to the maintenance of roads to the cities of refuge, and as to the division of the land, so that there should be a city of refuge in every third of the land.

Ver. 3.—**Thou shalt prepare thee a way.** In the East, the roads were for the most part mere tracks made by the feet of animals used as beasts of burden or for travelling; and this continues to be the case in Palestine and many other parts of the East even at the present day. That roads, however, properly so called, were not unknown to the Hebrews, even in early times, is evident, not only from this passage, but also from Lev. xxvi. 22; Numb. xx. 17; xxi. 22; ch. ii. 27; 1 Sam. vi. 12. The design of the injunction here was that every facility should be afforded to the fugitive to escape to the place of refuge. In later times, it was enacted that the roads leading to these cities should be repaired every year in the month Adar, and every obstruction removed.

Vers. 4—7.—(Cf. Numb. xxxv. 11, etc.)

Vers. 8, 9.—In case their land should be extended, in case they should come to possess the whole territory promised by God to the patriarchs, so that their domain should reach from the Nile to the Euphrates (Gen. xv. 18)—an event which should be realized only if they should continue steadfast in their obedience to all that God had enjoined upon them, and an event which in point of fact never was realized, for even under David and Solomon there were extensive territories within these limits which were not incorporated with the kingdom of Israel—in that case they were to add other three cities of refuge to those already appointed.

Ver. 10.—The design of appointing these cities was to prevent the shedding of innocent blood, which would be the case were the unintentional manslayer killed in revenge by one of the relatives of the man he had slain; in this case the guilt of bloodshed would rest upon the nation if they neglected to provide for the escape of the manslayer.

Vers. 11—13.—These cities, however, were not to be places of refuge for murderers, for those who from hatred and with wicked intent had slain others; if such fled to one of these cities, they were not to be suffered to remain there; the elders of their own city were to require them to be delivered up, that the avenger might put them to death (Numb. xxxv. 16—33, etc.). In the earlier legislation, it is enacted that the congregation shall judge in such matters, and that by their decision it should be determined in any case whether the person who had slain another was to be allowed to remain in a city of refuge or be delivered over to the avenger of blood. With this the ordinance here is not inconsistent; the elders were not to act as judges, but merely as magistrates, to apprehend the man and bring him to trial.

Ver. 14.—To the ordinance concerning cities of refuge Moses appends one prohibiting the removing of landmarks; if these had been placed by a man's ancestors to mark the boundaries of possessions, they were not to be surreptitiously altered. Landmarks were held sacred, and a curse is pronounced against those who remove them (ch. xxvii. 7; cf. Job xxiv. 2; Prov. xxii. 28; xxiii. 10; Hos. v. 10). Among other nations also landmarks were regarded as sacred (cf. Plato, 'De Legibus,' viii. p. 842; Dionys. Halic. ii. 17; Plutarch, 'Numa,' 16; Ovid, 'Fast.,' ii. 639).

Ver. 14.—**They of old time;** i.e. those of a former age (רִאשֹׁנִים, earlier ones, ancestors, predecessors). The word does not necessarily imply that the age described as "former" was removed at a great distance in the past; it might designate men of the immediately preceding age. The LXX. have here οἱ πατέρες, and the Vulgate *priores.* That the law here given was uttered whilst Israel was yet outside of Canaan, is evident from what follows in this verse.

Vers. 15—21.—To secure against injury to life or property through inadequate or false attestation, it is enacted that more than one witness must appear before anything can be established; and that, should a witness be found on trial to have testified falsely against his neighbour, he was to be punished by having done to him what he thought to have done to his neighbour (cf. ch. xvii. 6; Numb. xxxv. 30).

Ver. 15.—The rule in ch. xvii. 6, regarding accusations of idolatry, is here extended to accusations of every kind before a court of justice; a single witness was not to be admitted as sufficient to convict a man of any offence, either civil or criminal.

Ver. 16.—To testify against him that which is wrong; literally, to testify against him defection, i.e. from the Law of God. The speaker has apparently in view here all such defections from the Law as would entail punishment on the convicted offender. In ch. xiii. 5 [6], indeed, the crime described here as "that which is wrong" (margin, "falling away") is specially the crime of apostasy to idolatry; but the word (מָרָה), though usually expressing apostasy

from Jehovah, has properly the general sense of a deflection from a prescribed course (from סוּר, to go off, to go aside), and so may describe any departure from what is constituted right.

Ver. 17.—Both the men, i.e. both parties at the bar, shall stand before the Lord; i.e. shall come to the sanctuary where Jehovah had his dwelling-place in the midst of his people, and where the supreme judges, who were his delegates and representatives, held their court (ch. xvii. 9).

Ver. 19.—Thought. The verb here used (זָמַם) means generally to meditate, to have in mind, to purpose; but it frequently has the subaudition of meditating evil (cf. Ps. xxxi. 37; xxxvii. 12; Prov. xxx. 32, etc.).

Ver. 20.—(Cf. ch. xiii. 12.)

Ver. 21.—The lex talionis was in this case to be observed (cf. Exod. xxi. 23; Lev. xxiv. 20). Practically, however, a pecuniary compensation might be accepted for the offence (cf. Josephus, 'Antiq.,' iv. 8, 35).

HOMILETICS.

Vers. 1—13.—The cities of refuge. The appointment of cities of refuge by Moses is of great interest, as yielding a study in Jehovah's ways of educating his people, and of giving light and truth to men. We will see—

I. THE PLACE THIS INSTITUTION OCCUPIES IN HISTORY.[1] So far as we are aware, there is nothing just now existing among civilized nations with which it is altogether analogous. The most recent regulations which seem to be a kind of reflection of it from afar, are those in the mediæval Church, called "the right of sanctuary." Ecclesiastical historians inform us that the right of refuge in churches began as early as the days of Constantine; that at first only the altar and the interior of the Church was the place of refuge, but that afterwards any portion of the sacred precincts availed. This privilege was "not intended to patronize wickedness, but to give a place of shelter for the innocent, or, in doubtful cases, to give men protection till they could have a hearing, and to give bishops an opportunity of pleading for criminals." These refuges allowed thirty days' respite, though under the Anglo-Saxon law of King Alfred but three days were granted. It speaks but little for the advance of opinion then that the right of refuge was denied, not only to the openly wicked, but to heretics, apostates, and runaway slaves. In after times this right of sanctuary was granted even to notorious criminals, not excepting such as were guilty of treason. In early ages there were asyla among the Germans. Before that, among the Romans. In founding Rome, Romulus made it a place of refuge for criminals from other states, for the purpose of peopling the city. Further back, in the Greek states, the temples, altars, sacred groves, and statues of the gods possessed the privilege of protecting slaves, debtors, and criminals. And, if we go back further still, we find among Oriental peoples a custom known by the uncouth term, "blood-revenge," according to which, if a murder had been committed, the nearest of kin to the murdered man had a right to pursue the murderer and take

[1] Scripture passages: Exod. xxi.; Numb. xxv.; Josh. xx. The student will find much help on this subject by consulting Herzog's 'Encyc.,' art. 'Blood Revenge;' Bingham's 'Eccl. Hist.,' ii. 565, et seq.; art. 'Asyla,' Smith's 'Dict. Ant.;' Keil on Joshua, ch. xx.; Calvin; 'Speaker's Comm.,' and Jameson's ditto, in loc.; art. 'Asylum,' 'Encyc. Brit.;' Dr. Beard's art. 'Cities of Refuge,' in Alexander's Kitto's 'Bibl. Dict.;' Wines' 'Comm. on the Laws of Moses;' Langhorne's 'Plutarch,' i. 52; Wilkinson's 'Ancient Egyptians;' Lane's 'Modern Egyptians,' i. 145, 270—272; Gesenius and others, sub verb. גֹּאֵל (Göel).

vengeance on him.   It is said that among the Arabs this right exists to the present day.   In what form it existed among the ancient Egyptians we are able to infer from Mr. Lane's statement that it exists in almost savage wildness among the moderns.   And we might gather, from the way in which Moses uses the term "avenger of blood," that the Hebrews may have been familiar with it, as having seen it practised in Egypt, or as having received the custom from the nations among whom their fathers dwelt prior to going down into Egypt.   This right of the nearest of kin to avenge a murder in a family is called *goelism*, from the word "göel," which has the two apparently incompatible meanings of "next of kin" and "avenger of blood."   So that there are actually two institutions known of, in the light of which we have to look at these cities of refuge.   One, goelism; the other, the right of sanctuary.   Each of them was open to abuse.   If the former had unrestricted sway, private revenge might bear very hardly on one who had accidentally killed another.   Supposing the second to be left without guard, it might become the means of screening from justice criminals of the worst type. The first abuse was common among Oriental nations; the second, amongst Greeks, Romans, Anglo-Saxons, and the mediæval sanctuaries of Europe.   And it is only as we set the Mosaic institution in the double light of the earlier ones out of which it came, and of the later ones which came out of it, that its real value can be seen.   Hence we see—

II. THE PURPOSE IT SERVED IN THE MOSAIC LEGISLATION.   There is one fundamental principle on which the Mosaic civil code is based, *i.e. the value of patient culture.* Moses found certain abuses existing.   He did not sweep them away at once, but aimed at educating the people out of them.   With regard to this right of revenge, he established such a remarkable system of checks and counter-checks as surely only a superhuman wisdom could, in that age, have devised.   Our space will only allow us to indicate these very briefly.   1. Moses recognizes the sacredness of human life, both to God and to man.   2. He provides that, when a wrong is done to society, it should be in some way recognized, and that society should have its own safeguard against the repetition thereof.   3. A great step would be gained if such reparation for the wrong as is needed for the sake of security could be gained without any peril of the wild play of private revenge (ch. xix. 6; Numb. xxxv. 24).   4. A broad distinction is to be made between wrongs (Numb. xxxv. 25).   5. The examination of the case and the decision upon it were put into the hands of the people through their elders and judges. 6. The cities of refuge were selected where justice was most likely to be done; even from the cities of the Levites.   7. All this was doubly fenced from abuse.   For (1) No murderer was to be screened (Numb. xxxv. 31).   (2) No one was to be reckoned as a murderer on the unsupported testimony of one man.   So that the goel had no power except there were corroborative evidence of guilt.   8. The reason is given in Numb. xxxv. 33, 34.   Now, when we know that all legislation has to be tested, not by the question, "What is absolutely the test?" but by "What is the best the people can bear?"—surely these laws give indications of a guidance and wisdom not less than Divine.

III. THE TYPICAL FORESHADOWINGS IN THIS INSTITUTION ARE NOTEWORTHY.   They are many.   The preacher may well luxuriate in working them out.   1. Outraged right requires vindication.   2. In vindicating the right and avenging the wrong, equity and kindness are to be studiously guarded.   Grace is to reign through righteousness. 3. God, in his kindness, provides a refuge from the haste or excesses of private revenge.   4. God gives special directions concerning them.   There was to be one in each district, so that the fleeing one might not have too far to go.   The place was to be accessible; good roads thither were to be made.   The Jews caught the spirit of the directions, and had direction-posts put at the corners of roads, with the words "Refuge! refuge!" plainly put thereon.   The same rule for a Hebrew applied to the stranger and foreigner.   The refuge did not avail if a man did not flee thither.   And there were sins for which it did not avail at all (see vers. 11, 12, and Numb. xxxv. 29—34); and where the refuge did avail it was only the death of the high priest which set a homicide entirely free from the consequences of his blood-shedding.

IV. THERE ARE SOME RELATED TRUTHS IN THE GOVERNMENT OF GOD WHICH ARE NOT FORESHADOWED IN THESE CITIES OF REFUGE.   Two of these there are, and those so remarkable, that it is not surprising if some do not regard the cities of refuge as being typical at all. 1. Though the manslayer was to flee *to* the city, yet he was to flee *from* the goel. The opposite is the case under the gospel. We said that the word "goel" had two meanings, viz. that of "nearest of kin" and "avenger of blood," because the nearest of kin *was* the avenger of blood. But as the student traces the Bible use of this word, lo, it has a third meaning, even that of *redeemer* (Isa. xli. 14; xliii. 14; xliv. 24; xlviii. 17; liv. 5, 8; lx. 16). *Jehovah is the Goel.* The Lord Jesus Christ is our next of kin, the avenger of wrong, the Redeemer. He has vindicated the majesty of Law by bearing the stroke, that it may not be inflicted on the penitent. He is at once our City of Refuge and our Göel. We flee to him, not from him. 2. The refuge was provided for the delay of judgment till the case was examined. Here, refuge is for the penitent, that he may never come into judgment at all. He may say and sing—

> "Should storms of sevenfold thunder roll,
> And shake the globe from pole to pole,
> No flaming bolt shall daunt my face,
> For Jesus is my Hiding-place."

HOMILIES BY VARIOUS AUTHORS.

Vers. 1—13.—*Cities of refuge.* The institution of cities of refuge (cf. ch. iv. 41—43) seems to have been peculiar to the legislation of Moses. It is an institution reflecting strong light on the wisdom, justice, and humanity of the Mosaic code. The system of blood revenging, while securing a rude kind of justice in communities where no proper means existed of bringing criminals to public trial, was liable to great abuses (ver. 6). The usage was, however, too deeply rooted to be at once abolished, and Moses, by this ordinance, did not seek prematurely to abolish it. The worst evils of the system were checked, and principles were asserted which were certain in course of time to lead to its abandonment. In particular the two principles were asserted: 1. The distinction between accidental homicide (vers. 4, 5) and intentional murder (ver. 11). 2. The right of every criminal to a legal trial. It is a proof of the wisdom of the institution that, under its operation, blood avenging seems very early to have died out in Israel.

These old cities of refuge, though their grey walls have long since crumbled to decay, have still much about them to interest us. We can scarcely regard them as ordained types of gospel realities, but they certainly furnish valuable illustrations of important gospel truths. To a reader of the New Testament, Christ is suggested by them, and shines through them, and the best use we can make of them is to learn from them the need of seeking a like security in Christ to that which the manslayer found in his strong city (see *infra*).—J. O.

Vers. 1—13.—*The cities of refuge as types.* Using the word in a popular and not in a theological sense, we may speak of them in this way. We have in the law ordaining them—

I. A VIVID PICTURE OF THE DANGER OF THE SINNER. In certain points the contrast is stronger than the resemblance. 1. The manslayer might be guiltless of the crime imputed to him. His act may have been unintentional. He had in that case done nothing worthy of death (ver. 6). To slay him would have been to shed "innocent blood." The sinner who seeks refuge in Christ cannot enter this plea. His sins are only too real and inexcusable. 2. The avenger of blood may have pursued the manslayer unjustly. He may have sought his death in blind fury and passion. His hot heart would make no distinctions. The Avenger whom we have to fear is holy and just. His breast harbours no vindictiveness, nor does he pursue without just cause. Yet he does pursue, for sin is the one thing which God cannot tolerate in his universe, and he will not allow it to pass unjudged and unavenged. These are points of difference, but in the one point of awful and immediate danger, the parallel is exact. Outside the walls of the city of refuge the manslayer knew that there was no safety for him. A sword was unsheathed which would certainly drink his blood, if the pursuer could but overtake him. Delay meant death, and he would not tempt it by pausing one instant in his flight. Is the situation of the sinner out of Christ any less perilous? "The wrath of God abideth on him" (John iii. 36). The sword of justice is unsheathed against him. Whither shall he flee to escape his danger? Concealment may have been possible from the avenger of blood, but it is not possible from God. Nor will any other refuge than Christ avail. The man in shipwreck, who scorns to avail himself of the lifeboat, but prefers to cling to the solitary hulk, filling with water, and doomed soon to go to the bottom, is not more certain of his fate than is the transgressor of God's Law, rejecting Christ, letting his day of grace slip past, and clinging vainly to his own righteousness or to any other mocking hope. "Neither is there salvation in any other," etc. (Acts iv. 12).

II. A VIVID PICTURE OF THE SECURITY OF THE REFUGE PROVIDED IN CHRIST. In Christ, our Saviour, God has provided a secure and accessible refuge for the sinner. Here again there is a point of contrast as strongly marked as is the feature of resemblance. The refuge city was, after all, only a refuge for the innocent. The manslayer may have been rash and careless, and in that sense blameworthy, but he was not a wilful murderer. For the deliberate murderer there was no asylum (vers. 11—14). He was to be taken even from God's altar, and put to death (Exod. xxi. 14). In this respect the gospel presents features different from the refuge of the Law. It is true that even in Christ there is no refuge for sinners wedded to their sins. If murderers may come to him, it is no longer with murderous, impenitent, unbelieving hearts. But, on the other hand, of those who turn to him in penitence, there is none whose sins are so black that the Saviour will not take him in. The guiltiest and most red-handed may wash in his blood, and be cleansed from their stains (1 John i. 7). This is the peculiarity of the gospel that as, on the one hand, it proclaims the absolute need of salvation to those who may think themselves too good for it; so, on the other, it holds out welcome to those who might be tempted to think themselves too bad for it. There is none beyond the pale of God's mercy save he who puts himself beyond it by his own unbelief. Christ is a Refuge for sinners: 1. In virtue of the offices he sustains. 2. In virtue of the work he has accomplished. 3. In virtue of the position he occupies—appearing in heaven in the presence of God for us. In him believers are safe. They are freed from condemnation (Rom. viii. 1). They are justified—saved from guilt and wrath—under Divine protection, and certain of acquittal in the judgment (Rom. v. 1, 9, 10; viii. 31—39). They "have a strong city; salvation will God appoint for walls and bulwarks" (Isa. xxvi. 1).

III. A VIVID PICTURE OF THE SIMPLICITY OF THE WAY OF SALVATION. The way to the city of refuge was direct and plain. The roads were kept in good repair. A sufficient number of cities was provided to make the refuge readily accessible from every part of the land. It was God's desire that men should reach the refuge, and every facility was afforded them for doing so which the case admitted of. How fit an image of the simplicity and directness of the gospel method of salvation through *faith in Christ!* "Believe on the Lord Jesus Christ, and thou shalt be saved" (Acts xvi. 31). "It is of faith, that it might be by grace; to the end the promise might be sure to all the seed" (Rom. iv. 16). Faith includes the three ideas of believing in, accepting of, and resting in Christ. Doubtless, to some, faith seems anything but easy. Carrying with it the surrender of the heart to Christ, it is, in one view of it, the hardest of all conditions. But it is hard only to those who love sin more than they desire salvation. The soul that sees the evil of its sin, and has a deep desire to escape from it and to be reconciled to God, will never cease to wonder at the simplicity of the way by which its salvation is secured.

IV. AN ILLUSTRATION OF THE NECESSITY OF ABIDING IN CHRIST FOR SALVATION. The manslayer had to abide in the city till the high priest's death. If he went beyond it he was liable to be slain (Numb. xxxv. 25—29). Our High Priest never dies, and we must abide in our city if we would be safe (John xv. 4; Col. i. 23; Heb. iii. 14; x. 38, 39). The conclusion of the whole is, the duty of availing ourselves at once of this Refuge "set before us" (Heb. vi. 18).—J. O.

Ver. 14.—*Removing the landmark.* 1. A dishonest act. 2. A deceitful act. 3. A covetous act. 4. An injurious act. Nothing would as a rule be more keenly resented than this mean attempt to rob the owner of land of a bit of his ancient possession. —J. O.

Vers. 16—21.—*False witness.* God's brand is here placed upon the crime of false witness. It was to be severely punished. Every one is interested in the suppression of such a crime—the parties whose interests are involved, society at large, the Church, the magistracy, God himself, of one of whose commandments (the ninth) it is the daring violation. The rules here apply primarily to false witness given in courts of justice, but the principles involved may be extended to all forms of the sin.

I. FALSE WITNESS IS IN GOD'S SIGHT A GREAT EVIL. 1. It indicates great malevolence. 2. It is grievously unjust and injurious to the person wrongfully accused. 3. It is certain to be taken up and industriously propagated. A calumny is never wholly wiped out. There are always found some evil-speaking persons disposed to believe and repeat it. It affixes a mark on the injured party which remains on him through life.

II. FALSE WITNESS ASSUMES MANY FORMS. It is not confined to law courts, but pervades private life, and appears in the way in which partizans deal with public men and public events. Persons of a malicious and envious disposition, given to detraction, can scarcely avoid it—indeed, live in the element of it. Forms of this vice : 1. Deliberate invention and circulation of falsehoods. 2. Innuendo, or *suggestio falsi.* 3. Suppression of essential circumstances—*suppressio veri.* 4. The distortion or deceitful colouring of actual facts. A lie is never so successful as when it can attach itself to a grain of truth—

> "A lie that is all a lie may be met and fought with outright;
> But a lie that is part of a truth is a harder matter to fight."

III. THE FALSE WITNESS BORNE BY ONE AGAINST ANOTHER WILL BE EXPOSED AT GOD'S JUDGMENT SEAT. The two parties—he who was accused of bearing false witness and he who alleged himself to be injured by it—were required to appear before the Lord, and to submit their cause to the priests and judges, who acted as his deputies (ver. 17). It was *their* part to make diligent inquisition, and, if the crime was proved, to award punishment (vers. 18, 19). The punishment was to be on the principle of the *lex talionis* (vers. 19—21). So, at Christ's judgment seat, the person who has long lain under an undeserved stigma through the false witness of another may depend on being cleared from wrong, and the wrong-doer will be punished (Col. iii. 25). Meanwhile, it is the duty of every one to see to the punishment of this crime, not only in cases of actual perjury, but in every form of it, and not only by legal penalties, but—which is the only means that can reach every case—by the emphatic reprobation of society, and, where that is possible, by Church censures.—J. O.

Vers. 1—13.—*The cities of refuge.* The blood-feud, as we know, was carried out remorselessly among nomadic nations, the manslayer having to be slain, even though his manslaying were purely accidental. In other words, there was no distinction made between *manslaughter* and *murder* by the nomadic nations in the rude early ages. But, by the Lord creating the cities of refuge, three on each side of the Jordan, to which the manslayer could repair, and where, if it was manslaughter only, he could remain without molestation till the death of the high priest, a distinction between these two crimes was carefully made.[1] The city of refuge was a divinely ordained place of peace for the person who had only slain his neighbour accidentally. In case of premeditated murder, the person was to be taken even from God's altar and executed.

I. THE CHILDREN OF ISRAEL WERE HEREBY TAUGHT THAT ALL SINS ARE NOT EQUALLY HEINOUS IN GOD'S SIGHT. Morality must differentiate and distinguish, not treat sin in the lump. Morality is undermined where revenge treats manslaughter and murder alike. The Old Testament morality was thus a great advance on the morality of the time.

II. THIS ARRANGEMENT ABOUT THE CITIES OF REFUGE SHOWED THAT THERE WAS A WAY OF PARDON PROVIDED FOR AT LEAST SOME SINNERS UNDER THE LAW. The Law is sometimes regarded as merciless rigour, whereas its sacrificial ceremonies and such an arrangement as this before us proclaimed pardon and escape for some sinners. An undertone of mercy was heard underneath the thunder of its wrath.

Now, the way of pardon is instructive. It was to be *prepared.* Towards the cities of refuge the best roads of the country converged. Directions were given to keep them

[1] Cf. Mozley's 'Ruling Ideas in Early Ages,' pp. 200—221.

clear, that the man who was fleeing for his life might have his fair chance of escape.

And what *agony* must have been experienced along that way! The possibility of being overtaken, and having the life taken away, must have made the race to the city a desperate ordeal.

And then the imprisonment there till the death of the high priest must have made the manslayer walk very softly all those days. When at last the high priest died, he was free!

Now all this, we believe, is typical of the gospel. The soul is, like the manslayer, guilty of shedding innocent blood. Doubtless not intentionally, but much evil is wrought by want of thought, as well as by want of heart. We are *all* guilty. But a way has been provided for our safety. It is a way of anxiety, of solemn thought, and eventually of peace through the death of him who is our High Priest. Safety in the city of refuge is the symbol of safety in Jesus Christ; while he is also the High Priest whose death delivers and restores the exile. It takes the two things, the city of refuge and the death of the high priest, to bring out all that Jesus is to sinful men.

III. THERE WAS UNPARDONABLE SIN UNDER THE LAW, AS THERE IS UNDER THE GOSPEL. The murderer was not protected in a city of refuge, but delivered up to execution. Murder was one of the sins which the Law deemed unpardonable. We mean, of course, unpardonable so far as this life and world are concerned.

Now what we have to notice is that, under the gospel, there is an unpardonable sin (Matt. xii. 31; Mark iii. 28, 29). And about this sin our Lord is very explicit. It is *unforgivingness*, the perpetuation of the murderous spirit in impenitent mood. We do not hold that the blood of Jesus Christ is insufficient to cleanse away all sin (1 John i. 6, 7)—the very opposite. But so long as a soul regards others with an unforgiving temper, it is manifest that the Divine grace has been kept at bay. God will not forgive those who are not forgiving. Forgivingness and forgiveness are twin sisters, and they visit the soul together. If God has really forgiven us, we shall find ourselves in a forgiving mood, the least we could do in the circumstances; but conversely, if we continue in hard, unforgiving mood, it is proof positive that we have not yet experienced God's forgiveness. How deeply the gospel probes our carnal nature, and conquers it!

IV. VENGEANCE CANNOT BE DISPENSED WITH IN GOD'S GOVERNMENT, AND WE NEED NOT CALCULATE UPON SUCH A DISPENSATION. The avenger of blood was the officer for the time being of public justice. It was a public duty he was called to discharge. And public justice still has its revenges, and will, as long as criminals continue. It is the same with God. "Vengeance is mine; I will repay, saith the Lord." The weapon is a dangerous one for us to handle, but God will take charge of it, and will use it as the interests of good and all-wise government require.—R. M. E.

Vers. 14—21.—*The law of·retaliation.* When we consider "retaliation," we find that it is the converse of the "golden rule." In fact, it is giving back to a person his breach of that rule to see how he likes it. It is just a rough method of teaching rude, selfish souls that there is retribution in all selfish practices; the gun may be fired maliciously, but it sooner or later lays the sportsman in the dust. Now, it is morally right that those who do to others as they do not wish others to do to them should have precisely their own paid back to them. It is simple justice.

I. PUBLIC JUSTICE MAKES PROVISION FOR THIS IN EVERY CIVILIZED COUNTRY. When Jesus directed his disciples not to retaliate, but to cultivate the spirit of non-resistance to evil (Matt. v. 38—42), he did not wish them to take the law into their own hands, but to leave to *public justice* what in the olden time had to be settled privately. He certainly did not mean that his disciples should screen men from the processes of public law, when they had made themselves amenable thereto. His advice regarded the edifice of public justice as raised by advancing civilization, and taking up consequently many matters which private parties in a ruder age had to deal with.[1]

II. RETALIATION WAS IN THE EARLY TIME A DUTY WHICH INDIVIDUALS OWED TO

[1] Cf. Mozley's 'Ruling Ideas in Early Ages,' p. 184, etc.

THE PUBLIC. It is too often supposed that revenge is such a gratification that men need no exhortation to take it. But we find men that are too cowardly to retaliate, men who would rather let the greatest ruffians escape than risk anything in giving them their desert.[1] Before the erection of public justice, therefore, as a recognized and well-wrought institution, it was necessary to sustain the courage of the people against lawlessness by making retaliation a public duty. The avenger was not a man thirsting for blood, but one who would very likely have remained snugly at home instead of risking his life in retaliation. Men have to be "whipped up" oftentimes to the requisite courage for public duty.

III. RETALIATION, WHEN FAITHFULLY CARRIED OUT, WAS A CHECK ON SELFISH CONDUCT AND A HELP TO A HIGHER MORALITY. The golden rule of doing unto others as we would that they should do to us was the goal at which the morality of the Old Testament was aiming. One way of leading up to it is by carrying out its opposite, and giving to the wrong-doer an idea of what it is to receive what we do not desire. We have to practise this in the correction of children. When they act a cruel part by others, they get a taste of suffering themselves, just to let them know what it is like.

IV. AT THE BACK OF ALL GOD'S MERCY THERE IS THE ALTERNATIVE OF STRICT JUDGMENT IN CASE HIS MERCY IS REFUSED. The gospel is the golden rule in its highest exemplification. It is God doing unto man as he would have man do unto him were he in such circumstances. But if men reject the Divine mercy, and will not receive God's love, then there is no other alternative but strict justice. And strict justice means retaliation. It is giving back to man what he dares to give to God. If man refuses God's love, and, instead of accepting and returning it, gives to God hate; then it is only right, eternally right, that he should receive what he gives. God cannot but hate as utterly abominable the soul that hates him who is essential Love. Wrath is the "love-pain of God" (*Liebes-schmertz Gottes*), as Schöberlein has called it. It is forced on him by the action of his creatures. They have had the opportunity of love, but, since they refuse it, they must be visited by wrath.

Hence there is nothing weak about the Divine administration. Its backbone is justice; but special arrangements were made in the atonement of Jesus to allow of God being "justly merciful;" when, however, this just mercy is rejected, God must return to the stricter lines, and deal with the ungrateful as they deserve. In the retaliation of God there is, of course, nothing mean and nothing selfish. His vengeance is in the interests of public morals, and a necessary part of a wise administration. There should be no trifling, then, with the Divine offer; for, if it be not accepted, men must prepare for wrath.—R. M. E.

Vers. 1—10.—*The cities of refuge.* The territory of Canaan was allotted to the Jews for *this* special end, that the principles of the heavenly kingdom might be practically unfolded on earth. In the Divine treatment of men, as members of the body politic, justice and mercy were to be harmoniously blended. Human life was uniformly treated as precious, but righteousness was revealed as more precious still.

I. SEVERE INJURY TO MEN MAY BE WROUGHT SIMPLY BY THOUGHTLESS INADVERTENCE. The physical laws of nature are stupendous forces, which man must well investigate and comprehend, if he would wisely control. They are evidently intended for the welfare of mankind, and prove very useful servants, but very dangerous masters. In the infancy of science and technical skill, great peril arises to human life from gigantic forces which we have not learnt to command. The fall of an axe, the course of a projectile, is according to the operation of fixed law. Careful observance of this law is life; heedlessness is death. "Evil is wrought by want of thought, as well as want of heart."

II. THE DUTY OF THE STATE POLITIC TO PROVIDE FOR THE NECESSITIES OF THE UNFORTUNATE. Before the Jews entered into possession of the promised land, God gave them instruction how to fulfil responsible duties. If it was a claim of justice that refuge cities should be provided for unwary manslayers, then justice would equally require that provision should be made for all sorts of unfortunates and afflicted ones. To stay the hand of private revenge—to prevent the effusion of innocent blood—

[1] Cf. Mozley, *ut supra*, p. 185.

private vigilance does not suffice; it must be the business of the State. The whole community is addressed by God, as if it were a single person. In some respects, each man and each woman has to act separately and alone; in some respects, they have to merge self into the family, and the family into the nation. Man must learn to act as part of a greater whole.

III. THE FAMILY TIE IS ALWAYS STRONGER THAN THE NATIONAL TIE. It is obvious that this is the natural order. If a man was inadvertently killed, some blood relation would, in all likelihood, espouse the cause of the injured, and thirst to avenge the injury. Men feel bound to protect each the other against the assaults of violence. There is an understood compact for mutual protection. But, in proportion as affection becomes diffused and spreads over a larger area, so it becomes attenuated. What it gains in extension it loses in intensity. Therefore checks and restraints are needed for immoderate family feeling.

IV. HUMAN FEELING IS MORE RAPID IN ITS MOVEMENTS THAN THE JUDGMENTS OF REASON. On the whole it is best that it should be so. Self-preservation often depends on the spontaneous movement of instinct. But whenever human life is not in imminent peril, it is becoming that sane men should reflect and ponder before they yield to vindictive feeling. It is quite possible that the man killed was the more blameworthy; perhaps the only blameworthy of the two; yet the vengeful blood of neighbour or friend of the dead waits for no inquiry, but rushes off to add another to the tenants of Hades. This also is the work of the devil, and must be resisted. We must learn to bring all instincts and feelings under the sceptre of reason and love. Haste usually is a mark of weakness or of madness.

V. REVENGE IS INVIGORATING : SORROW AND FEAR ARE ENERVATING. If, under ordinary circumstances, two men were well matched in strength and courage, the one who has unwarily killed a neighbour is so enfeebled by sorrow or by fear (or by both), that he is no longer a match for the other. On the other hand, the man who undertakes to champion the cause of the dead is lifted into almost superhuman stature and strength. For the moment he feels as if girded with omnipotence, and acquires fleetness, courage, and strength over the quailing person of the manslayer. Therefore, every possible facility must the state politic afford for the relief of the manslayer against the avenger.

VI. TERRITORIAL PROPERTY CARRIES WITH IT RESPONSIBLE DUTIES. Material property has its dark side as well as its bright. It brings burdens as well as enjoyments. With every increase of territory, God required that there should be increase of refuge cities, and that roads should be prepared along which the unsinning manslayer should flee. All earthly blessings have their drawbacks, but heavenly possessions are unalloyed. They are pure gold without admixture, sun without shade, summer without winter.

VII. RELIGION ENNOBLES AND BEAUTIFIES EVERY EARTHLY LOT. The land which we inherit, or which furnishes for us a temporary home, is a gift from God. He has not parted with the freehold. It is *his* absolutely, and in the use of it his will is ever to be consulted. We have but a life enjoyment in it. As it is a free gift from him, we are bound to respect all the clauses he embodies in the trust. He is to be recognized and revered perpetually. The refuge cities were the residences of the priests; the elders of these cities were priests of Jehovah, therefore they were representatives of Jehovah's mercy. These cities were emphatically "cities of salvation." Their walls were deliverance; their gates, praise. They were symbols of Calvary—types of the great redemption.—D.

Vers. 11—13.—*Lex talionis.* The refuge provided by mercy is open to abuse. The perversity of man will poison the streams from the heavenly fountain. But in this city of peace none shall abide except those who have clean hands. False hopes are doomed to crushing disappointment. Even from the gate of heaven there is a back way to the prison-house of hell. The man of blood eventually destroys himself.

I. HATRED IS INGENIOUS IN ACCOMPLISHING ITS NEFARIOUS ENDS. Hatred has an insatiable appetite. It drives a man in whom it dwells, as with a slave-master's whip, to do its base behests. It robs him of his sleep at night, that he may lie in ambush for some innocent victim. All day long he is driven to most odious tasks by this spirit of mischief. Without interruption, hatred holds its busy conclave in the dark caverns of the soul, and presses into service every faculty of the man, until it has clutched its prey.

II. THE MURDEROUS MAN FLATTERS HIMSELF THAT HE SHALL BE SAFE. He is conscious that vengeance is in store for him. No sooner is the deed done than cowardly fear seizes him. The righteousness of God has fleet-footed detectives in its service. Nevertheless, cunning falsehood comes to him as the devil's comforter. Though his hands be stained through and through with blood, he will wear gloves of innocence, a mask of pretence. It were a [nobler thing to brave the matter out, and defy all opposition. But this the sinner cannot do. He quails before the omniscient eye; and, however insecure the hiding-place, he cheats himself with the hope of escape. Guilty as his conscience affirms him to be, he seeks a place among the innocent. For the sinner no refuge can be found. The earth shall cast him out.

III. THE POWER OF DEATH IS A SOVEREIGN FUNCTION OF THE STATE. "The elders of his city shall send and fetch him thence." Human life is too precious to be placed at the disposal of private revenge; therefore the chief province of the state politic is to protect life against violence. *Unbiased* natures are the only proper judges of right and wrong. Justice will speak only in the calm atmosphere of sincerity and truth. The representative power of the whole community is the only power which fully suffices to vindicate the claims of righteousness. This is God's vicegerent upon the earth. Hence magistrates are described as "gods."

IV. RIGHTEOUSNESS IS NOBLER THAN PITY. There are circumstances in which Pity must not speak—a time for her to be silent. "Thine eye shall not pity." There are some situations in which her presence would be out of place, her action injurious. But Righteousness must never be absent. The very atmosphere in God's kingdom is penetrated with her vital breath. Her sceptre is the sceptre of God, and exerts a potent influence over every department of human life. Righteousness is the soul's proper robe, and without it she can nowhere fitly appear. All true prosperity is the fruit of righteousness. It cannot go well with any nation, nor with any man, until guilt is put away. Even compassion for others must be a righteous compassion.—D.

Ver. 14.—*Caution against fraud.* Nothing that concerns man's welfare and joy is beneath God's care. The vast extent of his kingdom hinders not his guardianship ever every minute interest of his creatures. Even landmarks, boundary stones, are under his protection.

I. GOD IS TO BE RECOGNIZED AS THE ABSOLUTE PROPRIETOR OF ALL THINGS. As the Creator and Upholder of the universe, he has supreme claim to this solid globe. "The earth is the Lord's." Nor has he ever parted with his rightful claim, for he keeps the globe hourly in existence, and so continually proclaims his control over it. It is his gift to men, not in the sense that he has transferred all his rights to others, but only in the sense that we were unable to purchase from him. We hold every possession from him in trust, and are bound by such terms and conditions as his will may impose.

II. IT IS GOD'S WILL THAT LAND SHOULD BE DISTRIBUTED AS PERSONAL ESTATE. Although evils result from the division of the land into personal property, greater evils would result from communal or indiscriminate possession. The fields would not be well cultured. The land would not yield her prolific plenty. Dispute and strife would be the chronic state of society. Personal property is essential to healthy life in the State. Yet men are stewards, and not absolute proprietors.

III. BOUNDARY LINES BETWEEN OUR OWN AND OTHER'S POSSESSIONS ARE TO BE SCRUPULOUSLY RESPECTED. The arrangements of personal property offer a fine field for self-restraint, as well as for neighbourly kindness. If we had been destitute of all possessions, we should be denied the enjoyment of helping others. A man who has regard for the health of his own soul, will not remove his neighbour's landmarks by so much as a single inch. He will rather lose a pound than take by fraud a penny. This Divine command is but a tiny branch springing out of the root principle, "Thou shalt love thy neighbour as thyself."—D.

Vers. 15—21.—*Bulwark against perjury.* "The tongue is an unruly member, and cannot easily be restrained." Private slander is base enough, but its basest utterance is when, in the sacred halls of justice, it swears away a man's reputation or his life. It is doubtful if a deed so black is done in hell.

I. PERJURY IS SO COMMON AS TO NECESSITATE A PUBLIC STIGMA ON HUMANITY. "One witness shall not rise up against a man." If every man had been known as truthful, the testimony of one witness on any accusation would be ample. The narration of *one* eye-witness or ear-witness ought to be enough. For a truthful man would always speak within the limits of truth, and would promptly express his doubt, if certainty could not be reached. But the common experience of humanity has been that the bulk of men will prevaricate and conceal the truth, even under the solemn sanction of an oath. Hence it has been found wise to condemn no man judicially, unless more than one witness can be found. Cumulative evidence is required to obtain a valid sentence. This can be interpreted in no other way than a public testimony to the depravity of man. The prisoner obtains the benefit.

II. PERJURY IS A CRIME, TO BE TRIED IN THE HIGHEST COURT OF THE REALM. The accused and the accuser in such a case shall "stand before the Lord." This is not so much a sin against man as a sin against God. The sacred person of Truth has been publicly violated, and the wisest and holiest in the land are commissioned by God to be the judges. As often as we violate the truth, we insult the God of truth, and stand before God for judgment. Hence it is of the first importance that we cultivate truthfulness in our thoughts and in our speech.

III. IN PROPORTION TO THE GRAVITY OF THE CHARGE SHOULD BE THE THOROUGHNESS OF THE SCRUTINY. Although we may expect to know the will of God in any particular case by laying our own minds open to the action of God's Spirit, we are still bound to pursue the most diligent and thorough inquiry. God rewards, not the indolent, but the patient searcher after truth. He that *does* the truth will discover the truth. "God helps those who help themselves."

IV. INTENDED MISCHIEF IS TREATED AS ACTUAL CRIME. The character and quality of a deed depend upon the moral intention. Whether the intention becomes an overt act will often depend upon outward opportunity and circumstance. But God sees the incipient motive and purpose; in his court, judgment passes upon the offender. Human courts are to be, as far as possible, copies of the court of heaven. Hence the perjured witness, who seeks to visit judicial penalties upon the head of the innocent, is himself as guilty as if his base project had succeeded. "Into the pit which he had digged for another he shall fall himself." The gallows which Haman prepared for Mordecai, served for his own doom. This is God's law of retribution.

V. THE END SOUGHT IN THIS JUDICIAL EXECUTION IS THE PUBLIC GOOD. The sacrifice of one life is intended to bring advantage to the many. The moral effect is most precious, viz. regard for righteousness—public abstinence from crime. Every man should be filled with *this* patriotic sentiment—the higher virtue of the nation. We may do good in our circle, either intensively on the minds of a few, or extensively on the minds of the many. In doing good to others we do good to ourselves. "We are members one of another."—D.

EXPOSITION

CHAPTER XX.

DIRECTIONS CONCERNING WARFARE IN GENERAL, AND FOR THE BESIEGING OF CITIES IN PARTICULAR.

Vers. 1—20.—The instructions in this chapter are peculiar to Deuteronomy. As the people of God, Israel was not a warlike nation; they were rather to abstain from warfare, and as a general rule to cultivate the arts of peace. But they had before them at this time the prospect of a serious and protracted conflict before they could occupy the land which God had assigned to them; and they might in future years have to go to war to maintain their independence and repel aggression. In view of this, instructions are here given regarding the conducting of military service.

Ver. 1.—When they found themselves opposed by an army more numerous than their own, and better furnished with the material of warfare, they were not to be afraid or discouraged, for Jehovah their God, who had brought them out of Egypt, would be with them to protect and help them (cf. Ps. xx. 7). **Horses and chariots.** In these, which constituted the main strength of the nations with which they would have to contend, the Israelites were deficient; and to them these were always objects of terror in war (Josh. xi. 4; xvii. 16; Judg. i. 19; iv. 3; 1 Sam. xiii. 5). Ver. 2.—**The priest.** Not the high priest or any one of the priests, but the military priest, the priest appointed to accompany the army, "the anointed for the war;" משיח המלחמה, as the rabbins designate him (cf. Numb. xxxi. 6; 1 Sam. iv. 4; 2 Chron. xiii. 12). His business was to exhort the people, and to encourage them by reminding them that the Lord was their Leader, and would help them in the conflict. The formula of his exhortation is given in vers. 3, 4.

Vers. 5—7.—**The officers;** *the shoterim,* the keepers of the genealogical tables (ch. xvi. 18). It belonged to them to appoint the men who were to serve, and to release those who had been summoned to the war, but whose domestic relations were such as to entitle them to exemption. If there was one who had built a house, but had not dedicated it, *i.e.* by taking possession of it and dwelling in it; or if there was one who had planted a vineyard and had not eaten of the fruit thereof; or if there was one who had betrothed a wife, but had not yet married her;—such were to be allowed to return home, lest they should die in battle, and it be left to others to consummate what they had begun. According to Josephus, this exemption was for a year, according to the analogy of ch. xxiv. 5. **Dedicated;** probably formal possession was taken of the house by some solemn ceremony, followed by a festive entertainment. **Vineyard.** The Hebrew word (כֶּרֶם) here used designates "a field or park of the nobler plants and trees cultivated in the manner of a garden or orchard" (Ges.); so that not vineyards alone, but also oliveyards and plots of the more valuable fruit trees may be intended. **Hath not eaten of it;** literally, *hath not laid it open, made it common,* i.e. begun to use it, to gather its produce for common use (cf. ch. xxviii. 30; Jer. xxxi. 5). Trees planted for food were not to be used before the fifth year of their growth (Lev. xix. 23, etc.; cf. ch. xxiv. 5).

Ver. 8.—The *shoterim* were also to allow any that were naturally timid and faint-hearted to return to their homes, lest, if they remained with the host, others, infected by them, should lose courage and become unfit for service. **His brethren's heart faint;** literally, *flow down* or *melt* (cf. Josh. vii. 5). In ch. i. 28, this verb is rendered by "discouraged."

Ver. 9.—The next thing the *shoterim* had to do was to appoint captains to head the people who were going to war. The army was divided into bands or companies, and over each of these a captain was placed, whose it was to command and lead (cf. Numb. xxxi. 14, 48; 1 Sam. viii. 12; xxii. 7; 2 Sam. xviii. 1). **Captains of the armies.** The phrase, "captain of a host" (שַׂר צָבָא), usually designates the general or commander-in-chief of the entire army (Gen. xxi. 22; 2 Sam. ii. 8; 1 Kings xvi. 16, etc.); but here the phrase is used in the plural of the chiefs of the companies or detachments of which the whole was composed.

Vers. 10—20.—*Directions concerning the besieging of towns.* In the case of a town at a distance, not belonging to any of the Canaanitish tribes, on advancing against it they were first of all to summon the inhabitants to a peaceable surrender and submission (cf. Judg. xxi. 13). If this was complied with, the inhabitants were to become tributary to the Israelites and serve them; but if this was refused, the town was to be besieged, and, when taken, all the males were to be slain, and the women and children, as well as all the booty that was in the place, were to be taken as the prey of the conquerors, who were to appropriate the spoil to their own use.

Ver. 10.—**Then proclaim peace unto it;** *i.e.* invite it peaceably to surrender.

Ver. 11.—**Shall be tributaries unto thee, and they shall serve thee;** literally, *shall be to thee for tribute and service.* The word rendered by "tribute" (מַם) denotes properly tribute service, service rendered as a tribute, whether for a season or in perpetuity (cf. Gen. xlix. 15; Judg. i. 30, 33, 35; 1 Kings v. 13; ix. 21; Isa. xxxi. 8 [Authorized Version, "discomfited"]).

Ver. 14.—**Shalt eat the spoil;** consume it for thine own maintenance.

Vers. 16—20.—This was for cities at a distance; it was to be otherwise with the cities of the Canaanites. To them no offer of peaceful submission was to be made, and when the city was taken, all the inhabitants without reserve were to be destroyed. This was in accordance with God's command to Israel (Exod. xxiii. 31—33; xxxiv. 11—16; ch. vii. 1—3), and as a precaution against the risk of the people being seduced into idolatry by the heathen should they be allowed to remain in the land. But whilst engaged in besieging a town, they were not to destroy the fruit trees that were outside the walls;

but trees that were not for food they might cut down and use in their operations against the city.

Ver. 19.—**To employ** them **in the siege**; literally, *to come*, i.e. *that they should come into the siege before thee*, i.e. either as thine adversary or to be used by thee for the siege. **For the tree of the field is man's** life. This may mean that the tree supplies food for the sustenance of man's life. But as the words stand in the text, they can only be rendered thus: "For the man *is* a tree of the field." This gives no good sense, or indeed, any sense at all; and hence it is proposed to alter the reading of the text so as to produce a meaning that shall be acceptable. From an early period the expedient has been resorted to of reading the clause interrogatively, and, instead of regarding it as parenthetical, connecting it with the following words, thus: "Is the tree of the field a man to come into siege before thee?" So the LXX., Rashi, etc. It has been thought that only a very slight change in the punctuation is required to justify this rendering (הָאָדָם instead of הָאָדָם); but more than this is acquired: the subject and object are hereby reversed, and this is more than can be allowed. From an early period also it has been proposed to read the clause as a negation, "For the tree of the field is not a man to come into siege before thee." So the Targum of Onkelos, Abarbanel, Vulgate, etc. The sense here is substantially the same as in the preceding, and the same general objection applies to both. To both also it may be objected that by this way of taking the passage Moses is made to utter a sentiment at once puerile and irrelevant; for what need to declare formally, or in effect, that a tree is not a man? and what reason is there in this for not cutting down fruit trees any more than other trees? In the margin of the Authorized Version an alternative rendering is proposed, "O man, the tree of the field is to be employed in the siege." But admitting this as a possible rendering, it is exposed to the objection, on the one hand, that it is improbable that in a prosaic address like this an explanatory appeal would be introduced; and on the other, that it is inconceivable that Moses would in this casual and startling way anticipate what he goes on in the next sentence to express deliberately and clearly. The passage has probably suffered at the hands of a transcriber, and the text as we have it is corrupt. The sense put upon it in the Authorized Version is that suggested by Ibn Ezra, and in the absence of anything better this may be accepted. The fruit tree is man's life, as it furnishes that by which life is sustained, just as, in ch. xxiv. 6, the millstone is called a man's life, inasmuch as it supplies the means of life.

Ver. 20.—**And thou shalt build bulwarks against the city . . . until it be subdued**; literally, *That thou mayest build a siege*—i.e. an instrument for besieging, a rampart, or bulwark—*against the city, till it come down* (cf. ch. xxviii. 52).

HOMILETICS.

Vers. 1—20.—*Wars to be regulated by Divine precepts.* The directions given by Moses in this chapter may serve to show the spirit in which wars should, if undertaken at all, be entered on and prosecuted. We are not called upon here to moot the question whether war is under any circumstances justifiable; since the principle on which the Hebrew lawgiver proceeds is that of tolerating for a while certain socially accepted customs, mitigating whatever in them is evil, and gradually educating people out of them altogether. In order to estimate the value of this chapter, it should be compared with the war customs of the nations round about. Dr. Jameson's "Commentary" has some valuable references thereon. Here are directions: First, as to the men who are to serve. They are to be sifted. In each of the four cases of exemption there is an obvious significance. Having been chosen, they are then to be organized. And their attitude and courage in the war were to be those of men who knew that the Lord their God was with them. Note: *No war should be entered on in which the presence and help of God cannot be expected and implored.* Secondly, as to the mode of carrying on or entering on war. The nations of Canaan are to be "stamped out," that a great pollution may be driven from the world. With this exception the Hebrews are to avoid war, if possible (ver. 10), and are only to engage in it if forced thereto by the people by whom they were opposed. When in war, no wanton destruction was to be allowed. They were to build bulwarks against invaders, but were not to destroy the subsistence of a people by cutting down fruit trees, etc. How wonderfully humane and even tender are these regulations compared with the customs of other nations at that time!

By them, in fact, the old pagan war spirit is repressed, and a war policy discouraged. The main pursuits of their life are to be found in the tillage of the soil. A standing army was unknown among them. War was not to be encouraged by an indiscriminate levy of men, nor was it to be pursued at the cost either of the industrial pursuits or of the domesticities and sanctities of life. If even in those days the war spirit was to be kept in subjection, much more should it be so now! The preacher may at appropriate times and seasons develop herefrom Bible principles respecting war. 1. War itself, in any form, is regarded in the Word of God as but an accompaniment of a transition state of things. It is not to last always (Ps. xlvi.; Isa. ii.; Luke ii.). Hence all should desire and pray that it may speedily come to an end. 2. Aggressive and unprovoked war for the mere purposes of conquest, finds no sanction whatever in the Word of God. Israel's wars of conquest were to be limited within assigned bounds. 3. War should never be resorted to except in a case of stern necessity. Israel was to make the effort to avoid war, if possible. 4. Supremacy in war should never be the chief care of a people. It should at all times regard war as but an occasional and awful necessity, and should see more glory in avoiding it than in conquest. 5. When war is engaged in simply from sheer necessity, its horrors should be mitigated by a humane regard for the enemy's welfare. There is more honour in kindly consideration for an enemy than there is in crushing him. To deprive him of the means of livelihood is a barbarity infinitely to be condemned. 6. When war becomes a stern necessity, so that it cannot righteously be avoided, it may then be invested with religious sanctions, and the blessing and help of God may be expected, asked for, and relied upon; then a people may say, "In the Name of our God we will set up our banners" (Ps. xx.). For success in such a war, a united people may look up to their God, and they will find that Jehovah hears. There can be no finer instance of this than the one recorded in 2 Chron. xx. The prayer of Jehoshaphat is sublime. The answer came. 7. When thus a people can confidingly look up to the Most High, and in the full assurance of being right can ask his blessing, there should be no faint-heartedness known among them. They may be strong and of a good courage. The Lord God goeth with their armies, and he will give them success.

HOMILIES BY VARIOUS AUTHORS.

Vers. 1—5.—*War.* The wars of the world form a large part of its history. Savage nations delight in war, revel in its bloodshed and barbarities. Their heaven is a Valhalla. Civilized communities, while averse from having wars waged on them, are not always so averse from waging war on others. Military ambition, lust of conquest, hope of enrichment by pillage, the wiping out of old grudges, may instigate them to this course. Wherever or however waged, wars are a source of incalculable misery. It may be said of them, "It must needs be that wars come, but woe to that man by whom the war cometh!" War is not to be sought, it is to be by every legitimate means avoided, but it may become a necessity. In this case it must be bravely undertaken, and our trust placed in God for his help.

I. RELIGIOUS COURAGE NEEDED IN WAR. It is a not uncommon idea that the influence of religion is adverse to the hardier elements in character. The Christian faith in particular is thought to inculcate a meek passivity of disposition, which, if not absolutely inconsistent with patriotism, courage, and other soldierly virtues, is at least unfavourable to their development. The man of spirit and the devout man are supposed to represent two opposite and incompatible types of character. This idea is strange, when we remember how largely the images and illustrations of the Christian life in Scripture are drawn from warfare. But it is sufficiently refuted by reference to facts. The meekness and unwearied forgivingness which is to characterize the Christian in his private relations is perfectly compatible with the most unflinching heroism in the discharge of public duty, and in the service of his country in her appeal to the God of battles. Christian meekness is not softness or effeminacy. On the contrary, it is an aspect of the highest courage, and develops moral qualities which make it easier to act courageously in any circumstances in which the individual may be placed. Civil liberty has seldom fared better than in the hands of God-fearing men. Instead of being the worst, they make the best soldiers. An army of soldiers, God-fearing and thoroughly disciplined, has usually proved more than a match for vastly superior forces of the enemy: Cromwell's Ironsides, the Scotch Covenanters, the Cameronians. As fine examples of the soldierly character, we may name Colonel Gardiner, Sir Henry Havelock, Captain Hedley Vicars. It would be the life and strength of our armies were they composed of such men from the top to the bottom of the scale.

II. WARLIKE COURAGE NEEDED IN RELIGION. We may apply the exhortations of these verses to the spiritual warfare. The gospel summons us to warfare. 1. With evil within us. 2. With the spiritual forces of evil around us. 3. With the hydra-headed incarnations of that evil in the institutions and customs, sins and follies of society. It would be well if, in this campaign against evil, we could command in our ranks the same union, the same strict discipline, the same steadiness of action, above all, the same heroic bravery and endurance and preparedness to face the worst, which are often seen in earthly armies. Courage and readiness to sacrifice for Christ all that his cause demands, is a first condition of success in the spiritual warfare. There must be faith in the cause, devotion to the Leader, enthusiasm in his service, and the spirit of those who "love not their lives unto the death" (Rev. xii. 11). Instead of this, how often, when the battle approaches, do our hearts faint, fear, tremble, and are terrified because of our enemies! Victories are not thus to be gained. We forget that he who is with us is more than they who are against us. The Lord is more to those in whose midst he is than all the horses and chariots and multitudes of people that can be brought against them.—J. O.

Vers. 5—10.—*Exemptions* Three classes were exempted from service in war, and one class was forbidden to take part in it. The exempted classes were: 1. He who had built a house, but had not dedicated it. 2. He who had planted a vineyard, but had not eaten of its fruit. 3. He who had betrothed a wife, but had not married her. The class forbidden to engage in the war was the class of *cowards* (ver. 8). These regulations—

I. HAD AN IMPORTANT BEARING ON THE STABILITY OF SOCIETY. War has naturally a disturbing effect on industry and commerce. It unsettles the public mind. It creates a feeling of insecurity. It prevents enterprise. These evils would be intensified in a state of society where, besides the danger of the country being overrun by hostile armies, each adult male was liable for service in the field. In such a condition of society there would obviously be a disinclination, when war was imminent, to acquire property, to institute improvements, or to enter into any new engagements. The man who built a house would not be sure that he would live to dedicate it; the man who planted a vineyard, that he would live to eat of it; the man who betrothed a wife, that he would be spared to take her. This provision of the Law was therefore calculated to have a reassuring and tranquillizing effect, and would so far counteract the tendency of warlike rumours to paralyze industry and the arrangements of domestic life.

II. WERE AN IMPORTANT ALLEVIATION OF THE EVILS OF WAR. They aimed at exempting those who, from their circumstances and prospects, would feel most keenly the hardship of a call to service. Ver. 7 connects itself with the importance attached in ancient nations to the perpetuation of the house. "According to modern notions, a forlorn hope would naturally be composed of men who had not given hostages to fortune. Such, however, was not the light in which the matter presented itself to the Greek mind. The human plant had flowered. The continuance of the house was secure. It was therefore comparatively of little moment what befell the man whose duty to his ancestors had been fulfilled" (Renouf). The sentiment here expressed was that of ancient nations generally.

III. WERE OF GREAT IMPORTANCE IN SECURING EFFICIENCY IN THE ARMY. The army was plainly better without the cowards than with them. One coward may do harm to a whole company. But, besides these, it was likely that persons serving by compulsion, in a spirit of discontent at disappointed prospects, and for the sake of their prospects unwilling to part with their lives, would prove but inferior soldiers. At any rate, there was policy in recruiting the army only from those who had a fixed stake in the welfare of the nation. The man with house, wife, and vineyard was more likely to be ready to shed the last drop of his blood in defence of his treasures than one wholly unattached, or attached only in hope.

LESSONS. 1. Those entering the Christian warfare need to count the cost (Luke xiv. 25—34). 2. In Christ's service there are *no* exemptions. 3. Nevertheless, consideration should be shown in the work of the Church for those who are peculiarly situated. 4. The danger of being entangled in spirit in Christ's service (2 Tim. ii. 4). 5. The faint-hearted are no strength to a cause (Judg. vii. 3). 6. Numbers are not the only thing to be considered in reckoning the efficiency of a Church or of any body of spiritual warriors.—J. O.

Vers. 10—20.—*Forbearance and severity.* If these rules embody a severity happily rare in modern warfare, they also exhibit a forbearance which many modern nations might well learn from. We have here—

I. WAR'S HORRORS MITIGATED. 1. *Peace was invariably to be offered before attack to a foreign city* (vers. 10, 11). It is presumed that the war was just, and undertaken with the sanction of Jehovah. If peace was accepted, no one was to be injured, but only tribute imposed. The peacemaking spirit is pleasing to God (Matt. v. 9; Rom. xii. 18). 2. *In the case of a city taken by storm, no women, children, or cattle were to be destroyed* (ver. 14). The amount of self-restraint which this implies can only be appreciated after reading the accounts of warfare as anciently conducted. But we may get some light upon it by studying the horrors of the sack of a city, even in modern times, and under European, or even British, generalship (see histories of the Peninsular wars). 3. *In the sparing of trees useful for food* (ver. 19). War conducted on these principles, however severe in certain of its aspects, cannot be described as barbarous.

II. WAR'S SEVERITIES EXEMPLIFIED. 1. *The resisting city, if foreign, was to be punished by the slaughter of its adult males* (ver. 13). This, which sounds so harsh, was perhaps a necessity from the circumstances of the nation. It certainly typifies the "utter destruction" which shall fall on all resisting God's will, and placing themselves in an attitude of hostility to his kingdom on the earth. 2. *The Canaanites were to be completely exterminated* (vers. 16—18). This case differs from the other in being the execution of a judicial sentence, as well as an indispensable means to their own preservation against corruption (ver. 18). A general type of the fate which shall overtake the ungodly.—J. O.

Vers. 1—20.—*Religious wars.* We have in this chapter an instructive direction about the prosecution of a religious war. For, after all, *war* may be the only way of advancing the interests of nations. Disputes become so entangled, and great principles become so staked in the disputes, that war is welcomed as the one way to peace and progress. It is an awful expedient, but there are worse things than war. "Cowardice," said Rev. F. W. Robertson, of Brighton, "is worse. And the decay of enthusiasm and manliness is worse. And it is worse than death, ay, worse than a hundred thousand deaths, when a people has gravitated down into the creed that 'the wealth of nations' consists, not in generous hearts—'Fire in each breast, and freedom on each brow'—in national virtues, and primitive simplicity, and heroic endurance, and preference of duty to life;—not in *men*, but in silk and cotton and something that they call 'capital.' Peace is blessed. Peace arising out of charity. But peace springing out of the calculations of selfishness, is not blessed. If the price to be paid for peace is this, that 'wealth accumulate and men decay,' better far that every street in every town of our once noble country should run blood!" From the directions in the chapter before us, we learn such lessons as these—

I. THE RIGHTEOUSNESS OF THE CAUSE, AND NOT THE NUMBERS IN THE FIELD, IS TO BE THE FOUNDATION OF TRUST. The Jews were going into Palestine as the Lord's host, and, even though a minority sometimes, they were sure to win. "If God be for us, who can be against us?" was to be their ground of confidence. And our Lord contemplated the victory of a minority in his illustration about calculating the cost. "Or what king, going to make war against another king, sitteth not down first, and consulteth whether he be able with ten thousand to meet him that cometh against him with twenty thousand?" (Luke xiv. 31). A good cause, like a good king, is worth ten thousand soldiers (2 Sam. xviii. 3). David's great sin was trusting in *numbers* and not in *God* (2 Sam. xxiv. 2, etc.).

II. A RIGHTEOUS CAUSE ADMITS OF THE WAR BEING ENTERED UPON RELIGIOUSLY. The priest was to give them an oration before the battle, showing that they were going to fight the Lord's battles, and that he would be with them (vers. 2—4). Of course, this has been imitated often by those who had *not* right on their side. Yet the hypocrisy of a party or people is in itself a testimony to the need for a religious spirit characterizing combatants. The most depraved feel somehow in the tremendous game of war that they are appealing to the God of battles, and should at least acknowledge him in entering the contest.

III. THE ARMY SHOULD BE WEEDED OF THE CAREFUL AND THE COWARDLY. Provision is here made for the dismissal home of those who are careworn about an undedicated habitation (ver. 5), or about a newly acquired vineyard (ver. 6), or about a betrothed wife (ver. 7), and also for the dismissal of those who are faint-hearted (ver. 8). The combatants should be as free as possible from care, and from the infection of cowardice. They might have sung, with the modern minstrels—

> " We want no cowards in our band,
> 　　That from their colours fly ;
> 　We call for valiant-hearted men,
> 　　Who're not afraid to die."

IV. IN ORDINARY CONQUESTS, PEACEFUL PROPOSALS ARE FIRST TO BE TRIED. (Vers. 10—15.) If these are entertained, well and good; if not, then the conquest will be all the surer of having shown the preliminary consideration. This was to regulate any foreign conquest into which they might be forced. When the victory was won, the male adult population were to be put to the sword, because they had forfeited their lives by rejecting the peaceful proposals; but the women and children and property were to be the prey of the invaders. We have here the suggestion of arbitration, from which much is properly hoped in mitigation of war.

V. BUT IN THE CONQUEST OF THE IDOLATROUS NATIONS OF CANAAN, EXTERMINATION WAS THE ONLY SAFETY FOR THE INVADING HOST. By their abominable idolatries they had forfeited all right to life, and their continued existence would only have been a snare to Israel. Children and women as well as adult males were to be included in the desolation. This apparently harsh decree has its counterpart still in the government of the world. A storm or pestilence does not respect children any more than men. It shows that the Great Ruler does not intend the present state of things to be *final*. A judgment to come is surely the logical lesson of such a feature of war and of providence. The innocent who suffer with the guilty shall get their compensation in the other life.

VI. THE RAVAGES OF WAR ARE TO BE KEPT WITHIN AS NARROW LIMITS AS POSSIBLE. This seems to be the lesson in this arrangement about the protection of fruit trees in the siege (vers. 19, 20). The future peaceful and prosperous state of things is to be considered, and no more harm done by the stress of war than is absolutely unavoidable.

We have thus great principles applicable to all the warring period of human progress. Wars are still desperate remedies. A time is coming when " the war-drum shall throb no longer ; " but meanwhile, let wars be prosecuted in a religious spirit and with all religious precautions, when they must be engaged in. A noble illustration of what may be done in war-time by Christian men is afforded by the "Christian Commission" in the United States. Its 'Annals,' written by Rev. Lemuel Moss, Home Secretary of the Commission, Philadelphia, 1868, form a handsome volume of 752 pages, which amply repay perusal. We must *fight* for principle, if we cannot secure its triumph by more peaceful means; but one day all will submit to it, and war be needed no longer. May God hasten the happy day !—R. M. E.

Vers. 1—9.—*Military service to be voluntary.* In war, forced service is worse than useless; it is a source of weakness—a cause of defeat. For successful warfare, all the skill and energy of every soldier is demanded ; and unless the hearts of the warriors are in the conflict, no triumph can be anticipated.

I. TO BE LOYAL FRIENDS OF GOD, WE MUST SOMETIMES TREAT MEN AS FOES. If we are truly God's children, we must count God's friends to be our friends, God's foes to be our foes. We are not our own. We cannot expend life according to our personal will.

We are the property of another—the Supreme King. Therefore we must do his work and fight his battles. Our notion of what is right and just must be made subordinate to *his*. Our minds are often too much biased with selfish feeling to judge what is right, if left to ourselves; but we shall not err if we closely follow the precepts of our God. The interests of God's kingdom are to be held by us as paramount over the interests of man's kingdom.

II. GOD'S PRESENCE IN BATTLE OUTMATCHES ALL HUMAN FORCES. The source of conquest is not in the visible material of war. Victory is *not* on the side of the largest battalions. This is the creed of the infidel. If there were no God, it might be true. Mere numbers of combatants have as often hindered triumph as helped it. If God be ranged on the one side, it is a most unequal contest. The issue is a foregone event. Multiply human weapons or develop human skill as much as you please; let all the powers of arithmetic be exhausted in the computation; and still the finite is confronted by the Infinite. " Before him the inhabitants of the world are as grasshoppers." " If God be for us," vain is all opposition. Simple faith is the best equipment.

III. GOD'S PRIEST IS THE INSPIRER OF TRUE COURAGE. The sanctions and the inspirations of religion may be obtained for the business of war. The true priest will not heedlessly lend his sanction to *any* emprise of war, nor will he withhold his benediction from a righteous contest. By virtue of his office, he is the messenger from God to the royal court, as well as to the people. If ever the oracle of the sanctuary should be consulted, it is when war is imminent. It is not the business of the priest to initiate war; but if war becomes a duty, it is the business of the priest to encourage and inspire the host of God's elect. The true priest is in close accord with God. God's heart beats within his heart; God's will finds prompt response in him. Hence the priest's voice is the human exponent of God's thought. God's strength is through him conveyed to the mailed warriors, for he speaks with just authority.

IV. GOD WILL ACHIEVE VICTORY ONLY THROUGH THE RIGHT-HEARTED. Unless the soldier's mind and heart and soul be in the conflict, he had better tarry by his fireside. A few earnest, ardent warriors are preferred to mere array of numbers. If any soldier found more delight in his habitation or in his vineyard than in the success of battle, he might forthwith return. With the double-minded and the half-hearted God does not work. The channel must be emptied of self if Divine energy is to pass through it. We are not to conclude that God prefers the few to the many. But he will have the *right* kind of agents, or he will not work through them. The thirsty man does not prefer one drop of water to ten; but he does prefer one drop of wholesome water to a gallon of poisonous beverage. God works according to wise methods, and sends help through fitting channels. The best media through which he conveys military conquest is unselfish devotion to his cause. The consecrated soldier is the predestined conqueror.

V. LEADERS IN GREAT ENTERPRISES ARE TO BE SELECTED FROM THE COURAGEOUS FEW. Men will most faithfully follow those leaders whom they have themselves chosen. As the faint-hearted were unfit to go to the battle, so were they unfit to choose captains over the host. The courageous are also the most judicious. Accurately measuring the work that has to be done, they can the better judge who are the most competent to do it. The brave heart and the clear eye go together. These captains, so appointed, would be strong in the consciousness that they enjoyed the esteem and support of the troops. Such an arrangement gives the best guarantee for efficient leaders. On the same ground, the rulers of the Church should be chosen on the ground of spiritual fitness—solely on the ground of moral qualification.—D.

Vers. 10—20.—*The terrible side of human duty.* Sin has made such fatal havoc in our world, that the most severe remedies have to be applied. In the administration of these remedies God has chosen to employ men. Thus he allies himself with us and makes us partners with him in the administration of his kingdom. " Such honour have all his saints."

I. THE AIMS OF THE DIVINE GOVERNMENT MUST BE ACCOMPLISHED. Every aim which is formed in God's mind is a seed of righteousness. Therefore it *must* grow and come to perfection. Necessity enters into its very essence. No power on earth or in hell is able to hinder its accomplishment. Who shall withstand the will of Omnipotence? Righteousness shall, sooner or later, be triumphant. All opposition to Jehovah's will shall eventually be crushed out. He who created is able also to destroy. For the present his patient love provides other remedies; and if remedial measures fail, then fell destruction shall sweep into eternal darkness all opposition to his supreme will.

II. THE ENDS OF RIGHTEOUSNESS MAY BE ATTAINED BY PEACEABLE MEANS IF MEN WILL SUBMIT TO GOD'S TERMS. (Ver. 10.) Terms of peace were to be offered by the Hebrews in their wars with outlying nations. The main condition of peace and friendship was the relinquishment of idolatry. If men will fear and serve God, they shall live. To know God as *our God* is life eternal. If men *will* turn their backs upon the sun, they must dwell in shadow; so if men will sever themselves from the Source of life, they inevitably die. Not once, but often, does God offer to us reconciliation, blessing, peace. By every method of persuasion and entreaty the Father of our spirits has endeavoured to win us to paths of righteous obedience. His will is our sanctification; purity or perdition—here is the alternative!

III. THE EXECUTORS OF JEHOVAH'S WILL SHALL BE AMPLY REWARDED. "All the spoil thereof shalt thou take unto thyself" (ver. 14). The harder the work, the more abundant shall be the reward. God's remuneration is ever ample and munificent. Most carefully does he weigh every hardship we endure for him. Our every tear he puts into his bottle. Blind unbelief may count him an "austere Master," who requires irksome and painful work; but the man of filial temper will run on most difficult errands, and his language is uniformly this, "I do always the things that please him;" "They who suffer with their Lord now shall be glorified by-and-by together."

IV. EXCESSIVE WICKEDNESS INVOLVES MEN IN COMPLETE DESTRUCTION. Terms of peace were offered to less guilty nations lying in Israel's vicinity, but for the inhabitants of Canaan—such was their moral rottenness—there was no alternative but destruction. "Thou shalt save alive nothing that breatheth" (ver. 16). It is well for us to learn that there is a stage in our moral disease when the remedy of mercy ceases to take effect. It becomes "a savour of death unto death." "With the breath of his mouth shall he slay the wicked." When the heart has become identified with rebellion, when *all* feeling is averse from God, when total depravity has set in,—then God abandons the man to his inevitable doom. "Israel would have none of him, . . . so he gave them up to their own hearts' lust." This is man's blackest doom. Yet this is mercy for others.

V. THE WORK OF DESTRUCTION SHOULD BE BLENDED WITH PRUDENT KINDNESS. In laying siege against a city, not an axe was to be laid upon any fruit tree. Here we have a sample of God's thoughtful and generous love for men! Whatever can minister to the need and comfort of his servants shall be secured to them. Though engaged in the awful work of destruction, he does not forget mercy; he is planning all the while for his servants' good. Though a frown is upon his face, tenderest love is active within his heart. More careful is he for us than we are for ourselves. Not a want, however minute, is by him overlooked. The desolating flood is upon the earth, but an ark is provided for Noah. The rain of fire is consuming Sodom, but Lot is safe in Zoar. "Even the hairs of your head are all numbered."—D.

EXPOSITION.

CHAPTER XXI.

EXPIATION OF UNCERTAIN MURDER. TREATMENT OF A CAPTIVE TAKEN TO WIFE. RIGHTS OF THE FIRSTBORN. A REBELLIOUS, REFRACTORY SON TO BE JUDGED AND PUNISHED. A MALEFACTOR WHO HAS BEEN HANGED TO BE BURIED ERE NIGHTFALL.

One general idea, viz. the sacredness of human life and of personal rights, connects the laws in this chapter together, as well as connects them with the laws in the two preceding chapters.

Vers. 1—9.—If a body was found lying dead from a wound, and it was not known by whom the wound had been inflicted, the whole land would be involved in the guilt of the murder, unless it was duly expiated as here directed. First, the elders and judges (presumably of the neighbouring towns;

cf. Josephus, 'Antiq.,' iv. 8, 16) were to meet, the former as magistrates representing the communities, the latter as administrators of the law, and were to measure the distance from the body of the slain man to each of the surrounding towns, in order to ascertain which was the nearest. This ascertained, upon that town was to be laid the duty of expiating the crime.

Ver. 3.—An heifer, which hath not been wrought with, and which hath not drawn in the yoke; a young cow which had not been rendered unfit for consecration, nor had its vital force impaired, by being subjected to forced labour (cf. Numb. xix. 2).

Ver. 4.—A rough valley; literally, a stream of perpetuity, a perennial stream (cf. Ps. lxxiv. 15, Authorized Version, "mighty rivers;" Amos v. 24); but here rather the valley or wady through which a stream flowed, as is evident from its being described as neither eared—that is, ploughed (literally, wrought, tilled)—nor sown; a place which had not been profaned by the hand of man, but was in a state of nature. "This regulation as to the locality in which the act of expiation was to be performed was probably founded on the idea that the water of the brook-valley would suck in the blood and clean it away, and that the blood sucked in by the earth would not be brought to light again by the ploughing and working of the soil" (Keil). Strike off the heifer's neck there in the valley; rather, break the heifer's neck. As this was not an act of sacrifice, for which the shedding of blood would have been required, but simply a symbolical representation of the infliction of death on the undiscovered murderer, the animal was to be killed by breaking its neck (cf. Exod. xiii. 13).

Ver. 5.—And the priests the sons of Levi shall come near. The presence of the priests at this ceremony was due to their position as the servants of Jehovah the King of Israel, on whom it devolved to see that all was done in any matter as his Law prescribed. The priests present were probably those from the nearest Levitical town. And by their word shall every controversy and every stroke be tried; literally, And upon their mouth shall be every strife and every stroke, i.e. by their judgment the character of the act shall be determined, and as they decide so shall the matter stand (cf. ch. x. 8; xvii. 8). In the present case the presence of the priests at the transaction gave it sanction as valid.

Ver. 6.—The elders of that city. The elders, by the significant act of washing their hands, indicated that they threw off from them, utterly repudiated, the charge of blood-guiltiness on the part of the town which they represented (cf. Ps. xxvi. 6; lxxiii. 13; Matt. xxvii. 24).

Vers. 7, 8.—This act they were to accompany with a solemn declaration of their innocence of this crime, and of their entire ignorance of the perpetrator of it; and with an earnest cry to God that the sin which had been done might be forgiven. Be merciful... unto; be propitiated towards (literally, cover, כַּפֵּר לְעַמְּךָ; for the phrase, כַּפֵּר לְ, see Lev. i. 4). And lay not innocent blood; the blood of the innocent man who has been slain.

Ver. 9.—In this way they were to deliver themselves as a nation from blood-guiltiness. "Expiation was made by the killing of the transgressor when he could be found (ch. xix. 13; Numb. xxxv. 33); when he was not known, by the process here described. Of course, if afterwards he were apprehended, he would suffer the penalty he had incurred" (Knobel); so also Keil, Herxheimer, etc., after the Talmud ('Sota,' ix. 7).

Vers. 10—14.—If an Israelite saw among captives taken in war a woman fair of aspect, and loved her, and took her to be his wife, he was to allow her a full month to mourn her lost kindred, and become accustomed to her new condition, before he consummated his union with her. This refers to captives from other nations than those of Canaan, with whom the Israelites were to form no alliance, and whom they were not to take captive, but either wholly destroy or render tributary (cf. ch. vii. 3; Numb. xxi. 1, etc.; Josh. xi. 19).

Ver. 12.—She shall shave her head, and pare her nails. The shaving of the head and the paring of the nails, as well as the putting off of the garments worn when taken captive, were signs of purification, or separation from former heathenism, preparatory to reception among the covenant people of Jehovah (cf. Lev. xiv. 8; Numb. viii. 7). Pare her nails; literally, make or prepare her nails, i.e. by cutting them down to a proper size and form (cf. 2 Sam. xix. 25, where the same word is used of dressing the feet and trimming the beard). The Targum of Onkelos takes this in quite an opposite sense, rendering, as in the margin of the Authorized Version, "suffer to grow," and the rabbins who adopt this meaning suppose that the design of the prescription was that the woman, being rendered unlovely, the man might be deterred from taking her to be his wife. But this is altogether alien from the spirit and scope of the passage.

Ver. 13.—The raiment of her captivity; i.e. the raiment she had on when taken captive; this she was to lay aside, that she might put on garments of mourning. **A full month**; literally, *a month of days ;* the period of mourning was forty days (cf. Gen. l. 3).

Ver. 14.—Should the man afterwards come no longer to have pleasure in her, he was to let her go whither she would, but he was not to sell her for money or use any violence to her. **Thou shalt not make merchandise of her.** The verb in the form here used occurs only here and in ch. xxiv. 7; derived from a root which signifies to gather or press, it properly means to press for one's self, to lay hands on one, to use violence to one.

Vers. 15—17.—If a man have two wives, one of whom is a favourite and the other disliked, and if his firstborn son be the child of the latter, he is not to allow his love for the other to prejudice the right of the son, but must allow him, both in his own lifetime and in the disposition of his property after death, the full privilege and right of a firstborn son.

Ver. 16.—**He may not make;** literally, *is not able to make ;* i.e. is legally incapable of making.

Ver. 17.—**A double portion;** literally, *a mouth of two ;* i.e. a portion (so "mouth" is used in 2 Kings ii. 9; Zech. xiii. 8) equal to that of two; consequently, the firstborn inherited twice as much as any of the other sons. Amongst all nations and from the earliest times, the right of the eldest son to pre-eminence among his brethren has been recognized; and in legislating for Israel, Moses so far simply sanctioned a usage he found already existing; the assignment, however, of a double share in the inheritance to the eldest son is a new and special provision, mentioned only here. **Beginning of his strength** (cf. Gen. xlix. 3).

Vers. 18—21.—If a son was refractory and unmanageable by his parents, if, given to sensual indulgence, he would yield neither to reproof nor to chastisement,—the parents were to lay hold on him, and lead him to the elders of the town, sitting as magistrates at its gates, and there accuse him of his evil ways and rebelliousness. The testimony of the parents was apparently held sufficient to substantiate the charge, and this being received by the elders, the culprit was to be put to death by stoning.

Ver. 20.—**He will not obey our voice;** he is a glutton, and a drunkard. Gluttony and drunkenness were regarded by the Hebrews as highly criminal. The word rendered by "glutton," however (זוֹלֵל, from זָלַל, to shake, to shake out, to squander), includes other kinds of excess besides eating. It designates one who is prodigal, who wastes his means or wastes his person by indulgence. In Prov. xxiii. 30, the whole phrase (וְזֹלְלֵי בָשָׂר) is given—squanderers of flesh, *i.e.* wasters of their own body, debauchees. In Prov. xxviii. 7, the word is translated "riotous men" in the Authorized Version. Disobedience to parents was deemed an offence which struck at the roots of the whole social institute.

Ver. 21.—The penalty of such crimes was death; but the power of inflicting this was not among the Hebrews—as among some other ancient peoples, the Greeks and Romans, for instance—left with the father; the punishment could be inflicted only by the community, with the sanction of the magistrate. A Hebrew parent might chastise his child with severity, but not so as to affect his life (Prov. xix. 18, "Chasten thy son while there is hope, but raise not thy soul [let not thy passion rise so high as] to slay him"). While parental authority was sacredly preserved, a check was by the Law imposed on hasty passion.

Vers. 22, 23.—When a criminal was put to death and was hanged upon a tree, his body was not to remain there over-night, but was to be buried the same day on which he was executed.

Ver. 22.—**If a man have committed a sin worthy of death;** literally, *If there be on a man a judgment of death ;* if he lie under sentence of death. **Hang him on a tree.** This refers not to putting to death by strangling, but to the impaling of the body after death (cf. C. B. Michaelis, ' De Judiciis Pœnisque Capitalibus in Sac. Script. Commemoratis,' in ' Sylloge Commentt. Theolog.,' edita à D. J. Pott, vol. iv. p. 209). This was an aggravation of the punishment, as the body so impaled was exposed to insult and assault (cf. Numb. xxv. 4; Gen. xl. 19).

Ver. 23.—**He that is hanged is accursed of God;** literally, *a curse of God.* Some take this as meaning an insult to God, a contemning of him, "since man his image is thus given up to scorn and insult" (Rashi). But the more probable meaning is "a curse inflicted by God," which the transgressor is made to endure (cf. Gal. iii. 13). **That thy land be not defiled.** The land was defiled, not only by sins committed by its inhabitants, but also by the public exposure of criminals who had been put to death for their sins (cf. Lev. xviii. 24, 25; Numb. xxxv. 33, 34). On this law Joshua acted (cf. Josh. viii. 29; x. 26, 27).

HOMILETICS.

Vers. 1—9.—*The preciousness of one human life in the sight of God*. The value of this paragraph can be duly appreciated only as the indifference with which pagan nations of old regarded human life is studied and understood. As a piece of civil legislation, it is far superior to anything in the code of the nations around at that time. Dr. Jameson remarks that in it we have undoubtedly the origin or the germ of modern coroners' inquests. The following points in it are worthy of note. 1. It is a rule to be observed when they should be settled in the land of Canaan. 2. It indicates that from the first, each human life should be regarded as an object of common interest to the whole people, and that it was to be one of their prime points of honour, that no human life could be tampered with without arousing national indignation and concern. 3. God would teach them, that if it should be found that any one's life had been trifled with, it was a sin against Heaven as well as a crime against earth. 4. That this sin would be laid at the door of all the people if they were indifferent to the fact of its commission, and if they did not make full inquiry respecting it, and solemnly put it away from among them. At the back of this piece of civil legislation, yea, as the fount from which it sprang, we get this beautiful, sublime, and comforting truth— "*Each human life an object of Divine concern.*"

I. IN WHAT WAY HAS GOD MANIFESTED HIS CARE FOR THE INDIVIDUAL? 1. *This* passage is pregnant with blessed teaching thereon. We have: (1) The fact of man's ill-treatment of men recognized. (2) Rebuked. (3) Marked out as a brand of shame on any community which tolerates it. (4) In demanding an account thereof, God foreshadows his own coming judgment. 2. The Lord Jesus Christ taught it in terms more beautiful, more clear (Luke xii.; Matt. xviii.; Luke xv.). How often does Christ lay stress on "one"! 3. The death of the Lord Jesus Christ for every man, is a standing proof of every man's worth before God; so the apostle argues (2 Cor. v. 16). 4. The Spirit of God stirreth in every man to move his sluggish nature that it may rise toward heaven. Materialism merges the man in his accidents. Pantheism drowns him in the All. Deism hides him in vastness. Ultramontanism smothers him in the Church. Cæsarism makes the State all, the individual nothing. Christ rescues the one from being lost in the many, and cries aloud, "It is not the will of your Father in heaven that *one* of these little ones should perish."

II. WHAT SHOULD BE THE EFFECT ON US OF GOD'S CARE FOR THE INDIVIDUAL? 1. It should fill us with intense thankfulness that we are not lost in the crowd (see Isa. xl. 27). We are so apt to say, "God has too much to do to think of us," that we need to meditate often on the words, "He careth for you." 2. It should impress us with the dignity of man. When God fences every man round with such a guard against ill treatment from others, it may well lead us to "honour all men." 3. It should teach us the solidarity of the race. The weal of one is a concern to all. 4. It should teach us to cultivate the spirit of a universal brotherhood. "Have we not all one Father?" 5. It should lead us to aim at saving man. If God cares for all, well may we. 6. It should make us very indignant at any doctrines concerning the constitution and destiny of man, that would put him, or even seem to put him, on a level with the brute creation. 7. We should take every opportunity of warning men that, if ever they trifle with the interests and destinies of their brother man, God will call them to account at his bar. The voice of Abel's blood cried unto God from the ground. If a neglected, mutilated, slain body of any one, however obscure, was found in Israel's fields, they were responsible to the God of nations for inquiry and for expiation. No one is at liberty to cry, "Am I my brother's keeper?" When he maketh inquisition for blood, he forgetteth not the cry of the humble (see Ps. xciv.). And terrible beyond all power of expression, will be the shame and dismay, at the bar of God, of those who have trifled with human interests, and who go into eternity laden with the guilt of their brothers' blood!

Vers. 10—14.—*The female captive; or, Divine regard for woman's safety and honour.* Any one who is acquainted with the fearful licence practised among many nations towards female captives taken in war, can surely appreciate the humanizing influence which the injunction in this paragraph was intended to exert. The law here laid down may or may not be abstractly the best; but if it was the best that the people could bear: if it would certainly lift up the people a step higher in their regard for womanly honour: if, moreover, it would have the effect of enforcing a restraint upon the passions of men at that most perilous of all times, even that of war,—then the hallowed influence which was shaping Hebrew legislation becomes clearly manifest. A woman taken captive as a prisoner of war was not to be a plaything of passion, but was to be dealt with honourably; to feel that she might part with the symbols of slavery, enter into relation with the covenant people, become invested with the rights of a daughter of Israel, and learn to worship, love, and glorify Israel's God! (For details, see the Exposition, and also valuable remarks in Keil and Jameson.) And if, in the issue, there was no true and proper home for her, she was to have that most precious of blessings—liberty! In opening up the theme suggested here—*Divine care for woman's safety and honour*—some seven or eight lines of thought may be taken up and worked out by the preacher. 1. Here is a Divine protest against the tendency of men to make woman a mere tool of passion. This book is the charter of woman's honour and happiness. 2. Our God would aim at bringing about the true nobility of woman, by means of educating the people up to the standard at which it shall be a point of honour with them to insist upon it. 3. To secure this end, State laws should be stringently framed. 4. Not even in war-time, nor in connection with our soldiery, is it ever to be tolerated that woman should be at the mercy of the stronger sex. 5. The right place of woman is in the love and protection of one to whom she is dearer than his own soul; and no more honourable place need she desire than that assigned her by Solomon in his description of "a virtuous woman." Many of the holy women of Scripture illustrate this. 6. Under the gospel, woman's position is yet more strikingly asserted. "In Christ Jesus there is ... neither male nor female." In religious relationship man and woman are, *cæteris paribus*, on an equal footing. 7. While, in the home, the wives are to be in subjection to their own husbands, yet the sway of the husband is to be with a love pure and tender, like that of the Lord Jesus Christ. And it is only where the purifying and love-creating power of the gospel is known, that woman rises to her right position in the home, the family, the social circle, and the nation. The legislation on her behalf, which Moses began, has been going on under Judaism and Christianity for long ages, with what results we know in our happy homes. But how much we are indebted for these happy homes to the influence of Jewish and Christian law, can best be told by those who know the dark places of the earth, still "full of the habitations of cruelty."

Vers. 15—17.—*Home partialities never to warp home justice.* This paragraph indicates deep insight into human nature, and a far-seeing wisdom which surely indicates its superhuman origin. It is designed to restrict the action of the father with reference to the inheritance of the children, in cases where there were two families, not, apparently, by two wives living at the same time (as if the passage favoured polygamy), but rather by two of whom the second became the wife after the death of the first (comp. Jameson and Keil). It would probably, nay, almost certainly, occur, that one of the two would be thought more of than the other; the influence of the second wife, being later and withal continuous, might be exerted with the husband in favour of her own children, to the detriment of his by the former wife. And thus a son who was the father's firstborn might be put at a disadvantage through later preferences coming athwart his proper claims. Moses here teaches that he may not be dispossessed of the right of the firstborn, even though another should come on the scene who should be the firstborn in a second family. The principle on which this is based is indicated in the title of this Homily—"*Home partialities never to warp home justice.*" The following lines of thought may serve as a plan on which to enforce this principle.

I. It is an acknowledged duty of parents to care for the temporal weal of their children (see 2 Cor. xii. 14). There is indeed, on the part of some, a consuming desire to leave large fortunes to their families—a desire so great as to be inconsistent with faith in God's care. This is to be avoided on the one hand, while at the same time the opposite extreme is to be shunned on the other.

II. There are certain rights which belong to the children, supposing their father is possessed of an inheritance which he *can* leave them. Of course, if he has none, this paragraph in detail does not apply. Even in such a case, however, a parent owes it to his family to leave them the best of all heritages—a holy example, God's blessing, and a father's prayers! If he leaves them this, they will not want.

III. It is not impossible, nor even improbable, that circumstances may occur giving rise to partialities in a parent, which may lead him to consult the interest of some of his children to the detriment of that of others. Cases like that named in this paragraph are notoriously fraught with peril in this respect. And where such is the case there should be a special guard.

IV. These partialities are dangerous. They are so even during the father's life-time, but the results thereof after his death are likely to be serious and even disastrous. It is not possible to calculate the mischief wrought upon children, when the earthly name which should ever stand to them dearest in affection and highest in honour, is associated with an inequality by which some are advantaged and others wronged. No bitterness of feeling can surpass that which is thus engendered. It will wrap in shade an otherwise most venerated name.

V. God would teach us that *he* is ever watchful over the right in families, in every respect. The same Being who says to the children, "Honour your parents," says also to the parents, "Honour your children." As he would guard the heads of the house from being trifled with by the sons, so would he guard the sons from any injustice on the part of their parents. A wrong on either side towards the other is a sin against God. And so largely does the observance of the right in the family concerning money and property, affect the well-being of the State, that it is here made a part of the civil code of the " commonwealth of Israel," that no parent shall be at liberty, whatever his preferences, to ignore the standing claims of his children.

Vers. 18—21.—*A bad son a State peril.* This is a very remarkable provision. It is based on the well-known fact that there are some who need a strong deterrent to keep them from being a plague and peril to a State, and also on the all-important principle, that whoever is a pest and nuisance in the home, is the bane of the commonwealth to which he belongs. Moses had just laid down the duty of the parent to deal justly with his sons, whatever his personal partialities might be. He now lays down the extent and limits of parental authority over the son. He does not give the father the absolute power of life and death in reference to the child, as some ancient codes did, but, without abolishing that power altogether, he places such checks upon it that while, on the one hand, if a bad son became so outrageous that his life was putting others in peril through its poisonous influence, he would have before him the possibility of capital punishment; yet, on the other hand, this penalty could only be inflicted with the sanction of the elders of the city; the consent of both parents was required ere he could be brought before them; and they (the parents) were expected to be able to say that they had exhausted every known means of reclaiming him before they brought him to that tribunal. It is evident that the law is enacted with the intention of being so deterrent that it may never need to be put into execution. And thus indeed it seems to have proved. For there is no known instance in Jewish history of its having been carried out.[1] Forming part, as it did, of an ancient civil code for the Hebrew nation only, it is not in force with us now, and we are not called upon to appreciate its real worth as a guard to the stability of the Hebrew nation. But here, as elsewhere, even in obsolete statutes, we discover permanent principles, which it behoves preachers to develop and enforce, if they would not "shun to declare the whole counsel of God." The truth here taught is this—*A bad son is a State peril.* Five lines of thought may with advantage be followed out here, with the view of impressing this truth upon the hearts of the people.

I. A STATE IS WHAT ITS HOMES MAKE IT. It cannot be otherwise. It is made up of its own cities, towns, villages, and hamlets. Each one of these is made up of its homes. If they are all good, little legislation will be required; if they are

---

[1] Josephus ('Ant.,' xvi. ch. xi. § 2) gives an instance in which Herod the Great availed himself of it. (See Jameson, *in loc.*)

all bad, no legislation will avail, even if it could be secured. And according as the good or bad element preponderates, will a State be secure and prosperous or otherwise.

II. AN INCORRIGIBLE SON IS THE BANE OF ANY HOME. It is not within our present province to illustrate or even take up the truth that it is extremely unlikely any son will become incorrigible, unless there is some grievous failure in duty on the part of the parents in not correcting him betimes, and in not keeping the reins in their own hands. It is, unhappily, too often true—"his sons made themselves vile, and he restrained them not." But, however it may come about, the truth is the same, that where a son hearkens not to the voice of his father, and despises to obey his mother, there will be in any home in which such is the case, a source of deep sorrow and indescribable misery ; there will be an example fraught with evil influence to the other members of the family. "One sickly sheep infects the flock."

III. SUCH A HOME, SO POISONED, MAY BECOME A CENTRE OF UNSPEAKABLE MISCHIEF. For the sons who act so mischievously in the house are, as a rule, those who wander far and wide in pursuit of forbidden pleasure, giving way to the lusts of the flesh, and to sins of the tongue, polluting others wherever they go. Thus a moral miasma, pestilential and even deadly, may be carried from street to street, and from town to town.

IV. THOSE THUS POLLUTED WILL TAKE THE POISON TO OTHER HOMES. One home will infect others. Each infected home will spread the contagion. And so the evil will spread far and wide, not only in an arithmetical, but in a geometrical progression, till even in the course of one or two generations, it will assume a proportion which baffle all powers of calculation to formulate it, and a virulence which may defy the most powerful legislation to arrest it.

V. HENCE THE VERY EXISTENCE OF SUCH A CENTRE OF EVIL OUT OF WHICH SUCH COMPLICATED AND WIDESPREAD MISCHIEF MAY ARISE, IS A SOURCE OF GRAVE PERIL TO ANY COMMONWEALTH IN THE WORLD! It may not be seen nor even suspected when in germ. But germs of evil are fraught with all the evil of which they are the germs.

1. Learn how far-seeing are the provisions of this Mosaic law! What seems severity to the individual is really mercy to the nation. Preventive measures, though severe, may be most genuinely philanthropic. 2. Learn how great is the importance of wisdom and firmness in maintaining parental authority. 3. Learn the need of early habits of obedience to parents. An obedient son is a joy and honour to his parents, a credit to the home, an element of safety in a State. But "God never smiles on a boy that breaks his mother's heart." So said Richard Knill. Finally : What we have said thus far is valid, even if this life were all. But if to this life we add on the next, and bethink us of the amazing issues projecting themselves from time into eternity, who can adequately set forth the importance of taking heed to those early steps on which depend the direction of this earthly life, when on it depends the weal or woe of the life which is to come ?

Vers. 22, 23.—*Upon the tree!* These words form part of the criminal code of the Hebrews, and though as such they may be regarded as practically obsolete, yet they contain principles which will never wax old, and are, moreover, so frequently alluded to in the New Testament, that they furnish us with a starting-point of no mean interest for a devout Christian meditation. The case supposed in the text is not that of a man being put to death *by* crucifixion, but of his having suffered capital punishment, and of his body being afterwards hung upon a stake and put to an open shame by the exposure, as having been one of the vilest of criminals. Such an exposure after death was to be, so to speak, the expression of the execration of the people. It would be their public brand upon detestable guilt. And, when thus the public detestation and horror of wickedness had been expressed, that accursed thing was to be taken down that night and buried out of sight for ever, as a sign that the curse had spent itself. This *vox populi* was *vox Dei.* "He that is hanged is accursed of God."

Now, it may be asked, "Why take up the time of a congregation by recalling an obsolete enactment like this?" Our reply is, Let us now turn to Acts v. 30. Peter knew how the Jews would regard these words—"whom ye slew *and hanged on a tree.*" They would understand their significance to be, "You put him to an open shame, as though he, the best of men, were one of the vilest malefactors." Shall we call this the "irony of history"? How was it that God let the treatment of the basest of criminals be accorded to the holiest of our race? We often speak of it as a "mystery of Providence" when some great trouble befalls a good man. But of all such mysteries there is none so great as this. As a bare piece of history unexplained, there is no fact which in all its surroundings is so inexplicable as this, that Jesus Christ of Nazareth should have died amid such deep disgrace and shame. "Hanged on a tree!" Let us go further on. Read 1 Pet. ii. 24. Note the emphasis, "who his own self bare our sins in his own body *on the tree*." Here is an explanation of the strange fact. He was pressed down with others' woes, and burdened with the guilt of others' sins. And why? What was the effect of all? Read again. In Gal. iii. 13, 14, the apostle, quoting these words of Moses, shows us that in the fact of the ignominious death of the Lord Jesus Christ upon the tree, we are to see at once (1) the Divine execration of sin, and (2) the Divine redemption of the sinner.

I. Under a moral government, a righteous governor will, yea, must append blessing to good, and affix a curse to evil. If any one asks *Why?* we do not know that any one can answer further than to say that suffering is the desert of ill, and gladness the appropriate consequence of well-doing. No other theory would be workable in any well-ordered family, or nation, or city. In the family, paternal punishment expresses the father's sense of wrong done. In the State, punishment marks the nation's sense of wrong done. And these are but echoes of that Divine disapproval of sin to which the conscience of man with certainty points. And it is well known and understood that the disapproval and condemnation of wrong on the part of any government is never to be confounded with, but is very far removed from, personal vindictiveness. No government, indeed, would command the confidence of the people under which crime could be carried on with impunity. Without branding crime against a State, no government could long exist. That brand is "the curse of the law."

II. There is a law above all human laws. The latter are partial and defective, and may become obsolete. The everlasting law of righteousness is co-eternal with the Great Supreme. He judges the world in righteousness. Every child of man is answerable to his tribunal. Every deed, word, and thought are scanned by his all-seeing eye, and are estimated rightly by his unerring judgment. And he, the Great Judge, brings against each and all the charge of being law-breakers (see Rom. i., ii.). The Jew is so because he has broken a written Law; the Gentile, because he has broken an unwritten one. All the world is guilty before God. Under such circumstances, what is a righteous Being to do to secure the stability of his throne? To connive at sin? To pass it by, and take no notice of it? To let the sinner have the same grace as if he had never sinned? No; there must be a declaration, a demonstration, of his righteousness, as Paul calls it. And the demonstration of righteousness certainly involves the condemnation of sin.

III. If we are sinners, as we are, the Divine condemnation of sin places us under a curse. We must be careful to understand that in the Divine curse there is nothing vindictive, excessive, defective, or ineffective; there is nothing in it out of harmony with the everlasting love of righteousness which is the bulwark and safeguard of the Divine government of souls. As many as are of the works of the Law are—continue to be —under the curse. As long as a man's life is unright, by God's law he abides under condemnation.

IV. Guilty men *are* under the curse; a Guiltless One *comes* under it. So Gal. iii. 13, "being made a curse for us," rather, "having become a curse." (Let the student note here, as in John i., the careful use of, and the distinction between, the words for "being" and "becoming.") The Son of God, the Law-maker, comes and dwells with the law-breakers, and becomes as one of them. Joyfully taking their place, he bears their burdens and accepts their liabilities as if they were his own! He is pressed down as with a great weight. His sweat is as it were great drops of blood. He goes to *the tree*. The deepest indignity the Law knows is his. He is numbered with the transgressors. He is put to "an open shame." He dies as the worst of malefactors died—*on the tree!* The One who stands pre-eminent among men for the purity of his life stands out also conspicuously among men for the humiliation which attends on his death! He hangs on a tree, as if accursed of God!

V. Our Lord Jesus Christ then represented our race, and for them had become a curse. A stupendous transaction was then and there effected, to which we know of no parallel in heaven or on earth (cf. Matt. xx. 28; 1 Pet. ii. 24; 2 Cor. v. 21; John i. 29). Note: 1. He was of such dignity that he *could* represent the race. 2. His act was entirely spontaneous; he *willed* to do it. 3. It was the Father's appointment that he *should* do it. 4. Foreseeing the result of his work, he *rejoiced* to do it (Isa. liii. 11 (Hebrew); Heb. xii. 1, 2). Amid the external humiliation, the thought of saving men thereby, bore him on and bore him through.

VI. By bearing the curse on himself upon the tree he bore it off from us. He has redeemed us therefrom. He has bought us up out of it. He who deserved it not, was pressed down by it, that we who deserved it might be lifted up out of it. Sin having been, in him, condemned—once, completely, righteously, eternally—the righteousness of the Lawgiver was demonstrated. Then was his love free to act towards us apart from Law, on the principle of grace.

VII. The curse being thus rolled away, the way is prepared for the coming in of the blessing. However fully and freely infinite love now heaps blessing on blessing on the vilest sinner, not from one quarter of the universe can the murmur rise up that God thinks lightly of sin, when, in order to lift its weight off the guilty sinner, the Infinite Son of God has taken the whole load upon himself, and atoned for sin by his own sacrifice!

VIII. The blessing comes to men when they repent and believe. So argues Paul in both his Epistles to the Romans and Galatians. See especially Rom. iv. 16, and the wonderful parallel between the first and the second Adam in Rom. v.

IN CONCLUSION. 1. Let us adore and magnify the grace and righteousness of God in the atoning work of Christ on the tree. The manifold perfections of the Divine nature shine forth here in combined lustre. Thousands have objected to the doctrine of the atonement. No one ever objected to it who did not first misapprehend it. 2. Let us cultivate deep, serious, and earnest thinkings as to the evil of sin, thus branded with the curse of God. Only low moral conceptions can consist with the denial of the necessity for an atonement. 3. Let us see that we rely entirely and penitently on the work of the Son of God on our behalf. 4. Let us defend the manifold glories of the cross against all deniers and opponents. 5. Let us, before whom this Divine act of self-surrender stands as the warrant of our hope, have it ever before us also as the model and standard of our life. And, in studying ever more and more fully the meaning of Christ's self-surrender to God for us, shall we find the inspiration of our self-surrender to God for others!

HOMILIES BY VARIOUS AUTHORS.

Vers. 1—9.—*Atonement for unknown sin.* We have here a ritual applicable to cases where murder has not been expiated by the apprehension and execution of the murderer. The mystery has remained unravelled. The elders and judges, in such a case, are to come and measure which city is nearest the slain man, and the elders of that city are then required to take the heifer prescribed and make atonement, that the country may be delivered from the guilt of innocent blood. The heifer is to be one in the full vigour of life, which has not been wrought with, and consequently expressed in the fullest form the life-producing power to which the violent death stood as a contrast.[1] She is to be taken down into a "rough valley," or, as the words (נַחַל אֵיתָן) more accurately mean, "a perennial stream," and there is her neck to be struck off, and the blood thus violently shed is to pass away in the never-failing stream. While this is taking place, the elders of the city are to wash their hands over her, in protestation of their innocence, and to pray for deliverance from the guilt, and it shall be forgiven them.

I. AN UNDISCOVERED MURDER IS PROPERLY IMPUTED TO THE DISTRICT WHERE THE VICTIM HAS BEEN FOUND. In a well-ordered society life should be safe. When it is

---

[1] Cf. Kurtz's 'Sacrificial Worship of the Old Testament,' p. 427.

proved unsafe, society cannot plead " Not guilty." Locally, it must be allocated, and so the city nearest the victim has the crime *imputed* to it. The sense of guilt is distributed territorially, and the elders, or representatives of the people, are required to clear themselves by the special rite here described.

Sin has thus wider relations than to the individual who has committed it. It may lie at the door of a city, or of a neighbourhood, and in their collective capacity they may be required to deal with it.

II. THE DISTRICT THUS GUILTY THROUGH IMPUTATION IS MOST PROPERLY SUMMONED TO A RELIGIOUS SERVICE. It is surely a matter for general humiliation that such a crime could be secretly committed, and the murderer escape. It should lead to special religious exercises. It would be a very seemly thing if neighbourhoods where great crimes have gone undiscovered were to unite in supplicating God's mercy, in view of the guilt thus contracted.

III. A WAY OF DELIVERANCE FROM THE IMPUTED GUILT IS GRACIOUSLY PROVIDED. It consisted of the following elements.

1. The *violent death of an innocent and full-blooded animal*. The cruel killing of the heifer was a repetition of the tragedy, and was well fitted to bring its guilt before them. Thus was a sense of sin deepened.

2. *Its shed blood was carried away on the surface of the never-failing stream*. In this beautiful, poetic way, the providential removal of innocent blood, did God convey the idea of removing the guilt from the district concerned.

3. *Over the heifer so slain the elders were to wash their hands and protest their innocency*. In this way the most solemn sanctions were associated with their plea of " Not guilty."

4. *And they were further to intercede for the removal of the imputation against Israel*. Only after this minute ritual had been gone through was the assurance of forgiveness pronounced by the priest.

IV. IN THIS WAY WE DISCOVER A TYPIFICATION OF THE PARDON PROVIDED BY CHRIST. And here we do well to notice, as facts incapable of dispute—

1. That *people who are innocent have often to incur imputation along with the guilty*. The children of evil-doers incur an evil repute, although they may be perfectly innocent. It is a law of society as at present constituted—the innocent are grouped with the guilty.

2. *Jesus Christ is One who has voluntarily accepted of the imputation of sin, though innocent, and suffered in consequence*. Just as the innocent heifer was paraded with the guilty district, and alone suffered because of the committed and undiscovered sin, so Jesus takes up his position in the sad procession, and is the selected, yet voluntary, Victim.

3. *The Holy Spirit, as a perennial stream, carries the sense and sight of blood-guiltiness away*. For, without the Spirit's help, the shed blood of Jesus might only increase human guilt; with his help it takes all the guilt away.

4. *Those who wish pardon must not be too proud to ask for it*. " If we confess our sins, he is faithful and just to forgive us our sins, and to cleanse us from all unrighteousness." So have we the gospel vividly presented to us.—R. M. E.

Vers. 10—14.—*Through love to liberty*. We have here a regulation or law of war. Captives might be sold as slaves, but through love they might reach the position of a wife in a Jewish household, and if she did not please her conqueror, then she was to be made free again. So that the possible fate of the captive was "through love to liberty."

I. LOVE IS THE BEST CURE FOR THE ILLS OF WAR. The men were to be slain: women might be kept as a prey (ch. xx. 14). It was a blessed issue when the conqueror was himself conquered by his captive. Then slavery was over, and love brought liberty. The passion of hate had given place to the passion of love. The better time had come.

II. BUT THE PASSION MUST BE SUBJECT TO WISE RESTRAINT. A month's mourning is allowed the beautiful captive, during which her person is sacred in the house of her captor. She bids farewell to her relations, whether living or dead, for she is going to be the wife of a Jew; and her intended husband has time to think quietly over his passion of love, and to see whether it is lasting or no.

III. HER PRIVILEGE WAS TO BECOME THE FREE WIFE OF HER JEWISH LORD. If a happily ordered marriage, it must have been a joyful issue of the war. The terrible ordeal had proved to her the path to honour and social blessedness and peace. All the agony had given place to enlarging love.

IV. AT THE VERY WORST, SHE REGAINED HER LIBERTY. The love had in this case proved transient—she had not pleased him—they would not be happy together. In such a case she was given a legal title to liberty. If not loved, she had the next best privilege of being free.

In this arrangement, consequently, we have love and liberty in the house of a husband ; or liberty, if the love proves fickle and the match ill arranged. This was a beneficent arrangement compared with the licentiousness which usually accompanied war.

V. WE MAY CONTRAST THIS WITH THE LOVE AND LIBERTY GUARANTEED US BY CHRIST JESUS. Our Lord, in fact, offers us his love, oh, how strong and how true! And in his love there is liberty, the liberty wherewith he makes his people free. No uncertainty hangs over his offer to us ; no slavery is possible in his house. We shall, in fact, have reason to bless him for conquering us for loving purposes, and any anguish his conquest may have cost us, will be amply compensated in his royal and limitless love.

Conquest, love, and liberty for ever is the experience through which we pass in the hands of Jesus, the Conquering Hero, and no one ever regrets entering upon it, for it is enjoyment indeed !—R. M. E.

Vers. 15—17.—*The rights of the firstborn in the house of a bigamist.* Bigamy was not encouraged by the Mosaic Law. Where it took place in man's passion, the Law stepped in to regulate the relations in the household impartially. The house of a bigamist may be the scene of sudden jealousies and dispeace, but God steps in to forbid it being the scene of injustice. The discomfort is providentially inseparable from the bigamy—it would have been a pity had it been otherwise! But the Lord steps in to prevent flagrant injustice being done to the children solely through the father's caprice. Caprice may be permitted up to a certain point, with all its painful checks, but it will not be suffered to perpetuate undeserved wrong.

I. THE RIGHTS OF THE FIRSTBORN CONSISTED IN A DOUBLE SHARE OF THE FAMILY PROPERTY—TWICE AS MUCH AS THE OTHER CHILDREN. This was that he, as the beginning of his father's strength, and as acknowledged head of the family, might be able to sustain its honour properly. It was for this portion Elisha prayed when he desired a double portion of Elijah's spirit; not twice as much, but twice as much as the other sons of the prophets (2 Kings ii. 9). And this is what Jesus gets from the Father, according to the promise, " I will make him my Firstborn, higher than the kings of the earth " (Ps. lxxxix. 27). There was another right of the firstborn, in having a seed raised up for him in case of his premature decease. This also has its import in the case of Jesus.

II. BECAUSE A FIRSTBORN'S MOTHER WAS HATED WAS NO REASON WHY HE SHOULD BE DENIED HIS RIGHTS. The dark cloud of hate was not to envelop him, and keep him out of his double portion, or his right to a seed, if he prematurely died. And yet this was what Jesus received in the way of treatment. " He came unto his own, and his own received him not." As the Firstborn of humanity, he deserved the double portion, yet had not where to lay his head. He was denied his rights among men.

III. FROM THE CAPRICE OF MEN WE MAY ALWAYS LOOK UP TO THE IMPARTIAL JUSTICE OF GOD. This was the protection of the firstborn in the house of a bigamist. God was on his side. This was the protection of Jesus amid the injustice of men—the Father was along with him. He always did what pleased him. And whenever we feel aggrieved through the capricious conduct of our fellows, let us always look up confidingly to our Father above.

The Lord is just, at all events. We may rely on his vindication of our case in the great day, if not before.—R. M. E.

Vers. 18—23.—*Parental authority enforced.* It is plain that parents are to deal with their children to the best of their ability : but in case a stubborn and rebellious son would not hearken to father or mother, would not appreciate chastisement, and had become a drunkard and glutton, then the parents were directed to bring the case before the elders of the city, and the impenitent, licentious son was to be taken away from the earth by public stoning. The public law was thus, in the last resort, to back up parental authority and to remove the " scapegrace."

I. PARENTAL AUTHORITY IS TO BE EXERCISED TO THE UTMOST. Father and mother are both to do their best to save their son from being a public disgrace. They are to use the rod, to chasten him, if nothing milder will do. Only after they have prosecuted their parental authority to the last degree are they to seek the public officers.

II. GLUTTONY AND DRUNKENNESS ARE TREATED AS CAPITAL OFFENCES UNDER THE THEOCRACY. They are incompatible with membership in God's kingdom. Hence they are deemed worthy of death. Because they are not now so severely visited by public law does not imply that they are less heinous in God's sight than they were then.

III. IT MUST HAVE BEEN THE LAST RESORT WHEN PARENTS WOULD BRING FORTH THEIR SON FOR PUBLIC EXECUTION. What a wearying of love and patience there must have been before such a commandment as this would be carried out! The father and mother would bear long before they would bring themselves to make of their child a public infamy.

IV. THE EXECUTION OF THE SCAPEGRACE WAS A SOLEMN DEDICATION OF HIM, BY IMPOSITION OF HANDS, TO DEATH BY STONING. Such a public disgrace must have had a very wholesome effect in deterring reckless children from self-abandonment. We do not hear of any instance of such an execution. Drunkenness and gluttony were not common crimes in Israel.

V. IT WOULD SEEM THAT GIBBETING WAS ADDED TO THE STONING, TO EMPHASIZE STILL MORE THE DISGRACE IN SUCH CASES. When this was carried out, it was understood that the gibbeted person was taken down at sundown, so as not to defile the land, and was buried without delay. As accursed of God, the corpse was as soon as possible put out of sight into the tomb.

VI. IT IS INSTRUCTIVE TO THINK OF JESUS CHRIST BEING EXPOSED TO JUST SUCH A PUBLIC INFAMY. He was made a curse for us. He was hanged on a tree, gibbeted as a malefactor. What love led him to place himself in such a position! The authorities took him, and in his Father's and mother's presence they did him to death, as if he had been a disobedient and disgraceful Son. Thus did he deliver us from the curse of the Law. We receive honour because he accepted shame. The "holy Child Jesus" was nailed to the cross, was suspended on a tree, as if he were accursed of God. May we all profit by his voluntary humiliation, and imitate him as the holy, consecrated Child!—R. M. E.

Vers. 1—9.—*Purification from guilt of an uncertain murder.* The explanation commonly given of this peculiar ceremony seems unsatisfactory. Keil's view, that "it was a symbolical infliction of the punishment that should have been borne by the murderer, upon the animal which was substituted for him," is contradicted by the fact that, for deliberate murder, the Law, as he admits, provided no expiation, while the object of this ceremony was plainly in some way to remove blood-guiltiness. Fairbairn's explanation (in his ' Typology ') is even more far-fetched, that the heifer was "a palpable representative of the person whose life had been wantonly and murderously taken away." The key to the ceremony is, we think, to be sought for in another direction. The central idea is that a responsibility attaches to a whole community for crimes committed in its midst. The members of the community are implicated in the guilt of the murder till they absolve themselves by bringing the murderer to justice (vers. 8, 9). In the case here treated of, the murderer is unknown, and a rite is appointed by which the share of the community in his blood-guiltiness, which cannot be removed in the ordinary way, by executing justice on the criminal, is otherwise abolished. The heifer, in this view, represents neither the murdered man nor his murderer, but the people of the city, who seek to purge themselves from guilt by putting it to death. It is their own guilt they seek to get rid of, not the criminal's. Expiation was not admitted for the actual murderer, but the responsibility for the crime, which, failing the visitation of justice on the criminal, devolved on the community —for that, expiation was admitted. The animal, suffering vicariously, in full possession of its vital powers, while the elders of the city washed their hands over it, and declared their innocence of all knowledge of the murder, sufficed to secure that "the blood should be forgiven them"—forgiveness implying previous imputation. The valley, "neither eared nor sown," was, in its desolation and sterility, a fit place for such a transaction, which, while it cleansed the city, left the curse upon the murderer, and indeed made the spot a sort of witness of his yet unexpiated guilt. We learn : 1. That responsibility attaches to each and all in a community for crimes committed in its midst. 2. That the community is not absolved till every effort has been made to discover the perpetrators of crime and to bring them to justice. 3. That the punishment of murder is death. 4. That to ignore, connive at, or encourage crime in a community, involves the authorities in the criminality of the deeds connived at. 5. That all parties, the people (represented by the elders), the magistrates (judges), the Church (priests), are alike interested in bringing criminals to justice.—J. O.

Vers. 10—15.—*The captive wife.* The kindness, thoughtfulness, and strict justice of the Mosaic laws is very striking. The Law here interposes to secure—

I. CONSIDERATE TREATMENT OF ONE BEREAVED. (Vers. 10—14.) The case supposed comes under the law of ch. xx. 14. The woman was a captive in war and a heathen, yet the Israelite is required to respect her chastity, and, if he conceive a passion for her, must not only make her his wife in a proper manner, but must allow her a full month to bewail her dead relatives. The question of religion is a difficult one in such cases, but we may suppose that no force was applied to captives and strangers further than forbidding to them the outward practice of idolatry. The laying aside of the symbols of captivity, and the purificatory rites of cutting the hair and nails, could only imply reception into the fellowship of the covenant nation in the event of the woman freely accepting Jehovah as her God (cf. Ruth i. 15, 16). Learn : 1. That the tumult and disorder of war is no excuse for immoral licence. 2. We are to consider the situation and feelings of those whose circumstances place them at our mercy. 3. Natural affections are to be respected underneath all differences of creed and race.

II. PROTECTION FOR ONE UNFRIENDED. (Ver. 14.) The captive stranger wedded to an Israelite was not left to be treated by him as he listed. Her unfriended position exposed her to the risk of suffering from her husband's caprice and unfeelingness. While, therefore, he is permitted, if he lose delight in her, to divorce her—for the "letting her go" must be construed in the light of ch. xxiv. 3—he must on no account sell her or detain her as a captive. Another instance of God's care for "the stranger." Hasty marriages, founded on passion inspired by mere external attractions, seldom result in lasting happiness.—J. O.

Vers. 15—18.—*The firstborn of the hated wife.* The firstborn, in patriarchal and tribal societies, had recognized rights and honours, correlative with the duties and responsibilities which his position as prospective head of the household entailed on him. The principle is here asserted that individual preferences and partialities are not to be allowed to set aside the rights of the son who is lawfully the firstborn. Men would fain, sometimes, bend justice to their likings. Where an Israelite had two wives, either together or in succession, the one loved and the other hated, he might be tempted to pass by the son of the hated, and confer the rights of the firstborn on the son of the wife whom he loved, though it was the son of the hated wife who was entitled to that honour. With strict impartiality, the Law steps in and forbids this act of injustice. It demands that the son of the hated wife have all his rights. It will tolerate no tampering with them. Lessons : 1. The evils of polygamy. 2. The sin of allowing likes and dislikes to influence us to acts of injustice. 3. The danger of natural preferences degenerating into blameworthy partialities. 4. The duty of doing always what is right, whatever the bent of our private inclinations.—J. O.

Vers. 18—21.—*The rebellious son.* A law of this kind, which left it to the parents themselves to impeach their disobedient son, while ordaining that, when the charge was proved against him, and it could be shown that the parents had duly corrected him, the offender should be put to death, would, we may believe, very rarely be enforced.

In cases so aggravated that its enforcement was necessary, the penalty, judged by the usages and state of feeling of the time, would be thought anything but severe. The law, whether enforced or not, was a standing testimony to the enormity attaching in the eyes of God to the sin of filial disobedience. We learn—

I. INSUBORDINATION TO PARENTS IS A GRAVE OFFENCE AGAINST SOCIETY. It is treated here, not simply as a private wrong, but as a crime. Hebrew society rested so largely on the patriarchal basis that the due maintenance of parental authority was a necessity of its existence. The theocratic principle, according to which parents were invested with a peculiar sacredness as representatives of God, likewise called for the repression of incorrigible disobedience. But, whatever the form of social order, a spread of the spirit of insubordination to parents is the invariable prelude to a universal loosening of the ties and obligations of corporate existence. "It has been found," says Dr. Fleming, in his 'Moral Philosophy,' "in the history of all nations that the best security for the public welfare is a wise and happy exercise of parental authority ; and one of the surest forerunners of national degradation and public anarchy and disorder is neglect or contempt of domestic happiness or rule."

II. PARENTS ARE NOT ENTITLED TO COMPLAIN OF THE DISOBEDIENCE OF CHILDREN, SAVE WHERE THEIR OWN DUTIES TO THEIR CHILDREN HAVE BEEN FAITHFULLY DISCHARGED. To secure a conviction, the parents had to show, not only that they had done their best to bring the son up in right ways, but that they had corrected him, and otherwise endeavoured to reclaim him from his vices. Before parents are entitled to complain of the disobedience of children, they must have done their utmost (1) by instruction, (2) by admonition, (3) by correction, (4) by example, (5) by a firm assertion of parental authority generally, to keep them from error. Parents who neglect these duties have little cause to wonder at a son turning out ill; the wonder would be if he should turn out well. It is they, as much as the son, who deserve blame. Lesson : Compare with the behaviour of this rebellious son our own treatment of our heavenly Father.—J. O.

Vers. 22, 23.—*Accursed of God.* The criminal who had committed a sin worthy of death, and was put to death under the law, was viewed as dying under the ban or curse of God. When the crime was very execrable, and the criminal might be regarded as perishing under God's most awful curse, the fact was intimated by exposing the body on a tree. Compare the old custom of hanging a notorious criminal in chains. The placing of the body on a tree was not that which made the person accursed, but was an external sign or token of his being an accursed one. It was, therefore, a singular and striking feature in God's providential arrangements, not only that the death of Christ should be brought about as a result of judgment passed on him by the constituted authorities of his nation, pronouncing him guilty of the worst of all crimes under the theocracy, that of blasphemy, but that in the manner of his death even this external token of ignominy should not be wanting. In this act, the placing of Jesus on the cross, the sin and madness of the world were overruled, as in several other instances (Matt. xxvii. 25, 29, 42 ; Mark xv. 27, 28; John xi. 50), to give unwitting expression to the highest truth. "Christ hath redeemed us from the curse of the Law, being made a curse for us ; for it is written, Cursed is every one that hangeth on a tree" (Gal. iii. 13). The crucifixion of Jesus signifies to us : 1. *The world's judgment upon Christ.* It put him to death as one accursed of God. It treated him as the worst of malefactors, and interpreted his death upon the cross as a sure token of God having forsaken him (Matt. xxvii. 43). To many it may have appeared as if the inference were just. The Sanhedrim had convicted him of blasphemy, and their verdict seemed confirmed by the failure of Christ to deliver himself out of their hands. A true Christ would not thus have succumbed before his enemies. The cross was the refutation of his claims, and the proof of his being an impostor, justly doomed to die. "We did esteem him stricken, smitten of God, and afflicted" (Isa. liii. 4). The world was wrong, for Jesus was never dearer to his Father than in that hour when he hung upon the tree ; but, in a sense unknown to itself, it gave utterance to a truth. 2. *Christ's submission to a cursed death for the world.* The subjection of the sinless Christ to the death of the cross is a fact which requires explanation. If the world put him to death as one accursed, it is none the less true that he voluntarily submitted to this suffering and ignominy, and that the Father permitted him so to be "made a curse." A yet more mysterious feature in the death of Christ is that, in the direst hour of his agony, the Father seemed to side with the world, by withdrawing from him the light and comfort of his presence (Matt. xxvii. 46). Christ was dealt with by Heaven, not less than by men, as One under a curse; if not a sinner, he was treated as if he were one. The apostolic writings lay stress on this as a fact of essential importance in the work of Christ for man's salvation (2 Cor. v. 21; Gal. iii. 13). Subjection to the curse of the Law in the name of the world of sinners with whose lot he had identified himself, was not *all* that was necessary for their redemption from that curse, but it was involved in what was necessary. Any theory of atonement which leaves out the recognition of Christ "made sin" for us by voluntary endurance of sin's doom, must, on scriptural grounds, be pronounced at least incomplete.—J. O.

Vers. 1—9.—*The creation of righteous, public sentiment.* The influence of man upon man is omnific; it touches him at every point. The potency of influence depends on character, rank, age, station. The character of kings is soon reflected on their courtiers. From this principle is born the adage, "Like priest, like people." Crimes proceed from depraved sentiment, and sentiment can be purified by righteous influence.

I. CRIME COURTS CONCEALMENT. All crime is cowardly, base, mean. It fears the light. This may furnish a test for acts that lie near the boundary lines of morality, and admit of question. If the fierce light of righteous opinion is dreaded, the thing is already condemned. So lacking in fortitude and courage is the murderer, that he will seldom confess the truth unless conscience scourges him with intolerable remorse. Yet it is, in well-organized society, an exceptional thing if the murderer escapes. The movements of Divine providence usually furnish some clue to the red-handed man. Still, if amid the infirmities of human government the culprit should escape, he is amenable to another jurisdiction where concealment is impossible. Every crime shall eventually be seen in a blaze of noontide light.

II. MAGISTERIAL RESPONSIBILITY IS INDICATED. Crime is not merely injury against an individual, it is an assault upon society. If murder pass with impunity, no life will soon be safe. In the human race there is a solidarity of interest. Men constitute a *family*. Cities have a character as well as persons. The real leaders in society are laden with heavy responsibility. It is their paramount duty to foster healthy public sentiment; and if this sentiment does not penetrate far enough to prevent crime, it should penetrate far enough to detect crime. Every man can contribute something to influence public morals, and magistrates should lead the way.

III. PUBLIC ABHORRENCE OF CRIME IS IMPRESSIVELY SHOWN. The minds of men are more impressed by deeds than by words, especially by symbolic acts surrounded by the sanctions of religion. It was of the first importance that the city elders should be beyond any suspicion of connivance with the deed. Therefore they must publicly purge themselves by solemn attestation. A valuable heifer was to be selected, and the elders were required to decapitate the victim—a public protest that this would be their own desert if in any degree they had been accessories to the crime. The natural scene selected for this rite was significant. It was to be done in a rugged valley given over to barrenness or natural desolation; being an impressive picture of sin's effect. Accompanying this solemn immolation—this appeal of innocence to Heaven—there was the most explicit utterance of words; so that the honour of the rulers might shine out clear and bright. Magisterial authority is founded on public regard. It was, moreover, a representative act. Every citizen spoke through these elders.

IV. MEDIATION IS HERE FORESHADOWED. It is possible by our thoughtlessness to "become partaker of other men's sins." We all share, in greater or lesser measures, in the guilt of the race. There are sins of ignorance, and to these a measure of culpability belongs. Evils might have been prevented if we had been more faithful. But, by God's appointment, substitution is permitted. Other blood may be shed, by virtue of which we may be redeemed. "The blood of bulls and goats can never take away sin;" nor can the blood of man. No material compensation can be made for moral wrong. But moral effects may be produced by substitution, which shall be equally just and more beneficent. As the priests of olden time were mediators between God and the Jews, so we have a Great High Priest, who is a *real* Mediator, having royal interest for us with God.

V. PENITENCE AND PURITY ARE TWIN SISTERS. (See ver. 9.) There is an appeal for mercy: "Be merciful, O Lord, unto thy people Israel." Some measure of culpability must be felt in every solicitation of mercy. For mercy is that principle in God which conveys blessing when no merit exists. And if true penitence moves in the breast, it is the parent of reformation; its purpose is amendment. It seeks not only removal of burdens, but the destruction of the evil thing. In the hour of penitence, new love and new hate are born. Unless fruits of righteousness appear, penitence is only pretence. The sincere cry for mercy is always followed by "doing that which is right in the sight of the Lord."—D.

Vers. 10—14.—*The captor captured.* God's laws are accommodations to human infirmities. To require from men summarily, and as the result of law, perfect conduct of life is impracticable. Hence legislation, to be successful, must be adapted to the case, and must lead by gradations to a nobler life. This law, though tolerant of lesser evil, is a marked amelioration of earlier custom—a step towards order and purity.

I. FEMALE BEAUTY WINS THE HEARTS EVEN OF WARRIORS. There are other conquests, and nobler, than military conquests. Beauty snatches the palm from strength. In the very hour of victory the conqueror has laid all his spoils at the feet of a gentle woman. Love rules the camp. External beauty has its uses. Real beauty is the exponent of some hidden worth. It eloquently says, "There is some goodness here: search and find it out." And beauty has its perils too—it may excite sexual passion which cannot be controlled.

II. CONJUGAL UNION IS TO RESULT, NOT FROM SUDDEN PASSION, BUT FROM WELL-TRIED LOVE. This sudden desire to have his captive as his wife was required to be tested by time. Calm reflection is to precede a union so full of possible results. Beauty may fling her robe of colour about the haze of dawn, but the gay haze of dawn does not constitute the day. Mere bloom on summer fruit will not meet the hunger of the man. Marriage is a temple of God, and must not be built on an imaginary foundation. The charm of the fair captive's locks was to be temporarily removed, so that the lover's desire might rest, not on fleeting accessories, but on personal worth. Ill-assorted marriages are a fertile curse. Sympathy in religion is essential to a prosperous marriage union.

III. THE NATURAL FEELINGS OF WOMAN, AS WOMAN, ARE TO BE SCRUPULOUSLY RESPECTED. We may not understand all the purposes this Jewish law was designed to serve; but certain it is that, though a captive, the natural feeling of filial sorrow was to be allowed, yea, expected. To repress or root out the affectionate feeling of a daughter would be mutilation of the soul. A forgetful daughter will never be a worthy wife. Nothing in our external fortunes—not even success in war—warrants our playing the tyrant. It is for the benefit of the human race that woman should be treated on equal terms. Her fine endowments have a noble part to play in the culture of humanity.

IV. MARRIAGE HAS ITS DUTIES AS WELL AS ITS ENJOYMENTS. By the custom of that barbarous age, the captive, whether male or female, became the absolute property of the captor. He could reduce her to slavery. But if he chose to make her his wife, he conveyed to her rights which could not be alienated. It became henceforth his duty to protect her and all her interests. She was secure against the lust of avarice. God threw around her the shield of his sacred Law. But the very necessity for this commandment disclosed the rampant greed for gain which rules in some men. Thankful ought we to be that God removes such a possible temptation out of our way. Not by God's consent is marriage ever contracted or terminated for the sake of money gain.—D.

Vers. 15—17.—*Monogamy essential to domestic peace.* Every indication of God's will is a finger-post to felicity. A wise man will not wait for peremptory law. The faintest whisper of Jehovah's will is law to him. Without doubt, that each man should be the husband of one wife was the ordination of God.

I. THE FIRSTBORN SON IS PLACED IN A POSITION OF SPECIAL PRIVILEGE AND POWER. All human government is built upon the model of the family. Within the compass of the family the firstborn was a sovereign, had sovereign rule and responsibility. In families like Jacob's, where there were many children and dependents, *this* was a position of eminence and power. In every case, special duties devolve upon the first-born. He has often to act as the representative of the family, and to defend family rights. He becomes the natural arbitrator in family disputes. His influence, for good or for evil, is great. Therefore, to sustain his position and power, a double portion of the ancestral estate was his.

II. THE PRIVILEGE OF THE FIRSTBORN IS INALIENABLE. For a time the firstborn son is sole heir to his father's rank and riches; hence, for reasons external to him, it would be unjust to depose him. And injustice always leads to strife, disorder, and mischief. Filial reverence would be undermined. Seeds of hatred would be sown. The removal of the father's authority by death would be the sign for feud, litigation, and waste. What God has ordained let not man disturb. Our earthly possessions are entrusted to us temporarily by God, and the entailment has been determined by the Divine Proprietor. For the just management of our secular estates and of our family concerns, we are accountable at the great assize. Favouritism among children is a prolific evil.

III. THIS PROSPECTIVE MISCHIEF ISSUES FROM A PLURALITY OF WIVES. God has often tolerated among men what he has not approved. He does this, in some respect, every day. If he had imposed capital punishment upon the violation of monogamy, the effect, in many cases, would have been unchastity. Law, in order to be effectual, can never transcend the highest level of moral sentiment prevalent in the age. Otherwise judges themselves would be culprits, and no one could be found to administer the law. But the family intrigues, quarrels, and miseries which spring from a plurality of wives are God's visible brands and scourges on disobedience. What works best for society, for the human race, is (in the absence of other instruction) the revealed will of God. Wherever there is more than one wife there must be divided affection, divided interests, divided authority. The house is divided against itself.—D.

Vers. 18—21.—*A slippery path to ruin.* It is of the first importance that a child should begin life well. A twist in the young stem will develop into a gnarled and crooked tree. A slight divergence at the outset of a voyage may end in a complete reversal of the ship's course. Early obedience is the pathway to a prosperous life; disobedience leads to death. The tongue that curseth its father shall be scorched with devouring flame.

I. SELFISH INDULGENCE DESTROYS FILIAL REVERENCE. The human body is to be the servant of the mind. If the appetites and lusts of the body are allowed to rule, the mind becomes a slave, and all the better principles are manacled and enfeebled. We begin life as dependent children, and the fresh sense of loving obligation should be an antidote for selfishness. But if we set out in life with a resolve to please self, we are already on the way to ruin. Reverence for the parental character, and regard for parental authority, are the only solid foundations for a noble life. To feed unduly the body, and for gratification alone, is to starve the soul. Sensuality fosters self-will.

II. REBELLION IN THE CHILD DESTROYS SONSHIP. Disregard of authority soon chokes and strangles filial feeling. The tie of sonship is snapped. The qualities and attributes of a son are wanting. There is a relationship of body, but no true relationship of soul. Alienation has sprung up instead of vital union. The lad may dwell under the old roof-tree, but in reality there is a great gulf between him and his parents: he is a descendant, but not a son. To be the children of God there must be resemblance of character.

III. UNFRUITFUL CHASTISEMENT IS A TREMENDOUS CURSE. The medicine that does not do good, does harm. The flame that does not melt, hardens. Parental chastisement, when needed, is an imperative duty, but should be administered with wisdom, self-restraint, and pity. The obstinacy of the son is not unfrequently due to the foolish leniency or unrestrained severity of the parent. Chastisement is a serious experiment, and always produces some effect, either favourable or unfavourable. We are not the same men after trial or pain that we were before.

IV. THE STATE MUST SUPPORT PARENTAL AUTHORITY. So valuable is human life that the State wisely claims the sole power of capital punishment. If the disciplines and chastisements of home have failed to produce a virtuous citizen, the whole community must deal with the incorrigible reprobate. The State cannot afford, for its safety's sake, to allow a firebrand to be let loose in its midst. The example and influence of such a miscreant would be fatally mischievous. The whole State has vital interests to serve, and it would be sheerest folly to sacrifice them to a drunken madman.

V. PERSISTENT REBELLION LEADS TO AN IGNOMINIOUS END. It must be a duty, the most painful for human nature to perform, to surrender a son to public execution. Yet it sometimes *is* a duty. The hope of amendment has been quenched. To continue such a one in life has become a bane to himself and to others. If all remedies have failed, destruction must ensue. All the men of the city shall put their hand to the deed. This may be done by personal service or by representation. The mad career of the culprit ends in pain, loss, and perpetual disgrace. It is a symbol of the great judgment doom.—D.

Vers. 22, 23.—*The doom of law the embodiment of Divine curse.* The suspension of a human body on the gallows-tree is the utmost climax of ruin and disgrace. It is the fullest exponent of the public detestation and horror for the deed. In this case the curse of men is the curse of God. But this curse was not to continue. Blessing was to be perpetual, abiding, uninterrupted; but the curse was to endure for a moment. The body so accursed was to be buried before sunset. Many reasons have been assigned for this.

I. BECAUSE VINDICTIVE ANGER SHOULD BE KEPT WITHIN DUE BOUNDS. Anger against monstrous crime is a great assistance in the performance of painful duty. We are braced to do under stress of anger what we could scarcely do in calmer moods of feeling. Anger has its use, but should not be prolonged. When the painful deed is done, vengeful passion should cease. To this end let the lifeless body be buried out of sight.

II. BECAUSE THE HUMAN FORM IS SACRED AS GOD'S TEMPLE. The temple may be in ruins, yet sentiments of veneration hover round the ruined shrines. We know that yonder executed man was the workmanship of the living God. Every vein, and artery, and muscle, and nerve in that mutilated body was the handiwork of God. With that man's history God had taken pains; and over his mistaken course God had grieved. We think of what that man might have been, how fruitful in goodness and virtue! how meet for Divine service and honour! And the spectacle of that man's doom should arouse our fear. We may well stand in awe of sin. To commit such a corpse with gentle pity to the grave will do us good.

III. BECAUSE MORAL DEFILEMENT WOULD OTHERWISE RESULT. The exposure of a dead body in that climate beyond a single day would taint the atmosphere and damage health. But to accustom the minds of men to such a ghastly spectacle would tend to moral defilement. It would serve to harden their better feelings, and make too familiar the exhibition of Jehovah's curse. In our present condition sacred things may become too common. Here especially "familiarity breeds contempt." No greater evil can befall the soul than when it becomes heedless of Divine judgments.—D.

EXPOSITION.

CHAPTER XXII.

REGULATIONS REGARDING CATTLE STRAYED OR THINGS LOST, THE APPAREL OF THE SEXES, THE TAKING OF BIRDS, AND THE CONSTRUCTION OF HOUSES. CONFUSIONS TO BE AVOIDED. FRINGES TO BE MADE ON VESTMENTS. PUNISHMENT OF WIFE-SLANDER, ADULTERY, RAPE, FORNICATION, INCEST.

Vers. 1—4.—Moses repeats here the law

formerly given (Exod. xxiii. 4, 5), with additional details. Not only the ox or the ass that had strayed was to be taken and restored to its owner, but articles of raiment, and, in short, anything that had been lost was, when found by another, to be carefully kept until it could be restored to the person to whom it belonged.

Ver. 1.—Go astray; wandering at large. The Hebrew verb means primarily to seduce, draw aside, or entice (cf. ch. xiii. 6); and in the passive conveys the idea of wandering through being drawn away by some enticement. **Hide thyself from them**; *i.e.* withdraw thyself from them, avoid noticing them or having to do with them. **In any case;** certainly, without fail.

Ver. 4.—An animal that had fallen was also to be lifted up, and the owner was to be assisted to do this. In Exodus, it is specially declared that both these services are to be rendered, even though the parties are at enmity with each other, and the one is the object of hatred to the other.

Ver. 5.—The divinely instituted distinction between the sexes was to be sacredly observed, and, in order to this, the dress and other things appropriate to the one were not to be used by the other. **That which pertaineth unto a man**; literally, *the apparatus* (כְּלִי) *of a man*, including, not dress merely, but implements, tools, weapons, and utensils. This is an ethical regulation in the interests of morality. There is no reference, as some have supposed, to the wearing of masks for the purpose of disguise, or to the practice of the priests at heathen festivals of wearing masks of their gods. Whatever tends to obliterate the distinction between the sexes tends to licentiousness; and that the one sex should assume the dress of the other has always been regarded as unnatural and indecent (comp. Seneca, 'Epist.,' 122, "Nonne videntur contra naturam vivere qui commutant cum feminis vestem;" and Juvenal, 'Sat.,' vi. 252—

"Quem præstare potest mulier galeata pudorem

Quæ fugit a sexu?")

Such a change of vesture is here declared to be an abomination to the Lord, because of its tendency to immorality.

Vers. 6, 7.—(Cf. Lev. xxii. 28; Exod. xxiii. 19.) These precepts are designed to foster humane feeling towards the lower animals, and not less to preserve regard to that affectionate relation between parents and their young which God has established as a law in the animal world. **That thou mayest prolong thy days** (cf. ch. v. 16; Exod. xx. 12).

Ver. 8.—Still less was human life to be exposed to danger through neglect of proper precautions. The houses in Palestine, as in other parts of the East, had flat roofs, and, as these were much frequented by the inhabitants for various purposes (cf. Josh. ii. 6; 2 Sam. xi. 2; xviii. 24; Neh. viii. 16; Matt. x. 27; Acts x. 9), it was necessary that a battlement or balustrade should surround the roof, in order to prevent persons falling over. Hence the direction here given.

Vers. 9—11.—(Cf. Lev. xix. 19.) God has made distinctions in nature, and these are not to be confounded by the mixing of things distinct. The ox and the ass were chiefly used in husbandry; but, as they were of different size and strength, it was not only fitting that they should not be yoked to the same plough, but it might be cruel so to yoke them.

Ver. 11.—**A garment of divers sorts;** *sha'atnez*, a kind of cloth in which threads of linen and threads of woollen were interwoven. The meaning of the word is uncertain. The LXX. render by κίβδηλος, "spurious, bad;" Aquila, by ἀντιδιακείμενον, "variously disposed, diverse." No Semitic etymology can be found for the word, and as the Hebrews derived the textile art from Egypt, the home of that art, the word is probably of Egyptian origin.

Ver. 12.—(Cf. Numb. xv. 38.) **Fringes;** properly, *tassels*. The tunic of the Hebrews appears to have been divided at the bottom in front, and back, so that four corners or wings (כְּנָפוֹת) were made, to each of which a tassel was appended (Greek, κράσπεδον, Matt. ix. 20; xxiii. 5, etc.).

Vers. 13—29.—The laws in this section have the design of fostering purity and fidelity in the relation of the sexes, and also of protecting the female against the malice of sated lust and the violence of brutal lust. (For the case supposed in ver. 13, cf. 2 Sam. xiii. 15. On the whole section see Michaelis, 'Laws of Moses,' pt. ii. § 92; Niebuhr, 'Description de l'Arabie,' ch. viii.; Burckhardt, 'Bedwins,' p. 214.)

Vers. 22—29.—Four cases are here distinguished. 1. That of a married woman who has been unfaithful; in this case both the woman and her paramour are, when detected, to be put to death (ver. 22). 2. That of a virgin betrothed who is assailed in a town, where she might have cried for protection, but did not; in this case also both were to be punished with death as adulterers (vers. 23, 24). 3. That of a virgin betrothed who has been forcibly violated in the field, where, if she cried for help, her cry was in vain; in this case only the man should be liable to be put to death, whilst the woman was to be held innocent (vers. 25—27). 4. That of a virgin not betrothed with whom a man has had carnal intercourse; in this case the man should be required to pay a fine of fifty shekels of silver to the damsel's father, and to take her to be his wife, from whom he could not be separated during life (vers. 28, 29).

Ver. 30.—To these is appended a general prohibition of incestuous connections, the first provision in the earlier law being cited as a sort of index to the whole (Lev. xviii. 7, etc.).

HOMILETICS.

Vers. 1—4.—*The duty of cultivating neighbourly kindness.* It will be a valuable study in Divine ethics if we first of all show what it is which is here required of the Hebrews, and then, with the Mosaic teaching for a starting-point, advance further and see how far in Christian ethics there is incorporated all that was valuable in the Mosaic, while there is added thereto that which belongs peculiarly to the law of the gospel.

Moses, in this paragraph, enjoins acts of neighbourly kindness. To whom is this kindness to be shown? To "thy brother." He may be (1) a brother by kinship, (2) an unknown individual (ver. 2), or (3) an enemy (cf. Exod. xxiii. 4). In either case a like kindness is to be shown. There is contained in Lev. xix. 18 the general precept out of which these details of kindness would come. "Thou shalt love thy neighbour as thyself." This was to be the human aspect, the social side of a godly life. The basis of love to man would be found in loving God with all the heart, and soul, and mind, and strength. And as God had redeemed the people from Egypt, that they might be to himself a peculiar people to show forth his praise, they were to regard this redemption as uniting them in one bond of brotherhood, with interests and aims in common; hence each was to regard another's good as being as dear to him as his own. From this point let us now proceed to develop in outline the Christian law of kindness to others.

I. THE LORD JESUS CHRIST ENFORCES THE LAW OF KINDNESS ON HIS OWN AUTHORITY. (Cf. Matt. v. 43.) He not only reproduces the old law, but clears it from the ambiguities and disfigurements with which rabbinical teaching had obscured it. "Ye have heard that it hath been said, Thou shalt love thy neighbour, and hate thine enemy." Moses had said the first, the rabbis had added the second. Christ tears off this addition. Again, when the lawyer said, "And who is my neighbour?" Christ gave him the parable of the good Samaritan, in which he virtually said, "That depends upon yourself; whoever cherishes a kindly spirit to all, he is the neighbour, however far off in place or nation." The Christian law is, "As we have opportunity, let us do good unto all men." We are to know no barriers in race, colour, or clime; no, nor is even hatred or ill will on the part of others to prevent our seeking their good.

II. THIS KINDNESS TO OTHERS IS NOT THE WHOLE OF RELIGION, BUT ONLY THAT PART OF IT WHICH HAS TO DO WITH MAN. Love to God is the first command. This is the second. Benevolence without religion is incomplete; religion without benevolence is vain. Both must abound in the truly Christian life.

III. THE REASON OF BOTH IS TO BE FOUND IN THE DIVINE LOVING-KINDNESS TO US. See Matt. vii. 12: note the force of the word, "therefore," in the latter verse. Because God is so ready to bless you, be you ready to bless others. This great redeeming love of God for our race should lead us to see in all men members of one vast brotherhood, which God would encircle in his girdle of love, and draw together by the thought that, as he cares for all, each should care for the other! "Let no man seek his own, but every one another's wealth" (1 Cor. x. 24).

IV. THE INSPIRATION TO BOTH IS TO BE FOUND IN THE CROSS OF OUR LORD JESUS CHRIST. Here, here are we to find the love that must kindle ours. "When we were enemies, we were reconciled to God by the death of his Son." If we owe so much to redeeming love, ought we not to show a corresponding love for others? What said Paul? "If we be beside ourselves, it is to God; if we be sober, it is for your cause, for the love of Christ constraineth us." "If God so loved us, we ought also to love one another."

Vers. 5, 13—21, 22—24, 25—27, 27—29, 30.—*Divine care for sexual honour.* In these, as in so many of the precepts of this book, we find civil precepts invested with religious sanctions. Nothing is more important for the honourable maintenance of social life, than that both men and women should honour each other's sex as well as their own. Those that do otherwise are an abomination to the Lord their God. There are five or six different cases supposed in the verses referred to at the heading of this

Homily: (1) clothing (ver. 5); (2) impeached or impaired reputation (vers. 13—21); (3) adultery (vers. 22—24); (4) rape or seduction (vers. 25—29)—two cases; (5) unlawful marriages (ver. 30). Such sins would have been thought nothing of among the Canaanites. God would have his people lifted up above them. Hence it is needful that they should be specifically named, and that the people should be solemnly told of the odiousness of these sins in God's sight, that thus they might become odious also in their eyes. While all will feel that such subjects need great wisdom in handling them, yet undue reticence thereon may work direful harm. Many need to be told with great plainness of speech, "He that breaketh a hedge, a serpent shall bite him." Our theme is—"*Sexual dishonour odious in the sight of God.*" The following lines of thought suggest themselves.

I. God has made our nature, in every part thereof, for himself.

II. In making man, male and female, God has opened up to each wondrous possibilities of love, of holiness, of usefulness, by each rendering to the other due honour in accordance with Divine Law.

III. By as much as the joy and culture are great when God's sexual laws are obeyed, by so much are the misery and debasement great when they are disobeyed.

IV. He who trifles with himself or with others in regard to the holiest of all human relations, will find that sins of impurity nip his nature in the bud, embitter life beyond all power of expression, and render true greatness altogether impossible. One sin will drag the whole man after it. Hence our Lord's solemn warnings in Matt. v. 29, 30; Mark ix. 43, 45, 47. Hence—

V. We should look upon God's order in nature with devout and reverent regard.

Vers. 6, 7.—*Kindness to animals a religious duty.* There is a most valuable note in Dr. Jameson's 'Commentary' on this passage. "The Hebrews," says Trapp, "reckoned this commandment the least of all in the Mosaic Law, yet is there such a promise attached thereto." "This law," says another annotator, "teaches a spirit of mercy; it would also tend to prevent the extirpation of any species of birds which in a country producing many snakes and insects might cause serious injury." And, on the other hand, the permission here given might also tend to prevent too rapid increase. And manifestly, here is a check put on the destructive and plundering tendencies of man, and a quiet lesson taught them that they are to regard as sacred the affectionate relation between parents and their young, which God has established in the animal world. It is not a little remarkable that we find a like promise attached to this precept as to the fifth commandment. How is this? May not the reason be thus stated? It is a duty to cultivate kindness of disposition in all respects and towards all beings. The cultivation of uniform kindliness, whether to man or beast, will have a marked effect in the elevation of personal character, and in sweetening the surroundings of life. And he who out of pure love and obedience to God shows mercy everywhere, will be himself a partaker of mercy. The following may serve as starting-points of thought. 1. The lower creatures are put at the service of man. He is permitted to have service from them and enjoyment in them. 2. This enjoyment and service which man desires in and from them are to be had only in harmony with due regard to them as the creatures of God. 3. The cultivation of kindness to all creatures is, therefore, a religious duty. And the duty of so cultivating it is not only a part of the morality of the Law, but a part of the morality of that gospel which is for every creature. 4. Where such benevolence is universally cultivated, the seal and sign of God's approval thereof will be enjoyed.

[Note the command in ver. 10, "Thou shalt not plow with an ox and an ass together." This prohibition prevented great inhumanity (see Jameson, *in loc.*). See also marginal reference for another possible intent thereof.]

Ver. 8.—*Risks to human life to be minimized.* It is well known that "the roofs of the Israelitish houses were flat, as they mostly are in the East;" the inhabitants often walked upon them. Hence it is easy to see that a danger might exist of one falling off a house, if there were no battlement, parapet, or guard of some kind around it. And against this Moses is taught of God to warn the people. In the structure of their habitations the safety of the indwellers is to be rigidly consulted; and any trifling with human life, by the erection of insecure buildings, would expose the builder to blood-guiltiness in the eye of God.

I. There is in the social world a mutual interdependence of man upon man. "We are members one of another."

II. This fact renders it possible for each man in his own department greatly to help or seriously to injure others. In no sphere is this more manifest than in house-building; in attention to the details, the health and comfort of multitudes are concerned.

III. God charges upon each one a due regard to the well-being of others, in distinction from a selfish absorption in his own imaginary interests.

IV. Wherever, through neglect in his own department, of another's good, the health, comfort, or life of men are threatened or injured, God holds the man accountable for any mischief which may accrue. Other men may or may not be able to bring the sin home to the defaulter. But "God shall bring *every* work into judgment; with *every* secret thing, whether it be good, or whether it be evil."

Vers. 9, 11.—*Evil associations to be avoided.* "The essence of the crime (Zeph. i. 8) consisted, not in wearing a woollen and linen robe, but in having it in a particular form according to a favourite superstition of ancient idolatries" (Lev. xix. 19). So also as to sowing with divers seeds; it was a superstitious custom of the idolaters, and hence it is to be avoided. Note: *Evil associations* may *make* it wrong to follow or observe that which is *in itself* harmless. With the principle which underlies this passage thus stated, compare 1 Cor. x. 23 to end.

I. God, having called his people out of the world, would have them distinct from the world.

II. In carrying out this distinction in practice, Christians are bound to regard the *influence* which their practice will have upon others, as well as the practice itself.

III. It is quite possible that (as in the case of eating meats offered to idols) there may be rites, customs, habits, in which this or that Christian could indulge without injury to himself, and yet which, owing to the force of public sentiment and opinion, would tell prejudicially upon him, and lower his influence for good.

IV. When such is the case, he is to take the higher ground, not shrinking from being deemed puritanic—and to abstain not only from that which is wrong in itself, but from much which, owing to evil associations, has about it a suspicious look of worldliness and self-indulgence.

HOMILIES BY VARIOUS AUTHORS.

Vers. 1—4.—*Love unfeigned.* The precepts in these verses fairly anticipate the gospel love of one's neighbour, and even its inculcation of love to enemies (cf. Exod. xxiii. 4, 5). Whatever authority the scribes in Christ's time imagined themselves to have for their saying, "Thou shalt hate thine enemy" (Matt. v. 43), they did not find it in the Law. Even towards the heathen—save in the sense in which each nation desires the destruction of its enemies in war—they were not taught to cherish feelings of bitterness and hostility. Ch. xxiii. 6 forbids seeking the welfare of Moab and Ammon, but this does not amount to hatred of these peoples (cf. ch. ii. 9, 19), while the command to "blot out the remembrance of Amalek from under heaven" (ch. xxv. 19) is, like the command to exterminate the Canaanites, grounded in special circumstances, and is to be regarded as exceptional. Those who express horror of the sanguinary spirit of the Mosaic code should study the precepts before us, and reflect how far the race is from having yet risen to the height of them. They forbid—

I. SECRET REJOICING IN ANOTHER'S MISFORTUNE. Such rejoicing may have its source in: 1. *Enmity.* The statute in Exodus particularly specifies the ox and ass of an "enemy" (Exod. xxiii. 4). The enemy is further defined, not as one whom we hate, but as one who hates us (ver. 5). Yet if his ox, or sheep, or ass is seen going astray, we are not to hide ourselves or forbear help, but are to bring it back to him. So with all his lost property—we are to take it home and keep it for him. Or, if his ass fall under a burden, we are to help him to lift it up. How natural the disposition to act otherwise! No one knows that we have seen the stray beast. We may reason that we are not bound to interfere. A secret joy, even, may steal into our minds at the thought of an enemy's misfortune. The Law taught the Israelite to think and act very differently. It gave him the lesson of forgiving injuries, of loving enemies, of returning good for evil. 2. *Envy.* The precept in this passage speaks merely of a "brother." Through envy or some other wicked feeling, even where there is no enmity, we may be tempted to rejoice in the lessening of another's prosperity. But neither is this hateful principle to be allowed to sway us. 3. *Malice.* This is the disposition which delights in what injures another for its own sake. So diabolical a state of feeling might be deemed impossible did not experience of the world afford too many proofs of its existence. There are unquestionably malicious and spiteful natures who, irrespective of any personal interest in the matter, derive an absolute gratification from seeing misfortune overtake those around them. The faintest beginning of such a spirit ought surely to be most jealously guarded against.

II. SECRET RETENTION OF ANOTHER'S PROPERTY. What is found is not to be appropriated or concealed. If the owner is unknown, the beast or lost article is to be taken home, and kept till he can be discovered. Though he is an enemy, his goods are to be faithfully restored to him. This, again, is a form of virtue which only strength of moral principle will enable one always to practise.—J. O.

Ver. 5.—*Man and woman.* Woman has her rightful place and function in society. So has man his. Their places, while complementary, are distinct. In modern society, a variety of influences—competition in business, difficulty of finding suitable employment, the levelling tendency of the age, which is impatient even of distinctions that have their ground in nature—combine to thrust women into spheres and work not in keeping with womanly character. The distinction of the sexes is to be preserved: 1. In *dress.* 2. In *manners.* Unwomanly boldness and assertiveness in company or before the public is as unpleasant as foppish effeminacy is in men. 3. In *occupations.* Few would like to see women jostling men in the Exchange, pleading at the bar, or sitting in parliament. The feeling is not one of mere sentiment, but rests on inherent differences in the calling of the sexes. It deserves to be considered whether the line is not unduly crossed as it is in many forms of female occupation. It is certainly so crossed in some: barmaids; occupations involving an excessive tax on the female strength; manufactory work, where the system allows of the mingling of the sexes under conditions certain to demoralize, etc. (see Lecture on 'Sex in Industry,' by Joseph Cook—' Monday Lectures ').—J. O.

Vers. 6—12.—*The minutiæ of conduct.* The Law descends to very slight points of conduct. It keeps in view that character is made up of the result of our actions in the million trivial details of life. "Trifles," said Michael Angelo, when a friend thus characterized the slight finishing touches he was giving to a statue—"trifles make perfection." Matters which in themselves are of little moment acquire importance from the associations they awaken, the ideas they suggest, the consequences they lead up to. Little traits of humane behaviour (vers. 6, 7), the habit of considering the bearings of what we do on others (ver. 8), respect for the ordinary and obvious distinctions of creation (ver. 9), etc., have all their influence on character, their effect in making us what we ultimately become. We may suggest, as lessons from these verses, that our conduct is to be marked: 1. By *humanity.* (1) To animals. (2) To our fellow-men. In vers. 6, 7, the act forbidden is one akin to killing a cow and calf on the same day, or to seething a kid in its mother's milk (cf. on ch. xiv. 21)—an unfeeling violation of the sacredness of the relation between parent and offspring. Or the parent bird may be presumed to be taken only in wantonness, the young ones being really of service. This would be an act of cruelty. Humanity may be a motive in the precept of ver. 10 —" ox " and " ass " being obviously " unequally yoked together " (cf. Paul's allusion with application to marriage with unbelievers, in 2 Cor. vi. 14). 2. By *caution.* This is strikingly inculcated in ver. 8. How many accidents might be avoided if greater conscientiousness and caution prevailed in the different departments of labour! A shipbuilder puts in the side of a ship one wormy plank, and years after this costs the whole ship's crew their lives. 3. By *simplicity.* This is a lesson which may be learned from the precepts against mixing kinds (vers. 9, 11). 4. By *mindfulness.* The law of fringes in Numb. xv. 38—if this refers to the same thing—was intended to aid memory In another view of the precept, it inculcates decency and propriety.—J. O.

Vers. 13—30.—*Chastity.* The Mosaic Law is strict and stern in its requirement of purity in all that pertains to the marriage relation. Its strictness, however, is united with a fine sense of justice, and its shield is, as usual, extended for the protection of the innocent.

I. THE DEFAMED WIFE. (Vers. 13—19.) No act can be conceived more cruel or dastardly than that of a man who groundlessly assails his wife's character, accusing her of ante-nuptial unchastity. As the matter was one proof of which was not directly possible, and the man's word was all that could be adduced on his side, the Law threw the onus of clearing herself upon the woman through her parents, and indicated the mode of doing so. The "forty stripes save one" was a punishment not too heavy for this sort of false accusation.

II. THE UNCHASTE WIFE. (Vers. 20—24.) Three cases are distinguished, each punishable with death. 1. A woman found to be unchaste at time of marriage (vers. 20, 21). 2. Adultery after marriage (ver. 22). 3. A betrothed woman ravished with her implied consent (vers. 23, 24). In the last two cases, the partner in guilt dies also. In the first, he only escapes, because he is unknown. Yet that unknown seducer, the cause of the woman's fall—a fall which shame subsequently tempted her to conceal—was not lost to the eye of him who sees secret crime, and will repay it. Little do such seducers think of the life-long shame and sin and misery to which they may be dooming the unfortunate victims of their wiles. God knows it, and will bring them to account. The severe penalties attached to conjugal unfaithfulness place in a startling light the gravity of the offence in the Divine esteem, and form a striking contrast to the light tone adopted about such matters in society.

III. THE WOMAN RAVISHED. (Vers. 25—29.) The cases specified are those of rape. 1. If the woman was betrothed, and could not save herself, she was to be held innocent, but her violator was to be punished with death. 2. If she was not betrothed, the man who had injured her was heavily fined, and was compelled to take her to wife, with no right of subsequent divorce. Possibly our own law might fitly imitate that of ver. 29.—J. O.

Vers. 1—4.—*Consideration for man and beast.* We have here such express directions given as should have made of the Israelites a most neighbourly people. The finding of lost oxen, or sheep, or asses, or raiment, is here made to carry with it the obligation of brotherly kindness; the animals or lost property must be restored to the owner, if he be known, or kept until he makes himself known. It is the law of love in practice.

I. THERE IS A NATURAL INCLINATION TO SHIRK ALL POSSIBLE TROUBLE. There is a drop of laziness in all of us, and, if indulged, it will lead to many an unbrotherly act. In the case supposed there is no witness present; the lost property is unexpectedly found; how much trouble it will save to pass on and leave it to its chances in the hands of others! And so we are tempted to array ourselves in the cloak of selfishness, and to spare ourselves all possible trouble.

II. THE CASUAL DISCOVERIES OF DAILY LIFE CONSTITUTE DUTIES LAID BY THE OMNISCIENT ONE TO OUR HANDS. There is no such thing as chance so far as God is concerned. Much has the *appearance* of chance to us, but, when reconsidered, it is the all-wise arrangement of God. "For what is this chance?" says a very able writer. "It either has a real existence or not. If it has no existence, then when you say that a lot is determined by chance, you say that it is determined by nothing; that is, you say, Here is a sensible effect produced by no cause at all. This is pure nonsense. If your chance is a real being, what sort of being? Either it has life, intelligence, and power, or not. If not, then you say that millions of effects (for there are millions of lots in the world) are produced by a cause which has neither power, nor intelligence, nor life; that is, you say that millions of actions are performed by an agency which is essentially incapable of any action whatever. And this is as pure absurdity as the former. If you say that your chance is a living, intelligent, and active being, I ask who it is? and how you get your knowledge of it? You certainly imagine it to possess omnipresence and omnipotence; for you suppose it capable of producing, at the same moment, millions of effects in millions of places; and thus you have found out a being that displays perfections of God, and yet is not God. This conclusion is as blasphemous as the others are insane. There is no retreat. Survey the subject in any possible light, and you are driven to this issue, that the lot is, by the very nature of the case, a direct appeal to the living God, as Governor of the world" (Dr. J. M. Mason's 'Considerations on Lots'). Hence discoveries, however casual, which throw us into new relations to persons, animals, or things, should be accepted as Divine duties laid to our hands. God's call is in them to be faithful and brotherly.

III. THE SHIRKING OF RESPONSIBILITY AND TROUBLE IS REALLY REBELLING AGAINST AN ORDINANCE OF GOD. If we have found the missing property, we have really been sent of God to be its stewards. To hide ourselves in our self-care is to rebel against his ordinance, and do despite to his gracious arrangements. It is to make self-pleasing the rule of life, instead of the pleasing of God. And as a rule it will be found that the person who thus caudles himself and passes on trouble to others becomes heir of unexpected vexations himself.

IV. A THOROUGHLY OBLIGING AND HELPFUL SPIRIT HAS A WORLD OF COMPENSATION IN THE APPROVAL OF HIS OWN CONSCIENCE, IF NOT IN THE GRATITUDE OF MANKIND. Benevolence is its own reward. The kindness lavished on man and beast carries its own compensation with it. The sense of being brought to the opportunity of brotherly kindness by a gracious God, and of being his servant in showing his spirit, is surely worth all the trouble our kindness costs. So that, even supposing the recipients of our kindness were ungrateful, the kindness would still be well worth doing for its own sake.

But then gratitude is not so rare a thing as people would suppose. It is entertained often when not very eloquently expressed. It is sometimes too deep for utterance. And to think that we have become creditors of our fellows, so as to deserve their gratitude, is satisfaction indeed.

> " For merit lives from man to man,
> And not from man, O Lord, to thee."

If we have any wisdom, therefore, we shall gladly cultivate the brotherly kindness here inculcated, for life becomes by it more blessed and more noble.—R. M. E.

Ver. 5.—*The philosophy of clothes.* We have here particular directions as to the maintenance of the distinction of dress between the sexes. On the termination of what Carlyle calls " Adamitism," in his 'Sartor Resartus,' when through the fall of man fig leaves were first resorted to, it is evident that the Lord was not content therewith as the device of self-conscious modesty, but gave them " coats of skins." These "coats," we can well believe, were differentiated, so that Eve's was in some particulars distinct from Adam's. This distinction in dress between the sexes, begun, let us suppose, immediately after the Fall, is designed by God to continue ; and we have here the law prohibiting any exchanges of apparel, so as to conceal one's sex. It is, in fact, an earlier " philosophy of clothes " than Carlyle has given us.

I. THE PROMISCUOUS INTERMINGLING OF THE SEXES IS MOST UNDESIRABLE. Of course, this is quite another thing from the entire separation of the sexes as it prevails among Orientals. The latter custom proceeds on the supposition that there can be no social intercourse between them except licentious intercourse; and is the poor precaution of deep depravity. But suppose that men and women were wont to dress alike, there could be no enforcement of decorum such as difference in dress renders possible. The sexes are intended to be distinct, and cannot profitably be intermingled.

II. IT IS A DEEP INJURY TO BOTH SEXES TO OBLITERATE THE DISTINCTIONS PROVIDENCE HAS MADE. Whatever tends to render the male sex effeminate and the female sex masculine, is an injury to both. The tendency of the times is in this direction; women are being introduced to fierce competitions with men : we have had women, forgetful of their sex, even entering the prize-ring, to afford amusement to brutal onlookers ; we have women persistently knocking at the door of professions fit for men only ; while, on the other hand, we have a number of occupations, which will readily occur to every one, where men are made effeminate, and which could be most fitly discharged by women ; and those reformers are not friends of either sex who try to break down the barriers between them.

If Providence has made the one sex different from the other, then it is idle by any manipulation of ours to obliterate the distinction.

III. At the same time, it is a deep wrong to exaggerate the defects which Providence has allotted to each by enlightened ,systems of education. We thoroughly sympathize with the effort to do away with the exaggerated "subjection of women," upon which Mr. Mill in his book has so ably insisted. The education of each sex should be as broad and liberal as possible. But no education can ever remove the inequality which naturally obtains between the sexes.[1] Let education consider the providential purpose of sexual distinctions, and work on these lines, and then, and then only, need we expect permanent amelioration for oppressed sisters.

IV. Modesty is one of those social graces which should be fostered and not restrained. We have heard of men whose command of their emotions was so perfect as never to allow their modesty to appear by any chance. It may be harmless or ludicrous in men; but it is ruin to women, and whatever tends to make them "Amazons" or "Trojans" is to be reprobated most earnestly.

V. It takes the two sexes combined to give a complete image of the Divine nature. When God said, "Let us make man (אָדָם) in our image, after our likeness," he used the generic term, and hence immediately resorts to the plural verb, "and let them have dominion (יִרְדּוּ),", etc. (Gen. i. 26). The idea is that it takes the female with the male to complete the Divine image. There is a *maternal* element as well as a *paternal* and a *filial* in the Divine nature (cf. Isa. xlix. 15 with Ps. ciii. 13 and John viii. 29). And it is interesting to notice among the theological vagaries and conceits of such a man as Theodore Parker, that he was forced to call his God,"Infinite Father and Infinite Mother," a set-off to his dreary unitarianism.[2] If then we find the sexual distinctions to be but the reflection of elements in the Divine nature, then a halo of true glory is thrown around each. In their respective spheres the sexes are exhibiting traits of divinity, and all effort at obliterating the distinctions through artificial means, will be found only to obliterate the Divine. Father, Son, and Holy Ghost have their counterparts in the development of humanity, and it is well clearly to see this. May the sexes carry on their respective missions so faithfully that earth may soon reflect in undimmed lustre the various qualities of God!—R. M. E.

Vers. 6, 7.—*Birds' nests.* The command to spare the mother bird while the young might be taken, comes in significantly after the law distinguishing the sexes. The female sex is intended for motherhood; it "binds the generations each to each," as our Laureate says. On the exercise of this function the continuance of the species depends. Hence the command here is at once humane and intended to ensure the continuance of the species. Birds are very needful to keep down grubs and insects, and give the land a chance of due fertility. Hence the sportsman's enthusiasm was thus kept in proper check.

I. While God gives the animals to man for food, he would have the sacrifice of life thoughtfully made. There must be thought and deliberation about the selection of the young birds, about the pouring out of the blood, etc. All this introduced a humane element into the act.

II. The freedom of the dam was ensured by the sacrifice of the young— a perpetual lesson about substitution and sacrifice. As the mother received liberty, the Jewish sportsman would be led to think of the law of substitution and of sacrifice upon which all his religious hopes were built.

III. Motherhood was thus rendered sacred in the eyes of the Jews. The idea, sacred in the woods among the wild birds, would become sacred elsewhere. "The mothers in Israel," instead of being sacrificed *to* their children, would be honoured *by* them, which is the Divine order. The young generation should bear the burden rather than the old. To such a line of thought the law about birds' nests would naturally give rise.—R. M. E.

[1] Cf. Huxley's article on 'Emancipation, Black and White,' in his 'Lay Sermons,' pp. 23—30.

[2] Cf. Frothingham's 'Life of Theodore Parker,' pp. 283, 529.

Vers. 8—12.—*Linsey-woolseys.* The different directions here given may be reduced to one idea, that of *genuineness.* The houses were to be substantial edifices, not endangering the lives of others by defective buildings or deficient battlements. The vineyards were to be sown with pure seed, that the plants might have a fair chance of growing luxuriantly. The ploughing was not to be done by an ox and ass together, for though the oxen are so small in Palestine as to be yokable with an ass, the contrariety in temper and inequality in power would prevent good work. Linsey-woolsey was to be avoided as poor stuff compared with either woollen or linen alone. And finally, the fringes were to be made upon their garments, to be at once a finishing and a distinction in the clothes of the chosen people. God gave them thus a *uniform.* The great idea here, consequently, is that God's people should be distinguished by the *genuineness* and honesty of their life-work.

Carlyle's preaching against *shams* is here forestalled, and we may surely learn from the directions here such lessons as these—

I. To be thorough in all our work. This is God's great lesson for us in his own government of the world. The beauty of the flower of the grass, which is to perish and be cast into the oven so soon, tells us to be microscopically minute and thorough in the most transient work. There are no short cuts through " shoddy " to real worth and real usefulness; but all should be genuine if we would serve our generation by the will of God.

II. Let us not be ashamed to be called God's people amid life's hard work. The Israelites were to wear their fringes, to go in uniform, and be *pious peasants.* The linking of genuine work with professed piety is altogether admirable. " Sublimer," says Carlyle, " in this world know I nothing than a peasant saint, could such now anywhere be met with. Such a one will take thee back to Nazareth itself: thou wilt see the splendour of heaven spring forth from the humblest depths of earth, like a light shining in great darkness." [1] What we need is genuine piety to secure conscientious work. We shall not have better work till we have better men. Saintly workmen would discover for us the way back to Eden.

III. Let us follow the example of the Peasant of Nazareth. For our Lord became poor, and wrought as an artisan, and lived with the common people, to make a life of labour for ever glorious. Nowhere do pride and vanity receive such reproof as in the life of him who wrought so nobly in Nazareth. And when he exchanged the carpenter's bench for the work of the ministry, it was only to work harder than before. " He went about doing good." " He had no leisure so much as to eat." So busy was he that he had frequently to steal from sleep the time for prayer. In his example we have the ideal of genuine, hearty labour, and so far as we follow him shall we be safe and happy.—R. M. E.

Vers. 13—30.—*Expedients to secure purity.* We have here various wise expedients to control the licentiousness of the people, and secure, so far as possible, social purity.

I. Defamation of character was severely punished. A husband could not, with impunity, defame a newly married wife; for should there be proof forthcoming that his charge was false, he was to be publicly chastised, to pay a fine of one hundred shekels of silver to his father-in-law, whose good name and peace he had threatened, and to be bound to his wife all his days.

II. Whoredom was made a capital crime. If the charge made against his wife prove true, then she is to be stoned to death for her sin. Immorality was really treason towards the Divine King, it was incompatible with his kingdom, and so was put into the category of capital crimes. The *morale* of the theocracy was really higher in idea than that of any other kingdom then or now existing.

III. Adultery was also a crime for which both offenders must suffer death. Here the two parties are criminals against the theocracy, and such a flagrant crime cannot be tolerated within it. The morality is severe and wholesome.

IV. Adultery committed with a betrothed damsel is treated just as adultery with a married woman, for she is as good as married. Both parties

---

[1] ' Sartor Resartus,' Library Edition, p. 221. These words were written, it is now believed, with the ideal of his father before him.

in this case also must pay the penalty of death. Such severe measures were the wisest expedients in the end.

V. IN CASE OF ADVANTAGE BEING TAKEN OF A BETROTHED DAMSEL, THE RUFFIAN IS TO PAY THE PENALTY OF DEATH. If the taking away of life is justly punished with death, so should the murder of virtue. As a rule, our laws are too lenient towards ruffians that ruin women. Were a few of them sent to the gallows it would be no more than they deserve.

VI. IN CASE OF A VIRGIN THAT IS NOT BETROTHED, THE MAN WHO TAKES ADVANTAGE OF HER IS COMPELLED TO MARRY HER, AND TO PAY TO HER FATHER A SUBSTANTIAL FINE. The case thus dealt with is different from the preceding. It proceeds upon inquiry. The man is not carried by his passion into an act of great wrong towards one whom he can never hope to have as his wife, which was the last case; but he takes the case into his own hand, where no previous betrothal bars the way. He can make reparation, and he is compelled to do so. Again we say that our laws would be greatly improved if a spice of the severity of the Jewish law went to make the cowardly ruffians who disgrace society suffer more severely for their deeds.

VII. INCEST WAS FORBIDDEN. There is no mincing of matters, since all these abominations abounded among the Canaanites, and must be checked in Israel.

VIII. PURITY IS THUS SEEN TO BE GOD'S AIM. "Be ye holy; for I am holy," is God's direction. We must be as "chaste virgins" presented unto Christ. The social purity of Israel was only to reflect their spiritual purity as towards God. Our own lesson in these regulations is clear. We must not even in the slightest thought prove unfaithful to our Saviour and Lord. He is the Husband of the Church, and requires a faithful wife.—R. M. E.

Vers. 1—4.—*Brotherly service in daily life.* In a healthy state, our souls should so overflow with love, that every neighbour should be regarded as a brother. If the esteem should not at first be reciprocated, our kindness would soften his asperity and make him a better man. In the long run, kindness will produce kindness.

I. PROPERTY HAS ITS CARES AS WELL AS ITS ADVANTAGES. Our earthly possessions have many drawbacks, and are always subject to injury and loss. Hence it is wisdom to hold them lightly, and to grieve little over their diminution. This insecurity is an indication of their inferiority. But the possessions of the soul, viz. wisdom, righteousness, faith, love, patience, are inalienable. The "things unseen are eternal."

II. EARTHLY LIFE IS A FINE FIELD FOR KINDLY SERVICE. The ills and trials which are incident to the present life provide full scope for active sympathy and help. We can scarcely imagine a condition of life in which could be afforded such room for the culture and discipline of the best affections. Every station in life gives opportunity for doing service to others. Every day we hear some new call to duty. We thus train ourselves for higher service. We become more qualified to do good on a large scale, are qualified to rule.

III. NEGLECT TO SHOW KINDNESS IS A SIN. 1. It is sin, inasmuch as it is a plain violation of God's command. As Creator and King, he has a right to make law and to enforce it. 2. It is sin, inasmuch as it is disloyalty to our best feelings. The instinct to show kindness is a part of our constitutional nature. 3. It is sin, inasmuch as it consciously allows injury to be done. The ox or ass that has wandered to-day, will have wandered further (if not recovered) to-morrow; may be irrecoverable then. The gold that is not occupied rusts. To hide our light under a bushel is sin.

IV. GENEROUS KINDNESS IS MORE REMUNERATIVE THAN SELFISHNESS. Generous and self-forgetful kindness brings returns of blessing to the soul. The treasury of the heart is enriched. We gain wealth that is imperishable. We obtain a good name among men, and live in their affectionate memory. We secure, in some measure, the favour of our God. We are in truth, by kindly service, laying up large store of good for coming days. "Blessed is he that considereth the poor; the Lord will deliver him in the time of trouble. The Lord will preserve him, and keep him alive."—D.

Ver. 5.—*Against deceptions in dress.* Truthfulness in act is as needful as truthfulness in speech. Our very dress is a manifesto of truth or of falsehood. God has stamped a visible distinction in the appearance of the human sexes, and it is fraudulent to obliterate them.

I. SIN OFTEN ROBES ITSELF IN A FOREIGN GARB. If sin always appeared in her true habits, but few would court her society. It is her plan to put on a false appearance. Vice usually succeeds because she wears the semblance of virtue. It is the policy of the devil to hide the real nature of sin. Her native blackness would alarm many, if it were seen. The felon flatters himself that it is all fair game. Murder is palliated as just revenge. Profligacy is defended as the impulse of nature. Unchastity paints her face, and robes in others' dress.

II. THE SLIGHTEST APPROACH TO SIN SHOULD BE SHUNNED. The Bible nowhere frowns on innocent merriment. But frolics, that lead to sin, are to be branded as detestable. A wise captain will give a wide berth to perilous quicksands. We cannot keep the sparks too far away from a cask of gunpowder. It is wise to close both ears to the bland voice of the guilty enchantress. Avoid the first step of temptation.

III. DECEIT IN ANY FORM IS DETESTABLE BEFORE GOD. We cannot too highly value a true standard in moral conduct. 'Tis more precious far than a standard for purity of gold or for correctness in speech. Such a standard God has furnished us in his own feelings and judgments. Pretence of any kind is as smoke in his eyes. He is light, faithfulness, and truth. To be transparent, candid, straightforward, is to be Godlike.—D.

Vers. 6, 7.—*God's care for birds.* God's tender care extends to microscopical insects. Nothing is too minute to escape the notice of his eye. "Not a sparrow falls to the ground" without attracting his regard. In proportion as we become conformed to God's image, we shall cherish tender feeling for every living thing.

I. FOR MAN'S GOOD BIRDS LIVE AND BREED. They please the eye with their gay plumage. They regale our ears with pleasant song. They furnish our tables with food. They teach us lessons of cheerful trust. Devoid of anxious care, they daily feast upon the Divine bounty; and a ray of sunshine is repaid with melodious song. They fulfil a mission as the teachers of mankind. To birds we are indebted for considerable pleasure. For us they live: be ours no wanton cruelty.

II. IN THEIR MATERNAL CARES THEY APPEAL FOR GENTLE CONSIDERATION. We may wisely learn a lesson from their maternal affection, from the exposure of their own lives to defend their young. It will foster tender feeling in us to observe this self-forgetfulness in mother birds. But to take advantage of this self-exposure—this noble defence of their offspring—for the purpose of capturing the parent, will deaden and demoralize our own sensibilities. We may furnish a meal for our bodily appetite; but we shall at the same time injure our nobler parts, strangle our nobler feelings.

III. FUTURE PROSPECTS ARE TO BE PREFERRED TO PRESENT PLEASURE. It is a short-sighted policy to use for present need everything within our reach. It is wholesome discipline to deny one's self now, in the hope of greater future good. The farmer foregoes the sale or the use of his grain, that he may have wherewith to sow his fields in the coming season. So to spare the life of the parent bird is to secure in return many other lives. A source of future profit should not thoughtlessly be destroyed. Self-restraint is an exemplary virtue.—D.

Ver. 8.—*The perils of inadvertence.* Thoughtlessness is the parent of much mischief. To reach a state of security and bliss, there must be life in our every part—in intellect, foresight, prudence.

I. MAN IS EXPOSED TO MANY NATURAL EVILS. Although lord and interpreter of nature, nature afflicts him in many ways. She scorches him with heat, freezes him with cold, pierces him with pain. Man has skill and power to bring nature under his dominion, if he will duly exert himself for this purpose. Nature is willing to be ruled, and to become the servant of man; but consents to be ruled only in accordance with Divine law. Our duty is to examine these laws, and to bring her into subservience to our true interests. Herein lies scope for the training of mind, heart, conscience, will—training for a higher sphere.

II. NATURAL LAW IS NEVER SUSPENDED TO SUIT MAN'S IMPRUDENCE. Be a man ever so pious, or be he engaged in work ever so benevolent, a moment's imprudence may cut short his life. He may mistake poison for medicine; he may leave open a gas-tap;

he may imprudently trifle with some natural force; and pain or death will result. If he build a house, in order to protect himself and family from the rigours of the climate, any imprudence in the erection may bring on him heavier evils than those he thought to avert. The want of a parapet on the roof may expose his children to a sudden and painful death. We cannot too much admire God's thoughtful care in prescribing such regulations as these.

III. INADVERTENCE MAY PRODUCE GIGANTIC MISERY. It is not enough to have good intentions or gracious dispositions; mind, as well as heart, must be in active exercise. A foolish man is a curse to society. Wisdom is greatly needed to produce a prosperous life, and to make a man useful to others. Eli was a good man, but exhibited great folly in the management of his sons, and disaster came thereby upon Israel. Reason is entrusted to every man to be used, and if the powers of intelligence are allowed to rust, the result is loss to ourselves and calamity to others.—D.

Vers. 9—12.—*Directions in minor matters.* What was, in primitive days, matter for direct revelation from God, is now ascertained by scientific observation. Herein we learn that revelation and science spring from one origin and subserve one end—the good of men. And herein we may learn God's fatherly care for his children in the days of their infancy.

I. GREATEST FERTILITY IN NATURE IS TO BE SOUGHT. It is man's province to bring out the greatest productiveness in fields and fruit trees. Pruning, manuring, and grafting are essential. The vine needs especial care, and is susceptible of great increase of fruitfulness. So delicate is the blossom of the vine that the pollen of other plants in the vicinity, coming into contact, injures the formation of the fruit. It is a joy to God to see the trees of the field fruitful; how much more to see abundant fruitfulness in us! "Herein is our Father glorified." The least of God's commandments is profitable to observe.

II. NEEDLESS BURDENS ON ANIMALS FORBIDDEN. Every beast is appointed to be the servant of man; but man is required to act towards the inferior creation in God's stead. The burden of service laid upon oxen and asses is heavy enough; let it not be wantonly increased. Both the ox and the ass suffered from an unequal yoking in the plough. God saw the painful effect, and felt grieved. Animal feeling is a gift from God, and is intended to be for enjoyment. We may act in harmony with God, and increase that enjoyment; or we may, in part, frustrate his plan. In every act of man God takes lively interest. All day long he is approving or censuring.

III. OUR PIETY IS TO BE SEEN IN OUR RAIMENT. It is very probable that this prohibition about dress was to counteract a custom among idolaters—a custom which led to superstitious feeling. Some solid reason was at the root of the counsel, whether we can discover that reason or not. Our raiment is in some measure the exponent of our religion. If "Holiness to the Lord" is predicted as the motto to be found on the bells of the horses, so, and much more, should consecration to God be conspicuous on our dress and demeanour. Our raiment often serves as an ensign, and denotes to what party we belong—the Church or the world. If simplicity, modesty, beauty, sterling quality, be in our dress, these are ornaments of our holy faith. Whatever we do, or however we dress, be this our aim, to please God. A child will never be ashamed to acknowledge its father.—D.

Vers. 13—21.—*Slander, unchastity, and fraud.* No blame can lie against the Scriptures because they legislate on such detestable matters. The blame must lie at the door of depraved humanity, which perpetrates such deeds and makes Divine legislation necessary. The obscenity appertains to the vices, only praise belongs to the remedy.

I. A WOMAN'S CHASTITY IS HER MAIN DOWRY FOR LIFE. If she possess not this virtue, she is worse than worthless; she is a plague and a pest—a moral dunghill. Apart from chastity, she can fill no proper place in society. Her true function is ended. She is only a discredit to the human name. Her light is dense darkness. The streams of life are polluted. The fountain of bliss is corrupted at its source. Rottenness is at the core of society. No language can exaggerate the evil.

II. SLANDER AGAINST A WIFE'S CHASTITY IS THE BLACKEST OF SINS. In proportion to the vileness of the sin and the severity of the penalty, is the baseness and guilt of the man who makes the accusation falsely. This is a climax of sins of speech, which nothing can surpass. Slander of any sort is heinous sin, and slander against an intimate friend is more heinous yet; but slander against one's wife—and against her chastity— is most heinous of all. Fines and scourging are lenient punishment for such a monster.

III. THE PENALTIES OF SIN ARE IN PROPORTION TO INJURY DONE. On the principle laid down in a previous law, the penalty for false accusation was fixed according to the nature of the deed falsely alleged to be done. In this case, the slanderer well deserved such a result. But then the injured wife would be injured all the more. In the dread penalty imposed on him, she would have to share. Hence, for her sake, the husband's life is spared. To calculate all the effects produced by one act of sin is impossible to the finite mind of man; yet (unless pardon, full and complete, be enjoyed) in proportion to these perpetuated effects will be the penalty meted out to the sinner. We may well " stand in awe."—D.

Vers. 22—30.—*Various penalties for unchastity.* Purity in domestic life is at the root of national prosperity.

I. THE NEGLECT OF VIRTUE'S SAFEGUARDS IS GUILT. (Ver. 24.) If a sentinel reck- lessly leave open a portal in the beleaguered city, it is treason; it is as if he had betrayed his king. To see a house on flame, and to give no warning, is to become accountable for the destruction of a city. To neglect the physician's counsel in time of disease is to be guilty of death. So to make no resistance to the tempter is to court his approach. To go to the battle without sword, or spear, or shield is to invite defeat. Idle women may be said to tempt the devil.

II. NEGLECT OF DUE PRECAUTIONS OFTEN LEADS TO A TERRIBLE SURPRISE. Oftentimes we underrate what strength the tempter has until we are in his clutches. So long as we knew temptation only by hearsay, we imagined it easy to escape or to overcome; but when brought suddenly under its subtle, wily influence, we are surprised how easily we are overcome.

III. THE CONSENT OF THE WILL IS NEEDED TO CONSTITUTE A SIN. Whatever we are compelled to do by an external power, and against all the opposing force of our own will, this is not sin. Injury and loss may follow, but unless the will consents there is no moral culpability. The essence of sin lies in the inclination. A man may violate all the precepts of the Decalogue by a glance of his eye—ay, by a volition of his will. Whether the overt act follow or not may depend on favourable or unfavourable outward circumstance. The same mischievous effects will not follow, but the sin is there. Therefore, " Keep thy heart with all diligence."

IV. GENEROUS MINDS WILL PUT THE BEST POSSIBLE CONSTRUCTION ON HUMAN CONDUCT. (Ver. 27.) How generously minded a man may be, he is bound to be true. He cannot dissemble facts. He is under obligation to condemn the slightest sin. With the evil thing there must be no connivance. But if it be possible, with due regard to virtue, to give two interpretations on a deed, fairness to the doer requires that we give the inter- pretation the most favourable and generous. To a prisoner at the bar, the judge gives the full benefit of any doubt; and equal justice should be dealt to men in all our judgments upon them. If there be bright spots in their character and deeds, let us fasten our eyes upon these. It will do us good. To search out the diseased parts of humanity, and to find secret pleasure in contemplating these moral sores,—this will do us harm. As we measure our sentiments and judgments out to men, they will measure to us again. We may be blind to our own blemishes—we usually are; but others will readily find them out; and if we are harsh and ungenerous in our estimate of men, they will return the treatment, perhaps with compound interest. It is wise, every day, to foster in our breast the charity " that believeth all things, hopeth all things, endureth all things."—D.

EXPOSITION.

CHAPTER XXIII.

CIVIL RIGHTS. WHO MAY AND WHO MAY NOT ENTER INTO THE CONGREGATION. UN-CLEANNESS IN THE CAMP TO BE AVOIDED. RECEPTION OF FUGITIVE SLAVES. LICEN-TIOUS PERSONS TO BE REMOVED, AND GIFTS THE PRICE OF IMPURITY TO BE REFUSED. LAWS REGARDING USURY, VOWS, AND CER-TAIN DUTIES OF CITIZENSHIP.

Vers. 1—8.—Five classes of persons are here excluded from the congregation of the Lord.

Ver. 1.—Mutilation was performed by the two methods here specified—crushing and excision. The exclusion of persons who had suffered this from the congregation, i.e. from the covenant fellowship of Israel, the πολιτεία τοῦ Ἰσραὴλ (Eph. ii. 12), was due to the priestly character of the nation. Israel was a kingdom of priests (Exod. xix. 6), and the admission into it of one in whom the nature of man, as made by God, had been degraded and marred, would have been unfitting; just as all bodily blemish un-fitted a man for being a priest, though other-wise qualified (Lev. xxi. 16—24). This law, however, was one of the ordinances intended for the period of nonage; it had reference to the outward typical aspect of the Israelitish constitution; and it ceased to have any significance when the spiritual kingdom of God came to be established. Even under the theocracy, eunuchs were not excluded from religious privileges; they could keep God's sabbaths, and take hold of his covenant, and choose the things pleasing to him, and so be part of the spiritual Israel, though shut out from the fellowship of that which was outward and national (cf. Isa. lvi. 4).

Ver. 2.—A bastard; one born of a harlot; so the Hebrew word (מַמְזֵר), which occurs only here and in Zech. ix. 6, is said to mean; LXX., ἐκ πόρνης: Vulgate, de scorto natus; the Talmud and the rabbins represent the word as denoting one begotten in adultery or incest (Maimon., 'Issure Biah.,' c. xv. §§ 1, 2, 7, 9); so also the Syriac bar gamo, "son of adultery." To his tenth generation; i.e. for ever, ten being the number of inde-finiteness (cf. Gen. xxxi. 7; Numb. xiv. 22; Job xix. 3; Ps. iii. 6, etc.).

Ver. 3.—As Ammon and Moab had met the Israelites with hostility, and had brought Balaam to curse them, a curse had thereby been brought upon themselves, and they also were to be for ever excluded from the con-gregation of Israel.

Ver. 6.—Israel was not to seek, i.e. care for and use means to promote, the welfare of these nations. Individuals, however, of these nations might be naturalized in Israel, and as proselytes enter the congregation, as the case of Ruth proves. It was against the nations, as such, that this ban was directed, and this they had brought on themselves by choosing to be enemies of Israel when they might have been friends and allies.

Ver. 7.—It was to be otherwise with the Edomite and the Egyptian; though the former had refused permission to the Israel-ites to pass through their land, and the latter had oppressed and wronged the nation, yet as the former were connected with Israel by a bond of kindred—for he is thy brother —and the latter had received Israel to so-journ in their land, where, notwithstanding the oppression which clouded the later times of their sojourn, they had reaped many benefits, they were not to abhor these nations or place them under a ban of perpetual ex-clusion; descendants in the third genera-tion of an Edomite or Egyptian might be naturalized in Israel.

Vers. 9—11.—When the people went forth to war, all impurity and defilement was to be kept out of their camp. When the host goeth forth; literally, when thou goest forth as a camp or host. As in the wilderness the camp was to be kept pure (Numb. v. 2, etc.), so also in the future, when they went out to war, all defilement was to be removed from their host. Every wicked thing; rather, every evil thing, evil in the sense of blemish or uncleanness (cf. ch. xvii. 1).

Ver. 13.—A paddle upon thy weapon; rather, a small spade (the word properly means a pin or nail) among thy furniture, or, according to another reading among thy implements or accoutrements; they were to carry with them along with their imple-ments of war a tool for digging in the earth.

Ver. 14.—The camp was to be kept holy, because God went forth with their armies, and in his presence there must be nothing that defileth or is unclean. That he see no unclean thing in thee; literally, nakedness, shamefulness of a thing, i.e. anything that one would be ashamed of.

Vers. 15, 16.—A slave that had escaped from his master was not to be given up, but allowed to dwell in the land, in whatever part he might choose. The reference is to a foreign slave who had fled from the harsh treatment of his master to seek refuge in Israel, as is evident from the expression, בְּאַחַד שְׁעָרֶיךָ, "in one of thy gates," i.e. in any part of thy land. Onkelos, עֲבַר עַמְמִין, "a slave of the Gentiles." His master; the word used is the plural *adonim*, masters. The use of this for a human master or lord is peculiar to the Pentateuch (cf. Gen. xxiv. 9, 51; xxxix. 2; xl. 1; Exod. xxi. 4, 6, 32, etc.). In this use of the term there is no reference to severity of rule, as if this were a plural intensive.

Vers. 17, 18.—Amongst idolatrous nations prostitution was in certain cases regarded as an act of religious service (cf. Herod., i. 199), and both males and females prostituted themselves especially in the worship of Astarte. All such abominations were to be unknown in Israel (cf. Micah i. 7). **Whore;** *kedêshah* (קְדֵשָׁה), a female who prostituted herself in the worship of an idol. **The price of a dog;** not money obtained from the sale of a dog, but the gains of the *kadesh*, or male prostitute, here called a dog, as the type of all uncleanness (cf. Rev. xxii. 15).

Vers. 19—25.—Certain civil rights and duties are here prescribed.

Vers. 19, 20.—An Israelite might lend on interest money, or victuals, or other property, to a foreigner, but of one of his own people he was not to take interest for a loan (cf. Exod. xxii. 24; Lev. xxv. 36, 37).

Vers. 21—23.—A vow to the Lord, once made, was to be religiously kept; the Lord would require it, and to refuse or neglect to pay it would be held a sin. No one, however, was under any obligation to vow— that was to be a purely voluntary act. **That which is gone out of thy lips thou shalt keep and perform; . . . according as thou hast vowed unto the Lord thy God of free-will** (נְדָבָה, spontaneously). (For the law concerning vows in general, see Lev. xxvii. and Numb. xxx.)

Vers. 24, 25.—In the vineyard or corn-field of a neighbour they might eat to appease hunger, but no store of grapes or of grain might be carried away. **At thine own pleasure;** literally, *according to thy soul*, i.e. desire or appetite (cf. ch. xiv. 26). **Pluck the ears with thine hand** (cf Matt. xii. 1; Luke vi. 1). Among the Arabs of the present day the right of a hungry person to pluck ears of corn in a field and eat the grains is still recognized (Robinson, 'Bib. Res.,' ii. 192; Thomson, 'Land and the Book,' ii. 510).

HOMILETICS.

Vers. 1—8.—*Stern safeguards sometimes needed.* It was no small part of the education of the Hebrew people at once to stamp as disreputable the practices of bodily mutilation which were common enough among heathen nations. The honour of the congregation of the Lord was bound up in its freedom from complicity therewith. Eunuchs and illegitimate offspring were excluded from the congregation of the Lord, lest the moral virus connected with the associations of their life should be as poison in the camp. Hence this shield against its poisonous influence is to be preserved down "to the tenth generation," both as a brand on former sin and as a guard against future evil. Sentence of exclusion is also passed on the Ammonites and Moabites (see Gen. xix. 36—38). The stain on the origin of these races is grievous. And the new generations had, by their hostility to the people of God, and because of their superstitious arts, shown that nought but peril could attend their admission, for a long time to come. To seek "their peace and prosperity" would have been an increase of peril, as well as a connivance at wrong. Hence it was forbidden (ver. 6). That this, and not the cultivation of needless hostility or revenge, was intended by these prohibitions is clear from vers. 7, 8. Two extremes are to be avoided. No rancour or grudge is to be cherished over past ills inflicted, and yet kindliness of feeling is not to be allowed to degenerate into even apparent friendship with ungodliness and sin. In these facts and precepts the following teachings are included or suggested.

I. The perfection of social life can only be secured when the several members of any society are holy unto the Lord.

II. The outside world presents very much that is the reverse of this, even all kinds of spiritual and sensual wickedness.

III. While it behoves us to cherish a spirit of true benevolence towards all, yet we may never wink at sin.

IV. It may be necessary for us to adopt stern measures towards others, even that of banishment (1 Cor. v. 6, 13), in order to avoid contamination.

V. We may well cherish, and teach others to cherish, a special hatred of sins of the flesh, since it may not be for many, many generations that blood-poisoning thereby ceases to corrupt or taint the life.   Surely men would more frequently check themselves in sin if they would remember for how long they may enfeeble the constitutions and embitter the lives of those who may hereafter owe their existence to them.

Vers. 9—14.—*Cleanliness a religious duty.*   The Law of Moses may be regarded as fourfold—moral, ritual, civil, and sanitary.   The precepts in this paragraph are an example of the last-named part thereof.   They refer to the inculcation of cleanliness, both in camp and in person.   And not only so, but to the observance thereof in time of war.   While, perhaps, at such times special evils would result from the neglect of such regulations, yet, on the other hand, it would be precisely when movements were irregular, uncertain, and attended with much excitement, that there would be the strongest tendency to fail in their observance.   But no amount of war-pressure would be any excuse for uncleanliness.   We get here, moreover, an illustration of that which so often occurs in the Law of Moses, viz. that duties of the lowest, humblest, and most common order are urged on the people by the highest and noblest sanctions; and many a teacher may find reason for urging to cleanliness of habit from such a text as ver. 14, "The Lord thy God walketh in the midst of thy camp; . . . therefore shall thy camp be holy."   The precise application of the text must, of course, vary with locality and circumstance; but the principle of it includes the following.
1. The presence of the Lord God is everywhere.   2. He is in the "camp" of his people as a special light and guard.   3. Hence every such home may be regarded as a temple of God, the palace of the Great King.   4. In such homes the most menial acts may be acts of service done for God: common work may be dignified by great motives.   5. It will be regarded by a wise Christian man as a part of his duty which is by no means to be neglected, to maintain order and unsullied cleanliness in person and home.   This will be part of his life-worship—the living translation of "*laborare est orare.*"   This duty needs special enforcement in some quarters.   Many a humble Christian cottager elevates his home and all therein, by having it so beautifully clean that, on every piece of furniture, on every wall, on every floor, it seems as if the words were graven, "*Holiness to the Lord.*"

Vers. 15, 16.—*Israel's land a refuge for the oppressed.*   (For "the Mosaic treatment of slavery," see Homily on ch. xv. 12—18.)   To the features of his legislation thereon this must be added that, as soon as ever a foreign slave set foot on Hebrew soil, he was free.   Israel's land was for him the land of liberty!

Vers. 17, 18.—*Unholy wealth may not be put to Divine uses.*   (See Homilies on ch. xv. 1—6; xiv. 22—29.)   The same law which regulates the appropriation of wealth rightfully gained forbids the dedication to any holy use of wealth sinfully gained.

Vers. 19, 20.—*The opposite working of like principles.*   The difference here permitted between lending to brethren and to strangers resembles that allowed in ch. xv. 1—6 (see Homily thereon).

Vers. 21—23.—*Vows to God to be performed.*   The vow here made is supposed to be entirely voluntary.   It was "a free-will offering."   In Numb. xxx. 3—8, abuse is guarded against.   Vows made without the knowledge or consent of the father or husband were to be of no force.   No priest had any warrant from the Mosaic institutes to come between a young woman and her father, or between husband and wife.   Vows to God were to be completely spontaneous, as between the soul and God.   They were not to be extorted by others, nor yet to involve the entanglement of others.

Vers. 24, 25.—*Kindliness to neighbours a duty of the holders of property.*   This is a very instructive precept.   "In vine-growing countries grapes are amazingly cheap; and we need not wonder, therefore, that all within the reach of a passenger's arm were free.   The quantity plucked was a loss never felt by the proprietor, and it was a kindly privilege afforded to the poor and wayfaring man" (Jameson).   "Thou mayest take for necessity, not for superfluity" (Trapp).

HOMILIES BY VARIOUS AUTHORS.

Vers. 1—8.—*The excluded from the congregation.* Certain principles underlie these exclusions which it is worth our while to note. It will be seen that, though bars of this kind are done away in Christ, there was a fitness, under the theocracy, in the exclusion of the classes specified from full participation in covenant privilege, such exclusion being in harmony with the idea of "a holy nation"—type in earthly mould of the ideal kingdom of God.

I. THE EXCLUSION OF THE MUTILATED. (Ver. 1.) The idea here is that the preservation of the body in its vigour, and in the entirety of its functions, is a duty which we owe to God; that mutilation of it or dishonour done to it is dishonour done to him—a species of profanity. Those in whom this work of dishonour had been wrought, unfitting them for the discharge of the distinctive functions of their manhood, were barred from entrance to the congregation. The ban is removed under the gospel (Isa. lvi. 3—5).

II. THE EXCLUSION OF THE CHILDREN OF INCEST. (Vers. 2, 3.) "To the tenth generation" seems to be a periphrasis for "for ever" (Neh. xiii. 1). The rabbins take the term "bastard" to refer to children born of incest or adultery. These were to be excluded through all their generations. This principle, irrespective of the ground stated in ver. 4, would have sufficed to exclude Moab and Ammon. The truth conveyed is that the impure are unalterably debarred from membership in God's kingdom. God's kingdom is a kingdom of purity. In its final form nothing of an impure nature will be found in it. Impurity of heart and life exclude from inward membership in it now, and will do so for ever. Known impurity should exclude from Church fellowship on earth (1 Cor. v. 1, 2). The outward bar no longer exists, and the offspring of impure connection, if children of faith, are welcomed to the spiritual fold. But the *tendency* of sins of parents still is, as of old, to exclude children from the fellowship of believers. The unchurched little ones grow up outside the pale of ordinances, and tend, in course of generations, to become increasingly estranged from the means of grace. Parents who sin themselves out of Church fellowship thus do their children, as well as their own souls, an irreparable injury.

III. THE EXCLUSION OF THE UNMERCIFUL AND OF THOSE WHO SHOWED HATRED TO GOD'S PEOPLE. (Vers. 4—6.) The principle here is obvious. Christ expressly excludes the unmerciful from all participation in his kingdom (Matt. xxv. 41—46). And there can be no "peace" and no "prosperity" to those who are actuated by hostility to God's kingdom. So long as they retain this character, we cannot wish it for them. Hostility to Christ's people is hostility to Christ himself (Acts ix. 4, 5), and reacts fatally on the soul (Matt. xxi. 44). It draws upon it God's indignation, and ends in final exclusion from heaven.

IV. THE ADMISSION OF THOSE WHO SHOW KINDNESS TO GOD'S PEOPLE. (Vers. 7, 8.) The Edomite and the Egyptian were not to be abhorred; their children *might* be admitted in the third generation. The Edomites had not been as friendly as they might have been, but they had at least furnished the Israelites with victuals in their march, while the Egyptians had for a long time shown them kindness and hospitality. For these things they "had their reward." Acts of kindness to God's people do not entitle to admission into God's kingdom, but they show a "nighness" of spirit to it, and are remembered in God's dealings with the doers of them, and may issue in their final salvation (Matt. x. 42). Note: Past kindnesses are not to be forgotten because of a late change of disposition. The Egyptians were kindly remembered, though their treatment of the Israelites had latterly been very cruel. It is to be remarked also that the tone in which Edom is uniformly referred to in this book does not in the least harmonize with the late date assigned to it by many critics. Edom, in the time of the prophets, had become Israel's implacable foe.—J. O.

Ver. 5.—*The curse turned into a blessing.* No enchantment, no curse of evil men, can prevail against the people of God. Contrariwise, God will turn the curse into a blessing. In Malachi, on the other hand, he threatens to "curse the blessings" of the wicked (Mal. ii. 2). How does God turn the curse into a blessing? 1. Directly, *by substituting a blessing for a curse*. The curse is not merely not allowed to take effect for harm, but God puts a blessing in its stead. A Divine law of compensation comes into operation. The wicked is punished, and the object of his unrighteous hatred consoled and rewarded, by the curse being read backward, and made a reason for conferring blessing. The very curses of the wicked are thus a means of enrichment to the good. Balaam's curses were thus changed into blessings (Numb. xxiii., xxiv.). 2. Providentially, *by overruling the designs of evil men for their own confusion, and for his people's good*. We have examples in the histories of Joseph (Gen. l. 20), of Mordecai and the Jews (Esth. vi.—x.), of Daniel (Dan. vi.). The persecutions of the Church have thus been overruled for the extension of the gospel (Acts xi. 19). The highest example is the crucifixion of Christ (Acts iii. 13—19). 3. Spiritually, *by turning outward afflictions into means of spiritual good*. (1) Afflictions humble, chasten, purify (Job xlii. 4, 5; Ps. cxix. 71). (2) God can turn afflictions into sources of comfort and joy, into occasions of higher glory to himself, into means of salvation and glory to the saint (Acts xvi. 25; Rom. v. 3; 2 Cor. xii. 9, 10; iv. 17; Phil. i. 19). (3) God can overrule even punishment of sin for our ultimate good. Levi (Gen. xlix. 7).—J. O.

Vers. 9—14.—*Purity in the camp*. The camp was to be free from: 1. Moral pollution (ver. 9). 2. Ceremonial pollution (vers. 10, 11). 3. Natural pollution (vers. 12, 13)—M. Henry. This, because God was in its midst. He was there to work for their deliverance and for the confusion of their enemies. We are taught—

I. THAT MILITARY LIFE IS NO EXCUSE FOR LAXITY IN MORALS, OR FOR A LOWERED STANDARD OF PROPRIETY IN CONDUCT. The opposite opinion too commonly prevails. Immoralities are winked at in soldiers and sailors which would not be tolerated in ordinary society; nay, are sometimes half justified as a necessity of their situation. When public opinion is in this easy state, we cannot wonder that the individuals themselves are not very strict about their behaviour. They find Acts passed, *e.g.* to protect them in their evil courses, and they naturally suppose that they have a kind of sanction for their immorality. Officers do not always set the men the best example. This is in every sense to be deplored. Immorality does not change its nature in the barrack-room or on the march. Rather, when "the host goes forth" we should try to put away from us "every wicked thing." Only then can we confidently expect God's presence to go with us, or look to him for aid in battle. Compare Carlyle's account of Cromwell's army ('Cromwell,' vol. ii., at end), and the "prayer-meeting" of the leaders. See also Baillie's account of the encampment of the Scotch Covenanters at Dunse Law ('Letters,' i. 211).

II. THAT PURITY IS REQUIRED IN THE CAMP OF THE CHURCH, IF HER WARFARE IS TO BE SUCCESSFULLY ACCOMPLISHED. In spiritual conflicts, above all, we must look to spiritual conditions. The Church is an army of Christ. She is organized for aggressive and defensive warfare. Her only hope of success lies in the presence of the Lord with her. But can she hope for this presence if she is not careful to maintain her internal purity? True, she has no commission to search the heart, and must be content to allow tares to mingle with the wheat (Matt. xiii. 24—31). But it is within her province, in the exercise of discipline, to remove obvious scandals, and by rebuke and censure, as well as by positive teaching and persuasion, to keep down worldliness, irreligion, and sensuality, when these make their appearance in her midst. She ought to pray, labour, and use her authority for the maintenance of her purity. The purer she is internally the more resistless will she be in her assaults on evil without.—J. O.

Vers. 15—23.—*Various precepts*. No very close connection exists between the precepts in these verses, yet they are variously related, and suggest by their juxtaposition lessons of importance. We have—

I. A WORD SPOKEN IN THE INTERESTS OF LIBERTY. (Vers. 15, 16.) 1. The fugitive slave is not to be given back to his master. The case is that of a slave escaping from a heathen master. The *spirit* of the Mosaic Law is wholly opposed to slavery. This precept anticipates our own law, that a slave setting foot on British territory is free. 2. Every encouragement is to be given him to settle in the land. He is not to be oppressed or treated with unkindness, but is to be allowed to settle where he pleases. The holy land was thus a true asylum for the oppressed.

II. A BLOW STRUCK AT LEWDNESS. (Vers. 17, 18.) The lawgiver alone, so far as we know, among ancient nations, lays his axe at the root of this great evil. He refuses to it the least toleration. He is right. The prevalence of lewdness in a land blights and withers everything good. It saps the manhood of the nation, destroys its love of liberty (2 Pet. ii. 19), turns religion to hypocrisy (Matt. xxiii. 25—29), kills humane feeling, dissolves domestic ties, and degrades the wretched victim of it to the lowest point of brutishness—

> "It hardens a' within,
> And petrifies the feeling!"
>
> BURNS.

The contrast between the noble severity of the Bible teaching on this subject, and the wretchedly low tone of the teaching of such writers as Bolingbroke, or even of Hume, is very noteworthy.

III. CHECKS IMPOSED ON COVETOUSNESS. 1. The lender is not permitted to exact usury from his brother (vers. 19, 20). That the taking of interest was not regarded as in itself sinful is plain from the permission to take usury from a stranger. But in the circumstances of the time, and in view of the design of the lawgiver to check rather than to encourage extensive commercial operations on the part of the Jews, the law was a wise one, and tended to repress covetousness in a form which would very readily have developed itself. Lending was to be free and cordial, and God's blessing, the best usury, was promised in return. 2. Vows were to be faithfully performed (vers. 21—23). This checked covetousness, so far as that might prompt the person vowing to grudge payment when the time for paying his vow arrived. The vow was in his own choice, but, if made, it was to be religiously performed (Eccles. v. 4, 5). It is easier to vow than at the proper time to make the sacrifices which the vow demands.—J. O.

Vers. 24, 25.—*The vineyard and corn-field.* This law may be regarded: 1. As another check on covetousness. It restricted the operation of covetousness in the owner, and taught him to be generous and charitable. 2. As part of the Jewish provision for the poor (cf. ch. xxiv. 19, 20). 3. As a lesson in honesty. It taught those who used the privilege to restrain themselves to their immediate wants, and to respect on principle the rest of their neighbour's property. It taught them to be honest by trusting them. 4. As giving every one an interest in the fruitfulness of the land. Custom and the force of public opinion would guard the law from abuse.—J. O.

Vers. 1—8.—*The congregation of the Lord jealously guarded.* There has been considerable controversy about what the term " entering into the congregation of the Lord " signifies. It cannot be the Old Testament equivalent for our " communicants," or " Church members;" for it would seem from Exod. xii. 48, 49, that Jewish privileges were open to strangers on condition of their circumcision. Nor need we interpret it as merely indicating the marriage connections which Israelites were to avoid. We are satisfied with the interpretation, received by many, that the congregation (קהל) does not always signify the sum total of the people, but the great assembly of elders. The prohibitions in this passage would, therefore, mean prohibitions from holding office in the theocracy; in fact, they show those who were ineligible to the Jewish eldership. The ineligible parties are—

1. *Eunuchs.* For physical perfection was indispensable in a kingdom typically and ideally to be perfect. Besides, it has been said that this excluded class are deficient in courage, which the elders required.[1]

2. *Those whose family had the " bar sinister" within ten generations.* This was a great penalty against concubinage, and must have made the Jews most particular about the legality of their marriages.

3. *Amorites and Moabites.* They are treated like those with the " bar sinister," as

---

[1] Cf. Jennings's ' Jewish Antiquities,' p. 97.

a judgment on their inhuman treatment of Israel. So that there was caution to be exercised in the admission of outsiders to the honours of the Jewish commonwealth.

4. *Edomites and Egyptians.* They could not enter themselves, but their *grand-children* were eligible. They were not kept waiting so long at the door as those previously mentioned. This jealous guarding of the gate is surely instructive.

I. IT SHOWS US THE DUTY OF LAYING HANDS SUDDENLY UPON NO MAN. This was Paul's direction to Timothy regarding the ordination of elders (1 Tim. v. 22). Their selection was so important, that it should not be hastily or carelessly done. They should get time to prove themselves as worthy. And our ideal of Church officers should be so high as to allow of the introduction of no ill-qualified person through our haste or careless selection.

II. A CHURCH SHOULD MAINLY PRODUCE ITS OWN OFFICERS. Just as breeding is so important physically, so is Church training spiritually. It is the children in the tenth generation of the bastard who are, so to speak, by their ecclesiastical development through nine previous generations in ecclesiastical connection, to wipe out the ill effects of the " bar sinister." The grandchildren of the Edomite and Egyptian are to be eligible, because for three generations connected with the Church. That Church will be strong who can train up from among her own children the officers she needs.

III. OFFICE IN GOD'S CHURCH SHOULD BE THE HIGHEST AMBITION. For people are not in a wholesome state when they place offices in the world before those in the Church. God's service is *highest* service, whatever current opinion may be. Let the thought of holding office in the Church of God be held before Church members as the very noblest ambition for themselves or their children, and then shall the Church be placed upon the pinnacle it deserves.—R. M. E.

Vers. 9—14.—*A pure camp for a pure King.* After insisting on purity giving power in war (ver. 9), and giving direction to men about putting away uncleanness which may be due to natural causes, Moses urges the precaution, because the All-seeing One walketh through the camp, Inspector of all their ways (ver. 14). The directions here given might have been urged on *sanitary* grounds, but Moses puts them deliberately upon *religious.* For the experience among Orientals and Occidentals is that something more than sanitary reasons is needed to overcome man's indolence and keep him clean.

I. CLEANLINESS MAY BE RAISED INTO A PHASE OF GODLINESS. In the proverb is is said to be next to godliness; but here Moses makes it a part of godliness. Religion comes to the aid of science, and helps by its sanctions the wise regulations suggested by science. Witness how painfully slow remedial and sanitary measures are in getting adopted. It would be well if religion could aid the civil power in making sanitation a sacred thing in the eyes of the people.

The reason why cleanliness is not more sacred than it is is a latent Manichæanism, which seems to lurk in human nature; as if matter were essentially unholy, and could not be made sacred. But the religion of Christ lays hold of body as well as soul, and urges a *mens sana in corpore sano*, and promises the perfection of its idea in a bodily resurrection. There is, consequently, a physical side to our religion, which should find expression in the consecration of cleanliness, and divers washings, and food and drink; all that religion may be a more manly and efficient thing. We believe thoroughly in the religious duty of denouncing dirt.

II. RELIGION IS LIFE SPENT IN THE REALIZED PRESENCE OF GOD. " Thou God seest me " is the watchword of religion. When all our life is brought under his eye, when we believe that the commonest and most trivial things are not beneath his notice, when we desire to hide nothing from him by night or by day,—then the light of his pure being illumines and regulates all, and the highest purity is reached. " Muscular Christianity " is a good idea, if by it we mean that Christianity has a physical as well as spiritual sphere. No efforts of our own, muscular or otherwise, will ever save us; but, being saved by Divine grace, our whole being, muscles and all, is at God's service. Religion in everything is the sense of God all through, and this should be our aim.

III. GOD IS THE CAPTAIN ONLY OF THE PURE. A holy camp is the preliminary to God leading Israel successfully against the enemy (ver. 14). The pure in heart see God and follow him to victory. It is the state of the camp of Israel, not the state of their enemies, that is all important. If Israel is impure, it will soon prove impotent. The pure are, in the long run, the powerful. God is on the side, not of the heaviest, but of the purest battalions. Really religious men are ultimately, under God, victorious.—R. M. E.

Vers. 15, 16.—*The Hebrew fugitive law.* We have here a most remarkable law, entirely in the interests of the slave, and showing conclusively that no such thing as property in mankind was recognized in the theocracy. When a slave ran away, the person to whom he repaired is directed to harbour him and give him a place with his servants, but *not* to restore him to his former master. Here, then, is a fugitive law such as permitted no such monster as a slave-hunter to defile the land of Palestine.

I. THE BIBLE RECOGNIZES NO PROPERTY IN MAN. We cannot do better than quote from Dr. Cheever's 'God against Slavery.' He says, "The Jewish Law strictly forbade any one from ever returning unto his master that servant that had fled from his master to him. If an ox or an ass had strayed from its owner, any one finding the beast was commanded to restore it to its owner as his property; but if a man's *servant* had fled away, every one was in like manner *forbidden* to restore him, demonstrating in the strongest manner that a servant was never regarded as property, and could not be treated as such. A man's ox belonged to him, and must be restored to him as his property; but a man's servant did not belong to him, and could not be his property, and, if he chose to take himself away, was not considered as taking away anything that belonged to his master or could be claimed and taken back by him. It is not possible for an incidental demonstration to be stronger than this."

II. RUNAWAY SLAVES ARE ENTITLED TO AN OPPORTUNITY OF EARNING A LIVELIHOOD. Not only is he *not* to be restored, but he is also to be allowed a place in the establishment to which he has escaped. Doubtless he had a good idea of a vacancy being there, and the need for an extra servant. In such a case he is to get his chance, and be allowed without oppression to earn his livelihood. We do not assert that every human being, no matter how "heart-lazy," has a right to a living; but every one has surely a right to a livelihood. It is the organization of labour and livelihoods, rather than poor-laws, that should engross the attention of philanthropists.

III. WHILE MEN HAVE NO RIGHT TO OUR PERSONS, GOD HAS—WE ARE HIS. We are God's slaves. "We are bought with a price," and therefore bound to glorify him with our bodies (1 Cor. vi. 20). He has a title to us by virtue of *creation*; but for him we should not have existed. He has a title to us by virtue of his *providence*; for in him we not only live, but move and have our being. He has a title to us by virtue of *redemption*; for he has redeemed us at no less a cost than the blood of his Son. He has a title to us by virtue of his *inspirations*; for any good and holy desires and aspirations we entertain are through the indwelling of his Spirit. If we intelligently recognize our position, we shall own our obligations to him, and acknowledge we are slaves of God. But his slavery is "perfect freedom." Better to be the Lord's slave than the world's freeman. His Law is "the perfect Law of liberty," and when under it we are realizing that broadest phase of freedom which has made his slaves the mightiest of men.—R. M. E.

Vers. 17—25.—*Money-making must be above suspicion.* We have in these verses an excellent lesson upon mercantile morality. There are too many people in this world who are not at all particular how money is made, if only it be made. "The wages of iniquity" are as welcome to them as to Balaam. But it is plain from these verses that the Lord does regard the way money is won, and will not handle what has come licentiously himself, nor give any countenance to his people in doing so.

I. MONEY MADE BY WICKEDNESS IS ABHORRED OF GOD. The wretched woman who lives by her own dishonour, the wretched man who lends himself to licentiousness, are both intolerable to the Divine King. The idols of the heathen may receive the wages of licentiousness, and be served by lewd women, as the history of heathenism shows, but God will have no such dedications polluting his house. As the Holy One, he will not be served by the deliberately unholy and profane.

II. MONEY MADE OUT OF THE NEEDS OF THE POOR SAINTS IS ALSO AN ABOMINATION TO GOD. It was a noble law that Jew was not to play the money-lender to Jew. To extort from a brother what his needs can ill afford to pay, is forbidden. The Jews were to be brothers indeed, in readiness to lend without hope of recompense. And although this arrangement may not be literally binding under this dispensation, there is a general idea abroad of the undesirableness of making money out of God's poor people. There is to be special consideration shown surely to those who are of the household of faith (Gal. vi. 10). We should suspect a man of worldliness who extorted big interest from a struggling Church, when well able to advance the desperately needed loan.

III. A SPHERE FOR USURY IS RECOGNIZED BY THE LORD. The stranger may borrow under an engagement to pay interest. This is only right. If usury were universally forbidden, the world of commerce would come to a standstill. Capital would not accumulate if it had no reward awaiting it. The stranger, consequently, comes and asks the favour of a loan. He has no claim on you for it, but he is willing to pay a fair price for the obligation. The whole edifice of commerce rests upon the legality of such a transaction. It is a mutual benefit.

At the same time, there may be extortion and speculation in usury, just as in other lines of business; and God shows that "extortioners" (1 Cor. vi. 10) have no part in his kingdom. It is *selfishness* pure and simple, and in its most tyrannical and despicable form.

IV. ALL VOWS REGISTERED IN CONNECTION WITH OUR MONEY-MAKING MUST BE FAITHFULLY PERFORMED. It is almost a natural instinct that vows should be made unto the Lord in connection with our prosperity. Often a person struggling to realize an "honest profit," while the transaction is only in progress, and the issue is still uncertain, dedicates a proportion, if the Lord send him success; or a proportion of a new crop, if it be a good one. Such vows must never be recalled, but always honourably met. "Better is it that thou shouldest not vow, than that thou shouldest vow and not pay" (Eccles. v. 5).

V. THE RIGHTS OF THE HUNGRY SHOULD ALSO BE RESPECTED IF A LAND IS TO ENJOY SUCCESS. The vines are so productive in Palestine, when properly cultivated, and the vineyards so unprotected, that a hungry passenger may fill himself and no one be a bit the poorer. Or he may enter the field of standing corn and make what use he can of his hands. In other words, the hungry was regarded as having a right to satisfy the cravings of nature and to pass on.

And when it was placed on the statute-book as a *right*, it saved the poor man's self-respect and never interfered with his personal freedom. This "poor-law" gives man his need without asking him to surrender his liberty. This is its beauty, it meets the pressing necessity without destroying the person's legitimate self-respect. Liberty is more precious to any upright soul than bread; and it is a wholesome instinct which, as far as possible, should be respected in any beneficent national arrangement.—R. M. E.

Vers. 1—6.—*Loss of sacred privilege a grievous penalty.* In such passages as this, very much more is intended than is expressed. We have to read between the lines, for only they who lived in those days of Jewish life could comprehend the shadowy hints, the pregnant suggestions, which are here reduced to words.

I. THE ABUSE OF REPRODUCTIVE VITALISM IS A GIGANTIC SIN. The law of the natural kingdom, with regard to every species of life, that its "seed should be in itself," obtains in man its highest form. But here human inclination, passion, will come into play. It is an honour which God has conferred upon us, in that he has made us agents co-operating with him in the perpetuation of the human race. And the abuse of this function is followed forthwith by the Divine censure. In many cases, judgment swiftly follows upon the heels of the sin. As at Bethpeor, sudden and overwhelming penalty fell upon the Jewish culprits who yielded to the seductive snares of the Moabite women, so that there fell of the Hebrews four and twenty thousand men; so summary vengeance falls upon such transgressors still. Adultery and incest are stamped with the red brand of God's hottest wrath. One feels in reading the shameful narrative of Lot's incest at Zoar, as if the historian had not left on it the burning stigma of indignation; but we may draw no such conclusion from his silence. In this chapter we perceive how the blank is filled. The issue of that incestuous intercourse are branded with perpetual shame.

II. This gigantic sin begets a series of gigantic evils. 1. *It begets callous selfishness in posterity.* God did not forget that the Moabites and Ammonites refused the common necessaries of life to the Hebrews, who sought nothing more than a friendly passage through their territory. Although this sin was a branch and offspring from the first, it was something new, and demanded fresh chastisement. For every offence in God's kingdom there is prepared a just measure of retribution. 2. *It begets malicious opposition.* They hired, in their blindness, the services of Balaam, the sorcerer, in the hope that he would blast and ruin them with his witchery and curse. The end was frustrated. The purchased curse was changed into blessing. Nevertheless, the intention was criminal. The hearts of the Moabites burned with hate for their kinsmen; and base intentions shall be scourged. 3. *It begets idolatry and blind fanaticism.*

III. Such evils culminate in justest punishments. Suitable penalties begin to appear in this life. 1. *There is the loss of external privilege.* Such "shall not enter into the congregation of the Lord." What! not when the present generation has passed away? No; not to the tenth generation! No; not for ever. Possibly the culprits despised the privilege, mocked at the loss. But none the less was it an immeasurable loss, a terrible privation. It is not said that a penitent Moabite should not be forgiven —should not obtain eternal life. Yet the loss of external instruction and help lessened the probability that penitence would visit the soul. We do ourselves wrong when we contemn religious privilege. 2. *There is the loss of friendly intercession.* "Thou shalt not seek their peace nor their prosperity . . . for ever." Prayer for such is interdicted. Brotherly sympathy is denied. The Hebrews were ordained to be a nation of priests. The intention was that, by virtue of their growing piety, they should be, as an entire nation, the priests of the Lord, while foreigners should immigrate to be their husbandmen and vine-dressers. By reason of the Jew's superior knowledge of God, they might be successful intercessors for other nations. But from this gracious privilege the Moabites and Ammonites were permanently excluded. Despise not the prayers of the devout.—D.

Vers. 7, 8.—*Terminable chastisements.* The sting in God's curse is its irreversibleness. The bitter draught is dashed with mercy when we have prospect that it shall cease.

I. The conduct of some men is a strange admixture of good and bad. There were some fine traits in Esau's character commingled with coarse and selfish obstinacy. Light was interfused with darkness. The treatment of Israel by the Edomites was not the most friendly, nor was it decidedly hostile. It was marked by haughty reserve rather than by malignant hostility. So also the Egyptians were not wholly antagonistic to Israel. For more than four hundred years the Hebrews had found sustenance and shelter in Goshen. If the last Pharaoh had oppressed them with bitter bondage, a former Pharaoh had blest them with unusual kindness. From desolating famine, Egypt had shielded them. This shall not be forgotten; it shall temper chastisement. The remoter peoples shall be admitted to God's kingdom, while those nearer at hand shall be excluded.

II. Such conduct receives due measure of chastisement. It is impossible to entertain the best feelings of affection towards such persons. Yet we are to be just in our estimate of them. We are not to fasten our eyes only on the dark side of their characters. As far as it is possible we should be generous in feeling. "Thou shalt not abhor them." The present generation of such, and their children, shall be excluded from the privileges of the righteous. But *there* the ban shall terminate. If children of wisdom, we shall endure such chastisement with patient resignation—

> "For patient suffering is the link
> That binds us to a glorious morrow."

III. The inheritance of blessing is in reversion. "Weeping may endure for a night: joy cometh in the morning." The night is temporary; the day will be eternal. However dark be their present lot under the frown of Jehovah, the light of hope shines beyond—lights up the future. We live in our children. It alleviates our present burden when we are assured that our children shall be exempt. More often should we stand in awe of sin, if we did but perceive the miseries we were entailing on posterity. The revelations of the future are a valuable guide for the present.—D.

Vers. 15, 16.—*Sympathy for the oppressed.* It is supposed that oppressive forms of slavery existed among the neighbouring nations; and it might be anticipated that the oppressed would seek asylum among the people of God. The social atmosphere was to be that of healthful freedom, which is fatal to inhuman thraldom.

I. WE SEE SOCIAL RELATIONSHIP IN ITS EXTREME LIMITS. One is a master; one is a slave. One has risen to power; one has sunk into weakness. Humanity has immense capacity for rising and falling. Such abject dependence may be the result of external calamity, or it may be the effect of culpable folly.

II. THIS PROPRIETORSHIP IN MAN IS CAPABLE OF GREAT ABUSE. A slave-master must have great self-restraint if he does not abuse his purchased power. To no man ought irresponsible control over his fellows be entrusted. The temptation to encroach on human rights is too great to be put within any man's reach. Good men will use every position they occupy so as to do good to others; and even a slave-holder may be a source of large blessing. On the other hand, coarse and cruel men can turn the institution into a nest of villainy.

III. ABUSE OF SLAVERY MAY BECOME SELF-CURATIVE. A reflecting master will calculate that, if he injure his slave, he injures his property—he injures himself. But in moments when passion is dominant, a reckless slave-holder will think nothing about consequences. Yet his slave may flee. The common instincts of humanity will impel disinterested persons to aid the fugitive. And the successful flight of one will encourage others to make the attempt.

IV. THE OPPRESSED HAVE A CLAIM UPON OUR PRACTICAL SYMPATHY. The Hebrews could not easily discover the real merits of quarrel between a foreign slave and his master. But they would know that a slave would not leave his master and his home without sufficient cause. It was a precarious chance how an alien slave would find a livelihood. Therefore the refugee had a claim upon the Hebrews' sympathy. The oppressed of every land have a large place in the heart of God, and every friend of God will strive to imitate his deeds. Emmanuel's land is to be the land of liberty. Liberty may not suddenly be given to every man, in any condition of mind; yet liberty is man's birthright—his true inheritance; for this he is to prepare. A man is dwarfed, stunted, deformed, if he be not free.—D.

Ver. 18.—*Unacceptable offerings.* The value of religious offerings in God's sight is not measured by their magnitude, nor by splendour, but by the spiritual motive that originates them.

I. GOD HAS NO NEED OF HUMAN OFFERINGS. He is absolutely independent of his creatures. "The gold and silver" are already *his.* If he had need of these things, he would create them. The advantage of religious offerings belongs to man. The offerer is the party blest. Spiritual benefits (not to be measured or weighed in earthly balances) are obtained in exchange.

II. ILL-GOTTEN GAINS ARE BY HIM REJECTED. To accept such would be to connive at wickedness. It is often for this profane end that men bring them. They hope thereby to make the residue the more safe, and a base calling the more respectable. In a word, they desire to take God into unhallowed partnership with themselves. To him this can be only abomination—a stench in his nostrils.

III. RELIGIOUS OFFERINGS ARE MEASURED BY THEIR MORAL WORTH. The mite of the widow was estimated by the genuine love that inspired it. It was a solid nugget of spiritual affection. Seldom has the love of the human heart been so completely converted into a material gift. It was but one remove from creation. That widow would have poured out her very soul in creating gifts for God if she might. It is this sterling and practical love which God values. Offerings that are not the exponents of grateful feeling are nothing worth. God has a scale of moral arithmetic, and all religious offerings are placed in the balances of the sanctuary.—D.

Vers. 19, 20.—*Usury lawful and unlawful.* From all conduct the element of selfishness is to be eliminated. All forms of honourable commerce are permitted, because, while the end is gain, it is not solely gain; seller and buyer both obtain advantage.

I. OUR CONDUCT IS TO BE REGULATED BY RELATIONSHIP. Kindly feeling is due unto all men. We should honour man *as man*. Yet the conduct which is commendable to a stranger is not commendable to a father. According to the degree of propinquity should be the degree of affection. A brother has claims upon us which a stranger has not. Our stock of affection is limited; we are to bestow it on most suitable objects. Our capacity for doing good is measurable; we must expend it with care.

II. MONEY GAIN IS NOT THE BUSINESS OF LIFE. There are occupations nobler than money-getting. Contentment is better than gold. The culture of the mind is better. The discipline of the moral powers is better. Brotherly kindness is better. The diffusion of knowledge is better. Earthly prosperity is to be hailed especially as a condition for doing good. To have, and yet to refuse to help, is a sin. That man's gold is a curse.

III. YET MONEY GAIN, WITHIN PROPER LIMITS, IS WISE AND HONOURABLE. Properly viewed, moderate usury is but a species of commerce. If with my loan of a thousand pounds a shrewd merchant makes a gain of a hundred pounds in addition, it is just that I should receive a part thereof, as the earning of my loan. If one has money capital and another has skill and a third has time, it is simply equitable that the temporal earnings of the partnership should be divided, in some proportion, among all. If I obtain fair usury for the use of my money from honest traders, I have power to help impoverished brethren to an extent I could not otherwise. God had not intended that the Hebrews should be a commercial nation. Their business was to be witness-bearers to the world of heavenly truth.—D.

Vers. 21—23.—*The place of vows.* It is not obligatory to make vows; it is obligatory to fulfil them. We are often free to contract an obligation; we are not free to violate it. A man is not bound to marry; having married, he is bound to cherish his wife.

I. VOWS IMPLY SPECIAL ACTS OF KINDNESS ON THE PART OF GOD. The ordinary course of God's bounty baffles verbal description. The forethought, the active energy, the well-laid plans, the unslumbering attention, the changeless affection, which are required for the preservation of human life, no language can express. But this is not all that God does for us. In times of unusual perplexity, special guidance is often vouchsafed to us. When surrounding events seemed most adverse to our interests, in answer to prayer, sudden deliverance has come. A precious life was in jeopardy: human help was unavailing; but God graciously interposed, and midnight suddenly became a summer noon.

II. VOWS IMPLY, ON OUR PART, DEFECTIVE PIETY. Vows are made under the influence of excessive fear or from an influx of sudden joy. In a time of sharp distress, a man will put himself under special obligation, if God will grant his request. Or, when some expected good has fallen to one's lot, in the impulse of sudden gladness we vow to devote some special offering unto God. Now, this is not wrong. Still there is something better. It is better to be always in a frame of trustful feeling, so that we may welcome whatever God ordains, and realize that what God does is best. It is better to rely upon his promise that help shall come in times of need! It is better to cultivate the habit of frequent offerings to God's cause, so that no vow is needed to prick us up to the full discharge of duty. The vow implies that we cannot trust ourselves *at all times* to give to God his due. Therefore our endeavour should be to cultivate a childlike and a steadfast faith. It is good that the "heart be established with grace."

III. VOWS CREATE FOR US A NEW OBLIGATION. Having made a debt, we are bound to pay it; but it is better not to accumulate a debt. Men lay a trap to catch themselves. Conscious of deficient trust and love towards God, they take advantage of some favourable state of feeling to make new obligations from which it shall be difficult to escape. In their better moods of mind they create new motives and new sanctions for religious conduct, which they cannot remove when the better feeling has vanished. They use the rising tide to bear their barque away. They utilize summer piety to provide for winter coldness. But having framed a religious vow, truth requires that it should be scrupulously kept. To violate a vow would injure our own soul's life—

would deaden and stupefy conscience, would justly provoke our God. No common sin is this.—D.

Vers. 24, 25.—*Possession of earthly things only partial.* The mode and condition of human life in this world serve a moral purpose. A material body requires material food; material food implies material possessions. The use of these affords fine scope for the development of many virtues. Without material possessions, selfishness would scarcely be possible; nor could some moral qualities, as generosity, find a field for exercise.

I. EARTHLY ESTATE ADMITS ONLY OF A PARTIAL POSSESSION. We cannot retain for our exclusive use the beauty of the hills, or the fragrance of the flowers within territory called "our own." It is not possible for us to appropriate to our personal use all the products of our fields. Restrict the enjoyment as we may, we can succeed only to a limited extent. And why should we make the attempt? It adds immensely to our real pleasure to share the products with others. Indiscriminate appropriation of harvests would do good to no one. It would diminish productiveness. It would create waste; it would promote idleness. But profuse generosity is not only pleasurable: it is profitable. We gain the esteem of men. The whole community bands together to protect our crops. God smiles on our fields and our toil.

II. HUNGER HAS UNQUESTIONABLE CLAIM ON NATURE'S PRODUCTS. Be our skilful labour to secure a harvest what it may, the largest possible, yet we cannot forget that God too has contributed largely to make our fields productive. In God's contribution to the result, his poor ones ought to share. Lest the ordinary philanthropy of men might not suffice for this need of poverty, God himself has taken the poor under his sheltering wing; he has become their Champion, he has proclaimed a law for the protection of the needy. Inasmuch as God retains absolute proprietorship over all created things, and counts the richest men as his chief stewards, he has fullest right to determine on what conditions his bounty shall be enjoyed. When man has added his labour to the result, when he has garnered his crops, the condition is changed; but so long as it is standing in the field, hunger may find a meal.

III. THOUGH HUNGER HAS A CLAIM, COVETOUSNESS HAS NONE. The labourer or the weary traveller had a statutory right to relieve his existing hunger; he had no right to carry any fruit or corn away. This would be to abuse a precious privilege. "Thus far might they go, and no farther." The path of obedience always has been narrow. Here was a test of trust in God. He who has provided a meal for the hungry man to-day can also provide another meal to-morrow. Or, if one door is closed, cannot God open another? Covetousness is suicidal. In the long run it defeats its own ends. Careful obedience is a firstfruit of genuine trust. Give a bad man an inch, and he will take an ell. By this he may be known. But a good man is as careful of another man's possessions as of his own. This is but another outcome of the command, "Thou shalt love thy neighbour as thyself."—D.

EXPOSITION.

CHAPTER XXIV.

LAWS RESPECTING DIVORCE, AGAINST MAN-STEALING AND INJUSTICE.

Vers. 1—4.—*Of divorce.* If a man put away his wife because she did not any longer please him, and she became the wife of another man, by whom also she was put away, or from whom she was severed by his death, the first husband might not remarry her, for that would be an abomination in the eyes of the Lord, and would bring sin on the land. This is not a law sanctioning or regulating divorce; that is simply assumed as what might occur, and what is here regulated is the treatment by the first husband of a woman who has been divorced a second time.

Vers. 1—4.—These verses should be read as one continuous sentence, of which the protasis is in vers. 1—3, and the apodosis in ver. 4, thus: "If a man hath taken a wife, and married her, and it come to pass that she doth not find favour in his eyes, because of some uncleanness in her, and he hath written her a bill of divorcement, and given it in her hand, and sent her out of his house;

and if she hath departed out of his house, and hath gone and become another man's; and if the latter husband hate her, and write her a bill of divorcement, and give it in her hand, and send her out of his house; or if the latter husband who took her to be his wife, die: her former husband, who sent her away, may not take her again to be his wife," etc.

Ver. 1.—**Because he hath found some uncleanness in her**; literally, *a thing or matter of nakedness*, i.e. some shameful thing, something disgraceful; LXX., ἄσχημον πρᾶγμα: Vulgate, "aliquam fœditatem." In the Targum of Onkelos, the expression is explained by עֲבֵירַת פִּתְגַם; "aliquid fœditatis" (London Polyglot); "iniquitas rei alicujus"(Buxtorf); "the transgression of a [Divine] word" (Levi). On this the school of Hillel among the rabbins put the interpretation that a man might divorce his wife for any unbecomingness (Mishna, 'Gittin,' ix. 10), or indeed for any cause, as the Pharisees in our Lord's day taught (Matt. xix. 3). The school of Shammai, on the other hand, taught that only for something disgraceful, such as adultery, could a wife be divorced (Lightfoot, 'Hor. Heb. et Talm.,' on Matt. v. 31, Opp., tom. ii. 290). Adultery, however, cannot be supposed here because that was punishable with death. **A bill of divorcement**; literally, *a writing of excision*; the man and woman having by marriage become one flesh, the divorce of the woman was a cutting of her off from the one whole. Lightfoot has given (*loc. cit.*) different forms of letters of divorce in use among the Jews (see also Maimonides, 'De Divortiis,' ch. iv. § 12).

Ver. 4.—The woman was held to be defiled by her second marriage, and thus by implication, the marrying of a woman who had been divorced was pronounced immoral, as is by our Lord explicitly asserted (Matt. v. 32). The prohibition of a return of the wife to her first husband, as well as the necessity of a formal bill of divorcement being given to the woman before she could be sent away, could not fail to be checks on the licence of divorce, as doubtless they were intended to be.

Ver. 5.—A man newly married was to be exempt from going to war, and was not to have any public burdens imposed on him for a year after his marriage. **Charged with any business**; literally, *there shall not pass upon him for any matter*; i.e. there shall not be laid on him anything in respect of any business. This is explained by what follows. **Free shall he be for his house for one year;** *i.e.* no public burden shall be laid on him, that he may be free to devote himself entirely to his household relations, and be able to cheer and gladden his wife (comp. ch. xx. 7). "By this law God showed how he approved

of holy wedlock (as by the former he showed his hatred of unjust divorces) when, to encourage the newly married against the cumbrances which that estate bringeth with it, and to settle their love each to other, he exempted those men from all wars, cares, and expenses, that they might the more comfortably provide for their own estate" (Ainsworth).

Vers. 6—14.—*Various prohibitions.*

Ver. 6.—**No man shall take the nether or the upper millstone to pledge**; rather, *the handmill and the upper millstone* (literally, *the rider*) *shall not be taken* (literally, *one shall not take*) *in pledge.* Neither the mill itself nor the upper millstone, the removal of which would render the mill useless, was to be taken. The upper millstone is still called the rider by the Arabs (Hebrew *rechebh*, Arabic *rekkab*). **Fór he taketh a** man's **life to pledge**; or *for* (thereby) *life itself is pledged;* if a man were deprived of that by which food for the sustaining of life could be prepared, his life itself would be imperilled (cf. Job. xxii. 6; Prov. xxii. 27; Amos ii. 8).

Ver. 7.—*Against man-stealing:* repetition, with expansion, of the law in Exod. xxi. 16.

Vers. 8, 9.—The law concerning the leprosy is in Lev. xiii., xiv. By this law the priests are directed how to proceed with those afflicted with leprosy; and here the people are counselled by Moses to follow the directions of the priests in this case, however painful it might be for them to submit to the restrictions that would be thereby imposed upon them, remembering what the Lord did to Miriam the sister of Moses, how even she was separated from the camp by the express command of God until she was healed (Numb. xii. 14). Michaelis, Keil, and others, following the Vulgate ("Observa diligenter ne incurras plagam lepræ sed facies quæcunque docuerint te sacerdotes"), understand this passage as inculcating obedience to the priests, lest leprosy should be incurred as a punishment for disobedience. But it is improbable that a general counsel to submit to the priests should be introduced among the special counsels here given; and besides, the formula הִשָּׁמֶר בְּ means, "Take heed to yourself in respect of" (cf. 2 Sam. xx. 10; Jer. xvii. 21), rather than "Beware of," or "Be on your guard against."

Vers. 10—13.—If one had to take a pledge from another, he was not to go into the house of the latter and take what he thought fit; he must stand without, and allow the debtor to bring to him what he saw meet to offer. He might stand outside and summon the debtor to produce his pledge, but he was not insolently to enter the house and lay hands on any part of the owner's property. To stand outside and call is still a common mode of seeking access to a person in his own house or apartment among the Arabs, and is regarded as the only respectful mode. There would be thus a mitigation of the severity of the exaction, the tendency of which would be to preserve good feeling between the parties. If the debtor was needy, and being such could give in pledge only some necessary article, such as his upper garment in which he slept at night, the pledge was to be returned ere nightfall, that the man might sleep in his own raiment, and have a grateful feeling towards his creditor. In many parts of the East, with the Arabs notably, it is customary for the poor to sleep in their outer garment. "During the day the poor while at work can and do dispense with this outside raiment, but at night it is greatly needed, even in summer. This furnishes a good reason why this sort of pledge should be restored before night" (Thomson, 'Land and the Book,' i. 192, 500). The earlier legislation (Exod. xxii. 25, 26) is evidently assumed here as well known by the people. **It shall be righteousness unto thee** (see on ch. vi. 25).

Vers. 14, 15.—The wage of the labourer was to be punctually paid, whether he were an Israelite or a foreigner (cf. Lev. xix. 13; the law there is repeated here, with a special reference to the distress which the withholding of the hire from a poor man even for a day might occasion).

Ver. 16.—Among heathen nations it was common for a whole family to be involved in the penalty incurred by the head of the family, and to be put to death along with him (cf. Esth. ix. 13, 14; Herod., iii. 118, 119; Ammian. Marcell., xxiii. 6; Curtius, vi. 11, 20; Claudian, 'In Eutrop.,' ii. 478; Cicero, 'Epist. ad Brut.,' 12, 15). Such severity of retribution is here prohibited in the penal code of the Israelites. Though God, in the exercise of his absolute sovereignty, might visit the sins of the parent upon the children (Exod. xx. 5), earthly judges were not to assume this power. Only the transgressor himself was to bear the penalty of his sin (cf. 2 Kings xiv. 6).

Vers. 17, 18.—The law against perverting the right of strangers, widows, and orphans is here repeated from Exod. xxii. 20, 21; xxiii. 9, with the addition that the raiment of the widow was not to be taken in pledge. To enforce this, the people are reminded that they themselves as a nation had been in the condition of strangers and bondmen in Egypt (cf. Lev. xix. 33, 34).

Vers. 19—22.—(Cf. Lev. xix. 9, 10; xxiii. 23.) Not only was no injustice to be done to the poor, but, out of the abundance of those in better estate, were they to be helped.

Ver. 21.—**Thou shalt not glean it afterward**; literally, *Thou shalt not glean after thee*, i.e. after thou hast reaped and gathered for thyself. It is still the custom among the Arabs for the poor to be allowed to gather the berries that may be left on the olive trees after they have been beaten and the main produce carried off by the owner. All the injunctions in this section are adapted to preserve relations of brotherliness and love among the people of the Lord.

HOMILETICS.

Vers. 1—5.—*Permissive legislation.* No treatment of this passage can be appropriate which does not set it in the light thrown upon it by Matt. xix. 1—12. The heading we have given to this outline indicates a point on which special stress should be laid whenever an expositor has occasion to refer to it. In the course of time, men had come to regard this passage in the light of a *command.* Hence the wording of the question in Matt. xix. 7. But our Lord informs us that it was simply *permissive.* Divorce, under the circumstances here named, was tolerated a while by Moses owing to "the hardness of men's hearts," but that the original Divine arrangement contemplated the indissolubility of marriage. The entire principle of the Mosaic Law was that of educating the people out of a semi-degraded state into something higher. Its method of doing this was by giving the people the best legislation they could bear; tolerating some ill for a while rather than forcing on the people revolutionary methods. The more gentle and gracious, though the slower process, was to sow the seed of higher good, and to let it have time to grow. The following Divine teaching on marriage may well be brought forward with this passage as a basis.

I. That the marriage bond is holy in the eye of God, and ought ever to be recognized as very sacred by man.

II. That by God's own declared appointment this most sacred of all nature's ties is indissoluble.

III. That however, owing to the degeneracy of national habit and thought, civil legislation may suffer the legal cessation of the marriage bond, yet it can in no case be severed, save by death, without heinous sin on one side or on both.

IV. That the claims of married life are such that, with them, not even the exigencies of military service are unduly to interfere (ver. 5).

V. That the highest and purest enjoyments of wedded life come to perfection only when it is entered on and spent in the Lord Jesus Christ. The law was but a παιδαγωγός εἰς Χριστὸν (see 1 Cor. vii. 39).

Vers. 6—22.—*Neighbourly love and good will to be cultivated in detail.* One golden thread runs through all the varied precepts of this chapter. They are most interesting illustrations, one and all, of the spirit of humanity and of far-reaching wisdom which pervades the Mosaic Law. The following headings include the gist of the several injunctions here given, and show also their relation to each other. 1. Man's "inhumanity to man" is sternly restrained. No Israelite, however poor, is to be kidnapped and sold into foreign slavery (ver. 7). 2. No one might be deprived of the machinery, tools, or implements on the use of which his daily bread depended, for a pledge (ver. 6). It is doubtless to this humane regulation that we owe the ancient common law of this realm, that no man shall be distrained of the necessaries of his trade or profession as long as there are other things on which the distraint can be made. 3. A man's house is to be his castle. No one may enter it, even to fetch a pledge (vers. 10, 11). The exception to this is in the case of leprosy, in which instance the priest had a right to enter a man's house to see into the state of things, *i.e.* home is to be inviolable save where the public security demands it otherwise. Hence a special caution is given to avoid anything which might bring such a plague upon them. The case of Miriam should be before their eyes (vers. 8, 9). 4. If the poor man has pledged that in which he needs to sleep, it is to be restored to him before sundown (ver. 13). 5. Hired servants were not to be oppressed, but were to have fair and even generous treatment (vers. 14, 15). 6. The spirit of the checks upon blood-revenge, which are found in connection with the cities of refuge (see Homily thereon), is never to be violated, and no one is to suffer any civil penalty on account of another's sin. Justice is to operate always (ver. 16). 7. No advantage is ever to be taken of the stranger, the fatherless, and the widow. They who are deprived of earthly helpers on whom they might lean are to find their safeguard in the sentiments of honour and benevolence which pervade the people (vers. 17, 18). 8. Not only is no wrong to be done to them, but their aid and comfort are to be specially studied, in the time of harvest, and in the gathering in of the olive and the grape (vers. 19—22). 9. The reason for such cultivation of kindness to others is that God had been kind to them (vers. 18, 22).

I. The requirements of God in the social relations of life are righteousness, justice, mercy, love, and good will to all.

II. God has fenced round the poor, the weak, the widow, and the fatherless with a special guard.

III. A wrong done by man to man is sin against God.

IV. The inspiring motive for our showing love to others is the love of God to us (cf. Micah vi. 8, 9).

HOMILIES BY VARIOUS AUTHORS.

Vers. 1—4.—*Divorce.* The Hebrew Law, "for the hardness of men's hearts," found it necessary to "suffer" many things not approved of absolutely (Matt. xix. 8). Divorce was one of these. It was permitted on grounds of strong personal dislike (ver. 3). The Law was inapplicable to adultery, that being judged a capital offence. While permitting divorce, Moses obviously aims at restricting it, and shows, by his modes of expression, how alien this rupture of the marriage bond is to the original institution. We may learn—

I. THAT THE RIGHT OF DIVORCE IS ONE TO BE STRICTLY GUARDED. Divorce, even where most justified, is a great evil. It is the rupture of a tie intended by the Creator to be indissoluble. Adultery warrants it, but it must be deemed not the least part of the evil that so unhappy a cause for the dissolution of marriage should exist. The revelations of the divorce courts are most injurious to public morality. Facilities for divorce, such as some advocate, would lead to serious mischiefs. Besides being wrong in principle, they would create inconstancy, lead to domestic unhappiness, inflict hardship on children, prevent efforts being made to mend matters by forbearance and compliance. Frequent divorces blunt the sense of the sacredness of the marriage union, and so lead to licentiousness. "At the time when divorces were most frequent among the Romans marriages were most rare; and Augustus was obliged, by penal laws, to force men of fashion into the married state" (Hume). Moses restrains divorce thus far that he requires it to take place: 1. By means of a legal document. 2. For reason given. 3. He debars the man divorcing from remarrying the woman divorced if, in the interval, she has been married to another. The Christian law recognizes no legitimate ground of divorce save adultery (Matt. v. 32).

II. THAT RIGHT VIEWS ON DIVORCE ARE CONNECTED WITH A SENSE OF THE INHERENT SACREDNESS OF THE MARRIAGE RELATION. This is suggested by the terms employed in ver. 4. A husband is prohibited from remarrying his divorced wife if in the interval she has been the wife of another, and the ground given for the prohibition is that "she is defiled." But why "defiled"? The expression could not have been used had the first marriage been regarded as perfectly nullified by the legal divorce. The statement that a divorced woman, remarrying, is "defiled," implies that deep view of the marriage relation given in Genesis (ii. 24), and reiterated by Christ (Matt. xix. 3—10). And it will be found, in practice, that light views of the sacredness of the marriage relation invariably work in the direction of increasing facilities for divorce. "The sceptical party in France not long ago proposed to make marriage dissoluble at the pleasure of the parties whenever the woman had passed the age at which child-bearing was no longer to be expected" (R. H. Hutton, in *Expositor*, January, 1881). The writer just quoted ably argues that strict views on marriage, and divorce, are not possible, save under the sanction of a supersensual morality.—J. O.

Ver. 5.—*The man newly married.* The precept is in addition to those in ch. xx. 5—8. It provides that the newly married man shall be left free to enjoy the relation into which he has entered for a whole year, not being required to serve in war, and not being liable to be called from home on public business. It may be inserted here as tending to prevent divorces. We learn: 1. That it is the duty of the husband to love and cherish the wife (Eph. v. 29). 2. That it is the interest of the State to do what it can to endear the marriage relation. 3. That laws should be framed in a spirit of kindness, and with consideration for the happiness of the subjects. This law shows kindly consideration for the wife, (1) in not depriving her of the husband of her youth in the months of their early love; (2) in allowing time for the husband's affections to become securely fixed, so preventing inconstancy.—J. O.

Ver. 8.—*Leprosy.* I. A JUDGMENT TO BE DREADED. Leprosy is viewed here, as usually in Scripture: 1. *As a stroke of Divine judgment.* It was not always such (Job ii.). Nor did the stroke of Divine judgment always take this form (Uzzah, Jeroboam, Ananias, etc.). But it was a frequent form of punishment for sins of a theocratic nature (Uzziah, Gehazi, etc.). It is seldom safe to interpret judgments (Luke xiii. 1—6), but we may expect God's stroke in some way to fall upon ourselves if we persistently despise his laws. 2. *As a symbol of spiritual corruption.* The worst penalty with which God can visit any one is to smite him with soul leprosy, to leave sin to have its natural dominion over him, to allow its corruption to work and spread through his inner man.

II. A WARNING TO BE PONDERED. They are bid remember the case of Miriam. We do well to lay to heart the instances we have known of sin working out punishment and death. Miriam's case suggests the additional thought of pardon on repentance, and of the prevalence of intercession in obtaining forgiveness for offences (Numb. xii. 9—16).—J. O.

Vers. 6—15.—*The treatment of the poor.* The helplessness and dependence of the poor expose them to much harsh treatment. The poor man has, however, his Friend and Judge in God, whose Law here steps in for his protection. It ordains—

I. THAT THE NECESSARIES OF LIFE ARE NOT TO BE TAKEN FROM HIM. The millstone (ver. 6). His raiment, which if taken in pledge is to be restored by nightfall (vers. 12, 13). These are considerate provisions. It is the excess of cruelty to press law against a man to the extent of depriving him of the necessaries of life. This would apply to needful clothing, to a bed, to cooking utensils, to the tools by which he earns his bread. It is nearly as bad to receive and keep these things in pledge or pawn. Help, free and ungrudging, should be forthcoming to all honest persons in need, without driving them to such straits. If men will not work, neither should they eat (2 Thess. iii. 10), but while this may be a reason for refusing to support them in their indolence, it can be no reason for helping them to strip themselves of the necessaries of their existence. Instead of taking a man's tools from him, he should rather be encouraged to retain and ply them, " working with his hands the thing that is good," that he may both support himself and " have to give to him that needeth " (Eph. iv. 28).

II. THAT HIS PERSONAL FREEDOM IS TO BE RESPECTED. (Ver. 7.) No strong or rich neighbour was to be allowed to steal, enslave, or sell him. The stealing of a man was punishable with death. And the spirit of the Law carries us beyond its letter. It requires that we respect the poor man's freedom in all the relations of his life. Whatever the degree of his dependence, it does not entitle another to force his convictions, or do aught that would interfere with the exercise of his rights as man or citizen. Yet how often is compulsion and intimidation applied to those in dependent situations to compel them to act, not as their consciences approve, but as their superiors desire! He who takes advantage of a man's weakness to do anything of the kind is a " man-stealer " in principle and at heart.

III. THAT HIS DWELLING IS NOT TO BE INVADED. (Vers. 10, 11.) The fine sense of justice, the delicacy of feeling, in these precepts, is certainly remarkable. The poor man's house is to be as sacred from invasion as the house of the wealthy. Even his creditor is to wait outside, and let the man fetch as his pledge what he can best spare. We are taught a lesson of respect for the domiciliary and proprietary rights of the poor. Many act as if the homes of the poor were not entitled to have their privacy respected in the same way as the homes of the rich. The Law of God teaches otherwise. We owe it to God, and we owe it to the humanity which is in our poorer brethren as well as in us, that we treat them and their belongings with precisely the same amount of respect that we would show to persons in a better social position.

IV. THAT HIS WAGES ARE TO BE PAID WITH REGULARITY. (Vers. 14, 15.) Every day, the text says, and in the East this was necessary. During the Indian famines it was found that the persons engaged on the relief works had to be paid in this manner. Great suffering was sometimes experienced from the neglect of the rule. The law extends to hired service of all kinds, and enjoins in principle regularity in payment of wages. A like principle applies to the payment of tradesmen's accounts. We have heard tradesmen complain bitterly of the inconvenience to which they were subjected from the singular want of consideration displayed by wealthy families in this particular. Accounts are allowed to run on, and payment is withheld, not from want of ability to pay, but from sheer indolence and carelessness in attending to such matters. While to crave payment would, on the tradesman's part, mean the forfeiture of custom.—J. O.

Vers. 16—22.—*Doing justice and loving mercy.* I. EACH SOUL IS TO BEAR ITS OWN SIN. (Ver. 16.) This verse lays down the rule of human jurisprudence. Loss and suffering to the innocent, as a result of the course of justice inflicting punishment on the guilty, cannot always be avoided. But this is an incidental, not a designed result. With those wider movements of Divine justice, which seem to turn on the federal constitution of the race, and involve different principles, human justice has nothing to do. The rule for us is that the punishment of crime, with loss and suffering resulting therefrom, is to be confined as much as possible to the guilty person.

II. JUSTICE IS TO BE DONE TO THE WEAKEST. (Vers. 17, 18.) The stranger and fatherless and widow are again taken under the Law's protection. Their right is not to be perverted. The widow's raiment is not to be taken in pledge. There should need no inducement to do what is right, but Moses reminds the Israelites of their own past condition as bondmen. Oppression is doubly disgraceful when those guilty of it are persons who have themselves tasted its bitterness, or who have themselves been mercifully dealt with (Matt. xviii. 23—35). We cannot sufficiently admire the combined justice and tenderness of these Mosaic precepts.

III. PROVISION IS TO BE LEFT FOR THE NEEDY. (Vers. 19—22.) These are beautiful rules. The Jews were under the Law, but it was a Law the fulfilling of which was " love." The variety of ways in which the Law seeks to instil love into the hearts of the chosen people would form a study eminently suitable for the pulpit. The poor we have always with us, and they should be often in our thoughts. (Southey's poem, ' The Complaints of the Poor.') In the corn-field, among the olives, in the vineyard, they were to be remembered. When the wealthy are gathering in their abundance, then is the time for remembering the needy. Thus will the heart be kept warm, covetousness checked, our own happiness best secured, the wants of the poor supplied, their blessing obtained, a treasure laid up in heaven. " There is that scattereth, and yet increaseth " (Prov. xi. 24).—J. O.

Vers. 1—6.—*The rights of women.* The tendency of the true religion has been to secure and respect the rights of women. Now, we have here women's rights brought under notice in two cases—in a case of separation, and in a case of war. Moses, " because of the hardness of their hearts," allowed divorce, because it prevailed to a lamentable extent in society in his time. He suffered them to divorce their wives, but insisted on a *written* divorce. Among other nations an *oral* divorce was sufficient, and so a divorce might be from the flimsiest caprice. Again, Moses forbade any coming together as man and wife again, a custom which prevails among the Arabs when the oral divorce is so lightly undertaken. Hence we notice in this law given by Moses—

I. THE DIVORCE OF THE WOMAN MUST BE DELIBERATE AND FINAL. Woman was not to be the toy of man's caprice; she was not to be lightly sent away, and, when sent away by the husband after deliberately writing her divorce, she was never to be taken back again. In this way Moses really consulted the rights of women. They had a right to a deliberate statement of the grounds of their divorce; they had also a right to be protected from further interference on the part of their former husbands. It was a wise expedient considering the degeneracy of the time. It is an improvement assuredly on the arrangements of Mahomet.

Our Lord still further secured the rights of women in ordaining that nothing but infidelity on the part of the wife should dissolve the marriage union (Matt. v. 32).

II. WAR MUST NOT ROB A NEWLY MARRIED WIFE OF HER HUSBAND ; SHE HAS A RIGHT TO HIS SOCIETY FOR A YEAR WITHOUT MOLESTATION. This was placing the interests of a single woman above the interests of the State. This was exalting the bride to a throne of highest honour surely. Other systems and the world as well may degrade woman, but God's Law elevates her and enthrones her.

III. NOR IS SHE THROUGH HER HUSBAND'S DIFFICULTIES TO LOSE EITHER OF HER MILLSTONES FOR THE GRINDING OF THE CORN. Here was another right of the housewife. No legal distraint could reach the little mill which ground the corn at home and kept the wolf from the door.

Thus in her sorrows and in her joys God stood her Friend, and insisted on her rights. A similar shield should be thrown over her still. It is by securing her in her rights at home that woman's cause shall be advanced. She is intended to be a queen in the household. Everything that makes her position there more secure, everything that makes the home sacred even from the intrusion of a national war at certain times, everything that makes her feel the foundation firm below her,—is in the interests of public weal. But if she is carelessly thrown into the competition with the stronger sex, she will get deteriorated. The rights of women constitute a much longer subject than even Mr. Mill has made it.[1] May the interpreter in due season appear!—R. M. E.

Ver. 7.—*Man-stealing a capital crime.* We have already noticed the merciful fugitive law which forbade any one to restore a runaway to his master. That was the *cure* of existing evil. Here we have the *prevention,* which is better still. For man-stealing and man-selling are the origin of slavery, and the Lord attaches to this the penalty of death. As Cheever said of it, " God be praised for this law! It strikes through and through the vitals of this sin."[2]

[1] Cf. his ' Subjection of Women.'   [2] ' God against Slavery,' p. 110.

I. LIBERTY MUST BE MAINTAINED UNDER THE PENAL SANCTION OF DEATH TO HIM WHO INVADES IT. The ruffian who would steal and sell a brother deserves to die. His treason against the liberty of his fellow is an unpardonable sin against society, and he should get no quarter. No wonder men have fought and died for liberty when God surrounds it with such tremendous sanctions.

II. How MUCH GREATER THE CRIME OF BRINGING MEN INTO SPIRITUAL BONDAGE! And this is done daily. What is the meaning of the power exercised by superstitious priesthoods over their devotees? Is it not "spiritual despotism"? And should not the crime of man-stealing awake a suspicion in such hearts that their procedure is the exact analogue in the spiritual sphere? It should be combated and resisted unto the death, as destroying that heritage of liberty with which the Lord has endowed all men. —R. M. E.

Vers. 10—22.—*Consideration for the poor and needy.* After giving a cursory reference to leprosy as a Divine judgment to be divinely removed and ceremonially purged away (vers. 8, 9), Moses enters in these verses into the consideration which should be shown to the poor and needy. The debtor is not to be pressed for his pledge, and, if raiment, it must be restored in time for him to sleep with due clothing. The hired servant, engaged for the day, is to get his pay punctually at sundown. The widow, fatherless, and strangers are to have justice dealt to them, and in harvest generous gleanings are to be left for them. The Law inculcates consideration and mercy.

I. THE GENEROSITY INCULCATED BY THE LAW MADE IT A MESSAGE OF MERCY TO ALL MEN. For even suppose no sacrificial system preached, typically, the Divine pardon and love, the mercy enjoined upon others argued mercy in the Lawgiver himself. He could not have commanded so much mercy, and manifested none.

II. THE POOR WERE SAVED FROM UTTER MENDICANCY BY THE LIBERALITY OF THE LAW. They got their need supplied by working for it. It was better to glean than to have it laid without any cost or trouble to them at their feet. They were free, and had to bestir themselves; thus self-respect was fostered, and real, wholesome work prescribed. No wonder that mendicancy was unknown. But nowadays things are made too easy for the " ne'er-do-wells," and a laziness that sacrifices self-respect and liberty on its altar is the blessed result!—R. M. E.

Ver. 16.—*Responsibility not to be transferred according to human caprice.* We desire to notice this interesting direction. It is a contrast to the second commandment. There God represents himself as " visiting the iniquity of the fathers upon the children." We see it also in the law of heredity operating in nature. But it is a weapon which God retains in his own hand. We may for wise purposes treat men in the lump, and blend in common consequences the innocent and guilty. But man in his judgments must be particular to execute only the guilty.

I. HUMAN JUDGMENTS MUST BE FINAL IN THIS WORLD SO FAR AS THE JUDGING IS CONCERNED. Men do not get the chance of setting matters right in another world. They judge once for all, and if they execute the innocent, they have no reparation in their power.

II. GOD'S IMPERFECT JUSTICE IN THE PRESENT WORLD IS THE CLEAREST INDICATION TO CONSCIENCE THAT THERE WILL BE A JUDGMENT IN THE OTHER WORLD. Were his justice here perfect, or were there no judgment at all, men would say there is nothing to arrange in another world. But now there is enough to show God reigns, and enough left over to indicate a judgment to come.[1]

III. GOD'S PREROGATIVE OF TRANSFERRING RESPONSIBILITY IS THE SECRET OF OUR SALVATION. For he has laid on Jesus, the Innocent One, the iniquity of us all. He has visited the iniquity of the children upon him who is called our " Everlasting Father." The consequence is we are saved, and in salvation there is ample compensation for all who have to all appearance suffered unjustly here.—R. M. E.

Ver. 5.—*Nuptial joy.* Joy has its special seasons. The year has but one spring.

[1] Cf. 'Wolfe's Remains,' 6th edit., pp. 325—327.

Human life has but one nuptial feast. The freshness and charm of a first marriage can never be repeated. Around this special joy God has thrown a wall of defence.

I. NUPTIAL JOY IS A CARE OF GOD. In every act of Jesus Christ's earthly life, he could have said, "He that hath seen me hath seen the Father." Thus, when he became a guest at the marriage feast at Cana, he appeared and spake and acted as his Father's Representative. His miraculous deed was the expression of his Father's pleasure. On every honourable marriage the sunshine of Jehovah rests. In all the beginnings of human life God's fatherly interest centres. That human life may be full of joy is his main concern.

II. NUPTIAL JOY IS SUPERIOR EVEN TO CARES OF THE STATE. The marriage union is the spring-time of a man's life; let no rough wind of war blast it! To spoil the nuptial joy is to spoil a man's life. Other things can wait; this fleeting season of a man's history cannot be recalled. Others can fight the battles of his country better than can he; for at such a time his heart will be elsewhere than the battle-field. To send such as he is to invite defeat. It is not simply a permissive law; it is obligatory: he *shall* not go. To be pressed into military service on his marriage day might sour his temper, exasperate his feelings, dissipate his young love, ruin his earthly home, and blast his domestic prospects. Pious homes are the nursery grounds for God's kingdom.

III. NUPTIAL JOY HAS ITS LIMITATIONS. Such exemption prevailed for a year: then it ceased. The fresh and fragrant spring must give way to fruit-bearing autumn. Joy is a preparation for arduous service. It is worse than useless, if it begets only indolence. It is the parent of new exertion. It recreates the mind. It braces and vitalizes all the active energies. As sleep prepares for labour, so pleasure equips us for higher attainments. We need the spirit of wisdom to use our joys to advantage.—D.

Vers. 6, 10—13.—*Prohibited pledges.* Wealth is power; in every nation we need the safeguards of law to prevent such power from becoming tyranny. The poor are ever liable to become the prey of voracious avarice.

I. A SEASONABLE LOAN IS A PRICELESS SERVICE. Men can render service one to another in a thousand different forms. Redundance of possession on the part of one may serviceably supply the deficiencies of another. One man has riches which he cannot profitably employ, another has trade for which his money capital is insufficient. One man has accumulated experience, another has penetrative wisdom, another has technical knowledge. All this is equipment for useful service. So, in the spiritual kingdom, one has tender feeling, another has gift of prayer or gift of speech, another has extended influence. All human endowments are a common fund to be distributed for the benefit of all. There are occasions in human life when a loan is more useful than a gift. Temporary exigencies sometimes arise, for which loan, on fitting security, is the wisest alleviation.

II. FOR LOANS SUITABLE PLEDGES SHOULD BE TAKEN. 1. *This serves as a check upon facile borrowing.* If loans are granted on too easy terms, we may encourage a man in reckless commercial speculation, or destroy the natural checks on personal extravagance. 2. *This serves to prevent strife.* Borrowers have ofttimes a short memory for liabilities. While human nature has its imperfections and society its scoundrels, it is wiser to have solid guarantee for the redemption of loans, and honest borrowers will not object to give suitable pledges for honesty. 3. *Pledges are needed on the ground of uncertain mortality.* "We know not what a day may bring forth."

III. PLEDGES WHICH TOUCH A MAN'S LIFE ARE PROHIBITED. Money-getting is never to be so pressed as to impinge on the domain of life. Human life is a sacred thing, and must not be trifled with. It has latent capabilities, and may yet become a source of blessing to myriads. Gain becomes as the small dust, an inappreciable thing, when placed in the balance against a human life. The gold of a continent is a bubble in comparison with a man's soul.

IV. GENEROUS SURRENDER OF POVERTY'S PLEDGES AN ACT OF PIETY. Pledges are telltales of common dishonesty. If truthfulness and honour were as prevalent as they ought to be, no pledge would be needed. A man's word ought to be as good as his pledge. It often does a man good if we make his honour the only pledge. He is ennobled by our confidence. He rises in self-respect. Debts of honour are often paid prior to those which have material security. If we form a high estimate of men, they will often strive to reach the ideal.

Generous treatment of the poor secures their warmest interest on our behalf. The poorest of the poor has still access to the audience-chamber of the heavenly palace. Their simple suit on our behalf will sometimes secure blessings which no arithmetic can measure. Deeds of kindness done to the indigent are done to God, for God identifies himself with them. " He that giveth to the poor lendeth to the Lord." If the concession be an act of sterling love, pure from the alloy of selfishness, it is an act of righteousness—the fruit of the Divine Spirit's grace. This is not self-righteousness, for genuine love to men is a gracious affection. It does not begin with self; it does not terminate in self. God is its object; hence it shall be counted for righteousness. As Abraham's faith counted for righteousness, so does also genuine love.—D.

Ver. 7.—*Slave-traffic a capital offence.* Slavery, in modified form, has always prevailed in Eastern lands ; and, with prudent limitations, was tolerated among the Hebrews. To promulgate laws for men, which transcended their moral sense, would defeat the ends of law. God has continually to lead men from lower levels to higher. A man may voluntarily sell his liberty for a time. But to deprive a man of liberty by violence is a scarlet sin ; and man-stealing is rightly branded with the deepest indignation of God.

I. LIBERTY IS ESSENTIAL TO MAN'S FULLEST LIFE. Any form of bondage is a curtailment of life, a mutilation of the man. His outward condition may be bettered. He may have more food and warmer clothing and a healthier home, but the real man is injured. He is not fully susceptible of self-development. The springs of life are poisoned. He learns to despise himself, and to despise oneself is a step on the slippery road to ruin. Yet liberty is a human right not well understood. It must be distinguished from licence. True liberty has its limits and its checks. A man is at liberty to part with his liberty for a time. Every man who toils for his bread is compelled to do this. Yet even this temporary cessation of his liberty must be voluntary.

II. TO DEPRIVE A MAN FORCIBLY OF HIS LIBERTY IS TO DEPRIVE HIM OF HIS LIFE. The life of the body is not the whole of a man's life. The intellect, affections, choice, will, have a life more precious than the life of the body. To steal a man or to kidnap a child is to interfere, wantonly and injuriously, with the proper life of the person. The outward conditions of training and probation are not such as God ordained. The man's eternal prospects, as well as his earthly possibilities, are blighted. And all this moral damage is done for paltry gain. The man who can lend himself to such a business as slave-mongering is lost to all goodness, lost to shame. He is a disgrace to the human species—a tool of Satan.

III. FOR SUCH A CRIME THE GOD-APPOINTED PENALTY IS DEATH. No heavier penalty is imposed by the civil magistrate, because no heavier penalty is possible. Such a monster must be removed from the scenes of human society, because his presence is pestilential, demoralizing, deadly. Where human judgment ends, God's judgment begins. Such a one is hurried before the higher court of heaven, is arraigned before the great white throne of the Eternal, and fullest justice will here be meted out. My soul, be thou free from such taint as this !—D.

Vers. 8, 9.—*Leprosy symbolic.* God has intended the material world to be a schoolhouse, and every event a vehicle of moral instruction. The sick-chamber may become an audience-room, where lessons of heavenly wisdom are conveyed by the Spirit of truth. Leprosy was singled out by God to be a visible picture of sin ; so that " out of the eater there might come forth meat." Out of seeming evil, good can be distilled.

I. LEPROSY HAD A RELIGIOUS CHARACTER. More was meant by the infliction than was seen by the bodily eye. It was mysterious in its origin, and irresistible in its progress. It gradually spread and covered the whole man. It touched and injured every faculty. The intention was salutary, viz. to lead the sufferer's thoughts to the discovery of a deeper malady, and to awaken desire for a more enduring cure. The outward is an index of the inward. Leprosy is a type and picture of sin.

II. LEPROSY REQUIRED RELIGIOUS TREATMENT. It was vain to seek the offices of an ordinary physician. Earthly remedy *was* and still *is* unknown. The sufferer was required to visit the priest. Direct application to God was to be made. Meanwhile, the leper was to be completely isolated. He might not consort with his fellows.

Hereby he might learn the disastrous effects of sin, viz. in disintegrating society; and hereby he might in solitude mourn over sin, and seek its cure. The only possibility of the removal of leprosy was in religious obedience. Every part of the prescription was furnished by God, and was to be applied by God's ministers. Completest submission was a condition of cure.

III. LEPROSY, IN ITS CAUSE AND CURE, HAD AN HISTORIC TYPE. This type was furnished by Miriam. Her specific sin was known; it was insubordination to authority. Her chastisement was sudden. It came direct from God in the form of leprosy. The injured man became her intercessor. God graciously responded to the suit of Moses. Temporary separation and strict seclusion were the method of cure. Golden lessons lie here. Every leper may confidently follow this indication of God's will. If he healed Miriam, can he not also heal me?

IV. LEPROSY HEALED WAS CHARGED WITH RELIGIOUS OBLIGATIONS. As a healed man will cheerfully recompense the physician for his pains, so God required the restored leper to express his gratitude in the form of animal sacrifice. His gratitude could not be expressed in empty words. He was not permitted to bring that "which cost him nothing." In the slaughter of the devoted victim, the grateful man would confess that he himself had deserved to die, and that God had permitted a substitute. If the man were fully penitent, the sight of the dying substitute would vividly impress his heart with a sense of God's mercy. In every arrangement which God made, the good of man was sought. The method will often seem strange to our dim vision, but respecting the beneficent end there can be no question.—D.

Vers. 14, 15.—*Omitted duty ripens into curse.* Thoughtlessness is a flimsy excuse for neglected duty. It is a sin to be thoughtless. One talent is buried in the earth. In proportion to the mischief produced is the punishment thereof.

I. WE HAVE HERE A CASE OF OBLIGATION FULLY MATURED. 1. The rich is debtor to the poor. Obligation between the several ranks of society is equal. The rich rely for many services upon the poor. The king depends upon the cook. The labourer gives his strength, the employer contributes his money. There is as much obligation on the one side as on the other. 2. At a fixed point of time the obligation is matured. Henceforth the neglect of the obligation becomes sin. My obligations to-day differ from those of yesterday. The element of time plays an important part. Obligations grow. 3. Obligations are implied as well as expressed. Custom is unwritten law. Riches carry with them no warrant for arrogance. Riches have cursed the man if they have made him churlish.

II. NEGLECTED OBLIGATION ENTAILS UNKNOWN MISERY. We cannot follow the effects of thoughtlessness into all their intricate ramifications and to their utmost issues. What would be regarded as a trivial disappointment on the part of one man may be an agony of pain to another. Wages expected and deferred may mean to a needy labourer pinching hunger, not only to himself, but to feeble wife and to helpless babes. A gloomy and sleepless night may follow. Bitter and angry feelings may be engendered. Faith in human integrity may be lost. Self-restraint may vanish. For want of a nail a shoe was lost, a battle was lost, ay, an empire fell!

III. NEGLECTED OBLIGATION MAY BRING HEAVY CURSE UPON THE CULPRIT. It is not safe to treat any human being with contempt, especially the poor. God is the avowed Champion of such. The command, "Honour *all* men," is as binding as "Thou shalt not steal." The cry of the injured man in his distress is sure to pierce the skies. The ear of God is specially attent to his children's suffering cry, even as a mother catches the plaintive wail of her firstborn infant. Swiftly God attaches himself to the side of the oppressed, and takes upon himself the burden. The injustice done to the man becomes an insult done to God. The deed alters in its character, intensifies in its immorality, becomes heinous sin. Vials of wrath are preparing for the head of the unthinking transgressor. It will be as the sin of blasphemy or of murder unto them.—D.

Vers. 16—18.—*Public justice to be pure.* Unseen principles of justice lie at the foundation of human society, and if rottenness and decay appear in these foundations, the social structure will soon topple and fall. Visible prosperity is built upon invisible justice. In the absence of justice, property becomes untenable, commerce vanishes, peace spreads her wings for flight. "If the foundations be destroyed, what can the righteous do?"

I. THE MAGISTRATE'S TEMPTATION. Human nature, at its best, is accessible by temptation; and it is well that from the eyes of the nation a fierce light beats upon the judicial bench. If only the ear of the judge be open to the fascinating voice of self-advantage, if his hand be open to a bribe, wickedness will put on the most ravishing charms to deflect him from his duty. Because he occupies a seat so conspicuous, temptation selects him as a special target for her poisoned arrows. Yet even for temptation he may rejoice, for according to his trials should be his moral triumphs. Avarice may tempt him. Love of ease may tempt him. His own tastes and predilections may tempt. The praise of the powerful may tempt. He will become either the stronger or the weaker for the discipline, will grow in moral courage or in cowardice.

II. THE MAGISTRATE'S QUALIFICATION. *The* qualification for the judicial throne is ardent love of justice. As only a wise man can be a teacher, so only a just man can be a true judge. No matter what may be the nationality of the litigants, no matter what their colour, social rank, or sex, every one has an inherent claim on public justice. To pervert judgment is to arouse all the elements of wrath in heaven and earth. The judge is the visible exponent of justice; he wears the garb of justice, and if in him there dwells not the soul of justice, he is a sham and a pretence. Heart devotion to public justice is the only anchor that can hold him fast amid those currents and whirlpools of evil influences which ever surge around him. Things unseen are the most potent.

III. THE MAGISTRATE'S RULE OF ACTION. This is clearly made known to him by God, viz. that punishment is to be personal, not corporate. The child is not to die for the father. Where there is corporate guilt there must be corporate punishment. But this is no contravention of the rule. The inducement is often great to release oneself from the pains of unravelling a complicated suit; or, if relatives of the accused seem to be accessories to an evil deed, a judge is often tempted to embrace all the suspected family in one punishment. The light of truth is to be his only guide; love of justice his compass; the revealed will of God his chart. To him human life is to be held a sacred thing; not one life is to be needlessly sacrificed. It is a sad fact that judges have been amongst the greatest criminals; they have slain many innocent men.

IV. THE MAGISTRATE'S INSPIRING MOTIVE. Many motives may wisely influence him. He, too, must appear before a higher tribunal, and submit his whole life to judicial light. But the motive here pressed upon him is gratitude derived from past experience. The history of his nation is to mould his character and to teach him the value of human justice. He is expected to sympathize with the oppressed, to enter into their griefs, because he is a part of a nation that has felt the sharp scourge of oppression. He has learnt by national experience that, when justice by man is denied, God appears in court and champions the cause of the oppressed. He is the representative of a nation that has been redeemed. He himself is a ransomed one, and is under peculiar obligation to serve his Deliverer. His time, his capacity, his legal knowledge, his influence are not his own; he is redeemed, and belongs to another. Past deliverances are not to be lost upon us, or *we* are lost. To forget the lessons of the past is self-injury, yea, is heinous sin. In every station and office fidelity is demanded.—D.

Vers. 19—22.—*Autumn generosity.* If a man is not generous towards his poorer neighbours in time of harvest, he will never be generous. If the profuse generosity of God be lavished upon him in vain, his moral nature must be hard indeed. As men "make hay while the sun shines," so should we yield to benevolent impulses while God surrounds us with sunshine of kindness. As we are undeserving recipients, we should share our unpurchased bounty with others.

I. WE HAVE HERE A FITTING OCCASION FOR GENEROSITY. God supplies us with fitting seasons for getting good and for doing good. It is not always autumn. We cannot gather corn and olives when we please. We have to wait the arrival of the season, and this season is God's provision. We must gather *then* or never. Opportunity can never be trifled with. If abundance has been put into our hands, let us forthwith use it well, or it may be suddenly taken from us. If an unusual generous impulse be upon us, it is wisest to respond to it freely, to give it largest scope, for this is a visit of God to us for good.

II. FITTING OBJECTS FOR GENEROSITY ARE PROVIDED. Were it not for the existence of the poor, there would be no outlet for generosity in a practical and material form. There would be no discipline for the best part of our nature. It would be a pain and a loss to us if the instinct of benevolence within us found no field for its exercise. Thankful ought we to be that the poor shall not cease out of the land. The fatherless and the widow come to us as the sent of God, to loosen the sluices of our generosity, and to do us good. We are almoners of God's royal bounty.

III. DELICATE PLANS FOR CONVEYING GENEROSITY. The finer forces of our bodily nature are conveyed to every part by most delicate, almost invisible, ducts. Nerve-power is distributed from the centre to the circumference by minutest channels. So, too, should we employ the most refined delicacy in relieving the necessities of the poor. Let not our gift be spoilt by any assumption of superiority, nor by any arrogant rudeness. It is a noble thing to respect the manly feelings of the poor, and to touch with fairy finger the sensibilities of the suffering. We are to study, not only how much we can give, but especially how best to give it. From the harvest-field and the olive-grove we may learn this delicacy of kindness. Both the quantity and the quality of our service are important in God's esteem.

IV. THE POTENT MOTIVE TO GENEROSITY. Remembrance of their own redemption was the mighty motive for all good deeds. This is the constant refrain of God's message. As God is not wearied in reiterating the lesson, neither should we be wearied in hearing it. We are the objects of God's tenderest love. He has set in motion his most prodigious energies to rescue us from misery. He has emptied his treasury of blessings so as to enrich us, and the end for which he has enriched us is that we may enrich others. Ye have been ineffably blessed, do you bless in return.—D.

EXPOSITION.

CHAPTER XXV.

LAWS RELATING TO CORPORAL PUNISHMENT, LEVIRATE MARRIAGES, AND WEIGHTS AND MEASURES.

Vers. 1—3.—The first and second verses should be read as one sentence, of which the protasis is in ver. 1 and the apodosis in ver. 2, thus: If there be a strife between men, and they come to judgment, and they (*i.e.* the judges) give judgment on them, and justify the righteous, and condemn the wicked, then it shall be, if the wicked deserve to be beaten (literally, *be the son of blows*), that the judge, etc. It is assumed that the judges shall pronounce just judgment, and apportion to the guilty party his due punishment; and then it is prescribed how that is to be inflicted. In the presence of the judge the man was to be cast down, and the adjudged number of blows were to be given him, not, however, exceeding forty, lest the man should be rendered contemptible in the eyes of the people, as if he were a mere slave or brute. This punishment was usually inflicted with a stick (Exod. xxi. 10; 2 Sam. vii. 14, etc.), as is still the case among the Arabs and Egyptians; some-

times also with thorns (Judg. viii. 7, 16); sometimes with whips and scorpions, *i.e.* scourges of cord or leather armed with sharp points or hard knots (1 Kings xii. 11, 14). Though the culprit was laid on the ground, it does not appear that the bastinado was used among the Jews as it is now among the Arabs; the back and shoulders were the parts of the body on which the blows fell (Prov. x. 13; xix. 29; xxvi. 3; Isa. l. 6). According to his fault, by a certain number; literally, *according to the requirement of his crime in number;* i.e. according as his crime deserved. The number was fixed at forty, probably because of the symbolical significance of that number as a measure of completeness. The rabbins fixed the number at thirty-nine, apparently in order that the danger of exceeding the number prescribed by the Law should be diminished (cf. 2 Cor. xi. 24); but another reason is assigned by Maimonides, viz. that, as the instrument of punishment was a scourge with three tails, each stroke counted for three, and thus they could not give forty, but only thirty-nine, unless they exceeded the forty (Maimon., 'In Sanhedrin,' xvii. 2).

Ver. 4.—The leaving the ox unmuzzled when treading out the corn was in order that the animal might be free to eat of the grains which its labour severed from the husks. This prohibition, therefore, was dictated by a regard to the rights and claims of animals employed in labour; but there is involved in it the general principle that all labour is to be duly requited, and hence it seems to have passed into a proverb, and was applied to men as well as the lower animals (cf. 1 Cor. ix. 9; 1 Tim. v. 18). The use of oxen to tread out the corn and the rule of leaving the animals so employed unmuzzled still prevail among the Arabs and other Eastern peoples (Robinson, 'Bib. Res.,' ii. 206, 207; iii. 6; Kitto, 'Bib. Cycl.,' i. 86).

Vers. 5—10.—*Levirate marriages.* If a man who was married died without issue, his surviving brother was required to marry the widow, so as to raise up a successor to the deceased, who should be his heir. The brother who refused this duty must be publicly disgraced. The design of this institution—which was not originated by Moses, but came down from early times (Gen. xxxviii. 8), and is to be found amongst other nations than the Jews, and that even in the present day—was to preserve a family from becoming extinct and to secure the property of a family from passing into the hands of a stranger. The notion that the usage "had its natural roots in the desire inherent in man who is born for immortality, and connected with the hitherto undeveloped belief in an eternal life, to secure a continued personal existence for himself and immortality for his name through the perpetuation of his family, and in the life of the son who took his place" (Keil), seems wholly fanciful.

Ver. 5.—**Dwell together;** *i.e.* not necessarily in the same house, but in the same community or place (cf. Gen. xiii. 6; xxvi. 7). **And have no child;** literally, *have no son;* but this is rightly interpreted as meaning *child* (so the LXX.; Vulgate; Josephus, 'Antiq.,' iv. 8, 23; Matt. xxii. 25; Maimon., 'In Jibbum.,' ii. 6—9); for, if the deceased left a daughter, the perpetuation of the family and the retention of the property might be secured through her (cf. Numb. xxvii. 4, etc.).

Ver. 6.—**Shall succeed in the name of his brother** which **is dead;** literally, *shall rise up on the name of his deceased brother;* i.e. shall be enrolled in the family register as heir of the deceased, and shall perpetuate his name.

Vers. 7—10.—If the man refused to marry the widow of his deceased brother, he was free to do so; but the woman had her redress. She was to bring the matter before the elders of the town, sitting as magistrates at the gate, and they were to summon the man and speak to him, and if he persisted in his refusal, the woman was to take his shoe from off his foot, and spit before his face, and say, **So shall it be done unto that man that will not build up his brother's house.** The taking off of the shoe of the man by the woman was an act of indignity to him; it amounted to a declaration that he was not worthy to stand in his brother's place, and was scornfully rejected by the woman herself. As the planting of the shod foot on a piece of property, or the casting of the shoe over a field, was emblematical of taking possession of it with satisfaction (Ps. lx. 8; cviii. 9); and as the voluntary handing of one's shoe to another betokened the giving up to that other of some property or right; so, contrariwise, the forcible removal from one of his shoe and the casting of it aside indicated contemptuous rejection of the owner, and repudiation of all his rights and claims in the matter. To walk barefooted was regarded by the Jews as ignominious and miserable (cf. Isa. xx. 2, 4; 2 Sam. xv. 30). The spitting before the face of the man (בְּפָנָיו, in front of him) is by the Jewish interpreters understood of spitting on the ground in his presence (Talmud, 'Jebam.,' 106; Maimon., 'In Jibbum.,' iv. 6—8). This seems to be what the words express (cf. ch. iv. 37; vii. 24; xi. 25; Josh. x. 8; Ezek. x. 8, for the rendering of בפני); and this, according to Oriental notions, would be insult enough (cf. Numb. xii. 14; Isa. l. 6; Niebuhr, 'Description de l'Arabie,' i. 49).

Vers. 11, 12.—But though the childless widow might thus approach and lay hold on the man, no licence was thus granted to women to pass beyond the bounds of decency in their approaches to the other sex. Hence the prohibition in these verses. The severe sentence here prescribed was by the rabbins commuted into a fine of the value of the hand.

Vers. 13—16.—Rectitude and integrity in trade are here anew inculcated (cf. Lev. xix. 35, etc.).

Ver. 13.—**Divers weights;** literally, *a stone and a stone*—a large one for buying, and a small one for selling (cf. Amos viii. 5). Both weights and measures were to be "perfect," *i.e.* exactly correct, and so just. (On the promise in ver. 15, see ch. iv. 26; v. 16.)

Ver. 16.—(Cf. ch. xxii. 5; xxiii. 12.) **All that do unrighteously;** equivalent to all that transgress any law.

Vers. 17—19.—Whilst in their intercourse

with each other the law of love and brotherly kindness was to predominate, it was to be otherwise in regard to the enemies of God and his people. Them they were to overcome by force; wickedness was to be removed by the extinction of the wicked. Moses has already repeatedly reminded the Israelites that they had utterly to destroy the wicked nations of Canaan; and he here closes this discourse by reminding them that there was a nation outside of Canaan which was also doomed, and which they were to root out. This was Amalek, which had attacked the Israelites in their journey at Rephidim, and had taken advantage of their exhausted condition to harass their rear and destroy those who, faint and weary, had lagged behind. For this they had been already punished by the Israelites, who, led on by Joshua, had turned upon them and discomfited them with the edge of the sword. This, however, was not enough; Amalek was to be utterly destroyed, and this the Israelites were to effect as soon as the Lord had given them rest in the promised land. It was not, however, till the time of David that this was done.

Ver. 18.—**And smote the hindmost of thee;** literally, *and tailed thee ;* i.e. cut off thy tail, or rear. The verb (זָנַב) occurs only here and in Josh. x. 19. It is a denominative from זָנָב, a tail, and, like many denominatives, both in the Hebrew and in other languages, it has the sense of taking away or cutting off the thing expressed by the noun from which it is formed, like the English verb *to skin,* for example.

HOMILETICS.

Vers. 1—3.—*Humanity to be respected in judicial inflictions.* This passage is an interesting illustration of the restraints which the Law of Moses puts on the Hebrews, as to the semi-barbarous customs of other nations. It is well known that punishment by bastinado was common among the ancient Egyptians. It would be not unnaturally adopted by the Hebrews. There are here three matters to be noticed. 1. Here is a principle to be recognized (ver. 1). 2. The punishment (1) is to be inflicted in the presence of the judge, and (2) is not to exceed forty stripes. 3. The reason given is very impressive, "lest thy brother should seem vile unto thee," *i.e.* lest he should be so excessively punished as to be afterwards unfit for service, and lest he should be the common butt of any one who chose to dishonour him. *Human nature is to be respected,* even in carrying out legal sentences on crime. Trapp says, "The Turks, when cruelly lashed, are compelled to return to the judge that commanded it, to kiss his hand, to give him thanks, and to pay the officer that whipped them!"

I. The sight of a human being coming under the sentence of criminal law is matter for intense sadness.

II. The punishment to be inflicted on him should be such in matter and degree as to assert right principle, but not such as needlessly to dishonour him. For—

III. Humanity, in spite of crime, has dignity about it still. Sin and the sinner are not inseparable. God can kill one and save the other!

IV. With a view to a criminal's salvation, whatever of honour remains in his nature should be carefully guarded and tenderly appealed to.

Ver. 4.—*Labourers to live by their labour.* The use of this verse by the apostle has brought it out of an obscurity to which it might have been relegated. It is quoted by Paul in 1 Cor. ix. 10, and is there applied by him as an illustration in the ancient Law of Moses of the same principle which our Lord affirmed when he appointed that " they that preach the gospel should live of the gospel " (see Matt. x. 9, 10). We can scarcely go so far as John Calvin in reference to Paul's allusion to it. He says that Paul here says, *God does not care for oxen!* Surely his meaning is simply that it was not merely from his care for oxen that God commanded Moses to pen such a precept, but that there was a common care of God for all his creatures, and that if he cared thus for the less, it was very certain he would care even more for the greater. Labour, moreover, is to be like all native growths—it is to have "its seed within itself." All who employ labourers are to see that their workmen are sufficiently well paid to enable them to live by their labour. Any one desiring to develop this truth in relation to spiritual toil would naturally rather take the New Testament texts referred to above. Keeping, therefore, simply to the earthly sphere, we remark: 1. No precept in this book which is connected with duty or character is too trivial to be "worthy of God." 2. An apparently small command may wrap up in it a great principle. 3. True benevolence will be kind and thoughtful to the humblest labourer even in minute detail. 4. God does not allow any one selfishly to monopolize the fruits of another's labour without giving the toiler adequate compensation for his toil. 5. The Great Defender of the rights of the working classes is—God! 6. It is a divinely appointed ordinance for ever that the power of toil is to be a means of self-support; that labour shall bring wealth to the labourer. Here is a blow struck at slavery.

Vers. 5—10.—*Family honour to be maintained.* This law supposes a state of society and a kind of public opinion which does not now exist, and in detail it is therefore obsolete. But the principle it involves is clear, viz. that in married life the honour of the family on both sides is an object of mutual interest and concern, not only during the events of life, but also in case of arrangements at and after death.

Vers. 11, 12.—*An offending hand.* This may be compared with Matt. v. 30. 1. Any member of the body may become an instrument of sin. 2. Where there is in any case special danger, there should a special watch be kept. 3. Favourite, yet sinful lusts *must* be crucified, whatever the cost may be.

Vers. 13—16.—*Righteousness in trade imperative.* This paragraph requires no preparatory elucidation. The topic for a Homily which it gives is one of the most important in the range of human ethics. It furnishes six lines of thought. 1. In the providence of God men are thrown together for the purposes of trade. 2. Opportunity is thus furnished for the exercise of right principles of mutual justice and equity. 3. There is often given an opportunity also of taking advantage of others by unequal weights and measures. 4. God requires of us absolute justice to others, always and everywhere. 5. No false maxims of men, such as "business is business," can ever exonerate us from obligations to justice. 6. Our duty to man in this respect is enforced by a double argument. (1) The neglect of it is an abomination to God (ver. 16). (2) The observance of it will tend to long life, prosperity, and peace (ver. 15).

Vers. 17—19.—*Kindness to enemies is not to degenerate into sympathy with or indifference to ungodliness.* God is kind. God is terrible. When he riseth up against sin to punish it openly, who—who can stand? The repeated injunctions in this book, of kindness to enemies, the prohibitions against private revenge, etc., should effectually guard any against attributing to Moses any incitement of the people to revengeful retaliation. He utters a prophecy, as a prophet. In Exod. xvii. 16, the LXX. read, ἐν χειρὶ κρυφαίᾳ, κ.τ.λ., "by an unseen hand the Lord will war against Amalek." In Numb. xxiv. 20, Balaam foretells Amalek's doom. In 1 Sam. xv., the execution of judgment on Amalek is recorded; and thus is the meaning of our present paragraph explained. Note: 1. It is a very dangerous thing for a nation to harass or injure the people of God. 2. Such a nation may seem to prosper a while, but judgment is "laid up in store." 3. The retribution will come sooner or later in God's wonder-working providence. "Their feet shall slide in due time." 4. Whatever sympathy we may rightly feel for individual sufferers, the fact that God will ultimately avenge his people's wrongs may fill us with grateful joy.

HOMILIES BY VARIOUS AUTHORS.

Vers. 1—3.—*The bastinado.* Professor W. R. Smith ('Old Testament,' p. 376) regards this law of stripes as indicating a late date for Deuteronomy. He argues from the customs of the free Bedouins. But it is perilous to reason from the customs of the Bedouins to the punishments in vogue among a people who had lived some centuries in Egypt, where, as is well-known, the bastinado was in constant use. The sculptures at Beni-Hassan represent the very scene here described. We learn—

I. THAT IT IS THE FUNCTION OF CIVIL MAGISTRATES TO PUNISH CRIME. (Vers. 1, 2.) They bear the sword for this purpose (Rom. xiv. 4; 1 Pet. ii. 14). The modern humanitarian spirit tends to exalt the reformatory and preventive ends of punishment, at the expense of the retributive. That every effort should be put forth for the reformation of the criminal which the case admits of, we cordially allow. But the danger is, in these matters, that sentiment degenerate into sentimentalism. Crime *deserves* punishment, and on that ground alone, were there no other, ought to receive it. No theory can be satisfactory which loses sight of retribution, and makes reformation and prevention the all in all.

II. THAT PENALTIES OUGHT TO BE SUFFICIENTLY SEVERE. (Ver. 2.) To be effective in early stages of civilization, penalties must be severe, prompt, and specific enough to be vividly conceived (cf. H. Spencer's 'Essays:' 'Prison Ethics'). The progress of society admits of the substitution of punishments appealing to a higher class of sensibilities. But even these ought adequately to express the measure of the criminal's desert. If Mr. Spencer were right, the slightest restraint compatible with the safety of the community, combined with compulsory self-support, would be punishment sufficient for the greatest crimes. The sense of justice in mankind rejects such ideas. Carlyle's teaching in 'Model Prisons' is healthier than this.

III. THAT PENALTIES OUGHT TO BE MEASURED. (Ver. 3.) It is difficult to believe that in our own country, at the beginning of this century, the theft of five shillings from the person was a crime punishable by death. Yet the statute-book bristled with enactments, of which, unhappily, this was not the worst. Such outrageous disproportion between crime and punishment must have robbed the law's sentences of most of their moral effect. Anomalies exist still, which it would be to any statesman's credit to endeavour to remove.

IV. THAT PENALTIES SHOULD NOT BE UNDULY DEGRADING. (Ver. 3.) Lest "thy brother should seem vile unto thee." The effect of excessive severity is to harden, degrade, dehumanize. It often drives the criminal to desperation. As a victim of the older criminal code expressed it, "A man's heart is taken from him, and there is given to him the heart of a beast." The tendency in modern feeling is toward the abolition of corporal punishments entirely, as degrading alike to him who administers them, and to those by whom they are endured. Observe: 1. The profound idea on which the law rested. The body, part of human nature, and sharing its dignity as made in God's image. 2. The best laws may be unjustly and cruelly administered (2 Cor. xi. 24, 25).—J. O.

Ver. 4.—*The oxen.* The apostle draws from this passage the general principle that the labourer is entitled to eat of the fruits of his labour (1 Cor. ix. 9, 10). His application teaches us to look for similar general principles wrapped up in other precepts of the Law. We learn—

I. ANIMALS ARE ENTITLED TO GENEROUS TREATMENT. The ox that trod out the corn was not to be muzzled. He was to be permitted to eat of the fruits of his work. Kindness to animals is a duty: 1. *Which man owes to the creatures.* Severe moralists, arguing that animals, being destitute of reason, are also destitute of rights, would bring all man's duties towards them under the head of duties to himself (*e.g.* Kant). Alford thinks this to be implied in Paul's language. But Paul's argument, if it is to be pressed in this connection, rather implies the contrary. It recognizes in the ox, on the ground of its being a labourer, a kind of right to be provided for. All that the apostle affirms is that the precept had an end beyond the reference to oxen, that the "care for oxen" was subordinate to the inculcation of a principle of general application. Our duty to the creatures rests on the ground that they are sentient beings, capable of pain and pleasure, and on the law of love, which requires us to diffuse happiness, and avoid inflicting needless suffering. 2. *Which man owes to himself.* For this view, while not the whole of the truth, is an important part of it. Leibnitz, in a small treatise written for the education of a prince, advised that, during youth, he should not be permitted to torment or give pain to any living thing, lest, by indulging the spirit of cruelty, he should contract a want of feeling for his fellow-men. Alford says, "The good done to a man's immortal spirit by acts of humanity and justice infinitely outweighs the mere physical comfort of a brute which perishes."

II. THE HUMAN LABOURER IS ENTITLED TO SHARE IN THE PROFITS OF HIS LABOURS. Theoretically, he does so every time he is paid wages. In the distribution of the fruits of production, the part which the labourer gets, we are told, is *wages*, the share of the landowner is *rent*, that of the capitalist is *interest*, and the Government takes *taxes*. Practically, however, wages are settled, not by abstract rules of fairness, but by competition, which may press so hard upon the labourer as (till things right themselves) to deprive him of his fair proportion of industrial profits. The wage system is far from working satisfactorily. As society advances, it appears to be leading to an increasing amount of bitterness and friction. Masters and men represent opposing interests, and stand, as it were, at daggers drawn. It is easier to see the evil than to devise a cure. Economists (Mill, Jevons, etc.) seem to look mainly in the direction of some form of co-operation. Their schemes are principally two: 1. Industrial co-operation. 2. Industrial partnerships—the system according to which a fixed proportion of profits is assigned for division amongst the workmen engaged in production.

III. MINISTERS OF THE GOSPEL ARE ENTITLED TO BE SUPPORTED BY THEIR FLOCKS. This is the application made by Paul (1 Cor. ix.; cf. Matt. x. 10—12; Gal. vi. 6). Christian ministers, labouring in spiritual things, and by that work withdrawn from ordinary avocations, are to be cheerfully supported. The text applies to this case more strictly than to the case of workmen claiming to participate in profits. The workman claims but his own. The right of the minister to support is of a different kind. He labours in things spiritual, but, it is to be hoped, with a higher end than the mere obtaining of a livelihood. While, therefore, his support is a duty, it is, like duties of benevolence generally, not one that can be enforced by positive law. The right to support is a moral, not a legal one. It creates an obligation, but, as moralists say, an indeterminate obligation. It is an obligation to be freely accepted, and as freely discharged.—J. O.

Vers. 5—10.—*The levirate law.* At the root of this law, which obtained widely in the East, we find ideas and feelings such as these—

I. RESPECT FOR THE HONOUR OF THE FAMILY. In the East, as is well known, childlessness is reckoned a calamity, almost a disgrace. Hence, as well as for other reasons, the severity of the law in ver. 11. Hence also this custom of marrying a brother's widow, in order to raise up seed to the brother. The motive is plainly to avert disgrace from a brother's house, to wipe out his reproach, to hand down his name in honour. We may respect the feeling while repudiating the form in which it embodied itself. What touches the credit of our families ought to be felt to concern ourselves. Not in the sense, certainly, of leading us to uphold that credit at the expense of truth and of justice to others; but in the sense of doing everything we can with a good conscience to maintain or redeem it.

II. DESIRE FOR A PERPETUATED NAME. The men of the old dispensation, as Matthew Henry says, not having so clear and certain a prospect of living themselves on the other side death as we have now, were the more anxious to live in their posterity. The principle is the same at bottom as that which leads us to wish for personal immortality. What man desires is perpetuated existence, of which existence in one's posterity is a kind of shadow, affording, in contemplation, a like "shadow of satisfaction" to the mind. Positivism, in falling back from a personal to a corporate immortality, is thus a movement in the wrong direction. The exchange it proposes is the substance for the shadow. The desire to exist in the remembrance of posterity, and to be well thought of by them, is, however, a legitimate principle of action. It should operate in leading us to live good and useful lives, which is the secret of the only lasting honour.

> "Only the actions of the just
> Smell sweet and blossom in the dust."

III. THE DISGRACE ATTACHING TO REFUSAL OF THE DUTIES IMPOSED ON US BY RELATIONSHIP TO THE DEAD. The disgrace in this case was emphatically marked (vers. 9, 10). The wishes of the dead should be very sacred to us. The duties which spring from the bond of relationship, or from express request, should, if possible, be faithfully discharged. Aiding in the settlement of affairs, seeing provision made for a widow and children, accepting and fulfilling trusts, etc.—J. O.

Vers. 13—16.—*Morality in trade.* The Hebrew lawgiver lays just stress on honesty in weights and measures. The general principle is that of honesty in trade. Weights and measures connect themselves intimately with the ideas of justice, rectitude, impartiality. Justice is represented by a figure with scales and weights. Falsification of weights and measures is thus a representative sin, one which corrupts integrity in man with peculiar and fatal rapidity.

I. An INJUNCTION MUCH NEEDED. Trade morality is at present at a low ebb. Mixed up with the thousands of honest transactions which no doubt take place every day, there must be admitted to be an enormous number which are more or less fraudulent. "On the average," says Mr. Spencer, "men who deal in bales and tons differ but little in morality from men who deal in yards and pounds. Illicit practices of every form and shade, from venial deception up to all but direct theft, may be brought home to the higher grades of the commercial world. Tricks innumerable, lies acted or uttered, elaborately devised frauds, are prevalent—many of them established as 'customs of the trade;' nay, not only established, but defended" ('Essays,' vol. ii., 'Morals of Trade;' cf. Smiles on 'Duty,' ch. iii.). The saddest feature in the outlook is the apparent prevalence of the feeling that trickery of this kind is absolutely essential to success—that a man can't get on without it.

II. An INJUNCTION WHICH OUGHT TO BE ENFORCED. But how? By a fearless exposure of dishonesties, and by a loud and firm demand on the part of every upright member of society for honest and truthful dealing. Only if the dishonest are a majority in society—a majority of overwhelming numbers—can they ultimately prevail against the honest. A determined combination on the part of persons of integrity would suffice to put them down. The man known to be honest should be supported, even at some pecuniary sacrifice. Custom should be unflinchingly withdrawn from men detected in tricks, and the stamp of public reprobation placed on such men and their doings. Means should be taken to diffuse information as to the arts and frauds by which dishonesty sustains itself. The causes of these dishonesties need also to be looked into—chiefly, according to Spencer, the indiscriminate respect paid to wealth. Love of the honour and position which wealth gives—the certainty of being looked up to, courted in society, applauded for success, with few questions asked,—this is the tap-root of the evil, and it is to be cured by distinguishing between wealth and character, and by honouring the former only when in alliance with the latter.

III. An INJUNCTION WHICH IT IS EVERY ONE'S INTEREST TO ENFORCE. Trade dishonesty should, if possible, be checked: 1. *In view of its inherent immorality.* Nothing can be more despicable, more mean and disgraceful, than the lies, frauds, briberies, malpractices, adulterations, which, if the witnesses are to be trusted, abound in all branches of trade. These things are a blot on our country, the shame of which touches all. 2. *In view of its corrupting effect on morals generally.* Its influence spreads beyond itself. It saps principle, eats out faith in virtue, unfits the individual for every moral task. 3. *In view of its effects on national prosperity.* These are ruinous. God's displeasure rests on the nation, and he is certain to chastise it. But the sorest whip he uses to chastise it is the scourge of its own follies. Our dishonesties lose us (are actually losing us) our markets; lower us in the eyes of foreign nations; destroy credit; engender a spirit of general distrust; still worse, by undermining principle, they destroy the power of steady application to work, and increasingly substitute the motives of the gambler for those of the merchant content with lawful gains. The inevitable end is impoverishment and disgrace. 4. *As a measure of self-protection.* Each individual suffers as part of the whole. He is frequently cheated, sometimes incurs serious losses. Hard-earned money finds its way into the pockets of clever but unscrupulous scoundrels, who as rapidly squander it in reckless living. —J. O.

Vers. 17—19.—*Amalek.* Moses, in calling the sin of Amalek to remembrance, and enjoining destruction of that people, was not speaking "of himself." He but declared the will of God, long before announced, and solemnly recorded in a book (Exod. xvii. 14).

It was not "after the spirit or mission of the Law," as has been well remarked, "to aim at overcoming inveterate opposition by love and by attempts at conversion. The Law taught God's hatred of sin and of rebellion against him by enjoining the extinction of the obstinate sinner" ('Speaker's Commentary'). The lessons from the command are these—

I. GOD KEEPS IN REMEMBRANCE INJURIES DONE TO HIS CHURCH AND PEOPLE. (Ver. 17.)

II. GOD SPECIALLY REMEMBERS INJURIES TO THE FEEBLE AND AFFLICTED. (Ver. 18.) The "fear of God," if nothing else, ought to restrain inhumanities. "Saul, Saul, why persecutest thou me?" (Acts ix. 4).

III. WRONGS TO THE CHURCH OF GOD WILL NOT PASS UNAVENGED. (Ver. 19.) Repentance, as in Paul's case, may reverse the sentence. If the sinner is obstinate, the doom will fall as certainly as in the case of Amalek (2 Thess. i. 9).—J. O.

Vers. 1—3.—*Earthly magistracy an argument for the heavenly.* It is not conceivable that God should have taken such pains, through Moses, to secure pure administration of justice in earthly courts, unless he had established a like court of judicature in heaven. So far as the will of God is embodied in the judicial procedure on earth, it is copied from the pattern of heavenly things.

I. A JUDICIAL COURT IS CREATED FOR THE DISCRIMINATION OF HUMAN CHARACTER. The purpose of all examination and testimony is to separate the evil from the good— to bring to light the righteousness and the wickedness of men. Justice delights more in vindicating and commending the righteous than in censuring and condemning the wicked. Justice found a nobler occupation in marshalling Mordecai through the city, and proclaiming his innocence, than in erecting the gallows for the execution of Haman. Human judges, however, can discern only what is palpable and conspicuous. They have not an organ of insight delicate enough to detect the lesser excellences and blemishes; nor can they penetrate into the interior nature of man. These institutions are only the *shadows* of heavenly things. But every man stands before the tribunal of a higher Judge, where not only actions, but motives, intentions, and feelings, are examined and weighed. Here, without the possibility of mistake, the righteous are justified, the wicked are condemned. Discrimination is perfect: separation will be complete.

II. A JUDICIAL COURT IS ORDAINED FOR THE PUNISHMENT OF EVIL DEEDS. 1. The true punishment is *measured by the scale of demerit.* It is enjoined to be "according to his fault." In God's sagacious judgment, every degree of blameworthiness is noted. Nothing appertaining to moral conduct is beneath the notice of God's eye. *We* value far too little moral qualities. As we grow like God, we shall gain in that penetrative power which discerns the beauty of goodness and the blackness of iniquity. 2. *Punishment is a loss of manliness.* "The judge shall cause him to lie down." His dignity shall be prostrate. Sin robs us of manliness, but the loss does not come into public view until punishment follows. To be righteous throughout is to be a man. 3. *Punishment is to be public.* The culprit is "to be beaten before the judge's face." This publicity is part of the penalty. It is summary—to be inflicted at once. And publicity is also a safeguard against cruelty and against excess. So God invites public recognition and public approval of his doings. The ransomed universe shall unite in the testimony, "Just and true are thy ways, thou King of saints."

III. A JUDICIAL COURT REVEALS THE VALUE OF A HUMAN LIFE. The penalties were to be moderate, "lest thy brother should seem vile unto thee." The first ends of punishment are the reformation and improvement of the offender. If it is possible to teach the culprit the value of himself, and inspire him with a hatred of sin, we have done him unspeakable good. We do not spend so much in cutting and polishing a common stone as we do a ruby or a sapphire. Let our treatment of men be as if we esteemed them the jewels of God.—D.

Ver. 4.—*Doing good inseparable from getting good.* Active exercise of our powers is a primary condition of getting good. Real service for others is destined to gain reward.

I. SERVICE CAN BE RENDERED TO MAN BY VERY INFERIOR NATURES. The whole animate creation waits upon man. Every living thing upon the earth is a servant and a lackey for men. He is a king here; and, if he have sufficient wisdom, he can rule all for his own advantage. Yet, in a higher sphere, man is only a servant. He who is served by all inferior beings is called to serve the Highest Being. The disparity between God and man is a disparity immeasurable; and yet God permits, yea, encourages, our intelligent and willing service. Inferior as we are to him, we can render efficient service to his kingdom and glory. This is man's truest honour.

II. SERVICE CONTRIBUTES TO PROVIDE AN ABUNDANT BANQUET. The labour of the oxen prepared the corn for men. So gross is our ignorance of the lower creation, that we do not perceive our indebtedness to the birds and insects, which play so useful a part in the preparation of our food. All well-directed service contributes something to the substantial advantage of man. There is a banquet of intellectual food, or a banquet for the æsthetic taste, or a banquet for the soul, resulting. Active labour serves both to create an appetite and to furnish a table.

III. SERVICE HAS CLAIMS UPON OUR GENEROUS RECOMPENSE. It would be nothing else than selfish cruelty to deny to the oxen a share in the result of their labour. Thus God cares for the oxen. Thus he cares for all the works of his hands. And does his kindly care for the inferior beasts diminish his tender regard for men? It immeasurably enhances it! Whoever or whatever does us useful service brings us under obligation. To the extent of our power we are bound to recompense such. This sense of indebtedness is a channel of blessing to the soul. The richest man is he who is the most generous. A muzzle is a shackle forged by wanton selfishness.—D.

Vers. 13—16.—*Religion inspires commercial life.* It is certain that God displays the liveliest interest in every department of human life. He is not only the God of the hills; he is God of the valleys also. He takes cognizance, not only of great things, but also of small. Can any man tell us what are small things? Not only on the portal of every church, but on the forefront of every shop—ay, on the beam of every balance, we ought to see the inscription, "To the glory of God alone!"

I. RELIGION CLAIMS A THRONE IN EVERY SHOP. True religion is the sunny smile from God's eye, and, as the common light of day penetrates into every nook and cranny of nature, so the light of God's love pierces into every interest of human life. It is not a romantic something which has merely to do with the region of existence beyond the grave; it is the life of our present life—the secret spring of every duty. Ordinary trade is a splendid field for the practical exercise of religious virtues, because the commercial activities of the age afford large facilities either for fidelity or for fraud. In every office and warehouse religion claims to set up her throne. In the smallest act of buying and selling she insists on having a voice.

II. RELIGION GOES TO THE ROOT OF THINGS—DETERMINES THE STANDARDS OF HUMAN ACTION. If the weight or measure be false, then every transaction will be false. Ingenious wickedness had invented two sets of standards—an over-large one for the man as buyer, an under-size for the same man as seller. This course of vile procedure carried the villainy into every item of the man's mercantile life. It is of the first importance that we set up right standards. The Pharisee in the temple was a perfect man, according to *his* standard. The rich young man who came to Jesus Christ for counsel was blameless, according to *his* standard. Men are prone to set up conventional standards, and measure themselves and every one one else according to *their* rule. Take heed that *your* standard is *God's* standard, "a perfect and just measure."

III. RELIGION IS BOTH DESTRUCTIVE AND CONSTRUCTIVE. "Thou shalt not have *this*; thou shalt have *that*." It first pulls down, then builds up. It first uproots, then plants. "Mortify your members, then add to your virtues." The old must be destroyed; the new must be sown and nursed. In our self-culture and in our training of others, it is not enough that we are repressive and prohibitive; the new growths will often cast off effete and injurious matter. Prune away barren boughs; encourage the development of the fruitful wood.

IV. RELIGION BRINGS COLLATERAL GAINS IN THIS LIFE. Her main reward is in the future, viz. possession of the Divine image; nevertheless, she confers many solid favours here and now. Real pleasure is her daily gift, and "length of days" is her special prize. "The wicked shall not live out half their days"—they die prematurely. Nor is long life on earth to be despised. There are, doubtless, moral advantages and gains obtainable in this life, which are not obtainable in the life to come. Many of the means of discipline and pruning and reformation will end with this life. We are placed here for probation; and (if well-used) long school-life is an advantage unspeakable. To be esteemed by God as "the apple of his eye" is better than an earthly coronet. To be regarded by him as "abomination" is "concentrated curse."—D.

Vers. 17—19.—*Cowardice and cruelty avenged.* The feeling of resentment must be classed "low" among the moral sentiments. But this command to remember and to avenge the conduct of Amalek is not resentment. Abundant time was allowed the Amalekites to abandon evil ways and to cultivate friendly relations with Israel. But they continued, century after century, godless and hostile: hence their extinction.

I. ATHEISM BREEDS IN MEN BOTH CRUELTY AND COWARDICE. Against Amalek the gravest charge is, "he feared not God." This is the root of all his wickedness—the source of his base hostility to Israel. Practical atheism is the prolific parent of hateful vices. There was not a trait of nobleness in Amalek's conduct. It was cowardly and cruel. He attacked Israel in the rear—"smote the hindmost" stragglers—fell upon those already half-dead from fatigue. For a moment he gloried in the inglorious massacre, but only for a moment. The prayer of one man was more than a match for Amalek. In every age it is found that he "who fears not God" has no "regard for man." The influence of a bad man is perilously contagious. The whole tribe is embraced under the character of one man.

II. CRUEL TREATMENT LEAVES AN INDELIBLE IMPRESSION UPON THE MIND. Human nature is so constituted that a wrong done to us or to our fathers is held tenaciously in the memory, and provokes all the feelings to avenge the deed. Herein the Word of God is in accord with our mental nature. Human nature says, "Remember!" The Scripture says, "Remember!" "Thou shalt not forget it." Incidentally, we have here a proof that the Creator of the human mind is also the Author of Scripture. Injustice rouses up all the moral forces in the universe to inflict a fitting retribution; and very often God employs as his ministers of vengeance the victims of former oppression. The increase, the strength, the organization of Israel were to be employed early upon *this* end, viz. to extinguish Amalek.

III. INHERITANCE FROM GOD CARRIES WITH IT AN OBLIGATION TO DO HIS WILL. Rest is given to prepare for more difficult service. "When the Lord thy God hath given thee rest, . . . thou shalt blot out Amalek." God never gives to men any inheritance for exclusive selfish enjoyment. If we are not disposed for service, and even for warfare, the only consistent course is to decline God's gifts. He has plainly made known to men the conditions of his bequests. Before Israel possessed the promised land it was clearly revealed what was expected from the occupants of that inheritance. Nor is the inheritance of heaven a state of indolent repose. The voice that says, "Enter into joy," says also, "Be thou ruler." We read of disputes between Michael and the adversary. Who shall say that God will not employ his ransomed ones to put down rebellion in some outlying province?—D.

Vers. 1—3.—*Corporal punishment.* We have here directions given for the punishment of criminals. As the Hebrews had no gaol system, a properly graduated corporal punishment supplied most effectively its place. Moses here directs the judges to look carefully into the case, and to assign a certain number of stripes, which are never to exceed forty, the chastisement being given in the presence of the judge. Thus the largest measure of equity was introduced into their penal system.

I. RETRIBUTION OF SOME KIND IS CONSONANT WITH OUR IDEAS OF RIGHTEOUSNESS. To be allowed to sin with impunity would be, we all feel, an immoral regulation under any government, and especially immoral under a theocracy. Punishment for sin is demanded by the human conscience. All quarrel with retribution as such argues a want of conscientiousness.

II. BUT RETRIBUTION SHOULD BE PROPORTIONAL TO SIN. This is what the law before us secured. The stripes were to be few or many, according to the crime, but never to exceed forty. The judgment was to be righteous and equitable all through.

III. WE LOOK INSTINCTIVELY FOR THE SAME EQUITY UNDER THE GOVERNMENT OF GOD. And this is exactly what we have. And here let us observe—

1. *Sin is not allowed to go unpunished under God's government.* It has been very confidently asserted that, if people are penitent, no atonement is needed to secure pardon. But, supposing penitence a possible experience apart from the spectacle of a pierced and atoning Saviour (Zech. xii. 10), should we not have "sin with impunity" under the reputedly just government of God? Those who glibly talk of penitence being all that is required, have formed no broad or consistent notion of the necessities of government.[1] Now, the Divine arrangement has been to lay the "stripes" we deserve upon his willing Son. "With his stripes we are healed" (Isa. liii. 5). The sin is punished in the person of a sinless and most willing Substitute, and the demands of justice met. We may be sure that, as the Father presided at the punishment, no more was laid on Jesus than the demands of simple justice and the exigencies of the government required. And—

2. *Unpardoned because impenitent sinners shall have their punishment graduated according to the strictest justice.* It has been asserted that punishment without end would be excessive for the sins of a short life on earth. But it is forgotten that "everlasting punishment" is the shadow simply of "everlasting sin." The latter, alas! is possible through the freedom of the creature; and as sin continues, so must punishment. At the same time, the graduation of punishment in the other world will be as accurate and as careful as the corporal punishment under the Law of Moses. In fact, it is this idea of stripes our Lord employs to express the truth. "And that servant which knew his lord's will, and made not ready, nor did according to his will, shall be beaten with many *stripes*; but he that knew not, and did things worthy of stripes, shall be beaten with few *stripes*. And to whomsoever much is given, of him shall much be required; and to whom they commit much, of him will they ask the more" (Luke xii. 47, 48, Revised Version). It is thus clearly seen that the utmost care will be taken to graduate the penalties in the hereafter, so that no one shall have the least ground of complaint. The vulgar revolt against the everlasting punishment revealed in Scripture is due to the idea that the criminals are thrown pell-mell together and punished in the lump. With far greater care, however, shall each impenitent one have his penalties meted out to him than prisoners have under the most conscientious judges.

IV. INSTEAD OF BANDYING ABOUT ARGUMENTS IN FAVOUR OF RELIEF UNDER PUNISHMENT, IT WOULD BE KINDER FOR CONTROVERSIALISTS TO INDUCE MEN THROUGH FAITH IN JESUS CHRIST TO ACCEPT OF PARDON AND SO ESCAPE PENALTY. The spectacle at present is a sad one. Writers are pursuing the phantom of remission of sins and of punishment in the other life, as a new gospel for sinners, instead of urging their fellows to flee at once to Jesus, the only Refuge. This much is certain, "Him that cometh unto me," says Christ, "I will in no wise cast out." Upon such a promise any soul may repose. But the uncertainty of speculation is proverbial, and can never be the sheet-anchor of any sane soul. Let men come to Jesus, and the question of punishment, so far as they are concerned, is settled for ever. Punishment gives way to pardon; while at the same time, it is felt that the sin has *not* gone unpunished.—R. M. E.

Ver. 4.—*The rights of labour.* The threshing in the East is done by oxen in many cases still, though horses, where procurable, are found more serviceable. While the animals were engaged in their weary round, they were never muzzled, but allowed to eat of the corn they were treading out.[2] It would appear, indeed, that it was the *straw* simply that they were to receive, and the *corn* was to be reserved for the men, their masters.[3] But the idea manifestly was the right of the patient animal to a share of the corn he was helping to thresh. It suggests the large subject of the rights of labour. Into this, of course, we cannot enter at any length. But we may observe—

I. THAT CO-OPERATION IN WORK HAS A RIGHT TO A SHARE IN ITS WAGES. This is recognized in the Mosaic Law regarding the lower animals, and the argument is cumulative with regard to man. "The labourer is worthy of his hire," said our Lord. "The workman is worthy of his meat" (Luke x. 7; Matt. x. 10).

[1] Cf. Hutton's 'Essays,' vol. i. p. 372; and 'Retribution in Relation to the Justice, Goodness, and Purpose of God,' by the Rev. F. L. Patton, D.D.
[2] Cf. Van Lennep's 'Bible Lands,' p. 81.
[3] Hengstenberg's 'Egypt and the Books of Moses,' pp. 223, 224.

II. THE SHARE SHOULD BE SUFFICIENT TO SUSTAIN LIFE. The ox was expected to pick up on his rounds as much as would keep up his strength for labour. And in the same way, the wages of a labourer should be sufficient to sustain him in the position he occupies in society. The economic laws about the "wages' fund" are not so inexorable as to prevent such a plain principle being evermore kept in view. There is a heartlessness attributed to the laws of wealth that belongs to the capitalists themselves.

III. THERE SHOULD BE SYMPATHY BETWEEN EMPLOYER AND EMPLOYED. The very oxen occupy a position where sympathy must obtain between them and their keepers, if the work is to be properly performed. How much more must this obtain when the workers are our fellow-men! The late Sir Arthur Helps, in one of his early and anonymous volumes entitled, 'The Claims of Labour,' refers frequently to this. "You must not be surprised," he says to the employer, "at the ingratitude of those to whom you have given nothing but money." "Fortunately," he says in another place, "the proneness of men to regard with favour those put in authority over them is very strong; and I have little fear of finding any large body of thoughtful and kind masters suffering from permanent indifference or ingratitude on the part of their dependents." Sympathy between masters and men is more important even than adequate wages.

IV. BOTH JESUS AND PAUL APPLY THE PRINCIPLE TO MINISTERIAL SUPPORT. In the passage already noticed our Lord does so (Matt. x. 9—11; Luke x. 7). Paul also, in 1 Tim. v. 17, 18, makes use of it, referring both to the passage before us in Deuteronomy and also to our Lord's deliverance. In placing the ministry upon the same ground as other workers, it is clear that it is to be no exception to the rule of proportional reward. Of course, it is not supported as other and meaner occupations are. Every other occupation is beneath it in dignity, but every other almost is above it in reward. Its *rights* must be advocated; its claims are valid, and men deny them at their peril.—R. M. E.

Vers. 5—10.—*The rights of the firstborn.* We have already observed that the firstborn had a right to a double share of the family inheritance (ch. xxi. 17). We have before us another of his rights—a seed was to be raised up unto him by his younger brothers, that his name should not be put out in Israel. In a peasant proprietary such as existed in Palestine, we can easily understand the importance of such a regulation. It was, moreover, esteemed a most disgraceful act to refuse to raise up seed unto a dead brother, and the man guilty of it had to suffer the indignity of being spat upon, and of having his shoe contemptuously loosed.

Now, there can be no question that Jesus Christ occupies the position of Eldest Brother in the family of God. Not only was it declared prophetically, "I will make him my Firstborn, higher than the kings of the earth" (Ps. lxxxix. 27), but he is expressly called "the Firstborn from the dead," "the Firstborn among many brethren," and "the Firstborn of every creature" (Col. i. 18; Rom. viii. 29; Col. i. 15). Undoubtedly, then, the rights guaranteed by Jewish Law to the firstborn were intended to illustrate the rights of Jesus Christ.

I. JESUS CHRIST, LIKE THE DEAD FIRSTBORN, HAS TO DEPEND ON OTHERS FOR A SPIRITUAL SEED. For in the nature of things it would have been incongruous for Incarnate God to have entered into marriage with any daughter of Adam, and to have become physically a father. His condescension was surely great enough in becoming man at all, and it could not be expected that he would enter into still closer relations to the race. None ever stood in the relation to physical children of Jesus Christ. It would have made a confusion in the contemplated spiritual relationship. Hence our Lord had to look to others to raise him up a seed.

II. IT LIFTS THE FAMILY RELATION INTO THE HOLIEST LIGHT TO THINK THAT WE MAY BE RAISING UP A SPIRITUAL SEED FOR JESUS. How holy all marriage relations become when it is felt to be possible to be providing the Great Elder Brother with a spiritual seed! The children sent of God are then regarded as Christ's; we dedicate them to him in prayer, and perhaps also in baptism; we handle them and rear them as consecrated things; we train them up in his nurture and admonition, and we feel honoured in having any part in the formation of "the mighty family."

III. IT LIFTS THE PASTORAL AS WELL AS PARENTAL RELATION INTO THE HOLIEST LIGHT. In Weemse's book on the 'Ceremonial Laws of Moses,' where "the privileges of the firstborn" are so fully discussed, the application is made to *preachers* rather than to parents. But we think that parents should feel the elevation of spirit and life which the idea of raising up a seed for Jesus is fitted to impart. And if parents should feel it, much more should pastors. We are meant to be the "spiritual fathers" of men. We have exceptional advantages in prosecuting the holy work. Oh, how glorious it is to think of adding by our faithful labours to the great family of God! It is the Name and honour of Jesus which we should seek to perpetuate by our pastoral labours. And so our aim is to have men born again through the incorruptible seed, the Word of God, which liveth and abideth for ever (1 Pet. i. 23).

IV. ANY REFUSAL TO RAISE UP A SEED FOR JESUS WILL BE VISITED BY GOD IN DUE SEASON WITH DIRE DISGRACE. For the spitting in the face and the unloosing of the shoe are but symbols of the dire disgrace which shall overtake all who will not engage in this holy work. It is a work for Church members as well as for ministers. It lies as a responsibility upon every one that names the Name of Jesus, and is a younger brother or sister in the family of God. Woe be to the person who is indifferent to this!

And surely it should stimulate us to remember that the great ambition of Jesus is to have "many brethren." The mightier the multitude of redeemed ones the better. The glory and honour of Immanuel shall thus be the more thoroughly secured. He has no desire to be the solitary and selfish heir; but the whole plan of redemption is to have as many as possible "joint-heirs" with him. As families and as Churches grow in numbers and in loyalty to Jesus, his rights as Firstborn are being regarded and secured (Rom. viii. 17).

We cannot picture the dire disgrace which the refusal to secure the rights of Jesus Christ will entail. But the selfish souls will be the offscouring of all things; angels will despise them as having highest honour within reach, and not having the heart to accept it. Oh, let every one that has a word to speak and a kindness to perform in the Name of Jesus, do it in the holy hope of increasing the spiritual seed of the great and loving Elder Brother!—R. M. E.

Vers. 11—16.—*Honesty the best policy.* We have first a law of purity, which needs no exposition, but in its holy severity (vers. 11, 12) was fitted to check all tendency to lewd practices among the women of Israel. Then Moses passes on to speak of the crime of having divers weights and measures, and the effort to make money by dishonest practices. No blessing from God can rest upon such wilfully dishonest ones; if his blessing is to be experienced, it must be by a policy of honesty all round.

I. IT IS APPARENTLY EASY TO MAKE MONEY BY LIGHT WEIGHTS AND SHORT MEASURES. It is not only securing the ordinary profits, but gaining by the deficiency palmed off for the perfect measure. It is a gain by quantity as well as by price. And plenty of people who look only at the surface imagine that they can easily enrich themselves by a little dishonesty, which will never be detected. Inspectors of weights and measures are the embodiment of the suspicions of society.

II. IT IS A SYSTEM OF BUSINESS UPON WHICH NO DIVINE BLESSING CAN BE ASKED. No better test of the propriety of our procedure can be found than this. Will it stand the test of prayer? Can God, the All-holy One, be expected to bless it? Now, his whole Word shows that such practices are abominations to him. The stars of heaven will at length fight against such a policy.

III. NO TEMPORARY SUCCESS CAN COMPENSATE FOR AN UNEASY CONSCIENCE. Suppose that success waited on dishonesty invariably and proved lasting, life would be made miserable by the uneasy conscience. Stifled for a time, it rises like the furies at last, and makes life a lasting misery. No man ever trifled with conscience and did not suffer for it. Success becomes in such a case but a whited sepulchre; the experience within is but the rottenness of the tomb.

IV. HONESTY IS THE BEST POLICY FOR PERSONAL PEACE AND FOR DIVINE BLESSING. We say that no man should so far outrage his conscience as to be dishonest. Honesty is a policy to be pursued for its own sake, as the only condition of personal peace. Were there no Divine blessing in question at all, conscientious men would be as honest as they are now.

At the same time, it makes the honesty all the happier that it lies in the sunshine of the Infinite Presence, and that his radiant smile is on it. There is no danger of a mercenary spirit entering into such a relation with God. He so wraps us round that in his circle of love it would be most ungrateful and most dissonant to practise dishonesty.

With people under a theocracy, or reign of God, we should expect to find just weights and full measures. ·The visits of the inspectors should prove superfluous with all those whose life lies open as the day to the inspection of their King.—R. M. E.

Vers. 17—19.—*The extermination of the merciless.* The crime of the Amalekites was falling upon the hindmost, who were faint and weary. It was an act of judgment untempered by any mercy; and the decree of God is their extermination because they were merciless. Just as we see in another place that God won't forgive the unforgiving, so here we see that he will blot out the merciless from under his merciful heaven. " For he shall have judgment without mercy, that hath showed no mercy " (Jas. ii. 13).

I. THE MERCILESS DESERVE NO MERCY. In the case before us there was everything calculated to stir up mercy. The rearguard was feeble and faint and weary. Surely these Amalekites will pity the poor pilgrims, and show them some mercy. But no, they think they are all the better prey, and so they smite the people of God most mercilessly. In their heartless act they put themselves beyond the pale of God's compassion. He consigns them to extermination under the swords of Israel. Our conscience says, " Amen " to this decree. The Amalekites deserve destruction for their heartlessness.

What a word of warning to heartless people still! Let it be carried to a certain point, and God will hand them over to deserved destruction.

II. THE REARGUARD IS ALWAYS AVENGED. The tribe of Dan was directed to go " hindmost with their standards " (Numb. ii. 31). And it must have seemed a trial to be always in the rear and never in the van. But they were here taught that they had in God a special Avenger. He espouses their cause, and will bring forth their righteousness as the light, and their judgment as the noonday (Ps. xxxvii. 6).

III. LET US CONTENTEDLY TAKE THE HINDMOST PLACE IF GOD GIVES IT TO US. All cannot be in the van, and the faithfulness of the rearguard is as much a matter of Divine observation as is the dash and courage which characterize the van.—R. M. E.

EXPOSITION.

CHAPTER XXVI.

THANKSGIVING AND PRAYER AT THE PRE-
SENTATION OF FIRSTFRUITS AND TITHES.

As Moses began his exposition of the laws and rights instituted for Israel by a reference to the sanctuary as the place which the Lord should choose, and the place where religious service was to be rendered (ch. xii.), so here he follows up his address by a reference to the same. Of the gifts which had to be presented at the sanctuary there were two specially connected with the social and domestic life of the people, viz. the firstfruits and the second tithe. To these, by a natural transition from the preceding discourse—occupied as that is with injunctions regarding their social and domestic relations—Moses here refers for the purpose of prescribing certain liturgical forms with which the presentation of the gift was to be accompanied by the offerer.

Vers. 1—11.—Of the firstfruits the Israelite was to take a portion, and placing it in a basket, to bring it to the place of the sanctuary, where it was to be received by the attendant priest. The offerer was to accompany his presentation with the declaration, " I profess this day unto the Lord thy God, that I am come unto the country which the Lord sware unto our fathers for to give us ; " and the priest having set the basket down before the altar, the offerer was to make confession and prayer, gratefully acknowledging the Divine favour showed to Israel in choosing them to be a great nation, in delivering them out of Egypt, and bringing them into a rich and fertile land ; and along with this his bounty to the individual who now presented the firstfruits of his land unto the Lord.

Ver. 2.—**The first of all the fruit of the earth.** (On the law of the firstfruits, see Numb. xviii. 12 ; ch. xviii. 4.) A basket; טֶנֶא, a basket of wickerwork.

Ver. 3.—**The priest that shall be in those days**; not the high priest, but the priests collectively, or the individual priest whose function it was to officiate on the occasion. The fruit presented was the sensible proof that the land was now in their possession, and the confession made along with the presentation was an acknowledgment of their unworthiness, and of the Divine favour as that to which alone they were indebted for the privileged position in which they were placed.

Ver. 5.—**A Syrian ready to perish was my father.** The reference is to Jacob, the stem-father of the twelve tribes. He is here called a Syrian, or Aramæan, because of his long residence in Mesopotamia (Gen. xxix.—xxxi.), whence Abraham had originally come (Gen. xi. 31), and because there the family of which he was the head was founded. The translation "ready to perish" fairly represents the Hebrew; the verb אָבַד means not merely to stray or wander, but also to lose one's self, to perish, to be in danger of perishing (cf. ch. iv. 26; Job xxix. 13; Prov. xxxi. 6, etc.). Different renderings of this clause have been given. The Targum, Vulgate, Luther, etc., have, "The Aramæan (i.e. Laban) oppressed my father;" The LXX., Συρίαν ἀπέλιπεν ὁ πατήρ μου ("My father left Syria"); others, "To the Aramæan my father wandered." But these either follow another reading than that of the received text, or they are expedients to soften down the apparent ignominy of the description. The probable allusion to the wandering, nomadic life of the patriarch, however, is not to be lost sight of. **With a few**; literally, *in men of few;* i.e. consisting of few men, as a small company; the father and head of the tribe is named for those belonging to him (cf. Gen. xxxiv. 30; xlvi. 27). **A great nation,** etc. (cf. Exod. i. 7, 9).

Ver. 6.—**The Egyptians evil entreated us** (cf. Exod. i. 11—22; ii. 23, etc.).

Ver. 8.—(Cf. ch. iv. 34.)

Ver. 10.—**Thou shalt set it,** etc.; either a general concluding remark, taking up the statement of ver. 4, or the offerer may have resumed hold of the basket, and after holding it in his hand while offering prayer, would solemnly deposit it before the altar.

Ver. 11.—**And thou shalt rejoice in every good** thing, etc.; *i.e.* with these bounties of God's providence make a feast for yourself and your household, and omit not to invite the Levite and the stranger to partake of it with you. As with the yearly tithe (ch. xiv. 23) and the firstlings (ch. xv. 20), so with this portion of the firstfruits, a festive meal was to consummate the service. According to the Law, the firstfruits were the perquisite of the priest (ch. xviii. 4; Numb.

xviii. 12, etc.); but of these a portion was to be taken for this special service, and of that a feast was to be made.

Vers. 12—15.—On the occasion of presenting the tithes, a special service was also to be made. The tithe here referred to is the vegetable or predial tithe, which, at the end of each third year, as here prescribed, was to be converted into a gift to the poor and needy. This, properly the second tithe (LXX., τὸ δεύτερον ἐπιδέκατον), but usually called the third tithe (Tobit i. 7, 8; Josephus, 'Antiq.,' iv. 8, 22), is quite distinct from the Levitical tithe prescribed in Lev. xxvii. 30—33 and Numb. xviii. 21—32; and it is a mistake to suppose that the law here was designed to contravene or supersede that in the earlier books (see Kitto, 'Bibl. Cycl.,' iii. 1010). As this tithe completed the triennial series of tithes which the Israelites had to offer, it was fitting that in presenting it a solemn declaration should be made by the offerer to the effect that he had honourably and conscientiously discharged all the obligations in this respect which the Law laid upon him.

Ver. 12.—**The third year,** which is the **year of tithing.** As each week ended with a sabbath, so a sabbatical year ended each cycle or week of years; and as on it no tithes were levied, "the year of tithing" here specified would be the third and the sixth years in each septennial period.

Ver. 13.—**Say before the Lord;** *i.e.* address him as present and ready to hear. The expression, "before the Lord," does not necessarily imply that it was in the sanctuary that the prayer was to be offered. Isaac proposed to bless his son "before the Lord," *i.e.* within his own house or tent (Gen. xxvii. 7); and so the Israelite here might in his own home make his prayer to the Omnipresent Jehovah. **I have not transgressed thy commandments,** etc. This is not a self-righteous boast; it is rather a solemn profession of attention to duties which might have been neglected, and refers, not to the keeping of every commandment, but to the having faithfully done all that the Law required in respect of tithes.

Ver. 14.—**In my mourning;** *i.e.* while ceremonially unclean (cf. Lev. vii. 20; xxi. 1, etc.). **Neither have I taken away** ought **thereof for** any **unclean** use; rather, *Neither have I removed ought of it being unclean;* i.e. he had not only not eaten of it, but he had not removed any part of it from his house (ver. 13) while he was ceremonially unclean, in which state it was unlawful to touch what was hallowed (Lev. xxii. 23). **Nor given** ought **thereof for the dead**; *i.e.* on account of the dead; he had not sent any part of it to where there was one dead, according to the custom for friends and relations to send to a house of mourning provisions for the mourners (2 Sam. iii. 35; Jer. xvi. 7; Hos. ix. 4; Tobit iv. 17). Or the reference may be here to the expenses incurred by the death of one for whose funeral the individual had to provide. This view is adopted by Dr. Thomson, who, re-marking on this passage, says, " This was the strongest possible protestation that he had dealt faithfully in the matter of tithing and consecrated things and in charities to the poor. He had not allowed himself to divert anything to other uses, not even by the most pressing and unforeseen emergen-cies. It is here assumed, or rather implied, that times of mourning for the dead were expensive, and also that the stern law of custom obliged the bereaved to defray those expenses, however onerous. . . . The temptation, therefore, to devote a part of the tithes, hallowed things, and charities to defray these enormous, unforeseen, and providential expenses would be very urgent, and he who stood faithful at such times might safely be trusted on all other occa-sions " (' Land and the Book,' i. 149). The LXX. rendering, τῷ τεθνήκοτι, " to the dead," has led some to suppose that the reference here is to the placing of articles of food in the tomb along with the corpse; but though this custom prevailed among the Jews in later times, as well as among other peoples, there is no ground for supposing it to be referred to here. As all connected with a dead body was held to be unclean, as well as the body itself, a house of mourning with its inhabit-ants was held to be unclean, and into it, therefore, nothing that had been hallowed might be lawfully carried.

Ver. 15.—(Cf. Isa. lxiii. 15; lxvi. 1.)

Vers. 16—19.—Moses winds up his address by a solemn admonition to the people to keep and observe the laws and command-ments which the Lord by him had laid upon them, reminding them that they had entered into covenant with God, and had thereby pledged themselves to obedience to all that he had enjoined, as he on his part had pledged himself to be their Benefactor, who would fulfil to them all his gracious promises, and would exalt them above all the nations of the earth.

Ver. 16.—**This day.** This refers gene-rally to the time when this discourse was delivered.

Ver. 17.—**Thou hast avouched,** etc.; lite-rally, *Thou hast caused Jehovah this day to say to be a God unto thee;* i.e. thou hast given occasion to him to declare himself to be thy God, and (as a consequence of this) that thou shouldest walk in his ways and keep his commandments. In declaring that he was their God, he virtually declared also that they were to be wholly obedient to him.

Ver. 18.—So, on the other hand, God had given Israel occasion to say that they were his special people, his treasured pos-session (cf. Exod. xix. 5, 6), whose it was, as such, to keep all his commandments, and to whom he would be faithful to fulfil all that he had promised.

Ver. 19.—(Cf. Jer. xiii. 11; xxxiii. 9; Zeph. iii. 19, 20.) **An holy people** (cf. Exod. xix. 5, 6). " The sanctification of Israel was the design and end of its election of God, and would be accomplished in the glory to which the people of God were to be exalted " (Keil).

HOMILETICS.

Vers. 1—11.—*Joy in the use of temporal mercies; or, sanctification of our possessions to God warrants a holy joy in the use of them.* The order of thought is this: 1. In due time Israel would be in possession of the land which the Lord promised to give them. 2. Of this comfortable possession the gathering of the fruits thereof would be the proof and sign. 3. In accordance with a well-understood law, the firstfruits were to be offered to God (see reference). 4. In thus offering the firstfruits, the offerers were to go up to the house of the Lord, and present them to the priest, who was to lay them before the altar as offerings to the Lord. 5. This being done, there was to be an oral avowal of Divine mercy in pitying " the perishing Aramæan " from whom they were descended, in watching over the growth of their nation, in delivering them from Egypt, in giving them the good land, and in permitting it to yield them its fruit. 6. This being done, they could then rejoice before the Lord their God in the sacrificial meal which followed, in the companionship of friends invited to share with them the joy of harvest, and in the after use of the bounties of God's providence. For they would be doubly blessed, as, over and above the temporal mercies themselves, they would share the benediction of him who gave them all things richly to enjoy. Good Bishop Wordsworth remarks that this passage exhorts to harvest thanksgivings in the Christian Church. Such services are undoubtedly fully in harmony with the spirit of the chapter. But it seems to us to contain principles of far wider scope, and of everyday application. They are four in number.

I. OUR GOD WOULD HAVE US RECOGNIZE HIM AS THE AUTHOR OF ALL OUR MERCIES. For such he is. Without him no land would yield its increase, nor would man have power or skill to cultivate the soil. Without him no sun would shine nor rain descend. It is easy to say that such and such a harvest came in the ordinary course of law. We at once press the questions, Who ordained these laws? Who causes forces to act according to them? For no law ever did or could make itself. "Law" is a purely mental conception. It is not an entity, save as mind ordains it, and it only operates as energy works by it. It is unsound in philosophy, as well as rotten in piety, if we fail to acknowledge God in all. Nor is it bare power that we have to recognize; but goodness, mercy, loving-kindness. And all these kindnesses of God he would have us acknowledge: 1. By a confession of our entire dependence upon him. 2. By grateful retrospect of the past; remembering and recalling through what scenes God has brought us year by year. 3. By grateful survey of the blessings which are around us now. Nor should we ever leave out of account that which is the substratum of this chapter (and indeed of all the chapters in this book), though not here specified in words, viz. that, as sinful beings, our natural claims on the Great Being as his dependent creatures have been forfeited by sin, and that the continuance to sinful beings of such heaps of mercy is due only to, and is indeed a part of, that redemptive grace which to Israel was disclosed in germ, but to us in its fulness through Jesus Christ our Lord. Such thanksgivings as we owe may well even now be offered in the house of the Lord; but they should daily be the promptings of grateful and devoted hearts. In private and in the family circle our song should be, "What shall we render to the Lord for all his benefits toward us?"

II. THE THANK OFFERING SHOULD NOT ONLY BE VERBAL BUT PRACTICAL. There was to be the offering of the firstfruits to the Lord (see Homily, ch. xiv. 22—29). When God gave all, what precept could be more appropriate? What can be more becoming than to let God have the first of everything? This is the principle which ran through these varied regulations as to firstfruits and tithe. Jacob spontaneously said, "Of all that thou givest me, I will surely give the tenth unto thee." Solomon urges, "Honour the Lord with thy substance, and with the firstfruits of all thine increase." We have no distinctive proportion laid down in the New Testament as to our offerings to God. Yet the conscientious Christian should require no further hints than such as are found in 2 Cor. viii. 7—9; 1 Cor. xvi. 2. Circumstances have changed. Details will vary. Yet the great and mighty cause of God, even that of righteousness, truth, and love, has to be maintained and spread in the world by the efforts and offerings of those "put in trust with the gospel." And it will not be possible to be faithful to the claims of God and the demands of the times without a conscientious, systematic, proportionate giving of our gains to the Lord. Christians should never suffer the absence of detail in New Testament precepts on the subject of giving to the Lord, to be taken advantage of to the weakening of his cause who trusts our spontaneity. Let us not abuse God's confidence. Let the love of Christ constrain us.

III. THE GIVING OF THE FIRSTFRUITS TO GOD IS A TOKEN OF THE SANCTIFICATION OF ALL WE HAVE TO RIGHT AND HOLY USES. There is no better guarantee of a wise and right use of our substance than the conscientious dedication of firstfruits to our God. He who is conscientious enough in this respect may be safely relied on to spend rightly the rest of his gains, because the same conscientiousness which marks his first spendings will mark all the others.

IV. WHEN OUR GAINS ARE THUS RECEIVED IN A RIGHT SPIRIT, AND SPENT IN A RIGHT WAY, WE MAY REJOICE THEREIN BEFORE THE LORD. God hath given us "all things richly to enjoy." And men who know nothing of the Christian consecration of all things to God do not know how to enjoy what they possess. If men rejoice in earthly good for its own sake, it will soon cease to yield delight. "The world passeth away, *and the lust thereof.*" But when regarded, received, and spent in the way we have already pointed out, it may yield a pure delight. For: 1. It will be enjoyed, as the gift of One who is our redeeming God, in covenant relation to us, and with whom we are at peace. 2. It will be enjoyed with a sense of *rectitude* which only those can have who have been severely right in the regulation of their gettings and givings. 3. It will be enjoyed, because gains so acquired and spent will be a means of grace to a man. Riches in such a case will expand the heart. 4. It will be enjoyed, because such a man will bear about with him the holy and blessed consciousness that he is fulfilling God's will and spreading God's cause in the right use of his gifts. 5. It will be enjoyed, because such a one knows that God's blessing is resting on him and on all he has, that, rich as may be his earthly good, though he enjoys it while it lasts, yet he can afford to hold it with a loose hand, for it is not his all, and that when he is called to part with it, he will find richer treasure still laid up for him in heaven, for when " flesh and heart fail, God will be the strength of his heart, and his portion for ever."

Thus and thus alone is it possible to extract from earthly good the full delight it is calculated and intended to yield. If we make worldly possessions the food of our souls, they will turn to ashes in the mouth. They bring no blessing with them. They will disappoint, and if they take their flight, as they so often do, we shall be left miserably poor. But if through the grace and Spirit of our God we are led first to choose God as our *all*, and then to use our all for God, we shall enjoy the life that now is, and enter on a fulness of joy in that which is to come.

Vers. 12—15.—*Integrity in the will a condition of acceptable and successful prayer.* We do not recall any passage in this book, on which we have as yet touched, that conveys a more striking impression than this of the purity and heart-searchingness of the Law of God. For elucidation of the several points of detail, the reader may consult the expository section. For our purpose now it is enough to say that it is assumed that the people will faithfully carry out the precepts and ordinances of God with regard to the tithes, to the offerings, to the poor, the fatherless, and widow, and the specific injunctions with respect to ceremonial purity. When this is done, *so that they can declare it before the Lord*,[1] then they may also plead with God for a blessing. They, having, with a clear conscience and an upright will, fulfilled to the extent of their knowledge the requirements of their holy religion, may then come and entreat their God for his benediction and smile, according to his promise. Hence we have presented to us for homiletic teaching the all-important topic—*Integrity in the fulfilment of Divine commands a condition of acceptable prayer.* We propose to show how constantly this principle is recognized in the Word of God, by a comparison of Scripture with Scripture.

Prayer is an inestimable privilege. That weak and sinful man should be permitted to unburden his spirit to the Father of spirits is a mercy so great, that no words can adequately express it. It is only on the ground of the One Sacrifice of Christ, of which the Hebrew sacrifices were but foreshadowings, that such fellowship between God and sinful man is vouchsafed. We may pray, because we "are not under Law, but under grace." But though through the aboundings of mercy sinful men are permitted to pray, yet it is on the understanding that they repent of their sin. And true though it be that we are under grace and not under Law, yet grace brings with it its own law; it is no licence to lawlessness. Throughout the Word of God this precious privilege is guarded from abuse. Prayer is not thrown open promiscuously. The shriek of a terrified man or the query of an inquisitive man is not prayer. "The fear of the wicked, it shall come upon him; but the desire of the righteous shall be granted." "The sacrifice of the wicked is an abomination to the Lord; but the prayer of the upright is his delight." Let us trace the recognition of this chronologically.

I. JOB KNEW OF IT. He asks in xxvii. 9, concerning a hypocrite, "Will God hear his cry when trouble cometh upon him?"

II. DAVID TEACHES IT LIKEWISE. In Ps. lxvi. 18, "If I regard iniquity in my heart, the Lord will not hear me." He expects no answer to his prayer if in his inmost soul there is any tolerance of sin.

III. SOLOMON INDICATES THIS TRUTH. In the prayer at the dedication of the temple,

---

[1] See Keil on this phrase in ver. 13.

1 Kings viii. 35, 36, " If they pray towards this place, and confess thy Name, *and turn from their sin* . . . then hear thou," etc.   In the Book of Proverbs the same truth is repeatedly taught (xi. 20; xv. 8, 29; xxi. 13, 27).   True penitence and integrity of will are necessary conditions of appropriate prayer.

IV. ISAIAH IS BIDDEN TO PROCLAIM IT.   In i. 18, there are words of priceless worth, which may well be a comfort to every penitent; but they are often quoted without sufficient prominence being given to the words which precede : " Wash you, make you clean; put away the evil of your doings from before mine eyes; cease to do evil; learn to do well," etc.; *then* follow the words, " Come now, and let us reason together," etc. Past sin is forgiven when it is forsaken, and only then.

V. EZEKIEL DECLARES THE SAME.   There came to him certain of the elders of Israel, and stood before him to inquire of the Lord (see xiv. 1—11).   Ezekiel is bidden to tell them that it is useless to inquire of God if they were cherishing any hidden sin ; it would be a stumbling-block of iniquity, that would prevent any answer coming from God.   How grievously the disheartened Saul found this out ! (1 Sam. xxviii. 6.)

VI. MALACHI DECLARES THE LIKE LAW.   He tells the people that they have withholden the tithes from God, and that consequently God is withholding the blessing from them (iii. 1—12).   Thus in the varied ages of the Jewish Church this truth is uniformly taught, that cherished sin will block up the way of an answer to prayer.

VII. NOR IS THIS PRINCIPLE REPEALED UNDER THE NEW ECONOMY. Our Lord taught it.   See Matt. v. 23, 24, in which we are forbidden to present any offering to God while anger towards a brother is cherished in the heart.   In Matt. vi. 15, we are assured that he who forgives not is not forgiven.   In John xv. 7, 16, our Lord shows his disciples that the condition of their freedom and success in prayer is fruitful obedience.   The Apostle James also warns those to whom he is writing that the non-success of their prayer is owing to impurity in the will, and if they would that God should draw nigh to them, they must return unto him (Jas. iv. 3—8).

Possibly at this stage, or earlier, a difficulty may have suggested itself.   It may be said (cf. Luke xviii. 11, 12) in that passage the Pharisee, who had been most punctilious in his discharge of sundry obligations, and most austerely proper in his outward conduct, is yet rejected.   How is this?   The reply is threefold.   1. He did not pray at all.   Not one petition did he offer.   2. He thanked God *he was so good !*   As if there were any merit in simply doing one's duty, or any cause for self-gratulation.   3. He looked down with scorn on others.   He " exalted himself."   His spirit was wrong, though his observances might be right.   *Conscious rectitude of purpose, and self-complacency over performances, need never be confounded,* and only where they are so can this difficulty arise.   In conclusion—

1. While we thank God for permission to pray, let us ever guard the dignity of prayer.   2. The mournful thought ·is suggested, How many there are who seem to be doing what they can to make it useless for them to pray !   A man who tells lies over the counter cannot pray.   A man who bribes or who accepts a bribe cannot pray.   A man who forgives not, asks uselessly for forgiveness.   The only advice to be given to such is to repeat the apostolic demand, " Repent, therefore, of this thy wickedness, and pray."   3. How diligently should we, at times, search into our own hearts, to see if we are zealously putting away " the leaven of malice and wickedness"!   The possibility that any secret sin may be shutting off any answer to our prayers should make us cry fervently, " Search me, O God, and know my heart; try me, and know my thoughts; and see if there be any wicked way in me, and lead me in the way everlasting."   4. Let none rush to the opposite extreme.   Let none be disheartened at the stringency of the demands of God's grace; rather let the heart be unreservedly opened to God in gratitude for his holiness, and for his desire for the absolute purity of his people; rather let us be supremely solicitous to be " upright in heart."   It is not where there is a distressing consciousness of falling in execution below our desires and yearnings that prayer is blocked out.   Far from this.   But the desire to cherish sin, or the refusal to do *the whole* will of God, makes prayer itself useless and sinful, because the heart does not submit entirely to God.

Vers. 16—19.—*The golden chain.*   The end of the career of Moses was drawing nigh. Nothing could be more natural than that he should gather up all his powers to remind the people of their solemn vows, and to repeat in their hearing the sum and substance of that code which was to regulate their personal life, their religious service, and their judicial procedure. Having done this, he closes with a brief but very earnest appeal to the people's heart and conscience. In it there is much that has, primarily, an historical and local bearing, but the principles included therein have a far-reaching, a worldwide, a permanent significance. The phrases used here are reproduced by the Apostle Peter (1 Pet. ii.), and are applied by him to Christians. What Israel then was, locally and theoretically, believers are now spiritually. The words here uttered by Moses form a golden chain, which we will examine link by link. We may thus come to see that, notwithstanding the lapse of ages and the advance of the world, this golden chain is as real and as complete as ever. With God the first link begins; with God is the last. The chain is on this wise: God sends a Law; this Law is accepted by the people; so accepting the Law they are received in covenant; people loyal to God are elevated among men; they are thus for a praise and honour and glory;—and all this is according to the word of the Lord, "as he hath spoken." Thus that which goeth forth from his lips as a declaration cometh back to him as a fulfilment.

First link : HERE ARE COMMANDMENTS, STATUTES, AND JUDGMENTS APPOINTED BY GOD. From beginning to end this is the distinct declaration of Moses and the postulate of the Hebrew faith. That the Law *was* received from Sinai is, historically, as indisputable as that the battle of Waterloo was fought. That this Law was of God was the proclamation from the first; while our homiletic studies in this book have, we trust, deepened our conviction that from none but God could aught so holy with such a claim have proceeded, and that this commandment, which is holy and just and good, does disclose the exceeding sinfulness of sin in a way which could only have been done through one taught of him who is the Lord of consciences and souls. This effort to educate the people in righteousness was the most startling stride in morals which the world had ever known. It was then, and remains still, the only attempt ever made to start into being a new nation with God alone for its acknowledged King, righteousness alone for the corner-stone of its polity, and a free and holy brotherhood alone for its citizenship. In reference to worship, there was the revealed law of sacrifice as the ground of acceptance. In regard to life, the rule was, "Love to God and love to man." It is precisely so now. Just as beneath the Law there lay unrepealed the Divine Abrahamic promise, so along with the gospel there is the rule unrepealed, "Be ye holy, for I am holy." There was a gospel with the Law ; there is a law with the gospel.

Second link : THE PEOPLE HAD VOWED UNTO GOD THAT THEY WOULD OBEY HIS VOICE. (Ver. 17.) It is not noted, perhaps, with sufficient frequency and force how often, even amid the terror, thunder, and smoke of Sinai, the Lord threw the decision of this question upon the people's free consent. Not even their response in the moment of glad freedom and terrible awe was sufficient. God would not take the people by surprise nor fasten them unawares to an engagement they did not understand. They gave their assent, first to an oral inquiry, then to the Law when written in a book and read in their hearing, then to the covenant sealed with blood. So now. While, in one sense, God is Sovereign over us by a right none may dispute, yet there is another sovereignty to which he asks our willing, loving consent (Rom. xii. 1). He stoops to ask of us the love of our hearts.

Third link : THE COVENANT THUS ENTERED INTO BY LOVING CONSENT TO DIVINE SWAY IS DIVINELY RECIPROCATED. (Ver. 18.) "And the Lord hath avouched thee," etc. We must be careful, however, how we set this, or we shall obscure the gospel in the act of endeavouring to set forth its most priceless relations. We must not put the matter thus: "God loves us because we love him;"—that would be an entire reversal of the revealed order of things. But rather thus: "God loves first." When we respond to his love and are saved by it, he rejoices over us. The love of compassion becomes a love of complacency, and the Lord avouches us to be his "peculiar people." The Apostle Peter applies precisely this phrase to all believers (1 Pet. ii.). But, to an ordinary reader, the English phrase would not yield an approximation to its true meaning, which may be shown thus : the word *pecus*, cattle; *peculium*, property in cattle, private property, that which has been bought for one's self; and thus the phrase, "peculiar people," means a people whom God has secured as his own by purchase. Hence the New Testament phrases, "Ye are bought with a price," etc. God's satisfaction in man is complete only when man finds his home in God.

Fourth link : WHEN A MAN IS FOUND OF GOD, HE IS DESTINED FOR HONOUR AMONG MAN. (Vers. 18, 19.) "Then," says David, "shall I not be ashamed when I have respect unto all thy commandments." And whenever the citizens of a state are loyal and obedient to God, the state which is leavened by them will certainly rise to honour and renown.

Fifth link : SUCH A LIFE WILL BE FOR A PRAISE AND A NAME AND AN HONOUR. For whose? Certainly God's (cf. Isa. xliii. 1, 21). A holy man is the noblest work of God on earth. The life he lives among men is, in its way, a revelation of God, and reflects honour on him.

Sixth link : This glory, being thus brought to God through the power of holy lives, will be best confirmation of the origin, meaning, and power of the written Word. "As he hath spoken" (ver. 19). The Word regulates the life; the life confirms the Word.

Note—Christian people have the vindication of the faith in their own hands. Argument may do much, but holiness will do very far more.

HOMILIES BY VARIOUS AUTHORS.

Vers. 1—11.—*The presentation of the firstfruits.* This interesting ceremony : 1. Reminded the individual that the land and its fruits were God's. 2. Required from him a devout acknowledgment of the fact, with a gift in which the acknowledgment was suitably embodied. 3. Threw him back on the recollection of God's former mercies to his nation. 4. Secured a confession and rehearsal of these from his own lips. It served : 1. To create and deepen religious feeling. 2. To quicken gratitude. 3. To encourage free-will offerings. Two main points—

I. GOD'S MERCIES ARE TO BE GRATEFULLY REMEMBERED. These mercies are many and wonderful (Ps. xl. 5). The points dwelt on in this declaration are God's fulfilments of his promises in the increase of the nation (ver. 5), the deliverance from Egypt (vers. 6—8), and the bringing of the people into the land of Canaan (ver. 9), part of the firstfruits of which the worshipper now presented (ver. 10). We have here : 1. *National* mercies. Since in Israel Church and nation were one : 2. *Church* mercies. 3. *Personal* mercies. A similar review befits every Christian. What causes of thankfulness has he, not only in the remembrance of God's loving-kindness to him personally (Ps. xl. 1—4; cxvi. 1—19), but in the review of God's dealings with his nation, and still more in the consideration of his mercies to the Church! On the one side, our noble constitution, our just laws, our civil and religious liberties, our immunity from war—the fruits of long centuries of struggle and progress. On the other side, the facts on which the Church's existence is founded—the Incarnation; Christ's life, death, resurrection, and ascension; the gift of the Spirit: and the events of her extraordinary history—the progress she has made, God's goodness in preserving and protecting her, in raising up teachers and leaders, in purifying her by persecutions, in granting revivals, times of reformation, etc.; with the consideration of how in all promises have been fulfilled, prayers answered, deliverances vouchsafed, blessings bestowed, increase made.

II. GOD'S MERCIES ARE TO BE SUITABLY ACKNOWLEDGED. 1. *By recital of them before God himself.* Acknowledgment of mercies is as much a part of devotion as praise, confession, petition, or even adoration. The value of liturgical forms (within due limits) for purposes of prayer and acknowledgment, is not to be disputed. They (1) aid memory, (2) secure comprehensiveness, (3) guide devotion, (4) prevent irrelevancy, (5) create a bond of unity. Like hymns, they testify to the Church's catholicity amidst diversities of creed and polity. Their disadvantage, if preponderant in worship, is that they check too much the element of spontaneity. They discourage freedom and naturalness in the expression of the heart's feelings. The best form of Church order would probably be a combination of the liturgical with the free and spontaneous elements in worship—the latter decidedly predominating. 2. *By free-will offerings.* These are needed more than ever. The sphere of the Church's operations is yearly widening. 3. *By hospitality and charity* (ver. 11). Underlying all there is, of course, to be personal consecration in heart and life. It is *self* God wants—the love, reverence, service, devotion of self; not a mere share in self's possessions. Confession (ver. 3), gifts (ver. 10), worship (ver. 10), joy (ver. 11), have their rightful place after that, and as the outcome of it.—J. O.

Ver. 12.—*The year of tithing.* Why so called? A double tithe was taken each year—the ordinary Levitical tithe (Numb. xviii. 21—28), which Deuteronomy, without mention, takes for granted; and the festal tithe, ordained as a provision for the sanctuary feasts (ch. xiv. 21—27). On the third year a tithe was to be devoted to festivities at home (ch. xiv. 28, 29). It is usually, but too hastily, assumed that this third tithe was but the second diversely applied. That in itself is unlikely, as the feasts at the sanctuary required to be held on the third and sixth years, as well as on the others, and the provision for these could not well be dispensed with. Neither does it explain the expression, "year of tithing;" for while, on this supposition, the tithe was differently applied, there was nothing unusual in the manner of taking it. Each year was a year of tithing (sabbatical years excepted), and this no more than the rest. The ordinary view, besides, is directly in the teeth of the testimony of Josephus, who may be supposed to have known the practice of his time. His statement distinctly is that one-tenth was to be given to the priests and Levites; one-tenth was to be applied to feasts at the sanctuary; and a tenth besides was, every third year, to be given to the poor. If this was so, we have a natural explanation of the phrase, "the year of tithing," and self-consistency is introduced into the laws. The tithe-laws in Deuteronomy are often represented as if in conflict with those in Leviticus and Numbers. Part of the plausibility of the objection lies in the use of the definite article in the English version—"all *the* tithe" (ch. xiv. 28; xxvi. 12)—which gives an impression of allusion to the *ordinary*, the *well-known* tithe. That impression is not created if we take the plain Hebrew—"a whole tithe"—which by its very nakedness suggests a new regulation. Deuteronomy legislates for its own purposes in connection with the centralizing of the worship at the sanctuary. The newer criticism seems to have abandoned the old ground, which made the Levitical laws the earliest. It assumes that the distinction of priests and Levites, with the body of legislation based on that distinction, took shape not earlier than the exile—a view hopelessly in conflict with the histories of the return. Indeed, so great was the disproportion in the numbers of priests and Levites returning with Zerubbabel—twelve or thirteen priests for every Levite—that the Levitical laws could only have been put in force with material alterations and modifications. They are in some respects singularly inapplicable to the very times in which they are supposed to have originated.—J. O.

Vers. 12—15.—"*A good conscience toward God.*" This solemn avowal, ordained to be made at the completion of the round of tithe obligations, was a wise safeguard against unpunctuality and neglect. The subject suggested is—*The importance of self-examination in respect of the fulfilment of duties of religion.*
I. SELF-EXAMINATION A DUTY. The text suggests that we examine ourselves: 1. As to religious givings. 2. As to our fulfilment of the duties of hospitality and charity. 3. As to the condition in which these duties have been performed—whether from the right motive (regard to God's commandment), and in a right state (the state of sanctification). Extend the principle to all duties of religion. Self-examination, to be of service, should be: 1. *Comprehensive.* 2. *Conscientious*—as "before the Lord thy God" (ver. 13), who cannot be deceived. 3. *Periodical,* as: (1) At the end of a year. (2) The close of a *financial* year. (3) Birthdays. (4) Even the end of a week. A review of this kind not an unsuitable sabbath day's employment.
II. SELF-EXAMINATION A SAFEGUARD. 1. *Prevents neglect.* Things which we ought to do—which, at bottom, we are willing to do—get frequently overlooked: (1) From inadvertency. (2) From unpunctuality. (3) From habits of procrastination. A review of the kind proposed would bring many of these forgotten duties to recollection, and would act as a check on the causes of forgetfulness. 2. *Brings practice into comparison with the standard of obligation.* When duty is known, it does not follow that it is always done, or that we are always aware of the extent of our shortcomings. We may be greatly deceiving ourselves in this very particular. There may grow upon us the vicious habit of comparing ourselves with others rather than with the standard of the Divine Law. And nowhere is self-deception more common than

in the matter of religious and charitable givings. People will be heard expatiating on the vexatiousness of the calls of this kind made on them, who, were they to put their givings all together, would find that they did not amount to so much as they have often spent on the gratification of some whim, perhaps on a single dinner-party. Self-examination would counteract the tendency to take our performances of duty so readily for granted. It would *e.g.* require the rich man to measure his givings directly with his income, and with the proportion of that income which he felt to be due to God. 3. *Reminds us of the obligations themselves.* For, besides the shortcomings in practice referred to, there is often no little danger that the standard of duty itself may get to be lost sight of. 4. *Makes hypocrisy more difficult.* The withholder of the tithes would scarcely venture to stand before God and make this solemn declaration. His tongue might well cleave to the roof of his mouth if he attempted it. He would feel that he must either go and do what he ought or hold his peace. The hypocritical professor shuns self-examination. Two thoughts in closing: 1. We cannot expect blessing, save as duties are honourably fulfilled (ver. 15). 2. Reflecting on fulfilled duties, we need to beware of Pharisaic pride (Luke xviii. 11, 12).—J. O.

Vers. 16—19.—*Avouching extraordinary.* A wonderful sight! Israel and God exchanging pledges, plighting troth, "avouching" fidelity each to the other. The people, by the heed they had given to Moses' exposition of the Law, perhaps by signs made as he proceeded, had avouched their willingness to abide in the covenant. God, in turn, had renewed his promises and pledges towards them. The covenant thus renewed was the same in essentials as that made with believers.

I. COVENANT WITH GOD INVOLVES ENGAGEMENT TO OBEDIENCE. (Ver. 17.) It did so under the Law. It does so under the gospel. The gospel exhibits grace, and involves at the outset the reception of that grace. Nevertheless, obedience is required of us. It is the end of our redemption. We die with Christ that we may rise with him to newness of life (Rom. vi. 4). "New obedience" is the proof of true discipleship. Every real believer will seek to render it. It is a condition of ultimate salvation (Rom. ii. 6—12).

II. COVENANT WITH GOD INVOLVES A RELATION OF PECULIAR NEARNESS. (Ver. 18.) This is borne out by all Scripture. God chooses us, in Christ, to a relation of nearness so remarkable that it has no counterpart, save in the Son's relation to the Father (John xvii. 21). The saints are his peculiar treasure (1 Pet. ii. 9, 10). He is their "Shield," and their "exceeding Great Reward" (Gen. xv. 1). They are nearer to him than the angels—

> " Near, near, so near,
>   I cannot nearer be ;
> For in the person of his Son
>   I am as near as he."

III. COVENANT WITH GOD SECURES HIGH HONOUR AND BLESSEDNESS. (Ver. 19.) Great distinction was in store for Israel, should it prove obedient. God says he will make it high above all nations, "in praise, and in name, and in honour." Its honour would consist: 1. In the proud distinction of being God's people (ch. iv. 7). 2. In its high moral repute (ch. iv. 6). 3. In the material pre-eminence to which obedience would be certain to raise it (ch. vii. 12—16). Obedience, honour, blessedness, are three ideas ultimately inseparable. The "glory, honour, immortality" of heaven are for those who persevere in well-doing (Rom. ii. 7), for "an holy people." The honours in store for obedient Israel, great as they were, are not to be compared with the "exceeding and eternal weight of glory" now revealed as the inheritance of believers (2 Cor. iv. 17).—J. O.

Vers. 1—11.—*Commemorations of national deliverance.* An instinct in man impels him to dwell with pleasure on his national beginnings and growth; and, in cases where that beginning sprang out from a specific event, that event has been the subject of public commemoration year by year. Of this Rome is a conspicuous instance. But the Jews were designed to be eminently a religious people; hence this commemoration was to be a simple act of piety—the presentation of firstfruits.

I. MAN IS THE OBJECT OF GOD'S LAVISH GENEROSITY. Everything round the Hebrew in his home reminded him of the exuberant kindness of his God. The land which he possessed was land which Jehovah had given him. The temple was the place which Jehovah had chosen "to place his Name there." The priest was God's gift. The corn and fruit of the land were produce "which the Lord thy God giveth thee." Each man was taught to look on himself as belonging unto God. Of everything the absolute Proprietor was God. Their history, their deliverance, their security, their renown, were all due to God. Behind every visible object, behind every visible event, they discerned God.

II. REMEMBRANCE OF GOD'S DELIVERANCES WAS TO BE PERPETUATED. It is vital to the interests of a man that he should know the "rock whence he was hewn, and the hole of the pit whence he was digged." Are we from above, or from beneath? Are we the creatures of fortuitous circumstance, or has our life been planned by a Divine Artificer? Are all the forces and energies of life within ourselves, or are we dependent upon the will and the resources of another? 1. It is salutary to remember our original. "A Syrian ready to perish was my father." It will serve to beget in us humility. It will make us hopeful; for if we have risen so much, may we not rise higher yet? 2. It is salutary to remember the oppressions of men. "The Egyptians evil entreated us." Poor, selfish, changeful man can never be relied upon. Friendly to-day, they turn to be bitterly hostile to-morrow. "Cease from man, whose breath is in his nostrils." 3. It is salutary to remember the efficacy of prayer. "We cried unto the Lord." His ear is always open to human solicitations. The affairs of this universe do not unfit him to attend to our need. True prayer is never in vain. 4. It is salutary to remember God's interpositions. "He looked. He brought us forth. He hath given us this land." The affliction was essential to fitness for Canaan. Winter is essential to the fruitfulness of spring. When God begins to bless us, what limit shall there be? What? Only that which our incapacity to receive may impose! Being redeemed, our expectations are infinite.

III. GRATITUDE FOR GOD'S GIFTS MUST BE PRACTICAL. Words of thankfulness are cheap, unless accompanied by deeds. Songs of praise are sweet minstrelsy in the ear of God, but they must spring from the heart; and if the heart is grateful, the hands will be full of offerings. The firstfruits of all our increase belong to God as a matter of right. But duty is delight. This requirement is representative. We may not be husbandmen; still our firstfruits are due. The firstfruits of our time belong to God— the fresh dewy hours of every day. The first of our gains belong to God. Say not, "They are mine." Nay! they are *his*. The firstfruits of mental strength—our youth; the best of all we have belong to him. To secularize these is sacrilege.

IV. THROUGH ALL GOD'S GIFTS HIS INTENTION IS HUMAN GLADNESS. This gladness is fostered and fed by proportionate offerings. For this habit of religious offering will serve to draw away our confidence from our material possessions, and place it in the living God. This will strengthen and establish joy. It is surely better to trust the Fount than the channel—the Source than the stream. If every man on earth is not brimful of joy, it is not God's fault. To rejoice in God is our duty and our privilege. And this joy is contagious. "Thou shalt rejoice, . . . thou, and the Levite, and the stranger that is among you." Joy makes men generous, and the recipients of our generosity will share our joy. There will be joyous action and reaction. We are to be the channels through which God will pour his joy into others' hearts. In return they will give us their prayers.—D.

Vers. 12—15.—*Complete consecration a condition of continued blessing.* The system of social dependence is ordained of God. By a deliberate act of wisdom, God devoted the Levites to poverty, or rather to an equitable interest in the whole land. The necessities of some are created as the most fitting outlets for the charity of others.

I. MEN ARE APPOINTED TO BE GOD'S ALMONERS. Not more really does the sovereign of an empire employ persons of rank to be his stewards and almoners than God employs us. To expend upon ourselves the whole of our earthly possessions is sin—is the worst of sins—is sacrilege. We hold in our keeping God's property. We are not at liberty to use it as we please. Nor is the amount which appertains to God determined by the caprice of human inclination. A definite portion is God's, and becomes in the highest sense trust property. One-tenth of all our gains is the fixed proportion claimed by God. God identifies himself with the Levite, the widow, the fatherless. The Levites are his messengers. The poor are his friends. To deny them is to wrong him; and he will surely avenge the insult. On stated occasions, viz. triennially, each proprietor was required to render an account of his stewardship, and to make a solemn declaration that he had faithfully discharged his momentous trust. As often as we supplicate new favours we virtually protest our faithfulness.

II. SURRENDER TO GOD A CONDITION OF SUCCESSFUL PRAYER. In this passage the Hebrews were taught not to ask for God's blessing upon their land until they had confessed their complete surrender to God's revealed will. Pride bars the door which keeps out Divine favours. Pride chokes the channels so that the stream of God's bounty cannot flow. In like manner God acts in our earthly life. He will not give health except through the channel of food. He will not give strength except through the channel of exercise. He will not allow us to use steam or electricity except by surrender to his material laws. We do not really pray so long as any part of our nature is rebellious against his will. Lip-prayer is counterfeit. Genuine prayer is the up-going of the whole man.

III. GOD'S SOLEMN PLEDGES ARE CONDITIONED BY EARNEST PRAYER. God had sworn to the patriarchs to give this goodly land to their seed, yet his oath implied trust, surrender, prayer, upon their part. Indeed, if these things had been wanting in the Hebrews, no external possession would have been a blessing: Canaan would have been a curse. Material light is no boon unless there be an organ of human vision to enjoy it—unless the eye be open. Nothing really benefits a man until it actually enters his nature and becomes a part of himself. This is God's efficient act. "Ask, and ye shall receive." For all things promised of God, "he will yet be inquired of." Prayer gives the final fitness to receive.—D.

Vers. 16—19.—*The spiritual creation.* In the creation of the material world, " God spake, and it was done." But in dealing with rebellious men, obedience does not spontaneously follow on command. God has called into existence a substance that cannot arbitrarily be controlled—a human will. Therefore, to gain loyal response from human nature, God makes known himself as infinitely worthy of man's regard, indicates his authority, and sets forth the high advantages of his friendship. The largest obedience is man's real interest. It is the only path to promotion.

I. WE HAVE HERE GOD'S REVELATION OF HIS KINGLY AUTHORITY. It is his part to command—man's to obey. We cannot reverse or disturb this order without introducing anarchy and sorrow. 1. This revelation of God is always new. " This day " thy God hath commanded thee afresh. New discoveries of the extent, the wisdom, the graciousness, of God's sovereignty may be made to us every day. Every morning the voice of heavenly authority speaks to us afresh. 2. The spirit of wise authority is very imperative. " Thou *shalt* keep and do." It would not be safe for God to abandon any part of his prerogative. It would not be safe to allow men to diminish his sovereignty. We are creatures: he is Creator; hence it is supremely fitting that he alone should rule. 3. His commands are irrevocable. They are well designated "statutes," *i.e.* things well established. In the material world men are discovering how fixed and uniform are all God's laws. No deviation is allowed. Nor is it tolerated in the spiritual realm, and every new-born man says, "I will keep thy statutes with my whole heart." 4. Obedience embraces the whole man. Outward and ostensible service does not satisfy God, because they will bring no blessing to his creature man. These commands are for man as a spiritual being; and mere external service is hypocrisy. No fragrance is in our obedience unless heart and soul go out in our deeds. Obedience, to have any worth with God, must be the efflorescence of our love.

II. WE HAVE HERE MAN'S WILLING ACCEPTANCE OF THE COVENANT. The Jews, as one man, chose God to be their King, and swore to be loyal subjects. " Thou hast avouched the Lord to be thy God." 1. It must be an act of personal choice. Whether we perceive it or not, our course in life is our own choice. We may never consciously have faced the question, nor put into words our decision; yet our life plainly shows that some decision has been made. Happy the man who, after due reflection, can calmly say, " The Lord is *my* God !" 2. The language indicates progressive obedience.

The loyal servant "*walks* in God's ways." He is not content with standing still. In proportion as he obeys, he sees more clearly the wisdom of the command—he finds more pleasure in loyal service. At first he obeyed because it was a plain duty; now he responds because it is a delight. "He loves the Law." 3. And hearty obedience brings clearer knowledge of our Master's will. Having learnt the wisdom and the pleasure of obedience, he is more eager to hearken to the Divine voice. His ears have been opened. He can hear the soft whispers of a voice which is unheard by others. He loves to hearken. "The secret of the Lord is with them that fear him."

III. WE HAVE HERE GOD'S GENEROUS PLEDGE OF LARGER GOOD. 1. Here is adoption. He solemnly avers them to be "his peculiar people." He gives them a special place in his regards. Before the intelligent universe he espouses them as his own. "He is not ashamed to call them brethren." All his power is pledged for their protection. All his possessions become theirs. 2. He gives them an obedient disposition. His blessing can reach the interior will. If we have made a general surrender of ourselves to him, he imparts gracious strength to every energy of our souls. In response to our desire he makes us willing. "I will pour out my Spirit upon them, and cause them to walk in my statutes, and they shall keep my judgments, and do them." When men have embraced his external and written covenant, then "he makes a new covenant, and writes it upon their hearts." First there is what is natural, afterward that which is spiritual. 3. Here are eminence and honour secured. "To make thee high above all nations." Real glory is God's gift to his chosen. False honour and glitter Satan scatters abundantly among his votaries; but these are superficial and ephemeral. Satan cannot give what he does not possess. All honour belongs to God; and the dignities and eminence and glory which are God's, he has chosen to share with his saints. "Where I am, there ye shall be also." 4. Man's crown of beauty is promised: "that thou mayest be holy." Purity is the perfection of humanity. For this our spirits thirst. No external honour or greatness will satisfy us if we are not internally holy. And the purpose of God in our redemption is "that we may be conformed unto the image of his Son." "Then shall I be satisfied, when I awake in thy likeness."—D.

Vers. 1—11.—*The dedication of the firstfruits.* A beautiful religious service is here associated with the dedication of the firstfruits. It was to be an act of worship. There was to be the appearance before the priest, the acknowledgment of God's great bounty to the forefathers as well as to the worshipper himself, the presentation of the firstfruits as a return of God's gifts to him, the setting of the basket before God, and the rejoicing in the Divine presence. All this is surely typical.

I. JESUS CHRIST IS THE PRIEST TO WHOM WE SHOULD BRING THE FIRSTFRUITS OF ALL OUR INCREASE. In other words, we should bring our systematic beneficence before Christ, and prayerfully deal with it before him. He is the Mediator for our liberality, as well as for every other blessing.

II. WE NEED CHRIST'S MERITS TO RENDER OUR LIBERALITY, AS WELL AS EVERY OTHER GRACE, FRAGRANT BEFORE GOD. For we should never forget that no single grace is really fit in its naked imperfection to be presented to God. It requires to be performed with the merits of our adorable High Priest. There should be no boasting about it, as if it could stand alone.

III. OUR LIBERALITY SHOULD BE THE OUTCOME OF OUR GRATITUDE FOR FAVOUR SHOWN TO THE FATHERS AS WELL AS TO OURSELVES. The Jew reviewed gratefully the national history, the Syrian origin, the Egyptian bondage, the Exodus, the entrance into Canaan, and the fruitfulness of the land of promise. All this history of God's goodness made the firstfruits simply the expression of gratitude.

It is on this grace that systematic beneficence is to be built. Nowhere else can a fitting foundation be found.

IV. OUR LIBERALITY SHOULD BE ASSOCIATED WITH AN ACT OF JOYFUL WORSHIP. In no other way can liberality be sustained. "On the first day of the week let every one of you lay by him in store, as God hath prospered him" (1 Cor. xvi. 2). Why on the first day of the week? Manifestly to associate the grace with the religious services of the resurrection day. No week-day liberality will last long—it requires a Lord's day, with all its holy associations and sanctions, to sustain the liberality of the people.

And this saves the spirit of liberality from the grudging that is so vexatious and so worldly. "The Lord loveth a cheerful giver," and so he draws the giver into his own presence, and makes him joyful there, that he may offer in his liberality a "sacrifice of joyfulness."

V. The joy reached through liberality is to be carried into the social circle, to make home truly happy. The Jew, after presenting his firstfruits, was to rejoice in every good gift of God, along with the Levite and stranger who formed part of his household. A cheerful giver is the secret of a happy home. His relations with his Lord being bright and beautiful, he brings the fragrance home.—R. M. E.

Vers. 12—19.—*Looking up for the blessing.* The interests of the dependent classes, "the Levite, the stranger, the fatherless, and the widow," being considered and secured by the tithing of the third year, the Jew was directed then to look up for the Divine blessing on the land. The tithe was first paid, and then the blessing sought.

I. Systematic beneficence should be the preliminary of supplication for blessing, and not conditioned upon it. There is a temptation to make liberality a matter of speculation, to vow a certain portion if a certain blessing is conferred. Now, this may be all very well regarding what is beyond a tithe, but the tithe is a settled proportion to be promptly and gratefully paid, and the blessing can then be honestly asked when the debt to God has been discharged.

II. The truly liberal will look for spiritual blessing for his country, and not be content with temporal. In fact, it was revival, as we should now call it, that the Jew after his tithing sought. And systematic beneficence should be regarded as the indispensable preliminary of revival, if Mal. iii. 10 has any meaning. It is manifest that illiberality may hinder spiritual blessing, and consequently liberality should be fostered as the manifest test of sincerity regarding blessing. If one is not willing to pay his share that every hindrance of blessing may be removed, he cannot be in earnest about it.

III. Moses, as the mediator, guarantees the covenant blessings to the covenant-keeping people. God had brought Israel out of Egypt, and was about to introduce them to the land of promise, that they might prove his "peculiar people," and be "high above all nations which he hath made, in praise, and in name, and in honour," and above all, be "an holy people." This was his covenant engagement. Hence Moses urges them to keep the commandments God has given them with all their heart and soul, and they shall find how faithful God is.

Obedience is consequently to be the manifestation of their faith in God as "Faithful Promiser." If he gave the blessings in all their fulness first, faith would have no room to grow, and his people would be able to live well enough by sight. But when they are asked to obey and be blessed in and through their obedience, faith has its beautiful sphere.—R. M. E.

PART III.

THIRD DISCOURSE OF MOSES. THE COVENANT RENEWED.

CHAPTER XXVII.—CHAPTER XXX.

EXPOSITION.

CHAPTER XXVII.

Instructions as to the Publishing of the Law in Canaan.

Having set forth the laws and rights of Israel with special reference to the settle-

ment of the people in Canaan, Moses proceeds to dwell more particularly on the sanctions by which obedience to the Divine institute was enforced. Before entering on these, however, he gives some instructions regarding the setting up and proclamation of the Law when they should have entered Canaan. These instructions Moses gives in conjunction with the elders of Israel, who are associated with him here, because on them would devolve the obligation to see to the fulfilment of what the Law enjoined after Moses had ceased to be the ruler and leader of the people.

Vers. 1—8.—The first instruction respects the setting up of pillars on which the Law was to be inscribed. Such a mode of publishing laws or edicts was common in ancient times. Pillars of stone or metal, on which laws were inscribed, are frequently mentioned by the classical writers. Lysias quotes a law from such a pillar in the Areopagus at Athens ('Eratosth.,' 31, 12); at Eleusis there were pillars on which laws were inscribed (Pollux, 10, 97); Plato speaks of pillars set up in the market-place, on which were laws for the regulation of traffic ('De Legg.,' xi. p. 916 E); and Polybius even uses the word "pillar" (στήλη) as synonymous with "law" or "conditions of treaty" ('Hist.,' xxiv. 4, 12; xxvi. 1, 4, etc. Comp. also Plato, 'Crit.,' p. 119 C, E; 120 A; Ps.-Demosth., p. 1370, 25; 1381, 10; Cicero, 'Cat.,' iii. 8; 'Phil.,' xiii. 3; 'Fam. Epp.,' xii. 1; Ovid, 'Met.,' i. 3).

Ver. 1.—All the commandments, etc.; all that up to this time I have enjoined upon you. The reference is to the entire Law as given by Moses.

Ver. 2.—On the day when ye shall pass over Jordan; i.e. at the time; "day" is here used in a wide sense (cf. Gen. ii. 4; Numb, iii. 1; 2 Sam. xxii. 1; Eccles. xii. 3; Isa. xi. 10, etc.). Thou shalt set thee up great stones, and plaister them with plaister. The stones, the number of which is not specified, were to be large, because much was to be inscribed upon them, and they were to be covered with a coating of lime or gypsum (שִׂיד), in order to secure a smooth white surface on which the inscription might be clearly depicted. That the words were not, as Michaelis, Rosenmüller, and others suppose, cut in the stone, and afterwards covered with plaster in order to preserve them, is plain from its being enjoined that they were to be written upon (עַל) the stones so prepared; and besides, as this was intended to be a proclamation of the Law, the main purpose of the erection would have been frustrated had the inscription been concealed by such a covering as that supposed. Among the ancient Egyptians the practice of depicting records on walls or monuments covered with a coating of plaster was common (see Hengstenberg, 'Authentie des Pent.,' i. 464, English translation, i. 433); from them, doubtless,

it was borrowed by the Hebrews. It has been suggested by Kennicott that the writing was to be in relievo, and that the spaces between the letters were filled up by the mortar or cement. This is possible, but it is not such a process as this that the words of the text suggest. "A careful examination of ch. xxvii. 4, 8, and Josh. viii. 30—22, will lead to the opinion that the Law was written upon or in the plaster with which these pillars were coated. This could easily be done, and such writing was common in ancient times. I have seen specimens of it certainly more than two thousand years old, and still as distinct as when they were first inscribed on the plaster" (Thomson, 'Land and the Book,' ii. p. 204).

Ver. 3.—All the words of this law; i.e. all the purely legislative parts of the Mosaic institute. By the "Law" here cannot be intended merely the blessings and the curses afterwards mentioned (vers. 14—26); nor is there any reason why this term should be restricted to the precepts of this Book of Deuteronomy, as if they only were to be inscribed on the stones: the term must be extended so as to cover all that Moses had at any time delivered to Israel as a law from God. It is not necessary, however, to suppose that all the reasons and exhortations with which the delivery of these, as recorded in the Pentateuch, was accompanied were to be inscribed along with the Law; still less that the historical details amidst which the record of these laws is embedded should be given. It may be questioned even whether each and all of the legislative enactments of the Torah, reckoned by the Jews to be 613, were to be recorded; for it might be deemed enough that the substance and essence of the Law should be thus presented. But even if the whole was to be inscribed, there would be no serious difficulty in the way of carrying this into effect, seeing there is no limitation as to the number of the stones to be set up.

Ver. 4.—The stones were to be set up on Mount Ebal (cf. ch. xi. 29). The Samaritan Codex and Version have Gerizim here, in place of Ebal; but though some critics have accepted this, it is generally regarded as an arbitrary alteration introduced to favour Samaritan pretensions (see the exhaustive and conclusive Dissertation of Gesenius, 'De Pentat. Samarit.'). All the ancient versions, as well as all the Hebrew manuscripts, support the received text.

Vers. 5—7.—Besides the monumental stones, an altar of whole stones, on which no tool had passed (cf. Exod. xx. 22) was to be erected, and burnt offerings and peace offerings were to be presented as at the establishment of the covenant at Sinai, followed by the statutory festive entertainment (cf. Exod. xxiv. 5).

Ver. 8.—The injunction to write the Law on the stones is repeated, with the addition that it was to be done **very plainly** (LXX., σαφῶς σφόδρα: Vulgate, *plane et lucide*), which shows that the main purpose of setting up the stones was that the Law might be easily known by the people (cf. Hab. ii. 2). The stones and the altar were fittingly placed on Ebal, the mount of cursing. For the setting up of the stones on which the Law was inscribed, and the building beside them of the altar, was the symbolical renewal of the covenant of God with Israel, and the establishment in Canaan of that dispensation which was "the ministration of condemnation and of death" (2 Cor. iii. 7, 9), and of that Law which, though in itself "holy, just, and good," can only, because of man's perversity and sinfulness, bring on those who are under it a curse (Gal. iii. 10).

Vers. 9, 10.—When Israel renewed the covenant with the Lord, by solemnly setting up the Law in Canaan, it became thereby the nation of God, and bound itself at the same time to hearken to the voice of the Lord, and keep his commandments, as it had already done (cf. ch. xxvi. 17, 18; Micah iv. 5).

Ver. 9.—**Take heed**; literally, *Be silent;* LXX., σιώπα, with silent attention listen (cf. Zech. ii. 13).

Vers. 11—14.—Having set up the Law and renewed the covenant in Canaan, Israel was to proclaim upon the land the blessing and the curse of the Law, as already commanded (see ch. xi. 29). For this purpose six tribes were to station themselves on Mount Gerizim, and six on Mount Ebal, the former to pronounce the blessing, the latter the curse. (On the situation of these two mountains, see at ch. xi. 29.) The six tribes by whom the blessing was to be pronounced were Simeon, Levi, Judah, Issachar, Joseph, and Benjamin, all descended from the two wives of Jacob—Leah and Rachel. The tribes by whom the curse was to be uttered were those descended from Zilpah, Leah's maid, viz. Gad and Asher; those descended from Bilhah, Rachel's maid, viz. Dan and Naphtali; with Zebulun and Reuben, both descended from Leah. As, in order to obtain a division of the tribes into two equal portions, two of the sons of Leah must be assigned to the second half, Zebulun and Reuben were chosen, probably because the former was the youngest of Leah's sons, and

the latter had by his sin forfeited his birthright (Gen. xlix. 4).

Ver. 13.—**These shall stand upon mount Ebal to curse**; literally, *These shall stand upon the curse on Mount Ebal;* i.e. it shall belong to them to utter the curse.

Ver. 14.—The Levites—standing probably in some convenient spot midway between the two mountains (cf. Josh. viii. 33)—were to pronounce with a loud voice the blessing and the curse, so that all might hear; and the people were to give their assent, and take to themselves, as it were, the blessing or the curse as uttered, by a solemn **Amen**. By the Levites here are intended, not the sons of Levi generally, but that portion of them which belonged to the priesthood, and bare the ark of the covenant (cf. Josh. viii. 33).

Vers. 15—26.—The curses to be pronounced were twelve in number, probably to correspond with the number of the tribes. The blessings are not here recorded; but when the injunction here given was fulfilled by Joshua, the blessing as well as the curse was pronounced (Josh. viii. 34). And probably, as the Jews report, each, the blessing and the curse, was pronounced alternately (Talmud Bab., 'Sotah,' c. 7; Targum Hieros., *in loc.*; Surenhus., 'Mishna,' iii. 262). It has sometimes been doubted whether any human voice could be audible over so wide a stretch as that between these two mountains; but this need be no longer matter of doubt, for the experiment has been repeatedly tried in recent times with success (Tristram, 'Land of Israel,' p. 150; Bonar, p. 371; Stanley, 'Syr. and Pal.,' p. 13). In the clear atmosphere of the East sounds travel far. It is to be borne in mind also that it was not a single voice that had to make itself heard across the valley on this occasion, but a chorus of voices proceeding from a body of priests stationed apparently in the midst between the two companies (cf. Josh. viii. 33), and chanting in unison the words of each blessing or curse.

Vers. 15—26.—Each of the first eleven curses is directed against some particular sin already denounced in the Law. The twelfth curse is directed generally against all breaches of the Law, against those who fail or refuse to set up the whole Law and follow it as the rule of life and conduct. This shows that the sins specially denounced are selected by way of specimen, and also, perhaps, because they are such as could for the most part be easily concealed from judicial inspection.

Ver. 15.—(Cf. Exod. xx. 4; Lev. xxvi. 1.)
Ver. 16.—(Cf. Exod. xxi. 17.)
Ver. 17.—(Cf. ch. xix. 14.)
Ver. 18.—(Cf. Lev. xix. 14.)
Ver. 19.—(Cf. ch. xxiv. 17.)
Ver. 20.—(Cf. Lev. xviii. 8; ch. xxii. 30.)

Ver. 21.—(Cf. Lev. xviii. 23; xx. 15.)
Vers. 22, 23.—(Cf. Lev. xviii. 9, 17.)
Ver. 24.—(Cf. Exod. xx. 13; Numb. xxxv 16, etc.)
Ver. 25.—(Cf. Exod. xxiii. 7, 8.)
Ver. 26.—(Cf. ch. xxviii. 15; Jer. xi. 3, 4.)

HOMILETICS.

Vers. 1—10.—" *Very plainly.*" These words, " very plainly," suggest three lines of thought.

I. THEY SHOW SOMETHING THAT WAS ORDERED TO BE, viz. that the Law of God was to be written very plainly, as the permanent, standard expression of right, to which the people might appeal. It was not to be left to a floating tradition. To no such risks would God expose his teaching. There was no priesthood in Israel which had any monopoly of knowledge. The words were to be so clearly and accurately recorded that, upon all that pertained to life and godliness, the people might see for themselves what the Lord had spoken, and not be dependent on any sacerdotal interpretation whatever. How clearly does this fact indicate the mind and will of Jehovah concerning our race! God would not have us walk uncertainly. He would have the way of life so plain, that the " wayfaring men, though fools," need not err therein.

II. THEY SHOW SOMETHING WHICH HAS BEEN. The injunction has been carried out, not only in the matter here specially referred to, but in God's later disclosures also. 1. In the books which Moses left behind him there was a revelation of the Divine mind and will so clear and distinct, that no one reading even the Pentateuch with a loyal faith need ever have been at a loss to know that the ground of his trust was the forgiving love of God, and that the duty of life was summed up in love to God and love to man. 2. Later teachings are given with equal, yea, with increasing clearness. (1) Those of the prophets. (2) Of our Lord. (3) Of the apostles. In all, the main teachings are given " very plainly." Note: The plainness of Scripture is not of that kind which men outgrow as they get older. Those very passages which charm childhood with their simplicity, do come to have a fuller and deeper meaning for the " old disciple."

III. THEY SUGGEST SOMETHING WHICH SHOULD BE. 1. Let us ever regard the Bible as a Book for the people, and let us insist on its being made the ultimate standard of appeal. 2. Let us use it as God meant us to use it, not as *a* book, but as *the* Book; not as man's, but as God's. 3. With such a Book before us, let us walk (1) intelligently, as if we understood the meaning of life; (2) thankfully, as if we apprehended the glory of life; (3) earnestly, as if we knew the solemnity of life; (4) hopefully, as those who are advancing towards the goal of life.

Vers. 11—26.—*A grand " Amen!"* It is more than possible that, with the strong disposition there is nowadays to look on Judaism as obsolete, the chapter before us may be very frequently passed over as if full of curses that no longer have any effect; especially as Paul, in Gal. iii., says, "Christ hath redeemed us from the curse of the Law." But we are apt, perhaps, in dealing with the doctrinal aspect of these curses of the Law, in reference to the Atonement, to lose sight of their primary historical aspect in reference to Israel. But the significance of both altar and pillar, pillar and altar, should be taken into account. Here, in the valley between Gerizim and Ebal, the grandest assembly met that was ever convened. The Law was read in the people's hearing, and the people were to declare themselves ready to brand sin with their curse, as God branded it with his. In a word, they were in a glorious league with the Great King of heaven and earth, that, whatever he disapproved, they would combine to brand with the infamy of eternal shame. As Israel was expected then to be in league with God in denouncing wrong, so are Christians expected by the holy cross to swear eternal war against sin. This may be worked out in seven consecutive lines of thought.

I. God's people now are a divinely chosen commonwealth.

II. In subjection to God alone, this commonwealth is a self-governing body.

III. The only law for life which they accept is that of righteousness—righteousness, of course, *all round*, both as regards God and man.

IV. It was for this very purpose Israel had been chosen out of the peoples that, for the world's sake, there might be one nation in which righteousness was the supreme law.

V. Side by side with the records of a Law which demands perfect righteousness, there is the altar and its sacrifice thereon, speaking to the people of a Divine provision for forgiving the penitent.

VI. The penitent is set free from the curse of Law, that he may ever after co-operate with God in honouring the Law from whose curse he has been redeemed.

VII. The passionate concern for holiness, and the delight in a holy Law, which are begotten in them who are of " the commonwealth of Israel," ensure their entire sympathy with God in the everlasting curse pronounced against all unrighteousness.

VIII. Thus the pure and just Law of God may serve believers as an educatory force throughout their whole life. And in their incessant hatred and condemnation of evil is the saying true in the highest sense, *Vox populi, vox Dei.*

HOMILIES BY VARIOUS AUTHORS.

Vers. 1—8.—*The stones on Ebal.* This chapter is significant, as letting in light on the design of the Law, and on the nature of the Jewish covenant. We see from it: 1. That the Law could not give life. 2. That it was not designed to give life. 3. That its real aim was to convince of sin, and so to shut men up to the faith that would afterwards be revealed (Gal. iii. 23). Three topics in these verses—

I. THE ERECTION OF THE STONES. (Vers. 2, 3.) Stones were to be set up, coated with plaster (a custom of Egypt), on which were to be written, " very plainly," " all the words of this Law " (ver. 8)—either the Law in Deuteronomy, or the Pentateuchal laws generally. The stones were: 1. Significant reminders of the tenure on which the land was held. 2. Witnesses against the people in case of disobedience. 3. A testimony to the plainness with which the Law had been made known to them. The last point reminds us of our own privilege in possessing a clear and full revelation of the will of God in the Bible. Copies of the Bible are like these stones, witnesses against us if we disobey the gospel. "Light has come into the world " (John iii. 19). We are not left to the natural conscience, sufficient though that be to convict men of sin (Rom. ii. 14, 15). We are servants who know our Lord's will (Luke xii. 47). We have the light both of Law and gospel. Supremely great are our privileges, and equally great are our responsibilities.

II. THE STONES ERECTED ON EBAL. (Ver. 4.) But why on Ebal? Why on the mount of cursing? Had there been a Law which could have given life, " verily," Paul says, " righteousness should have been by the Law " (Gal. iii. 21). In that case, the appropriate place for the erection of the stones would have been Gerizim—the mount of blessing. But the Law could not give life. In itself considered, as requiring perfect obedience, it could only condemn. Its principal function—its economic scope and purpose—was not to bless, but to give " knowledge of sin " (Rom. iii. 19, 20 ; vii. 9—14; Gal. iii.). Hence the appropriate place for the stones being planted was on the mount of cursing.

III. THE ACCOMPANYING SACRIFICES. (Vers. 5—7.) 1. As the Law testified to sin, so the sacrifices testified to grace—to the provision in mercy which lay within the covenant for the removal of guilt. Burnt offerings and peace offerings, as well as the sin offerings, included the idea of propitiation. This was shown at the first forming of the covenant by the action of sprinkling the blood (Exod. xxii. 6—8; cf. Heb. ix. 19—23). Without sacrifice, without the means of removing, or at least covering guilt, Israel's position under the Law would have been a mockery. 2. The altar of unhewn stones testifies to the subordinate place which art ought to have in the worship of God. There was a special suitableness in the altar of propitiation being built of undesecrated materials. Himself sinful, man's art would have polluted it. Only when propitiation had been made was art permitted to resume its function of ministering to the beauty of Divine service. But art, in religion, needs to be carefully guarded. It is false art when it drowns other thoughts in admiration of the finish, injuring worship by that which draws away the mind from worship. 3. The burnt offerings and peace offerings testified—the one to the entire consecration of heart and life which is the condition of acceptable service; the other, to the peace and fellowship with God which, on the ground of sacrifice, are attained through consecration and obedience.—J. O.

Vers. 9, 10.—*A people of God.* I. A PEOPLE BOUND TO GOD BY MANY TIES. Both by what God had done for them, and by the vows which, on different occasions, they had taken on themselves. They were his by covenant with the fathers. He had made them his by redemption from Egypt. He had covenanted with them at Sinai. The covenant being broken, he had, at Moses' intercession, graciously renewed it. He had kept covenant with the children, even when rejecting the fathers. Thirty-eight years he had led them in the wilderness, and once more had gathered them together, to hear them renew their vows of obedience. Which things are a figure. They remind us of the many bonds by which numbers of Christ's people are bound to his covenant. By redemption, by dedication of parents, by personal choice of the Saviour, by public profession, by repeated visits to his table, by special vows, etc.

II. A PEOPLE REAFFIRMED TO BE GOD'S BY RENEWAL OF COVENANT. We "become" the Lord's by revival and renewal of profession, as well as by original entrance into grace. As Christ's Sonship is from eternity, yet is dated from successive epochs—his birth (Luke i. 32, 35), his resurrection (Acts xiv. 33; Rom. i. 4)—so each new act of self-dedication, each new approach of God to the soul, each renewal of covenant, may be taken by the Christian as a new date from which to reckon his acceptance.

III. A PEOPLE UNDER WEIGHTY RESPONSIBILITIES. The believer's relation to God entails a solemn obligation to obedience. The very name, "people of God," reminds us of our "holy calling"—of the obligation resting on us to be holy as God is holy (1 Pet. ii. 15, 16); exhibiting to the world a pattern of good works, and proving our discipleship by likeness of character to him whose Name we bear.—J. O.

Vers. 11—26.—*Ebal and Gerizim.* This ceremony turns on the idea of the Law as primarily entailing a curse. Blessings and curses were both to be recited (vers. 12, 13). But the curse seems to have been first pronounced, and it only is given in the record. It has the lead in the transaction. The explanation is obvious. Ver. 26 shows that, in strictness, none can escape the curse (Ps. cxxx. 3; Gal. iii. 10). A blessing is pronounced from Gerizim, but it is abortive, as depending on a condition which no sinner can fulfil. Hence: 1. The stones are all placed on Ebal. 2. All the sons of the bondwomen are placed on that mount (cf. Gal. iv. 21—31). This is preferable to supposing that prominence is given to the curse, inasmuch as, under law, fear rather than love is the motive relied on to secure obedience. The appeal to fear is itself an evidence that "the law is not made for a righteous man" (1 Tim. i. 9). It brings strikingly to light the inherent weakness of the economy (Rom. viii. 3). When a Law, the essence of which is *love*, requires to lean on *curses* to enforce it, the unlikelihood of getting it obeyed is tolerably manifest. As an actually working system, the Mosaic economy, while availing itself of the Law to awaken consciousness of sin and to keep men in the path of virtue, drew its strength for holiness, not from the Law, but from the revelations of love and grace which lay within and behind it. We learn—

I. THAT THE LAW IS COMPREHENSIVE OF EVERY PART OF OUR DUTY. A variety of sins are mentioned as examples. They relate to all departments of duty—duty to God and duty to man. The list is avowedly representative (ver. 26). Note: 1. *That it covers a large part of the Decalogue.* The first table is fairly represented by the second commandment, and a curse is pronounced on the making and worshipping of images (ver. 15). The precepts of the second table are involved in the other verses— the fifth commandment in the curse on filial disrespect (ver. 16), the sixth in the curse on murder (ver. 24), the seventh in the curses on the grosser forms of uncleanness (vers. 20—23); the eighth in the curse on removing the landmark (ver. 17); the ninth in the curse on slaying another for reward, which may include perjury (ver. 25); while vers. 18, 19 may be viewed as forbidding breaches of the law of love generally. 2. *That the sins against which the curses are directed are mostly secret sins.* The Law searches the heart. 3. *That the usual care is shown for the interests of the defenceless* (vers. 18, 19). It is touching, in the heart of so awful a malediction, to find this tender love for the blind, the stranger, the fatherless, the widow. Wrath and love in God are close of kin.

II. THAT A CURSE WAITS ON EVERY VIOLATION OF THE LAW'S PRECEPTS. The position of Scripture is that every sin, great and small, subjects the sinner to God's wrath and curse. It derives this truth, not, as some have sought to derive it, from the metaphysical notion of sin's infinite demerit, as committed against an infinite God; but from its own deep view of sin, as involving a change, a deflection, an alteration, in its effects of infinite moment, in the very centre of man's being. There is no sin of slight turpitude. A holy being, to become capable of sin, must admit a principle into his heart totally foreign to the holy condition, and subversive of it. In this sense, he that offends in one point is guilty of all (Jas. ii. 10, 11). Sin is in him, and on a being with sin in him the Law can pronounce but one sentence. His life is polluted, and, being polluted, is forfeited. The curse involves the cutting of the sinner off from life and favour, with subjection to the temporal, spiritual, and eternal penalties of transgression. The denial of this article leaves no single important doctrine of the gospel unaffected; the admission of it carries with it all the rest. It gives its complexion to a whole theology.

III. THAT THE SINNER MUST ACKNOWLEDGE THE JUSTICE OF THE LAW'S CLAIMS AGAINST HIM. The people were required to say, "Amen." This "Amen" was: (1) An assent to the conditions of life proposed. (2) A recognition of the righteousness of them. The Law declares God's judgment against sin. And this: 1. *Is echoed by the conscience.* Fitfully, reluctantly, intermittently, yet truly, even by the natural conscience. The "Amen" is implied in every pang of remorse, in every feeling of self-condemnation. Every time we do that we would not, we consent unto the Law that it is good (Rom. iii. 16). The very heathen know the "judgment of God, that they which commit such things" as are here specified "are worthy of death" (Rom. i. 32). But it needs the spiritually convinced heart to render this "Amen" hearty and sincere. The true penitent justifies God and condemns himself (Ps. li.). 2. *Was acknowledged by Christ as our Sin-bearer.* In Christ's atonement, it has been truly remarked, there "must have been *a perfect ' Amen' in humanity to the judgment of God on the sin of man.* Such an ' Amen' was due to the truth of things. He who was the Truth could not be in humanity and not utter it—and it was necessarily a first step in dealing with the Father on our behalf" (J. McLeod Campbell). 3. *Will yet be joined in by the whole universe* (Rev. xv. 2; xvii. 1, 2).

CONCLUSION. "Christ hath redeemed us from the curse of the Law, being made a curse for us" (Gal. iii. 13). In him no condemnation (Rom. viii. 1).—J. O.

Vers. 1—10.—*Safeguards for obedience.* The enthusiasm of Moses for God's Law is admirable, and no less admirable is his earnest desire for Israel's prosperity. That self-forgetful zeal for others' good was one main qualification in Moses to be the vehicle of God's revealed will. With singular sagacity, Moses presses into the earliest service, for the promulgation of Divine Law, the people themselves. The very stones of Canaan were to be written over with the substance of the Law, and in this way were to become monuments of the covenant between God and Israel. The people who had taken an active part in publishing that Law would feel bound in self-consistency to maintain it. Their title-deeds to Canaan they set up in sight of heaven and earth; and if afterward they should be disobedient, the very stones of the land would cry out against them.

I. AN OBEDIENT SPIRIT DELIGHTS TO EXALT AND PERPETUATE GOD'S LAW. Moses, instructed by God, was a wise observer of human nature; hence he engages the cooperation of the people in proclaiming the Law in the first flush of conquest. The first stones they touched with their feet on the other side Jordan were to be consecrated to the service of God's Law. Deficient in tools, they were not expected to grave them in stone, but to write them on plaster. This could be expeditiously done, and might serve to remind them how easily were the Divine commands effaced from human hearts. As soon as God had begun to fulfil his part of the covenant, man must fulfil his. The people were to write "all" the precepts; for not one of them, however minute, was needless. What was sufficiently important for God to reveal, we may be sure was important enough for man to preserve. These stones, when inscribed with Divine legislation, were to be set up on a mount central in the land, to indicate the universal honour to which they were entitled. And probably Ebal was selected that the people might be awed by the curses which sprang from disobedience. To magnify the Law of the King is the loyal subject's delight. "Oh, how I love thy Law!"

II. AN OBEDIENT SPIRIT IS QUALIFIED TO ENTER UPON A LARGER INHERITANCE. (Ver. 3.) The language is significant. Having passed over Jordan, they were to select and prepare these monumental stones, to the end "thou mayest go in unto the land." Various measures of success were possible. They might destroy the Canaanites, and yet find little advantage or comfort from the inheritance. God could give with one hand and blast with the other. Though in the land, it might not yet open out its resources to them as a "land flowing with milk and honey." Every day they tarried in the land, they might pass into an inner circle of blessing. New waves of sunshine and blessing might sweep over them, so that every morning the inheritance might be to them new. Nature, in its beauties, its wonders, its products, is inexhaustible. With God as our Friend and Teacher, we may find accessions of good and gladness perpetually. Obeying his voice, we enter in; and still, as obedience grows, we enter into fuller possession increasingly.

III. AN OBEDIENT SPIRIT OBTAINS QUICKENING AND STRENGTH AT GOD'S ALTAR. It was forbidden the Hebrews to erect an altar for burnt offering anywhere except the place which God should choose for his abode. So vital, however, to the interests of the nation was this act of proclaiming the Law, that an exception was made in its favour. In the presence of the Law, men would feel their deficiencies and offences; hence provision was specially made for the confession of sin, for the presentation of sacrifice, and for the assurance of mercy. At the altar of burnt offering God and guilty man could meet; here reconciliation could be effected, and here new grace could be obtained. In the sombre light of the burnt offering, men would read the august meaning of the Law, and learn to cover that Law with honour.

But why must the altar be built of unhewn stones? We can only conjecture. Was it to symbolize the fact that God can allow no human interference or co-operation in the work of atonement? Was it to indicate that every part of God's will and Law must be kept perfectly intact, if man would be the friend of God? Was it to prevent any kind of graven work, the craft of human imagination, from adorning the altar of God; by which the minds of worshippers might be diverted from the one solemn act to be performed? There may be an element of truth in all these surmises.

IV. AN OBEDIENT SPIRIT FINDS UNEXPECTEDLY A BANQUET OF JOY. "Thou shalt eat, and shalt rejoice before the Lord thy God." On all sides God has provided the materials for a splendid repast, where every desire of the soul may be satisfied; but the pathway to that sumptuous feast is the pathway of hearty obedience. We can secure the annual harvest only by acting along the line of God's law in nature; and active co-operation with the Divine will is essential to our soul's satisfaction. The joy that thrills the heart of God he desires to share with us, but self-will too often robs us of the boon. "The meek shall eat and be satisfied."

V. AN OBEDIENT SPIRIT RECEIVES INSPIRATION FROM THE HIGHEST SOURCE. "Thou art the people of the Lord thy God; therefore thou shalt obey" his voice. Service which is done from motives of advantage—to gain favour or promotion from God—is mercenary. A selfish end is in view. The favour of the Most High is not merely the *end* we seek; it is the *source* whence all right desire and exertion spring. Thou art the Lord's: this is the chief inspiration of effort. Thou art the Lord's; therefore live as becometh such royal rank. Thou art the Lord's; therefore all his stores of help are at thy command." "Greater is he that is for us than all who can be against us."—D.

Vers. 11—26.—*The Decalogue nationally reciprocated.* It is obvious that the same God who prescribed its Jewish Law is the Creator also of the human conscience; for, just as the sword fits its scabbard, or as cog corresponds with cog in the mechanical wheel, so accord Mosaic Law and human conscience. They are natural counterparts.

I. MEN ARE RULED BY A SYSTEM OF REWARDS AND PUNISHMENTS. Notwithstanding the development of the human mind, and the progress of civilization since Moses' day, human nature is still in its minority, still in a state of childhood. We do not yet see into the interior nature of spiritual realities. We do not see the inherent excellence of righteousness. We do not see the native beauty of obedience. Hence we need to be attracted by rewards and awed by punishments. We perceive the glory or the shame of moral conduct chiefly by its fruits. As we grow in piety, we shall value virtue and holiness for their own sakes, and think less about remote effects and consequences. At present we need the attendant pleasure and pain, the promises and threatenings.

II. FINAL SEPARATIONS OF MANKIND ARE HERE PREFIGURED. As the twelve tribes were here divided into two distinct groups, divided by the vale of Shechem; so all the tribes of men shall eventually be separated, and that by an impassable gulf. The principle of classification on Ebal and Gerizim was not personal merit or demerit (as it will be at the final assize), yet even this ultimate principle of separation seems to have been foreshadowed there. Only children of Jacob's married wives were placed on the mount of blessing; but Reuben, the firstborn, had forfeited this privilege by reason of his sin. As yet, the evil could be averted—the positions might be reversed; these dramatic proceedings were omens both of good and of evil, and were intended to arouse a torpid conscience. To heaven or to hell each man hourly gravitates.

III. GOD'S BLESSING OR CURSE TAKES EFFECT FROM CENTRE TO CIRCUMFERENCE. These mountains were situated almost central in the land. Soon this vast congregation would be scattered to their allotted homes, and thus the influence of this scene would be transmitted all over Canaan. Even this external transmission was typical. The blessing and the curse touched every interest and relationship of Jewish life—religion, home, society, government. The curse was invoked upon idolatry, undutifulness, avarice, oppression, unchastity, insubordination. It began in the inner chamber of the heart, and extended to the outermost circle of the social system. It begins at once, follows the crime as the shadow does the object, until it reaches into the most distant cycles of eternity.

IV. THE HUMAN CONSCIENCE IS THE RECIPROCAL OF THE MORAL LAW, THE ECHO OF ITS SANCTIONS AND ITS PENALTIES. Every healthy conscience utters its sincere "Amen" to every dictate of God's Law. When free from the mists and storms of guilty passion, it reflects, with the fidelity of a mirror, the decisions of God's royal will. Even when a man is the victim of judicial sentence, his conscience admits the justice of the doom. The culprit, in his calmer moods, is self-convicted and self-condemned. When God, by the lips of Moses, required all the tribes to affirm thus solemnly the curses due to disobedience, he knew that every man would heartily take his part in that august deed.

V. MEN BECOME THE ADMINISTRATORS OF GOD'S LAW. We cannot doubt that one reason why God required this public assent to the sanctions of his Law, was that each man might feel more deeply his responsibility toward himself and toward his neighbours. In proportion to our reverential regard for God becomes our concern for others' obedience. The Levites more than once had girded on their swords, and, fired with zeal for their God, had slain their own countrymen. No resistance was attempted, for conscience had made cowards of the culprits. To the same end, David prays, "Let the righteous smite me; it shall be a kindness." Moved by this impulse, men would seek "to please their neighbours for their good *unto edification*." Possessed with a pious disposition, they endeavour to make known on every side God's will, to preserve its remembrance among those disposed to grow oblivious, and to exalt its authority on every hand. Self-consistency required that those who had publicly pronounced the curses of the Law should jealously watch their own conduct—should tenderly caution others!—D.

Vers. 1—10.—*Law-abiding people.* We have here a direction about writing, upon great stones in Mount Ebal, the words of the Divine Law. Whether this meant only the blessings and curses, as Josephus thinks, or an abstract of Deuteronomy, or only the ten commandments, we cannot tell. But the idea implied is similar to the writing of the Decalogue in stone; it was to render *fixed* the Law on which the national policy was to rest. In other words, it was a symbolic way of declaring that Israel will be a Law-abiding people. In connection with this display of the Law, there was to be an altar erected, on which burnt offerings and peace offerings were to be presented, and the people were to realize, as they had never before done, that they have " become the people of the Lord their God." The following ideas are, among others, suggested :—

I. THE LORD'S PEOPLE WILL GREATLY HONOUR HIS LAW. All disrespect shown to the Divine Law argues superficiality both in thought and in feeling. Even suppose it were not most practical and just and good, it ought to be held in high honour as proceeding from the Lord. How much more when it is so wise and so thorough in dealing with human and national life! The great business, therefore, of getting the Law written on the rocks of Mount Ebal must have impressed its sacredness upon the people, and have constituted a standing witness of their undertaking to obey it. It was the acceptance and the publication of Divine Law as that by which, as a nation, they would abide.

II. THE BURNT OFFERINGS INDICATED THEIR PERSONAL CONSECRATION TO GOD. A reference to this sacrifice [1] will show that the idea emphasized in the burnt offering is consecration. The fire is emblematic of the sublimating influence of the Holy Spirit, by which the whole being, the entire personality, is lifted heavenward. When, then, the Israelites gathered round the altar between Mount Ebal and Mount Gerizim, and had plentiful burnt offerings presented by their priests, it was surely dedicating their persons unto God, vowing to be a holy people unto him. Just as the burnt offering comes first in Leviticus to indicate the consecrated attitude of a people redeemed from Egyptian bondage, so it comes first on their entrance into the land of promise. It was Israel asserting that they were not their own, but "bought with a price," and therefore bound to glorify God with their bodies, and their spirits, which are God's (1 Cor. vi. 20).

III. THE PEACE OFFERINGS INDICATED FELLOWSHIP BEFORE GOD. After the burnt offerings came the peace offerings, part of which was laid on the altar, part appropriated by the priests, and the remainder the portion of the people. It was a feast of fellowship between God and his people. It was the sacrament of the land of promise. It indicated peace and unity between God and man. What a precious and interesting service it must have been! The most magnificent congregation the world ever saw, and the most impressive service! Communion is based upon unity of mind and of will on the part of the covenant-keeping God and his Law-abiding people.—R. M. E.

Vers. 11—26.—*Responses.* After the writing of the Law, and the sacrifices, there was to be a great congregation, and half of the people were to assemble on Mount Gerizim to bless, viz. Simeon, Levi, Judah, Issachar, Ephraim, Manasseh, and Benjamin; while the other half were to assemble on Mount Ebal to curse, viz. Reuben, Gad, Asher, Zebulun, Dan, and Naphtali. Now, we know from Numbers that the order of march was this: Judah, Issachar, Zebulun, Gershon and Merari with the tabernacle, Reuben, Simeon, Gad, Kohath with the sanctuary, Ephraim, Manasseh, Benjamin, Dan, Asher, and Naphtali. The order for the arrangement, therefore, was that the van, consisting of Judah and Issachar, marched to Gerizim; then Zebulun, the next tribe, marched to Ebal; then the Gershonites and Merarites marched to Gerizim; then Reuben to Ebal; Simeon to Gerizim; Gad to Ebal; the Kohathites to Gerizim; followed by Ephraim, Manasseh, and Benjamin, who were the followers of the ark; and lastly the rearguard, Dan, Asher, and Naphtali, to Ebal. No commander-in-chief ever disposed of his men more impartially than did Moses in this address beyond the Jordan. Now, we have one or two remarks arising out of this arrangement.

I. THE TRIBE OF LEVI, WITH ALL THE APPOINTMENTS FOR SACRIFICE, PASSED TO GERIZIM TO BLESS. In the march Levi was divided into two parts—the Gershonites and Merarites going fourth with the tabernacle furniture, while the Kohathites went eighth with the ark and sanctuary. But they unite at Mount Gerizim. Nothing could more clearly indicate the mercy and blessing embodied in the whole ceremonial law which the Levites represented. The Law in its judicial aspect might have its penalties and judgments, but it had its ceremonies of mercy to counterbalance these.

II. THE WEIGHT OF THE NATION STOOD ON MOUNT GERIZIM. When we consider

[1] 'Pulpit Commentary,' on Lev. i., Homily by the present writer

the tribes that defiled upon the mount of blessing, we see that they absorb the heroic in Israel. Reuben, Gad, Asher, Dan, Zebulun, and Naphtali were nobodies, so far as national heroism is concerned; whereas the other tribes became famous in the history of Palestine. It is surely significant that the weight of the nation is assigned to the mount of blessing.

III. The people had to say "Amen" to the curses as well as to the blessings pronounced in the Name of God. Some are ready with their responses to the blessings; they cannot get too much of them. But they demur to any curses issuing from God. They think they are unworthy of him. It so happens, however, that, in the great congregation between the mountains, the curses of Ebal had precedence of the blessings of Gerizim. The emphasis chronologically was given to the *curses*. And our consciences must acknowledge that the Law of God must carry out its penalties punctually, or it will forfeit all respect.

IV. A review of the curses here uttered shows that they all rest upon right. No one dare take up one of these curses and suggest its omission or alteration. It is absolute morality which assigns a malediction to such crimes as these. They have the hearty "Amen" of every unbiassed conscience.—R. M. E.

EXPOSITION.

CHAPTER XXVIII.
The Blessing and the Curse.

Having enjoined the proclamations of the blessing and the curse on their entering into possession of Canaan, Moses, for the sake of impressing on the minds of the people both the blessing and the curse, proceeds here to dilate upon both, dwelling especially upon the latter as that which the people the more needed to have brought home to them. As he proceeds, the language of terrible denunciation passes into that of no less terrible prediction, in which the calamities that should come upon the nation because of their apostasy and rebellion are clearly and pointedly foretold.

Ver. 1.—*The blessing.* The condition *sine quâ non* of all enjoyment of the Divine bounty was obedience on the part of the people to the word and Law of Jehovah their God. This rendered, the blessing would come on them rich and full, and abide with them (cf. vers. 2, 9, 13, 14).

Ver. 2.—The blessings about to be specified are represented as personified, as actual agencies coming upon their objects and following them along their path.

Vers. 3—7.—The fulness of the blessing in all the relations of life, external and internal, is presented in six particulars, each introduced by the word "blessed." Israel should be blessed in the house and in the field, in the fruit of the body, in the productions of the soil and the increase of herd and flock, in the store and in the use of what nature provided,—in all their under-takings, whether in peace or in war, at home or abroad. **Basket and thy store;** rather, *basket and kneading-trough* (see Exod. viii. 3; xii. 34); "the basket" representing the store in which the fruits of the earth were laid up, the "kneading-trough" the use of these for the supply of daily needs (ver. 6; cf. Numb. xxvii. 17; Ps. cxxi. 8).

Ver. 8.—The effect of the blessing should be seen, not only in the supremacy of Israel over all opposition, but in the abundance of their possessions, in the success of their undertakings, and in the respect in which they should be held by all nations. **Storehouses.** The Hebrew word (אֲסָמִים), which occurs only here and in Prov. iii. 10, is properly thus rendered. It comes from a root which signifies to lay up.

Ver. 9.—The Lord would establish them to be a people holy unto himself, in whose blessed condition all would see that they were indeed his people, favoured by him.

Ver. 10.—**Thou art called by the name of the Lord;** rather, *the Name of Jehovah is called upon thee.* The Name of God is God himself as revealed; and this Name is called or named upon men when they are adopted by him, made wholly his, and transformed into his likeness. This blessing Israel enjoyed as a nation—"Theirs was the adoption and the glory" (Rom. ix. 4)—but it was theirs only in symbol and in shadow (Heb. x. 1); the reality belongs only to the spiritual Israel, and this came to men in all its fulness when he who is "the image of the invisible God" appeared and set up his tent among men, full of grace and truth (John i. 12, 14).

Ver. 11.—**The Lord shall make thee plen-**

teous in goods; literally, *shall make thee to abound for good*; i.e. shall not only give thee abundance, but cause it to redound to thy felicity.

Ver. 12.—**His good treasure**; equivalent to *his treasure-house*, i.e. heaven, whence blessing should be poured out upon them (cf. ch. xi. 14; Lev. xxvi. 4, 5). He would so fructify their ground, and so bless their toil in cultivating it, that they should become rich, and be able to lend to other nations, and not need to borrow.

Ver. 13. — They should be manifestly superior to other nations, heading them and being above them, their leader and not their subject or follower (cf. Isa. ix. 13). Note the contrast in vers. 43, 44.

Ver. 14.—(Cf. ch. v. 29; xi. 28.) Moses ends as he began, by reminding them that the condition of enjoying the blessing was obedience to the Divine Law, and steadfast adherence to the course in which they were called to walk.

Vers. 15—68.—*The curse*. In case of disobedience and apostacy, not only would the blessing be withheld, but a curse would descend, blighting, destructive, and ruinous. As the blessing was set forth in six announcements (vers. 3—6), the curse is proclaimed in form and number corresponding (vers. 16—19). The curse thus appears as the exact counterpart of the blessing. The different forms in which the threatened curse should break forth are then detailed in five groups.

Vers. 20—26.—*First group*. The curse should come upon them in various forms of evil, filling them with terror and dismay, and threatening them with utter ruin (cf. Mal. ii. 2).

Ver. 20.—**Vexation**; rather, *consternation*; the deadly confusion with which God confounds his enemies. The same word is used in ch. vii. 23; 1 Sam. xiv. 20. **Rebuke**; rather, *threatening*.

Vers. 21, 22.—The afflictive visitations here named are such as destroy life; but the distinctive character of each it is not easy exactly to define. The **pestilence** is probably a generic term for any fatal epidemic. In the LXX. it is usually represented by the general word θάνατος, death. **Consumption**; literally, *wasting*; the designation of any species of tabes or marasmus. **Fever** (דַּלֶּקֶת, from דָּלַק, to be parched, to glow); **inflammation** (חַחְתֻּר, from חָרַר, to burn); **burning fever** (קַדַּחַת, from קָדַח, to kindle): different species of pyrexia, the distinction between which has not been determined. **The sword**. Instead of חֶרֶב, sword, the Vulgate, Arabic, and Samaritan adopt the reading חֹרֶב, heat, drought (Gen. xxxi. 40); but all the other versions support the reading

of the received text, and there is no reason why it should be departed from, more especially as drought is threatened in the verse that follows. **Blasting and with mildew**; diseases that attack the grain (Amos iv. 9); the former (שִׁדָּפוֹן, from שָׁדַף, to scorch, to blast) a withering or scorching of the ears caused by the east wind (Gen. xli. 23); the latter (יֵרָקוֹן, from יָרַק, to be yellowish) the effect produced by a hot wind, which turns the ears yellow, so that they are rendered unproductive.

Vers. 23, 24.—Terrible drought is here threatened; no rain should fall (cf. Lev. xxvi. 19); but instead thereof dust, both light as powder and heavy as sand, should fall upon them. The allusion is probably to those clouds of dust and sand which often fill the air in Palestine, when the heat is intense and there has been no rain for a season; the wind then becomes a vehement sirocco, and the air is filled with sand and dust, and is like the glowing heat at the mouth of a furnace (Robinson, 'Bib. Res.,' ii. 123; Thomson, 'Land and the Book,' ii. 311).

Vers. 25, 26.—Utter defeat in battle (the opposite of the blessing promised, ver. 7) and dispersion among the nations are threatened, with the utmost indignity to those who were slain, in their bodies being left unburied to be devoured by birds of prey and wild beasts (cf. 1 Kings xiv. 11; Ps. lxxix. 2; Jer. vii. 33; xvi. 4, etc.). **Shalt be removed into all the kingdoms of the earth**; literally, *shalt be a tossing to and fro to all the kingdoms*, etc.; "a ball for all the kingdoms to play with" (Schultz; cf. 2 Chron. xxix. 8; Jer. xv. 4; xxiv. 9; xxix. 18, etc.).

Vers. 27—34.—*Second group*. The Lord should afflict them with various loathsome diseases, vex them with humiliating and mortifying calamities, and give them over to be plundered and oppressed by their enemies.

Ver. 27.—**Botch of Egypt**; the form of leprosy peculiar to Egypt (Exod. ix. 9, etc.), *elephantiasis*, "Ægypti peculiare malum" (Pliny, 'Nat. Hist.,' xxvi. 1—5). **Emerods**; tumours, probably piles (cf. 1 Sam. v.). **Scab**; probably some kind of malignant scurvy. **Itch**; of this there are various kinds common in Egypt and Syria.

Vers. 28, 29.—Besides bodily ailments, mental diseases should come upon them—insanity, incapacity, confusion of mind, so that even at midday they should grope as a blind man gropes, *i.e.* under the most favourable circumstances they should be unable to find the right path, to hit on the right and safe course. It is of mental blindness that the word is here used (cf. Isa. xlii. 19; Lam. iv. 14; Zeph. i. 17;

Rom. xi. 25; 2 Cor. iv. 4). **Thou shalt grope** (cf. Isa. lix. 10). Thus afflicted in body and mind, their state should be one only of oppression and calamity, with no hope of deliverance.

Vers. 30—34.—The spoliation of them should be utter. All most dear and precious to them should be the prey of their enemies. Wife, house, vineyard, herd, and flock should be ruthlessly taken from them; sons and daughters should be carried into captivity, and their eyes should look for them in vain, with constant and wasting longing (cf. Jer. viii. 20; Amos v. 11; Micah vi. 15; Zeph. i. 13; 2 Chron. xxix. 9; Neh. xi. 36; Jer. v. 15).

Ver. 30.—**And shalt not gather the grapes thereof**; margin, "Hebrew, *profane*." This is the literal rendering of the verb; the meaning is that given in the text. A vineyard was, for the first three years after it was planted, held sacred (Lev. xix. 23); after that, its consecration ceased, and the fruit might be gathered for common use (cf. ch. xx. 6), and it was said to be profaned.

Ver. 32.—**And there shall be no might in thine hand.** Keil proposes to render here, "Thy hand shall not be to thee towards God;" and others, "Thy hand shall not be to thee for God," *i.e.* instead of God. But אֵל here is not "the Mighty One, God; but simply "might, strength, power," as in Gen. xxxi. 29; Prov. iii. 27; Micah ii. 1. Literally rendered, the words are, *And not for might is thy hand*, the meaning of which is well expressed in the Authorized Version.

Vers. 35—46.—*Third group.* Moses reverts to the calamities already threatened (ver. 27), for the purpose of leading on the thought that, as such diseases separated the sufferer from the society of his fellows, so Israel should be separated from God and brought under the dominion of strangers as a punishment for rebellion and apostasy.

Ver. 35.—**A sore botch**; an incurable leprosy, affecting not merely the joints and extremities, but the whole body. Such an affliction would exclude a man from all fellowship and from all covenant privileges of the nation. So Israel, rendered unclean by their sin, should be cut off from covenant union with God.

Vers. 36, 37.—As a consequence, God would bring them under subjection to a foreign power, and they should be made to serve other gods, wood and stone (ch. iv. 28), and would become an object of horror, a proverb, and a byword among the nations (cf. 1 Kings ix. 7; Jer. xxiv. 9).

Ver. 38.—Even in their own land the curse would overtake them and rest upon them in all their interests and relations.

Ver. 39.—**Worms**; probably the vine weevil, the convolvulus or involvulus of the

Latin writers (Pliny, 'Nat. Hist.,' xvii. 47; Cato, 'De Re Rust.,' c. 95; Plaut., 'Cistell.,' iv. 2), the ἴξ or ἴψ of the Greeks (Bochart, 'Hieroz.,' pt. ii. bk. iv. c. 27).

Ver. 40.—**Thine olive shall cast his fruit.** Some would render here "shall be plundered or rooted out," taking the verb יִשַּׁל as the Niph. of שָׁלַל; but the majority regard it as part of the verb נָשַׁל, and render "shall drop off," or as in the Authorized Version. There is some doubt, however, whether the verb נָשַׁל can be used intransitively.

Ver. 42.—**Consume**; literally, *take possession of.* The name given here to the ravaging insect is not the same as in ver. 38; but there can be no doubt it is the locust that is intended.

Vers. 43, 44.—(Cf. vers. 12, 13.)

Ver. 46.—These curses would be for a sign and for a wonder, exciting astonishment and dismay in the beholder, and showing that it was indeed the hand of God that was upon the rebellious nation. **For ever.** This, though it may imply the final and utter rejection of Israel as a nation, does not preclude the hope of restoration of a part of Israel as individuals, or as a remnant remaining in or returning to faith and obedience (cf. Isa. x. 22; vi. 13; Rom. ix. 27; xi. 5).

Vers. 47—57.—*Fourth group.* In order still more to impress on the minds of the people the evil and danger of rebellion and apostasy, Moses enlarges on the calamities that would ensue on their being given up to the power of the heathen. Because they would not serve Jehovah their God, they should be delivered to be servants to their enemies.

Vers. 49, 50.—The description here given of the enemy to whom Israel was to be subjected, applies more or less closely to all the nations whom God raised up from time to time, to invade Israel and chastise the people for their rebellion—the Chaldeans (cf. Jer. xlviii. 40; xlix. 22; Ezek. xvii. 5—7; Hab. i. 6, etc.), the Assyrians (cf. Isa. v. 26; xxxviii. 11; xxiii. 19), the Medes (Isa. xiii. 17, 18); but there are features in the description which apply especially to the Romans; and the horrors delineated in the latter part of the section (vers. 52—57) carry one's thoughts immediately to the terrible scenes which transpired during the wars of Vespasian and Titus with the Jews as narrated by Josephus ('De Bell. Jud.,' vi.; see Milman, 'Hist. of the Jews,' bk. xvi.).

Ver. 49.—**As the eagle flieth.** The eagle was the common ensign of the legion in the Roman army; and by the Latin writers *aquila* (eagle) is sometimes used for a legion (Cæs., 'Hisp.,' 30; cf. Matt. xxiv. 28).

Ver. 50.—**A nation of fierce countenance;** literally, *firm* or *hard of face;* i.e. obdurate and determined (cf. Prov. xxi. 29; Dan. viii. 23).

Vers. 52—57.—(Cf. Lev. xxvi. 29; 2 Kings vi. 24—30; Jer. xix. 9; Lam. ii. 20; iv. 10.)

Ver. 56.—So intense should be the hunger, that the delicate and sensitive woman, brought up in luxury, and who would not set her foot on the ground lest she should be fatigued by the exertion or offended by coming in contact with the base soil, but when she went abroad must be carried in a litter or borne by a camel or an ass,—even she should break through all restraints of delicacy and affection, and would secretly devour the very infant she had borne during the siege.

Ver. 57.—**Her young one;** literally, *her after-birth.* The Hebrew suggests an extreme of horror beyond what the Authorized Version indicates.

Vers. 58—68.—*Fifth group.* Even these fearful calamities would not be the consummation of their punishment. If they should be obstinate in their rebellion; if they would not observe to do all that the Law delivered by Moses enjoined on them; if they ceased to reverence and obey Jehovah, their God;—then should come upon them the curse in full measure, and long-continued chastisement should show how grievous had been their sin.

Ver. 58.—**This book.** Not the Book of Deuteronomy, which was not then written, but the Book of the Law, the Torah, delivered by Moses to Israel from God; and of which he had been, in his addresses to the people, recapitulating some of the principal points (cf. vers. 60, 61). **That thou mayest fear,** etc. It was not mere outward observance of the Law, not the mere "doing" of what was enjoined that was required, but the doing of it heartily and sincerely in the fear of the Lord, in the fear of him who had revealed himself to them by the glorious and awful Name, Jehovah, their God (cf. Lev. xxiv. 11).

Vers. 60, 61.—**The diseases of Egypt** are the plagues sent on Pharaoh and his people, as recorded in Exod. vii.—xi. Besides these, other plagues, not recorded in the Book of the Law, should come on rebellious Israel, so that they should be almost utterly destroyed.

Ver. 62.—(Cf. ch. iv. 27; x. 22; Neh. ix. 23.)

Ver. 63.—(Cf. ch. xxx. 9; Jer. xxxii. 41.) He, whose joy it had been to do them good, should rejoice over their destruction (cf. Prov. i. 26).

Ver. 64.—Those of them that survived the plagues that should come upon them, and the horrors of the siege, should be scattered amongst all nations to the ends of the earth, and there subjugated to the utmost indignities and sufferings.

Ver. 66.—**Thy life shall hang in doubt before thee;** literally, *Thy life shall be hung up before thee;* i.e. shall be like an object suspended by a thread which hangs dangling before the view, ready to fall or to be cut down at any moment. Comp.—

" Omnia sunt hominum tenui pendentia filo
Et subito casu quæ valuere ruunt."
(Ovid, ' Epp. ex Ponto,' iv. 3, 35.)

Ver. 68.—Worst of all, they should be again reduced to bondage, carried back to Egypt, put up for sale as slaves, and be so utterly despicable that no one would purchase them. **Bring thee into Egypt again.** "If the Exodus was the birth of the nation of God as such, the return would be its death" (Schultz; cf. Hos. viii. 13; ix. 3). **With ships.** They came out of Egypt by land, as free men; they should be carried back imprisoned and cooped up in slave-ships. **By the way whereof I spake unto thee, Thou shalt see it no more again.** This does not refer to their being carried to Egypt in ships as different from the way by which they had come out from it, but simply to the fact that they should be carried back thither, contrary to what was expected when they so triumphantly came forth from it. **There ye shall be sold;** literally, *shall sell yourselves;* i.e. give yourselves up to be sold as slaves. Egypt may be here, as Hengstenberg suggests, "the type of future oppressors;" but there seems no reason why the passage should not be taken literally. It is a fact that, after the capture of Jerusalem by Titus, the Jews were in large numbers carried into Egypt, and there subjected to most ignominious bondage; and in the time of Hadrian, multitudes of Jews were sold into slavery (Josephus, ' De Bell. Jud.,' vi. 9, 2; cf. Philo, ' Flacc.' and ' Leg. ad Caium.').

HOMILETICS.

Vers. 1—14.—*God's blessing promised to the obedient.* The aged lawgiver was finishing his course. Ere the end comes he would open up to the people once more the dread alternative of blessing and cursing, and would show them that they must accept either one or the other. And so, before the Holy Land is taken possession of, they are reminded how very much the realization of the promises of temporal good depends on what they are. We cannot be too frequently reminded of the fact, however, that, though *primâ facie* this chapter looks as if people were then under Law; yet it was not so in reality. They were being educated by *the* Law; but under it the Abrahamic promise lay as firm as granite (Gal. iii. 17). This is seen by the fact that God speaks to them as their God. This was of his free grace. But, though this educatory law is based on grace, grace must bring with it its own law. Grace never gives the reins to lawlessness. But it teaches us that one of the motive forces by which God would quicken men to righteousness and educate them in it, is found in showing them that his providential arrangements are such that the shaping of their earthly destiny is, in some sort, in their own hands. "Of their *earthly* destiny," we say. For it is a well-known fact that Moses seldom, if ever, refers to the next state of being. The rewards and punishments known to the Pentateuch are almost entirely connected with this earthly state. Of course, there is nothing like a denial of a life beyond the grave. But it did not fall within the scope of the revelation given through Moses that another world should be brought clearly into view. We doubt not that there was mercy as well as wisdom in this arrangement; the people had as much revealed to them as they could bear, and more than they knew how to improve. There is a world of deep meaning in the disclosure of the laws of God's providence which are unfolded to them here. One would think that such promises as are made to the obedient would have been enough to win them to follow the will of God; and that the long-continued, terrific, appalling statement of what would follow on their disobedience would have been enough to dissuade them by "the terrors of the Lord" from venturing on the highway of evil. It would be easy to write a separate Homily on each verse in this paragraph, but, with such expansion, our work would extend to a most inordinate length. We will but suggest, and leave the expansion to others. We have but one more proviso to make before coming to our main divisions; that is this: Barring the special complexion here given to the chapter, owing to the peculiar feature of Israel's national constitution, the main laws of providential administration which were disclosed by Moses are still in force. Even now it is true, "Godliness is profitable unto all things: having promise of *the life that now is.*" And this is the truth which, in varied forms, is set forth here. Let us observe—

I. A MAN'S EARTHLY DESTINY IS, IN SOME SORT, IN HIS OWN HANDS. (Vers. 1, 2.) "*If thou shalt hearken to the voice of the Lord thy God,*" such and such blessings shall "come upon thee, and overtake thee." If Israel sought success for its own sake, irrespectively of the rightness or wrongness of any methods adopted to secure it, there would be no guarantee whatever of their securing the end at which they aimed; and even if they should, the results would be fraught with evil; for "the prosperity of fools would destroy them." But if their supreme, their sole aim, was to do right, to serve and please the Lord, then the Divine blessing would be sure to follow them. "'Tis ours to obey, 'tis his to provide." If we do right, and leave the issues with God, we shall not be left without tokens of his approving smile (Matt. vi. 33). There may be large temporal gains, or there may not; but, with the much or with the little, that blessing will come which maketh rich; and he addeth no sorrow therewith.

II. THE BLESSING ENJOYED BY THE OBEDIENT MAN WILL REST ON EVERYTHING WHICH HE HAS, AND WILL FOLLOW HIM EVERYWHERE. Let every clause in the paragraph be separately weighed. Would we set this in gospel light, if any one were to ask the question, "What are the signs of God's blessing which God's faithful ones enjoy, even in this life?" we would enumerate six of them. 1. They have peace with God through the Lord Jesus Christ. 2. They have a clear conscience; they know that the aim of pleasing God is right, whatever difficulties it may involve. 3. They enjoy what they have as from God, and as the loving gifts of a Father's hand. 4. If much be given, they delight to use it for God. 5. If little be theirs, they know that a little that a righteous man hath is better than the riches of many wicked. 6. And, above all, the supreme proof of God's blessing is that gains and losses, joys and cares, health and sickness, do "all work together for good" to them; they minister to the growth of character, and help to make them better, wiser, and holier men.

III. THERE IS A SPECIAL LAW OF GOD'S PROVIDENTIAL GOVERNMENT WHICH ENSURES

THIS BLESSING TO THE OBEDIENT. (Ver. 12.) It may, at first sight, seem to be an antiquated setting of things which we find in this verse, in which it is said, virtually, that the amount of rain will depend on the amount of virtue, and that the accumulation of men's possessions will depend on their fidelity to God! The second sentence we can understand, since fidelity to God implies, among other things, fidelity in the use of God's appointed means of success; so that this is only saying, Use the right means rightly, and you will gain your end. But as to the former, who *can* understand it? *The amount of rain dependent on the measure of virtue*—how *can* such a thing be? We ask, first of all, *Hath the rain a father?* The reply is, *Yes*, beyond all question—God. But then God is the Father of spirits also. That is to say, there are two spheres: that of matter and force, and that of spirit; the one governed by physical laws, the other by laws which are spiritual; but all laws, whether physical or spiritual, are ordained and regulated by one Supreme Being, and in his hands there is unity of action therein. So that, concerning these two as governed by one God, we ask, Is there any relation at all between them? Does the fact of both sets of laws originating with the same Being give them a point of contact, or does it not? In a word, Is the world of physical forces governed without the slightest reference to the government of souls? or is it so governed as to help on the training of souls?—which? If the first alternative is true, the doctrine of ver. 12 is shut out. But who can believe that the Great Father, in governing the less, ignores the greater? We, at any rate, recoil in horror from a view so unworthy of God. We fall back, therefore, on the second alternative, which alone is reasonable, that the less is governed in the interest and on the behalf of the greater; that *things* are for spirits. But this principle allows room for the point of detail in ver. 12, and for ten thousand more details in the physical sphere. God would make the natural world a theatre for, and a means of, the evolution of principles and the growth of souls (cf. Amos iv. 6—13; Ps. cvii. 33—43). (See Homily on ch. xi. 10—17.)

IV. LOYALTY TO GOD TENDS, NOT ONLY TO TEMPORAL SUCCESS, BUT ALSO TO HONOUR. (See end of ver. 12 and ver. 13.) 1. Individually; men, in the long run, go pretty much for what they are worth. Faithful fulfilment of duty to God and man *must* tell, and will. "Seest thou a man diligent in his business; he shall stand before kings, he shall not stand before mean men." 2. And collectively; if a nation has in it a preponderance of wise, true-hearted, upright men, such as fear God, love righteousness, and hate iniquity, nothing can prevent such a nation rising in the scale. Its prosperity will be manifest in its inward peace, in the readiness of other nations to deal with it by opening up commercial relations, and in the good will of other nations which it will certainly share. It will have the armour of light. Its virtue will be a wall of defence. "Its land will yield her increase; and God, even its own God, will bless it." "Happy is the nation that is in such a case; yea, happy is that people whose God is the Lord." To such a nation it may well be said, "Blessed is he that blesseth thee, and cursed is he that curseth thee" (Numb. xxiv. 5—9).

Vers. 15—68.—*Love veiled in frown.* Probably many may think that this is one of the most awful chapters in the Word of God. Certainly we are not aware of any other in which there is such a long succession of warnings, increasing in terror as they advance. In fact, Matthew Henry tells us of a wicked man who was so enraged at reading this chapter that he tore the leaf out of his Bible! Impotent rage! Impotent as if, when a man dreaded an eclipse of the sun, he were to tear up the announcements thereof. *It would come for all that!* So here; there are two historical facts, viz. that the children of Israel *did* depart from their God, and, that all these curses *did* befall them. Some are unspent even yet. Hence this chapter is a standing proof of the accuracy of the foresight which dictated its prophecies. But while we thus get, on the one hand, a verification of the words, and so a proof of their Divine origin, another question is raised, viz. How are all these terrible realities consistent with the love of God? Now, far be it from us to attempt any vindication of the ways of God. He is infinitely beyond any need of that. What he does is right, whether we can see it to be so or no. One thing only do we aim at now: that is, to guard men against any misinterpretation of those ways, and to point them to such teachings concerning them as God has given to us. Our theme is—*Love veiled in frown; or, the terrors of the Lord a necessity of his infinite love.*

I. There are some in every nation whom it is absolutely necessary to sway by deterrents, and in the infancy of a nation fear is more potent than faith.

II. God has a curse as well as a blessing. His love is not a mere desire to make men as easy as possible. It is, first of all, a righteous love. When love has to deal only with righteousness, its benevolent aspect only will be seen; but when sin has to be dealt with, the case is very different.

III. It should be deeply graven in our souls that the black-looking and lowering storm-cloud of Divine wrath, though we call it "the curse of God," must never be thought of in any way which would be inconsistent with his pure and perfect love. The wrath of God is holy love frowning on wrong.

IV. When once the wrath of God is incurred, the sinner cannot elude it, any more than he can retreat from his own shadow.

V. Given the actuality of sin, and a far-seeing eye can with certainty descry some of the consequences thereof; an infinite eye can discern them all. (The list of predicted evils in this chapter may with great advantage be arranged and classified. All have been realized. See also the *Times*, November 18, 1880, for an account of the present anti-Semitic agitation in Germany.)

VI. We know that God has no pleasure in the death of the wicked, but his vindication of his own laws is essential to guard righteousness as with a wall of fire! Hence—

VII. The truest kindness is seen in the enunciation of the most alarming warnings which can be given. The truest love is that which is most faithful. Hence it will often seem the most stern.

VIII. A like holy guard to that which is here thrown around the Law of God is also thrown around the gospel. Just as, on the one hand, this Law did not and could not annul the promise which had been made to Abraham and his seed, even so, on the other hand, not even the richness and glory of the gospel of our Lord Jesus Christ can ever annul the action of these stern, retributive laws of God's providence on those who continue in sin, and who reject the redemption brought in by the Son of God (see Heb. ix., x.).

HOMILIES BY VARIOUS AUTHORS.

Vers. 1—14.—*The blessing.* Blessing and curse, as Keil says, are viewed in these verses "as actual powers, which follow in the footsteps of the nation, and overtake it" (vers. 2, 15, 22; Zech. i. 6). The blessing of God is a *vera causa* in human life. It is not to be resolved entirely into natural tendencies. A cheerful mind conduces to health; virtuous habits tend to prosperity, etc. But this is not the whole. Conspiring with natural tendencies, we must recognize a special providence, a designed direction of the beneficent powers of nature and life, so as to pour treasures of goodness on the favoured individual. Virtue has its natural reward in the approval of conscience; but it would not of itself suffice to bring about the exceptionally fortunate condition in the outward lot which these verses represent. So strongly was this felt by the philosopher Kant, that, as is well known, he postulates the existence of God, for the express purpose of bringing about an ultimate harmony between virtue and felicity.

I. THE SPHERE OF THE BLESSING. The covenant rested largely on temporal promises. Jehovah was doubtless felt by the believing soul to be a better portion than any of his gifts (Ps. xvi.; lxxiii.), and the relation which he sustained to his worshipper could not but be thought of as subsisting beyond death, and yielding its appropriate fruit in a future life (Ps. xvi. 11; xvii. 15; xlviii. 14; xlix. 14, 15; Heb. xi. 9—17). Yet, inasmuch as "life and immortality" had not been clearly brought to light (2 Tim. i. 10), his favour was specially exhibited in the abundant communication of earthly blessings. A higher order has supervened, and the temporal promises of these verses are swallowed up in better and more enduring ones (Heb. viii. 6). The gospel does not sever the connection between godliness and prosperity. It gives it a new sanction (1 Tim. iv. 8). Were the obedience of God's children more uniform and perfect, and piety more widely diffused in communities, the connection would be more manifest than it is. But on the whole, temporal prosperity occupies a lower relative place in the New Testament than in the Old. 1. The spiritual man, serving Christ, and witnessing for him amidst the evil of the world, is more frequently exposed to persecution (Matt v. 11; x. 24, 25; John xv. 15—21). He has more occasion to take up the cross (Matt. xvi. 24). He may require to sacrifice all he has, with life itself, for Christ's sake and the gospel's (Mark x. 29, 30). 2. Temporal prosperity is in every case subordinated to spiritual good (2 Cor. xii. 7—10; 3 John 2). Bacon's saying has, therefore, truth in it, " Prosperity is the blessing of the Old Testament; adversity is the blessing of the New, which carrieth the greater benediction, and the clearer revelation of God's favour." Adversity, however, even in the New Testament, is but a step to something higher. Spiritual compensations now; hereafter, " a far more exceeding and eternal weight of glory " (Mark x. 30; 2 Cor. iv. 17).

II. THE OPERATION OF THE BLESSING. It is viewed as pervading every department of the earthly life. It mingles itself with all the good man is, with all he does, with the circumstances of his lot, with the powers of the natural world which constitute his environment. It rests on his person, on his household, on his possessions. It helps him against his enemies, making him wealthy and powerful (Abraham, Job), and exalting him to a position in which others are dependent on him. It attends him in city and field, in his coming in and going out, so that whatever he does prospers (Ps. i. 3). These promises demonstrate: 1. That the providence of God, in the sphere of the outward life, is free, sovereign, all-embracing. 2. That there is under this providence a connection between outward events and circumstances and spiritual conditions. 3. That, subordinately to higher ends, piety and virtue, under this providence, will be rewarded by prosperity. (See a valuable treatment of this subject in M'Cosh's ' Method of the Divine Government,' bk. ii. ch. 2.) Yet glorious as these promises are, they "have no glory in this respect, by reason of the glory that excelleth " of the promises of the New Testament. Promises: 1. Of salvation (Rom. v. 9, 10). 2. Of spiritual blessings (Eph. i. 3). 3. Of a heavenly inheritance (1 Pet. i. 3, 4). 4. Of " riches " of goodness which will remain unexhausted through eternal ages (Eph. ii. 6, 7). 5. Of perfected transformation into the moral image of God (Ps. xvii. 15; 1 Cor. xv. 49; Col. i. 22; 1 John iii. 2).

III. THE CONDITION OF THE BLESSING. Obedience (vers. 1, 2, 9, 13, 14). 1. Legally, perfect obedience. 2. Evangelically, obedience habitual and sincere, albeit imperfect. The *meritorious* ground of a believer's acceptance, and of the blessings he receives, is the obedience unto death of Christ (Rom. v. 19—21). Christ expiates his sins, and fulfils *de novo* the condition of the covenant. It is well to remember, as explaining anomalies in the histories of righteous men under the old covenant, that the promises in these verses were primarily *national*. They could be realized to the individual only in connection with the obedience of the nation as a whole. When apostacy provoked God's judgments, pious individuals suffered in the general calamities. They suffered, too, as drawing upon themselves the hatred of the wicked. Hence the development in the Psalms and Prophets of the idea of the " Righteous Sufferer "—One whose afflictions are entailed on him by the hatred and injustice of the wicked, or who, innocent himself, suffers as a member of the body politic. This idea, which has throughout a Messianic reference, culminates in the prophecy of the " Servant of Jehovah " (Is. lii., liii.), who, by the holy endurance of sufferings for others, makes their sin his own, and vicariously atones for it.—J. O.

Ver. 8.—*The blessing that maketh rich.* I. FULL STOREHOUSES, WITHOUT GOD'S BLESSING, ARE NOT RICHES. God does not count a man rich further than the good things he has are of real and lasting benefit to him. Wealth unblessed of God is not to be desired. 1. Unblessed good *is* ill (Eccles. v. 10—15). 2. It *turns* to ill—is not enduring (Prov. xiii. 22), takes wings and leaves, is a curse to offspring (Eccles. v. 14, 15; vi. 2; Jas. v. 1, 2).

II. GOD'S BLESSING, WITHOUT FULL STOREHOUSES, MAKES RICH. 1. It enriches the little we have. A man with a moderate competence, and peace and comfort in the use of it, may be richer than the man whose means are tenfold greater (Ps. xxxvii. 16). 2. It makes adversity a means of spiritual enrichment. 3. It is itself the best of all riches (Hab. iii. 17—19).—J. O.

Ver. 9.—*Established.* Probation, in the case of the faithful, ends in establishment. If Israel would keep the commandments, God would "perfect, stablish, strengthen, settle " them as "an holy people " to himself, and so confirm the promises made to the fathers. A like promise to the Church and to Christians (Acts xvi. 5; Rom. i. 11; Col. ii. 7; Heb. xiii. 9; 1 Pet. v. 10; 2 Pet. i. 12). Establishment is: 1. Unto holiness. 2. A result of God naming his Name upon his people (ver. 12, Hebrew), *i.e.* dwelling with them, and revealing his attributes in saving, sanctifying, blessing, and exalting them. 3. The reward of fidelity. 4. A proof of God's fidelity. God "hath sworn" to fulfil his word (Heb. vi. 17, 18; cf. 1 Cor. i. 9; Phil. i. 6).—J. O.

Ver. 10.—*The world afraid of the godly.* I. GOD'S PEOPLE CALLED BY HIS NAME. God calls or names his Name upon them, *i.e.* distinguishes, owns, chooses, recognizes them as his, by dwelling among them (2 Cor. iii. 16), by causing his blessing to rest upon them, by answering their prayers, by favouring their cause, by establishing their work (Ps. xc. 13—17). "God is love" (1 John iv. 8). His "Name" expresses pre-eminently that attribute of his character (Exod. xxxiv. 6, 7). It can, therefore, be revealed only upon or in relation to his own people.
II. NOMINAL AND REAL CALLING. "They are not all Israel which are of Israel" (Rom. ix. 6). Real, as distinguished from nominal, saints are marked: 1. By obedience to the Divine commands (ver. 9; Matt. vii. 22). 2. By separation from the world (2 Cor. vii. 17, 18). 3. By the power of holiness dwelling in them. 4. By manifold tokens of the Divine favour. Thus the world "sees" them to be what they are (Acts iv. 13).
III. THOSE KNOWN TO BE CALLED BY GOD'S NAME ARE FEARED. Worldly men fear them. They fear the holiness that resides in them. They fear their prayers. They fear their power with God. They feel that there dwells in them a Presence whom they have every reason to dread (Acts ii. 43).—J. O.

Ver. 13.—*Moral gravitation.* In studying the histories of the good men of the Bible, we notice how, notwithstanding the numerous causes which act adversely to their fortunes, the constant tendency of their piety is to lift them upwards. A law is none the less a law because other laws come in to interfere with, modify, suspend, or counteract its operation. A cork or other light body may be pushed under water, but the law of its nature is to rise to the top. Violence may abnormally depress the righteous man's fortunes, but the "law" of piety is to elevate them. Mingle lighter and heavier bodies in water, and the heavier gradually sink, while the lighter mount surfacewards. So piety, both from its own nature and by the blessing of God upon it, tends to raise a man in favour and influence, and gradually to improve his fortunes; while ungodliness as invariably drags him down. The good man gains ground; his enemies lose it. He mounts to be the head, and they sink to be the tail. He is uppermost; they are undermost. Illustrate from the histories of Joseph, David, Daniel. It is the same to-day. As years advance, the good man grows in influence; slowly but surely overcomes his first difficulties; is trusted, sought after, looked up to; rises in social position; ultimately occupies the seats of honour; while those who started life with him, but took a different course, gradually lose their advantages, fall one by one out of rank, and are driven to the wall (cf. Prov. iv. 8; xiii. 22, etc.).—J. O.

Vers. 15—48.—*The curse.* Like the blessing, the curse is a reality. It cleaves to the sinner, pursues him, hunts him down, ruins and slays him (ver. 45). Does some one say, "An exploded superstition"? If so, it is a superstition in the belief of which mankind has shown itself singularly unanimous. View its reality as attested: 1. By *conscience.* The criminal cannot divest himself of the belief that avenging powers are following on his track. 2. By *experience.* "Rarely," says Horace, "has Punishment, though lame, failed to overtake the criminal fleeing before her." Greek tragedy rests on an induction from the facts of life. 3. By *mythology.* It was a conviction, true alike to conscience and the facts of life, which the Greeks sought to personify in the Erinyes, in Nemesis, and in Até, who clung to a man or to a family in punishment for some half-forgotten crime. 4. By *literature*, which is full of the recognition of avenging powers. The Bible confirms the substance of this varied teaching, but lifts the subject out of the region of mythology. Jehovah alone has power to bless and curse. The blessings and curses of men have no efficacy save as he gives it to them. His blessings and curses are part of the moral government of the world, and turn exclusively on moral conditions. This is the contrast between the Bible and the heathen idea of a curse. The curse was a prominent part of heathen sorcery, but was wrought with charms and incantations. Protection against it was sought, not in a life of virtue, but in counter-charms and amulets—in conjurations more powerful than those of the enemy. The Bible countenances no such superstitions. Incantations are value-less. A curse is futile against those whom God has blessed (Numb. xxiii. 20—23). The Bible doctrine is: 1. Simple. 2. Rational. 3. Ethical. That of heathenism (with its modern survivals, the evil eye, charms, witches, etc.) is conspicuously the reverse.

I. The curse in its nature. 1. *A natural fruit of sin.* Natural process is not the whole. But a larger place may be allowed it than it had in the blessing. The blessing is "gift;" sin's fruit is of "debt"—"wages" (Rom. vi. 23). Conceivably, yet without miracle, God might have withheld from virtue its appropriate outward reward. But no power, even that of God, could prevent the sinner from reaping wretchedness and woe as a result of sin. "The righteous shall be recompensed in the earth; *much more* the wicked and the sinner" (Prov. xi. 31). The wiser course is not to oppose God to the laws of our moral nature, but to recognize him in them, and to draw from them a knowledge of his character and will. These, like all punitive laws, are the executors of his judgments. The sinner, having placed himself in conflict with the laws of life, of society, and of the outward universe, necessarily suffers in mind, body, and estate. Sin introduces discord, disorder, lawlessness, into the *soul*. It blinds and infatuates (vers. 28, 29). It makes wretched. This wretchedness is aggravated: (1) By remorse and self-reproach. (2) By sense of Divine anger. (3) By opprobrium of society. (4) By imaginative terrors. Sin poisons the fountains of *health*, and induces diseases (vers. 22, 27, 35). The internal anarchy spreads outwards. The bonds of *society* are loosened; wealth accumulates in the hands of the few; the unhappy toilers, oppressed and spoiled, sink deeper and deeper in debt and wretchedness. At this stage the nation becomes an easy prey to the first strong power that cares to pounce upon it (vers. 29—38). 2. *An effect of hostile action on the part of God.* We fail of a complete view if we look only at the hostile relation of the sinner to God, and leave out of account the hostile relation which God assumes to the sinner. It is not merely that the sinner gets into conflict with himself and with the world around him, but nature and providence, under the direction of a hostile will, take up an antagonistic relation to him. Their movements are no longer for his good, but hostile and retributive (vers. 20—24). So the *mental* maladies of ver. 28 are more than the merely natural effects of sin (cf. 1 Kings xxii. 22). "The inquiring mind," says Dr. M'Cosh, "will discover designed combinations, many and wonderful, between the various events of Divine providence. What singular unions of two streams at the proper place to help on the exertions of the great and good! What curious intersections of cords to catch the wicked, as in a net, when they are prowling as wild beasts! By strange but most apposite correspondences, human strength, when set against the will of God, is made to waste away under his indignation, burning against it, as, in heathen story, Meleager wasted away as the stick burned which his mother held in the fire." Laws of nature are the warp, Divine providence the woof, of this awful garment of the curse with which the sinner clothes himself.

II. The curse in its operation. Pictured in these verses in ample and vivid detail. The counterpart of the blessing (vers. 15—26). Takes effect in misfortune (ver. 20), sore diseases (vers. 21, 22), scourging by natural agencies (vers. 23, 24), invasions by enemies (vers. 25, 26). Action and reaction lead to the reproduction of these evils in aggravated forms. To worse bodily plagues (ver. 27) are superadded mental maladies (vers. 28, 29), issuing in renewed panic and defeat in war (ver. 29), with innumerable resultant calamities (vers. 30—33). Confusion and anarchy unite with oppression to produce madness of heart (ver. 34), disease pursues its ravages in forms of increasing malignity (ver. 35), and the nation ultimately sinks in total ruin (vers. 36, 37). Meanwhile, co-operating with these causes to reduce it to subjection, the curse has been working in all labour and enterprise, thwarting, blasting, destroying (vers. 43, 44; cf. Amos iv. 6—12; Hag. i. 5—12; Mal. ii. 2). The full terribleness of the Divine curse, however, is only brought out in the New Testament. As the relation of God to the soul goes deeper than life in the world, so it extends beyond it. The worse part of the curse is the sinking of the soul in its own corruptions, with the drying up of its possibilities of life, peace, and joy, under the weight of the Divine displeasure—an experience of "indignation and wrath, tribulation and anguish, upon every soul of man that doeth evil, of the Jew first, and also of the Gentile" (Rom. ii. 8, 9). Happily, no man in this life knows what the full extent of that curse is (Isa. lvii. 16). A remedial system is in operation, in virtue of which no soul is utterly deserted of grace, and even the natural workings of sin are manifoldly checked, limited, and counteracted. Space is thus given for repentance, and salvation is possible. The end, however, if the riches of this goodness and forbearance are despised, will only be the more terrible (Rom. ii. 3—10).

III. THE CURSE IN ITS CAUSES. Sin, disobedience (vers. 45, 46). The curses written in this book were literally fulfilled. Israel would not serve the Lord with joyfulness and gladness of heart, therefore—sad retribution!—she had to serve her enemies "in hunger, and in thirst, and in nakedness, and in want of all things" (ver. 48; cf. the prodigal son, Luke xv. 14—17). All sin ends in bondage. Nations that imitate Israel in her sins may expect to be made like her in her punishment.—J. O.

Vers. 37—42.—*God, Ruler in nature.* I. NATURAL OBJECTS ARE OF HIS CREATION. The Psalmist bids us lift up our eyes to the hills, and seek help from God, "who made heaven and earth" (Ps. cxxi. 2). It is this which enables him to help us, and makes it reasonable in us to implore and trust in his assistance; as well as leads us to fear his displeasure. Seed, vineyards, olive trees, are his creatures, and subserve his purposes. He who made can destroy.

II. NATURAL AGENCIES ARE UNDER HIS CONTROL. The *greater* agencies of nature—rain (vers. 23, 24), pestilence (ver. 21), diseases (vers. 27, 35). The *lesser* agencies—locusts (vers. 38, 42), worms (ver. 39), "powder and dust" (ver. 24). He marshals these agencies at will, appoints them their work, superintends them in the doing of it. He brings strength out of weakness, making the feeblest creatures the instruments of his most terrible strokes of vengeance.

III. THE FRUITFULNESS OF THE EARTH IS DEPENDENT ON HIS BLESSING. He gives, and he can at will withhold. It is a false science which sees only "laws" in the productiveness of nature, and ignores the hand and blessing of a living God.—J. O.

Vers. 49—59.—*The extremity of the curse.* A truly appalling description of the evils which would overtake apostate Israel; one, too, not more remarkable for the sustained vehemence and energy of its thought and diction, than for the minuteness and literality with which its predictions have been fulfilled.

I. THE PROPHECY IN THE LIGHT OF ITS FULFILMENT. The wonderfulness of these predictions is not removed by any date we may assign to the Book of Deuteronomy. For: 1. It is certain that the Assyrian and Chaldean invasions—to which a reference is no doubt included (Jer. iv. 13; v. 15)—fell far short of what was necessary for their complete fulfilment. (1) The Babylonian Captivity was only of seventy years' duration. (2) The Jews returned and remained long afterwards in possession of their land. 2. It is equally certain that, in the subsequent conquest of the nation by the Romans, with the dispersion that followed, and which lasts to our own day, every feature in the prophecy *has been* exhaustively fulfilled. (1) The Romans agree better than either Assyrians or Chaldeans with the description of the foreign foes in vers. 49, 50. (2) The sufferings of the siege (vers. 52—57) had their literal fulfilment in the Roman wars, and especially in the siege of Jerusalem under Titus (cf. Josephus, 'Wars of the Jews,' bk. v. 10, 3; vi. 3, 3, 4; vi. 8, 2). (3) "Hundreds of thousands were sold as slaves" (cf. ver. 68); "and the whole people were cast forth as wanderers among the Gentiles; and they have ever since remained a nation of exiles, unsettled, harassed, and oppressed, in many instances most cruelly, not only by pagans and Mohammedans, but also (to our shame be it spoken) by Christian nations; and still remaining a distinct people, though without a home" (Whately, 'Evidences'). (4) "To serve other gods" may mean no more than to be banished from the territory of Jehovah, and to dwell in and be compelled to conform to the laws of a country where other gods are recognized (cf. 1 Sam. xxvi. 17). It is also true that, to shield themselves from persecution, the Jews have too often been willing to dissemble and conform to worships which their hearts abhorred (saint and image worship: adoration of the host, etc.); while in idolatrous countries their religion is frequently so corrupted as to be scarcely recognizable. The Beni-Israel, near Bombay, *e.g.* remain a distinct people, but, together with Jehovah, worship the gods of the Hindus. Predictions (1) so minute, (2) so extensive in their range, yet (3) so exhaustively verified by events, cannot be ascribed to accident, but constitute an irrefragable proof of the inspiration that dictated them. Their fulfilment converts the very unbelief and rejection of the Jews into a powerful argument for Christianity.

II. Lessons from the prophecy. 1. *The severity of God.* If the fulfilment of these predictions teaches anything, it is that God will not shrink from the punishment of sin. We shudder as we read the details of these curses—"plagues wonderful, . . . great plagues, and of long continuance, and sore sicknesses, and of long continuance" (ver. 59), and ask ourselves, Can God really tolerate the sight of, not to say inflict, such incredible sufferings? Yet we find that not one of these curses failed of its accomplishment. So solemn a fact bids the sinner pause and ponder *his* chance of escaping in the great "day of wrath, and revelation of the righteous judgment of God" (Rom. ii. 5). 2. *The self-ruinous character of sin.* The fulfilment of these threatenings was largely, though not wholly, brought about by simply giving sin scope to work out its own evil results. The bitterest element in retribution must be the feeling which the sinner has of self-wrought ruin. "He that soweth to the flesh shall of the flesh reap corruption" (Gal. vi. 8). Like water, which, left to itself, will not cease running till it has found its level; like a clock, which, left to itself, will not cease going till it has run itself completely down; like a tree, which, left to grow, cannot but bring forth its appropriate fruit;—so sin has a level to seek, a course to run, a fruit to mature, and "the end of those things is death" (Rom. vi. 21).—J. O.

Ver. 52.—*The high and fenced walls.* God's enemies will ultimately be driven from all their defences. Cities "great and fenced up to heaven" will be no defence to them, any more than they were to the Canaanites (ch. ix. 1). Horses and chariots (Ps. xx. 7), numbers, prowess, wealth (Prov. x. 15), arts of policy, leagues with foreign powers (Isa. xxx.), afford no protection when God is the besieger. Spiritually, the sinner will ultimately be driven out of every "refuge of lies." 1. Self-righteousness; every mouth shall be stopped (Rom. iii. 19). 2. False trusts (Matt. iii. 9; vii. 22). 3. Evasions and excuses (Matt. xxv. 26; Luke xiv. 18).—J. O.

Vers. 56, 57.—*The delicate lady.* (Cf. Isa. iii. 16—26.) The queens of select society have little reason to be vain of their excessive and artificial delicacy. They need not pride themselves in it, or think that it entitles them to look haughtily on others. For—
I. Delicacy is not character. It is consistent with a vain, light, scornful, wicked disposition. The tender and delicate lady in this verse is one of the enemies of God. The purest types of female character avoid those extravagances of delicacy which, indulged in, become second nature. Character alone entitles to respect. To be vain of beauty or breeding, when the heart is false and the life untrue to God, is to be vain of an ornamented husk within which lies rottenness. "'Tis only noble to be good."
II. Delicacy is an accident of fortune. It is adventitious—an accident of position. Born in another sphere, she who boasts of it would not have had it. It is the product of artificial conditions, of which she reaps the benefit, but which she had no part in creating. It is not gained by her own exertions, or attributable to her worth or merit. If she values it, let her at least not despise others. She might have been the cottager, the cottager the lady.
III. Delicacy is valueless when fortune ceases to smile on its possessor. No change of circumstances can rob of its value the possession of knowledge, talents, virtue, good breeding, or refinement. These will grace the humblest home, will

prove a passport to respect in any society. It is different with the fastidious and excessive delicacy of the belle. So entirely is this an appendage of a certain social position that, when that is gone, it perishes like a crushed flower. The admirers of the delicate lady have deserted her. She is treated with coldness, even rudeness. No one so helpless, so dependent, as she. She shone, like the moon, in a reflected brightness, and, foolishly inconsiderate, gloried in it as something of her own.

IV. DELICACY MAY BE COMPELLED TO STOOP TO THE BITTEREST DEGRADATIONS. This is the lesson of the verses before us, and we need not dwell upon it. But the thought of such possibilities should quell pride and awaken awe. The depths of want and woe to which the most delicately nurtured may sink, are only paralleled by the possibilities of joy that lie hidden in the most wretched souls, if they will but forsake sin and give themselves up to Jesus and the guidance of his Spirit.—J. O.

Ver. 63.—*God rejoicing in judgment.* The language in this verse is bold, almost beyond example. It jars with our conceptions of the Divine Being to think of him as "rejoicing" in the destruction of even the most obdurate of sinners. He declares that he has no pleasure in the death of him that dieth (Ezek. xviii. 32). Christ predicted Jerusalem's fall, but "wept over it" (Luke xix. 41). The language is best interpreted, not of actual joy felt by God in the execution of his judgments, but anthropopathically of the certainty, rapidity, and unsparingness with which, like waves chasing each other to the shore, strokes of judgment would descend, *as if* God took pleasure in inflicting them. The figure is derived from God's joy in the communication of blessings. As God's joy—in this case a real joy—was shown in the number and accumulation of the blessings, so would it be with the judgments—he would appear to rejoice in the sending of these also. We do not, however, ignore the fact that God must approve of, yea, rest with satisfaction in, every exercise of his perfections, even in the infliction of judgment. The verse, in any view of it, is a very terrible one in its bearings on the prospects of the wicked.—J. O.

Vers. 65—68.—*Mental torture as a result of sin.* The picture here drawn is true in an especial sense of the Jews in their state of exile, maddened, affrighted, and kept in continual torture and suspense by the persecutions and miseries they have been made to endure. We apply it to the state of the ungodly generally—a state of internal misery resulting from transgression.

I. UNAPPEASABLE RESTLESSNESS. (Ver. 65.) The sinner is destitute of peace (Isa. lvii. 21). 1. There is nothing to give it. No inward source of comfort. No perennial spring of satisfaction. 2. There is everything to take it away. (1) An evil conscience. (2) Sense of God's displeasure. (3) Inward disunion and anarchy. The consequence is that the sinner cannot settle. He does not feel at rest. He cannot be happy or contented in any place or occupation. Like a patient tossing under fever, he thinks that his uneasiness arises from his position, whereas it is his disorder. (Cf. 'Childe Harold,' i. 4, 5; or words of Tiberius to his senate—"What to write to you, conscript fathers, or how to write, or what *not* to write, may all the gods and goddesses destroy me worse than I feel that they are daily destroying me, if I know.")

II. FEAR AND TREMBLING OF HEART. (Vers. 65, 66.) "The wicked flee when no man pursueth" (Prov. xxviii. 1). The guilty conscience is full of terrors. It "does make cowards of us all." Gives rise to groundless fears (Joseph's brethren, Gen. xlv. 3; l. 15). Morbid working of imagination—starting in sleep (Richard III.), fancying sounds and movements (Macbeth). Works despair (Saul, 1 Sam. xxviii.). It unnerves and unmans.

III. LOATHING AND WEARINESS OF LIFE. (Ver. 67.) A sated despairing feeling, incapable of removal or alleviation. Ennui. Unbearable dragging on of time. "I may say that in all my seventy-five years I have never had a month of genuine comfort. It has been the perpetual rolling of a stone, which I have always had to raise anew" (Goethe). Cf. 'Childe Harold,' as above—

"He felt the fulness of satiety,
Then loathed he in his native land to dwell:"

or Matthew Arnold's lines—

> " On that hard pagan world disgust
> And sated loathing fell;
> Deep weariness and sated lust
> Made human life a hell," etc.

J. O.

Vers. 1—14.—*The purpose of temporal blessing.* After the " Amens " from Mount Ebal had been faithfully given, the Levites turned to Gerizim with the detail of *blessings,* and received from the assembled thousands the grand "Amen." We have in these verses before us the purpose of the blessing. The children of Israel had been brought out of Egypt by a Divine deliverance, they were about to settle in Canaan as the people of the Lord. They were a spectacle, therefore, to the rest of the world of how a people fared at the hands of the Lord in obedience or in disobedience. We must regard Israel as a visible experiment, so to speak, for the instruction of the rest of mankind. Now, the rest of mankind at this early stage could only appreciate such a reward as *temporal* blessing. Spiritual blessing would have been no demonstration to them, and have made no impression upon them. Hence it was temporal blessing which God in the *main* gave them. Of course, we do not at all accept the special pleading of Warburton, in his 'Divine Legation of Moses,' in favour of temporal rewards and punishments being *all* that the Law of Moses contemplates. There are significant references to a future life in the Mosaic books, but for the reason now stated, God was mainly working in the temporal sphere. Let us notice some of the particulars in which an *obedient* people were to experience blessing.

I. CITY LIFE was to be blessed. It has been said that " God made the country, but man the town." And doubtless the concentration of population in cities is fraught with peculiar temptation and danger. Yet God's Law is sufficiently " broad " to secure right order and government in cities as well as in country districts. If men would only carry out the law of love, if they would live by the golden rule, then cities would soon put on an air of holiness, and wickedness within them would hide its head. It is through the conscience and heart God's Law works, and city life can alone be elevated and regenerated thereby. If we had pious mayors, aldermen, and councillors, pious high sheriffs and officials, then corruption, rapacity, and self-seeking would disappear through a general and conscientious desire for the public good.

II. AGRICULTURE was to be prosperous. Palestine was intended to be occupied by a pastoral people, and peasant proprietors were to fill the land. It was to flow with milk and honey if man co-operated with God, and did his share honestly. The conditions of the country, as already remarked (cf. Homily on ch. xi. 10—17), fostered faith in God, and success was the outcome of constant dependence upon him. A dependent people wrought diligently and received the blessings of nature as the gifts of a faithful God. There was to be increase of cattle, of kine, of sheep, of the fruit of the field, and of all that is implied by " basket and store." In the basket, as Van Lennep somewhere observes, grapes, olives, and the like are collected, and so the blessing on the basket means general agricultural prosperity.

Now, there can be no doubt that piety is an excellent handmaid to agriculture. All the *cant* now talked in the name of science about God's practical exclusion from the "reign of law," is insufficient to overturn the plain truth that those who try to keep his commandments and live in his fellowship are more likely than others to fulfil the conditions of agricultural prosperity.

III. POPULATION will increase. The fruit of their body was also to be blessed. We can understand how important numbers are to national power. When the population advances in the sunshine of advancing prosperity, the elements of national greatness are secured. The *Malthusian* scare introduced into political economy was an exaggerated lesson upon prudence. Population progresses with sufficient check upon it in the ordinary struggles of life, without requiring such prophets of evil as the Malthusians have been. The prudence fostered, being of a worldly character, has degenerated, it is feared, in many cases, into licentiousness as legitimate, when marriage, except in most favourable circumstances, is deemed imprudent.

Now, it is well known that Palestine must have been very populous, containing about as many human beings to the square mile as the most densely populated countries at the present time,[1] and in its densely filled country districts testified to the general security which then existed.

IV. They will be VALIANT IN REPELLING INVASION. It is noticeable that foreign conquest is not contemplated when they are settled in the land. It is when the enemies rise up against them that the Lord will give them, as obedient people, the power to disperse them. The invasion may take place in one way, but their rout will be complete, they shall flee before Israel seven ways (ver. 7)—the perfect number indicating perfect defeat. The Lord will not encourage them in a "spirited foreign policy," but will make them invincible defenders of their hearths and homes.

V. They shall be in a position to LEND UNTO SURROUNDING NATIONS. Not only would they repel successfully all invasion, but be able to lay other nations under obligation. Now, we see that, in being able to *serve* others in this way, lies the secret of sovereignty and influence. The thrifty nations that can lend to others, so far get these others into their power. In the lending power God promises to Israel, if obedient, we see the germ of undoubted ascendancy.

No wonder, then, that other nations are to fear and to honour them, if this is to be their career. No wonder they are to be the head, and not the tail; to be above only, and not beneath. Obedience will prove the one condition of ascendancy.

Now, it is true that the world can think better in these latter days than it did in the days of Moses. Religion does not now need a demonstration of temporal prosperity nor a favoured nation. Religion now demonstrates its reality and sustaining power in making poor saints bright and joyful; in making suffering saints patient and hopeful; and in making the sorrowing ones resigned and confident of reunion. These are the "martyrs" now, and the seed of the Church. At the same time, it may be seen written clearly on the order of providence that "righteousness exalteth a nation;" that the religious nations, other things being equal, are the more prosperous. It cannot but be so. As nations get no resurrection as nations, only as individuals, it then comes to pass that as nations they must be judged in this world, and get their reward or punishment, as the case may be, while the individuals composing the nations may be asked in many cases to wait for their compensation and reward in the world to come. —R. M. E.

Vers. 15—68.—*A nation becoming a beacon.* If Mount Gerizim had the weight of the people on the side of the blessing, Mount Ebal had certainly the weight of the deliverance. No wonder the Law was to be written on its rocky tablets, since the major part of the Law consists in such denunciation of possible disobedience as might serve to render it improbable. As Dr. Arnold has said, "As if, too, warning were far more required than encouragement, we find that the blessings promised for obedience bear a small proportion in point of length to the curses denounced against disobedience."[2] We shall try to sum up the evils here threatened against Israel in case of their disobedience, and then point out their practical and present application.

I. DEGRADATION OF CITY LIFE. If the massing of people gives advantages to religious effort, it gives corresponding advantages to sin. Temptation becomes intensified. The leaven of corruption gets speedily through the compacter mass. The very mention of the city and its sins and sorrows brings a frightful panorama before us. Ignorance, drunkenness, irreligion, licentiousness,—all these are found in their most fearful forms in cities. No wonder that such a man as Dr. Guthrie delivered a series of special sermons on the subject.[3] Now, the Jews are threatened with a curse upon their city life in case of their disobedience. Chorazin, Bethsaida, and Capernaum are but samples of doomed cities through the disobedience of the people (Matt. xi. 20—24).

II. AGRICULTURE will be cursed because of their disobedience. The land of promise

[1] Cf. Geikie's 'Life and Words of Christ,' vol. i. p. 22.
[2] Cf. 'Sermons on the Interpretation of Scripture,' pp. 44—50.
[3] Cf. 'The City: its Sins and Sorrows,' by Thomas Guthrie, D.D. See also a more formidable book, 'The Age of Great Cities,' by Robert Vaughan, D.D., where the bearings of modern civilization are carefully sketched.

will become, through drought and carelessness, a barren waste, like the worn-out lands of slave-holding people, which once were glorious virgin soil. And travellers have no difficulty in believing that Palestine is under the curse of God.[1] The threat of Deuteronomy has become a sad reality, and the land stands as a witness to the faithfulness of God to his threatenings.

III. A curse was to rest upon THEIR CHILDREN. No more terrible form of judgment can be supposed than this. Parents are touched deepest in their children. Hence it must have been a great trial for the wayward Jews to find their children deteriorating through their sin, and carrying in their persons the curse of God. Population dwindled, and instead of being the countless people they once were, they have become so small that it is one of the wonders of the world that they maintain their separate existence.

IV. DISEASES of the most frightful kind were to come upon them. Now, it would seem that certain diseases were peculiar to Egypt, and of these the Israelites were particularly afraid. Now, the Lord threatens them with all the diseases of Egypt, of which they were so afraid (vers. 27, 35, 60). The diseases with which the human frame is visited are certainly manifold and terrible. To attach them to sin in a way of natural law only makes the judgment the more terrible. Of course we cannot say special sickness is proof positive of special sin; but we can say that but for sin there would have been no suffering and no sickness; and that sin deserves all that is sent. The frightful character of the sickness and sorrows God sends is the expression of his detestation of man's sin.

V. FAMINE was a still worse curse. To perish with hunger because of the scarcity of food is terrible. To waste away for want of due nourishment is terrible. Yet this the Lord threatened, and ultimately sent as the history tells us.

VI. WAR AND SIEGE. The worst enemy of mankind is man. Of all judgments war is worst. And the siege endured in Jerusalem twice over transcends all others recorded in history. Of minor sieges at Samaria and elsewhere we need not speak. According to Josephus, eleven hundred thousand Jews perished in the course of the siege of Jerusalem under Titus by sword, pestilence, or famine. " Besides these eleven hundred thousand, ninety-seven thousand were taken prisoners; and these were reserved, not for the light sufferings commonly undergone by prisoners of war in our days, but for the horrors of the slave-market, and for a life of perpetual bondage."[2] It is believed that direct reference is made to the Roman eagles in vers. 49, 50, etc., and it is known that women ate their children in the terrible siege.

VII. DISPERSION AND BONDAGE. To those with national spirit dispersion must have been terrible. Emigration is now deemed bad enough, even though it may be to a better inheritance. But the Jewish dispersion threatened was captivity which we know came upon them at different times. The Babylonish Captivity was acknowledged by them to be in consequence of their sins, the recognized curse of God. And even after their return in part to Palestine, they came in for bondage to the yoke of Rome, and felt the yoke of iron on them.

VIII. The OFFSCOURING OF ALL THINGS unto this day. The Jews were threatened with such a scattering among the nations as would make them universally despised. And they have become so. Even yet, notwithstanding toleration and Jewish money-grubbing, the nation has not secured the respect of mankind. As Byron wrote—

> " Tribes of the wandering foot and weary breast,
> How shall ye flee away and be at rest!
> The wild dove hath her nest, the fox his cave,
> Mankind their country—Israel but the grave ! "

Such in brief are the judgments threatened, and, as history shows us, faithfully executed. The nation constitutes the *beacon* of history—the most terrible evidence of the perils of disobedience! The following lessons of a practical character are surely taught :—

1. *Of those to whom much is given shall much be required.* No nation was so favoured;

---

[1] Cf. ' The Land and the Book,' by Dr. W. M. Thomson, edit. of 1860, p. 341 ; Stanley's 'Sinai and Palestine,' pp. 117—123 ; Kitto's ' Physical History of Palestine,' p. cxx., etc.

[2] Dr. Arnold, *ut supra*, p. 47.

but, neglecting its opportunities, no nation has been so cursed. It has been more tolerable for Tyre and Sidon, and for Sodom and Gomorrha, than for the Jews.

2. *It is terrible when judgment has to begin at the house of God.* This is the meaning of the melancholy history. It is a tragedy at the house of God (1 Pet. iv. 17). "Let him that thinketh he standeth take heed, lest he fall."

3. *The prophetic threatening did not prevent their apostasy.* Though as we believe, having their possible career through disobedience to direct judgment so carefully sketched, the prophecy lay for ages as a sealed, if not a neglected book.[1] We think, with the rich man in Hades, that categorical warning would reform any of our brethren, no matter how abandoned, but find it a mistake (Luke xvi. 27—31). He who knows the end from the beginning has by his prophecy demonstrated that warning is often despised just in proportion to its particularity and faithfulness.

4. *The judgment on earth is an image of a more terrible judgment beyond.* "For us, each of us," said Dr. Arnold, "if we do fail of the grace of God, . . . there is reserved a misery of which indeed the words of the text are no more than a feeble picture. There is a state in which they who are condemned to it shall for ever say in the morning, Would God it were even! and at even, Would God it were morning! for the fear of their heart wherewith they shall fear, and the sight of their eyes which they shall see." In forecasting what the doom of the impenitent shall be, we would do well to remember what God has done to sinners in the present life. Imagination may picture *post-mortem* pardons and insist on sentiment determining the doom of disobedience, even when perpetuated; but the history of judgment here on earth should make every sane man fear to speak lightly of the judgment beyond. May God preserve us all from such an experience, through the blood and merits of Jesus!— R. M. E.

Vers. 1—14.—*The present portion of a good man.* The natural world may be fitly regarded as the visible symbol of the spiritual world, the earthly state a lower copy of the heavenly. The order of cause and effect is as uniform in the spiritual sphere as in the material. Fire in contact with gunpowder will result in explosion. True seed in fitting soil will bear fruit. "Whatsoever a man sows that shall he also reap."

I. WE HAVE HERE A DESCRIPTION OF A GOOD MAN. 1. He is described by his teachableness. He "hearkens diligently unto the voice of the Lord." This is a trait of a true child. He has a sense of need, a sense of dependence upon another. He admits God's right to instruct and to command. He inquires after God, and reverently listens to his voice. It is his delight to hear the wise precepts of the unerring God. 2. He is described by his circumspection. He is observant of God's ways, discovers manifold and hidden indications of his will. Not only is his ear intent to the whispers of his Father, but his eye is open too. Blindness of mind has gone. 3. He is described by his completeness of obedience. He practically "does *all* the commandments of God." These came of old by the agency of Moses; but a good man detects within the human voice the Divine message—the authority of Heaven. And his entire conduct is determined by the known will of God.

II. GOODNESS IS ALLIED TO GREATNESS AS SURELY AS CAUSE TO EFFECT. "The Lord thy God will set thee on high above all nations of the earth." As in nature it is certain that all botanical life shoots upward, or that gases, as they expand, also ascend; so in the spiritual kingdom it is certain that goodness will grow into eminence. 'Tis not merely an arbitrary decree of God; 'tis the outcome of the very constitution of the universe. The character of Jehovah is a guarantee that the constitutional principles of his empire do not change. Hostile influences and powers may for a time prevent goodness from receiving its due reward—just as superincumbent clay may prevent the young plant from shooting upward, but the final issue is certain. Faithful service shall be crowned with honour.

III. THE REWARD OF GOODNESS IS ITS OWN PERMANENCE. "The Lord shall establish thee an holy people" (ver. 9). "And thou shalt not go aside from any of the words which I command thee." In the life of obedience "God helps those who help themselves." Separate acts become easier by repetition. They evolve into habits. Habits

---

[1] Cf. W. Robertson Smith's 'Old Testament in the Jewish Church,' p. 363, etc.

tend to permanence and constitute character and foreshadow destiny. All proceeds by virtue of an eternal law : "God helps those who help themselves." It is easier for a good man to resist temptation now than it was in the first stages of his Christian life. Devotion has become the natural outflow of his soul, the fruitage of his new life.

IV. BEHIND ALL FORMS OF BLESSING A PERSONAL GOD MAY BE SEEN. The material food does not sustain bodily life; it is God acting through the food. Neither fertile land, nor good husbandry, nor auspicious weather, nor all combined, will in themselves secure a copious harvest; it is God acting through natural forces. "The Lord shall command the blessing." However riches may increase, if God smile not, there will be no joy. The house may be full of children; yet instead of ruddy health there may be wasting sickness—instead of intellectual vigour, imbecility—instead of laughter, weeping : the blessing of God is wanting. We may possess substantial homes, yet no security ; marauders and incendiaries may infest the land. True prosperity is a Divine Father's benediction.

V. A GOOD MAN DELIGHTS IN DISTRIBUTING GOOD. He himself becomes an inferior God, a lesser source of blessing. " Thou shalt lend, and shalt not borrow." The Name of God is put upon him. He acts in God's stead, and imitates God in all things. The result of the Divine favour will be conspicuous. All people shall see the gracious distinction which marks and signalizes the friend of God. All his beneficent deeds will be covered with a glory not born of earth. His mysterious influence will spread far and wide. He becomes a " burning and a shining light; many will rejoice in his light."—D.

Vers. 15—44.—*The Nemesis of disloyalty.* It is instructive that Moses dilates with far greater fulness on the curses attached to disloyalty than on the rewards of disobedience. In the childhood of the world people were more under the influence of fear than of hope, more deterred by threatening than drawn by promise. The message of Moses was admirably adapted to the people's need.

I. THE EQUITY OF THESE CURSES. 1. Disobedience under such circumstances of privilege was eminently *base and blameworthy*. Disloyalty had no excuse. To refuse to hearken to the Creator's voice was sheer obstinacy, which could plead no extenuation. 2. *It was perjury.* They had sworn to be loyal subjects. They had acknowledged the just terms of the covenant, and had entered Canaan on the terms of pledged obedience. 3. *It was rebellion against their accepted King.* If such flagrant rebellion escaped with impunity, God would be dishonoured in the eyes of the universe. 4. *The curses were their own choice.* They knew clearly what the fruits of disobedience were. They had seen the fruits in others' fate—in the Egyptians, in their brethren, in the Canaanites. If they should choose other gods, they should be led into captivity, and *there* they should "serve other gods, wood and stone." 5. *The curses were the natural evolution of their crimes.* Sin is the seed of which penalty is the fruit. If they forsook God; God would forsake them. What could be more equitable? Men say, "Depart from me; I desire not the knowledge of thy ways." God says, "Depart from me; I never knew you."

II. THE EXTENT OF THE CURSE. 1. *It is a complete reversal of the purpose of God.* His purpose had been to bless—to bless abundantly. But sin changes the light into gloom, sweetness into bitterness, summer into winter, food into poison. At every point and through every moment the sinner is in direct and absolute antagonism with God. 2. *Every earthly possession becomes an instrument of pain.* The body, which is the organic instrument by which the soul has intercourse with the material world, furnishes a thousand avenues for pain. Our children are intended as channels of joy ; they become channels of sorrow. Every possession becomes a source of anxiety and care. Every occupation bears a harvest of disappointment. Blight is upon all the summer fruit. Black portents fill every quarter of the sky. 3. *The natural elements become agents of woe.* The sun becomes as a fiery oven, while no cloud tempers the scorching heat. Fierce winds fill the heated air with fine dust, which afflicts the eye with disease and blindness. Inflammation of the blood and fever follow. The air is charged with pestilence, and men breathe it with every inspiration. Material nature fights for God. 4. *The curse includes disordered reason.* Nor can we wonder. The delicate organs of the mind are sustained in vigour by God, and if he withdraw his hand, madness swiftly follows. 5. *In proportion to the previous exaltation becomes the degradation.* It is better not to be raised to eminence than to be lifted up and then cast down. This would be a stigma of reproach in the eyes of all the nations.

III. THE CERTAINTY OF THE CURSE. "It shall come to pass." 1. *It is fixed by an inherent necessity.* The law of Nemesis is embedded in the constitution of the universe. As surely as night succeeds to day, as surely as fire melts wax, so surely does penalty follow sin. Every dynamic force in nature is in league with righteousness against sin. 2. *It is made certain by Jehovah's word.* His word is a part of himself; and as his nature is unchangeable, so no word of his can ever be revoked. This is his prerogative: "I am Jehovah; I change not." 3. *It is made sure by the holiness of God.* For God to treat sin with levity or with impunity would be to do violence to his own nature—would be to act against himself. In the light of holiness sin must be consumed; and if it inhere ineradicably in the sinner, then must the sinner be consumed likewise. So long as God is holy he must, by the essential quality of his nature, pursue sin unto the death.—D.

Vers. 45—68.—*The remoter consequences of rebellion.* The evil if uncured aggravates itself—develops new symptoms; and as the evil grows, so misery increases likewise. The man of God forsees a yet further stage of misery in the distant future. His predictions of woe plainly point to the domination of the Roman eagles, and to the miseries consequent upon the final dispersion of the Jews. To the eye of God's prophet the long procession of coming woes is clearly revealed—a series of miseries stretching away through milleniums of years.

I. IT IS A NECESSITY THAT GOD'S RULE SHALL BE MAINTAINED. So long as the universe continues, the Creator must be King. Our only choice is whether we will have him as our Friend or as our Foe. "For he must reign." We must serve (ver. 47). To forsake God is not to gain liberty; it is only the exchange of a noble Master for a thousand petty tyrants. "Because thou servedst not the Lord thy God with joyfulness, . . . thou shalt serve thine enemies in hunger, and in nakedness." This is the only alternative. We oscillate like a pendulum between these two points—serving God and serving our enemies.

II. IN PROPORTION TO THE GOODNESS ABUSED IS THE CURSE THAT FOLLOWS. The language in the earlier part of these comminations clearly points to the overthrow of the people by the Assyrians. That calamity and the consequent captivity were the chastisements of wisdom—were part of the costly training by which Israel might have been recovered to the Divine favour. But even that severe correction soon lost its purifying effect. Another overthrow, more complete and galling yet, was therefore approaching. A yoke of iron was preparing for their neck, which should destroy their national life. More ruthless treatment should be endured under the Romans than under the Chaldeans. The sufferings in the siege were to be unparalleled. Mutual hate and rage would prevail. All the love of human nature would be turned into hateful selfishness. It would be the reign of hell upon the earth.

III. THE FATHERLY KINDNESS OF GOD IS DISPLAYED IN THIS FORECAST OF SIN'S EFFECTS. It must have been a pain to the heart of Moses (and greater pain still to the heart of God) to dwell on the terrific consequences of possible disobedience. It would have been more pleasant employment to have sketched out the prospects and rewards of righteousness. Yet in proportion to the pain felt in anticipating the desolation and misery of Israel, was the ardent love for Israel's good. If affection could erect beforehand any barrier which could withstand the torrent of evil, that barrier shall be erected. If love can abolish hell, it will. What language can measure the Divine love which thus pleads with men to eschew sin? Even a present sight of coming war does not deter men from sin.

IV. THE FULFILMENT OF GOD'S THREATENINGS ARE A SIGN FOR FUTURE GENERATIONS. A thousand years elapsed before the woes foreshadowed were inflicted. With the Lord, "a thousand years are as one day." Nevertheless, every word spoken by Moses became a fact. The prophecy has been turned into history. In part, those prophecies are fulfilled to-day before our eyes: "Ye shall be plucked from off the land whither thou goest to possess it;" "the Lord shall scatter thee among all people, from the one end of the earth even unto the other;" "among these nations shalt thou find no ease, neither shall the sole of thy foot have any rest." The present condition of the Jews is a signal proof of the divinity of Scripture, an impressive symbol of the crushing judgments of God. Who can trifle with such a Being? Wisdom says, "Stand in awe, and sin not!"—D.

EXPOSITION.

RENEWAL OF THE COVENANT IN THE PLAINS OF MOAB.

(Ch. xxviii. 69—Ch. xxx.)

CHAPTER XXIX.

The first verse of this chapter is placed in the Hebrew text at the end of ch. xxviii., but in the LXX. and Vulgate the arrangement is as in the Authorized Version, where it appears as the title of the section that follows. In that section is contained an address to the people by Moses, in which he appeals to them to enter anew into the covenant with the Lord, which had been before concluded at Horeb; denounces apostacy as what would lead certainly to their being rejected of God; assures them at the same time of God's readiness to restore them should they sincerely repent and return to him; and once more sets before them the blessing and the curse, and adjures them to choose the blessing.

Ver. 1.—**Beside the covenant which he made with them in Horeb.** This was not a new covenant in addition to that made at Sinai, but simply a renewal and reaffirmation of that covenant. At Sinai the covenant was, properly speaking, *made;* sacrifices were then offered, and the people were sprinkled with the sacrificial blood, whereby the covenant was ratified (Exod. xxiv.; cf. Ps. l. 5); but on the occasion here referred to, no sacrifices were offered, for this was merely the recognition of the covenant formerly made as still subsisting.

Ver. 2.—Moses addresses the nation as such, and reminds them of their dulness to apprehend the manifestations of God's grace which had been so abundantly afforded in their past history, in order that he may arouse them to a better state of mind, and stimulate them to hearken to the voice of God in the future.

Ver. 4.—**The Lord hath not given you an heart to perceive,** etc. Moses says this "not to excuse their wickedness, but partly to direct them what course to take, and to whom they must have recourse for the amending of their former errors, and for a

good understanding and improvement of God's works; and partly to aggravate their sin, and to intimate that, although the hearing ear and the seeing eye and the understanding heart are the workmanship of God (Prov. xx. 12), and the effects of his special grace (ch. xxx. 6; Jer. xxxi. 33; xxxii. 39, etc.), yet their want of this grace was their own fault and the just punishment of their former sins" (Poole). As they would not attend to God's word, as they had shut their eyes and their ears, that they might not see, or hear, or learn what God was teaching them by his conduct towards them, they had been left to themselves; and, as a necessary consequence, they had become as persons who had no eyes to see, or ears to hear, or heart to perceive what was set before them for their learning.

Ver. 5.—Having referred to the gracious dealing of God with them in the wilderness, Moses introduces Jehovah himself as speaking to them (cf. ch. xi. 14). (On vers. 5 and 6, see ch. viii. 3, 4; and on vers. 7 and 8, see ch. ii. 26, etc.; iii. 1, etc.)

Ver. 9.—**That ye may prosper in all that ye do.** The verb here used (הִשְׂכִּיל) means primarily to look at, to consider or attend to, hence to become intelligent, to be prudent, to act wisely, and so to have success, to prosper. It is the prosperity which comes from wise and prudent action that God commends to his people (cf. Josh. i. 7, 8).

Vers. 10—15.—*Summons to enter into the covenant of the Lord with fresh ardour and cordiality.*

Ver. 10.—Translate: **Ye stand this day all of you before Jehovah your God, your chiefs, your tribes, your elders, and your officers, every man of Israel.** The two members are parallel: the heads or chiefs are the elders and officers, the tribes are all Israel. The Authorized Version follows the LXX., but against the idiom of the Hebrew. Ibn Ezra says רָאשֵׁיכֶם is instead of רָאשׁ, but this can hardly be.

Vers. 11—14.—The covenant was a national engagement, and as such included not only the adults and existing generation, but the little ones, the strangers resident in Israel, the lowest menial servants, that is, all the elements of which the nation was composed, as well as their posterity in coming generations. **That thou shouldest enter into covenant.** The expression in the Hebrew is a strong one, indicating not a mere formal engagement, but a going thoroughly into the covenant; the phrase is used of the sword going through the land (Lev. xxvi. 6), and of one going into the pit (Job xxxiii. 28). **Into his oath.** Covenants were confirmed by oath (Gen. xxvi. 28; Heb. vi. 17); hence in Scripture the covenant of God is sometimes called his oath (ver. 14; 1 Chron. xvi. 16; Heb. vii. 28). (On ver. 13, cf. ch. xxviii. 9; xxvii. 9; Exod. xix. 5, 6.)

Vers. 16—29.—The summons to renew the covenant is enforced by a fresh exposition of the evil and danger of apostacy from the Lord. This is introduced by a reference to the experience which the people already had of idolatry in Egypt, and among the nations with whom they had come in contact during their march through the wilderness, from which they must have learned the utter worthlessness of all idols, that they were no gods, but only wood and stone.

Vers. 16, 17.—These verses are not a parenthesis, as in the Authorized Version. Ver. 18 is connected, not with ver. 15, but with ver. 17; there should be a full stop at the end of ver. 15. **Their idols**; literally, *their blocks* or *logs* (גִלּוּלִים, from גָלַל, to roll something too heavy to be carried), a term of contempt used frequently in Scripture of idols.

Ver. 18.—**Lest there should be among you;** rather, *See that there be not among you,* etc. The part. פֶּן, *lest,* at the beginning of a sentence, sometimes implies a prohibition or dissuasion, as Job xxxii. 13, "say not;" Isa. xxxvi. 18, "beware of saying" (Gesenius, Noldius *in voc.*). **Gall.** The Hebrew word so rendered (רֹאשׁ) is supposed by Gesenius to be the poppy plant, by Celsius to be the hemlock (it is so rendered, Hos. x. 4; Amos vi. 12), and by Œdman to be colocynth. It is probably a general name for what is poisonous and bitter; for it is used of poison generally (ch. xxxii. 32) and of the venom of asps (ch. xxxii. 33; Job xx. 16), as well as of poisonous roots and bitter fruits (see Kitto, 'Bibl. Cycl.,' iii. 701). Coupled here with **wormwood,** it must be a plant that is referred to; and the union of the two affords "a striking image of the destructive fruit borne by idolatry" (Keil).

Ver. 19.—**That he bless himself in his heart;**—congratulate himself—saying, I shall have peace—*i.e.* all shall be well with me—though—rather, *for*—I walk in the imagination of mine heart; literally, *in the firmness or hardness of my heart,* (שְׁרִירוּת, from שָׁרַר, to

twist together, to be tough or firm); the word is always used in a bad sense in Hebrew, though not in Aramaic (cf. Ps. lxxxi. 13 [12]; Jer. iii. 17; vii. 24; ix. 13 [14]; xi. 8). **To add drunkenness to thirst;** a proverbial expression, of which very different explanations have been given. It is now generally admitted that the verb (סָפוֹה) cannot be taken here in the sense of "add," but has its proper sense of pouring out, pouring away, destroying. The word rendered "drunkenness" (רָוָה, from רָוָה, to be sated with moisture, to be drenched) means rather "sated, drenched, well-watered;" and the word rendered "thirst" (צְמֵאָה, from צָמֵא, to thirst) is properly thirsty, and is used of dry land (Isa. xliv. 3); both are adjectives, and a substantive is to be supplied. Some supply נֶפֶשׁ, soul or person; others, אֶרֶץ, land. The former render, "The full [soul] with the thirsty" (Gesenius); or, "Them that are sated with them that are thirsty," *i.e.* as well those who have imbibed the poison as those who thirst for it (Knobel); or "That the sated [soul] may destroy the thirsty," *i.e.* that the impious one, restrained by no law and, as it were, drunk with crime, may corrupt others, also prone to evil, and bring on them destruction (Maurer). Those who supply " land," render "To destroy the well-watered [land] with the dry." This last seems the preferable rendering; but the general meaning is the same in either case, viz. that the effect of such hardness of heart would be to destroy one and all. " The Orientals are fond of such bipartite forms of expressing the whole (cf. Gesenius, 'Thes.,' p. 1008)" (Knobel; cf. ch. xxxii. 36).

Vers. 20, 21.—Though the sinner fancies all is well with him, and is hardened in his iniquity, and is leading others astray by his example, the Lord will not suffer him to rest in impunity, but will send on him terrible punishments. **The anger of the Lord and his jealousy shall smoke,** *i.e.* shall break forth in destructive fire (cf. Ps. lxxiv. 1: Isa. lxv. 5; Ps. xviii. 8). **The Lord shall blot out his name from under heaven** (cf. ch. xxv. 19; Exod. xvii. 14). **The Lord shall separate him unto evil out of all the tribes of Israel,**—so that, excluded from the covenant nation, and placed beyond the sphere over which rests the salvation of the Lord, they will be exposed to destruction—**according to all the curses of the covenant that are written in this book of the law;** rather, as in the margin, *is written;* the participle agrees with " covenant."

Vers. 22—24.—Future generations and foreign visitants, seeing the calamities with which the rebels had been visited, nay, all nations, should ask, in astonishment and

horror, **Wherefore hath the Lord done thus
unto this land? what meaneth the heat of
this great anger?** It is evident from this
that Moses contemplates, and in fact here
predicts, a defection, not of individuals or
families merely, but of the nation as a whole
from the Lord, and the punishment which
came in consequence upon the nation. The
words from "when they see" (ver. 22) to
"wrath" (ver. 23) are a parenthesis, in which
a reason for the main thought is given in a
circumstantial clause; and the "say" of
ver. 22 is resumed by the "say" of ver. 24.

Ver. 23.—**And that the whole land thereof
is brimstone, and salt, and burning,** etc.;
rather, *sulphur and salt, a burning the whole
land thereof, it shall not be sown,* etc. The
words "sulphur," etc., are in apposition to
the "plagues and sicknesses" of ver. 22,
and thus so far depend on the "see."
The description here is taken from the
country around the Dead Sea, to which
there is an express allusion in the close of
the verse (cf. Gen. xix. 23, etc.). As this
country, which before had been as the garden of the Lord, became, when the wrath of
God was poured upon it, utterly desolate
and waste; so should it be with the land of
Israel when the plagues and sicknesses
threatened were laid on it by the Lord.

Ver. 24.—**What meaneth the heat of this
great anger?** The reply to this question
comes in what follows (vers. 25—28).

Ver. 26.—**Gods . . . whom he had not
given unto them** (cf. ch. iv. 19).

Ver. 27.—**All the curses;** literally, *every
curse,* or *the whole curse* (cf. Dan. ix. 11, etc.).

Ver. 28.—**And cast them.** In the Hebrew
the word *cast them* (וישלכם) has one of

its letters, the ל, larger than the rest, and
another letter, י, which should be after the
ל, is omitted; on which "Baal Hatturim
noteth, There is a great *lamed* and a want
of *yod,* to teach that there is no casting away
like that of the ten tribes" (Ainsworth).
According to Buxtorf, the large *lamed*
represents the first letter of *l'olam,* for ever,
and the *yod,* the numeral 10, represents the
ten tribes, whose perpetual omission from
the nation of Israel is thus indicated
('Tiberias,' I. c. 14, p. 157).

Ver. 29.—**By secret things,** here, some
understand "hidden sins," which are known
only to God, and which he will punish
(Targum Jon.); but the meaning rather is,
things in God's purpose known only to
himself: these things, it is affirmed, belong
to him, are his affair, and may be left with
him. On the other hand, the things revealed are the things made known by God
to man in his Word, viz. his injunctions,
threatenings, and promises; and with these
men have to do. This verse is by some
regarded as part of the answer given to the
question of ver. 24; but others regard it as
a general reflection added by Moses by way
of admonition to his previous discourse.
This latter view is the more probable, and
the scribes may have had this in their mind
when they distinguished the words, **unto us
and to our children,** by placing over them extraordinary points (לנו ולבנינו עד), in order
to emphasize them, though by many this is
regarded as a mere critical notation, indicating a various reading (Buxtorf, 'Tiberias,'
I. c. 17, p. 179; Hävernick, 'Introd.,' p.
281; Bleek, 'Einleit,' p. 799).

HOMILETICS.

Vers. 1—6.—*Witnessing without seeing.* There is an instructive note on this passage
in Dr. Jameson's 'Commentary.' For nearly forty years the people had been witnesses of the extraordinary care of God in watching over them, in supplying their
wants, and in conducting them through the wilderness; and yet the constant succession
of mercies had had no proper effect on them. They did not read the loving-kindness of
God in all as they should have done. Having eyes, they saw not; having ears, they heard
not. The form, however, in which Moses here throws this is remarkable. If his words are
not understood, he may seem even to cast a reflection on God, for having given them
such great mercies, while at the same time he withheld the one mercy which would
make blessings of all the rest. Yet we cannot for a moment think that Moses intended
anything of the kind. He evidently reproaches the people for their dulness. If there
had been an earnest desire to understand the deep meaning of God's dealings with
them, certainly the needful light and wisdom would not have been withheld. Our
subject of thought arising hence is—*Spiritual stolidity; or, witnessing without seeing.*
The following passages of Scripture should be studied in regard to this theme :—Isa. vi.
9, 10; lxiii. 9, 10, 17; Jer. v. 21; Ezek. xii. 2; xiv.; Matt. xi. 25; xii. 24; xiii. 14, 15;
xv. 16; xvi. 9; xxi. 27; Mark iii. 5 (Greek); v. 23; vi. 52; viii. 10—13, 21; Luke
vii. 29—35; xii. 56, 57; xix. 42; John iv. 33; vii. 17; viii. 31, 32, 47; ix. 39—41;
xiv. 9, 22; 1 Cor. ii. 14; 2 Cor. iii. 14, 15; Ps. xxv. 14. Observe—

I. THERE IS A MEANING, RICH AND FULL, IN THE INCIDENTS OF LIFE. Each one's life is full of incident, from morning till evening, from the beginning of the year unto the end of it. There may not have been the succession of what is startling and striking, as there was in the case of Israel, but simply common mercies coming speedily and without pause, just as they were needed; the mercies one by one, fitting exactly into place, *as if* a gracious care had provided all. *As if*—do we say? That is it. A gracious care *has* provided all. That is precisely our present postulate. We should as soon think that the letters in a printing office would spontaneously arrange themselves into order for a printed book, as that the constant succession of our comforts in life should come as they do without any prearrangement. 1. Life's comforts and supplies are a constant disclosure of Divine loving-kindness. They reveal God (Ps. cvii. 43). 2. They are intended to help on the culture and growth of character. Even supplies which come in the physical region, when granted to moral beings, have a moral significance in them. 3. By winning us to God, his mercies are intended to lead us to repentance, and thus to open up to us a glorious goal in character and destiny.

II. THIS DIVINE MEANING IN THE MERCIES OF LIFE IS OFTEN MISSED BY THOSE ON WHOM THOSE MERCIES ARE BESTOWED. Of how many it may still be said, "Having eyes, they see not; and having ears, they hear not"! This may arise from one or more of several causes. 1. There may be some preconceived assumption or foregone conclusion which, if indulged in, will shut out all acceptance of any thought of God's loving-kindness in common life, or anywhere else. Some "high thought" may exalt itself against the knowledge of God. 2. There may be the lack of a spirit of loyalty, so that the individual is indisposed to read aright the messages of his Father's goodness. 3. There may be a misuse or non-use of the organs and faculties by which spiritual knowledge may be acquired. See 'Candid Examination of Theism,' by Physicus, which is a striking example of total failure in this respect. 4. There may be distraction of heart and soul by the whirl and rush of life, so that the spirit has no leisure therefrom to learn of God in "secret silence of the mind." 5. There may be entire indifference concerning the higher meaning of common things. Any one of these five causes will amply account for a man failing to learn of God through the experiences of life.

III. THERE IS NO ADEQUATE REASON WHICH CAN JUSTIFY SUCH A FAILURE TO LEARN LIFE'S LESSONS. For: 1. We have a revelation of God given to us in the Book, whereby we may come at the true interpretation of life. Israel had their Law, by which they might read their life. We have both the Law and the gospel. And the preciousness of human life in the eye of God is taught us in Luke xv., and in the light of such a chapter should the mystery of human life and Divine care be studied. 2. We have a distinct disclosure to us of the one condition on which religious knowledge and certitude can be acquired (John vii. 17; Ps. xxv. 8, 9, 14). 3. There is a direct and clear promise of wisdom to those who lack it and seek it (Jas. i. 5—7). The promises given by our Lord are also abundant. 4. There is the testimony of the experience of such as are taught of God. They can tell of his mercies, and sing aloud of his righteousness (Ps. xxxiv. 6; lxvi. 16). And such experience is or should be an invaluable help to those who have yet to learn "the secret of the Lord." Now, with this fourfold clue, it is altogether needless for any to misunderstand life's mystery and meaning. So that it follows—

IV. THAT TO BE AND TO REMAIN WITHOUT SPIRITUAL PERCEPTION IS MATTER FOR SERIOUS REPROACH AND REBUKE. It is not against God that the words of ver. 4 are spoken. He would have given them eyes to see, had they desired and sought that blessing. And so he will now. Hence there is a fivefold injustice done by us if we remain without the true knowledge of the rich meaning in our mercies. 1. There is injustice to the Word of God. 2. There is injustice to the God of the Word. 3. There is injustice to ourselves. 4. There is injustice to the mystery of life. 5. There is injury to our future and eternal destiny.

Well may we adopt for ourselves, on our own behalf, as well as on that of others, the prayers of the apostle for spiritual enlightenment (Phil. i. 9—11; Col. i. 9, 10; Eph. i. 15—18). For as we understand the mystery of God in Christ will all minor ones have the light of heaven poured upon them.

Vers. 10—21.—*Apostacy in heart a root of bitterness.* In the midst of this paragraph there is an expression of which the writer to the Hebrews makes use as a warning. It is found in the eighteenth verse : " Lest there should be among you a root that beareth gall and wormwood." In the Epistle to the Hebrews xii. 10, the sacred writer says, " Looking diligently . . . lest any root of bitterness springing up trouble you, and thereby many be defiled." The root bearing gall and wormwood which Moses deprecates is, Apostacy from God who has revealed his will through him. That which the New Testament writer dreads, and to ward off which his whole Epistle was written is, Apostacy from God who has revealed his will through his only begotten Son. The parallels between the two possibilities would furnish a most instructive theme for the preacher ; so likewise would the contrasts. We propose now to suggest a line of thought which may " open up " and impress on the heart and conscience the truth that heart-apostasy is a root bearing gall and wormwood.

I. THE CHRISTIAN, LIKE ISRAEL OF OLD, IS SURROUNDED WITH INFLUENCES THAT ARE UNFAVOURABLE TO FIDELITY TO ALL THAT HE BELIEVES AND HOPES. Israel was in the midst of other nations, who had a greatness and pomp with which they could not vie, who had a religious worship other than theirs, and a literature and learning which were greater than theirs ; and it was not at all unnatural that now and then, at any rate, they should cast a longing look at them, and cherish a wish to rival them. And as their acquaintance with other nations increased in the course of the ages, it cannot be wondered at if they were tempted to depart from the simplicity of their monotheistic faith and worship. And now, the parallel between them and us is closer than ever it has been. Increasing research has brought to light much religious literature in the world, which pertains to varied religions, in which even fifty years ago our fathers thought there was nothing good. The great religions of the world—Brahmanism, Buddhism, Confucianism, Mohammedanism—were looked on by some as almost totally bad. And now, some are so elated by the features of excellence that may be traced in one and another, and so startled by some parallels between the Christian religion and others, that they are tempted to indulge the thought that our faith is but one among many—the best, perhaps, of all the varied religions in the world, but yet differing from others rather in its superior measure of excellence, than in any features altogether and absolutely unique and incomparable. Hence—

II. THERE IS A DANGER OF APOSTACY OF HEART FROM THE LORD JESUS CHRIST, ANALOGOUS TO THE PERIL WHICH BESET ISRAEL OF OLD. The peril to which Christians are now exposed is not merely the ordinary one arising from the fickleness of the human heart, and from the subtle temptations and fiery darts of the wicked one. With the larger knowledge just referred to of whatever excellence other religions may have, a new temptation is presented to the understanding, no longer to regard our Saviour as the one and only Redeemer, but as simply the Highest and Best of the Religious Teachers of the world. And so far as this temptation is yielded to, there may come a defection from the faith on any one or more—or all—of the five following points:—1. Christ may cease to be regarded as the only begotten Son of the Father. 2. His Godhead, and therefore his incarnation, may come to be denied, or at least may cease to be held as a part of the " faith once [for all] delivered to the saints." 3. His redemption, as at once furnishing us with a gospel of deliverance and a gospel of power, may be lost sight of as the distinctive feature of his work, to which no religion in the world can furnish a parallel or point of comparison. We have many religions in the world ; there is but one gospel. 4. His example may come to be regarded as simply one that towers above that of other men, and as unattended with any power of lifting the world up to his own level. 5. And with all this, the dread and august majesty with which he, as the Mediator of our race, exercises all power in heaven and on earth, may be thrown into the background, and may thus cease to sway the heart and life. No one who understands the times can fail to see the reality of these dangers, and the serious proportions they are assuming. That amid the storm, the kingdom of Christ will be shaken, we have no fear whatever, but many may depart from the faith meanwhile.

III. SUCH APOSTACY WOULD BE A ROOT OF BITTERNESS. This of itself would require an entire homily to do it justice. We can but hint in outline. 1. If thus the heart loses its hold of Christ as a Redeemer, the attainment of salvation will henceforth become impossible. 2. If once the power of Christ ceases to renew, the old self will reign, and evil passions be under no adequate control. Inferior power may curb the manifestation of passion, but only Divine power can tear up its roots. 3. Such defection from the faith will "defile" many. The evil will not stop with one. It will be infectious. 4. Such dishonour done to the Son of God will bring upon those who are guilty thereof the Divine displeasure. 5. The sure effect will be the breaking up and disbanding of the Churches which are poisoned thereby. There will be no reason why Churches *should* hold together, if their Divine Christ is gone, and there will be no power that *can* keep them together, if his Spirit is grieved and departs.

IV. HENCE AGAINST SUCH A GRIEVOUS RESULT CHURCH MEMBERS SHOULD CARE-FULLY GUARD. "Looking diligently lest," etc. 1. They should watch the signs of the times, in order that, as far as in them lies, they may guard the Church to which they belong from the dangers with which the changeful currents of human thought may threaten them. 2. They should seek so to quicken the zeal and inflame the fervour of piety around them, that temptations to apostatize may have no power. 3. They should cherish a loving solicitude, and fervently pray, for each other, that mutual care and prayer may be an effectual guard against the approach of disloyalty in faith or even in thought. 4. Each one should be very jealous over his own heart. In others we can discern only fruit; in ourselves we can detect the root, of evil. Hence this watchfulness over our own spirits is doubly important, since it may be doubly effective. Even in others we may perhaps lop off the evil fruit, but in ourselves we can see that even the root is plucked up. For this, the only radical, certain, and absolute preventive of apostacy, the Spirit of God can effect, and he will, if we resign ourselves to his almighty hands. He can so renew and sanctify the heart that no "root of bitterness" can find any hold. He can make the soil so receptive of truth that any living seed of righteousness will at once germinate, and yet withal so destructive of error that any seed of evil casually dropping in will perish in its fall. Happy man, whose heart is in the effectual keeping of the Holy Ghost, and who is so sanctified that no germ of ill can find even a momentary home!

Vers. 22—28.—*Historical witnesses to the wrath of God.* The chapter preceding this is shaded, yea, dark indeed. Nevertheless, it is an exact forecast of the state of Israel at this very day. In fact, the comparison between the state of the land of Palestine and the words of the Book, suggests two lines of instructive thought.

I. HOW MANIFESTLY, IN THE DESOLATION OF THE HOLY LAND, IS SEEN THE EFFECT OF THE WRATH OF GOD! To this even Volney bears witness. He asks, "From whence proceed such melancholy revolutions? For what cause is the fortune of these countries so strikingly changed? Why are so many cities destroyed? Why is not that ancient population reproduced and perpetuated? A mysterious God exercises his incomprehensible judgments. He has doubtless pronounced a secret curse against the land. He has struck with a curse the present race of men in revenge of past generations" (quoted by Jameson, *in loc.*).

II. HOW IS THE ACCURACY OF THIS PART OF THE OLD BOOK THEREBY CONFIRMED! It is now a favourite canon of scientific men, that whatever cannot be verified must be relegated to the past and forgotten. To this there can be no objection, if those who insist on this negative will insist equally on the reciprocal positive, and say that whatever *can* be verified must be accepted. For it would be simply a proof, either of discreditable ignorance or of perversity, if men were to deny or to spurn the repeated verifications of the words of Moses in the subsequent course of history.

And it is of no use for men to declaim against the possibility of miracles, when there is the standing miracle before our eye, of some superhuman knowledge having forecast, three thousand years ago, precisely the line along which Hebrew history would move, down till the present day. While there is also this difference between miracle in mighty works, and miracle in prophetic words: The proof of the works is most clear to those who see them at the time; it may possibly diminish with the lapse of years. That of a prophetic word is *nil* at the time: it awaits confirmation from the lapse of years. And as long as our present historical records stand, so long will there remain the confirmation of the precision with which Israel's lawgiver, speaking in the name of Jehovah, laid down beforehand the lines along which the Jewish nation should move for thousands of years. When we put together the land and the Book, the work and the word, and see the correspondence between them, we cannot but say, " This is the finger of God ! "

Ver. 29.—*Secret things.* " Secret things belong unto the Lord our God." So says the great lawgiver. On a not dissimilar topic, Bishop Butler says, " We do not know the whole of anything." Is it not so? Who can tell *all* about a stone or about a blade of grass? Who can aver that the furthest star has been yet discovered, or tell us what lies beyond it? There are secrets among the minute; there are secrets among the vast.

I. LET US MAKE A DISTINCTION AS TO THE MANNER, KIND, OR DEGREE OF SECRECY. 1. Some things are secret, awaiting fuller discovery to reveal them. 2. Some things are secret, but await the unfolding of events in God's providence. 3. Some things are secret in one sense, but not in another. We often know manifestations, but not essences; phenomena, but not noumena; facts, but not modes or reasons. 4. There are some secret things which are altogether unknowable, and must long remain so; *e.g.* Who can give an account of the reason why sin was permitted to enter? Who can tell whether it will always exist? Who can explain the doctrine of the Trinity? Who can descry the reason why this man had such and such suffering? etc., etc. How soon, when we come to ask questions like these, are we in " a boundless deep, where all our thoughts are drowned " !

II. LET US INQUIRE, IN WHAT RESPECT DO SECRET THINGS BELONG UNTO GOD? They belong unto him: 1. To conceive them. 2. To will them. 3. To originate them. 4. To comprehend them. 5. To overrule them. 6. To conduct them to their final issue.

III. LET US ASK, WHAT EFFECT SHOULD THE FACT THAT SECRET THINGS BELONG UNTO GOD HAVE UPON US? 1. It should humble us to find out how incompetent we are to scan the Divine works and ways. 2. It is obvious that we *must* leave secret things with him to whom alone they belong. 3. It is manifestly *right* to leave them with him. 4. It should give us no uneasiness to leave them there. 5. We should be fully content to leave them there. For we have (1) a revealed will of love; (2) plain and straightforward duty to discharge; (3) a full gospel of redeeming mercy; and (4) a good hope through grace. What more can we want? 6. We should be adoringly thankful that God keeps in his own hands what we could not understand, and entrusts us only with what we can. 7. Thankfully leaving in God's hands what belongs to him, let us lovingly attend to that which belongs to us.

Ver. 29.—*Revealed things.* This verse is so full of meaning that it is not easy to do even approximate justice to it in one discourse. Hence we have reserved the latter part thereof for a suggested outline of a distinct homily: " Those things which are revealed belong unto us and to our children for ever, that we may do all the words of this Law." The statement here made concerning the Law of God in particular, is true of the entire Word of God as the regulator of faith and life. Three lines of thought here naturally follow on each other.

I. WITHIN THE WORD OF GOD WE HAVE THE REVEALED MIND AND WILL OF GOD. He made known his ways unto Moses, etc. And now he hath spoken to us in his Son. The sum and substance of the Divine message is, " Where sin abounded, grace did much more abound."

II. THE MANIFEST OBJECT OF THIS REVELATION OF AND FROM GOD IS THAT WE MAY THEREBY HAVE AN ADEQUATE GUIDE FOR FAITH AND LIFE. " That we may do all the words of this Law " is the Old Testament form of setting this. The New Testament form is, " Preaching . . . repentance towards God, and faith towards our Lord Jesus Christ."

III. IN THIS RESPECT THE WORD OF GOD IS, EMPHATICALLY, " OURS." " Those things which are revealed belong unto us," etc. 1. They belong to us—our treasury of wealth. 2. They belong to us—our measure of responsibility. 3. They belong to us—our rule by which we shall be finally tried (Rom. ii. 1—16).

HOMILIES BY VARIOUS AUTHORS.

Vers. 2—9.—*Seeing, yet not seeing.* The Israelites had seen God's mighty works (ver. 9), yet God had not given them a heart to perceive, nor eyes to see (ver. 4).

I. NATURAL SIGHT WITHOUT SPIRITUAL DISCERNMENT. Moses accuses the people of blindness to the facts of their own history. These facts included: 1. God's mighty works in Egypt; here, as in ch. iv. 34; vii. 19, classified as temptations, signs, and wonders (vers. 2, 3). 2. God's guidance of the people in the desert, which also was rife in signs and wonders (vers. 5, 6), and was a course of discipline (temptation, in sense of trial) throughout. 3. The victories over Sihon and Og (vers. 7, 8). No people ever saw so many miracles or passed through so extraordinary a curriculum as Israel did. Yet Moses says they had failed to apprehend the lessons of their history. Seeing, they saw not (Matt. xiii. 10—16). That generation may not have been so dull as the one which had preceded it, but even it had shown by recent rebellions (Numb. xx., xxi.) how far it was from having laid earnestly to heart the lessons of God's dealings with it. A like vail lies on every unspiritual mind (2 Cor. iii. 13—18). The Bible is a book of riddles to it (Luke xxiv. 25—27, 44—46). Christ is known only after the flesh (2 Cor. v. 16). The lines of a Divine leading in the events of life are not recognized. Warnings are scorned; prosperity is misused; adversity hardens. There is outward experience of facts, but, as in Israel's case, the Word preached does not profit, not being mixed with faith in them that hear it (Heb. iv. 2).

II. SPIRITUAL DISCERNMENT IS FROM GOD. Yet not arbitrarily given or withheld. It is given to those who feel their need of it, who seek it, and who act in faithfulness to the light already possessed (Ps. xxv. 9, 12, 14; cxix. 18; Matt. xiii. 10—16; John vii. 17). From none such will God withhold the " heart to perceive, and eyes to see." On the other hand, Divine illumination is indispensable to the knowledge of spiritual truth (cf. John vi. 45; 1 Cor. ii. 12—16; 2 Cor. iv. 6; Eph. i. 17). As the poet's eye is needed for the discernment of the poetic suggestions and analogies of nature, so is the spiritual eye needed to penetrate " the secret of the Lord." The eye in this case, as in the other, " sees only what it brings with it the power of seeing." And to gain this seeing eye, there must, as before remarked, be prayer—prayer and *obedience.* Without these two golden keys, no thought, no labour, no learning, no cleverness, will enable us to force the gates of the inner sanctuary of truth. God's world, God's Word, God's providence, will be alike mysterious; if spiritual instruction is offered, the reply will be " Doth he not speak parables ? " (Ezek. xx. 49).—J. O.

Ver. 3.—*Temptations, signs, miracles.* (Cf. ch. iv. 34; vii. 19.)

I. THE RELATION OF THE TERMS. " Temptations " is a wider category than " signs," and " signs " is a wider category than " miracles " or " wonders." All " wonders," however, in the kingdom of God have the moral significance of " signs; " and all " signs and wonders " are " trials " of the disposition.

II. THE APPLICATION OF THE TERMS. 1. *Wonders,* meaning strictly, supernatural occurrences. 2. *Signs.* Anything is a " sign " which indicates God's presence (Luke xi. 20), which discovers a law of his working, which is a pledge of his grace, which furnishes a symbol of a spiritual reality. Miracles were " signs." Nature is a " sign " in her order, regularity, and invariableness (Gen. i. 14; viii. 22; ix. 13; Ps. cxix. 89—92; Jer. xxxiii. 25; Acts xiv. 17; Rom. i. 20). Every answer to prayer, every deliverance from trouble, every indication of the Divine will in providence, every specific warning and encouragement, is a " sign." 3. *Temptations,* i.e. tests or trials. " Trial " is a word of wide scope, for God tries us every moment, as well by things little as by things great. Every event in providence contributes to the formation, testing, and discipline of character. Naturally, however, we give the name " trials " to the harder and more severe experiences of life—those which most throw us back on our true selves, and reveal or determine character.—J. O.

Vers. 10—15.—*National covenanting.* This covenant—

I. WAS MADE WITH THE NATION AS SUCH. National covenanting finds modern exemplifications in the Scotch covenants, and in the "Solemn League and Covenant" of 1643–44. Irrespective, however, of the particular stipulations of these covenants, the propriety of such engagements must be pronounced doubtful. The case of Israel can scarcely be pleaded as a precedent. Certainly, were God to reveal himself to any nation now as he did to that chosen race, grant it a revival of religion, give it laws and judgments, and summon it by positive command to an engagement of the kind, it would, as of old, be its duty to obey. Even then: 1. The covenant would involve a remodelling of the constitution of the State. It would be meaningless save on a theocratic basis, Church and State merging in one body, and breaches of covenant obligation being regarded and punished as crimes. 2. The arrangement would require for its successful working conditions of strictest isolation—such conditions as God in his wisdom devised for Israel. The difficulties in the way of such a covenant amount now practically to impossibility. In ancient times, the units of society were families, tribes, nations, the sense of individuality being comparatively weak; now the sense of individuality is strong, and every arrangement must take large account of the individual conscience. In Israel, again, Church and State were one, but they are so no longer, Christ's kingdom refusing to identify itself with any earthly polity. The modern state, based on popular representation, and declining to take cognizance of differences of creed, is least of all favourable to the coalescence of civil with spiritual functions. Oaths are to be deprecated in any case, save where absolutely called for. They ensnare consciences, and lead to profanation by the disregard of them by the irreligious. Large sections of the community must always be left outside of such covenants, and in so solemn a transaction, the right of the majority to bind the minority, and still more to bind posterity, must be questioned. The covenants, in Scotland especially, were the source of great religious inspirations, but the good was not unmixed with evil. On the other hand, the fact of such obligations being freely undertaken by a nation must be admitted to involve it in grave responsibility, and greatly aggravates the guilt of subsequent apostasy.

II. INCLUDED ALL CLASSES, AND HAD RESPECT TO POSTERITY. 1. *It included children* (ver. 11). Whatever may be said of national covenants, it is undoubted that, in the *spiritual* sphere, parents and children stand in very close relation. The act of a parent, himself in covenant with God, in dedicating his child to God—probably naming the Name of God upon it in baptism—entails on that little one the weightiest responsibilities. It is a child of the covenant, stands within its bonds, and is pledged to love, serve, and worship the God of its fathers. 2. *It bound posterity.* Covenanting apart, the people that is faithful to God and zealous for his glory, abounding in fruits of righteousness, may expect his blessing to distant generations; whereas the nation that forgets him, and abounds in impiety, infidelity, and wickedness, with equal certainty provokes his indignation, brings down his scourge, and bequeaths to posterity the inheritance of a curse.—J. O.

Vers. 16—21.—*The lying hope.* We have here—

I. INEXCUSABLE UNBELIEF. (Vers. 16—18.) The man who, turning from Jehovah, went after the gods by the nations, was doubly inexcusable. 1. The true God had been revealed to him. 2. The worthlessness of heathen idols had been demonstrated. He had the light, and could compare it with the darkness of the nations around. If not himself, a witness of God's mighty works in Egypt and in the desert, he had heard of them from his forefathers, or could read of them in his Scriptures (ver. 20). The existence of the nation was a proof that such things had been done. Unbelief is not less inexcusable in us: 1. With the Bible in our hands. 2. With so large a body of evidences of Divine truth. 3. With centuries of experience of the regenerative influence of Christianity. 4. With a wide knowledge of heathen nations, discovering to us by contrast our own advantages. Unbelief may be: 1. Speculative. 2. Practical. It is enough that our practice be shaped on the hypothesis of the untruth of God's Word, to constitute us unbelievers (1 Tim. v. 8).

II. GROSS SELF-DECEIT. (Ver. 19.) The act of this wicked man is very remarkable. He blesses himself in his heart, and says, "I will have peace," at the very time that God's curses are being read out to him. Yet his case is not a solitary one. He does no more than men do every day in the teeth of the threatenings of the Bible.

Satan whispers, "Ye shall not surely die" (Gen. iii. 4); "Be it far from thee: this shall not be unto thee" (Matt. xvi. 22); and Satan, not God, is believed. We may explain this self-deceit: 1. From *want of consideration* (cf. Isa. i. 3). The wicked man does not really trouble himself about the curses. They are mere words to him. The mind makes no application, scarcely even asks the meaning, of what it hears. The oracle with which the wicked man consults is in his own heart (Ps. xxxvi. 1—5), and the "oracles of God" get no attention. 2. From *want of faith*. God's Word, even if attended to, could not compel belief in a heart already possessed by an opposite set of beliefs, and determined not to part with them. 3. From *self-will*. Will enters into the question of our beliefs; so long as it can twist evidence, resist unwelcome conclusions, find evasions and pretexts, it will not accept what is contrary to its ordinary bent. While, if the worst comes to the worst, it can cut the knot by a simple "I won't," and obstinately refuse to believe aught but what it likes. The account of the sinner's unbelief and self-deceit is therefore this: 1. He has not liked to retain God in his knowledge. 2. Unwelcome subjects have been banished from his mind. 3. Through unfamiliarity to his thoughts, the supersensual world has become less and less a reality to him. 4. He acquires the power of ignoring it, and ends by disbelief in it.

III. UNUTTERABLE FOLLY. (Vers. 20, 21.) Unbelief, unhappily for the sinner, cannot alter the actual state of the case. God's anger smokes against him, and will certainly destroy him. His sin, agreeable as it may appear at present, will yield at last gall and wormwood. Contending with the Almighty, he rushes on his ruin. The curses written in the Book will not fail to overtake him. It is easy for sinners to "laugh now" (Luke vi. 25), but there awaits them a terrible undeceiving—a day when they shall "mourn and weep."—J. O.

Vers. 22—28.—*The stranger's wonder.* The state of the Holy Land—

I. AN EVIDENCE OF THE TRUTH OF REVELATION. The sterility of Palestine has been urged in disproof of Bible representations of its former fruitfulness and plenty. It should rather be remembered that, were the Holy Land in a less desolate state than it is, Bible predictions would not have been fulfilled—revelation would have been discredited.

II. A WONDER TO THE STRANGER. "Great God!" exclaims Volney, the unbeliever, "from whence proceed such melancholy revolutions? For what cause is the fortune of these countries so strikingly changed? Why are so many cities destroyed? Why is not that ancient population reproduced and perpetuated?" ('Ruins,' ch. ii.)

III. A JUST RETRIBUTION FOR SIN—pointing a warning to ourselves.—J. O.

Ver. 29—*Secret things.* The "secret things" of this verse were the things which God had *not* revealed regarding Israel's future—especially the time and manner of the fulfilment of those promises and threatenings which were made contingent on their obedience or disobedience. The things which *had* been revealed whetted their appetite to know more (cf. Dan. xii. 8; John xxi. 21). Moses in this verse discourages the prying of a too eager curiosity into things purposely kept secret, while directing the people to the things revealed as containing all that was necessary for the doing of their duty. The truth to be drawn from the passage is, that *the Bible is primarily a Book for practical guidance, not for solution of speculative difficulties or gratification of a vain curiosity.*

I. DUTY, NOT CURIOUS SPECULATION. The difficulties and mysteries inherent in the scheme of revelation are acknowledged. They may be usefully distributed into three classes. 1. *Those which are not peculiar to the Bible,* but inhere in all our thinking about the facts of existence. The Bible did not create, if it does not undertake to solve, the mysteries of the origin and existence of evil, of the suffering of the innocent with the guilty, of free-will and necessity, of the reconcilability of man's freedom with God's foreknowledge and foreordination. These are difficulties of all religion and philosophy, as well as of the Bible. 2. *Those which are peculiar to the Bible*—which emerge in connection with the scheme and process of revelation itself. Such are the doctrines of the Trinity, of the incarnation, of the atonement, of regeneration—doctrines all light and comfort to us on the practical side, and yet on the speculative side involving much that is baffling to the reason. 3. *Those which arise from our imperfect apprehension of the facts revealed*—from the overlaying of them with mistaken theories and false interpretations. This last class of difficulties does not concern us here. If we ask, *Why* should so much be left unrevealed in Scripture? the answer is: 1. There is much that *cannot* be revealed—would not be intelligible to us. 2. The purpose of Scripture *does not require* more to be revealed than suffices for our guidance. 3. The existence of unsolved difficulties *acts as a moral test*, and aids the development of faith—faith, viz. as a practical principle, believing and trusting in God on the strength of what *is* revealed, difficulties notwithstanding (John xx. 29). This gives the key to our duty, in presence of these difficulties. We do not forget: 1. That things once kept secret are now revealed (Col. i. 26). 2. That in the course of ages God is ever making his counsels clearer. 3. That it is the privilege and duty of the Church to be always making progress in the knowledge of God's will, as far as he has chosen to reveal it (Eph. i. 17, 18; iii. 18, 19; Col. ii. 2). Nevertheless, it is the condition of earthly existence that "we know" only "in part" (1 Cor. xiii. 9). Our duty, therefore, plainly is, not to neglect the light we have in vain beating against the wires of the cage that confines us; but diligently to improve that light as the likeliest means of getting more. It is more important to get a fire put out than to know exactly how it originated; more important to escape from the burning building than to know exactly the course which the flames will take after we have left. We are not to forego prayer because it is mysterious to us how God can answer prayer; to forbear fleeing to Christ because we cannot frame a theory of the atonement; to renounce activity because we cannot reconcile free-will and Divine foreordination. Revelation resolves the central difficulty, how God can be just, and yet the Justifier of the ungodly; it gives light in abundance on the character of God, the way of salvation, the requirements of holiness; it makes much certain that to the natural reason must ever have remained doubtful. What folly, then, to make duty wait on the solving of speculative difficulties, many of which will probably never be solved on earth!

II. DUTY, NOT ANXIOUS PRYING INTO THE FUTURE. The "secret things" in regard to that also belong unto the Lord. His Word teaches us in a general way the issues of particular lines of conduct, but it lies with God to determine the when, how, what, and where of the actual event. His providence is a mystery unfathomable by all but himself. This, however, need not disquiet the children of God. He is their Father, and they can confidently trust their future to his wisdom and his love (Matt. vi. 26—34). Of little use is it to fret ourselves with fears and cares about what may possibly befall us. Do duty, and leave the issues to him who is above. Duty, not calculations of expediency. Those who steer by expediency rather than duty, in the hope to avoid evils, split on a worse rock than the one they shun.—J. O.

Vers. 1—13.—*The renewal of God's covenant with Israel.* Every act of obedience is a step of the soul upward. It leads us into clearer light and into purer air. The man is braced by the exercise. On the other hand, the neglect of a great occasion of blessing is an irreparable loss.

I. NOTE GOD'S GRACIOUS ACTIVITY ON BEHALF OF HIS COVENANT PEOPLE. Ancient Israel was sadly prone to forget what God had done for them. Ingratitude is base. It injures greatly the man who is guilty of it. We lose immensely by our obliviousness of God's kindness. For the Hebrews, God had exerted his power and pity in methods unprecedented. Almost every act of his for their deliverance was a miracle. The crops of Egypt were blasted in order to rescue the sons of Abraham. The firstborn of Egypt, of man and of beast, were slain to emancipate Israel. The king, his courtiers, and Egypt's military were submerged in the sea to deliver the Hebrews. For forty years they had been miraculously led and miraculously fed. For forty years their clothes had resisted all decay, and their sandals had not yielded to wear. Without ordinary bread—without wine—they had been kept alive; yea, had become robust and irresistible. Conquest over foes was already theirs, and Canaan itself was, in part, possessed. Never before—never since—has God so set aside his ordinary methods of providing for men, and revealed himself as the personal Friend of his people.

II. THIS GRACIOUS ACTIVITY CONTAINED PREGNANT PLEDGE OF HIGHER GOOD. Wondrous as were these acts of Divine kindness, they did not terminate in themselves. They were the earnests of something more—something higher. Every gift in the desert and every conquest in Canaan contained a kernel of spiritual promise. These events through which the Hebrews passed, both prosperous events and adverse, were "temptations," or tests, by which to develop their faith and fortitude. Every carnal battle was drill and discipline for spiritual conflict. Very instructively are the miraculous deliverances here called "signs" (ver. 3). For signs and symbols they were of realities in the spirit-realm. The redemption from Egypt was the sign of a better redemption for the soul. Sinai foreshadows Calvary. The smitten rock prefigured Christ. The desert life was a type of the earthly pilgrimage. The brazen serpent symbolized the remedy for sin. By new and singular methods was the host of God's elect daily fed, and Moses plainly indicates the gracious intention of the plan, viz. that " *Ye might know that I am the Lord your God.*" The descending manna was an object-lesson. Every meal was a revelation of God. Within the food for the body was to be found richer food for the soul.

III. WE SEE MAN'S INSENSIBILITY TO THE GRACIOUS INTENTION OF GOD. In this address of Moses we discover an *apparent* contradiction. "Ye have seen," he says, "all that the Lord did" (ver. 2). " Yet," he adds, "the Lord hath not given you eyes to see" (ver. 4). But the contradiction is only on the surface. They saw, and yet they did not see. They saw the external event; they did not perceive the interior meaning. They had no eye for spiritual penetration. They had not the pureness of heart by which they might have seen God. And the blame of non-possession does not rest on God. Some gifts he bestows unasked. "He sendeth rain on the just and on the unjust." But the higher gifts for the soul he grants only to the meek and the prayerful. "Ask, and ye shall receive." "Open thy mouth wide, and I will fill it." The Hebrews saw the cloud, but did not see the God within the cloud. They saw the splendid coruscations of his glory, and they entreated that the vision might not be repeated. Their mouths were filled with material food, but they had no eye to discern the love which supplied it. They remained deaf to the soft whispers of the Divine voice—the voice within the human voice. They were too carnal to perceive the illustrious vocation to which they were called, or the magnificent destiny that lay in their path. Jehovah offered to be " their God."

IV. WE SEE A FRESH OPPORTUNITY FOR COMPLETE CONSECRATION. On the threshold of the promised land God summoned a halt. He reviews, by the mouth of Moses, their past history, reminds them of their mistakes, reproves their obtuseness of mind, and invites them to a renewal of the sacred covenant. Another chance was given them for spiritual reformation. Here was the commencement of a new epoch. Again, as in Horeb, God bids for man's allegiance. He renews his pledge to be in Canaan what he had been in the desert—their special Friend, their God. In this compact all the resources of God were secured to Israel. His power, his glory, his life, his home, were conveyed to them. All was to be theirs; but on *one* condition—and that condition was a necessity—that they should be loyal and true to him. What a splendid opportunity was there for a new beginning—for a fresh departure! So ever and anon God comes near to us, and offers to make a covenant with us—to be our Friend and God for ever. On the morning of every day—on every returning sabbath—he appeals to us afresh to make consecration of ourselves. If we will be indeed his people, he will be most truly our God. We too may " enter into his oath."—D.

Vers. 14—28.—*The government of God all-embracing.* The detective force in God's kingdom is perfect. Escape through the meshes of his Law is an impossibility. Every defaulter is within the custody of the Omniscient Eye. Arraignment, conviction, and execution proceed (sometimes leisurely) with the precision and certitude of irresistible law. In this paragraph—

I. WE LEARN THE ORGANIC UNITY OF THE NATION. Every individual is a member of the community—an integral part of the kingdom. "No man liveth unto himself." A citizen of an empire cannot demean himself as he please. He is bound to consider the well-being of the body politic. Hence Moses affirmed that the covenant made with the elders and officers present was a covenant also made with those not present. Whoever elected to share in the security and triumphs of the nation was bound to share in its obligations. We cannot belong to society and claim exemption from its laws. The individual is bound by the decisions of the nation.

II. WE LEARN THE GREAT USES OF EXPERIENCE. "Ye have seen their abominations." To a generation that had not seen the obscenities, impurities, and social corruptions of idolatry, it would be difficult to convey an adequate idea of the evil. It was, therefore, of the first importance that the experience of the Hebrews who had come up from Egypt should mould and inspire the convictions of the younger generation. Those who had seen the abominations of Egypt, felt its oppressions, and taken part in uprooting the corrupt races of Canaan, ought to have cherished a deep sense of the value of this covenant with God. The evil against which they solemnly leagued they knew to be a curse to men and an abhorrence to Jehovah. If only the treasures of experience were garnered and utilized, they would be worth more than mountains of silver and gold.

III. WE LEARN THE DECEPTIVE FLATTERIES OF SIN. "I shall have peace, though I walk in the imagination of mine heart." 1. *The transgressor is intensely selfish.* He plots for himself, and thinks only of his comfort. "I shall have peace." 2. *The transgressor is essentially blind.* He imagines that although all others may be detected, he shall escape. He sees no immediate danger. He vainly fancies that his evil course is sagacious, and will bring prompt returns of advantage. 3. *The transgressor is a practical atheist.* Because human magistrates or human witnesses may not discover his crime, he concludes that God will not. In fact, he leaves God out of the calculation. He lays his plans and carries them as if there were no God. The great sin of men is *this*, viz. that "God is not in all their thoughts." Sin seldom appears in its true colour in this life. It is ashamed of its own fruits. It promises its dupes the fruits of righteousness. The creed of this world is that men "*may* gather grapes from thorns, and figs from thistles."

IV. WE LEARN THAT GOD'S DETECTIVES NEVER FAIL. "The Lord will not spare him." The secret conspiracy of the heart shall be proclaimed upon the housetops. If the culprit hide in the darkest den of a populous city, thence will Jehovah's arm drag him forth. "He besets us behind and before." If he be alone in his guilt, he is the more to blame, since he has no help or encouragement from others. All social influences have been deterrent from evil; but he has resisted them all with his obstinate folly. He has been singular in his sin; he shall be singular in his suffering. Against him the anger of Jehovah will burn with a white heat of justice. All the vials of righteous wrath shall be emptied on that guilty head. His name shall perish. He shall be "separated unto evil." The nation shall loathe him. The universe shall be banded together to punish him.

V. WE LEARN THAT THE EFFECT OF PUBLIC RETRIBUTION IS TO MAKE LUMINOUS GOD'S RIGHTEOUSNESS. God delights in earth's fertility. He finds pleasure in fruits and flowers. But his delight in the fruits and flowers of the soul is so much greater, that he will blast all the beauty and fertility of earth in order to produce in men the fruits of holiness. His police force is enormous. Pestilence and earthquake, volcanic flame and electricity, human armies and microscopic insects, execute his judicial word. And the effect upon mankind is to excite inquiry. Wherefore this demolition and curse? Some solid reason must exist for this complete reversal of former blessing. The contrast is eloquent with meaning. The flames of Sodom shed a lustre on the Divine righteousness. The barren hills, with mute yet mournful tongue, declare God's faithfulness. A broken covenant explains it all! The hills shall flee; the stars shall fade; but not a word from Jehovah's lips shall ever miscarry. The sleepless sword of judicial vengeance shall pursue to the death every false thing.—D.

Ver. 29.—*The purpose of Divine revelation.* Taught by God's good Spirit, Moses discerned that the purpose of Divine revelation was not to gratify intellectual curiosity, but to qualify for practical obedience.

I. REVELATION IS THE ONLY SOURCE OF SAVING KNOWLEDGE FOR GUILTY MEN. Knowledge of God, his attributes, and methods of operation may be obtained from investigation of man and nature. But the special knowledge of God's merciful dispositions and purposes respecting sinners can be acquired only from the direct revelation he is pleased to make. Whether rebellious men can be reconciled to God, and by what method; how the injured nature of man is to be renovated; whether any existence, or service, or promotion is possible beyond the grave;—these and other vital questions can be answered only by the voice from heaven.

II. REVELATION IS NOT COEXTENSIVE WITH REALITY AND FACT. There is yet a realm of the unknown which God has not disclosed to men. The class of "secret things" is in God's keeping. Such confidence have we in the benignity of the Most High, that we anticipate further revelations, yea, an unending series of disclosures; but the time and method of these gradual unveilings God has wisely reserved unto himself. One thing inspires a hope of increased knowledge: we have a Divine promise that what we know not now we shall know hereafter. Compared with the unknown, the known is a speck, an atom, an alphabet only. The universe of knowledge is still beyond us, enticing our inquiry.

III. REVELATION IS A RESPONSIBLE TRUST TO ITS POSSESSOR. The "things which are revealed belong unto us and to our children for ever." So long as this revelation is quite external to us it cannot be said to be ours. To possess it, it must fill the understanding, move the affections, quicken the desires, cheer the conscience, mould the character. Then only does it "belong to us." Thus we are to conserve it, viz. by a wise appreciation and by practical use. It is to be handed down to our children intact; i.e. not the written scroll so much as the living belief. We are so to prize and practise this revelation that our children shall see it is our precious treasure, our anchor in trouble, our pole-star in darkness, our daily chart and guide. It belongs to us; therefore as wise men we should use it, yea, extract from it all the advantage we can. For the right improvement of the written Word we shall be counted responsible. We "are stewards of the mysteries of God."

IV. REVELATION IS MEASURED OUT FOR PRACTICAL USE. It is given to us "that we may do all the words of this Law." It possesses regal authority, for it is a "Law." In giving us this Law, God deals with us as with intelligent beings, capable of understanding his will, capable of rendering him efficient service. There is no niggardliness in any of God's gifts. As soon as we have improved to the utmost our knowledge of God's will, we shall receive more. "The secret of the Lord is with them that fear him." "Then shall we know if we follow on to know the Lord." Honest obedience enlarges the capacity of knowledge; it whets the appetite for higher spiritual acquisition; it awakens expectation. To know God and his Son Jesus Christ, this is life; this is an ever-expanding life—life eternal.—D.

Vers. 1—9.—*Time-defying habiliments.* After the extensive list of curses to be recited amid the mountains, Moses proceeds to speak of the perfect providences of the pilgrimage as a loud call to obedience out of gratitude. He points out not only the miracles connected with the Exodus, but also the arrangements of, as we should say, the commissariat. They had not to manufacture bread, for the manna fell from heaven; they had not to carry with them wine or strong drink, for the pure water out of the smitten rock followed them all the way. Nor had they to concern themselves about clothing, for their clothes defied the march of time, and their shoes stood intact all the rough journey of the wilderness. We have only to consider what such an arrangement saved them, and how at the end of the forty years' march, instead of "ragged regiments," they presented themselves in bright and impressive array, to conclude that this merciful care of their clothing as well as of themselves was a crowning experience of the wilderness. It has indeed been suggested that all here implied is a providential blessing upon their ordinary endeavours and barters with the surrounding tribes;[1] but we imagine there is much more in this reference to their time-defying garments. We are led to speak again of the "philosophy of clothes" (cf. ch. xxii. 5).

I. THE PURPOSE OF CLOTHES IS TO COVER OUR NAKEDNESS. This was shown in Eden, and as Carlyle says about his *alter ego* (*Teufelsdröckh*), "The utility of clothes is altogether apparent to him; nay, perhaps he has an insight into their more recondite and almost mystic qualities, what we might call the omnipotent virtue of clothes, such as was never before vouchsafed to any man. . . . Society, which the more I think of it astonishes me the more, is founded upon cloth."[2] And into this most proper purpose of hiding our nakedness, let us observe, the Lord entered in Eden and afterwards. Man is a spirit, but it is also evident that in this present world he was meant to wear clothes and to conform to decency thereby.

---

[1] Kitto's 'Pictorial Bible,' *in loco.*   [2] 'Sartor Resartus,' pp. 58, 59.

II. There is no virtue in raggedness. In fact, one of the prophets, in order to convey impressively the worthlessness in God's sight of our self-righteousness, uses this very figure: " But we are all as an unclean thing, and all our righteousnesses are as filthy rags; and we all do fade as a leaf; and our iniquities, like the wind, have taken us away " (Isa. lxiv. 6). Suppose that Israel had reached the land of promise in desperate raggedness; it would have been no credit to themselves or to their God. It would, on the other hand, have made the invasion more perilous. But when, instead of " ragged regiments," they came with unworn uniforms from the wilderness, the very freshness of the appearance of the host struck terror into their adversaries.

III. The fact had evidently failed to strike the Israelites as it ought to have done. " Yet the Lord," says Moses, " hath not given you an heart to perceive, and eyes to see, and ears to hear, unto this day " (ver. 4). The unchanging, well-appointed host had ceased to be a marvel to itself, although it must have been a marvel to all other observers. The bright, unfading, well-kept dresses continually before their eyes failed to make adequate impression. They took God's goodness, as we are too prone to do, as a matter of course.

IV. God's provision for man's body was a type of his provision for man's spirit. The spirit of man has its hunger and thirst and nakedness, just as well as the body. And we are accustomed to see in the *manna*, which satisfied the hunger of the Israelites, a type of him who, as the Living Bread, came down from heaven (John vi. 49, 50); in the *water* from the smitten rock, which satisfied their thirst, a type of the Spirit, proceeding from the Son, to refresh the souls of men (John vii. 37—39). And why, we ask, should we not discern in the time-defying *garments*, which God so wonderfully preserved, a type of that righteousness with which he clothes our spiritual nakedness, which is unto all and upon all them that believe (Rom. iii. 22)? Round the human spirit, as Carlyle has put it, there lies a " garment of flesh contextured in the loom of heaven . . . it is sky-woven, and worthy of a God; " but around it he is pleased to place another garment, of which the unworn uniforms of Israel were types, the righteousness of Jesus Christ, which is sufficient to cover all our nakedness, and which stands defiantly against the powers of time. It is in this array and panoply that, as pilgrims, we shall reach the land of eternal promise. Vicissitude and change will work no havoc in this garment of God. In contrast to all man's "shoddy" and "ragged righteousness," it stands in perennial brightness, the time-defying clothing out of the commissariat of God. May we all be arrayed in none other as we approach the Jordan!—R. M. E.

Vers. 10—28.—*The land of promise becoming accursed.* Moses has tried the principle of *gratitude* with the Israelites, urging obedience from a sense of the great goodness of the Lord. And now he turns to the other principle of *fear*, which cannot be dispensed with in religion,[1] and urges obedience out of respect for the promised land, since if they are disobedient it will be turned to a land accursed. The land will in such a case become a witness to the curse of God, instead of continuing a standing evidence of his love; a beacon instead of a type; a wilderness instead of a paradise. And it is instructive to notice the exact danger Moses meets in this passage. The curses have already been pronounced; but it is just possible for some one to say that the curse is levelled at collective sin. National apostasy is contemplated, but an *individual* will never be noticed in his course of licentiousness. The wholesale is judged; the retail may escape. This is the idea that Moses here refutes. He shows that the individual shall be judged, and the land become accursed through the apostacy of individuals. We remark, then—

I. The nation apostatizes through the apostacy of individuals. No nation as a public act apostatizes, but it gets rotten through individual action. When then a number of units, under the delusion that as units they shall escape, betake themselves to evil courses, blessing themselves in their hearts, saying, " I shall have peace, though I walk in the imagination of mine heart, to add drunkenness to thirst," then does rottenness enter into the state of Denmark! It is well for units not to pretend to under estimate their influence as an excuse for living as they please. The nation

[1] Cf. Mozley's ' Sermons Parochial and Occasional,' pp. 322—329.

suffers through the deterioration of its component particles. If the individual withers, the nation withers too.

II. INDIVIDUAL WAYWARDNESS MAY WORK THE RUIN OF A LAND. When we look into the admirable work of Van Lennep, we find him ascribing the barrenness of Palestine at present to the cutting down of forests, the fall of terraces, and the consequent want of rain.[1] A land thus lies at the mercy of individuals much more than we imagine. An individual may cut down the trees on his patch of freehold, and his neighbour follow his example, to carry on his self-indulgence with the proceeds, and the result may be the change of climate which turns a paradise into a waste. We have already seen that Palestine was peculiarly dependent upon bountiful provision in the shape of the early and latter rains; and if individuals, through the necessities begotten by their self-indulgence, outrage the arrangements of providence, the land becomes of necessity accursed.

III. AS A MATTER OF FACT, THE HOLY LAND IS NOW AN EMBODIMENT OF THE CURSE OF GOD. Travellers are struck with the brown and barren aspect of the whole land. Spots here and there, of course, burst into beauty through the gift of rain, but as a whole the land is no longer "with milk and honey blessed," but under the anathema of Heaven. How much longer this blight is to rest upon its bloom we cannot say, but the fact is patent to all observers.

IV. THE MUTE APPEAL OF A STRICKEN LAND SHOULD NOT BE LOST UPON THE OBSERVERS OF IT. When the question of slavery was being discussed, before God settled it by permitting the American civil war, attention was directed to the "waste lands" created by the slave-labour. It was shown that the iniquitous system made virgin and splendid soil in the course of years, through monotonous cropping, a wilderness, and that the spectacle of the deterioration of the earth should weigh with thinkers.[2] And Nature is surely meant to speak to man's spirit by her deformities as well as by her beauties; by her manifest wrongs as well as by her manifold bene- dictions. Such a man as Ruskin, considering the question as art critics will, pleads eloquently for the natural beauty which the advancing needs of railway and of manufacture threatens with desolation. But such a wilderness as Palestine now is, such a wilderness as the slave states of America were becoming, speaks to the conscience of observers, and calls for penitence and tears. The muteness of the appeal, the golden silence, which characterizes such impressive scenes, should make each witness of the waste a penitent worshipper!

V. OBEDIENCE TO GOD WILL YET REGENERATE NATURE. We see the reverse of the disaster in Ps. lxvii. 5, 6, "Let the people praise thee, O God; let all the people praise thee. Then shall the earth yield her increase." The wilderness shall yet blossom as the rose when the children of men shall learn their privilege and duty as children of God.—R. M. E.

Ver. 29.—*The purpose and limits of revelation.* This passage states fairly both the purpose and limits of revelation.

I. THE PURPOSE OF REVELATION. It is not to gratify curiosity, but to secure obedience in the successive generations. In other words, it is not speculative, but practical.

1. The objections urged against revelation largely consist in the *disappointments of speculative curiosity.* Because God did not inform man scientifically about the creation of the world; because he did not deliver an articulated theological system; because he did not compose a philosophical text-book;—therefore this popular, miscellaneous, and discursive Book cannot be Divine. But so far from such arguments being valid, they go to substantiate the Divine character of the Book. For—

2. It is *an intensely practical Book, inculcating on parents and children obedience to God.* It takes up man in the family, and urges him to obey God and try to get his children to obey him. It reveals God as a Father seeking the obedience and trust of his human children, and inviting them to the heaven of obedience to his command- ments. It makes man understand sufficient about God to know the duty and the blessedness of obeying him. And here let us notice two important positions taken up

---

[1] Van Lennep, *ut supra*, p. 26.   [2] Cf. Cairnes' 'Slave Power,' p. 77, etc.

by the revelation. (1) It declares that we have been made in the Divine image. Let men make us out to be physically in the image of the beast, we are spiritually in the image of God. And (2) it declares that for man's salvation God became incarnate. Mutual acquaintance and understanding are manifestly possible and practicable upon these terms. Man can reason upwards from his own nature, which, as Carlyle said, after Chrysostom, is "the true Shechinah;" and man can appreciate Godhead when revealed through a sinless human life. As a revelation, then, it is most reasonable.

II. THE LIMITS OF REVELATION. It leaves a realm of secrecy to God. That is, it does not profess to reveal God fully, for "he cannot, on account of his incomparable greatness and excellence, bring his plans and operations within the comprehension of his creatures."[1] The finite cannot take in the infinite. We only know in part. But we *know*. To doubt the possibility of knowing God would lead us straight to universal scepticism. Agnosticism has no logical halting-ground on this side of universal doubt.[2] Hence we venture not beyond the assigned limits of the knowable. We take all that God gives and use it reverentially. At the same time, we recognize a world beyond our ken, of essence and of purpose and of perception, which is God's alone. Our pride is broken; we are penitent before him, and we adore.—R. M. E.

EXPOSITION.

CHAPTER XXX.

Vers. 1—10.—Though rejected and exiled because of rebellion and apostasy, Israel should not be absolutely or for ever cast off. When dispersed among the nations, if the people should return to Jehovah their God, he would again receive them into favour and gather them from their dispersion (cf. ch. iv. 29, etc.; Lev. xxvi. 40, etc.). Moses, looking into the future, anticipates that both the blessing and the curse would come upon the people according as they were faithful to their covenant engagement and obedient to God's Law, or were disobedient and unfaithful. But even when the curse came upon them to the full, this would not amount to final rejection; but God would, by the discipline of suffering, lead them to repentance, and then he would again bestow the blessing (cf. Neh. i. 9).

Ver. 1.—**Thou shalt call them to mind** (cf. 1 Kings viii. 47, where the same expression is rendered by "bethink themselves"). This is the meaning here also; it is not the mere recollection of the curse and the blessing that is referred to, but a general consideration of their own condition and conduct.

Ver. 2.—**And shalt return unto the Lord thy God**; return from the worship of false gods to worship and serve Jehovah the one true God, the God of their fathers, and the God whom as a nation they had before worshipped (cf. Neh. i. 8, 9).

Ver. 3.—**The Lord thy God will turn thy captivity.** This does not mean will cause thy captives to return, for (1) the verb in Kal (as it is here, שׁוב) never has the force of the Hiph.; and (2) the returning of the dispersed is afterwards referred to as consequent on the turning of the captivity. The plural is used here as elsewhere to indicate the cessation of affliction or suffering (cf. Job xli. 10; Ps. xiv. 7; lxxxv. 2; cxxvi. 1, 4; Jer. xxx. 18; Ezek. xvi. 53). The rendering of the LXX. here is noticeable, καὶ ἰάσεται Κύριος τὰς ἁμαρτίας σου: "and the Lord will heal thy sins," *i.e.* will remit thy guilt and will deliver thee from the pernicious and destructive power of sin (cf. Ps. xli. 4; Jer. iii. 22; xvii. 14; Hos. xiv. 4; Matt. xiii. 15, etc.).

Vers. 4, 5.—Consequent on this deliverance would be the gathering of Israel from all the places of the dispersion and their return to possess the land which their fathers possessed, in greater numbers than their fathers were. This last statement suggests doubt as to the literal interpretation of this prediction, for, as Keil remarks, "If there is to be an increase in the number of the Jews when gathered out of their dispersion into all the world, above the number of their fathers, and therefore above the number of the Israelites in the time of Solomon and the first monarchs of the two kingdoms, Palestine will never furnish room enough for a nation multiplied like this." The reference in the following verse to a spiritual renewal suggests the inquiry whether the reference here is not to such a gathering and restoration of Israel as that

---

[1] Cf. Robert Hall's 'Works,' vol. vi. p. 54, etc.
[2] Cf. B. P. Bowne's 'Studies in Theism,' ch. i., etc.

which St. Paul describes in Rom. xi., when the branches that had been broken from the olive tree shall be again grafted into it, and all Israel shall be saved after the fulness of the Gentiles shall be brought in. To Moses, and indeed to all the Old Testament prophets and saints, the Israel of God presented itself as a nation dwelling in a land given to it by God; but as the national Israel was the type of the spiritual Israel, and as Canaan was the type of the spiritual kingdom of God, the full import of what is said concerning the former is only to be perceived when it is viewed as realized in the latter. Certain it is that it was on this principle that the apostles interpreted the fulfilment of the Old Testament declarations concerning Israel, of which the explanation given by St. James of Amos ix. 11, 12 may be noted as an instructive example (Acts xv. 15—17). If the rebuilding of the ruined tabernacle of David is to be effected by " the residue of men " being brought to " seek after the Lord, and all the Gentiles upon whom his Name is called," we need not shrink from interpreting this prophecy of Moses as referring to the restoration of Israel by the bringing in of Jew and Gentile into the one fold under the one Shepherd, the Shepherd of Israel (John ix. 16).

Ver. 6.—**The Lord will circumcise thine heart;** " when thou *wilt* become better, God will help thereto (cf. ch. x. 16)" (Herxheimer). When Israel should return to the Lord, he would take away from them the evil heart of unbelief, and give them the new heart and the right spirit. " Qui pravis affectibus renunciat is circumcisus corde dicitur" (Rosenmüller. Cf. Jer. xxxi. 33; xxxii. 39; Ezek. xi. 19, etc.; xxxvi. 26; Rom. ii. 29; Col. ii. 11).

Vers. 8, 9.—**Thou shalt return and obey;** *i.e.* thou shalt again hearken (see ver. 9, where the same expression is thus rendered). These two verses are closely connected, the former expressing the condition on which the aspect expressed in the latter depends. They should be rendered accordingly, **If thou shalt return . . . then the Lord thy God,** etc. (comp. Gen. xlii. 38; Exod. iv. 23, where a similar construction occurs).

Ver. 10.—Israel would then be restored to the full enjoyment of privilege, would again enter into covenant union with the Almighty, and would be enriched with all the blessings of his favour (cf. ch. xxviii. 11, 63); only, however, on the indispensable condition of their hearkening to the voice of God and being obedient to his Law.

Vers. 11—14.—The fulfilment of this condition was not impossible or even difficult; for God had done everything to render it easy for them. The commandment of God was **not hidden from them**; literally, *was not wonderful to them*; i.e. hard to be understood or to perform (see the use of the Hebrew word in Ps. cxxxi. 1; Prov. xxx. 18); nor was **it far off; it was not in heaven**—*i.e.* though heavenly in its source, it had not remained there, but had been revealed—so that there was no need for any one to say, **Who will ascend to heaven, and bring it down to us, that we may hear it, and do it ?** The idea is not, as Keil suggests, that of "an inaccessible height" which none could scale; nor is it, as suggested by Knobel, that of something " incomprehensible, impracticable, and superhuman ; " it is simply a statement of fact that the Law had not been retained in heaven, but had been revealed to men. Nor was this revelation made in some far distant place across the sea, so that any need say, **Who will go over the sea for us, and bring it unto us, that we may hear it, and do it ?** On the contrary, it was very near to them, had been disclosed in words so that they could utter it with their own mouth, converse over it, and ponder it in their hearts (cf. Isa. xlv. 19; Jer. xxiii. 28; Rom. x. 6). In the allusion to the sea, the representation is not that of depth (Targum Jon.), but that of distance.

Vers. 15—20.—Moses concludes by solemnly adjuring the people, as he had set before them, in his proclamation of the Law and in his preaching, good and evil, life and death, to choose the former and eschew the latter, to love and serve the Lord which is life, and to shun apostasy and disobedience which are death (cf. ch. xi. 26, 27).

Ver. 17.—(Cf. ch. iv. 19.)

Ver. 19.—(Cf. ch. iv. 26.)

Ver. 20.—**For he is thy life;** rather, *for this is thy life ;* to love the Lord is really to live the true, the higher life (cf. ch. iv. 40; xxxii. 47).

HOMILETICS.

Vers. 1—10.—*Dispersion not rejection.* It is very comforting to pass from so gloomy a chapter as the twenty-eighth to such a paragraph as this. In this thirtieth chapter, the onlook and outlook of Moses are much more extended than before. So distantly is his eye cast now, that he actually looks to the further side of the gloomy scene he had so recently sketched, and sees in the horizon a belt of glory bounding his view (ver. 9). So that, although the present darkness and distress into which the scattered nation is plunged are the exact fulfilment of the Word of God, yet that same Word declares this to be a transition, and not a final state of things. " *God hath not cast away his people.*" Concerning them there is a twofold promise : (1) of their conversion to God ; (2) of their restoration to their land. Both are certain. Both will be fulfilled. The first, in their conversion to the Lord Jesus Christ. The second, in whatever sense the Holy Ghost used the words, but what that sense is is not so clear. There had been a promise made to Abraham (Gal. iii. 8). The Law did not annul that (Gal. iii. 17, 18). Now, if we turn to the promise to Abraham, we find (Gen. xii. 1—8) there are three parts in it : (1) that Abraham should have a seed; (2) that his seed should bless the world; (3) that they should inherit the land. Now, when Paul expounds this Abrahamic promise, he shows : (1) that all who are Christ's are Abraham's seed (Gal. iii. 26); (2) that the promise made to Abraham was " the gospel " (Gal. iii. 8),—it was made to him, " foreseeing that God would justify the nations through faith." But since the promise swells out to the full gospel, since the expression " Abraham's seed " includes all who are Christ's,—may not, yea, must not, the land-promise also swell out into something proportionately larger and grander ? Such is the question.

Further. The same apostle not indistinctly teaches that, within the lines of his own exposition, there is mercy in store for Israel. What are these lines of exposition ? 1. That Jew and Greek are one in Christ Jesus. 2. That the Jewish rites and ceremonies are for ever abolished. 3. That the commonwealth of Israel now is made up of men of every kindred, and tongue, and people, and nation.

In the application of these principles, the following steps of thought, *taken in order*, will enable us to summarize Scripture teaching thereon :—

I. There is a condition laid down in ch. xxx. 2.

II. The Lord Jesus has come, laden with blessings for Jew and Gentile (Rom. xi. 26).

III. As the Gentile obtained mercy through Jewish preaching, so the Jew is to obtain mercy through the instrumentality of the Gentile (Rom. xi. 30, 31).

IV. The Lord Jesus Christ declares (Luke xxi. 24) that Jerusalem shall be trodden down of the Gentiles, till the times of the Gentiles be fulfilled.

V. The apostle declares (Rom. xi. 25) that blindness in part is happened to Israel, till the fulness of the Gentiles be come in.

VI. A time is foreseen when Israel shall " turn to the Lord " (2 Cor. iii. 15, 16). They will yet see Jesus as their Messiah.

VII. The prophets also speak of their conversion to God (Ezek. xxxvi. 21—32).

VIII. Then, too, will such predictions as Ezek. xxxvi. 24, 28, 34, 35, etc., be fulfilled, but whether in the literal or in the larger sense indicated above, we leave for the providence of God to show.

IX. The same Book which predicts all this tells us also of the means and agencies by which it shall be brought about. There will be providential movements (Ezek. xxi. 27). But the supreme agency will be the power of the Holy Ghost (Ezek. xxxvi. 25—27 ; xxxvii. 1—14; Zech. xiii. 10. For the means to be used by us, see Ezek. xxxvi. 37).

X. The reason or ground of all will be the sovereign good-pleasure of God (Ezek. xxxvi. 32 ; cf. Isa. xliii. 25).

XI. When Israel is thus restored, it will be like " life from the dead " (Rom. xi. 15). When the long-lost nation is thus regathered, when it returns with weeping and supplication to the Saviour, and, saved by him, sings the songs of Zion, then will it become by its evangelistic zeal what it now is by its sacred literature—a priesthood for the world !

XII. Concerning all this, the fulfilment of past prophecy is a prophecy of future fulfilment !

IN CONCLUSION. 1. Let us ever hold the Hebrew race in high honour. " Salvation is of the Jews." 2. Let us bear them on our hearts in prayer. 3. Let us watch the movements of God's providence. 4. Let us heed the cautionary words in Rom. xi. 18—21.

Ver. 6 (comp. with Jer. xxx. 31—34, and Heb. viii. 6).—*The old and new covenants.* It may not be uninstructive at this stage of homiletic teaching upon this book, to place on record the points of comparison and of contrast between the old and new covenants; *i.e.* between the covenant made through Moses and that propounded and sealed through the Lord Jesus Christ.

I. LET US NOTE THE POINTS OF COMPARISON. 1. Both are made with a people formed for God (Isa. xliii. 21; 1 Pet. ii. 9). 2. Both make God all in all (ch. xiv. 2; 1 Cor. vi. 20). 3. Both inculcate holiness (ch. vii. 6; 1 Pet. i. 15). 4. Both of them are based on sacrifice (Heb. ix. 22, 23). 5. Both teach a mediatorial administration (Lev. xvi.; Heb. viii. 6). 6. Both set before the people a future inheritance (ch. xii. 1). 7. Both urge to duty by the impulse of gratitude (ch. v. 6; Heb. iv. 9). 8. Both appeal to fear as well as to hope (ch. xi. 16; Heb. iv. 1).

II. THERE ARE ALSO POINTS OF CONTRAST. 1. In the form of the covenants. (1) They differ as to the extent of their compass. One includes a nation, the other men of every nation. (2) The spirituality of its genius, and paucity of definite rules and ritual is another mark of the New Testament covenant (cf. Rom. xiv. 17). (3) The new covenant has clearer revelations: (*a*) Of the law of sacrifice (comp. Leviticus with Hebrews). (*b*) Of the Divine character (Heb. i.). (*c*) Of the destiny of mankind (Heb. x. 25—31). (*d*) Of the tenderness of the Divine concern for man as man (Luke xv.). 2. In their promissory grounds they differ quite as widely. (1) The old covenant ensures objective good, if there is a subjective fitness for it; the new covenant promises subjective fitness that objective good may be secured. The one says, "Do this, and thou shalt live." The other, "Live, and you will do this" (ch. xxx. 6). (2) The security for the fulfilment of God's promises to us is far more strikingly seen in Christ than it could possibly be under Moses (2 Cor. i. 20). (3) The certainty of the fulfilment of the conditions of the covenant by those who are included in it, is provided for under "grace," as it was not under "Law." *This* covenant is "ordered in all things and sure," and is in no way contingent on the fickleness of human will. It is a "better covenant," and is "established upon better promises." And the reason of the difference is found in the fact that the first covenant was intended to serve an educational purpose, and so to prepare the way for the Lord Jesus Christ to bring in a greater and larger one, under which regeneration unto salvation should be certainly secured (John vi. 37—40).

Vers. 11—14 (comp. with Rom. x. 6—13).—*The word of faith.* No Christian preacher is likely ever to deal with these words of Moses without setting by the side thereof the words of the Apostle Paul respecting them, in which, indeed, we have the best possible exposition of and commentary upon them. We propose to give an outline Homily thereupon.

I. THERE IS A "WORD OF FAITH" WHICH, THOUGH ANTICIPATED IN THE OLDEN TIME, IS NOW MADE THE BURDEN OF CHRISTIAN PREACHING. 1. There is a grand thesis to be maintained throughout all time, viz. that Jesus is Lord (Rom. x. 9; 1 Cor. xii. 3; Phil. ii. 11). 2. There is a twofold duty required with reference thereto. (1) Believing. (2) Confessing, *i.e.* (*a*) letting the faith cherished in the heart become a practical power in the life; (*b*) letting the tongue speak for him; (*c*) letting the noblest energy be spent for him. We see why these two and just these are named. Believing is the attitude of the soul Godward. Confession is the attitude of the life manward. Both are required. A faith which can content itself without a confession, and a confession which has not its root in faith, are alike valueless. 3. There is a double effect of this double act. (1) Faith—the Godward act—is followed by "righteousness," *i.e.* in Pauline usage, justification. (2) Confession—the manward life—issues in "salvation," *i.e.* the sound use of all our spiritual powers (cf. Acts iv. 9—12 (Greek) and 1 John i. 7). The effects are as the duties. Justification is a right-setting before God. Salvation, a transformed life before man. 4. For all this we have the sure guarantee of God's own Word (Rom. x. 11—13).

II. THERE ARE SOME NOTEWORTHY FEATURES ABOUT THIS "WORD OF FAITH." Moses had said, "It is not too hard, nor too high, nor too far off (cf. Hebrew), but it is very near," etc. Paul quotes this with some variation, saying: 1. "It is near." It speaks to man's inner self—to his conscience. 2. "It is in thy mouth." In words which can be uttered to the people and by them. 3. "It is in thine heart." The word "heart," being quoted from Moses, we take rather in its Hebrew sense, as meaning "understanding," and thus the phrase would signify, "It is intelligible to you." Being thus near, we have not to go to heaven to fetch a Saviour, nor to the grave to fetch him from the dead.

He came. The work is done—done for all, without distinction of persons. Done—once and for ever,

Hence—1. How large the encouragement to call on the Lord Jesus and be saved! 2. Men need not remain unsaved. 3. Men ought not to remain unsaved.

Vers. 15—20.—*A dread alternative.* While handling substantially the same momentous themes, the aged lawgiver, as if the thought were oppressing him that he should very soon speak his last word, becomes more and more intensely earnest, and mingles a solemnity and pathos which may well be followed by those whose work it is to "*warn* every man, and teach every man in all wisdom," that they may "present every man perfect in Christ Jesus." Here is presented to us a series of considerations, which are cumulative in their force, and which should be deeply pondered in strict order of progress.

I. HERE IS A GREAT MASS OF TRUTH SET BEFORE MEN'S CONSCIENCES AND HEARTS. There are a few words and phrases here given, in form most short and simple, yet in meaning how august! how deep! how high! They are such as these—God,—the Lord thy God,—good,—evil,—life,—death,— blessing,—cursing. "Dread words! whose meaning has no end, no bound." There are immeasurable, yea, infinite realities behind them. And having once been lodged in the conscience with the significance which is theirs, no power can dislodge them, nor can any one cause it to be to the man as if he had never heard them.

II. THERE IS A GREAT DUTY WHICH PRESSES ON MEN WITH WHOM THIS TRUTH IS DEPOSITED. (See vers. 16, 20.) To love the Lord, to obey him, to cleave to him, to walk in his ways, and to keep his commandments, and his statutes, and judgments,—this is obviously the right course for men to follow. On many grounds. 1. The Lord God is holy, and all his commandments are so too; and it is intrinsically and manifestly right to follow what is holy. 2. As our Maker and Preserver, God has supreme claims on our loyalty of heart and life. 3. As our Lawgiver, he has the infinite right to require our obedience. 4. As our Infinite Benefactor, having commended his love towards us, having bought us with a price, he has a claim of love as well as a right of law. And it is not possible for a man to dispute this claim unless his nature is becoming so perverted that he begins to call evil good, or good evil.

III. THERE IS A GREAT BLESSING WHICH WILL FOLLOW OUR LOYALTY AND OBEDIENCE. This is so under the gospel, as really as under the Law. For the Law rested on a basis of gospel, and the gospel brings with it its own law. How can it be otherwise? The gospel call is, "Repent, believe, obey." This is the precise and immutable order. The grace of God teaches us that "we should live soberly, righteously, and godly in this present world, looking for that blessed hope," etc. And we know what is the promised issue: "Godliness . . . hath promise of the life that now is, and of that which is to come." "For God is our life and the length of our days." Peace, joy, hope, and all joyful graces and blessings attend on a life which is in accordance with God's will.

IV. IT IS NOT POSSIBLE THAT OPPOSITE MORAL COURSES SHOULD HAVE LIKE ISSUES. Men going in opposite directions, in a right line, on a plane surface, from the same point, can never meet. If to love and obey God be good and tends to good, then the reverse must be evil, and can work nothing but evil. And such ill effects must, for aught we know, go on for ever and ever, unless something or some being interposes (ver. 18). The prolongation of Israel's life in the promised land, even though they reached it in peace, would depend on the continuity of their obedience to their God. They rebelled. Their kingdom was broken up; their people were carried captive; and the sad story already rehearsed became theirs. And if now men quit the leadership of the Lord Jesus Christ, there will be—there must be, a sorer condemnation than for those who rebelled against the Law of Moses (Heb. vi., ix., x.; John iii. 36). The outlook for the despisers of Christ, in the next life, is darkness without a gleam of the light of hope in the distant horizon. And even in this life nothing but woe can possibly be to him who striveth with his Maker.

V. THERE ARE WITNESSES THAT WE HAVE NOT BEEN LEFT UNDIRECTED AND UN-WARNED. (Ver. 19.) Compare with this solemn adjuration of Moses that of Paul in Acts xx. 26, 27; Phil. i. 8. "Heaven" was witness. For every warning given to men in God's Name is known and received on high. "Earth" is witness, for the record of the warning is published to the world. And the warning itself was heard by thousands of ears, and was heard of by many thousands more. By the very directions of our Lord, we are to proclaim to the many, not to whisper to a few.

VI. SUCH OPEN HERALDING SHOULD PREVENT ANY ONE WHO HEARS THE MESSAGE FROM CHERISHING THE HOPE OF SCREENING HIMSELF UNDER FALSE PRETENCES. The following passages may be compared with our text:—Ezek. xxxiii. 2—5, 9 ; Matt. xii. 41, 42; viii. 11, 12. If any one, having heard the gospel message in all its fulness and freeness, should ever attempt to throw the blame of his destruction upon others, the light of eternity will be to his complete unmasking and discomfiture. No false pretences will stand in the judgment (Ps. i.).

VII. AN OUTLOOK SUCH AS THIS MAY WELL GIVE A DEEP AND DEEPENING EARNESTNESS TO A PREACHER'S TONE. Specially : 1. If he is nearing the close of his course. 2. If a year is approaching its close. 3. If he realizes the thought that soon, very soon, some of his hearers may be in the eternal world. 4. If he gives due heed to the thought that, even apart from the possible nearness of the next life, the accidents of time may make the period exceedingly short for teaching and warning any one individual.

VIII. AFTER ALL, THERE IS A LIMIT BEYOND WHICH NO HERALD FOR GOD CAN GO. He may teach and warn and plead, but when he has done that—*where his responsibility ends, that of the hearer begins*; ver. 19, " therefore choose life." The preacher witnesses. The hearer must be left alone with God and his own conscience to decide the all-important question, on which a whole eternity depends. Man can direct his fellow-man to God. He may plead and beseech, even weeping. He may, as in Christ's stead, pray, " Be reconciled to God." But on the hearer *alone* the full responsibility for the final step must rest. We may point to God : but we cannot come between the soul and God. We can herald the way : but we cannot lead the soul along the paths of righteousness (Ezek. xxxiii. 4). Hence the final word *must* be, " Choose life." " Choose ye this day whom ye will serve." With the power of free choice man cannot interfere. With it God will not trifle. And what should be the effect of such an appeal, but to shut the sinner up alone with his God, that between him and Heaven the great matters of life and death may be decided, and that, with the judgment seat alone in view, in full sincerity of soul, the sinner, pressed with the weight of the Divine claims, may then and there " repent," and " yield himself unto God " ? And if then, conscious of the feebleness of a will weakened by so oft determining on the wrong side, he cries, " Lord, help me, and I will be thine for ever," a regal love shall cancel past sin and completely forgive; and a gracious power shall cure the weakness and perfectly restore !

HOMILIES BY VARIOUS AUTHORS.

Vers. 1—10.—*Israel's restoration.* The blackness of the picture of Israel's rejection and desolation is relieved by this rim of gold on the further edge. The verses seem to teach, not only that *if* Israel repent, mercy awaits it, but that Israel *will* repent; that a day of repentance is ordained for it—a day in which the veil that has been so long left lying on Jewish hearts will be lifted off, and the nation will mourn for him whom it has pierced and has so long rejected (Zech. xii. 9—14; Rom. xi. 25—33 ; 2 Cor. iii. 14—16). The result will be the incorporation of the Israelitish people into Christ's kingdom, with *possibly* restoration to the land given them as a national possession, and blessings, temporal and spiritual, beyond those bestowed upon their fathers (ver. 5). In a wider regard, the passage teaches—

I. THAT IN MAN'S CONVERSION, IT IS THE SINNER, NOT GOD, WHO CHANGES. Israel is saved at last, not by any lowering of the standard of holiness, or by any change in God's requirements, or by any new and easier way of life being discovered than that originally provided, but by Israel coming round to God's way of thinking, and doing in the end what God pleaded with it to do at first (ver. 2). After all their sorrowful experiences, the people are brought to this : that they must submit to do what they were told in the beginning that they ought to do. It is so always. There can be no change on God's part. If the sinner is to be saved, it is he who must forsake *his* thoughts and *his* ways (Isa. lv. 7). He must do at last what he now feels he has not the least inclination to do—what, as years go on, he is getting the more disinclined even to think about. Will he do it? Is it likely? Is it certain? If ever it is to come about, what agonies of soul must be gone through before so great a revolution can be produced!

II. THAT CONVERSION IS SOMETIMES A RESULT OF THE EXPERIENCE OF THE HARD-NESS OF TRANSGRESSION. It is in the far-off country, broken, peeled, and scattered, that Israel, like the prodigal (Luke xv. 14—19), remembers the Father's house. Is not this a reason why God sometimes leaves a sinner to eat of the fruit of his own devices—to take the reins upon his own neck, and plunge wildly away into sin's wildernesses?—that he may taste the hardness of such courses, the bitterness, the emptiness, the essential unsatisfyingness of a life of evil, and so, if by no gentler methods, be brought back to ways of righteousness? The penalties which attend sin are, while retributive, also designed in this world for the sinner's correction (Hos. ii. 6—23; xiv.).

III. THAT THE MOMENT THE SINNER RETURNS, GOD IS READY TO FORGIVE HIM. We must not, indeed, post-date the mercy of God, as if that waited on the sinner's self-moved return as a condition of showing him any kindness. God's gracious action goes before conversion—leading, drawing, striving, enlightening, aiding; nay, it is this gracious action which leads to conversion. This is of itself a pledge that when conversion comes, he who has thus drawn us to himself will not say us "nay." But we have express assurances, backed by numerous examples, that whoso cometh he will in no wise cast out (Ps. xxxii. 5; John vi. 37; 1 John i. 9). There is: 1. Forgiveness, with reversal of sentence of rejection (ver. 3). 2. Redemption from bondage (vers. 3, 4; Col. i. 13). 3. Restoration to inheritance (ver. 5; Eph. i. 14). 4. A new heart and spirit (ver. 6). 5. Deliverance from enemies (ver. 7; 2 Thess. i. 5, 6). 6. Untold blessings (ver. 9; Eph. i. 3).—J. O.

Vers. 11—14.—*The word of faith.* Paul, in Rom. x. 6—10, applies these words to the "righteousness of faith," and contrasts them with the voice of the Law, which is, "The man which doeth those things shall live by them" (Rom. x. 5). That this application is not a mere accommodation of the words of Moses to a new subject, will be evident from a brief consideration.

I. ISRAEL AND THE "RIGHTEOUSNESS OF FAITH." The constitution under which Israel was placed, while formally a *legal,* was practically an *evangelical* one. On the legal footing, on any other footing than that of the "righteousness of faith," the statement that the commandment was neither far to seek nor difficult to obey would not have been true. The Law, as requiring perfect holiness, obedience unvarying and uninter-rupted, prescribed as the condition of life (Rom. x. 5) that which no one on earth, saint or sinner—the sinner's Saviour only excepted—has ever rendered. It was certainly "nigh," but, as a "ministration of death"—"of condemnation" (2 Cor. iii. 7, 9), its nighness was no boon. How, then, was the curse averted or acceptance made possible? Not by the ability of the Israelite to yield an obedience adequate to the Law's requirements, but by the introduction of the principle of grace. Sin was forgiven, and, shortcomings notwithstanding, the sincere worshipper accepted in "his full purpose of, and endeavour after, new obedience;" or rather, in view of his faith, of that spiritual trust in Jehovah in which these strivings after obedience had their origin (Gen. xv. 6; Ps. xxxii. 1, 2). The hidden ground of this acceptance was Christ, now manifested in the preaching of the gospel (Rom. x.). From this point of view, the commandment no longer towered above the Israelite, stern and forbidding, launching out curses against him, and filling him with dread and dismay; but its precepts were sweet and consolatory to him, and only filled him with the greater delight and love the longer he meditated on them or practised himself in obeying them (Ps. xix. 7—14; cxix.). It is in this evangelical spirit we are undoubtedly to read these exhortations of Moses, whose standpoint, therefore, essentially harmonizes with that of Paul.

II. ISRAEL AND THE NIGHNESS OF THE COMMANDMENT. "He hath showed thee, O man, what is good" (Micah vi. 8). God had written to Israel the great things of his Law (Hos. viii. 12). He had made known his Name, his precepts, the conditions of acceptable service, the way of life; had given that people a revelation, full, clear, adequate, adapted to their mental stature, and to their condition as sinners. This takes for granted the underlying evangelical element above referred to. Without that, the "commandment" would but have mocked their weakness. And it is this evangelical element in Moses' "commandment" which comes clearly to light in Christ, and which is embodied in Paul's doctrine of the "righteousness of faith." The words of this passage apply with increased force to the historical revelation of the Saviour. They strikingly suggest: 1. That man needs a revelation. 2. That he instinctively craves for one: "Who shall go up?" etc. 3. That he would sometimes make great sacrifices in order to get one: "Go up to heaven;" "go over the sea." But the revelation which man needs most of all is the revelation of a Saviour. He wants to know how he can escape from sin, from guilt, from wrath, from bondage; how he can be restored to holiness, to peace, to blessedness. The "commandment," in its wider sense, gave him this knowledge in part; the full discovery is in the gospel. The Word, in the preaching of this gospel, as well as in the circulation of copies of the Scriptures, and the innumerable opportunities enjoyed in Christian lands of getting acquainted with the way of life, has now come very nigh to us. It is in our mouths and in our hearts, while the salvation which the Word makes known is as readily available as the Word itself is simple and intelligible. "If thou shalt confess," etc. (Rom. x. 9).

III. ISRAEL AND THE PRACTICABLENESS OF OBEDIENCE. The word which Moses gave was one which *could be obeyed*—nay, obedience to which was easy. Only, however, provided there was circumcision of heart (ver. 6)—a sincere willingness to know and to do God's will (John vii. 17). To the natural heart the commandment is hard, and must always remain so. This, again, shows that the obedience Moses has in view is the spiritual, though not faultless, obedience of the believing and renewed heart—the result of possession of and standing in the righteousness of faith. Only through faith relying on a word of grace, and apprehending mercy in the character of God, is such obedience possible. Ability to render it is included in that "being saved," which Paul posits as a result of believing with the heart in the crucified and risen Christ (Rom. x. 9). Observe, further, how the Law, with all its apparent complexity and cumbrousness, resolves itself in Moses' hands into one "commandment" (ver. 11). It is this which makes the Law simple, just as it is the simplicity of the gospel that it reduces all "works of God" to the one work of "believing on him whom he hath sent" (John vi. 29). Amidst the multiplicity of commands, there was but one real command—that of loving the Lord their God (ch. vi. 4; x. 12; vers. 6, 10, 16, 20). In love is implied faith—the knowing and believing the love which God has to us. Love is faith's response to the revelation God makes of himself to man. Faith is thus the condition: 1. Of justification. 2. Of acceptableness in obedience. 3. Of power to render obedience.—J. O.

Vers. 15—20.—*A last word.* I. AN ALTERNATIVE. Life and death; good and evil (ver. 15); blessing and cursing (ver. 19). An alternative for the nation, but also for the individual. "Life" is more than existence—it is holy and happy existence. "Death" is not equivalent to non-existence. As respects the natural life, it is the separation of the living, thinking principle from the body, and is compatible with the survival of the soul in a future state. As respects the spiritual life—that life which the believer *has*, and the unbeliever *has not*, even now, while yet both have conscious being (1 John v. 12)—death is the cessation in the soul of all holy, spiritual functions, implying, indeed, a state of moral ruin, destruction, and disorganization, but by no means the wiping out of consciousness. "Eternal death"—a phrase not scriptural, though "eternal punishment" is (Matt. xxv. 46)—is not held by any one to *mean* "eternal existence in suffering;" but it is believed that a being who exists eternally, and exists consciously, whether in actual suffering or not, may yet in a very true sense be "dead." "Death," in this verse (ver. 15), is deemed compatible with experience of "evil." How strange that between *such* alternatives there should be a moment's hesitation!

II. A WARNING. (Vers. 17, 18.) If the heart is drawn away from God, and turns to idols, *i.e.* sets up any other objects in God's place, and forbears to give to God his proper love and honour, he whose heart does this, or the nation if it does so, shall surely perish. 1. An *awful* end. 2. A *certain* end. 3. An end of which *due warning* has been given.

III. AN APPEAL. (Vers. 19, 20.) "Therefore choose life," etc. On which note : 1. That choice or moral determination underlies our salvation. 2. That choice underlies the possibility of love to God. 3. That one deep choice in the heart's centre underlies all the separate acts of choice involved in a life of obedience. 4. That the choice God wishes involves the choosing of himself, with a view to love him, to obey him, and to cleave to him. 5. That the choice of God is the choice of life, and carries all lesser good with it.—J. O.

Ver. 19.—*Nature a witness.* (See for other instances, ch. iv. 26; xxxi. 28; xxxii. 1; Isa. i. 2.) The invocation of heaven and earth as witnesses turns on deep principles. They are " called to record "—

I. BECAUSE THE MIND RECOGNIZES THEIR PRESENCE AS WITNESSES OF ITS TRANSACTIONS. It projects its own consciousness on its surroundings, and feels as if earth and sky, sun, moon, rock, river, tree, mountain, were not inanimate but animate and sympathetic witnesses of its doings. It attaches its own thoughts to the outward objects. In presence of the scene of any great transaction, it feels as if the place retained its memory ; still spoke to it of the past; thought, felt, rejoiced, accused, praised, according to the nature of the deed. Define as we will this feeling of a " Presence " in nature— this " sense of something far more deeply interfused," which we inevitably carry with us into our relations with the outward universe—it is a fact in consciousness, and furnishes a basis for such appeals as those of Moses.

II. BECAUSE GOD IS PRESENT IN HEAVEN AND EARTH AS A WITNESS OF WHAT IS DONE. (Cf. Matt. v. 34, 35.) Heaven is his throne; earth, his footstool. He is present in them, upholding them by the word of his power, and through them is a true witness of all we say and do.

III. BECAUSE HEAVEN AND EARTH ARE CREATURES THEMSELVES CONSPICUOUSLY FULFILLING THE ENDS OF THEIR CREATION. The universe as a whole is thus a standing protest against the apostacy and self-willedness of the sinner (Isa. i. 1, 2). It bears witness against him by its very fidelity to its Creator. "They continue this day according to thine ordinances, for all are thy servants" (Ps. cxix. 91).

IV. BECAUSE HEAVEN AND EARTH ARE SIGNAL MONUMENTS OF THE DIVINE FAITH-FULNESS AND IMMUTABILITY. (Ps. cxix. 89, 90.) They testify to the reign of law, to God's constancy of purpose, to the uniformity and inflexibility of his rule. They dash the sinner's hopes of his Word failing, of his threatenings not being put in force.

V. BECAUSE HEAVEN AND EARTH RETAIN AN ACTUAL RECORD OF WHAT IS DONE IN THEIR PRESENCE—a record which may admit of being produced. This is simple truth of science.

VI. BECAUSE HEAVEN AND EARTH ARE INTERESTED SPECTATORS OF WHAT IS BEING DONE. They have shared in the consequences of man's transgression; they will share in the glory of the manifestation of the sons of God. They wait the day of their redemption with earnest expectation (Rom. viii. 19—23).

That Moses, in connection with his appeal to the people, summoned heaven and earth to witness, was an evidence : 1. Of the *solemnity* of this appeal. It must be a matter of momentous importance when the universe is called in to witness it. 2. Of the *rationality* of this appeal. Nature and nature's God were on his side. He had the universe with him, though a foolish people might reject his counsel. 3. Of the *enduringness* of the issues which depended on this appeal. Neither the blessing nor the curse would work themselves out in a day. It needed *lasting* witnesses to take account of the fulfilment of God's words.—J. O.

Vers. 1—10.—*Divine discipline founded on known principle.* Human anger is often an uncontrollable passion. God's anger is directed, not so much against the man, as against his sin. God's anger is the acting of sound principle—a part of his righteousness. Hence, as soon as chastisement produces its designed effect, it ceases. Instantly that the wayward child turns to its Father, the Father turns to his child.

I. REPENTANCE OFTEN SPRINGS OUT OF THE BITTER EXPERIENCE OF TROUBLE. 1. Disobedience brings degradation. Moses foresaw that the elect of God would become, for their sin, captives in a foreign land. No chastisement would be more galling to their pride. Their renown as conquerors had spread far and wide. To be crushed, enchained, and exiled was humiliation unspeakable. Such degradation is the native fruit of sin. 2. The curse would be felt the more as a contrast to former blessing. The ploughboy does not bemoan his lot, but for a prince to be tied to a plough would be a galling pain. So the prodigal boy, in the parable, was stung by the remembrance of former plenty. 3. Impression would be deepened by the recollection that this misery had been predicted. It was evidently no casual occurrence. They had brought the disaster upon themselves. They could lay the blame nowhere but on their own folly. Unless the moral nature be utterly dead, such experiences often lead to reflection, sorrow, and repentance.

II. REPENTANCE INCLUDES PRACTICAL REFORMATION. Repentance that expends itself in idle grief is a counterfeit. True repentance takes instant decision to retrace false steps. Darkness had come by turning away from the sun; now the penitent man turns fully toward it. He does not wait for others to act. He is not going to be deterred by others' indifference or by noisy ridicule. Call him "turncoat," if you will; there are worse characters in the world than turncoats. He is more afraid of God's anger than of man's paltry spleen. It is not only a halt in the downward course, but "right-about face." He returns unto the Lord. He now docilely listens to his voice; he honestly endeavours to practise all the Father's will. "Lord, what wilt thou have me to do?" is his daily prayer. His whole heart goes out in repentance. To repair past follies—this is his special work. So earnest is he in his new life, so marked a change and so beneficent is there in his character, that his children feel the impression, and catch the blessed contagion. As formerly his influence over his family was most baneful, so now it becomes vernal sunshine, like the fragrance of sweetest flowers.

III. REPENTANCE SECURES THE REVERSAL OF THE CURSE. No sooner do men return to God than God returns to them. Only level the barrier which sin has set up, and reunion of man with God is restored. The return of favour shall be most complete. No matter how far the curse had taken effect; no matter how far the separation had proceeded; no matter to what extremity of woe the rebels have been driven;—from thence will Jehovah gather them,—reconciliation shall be thorough. Omnipotence will outpour itself in benedictions. Let the frost of winter be ever so severe, the summer sun shall melt it. He who created the universe out of nothing can reverse all the wheels of adversity; and, out of ruins, rebuild a glorious city. As sin is the only source of disorder and woe, so repentance is the extinction of the cause of woe. If God takes in hand to restore his people to peace, all opposition is vain. The thing is done.

IV. REPENTANCE LEADS TO ENTIRE RENEWAL OF A MAN'S NATURE. "The Lord thy God will circumcise thine heart, and the heart of thy seed." Honest endeavours after a righteous life shows to us a corrupt heart—a heart prone to love evil. The man who begins to pray for pardon soon learns to pray for purity. Nothing will satisfy the mind (when divinely illumined) short of complete regeneration. The repentant Jew discovered that the circumcision of the flesh effected nothing to deter from sin; *now* he perceives that circumcision of heart is the only real safeguard. At a later day, this inward change was more clearly pictured: "I will take away the stony heart out of your flesh." To the same effect Jesus promised: "If ye . . . keep my commandments, I will send you another Comforter, even the Spirit of truth, who dwelleth with you, and shall be in you."

V. REPENTANCE IN MEN AWAKENS PUREST JOY IN GOD. "The Lord will again rejoice over thee for good." So Jesus himself affirmed: "There is joy in heaven over one sinner that repenteth." For reasons which we cannot fathom, the well-being of man is a matter of the liveliest interest with God. Union of nature, and of interest between man and God is intimate. "His glory is great in our salvation." To bring all his purposes and enterprises to a successful issue—this is a source of loftiest joy to God. "He will rejoice over us with singing." The gladness of Jehovah at the completeness and beauty of creation was great; a hundredfold greater will be his joy at the final success of redemption. Messiah will "see of the travail of his soul, and shall be *satisfied.*"—D.

Vers. 11—14.—*Revealed truth clear and available.* Dishonest minds are wont to plead that religious truth is recondite, self-contradictory, hard to be understood. Its obligations too, they aver, are impracticable, beyond the power of man to fulfil. Self-indulgence and impiety have never yet failed to frame excuses for their rejection of the Divine Word. But excuses avail them nothing. The indolent man has for long ages past learnt to say, "There is a lion in the path." Honest investigation soon finds the truth of God " worthy of all acceptation."

I. OBSERVE THE AUTHORITY OF GOD'S WORD. It is a " commandment." It comes to men with all the character of a law. It is not possible that we should treat it as we please. We are not permitted to mutilate or dismember it—not permitted to accept a part and reject a part. As in a tree the living sap runs into every branch and twig and leaf, so that we cannot pluck the tiniest part without breaking the vital current; so every part of God's Scripture is instinct with high authority, nor can we neglect the least commandment without defying the majesty of heaven. We are bound to bow our wills to it; it will, in no degree, bend its requirements to suit our tastes.

II. THE PERSPICUITY OF GOD'S WORD. Its essential truths are within the compass of every mind. Every man knows what it is to love; that love is due from each man to his Maker. Every child knows what obedience means; *that* obedience is due to the Father of our spirits. Truly, some facts concerning the eternal world are so profound that, like ocean-depths, human reason cannot fathom them. But these are not the facts which lie at the foundation of man's safety and hope. The practical duties which appertain to virtue and well-being are so plain that even a child may understand. Whatever difficulty lies in the way of human obedience, it does not lie in the haze or uncertain meaning of the revelation. The difficulty is *within* a man, not without him. The objects of faith are clearly revealed; we want only an eye to discern them.

III. THE ACCOMMODATENESS OF GOD'S WORD. On the part of scriptural truth, there is an exquisite fitness to meet the capacity of men's minds and the needs of their souls. "The word is nigh thee; yea, in thy very heart." There is perfect accord between the constitution of the man and the contents of revelation. The Bible is the counterpart and complement of conscience. It is obvious that the Lord of conscience is Lord of Scripture also. The Bible says, " Thou hast sinned; " and conscience admits the fact. The Bible says, "Thou art helpless to save thyself; " and conscience knows it true. The Bible declares that happiness is inseparable from obedience; and con-science feels that it is so. There is a living witness in every man (until gagged by sin) which testifies to the authority and necessity and reasonableness of God's Law.

IV. THE PRACTICALNESS OF GOD'S WORD. " That thou mayest *do* it." Religious truth is not revealed to gratify a prurient curiosity, not to afford matter for specula-tion, but solely to promote obedience. To *know* God's requirements will bring us no advantage unless we heartily and loyally *do* them. Accurate and orthodox beliefs convey, in themselves, no life nor joy. Right belief is barren and abortive until it brings forth active obedience. We are not to be judged at God's tribunal for our opinions or theories, nor for our religious creeds; we are to be judged of " the *deeds* done in the body." " I was hungry, and ye gave me meat," will be the grounds of the judicial verdict. Practical service is the end and purpose of Divine revelation.—D.

Vers. 15—20.—*An alternative choice.* The prophet's power to persuade and in-fluence a people is great—unspeakably great; yet it is not irresistible. It has its limits. After all that has been said to him, a man feels that the determination and choice rest within himself. Reason may be convinced; judgment may give a decided verdict; still inclination may inordinately lean to the weaker side, and baffle all prudent cal-culations. The intense eagerness of Moses for the people's weal is a sublime spectacle of generous devotement—an unparalleled instance of ardent patriotism. Calling up all his powers of persuasive and passionate appeal, he makes a final effort to win the tribes for God. We have here—

I. ALTERNATIVE LINES OF CONDUCT. All possible courses of life are reduced to two —*one* of which every man must take; a third course is excluded. The two are separately described. 1. The course of loyalty is described: (1) *By the man's state of heart.* " To love the Lord thy God." This determines all that follows—the root out of which all flowers and fruits of obedience spring. This love arises from a right appreciation of God. " He is thy life," yea, the life of thy life. Without him, life is a shadow—a dream—outside show. " In him we live." " Christ is our life "—the Source of all strength and goodness and joy. This love arises from near relationship. He is *our* God ; he has entered into loving covenant with us—joined for ever his interests with ours. (2) *By the man's habit of life.* He "walks in God's ways." In those ways he finds God. It is the King's highway. He has daily companionship with Jehovah. All his tastes and wishes are gratified. His will is sweetly acquiescent in God's will. He steadily makes advancement in the beauteous life. He does not halt ; he walks. (3) *By his practical obedience.* "He keeps his commandments and his statutes." He keeps them in memory, and has regard to them in every step he takes. They are written upon the tablet of his heart; they shine out in lustrous characters in all his actions. He guards them fron the assaults of others. As the stone tablets of the Decalogue were preserved in the ark of the covenant, so in the more capacious ark of a good man's heart, the commandments of God are kept. 2. So, also, the course of disloyalty is portrayed : (1) *As a dislike of God.* "If thine heart turn away." Through ignorance, or prejudice, or pride, or sensual indulgence, men grow in dislike of God, until his very Name is odious—his presence a very hell. Repugnance to God is the livery they wear. (2) *As wanton deafness.* "So that thou wilt not hear." The ear is only an instrument; the effective power comes from a deeper source. We gradually bring ourselves into a condition in which we hear only what we wish to hear. The bulk of men have made themselves deaf to God's voice. (3) *As weak compliance to temptation.* Thou "shalt be drawn away." The habit of most men is to float with the stream. They yield thoughtlessly to the influence of public example. They do as others do, speak as others dictate. (4) *As ignoble service of idols.* "And worship other gods." Man must worship somewhat. It is a necessity of his being. He is not self-contained ; nor can he be satisfied out of himself. He worships power, wealth, fashion, social fame, fate, the devil.

II. ALTERNATIVE EXPERIENCE. 1. The course of loyalty secures: (1) *All real good.* The good is not always apparent—not always immediate. Yet even the experiences of pain and calamity prove ultimately to the obedient soul a real good. The storms of winter are as needful to the best life as the warm breath of spring. All that is wise, pure, excellent, elevating, noble, useful, is to be gained in the pathway of obedience. Every stage accomplished is a new instalment of good. (2) *It secures increase of numbers.* Rapid multiplication was, humanly speaking, Israel's security. By this means, they could outnumber their foes. Through our children, blessing and glad-ness come. So is it in spiritual things. We taste the highest joy when we become the channels of Christ's life to men. We long to have many genial companions in the road to heaven. (3) *It secures Divine blessing.* "The Lord thy God shall bless thee." External possessions contain no blessing in themselves. The richest lands—the fairest scenes on earth, are stripped of charm, so long as they are enveloped in absolute dark-ness. It is the light of God's favour that converts possession into blessing. Hence the *little* of the righteous is better than the abundance of the wicked. If God's blessing be on our estates, *that* makes them secure. *That* blessing is the core and marrow of true prosperity. That blessing alone gives fragrance and gladness to life. This blessing is secured by the oath of God. 2. But the course of disloyalty is marked by the opposite experience. (1) *It is an experience of evil.* The table may groan under the pro-fusion of dainty food, but there is a scarcity of food for the soul. The body may be pampered, but there is leanness in the spirit. Riches may increase, but they daily corrupt the mind. There may be noisy laughter, but it only covers inner sadness and hidden grief. No sorrow is sanctified. The real man is starved and ruined. (2) *There is distressing insecurity.* We are rich to-day ; we may be paupers to-morrow. "Ye shall not prolong your days in the land." Apart from God's favour, we have not a day's lease of life—not the certainty that any possession of ours shall continue. We dwell on the verge of a volcano. The earth quivers under our feet. (3) *There is a sense of the Divine curse.* A life of disloyalty is a life of constant warfare with God—a conflict with Omnipotence. Every plan which impious men make is a plan to elude and defeat God. And they know they cannot permanently succeed. There is a dark pall over-hanging every prospect—a night of gloom closing in their little day. The curse of a good man is an awful calamity : what must God's curse include ?

III. ALTERNATIVE DESTINY. 1. *The destiny of the good man is life.* This means life in its fullest measure, in its highest form, in its perpetual developments. Gradually all the elements of weakness and pain and decay shall be eliminated. Compared with the future life of the righteous, the present life is but childhood—the feebleness and ignorance of infancy. The life which is promised to the righteous is nothing less than the life of God. " We shall be like him." 2. *The destiny of disloyalty is destruction.* " Ye shall surely perish." This includes disappointment—the sudden collapse of all earthly hopes. It embraces shame and public reproach. The disloyal will be the laughing-stock of the universe. They shall be covered with confusion. This dark destiny includes poignant remorse. The unrighteous will know, to their deepest grief, that they might have been saved if they would. Such despair baffles all description.

IV. INSTANT CHOICE DEMANDED. We cannot do other than admire the condescension of God in pleading so pathetically with men. 1. *There is full instruction.* "I have set before thee life and death." Every element of needed information is furnished ; and personal examination of spiritual facts is expected. Every man is bound to investigate, to ponder, to judge. 2. *There is authoritative command.* "I command thee." On the side of righteous precept there is supreme authority. Every appeal of God is an appeal to the noblest part of our nature—to conscience. Every solicitation of the tempter is an appeal to appetite and passion. 3. *There is tender entreaty.* To the activities of wisdom and authority is added the impulse of love. If man's benevolent love prompt him to use all measures to turn the disloyal unto God ; how much deeper must be the love of God, of which man's affection is but a faint adumbration ! With all the pathos which human sympathy can lend to entreaty Moses pleads, "therefore choose life." 4. *Heaven and earth are summoned to hear the solemn charge.* Angels note the fidelity of God's prophets. All heaven is interested in man's obedience. The joy of heaven rises to new heights with every accession of loyal subjects. And all the inhabitants of earth are interested in our obedience, whether they feel that interest or not. The future history of this world is in our hands—is being moulded by our deeds. What we are to-day determines what the next generation will be. Each man who hears the heavenly summons makes decision straightway, if not in form, yet in reality. Each man is writing the epitaph for his tomb—preparing his verdict for the last assize ! Can we not to-day forecast our final destiny ?—D.

Vers. 1—10.— *The restoration of the Jews.* So certain is the apostasy and the judgment on the land, that Moses assumes it as an accomplished fact, thereupon proceeding to predict a restoration of the "scattered nation " in case of their repentance. There must be the penitent return to God, and then God will restore them and bless them abundantly. It was this principle which was carried out in the restoration from Babylon, and which will be carried out in any future restoration of Israel. We have here the *raison d'être* of Jewish missions.

I. THE PENITENCE OF ISRAEL IS THE PRELIMINARY TO THIS RESTORATION. Their captivity and dispersion having arisen from their forsaking God, it is only reasonable that their penitence should precede their restoration. Into the question of the re-establishment of the Jews in Palestine we need not here enter. Dr. Brown, who has written so well on *the second advent,* and shown conclusively, we think, that it will not be premillennial, has also advocated a restoration of Israel to their own land.[1] However this may be, of one thing we may be certain, that the *spiritual* restoration of Israel will precede any *local* restoration. They will be restored to *God* before being restored—if restored they are to be—to Palestine.

II. TO THE EVANGELIZATION OF THE JEWS CHRISTIAN CHURCHES SHOULD INTELLIGENTLY DEVOTE THEMSELVES. The winning of them by and to the gospel is the most important service we can render them. No movement of the political chess-board is half so important as the winning of them back to God. When, moreover, the local restoration is problematical, while the spiritual restoration is the indispensable preliminary to any further good fortune,—the duty of Christians is most clear. The gospel of Jesus must be adapted to the peculiar circumstances of Israel, and pressed upon their attention with all the sweet persuasiveness Christian grace ensures.

III. JEWISH MISSIONS ARE THE TRUE COMPENSATION FOR THE PERSECUTION OF THE

---

[1] 'The Restoration of the Jews: the History, Principles, and Bearings of the Question,' by Dr. David Brown. Edinburgh : 1861.

JEWS, TO WHICH, ALAS! THEY ARE STILL IN SOME QUARTERS SUBJECTED. For it must be remembered that the persecution of Israel, though allowed as a just retribution for their rejection of God, may be prosecuted in such an unholy spirit as to entail upon the persecutors the merited curse of God. Because there may be Shylocks among the Jews is no reason why men should wreak their vengeance on them. Indeed, the Lord threatens to put the curses upon their persecutors, when *they* have turned unto him.

If this be so, then it is the duty of Christian people to repudiate all persecution of the Jews as such, and to organize such mission work as may bring the truth and claims of God before the mind and heart of his ancient people. This will prove the true compensation to them. It will solace them under suffering and trial, and enable them to forget in the joys of a new life the pains and judgments of the old. Besides, the mission work undertaken by God's people may avert the judgments of Almighty God deserved by the nations that have persecuted the Jews. It is a matter of great thankfulness that England and America have an open door for Israel, and no sympathy with their present oppressors.

IV. THE FUTURE OF ISRAEL IS TO EXCEED IN GLORY THE PAST. This seems clear from this passage. The Jewish development is to exceed all past developments. They are to have a mighty population, great wealth, and God is to rejoice over them for good again. We do not regard a national organization as essential to influence. Christianity is now, for example, the mightiest factor in human society, and yet it is not organized *nationally*. Should the Jews by their rare linguistic powers, by their patient courage, by their singleness of aim, become when converted to Christianity the predominant missionary factor in the world, then we can see in such a restoration a more powerful and blessed influence than if they furnished to the world a new line of famous kings. It is not dynasties, but the devotion of the people, which goes to make a people mighty. The kingdoms over which men rule may not be defined in statute-book or in treaties. There are kingships exercised by humble, devoted, cross-bearing men, which explain the kingship of the crucified Nazarene. It is to this spiritual domination that we trust Israel shall yet come.

And this shall prove its glory. For glory consists not in the employment of physical and mechanical force, but in the exercise of self-denial and devotedness of spirit. As Carlyle has said in 'Sartor Resartus,' "The first preliminary moral act, annihilation of self (*Selbst-tödtung*), had been happily accomplished; and my mind's eyes were now unsealed and its hands ungyved." It is they who have realized this who are on the path of real glory. From their money-lending and money-grubbing the Jews, by Christianity, shall yet be delivered, to devote themselves in a more excellent way to the interests of mankind.—R. M. E.

Vers. 11—14.—*The revelation at man's door.* We have a very beautiful thought inserted by Moses regarding the proximity and handiness—if we may be allowed the thought—of God's commandments. It is used by Paul in the same connection, and so adapted to the gospel as to show its practical tenor (Rom. x. 6—9). And here we would observe—

I. EXTRAVAGANT NOTIONS ARE ENTERTAINED OF WHAT A DIVINE REVELATION OUGHT TO BE. It is thought that it should be some far-away affair, to which none but seraphic spirits could soar; as high as heaven, and requiring vast powers and efforts to reach. Or it is thought to be as recondite as matters lying in the deep-sea bed, demanding such diving apparatus as practically to put it out of reach of ordinary mortals. This is the favourite notion of the self-confident critics, that a Divine revelation must be something attainable only by scholars, appreciable only by the geniuses of mankind.

II. BUT AS A MATTER OF FACT, GOD'S REVELATION COMES DOWN TO EVERY MAN'S DOOR. God came down to Mount Sinai, and spoke to the people directly. The trouble then was that he was too near—too homely; they wished him further away. Then prophets came, and for fifteen hundred years the word was brought very nigh to men. At last God's Son became incarnate, and was each man's Brother, and brought the message so close to men that only the proud escaped it. The whole genius of revelation is contained in the remarkable words, " I thank thee, O Father, Lord of heaven and earth, because thou hast hid these things from the wise and prudent, and hast revealed them

unto babes. Even so, Father: for so it seemed good in thy sight " (Matt. xi. 25, 26).
The revelation is for babes; for men of a childlike—not a childish—spirit; for men who
have laid aside their pride and presumption, and can take truth trustfully from the
Infinite Father.

The idea is surely monstrous that God cannot break his Divine bread small enough
for his human children; that none but men of a certain mental calibre can get hold of
the food or digest it. It is surely a diviner plan to bring the truth so plainly home
that none have any excuse for rejecting it.

III. LET EACH OF US GIVE UP OUR GRAND EXCURSIONS BOTH SKYWARD AND SEA-
WARD, AND RECEIVE GOD'S MESSAGE BROUGHT NEAR US BY HIS SON. Pride is for
ever leading men upon some aerial or aquatic adventure, searching the heights of
heaven on the wing of fancy or of speculation, or exploring the deepest depths, professedly
to find truth and God. Philosophy is invoked, and everything brought to the test of
it. Now, all this must be sacrificed before we receive the truth. We must humble
ourselves, and recognize the truth brought in Jesus Christ to our very door. If we
required terrific effort to reach the truth, we would boast that we had succeeded through
that effort. If it depended on great mental powers and struggle, we would take credit for
both. But the fact is, it is brought so near to each of us, and so plainly home, that not
one of us can boast of our discovery, but only chide ourselves that it was so long near
us and so long overlooked!

IV. IT IS HERE THAT WE MUST BEGIN WITH THE JEWS. As a rule, they are so puffed
up with pride and self-importance, that the gospel is overlooked in its glorious proximity and adaptation. They think they are such linguists and such thinkers that none
can instruct them, and the result is that the simplicity of the gospel escapes their
notice altogether. The grandeur of what is simple and comprehensible by all who are
not too proud to consider it must be urged with earnestness. The apologetic now needed
is, not what follows speculation to its utmost height or utmost depth, and boasts itself of
learning as great as the objector has; but what takes its firm stand upon the *simplicity*
of revelation as the supreme proof that it is Divine. It seems to us that some of the
apologetic to which we are now treated is as pedantic as those it desires to convince, and,
in a contest of mere pedantry, it is sure to be defeated. Rather should we assure men
that it is pedantry and pride which keeps them from discovering the wondrous revelation that lies so near us. Let Gentile and Jew give up the weary wandering, the
" will-o'-the-wisp" work of pride, and recognize the God who is knocking at each man's
door.—R. M. E.

Vers. 15—20.—*Death and life set before the people.* In this earnest word which
concludes a section of his address to the people, Moses is summing up his deliverance.
It has been called by Hävernick "the classic passage " upon the subject of death and
life as understood in Old Testament times.[1] " Shut out from the true community of life
(*Lebensgemeinschaft*)," says Hävernick, " the sinner puts in only a pretended life (*Schein-
leben*), without God, enduring and promoting ruin in himself, until death physical, with
its terrors, overtakes him. The Divine penalty manifests itself to the sinner as death."
Let us consider what is here suggested. And—

I. GOD IS THE FOUNTAIN OF LIFE. He was before all things; in him they live and
move and have their being; by him all things consist. Life physical is from him; but so
also, and in a much fuller fashion, is life spiritual. The inner man is from him, and
depends upon him for sustenance. And when his only begotten Son came into the world,
he gave him to have life in himself (John v. 26), so that of him it could alone be said,
" In him was life, and the life was the light of men " (John i. 4). We recognize in God,
therefore, " the Fountain of living waters," from which, to their own great damage, men
are separating themselves, as if the broken cisterns of their own hewing could ever slake
their thirst (Jer. ii. 13).

II. LOVE ATTACHES US TO THIS SPIRITUAL FOUNTAIN. As we love God with all our
heart, and soul, and mind, and strength, we find that we have begun to live. On the
other hand, the loveless life is only a pretended life, and carries within itself the
" Anathema Maran-atha " (cf. 1 Cor. xvi. 22). Love places our heart at a level with

---

[1] Cf. Kahle's ' Biblische Eschatologie,' note p. 29.

God's, and the riches of his life flow into us. As Emerson, writing of *gifts*, says, "The gift, to be true, must be the flowing of the giver unto me, correspondent to my flowing unto him. When the waters are at a level, then my goods pass to him and his to me. All his are mine, all mine his." It is exactly in this magnanimous spirit God deals with those who love him. All his life and fulness flow down to us; we cannot, of course, take all in—our measure is a small one, but we are filled up to our capacity with all the fulness of God (Eph. iii. 18).

III. LOVE GIVES BIRTH TO NEW OBEDIENCE. If we love God, we shall keep his commandments (John xiv. 15). In the eye of love, his commandments are not grievous (1 John v. 3). Our meat is found in doing the will of him that sends us, and in finishing his work (John iv. 34). We say with the Master,"I delight to do thy will, O my God; yea, thy Law is within my heart" (Ps. xl. 8). And so, in the terms of the passage before us, we walk in God's ways, and keep his commandments and statutes and judgments.

Now, this obedience strengthens the spiritual life. Just as exercise invigorates the body, so work of a spiritual kind invigorates the soul. We not only find rest in coming to Jesus, but refreshment in taking on us his yoke and his burden (Matt. xi. 28—30).

IV. SUCH A LIFE OF ATTACHMENT AND OBEDIENCE UNTO GOD TENDS TO PERPETUATE OUR POWER AND EXISTENCE. Other things being equal, a religious life tends to perpetuate physical power. The calm which pervades the faculties, the wholesome exercise which devotedness to God administers, the deliverance from fear which religion bestows in face of all possible vicissitude and change,—all this favours health and longevity. Of course, Christianity does not need now such outward testimonies as these. Many saints are sickly, and die young; but religion never made their sickness a whit more serious, nor shortened their career by a single day. They would have been less easy in their sickness, and it would have cut their thread of life more quickly, had they been strangers to its solaces and joys.

V. SEPARATION FROM THE SOURCE OF LIFE IS DEATH INDEED. In this striking passage, while " good " and " life " go together, so do "death " and "evil." The idea in death is not cessation of existence, but separation from God. Adam and Eve died the day they doubted God's love and ate the fruit. They ceased not to exist that day, but died out of fellowship with God. Hence we are not to associate an *annihilation* view with the Biblical idea of death. Men die when they are separated from God as really as the branch broken from the stem. Sin is the mother of Death (Jas. i. 15). It brings it forth, because it separates the soul from him who is the Fountain of life.

The Jews found in their national experience how deadly a thing it is to disobey their God and to depart from him. Nor shall their calamities cease till they return to him. Meanwhile, may we see to it that we cleave trustfully and lovingly to God, and have increasing life in his favour!—R. M. E.

PART IV.

FAREWELL ADDRESS OF MOSES, WITH HIS PARTING SONG AND BENEDICTION.

CHAPTER XXXI.—CHAPTER XXXIII.

EXPOSITION.

MOSES had now finished his work as the legislator and ruler and leader of Israel. But ere he finally retired from his place, he had to take order for the carrying forward of the work by the nomination of a successor to himself in the leadership; by committing the keeping of the Law to the priests; and by anew admonishing the people to obedience, encouraging them to go forward to the conquest of Canaan, animating them with the assurance of the Divine favour and blessing, and pronouncing on them his parting benediction.

CHAPTER XXXI.

MOSES' FINAL ARRANGEMENTS AND HANDING OVER OF THE LAW TO THE PRIESTS.

Vers. 1—13.—*Last acts of Moses.*

Ver. 1.—And Moses went; *i.e.* disposed or set himself. The meaning is not that he "went away" into the tent of teaching, as one of the Targums explains it (London Polyglot, tom. iv. p. 377), which does not agree with what follows; nor is "went" merely equivalent to "moreover;" nor is it simply redundant;—it intimates that the speaking was consequent on Moses having arranged, disposed, or set himself to speak (cf. Exod. ii. 1 ; Josh. ix. 4 ; Job i. 4).

Ver. 2.—I am an hundred and twenty years old this day. When Moses stood before Pharaoh he was eighty years old (Exod. vii. 7) ; since then forty years had elapsed during the wanderings in the wilderness. **I can no more go out and come in;** I am no longer able to work among and for the nation as I have hitherto done (cf. Numb. xxvii. 17). This does not conflict with the statement in ch. xxxiv. 7, that up to the time of his death his eyes were not dim nor his natural strength abated, for this is the statement of an observer, and it often happens that an individual feels himself to be failing, when to those around him he appears to possess unabated vigour. There is no need, therefore, for resorting,

with Raschi and others, to the expedient of reading "for" instead of "and" in the following clause; as if the cause why Moses could no longer go in and out among the the people was God's prohibition of his going over Jordan. This is simply another and collateral reason why he had now to retire from his post as leader.

Vers. 3—6.—But though Moses was no longer to be their leader, he assures them that the Lord would fulfil his engagement to conduct them to the possession of Canaan, even as he had already given them the territory of the kings of the Amorites; and he therefore exhorts them to be of good courage and fearlessly go forward to the conquest of the land (cf. ch. i. 21; x. 3).

Vers. 7, 8.—Moses, having in view the appointment of Joshua as his successor, also encourages him to go forward on the strength of the Divine promise. **Thou must go with this people.** This is a correct rendering of the words as they stand in the Hebrew text. The Samaritan, Syriac, and Vulgate have, "Thou shalt bring this people ;" but this is probably an arbitrary correction in order to assimilate this to ver. 23. **And thou shalt cause them to inherit it;** *i.e.* shalt conduct them to the full possession of the land.

Vers. 9—13.—Moses turns next to the priests and the elders, and to them he commits the Law which he had written, with the injunction to read it to the people at the end of every seven years during the festival of the year of release, viz. at the Feast of Tabernacles (cf. Lev. xxiii. 34), when they appeared before the Lord. **At the end of** every **seven years** (cf. ch. xv. 1). The Law was committed to the priests and elders, not merely to preserve it in safe keeping, but that they might see to its being observed by the people; else why commit it to the elders whose it was to administer rule in the nation, as well as to the priests who alone had access to the ark of the covenant where the Law was deposited? Moses "entrusted the reading to the priesthood and the college of elders, as the spiritual and secular rulers of the congregation; and hence the singular, Thou shalt read this Law to all Israel" (Keil). By the Law here is meant the Pentateuch; but it does not necessarily follow that the *whole* of the Pentateuch was to be thus read. As the reading was to be only once in seven years, it may be concluded that it was not so much for the information of the people that this was done, as for the purpose of publicly declaring, and by a solemn ceremony impressing on their minds the condition on which they held their position and privileges as the chosen people of the Lord; and for this the reading of select portions of the Torah would be sufficient. The Feast of Tabernacles was appointed as the season for the reading, doubtless because there was a connection between the end for which the Law was read and the spirit and meaning of that festival as a festival of rejoicing because of their deliverance from the uncertainty and unsettledness of their state in the wilderness, and their establishment in a well-ordered state where they could in peace and quietness enjoy the blessings which the bounty of God bestowed. **When all Israel is come to appear before the Lord** (cf. ch. xvi. 16). **Thou shalt read this law** (cf. Josh. viii. 34; 2 Kings xxiii. 2; Neh. viii. 1, etc.).

Vers. 14—23.—After nominating Joshua as his successor, and assigning the keeping of the Law to the priesthood and body of elders, Moses was summoned by the Lord to appear with Joshua in the tabernacle, that Joshua might receive a charge and appointment to his office. At the same time, God announced to Moses that after his death the people would go astray, and turn to idolatry, and violate the covenant, so that God's anger should be kindled against them, and he would leave them to suffer the consequences of their folly and sin. In view of this, Moses was directed to write a song and teach it to the people, that it might abide with them as a witness against them, rising up, as songs will do, in the memory of the nation, even after they had apostatized from the path in which the author of the song had led them.

Ver. 14.—**The tabernacle of the congregation**; properly, *the tent of meeting* (cf. Exod. xxxiii. 7; xxxix. 32). **May give him a charge**; may constitute him (וְצַוֵּהוּ; cf. Numb. xxvii. 19; "and constitute him in their sight," Gesenius), appoint and confirm him in this office.

Ver. 15.—**The Lord appeared . . . in a** pillar of a cloud (cf. Exod. xxxiii. 9; xl. 38; Lev. xvi. 2; Numb. xii. 5).

Ver. 16.—**Behold, thou shalt sleep with thy fathers** (cf. 2 Sam. vii. 12; Ps. xiii. 3; lxxvi. 5; Dan. xii. 2; Matt. xxvii. 52; John xi. 11; 1 Thess. iv. 14). "The death of men, both good and bad, is often called a *sleep*, because they shall certainly awake out of it by resurrection" (Poole). **Go a whoring** (cf. Exod. xxxiv. 15; Judg. ii. 17) **after the gods of the strangers of the land**; literally, *after gods of strangeness of the land;* i.e. after gods foreign to the land, as opposed to Jehovah, the alone proper God of the land he had given to them.

Ver. 17.—**I will hide my face from them**; will not look on them with complacency, will withdraw from them my favour and help (cf. ch. xxxii. 20; Isa. viii. 17; lxiv. 7; Ezek. xxxix. 23).

Ver. 19.—**Write ye this song.** This refers to the song which follows in next chapter. Moses and Joshua were both to write this song, Moses probably as the author, Joshua as his amanuensis, because both of them were to do their endeavour to keep the people from that apostacy which God had foretold.

Ver. 23.—**And he gave,** etc. The subject here is God, not Moses, as is evident partly from ver. 14, and partly from the expression, **the land which I sware unto them; and I will be with thee** (cf. Exod. iii. 12).

Vers. 24—29.—After the installation of Joshua, only one thing remained for Moses to do that all things might be set in order before his departure. This was the finishing of the writing of the Book of the Law, and the committing it finally to the priests, to be by them placed by the ark of the covenant, that it might be kept for all future generations as a witness against the people, whose apostacy and rebellion were foreseen.

Whether this section is to be regarded as wholly written by Moses himself, or as an appendix to his writing added by some other writer, has been made matter of question. It is quite possible, however, that Moses himself, ere he laid down the pen, may have recorded what he said when delivering the Book of the Law to the priests, and there is nothing in the manner or style of the record to render it probable that it was added by another. What follows from ver. 30 to the end of the book was probably added to the writing of Moses by some one after his death, though, of course, both the song in ch. xxxii. and the blessing in ch. xxxiii. are the composition of Moses (see Introduction, § 6).

Ver. 25.—The Levites, which bare the ark; *i.e.* the priests whose business it was to guard and to carry the ark of the covenant; "the priests the sons of Levi," as in ver. 9. According to Numb. iv. 4, etc., it was the Kohathites who carried the ark on the journey through the desert; but they seem merely to have acted in this respect as the servants or helpers of the priests, who alone might touch the ark, and by whom it was carefully wrapped up before it was handed to the Kohathites. On special occasions the priests themselves carried the ark (cf. Josh. iii. 3, etc.; iv. 9, 10; vi. 6, 12; viii. 33; 1 Kings viii. 3).

Ver. 26.—In the side of the ark; *at or by the side of the ark.* According to the Targum of Jonathan, it was in a coffer by the right side of the ark that the book was placed; but the Talmudists say it was put within the ark, along with the two tables of the Decalogue ('Baba Bathra,' 14); but see 1 Kings viii. 8.

Ver. 27.—I know thy rebellion; rather, *rebelliousness,* i.e. tendency to rebel. In Numb. xvii. 25 [10], the people are described as בְּנֵי מֶרִי, "sons of rebelliousness;" Authorized Version, "rebels."

Ver. 28.—Call heaven and earth to record against them (cf. ch. xxxii. 1). **These words;** the words of his charge, and especially the song he had composed, and which it would be the business of these officers to teach to the congregation.

Ver. 29.—Ye will utterly corrupt yourselves; literally, *corrupting, ye will corrupt* (הַשְׁחֵת תַּשְׁחִתוּן, *sc.* דַּרְכְּיכֶם); i.e. *your ways* (cf. for the phrase, Gen. vi. 12). **The latter days;** *the after-time, the future,* as in ch. iv. 30; Numb. xxiv. 14, etc. **The work of your hands;** the idols they might make (cf. ch. iv 28). By some, however, the phrase is interpreted of evil deeds in general.

HOMILETICS.

Vers. 1—13.—*A new generation receiving the heritage of the past.* The closing scene of Moses' life is drawing nigh. The time is at hand when he and Israel must part, and the leadership must be undertaken by another. As far as can be done, two things have to be ensured—viz. the conservation of Israel's Law, and the conduct of the people to their goal. "God buries his ministers, but he carries on his work." Hence Moses first addresses all the people; then he turns to Joshua, confirming him as the future leader (vers. 7, 8); and finally to the priests, who are to be henceforth the custodians and guardians of the holy Law. Having thus handed over the leadership of an army, and the conservation of a faith, Moses has little else to do but to go up and die. Hence our theme—*A new generation entrusted with the heritage of the past.* Taking up this as a Christian preacher may be supposed to do, we find that seven consecutive lines of thought are suggested.

I. There has been given, prior to our time, a "precious faith," which has been handed down to the present day (vers. 12, 13).

II. Those who have been the leaders and warriors in God's Israel in past days have commended this faith to us, with all the earnestness created by their deep and strong convictions, which, in the hard school of experience and trial, were formed, fostered, and verified (vers. 3, 4).

III. The work thus entrusted to the men of the present is analogous to that which was required of the ancient people of God: (1) to clear the ground of alien faiths; (2) to occupy the ground so cleared; and (3) to maintain thereon pure worship, brotherly fellowship, and holy life.

IV. In the fulfilment of this work we shall enjoy the Divine presence (ver. 6).

V. God's providence will also go before us to clear the way (ver. 8).

VI. Consequently, it behoves us to go forward, to "be strong and fear not" (ver. 6); for—

VII. Where the responsibilities of the men of the past leave off, our responsibility begins.

Vers. 9—13.—*Importance of knowing the Word of God.* In resigning his commission into other hands, Moses had a double duty to discharge. There had been, in fact, a twofold responsibility resting on him more or less till the close of his life, which after his death would be divided. He was not only the leader of the people, but also the receiver, transcriber, and guardian of the Law. As the nation became consolidated, this double work would certainly become too heavy for one man to discharge. Hence he commissions one man to be the leader of an army, and another set of men to be the conservators of the truth. Joshua is leader. The priests are to be the keepers and teachers of the Law. It is one remarkable feature of the constitution of the Hebrew common-wealth, that such stress is laid upon popular education. This was again and again made matter of Divine precept. And about this there were two main regulations: one, that it was to begin at home; another, that it was to have as its one golden thread running through all, that the fear of the Lord was the beginning of wisdom. Over and above, however, the home teaching from childhood, there was to be at stated times a public reading and enforcement of the Law. At this public reading, the people were to be gathered together. "Young men and maidens, old men and children;" the stranger that was within their gates was not to be forgotten. All, *all* were to hear the Word of God, that they might learn, fear, love, and obey.

It is to secure this most desirable end that Moses, having written the Law, delivers it to the priests, the sons of Levi, and gives them the charge of which the paragraph before us is the sum. Our theme is—*The value of the Word of God as an educating power in home and nation.* The points to be noted in the words of Moses here given, are these: 1. That both young and old were to have ever before them the truth that their life was for God, was to be permeated by Divine influence, and regulated by the Divine will. 2. That the will of God, so revealed as to be the true and sufficient regulator of life, was to be found in the Book of the Law. 3. That all classes of the people, home-born and alien, freemen and slaves, were to be taught what was the Divine will concerning them. 4. That the object of the teaching was that they might grow up with an intelligent apprehension of the deep meaning of life. 5. That intelligence was intended and expected to blossom into piety. Men were to "fear" the Lord their God, and to "observe to do all the words of this Law."

Our purpose in this Homily is to inquire, How far does all this hold good at the present day? When Moses wrote the Law, it served, as it did for ages after, as the people's literature. It would take a like place with the people that our histories of England do now, and would, moreover, serve them as the story-book for children, and the statute-book for all. And there was a time when to large masses of our people the Bible constituted the chief literary treasure of the home. And ere the people could read, the exposition and enforcement of its truths from the pulpit formed the staple of their education. But things are changed now. The increase of literary material in every direction is amazing. The vastly wider field of natural knowledge takes so much time and energy for its exploration, that the Bible is in danger of being "crowded out." And what may be called in an intelligible sense the literary rivals of the Bible are "legion." We propose to suggest a few lines of thought which the Christian preacher may work out, with the view of showing that an intelligent acquaintance with the Word of God is, if possible, more important now than ever it was. Many reasons may be urged for this.

I. LET US CONSIDER THE VARIOUS ASPECTS IN WHICH THE BIBLE MAY BE RE-GARDED. We need scarcely observe (save for the sake of completeness of setting) that our Bible is much larger than Israel's was, and that therefore by so much as this is the case there is much more to be affirmed of it now than could be of the old Book of the Law. 1. In the Bible we have a trustworthy history of Judaism and Christianity, in their origin and meaning. Of the first we have an outline during the main periods of its constitutional history; of the second, during the first generation after its planting. And so important are these features of history, that apart from them the history of the world cannot be understood. 2. We have the noblest ethical standard in the world. The moral law cannot, even in conception, be surpassed. 3. We have a revelation of a great redeeming plan steadily unfolded from Genesis to Revelation. 4. We have a disclosure of God in the Person of the Lord Jesus Christ. 5. We have the manifesta-tion of power from heaven to begin a new creation of grace. 6. We have a body of doctrine for the life that now is. 7. We have glorious glimpses of the life which is to come. In all these respects the Book is unique. It has no compeer in any literature in the world!

II. AS THE CONTENTS OF THE BIBLE ARE UNIQUE, SO ALSO IS ITS OBJECT DEFINITE.

(See Ps. xix.; cxix.; John xxi. 31, *et al.*) That object is the regulation of life on earth, and the preparation of it for heaven. And the Book seeks to secure this by enforcement of duty, revelations of truth, disclosures of love, and offers of power.

III. No AMOUNT OF NATURAL LEARNING CAN EVER COMPENSATE FOR DEFICIENCY OF KNOWLEDGE OR FAILURE IN PRACTICE CONCERNING MAN'S DUTY TO HIMSELF, HIS FAMILY, HIS NEIGHBOUR, AND HIS GOD. If he fails here, he fails everywhere. The more splendidly a vessel is fitted up, the more costly the wreck if she dashes on the rocks. To teach natural knowledge and leave out religion, is to furnish the vessel but to fail to make any provision for steering it aright.

IV. NATURAL KNOWLEDGE IN THE HANDS OF OTHER THAN VIRTUOUS MEN MAY BECOME AN INSTRUMENT OF ENORMOUS MISCHIEF. The attempt to blow up the Winter Palace at St. Petersburg is an illustration of what science and skill may do in bad hands. The disclosures after the destruction of the Tay Bridge showed us how science, art, and skill may do their best, and yet the greatest efforts of great men may be blown away in an hour by a single blast, through the weak points which un-conscientious work had left, in the hope of being undetected.

V. THE GREATER THE STRENGTH THAT IS PUT FORTH IN ACQUIRING KNOWLEDGE, THE GREATER THE ENERGY DEMANDED IN ORDER TO USE SUCH KNOWLEDGE WELL. The larger the vessel, the more power is required to propel her. So the wider the culture, the stronger does moral principle need to be in order that natural knowledge may be not a veil to conceal, but a book to reveal the Divine.

VI. HENCE THE CONCLUSION FOLLOWS: So far from the accumulating mass of natural knowledge making the Word of God less necessary as a guide to living well and dying well, the fact is, that *the necessity of Bible study is greater than ever!* No book can take its place. No study can supersede that of the ways of God to man. Some of the wisest men of the age (so far as science goes) confess themselves hopelessly in the dark with regard to man's origin, nature, and destiny. Ah! in the Book of God, and in that alone, can man learn that which shall make him wise unto salvation. Here alone can we learn the mystery of God's will which was hidden from ages and generations, but now is made manifest. Here alone can he be taught that godliness which hath "promise of the life that now is, and of that which is to come."

Vers. 16—21.—*Faithful words silent accusers of those who heed them not.* In the several paragraphs of this chapter we find that Moses was borne along by the Holy Ghost to take a glance into the future. He had been instructed by God to give a charge to Joshua, and to surrender into his hands the leadership of the host. He had given to the priests their commission to guard the Law for the people. And now there remained but for him to give his final words to the people themselves. The Omniscient One foresaw that, after the death of their leader, they would become corrupt, forsaking the Lord, and ensuring for themselves and their children a heritage of woe. And hence it was mercifully provided that, even in the worst of times, their lawgiver's words should be for them a perpetual standard of appeal; so that, however the people might have fallen from the heights of virtue, they should still have the same trusty words to guide their path, and to direct and restore their life. While at the same time, these words would be a constant and silent witness against them for departing from the ways of the Lord. It is not at all unlikely that our Lord had this passage in mind when he said to the Jews, "Do not think that I will accuse you to the Father: there is one that accuseth you, even Moses, in whom ye trust." That very Book, which if rightly used is "a lamp" to the feet and "a light" to the path, becomes, if neglected, a perpetual and silent accuser. Very earnestly and solemnly may the Christian preacher press this home "to every man's conscience in the sight of God." That selfsame purpose which was answered by securing permanent records of the Mosaic legislation, is also answered by permanent records of the Christian redemption. The apostles and prophets of the New Testament, like the legislator of the old, spake and wrote as they were borne along by the Holy Ghost. It is, therefore, over the larger sphere that we propose now to illustrate and enforce the truth that *neglected teaching becomes a silent accuser.*

I. WHEN OUR GOD LODGED IN THE WORLD THE JEWISH AND CHRISTIAN FAITHS, HE LOOKED ONWARD AND FORESAW THE FEATURES OF THE COMING GENERATIONS. (Cf. vers. 16--18; see also Acts xx. 29, 30; 1 Tim. iv. 1—3; 2 Pet. iii. 3; Matt. xxiv. 24.)

Whatever developments of ungodliness or of unbelief, of immorality or of heresy, may develop themselves, are all known to him who seeth the end from the beginning.

II. WITH FUTURE EVIL FULL IN VIEW, GOD HAS HAD HIS OWN WORD PUT DOWN IN WRITING. The words of Moses, of the prophets, of the Lord Jesus Christ, and of his apostles are faithfully recorded. They have suffered no material change through all the accidents of transition (Phil. iii. 1). Paul felt what a safeguard it would be for after ages to have his words written down, and sent to the Churches, that they might be by them guarded, distributed, and taught (see ver. 19).

III. THE WORD OF GOD, SO RECORDED, IS A PERPETUAL STANDARD OF APPEAL FOR EVERY AGE. Whatever corruptions may enter into or fasten on the Churches; however oral tradition may change the original form of Divine communication,—the *written* Word changeth not. How very soon Churches as Churches may drift far away from the true in faith and the holy in life, the Epistles to the Churches in Galatia, Corinth, Ephesus, Pergamos, Thyatira, Laodicea, tell. We see by them how very soon our faith might be seriously obscured or impaired if dependent merely on the oral transmission of any Church.

IV. BY THE PURE WORD OF GOD, ABERRATIONS MAY FROM TIME TO TIME BE CORRECTED. It is by the Church that the Word of God is kept and transmitted. It is by the Word so kept and transmitted that the Church is to be tested. Hence, whatever respect it may be appropriate to pay to the decision of a Church or of Churches, those decisions are valid only as they harmonize with what the Lord hath spoken in his revealed Word. Whatever will not abide the test of an appeal to the Book of God, with it Christian Churches and people should have nothing to do. Of how much importance our Lord regarded this final test is seen by his frequent appeal to what is written. Whether he was in conflict with the evil one, or was himself exposing or denouncing evil, his ultimate reference was to what God had said.

V. CONSEQUENTLY, BY HAVING IN OUR HANDS A PERPETUAL STANDARD OF REFERENCE, WE HAVE A CONSTANT AND UNVARYING GUIDE TO WHAT IS RIGHT BOTH IN FAITH AND PRACTICE. The accounts which we get of the after history of the Hebrew nation show us plainly enough how far adrift the people might soon have gone, if their faith had not been once for all enshrined and guarded in a book. And so it is in the New Testament. For though we get therein hints of the Church's life for but little more than two generations after they were formed, yet the severe lashings and rebukes which the Churches in Corinth, Galatia, and Colosse required, as well as the seven Churches, show with equal distinctness that our most holy faith might soon have been all but unrecoverable from the mass of corruption, if it, too, had not been recorded in the writings of the apostles and evangelists. But thus recorded it was, and through all the ages it has been guarded for us as a perpetual standard of appeal.

VI. IF, HOWEVER, WE ARE GUIDED BY THE VARYING OPINIONS AND SINFUL PRACTICES OF MEN, AND SO NEGLECT TO TAKE HEED TO OUR STANDARDS, THEY WILL BE PERPETUAL WITNESSES AGAINST US. (Ver. 21.) So our Lord tells the Jews in reference to the departures from the faith and the corruptions in life which marked his time (cf. John v. 54). And thus it must ever be. The very fact of having a standard of appeal serves two purposes. Which of the two it will serve so far as we are concerned depends on the use we make thereof. If we abide by it and conform thereto, it will verify our belief and justify our life. But if we depart from it, it can only act as a witness against us to condemn us. *Every privilege is thus two-edged.* If used aright, it helps us; if disused or abused, it will be for a perpetual reproof. So it is with parental advice, with a teacher's counsels, with a pastor's pleadings, with a Saviour's invitations: accepted and heeded, they will be a perpetual joy; but if made light of, they will plunge daggers into the soul.

VII. THIS SILENT ACCUSATION GOING ON NOW, FORESHADOWS A MORE SERIOUS CRIMINATION AT THE JUDGMENT DAY. (Cf. Matt. xi. 22, 24; xii. 41, 42.) The whirl of life, and the surroundings of flesh and sense, conceal from many the spiritual world. *But it exists.* And when we are summoned hence we shall see it and know it. We shall feel ourselves with God—alone. And this—this will be the beginning of that awful process of judgment which, on the last day, is to be consummated and sealed. And what sore condemnation must await those to whom God has spoken in his Word for years on years, but in vain (see Ezek. xxxiii.)!

HOMILIES BY VARIOUS AUTHORS.

Vers. 1, 2.—*Moses the aged.* I. A MAN MAY BE IN HEALTH AND VIGOUR, YET PAST CAPACITY FOR A CERTAIN WORK. Moses' "eye was not dim, nor his natural force abated" (ch. xxxiv. 7), yet he felt that he lacked the fire, the activity, the youthful energy, the elasticity of mind and body, which would have made him a suitable leader for Israel in the new period of her history. Greatness is tested by the magnanimity with which a man long used to power is able to lay it down when he feels that his day for effective service is past. Moses had served his generation nobly. There arose none like him. But, as has been said of Luther, who reached his meridian at the Diet of Worms, and whose end, had Providence pleased to remove him then, would have been like an apotheosis, "It is a law of history that every personality bears within itself a measure which it is not permitted to exceed" (Hagenbach). A new age was opening, and new powers were needed to do justice to its calls. The lawgiver, the prophet, the leader of the desert march, the meek, long-enduring, deep-souled man of God must give place to one more distinctively a soldier. The calm gifts of the legislator and statesman were not those which were most required for the work of conquest and settlement. Moses felt this, and felt, too, that he was getting old. The old man cannot enter as a younger man would into the thoughts, circumstances, and feelings of a new time. He belongs to the past, and is limited by it. His powers have lost their freshness, and can henceforth only decay. This was Moses' situation, and he had the dignity and wisdom to acknowledge it, and to arrange for the appointment of a suitable successor.

II. WHEN A MAN'S DAY OF SERVICE IS PAST, IT MAY BE KINDNESS IN GOD TO REMOVE HIM FROM THE WORLD. Moses' removal was a punishment for sin, but there was mercy concerned in it also. Long life is not always desirable. Had Moses lived longer, he could never have been greater than he is. He might have seemed less. Shades appear in the character of Luther after it had reached its meridian above spoken of—things which disturb and annoy us. Certainly, Moses' position, with Joshua as actual leader in the field, would not have been an enviable one. Joshua must increase, he must decrease. The impetuous soldier, the able strategist, the hero of the battles, would have eclipsed him in the eyes of the younger generation. He would feel that he had overlived himself. Fitly, therefore, is he removed before the decline of his influence begins. The great thing is to have done one's work—to have fulfilled the ends for which life was given. That done, removal is in no case a loss, and in most cases a boon in disguise (2 Tim. iv. 6—9).

III. WHEN THE SERVICES OF ONE MAN FAIL, GOD WILL PROVIDE FOR THE CONTINUANCE OF HIS WORK BY RAISING UP SUCCESSORS. So Joshua was raised up to succeed Moses.—J. O.

Vers. 3—8, 23.—*Joshua.* Joshua a type of Jesus, the true Leader into the rest of God (Heb. iv. 8). God has given him, as formerly he gave the son of Nun, for "a Leader and Commander to the people" (Isa. lv. 4).

I. THE MAN. Joshua as leader was: 1. Divinely *appointed* (ver. 3). 2. Divinely *led.* "He doth go before thee" (ver. 8). The captain had a higher Captain (Josh. v. 14). 3. Divinely *assisted.* "He will be with thee" (ver. 8). Our Leader is Emmanuel—"God with us" (Matt. i. 23). 4. He was to be *strong and courageous* (ver. 7). The ground of true courage is God being with us. It is said of the Saviour, "He shall not fail nor be discouraged" (Isa. xlii. 4). The perseverance of the Saviour is as deserving of consideration as the perseverance of the saints.

II. HIS WORK. While Joshua's and the people's, it was still more God's work (vers. 3, 4). With Joshua as leader: 1. The enemy would be overthrown (vers. 3—6). 2. All opposition would be overcome. 3. He would conduct the people unto the land of their inheritance (ver. 7). 4. He would cause them to inherit it (ver. 7), *i.e.* settle them in their possessions. Christ in like manner has overthrown the enemy (Col. ii. 15); has won an inheritance for his people (Col. i. 12); in his victory they are enabled to overcome the world (John xvi. 33; 1 John iv. 4); his cause is steadily triumphing; he is conducting, and has already conducted, many sons to glory (Heb. ii. 10).—J. O.

Vers. 9, 24—26.—*The authorship of the book*. A clear testimony to the Mosaic authorship of the Book of Deuteronomy. The book, as Moses gave it to the priests, has plainly been re-edited, with the additions of Moses' song, Moses' blessing, and the account of his death; but only the wantonness of criticism can see "a different hand or hands" in ch. xii.—xxvi. from that employed upon the earlier chapters, or discern probability in the assumption that ch. iv. 44—xxvi. 19 once constituted a separate book. The unity in style and treatment is so conspicuous throughout—" the same vein of thought, the same tone and tenor of feeling, the same peculiarities of conception and expression "—that unity of authorship follows as a thing of course. The denial of it is incomprehensible. It is less certain whether the "Book of the Law" (ver. 26) comprehénds Deuteronomy only, or the bulk of the other books of the Pentateuch as well. That Deuteronomy is represented as existing in a written form is plain from ch. xxviii. 58, 61; xxix. 20, 21, 27; and Moses had probably the written discourses in his hand when he delivered them. But Deuteronomy, as a written book, rests so entirely on the history as we have it in the previous books; is so steeped in allusions to it; implies so full and accurate a knowledge of it, from the days of the patriarchs downwards;—that the presumption in favour of that history also existing in a written form, in authentic records, which subsequent generations could consult, is so strong as almost to amount to certainty. It is incredible that Moses should have taken pains to write out these long discourses—discourses based on the history, and inculcating so earnestly the keeping of its facts and lessons in remembrance—and yet have taken no pains to secure an authentic record of the history itself; that he should not have compiled or composed, out of the abundant materials at his command, a connected narrative of God's dealings with the nation, down to the point at which he addressed it; incorporating with that narrative the body of his legislation. Confining our attention to Deuteronomy, there can be no fair question but that it gives itself out as from the pen of Moses. This claim is disputed, and the book referred to about the time of Josiah on grounds of style, of discrepancies with the Levitical laws, and of laws and allusions implying the later date. On the contrary, we hold that the critical hypothesis can be shown to raise greater difficulties than it lays, and that the difficulties in the way of accepting the book as a composition of Moses have been greatly exaggerated. We glance at a few of these difficulties.

I. STYLE. Professor W. R. Smith ('Old Testament,' p. 433) notes as a crucial instance the laws about the cities of refuge in Numb. xxxv., and Deut. xix. These laws are supposed to have been penned by the same hand within a few months of each other; yet, it is alleged, the vocabulary, structure of sentences, and cast of expression widely differ. But allowance must surely be made for the difference between a careful original statement of a law, and a later general rehearsal of its substance in the rounded style of free, popular discourse. And what are the specific differences? Deuteronomy, we are told, does not use the term "refuge," but "the cities are always described by a periphrasis." But the Deuteronomist simply says, "Thou shalt separate three cities for thee in the midst of thy land" (ch. xix. 2); "thou shalt separate three cities for thee" (ch. xix. 7); "thou shalt add three cities more for thee "(ch. xix. 9); and *there is no periphrasis*. The phrase, "that every slayer may flee thither" (ch. xix. 3), "the slayer which shall flee thither" (ch. xix. 4), is derived from Numb. xxxv. 11, 15. But Deuteronomy and Numbers use different words for "accidentally." Admitted, but the words used are synonymous, and are only used in each case twice altogether—in Numb. xxxv. 11, 15, and in Deut. iv. 42; xix. 4. "The judges in the one are 'the congregation,' in the other 'the elders of his city.'" But Deuteronomy says nothing about "judges," and "the elders" who are once referred to in ch. xix. 12, plainly act in the name of the congregation. "The verb for 'hate' is different." Rather, "the verb for 'hate'" does not occur at all in Numb. xxxv., but the noun derived from it does (Numb. xxxv. 20), and is translated "hatred," while in vers. 21, 22, a different term, translated "enmity," is employed, which expresses nearly the same sense. Had these words appeared, one in Numbers and the other in Deuteronomy, instead of standing in consecutive verses of one chapter, they would doubtless have been quoted as further evidence of diversity of authorship. So one book uses the expression " to kill *any person*," while the other has " to kill his neighbour "—a difference surely not incompatible with identity of authorship. "The detailed description of the difference between murder and accidental homicide is entirely diverse in language and detail." But in Deuteronomy there is no "detailed description" of the kind referred to. There *is* in Numbers (xxxv. 16—24); but Deuteronomy confines itself to one simple illustration from concrete life, admirably adapted, it will be admitted, to the speaker's popular purpose (ch. xix. 5). The statement in Deuteronomy, it is evident, presupposes the earlier law, and is incomplete without it, occupying only a dozen verses, as compared with over twenty in Numbers, while even of the dozen, three are occupied with a new provision for the number of the cities being ultimately raised to nine (ch. xix. 8—10).

II. Discrepancies in laws. Considering the number of the laws, the alleged discrepancies are singularly few. On the "tithes," see ch. xxvi. 12; on the "firstlings," ch. xv. 20; "the priests' due," in ch. xviii. 3, seems, like the "fleece" of ch. xviii. 4, to be *in addition* to the provision in Numb. xviii. 11—18; the law of carrion (ch. xiv. 21) is slightly modified in view of the altered circumstances of settlement in Canaan (cf. Lev. xvii. 15); and so with other instances. The chief modifications arise from the new legislation in regard to the central sanctuary, with the permission to kill and eat flesh at home (ch. xii. 20—24). On this depends the new tithe-laws (provision for the sanctuary feasts), the additions to the priests' portions, and various minor changes.

III. Peculiarities implying a later date. We need not delay on stray phrases, such as "unto this day" (ch. iii. 14), or "as Israel did unto the land of his possession" (ch. ii. 12). The instances usually cited are not of great force, and are easily explicable as glosses. More important cases are: 1. *The central altar.* On this, see under ch. xii. It suffices to meet most objections to observe that, on the face of it, the Law bears that it was not intended to be put strictly in force till certain important conditions had been fulfilled—conditions which, owing to the disobedience of the people, who during the time of the judges so often put back the clock of their own history, were not fulfilled till as late as the days of David and Solomon. For thus it reads (ver. 10), "When ye go over Jordan, and dwell in the land which the Lord your God giveth you to inherit, and when he giveth you rest from all your enemies round about, so that ye dwell in safety; *then* there shall be a place, " etc. (cf. 2 Sam. vii. 1; 1 Kings iii. 2; v. 4). 2. *Priests and Levites.* The distinction between priests and Levites, which counts for so much in Leviticus and Numbers, is not, it is alleged, recognized in Deuteronomy. The phrase in use is not "priests *and* Levites" (which, however, as little as the other, occurs in the earlier books), but "the priests the Levites" (ch. xvii. 9, 18; xviii. 1; xxiv. 8; xxvii. 9). They are not distinctively "the sons of Aaron," but "sons of Levi" (ch. xxi. 5; xxxi. 9). "All Levites are possible priests." But the objection is deprived of its force when we discover, what any one can verify, that these same expressions were freely used, and used interchangeably with others, at a time when it is not doubted that the Levitical system was in full operation. This is the case in the Books of Chronicles, written, it is asserted, in the interest of that system, yet using this phrase, "the priests the Levites," without hesitation or sense of ambiguity (2 Chron. v. 5; xxiii. 18; xxx. 27). "The priests the Levites" mean simply the Levitical priests; and when the tribe of Levi as a whole is meant, it is either expressly designated as such (ch. x. 8), or the designation is appended to the other phrase as a wider denomination (ch. xviii. 1). Nor is the idiom a strange one. At first, the priests, "the sons of Aaron," stood out from the people with sharp distinctness, as alone invested with sacred office. The case was greatly altered after the separation of the tribe of Levi; when the designation "sons of Aaron" seems speedily to have been dropped for another identifying the priests more directly with their tribe. "Sons of Aaron" is not found in the latter part of Numbers. Priests and Levites had more in common with each other than either class had with the body of the people; and besides, the priests *were* Levites. So that to the popular eye, the tribe of Levi stood apart, forming, as a whole, one sacred body, engaged in ministering in holy things to God. Sacerdotal functions are attributed to the tribe, but not necessarily to all members of it (ch. x. 8; xviii. 7). (On the ministering of the Levites, comp. 1 Chron. xv. 2; 2 Chron. xxix. 11; xxxi. 2). The counter-theory, that this distinction had no existence under the kings, and first originated in the time of the exile, is without a jot of evidence in the Books of Kings, and only escapes foundering on the statements in Chronicles, Ezra, and Nehemiah, by robbing these books of their historical character. 3. *The position of the Levites.* Instead of being furnished with cities and pasturages, and enjoying an independent income from the tithes, they are represented as homeless and dependent, wandering from place to place, and glad to be invited, with the stranger, the widow, and the fatherless, to share in charitable feasts. (See on this, ch. xii. 19.) But if a time is sought for the composition of the book when this was the actual position of the Levites, no time is so suitable as that of Moses himself, before the tithe-laws had come into regular operation—when, in truth, there was little or nothing to tithe—and when the Levites would be largely dependent on the hospitality of individuals. The language would have a point and force to Moses' contemporaries, which it would have greatly lost had the circumstances of the Levites, at the time of his address, been more prosperous. They were dependent then, and might from very obvious causes come to be dependent again. Their state would not be greatly bettered in the unsettled times of the conquest. Nothing could be more appropriate in itself, better adapted to create kindly sympathies between Levites and people, or more likely to avert neglect of the tribe by withholding of their just dues, than the perpetuation of these primitive hospitalities. No doubt the Levites suffered severely in the days of the judges and under bad kings, but we are not to forget the power and splendour to which the order attained under David and Solomon, and the revivals it enjoyed under Hezekiah and Josiah. There is no evidence that their condition was so deplorably destitute in the later days of the kingdom as the critics represent. 4. *The law of the king* (ch. xvii.). The law, it is thought, is sketched in terms borrowed from the court of Solomon. The objection derives much of its plausibility from not observing that the description of Solomon's court in the Book of Kings (1 Kings x. 26—29; xi. 1—4) is, on the other hand, given in terms distinctly borrowed from this law. The familiarity of the writer of the Books of Kings with Deuteronomy is undoubted, and he plainly draws up his account of Solomon's luxury and splendour in such language as will impress the mind by its contrast to the law. We, on the contrary, reading the law, are apt to think of Solomon's reign as if *it* were the original, and the law the copy. Solomon did what Moses knew too well kings would be prone to do, and there was every reason for the warning that was given. The objections taken to the book cannot, therefore, be allowed to set aside its own decisive testimony to its authorship. If we adopt the hypothesis of the critics, we are involved in graver difficulties than those from which we flee. We must suppose a state of things as existing under the kings, in respect of the Levitical orders, which we have no reason to believe ever did exist, which there is great difficulty in believing to have existed, and which historical documents in the most express language tell us did not exist. We must suppose Josiah and his people deceived about the book, for they unquestionably took it for a veritable book of Moses, grieving that its words had been neglected by their fathers (2 Kings xxii.; xxiii.; 2 Chron. xxxiv.). We must explain away a multitude of the plainest allusions to the book, not simply in Joshua, but in the prophets, particularly in Hosea, whose pages are rich in such references (cf. ch. vii. 13; viii. 7—20; xi. 14—16, with Hos. ii. 8; xii. 8; xiii. 6; ch. xii. with Hos. viii. 11; ch. xviii. 18 with Hos. xii. 13; ch. xvii. 12 with Hos. iv. 4; ch. xxviii. 68 with Hos. viii. 13; ix. 3; ch. xxix. 23 with Hos. xi. 8; ch. xxx. 1—10 with Hos. xiv.; ch. xxv. 13—16 with Hos. xii. 7, etc.). We must suppose such a passage as Solomon's prayer at the dedication of the temple (1 Kings viii.), which is saturated with Deuteronomic language, to have been a free and unhistorical composition; though, if this be allowed for Deuteronomy, it need not trouble us with Solomon. Even then we are not out of difficulties, for the book itself is in many respects internally unsuitable to the times to which it is assigned; compare *e.g.* the mild tone of the book towards Edom—the kindly and brotherly relations which are enjoined—with the hostile tone to which we are accustomed in the prophets, where Edom is a sort of later Amalek, a standing type of implacable enmity to the people of God. If Deuteronomy is not by Moses, it bears false witness of itself, was misconceived by the writers of the later books of Scripture, imposed upon the Jews from the days of its first appearance, and has had its claims endorsed by Christ and his apostles in a way which makes them partners in the general delusion. —J. O.

Vers. 9, 24—27.—*The written Word.* The Law here put in writing and solemnly deposited in the side of the ark, is the foundation of our present Bible. All Scripture is built up upon it. On this consignment of the first instalment of the Word, we remark—

I. THE WRITTEN WORD EMBODIES AND IS THE VEHICLE OF AN AUTHORITATIVE REVELATION. The Law was first given, *thereafter* recorded. Revelation precedes the record of it. But this line must not be drawn too finely. The record is inspired (1 Tim. iii. 16), and is to us the revelation of the will of God. It *is*, as well as *contains*, the Word of God. The line must not be drawn too finely : 1. *Between revelation and its history.* The threads of revelation cannot be picked out from the texture of its history, and exhibited apart. They constitute one whole; the record embraces both. 2. *Between revelation and inspired prophetical discourses*—with psalms, poems, wisdom literature, etc., which unfold the principles of revelation, apply and enforce them, turn them into subjects of praise, or deal with them reflectively. For discourses, psalms, didactic literature, etc., *add* to revelation as well as unfold its meaning. 3. *Between revelation and the written Word.* For that, as above remarked, is the revelation to us. It is clothed with its own authority as inspired—an authority the nature and degree of which is a study by itself—and it is clothed with the authoritativeness (objective) inherent in the revelations of which records are preserved.

II. THE WRITTEN WORD IS NECESSARY FOR THE PERPETUATION OF REVEALED TRUTH. It embodies truth in a form which secures its transmission to posterity without material distortion or corruption. Tradition, however carefully guarded, would have been a most unsafe medium for the conveyance of important revelations. A body of facts and laws such as we have in the Pentateuch, or discourses like these of Moses, could not have been entrusted to it without certainty of mutilation. The Law, accordingly, was put in writing. A written revelation is one great proof of the wisdom and care of God. Variations in manuscripts rarely affect the substance of the message.

III. THE WRITTEN WORD IS A WITNESS FOR GOD AGAINST THE APOSTACY OF THOSE TO WHOM THE WORD IS GIVEN. (Ver. 26.) 1. If it does not prevent *corruption* of *doctrine*, it testifies against it. It was by appeal to the Scriptures that Josiah wrought his reformation in Judah (2 Kings xxiii.). It was by appeal to the Scriptures that the Reformers aroused Europe against the Church of Rome. 2. If it cannot prevent *apostacy in deed*, it remains as a witness against the apostates. It holds up the Law from which they have departed. It convicts them of rebellion. It denounces against them the penalties of transgression. While it invites them to repentance, and promises, if they return, healing of their backslidings.—J. O.

Vers. 10—13.—*Reading the Law.* (For an example of fulfilment of this command, see Neh. viii.) Observe—

I. IT WAS TO BE READ AT A RELIGIOUS FEAST. On an occasion of solemnity—at the Feast of Tabernacles (ver. 10). Our feelings in reading the Scriptures, or in hearing them read, ought always to be of a solemn and reverential kind. But it is well to avail ourselves of every aid which may lend solemnity and impressiveness to the reading of words so sacred.

II. IT WAS TO BE READ AT A TIME OF GENERAL LEISURE. In the sabbatical year— " the year of release." Leisure hours cannot be better employed than in making ourselves acquainted with " what God the Lord will speak " (Ps. lxxxv. 8). We should avail ourselves of the leisure of others to endeavour to instruct them.

III. IT WAS TO BE READ PUBLICLY. (Ver. 11.) The private reading of the Law would doubtless be attended to in many pious homes. But the practice would not be general (scarcity and expensiveness of manuscripts, want of education, religious indifference). The Levites were to teach Israel the Law (ch. xxxiii. 10; Lev. x. 11; Mal. ii. 7); but they might not do so, or the people might not wait on their instructions. The public reading of the Law, even once in seven years, was thus calculated to be of great advantage. As long as the practice was observed, multitudes would derive benefit from it. The reading was of the nature of a public testimony, but also, as we see in Neh. viii., for purposes of real instruction. The public reading of Scripture, with or without comment, is an important means of edification. Read with intelligence and judgment, the Word commends *itself*. And such readings are necessary. Many have Bibles, yet do not read them ; many read and do not understand.

IV. It was to be read for the benefit of old and young. (Ver. 12.) All are interested in listening to the Word of God. Men and women, little children, strangers, no class but has a concern in it. None but may be edified by it. Children ought to be more recognized than they are in religious services. Need for making them feel that they too are interested in what is being said; that the Bible has a message for them as well as for their elders.

V. The end of reading God's Word is that we may be enabled to obey it. (Ver. 13.)—J. O.

Vers. 16—22, 28—30.—*God's foresight of Israel's declension.* We learn—

I. That the future is perfectly unveiled to God. God claims this power as one of his prerogatives (Isa. xli. 22; xlii. 9; xliii. 25, 26; xlv. 20, 21). And no one can question but that these predictions have been strikingly fulfilled. The people *did* corrupt themselves and turn aside, and evil did befall them in the latter days (ver. 29).

II. That the plainest warnings are frequently disregarded. Israel was under no government of fate. Had the people repented, they would have been forgiven. The predictions are cast in absolute form, only because God saw that warning would not be taken. He would only too gladly have revoked his threatenings, had Israel, roused to alarm, turned from its evil (cf. the case of Nineveh). This, however, it did not do, but, with these woe-laden prophecies spread before it, rushed madly on, as if eager to fulfil them. How like sinners still! The plainest declarations, the most explicit warnings, the direst threatenings, are as little recked of as if no Word of God were in existence. Strange that God's Word should be so disregarded, and yet profession so often made of believing in it (cf. Jer. xxxvi.)!

III. That God's Word has its uses even though men prove disobedient. It is to be spoken to them and taught them, "whether they will hear, or whether they will forbear" (Ezek. ii. 7). It tells them the truth. It shows them their duty. It warns them of the consequences of disobedience. It upholds a witness for God in their apostacy (ver. 19). It renders them inexcusable. A solemn responsibility thus attaches to us in the possession of God's Word.

IV. That a time will come when the sinner will be forced to confess that God's words against him have all become true. (Ver. 17.) Only that time may come too late (ver. 18). "Missing God is not true repentance" (Keil).—J. O.

Vers. 1—8.—*The leadership made over to Joshua.* There is something wonderfully pathetic in the great leader, whose eye is yet undimmed, laying down his trust beside the Jordan. He is a hundred and twenty years old, but the Lord hath denied him the privilege of entering the land of promise. He now meekly resigns his command, and nominates Joshua as his successor. It might have discouraged the people, the loss of their great leader; but he points them upward to the Lord their God, who had been the real Leader in the Exodus and pilgrimage, and who was going at their head across the Jordan. Their faith in the invisible Leader is to be strengthened now that the visible and human leader is to be taken away from them. Besides, they are to have Joshua as the captain of the host. We notice here—

I. The men appointed by God to special office receive from him special preparation. Moses himself had received a wondrous preparation, first at his mother's knee, next in the palace of Pharaoh, and next in the solitudes of Midian. And Joshua, who is to succeed him as leader, though not as lawgiver, has also received important preparation. He is first associated with Moses in the mount, as he is receiving the Law. He is thus trained to firm faith in the invisible King, and accustomed to his wonders. He is next exercised in battle, leading the Israelites against Amalek, and proving himself skilful in the field. He had also, as a spy, become minutely acquainted with the land of promise, and brought up with Caleb an encouraging report. None was so fitted as he for high command. Just, then, as the twelve were carefully trained to be the apostles of the Church, so was Joshua trained, and so is every one selected for important work.

II. The assurance that God was associated with the invasion gave the invaders the best possible stimulus. God is to go with them; they need in such a case fear no evil. Their foes may be gigantic, but greater is he that is for them than all that can be against them. Their vantage-ground is that they can be "strong in the Lord, and in the power of his might."

And this is the one question to be asked always: Is God with us? If so, all is well. The work always succeeds of which he is the head.

III. The work before them is to be judgment. They are to enter Canaan as destroyers. It is *iconoclasts* that have been brought from Egypt. Their commission is death to the old religions of the country, and to the incorrigible devotees. They enter as "the scourge of God." And such a mission must have proved a warning to themselves. If called to be the executioners of the apostates of Palestine, they will surely guard against apostacy.

IV. In the invasion they must adhere to the letter of the commandments. It is a terrible mission; but God leaves no loophole for them to escape it. He leaves nothing to licence; he gives them strict orders, and these must be carried carefully out. Thus are the rigours of the invasion brought under the shadow of his throne, and he, who is Sovereign and legitimate Avenger, commissioned Israel to execute his orders amid the criminal population of Palestine.—R. M. E.

Vers. 9—13.—*The literary executors of Moses.* It must have been a solemn act on the part of Moses, after having nominated Joshua as his successor in the leadership of Israel, to summon the priests and the elders, that they might be the custodians of his manuscripts, and deal with them as he desired. It was to the ministers of religion, and to the rulers elected by the people and ordained of God, that he gave this important charge. Of course they could not, as nowadays, publish in multiplied copies the carefully written Law. But they were directed to have a great congregation every seven years, at the time of the Feast of Tabernacles, for the public reading of the Law. Hence in this sabbatic time, when no rain need be feared, but brightness and peace reigned by night and day in the land of promise, they were to make public, through reading, this important Law. This interesting arrangement suggests such lessons as these—

I. There is nothing so precious as God's Word. No wonder that special officers got special charge of it, when the first instalment was given and completed. It was a sacred deposit such as no other nation possessed. The Jew had surely a great advantage, inasmuch as there were committed to him " the oracles of God" (Rom. iii. 2).

II. The widest possible publication should be secured for it. No better arrangement in times before printing can be imagined than this one of a great congregation with perfect publicity thereat. What an audience every seventh year! And amid the solemnity of the year of release, the sabbatic year, when time lay plentifully on their hands, they could not better spend a portion of the year than in meeting together to learn God's Law. It was a splendid, periodic publicity.

And is it not typical of that wider publicity which the printing press is now giving to the Divine Word? Assuredly it is a striking fact that the circulation of the most successful human publication dwindles into insignificance compared with the circulation of the Word of God. Men are trying to make it as widely known as possible.

III. Special seasons for the study of God's Law are eminently desirable. Had this direction of Moses been faithfully followed, there would have been a revival of religion every seventh year. A new start would thus have been given to the study of God's will, and greater devotedness of spirit have been created throughout the many thousands of Israel.

Similarly, congregations and Churches should have grand assemblies for the express purpose of the public study of God's Law, not merely on the Lord's day each week, but at special and stated seasons. The "camp meetings" of America may have objectionable elements attaching to them; but it would be a good day for all the Churches, if some grand reunions could be devised, when the highest aim of mankind would be carried out in the study of God's Law.

IV. The children as well as adults should be made sharers in the special study and blessing. The purpose of the arrangement was not only to publish truths as widely as possible among the adult portion of the population, but to interest also the children in the doctrines and discipline of the Church. Hence the meeting was to be an aggregation of families. It was to be "a gathering of the clans;"

young as well as old were to hear the wonderful works of God and his gracious commandments.

The special religious service, then, which the Churches should aim at, will be of the widest character. It should contemplate the presence of the young as well as the old, and be adapted to the revival of the Lord's work in all sections of the Church. There is power in the aggregation of individuals for religious purposes. The children must be kept in view in every effort to extend the kingdom. The family must be lifted, if possible, all of a piece, as a unit of God's own making, and in the elevation of families will come the elevation of nations.

There is something peculiarly bright and happy in the picture. The sky is cloudless and the people are living in booths "without carefulness." They have met together for the purpose of celebrating a feast, but there is to be a special study of the Law for the benefit of young as well as old. Old heads and young are bowed before the Majesty of heaven, anxious to know his will and how to do it. In such circumstances surely religion must be promoted. May we have grace to imitate such an excellent example!—R. M. E.

Vers. 14—23.— *The Lord's charge to Moses and Joshua.* Moses, in making over the leadership to Joshua, was only anticipating a more formal assignment of it by God himself. He directs the old leader and his successor to repair to the tabernacle, and there to receive their respective charges. The Shechinah appeared to convince the people of the reality of the Divine interview with the leaders. Moses is first informed of his own approaching end, of the certain apostasy of the people, and of the desirability of laying before them a song which would testify to the wickedness of the apostasy when it took place. Then Joshua is encouraged by the Lord himself and promised his presence.

I. LET US NOTICE THE EXPRESSION THAT MOSES IS TO "SLEEP WITH HIS FATHERS." The words (שֹׁכֵב עִם־אֲבֹתֶיךָ) are literally, "lie down with thy fathers," and in this connection are surely significant. They point assuredly to fellowship and rest with the fathers in another life. They cannot refer to any depositing of the remains of Moses in the same tomb as his fathers. His sepulchre was solitary and sacred; his lying down with his fathers, therefore, can only refer to the fellowship in a future life. This is the only place in the Pentateuch where this particular expression occurs, although we meet it in the Books of the Kings no less than twenty-six times. It was undoubtedly an intimation to Moses that he was about to enter into restful fellowship with his fathers, and was most welcome consolation at this peculiarly trying time.

II. APOSTASY NEVER TAKES GOD BY SURPRISE. He foresees it and makes provision for it, preparing his servants for its appearance, and preparing a proper recompense for the apostates themselves. It must be a remarkable experience to be in such a position as God, and to have prevision of all the future, so that there can be no element of surprise for him. His resources are so adequate that he is outside the region of finite surprises and difficulties.

III. SCEPTICISM IS THE DAUGHTER OF ABUNDANCE RATHER THAN OF WANT. It will be, the Lord says, when Israel has entered into the promised land, and enjoyed its milk and honey, and when they have waxed fat, that they shall turn to other gods and be guilty of apostasy. In the same way, our modern sceptics are men for the most part in comfortable worldly circumstances, and out of these spring doubts about the existence of God and suspicions that we can do very well without him, and with minor majesties. "It is on the bed of luxury," says Mr. Martineau, "not on the rock of nature, that scepticism has its birth. . . . And while from the centre of comforts many a sad fear goes forth, and the warmest lot becomes often filled with the chillest doubts, hidden within it like a heart of ice that cannot melt, you may find toiling misery that trusts the more the more it is stricken, and amid the secret prayers of mourners hear the sweetest tones of hope."

IV. PROPHECY IS A WITNESS SUBPŒNAED BEFOREHAND AGAINST GOD'S ENEMIES. We have here God giving a certain song which is to be a witness against Israel in the coming apostasy. And prophecy is the retaining of a witness long beforehand for the coming trial. It is proof positive that no varying moods of men can ever surprise God or thwart his magnificent designs. The substance of this song we are presently to consider.

V. JOSHUA RECEIVES ENCOURAGEMENT ABOUT A SUCCESSFUL LEADERSHIP AND THE PERPETUAL PRESENCE OF GOD. This means immediate success as a set-off to the sad intelligence about ultimate apostacy. Joshua is assured that God will be with him and ensure the success of the invasion. Hence Joshua is only to be a *lieutenant-general* under the invisible Leader and King. And Joshua desired nothing higher. The great honour was in being a fellow-soldier with God. It was God's battles he was going to fight, and it would be God's victories which Israel would win.

VI. IT IS A GREAT BLESSING AT LIFE'S CLOSE TO HAVE A SUCCESSOR TO CARRY ON OUR WORK, AND AN ASSURANCE THAT WE OURSELVES ARE SAFE BEYOND THE BORDER. There was much sadness about the close of Moses' career. He was reminded of his sin in his exclusion from Canaan. But he had compensation in Joshua taking up his work, and in the assurance of "rest beyond the river." He was going over to a better land than lay beyond the Jordan. He was passing on to peace with the sainted fathers who had preceded him. He had thus calmness and blessing given in the midst of his pain.

May we have work worth carrying on after us, and some one to succeed us in it; and may we have rest like that of Moses after our demise!—R. M. E.

Vers. 24—30.—*The Divine testimony deposited in the ark.* Moses, being thus commissioned of God to utter the inspired warning, loses no time in summoning the congregation. But while doing so, he gives precise directions to the Kohathites, who had charge of the ark, to deposit his manuscripts within it. Is anything to be learned from this consignment of the sacred books?

I. THE SACRED BOOKS ARE NOT COMPLIMENTARY TO HUMAN NATURE. The Pentateuch, in its tremendous charges and indictments against mankind, is in unison with the rest of the Word. It is a sustained witness against the human race. "Others may perhaps suspect," says Henry Rogers, "that Jewish vanity led the writers thus to ignore or treat lightly the affairs of all nations *except their own.* The answer is concise, but conclusive. Let Jewish vanity in general be what the reader pleases, these writers would seem to have had none of it. If they have passed by the glorious achievements of secular history, they have recorded all the infamies of their own nation; and, indeed, their principal references to *other* nations are as 'scourges' of their own—scourges justly sent, they confess and avow, for apostacies which had wearied out the patience of Heaven!" The marvel is that the Jews and Christians should conspire to preserve what is a most humiliating account of the race.

II. THE ARK WAS THE TREASURE-HOUSE OF GOD PROTECTED BY HIS PRESENCE. It was the "safe" of Israel, not, alas! "fire-proof," like Milner's, as the Babylonians demonstrated, yet as durable and as sacred as the times allowed. It was fenced around by the holiest sanctions. Nowhere could the manuscripts be so safe. Now, the ark is regarded as a type of Jesus; and if so, then the depositing of the Law within the ark would convey the idea of the Law of God being within the heart of Christ (Ps. xl. 8). In other words, Jesus Christ embodies the Divine Law or will, and is at once its most brilliant exposition and the most tremendous indictment of human nature. The Jews were not so careful of the living Law as their forefathers were of the written Law. They recognized its charge against themselves: the charge had become oral; it walked before them; it was something that they could not shake off except through the desperate alternative of assassination. They killed in Christ their living Conscience.

III. WE SHOULD LEARN FROM THE EXAMPLE OF CHRIST TO TREASURE UP GOD'S LAW WITHIN OUR OWN HEARTS. We cannot have too much of the Bible in our minds and memories. The more we study it, the more like Christ shall we become. He whose "delight is in the Law of the Lord, and in his Law doth he meditate day and night," is blessed, and he shall be like the tree whose roots are in the waters, duly fruitful and ever green (Ps. i. 2, 3). His conscience shall be reinforced and become increasingly tender; his heart shall be elevated in its affections and longings; and his mind shall be trained to what is high and holy. Thus is the whole being enriched and the life enlarged. May we deposit the Word of God with as much care in our hearts as the Levites did the rolls of Moses in the ark!—R. M. E.

Vers. 1—8.—*Putting off the harness.* Faith in God anticipates every event without distress. If God's plan cut across the grain of our own inclination, faith inspires us to say, "His plan is best." By virtue of a living faith, we can face death without anxiety, and advance to meet the last foe. We see in this passage—

I. FAITH ACQUIESCENT IN BODILY DISSOLUTION. Splendid triumphs were in sight. The Jewish host was about to complete its conquest; just about to realize full success after forty years of patient trial. Such an hour is the most precious in a man's history. Yet the faith of Moses saw a nobler conquest yet—a conquest over self, a conquest over the unseen foe. A voice from within—the voice of failing nature—whispered that he was no longer equal to the fatigues of a military campaign. And a voice from above told him that his work was done; and, though high reward was in store, justice exacted satisfaction for an earlier misdeed. Even a single blemish in a good man's life entails on him loss. We cannot cheat God. Without a murmur, Moses, like a little child, yields to his Father's decree, and meekly prepares to die.

II. FAITH REJOICING IN OTHERS' PROMOTION. In every age, faith has worked to the production of love. It is the extirpator of selfishness. Moses found as much pleasure in announcing that Joshua should lead the people to conquest, as that he should himself lead. Indeed, Moses felt that Joshua could do better than he could. He had been emphatically a legislator; now a warrior was needed. If God removes one servant, he provides a better. The eye cannot say to the hand, "I am nobler than thou." Each man has a place and an office of his own. If only God's work is well and truly done, faith will rejoice in the means.

III. FAITH CONVINCED THAT GOD AND MAN MUST CO-OPERATE FOR THE TRIUMPH OF THE KINGDOM. "The Lord thy God, he will go before thee;" and "Joshua, he shall go over before thee" (ver. 3). The presence of man, in action or in warfare, does not exclude the presence of God. Joshua could gain no triumph if he had gone alone. God has chosen to work through human agencies. By his wise appointment, Divine and human co-operation is a necessity. "The Lord shall give them up before your face, that *ye* may do unto them according to his commandment" (ver. 5). Nor is Moses' power and influence to be quite absent from the conflict. Being dead, he yet acted. His commandment regulated their conduct. His word was still a mighty spell. Each man can add something to the aggressive activity of God's truth.

IV. FAITH ASSURED OF GOD'S SELF-CONSISTENCY. God had succoured Israel in the past; therefore he would succour them again. He had begun to dislodge the Canaanite kings before Israel, therefore he would go on until he completed for them the conquest (ver. 4). Jehovah had foreseen all the weaknesses and unfaithfulness of Israel and yet he had commenced to give them triumphs. On what reasonable ground would he do this, unless he purposed to repeat his favours, and to subdue for them every foe? Half a conquest would be no boon to them. This would be a vexation to Israel] and a dishonour to God. The man of faith knows that God can never be at variance with himself. When we have discovered the method of God's procedure, we should act along this line in order to enjoy his help. In his footsteps let us plant our feet.

V. FAITH IN ONE STIMULATING IN OTHERS LATENT QUALITIES OF ENERGY. Although it appears that Moses was lacking in martial skill and prowess, his faith in God enabled him to stir up the hidden gifts of others. Faith foresees the victory, and confident hope is a great inspirer of strength. Like new nerve-power, it interlaces and braces all the active energies of a man. The voice of robust faith has always a magical charm over us. We perceive forthwith that the demand is most reasonable, and that largest exertion is our highest glory. It is easy to be strong when Infinite Strength is awaiting us. Every endeavour we make enlarges our capacity to receive more strength. The weaker parts of our nature perish under the strain, but newer and nobler elements fill up the room. And if God be with us, then fear of man departs. Faith is a prolific parent of courage.

> "Fear him, ye saints, and ye will then
> Have nothing else to fear."

And God can never fail the man of faith. Having pledged his presence, we are well ensured. For him to forsake his friends is an impossibility. "The mountains may depart, and the hills be removed; but never shall the covenant of his faithfulness fail."—D.

Vers. 9—13, 24—29.—*The honour appertaining to God's Law.* As our Lord, in the near prospect of death, employed his thoughts in comforting and instructing others, so Moses, instead of centring his thought upon himself, is only more eager to provide for the people's future obedience. Inasmuch as his days on earth were now very few, he yearned to crowd into them as much counsel and kindly warning as it was possible. To be of service to Israel—this absorbed the passions and desires of his soul.

I. GOD'S REDEMPTIVE LAW IS EMBODIED IN A WRITTEN FORM. To Moses it had been revealed that it would not suffice to instruct the people *orally* in the lines of religious duty. So pregnant with importance is the Law of God, that it must be reduced to writing, and carefully preserved. God's law concerning our bodily life—how to use food, how to heal disease, how to prolong our days—all this is revealed in other modes: this Law is written by the finger of God on the very structure of man. In such matters, God's will is to be discovered by investigation and by experiment. But the law of the soul's life is disclosed to us in a different way. How sin can be pardoned; how reconciliation between a guilty man and his Maker can be secured; how inward purity can be gained, and immortality reached;—all this is disclosed by God through his prophets, and reduced to a written form. If a perverse disposition prevails in a man, he may refuse to read the record, and so "count himself unworthy of everlasting life."

II. GOD'S REDEMPTIVE LAW IS COMMITTED TO TRUSTY STEWARDS. The Law of God written by Moses, touching purification and obedience, was placed in the custody of the priests (ver. 9), and secured in the ark of the covenant. This was both a realized fact and a symbolic figure. That ark is an emblem of Christ's Church, and the sons of Levi were the early representatives of genuine believers. The Christian family has become a royal priesthood; and one of their delightful duties is to conserve God's Law so as to hand it on to coming generations. By the loving care of loyal disciples, the oracles of God have been preserved intact. The vigorous life of the Church to-day is displayed in revising the exact text, translating it into other tongues, and unfolding it to the understanding of the people. We are "stewards of the mysteries of God."

III. GOD'S REDEMPTIVE LAW IS TO BE PERIODICALLY EXPOUNDED. Moses required this to be done once in every seven years. By this method, the recollections of those who had heard it aforetime would be revived, it would be impressed on memory with fresh force, and many would rise to a higher understanding and appreciation of its meaning. The recurring period is symbolic. Once every seven days the privilege now returns. Nor have we to journey to some metropolis to hear the sacred record. Printing has multiplied the copies of God's Law on every side; and it would be spiritual obtuseness if we did not recognize this modern invention as a new agency in God's hands for enlightening the human race. The Law was ordained to be "read in the year of release, and at the Feast of Tabernacles." This was the anniversary of the Sinaitic revelation; this festival was signalized for its unusual joyousness. And this fresh revelation of God's truth, in each septennial period, would add new zest to gladness. Good men would say, "Thy words were found, and I did eat them, and they were to me as the joy and rejoicing of my heart."

IV. GOD'S REDEMPTIVE LAW IS TO BE BROUGHT WITHIN THE UNDERSTANDING OF ALL. The wisdom and the loving-kindness of God are displayed in his care for children. As he has abundantly provided for their bodily and mental wants in their long dependence upon parents, so too he provides for the enlightenment of their consciences by the ministry of his Word. Right impressions are very early made. It is the highest wisdom to entwine the tender affections of children around God and truth and heaven. Before they "know anything" else, God commands us to see to it that "they hear, and learn to fear the Lord our God." To neglect the religious training of the young is heinous sin. This is to deprive the host of God's elect of young recruits. "Instead of the fathers, must come up the children." God's will is abundantly revealed, to the end that we may do it.—D.

Vers. 14, 15, 23.—*The official investiture of Joshua.* It was fitting that a public transference of authority should be made from Moses to Joshua. The nobleness of Moses comes prominently into view. As John said of Jesus, so substantially Moses said of Joshua, " He must increase, but I must decrease."

I. THE OCCASION. The occasion had an aspect of mournfulness. Moses was about to die ; nevertheless, no tinge of grief is in his words. He contemplates the event with calm serenity. His chief concern is a competent successor. The good of others was still Moses' uppermost desire. Promptly he responded to the Divine call.

II. THE PLACE. God had appointed the meeting to take place in the tabernacle. All great enterprises should be consecrated in the sanctuary. Here we touch the fountain head of effectual blessing. God has engaged to be found by us here. " This is my rest for ever : here will I dwell ! "

III. THE APPEARANCE. " The Lord appeared in a pillar of a cloud." So ineffably dazzling is the native glory of God, that no mortal eye can look upon it. We should be blinded by the excess of light. In accommodation to human weakness, God tempers his brightness by an attendant cloud Such was the form in which he was pleased to appear upon the mercy-seat. Such was the mode of his manifestation on the Mount of Transfiguration. In our present imperfect state we need the intervention of the cloud.

IV. THE CHARGE. God's charge came to Joshua through human lips, yet none the less was it God's charge. We must suppose that Joshua was lacking that susceptibility of soul which is essential for the hearing of God's voice. Some can hear that voice direct ; some can hear it only through transmission of others' speech. God's charge and Moses' charge were one, " Be strong and of a good courage." What God commands, God first gives. Says he to men, " Here is my entrusted strength : use it well ! More is ready as soon as it is needed." Best of all, he adds, " I will be with thee."—D.

Vers. 16—22, 29.—*The last precaution against idolatry.* We cannot trace into all its ramifications the subtle influence of a good man's life. If it does not accomplish all that he has desired, it often achieves more than he imagines. It operates in directions he had not designed. The presence of a good man will often repress an evil which he cannot eradicate. All the faith and piety of Moses had hardly restrained the people from idolatry ; his removal will be the loosening of the flood-gates which had held in check the wayward passion. We have in this paragraph—

I. GOD'S FORECAST OF ISRAEL'S FUTURE SIN. " This people will rise up, and go a-whoring after the gods of the strangers " (ver. 16). Moses himself had surmised this result. With hidden sorrow, he had observed the base tendencies of the people towards idolatry. As he forecast the time when warfare should cease, and the tribes should find themselves among the relics of idols, he trembled for the result. And now this surmise on his part was confirmed by a revelation from God. It is now a foreseen reality : " They will forsake me, and break my covenant." Worldly success and self-indulgence would lead to impiety. Yet this foreknowledge of Israel's certain sin did not deter God from promising to Joshua military success, nor did it deter God from using all practical measures to dissuade from sin. We conclude that God sees it best to employ all remedial measures, even when it is known that in the chief end they will fail.

II. WE HAVE GOD'S ANNOUNCEMENT OF CONSEQUENT CALAMITY. " My anger shall be kindled against them, . . . and I will forsake them." The series of evils that would spring from idolatry is vividly set before them ; and no other motive can be conjectured for this than a generous desire to deter from sin. Love is more conspicuous in portraying the certain miseries of misconduct, than in promising the rewards of obedience. The former duty is done with personal painfulness ; the latter is a delight. And not only will the severity of the punishment be keenly felt, but the people will also apprehend the reason of the calamity. They will trace it up to God's displeasure ; yet will they not repent. Men are woefully blind to the iron force of sinful habit. To-day it is a silken thread ; to-morrow it is an iron chain.

III. GOD'S LAST EXPEDIENT TO PREVENT SIN. Moses, the servant of God, was about to die ; but his death was to be a sleep, and he should die with a song in his mouth. At first sight, it seems a strange expedient as a deterrent from sin. But the intention was, that by the sweet and flowing sounds of rhythm, the main facts of God's covenant might be kept vividly alive in the people's memory. In the absence of printing, and cheap circulations of written documents, poetic forms will live when prose is quite forgotten. God condescends to employ every possible method by which a sense of religious duty might be preserved and perpetuated. The song would live by the action of known law, when the full sense would be ignored. Thus the song of Moses, "familiar in their mouths as a household word," would be an abiding witness against them. Said God, "It shall not be forgotten." By such gracious methods the Most High would win men unto obedience and life. The mightiest power is in gentleness. If this fails, all fails.—D.

EXPOSITION.

CHAPTER XXXII.

Song of Moses and Announcement of his Death.

In accordance with the Divine injunction, Moses composed an ode, which he recited in the hearing of the people, and committed to writing, to remain with them as a witness for God against them. With this end in view, the ode is directed principally to a contrasting of the unchanging faithfulness of the Almighty with the anticipated perversity and unfaithfulness of his people. The poem may be divided into six parts. 1. An introduction (vers. 1—3), in which the importance of the doctrine to be delivered is announced. 2. The blamelessness and excellency of Jehovah are placed in contrast with the corruptness and perversity of Israel (vers. 4, 5). 3. The folly and ingratitude of the rebellious people is dwelt upon (vers. 7—18). 4. The purpose of God to punish and reject the rebellious generation is declared (vers. 19—23). 5. The fulfilment of this purpose in the judgments which should come upon the rebels, whilst mercy and favour should be showed to those that repented and were humbled under the hand of God (vers. 24—34). 6. And finally, the judgment which God would execute on the enemies of Israel, and the mercy he would show to his servants (vers. 35—43).

In this ode—"carmine plane divino" (Lowth)—Moses displays the genius of the poet, as in the other parts of this book he has showed the sagacity of the legislator and the skill of the orator. Vigour of diction, elevation of sentiment, vivacity of representation, beauty and sublimity of imagery, characterize this ode throughout. Nor is the piety less noticeable than the poetry; zeal for God, earnest desire for his honour, and devout reverence of his majesty pervade and inspire the whole. Remarkable also is this ode in relation to the later prophetic utterances in Israel. "It is the compendious anticipatory sketch and the common watchword of all prophecy, and stands related to it as fundamentally as the Decalogue to all laws, and the Lord's Prayer to all prayers. The legislator has here condensed in a song the prophetic contents of his last address (ch. xxvii.—xxviii., xxix., xxx.), wherewith he lives on in the memory and mouth of the people. He here sets before them their whole history to the end of the days. In this ode, each age of Israel has a mirror of its present condition and future fate. This mirror prophecy holds up before its contemporaries" (Delitzsch, 'Jesaias,' s. 33).

Ver. 1.—Heaven and earth are summoned to hearken to his words, both because of their importance, and because heaven and earth were interested, so to speak, as witnesses of the manifestation of God's righteousness and faithfulness about to be celebrated (cf. ch. iv. 26; xxx. 19; xxxi. 28, 29; Isa. i. 2; Jer. ii. 12; xxii. 29).

Ver. 2.—**My doctrine shall drop as the rain.** The Hebrew verb here and in ch. xxxiii. 28 is properly rendered by "drop;" it expresses the gentle falling of a genial shower or the soft distillation of dew. The clause is best taken imperatively, as it is by the LXX., the Vulgate, and Onkelos: *Let my doctrine drop as the rain, let my speech distil,* etc. The point of comparison here is not the quickening, fructifying, vivifying influence of the rain and dew, so much as the effective force of these agents as sent from heaven to produce results. So might his doctrine come with power into the minds of his hearers. **Doctrine** (לֶקַח, from לָקַח, to take); that which takes one (Prov. vii. 21, "fair speech," by which one is captivated), or which one takes or receives, viz. instruction (Prov. iv. 2; Isa. xxix. 24). **Small rain;** gentle showers, such as conduce to the growing of herbs. The Hebrew word (שְׂעִירִם) primarily means hairs, and is here used of rain coming down in thin streams like hair. Showers; *heavy rain* (רְבִיבִים, from רָבַב, to be much or many, equal to multitude of drops).

Ver. 3.—**I will publish the name of the Lord**; literally, *I will call*, i.e. *proclaim*, or *celebrate*, etc. **Ascribe ye greatness unto our God.** The hearers of the song are summoned to join in the celebration of the Divine majesty. The word rendered "greatness" occurs only in this book (ch. iii. 24; v. 21; ix. 26; xi. 2), and in Ps. cl. 2. It is the greatness of God as the Almighty that is here celebrated.

Vers. 4, 5.—**He is the Rock, his work is perfect;** rather, *The Rock! his work is perfect,* i.e. blameless, without fault. God is called "the Rock" (הַצּוּר), as the unchangeable Refuge and Stronghold of his people, by which they are sustained, and to which they can resort for defence and protection at all times. The epithet is applied to God four times besides in this song (vers. 15, 18, 30, 31); it occurs also frequently in the Psalms (cf. Ps. xix. 14; xxviii. 1; xxxi. 2, 3; lxii. 2, 7; etc.). The Hebrew word, *tsur, çur,* or *zur,* appears in several proper names of the Mosaic period, as *e.g. Pedahzur,* "Rock delivers" (Numb. i. 10), a name of the same import as *Pedahel,* "God delivers" (Numb. xxxiv. 28); *Elizur,* "God is a Rock" (Numb. i. 5); *Zuriel* (Numb. iii. 35) and *Zurishaddai,* "the Almighty is Rock" (Numb. i. 6; ii. 12). "If Jehovah," says Baumgarten, "is here called *Rock,* without any qualification, the reason is that he is the only true rock, and all the strength and firmness of earth's stones is but an ectype of his unchangeable faithfulness and rectitude. If one cleaves to the dualism of spirit and nature, and regards the figure as a merely subjective, arbitrary union of the two, such an expression is simply unintelligible; but if we would understand Scripture and religious speech, we must with all earnestness accustom ourselves to recognize the spiritual ground in nature, and apprehend this in the Biblical expression (comp. Steffens' 'Religionsphilosophie,' i. s. 101, 102)." It is remarkable that none of the ancient versions have retained this epithet here. The LXX. have Θεός: the Vulgate, *Deus* ("Dei opera"); the Targum of Onkelos, תַּקִּיפָא, "Mighty;" while the Peshito has simply the pronoun "his" appended to "works," ܒܥܒ̈ܕܘܗܝ. **For all his ways are judgment;** i.e. accordant with rectitude (cf. Ps. cxlv. 17). **A God of truth;** rather, *of faithfulness* (אֱמוּנָה, from אָמַן, to stay, or be stayed, to be firm). **They have corrupted themselves, their spot is not the spot of his children: they are a perverse and crooked generation.** Of this difficult passage the

following seems the best construction and rendering:—*A perverse and crooked generation—not his children,* [but] *their spot—has become corrupt towards him.* The subject of the verb at the beginning of the verse is the "perverse and crooked generation," at the end of it, and between the verb and its subject there is interjected parenthetically the clause, "not his children, but their spot." *Spot* is here used in a moral sense, as in Job xi. 15; xxxi. 7; Prov. ix. 7. These corrupt persons claimed to be children of God, but they were not; they were rather a stain and a reproach to them (cf. 2 Pet. ii. 13; Isa. i. 4). The rendering above given is substantially that of De Wette, Knobel, Keil, and Herxheimer, by all of whom the "perverse generation" is regarded as the subject of the sentence. This is the view adopted also in the 'Speaker's Commentary.' Some would make "God" the subject, and render, "He hath corrupted to him, or to himself" (margin, Authorized Version; Ibn Ezra, etc.). Others take "spot" as the subject, thus: "Their spot or blemish hath corrupted before him children not his" (Lowth, Dathe); but such renderings are forced, and proceed on constructions of the text which are illegitimate. Donaldson ('Jashar,' pp. 186, 223, edit. Sec.), following Lowth's construction, appeals to בָּנִים לֹא אֵמֻן בָּם (ver. 20) as a similar inversion. But the two cases are not parallel. To make them so, we must have here בָּנָיו לֹא מוּם בָּם, "his children in whom is no spot." Ewald takes מוּמָה as the noun here, instead of מוּם, and tracing it to the Syriac ܡܘܡܐ, *juravit,* renders "to him they, his not-sons, have corrupted their oath," *i.e.* have broken it; and this Fürst approves. But the phrase, "to corrupt an oath" is unexampled in the Old Testament, and there is no ground for changing the noun. The ancient versions vary considerably here: LXX., ἡμάρτοσαν, οὐκ αὐτῷ τέκνα μωμητά: Aq., διέφθειραν αὐτῷ οὐχ δι υἱοὶ αὐτου: Sym., διέφθειραν πρὸς αὐτὸν οὐχ οἱ υἱοὶ τὸ σύνολον: Vulgate, *peccaverunt ei et non filii ejus in sordibus*; Vet. Itala., *peccaverunt non ei filii maculati;* Syriac, "They corrupted but not him, children of defilement." These various renderings indicate that probably the text is and has long been corrupt. Some of the older English versions are worth noting on this verse. Rogers [Matthew], "The frowarde and overthwart generation hath marred themselves to himward, and are not his sonnes for their deformitie's sake;" Bishop's Bible, "Frowardly have they done agaynst him by their vices, not being his own children, but a wicked and froward generation;" Geneva Version, "They have corrupted themselves towards him by their vice, not being his children, but a froward and crooked generation."

Vers. 6, 7.—Instead of gratefully acknowledging the Divine beneficence, and dutifully obeying the Divine will, Israel had perversely and foolishly requited the Lord for all his benefits, by apostacy from him. Do ye thus requite? The verb here signifies primarily to do to any one either good or evil, whether in return for what he has done or not (cf. Gen. l. 15; 1 Sam. xxiv. 18; Prov. iii. 30); then, as a secondary meaning, to reward, repay, requite, as here and Ps. xviii. 21. To bring more forcibly to their view the ingratitude and folly of their conduct, Moses dwells upon what God was and had been to the nation: their Father, in that he had, in his love, chosen them to be his people (cf. Isa. lxiii. 16; lxiv. 7; Mal. ii. 10); their Purchaser, who had acquired possession of them by delivering them out of Egypt (cf. Ps. lxxiv. 2); their Maker, who had constituted them a nation; and their Establisher, by whom they had been conducted through the wilderness and settled in Canaan. Days of old; the times of Israel's deliverance from bondage, and the times during which successive generations had lived and experienced the goodness of the Lord. The form of the word rendered "days" is poetical, and is found only here and in Ps. xc. 15, which is also ascribed to Moses. The years of many generations; literally, years of generation and generation; "ætatum singularum annos" (Rosenmüller).

Vers. 8, 9.—From the very beginning, when God first allotted to the nations a place and a heritage, he had respect in his arrangements to the sons of Israel, who were his portion, and had as it were kept their interest in view in all that he appointed and ordered. According to the number of the children of Israel. When the Most High portioned out to the nations the heritage of each, he reserved for Israel, as the people of his choice, an inheritance proportioned to its numbers. The LXX. has "according to the number of the angels of God," an arbitrary departure from the original text, in accommodation, probably, to the later Jewish notion of each nation having its guardian angel. The Lord's portion is his people (cf. Exod. xv. 16; xix. 5; 1 Sam. x. 1; Ps. lxxviii. 71). The lot of his inheritance; literally, the cord, etc., the allusion being to the measuring of land by a cord, equivalent to the portion by measure which Jehovah allotted to himself as his inheritance (cf. Ps. xvi. 6).

Ver. 10.—God's fatherly care of Israel. In the desert land, and in the waste howling wilderness; literally, in the land of the desert, in the waste (the formless waste; the word used is that rendered, Gen. i. 2, "without

form"), the howling of the wilderness. "Israel is figuratively represented as a man without food or water, and surrounded by howling, ferocious beasts, and who must needs have perished had not God found him and rescued him" (Herxheimer). The apple of his eye; literally, the mannikin (אִישׁוֹן) of his eye, the pupil; so called because in it, as in a mirror, a person sees his own image reflected in miniature (Gesenius), or because, being the tenderest part of the eye, it is guarded as one would a babe (cf. Ps. xvii. 8; Prov. vii. 2; Zech. ii. 12). By Delitzsch and others this explanation of the word is rejected as not philologically justified, there being no evidence that the termination וֹן had a diminutive force; and as not in keeping with the earnestness of the passages in which this word occurs. They prefer the explanation man image to mannikin. Anyhow, the use of the word here must be taken as indicating that Israel is ever in the eye of the Lord, the object of his constant and tenderest care.

Ver. 11.—God's treatment of his people is compared to that of an eagle towards its young (cf. Exod. xix. 4). In the Authorized Version, the apodosis of the sentence is made to begin at ver. 12, and ver. 11 is wholly understood of the eagle and its young. To this arrangement it has been objected that it overlooks the fact that the suffixes to the verbs "taketh" and "beareth" are singulars, and are to be understood consequently, not of the eaglets, but of Israel. It has, therefore, been proposed to render the passage thus: As an eagle which stirreth up its nest, fluttereth over its young, he spread out his wings, took him up, and carried him on his pinions. The Lord alone did lead him, etc. The comparison is thus made to pass into a metaphorical representation of the Lord's dealing with Israel. One feels that there is something violent in this, for whilst God's care for Israel might be fittingly compared to that of an eagle towards her young, it is less fit to speak of God himself as if he were an eagle with wings which he spread abroad and on which he bare Israel. The rendering in the Authorized Version is on this account to be preferred, if it can be grammatically vindicated. And this it may on the ground that the suffixes may be understood of the "nest" as containing the young ("continens pro contento," a common rhetorical trope in Scripture; see Glass., 'Phil. Sac.,' p. 686; cf. Virgil, 'Æneid,' xii. 475, "nidisque loquacibus escam"); or the young may be referred to individually, "taketh it, beareth it," i.e. each of them; or, if the nest be understood, the whole body of them as therein contained. Stirreth up her [its] nest i.e. its nestlings; provocans ad volan-

dum pullos suos, Vulgate. This is the explanation usually given of the initial clause of this verse; but its accuracy has been questioned. Fürst would render the verb by "watches over;" but though הֵעִיר, as the Hiph. of עוּר, to watch, may have this meaning, it is undoubtedly used generally in the sense of rousing, exciting, stirring up. Knobel retains this meaning, but understands the clause of the exciting of the nestlings by the parent bird coming to them with food. This is certainly more in keeping with what follows; for when the eagle nestles or broods over her young, she does not excite them to fly. **Fluttereth over her young;** rather, *broods over, nestles,* or *cherishes* (יְרַחֵף). **Spreadeth abroad her wings,** etc. "I once saw a very interesting sight above one of the crags of Ben Nevis, as I was going in pursuit of black game. Two parent eagles were teaching their offspring, two young birds, the manœuvres of flight. They began by rising from the top of a mountain, in the eye of the sun;—it was about midday, and bright for this climate. They at first made small circles, and the young imitated them; they paused on their wings, waiting till they had made their first flight, holding them on their expanded wings when they appeared exhausted, and then took a second and larger gyration, always rising towards the sun, and enlarging their circle of flight, so as to make a gradually ascending spiral" (Davy, 'Salmonia;' see also Bochart, 'Hierozoicon,' ii. 181). The general reference is to God's fostering care of Israel, and especially his dealing with them when "he suffered their manners in the wilderness" (Acts xiii. 18), disciplined them, and trained them for what they were appointed to do.

Ver. 12.—**The Lord alone did lead him** (cf. Exod. xiii. 21; xv. 13). **With him;** *i.e.* along with Jehovah, as aiding him.

Ver. 13.—**He made him ride on the high places of the earth.** To ride over or drive over the heights of a country is figuratively to subjugate and take possession of that country (cf. ch. xxxiii. 29; Isa. lviii. 14). Israel, having subjugated Canaan, could eat of its produce, the increase of the fields, as his own. **Honey out of the rock, and oil out of the flinty rock.** Canaan abounded in wild bees, which had their hives in crevices of the rock, and in olive trees, which grew on a rocky soil; as is still the case in Palestine.

Ver. 14.—**Butter of kine.** The Hebrew word (חֶמְאָה) here used designates milk in a solid or semi-solid state, as thick cream, curd, or butter. As distinguished from this is the **milk of sheep;** where the word used (חָלָב) properly denotes fresh milk, milk in a fluid state, and with all its richness (חֵלֶב, fatness) in it (cf. Gen. xviii. 8; Isa. vii. 22).

Fat of lambs; lambs of the best, "fat" being a figurative expression for the best (Numb. xviii. 12). **Rams of the breed of Bashan;** literally, *rams, sons of Bashan;* i.e. reared in Bashan, a district famous for its cattle. **With the fat of kidneys of wheat;** *with the kidney-fat of wheat;* i.e. the richest fat, the best and most nutritious wheat. **And thou didst drink the pure blood of the grape.** The blood of the grape is the expressed juice of the grape, which, being red, is compared to blood. The rendering "pure" here is not inapt. The original word (חֶמֶר, from חָמַר, to boil up, to foam, to rise in bubbles) describes this juice as it appears when pressed into a vessel, when the surface of the liquid is covered with froth or foam. There is no ground for the explanation "fiery wine" (Keil); wine in such a state was never among the Hebrews counted a blessing. That they had and used fermented wine is certain; but what they specially esteemed as a luxury was the pure unadulterated juice of the grape freshly pressed out and drunk with the foam on it.

Vers. 15—18.—Israel's ungrateful return for the Lord's benefits.

Ver. 15.—**Jeshurun.** This name, formed from יָשָׁר, righteous, designates Israel as chosen to be a righteous nation; and in the use of it here lies the keenest reproach of apostate Israel, as fallen into a state the opposite of that to which it was destined. "By using the name *righteous* in place of *Israel,* Moses ironically censures those who had swerved from rectitude; by recalling to memory with what dignity they had been endowed, he the more sharply rebukes the perfidy which was their crime" (Calvin). This name appears also in ch. xxxiii. 5, 26, and in Isa. xliv. 2; but in these places without any implied censure. By some the word is regarded as a diminutive from שׁוּר, the same as יָשָׁר, in the sense of *rectulus, justulus,* "the good little people" (Gesenius); others as a diminutive from יִשְׂרָאֵל, Israel, as a sort of term of endearment (Grotius). But the latter of these derivations is impossible; and as to the former, there lacks evidence of the termination *un* having a diminutive significance in Hebrew. Besides, neither here nor in ch. xxxiii. 5 would a term of endearment be suitable. **Waxed fat, and kicked** (cf. ch. vi. 11; viii. 10; xxxi. 20). The allusion is to an ox that had grown fat through good feeding, and had become unmanageable in consequence (cf. 1 Sam. ii. 26; Hos. x. 4). **Lightly esteemed.** The Hebrew is strongly expressive here: *Thou hast treated as a fool* (נִבֵּל, from נָבָל, to be foolish (cf. Micah vii. 6).

Ver. 16.—**They provoked him to jealousy.**

God had bound Israel to himself as by the marriage bond, and they by their unfaithfulness had incited him to jealousy (cf. ch. xxxi. 16; Exod. xxxiv. 15; Isa. liv. 5; Hos. i., etc.). **Strange** gods (cf. Jer. ii. 25; iii. 13).

Ver. 17.—**Devils**; *shedim*, a word which occurs only here and Ps. cvi. 37. It stands connected with the verb שׁוּר, to rule, and means primarily "lords." The LXX. render by δαιμόνια, demons. In Assyrian it is said to be a name for demigods. **Not to God**; rather, *to a not-God*, a composite term in apposition to *shedim*; the meaning is rightly given in the margin of the Authorized Version, "which were not God." **To new** gods that came **newly up.** The word rendered by "newly" (קָרוֹב) properly means "near;" it is an adjective both of place and of time; here it is the latter, equal to of a near time, recently—gods recently invented or discovered.

Ver. 18.—Moses here returns to the thought of ver. 15, for the purpose of expressing it with greater force, and also of leading on to the description he is about to give of the Lord's acts towards the nation who had so revolted from him. **Thou art unmindful**; LXX., ἐγκατέλιπες: Vulgate, *dereliquisti*. The Hebrew word שִׁיָה occurs only here, and the meaning is doubtful. From the rendering of the versions, it would seem to be allied to the Arabic ساها, *saha, oblitus est*. **That formed thee**; literally, *that brought thee forth* or *caused thee to be born*; "qui te eduxit ex utero materno" (Jarchi). Cf. for the use of the verb, Ps. xxix. 9). In the Samaritan Codex, מהללך, "who hath glorified or praised thee," is the reading, instead of מחללך; and this the Syriac also expresses. The other versons, however, support the Masoretic reading.

Vers. 19—33.—Because of their rebellion. God would cast them off and visit them with terrible calamities.

Ver. 19.—When the Lord saw how they had departed from him to serve idols, he **abhorred** (rather, *spurned* or *rejected*) them in consequence of the provocation which their unworthy conduct had given him.

Ver. 20.—God himself comes forth to announce his resolution to withdraw his favour from them, and to inflict chastisement upon them; he would withdraw his protecting care of them, and see how they would fare without that; and he would also send on them the tokens of his displeasure. **A very froward generation**, etc.; literally, *a generation of perversities*, an utterly perverse and faithless race.

Ver. 21.—(Cf. ch. v. 16.) Because they had moved God to jealousy and provoked him to anger by their vanities, their nothingnesses, mere vapours and empty exhalations (הֲבָלִים; cf. Jer. x. 6; John ii. 8; 1 Cor. viii. 4); as they had forsaken him for a no-God, he would send retribution on them by adopting as his no-people, and giving to a foolish nation, *i.e.* a nation not before possessed of that true wisdom the beginning of which is the fear of the Lord, the privileges and blessings which Israel had forfeited by their apostacy. By "a no-people" is not to be understood a savage tribe not yet formed into a community, but a people without God, and not recognized by him as in covenant union with him (cf. Rom. x. 19; Eph. ii. 12; 1 Pet. ii. 10).

Ver. 22.—(Cf. Jer. xv. 14; xvii. 4; Lam. iv. 11.) **The lowest hell**; *the lowest sheol*, the uttermost depth of the under-world. The Hebrew *sheol* (שְׁאוֹל) answering to the Greek ᾅδης, by which it is usually rendered by the LXX., is a general designation of the unseen state, the place of the dead. By some the word is derived from שָׁאַל, to ask, because *sheol* is ever asking, is insatiable (Prov. xxx. 16); but more probably it is from a root signifying to excavate, to hollow, and, like the German *hölle*, means primarily a hollow place or cavern. The Divine wrath kindles a consuming fire, that burns down to the lowest depths—to the deepest part of *sheol*—consumes the earth's produce, and sets on fire the foundations of the mountains. This does not refer to any particular judgment that was to befall the national Israel, but is a general description of the effects of the Divine wrath when that is poured forth in judgments on men.

Ver. 23.—**I will spend mine arrows upon them**; I will inflict on them so many calamities that none shall remain. The evils sent on men by God are represented as arrows shot on them from above. (Cf. ver. 42; Job vi. 4; Ps. vii. 13; xxxviii. 2; xlv. 5; lviii. 7; Zech. ix. 14; Homer, 'Iliad,' i. 45, etc.)

Vers. 24, 25.—The evils threatened are famine, pestilence, plague, wild beasts, poisonous reptiles, and war. They shall be burnt with hunger, etc.; render : Sucked out by hunger, consumed with pestilential heat, and bitter plague; I will send against them the tooth of beasts and the poison of things that crawl in the dust. When hunger, pestilence, and contagious disease had wasted and exhausted them, then God would send on them wild beasts and poisonous reptiles. *Shall be burnt.* The Hebrew word occurs only here; it is a verbal adjective, meaning, literally, *sucked out, i.e.* utterly exhausted; LXX., τηκομένοι λιμῷ. *Tooth of beasts and poison of serpents;* poetical for ravenous and poisonous animals (cf. Lev.

xxvi. 22). **Shall destroy**; literally, *shall make childless, shall bereave*, viz. the land which is thought of as a mother whose children were destroyed. The verb is here *sensu prægnanti*, shall bereave by destroying, etc. (cf. 1 Sam. xv. 23; Lam. i. 20; Jer. xviii. 21).

Vers. 26, 27.—Israel's desert was to be utterly destroyed, but God refrained from this for his own Name's sake. **I said, I would scatter them into corners**; rather, *I should say, I will blow them away*, i.e. disperse them as by a mighty wind. The verb here is the Hiph. of פָּאָה, to breathe, to blow, and is found only here. The rabbins make it a denominative from פֵּאָה, a corner, and this the Authorized Version follows; others trace it to an Arabic root, אאפ, *amputavit, excidit*, and render, "will cut them off." The idea intended to be conveyed is obviously that of entire destruction, and this is not satisfied by the representation of their being scared or driven into corners. **Were it not that I feared the wrath of the enemy**. Various renderings and interpretations of this passage have been given. 1. *Were it not that I feared the provocation of the enemy*, i.e. that I should be provoked to wrath by the enemy ascribing the destruction of Israel to their own prowess. 2. *Were it not that I feared a wrath upon the enemy*, with much the same meaning. 3. *Were it not that I feared the fury of the enemy*, i.e. against Israel—feared lest the enemy should be encouraged to rise up against Israel and ascribe their destruction to their own valour. Of these that most generally approved is the first. (On this reason for sparing Israel, see ch. ix. 28; Exod. xxxii. 12; Numb. xiv. 13, etc.; Isa. x. 5, etc.; Ezek. xx. 13, 14.) **Should behave themselves strangely**; rather, *should mistake* or *falsely pretend*. The verb is the Piel of נכר, to look upon, to mark, and conveys the idea of looking on askance or prejudicially, hence being ignorant of, mistaking, feigning, or falsely pretending. **Our hand is high**; rather, *was high*, i.e. was mighty in power.

Vers. 28—33.—The cause of Israel's rejection was that they were a people utterly destitute of counsel and without understanding. Had they been wise, they would have looked to the end, and acted in a way conducive to their own welfare, instead of rushing upon ruin.

Ver. 29.—**Oh that they were wise**, that they understood this; rather, *If they were wise they would understand this*. They would consider their latter end! *i.e.* the end to which they were going, the inevitable issue of the course they were taking.

Ver. 30.—If Israel were wise, they could easily overcome all their foes through the help of the Almighty (Lev. xxvi. 8); but having forsaken him, they were left by

him, and so came under the power of the enemy.

Ver. 31.—The heathen had also a rock in which they trusted—their idol-gods; but even they knew and felt that their rock was not as the Rock of Israel, for, having often experienced the almighty power of God, they could not but acknowledge that he was mightier far than the gods whom they worshipped (cf. Exod. xiv. 25; Numb. xxxiii., xxxiv.; Josh. ii. 9; 1 Sam. v. 7). Moses is here himself again the speaker.

Ver. 32.—If the Rock of Israel was so much mightier than the rock of their enemies, how came it that Israel was beaten and put to flight by their enemies? The reason is here given: It was because Israel had become wholly corrupt and vitiated that they were forsaken of the Lord and left to the power of their enemies. **Their vine**; *i.e.* Israel itself (cf. Ps. lxxx. 9, etc.; Isa. v. 2; Jer. ii. 21; Hos. x. 1). **The vine of Sodom**. It has been supposed that there is reference here to a particular plant, and different plants have been suggested as deserving to be so named. But it is more probable that Sodom and Gomorrah are here advanced as types of what is depraved, and to the moral taste nauseous (cf. Isa. i. 10; Jer. xxiii. 14). **Gall** (cf. ch. xxix. 18).

Ver. 33.—The wine of these grapes is poison and venom. **Dragons**; *tannin* (cf. Exod. vii. 9, 10). **Cruel [deadly] venom of asps**. The *pethen*, one of the most poisonous of snakes, the bite of which was immediately fatal (Kitto, 'Bibl. Cycl.,' iii. 494; Smith's 'Dict.,' i. 21). These figures express the thought that Israel had utterly corrupted their way and become abominable; probably also it is intimated that, as they had imitated the impiety of the inhabitants of Sodom and Gomorrah, they deserved to perish as they did (J. H. Michaelis).

Vers. 34—43.—Notwithstanding the iniquity of Israel and the judgments that should come upon them, God would have compassion upon them for his Name's sake, and would appear for their vindication and defence. The "this" in ver. 34 is by some understood of the sinful doings of the Israelites which God should not forget or overlook. So the Targum of Onkelos: " Are not all their works manifest before me, kept against the day of judgment in my treasures?" So also Calvin, "Quanquam de pœnis hunc versum quidam exponunt, acsi Deus assereret diversas earum species apud se paratas esse, quas depromat quoties libuerit: rectius tamen est de sceleribus intelligere." But there is a more comprehensive reference here. Not only the deeds of the transgressors, but the judgments that should come on Israel, and also God's interposition on their behalf, *were laid up in store with him, and sealed up among his treasures.* All that had been done had been noted, and all that should happen was decreed, and should certainly come to pass. The "this" has thus both a retrospective and a prospective reference; it includes both the sin of the nation and God's dealing with them afterwards, as well as his judgments on their enemies.

Ver. 34.—**My treasures.** God's treasures contain not only a store of blessing, but also instruments of punishment, which as he sees meet, he sends forth on men (cf. ch. xxviii. 12; Job xxxviii. 22, 23; Ps. cxxxv. 7).

Ver. 35.—Render: **Vengeance is mine, and retribution for the time when their feet shall totter; for the day of their calamity is at hand, and that which is prepared for them maketh haste.** The tottering of the feet represents the incipient fall. God would manifest himself as the Avenger when their calamity began to come upon them.

Ver. 36.—**The Lord shall judge his people** (cf. Ps. cxxxv. 14; 1 Pet. iv. 17). **And repent himself for his servants**; rather, *and have compassion upon his servants.* **And there is none shut up, or left.** The words rendered "shut up or left" are a proverbial expression for "every one, men of all sorts" (cf. 1 Kings xiv. 10; xxi. 21; 2 Kings ix. 8; xiv. 26); but how the words are to be rendered or explained is uncertain. Rosenmüller renders as in the Authorized Version; Gesenius has, "the shut up and the let go free, the bond and the free;" so also Fürst and De Wette; De Dieu, "married and single, *conjugatus et cœlebs*," referring to the Arabic usage in support of his conclusion ('Animad. in Vet. Test.,' p. 114), and this Keil approves. Ewald has "kept in (by legal impurity) or at large." The explanation of Gesenius and Fürst seems best.

Ver. 37.—The Lord would show his people the utter worthlessness of idols, and bring them to acknowledge him as the only true God. **Their gods**; the idols to which Israel had turned, the strange gods which they had foolishly and sinfully preferred to Jehovah.

Ver. 39.—**See now that I am, even I am he.** The Hebrew is more expressive, *See now that I, I am;* LXX., ἴδετε, ἴδετε ὅτι ἐγώ εἰμι (cf. Isa. xli. 4; xlviii. 12; John viii. 24; xviii. 5). Their own experience of the utter impotency of these idol-gods to help them or to protect themselves from the stroke of the Almighty was enough to convince them that they were no gods, and that he alone was to be feared and worshipped.

Vers. 40, 41.—These verses should be read continuously: **For I lift up my hand to heaven, and say, As I live for ever, if I whet my glittering sword, and if my hand take hold on judgment; I will render vengeance to** mine enemies, etc. Lifting up the hand to heaven was a gesture intended to express that the person taking an oath appealed to God as a witness of his oath, and who would perish for falsehood (cf. Gen. xiv. 22); and "as the Lord liveth" was a common formula in taking an oath (cf. Numb. xiv. 21; 1 Sam. xiv. 39, 45; Jer. v. 2). As God could swear by none greater, he sware by himself (cf. Exod. vi. 8; Numb. xiv. 30; Isa. xlv. 23; Jer. xxii. 5; Heb. vi. 17), that if he did come forth to avenge himself of his enemies, he would not spare, but would do thoroughly what he had come forth to do. —*Glittering sword;* literally, lightning of sword (cf. Ez. xxi. 10 [15]).

Ver. 42.—**My sword shall devour flesh;** literally, *shall eat flesh;* "the edge of the sword is called its mouth, because, like a mouth, it is said to eat and devour" (Gesenius). **From the beginning of revenges upon the enemy.** Different renderings of this have been given: LXX., ἀπὸ κεφαλῆς ἀρχόντων ἐχθρῶν, "from the head of the hostile princes;" "from the head of the chiefs of the enemy" (Gesenius, Fürst, Rosenmüller); "from the hairy head of the foe" (Keil, Herxheimer, Knobel). פְּרָעוֹת, the plural of פֶּרַע, hair, locks, signifies primarily hairs, and a head of hairs, and may be taken as equivalent to "a hairy head;" but the word is also used in the sense of "princes" or "chiefs" (probably because such were distinguished by copious flowing locks; cf. Judg. v. 2); hence the rendering, "head of the chiefs." The former is to be preferred here, for why chiefs or princes should be referred to in this connection does not appear (cf. Ps. lxviii. 22). The rendering of the Authorized Version is wholly unauthorized. This verse presents an instance of alternate parallelism; each half falls into two members, and of the four members thus constituted, the third corresponds to the first, and the fourth to the second; thus—

a "I will make my arrows drunk with blood,
  b And my sword shall devour flesh;
a′ With the blood of the slain and the captives,
  b′ From the hairy head of the foe."

Ver. 43.—"As this song commenced with an appeal to heaven and earth to give glory to the Lord (vers. 1—3), so it very suitably closes with an appeal to the heathen to rejoice with his people on account of the acts of the Lord" (Keil). **Rejoice, O ye nations, with his people.** The Authorized Version here follows the LXX., εὐφράνθητε ἔθνη μετὰ τοῦ λαοῦ αὐτοῦ, and so St. Paul cites the passage in Rom. xv. 10. The Jewish interpreters generally render, *Praise his people, O nations;* and this several Christian interpreters adopt. But as Rosenmüller remarks, it is the Divine righteousness manifested in the vindication of his people from their enemies that is to be celebrated, and not the people themselves, as what follows shows. Here as elsewhere the *nations* and the *people* are in contrast.

Vers. 44—47.—Moses, having composed this song, came, accompanied by Joshua, and they together spoke it in the hearing of the people; after which Moses took occasion to urge upon them anew the importance of keeping the commandments of God.

Ver. 44.—**Hoshea the son of Nun.** Moses invariably writes this name *Jehoshuah* (Jehovah is help; cf. Numb. xiii. ; ch. xxxi. 3, 7, 14, 20, etc.). The use of Hoshea here is due to the fact that this account is part of the supplement added by another writer to the writing of Moses.

Ver. 46.—(Cf. ch. vi. 7; xi. 19.)

Ver. 47.—**It is not a vain thing for you; because it is your life;** these are not mere empty words; they are of vital import (cf. ch. xxx. 20).

Vers. 48—52.—On the day on which Moses rehearsed this song in the hearing of the people, his death was announced to him by God, and the command was again given to him to ascend Mount Nebo, thence to survey the promised land, and there to be gathered to his people. The same in substance, the command as given here differs slightly in form and in some minor particulars from that as recorded by Moses himself (Numb. xxvii. 12—14).

Ver. 49.—**Abarim** (cf. Numb. xxi. 10, 20). **Nebo** (cf. Numb. xxxii. 3, 38). An idol Nebo was worshipped by the Moabites (Isa. xlvi. 1).

Ver. 50.—**And be thou gathered unto thy people.** "To Abraham, Isaac, and Jacob. This signifies," saith R. Isaac, "that he should be associated and joined to the souls of the just who are called *his people.* For the people of Moses were not buried in Mount Abarim, and therefore he doth not speak of gathering his body to their bodies, but of his soul to their souls ('Chissute Emuna,' i. 11)" (Patrick).

Ver. 51.—(Cf. Numb. xx. 13, 24.) **Because ye sanctified me not** (cf. Numb. xxvii. 14; 1 Pet. iii. 15).

Ver. 52.—**Yet thou shalt see the land** (cf. Heb. xi. 13).

HOMILETICS.

Vers. 1—4.—*God the believer's Rock.* "Forms change: principles never." So have we had often to remark in discovering in and developing from this book the everlasting principles which are therein set in archaic forms. The song of Moses here recorded will yield us many illustrations of this kind of teaching. Its first four verses suggest three lines of thought.

I. THERE IS HERE A REVEALED DOCTRINE CONCERNING GOD. In the last song which the old man utters ere he climbs the mount of Nebo to die, he declares, "I will publish the Name of the Lord." 1. This Name is "*Jehovah.*" The word involves self-existence, self-sufficiency, immutability, pure being, personality. "I am that I am" expresses all this. It would be a burning shame for any one to apply the term "anthropomorphic" to such a revelation as this. Such a conception may be revealed *to* man, but assuredly it borrows nought *from* him. 2. To this Being, greatness is ascribed; *i.e.* royal magnificence and splendour. The sovereignty of heaven and earth is there! 3. All moral perfections are in the "Name" of God (cf. Exod. xxxiv. 6, 7). 4. His work is perfect. The revealed attributes of God warrant us in drawing this conclusion. The intention of Moses here is to set the perfection of God's work over against the sin of man's. 5. His ways are judgment; *i.e.* they are according to justice. 6. He is the *Rock.* This epithet is a "piece of Mosaic." It was indeed used by others long after. But the use of it began with Moses. On the *rocks* of Sinai was the Law proclaimed. In the *rock-cleft* was Moses hidden. From the smitten *rock* the waters gushed forth. How natural for Moses to apply this figure to the eternal God! In ver. 31, Moses speaks of God as "our Rock." He was known to Israel as theirs, their own firm, changeless ground of strength, through all the changing years!

II. THIS DOCTRINE OF THE LIVING GOD AS THE ROCK IS FRAUGHT WITH COMFORT AND REFRESHMENT FOR MAN (ver. 2); *i.e.* what the rain is to the herb, what the showers are to the grass, that is this teaching concerning God to the soul of man. 1. Our heart wants God (Ps. lxxxiv. 2). 2. *Such* a God—*this* God is as rain and as dew: refreshing, enlivening, restoring. 3. This doctrine of God is meant to make the heart productive of holiness. God's revelation of himself is meant to draw men to himself; in doing this God saves them!

III. THE DOCTRINE THUS PROPOUNDED DESERVES TO BE UNIVERSALLY HEARD, LISTENED TO, AND BELIEVED. (Ver. 1.) Moses would summon all to hear it. It is: 1. For all classes. 2. For all lands. 3. For all the ages. The day will never come when this doctrine of God will be obsolete—never!

Vers. 5—14.—*Ungrateful men interrogated.* In almost every clause of this paragraph there is some specific allusion, for the elucidation of which the reader will refer to the Exposition. The commentary of Dr. Jameson thereon is very valuable. Our aim is strictly homiletic. The central words around which the preacher's expository thoughts may gather are these—"Do ye thus requite the Lord?" Three main lines of illustration are suggested.

I. HERE IS A REHEARSAL OF THE DIVINE LOVING-KINDNESS AND TENDER MERCIES. 1. There is the mercy of *redemption.* "Is not he thy Father that hath bought thee?" 2. There is the mercy of Divine choice of Israel as a people. "Hath he not made thee, and established thee?" (see also vers. 7, 8). 3. There is Divine leadership. "He led him about," etc. 4. There is Divine guardianship. "He kept him as the apple of his eye." 5. There is Divine help and training of the most tender kind. A wonderful description is given thereof in ver. 11. 6. There is abundant Divine provision for the wants of the ransomed ones (vers. 13, 14). Each one of these six points may be enlarged upon, as applicable to present gospel blessings and providential mercies.

II. HERE IS A STRANGE RESPONSE TO SUCH ABOUNDINGS OF MERCY. The burden of Moses here is not unlike that of a far later prophet, even Isaiah (see Isa. i. 2—4). The moan of many of God's prophets has been the same ever since; it is so now. The contrast between God's bounty and man's perversity causes a grief almost too heavy to be borne. Here are at least five complaints. 1. They are corrupt. 2. They are perverse, or false. 3. They are crooked, twisted. 4. They are foolish, not acting as reasonable men. 5. Instead of being like his children, they are a spot upon them—a stain (see Hebrew). The question may fairly be asked, Who are they of whom similar complaints may be made now? We reply: 1. Those who profess to be the people of God, and who show no signs whatever that their profession is real. 2. Those of God's children who are but half-hearted in their love and zeal. 3. Those who are ready with lip-service, but are grievously defective in Christian morality. 4. Those who have neither yielded themselves to God nor yet made any profession thereof. Of all such, similar complaints may be made to those here laid against Israel of old.

III. HERE IS A REASONABLE QUESTION. It is, indeed, a reproachful one. And if ever the servants of God now take it up and apply it to the heart and conscience of their hearers, it should be done with the utmost tenderness, even unto tears; remembering, on the one hand, how infinitely greater the mercies of God are now, compared with aught that Moses knew; and also considering themselves, how often they have been as ungrateful Israel of old, and that, if it had not been for almighty grace, would have been ungrateful still. The solemn and sorrowful interrogative—"Do ye thus requite the Lord?"—may be pressed home in a series of cumulative inquiries. It may be asked: 1. Is this the *natural* return for mercies so great? 2. Do not such love and care *demand* a holy and grateful life? 3. Can any reason whatever *justify* so poor a response as God has yet received? 4. Have men no *remorse* in the review of the contrast between God's mercies and their sin? 5. Should not remorse lead on to *repentance?* 6. And shall not this penitent life begin *now?* It is quite certain that, though God is long-suffering, "not willing that any should perish, but that all should come to repentance," he will not always allow his mercies to be thus trifled with (see Amos. iv.). But why, why should men compel us to present thus "the terrors of the Lord"? He would rather win by love. Judgment is "his strange work."

Vers. 15—18.—*God provoked to jealousy by an unfaithful people.* (On the whole subject of "anthropomorphism," which is alleged against the Old Testament representations of the Divine Being, see the Homily on vers. 1—4 of this chapter, and also Homily on ch. iv. 21—24). This paragraph is a continuation of the same theme as that touched on in preceding verses. It not only sets forth the waywardness of the people retrospectively, but also prospectively. In fact, it is more of a prophetic forecast than otherwise. Moses sees the people in the enjoyment of all the blessings of

God's providence; he looks onward, and, with the seer's eye, he beholds them in the promised land, their wanderings over, and their marches hither and thither exchanged for a settled life in a land of plenty and of delight. There they are prospering abundantly; and if they only used their prosperity aright they would be doubly blessed, even with that blessing which "maketh rich, and he addeth no sorrow therewith." But, alas! how different is the picture here drawn! And how precisely did the after-reality answer thereto! There is in these verses a logical order of thought, in the sketch given, first, of Israel's downward course; and then, of the effect of that on the relations between them and their God.

I. HERE IS A GRIEVOUS PICTURE OF SPIRITUAL DEGENERATION IN THE MIDST OF WORLDLY PROSPERITY. There are four steps in the descent. 1. Prosperity generates wilfulness, and a resistance to the Divine claims. If men can have their own way entirely, for a while, and secure precisely their own ends, such success, if not sanctified, will but create a self-will and self-assertion stronger than ever. "Jeshurun waxed fat, and kicked." The restraints of duty, conscience, God, will be irksome, and will provoke to resistance. Men will "kick against the pricks." 2. Another stage will surely follow on. The irritation which was at first felt will subside, and insensibility will steal over the soul. "Thou art waxen fat, thou art grown thick." Stubborn obstinacy without the former stings of conscience. "Past feeling." The terrible symptom of a moral and spiritual paralysis! 3. To this there will follow a third stage. "He forsook God . . . and lightly esteemed the Rock of his salvation." Here there sets in a thinking lightly of God altogether, and a forsaking of him. How true is the picture here given to the actual progress of sin in the soul everywhere! 4. To this succeeds not only neglect of God, but *the substitution of other gods* (vers. 16, 17)! This actually came about (see Jer. ii., specially ver. 13). The heart of man must have a supreme object of love; and if God be not enthroned in the heart, some rival will be seated there.

Note—How very little all possible worldly good can do for a man unless there is a process of spiritual renewal and culture going on, which will enable him to sanctify all to the highest purposes! Yea, more. If worldly prosperity is not sanctified to God and by him, it will be as a dead weight upon the spirit. It will engender, first resistance, then deadness, then estrangement, then idolatry! This is the sure and certain effect of an accumulation of worldly good, when its possessor is not led by Divine grace to use it wisely and piously. It is an evil much to be lamented that so many glory in the accumulation of things, while neglecting the culture and education of their souls. Why, even in common life, there are no more awkward, ungainly, and impracticable beings than those who have grown rich while neglecting to educate themselves. They have acquired a prodigious strength of self-will, without the knowledge of self-government. And of all men in the world, they are of the least use to their generation.

II. HERE IS A STRANGE EFFECT OF SUCH DEGENERACY ON THE DIVINE BEING. "They provoked him to jealousy" (see remark in "anthropomorphism," *ut supra*, and also Homily on ch. iv. 24). Of all the attributes or epithets applied to God, there is no one which endears him to us more than this: "jealousy"! What does it mean? 1. That God has a heart of love. 2. That his love yearns to be reciprocated. 3. That the reciprocation of love for which he yearns is the whole undivided love of our hearts. 4. That if such devoted love is not accorded to him, he feels wronged. 5. That if supreme love is bestowed on any other than God, his holy love is outraged; his pure indignation is "jealousy." And consider how great the wrong is which is thus committed against a gracious God. What would an earthly father think if his children, who lived on his bounty, thought only of eating and drinking, and cared not for *him?* What if the children thought more of their toys than of their father? *Ought* he not to be jealous? Would he—could he be a good father, and not be jealous? Surely not. It is easy to apply this in such a case. Christ teaches us to learn of the heavenly Father by means of earthly ones. Consider, moreover, (1) the wrong done to God, (2) the misplacement of *things*, (3) the injustice and injury done to ourselves, and (4) the injurious effect of wealth, brought about by such misuse of God's benefits.

III. TWO INQUIRIES CANNOT BUT SUGGEST THEMSELVES. 1. *How may such evil be guarded against?* This question supposes that the evil has not yet been fallen into.

" Prevention is better than cure." (1) Let us regard ourselves as of infinitely more moment than our possessions. What we *are* is beyond measure of more concern than what we *have*. Our culture for eternity is of the first importance. (2) Let us from the outset of life regard God as the Author of all good, and as therefore having the first claim on our regard. (3) Let us cultivate the devotional habit of receiving all our temporal comforts as from God. If we have used means to secure them, he it is who has given us the means to use ; who has given us the power to use them, and who has made those means a success. (4) Let us seek wisdom from above to hallow all our good for God, and to " honour the Lord with our substance, and with the firstfruits of all our increase " (see Homily on ch. xiv. 22). (5) Conscious of the deceitfulness of the human heart, let us entreat our God to fill us with the power of the Spirit, as well as to give us providential mercies. Then, the first will ensure the sanctification of the second. The larger our possessions, the more we need of the Spirit of God, to ensure their becoming a blessing, and to prevent their becoming a snare. 2. *If we have fallen into such evil, how may we be recovered therefrom ?* (1) Let the very suggestion that a spiritual paralysis may have stolen over the soul, startle us into the inquiry, Is this the case with us ? (2) Let us inquire solemnly, " What shall it profit a man, if he shall gain the whole world, and forfeit his life ? " (3) Let us repent before God of the wrong we have done to him in seeking from creature comforts the joy which he alone can give. (4) Taught by long and sad experience how a perverted nature may pervert all things, let us implore his renewing and sanctifying grace to enlighten our understandings, to regulate our affections, to mould our will, to empower and transform our life. If God fills us by his grace, then will earthly good be sanctified. Our God will be our richest joy of all, and every worldly comfort will yield us double joy, when hallowed by him and for him.

Vers. 19—25.—*An unfaithful people provoked to jealousy by God.* This paragraph is the antithesis of the preceding one. In form the expressions are archaic. The principles underlying these ancient forms of expression are for all the ages. In fact, there are few of the Old Testament passages which are more pointedly referred to in the New Testament ; and none, the principles of which are more frequently reproduced. The various clauses are *seriatim* explained in the Exposition. We 'propose but to develop the main thought, which is indicated in the heading of this Homily. Its contents are fourfold. 1. God was provoked to jealousy by his people choosing a *no-God* instead of him. 2. The time would come when he would, as a punishment to Israel, choose a *no-people* instead of them. 3. Those who had been exalted in privilege should be deprived of their privileges, and should pass through the bitterest sorrows. 4. At the thought of their privileges passing away from them, and passing on to others, Israel should be provoked to jealousy.

Now, it would be a most instructive and impressive exercise to compare what is here said by God in his Word with that which actually came to pass. What does history say ? Does it not confirm Moses at every point ? The facts of history are these—

1. The people of Israel did fall away from the God of their fathers, and bring upon themselves the remonstrance of prophet after prophet, and were made in the course of God's providence to suffer sorrow upon sorrow.

2. The time did come when the kingdom of God passed away from them, and when they were no longer, as they once had been, the favoured people.

3. That kingdom of God passed over to the Gentiles.

4. At its so passing over, the Jews were exceedingly jealous and angry.

5. So much so was this the case, that Paul makes use of the fact in arguments to quicken both the Jew and the Gentile, as the case may be.

The following passages of Scripture should be carefully compared together, bearing as they do alike on the history, the principles involved therein, and their everlasting application :—Rom. x. 19 ; Matt. viii. 11, 12 ; xxi. 31, 43 ; Acts xiii. 46 ; Rom. ix. 30—32 ; xi. 11 ; Hos. i. 10 (latter part) ; Rom. ix. 25, 26 ; 1 Pet. ii. 10 ; Eph. ii. 11—13 ; Rom. xi. 13—25. From all which several all-important truths of permanent significance may be clearly deduced and powerfully applied.

I. THESE ARE TIMES OF GREAT RELIGIOUS PRIVILEGE WITH US. True, we are not *exclusively* a favoured race, in the same sense as was Israel of old. But our advantages are not less because others share them with us. We have *all* that Israel ever had, and vastly more. "The kingdom of God is come unto us." The "word of faith" is nigh us, in our mouth and in our heart. We are bidden to "Behold the Lamb of God, which taketh away the sin of the world," etc.

II. IF THESE PRIVILEGES REMAIN UNIMPROVED, OUR NEGLECT THEREOF WILL BE A GRIEVOUS SIN IN THE EYE OF GOD. We have but to read the Epistle to the Hebrews in order to find such an argument as this repeatedly presented, though in varying forms: If the Law of Moses was trifled with by any one, they did not escape punishment. But Jesus Christ is greater than Moses. By as much as he is greater than Moses, by so much are the sin and danger of neglecting him greater than those of neglecting the lawgiver of old.

III. BOTH CHURCHES AND NATIONS HAVE A DAY OF PROBATION GRANTED THEM, DURING WHICH THEIR PRIVILEGES ARE CONTINUED. (See Isa. xlix. 8; 2 Cor. vi. 2; Luke xiii. 6—9; Rev. ii. 5, 21; Luke xix. 42—44.) An unending probation is granted to no one.

IV. IF THE PERIOD OF PROBATION PASSES BY UNIMPROVED, OUR PRIVILEGES WILL BE TAKEN AWAY FROM US.

V. OTHER LANDS AND OTHER PEOPLES ARE READY, YEA, EAGER TO RECEIVE THE LIGHT WHICH SOME APPRECIATE SO LITTLE.

VI. MANY, MANY WILL COME FROM LESS FAVOURED LANDS AND FROM LESS CULTURED RACES, AND WILL STEP INTO THE KINGDOM OF HEAVEN AND BE SAVED; while many of the children of the kingdom will be cast out into outer darkness. Hear what our Lord says to the Pharisees: "The publicans and harlots will go into the kingdom of God before you."

Vers. 26—28.—*The Divine mind influenced by reasons.* Moses, in uttering this song, is "borne along" (2 Pet. i. 21) by a power working through him and yet not of him, to make a most remarkable assertion in the Name of Jehovah; viz. that Israel's Deliverer was moved *by fear of the wrath of the enemy* not to destroy them altogether! How is this to be understood? Some might perhaps pass it over as a piece of obsolete anthropomorphism. So will not we. To us, many a sentence in the grand old volume, which at first sight seemed uncouth and almost repellent in its archaism, has on further study yielded up treasures of delight with which we would not willingly part. Perhaps it may be so here.

Note—The verb "I said," in ver. 26, is rendered by Keil, "I should say." This shows the sense more clearly, "*I should say, I will blow them away, I will blot out the remembrance of them among men; if I did not fear wrath upon the enemy* [i.e. "displeasure on the part of God at the arrogant boasting of the enemy, which was opposed to the glory of God" (Vitringa, quoted by Keil, *in loc.*)] *that their enemies might mistake it, that they might say, Our hand was high, and Jehovah has not done all this. For,*" etc. If we analyze these words, we shall find that they are separable into six main thoughts, expressed or implied. 1. That Israel was a people void of understanding. 2. That they consequently tried the patience of God, as falling very far below his ideal and their duty and honour. 3. That it would have been no great loss to the world if they should therefore be blotted out of being, and should actually drop out of the remembrance of the nations. 4. That if this extreme punishment should be meted out, then the adversary would glory over them and against them, and say that Israel's God either could not or would not guard the people whom he chose: that their enemies were mightier than their Redeemer. 5. That such a result would veil the glory of Jehovah, and make men uncertain whether God had a special people in the world or no. 6. That consequently, *for his own sake,* God would punish, but in measure; he would scourge, but not destroy. Hence there stands forth this great and glorious truth, *God will so govern and discipline his people as to reveal his own glory in them and by them.* This is the thought we now propose to develop in a series of considerations arranged according to the structure of the text.

I. GOD HAS AN ISRAEL NOW. (Eph. ii.; Heb. xii. 18—28.) The redemption from Egypt, the march through the wilderness, the formation of a commonwealth, the inheritance of Canaan, are all at once symbolic and typical of a greater deliverance, a nobler commonwealth, a spiritual pilgrimage, a heavenly home.

II. During the march of the Church of God through the wilderness of this world, GOD'S PEOPLE OFTEN FALL VERY FAR BELOW THE IDEAL SET BEFORE THEM. They try the patience of God, and excite the wonder, the laughter, and the ridicule of man. Think of what has been done in the name of religion! Think of the sharp controversies, the angry words, and the prolonged strife of Christendom! Think of the number of inconsistent professors, who cause our enemies to laugh among themselves! etc.

III. SO GRIEVOUS HAVE BEEN THE STAINS AND BLOTS THUS BROUGHT ON THE CHRISTIAN NAME, THAT MEN HAVE BEEN TEMPTED EVEN TO THINK THAT GOD'S CHURCH WAS AN INCUBUS IN THE WORLD; yea, that it might, with advantage to mankind, have ceased to exist. For certain it is that the great God could, even if his Church should become extinct, create a purer and nobler people in their stead, who would honour him and bless the world!

IV. MANY OF THE ADVERSARIES ARE WISHING FOR AND SEEKING TO BRING ABOUT THE CHURCH'S EXTINCTION. They would destroy the fellowship by sapping the life thereof. They would sap the life by undermining the faith. And never more eagerly than now—they are at work to educate men into the belief that God never had a people, that the people never had a God, and that all the faith they have been cherishing for ages has been based on a delusion and a lie!

V. IF SUCH A RESULT WERE TO ACCRUE, HOW WOULD THE ENEMY GLORY! They would say, "Our hand is high, and the Lord hath not done all this." *If* only the Church should be driven from her moorings, *if* her anchor of hope should become unusable, and she should be difted out to a wild, pathless, shoreless sea,—what glorying there would be in the enemy's camp! "Ha, ha! so we would have it!" "How would the powers of darkness boast if but one praying soul were lost!"

VI. SUCH A POSSIBILITY IS GUARDED AGAINST IN THE DIVINE COUNSELS. It is just such a provision that is indicated in the text. God will not let the "*adversaries behave themselves strangely*" in this way. *They will never have the chance!* The Church is built on a rock, from which it can never be dislodged. The day will never come when it will cease to exist. And ever will God remember the word on which he has caused us to hope!

VII. GOD GUARDS AGAINST ANY SUCH POSSIBILITY, BY DOING WHAT HE DOES FOR HIS OWN SAKE. The revelation of his own honour and glory in the eyes of men is too precious in his eye for him to let things so move on that all trace thereof is lost *to his own people* (cf. Isa. xliii. 45; Ezek. xxxvi. 21, 22, 32; Ps. cvi. 7, 8; Ezek. xx. 9, 14, 22). See too what argument Daniel uses in prayer (Dan. ix. 19). David also (Ps. xxv. 11).

For the sake of his own honour, God will purify his Church from all corruption by the spirit of judgment, and by the spirit of burning; and while thus jealous for his people's purity, he will as jealously watch over them, so that "upon all the glory there shall be a defence" (Isa. iv. 2—6; cf. 1 Cor. xi. 32; 1 Pet. iv. 17).

IN CONCLUSION. 1. Let the righteous rejoice, yea, let them exceedingly rejoice. God's supreme aim is that his glory shall be revealed. The bringing of it forth to clear light is the aim and tendency of events, without let or pause. 2. Let all men clearly distinguish between the two providential processes which are ever, ever in process of fulfilment. One, the purification of the Church. The other, the condemnation and confusion of the world. 3. Let the wicked tremble. Or if they are too benumbed to tremble, let them at least cease to make merry over the corruptions of the Church. They may laugh now. They will not laugh always. The severing processes of God's judgment are going on now, and they will issue in "everlasting contempt" to the ungodly, and in the redemption of Israel from all his iniquities!

Vers. 29—35.—*The short-sightedness of sinners.* "Oh that they were wise, that they understood this, that they would consider their latter end!" Such is the moan with which this paragraph begins. By "this" is meant the consequence which will certainly follow on their departure from God. By "their latter end" is meant the latter days of their history, when sins which were beforehand in germ should have wrought out to full development. We need not again recount the historical aspects of this serious outlook. We will but note, in a series of consecutive thoughts, the truths which are here indicated, and which are of universal and perpetual application to individuals, families, and nations.

I. It is a mark of a vicious short-sightedness to take no heed to the consequences of a course of conduct. If men take no reckoning of their "latter end," it is the reverse of wise. Our Saviour asks, "What shall it profit a man?" etc. To take heed only to present appearances and to avoid all preparations for the future, is folly in the extreme.

II. Whether we will or no, certain consequences are bound up with conduct by a law which no created power can avert or modify. They may be "sealed up"—hidden from sight at present, but they are "laid up in store" (Rom. ii. 5; 1 Thess. v. 3).

III. The Most High reserves to himself the execution of his own laws. "To me belongeth vengeance." Vengeance cannot safely be entrusted to frail and passionate man. Only in the hands of "the Judge of all the earth" is there an absolute guarantee that in its infliction there will be neither excess nor defect. No weakness will cause delay or halt. No vindictiveness will induce any variation from the right.

IV. However long vengeance may be delayed, it will not be postponed too long. "Their feet shall slide in due time."[1] Time is on God's side. In the moral world there is not a moment's pause. Character is ripening for good or for ill, and great issues are working out at every tick of the dial.

V. In the ripening of character and the advanced issues of conduct there will be awful results on the side of evil. The figurative expressions in each clause are of terrific significance. They indicate: 1. The failure of the refuge to which they had fled. 2. The collapse of their strength in great emergencies. 3. Bitterness of misery. 4. Venomous poison as the fruit of their vine of Sodom. Now is the day for accumulating; hereafter will be the day for the manifestation, of these hidden treasures of ill.

VI. This day of awful recompense will come upon sinners suddenly. "The things that shall come upon them make haste" (cf. Matt. xxiv. 36—44; Mark xiii. 35—37; 2 Pet. iii. 10). It is one remarkable feature of the Mosaic outlook, that the lawgiver scarcely ever refers to another life, but to the working out of God's judgments in this. The future life comes into view in the New Testament. The law of sowing and reaping holds good for both worlds (Gal. vi. 7).

VII. With an outlook so grievous, the thoughtlessness of sinners is an evil greatly to be lamented. "Oh that they were wise!" etc. (cf. Jer. ix. 1; Ps. cxix. 136).

In conclusion. There is at least a threefold application of the text, which should be made use of to warn men against sin. 1. Those who have to direct or influence national affairs should remember that a wrong policy is a foolish one. No nation will continue to thrive that fights against God. 2. Heads of families should remember that, by a course of disloyalty to God, they are sowing the seeds of dishonour, grief, and shame in their families, and are entailing sorrow on the children of their care. 3. Let each individual learn that whatever a man soweth that shall he also reap, both in this world and in that which is to come. "Woe unto him that striveth with his Maker!"

Vers. 36—43.—*Jehovah reigns; be glad!* This paragraph has about it a remarkably martial ring. It is not to be looked at as bald and literal prose. It is part of a song; it is laden with imagery, in which the God of Israel is set forth as a mighty Warrior, whose march none can hinder, whose inflictions none can withstand or evade. The *style* of the song was precisely appropriate to the age in which it was composed, and suited to the people in whose hearing it was addressed. The *truths* clothed in such Oriental garb are for all lands and for all time. For though there is an abundance of figure, yet not all is figurative. There are at least two phrases which are plain in their phraseology, and which furnish us with the key for the right interpretation of the others. One of these is found at the beginning of the passage, the other towards its close. The first is in ver. 36, "The Lord shall judge his people." The other is in ver. 43, "Rejoice,

---

[1] See a sermon of great power on this text in President Edwards's works.

O ye nations—his people." [1]   The former assures us that all the various processes of judgment to which the seer's eye looks forward are in the hands of God.   The second calls upon the nations to rejoice therein.   *Between* these two, the varied details in the paragraph fall naturally into place.   Our Homily will, therefore, be mainly an answer to one inquiry, viz. *What materials for joy are here given us ?*

It is useless to bid any one to be glad unless a reason is given them why they should be so.   A somewhat careful study of the paragraph in hand will show at least eight reasons for holy and grateful joy.

I. It is matter for joy that God reserves in his own hands the judgment of his people (ver. 36).   Where else could it safely be?   Who else has the power, the wisdom, the justice, the kindness, the knowledge required?   If the sceptre of power were in any other hands, the guarantee of righteous administration would cease.

II. We may rejoice that in his judging processes God will convince his people of the folly of relying on any but on himself (vers. 37, 38).   The reason of the peculiar imagery in these verses every student knows.   The underlying thought is clear.   It may be a sharp, but it is a necessary discipline, that every prop should give way which would prevent us from leaning on God alone.

III. We may rejoice in the severity with which a righteous God will deal with sin. Severity against sin is mercy towards the sinner (ver. 42).   In the early conquest of Canaan, severity towards Achan and his accomplices was mercy towards Israel.   In the early Church, judgment on Ananias and Sapphira was mercy to the Church.   In both cases the canker of dishonesty and hypocrisy needed to be cut out by a strong and firm hand.

IV. We may rejoice that the ruling motive and the ultimate intent of God's dealings are love and mercy (ver. 43).   Beyond the blackest clouds Moses sees in the horizon light and glory.   The twenty-eighth and twenty-ninth chapters of this book, with all their threatenings, are followed by the thirtieth, with all its promises.   Wrath in the *process*, mercy as the *product*.

V. Let us rejoice that in this law of recompense there is mercy in the educational process therein ensured (see Ps. lxii. 12).   There is a wide difference between a fatherly correction and the infliction of a legal penalty.   It is the former which God metes out towards his people.   Their relation to him is one of grace, not of bare law.

VI. Let us rejoice that mercy will regulate the mode, the time, and the result of the chastisement.   *The mode :* "Their power is gone," *i.e.* their false props are destroyed. *The time :* "He will repent himself," *i.e.* he will not be wrath for ever; when the infliction has answered its end, he will change his dealings.   Though God never changes a plan, he may plan a change.   *The result :* "He will be merciful unto his land," etc., *i.e.* he will be propitious.   When his people are brought back from their wanderings, he will "cover" all their sin in eternal forgetfulness.

VII. Let us rejoice in the clear and perfect discrimination which will mark all the Divine dealings with his people and with his adversaries; ver. 43, "vengeance—mercy." Both form part of God's governmental methods.   How can it be otherwise in a world of sin?   The perfections of Jehovah guarantee that neither will infringe on the other. Tenderness will never weaken vengeance.   Vengeance will never lessen tenderness. God alone knows the absolutely perfect adjustment.

VIII. Let us rejoice that the eye of the seer beholds brightness in the far distance. The gloom does but intervene; it does not cover the whole canopy of heaven, nor darken all the outlook.   "Light is sown for the righteous."   "Joy cometh in the morning" (ver. 43).

Let all these several particulars be woven together, and they will make one glorious pattern—at the sight of which we may well shout aloud for joy.

Learn—1. In such a review of the methods and outcome of God's providential dealings only those who are at peace with God through our Lord Jesus Christ are in a position to understand them.   Enmity cannot understand love.   And where men are

---

[1] The Hebrew has not the word "with."   It reads, "Rejoice, all ye nations—his people." Is it not possible that here the aged lawgiver's prophetic eye was gifted with supernatural strength, and that he foresaw a time when "all nations should come in, and make one undivided fold"?

"enemies in their mind by wicked works," they are certain to misunderstand God's nature, and to misinterpret his ways. Man's *first* duty is to repent of sin and obey God. Till he does this the mysteries of God will not be unveiled to him. 2. When we understand something of the redemption which is in Christ Jesus, then the true key to the interpretation of providence is in our hands (Rom. viii. 34). Hence we can "rejoice in the Lord" (Ps. xxxiii. 1; Phil. iii. 1; iv. 4; Ps. xcvii. 1; xcvi.; xcviii.). 3. In proportion to the greatness of the love which furnishes the key for unlocking providential mysteries is the greatness of the sin which turns away from and finally rejects God. (See the use of this paragraph in Heb. x. 30, 31.) However deep the gloom which Moses depicts, he sees a rim of golden glory in the horizon, as if another dispensation were to follow. But the writer of the Epistle to the Hebrews sees no after-light for those who turn away from Christ. "For if we sin wilfully after we have received the knowledge of the truth, there remaineth no more sacrifice for sins, but a certain fearful looking for of judgment and fiery indignation, which shall devour the adversaries. . . . It is a fearful thing to fall into the hands of the living God." The contest of the sinner with God must end in the guilty one's ignominious and hopeless defeat; Amos iv. 12, "Because I will do this unto thee, prepare to meet thy God, O Israel."

Vers. 44—47.—*Life at stake!* This paragraph—concerning which Keil is probably right in his surmise, that it proceeds from an editor's hand—sets before us in a quiet and incidental way, one of the most important transitions Israel had yet experienced. We have seen in ch. xxxi. 7, 8, that Moses gave Joshua a charge, and told him that *he* must lead the people into the promised land. After that came the utterance of this song. When it was uttered, *Joshua stood side by side with Moses.* Thus, just for once, the two leaderships overlap. The joint presence of both the old and new leaders this signifying, that, though the earthly administration changed hands, the same message would be passed, and not a word of Jehovah's would be lost. There are six features about this closing public scene of the life of Moses, which open up an invaluable line of thought. 1. Here is an assembly, met to hear Moses' last song. 2. Though it is the last, there is in it nothing new. It is the one message—God's goodness, faithfulness, and love, calling for their reciprocation and obedience. 3. This old message is reimpressed on their hearts. 4. The people were to command their children to observe it. The children were, in their home life, to receive an education for God. 5. This is urged upon them by the consideration that all that is precious to them in life depends on their obedience to God's message. 6. Moses and Joshua appear together before the people, as if to declare to them that the same teachings which the aged leader had laid down, the younger one would accept, enforce, and transmit. There was a change in human leaders, but not in Divine laws or the Divine message. And to all the solemn sanctions with which Moses guarded the Law, Joshua here pledges himself before the people and before his God. Hence we get this theme—*Amid all changes we have an unchanging message from above, on the observance of which our life depends.*

I. Let us clearly declare and show that there is at this moment a message of law and a revelation of grace, which have come to us, not of man, but by the inspiration of the Spirit of God, by the manifestation of God in Christ, and by the power of the Holy Ghost on and since the day of Pentecost. This message is, in sum and substance, given in John iii. 16; 1 Tim. i. 15; Rev. xxii. 17; Titus ii. 11—13. This message is the development of that which through Moses was given but in germ (John v. 46, 47; Matt. v. 17).

II. Here past and present generations meet, giving out the same words. We have now "the faith once [for all] delivered unto the saints." Aged patriarchs in their declining years do reiterate the same message they gave when in the vigour of youth. And young men, filled with the same spirit, and having their hearts kindled with the same fire, take it up with the earnest hope and prayer that it may suffer no loss in their hands! Often have a Moses and a Joshua thus stood side by side.

III. The message now is far fuller and clearer than it was when given to Israel of old. *How* much, Christian preachers and teachers can tell. Yet in three respects they are similar. 1. Both reveal the love of God, and recount a great deliverance. 2. Both solicit, in Heaven's name, the response of the peoples' hearts (see Rom. xii. 1;

2 Cor. v. 14—21; Rom. v. 8). 3. Both require, on the ground of Divine love to man, love to the redeemed brotherhood, and good will to all men (1 Cor. xiii.; John iv. 10—19).

IV. The commanding force of the gospel message through our Lord Jesus Christ is far greater than that sent through Moses. True, there was terror at Sinai; there is tenderness in Calvary. Moses orders; Jesus pleads. Moses speaks in thunderings; Jesus with tears. Yet must we not mistake tenderness for weakness, nor gentleness for lack of authority or of power. (See the entire argument in the Epistle to the Hebrews.)

V. All that can give fullest value to this life and joy to the next, depends on how we treat this message from God. "It is not a vain thing for you; it is your life" (ver. 47). The expansion of this would require many Homilies. We can but hint. 1. The enjoyment of peace with God (Rom. v. 1). 2. The growth of character in holiness. 3. The true enjoyment and use of this earthly life, as families, as nations, as individuals, depend on loyalty to God. "Godliness is profitable unto all things; having promise of the life that now is." 4. All our hope for the next life depends on our response to God; hence the close of the verse just quoted—"and of that which is to come." Apart from the acceptance of Jesus Christ by faith, and a life of loyalty to God, there is not a gleam of light or hope for the next life (see Heb. ii. 3). If God did not allow his message through Moses to be slighted with impunity, certainly he will not suffer men to "trample under foot the Son of God," and then leave them unpunished!

VI. What dread, what awful possibilities as to the fate of immortal souls are trembling in the balance, while they refrain from "yielding themselves unto God"! How earnestly and frequently may we with reason reiterate the words, "*It is your life*"! All that ensures life here and hereafter being a blessing, depends on the way men treat Jesus Christ and his salvation.

VII. However many changes there may yet be in the bearers of this message, yet, down to the end of time, God will never send a greater. Moses and Joshua. The old generation passing away, the new coming on the stage. They meet and greet. The faithful and tried veteran passes on the word. The younger messenger, with solemn vow to God before his brother man, receives it, and swears before high heaven that he will maintain the message unimpaired, and in his turn "commit it to faithful men, who shall be able to teach others also."

> "Thus shall the bright succession run,
> Till the last courses of the sun."

Vers. 48—52.—*Death immediately in view.* The utterance of the sublime song which we have just treated on, was the last recorded public act of Moses. His work is all but done. He receives an intimation that the time is nigh at hand for him to "go up and die." The circumstances which gather round that death are most suggestive. The following passages should be compared together:—Numb. xx. 12; xxvii. 12—14; ch. i. 37; iii. 23—28; iv. 21, 22; Ps. cvi. 32. Historically, the following points are indicated in this paragraph :—1. Moses recognized the call to die, as well as the call to work, as from God; ver. 48, "*The Lord* spake," etc. 2. His joy in death would be checked by the remembrance of faults in life (ver. 51). It is by no means clear to us why so severe a sentence was imposed on Moses for one outburst of temper. Dr. Jameson suggests that there may have been other circumstances, which are unrecorded, to account for it. Possibly, however, the phrases, "for your sakes," "for their sakes," furnish a clue to the reason. The people might need thus to be guarded against presumptuous sin. 3. Visions of the glorious land in store for God's people would be granted him ere he quitted the earth. His joy would be rich, though not unalloyed (ver. 52). 4. The work which he had thus far carried forward must be completed by other hands. This is implied, and elsewhere expressed. 5. Moses, like the saints of God who went before him, must plunge into the unknown realm. He must "be gathered unto his people," as Aaron had been (ver. 50). 6. He would do so under the eye of the same God whom he so long had served. Till the very last he lives in fellowship with God. At the last he will die in fellowship with him.

No Christian expositor can fail to take note of the different aspect which death has to believers, since "life and incorruption" have been brought to light by Jesus Christ. The believer, at death, enters the invisible world. The names for it are "Sheol" and "Hades." The former is a Hebrew word, the latter Greek. Both mean (practically) the same, though they present the mysterious realm of the departed under different aspects. To the Hebrew it is the all-demanding world. To the Greek, the unknown region. In the New Testament (Revised Version) the word Hades is reproduced. But though *the word* is reproduced, *its meaning* is changed. The *heathen* view of Hades was that of a mysterious under-realm of the dead—gloomy and without hope. The *Jewish* view of Sheol (LXX. Hades) was also that of a mysterious under-realm—gloomy, but with a hope of glory "in the awaking" (Ps. xvii. 15). The *Christian* view of Hades is that of an invisible realm of departed souls, who are entirely under the mediatorial administration of the Son of God; a region without gloom, of perfect rest and of glorious hope for the believer. "Absent from the body: at home with the Lord." "Whether we live or die, we continue to be the Lord's." Let us thankfully make use of this new light which Christ has thrown on the death of believers, in meditating on "*Christian dying.*"

I. THE CHRISTIAN IS ABSOLUTELY AT THE DISPOSAL OF HIS LORD, FOR WORK OR FOR REST, FOR LIVING OR FOR DYING. (Rom. xiv. 9; Phil. i. 20.) He will be prepared to say, "Lord, it belongs not to my care, whether I die or live." Work is worth doing only so long as Christ has it for us to do. Life is worth living only as we can serve Christ thereby.

II. THE CHRISTIAN'S JOY IN DEATH MUST SURELY BE CHECKED AT THE THOUGHT OF NUMBERLESS DEFECTS, FAILURES, AND FAULTS IN LIFE. Whether or no there have been any such serious outbreaks as that of Moses, there must come rushing into memory so much defective work, so much mixed motive, such an utter lack of anything done or said which rose up to even his own ideal, that he would despair of his future, if it were not for the abounding grace of God; and even then, though this grace keeps him from sinking, and he may feel assured that his sin is forgiven, yet it must bring a shade over his spirit to think there has been so much for which he needed forgiveness!

III. ACTIVE WORKERS AND LEADERS IN GOD'S CHURCH OFTEN LAY DOWN THEIR WORK WITH A STRANGE FEELING OF INCOMPLETENESS. Moses had brought the people thus far, *just to the verge* of the promised land! He would gladly have finished the work. But it was well for Moses to feel how entirely the work was of God and not of man. How many a worker would like to see this or that controversy closed, this or that Church settled, this publication completed, this convert a little more established in the faith! But no. It is as God wills, and that will is best.

IV. THOUGH GOD SUFFERS THIS SHADE OVER LIFE'S CLOSING HOURS, YET HE OFTEN CHEERS HIS SERVANTS BY BRIGHT VISIONS OF THE GLORY WHICH IS IN STORE FOR THE PEOPLE OF GOD. Ver. 52, "Thou shalt see the land before thee." Yes, and Moses knew that, though he must leave the work incomplete, there was yet a great future for God's Church, when the wilderness life was over. And so now. However decided may be the sense of unfinished work, with which God's servants close their earthly career, they have no misgiving as to God's finding others by whom the work will be carried on, nor have they a doubt as to the future triumphs of Christ and his cause. From the top of faith's Pisgah, they "see the land before them," and though it lieth afar off, yet the sight ravishes them. Lo! "a new heaven and a new earth, wherein dwelleth righteousness."

V. MEANWHILE, THE SAINT MUST BREATHE HIS LAST BREATH, AND QUIT HIS HOLD OF EARTH, ENTER THE "GATES OF HADES" (Matt. xvi. 18, Greek), AND FIND HIS PLACE, TILL THE LORD COMES, IN THE INVISIBLE WORLD. Like Moses, he must be "gathered to his people;" but he knows a great deal more than it is probable Moses did, of what that means. The words in Rev. i. 18 are enough for faith, till God reveals the rest.

VI. HE WILL DO SO, LIKE MOSES, UNDER THE EYE AND CARE OF THE SAME GOD WHOM HE HAS SERVED IN LIFE. By directions from God, Moses would go up to die. And what he thought thereon may be gathered from the words of his own blessing. "The eternal God is thy refuge, and underneath are the everlasting arms." Moses would not—could not fail to take the comfort of all this for himself. We have a like comfort more clearly given (1 Thess. v. 10). Once Christ's we are *never* out of his hands!

HOMILIES BY VARIOUS AUTHORS.

Vers. 1—3.—*Beneficial teaching.* Moses was directed to instruct the people by composing for their use a song (ch. xxxi. 19, 21). A song is : 1. Memorable. 2. Easily handed down from mouth to mouth. 3. Of singular power to awaken sympathetic feeling (cf. influence of ballads, of Jacobite songs, of the 'Marseillaise,' of popular hymns). The action of song is not violent, but gentle and persuasive. It steals about the heart like rippling water or like sunlight, trickles into its pores, works as if by spirit-influence on its seats of laughter and tears, explores its innermost labyrinths of feeling. Here compared (ver. 2) to the gently distilling dew and rain.

I. THE DEW AND RAIN AS EMBLEMS OF THE TEACHING MOST LIKELY TO PROVE EFFECTIVE. Their action is : (1) gentle, (2) silent, (3) pervasive, (4) kindly ; yet : 1. *Invigorative.* They revive, refresh, stimulate. 2. *Powerful.* Rocks shattered by drops of water in their pores and crevices. 3. *Deep-reaching.* They act on plants by watering *their roots.* Take a lesson from them. It is not the best kind of teaching which is loud and violent, which tries to *force* men's convictions. Convictions must have time to grow. Teaching must be loving. The earthquake, the whirlwind, the fire, have their own place, but "the still small voice" is needed to succeed them. The Lord is peculiarly in that. Angry scolding, petulant rebuke, biting censure, clever satire, seldom do much good. Love alone wins the day.

II. THE DEW AND RAIN AS EMBLEMS OF THE TEACHING MOST SUITABLE IN THE INSTRUCTIONS OF RELIGION. Moses employed it here. Christ employed it. "He shall not strive nor cry," etc. (Matt. xii. 19). Paul commends "truthing it in love" (Eph. iv. 15). "The servant of the Lord must not strive ; but be gentle unto all men, apt to teach, patient, in meekness instructing those that oppose themselves" (2 Tim. ii. 24, 25). This kind of teaching harmonizes best : 1. With the *subject* of religion—"the Name of the Lord" (ver. 3). God had revealed his Name to Moses (Exod. xxxiv. 6, 7), and the attributes of mercy preponderate. 2. With the *end* of religion—the ascription of greatness to God (ver. 3). Religious teaching fails if it does not inspire men with such convictions of God's greatness as will lead them to fear, honour, worship, praise, and serve him. 3. With the special theme of the gospel—peace, love, good will to men. This song of Moses has to deal with stern truths, but even in its sternest passages it breathes the pathos of tender and sorrowful affection. It dwells largely on God's kindnesses and the people's ingratitude, and ends with loving promises. The song has numerous echoes in Isaiah.—J. O.

Ver. 4.—*God the Rock.* (Cf. vers. 15, 18, 31, 37.) This name for God occurs chiefly in this song of Moses, and in the compositions of David and of later psalmists. It was a name full of significance to those familiar with the desert. Rock—rock—rock—Israel had seen little else during the thirty-eight years of wandering. The older men could remember the seclusion and granitic sublimity of the rock sanctuary of Sinai. The congregation had mourned for Aaron under the shadow of Mount Hor, "rising high aloft into the blue sky, like a huge, grand, but shattered rock-city, with vast cliffs, perpendicular walls of stone, pinnacles, and naked peaks of every shape." They had witnessed the security of Edom in the hills in which now stand the wondrous rock-hewn ruin of Petra. They had traversed the defiles of the terrible and precipitous Arabah. When David was hunted in the wilderness, he, too, was often led to think of God, his Rock (Ps. xviii. 2 ; lxi. 2 ; lxii. 2, 7, etc.). It is wilderness experience which still makes the name so precious.

I. ROCK A NATURAL IMAGE OF DIVINE ATTRIBUTES. The image is not an arbitrary one. Nature abounds in shadows of the spiritual. It is what the mind puts into the objects of its survey which makes them what they are. "The Alps and Andes are but millions of atoms till thought combines them, and stamps on them the conception of the everlasting hills. Niagara is a gush of water-drops till the soul puts into it that sweep of resistless power which the beholder feels. The ocean, wave behind wave, is only great when the spirit has breathed into it the idea of immensity. If we analyze our feelings, we shall find that thought meets us wherever we turn. The real grandeur of the world is in the soul which looks on it, which sees some conception of its own reflected from the mirror around it; for mind is not only living, but life-giving, and has received from its Maker a portion of his own creative power" (Dr. John Ker). Rock is thus more than rock—its awfulness, grandeur, immovability, everlastingness, strength, are born of spiritual conceptions. These attributes do not in reality belong to it. Rock is *not* everlasting, moveless, abiding, etc. Old rocks are being worn away, new rocks are being formed; the whole system had a beginning and will have an end (Ps. xc. 2). It is not that these attributes belong to rock, and are thence by metaphor attributed to God; but these attributes of God, being dimly present in the mind, are by metaphor attributed to rock. We clothe the natural object with shadowy attributes of Deity. God is the *true* Rock, the other is the image. God is rock, in virtue of: 1. The eternity of his existence (Ps. xc. 2). 2. The omnipotence of his might (Dan. iv. 35). 3. The wisdom of his counsel (Isa. xl. 13). 4. The immutability of his purpose (Ps. xxxiii. 11; Isa. xlvi. 10). 5. The faithfulness of his Word (Ps. cxix. 89, 90). 6. The rectitude of his government (Ps. cxlv. 17). Whence: 7. The perfection of his work. Christ is like the Father, eternal (Rev. i. 11), unchangeable (Heb. xiii. 8), all-powerful (Matt. xxviii. 18), faithful (John xiii. 1; xiv. 18—20), righteous (Rev. xix. 11), wise (Isa. ix. 6).

II. ROCK A NATURAL IMAGE OF WHAT, IN VIRTUE OF HIS ATTRIBUTES, GOD IS TO HIS PEOPLE. 1. A shelter (Ps. lxi. 3). 2. A defence (Ps. xviii. 2; lxii. 6). 3. A dwelling-place (Ps. xc. 1). 4. A shadow from the heat (cf. Isa. xxxii. 2). 5. A moveless standing-ground (Ps. xl. 2). 6. A foundation (cf. Matt. vii. 24). The rock smitten in the wilderness furnishes the additional idea of: 7. A source of spiritual refreshment. Apply throughout to Christ, the Rock on which his Church is built (Matt. xvi. 18; 1 Cor. ii. 11), the smitten Saviour (1 Cor. x. 4; 1 John v. 6), the spiritual Refuge and Salvation of his people (Rom. viii. 1, 34—39). Toplady's hymn, "Rock of Ages." —J. O.

Vers. 4—7.—*God's righteousness and man's iniquity.* The sin of man is only fully seen in contrast with God's righteousness and love. The light is needed to bring out the depth of the shadow. It reveals the "spot."

I. GOD'S FAVOUR TO ISRAEL. God's dealings with Israel had been marked by: 1. *Rectitude* (ver. 4). He had done everything that was just and right to them. His ways had been equal. He had given them just statutes. His covenant-keeping faithfulness had been signally manifested. There was not the shadow of a pretence for accusing God of injustice or of infidelity to his engagements. 2. *Love.* Love and grace had been more conspicuous in his treatment of them than even justice. It was shown in their election, in the deliverance from Egypt, in the guidance of the desert, in pardon of offences, in the many and undeserved favours which had been heaped upon them (cf. vers. 9—14). Rectitude and love have reached their fullest manifestation in the gospel. The cross displays both. It harmonizes their apparently conflicting claims, and exhibits them in new glories. God's character, revealed in Christ, is the condemnation of an unbelieving world.

II. ISRAEL'S REQUITAL OF GOD'S KINDNESS. (Vers. 5, 6.) Their requital was an incredibly base one. They corrupted themselves. They wantonly departed from the ways of right. They behaved ungratefully. Instead of imitating God in the example of rectitude he had set them, and walking before him "as dear children," they flung to the winds the remembrance of his mercies, and brought disgrace upon his Name. He was their Father (ver. 6), but instead of reflecting the features of his image, they dishonoured and discredited it (cf. Isa. i. 2—4, which appears to be based on this passage). Their sin was: 1. *Self-caused.* There was nothing which they had seen in their God to cause it, to account for it, or to excuse it. 2. *Irrational.* Their powers, given by God, ought willingly to have been devoted in his service. Obedience is the normal condition. Heaven and earth, undeviatingly obeying the law of their existence, condemn man's apostasy (ver. 1). The very brute creation testifies against him (Isa. i. 3). 3. *Ungrateful.* God had bought them for himself, had made a nation of them, and established them in Canaan. Yet, without compunction, they cast off his yoke. 4. *Foolish;* for the way they chose was the way of death, whereas in God's favour was life (ver. 47), with every blessing that heart could wish for. The same remarks apply to sinners—despising the gracious overtures which God makes to them, with all the favours, temporal and spiritual, he has actually shown them, and careering on to their eternal ruin. "O foolish people and unwise!"—J. O.

Ver. 8.—*The world ruled for the benefit of the Church.* What this verse asserts is that in the providential distribution of the nations, and assignment to them of their special territories, respect was had from the beginning to the provision of a suitable dwelling-place for the chosen race. Our subject is—*The government of the world conducted with a view to the interests of the Church.*

I. A TRUTH FREQUENTLY TAUGHT IN SCRIPTURE. Both by facts of history, and by express statement. Israel's position brought it into contact, not only with petty neighbouring states, but with the mightiest empires of East and West. These appear in Scripture only as they affect the chosen race, but it is then made manifest how entirely their movements are directed and controlled by Divine providence. And the centre of God's purposes is always Israel. "For your sake," says God, "I have sent to Babylonia, and have brought down all their nobles, and the Chaldeans, whose cry is in the ships" (Isa. xliii. 14; cf. vers. 3, 4). Is Egypt visited with famines—with scarce years and good years? The design is the working out of a certain plan in the chain of God's appointments for Israel. Is a Cyrus raised up in Persia? God saith of him, "He is my shepherd, and shall perform all my pleasure," etc. (Isa. xliv. 28). So is it throughout. Egypt, Assyria, Babylonia, Persia, Greece, Rome, appear in all their relations with Israel as ministers of the Divine will, as simple executors of the Divine purposes, and their power is strictly limited by their commission. In harmony with this prophetic teaching are the express testimonies of the Epistles (*e.g.* Rom. viii. 28; Eph. i. 20—23; iii. 9—11). (1) Nature, (2) history, are ruled for the benefit of the Church.

II. A TRUTH IN ITSELF REASONABLE. Once admit the goal of history to be the establishment on earth of a universal spiritual kingdom—a gathering together in one of all things with Christ as Head (Eph. i. 10), and it is certain that herein must lie the key to all historical developments, the explanation of all arrangements and movements of Divine providence. The centre of interest must always be that portion of the race with which for the time being the kingdom of God is identified. "Just as, in tracing the course of a stream, not the huge morasses nor the vast stagnant pools on either side would delay us: we should not, because of their extent, count them the river, but recognize that as such, though it were the slenderest thread, in which an onward movement might be discerned; so is it here. Egypt and Assyria and Babylon were but the vast stagnant morasses on either side of the river; the Man in whose seed the whole earth should be blessed, he and his family were the little stream in which the life and onward movement of the world were to be traced. . . . They belong not to history, least of all to sacred history, those Babels, those cities of confusion, those huge pens into which by force and fraud the early hunters of men, the Nimrods and Sesostrises, drove and compelled their fellows . . . where no faith existed but in the blind powers of nature and the brute forces of the natural man" (Archbishop Trench).

III. A TRUTH FRAUGHT TO THE CHURCH WITH COMFORT AND ENCOURAGEMENT. 1. When the powers of the world are threatening. 2. In times of internal decay. 3. Under long-continued trials.—J. O.

Vers. 10—14.—*A panorama of grace.* How Israel was found, led, taught, kept.

I. WHERE GOD FOUND HIM. (Ver. 10.) Partly metaphorical—the state of Israel in Egypt being likened to that of a man perishing in the desert; partly literal—it being in the desert that God found the people when he took them into covenant. An image of the helpless and hopeless condition of the sinner. Cut off from life, without shelter, provision, resting-place, or final home.

II. HOW GOD DEALT WITH HIM. (Vers. 10, 11.) That Israel was kept in the wilderness so long was his own fault. But grace overruled the discipline for good. The long sojourn in the desert made Israel's case, also, a better type of our own. There are ends to be served by this sojourn (John xvii. 15). God showed himself: 1. Condescending to Israel's *feebleness* (Hos. xi. 3, 4). 2. Mindful of his *ignorance.*

"Instructed him." 3. Watchful of his *safety*. "Kept him." 4. Careful of his *training* (ver. 11). The love and solicitude implied in such phrases as, "kept him as the apple of his eye" (ver. 10), and "as an eagle stirreth up," etc. (ver. 11), specially deserve notice. The apple of the eye is a sensitive part, which we protect with the utmost care, and from the *slightest* injuries. (On the eagle, see below.)

III. WHITHER GOD CONDUCTED HIM. (Vers. 13, 14.) To a land of plenty and rest. Made his defence the munitions of rocks. Provided him with all that heart could desire. So does God bring the believer to a large and wealthy place—a place of "fulness of joy," of richest satisfactions, of most perfect delights. Spiritually, even here, where the most unpropitious circumstances yield him unexpected blessings. Eternally and in perfected form hereafter. Note: God *alone* did all this for Israel. (ver. 12).—J. O.

Ver. 11.—*The eagle.* "The description is of a female eagle exciting her young ones in teaching them to fly, and afterwards guarding with the greatest care lest the weak should receive harm" (Gesenius). In this picture of the eagle's treatment of her young, note—

I. HER AIM. She aims at teaching them self-reliance. It is not God's wish that his children should go in leading-strings. They must be trained to prompt, fearless, self-reliant action. This was an aim of the discipline of the wilderness. Our action is to be in a spirit of dependence, but it is to be *active*, not *passive* dependence.

II. HER METHOD. She stirs up her nest. She does not leave her brood to the ignoble ease they would perhaps prefer. So God rouses his people to action by making their place uneasy for them. By placing them in trying situations, by removing comforts, by the stimulus of necessity, by the sharp provocation of afflictions, he goads them to think, act, and put forth the powers that are in them. It is not for the good of Christians that they should have too much comfort.

III. HER CARE. The experiment is not carried to the point of allowing the young to hurt themselves. She hovers over them, supports them on the tip of her wings, etc. God tries us, but not beyond our strength.—J. O.

Vers. 15.—18.—*Jeshurun.* I. A GOOD NAME BELIED. Jeshurun, equivalent to righteous. An honourable name, but sadly falsified by the conduct described. How many Jeshuruns have thus forsaken the God of their early vows! Notice, a good name is of no account without the good character. Balaam praised Israel's righteousness, and wished to "die the death of the righteous" (Numb. xxiii. 10, 21); but it is the *being* righteous, not the being *called* so, which makes the happy deathbed.

II. AN EVIL EFFECT OF PROSPERITY. "Waxed fat—kicked." How common! The effect foretold or warned against in earlier chapters (ch. viii. 12—18, etc.). Prosperity, then pride, then stubborn self-willedness. The self-willed heart refuses to submit to God's government; throws off the memory of past obligations, and treats God with ill-concealed indifference and dislike; turns from the true God to gods of its own choosing. Two steps in the great apostasy—forsaking the fountain of living waters, and hewing out broken cisterns, etc. (Jer. ii. 13). Such conduct is (1) wicked, (2) ungrateful, (3) irrational, (4) fatal (vers. 22—25).

III. RESULT OF AN ITCH FOR NOVELTY. (Ver. 17.) The *newness* of the gods was a chief attraction. The worship of them was a change, a novelty. It pleased them by variety. 1. When God has been abandoned, men are at the mercy of the most trivial influences. "Itching ears"—"every wind of doctrine" (Eph. iv. 14; 2 Tim. iv. 3). 2. When God has been abandoned, novelty is greedily accepted as a substitute for truth, in theories, in creeds, in styles of worship, in religious nostrums. 3. Apostasy from God means transference of the affections to that which is degrading. In this case to "destroyers," so the word means; devils, malignant deities. But we worship devils, or *the* devil (Matt. iv. 9), when we bow in spirit to the world's modes and shows; when we serve gold, or fashion, or the opinion of society; when we are slaves to lust of power; when we bow to a false *gnosis*, etc.—J. O.

Vers. 19—27.—*A God provoked.* Consider here—
I. THE REALITY OF WRATH IN GOD. Let it not be minimized or explained away.

"Instead of being shocked at the thought that God is wrathful, we should rather ask, *With whom?* and *For what?* A God without wrath, and a God who is wrathful on other accounts than for sin, is not a God, but an idol" (Hengstenberg). It is only, as this writer observes, when "man himself is not displeased with sin, when it assumes to him the appearance of a bagatelle," that he no longer perceives why God should feel wrath at it. But man, we may observe, is by no means disposed to treat lightly sins *against himself.* He never feels that he does not "do well to be angry" on account of these or against the person who does them. A very slight wound to his honour makes him clamour for satisfaction. A God who is incapable of moral indignation would be equally incapable of moral love, and could not, with truth, be spoken of as dispensing mercy. Wrath and love are opposite poles of one affection. Where there is no offence, there needs no forgiveness.

II. WRATH IN GOD, WHEN IT BURNS AGAINST MEN, IS TERRIBLE IN ITS EFFECTS. Two aspects of its operation: 1. Leaving men to themselves (ver. 20). When God hides his face from them, there need be little doubt what the "end" will be. Yet can the sinner complain if he is at length permitted to eat the fruit of the devices which nothing will persuade him to give up? 2. Heaping on them positive inflictions (vers. 22—25). It is a fire, burning to destroy them. It is noteworthy that the conflagration of the Divine wrath is represented as not only taking in *sheol*, but as widening till it embraces the whole earth (ver. 22). This, in connection with the glimpse at the calling of the Gentiles in ver. 21, points to the future universal extension of the outward dispensation of grace. The extension of the kingdom of God brings all nations within the range of the Messianic judgment (Matt. xxv. 31). The wrath of God is not represented in less terrible colours in the New Testament than it is in the Old. The individualized description of these verses (vers. 24, 25) figures out terrors of a future life too painful to allow the mind to dwell upon them.

III. WRATH IN GOD IS, IN THIS LIFE, NOT DIVORCED FROM MERCY. Not at least so long as hope of recovery remains. He would fain make punishment subservient to conversion. This is the thought in ver. 21. Israel is not cast off for ever. God is seeking to provoke it to jealousy by a transference of his regard to the Gentiles. His retaliation has a merciful as well as a wrathful design. Mercy waits on every sinner, courting his repentance.

IV. THE MANIFESTATION OF WRATH IN GOD IS LIMITED BY REGARD TO HIS HONOUR. (Vers. 26, 27.) God is jealous of his honour. He will take from his adversaries the power of boasting against him, by marvellously restoring those who, had they received their full deserts, would have been utterly destroyed. This stays his hand from expending his wrath against them to the uttermost. We may read this otherwise, and say that zeal for his honour leads God to spare them, that he may glorify his Name by causing mercy to rejoice over judgment. There is more honour to God in saving men than in destroying them.

And what provokes this wrath in God? Sin—sin only. Most especially the sins of his own people. 1. "No faith"—want of fidelity to vows. 2. "Frowardness"—persistence in sin (ver. 20). Those who have stood in nearest relations to him, who have enjoyed most favours, are those who will be most severely punished (Amos iii. 2). —J. O.

Vers. 28, 29.—*The true wisdom.* Consider—

I. IN WHAT WISDOM CONSISTS. 1. The choice of right ends. 2. Of right means to secure these ends. 3. In harmony with a just and proportioned view of all the circumstances of our situation. When essential circumstances are omitted in the calculation, when the horizon is unduly narrowed, when all-important factors of the situation are left wholly out of account,—it is vain to speak of wisdom. Absolutely, and as regards our standing as moral beings, wisdom embraces: 1. *The choice of a true end,* i.e. the choice, as our end in life, of that end for which we were created. 2. *The practical shaping of conduct with a view to that end,* and in the way best calculated to attain it. And this: 3. *In view of all the circumstances of the case,* i.e. with right apprehensions of God, of the issues of moral conduct, of eternity. What wisdom is more to be desired than this? What efforts ought to be put forth to attain it! What incalculable value ought to be set upon it!

II. SIN IS THE ABSOLUTE UNWISDOM. 1. *For the true end of life it substitutes a false one.* The end for which we were made was holiness—the service of God with all our powers of soul, body, and spirit. In this consists our life, our happiness, our well-being. In pursuit of this end, our nature works harmoniously with itself, and with the general constitution of the world. But sin substitutes for this an end which violates, disturbs, perverts the harmony of every sphere of our existence. It asserts a false independence of the creature. It bids us use our powers for self, and not for God. It holds up as an end a shadowy good which is never realized. It cheats with insincere promises. By perverting the nature, it gives to fleshly lusts a tyrannical predominance, and degrades the spirit to the position of a bondservant. For unity there is thus established anarchy—each lust, as its own master, seeking an independent gratification. Life in this way falls asunder—it has a proper end no longer—and the strife continues till a new equilibrium is established by one lust or passion usurping the mastery over the rest. 2. *For the true conduct of life it substitutes a course of conduct resting on false bases.* The false end yields its natural fruit in false principles of life. The sinner's whole career, whatever he may think of it himself, is one tissue of errors and illogicalities. If measured by the end he *ought* to set before him, it is seen to be a course leading him wildly and hopelessly astray. The more skilfully and assiduously he applies himself to *his* ends, only the more conspicuously does he convict himself of folly. 3. *Instead of taking all the factors of the case into account, it usually leaves God and eternity out of it.* This is that which most convincingly brands the sinner's course as folly. If God exist, and if he have the power to bless or blast our schemes, and if in the end we have to meet him as our Judge,—it surely cannot be wisdom to leave this fact unnoticed. So, if we are beings made for eternity, destined to exist for ever, he must be a fool who makes preparations for everything but for eternity. If, again, the issues of obedience and sin are on the one hand life, and on the other death, he must be insane who deliberately makes a preference of the latter. Even if the choice is not deliberately made, but the eyes are kept closed to the issues, this does not alter the unwisdom of the choice itself. We can see, therefore, how a man may be most wise as regards this world, and yet the veriest fool as regards the whole scope of his existence. He may be gifted, talented, energetic, a shrewd man of the world, sagacious in pursuit of earthly ends, yet totally blind to his eternal interests. He may be neglecting the "one thing needful," making no preparation for a hereafter, missing the end of his existence, treasuring up wrath and sorrow for himself at the end. "Thou fool!" was the stern word of Heaven to a man who, in earthly respects, was probably deemed very wise (Luke xii. 20). Men *are* fools who neglect the voice of religion.—J. O.

Ver. 31.—*The superiority of the believer's Rock.* Few men but feel that they need a rock of some kind. Only when their mountain stands very strong do they feel as if they were absolutely secure and independent (Obad. 3, 4). Even then their trust is in acquired power and riches, which is a "rock" to them, though their confidence often proves delusive (Haman, Nebuchadnezzar, Wolsey). When men have lost faith in religion, they frequently take refuge in the "rock" of philosophy. The "rock" of the heathen is their idols and the arts of the soothsayer. Men tend to make a "rock" of those superior to them in power and wisdom. The "rock" of nations is too often their military and naval defences, with arts of diplomacy, and alliances with stronger powers (Isa. xxx.). The believer's Rock, which is the best of all, is God. I. THE SUPERIORITY OF THE BELIEVER'S ROCK EVINCED. 1. *From the nature of this Rock.* Grant that God *is*, a Being, infinite, eternal, and unchangeable, wise in his counsel, omnipotent in his power, faithful in his promises, righteous in his actions, infinitely gracious and merciful to those who put their trust in him, a "strong Rock," "an House of defence" to save them (Ps. xxxii. 7), a "Hiding-place" to preserve them from trouble (Ps. xxxii. 7),—and the superiority of this Rock to every other needs no further demonstration. It is self-evidently impossible to have a surer or a better. What can man ask more than that the "eternal God" should be his "Refuge," and that underneath him should be the "everlasting arms"? (ch. xxxiii. 27). 2. *From the advantages derived from this Rock.* These are such as no other can pretend to give. The believer's life being hid with God (Col. iii. 3) and guaranteed by the life of Christ in heaven (John xiv. 19), and his inheritance lying beyond death (1 Pet. i. 4), no hostility of man can reach either. No other "rock" can give the same security, the same peace, joy, shelter, strength, comfort, and refreshment, as the believer's. To which considerations add the following:—1. Many of these so-called "rocks" are *nonentities.* The idols of the heathen are of this description. So with the arts and charms of sorcery, prayers to the Virgin, etc. 2. The surest of these "rocks" are *not to be depended on.* "Wisdom is better than strength" (Eccles. ix. 16); but wisdom, strength, riches, rank, powerful friends, long-consolidated might,—all sometimes fail those who put their trust in them. 3. Not one of these "rocks" *can stand when God wills its overthrow.* God's help, on the other hand, is *real,* always *to be relied on,* and *invincible against opposition.*

II. THE SUPERIORITY OF THE BELIEVER'S ROCK CONFESSED. It is often confessed, even by the enemy. How often, *e.g.* have ungodly men expressed themselves envious of the religious trust and peace of the believer! How often have they admitted its superiority to anything possessed by themselves! How often, again, have they owned to their own "rocks" failing them in time of need! How often, even, when it came to the end, have they lamented that they had not sought the Rock of the believer! Philosophy is admitted, even by those who take refuge in it, to be but a sorry substitute for religion. Passages could be culled from current literature showing very distinctly this need of the believer's rock—the almost agonizing expression of a wish that belief were possible—the confession that in the surrender of Christian beliefs a large part of life's hopefulness and joy has gone for ever (see in Mallock's "Is Life worth Living?").—J. O.

Ver. 31.—*Our Rock.* Apply to the religion of the Bible. Proved to be superior to every other system: 1. In proofs of supernatural origin. 2. In moral and spiritual power. 3. In the privileges it offers. 4. In the prospects it holds out. Admissions and concessions on each of these points could be gathered from the writings of many of the most noted unbelievers.—J. O.

Vers. 32, 33.—*The vine of Sodom.* Emblem of fruit of sin. 1. Tempting. 2. Deceptive. 3. Ending in disappointment and disgust.—J. O.

Vers. 34—43.—*Retribution.* I. VENGEANCE A PREROGATIVE OF DEITY. As just Judge of the earth, God must avenge transgression. Vengeance is to be distinguished from personal vindictiveness. Of that God is incapable. But Scripture, supported by reason and conscience, attributes to him a holy and inflexible determination to punish sin—to visit on the wrong-doer the consequences of his transgression. The rule for individuals is, "Avenge not yourselves," etc.; but the reason for this is not that vengeance is unnecessary, but that God will avenge (Rom. xii. 18). Magistrates, however, bear from God a certain delegated power to punish public offences—to "avenge" evil (Rom. xiii. 4). He who "takes away vengeance from God, at the same time takes it from God's servant, the magistracy, which carries the sword of vengeance over evil-doers" (Hengstenberg). God has his own time, as well as his own way, of avenging sin, and it is not for man to anticipate this.

II. VENGEANCE ASSUREDLY IN STORE FOR GOD'S ENEMIES. However delayed by forbearance. Because judgment is not executed speedily, sinners take confidence (Eccles. viii. 11; 2 Pet. iii. 9, 10). But the sleepless eye of God is all the while upon them, and the stroke falls when they are least expecting it. Sooner or later, every transgression and disobedience will meet with its due recompense of reward, Note: 1. "Judgment begins at the house of God" (vers. 35, 36; 1 Pet. iv. 17). 2. It will ultimately extend to all who are God's enemies (vers. 41, 42). We are taught that the Messianic kingdom will be established on earth amidst mighty displays of judgment (Rev. xix. 11—21). There will follow the general judgment of quick and dead—"that day of wrath, that dreadful day"—which will complete the work. God's vengeance is: 1. *Assured.* "As I live," etc. (ver. 40). 2. *Terrible.* "My glittering sword;" "arrows drunk with blood," etc. 3. *No escape from it* (ver. 39).

III. JUDGMENTS EMPLOYED TO CONVINCE BACKSLIDERS OF THEIR SINS. They tend: 1. To break up false confidences (vers. 37, 38). 2. To create a feeling of the need of God's help (ver. 39). 3. To convince of the folly of past conduct. God compassionates even while he punishes (ver. 36). He would fain, through judgment, break a way for mercy. Illustrate this use of judgments from Israel in time of the judges, or from case of Manasseh (2 Chron. xxxiii. 11—14). This one use of the present exile. May we hope that the day of God's "repenting himself" toward Israel is drawing near !

IV. THE RECOVERY OF ISRAEL THE INAUGURATION OF A TIME OF BLESSING TO THE WORLD. The nations are to share in the joy (ver. 43). God is to be merciful to his land and people. The latter-day glory includes the conversion of the Gentiles (Rom. xi.).—J. O.

Ver. 47.—*Your life*. The doing or not doing of God's will, the obeying or not obeying of God's Word, is a matter of life and death to us. This is the simple and solemn and uniform testimony of Scripture from its first page to its last. The gospel, with its revelation of "life and immortality," only heightens the solemnity of the alternative. Instead of bare "life," it is now "eternal life" which is proposed for our acceptance, and which is lost or forfeited by sin. If "life" is the promise, the counter-alternative is death, and "death" accordingly is denounced against the sinner in gospel, as in Law. "The wages of sin are death" (Rom. vi. 23). Eternity is a factor to be taken into account here, as well as in the case of "life." Death, indeed, is not non-existence, but it is the loss of all that makes existence a boon; the extinction in the soul of holiness, happiness, and love. Whatever the final state of the lost may be, whether one of active torment or not, it will be true death. The man loses his "soul" —his "life"—"himself" (Matt xvi. 26; Luke ix. 25). Oh that men were wise, that they understood these things, and acted on their choice as wise men should !—J. O.

Vers. 48—52.—*Moses' end* (see ch. xxxiv.).—J. O.

Vers. 1—14.—*The fatherhood of God*. In this first section of the Divine song, the predominating idea is God's fatherhood. It comes out in ver. 6 in express terms; it is implied in the care that is attributed to him for his children of Israel; it passes into the still tenderer idea of motherhood in the illustration of the eagle (ver. 11); and may fairly be taken as the idea dominating the whole. It has been thought that the father-hood of God is almost altogether a New Testament idea; but we have it here expressly stated, and it underlies many portions of the Old Testament. This whole song is, in fact, a paternal expostulation with children that have been wayward in the wilderness, and will be more wayward still in the land of promise. We shall notice in order the ideas suggested by this section.

I. FERTILIZING DOCTRINE. Divine doctrine, even in its severest forms, has a gracious and fertilizing influence like rain or dew. It comes down upon the wilderness of human nature, and makes it a fruitful field. It comes down upon the tender herb of implanted graces, upon the grass of humble and useful piety, and makes all to grow more luxu-riantly. Nothing is so important as "good doctrine."

II. THE ROCK-STABILITY OF GOD. This is the first inquiry. Can God be trusted as truly stable? The answer is that he is a Rock, and that upon his veracity and justice and helpfulness we can constantly rely. Moses and the Israelites had ex-perienced this; as they wandered amid the rocky fastnesses of the desert, they had found him as firm and as reliable as the rocks. Up to this time, the figure had not been applied to God. The Israelites have, indeed, from the hard and flinty rock, had refreshing streams; the rock was to them a fountain of waters; and doubtless when here the figure is for the first time applied to God, they would find it delightful to associate refreshment and shelter with him. Then in course of time it became a favourite figure, as the Psalms in many passages show (cf. Ps. xxviii. 1; xxxi. 2, 3; xlii. 9; lxii. 2, 7; lxxviii. 20, 35; xcv. 1, etc.). And we rejoice to call our Redeemer "Rock of Ages," in the clefts of which, according to Toplady's idea, taken from Exod. xxxiii. 22, we can take shelter and feel safe.[1]

III. PATERNAL APPEAL. Although God is so worthy of trust, the Israelites have corrupted themselves; they are unwilling to have upon them the mark or spot of

---

[1] Cf. Gerok's 'Pilgerbrod,' p. 895; and his 'Evangelien-Predigten,' p. 720, for suggestive discourses on this text.

the children of God, but the mark of some other tribe;[1] and so as a *Father* he appeals to them because of their ingratitude. Has he not made them, bought them, and established them, and, in consequence, earned a right to different treatment from this? Fatherhood has rights by reason of service which no grateful child can overlook.

IV. PATERNAL FORESIGHT. He speaks next of the days of old, of the years of many generations, which the fathers and elders could testify about, during which time the Father was but evolving his glorious plan, separating and scattering the sons of Adam according to the interests and number of the children of Israel. At Babel and the subsequent migrations of men, " God so distributed the earth among the several peoples that were therein, as to reserve, or in his sovereign counsel to appoint, such a part for the Israelites, though they were then unborn, as might prove a commodious settlement and habitation for them."[2] Noble foresight, worthy of an everlasting and infinite Father.

V. PATERNAL INSTRUCTION. One element in fatherhood is a sense of possession in the children. The father rejoices that the children are his, and will not part readily with his portion. So with God. "The Lord's portion is his people; Jacob is the lot of his inheritance." Out of this sense of property comes the improvement of the children by faithful instruction. Hence Israel were led into the wilderness, and their Father found them there, and led them about, instructing them, and keeping them as "the apple of the eye." It was the Father educating them through his own companionship, and leading them onwards in safety towards their home.

VI. PARENTAL DISCIPLINE. The song introduces (ver. 11) the figure of the eagle, and the motherly discipline to which she subjects her brood. "Naturalists tell us that when her young are old enough to fly, the eagle breaks her nest in pieces, in order to compel them to use their powers of flight; fluttering over them, that by imitation they may learn how to employ their wings, but, when unwilling to fly, spreading abroad her wings, she bears them upwards in the air, and then shaking them off, compels them to use their own exertions."[3] From this Mr. Hull deduces the truth that "the Divine discipline of life is designed to awaken man to the development of his own powers." We see thus the kindness of the parental discipline, and that it takes *motherhood* as well as *fatherhood* to illustrate the Divine relation (cf. Isa. xlix. 15).

VII. PARENTAL BLESSING. Having exercised such parental care over the people, the result was abundant temporal success and blessing. This is beautifully brought out as a "riding upon the high places of the earth." And then the whole panorama of agricultural prosperity is presented, "the increase of the fields" providing *bread*, the rocks affording shelter for the bees which extracted abundant *honey* from the flowers, the olives clinging to the flinty rocks and affording abundance of *oil*, while the kine in the fat pastures gave *butter*, and the sheep *milk*, and the lambs were choice food, and the rams of the breed of Bashan, while the finest wheat and the purest wine made the lot of Israel princely. It was a land of promise surely which supplied their wants in such a fashion. God's goodness was exceeding great.

The "fatherhood of God" had thus its grand exemplification in the history of Israel. A Father who was firm as the rocky fastnesses around them and as reliable; who provided for his children long before they were born; who instructed and disciplined them, and brought them eventually to a splendid inheritance,—might well look for their trust and obedience. The Lord shows a similar fatherly care still to all men, even those who do not return a filial spirit; and if, in his grace, they yield at length to his paternal appeals, then he comes and gives them a [fellowship such as they never dreamed of. "He that loveth me," saith Jesus, "shall be loved of my Father, and I will love him, and will manifest myself to him" (John xiv. 21).—R. M. E.

Vers. 15—18.—*The danger of worldly success.* Success, when granted, bids for men's trust. They begin accordingly to insinuate that the reliable Rock who begat them is not

---

[1] Cf. 'The Land and the Book,' p. 67.
[2] So Bochart, as quoted in Jennings' 'Jewish Antiquities,' p. 562.
[3] Hull's 'Sermons,' 3rd series, p. 133.

the source of all success, and that the rill may be tracked to some nearer source. Hence new gods, novelties of man's imagination, or demons from the waste, grateful for even a false faith, are worshipped; and the ever-living and true God forgotten. Apostasy and scepticism, we would repeat, are born of luxury and success. Men think, because they are rich, that they can do bravely without God.

I. It is well to consider the danger of worldly success. Many a man was more religious when poor than after he became rich. Increase of riches needs increase of grace; and, if men are not watchful, riches only minister to backsliding. It is undesirable independence which proves independence of God. Better to trust God in the absence of wealth than to defy him or ignore him with it. Many a successful worldling would have had more success in a poor station, through increase of faith and of heart. The success was at the price of leanness being sent into his soul.

II. Those who will not sacrifice to God are always found sacrificing to their fears. The credulity of unbelief is one of the most curious questions of the time. When men deny God his due reverence and ignore his existence, their fancy haunts them with new gods, and powers whom they must propitiate—the luck and chance that they advance to the throne. The man alone is free from vain fears who trusts in the living God; all others sooner or later prove adepts at new religions, and are devotees at fancy shrines.

III. The Divine jealousy is justly provoked by such forgetfulness. Jealousy is the anger of ill-requited love. It is what has been called, as already observed, "love-pain," and is eminently worthy of him who is love itself. God cannot but feel he deserves man's love; he cannot but desire it; he longs for it more intensely than ever love-sick one among the children of men has longed; and when he sees the love he deserves made over to another, when he sees his life of love and death of love ignored, —is it not eminently reasonable that he should be jealous and have his holy anger stirred?

Herein lies the danger, then, of success. It may decoy the unguarded soul to mean fears and fancy shrines, and lead at length to the encountering of that jealousy which a God of love most justly entertains. Hence the prayer of souls should be that with success may come watchfulness; that with fatness may come faith; that out of goodness may come repentance. Then success may help and not hinder. Successful saints become a blessing to their kind, and make success a stewardship. "It takes a steady hand to carry a full cup;" so says the proverb. Blessed be God, amid many shaky hands, unequal to the task, there is a select few that carry their success in a cool, conscientious fashion!—R. M. E.

Vers. 19—47.—*Vengeance and recompense.* The reasonableness of the Divine jealousy being shown already, we can have little difficulty in recognizing the further reasonableness of the Divine vengeance. Paul's treatment of the question is concise and conclusive. "Is God unrighteous who taketh vengeance? (I speak as a man). God forbid: for then how shall God judge the world?" (Rom. iii. 5, 6). Vengeance is recognized, therefore, as belonging to God's justice, which shall be called into play as vengeance through the ingratitude and folly of many of mankind. Let us briefly indicate the course of the Divine vengeance as presented in the remainder of this song.

I. God proposes to move his ungrateful people by introducing Gentiles to their privileges. This is the first experiment of the holy jealousy, to see what effect the ingathering of the Gentiles will have. And to a Jewish mind there must be something striking and convincing in the history of Christianity. Surely the elevation and civilization of the heathen world must be due in large measure to that Divine favour which, as Jews, they despised and forfeited. Such a spectacle is calculated to lead them to earnest thought and deep contrition. Were their hearts not dull and gross, they would humble themselves before God, and acknowledge that they deserve other heirs to be put into their room.

II. The actualities of the Divine vengeance have been terrible. The Lord represents his anger as burning to the lowest hell (שְׁאוֹל תַּחְתִּית), reaching manifestly to that "under world," as Kahle would call it, where the spirits of the faithless are confined.[1]

[1] See his 'Eschatologie,' *ut supra*, pp. 37, 53.

But in the present life there is a foretaste given of the vengeance which embraces the life to come, which may be summed up, as given in these verses (vers. 23—25), in the terms *hunger, pestilence, wild beasts,* and *war.* The faithless nation experienced all these, as an earnest of the Divine vengeance which justly burns even to the lowest hell. The only limit to it is lest the enemies employed to execute part of the vengeance should say, " Our hand is high, and the Lord hath not done all this " (vers. 26, 27). The Lord will modify and limit his vengeance, lest his instruments should regard it as their work and not his.

III. The regret about possibilities thrown away will form part of the Divine vengeance. Very pathetically is this put in this song (vers. 29—31). The Israelites, though in a vast minority sometimes, had been carried by their most faithful Father and God to victory, and this would have still characterized them had they remained faithful to him. They would have proved his " invincibles." And no effort of faithless souls can keep regret at bay. We see Milton very properly putting it into the mouth of the archangel when he says—

" Farewell, happy fields,
Where joy for ever dwells ! "

and subsequently summons his associates from " the oblivious pool," where they are lying astonished. Unholy spirits may doubtless see the vanity of regret, but they cannot dismiss it. Indeed, it is one of the test struggles of the Christian life to put regret away. We need the rousing words of the poetess continually—

" Rise ! if the past detains you,
Her sunshine and storms forget ;
No chains so unworthy to hold you
As those of a vain regret.
Sad or bright, she is lifeless ever ;
Cast her phantom arms away,
Nor look back, save to learn the lesson
Of a nobler strife to-day."

How deep a sorrow this regret must be to all who despise God and reject his love we cannot in this life tell.

IV. Apparent prosperity will prove real disaster. Just as the *osher* plant, which flourishes best near the site of Sodom and Gomorrha, presents apparently most luscious and attractive fruit, which yet prove but bags of air and ashes, so the apparent prosperity of the faithless souls proves emptiness and bitter disappointment at last. All the investments, so to speak, which seem so fortunate turn into splendid mistakes and miseries. Upon the whole life, opposed as it is to God, there broods a curse.

V. The programme of vengeance is carefully prepared. This is the spirit of the remaining verses (vers. 35—43). God makes his calculations calmly and deliberately. The foot of his enemies shall slide in due time, and his work of vengeance, like all his other work, prove perfect. As God refuses to exercise " unprincipled mercy," so will he refuse to execute random wrath. The great Jonathan Edwards has a remarkable sermon on ver. 35, entitled ' Sinners in the Hands of an Angry God,' which may be distasteful to some easy-going theologians, but is nevertheless weighty with doctrinal and convincing truth. The idea should surely be got rid of that there is any difference in *principle* between the Old Testament and the New. The prerogative of vengeance so powerfully asserted in this song of the Lord, put into the mouth of Moses, has not been renounced nor laid down for an instant. The Lord still claims it, as Rom. xii. 19; Heb. x. 30, and other passages show.

VI. The policy of the Lord shall have a splendid consummation. After the cycle is complete, Jews and Gentiles, as ver. 43 distinctly indicates, shall be found rejoicing in concert before the Lord, who has shown himself merciful to his land and his people. We need not in this Homily enter upon the discussion of the great difference between the Hebrew of ver. 43 and the LXX. It does not affect the truth we draw from the remarkable passage. However the individuals may suffer through the Divine vengeance, it will not be lost as a lesson upon the race. Jew and Gentile shall alike recognize its justice and the compensating mercy which always lay for men in the tender hands of God. The vengeance is forced upon him—the judgment is his strange work; but he delighteth in mercy.

VII. MOSES SUMS UP THE LESSON OF THE SONG BY URGING OBEDIENCE UPON THE PEOPLE AS THEIR LIFE. And when we remember that God is the source of life; that spiritual life lies in his favour and fellowship; then it is clear that the Israelites had but one duty to discharge—to obey God and live. All the energy of Moses and all the urgency of God are devoted to secure this obedience. The remembrance of God's love, the recognition of his vengeance and deserved wrath, and the consummate wisdom manifested in the whole policy pursued, should move our hearts to love and obey. Let us accept of the mercy, and not force the Lord to judgment!—R. M. E.

Vers. 48—52.—*Death a judgment even to the most faithful servants of God.* After the solemn address to the people, God gives a personal address to Moses. It is about his approaching death. He is to see the land, but not to enter it, because he sanctified not the Lord at the waters of Meribah. It raises, therefore, the whole question of death as the portion even of the most faithful servants of God.

I. IT IS SURELY REMARKABLE THAT, WHEN SAVED THROUGH THE MERCY OF GOD IN CHRIST, WE DO NOT BECOME IMMORTAL. Salvation seizes on the spirit, it becomes life through the righteousness of Jesus, but the body is still dead (or mortal) because of sin (Rom. viii. 10). Why does salvation take our personality in instalments? save spirit first, and leave the body to the repairs of a resurrection? Can the procedure be vindicated? We think it can. For—

II. IF WE BECAME PHYSICALLY IMMORTAL THROUGH THE RECEPTION OF SALVATION, A MERCENARY ELEMENT WOULD BE INTRODUCED INTO OUR MOTIVES, AND MEN WOULD SEEK SALVATION TO ESCAPE THE PAIN OF DYING. Under the present arrangement, saint as well as sinner has to pass the dark portal. Dying is made the general lot of man, and, if salvation is desired, it is for spiritual purposes. Just as God does not promise immediate success to our efforts or our prayers, lest we should be tempted to live by sight and not by faith.

III. IT IS NOT DESIRABLE THAT, WITH PARDON, WE SHOULD ESCAPE ALL SUFFERING FOR OUR SIN. It is a wise arrangement on God's part, even when forgiving sinners, to take vengeance on our inventions (Ps. xcix. 8). For suppose that, in praying for pardon, we escaped all physical consequences of our sin, the result would be that pardon would be used as a great physical agent and factor, and the *physical* escape would be more thought upon than the spiritual. It is better, therefore, that things should take their course so far as the body is concerned, and that, meanwhile, the spirit should be the chief recipient of the benefit. God does not take the seeds of mortality, therefore, out of our bodies: he leaves them there as sin's own work; and he gives us the earnest of complete redemption in the resurrection and emancipation of our spirits.

IV. IT IS A SPLENDID TEST OF OUR FAITH IN GOD TO BE ASKED TO DIE. For up to the hour of death, we have found persons and things to lean upon in a measure; we have not as yet been left to lean on God alone. But when death comes, we are forced to lean on God only, if we are to have any support at all. God says, "Can you trust me, even when I take away your physical life?" "Though he slay me," said Job, "yet will I trust in him." Death brings us all to this test, and happy are we if we reach the same assurance.

> "The real is but the half of life; it needs
> The ideal to make a perfect whole;
> The sphere of sense is incomplete, and pleads
> The closer union with the sphere of soul.

> * * * * *

> "Then let us, passing o'er life's fragile arch,
> Regard it as a means, and not an end;
> As but the path of faith on which we march
> To where all glories of our being tend."

R. M. E.

Vers. 1—6.—*God's vicegerent as poet.* The true poet is God's messenger. He that sings not of truth and goodness is not a genuine poet; he is but a rhymester. As the swan is said to sing sweetly only in the act of dying, so, on the eve of his departure, Moses sings his noblest strains.

I. OBSERVE THE POET'S AUDITORY. He summons heaven and earth to hear. We read in ancient story that when Orpheus made music with his lyre, the wild beasts listened, and the trees and rocks of Olympus followed him about. This may serve as a just reproof to some men, who, having ears, act as if they had them not. 1. *Heaven and earth may denote both angels and men.* For even "the principalities of heaven learn from the Church the manifold wisdom of God." 2. *Heaven and earth may denote all classes of the people, high and low.* Frequently in Scripture great men are represented as the stars of heaven. The man of ambition is said to lift his head to the stars. The righteous are to shine as the brightness of the firmament. 3. *Heaven and earth may denote the intelligent and the material creation.* On account of man's sin, "the whole creation groaneth;" and the effect of man's obedience will be felt beneficially on the material globe. It will increase its fertility, its beauty, its fragrance, its music. "Truth" shall spring out of the earth, and righteousness shall look "down from heaven." "Then shall all the trees of the wood rejoice."

II. THE POET'S BENEFICENT INFLUENCE. "My doctrine shall drop as the rain," etc. (ver. 2). This imagery teaches us: 1. *The silent, unobtrusive power of truth.* It finds it way, quietly and unobserved, to the roots of human judgment and feeling. 2. *It is refreshing.* What a draught of clear water is to a thirsty man, truth is to a healthy, active soul. 3. *It is fertilizing.* It nourishes all good affections, and strengthens every virtue. 4. *It is most suitable.* No fitness can be more manifest than dew for tender grass. Poetic truth is suited to every grade of human understanding.

III. THE POET'S LOFTY THEME. His theme is God; but God is only known as he reveals himself in his Name. 1. He descants upon his majesty, his supreme power, and the splendours of his state. 2. He touches upon his eternal stability. What the unchanging rock is amid the shifting sands, God is—unalterably the same. 3. He dwells upon the perfections of his character ("just and right is he"); upon the perfection of his works, which are incapable of any improvement; upon the perfection of his government ("all his ways are judgment"); and upon the perfection of his speech. He is "a God of truth." He alters nothing, retracts nothing.

IV. THE POET'S MORAL PURPOSE. To restore harmony between man and God. 1. He proclaims man's fallen state: "they have corrupted themselves." Human nature is not as it was when it came from the hands of God. Man holds this tremendous power of ruining his own nature. 2. The mark of sonship has disappeared. "Their spot is not the spot of his children." Childlike docility and submissiveness form the family lineament. 3. This depravity has spread like the virus of disease. The whole race is infected. "They are a perverse and crooked generation." 4. Such conduct is suicidal folly. It is most antagonistic to self-interest. No madman could have acted worse. 5. Such conduct is the basest ingratitude. "Do ye thus requite the Lord?" Consider his claims. Did he not create thee? Has he not been a Father to thee? Has he not redeemed thee? Tender expostulation with the conscience is the poet's mission. For this vocation he has been specially inspired by God. A heavenly spirit breathes through his every word. No higher honour can man attain on earth.—D.

Vers. 7—14.—*History's testimony for God.* A defective character often results from mental indolence. Men do not use their faculties. Did they consider, reflect, and ponder, they would be better men. To call into activity all our powers is an imperative and sacred duty. For this purpose God has given them. Whose am I? whence have I come? what is my business in life? what are my obligations to my Maker?—these are questions possessing transcendent interest, and are vital to our joy. Ask intelligently and thoroughly; then act upon the answers. God's careful provision for Israel had been long-continued, thoughtful, special. No less, probably greater, has been his considerate and far-seeing provision for us.

I. WE NOTE A SPECIAL HABITATION PREPARED BY GOD. 1. Our earth has for untold ages been undergoing preparation as a suitable dwelling-place for man. Rocks have been formed for man's use, treasures of coal and metals have been stored up for his advantage. The soil has been pulverized to receive his seed. A marvellous and pains-taking preparation has been made. 2. Equally conspicuous is God's wisdom in selecting special territory for special nations. Amidst all the hurly-burly of war, the unseen hand of God has "divided to the nations their inheritance." Oceans and rivers, mountains and deserts, have been God's walls of partition. 3. All these selections have been subordinate to Israel's welfare. All the lines of God's government met here. To Israel's good everything was to bend. 4. The reason of this is declared. "The Lord's portion is his people." Some location on earth was to be reserved for Jehovah. He too had chosen a dwelling-place, an inheritance. And his habitation was in the hearts of his people Israel. "For to that man will I look, and with him dwell, who is of an humble and contrite spirit." "Jacob is the lot of his inheritance."

II. SPECIAL TRAINING BY GOD. 1. Apart from God, earth would be a barren desert. Man's environment, where God is not, would be discordant, unsuitable, painful. The flowers and fruits of life are divinely provided. 2. Inscrutable are the methods of God's training. "He led him about." A masterly hand is in the matter, and we are very incompetent critics. Those marches and counter-marches in the wilderness were all needful to nourish robust courage and simple faith in the Hebrews. In God's arrangements no waste is permitted. 3. Tenderest kindness is here expressed. "He kept him as the apple of his eye." We count the eye among our most precious endowments. It is protected by the most clever contrivances. No part of the body is so delicate or so susceptible of pain. So God regards his chosen people. As a man guards from harm his eye, so God guards his own. 4. Consummate skill was expended to develop the best qualities of Israel. This is set forth by a piece of impressive imagery. As the eagle knows the perils of indolence, and is anxious to train her young brood to early self-exertion, she breaks up the nest, takes the eaglets on her strong pinions, bears them heavenward, shakes them free, then, as they sink, darts beneath them, bears them up again, and encourages them to seek the sun; so, by a thousand kind devices, God taught his people "to seek the things which are above." So precious an end is worthy of the largest expenditure of means.

III. DOMINION OVER NATURE AND OVER MAN ACCORDED BY GOD. In proportion as man has loyally served his God, man has gained earthly dominion. To Adam was accorded sovereignty over all living things in air, or earth, or sea; and of the second Adam we read, "Thou hast put all things under his feet." 1. Victory over enemies is secured. "He made him ride on the high places of the earth." Every mountain fortress was, one by one, possessed. To ride is significant of military conquest. The triumphs of Israel were swift, signal, and complete. 2. The peaceful conquest of nature followed. To the arts of industry, the earth yielded in sevenfold profusion. The olives on the rugged hills filled their presses with oil. Wild bees toiled early and late to lay up stores of honey. Their cattle, plentifully fed, yielded butter and milk in abundance. Under the curse of civil strife and petty feuds of the Canaanites, crops had been devastated, and flocks had been destroyed. Now, peace reigned in every valley, and the very trees blossomed with ruddy gladness. Hill and plain poured their unceasing tributes at the feet of lordly man. 3. The sole Author of this splendid inheritance was God. "The Lord alone did lead him." The deities of the Amorites (if they had any power at all) had bestowed on their votaries an inheritance of lust and war and ruin. In whatever respect Israel's inheritance was a contrast, it was due to the beneficence of Jehovah. He had blessed them with an ungrudging hand. 'Twas the indulgence of his native instinct to give and to make glad. No sane man among them could reach any other conclusion than that Jehovah was the royal Giver of all. And with one voice they should have made the clear welkin ring with hearty hallelujahs: "The Lord hath done great things for us." The gift was unique. It was conspicuously a deed of grace.—D.

Vers. 15—25.—*Sowing and reaping.* The connection between sin and suffering is natural, organic, and universal. Suffering, in some form, is the proper development of sin. Like the plants of nature, sin has its seed within itself.

I. WE HAVE A CASE OF AGGRAVATED SIN. 1. *It was a wanton abuse of special kindness.* The splendid gifts of providence, which ought to have bound them by golden ties of obligation to God, were erected into barriers to shut out God from them. An inner principle of selfish perverseness turned all food into poison. Instead of gratitude, there was scoffing; instead of loyalty, there was insolence. So it often happens that earthly wealth is an injury instead of a benefit. It detains a man's faith and delight on itself. He exalts his riches into a god. Entering a man's heart, as his professed friends, riches become his secret foes : they sap the foundations of his piety ; they degrade and stultify the man. 2. *The flagrancy of sin is seen in the perversion of privilege.* The Hebrews had been chosen by God to a place of peculiar honour. They had been admitted to a nearer access to his friendship than any other nation. God had called them his sons and daughters. Nothing of good had God withheld from them. For these privileged persons to turn their backs on God, and act as traitors to their Lord, was sin of more than ordinary flagrancy. If such fall from their allegiance, how great must be their fall ! 3. *The course of sin proceeds by perceptible stages.* Sin often begins by culpable *omissions.* There is first negative good, then positive offence. The people began their downward course by being "unmindful" of their Maker. Their sense of dependence on God declined. Then they quite forgot the God who had so often rescued them. The next stage was openly to forsake God. They avoided his presence, neglected his worship. Soon they "lightly esteemed" their Deliverer. If they thought of him at all, it was only to look down on him—yea, to despise him. Yet in a condition of atheism they could not long remain. Their nature demanded that they should worship somewhat. So they set up strange deities ; they sacrificed unto demons. They provoked to jealousy, and to just indignation, the God of Israel. Beyond this it was impossible for human rebellion to proceed. 4. *Sin leads to a terrible alternative,* viz. the worship and service of devils. There is no middle place at which a man can halt. He either grows up into the image of God or into the image of Satan.

II. WE HAVE A CASE OF EQUITABLE PUNISHMENT. 1. *It was the reversal of former good.* He who aforetime had promised them prolific plenty now threatens to "consume the earth with her increase." Instead of the sunlight of his favour, he was about to "hide his face from them." The wheels of providence were to be reversed, and the effect would be to overthrow and to crush them. 2. *God's judgments are tardy.* He did not smite at once. His first strokes were comparatively light, and then he patiently waited what the effect might prove. "I will see what their end shall be." The long-suffering of God is an immeasurable store. He "is slow to anger." Attentively he listens, if so be he may catch some sigh of penitence. "I have surely heard Ephraim bemoaning himself." 3. *We may observe here the equity of God's procedure.* By making his punishments, in great measure, like the sins, the Hebrews would the readier detect their folly and guilt. They had forsaken God : therefore God will "hide his face from them." They had "lightly esteemed" God : therefore he will abhor them. They had "excited his jealousy," by choosing another object of worship : he will excite their jealousy by choosing another nation to fill their place. They had provoked his anger by their choice of vanities : he will provoke their anger by supplanting them with a "foolish nation." The emotions which exist in man have their correspondences in the nature of God. Thus, by stupendous condescension, God accommodates his messages to human understanding—employs a thousand comparisons by which to impress our hearts. 4. *God's agents to execute his behests are numerous and terrible.* A few only are mentioned here, but these may serve as samples of others. Material forces are pressed into service. The atmosphere will be a conveyer of pestilence. Fire is a well-known minister of God. Earthquake and volcano have often been commissioned to fulfil Jehovah's will. As a skilled warrior aims well his deadly arrows upon his foes, so God sends his lightnings abroad out of his quiver. Famine is decreed : "they shall be burnt with hunger." Sickness and fever shall follow : they shall be "devoured with burning heat." Pestiferous insects shall assail them, and wild beasts shall overrun the land. The sword of the invader shall fall with ruthless violence upon young and old—upon babe and veteran. They who escape from one peril shall fall under another. From the hand of God release is impossible.—D.

Vers. 26—29.—*The pleading of Divine wisdom.* The judicial anger of God is not an uncontrollable passion ; it acts in harmony with infinite wisdom. The vast and varied interests of all God's creatures are tenderly considered in the act of judicial retribution. We have here—

I. GOD'S ESTIMATE OF HUMAN DESERT. Were guilty men alone to be considered, no penalty would be too severe as the award for their high-handed offences. Every vestige of merit has disappeared. The consensus of all righteous beings requires unreserved condemnation. Nor can the condemned offender himself escape this conclusion. When his conscience awakes to ponder his guilt, he joins in his own condemnation; he confesses the justice of his sentence. If the demerit of the sinner were the only question to be solved, the answer would be at once forthcoming; the verdict would be complete destruction.

II. WE SEE GOD'S FORESIGHT EMBRACING WIDER INTERESTS. 1. *The advantage of other races is, by God, taken into the account.* What effect upon other nations will the condign punishment of Israel have? Will it make them self-confident, arrogant, defiant? The true king has at heart the well-being of all his subjects. 2. *The honour of God himself must be taken into account.* The public reputation of God is indissolubly bound up with the well-being of his intelligent creatures. His honour is dear to him; for his honour is nothing more than his native excellence illustrated and made known. 3. *How graciously the Most High accommodates his speech to suit the conceptions of men!* As a man may fear the wrath of his foes, so God (to bring his doings within the compass of the human understanding) speaks of himself as the subject of fear. In our present state, we cannot rise to the comprehension of God *as he is:* our knowledge of him is conditioned by our limitations of mind.

III. GOD'S GRIEF FOR HUMAN FOLLY. The tender affection of God in pleading with men to avoid sin is very impressive; but more impressive still are his exclamations of grief when the final step has been taken, and when, for many, recovery is impossible. Thus when Jesus looked down from Olivet upon the guilty metropolis, and knew that the die was cast, he nevertheless wept and said, "How often would I have gathered your children, as a hen her brood; but ye would not! Behold, your house is left unto you desolate!" So too in the Psalms God thus speaks, "Oh that my people had hearkened unto me! that Israel had walked in my ways!" The measure of God's love transcends all known limits; its forms are infinite in their variety! When every remedial measure has been tried in vain, love can only weep.—D.

Ver. 29.—*God's pathetic appeal to men.* Wisdom is far-seeing. Not content with estimating present experiences and fortunes, it embraces the remoter issues of our choice; it takes in all the possibilities of the future.

I. AS THERE HAS BEEN A BEGINNING OF THE PRESENT LIFE, SO THERE WILL COME AN END.

II. THE END OF PROBATIONARY LIFE DEMANDS OUR SERIOUS CONSIDERATION.

III. THE HIGHEST WISDOM FORECASTS THE WHOLE REACH OF LIFE, BOTH PRESENT AND FUTURE.—D.

Vers. 30—35.—*The devil's counterfeit coin.* It is not in the power of Satan to originate any new thing. Knowing that his power is restricted, the utmost he can do is to make spurious imitations of God's good things. His base purpose is to deceive man with spectral illusions. His nefarious design is to raise before the world's eye an empty mirage of a carnal paradise.

I. EVERY MAN CRAVES FOR SOME GROUND OF CONFIDENCE, EXTERNAL TO HIMSELF. To the men of the East, this external foundation of trust was best described as a rock. *What* the solid rock is amid the loose alluvial soil of Egypt, or amid the shifting sand of the desert, *that* God is designed to be unto every man. Complete independence is impossible to created man. He can never be self-contained nor self-nourished. Pure atheism has never been a permanent resting-place for the human heart. When the invisible God is forsaken, the human mind swings toward idolatry. The carnal mind finds delight in a ground of confidence that is visible and tangible. Some god we must have, if it be only the shadowy deity named Fate, or Law, or Chance.

II. COMPLETE CONTRAST EXISTS BETWEEN THE OBJECTS OF HUMAN TRUST. The only point of similarity is the *name.* The devil borrows this, so as the better to throw dust in the eyes of his followers. Our God is a Rock; the world also has its counterfeit rock. By the judgments and verdict of worldly men, *our* Rock differs *in toto* from theirs. Their rock, they acknowledge, is unstable and unreliable. They trust it simply because they know not a better. It is misnamed a rock. Their rock ofttimes deserts them in the hour of greatest need. Ah! fortune, say they, is *fickle*. Very tyrannical and self-willed is fate. But our God is a Rock in very deed. He never forsakes his liege disciples. In the darkest hour he is nearest—the "shadow of a great rock in a weary land." Their misnamed rock encourages them to enter the battle-field, and then forsakes them. They are "sold to the enemy."

III. NOTWITHSTANDING THE CONTRAST IN THESE OBJECTS OF TRUST, THE FALSE IS A CLEVER IMITATION OF THE TRUE. All through life, we find that the false counterfeits the true. The thief puts on the pretence of honesty. The villain trains himself to use fair speech. The adulterer wears the garb of virtue. Beauty is the robe of God, but the devil fabricates meretricious tinsel. He, too, has his "promised land," but it is a fool's paradise. He has his vine, but his vine is the vine of Sodom, which generates drunkenness and unchastity. He also has his fields, but they are fields of Gomorrah. The fruits are pleasant to the eye, but they turn to ashes in the mouth. There is the appearance of grapes, but lo! the juice is gall—the clusters are bitterness itself. And not only is the experience disappointing, it is even disastrous and deadly. This pretended wine is only poison, it is a gilded pill. Cruel deceit has provided this counterfeit banquet. Beneath the glamour of a fair exterior, there is the "serpent's venom." Thus fares it with all who leave their God. They find out the bitter mistake at last. So sang Byron in his last days—

> " The worm, the canker, and the grief
> Are mine alone."

IV. SUCH HUMAN EXPERIENCES OF THE FALSE, GOD USES IN THE GOVERNMENT OF THE WORLD. " Is not this laid up in store with me, and sealed up among my treasures ? " God knew well what the effects of an idolatrous course would be, what bitter vexation and disaster would come at last. But he foresaw that it was better for men that they should pass through this experience than that he should remove the possibility of it. He might have prevented, by exercise of power, the stratagems of the tempter. He might have curtailed Satan's freedom, and put on him chains of darkness from the first. But his infinite wisdom has decided otherwise. He foresees more glorious results from this method, so he patiently waits; he calmly watches the stages of the process. "Their foot," says he, "shall slide *in due time*." "The day of their calamity is at hand." *Now*, it is difficult to discern between a grain of living seed and a grain of dead sand; but put both into the furrowed field, and give them time, so when the day of harvest comes, the man who sowed the sand will be covered with shame, while he who sowed good seed will bear gladly his sheaves into the heavenly garner. Our business now is to discriminate between God's corn and the devil's chaff. " The day will declare it."—D.

Vers. 36—43.—*The final revelation of God's supremacy.* In this inspired song—an epitome of the Bible—Moses looks adown the long vista of history, and discerns what will be the outcome of the whole, viz. to establish on a safe basis the acknowledged supremacy of Jehovah. Truth shall eventually conquer, whatever be her present fortunes; and the supreme authority of Jehovah is a fundamental truth, which must in due time effectually shine forth.

I. HUMAN EXPERIENCE WILL ULTIMATELY CONFIRM THE VANITY AND FUTILITY OF IDOLATRY. Men will accept, at the close of a changeful and bitter experience, what they would not accept at the outset of their course, viz. that there is one God—invisible, supreme, eternal. In the conscious pride of self-will, men will sound all the possible problems of life. They will not at first accept, with the docility of a child-like nature, the *ipse dixit* even of God himself. But when all trust in self and in created power has proved a failure; when all power is gone, and we lie on the battle-field, wounded and helpless;—then we begin to give heed to the heavenly voice. Then the gentle message of God comes, with the charm of evening music, upon the ear—yea, as an anodyne and a balm upon the bleeding heart. In a mood of self-despair, we clutch the hope of the gospel, viz. God manifest to man. God invites us to earnest and profound inquiry. He asks us to give a mature deliverance touching the power and helpfulness of the God whom we have long trusted; and the final experience of men, in all lands and ages, is uniform. "The gods who have not created the heavens and the earth shall perish !"

II. HUMAN EXPERIENCE ATTESTS THE SUPREMACY AND TRIUMPH OF JEHOVAH. "*See* now, that *I*, even *I* am he, and there is no god with me." The eye of man can clearly discern the fact—the foundation-fact of all religion—so soon as the veil of prejudice and sin is removed. The revelation is clear enough, if only the organ of mental vision be in healthful vigour. Without question, God is the sole Arbiter of life and death. No other deity has ever assumed an act of creation. The powers of evil have flourished the wand of a necromancer, and have pretended to effect sudden changes in the conditions of nature; but not one has ever pretended to create a star or to produce a single human life. God is still left upon the throne, as sole and undisputed Monarch.

Eternal existence is another prerogative of Jehovah. Where are now the gods of the heathen? Who now worships Jupiter, or Dagon, or Isis, or Moloch? Their names are historic only. They had a passing popularity, but it has long since vanished. But with solemn form of adjuration, the Most High lifts his hand and swears, "I live for ever!" As in a court of justice men accept the testimony of a fellow-man, when that testimony is given under the sanction of a religious oath; so, in self-consistency, are we bound to accept the asseveration of the eternal God. In pity for his creatures, he also takes the form of oath, and since "he can swear by none greater, he swears by himself."

III. THE ROYAL SUPREMACY OF JEHOVAH IS A GROUND FOR HUMAN JOY. Every perfection of God is suitable material for grateful praise. His power is a security for good men. All our interests are safe, being under the protection of such a Friend. His holiness also affords distinct ground for gladness. Because he is holy, we can cherish a confident hope that we shall be holy too. Hence we "give thanks at the remembrance of his holiness." We rejoice to know that the sceptre of the universe is in the hands of a God who is absolutely and incorruptibly just. We know that "the right" will not long be trodden underfoot of the oppressor. We are assured that the malice and craft of Satan shall not triumph. We heartily rejoice that Jehovah is King of all the earth; for "all things must now work together for good to them that love him."

> "Truth, crushed to earth, shall rise again;
> The eternal years of God are hers;
> But Error, wounded, writhes with pain,
> And dies amid her worshippers."

Most of all, we rejoice in his mercy. "He will be merciful to his land and to his people." We are the very persons who need Divine mercy; for lack of that mercy we die. Not more urgently does the parched land need the liquid shower, than do we, who have so grossly sinned, need Jehovah's mercy. Yet not more sure is the need than the supply. That mercy is made amply secure to all who desire it. As certainly as light streams from the natural sun, so freely and copiously does mercy stream forth from Jehovah's heart. Therefore we do well to "rejoice and to be exceeding glad." For saith Jehovah, "I will pardon your unrighteousness, and your sins and your iniquities will I remember no more." God's revelation closes with the theme of mercy.—D.

Vers. 44—47.—*Religion a reality.* The bulk of men treat religion as if it were a fancy or a myth. They deem it useful for the sick, the aged, and the dying. But for the healthful man and the active man of business it is voted a bore. Now, Moses puts religion in its right place when he declares it vital to human interests—vital, in the highest and largest sense. "It is your life."

I. THE OBJECTS ABOUT WHICH RELIGION TREATS ARE REAL, NOT SHADOWY. "It is not a vain thing." The eye of man cannot embrace God's universe. The material kingdoms are not all. God's creation extends above and beyond the reach of mortal sense. With respect to much that God has made, "eye hath not seen, nor ear heard, nor mind conceived." Science deals with one class of objects, religion with another class. The subject-matter of religion is the most excellent, substantial, and enduring. It treats of God, heaven, eternity, the soul of man—its sins and sorrows, the way to holiness, the hope of everlasting life. These things come not under the cognizance of our sensuous organs; they are more substantial than the granite rocks—more real than jewels.

II. THE TRUTHS CONCERNING RELIGION ARE AUTHENTIC, NOT ILLUSORY. They come to us supported by abundant evidence, both internal and external. They come with a better title to belief than any books of equal antiquity. If we reject Moses and Isaiah, we are bound, in self-consistency, to reject Thucydides and Herodotos, Bede and Gibbon. But to every Christian, the most conclusive evidence is experimental. He has the "witness in himself." The truth, admitted to his mind, has elevated his tastes, enlarged his views, purified his affections, ennobled and beautified his whole nature. As light suits the eye and music the ear, so the truth of Scripture exquisitely suits the needs and aspirations of the soul. It meets a real want.

III. THE HUMAN INTERESTS, WHICH RELIGION PROMOTES, ARE REAL AND PRECIOUS, NOT VAPID OR FANCIFUL. These interests are internal and external; they reach to the family and to the utmost limits of human society; they embrace the present and the unbounded future. Reconciliation with God, the removal of sin, the development of man's best nature, the heritage of inward tranquillity, the conquest of care, the extraction of blessing out of sorrow, a hope that conquers death,—these are among the advantages obtained by religion. It makes men better husbands, better masters, better servants, better citizens, nobler, truer, wiser. It imparts a meetness for the society and the service of heaven. It brings advantage to every relationship and circumstance of human life. "It is not a vain thing;" it is life and health and joy.—D.

Vers. 48—52.—" *Obedient unto death.*" In Moses, Faith had achieved one of her most signal triumphs. From early youth to latest manhood, he had acted and "endured as seeing him who is invisible." No earthly or visible honour had ever enchanted his vision. He had lived very simply "in his Great Taskmaster's eye." Therefore it was that he submitted to be deprived of the earthly Canaan without a murmur, "for he looked for a city which had foundations, whose builder and maker was God." To him death was but a darksome passage to an enduring home.

I. THE GODLY MAN DIES AT GOD'S COMMAND. In this respect, Moses was a type of Christ, and has left us an example deserving our imitation. It should be enough for us to know that God requires it. It is no accident—no unforeseen event. Every circumstance touching the believer's death is wisely arranged by God. "Precious in the sight of the Lord is the death of his saints." Our Elder Brother has passed the dark valley before us, and his presence lights up the once gloomy way. "I will fear no evil, for thou art with me." At the girdle of our Captain hang "the keys of death and of Hades." "He opens, and no man shuts." To the genuine disciple death is no terror. "It is my Father's voice I hear. I see his beckoning hand. I feel his sustaining arm." "Death is swallowed up in victory."

II. THE GODLY MAN'S DEATH IS PARTLY JUDICIAL, PARTLY MERCIFUL. To the full-grown and ripe Christian, earth has little attraction. Its joys pall upon the taste. We aspire after nobler and better things. "I would not live alway." A time comes in the good man's history when he wishes the probation to close, and the real life to begin. The heir longs for his majority and for the ancestral heritage. The believer dies because death is the most convenient portal by which he can enter heaven.

Yet judgment is mingled with the mercy. Moses was on the tiptoe of earthly expectancy—on the threshold of a great success, when God required him to relinquish all for heaven. To him it was revealed, in clearest form, that earlier sin required this late correction. For Israel's sake, for the world's sake, and for Moses' sake, his trespass must bear fruitage in loss and sorrow. In the very nature of things, it is impossible that men can sin without privation of some kind. We may flatter ourselves, at times, that God has winked at our folly, and that no ill consequence has ensued. But judge not prematurely. Possibly, in our last hours of life, the remembrance of that sin will rob us of our peace, will impose some serious loss. In the moral realm, " whatsoever a man sows, that shall he also reap."

III. THE GODLY MAN DEPARTS THIS LIFE FROM THE MOUNTAIN-PEAKS OF PERSONAL ATTAINMENT. There were solid reasons in the Divine mind (partly hidden and partly revealed) why Moses should die upon the mount. He might have viewed the magnificent prospects, and then have descended to die. But mountains have often been selected by God as the scene of grand events. On the summit of a mountain we are inspired with a sense of awe. We take in the sense of the infinite. We are constrained to worship. Thence we are already half disposed to mount and soar to heaven. This is suggestive. When through much active energy of faith we have climbed the heights of practical holiness, we feel that the work of life is done. We have finished our course. There has been steady advancement thus far, and now, what next? We feel that the world is beneath our feet; and from this pinnacle of moral elevation we wait the revelation of the future, we prepare for the strange transition.

From such an elevation of faith, too, we clearly discern the scene of the Church's future conquests. The past is a light which irradiates the prospective triumphs of truth and holiness. "Much land remains to be possessed;" but the assurance of success is absolute. Already the foes of God are at our feet. "He must reign."

IV. THE GODLY MAN'S DEPARTURE IS NOT TO SOLITUDE, BUT TO SOCIETY. "Thou shalt be gathered unto thy people." Whatever thoughts, or hopes, or fears this language of God suggested to Moses' mind, it suggests to our minds one of the charms of heaven. We love to think of it as a home. Next to the ecstasy which God's presence shall inspire, is the rapture of reunion with departed friends. "In my Father's house are many mansions." No question need distress us touching mutual recognition. Moses and Elijah were recognized as such when they came down in glorified state, and conversed with Jesus on the mount. Not a faculty shall be wanting there which we possessed here. "Then shall we know, even as also we are known." If men from distant climes shall "sit down with Abraham, Isaac, and Jacob, in the kingdom of God," one main element of honour and of joy would be missed unless these illustrious patriarchs were known.—D.

EXPOSITION.

CHAPTER XXXIII.

MOSES' BLESSING.

Before ascending Mount Nebo, to take a view of the land he was not permitted to enter and then to die, Moses took farewell of the people he had so long guided and ruled, by pronouncing on them a blessing in their several tribes. This blessing was probably spoken on the same day as the song recorded in the preceding chapter, and to the same assembly. The one may be regarded as the counterpart of the other. In the song, Moses dwells chiefly on the calamities that were to befall the people because of their apostacy; in the blessing, he depicts the benefits that were to be enjoyed by them through the Divine favour. The tone of the one is sombre and minatory; the tone of the other is serene and cheering. The one presents the darker side, the other the brighter side, of Israel's fortunes. Both were fitting utterances for the occasion: the one the farewell warning, the other the farewell benediction, of him who had so long proved them and known their ways; who, whilst he desired their

welfare, feared they might forfeit this by their folly and sin; and who sought, both by warning and by blessing, to encourage them to pursue that course by which alone prosperity and happiness could be secured.

The blessing consists of a series of benedictions on the several tribes (vers. 6—25), preceded by an introduction (vers. 1—5), and followed by a conclusion (vers. 26—29).

Vers. 1—5.—*Introduction.* The blessing opens with an allusion to the making of the covenant and the giving of the Law at Sinai, when the Lord revealed himself in glory and majesty as the King of Israel, in order at the outset to fix the minds of the people on the source whence alone blessing could come to them. God's love to Israel is celebrated, and the intention and end of his choice and elevation of Israel to be his people is declared.

Ver. 1.—**Moses the man of God.** This appellation is applied to Moses only here and in Josh. xiv. 6 and the heading of Ps. xc. The phrase, "man of God," indicates one favoured with Divine communications, and employed as God's messenger to men (cf. 1 Sam. ix. 6; 1 Kings xii. 22). In this heading, the author of the blessing is clearly distinguished from the person by whom it was inserted in this place.

Ver. 2.—**And he said.** Here begin the words of Moses. He commences by depicting the majesty of Jehovah as he appeared to Israel when he came to make the covenant with them and give them his Law. **The Lord came from Sinai, and rose up from Seir unto them,** etc. *Seir* is the mountain land of Edom to the east of Sinai. **Mount Paran** is probably the range of lofty hills which form the southern boundary of the promised land to the north of the desert of Et-Tîh. These places are not mentioned as scenes of different manifestations of the Divine glory, but as indicating the extent to which the one manifestation given at Sinai reached. The light of the Divine glory that rested on Sinai was reflected also from the mountains of Seir and Paran (cf. Hab. iii. 3; Judg. v. 4). **He came with ten thousands of saints;** rather, *he came from ten thousands of holy ones;* literally, *out from myriads of holiness;* i.e. "from his celestial seat, where myriads of angels surround his throne" (Rosenmüller). The rendering "with," though that of the Targum, LXX., and Vulgate, cannot be retained; nor does Scripture represent God as attended by angels when he comes forth to manifest his glory to men. They are represented as surrounding his throne in heaven (1 Kings xxii. 19; Job i. 6; Dan. vii. 10), as his servants awaiting his behest, and his host that do his pleasure (Gen. xxviii. 12; xxxii. 2, 3; Ps. ciii. 21); and God is represented as dwelling in the midst of them (Ps. lxviii. 17). Hence he is represented here as coming forth from among them to manifest himself to his people. **A fiery law.** There is a various reading here; instead of אֵשׁ דָּת, fire of law, many codices have אשדת in one word, and this is supported by the Samaritan text and other authorities, and is accepted by most critics and interpreters. It is a fatal objection to the textual reading that דַּת is not a Semitic word, but one of Persian origin, brought by the Jews from Babylonia, and found only in the post-exilian books (Esth. i. 8, 19; ii. 8, 12; iii. 8, 14; iv. 11, 15; Ezra vii. 12, 21; viii. 36; Dan. ii. 9, 13, 15; vi. 5, 9, 13, 16); and in them as applied to the Law of God only by heathens. It is, therefore, altogether improbable that this word should be found in any Hebrew writing anterior to the Captivity. Besides, what is the sense of אֵשׁ דַּת, supposing דַּת to mean "law"? The words cannot be rendered, as in the Authorized Version, by "fiery law;" they can only be rendered by "a fire, a law," or "a fire of law," and what either of these may mean it is not easy to see. The ancient versions vary here very considerably: LXX., ἐκ δεξιῶν αὐτοῦ ἄγγελοι

μετ᾽ αὐτοῦ: Vulgate, *In dextera ejus ignea lex;* Targum of Onkelos, "Written by his right hand, from the midst of the fire, a law gave he to us;" Syriac, "With myriads of his saints at his right hand. He gave to them, and also caused all peoples to love them." The best Hebrew manuscripts have אשדת as one word. The Masoretic note is, "The *Chatiph* is one word, and the *K'ri* two." The word אשדת is best explained as a compound of אֵשׁ, fire, and שִׁרָא, an Aramaic word signifying to throw or dart; the Syriac ‎ܫܪܐ, or the Hebrew יָרָה, having the same signification, so that the meaning is "fire-dartings:" from his right hand went rays of fire like arrows shot forth (cf. Hab. iii. 4; Exod. xix. 16). **To them;** i.e. to the Israelites, to whom this manifestation was vouchsafed.

Ver. 3.—**Yea, he loved the people.** The proper rendering is, *he loveth peoples* (עַמִּים). This is generally understood of the tribes of Israel; but some would understand it of nations in general, on the ground that such is the proper meaning of the word, as in ch. xxxii. 8 and other places. A reference to nations at large, however, would seem incongruous here; and the use of the word in relation to Israel in such passages as Gen. xxviii. 3; Judg. v. 14; Isa. iii. 13; Hos. x. 14; Zech. xi. 10, justifies the taking it so here. **All his saints are in thy hand.** The people of Israel are here called God's saints, or holy ones, because they were chosen by and consecrated to him. It is not probable, as some suggest, that the angels are here intended. The change from the third person to the second is not uncommon in Hebrew poetry (cf. ch. xxxii. 15; Ps. xlix. 14, etc.). **They sat down at thy feet.** The verb rendered "sat down" here (תֻּכּוּ) is found only in this passage, and is of uncertain meaning. Kimchi explains it as "they *united* or *assembled together to follow thy steps;*" Knobel makes it "*they wandered at thy feet,*" and understands it of Israel's following the lead of Jehovah in the wilderness, when the ark of the covenant preceded them in their march; Gesenius and Fürst, "*they lie down at thy feet.*" This last is accepted by Keil, and seems to have most in its favour. **Every one shall receive of thy words.** Some render here, *they rise up at thy words;* but though the verb נָשָׂא is sometimes used intransitively, it is properly an active verb, and there seems no reason why it should not be so regarded here: *every one receives* [the singular, יִשָּׂא, used distributively] *thy words.*

Ver. 4.—Moses here, identifying himself with the people, uses the third person, and includes himself among those to whom the

Law was given; cf. Ps. xx., xxi., where David not only speaks of himself in the third person, but addresses such prayers for himself as could only be offered by the people for their king (cf. also Judg. v. 12, 15; Hab. iii. 19). **Even the inheritance of the congregation.** The "even," which the translators of the Authorized Version have inserted here, were better omitted; the words are in apposition to "law." The Law which Moses communicated to Israel was to remain with them as the inheritance of the congregation. The Bishops' Bible and the Geneva Version have, more correctly, "for an inheritance of the congregation."

Ver. 5.—Some refer this to Moses, but Moses was never recognized as king in Israel: he "was faithful in all his house as a servant" (Heb. iii. 5); but Jehovah alone was King (Exod. xv. 18; Ps. xlvii. 6, 7). **Jeshurun** (cf. ch. xxxii. 5). The gathering together refers to the assembling of the people at Sinai, when Jehovah came forth as their King to give them his Law.

Vers. 6—25.— *Blessings on the tribes individually.* With these may be compared the blessing which Jacob pronounced on his sons as representing the tribes of which they were the heads. The two resemble each other in many points; the differences are such as naturally arose from the different relations of the speakers to the objects of their address, and the changes in the condition and prospects of the tribes which during the lapse of centuries had come to pass.

Ver. 6.—**And let not his men be few.** The negative, though not expressed in the Hebrew, is to be carried into this clause from the preceding. Though the rights of primogeniture had been withdrawn from Reuben, and Jacob had declared that he should not excel, Moses here assures the tribe of continuance, and even prosperity. Their number was not to be small; which was, perhaps, said to comfort them, in view of the fact that their numbers had greatly diminished in the course of their wanderings in the desert (comp. Numb. i. 21 with xxvi. 7). At no time, however, was this tribe numerous as compared with the others; nor was it ever distinguished either by the enterprise of its members or by the eminence of any of them in the councils of the nation or the management of affairs.

Ver. 7.—The blessing on Judah is in the form of prayer to Jehovah. As Jacob had promised to Judah supremacy over his brethren and success in war, so Moses here names him next after Reuben, whose pre-eminence he had assumed, and prays for him that, going forth at the head of the tribes, he might return in triumph, being helped of the Lord. **Let his hands be sufficient for him**; rather, *with his hands he contendeth for it* (to wit, *his people*). רָב here is not the adj. much, enough, but the part. of the verb רִיב, to contend, to strive; and יָדָיו is the accus. of instrument. The rendering in the Authorized Version is grammatically possible; but the meaning thereby brought out is not in keeping with the sentiment of the passage; for if Judah's hands, *i.e.* his own power and resources, were sufficient for him, what need had he of help from the Lord?

Vers. 8—11.—The blessing on Levi is also in the form of a prayer. In Jacob's blessing, Simeon is joined with Levi, but Moses passes him over altogether, probably because, as Jacob foretold, he was to be scattered among his brethren (Gen. xlix. 7), and so lose his tribal individuality. Simeon, however, is included in the general blessing pronounced on Israel; and as this tribe received a number of towns within the territory of Judah (Josh. xix. 2—9), it was probably regarded as included in the blessing on that tribe. **Thy Thummim and thy Urim**; *thy Right and thy Light* (cf. Exod. xxviii. 30). The high priest wore the breast-plate on which these were placed when he went in before the Lord; and this is here represented as the prerogative of the whole tribe. **Thy holy one;** *i.e.* Levi, the tribe-father, representing the whole tribe to which the blessing applies; hence in the following verses the verb passes into the plural. For "holy one," it would be better to read "pious" or "godly one;" literally, *the man thy pious one.* Some would render "the man thy favoured one," or "the man of thy friendship;" but this is wholly arbitrary, the word (חָסִיד) has no such meaning. To explain this more particularly, reference is made to the trials at **Massah and the waters of Meribah** (strife), when the people rebelled and murmured against Moses and Aaron, whereby the piety of these men was put to the test, and in them, the heads of the tribe of Levi, the whole tribe was proved. (On Massah, see Exod. xvii. 1—7; and on the waters of strife, see Numb. xx. 1—13.) In these trials, Levi had proved himself faithful and godly, having risen up in defence of the honour of Jehovah, and in support of his covenant, though in the latter case both Moses and Aaron stumbled. **Who said unto his father and to his mother**, etc. This refers to what is narrated in Exod. xxxii. 26—29, when the Levites drew their swords against their brethren at the command of Moses, to execute judgment without respect of person, because of the sin of the people in the matter of the golden calf (cf. also Numb. xxv. 8, and, for the principle here implicitly commended, see Matt. x. 37; xix. 29; Luke

xiv. 26). Because of their zealous devotion to the claims and service of the Lord, the dignity of the priesthood had been conferred on this tribe; and to them belonged the high office of being instructors of the people in Divine things, and of presenting the sacrifices of the people to the Lord. For those entrusted with such an office, nothing was more to be desired than that they should be blessed with power rightly to discharge the duties of their office, that their service should be accepted with favour, and that their enemies and haters should be foiled and rendered impotent; and for this Moses prays on their behalf.

Ver. 12.—Benjamin, the beloved of his father, is also the beloved of the Lord, and would be cared for and protected by him. **Shall dwell in safety by him;** *shall dwell securely upon him,* i.e. resting on him. **Shall cover him.** The word rendered "cover" (חֹפֵף) occurs only here; construed with עַל, upon, it conveys the idea of sheltering: he continually is sheltering him. **And he shall dwell between his shoulders.** "To be between the shoulders" is to be carried on the back (cf. 1 Sam. xvii. 6); and as a father might thus bear his child, so should Benjamin be borne of the Lord. There can be no doubt that Benjamin is the subject of this clause; to understand it of Jehovah dwelling on the shoulders of Benjamin, in the sense of having the temple, the place of his rest, within the territory of Benjamin, is too violent and far-fetched an interpretation to be admitted. In the change of subject in the three clauses of this verse, there is nothing strange, since such a change repeatedly occurs, and is found even in prose, as e.g. 2 Sam. xi. 13. "To dwell upon God, and between his shoulders, means as much as to lean upon him; the similitude being taken from fathers who carry their sons while yet small and tender" (Calvin).

Vers. 13—17.—The blessing on Joseph by Moses closely resembles that pronounced by Jacob on his favourite son; he solicits for him the utmost abundance of temporal blessing, and the riches of the Divine favour. There is this difference, however, between the two blessings, that in that of the patriarch it is the growth of the tribe in power and might that is chiefly contemplated; whilst in that of Moses it is the advance of the tribe in wealth, prosperity, and influence that is chiefly indicated. "Jacob described the growth of Joseph under the figure of a luxuriant branch of a fruit tree planted by the water; whilst Moses fixes his eye primarily upon the land of Joseph, and desires for him the richest productions" (Keil). **For the precious things of heaven, for the dew.** Several codices, for מִטַּל, "for dew," read מֵעָל, above—"the precious

things of heaven above;" and this reading, some critics of eminence adopt. Probably, however, this is only a correction, to bring this passage into accordance with Gen. xlix. 25. The Targums and the Peshito combine both readings. Instead of "*for* the precious things," it is better to read "*with,*" etc., and so throughout vers. 13—16. Literally, it is *from,* etc.; מִמֶּגֶד, the מ expressing the instrumental cause of the blessing, of which the Lord is the efficient cause. The noun מֶגֶד, literally, *excellency, preciousness,* occurs only here and in Cant. iv. 13, 16 and vii. 13, where it is rendered by "pleasant." The precious fruit of the heavens is the dew, which, with the waters stored up in the recesses of the earth, furthers the growth of the earth's produce, ripened by the influences of sun and moon. **And for the chief things of the ancient mountains;** literally, *and from the head of the mountains of old.* The precious things of the mountains and hills are the vines and olive trees with which the lower slopes are adorned, and the forests that crown the loftier. **The good will of him that dwelt in the bush.** The reference is to the appearance of Jehovah to Moses in the bush at Horeb (Exod. iii.), when he manifested himself as the Deliverer of Israel, whose good pleasure it was that they should be redeemed from bondage and favoured with blessing. That was **separated from his brethren;** separated in the sense of *consecrated,* or *distinguished* (נְזִיר, from נָזַר, to consecrate), from among his brethren. **His glory** is like **the firstling of his bullock;** rather, *the firstborn of his oxen, majesty is to him.* The singular, שׁוֹר, is here used collectively, as in ch. xv. 19. The oxen are Joseph's sons, all of whom were strong, but the firstborn excelled the rest, and was endowed with majesty. It is Ephraim that is referred to, whom Jacob raised to the position of the firstborn (Gen. xlviii. 8, etc.). **His horns** are like **the horns of unicorns;** literally, *and horns of a reëm are his horns.* The reëm is supposed to be the aurochs, an animal of the bovine species, allied to the buffalo, now extinct, but which the Assyrian bas-reliefs show to have been formerly hunted in that region (cf. Job xxxix. 9, etc.; Ps. xxii. 22; Rawlinson 'Anc. Mon.,' i. 284). By his strong power, Ephraim should thrust down nations, even the most distant. **And they are the ten thousands of Ephraim;** *and these are,* etc.; *i.e.* in such might will the myriads of Ephraim come forth. To Ephraim, as the chief, the myriads are assigned; to Manasseh only the thousands.

Vers. 18, 19.—Zebulun and Issachar, the two last sons of Leah, are taken together by Moses; and Zebulun, though the younger son, is placed first, in accordance with Gen.

xlix. 13. Success in enterprise, and felicity at home, are assured to both. "Although 'going out' (enterprise, labour) is attributed to Zebulun, and 'remaining in tents' (the comfortable enjoyment of life) to Issachar, in accordance with the delineation of their respective characters in the blessing of Jacob, this is to be attributed to the poetic parallelism of the clauses, and the whole is to be understood as applying to both in the sense suggested by Graf, 'Rejoice, Zebulun and Issachar, in your labour and your rest'" (Keil). **They shall call the people unto the mountain;** rather, *they shall call nations to the mountain,* i.e. the mountain of the Lord's inheritance (Exod. xv. 17), the place of his sanctuary. **Sacrifices of righteousness;** *i.e.* sacrifices offered according to God's Law, and in a manner and a spirit well pleasing to him (Ps. iv. 6; li. 21). **They shall suck of the abundance of the seas,** etc. The treasures of both sea and land should be theirs. The Targumist Jonathan Ben Uzziel explains this as referring especially to the obtaining of the rich purple dye from the shell of the oyster (*murex Syrius*), and the producing of mirrors and glass vases from the sand. The existence of vitreous sand on the coast of Zebulun is attested both by Strabo (lib. xvi. p. 757) and Pliny ('Nat. Hist.,' lib. xxxvi. c. 286).

Vers. 20, 21.—As in the blessing of Shem by Noah, God is praised for Shem's prosperity (Gen. ix. 26), so here God is praised for the enlargement of the warlike tribe of Gad (cf. Gen. xlix. 19). **He dwelleth as a lion;** rather, *as a lioness.* Though the noun לָבִיא has a masc. termination, usage shows that it was the female and not the male that was thereby designated (see *e.g.* Gen. xlix. 9; Numb. xxiv. 9, where it can hardly be a mere synonym; and Job iv. 11; xxxviii. 39, where the reference to the young of the animal accords better with the lioness than with the lion, Gesenius). **Ver.** 21 refers to Gad's obtaining an inheritance for himself from Moses beyond Jordan. **And he provided the first part for himself;** literally, *and he saw for himself* (i.e. chose) *the first,* i.e. either the most excellent part or the firstfruits of the conquest. **Because there, in a portion of the lawgiver, was he seated;** rather, *for there the portion of the leader was reserved.* The word rendered "lawgiver," or "leader" (מְחֹקֵק), signifies primarily one who ordains or appoints, and is used in both the above senses (cf. Exod. xxxiii. 22; Judg. v. 14); it is here applied to Gad, because that tribe displayed such promptitude and energy at the head of the tribes in the conquest of the land, that it might be regarded as their leader. An entirely different view of the passage has been

taken by some, who by the *mechokek* understand Moses as the lawgiver, and his portion as the place of his grave, which was concealed, but was within the inheritance of Gad. But it is a fatal objection to this view that not only is the word rendered "portion" (חֶלְקָת) nowhere used of a grave, but the grave of Moses on Mount Nebo was in the territory of Reuben, not in that of Gad. Gesenius renders, "The portion of (assigned by) the lawgiver was preserved." But this does not tally with the immediately preceding statement, that Gad *chose* his portion for himself; at any rate, it could not be *because* of this that he chose it. Gad chose for himself a portion on the east of Jordan, and the portion he had chosen was sacredly kept for him, though he went with his brethren to the conquest of Canaan. **And he came with the heads of the people;** *i.e.* his place of marching was with the leaders; his place was at the head of the tribes (cf. Numb. xxxii. 17, 21, 32, and Josh. i. 14; iv. 12). **He executed the justice of the Lord,** etc.; *i.e.* he did what God required of him, obeying his commands, and thereby fulfilling all righteousness (cf. Matt. iii. 15; Phil. iii. 6). **With Israel;** in the fellowship of Israel.

Ver. 22.—Jacob compared Dan to a serpent that suddenly springs forth by the way, and bites the heels of a horse so that the rider falls backward. Moses here compares the tribe to a young lion that suddenly leaps from its lair in Bashan on the object of its attack. Both similitudes relate to the vigour and force which the tribe should display in conflict.

Ver. 23.—In Jacob's blessing, Naphtali appears invested with the attributes of freedom, gracefulness, and graciousness; here Moses assures that tribe of the Divine grace and blessing, and promises to it prosperity and felicity. **Possess thou the west and the south.** The word rendered "west" here (יָם) properly means sea, and came to signify "west" from the fact of the Mediterranean, or Great Sea, lying to the west of Palestine. The proper meaning of the word is to be retained here. As the territory of Naphtali lay in the north of Canaan, and was far from the sea, the blessing here pronounced upon him must be understood generally of prosperity and felicity. He was to possess riches as of the sea, and genial and fructifying warmth as of the south.

Vers. 24, 25.—Asher, the prosperous one, as his name implies, was to be rich, and honoured, and strong, and peaceful. **Blessed with children;** rather, *blessed among the sons;* i.e. either blessed more than the rest of the sons, or blessed by the sons who were to reap benefit from him. From what follows, the latter explanation seems the one to be preferred. The preposition מִן is constantly used as indicating the source whence anything proceeds, or the agent by whom anything is done. **Let him be acceptable to his brethren;** "iis e terræ suæ proventibus res optimas suppeditaturus; cf. Gen. xlix. 20" (Rosenmüller). This tribe should find itself in so advantageous and luxurious a condition that the other tribes should have delight and pleasure in it" (Knobel). Others render, "favoured among his brethren;" favoured, that is, by the Lord more than his brethren (Keil). But the former seems preferable. **And let him dip his foot in oil.** This points to a land abounding in olives, and generally richly fertile, a fat land and yielding rich dainties, such as Jacob promised to Asher (Gen. xlix. 20). **Thy shoes shall be iron and brass.** The word rendered "shoes" (מִנְעָל) occurs only here. It is a derivative from נָעַל, to bolt or shut fast, and is to be taken in the sense of a fastness or fortress, a place securely closed: *iron and brass shall be thy fortress;* i.e. his dwelling should be strong and impregnable. The rendering "shoes" is from a supposed derivation of the word from נַעַל, a shoe. **As thy days,** so shall **thy strength** be; literally, *as thy days, thy rest;* i.e. as long as thou livest, so long shalt thou have rest and quiet. The noun rendered "strength" (דֹּבֶא) in the Authorized Version, occurs only here, unless it be found in the proper name מֵידְבָא (*Medeba*), and has no cognate in Hebrew; but the Arabic supplies a root for it in دبى (*deba*), to rest. Fürst connects it with דֹּב, and the Targum with דְּוָא, to flow, and translates by "riches."

Vers. 26—29.—As Moses commenced by celebrating the glorious majesty of Jehovah when he appeared to establish his covenant with Israel, so he concludes with a reference to God as the eternal Refuge and the saving Help of his people.

Ver. 26.—**There is none like unto the God of Jeshurun.** The points and accents direct that this should be read, *There is none like God, O Jeshurun;* and though all the ancient versions read as does the Authorized Version, the Masoretic punctuation is vindicated here by the following **thy help,** which shows that Israel is here addressed.

Ver. 27.—God is the Refuge or Dwelling-place of his people, their Protection amid the storms of life, and the unfailing Source of comfort and blessing to them in their pilgrimage state. Over them is his sheltering protection, and underneath them the support of his everlasting arms.

Ver. 28.—The clauses of this verse are parallel to each other; their symmetry will be seen if we render and arrange thus—

> "And Israel dwelleth securely,
> Alone, the fountain of Jacob,
> On a land of corn and new wine;
> His heavens also drop down dew."

The **fountain of Jacob** is parallel to **Israel.** Israel is so designated because they came forth from Jacob as waters from a copious source (Ibn Ezra; cf. Isa. xlviii. 1; Ps. lxviii. 26).

Ver. 29.—"This concluding verse comprehends the whole blessing. Israel is to be congratulated and praised because, through the true God, it has unparalleled protection, salvation, and triumph" (Herxheimer). **Thine enemies shall be found liars unto thee;** literally, *shall feign unto thee;* i.e. shall pretend to be thy friends, in order to obtain favour with thee. The verb conveys the idea of fawning upon a person with a feigned humility and submissiveness (cf. Ps. xviii. 44; lxvi. 2; lxxxi. 15). **Thou shalt tread upon their high places;** *i.e.* shalt wholly subdue them and triumph over them (cf. ch. xxxii. 13); "arces eorum in montibus positas, loca eorum inaccessa victor calcabis, iis potieris; qua ipsa phrasi, Am. iv. 13, Mic. i. 3, superbe incedens victor describitur" (Rosenmüller).

HOMILETICS.

Vers. 1—5.—The general import of this paragraph is clear. Some of its phrases, however, are far from being so easy that we can be quite sure of their meaning. (For a discussion of the points in dispute, see the Exposition; also Keil, Lange, and a work far too little known, Barrett's 'Synopsis of Criticisms,' vol. i. pt. 2.) There is, however, quite enough that is sufficiently clear to furnish us with a topic for valuable pulpit teaching, albeit there may be, in this introductory paragraph and between each blessing, indications of an editor's hand. The whole paragraph has reference to God's august manifestation of himself at the delivery of the Law on Sinai. In it there are eight matters to be noted. 1. The new disclosure of God was as the rising of a bright light in the midst of the darkness (see Gesenius, *sub verb.* זָרַח (*zāh-ra‘gh'*), and *all* the uses of the verb in the

Old Testament). 2. The beams of the newly risen light flooded the region of Sinai, Mount Paran, and Mount Seir (ver. 2). 3. In the displays of his glory, Jehovah was attended by ten thousands of his holy ones (ver. 2). 4. From Jehovah thus attended there went forth a Law (ver. 2). 5. This Law thus given was the expression of Jehovah's love (ver. 3). 6. All the holy ones (English Version, "saints") thus surrounding Jehovah, were at his disposal, to serve the people of his choice, and reverently waited for his words of command (ver. 3). 7. The Law thus given in august majesty was the rich inheritance of the people (ver. 4). 8. On a people so honoured of God, the man of God is moved to utter a blessing, as his last act ere he quits the scene of toil for the realm of rest (ver. 1). The exposition and illustration of all this will furnish Christian preachers and teachers in every age with abundance of material for the understanding, heart, conscience, and life.

Ver. 6.—*The blessing of Reuben; or, life impoverished through ancestral sins.* For a blessing, there seems something unusually weak in that pronounced on Reuben. Continuance—a preservation from being blotted out of existence—is all that the man of God seems to hope or expect from him. The English reader may wonder to see that the word "not" is in italics, as not being in the Hebrew, but supplied by the translators. It is, however, wisely done in this case, as will be seen if the reader will put stress sufficient on the word "*not*" in the following rendering to carry the force of the negative on to the end of the sentence :—"Let Reuben live; and *not* die and his men be few;" *i.e.* if his men became a mere handful, the tribe would be virtually extinct; and Moses desires that this may not be the case; so that, according to English idiom, the insertion of the italic *not* is required to preserve the meaning of the original. The gist of the blessing then is, let not the tribe have such a paucity of men as to sink out of sight altogether. Bare continuance;—this is all that is prophesied concerning that tribe. This is, as far as we can follow its history, in strict correspondence with its after experience. There may be noted again and again a decrease in its numbers; cf. Numb. i. 21; xxvi. 7; 1 Chron. v. 18, from which it appears "that the tribe had decreased since the Exodus, and also that in later times its numbers, even when counted with the Gadites and the half of Manasseh, were fewer than that of the Reubenites alone at the census of Numb. i. They took possession of a large and fertile district east of Jordan. Occupied with their flocks and herds, they appear soon after the days of Joshua to have lost their early energy: they could not be roused to take part in the national rising against Jabin (Judg. v. 15, 16). They do not seem to have cared to complete the conquest of their own territory; and even the cities assigned them were wrested from them by the Moabites. While from this tribe no judge, prophet, or national hero arose" to redeem it from insignificance (see 'Speaker's Commentary,' *in loc.*, to which we are indebted for the above details). We are not at a loss to account for this. The gross wickedness of the head of this tribe left a stain upon its name which not generation after generation could wipe out, and "destroyed at once the prestige of birth, and the spirit of leader-ship" (J. L. Porter [1]). Hence our topic for homiletic treatment—a topic which no teacher who desires to declare the "whole counsel of God" can forbear to touch upon in due season. It is this—*Life impoverished through ancestral sins* (see Gen. xxxv. 22; xlix. 4).

I. THERE ARE CERTAIN SINS—SINS OF THE FLESH—TO WHICH MEN GENERALLY ARE LIABLE; WHICH TO SOME CONSTITUTIONS PRESENT THEMSELVES AS TEMPTATIONS SPECIALLY STRONG. In every one there is some weak point, at which seductive influences may easily enter: "Every one is tempted, when he is drawn away of his own lust (ὑπὸ τῆς ἰδίας ἐπιθυμίας) and enticed."

II. THERE ARE NO SINS WHICH WORK GREATER HAVOC IN A MAN THAN THOSE TO WHICH REUBEN GAVE WAY. The desperately wicked act recorded of him indicates with too much certainty a previously formed habit of self-indulgence, in which he had suffered the reins of self-control and self-respect to fall from his hands. The effect of such habits in a physiological point of view is disastrous. But more grievous still are their moral issues. They lower the man himself in his own eyes. They lower his view of mankind

---

[1] See Mr. Porter's valuable article on 'The Tribe of Reuben,' in Dr. Alexander's edition of Kitto's 'Bibl. Cyc.'

at large. They lead inevitably to the association of thought with what is lowest in human nature, rather than with what is highest and best. And, unless renounced, these sins will drag the whole man after them, and make of him a wreck and a ruin. Hence the terrific warning of our Saviour in Matt. v. 29. Nothing will sooner becloud and deaden the moral sense than indulgence in sensual sins.

III. THE EVIL EFFECT OF SUCH SINS STOPS NOT WITH THE MAN HIMSELF. With regard to those whose good opinion and respect are most worth having, it is impossible for them to look on one who indulges in such sins otherwise than with profoundest pity and shame, and even with disgust! They see that one who by his sex is meant to be the guardian of woman's purity, honour, and joy, is basely tampering with them all! Not even Jacob, though the tenderness of the old patriarch under such circumstances must have been at its height, could bring himself to pronounce a rich blessing even on his firstborn, whose life had been thus disfigured and disgraced. Reuben's whole family and tribe shared in the stigma of their father's sin; not as being guilty in like manner, but because the name of their sire could not henceforth be dissociated from the thought of base and treacherous lust.

.IV. NOR DOES THE ILL EFFECT OF SUCH SINS EXPIRE WITH THE GENERATION IN WHICH THEY WERE COMMITTED. The foul odour of Reuben's crime rises up before Moses. 'Tis not named indeed. But he has no blessing for his tribe of any richness or depth. "May he not become so weak as to be lost sight of altogether!" Such is the gist of it. The descendants of Jacob's firstborn were long, long under the gloomy shadow cast on them by the sins of their sire! There is nothing in this record of the Word of God which does not frequently find its counterpart in the generations of men now. Many, many there are who inherit some physical ill, some mental weakness, or some moral incapacity or obliquity, through a constitutional taint from sins long gone by!

Learn—1. We know not whence, on the physical and moral side of our constitution, a mightier argument can be drawn for purity of life and manners, than from such a theme as that suggested by the text. If men have little care for themselves, let them at least guard against shading with sadness or marring with weakness the lives of those who may hereafter owe their existence to them. 2. Maybe some who may read these words may be disposed to say, "If I may possibly be the possessor of an enfeebled constitution on account of some sins which preceded me, then how can I or any one judge of my measure of responsibility before God as to how far it is affected thereby?" We reply : (1) No living man can gauge exactly another's responsibility, or even his own ; *but God can*. He does, and he makes all allowances that equity requires. He who is most just is most kind. (2) God invites every man to come to him through his Son Jesus Christ, that sin, as guilt, may be forgiven ; and that, as disease, it may be cured. (3) Wherever God's invitation is accepted, his grace will cancel guilt and cure corruption ; thus imparting health and soundness for the life that now is, and promising the life to come. (4) To this each one may well be urged, not only on the ground of his individual well-being, but also on the ground that the streams of purifying grace, cleansing his nature, may do much to check the onward flow of the poison he inherits, and to help towards a sounder life in those who shall follow him.

Ver. 7.—*The blessing of Judah; or, help needed to fulfil destiny.* It cannot but suggest itself to the student to compare the blessing on Judah pronounced by Moses, with the renowned prophecy of Jacob concerning him and his tribe. That the patriarch's words declared the future pre-eminence of that tribe is well known ; consequently, it could not be surprising to the other tribes to find precedence given to Judah in the order of encamping and of marching (cf. Numb. ii. 1—4 ; x. 14). This thought of Judah's *firstness* gives its hue to the words uttered respecting him. They take the form of a prayer, which is at once the holy benediction of the dying leader, the pious breathing of the saint, and the prophetic fore-glance of the seer. It could not be a matter of doubt, that being in the front would involve not only eminence in honour, but also precedence in weight of responsibility ; and in order to sustain aright great responsibility, there is need for an unusual supply of Divine strength. This it is which forms the contents of the prayer. Jacob had said, "To him shall the gathering of the people be ;" Moses prays, " Lord, fulfil that prediction, and (1) sustain him ; so that he may be brought to his people ; (2) give him all the strength he requires to enable him to fulfil his high and holy destiny; ‘let his hands be sufficient for him;’ and (3) when the enemy would endeavour to overthrow him, let thine almighty aid be near; ‘be thou a Help to him from his enemies.’” That this prophetic blessing and prayer is, in the highest meaning thereof, Messianic, seems to admit of no question. Its complete fulfilment will be realized in the ultimate triumph of him who is at once “the Lion of the tribe of Judah,” and yet “the Lamb that was slain.” He will be brought “unto his people;” his hands have been and will be “sufficient for him;” and power no less than that of the eternal Father will ensure the defeat of the enemy and the enthronement of the Son, that “in all things he may become the pre-eminent One.” For this believers have prayed *implicitly* ever since the days of Moses; for this they have prayed *explicitly* ever since the day of Pentecost.

But there is another bearing of this blessing of Judah, perhaps less obvious, though not less real than the one already named; while it equally suggests a topic for pulpit teaching of no small interest and value, viz. *Divine help needed for man, that he may realize his true destiny.* The following line of thought may serve to press home this truth:—

I. The life of man has a noble destiny before it.

II. According to the greatness of destiny must be the measure of responsibility.

III. According to responsibility, so is the need of Divine help to give unity and directness to life. We need (1) strength: “let his hands be sufficient for him;” (2) protection: “be thou a help to him from his enemies.”

IV. That such Divine help may be granted may well be made matter of earnest prayer: (1) of pastors for people; (2) of parents for children; (3) of friend for friend.

V. It is a great stimulus to prayer, when the one prayed for is known to pray for himself. Moses was not praying for a prayerless tribe. “Hear, Lord, the voice of Judah.”

VI. When prayer has great promises to fall back upon, we may be absolutely sure of its success. The prayer, “Bring him unto his people,” was based on the promise, “To him shall the gathering of the people be.” It is equivalent to, “Lord, fulfil thine own promise.” The great Messianic promise was made through Judah, and through him and in him was it fulfilled.

Vers. 8—11.—*The blessing of Levi; or, entire devotion to God a necessary qualification for ministerial service.* Moses and Aaron were themselves of the tribe of Levi. Consequently, Moses is here speaking of his own tribe; he forecasts its future; he seems in a remarkable manner to revoke the harsh sentence of the patriarch Jacob upon it. Nor is this altogether unaccounted for. The tribe had manifested a genuine repentance by a remarkable zeal for God’s honour on several occasions. It was the tribe, moreover, which God had selected from the rest, to minister in holy things; and these facts, blending themselves with a painful reminiscence of his own breakdown at Meribah, give the character to the blessing of Moses. The points therein which furnish a basis for historic and homiletic teaching are these: 1. Here is an office divinely appointed and assigned to a particular tribe—“thy holy one” (ver. 8). 2. Here is a history, in some sort chequered and sad, connected with the tribe (ver. 8) —“Massah,” “Meribah” (Numb. xx. 1—13). There had been a grievous failure on Aaron’s part too, as well as on that of Moses (Exod. xxxii., xxxiii.). Still, as a whole, the tribe had been marked by great zeal for God, great concern for his honour, and great devotion to his service (ver. 9; cf. Numb. viii. 14—26; xxv. 1—15; Exod. xxxii. 26—28). The honour of God was deemed by this tribe paramount to all personal and family considerations. 3. Here is a commission for the discharge of varied duties resting on the tribe (ver. 10)—teaching, incense, sacrifice (see ch. x. 8; Mal. ii. 4—7). The duties of the priesthood were more varied than is generally supposed (cf. Dean Stanley on the Jewish Church, vol. ii. lect. xxxvi.). Whatever a man could be or do to help his people in prayer, work, war, worship, knowledge, or life,—all this was charged upon the priest. 4. Here is a danger espied to which the tribe would be liable (ver. 11) —“them that rise against him;” “them that hate him.” This hatred had already manifested itself in jealousy (Numb. xvi. 3, *et seq.*). It is very suggestive that we find one of the Reubenites, *a tribe which had lost its birthright,* concerned in that conspiracy.

There always has been and there will be jealousy and odium towards God's ministers, as "taking too much upon them." As Moses had found it out already, he knew by some experience what it was likely to be in the future. Hence: 5. Here is a prayer which takes its shape from a review of the varied facts named above (ver. 11), that a blessing might attend on their consecrated energies: "Bless, Lord, his strength;" that the work might be accepted in God's sight; and that the enemies and haters of the tribe, who rose up in jealousy against the office and those who filled it, might be put to utter shame![1]

Here is a mass of truth suggested of great interest and value.

I. There is a ministry appointed by God under the Christian economy.

II. To this office great honour now belongs.

III. Its faithful discharge makes varied demands on those who hold it.

IV. These demands cannot be rightly met without entire and unreserved consecration.

V. However faithful God's ministers may be, they will certainly meet with hatred and opposition.

VI. That their work may, in the midst of all difficulty, be divinely accepted and guarded, may well be made matter of earnest prayer.

Ver. 12.—*The blessing on Benjamin; or, safety in the sheltering care of Divine love.* Though not without difficulty in some points of detail, the general tenor of this blessing on Benjamin is tolerably clear. It is well known that Benjamin was the object of his father's special love. The expiring lawgiver seems to see in that a reflection of a tenderer and mightier, yea, a Divine love, which, as it had been manifest to the head of his tribe in time past, would also be manifest to the tribe itself in the ages yet to come. Benjamin had been and would be "the beloved of the Lord." The words, "he shall dwell between his shoulders," are variously interpreted (see the Exposition; also Keil, Calvin, Jameson, the 'Speaker's Commentary,' *et al. in loc.*). We prefer the simpler meaning accepted by Calvin, that the figure is that of a father carrying on his shoulders a young and feeble child (see ch. i. 31). During all the changes of Israel's history, a special lustre shone forth from this tribe. From hence its first king was chosen. On or by its territory was God's "foundation" in the holy mountains. And as far on as the time of the first century of the Christian era, Paul reckoned it as one of his points of native glorying that he was of the tribe of Benjamin (see Rom. xi. 1; Phil. iii. 5). Our topic for meditation is—*Safety in the sheltering care of Divine love, an inestimable blessing.*

I. THERE ARE THOSE WHOM GOD LOVES WITH A SPECIAL LOVE. They are, in a degree to which others are not, "the beloved of the Lord." No doubt there is a sense in which it is true that God loves all mankind. His love to our race is such that he has given us the noblest gift which even Heaven itself could bestow (John iii. 16; Rom. v. 8; Eph. ii. 4). This is a love of benevolence. But our Lord speaks of something further in John xiv. 21, 23; xvi. 27. And Paul the apostle, in describing the blessings of a justified life, speaks of the "love of God" being "shed abroad in the heart by the Holy Ghost," *i.e.* a pervading sense of that love.

But who are they who are thus specially loved of God? They do not belong, as such, to any nation, tribe, or tongue. They may be found in all of them. Those who are "in Christ," pardoned, renewed, accepted, justified, sanctified,—these, these are "beloved of God, called to be saints."

II. THEY CAN REJOICE "ALL THE DAY LONG" IN THAT NEW RELATIONSHIP WHICH IS THE CREATION OF REDEEMING LOVE. In the figure used in the text, and in a not dissimilar verse in ch. i. 31, there is the underlying thought of a gracious fatherly relation. That is also disclosed in the gospel; and in both cases it has its reciprocal—that of "son" (see Rom. viii. 14—17). This is *not* that general relation to God indicated in Acts xvii. 28; *that* is common to man as man. *This* is peculiar to those who are born again. The former may be and is marred by sin. The latter will never be; it is made possible through a propitiation for sin by the blood of Christ,

---

[1] On the prayer of Moses concerning the Urim and the Thummim, see Hengstenberg's 'Egypt and the Books of Moses,' pp. 149—153.

and made actual through the destruction of sin by the power of the Holy Ghost (1 John iii. 9). Hence in the perpetuity of this relationship there is matter of constant joy (Rom. viii. 38, 39).

III. IN CONNECTION WITH THIS RELATION THERE IS A CORRESPONDING CARE ON THE PART OF JEHOVAH. The father carries the child "between his shoulders," not only because the child is too young or too weak to go alone—true enough though that may be—but because he feels that the child's safety is its father's care. And the parent would feel it a reproach to himself if the weal of the child were not the care of his heart. Now, we know how our Lord permits, yea, teaches us to look up from human tenderness to the Divine, as if the lower were but the reflection (and consequently the image) of the higher (Matt. vii. 9—11). And St. Peter directly teaches the positive truth, "he careth for you" (1 Pet. v. 7). And so does Peter's Lord, in Luke xii. 6, 7, 22—30; Matt. xxi. 32, 33. How much of loving care is indicated in John vi. 38—40; x. 1—29, words would fail to tell. The believer may meditate thereon to his heart's delight, but he will find no words adequately to express the glories revealed to his faith in the infinite care for him of God the Father and the Son.

IV. HENCE THE BELOVED OF THE LORD ARE IN PERPETUAL SAFETY. "The beloved of the Lord shall dwell in safety by him"—"upon him" the word is: God bears him up; he rests safely on God. God is his "Shelterer" all the day long, without let or pause. The Old Testament saints felt this, or they could never have penned Psalms xxiii., xci., and cxxi. 1. They are safe in Divine love. None can wrest them thence. 2. They are safe at all hours. "He that keepeth Israel shall neither slumber nor sleep." 3. They are safe from all plots, snares, and fiery darts. 4. They are safe under all circumstances of duty, care, trial, affliction, bereavement, death. They may be tossed about on the Rock, but never from it.

IN CONCLUSION. 1. Let the believer rejoice in the Lord; yea, let him shout aloud for joy (Ps. xxxiii. 1; Phil. iii. 1; iv. 1). 2. If any ask us this question—"If the believer is so safe, how is it that one like Paul can write as he does in 1 Cor. ix. 23—27?"—the answer is, This is one way in which God secures the safety of loyal souls, by giving them to see the danger they are in from themselves, that they may look ever to the Rock that is higher than they are. For: 3. No such security is ever enjoyed as to warrant any departure from duty's path, or any presuming on God's providence. To a temptation in this direction, even our dear Lord was exposed, and his followers must not expect to be free therefrom yet awhile (see Matt. iv. 5—7). 4. The great reason why God takes our cares on himself is that he may set us free for the one business of life, which is in loyalty and love to do the work of the day in the day, and to leave all else in his hands. Let us say—

> "I have no cares, O Blessed Will;
> My cares thou makest thine.
> I live in triumph, Lord, for thou
> Hast made thy triumphs mine!"

And sooner shall heaven and earth pass than one such beloved one of the Lord shall ever be put to shame.

Vers. 13—17.—*The blessing of Joseph; or, God's favour the mercy of mercies.* We may see here a reflection of Jacob's blessing, both as in Gen. xlviii. 19 and also Gen. xlix. 25, *et seq.* In Dean Stanley's 'Sinai and Palestine,' pp. 226—250, there is much interesting information as to the correspondence between this prophecy of Moses on the one hand, and the extent of territory, the beauty and fertility of the district, the dignity, valour, and advance of the tribes of Ephraim and Manasseh on the other. (For an elucidation of each clause in this somewhat lengthened blessing, see the Exposition.) By way of "opening up," however, the theme of our Homily, we must call the readers' attention to the structure of the verses. We regard them as a blending at once of prophecy and prayer. Both the beginning and the close are prophetic. The beginning, from ver. 13 down to the word "thereof," in ver. 16; the ending in ver. 17. In the intervening clauses we regard (so Calvin, Keil, *et al.*) the word רְצוֹן (*rêtzōn*) as a nominative case. We read thus: "*And may the good will of him that dwelt in the bush come upon the head of Joseph,*" etc. It will be observed that in the

English Version the words " for " and " the blessing " are in italics, to show that they are added by the translators. And the fact that there is no " for " in the original at the commencement of this clause seems to show that it is not co-ordinate with the preceding ones, and so to mark a new starting-point; as if Moses had said, " He will have a noble territory, rich in all temporal wealth ; his tribe will be an enterprising, hardy, and pushing one ; may there be superadded to all, the favour of him who dwelt in the bush, to crown and glorify the whole."   The reader will find the varied scriptural senses of the word here translated " good will," in the following passages, where it occurs :—Exod. xxviii. 38 ; Lev. xxiii. 11 ; Ps. v. 12 ; xix. 14 ; xxx. 5 ; Prov. xv. 8 ; Isa. xlix. 8 ; lx. 7 ; lxi. 2.   If in addition to all that earth's varied wealth and tribal renown and conquest could yield, Joseph had the " favour " of the Lord, that would make him rich indeed.   Whence our theme suggests itself—*God's favour the mercy of mercies.*

I. THE STORE OF MERCIES WHICH ARE THE TEMPORAL GIFTS OF GOD'S HAND IS BY NO MEANS SMALL.   The land, with its wondrous capacities and its adaptation to this seed and to that ; the dew that gently distils, or the vapour that exhales ; the lakes that lie sleeping on the bosom of the hills ; the variety of beauty, fragrance, and fruitfulness coming through the sunbeams ; the produce of the several months, year by year ; the wealth stored up in the mountains and hills ; the varied productions of the soil ;—all these are referred to in the text ; and, in a few brief touches, what a conception they give us of the wealth with which God has enriched this globe, and of the series of constant adaptations with which it is made subservient to the use of man !   So great are all these blessings which go to make up the enjoyments of life on its temporal side, that meditation thereon may well call up from the soul a grand song of praise such as we find in Ps. civ.

Nor can we in such an age as this, leave out the additional fact that, owing to the rapid communication between the people of one land and those of another, the productions of one country supply the wants of another ; and thus the nations at large share the supplies sent them by a gracious God.

And be it remembered these supplies are not less from God because he uses means in sending them ; it is rather a proof of his care for the culture and education of man, that he makes him the means of the cultivation and tillage of the soil.   " Whoso is wise and will observe these things, even he shall understand the loving-kindness of the Lord."

II. THERE IS A FAR GREATER MERCY THAN ANY OF THESE—one which we have called " the mercy of mercies."   It is referred to in ver. 16, " The good will . . . may it come upon the head of Joseph."   Favour, mercy, on Joseph's head, is a boon greater far than plenty on his land !   There are three questions which we may appropriately ask concerning it.

1. *What is this " good will " ?*   It is not simply that benevolence to which our Saviour refers in Matt. v. 45.   In this sense God's goodness extendeth to all.   " His tender mercies are over all his works."   *This* good will is something special.   If the student will compare the several passages (those given *ut supra et al.*), in which the same word is used which is here translated "good will," he will see how much meaning it conveys.   It includes : (1) acceptance in God's sight—forgiveness, access ; (2) God's delight in the accepted one ; (3) the constant possession of God's special love, which enriches the accepted one with all spiritual blessings in heavenly places in Christ Jesus.

2. *How can this good will be assured to its possessor ?*   (1) There is a word of promise which assures us that it is made over to the believer in Christ (John i. 12 ; Gal. iii. 26).   (2) To him who believes, the Spirit is given, confirming to the soul its interest in Christ, and sealing it " to the day of redemption."

3. *Why is this the mercy of mercies ?*   (1) Because the possessor thereof can delight in God himself.   He can realize that in God he has One who is infinitely more than all his gifts, and who will be his joy when all earth's joys have lost their power to charm.   (2) Because all other mercies have new joy stamped upon them when they are enjoyed as coming from a reconciled God and Father.   (3) Because we are then enabled to use other mercies aright.   Surely that must be a crowning blessing which teaches the right use of every blessing.   (4) The conscious enjoyment of God's favour and love gives, as nothing else can, strength for the duties of life.   " The joy of the Lord

is your strength." (5) With such joy and strength life will be so sanctified as to be rich in influence for good. (6) God's favour and love will be a source of joy long after we have ceased to dwell below, yea, for ever and ever.

Oh, it is not—it is not merely having a wealthy land, or great estates, or splendid revenues, or military prowess, or pushing energy, that can make life a success. We may have all these, and yet life may be a miserable, an unredeemed and irredeemable failure. It may well be a matter for frequent wonder how parents who profess to aim at and to be living the higher life, do seek so earnestly to get the best situations in life for their children, yet never manifest half the same amount of anxiety that their loved ones may have " the good will of him that dwelt in the bush " resting on their heads. And yet, without God's favour, what is life, what is wealth, what are earthly friends, but blessings that disappoint our hopes, and prove, perhaps, anything but blessings in the end ?

FINALLY: THIS MOST NEEDFUL OF ALL BLESSINGS IS THE VERY ONE OF WHICH ALL WHO CRAVE IT SUPREMELY MAY MAKE MOST SURE. God may not give us much of this world's goods. He *will* give us himself. He waits to be gracious. He delights in loving-kindness. He will be the seeker's God for ever and ever; his Guide even unto death.

Vers. 18, 19.—*Trade and commerce subservient to evangelization.* There is room for considerable divergence of view with regard to some of the minutiæ of this passage, on which the reader will consult the Exposition, and may also refer with great advantage to Keil, Jameson, and Wordsworth, on the blessing of Issachar and Zebulun. The following points, however, stand out with a fair degree of clearness :—1. Zebulun and Issachar had the territory which corresponds to the Galilee of our Lord's time. 2. They had a fine piece of sea-board, which would enable them to open up traffic with other nations. 3. They had also a considerable space inland, reaching to the lake of Gennesaret. 4. With this double advantage, there would be scope for the development of foreign and home trade. 5. They, having the inestimable blessings of the knowledge of God, of a pure faith, and of a holy worship, would be in a far better position religiously than any of the nations with whom they would carry on intercourse for the purposes of trade. 6. They would be made rich by the treasures of wealth brought to them from afar. " They shall suck of the abundance of the seas," etc. 7. They would make their traffic with other peoples a reason for and an opportunity of inviting them to join them in the sacrifices of righteousness (see Gesenius, *sub verb.* זָבַח). As other nations enriched them in temporal things, they would enrich other peoples in spiritual things (see a fine suggestive note by Bishop Wordsworth, *in loc.*). This was fulfilled " when the apostles and evangelists of Galilee went forth to evangelize all nations in the ships of the Christian Church." The apostles, " men of Galilee," called all nations to the mountain of the Lord's house on the day of Pentecost. A greater fulfilment awaits this passage (see Isa. lx. 5, 6, 16 ; lxvi. 11, 12). Hence the Holy Ghost, by the law-giver, gives us here a great theme for homiletic teaching — *The development of commerce subservient to evangelization.*

I. The Church of God is here prospectively regarded as upon a " mountain " (ver. 19 ; see this figure carried out in Isa. ii. 2 ; Micah iv. 1).

II. From this mountain an invitation to the nations is to be sent forth ; ver. 19, " They shall call," etc. (cf. Isa. ii. 3 ; Micah iv. 2 ; Zech. viii. 20—23 ; Isa. lv. 5).

III. There will be such national intercommunication as shall help to forward these world-wide invitations (Isa. lx. 3, 4 ; Dan. xii. 4 ; cf. Acts ii. 5—11).

IV. The time will come when the Church of God shall be enriched by the glad inflowing of a people's wealth ; ver. 19, " For they shall suck," etc. (cf. Isa. lx. 9, *et seq.* ; Micah iv. 13).

V. The nations at large shall then " offer sacrifices of righteousness " (ver. 19 ; cf. Mal. i. 11 ; Rom. xv. 16 ; Heb. xiii. 15, 16 ; 1 Pet. ii. 5).

Learn—1. With what interest may believers contemplate the commercial progress of the age, and the increased facility of communication between people and people! Man is seeking to bring about all this, to serve himself. God overrules all for the higher purposes of his race, and governs the world in the interests of the Church. 2. How great a shame is it when men from Christian lands, in carrying on traffic with other nations, make such traffic a means of propagating corruption, lust, and crime ! 3. Commerce may be " holiness unto the Lord," and will never reach its true splendour till such is the case (Zech. xiv. 20). Its stainless purity is of infinitely more moment than its extent or amount.

Vers. 20, 21.—*Gad ; or, a place in the Church and the world for lionlike strength.* " The territory of Gad lay in the east of the Jordan . . . it included several cities remarkable in the history of the patriarchs and of the judges, as Mahanaim, Ramoth, Mizpeh, Succoth, and Peniel ; but it was pre-eminently remarkable because it contained the grave of the great general and lawgiver, Moses—a fact which so decidedly invested the province with a character of holiness that, though situated on the east of the river, it was regarded as one of the most honoured parts of the promised land, from which the leaders of the people might legitimately arise " (Kalisch on Gen. xlix. 19). The blessing of Moses, like that of Jacob, upon Gad, has a warlike ring about it. He is spoken of here as lionlike in courage and strength, and also as being charged with the execution of the justice of the Lord and his ordinances with Israel. " The clause, ' He came to the heads of the people,' expresses the thought that Gad joined the heads of the people to go at the head of the tribes of Israel (comp. Josh. i. 14 ; iv. 12, with Numb. xxxii. 17, 21, 32), to conquer Canaan with the whole nation, and root out the Canaanites " (Keil, *in loc.*). The character of this tribe is described with remarkable vividness in the Book of Chronicles. It was strong, hardy, fierce, warlike, magnificent in heroism, invaluable to friends, terrible to foes. Among them were " strong men of might, men of war for the battle, that could handle shield and buckler, their faces the faces of lions, and like roes upon the mountain for swiftness : " " the least of them more than equal to a hundred, and the greatest to a thousand " (1 Chron. xii. 8, 14). And amid all the conflicts which were inevitable to the Hebrews with the nations round about, such lionlike courage and hardiness would be invaluable in leading them on to victory, and in helping them through great crises of their political and military history. And when such courage and valour are animated by the right spirit, and engaged on the side of righteousness, upon them an aged saint may well pronounce his blessing. It is indicative of the spirit which pervaded this tribe that such men as Jephthah, Barzillai, and (probably) Elijah were of it. Our theme for homiletic teaching is—*That the special qualities of courage and strength have a valuable place in carrying out God's work both in the Church and the world.*

I. THERE ARE NOT UNFREQUENTLY GREAT CRISES WHICH ARISE IN THE CHURCH OR IN THE WORLD. Work has to be done which requires no ordinary amount of independence and assurance ; as *e.g.* when a way has to be opened up through new and untried districts ; or a step has to be taken on which the weal or woe of ages may depend. Sometimes in the military career of a nation a giant foe has to be grappled with, or, in the progress of a Church, some heresy has to be attacked, and battles, harder than any on a nation's battle-field, have to be fought in the name of the Lord of hosts. Perchance some Ahab with his pride and covetousness, or some Herod or Felix rioting in lust and splendour, may have to be sternly addressed for righteousness' sake. Or there may come a time when the flood-gates of iniquity are burst open, and sin rushes forth in torrents, and the wicked ride high and triumph over the righteous, and the greater part of men are cowed before the storm-blast.

II. THE WORK OF GOD AT SUCH TIMES MAY BE STERN AND HARD. It may be that some special form of service is just then imperatively needed. " Who will rise up for me against the evil-doers ? who will stand up for me against the workers of iniquity ? " The quiet souls, precious as they are, will seem to be at a discount then. There requires : 1. Leadership in the cause of the right. 2. Men who can venture all, to clear the way to an unknown region. 3. Men who can endure hardness as good soldiers of Jesus Christ. 4. Men who can fearlessly rebuke ill, and fear the face of neither man nor devil.

III. FOR THIS SPECIAL FORM OF SERVICE, ENTERPRISE, COURAGE, BRAVERY, AND THE STERNER VIRTUES ARE REQUIRED. Those who are naturally timid and retiring will probably be out of sight at such times. Their work, indeed, is not lost. Their sighs and cries and prayers do enter into the ears of the Lord of sabaoth. But still there then is need of the shaggier spirits to come to the front. There was time when evil so overspread Israel, and persecution was so sore, that it seemed as if virtue would soon become extinct unless God arose in his might. There were seven thousand souls hidden in obscurity. But one man, stern and strong, must be to the front. It was *Elijah* (cf. also John the Baptist).

IV. GOD IN MERCY, AS HE FORESEES THESE CRISES, PREPARES MEN FOR THEM. The Hebrews could not have dispensed with the men of Gad. Their *strength* was required as much as the sanctity of the Levites. Every virtue, every grace, has its own distinctive sphere of service. God gives some more of the kindlier graces, that they may be comforters; and others more of the hardier ones, that they may be awakeners. One is a Barnabas; another a Boanerges.

V. THEREFORE, WHATEVER OUR NATURAL GIFTS MAY BE, LET US BE SUPREMELY CONCERNED TO SANCTIFY THEM FOR GOD. Let no one regret that he cannot be anybody else. Rather, "as much as in him is," let him use his powers, whatever they may be, for his redeeming God. The meek, quiet, gentle, retiring souls have their work. The rougher, sterner ones have also theirs. "Each one in his place is best." Be it ours every day to ask, "Lord, what wilt thou have me to do?" In a great house there are not only vessels of gold and of silver, but also of wood and of earth; some to honour and some to dishonour. If a man, therefore, purge himself from these, he shall be a vessel unto honour, sanctified and meet for the Master's use, and prepared unto every good work.

Vers. 22, 23.—*The blessing of Dan and Naphtali; the satisfaction which accrues from the enjoyment of the Divine favour.* The word rendered "favour" in this verse, is the same as the one translated "good will" in the blessing of Joseph. (For several instances in which that word is used, see the Homily on that passage.) We are not going beyond the significance attached to the word in the time of Moses, in thinking of it as conveying to us the meaning of that favour, grace, and mercy of God which is the portion of those who are accepted in his sight. And the Mosaic expression, "satisfied with favour," suggests to us this theme for meditation—*Acceptance with God a matter for devout satisfaction.*

I. THE BLESSING HERE PRONOUNCED ON DAN AND NAPHTALI SPEAKS OF TEMPORAL MERCIES OF NO MEAN VALUE. To Dan is promised the strength and leaping freedom of young life. Samson was a mighty hero in this tribe. The historical details are not sufficient to enable us to compare the history of the tribe with the blessing upon it. Nevertheless, in general, it is sufficiently obvious that an amplitude of power is a great boon, if, indeed it be attended with the greater one, of wisdom to use it aright. Naphtali, too, was to enjoy "the sunny south" (see Hebrew). To be permitted to know this earthly life on its sunny side is indeed a mercy; how it sweetens our existence when, enjoying the warm sunbeams, we are permitted to feel that life is a privilege. Let such as have the earthly gifts bestowed on Dan and Naphtali— strength and sunshine—not be slow to perceive or to acknowledge their indebtedness and responsibility to God.

II. YET GREAT AS THESE TEMPORAL MERCIES ARE, BY THEMSELVES THEY WILL NOT YIELD SATISFACTION TO THE HIGHER NATURE OF MAN, HOWEVER ABUNDANT THE DEGREE IN WHICH THEY MAY BE POSSESSED. It is true that this is not so much expressed in the text as implied in the form of it. The satisfaction of which Moses speaks arises from something else which neither might nor brightness can secure.

III. THERE IS A GREATER BOON, even "*favour*"—acceptance with God. This the Hebrews enjoyed who had made a covenant with God through sacrifice. (For the blessedness of this in its ripest Christian form, see Rom. v. 1—11). Earthly blessings are the gifts of God's hand. Spiritual blessings are the outflowings of his grace (Eph. i. 1—3; ii. 1—6).

IV. THIS GREATER BOON IT IS WHICH YIELDS ENTIRE SATISFACTION. With God's "favour," all who possess it are abundantly satisfied. It must be so. For in this blessed state of acceptance, we enjoy what the Apostle Paul speaks of as a *resurrection life.* We are in "a new creation," "all things are become new." (1) The intellect is satisfied. For so much comes into view to delight the soul (1 Cor. ii. 9, 10). (2) The conscience is pacified. For the enjoyment of God's favour comes out of Christ's own reconciling work, and is attended with pardon and adoption. (3) The affections are satisfied. For Divine love is "shed abroad in the heart." Fellowship with God is ever maintained. (4) A double joy is put into the use of earthly gifts. They are received as a Father's tokens of love. They mean so much more than they can to others. (5) The expectations are satisfied. In God's love they have an enduring treasury of wealth.

> "... when all earthly pleasures fail,—
> (And fail they always will to every soul of man),
> He sends his hopes on high; reaches his sickle forth,
> And reaps the clusters from the vines of God."

Verily such a one is "satisfied with favour, and filled with the blessing of the Lord."

Vers. 24, 25.—*Asher's blessing; strength as the day.* There are several features in this blessing to Asher. He is to have a numerous seed: to enjoy above his brethren the favour of the Lord; to be surrounded with plenty; to be guarded with bars of iron and brass; and to have strength according to the days. (The Hebrew word translated "days" is so rendered or explained by the Targum, Boothroyd, and Parkhurst. The LXX. render it ἰσχυς: the French version has it *ta force*; Gesenius renders it "rest." In this Homily we follow the LXX., and accept our translation, "strength.") However great the temporal blessings may be which are here promised to Asher, this last-named one is surely the greatest of all, yea, greater than any merely earthly blessings could possibly be. And perhaps there is no promise of God's Word which has more deeply touched the hearts of his people, or more frequently proved itself a balm in care, than this one. For that it was made to Asher first, need not shut off any child of God from taking the comfort of it. There is a distinct promise made to Joshua, "I will not fail thee, nor forsake thee;" but yet the writer of the Epistle to the Hebrews bids the people whom he is addressing to make that promise their own. And so assuredly may the people of God in every age and land do with the promise before us. They have done so hitherto, and will do so till the end. Let us meditate on it now, presenting, as it does, this topic—*Strength promised for the day.*

I. WHAT DOES THE PROMISE INCLUDE? It suggests truths of which we are often reminded, viz.: That *we have to live by the day.* In one sense we can do no otherwise. We can never with certainty look over the rim of one day so as to see what will happen to-morrow. Then *each day has its own peculiar alternations and variations of light and shade.* One day all is smiling; the next, perchance, all is in gloom. Every hour, every place has "hues of its own fresh borrowed from the heart." Consequently, *each day brings its own demands with it.* And for each day we require new self-adaptedness. Moreover, *the strength of each day will not serve for the next.* Now, these are the facts which this promise is intended to meet. How does it meet them? 1. It assures us of strength *as varied* as the day. Whatever kind of strength is wanted, that kind of strength will be given—whether for work or war, pain or sickness, poverty or temptation, bereavement or death. "They that wait on the Lord shall renew [*i.e.* change] their strength." 2. It is a promise of strength *as sure as* the day. No day shall come without its due measure of might to enable us to meet its demands. He who hath taught his children to cry, "Give us day by day our daily bread," in teaching them so to pray reveals his purpose to fulfil the prayer he has taught. We shall never find a day when the Saviour's grace is a-wanting. 3. It pledges strength *as long as* the days shall last. So long as any demands are made upon us, so long will God's grace be sufficient to enable us to meet them. We need not look wistfully and anxiously ahead. Our Father cares. One whose words are more to us than thousands of gold and silver has said, "Take no thought for the morrow," etc. And an inspired writer has given us an impregnable argument, "He that spared not his own Son, but delivered him up for us all, *how shall he not* with him also freely give us all things?" But let us inquire—

II. WHAT IT IS WHICH GIVES THIS PROMISE A SPECIAL VALUE? "As thy days, so shall thy strength be." The words remind us of a picture drawn by Mrs. Stowe, in 'Uncle Tom's Cabin,' of a slave weary and worn with toiling in the sultry sun. One quotes the words, "Come unto me all ye that labour and are heavy laden, and I will give you rest!" "Them's good words," is the reply, "*but who says 'em?*" Obviously all depends on that. So it is here. The words are said—by 1. One who knows what our days will be. 2. One who orders our days. 3. One who measures our days. 4. One who loved us from everlasting days. 5. One whose love changes not with the days. 6. One who has infinite resources on which we can draw throughout the days. 7. One whose love as revealed in Christ is a pledge that he will be with us to the end of the days. Is anything wanting to heighten the value of a promise if it comes from such a Promiser?

III. OUGHT NOT SUCH A PROMISE TO HAVE GREAT POWER OVER US? Yea, verily. A triple power. 1. It should stimulate to holy obedience. 2. It should prepare us to look onward with holy calmness. "I will trust, and not be afraid." 3. It should embolden us to meet emergencies with a valiant heart. 4. It should lead us to look upward with a waiting, expectant eye.

Vers. 26—29.—*The glory of Israel's God, and the blessedness of God's Israel.* Ere Moses quite throws up his task, he gives us his view of Israel as a whole. He has had a word of blessing for tribe by tribe, and now he takes one last look at the whole nation, and viewing it in the light of that eternal world on which he is so soon to enter, his words are richer, riper, sweeter than any we yet have read. The name he gives to the people is very significant—"Jeshurun." The word is found but four times in the Scriptures, viz. in ch. xxxii. 15; xxxiii. 5, 26; Isa. xliv. 2. It seems to be a kind of diminutive from ישׁר, and in the passage before us it appears to be used as a term of admiration and endearment; some would think it equivalent to "a righteous little people" (see Gesenius). Anyway, the root-notion of the word is connected with righteousness. And the fundamental conception which Moses has of the nation is that it is a nation in covenant with Jehovah on the righteous basis of sacrifice, and that it is one, moreover, which has righteousness for the corner-stone of its constitution and polity. And he pronounces them blessed in two senses: they have a God who is infinitely greater than all gods; they have privileges which make them greater than all other peoples. Hence we have a double theme to meditate upon, from the evangelic standpoint.

I. NONE IS SO GLORIOUS AS ISRAEL'S GOD. It is one mark of Divine condescension that our God lets his people speak of him in language they can best understand; *e.g.* "None like unto the God of Jeshurun" is a phrase which would seem to imply that there may be some other gods, but none equal to the one God (cf. Micah vii. 18; 1 Sam. ii. 2), whereas in fact there is no other. Still, men of other nations worshipped other beings whom they deemed to be gods; and Israel's God, in his infinite condescension, suffers himself to be put in contrast from them, although he is God alone. 1. He is "the eternal God." The word rendered "eternal" here is one which refers to God's having existed from the eternal past. "From everlasting" he is God—he is Jehovah. He changes not. 2. He is one who "rideth above the heaven," etc.; he is over all. In the glory of his transcendent majesty, all things are under his feet. "He maketh the clouds his chariot; he walketh upon the wings of the wind." 3. He is one who bears up Israel and all things in his arms. "Underneath are the everlasting arms"—arms spread out, expanded with the intent of bearing all. "Everlasting arms," that will remain thus spread out and bearing all to eternity, without weariness, though they have borne the weight of all things from eternity. 4. He is one whose active energies are ever going before his people, to "thrust out" their enemies. Whatever would obstruct them shall be taken out of the way. 5. He himself is and will be the Dwelling-place in which his people can abide. "Thy Refuge" (see Ps. xc. 1; xci. 2, 9; Isa. iv. 6). It is not at all unlikely that the figure of God as a permanent Home to his people suggested itself to Moses by way of contrast, as the people had lived such a wandering life, and abode in tabernacles (so Keil).

Let these five features which mark Israel's God be put together. May we not well say, "Who is like to the God of Jeshurun?"

II. NONE CAN BE SO BLESSED AS GOD'S ISRAEL. This is seen whether we consider what God is to them, or what they have and are in, through, and from God. 1. *Their blessedness arises from what God is to them*; it is an incomparable blessedness. For: (1) Who else has an eternal God? (2) Who else has one so great in majesty? (3) Who else has one so strong to bear? (4) Who else has one so mighty to defend? (5) Who else has one in whom is such a home? Each of these five points, the correlatives of those under the first head, requires expansion. 2. *It arises also from what they have and are in and through God.* (1) They have security. "Israel shall dwell in safety." (2) Plenty shall be theirs. "The fountain of Jacob shall be upon a land of corn and wine." "They that fear the Lord shall not want any good thing." (3) They shall have refreshment. "His heavens shall drop down dew." God will be "as the dew unto Israel." (4) Victory shall be theirs. (*a*) "Thine enemies shall be found liars unto thee: *i.e.* they threatened to destroy, and they are proved false. (*b*) "Thou shalt tread upon their high places;" *i.e.* the high and fortified places in which they gloried shall be as ramparts over which you shall walk.

Who can desire to be more blessed than this? Yea, who can conceive of a greater blessedness? Is it not enough to set the heart a-longing? May not the remark be appropriately made in closing, that—

It behoves each one of us to make sure that we are of the Israel of God, so that we may know this blessedness is ours!

HOMILIES BY VARIOUS AUTHORS.

Ver. 2.—*A fiery Law.* The fieriness of the Law, significant: 1. Of the holiness from which the Law emanated. 2. Of the fiery sanctions by which it is guarded. 3. Of the threatening aspect which it wears to sinners. 4. Of the purifying effects which it exerts in the hearts and consciences of believers.—J. O.

Ver. 3.—*God's saints.* 1. Their *happiness*—loved of God. 2. Their *safety*—in God's hand. 3. Their *attitude*—sitting at God's feet—at the feet of God's Son (Luke x. 3, 9). (1) Willing to know God's will. (2) Seeking instruction in it. (3) Waiting on God for that instruction. (4) Their *duty*—to receive of God's words. The receiving to be of the practical kind of hiding God's words in the heart, and going on to put them in practice (Matt. xiii. 23).—J. O.

Vers. 6, 7.—*Reuben and Judah.* The tribe without a destiny and the tribe with one.

I. THE PRESERVATION AND INCREASE OF EVERY PART OF THE CHURCH IS OF INTEREST TO EVERY OTHER. Reuben's sins had incurred the forfeiture of privilege. His numbers were diminishing. It had been predicted of him that he would not excel (Gen. xlix. 4). But Moses desires that his tribe should not perish. He prays for its preservation and revival. Or, on another view, he prays that, though its numbers are few, it may not utterly die out. So ought we to pray for any part of the Church that seems in a dwindling condition.

II. THE STRENGTH OF THE STRONG IS STILL TO BE SOUGHT FROM GOD. Judah, though strong, with great promises behind and great hopes before, was yet to recognize that his help and sufficiency were of God. That there may be strength, there must be prayer, "Hear, Lord, the voice of Judah," etc.—J. O.

Vers. 8—11.—*Levi.* The priestly tribe. Its curse (Gen. xlix. 7) turned into a blessing. Repentance and zeal cut off the entail of a curse, or so transform it that out of the very curse God evokes a blessing (cf. Exod. xxxii. 29; Ps. cvi. 31).

I. THE GROUND OF THE BLESSING. 1. Levi's *fidelity* (ver. 8). "Among the faithless, faithful only he." The zeal and constancy of the tribe on critical occasions had been remarkable. Learn how the wicked, returning to God and proving zealous in his service, may retrieve past forfeitures and win great honour. 2. Levi's *renunciation of earthly ties* (ver. 9). Christ also requires that no earthly tie be allowed to stand between his disciples and the allegiance they owe to him (Matt. x. 37).

II. THE BLESSING ITSELF. 1. Great privileges were conferred. (1) Levi *was to be the medium of God's revelations.* Urim and Thummim (ver. 8). This privilege of the tribe receives its highest fulfilment in Christ—God's "Holy One," by pre-eminence, and the Revealer of all his counsel to men. Note: The Urim and Thummim is attributed *to the whole tribe,* equally with burning incense and offering sacrifice (ver. 10), though no one pretends that the prerogative of consulting through the oracle belonged to any other than the high priest. This shows the futility of the argument that in Deuteronomy all Levites must be held as priests because priestly functions are in ch. x. 8, etc., attributed to the tribe as such. (2) *They were to teach the Law to Israel* (ver. 10). This privilege now preserved by ministers of the gospel, and other teachers in the Christian Church. In Levi's fidelity and spirit of consecration we see the qualifications required for such work. (3) *They were to burn incense and offer sacrifice.* This privilege has its fulfilment in Christians in general, in whose personal consecration and offering of spiritual sacrifices, with the incense of prayers, the character of a " royal priesthood " is maintained (1 Pet. ii. 5, 9). Their sacrifices are acceptable through the High Priest, Christ. 2. Great promises were given (ver. 10). His substance would be blessed, and special protection afforded him. God's servants have all an interest in these promises, especially those whose sacred calling deprives them of the ordinary means of live-lihood.—J. O.

Vers. 12—17.—*Benjamin and Joseph.* The name given to one of these sons of Rachel (ver. 12) would apply to both—"Beloved of the Lord."

I. WHOM GOD CHOOSES TO PRESERVE NO FOE CAN INJURE. Benjamin would dwell in safety as between the shoulders of Jehovah (ver. 12). The Lord would cover him all the day long. This is true of every good man. No power can separate him from God's love. No enemy can reach him to harm him (Ps. cxxi.). Christ's sheep are in the Father's hand, whence no man can pluck them (John x. 29).

II. WHOM GOD CHOOSES TO BLESS ALL THINGS CONSPIRE TO POUR BLESSING UPON. (Vers. 13—16.) All things would "work together " for the good of Joseph—would combine to fill his lap with treasures. They would unite to benefit and enrich him. Precious things of heaven and of the deep, precious things of sun and moon, precious things of the hills, precious things of the earth, and with these " the good will of him that dwelt in the bush "—a better portion than all, would be multiplied to this favoured tribe. So all things in the spiritual respect work for the believer's good (Rom. viii. 28), even afflictions turning to his salvation through prayer and the supply of the Spirit of Christ Jesus (Phil. i. 19).

III. WHOM GOD CHOOSES TO HELP NO ADVERSARY CAN WITHSTAND. (Ver. 17.)—J. O.

Ver. 16.—*The good will of him that dwelt in the bush.* God chose a bush of the desert as the medium of his appearance to Moses (Exod. iii. 2), which, burning, was not consumed. A symbol: 1. Of *Divine condescension.* God stooping to dwell with men (1 Kings viii. 27), using humble and despised instruments (1 Cor. ii. 18—31; 2 Cor. iv. 7). The bush, "a neglected manifestation of God." 2. Of *indwelling presence.* A symbol of the Church, and of the individual believer, indwelt in by God. Inconspicuous and contemned, yet the seat of the Divine presence—a medium of the Divine manifestation. 3. Of *miraculous preservation.* 1. God's presence *is* a fire in the midst of his Church—flaming out upon the adversaries. 2. God's presence *preserves* the Church amidst fires of persecution and affliction.—J. O.

Vers. 18, 19.—*Zebulun and Issachar.* I. TWO FORMS OF THE BLESSING OF THE ALMIGHTY. 1. Commerce. 2. Agriculture (ver. 18). Note: 1. *Some are fitted for one kind of life, some for another.* Varieties of disposition and talent. Variety of situation, giving scope for innate gifts. Divine providence, as here in allotment of the tribes, fits the one to the other. 2. *God's blessing is needed in one kind of life as well as in another.* Neither in commerce nor in agriculture can that blessing be dispensed with. It may rest on us in both, both being legitimate lines of human activity. It is in both equally efficacious. 3. *Prosperity flowing to us from God's blessing is a just cause for rejoicing.* Unblessed prosperity is not to be rejoiced in, but prosperity with God's blessing attending it is riches indeed.

II. WEALTH DERIVED FROM GOD'S BLESSING IS TO BE SANCTIFIED TO HIS GLORY. (Ver. 19.) 1. *The nations are to be invited to share the blessing.* Note here: *Commercial* nations have peculiar opportunities for being *missionary* nations. Cosmo-politan in spirit. Come in contact with many nationalities. Usually possess the means. The preaching of Christ was largely in the region of Zebulun and Issachar, with that of Naphtali, who "giveth goodly words" (Gen. xlix. 21). Application to ourselves, and duty of consecrating wealth to missionary enterprise. 2. *Sacrifices of righteousness are to be offered* in: (1) recognition of God's gift; (2) dedication of wealth to God's service; (3) personal surrender of the offerer to God.—J. O.

Vers. 20—25.—*Gad, Dan, Naphtali, Asher.* The blessings on these tribes are connected with—

I. PROWESS. (Vers. 20, 21.) The chivalrous heroic spirit, which, as well as in bloodier conflicts, finds scope for its exercise in the battles of the cross, has here its appropriate recognition. A first portion is reserved for it.

II. ACTIVITY. Dan's characteristic was agility. In Genesis, the dart of the serpent (xlix. 17); here, the leap of the lion's whelp (ver. 22). A counterpart in minds of bold, nimble, adventurous type; prompt in decision, subtle in thought, swift in action. Such minds, if to the wisdom of the serpent is added the dove's harmlessness (Matt. x. 16), are of immense service in Christian enterprises needing bold pioneers or swift and decided action.

III. CONTENTMENT. (Ver. 23.) Naphtali was less active than receptive. Did less, but received more. Possessed a region of great sweetness and beauty, and dwelt in it with unambitious satisfaction. Such dispositions are needed as a balance to the others.

IV. SKILL IN THE ARTS. (Vers. 24, 25.) Iron and brass. Asher appears to have wrought these metals, whether from mines in its own district or brought from a distance does not appear.

Lessons—1. Talents are diverse. 2. All have their place. 3. A community needs all. 4. The blessing of God rests on a faithful use of all. 5. All should co-operate.—J. O.

Vers. 26—29.—*Israel's happiness.* A noble climax! The round of blessing has been completed, and the dying lawgiver revels in the thought of the greatness and felicity thence resulting to favoured Israel. One by one the tribes have passed before his eye, and he has sketched in outline, not indeed their actual future, but what might have been, what would have been their future, had they remained faithful to their God. The picture is largely an ideal one, though in the after-history of the tribes, in the lots assigned to them in Canaan, in the types of character exhibited by them, in the variety of their callings and destinies—as in the ruins of a temple we may trace something of its original design—we discern the fulfilment of many features of the prophecy. Moses' blessing on the tribes is at once a wish, a prayer, and a prediction: a wish that certain blessings may be theirs; a prayer that the blessings may be given; and a prediction of what, conditionally on obedience, would actually be realized. Reading the blessings, we think, as in the parable, of servants entrusted with certain talents to be used in their Lord's service, but capable of making a bad as well as a good use of them (Matt. xxv. 14—31). The tribes, speaking generally, used theirs badly, and the blessings were not fulfilled. What applies to the blessing as a whole applies especially to this magnificent concluding passage. It is the ideal, not the actual Israel which stands here before the great lawgiver's eye, and the language applies to the actual, only in so far as it was also the ideal, people of Jehovah. Its full application is to the Church of Christ—the Church catholic and invisible.

I. THE BASIS OF ISRAEL'S HAPPINESS, viz. the relation which the tribes sustained to the eternal God. He was the God of Jeshurun—of the righteous people. He was a God bound to them by covenant. They had been saved by him. He was their changeless Dwelling-place, Defender, and Support. All power in heaven and earth was at their service, and engaged for their defence. They had nothing to fear with a Protector so almighty; they had everything to hope for from one so able to save and bless. Precisely similar is the relation of God in Christ to the Church of believers.

II. THE GREATNESS OF IT. 1. *Complete as regards its elements.* No element of good a-wanting. Rising from natural blessings, and safety and protection against enemies, they had also, in the favour of God and communion with him, every pledge of spiritual blessing. 2. *Permanent.* Enduring as the eternal God. 3. *Exalting and ennobling to the soul of its possessor.* Such a relation to God as Israel sustained should have wrought in the people, did in part work in them, a surpassing elevation of consciousness; was fitted to raise thought and feeling to the pitch of sublimity; should have made of them a *great* nation, in the best sense of the words, a nation great in thought, aspiration, and endeavour—*heroically* great. A like elevation of spirit should characterize the people of Christ.—J. O.

Ver. 27.—*The eternal God a Refuge.* I. THE SUBLIMITY OF THIS PROMISE. Is there one who can open his mind sufficiently to take in anything like the grandeur of this thought? To think realizingly of God at all is to many a difficulty. It shows how little we do think of him; how habitually our minds are occupied with other objects; that when we wish to bring even his *existence* clearly before our minds, we find it difficult to do so. It is not a difficulty which would be felt if our relations with God were close and intimate, if our communion with him was habitual, if we were trying to live continually as in his presence and under his eye. "I believe in God the Father Almighty!" Is not that just what most of us do *not* do? Is there one who would not tremble far more in the presence of many of his fellow-mortals than he ever does at the thought of standing in the presence of his God? What sort of a belief is it which leaves us so destitute of all real apprehension of *what* God is, and even of a habitual realization of the feeling *that* he is? We think of him, but often how coldly, how distantly, how notionally, how unbelievingly! We speak of "revivals," but, sooth to say, we need a revival of living belief in the first article of the Creed. We need to have our eyes opened, thought set to work, faith made more real. If that were given, then should we know, as we had never known before, how wonderful, how sublime, how infinitely grand a thing it was to have this God as our Refuge, and to know that underneath us were these everlasting arms. If it is difficult to attain to a steady persuasion even of God's existence, vastly more difficult is it to frame a just conception of his *eternity*. Before worlds were, God existed; when they shall have waxed old and disappeared, he shall exist still. Time flows, but, like the rock in the midst of the stream, which, from its stable base, laughs at the flood whose impetuous course it overlooks; so, amidst the flow of ages, God *endures*, "the same yesterday, to-day, and for ever." Does it not, then, seem as something incredible that this eternal God should constitute himself a Home and Refuge for weak, sinning, mortals; should even stoop to press himself on such mortals as a Friend, Saviour, Protector, Support, Helper? If we see nothing strange in this, it is impossible that anything should seem strange to us; if we can believe this, we need not stumble at much else in revelation. For this is just the central truth the Bible has to tell. It tells of a God, infinite, everlasting, almighty, inflexibly righteous, unutterably pure, incomprehensibly great and wise and good; from whom men have indeed wandered in numberless paths of error; but who has revealed himself for the very purpose of bringing them back to himself, that they may be saved from death and may enjoy eternal life; who will by no means clear the guilty, but who waits to be gracious to every penitent sinner returning to his care; and who has provided all means for that return in the atonement of his Son, our Saviour Jesus Christ, and in the grace of his Holy Spirit. That is the message the Bible has to bring, and it is nothing else than the almighty and eternal God offering himself, in his grace, as a Refuge for our otherwise defenceless souls; stretching out those everlasting arms of which the text speaks, to draw us to himself and save us from otherwise inevitable ruin. Say not, you do not need this refuge! The son of man is not yet born who does not need it, and who will not one day, whether he does so now or not, acknowledge that he needs it. And say not, you will delay in seeking it! for even could a day or a year be guaranteed in which to rethink the question now proposed, it is plainly folly in itself, and grievous dishonour done to God, that so vast and glorious an opportunity should stand for a single day unimproved; that God should sue to you, and you refuse his gracious invitations. Rather, " seek the Lord while he may be found," etc. (Isa. lv. 6).

II. THE COMPREHENSIVENESS OF THIS PROMISE. View it in three relations. In relation : 1. To *our temporal existence.* Having God as our Refuge does not indeed imply that we are to have a great abundance of this world's possessions, or be absolutely free from cares and sorrows. It does not secure that we are to be either the richest or the least tried of all around us. God knows how often it is otherwise. Some of the best of God's saints have been, like Paul, the worst off of humankind.

"They were stoned, they were sawn asunder," etc. (Heb. xi. 37). Was God therefore not the "Refuge" of those saints because they were so ill off in this life, or did the "everlasting arms" not sustain them? Or was it not in the midst of these "great fights of afflictions" that they first realized how true a Refuge God was to them? When Paul was at his work, "in journeyings often, in perils of waters, in perils of robbers, in perils of his countrymen, in perils of the heathen, in perils of the city, in perils of the wilderness, in perils of the sea, in perils of false brethren; in weariness and painfulness, in watchings often, in hunger and thirst, in fastings often, in cold and nakedness" (2 Cor. xi. 24—28), had God in these circumstances falsified his promise, and failed to be a Refuge to him? The question needs only to be put to be its own answer. Yet it is certain that, even in outward things, God is a Refuge for his people, and that under his care they ordinarily enjoy both unusual blessing and a quite especial protection. Jesus teaches us to trust our Father in heaven, while of course using the means he gives us, for all our temporal necessities (Matt. vi. 25—34). He pledges himself that, so long as it is the Father's will that we should live in the world, we shall be protected from harm, and suitably provided for. This was David's confidence, expressed in many of the psalms, and it has been the confidence of all God's people. Experience verifies that the good man's dwelling is the "munitions of rocks;" his bread is given him, his water is sure (Isa. xxxiii. 16). 2. To *our spiritual existence*. God is the soul's (1) spiritual Saviour. Though our Lord and Judge, it is only in his bosom, in his forgiving grace, we can find refuge from our sins, from the unhappiness they cause us, and from the ruin they have brought upon us. The child that has offended his parent may seek the whole world through in vain for the rest he can find at once by coming back, confessing his sin, and being forgiven. God has devised means "that his banished be not expelled from him" (2 Sam. xiv. 14). The way is open. "O Israel, thou hast destroyed thyself; but in me is thy help" (Hos. xiii. 9). (2) Unfailing Retreat in trouble. No matter what storms beat without, what blessings of an outward kind are given or withheld, what threatening forms the enmity of man may assume, the soul has in God a Retreat, a place of resort and Refuge, which never fails it. There it dwells in a region of love, breathes an atmosphere of peace, holds a communion with the Father of spirits, which only grows the sweeter the longer life lasts, and the more the outward cup is bitter to the taste. In this inward home of the spirit it renews its strength and drinks of living waters, has meat to eat which the world knows not of, finds satisfaction for its deepest needs (Hab. iii. 17, 18). (3) Unfailing Support. He upholds the soul. Has the believer trials to come through? He is upheld to bear them. Has he temptations to face? He is upheld to conquer in them. Has he work to do? He is upheld and strengthened to perform it. Has he enemies to fight? His courage is sustained, and he is made "more than conqueror." But for the upholding of the "everlasting arms," how many of God's saints would never have come through what they have experienced! 3. To *our eternal existence*. "The *eternal* God," etc. Heavenly and eternal existence are wrapped up in this promise. God does not make his eternity a refuge for beings of a day. There would be an utter disproportion between an everlasting dwelling-place and a creature of some three score years and ten. All eternal good is here implied, and this crowns the promise and carries it beyond all comprehension of its greatness. "Eye hath not seen," etc.—J. O.

Vers. 1—5.—*The King and his viceroy*. Moses, having received the direction about his death, proceeds next to formally bless the tribes. We have in these verses the introduction to the blessing. It brings under our notice the Great King himself, and the minor king, Moses, the viceroy. As the parting blessing of him whom God had made "king in Jeshurun," it has more weight and significance than anything which ever came out of the lips of kings. Even David's dying words are not so sublime as these of Moses (cf. 2 Sam. xxiii. 1—7). Let us look first at the Great King, and then at his viceroy who reigned in Jeshurun. I. THE ADVENT OF GOD. He is represented as rising at Sinai, as scattering rays from Seir, and as riding forth in sunlike majesty from Mount Paran. The idea is borrowed from the dawn. Just as, before the sun appears in splendour, the mountaintops are tipped with gold, and then the dawn gathers into glory, and the sun at last steps forth in might, so the Lord made his proximity felt on the top of Sinai; there was a still greater impression made at Seir, with the mercy of the brazen serpent ; and last of all in Paran, in whose wilderness was Kadesh, the scene of chequered experience and yet abundant blessing, the sunlight having then fully come. God had come as the Light-giver. " God is light, and in him is no darkness at all " (1 John i. 5).

Next let us notice his *court*—" myriads [רִבְבוֹת, which may mean *a million*] of saints." This cannot refer to Israel, as some suggest, but to the holy ones accompanying the Lord from heaven. What a magnificent array ! Only the holy can stand in his sight or constitute his train.

Next let us notice his *gift* to men—" from his right hand went a fiery Law for them." This fiery Law can only mean that *moral law* which penetrates unto the heart with its fiery heat.

And all was in *love* (ver. 3), for the God who is light and fire is also love. The saints are safe in his hand, and they gather round his feet.

II. THE VICEROY. He is called here " the man of God," and justly so. He was the man who recognized himself as God's property, as God's servant, as God's minister.

And this is why he was " king in Jeshurun." It is consecration to God's glory which secures the real kingship. No kingship is worth the name which consists not in holy influences ; and every man is a " king of men " who reigns over them by the sovereignty of intelligent consecration.

In these respects Moses was a type of Jesus. Pilate could not understand his kingship through truth ; but the world recognizes it. He was so devoted to the Father's glory, and so bent on the good of men, that increasing multitudes every year are owning his sway and accepting of the Law at his mouth. Fiery it is doubtless, fitted to kindle the coldest heart to rapture. As it dwells within us, it moulds to highest good the life.—R. M. E.

Vers. 6—25.—*Watchwords for the tribes.* The blessings authoritatively pronounced by these old worthies amounted to watchwords for their future development. They were divinely suggested ideas regarding their future courses. We shall look at the ideals thus presented in their order.

I. THE UNOSTENTATIOUS DEVELOPMENT OF REUBEN. Deposed from the primacy among the brethren, because of his self-indulgence, he is to content himself with pastoral progress amid the mountains of Moab. The blessing is a good one, quiet life and progress.

II. THE SOVEREIGNTY THROUGH SUFFERING OF JUDAH. In ver. 7 we have clearly the regal strain. It is the struggle and the victory and the reign. The brunt of battle is to fall on Judah, and the sovereignty in the end. That it refers to Messiah ultimately is, we think, quite reasonable. Indeed, Kennicott regards ver. 5 as referring to the Messiah and not to Moses, and consistently therewith he would have the words " bring *him* to his people " to refer to the king, Shiloh, of Judah's tribe. However this may be, we can discern in this watchword of Judah the key-note of the Saviour's suffering life.

III. THE SELF-DENIAL AND DEVOTEDNESS OF LEVI. The treasure of the oracle was to be with the Levites, and, in prosecuting the work of God, they were to show that they loved their Master more than even father or mother, sister or brother, sons or daughters. In prosecuting their ministerial work, they were to illustrate discipleship as a giving unto God the first place above the nearest and the dearest (cf. Luke xiv. 26). Moreover, in this holy work the sons of Levi shall need the Lord's blessing on their substance, since they lived by voluntary contributions, and the Lord's help against calamities. A special blessing is thus looked for in connection with special work, of a self-denying character. And the same is applicable to the ministry still.

IV. THE SHADOW OF GOD FOR BENJAMIN. This powerful tribe was to afford shelter to the central government and worship in the time of the monarchy. The Divine presence thus was specially to overshadow the descendants of Benjamin. As Joseph so tenderly overshadowed his brother, so will the central government and worship his seed.

V. THE SPLENDID SUCCESS AND PROWESS OF JOSEPH. All the fatness of the earth and the favour of God and the power to push successfully their way against all opposing forces are to belong to Ephraim and to Manasseh. From Joppa unto Carmel, on the sea across to the pastures of Gilead, the two half-tribes were destined to hold sway, and to enjoy all the wealth this encircled. It was the magnificent central province of Samaria, with any amount of pasture-land beyond the Jordan.

VI. THE HIGHWAY OF ZEBULUN. Its outlets are to be peculiarly important, as we know they proved between the Great Sea and the sea of Tiberias. Through Zebulun the traffic passed from the great Eastern kingdoms. Their situation, mercantilely regarded, was superb.

VII. THE CONFIDENCE AND CONSOLIDATION OF ISSACHAR. Settled beside Zebulun, with a series of mountain fastnesses behind, and Esdraelon's plain down to the sands of the Mediterranean as their coast, the children of Issachar were to feel settled and secure in their tents. The mountain tracts will nurse the piety of the people, while the sea shall yield its abundance, and the sand become a source of treasure. No better home could be found for a trading, manufacturing people.

VIII. THE VANTAGE-GROUND OF GAD. This tribe is represented as hemmed in like a lion at bay, and thus compelled to take a prominent part in critical affairs. Lying between the mountains and the Jordan, it became the battle-ground of the monarchy, and at Ramoth-Gilead and Mahanaim important issues were decided. The watchword was vigilance, because of the vantage-ground.

IX. THE COURAGE OF DAN. He is represented as a lion's whelp, full of courage, though small in size. Leaping from Bashan, he made his lair northwards, but ever ready to shift to better quarters if he heard of them. He found a lair too at the sea, in the borders of Philistia.

X. EASY-GOING NAPHTALI. This tribe is represented as taking a south-west location after the northernmost Danites, and as rejoicing there in the manifold goodness of God.

XI. BLESSED BY NAME AND NATURE AS ASHER. This tribe is to be blessed, as the very name implies, in domestic relations, in fraternal relations, in the olive-yards yielding such magnificent oil, and in the iron and brass with which, instead of the ordinary wooden bars, they could protect themselves. To this tribe was given the oft-quoted promise, "As thy days, so shall thy strength be." They were to have "strength proportioned to their work."

It does not appear why to Simeon no blessing is assigned; and yet it is noticeable that this tribe played but a small part in the drama of Israelitish history.—R. M. E.

Vers. 26—29.—*The incomparable Saviour.* In finishing the blessing of the people, Moses cannot refrain from bursting into a tribute of admiration for him who had brought them thus far. He speaks of God's incomparable excellency, and how happy Israel was in relying upon his power. We shall notice the two thoughts in this order as cause and effect.

I. THE INCOMPARABLE EXCELLENCY OF GOD. This is brought out in several particulars. And: 1. God is *incomparably excellent in himself.* He "rideth upon the heaven in his help, and in his excellency on the sky." The reference is believed to be to the Shechinah cloud, which passed in calm majesty along the upper heavens to indicate to Israel, or "Jeshurun," as Israel is here called, the way they should take. In no more beautiful way could God's essential sovereignty be brought out. He moves in calm majesty among the spheres, the Ruler because Maker of them all. No one can for a moment be compared with him. 2. God is *incomparably excellent as the Saviour of his people.* Israel experienced his help in the deliverance from Egypt, in the pilgrimage to Palestine, and they were about to experience still further favour in the success of the invasion. The language is most beautiful by which all this is conveyed. "The eternal God is thy Refuge;" to him who dwells in the *eternities* and who orders their processions, the difficulties of *time* must be as nothing. "Underneath are the everlasting arms," no weariness ever overtaking arms which are full of everlasting strength. "He shall thrust out the enemy from before thee; and shall say, Destroy them." Now, in all this we have a figure of the salvation which God extends still to men. (1) He delivers us from the *bondage of sin*; (2) he *justifies* us freely from all things; (3) he *sanctifies* us by his Spirit; (4) he *protects* and delivers us from all our enemies.

II. THE CONSEQUENT HAPPINESS OF ISRAEL. What distinguishes Israel and renders them a happy people is the possession of such an incomparable Saviour. It is not in Israel themselves, but in their God, that the cause of their happiness dwells. And it is well to remember this. 1. *Frames and feelings are no proper foundation for our spiritual confidence.* Anxious souls prolong their anxiety and postpone their peace by excessive introspection. Instead of occupying themselves with the incomparable excellency of their Saviour, they occupy themselves with the incomparable vileness of their own hearts. No peace and joy can come from within. 2. *The changeless Saviour is a true Foundation for our confidence and hope.* It is "Jesus Christ, the same yesterday, to-day, and for ever," in whom we are asked to confide. He has every excellency which our necessities demand. He has the atonement and the sympathy and the intercessory powers we need to free us from deserved penalties and fit us for undeserved blessing. 3. *We stand in consequence as an expectant people awaiting our entrance to the land of promise.* For it is to be noticed that Israel were not only happy in their experience, but happy also in their hopes. They were about to enter the promised land. There they were to dwell safely alone, like the heavenly state where "the wicked cease from troubling and the weary are at rest." They are to have plenty of corn and wine, as the redeemed have in heaven, where they eat angels' food and drink the new wine of the kingdom. They are to dwell under the fertilizing dews of heaven, as the redeemed shall under the benedictions of God. In hope, then, Israel was happy : and we too may "rejoice in hope of the glory of God."—R. M. E.

Vers. 1—5.—*The Godlike act of blessing.* Moses is finely described as "the man of God." Among his contemporaries there was no man who bore so much of the Divine image. In character, in office, in deed, he was eminently Godlike. As his earthly life drew to a close, the real man came more fully into view. Death is a clever unveiler of a man—it strips off shams and masks, it discovers the reality. Like his great Antitype, Moses forgets himself in the crisis of death, and concerns himself about others. As his hours are few, he will crowd into them as many acts of blessing as he can. It is in the power of one man to bless many. This is Godlike.

I. BLESSING CAN COME TO MEN ONLY THROUGH THE CHANNELS OF LAW. It is useless to wish a man some good fortune, unless he is prepared to follow the lines along which good fortune comes. It is useless to wish a man health, while we know that he is wedded to the wine-cup. The only real blessing we can confer is to put men into connection with God's channels of blessing. The man who unveils to us the law of God respecting the expansion of steam, confers real blessing on the race. Similarly, the man who reveals to us the law, or method, through which God's favour flows to sinners, imparts solid blessing. Respecting blessing, God is the only primal Source, but men can be subordinate agents in distributing it. "Order is Heaven's first law ; " and, in blessing others, we must observe God's order of procedure. Submission to law is an essential condition of blessing.

II. BLESSING TO MEN HAS ALWAYS BEEN THE PURPOSE OF GOD'S SUBLIMEST MANIFESTATIONS. Desiring to bless the tribes, Moses at once reverted to Sinai, and to God's grand plan for blessing men. Heart and soul, Moses was a legislator. He saw the grandeur, the eternity, the utility of Law. The "ruling passion was strong in death." The splendid manifestation of God's majesty at Sinai again passed before the eye of memory. All those splendours of royal state were destined to illustrate the intrinsic majesty of Law. That magnificent retinue of consecrated ones illustrated the native glory of the Divine Law. That entire epiphany of God culminated in this significant act : "from his right hand went a fiery Law"—a Divine force to soften, melt, purify, and consume. Those honoured beings that found a place in the retinue of God received that exaltation and that office by virtue of submission to Law; "they sat down at thy feet." To reveal to men his Law is a Divine equivalent for largest blessing. God's Law is the outcome of his love. The spring and motive of this stately display of Law is deep and generous love. "Yea, he loved the people."

III. TO BLESS MEN, THROUGH THEIR OBSERVANCE OF LAW, IS THE AMBITION OF EVERY REAL KING. God is supreme Sovereign of all intelligent beings. The supreme Monarch manifests irrepressible desire to bless his subjects. Amidst impressive solemnities, he declares that blessing can only come through the channels of righteous Law. Moses, too, is a subordinate king—king in Jeshurun—God's vicegerent. Moses, too, desires to bless the people. His life had been spent in their interests. Even during the forty years he spent as a shepherd in Midian, he was undergoing preparation for his great undertaking. But Moses likewise knew that the greatest blessing he could confer on Israel was love of God's Law. No wishes, or hopes, or aspirations, which he could cherish for them would be of any practical value apart from their dutiful obedience to God. Therefore, his legacy was counsel and prayer : " He commanded a Law, even the inheritance of the congregation of Jacob." This is the richest heritage we can acquire on earth, viz. God's Law enshrined in the heart. Then are we living temples, the " habitation of God through the Spirit."—D.

Ver. 6.—*A prayer for the firstborn.* The personal character of Reuben had not been exemplary. His salient features were coarse. Moral qualities were entailed to posterity ; and the tribe, generation after generation, occupied a low place in the history of the nation. Nothing noble seems ever to have been achieved by it.

I. PRIORITY OF PLACE DOES NOT ENSURE NOBLENESS OF CHARACTER. Reuben was, in Jacob's household, *first* in the order of time, but not first in native dignity. "Many that are first shall be last." The king has not always the most royal character in the empire. The palace does not always contain the noblest society. The most obscure may yet become the purest and the best. Moral rottenness has often been on the throne, and real royalty on the gibbet.

II. PRESENT LIFE DOES NOT SECURE CONTINUOUS LIFE. Human life is not self-created; it is sustained through every hour by a Divine hand ; and whenever Divine wisdom sees best, that life is brought to a close. As life, with all its advantages, is a trust from God, which may be terminated any moment, we should use every moment well, in order to deserve its continuance. In proportion to the precariousness of life is the value of every moment increased. So, too, in the life beyond the grave, the same dependence on God remains. We hang on him for continued life. Christ is our life. Through eternity we live (if we live at all) by faith on the Son of God. Hourly the prayer ought to ascend, " Let me live, and not die."

III. PRESENT UNITS MAY BECOME FUTURE MYRIADS. At the time of Moses' dissolution, the number of Reuben seems to have been small. Possibly this may have been a penalty for Reuben's incest. In this case it would be an appeal to God's mercy to remove the curse. Beneath the benediction of God, "a little one soon becomes a thousand." Prolific increase is a sign of Divine approval. All the oak forests on the globe sprang from a single germ.—D.

Ver. 7.—*The royal house of Judah.* The name Judah signifies praise. Here Moses represents Judah as the praying tribe—in this respect inheriting the spirit of its great father, Jacob. Prayer and praise usually wed ; they make a happy pair in the habitation of the heart, and the offspring is royal nobleness.

I. TRUE PRAYER PLEADS FOR AN APPOINTED DESTINY. What God has designed and destined for us—*this* is a proper object of prayer. For although God has designed some good for us, our prayer is the last link in the succession of causes which brings us into actual possession. "For all these things," saith God, "I will be inquired of . . . to do it for them." Prayer has respect to the will of God. The purpose and oath of God have prepared the blessing. The hand of faith is stretched forth to take it.

II. TRUE PRAYER IS SUPPORTED BY OTHERS' INTERCESSIONS. The prayer of a good man on our behalf is an inestimable boon. Here Moses prayed that Judah's petition might be heard. Example is contagious. When good men see us praying, they will pray with us, and for us too. If only combustible material be at hand, the fiery flame will spread. It is always an inspiration to us, if we remember that while we pray, Christ our Elder Brother is praying for us above.

III. TRUE PRAYER IS ALWAYS SECONDED BY PERSONAL ENDEAVOUR. "Let his hands be sufficient for him." What we can do to gain the blessing, God will not do for us. What we cannot do, God will, if we meekly ask him. Prayer without effort is hypocrisy. We are not sincere in our request. Labour without prayer is stark atheism. The boat of human progress must be rowed with two oars—prayer and effort. Unless both wings are in motion, the eagle cannot rise.

IV. TRUE PRAYER OBTAINS THE HELP OF GOD. It obtains help for every undertaking —husbandry, commerce, art, and war. Prayer always has prevailed—it always will. Prayer and painstaking can accomplish anything. Prayer secures for us the best help, the presence of God himself. "Be thou a Help to him." This is an Ally worth having —an Ally who, by a breath, secures success. If the Lord be our Helper, we can wisely speak the challenge, "What can man do unto me?" God with me, God *in* me, inspiring every thought, and purpose, and desire and deed,—*this* makes a mean man royal indeed. Thus we may all obtain a place in the honoured tribe of Judah, and be "kings unto God."—D.

Vers. 8—11.—*The priestly tribe.* The abuse of the priestly office has brought the name of priest into contempt. Best things, when corrupt, become the worst. Sour milk and rotten grapes and stained snow are things most obnoxious. Yet a true priest is the noblest form of man—the greatest benefactor of his species. A pompous, bedizened, arrogant ecclesiastic, is not a true priest. God's priest is meek, self-forgetful, saintly, Christlike.

I. PURITY AND CONSECRATION ARE THE ESSENTIAL QUALIFICATIONS FOR THE PRIESTHOOD. Levi is here described as "thy holy one." This was God's ideal, though never fully realized except in Christ. If there was not perfect purity of character, there was the nascent germ within—the inner yearning and desire after holiness. Levi was the rude type, the rough outline of the perfect priest. *A further qualification was consecration.* This personal righteousness was to be practical. It was required to be actively devoted to the service of God. Regard for God was to dominate regard for earthly relatives. When called to God's service, the Levite was to regard his parents as if he had them not; he was to forget his brethren and his father's house; yea, he must love his children as though he loved them not. *God first;* every one else must find a subordinate place (ver. 9). Here we have the forecast of Christ's axiom, "He that loveth father or mother more than me, is not worthy of me." *Further, this character was a tested one.* To an office so responsible, God does not admit a novice. Mere innocence is not a qualification. There must be tried and tested character— character tried in the furnace of temptation. So with respect to this tribe of Levi; him "thou didst prove at Massah," with him "thou didst strive at the waters of Meribah."

II. PRIESTLY CONSECRATION IS A CONDITION FOR RECEIVING REVELATION FROM GOD. "Let thy Thummim and thy Urim be with thy holy one." Although it is confessedly difficult to determine precisely what the Urim and the Thummim were, it is obvious that it was God's ancient method for revealing his will to Israel. In emergencies, whether personal or national, it was the practice to ask counsel of God by means of the Urim and Thummim. It is a necessity that there should be internal fitness in order to receive and transmit the will of God. Light can only circulate through a fitting medium. Music can only be transmitted by a specific conductor. As it is in the natural world, so in the spiritual, only the pure in heart can see God. His will is revealed only to the dutiful. "The secret of the Lord is with them that fear him." On this account, God's priests have often been God's prophets; *e.g.* Jeremiah, Ezekiel, Samuel, and John the Baptist. Moses too belonged to the tribe of Levi.

III. PRIESTLY CONSECRATION INCLUDES SERVICE GODWARD AND MANWARD. (Ver. 10.) Every true priest is a mediator between God and men. He receives of God and imparts to men; he receives from men and presents unto God. The only perfect Mediator is the "Son of the Highest;" but, in a humbler sphere, earthly priests are also mediators. They receive God's Law from the fountain of his lips, and they convey it unto their brethren. Every real teacher is a real mediator. He delivers unto others that which he has first received. The priest has also a service to perform *Godward.* He brings human offerings before the Most High—the offerings of gratitude and praise. But men have sinned, and this sad fact must be recognized. They stand in urgent need of Divine mercy. Hence substantial proofs of penitence and confession are required. God has a proper and prescribed method for conveying his mercy. He will be approached in the way of sacrifice, and it is part of the priest's vocation to present "whole burnt sacrifice upon God's altar."

IV. COMPLETE CONSECRATION ENSURES COMPLETE SALVATION. Salvation is many-sided; it is negative and positive. It embraces deliverance from every evil, present and future; it embraces every good that can enrich and ennoble the man. While we care wholly for God's interests, he will most completely care for ours. No external substance will bring us any real advantage unless God's blessing be upon it, ay, pervade it. The Levites were compelled by official duties to be often absent from their families and homesteads, which needed therefore special protection from God. "Bless, Lord, his substance." But more important yet was it for the whole nation that the offerings and intercessions of the priests might find acceptance with God, If anything upon their part should nullify the offices of religion, the effect would be unspeakably disastrous. Therefore, looking along the vista of the future in fervent anticipation, Moses prays, "Accept the work of his hands." It is as if he had said, "Let thy gracious plan for pardoning and saving men completely succeed!" And lastly, he prays for the priest's security against all foes. We may not here confine our thoughts to foreign adversaries. The true and faithful priest will always find enemies in proportion to his fidelity. His foes shall be those of his own household. They will assail his earnestness, suspect his motives, attack his reputation. But God shall undertake his servant's cause. He will, in his own way, so smite his foes, that they shall be completely silenced; "they shall not rise again."—D.

Ver. 12.—*God's fatherly interest in Benjamin.* The circumstance of Benjamin's birth has a melancholy interest. His birth was the occasion of Rachel's death. If we may argue back from the qualities of Rachel's children to the qualities of Rachel, she must have been a woman deserving high esteem. Rare excellences embellish the characters of her sons. To Joseph and to Benjamin were assigned territory in the very heart of Canaan. In the benediction of Moses we have—

I. An endearing name. A name given by God is pregnant with meaning. It is no empty compliment. If God regarded Benjamin as his "beloved," there was sufficient ground and reason for it. This tribe may not have been conspicuous for robust energy or for martial enterprise, but it was distinguished for its genuine piety and its devout attachment to the cause of God. If we cannot all be great, we can all be good. To be consistently and thoroughly pious is within the reach of all. Each of us can be knighted and ennobled with this title, "The beloved of the Lord." We have indicated here—

II. The best society. "He shall dwell in safety by him." This promise, in all likelihood, alludes to the position of Benjamin's inheritance. His portion in Canaan included the hill of Moriah, on which, in later days, the temple was erected. This was no insignificant honour—no mean token of Jehovah's favour. The successive generations of Benjamin would dwell in closest vicinity to the oracle of God, and would enjoy easy access to the public ordinances of worship. So long as man needs the aid and inspiration of external ordinances, so long will this vicinity to the temple be a real advantage. In our folly we may despise the privilege, but this foolish contempt no way derogates from its value. They who most prize the house of God most prize God himself. We have also—

III. Complete protection promised. "The Lord shall cover him all the day long." God was pleased, in a very remarkable manner, to disclose himself to the Hebrews by metaphors easily interpreted. In a climate where men suffered most from a scorching sun, a covert from the burning heat was most appreciated. Therefore God was to them just what they needed, "the shadow of a great rock in a weary land." The fervent heat was tempered with a cloud. From every evil thing God covers his saints —from the heat of trial, sorrow, care, excessive prosperity. He never fails as does a passing cloud. He covers his chosen "all the day long." We have promised likewise—

IV. Unerring guidance. "He shall dwell between his shoulders." As the temple of God was to rest on Moriah, and the visible Shechinah be enshrined within, this would properly seem as a crown of glory on the head of Benjamin; or, what the head is to the human body, *that* God would be to this favoured tribe. The head informs, enlightens, directs the whole body; so, saith God, "I will guide thee with my eye." That man has reached the perfection of being when Christ dwells in him, as "wisdom, righteousness, sanctification," life. To be most godly is to be most manly.—D.

Vers. 13—17.—*Royal donations on Joseph.* It is instructive to observe with what loving ardour Moses speaks of Joseph. No sooner does he mention this name than his tongue, the ready servant of his heart, gives vent to a flood of eloquence. No good is too great to predict for Joseph. No benediction is too costly for him. The finest imagery that his fancy can invent is employed to foreshadow his greatness. The imagination of the dying saint fondly revels in the prospect of Joseph's prosperity and power. Touching Joseph, we have mentioned—

I. HIS FAITHFUL IMPROVEMENT OF TRIAL. The description of Rachel's firstborn is truly pathetic. He is pictured to us as he "that was separated from his brethren." In a sense he had always been separate. In youth, his temper and tastes and predilections were all superior to theirs. They were coarse, vulgar, cruel; he was refined, thoughtful, gentle—cast in a nobler mould. But the reference made by Moses to separation is, doubtless, to that violent and murderous separation, when by his brothers' hands he was sold as a bond-slave and carried into Egypt. How nobly he had borne that treatment is a matter of historic fact. How Joseph's behaviour in captivity had led to the development of Israel's fortunes could never be erased from Jewish memory. His affectionate treatment of his aged father, and his generous forgiveness of his brethren, marked him as "separate" from the common herd of men. This is a kind of separateness we may aspire to emulate. Here is a pattern man.

II. HIS FORESEEN PROSPERITY. This forecast of prolific prosperity was founded on a double basis, viz. on the native resources of the district which was to be his favoured portion; and on the abiding benediction of Jehovah. Yet these two sources of prosperity were in reality one—one source flowing through many channels. His hills should laugh in fertility and gladness beneath the sunny smile of God. The vale of Shechem has always enjoyed a wide celebrity for its beauty and fruitfulness. Samaria was the paradise of Canaan. Its hills were covered with olives and vines and figs. Its valleys waved with golden corn. One natural source of abundance is its perennial fountains and flowing streams—the "deep that coucheth beneath." Here it was that Jacob made his first purchase of land, and here he digged the well which to this hour bears his name. To this verdant district Jacob's sons led their flocks when drought and barrenness covered the land. And in this district occurred the shameful deed when Joseph was imprisoned in the pit and then sold to Ishmaelites. By a generous retribution of God's sagacious providence, Joseph obtained his permanent portion in this very territory, and with all the energy of his soul Moses prayed, "Blessed of the Lord be his land."

III. HIS FUTURE POWER. A double portion of property and power fell to Joseph. By the dying bequest of his father Jacob, each of Joseph's sons, Manasseh and Ephraim, was to rank in the first degree, adopted by Jacob in the place and rank of his own. Yet the two sons were destined not to grow in the same proportion of power. While there were to be the "thousands of Manasseh," there were to be the "ten thousands of Ephraim." God "divideth to every one severally as he will." The glory of these young men was to be "their strength," and this would be fostered by the fatness of their land. Yet their strength was not pictured under the image of a lion or an eagle. It was to be rather the quiet, patient strength of the ox—the strength which endures, as did Joseph's in the land of Egypt. Horns are the bullock's natural weapons of defence, and these are significant emblems of power. But Joseph's horns were to be like those of the unicorn. His was to be royal authority and strength. Evidently Moses foresaw the day when the sovereignty of the Hebrews would be divided, and when Joseph should wield a sceptre in Israel. The royal emblazonry of Britain thus corresponds, in part, with the heraldry of ancient Samaria. "With the horns of unicorns" he was destined "to push the people together to the ends of the earth." His "horn God exalted unto honour." To this hour, a remnant of Joseph's power remains in Samaria. *There* still in the synagogue is enshrined the ancient Law, and *there* yet is observed the Paschal feast.—D.

Vers. 18, 19.—*Combined work and worship.* Some tie of affinity bound these two tribes in peculiar intimacy. We cannot find this cementing link in the fact that their lands lay in close contiguity; this fact was not unique. Other tribes bordered on their coasts, with whom no such intimate alliance prevailed. Neither were their secular occupations alike. It was an affinity springing out of congenial character. The same tastes and purposes and aims were dominant in both. To their honour, it is handed down to distant posterity that they were zealous for the worship of God.

I. SECULAR PURSUITS SHOULD BE FOLLOWED IN A SPIRIT OF GLADNESS. The man of God leaves it as a charge upon these tribes to rejoice in their several avocations. The earthly callings of Zebulun and Issachar seem to have been quite distinct the one from the other. Zebulun's territory abutted on the sea-coast, and enjoyed the advantage of a small harbour under shelter of Mount Carmel. Hence the people had access to the sea; they had a fishery; they possessed opportunities for commerce. Though they had no maritime tastes (like the Phœnicians), yet the ships of other nations would visit their coast, and the merchandise of distant lands would find their way thither. "They shall suck of the abundance of the seas." Issachar was an agricultural tribe. The people dwelt in tents, and their possessions consisted in flocks and herds. But whatever their occupation, it ought to be an occasion for joy. It gave scope to the pleasant exercise of their powers. It furnished them with the means of family subsistence. It was a fine field for the discipline of their virtues, for the exercise of brotherly help and mutual kindness. It enabled them to trace in their daily walk the footsteps of Jehovah, and provided material for daily praise. Whatever our work be, it should be fulfilled with gladness. Happy is the man who sings at his work.

II. SECULAR PURSUITS ARE NOT INCOMPATIBLE WITH DIVINE WORSHIP. "They shall call the people unto the mountain." Although their abodes were far away among the northern hills, they did not hold themselves free to abstain from public ordinances of worship. Yea, not only did they stir themselves up to this delightful duty, but they summoned the surrounding tribes also to keep the sacred festivals. In the absence of modern reminders of the seasons—in the absence of almanacks and clocks—these twin tribes noted the revolutions of sun and moon, became the timekeepers of the nation, and called the tribes to prayer and sacrifice. Probably their secular duties as fishermen and as shepherds furnished the opportunities for observing the phases of the moon. New moon or full was the signal in the heavens for the recurrence of the special festivals; *then* the silver trumpets would ring out the summons from hill to hill, and from hamlet to hamlet. If there be the disposition to worship God, facilities will be found or *made*.

III. SECULAR PURSUITS FURNISH THE MEANS FOR ACCEPTABLE SACRIFICE. "They shall offer sacrifices of righteousness." Secular pursuits will never satisfy all the yearnings of the human heart. There is a hunger within which no material banquet can relieve. There is a thirst of soul which can be slaked only by the water of eternal life. To gratify all the cravings of the mind we must come to God. But he will be approached by means of sacrifice. This furnishes a test of our sincerity. This awakens a sense of our deepest need. This provides a channel for our highest joy. Whatever form our sacrifices may take—whether corn, or oil, or fruit—whether lambs or doves—whether contrition, praise, or gratitude—it must be a sacrifice of righteousness, or it cannot be accepted. As the act of devout obedience to Divine command, or as the outgoing of desire after holiness, or as the expression of righteous obligation, it will find acceptance on God's altar.

IV. SECULAR SUCCESS IS PROMOTED BY GENEROUS CONSECRATION OF SUBSTANCE TO GOD. "Them that honour me I will honour." God is the most generous of Masters, but he hates empty pretensions of loyalty. He will not accept words where deeds are possible. The honour is conferred, not on the God who receives, but on the man whose gift finds acceptance. "It is more blessed to give than to receive," is a lesson not easily learnt—an experience not common enough. This is not a firstfruit, but one of the latest fruits of Christian living. Yet without the favouring smile of Jehovah no secular pursuit can succeed. Men often sow a bushel and reap a peck. But when God is on our side, our seed multiplies a hundredfold: "a little one becomes a thousand;" "godliness is profitable unto all things." The only real insurance for successful enterprise is the benediction of God. The treasures remain in the land (ver. 19) until God teaches us how to draw them forth. The eye of faith is clearer-sighted than the eye of expediency.—D.

Vers. 20, 21.—*Gad's valour and chivalry commended.* Gad had been prematurely hasty in seeking an allotment in Canaan. When the heads of this tribe perceived how suitable were the hills of Gilead for pasturing their extensive flocks, they clamoured at once for this possession, ere yet an inch of land had been gained on the west of Jordan. Moses yielded to their request, on condition only that they should go over Jordan armed with their brethren, and should fight in the front of battle. This they nobly did, and returned to their families and flocks only when Joshua released them from further service. We see—

I. A HASTY CHOICE OVERRULED FOR GOOD. There can be little doubt that selfishness was the originating motive for this choice. The well-being of other tribes was not, for the time, weighed. Yet it was a choice beset with perils. The district coveted lay on the borders of the wilderness, and was exposed to raid and depredation from foes. It is wiser always to look heavenward and to say, " Thou shalt choose our inheritance for us." Yet, though selfishness was for the hour dominant, other and better qualities dwelt in the tribe. As often happens, God allowed their choice, and then led them through severe discipline to enable them to enjoy it.

II. THEIR CHOICE WAS PURCHASED BY HARD AND PERILOUS WARFARE. " He came with the heads of the people, he executed the justice of the Lord, and his judgments with Israel." To acquire this territory, Moses stated at once the simple condition, viz. that they should fight in the van of Israel's battalions. This condition they accepted, and bravely they acquitted themselves. The event taught them valuable lessons. It taught them that they were an integral part of a great commonwealth, and could not separate themselves, without injury, from it. It taught them to look, not only on their own welfare, but also to consult for the welfare of others. It taught them that rest and quiet possession were more valued after a hard-fought campaign than before.

III. THEIR CHIVALROUS CONDUCT DEVELOPED THEIR LATENT QUALITIES OF MARTIAL PROWESS. The greatest advantage resulting from their military encounters was the personal strength and heroism which were developed in themselves. They were better, braver, nobler men afterwards than ever before. Now, and not till now, they were qualified to protect their own hills and flocks. This advantage they had not foreseen, yet it was the best and most enduring. Now the men of Gad " dwelt like a lion " in fearless possession ; now they were able, when assailed, " to tear the arm " of a foe, " with the crown of the head." This heroic quality reappeared, in brighter form, in the person of Elijah, and probably also in the forerunner of our Lord.

IV. THIS FEARLESS COURAGE OBTAINS A PRAYER FOR STEADY ENLARGEMENT. "Blessed be he that enlargeth Gad." It was a boon to the whole of Israel to have such a martial tribe occupying an outpost in the land. To enlarge and strengthen Gad was to strengthen their military defence, was to increase their own safety, was to perpetuate their own peace. So long as the lion-hearted tribe of Gad had a numerous generation, no foe could invade Israel from that side. The very reputation of Gad eastward kept the nations in salutary awe. The welfare of Gad was the welfare of all.—D.

Ver. 22.—*The blessing of strength.* From the tribe of Dan sprang Samson, whom we may regard as a typical child of Dan. In all probability the whole tribe was noted for strong men, and their pride was to cultivate and increase muscular strength. We have here promised—

I. YOUTHFUL STRENGTH. This is confessedly not the highest form of blessing; yet, in some conditions of civic society, it is essential to the preservation of independence, property, and life. The picture is that of a young lion.

II. DESTRUCTIVE STRENGTH. This has its place in God's kingdom. The destructive strength of Samson was an inestimable boon, when the Philistines threatened to overwhelm the land. We cannot otherwise regard the prodigious strength of Samson but as God's scourge for the chastisement of gross idolaters. Yet, what prodigies of good might such strength accomplish if directed into beneficent channels !

III. STRENGTH UNDER THE DIRECTION AND CONTROL OF SAGACITY. " He shall leap from Bashan." Strength is ofttimes wasted from want of prudence. The strength of Dan was reserved for suitable occasions. It displayed itself in forms surprising and unexpected. The close vicinity of the Philistines to one part of Dan's allotment necessitated this training of muscular strength. It is instructive to note what latent energies there reside in man, which come into view only when great occasions require.—D.

Ver. 23.—*Naphtali's goodly choice.* Naphtali's position was in the north of Canaan, and had its southern border adjacent to the sea of Galilee. A large proportion of our Lord's ministrations were bestowed on the inhabitants within this district. Obviously the heads of this tribe in Moses' day aspired after the best possessions.

I. WE OBSERVE HERE THE BEST HUMAN AMBITION. "Satisfied with favour." It is scarcely conjecture that imports into Moses' words the meaning, "the favour of God;" for in the next clause he mentions distinctly the "blessing of the Lord." No other favour can satisfy save the "favour of Jehovah." This is all-sufficient—an ocean, in which the soul of man can bathe itself with amplest delight. This phrase, "the favour, or grace, of God," includes everything which God can supply for human need. In it is embraced light, pardon, Divine friendship, purity, peace, strength, liberty, rest. A comprehensive prayer is *this*, "Oh, satisfy me early with thy mercy!"

II. WE NOTE THE BEST AMBITION SATISFIED. "Full with the blessing of the Lord." We often desire inferior good, and desire in vain. The love of God is too deep and wise to indulge our foolish requests. But when we ask for highest good, and desire it earnestly, we never fail to obtain. What man ever sued for grace and was sent empty away? No; God's chief complaint is that we come too seldom, and ask too little at his hands. Still he says to us, "Open thy mouth wide, and I will fill it." The possession and wise use of God's grace enlarges our capacity to receive. It is a cure for all murmuring and discontent.

III. WE SEE HOW, WITH THE HIGHEST BLESSING, GOD GIVES THE LOWER UNASKED. Naphtali desired to be satisfied with the Divine favour; and a voice was commissioned to say, "Possess thou the sea and the south." It is a recognized method of God's procedure that when men ask for spiritual riches, God grants both spiritual and temporal good. In Gibeah, God appeared to Solomon, and proposed to him, "Ask what I shall give thee;" and when Solomon craved to possess the gift of wisdom, his generous God assured him that not only should wisdom be his, but things he had not asked—even unprecedented riches and honour. To the same effect, our Lord affirmed, "Seek ye first the kingdom of God, and his righteousness, and all other (needed) things shall be added unto you." He is "able to do for us exceeding abundantly above all that we can ask or think."—D.

Vers. 24, 25.—*The comprehensive benediction of Asher.* No one can read this series of poetical benedictions without cherishing the conviction that Moses "spake as moved by the Holy Ghost." The peculiar fitness of his aspirations for the future exigencies of the tribes, and his clear foresight of their distant fortunes, indicate unmistakably that a supernatural light suffused his understanding. This benediction of the dying prophet foretokens—

I. NUMERICAL INCREASE. By a natural law of God's providence, rapid increase of the people is a fruit of material prosperity. When scarcity of food is a permanent condition, infanticide prevails, or children perish for lack of nutritious food. This increase of children was, in former times, a distinct token of God's favour, and a frequent subject of promise. As the numbers of Israel increased, so would their strength to resist aggression. It was when Israel's numbers were diminished by intestine wars, that the Eastern potentates gained decisive triumphs. Occupying, as Asher did, the extreme north-west of Canaan, numerical increase was a source of defensive strength. To the Christian parent—to the Church, children are a blessing. "Happy they who have their quiver full" of these Divine arrows.

II. THERE IS SET FORTH SOCIAL REPUTATION AND GOOD WILL. "Let him be acceptable to his brethren." So long as the tribal relationship was maintained in strength, there was a constant danger of mutual jealousies and animosities. Occasionally this evil passion took fire and broke into open flame. From tribal suspicion and dislike Asher would be free. It is an honour and a joy to live in the esteem and good will of brethren. The outward reach of influence is enlarged. Life is felt to have nobler interests. The better part of human nature finds development.

III. THERE IS FORESHADOWED AGRICULTURAL PROSPERITY. Upon the northern hills of Palestine the olive tree flourishes, and authorities affirm that no agricultural produce is so abundant and so remunerative as that of the olive. It is hardy, will flourish in rocky soil, and attains venerable age. Its fruit is valuable, is utilized for domestic purposes, and has always been a staple commodity of commerce. So prolific were the olives of Asher to become, that the people should have, not only the head, but the feet also, in the abundant oil; or the language may be designed as a bold figure, to indicate that so full should be the oil-vats at the base of every olive-clothed hill, that the very land should seem to be foot-deep in golden oil.

IV. THERE IS PREDICTED IMPREGNABLE DEFENCE. The poetical imagery here may be better translated, "Thy bars shall be iron and brass." It may be that these metals were found in veins among the hills, or rather iron and copper. It may that the gates of their cities were, in some cases, fashioned with these metals. Doors and gates of iron are still to be seen in the district of Bashan. But it is better to treat the language as elegant imagery, to indicate the matchless strength of Asher's fortresses. Over all her internal wealth there shall be a sure defence. The Chaldee paraphase reads, "Thou shalt be strong and bright, like iron and brass."

V. THERE IS PLEDGED INTERNAL STRENGTH PROPORTIONED TO NEED. "As thy days, thy strength." A precious promise this of universal application. Our days are under Divine inspection ; our circumstances are under Divine control. It is better for the man every way that his strength should be increased than that the trial should be abated. The outcome is that the man emerges stronger, nobler, more highly developed. The supply is always adjusted to the particular need. God is the model of frugal economy. In his administration there is no waste. But there would be waste if the supply of strength daily given were in excess of the requirement. This would be a blot upon his wisdom. What should we say of the water company that sent daily into our houses ten times the quantity of water that is required ? Or, what advantage would it be to us if the supply of light from the sun daily were a hundredfold in excess of this world's need ? Our God is perfect wisdom, as well as infinite love. Strength shall be supplied, not in superabundant waste, but in exact proportion to our need. "As our days, our strength." The infant would be crushed with the strength of the full-grown man.—D.

Vers. 26—29.—*God, the crown of Israel's glory.* As soon as Moses touches upon this theme, language seems too poor to express the greatness of his thought—too cold to convey the glowing ardour of his love. Here all metaphors fail; all comparisons are vain. God is above all imagery, or metaphor, or illustration. As there is none like him, so nothing can fitly express his deeds towards his chosen. His conduct is, like himself, ineffable. As heaven is loftier than earth, so do God's thoughts and ways transcend human conception.

I. OBSERVE ISRAEL'S SOURCE OF GREATNESS. Without question, Israel's source of greatness is *God.* Inconceivable as it is to mortal minds, the eternal Sovereign of the universe has come into intimate alliance with his chosen people. He is not simply God —the abstract Deity—he is the "God of Jeshurun." His eternity is brought into human use—is available for human needs. In the eternal and unchangeable God we may dwell. He is our Refuge, our Dwelling-place, our Sanctuary. All the resources of his omnipotence are for us : beneath us "are the everlasting arms." But hath God arms ? Hath he human members and organs ? "He that formed the eye, shall he not see ?" He that fashioned our arms and hands, hath he no instruments with which to support our sinking frame ? Yea, "in him we live."

All the activities of his providential government are *for us.* "He rideth upon the heavens," like a king in his chariot, for our help. This is true, both for Israel collectively, and for every individual believer. In every decree that issues from his throne, he has *us* in view. All the machinery of his extended providence works with one design, viz. our advantage. He thinks, and plans, and executes, and overturns for one main end—the final redemption of his people. God and we are one.

II. ISRAEL'S SAFETY. "Thou shalt dwell in safety alone." From the foregoing premiss, this is a sound and certain conclusion. "If God be for us," who can assail us successfully ? What can prevail against omnipotence ? What can penetrate the thick bosses of Jehovah's shield ? Fear in such a case is unreasonable disloyalty. This globe must be shivered into a thousand atoms, all the forces in God's universe must be rendered powerless and ineffective, the sceptre of Jehovah must be broken, before any danger can touch the elect of God. Safe, beyond the spectre of a fear, are hose whom God defends.

III. ISRAEL'S ABUNDANCE. "The fountain of Jacob shall be upon a land of corn and wine." Jacob is represented as the fount or source of many people, all of whom shall find an abode in the land of corn and wine. Every want shall be met. In this "mountain, shall the Lord of hosts prepare a feast of fat things." In the paradise of God there flourishes on both sides of the stream, the tree of life, which bears twelve manner of fruits, and yieldeth her fruit every month. Here is a perennial supply and satisfying variety. And though this is expressed by material images, it sets forth substantial and eternal truth—the very truth of God. In the kingdom of God there is provided whatever can please the eye, delight the ear, regale the appetite, relieve a need, gratify a sense. For perpetually does the voice of the King ring out a hearty welcome, "Eat, O friends; yea, drink abundantly, O beloved."

IV. ISRAEL'S TRIUMPH. God's triumph is Israel's triumph also. God will not dissociate himself from his people. "His covenant is an everlasting covenant, ordered in all things and sure." Yea, God's conquests are not separate and distinct from ours. He conquers through us—yea, by means of us. If we belong to the true Israel, God's foes are our foes, God's weapons are our weapons, God's interests are our interests. Our excellent Sword in this warfare is God; he himself is "the Shield of our help." The contest may be protracted, severe, wavering; success may seem to hang in suspense; but beyond the smoke and dust and uncertainty of battle, faith clearly sees the final triumph, and hears the immortal pean: "Thou shalt tread upon their high places."

V. ISRAEL'S TRANSCENDENT HAPPINESS. "Happy art thou, O Israel; who is like unto thee?" Surely, their happiness is complete, and impossible of enlargement, who repose themselves in the very heart of God, and dwell perpetually in his love! The utmost capacity of human speech is impotent to express their deep and satisfying joy. It is a thing to be experienced, not expressed. Such joy hath no vocabulary, no tongue. It is "joy unspeakable, and full of glory." What the noonday sun is to a glowworm's spark, so is the joy of the righteous compared with the joys of earth. God's own joy is conveyed to godly hearts.—D

EXPOSITION.

CHAPTER XXXIV.

DEATH, BURIAL, AND ENCOMIUM OF MOSES.

After blessing the people, Moses, in obedience to the Divine command, ascended Mount Nebo, the highest peak of the Pisgah range, and thence surveyed the whole land of Canaan, from north to south, and from east to west, as well as the district on the east of the Jordan, not included in Canaan proper.

Ver. 1.—**Unto the mountain of Nebo, to the top of Pisgah**; rather, *unto Mount Nebo, the summit of Pisgah*. **Gilead unto Dan.** Not Dan Laish, near the central source of the Jordan, which was not in Gilead, but another Dan in Northern Perea, the site of which has not yet been discovered (cf. Gen. xiv. 14).

Vers. 2—4.—**Unto the utmost sea**; rather, *the hinder sea*, viz. the Mediterranean (cf. ch. xi. 24). **The south**; the Negeb, the pasture-land in the south, towards the Arabian desert. **The plain of the valley of Jericho**; the extensive plain through which the Jordan flows, extending from Jericho to Zoar, at the south end of the Dead Sea. This wide prospect could not be surveyed by any ordinary power of vision; so that Moses must for the occasion have had his power of vision miraculously increased. There is no ground for supposing that he saw the scene in an ecstatic vision, and not with his bodily eyes.

Ver. 5.—**According to the word of the Lord**; literally, *at the mouth of the Lord*. The rabbins interpret this, "by a kiss of the Lord" ('Baba Bathra,' 17 a); *i.e.* as Maimonides explains it ('More Nevoch.,' iii. 51), Moses "died in a moment of holiest joy in the knowledge and love of God." The phrase, however, simply means "by or according to the command of" (cf. Gen. xlv. 21; Exod. xvii. 1; Lev. xxiv. 12; Numb. iii. 16, etc.).

Ver. 6.—**The valley in which God is supposed to have buried Moses was probably some depression on the Pisgah range, upon or close by Nebo. The rabbins say that Moses was buried by retiring into a cavern, where he died and where his body remained. It is probable that, like Enoch and Elijah, he was transferred to the invisible world without seeing corruption. Hence his appearance along with Elijah in bodily form on the Mount of the Transfiguration; and hence also, perhaps, the tradition of the contest for the body of Moses between Michael and Satan (Jude 9). If the body of Moses was actually buried, the concealment of his grave so that no man knew of it may be justly regarded as "the first instance on record of the providential obliteration, so remarkably exemplified afterwards in the gospel history, of the 'holy places' of Palestine; the providential safeguard against their elevation to a sanctity which might endanger the real holiness of the history and religion which they served to commemorate" (Stanley). The reverence which the Jews paid to graves shows that there was no small danger of their coming under a superstitious regard to that of Moses had it been known.

Ver. 7.—Though Moses had reached the age of a hundred and twenty years, his eye had not become dim, nor were the juices of his body dried. **Natural force.** The word so rendered (לֵחַ) occurs only here; but it is doubtless the subst. connected with the adj. לַח moist, fresh (cf. Gen. xxx. 37; Numb. vi. 3), and properly means moisture, freshness. It is used here of the natural juices of the body.

Ver. 8.—The people mourned for Moses thirty days, as they did for Aaron (Numb. xx. 29).

Ver. 10.—(Cf. Exod. xxxiii. 11.) **Whom the Lord knew.** "For the Lord was revealed to him face to face" (Onkelos). The knowledge here referred to was not merely that cognizance which God as the Omniscient has of all men, but that special knowledge by which men, being known of God, are made to know him (cf. 1 Cor. viii. 3). The statement in this verse could only have been inserted some time after the death of Moses, and after the people had had manifestations of God's presence with them, both by communications from him through the prophets and by the successes which he had given them over their enemies. But it is not necessary to suppose that a long period during which a lengthened succession of prophets had arisen had elapsed. "Moses was the founder and mediator of the old covenant. As long as this covenant was to last, no prophet could arise in Israel like unto Moses. There is but One who is worthy of greater honour than Moses, namely, the Apostle and High Priest of our profession, who is placed as a Son over all the house of God, in which Moses was found faithful as a servant (comp. Heb. iii. 2—6 with Numb. xii. 7), Jesus Christ, the Founder and Mediator of the new and everlasting covenant" (Keil).

HOMILETICS.

Vers. 1—9.—*The last journey.* (For other aspects of the death of Moses, see Homily on ch. xxxii. 48—52.) We have come at last to the closing scene. It is evidently recorded by other hands; for "Dan" (ver. 2) did not exist by that name till a much later period (see Judg. xviii. 1, 27—29). Vers. 10—12 indicate, moreover, a period later still; very possibly, it may have been as far on as the time of Ezra when those verses were added. And whoever will make use of the formula,— "early authorship, late editorship," as applicable to the Book of Deuteronomy, will have in his hands a key which will enable him to unlock many of the intricacies with which unbelieving writers seek to worry us. In all probability there was an ample supply of men in the later schools of the prophets who would be quite equal to editorial work; and most assuredly, Ezra would not be lacking in fitness for such service. It is altogether gratuitous and unnecessary to attempt to lower the value of the book in the eyes of others on account of the manifest touches of a later age. The revision of an ancient book, freeing it from archaisms, and, as we should say, "posting it up to date," would increase, not diminish its value.

By whomsoever written, this closing chapter is a fitting appendix to the words of the lawgiver himself. For homiletic use it is exceedingly suggestive.

I. MOSES HAS TO TAKE A REMARKABLE JOURNEY. (Vers. 1, 5.) He has to go up and die. In one sense this is true of us all. We are all on a pilgrimage, at the close of which, on its earthly side, there must be the act of dying. But in two respects there is a notable element in the journey of the aged lawgiver: in one of these it was unique. 1. His act of dying was, as much as his acts in life, one of conscious and intentional obedience to the will of God. He knew that he held his life absolutely at the disposal of another, and he would not, if he could, have prolonged it beyond its appointed time.

In this respect believers now are in full sympathy and accord with him. For them to live is Christ. Their supreme desire is that Christ may be magnified in their body, whether by life or by death. They desire to honour their Saviour in their dying as well as in their living work. "Whether" they "live" they "live unto the Lord; and whether" they "die" they "die unto the Lord; whether" they "live therefore or die," they "are the Lord's." 2. Moses, however, takes a journey, knowing just *when* and *where* he should die. It is not easy for us to enter into his feelings then. The time and place of our death are entirely unknown to us. How could we bear it if it were otherwise? Or if we could, how could our fondest ones on earth? We are often glad to throw ourselves anew on God, in thankfulness at the uncertainty which shrouds the future. We cheerfully say—

> "Lord, it belongs not to our care
> Whether we die or live."

But what a pall would seem to be thrown over the home, if it were disclosed when we should be called away! The holier and more beautiful the life, the more painful would the thought of parting with it be.

II. ERE HE DEPARTS, VISIONS OF GLORY ARE VOUCHSAFED. (Ver. 2.) "The Lord showed him all the land." The vision was in part physical, but that which faith beheld in the glorious future which was assured to the people of God, was by far the most precious part of the sight—incomparably so. Thus the Lord was merciful to Moses, in that, though his joy in death was checked by the sense of his own defect and failures, he would, on the other hand, be borne up by the thought that *God never had failed, and never would.* The future, from which he was cut off, would assuredly develop gloriously under the care and grace of Israel's covenant God. Even so, when God's heroes sink in death, they know that, though they die, God's Church will live on, and that the promised inheritance will yet be theirs. And many, many a believer has had a vision, in death, akin to that of Stephen, and, though appalled at his own shortcomings, has been borne up by a sight of Jesus, as "mighty to save," and as the Captain of salvation, who will bring the Church onward to the fulness of redemption.

III. WHEN THESE DEATH-SCENES ARE WITNESSED THE SOUL WILL BE ABSOLUTELY ALONE WITH GOD. Moses lay himself down to die, without any attendant by his side. However many there might have been around, between himself and God no one could possibly come. He must die alone; so must we. Alone must we pass through "death's iron gate," save as we can use the words in Ps. xxiii. 4. There is but One whose real presence can comfort us then.

IV. THE BODIES OF GOD'S SAINTS ARE NOT OVERLOOKED BY HIM. (Ver. 6.) "The Lord buried him," says the editor, "and no man knoweth of his sepulchre unto this day." Some have assigned it as a reason for the concealment of the body of Moses, "that his tomb might not become the occasion of idolatry or superstition." Others, rejecting this as inconsistent with the known fact that in the eye of the Hebrews every dead body was unclean, have sought for a reason by comparing Jude 9 with Matt. xvii. They deem it not improbable that there might be some change in the body of Moses in death, which would account for his appearing in the Transfiguration scene with another, who was taken up to heaven without dying, and also for the mysterious conflict over the body, of which Jude informs us. This may have been, but we can go no further than the text takes us by the hand. It suffices to know that God cared for Moses' body as well as for him. The body of believers is now the temple of the Holy Ghost. Christ is "the Saviour of the body." The Spirit who dwells in us will quicken the mortal body at the resurrection.

V. THE WORK WHICH MOSES HAS DONE IS ONE WHICH WILL FIND NO PARALLEL TO IT. (Ver. 10.) (See next Homily.) Every worker for God has his own distinctive work, which only he can do.

VI. GOD HAS ALREADY RAISED UP ONE TO CARRY ON THE WORK OF MOSES, SO THAT IT WILL NOT FALL TO PIECES WHEN HE DIES. (Ver. 9.) Joshua is ready. So that there are no chasms in the service.

VII. THE INCOMPLETENESS OF MOSES' WORK IS NOT ONLY A HISTORICAL BUT A SYMBOLIC FACT. It is not a lawgiver alone who can lead the Church on to Canaan, but a Joshua—Jesus, a Saviour. "The Law was given by Moses, but [the] grace and [the] truth came by Jesus Christ." Moses had propounded truth in his legislative precept and teachings. He had taught God's grace in the institutions of sacrifice, and in the ordinances of worship, prayer, and praise. But *the* truth he disclosed, *the* grace he declared, were brought in by another, long ages after, for whose work he was intended to prepare the way. "The Law was a child-guide until Christ." Happy are they whose life-work is in harmony with the plan of him who seeth the end from the beginning! Happy they, whether in more prominent or more obscure positions, who are in their Lord's own appointed way workers together with him!

Vers. 10—12.—*The distinctive greatness of Moses.* These closing verses do not touch upon the character of Moses, but upon his unique position as a prophet. "There arose not a prophet since in Israel like unto Moses," etc. (ver. 10). This does not exactly ascribe inferiority, but rather dissimilarity to all who had followed, up to the date of this editorial postscript. "Nothing can have two beginnings;" and in this lies the one and sufficient reason why Moses could not be followed in the after ages by any one who took a like position with his own. Purposely avoiding any outline of the character of Moses, we propose to enumerate a few of those features in which the work of Moses was altogether unique, and ever must so remain.

I. MOSES WAS THE FIRST TO DISCLOSE THE GLORIOUS NATURE OF GOD AND HIS GRACIOUS RELATIONSHIPS TO OUR RACE, AS THE CORNER-STONE OF A GREAT COMMONWEALTH.

II. HE WAS THE FIRST TO PROCLAIM, BY HIS SACRIFICIAL INSTITUTES AND TEACHINGS, THE ONE PRINCIPLE THAT "WITHOUT SHEDDING OF BLOOD IS NO REMISSION." Sacrifice was adopted in other nations as a human expedient for appeasing Divine wrath; Moses declares it to be a Divine appointment for the acknowledgment of human sin and of the Divine holiness.

III. HE WAS THE FIRST TO PROCLAIM THE ELEMENTARY PRINCIPLES AND THE TRUE BASIS OF THE NOBLEST HUMAN ETHICS : "BE YE HOLY : FOR I AM HOLY."

IV. HE WAS THE FIRST TO REQUIRE OF A PEOPLE LOVE TO GOD AS THE SPRING OF ALL OBEDIENCE, AND TO ASSIGN AS THE REASON FOR THEIR LOVE THE CARE OF GOD TO THEM. (Ch. v. 6 ; vi. 5.)

V. HE WAS THE FIRST, YEA, THE ONLY ONE IN ALL HISTORY, TO DEMAND OF A TYRANT THE LIBERATION OF AN OPPRESSED PEOPLE, AND TO FORM THEM INTO A NEW COMMONWEALTH, WITH THE AVOWED AIM AND PURPOSE OF PLANTING IN THE WORLD A NEW RELIGIOUS FAITH AND LIFE. (Ch vii. 1—11 ; ix. 1—6.)

VI. HE WAS THE FIRST WHO MADE PROVISION FOR THE EDUCATION OF A WHOLE PEOPLE IN THE THINGS OF GOD; WITH VIRTUE AND PIETY FOR ITS LESSONS, AND THE HOME FOR ITS TRAINING-SCHOOL. (Ch. xxxi. 12, 13 ; vi. 1—9 ; x. 12—22 ; xi. 18—21.)

VII. HE WAS THE FIRST WHO AIMED AT EDUCATING A PEOPLE TO SELF-GOVERNMENT. They were to choose their own officers, judges, and magistrates, according to principles of righteousness. And (as we have shown *in loc.*) even the government of Jehovah was not forced upon them. Their consent was asked again and again; and their solemn, loud "Amen" was required, confirming the sentence of God as if it were their own. Thus from the first the people were made "workers together with God."

Others might follow on in all these respects, but no one else ever could be like Moses in *starting* all this new national life, thought, and virtue, in organized form. And yet how much more than one like Moses do we need for a world's regeneration and a Church's education! "If there had been a Law given which should have given life, verily righteousness should have been by the Law." But "what the Law could not do," God has done through our Lord Jesus Christ. Moses can give rules. Only the Lord the Spirit can give life. A Greater than Moses has come, and has created by his power a new commonwealth, whose πολίτευμα is in the heavens. In this "new Jerusalem, which cometh down from God out of heaven," lo! "all things are made new."

Ver. 10.—"*Face to face ;*" or, *the secret of power.* "Whom the Lord knew face to face." Such is the remarkable expression used with regard to Moses. This certainly implies that there was in his case unwonted closeness of fellowship with God. There are expressions not dissimilar in Num. xii. 7, 8, but yet we must make allowance for the prevalence of the vividness of Eastern imagery, and not press the literalness of the words too closely. In fact, we are guarded against that by the words in Exod. xxxiii. 20.

To what extent Moses saw any manifested form, it is not likely we shall ever in this state of being, be able to tell. It is the duty of thoughtful men to penetrate beneath the archaisms and Orientalisms of the ancient text, and to seize the permanent truth which underlies them. The thought which we here detect as that which is under the surface is this—that Moses had very close communion with God.

Every spirit which yearns after God may hold communion with God. And inasmuch as "every man's life is a plan of God," God may make that fellowship serve any purposes he has for the man to fulfil. By such communion there may be: (1) an inner life of devotion and an outer life of godliness to be nurtured and sustained; or there may be (2) a spur and a pressure applied to high and holy service in one specific direction,— this is the case where men are borne along to the fulfilment of a special mission; or there may be (3) some new truth or clearer light which God wills to impart to and through the soul so communing with him.

Now, there is a specific term for each of these three effects of communion with God. When it simply subserves the life of holiness which all may lead, we call it *religion*; when it is made tributary to a special form of service, we call it *inspiration*; when it is made the means of causing new truth to appear, we call it *revelation*.

The latter has been realized by those few—extremely few—of the human race by whom God has unfolded new truth. The medial one has been experienced by the more numerous souls who have been borne along as by a special outside force to the fulfilment of a great mission. The first-named is the common privilege of all God-fearing souls.

Moses was one of the very few who enjoyed the privilege of "seeing the Unseen One" for all three purposes; and the four following sentences will sum up his life :—

I. By the power of RELIGION he lived the life of the saint.

II. By that of INSPIRATION he discharged the functions of leader, administrator, and recorder.

III. By that of REVELATION he had the visions of the seer.

IV. COMMUNION WITH GOD was the secret of all: "face to face."

To those who understand communion with God, either of the three will be regarded as in the highest degree reasonable, intelligible, and credible. Those who do not know what it is to pour out the soul unto God, may indeed accept all three in a formal manner, but they can go no further. And if such formal believers should chance to be subject to the fierce storms of modern criticism, there is no telling but they may come to deny them all; yea, they may come to think that religion, inspiration, and revelation are swept clean away; and all because they understand nothing of man's highest privilege—*Communion with God!*

HOMILIES BY VARIOUS AUTHORS.

Vers. 1—12.—*The death and burial of Moses.* We have in this concluding chapter the remarkable account of the death and burial of Moses. He had, as we have seen, blessed the tribes; he had laid his hands on Joshua (ver. 9), and thus ordained him, so to speak, to the leadership; he had given his manuscripts to the priests to be deposited in the ark; and now all that remains for him to do is to take the course God indicated to the mountain-top, see the promised land, and die. It has suggested some noble sermons, to which we would at once refer before proceeding with a few observations suggested by the history.[1]

I. LET US NOTICE THE VIEW OF CANAAN AND OF LIFE FROM THE MOUNTAIN-TOP. It is evident, we think, that Moses went up the mountain without an escort. He was going up to hold high communion with God, as he had done on Siani. Mountain-tops

[1] Cf. Bersier's 'Sermons,' tom. ii. p. 125, a very fine sermon on 'La Terre Promise;' Ker's 'Sermons,' p. 153, a sermon equally fine on 'The Burial of Moses: its Lessons and Suggestions;' and Hull's 'Sermons,' 3rd series, p. 119, a very suggestive though short discourse on 'The Death of Moses.'

are favourite places for communion with God in the case of busy men like Moses and our Saviour (cf. Luke ix. 28). It was a sublime solitude, filled with the presence of God. Sooner or later, God draws his servants upwards out of the bustle of life to have special communion with him and finish their course with joy.

Moses, moreover, had an undimmed eye at this time, and his natural force was in no wise abated. His outlook was consequently clear. The land of promise lay out before him in all its attractiveness, and he could have wished to cross the Jordan and see it, and the goodly mountain, Lebanon. But the view of it, clear and glorious, is all that in the present life he is to receive.

Now, it is sometimes insinuated that saintly, self-denying men, whose lives according to worldly notions have been incomplete and unsuccessful, are unable to form a proper judgment about their careers, and must regret them. But as a rule, God gives in life's last hours the "undimmed eye," and his servants are enabled to see life's relations clearly, and the land of promise under the sunset glow. They regret their incomplete lives as little as Moses did his from the mountain-top.

Jonathan Edwards notices, in his 'Notes on the Bible,' that "God ordered that Aaron and Moses should go up to the tops of mountains to die, to signify that the death of godly men is but an entrance into a heavenly state;" and Baumgarten has made a similar remark regarding the death of Aaron. "The circumstance that it was expressly fixed that Aaron should die upon a mountain, and so upon a place which through its very nature points to heaven, the seat of Jehovah, throws into the darkness of his death a ray (*Strahl*) of hope."[1] The mountain-tops to these great brothers were indeed the gate of heaven, whence clear views of life and of the hereafter were obtained.

II. THE CIRCUMSTANTIALS OF THE DEATH OF MOSES ARE UNIQUE IN THEIR SIMPLE MAJESTY. It has been said that the presence of Moses on the mount of Transfiguration must have suggested a contrast between his death on the top of Pisgah and our Lord's approaching death amid the mocking crowds at Jerusalem.[2] And what a contrast there is between the two departures! In the one case, the servant of God dies amid the solemn grandeur of the hills, with the sunset glow around him—dies, as some Jewish doctors say, "of the kiss of the Eternal;" in the other case, our Lord dies amid the ribaldry and scoffing of overcrowded Jerusalem. There may have been an element of sadness in Moses dying on the threshold of the promised land; but there was an element of glory in the death-bed among the mountains.

III. GOD IN HIS LOVE NOT ONLY TOOK CHARGE OF THE DYING BUT ALSO OF THE DEAD. He died with God; and God buried him. No wonder the poetess calls it "the grandest funeral that ever passed on earth."

> " And had he not high honour?—
>   The hill-side for his pall;
> To lie in state, while angels wait
>   With stars for tapers tall;
> And the dark rock-pines, like tossing plumes,
>   Over his bier to wave;
> And God's own hand, in that lonely land,
>   To lay him in the grave!"

This disposal of the body, as well as of the departed spirit, was surely a significant act on the part of God. He took the matter as completely out of the hands of Israel, as in the Resurrection our Lord's body was taken out of the keeping of the Roman guard. Was it not to indicate that the body as well as the soul is to share in the redeeming care of God, and so far an earnest of the resurrection?

IV. THE PRIVACY OF THE TOMB IS ALSO INSTRUCTIVE. Manifestly all Israel *saw* was the retirement of Moses to the mount; for the rest, his death and his Divine burial, they were dependent upon *faith*—they believed him when he told them he was going away by death, and that they need make no preparations for him, as God would bury him. Had it not been for his prophetic notice, they might have concluded he was

---

[1] Quoted in Kahle's 'Eschatologie,' note p. 48.
[2] Cf. Godet sur 'L'Evangile de Saint Luc,' ch. ix. 30—32.

translated. It was a matter of *faith entirely*, and no searching could bring it within the range of sight. The privacy of the tomb compelled them to take the funeral and burial on trust. The mourning and weeping for a month arose really from faith; Moses was not—God took him; but they had only Moses' word for it that he was to die with God, and be buried by him.

And God's dealing with our dead must remain still a matter of faith to us, though of fruition unto them. We believe the very dust of the saints is dear to God, but we have to put their remains in a coffin, and deposit them amid common clay. We believe their spirits are in his safe keeping, but they send no messages and make no sign. If sense is the measure of our knowledge, then assuredly we may put Christian hope into the realm of beautiful dreams, of which there is as little sensible evidence as of Moses' tomb. But there are "foundations of faith" as strong as those of sense and sight.[1] In such assurance, we believe that God took charge of Moses, body and soul, and will take as real and as faithful charge of us.—R. M. E.

Vers. 1—8.—*The calm sunset of an eventful day.* A man's death is in keeping with a man's life. You cannot have a tropical sunset in an arctic zone. It is vain to live the life of the voluptuous, and desire "the death of the righteous." Enoch's death corresponded with Enoch's life. The spirit of Elijah was characterized by heavenly fire: he ruled men with burning words of truth; it was, therefore, meet that he should depart as a king, "in a chariot of flame." Our Lord's whole life was a crucifixion—sublime self-sacrifice; it was fitting, then, that he should die upon a cross. Moses was transcendently great; in native grandeur he towered like a mountain above his brethren. To be in the society of God was his delight; hence there was a propriety that he should die alone, and upon the mount with God.

I. THE DEATH OF A GOOD MAN HAS MANY GRACIOUS MITIGATIONS. It is not unmingled sorrow. The evil in it is reduced to an infinitesimal point. It is a passing cloud, while the sun in its strength shines on the other side, and often penetrates the thin vapour. It is not the valley of humiliation, but the mount of communion. Visions denied to us before are vouchsafed to us now. God is nearer to us than ever yet; and though earthly friends cannot accompany us along the mystic path, strong angels are at our side to bear us on their wings to the glory-land.

> "The chamber where the good man meets his fate
> Is privileged above the common walks of life;
> Almost upon the very verge of heaven."

II. DEATH OFTEN REVEALS TO US WHAT WE MIGHT HAVE ATTAINED. In the hour of dissolution, Moses saw what he might have enjoyed if he had neglected no opportunity in the past. That faulty past is irrecoverable. We may obtain pardon the most ample and complete; but we cannot regain lost ground. Well for us if, on our death-beds, we have only one fault to bemoan; and yet one fault may entail immeasurable loss. When we stand face to face with death, we shall see the value of life as we have never seen it yet; we shall lament our negligences as we have never lamented them before. What illustrious characters we might have acquired! What conquests of good we might have won! What service for God we might have wrought! Alas! some well-meant purpose still remains immature!

III. DEATH TO A GOOD MAN IS NEEDFUL FOR FULL POSSESSION. The land which God had sworn to give to Abraham and his seed, Moses was permitted to see, and in part to possess. Yet, had he gone over Jordan and endured the fatigues of battle and dwelt in the land, his soul would not have been satisfied therewith. As his powers of soul matured and ripened, he would have desired a better inheritance than Canaan could yield. The old yearning would have come back again, "I beseech thee, show me thy glory." The soul yearns for knowledge which earth does not permit. We long to pass the barriers of darkness and tread the plains of everlasting light. Impatiently the spirit beats against the bars of this fleshly cage, and longs to find her proper wings. We must pass through the dark gateway of death ere the soul can enter upon the full "inheritance of the saints."

[1] Cf. Professor Wace's 'The Foundations of Faith,' *passim*.

IV. THE DEATH OF A GOOD MAN IS IN PART THE PROCESS OF NATURAL LAW, IN PART THE PENALTY OF MORAL LAW. So far as man partakes of animal life, so far he is under the law which rules animal natures. In every animal species we discern the stages of birth, growth, maturity, decay, death. But man is endowed with regal powers, which give him, in some measure, dominion over his animal nature. Yet, as a fact, men die before their physical powers have decayed. In earlier ages of human history, human life reached to centuries, while now barely to four score years. Moses was called to die, but "his eye was not dim, nor had his natural force abated." In his case we are authoritatively informed that his premature decease was due to guilt. The moral conduct of men does operate, then, in modifying the laws of nature. There is an unseen law—a law of God—which interlaces the laws and forces of the visible world, just as the system of nerves interlaces and animates the muscles of human flesh. The time and the mode of the believer's death are not the outcome of natural law; they are fixed by the wisdom and the kindness of our personal God.

V. THE LIFELESS BODIES OF THE SAINTS ARE THE ESPECIAL CARE OF GOD. "God buried him in a valley in the land of Moab." There is a secrecy and a mystery about Moses' burial, which it would be profanity to attempt to penetrate. On a later page of Scripture we read that, respecting this body of Moses, Michael had a serious dispute with the devil. We feel bound to connect this mysterious disposal of Moses' lifeless body with the appearance of the same glorified body on the Mount of Transfiguration. But the point which concerns us at present is *this*; God has manifested in various ways his tender regard for the mortal remains of his servants. The elementary particles may dissolve, but the personal organization shall survive. "It is sown a natural body; it is raised a spiritual body." Yet, by the conserving power of Deity, it is a body still, though fitted more completely in the future as a vehicle for perception, intercourse, motion, and free activity. We can be well content to entrust every interest we have in life with him "who counts the very hairs of our head."

VI. THE DEATH OF A GOOD MAN IS AN OCCASION FOR EXTENSIVE SORROW. "The children of Israel wept for Moses in the plains of Moab thirty days." Although he had often severely censured them, exposed faithfully their faults, and denounced their vices, they knew they had lost a genuine friend. Never would they look upon their noble leader's face again. His fatherly interest in them could never be replaced. Not till he was gone did they learn what a fount of blessing he had been. Had this coming event been steadily kept before them, they would have treated him with more generous esteem, and would have rendered to his counsels a more loyal respect. Now they lash themselves with just remorse. A good man's departure leaves a great vacancy in the Church and in the social circle. Shall we be thus missed when death hath laid us low?

Yet the days of mourning even for a good man must cease. There are sterner duties in life demanding unceasing care, and our sorrow for the departed ought to qualify us for future service.—D.

Ver. 9.—*Posthumous influence.* Although dead, Moses still ruled. His spirit reappeared in his successor. The principles of Moses had been planted in the nature of Joshua: these had flourished and come to maturity. The memory of Moses was still a mighty power in Israel, and they "did," all through the days of Joshua, "as the Lord commanded Moses." The legislator had moulded and trained the warrior. Moses was promoted to higher honour, because Joshua was better qualified for this new work —the realization of Israel's destiny.

I. NOTE THE HIGH QUALIFICATION OF JOSHUA. He was "full of the spirit of wisdom." This is a rare gift. By nature he had been endowed with strength and fearless courage, so that he had been military lieutenant to Moses all through the desert. He was illustrious also for diligence and fidelity in a long career of service. Among the spies despatched to Canaan, he (in company with Caleb) had been "faithful among the faithless found." Now to courage and unbending loyalty there was added another endowment, and this in amplest measure: he was "filled with the spirit of wisdom." "To him that hath, it shall be given."

II. OBSERVE THE METHOD BY WHICH THIS WISDOM WAS ACQUIRED. "Moses had laid his hands upon him." We need not limit our thoughts to a solitary act, even though it might be a solemn and religious act. We may rather think of the plastic, formative influence which Moses had exerted over the growing character of this young man. It is astonishing what immense power God has entrusted to our hands for fashioning and embellishing the spiritual nature of men. By a wise employment of spiritual energy, we can direct into right channels the lives of many; by implanting right principles into youth, and by awakening into vigorous activity the latent forces of character, we may elevate a city—we may influence the destinies of the world.

III. MARK THE BENEFICIAL EFFECT. "The children of Israel hearkened unto him." Moses influenced for good his servant Joshua. Joshua influenced for good the nation of Israel. The twelve tribes felt the force of Joshua's character, and yielded to the wisdom which he displayed. They were a different people as the consequence of Joshua's leadership. He touched, through Israel, the fortunes of the world. The high example of Joshua provoked the imitation of the tribes. His combined wisdom and energy led them on to triumph. By virtue of his superlative wisdom he became, in God's hands, a Saviour, and remains, in name and office, the type of the world's Redeemer.—D.

Vers. 10—12.—*Communion with God the secret of real power.* Leaving out of view our Lord Jesus Christ, there is no man who has left so deeply the impress of his character upon the world as the Jewish legislator. By no man have so many and such mighty works been achieved. By no man has such wise legislation been devised for the government of human society. By no man has a great national emancipation been so skilfully and successfully executed. At the time of our Lord, Moses still wielded a mighty sceptre among the Jewish nation; and from that day to this, the influence of Moses has been powerfully felt. The history of the Western world would have been very different from what it is, if Moses had found an early grave among the rushes of the Nile. The secret of it is—he was a "man of God."

I. COMMUNION WITH GOD IS THE HIGHEST ADVANTAGE MAN CAN ENJOY. The friendship of a wise and great man is an inestimable boon. To be in the society of a good man for an hour leaves a purifying and an elevating stimulus behind. We feel better and nobler for the contact. And if the friendly influence of a good man can find its way to intellect and conscience and feeling, how much more can the influence and energy of God! There is no doubt that God can find access to the nature he has made, and can enrich it with all good. The question is whether, considering our great demerit, Will he? This question also is completely answered by himself. He invites us to the closest friendship—welcomes us to fullest intimacy. The words of Jesus Christ suffice to allay all doubt, "If any man love me, he will keep my words: and my Father will love him, and *we* will come unto him, and make our abode with him." We may not have visions of God precisely after the form and fashion that Moses had: *these* were adapted to a particular state of human development; but we may have contact with God as close—communion as sweet and tender, as ever Moses enjoyed. "The fellowship of the Holy Ghost" is our special privilege. To us "the Spirit of truth" is given. And "truly our fellowship is with the Father, and with his Son Jesus Christ."

II. COMMUNION WITH GOD PRODUCES REAL GREATNESS OF CHARACTER. As a result of the intimacy between God and Moses, we read, there "arose not a prophet since in Israel like unto Moses." Intercourse with God purifies every feeling, elevates every aspiration, energizes every sterling principle, ennobles the whole man. The creative influence of the Almighty renews our innermost life. In the presence of God we become ashamed of our meanness and pride and folly. We see and feel how noble it is possible to become. We confess into his fatherly ear our sin: we resolve to do better in the future. The assurance of his sympathy and aid encourages us. We grow up into his image; we gradually find that this is our proper destiny—"to be conformed to the image of his Son."

III. COMMUNION WITH GOD GIVES US POWER OVER NATURE AND OVER MEN. It is admitted by scientists that the human will is the greatest force known, save the power of God. Now, fellowship with God strengthens that will. To his chosen friends, God conveys new power. On man was originally bestowed complete dominion over nature; and this prerogative is to be restored through the man Christ Jesus. Thus the prodigies wrought by Moses are declared to be signs—symbols of greater things yet to be achieved. Our Lord has taught us that true faith can overturn the mountains. The possessor of faith is predicted to outstrip even Christ in mighty deeds.—D.

Vers. 1—4.—*Moses' vision.* The end of Moses, viewing the land to which he had so long and so painfully been leading the people, yet not permitted to enter it—dying on the threshold of the accomplishment of all his hopes, and leaving Canaan to be won by his subordinate minister, Joshua,—has often been likened to the common fate of the highest characters in history, "removed from this earthly scene before their work has been appreciated, and when it will be carried on, not by themselves, but by others." (See the development of the thought in Stanley's 'Jewish Church,' vol. i. p. 175, with the application to Lord Bacon by Macaulay.) Often, also, it has been likened to the visions of the "land beyond the flood" received through faith by dying Christians. They, however, see a land into which they are soon to enter; Moses looked on one from which he was debarred. This vision was—

I. A COMPENSATION FOR A GREAT LOSS. Not permitted to enter Canaan, Moses was yet permitted to see it. His eyes were strengthened to take in the vision of its goodliness from north to south, from east to west. How his spirit must have feasted on the widespread prospect! This compensation, we remember, was won from God by prayer (ch. iii. 23—39). We cannot always gain reversal of our punishment of loss; no, though we seek it carefully, with tears (Heb. xii. 17). But, while the losses remain, they may be sanctified to us, and, in answer to prayer, gracious compensations and mitigations granted.

II. A PERFECTING OF HOLY RESIGNATION. Then, no doubt, while looking on that good land, and feeling that he could not enter it, would Moses have his last struggle, and conquer his last lingering wish to have it otherwise than as God willed. We know how sore the struggle in his mind had been, how earnestly he had wrestled with God to have the sentence reversed (ch. iii. 23—29). But it was not to be, and Moses must learn to say, as the Greater than Moses said long after, "Not my will, but thine be done!" (Luke xxii. 42). Who doubts but that the sacrifice was made? that Moses was brought to the point of perfect aquiescence before he died? And that in truth was a greater compensation than the other. The achieving so great a spiritual victory was well worth the surrender of the land. That victory, too, would take the sting of the trial away. The worst part of a trial—nearly all that is bitter in it—is past, when we are brought to the point of embracing the Divine will in it.

III. A TRANSITION TO A HIGHER HOPE. Is it possible to think that Moses, in laying down his life on that mountain summit, believed that he was laying it down for ever? Could he believe, after all the relations of friendship which had subsisted between him and Jehovah, in view of that land of promise from which he was debarred, and at this very moment of his greatest spiritual triumph,—that his death ended all? that there was no hereafter? that there was no compensation beyond? We may rather believe that, in this very perfecting of his soul in its holy acquiescence in the Divine will, there would spring up in his mind a holier hope—a trust and assurance that all he now surrendered would be made up to him in some better form in heaven. What we part with on earth for Christ's sake are our ultimate gains.—J. O.

Vers. 5, 6.—*Moses' death and burial.* Lessons from it—

I. GOD WILL HAVE NO ONE, LIVING OR DEAD, TO STAND BETWEEN HIS CREATURES AND HIMSELF. "He dies apart, and is buried in secret, where his grave can be dishonoured by no pilgrimage, and where no false veneration can rear altars to his memory."

II. GOD WISHES MEN TO SEE SOMETHING MORE LEFT OF HIS SERVANTS THAN THE OUTWARD SHRINE. They had the life and words of Moses, which his shrine might have obscured. It was expedient that even Jesus should go away, that his spiritual presence and the spiritual significance of his work might be fully realized (John xvi. 7).

III. GOD TAKES THE HONOUR OF HIS SERVANTS INTO HIS OWN KEEPING.

IV. GOD WOULD TEACH MEN THAT HE HAS A RELATION TO HIS SERVANTS WHICH EXTENDS BEYOND DEATH. "Can the Maker put so disproportionate an estimate upon his own handiwork, as carefully to store up the casket and throw away the precious jewel which it held?"

V. GOD WOULD TEACH MEN THAT HIS REGARD IS NOT CONFINED TO ANY CHOSEN SOIL. "In a valley in the land of Moab." We have one more lesson from the New Testament—

VI. THAT THE SEEMING FAILURE IN A TRUE LIFE MAY AT LAST HAVE A COMPLETE COMPENSATION. Moses did at last, with Elias, tread the soil of Palestine, and there see "the King in his beauty" (Matt. xvii. 3). (Dr. John Ker.)—J. O.

Vers. 10—12.—*The greatness of Moses.* It was a greatness entirely unique. "There arose not a prophet," etc. (ver. 10). His greatness lay largely in character. As a man —in respect of qualities of character—Moses was one of the greatest men who have ever lived; perhaps, all things taken together, *the* greatest next to Christ. But so entirely is Moses the *man* lost in his relation to God as instrument of *his* will and work, that his greatness in the former respect is not in these verses even referred to. Moses is overshadowed by the God of Moses, whose power he wielded, and in whose Name alone he wrought. This greatness of Moses arose—

I. FROM THE RELATION OF PECULIAR INTIMACY HE HELD TO GOD. "There arose not a prophet since in Israel like unto Moses, whom the Lord knew face to face" (ver. 10). In this greatness Moses stood alone till there arose that greater Prophet, whose advent he had predicted (ch. xviii. 18).

II. FROM THE GREATNESS OF HIS WORK. (Ver. 11.) He was sent to Egypt to deliver Israel. In this also a type of Christ.

III. IN THE POWER OF GOD PUT FORTH THROUGH HIM. (Vers. 11, 12.) True greatness therefore lies : (1) in power of near approach to God; (2) in great work done for God; and (3) in spiritual power exerted through God acting in and with us.—J. O.

HOMILETICAL INDEX

TO

THE BOOK OF DEUTERONOMY

CHAPTER I.

THEME   PAGE

The Word of God Full of Hidden Treasure 7
The Hebrew Right to Canaan ... 8
Rules to be Observed in Choosing Rulers 9
Divine Covenant and Human Conduct 10
The Blessing of Good Government ... 11
The Deuteronomic Discourses ... 12
The Might-have-beens of Life ... 13
A Summons to Advance 13
Israel's Increase 14
Division of Labour 14
Judging 14
The Impartiality of God to be Reflected in the Judges of His People ... 15
Sending the Spies 19
The Grievous Consequences of Unbelief 21
Forced Back ! 22
Irrecoverableness of Wasted Opportunity 23
"That Great and Terrible Wilderness" 24
Courage 25
The Mission of the Spies 25
Love in the Wilderness 26
The Excluded and the Admitted ... 26
Tardy Repentance 27
The Unbelief in Sending out and in Hearkening to the Spies ... 28
The Heirs of Promise 28

CHAPTER II.

God's Knowledge of Our Pilgrimage 34
International Relationships ... 35
Warrantable Warfare 36
Edom, Moab, Ammon 38
The Emims, Horims, Zamzummins, etc. 39
Dying out 39
The Effects of Israel's Conquests ... 40
The Conquest of Sihon 40
God's Faithfulness in Dealing with Nations outside the Covenant ... 41
The Wasting of the Warriors ... 42
The Destruction of Sihon, King of the Amorites 42

CHAPTER III.

The Last of the Giants 47
Self-Propagating Conquest ... 49
Prospect of Death 50
The Conquest of Og 51
The Destruction of the Populations ... 52
Distribution of Territory 53
Encouragement 53
God's Refusal of Man's Wishes ... 53
The Destruction of Og, King of Bashan 54
The Pioneers of the Invasion of Palestine 55
Moses' Longing to Enter the Promised Land Refused 56

CHAPTER IV.

Life and Prosperity Dependent on Obedience to God 60
National Greatness Dependent on Obedience to God 62
Israel's Peculiar Relation to God ... 63

THEME	PAGE
God a Consuming Fire	65
The Sacredness of the Divine Law ...	67
The Curse of Idolatry	68
Acceptable Obedience	69
A Nation's Glory...	69
The Religious Education of Children	70
The Revelation at Horeb ...	70
Warning against Heathenish Idolatry	71
The Iron Furnace	71
Obedience the Secret of Success ...	71
The Divine Jealousy of Graven Images	72
National Backsliding	76
The Wonderfulness of Israel's History	77
Beloved for the Fathers' Sake ...	78
The Mercy of God	78
The Cities of Refuge (see also ch. xix.)...	79, 82
Judgment Leading to Mercy ...	80
The Deliverance of the Lord's People Unparalleled	81
The Circumstances under which the Law was Reiterated	82

CHAPTER V.

The Divine Law Based on a Divinely Revealed Relationship	86
The First Commandment	87
The Second Commandment ...	89
The Third Commandment	91
The Sabbath, or a Rest-Day for Man	93
The Fifth Commandment	95
The Sixth Commandment	97
The Seventh Commandment ...	99
The Eighth Commandment ...	101
The Ninth Commandment... ...	103
The Tenth Commandment... ...	104
The Law as a Whole, and its Effect upon the People	106
The Abrahamic Covenant Renewed...	108
The Divine Plan for the Conduct of Our Life on Earth	109
Character Determines Environment	110
Reminiscences of Horeb	112
The Covenant at Horeb	112
Mediation	113
The Iniquity of the Fathers Visited on the Children	113
The Sabbath	114
Honour to Parents	115
Moral Law	115
The Element of Terror in Religion ...	115

THEME	PAGE
God's Desire for Man's Good ...	116
The Decalogue	116
How Moses became Mediator ...	117

CHAPTER VI.

Obedience to God Conducive to the Highest Good	120
Truth and Godliness to be Perpetuated by Means of Home Training ...	122
"Dangers Ahead! Beware!" ...	123
The Value of History in Parental Teaching	125
"Obedience the End of Law" ...	127
Love, the Root-Principle of Obedience	128
The Peril of Prosperity	129
The Parental Office	129
Descending Obligations	130
The Great Commandment	131
The Religious Education of Children	131
God's Words to be Valued... ...	132
The Creature Displacing the Creator	132
Tempting God	132
Our Righteousness	133
The Essence of the Decalogue is Love	134
Family Training is to Propagate the Law	134

CHAPTER VII.

A Holy People's Policy of Self-Preservation	137
Temporal Prosperity a Result of Obedience to Divine Law	139
An Anxious Question, or Dreading Difficulties	141
Israel's Iconoclastic Mission ...	142
Reward in Proportion to Arduous Service	144
Judgment without Mercy	145
Marriage in the Lord	146
Reasons for Non-Conformity to the World, and for Aggression on Its Evil	146
Lessons from History	147
The Rewards of Obedience ...	147
God for Us	148
The Cursed Thing	148
Extermination with a Moral Purpose	149
On the Election of Nations ...	149
The Divine Veracity	150
Canaan Gradually Won	151

CHAPTER VIII.

THEME	PAGE
Life's Meaning Discerned by the Retrospect of it	154
The Duty of Thankfulness for the Bounty of God in Nature ...	156
Danger of Self-Glorification ...	157
The Moral Uses of Memory ...	158
Wealth Perilous to Piety	159
The Uses of Adversity	161
Not Bread, but God's Word ...	161
God the Chastener	162
The Good Land	162
The Dangers of Wealth	162
The Blessing of a Thankful Spirit ...	163
Good at the Latter End	163
The Lessons of the Wilderness ...	164
God Forgotten amid Second Causes...	164

CHAPTER IX.

A Six-Weeks' Religion; or, Emotional Religiousness not Vital Godliness	167
True Greatness Manifested in a Great Emergency, by Self-Sacrifice	169
Self-Righteousness	171
The Sin at Horeb	172
Moses' Intercession	173
Against Self-Righteous Conceit ...	173
Human Memory a Repository of Guilt	174
The Place of Human Mediation ...	175
The Policy of Reprobation ...	177
Humiliating Memories	178

CHAPTER X.

The Results of the Intercessory Prayer of Moses	180
Israel's Duty Summed up and Touchingly Enforced...	183
God no Respecter of Persons ...	184
Tokens of Mercy...	186
The Supreme Requirement ...	186
The Supreme Persuasive	187
Heart Circumcision	187
Love the Stranger	188
Religion in Brief...	188
The Law Deposited in the Ark ...	188
Progress	189
Knowledge of God the Parent of Obedient Faith	190
The Covenant Renewed	192
The Separation of the Sons of Levi...	192
New Obedience	193

CHAPTER XI.

THEME	PAGE
The Voice of God in Passing Events to be Heeded, Interpreted, and Obeyed	196
The Order of Nature Subservient to Moral Purposes	198
The Moral Power of National Righteousness	200
The Dread Alternative before every Man	201
Obligations Arising from Personal Experience	203
Canaan and Egypt	204
The Great Alternative	205
Vastness of Promise	205
Gerizim and Ebal	206
Ocular Demonstrations of God's Nearness Increase Human Responsibility	206
Obedience Leads to Prolonged Possession	207
Valuable Possessions Reserved for the Righteous	207
God's Word Potent to Dominate the Whole Life	208
He who best Serves is most fit to Rule	208
Startling Alternatives	209
Divine Judgments upon Others, to Ensure Obedience in Us ...	209
The Land of Promise	210
Family Training an Element of Success	211
Life's Solemn Alternative	213

CHAPTER XII.

Regulations for Divine Worship; Specific Rules Embodying Permanent Principles	217
Destruction of Monuments of Idolatry	219
The Central Sanctuary	219
Public Worship	220
The Divine Regulation of Food ...	221
The Levite	221
Unworthy Inquiries	221
The Invasion a Religious One ...	222
Centralization in Worship	223
Private Worship not the Substitute for Public	224
The Sanctity of Blood	225
The Doom of Idolatry	225
Characteristic Signs of Jehovah's Worship	226
The Subtle Ensnarement of Idolatry	227

CHAPTER XIII.

THEME	PAGE
Temptations to Depart from God to be Resisted at all Costs	229
False Prophets	231
God or Our Brother	232
A City under Ban	233
Idolatry to be Treated as a Capital Crime	234
God's Executioners upon Idolaters ...	235

CHAPTER XIV.

The People of God when Death is in the Home	238
The People of God at Their Own Table	240
A Threefold Cord ; or, the Triple Use of Property	241
Self-Respect in Mourning... ...	243
Clean and Unclean	243
Seething a Kid in Its Mother's Milk	244
The Second Tithe	245
Sorrow is to be in Holy-Hopefulness	246
A Holy People will Eat Sanctified Things	247
Systematic Provision for Fellowship with God	248
Against Conformity with Heathen Customs	250
Discrimination in Meats ...	250
God's Claim upon Our Money Gains	251

CHAPTER XV.

Divine Checks on Human Greed ...	254
The Duty of Kindness to the Poor ...	256
The Rights of the Slaves ...	258
Sacrifices to be without Blemish ...	260
"The Lord's Release"	261
The Poor in the Land	262
Bondmen	263
The Firstlings	263
The Year of Forgiveness ...	263
Open-Handedness	264
The Freedom of the Slave	265
The Firstlings for God ...	267
A Bulwark against Cupidity ...	267
Slaves to be Regarded as Brethren ...	268
The First for God	269

CHAPTER XVI.

The Feast of the Passover... 272, 276, 282
The Feast of Weeks, or of Harvest ...	274
Pentecost 277, 280

THEME	PAGE
Feast of Tabernacles, or of Ingathering 276, 278, 283
Model Judges	279
The Passover a Memorial of Deliverance	279
The Feast of Tabernacles—Life a Tented State	281
Impartial Judges	282
The Administration of Justice ...	284
The Pathways to Temptation to be Shunned	285

CHAPTER XVII.

The Sacredness of Personal Reputation Seen in the Regulations Concerning Human Testimony ...	287
Religion the Guard of Justice ...	288
Kings Subject to the King of Kings	290
"No Retreat!" or, "The Gate Behind Us Closed"	291
The Blemished	292
Sabæism	292
Criminal Procedure	293
The Priest and the Judge	293
The King in Israel	294
Idolatry a Capital Crime	295
The Ruling Power of the Priests in the Jewish Church	296
The Limitations of Monarchy 297, 300
The Prevention of Religious Fraud ...	298
Idolatry a Crime against Society ...	299
High Court of Appeal	299

CHAPTER XVIII.

The Support of the Ministry the Duty of God's People...	305
"Spiritualism" condemned ...	306
God Speaking to Man through Man	308
God's Provision for the Priests and Levites	310
Divination Forbidden	311
The Promised Prophet	311
The Lord Our Inheritance	312
The Priesthood	313
Love to the Sanctuary	313
Magic	313
Prophecy	314
The Prophet like unto Moses ...	315
The False Prophet	315
The True Priest is the Highest Type of Man	316

THEME	PAGE
Gross Superstition the Alternative of True Religion	317
Presages of the True Prophet ...	317

CHAPTER XIX.

THEME	PAGE
The Cities of Refuge 320, 322, 324, 326	
Removing the Landmark	323
False Witness	324
The Law of Retaliation	325
Lex Talionis	327
Caution against Fraud	328
Bulwark against Perjury	328

CHAPTER XX.

THEME	PAGE
Wars to be Regulated by Divine Precepts	331
War	332
Exemptions	333
Forbearance and Severity	334
Religious Wars	334
Military Service to be Voluntary ...	335
The Terrible Side of Human Duty ...	336

CHAPTER XXI.

THEME	PAGE
The Preciousness of One Human Life in the Sight of God	340
The Female Captive; or, Divine Regard for Woman's Safety and Honour ...	340
Home Partialities never to Warp Home Justice	341
A Bad Son a State Peril	342
Upon the Tree !	343
Atonement for Unknown Sin ...	345
Through Love to Liberty	346
The Rights of the Firstborn in the House of a Bigamist	347
Parental Authority Enforced ...	347
Purification from Guilt of an Uncertain Murder	348
The Captive Wife	349
The Firstborn of the Hated Wife ...	349
The Rebellious Son	349
Accursed of God	350
The Creation of Righteous Public Sentiment	351
The Captor Captured	352
Monogamy Essential to Domestic Peace	352
A Slippery Path to Ruin	353
The Doom of Law the Embodiment of Divine Curse	354

CHAPTER XXII.

THEME	PAGE
The Duty of Cultivating Neighbourly Kindness	356
Divine Care for Sexual Honour ...	356
Kindness to Animals a Religious Duty	357
Risks to Human Life to be Minimized	357
Evil Associations to be Avoided ...	358
Love Unfeigned	358
Man and Woman	359
The Minutiæ of Conduct	359
Chastity	360
Consideration for Man and Beast ...	360
The Philosophy of Clothes ...	361
Birds' Nests	362
Linsey-Woolseys	363
Expedients to Secure Purity ...	363
Brotherly Service in Daily Life ...	364
Against Deceptions in Dress ...	364
God's Care for Birds	365
The Perils of Inadvertence	365
Directions in Minor Matters ...	366
Slander, Unchastity, and Fraud ...	366
Various Penalties for Unchastity ...	367

CHAPTER XXIII.

THEME	PAGE
Stern Safeguards sometimes Needed	369
Cleanliness a Religious Duty ...	370
Israel's Land a Refuge for the Oppressed	370
Unholy Wealth may not be Put to Divine Uses	370
The Opposite Working of Like Principles	370
Vows to God to be Performed ...	370
Kindliness to Neighbours a Duty of the Holders of Property ...	370
The Excluded from the Congregation	371
The Curse Turned into a Blessing ...	371
Purity in the Camp	372
Various Precepts	372
The Vineyard and Corn-Field ...	373
The Congregation of the Lord Jealously Guarded	373
A Pure Camp for a Pure King ...	374
The Hebrew Fugitive Law ...	375
Money-Making must be above Suspicion	375
Loss of Sacred Privilege a Grievous Penalty	376
Terminable Chastisements	377

THEME	PAGE
Sympathy for the Oppressed	378
Unacceptable Offerings	378
Usury Lawful and Unlawful	378
The Place of Vows	379
Possession of Earthly Things only Partial	380

CHAPTER XXIV.

THEME	PAGE
Permissive Legislation	382
Neighbourly Love and Good Will to be Cultivated in Detail	383
Divorce	383
The Man Newly Married	384
Leprosy	384
The Treatment of the Poor	384
Doing Justice and Loving Mercy	385
The Rights of Women	386
Man-Stealing a Capital Crime	386
Consideration for the Poor and Needy	387
Responsibility not to be Transferred according to Human Caprice	387
Nuptial Joy	387
Prohibited Pledges	388
Slave-Traffic a Capital Offence	389
Leprosy Symbolic	389
Omitted Duty Ripens into Curse	390
Public Justice to be Pure	390
Autumn Generosity	391

CHAPTER XXV.

THEME	PAGE
Humanity to be Respected in Judicial Inflictions	394
Labourers to Live by their Labour	394
Family Honour to be Maintained	395
An Offending Hand	395
Righteousness in Trade Imperative	395
Kindness to Enemies is not to Degenerate into Sympathy with or Indifference to Ungodliness	395
The Bastinado	395
The Oxen	396
The Levirate Law	397
Morality in Trade	398
Amalek	398
Earthly Magistracy an Argument for the Heavenly	399
Doing Good Inseparable from Getting Good	399
Religion Inspires Commercial Life	400
Cowardice and Cruelty Avenged	401
Corporal Punishment	401

THEME	PAGE
The Rights of Labour	402
The Rights of the Firstborn	403
Honesty the Best Policy	404
The Extermination of the Merciless	405

CHAPTER XXVI.

THEME	PAGE
Joy in the Use of Temporal Mercies	407
Integrity in the Will a Condition of Acceptable and Successful Prayer	409
The Golden Chain	410
The Presentation of the Firstfruits	412
The Year of Tithing	413
"A Good Conscience toward God"	413
Avouching Extraordinary	414
Commemorations of National Deliverance	414
Complete Consecration a Condition of Continued Blessing	415
The Spiritual Creation	416
The Dedication of the Firstfruits	417
Looking up for the Blessing	418

CHAPTER XXVII.

THEME	PAGE
"Very Plainly"	421
A Grand "Amen!"	421
The Stones on Ebal	422
A People of God	423
Ebal and Gerizim	423
Safeguards for Obedience	424
The Decalogue Nationally Reciprocated	425
Law-Abiding People	426
Responses	427

CHAPTER XXVIII.

THEME	PAGE
God's Blessing Promised to the Obedient	431
Love Veiled in Frown	433
The Blessing	434
The Blessing that Maketh Rich	435
Established	436
The World Afraid of the Godly	436
Moral Gravitation	436
The Curse	436
God, Ruler in Nature	438
The Extremity of the Curse	438
The High and Fenced Walls	439
The Delicate Lady	439
God Rejoicing in Judgment	440
Mental Torture as a Result of Sin	440
The Purpose of Temporal Blessing	441

THEME	PAGE
A Nation Becoming a Beacon	442
The Present Portion of a Good Man	444
The Nemesis of Disloyalty	445
The Remoter Consequences of Rebellion	446

CHAPTER XXIX.

Witnessing without Seeing	449
Apostacy in Heart a Root of Bitterness	450
Historical Witnesses to the Wrath of God	452
Secret Things	453, 456
Revealed Things	453
Seeing, yet not Seeing	454
Temptations, Signs, Miracles	454
National Covenanting	454
The Lying Hope	455
The Stranger's Wonder	456
The Renewal of God's Covenant with Israel	457
The Government of God All-Embracing	458
The Purpose of Divine Revelation	459
Time-Defying Habiliments	460
The Land of Promise Becoming Accursed	461
The Purpose and Limits of Revelation	462

CHAPTER XXX.

Dispersion not Rejection	464
The Old and New Covenants	465
The Word of Faith	466, 469
A Dread Alternative	467
Israel's Restoration	468, 475
A Last Word	470
Nature a Witness	471
Divine Discipline Founded on Known Principle	471
Revealed Truth Clear and Available	472
An Alternative Choice	473
The Revelation at Man's Door	476
Death and Life Set before the People	477

CHAPTER XXXI.

A New Generation Receiving the Heritage of the Past	481
Importance of Knowing the Word of God	481
Faithful Words Silent Accusers of Those who Heed Them not	483

THEME	PAGE
Moses the Aged	485
Joshua	485
The Authorship of the Book	486
The Written Word	489
Reading the Law	489
God's Foresight of Israel's Declension	490
The Leadership Made over to Joshua	490
The Literary Executors of Moses	491
The Lord's Charge to Moses and Joshua	492
The Divine Testimony Deposited in the Ark	493
Putting off the Harness	494
The Honour Appertaining to God's Law	495
The Official Investiture of Joshua	496
The Last Precaution against Idolatry	496

CHAPTER XXXII.

God the Believer's Rock	504
Ungrateful Men Interrogated	505
God Provoked to Jealousy by an Unfaithful People	505
An Unfaithful People Provoked to Jealousy by God	507
The Divine Mind Influenced by Reasons	508
The Short-Sightedness of Sinners	509
Jehovah Reigns; be Glad!	510
Life at Stake!	512
Death Immediately in View	513
Beneficial Teaching	515
God the Rock	515
God's Righteousness and Man's Iniquity	516
The World Ruled for the Benefit of the Church	517
A Panorama of Grace	517
The Eagle	518
Jeshurun	518
A God Provoked	518
The True Wisdom	519
The Superiority of the Believer's Rock	520
Our Rock	521
The Vine of Sodom	521
Retribution	521
Your Life	522
The Fatherhood of God	522
The Danger of Worldly Success	523
Vengeance and Recompense	524

THEME	PAGE
Death a Judgment even to the Most Faithful Servants of God ...	526
God's Vicegerent as Poet	526
History's Testimony for God ...	527
Sowing and Reaping	528
The Pleading of Divine Wisdom ...	529
God's Pathetic Appeal to Men ...	530
The Devil's Counterfeit Coin ...	530
The Final Revelation of God's Supremacy	531
Religion a Reality	532
"Obedient unto Death"	533

CHAPTER XXXIII.

The Blessing of Reuben; or, Life Impoverished through Ancestral Sins	540
The Blessing of Judah; or, Help Needed to Fulfil Destiny ...	541
The Blessing of Levi; or, Entire Devotion to God a Necessary Qualification for Ministerial Service ...	542
The Blessing on Benjamin; or, Safety in the Sheltering Care of Divine Love	543
The Blessing of Joseph; or, God's Favour the Mercy of Mercies ...	544
Trade and Commerce Subservient to Evangelization	546
Gad; or, a Place in the Church and the World for Lionlike Strength ...	547
The Blessing of Dan and Naphtali; the Satisfaction which Accrues from the Enjoyment of the Divine Favour	548
Asher's Blessing; Strength as the Day	549
The Glory of Israel's God, and the Blessedness of God's Israel ...	550
A Fiery Law	551
God's Saints	551
Reuben and Judah	551

THEME	PAGE
Levi	551
Benjamin and Joseph	552
The Good Will of Him that Dwelt in the Bush	552
Zebulun and Issachar	552
Gad, Dan, Naphtali, Asher ...	553
Israel's Happiness	553
The Eternal God a Refuge ...	554
The King and His Viceroy ...	555
Watchwords for the Tribes ...	556
The Incomparable Saviour ...	557
The Godlike Act of Blessing ...	558
A Prayer for the Firstborn ...	559
The Royal House of Judah ...	559
The Priestly Tribe	560
God's Fatherly Interest in Benjamin	561
Royal Donations on Joseph ...	562
Combined Work and Worship ...	562
God's Valour and Chivalry Commended	563
The Blessing of Strength	564
Naphtali's Goodly Choice	565
The Comprehensive Benediction of Asher	565
God the Crown of Israel's Glory ...	566

CHAPTER XXXIV.

The Last Journey	568
The Distinctive Greatness of Moses	570
"Face to Face;" or, the Secret of Power	570
The Death and Burial of Moses ...	571
The Calm Sunset of an Eventful Day	573
Posthumous Influence	574
Communion with God the Secret of Real Power	575
Moses' Vision	576
Moses' Death and Burial	576
The Greatness of Moses	577

JOSHUA

INTRODUCTIONS BY

A. PLUMMER   J. J. LIAS

EXPOSITION AND HOMILETICS BY

J. J LIAS

HOMILIES BY VARIOUS AUTHORS

E. DE PRESSENSÉ   R. GLOVER

J. WAITE   W. F. ADENEY

S. R. ALDRIDGE

INTRODUCTION

TO THE

HISTORICAL BOOKS: JOSHUA TO NEHEMIAH.

BY

THE REV. A. PLUMMER, M.A.,

MASTER OF UNIVERSITY COLLEGE, DURHAM.

In tragic interest alone the history of the children of Israel during the period before us—from Joshua to Nehemiah—is unique.* Perhaps some of us in the experience of life have known what it is to see a young man of good birth and ability enter upon a noble inheritance which has long been waiting for him, and for the management and enjoyment of which wise and affectionate friends have been giving him the best training and preparation in their power. Such a sight kindles a hopeful enthusiasm, which, however, in thoughtful minds will be tempered with something of anxiety. Perhaps we have known also what it is in such a case to have our enthusiasm kept up but for a very short time, our hopes only very partially fulfilled, while our anxiety is more than justified. The fair inheritance, during a career of some brilliancy, chequered by grievous mistakes, is ruinously mishandled, and at last lost altogether ; and the gifted owner, soured by disappointment and vitiated by reckless misconduct, becomes an outcast—almost a beggar. Such things are not uncommon. And there are cases not frequent, but often possible, where, after weary years of struggling, the ruined outcast wins his way back to the possessions which he had (mainly by his own fault) lost. What a contrast between the first taking possession and the second! The brightness of the inheritance is gone, and still more the brightness of him who enters upon it. Heavier work, heavier responsibilities lie before him ; and he has only crippled resources, in health, in energy, and in fortune, for meeting both. The task which confronted him at the beginning of life confronts him again at the end of it. But the work has waxed while he has waned ; and he has all his work to do with cold and palsied hands. There is still much to hope for, much to be thankful for ; but more to regret, still more to fear. The joy of returning is almost counterbalanced by the misery of contrasting the past with the present, and what is with what might have been (Ezra iii. 12, 13).

An instance of this kind awakens keen interest and sympathy when we witness it in the case of an individual. How much more, then, when the chief actor is not an individual, but a whole people, and that people one of the leading, one of the

---

* In writing this Introduction the works of the following writers among others have been used :—Edersheim, Ewald, Perowne, Smith, Stanley; together with articles in the 'Dictionary of the Bible' and various commentaries.

typical nations of the world! The remark, therefore, which was made at the outset seems to be justified; that in tragic interest alone the history of the Israelites from Joshua to Nehemiah is unique. And of course for the philosophic student, and still more for the Christian student, the dramatic element in the history of the Jews is far from being either the most interesting or the most important. Whether the religion be regarded as true or false, this much must be admitted by the philosopher; that to Judaism we owe the spirit of religion, as to Greece that of culture and philosophy, and to Rome that of order and law; and these things combined make up nearly the whole of what is really precious in civilisation. If again, as St. Ambrose says, *Novum testamentum in vetere latet, vetus testamentum in novo patet;* and if, as many of us know from the deepest experience, our own spiritual vicissitudes, both as a Church and as individuals, are writ large, for guidance and for warning, in the chequered history of the Chosen People; then for the Christian this history must ever have an interest, which, for profundity and extent, is absolutely without a rival.

A comparison between the two chief figures which stand, the one at the beginning, and the other at the close of our period, will be suggestive and instructive. Joshua and Nehemiah seem to be alike in this, that both were born in the land of captivity, and both were taught by serving in youth how to command in manhood. Joshua was born in Egypt, "the house of bondage," and had reached middle life before he quitted it; and we first catch sight of Nehemiah as cupbearer to Artaxerxes Longimanus, king of Persia, in the winter palace at Shushan. But how different was the condition both of their servitude and of their command! Joshua's servitude was one of suffering and degradation, Nehemiah's of luxury and honour. Yet, if Joshua was braced by his lot, Nehemiah would seem to have been in no wise enervated by his. And if the effortless overthrow of the walls of Jericho is in strange contrast with the painful rebuilding of the walls of Jerusalem, and the six years' rapid conquest of six strong nations, with the tedious watching against treacherous foes, yet the two great leaders are splendidly alike in the disinterestedness of their motives and the integrity of their conduct. Joshua, after forty years bondage in Egypt and forty years wandering in the wilderness, might have claimed, at the age of fourscore years and over, to be allowed to hand over to one of a younger generation the toils and responsibilities of an invading general, to be succeeded by the invidious labour of dividing the conquered land. But no such plea ever crosses his lips. Nehemiah gave up a post of influence and emolument at the first court in the world in order to rescue his defenceless fellow-countrymen from the misery of a ceaseless menace. And in the discharge of the difficult offices which they undertook this may be said of both—and it can be said of very few leaders of whom we know so much—that there is not a single blot upon their character. If Nehemiah is somewhat self-conscious, while Joshua seems to have all the simplicity of a child, yet in both we have the beautiful spectacle of great ability and great authority employed without any taint of selfish aims. It may well add to our pleasure in studying the period which lies before us to find that it begins and ends with so conspicuous an example of true patriotism and disinterested statesmanship.

THE CONQUEST OF CANAAN.

"Moses My servant is dead." Such is the Divine greeting to the already aged Joshua with which the book that bears his name opens. It was a message that must have tried even his fortitude; and it came from Him who alone could send it with assurance of perfect certainty. Moses was dead—just at the very moment, it would seem, when his people and those who had helped him to lead them needed his guidance most. The ascent of Pisgah was not to be, like the ascent of Mount Sinai, followed by a return, after which their leader was even more divinely illuminated than before. They were never to see him again, nor even to know where his bones were laid. Henceforth they must be content with the guidance of "Moses' minister" (Exod. xxiv. 13; Num. xxvii. 18; Deut. i. 38). It would seem as if they loyally accepted Joshua. Certainly he accepted with childlike trust and simplicity the high but heavy charge that was thus suddenly laid upon him. Neither elated nor depressed by it, he at once set to work to carry out the Divine command. The remaining thirty years of his life are a calm, unwavering response to the exhortation of Jehovah : " Have not I commanded thee ? Be strong and of a good courage ; be not afraid, neither be thou dismayed : for the Lord thy God is with thee whithersoever thou goest " (Josh. i. 9).

It is easy for those who have laid down for themselves as an axiom, that a miracle is an impossibility, to set aside the Book of Joshua as unhistorical, because of the large amount of miraculous details contained in it. Even if the miracles of the Book of Joshua stood alone, we might fairly protest against so summary a mode of dealing with what bears all the impress· of historic reality. But the miracles which attended the conquest of Canaan stand or fall with all those which have marked God's dealings with His Chosen People, whether under the Law or under Gospel ; and to a fair mind these are simply a question of evidence. The simple truthfulness of the author of the Book of Joshua, and the worthiness of the object for which the miracles which he records are wrought, may rightly be allowed to tell for, rather than against, the truth of miracles as a whole.

It is also possible from another point of view to do but scant justice to the contents of the Book of Joshua. What (it might be asked), at this distance of time and space, have we to do with the invasion of an insignificant tract of country, less than half as large as Scotland, by one of the endless swarms of nomads that find a home in Asia? But even from this limited point of view the conquest of Palestine by the Israelites is by no means devoid of interest or significance. It fills an important place in a long series of invasions of the same tract of country, which occupy the pages of history almost from its earliest chapters down to our own day. What conquests may have preceded those of the Philistines we hardly know. It is likely enough that those whom they displaced were themselves invaders ; but that old race of " giants," who seem to us like the traces of a primæval age preserved in shadowy outline in the rocks, is too little known to us for anything to be asserted positively as to their origin. The Semitic Ammonites, Moabites, and Edomites contributed with the Philistines to the destruction of these primitive populations. After them come the children of Israel ; to be followed in a long train through three thousand years of history by Egyptians, Assyrians, Babylonians, Greeks, Romans, Arabs, Saracens, Crusaders, French, and English. And who will venture to say that the list of invaders is closed ?

But it is a very narrow view to take of the conquest of Canaan by Joshua to regard it merely as one of a series of more or less similar invasions of the same territory. In its most important aspects the conquest under Joshua stands quite apart from most of the other conquests of Palestine, and in some aspects stands alone. Along with those of the Assyrians, Babylonians, and Romans, it was the fulfilment of declarations made by the Almighty beforehand ; but whereas they took place in fulfilment of a threatened punishment, it was the fulfilment of a promised blessing. And the victories of Joshua were not only the subject of prophecy, they were a prophecy themselves—a type and an earnest of the blessings which Jehovah had in store for His people, and on their darker side a type and an earnest of His judgments upon those who refuse to know Him and fight against Him.

In the plan of the campaign against the Canaanites we see that it was a sagacious appreciation of ability which caused Moses to select Joshua as a commander in the battle with Amalek at Rephidim, where he won his first victory some years before. Joshua certainly had some, if not most, of the qualities which make a great general—firmness and gentleness, winning ready trust and obedience from his men, decision and rapidity, whereby the enemy was sometimes virtually defeated before the action began. The plan of the invasion shows true military skill. Joshua succeeded in doing what French generals attempted and signally failed to do in the recent war with Germany. He chose a weak point near the middle of the frontier and pushed on to the centre of the country and beyond it, thus cutting the invaded land in two. The southern half was conquered or won over before the northern half had quite recovered from its panic, or could agree what to do against the invaders. The south being successfully subdued, the north was then conquered in like manner. The Canaanites were beaten in detail. From the miraculous ford at Jordan he pushed on to Jericho, from Jericho to Ai, from Ai to Gibeon, and from Gibeon to the Beth-horons, where his first great decisive battle was fought and won against the five kings of the Amorites, on the same spot where Judas Maccabæus more than twelve centuries later as triumphantly vanquished the Syrian army under Seron. There is no need to trouble ourselves with speculations as to the *way* in which the standing still of the sun and moon at the prayer of Joshua are to be reconciled with modern science. The mode of *all* miracles eludes us: the fact is all that concerns us to know. And if we cannot know the way in which something is created out of nothing, water becomes wine, and the like, it is idle to ask how that way is to be reconciled with other things. The rising and setting of the sun is always an illusion to our sight, for light takes time to travel. Science itself tells us that under certain conditions light travels more slowly than at other times, and those conditions are in the Almighty's control. He who said, "Let there be light," can still make the light do His bidding, and did so in a signal manner at Beth-horon, that His servants might once more be assured that He was with them and fought for them, and that the foul inhabitants of Canaan might be dismayed.

The victory on the road between the two Beth-horons was soon followed by the others. Makkedah, Libnah, Lachish, Eglon, Hebron, and Debir (Kirjath-sepher), were captured one after another. And as it is said of Lachish alone that Israel "took it on the *second* day" (Josh. x. 32), we are perhaps to understand that a single day sufficed for the capture of the other cities, so irresistible did the Israelites under Joshua appear to be. "So Joshua smote all the country of the hills (the mountain district of Judah), and of the south (the *negeb*, a limestone tract, half wilderness), and of the vale (the lowlands, or "plain of the Philistines"), and of the springs (or perhaps the slopes, *i.e.*, the swelling uplands between the "vale" and the "hills"), and all their kings: he left none remaining, but utterly destroyed all that breathed, as the Lord God of Israel commanded (Josh. x. 40).

Thus, in a campaign of a few weeks at the most, the conquest of the south was accomplished. But even when we have recognised the excellence of the plan of the campaign, and the rapidity with which Joshua carried it out, we might still be surprised at his almost unbroken success, if it were not for the fact that "the Lord fought for Israel," and gave to them the elements as their allies. This southern portion of Palestine, Judah, Benjamin, and Ephraim, are strategically very strong, and capable of being obstinately defended. The deep valleys of Judah, and the ravines of Benjamin, running right and left from the central backbone, cut up the country into a number of more or less isolated eminences, equally suggestive of a hill-fort for defence, or a "high place" for worship. The very names Gibeon, Gibeah, Geba, which all mean "hill," point to the physical character of the district. It shows what a panic had fallen upon the inhabitants that these natural defences were not utilised in withstanding the invaders. The fate of Bavarian armies in the Tyrol in the present century sufficiently illustrates what would be the probable result of an invasion of southern Palestine, if the country were stoutly defended by the population. But in this case the inhabitants were "discomfited" (ch. x. 10; comp. Judges iv. 15; 1 Sam. vii. 10; 2 Sam. xxii. 15); troubled and dismayed by God, so that they could not hold together and organize a systematic resistance.

The conquest of northern Palestine follows. The combination of the five kings in the south arranged by Adoni-Zebek, king of Jerusalem, is imitated by Jabin, king of Hazor, who hopes to make a more successful combination of native sovereigns in the north. To strengthen it he tries to include such of the northern tribes also as would venture to try their fortune again—the Amorites and the Hittites, with the still unconquered Jebusites. The attempt is so far successful that he gathered together "much people, even as the sand that is upon the sea shore in multitude, with horses and chariots very many" (Josh. xi. 4). But once more the promised help of Jehovah and the rapidity of Joshua's movements secure the victory for Israel. Without waiting to be attacked, "Joshua came, and all the people of war with him, against them by the waters of Merom *suddenly;* and they *fell upon them*" (ch. xi. 7). The result was the utter defeat of the confederates, a defeat which carried with it the submission of the north, as that at the Beth-horons had decided the fate of the south. The extermination of the Anakim followed, that old giant race of which we know so little; and then "the land rested from war" (ch. xi. 23). The conquest of Palestine, *so far as it required the united forces of all Israel,* was over; not that there was not an immense deal still to be done in putting down risings, in consolidating what had been won, in capturing isolated and still unconquered cities; but this was left for the most part to the energy of the tribe to which the territory in question was assigned. The warlike half of Joshua's great task was accomplished: the more peaceful work of dividing the conquered territory between the victorious tribes remained. The second half of the Book of Joshua (chs. xiii.—xxii.), the Domesday Book of Palestine, is mainly taken up with the details of the distribution. They are no less honourable to the man who carried them out than the details of the campaign which rendered them possible. The division of Palestine among the tribes will bear comparison for equity, sagacity, and permanent results with perhaps most divisions of conquered territory in modern times, from the Norman conquest of England downwards. With characteristic unselfishness he waited until every one else had received their share before asking anything for himself; and then it was but a small portion in the rough mountain country that had been assigned to his own tribe of Ephraim. Here he built the city of Timnath-Serah, and spent the remainder of his days.

How long he enjoyed the rest which something like a century of toil had earned, we do not know, for there is no clear indication of the number of years occupied by the conquest and division of the land. But he reached the age of a hundred and ten, and the end of his life was in harmony with the rest of it. His last public act was to summon the tribes with their officers to Shechem, already a place of solemn associations (Josh. viii. 30—35 ; Gen. xii. 6, 7 ; xxxiii. 18—20 ; xxxv. 2, 4), and the destined resting-place of the bones of Joseph (Josh. xxiv. 32), and gave them a farewell charge to remain ever faithful to Jehovah. It might seem as if such a charge could scarcely be needed ; self-interest alone would suffice to secure fidelity ; for never before or since has an invading force had such manifest help from Heaven. But Joshua knew his own nation. The murmurings and rebellions and idolatries in the wilderness were still fresh in his memory ; and therefore, almost with his last breath, he exhorted them to beware of the abominations with which they had come in contact, and reminded them of the consequences both of obedience and disobedience. It is not as a warrior that the aged commander addresses them : it is not to talk over old campaigns, or to stir them up to future conquests, that he has sent for them : rather as one on the brink of the grave he would speak to them of the one thing needful—holiness and the fear of the Lord. "And it came to pass after these things, that Joshua the son of Nun (no longer "Moses' minister," but now like Moses) *the servant of the Lord,* died, being a hundred and ten years old" (Josh. xxiv. 29). Thus, in the simplicity of mind in which he had lived, and fought, and ruled, this aged servant of the Lord passed away to that better country, of which the one which he had conquered was but a figure, and to a closer know-ledge of Him under whose visible command he had fought at Jericho (ch. v. 13— vi. 5), and of whom he had through life in so many particulars been a type.

The writer of the Epistle to the Hebrews (ch. iv. 8) seems to direct our attention to *Joshua as a type of the Saviour* (comp. Acts vii. 45). Certainly Christian writers outside the New Testament, from Justin Martyr downwards, have delighted in this aspect of the son of Nun. The very name suggests it, although in interpreting Scripture we must be on our guard against fanciful ideas suggested by names. Hoshea (salvation) became Jeho-shua, or Joshua (God's salvation, or God the saviour). See Num. xiii. 16 ; xiv. 6, 30. And in the LXX. the Greek translation of the name is Ἰησοῦς (Jesus), the form which the name assumes in the New Testament, where our translators have unfortunately retained the Greek, instead of returning to the Hebrew form (Acts vii. 45 ; Heb. iv. 8). The following points seem in this case to justify our accepting the name as "*nomen et omen*" of a career full of blessed meaning. (1) Joshua began his life by sharing the sufferings of his brethren in Egypt ; so Jesus took upon Him the form of a servant, and shared the lot of His brethren. (2) The imperfect work of Moses was taken up and completed by Joshua : in a far higher sense it was taken up and completed by Christ ; the Law was perfected in the Gospel. (3) In accordance with their common name, both saved the people given to them by the Father from their enemies. (4) Both "went forth conquering, and to conquer ; " and both conquered after being at first apparently defeated through the sins of others. (5) Joshua brought the Chosen People into the Promised Land, and gave them rest and a home in it. Jesus brings the elect into the kingdom prepared for them, and gives them rest and an eternal home in the "many mansions" of the Father. Other analogies in matters of detail are at least interesting, although to some they may seem less certain than those already noticed. (6) Both entered on their ministry on the banks of Jordan.

(7) Under Joshua the passage of Jordan as the road to the Land of Promise was freed from difficulty and danger. The river of death by which we must enter into our rest has been robbed of its terrors by Christ. (8) The twelve stones taken from the bed of Jordan and set up as witnesses to the people of their deliverance may represent the twelve living "witnesses of His resurrection," and of our deliverance through His resurrection appointed by Christ. (9) Joshua, when he had completed his work, ascended the mountain of Ephraim, and dwelt in security from his enemies. Jesus, having finished the work which the Father gave Him to do (John xvii. 4), ascended up on high and sat down on the right hand of God; from henceforth expecting till His enemies be made His footstool (Heb. x. 12, 13).

From very early times *the extermination of the Canaanites* in obedience to the command of God ("Thou shalt save alive nothing that breatheth; but thou shalt utterly destroy them"—Deut. xx. 16, 17; comp. Num. xxi. 2, 3, 35; xxxiii. 52–54), has been urged as an objection against the morality of the Old Testament. Is such cruel severity in harmony with the Divine attributes? This question seems to call for some notice here. The following considerations are of importance in forming a judgment on it:—(1) The age was one of imperfect knowledge of God, and consequent imperfect morality. "Because of the hardness of men's hearts," acts were allowed and even commanded under the Law which are discouraged or forbidden under the Gospel. (2) It was also an age in which the idea of individual rights and individual responsibility was very imperfect. Property belonged to the community, not to the individual. Communities were held responsible for the acts of individual members, and, conversely, communities exacted retribution for wrongs done to individual members. The punishment of a whole nation was therefore quite in harmony with the prevailing sentiment of justice. (3) It was more important that this strong sentiment of justice should be turned in the right direction, viz., against the worst forms of sin, than that in its exercise it should carefully discriminate between a criminal and his connections. God's revelations are gradual; and as man could not learn the morality of the Gospel all at once, the most necessary elements were insisted on first. (4) Although it would have been possible to punish the Canaanites, as Sodom and Gomorrha were punished, without employing the sword of Israel, yet this would have been less generally beneficial. The Israelites were the trustees of the morality of the world. If they had lost their sacred deposit in the abominations of Canaan, the whole human race might have sunk to the level of Sodom. Warnings, like the fate of Korah and his company, lost their effect in time. Nothing could impress the hatefulness and peril of sin so strongly upon the Israelites as to make them themselves the instruments of God's vengeance on those who persisted in sin. These considerations will go far to explain God's command so far as it affected those who had to execute it. With regard to those on whom it was executed we must remember further: (5) That it was a punishment for sins of the most abominable and contagious kind. (6) That the Canaanites were not only heinous sinners, but sinners against light: they had had the pure lives and pure worship of the patriarchs among them for generations. (7) They had had the warning of the fate of the cities of the plain at their very doors, even if the tradition of the flood had perished among them.

It remains to say a few words about the book in which the history of these great types and warnings is contained. Its single and inartificial style leads us to place it earlier than the less archaic Books of Kings and Chronicles. The Jews believed it to be written by Joshua, and this view was followed by the Fathers, and as regards much of the book, at any rate, is still advocated by some modern critics. It is clear that the account of Joshua's death, and the statement that "the Jebusites dwelt with the children of Judah at Jerusalem" (ch. xv. 63), point to a date later than Joshua. Moreover, the conquests of Hebron by Caleb, of Debir by Othniel, and of Laish by the Danites, were almost certainly not completed until after the death of Joshua (comp. Josh. xv. 13—20, and xix. 47 with Judg. i. 10—15, and ch. xviii. 7). On the other hand, the book seems to be written during the lifetime of Rahab (ch. vi. 25), and by one who took part in the campaign (ch. v. 1), and must certainly be earlier than the time of David (ch. xv. 63). The hypothesis that it was written, or at least completed, after Joshua's death by some one who obtained a great deal of material from Joshua himself, seems to harmonize with all these points, and also to account for the great minuteness of detail which characterizes portions of the books. Its contents are alluded to in the Psalms (xliv. 2, 3; lxviii. 12—14; lxxviii. 54, 55), in the Prophets (Isa. xxviii. 21; Hab. iii. 11—13), and in the New Testament (Acts vii. 45; Heb. iv. 8; xi. 30—31; James ii. 25); and its canonicity has never been disputed either among Jews or Christians. It stands in somewhat the same relation to the Pentateuch as the Acts of the Apostles to the Gospels. While the Pentateuch gives the origin and principles of Judaism, and the Gospels those of Christianity, in the Books of Joshua and of the Acts of the Apostles we see those principles in action. The two books give us the youth—the one of the Jewish and the other of the Christian Church. In each case we are introduced to the first beginnings of ecclesiastical history. It is important to keep this aspect of the Book of Joshua constantly in view, in order to retain an adequate appreciation of its significance. Neither the Pentateuch nor the Gospels are primarily historical. They are rather the text-books of the Old and New Covenant; and the historical elements which they contain is there not so much as history as in order to explain the origin, and illustrate the meaning, of the covenant in each case. The Book of Joshua and the Acts *are* primarily historical. There object is to show how the promises made to the Church were in the first instance fulfilled, and how provision was made for a still larger fulfilment in the future. If this estimate of the two books is correct, we must at once give up the notion that the Book of Joshua is a mere appendix to the Pentateuch, possibly by the same hand. It would be more reasonable to regard it as a preface to the books that follow. Yet, strictly speaking, it is neither; it is a complete whole in itself, a necessary link in the great chain of events by which the Jewish dispensation prepared the way for the Gospel.

THE AGE OF THE JUDGES.

Although, in one sense, we are still in the same period of Jewish history, that which is commonly called the Theocracy, yet we feel that we have passed into a different atmosphere when we pass from the rule of Joshua to the rule of the Judges. It is something like passing from the age of heroism to the age of chivalry; from an age in which the chief figures seem to be far above us, and almost to belong to another world, to one in which we feel at home, because the prominent characters both in their strength and in their weakness are like ourselves. Where they are great, it is not an unapproachable grandeur, but one that we could imagine to belong to our own generation; and they are not always great. When they fall they prove to us that the age of chivalry is not very far removed from that of barbarism, and even contains some taint of savagery in itself. Something of this kind may be in our thoughts when we leave the calm, majestic guidance of Moses and Joshua for the turbulent rule of Gideon, Jephthah, and Samson.

Of all the books in the Bible the Book of Judges is perhaps the most human. In most of the books the Divine element is so strong, or we are in the habit of keeping it so constantly in view, that we are apt to forget that the actors in the various scenes are not merely instruments in the hands of the Almighty, but men and women with wills and passions like ourselves. In the history of the Judges it is impossible to forget this. The difficulty is rather the other way : viz., to understand how men so faulty, so barbarous, one might almost say, so brutal, came to be chosen by Almighty God as the deliverers and rulers of His people. In this respect the Book of Judges and the Book of Ruth may go together. The one gives the roughness and wildness, the other the sweetness and tenderness of life ; but both in their way are intensely human. There is manifest gain in this, and it may be one of the special lessons intended to be conveyed by these two writings. Just as in the case of Jesus Christ Himself it is possible to lay so much emphasis on His Divinity as to lose sight of His perfect humanity ; so also in the revelation which He has granted to us, of His dealings with mankind, it is easy to fix our eyes so continually on the Divine decrees and their fulfilment, as to forget that throughout it all man's will was free, and that God worked not with soulless machines, but with persons who had the terrible privilege of being able to follow their own wills rather than His, if they so pleased. This is everywhere apparent in the Book of Judges. Not only is God's Chosen People as a whole frequently in rebellion against Him, but those who were specially selected out of them (ἐκλεκτῶν ἐκλεκτότεροι), as agents peculiarly set apart to carry out His purposes, are wayward to a degree that makes the question, "Quis custodit ipsos custodes," eminently pertinent respecting them.

There is a wild freshness about the Book of Judges which tells of youth and independence, and freedom from restraint and care : the freshness of nature and the freshness of human life. It is mountain and woodland scenery filled with the thrilling incidents of the romances of chivalry. It is a tale of ancient times, and therefore it has all the interest of what lays outside our own everyday experience. It is a tale of men and women like ourselves, and, therefore, we can realise it all. But the freshness and the independence have their dark side. It is an age in which freedom too often means license, and anarchy, and violence. What is human is too often barbarous, even savage and bestial. The lower part of man's nature is ever coming to the front and often takes the upper hand. Hence the story is no mere idyll of pastoral brightness, no mere epic of the triumph of what is noble and pure. The cry of suffering alternates with the cry of victory, and the tragic element is not wanting ; the right is too often a "random right," and there is abundance of "random wrong." Thus the pathos of tragedy and the brilliancy of romance go hand in hand. There is yet another element, not prominent but distinctly present here and there, which must not be passed over, because it makes the picture all the more true to life. A vein of humour, almost of drollery, comes to the surface at times, making us feel still more at home with those of whose doings we read. We almost see the twinkle in the eyes of the men of Dan as they say to their brethren, "Do ye know that there is in these houses an ephod, and teraphim, a graven image, and a molten image? now, therefore, consider what ye have to do" (ch. xviii. 14). And, again, when they have carried off these things, and the owners come after them to complain, there is the same spirit of fun in their question, "What aileth thee that thou comest with such a company?" (ver. 23). This element is specially strong in the history of Samson, whose exploits have a rollick-ing air about them, which appeals at once to the spirit of adventure and mischief with which we all of us have more or less sympathy. Note especially the grim humour with which, in the last terrible scene, he prays to be avenged "for *one* of my two eyes," according to the emended translation.

It is not difficult to catch the narrator's own point of view. Four times in the course of his narrative he reminds us that "in those days there was no king in Israel" (ch. xvii. 6; xviii. 1; xix. 1; xxi. 25), and twice he adds, as the natural consequence of this, "every man did that which was right in his own eyes." This is the refrain, the echo of which resounds throughout the whole book. And what was the result of every man doing that which was right in his own eyes? In a sentence of still more ominous frequency (chs. ii. 11; iii. 7, 12; iv. 1; vi. 1; x. 6; xiii. 1), he tells us again and again that "the children of Israel did evil in the sight of the Lord," "the children of Israel *again* did evil in the sight of the Lord." Thus we have a regular cycle of cause and effect—sin produces punishment, and punishment amendment, and amendment deliverance, and deliverance presumption with fresh apostacy and sin, with which the cycle begins again. So long as Joshua and his contemporaries lived (ch. ii. 7, 10), the Israelites remained faithful to Jehovah; but after them arose a godless generation who fell into the snares of which Joshua had warned them (the seductive idolatries of the nations round about them), and served Baal and Ashtoreth. The period is one of transition; the old rulers, Moses and Joshua, have passed away and kings have not yet arisen. And now that the external pressure of common dangers is removed, another great bond of union is taken away. The nation is in danger of disintegra-tion almost before it is formed, and is falling apart into tribes, or at most groups of tribes, each with separate, and sometimes, conflicting interests. This is the peril from within. And there is peril also from without. The conquered populations are neither expelled, nor absorbed, nor perfectly subdued. Like the Britons under the Saxons, and the Saxons under the Danes and under the Normans, they still kept possession of large districts and important points. They were biding their time, and perhaps, like the Saxons in the case of the Danes, might still get the upper hand. Moreover, the nations outside Palestine were not friendly to the invaders, who might any day cross the border and turn against them. Thus a great deal of the work of Joshua had to be done over again. Cities and districts had to be reconquered; and where the Israelites had fallen away into idolatry, there was reconquest on the side of the Canaanites. What with division and apostasy within, seduction and hostility without, it looked as if the possession of the Promised Land by the Israelites was destined to be very brief.

Yet, although in certain respects the period under the Judges is retrograde, it is retrogression preliminary to and possibly necessary to further advance. The tide was advancing, though the waves frequently went back; and human progress is no river, but a tide that ebbs and flows and moves in circles fitfully. In two marked particulars this time of apparent disintegration and anarchy had great influence on the future development of the nation. First, the Israelites were passing through the all-important change from a nomad to a settled life; they were ceasing to be mere herdsmen, and were becoming agriculturists. Secondly, the isolation of the wilderness was at an end; they were becoming rapidly acquainted, both for good and for evil, with other civilisations besides their own.

The change from a wandering to a stationary life was not made suddenly.

During their long halts in the wilderness there had been some preparation for it; and a fertile tract will tempt even permanently nomadic tribes to settle long enough to sow and reap a harvest. And now that the Israelites had reached their goal, and looked forward to no more wandering, we need not suppose that the wanderers settled down at once, each on his own allotment. Within the limits of each tribe there would be room enough for much changing before a permanent home was made; for the theory that the divisions of property made by the Canaanites were adopted, just as they stood, by the Israelites cannot be regarded as probable, or more than in a very remote degree possible. Everything Canaanitish was an abomination. Be this as it may, the important fact remains that during this period a large portion of the Israelites became agricultural.

The change from a life of isolation to one of constant intercourse with others was scarcely less pregnant with results. The hermit-nation had returned after long years of solitude into the world; and had at once come in contact with nations whose language was near enough to their own to render intercourse easy, and moreover who, in trade, and art, and civilisation generally, were greatly in advance of themselves. As we might expect, this was specially the case with the nations who inhabited the sea-board of Palestine, and whose opportunities for commerce were the greatest—the Phœnicians and the Philistines. Tyre and Sidon had already reached a condition of strength and prosperity, and seem, like the nation of traders that they were, at once to have made the coming of the Israelites a mere matter of business. Neither side appears to have attempted to molest the other, and commercial relations soon began to exist between the Phœnicians and the Israelites. It would seem that the easy-going life of the Sidonians had passed into a proverb (Judg. xviii. 7); the fact probably being that, so long as their commerce was secure, they never troubled themselves to fight for anything;—the "peace-at-all-price" policy of a mercantile nation. It was very much otherwise with the Philistines. Their intercourse with the Israelites was by no means of so friendly a nature. Immigrants like the Phœnicians and the Israelites, but at a very early age, they were much less disposed than either to rest peaceably within the limits of the territory which they had occupied. They were a warlike rather than a commercial people, and seem to have possessed a considerable military organization. Their five confederate cities, Gaza, Askelon, Ashdod, Gath, and Ekron, were strong enough to dispossess Dan, to conquer Judah, and towards the end of this period to make their heavy hand felt in other tribes as well. While the Phœnicians remained friendly or indifferent towards the new-comers, the Philistines were actively aggressive. The attitude, therefore, of these two important nations towards the Israelites may serve very well as samples of the varied influences to which the Chosen People were subjected now that they had come into contact at every corner of the land, and here and there in the very centre of it, with strangers. Roughly speaking, the Israelites held the hill-country while the Canaanites held the plains. The Israelites had hardly anything but infantry, and in the plains, where cavalry and chariots were most effective, they were at a great disadvantage against the Canaanites, who were often very strong in both. It is scarcely too much to say that throughout the greater part of their sojourn in Palestine, the Israelites were not masters of their own plains; these were so constantly at the mercy of either Canaanites or Syrians.

These two facts—the change from a nomadic to a stationary and generally an agricultural life, and the intercourse, friendly or hostile, with other nations—are

among the chief forces which are at work during the period of the Judges to mould
the nation into the form in which we find it under the early kings. And indeed,
other seed is being sown to bear fruit in a still more distant future. In the selfish
indifference with which one tribe regards the calamities of another, in the jealous
rivalry which shows itself between them, especially between the more powerful
tribes, we see the first beginnings of the strife which was to end in the permanent
disruption of the nation. Deborah complains bitterly of the apathy of Reuben,
Dan, and Asher, during the oppression of Zebulon and Naphtali; and any joint
action between Judah and Ephraim was evidently not looked for. Judah is not
even mentioned, as if its absence on such an occasion was a matter of course.
This silence respecting Judah is not confined to the Song of Deborah. During the
whole period there is very little mention of this tribe. On the principle that happy
is the nation that has no history, we may consider this silence as being to the
credit of those whose doings are left unrecorded. Simeon, the neighbour of Judah,
shares this honourable obscurity. We can only conjecture the cause; but it is not
improbable that these two tribes, secure in their mountain fastnesses, remained
aloof from the others, neither mixing in their squabbles nor sharing their dangerous
intercourse with the heathen. Omitting Ibzan and Shamgar as doubtful, only one
of the numerous Judges belonged to Judah—Othniel, who was perhaps the first of
the Judges. The reason may have been that, being comparatively free from the
disorders which troubled the rest of the Israelites, these two southern tribes had no
need of exceptional deliverers and rulers. And even Othniel was not in the
strictest sense of Judah. He is called "son of Kenaz" (ch. i. 13), and his elder
brother Caleb is described both as a "Kenezite" (Num. xxxii. 12), and also of Judah
(Num. xiii. 6). The Kenezites belonged to the old inhabitants (Gen. xv. 19), so
that some of them at any rate must have been allowed to unite with the tribe of
Judah, and to be counted as members of the tribe. This remarkable adoption by
so exalted a tribe as Judah is of great interest, and has a parallel in the case of the
Kenites. Kenaz was a descendant of Esau; and if the Kenites were Midianites,
they also sprang from Abraham; so that the Kenezites and Kenites, though not
Israelites, were not absolute aliens. The fact that Othniel, the Kenezite, delivered
Israel from an invasion which came from the north, seems to show that in this first
oppression, and probably in this one only, the whole land was overrun. From
most of the troubles of this period Judah remained exempt; and we have some
evidence that this was due to its own good conduct. First, we have the beautiful
picture of quiet and pure domestic life preserved for us in the Book of Ruth, in
tremendous contrast to the episodes of Micah and the Danites, the men of Gibeah
and the Benjamite war, the act of Jael, and the whole history of Samson and of
Jephthah. Secondly, there is the evident superiority of the tribe of Judah, so soon
as it emerges from its obscurity under David. True that Judah did not altogether
escape the oppression of the Amorites, and still less that of the Philistines; yet
they were not ground down as were other tribes by these oppressions; and in
David's time they more than paid their debt to both. The remainder of the tribes
on the west of Jordan were far from united among themselves; but the tendency
was to acquiesce in the pretensions of Ephraim, which lost no opportunity of
asserting itself. Thus the way was steadily being prepared for the future division
of the kingdom. The two-and-a-half tribes on the other side of the Jordan were
cut off by this natural barrier from much intercourse with their brethren. Nor
were they united among themselves. Here also, as on the west bank, the southern-

most remained aloof. But the isolation of Reuben was far less honourable than that of Judah. Reuben, the first-born, sinks down into an obscurity from which it never emerges. Out of Reuben arises no judge, no hero, no prophet. Deborah singles it out for scornful reproach, and this is almost the last mention of the tribe. While Gad and Manasseh produced valiant men, and sometimes gave a refuge to their suffering brethren from the western bank, Reuben remained apart in well-to-do repose, absolutely cut off from Judah by the Dead Sea, and not having much intercourse even with Gilead.

Thus, then, the nation which had entered Canaan in the strength of internal purity and union under one leader, had fallen apart into at least four unequal and irregular groups, two on each side of the Jordan. On the west bank (1) Judah and Simeon, probably far the best representatives of the old purity and discipline, and for this reason, as well as from the character of their territory, the strongest of the groups. (2) The remainder of the tribes on this bank, not really united, but all more or less acquiescing in the precedence claimed by Ephraim. On the east bank (3) half Manasseh and Gad, on fairly good terms with the western tribes, but prevented by the Jordan from being very intimate. (4) Reuben, in comfortable and ignoble solitude.

It would have gone very hard with the Israelites during this period of serious dismemberment if something of the same kind had not prevailed among the Canaanites also. We have seen the ill-success of the hastily formed leagues, first in the south and then in the north, against Joshua. A successor, and possibly a descendant of the Jabin, king of Hazor, who formed the northern league on that occasion, was the author of the twenty years of oppression from which Deborah and Barak delivered Israel. Only so long as his general Sisera kept the key of the position with his 900 chariots at Harosheth of the Gentiles, could the domination of Jabin be maintained. If the various Canaanite cities (which still remained scattered about like so many dark islands, in the midst of the tribes) had combined with Jabin, the Israelites would have been enclosed in a network of hostile fortresses, from which it might have required another miraculous campaign, like that of Joshua, to free them. Gezer in Ephraim, Jebus in Benjamin, Bethshean, Ibleam, Taanach, Megiddo, and Dor in Manasseh, Kitron and Nahalol in Zebulon; while in the case of Asher and Naphtali the proportion of Canaanites was so large that, whereas of other tribes it was said that "the Canaanites dwelt among them," of them it was said that "they dwelt among the Canaanites" (Judg. i. 32, 33). The map will show how these facts illustrate the statement made above, that the Israelites could not gain possession of the plains. Gazer and Dor are in the plain of Sharon; Bethshean, Megiddo, and Taanach in the plain of Esdraelon. Nahalol was probably in the plain of Esdraelon also, but neither the name nor the situation of the city can be determined with certainty. During Jabin's domination the northern tribes were practically prisoners in their own land; and had these constellations of Canaanite cities joined vigorously with him his success would have been still greater, and might have been indefinitely prolonged. But Jehovah had willed it otherwise. Even as it was, these Canaanites cities worked disaster enough : they were permanent centres of religious and moral corruption.

Thus far, then, we have arrived at these characteristics of the period under consideration. (1) It was a time of great freedom tending to anarchy. The paternal rule of Moses and Joshua was removed, and the tribes resorted to democratic government before they were in the least degree ripe for it. The result was that there was very little government at all. (2) A large proportion of the nation was rapidly changing from the pastoral to the agricultural state; an advance without which the future development of the nation would have been impossible. (3) Both inside and outside Palestine the Israelites were abandoning a condition of isolation for one of contact and intercourse with a variety of nationalities, in culture superior, in religion and morality vastly inferior, to themselves; a change productive of calamitous results, but not unmixed evil. (4) The external pressure of a common and imminent danger being removed, and the bulk of the territory being conquered, the tribes were falling apart from one another, each following its own selfish interest. A common danger at times reunited those who felt its pressure; but generally there was a tendency to separate into loosely connected groups. The worship of Jehovah was to a large extent deserted for Canaanitish idolatries, and thus the highest of all bonds of union was lost. Hence (5) their various enemies gained strength and subjugated large portions of the country from time to time. Had their enemies been united among themselves, and had the suffering which they inflicted failed to check the canker of political and religious disintegration which was ruining Israel, the land would probably have relapsed into the hands of its former owners, and the Israelites would have been reconquered and absorbed. But the sharp medicine administered again and again at last did its work: and after a long and uneven struggle the purer religion and the nobler race prevailed.

But meanwile the purer religion was almost lost. In the wilderness the Israelites had lived, as it were, in a religious hothouse. They had been kept apart from the common atmosphere, and had lived in a world of their own. In this way they had been brought up to a spiritual elevation, which was partly supernatural and partly artificial. The supernatural influences of perceptible communication with Jehovah had ceased; the artificial restraint of complete isolation had been thrown aside; and they appeared to be left to do "what seemed good in their eyes." The result showed that they were quite unequal to so severe a trial. Those who lived at a distance from the tabernacle at Shiloh at most went up to it only once a year, probably for the most attractive and joyous of the feasts, that of Tabernacles. What was out of sight soon went out of mind, and the ordinances of religion were one by one forgotten. With no one to read the Law to them, with no religious ceremonial to teach them by the eye, large numbers grew up in the grossest ignorance as regards creed and worship. Superstitious observances grew up under trees and in high places. Jehovah was represented by images. This soon led to a still graver profanation. The image of Jehovah became only one of many, and His worship was mingled with that of heathen deities. In many cases the last and final step was taken, and the worship of the one true God was entirely abandoned for that of Baal and Ashtoreth. Thus the belief of Abraham, Isaac, and Jacob in the unity of God, the creed which had ennobled and sustained Israel through so many generations, was tampered with, and corrupted, and in many cases lost. Such was the price which Israel paid for premature intercourse with higher civilisations.

And thus, as in the case of Paradise, the Divine ideal had been frustrated by the free-will and self-will of man. Had God's commands been obeyed, the polluting influence of the Canaanites would have been expelled or extinguished, and His people would have been free to receive and cherish and develop, in His own good time, the revelation which He had partly given and partly had still in store for them. Secure from seductions and hindrances from without, bound together by their common privileges within, they would not only have preserved their old level of spiritual enlightenment, but would have risen steadily to a still higher one. But, as of old, the forbidden fruit seemed "good for food," and "pleasant to the eyes," and a thing "to be desired to make one wise;" and when once it was tasted the mischief was done. The whole Jewish race from that day to this has paid the penalty; just as the whole human race has paid the penalty of Adam's transgression. The two Captivities with their lasting consequences were the direct result of the idolatry which dates from this forbidden intercourse with the Canaanites. The lesson is similar to that taught in Eden. Man's free-will involves the possibility of a fall, and one fall renders another fall probable. Man's fallen nature can be regenerated only through suffering: and thus, what was in the first instance a punishment, by God's mercy becomes in the end a blessing. The certainty of punishment for sin, the possibility of repentance, the discipline of suffering—these are the great lessons of the Book of Judges.

The period has been compared with the heroic age in Greece and other pagan lands. The analogy holds good in several interesting points. In both there is an invasion of new territory, and the prowess of the heroes is exhibited in the struggle with the primitive inhabitants for possession. In both there is a startling mixture of virtue and vice, of what is noble with what is vile, of splendid self-sacrifice and bravery with savagery, treachery, and lust. The analogy fails, however, in one most important particular. Even in the wildest of the Jewish heroes we find a consciousness of a divine mission, and a reliance on God, of which pagan heroes show little trace. And although brutal acts of licentiousness and cruelty are only too frequent amongst both, yet the popular conscience regards them with abhorrence in the one case, while it applauds them or looks upon them as a matter of course in the other. A truer analogy seems to be found in the age of Christian chivalry; *e.g.*, in the Crusades, a struggle for the same territory. There also we find a hideous amount of evil mixed with the good; there also the evil too often triumphed while the good failed: but this must ever be the case where an appeal is made on a large scale to force. Yet there was the moral, the religious purpose at bottom, however much it might be alloyed or overlaid with ignoble motives. And in the general outcome of the period of the Judges, as of the Crusades, the world has been greatly the gainer. Along with a mere love of adventure, which is neither right nor wrong, along with treachery and cruelty and other grievous crimes, committed both in the name of and in defiance of religion, there was a power and a reality in both, calculated to bring out all that is heroic in human nature: love of liberty, admiration of prowess, sympathy with suffering, patient endurance when hope seemed gone, perseverance to the end

The chronology of the period is involved in obscurity, but this need not cause any serious difficulty. Chronology is not what the compiler of the various narratives aimed at giving us; and therefore we need not be surprised that clear marks of time are wanting. The whole period is perhaps about a century and a half, as seems to be indicated by the genealogies. To add up the years of alternate oppressions and rests given in the book itself would only lead us astray: for (1) the narratives possibly run parallel to one another in certain cases, being accounts of what was going on in different parts of Canaan at one and the same time; (2) no great reliance can be placed upon the frequently recurring numbers, twenty (chs. iv. 3; xv. 20; xvi. 31), forty (chs. iii. 11; v. 31; viii. 28; xiii. 1), eighty (ch. iii. 30), which may be round numbers with no pretension to exactness. Modern chronologers vary from 150 to 300 years; ancient writers give double that amount; *e.g.*, Josephus 592, Eusebius 600. The date of the compilation of the book and the name of the compiler are both unknown. In its present form it must be comparatively late, for in what is sometimes called the Appendix (chs. xvii.—xxi.) the writer shows that not only Shiloh has ceased to be the seat of the tabernacle (ch. xviii. 31), and that there have been kings in Israel (chs. xvii. 6; xviii. 1; xix. 1; xxi. 25), but also, according to the more probable interpretation, that the Assyrian captivity has taken place (ch. xviii. 30). This would place the writer of this portion after B.C. 721, and probably a still later date must be taken for the final redaction in its existing form. But the best scholars are not agreed on the subject; and for ordinary students of the Bible to attempt to pronounce an opinion on these different theories is perhaps not a profitable exercise. It will be wiser for us to study what this unknown writer has preserved for us, and to be thankful to Him through whose providence it has been preserved.

There are no quotations from the Book of Judges in the New Testament, but there are references to its contents in Acts xiii. 20 and Heb. xi. 32. Allusions in the Psalms and in the Prophets are frequent.

The *Book of Ruth*, as already indicated, may be considered as another Appendix to the Book of Judges. It gives us the other side of the picture; natural affection, domestic piety, gentleness, and quietude, in contrast with the troubled scenes in which Gideon, Jephthah, and Samson move. Probably neither Appendix is in its proper chronological position; but the effect is for that very reason all the more striking. From the hideous deed of the men of Gibeah and its bloody consequences, we turn with relief and refreshment to the beautiful devotion of Ruth the Moabitess, and to the sunny corn-fields of Bethlehem. Besides this the book contains the genealogy of David, from the time of the patriarchs onwards; from Pharez, the son of Judah and Tamar, to Jesse the Bethlehemite. This genealogy is of great historical value, not only as a portion of the genealogy of the Messiah, and as containing that portion of it which marks the founding of the house at Bethlehem, but also as a guide to the chronology of the period. Salmon, the husband of Rahab and first proprietor of Bethlehem, is the grandfather of Obed, the grandfather of David; *i.e.*, three, or possibly four, generations cover the period of the Judges. Excepting so far as this genealogy agrees with those in St. Matthew and St. Luke, and may be one of the sources used by the Evangelists, there is no quotation from the Book of Ruth or any reference to it in the New Testament. The typical character of the book must also be borne in mind in connexion with the lineage of the Messiah. The union of Ruth the Moabitess with a man of the tribe of Judah foreshadows that union of Jew and Gentile in Him who sprang from this marriage. Those who are admitted to the high honour of being ancestors of Christ, are an earnest of the all-embracing character of His kingdom. If among them are included the incestuous Tamar, the harlot Rahab, and the Moabitess Ruth, there are none who may not hope, by doing the will of God, to be equal to His brother, and sister, and mother (Mark iii. 35).

The Last of the Judges. Eli.

At first sight it may appear strange that the two last who held the office of Judge in Israel are not included in the Book of the *Judges*, but are noticed at the beginning of a series of books, which in the Vulgate bear the appropriate names of the First, Second, Third, and Fourth Books of *Kings*. The common titles, derived from the printed Hebrew Bible, are less appropriate, for of the First and Second Books of Samuel only part of the First Book tells of Samuel, all the remainder of the two

Books being filled with the reigns of Saul and David. The including of Eli and Samuel in this series rather than in the Book of Judges would seem all the more strange, if (as some suppose) all these five books were compiled about the same time, and possibly by the same hand. And yet the arrangement is perhaps not only a justifiable one but the best that could have been made. For (1) the judgeship of Eli and Samuel is a very different office from that which was held by Gideon, Ehud, or Samson; (2) the importance of Samuel does not consist in his closing the list of Judges, but in his preparing the way for the monarchy, and in particular for David, the type and most notable progenitor of the Messiah.

The judgeship of Eli and Samuel was permanent, sacerdotal, and perhaps, in virtue of its connexion with the sacerdotal office, was intended to be hereditary. The office of the earlier judges was the reverse of all this. It was exceptional and provisional; like the dictatorship among the Romans, a temporary concentration of the power in the hands of one man in order to meet a crisis. Moreover, it had no connexion with the priesthood; not one of the earlier Judges was of priestly descent. The attempt of Abimelech, the son of Gideon, to inherit some of his father's power failed. In what way the office became so changed as we find it in Eli's hands is unknown. Between Samson's overthrow of the Philistine temple at Gaza and the Philistines' overthrow of the sanctuary at Shiloh, there is a blank in the sacred narrative which we cannot fill. How did Eli, who belonged to the family of Ithamar, Aaron's second son, become high-priest, although the line of Eleazar, the eldest son, was not extinct? How did Eli come to be both high-priest and judge? These are questions which we can only answer conjecturally. But it may easily have been the case that Eli was elected judge for exploits against the Philistines early in life, and that, being a descendant of Aaron, the fact of his being judge led to his obtaining the high-priesthood also. The kind-hearted old man whom we find sitting at the entrance to the sanctuary of Shiloh, when the narrative begins again, can scarcely be one who gained office by violence or fraud. Nothing of the kind is laid to his charge, when for his sons' iniquity and his weakness in not restraining them his family is brought to ruin. But the great influence which he enjoyed is shown by the fact that, even after the heavy blow fell upon his house, we find his descendants, Ahijah with Saul, and Abiathar with David, in honourable priestly offices.

Nothing shows more clearly the depth of the moral degradation into which the people had fallen during the time of the Judges than the conduct of Eli's sons. In the very sanctuary itself, and in the ministers to it, we find the most barefaced cupidity and wantonness. Hophni and Phinehas are the prototypes of grasping and sensual ecclesiastics throughout all ages; and the consequences of their sins, to the congregation, to the sanctuary, and to themselves, are warnings of the judgment which must fall sooner or later upon corruption and profligacy in high and sacred places. Micah's Levite in the Book of Judges is a similar though less glaring instance. And yet, great as the plague-spot is, one sees that Israel is still sound at heart. The conduct of the priests is felt to be a scandal; it is not ignored or laughed at: " men abhorred the offerings of the Lord." The depth has not yet been reached when " My people love to have it so " (Jer. v. 31).

The superstitious carrying of the ark of the covenant into the field of battle is another sign of the corruption of the times; and it again has its counterpart in more modern times in the carrying of the consecrated host as a sort of charm against danger. The guilty priests, having no spiritual or moral influence with the people, resort to this material emblem as a means of inspiriting the disheartened troops. The battle-field of Aphek, close to the scene of happier auspices, Beth-horon, and itself the scene of a victory a few years later (1 Sam. vii. 12), was to decide whether the Philistines should be the slaves of the Hebrews, or the Hebrews of the Philistines. " On the success of this wager of battle the priestly rulers of the nation had staked the most sacred pledge of their religion." Staked and lost both it and the sanctuary, and their own miserable lives also. The Philistines, believing that they were contending against terrific odds, and that the God of the Hebrews was in the ranks of their opponents, fought with the courage of despair. We read of the capture of the ark and of the death of Eli ; but of what must have followed soon after, the violent overthrow or rapid decay of the sanctuary of Shiloh, we are not told. But its desolation passed into a proverb as a monument of Divine judgment. " Go ye now unto My place which was in Shiloh, where I set My name at the first, and see what I did to it, for the wickedness of My people Israel " (Jer. vii. 12). " Then will I make this house like Shiloh, and will make this city a curse to all the nations of the earth." " This house shall be like Shiloh, and this city shall be desolate without an inhabitant " (Jer. xxvi. 6, 9). Still more striking, because so incidental, is the notice of it at the end of the Book of Judges. " Shiloh, which is in the land of Canaan." " Shiloh, which is in the north side of Bethel, on the east side of the highway that goeth up from Bethel to Shechem, and on the south of Lebonah " (ch. xxi. 12, 19). At the time when this was written the very site of Shiloh was so little known that it needed to be thus minutely described ; and this exact description enabled Dr. Robinson in 1838 to discover the site. He found the name still surviving among the shepherds of the neighbourhood as Seilûn.

Each of the three great epochs in the history of the Jews ends with the destruction of the visible sanctuary. The fact may teach us, as Ewald points out, that the history of Israel is the history of a religion rather than of a nation. " They are not all Israel which are of Israel ; " and " he is not a Jew which is one outwardly " (Rom. ix. 6 ; ii. 28). The Theocracy ended with the downfall of the sanctuary at Shiloh, directly or indirectly through the spoliation by the Philistines. The monarchy ended with the destruction of the first temple of Jerusalem by the armies of Babylon. The period after the Captivity ended with the destruction of the last temple of Jerusalem by the armies of Titus. Each overthrow was worse than the previous one, and each might have warned the Jews that along with their sanctuary a period of probation had passed away. The destruction by the Chaldeans prepared the deathbed, the destruction by the Romans prepared the funeral, of the Jewish religion. The glory of it departed with the one, the very possibility of life was extinguished by the other. Since the ruin wrought by Titus the keeping of the law has been a physical impossibility. But the overthrow of the first sanctuary was a judgment that was turned into a blessing. It inspired a yearning and prepared the way for something higher — for a more glorious sanctuary on a nobler site, where a renovated priesthood should minister to a chastened and purified people.

The Last of the Judges. Samuel.

Samuel, like the Baptist, closes one great era and inaugurates a new one ; like the Baptist also, he nominates a successor greater than himself. Both men, grand in themselves, the one at the beginning, the other at the end of " the goodly fellow-ship of the prophets," derive their chief importance from that which they inaugurate rather than from that which they are, or do, themselves. Samuel has this further characteristic peculiar to himself; he inaugurated the new system against his own previous convictions. He himself regarded the new departure as a lamentable abandonment of what had hitherto been the ideal, the ideal of Sinai and of Ebal and Gerizim. And yet, as soon as he saw that the change was inevitable, with all the generosity and wisdom of a noble nature and an open mind, he flung himself into the new movement, if not with enthusiasm, at least with energy and devotion. If a new constitution must come, it should be the very best that he could make it. The people had refused to listen to him and had insisted on their own cravings ; that should not make him stand moodily aloof while they blindly followed the evil models of Canaanitish monarchies. At first he did his utmost to make the old system meet the requirements of the age ; when he found out that this was impossible, he had the courage to own it to himself, and the nobleness to transfer his energies to the movement which he personally disliked. As was natural, his interest in it grew with the work ; and that which at first he would have prevented from existing, he before long loved and fostered as his own child.

The judgeship of Samuel resembles that of Eli more than that of the previous Judges, but it was not the same. Samuel and Eli were alike in this, that both were ecclesiastics holding the highest civil office, and that the office was permanent and not provisional. But Samuel, though a Levite and a Nazarite, was not of the family of Aaron, and therefore could not be, as Eli was, high-priest. On the other hand, Samuel was what Eli was not, a prophet, and from the first was recognised as such (1 Sam. iii. 19—21). This supernatural fact a great deal more than compensated for his not holding a high-priestly office. Indeed, in Eli's time, the priesthood had fallen so low that probably the office gained far more influence from his personal character and civil dignity than it conferred by its peculiar sanctity. On the whole, the history of the Jewish priesthood, from Aaron to Caiaphas, is the history of a tremendous failure ; a conspicuous illustration of the maxim, *corruptio optimi fit pessima*.

A Levite by birth, a Nazarite by the devotion of his parents, judge by the election of the people, prophet by the consecration of Jehovah, Samuel united in himself all the moral and spiritual gifts by which he could most powerfully influence the people whom he had to rule. How long an interval elapsed between the death of Eli and the election of Samuel we do not know ; but the trouble into which the victory of the Philistines at Aphek plunged the land would make the people soon feel the need of another ruler : and the fact of Samuel being already recognised as a prophet would point him out as the man. Nor is it quite certain whether his being judge led him to assemble the people at Mizpeh, or whether his victory led to his being elected judge. Be this as it may, on the very same field of Aphek, he so broke the power of the invading Philistines that for years they never again crossed the frontier, and moreover had to surrender the cities near the frontier which they had won from the Israelites. The warlike Amorites also, in the western mountains of Judæa, now withdrew from their connexion with the Philistines, and accepted the protectorate of Israel. But we are, perhaps, not to suppose that the Philistine yoke was absolutely thrown off ; at any rate, perfect liberty, if it was regained for a time, was lost again before long. The shameful state of subjugation in which we find the Israelites in the second year of Saul's reign (1 Sam. xiii.) must have begun under the rule of Samuel.

In his character of Nazarite it is natural to compare Samuel with the predecessor who was, like him, both Nazarite and judge, Samson. The birth of both was promised beforehand. Both were dedicated as Nazarites from their birth; not (according to the common Nazarite vow) for a limited period, but for life. Both, in their way, prevailed. But here the likeness ends. Samson was a Nazarite in the letter, but knew nothing of the Nazarite's spirit; Samuel was a Nazarite in heart and in life. Samson prevailed by superhuman strength over men's bodies; Samuel influenced their minds. The work of the one was to destroy and to slay; the work of the other to restore and to create. In Samson we see how a work, most manifestly blessed by God, may be marred by the self-will and self-indulgence of man; in Samuel we see what divine things can be wrought when a man of great gifts yields himself with self-sacrifice and devotion to work under and with the Almighty.

It was the high privilege of Samuel to effect two reunions, impossible to over-rate in importance. He reunited the tribes among themselves; he made united Israel once more at one with Jehovah. Under his leadership even Judah and Ephraim work together; at his urgent exhortation "the children of Israel did put away Baalim and Ashtaroth, and served the Lord only" (1 Sam. vii. 4). Thus what had been the weakness and curse of Israel under the earlier Judges, the political and religious dissolution was for the time at least cured. It was, possibly, to typify this new birth of the nation that Samuel "took a *sucking lamb*" as his first public sacrifice on behalf of the people. It was in contrast to the sacrilegious greed of Hophni and Phineas that he "offered it for a burnt offering *wholly* unto the Lord" (1 Sam. vii. 9). The answer was the victory of Aphek, or Ebenezer, already noticed. In the presence of this prophet, who received such immediate and visible answers to his prayers, reunited Israel knew that it once more had the minister of Jehovah living among them. The dreary interval during which God's voice had been heard so seldom had passed away, and as in the days of Moses their heavenly King in the person of His prophet was ever present to His people. At Ramah, his birthplace, which he fixed upon as his abode, he "judged Israel all the days of his life," making circuits every year to the sacred centres of Bethel, Gilgal, and Mizpeh, and thence returning to Ramah. For as yet there was no national centre; each judge fixed his own for himself. Personal and family ties were still paramount; a fixed national metropolis arose first under the monarchy. Thus he continued, "spending and being spent" for Israel, with the care both of the whole Jewish Church and of the whole Jewish nation on his shoulders. As prophet he was the centre and organ of the religious life, as judge he was the centre and organ of the political life of the people. What many popes have claimed to be, what a few of the greatest of them have earnestly striven to be, Samuel, without any self-seeking or lust of power, was.

We shall be altogether mistaken if we regard any portion of the Books of Samuel as a biography of the prophet whose name they bear. They are not that any more than the Book of Joshua is a biography of Joshua, or the Book of Judges a series of lives of Jewish leaders. None of the books of the Bible are that. The historical books both of the Old and New Testament are all alike in this, that they are histories not of individuals but of the kingdom of God. Hence, among other characteristics, the comparative neglect of chronology; for it is the exception when chronology has importance in the history of His kingdom, with whom "one day is as a thousand years, and a thousand years as one day" (2 Peter iii. 8). We are once more without a date in the sacred narrative, and we once more have a blank which we can fill only tentatively. Just as in the Gospels, "He went down with them, and came to Nazareth, and was subject unto them," and "increased in wisdom and stature, and in favour with God and man " (Luke ii. 51, 52), is all that we know of the Messiah's life during an interval of about seventeen years, so here, " Samuel judged Israel" covers an interval of perhaps nearly double that duration. We leave him a young man setting up the memorial stone of Ebenezer ; and when the narrative begins again he is old and failing in strength, and has made his sons judges to help him. During the interval the political atmosphere has become more and more heavily charged with the desire for a change of government, and a comparatively small thing precipitates it. Joel and Abiah, the two sons of Samuel, are not satisfactory as judges. They are not scandalously wicked, like Hophni and Phinehas, but they are tainted with what has ever been the plague-spot in the administration of justice in the East—bribery—and also with exorbitant usury. "They turned aside after lucre, and took bribes, and perverted judgment" (ch. viii. 3). Samuel's uprightness is wanting in his sons, just as Eli's piety in his, to the sorrow and shame of the parents. And thus the proverb against which Ezekiel protests so emphatically is reversed: "The children eat the sour grape and the fathers' teeth are set on edge." The "elders of Israel" come to Samuel and formally request him to nominate a king. Whether the judgeship as administered by him had been adequate to their needs or not, certainly it was not at all so as administered by his sons. The old evils would soon be coming back again ; the tribes would be falling away into their fatal state of division and isolation, if there were not some central power, which all could respect, to hold them together. Even as it was, the Philistines were still in the land, and had been so for years, because there was no one to take the lead in driving them out. This feeling had been in the air at least since Abimelech, the son of Gideon, made his ill-advised attempt at royalty (comp. Judg. viii. 22) ; and it had evidently been increasing. The miscarriages of justice in the hands of Samuel's sons brought matters to a crisis. The wave of national despair at the loss of the ark, and the still more powerful wave of national enthusiasm at its recovery, which had carried Samuel to the high position in which his great gifts had since then maintained him, had by this time subsided ; and popular discontent now made itself formally heard. It had been proved by the sad experience of centuries that the Theocracy under a republican form of government was too high an ideal for the Israelites ; experience of so stern a kind must not be thrown away, and the time had now come for a change to a constitution which, if less lofty in conception, would be more beneficial in fact.

" But the thing displeased Samuel." The demand shocked him, not so much because it was a revolution as because it was a revolt; a revolt against Jehovah. The Almighty sanctioned this view ; but at the same time instructed Samuel to yield to the demand. He was first to explain to the people what monarchy meant, and then, if they still wished for it, to comply.

The case reminds us of that of Balaam. In both the Almighty grants a petition with which He is displeased ; and inasmuch as He granted what was asked, the thing asked for cannot in itself have been wrong. What then displeased Him in the petition ? The answer seems to be the same in both cases—the spirit which dictated it. It was lawful for Balaam to go to Balak; but to do God's will, not his own. A rebellious hope of being able to get his own way, at least in part, lurks in Balaam's mind to the last. It was lawful for Israel to have a king. It had been promised to Abraham that *kings* should come out of him (Gen. xvii. 6) ; Jacob had foretold that the *sceptre* should not depart from Judah till Shiloh come (Gen. xlix.

10) ; and the Law itself expressly provided for the possibility of a regal form of government (Deut. xvii. 14—20). But the spirit in which it was demanded was faulty. It implied that their invisible King was unable to go out before them and fight their battles, to free them from the Philistines, and protect them against the Amorites (1 Sam. xii. 12) ; they must have a visible king. In other words, there was no faith in their request ; it was a desire not so much to know God's will as to obtain their own. The very wording of their reiterated demand seems to show this, " Nay, but we will have a king over us ; that we also *may be like all the nations ;* and that our king may judge us, and *go out before us,* and *fight our battles* " (1 Sam. viii. 19, 20). The picture which Samuel faithfully drew of Oriental despotism, as it existed all around them, had an effect the exact opposite of which he had intended. " Nay, that is the very thing we want ; the pomp to dazzle, and the strong hand to rule."

Thus Samuel " stood between the dead and the living," between the dead past, with which all his affections were buried, and the living future, in which hope had scarcely begun to shine. But God's command was enough for him, little as he might understand it. Had he been " seeking the living among the dead " ? and were the people right, after all ? Or was God " giving them a king in His anger," as He gave them flesh to eat in the wilderness ? At any rate, the course of His prophet was clear : henceforth to devote his thought and care to the moulding of this new form of government, to directing the stream of the current which he was powerless to stem.

There is something inexpressibly touching in Samuel's complete surrender of the convictions and aspirations of a lifetime. After growing gray in a devoted effort to make the system committed to him meet the needs of the people over whom he ruled, he was suddenly called upon to break with the past, and not only give up his own supremacy in the civil government, but himself inaugurate the system that was to supersede him. It was not merely as if what was nearest and dearest to him was slain before his eyes ; it was not merely as if, like Abraham, he was ordered to strike the fatal blow himself. He was called upon to do this and more ; to take a stranger to his bosom in the place of the slain, and to foster him as his own son. We shall measure the sacrifice of will better if we compare it with another ; and we shall at the same time measure the difference in power between the philosophy of a pious heathen and the faith of a pious Hebrew. When the un-welcome truth was forced upon Cato that the republic to which he had devoted his life was dead, his religion allowed him, and his philosophy counselled him, to die with the political system for which he had striven in vain. And so the last upholder of the old Roman republic committed suicide at Utica. It never occurred to him that Heaven and his country still claimed services which it was no longer possible to render to a particular system; or that Heaven had better things in store for his country under a new *régime.* To transfer his energies to the side of Cæsar in order to make the new *régime* as beneficial as possible would to Cato have been inconceivable. And this is precisely the kind of sacrifice, intensified by being a sacrifice of religious as well as of political conviction, that Samuel without a murmur made. It would take time to work out, but it should be done. There is a bursting, as of heart-strings, a wrench, as of one who is parting from what is dearer than life, in the simple utterance with which the discussion ends : " And Samuel said unto the men of Israel, Go ye every man unto his city " (ch. viii. 22). There was no power to say more.

The Monarchy. The First King. Saul.

It was by a Divine revelation that Saul, the son of Kish, a Benjamite, was pointed out to Samuel as the future captain over Israel, to save the people out of the hand of the Philistines ; but we may reverently notice the wisdom of the choice. The danger being from the Philistines and the Ammonites, the king must be from one of the southern tribes. A king from the northern groups would, perhaps, have been negligent of pressure and danger in the south, or at least would have known less well how to deal with it. Of the southern tribes Simeon or Benjamin would be preferable to Judah or Ephraim ; for had the first king been taken from either of the two great rival tribes, only too probably the other tribe would have yielded a very imperfect allegiance. As between Simeon and Benjamin, there was not much to recommend the first and a great deal in favour of the second. Of the southern tribes Benjamin was the most central. It contained Bethel, perhaps of all the sanctuaries of Palestine the most ancient; Mizpeh, where the great assemblies of all Israel took place (Judg. x. 17; xi. 11; xx. 1; 1 Sam. vii. 5); and Gibeon, "the great high place." It had had the honour of sheltering the ark at Kirjath-jearim, perhaps also of being the home of Samuel; but the situation of Ramah is uncertain. It was warlike and powerful, quite out of proportion to its members or the size of its territory. The dying patriarch foretold that "Benjamin should ravin as a wolf;" and the way in which it defended itself against the rest of Israel, in vindication of the horrible deed of the men of Gibeah, is one of the most extraordinary things in the military history of the Jews. Among this tribe of warriors Kish, Saul's father, was a powerful chief; and Saul himself was in stature almost gigantic, with strength and activity equal to his frame (2 Sam. 1. 23). All these details are very significant, and help us to understand the meaning of God's dealing with His people in yielding to their importunity, and granting a king. The gift was at once a judgment and a blessing. It punished the people for the wrong spirit in which they had demanded a king, and at the same time disciplined them for the future, so that when a worthy king was found, a people worthy of him was ready. In some sense Saul was the chosen of God, in the fullest sense he was not. God pointed him out to Samuel as the future king ; not, however, as being His own choice (1 Sam. xv. 11, 35), but as being such as the people would desire. David was the "man after God's own heart;" Saul was rather the man after Israel's own heart. The Almighty was giving them a king such as they had longed for, the goodliest man in all the land; perhaps to show them that, although when such men have His blessing they succeed, yet without it they are powerless as the smallest child, whether against His friends or His enemies. Saul might be "swifter than an eagle, and stronger than a lion;" but when the Lord was no longer with him, "the race was not to the swift, nor the battle to the strong."

"And it was so, that when he had turned his shoulder (that great shoulder by which he was afterwards so conspicuous) to go from Samuel, God gave him another heart" (ch. x. 9). In other words, like his far greater namesake in the New Testament, Saul was an instance of what we are accustomed to call "sudden conversion." From this, as well as from the expression of astonishment, which has since become a proverb, "Saul also among the prophets !" we gather that in his earlier life he had been by no means a very religious man. In this, as in so much else, Saul was a great contrast to the ruler whom he superseded. From his childhood upwards Samuel had "ministered unto the Lord," and "the Lord had been with him" (ch. iii. 1, 19). There has been no sudden change, but a steady growth in holiness. Hence the calm steadfastness, the " sweet reasonableness" of all his conduct, even under the gravest provocation. He can be tender, and he can be severe, but he is never fanatical. With Saul it is otherwise. A novice in religion, his spiritual experiences are a series of surprises to him and throw him off his balance. There is excitement and fanaticism in his religion almost from the first; and as he takes little pains to deepen and make sure the change of heart which had been granted to him, what is left of religion in him becomes for the most part superstition mixed with a strong kind of frenzy, which may have been something akin to religious mania. We see the want of judgment and of reasonableness in his " forcing himself" to offer sacrifice, in his ill-advised adjuration, in his sparing the best of the Amalekite spoil for sacrifice, in his fierce extermination of wizards, and in his himself inquiring of the Lord through a witch. His career is a standing warning to those who presume upon great spiritual blessings which they take no pains to appropriate and secure; from such an one "shall be taken away even that which he hath." So it was with Saul. The modest, retiring conduct which charms us so much at the outset is quite wanting in his later life; instead of it we have his ostentatious triumph over the Amalekites (Agag was spared to grace the procession) and his envy of David's praises. The clemency which he shows at the outset to the men of Belial, who scoffed at his election, is forgotten in his slaughter of the Gibeonites (2 Sam. xxi. 1), and the savage massacre of the priests with all their families (1 Sam. xxii. 17—19). In this he reminds us of our own King Henry IV. The sullen sternness at the close of life is so unlike the bright generosity at the beginning of it. The explanation in both cases is perhaps the same: disease, both of body and mind, coupled with the reproaches of an ill-informed conscience. But, *nemo repente turpissimus:* almost to the last Saul has his better moments, and in these nothing is more conspicuous than his tenderness for David, whom at other times he had come to regard with frantic hatred. In the whole of the Old Testament there is no biography more tragic: the nearest to it, perhaps, is that of Samson. In both we see the utter wreck of great powers through the indulgence of an unbridled will.

It is a relief to turn from the lurid lights and deepening gloom of Saul's last years to the last years of the man with whom we have contrasted him. In spite of the bitter trial which the establishment of regal power was to him, and the bitter disappointment which the first king's recklessness caused him, Samuel remains calm and steadfast to the last; steadfast alike in his loyalty to God, to the heedless king, and to suffering Israel. For a time he shared the supreme power with Saul (ch. xi. 7). After the confirmation of the regal power, in the enthusiasm caused by Saul's victory over the Ammonites (ch. xi. 14), he made his great testimony before the people (ch. xii.), and then seems to have retired somewhat from the conduct of affairs, retaining, but perhaps without being often called upon to exercise, his office as judge (ch. vii. 15), and appearing chiefly in his character as prophet. It is in his character as prophet and as the anointer of David that his importance in the history of the kingdom of God chiefly consists. The first point might have been noticed earlier in the section specially devoted to Samuel; but the second must have remained over until now in order to avoid confusion. To consider the two points together adds to the significance and impressiveness of each; and with them we may bring this section to a close.

As prophet, Samuel has mainly two aspects: (1) he is the founder of the schools of the prophets; (2) he is the inspired exponent of the will of God.

(1) Although there had been prophets, and at least one great one before Samuel —Moses, Miriam, Balaam, Deborah, and others (Num. xi. 25; Judg. vi. 8)—yet he was the *first of the regular succession of prophets*, which extends throughout the whole period of monarchy. St. Peter seems to express this fact in his address to the people in Solomon's Porch, "All the prophets from Samuel and those that follow after" (Acts. iii. 24). Henceforth we begin to read of those societies called the "company of the prophets," and the "sons of the prophets" (1 Sam. x. 5, 10, &c.), over which Samuel presided (ch. xix. 20). These schools, in which sacred dance and music, both vocal and instrumental, were studied, together with the law and prophetic utterances, have been compared with mediæval universities. Their appearance precisely at this time, and their having their first seat in Ramah, Samuel's own dwelling-place, leaves little doubt that he was the founder of them. No one more fitted to found them could have arisen, for he had been a prophet from childhood; and this, so far as we know, was true of no other prophet until the time of Isaiah.

(2) The law, in spite of the number of its enactments, could not possibly cover all cases in the infinite complexity and variety of life. Moreover, the law was but imperfectly known, and when known it was often neglected. Hence there was abundant of room, side by side with the law, for an authoritative statement of the Divine will; and indeed, in the numerous crises through which the Chosen People had to pass, there was a crying need from time to time for such a statement. To make it, to interpret God's dealings to man, to declare His counsels, to exhort and warn in His name, were the functions of the prophet. The law might instruct them about sacrifices, and purifications, and the elements of justice and charity; but it required the trumpet-voice of the prophet to remind king and people alike that an obedient spirit is better than sacrifice (1 Sam. xv. 22), and that what the Lord requires is not a self-satisfied conformity with written enactments, "but to *do* justly, and to *love* mercy, and to walk *humbly* with thy God" (Micah vi. 8). The eternal principles of right and wrong, the *unwritten* law of God, these are the subjects of the prophet's utterance from Samuel to Malachi.

The Christian poet Keble ('Christian Year,' Second Sunday after Easter) longs for "a sculptor's hand" to set forth in stone the wild figure of Balaam uttering his compulsory blessing over Israel. A subject that might make one yearn for a painter's skill is that of the aged Samuel uttering his sorrowful denunciation of the king that he had himself anointed. The long, flowing locks, across which no razor had passed, now snow-white with age, the spare, austere figure, the judge's bearing, the prophet's eye, the long, flowing mantle, by which Saul tried to stay him, and by which he recognised his apparition on the eve of his own death; all these form a picture, the majesty of which, if we cannot see it for ourselves, we gather from the exclamation of the woman of Endor, "I see a *god* ascending out of the earth" (1 Sam. xxviii. 13). To her the form seems superhuman and Divine.

It remains to notice Samuel as the anointer of his still greater successor, David. This is his importance in the long prelude to the kingdom of the Messiah; he is the "spiritual father" of the greatest of the Messiah's progenitors. He not only inaugurated the monarchy which typified Christ's kingdom, but he lived to supersede the first unworthy king and to elect the man after God's own heart, the lion of the tribe of Judah, the sweet Psalmist of Israel. Both the people's king and the Lord's king receive their consecration from his hand; and, therefore, whether we trace the kingdom of Israel to the beginning of the monarchy, or the royal line of Christ to the beginning of its royalty, we come to Samuel as the vicegerent of Jehovah in instituting it.   But this shows that, great as Samuel is in himself (and he is one of the grandest figures in the Old Testament), yet in his chief aspect his greatness is relative.   He is great chiefly because he prepares the way for David, just as the Baptist is great chiefly because he prepares the way for Christ.   Thus we see that the arrangement and division of the Books of Samuel are fully justified.   Eli and Samuel are too closely connected to be severed, and as Samuel's place in the history is that of the inaugurator of the kingdom and the anointer of David as king, it follows that the notices of Eli and Samuel must come as a prelude to the history of the Kings rather than as a conclusion to the history of the Judges.   This fact will also explain the omission of nearly the whole of Saul's reign except the beginning and end of it.   It is immaterial to the history of the kingdom of God.

"And Samuel died ; and all the Israelites were gathered together, and lamented him, and buried him in his house at Ramah " (1 Sam. xxv. 1).   Such is the simple but pregnant account of the end of the grandest figure in Jewish history from the conquest to the captivity.   "*All* the Israelites were gathered together," a fact to which the narrator a second time directs our attention.   "Now Samuel was dead, and *all* Israel had lamented him, and buried him in Ramah, even in his own city " (ch. xxviii. 3).   With one voice they had responded to his challenge respecting his integrity " (ch. xii. 5) ; with one voice they had all entreated him to pray for them, when he brought home to them their sins in demanding a king (ch. xii. 19) ; and now with one voice they lamented him, and sent representatives from all parts of the land to pay the last tribute of respect to him.   Ramah, his birthplace and his dwelling-place, became his tomb; but inasmuch as the site of Ramah remains unknown, it may be said of him, as was said of Moses, " No man knoweth of his sepulchre unto this day."

The First King of the Line of Judah.   David.

We once more have to admire the infinite variety of Scripture.   It has been noticed as one of the various ways in which " the Spirit bloweth *where it listeth*," that we have this wonderful variety in the Bible.   Had the Bible (which, be it remembered, is an inspired *library* rather than an inspired *book*) been put together by men, no matter how learned and holy, this variety would have been wanting. We should have had a more or less useful and edifying, but probably more rather than less insipid, volume, suited at best to the needs of the generation in which its compilers lived, and probably of only a limited portion of that.   Instead of this, we have, both in form and in matter, a many-sidedness and variety of which the world has never wearied, and in which every person can find something to delight his taste, and every soul something to satisfy its needs.   Side by side with the stormy and blood-stained pictures of the Book of Judges we have had the bright oasis of the Book of Ruth ; the vile conduct of the sons of Eli is narrated in the same chapter with the sweet innocence of the child Samuel ; and here, as the reign of Saul darkens through his withdrawing more and more from God, and God at last withdrawing His Spirit from him, we have bright lights constantly breaking in from the life of the young son of Jesse.   His guileless youth, the gloomy king's love for him, never quite quenched even in Saul's darkest days (1 Sam. xxvi. 25) the touching friendship with his persecutor's son, the exquisite lament over Saul and Jonathan, all these things are a relief and a refreshment in the midst of such scenes as Saul's bloodthirsty hunt after David (madness, as often, turning love into hate), the massacre of the priests, the night visit to Endor, the suicide on Mount Gilboa.

In treating of David in a summary of the present kind, the difficulty is to keep within bounds, so rich are our materials. The age of David seems to have been recognised almost at once by the Jews themselves as the grandest epoch that the nation has as yet known ; as we can now see that it has never since been surpassed. Hence the record of it has been preserved with a fulness of detail found nowhere else in the historical books of the Bible. The narrators pour forth their knowledge with a buoyant exuberance that is never weary and has no fear of wearying others. Everything is of interest that belongs to that glorious time ; every one is of import- ance whose fortunes are entwined with the career of that glorious king. Hence we have a full account, not merely (as in the case of Saul) of the opening and close of his reign, but of the whole of it. Hence also we have (what is wholly wanting in the history of Saul) a very vivid account of a great deal of David's life previous to his ascending the throne. And it is probably owing to the fact that the earlier portion of David's life is so much bound up with the latter days of Saul, that we know as much as we do about those gloomy days. They derive their importance not from the reigning, but from the future king. And it is not only that our materials respect- ing this period as a whole are specially full ; our means of knowing the central figure of it are in the Old Testament unique. As in the case of St. Paul, and to a much more limited extent of St. Peter and St. John, " we have the advantage of comparing a detailed narrative of his life with undoubted works of his own com- position ; and the combined result is a knowledge of his personal character, such as we probably possess of no historical personage before the Christian era, with the exception of Cicero, and perhaps of Cæsar " (Stanley). Plato and Aristotle, like St. John, we know more from their own writings than from what others have written about them ; and, if the choice had to be made in the case of David, it is the Psalms that we should keep while we let the history go. In them we have the outpourings of his spirit and the secret workings of his soul, the key not only to that age and that reign, but to the human heart throughout all ages. But God's providence has preserved both for us ; and we have the rare privilege of comparing the picture unconsciously drawn by himself in his songs with that which the native historians give us of him. Thus we are able to penetrate to the springs of the actions which they record, and also to judge how the events in which he shared told on that noble and tender spirit.

As in the case of Saul, the anointing of the future king is preceded by a sacri- ficial feast. And here we once more have an opportunity of observing how, in spite of their frequent aberrations into idolatry, and their constant neglect or ignorance of God and His law, the Israelites ever remained *a religious people at heart.* In their hour of darkest need they ever " cried unto the Lord," and in their victories they thanked Him. Trouble and blessing alike are recognised as coming from His hand. A summons to a great sacrifice is never made in vain ; and although the sanctuary at Shiloh is in ruins, and the ark has no proper home, yet the worship of God continues at local centres and in the family circle. It is in the complete family circle at Bethlehem, gathered together for an act of solemn worship, rendered specially solemn by the unexpected presence of the prophet, that we are first introduced to the future king. His name (David=beloved) may perhaps indicate that, like Joseph, he was his father's darling. Certainly, like Joseph, he seems to have been estranged from his brethren (1 Sam. xvii. 28) : and in the solitary life which he lived, tending the flocks apart from them, much of the foundation of his future life was laid. The impress which this period left upon his mind is clearly traceable in the Psalms (viii., xix., xxiii., xxix., lxxviii. 70, 72, &c.); and the devotion with which he guarded his sheep at the risk of his own life (1 Sam. xvii. 34, 35) was an earnest of the self-sacrificing spirit in which he would rule over Israel.

It would seem as if David himself remained in ignorance of the meaning of his anointing by Samuel. No explanation is recorded, and no signs are given, as there were to Saul, to confirm the anointing. When the young Psalmist was summoned to exercise his skill in music on the vexed spirit of the king, he probably never dreamed that he was to succeed him; and when he went out to risk his life against the giant of Gath, he knew not that he was risking his own kingdom along with it. Still less did Saul know that the stripling before him was his successor; at Samuel's entreaty that had carefully been avoided (ch. xvi. 2). And so much had his mental depression and temporary derangement affected Saul's faculties, that on the battle-field of Ephesdammim he did not recognise the skilful young harper in the slayer of Goliath.

"David lost nothing by his encounter with the giant, not even his temper" (Jacox). Let those who think this latter point small praise consider what a trial it is to a high-spirited young man, conscious of strength and activity, to be twitted with his youthfulness as a boy unworthy of notice. He lost nothing, but he gained much; he gained his entrance into an entirely new sphere of life, which was to be his second school of preparation for the throne. The victory over the giant was thus a crisis in his life; it "took him away from the sheepfolds" and introduced him to court life.

His character suffered nothing in consequence; on the contrary, it developed rapidly. His promotion was rapid, but it did not turn his head. He became the king's armour-bearer, the bosom friend of the king's son, the accepted lover of the king's daughter. In the midst of this success, jealousy of his praises, combining with Saul's mental derangement, turned the favour of the king into hatred. Henceforth David's position became one of the utmost delicacy. It was scarcely possible to be loyal at once to Saul, to Michal, and to Jonathan. But David, who as a lad had proved himself to be "prudent in matters" (ch. xvi. 18), in this difficult position also "behaved himself wisely in all his ways" (ch. xviii. 14). He won Michal's hand, he retained the love of Jonathan, and he escaped the murderous frenzy of Saul.

He had yet another school to go through before his education for the leadership of God's people was complete—the school of adversity. The faithful shepherd had become the prudent courtier: he must now become the vigilant, active, enduring outlaw. This phase of life helps still further to ripen his character, specially in two directions—chivalrous generosity and reliance upon God. His harp accompanies him here also, and no doubt shared many a sad hour in the caves of Engedi, or on the slopes of Mahanaim. There is the true spirit of chivalry in his sparing Saul's life twice when others would have taken it, in his readiness for reconciliation, in his burning protestation of his own innocence. "Jehovah, my God, if I have done this; if there be iniquity in my hands; if I have rewarded evil unto him that was at peace with me; yea, rather, I have delivered him that without cause is my enemy. Let the enemy persecute my soul, and take it; yea, let him tread down my life upon the earth, and make my glory abide in the dust" (Psa.

vii. 3—5). The same psalm opens with a declaration of trust in God: "Jehovah, my God, in Thee have I found my refuge." The hunted outcast, seeking shelter among the crags and rocks, and sometimes only escaping through his nimbleness and fleetness of foot, sings how Jehovah had "made his feet like hinds' feet, and set him on His high places" (Pss. xviii. 33). Jehovah is his "rock," his mountain fastness, where he is safe (Psa. xviii. 1, 2, 30, 31, 46; lxii. 2, 6, 7); "His right hand holds him up;" "He makes room for his steps under him, that his ankles do not slip." Such passages might be multiplied largely. And here we may remark two things with regard to the Psalms, which tell of his sufferings and persecutions, whether at this period or later on in his life. (1) They contain imprecations on his enemies painful to read, so wanting is the spirit of forgiveness, the spirit that prays for enemies. This is the particular in which the Psalms fall so immeasurably short of the Gospel. Otherwise in reading them, one sometimes feels inclined to ask, What has Christianity to give that is higher and nobler than this? (2) On the other hand, his enemies are never named: the denunciations are general, not special. There is no mention of Saul, or Doeg, or Ahitophel, or Shimei. And in this also, no doubt, he was ruled by the Spirit. Songs that were to be the heritage of religious souls throughout all ages could not be marred by personal animosities. And words which were launched against the head of David's persecutors, Christians may utter as against the opponents of Christ.

The moment when the crown passes into the hands of the man who had gone through this long and diversified training for it, is one of the strangest complication. David, with a formidable force of 600 men, has crossed the border, and taken service under the Philistine king, Achish. Ziklag is granted him for an abode, and he remains there sixteen months. And it is significant of the national feeling respecting him, that a contingent from Saul's own tribe comes over to him here (1 Chron. xii. 1—7). But the lords of the Philistines did not share Achish's trust in David, and would not let him march with them against Israel. Thus David was spared the misery of having to choose between faithlessness to Achish or treason against Saul. He returned to find that Ziklag had been plundered by the Amalekites, and while he was taking vengeance on them, and recovering captives and spoil, the fatal battle of Gilboa was fought, and the first news that greeted him after his return to Ziklag was that Israel had been defeated by the Philistines, and that Saul and Jonathan were slain. The noble ode which celebrates their memory, royal in its generosity, in its tenderness, and in the beauty of its language, is in every way worthy of its subject and its composer. Perhaps there is no finer elegy in any language. Its echoes had scarcely died away, when its author was called upon to fill the vacant throne.

It augurs well for the new king's rule that he is no way eager to seize the crown. The kingdom sought him, not he the kingdom. "For at that time day by day there came to David to help him, until it was a great host, like the host of God" (1 Chron. xii. 22). But not until "the Lord said unto him, Go up" (2 Sam. ii. 1), did David cross over into Judah, and by His special direction fix his seat at Hebron, the ancient sacred city of the tribe, the tomb of the patriarchs, and the lot of Caleb. Here he was anointed king, and reigned over Judah for seven and a half years. It shows how entirely he submitted himself to the Divine guidance, that he made no attempt to grasp the rest of the kingdom, and did not oppose the setting up of Ishbosheth as Saul's successor, but waited for God to give him the kingdom in His own way. In this respect David is a striking contrast to Jeroboam and Jehu.

The victory of the Philistines had given them the central part of western Palestine, and they very possibly conquered the north also: but in any case the north was cut off from David's kingdom in the south. In eastern Palestine, Abner, Saul's cousin and commander-in-chief, seems to have established himself with Ishbosheth, the only surviving son of Saul. Gradually they won back territory from the Philistines; then Ishbosheth was proclaimed king, and by the end of five years was recognised as king by all but Judah. He, like David, chose an ancient and sacred city as his seat of government—Mahanaim, on the borders of Gad and Manasseh. The war between the rival kings was none of David's seeking. Abner provoked it by trying to gain possession of "Gibeah of Saul" in Benjamin, as a capital for his puppet, Ishbosheth, no doubt with a view to ousting David, and ruling over all Israel in Ishbosheth's name. This bold stroke proved the ruin of himself and the house of Saul: and after his and Ishbosheth's death (murders of which David was wholly guiltless, and which he publicly condemned) there was no other claimant to the throne. David was rewarded for his trust in God's promises, and for his chivalrous conduct towards the house of Saul, and became undisputed king of all Israel.

During this brief period of limited rule over Judah, amid much that is promising, we notice the beginning of two evils which are among the curses of Oriental monarchies. (1) In order to strengthen himself, he seeks or accepts connexions by marriage with various powerful families. To Ahinoam and Abigail he adds four new wives, and as a hold upon Abner, when he was willing to desert Ishbosheth, he demanded back Michal, whom Saul had taken from him. Thus a harêm, with all its baneful influences, was begun. (2) Being not yet firmly established, he was obliged to humour his powerful relatives. Men whom he could not do without, and whom he could only imperfectly control, acted without consulting him, or in defiance of his wishes. His passionate lament over the murder of Abner, which he could neither prevent nor punish, is the beginning of an enforced nepotism, which throws a shade over the whole of David's reign.

All Israel now recognised the claims of the man, who, even in Saul's lifetime, had ever led them to victory, and to whom Jehovah had said, "Thou shalt feed My people Israel:" and he was anointed king in Hebron. He belonged to them all, not to Judah alone. "*All* the tribes of Israel came to David and spake, saying, Behold, we are thy bone and thy flesh" (2 Sam. v. 1). There had been no such unanimity since the burial of Samuel, and it anticipates the feeling when in after years David was recalled to the throne: "We have ten parts in the king, and we have also more right in David than ye" (ch. xix. 43). Seldom, perhaps, has a king been welcomed with greater enthusiasm than David. For long it had been true of him, that "whatever the King did, pleased *all* the people" (ch. iii. 36), and it remained true of him through nearly the whole of his reign. He was "as an angel of God" (ch. xiv. 17, 20; xix. 27) in their eyes; he bowed their hearts "as the heart of one man" (ch. xix. 14); he was "the light of Israel" (ch. xxi. 17). And the enthusiasm was well founded. Like the greatest of our own kings, Edward I., David came to the throne thoroughly understanding and thoroughly disciplined for the task that lay before him. In both cases there was a kingdom needing an adequate organization for preserving internal unity and effective means of national defence. Both rulers had learned much from the errors of the previous reign; and both knew that only with the sympathy and help of the people whom they ruled could the great needs of the kingdom be supplied. Both had enlarged their political and military experience by service abroad; and David probably learned much from the excellent military system of the Philistines. One more point of resemblance, and it is the highest of all. Both kings were qualified for doing far more than restoring unity and energy to a disorganized and disheartened people: they were fit and ready to start then on a new career of order, and hope, and progress.

Thus, without any advantage of birth, without any dexterous scheming or violent revolution, in ripeness of mind and body, at the moment when he was most needed, the greatest man of the age reached the highest position in it, the headship over the whole of God's Chosen People. The shepherd-lad, musician, courtier, warrior, poet, outlaw, and tribal king, had reached a pinnacle to which no one had risen before, the throne of united Israel. He had experienced the trials of solitary watching in the wilderness, of jealousies and plots at court, of being hunted like a wild beast in the mountains, of being an exile in the land of Israel's deadliest enemies. There remained the severest trial of all, the possession of supreme power. It remained to be seen whether one who had met with such transcendent success would now lose his reliance on Jehovah, and begin to trust in himself.

His first exploit is strong proof both of his sagacity and of his vigour. As king of all Israel he could not remain at Hebron, it was not nearly central enough. On the other hand, it would have affronted his own tribe to seek a capital entirely away from Judah. Therefore some strong place on the northern frontier of Judah was wanted. Jebus fulfilled all these conditions, and the fact that the Canaanites had been able to maintain themselves there for centuries, was evidence of its value as a stronghold; indeed, they scoffed at the notion of its being taken. Joab won the post of commander-in-chief by being the first to scale the rocky side of the fortress, a fact of no small influence on David's reign; and then the citadel of Zion, now first named in history, was soon taken.

Here David established his seat of government, and centuries of history have ratified the wisdom of his choice. The creation of the national capital is therefore contemporaneous with the establishment of the monarchy in its complete form, and both are the work of David. That it should be called "the city of David" was doubly justified by his having captured it, and by the use he made of it. It commands the country as no other place does; for it stands on the broadest ridge of the network of hills which runs through Palestine, from Carmel to the wilderness of Paran, forming the watershed between the Great Sea and the Jordan. Strategically its position is very strong. Most of the approaches to it are too intricate and precipitous for large armies; and the one that is least so, the one that has almost invariably been used by hostile armies, is very circuitous—from Jaffa and Lydda, over the pass of the Beth-horons to Gibeon, and thence over the hills to the north side of Jerusalem. History shows that the armies of Egypt and Assyria often marched by along the plain, and sometimes fought there, without in any way interfering with Jerusalem.

The moral effect of the capture was immense. All the surrounding nations waited in suspense to see what the conqueror would attempt next. The effect was felt as far as Tyre, for Hiram sends workmen and cedar-wood to build a palace for David in his new capital. The palace was built; and we once more see the weakness of frail humanity in David's great work, in his violating the law (Deut. xvii. 17), by multiplying wives to himself; though he never seems to have done as Solomon did to his own ruin, take wives from heathen nations. The Philistines also were moved by the capture of Zion, and did not wait to be attacked, but invaded the land and were twice utterly routed. The friendship of Hiram and the defeat of the Philistines secured peace for Israel along the whole of the sea-coast.

Thus far David had been urged on by political necessity: it was impossible to undertake higher work till a seat of government was established and a prospect of peace secured. But his heart had been elsewhere throughout. For fifty years or more the ark of God had been homeless. It was still in its temporary resting-place at Kirjath-jearim; it must be brought to Zion and a new house built for it. First the Philistines' inroad and then the death of Uzzah—a terrible warning to those who irreverently seek God "not after the due order" (1 Chron. xv. 13)—caused delay: but at last the half of David's wish was accomplished, and the ark was brought up to Jerusalem; the other half, of building a house for it, he was commanded to leave for his son. It is one more proof of the irreligiousness of the court of Saul that his daughter Michal considered the prominent part which David took on this joyous occasion nothing but a shameful lowering of the royal dignity. Her father had known how to keep priests in order, and now her husband was making himself as one of them: and " she despised him in her heart."

Various psalms bear strong evidence of having been composed for this great festival. Chief of these are Psalms cxxxii., lxviii., and xxiv.; to which xv., ci., and perhaps xxix. and xxx., may be added.

The seat of empire and the seat of worship being thus secured and united, David proceeds to consolidate his kingdom both within and without. The details of his military and civil administration, and of his religious institutions and successful wars, are told us at great length. His victories, celebrated in Psalms lx. and cx., carried the frontier of Israel to its furthest limits (limits maintained for little over half a century), and then the brightest portion of his reign is over. His great sin, the adultery with Bathsheba and murder of Uriah, follows and clouds the rest of his life. Immediately before it we have a fair spot to rest on for a moment, his tender kindness to Mephibosheth, the crippled son, and apparently the only child of Jonathan. Now that the most pressing work of his reign is completed, David remembers his compact with Jonathan, that "Jehovah should be between them and their seed for ever," and that " he would not cut off his kindness from Jonathan's house for ever " (1 Sam. xx. 42, 15). He makes inquiries for the descendants of Saul, hears of Mephibosheth from the crafty Ziba, and generously provides for the depressed and timid prince, who, but for his grandfather's sins, might have been king of Israel. It is the last unclouded spot in David's life.

" Be sure your sin shall find you out " (Num. xxxii. 23). The rest of the life of David is one long commentary on the solemn text. In tragic horror and pathos, in psychological interest, in spiritual instruction, the history of David's sin and repentance and punishment has scarcely an equal. Lust and murder, the common sins of Oriental despotism, may be traced in part at least as the natural outcome of what has already been pointed out as the plague-spot in David's royal state. No consideration of prudence, or honour, or gratitude, no fear of God hold's him back. Bathsheba was the granddaughter of Ahitophel his counsellor; Uriah was one of his " thirty mighty men," and was at that very moment risking his life for David. It seems to show how prosperity and luxury had weakened David's character that he remained indolently at Jerusalem while all Israel was in arms against Ammon and Syria. The sending of the ark to Rabbah seems also to indicate a change for the worse. The king's attempt to cover his crime shows the nobility of Uriah's character, and as a reward for it he is made to carry his own death-warrant back to the war. The atrocity of David's plot is scarcely excused by the fact that a similar one had been laid against himself by Saul; and the empty commonplace with which David answers the message that there has been heavy loss of life, including that of Uriah (2 Sam. xi. 25), is evidence of the slumber in which his conscience is lulled. But there was soon to be a full awakening.

It is one more evidence how morally sound the Chosen People were at heart, that the sin even of one so exalted, of one so dear to them, was not in any way palliated wherever it became known; and it is proof of how truly, in spite of it all, he was "a man after God's own heart," that *he* made no attempt to excuse it, but at once admitted it in its true colours. The noble courage of Nathan in rebuking his sovereign is equalled by the nobility of David's complete confession and submission. "*O felix culpa!*" one is almost tempted to exclaim, when one reads the history of David's penitence, and still more when one appropriates the passionate outpouring of remorseful struggle, of sense of guilt, of sorrow for sin, of yearning for purity, of submission to God, of joy for the peace of reconciliation, in which he has given a voice to the penitence of the whole world from that day to this (Psalms xxxii. and li.).

Sin has three consequences in this world—weakening of the sinner's own character; the force of bad example to others; misery entailed on the sinner and those connected with him. Every one of these can be distinctly traced in the case of David's sin. For evidence of the first there is the cruelty to the conquered Ammonites (2 Sam. xii. 31), the leaving Amnon unpunished, and the other great sin of numbering the people; for the second there is the outrage on Tamar, the murder of Amnon, the revolt of Absalom, with the treatment of David's concubines; for the third there is the death of Bathsheba's first child, the efficient aid given by her grandfather to Absalom, the immense power over David which complicity with the murder of Uriah gave to the headstrong and impetuous Joab. No one can consider these facts in themselves and in their pregnant consequences, and then think, because of Nathan's declaration, "The Lord also hath put away thy sin; thou shalt not die," that God spared sin in the man after His own heart. There is no royal road to forgiveness. And if any one thinks that David's sins are any excuse for his own, let him first try to measure the difference between the Law and the Gospel, and then measure his own by David's repentance.

It is among the many curses of polygamy that the children of the different wives grow up from the first in an atmosphere of sensual indulgence; secondly, that there is sure to be rivalry between them, and intriguing among their mothers, with a view to their father's favour and the succession to his property. All this is abundantly illustrated in the history of David's children, especially of Amnon, Absalom, and Adonijah.

Absalom, the Hebrew Alcibiades, beautiful and bad, fascinating in manner and hollow of heart, is the instrument by which the curse pronounced by Nathan was fulfilled, "Behold, I will raise up evil against thee out of thine own house" (ch. xii. 11). The warnings taught by the troubles of Eli and Samuel seem to have been unheeded; for his children also grow up unchastened and unrestrained. It is significant of the corrupt atmosphere of the harêm that Tamar thinks that David will consent to an incestuous marriage between her and her half-brother (ch. xiii. 13). The murder of Amnon, similar to that of Shechem by Simeon and Levi, probably left Absalom eldest son. In the irksome idleness of his enforced exile he conceived bold schemes of self-advancement, and after four years of skilful preparation, flung himself into civil war with a light heart. His complete success, especially in Judah, points to some falling off in David's popularity, the result, perhaps, of his conduct in the Ammonite war, especially in the matter of Uriah. But both Absalom's success and Absalom's overthrow were alike full of misery for David; probably the heaviest blows that had ever fallen on him in a long life of adventure and trial. Psalm iv. seems to have been written for the evening, and Psalm iii. for the morning after David's flight from Absalom; Psalm xlii. may possibly refer to the exile beyond Jordan; Psalms lv. and cix. are believed to point to the treachery of Ahitophel. David's return was marred by an ominous quarrel between Judah and the rest of the tribes. The rebellion lingered on in the north, but was quelled by the vigour of Joab. Once more the kingdom and its troubled king had peace.

We pass to the last period of David's life. It has only one strongly marked incident, and that a sad one, the numbering of the people—at the suggestion of Satan, as we are expressly told (1 Chron. xxi. 1). The idea would seem to have arisen from a proud desire to revel in the knowledge of the forces which were at his command, the result of his own new military system. If so, it would be similar to that which brought a judgment on Nebuchadnezzar. "Is not this great Babylon, that I have built for the house of the kingdom by the might of my power, and for the honour of my majesty?" (Dan. iv. 30.) The thing was so hateful even to the not too scrupulous Joab, that he left out the tribes of Benjamin and Levi, and would not complete the census. This time David was permitted to choose his own punishment; three years of famine, three months of flight before his enemies, or three days of pestilence. He had already experienced three years' famine in punishment for the "bloody house" of Saul; and three months' flight before Absalom, in punishment for his own sin with Bathsheba. He chose three days of pestilence. And thus, as if to teach us the vanity of all that is mortal because of the taint of sin, this threefold τρικυμία κακῶν, these three triplets of woe form the landmarks in the reign of the greatest king that ever ruled over Israel. The three years' famine had taught that God is "a jealous God, visiting the sins of the fathers upon the children." The three years' flight had shown that God visits the sins of the fathers on the fathers through the children. The three days' pestilence would prove that the sins of a prince may be the scourge of a whole people, that the Lord gives and the Lord takes away, and that He who could make Israel as the stars of heaven or the sand of the sea for multitude could also unmake the nation with a word.

The rebellion of Adonijah, the eldest surviving son of David, who, with the aid of Joab and Abiathar, tried to secure the throne for himself, troubled the last days of the reign. But the aged king showed that his infirmities had not robbed him of the power to rule. Solomon was solemnly proclaimed king, and the chief conspirators took sanctuary.

The end of this life of almost ceaseless change and eventfulness was one of peace. David gave his last charge to his successor, and then "died in a good old age, full of days, riches, and honour." It is characteristic of the age rather than of the man that his last recorded words are words of vengeance. We see in this, as already noticed respecting the Psalms, how very far short of the Gospel was the very best that the Law could produce. In sparing Shimei's life during his own lifetime, David was above the moral level of his age; but with regard to Shimei, as with regard to Joab, he leaves to his son Solomon a legacy of vengeance, as though he repented of his own lofty clemency. It almost shocks us to find the sweet Psalmist of Israel ending his life, not with a *Nunc dimittis*, but with the charge, " His hoar head bring Thou to the grave with blood."

In the varied elements of his life and character there is no one in the whole of the Bible like David. A life teeming with vicissitudes, with romance, with pathos, and those startling changes of fortune which make history so much stranger than fiction. What drama is equal to it for tragic and romantic interest alone, to say nothing of instruction? His character is as varied as his life. It reminds to no small extent of him whose writings in the New Testament hold somewhat the same place as the Psalms in the Old, the Apostle St. John. In both there is all the strength of man with all the tenderness of woman. In both there is the same intensity—intensity of action, intensity of thought and word, intensity of love and hate. They could hate with the same fervour that they loved. They abhorred that which was evil in cleaving to that which was good ; the one implied the other. But, as we might anticipate from the difference of the dispensations under which they lived, the indignation which St. John feels for the wrong done to his Lord, David often feels for the wrong done to himself. He has strong words, and strong deeds sometimes, for those who treat him ill. With the exception of his dastardly conduct to Uriah there is no meanness about him. There is nobility even in his faults ; and certainly his repentance is noble. Is there any one in the whole of the Old Testament of whom we know so much, and yet find so much to admire, and praise, and love ? With his chivalry and generosity, with his passionate love for his friend and for his son, with his sweetness and delicacy, his energy and courage, do we not feel him to be a man after *man's* own heart as well as after God's ? Whether we take the world's rough measure and judge him by what he *did*, or look deeper and judge him by what he *was*, we must admit that in him we have a king who was at once a true hero and a true saint.

He was buried " in the city of David," *i.e.*, on Mount Zion, in a tomb which he had probably prepared for himself. Even the site of it is now unknown. But he had reared himself another monument far more lasting in those imperishable hymns which have secured him a memorial in the hearts of all mankind. Of course not all the Psalms are his ; perhaps by no means all of those which bear his name. But they are his in spirit, if not in fact: the Divine inspiration flows through him to those who were moved to imitate him. They belong to no Church, eastern or western, not even to Christianity itself, although the Gospel alone can give them their full meaning. They are the possession of the whole human race wherever it knows its God. Since the day on which he gave them to the world, the Psalms of David have never ceased to rise to the eternal throne.

It may be thought that this survey of the life of David is in extent out of all proportion to the remainder of the summary. But the example of Scripture itself would seem to show that this is not so. Whether we regard the influence of David himself upon the people he ruled, or the growth and development of the people under his guidance, or the instruction which his life supplies for each individual soul, or the deep analogies which lie between the history of Israel at this its most glorious period and the history of the Christian Church, the age and reign of David stands alone in the history of Israel. If Samuel had founded a school of prophets, David had founded a school of heroes, a nation of warriors, consecrated, like a great military order, to the work of fighting for the Lord against the heathen, for Him who now first begins to be commonly known as " the Lord of hosts." Coming, like Joan of Arc, from deep pastoral solitudes to take the lead in armies and stand at the right hand of kings, he had reanimated and raised from disgrace to glory a noble but disheartened nation. A man of the people himself, and owing nothing to his birth, he was a living witness to all, that the very highest advancement was possible to every man who worked with the blessing of Jehovah. Thus the whole nation felt itself ennobled in him, and reverenced him with an enthusiastic devotion both on the throne and in his grave. This enthusiasm was not the creation of David: it met him half way, and was the greatest of all his advantages; second only to the aid of Jehovah Himself. Thus he and his people mutually acted and reacted on one another, a type and an earnest of the relations between Christ and His Church. He abode among them, and they were represented and glorified in him, each rendering still further advance more possible for the other. From that uncertain period, which is neither childhood nor manhood, the nation had emerged into the strength and self-possession of the prime of life. How long will it remain there? For the prime of a nation's life has no necessary limits. If the right conditions are there, the limits may be extended indefinitely. This question will find an answer only too soon in the history of the next reign.

The Last King of United Israel. Solomon.

We pass from the deathbed of King David to a scene of almost dazzling splendour. The few detailed narratives that have come down to us of events in the reign of Solomon are enough to show us that: and fresh from the abundance of information preserved for us respecting David, we are perhaps surprised that comparatively so little is told us about the son who succeeded to all, and more than all, his grandeur. The fact of this almost sudden check in the full stream of the history is evidence of one thing at any rate—that, whatever may have been the opinion of his own age with regard to Solomon, later generations did not find the picture of his reign so delightful to dwell on as that of his father's era: and it was they, and not the contemporary writers, who had to decide what should be preserved and what not of the annals of those times. It was pleasant to remember Solomon's miracles of wisdom, the treasures he accumulated, the splendour of his court, and the extensiveness of his commerce. His temple, his palaces, and his public works remained as lasting evidence of all this magnificence. But at the same time men had come to know by profound experience how dearly the magnificence had been bought. Israel throughout long generations was paying the cost of Solomon's glory. Limitation of liberty and heavy taxation at the time, followed in the next reign by a permanent schism; this was the heavy price. It might be worth while for Judah and Benjamin, who had this magnificence and its accompanying expenditure in the midst of them, to submit to some loss of freedom and to taxes which came back to them in trade; but what had Ephraim and the other tribes to gain by it all? Moreover, not even in Solomon's day had the kingdom been preserved in its full integrity. Contrary to the law (Lev. xxv. 13—34), he had given away a portion of the inheritance of Israel to Hiram, king of Tyre (1 Kings ix. 11).

These considerations will explain to us why our materials for the reign of Solomon are comparatively so scanty. No doubt there are higher causes still. In making their compilations the sacred historians were guided to the preservation of what was of permanent value for the history of the kingdom of God. Mere worldly opulence and splendour has little instructiveness about it. A prolonged narrative of Solomon's magnificence and power would have had scarcely a higher moral value than the "Thousand and One Nights." Enough is told us to enable us to appreciate God's bounty to the young man who deliberately preferred wisdom to wealth and power, and to see the powerlessness of mere wisdom and culture, even of the highest kind, when dissevered from the fear and love of God, against human passion and human pride. Under Solomon the star of Israel continues still to rise for a time, and under him the zenith of the nation is reached. Yet his reign is not on that account greater than his father's, which was a continual growth from first to last. On the contrary, it is the lamentable distinction of Solomon's reign that with him, and largely in consequence of his faults, begins a decline which was never really arrested and which in the end proved fatal. The lesson of his life is to a large extent that of Samson's and of Saul's combined : miraculous powers neutralised by self-indulgence ; great natural gifts rendered baneful by desertion of God. Therefore a few scenes of splendour, the canker, and its consequences, are all that are needed to be told. The remainder, however flattering to himself and his age, has little instruction for us.

Solomon seems to have been one of those men who try to serve God with one hand and themselves with both. The one hand soon becomes weary of its double duty, and the end is devotion to self alone. Unlike his father, he was born in the purple, and had never known the bracing influences of difficulty or adversity. Brought up in the constant society of his mother, of whom we know much evil and no good, and in expectation of a glorious crown, we can hardly wonder that his character does not bear the strain of the possession of enormous wealth and power. Nothing had occurred to prove to him his entire dependence on God. His prayer at Gibeon, high and noble as it was, and "pleasing to the Lord," was not the highest. It is the prayer of the Stoic rather than of the saint, of one who seeks to be self-sufficing rather than of one who feels that dependence on God is his only hope and stay. What would David have asked for had he had the choice ? His psalms leave the answer scarcely doubtful : to be delivered from his transgressions, to have a clean heart and a right spirit, to hold fast by God ; or, in one word, holiness. The widest range of wisdom without that was worthless, not only in God's eyes but for bringing peace to the heart. This truth, Solomon, with all his varied knowledge, did not know ; and had to learn it through a dreary round of the bitterest disappointments.

Solomon began well. He "loved the Lord, walking in the statutes of David his father" (1 Kings iii. 3), and almost his first care is to accomplish the desire, inherited from his father, of building "the house of the Lord," for which David had long since been collecting materials. But even at this early date, when all seems so fair, the germs of evil are not wanting. There is something astounding in finding that one of his first acts was to seek a wife out of Egypt, the house of bondage. Since the Israelites "spoiled the Egyptians" there had been no intercourse between the two nations. Solomon's marriage was probably a diplomatic one, to gain the aid of Pharaoh against Edom, or at least to withhold him from helping Edom. It was the beginning of those many unions with strange wives who in the end led him into abominable idolatries. But he is nowhere said to have built altars to any Egyptian god, so that we may perhaps conclude that Pharaoh's daughter became a proselyte, and that for this reason the marriage was not specially condemned. But the connexion with Egypt, if it did not lead to idolatry, led to another violation of the law. In direct contravention of Deut. xvii. 17, Solomon had horses brought out of Egypt (1 Kings x. 28). Again, the oppressive slave-work to which not only the surviving Canaanites, but even free-born Israelites, were subjected in building the temple (1 Kings v. 13, 14) is an unpleasing feature in the work. The prophecy of Samuel (1 Sam. viii. 16) was being abundantly fulfilled. It has been suggested that it was partly in order to keep out of sight and hearing the misery that he was causing to these huge gangs of enslaved Israelites and Canaanites, that Solomon had every-thing made ready for the temple before it was brought to the site, so that it could be put up there with little trouble and noise. Be this as it may, it is not improbable that in the superb magnificence with which he adorned the house of God, Solomon found salve for a conscience disquieted by his luxurious self-indulgence. If the Lord had a large share of his opulence he might safely enjoy the rest.

In his temple, and in the prayer with which he dedicates it, Solomon appears as a man with an ideal far above that which he actually practised. There is no harm in this; nay, it is what must be the case with all ideals, especially with ideals in religion. The fatal thing is when there is no effort to make the practice approach to the ideal; when a man rests content with having set up a high standard which he does not strive to reach. This comes to be the case with Solomon; and the solemn warning which he receives immediately after the dedication leads us to suppose that something is amiss already (1 Kings ix. 6—9). It would be startling to turn from the eighth to the eleventh chapter of the First Book of Kings, if such inconsistencies and falls were not among the common experiences of life. First, the multitude of sacrifices, and then the multitude of wives: first, the temple to the Lord God of Israel, and then the high places for Chemosh and Molech and Ashtoreth. The God of light, and love, and purity is supplanted in the heart of the wisest of men by the deities of darkness, and cruelty, and lust. Whether the idolatry, which Solomon certainly aided and appears to have shared, was the result of an unwise toleration ; or of weak indulgence to his wives ; or of his great knowledge of nature, leading him to seek forbidden ways into her mysteries ; or of his foreign policy, which might seem to make the permission and even support of foreign religions a political necessity ; or of several of these combined—we cannot decide. Certain it is that he was dragged down from the high spiritual level on which he started, and that the nation was dragged down with him. In David's time monarch and people mutually helped one another to rise. In the latter half of Solomon's reign the reverse is the case, although for awhile the dazzling brilliancy of the age prevented the germs of evil from being seen. Long peace gave a sense of security; increased commerce encouraged luxury and indolence ; and there was the king himself show-ing them the way to enjoy them. They were forgetting Him who had given and could take away ; and this was in itself a half-way house to idolatry, with which their foreign trade was again making them dangerously familiar. While this was true of the more prosperous half of the people, the rest were being ground down by Solomon's oppressive taxation and task-work, which were preparing a seething mass of discontent ready to boil up at any moment. Thus David's nation of devoted warriors was on the road to becoming a nation of mingled voluptuaries and serfs. And if Solomon did not raise his people to a higher moral level, but rather the con-trary, neither did his people help to raise him. They did not meet him, as they did his father, with a warm and enthusiastic sympathy. There is enthusiasm about him at first, but it is for his father's son rather than for himself ; and if for himself, rather for the beauty of the young king's form, and for the intellectual delight afforded by his conversation, than for what he did *with* them and *for* them. He was not, as David had been, one of themselves. They were not so sure of his sym-pathy, of his being able to understand them. Above all, it would seem as if he had little hold over their moral and spiritual life. Of his thousand and five songs (1 Kings iv. 32), not one gained hold enough on the people to live; and if they expressed the life which is lamented over in the Book of Ecclesiastes, it is as well that they have perished. Of the Psalms, only two by the Hebrew titles bear his name (lxxii. and cxxvii.), and of these the former is possibly, and the latter probably, not his. Thus what was one of the strongest links between David and his people was altogether wanting in the case of Solomon.

But there was not merely an increasing want of union between the sovereign and the nation, there was also an increase in the old evil of disunion in the nation itself. Its chief bond of union lay in its religion; and through the royal tolerance and support of idolatry the religious tie was being rapidly weakened. Would religious men make pilgrimages to Jerusalem for the feasts only to be scandalized when they arrived there by high places for Chemosh and for Molech, "on the hill that is before Jerusalem," within sight of the temple itself? (1 Kings xi. 7.) And if Jerusalem was an offence to them, why should it remain their capital? And what offended religious Israelites did not attract others; for those who lapsed into idolatry could have their own impious altars at home. There was no need to go to the Mount of Olives to worship. Thus for all classes, religious and irreligious alike, the tie that bound them to the capital was fast becoming weaker, and in the next reign it snapped altogether.

Of Solomon's last days and death we know nothing. If the traditional belief, that the Book of Ecclesiastes is his confession of the vanity of his life, is correct, we are still far from knowing in what state he died. The book itself is an enigma. But whatever be the interpretation of its half-melancholy, half-scornful estimate of life in general, and specially of the Preacher's own, how different is it from the fifty-first Psalm! In his persistency in sin and in the gloominess of his repentance Solomon is utterly unlike his father. There is a calculating reflectiveness about the Preacher's recantation, as apparently also about his sins, which forms the strongest contrast to the passionate yearning with which the Psalmist flings himself and his sin before Jehovah, and leaves all to Him.

This, then, is the mournful conclusion: the wisest, wealthiest, and most powerful king of the noblest nation—at that time the only noble nation—in the world, at the most glorious period of its career, writes this at the end of a long life and reign as the sum of his experiences: "All is vanity."

Before passing on, let us remind ourselves that we are following not so much the history of a people or the lives of individuals, as the history of a religion, the history of the kingdom of God. The history of the people and of its leaders is real and not fictitious; but at the same time it is typical, and was divinely ordered throughout to be so. The history of the people shows forth in a figure the mysteries of redemption, and both in figure and in fact God's moral government of the world. The lives of the representative leaders set forth in a figure each some fragment of the life of Christ. The Messiah is Priest, Prophet, and King. All these great offices of the Theocracy find their highest representative in Him: all, therefore, who held these offices under the law were each in their measure types of the Messiah. In the supreme rulers of united Israel we have just had examples of all three: Eli the priest, Samuel the prophet, Saul, or David, or Solomon the king.

The high-priest was the representative of the people before God, the intercessor between God and man. He went into the holy of holies once a year to make atonement for sin with blood. But the holy of holies was no perfect sanctuary, for it was made with hands. The atonement was no perfect atonement, for it needed to be repeated. The sacrifice was no perfect sacrifice, for it was the blood of a brute beast, which can never take away sins. Above all, the priest was no perfect priest, for he had to make atonement for his own sins before he interceded for the people. All the ordinances respecting him and his sacrifice proved to the people that though he was divinely ordained, and a true type, yet he was no more than a type. They must look elsewhere for the true Priest, and true Intercessor, and true Representative, who would offer one perfect sacrifice for ever putting away sin.

As the priest represented man to God, so the prophet represented God to man. He came to declare God's will: His commands, His promises, His judgments. He came to denounce the priest, who forgot his high calling and profaned the sanctuary or allowed others to do so; to warn the people who forgot that the Lord was their King, and that the Lord was their God; to rebuke the king who forgot that he had to obey as well as to rule, and that for him too there were punishments for wrongdoing. But the prophet, though he had a Divine commission, which was often attested by miraculous powers, was manifestly not perfect. He declared at best only a fragment of the truth; and he often uttered that fragment so dimly and obscurely that it was hard to gather his meaning; sometimes he himself did not understand the meaning of his own message. Therefore he too, though a true prophet sent from God, was but a type and an earnest of the perfect Prophet, who should not only teach what was true, but Himself be the Truth; who should not only declare God's word, but Himself be the Word of God.

But, while the prophet declared God's will, he had no power to enforce it: he did not rule, he did not govern. There needed, therefore, to be yet another representative of God in the Theocracy; one who should represent not so much His will as His authority. This was the king, the vicegerent of Jehovah, "the Lord's anointed." He represented "the Lord of Hosts" as "Captain over His people" (1 Sam. ix. 16; x. 1; xiii. 14; 2 Sam. v. 2; 2 Kings xx. 5); he represented "the Judge of all the earth," as appointed to execute judgment and justice between man and man. But in giving this lofty type of royalty to His people, God showed to them that it was a type and no more: for their captain could not promise them victory, and their judge was not infallible in judgment. The perfect King, the great Anointed One, was still to come. (See Perowne 'On the Psalms,' i. pp. 49—52.)

And if it was clear from the very nature of the offices themselves that they were only types of something more perfect, still more clear did this become when the people had experience of the men who held the offices. Each of these offices had in turn come to be supreme in Israel; and therefore it might perhaps have seemed as if the great representative of each had come. But it was impossible that Eli, whose weak fondness had tolerated the enormities of his sons, and who had himself been rebuked for his shortcomings, could be the perfect priest. It was impossible that Samuel, who also was discredited in his sons, who feared to do God's bidding lest Saul should kill him, who mistook Eliab for the Lord's anointed, who was bidden to set another in his own place as supreme ruler, could be the perfect prophet. It was impossible that Saul the strong, or David the well-beloved, or Solomon the magnificent, could be the perfect king; for was it not also true to call them, Saul the suicide, David the adulterer and murderer, Solomon the idolater? From the men themselves, therefore, as well as from the nature of the offices which they held, it was manifest to all that the true Priest, Prophet, and King was not yet given to Israel. It was their duty still to watch, still to prepare for Him.

The time of waiting was long and dark. The types, especially in the permanent offices of priest and king, grew less rather than more perfect, as the men who held them grew less worthy of them. The kingdom was rent in twain, and in the true sense of the title there was no king of Israel, no captain of the Lord's people. "The prophets prophesied falsely, and the priests bare rule by their means." And, worst of all, the "people *loved* to have it so." Well might the prophet ask, "What will ye do in the end thereof ? "

THE DIVIDED KINGDOMS OF JUDAH AND ISRAEL.

We may pass on rapidly now. In a sketch of this kind it would not be possible, nor if possible be worth while, to give a detailed notice of each of the kings that for a time reigned over the divided kingdoms of Judah and Israel. It will suffice to state the general characteristics of each kingdom, and to trace the tendencies in each from the division of the monarchy to the Captivities. There is a dismal monotony about many of the reigns, especially in the northern kingdom. The special features of each, and the lessons which they seem to inculcate, will be found in the commentaries on the Books of Kings and of Chronicles.

Sometimes a weak rule following a strong one is a clear gain : the nation is able to advance more firmly, and develope more freely, for the relaxation which follows after discipline. Such might possibly have been the case had Rehoboam made wise concessions to the reasonable demands of his subjects. As it was, there was an unhealthy reaction, a severing of ties both political and religious in a way that almost precluded the possibility of reunion. It was a severing of ties which had long fretted some of those who were bound by them, and who were therefore all the less likely to seek to be reunited. The rivalry between Ephraim and Judah has been compared to that between the houses of York and Lancaster in our own history ; but the parallel fails in several obvious particulars. In England we had not the miserable result of two rival kingdoms perpetuated for centuries. Again, the contest was between two royal families and their followers ; there was no deep cleft running through the whole nation. When the families ceased to quarrel, the nation at once reunited. Lastly, our civil war was not embittered by differences of religion : neither party set up a religious as well as a political schism. From the time of the conquest of Canaan the leadership of Israel had been more or less with Ephraim. Joshua had belonged to it, and Ephraim held his tomb. Shechem with the two sacred mountains, and Shiloh the ancient sanctuary, were within its borders. The territory of Ephraim was both rich and secure. Its fruitful plains could scarcely be approached by an army either from the east or from the west, and no attack from either quarter is on record. Its vulnerable, though not very vulnerable, side was the north, and here, from the plain of Jezreel, Shalmaneser invaded it. These advantages fostered the haughty spirit which was natural to the tribe. Hence their jealous complaints against Gideon (Judges viii. 1), against Jephthah (Judges xii. 1), and against David (2 Sam. xix. 41). The death of Ishbosheth and the personal popularity of David staved off the rupture for a time, and retained Ephraim in uneasy union with Judah : but the success of Absalom's revolt shows how insecure the tie between the rival tribes was. Had Solomon succeeded in killing Jeroboam (1 Kings xi. 40), the union might possibly have continued for some time longer for want of a sufficiently able leader to head the secession. Rehoboam's selecting Shechem rather than Jerusalem for his coronation shows that he was not disinclined to recognise Ephraim's claims on the reigning house. But it was far too late for a trifling concession of this kind to do much towards soothing angry and ambitious Ephraimites. It might even irritate them by flaunting a pomp before them which they knew was to be paid for by oppressive taxation: and Rehoboam was the last king of Judah who visited Shechem as part of his own dominion; the last also who, having ventured so far, returned home unmolested.

The history of the kingdom of Israel is mainly the history of the tribe of Ephraim; and some of the prophets call attention to this fact by calling the kingdom not "Israel," or "Jacob," or even "Joseph," but simply Ephraim (Hosea iv. 17; v. 3—14, &c.; Isa. vii. 2—17; ix. 9, 21, &c.; Zech. ix. 10, 13). "The ten tribes" was a geographical rather than a political expression. Of the northern tribes it still remained true that they "dwelt among the Canaanites" (Judges i. 32, 33), rather than the Canaanites among them; and the tribes east of Jordan remained, as before, very much cut off from their brethren. Simeon and Dan gravitated towards the kingdom of Judah, together with the greater part of Benjamin; so that the kingdom of Israel is mainly the lot of Joseph; i.e., Ephraim and Manasseh. This fact must be borne in mind in considering the nature of the disruption. Here, as so often, we are in danger of confounding occasions with causes. It was not the ambition or ability of Jeroboam, it was not the task-work and taxation of Solomon, it was not the folly of Rehoboam, which were the causes of the rupture. All these things combined made a very favourable *opportunity* for it: but the real causes lay deeper; viz., in the ambition of Ephraim stimulated by its undoubted advantages and its jealousy of Judah, a jealousy of 400 years standing.

The kingdom of Israel had a grand opportunity of justifying the secession. It might resolutely have set to work to avoid and to remedy the grievous errors which had disfigured the latter part of the reign of Solomon. The fatal mistake consisted in supposing that these could be avoided by mere severance from the house of David, and that no remedy was needed. Had Jeroboam and his successors honestly laboured to abolish idolatry, to moderate taxation, and to strengthen the frontier, they would have retained the alliance of the prophets, the most powerful moral force of the age, and would have won the respect and lasting affection of the tribes. But they cared for their own dynasty much more than for the true religion, and to surpass Judah much more than to put down and thrust back the heathen. Thus even in the first period (from Jeroboam to Ahab, B.C. 975—900), which is one of hostility between two kingdoms, although Israel gains considerable advantages over Judah, yet what advance is made is wholly in the southern kingdom, while the northern simply goes back. Jeroboam, in order to make the break with the capital of Judah as decided as possible, made a clean sweep of all that could remind his subjects of the glory of David and Solomon, and with it of a large portion of the existing civilisation. Thus his kingdom was at once sent back to the rudeness of the age of Saul; and before long was plunged in the anarchy and consequent weakness which had distinguished the age of the Judges. Hence in the kingdom of Israel there seems to be nothing to compensate for the evil of division. For the evil of division in an empire is by no means necessarily unmixed. Sometimes the several portions develope all the more healthily for being independent, if only they have sufficient internal force and sufficient scope for action. The kingdom of Israel was deficient in both; and the force which it possessed was misdirected, so that what scope it had was thrown away.

In the kingdom of Judah the schism was by no means all loss, although the balance was on that side. It lost seriously in prestige and population, but it gained in compactness. It had the incalculable advantage of *preserving the true religion*. It possessed the temple, and (thanks to the wicked and shortsighted policy of Jeroboam) it possessed the sympathy and support both of the hierarchy and of the prophets. Jeroboam's idolatrous sanctuaries at Bethel and Dan drove all the priests and Levites to Judah, and threw the prophets into irreconcilable opposition: and although the southern kingdom remained by no means free from the abominations of idolatry, still these existed side by side with the worship of Jehovah, and not (as in the northern kingdom) in place of it. Of the prophets whose writings have been preserved, only three seem to have ministered in the northern kingdom —Jonah, Hosea, and Amos; and of these Amos was a native of Judah.

These advantages and disadvantages on the one side and on the other existed from the first; others showed themselves in the course of time. In the kingdom of Judah the crown remained in one family, the house of David, which possessed the enormous prestige of the promise of the Messiah. In Israel, on the contrary, a dynasty never lasted for more than a few generations, and a new dynasty was generally introduced by a bloody revolution. Thus in the two centuries and a half, during which the kingdom of Israel lasted, it had nineteen kings, while Judah in the same period had only twelve. This of course was the result of the violent deaths which generally marked a change of dynasty in Israel. Israel in this respect sunk to the level of ordinary Oriental kingdoms, while the permanence of the house of David was probably absolutely unparalleled, and was therefore perpetual evidence of God's blessing. We have seen that the period of the Judges is summed up in the statement that "in those days there was no king in Israel, but every man did that which was right in his own eyes" (Judges xvii. 6). Similarly the history of the kingdom of Israel may almost be summed up in one simple and typical narrative; "the people that followed Omri prevailed against the people that followed Tibni: so Tibni died, and Omri reigned." Might is right, and the weakest goes to the wall; but the mere change of names in the rivals adds nothing to the interest or instructiveness of the history. It is a dreary round of tyranny overturned by violence and succeeded by tyranny again.

Along with this contrast as regards the stability of the reigning house a contrast soon showed itself between the individual sovereigns in each kingdom. Israel produced a few kings who deserve to be called successful rulers, *e.g.*, Jehu and his descendant Jeroboam II., but not one who was morally even respectable. Jehu's "zeal for the Lord" was apparently sheer hypocrisy: he put down Baal-worship because political capital might be made out of such an *auto-da-fè*, while he retained the worship of the calves because it appeared to be politically expedient to do so. In Judah, on the other hand, although there was abundance of idolatry and other wickedness among the kings, and although Solomon's erections on the Mount of Olives to Chemosh and Moloch remained, and probably were used, for four centuries, yet upright and even holy kings were not wanting, some of whom carried out very thorough reforms, *e.g.*, Asa, Jehoshaphat, Jotham, Hezekiah, and Josiah.

After a consideration of all these differences between the two kingdoms, and others might be added (*e.g.*, fixedness of the capital on one side, and change on the other; subordination of the army in the one case, insubordination in the other), we are prepared for the final result—that the kingdom of Judah lasted for 130 years longer than that of Israel, and that its punishment was limited in duration, whereas that of Israel continues to this day. No doubt a considerable number of the captives from Israel shared in the restoration of Judah, but the bulk of them have been merged in Oriental populations. The astounding fiction that the English nation is descended from the lost ten tribes contradicts the very first principles of history, ethnology, and philology; and even if it were true would be worthless for the purposes which it is supposed to serve; for the promises made to the patriarchs and their descendants are now transferred to the Christian Church. Not Jews, whether known to be so or not, but Christians are heirs to the promise. If this remains doubtful, surely St. Paul has written in vain. But of this more hereafter.

A more profitable question remains: *Was the disruption of the kingdom unfavourable to the special mission of the Jewish Church?* That mission was to keep religious truth alive in the world, to preserve the worship of the one true God, and to prepare a field for the Gospel. Even if united Israel, had it remained true to its calling, would have fulfilled the Divine purpose in the best way possible, yet it is not difficult to see how, under the conditions existing in the reign of Solomon, this purpose may have been better accomplished by the kingdom of Judah than by the whole nation. Let us remember that the Canaanite was *still* in the land, in the northern tribes perhaps still in a majority; that there was extensive commerce between Tyre and the northern tribes, and that this promoted idolatry and its attendant corruptions; that Syria, conquered and garrisoned by David (2 Sam. viii. 6), had under Rezon begun to shake itself free (1 Kings xi. 23—25), and to produce a baneful effect upon the north of Israel. From all these evil influences the kingdom of Judah was very considerably protected by the barrier of the northern kingdom. Again, the expulsion of the priests and Levites from Israel, and their concentration in Judah, helped the cause of true religion in that kingdom. For, however much the hierarchy may have fallen below the level of their sacred office, they at least kept alive a knowledge of Jehovah and of His worship, wherever they were; and Judah now possessed the whole of this teaching, which before had been diffused through all the tribes. Above all, the kingdoms being two instead of one, it was possible for one to be a lesson and a warning to the other. This was certainly the case latterly, to the great benefit of the true religion in Judah. Would Hezekiah's reign have been as godly, would Manasseh have repented, would Josiah have been able to carry out his pious reforms, had there not been before the eyes of all the awful judgment which had overtaken the sister kingdom of Israel? Add to this the notable fact that precisely the period when Judah has friendly relations with Israel, and the two kingdoms are to some extent reunited, is perhaps the very worst period both morally and politically in the history of Judah. For all these reasons we may believe that, although the disruption of the monarchy was an abandonment of the highest ideal, yet in God's Providence good was brought out of evil; and, as in the earliest disruption of all, when the patriarchs broke their family bond by selling Joseph into Egypt, the wrong-doing of the few was turned into a blessing for many, including in the end even the wrong-doers themselves.

The Captivity of Israel.

After a duration of 255 years the kingdom of Israel came to an end in the reign of the nineteenth king, Hoshea. He was the last and the best of that unholy and irregular line of monarchs. It might perhaps surprise us that the annihilating blow should fall in the reign of the best king. But "the best king of Israel" is an expression of diminished blame rather than of praise. "He did evil in the sight of the Lord, but not as the kings of Israel that were before him" (2 Kings xvii. 2),

He is not good, but somewhat less abominable than his predecessors. We are not told in what this diminution of wickedness consisted. We may conjecture that when the golden calves were carried away, the one at Dan by Tiglath-Pileser, and the one at Bethel by his son Shalmaneser, Hoshea did not set them up again, nor enforce the policy of the arch-apostate, of preventing his subjects from going up to Jerusalem to worship. It is not said of him, as of nearly all of his predecessors, that "he departed not from the sins of Jeroboam, the son of Nebat, who made Israel to sin." Even had Hoshea been like his contemporary Hezekiah, we may doubt whether the fate of Israel would have been averted. There is a point in the character of nations, as of individuals, at which gravitation acts irretrievably, and at which there is no possibility of redemption *in the natural order of things.* God may work a miracle of grace and turn the course of nature, but we have no right to expect Him to do so, even in answer to prayer, any more than to expect Him in answer to prayer to stop the avalanche which we have set rolling; and in this case there would seem to have been no prayer. If this is true of character, much more is it true of the natural results of character, the miseries which follow in the train of persistent wrong-doing. Repentance may be granted, but it may come too late to avert any of the *temporal* consequences of sin. "The case is become desperate: and poverty and sickness, remorse and anguish, infamy and death, the effects of their own doings, overwhelm them, beyond possibility of remedy or escape" (Butler, 'Analogy' I. ii.). Or, as the contemporary prophet Hosea testifies (ch. vii. 1, 2), "When I would heal Israel, then the iniquity of Ephraim is discovered, and the wickedness of Samaria: for they commit falsehood; and the thief cometh in, and the troop of robbers spoileth without. And they consider not in their hearts that I remember all their wickedness; *now their own doings have beset them about;* they are before My face." The next verse seems to imply that, whereas in former times it was the kings that "made Israel to sin," in this last reign it is the people that take the lead in iniquity. "They make the king glad with their wickedness, and the princes with their lies." Thus the unrighteousness of sovereigns and their subjects acts and reacts one upon the other. Israel's wounds were incurable (Micah i. 9), her cup of iniquity, bloodshed, idolatry, and impurity was full, and the only cleansing that remained was that they and their sins should be swept away together.

Although the reign of the last king was morally superior to that of the others, yet politically the monarchy preserved its irregular character to the last. Like exactly half his predecessors, Hoshea was an adventurer, who gained the throne by the slaughter of his sovereign. In nineteen kings we have nine different dynasties, four of which end with the conspirator who founded it; among the whole nineteen "not one calling upon the Lord" (Hosea vii. 7). And thus the Lord was ever giving Israel a king in His anger, and taking him away in His wrath (ch. xiii. 11).

The last terrible end did not come without warning. Over and above the permanent declarations of the Law, and the frequent denunciations of specially commissioned prophets, two lighter calamities heralded the coming of the final blow. In the last reign but one, Tiglath-Pileser (B.C. 740) had carried into captivity the three tribes east of Jordan (1 Chron. v. 26), "and Galilee, and all the land of Naphtali" (2 Kings xv. 29). At the beginning of Hoshea's reign Shalmaneser made an attack on Phœnicia and terrified the new king of Samaria into becoming tributary without a contest. All Phœnicia was conquered except Tyre; and its success in holding out perhaps encouraged Hoshea to endeavour to throw off the yoke which he had accepted. To strengthen himself he made an alliance, not with Hezekiah, who also was revolting, but one forbidden by the law, with So king of Egypt, probably the Sabaco of Herodotus or the Sevechus (Sevichos) of Manetho. Thus the same dark power which had tried to strangle the Chosen People at its birth, which had lent its sinister aid to the founding of the schismatical kingdom of Israel, now by once more lending aid contributed to its final overthrow. So truly was Egypt like the reeds of its own river, "on which if a man lean, it will go into his hand and pierce it" (2 Kings xviii. 21). The alliance was made known to Shalmaneser, who at once called Hoshea to account and put him in prison. And thus Samaria's king "is cut off, like a chip upon the water" (Hosea x. 7). Samaria held out stubbornly, like Jerusalem after it, defending its walls, its "crown of pride" (Isa. xxviii. 3), with the courage of despair. This death-struggle, the last of an expiring people, lasted three years; at the end of which the place was taken by Sargon, the successor of Shalmaneser. His "*veni, vidi, vici*" is still in existence: "Samaria I looked at, I captured: 27,280 who dwelt in it I carried away." This was the common policy of Oriental conquerors—to transplant the inhabitants of conquered territories, and occupy their land with other populations. This served various purposes. It weakened both of the nations interchanged, and kept them for a time at least submissive; for their energy would be expended in settling in their new home. Sometimes a trustworthy people near at home was exchanged with a troublesome nation near the frontier: this was precisely the case with the Israelites. Sometimes a more advanced people were planted as a centre of civilisation in the midst of ruder tribes. The Israelites were not only transported but dispersed, no doubt with a view to prevent concerted action in the future, a policy which has been entirely successful (2 Kings xvii. 6; xviii. 11). A few may have escaped the Assyrian net and remained in Samaria, or have returned thither afterwards, to mingle with the Samaritans. A few returned with the Jews and became merged with them in Judæa. Many would coalesce with the Jews in Babylon and become part of the "Dispersion." It is worth noting in reference to the last two cases that Ezekiel, after the captivity of Judah, speaks of the captives as *Israel* (ch. ii. 3; iii. 1—7; iv. 3, 13, &c.). The bulk probably carried their habitual love of idolatry with them into exile, and became lost by intermarriage with the heathen populations of Assyria. The imagination of Jews and Christians alike has tried to pierce the veil which history has drawn over their ultimate fate. The black Jews of Malabar, the Red Indians of North America, Afghan tribes, Himalayan tribes, the Nestorians, have all had their advocates as the representatives of the lost tribes. It was reserved for the present generation to suggest and maintain almost as an article of faith, or even as the announcement of a new gospel, the most wildly impossible theory of all, that the present descendants of these Semitic ancestors are the Aryan inhabitants of Great Britain. To some persons this astonishing hypothesis seems too absurd to be worth combating, while others allow it to pass as a harmless delusion.

The following questions demand a clear and reasonable answer from all those who advocate the doctrine:

(1) If Anglo-Israelism is true, *how is that not a single theologian, or historian, or philologist of any eminence has accepted it*, or even admitted its possibility? True that the Gospel was in the first instance hidden from the wise and prudent and revealed to babes; but it does not therefore follow that what the wise and prudent reject, and babes accept, is true. Moreover, the wise and

prudent accepted the Gospel when it became known to them. Here the wise and prudent disbelieve, not because things are hidden from them, but because they are known. It is those who do not know all that their own theory involves who believe.

(2) The change of a Semitic race into an Aryan race, of a Semitic language into an Aryan language, would be a miracle of the very highest order. *Where is the evidence of the miracle?* It is trifling with faith to believe in a miracle utterly unsupported by evidence. A nation disappears from history; after a lapse of many centuries another nation, entirely different in type and language, grows up in quite a different part of the globe; and we are asked to believe, without anything that can seriously be considered evidence, that the one has become the other. We might as well believe that the rose-trees in the Temple gardens sprang from the olive-trees of Gethsemane, through cuttings brought home by the Crusaders.

(3) Even if the theory were true, *what would be its value?* As already stated, the blessings promised to Abraham, Isaac, and Jacob have passed over to the Christian Church. "He is not an Israelite who is one outwardly." Human generation has nothing to do with spiritual regeneration. "If righteousness comes by the law," if spiritual blessings depend on descent from Abraham, "then Christ died for nothing" (Gal. ii. 17).

Thus much with regard to the past seems to be in place and necessary in the present historical sketch. It would be altogether out of its scope to inquire into the future by discussing the hidden meaning of unfulfilled prophecy. We may leave on one side, therefore, the controversy as to *the restoration of Israel.* The prophesied restoration has been at least in part fulfilled by the share which Israel took in the return of Judah; and St. Paul seems to intimate (Rom. xi.) that henceforth the restoration will be spiritual, not literal. The Holy Land to which Israel needs to return is not that which once flowed with milk and honey, but the kingdom of God.

One other point remains to be noticed—the condition of the land from which the captive Israelites were withdrawn. The matter is one of considerable obscurity as regards details, but the general outlines are clear. That the bulk of the Israelite population was withdrawn, that heathen populations were put in its place, and that these formed the large majority, is manifest. It is also certain that it was Tiglath-Pileser who carried away much people from Reuben, Gad, eastern Manasseh, Naphtali, and Galilee (2 Kings xv. 29; 1 Chron. v. 26), and Sargon, who carried away a great many more from Samaria (2 Kings xvii. 6). Again, it is certain that it was Esarhaddon, Sargon's grandson, who planted heathen colonists in place of the captive Israelites (Ezra iv. 2), and that a great variety of such colonists came under the leadership of "the great and noble Asnapper" (Ezra iv. 10). What is uncertain is, whether Sargon literally depopulated the country, or left a large number in the rural districts, how long an interval elapsed between the deportation under Sargon and the first importation, whether there was any importation previous to that under Esarhaddon, whether the immigrants led by Asnapper were those whom Esarhaddon sent or others. But none of these details are of serious moment. We know that the new inhabitants of central Palestine are heathens to so complete an extent that a Hebrew priest with assistants has to be sent back from Assyria, in order to "teach them the manner of the God of the land" (2 Kings xvii. 27), so that the Israelites left behind by Sargon, if numerous, must have been grossly ignorant. We also know that the nation which grew out of these varied heathen elements and this insignificant Israelite element became hostile to the Jews on their return from captivity (Ezra iv. 1, &c.), continued so during New Testament times (Matt. x. 5; Luke ix. 53; John iv. 9; viii. 48), and remain so to this day. The religion which prevailed among the Samaritans was at first as mixed as the nation themselves. The priest sent back from Assyria would almost certainly be one of those instituted for the worship of calves, for the original priesthood had from the first retired to the southern kingdom. His settling at Bethel, the chief seat of Jeroboam's calf-worship, confirms this; and his teaching the new inhabitants to worship after the manner of the land can hardly mean anything but that he taught them to worship Jehovah under the image of a calf, which had been the manner of the land for two centuries and a half. The study of the Pentateuch and the proximity of the Jews after the return would tend to purify the religion of the Samaritans more and more until at last idolatry died out altogether. A people who claimed to keep the Law more strictly and have a purer worship than the Jews themselves would have made themselves ridiculous if they had tolerated idolatry; and this claim the later Samaritans made. But at first the hybrid nation not only worshipped God in a very imperfect, ignorant way, but were idolaters as well: "they feared Jehovah, and served their own graven images" (2 Kings xvii. 33, 41). Thus the goodly heritage of Ephraim, with its sacred spots and associations—Jacob's well, Ebal and Gerizim, Joshua's tomb, Shiloh, and Shechem—passed into the hands of strangers. What a glorious past! "When Israel was young then I loved him, and out of Egypt I called my son." What a miserable present! "Israel is swallowed up: now are they among the Gentiles as a vessel wherein is no pleasure." Yet there is still some hope in the future: "I will heal their falling away, I will gladly love them: for my anger is turned away" (Hosea xi. 1; viii. 8; xiv. 4).

The Captivity of Judah.

There was a moment when the two kingdoms of Israel and Judah were in a condition of great prosperity together. The reign of Jeroboam II. was the most prosperous period of the kingdom of Israel. When it was half over, the youthful Uzziah came to the throne of Judah, which he was destined to fill for half a century. He was one of the ablest of the kings of Judah, victorious over Edomites and Philistines, fortifying the capital and the country round it, and promoting agriculture. It was at this time, towards the close of the reign of Jeroboam II., that Hosea began to prophesy, and he looked with longing eyes toward Judah, and dared to hope that even yet the children of Judah and the children of Israel might be gathered together under one head (ch. i. 7, 11). Uzziah had the happiness of being succeeded by a son equal to himself as a ruler, whereas Jeroboam's success ended with himself. But under Jotham the general prosperity produced a love of luxury and wantonness of life against which Isaiah pronounced strong denunciations. Hence when the weak and wicked Ahaz succeeded the virtuous Jotham, he found a people only too ready to be pleased with him. The idolatrous party in the state now came to the top, and even heathen rulers were invited from abroad to take office. The grandest utterances of the grandest of the prophets seem to have had no lasting effect, and he continued his wicked course to the end. The group of righteous men that had gathered round Isaiah were cheered in spirit by a change of ruler. Wicked kings were still the exception rather than the rule in Judah, whereas Israel, now just at the close of its career, had never known a good king.

At the time when Israel was swept into captivity, Hezekiah was reigning in Jerusalem, the noblest prince that ever sat on the throne of David. Not only was it said of him, that he "did that which was right in the sight of the Lord, *according to all that David his father did*," praise that had not been given for nearly two centuries, but "he trusted in Jehovah, God of Israel; so that after him was none like him among all the kings of Judah, nor any that were before him." Solomon, Asa, Jehoshaphat, Joash, and Amaziah had fallen away in their latter days; Uzziah had been guilty of gross profanity; but Hezekiah "clave to Jehovah," and as a consequence of this "Jehovah was with him" (2 Kings xviii. 1—7). This had been said of no king since David (2 Sam. v. 10). His fidelity was not untried. Assyria, having punished Samaria for its alliance with Egypt, prepared for taking vengeance on Egypt also. In such a struggle the little kingdom of Judah might be crushed as a pebble between two millstones. Repulsed from Egypt, Sennacherib fell back on Jerusalem. A victory there would cover his failure. It seemed an hour of the utmost danger for Jerusalem, and Hezekiah tried to buy the invader off. Sennacherib took the treasure, but still continued to march on Jerusalem; for the treasure increased his desire to capture the city. Thus was Hezekiah punished for trusting even for a moment in bribes rather than in Jehovah. Isaiah, in a strain of magnificent defiance (2 Kings xix. 21—34), brought the king and the people round again to the attitude of supreme confidence in the Lord of Hosts; and just at the moment when the king of Assyria appeared about to swallow up the city, two irresistible disasters annihilated his huge army—panic and plague. In a single night thousands died by the visitation of God. The rest returned with their crest-fallen king to Nineveh. No deliverance like it had been known since the death of the first-born in Egypt.

The strain and excitement of the crisis brought Hezekiah to death's door; but at his passionate entreaty fifteen years were added to his life. The psalm of thanksgiving which he composed on his recovery shows that he too, like the king whom he resembles, was a true poet and a pious one; but it also shows the dreary, hopeless horror which crushed out every other thought in the mind of even a saintly man in the expectation of death. In the case of the sweet Psalmist of Israel we have noticed how the want of the spirit of forgiveness makes the Psalms so different from the Gospel. In the case of his great successor we notice another point of inferiority—the attitude of mind in the contemplation of death.

Hezekiah was the last king of Judah who did not outlive his felicity: he was prosperous to the last. His enemy, Sennacherib, died about the same time as Hezekiah, and along with them the man who had exercised such an influence over the lives of both, the prophet Isaiah. When Isaiah's voice was silenced by death, and the godly Hezekiah was succeeded by the impious Manasseh (Commodus succeeding Marcus Aurelius), it might well seem as if the star of Judah had set, and as if the fate that had just overtaken Samaria must soon overwhelm Jerusalem. The prophets uttered the severest warnings, and Manasseh, unable to intimidate them, silenced them by death; among them, according to tradition, the aged Isaiah. This was the crowning act of iniquity which sealed the doom of the kingdom of Judah. "He filled Jerusalem with innocent blood, which *the Lord would not pardon*" (2 Kings xxiv. 4). The crisis to some extent resembles that of the struggle between Ahab and the prophets. There, however, the prophets in the person of Elijah were victorious; but a decline in the spirit of prophecy in the northern kingdom may perhaps be traced from that victory. In this later struggle in Judah the persecutor was for the time at least successful (Jer. ii. 30; Zeph. iii. 4); and it may be doubted whether the prophets ever regained their former position. They appear no more in the history of this long reign. But the truths to which they had borne witness, both in life and in death, were eternal and could not lose their power. And this horrible period, equal in its abominations and cruelties to the reign of a Caligula or a Nero, forced home two truths upon the few who in sorrow and indignation remained true to Jehovah; (1) that the Messianic hope, the salt of the kingdom of Judah, must now be transferred to a remote future; (2) that there must be a reward *hereafter* for those who had suffered so terribly for the truth in this life; their bodies might perish, but their souls were indestructible: if in this life only they had hope in Jehovah, they were of all men most miserable (1 Cor. xv. 19). They saw, however, that even in this life Manasseh's wickedness brought its proper punishment. Esarhaddon's army found Jerusalem so weakened by the tyrant's enormities that it could make no resistance, and Manasseh was carried away to repent in the prisons of Babylon. When he was allowed to return, there was a great change for the better in his government: the altar of Jehovah was restored, and foreign idolatry was to some extent put away, although not the forbidden worship in the "high places." But the evil had eaten too deeply into the heart and intellect of the people to be cured by a partial reform of this kind, or even by the more searching reformation under Josiah. The bright gleam which is again shed over Jerusalem during the reign of this young reformer extended even to the inhabitants of the northern kingdom. His orders for the extirpation of idolatry were obeyed throughout Palestine, and it might even appear as if the time were coming when the whole land should be once more under the rule of one king, a righteous prince of the house of David. These bright hopes were quenched by the untimely death of the virtuous king: the random arrow of an Egyptian ended the life of the best-beloved sovereign that had reigned since David. His loss was bewailed with the profoundest lamentations by his heart-broken people.

The eye finds nothing pleasing to rest upon in the reigns of his four miserable successors. Their faithlessness and imbecility placed them at the mercy of the Assyrians, who never wanted a fair pretext for attacking them or an excellent prospect of success. Troop after troop of captives was carried away (2 Kings xviii. 13; xxiv. 14; xxv. 11; 2 Chron. xxxvi. 20; Jer. lii. 28, 29; Dan. i. 2, 3). The final blow fell when Zedekiah, the last king of Judah, was led away, childless and sightless, to Babylon, when the walls were broken down, the temple laid in ruins, and all but a scanty remnant of the surviving population carried into captivity. It was the sad fate of Jeremiah to witness the complete fulfilment of his darkest prophecies. He survived the city whose overthrow he had predicted; survived to lament over it in elegies which for pathos and beauty are perhaps without an equal in literature. They remind us of David's lament over Saul and Jonathan; but with this great difference; that whereas David finds comfort in the former glory of the fallen, this to Jeremiah is but an aggravation of his sorrow, so full is his mind with every detail of the unspeakable calamity that has fallen upon the guilty city. King and people, temple and priest, were involved in a common ruin; and the worst feature of all was that the ruin was more than deserved. It was but the inevitable outcome of a long series of royal and national and sacerdotal sins.

If the miserable apostasy and consequent overthrow of the two kingdoms of Israel and Judah might lead us to question whether after all this renegade and ruined nation was the Chosen People of Jehovah, the history of the Jewish exiles in Babylon might reassure us of the fact. It is marvellous that the Jews still retained their nationality; still more marvellous that they continued to cherish hopes of a return and of a happy future under the promised Messiah. Their removal to a strange land, amid strange people and strange rites, the knowledge that their city was a ruin, their king a captive, their kinsmen slaughtered, failed to destroy either the one or the other. Even in the hour of His wrath Jehovah would still remember His covenant with Abraham and David. This they believed; and He alone could have kept alive such a belief under conditions which seemed emphatically to give the lie to it. They had one great assurance that their Divine King had not entirely deserted them. In this hour of their sorest need the voice of prophecy, so far from being silenced, was heard all the more clearly. Of the four " Great Prophets," three fall within the period of the exile. From Egypt, during the first period of the Captivity, Jeremiah continued the strong warnings and protests which had been the forerunners of the city's fall. In the land of exile itself Ezekiel and Daniel continued to make known the judgments of God to the captives and their conquerors. This alone sufficed to prove that Jehovah had not utterly forsaken His people. Moreover, their conquerors were moved to treat them kindly. They became not slaves but colonists; they were allowed to preserve their own laws and customs, their distinctions of rank and family; they might even rise, as Daniel did, to high office in the state. Lastly, there was a conspicuous contrast between their fate and that of the nations round about Judah, who had exulted over the downfall of their hereditary foe, Edom, Ammon, and Moab. These also, before long, felt the heavy hand of Nebuchadnezzar, and it crushed them utterly. As Jeremiah had foretold even before the destruction of Jerusalem: " Fear thou not, O Jacob my servant, saith Jehovah, for I am with thee : for I will make a full end of all the nations whither I have driven thee : but I will not make a full end of thee, but correct thee according to justice; but I cannot leave thee wholly unpunished " (Jer. xlvi. 28).

These words of Jeremiah, and others like them, would be in the minds of the Jews when they saw the armies of Cyrus pouring through the streets of Babylon ; and it must have been with hope and pride that they noticed how, amidst all the changes of sovereigns, it was still a Jew who was foremost among the statesmen at their court. Under Nebuchadnezzar, Belshazzar, Darius the Mede, and Cyrus, Daniel is constantly prominent and always prosperous ; and we may confidently attribute it to his influence that one of the first acts of Cyrus, when he began to reign alone in Babylon (B.C. 536), was to issue a decree for the restoration of the Jews to their native land, and for the rebuilding of the temple.

THE RETURN FROM CAPTIVITY.

It is remarkable that the author of the Book of Ezra makes no mention of Daniel in connexion with the decree of Cyrus for the restoration of the Jewish nation and temple; he simply says, " that the word of the Lord by the mouth of Jeremiah might be fulfilled." The decree states that God had charged Cyrus to build Him an house at Jerusalem, which implies a knowledge of the prophecy of Isaiah (xliv. 28) ; and no one is more likely than Daniel to have told Cyrus of the prediction. Moreover, the parenthetical " He is the God " (Ezra i. 3) recalls Dan. vi. 26.

It shows how well they had been treated in the land of their exile that only about 50,000 were found willing to avail themselves of the offer. The bulk preferred to remain in their new homes. Of these, some followed later ; the rest formed the

Babylonian branch of " the Dispersion," a very numerous branch, as the Book of Esther shows. Just as the whole nation had emerged from its first captivity in Egypt laden with the silver and gold of their panic-stricken taskmasters, so now this remnant goes forth from their second captivity, strengthened with the gifts not only of their brethren who remained behind, but of the heathen population also. Perhaps those who declined to leave their comfortable settlements for the chance of returning to the ruined Jerusalem eased their consciences by contributing to help those who were more willing to make sacrifices for Zion and for the glory of Jehovah.

With what thoughts did Zerubbabel and this band of exiles recross the Jordan on the way to regain their desolated homes! We have no record of the journey; but at this point the imagination would gladly picture something of the scene. The place, the crossing, the name of the high-priest who accompanied them, could scarcely fail to remind them of that first triumphant crossing under Joshua 900 years before. This wreck of the nation was standing just where their ancestors had stood before them: but with how different a past, with how different prospects! *Then* Israel had been triumphantly wrested out of the hands of tyrannical oppressors; had vanquished all who came in contact with them in their long journey from Egypt, so that all the surrounding nations trembled at their approach; had before them the Promised Land flowing with milk and honey. *Now* the remnant of a few tribes had been condescendingly allowed to depart out of the land of their half-pitying, half-contemptuous masters; had passed unopposed through the intervening populations; and now stood on the threshold of their own home in fear and dread lest any of the surrounding nations should forbid them to enter it. Before long their fears were realised. No sooner had they begun to rebuild the temple than the Samaritans asked to take part in the work. To have allowed this would have been to risk the purity of the religion, for polluting which they had already suffered such punishment; and Zerubbabel and Jeshua refused. By machinations at the Persian court the Samaritans succeeded in discrediting the Jews, and the work was stopped by order of " Artaxerxes," who is possibly Gomates, otherwise known as Pseudo-Smerdis in profane history.

Once more we see how readily men acquiesce in a bad state of things so long as their own personal comfort is not at stake. We have just seen how the bulk of the exiles were content to remain with maimed rites and ceremonies, cut off from Mount Zion and the worship of the temple, cut off from the Land of Promise, with all its sacred associations, in a heathen land, where they lived on sufferance at the mercy of an idolatrous sovereign; and all because they had obtained comfortable settlements, which they did not care to sacrifice. Now we find that those who rose above that temptation are in danger of falling victims to a similar snare in the home which they have recovered. The prophet Haggai rebukes them in the sternest language for their readiness to leave God's house desolate if only their own houses were built and properly adorned. "Is it time for you to dwell in your inlaid houses, and this house lie waste?" "Mine house is laid waste, and ye run every man for his own house" (ch. i. 4, 9). Thus, under the constant exhortation of Haggai and Zechariah, the work went on; and the second temple was finished in the sixth year of Darius, 21 years after its commencement, and about 70 years after the destruction of its predecessor. At the dedication offerings were made for *all twelve tribes;* those who had returned being considered the representatives of all Israel. Here again we notice a mournful contrast with the glories of the past. The new temple had less lofty dimensions and was far less magnificently adorned. It had no Shechinah. Of the 24 orders of priests only four were there to conduct the services. And compare the 712 animals offered at this dedication with the thousands sacrificed by Solomon!

It is here, probably, that we may insert the episode contained in the *Book of Esther*, the most purely historical Book in the whole Bible. Of course it may be used to point a moral—whether that "blood is thicker than water," or that "pride goes before a fall:" but the main purpose of the book is simply to give an historical account of the origin of the feast of Purim. That the author has no religious object in view may be inferred from the fact that God is not even mentioned; nor is there any allusion to His worship, or the temple, or Jerusalem. The absence of these is a guarantee for the truth of the narrative. Had the whole been a fiction for the glorification of Esther, or Mordecai, or the Jews, the author would scarcely have omitted to give us some reflections on the providential character of the whole. As it is, the story is left to speak for itself. Only once, and then quite incidentally, the spirit of the author appears; and it is wholly in accordance with the spirit of Scripture generally: " Who knoweth whether thou art come to the kingdom for such a time as this? " (ch. iv. 14.) Just as the Book of Judges teaches us that God often selects very faulty and imperfect men to be His special instruments, that He can work with a Samson or a Jephthah no less than with a Moses or a Daniel, so the Book of Esther teaches us that in the ordinary careers of individuals and of nations, in which no miraculous element is present, no supernatural direction visible, it is still God's hand that combines, His providence that guides, the endless complexities of human life. We call it chance that the king could not sleep, that he preferred reading to wine or music, that he asked for the chronicles rather than poetry, that the reader came upon the account of Mordecai's services, that Haman entered the court at that moment, and that the king heard him, &c. But chance is only the name under which we hide our ignorance of causes, or our indifference towards them: and in all these " chances " Jew and Christian alike will trace the directing hand of God. The senseless caprices and fitful passions of Xerxes may work His will no less surely than the conscious and willing service of Joshua or Samuel. The burning bush and the dry or dripping fleece may be granted to Moses and to Gideon: but although we have them not, it may still be true of each one of us in the place to which we have been called, that we " have come to it for such a time as this." And if it be so with men's work and duty, so also is it with God's blessing and protection. Though there is no drying up of the Red Sea or of Jordan, no falling down of the walls of Jericho, yet evil does not therefore prevail. He who by miracles delivered His people from Egyptians and Canaanites can without miracles deliver them from Haman.

We return from this episode respecting the Jews of the Dispersion in Persia to those who had returned to Judæa. Their children had not kept up to the moral level of the devoted band who had left their prosperous settlements to rebuild Jerusalem. True, that the old fatal plague of idolatry was utterly eradicated, and a deep reverence for the law had taken its place; but the first enthusiasm of the return had passed away. Zerubbabel's descendants and the house of David had sunk into obscurity; the change of language from the old Hebrew to the Chaldee caused the bulk of the people to be strangely ignorant of the Law: many abuses crept in; marriages with the heathen, usury, neglect of the sabbath, and the like. When Ezra, under the favourable rule of Artaxerxes Longimanus, Xerxes' successor on the Persian throne, led a fresh caravan of returning exiles to Jerusalem, he found much work necessary in the way of reformation. This was specially the case with regard to marriages with the heathen, by which the pure descent not merely of the nation but even of the priests was being contaminated. We could hardly have a stronger proof of the change wrought by the Captivity, in turning the people from love of foreign idolatry to devotion to their own law, than the fact that they consented to snap the strong ties of wedlock and fatherhood, when they became convinced that the law required it of them.

We need not suppose that the decree of Cyrus allowing the Jews to return and rebuild the temple and Jerusalem was an act of wholly unmixed generosity. There was probably something of Persian statecraft in it; viz., the wish to place a nation bound by ties of gratitude to Persia, for delivering them from Babylon and letting them go free, on the dangerous frontier that looked towards Egypt. At any rate, the generosity of the Persian kings had thus far been limited by their jealousy of possible rivals or rebels; and they had hitherto not allowed the Jews to rebuild the walls of a place strategically so strong as Jerusalem. The fortifications and gates of the city were still in the same ruined state to which they had been reduced by the armies of Nebuchadnezzar. Consequently the Jews lived in constant dread of falling victims to the avarice, or jealousy, or animosity of their neighbours. A deputation was sent to the Persian court, where Nehemiah, a Jew holding high office among the great king's personal attendants, became their spokesman. Here again, as in the history of Esther, we may trace the workings of Providence in the political history of the world. Previous events had contributed not a little to predispose Artaxerxes to listen to Nehemiah's trembling request. The Persian empire had just received heavy blows from the Athenian admiral, Cimon. His victories, especially the last, in the midst of which he died, compelled Persia to abandon all attempts at aggression and to adopt a defensive position. She bound herself not to allow her armies to approach within three days' march of the sea. Jerusalem, being just about this distance, became a military position of the highest importance: and as risk must be run somewhere, it was better to allow Persian vassals under a native officer of tried fidelity to fortify it than to risk its falling into the hands of the enemies of Persia. Hence the secrecy with which Nehemiah acts, not only in the interests of the Jews but of the Persians. However, in spite of the active opposition of the Ammonites, Arabs, and Samaritans, the fortification of Jerusalem was successfully completed. And then Nehemiah, like Ezra, had to direct his attention to internal reforms. Abuses of the grossest kind, especially in the way of cruel oppression of the poor by the rich, had again crept in. By example and sharp exhortation Nehemiah rectified this, and, in conjunction with Ezra, renewed the often forgotten covenant between the people and Jehovah; after which he returned to the Persian court (c. B.C. 433).

It must have made this self-denying and generous statesman indeed sick at heart to find on his return to Jerusalem, after some years of absence, that he had all this miserable work to do over again. The solemn covenant had been forgotten as soon as his back was turned. The high-priest himself had profaned the temple; the sabbath was systematically violated; and mixed marriages had again taken place, the grandson of the high-priest being one of the offenders. It is in the midst of the reformation of these evils that we lose sight of Nehemiah. His concluding prayer has been heard; he has been " remembered for good " (ch. xiii. 31, 14). His good deeds have not been wiped out, but are preserved in the canon of Scripture for a memorial and an example for ever.

Here the historical books of the Old Testament come to an end. The figures which fill the narratives contained in them have passed before us in their marvellous variety of office and character, of greatness and littleness, of virtue and vice; commanders and judges, priests and prophets, warriors and poets, kings and subjects. But their doings have been presented to us not for their own sake, but as indications of the working of those great principles upon which the moral government of the world in general, and more especially God's dealing with His Chosen People, depends. We have seen that every great crisis in the life of the children of Israel has turned mainly on this one point of supreme importance—the relation existing between the nation and its invisible King. Other factors have had great power—the relations between the people and its rulers, between the rulers and the prophets, between tribe and tribe. But the main importance of all these has lain in the influence which they have exerted on the chief question of all—the attitude of the whole people towards Jehovah. Great men influence critical conjunctures, but they do not create them. It would be more true to say that the conjunctures create the great men; at any rate, they give such men an opportunity of proving their greatness. Their influence is of the most diverse kind. Sometimes, like Jeroboam or Jehu, they may precipitate a crisis; sometimes, like Hezekiah and Josiah, they may retard it. The greatest, such as Samuel and David, strive to guide the nation through the critical period. Of others it may at least be said that they have " come to the kingdom for such a time as this; " and of none perhaps may this be affirmed with more certainty than of the two leaders who stand, the one at the opening and the other at the close of our period—Joshua and Nehemiah. But whatever be the influence of such leaders, it is not with them that the student of sacred history has principally to deal, but with principles and institutions. The leaders, great or small, obtain significance mainly as illustrating the principles and working the institutions. Neither the principles nor the institutions were perfect, but progressive; they pointed to something nobler in the future, for which they were preparing the way. In their origin they were manifestly Divine; for (1) they were frequently authenticated and sanctioned by exhibitions of miraculous power; (2) they were immeasurably superior to those of other nations, who in culture and material civilisation stood on a much higher level. But although Divine, they were socially, morally, and spiritually imperfect. It is of the utmost importance to recognise this fact and keep it constantly in view. Without it the history of the Chosen People is worse than unintelligible; and what ought to be a pillar of fire to give light by night becomes a cloud and darkness. Life is full of mysteries, which we shall never explain on this side of the grave: while they awe and sober us, they need not confuse us. But let us beware of adding to them by enigmas and perplexities of our own making: and to refuse to acknowledge that the Almighty and Omniscient Ruler of the universe works out His purposes by means which, though relatively good, in themselves are imperfect and even evil, is to make not only the historical part of Scripture, but all history whatsoever, a hopeless riddle. Nothing is gained by foisting upon Divine institutions a perfection which does not belong to them; this is not humbly to honour God, but ignorantly to flatter Him. What would be miserable fare, or even slow poison, to a healthy man, may be the best diet for a sickly child; and this applies to moral laws no less than to doctrine. God could, if it had pleased Him, have antedated Pentecost by fifteen hundred years, and have revealed to Moses what He revealed to St. John; just as He might at any moment restore the whole human race to Paradise with a word. But this would be to destroy the educational progress of mankind, or, in other words, to eliminate the moral element from history.

Study of the past is generally our best, sometimes our only, guide to understanding and using the present. But the study must be reverent and patient, or it will be misleading. The question is not what God *must* do (according to our preconceived notions), but what He *does ;* and "His thoughts are not as our thoughts, nor His ways as our ways." Bearing this in mind, we shall find much comfort and guidance in dealing with the difficulties which confront Christians and Churchmen in our own day by studying those which beset the chosen people and the chosen tribe three thousand years ago. This much at least has been demonstrated by all the experience of Israel—that belief in a Personal God, who has given men a law to live by, and to whom they must give account, is of all influences that have ever been tried, the only one that can tame and ennoble the fallen nature of man. In spite of the hopeless failure of Solomon, and the ruin of Israel and Judah, we are again being told that culture may be made a substitute for conscience, and that responsibility has no higher meaning than self-respect. In spite of the indelible stigma which Scripture has written as the epitaph of Jeroboam, " who made Israel to sin," and the steady degradation of the kings and the kingdom of Israel, we are still assured that schism is a valuable expression of liberty, and that unity of doctrine and of worship means tyranny or narrowness of mind. There are errors in quite another direction also, for which the historical books of the Old Testament contain a cure. There are Christians who are staggered at the slow progress which the Gospel has made after eighteen centuries of preaching, at the slow progress which, with all its enormous advantages, it continues to make still. Were the prospects of truth, especially when seen in the light of the past, more hopeful, when Jeremiah uttered his solemn protests in Egypt, or Ezekiel his unflinching rebukes in the land of the Chaldæans? The Divine light, instead of spreading, however slowly, seemed on the eve of being utterly extinguished. And yet, all the while, the road for the Gospel was being surely though darkly prepared. Again, there are Churchmen who are chafed and irritated, even if they are not utterly perplexed, at finding the Church as it now exists so wofully unlike the ideal which they find in Scripture, or which they have constructed for themselves. Some men in their uneasiness shift from one branch of the Church to another, often with the result of finding their disquietude increased rather than allayed : others, in despair, go out of their own communion and enter no other ; so intolerable do external interferences or internal scandals appear to them, so incompatible with their idea of a true Church. When we are disposed to think " the tyranny of the state," whether it comes from " secular courts," or from a " non-Christian parliament," to be fatal to the very existence of a church, let us think of Manasseh's infamous persecution, and be patient. Perhaps there never has been an age when the Church, whether Jewish or Christian, has not had much to bear from the powers that be. And why should she not? Why should she in this fare better than her Divine Head? And why should this age claim to be exempt? Again, when some grievous scandal, whether of simony or sacrilege, or false doctrine openly taught, makes men inquire whether a communion in which such things are possible can be a branch of the Church at all, let us remember the idolatrous erections of Solomon, tolerated within sight of the temple for four hundred years, and again be patient. But just as there are persons who take pride in making out that their own particular maladies or troubles are in excess of those of their neighbours, so each generation flatters itself that it is passing through a great crisis, and that society, or religion, or the Church, was never in such peril before. It is never our duty, of course, to blind ourselves as to the existence of evil; but there are cases in which to ignore evil is less disastrous than to exaggerate it. The one need not interfere with the accomplishment of a great deal of good; the other by causing a panic is almost certain to do so. "In quietness and in confidence shall be your strength."

At the close of this historical section of the Pulpit Commentary it may perhaps be permitted to offer a suggestion for the consideration of preachers. It is in the historical portion of Holy Scripture that the most generally useful material for the preacher's purpose may be found: yet on the whole it is very much neglected, greatly to the loss of congregations; especially of uneducated congregations. There are many who cannot understand—or, if they understand, take but a languid interest in—abstract theology, or abstract morality, who yet will listen with intelligence and eagerness when the doctrine or the morality are clothed in flesh and blood. The variety of character and incident given us in Holy Scripture is practically unlimited; and there is perhaps scarcely a doctrinal truth or ethical precept that could not be illustrated from some event or biography in the sacred narrative. The example of Scripture itself would seem to give us a guide in this matter: the historical element greatly predominates over the didactic in the Old Testament and somewhat predominates in the New. Or, to take higher ground still, that which is given us in the Gospel for our instruction and guidance is not so much a code, or a creed, as a *life;* a life involving both definite rules and definite beliefs, no doubt; but still it is the *pattern life* that comes first. "Though ye believe not Me, believe *the works*" (John x. 38): that is the first step. And the second is on the same ground: "Believe Me for the very *works'* sake" (ch. xiv. 11). It is with what Christ *does*, that is, with His *life*, that we must begin. And this applies in a lower degree to all the lives that are set before us in Scripture for instruction and warning. It is but an illustration of the well-worn saying, that "example is better than precept." People can comprehend and will listen to the encouragements and cautions to be derived from the doings and sufferings of men and women like themselves, who would carry nothing away from eloquent dissertations on virtue and vice. The command, "Go, and do thou likewise," the home-thrust, "Thou art the man," will go direct to the heart in many a case in which the Decalogue, or any part of it, would never pass beyond the ear.

The following tables, drawn from the portion of the Old Testament which we have been considering, will illustrate the suggestion just made. They could be greatly enlarged even within the limits of this portion of Scripture. Of course, if the whole of the sacred history were placed under contribution, the illustrations might be increased and improved to a very large extent. But a stronger case is made out by showing how much may be done with no more than the section of the Bible immediately before us.

THE DIVINE ATTRIBUTES.

Power. . . . . . $\left\{\begin{array}{l}\text{The cutting off of Jordan.} \\ \text{The walls of Jericho.} \\ \text{The destruction of Sennacherib's army.}\end{array}\right.$

Mercy. . . . . . $\left\{\begin{array}{l}\text{The forgiveness of David.} \\ \text{The respite granted to Ahab.} \\ \text{The sparing of Nineveh.}\end{array}\right.$

Justice . . . .
- The punishment of David's sins.
- The miserable ends of the disobedient prophet, of Jezebel, and of every dynasty in the kingdom of Israel.
- The different fates of the kingdom of Israel and the kingdom of Judah.

Longsuffering
- The whole period of the Judges.
- The many opportunities granted to Saul.
- The many opportunities granted to the kingdoms of Israel and Judah.

Truth. . . . .
- The covenant kept with David.
- The fulfilment of prophetical warnings and blessings.

THE TEN COMMANDMENTS.

First. Elijah and the prophets of Baal.

Second. Jeroboam and the worship of the calves.

Third
- Saul's sacrifice.
- Saul's ill-advised adjuration.
- Saul's inquiring of the Lord by a witch.

Fourth. Nehemiah and the sabbath-breakers.

Fifth. Ruth's filial piety. Absalom's rebellion.

Sixth. The cruel vengeance of Joab and of Jehu.

Seventh. Bathsheba.

Eighth. Micah robbing his mother, and robbed by the Danites.

Ninth. Ziba and Mephibosheth. Jezebel and Naboth.

Tenth. Achan. Gehazi.

THE THREE THEOLOGICAL VIRTUES.

Faith. The widow of Zarephath.

Hope. Hannah.

Charity. Rizpah, the daughter of Aiah.

THE FOUR CARDINAL VIRTUES.

Justice. Solomon's early administration.

Prudence. David at the court of Saul.

Temperance. Josiah. The Rechabites.

Fortitude. Deborah. Esther.

THE SEVEN DEADLY SINS.

Pride. Nebuchadnezzar. Haman.

Covetousness. Ahab and Naboth's vineyard.

Lust. The men of Gibeah. Samson. Amnon.

Envy. Saul and David. Haman and Mordecai.

Gluttony. Hophni and Phinehas.

Anger. Saul and the priests.

Sloth. Eli. Joash and the arrows.

It would not be difficult, especially if the Pentateuch and New Testament were added, to illustrate in this way the Creed, the Lord's Prayer, and the Sermon on the Mount.

THE BOOK OF JOSHUA

INTRODUCTION

§ 1. Origin and Date of the Book of Joshua.

Except, perhaps, the Book of Daniel, there are no parts of Holy Scripture concerning the date and authorship of which so lively a controversy has raged as the first six books of the Old Testament. To mention all the various theories that have been advanced would be impossible. We will give a brief sketch of some of the most noticeable, and then proceed to examine more in detail the arguments which have been advanced to support them.

1. There is the view that the book is a contemporary document. This is the early Jewish tradition. The Talmud states that it was written by Joshua himself; that Eleazar wrote the account of Joshua's death, and that Phinehas added the verses containing the narrative of the death of Eleazar.* This view has been maintained, among later authors, by the learned Hävernick, at least in its main features; for he holds that the first part of the book, up to ch. xii., and the last chapters, were written by Joshua, the passage relating to the deaths of Joshua and Eleazar having, of course, been added by a later hand.

2. Keil and others regard it as a treatise of somewhat later date than the time of Joshua, composed about twenty-five or thirty years after his death.

3. Ewald's theory is a very elaborate one. He regards the book as a composition of the Deuteronomist in the time of Manasseh. This conclusion he bases on the very slight foundation that there is an allusion in Deut. xxviii. 68 to the condition of Judæa in the time of Manasseh, or even later. This argument, again, rests upon the assumption that prophecy is

---

* We read in the Babylonian Talmud (Nedarim, fol. 22 в), that had the Israelites not transgressed the law they would have needed no other canonical books than the Pentateuch, to which the Book of Joshua must be added, because it contains the account of the settlement of the tribes in the Land of Promise. In the same Talmud (Baba Bathra, 15 a), we are told that Joshua wrote the book which goes by his name, as well as the last eight verses of Deuteronomy (see note on ch. i. 1).

impossible, a postulate which many will be indisposed to grant. But his method is, as he states, "scientific," which seems to mean that he takes everything for granted which is necessary to establish his theory. The many indications of earlier origin and authorship he quietly disposes of by assuming that they were portions of some earlier work, imbedded precisely as they stood in the mass of fiction which the writer of later times has evolved from his own moral consciousness. Not only so, but scientific criticism, he believes, can disintegrate these fragments with unfailing accuracy, and assign them to their proper owner. There are thus, he holds, (1) a few fragments of contemporary works inserted *verbatim* in the midst of the mass of later history or tradition. These consist (*a*) of a book quoted by name in Num. xxi. 14, " The Book of the Wars of Jahveh," or Jehovah ; (*b*) the Biography of Moses ; and (*c*) the Book of Covenants, from which all the legal or quasi-legal matter is derived ; written, as he says, in an age of confusion, when men tried to secure themselves by covenants with their neighbours. Then (2) about the time of David comes the great Book of Origins (Tol'doth—the use of this word frequently marking the extracts from the book). Lastly (3) we have the prophetic narratives, written by the prophets subsequently to David's time. Among these we have a *third, fourth,* and *fifth* narrator, and finally, the Deuteronomist of a time later than the reign of Manasseh, who reduced the whole into shape,* not by re-writing the whole from the materials before him, but by inserting bodily into his compilation passages from older authors, and adding his own generally fictitious narrative, composed with a view of imposing the author's own view of the law of Moses upon a corrupt and decaying people.

4. Ewald has found various imitators, among whom the principal is Knobel. Adopting De Wette's view of the discrepancies in the text of the Pentateuch and Joshua, and Ewald's general method of explaining it, Knobel nevertheless proposes a different arrangement of the original materials from which the supposed mosaic of the Pentateuch and Joshua is made up. Knobel, like Ewald, also finds it possible to assign each of the various extracts of which the Pentateuch and Joshua are made up to their respective authors. But he has not only discovered by his analysis different authors to Ewald, but he assigns different portions to them. Ewald's system he pronounces " so complicated and obscure a fabric," so devoid of all tenable hypotheses, that it fails to convince (p. 496) ; while he complains that critics like Hengstenberg and Hävernick and Keil, because they do not accept his methods, " convert a scientific inquiry into a theo-

* Or rather, out of shape ; for the whole narrative in its present condition, we are told, teems with the most obvious blunders and inaccuracies, while its style would resemble an English history made up of extracts from Robert of Gloucester, Mandeville, Wiclif, Lord Herbert, Hume, and Macaulay.

logical controversy." Therefore he plays the part of Tycho Brahe to Ewald's Ptolemy, and invents a theory which renders a few of the latter's epicycles unnecessary. Thus there is (1) an Elohistic document, clear, orderly, and historical, free from the marvellous occurrences in which the later works abound, which constitutes the groundwork of the whole narrative. Then follows (2) a Book of Laws or first Jehovistic source. Then (3) the Book of Wars, or second Jehovistic source. Then we have (4) the Jehovist himself. Lastly (5) the Deuteronomist appears, to whom all Deuteronomy, with the exception of certain specified portions, and all the parts of Joshua which refer to Deuteronomy belong.

5. Nöldeke subjects Knobel to a similar simplifying process to that which Knobel subjects Ewald. According to Nöldeke, there are two sources ; (1) an outline history (Elohistic), and (2) a history filling up that outline ; composed (a) by the second Elohist, and (b) by the Jehovist. Lastly, we have two editors. The first combined these into a consistent whole. The second added Deuteronomy and remodelled Joshua, bringing it into accordance with his fictitious additions to the Mosaic narrative.

6. Bleek feels himself compelled to still further reduce the number of histories, and thereby approaches nearer to a consistent and rational explanation of the facts. Documents existed, he believes, at an earlier period. But the first author, whom he calls the first Elohist, appeared at the time of Saul, and his history contains the greater part of Joshua. In the time of David appeared the Jehovist, who revised and re-wrote, with the aid of earlier documents then existing, the greater portion of the Elohist. Lastly, at the time of Manasseh, or thereabouts, arose the Deuteronomist, who reduced the book into its present shape.

Such is an abstract of some of the chief theories which have been put forward regarding the authorship of Joshua. It is needless to say that the opponents of the authenticity and single authorship claim for their methods the exclusive title of scientific investigation. Ewald, with lofty infallibility, places Hengstenberg, Keil, Delitzsch, Kurz " outside of all science." But those who adopt his method, and venture only to question its application, fare scarcely more favourably at his hands. Thus, when he commences his researches, he examines what has been before written in the direction in which his predilections lead him. He finds that Ilgen takes a step on the right road, but always loses it again. " There was," he complains, " much perversity of attempt and aim mingled with" the otherwise praiseworthy attempts of these early investigators. They " were too easily satisfied with hunting out mere contradictions in the books and resolving everything into fragments," and were " unable to distinguish a real incongruity from a merely apparent discrepancy" (p. 61). Nor do his successors in the investigation please him any more than the pioneers who preceded him. Hupfeld and Knobel, we learn from a note to a later addition, are "unsatisfactory and perverse." We have already seen what Knobel's opinion of Ewald is. It may, therefore, not be entirely unscientific if we venture to suspend our judgment, and examine the facts anew, with the desire to arrive at a satisfactory conclusion.

For first of all it may be remarked that the conclusions of writers like Ewald, Knobel, and Nöldeke are extremely improbable in themselves, and would require very clear and cogent evidence before a truly scientific mind could be induced to adopt them. We are required to believe that in a nation which had early reached a high degree of civilisation, which in the days of Solomon had added to that civilisation a considerable amount of material prosperity,* which even in its decline maintained no small amount of intercourse with the great nations around it (see, for instance, 2 Kings xx. 12), which still possessed great wealth and resources (Isa. ii. 7 ; iii. 18—23 ; vii. 23), a historical document came into existence which at once obtained credit, and superseded the regular chronicles which, we are repeatedly assured, were regularly kept in those days. This document was made up of disconnected fragments of earlier compositions of various dates, and thrown together without the slightest attempt to fuse together differences of style, or to harmonise the most glaring contradictions. So badly was the work done that it is possible, after a lapse of 2,500 years, to disintegrate the whole and to assign the various fragments, with an accuracy beyond dispute, to their respective authors. Yet neither the patchwork character of the history, nor its frequent and palpable contradictions, were able, in an age of some pretensions to cultivation, to hinder its immediate reception as authentic and even inspired history. All this is necessary to the theory ; and we have also to explain the very remarkable historical and psychological fact that the law, to which the Jews have for centuries cherished so profound and even passionate attachment, and for the neglect of which they conceive their banishment from their own land to be owing, never, according to this theory, existed at all, but was the invention of the priests in the hour of national degradation, to account for the miseries suffered by the people, and that this fable was greedily swallowed, and has ever since been most firmly believed among them. Surely so unique a fact in the world's history ought to be established on better evidence than this.

The industry and research which has been expended upon the task of establishing these theories is beyond all praise. Knobel, especially, has devoted the most minute attention to the words and phrases of the Hebrew Scriptures. But the objection is made, not to the utmost possible minute-

---

* Pax alma et commercium dona sua ubique largiebantur. Inter tot humanitatis et opulentiæ emolumenta procul dubio litteræ et poesis non sordebant. (Donaldson, 'Jashar,' p. 25.)

ness of study of the phrases of Holy Writ, but to the method pursued by the observers. In minuteness of observation the German critics have been anticipated and surpassed by the Rabbis, in whose hands this minute observation yields results in precisely the opposite direction. It is not mere minute observation, but the use that is made of it, which is required. And this so-called " scientific " criticism is carried on by methods diametrically opposite to all which science has hitherto recognised. For if there be one principle better established in science than another, it is that in scientific processes nothing must be taken for granted but the most self-evident truths.

Now the " scientific" critics of the Old Testament proceed upon two assumptions which can by no means be regarded as self-evident truths. First, they assume that there is no such thing as the supernatural in revelation, that all prophecies were written after the event, and all miracles are the result of legends gradually gathering round the facts of history in later ages. And next, they assume that it is possible, on purely subjective grounds, to determine without risk of error the authors of the respective fragments of which the Hebrew Scriptures are composed. But it may be observed, in reference to this second point, that in no two hands do the same premises yield the same results, a fact which in any other branch of science would lead us to suspect the accuracy either of the data or of the method. As to the method itself, when we find Knobel assigning, for instance, without the smallest doubt or hesitation, a passage in which בַּעֲבוּר occurs to one author, בִּגְלַל to another, and עַל־אֹדֹת to a third, we are naturally driven to ask what would be the result if a similar process were applied to an English author who uses indifferently the phrases *on account of*, *because of*, *by reason of*, and the like. Again, in science it is usual, when a law is believed to be established by a sufficiently wide induction, to reverse the process, assume the truth of the law, apply it to known facts, and see if the results correspond to observation.* Have the so-called " scientific " critics of the Old Testament done this ? Will their methods enable us to analyse historians like Motley or Macaulay, and to assign without fail the various portions of their history to the sources from which they have avowedly obtained them ? Is there any method in existence which will enable us, without risk of error, to assign to Shakspere and his contemporaries the various portions of the works known to have been written by them in common ? And if no method has been discovered which

---

* Whewell, 'Philosophy of the Inductive Sciences,' ii. 440. This was Newton's method. Bacon, in the first book of his ' Novum Organum,' speaks of science ascending " continuously and by degrees " to the discovery of general laws. The brief abstract given above of German criticism on the Hebrew Scriptures, shows that what has been called scientific criticism has had to recede " continuously and by degrees " from the hasty generalisations to which it at first committed itself.

will enable us to do this in the case of authors whose works we know, and who wrote in a language we are daily using, how shall such a method be infallible when applied to records written thousands of years ago, in a dead language, and when a million helps to the right understanding of the history have irrecoverably perished?

It must be confessed that these "scientific" theories, if not sound, are extremely ingenious. It is very difficult to reply conclusively to a critic who has a theory ready made to meet every emergency. Thus, if the author of the Book of Joshua displays an accurate and minute acquaintance with his subject, he is quoting an early and authentic document. If he states anything which is not at first sight easily reconcileable with what he has stated elsewhere, he has taken it out of another less early and less authentic one. If he quotes the Book of Deuteronomy, which according to all the laws of literary criticism proves it to have been in existence when he wrote, he was himself the author of it, and was engaged in the task of mingling its contents with real and veracious history. If a 'Book of the Wars of Jahveh' is quoted, as in Num. xxi. 14, 15, it is an older document. If a 'Book of the Law of Jahveh,' he wrote it himself. This is not to inquire, it is to make inquiry impossible. It is to substitute dogma, the dogma of the destructive school, in the place of the dogma they have so persistently decried, which assumes that the books of Scripture, as a rule, were written by the persons whose names they bore. Is the one dogma one whit more scientific than the other?

The authenticity of the Book of Deuteronomy is a question on which we are of course precluded from entering. But the question of the hand the Deuteronomist had in the compilation of the Book of Joshua is one which falls within our limits. There is not the slightest evidence in the book itself to lead to the conclusion that it was a production of the time of Manasseh, a conclusion which the opponents of the genuineness of Deuteronomy have based upon the very slender foundation of the prophecy in ch. xxviii. 68. If, as is assumed, the Deuteronomist embodied the references to his own work into the Book of Joshua, in order to facilitate the reception of his pretended laws of Moses, the question forces itself irresistibly upon us, Why did he not introduce more of them? Why did he confine his extracts from the 'Book of the Laws of Jahveh' to the passage at the end of ch. viii., and a few exhortations to "be strong and of good courage," and the like, which is all we find elsewhere? These extracts are not enough for his purpose, were he introducing them for the purpose of gaining acceptance for the precepts he was desirous of enforcing.

We proceed briefly to notice some objections to the narrative of Joshua which meet us in the pages of Ewald, Dr. Davidson, and others. Ewald supposes Joshua to be the "ideal king" of the times of the Deuteronomist

('History of Israel,' i. 116). Now there is not one single trace of the kingly idea throughout the Book of Joshua. The severe simplicity of his life, the remarkable absence of anything like kingly claims (see especially ch. xix. 49, 50), is one of the most striking features of the book. As well could we suppose the characters of Brutus or Cincinnatus to have been ideals of civic virtue called up to animate dying Roman patriotism in the days of Elagabalus, as to suppose that the writer of the Book of Joshua had the Oriental type of king before his eyes, such as existed in Judæa and the neighbourhood in the reign of Manasseh.

Next, Ewald remarks on the archaic character of Josh. xvii. 14—18, which he describes as "rough and hard as a stone." Yet Knobel, who was no mean Hebraist, assigns the passage to the "first Jehovist." And if Ewald's view be right, the passage may easily be explained on the hypothesis that we have here the *ipsissima verba* of Joshua himself.

In the pages of Dr. Davidson's well-known work other objections will be found. They are open to the same reproach that we have already brought against the other productions of his school, namely, their unduly dogmatic tone. And this is adopted, not merely towards those of an opposite school, but to his own allies. Thus (i. 424) he complains that Knobel "has un-warrantably robbed the Deuteronomist of his due," a statement which we are apparently to take on Dr. Davidson's authority, since he vouchsafes no proof of it. But to proceed with his objections to the authenticity of the Book of Joshua as it stands, he tells us that the narrative at the end of ch. viii. has got into the wrong place, and triumphantly asks, How, then, can the genuineness of the book be maintained? as if such a supposition as an error of the copyist were quite out of the question. A similar use is made of the discrepancy in numbers between ch. viii. 3 and ch. viii. 12, as though here again (see notes on the passage) a slip of the pen in very early times might not have caused all the confusion. Then we are told that the Levites in the historical portion of the book are called "the priests, the Levites," while in the geographical they are called "sons of Aaron," and that the former is a Deuteronomistic, the latter an Elohistic expression, as though the expression "sons of Aaron" in ch. xxii. were not clearly opposed to "sons of Kohath, Gershom, and Merari." Ch. vi. 26 contains, on the sup-position of the early date of Joshua, the record of a prophecy fulfilled long afterwards. It is assumed that the prophecy was invented after its sup-posed fulfilment. Yet, unless the writer of the book were a deliberate im-postor, endeavouring to palm off his work as one of an earlier date—a rather strong supposition—is it conceivable that he would have avoided all mention of the fulfilment of the prophecy in this place? Again, we are told that the twelve stones could never have been placed in the middle of the Jordan. Ordinary attention to the words of the passage (see notes on ch. iv. 9)

would show that they never were said to have been placed in the middle of
Jordan, at least as we understand the words. The etymology of the word
Gilgal, again, presents some difficulties (see note on ch. v. 9). But it is
surely cutting the Gordian knot in a very summary manner to assume that
this etymology was invented at the time of Manasseh. The placing the
tabernacle at Shechem is, we are told, another instance of inaccuracy. But
without resorting to the hypothesis of a copyist's blunder again here, though
it is less violent than Dr. Davidson's, is it quite inadmissible to adopt the
explanation that the author was narrating facts, and did not stop to consider what difficulties his simple narrative might present to those who, many
centuries after, were not in full possession of the details? Is not this far
more probable than the theory that the redactor, or inventor, or by whatever
name he be called, had quite forgotten, or never observed, what he had
stated six chapters previously? Are we to believe that the compiler of the
time of Manasseh never took the trouble to read over his own work, or that
no one in his own day was likely to ask the questions which occur at once
to every reader now? The Shoterim, again, we are told (see note on ch. i.
10), were an institution of later date, and their place in Joshua's time was
supplied by the fathers and heads of the tribes. No proof of this assertion
is given. But is it credible that a vast invasion, in which their wives and
families accompanied the warriors, can have been conducted without a considerable organisation, or that the Israelites could have lived in a civilised
country like Egypt without being familiar with that principle of division
and subdivision of labour without which no great undertaking can possibly
be carried out? Then we are asked to observe the discrepancies between
ch. xi. 16—23 and ch. xiii. 1—6; between chs. x. 36, 38; xi. 21; xv. 14—17,
and Judg. i. 10, 11; and between chs. xv. 63; xvi. 10, and 1 Kings ix. 16.
These questions will be found fully discussed in the notes. The only question
which will be asked here is this. We have supposed that the later, or geographical, portion of the book is the expansion of the passage in ch. xi. 23,
which concludes the historical portion. But if this explanation be not
accepted, how comes it, we ask again, that such a bungling mass of contradictions could have been accepted in a civilised age like that of Manasseh,
when *ex hypothesi* a large body of literature was in existence? There were
the Chronicles, as we have seen, of the Kings of Israel and Judah. There
was, according to Knobel, the " clear and orderly " narrative of the Elohist.
The historian's calling, if we may trust Ewald, had become a special art
(' History of Israel,' i. 59) which " needed ability and dexterity " (ib.), and
the result is described as "elegant and perfect " (p. 60). The perfection of
a method which gives, as we are required to believe, three inconsistent
versions, from various sources, of the conquest of Hebron, Debir, and the
Anakim, which describes the country as completely subdued when the work

of subduing it had hardly begun, which displays so little literary skill as to copy out of an old record a statement (ch. xv. 63) which had ceased to be true for three centuries and a half, may seem a little doubtful. But if this be a mere question of taste, the more formidable difficulty remains behind, how such a narrative ever came to be received, in the later days of the Jewish kingdom, as authentic history.

It is not contended that no difficulties are presented by the history as it stands. What is denied is that what has been called the "destructive criticism" has found a way out of them. On the contrary, it involves us in far greater difficulties than it removes. When dealing with a narrative of such remote antiquity, which does not pretend to be an exhaustive record of everything that happened, it would be strange indeed if we did not find difficulties. And we must be content to leave them unsolved, for the simple reason that we have not sufficient information at hand to explain them. The theory that some of the passages that suggest a later date were interpolations is an arbitrary one. But it cannot therefore be dismissed, as is dismissed with lofty scorn by Ewald, as entirely untenable. It offers at least a possible solution of some of the difficulties that beset us. And it is by no means impossible that the greatest difficulty of all in the way of the earlier origin of the Book of Joshua, the citation of the Book of Jasher, may be thus explained. The most natural interpretation of 2 Sam. i. 18 would lead us to conclude that the Book of Jasher was not composed till the time of David. Therefore its citation in Joshua proves that book not to have been written earlier than the time of David, unless we believe the passage to have been an interpolation. The only other alternative is to adopt the explanation of Maurer and Keil, that the Book of Jasher was a collection of national songs, to which additions were made from time to time.*

We proceed to enumerate the reasons for believing that the Book of Joshua was composed at an early date. The first is, the entire absence of any allusion to the later condition of Israel in it. We have already noticed how entirely the idea of regal pomp or authority is absent from the whole conception of Joshua's character, and from the whole treatment of the subject. That it was written before the time of David seems clear from the statement (ch. xv. 63) that the Jebusites dwelt among the children of Israel "until this day." The mention of the place which Jehovah "should choose" implies, not only that the temple was not yet built, but that its site had not yet been fixed upon. The mention of the Gibeonites without any reference to Saul's neglect of the solemn promise made to them in God's name would lead to the belief that it was written before the time of Saul. We have a yet more distinct intimation of an early date in ch. xvi. 10. It could hardly

* See notes on ch. x. 12—15.

be said that the inhabitants of Gezer serve under tribute "unto this day" when Israel was groaning under Canaanitish oppression. Such language could hardly have been used, at least after the time of Othniel. Nor do the other occasions on which the words "unto this day" are used of necessity imply a very remote future.* Again, it is not denied that the author of the book, whoever he was, must have had access to authentic contemporary information. Is it probable that information of the precise, yet by no means minute, character that the book contains could have been drawn up in its present form four or five hundred years after the events recorded, when Israel and Judah had been long divided, when the former kingdom had been carried away captive, and when confusion and disorder reigned in the latter? The last half of the book points clearly to an earlier period, and, whether we admit occasional interpolations or not, must have existed at that early period in something very near its present form.

The style of the book strongly supports this conclusion. Even those who study it in a translation only cannot fail to be struck with one characteristic it has in common with the books of Moses. This is the peculiar habit the author has of repetition, which marks an age of great literary simplicity. We lose this feature to a very great extent in the later historical books. As greater polish of style was attained, the writer learned how to impart emphasis to his sentences by other means. This repetition is chiefly found in the earlier portion of the book, which, tried by this test, should be pronounced the older portion. But it may also be detected in the later.†

Verbal criticism is a more difficult task. Yet though we may safely take exception to the theory that it is possible by verbal criticism alone to resolve the Book of Joshua into its component parts, yet there is a whole class of phenomena which have been somewhat unjustly passed over by those who have devoted most time to a verbal analysis. No satisfactory attempt has been made to explain the fact that in the Pentateuch there is but one form for the masculine and feminine of the demonstrative pronoun הוא, and that the feminine form first presents itself in Joshua. A more interesting instance of the gradual development of the inflexions of a language can scarcely be found. In the Pentateuch, the archaic form אל (these) is often met with for אלה. This ancient form leaves us in Joshua. It may also be asked, if Joshua be a redaction of earlier documents by the hands of the Deuteronomist, why he always used ירחו for Jericho in the Pentateuch and the fuller form יריחו in Joshua? So we have ממלכת and קנא in the Pentateuch and ממלכות and קנוא in Joshua. הצית for "to kindle a fire," and

---

* Ch. iv. 9; vi. 25; vii. 26; viii. 28; ix. 27; xiv. 14.

† Cf. ch. xi. 17 with xii. 17; xiv. 13—15 with xv. 13, 14; ch. xxi. 43—45, and the threefold repetition concerning the inheritance of Levi.

צנח, " to alight," are not found in the books of Moses, nor is the term קצין for a prince or captain. Such phenomena as these cannot justly be left out of the account in a full investigation of the question of the authorship and date of this book. And their force is being silently recognised in Germany. Later writers, like Stähelin and Bleek, have been forced considerably to modify the violent theories of Ewald and Knobel, and the former, so Keil tells us, in the later editions of his work, has quietly dropped out much which he had embodied in the former. We may regard this as the earnest of a time rapidly approaching, when the advance of criticism in England shall have produced the same result among ourselves.*

But we are not without some nearer indications of authorship. The far greater familiarity displayed with the concerns of the tribe of Judah than any other indicates that the author was resident within the limits of that tribe. And not only so, but his acquaintance with the personal history of Caleb (ch. xiv. 13—15; xv. 13—19), and with the city of Hebron in particular (ch. xxi. 11—13), seems to mark him out as a resident there. But Hebron was one of the priestly cities. Combining this with the repeated mention of the fact that no inheritance was given to the tribe of Levi, we infer that the writer was himself a priest. He was not Phinehas himself, for we find by ch. xxiv. 33 that Phinehas dwelt in Mount Ephraim. But the writer may well have been intimately acquainted with him. He refers to the settlement of the Danites at Laish (ch. xix. 47), with the events resulting from which we know, from the last three or four chapters of the Book of Judges, Phinehas was largely mixed up.† His description of the scene between the tribes on the occasion of the erection of the altar bears evident tokens of the presence of an eyewitness. And such we know Phinehas was; and our author may have heard the story from his lips. Living at Hebron, the author would no doubt have been on terms of friendly intercourse with Othniel, and from him had heard the story of the allotment of the springs to Achsah.

On the whole, therefore, we conclude, as well from the arbitrary assumptions to which those are driven who assign the book to a later date, as from the internal evidence of the book itself, that it was written within forty or fifty years at the least of the death of Joshua; that its author was one of the priestly race; that he dwelt in the tribe of Judah, and most likely in the city of Hebron; that by his family connection with Phinehas, and his residence among the relatives of Caleb, he had the fullest opportunity of acquainting himself with the facts; and that we have therefore in this book

---

* For various indications of minute personal knowledge of the events described, which are hardly compatible with a later date, see notes on ch. ii. 14; ix. 10; x. 2, 4, 6, 18, 33.

† This alone, unless the passage be interpolated, disposes of the theory of Joshua's authorship.

an authentic account, by one every way qualified to write it, of the conquest and occupation by the Israelites of the Promised Land.

II. On Difficulties in the Book of Joshua.

The principal objections which have been made against the Divine inspiration of the Book of Joshua are of two kinds, moral and scientific. The first class of objections is raised against the slaughter of the Canaanites as inconsistent with the goodness and mercy we know to be attributes of the Divine Being. The second class take their stand on the inconsistency of miraculous parts of the history with the known laws of nature as revealed by science.

I. The moral objection admits of a very simple answer. How, it is asked, could the revolting and cruel command have been given by the God of love and mercy to Moses and Joshua, to massacre an unoffending population under circumstances of the grossest barbarity; involving aged men, weak women, and harmless children in the same slaughter with the warriors and leaders of the people ?

(1) We reply, in the same spirit as Bishop Butler, that, whatever objection applies to the God of Revelation on this ground applies equally to the God of Nature. If it be of any force at all, it proves that the Supreme Being is a cruel being.* For it is one of the most palpable facts of history that He has permitted such massacres to take place throughout the whole course of the world, from the beginning until our own time. And not only so, but massacres with wicked refinements of cruelty which cannot be charged against the Jews. We may go further still. The God of Nature has not merely permitted such atrocities, He may be said, in a sense, to have enjoined them. For it has been an invariable law of His providence that when civilised peoples steeped in luxury, vice, and immorality have become the prey of peoples simpler and purer than themselves, these cruelties, and far more than these, have always taken place. Assyrian, Babylonian, Persian conquerors were not more, but far less merciful than Joshua. The Greeks and Romans alone can be said to have been milder; but even the progress of their arms has not been unstained by crimes from which Joshua was wholly free. The violation of women and children, and even crimes of a fouler kind, have not been unknown. The dedication of captives to the impure worship of Mylitta or Aphrodite (see 'Records of the Past,' iii. 36, 39—50) †

---

* The force of this argument has been felt by so keen a reasoner as John Stuart Mill. In his Essay on Nature he accepts the position. He regards nature as immoral and imperfect, asserts that " blind partiality, reckless injustice, atrocious cruelty, abound to excess in the commonest phenomena of nature," and regards nature and life as "the product of a struggle between contriving goodness and an intractable material," the ὕλη, in fact, of the Gnostics and Manicheans.

† The Moabite stone, too, tells us how Mesha devoted the pure virgins of Israel to the foul orgies of Chemosh.

was almost universal. And it is quite possible that death itself may have been preferable—and by many it was regarded as preferable—to a life-long bondage. The miserable condition to which such slaves were often reduced is touchingly represented in the Hecuba of Euripides, where the desolate mother, once a queen, now bereft of husband, sons, friends, a bondslave in a foreign land, is driven in her desperation to appeal to the only hope left, her daughter, who is permitted, though not a lawful wife, to share the bed of Agamemnon. And though this is but fiction, we can hardly doubt that it is fiction in which fact is not too highly coloured. But if Roman and Greek ambition had learned that extending privileges of citizenship to the vanquished would largely increase the power of the victor, we have a return, and more than a return, to the older order of things at the downfall of the Roman Empire. The worst atrocities of the early ages found a parallel in the scenes of bloodshed, lust, and rapine which marked the steps of the barbarian swarms who destroyed the remains of Roman power. Goths, Vandals, Huns, Lombards, Franks, Saxons, Bulgarians, and Turks vied with one another in pitiless cruelty. Even later times still have known a "Spanish fury" and a sack of Magdeburg. And were civilisation again to fall into decay, and the savage tribes of Africa or Asia once more to gain the mastery, the old law would once more assert its force, and the sins of races enervated by luxury would receive their usual punishment. Thus, then, we are face to face with the same vast difficulty whether Joshua received any command from God or not. We have the same question to answer, how God could permit, nay, even apparently arrange for the commission of, these awful crimes, with the intense suffering which they must necessarily bring in their train,[*] and yet retain His character for mercy and loving-kindness. And the only answer that can be found is that there is another order of things in the future, whereby it is His will to remedy whatever inequalities He has permitted to exist here.

(2) But we may carry the argument a step further. The conception of God which we now put forward as an objection to the morality of the Old Testament is derived from the teaching of the New. No such idea of God as that which we now entertain was entertained by earlier ages. Why this was the case we cannot tell. That it is a fact can hardly be denied. It can be no matter of wonder if men in those days acted according to their belief. They conceived of God as a God of strict and vigorous justice. No other view of Him had been as yet made known. Where is the inconsistency of their considering themselves, and acting as, the ministers of One who has shown, both before and since, that He does take terrible vengeance

---

[*] There is a remarkable passage in the Saxon Chronicle on the miseries suffered by English people during the reign of Stephen, when the Norman barons worked their will, unchecked by authority, " when men said openly that God and His saints slept."

upon the sins of men? For more than four thousand years men were ignorant of the conception of God with which we are now familiar. This is an undeniable fact in the economy of Providence. It is surely unreasonable to require men to act upon any other principles than those which God had then permitted to be known.

(3) For it must be remembered that the severe punishment inflicted by Joshua upon the Canaanites who fell into his hands was not a mere outburst of savage cruelty. The institutions and principles of the Jews were far more humane than those of any other nation in those early times.* The precept to exterminate the Canaanites owed its origin to a stern indignation against vices which were sufficient of themselves, according to God's righteous order, to destroy by a more lingering, and therefore a more cruel, death any nation who yielded to them. It was a part of God's curse against that sin, the existence of which has been in many ways man's greatest difficulty in comprehending God. The awful catalogue of abominations which we scarcely venture to read in Leviticus xviii.—xx., are distinctly said to have been committed by " the men of the land" (ch. xviii. 24—30 ; xx. 23), and the land was " defiled " therewith, and God " abhorred " it. The power of grown-up women to lead the Israelites into such sins had been already fatally proved (see Numbers xxvi.). In days before men were endowed with supernatural strength from on high, there seemed no safeguard against the seductive influences of the sensual creed of Palestine but the destruction of those who professed it. The neglect to to carry out the command was at once followed by a relapse into these abominable idolatries, and as lust and cruelty are strangely and nearly allied, the land was filled with bloodshed, and injustice, and crime, culminating in the atrocious custom of the sacrifice of innocent children at the altar of the infernal Moloch. It may even be questioned whether, in view of the inevitable results of a *cultus* like that of Palestine, severity might not have been, as it often is, the truest kindness; whether, had the Jewish law been fulfilled, the Canaanites extirpated, and Jewish ascendancy been established from Lebanon to the wilderness, from Euphrates to the river of Egypt, the principles of humanity now gaining ground among us might not have been antedated, and the inhabitants of Palestine have been socially and politically almost as much gainers by the Jewish polity as the world at large by the religion of Christ.

(4) We are entitled, besides, to remember that the revelation of God through Moses *was* an immense advance in the moral education of the world. Perhaps we have been too much absorbed in its visible failure as regards the many, to observe that, as regards the few, it was as conspicuous a success.

---

* This is not the place for a detailed examination of the statement. It properly belongs to the treatment of the Pentateuch.

Our minds have been so occupied with St. Paul's view of it as demonstrating to man his utter inability to satisfy God by exact compliance with the conditions of a rigid covenant of law, that we have omitted to notice what a vast stride it was in the moral education of the world. The history of the conquest of Palestine can compare favourably with the history of any other conquest the world has known, in the simplicity and absence of personal aims of its leader, in the absolute fairness and equity of his conduct, in the wisdom and humanity of the institutions it established, in the provision, not only for religious worship, but for the moral instruction of the people. The dispersion of the Levites throughout the ten tribes, with the duty of expounding and enforcing the Jewish law, was a means of moral elevation greater than any other nation possessed. Nor, though it did not succeed in securing the obedience of the nation at large, can it be held altogether to have failed. The schools of the prophets raised up men who for their energy, courage, moral grandeur, and sometimes (as in the case of Samuel) political capacity and honesty, can challenge comparison with any great men that have been produced elsewhere. David was a monarch of a type unknown to the world in that or even in far later times, and the one crime into which he was betrayed by irresponsible power would not have excited equal reprobation in an Alexander, a Cæsar, a Charlemagne, a Charles V., or a Napoleon; though an honest and independent prophet could foresee that it would "cause the enemies of the Lord to blaspheme" when committed by "the sweet Psalmist of Israel," the man who in his ingenuous youth was the "man after God's own heart." Thus the objection that Moses and Joshua were not in every respect in advance of their age would seem inconclusive, when weighed against the fact that in so many respects they *were* in advance of it. So far from the Jewish religion having introduced barbarity into the world, it greatly mitigated such a spirit, while the Jewish law was the seed-plot from whence sprung that vast improvement, both in humanity and morality, which has contributed not a little to the happiness and the excellence of mankind.

II. A more formidable objection by far is raised to the miraculous portion of the Book of Joshua. The progress of modern physical science has altogether altered the position of miracles among the evidences of Christianity. In earlier ages the marvels that were believed to have been wrought by God at the inauguration both of the old covenant and the new, were regarded as among the most conspicuous proofs of the Divine origin of both. Now these very miracles are the greatest difficulties in the way of the reception of Christianity. The discovery of the laws of force by which the universe is governed, and the apparent invariability of their action, is calculated to throw considerable doubt on the accuracy of a narrative which records so startling a departure from the ordinary course of nature. The more what used to be considered wonders or portents in nature are brought within the range of nature's ordinary laws, the harder it becomes to believe that on some special occasion, and for special reasons, those laws were altogether set aside. And this view of things derives additional strength from two important facts : first, that, in the infancy of all nations alike, the occurrence of prodigies of the strangest nature was devoutly believed ; and next, that, down to our own day, in countries where superstition is predominant, the same childish tendency to the marvellous is constantly observed. If we are to believe the stories of the miraculous passage of the Red Sea or of the Jordan, it is asked, If you wish us to accept the story of the appearance of the angels to the shepherds, or of the performance of a number of extraordinary miracles in Palestine at a certain epoch, on what grounds can we withhold our credence to the visions of Lourdes and La Salette, or the apparitions at Knock ? And if every man of common sense rejects the latter, on what principles can the former be defended ?

It cannot be denied that there is force in this argument. For if the facts of Jewish history are guaranteed by the festivals of the Jewish nation, by the evident sincerity and steadfastness of its belief, which has survived the lapse of time, and a long course of trials and vicissitudes which might have shaken the stoutest faith ; if the truth of the Christian miracles be confirmed by the Christian sacraments,* and attested by the affirmations of competent witnesses, we have also respectable evidence for a long list of cures at Lourdes, La Salette, Knock, and elsewhere ; and we find in the pilgrimages to these places the clearest proof that the evidence for them has secured acceptance at the hands of some of the most cultivated and intelligent persons in Christendom. And nothing makes it harder to defend revelation, whether under the Old Covenant or the New, than these eccentricities of its professed allies. Yet it is only fair to notice that the cases are not exactly parallel. Paley's argument that miracles are the only way in which a revelation can be shown to be such, if over-stated, is not without its force. At least those who impugn it ought to state how, in their judgment, a revelation could be recognized as such without the aid of miracles. This, so far as we know, they have never done. If, then, Mosaism and Christianity were both special interventions of God in the moral and spiritual order of the world—and this, though denied, is not disproved—it seems at least highly probable that they would be attested by some miraculous occurrences, some signs of a Hand overruling the natural, as these revelations have unquestionably largely affected the moral and spiritual order of things. It will be observed, in conformity with this view, that the promulgation of the Mosaic law and the settlement of Israel in Palestine were attended with a greater display of the miraculous than at

* See Dr. Maclear's Boyle Lectures.

any earlier or later period in Jewish history. That the miraculous element was not entirely withdrawn throughout the greater part of the Jewish history previous to our Lord's coming, that portent and prophecy were still to be met with, may be accounted for by the unique position of the Jews as the only people to whom a revelation had been vouchsafed, and the necessity of extraordinary aids to sustain the faith of a people placed in so peculiar and difficult a position. The renewed manifestation of the miraculous which attended the preaching of the Gospel has in it nothing surprising, if our Lord were really what He represented Himself to be—the Eternal Word of God, by whom all things were created. On the contrary, we could not expect so exalted a Being to manifest Himself without a display of the power inherent in Him. The gradual cessation of the miraculous after His ascension is satisfactorily accounted for by the fact that this was the last manifestation of His will. All that was necessary for the salvation of man had now been given, and since faith was to be the transforming power which was to fit men for their eternal inheritance, all further appeals to the senses would be out of place. No such reason exists, or is assigned, for the modern miracles of the Roman Catholic Church. It is not pretended that the perpetual visible appearance of God the Son on earth is necessary for the success of His scheme of salvation. It is not contended, even by themselves, that the principle of salvation by the operation of faith needs the perpetual visible intervention of the objects of faith, still less of any subordinate assistants in the work, if indeed the Virgin Mary and her husband Joseph can be said any longer to be subordinate agents in the work of salvation. * Nor are the nature of the prodigies the same. The miracles of the Old Testament and the New were at least palpable undeniable facts, if we can believe the accounts that have been handed down to us. If there were any apparitions of celestial beings in a blaze of light, it was but to herald the appearance of One who, whatever may be thought of Him, was undeniably an historical personage. Nor, again, is the kind or the concurrent weight of such testimony the same. It is obviously suicidal, with the late Professor Mozley, to hold that, " if we hold certain doctrines to be false, we are justified in depreciating the testimony of their teachers to the miracles worked in support of them.† For then those who believe revealed religion to be false have as much right to reject without examination the Christian miracles as we those of the Roman Catholic Church.

---

* Liguori's ' Glories of Mary ' is notorious enough for the almost, if not quite, Divine honour it pays to the Blessed Virgin. It is not, perhaps, so generally known that St. Joseph is now acknowledged to be the universal patron, protector, and guardian of the whole Church, and that the new trinity of " Jesus, Mary, and Joseph " has almost, if not quite, usurped the place of "Father, Son, and Holy Ghost."

† Bampton Lectures, Lect. viii.

But in truth there is the utmost difference possible between the two cases. In the Roman Catholic Church we have an already existing institution, with a priesthood whose sacerdotal pretensions have received an altogether abnormal development, who are not entirely beyond the suspicion of pious fraud,* who rest mainly upon the support of a people credulous almost beyond belief,† and who resort to every expedient to maintain their influence over such people in order to hold their ground against the opposing forces of Protestantism and infidelity. If we inquire into the character of those on whose testimony these apparitions are believed, we are referred to a few children, not over-distinguished for truthfulness, or an Irish housekeeper, who can scarcely be regarded as a first-rate judge of evidence, backed up by the stout affirmations of a peasantry not regarded as altogether the most enlightened in Europe. And the Roman Catholic Church has invariably a reserve of enthusiasm to fall back upon ready to welcome any prodigy, however improbable, which might redound to the honour of their Church. The circumstances under which the Jewish and Christian miracles were worked was in every way different. In the latter case there was no reserve of enthusiasm to fall back upon, for the founding of the Christian society, even with the alleged support of these miracles, was a task of the utmost difficulty, and all the miracles were worked under the eyes of a band of prejudiced and most watchful opponents. The miracles themselves were of an altogether different character, such as precluded altogether the possibility of mistake. Even if we give up all the miracles of healing as due to the influence of imagination, there remains a host of others which cannot be so disposed of. And lastly, the character of the witnesses is altogether different. Not only had they every inducement to disbelieve what they saw, or to say they disbelieved it if they did not; not only did they gain no personal ends by maintaining to the last the truth of their story, but their whole subsequent career shows that we have in them no half-crazy fanatics who were ready to throw away their lives for an idea, but hard-headed men of business, who set to work with the utmost cool-ness and shrewdness to attempt the morally impossible, and by dint of patience and practical tact, added to the force of an assured conviction, actually accomplished it. The miracles of the Old Testament are distinct either from those of the New or from the prodigies of later times. The evidence for them is more distant, the period one of less enlightenment.

* Some curious stories are told of pilgrimages to Rome on the part of poor working people who had seen the straw on which the poor "prisoner of the Vatican" reclined, and of their astonishment at contrasting what they had been told with the reality.

† See Professor Reusch's crushing *exposé* of German superstition in his 'Die Deutschen Bischöfe und der Aberglaube.' Professor Reusch is no prejudiced antagonist. At present he holds a position midway between the Old Catholics and the Roman Catholic Church.

But if we may trust our histories, they were worked for a definite purpose, in the eyes of a whole people, and in a manner which admits of no mistake. They were no apparitions seen, or believed to be seen, by a few ignorant and credulous people ; they were marvels publicly wrought on behalf of a nation in arms, and they facilitated one of the most memorable conquests to be found in all history. The evidence for them rests upon the credibility of the documents that relate them. And if we are not entitled to assume that these were contemporary documents, we have no right, on the other hand, to assume that, from the mere presence of the miraculous in them, they must be relegated to a later date. If the events related will generally stand the test of criticism, we cannot detach the miraculous portions from the remainder. The evidence that the writer had access to authentic information in one part of his work gives him at least serious claim on our attention throughout. At least, therefore, we are entitled to contend that the Scripture miracles must be allowed to stand on an altogether different basis than occasional apparitions to women and children, occurring for reasons of which it is impossible to give a rational explanation.

It is with pain that in the foregoing remarks we have felt ourselves compelled to reflect with severity upon the religion of a vast number of our brethren in Christ. No good can be done by going out of the way to attack the belief of one's neighbours. And nothing but a deep conviction of the cruel injury done to the cause of revealed religion among the thoughtless and superficial by this endless crop of spurious wonders would have justified these reflections. But in view of the way in which these supposed miracles have been used to discredit revelation, it has become necessary to show that the miracles of the Bible rest on altogether different grounds to those of the Roman Catholic Church. It remains to deal with an objection to the miracles of the Old and New Testament alike, that they are contrary to the laws by which modern discovery has proved that the physical universe is governed. Those laws, we are told, are invariable, and any statement, it is added, asserting that their action has been suspended must be discredited. It would lead us too far were we to enter upon the full consideration of this question. The question of the possibility of the miraculous has been ably dealt with by others.* Suffice it here to say that science has not only proved the invariability of forces and their laws, it has proved much more. It has proved that invariable forces, acting by invariable laws, are the most plastic instruments possible in human hands. The most extraordinary physical and moral results are being produced upon the face of the globe by the moral agent *will*, when at work upon the physical agencies whose action is said to be invariable. All that is claimed for God in these

* See, for instance, Dr. Mozley's Bampton Lectures, and Dean Mansel's Essay in 'Aids to Faith.'

pages is the possession of what is unquestionably possessed by man, the power, without suspending the action of a single force, so to control its operation as to produce the results He desires. If man can drain marshes at his will, and turn them into fruitful fields, why should not God be able, at His will, to make a path across the sea, or arrest the course of a river? If man can, by touching a wire, cause an explosion that might lay half London in ruins, how can we assert it to be impossible for the Creator of heaven and earth to bring the walls of Jericho to the ground by means the secret of which is known to Him, but which is, and may for ever remain, hidden from us? So far from the discoveries of science rendering the belief in miracles impossible, it is, in fact, supplying the defenders of revelation with the strongest evidence in the opposite direction. For if during the last few years man has become possessed of powers the existence of which, previous to their discovery, would have seemed in the highest degree incredible, there is the best reason for believing that Nature possesses powers and possibilities yet unknown, which, in the hands of the Author of Nature, may produce results which appear to us beyond measure extraordinary and portentous.

It now remains to consider the vexed question of Joshua's command to the sun and moon to stand still, which has been so great a difficulty, not only to commentators, but to all apologists of revealed religion. It may be well first to state the various interpretations which have been given of the passage, before discussing it more particularly. Maimonides (a mediæval writer, be it remembered), whom Rabbi ben Gerson among the Jewish, Grotius * and Masius among the earlier, and Hengstenberg among the later Christian commentators follow, regards it as simply a poetic way of saying that the day was long enough to enable the Israelites to complete the slaughter of their enemies. We read in his 'Moreh Nevochim' (ii. 35) : "Sicut diem integrum mihi videtur intelligi dies maximus et longissimus (*Thamim* enim idem est quod *schalem*, perfectus), et idem esse si dixisset quod dies ille apud ipsos in Gibeone fuerit sicut dies magnus et longus in æstate." Masius is very confident in this view, and says that if Kimchi thinks otherwise, it is only a proof how little the Jews of his day knew of their own scriptures. The earlier Rabbis are unanimous that the sun literally stood still, though they differ, like the Fathers, as to the time that it remained above the horizon. David Kimchi thought that the period was twenty-four hours, and that after the sun had set, the moon still remained stationary that

* Keil represents Grotius as being in favour of the notion of a refraction which kept the sun's appearance above the horizon long after it sank below the horizon. But his interpretation is the one stated above, although he adds, " quanquam impossibile Deo non est solis cursum morari, aut etiam post solis occasum speciem ejus in nube super horizontem exstanti repercussum ostendere."

Joshua might complete the slaughter of his foes.* The Fathers generally take the literal view of the passage, and suppose the sun to have literally stood still in the heavens, some for a longer, some for a shorter period, some supposing it to be forty-eight, some thirty-six (so Justin Martyr, 'Dial. Tryph.' 132), some twenty-eight hours (as Cornelius à Lapide, whose commentary is of course based on the patristic writings). Keil seems finally to have decided in favour of what he calls a " subjective " lengthening of the day. He believes that the day was supposed by the Israelites to have been lengthened, they being too fully engaged in the conflict with their enemies to take any very accurate note of time. Curiosities of interpretation, such as that of Michaelis,† who supposed that the lightning which accompanied the hailstorm was prolonged far into the night; or that of König,‡ who supposes that the ·hailstorm which, according to the history, preceded the standing still of the sun, was a consequence of that occurrence, need only be noticed to be rejected.

We come next to inquire which of these views is the most probable. And here, with Keil and Grotius, we may dismiss all notions from our mind of the *impossibility* of the miracle. He who holds the heavens in the hollow of His hand could arrest the revolution of the earth and prevent all the tremendous consequences (as they seem to us) of such a cessation, as easily as a man can arrest the progress of a vast machine more than ten thousand times as powerful as himself. The former event is not more antecedently incredible than the latter, but the contrary. But though it seems eminently unreasonable to doubt the possibility of such an occurrence, we may, with far more reason, doubt its probability. It is a fair question whether a miracle of so stupendous a kind were really worked for such a purpose by Him, the economy of whose means to His ends is one of the most striking features of His works. It may be reasonably doubted whether He who de-

---

* The following specimens, for which I am indebted to the kindness of a well-known Rabbinic scholar, of the way in which this subject is treated in the Rabbinical writings will not be without interest. In the Midrash on Genesis (Bereshith Rabba, cap. 6) we read that the Book of Deuteronomy was Joshua's banner. When God spake to him as recorded in Josh. i. he had the Book of Deuteronomy in his hand, and he was bidden (says R. Simeon ben Jochai) not to let it depart out of his hand. Thus, in the thick of the fight at Beth-horon, he raised the Book of Deuteronomy on high, and said, "As I never ceased (דוּם) to study this book, so do thou stand still (דוּם) in the heavens." R. Isaac says that Joshua addressed the sun as follows: " Thou wicked servant, art thou not the slave of my father (Joseph)? . Did not my father see thee thus in a dream?" Others held that the standing still of the sun and moon, and the retiring of the waters, were part of the original compact with them at the beginning of the world.

† J. D. Michaelis, 'Deutsche Uebersetzung des Alten Testaments, mit Anmerkungen für Ungelehrte.' 1774.

‡ Cited by Keil, who is, however, very inaccurate in his representations of the views of the authors he mentions.

clined, at the suggestion of the tempter, to suspend the laws of nature that He might be fed, who never has suspended those laws in such a manner for the benefit of His creatures, would have suspended them for their slaughter. And while steadfastly maintaining the genuineness and authenticity of the Scriptures, and their accuracy on all the main points of their narrative, it has never yet been authoritatively decided that they were free from error on every point. From the time of St. Jerome downwards it has been held that mistakes in minor points might be admitted in them without invalidating their claim to be regarded as authoritative exponents of the will of God. Thus, then, the writer will have satisfied all the conditions of authentic history, if he tells us what was the current belief in his own day. The success of the Israelites was so far beyond their expectations, the slaughter of their powerful enemies so immense, that it may have been their firm belief that the day was miraculously lengthened on their behalf. But we are not driven to this view of the case. The quotation has an obviously poetic form, as every one must admit. The Book of Jasher (although Jarchi, as well as Targum, thinks it is the Pentateuch, and other Rabbis believe it to be the Books of Genesis and Deuteronomy respectively) has been very generally supposed to be a collection of national songs existing in early days, and receiving additions from time to time. This is Maurer's belief, and it has been adopted by Keil and others. We are not compelled therefore to regard Joshua's prayer and the whole paragraph as more literal than the apostrophe of Isaiah, " O that thou wouldst rend the heavens and come down, that the mountains would flow down at Thy Presence," or the statement of Deborah and Barak that "the stars in their courses fought against Sisera." But, again, the words of the original have been singularly exaggerated. Literally translated (see notes on the passage) they amount simply to this: " Then spake Joshua to (or *before*, as Masius) Jehovah in the day when Jehovah gave the Amorite before the sons of Israel. And he said before the eyes of Israel, Sun, in Gibeon be still, and moon, in the vale of Ajalon. And the sun was still, and the moon stood till a nation was avenged of its enemies. Is not this written in the book of the upright ? And the sun stood in the midst of heaven, and did not haste to go down, as (or *like*) a perfect day. And there was not a day like that before or after it, for Jehovah to hearken to the voice of a man, for Jehovah fought for Israel." It is obvious that the actual meaning of the author is involved in much obscurity. It is certainly not asserted that the sun remained in the heavens twenty-four, or twelve, or even one hour beyond its usual time. All that is stated is that Joshua in impassioned words demanded that the sun and moon should not set until his work was done, and that this (to the Israelites) extraordinary request was fulfilled. He had perfect day until Israel was avenged of their enemies. A vast league of civilized states, with all the best appliances of warfare banding together to resist a nation unused to military exploits, defeated with tremendous slaughter, and annihilated in a single day, would doubtless seem to Israel a stupendous work of God's hand. Well might they embody it among their national songs, and relate for ever after how the sun remained above the heavens until the victory was more than complete, and how the moon continued to give her light until the scanty remnant of the mighty host were pursued to their strongholds. Nor is this view of the passage without corroboration. Hengstenberg ('Geschichte des Reiches Gottes,' p. 231 sqq.) does not fail to notice the fact that in all the allusions — and they are many—to the great things God had done for Israel, *not one* is found to this supposed miracle, until the time of the son of Sirach (ch. xlvi. 4), save a very doubtful passage in Habakkuk iii. This is surely decisive as to the view Scripture itself has taken of the passage, and it is as true of the New Testament as of the Old. Thus, therefore, we conclude that the whole passage is so obscure and difficult, besides being very probably a quotation—perhaps even an interpolation—from another book, that we are at least justified in considering its importance to have been exaggerated both by assailants and defenders. The interpretation which supposes it to refer to a vast natural convulsion, wrought by the Almighty in order to complete the defeat of the Canaanites, though a possible, is, as has been shown, by no means the *only* possible explanation of the words of the narrative. And this position once established, the whole fabric of controversy that has been raised on this much-vexed passage falls to the ground.

§ III. The Original Inhabitants of Palestine.

The people who inhabited Palestine at the time of the Israelite invasion are regarded in history from two very opposite points of view. To the Israelites, in whom the moral sense strongly predominated over culture, they appeared as monsters of iniquity, deserving of nothing but absolute extirpation. To profane history, regarding mankind from a more material point of view, they appear as the parents of civilization, the founders of literature and science, the pioneers of commerce, the colonists of the Mediterranean. These views may be to a certain extent harmonized. It is not necessary to regard the Jews as the opponents of all culture, because they were stern avengers of moral depravity. The time when the Phœnician power attained its utmost height was coincident, as recent discoveries show, with the time of the Israelite sojourn in Egypt. Civilization, as it usually does, brought luxury, and luxury demoralization; and the same fate attended the Phœnician supremacy which attended the supremacy of all the great empires of the ancient world, a dissolution of morals and consequent decay. The severe lesson taught by Joshua's invasion seems not to have been without its effect upon the Sidonians and Tyrians, who retained their commercial pre-eminence to a considerably later date.* But the rest of Phœnicia seems gradually to have sunk from that time, and her supremacy in literature and the arts was irrecoverably gone.

Modern research has only just recovered for us a great deal of the history of the Phœnicians which had long been lost. We knew of them as the race who introduced letters to the Greeks from the legend of Cadmus, and the ancient Hebrew letters were no doubt borrowed from their system. We knew that Phœnician colonies had been found at Cyprus, Rhodes, Crete, Asia Minor, Sicily, Sardinia; and that Carthage derived its appellation of Punic, and even its language, from them.† We knew from the Bible that they were a Turanian race.‡ But what we did not know was that under the name of Hittites, or rather Chittites (a name preserved at the town of Citium, now Chitti, in the Phœnician colony of Cyprus, the abode, according to Scripture, of the Chittim), they were among the leading peoples of the world at an early period; that Carchemish was their capital, and that they had there held a position of equality both with the Babylonian and Egyptian powers. The recent researches at Carchemish, discovered in 1874—75 by Mr. Skene, the British consul at Aleppo,§ on the west bank of the Euphrates, have established this fact. Previous to these discoveries the only authentic account of them, as distinct from tradition, was to be found in the monuments and records of those who had subdued them.‖ They appear to have been originally known to the Egyptians as Ruten or Rutennu.¶ Afterwards they were known as the Kheta or Khatti, and many fierce and destructive wars were waged against them by the Babylonians and Egyptians.**
Their power received a rude shock in the occupation of the south-western portion of their empire under Joshua, and the final blow to their pre-eminence

* See notes on Tyre and Sidon (ch. xix. 29, and xi. 8).

† Kenrick, 'Phœnicia,' chs. iv., v., Movers, 'Die Phönizier,' ii. 2. Inscriptions have been found in Greece, Malta, Carthage, in precisely the same alphabet and language as is found on the Moabite stone. And the Carthaginian passage in the Pœnulus of Plautus, though wofully disfigured by transcribers, is easily translatable, as Movers has restored it, when written in the Hebrew character. See a paper on this passage by Mr. Rodwell in the 'Trans. Soc. Bibl. Archæol.,' ii. 235.

‡ Gen. ix. 18; xl. 15—18. Whether this be regarded as an ethnological or geographical view of these nations, the Scripture clearly regards them as Turanians.

§ See Times of Aug. 19, 1880. Mr. George Smith fully concurred with Mr. Skene in identifying the ruins as those of Carchemish.

‖ See the great expedition of Thothmes III. against Carchemish, which took place during the life of Moses and before the Exodus ('Records of the Past,' ii.).

¶ 'Records of the Past,' ii. 31 sqq. Thothmes III. speaks of the Syrians as Kharu, and in one place as Katu, according to the translation of the account of the battle of Megiddo. Palestine is spoken of as Taneter and Kefa, and its inhabitants as Kefau (ibid. p. 39 sqq.).

** 'Trans. Soc. Bibl. Archæol.,' iii. 83 sqq.

was dealt by Rameses II. in his expedition against the Syrians.* Their Turanian origin cannot be said to be disproved by their adoption of the Semitic language. In whatever difficulties such a theory may involve us, we are not entitled to contradict the plain assertion of Scripture (see above). It is corroborated by the fact that traces of a Turanian occupation of Palestine are to be found in Phœnician words.† Moreover, that Turanians and Semites were much intermingled in those regions is an admitted fact. Recent investigation has conclusively established the truth of the Scripture statement, that Babylon was originally inhabited by a Turanian race,‡ and that this race was afterwards subjugated by a Semitic one.§ Instances of nations abandoning their language and adopting another are not unknown. The Bulgarians and the Northmen are cases in point.|| Lenormant ¶ thinks that though their language can scarcely be distinguished from Hebrew, it was not necessarily confined to the Semitic races, and he remarks on similar phenomena, as they appear to him, in the languages of ancient Babylonia. Movers, who inclines on the whole to regard them as the primitive inhabitants of the land, in spite of the Greek traditions which speak of their having emigrated from the shores of the Red Sea, notices that they were not connected together by any very close genealogical ties.** He remarks †† that the fact that the Israelites, while they speak of the B'ney, or sons of Israel, Moab, Ammon, always, with one remarkable exception, speak of the inhabitants of the land as the Canaanite, Amorite, Jebusite, &c. The one exception is the B'ney Khet, or Heth, which is in accordance with what we know from other sources, that they were a powerful people beyond the borders of Palestine. This view is confirmed, he believes, by the thirty-one kingly cities which are mentioned in ch. ii. 9—24, as having been taken by Joshua.

* See note on ch. i. 4, and 'Records of the Past,' ii. 65 sqq.; iv. 25. Carchemish was finally conquered by Sargon I., and it afterwards became the great mercantile emporium of the East.

† Tomkin's 'Studies on the Time of Abraham,' p. 95.   ‡ Gen. x. 6—10.

§ The early language of Babylon, the Accadian, was a Turanian one. See Smith's 'Notes on the Early History of Assyria,' pp. 3—16 ; Sayce, 'Babylonian Literature,' p. 6 'Trans. Soc. Bibl. Archæol.,' i. 298.

|| See Freeman's 'Hist. of the Norm. Conq.,' i. 196; Gibbon's 'Decline and Fall,' ch. xlii., and Smith's notes on ch. lv.

¶ 'Manual of the Ancient History of the East,' i. 72.

** Lenormant, on the contrary, thinks that they were preceded by the Horites, Rephaim, and others. But Movers remarks on the uncertainty of the Greek traditions which may (1) have originated from a misapprehension of the origin of the word *Phoinix*, and (2) may have been founded on (*a*) the Israelitish, (*b*) the Philistine, or (*c*) the Assyrian (see 2 Kings xvii. 24) inhabitants of Canaan. Moreover, he shows from Deut. ii. 20—23, that the Moabites, Ammonites, Edomites, and Philistines were later invaders of Canaan, but there is no trace of any conflict between the Canaanites or Hittites and the aborigines. The Babylonian myths represent the Phœnicians to have had their origin in Mesopotamia, the cradle of the human race.   †† 'Die Phönizier,' II. i. 3.

It is still further confirmed by the fact that Gibeon was differently governed from the rest,* as well as by another fact which Movers points out, that the Hivites were scattered over Palestine.† The term Canaanite is regarded by Movers as referring, not to a genealogical descent, but to the situation of the inhabitants in the lowlands of Palestine, while Perizzite in his opinion means the *separated* or scattered agricultural families (see ch. iii. 10). Thus it seems not at all improbable that a variety of races may have emigrated to the shores of the Mediterranean, have adopted the same language, manners, and religious customs, ‡ and constituted what has been known to history as the Phœnician people.

The Phœnician religion seems to have been the parent of the religions of Greece and Rome. Baal seems to have been equivalent to Zeus, and Ashtaroth § to have combined the characteristics of Artemis and Aphrodite. Asherah was the prototype of Rhea or Cybele, and her rites seem to have consisted in a combination of the phallic worship with the idea of the fecundity of nature. The worship of Moloch was not known to the Israelites till later times, and he is thought by some to have been an Ammonite deity and identical with Milcom. Yet it is probable that in the worship of the Phœnician representatives of Cronos, the bloody rites ascribed in the Scripture to Moloch were observed.‖ Thammuz,¶ known later as Adonis, was fabled to have died on Lebanon, and the temple at Apheka, or Aphaca, was dedicated to the mourning Aphrodite. The remainder of the chief deities known to Greece had their place in the Phœnician, as they appear to have done also in the Babylonian, pantheon. The general character of the worship, as described by Lenormant in his ' Manual of the Ancient History of the East,' fully justifies all that is said of it in the books of Moses. "The Canaanites," he says, " were remarkable for the atrocious cruelty that stamped all the ceremonies of their worship, and the precepts of their religion. No other people ever rivalled them in the mixture of bloodshed and debauchery with which they thought to honour the deity. As the celebrated Creuzer has said, ' Terror was the inherent principle of this religion ; all its rites were bloodstained, and all its ceremonies were surrounded by bloody images.' "**

Of their political institutions we know but little. They seem, like ancient Greece, to have been split up into a number of separate states, the great majority of which seem to have adopted a monarchical, but some, as

---

* See notes on ch. ix. 3 ; x. 2. † See note on ch. iii. 10.

‡ Movers does not fail to remark that the Moabites and Ammonites, though Semitic peoples, adopted the Phœnician religion. It was difficult, he might have added, to prevent the Jews from doing the same. § See note on Ashtaroth, ch. xii. 4.

‖ Kenrick, 316. Lenormant thinks he was originally the fire-god. Movers identifies him with Heracles and Ares, as well as with the fire-god or destroying principle.

¶ Ezek. viii. 14. * Vol. ii. p. 223.

Gibeon, a republican government. Society, as has been intimated, was highly organized among them. They had already reached a high degree of civilization and culture. The land had long fallen into the hands of private landholders. The slight glimpses we get (as in chs. ii. 1, 2 ; ix. 1 ; x. 1, 3, 5 ; xi. 1, 2) into the interior life of the cities leads us to believe that the kings possessed autocratic power, nor do we read of any assembly of their people in the Book of Joshua. This agrees with the picture of a king given in Deut. xvii. 14—18, taken, no doubt, from the kings of Canaan. The character of the inhabitants seems on the whole to have been peaceful, as we might naturally expect from their mercantile pursuits,* though there seems to have been considerable cohesion among them, since the leagues formed by the northern and southern tribes after Joshua's invasion were apparently formed without any difficulty. This slight tendency to defection, however, may have been due to Joshua's unconcealed purpose of exter-mination, of which the Gibeonites were obviously aware. It seems probable that the kings of Palestine had owed a sort of feudal allegiance to their Hittite head at Carchemish. But he seems to have had no power to aid them in the time of Joshua. Possibly, therefore, the great Hittite power was already on the wane. The centre was losing its hold on the extremities, and the confederacies of which Jerusalem and Hazor were the heads had become in a great measure independent of the central power. This accounts for the fact which otherwise would be surprising, that no attempt was made by the Hittites beyond Palestine to regain their lost territory. Of their literary activity we know but little. Yet the legend of Cadmus, the ancient name of Debir, Kirjath-Sepher, the city of the book, as well as the recent discoveries at Carchemish, prove them to have attained a high pitch of cultivation. Their commercial achievements are better known. Tyre and Sidon retained (see note) to a much later period their mercantile pre-eminence. The colonial development of the Phœnicians arose out of the commercial. It was for trading purposes that these settlements were formed. And so enterprising were they, that while other nations— the Jews among the rest—sought the seas with fear and trembling, the Phœnicians ventured beyond the Pillars of Hercules, and set on foot a brisk trade with the inhabitants of these otherwise unknown islands for tin and other metals. Against such a people was Joshua's memorable expedi-tion directed. Of its leader, and the singular military skill he displayed in the choice of a spot for the invasion, and in his conduct of the enterprise,

---

* Movers, ii. book i. 2 section 2, remarks on the absence of any signs oi a warlike cha-racter among them in the Book of Genesis, and on their peaceful reception of strangers, as evidenced by the whole narrative. But society was evidently far more highly organized in the time of Joshua, and, as a natural consequence of the wealth gained by commerce, not less peaceful, but infinitely more corrupt.

nothing need be said here. Those subjects will be found fully discussed in the notes. The moral aspect of the invasion has already been considered. It remains only to add that, many as are the memorable conquests on record, conquests whose results have had an abiding influence upon after ages, this one is the most memorable of all. The occupation of this small strip of territory scarcely larger than Wales, though it led to no further results in the way of conquest, has nevertheless to a great extent moulded the moral and religious history of the world. Christianity and Moham-medanism have alike sprung from it; and though at first the latter seemed to have surpassed the former in political and warlike activity, supremacy has at length fallen unchallenged into Christian hands. Thus the Israelite conquest of Canaan was in fact an event of primary importance to man-kind. It was one which might well have been ushered in with portent and prodigy, and certainly it was one which will always occupy a foremost place in men's minds. No amount of destructive criticism can dispose of the fact that the subjugation of Palestine was achieved by a people without a rival in the influence it has exerted on the destinies of the human race.

§ IV. The Settlement of Palestine.

A few remarks on the landed and governmental system of Palestine may not be out of place. The institutions of the people as a whole may of course best be studied in the Mosaic law, but it is not unimportant to endeavour to gain from the condition of Palestine after the conquest some idea of the way in which it was originally designed that this law should be administered. This question divides itself into two heads, the system of government and the tenure of land.

I. What the system of government was in Joshua's time is clear enough. It was virtually what we now call a constitutional monarchy, though rather of the type which such a monarchy took at the time of William III. than that which exists among us at the present day. Joshua was supreme, yet simply by force of character, not from any supposed inherent right he possessed to such supremacy, still less, like many successful soldiers, by a military despotism. For great as his authority unquestionably was, he never acted alone. Whenever we see him discharging the functions of chief magistrate, he reminds us of an early Anglo-Saxon sovereign. His Witenagemot, his council, the representatives of the tribes, the high officers of Church and State, were always around him (ch. viii. 33; xviii. 1; xxii. 11—14; xxiii. 2; xxiv. 1). But after his death the tribes assumed a form more like the United States in Holland and America. Each one had its own defined portion of territory, apportioned to it by lot, and was sovereign within its own borders, but common dangers and common interests were discussed at a general assembly. There appears, however, to have been no organized system of united action, no fixed time for the general assembly to meet, but such assemblies were only held under the pressure of extraordinary need (Judg. xx. 1). Therefore, when the personal influence of the "elders that over-lived Joshua" was removed, the acknowledgment of the theocracy, the provision for united worship, was not found sufficient to band the tribes together, and the once formidable confederacy soon fell to pieces. Its integrity was seriously threatened as early as the events recorded in Judges xx. It had already ceased to exist in the time of Deborah and Barak. The internal unity of each tribe or *clan* was much better preserved. Its organization was extremely complete. The tribe was divided into its מִשְׁפָּחוֹת or septs, its בֵּית־הָאָבוֹת or families, and its גְּבָרִים or heads of households. The אֲלוּפִים or thousands, which have been held to correspond to the מִשְׁפָּחוֹת, were probably a military division parallel to, but independent of, the genealogical one, and bore some analogy to the *hundred* or *wapentake* of our own island. The question which has been learnedly argued concerning Anglo-Saxon institutions, whether the national system was one of aggregation or subdivision, does not arise here. For Israel was, as the name implies, a *family*, the family of Jacob. From hence the minor divisions arose by subdivision, the tribe into the sept, the sept into the family, the family into the household. Thus the political unit, which in early English society was the mark or village, in Palestine was the tribe. The government thence arising was partly aristocratic, partly representative. The heads of the tribes had no doubt to summon to the council all the heads of the households,* but they themselves, as the lineal descendants of the eldest son, had the greatest weight in the decision (see Josh. xxii. 14). The powers of the head of a household were great, though by no means so absolute as in many of the primitive Aryan communities,† where the house-father had an absolute power of life and death. The Mosaic law knew nothing of the fierce rigours of this patriarchal tyranny. It did not subsist in the households of Abraham, Israel, and Jacob. If it had had a tendency to grow up in Egypt, the Mosaic law would have checked it. It is clear from Exod. xxi. 15—17, from Levit. xx. 9, from Deut. xxvii. 16, and above all from Deut. xxi. 18—21, that the Jewish head of a household had not, like the Aryan house-father, the power of life and death over his children. Though the members of his family had no representative at the general council of the tribe, he was responsible for his treatment of them to the laws of the land. By whom those laws were administered we know not. The judges were originally (Exod. xviii. 25)

---

* Sometimes, as in ch. xxi. 1, only the heads of the *families* were present. Compare the greater and lesser Skuptschina in Servia.

† As in India (see Maine, 'Village Communities,' Lect. iv.). And in Greece and Rome (see Hearn, 'Aryan Household,' ch. iv.).

appointed by Moses. No doubt Joshua continued to appoint them during his lifetime. But we hear of no provision for their appointment after his death. Possibly they were appointed by the general assembly of the tribe, but in the rapid disintegration of Jewish institutions which followed, we find their office usurped by the military leader who had for a time retrieved the fallen fortunes of Israel.

II. The land system of Israel differed much from the Aryan land systems. There, originally, land appears to have been held in common by the inhabitants of the mark, and to have been divided into three parts, for wheat, spring crops, and fallow, beside the pasture grounds; and originally to have been shifted from time to time, when exhausted. * The Semitic and Turanian tribes seem to have differed from the Aryans in having grasped much earlier the idea of private property in land. The Egyptians, by Joseph's advice, had converted the vast bulk of Egyptian proprietors then existing into the tenants of the crown. In Palestine, as early as the time of Abraham, the Hittites appear also to have recognized the rights of private proprietors. It is impossible to read the narrative of Gen. xxiii., † and fancy that we are reading of an account of the permanent acquisition by Abraham of a portion of the *ager publicus*.‡ The ground was evidently the property of Ephron, and the other children of Heth were but the witnesses and guarantors of the legality of the transaction. A similar purchase is recorded in Gen. xxxiii. 19.§ But the land system of Palestine received a remarkable modification when it fell into the hands of the Jews. Jehovah Himself became the actual owner of the land; each head of a household received his inheritance in fief and in perpetuity from Him. The institution of the year of release secured that no property should be permanently alienated from its owner. Thus every Israelite was a landed proprietor; and not only so, but a landed proprietor in perpetuity. Each had, therefore, an equal stake in the community. No system could be better adapted to the stability of the commonwealth. But there is reason to suppose that it

---

* " Neque quisquam agri modum certum aut fines habet proprios." Cæsar, ' De Bello Gallico,' vi. 22 ; Tacit. ' Germ.,' 26 ; Stubbs, ' Constitutional History,' vol. i., ch. ii ; Freeman, ' Norman Conquest,' ch. i. pp. 89, 90. The Germans seem to have acquired some notions of private property in land between the time of Cæsar and that of Tacitus. It appears clear that they brought the idea with them to this country. But much of the land was still held in common at that time (see Stubbs, ' Constitutional History,' vol. i., ch. v.).   † Especially vv. 8, 10, 14, and 17.

‡ This view is taken in an article on the land tenure of Palestine in the *Church Quarterly Review*, October, 1880.

§ Here again I am unable to follow the reviewer. Jacob, we are told in the Hebrew, obtained the allotment of the field where he had pitched his tent. There is no hint that the *sadeh* here was the *ager publicus*. If so, how could it be alienated, and how was it that if private property in land were unknown among the Hivites, Jacob so easily obtained it for himself ? (See also Josh. xxiv. 32.)

was not long maintained. First, the repeated invasions of Israel, and next the usurpations of kings (1 Kings xxi. 3), destroyed it, and in the later days of the Jewish history we find that even the person of the Israelite was no longer sacred from slavery (Jer. xxxiv. 8—11).

One feature of the Jewish land system seems to have approximated to the Aryan custom. A certain amount of pasturage (see note on מִגְרָשׁ "suburbs," ch. xxi. 2) was reserved for the Levites in the neighbourhood of the cities assigned to them. It seems to have been used in common by them, and not to have been accompanied by any assignment of arable land. As the Levites, we are frequently told, had no inheritance with the rest of their brethren, the view taken in the notes seems the most probable one, that they dwelt in the cities with their brethren of each tribe, the right of pasturage for their cattle being the only right reserved to them. The rest of their subsistence they derived from the offerings of the people (see ch. xiii. 14).

§ V. CONTENTS OF THE BOOK.

As has been already said, and as will be found in the notes on ch. i. 1, the Book of Joshua is clearly a continuation of the Book of Deuteronomy. It commences (ch. i. 1—9) with God's charge to Joshua, embracing (1) the extent of the dominion to be given to the children of Israel, and (2) instructions to himself as to the grounds of his confidence, and the way in which he is to seek it. He is to be successful, *if* he studies and keeps the law of God.

In ch. i. 10—15 we have Joshua's instructions to the people, (1) to the officers to see that the necessary preparations were made, and (2) to the tribes who had already received their inheritance, concerning the part they were to take in the impending struggle. Vers. 16—18 contain the people's acceptance of Joshua as leader in the place of Moses, and their promise of a most implicit obedience.

Ch. ii. (see notes) is parenthetical. It contains the preparations Joshua had already made for the invasion of Canaan, by sending spies to reconnoitre the first city he intended to attack. They excited the suspicion of the king, and had to take refuge in the house of Rahab. There they learn the terror which the news of their approach had inspired in the hearts of the Canaanites, as a people believed to be under the protection of a mighty deity. They were hidden by Rahab under the stalks of flax (it being the time of the earlier harvest), were then let down the city wall, after having promised to save Rahab and her family in the sack of the city. Certain tokens were agreed upon for the performance of this promise, and then the spies departed, hid themselves in the mountains, thus escaping pursuit, and finally returned in safety to Joshua.

Ch. iii. contains the narrative of the crossing of the Jordan. The people followed the ark at a fixed distance, until they had reached the place appointed for crossing. The waters, as usual at the time of barley harvest, had overflowed the banks. The priests bearing the ark dipped their feet in the brim of the water at the point to which the waters had then reached; the course of the river was at once arrested and the Israelites crossed on dry land.

Ch. iv. contains the continuation of the narrative. Joshua gives orders for the erection of two memorials, one on the Canaan side of Jordan, where they first rested for the night, the other on the eastern side, at the spot on the brink of the swollen river where the priests had stood during the crossing. The first memorial consisted of large stones taken out of the bed of the Jordan. The others (whence they came we are not told) were set up in the shallow water where the priests had stood. The crossing complete, the priests cross with the ark, and as soon as they have reached the dry land on the other side the waters flow as before. The memorial is then set up at Gilgal, and its purpose is explained.

Ch. v. 1—9 relates the formal renewal of the covenant by the rite of circumcision, which appears (see notes) to have been suspended since the rejection of the people in Num. xiv. In vers. 10, 11 we read of the keeping of the passover, which may have been intermitted altogether, but had certainly not been kept by the whole nation for thirty-eight years. Ver. 12 notes the cessation of the manna.

We come next (ch. v. 13—vi. 27) to the taking of Jericho. Joshua was near Jericho, either engaged in meditation or in reconnoitring the city, when a vision (ver. 13) appears to him in the shape of a man with a drawn sword, who (ver. 14) announces himself as the " captain of the Lord's host " and (ver. 15) as a Being of Divine nature. This Being proceeds to give directions for the capture of the city (ch. vi. 2—5), which, as the first step in the conquest of Canaan, was to be of an entirely supernatural character. The directions are abbreviated in the narrative, but we afterwards learn more fully what they were. The men of war, followed by seven priests bearing seven trumpets and the ark, and they, in their turn, by the rest of the people, were to march round the city once for six days. On the seventh they were to march round it seven times. Then a prolonged blast was to be blown on the trumpets, the people were to raise the shout of victory, and the wall of the city would fall down and the people delivered into their hands. The spoil of the city was to be solemnly devoted to God. These directions (vers. 6—21) were fulfilled, and the result was as had been promised. We next (vers. 22—25) read of the destruction of the city and the fulfilment of the promise to Rahab. Verses 26, 27 relate the curse pronounced against any one who should rebuild Jericho, and the effect of its fall upon the rest of the people of the land.

Ch. vii. brings us to the episode of Achan. Joshua sent a small detachment to effect the capture of Ai, following the advice of his scouts, who pronounced it to be an insignificant place. The result was a slight repulse. This produced an effect on Joshua and the people which would have been altogether disproportionate had it not been regarded as a sign of Jehovah's displeasure (vers. 2—5). Joshua prays to God, and is told that such was actually the fact, for the ban on the spoil of Jericho had been transgressed. He was ordered to take the tribes, families, households, and lastly individuals by lot, and to burn the transgressor for his sin (vers. 6—15). Joshua fulfils the injunction (vers. 16—19) and Achan is discovered to be the transgressor (ver. 8). Adjured by Joshua, he confesses his misconduct, which is placed beyond doubt by the discovery of the secreted goods (vers. 19—23), and Achan is burnt, with all his family and goods, and a monumental heap raised to commemorate the event (vers. 24—26).

Joshua next (ch. viii.) proceeds to the capture of Ai. He now regards it as a task of importance sufficient to employ his whole force, and is instructed by God to do so (vers. 1—3). He gives directions for the attack, which was to consist of a feint by the main body of the Israelites to draw the defenders away from the city, while the real attack was to be made by a detachment placed in ambush (vers. 4—9). The stratagem succeeded. The detachment in ambush occupied the city, thus denuded of its defenders, and set it on fire, while the warriors of Ai, with the Israelite host turning upon them in front, and their city in flames in their rear, were seized with a panic, and were unable to offer any effectual resistance. Ai, its king and people, were utterly destroyed, and the city made a heap of ruins (vers. 10—29).

It is here that the majority of MSS. place the fulfilment of the instructions of Moses in Deut. xi. 29 and xxvii., to inscribe a copy of the law upon the altar at Ebal (ch. viii. 30—35), which was fulfilled in the presence of the people.

In ch. ix. we read of the effect of these successes upon the people of the land. While they stirred the kings to resistance (vers. 1, 2) they induced the Gibeonite republic to prefer an accommodation. Aware, by some means, that the inhabitants of Canaan were doomed to destruction, they resorted to the expedient of representing themselves as a distant people, and the artifices are recorded whereby they sought to gain credence for this statement (vers. 3—13). The Israelites, not regarding the matter of sufficient importance to refer to Jehovah, fell into the trap. They afterwards discovered the fraud, and doomed the Gibeonites to perpetual servitude, sparing their lives on account of the oath they had taken to do so (vers. 14—27).

This submission of the Gibeonites appears to have disconcerted the preparations which were making for a general league of all the sovereigns of Palestine against the invaders. Startled by the imminence of the danger, the kings of southern Palestine hastily gathered their forces together, not to attack Joshua, but to reduce Gibeon (ch. x. 1—5). Their plans are disconcerted by the celerity of Joshua, who, on the receipt of tidings of the attack on Gibeon, falls suddenly upon the allies in the morning, and routs them with immense slaughter (vers. 6—10). A violent storm (ver. 11) assists in the discomfiture of his enemies, and Joshua adjures the sun and moon not to go down until his victory is complete, an adjuration which is fulfilled (vers. 12—14). We next read (vers. 16—27 : for ver. 15 see notes) of the death of the five kings, and the pursuit of the flying enemy. Then come a series of sieges (vers. 28—43), those of Makkedah, Libnah, Lachish, Eglon, Hebron, and Debir, as well as the annihilation of an expedition from Gezer, with the view of forcing Joshua to raise the siege of Lachish (ver. 33). The result of this was the subjugation of the country from Gibeon to Kadesh-barnea and Gaza.

Ch. xi. brings us to a combination of the cities of northern Palestine, under Jabin king of Hazor, to resist the progress of Joshua. The rendezvous appointed was at the lake Merom, not far from the Anti-Lebanon range (vers. 1—5). But once more the danger was averted by the promptitude of Joshua, who fell upon them before their preparations were complete, and totally routed them, and destroyed many of their cities (vers. 6—14). But the reduction of northern Palestine was a more serious matter than that of the south. We are expressly told that Joshua made war a long time with those kings (ver. 18). But the result was the reduction of the whole country with certain exceptions, of which we afterwards read (ch. xvii. 12). The supremacy of Israel was, however, not contested, as the payment of tribute shows (vers. 15—20). In vers. 21—23 we read of the destruction of the Anakim, who had probably taken refuge in Philistia, but who had clearly taken advantage of Joshua's prolonged campaign in the north to repossess themselves of their cities. It was not until a later period that this territory was given by lot to Judah, for this tribe must have been engaged with the rest in the campaign in the north. The reduction of the Anakim, exhausted by their previous defeats, does not seem to have been a difficult task.

Ch. xii. commences the second portion of the book, which relates to the territory conquered by Israel, and its distribution among the tribes. The district beyond Jordan, inhabited by Reuben, Gad, and the half-tribe of Manasseh, is first mentioned (vers. 1—6). In the remaining verses the territories of thirty-one kings are mentioned as conquered by Joshua.

Ch. xiii. commences with the mention of the portions of Palestine as yet unconquered, and proceeds to a more minute specification of the conquered territory eastward of Jordan. The unconquered territory consisted (1) of Philistia (vers. 2, 3) ; (2) of the lowlands bordering on Sidon (see notes) (3) the country near Aphek ; (4) the land of the Giblites ; and (5) the extreme northern portion of Palestine, including the great Lebanon range (vers. 4—6). Joshua is now commanded to assign the land beyond Jordan, which is described in detail, with occasional references to the condition of the country when the book was written, and the remark, several times repeated, that the Levites had no share in the allotment (vers. 7—14). Then follows a still more detailed account of the territory beyond Jordan, and the races displaced (vers. 15—33).

Ch. xiv. tells us that the inheritance was made by lot, and repeats, after the author's manner, the statements that the country beyond Jordan was given to the two and a half tribes, and that the Levites had no part in the distribution (vers. 1—5). The remainder of the chapter (vers. 6—15) is devoted to Caleb's request, and its fulfilment.

Ch. xv. divides itself into three parts. The first (vers. 1—12) traces out the border of the tribe of Judah. The second (vers. 13—19) narrates an interesting incident in the family of Caleb. The third (vers. 22—63) enumerates the cities of Judah.

Ch. xvi. describes the border of Ephraim.

Ch. xvii. begins by mentioning the families of the portion of the tribe whose inheritance was west of Jordan (vers. 1—6), specially noting the fact that "Manasseh's daughters" had an inheritance with his sons. Vers. 7—11 give a very imperfect outline of the territory of Manasseh. Vers. 12—18 record the complaint of Ephraim and Manasseh, that the portion allotted to them was not sufficient, and Joshua's answer.

Ch. xviii. gives the account of the fresh survey ordered by Joshua (vers. 1—9), and the fresh division (ver. 10) in consequence. In ver. 11 begins the description of the border of Benjamin, which is continued to ver. 20. Then follows (vers. 21—28) an enumeration of the cities of Benjamin.

Ch. xix. 1—9 names the cities in the territory of Simeon. The border of Zebulon follows (vers. 10—16), and is succeeded by the border of Issachar (vers. 17—23); Asher (vers. 24—31) follows; then Naphtali (vers. 32—39); and lastly (vers. 40—48), Dan, whose later migration northward when they found the territory too small for them, is here recorded. When all the allotments had been made, Joshua himself received his portion (vers. 49—51).

Ch. xx. contains the appointment of the cities of refuge; and ch. xxi. that of the Levitical cities.

In ch. xxii. the history is resumed. The two and a half tribes on their return, after a solemn farewell from Joshua, to their inheritance, fearing that they shall be regarded as outcasts beyond Jordan, erect an altar on their way homeward, as a token of their connection with Israel (vers. 1—10). The remaining tribes, regarding this act as an infraction of the law of Moses, gather together in assembly, prepare for war, but first send an embassy, consisting of the heads of the nine tribes and a half westward of

Jordan, accompanied by Phinehas, as the representative of the priesthood, to remonstrate (vers. 11—20). They receive the unexpected reply that, so far from the erection of this altar being significative of an intention to break the law of Moses, it had precisely the contrary object, and was intended to show their deep reverence for that law, and an evidence of the right they had to consider themselves subject to it (vers. 21—24). The reply is regarded as eminently satisfactory (vers. 30—34), and is received with deep thankfulness by Israel at large.

Ch. xxiii. relates a charge given by Joshua to the children of Israel when advanced in age. He first (vers. 3—5) reminds them of what God has done and promises to do. Then (vers. 6—11) he reminds them of their duty in consequence, and warns them (vers. 12, 13) of the danger of neglecting it, concluding with a final appeal in which he alludes to his long career, in which God has signally fulfilled His promises, and his approaching death.

Ch. xxiv. contains the history of another great gathering, following, no doubt, closely on the former, in which Joshua seeks to bind the Israelites once more before his death, by a solemn ceremony, to their duty of obedience to God. He commences with a brief summary of the history of Israel (ver. 2—13), and while bidding them choose their gods for themselves, declares his fixed determination to serve Jehovah only (vers. 14, 15). The people reply by declaring that it is impossible for them to serve another god (vers. 16—18). Joshua reminds them of the difficulty of the task, yet without shaking their purpose (vers. 19—21). He calls them to witness against themselves that they have made the promise, to which they assent, bids them put away all strange gods, and writes the covenant then made in the book of the law, and places a great stone as a memorial of the event, after which the people separate (vers. 22—28). In the remaining verses we read of the death and burial of Joshua (vers. 29, 30), of the faithfulness of the children of Israel after his death (ver. 31), of the interment of the bones of Joseph (ver. 32), and lastly (ver. 33), of the death and burial of Eleazar.

§ VI. Critical and Exegetical Helps.

Those who find it easy to consult authors in the learned languages will find much help in Origen's 'Homilies on Joshua,' which we have in a Latin dress. These, with the 'Questions' of Theodoret and Augustine, may be found in various editions. The commentary of Rabbi Solomon Jarchi (Rashi) originally written in Rabbinic, has been translated into Latin, and is very brief, and often much to the point. Calvin's Commentary may be found in Latin and French, and an excellent English translation has been issued by the Calvin Society. His treatment of Joshua is neither so striking nor so suggestive as his works on the New Testament, but his sound masculine understanding is often displayed in valuable thoughts. Masius,

GROTIUS, and others may be consulted in the ' Critici Sacri,' and the learning and industry of ROSENMÜLLER, as well as the brief and pregnant, though often hazardous, suggestions of MAURER, may either be consulted in their own works, or in BARRETT's ' Synopsis.' CORNELIUS À LAPIDE is a most favourable specimen of the Jesuit commentator, and is terse, pointed, and acute. MICHAELIS' ' Anmerkungen für Ungelehrte' are in German. There is a learned Commentary by CALMET. POOLE's ' Synopsis' combines many of the older commentators with skill and accuracy. Of later aids to the critical study of the Book of Joshua we may mention KEIL, FAY (in Lange's Commentary), and the abbreviated and often improved edition of Keil in the volume containing Joshua, Judges, and Ruth, by Keil and Delitzsch. All these have been translated in Messrs. Clark's Series. KNOBEL's learned and most valuable work can only at present be consulted in the original. BLEEK's ' Introduction to the Old Testament' has been translated by Mr. Venables (Bell and Co.). Dr. DAVIDSON's ' Introduction' contains much valu- able matter, but the student must expect to find the " destructive criticism " in his pages. In EWALD's ' History of Israel' the reader will find much light thrown upon the history of the period. The geography of Palestine has been profusely illustrated. The best known works are those of Dr. ROBINSON, Dean STANLEY, Mr. J. L. PORTER, and Canon TRISTRAM, while the latest information is to be found in the publications of the Palestine Exploration Fund. The Book of Joshua, by Dr. ESPIN, in the ' Speaker's Commentary,' contains the latest information to be obtained on the subject, while of smaller works much geographical and general information may be found in Dr. MACLEAR's ' Joshua,' in the Cambridge Bible for Schools.

The Book of Joshua does not seem to have been a favourite one for homiletic treatment, but much may be gathered in this department from the works of ADAM CLARKE and THOMAS SCOTT, and above all, from the pious and thoughtful labours of MATTHEW HENRY. HALL's ' Contemplations' are a perfect mine of reflections on the particular points selected, while Dr. VAUGHAN's ' Heroes of Faith,' and the late BISHOP WILBERFORCE's ' Heroes of Hebrew History,' will also be very useful to the preacher.

Note A., Introduction, p. xi.

The number of expressions found in Joshua and not in the Pentateuch given in Section I. is incomplete. We may add the peculiar form of the infinitive in ch. xxii. 25, where see note. The word דְּאָגָה occurs first in ch. xxii. 24, though many words for anxiety and fear are to be found in the Pentateuch. The use of חֶרֶשׁ adverbially occurs only in Josh. ii. 1. The word תּוֹדָה occurs first in ch. vii. 19. If the word signifies *praise* here, as it does elsewhere (as in Psa. xxvi. 7, &c.), the use of the word is a very decided indication of different authorship from the Pentateuch.

And the sense *confession* appears to be quite a later one. It is only found in Ezra x. 11. The Hiphil of יצק in the sense of setting up, in the place of the original meaning, to pour out, is first found in Josh. vii. 23. This use is only found elsewhere in Job, where it frequently means " molten," and thence " hard," " firm." The adverbial use of the infinitive הבן or הבין is peculiar to Joshua. The כידון or lance is first mentioned there. The Pentateuch has another word, רמח. מאפל for darkness is only found in ch. xxiv. 7. The word נכם for " goods " is almost peculiar to Joshua, and is described by Gesenius as a " word of the later Hebrew." But why it is found in Joshua and not in the Pentateuch is hard to explain on the Deuteronomist revision theory. It only occurs elsewhere in Chronicles and Ecclesiastes. Another word occurring first in Joshua is סרני for the lords of the Philistines, implying that now, for the first time, the Israelites had come in contact with them, and therefore a strong argument for the early date of Joshua and for the Pentateuch having been written before the invasion of Palestine. Other words not found in the Pentateuch are ציר (or if we read the Hithpahel of ציד the word is still, in this form, peculiar to Joshua—see note on ch. ix. 12), פשתי עץ stalks of flax ; תקוה cord. The phrases פנה ערף and הפך ערף appear first in Joshua, and so does the verb תאר applied to a boundary line. But this last can hardly be quoted as in any way assisting to determine the date of the book, since the Pentateuch has little or nothing about boundaries, and that the word was previously in existence is shown by the noun תאַר, which is found in Genesis. On the whole the linguistic phenomena of Joshua are strongly corroborative of the view taken in Section I. The number of words occurring for the first time are few. Nearly ten times as many occur for the first time in Judges. But (1) the Book of Joshua is a brief historical narrative, in which few unusual words would be likely to occur; and (2) if written soon after the Pentateuch, when that was the only book of importance Hebrew literature possessed—a book, moreover (Josh. i. 8), which was held in the highest reverence—it would be likely to agree in its main features with the diction of its predecessor. Long settlement in Palestine, with a life of much greater liberty and dignity, would bring many new words into use. And such words we find in unusual numbers in the comparatively small Book of Judges.

Note B., p. xi.

To the passages indicating minute personal knowledge on the part of the author of the events he was describing, ch. xvii. 14 ; xx. 7 ; xxi. 2, 4 ; xxii. 3, 17, 22, may be added, beside many others ᵣeferred to in the notes.

Note C., pp. xxiv., xxvii.

The conclusion to which a perusal of the latest authorities would lead the student is that Palestine was a congeries of nationalities gathered together for commercial purposes, that the Hittite element formed the larger portion of the people, and that in some way or other these independent communities had managed to escape subjection to the Hittite monarch at Carchemish, as also to Egypt.

General Note.

It has been the object of the writer of the following exposition to gather together the notices of locality to be found in the Old Testament, so that if a preacher finds a name mentioned elsewhere he may turn to the Book of Joshua for additional information (see Geographical Index)

THE BOOK OF JOSHUA

———————

EXPOSITION.

CHAPTER I. 1—4.

JOSHUA'S COMMISSION. — Ver. 1. — **Now after the death of Moses.** The form of the Hebrew is the usual historical one for the continuation of a narrative before commenced. The Book of Joshua is thus shown to be, and to be intended to be, a continuation of the Book of Deuteronomy, which ends with the death of Moses (see Speaker's Commentary *in loc.*). This link of connection is lost in the English version. The question forces itself upon the critic, At what time was this consecutive narrative—written, as is admitted, in various styles, in the language of obviously distinct periods—first composed and palmed off upon the Jews as the genuine work of a writer contemporary, or nearly contemporary, with the events he describes? **The servant of the Lord.** This term (Keil) is applied to the heavens and the earth (Psa. cxix. 91), to the angels (Job iv. 18), to the prophets (Jer. vii. 25, &c.), to Abraham, Isaac, and Jacob, to the Jewish people (Exod. xix. 5), to Zerubbabel (Hag. ii. 23), and even to Nebuchadnezzar (Jer. xxv. 9, &c.), as the appointed minister of God's wrath, and to pious men in general (Gesenius; see Psa. xxxiv. 23, &c.). It is also applied to the Messiah (Zech. iii. 8 ; comp. the word παῖς similarly applied in Acts iv. 27). It originally implies the position of a *slave*, whether born in the house or bought with money (see Levit. xxv. 39 ; and Gen. ix. 25 ; Exod. xiii. 3, 14). In all cases it expresses a closer and more familiar relation than the term *minister* below. Keil says that it is applied so frequently to Moses that it has become almost his " official title " (see Deut. xxxiv. 5, and the Book of Joshua *passim*, and cf. Heb. iii. 5). It is, however, still more fre-

quently applied to David. But it suits well with the special and peculiar mission which Moses had above the rest of mankind. He was, as it were, the household servant of the Most High, His steward and representative, ruling over the family of God in His name, and giving to them the directions of which they stood in need. **That the Lord spake unto Joshua.** Either by *Urim and Thummim*, which seems at least probable (see Num. xxvii. 21, and Josh. ix. 14). But the great majority of commentators prefer the idea of an inward revelation, since the words are frequently used in this Book of God's revelations to Joshua (Josh. iii. 7 ; iv. 1, 15 ; v. 2, 9 ; vi. 2, &c.). The manner of these inward revelations is also a matter on which much difference of opinion exists. They, no doubt, were frequently made through a vision or dream, as to Abraham at Sodom (Gen. xviii. 1), Jacob at Bethel, and Joshua himself (ch. v. 13). But it is by no means clear that they were *always* so. The voice of God in answer to prayer is recognised by Christians in a strong inward persuasion of the desirability or necessity of a particular course. Of this kind would seem to be the answer to St. Paul's prayer in 2 Cor. xii. 9. And it is quite possible that in passages such as Gen. xii. 1, xxii. 1, 2, nothing more is meant than that the persuasion, by God's permission or inspiration, was strongly felt within. And so it is possible that one so specially and divinely commissioned as Joshua discerned, in a strong and apparently irresistible conviction, the voice of God (cf. Acts xvi. 7 ; 2 Cor i. 17). *Joshua's* name was originally *Hoshea* (like the prophet and the Israelitish king of that name). The name originally meant *salvation*, or *deliverance*, but it was changed, either when he entered into Moses' service, or when he was about to fight the Amalekites (Num. xiii. 8, 16; Deut. xxxii. 44), into Jehoshua, or Joshua (either "God shall save," or "God's salvation "). It is not stated in Holy Writ *when* the name Joshua was given. In Exod. xvii. 9, where Joshua is named for the first time, he is called by the name Moses gave him, and is mentioned incidentally as a person well known to the writer and his readers. The reader need hardly be reminded that in the form Jeshua (Gr. 'Ιησοῦς) it was the name of our Blessed Lord Himself, and that the Name which is now above all other names is used of Joshua in two places in the New Testament, in Acts vii. 45, in Heb. iv. 8. It was a common name in later times, as Col. iv. 11 and Acts xiii. 6 will serve to show. In later Hebrew, as in Neh. viii. 17, Joshua is called Jeshua, and the names of Joshua and Jeshua are given indiscriminately to the high priest, the son of Josedech, who was contemporary with the building of the second temple. For Joshua as a type of Christ the reader may consult a deep passage in 'Pearson on the Creed,' Art. II., from which some of the most striking parts are here quoted:—"First, it was he alone, of all which passed out of Egypt, who was designed to lead the children of Israel into Canaan, which land, as it is a type of heaven, so is the person which brought the Israelites into that place of rest a type of Him who only can bring us into the presence of God, and there prepare our mansions for us. Besides, it is further observable, not only what Joshua did, but what Moses could not do. The hand of Moses and Aaron brought them out of Egypt, but left them in the wilderness. Joshua, the successor, only could effect that in which Moses failed. Moses must die that Joshua may succeed (Rom. iii. 20—22). The command of circumcision was not given to Moses, but to Joshua; nor were the Israelites circumcised in the wilderness under the conduct of Moses and Aaron, but in the land of Canaan under their successor. Which speaketh Jesus to be the true circumciser, the author of another circumcision than that of the flesh (Rom. ii. 29; Col. ii. 11). If we look on Joshua as the 'minister of Moses,' he is even in that a type of Christ, 'the minister of the circumcision for the truth of God.' If we look on him as the successor of Moses, in that he represented Jesus, inasmuch as 'the law was given by Moses, but grace and truth came by Jesus Christ.' If we look on him as judge and ruler of Israel, there is scarce an action which is not predictive of our Saviour. He begins his office at the banks of Jordan, where Christ was baptized and enters upon the public exercise of His prophetical office; he chooseth

there twelve men out of the people to carry twelve stones over with them, as our Jesus thence began to choose His twelve apostles, those foundation-stones in the Church of God (Rev. xxi. 14). Joshua smote the Amalekites and subdued the Canaanites, by the first making way to enter the land, by the second giving possession of it. And Jesus in like manner goeth in and out before us against our spiritual enemies, subduing sin and Satan, and so opening and clearing our way to heaven; destroying the last enemy, death, and so giving us possession of eternal life." Pearson quotes Justin Martyr, Tertullian, Theodoret, and others as justifying his view of the history. Theodoret, moreover, in his 'Questions on Joshua,' remarks on the coincidence between Josh. i. 17 and John v. 46. And Origen, in his first 'Homily on Joshua,' remarks on the fact that the first time the sacred name meets us in the Book of God, it is as the leader of an army (Exod. xvii. 9). Another way in which Joshua was a type of Christ is this. Under Moses there are constant murmurings and disputings, for "the law made nothing perfect" (Heb. vii. 19). Under Joshua all is confidence and triumph, for "by one offering Jesus hath perfected for ever them that are sanctified " (Heb. x. 14). **Moses' minister.** This word is principally used of service in the house of God. Thus it is used of Aaron and his sons, Exod. xxviii. 43; xxxix. 41, &c.: of Samuel, 1 Sam. ii. 11; iii. 1, &c.: of the priests and Levites, 1 Chron. vi. 32; xvi. 4; Ezek. xiv. 5; Joel i. 9, &c. In these places it seems to be equivalent to the LXX. λειτουργός. But it is by no means confined to such service. In Exod. xxxiii. 11, where it is applied to Joshua, it is rendered in the LXX. by θεράπων, and it is quite clear that Joshua's service to Moses was not exclusively of a religious character. Some commentators have suggested the word *aide-de-camp*, but this would be equally incorrect in the opposite direction, since Joshua's services (see Exod. xxiv. 13; xxxiii. 11) were clearly not rendered only in time of war. The word is used of Abishag the Shunamite, 1 Kings i. 4, 15; and of Elisha, 1 Kings xix. 21.

Ver. 2.—Moses my servant is dead. "When you see Jerusalem overthrown, the altar forsaken, no sacrifices, no holocausts, no drink offerings, no priests, no Levitical ministry, when you see all these things cease, say it is because Moses the servant of God is dead, and Jesus the Son of God obtains the leadership" (Origen, Hom. 2 on Josh.). **This Jordan.** Called "this" because it was now close to them, just as we have "this people," "this Lebanon " (see note on ver. 4), &c. The name Jordan signifies "Descender," from the verb יָרַד to descend. The word fitly describes the head-long current of the river, which, according to Mr. Macgregor ('Rob Roy on the Jordan,' p. 282), has a fall of fifteen feet per mile, and if we subtract the Lake of Gennesareth and the lake and attendant marshes of Huleh, of thirty feet. Between the Sea of Galilee and the Dead Sea, however, the average fall is much less. Just after leaving the Sea of Galilee its fall is over forty feet. (Conder, 'Handbook,' p. 216). It may be interesting to compare with this the average inclination of some of our own English rivers. The swiftest is the Dee, in Aberdeenshire, which has a fall of 16·5 ft. per mile. The Tweed and Clyde have a fall of 16 ft. and 14 ft. respectively, while the Severn has but 26¼ in., the Thames 18 in., and the Shannon 9 in. per mile. This comparative table will give the best idea of the rapidity of the Jordan. The various explorers bear testimony to the swiftness of its current. Thus Robinson, in his 'Biblical Researches,' says, "The current was so strong that even Komeh, a stout swimmer of the Nile, was carried down several yards in crossing." "It was so swift," says Dr. Bartlett ('Egypt and Palestine,' p. 452), "that a gentleman of another company, who went to bathe, was not suffered by his friends to do so without a rope most un-romantically attached to his person." This was in March, at the time of the overflowing (see chap. iii.), and he adds, "the turbid stream rushed along like a mill-race." Canon Tristram, visiting it in April, describes it as "rushing with tremendous force." It rises among the snows of Hermon, dashes down headlong into the lake Huleh, the Merom of the Book of Joshua, and thence, with a descent of 60 ft. per mile, into the Sea of Galilee. Thence it shapes its course, as we have seen, with greatly diminished velocity into that strange depression where the Dead Sea lies, at a level of 1,290 ft. beneath the level of the Mediterranean. I **do give**, literally, *I am giving ; i.e.*, at this moment, when you are preparing to enter it.

Ver. 3.—**Every place that the sole of your foot doth tread upon.** These words are a quotation, almost word for word, from Deut. xi. 24, but the original promise is to be found in Gen. xii. 1—7, with which we may compare Gen. xiii. 14—17; xv. 18; xvii. 8. Comp. also Josh. xiv. 9 ; Exod. xxiii. 30, 31, &c. It was God's *purpose* that the whole land should belong to the children of Israel; a purpose which, as usual in Hebrew prophecy, is signified by the use of the perfect tense here. The conquest was intended to

be complete. Not a foot's breadth was to rest in the hands of its former owners. But here, as elsewhere in Holy Writ, we may mark the way in which man's sin and want of faith has marred the purposes of God. In the Book of Judges we read that the Canaanites were not only not driven out, but that the children of Israel made marriages with them, worshipped their gods, and practised their abominations. Jerusalem remained in the hands of the Jebusites until the time of David, while the Philistines remained in possession of their portion of Palestine until it was reduced under the power of the king of Babylon. We may observe that, according to all the ordinary laws of criticism, this citation of Deuteronomy is a proof that that Book existed when the Book of Joshua was written. For the cumbrous scheme of Elohists, Jehovists, Deuteronomists, and the like, by which this natural conclusion is overruled, see Introduction. **Have I given it.** The preterite here denotes God's purpose (cf. Gen. i. 29).

Ver. 4.—**From the wilderness and this Lebanon.** The words suppose a line to be drawn from the desert of Arabia on the south and the range of Lebanon on the north, to the River Euphrates on the one hand and the Mediterranean Sea on the other, including the land of the Hittites (see 1 Kings iv. 24 ; 2 Chron. ix. 26). Tiphsah, the later Thapsacus, was far north of the utmost limits of Palestine, and almost in the latitude of Antioch. Azzah is generally termed Gaza in our version. See note on chap. xi. 22. The land of the Hittites here (Keil) seems to be taken for the land of Canaan in general (see 1 Kings x. 29 ; 2 Kings vii. 6; Ezek. xvi. 3), but extending far beyond their border, and including Syria, Moab, Ammon, the land of Bashan, and part of Arabia. This was never actually in the hand of the Israelites save during the reigns of David and Solomon, when these regions were either tributary to them, or had been actually reduced under their immediate sway. "The promise," says Theodoret, "was not undefined, but ' if ye shall keep my commandments and ordinances' (Deut. xi. 22, 23). But they, inasmuch as they immediately transgressed the law, did not obtain the perfect promises. The Divine Apostles, on the contrary, not only conquered those places on which they set their foot, but even those in which their all-wise writings were read ; and the land that was before a desert they displayed as a Divine Paradise." **This Lebanon.** This expression is no doubt used because Lebanon was visible from the spot where Joshua was standing. There is nothing surprising in this. We learn from travellers that its range, which there is no doubt included that of Anti-

Lebanon, with its lofty peak Hermon, the highest point in Palestine, is visible from all parts of the Holy Land, even from the depths of the Jordan valley near the Dead Sea. Dr. Thomson ('Land and the Book,' p. 2) says that it is visible from Cyprus. Canon Tristram ('Land of Israel,' p. 609) tells how he had seen Hermon from Tyre, Sidon, Carmel, Gerizim, from the neighbourhood of Jerusalem, from Gilead, from Nebo, and from the Dead Sea. The name Lebanon, derived from לָבָן to be white, like the Arabic *lebanon*, milk, is supposed by Robinson to have been given from the whitish colour of the chalk or limestone rock (so Conder, 'Handbook,' p. 206). But it is at least equally probable that it derives its name, like Mont Blanc in Savoy, from its snowy peaks. Hermon is still called by the Arabs Jebel-el-Thelj, or "the snowy peak." The Jordan, the river of Palestine *par excellence*, derived its copious and everflowing streams, so essential in that "thirsty land," from the Anti-Lebanon range. "Abana and Pharpar, rivers of Damascus," as well as the Orontes, and the Litany or Leontes, derive their waters from the same source (see Tristram, 'Land of Israel,' chap. xxv.; Thomson, 'Land and the Book,' pp. 172, 173). We have a vivid description of the region of Lebanon and the adjacent range of Anti-Lebanon and Hermon, in the spring, at the time of the melting of the snows, in the 42nd Psalm. There David, recalling to mind his sojourn in the "land of the Jordan," and of Hermon, speaks of the "deep calling unto deep," of the noise of the cataracts as they dashed from rock to rock and foamed along the mountain sides; and he describes his sorrows as overwhelming him by their number and magnitude, just as the multitudinous torrents that rose in that snowy region threatened to engulf the unwary traveller in their onward sweep. The far-famed cedars of Lebanon are indigenous to this region, and to it alone, but the climatic changes which Palestine has undergone have reduced their number largely, and comparatively few specimens now remain, in a wild condition, of that noble tree, once the pride of the dwellers in the land. "We cannot study all the passages in the Old Testament which refer to the cedar, without feeling certain that in ancient times it was a far more conspicuous feature in the landscape than it is now" (Tristram, 'Land of Israel,' p. 631). **The great river, the river Euphrates.** *Das grosse Wasser Phrath* (Luther). The Hebrew name is as Luther gives it. The Greeks added the euphonic syllable at the commencement, according to those who assign to the word a Semitic

derivation. Others, however, derive it from an Aryan source, and regard it as equivalent to "the flowing river." This mighty stream, especially after its junction with the Tigris, far transcended in size any other with which the Israelites were acquainted. The plains of Mesopotamia, even as far as Nineveh and Babylon, were destined to have been occupied by the Jewish race, had not their impiety and rebellion prevented; and the world-empire obtained by Nineveh and Babylon might, and had they been obedient would, have been theirs. **All the land of the Hittites.** The Hittites, or Chittites, seem to have been the most considerable of the tribes which inhabited Canaan. We find them in possession of Hebron in the time of Abraham (Gen. xxiii.), but their more usual dwelling-place was in the valley. They appear from the narrative above quoted to have been a peaceable people. We have records of them in Egyptian and Assyrian inscriptions. Thus we hear of the Khita in the inscriptions of Rameses II., who reigned between 1383 and 1322, B.C.; that is, about the time of Deborah and Barak ('Records of the Past,' ii. 67—78; iv. 25—32). They were the inhabitants, however, of a region further to the northward, beyond the borders of the Holy Land, on the banks of the Orontes. So a Mohar, or scribe, of Rameses II., in an account of a tour in Palestine, in which he mentions Kirjath Anab, Achsaph, Megiddo, and the land of Hamath, describes Khita as to the north, bordering on this latter territory ('Records of the Past,' ii. 106). The various translators of the Assyrian inscriptions of Assur-bani-pal, Tiglath Pileser, Shalmaneser, and Sennacherib recognise the Hittites in the people mentioned as dwelling to the north of Palestine (*ibid.* iii. 52; v. 21, 32, 33; vii. 61), though Ewald thinks that the Khatta there mentioned must be sought still further north. Prof. Sayce, in a recent lecture, regards the Hittites as having occupied a large portion of Asia Minor, and as having had great influence upon early Greek art, and adds, "Till within the last few years the Bible alone has preserved the name of a people who must have had almost as great an influence on human history as Assyria or Egypt." Shalmaneser mentions the kings of the Hittites, just as they are mentioned in the later narratives of Kings and Chronicles (see note on chap. iii. 10). **Unto the great sea.** As the Euphrates was the greatest river, the Mediterranean was the greatest sea, known to the Jews. Unlike the race they displaced, the Canaanites—or, to call them by a title by which they are better known to profane history, the Phœnicians—the Jews were no sailors. It may have been even before the conquest of Canaan under

Joshua that the Phœnician fleets sailed out beyond the pillars of Hercules, and brought back tin from the British isles. For Canaan, or Phœnicia, was a powerful and civilised country when conquered by the Jews. But whether it were before this period that Britain was discovered, or whether the fleets of Tyre and Sidon first sailed thither at a later period, to the Jews the Mediterranean still remained the great sea. They knew nothing of the vaster ocean into which it flowed. It seems strange that, with the example of Tyre and Sidon before them, the Israelites should have been so indifferent to navigation. Even in the time of David, it was Hiram's ships that brought him his treasures and building materials. The later navies of Solomon and Jehoshaphat did but coast along the Red Sea and the Persian Gulf to Ophir, which has been identified with India, or more probably with Arabia.

HOMILETICS.

Vers. 1—4.—*Joshua's Commission.* This passage may be viewed under two main aspects : (1) regarding Moses as the type of Christ and Joshua of His ministers ; and (2) regarding Joshua as himself the type of Christ. As these points of view suggest two perfectly distinct and independent lines of thought, it is obvious that they are better fitted for two separate discourses than for being combined in one.

I. JOSHUA AS THE TYPE OF GOD'S MINISTERS.

1. *After the death of Moses, the task devolves upon his minister.* So after the death of Christ, the task of conquering the world devolved upon His apostles, His " ministers." They who waited on Christ during His human life, who were with Him in His temptations, were the men appointed to carry on His work when He had gone hence.

2. *By the express command of God.* So the apostles not only had Christ's commission, " Go ye into all the world and preach the gospel to every creature" (Mark xvi. 15 ; xxviii. 19), and " As my Father hath sent me, even so send I you " (John xx. 21), but they were bidden to wait till the time was fixed (Acts i. 4), and the Spirit poured out upon them from on high (Acts ii. 4). Hence we learn that no work, however high and holy, should be undertaken without the express intimation that it is God's pleasure we should attempt it ; that no motives, however pure, will justify us in putting our hand to the ark (2 Sam. vi. 6, 7) unless we are ordained by God to touch it. And if we ask how we are to know when we are so ordained, the answer—is (*a*) by seeking counsel of God ; (*b*) by scrutinising carefully the purity of our own motives, lest we may have mistaken pride or self-interest for the voice of God. That intimation will be given in various ways. We know not how (see note on v. 1) Joshua was stirred up by God. But men are marked out for special tasks in three ways : (1) by *circumstances.* Thus Joshua, as the minister of Moses, most closely acquainted with his modes of thought and course of action, became naturally his successor. So Timothy takes the place of St. Paul (2 Tim. iii. 10). (2) By *external authority ;* that of those who have a right to exercise it, like the high priest when he sought counsel of God by Urim and Thummim. (3) By *inward intimations* of God's Spirit, which cannot be mistaken, save by those who have blinded their own eyes by self-seeking and self-conceit.

3. *The command is based upon Moses' death.* So all the work of God's ministers derives its energy from the death of Christ. It was the one all-sufficient sacrifice and satisfaction for the sins of the whole world that was the salt of the Apostles' mission. It is that same atonement which gives power to their successors now.

4. *The work is of God, but the ministers are human.* God *might* have performed His work without the intervention of means. But He has chosen to act through human instrumentality. Thus He magnifies His greatness even more than if He had done the work Himself. For human infirmities sorely mar the work of God. And yet that work goes on, and even human infirmity is overruled to God's glory (1 Cor. ii. 4, 5 ; 2 Cor. iv. 7 ; xii. 9). So it was with Joshua's error in judgment regarding the Gibeonites (ch. ix. 14), and so it often is with our own.

5. *Difficulties often present themselves, insuperable but by the hand of God.* " Go over this Jordan." But how? The river was full to overflowing, the

passage dangerous; in fact, for the whole multitude, in the face of the enemy, impossible. Yet the hand of God was stretched out, the river dried up, and what would have been a task of the greatest peril to themselves was instead a source of terror to their adversaries. So at the outset of great spiritual undertakings we are often confronted with difficulties far beyond our power to overcome. But "God showeth his voice," and they "melt away."

6. *The result, possession of the promised land.* The land promised to the Israelites was a limited space, but the spiritual Israel has the promise of the whole earth (see Gen. xii. 3; Psa. ii. 8; Isa. xi. 9; Dan. ii. 35, &c.).

II. JOSHUA AS THE TYPE OF CHRIST.

1. *After the death of Moses.* The law could never give us our inheritance (Heb. vii. 19); therefore Moses must die and Joshua arise. Again: the law was crucified together with Christ (Rom. vi. 6, 10; vii. 4; Gal. ii. 19; v. 24; Eph. ii. 15, 16; Col. ii. 14; also 2 Cor. iii. 14 in the Greek). As long as the law existed, man could only dwell in the wilderness, be dead in trespasses and sins, wander about without power to enter the promised land. He was continually confronted with a standard of holiness utterly beyond his strength to reach. But when Moses —*i.e.*, the law—is dead, the true Jesus arises and leads His people into their inheritance, giving them the power to fulfil a law which He has written within.

2. *Joshua was Moses' minister.* So Christ was "made under the law" (Gal. iv. 4), and was bound, by His Father's will, to keep it. By His obedience alone was His sacrifice made acceptable to His Father. The law could but condemn us for being "weak through the flesh" (Rom. viii. 3); we could not fulfil its precepts. But Christ condemned sin (1) by His perfect fulfilment of God's law, and (2) by submitting to death, as the "wages" of that sin which mankind, whom He represented, had so fully deserved. Thus did He gain the right to be our leader into the inheritance God had promised us.

3. *Jordan must be crossed; i.e.,* Jesus must die. As our representative, He dies once for all to sin, and His death translates us into a new life. Henceforth, by virtue of His atonement, "sin has no more dominion over us," and we are, under His leadership, to destroy its empire for ever. And we must follow Him through Jordan; that is, we too must die to sin and rise again unto righteousness. The river which divides our old condition from the new, which separates the wilderness from the promised land, is an eternal boundary between our condition by nature and our condition by grace. The waters of Jordan are likened by some to the waters of baptism, whereby we are "baptized into Christ's death;" and by others to the moment of conversion, when, by the power of God alone, we are changed from wanderers and outcasts into the covenant people of God.

4. *The land must be conquered.* It was a wicked land; a land the sins of whose inhabitants contaminated it by their example; a land which called for condign chastisement from on high. The land with which Christians have to do is either (1) the whole world, or (2) the human heart. In the first case it is the duty of the Church, in the second of the individual, in each case under Christ as a leader, to wage unceasing warfare against evil, in whatever forms it may be found. The character of that warfare will be indicated later. At present it will be sufficient to remark that the nature of the warfare itself is not changed, though its conditions are. The servants of God are eternally pledged to root out evil without compromise, and without mercy.

5. *It was a land flowing with milk and honey.* Every blessing was to be obtained there. Not only food, but delights. It is called emphatically "the good land" (Deut. iii. 25; iv. 22). It contained every good thing man could desire (Deut. viii. 7—9). So the steadfast determination to follow Christ, to him who is resolved to do so, insures us every blessing we need—the supply of our wants, means of defence against our enemies, and the means, moreover, of happiness and enjoyment—provided always that we do not cease the combat until all our enemies be destroyed.

HOMILIES BY VARIOUS AUTHORS.

Vers. 1, 2.—*Consolation for bereaved workers.* In these words, addressed to Joshua, we have the most effectual consolation that can be offered to believers, when one has been taken away from their midst whose life seemed indispensable to the work and service of God. They are words applicable to the family no less than to the Church. Moses had just been taken from the people, from his friends, from Joshua his faithful servant. The great leader of Israel through the wilderness journey, the captain who had gone forth with their hosts to battle, the medium of the highest revelations of God to the nation, had vanished from among them. Israel would look no more on that noble face which had caught and kept the brightness of the glory of God revealed upon Sinai. The prophetic voice of him who had talked with God as a man talketh with his friend was hushed in lasting silence. He had been struck down on the very borders of the land of promise, to which he had safely led the sons of Abraham, Isaac, and Jacob. There was a peculiar sadness in the death of Moses just at this time. Have we not often felt the same when we have seen the strong man fall at the very moment when he was about to reap the fruit of his patient labours, and to win the hard-fought fight? The words spoken by God Himself for the consolation of Israel may suggest thoughts helpful to us under similar circumstances.

I. GOD'S WORK DOES NOT DEPEND ON ANY ONE WORKER, EVEN THE GREATEST. It goes on, uninterrupted by the strokes of death. "Go over this Jordan, thou and all this people, unto the land which I do give to them, even to the children of Israel." Thus the cause still advances. Moses may die; his work cannot. Nay, it is extended, and assumes new developments. Moses has led the people to the verge of Jordan. Joshua will carry them over. Both Moses and Joshua are only instruments which may be broken and laid aside; but He who uses them will never be stopped in His work of love. "My Father," says Jesus Christ, "worketh hitherto" (John v. 17).

II. As GOD ONLY WORKS BY HIS SERVANTS, THESE MUST NEVER REST IN AN IDLE RELIANCE ON HIS POWER; THEY MUST TAKE UP THE WORK JUST WHERE IT IS HANDED OVER TO THEM, EVEN THOUGH THEIR HEARTS MAY BE BROKEN BY SORROW. Thus the Lord says to Joshua: "Arise, go over this Jordan." We may not sit still mourning even over our beloved dead; we are to arise and take up their work. To carry it on is a sweet consolation; we feel ourselves still linked with the departed as we trace their blessed footsteps, and deepen the furrows they have already made. It brings us into closer fellowship with them. Joshua, as he took up the charge laid down by Moses, was more than ever brought into oneness of spirit with him.

III. GOD, IN SPEAKING OF MOSES AS HIS SERVANT, GIVES TO THE SURVIVORS THE SWEET ASSURANCE THAT HE HAS TAKEN HIM TO REST IN HIS OWN PRESENCE. The recognition of his faithful service implies that of his sure reward. Undoubtedly he, like all the sons of men, was an unprofitable servant, but he nevertheless received from God that grand word of commendation, "Well done, good and faithful servant;" and this is the word which sets before him who receives it an open heaven. Thus to know that God never leaves His work incomplete, that He gives it to us to carry on, and that those who have gone before us have entered into His rest, while we take up their unfinished task—this is the threefold solace of the sorrows alike of the Church and of the Christian family. Thus both "he that soweth and they who reap rejoice together" (John iv. 36).—E. DE P.

Vers. 2, 3.—*God's gift to the Church.* The loss of a privilege teaches us how inadequately we have appreciated its worth. The removal of an honoured servant of God often awakens a deeper sense of the blessing that has been in our midst. And sometimes a tendency is thus created to dwell unduly on the past, to become morbid, and to neglect the present, undervaluing what still remains to us. Mourning has its proper limits. In the text God impresses on the people the duty of recognising facts. "Moses is dead." True, you will never look upon his like again;

but also true, that all your regrets will not restore him to his wonted place. There is to be no standstill in the kingdom of God. A new leader is summoned to the front. Joshua must succeed to the vacant post.

I. We have A NEW LEADER AND A FRESH START. As if to magnify Joshua in the eyes of the Israelites, the command is at once given to prepare for that entrance into the land of promise which Moses had so ardently longed for but was not permitted to witness. "One soweth, another reapeth." The law paved the way for the gospel. It is well to follow a period of inaction by vigorous measures. Active employment would turn away the people's thoughts from unduly dwelling upon the absence of Moses, and would prove that all wisdom and energy had not died with him, nor had God also perished in His servant's death. And so to-day the class in the Sunday-school shall continue its training, though the much-loved teacher has been compelled to renounce his work; the congregation shall be instructed as heretofore, though by a different voice. Let class and congregation rally around their new chief. The appointment of a new leader should be the signal for a fresh advance. Let "Onward!" be the cry.

II. THE TITLE OF POSSESSION. The real claim of the Israelites was grounded on the gift of God. Consider the earth (a) *Materially*, as belonging to God. "The earth is the Lord's." Men are but His tenants-at-will. The justification of the Israelites in driving out the Canaanites is to be sought in the fact that the inhabitants had made an ill use of the land. He who owned it had revoked His grant, and conferred it on His chosen people. The lesson enforced by our Lord in the parable of the talents is of wide application. Not only agriculturists but merchants must regard their property as held at the disposal of the Creator. Nevertheless there is something in the possession of a "foot of ground" which seems to connect us immediately with the Lord of the earth, and renders impiety amid scenes of nature the more guilty. (b) *Spiritually*, as given through Christ to the Church. The commission of Christ to the disciples embraced the whole world. Every nation of right belongs to God, and the establishment of missions is but claiming the land for its Great Owner. God hath given to every company of believers a "land" to possess, a neighbourhood to be evangelised, cruelty and vice and selfishness to be expelled, that peace and love and righteousness may dwell in the conquered territory. The text may remind us, therefore, of the aggressive measures which the Church of Christ is required to undertake.

III. THE DIVINE GIFT NO SUPERSESSION OF HUMAN EFFORT. First the Israelites must cross the river Jordan, and then seize the gift offered. They had literally to tread with the "sole of the foot" upon the land they desired to receive from God. Every promise of Scripture is intended not as a sedative, but as a stimulus, to exertion. We have to "*labour* to enter into the rest." There is a Divine law, "Seek and ye shall find; knock and it shall be opened." The redemption that is in Christ will not benefit unless appropriated. The "treasures of wisdom and knowledge" will be ours by taking them in Christ from the outstretched hands of God. In all church operations we must be mindful that "Christ expects every man to do his duty." The heathen are His inheritance, but will be made His only as the Church is stirred up to diligent activity in moral conquest. Thus the gifts of God are conditional upon human service. Not, of course, that God simply allocates the land as did the Popes formerly, expecting the grantees to secure it for themselves; for He helps us, and without Him our efforts would be vain.

IV. THE RECORDED PROMISE INTENDED FOR ALL GENERATIONS. "As I said unto Moses." There is evident reference to the utterance of Jehovah forty years before (Exod. xxiii. 31). He had not forgotten His word. Should the unbelief of the people make His "promises of none effect"? That Moses had not allowed the declaration to slip from his memory is seen in Deut. xi. 24. Intervening years do not render the fulfilment of God's promises less sure. Thousands of years rolled away between the first prediction of a Messiah and His actual appearance. Let not our hearts fail to trust in God. "As I said unto Moses" may be turned into a general promise, as the Epistle to the Hebrews did with the specific utterance of ch. v. 5 to Joshua (Heb. xiii. 5). It may be kept before us as a message of hope and assurance.
—A.

Vers. 1—9.—*Joshua the successor of Moses.* The very name *Joshua, Jesus,* " *God's salvation,*" is enough of itself to awaken special interest in the man who, on the page of Scripture, first bears it. It is suggestive at once of the nature of his life-work, and it leads us to anticipate some points of analogy between him and the Saviour of the world. Joshua is one of the few Old Testament characters against whose name there is no reproach. Not that this Book presents any formal delineation of his character or pronounces his praise. It is but a simple, matter-of-fact record of great events in which he took a leading part. His illustrious deeds are their own eulogium. He stands before us as the type of a godly warrior, reverent in spirit yet full of practical energy, blameless and fearless, gentle and strong, spending a long life in unselfish and unwearied devotion to the cause of the people and of God. He was the brave soldier whose work, dark and terrible as it was, was consecrated by the inspiration of a Divine call and of a beneficent purpose. A general view of Joshua's position in the annals of the Hebrew race is suggestive.

I. IT REMINDS US HOW, AT CRITICAL PERIODS IN HUMAN HISTORY, GOD RAISES UP MEN AS FITTING INSTRUMENTS FOR THE ACCOMPLISHMENT OF HIS PURPOSES. The death of Moses marks a crisis in the career of the chosen people. He who has been their "leader and commander" through all the forty years' wandering in the wilderness and has brought them to the borders of the land of promise, is taken from them just when they seem most to need him. Only Jordan now rolls between them and the fruition of their hopes; the prize is within their reach. Shall they fail, and, after all, come short of it? They would have failed if God had not been with them, moving, working among them, fulfilling His own will, magnifying His own name. Joshua's uprising is itself a Divine interposition. He is not the product of the mere natural working of events and second causes. He is a deliverer whom God has provided, well named *God's salvation.* The lesson is an important one. When God has any great work for men to do, He never fails to call forth those who can do it. The history of the Church, the general course of the world's life, establish this law. The demand and the supply, the hour and the man, always meet. When those who are in the high places of the field fall, others step forth, often from very unlikely quarters, to fill the gap and carry on the work to riper issues. This continuity of the Divine purpose and of the path of its development is very wonderful—

> " The voice that from the glory came
> To tell how Moses died unseen,
> And waken Joshua's spear of flame
> To victory on the mountains green,
> Its trumpet tones are sounding still,"

kindling our expectations, rousing our energies, rebuking our distrust. Through the shifting clouds of circumstance we catch " glimpses of the unchanging sky." God's redeeming purpose shines on through all human and earthly changes. We need not fear but that He " will plead his own cause," and when new emergencies arise provide some new instrument or agency to meet them.

II. IT REMINDS US OF THE PROCESS BY WHICH GOD IS WONT TO PREPARE MEN FOR THE WORK HE HAS FOR THEM TO DO. Joshua was a divinely chosen and ordained deliverer (Num. xxvii. 18—23; Deut. xxxi. 14—23). But God's choice is never arbitrary, reasonless. There is generally some native quality, or circumstantial advantage, that makes the chosen man the more fitting instrument. (Examples: Moses, David, Cyrus, Paul, Luther.) Joshua grew up as a slave in the brick-fields of Egypt. Born about the time when Moses fled into Midian, he must have been forty years old at the exodus. It may seem strange that such greatness as his should have been nursed amid such associations. But when God has fixed His choice on a man He can make what seem to be the most adverse conditions a school of preparation. And, perhaps, the rough influences of such a lot were, after all, the best school. In servitude as a youth, he learnt how to command as a man. No doubt sudden emergencies have often developed unlooked-for qualities in men. Tender spirits, nursed in the lap of luxury, have been found calm in danger, brave in battle. Still, as a rule, to "bear the yoke in one's youth" is the best preparation for the stern struggle of after life. Moreover, the trials and responsibilities of life are graduated. The right discharge of lesser duty qualifies for higher positions of trust. Joshua proved, in the previous expeditions on which Moses sent him (Exod. xvii. 9; Num. xiii. 17), his fitness to take the place of the great leader. "He that is faithful in that which is least is faithful also in much." "If thou hast run with the footmen," &c. (Jer. xii. 5). Again: other circumstances of a different kind—miraculous manifestations, Divine revelations—had their part in Joshua's preparation. He had witnessed the wonders in Egypt and at the Red Sea, had been with Moses in the mount, had had direct communication from God to himself (Deut. xxxi.). We are reminded of the higher, diviner influences that help in the formation of all noblest human character; there is always the blending of natural and supernatural elements, ordinary associations of life mingled with direct heavenly visitations, innate qualities sanctified and glorified by special ministries of the grace of God.

III. IT ILLUSTRATES THE HEROISM THAT SPRINGS FROM FAITH. Faith, the faith that brought him into personal contact with the living God, was the spring of all Joshua's strength and courage. He had no prophetic gift as regards the vision of the future, for it was through the priest Eleazar, "after the judgment of Urim," that he was to ask counsel of the Lord (Num. xxvii. 21). But as military leader of Israel he was divinely inspired; and his inspiration was the energy of faith. This has ever been the prolific root of the noblest forms of character and deed. By it "the elders," whose names shed lustre on the ages of the past, "obtained their good report." And so it always will be. There is no heroism like that which springs from the soul's living hold on the unseen and eternal. The hope of the world for deliverance from the ills that afflict it, and its being led into the heritage of a brighter future, is in the men of faith. And he is an enemy to his race who would attempt to dry up this spring of power. "This is the victory," &c. (1 John v. 4).

IV. IT PRESENTS US WITH AN INTERESTING HISTORIC TYPE OF GOSPEL SALVATION. Many points of typical resemblance have been traced. This, at least, is clear,— as Joshua, "Moses' minister," consummates his work, leads the people into the promised land, divides to them their inheritance; so Christ, "made under the law," brings in the richer grace. He is the "end of the law for righteousness," &c. (Rom. x. 4). The Captain of salvation leads many sons, His redeemed ones, to glory and eternal rest.—W.

EXPOSITION.

CHAPTER I. 5—9.

THE SOURCE OF JOSHUA'S CONFIDENCE.— Ver. 5.—**There shall not any man be able to stand before thee.** Literally, *no one shall set himself up against thee, i.e.,* successfully resist thee (ἀντιστήσεται, LXX.). **As I was with Moses.** Literally, *as I have been* with Moses: that is to say, was with him and remained with him unto the end. The continuity of the work of God under the old dispensation is thus as clearly marked as that of the new in Matt. xxviii. 20, and John xx. 21—23. The promises made to Abraham, the law given to Moses, the gift of a new life in Christ, are so many parts of one great work, and that work the regeneration of mankind. **I will not fail thee.** Literally, I will not *be weak* towards thee,

relax towards thee. God is ever the same, If His attitude to us be altered, it is not He who has changed, but ourselves.

Ver. 6.—**Be strong and of a good courage.** Literally, *be strong and vigorous.* The word does not refer so much to the *character* of Joshua as to his actions. He was to be a man of action, alert, prompt, ready to act when occasion demanded (see Deut. xxxi. 6, 7, 8, 23). **Which I sware unto their fathers** (see note on ver. 3).

Ver. 7.—**Be very courageous.** The word is the same as is translated "be of good courage" above. Knobel remarks that the phraseology here is similar to that of Deuteronomy, but "strange to the other Books" of the Pentateuch. This may be from the fact that Deuteronomy is throughout hortatory, while the other Books are historical. But the recurrence of the hortatory phrases of Deuteronomy here is at least remarkable (see ver. 3). **Prosper.** Rather, perhaps *be wise* (cf. Deut. xxix. 9, though, according to Calvin, the word means, "not only to act prudently but successfully"). The only true wisdom is that obtained from God, whether in answer to prayer, or in meditation on His law (see 1 Cor. i. 17—31; ii. 12—16; iii. 19). Ver. 8.—**This book of the law.** The law was, therefore, embodied in a written document when the Book of Joshua was written; and as the antiquity of this Book may be regarded as proved, we may quote thus an early authority for the genuineness of at least some portions of the Pentateuch. There was a "book of the law" in Joshua's time, according to this early testimony, and we may conclude from vers. 3—7 that Deuteronomy formed a part of it (see also Deut. xvii. 19 for a similar precept. And for the fact see Deut. xxxi. 24—26). **Meditate therein** (cf. Psa. i. 2, lxiii. 7,

cxliii. 5, in the original. Also Deut. xxxi. 26). **Observe to do.** Literally, *keep to do*, thus impressing on us the care necessary in deciding on our actions. **All that is written therein** (cf. for the expression Deut. xxviii. 58, 61; xxix. 19, 20, 26; xxx. 10). **Shall have good success.** The word is the same as is translated "prosper" above, and *not* the same as that rendered "prosperous" in this verse. "Men," says Calvin, "never act skilfully, except in so far as they allow themselves to be ruled by the Word of God." **Have I not commanded thee?** "An emphatic inquiry is a stronger form of affirmation, and is generally employed by those who wish to infuse into another courage and alacrity" (Michaelis). Moreover *repetition* is a remarkable feature of Hebrew composition, as we may observe from the second chapter of Genesis onward, and is designed to give emphasis to what is commanded or related. Calvin would lay stress on *I:* "Have not *I* commanded thee?" But this is not borne out by the Hebrew.

HOMILETICS.

Vers. 5—9.—*The source of Joshua's confidence.* I. HE HAD BEEN CHOSEN BY GOD. Moses was dead, and Joshua's heart might well have failed him. For the great lawgiver had found the task of leading the Israelites from Egypt to the borders of the promised land too much for his strength and spirit (Exod. xviii. 13—17; Num. xi. 11—17; Deut. i. 9—15). Constant rebellions and murmurings had weakened his hands. "They provoked his spirit, so that he spake unadvisedly with his lips (Psa. cvi. 33), and in consequence he was not permitted to lead them into Canaan. To Joshua a harder task was assigned. He was not only to lead the Israelites, but to lead them in battle, and against foes more numerous and better prepared for war than themselves. Yet the sense that he had been marked out for the task, as well as his determination to obey the orders he had received, sustained him. He was never known to waver but once (ch. vii.), nor did the confidence of his followers in him ever falter. So may all those who have received a charge from God rest assured that they will be able to execute it.

II. HE REPOSED UPON GOD'S PROMISE. He "believed God," and it was not only "counted unto him for righteousness," but his faith led him to victory. Nothing could have nerved him for such a task but the consciousness that God was with him. For he had no personal ambition (ch. xix. 49), such as often stimulates men to great tasks. Thus the Christian warrior of to-day, who contends not for himself but for his Master, may emulate Joshua's courage and confidence, for the same promises are his as were Joshua's (Heb. xiii. 5, 6; Eph. vi. 10; 2 Thess. iii. 3).

III. HE WAS DILIGENT IN THE STUDY OF THE SCRIPTURES, AND HE GUIDED HIMSELF BY THEIR INJUNCTIONS. He had only the law of Moses, but he kept it (ch. v., vi., vii.). He had been warned to extirpate the Canaanites, and he obeyed the command to the letter (ch. x., xi. 15). The Christian who would conquer in his conflict with the powers of evil must be diligent in his study of God's Word, and careful to frame his life by its precepts. He must "meditate therein day and night (cf. Psa. i. 2; cxix. 1; 97—99; also Deut. iv. 9; xi. 18—20; xvii. 18, 19), and must take heed to carry out the lessons he has learned.

HOMILIES BY VARIOUS AUTHORS.

Vers. 6—9.—*A renewed covenant.* The covenant made with the patriarchs, and afterwards with their descendants when they came out of Egypt, is here renewed in almost the same words. The promises are identical (vers. 4, 5), and also the conditions of their fulfilment, which are summed up in fidelity and obedience: "*Observe to do according to all the law which Moses my servant commanded thee*" (vers. 7, 8). This renewal to each generation of the covenant between God and His people is a law of religious history. It results both from the nature of that covenant and from the character of those who enter into it.

I. This alliance is, in its essence, THE RESTORATION OF THE BOND OF LOVE BETWEEN MAN AND GOD, by the obedience of faith. Now love is a feeling which needs to be constantly renewed. The love of one generation will not avail for the next. It must be rekindled and find fresh expression.

II. The covenant must be made between the true God and man made in His image; IT MUST BE SPIRITUAL AND SPONTANEOUS IN ITS CHARACTER. It cannot be signed upon parchment or graven in the insensate stone; it must be written upon living hearts. Hence it ought to be perpetually renewed, though it gladly avails itself of the strengthening influence of its glorious antecedents. It recognises as its essential principle the free and sovereign initiative of Divine love. "We love him because he first loved us" (1 John iv. 19). Nor is it enough that this Divine covenant be renewed with each successive generation; it must be entered into by every individual soul. This was true, indeed, in relation to the higher religious life, even under the old covenant. How much more under the new—the covenant of the Spirit—which is ratified not by circumcision but by conversion. "Except a man be born again he cannot see the kingdom of God" (John iii. 3).—E. DE P.

Vers. 5, 6.—*The leader's promise.* Such is God's word to Joshua when commencing his great task. He needed the urgent precept and the supporting promise. He was no youthful dreamer, but one long past middle life, who had no exaggerated estimate of Israel's faithfulness, and no illusions about its task. He needed, and here he gets, the quickening influence of a sacred charge. As God spake to him, so he would speak to all who are constrained by a sense of duty to God or man to undertake some task that seems beyond their powers. Let us take its general lessons to all.

I. HEROES PASS AWAY, BUT THE POWER THAT MADE THEM STILL REMAINS. When Moses left his task it seemed as if the work must come to a stand. Where should they find such grace again? or how could they do without it? Such a combination of courage and meekness, faith to follow anywhere, patience with those who had hardly faith to follow at all; such wisdom, such love—could it be repeated? could it be dispensed with? Especially now, when the finish of their great enterprise was so full of difficulty. They know little of the human heart who imagine that Joshua could gaily assume the responsibilities of his command. They who enter into great wars "with light heart" do not take long to gather heaviness. And Joshua, advanced in life, acquainted with the difficulties of his task, doubtless was tempted to feel that with Moses the heroic age had ended, and prosaic common life alone remained. Probably the people shared this feeling; and with the departure of this great hero there was the feeling that all greatness and glory was gone. The first thing that will quicken men with hope is this—heroes leave us, but God remains. Before the special promise will operate its special comfort there must be this general thought of comfort cherished and realised. And we all shall be prepared to realise the promises which suit ourselves, if we realise that amidst all changes God remains unchanged, and whatever leaves us He abides. We are all apt to say that former times were better than the present; to imagine that former greatness cannot be grown now; that grandeur of thought, saintliness, courage, will come no more " to dignify our times; " that there was special grace vouchsafed to past ages which made them rich, and which has evaporated long ago. Churchmen look back to the Fathers; Dissenters to the Reformers of the Church. Now the martyrs of the ancient days, now the stalwart heroes of Puritan times, are gilded with our reverent memory; and then rises the pensive thought that "the tender grace of the day that is dead" will never return. "As I was with Moses, so will I be with thee." Revere the saintly past, but recognise the Divine present. The great ones have gone; that which made them great remains. The fixed constancy of their maturer service makes us forget with what gradualness their characters grew. How by lowly ventures, by difficult waiting, by support only sufficient to prevent despair, they rose step by step; God's grace entering them ever the more largely and obeyed ever the more fully. So, blade to ear, ear to full corn in the ear, their character grew; and so may ours. To-day the Spirit of all grace broods on humanity, kindling all wakeful spirits, entering and employing them. Still Christ's love helps and harbours all. The peculiarities of the nineteenth century do not enfeeble God. And He is here, fresh and strong to-day. He will hallow, not equalise, varieties of constitution; will not make a Joshua into a Moses, nor an Elisha into an Elijah; but with special grace for their special task will equally endue each. Despair not of God's Church; tremble not for the ark of God; despair not of our country, or of mankind. Whoever, whatever has gone, God remains. "As He was with our fathers, so He will be with us."

II. WITH EVERY DUTY COMES THE POWER TO DO IT. "I will not fail thee, nor forsake thee." If the first clause of the text promised the presence, the second pledges the power and help, of God. He will be with Joshua—not merely in sense of ubiquity, but in sense of interest; not to watch faults and failures, but to prevent them. There was the fear that in this enterprise many things might "*fail*" them. The people's courage might fail; they might withdraw from allegiance to him; his wisdom might be at fault, his endurance might fail. But God comes in and says, "I will not fail thee." Will disappoint no expectation, withhold no needed help; will not fail you when you are weak, nor forsake you when you are faulty. With the duty there will be the power, for God will not fail us. There is no part of the gospel more necessary or more sweet than this—that with duty power always comes; they walk hand in hand. The moment the Saviour's precept makes it the man's duty to stretch forth his hand, that moment he has power to do it. When the disciples are bidden to feed the multitude they have power to do so. The acceptance of a charge opens the heart to God, and He floods it with His grace. If the disciples are sent out to cast out devils they have the power to do so, for God does not fail them. They never get power apart from Him, of which they can be conscious and proud. But He is there—by them, in them; and when they are feeling all weakness, and unfitness, He, not failing, charges them with all the grace they need. You are called to confess Christ; to forsake some pleasant or profitable course of evil; to stand alone; to take up some forlorn hope of philanthropy. . . . and you feel no strength, energy, vigour for your task. Take this comfort: with duty there invariably comes the power to discharge it. "I will never fail thee, nor forsake thee." Observe lastly—

III. COURAGE IS THE SUPREME REQUIREMENT OF GOD'S SAINTS, AND STRENGTH GOES WITH IT. "*Be strong and of a good courage.*" It is striking how large a place exhortations to courage hold in all the Bible. "Add to your faith, *courage*" (not *virtue*), says Peter; and so saying sums up many testimonies. You cannot easily count the "fear nots" of the Bible. And these are not merely soothing words, calming solicitude, but quickening words, calling to conflict and to victory. Take the eleventh chapter of Hebrews, and you will find that in almost every instance in which the writer attributes men's greatness to their faith he might have done so with equal truth to their courage. Fear is the parent of every kind of vice; fear of conflict, fear of shame, fear of failure, fear that God will leave fidelity unrewarded and prayer unanswered. "They were afraid to confess him," says the Evangelist of those who sold their birthright for a mess of pottage. "I was afraid and went and hid my talent." Fear exaggerates difficulties, murmurs at duties, shrinks from reproach, postpones duty, then neglects it, and then hates God with the bitterness of despair. *Be of good courage.* If seeking God, seek hopefully, expecting to find Him. If distressed with doubts, face them bravely, and calmly wait the rising of the broader light which will include all that is best of old and new. Are you afflicted, bereaved, and broken? Be brave and of good courage. Look the grave in the face, and summon your energy to meet the falsehoods of despair. Are you failing— "feet almost gone," "perplexed," and all but in despair? Be of good courage, for hardihood of spirit, while it is needed, is sufficient for what you have to do. *Strength goes with it.* The momentum of a projectile is the product of its mass and velocity; and a lighter ball, if driven with greater force, will do all the work of a heavier one that moves more slowly. And this law of mechanics is true of souls. There is many a soul light, fragile, weak, but which hurls itself with energy against resisting forces, which has a power of overcoming far in excess of that possessed by many stronger and lordlier natures. Be strong and of good courage. If God appoints the task and leads the way, you are in a course in which fear of failure is superfluous. Let the eye be brighter; go not to your task burdened with melancholy of dark foreboding. Courage gladdening, strengthening you is duty and strength in one. Joshua obeyed the precept, and exceedingly abundantly above all he thought realised the promise. Let us act like him, and then from a pinnacle of high performance and blest success we shall look back and praise our God for the "faithful word on which he caused us to hope."—G.

Ver. 8.—*The study of the Bible.* Who without secret misgiving could succeed to the position of Moses, that large-hearted, clear-sighted, faithful servant of God? How overwhelming the anxiety of him who would aspire to be leader of the Israelites; a fickle people who, "like bees about to swarm, were ready to alight on any bough." He who summoned Joshua to occupy the vacant post promised to stand by and strengthen him. He gave him the direction contained in the text, to study well the book of the law. He seemed to say, "Take it; it shall be thy food, live upon it: carry it as a torch, and it will illumine thy pathway in the thickest darkness: in the vigour of thy manhood it shall be thy wand of truth to scatter doubt and error from before thee, and it shall be a staff to sustain thee in the decrepitude of age." Surely the advice given to Joshua is applicable to all who are in positions of responsibility or perplexity. How fitted for the young! What better can any of us do than seek wisdom at the oracles of God? Let us group our thoughts under three headings.

I. MEDITATION.

1. *Its subject-matter.* "This book of the law." This recommendation stamps the Pentateuch with authority. Joshua was favoured with direct communications from the Almighty, sometimes by an inward revelation, sometimes by the appearance of an angel in visible form. He could also consult the wishes of God by means of the high priest's Urim and Thummim. Yet was he to study the written word. Meteoric flashes were not to make him careless of the steady light that burned in the lamp of God's truth. Provision was made for a public rehearsal of the law every seven years, at the Feast of Tabernacles (Deut. xxxi. 10), and it was the duty of a king on ascending the throne to write out a copy of the law (Deut. xviii. 18). How intense should be the eagerness with which we meditate on the whole Bible. The rapturous strains of the Messianic prophets, the simple and sublime gospel narratives, the epistles—those commentaries on the preparatory dispensation and on Christian doctrine—do not all these "testify" of the Saviour? Well may we "search the Scriptures." Consider the fitness of the Bible to be a general text-book. It contains lessons suited to all capacities; the flowing river for the man, the purling brook for the little child, doctrines for the learned, pictured stories for the common people. It contains all truth needful to make us "wise unto salvation," and contains it in a compact form, so portable that each may have a Mentor always at his side. It tells us things of the utmost importance which we could not know without it; and it comes in to verify the conclusions of our reasoning. It lends to the utterances of conscience the might of Divine testimony.

2. *The character of the meditation enjoined.* Constant—"day and night." So close a companion that it was not to "depart out of his mouth." It should become his mother-tongue; his speech should be redolent of the law. Constant reading alone

can make us familiar with the contents of Scripture, so as to be well equipped at all points for the Christian warfare. Many knotty questions would Joshua have to decide; and many are the occasions on which men err grievously through "not knowing the Scriptures." The command of the text implies that it was to be no formal perusal, but an endeavour to grasp the real meaning of the law. Glancing at the pages of the word can do little good; we want to enter into and imbibe the spirit of that we read. A good plan to read the Scriptures regularly through. There will be many an oasis in what we called a desert, and many a pretty flower on what we deemed only a sterile rock. It is profitable to read "at morning and at night." He is well armed for his struggle with temptations and annoyances who goes to his work fortified by previous study of the Scriptures; and after the battle of the day is over, when the shadows of evening surround him or the gloomier shadows of trouble threaten to enclose him, there is naught so effectual to dissipate the darkness as the kindled rays of the heavenly lamp. Then "at evening time it shall be light."

II. ACTION. Meditation is to be followed by appropriate conduct. "That thou mayest observe to do according to all that is written therein." The inference is plain—that the law contains, as we should expect in a law, precepts to be observed. And the whole Bible may be considered as a law. There are general regulations and positive institutions. "This do and thou shall live" is common both to the Old and New Testament, the difference being in the things to be done, and the spirit that is to characterise the doing thereof. *We may test the value of our meditation* by the obedience which results. Obedience is a proof of holding the things read in due estimation. "Why call ye me, Lord, and do not . . . . say?" Obedience springs from faith, a hearty acceptance of the will and ways of God. Obedience brings its own confirmation of the truth. "If a man love me, he will keep my words, and my Father will love him, and we will come unto him." "If any man will do his will, he shall know of the doctrine whether it be of God." "Hereby we do know that we know him if we keep his commandments." *Obedience is to extend to the smallest matters.* "Observe to do according to all." The only question with Joshua to be, "What is written in the law? how readest thou?" We do not plead for the "letter" as against the "spirit," nor forget that many Scripture precepts are expressed in a general form, and one must be compared with another to ascertain the intention of our Lawgiver. But many persons are for drawing distinctions, for keeping greater and violating lesser commandments. Some will compound with God. These ordinances they will observe, those they will neglect. Such resemble the strangers imported into Samaria, who "feared the Lord and served their own gods" (2 Kings xvii. 33). A little Christian service and a little idolatry, a little self-denial, and a little worldliness to make the former palatable. We see *the necessity of the frequent injunction*, "Be strong, very courageous." Joshua would have often to act in opposition to the prejudices and desires and clamours of the multitude. He who will follow Christ must "be courageous," must be prepared to act in the teeth of worldly wisdom, to forego "good openings," to refuse to give dishonest measure, though his gains be thereby slow in accumulating. We want a knowledge of the Bible, not merely as words and sentences but as influential principles. Not the Hebrew and not the Greek do we want so much as a translation of them into thought and feeling and conduct. He has not read his Bible to good purpose who has not repented of sin and thankfully accepted God's well-beloved Son as his Saviour, his Redeemer "from all iniquity."

III. PROSPERITY. The reward of obedience. 1. Regard prosperity, first, as *the natural consequence of acting on good advice.* The rules framed for the guidance of the Israelites evince consummate wisdom. Experience proved how disastrous was any attempt to depart from the lines of procedure there laid down. And many familiar instances show that, in modern days, he who steers by God's compass and chart is preserved from many rocks and shallows, and is most likely to reach the haven of his legitimate desire. A pure, temperate Christian life is likeliest to win real success in any department of activity. 2. Regard prosperity as a *promised result.* He who consults Omniscience is helped by Omnipotence. A finger-post may indicate the way, it can do no more. God is a living Guide ; He has written directions and He aids in the performance of them. " No good thing shall fail of all that he has promised concerning us." " Seek first the kingdom of God, and all other things shall be added unto you." Blessed is the man whose " delight is in the law of the Lord," so that " in it he doth meditate day and night. He shall be like a tree . . . . shall prosper " (Psa. i. 2, 3).—A.

EXPOSITION.

CHAPTER I. 10—15.

JOSHUA'S COMMAND TO THE PEOPLE. — Ver. 10. — **Then Joshua commanded the officers of the people.** The *Shoterim*, a term derived from the same root as an Arabic word signifying " to write." Different ideas have been entertained of their duties. Keil, Jahn (*Hebrew Commonwealth*), and others believe that they were genealogists ; but it seems more probable that their original duties were to keep processes and minutes, and that, like our Indian " writers " and the " Master of the Rolls " at home, they exercised some kind of judicial functions, with which, moreover, active duties were sometimes combined. The idea that they were genealogists is contrary, as Gesenius shows, to the context in many places. Thus in Exod. v. 6—19, they seem to have had to see that the specified tale of bricks was delivered up ; and we know from the recently deciphered Egyptian inscriptions that very accurate registers of such matters were kept. In Deut. i. 16 (cf. Deut. xvi. 18 ; Josh. viii. 33 ; xxiii. 2 ; xxiv. 1, &c.) they appear to have exercised judicial functions in connection with the " princes " (not " captains," as in our version, which would lead to the idea that they were military officers). In Num. xi. 16 they are connected with the elders. In 1 Chron. xxvi. 29 they seem again to have exercised judicial functions, whereas in 2 Chron. xxvi. 11 their duty appears to have been to keep the muster rolls. In Prov. vi. 7 we find them once more with active duties as in the text. The LXX. equivalent, γραμματεύς, is rendered in Acts xix. 35 by " town-clerk," an officer with active as well as merely secretarial duties. Here they seem to have acted as officers of the commissariat, civil and military functions being naturally largely interchangeable in the then condition of the Israelitish people, just as they were in the early days of our Indian empire.

Ver. 11.—**Prepare you victuals.** Literally, *game*, the term being applied to meat obtained by hunting. Thus it is applied by Isaac to Esau's venison in Gen. xxvii. Here it means *food of any kind*, but especially animal food. It is therefore obvious that the miraculous supply of manna was soon to cease (cf. ch. v. 12). **Within three days.** Much difficulty has been created here by the fact that another three days are mentioned in chap. iii. 2 as elapsing after the return of the spies, which has been supposed to have taken place between this command and the period then mentioned. Three more days were spent (ch. ii. 22) by the spies in eluding the pursuit of the men of Jericho— one day in going thither, and one more in returning to Moses. Consequently eight days, if not more (see ch. iii. 7), must have elapsed between this proclamation and the actual crossing of the Jordan. But when we remember that the Hebrew language possesses no pluperfect tense, that there are many instances, such as (very probably) Gen. xii. 1, and more certainly Gen. iii. 1, vi. 6, xx. 18, xxvi. 18, 32, where the Hebrew narrative has clearly departed from the chronological order, and that the chronology is obscured by this chasm in the Hebrew linguistic system, we may suppose that the narrative in the second chapter is parenthetical, and relates to events which occurred before the occasion now spoken of. This is the view taken by Josephus and the Rabbis, and our translators have adopted it in the margin—a proceeding which, as their preface shows, may frequently be held to imply that in their opinion it is the preferable interpretation. It is energetically impugned by Keil, who maintains that there are insuperable difficulties in the way of this arrangement. He does not, however, make out a very powerful case against the simple explanation of Cornelius à Lapide, that the spies left the camp on the 3rd Nisan, returned on the 6th, that Joshua gave his order on the 7th, and that on the 10th (ch. iv. 19) the crossing was effected. Stripped of all verbiage, Keil's argument appears to amount simply to this, that it was not likely that the account of the narrative would be thus interrupted by an account of a transaction out of its proper chronological order. It may be added that it seems doubtful whether we must not render the word יֹּאמֶר in ver. 12, by the pluperfect, for it seems very probable that the word of command to the two tribes and a half who had obtained their inheritance beyond Jordan had been given before this, and that therefore it may have preceded the command given to the spies, in which case one of Keil's chief objections falls to the ground. Other explanations than that of Cornelius a Lapide have been suggested. Thus Kimchi supposes that the spies left on the 5th Nisan and returned on the 8th ; while Masius supposes that they were sent out simultaneously with these orders. Augustine's explanation, that Joshua did not speak by revelation, but was influenced by human hope, is noticeable, as proving that the early fathers did not always take the strictest view of inspiration.

Ver. 12.—**And to the Reubenites, and the Gadites, and the half-tribe of Manasseh** (see Num. xxxii. 1—33). We have here a remarkable instance of undesigned agreement between the various books of the Old Testament : one of those signs of the genuineness of the narrative which would be almost impossible to a compiler of fictitious records. We are told in the passage just cited that the reason why these particular tribes desired an inheritance on the other side Jordan was because they were particularly rich in cattle. Now we learn from other passages that this region was—and travellers tell us that it is to this day—a region particularly suited for pasture. The 'Jewish Chronicle,' in December, 1879, mentions a scheme projected by Mr. Laurence Oliphant for colonising this district for agricultural purposes under the auspices of a company. The "fat bulls of Bashan" were almost proverbial in Scripture. Mesha, king of Moab, was a "sheep-master," we read (2 Kings iii. 4), and his tribute, rendered in sheep to the king of Israel, was a very large one; especially when we remember that Moab was at that time but little larger than an ordinary English county (see also Deut. xxxii. 14 ; Ezek. xxxix. 18). The land to the east of Jordan bore the name Mishor, or level land, as contrasted with the rocky region on the other side of Jordan.

Ver. 13.—**Remember the word.** The substance, and not the *ipsissima verba*, of the directions of Moses in Num. xxxii. is here given (see also Deut. iii. 16—20). **Hath given you rest.** Perhaps, rather, hath *caused* you to rest—hath permitted you to settle ; though the LXX. here has κατέπαυσεν, and the Vulgate, *dedit vobis requiem* (cf. Heb. iii. 11—18 ; iv. 1—11 ; and Psa. xcv. 11). **This land,** *i.e.*, that in which they then were, on what we call the further side of Jordan.

Ver. 14.—**Armed.** This word, translated *harnessed* in Exod. xiii. 18, only occurs besides here in ch. iv. 12, and in Judges vii. 11. In the first cited of these passages it has given rise to much discussion among those whose studies have been confined to the text of the English Bible, excluding even the margin. But its meaning is much debated among scholars. There seems no authority whatever for the translation *armed* or *harnessed*. We must either take it (1) to mean *in five divisions*, the usual manner of marching under Moses (see Num. ii.), "divided into centre, right and left wings, van and rear guard " (Ewald) ; or (2) *fierce, eager, brave*, from a Semitic root found also in the Arabic. So Rosenmüller and Genesius—who does not, however, as Keil asserts, derive the word from חָמֵשׁ to be fat, but from a root akin to חָמָס violence, and חָמֵץ to be pungent. The former refers to the parallel passage in Num. xxxii. 17, where for חֲמֻשִׁים we find חֻשִׁים *quick*. The first interpretation is rendered probable by Num. ii., where the order of march is described as a fivefold order, and by the similarity of the word to חָמֵשׁ five, and is not excluded by Judges vii. 11, where the army, though disorganised, may have still been arranged in its fivefold divisions. The fact that there is an Arabic word, almost precisely similar, which is applied to the fivefold division of an army, makes it almost certain that this is the true meaning. But some scholars prefer to render it " brave," or " eager for war " (cf. חֲלוּצֵי Josh. iv. 13). This last word is also found in the parallel passages in Num. xxxii. and Deut. iii. 18—20. Its original meaning is *expeditus*—unencumbered. See note on the last-mentioned passage. **All the mighty men of valour.** The number of fighting men in these tribes would be, from a comparison of Num. xxvi. 7, 18, 34, remembering that *half* only of the tribe of Manasseh must be counted, between 110,000 and 111,000. But we read in Josh. iv. 13 that 40,000 only of them went over. Above 70,000 must have remained behind to guard their women, children, and flocks, a precaution both reasonable and necessary. So indispensable, in fact, was it, that in this apparent discrepancy we may find one of the strongest proofs of the genuineness of our narrative. For, as Calvin remarks, in a country not yet pacified, all the women and children would infallibly have been massacred had they been left unprotected.

HOMILETICS.

Vers. 10—15.—*Joshua's command to the people.*

I. WE MUST WORK WITH THE GRACE OF GOD. All these promises of God were not intended to supersede human effort. God had promised to be with Joshua, but Joshua must act on the promise. He had promised to plant the people in the Holy Land, but not without exertion on their part. Where their own action was impossible, as in crossing the Jordan, He did all for them. When a sign of His presence with them was necessary, as at Jericho, He did likewise. But in the rest of their warfare He did but prosper their own endeavours. So we are both to pray and work, save in cases where to work is denied us, and then our weapon must be prayer alone.

II. WE NEED PROVISION FOR THE WAY. Without meat we should "faint by the way." But we have "meat to eat" that the world "knows not of," even the flesh and blood of Christ. And this we must "prepare;" that is, we must take pains to obtain it. "This kind goeth not forth but by prayer and fasting," and by endeavours to serve Christ. Whether in the sacrament of His love, or in any other way in which He vouchsafes to impart His humanity to us, there needs on our part (1) an earnest petition for the gift; (2) steady self-denial in our lives; (3) steadfast efforts to do His will. It is remarkable that the miraculous provision failed as soon as there was no more need for it. So exceptional provision for our spiritual needs is withdrawn so soon as we find ourselves within reach of the means of grace. These we must use with due diligence and forethought if we would derive benefit from them.

III. WE FIGHT, NOT FOR OURSELVES ALONE, BUT FOR OTHERS. The two tribes and a half had received their inheritance, yet they were not allowed to settle down in it. They had been solemnly bound to help their brethren. Nor may we Christians sit down in the exclusive possession of religious privileges, but must impart them to our brethren, whether (*a*) by nature, as the heathen, or (*b*) by grace, as in the case of Christians less favoured than ourselves. We cannot cease our labour till they are as well off as we. Thus the duty is incumbent upon us of co-operating in every good work, whereby the temporal or spiritual benefit of others is attained.

IV. EACH HAS HIS APPOINTED TASK. As Christ gave to His disciples to set before the multitude (John vi. 11, &c.), so Joshua "commands the officers" to "command the people." All are not apostles or prophets, but each has his proper office in God's Church. Some are set over the flock to guide and exhort them, while others have to listen and carry out the voice of exhortation. They were to go up *chamushim*, in battle array (ver. 14), with van and rear, with wings and centre, each in his appointed rank. And we, too, shall only throw the army of Jesus into disorder if we fail to keep the place which God's providence has assigned us.

V. SOME, BY THEIR POSITION, ARE DENIED A PART IN THE GENERAL CONFLICT. As Christ forbade the demoniac to attach himself to His person, but bade him "go home to his friends" (St. Mark v. 19), so there are those, like the women and children here, whose work for Christ is the simple discharge of domestic duties, whom Christ has not called to any more public efforts in His cause.

HOMILIES BY VARIOUS AUTHORS.

Vers. 10—18.—*Joshua and the Reubenites.* The Reubenites and Gadites had already settled on the banks of the Jordan. They were at rest; they had not to await the ordeal of the conquest. As far as they were concerned, they had already received the promise. And yet they were not to be allowed to remain in idleness, and in selfish enjoyment of their own good. They were not to forget their brethren. "Ye shall pass before your brethren armed," said Joshua, "and help them." "And they answered Joshua, saying, All that thou commandest us we will do." Such was the response of these valiant and true-hearted men. We have here an admirable illustration of the great bond of solidarity which makes all the people of God one.

I. IN REALITY, NO SECTION OF GOD'S PEOPLE CAN LIVE AN ISOLATED LIFE. It would be vain for the Reubenites to dream that they could rest at ease under their vines and fig trees. The defeat of their brethren would recoil upon them, and should the Canaanites be victorious the Reubenites would quickly find themselves driven out of the land. And it is the same with the Church—*each for all, and all for each;* this is the Church's motto. Therefore it is that all should rally round the great standard of the army.

II. FOR ANY SECTION OF GOD'S PEOPLE TO ISOLATE THEMSELVES in their prosperity is not only the sure way to impoverish and ultimately to ruin themselves, but it IS TREASON TO THE KING OF THE SPIRITUAL KINGDOM; for it implies that the first object of desire is prosperity for themselves, not the glory of the King; that He is loved, not with a pure, but with a selfish love.

III. SUCH ISOLATION HARDENS THE HEART. It is a violation of the first law of the kingdom—the law of love. Its tendency is, as far as possible, to obliterate that law. It ignores the fact that we receive only to give again. Let us fully grasp, then, this great truth, that every blessing received is a trust placed in our hands only that we may diffuse it among our brethren. The applications of this great precept of Christian love are innumerable. Do we possess in large measure the good things of this world? It is that we may communicate to our less favoured brethren. Are we rich in spiritual gifts? It is that we may impart to those less privileged and of fewer opportunities than ourselves. And as we are indebted to the Church, so are we also to humanity, for are we not all one flesh? Hence the claim of missions, both at home and abroad, as a means of imparting the gifts of God already received by us to those who as yet are ignorant of them. Nor is this all. After having won the victory for ourselves, we have to begin the battle over again, and to suffer in sympathy with those who have yet the Jordan to cross. Let us never forget Him who left the blessedness of heaven to undertake our cause, and who, though He was rich, yet for our sakes became poor.—E. DE P.

Vers. 12—15.—*Duties of brotherhood.* We have here a fine appeal, and a fine answer to that appeal. Arrived at the Jordan, they are about to make that invasion of Palestine which gave the Church of God a country and truth a home. At first the settlement of all the twelve tribes in the country between the Jordan and the sea seems to have been the design of Moses. But "the region beyond Jordan" was fertile—a finer land for flocks than Canaan itself. It was not surprising, therefore, that the pre-eminently pastoral tribes of Reuben, Gad, and Manasseh should desire to settle there. And when the opposition of Og, king of Bashan, and Sihon, king of the Amorites, necessitated war, and ended in their defeat, the desire of these tribes found expression in a formal request. On the condition that their settlement on the nearer side of Jordan was not to be a "secession," and that they would help their brethren in the conquest of the whole land, Moses had granted their request, and divided the territory between them. Now Joshua, on the death of Moses, requires their fulfilment of their pledge. Rest would have been pleasant, and selfish reasons in plenty forthcoming for evading the fulfilment of their promise; but the claim for brotherly help was made to men of brotherly nature. This chapter shows their prompt response, and the remainder of this Book shows— one might almost say all the subsequent books of the Bible do so—the splendid results of their brotherliness. I find a very perfect illustration of a great theme, viz., the duty and blessedness of the more favoured helping their less favoured brethren. Observe—

I. THE DUTY OF THOSE MORE EARLY, OR MORE RICHLY BLESSED, HELPING THEIR LESS FAVOURED BRETHREN. There are those more and those less favoured. Those that attain the desire of their hearts much earlier and much more fully than their brethren. God does not divide His favours as a communistic philosopher would do. All are largely, but all unequally and diversely, blessed. So it happened here. The two and a half tribes had got all their fighting over before the others had well begun. Had Israel entered the land of Canaan by the south, as they probably would have done if they had not shrunk from the enterprise on the return of the spies, then

Judah would have been the first to find its home secure; and Reuben, Gad, and half Manasseh would have been the last if they still desired the district of Gilead. It is not the peculiar virtue of the latter that it should be earlier, nor any fault of the former that it should be later. It is due simply to their entering now from the east instead of from the south. So in the contrasted condition of these tribes we have but a type of the contrasted conditions of men. There are some have made their fortune by the time others are just beginning to struggle for it. To some, truth comes with clear evidence as a bright heritage of their youth, while others only reach it with protracted struggle. Some are favoured with a knowlege of the gospel, while others are in densest ignorance. Some nations have vast wealth of liberty and justice, when others are just beginning to achieve the first sweets of freedom. And in such circumstances the more fortunate are very apt to enjoy their comforts, regardless of the struggles of their brethren; just as these tribes might have argued with plausible ingenuity that they should be excused from rendering assistance to their brethren. The struggle with Bashan—that district which rises like an island of rock from the pastoral plains, and which is the great natural fortress, the "keep" of the whole district—had been arduous. The remains of the cities of Bashan, so strongly built that three thousand years has not been able to reduce them to ruins, show the energy and developed civilisation of their foes. There are not a few indications that the stress of the conflict fell on the two and a half tribes. How easily they might have been tempted to settle down, indifferent to their brethren's welfare. Besides, they had respectable excuses. Who would defend their wives and children when all their mighty men were across the Jordan? What would become of their cattle? What security was there against the Bedawin, then, as now, roving about intent on spoil? Might they not act as rear-guard, and keep the communications open— secure a safe retreat? But Moses, Joshua, God, all expect the more to help the less fortunate, and the generous instincts of their own hearts assent to the doctrine, and the nobility of their action testifies to all posterity that privilege carries responsibility, and that all who have are bound to aid all who lack. "Go forth before your brethren armed, till the Lord hath given them rest." Let the upper classes of our country share rather than monopolise education, power, enjoyment of life. Let the rich aid the poor; the strong free the weak. Let those who have the gospel help those who are in darkness to attain its light. The successful have a duty to the struggling to aid them, not feebly, but with their full strength. If this example illustrates the duty of the more helping the less favoured, it illustrates with equal clearness, secondly—

II. THE BLESSEDNESS OF DOING SO. One does not like to contemplate what would have been the results had they withheld their help. The Amorites, strong in their mountain fastnesses, the Canaanites—the race we know better under the name of Phenicians, strong in their civilisation, wealth, commerce, maritime enterprise, inhabiting the sea-board plains—were not enemies to be lightly overcome. Ten out of the twelve spies—all brave men—reported the conquest impossible; and the other two hoped for it only because they had the faith that remembered nothing was impossible. What would have been the effect on the world if Phenician religion, with its unutterable vileness and cruelty, destruction of morality and virtues in all their forms, had extirpated Hebrew religion, with its inspiration of virtue, truth, liberty, and all things high, one is content to leave unguessed. But Israel was fighting the world's battle of truth and righteousness against enormous odds, and the two and a half tribes nobly taking their share in the conflict. Observe what blessed results followed.

1. *They had the reward of being grandly useful in the service they rendered.* They did not fail, nor were discouraged until, as the result of three or four years of war, the whole land from Hebron in the south to Baal Gad in Lebanon was theirs. And God's people, God's Church, and God's Truth had an earthly house. The candle was set on a candlestick, and gave light to all surrounding nations and succeeding ages. Thy brotherly help, in whatever direction rendered, will never be in vain. Nothing has such success and so little failure as kindly help.

2. *Their service resulted in the development of a finer brotherhood.* Not a perfect one, as there will be too much occasion to mark, but yet a relationship in which there was on the one hand the genial interest we always take in those we help, and on the other there was the gratitude always felt where service is promptly and freely given. They know not what they lose who never render help. Serve and love your brethren and they will pray for you and love you, when perhaps their love and prayer will turn the scale between hope and despair.

3. *There was developed in these tribes a noble sentiment of heroic patriotism.* We make our acts: but our acts make us. And a noble deed increases the nobility of nature from which it sprung. The service now rendered by the tribes inhabiting Gilead lived in their memory, an inspiration to similar service. Gideon and Jephthah headed the tribes, and twice over delivered Israel from her oppressors. And in later times this same region gave Israel her grandest prophet—the great Elijah—who restored pure and undefiled religion to its throne. The service you render ennobles you, and makes you more capable of nobler service in all time to come.

4. There was the direct outward reward. They lost nothing by it even in material wealth. No enemy attacked their families. They brought back great store of spoil, more wealth than herding could have given them in the interval. And through all their future history the service now rendered by them was repaid to them. So that, though exposed in situation, the first to feel the brunt of the attacks of Syria and Ammon, they retained, by help of their brethren, their possessions and their freedom, right down to the days of Ahab. It is no slight reward which waits on brotherly kindness and charity, but one which makes men richer than with any wealth of selfishness they could possibly be. Go thou, and in thy sphere do as these tribes did—render prompt, willing, rich, lengthened service to your less favoured brethren, and "exceedingly abundant above all you ask or think" will you find your reward in heaven.—G.

Ver. 13.—*An agreement remembered.* The latter part of this chapter recounts the preparations made for the entrance of the Israelites into Canaan. Joshua was already showing himself "the right man in the right place." Having given orders with respect to the food necessary for the next march, he now addresses the tribes who had been permitted to choose an inheritance on the east of the Jordan. He reminds them of their promise to send their armed men as a van-guard to the people. Though under the sheltering wings of the Almighty no prudent precautions must be neglected, no vigilance relaxed, the honour of God demands that reasonable care should be exercised to prevent surprise and the consequent disgrace that would attach to His holy name. God helps us not only outwardly but inwardly, teaching us how to live a sober, righteous, and godly life, and so to vanquish the machinations of the enemy.

I. A COVENANT REMEMBERED. If the Reubenites and Gadites had forgotten it, not so Joshua. Nor does God fail to recollect the vows we have made. As He recalled Jacob to a sense of his ingratitude and remissness (Gen. xxxv. 1), so He will not have us treat our promises lightly. It is part of the functions of a faithful leader to bring to light forgotten duties. A minister reminds his people of their engagements. What declarations of devoted adherence to Christ were uttered at conversion! how they bound themselves henceforth to live to the glory of God! The people's promises to God must be insisted on, as well as the cheering promises which God has made to them. Let us not be angry nor revile such admonitions as the preaching of the law instead of the gospel. An appeal was made to authority. The agreement had been a commandment on the part of Moses. Joshua enforced compliance therewith. On the same grounds we draw attention to the precepts of prophets and apostles, as well as to the direct dictates of the Lord. These holy men were inspired, and to dispute their utterances is to call in question the authority of the Master whose servants they were. Joshua thus sanctioned Moses as Peter afterwards bore witness to Paul (2 Pet. iii. 15).

II. PRINCIPLES RECOGNISED IN THE COVENANT.

1. *Favours merit some grateful return.* The land of Gilead and Bashan was

desired by these two-and-a-half tribes on account of its fruitful pasturage. It was adapted for flocks and herds, and the sight of such fertile territory caused the owners of much sheep and cattle to be willing to settle down at once, rather than to occupy soil in the "land of promise" itself. Their request was not pleasing to Moses, as it seemed to put a slight upon Canaan, and to threaten a relapse into idolatry, beside the imminent danger of discouraging the rest of the Israelites, and so effecting by the wrath of God the utter extinction of the nation. Yet on the condition to which reference has been made the petition was ultimately granted. As they had achieved their desire it was rightly expected that they would render some proportionate recompense. And in similar method our heavenly Father deals with us to-day. We must be ready to cry with the Psalmist, "What shall I render unto the Lord for all his benefits toward me?" If more than others we have received, of us will more be required. Health and strength, wealth and position, learning and influence—not one of these gifts but entails a corresponding responsibility. If the conditions have not been stated in so many words, yet they are easily discoverable.

2. *The priority of duty to pleasure.* Before these armed men could lawfully enjoy their inheritance they must fulfil their engagement. We do not oppose duty to pleasure, strictly speaking, for it is obvious that only when mindful of the former can the latter be truly known. But the two may be distinguished, and it is clear that there are cases in which selfish inclination would lead one way and obligation calls us another. The rule to be adopted is plain. Listen to "I ought," and follow whither it directs; there will be a satisfaction gendered which will go far to repay us for any sacrifice; and then when the period of relaxation has really arrived our delight will be embittered by no stings of reproachful conscience, but enhanced by the remembrance of duty discharged. Let this be noted and acted upon by the young, and there will be fewer wasted lives. Let Church members consult their obligations before their convenience and there will be fewer vacancies crying out for occupants.

3. *The obligations of fraternal love.* The dislike of Moses to the request of these tribes was akin to the grief of a father who witnesses the separation of some members of the family from the rest. The river Jordan was in itself but a small dividing line, but it might be significant of a wide and deep estrangement. Evidently perceiving the fear of Moses, the Reubenites, &c., offered to prove by their conduct that they were still at one with their brethren and intended so to remain. The offer was approved of and established as a covenant between the whole nation and these special tribes. It affirmed a participation in the common hopes and risks. The New Testament speaks not less clearly of the relationship between all the children of God. The members of the body of Christ are bound to feel with and for one another (1 Cor. xii. 25, 26). "Let brotherly love continue." So forcible was the impulse of the first preaching of the gospel that it led the Christians of Jerusalem to a commonalty of goods. It is required of the rich to help the poor, the strong must assist in bearing the burdens of the weak, the settled in position and faith must stretch out the hand to those who are still searching for a place of rest, and those who have leisure must devote a portion at least to the succour of the busily employed. The Jewish Paul having obtained the privileges of Christianity could wish himself to be "accursed for his brethren, his kinsmen according to the flesh." We are selfish indeed if we pray not and labour not for the salvation of our friends till they become possessed likewise of an eternal inheritance. Briefly note—

III. THE RATIFICATION OF THE COVENANT. The covenanters assented immediately to the command of Joshua. They were ready to keep their word. No excuses urged, no pleas of misunderstanding, no subtle equivocations, no attempts to secure a remission of their engagement, but downright honest confirmation of their pledged promise. They did not desire their sin to find them out (Num. xxxii. 23). The covenant had been really made with the Lord, and He would be certain to punish its violation. God give us grace to imitate their example! Like Jephthah, we have "opened our mouth to the Lord and cannot go back." We have declared that our bodies shall be living sacrifices, that our mouths shall show forth the Redeemer's praise, that as for us we will serve the Lord. Very shame should bind us to our word; we must not, dare not, "keep back part of the price." And love to God and man draws us onward to our "reasonable service."—A.

EXPOSITION.

CHAPTER I. 16—18.

THE PEOPLE'S ANSWER. — Ver. **16.** — **And they answered Joshua, saying.** We may compare this joyful willingness with the murmurings of the people in the wilderness, and their rebellion after the death of those who led them into the promised land (cf. Joshua xxiv. 31 with Judges ii. 10, 11, &c.). Obedience is easy when all goes well with us, and when it makes no demand upon our faith. The Israelites murmured when the promise was as yet unfulfilled. They rebelled against God when obedience entailed self-sacrifice. But now all was hope and eagerness. So it is often with the young Christian at the outset of life's battle, before he has begun to realise the exertion and self-denial that can alone ensure him victory.

Ver. 17.—**As we hearkened unto Moses.** Calvin remarks that the Israelites did *not* hearken unto Moses, but replies that, compared with the conduct of their fathers whose bodies lay in the wilderness, the conduct of this generation was obedience itself. It certainly appears as though for the last two years of the wandering in the wilderness there was far less rebellion against Moses than before; and after the solemn repetition of the precepts of the law to the new generation which had arisen, given in the Book of Deuteronomy, there seems to have been no rebellion at all (see Num. xxvi. 63).

Ver. 18.—**Whosoever he be that doth rebel against thy commandment.** A striking fulfilment of this promise appears in the case of Achan, who was put to death by the act of the whole congregation (see ch. vii. 25; and cf. Deut. xvii. 12). **Only be strong and of a good courage.** The task of a leader in Israel is easy when he is sustained by the prayers of his people, and when their exhortations are an echo of the words of God (see vers. 6, 9).

HOMILETICS.

Vers. 16—18.—*The people's answer.* This passage can only be interpreted of Jesus, of whom Joshua was the type. Implicit obedience is no longer due to any human leader, nor has been since Joshua's death. Even a St. Paul can say, "I speak as to wise men, judge ye what I say" (1 Cor. x. 15). And St. Peter urges the clergy to remember that they are not "lords over God's heritage" (1 Pet. v. 3). And this because we each "have access by one Spirit to the Father by the faith of Jesus Christ" (Eph. ii. 18; iii. 12). We may remark—

I. THAT EVERY CHRISTIAN IS BOUND BY A VOW OF OBEDIENCE. Jesus is the Captain of our salvation. He leads us in the warfare against every kind of evil. To disobey is to mutiny, and mutiny in every army is a capital crime. Yet here we may remark on the forbearance of our Joshua. *All* his troops are more or less guilty of this crime. Yet (1) He pardons it, and (2) with His mutinous troops He has achieved, and will achieve, many a glorious victory. But there is a limit to His patience (see below). Though we sin often we must take heed to repent as often, and strive to do better for the future. "If any man have not the Spirit of Christ," at least in such a manner as to make him strive sedulously after obedience, "he is none of his" (Rom. viii. 9). The best we can do is to ask Him to "renew our will from day to day," that so, after each of our frequent falls, we may brace ourselves up to a renewed obedience. And thus, by virtue of His merits, not of our own, shall we be recognised as faithful soldiers of the true Joshua—Jesus Christ.

II. THAT THE LAW IS STILL "OUR SCHOOLMASTER TO BRING US TO CHRIST." We must still "hearken to Moses" before we can hear the voice of Christ. Still in our childhood must we be subject to law, be under tutors and governors, have duties prescribed for us, obey precepts "contained in ordinances," before we reach the "glorious liberty of the children of God," before we find the law "written in our hearts," and a power existing within us prompting us to a spontaneous obedience.

We must all know the period of struggle, when, "after the inward man," we "de-light in the law of God" (Rom. vii. 22, 23), but find another law in our members at conflict with it. So must we learn to find the only deliverance from "the body of this death," in Jesus Christ our Lord, just as to follow Joshua was the only escape from the wilderness. And if we live up to the law that is set before us, we shall find through it a pathway to a better land, the land of promise (Gal. iii. 18). For "the law is not against the promises of God, God forbid" (Gal. iii. 21). It is "holy, and the commandment holy, just, and good" (Rom. vii. 12). But its object was to show us "the exceeding sinfulness of sin," and the terrible reality of our bondage to it, that we might learn the infinite value of the reconciliation which has been effected for us in the Person and work of Jesus Christ.

III. "THE WAGES OF SIN IS DEATH." This is recognised as a fact by the fol-lowers of Joshua. So the followers of Jesus must acknowledge the fact that to sin against Him, to refuse to obey His words, leads to destruction. And they must separate themselves from all that "walk disorderly" (2 Thess. iii. 6; 1 Tim. vi. 5; 2 Tim. iii. 5). For they only who do His commandments "have right to the tree of life." All they that do otherwise are "without," shut out from the joys of eternal life, and condemned to the "second death" (Rev. xxi. 8; xxii. 14, 15).

HOMILIES BY VARIOUS AUTHORS.

Vers. 16—18.—*Loyalty.* A demand had been made that the "men of valour" of these tribes should leave their relatives and property in the fenced cities of their inheritance, and head the advance of the Israelites into Canaan. A call to a dangerous position, to bear, as it seemed, the brunt of the enemy's attack; a sum-mons to exercise self-denial in absence from home and possessions; the precept issuing, too, from unaccustomed lips, those of a new general. These verses record a courageous, generous response, which may well furnish matter for meditation and imitation.

I. A DECLARATION OF OBEDIENCE.

1. *A prompt assent.* No time for thought and preparation asked for. No reasons invented for delay.

2. *A hearty assent.* It is expressed in three forms: a promise to do what is com-manded, to go where sent, and to hearken when addressed. These phrases cover all possible kinds of precepts.

3. Promise of *unreserved obedience.* "All," "whithersoever," and "in all things," thus blocking the smallest loophole of escape in each case. No picking and choosing here of the mandates to which they will conform.

Such complete acquiescence as this can be required of us only with respect to Him who is the Captain of our salvation. With regard to other subalterns of His, and to the national sovereign, there are occasions on which refusal and resistance are justifiable. Consider the grounds on which we owe fealty to Jesus Christ. He is our Lord as Creator, "by him were all things made," and as Redeemer, "that they which live should not henceforth live unto themselves," &c.

II. A PRAYER OFFERED FOR THE LEADER. "Only the Lord thy God be with thee as he was with Moses." 1. This petition *recognised the fount of authority.* The warriors readily complied with the demand of Joshua because they believed that he was appointed to occupy the place of Moses. Joshua was henceforth to receive and utter the directions of the Almighty, to be His vicegerent to the Israelites. And on this foundation Jesus Christ often based His claims to be heard by the Jews, viz., that He was sent from God and spoke the words of God. He pointed to His mighty works in evidence of the truth of His pretensions. Nicodemus declared, "No man can do these miracles that thou doest except God be with him." The Father openly signified His approval of the Son's mission, "This is my beloved Son, hear ye him." The Jewish king was the "anointed of the Lord. "The powers that be are ordained of God." Pastors under the Christian dispensation are "over" men "in the Lord." "Remember them who have the rule over you, who have spoken unto you the word of God." "Obey them that have the rule over you, and submit yourselves, for they watch for your souls as they that must give account."

2. The prayer invokes *the presence of God as the leader's source of strength.* By prayer we can commend to Divine grace "all that are in authority." How the Apostle Paul reiterated his request that the readers of his epistles would earnestly pray on his behalf! When Peter was miraculously released from prison he found "many gathered together praying." Thus may the people aid their minister, as Aaron and Hur upheld Moses' hands. There were seasons when the commands of the great legislator were received with murmuring, and when his right to rule was called in question. These Reubenites had not "in all things" hearkened unto Moses. Yet now they spontaneously avow that he had been supported by God. The death of a celebrated man calms passion, removes prejudice, and purges the vision.

III. A STERN RESOLUTION. To inflict the punishment of death on any recalcitrant offender. Presumptuous refusal to hearken to the priest or judge was to be visited with this severe penalty (Deut. xvii. 12). This declaration by these tribes evinced their firm determination to abide by the decrees of their new ruler. Rebellion is treated as one of the worst crimes, inasmuch as whilst some illegal acts are only indirectly subversive of government, this strikes a blow at the very seat of authority, and endangers all order. Nor is it a matter of small moment whether men bow or not to the rule of Christ. Peter quoted the prophecy of Moses in reference to Christ and the terrible threat annexed, "Every soul which will not hear that prophet shall be destroyed from among the people." Our Lord, in the parable of the pounds, represents Himself as saying, "But those mine enemies . . . and slay before me."

IV. ADMONITORY ADVICE. In olden days servants were much freer in speaking their mind to their masters, and soldiers to their generals. But Joshua's humility in listening to this exhortation is worthy of being copied. The wisest may learn from the ignorant, and the meanest of the flock may sometimes suitably address their pastor. Nor need any of us be above accepting good counsel, from whatever quarter it proceeds. There is *no intimation of weakness*, but only that these tribes perceived the weighty enterprise in which Joshua was engaged, and the necessity of his exhibiting a fearless demeanour. They sympathised with him, and wished to inspirit him for his arduous, honourable work. They knew how much commonly depends on the leader's courage, and how quickly his fear would affect his subjects. It was *advice in full accordance with their actions.* They had gone the right way to strengthen Joshua by their instant submission to His will. They did not try to cheer him with words after having previously knocked the breath out of him with their deeds. Speech and conduct were in harmony, and lent each other force. Marvellous is the effect of an encouraging word! Is there not some one whom we can thus send to his post with augmented zeal and hope? *Conclusion.* Whom are we serving? Under whose banner enlisted, and what wages, what reward do we anticipate? The true Joshua, even Christ, demands, invites, yea, entreats our faithful adherence.—A.

EXPOSITION.

CHAPTER II. 1—12.

RAHAB AND THE SPIES. — Ver. 1. — **And Joshua the son of Nun sent.** Rather, as margin, *had* sent (see note on ch. i. 2). It might have been at the very time when the command was given to the Israelites, for, according to a common Hebrew manner of speech (see, for instance, 1 Sam. xvi. 10), the three days (ver. 22) may include the whole time spent by the spies in their exploring expedition. **Out of Shittim.** Literally, *from the valley of acacias.* It is so called in full in Joel iii. 18. This place (called Abel-Shittim in Num. xxxiii. 49), in which the Israelites had sojourned for some time (see Num. xxv. 1 ; cf. xxii. 1), seems to have been "in the plains (עֲרָבָת see note on ch. iv. 13) of Moab, by Jordan, opposite Jericho" (Num. xxxiii. 48, 49, 50 ; xxxvi. 13 ;

cf. Deut. i. 5). It was "the long belt of acacia groves which mark with a line of verdure the upper terraces of the valley." (Stanley, 'Sinai and Palestine,' p. 298). The word Abel, or meadow, signifying the long grass with its juicy moisture, points to it as a refreshing place of sojourn and pasture for flocks, after the weary wandering in the wilderness. The acacia, not the *spina Ægyptiaca* of the ancients, the *mimosa Nilotica* of Linnæus, but the acacia Seyal, a tree with a golden tuft of blossom, which is still (Tristram, 'Land of Israel,' p. 524) to be found on the spot, very hard dark wood, of which much use was made in the tabernacle and its fittings (see Exod. xxv., xxvi., xxxvi., xxxvii., &c.). The name Abel was a common one in Palestine, and is the same as Abila, from whence comes Abilene (Luke iii. 1). We may add that it has nowhere been said that they *were* at Shittim. We find this out from Num. xxv. 1. This undesigned coincidence is beyond the power of an inventor, and far beyond the power of a compiler who was not only untrustworthy, but so clumsy that he made the most extraordinary blunders in the management of his matter (see note on next verse, and also on ch. i. 11). **Two men.** *Young men*, as we are told in ch. vi. 23, and therefore active, fleet of foot as well as brave and prudent. All these qualities, as the subsequent narrative shows, were urgently required. "Joshua himself was full of God's Spirit, and had the oracle of God ready for his direction. Yet now he goes, not to the Propitiatorie for consultation, but to the spyes. Except where ordinarie meanes faile us, it is no use appealing to the immediate helpe of God; we may not seek to the posterne, but where the common gate is shut. It was promised Joshua that hee should leade Israel into the promised land, yet hee knew it was unsafe to presume. The condition of his provident care was included in that assurance of succésse. Heaven is promised to us, but not to our carelessnesse, infidelitie, disobedience" (Bishop Hall). **Secretly.** Literally, *dumbness* or *craftiness* (the noun being used adverbially), implying the silence and skill required for the task. He who knows how to be silent possesses one at least of the elements of success. The necessity of silence and secrecy may be inferred from ch. vi. 1. Keil, however, following the Masoretic punctuation, regards "secretly" as referring to the Israelites, and the spies as sent unknown to the army, that no depressing report might damp their courage. **Jericho.** "The city of fragrance" (from רוח to breathe, and in the Hiphil, to smell a sweet odour), so called from its situation in the midst of palm trees, from which it was called "the

city of palm trees עִיר הַתְּמָרִים in Deut. xxxiv. 3, 2 Chron. xxviii. 15; cf. Judg. i. 16. The vast palm grove, of which relics are even now occasionally washed up from the Red Sea, preserved by the salt in its acrid waters, has now disappeared. We read of it as still existing in the twelfth century, and indeed traces of it were to be seen as late as 1838. A dirty and poverty-stricken village called Riha, or Eriha, is all that now marks the site of all these glories of nature and art, and the most careful researches have until lately failed to discover any remains of the ancient city. It is doubtful whether the ruins observed by Tristram ('Land of Israel,' p. 216) are not the ruins of some later city, built in the neighbourhood. Bartlett, p. 452, believes Riha to be the site of the later Jericho of our Lord's day, but Tristram would, with less probability, identify Riha with Gilgal. They both, however, place the site of ancient Jericho about a mile and a half from Riha. Conder thinks its true position is at the fountain Ain-es-Sultan. Lenormant, in his 'Manual of Oriental History,' remarks on the skill of Joshua as a military tactician. Whether he followed the advice of his experienced leader, or whether we are to attribute his success to special guidance from above, he certainly displayed the qualities of a consummate general. "Jericho," says Dean Stanley ('Sinai and Palestine,' p. 305), "stands at the entrance of the main passes from the valley of the Jordan into the interior of Palestine, the one branching off to the south-west towards Olivet, the other to the north-west towards Michmash, which commands the approach to Ai and Bethel. It was thus the key of Palestine to any invader from this quarter." He illustrates by *Chiavenna* (or the key-city, from its situation), in Italy. Lenormant remarks that from an ordinary historical point of view the strategy of Joshua is worth notice. It was the practice ever followed by Napoleon, and, he adds, by Nelson also, to divide his enemies, and crush them in detail. Had Joshua advanced upon Palestine from the south, each success, as it alarmed, would have also united the various communities of the land, under their separate kings, by the sense of a common danger. Thus each onward step would have increased his difficulties, and exposed him, exhausted by continued efforts, to the assaults of fresh and also more numerous enemies, in a country which grew ever more easy to defend and more perilous to attack. But by crossing the Jordan and marching at once upon Jericho, he was enabled, after the capture of that city, to fall with his whole force first upon the cities of the south, and then on those of the north. The political condition of Palestine at that time (see Introduction) did not permit of a resistance by the whole force of the country under a single leader. A hasty confederation of the kings of the south, after the treaty with Gibeon, was overthrown by the rapid advance of Joshua and the battle of Beth-horon. By this success he was free to march with his whole army northward, against the confederation of tribes under the leadership of the king of Hazor, whom he overcame in the decisive battle of Merom. There is no hint given in the Scripture that in this strategy Joshua acted under the special guidance of the Most High. The probability is, that in this, as in all other of God's purposes effected through the agency of man, there is a mixture of the Divine and human elements, and that man's individuality is selected and guided as an instrument of God's purpose, which, in this instance, was the chastisement of the Canaanitish people, and the gift of the Holy Land as a possession to the descendants of Abraham. That Joshua was not indifferent to human means is shown by this very verse. **Into a harlot's house.** Many commentators have striven to show that this word simply means an innkeeper, an office which, as Dr. Adam Clarke proves at length, was often filled by a woman. It has been derived from זון to nourish, a root also found in the Syriac. The Chaldee paraphast and many Jewish and Christian interpreters have adopted this interpretation, in order, as Rosenmüller remarks, "to absolve her from whom Christ had His origin from the crime of prostitution." But St. Matthew seems to imply the very opposite. The genealogy there contained mentions, as though of set purpose, all the blots on the lineage of Christ as was fitting in setting forth the origin of Him who came to forgive sin. Only three women are there mentioned: Tamar, who was guilty of incest; Rahab, the harlot; and Ruth, the Moabitess. And the LXX. render by πόρνη. Calvin calls the interpretation "innkeeper" a "presumptuous wresting of Scripture." Hengstenberg ('Geschichte des Reiches Gottes,' p. 197) also rejects the interpretation "innkeeper," and maintains the right of the spies, who, he says, were no doubt chosen by Joshua for their good character, to enter a wicked woman's house for a good purpose. It does not appear that the spies entered the house of Rahab with any evil intent, but simply because to enter the house of a woman of that kind—and women of that kind must have been very numerous in the licentious Phœnician cities—would have attracted far less attention than if they had

entered any other. Even there it did not escape the notice of the king, who had been thoroughly alarmed (ver. 9) by the successes of Israel eastward of Jordan. Origen, in his third homily on Joshua, remarks that, "As the first Jesus sent his spies before him and they were received into the harlot's house, so the second Jesus sent His forerunners, whom the publicans and harlots gladly received." **Named Rahab.** Origen (Hom. 3) sees in this name, which signifies *room* (see Rehoboth, Gen. xxvi. 22), the type of the Church of Christ which extends throughout the world, and receives sinners. **And lodged there.** Literally, and *lay* there, perhaps with the idea of lying hid, for they did not (ver. 15) spend the night there.

Ver. 4.—**And the woman took the two men.** The majority of commentators are of opinion that here, as in ver. 1, we must render by the pluperfect. For, as Calvin remarks, Rahab would hardly have dared to lie so coolly had she not previously taken precautions to conceal her guests. And therefore she must have told a twofold falsehood. She must have discovered, or been made acquainted with, their errand, and therefore have "known whence they were," in addition to her assertion that she did not know where they were now. **And hid them.** The original is remarkable and very vivid. *And hid him, i.e.,* each one in a separate place. No doubt the detail comes from an eye-witness, so that if the Book of Joshua be not a contemporary work, the writer must have had access to some contemporary document.

Ver. 5.—**I wot not.** Much has been said about Rahab's falsehood which is little to the point. The sacred historian simply narrates the fact, and makes no comment whatever upon it. But the fact that Rahab afterwards became the wife of Salmon, a prince of the tribe of Judah, as the genealogy in St. Matthew informs us (though Knobel denies this, asserting that between Joshua and David there were more than three generations, forgetting that Boaz, when he married Ruth, was an old man, see Ruth iii. 10), shows that neither her falsehood nor her mode of life excited much disapprobation among the Jews. Nor need this surprise us. There is no need, with Keil, to repudiate energetically the assertion of Hauff that the author of this Book regarded Rahab's deception as not only allowable, but praiseworthy, any more than we need scruple to confess that Jael's base treachery met with the approval of Deborah and Barak. The tone of feeling in Jewish society in Rahab's day must have differed enormously in many respects from what obtains in our own time, in the light of the dispensation of the Spirit. We may take, as an instance of what that tone of feeling was, even before Israel had been corrupted by their sojourn in Egypt, the narrative in Gen. xxxviii. And we may be sure that in a Phœnician city the tone was many degrees lower still. Rahab, therefore, was no doubt absolutely ignorant that there was any sin, either in her mode of living or in the lie she told to save the men's lives. She acted from a twofold motive, and her course, both of thought and action, was a most surprising instance of faith and insight, in one brought up as she had been. She not only followed an instinct of humanity, at a time when human life was thought of little value, in preserving the lives of the men who had sought shelter under her roof, but she could discern in the wonderful successes of Israel the hand of a higher power than that of the gods whom she had been brought up to worship. In her subsequent conduct she betrayed an affection for her kindred somewhat uncommon in persons situated similarly to herself. And we may be sure, from the fact that she was chosen to be a "mother in Israel," that she forsook the sins of her country and her education as soon as she came within the range of a higher light (see Heb. xi. 31 and James ii. 25). From what has been said we may learn that, though Rahab's faith was "as a grain of mustard seed," her conduct showed that she possessed it; and in hers, as in every case, to walk by the light she had was a sure prelude to the possession of more. And as regards her departure from truth here, it must be shown, before she can be blamed, that she had any idea that truthfulness was a duty. Such a duty does not appear to have been clearly recognised until He who was Himself the truth came among men. "However the guilt of Rahab's falsehood may be extenuated, it seems best to admit nothing which may tend to explain it away. We are sure that God discriminated between what was good in her conduct and what was bad; rewarding the former, and pardoning the latter. Her views of the Divine law must have been exceedingly dim and contracted. A similar falsehood, told by those who enjoy the light of revelation, however laudable the motive, would of course deserve a much heavier censure" (Matthew Henry). So also Calvin *in loc.*, "Vitium virtuti admistum non imputatur."

Ver. 6.—**But she had brought them up.** Literally, *and she caused them to ascend;* but our version has very properly (see ver. 4) given the preterite the pluperfect sense here. "Two strangers, Israelites, spies, have a safe harbour provided them, even amongst their enemies, against the proclamation of a king." "Where cannot the God of heaven

either find or raise up friends to His own causes and servants?" (Bp. Hall.) **To the roof of the house.** The flat roofs of Oriental, and even of Greek and Italian houses, are used for all kinds of purposes, especially for drying corn and other things for domestic use (see 1 Sam. ix. 25, 26; 2 Sam. xi. 2; xvi. 22; 2 Kings xxiii. 12. Also Acts x. 9, where the roof is used as a place of retirement and repose). **Stalks of flax.** Literally, *flax of the tree.* The word translated flax is used either of the raw material or of the linen made from it. Here it must mean flax as it came cut from the field; that is, as our version translates it, the stalks of flax (λινοκαλάμη, LXX.), which grows in Egypt to a height of three feet, and may be presumed to have attained a height not much less at Jericho. The word עָרַךְ which signifies to *lay in a row*, and is used of the wood on the altar in Gen. xxii. 9, and of the shew-bread in Levit. xxiv. 6, confirms this view. It is obvious that this would have formed a most sufficient hiding-place for the fugitives. "Either faith or friendship are not tried but in extremities. To show countenance to the messengers of God while the publique face of the State smiles upon them, is but a courtesie of course; but to hide our own lives in theirs when they are persecuted is an act which looks for a reward" (Bp. Hall).

Ver. 7.— **Unto the fords.** There were several of these fords. One near Jericho (cf. Judges iii. 28; xii. 5, 6; 2 Sam. xvii. 22, 24; xix. 16, 19, 39); one at Bethsean, now Beisan, leading to Succoth (Judges viii. 4; cf. Gen. xxxii. 22; xxxiii. 17. See Robinson, 'Biblical Researches' ii. 497; Ritter, 'Geography of Palestine'); beside others not mentioned in Scripture. A vivid description of the crossing the Jordan at the fords near Jericho is to be found in Tristram's 'Land of Israel,' p. 520. The ford is almost certainly the one mentioned here, since an hour or two's ride brought the party to Shittim. These fords were easy to cross save when the Jordan, as was now the case (ch. iii. 15), overflowed its banks. This may have been the reason why the pursuers did not cross the fords, but they pursued the spies to the fords, hoping to find their retreat cut off. This is rendered more probable by the fact (ver. 22) that the pursuers appear to have continued their search after leaving the fords.

Ver. 8.—**And before they were laid down,** *i.e.,* to sleep on the roof, a common practice in the East in summer.

Ver. 9.—**Hath given.** Rahab's faith is shown by this expression. What God willed she regarded as already done. To speak of the future as of a past already fulfilled is the usual language of the Hebrew prophets. **Faint.** Literally, *melt;* cf. Exod. xv. 15, 16, which is thus shown to be not poetic license, but sober fact. For we may take the future in the passage just cited as a present, and translate, " All the inhabitants of Canaan melt away; fear and dread are falling upon them " (cf. Deut. ii. 25; xi. 25).

Ver. 10.—For we have heard how the Lord dried up the water of the Red Sea for you. Rahab uses the word יְהוָה. Whether this name were known to her or not, she knew what was signified by it, the one only self-existent God (since יהוה is clearly derived from הָיָה or הָוָה *to be*), the Author of all things, visible and invisible (see ver. 11). **The Red Sea.** Brugsch, in his ' History of Egypt, denies that יַם־סוּף should be rendered ' Red Sea,' and affirms that this error of the LXX. interpreters has been the source of endless misapprehensions. סוּף is an Egyptian word signifying flags or rushes, which abound not only in the Red Sea, but in the marshes on the shores of the Mediterranean, as, in fact, in all low-lying lands. It is here, according to Brugsch, in a treacherous and well-nigh impassable country, near that Serbonian bog, " where armies whole have sunk " (Milton, ' Paradise Lost,' Book II., line 594), that we are to look for the victorious passage of Moses, and the destruction of Pharaoh and his host. The סוּף or rushes were to be found in the Nile, as Exod. ii. 3, 5 shows (cf. Isa. xix. 6). So that יַם־סוּף by no means necessarily implies the Red Sea. Yet on the other hand we may remember, with the Edinburgh Reviewer (July, 1879), that the coast-line of Palestine and of the delta of the Nile has undergone considerable changes during the historic period, and that the land has, during that period, largely encroached on the sea. **Sihon and Og.** As we read in Num. xxi. and Deut. ii., iii. **Whom ye utterly destroyed.** Rather, *devoted to utter destruction* (see ch. vi. 21). Rahab

seems to be aware that the extermination of these nations was in fulfilment of a Divine sentence.

Ver. 11.—Melt. The word in the Hebrew is a different one to that used in ver. 9, but it has a precisely similar meaning. There seems no reason why the destruction of Sihon and Og should have inspired such terror into the hearts of the powerful Phœnician tribes. But the miracle of the drying up of the Red Sea was an event of quite another order, and eminently calculated to produce such feelings. Nothing but such an occurrence could have explained Rahab's language, or the anxiety which the near approach of the armies of Israel inspired in those " cities, great and walled up to heaven," with their inhabitants of giant-like stature and strength. **Courage.** Literally, *spirit.* The word רוּחַ seems to have been used in the Hebrew in just the same senses as our word *spirit*, and it signified *wind* also (see 1 Kings x. 5). **For the Lord your God, he is God.** Literally, *for Jehovah your God.* This declaration, bearing in mind the circumstances of the person who uttered it, is as remarkable as St. Peter's, " Thou art the Christ, the Son of the living God." How Rahab attained to this knowledge of God's name and attributes we do not know. It is certain, however, that under the circumstances her knowledge and spiritual insight are as surprising as any recorded in Scripture, and are sufficient to explain the honour in which her name has been held, both at the time and ever since. " I see heere," says Bp. Hall, "not only a disciple of God, but a prophetesse." Keil argues that Rahab regards God only as *one* of the gods, and supposes that she had not entirely escaped from polytheism. But this view does not appear to be borne out by the form of her expressions. We should rather, in that case, have expected to find "he is *among* the gods," than *He is God*, which is the only possible rendering of the Hebrew.

HOMILETICS.

Vers. 1—12.—*Rahab and the spies.* Three points demand our attention in this narrative. First, the conduct of Joshua; secondly, of the spies; and thirdly, of Rahab.

I. JOSHUA'S CONDUCT. Here we may observe that—

1. *He does not despise the use of means.* He was under God's special protection. God had promised (ch. i. 5) that " he would not fail him nor forsake him." He had seen miracles wrought in abundance, and was destined to receive other proofs of God's extraordinary presence with him. Yet he does not rely on these, where his own prudence and diligence are sufficient. We must learn a similar lesson for ourselves—*(a)* in our external undertakings, *(b)* in our internal warfare. In both " God helps those that help themselves." We must " work out our own salvation," *because* it is " God that worketh in us," by ordinary as well as by extraordinary

means.   To pray to God for special help or direction, without doing our best to use
the means placed within our reach, to exercise our reason, and to see His directing
hand in the external circumstances of our lives, is mere fatalism.   To expect to be
freed from besetting sins, to triumph over temptations without effort on our own
part, to have victory without struggle, perfection without perseverance, is mere
selfishness and indolence.

2. *The use of ordinary means, where possible, is a law of God's kingdom.*
God might have written His gospel in the skies.   He might have proclaimed
and might re-proclaim it in voices of thunder from heaven.   He might make it an
irresistible influence from within.   But He does not.   He uses human means.
Jesus Christ, like His prototype, sent His disciples two and two to go before Him.
(Mark vi. 7; it is implied in Matt. x. 1; Luke x. 1).   Human influence has ever
since been the means of propagating Divine truth.   And not only so, but to use
extraordinary means when ordinary would suffice was a suggestion of the devil,
peremptorily rejected twice by Jesus Christ (Matt. iv. 4, 7; Luke iv. 4, 12); and this,
because this world is God's world as well as the other: reason and prudence,
though subordinate in importance, yet are as much God's gifts as faith.

II. THE CONDUCT OF THE SPIES.

1. *They preferred duty to reputation.*   The only house they could enter without
suspicion was a house whither, under ordinary circumstances, it would have been
impossible for them to go.   So Christ's disciples must not fear the comments of the
evil-minded when duty calls upon them to incur suspicion.   To give needless cause
for slander is a sin: to shrink from seeking the lost for fear of it is a greater.
Compare Boaz (Ruth iii. 14) with the spies here, and both with Jesus Christ
(Luke vii. 37, 38).   Ministers of religion, physicians, and the purest-minded
Christian women do not fear to visit the lowest haunts of vice for the temporal or
spiritual welfare of those who inhabit them.   It is well that their garb should proclaim the fact that they are on an errand of mercy. All needful precautions should be
taken to preserve their reputation.   But often they will have to put reputation and
all in God's hands, when duty calls, and they may be sure that all is safe with
Him.

2. *They went unmurmuring on a task of the utmost peril.*   So must God's
messengers now take their lives in their hands when they visit the sick, either to
serve their bodies or their souls.   The missionary confronts a similar risk when he
carries to savage nations the good tidings of salvation by Christ.   If He preserve
them alive, they thank Him for His goodness; if not, the blood of such martyrs is
still the seed of the Church.   Men do and dare all for the sake of the temporal
reward of the Victoria Cross.   The messengers of Jesus Christ ought not to be less
willing to risk all that is worth having in this life for the Eternal Crown.   How
rare is this spiritual gallantry, as we may call it!   Yet it is rare only because
genuine faith is rare.   We believe in rewards that we can see.   The unfading
crown excites few longings, because it is of faith, not sight.

3. *They did not recklessly expose themselves to danger.*   When Rahab bid them
conceal themselves, they did so.   They willingly accepted her aid in letting them
down from the wall, and her advice in concealing themselves in the caves of the
mountains.   In so doing they did but anticipate the command, "When they
persecute you in one city, flee ye into another" (Matt. x. 23).   Thus St. Peter concealed his residence from the disciples (Acts xii. 17); St. Paul was let down in a basket
from the walls of Damascus (Acts ix. 25; 2 Cor. xi. 33); St. Cyprian retired from
his see for awhile that he might still continue to guide it while his guidance was
needed.   So now, to expose one's life unnecessarily is suicide, not sanctity.

III. RAHAB'S CONDUCT.

1. *Her faith.*   This is commended in Heb. xi. 31.   It was manifested by her
conduct, as St. James tells us in ch. ii. 25.   For (*a*) she incurred danger by acting
as she did.   This was a proof of the sincerity of her profession.   For no one
willingly incurs danger for what he does not believe.   And (*b*) the reason for her
acting as she did was faith in God.   It might not have been a strong faith.   It was
certainly a faith which had not had many advantages.   She could have *known* little

about Jehovah ; but she recognised His hand in the drying up of the Red Sea and the discomfiture of Sihon and Og. Then (c) she seems to have lived up to her light. To be a harlot was no very grievous offence in the eyes of a people who regarded that profession as consecrated to the service of the gods, as was the case in Babylonia, Syria, Cyprus, Corinth, and a host of other places. Yet she was not idle, as the stalks of flax imply, and perhaps, in spite of her impure life, the guilt of which she had no means of realising, she might have been one of those (Prov. xxxi. 13) who " seeketh wool and flax, and worketh willingly with her hands." And so she was permitted to "feel after God and find him" as other sinners have been, through His merits who cried, "Father, forgive them, for they know not what they do."

2. *Her unselfishness.* She receives the men, knowing the danger she was in. She risks her life rather than give them up. She takes every care for their safety by her prudence and the excellent advice she gives them. As the next section shows, she had a regard, not merely for her own safety, but for that of her kindred. And this is a proof that she had striven to a degree after better things. For it is well known that nothing more deadens men and women to the gentler impulses of our nature, nothing has a greater tendency to produce cruelty and callousness to suffering, than the systematic indulgence of sensual passion.

3. *Her falsehood.* As the notes have shown, this was of course a sin, but in her case a venial one. Even Christian divines have held it to be a debatable question whether what Calvin calls a *mendacium officiosum*, a falsehood in the (supposed) way of duty, were permissible or not. And though this casuistry is chiefly that of Roman Catholic divines, yet Protestants have doubted whether a lie might not lawfully be told with the intent of saving life. In Rahab's time the question had never arisen. Heathen and even Jewish morality had hardly arrived at the notion that the truth must in all cases be spoken. Sisera requested Jael, as a matter of course, to do what Rahab did. Jonathan deceives his father to save David's life, and he is not blamed for doing so (1 Sam. xx. 28, 29). David deceives Ahimelech the priest (1 Sam. xxi. 2). Even Elisha appears not to have adhered to strict truth in 2 Kings vi. 19, and Gehazi is not punished so much for his lie as for his accepting a gift which his master had declined. Jeremiah, again, tells without hesitation the untruth Zedekiah asks him to tell (Jer. xxxviii. 24—27). How, then, should Rahab have known that it was wrong of her to deceive the messengers of the king, in order to save the spies alive ?

4. *Her treachery to her own people.* This, under ordinary circumstances, would also have been a sin. But here the motive justifies the act. It was not the result of a mere slavish fear of Israelite success. It was due to the fact that she recognised the Israelites as being under the protection of the true God, who would punish the idolatry and impurity of the Canaanites. Resistance, she knew, was vain. Jehovah had given them the land. There could be no harm in delivering her own life, and and the life of those dear to her, from the general slaughter. Besides, neither as a probable consequence nor in actual fact did the escape of the spies, through Rahab, affect the fate of Jericho. Not as a thing probable from her action, for the report of the spies, though it might supply Joshua with valuable information, could not bring about the fall of Jericho. Her conduct was not like that of Ephialtes at Thermopylæ, or of Tarpeia at Rome. Nor did the report of the spies actually bring about the fall of Jericho, for it was effected by supernatural means. In conclusion, it may be remarked that Rahab was in a sense the " first fruits of the Gentiles." She was justified by faith, not by works, in the sense in which St. Paul uses the words. That is to say, her former life had not entitled her to the favour of God, though her work in saving the spies was effectual as an evidence of her faith. She was forgiven, saved, numbered among faithful Israel, and became a " mother in Israel." And as a " woman that was a sinner," she was a type of those whom Jesus Christ came to save, who, " dead in trespasses and sins, were quickened " by the grace and mercy of the true Joshua, our Lord Jesus Christ.

HOMILIES BY VARIOUS AUTHORS.

Ver. 1.—*Forethought.* Let us play a little with this word. It has more in it than a good example for a military commander. And its side suggestions as to what is wise in all conflicts are many and valuable. Generalise the action of Joshua here, and its gives you some lesson of prudence in all departments of life. Let us gather a few of these.

I. Look before you leap. Always and everywhere do so. Many definitions have indicated the difference between man and the lower animals. One says, man is an animal that can strike a light; another, one which has language; another, one that can form abstract ideas. A very profound thinker recently taught us, "Man is an animal that knows what's o'clock," *i.e.*, that takes note of time. It is perhaps only an amplification of this last idea to add, man is an animal that thinks of to-morrow. The vegetable, in its vocabulary of time, knows only the word to-day; the animal knows yesterday and to-day; man alone lives in a yesterday, to-day, and to-morrow. He belongs to to-morrow as much as to to-day: is a sort of amphibious animal, living on the dry land of to-day and in the watery element of to-morrow. From to-morrow springs hope, fear, rest, distress. Man never is—but always *to be* blest. This instinct of anticipation is natural because it is necessary. We cannot get on without " sending out spies." Unless we forecast what is coming we cannot prepare for it, enjoy it, or secure it. If we advance without forecasting, we find ourselves perplexed in simplest circumstances; helpless, though possessed of abundant resources; weak, though endued with force of character; unready, though competent and resolved. There are some who never seem taken at a disadvantage; they have their wits about them; have presence of mind to do the wise thing, and presence of heart to do the right. Their difficulties kindle elation, and always end in advantage. There are others who move like a worm cut in two, their reasoning and acting powers always lagging behind themselves. An opportunity only agitates them; a duty disturbs them; a difficulty deters them from any further advance. All their wise thoughts come in the shape of resolutions which are not acted on, or regrets which are enfeebling. The difference between these two classes of men arises from this. The former send out spies, and are prepared; the latter take no trouble to forecast wisely—are always, therefore, taken by surprise. See that you look out well. Christ did not forbid thinking, but anxious thinking of to-morrow. Think what duties may come, and get ready, by prayer and self-denial, the strength to do them. Think of opportunities, and get ready the clearness of view which will let you embrace them. Think of temptations, and by prayer protect yourself. Happy is the man who can so wisely anticipate that every duty, difficulty, danger, as it comes, finds him ready. Therefore, look before you leap, and send out spies.

II. Do not send forth too many spies, nor send them forth too far. Here Joshua sent two men to Jericho—say ten miles away. There are some send all their forces out to spy, like a general who reconnoitres in force and does nothing else. They are always prospecting with all their powers. Their whole energies are given up to the guessing of the future. Reason, imagination, conscience, all are engaged in anticipation. So busy are they with to-morrow that they have but little strength left for to-day. Joshua did not reconnoitre in force, nor did he send out many to spy the land. He sends only two. Do not be always thinking on what is before you; it will become brooding, and when we brood our forecast is equally erroneous and enervating; nor let your whole soul go out into the to-morrow. To-day needs the bulk of your powers. To-morrow cannot claim so much. And doing to-day's work well, while not the whole, is yet nine-tenths of preparation for the morrow. A little thought, a little care, a little preparation, is the lesson of Joshua's two spies. And if we should not send forth too many, neither should we despatch them too far. Joshua limits his scrutiny to the immediate struggle before him. About to assail Jericho, he seeks all the information he can get on it. So ought we to put a limit to our prospects. The distant advantage should be excluded from our dreams, and the remote danger from our apprehensions. What is immediately before him is a wise man's care. And to take each stage as it comes into sight and provide for it is safety and wisdom alike. It is the golden mean between the levity of indifference and the torture of anxiety. Not too many spies must be sent out, nor too far afield.

III. SEE THAT YOUR SPIES ARE FIT FOR THEIR TASK. It is not every soldier who will make a scout; for his task there is needed endurance, resource, coolness, daring, quickness of perception and of purpose, in their highest form. I assume that Joshua chose two fit men; partly because he had seen the invasion of Canaan postponed for forty years through the unfitness of the spies then sent, and also because the few glimpses we have of them show them to have been the right sort of men. We can see that they had the agility of youth (ch. vi. 23) and the daring of faith (ch. ii. 24), and doubtless they had other qualities beside. See that the *spies you send out are fit for their work.* Some people employ their *Wishes* in this work, and these return with tale more flattering than true; some their mere *imagination*, which takes in all that may, can, or will happen; some send forth their *fears*, which return telling of countless lions in the way, and some their *superstitions*, which read auspices of good or omens of evil fortune in the simplest and most meaningless experiences. *They choose unfit spies.* If you are to send two, who shall they be? Of the first one there can be no doubt—it must be *faith*, for faith has clearer eyesight than anything else. It sees the invisible. It beholds God as well as man; sees His moral as well as material laws at work; sees the elements of hope which He brings with Him into every scene; is the attribute of daring; can always find or make a way out of difficulties. Let faith have the forecasting as its charge. And if faith should be invariably one of the two spies, *consecration* should be the other. Spy out the future, not simply to know it, but with desire to use it. And to that end scrutinise the future with the eye of consecration, with the desire to see the opportunities of doing good, of growing in grace, of honouring God, of blessing man. Happy the man who chooses his spies well, and sees with trustful eye the help, and with loving purpose the opportunities, which lie before him. Lastly—

IV. SEND YOUR SPIES ACROSS JORDAN BEFORE YOU YOURSELF MAKE THE PASSAGE. It is not by accident of poetic fancy merely that the Jordan, dividing the land of sojourn from the land of rest, has been taken as an image of that " river without a bridge," across which is the better land. Of course like all analogies it is imperfect, for while God's Israel finds rest in the heavenly Canaan, it finds no Canaanite to dispute the enjoyment of it. Still it is a suggestive emblem of the rugged, forbidding boundary beyond which is our land of milk and honey. And if our wisdom exercises itself in surveying every stage in advance and preparing for it, it certainly will find a special reason for surveying, and preparing for what is on the other side of the great dividing line between him and eternity. Have you sent out your spies there? Do you know exactly the sort of experience which is before you? Could you confidently pass over Jordan? Through your Saviour is it the abundant entrance that is waiting you? Do not confine your thoughts to Shittim, however sweet its shade of acacias may be; but prepare for what is beyond, and face the passage of the Jordan with the full knowledge and firm faith which would make your rest in Canaan sure.—G.

Ver. 1.—*A brand plucked from the fire.* This strange and somewhat romantic story of Rahab and the spies forms an interesting episode in the Scripture narrative. The special interest lies in the nature of the incidents and the character of the chief actor. Nothing is told us as to any definite result from the visit of the spies affecting the after siege and capture of the city, except so far as this, that they learnt from Rahab the alarm of the inhabitants at the approach of the Israelitish host. It shows, however, that, confident as Joshua may have been that the Lord was fighting on his side, he did not abstain from taking all proper precautions to ensure safety and success. God commonly works by the use of means and instruments, and they who have most living faith in His protecting and delivering power will be most careful to be co-workers with Him in all prudent forethought and diligence. We may, per-haps, best develop the moral teaching of this narrative by keeping the conduct of Rahab most prominently in mind. Her honourable distinction is that, as far as we know, she alone in all that dark, guilty land of Canaan was disposed to recognise the divinity that guided the onward march of the Israelites, and to welcome them to their destined inheritance. Certain moral difficulties have been felt by many in reference to the honour given to her name in Scripture. Her character and mode of life has been felt to be a difficulty; attempts have been made to show that "harlot" may simply mean "innkeeper." But this interpretation will not hold good. Much of the point and worth of the narrative depends on our regarding her as one of a class on whom Christ bestowed His pity; "a woman that was a sinner." Her treachery to her own people is condemned; but this, despicable as under ordinary circumstances it may be, is to be justified on the ground of loyalty to the God of Israel. It is a Christian principle that the claims of God are supreme over all other claims, even those that spring out of the ties of nature and of nationality. Her falsehood is a difficulty. No need to attempt to justify this. A low moral standard and the pressure of circumstances may palliate it, but cannot excuse. A lie must always be offensive to a God of truth. No skilful casuistry can make this aspect of her conduct right. But she is commended in Scripture, not for her treachery or falsehood, but for her *faith* (Heb. xi. 31; James ii. 25)—for the fact that, hearing of the wonders wrought by Jehovah, she believed Him to be the only true and living God, and so was moved to escape from the corruption of her own doomed city and cast in her lot with His people. The following lessons seem to be suggested:

I. THE SIGNALS OF GOD'S GRACE MAY BE FOUND UNDER VERY UNLIKELY CONDI-TIONS. Here is a gleam of light in the midst of gross heathen darkness; a sus-ceptibility to Divine impressions where it might least have been expected. The report of Israel's successes could scarcely of itself have produced it. In her that report awakened faith and the desire for a purer life, but in her neighbours it only roused the recklessness of despair. It moved her to seek deliverance: it made them only the riper for their doom. Why this difference? We trace here the secret working of that Spirit from the Lord who prepares the souls of men for higher revelations of truth. God directed the spies to her house because He had first put it into her heart to receive them kindly. Thus within the vilest and the most degraded there may be latent possibilities of good that only need the outward incentive to call them forth. God is often nearer to men, and they are nearer to "the kingdom," than we suppose. He who came "to seek and to save that which was lost" made Himself the "friend of publicans and sinners," not only because they most needed Him, but because He saw that they were most ready to welcome Him. His word awakened an echo in their hearts, when proud Pharisaic hearts were hope-lessly closed against it. It discovered and quickened germs of better life in the midst of corruption and death. It kindled hope in the region of despair. To the self-satisfied rulers of the people He said, "The publicans and the harlots go into the kingdom of God before you."

II. REPENTANCE MAY TRANSFORM A LIFE OF SIN AND SHAME INTO ONE OF HONOUR AND RENOWN. Rahab's sin was forgiven as soon as her heart turned to the Lord. There is a place for her in the commonwealth of Israel. Her faith saved not only herself, but her whole household (vers. 12, 13). She became the wife of Salmon, mother of Boaz, and thus ancestress of David and of Christ (Matt. i. 5, 6). A suggestive hint of the way in which the grace of God can "graft the wild olive tree in among the natural branches," and make it abundantly fruitful to His praise. It not only wipes out the reproach of the past, but developes from it a rich and glorious future. Faculties that have been wasted in the service of sin become effective instruments of righteousness. The history of the Church is full of examples. As in the case of Saul of Tarsus, so in less conspicuous instances, God has often entered the ranks of the enemy and brought forth from them living trophies of His power, who have henceforth served nobly the cause that once they destroyed.

III. The reward of generous trustfulness. It is remarkable that this Canaanite woman should have had such confidence in the sanctity of a promise and oath (ver. 12). It is significant of eternal principles enshrined in the heart of man, which the most degrading conditions cannot wholly obliterate. Note here, not only a Divine Providence, but a law of human nature. There is trust on both sides. The woman meets the spies with generous kindness, takes their life under her protection, and they in return keep sacred watch and guard over hers. It is a valuable lesson for all time. "With what measure ye meet," &c.; "Blessed are the merciful," &c. The trustful soul is trusted. Love begets love. "For a good man some would even dare to die." Whatever noble quality you cherish and practically exemplify has power to awaken something similar to it in others. It propagates and multiplies itself, and that is its reward.

IV. In the deliverance of this Canaanite family from the destruction of the doomed city we see a type of Gospel salvation. The Fathers, as usual, have carried the principle to a fanciful extreme in their use of these incidents. But the general features of the analogy are too plain to be overlooked. The rescue of Rahab and her kindred is certainly dimly prophetic of the gathering of a redeemed Church out of the Gentile world; and in the "scarlet cord," the sign of the covenant and the means of deliverance, we can scarcely help seeing a hint both of the blood of the passover and the "blood of the cross." How blessed the security of those who are under the protection of that sacred sign, that "true token!" In the "day of wrath and revelation of the righteous judgment of God," with what joy will they lift up their heads, knowing that their "redemption draweth nigh."—W.

Ver. 4.—*The harlot Rahab.*—A peculiar interest has always attached to this woman's case. Of the doomed nations with whom Israel came into collision, she is the first to be known, and the first to escape the doom ordained for them: an early type of the calling of the Gentiles; a whisper that the faith which was a sacred secret for Israel would yet become the heritage of the world; a study for early theologians on the sovereign grace of God, which can call those farthest off and make them vessels of His grace and mercy. While theologians learnt charity and hope from her experience, the historian and the patriot looked back with hardly less of interest to her, as to one whose simple service and womanly hospitality were a national boon. At the moment when the difficulties and perils of their undertaking were conspicuous, when the bravest people might have shrunk from an encounter with such foes, Rahab's greeting heartened them. Like the Midianite's dream of the cake of barley bread which heartened Gideon, so this woman's acknowledgment of Israel's God, and prediction of their success, was itself an inspiration. "A cup of cold water" given in the name of Jehovah, her act refreshed a nation. And so her name, cleared of the dishonour which had clung to it, was enrolled amongst those of the worthies who had deserved well of Israel. And all the thoughtful, whether their interest lay in creed or country, were glad to note that "a great reward" was given her by the God under whose wings she had come to trust. The deliverance of herself, of her family; a noble marriage, a royal progeny—these were dwelt upon by the devout of Israel, as examples of what all might expect who lived for the service of the Lord. Let us consider her story.

I. The waking of the soul. There has been an attempt made to take off the stigma which, to point the marvels of grace, all the centuries had attached to her. One of the earliest versions of the Jewish Scriptures renders the word which describes her calling—innkeeper. And one commentator (Adam Clarke) shows that women were the tavern-keepers in Greece and Egypt in ancient days; and points out many items in the narrative which would comport with such a view. We adhere more strictly to both letter and spirit of the narrative when we accept the usual rendering, and seek for mitigation of her ill-repute in other less questionable considerations. It is right to remember that amongst her own people, probably, there was no stigma in the name; that she was probably a priestess of the Phœnician Venus, like the priestesses of Bhowani, in India, to-day, consecrate to the goddess; that she was hard-working, attached to her kindred, and apparently treated with respect by her people.   But applying such considerations to modify the revulsion which every pure mind feels at the name given her, we still cannot avoid feeling that there is a vast gulf between Rahab as she had been, and the Rahab that can say, "Jehovah, your God, He is God in heaven above and in earth beneath."   A former faith—for the heathen have faith—had disappeared; in stern and terrible questionings it had broken up and melted away; a new God had risen on her soul; a deity of indulgence had sunk into the disregard of true repentance, and *the Jewish deity of mercy and of duty* had risen on her heart.   For us to change one thought about our God for another involves often a painful and protracted embarrassment; but for one to change her goddess in spite of all the centuries of tradition commending her—her acceptance by the people, and to be in Jericho a solitary believer in Jehovah—such a change was not wrought easily or lightly, and was not wrought out, one fancies, while she still pursued a course of wrong.   "The fountains of the great deep were broken up," and her soul went through the experience of earthquake and fire, before the small still voice could calm her into faith.   *This was a soul waking.*   How it came about none can tell. The external influences that prepare for such changes may be roughly traced, but the inward "moving" is too deep and subtle to be seen.   Jericho lay on the route of a caravan trade, which was even then carried on between Babylon and Egypt (see Babylonish garment, ch. vii. 21).   And so she had heard of all God's wonders in Egypt, and of "the strong hand and mighty arm" with which He had brought them out.   The overthrow of the inhabitants of Bashan and the Amorites, the war-like people—the remains of whose cities excite the marvel of all to-day—had seemed too wonderful to be the result of unaided human strength or skill.   And these, likely enough, started the deeper thoughts.   But they only occasioned, they did not produce them.   There must have been a deeper work going on.   Dubiety had risen in her about the Godhead of Deity that sanctioned the life she led; a sense that her country's gods exerted no hallowing or elevating influence—that they sanctioned all vile indulgences, but inspired no virtue; she had grown weary of worldliness; restless with the longing for a God pure and strong enough to trust. The God of Israel—who alone among all deities then worshipped, stood forth as the God of help and duty—looked in her face, breathed on her heart, and she was His. We must not miss the lessons of such a waking.   We must despair of none.   The soul, like the body, may sometimes be easily killed, but sometimes it takes a great deal of killing.   And from sins, and vices, and unbelief, which wound the soul and apparently leave no chance of life, ofttimes it will recover, and its health will come again like the health of a little child.   God can travel where no teacher comes, and can enter where no truth is known, and can commend Himself to hearts that seem incapable of appreciating His charms.   And so here, without guide, teacher, or companion, she rises to the light of God.   Have you waked thus to the greatness, the nearness, and the claims of a redeeming God?   Observe secondly—

II. THE ACTION OF FAITH.   Here we have not quite so easy a theme; for the mixture of good and evil which always marks human action is provokingly obvious here.   With clear faith falsehood is mingled; with devotion to Israel, something like treason to her people.   And persons who can do addition, but cannot balance accounts, are apt to reject her altogether.   They forget that morality has its chronology, and that the sanctity of truth dates from the Christian era.   They forget, too, what ought to be obvious, that the charge of not doing all she can to save her country hardly lies against a person who has the conviction that her country cannot be saved, and that her city is for its sins a very City of Destruction; and that in rewarding her, God rewards, not her lie, but her hospitality, her courage, her taking the part of Israel, her confession of His name; and that what we have here is not nineteenth century Christianity, but incipient Israelitism.   Considering these things, mark the action of faith in her case.   When these considerations have their weight, it is very striking how many of the characteristics of Christian faith are found here.

1. *Her faith sees clearly all that it is needful to see.*   She has the purged eye which discerns the great lines on which God works, and the great lines on which

our safety and bliss are to be found. Fortune and probabilities fade from her view, and she sees all things depending on God, and all bliss depending on following Him.

2. *Her faith braves every danger in the way of duty.* Think you a weak or timorous woman would have risked her life as she did? The King was nearer than the hosts of Israel: it were easy to have her falsehood discovered; and if so she dies. But faith dares what nought else dares. An inward moral courage is its continual mark, and at the risk of life she makes her choice.

3. *Her faith leads her to cast in her lot with the people of God, and seek to share their fortune.* An earthborn faith makes a person trim and endeavour to stand neutral—to avoid the fate of Jericho without identifying one's self with the fortunes of Israel. But she says in effect to the men, "Your people shall be my people, and your God my God." And by hiding them, aiding their escape, counselling for their safety, entering into covenant with them, she chooses her part with the people of God. To this she may be moved by fear more than by love. And love is better than fear. But the fear of God is infinitely better than listlessness, and is the beginning of wisdom. Happy they who see with the clearness, who venture with the courage, who choose with the piety of God's believing people. Shrink thou from no risk in following Christ. Choose thou the heritage of the people of God: His grace, His pardon, His eternal love. Lastly, observe—

III. THE REWARDS OF HER FAITH. Faith has always an exceeding great reward. It passes tremblingly along its anxious path to peace and rest. And so here. Observe how, answering the workings of her heart, God brings nigh His help. 1. She has an open door set before her. Not casually, but by God's guidance, the spies come for lodging to her house. 2. All needed wisdom is given where she has the will to use it. 3. She is kept safe from the men of Jericho by God. 4. While miraculous incidents in the destruction of Jericho leave her no room for thought of having helped it, she is herself saved, with her father, mother, brethren, and all that she had. 5. An honoured guest of Israel, she becomes the wife of the head of the tribe of Judah, Salmon. Probably he was one of the two spies, Ephraim and Judah being the leading tribes, and heads of the tribes being chosen for such work. 6. Her child was *Boaz*, one of the brightest and most honourable of Israel's saints; her daughter-in-law, Ruth the Moabitess; her grandchild's grandchild, David; and Jesus of Nazareth had her blood in His veins. How little she had dreamt of all that satisfaction, that gracious wealth, and sweet renown! And so it ever is! Cast in thy lot with the people of God. Like them, follow Him, His conscience-oracle, and there will be a growing benediction on your life, a various mercy—pardon, peace, joy of His love, hope of His heaven—till, so exceeding and abundantly above what you asked or thought, His mercy will come to you, that you will be "like them that dream;" and when others say, "The Lord hath done great things for us," your heart will reply, "The Lord hath done great things for us, whereof we are glad."—G.

Ver. 9.—*Rahab's faith.*—Since the time when Moses despatched twelve spies to inspect the land, the fame of the Israelites had spread amongst the inhabitants of Canaan. They were on their guard, and it was necessary to act with caution. Joshua sent, therefore, only two men, and that "secretly." The few are sometimes better than the many. Arriving at Jericho towards evening, they entered into Rahab's house, there to spend the night. As Rahab is honourably mentioned in the Epistle to the Hebrews as an example of "faith," and in the Epistle of James as an illustration of the "works" that result from faith, let us consider her faith so far as it is worthy of imitation.

I. IT WAS A FAITH THAT REASONED. It based itself on facts. She mentioned two striking events, the passage of the "sea of weeds," and the overthrow of the two kings of the Amorites by the Israelitish nation. From these she argued that the God of Israel must be mightier than the gods whom her country worshipped, that He was "Lord in heaven and earth," and that He would procure for His people the land of Canaan. Thus she took to heart the lessons of the past. Prejudice is strong. It could not have been an easy matter to renounce belief in her own deities, and to acknowledge the supremacy of an enemy's God. If men consult history they find therein ample evidence of a "power that maketh for righteousness." And further, the hand of God can be seen as the power that upholdeth righteousness. The history of the Jews is itself a witness to the truth and might of God. The spread of Christianity cannot be accounted for except on the supposition that it was "the work of God." What the keenest shafts of philosophical ridicule and reasoning failed to accomplish, that the "religion of the fishermen" soon achieved. It released men from the bondage of grossest idolatry and foulest sin. We may reasonably demand that men should pay to the "God of the Christians" that homage which is His due. We only ask that they will allow facts of religion to press upon them with their proper weight. The wicked may well feel downcast, for the chaff shall be blown away before the wind of judgment. "Who is on the Lord's side?'

II. IT WAS A FAITH THAT LED TO THE ADOPTION OF PRACTICAL MEASURES. (a) She hid the messengers. With the proverbial ingenuity of woman, she concealed them behind the stalks of flax piled upon the roof. Possibly the Eastern law of hospitality had some influence upon her conduct, but the narrative shows that Rahab was *willing to undergo present risk for the sake of future preservation.* Had the spies been detected in her house, death was sure. We do not excuse the falsehoods she told, nor are they commended in Scripture. They were an outcome of her degraded state, and an infirmity which was graciously overlooked by reason of her faith. To have respect to a future good is the duty of every man. The obstacle in the path of many is that they cannot forego present enjoyment. Religion requires us to endure "as seeing Him who is invisible," to "look at the things unseen." (b) She bound the scarlet line in the window. Before letting the men down by a cord, she demanded " a true token " that should assure her of security in the day of assault. The spies gave her an oath pledging their life for her safety, but coupling with the oath certain conditions to be fulfilled on her part. Here again is Rahab a *model of appropriate action.* God binds Himself by a covenant to forgive men if they respect the terms thereof. He confirmed His declaration by an oath (Heb. vi. 17). But only those can be said to " believe " who actually "flee for refuge to lay hold upon the hope set before them." The Israelites were required to sprinkle the blood upon the lintel of the door-post, and similarly must the blood of Christ be sprinkled upon our consciences if we would be unharmed when the destroying angel passes by. Our foreheads must be sealed (Rev. vii. 3), but not with the mark of the beast (Rev. xx. 4). If the promises of God are to have effect, we must observe the conditions. Herein many are found wanting. They listen, hesitate, think, but there is no practical faith, no actual recognition of God's love by accepting His gracious offers. Let the "scarlet line " be visible forthwith! then in the sifting day our interests will be secure. Though the elements crash all around, for us there will be " perfect peace."

III. A FAITH THAT CARED FOR THE WELFARE OF FRIENDS. Natural affection had not been extinguished by her wretched life. Her trust in the God of Israel brought into clearer light her love for her relations, and she desired their safety. And how can Christians enjoy their salvation without being deeply concerned for the state of those dear to them? As Rahab *implored protection for her kins-folk,* so will the followers of Christ commend to their Saviour's care those whom they love. Rahab's was intercessory prayer. It is related of a dumb son of Crœsus that when he saw a soldier about to kill his father, he burst forth into the utterance, "What! will you kill Crœsus? " Moreover, it was required of Rahab that when the siege commenced she should *gather her friends within the shelter of her own domicile,* otherwise they could not be recognised and saved. It is not sufficient merely to plead with God on behalf of those we love; He expects us to use all possible efforts for their moral safety. It was impossible for Rahab to preserve the whole city. Love dictated the enlargement of her sphere, prudence set reasonable bounds to it. The inhabitants would doubtless have resented her action and advice, and death would have ensued. There is no need for us to seek to justify all that

Rahab did. We are only concerned to imitate her in so far as she is presented to us as a model of faith.—A.

Rahab and the spies. The history of the escape of the Israelitish spies through the assistance of Rahab the harlot, and the reward given her for her services, in the sparing of her life when all her townsfolk perished, is one which presents many moral difficulties. To help the enemies of one's country is an act severely and justly reprobated by all nations. That which is in itself evil cannot be transformed into good because it is done for a good cause ; otherwise we ought to give plenary indulgence to the Society of Jesus. We must beware, then, of extolling the wrong thing which Rahab did. But at the same time we must recognise that she was prompted to it by a nobler motive than that of securing her own safety. Faith in the true God had taken rough possession of this ignorant soul. She had heard of the miracles by which Israel had been brought out of Egypt and led safely through the perils of the wilderness. She says, " We have heard how the Lord dried up the water of the Red Sea for you when ye came out of Egypt, and what ye did unto the two kings of the Amorites," &c. It is clear, then, that the Canaanites knew enough to acknowledge with Rahab, that " the Lord the God of Israel was God in heaven above and in the earth beneath ; " and therefore that they were sinning by still cleaving to their false gods, whose worship was an abomination to the only living and true God. It cannot be denied, therefore, that Rahab gave a proof of faith in the choice which she made between her own people and the people of God. It is this aspect of her conduct alone which is commended in the Epistle to the Hebrews (ch. xi. 31). We must be careful, moreover, not to exaggerate what she did. She did not betray the secret of her people, she simply preserved the lives of the representatives of the nation which she knows to be enrolled under the banner of the true God. This act of faith saved her, and even won for her the honour of a place in the genealogy of Messiah (Matt. i. 5). We occupy a very different position from that of Rahab. No such conflict can arise in our case between duty to the earthly and to the heavenly fatherland, because the weapons of our warfare are not carnal but spiritual. Let it be ours to have the faith of Rahab in the victory of our Divine Head; and let us hold fast this confidence, especially in view of the great conflicts that are before us, between the Captain of our salvation and an unbelieving world. Have we not as much to rest our faith upon—nay, far more than Rahab had—in the great victories of the past? We are the soldiers of a General who said, " Be of good cheer, I have overcome the world " (John xvi. 33). To be confident of victory is to have already conquered.—E. DE P.

EXPOSITION.

CHAPTER II. 12—25.

THE OATH OF THE SPIES.—Ver. 12.—**Kindness.** The original is perhaps a little stronger, and involves usually the idea of mercy and pity. This, however, is not always the case (see Gen. xxi. 23 ; 2 Sam. x. 2). " It had been an ill nature in Rahab if shee had been content to be saved alone: that her love might be a match to her faith, she covenants for all her family, and so returns life to those of whom shee received it" (Bp. Hall). **A true token.** Literally, *a token of truth.* The construction is that in which the latter noun often stands in Hebrew for an adjective. Here, however, it would seem to be a little more, *a token of truth*—a pledge, that is, of sincerity. Rahab wanted some guarantee that her life and the lives of her kindred would be saved. The bare word of the spies would not suffice, for how could she and her kindred be identified in the confusion attending the sack of the city? But if the spies would agree upon some sign by which she could be recognised, it would at once be a pledge that they intended to keep their word, and a means of protection in the approaching downfall of the city.

Ver. 14.—**Our life for yours.** Literally, *our souls* (נַפְשֵׁנוּ, answering to the Greek ψυχή —the principle of life in men and animals) *in the place of you to die ; i.e.,* may we die if you are not preserved safe and sound. A similar expression is used by Ignatius, ad Eph. i., ad Polyc. 2, 6, &c. **If ye utter not,** *i.e.,* Rahab and her kindred (Rosenmüller).

Many MSS., however, read "if *thou* utterest not."

Ver. 15.—**Then she let them down.** The conversation which is related afterwards, no doubt occurred afterwards, as is proved by the use of the perfect הוֹרַדְתֵּנוּ in ver. 18. There is no reason to suppose the window by which she let them down to have been so distant from the ground as to preclude a conversation, and it is quite possible that Rahab's house may have been in a situation in which such a conversation could be carried on without interruption. There are continental cities now surrounded by walls, in which such a conversation would involve no difficulty whatever, especially if the house from which such a conversation was carried on happened to stand a little apart from other houses. And though the spies sent by Moses described the walls of the Phœnician cities in hyperbolical language, it is highly improbable that their fortifications were stronger than those of mediæval times. The little town of Ahrweiler, in the valley of the Ahr, near Remagen, may serve as an instance in point. It would once have been called a strongly fortified town, but the walls are of no great height, and the houses are built upon them. The same may be seen at Bacharach and Oberwesel, and other well-known places where the fortifications have not been modernised. With the escape of the spies we may compare the escape of St. Paul from Damascus, as is recorded in Acts ix. 25, and 2 Cor. xi. 32, 33.

Ver. 16.—**Get you to the mountains.** No hint is given *why* the mountains were to be so safe a refuge. But a reference to the geography of the district will supply the reason. Any mountain district is usually less accessible and less thickly inhabited than the plains. But within five miles of Jericho lay the remarkable range called Quarantania, or Kuruntûl, which is literally honeycombed with caves, so that a man might be concealed for months in the immediate neighbourhood of Jericho with a very slight risk of discovery. It is obvious how strongly this fact confirms the accuracy of the narrative. An inventor would have been certain in some way or other to draw attention to a statement intended to give an air of probability to his narrative. But there is nothing of the kind here, and yet the narrative displays a thorough acquaintance with the geographical features of the neighbourhood. Canon Tristram ('Land of Israel,' p. 207, *sqq.*) carefully explored the caverns. On one face of the rock, which is perpendicular, he found "some thirty or forty habitable caves," and on the southern face, towards Jericho, he supposed

there were a good many more than this. The scouts of the king of Jericho might be excused a very diligent search, for we are told that the "foot-hold was hazardous and the height dizzy." From the days of the spies till long after the Christian era, these caves have been in existence. They have been tenanted by Greek, Syrian, and even Abyssinian monks, and Canon Tristram found many Greek and Ethiopic inscriptions, as well as figures of our Lord and the saints. The Abyssinian Christians make a yearly pilgrimage there even now. The reason of the reverence in which the place is held, is the tradition (not, however, eight hundred years old, see Ritter, iii. 37) that, as the name Quarantania implies, the forty days' fast of our Lord took place there. As a specimen of the mystical interpretations in which the Fathers indulged. we find Origen expounding the advice, "Get you to the mountains," as follows: "Humilia et dejecta refugite, quæ excelsa sunt et sublimia, prædicate."

Ver. 17.—**We will be blameless.** Perhaps "we *would be* blameless," and therefore we make the conditions which follow. Something must be supplied to fill up the sense. The most ordinary rule would be to translate "we *are* blameless," *i.e.*, by making these conditions. But the former yields a better sense.

Ver. 18.—**This line of scarlet thread.** Rather, this *rope*, from קָוָה to twist. It is described as made of sewing-thread (חוּט), because no doubt it was formed of several such threads twisted into a rope. The scarlet (שָׁנִי), or rather *crimson*, was produced from the dried bodies as well as the eggs of the cochineal insect, called in Arabic, kermes (whence our word crimson, and the German *karmesin*). This line of scarlet thread is regarded by the Fathers generally, and by our own divines, as Bishop Hall and Bishop Wordsworth, as symbolical of the blood of Christ (see Clement of Rome, 'Epistle to Corinthians,' 12 ; Justin Martyr, 'Dial. Tryph.' 111 ; Iren., 'Adv. Hær.,' iv. 37 ; Orig., 'Hom. 2 on Joshua.' "Coccineum, quod sanguinis formam gerebat." See also Bp. Hall, 'Contemplations,' Book viii. ; and Levit. xiv. 4, 6, 42, 51).

Ver. 19.—**His blood shall be upon his head** (cf. Levit. xx. 9). "If we will wander out of the limits that God has set us, we cast ourselves out of His protection." (Bp. Hall).

Ver. 20.—**And if thou utter this our business.** This was an obvious condition. Rahab's betrayal of the spies could not save Jericho, but it would destroy them, or at least expose them to imminent danger.

She would, therefore, by mentioning the matter, deprive herself of all title to protection.

Ver. 21.—**And she bound the scarlet cord in the window.**—Not necessarily at once, but when the time for the precaution arrived.

Ver. 23.—**And passed over.** The sacred historian does not say how. But it is improbable (see ver. 7) that they forded the river. They probably swam across, as they were no doubt unarmed (cf. 1 Chron. xii. 15). **That befel them.** Literally, " that *found* them."

Ver. 24.—**For even all the inhabitants of the country do faint because of us.** "For even" is literally "and also." As Keil remarks, this information concerning the feelings of the Canaanites was the one great thing they had been sent out to discover.

HOMILETICS.

Vers. 12—24.—*The oath of the spies, and their return to Joshua.* This passage suggests considerations of various kinds, historical, practical, and allegorical.

I. THE TRUSTWORTHINESS OF THE SPIES. They had, no doubt, been specially selected by Joshua for this purpose, and they show themselves worthy of his choice. (1) They are *scrupulously honest.* They enter into an engagement with Rahab, and that engagement is faithfully kept. They are anxious that the tenor of their engagement should be thoroughly understood on both sides, so that there may be no reproach cast upon them for not observing conditions which it would be impossible to fulfil. And they are also (2) *men of foresight.* They do not give their word rashly, without having considered to what they are pledging themselves. They see beforehand how impossible it would be, in the confusion attending the sack of the city, to ensure the safety of those in whose welfare Rahab is interested. Thus they suggest the twofold precaution that Rahab's relatives should be collected together in Rahab's house, and that Rahab's house should be plainly indicated by the scarlet cord. And (3) they are *grateful.* They might have left matters as they were, and taken no trouble to point out to Rahab the risk she was running, in the absence of some definite agreement as to the way in which the promise should be carried out. They might have excused themselves afterwards by saying that it was not their business, but Rahab's, to secure the identification of herself and her kindred. But they took every care and trouble possible to show their sense of the obligation they were under to a stranger who had thus generously interested herself in their safety. Such are the men who ought to be singled out for special work in God's Church, scrupulous, thoughtful, frank, generous, grateful men, who make it their first care to deal with others as they would desire to be dealt with themselves.

II. THE SCARLET CORD A TOKEN OF SALVATION THROUGH CHRIST. For scarlet, or rather crimson (see note), is the colour of blood. The scarlet cord had been the salvation of the messengers. It was now to be the means of salvation to her who had received from them the assurance of deliverance from the wrath to come. Like the blood upon the door-post, it was to be the sign which the destroying messengers of God's vengeance were to respect and pass by. That scarlet cord alone could ensure safety. And it could ensure the safety only of those who trusted in it alone. It must be taken, therefore, as the type of salvation through the blood of Christ alone.

III. EXTRA ECCLESIAM NULLA SALUS. Like St. Paul's "Except these abide in the ship, ye cannot be saved" (Acts xxvii. 31), so the spies here declare that to abide in Rahab's house is a necessary condition of safety. The house here is a type of the Church of Christ, not necessarily of external communion with any particular branch of it, but of actual internal membership in the mystical body of Christ, of which, ordinarily speaking, Baptism and the reception of the Sacrament of the Lord's Supper are the outward tokens. "Holy Scripture," says the 18th Article of the Church of England, "doth set out to us only the name of Christ, whereby men must be saved." And we must unite ourselves with Him by faith and obedience. We must enter into the "House of God, which is the Church of the Living God, the pillar and ground of the truth" (1 Tim. iii. 15). We must keep up a " continual remembrance of the sacrifice of the death of Christ." Our scarlet cord must be bound prominently in the window. Those who wander recklessly from the fold, who are carried about to " erroneous and strange doctrines," who follow their own wills instead of abiding by the covenant of salvation in Christ, cannot expect the deliverance which comes only to those who confess Christ openly before men, and declare plainly their union with those who fight under His banner.

IV. THE SPIES WHO FAITHFULLY DISCHARGE THEIR DUTY HAVE THEIR REWARD IN BRINGING GOOD TIDINGS. We have seen what the conduct of the spies has been. And now they return to reanimate their brethren. Their report is, that already their enemies are disheartened and dispirited at the thought of the Great Name under the protection of which the Israelites fight. So does the faithful soldier of Christ ever become a source of encouragement to his brethren. He who trusts in the Lord, and goes steadfastly about His work, never fails to find the enemies of the Lord " fainting because of " His soldiers. It is only the cowardly and distrustful who find the " children of Anak," and " cities walled up to heaven "—that is, insuperable difficulties and tasks beyond their powers. They who set themselves in earnest to combat the enemies of God, and will neither make a compact with them, nor be " afraid of their faces," are sure of victory. Sometimes the walls of some fortress of sin will fall as if by miracle. Sometimes the enemy will only be discomfited after the prolonged and exhausting efforts of a battle of Beth-horon. But the servants of God on the eve of a new conflict with the powers of evil may safely address their fellow-warriors in the words, " Truly the Lord hath delivered into our hands all the land."

EXPOSITION.

CHAPTER III. 1—6.

THE COMMAND. — Ver. 1.—**And Joshua rose up early in the morning**, *i.e.*, after the return of the spies, and most likely (see ch. i. 10, 11) on the morning on which the announcement was made to the children of Israel that they were to cross the Jordan. " This newes is brought but over-night, Joshua is on his way by morning, and prevents the sunne for haste. Delays, whether in the business of God or our owne, are hatefull and prejudiciall. Many a one loses the land of promise by lingering; if we neglect God's time, it is just with Him to crosse us in ours " (Bp. Hall). **And they removed from Shittim.** Literally, *from the acacias* (see note on ch. ii. 1). To do this completely, and to be quite ready for the crossing, would, as Rosenmüller thinks, require the greater part of three days. But it adds that " they lodged (ןילָ) there before they passed over." But this need be no difficulty. The great mass of the people could easily leave the acacia meadows on the higher ground, and encamp on the brink of the Jordan, while the remaining two days might be spent in making the necessary arrangements for the crossing. For we must remember (as Keil observes) that, not only a body of armed men, but their women and children, and all their possessions, had to be led safely across.

" Though they were not told how they should pass the river, yet they went forward in faith, having been told (ch. i. 11), that they should pass it " (Matthew Henry).

Ver. 2.—**The officers.** LXX., γραμματεις (see ch. i. 10). This is evidently the history of the fulfilment of the command there given by Joshua. There he orders the officers to pass through the host; here the command is fulfilled. There is no reasonable doubt that the spies had returned before the order recorded in ch. i. 10 had been given. Many commentators have raised objections to the order of the narrative in this and in the following chapter; and commentators like Houbigant, Masius (who says, " Narrationis ordo admodum perturbatus "), and Bishop Horsley, have suggested a different order of the verses. But Delitzsch has observed that the narrative is drawn up in a threefold order. First, the commencement of the crossing is detailed, from vers. 7—17 of this chapter; then (ch. iv. 1—14), its further progress; lastly (ch. iv. 15—24), its conclusion. And in each separate paragraph we have (1) God's command to Joshua; (2) Joshua's command to the people; and (3) their fulfilment of his command. Thus the Divine command, the human leadership, and the measures taken in obedience to that leadership are kept in close connection throughout. We need not suppose (he adds) that each separate act was enjoined at the moment when the necessity for the injunction arrived. Nor, we may add, is it necessary to suppose that every intimation given by God to Joshua is necessarily recorded in chronological order (see note on ch. ii. 1.) We are only to understand by the order followed by the sacred historian, that he desires to impress fully upon his readers how entirely every step taken by Joshua was taken at the express command of God. The idea of Paulus, Eichhorn, Ewald, Knobel, and others, that this account is compiled from two or more different documents, would not only require us to suppose great clumsiness in the compiler, if their view of his work be true, but is wholly unnecessary. The text involves no contradictions; only an amount of repetition, which is an essential feature of all the early Hebrew historical narratives, as is evident to the most casual observer, and is a proof, not of compilation, but of the antiquity of the document, and the simplicity and absence of art of the writer. Ewald has remarked that it is characteristic of the Hebrew historians to mention the termination of the event as soon as possible, and then to fill in their outline by the narration of intermediate circumstances (see chs. i., iii., vi., vii. of the Book of Joshua). As a specimen of the way in which contradictions are manufactured, we may take Knobel's assertion that the two statements that the people came to Jordan, and that there was a space of 2,000 cubits between them and the priests, are irreconcilable. As though it were not possible that the 2,000 cubits were to be measured *along the river*, and that the priests were ordered to walk along the bank until it was signified to them that they had arrived at the place of crossing. For we are plainly told that this distance was to be preserved that the people might "know the way which they must go" (ver. 4).

Ver. 3.—**And they commanded the people, saying.** These words are interesting as showing that all was orderly in the Israelitish camp. Everything was carried on according to the strictest rules of military discipline. The removal of the ark was to be the signal for the advance of the whole host. **The ark of the covenant.** We may with advantage compare the *religious* use of the ark here and in ch. vi., with its *superstitious* use in 1 Sam. iv. 3, 4. We do not read that when the Israelites were defeated at Ai, Joshua took the ark with him in a march to repair the disaster. Such a misuse of the symbol of God's Presence was only possible in days when faith had grown cold. When the Israelites had need of supernatural guidance, when they were placed in circumstances where no use of

their own unaided powers could guide them, *then* they must repair to the ark of God. There they must seek counsel, this they must set before them to guide their ways. But to regard it as a charm which could possibly atone for their want of faith and their lack of obedience, was to profane it. Such temptations as these Jesus Christ resisted in the wilderness; such temptations Christians must resist now. We have no right to seek for supernatural aids where natural ones will suffice us—no right to invoke the special intervention of God till we have exhausted all the means He has placed at our disposal. Above all, we have no right to expect Him to save us from the consequences of our own sin and disobedience except on His own condition, that we shall truly repent. We may further remark that the Pillar of the Cloud and the fire, like the manna, had ceased, and even the ark of the covenant only preceded the Israelites on special occasions. **The priests the Levites.** This phrase has given rise to some discussion. Some editions of the LXX., as well as some Hebrew MSS., read, "the priests *and* the Levites." The Chaldee and Syriac versions have the same reading. The Vulgate—more correctly, as it would seem—renders "sacerdotes stirpis Leviticæ," *i.e.*, "the priests who are of the tribe of Levi" (see ch. viii. 33, Num. iv. 18, and Deut. xxxi. 9). Keil's explanation that this expression must be taken in opposition to non-Levitical and, therefore, unlawful priests, seems hardly satisfactory. It is not till much later—in fact, till the time of Jeroboam—that we hear of unlawful priests. It is more probable that it is intended to emphasise the position of Levi as the sacerdotal tribe, the one tribe which had no share in the operations of the war. So Rabbi Solomon Jarchi explains it, citing the B'reshith Rabbah, which states that the phrase is found in forty-five places in the Bible, with the meaning that the priests are of the tribe of Levi.

Ver. 4.—**There shall be a space between you and it.** Perhaps in order that they might keep it in view. This agrees best with the remainder of the verse, "that ye may know the way by which ye must go." Keil remarks that, had the Israelites pressed close on the heels of the priests who bore the ark, this would have defeated the very object with which the ark was carried before the people, namely, to point them out the way that they should go. But Cornelius à Lapide among the earlier commentators and Knobel among the moderns hold that it was the sacredness of the ark which rendered it necessary that there should be a space of more than half a mile between it and the Israelites. Jarchi says the space was "in honour of God." We may learn hence that irreverent familiarity with sacred things is not the best way to obtain guidance in the way in which God would have us walk. "What awfull respects doth God require to be given unto the testimony of His presence? Uzzah paid deare for touching it; the men of Bethshemesh for looking into it. It is a dangerous thing to bee too bold with the ordinances of God" (Bp. Hall). "Neither was it onely for reverence that the arke must be wayted on afarre, but for convenience" (*Ibid.*). "The work of ministers is to hold forth the word of life, and to take care of the administration of those ordinances which are the tokens of God's presence and the instruments of His power and grace, and herein they must go before the people of God in their way to heaven" (Matthew Henry *in loc.*). (Cf. Num. iv. 19, 20; 1 Sam. vi. 19; 2 Sam. vi. 6, 7; also Exod. xix. 21.) The original here is more emphatic than the translation. "Only there shall be a distance (LXX. μακρὰν ἔστω) between you and it." **Ye have not passed this way heretofore.** Literally, *ye have not crossed since yesterday, the third day.* Paulus would translate this "*lately*," and thus get rid of the miracle, regarding it as an intimation that they were crossing at one of the fords. But they had not crossed the Jordan *at all* before. Consequently the translation *lately* is inadmissible. And even if they had been crossing Jordan by one of the fords, there is, as we have seen, a wide difference between crossing at the ford in ordinary times and crossing it when Jordan had overflowed its banks. This is a fair sample of the criticism which seeks to explain away miracles, as well as finds discrepancies where there are none.

Ver. 5.—**Sanctify yourselves.** The Hithpahel, which is used here, is frequently used of ceremonial purification, as in Exod. xix. 22; 1 Chron. xv. 12, 14; 2 Chron. v. 11; and especially 2 Sam. xi. 4. It is also connected with purification, but ironically, in Isa. lxvi. 17. **To-morrow.** These words were uttered while all was in preparation. We learn from ver. 7, though it is not expressly stated, that the actual crossing took place the next day. We ought, probably, to place this verse in a parenthesis, and to translate "Joshua *had* said," because the sanctification (see Exod. xix. 10, 14) involved some definite period. Knobel, however, assumes, as usual, that there is at least a faulty arrangement here. **Wonders,** or rather, *miracles,* from פָּלָא to *separate, distinguish.* They were, therefore, acts distinguished from the ordinary course of God's providence. We may observe that, while among the Canaanites all was terror and confusion, in the camp of Joshua all was confidence and faith. "Either successe or discomfiture begins ever at the heart. A man's inward disposition doth more than presage the event. If Satan see us once faint, he gives himselfe the day. There is no way to safety, but that our hearts be the last that shall yield" (Bp. Hall).

Ver. 6.—**And Joshua spake.** We return now to the ordinary course of the narrative. **To the priests.** This was because the occasion was an extraordinary one. On ordinary occasions this was the duty of the Kohathites (Num. iv. 15). **And went before the people.** The people were to "follow the priests as far as they carried the ark, but no further; so we must follow our ministers only as they follow Christ" (Matthew Henry).

HOMILETICS.

Vers. 1—6.—*The command to cross Jordan.* We have here a chapter replete with instruction, whether we take the words in their natural and literal or in their figurative and allegorical sense. The instruction is of a kind which it is difficult to gather up into one point of view, so various and many-sided is it. It will be best, therefore, to follow the events of the narrative *seriatim*, and endeavour to notice the various points which may be observed for instruction and exhortation, rather than to gather up the whole into the materials for one or two separate discourses. We may therefore observe—

I. That Joshua was an example of diligence and promptitude. This is urged upon us in matters (1) of this world; (2) of the soul. The maxim (1) as regards the affairs of this world, "Whatsoever thy hand findeth to do, do it with thy might," has been exemplified in the history of God's servants in all ages. They have not been wont to let the grass grow under their feet. "Not slothful in business," is the precept of St. Paul, and he laboured energetically at his craft while he preached the gospel. When we have a work to do, it is our duty to do it, and not to take our rest till it is done. Procrastination is not only foolish, it is wrong.

Habits of industry, punctual attendance to duty, *business-like* habits, as they are called, are required of every Christian by his profession. And it is remarkable that in no other saint of the Old Testament do we find that virtue so conspicuous as in the great captain, who alone among them was privileged to bear the Saviour's name. (2) This is also the case in the affairs of the soul. It is our duty to wait until the will of God is made known. So Samuel waited (1 Sam. xiii. 10), and Saul for his unwise haste was censured. But when it is made known, there should be no hesitation, no delay. By such hesitation Moses provoked God's wrath (Exod. iv. 10—14). It is a question whether Gideon did well to prove the Lord repeatedly (Judges vi. 36—40). Balaam was involved in the most grievous sin by not being content with God's decisive answer to his prayer (Num. xxii. 12). Many a good man makes shipwreck of his work, and some of their faith also, by hesitating to carry out a plain command of God, by waiting for some additional manifestation of His pleasure, or some opportunity to do that for which an opportunity should be made. The time of waiting in Joshua's case was over. The spies had brought back their report; the way was open; the command clear. The very next morning, and that *early*, the preparations were made for the decisive step which committed Israel to the struggle which lay before them. So in the work which God has set us. When the path of duty is clear, we are bound to enter upon it at once.

II. OBSERVE THE FAITH OF THE CHILDREN OF ISRAEL. They implicitly obeyed Joshua's command, though it seemed the very height of folly. Jordan was overflowed; the ordinary fords were impassable; there was no way through the river. They had been told that "within three days they should cross Jordan, and there is neither murmuring nor disputing. So we ought to follow the directions of our Joshua, even where success seems hopeless. It is want of faith alone which hinders us from performing like impossibilities now. The mountain of difficulty will ever be removed by the purpose of faith. When a duty lies before us, we must set about performing it as far as our human strength goes. What lies beyond it, we must leave to God. And we shall find that the same power which rolled back the waves of the Jordan can arrest the overrunning flood of ungodliness, the headlong stream of the opposition of evil men. Where no way appears to human eyes, there can He make one when He pleases, "Whose way is in the sea, and His path in the great waters."

III. THE ARK OF THE COVENANT MUST GO BEFORE, *i.e.*, the visible signs and symbols of God's presence. The ark contained the law of God and the manna—that is, God's Word, and His sacraments and ordinances. Over it was the mercy-seat, the token of the presence of Christ, in whom sin and pardon meet. We can but go in the path marked out for us by these. His Word is "a lantern to our feet, and a light unto our paths." His earthly life has been lived as a pattern to us. His presence is "with us always, even unto the end of the world," to animate and to guide. The visible signs and tokens of His presence among us are to be reverenced and kept in view, lest the "remembrance of Him," which He ordered to be kept up, should perish from off the earth. By thus keeping Him ever in view, in public as well as in private, in the visible sanctuary as well as in the sanctuary of our own hearts, we shall pass through the "waves and storms of this troublesome world," and attain to the eternal rest at last.

IV. THERE MUST BE NO UNDUE FAMILIARITY WITH SACRED THINGS. A space is kept between the people and the ark. So between His perfect example and our imperfect obedience there is a gulf which cannot be passed over. We are ever pressing forward in the direction of it; we never thoroughly attain to it (Phil. iii. 13, 14). Again, we learn that reverence is the best means towards knowledge of spiritual things. "Not to be wise above what is written" is good advice. The mysteries of the kingdom of God are hidden from the "wise and prudent" in their own estimation, and are "revealed unto babes" (cf. 1 Cor. ii.). This is true, both in opinion and in action. Those who think that all the deepest questions that concern humanity are to be settled by argument and logic, rather than by teachableness, experience, and prayer, are likely to end with a very moderate acquaintance with the "deep things of God." Those who look upon God's Word as a common book, or Christ's sacraments as simple symbols, without any mystery about them, even to the faithful worshipper, are likely to deprive themselves of a very necessary help and guidance in their way through the world. Awe, and reverence, and a sense of the mystery as well as the nearness of the Unseen, are among the most necessary features of a life that seeks aright after the perfection of man's nature.

V. THE MINISTERS MUST LEAD THE WAY. Without any undue sacerdotal pretensions, it may at least be said that if the ministers of Christ's Church be not the guides and teachers of the people, we were better without them. Yet, as Matthew Henry remarks, we are only to follow them when they follow Christ. Nor is there any contradiction in this. It is our duty ever to " search the Scriptures, whether these things are so." We are to " prove all things," to "hold fast " only " that which is good." But it is the duty of those whose province it is to " rule the Church of God" to be ever foremost in every good work. It is idle to preach if we do not practice. It is useless to exhort men to follow the right path, unless we ourselves go before them in the way. An officer cheers his men into action not from behind, but from the front. So the officers of God's army should be in the van of its progress. Therefore in all things which become the Christian, the Christian minister must set the example. In zeal for his Master's cause, in unwearied efforts to promote it, in purity of life, in acts of love to the sick and aged, to the young and tender, in kindness to all, in public spirit moreover, and regard for the general welfare, in honour, in truth, in prudence, in self-command, in self-abnegation, the ordained servant of God should be in the fore-front of the grand army. But the army must follow its leaders. It is not sufficient to lay down a high ideal for our officers, and to consider that the part of the privates is to criticise sharply and closely the actions of those who are set over them. Whatever they do, we must do also. Where they go, we must go too. We are all pledged to the same work, and, taking our tone from those who are appointed to lead us, we must lead a life animated by the same spirit as theirs, the Spirit of the living God.

VI. A SPECIAL WORK REQUIRES A SPECIAL PREPARATION. Joshua bids the Israelites " sanctify themselves " because God was about to " do wonders among" them. So when we set about any work of more than ordinary importance, be it sacred or be it secular, we are bound to prepare ourselves by prayer, by meditation, by reception of the Holy Communion, by a special study of God's Word, by a cessation, as far as possible, of ordinary cares and engagements, for the task that awaits us. Thus Jesus Christ spent the night before choosing His apostles in prayer to God. Thus before His Passion He withdrew Himself for a while from the concourse of men. Thus the apostles waited in silence at Jerusalem for the descent of the Holy Spirit. Thus St. Paul spent three years in Arabia communing with God before he entered on his life-long work. God's Spirit is ever near us, but at special times He requires to be specially sought. And he who never permits himself a moment's retirement from the ordinary business and amusements of life may well doubt whether God's Spirit have really a hold on his soul.

HOMILIES BY VARIOUS AUTHORS.

Ver. 16.—*The crisis of life.*—There is only one date in history transcending this in importance—the date when, across a vaster Jordan, the dividing line between heaven and earth, God came in the person of a little babe to make a conquest of a world of promise. The year of the founding of Rome, the flight of Mohammed, the invasion of the Saxons, the irruption of the Gauls into Italy, the Norman Conquest, the War of Independence in America, the French Revolution—what date can compare with this crossing of the Jordan by a people only a generation free from slavery, ignorant of their own destiny, crossing with a hope of finding an earthly home, but with no dream of the world-wide usefulness which would crown their history ? The beginning of the history of Canaan ! Invasions do not generally contribute much to the well-being of mankind, and frequently are as evanescent in their results as they are disastrous in their immediate miseries. Successive invasions of the great monarchies of Persia and Babylon have left little but a lesson on the vanity of human glory. Successive invasions of India have left their traces chiefly in those caste distinctions, each step of which tells of a class lorded over by a class above it on the strength of a conquest completely made and long enforced. But the invasion of Canaan hallowed a land, gave God an earthly throne, started what was, with all its faults, a model commonwealth, and gave a home to a people which, with all its backslidings, was still " a kingdom of priests " to mankind. Consider a few features of this great event. And first consider the illustration afforded here of—

I. THE CRISES OF LIFE.—Our life is built up of acts, every one of them important. They, made by our character, react on our character and make it. And in the sense that it contributes to an enduring result in character, no act is little. But there are times specially solemn in our life, when the roads which invite us diverge at a large angle, and are such that each step we take on the one makes return to the other more difficult. And if a man is made by his ordinary acts, much more is he made by his crisis acts. If a nation's character is moulded by its acts, much more by its crisis acts. Here there is a crisis reached in Israel's history very analogous to the first great crisis, when they passed the Red Sea. Shall they or shall they not commit then selves to the struggle with the seven nations of Canaan— some with what seemed impregnable fastnesses, some with chariots of iron, some conspicuous for gigantic stature ? Jordan accentuates the question. To cross it is to commit themselves to a course condemned by ten out of twelve of the spies sent out forty years before, is to hazard everything on the chance of battle, is to have no retreat, is to win or lose all things. It was a crisis on which their national future hung. It needed crisis virtue. Let them hang back and their enthusiasm would evaporate, their unity break up ; they would fall off into a number of nomadic tribes, and probably degenerate into a people like the Ishmaelites, without any of that consecutive progress and self-contained strength that constitutes a history. Let them go forward, and to remotest ages and countries mankind is blessed by the national history that takes a forward stride and reaches a stouter solidity by their new departure. *Happily, they had crisis virtue ;* at least, a sufficient amount of faith to let them venture—to make them obedient to faithful leaders, and united in their purpose to obey the guidance of their God. And meeting the crisis, they accepted its duty, with results of perpetual usefulness, and left us a testimony as to the solemnity of all such junctures and the blessedness of meeting them aright. The kind of juncture that comes to us you will recognise from your own experience. They vary in their kind, but all have this in common, that they summon a man to some higher duty, some better life, some bolder enterprise, and put before him "an open door ;" that to decline them is to degenerate into a poorer character and more sordid life, while to accept them is to rise to "newness of life." Their variety, indeed, is striking. Sometimes it is a great mercy that comes to a man, meant to wake him to a sense of the fatherliness of God, and to win him by the gentle constraints of gratitude to filial duty ; to cure grumbling or to destroy despair. If he meets this crisis well, he passes to a higher level of gentler, kinder, gracious thoughts and purposes ; and a sense of debtorship to man and an overflowing gratitude to God are the abiding results of the crisis of a great mercy. Sometimes the crisis is the revelation of a duty. Some sudden turn in our experience devolves on us a duty hitherto discharged by others ; or some new duty arising from a fresh contingency. It may be a duty of Christian mercy to some overtaken in calamity. It may be that a slumbering conscience or an indolent mind has been awaked to the discernment of God's requirements. It may be that with some growth of years or development of thought and feeling we see we owe some duty to our Saviour and our fellow-men hitherto not due from us or not known to us. This is a crisis not to be overlooked. Hitherto there was comparative unimportance in the neglect of this duty. It was a " time of ignorance God winked at." But to neglect it now, when it stands out eminent and clear, would be to cast off the Divine Master, and to be guilty of unfaithfulness to the Lord that bought us ; while to do this would strengthen the bond that binds you to God and man, would result in enlargement of heart, ennoblement of purpose, strengthening of conscience, and enjoyment of peace. Sometimes the crisis is a temptation, pressing on the spirit on every side, and by guile, clamour, terrors, and allurements compelling its divergence from the path of duty. I need not enumerate other kinds of crises. Let me only urge that, in whatever way the crisis come, we meet it manfully. When you come to Jordan see that you cross over it. God will not fail you if you do not fail yourself.

II. I ask you to observe, secondly, THE CREED FOR A CRISIS. It is given us here: one of those beautiful instances of faith in which noble hearts find at once their expression and their sustenance. Here is one couched in a name of God. Here are two significant titles, neither of them in common use previously: He calls God "the living God," and "the God of the whole earth." Once only is the former of these names found in Scripture before this use of it, and the other is not found in use until long after. They are, therefore, not traditional words a parrot might have used, but great original words which register the truth Joshua had conquered for himself. And if we would meet our crisis, when it comes, as nobly and grandly as Joshua met his, we must try and get his creed of two articles.

1. We must believe God is *the living God,* for all do not believe that; not that they would formulate the idea that on such a day God died, and has not been heard of since. But the general feeling is, He is as good as dead. A distant God, without living eye to mark our necessities, without living hand to help us, without a living heart to feel for our distresses. And if Joshua had been of that creed there would have probably been no passage of the Jordan, and no victory of Jericho, and no conquest of the land. But by the ever-extending obedience or experiences of his life he had learned this mighty secret—that God is *alive*, is here, gives their bias to all events, can hear a prayer, can save a soul, can cleave a passage through sea or river.

2. And the second was like to it. He deemed God " *the Lord of all the earth.*" No local deity, like those heathen deities whose sovereignty was often as limited as a German duchy; no limited being; but master of all powers of nature, master of all tribes of men, with the government upon His shoulder of all things; able to open a path where all passage seemed denied; so that his and Israel's future would not depend on their own wisdom, strength, or fortunes, but would depend supremely on the favour of God. Aye, and that is the sort of creed which we all need for the crises we have to face. God living and reigning; earth alive with His presence and His work; all events dependent on His will. Oh, let us catch from heroic souls at least their creed. Their faith, which works such wonders, must be the true faith. *God* IS *living*, His heart is alive with tenderness. He is not the great grave into which all things fall, but the great fount of life from which all things live. So alive that He could become incarnate and take infinite trouble to redeem us. So alive He is here to-day, ready to help us. If you suspect the creed of priests, here is a layman, a soldier, a hero; this is the first article of His creed. Have you that creed? If not, pray for a large enough heart to hold it. And especially if you are in any crisis of your life; for if in any crisis of our life we assume in our despair that, so far as we are concerned, God is dead, or unable to control the elements of nature, the fair results of all opportunity are lost because it passes unused. If you have come to Jordan, cross over it; and if you want strength to do it, find it in this creed: God is the living God, and the Lord of all the earth. And observe lastly—

III. CRISIS GRACE comes wherever there is crisis faith and obedience. It is a strange story, in its circumstantiality, that of the dividing of the Jordan. The baring of the bed of the river, the water gathering for thirty miles up by the sudden arrestment of its flow into a lake like Loch Lomond in size and form, while below the point of transit it flows away as if its career was ended. There is interest in all explanations that are suggested; in that, for instance, which, combining the destruction of the walls of Jericho with this dividing of the river, and both with the numerous traces of volcanic action in the neighbourhood, and demonstrable changes in the river bed, sees here the action of an earthquake, upheaving the bed, and thus for a day or so making of all the deep valley of the Jordan above it a temporary lake.   But there is more importance in our marking the fact and its lessons than in our being able to explain the mode.   Does Joshua believe God to be the living God?   " According to his faith it is Him."   And with all Divine energy of love He comes nigh to help them that trust in Him, laws of nature and forces of nature notwithstanding.   Such faith never goes dishonoured ; and we ought to mark it for our comfort in life.   God is not dead ; He is living still, as fresh for working miracles as when He divided Jordan, and as sure to open up our way, and to lend supernatural aid to simple faith, as when Israel halted before Jordan.   Our hope must not be limited within the sphere of what is obviously possible according to laws of nature.   I should think God never in any miracle broke the usual laws, but only employed unusual forces.   And He does the impossible still—making weakness strong, despair victorious ; healing the sick, saving the lost, giving victory and success.   The supernatural is not contranatural, but blends kindly with nature ; and whenever in the crises of our life there is the obedience which honours God and the faith that trusts Him, there is specifically supernatural help and grace making the grandest deliverance and achievements possible.   Our lives might be perpetual miracles, and every day behold the impossible achieved, and the insurmountable surmounted with blessed ease.   Is there some stern crisis on you now?   Do not faint.   There is crisis grace for all who have faith enough to admit and act on it. Let it in, and even though Jordan be at the flood you will pass over as on dry land.—G.

Ver. 5.—*Preparation for beholding displays of Divine power.*   With what longing eyes must the Israelites have looked upon the river which they were soon to cross.   Hope had been deferred for years.   The promised land, fertile and beautiful, seemed to disappear from their sight, as did the fruit and water from the eager hands and parched lips of Tantalus.   Could it, then, be really true that on the morrow the boundary-line would separate them from their inheritance no more ? By the Jordan the Israelites were encamped, and the command of the text sounded in their ears, " Sanctify yourselves."   This was to be THE PEOPLE'S PREPARATION FOR GOD'S WORK AMONGST THEM.   Probably the injunction respected rather the hearts than the dress and bodies of the people.   It invoked a seriousness of deportment befitting the solemn ceremony of the coming day, an examination of themselves, a recalling of the facts of their past history, a mourning over their numerous transgressions, and a resolve henceforth to serve the Lord.   We believe that in endeavouring to ascertain the reasons which dictated the advice of the text, we shall be meditating on truths profitable to our own souls.

I. SANCTIFICATION WOULD FIT THEM TO BEHOLD THE MANIFESTED PRESENCE OF GOD. Emblem, ritual, and precept were unceasingly employed to remind the Israelites of the holiness of God.   They were to observe the sanitary regulations, because " the Lord thy God walketh in the midst of the camp."   Before their offerings could be accepted they must purify themselves with ablutions.   And, above all, they were excluded from the tabernacle where God's dwelling was, and into the Holiest only the high priest could enter once a year.   Now every prodigy was the special coming of Jehovah into the midst of Israel.   Whilst really present in the unceasing operations of nature, nevertheless it was on the occasion of the miraculous that God seemed to put aside the veil and to draw nigh in person.   Hence the need that the Israelites should be sanctified.   Holiness consumes impurity as light destroys darkness.   The people must prepare themselves to stand in the glory of God's presence. So was it required at the appearance of the Almighty on Sinai, and before the wondrous shower of quails, and so afterwards for the battle of Ai ; otherwise would " the Lord break forth upon them."   Whilst we are not under the terrors of the law, yet reverence beseemeth us in our approach to the " Father of our spirits." We would not rush heedlessly to communion with Him, nor fall into levity while upon our knees.   With us, too, there are times when we must sanctify ourselves for the special manifestation of the Divine.   Sin amongst Christians is a chief obstacle to the accomplishment of signs and wonders in the name of Jesus.

II. SANCTIFICATION WOULD PREPARE THEM TO APPRECIATE THE GREATNESS OF THE

MIRACLE. As was the case with the "mighty works" of our Lord, these wonders of the Old Testament were not wrought simply to assist men in their straits and feebleness, but to exert an ethical influence upon them, teaching the power and love of God. Now that the Israelites were about to enter upon their inheritance, the time was a fitting one for signal marks of Divine favour and might. But in order that the miracle have due weight, previous reflection and expectation were essential. The Israelites were as children whose curiosity must be aroused and excitement intensified by stimulating annunciations. Then, when the notable day dawned, attention would be drawn to every detail, every occurrence, and the more vivid and lasting would be the impressions produced. A miracle silently and suddenly performed would fail of the results intended. Preparation befits our solemn engagements, qualifying us the more quickly to hear the " still small voice," and to note the " way of God" amongst men. It is well for the passions to be quieted, and the common duties dismissed from the mind, as we near the sacred operations of God. Of what abiding influence would the services of the Lord's day be capable, if it were possible to spend the previous evening in preparing the mind to say, " Speak, Lord, for thy servant heareth " ! Fully to reap benefit from witnessing a " sign," or from perusing an account thereof, demands of us the same sanctification of heart.

III. SANCTIFICATION WOULD AFFORD EVIDENCE OF FAITH IN THEIR LEADER AND IN GOD. What folly to trouble about purification unless they believed that the promise would be fulfilled. The miracle was to be eminently a proof of the love of God. His honour demanded that the people should show themselves to be in some degree worthy of His favour. Jesus inquired of the applicants for relief whether they had faith in His ability to heal them ; and we read of places where " he did not many mighty works because of their unbelief." Unbelief is the great hindrance to the progress of religion, both in the individual and in the world. We block the only avenue by which heavenly blessings can come to us; we shut the gates, and wonder why our city is not thronged with angelic visitants. *Faith in preparation would lead to augmented faith in the time of action.* Soon was coming the hour of trial. How would the people venture between the dangerous heaps of water ? Here would be reaped the advantage of previous thought. Faith grows by exercise. The conquest of one difficulty opens the way for subsequent victories. If the Church of Christ is paralysed by secret disbelief of the efficacy of God's Word and Spirit to convert men, how can she expect great awakenings ? " According to our faith " is it unto us. And if there is not sufficient faith to lead to the making of the necessary arrangements, where shall be the faith to enable us to rejoice in the evident tokens of God's presence ? Let us " lift up *holy* hands without wrath and *doubting*." —A.

Ver. 3.—At this decisive moment, when the people of Israel were about to enter on the great conflict which was to secure the possession of the land of promise, the command was given to gather themselves together around the ark of the covenant, as their banner. This indicates the great central truth of the history of Israel. The focus of its national life is the law of its God. It is for this it is to fight and overcome, and not merely that it may gain possession of a rich country and develop its material resources. In its fidelity to the ark of the covenant, lies moreover the secret of its success. This sacred memorial of its religious faith must be its great rallying point in the day of battle. This is a principle applicable to the people of God in all ages, and equally true of their individual or collective life.

I. For mankind at large, as for Israel, there are two aspects of all the great phases of its history. ONE DIRECT, TEMPORAL, TERRESTRIAL, LIKE THE CONQUEST OF A FRUITFUL LAND for Israel ; the other higher, more comprehensive, more Divine— THE FULFILMENT OF A DIVINE PURPOSE ENTERING INTO THE PLAN OF REDEMPTION. Such was the double significance to the descendants of Abraham, of the conquest of the land of promise, the land in which their religious destinies were to be fulfilled, where the ark of the covenant was to find its resting-place, and to become the centre of the theocracy. So is it in all our lives. Everything that befals us in our private and domestic life has a twofold bearing. It has an earthward aspect ;

and marriage, the birth of children, the acquisition or loss of property, affect primarily our temporal estate. But these same results have also a heavenward side; they tell upon the higher life within, and help to work out our eternal destinies. Their true intention is to develop our higher life, and to establish within us the reign of righteousness, of which the ark of the covenant was the emblem to the Israelites.

II. It is not enough that we believe in this realisation of our higher destiny through the events of life; WE MUST OURSELVES DIRECTLY AID IN ITS FULFILMENT. We must make this our first consideration, and rally round the ark of the covenant in order to fight the battles of the Lord. This is our duty, as members, or, to speak more truly, as soldiers of the Church. The same obligation rests upon us in our individual life. Through all its varied phases it should be our aim to hold high our sacred banner, and to conduct ourselves valiantly under all circumstances as the soldiers of Christ. Let us carry into all our life the thought of immortality. Let us be ever watching, ever fighting, and let the ark of the covenant be that around which centres all our public and private life.—E DE P.

Ver. 5.—*God's wonders.* "Sanctify yourselves, for to-morrow the Lord will do wonders among you. These words admirably express the conditions of all blessing for the people of God. Those conditions are at once Divine and human. The Divine is the essential; the human can only be realised through it.

I. GOD WILL DO WONDERS. This is a true description of all God's works of deliverance, and primarily of His great miracle of pardon. For, of all the marvellous things which He does, the most amazing is that He should have pity upon us, and should come back to us after we have forsaken Him. Grace is the crowning miracle. Never discouraged, it is perpetually triumphing over all obstacles, breaking down all that opposes its designs, bidding the mountain to become a plain, and magnifying itself in our infirmities. There are periods in the history of the race, and in that of individuals, when this miracle of constant recurrence is made yet more emphatic, as though to hasten on the purpose of eternal love. So was it at the time of the conflict between Israel and the Canaanitish nations. So was it at the birth of Christianity. So is it at the time of the beginning of the new life in the individual soul. The free and sovereign grace which *does wonders* is thus the necessary, antecedent Divine condition.

II. THE HUMAN CONDITION IS CLEARLY EXPRESSED IN THESE WORDS OF JOSHUA. "*Sanctify yourselves.*" We repeat, this condition cannot be fulfilled unless Divine grace have renewed our heart, and given us strength to sanctify ourselves. But our duty is none the less positive, imperative, sacred. God does not treat us as passive, inert beings, but as free agents made in His likeness. It behoves us, then, to respond to His grace. Hence the necessity to sanctify ourselves, in order that we may be partakers in the wonders He will work. This is all the more necessary since God will not work these wonders without us, but, by us and with us, calling us to be fellow-workers with Him. Israel must prepare itself for victory by sanctifying itself. To sanctify ourselves is to put away all that is alien to the Divine life; to consecrate ourselves unreservedly to God; to give ourselves to Him; to bring Him our heart that He may fill it. It is to yield ourselves to Him as willing instruments in His hand; so that we are never better workers with Him than when we allow Him to work in us. To let Him work, this is our best way of serving. Do we desire that He should again "do wonders" in our age, in these days of final conflict between the gospel and antichrist? Let us, then, sanctify ourselves, like the children of Israel on the eve of battle with the Canaanites, and so will be fulfilled the twofold condition of all spiritual blessing so well set forth by St. Paul in the words: "Work out your own salvation with fear and trembling, for it is God which worketh in you to will and to do of his good pleasure" (Phil. ii. 12, 13).—E. DE P.

EXPOSITION.

CHAPTER III. 7—17.

THE PASSAGE OF THE JORDAN.—Ver. 7.—
This day will I begin to magnify thee.
"Neque enim ante mysterium baptismi exal-
tatur Jesus, sed exaltatio ejus, et exaltatio
in conspectu populi, inde sumit exordium"
(Orig., Hom. 4 on Joshua. Cf. Matt. iii. 17;
Luke iii. 22).

Ver. 8.—**And thou shalt command the
priests.** We have not here the whole command. That is to be found in ver. 13. **To
the brink.** עַד־קְצֵה. Literally, *to the end,*
i.e., the end or brink of the waters at the
eastern side. There they halted, and as
long as the ark remained there, the waters
of Jordan ceased to flow.

Ver. 10.—**That the living God.** Rather,
perhaps, that *a* living God, *i.e.,* that you
have not with you some idol of wood or
stone, or some deified hero, long since
passed out of your reach, but a living, working, ever-present God, who shows by His
acts that your faith in Him is not vain.
The phrase is a very common one as applied to God in the Old Testament. In the
New, Christ is frequently referred to as the
source of life. **Is among you.** The original
is stronger, *in the midst of you.* **The Canaanites.** The descendants of Canaan, the son
of Ham (Gen. ix. 18). The word which
signifies "low" is by some supposed to signify the same as lowlanders, because the
Canaanites inhabited the less mountainous
portions of Palestine, by the sea (Num.
xiii. 29; Josh. v. 1), and by the side of Jordan (Num. xiii. 29). According to Ewald,
their territory extended along the west
bank of the Jordan as far as the Mediterranean Sea. Canaan has also been held to
signify *bowed down, depressed* (see Gen. ix. 25).
But St. Augustine, in his exposition of the
Epistle to the Romans (sec. 13), says that
the country folk of the neighbourhood of
Carthage, a Phœnician colony, as the name
Punic implies, called themselves *Canani,*
which they would hardly have done were
the name a badge of servitude. Whether we
are to attach much importance to this statement or not, it is certainly a remarkable
coincidence. The story told by Procopius
(' De Bello Vandalico,' ii. 10 ; see also Suidas,
s. v. χάνααν) of two pillars of white stone
near Tangier, with the inscription in Phœnician, "We are those who fled from the face
of the robber Joshua, the son of Nun," is
obviously not to be depended upon. Even
if the inscription existed it was not likely to
be of ancient date. And as Kenrick remarks (' Phœnicia,' p. 67), those who erected

the pillars were not likely (1) to represent
themselves as fugitives, and (2) to speak of
Joshua as the "son of Nun." He further remarks that, while the oldest genuine Phœnician inscription is not more than four
hundred years before Christ, this, if genuine,
must have been erected nearly a thousand
years earlier still ; and he further observes
on the impossibility of its having been deciphered by the scholars of Justinian's day.
The story, no doubt, had its origin in the
Rabbinical tradition, mentioned by Jarchi
in his Commentary, as well as by Kimchi,
that Joshua wrote three letters to the
Canaanites before invading Palestine : the
first inviting them to make peace ; the
second, on their refusal, proclaiming war ;
the third, to those who feared the wrath
of Jehovah, warning them to depart *to
Africa* — advice which, Jarchi adds, was
actually taken by a great many. Concerning these seven nations more will be found
in the Introduction (see also Gen. x. 15—18 ;
xv. 19—21; Exod. iii. 8, 17, &c.). That a
Hebrew signification is found for Phœnician words need not surprise us. The
descendants of Ham, when "dwelling in the
tents of Shem," might have formed for
themselves a similar language. But that the
Aramaic, which was spoken throughout
Syria and Palestine, was closely similar to
the Hebrew, we have overwhelming evidence.
Not only is there clear proof that Abraham
and the Canaanites spoke the same language,
not only are all the ancient names of places
and persons of Hebrew origin, but even the
Carthaginian language is pronounced by
Jerome, a competent judge, to be cognate
to the Hebrew (see Hävernick, Introduction,
sec. 21). **The Hittites.** The Hittites
(Hebrew, Chittim) were out of all proportion
the principal tribe in Palestine at this time,
as we have already seen (ch. i. 4). They
were the descendants of Heth or Chet (Gen.
x. 15), who dwelt in the neighbourhood of
Hebron in the days of Abraham (Gen. xxiii.
19 ; xxv. 9). At that time they do not
appear to have attained the importance
which they afterwards reached (Gen. xii. 6 ;
xiii. 7; xxxiv. 30), though this is perhaps not
altogether a safe inference (cf. Judges i. 4,
5). For the mention of the Canaanites in
Gen. xii. 6 *without* the Perizzite might lead
to a similar inference with regard to the relative importance of these two tribes, whereas
in the other two passages they appear on a
level. Be this as it may, we find the Hittites occupying a prominent position in Canaan at this time, not only in the Book of
Joshua, but on the Egyptian monuments,

" Before the exodus the Kheta had become the terrible rivals of Egypt, and had mingled their genealogy with that of the renowned Pharaohs of the nineteeth dynasty " (Tomkins's 'Studies on the Times of Abraham,' p. 89). It is worthy of remark, however, that on the Egyptian monuments their leaders are spoken of as chieftains (see note on ch. ix. 3, and 'Records of the Past,' ii. 67—78). In later times they had attained to regal government (1 Kings x. 29 ; 2 Kings vii. 6 ; 2 Chron. i. 17). It is, however, possible that the proud monarch of Egypt would not admit the petty kings of the Hittites to an equality with himself (see also note on ch. i. 4). Moses connects the Chittim (Num. xxiv. 24 ; Isa. xxiii. 1 ; Ezek. xxvii. 6), or the inhabitants of Cyprus, with the Hittites. Since these words were written an able article appeared in *The Times* of Jan. 23rd, 1880, on the Hittite Empire. Carchemish, on the Euphrates, and Kadesh, or the Holy City, on the Orontes, appear to have been the chief centres of the Hittite power. They were "powerful enough to threaten Assyria on the one hand and Egypt on the other, and to carry the arts and culture of the Euphrates to the Euxine and Ægean seas." Professor F. W. Newman, finding no mention of their existence in profane histories, came to the usual conclusion of his school, that where the Bible mentioned persons or nations and profane history did not, it was quite clear that such persons or nations never existed. The cases of Sargon and the Hittites may perhaps induce critics of this school to be a little less hasty henceforth in dismissing the statements of Scripture. The site of ancient Carchemish has lately been discovered on the western bank of the Euphrates. **The Hivites,** or rather *Hivvites.* The name of this tribe is not found in the first enumeration of the nations of Canaan (Gen. xv. 19—21), but we find the name in the list of Canaan's descendants in Gen. x. 17 and 1 Chron. i. 15. Shechem, the prince of the city of that name, was a Hivite (Gen. xxxiv. 2), though some copies of the LXX. read Horite for Hivite without authority. The Hivites then (Gen. xxxiv. 10—21) seem, as afterwards in the case of the Gibeonites, to have been a peaceful, commercial race. The character of the Shechemites afterwards seems to have been unwarlike. At least they were neither very spirited nor successful in their military enterprises, as the narrative in Judges ix. shows. The voluptuous beauty of the place, testified to by so many modern travellers, such as Robinson, Vandevelde, &c., falls in well with the character of the inhabitants. A colony of Hivites seem to have dwelt in the north, in the highlands beneath Mount Hermon,

a country to which the name of Mizpeh, or *watch-tower,* seems to have been given, no doubt from its elevation. This must not, however, be confounded with Mizpeh in the land of Benjamin (see ch. xi. 3). In 2 Sam. xxiv. 7 they appear to have been found in the neighbourhood of Tyre, though this is by no means clear. The derivation of the word is uncertain. Ewald would explain it "midlander;" Gesenius explains it by " village," from חָיָה to live, breathe. That חַוָּה signifies a town or village we may learn from Num. xxxii. 41, Deut. iii. 14, Josh. xiii. 30, Judges x. 4, 1 Kings iv. 13. The mention of their city so early as the time of Jacob, the description given of their character in that narrative, and the characteristic astuteness of the Gibeonites as well as their unwarlike conduct, would lead to the conclusion that they dwelt in settled habitations, not nomadic encampments, and that they gained their living chiefly by commerce. We ought not to quit the subject without the remark that all we learn from Scripture concerning the Hivites is remarkably consistent, and bears testimony to the scrupulous accuracy of the writers. **The Perizzites.** The word Perizzite signifies countryman, as distinguished from the dwellers in houses. Thus the word signifies "unwalled," or "open," in Deut. iii. 5, 1 Sam. vi. 18, and in the Keri of Esther ix. 19. Perhaps the reason of the omission of their name in Gen. x. and 1 Chron. i. may justify the supposition that they were of no particular tribe, but were a collection of men from every tribe engaged in agricultural pursuits. Redslob (see art. in 'Dictionary of the Bible') suggests that the Havvoth (ch. xiii. 30) were pastoral, the Perazoth agricultural villages. This is to a certain extent borne out by the fact that Havvoth signifies " living places," and Perazoth " places spread out," as well as by the fact that the trans-Jordanic tribes were specially pastoral in their habits. Passages such as 2 Sam. v. 20, vi. 8, 1 Chron. xiv. 11, Isa. xxviii. 21 are cited as illustrative of this word, but erroneously, for in the Hebrew the letter is Tzade, and not Zain, as here. Ritter regards the word as analogous to Pharisee, from *pharash,* to separate, and regards them as nomad tribes. But the authority of Ewald and Gesenius must outweigh his. **The Girgashites.** They are not mentioned in Scripture, save in Josh. xxiv. 11, Gen. xv. 21, Deut. vii. 1. They were therefore no doubt a small tribe, inhabiting, it has been supposed, the country of Gergesa or Gerasa (as some editions read in Matt. viii. 28) upon the lake of Gennesareth. But this was on the other side of Jordan. If therefore there be any connection between Gergesa or Gerasa and the Girgashites, there must have been a small settlement of them on the eastern side of the lake of Gennesareth. **The Amorites.** These were the most powerful of the Canaanitish peoples (see Amos ii. 9). They not only inhabited the mountains (Num. xiii. 29; Josh. xi. 3), but crossed the Jordan and wrested the country from Arnon to Jabbok out of the hands of the Moabites (Num. xxi. 13, 24, 26), and dwelt there until dispossessed by Moses. In Gen. xiv. 9 we find them west of Jordan, near Engedi, on the shores of the Dead Sea. Thence crossing Jordan they seem to have spread eastward. They are found in the Shephelah, on the borders of Dan (Judges i. 34), and even in the mountain district near Ajalon. But (ver. 35) they seem to have been driven out of Judah, and to have occupied a small portion of the Arabah south of the Dead Sea (cf. Josh. xv. 3). Ewald, as well as Gesenius, regards the word Amorite as signifying highlander, and he quotes Isa. xvii. 9, where Amir signifies the highest part of anything, as of a tree. So the Syriac Amori signifies a hero, and the Arabic Emir signifies a ruler. With this we may compare the term Ameer of Afghanistan, no doubt derived from a similar root. See also Isa. xvii. 6, and the Hithpahel of אמר in Psa. xciv. 4, with the meaning to exalt one's self. Shechem, though a Hivite settlement, is spoken of by Jacob (Gen. xlviii. 22) as an Amorite city, and in ch. x. 6 the sovereigns of Jerusalem and the neighbour cities are spoken of as Amorite monarchs. This would suggest that the words applied to the inhabitants were to a great extent convertible terms, just as we apply the term Celt, Gael, Highlander indiscriminately to the inhabitants of the north of Scotland, Dutchman and Hollander to the inhabitants of Holland, and as Scotus and Erigena were both applied to Irishmen up to the 10th century. **The Jebusites** were in possession of the central highlands around Jerusalem, their stronghold. They retained possession of this until David dislodged them (2 Sam. v. 6—8. See note on ch. x. 1).

Ver. 11.—**The Lord of all the earth.** As He was about to prove Himself to be by the mighty miracles He wrought to establish the Israelites in their land and thus fulfil His promise. The Israelites needed to be reminded of this to support them during the crossing of the Jordan. The translation of the LXX., though rejected by the Masorites, who separate the words "covenant" and "Lord," is admissible here, "the covenant of the Lord of all the earth." If we follow the Masoretic punctuation, we must supply the word "ark" again, and

translate "the ark of the covenant, the ark of the Lord of the whole earth."

Ver. 12.—**Take you twelve men.** Joshua commands the election of twelve men previous to the passage of the Jordan, and in pursuance of the command he had already (ch. iv. 2; cf. note on ver. 2) received from God. The reason for which they were to be chosen was probably not communicated to the Israelites till after the passage had taken place. Masius thinks that it would make the narrative clearer, "si proximum is versiculum sequeretur." But see note on ch. i. 1.

Ver. 13.—**The Lord, the Lord of all the earth.** The original is, *Jehovah, the Lord of all the earth.* **That the waters of Jordan shall be cut off.** The construction here seems to have perplexed the LXX., Vulgate, and English translators. The former have given the sense, but have changed the construction. The second have supposed יִכָּרֵתוּן to mean *fail,* and to refer to the waters *below* the place of crossing. The third have interpolated the word "from." The words "the waters descending from above" are in apposition to, and explanatory of, the words "the waters" above. If for "from" in our version we substitute "namely," we shall express the meaning of the original. The Masorites point thus, dividing the verb from what follows by Zakeph Katon. **A heap** (cf. Psa. xxxiii. 7). The original is picturesque, "and they shall stand, one heap."

Ver. 14.—**Removed from their tents.** The word used for "removed" in this chapter is the same as is used of Abraham's removing. It is appropriate to the nature of the removal, for it signifies originally to pull up stakes or tent-pins, and has reference, therefore, to the removal of a people who dwelt in tents.

Ver. 15.—**Brim.** The water's edge is meant here, as in ver. 8, where the same word is translated *brink* (see note on ver. 17, and on ch. iv. 19). **Jordan overfloweth all his banks.** Some commentators translate here, *filleth all his banks* (ἐπληροῦτο, LXX.). But this rendering is contrary (1) to the Hebrew, and (2) contrary to fact. The literal rendering here is, "filleth or (or *upon*) all its banks." In ch. iv. 18 we read that Jordan goeth *over* all its banks. And that the Jordan is not merely full, but full to overflowing, at the harvest season, is proved by the statements of many travellers. Take, for instance, Canon Tristram ('Land of Israel,' p. 223), who describes his visit to the Jordan as occurring just after it had been overflowing its banks, and the lower level of the valley as filled with "a deep slimy ooze." He adds that, by measurement, the river was found to have been fourteen feet above the level at which he found it, and it was then quite full. Bartlett ('From Egypt to Palestine,' p. 451) remarks, "We were fortunate enough to see it in the state in which it is described in Joshua, 'overflowing all its banks'—that is, the whole line of its banks. The turbid stream rushed along like a mill-race, and though it had fallen from its greatest height, the proper banks of the channel were invisible, and indicated only by lines of oleanders and other shrubs and trees." This was on the 22nd of March. This overflowing is caused by the melting of the snows of Hermon, which then rush down, fill Lake Huleh and its marshes, as well as Gennesareth, and cause the "swelling of Jordan" (Jer. xii. 5; xlix. 19; l. 44), which drives the wild beasts from their retreats on its banks (see also 1 Chron. xii. 15). Some travellers have boldly asserted, in spite of this concurrent testimony, that Jordan does not overflow its banks at the time of harvest. But they have mistaken the wheat for the barley harvest, forgetting that in Palestine the latter precedes the former by six or seven weeks. By the time of wheat harvest Jordan has returned to its normal condition, and all traces of the inundation have passed away (see Thomson, 'Land and the Book,' pp. 618—621). **The time of harvest**, *i.e.*, the barley harvest, which took place about the 10th Nisan, or Abib, when the Israelites crossed. The wheat harvest was about Pentecost, or seven weeks later (Exod. xxxiv. 22). An important argument for the genuineness of the narrative (and much the more important as its chief incident is miraculous) is drawn from this passage by Blunt in his 'Undesigned Coincidences.' He remarks that in Exod. ix. 31, 33 the barley and flax are said to have ripened together. Therefore the time of the barley and flax harvest would be identical. Accordingly we have Rahab, three days before the event here recorded, in possession of the as yet undried stalks of flax which had just been cut. Nothing could be a more satisfactory proof that the narrative we have before us comes from persons who were accurately and minutely informed concerning the circumstances of which they tell us.

Ver. 16.—**Stood and rose up upon a heap.** Literally, "stood—they rose up, one heap." The narrative assumes a poetic form here (cf. Exod. xv. 8, 9; Judges v. 27). **Very far from the city Adam.** The Masorites have corrected the text here. The original text has בְּאָדָם for which the suggested Keri is מֵאָדָם. But the correction is needless. It is better to render, "they rose up, one

heap, very far off, at the city Adam." The city Adam is nowhere else mentioned in Scripture. The LXX. appears to have read מְאֹד מְאֹד instead of מְאֹד מֵאָדָם, for it translates σφόδρα σφοδρῶς. This reading of the LXX. shows that the correction, though it obscures the sense, is of great antiquity, and that the site of Adam was then quite unknown. Knobel would place it either just south of the Jabbok, where the ford *Damieh* now exists, or at *Eduma*, now *Daumeh*, twelve German miles east of Neapolis. The former is generally accepted now, and Conder ('Handbook,' p. 241) identifies it with Admah (see Gen. xiv. 2), in the plain or ciccar of Jordan. **That is beside Zaretan.** Called Zarthan in the original (cf. 1 Kings iv. 12; vii. 46), and Zeredatha, in 2 Chron. iv. 17. Some read Zeredatha for Zererath in Judges vii. 22. Knobel supposes, and not without some probability, that Zereda, Jeroboam's birthplace, is the same as this. It was in the plain of Jordan, not far from Succoth, at the mouth of the Jabbok. The LXX. here reads Καριαθιαρείμ, *i.e.*, either Kiriathaim or Kirjath-jearim, but without authority. Delitzsch and Knobel suppose the spot to be Kurn, or Karn (*i.e.*, *horn*) Sartabeh, near the ford *Damieh*, where the Jordan valley is at its narrowest, and the rocks stretch forward so as almost to meet. They fix on this spot, partly from the suitability of the situation for such an arresting of the waters, partly from its agreement with the situation of Zarthan, as described in the Scriptures. Vandevelde agrees with them. There was an Adami and a Zartanath higher up the river near Bethshean, which some have supposed to be meant (see ch. xix. 33; 1 Kings iv. 12), but these lay entirely out of Joshua's line of march. **The sea of the plain.** Rather the sea of the עֲרָבָה (θάλασσαν Ἄραβα, LXX.), or desert (so Deut. iii. 17; iv. 49; 2 Kings xiv. 25; see also Deut. i. 1). The term is applied by the Hebrews and Arabs to any sterile region, and thence to the sterile depression which borders on the Jordan, extending from the lake of Tiberias southward. The Arabs now apply the term *el ghor* to the part between Tiberias and the Dead Sea, and reserve the term Arabah for the desert valley, or wady, which extends thence to the Red Sea. So Gesen., 'Thesaurus,' *s. v.*; and Robinson, 'Bibl. Res.' The word translated *plain* in Gen. xiii. 10 is כִּכַּר, a word of very different signification (see also 'Shephelah' and 'Emek,' ch. x. 40; xi. 2). **The salt sea.** This sea is called the Dead Sea from the immobility of its waters, as well as from the apparent absence of all life within them. " Some of our party," says Canon Tristram, "employed themselves in searching, but without avail, for life in the Dead Sea." It lies at a level of more than 1,300 feet below the level of the Mediterranean. Its waters are thus described by Dr. Thomson : " The water is perfectly clear and transparent. The taste is bitter and salt, far beyond that of the ocean. It acts upon the tongue and mouth like alum ; smarts in the eye like camphor ; produces a burning, pricking sensation." The specific gravity of its waters is very great, and bathers find a great difficulty in swimming in it from the unusual buoyancy of the water. This is caused by the very large quantity of saline matter held in solution from the salt hills in the neighbourhood. One of them, Jebel Usdum, is described by Canon Tristram as "a solid mass of rock salt," and the water in its vicinity as " syrup of chloride of sodium," that is to say, of common salt. So also Bartlett, ' Egypt and Palestine,' p. 451. The statement that no bird can fly across its waters is a fable. The fullest account of the various attempts — some of them fatal—to explore the Dead Sea are to be found in Ritter's ' Geography of Palestine,' vol. iii. Canon Tristram explored the western side thoroughly, while Mr. Macgregor's canoe voyage, described in his ' Rob Roy on the Jordan,' gives a number of most interesting details. In Ritter's work will also be found some valuable observations on the physical geography of the district, on the geological formation of the basin of the Dead Sea, together with two papers, one by M. Terreil and the other by M. Lartet, on the chemical composition of the Dead Sea waters. **Failed and were cut off.** Literally,

were completed, were cut off, i.e., were completely cut off, so that the supply of water failed, and the channel of the Jordan to the southward, and to the northward as far as Zaretan, became dry ground (see also Psa. cxiv. 3).

Ver. 17.—**Firm.** The LXX. does not translate this. The Vulgate renders *accincti*. The original, literally translated, means *to cause to stand upright*. **In the midst of Jordan.** That is, they stood surrounded by water, but not in mid-stream, which would be expressed by בְּקֶרֶב as in ver. 10, where our version has " among " (see note on ch. iv. 9). So Drusius: "In medio Jordanis ; *i.e.*, intra Jordanem. Sic Tyrus legitur sita *in corde maris ; i.e.*, intra mare nam non procul abest a continente." **Clean over.** The word is the same as that translated " failed " in the last note. It means *completion*—" till the people had entirely finished crossing." Origen thus explains, in his fourth homily on Joshua, the mystical signification of this crossing the Jordan : " Cum catechumenorum aggregatus es numero, et præceptis Ecclesiasticis parere cœpisti digressus es mare rubrum, et in deserti stationibus positus, ad audiendam Dei legem, et intuendum Mosei vultum per gloriam Domini revelatum quotidie vacas. Si vero ad mysticum baptismi veneris fontem, et consistente sacerdotali et Levitico ordine initiatus fueris venerandis illis magnificisque sacramentis quæ norunt illi quos nosse fas est, hanc etiam sacerdotum ministeriis Jordane digresso terram repromissionis intratis, in qua te post Moysen suscipi Jesus, et ipse tibi efficitur novi itineris dux."

HOMILETICS.

Vers. 7—17.—*The passage of Jordan.*

I. THE MINISTRY OF JOSHUA AND JESUS BEGAN AT JORDAN. As with Joshua at his crossing, so with Jesus at His baptism, God marked the moment of their coming to Jordan with a special favour. For as the waters of the Red Sea (1 Cor. x. 2), so the waters of Jordan are the type of Christian baptism. In connection with the wandering in the wilderness, the stream of Jordan is the type of death, which admits us to the promised land. But in connection with the conflicts in Canaan, to which it was the introduction, it is a type of the commencement of the spiritual life. For in it we are dedicated to our Joshua—we begin to follow our Leader. In it He was first "marked out to be the Son of God" (Matt. iii. 17) ; and in it He shows to us the power of God in delivering us from our wanderings in the wilderness of evil, and translating us into the regions of His promises. In baptism we enter into covenant with God, and receive His blessings and gifts, as well as declare our resolution to serve Him. Thus it is the turning-point of our lives whenever we receive it. It places us in a new covenant-relation to God. It introduces us into new obligations, and entitles us to new blessings. It gives us the right to claim the aid of God in our conflict with evil ; in other words, it is the

starting-point of our sanctification. And the work is all of God. He alone parts
the waters for us to cross from the world into His kingdom. Jordan is overflowed.
No passage is possible by human means; that is, no works of our own can avail to
place us where we may hope to carry on a successful war against our own and God's
enemies. "Not of works, lest any man should boast," but "by grace are ye saved
through faith, and even that (*i.e.*, faith) not of yourselves, it is the gift of God." We
attribute no magical power thus to the sacrament of baptism. It derives its sole
power from being the means appointed by Jesus Christ Himself whereby we enter
into covenant with Him.

II. IT WAS NO LONGER THE PILLAR OF CLOUD THAT GUIDED THEM, BUT THE ARK
OF THE COVENANT. That is, the mystery of the law was unveiled in the gospel.
Like the veil on the face of Moses (2 Cor. iii.), so this figure teaches us that what
was dark under the Mosaic dispensation should be made clear by Jesus Christ.
"For the law made nothing perfect, but the bringing in of a better hope did" (cf.
also Heb. xii. 18—24). The law guided through the wilderness; the gospel, into
the promised land. The law, which was enshrouded in darkness, led man only in
uncertain wanderings; the gospel led them to favour and victory. God was with
them, no longer by cloudy tokens in the skies, but by the visible symbols of His
presence. And so the God who leads us now is no longer a God who hides Himself,
but God manifest in the flesh; God clothed in a visible form, that thus we might
see Him who is invisible. The humanity of Jesus is at once the revelation of
God, and the perfection of man. Following Him, though at a respectful distance, beholding Him, though not too nigh, we enter into the enjoyment of the
promise.

III. JORDAN WAS CROSSED AT THE TIME OF ITS OVERFLOWING. Thus God manifests His own glory and man's insufficiency. The miracle was the greater in that
it was performed at such a time. So God always deals with His people. The time
of trouble is the time when He manifests His power. It is then that He makes our
way most "plain before our face." Both Churches and individuals are apt in their
prosperity to say, "I shall never be removed." But in adversity they betake themselves in all humility to God, and He makes them a way through the deep waters.
"The swellings of Jordan" abate at His presence; "the overflowings of ungodliness" give ground at His word. When He speaks, sorrow and distress flee away
"far off," and they whose "treadings had well-nigh slipt," who were "grieved at
the wicked," or at the seeming tokens of God's wrath, find that He has made
"straight paths for their feet" where all had seemed disappointment and despair.

IV. HELP AND STRENGTH ARE TO BE FOUND IN THE ORDINANCES OF RELIGION.
When the priests' feet touched the brink of the waters they fled away. And is it
not a spiritual fact that the consolations and helps of religion are to be found at the
hands of the ministers of religion? How often did the exhortations of a Moses,
a Joshua, or Samuel revive the drooping spirits of God's people? How often were
the first converts of the gospel "provoked unto love and good works" by the mouth
of a St. Peter or St. Paul! How many date their first serious impressions of Divine
things from an earnest sermon, or a few words of loving counsel spoken by a minister
of Christ! How many have felt kindled to love and devotion by the prayers
reverently offered up in the sanctuary, where the sacred fire spreads from soul to
soul till it has enkindled the warmth of zeal in all present! How often has the
worshipper, either in the congregation or on the sick bed, been moved to tears and
stirred to the depths of his soul by the "blest memorials of a dying Lord," consecrated and administered according to His word! It is one of the privileges of the
Christian ministry of the New Covenant, when faithfully carried on, as of the priests
at the command of the Jesus of the Old Covenant, that as their feet touch the
swelling waters of neglect, thoughtlessness, and indevoutness, they subside, they
flee far off, at least when, at the root of the individual life, there lies the spark—
even though almost quenched—of faith. Not that the ministers are to take credit
to themselves for this. They are but the organs of the Spirit of Christ. As Matthew
Henry remarks, "God could have divided the river without the priests, but they
could not do without Him." But He is pleased to use human means, and He

blesses them. Though the "treasure is in earthen vessels," yet the "excellency of the power is of God."

V. THE PRIESTS STOOD FIRM. They were "caused to stand upright," as the Hebrew says; that is, there was no faltering or wavering. Had they drawn back after entering Jordan, had they shown signs of uncertainty, the waters would have returned, or the people had never dared to cross. So great is the responsibility that rests on God's ministers. The people look to them for guidance—for encouragement. If they "faint by the way," if they falter in their work of contending for the faith, of promoting the spread of Christ's Gospel, if their trumpet gives an uncertain sound, or if they retreat from their appointed task, the conflict with evil stands still; the pathway for God's Church to proceed to further conquests is not opened. How many great works for the spread of Christ's Gospel, for the proclamation of His truth, for the victory of His cause among men, have failed because the "priests" have not "stood firm" in the waters of Jordan; because timidity, half-heartedness, divided counsels, profitless controversies have obscured the witness for God's truth! If "the kingdoms of this world" have not "become the kingdoms of our God and of His Christ," if the number of Christ's elect is not yet filled up, if the pathway to the final fulfilment of God's promises be not yet open, how much of it is because His ministers have not yet learned to "stand firm in the midst of Jordan"?

HOMILIES BY VARIOUS AUTHORS.

Ver. 11.—*The passage of the Jordan.* The lessons of importance are not exhausted in those already suggested in this passage of the Jordan. A deed so great, so solemn, so vast in its results, has many sides, and many subordinate points of interest. I gather up in this second homily a few of those points of interest and instruction. And first observe—

I. THE SIGN OF GOD'S PRESENCE WITH ISRAEL IS TEMPORARY, BUT THE PRESENCE ITSELF IS PERMANENT. This lesson arises at once from the fact that the pillar of cloud which hitherto had led them does not precede them now. To its guidance hitherto they had marched, and under its shadow rested. And the sign of God's presence had been a sweet assurance and a constant augury of success. Now it disappears altogether from the history of Israel. They will cross Jordan under the guidance of the ark, and of that alone. God's presence remains with them, but the sign of it is withdrawn. There were doubtless many who regarded such a loss as an omen of sinister significance; and many who, mixing devotion and superstition, would deplore that when the great crisis of the enterprise was come, their usual assurance of God's presence failed them. But there were some that had looked not to but through the sign, and built their hopes on the living God. And they, Joshua leading them, trusting in the love and faithfulness which they felt must be His character, were ready to venture without their sign. And venturing, they found God there, though the cloud of His presence had been withdrawn, and they got a notable lesson in walking by faith rather than by sight. We need few lessons more than this: That God's presence or absence is not to be concluded from the presence or absence of the sign of it. We are all Jewish enough to "require a sign." We want some assurance of acceptance over and beyond what gospel words convey. We want some "leading of Providence" in addition to the sense of duty before we feel comfortable in starting on any course. Raptures, mystic whisperings of God's consolation, special experiences not granted to others—these are apt in the regard of all of us to assume too much importance. We are apt to make the same mistake concerning these which some in Israel doubtless made concerning the pillar of cloud and fire; namely, to imagine them a special crown, a testimony to our unusual sanctity, instead of a gracious condescension to our weaknesses and to the fears which mark our setting out on a pilgrimage. Just escaping from slavery, Israel needed signs; now, maturer in experience and stronger in faith, the signs are no longer needed. Probably in all cases it will be found that signs belong to the earlier stages of the experience either of the community or the individual.

When experience and faith are strong, they are withdrawn. Put not a dark construction on any mere want of signs, for while the sign of the presence is temporary, the presence itself is permanent with all God's people. Growing out of this a second lesson suggests itself, viz.:

II. THEY ARE WELL LED WHO ARE ARK LED. Israel no longer had the pillar of cloud and fire, but they had the ark of God, and, as the event proved, the ark led them just as wisely as the pillar; and in following it they found just the same help of miraculous power. What was this ark of the covenant? A wonderful piece of sacred symbolism. Over it—in fact, forming the lid of it—was what was named *the mercy-seat*, God's earthly throne. Within it were the ten commandments, written on two tables of stone. This combination of symbols of law and mercy belonged to no religion but that of Israel. The gods of other nations required but little duty, and were hardly expected to show mercy. But the symbolism of the ark and the whole Mosaic economy projected these thoughts before the minds of Israel: The true God is a God of mercy. But at the same time He insists on duty. The ark proclaimed Him the God of mercy and of law; of gracious promise, of ennobling precept; delivering men by the grace He gave, dignifying them by the duty He exacted. This was the God of Israel. And now, in lieu of signs, the symbol of mercy and of duty was to lead the way. *Not eagles*, symbols of victorious power, but *tables of stone* led them, and "marshalled them the way that they were going." And their successful following of this lead suggests that when any one marches to the lead of the ten commandments, or of the promises of God, he is as well led and as grandly succoured as when some cloudy pillar moves before him. There is importance in this. Often our signs are withdrawn; as with the community of Israel so with us, it is probably the case that *signs* grow fewer and that special experiences grow more rare as character matures. Then comes a time, more or less clearly definite, when, instead of mysterious movings felt to be Divine, the guidance of the Lord is given, through *a testimony of mercy and of duty*. Before you goes the symbol of heavenly love and of earthly duty. And you have to march, coldly as it may seem, to the lead of tables of stone and verbal assurances only of God's care. Murmur not at this; a hope and a duty are guides sublime. The ark is just as good as the cloud. If you had the choice of an enlightened conscience or a special angel to be your guide, you would do wisely to choose the conscience in preference to the angel. You may mistake the reading of your signs—you rarely will your duty. Next to His redeeming grace, the richest mercy He gives us is a "word behind us," or within us, "saying, this is the way, walk ye in it." And the grandest spirits of mankind—in their pilgrimage from victory to victory—have marched under the lead of nothing grander than some ark, something that whispered hope and demanded duty. Thus led, did Israel lose? Nay, as before the cloudy pillar the sea divided, so before the sacred ark did Jordan. If you have something like what the ark embodied—a promise and a precept—ask no more; where the tables of the covenant lead you, there follow. Few get more, and none get anything better, than these. God guides through enlightenment of conscience, or Bible precept, or the devout example which you instinctively perceive is a pattern to be followed. Seek not any sign; God's presence will ever be with all those that keep His precepts. If the ark of God, as replacing the pillar of cloud, has such suggestions, observe thirdly—

III. GOD'S HYDRAULICS ARE NEVER FAULTY. In the West of England just now there is considerable discussion about "dockising" the river Avon, *i.e.*, so throwing a dam across the mouth that all the river up to Bristol would be converted into one huge dock. And in the discussion the strength of such a dam, its cost, its leakage, the right place for it, how to provide for the outlet of all water above a certain level, are canvassed by all. Here we have the "dockising" for a day or two of the river Jordan, a very much larger river than the Avon, one whose very name suggests the swiftness of its current. And the dam that effects this great collection of the waters is "the ark of God," set down in the midst of the Jordan bed, with the priests grouped on either side. How would the philosophers of that day criticise that dam, and express with assumed anxiety their fears that the law of gravitation and the law that governs the flow of liquids would prove too much for the legs of the priests, and even for the weight of the tables of stone. But whatever fear might be entertained by the people before the ark entered Jordan, and whatever misgivings by the priests when they were standing in its pebbly bed, there was a power which operated from that ark which dammed the river as no engineer could have done it. So that instead of reading of struggling with the water, of multitudes carried down the stream, of hairbreadth escapes, of multitudes left behind, all got safely across. And here, I think, we have a specimen of what is everywhere to be seen; *the efficiency of spiritual barriers against all assailing forces.* We see them on all hands; we dread lest they be overborne by some strong current bearing down against them. But lo! they stand against all force that threatens them. God's truth is such a barrier. With error like a huge river rushing down upon it, it seems as slender and insufficient as was the barrier of the ark. Science is so arrogant and captious, chronology so sure, metaphysics so disputatious, error so agreeable to the natural man, that it seems as if there could be no standing. But the Jordan of all the philosophies and all the heresies threaten in vain, and God's ark of truth is sufficient to withstand them. God's grace in the heart is such a dam; nothing seemingly more feeble, nothing really more strong, against the swelling tides of inward corruption and outward temptation that assail the character. Sometimes prayer shields a distant boy, an erring friend, and protects them with a guard as really omnipotent as it appears feeble. Judge not by the outward appearance. The clock is not about to go backward, nor error usurp the place of truth. Don't tremble for the ark of God, as did Eli. Whatever God wants guarded, it is omnipotent to guard. So that, amongst other lessons, this sweet one comes to us that we are guarded better than we think. And what seems God's weakness is mightier than the strongest strength which can come against us.—G.

Vers. 14—17.—*The division of the waters.* The passage of Jordan, like that of the Red Sea, marks a momentous crisis in the career of the chosen people. The events are similar in their general character as Divine interpositions, but there are notable points of difference. In the first case there was haste, confusion, and alarm; the people fled precipitately, the noise of the Egyptian host behind them, the mountains shutting them in, the sea an object of terror before them; they cried unto the Lord, in their distress. Even Moses seems to have had his misgivings. "Wherefore criest thou unto me?" &c. (Exod. xiv. 15). But here, apparently, all is tranquillity and order. The territory on which they stand has been subdued and is their possession, and they move deliberately, under the direction of Joshua, down to the brink of the river, waiting in calm expectancy for the salvation of the Lord. In the former case, the region beyond the sea was a dread mystery to them. It was a waste, howling wilderness, towards which they could not look without sad forebodings. But here the hills, and forests, and fertile plains of the land of promise are actually in sight, and though they know that they are not destined to enter at once into peaceable possession of it, the vision gives such stimulus to their faith that it is as if the inheritance were already theirs. Let us look at this event—(1) as a revelation of God; (2) as a chapter in the moral education of the people.

I. As a REVELATION OF GOD. The miraculous, supernatural character of the event we take to be beyond all reasonable doubt. It is impossible to explain it on mere natural grounds. The spies, like David's "mighty men" at a later period (1 Chron. xii. 15), probably swam the flood. But, considering the condition of the river at the time (ver. 15), it is incredible that so vast a host, with women and children, should have passed over except by a miraculous division of the waters. In the passage of the Red Sea an intermediate agent was employed to bring about the result. "The Lord caused the sea to go back by a strong east wind" (Exod. xiv. 21). But there is no indication of anything of this kind here. It is a direct exercise of the wonder-working hand of God. In the one case a natural agent is used supernaturally; in the other nothing intervenes between the supernatural cause and the visible effect. Note—

1. God's control over nature. All miracles in the physical realm are an assertion of the absolute sovereignty of God over the things He has made and the laws
He has ordained. The possibility of miracles springs naturally from the fact of the
existence of a "living God," who is "Lord of all the earth." Whether any
particular miracle is credible must depend on the force of evidence, and in this
evidence the moral end to be answered plays an important part. But to deny its
possibility is to deny the Divine sovereignty. It is absurd to suppose that the
order of nature which God Himself has established limits His own freedom. The
power that created it must ever be Lord over it. Consider how this truth of the
supremacy of the living God is the basis of our faith in a controlling Providence
and in the efficacy of prayer. How the Divine will may work freely *within the
bounds of natural order* we know not. But once grasp the principle that the
forces and laws of nature are not fetters imposed on the freedom of Divine power,
but instruments by which that power may accomplish the purposes of love as it
pleases, and you have no longer any difficulty in believing in a fatherly Providence
in which you can trust and to which you can appeal in time of need.

2. God's control over the nations. This miracle is to the people a prophecy and
pledge of victory in their conflict with the Canaanites. "Hereby ye shall know," &c.
(ver. 10). The power that rolled back the waters of the rushing river could roll
back the force of the barbarous tribes beyond it. The opening for the chosen
people of a pathway across the stream would be a doubtful benefit unless they
could take it as the pledge of the presence of that power with them afterwards.
Moreover, shall not He who planted the nations be able to uproot them? Shall
not He who "determined for them the times before appointed and the bounds of
their habitation," &c., be able to change their boundaries as He pleases, and to
destroy them when they fail to fulfil the ends for which He gave them their local
habitation? This is a very different thing from saying that the strong have license
to oppress and exterminate the weak. It may be perfectly true that there is a
process ever going on among the peoples of the earth, by virtue of which those that
have risen higher in the scale of humanity thrust out the lower, a "survival of the
fittest." But this in no way overrides the law that the oppressor and the spoiler
must, sooner or later, suffer a righteous retribution. "Woe to thee that spoilest,"
&c. (Isa. xxxiii. 1). God may use one nation as the scourge of another, and the
avenger of His own abused authority. But let none think to move in this path
without a very distinct and definite Divine call. "Vengeance is mine," &c. (Rom.
xii. 19). This violent seizure of the land of Canaan by the Israelites can be
justified only on the ground of a direct Divine commission, and of that commission
the miraculous passage of Jordan was the seal and proof.

II. A CHAPTER IN THE MORAL EDUCATION OF THE PEOPLE. AN EDUCATION IN
FAITH, AND IN THE COURAGE THAT SPRINGS FROM FAITH. Their whole career in
the wilderness had been marked by signal Divine interpositions. "The Lord alone
did lead them, and there was no strange God with them" (Deut. xxxii. 12). They
specially needed to have this impressed on them now, entering as they were on a new
stage in their national history, new situations, new responsibilities; coming as an
organised commonwealth into contact with the corruptions of Phœnician idolatry.
This miracle was intended also to give them confidence in their leader: "This day
will I begin to magnify thee," &c. (ver. 7). And the calm strength of Joshua's faith
was fitted to inspire them with the same spirit.

Lessons suggested: (1) Life to most of us is a succession of trials of faith and
fortitude. "Ye have not passed this way before." We are continually entering on
new ground, new phases of experience, unknown difficulties and dangers. Our
only security is the consciousness of the Divine presence, the faith that lays hold on
the strength of God. (2) The inspiring effect of a noble example. "It does a wrestlin/
man good to be surrounded by tried wrestlers." He is most honoured of God wh
has most power to awaken in his fellows faith in God. (3) The conditions of victo
in the last emergency of life. Though there may be nothing in Scripture teach
to warrant it, it is not without reason that, in hymns and allegories, the Jorda
regarded as a symbol of death. The dark river rolls between us and the lan

promise ; how shall we cross it in safety? "Yea, though I walk through the valley," &c. (Psa. xxiii. 4). Let us hear the voice of the Captain of our salvation, and we shall not be afraid. The ark of the covenant will open for us a sure pathway through the deep.—W.

EXPOSITION.

CHAPTER IV. 1—24.

THE MEMORIAL.—Ver. 2.—**Twelve stones.** The commemoration of events by the setting up of huge stones was by no means peculiar to the Jews, though it was often used by them, as, for instance, Gen. xxviii. 18., xxxv. 14, 1 Sam. vii. 12. Almost every nation has adopted it. The Egyptian obelisks, the stones at Hamath, supposed to be of Hittite origin, the dolmens and other megalithic monuments of the Celts, the Logan or rocking-stones, are cases in point. The Scandinavians filled their country with them. Our own Stonehenge and the Avebury stones are supposed by some to be, not temples nor burial-places, but memorials of some battle. The command here given to Joshua was regarding what was to be done by the twelve men, who (v. 4; cf. ch. iii. 12) were already chosen. The form of the command is merely another instance of the common Hebrew practice of repetition.

Ver. 3.—**Stood firm.** Much discussion has taken place about the proper rendering of the word הֵכִין which the LXX. translates ἑτοίμους, and the Vulgate *durissimos*. It seems best to take it, as our version does, as the infinitive absolute, and to translate as in ch. iii. 17. But the punctuation of the Masorites separates it from מֻצָּב. They would apparently render "to set up."

Ver. 4.—**Prepared.** Literally, *appointed*.

Ver. 6.—**That this may be a sign unto you.** There was for many years a *visible memorial* of the miracle. **When your children ask their fathers in time to come** (cf. Exod. xii. 26; xiii. 14; Deut. vi. 20). The passover, the law itself, as well as certain outward and visible memorials, were to be the guarantees to future ages of the truth of the history related in the Books of Moses and Joshua. The monument has disappeared, but the observance of the passover and the whole law by the Jews now, more than 3,000 years after the events related in these books, is a perpetual standing witness of the truth of the record. In like manner the Christian passover, the sacrament of the Lord's Supper, is appealed to by Christians of every denomination as a proof of the substantial truth of the narrative of the Gospels.

Ver. 9.—**And Joshua set up twelve stones in the midst of Jordan.** A great deal of ingenuity has been wasted over this passage. Kennicott would read " *from* the midst," instead of " *in* the midst;" but this purely conjectural emendation is contrary to the fact that these stones were to be set up where the priests bearing the ark stood, while the others were to be set up where the Israelites rested for the night. Again: it has been asked why stones should be placed as a memorial in the Jordan itself, where no man could see them. The answer is a simple one. They were not placed in the Jordan, but at some distance from its banks. They were placed where the priests stood, *i.e.*, at the *brink* of the Jordan (" juxta ripam," Jarchi), which at that time had overflowed its banks (ch. iii. 15). It is no reply to this to observe with the translator of Keil that the stones would by this interpretation be left high and dry for the greater part of the year, for this would be the very reason why that precise spot was fixed upon for a memorial. Nor does the word בְּתוֹךְ in the midst, constitute any valid objection to this interpretation, for the same word is used in ch. iii. 17, although two verses previously we are told that the priests stood at the brink of the swollen river with the soles of their feet just dipped in the water (see note there). Thus while the Vulgate translates "in medio Jordanis alveo," the LXX. renders more accurately by ἐν αὐτῷ τῷ Ἰορδάνῃ. Thus Rosenmüller's objection to the two monuments, namely, that such monuments would never be placed in a rapidly flowing stream like the Jordan, vanishes; while, as Poole suggests, these stones might be heavier, and form even a more enduring memorial than that of the first resting-place of the Israelites, constructed as it were of stones which were not beyond the power of one man to carry. After all, it may be asked whether it is more probable that this passage is an insertion from another, and an irreconcilable account (Meyer, Knobel), or that it is a later gloss (Rosenmüller, Maurer, &c.), or that two monuments of so mighty and memorable a miracle should have been set up, one at the place where the priests stood, and the other where the Israelites rested after this wonderful interposition of God on their behalf. So Hengstenberg 'Geschichte des Reiches Gottes,' p. 203. The Syriac version only supports Rosenmüller's view. The LXX. and Vulgate render " twelve other stones." The supposition that the sacred historian gives all the commands of God to Joshua, and that therefore such parts of the narrative as are not contained in these commands are to be rejected, is refuted by a comparison, for instance, of ch. iii. 7, 8, with vers. 13, 17.

Ver. 10.—**For.** Rather, *and*. This verse does not give a reason for the last. **The priests which bare the ark stood.** This must have been a majestic sight. While the people " hasted " to cross, either that they might effect the passage during the day, or, more probably, because they crossed in fear and trembling, partly in spite of, and partly because of, the miraculous interposition on their behalf, the priests bearing the ark of God, the visible symbol of His presence, stood solemnly still at the brink of the river, nor did they stir until every one of that mighty host had passed over. Then, when all had safely crossed, the ark of God was borne across the bed of the river, and as soon as the soles of the priests touched the highest point that the waters had reached on the other side, they returned to their place, and all was as it had been before. Well might the Israelites erect a double memorial of a scene so wonderful as this! **All that Moses commanded Joshua** (Deut. xxxi. 23). **And the people hasted and passed over.** " Unde et ego arbitror, quia nobis quoque venientibus ad baptismum salutarem, et suscipientibus sacramenta Verbi Dei, non otiose, nec segnitur res gerenda est, sed festinandum est, et perurgendum " (Orig., Hom. v.).

Ver. 12.—**Armed** (see ch. i. 14). **Before the children of Israel.** Not necessarily " in front of," but " in the sight of," as in Num. viii. 22. The Israelites were witnesses of the fulfilment of the pledge given them by their brethren. But the usual place of these tribes was not with the vanguard. See last verse, where the same words are translated " in the presence of."

Ver. 13.—**Prepared for war.** εὔζωνοι, LXX. Literally, *disencumbered*, like the Latin *expeditus*. Unlike Num. xxxi. 5, the Hebrew has the article here. The meaning therefore may be " equipped men of the host," *i.e.*, the light - armed and active among them. If we translate thus, it is clear that all their armed men did not go over Jordan. The *impedimenta* were left behind, under a strong guard (see notes on ch. i. 14). **The plains of Jericho.** Here the LXX. and Theodotion have τὴν Ἰεριχὼ πόλιν, Symmachus renders by ἀοίκητον, the Vulgate by *campestria*. The original is עֲרָבוֹת literally, the *deserts* or *uncultivated lands* (see note on ch. iii. 16). They formed

a "low-lying plain about four hours' journey in breadth," at that time largely covered with palm trees and thorny acacias, but apparently not cultivated. Since that time, the palms having disappeared, the plain has become " a very picture of fertility," " covered with luxuriant vegetation " (Bartlett, ' From Egypt to Palestine,' p. 453. See also note on ch. iii. 16). The valley narrows to a gorge at Jericho, through which the Kelt, according to Robinson the ancient Cherith, flows, the source of all the verdure which once bloomed around the city. The gorge of the Kelt Canon Tristram describes as " tremendous," but he believes the Cherith to have been eastward of Jordan, following Mr. Grove, who is here disposed to accept the tradition of Eusebius and Jerome.

Ver. 14.—**On that day the Lord magnified Joshua.** This was not, as Calvin remarks, the chief aim of the miracle. But it was, nevertheless, one important result of it. Joshua was the appointed leader of the Israelites, and he was under God's special protection and guidance. But however much God may overrule our human nature to His own purposes, He never abrogates the laws of its working. Confidence in a leader, from a human point of view, is one of the most essential requisites for success in war. Therefore in the crossing of the Jordan we find Joshua directing all the operations, though the direction of affairs might have been put into other hands, that of Eleazar the high priest, for instance. But this was the public attestation of the secret intimation God had given Joshua (ch. i. 5) : " As I was with Moses, so will I be with thee : I will not fail thee nor forsake thee." From this point onward we see no signs of hesitation on the part of the Israelites ; nothing but the most unwavering confidence in the Divine mission, as well as in the extraordinary natural gifts, of their leader.

Ver. 15.—**And the Lord spake unto Joshua, saying.** Meyer and others, according to the method of a certain school, regard this as an extract from another document, which is equivalent to saying that the Book of Joshua is a compilation of the most unintelligent kind, a conclusion which is refuted by every line of the Book. A vivid and picturesque narrative, such as we have before us, could hardly have been brought together by the liberal use of scissors and paste, with utter disregard of the coherence of the extracts. It is not denied that the writer of the Book of Joshua may have compiled his history from contemporary documents (see Introduction). All that is affirmed is that in so doing he used his materials with ordinary common sense. As has been before remarked, a marked feature of early Hebrew composition was repetition; repetition with additional details to add to the completeness of the narrative, but designed principally to emphasise the principal facts. Thus we are now told that it was at the command of Joshua, on God's express intimation, that the priests left their post. And to mark more clearly the historian's sense of the importance of the miracle, it is added that, as soon as the priests' feet had left the channel in which the waters had flowed up to the moment that they entered the waters of Jordan on the other side, the waters which had been cut off returned, and flowed exactly where they had done before. This additional fact, supplementing as it does the briefer detail in ch. iii. 17 and ch. iv. 11, must be therefore regarded as a record of the solemn conviction of the historian that in the events he is narrating he recognised a special interposition of the hand of God (see vers. 23, 24), in which in like manner we find a repetition in fuller detail of the command concerning the stones, designed to mark more clearly the sense the historian wishes his readers to have of the direct interference of God in what he has recorded.

Ver. 16.—**The testimony.** The word עֵדוּת though derived from the same root as עֵד witness, would seem rather to have the sense of *precept*, from the idea of repetition contained in the root. Compare the well-known Hebrew particle עוֹד again. It must refer to the two tables of the law which (Heb. x. 4) were placed in the ark (see Deut. x. 5, and comp. Exod. xxv. 16, 21, 40, Num. xvii. 10, where this is said to be the testimony. Other things were placed in the ark, such as the manna, Aaron's rod, and these, no doubt, were for a witness to the facts of the Mosaic record. The LXX., however, consistently render this word by μαρτύρια, μαρτύριον. The Vulgate here has *arcam fœderis*.

Ver. 18.—**When the priests . . . were come up.** There is a difference of reading here. The Masorites read as our version. The Hebrew text implies that the waters began to flow from the very moment that the priests' feet left the channel of the Jordan. **Were lifted up.** The original is more vivid, and marks the authentic sources from which this history is derived. *Were plucked up*, *i.e.*, out of the soft adhesive mud in the channel of the river. The construction of the original is a *constructio prægnans*. They dragged their feet out of the mud, and planted them on dry ground.

Ver. 19.—**On the tenth day of the first month.** This statement, compared with

ch. v. 10, will bear close analysis, and refutes the clumsy compiler theory. There was just time between the tenth and fourteenth day of the month for the events described in the meantime. And the scrupulous obedience to the law, the provisions of which, we are expressly told, had been of necessity neglected hitherto, is a fact closely in keeping with the character of Joshua, and the whole spirit of the narrative. **Gilgal.** *The Gilgal*, according to the Masorites, no doubt from its being a circular encampment. Not as yet, however, called by this name (see ch. v. 9). It was "about five miles" (50 stadia, according to Josephus), "from the river banks" (Stanley, 'Sinai and Palestine,' p. 307). We gather from ch. v. 3 that it was a rising ground, but it is impossible to identify the spot, since there never existed any town or village there. A spot is shown by the inhabitants about two miles from Jericho, which is held by them in great reverence, but this is further from Jericho than Josephus imagines it to be, for he places it about a mile and a quarter from Jericho. Tristram ('Land of Israel,' p. 216) identifies Riha (see note on ch. ii. 1) with Gilgal, but Bartlett (p. 452) places it "a mile east of Riha," "some three miles or more from the fords." It is hardly probable, however, that the Israelites, in their then unprepared condition (see next chapter, and cf. Gen. xxxiv. 25), encamped so near the city, even though they were conscious of Divine protection, as Josephus would have us suppose. It has been denied by some that the Gilgal mentioned in ch. ix. 6, x. 6 is the same as this one (see notes there, as well as the Masoretic translation above). The reverence for sacred places, such as Gilgal, degenerated in the course of time, according to a well-known law of humanity, into superstition—a superstition severely rebuked by the prophets (Hosea iv. 15; ix. 15; Amos iv. 4; v. 5). We may compare the idolatrous worship of the brazen serpent (2 Kings xviii. 4). It is sometimes contended by Roman Catholic commentators that no approval of the conduct of Hezekiah is here expressed; but a comparison of this passage with those above cited will show in which direction the minds of inspired men tended. Other places seem to have been similarly regarded with superstitious reverence. Not only do we find Bethel mentioned among such places as we might well expect from Jeroboam's idolatrous worship there, but Beersheba also seems to have become a seat of this misdirected devotion (see Amos v. 5; viii. 14)

Ver. 21.—**When.** Heb. אֲשֶׁר. The relative pronoun here is sometimes equivalent to "when," as in Deut. xi. 6; 1 Kings viii. 9. Gesenius would translate "if that," and Keil would render by *quod*.

Ver. 23.—**For.** The original here again is אֲשֶׁר, with the meaning *because*.

Ver. 24.—**The hand of the Lord, that it is mighty.** "Thus the river, though dumb, was the best of heralds, proclaiming with a loud voice that heaven and earth are subject to the Lord God of Israel" (Calvin). **That ye might fear.** The construction here is unusual. Instead of the imperfect or infinitive with לְמַעַן we have the perfect. Therefore Ewald, Maurer, and Knobel (who says that the second member of the sentence ought to correspond with the first) have altered the pointing in order to bring this passage into conformity with the supposed necessities of grammar. In so doing they have robbed it of its picturesqueness and its meaning. For the object is clearly to show the lasting nature of the fear, "that ye might recognise now the hand of the Lord, that ye might have a thorough and lasting fear of his name." We may here remark on the necessarily miraculous character of the whole narrative of the crossing the Jordan. It admits of no explaining away. The account must either be accepted or rejected *en bloc*. First we have the specific declaration of Rahab in chap. ii. 10, that Jehovah dried up the Red Sea, and that this proof of the peculiar protection of Israel by the Most High had struck terror into the hearts of the inhabitants of Canaan. Next we have the fact that Jordan had overflowed its banks. The dangerous nature of the crossing, even at ordinary times, has been mentioned already. Lives are frequently lost in the attempt, as recent travellers with one voice declare. At the time when the waters were out such a crossing was practically impossible to a host like the host of Israel. Nor can there be any mistake about its being the period of the overflowing of Jordan, for the time of the crossing is mentioned. It was the time of harvest—that is, of the barley harvest. This is confirmed by the fact that the recently cut flax was now lying on the roof of Rahab's house, and by the fact that the barley and flax ripened together, a coincidence which we have already mentioned in the note on chap. ii. 6. The time is yet further defined. It was the "tenth day of the first month." We learn, moreover, from Levit. xxiii. 9—15 and Deut. xvi. 6 that this was the time when the first-fruits were offered, from which seven weeks were reckoned to the beginning of wheat harvest (Exod. xxxiv. 2). Moreover, the passover was kept immediately afterwards (chap. v. 10), on "the fourteenth day of the

first month." Thus the date of the crossing, which is accurately fixed by a variety of circumstances, is clearly proved to correspond with the time of Jordan's overflow. We next come to the measures taken to secure the crossing. There is likewise no mistake here. Not one single intimation is given of an endeavour to break in any way the force of the current, or to preserve the Israelites, either men, women, or children, from the imminent risk they ran of death by drowning. Not only are no other expedients resorted to, but no animals seem to have been prepared to transport them over. Nor, again, were any means used to elude the vigilance of the inhabitants of Canaan. Readers of Xenophon's 'Anabasis' will not fail to notice how often the passage of the rivers was a matter of the utmost difficulty to that expedition, and how fiercely attempts at crossing were disputed by the half-savage tribes of Asia Minor. How are we to account for the fact that no opposition was offered to Joshua's passage by the highly-civilised nations of Palestine? According to the narrative before us it was effected in the most leisurely and peaceful manner. What other explanation is possible than that offered in the text, that when the feet of the priests bearing the ark touched the waters, those waters were cut off by supernatural power, and a way was miraculously made for the people of God through the midst of Jordan? The crossing was remarkable enough, we are told, to have been commemorated by a double memorial (vers. 8, 9). If it had taken place through an unusually easy ford there would have been nothing remarkable about it. Therefore it is clear that the whole narrative of the crossing is either absolute fable or strictly and historically accurate. Let us conclude by summing up the several reasons which make the former alternative inadmissible. The first is the precision with which the date is fixed, and the fact that the correctness of this date is confirmed, as we have seen, by a variety of corroborative evidence. The next is the simplicity and artlessness of the narrative, and its appeal to still-existing monuments as confirmatory of the facts recorded. The third is that no account of a battle at Jordan is even hinted at by the Hebrew or any other historian, a battle which must infallibly have taken place had the Israelites attempted to enter Palestine in any ordinary manner; for the supposition that the waters of the ford at Jericho were unusually low at this time is quite inadmissible for the reasons given above; nor can it be supposed that the Israelites crossed the river by any other ford without rejecting the whole history of the conquest. The last reason is the touch of detail given in the word נִתְּקוּ which seems to mark the transition from the soft adhesive mud of the river to the firmness of the dry land beyond (for the word translated "dry land" in chap. iii. 17 only means that it was land and not water. Gesenius). Our witness, in fact, can be subjected to the severest cross-examination without shaking his testimony. And we are thus compelled to choose between accepting the literal correctness of the narrative as it stands, or crediting the author with a skill in constructing a work of fiction which itself scarcely falls short of the miraculous.

HOMILETICS.

Vers. 1—24.—*The memorial.* From this chapter we learn several lessons.

I. THE DUTY OF COMMEMORATING, BY A PIOUS MEMORIAL, THE GOOD THINGS GOD HAS DONE FOR US. The memory of events under the law was ever kept up in this way. The memorials of God's mercy we read of in the Old Testament are innumerable. There was circumcision, the memorial of God's covenant with Abraham; the stone set up at Bethel, the memorial of Jacob's vision. There was the passover, the memorial of the deliverance from Egypt; the manna and Aaron's rod in the ark; the memorial of the miraculous feeding of the Israelites in the wilderness; and the selection of the progeny of Aaron for the high-priesthood. Thus we have the memorial here mentioned of the passage of Jordan, and the memorial of the victory over the Philistines in 1 Sam. vii. 12. National deliverances also were commemorated by annual feasts. Such was the feast of Purim, the establishment of which is recorded in Esther ix. 20—32. Our Lord gives His sanction to the principle in the institution of the sacrament of Holy Communion, and the Christian Church has made it her own by the establishment of festivals like Easter, Whitsuntide, Christmas, and the like. The same principle is at work in the erection of memorial churches and other means of commemorating great mercies, or the lives of good men. But the principle is capable of extension. It seems a little ungrateful that we as a nation, or even the members of our religious bodies, think so little of commemorating God's signal mercies and deliverances by special days of thanksgiving. The observance of such days as January 30th, May 29th, November 5th may have assumed too political and party a character, but there are surely other days of national blessings which, if observed as days of thanksgiving, would not be open to the same objections. At least we may go so far as this. Gratitude, in the Old Testament, was testified by outward signs. Where those outward signs are wanting among ourselves, it is to be feared that the gratitude is wanting also. The country ought to be covered with memorials of national and local as well as individual mercies. Days of recognition of such mercies to the empire, or particular parts of the empire, should be more common than they are. Our unhappy divisions, or even the fear of aggravating those divisions, should not withhold us from publicly recognising what in our hearts we believe to be acts of God's gracious providence over us. A stranger going through our country should have frequent occasion to ask, "What mean these?" and should repeatedly receive the answer, "These are the memorials of the great things God did for us in our fathers' days, and in the old time before them."

II. THESE MEMORIALS TEND TO STIR UP A SPIRIT OF PIETY AND GRATITUDE. There is no more frequent speech recorded in connection with memorials, whether buildings or festivals, than the supposition of an inquiry regarding their nature on the part of the young, and of an answer on the part of parents explaining it. Now the abstract facts of history make but a faint impression on the young, while a noble building or a remarkable observance attracts their attention at once. It is an old heathen proverb, "Segnius irritant animos demissa per aures quam quæ sunt oculis subjecta fidelibus." It is surely a matter of Christian prudence to stir up as early as possible in the minds of the young an interest in the truths of religion, and of the history of their country and Church. This is done, as regards Christian doctrine, by the increased attention given to the commemoration of the chief events in the life of Christ at the great Christian festivals. But much more might be done. How much of our decreasing respect for the Reformation may be traced to our neglect of some sort of yearly commemoration of those who laid down their lives for it, is a question. How much our very faint sense of the mercies of God to this country, and in particular to the wonderful salvation God vouchsafed to us in the destruction of the Spanish Armada, is due to the same cause, may also be a question. As regards the latter, it is perhaps not too much to say that scarcely one educated Englishman out of ten, and no uneducated one, has any idea from what vast perils we, as a nation, have been delivered by that one event. And in spite of the many signal mercies we have received, and in spite of the great things God has wrought for us in granting us the character we enjoy for fairness, uprightness, respect for liberty and law, and in spite of the vast and extended dominion He has placed in our hands, our sense of gratitude to God for these things seems diminishing daily. We shall do well to ask ourselves how much of it is due to a neglect of the principle laid down in this chapter regarding the wisdom of memorials of past blessings which shall induce the young to ask what they mean, and shall enable us, in reply to their question, to incite them to "praise the Lord for his mercies. and declare the wonders that he doeth for the children of men."

III. EVERY TRIBE TOOK PART IN THE WORK. The principle above contended for is capable of misapplication. The multiplication of party or sectarian memorials of animosity and ill-feeling would be an evil, rather than a blessing. Even memorials of the Reformers, or of so great a national deliverance such as that to which we have just referred, might easily, as is the case in Ireland, be made occasions of strife. But this applies rather to the abuse than the use of them. In modern days of freedom of thought there could hardly exist a single anniversary the propriety of which would be questioned by no one. To keep only such anniversaries as no one objected to, would be to keep none at all. But care should be taken that all memorials of this kind should be (1) so kept as not wantonly to insult the prejudices of others, and (2) should be confined to events in which the community as a whole had a share. The victory of Israel over Benjamin was not commemorated by a memorial, though it was doubtless a real national blessing. Only such events as can be commemorated by taking " out of every tribe a man" are intended by the foregoing remarks.

IV. WE ARE ALL EQUALLY BOUND TO DECLARE WHAT GOD HAS DONE FOR US. The duty of erecting the memorial was not confined to the priests or Levites. So now, it is not the clergy only who are to proclaim God's "noble acts." All, in their several spheres, are to make known the great things He has done, and to take part in the public commemorations of them. The Church does not consist of clergy only, but of clergy and laity. So, too, the duties of a public recognition of the goodness of God are as incumbent on the laity as on the clergy. The laity are to bear the stones on their shoulders, and to deposit them where the people rest for the night. It is not well when they leave these duties to women and children, or to those whose duty it is to bear the ark. The duties of worshipping God in the sanctuary on other days beside Sunday, of promoting religious works and religious societies, is often left to the clergy by those who have plenty of time, if they preferred to spend their leisure hours in work for the benefit of others rather than in regarding their own comfort.

Other points in the narrative are worthy of mention.

I. THE PEOPLE HASTED AND PASSED OVER. They hasted (1) because they feared the waters might return and overflow them. So, even when we are experiencing a deliverance by the mighty hand of God, ought we to be watchful and trembling lest we be again overtaken by sin. Want of watchfulness in the hour of triumph has been the occasion of many a fearful fall. Or they hasted (2) because they were anxious to enter the promised land. Would that all Christians were as full of a chastened eagerness to enter upon the conflict with evil, which they only can do who are delivered from the power of Satan and of sin. Would that they were as anxious to "forget" the days of sinful indulgence they have "left behind," and to "reach forward" unto the time of victory and triumph, which to faith appears clearly "before." Lukewarmness in the Christian course is the forerunner, not of victory, but of disgrace. Or (3) they hastened that they might not try the patience of God. He only works miracles when natural means are insufficient. If we expect Him to stay the waters of Jordan to suit our convenience, to preserve us from temptation when we ought to have removed ourselves from its influence, to guard us by His special providence from dangers from which ordinary care and watchfulness would have preserved us, we shall be mistaken. We ought not to keep the priests standing in the Jordan one minute longer than is necessary.

II. THE ISRAELITES WENT OVER "PREPARED FOR WAR." This was true, not only of the two-and-a-half tribes, but of the other tribes also. (1) *The Christian must be ready for a conflict.* His Master forewarned him that He came to send "not peace, but a sword," upon the earth. We have to "fight the good fight of faith," to "wrestle against principalities, against powers, against the rulers of the darkness of this world, against spiritual wickedness in high places." We do not enter the land of promise to be idle. A conflict against evil awaits us, both within our own hearts and in society around. A man who leads a life of inaction against evil within or in society around him is a traitor to the cause. We should deceive him were we to lead him to suppose that he should enjoy the milk and honey, the pleasures and consolations of religion, till he had undergone its perils and its struggles first. And (2) *preparation for war involves self-discipline.* The word in the original means "disencumbered." The impediments to action were to be removed; that is, habits, social customs, business engagements, which fetter us in our conflict with evil, must be given up. Even the ties of affection must not be suffered to hamper us in the discharge of our duty. The most innocent amusements, if incompatible with effectual action against God's enemies, must be cast aside. Like the runner in the race, we must "lay aside every weight, and the sin which doth so easily beset us." So, and so only, must we enter into the enjoyment of God's covenant, and fit ourselves for the unspeakable blessings which God has prepared for those who are "faithful unto death."

HOMILIES BY VARIOUS AUTHORS.

Ver. 6.—"That this may be . . . . stones.' *The children's question.* That life is intended to be a school of instruction to us we see plainly from the many directions given to the people of Israel. For they were under the immediate government of God; He blessed them with special favours, was ready also to reprove their faults, and omitted no method of inculcating the lessons which the events of their lives were calculated to teach. Christians are "led by the Spirit of God;" their eyes should be open to see, and their ears uncovered to hear, the meaning of providential dispensations. In the instructions conveyed by God through Joshua, posterity was not forgotten. Provision was made for handing down to following ages a record of God's dealings with His people. With that provision our text is concerned.

I. THE INQUIRY. "What mean ye by these stones?"

1. *By what suggested?* A representative from each tribe selected a large stone from the bed of the river Jordan, and these twelve stones were set up in Gilgal, where the people spent the first night after the crossing. The importance of erecting this memorial is indicated by the number of times it is referred to in these chapters (iii. 12; iv. 5; and iv. 20). A conspicuous heap of stones was the customary method of directing attention to a particular scene of some remarkable occurrence, and accordingly stones were also placed in the Jordan where the priests' feet had stood. But the memorial at Gilgal would be more enduring, and could not fail to excite attention each time that the national assembly was held there, as was frequently the case (See 1 Sam. xi. 15, and 2 Sam. xix. 15). It was contrary to the law to erect a carved image, for fear of idolatrous practices, but rude stones served the purpose. The "sensible" is more impressive than the abstract. Ignorant persons and children who had not yet learned to read, to whom writing would be useless, could appreciate the significance of such a memorial.

2. *By whom asked?* It is the question of children whose curiosity has been

awakened. What child in Altorf but must have inquired respecting the statue of William Tell, or in Lucerne about the lion sculptured by Thorwaldsen to commemorate the deaths of the Swiss guards? Young people are not to be discouraged, but stimulated to put questions for information. The test of a good teacher is found in his ability to induce his pupils to make inquiries spontaneously. And the lesson may be of use to older people, not to be ashamed to confess ignorance, but to ask for enlightenment.

3. *By whom answered?* The fathers are to make the reply, explaining the intention of the "sign" to their interested children. Parents are the proper persons to satisfy the inquiries of their offspring. There is an implicit trust reposed in their statements which is not so readily accorded to strangers. The remarks of Joshua illustrate the necessity of parents attending to the religious training of their children. Can it be deemed sufficient merely to provide food and clothing for the body, and secular learning for the mind, and to allow the moral and spiritual faculties to be neglected? "Godliness is the best learning." Joshua knew that the deepest impressions are often created in childhood. The clay is then easily moulded; the tree has not yet grown stubbornly crooked, and can be straightened; the white paper, if not quite a blank, has still much space left for godly teachings. A sculptor once engraved his own name at the base of a statue, and covering this with plaster, cut therein the Emperor's name and titles, knowing that as years went on the plaster would vanish, and the first inscription become legible. So does early piety become dimly observable sometimes in the rush of pleasure and the turmoil of business, and then the storms of life sweep away the overlaying strata, and the desires of childhood, the gospel learnt at a mother's knee, the prayer offered to the God of his fathers, these stand out in all their vividness as in the former days.

II. GENERAL LESSONS TO BE DERIVED.

1. *The wondrous works of God are for all time.* Their impressiveness and utility are not intended to terminate with their immediate effects. They exemplify His power, and teach all men reverence (ver. 24). Of no avail to plead absence, the recital to us is sufficient to move our hearts. The demand for a repetition of miracles in order to convince each generation in its turn is extravagant and unreasonable. These works of God exhibit also His favour to His people, and incite to trust and love, if we can declare, "This God is our God for ever and ever."

2. *The importance of studying Scripture history.* Not that we would insist so strongly on the distinction between "sacred" and "profane" history. For all history is sacred, all events being under the control of the Almighty, and evincing His moral administration of the world. Yet Scripture is authoritative, presents us with inspired comments on character and actions, and in many places strips off the the veil and affords us clear and certain glimpses of the movements of Deity. As distinguished from mere declarations of the nature of God's attributes, history shows us God in operation, and the picture is helpful to true and definite conception. It furnishes us not merely with a statement, but with an illustrative proof.

3. *God expects men to propagate His fame*

4. *The use of a memorial.* The stones were for a "sign" to excite inquiry and to prevent past history from sinking into utter oblivion. Events the most illustrious are easily forgotten. There is need of enshrining their remembrance in some permanent form. Read the mournful tale of Israel's ungrateful want of recollection in Psa. lxxviii. Again and again "they forgat his works and the wonders he had showed them." Writing has been the chief method of preserving the memory of famous deeds. When resorted to in time it forbids suspicion of legendary exaggerations, and there is not the temptation to relic-worship which "signs" foster. The Jewish dispensation was emphatically the age of symbols, but the gospel has dispensed with them almost altogether. Of the miracles of Christ there are no genuine memorials, save the narratives of the Evangelists and the Christian Church itself. What has been the effect upon ourselves of a perusal of the Gospels? Are they merely "idle tales," or have they revealed to us the love of God, and His willingness to receive His erring children?—A.

Vers. 6—22.—*Memorials.* The crossing the Jordan dry shod was the first miracle which marked the entrance of the people of Israel into the land of Canaan. It was God's purpose that this should be held in perpetual remembrance. Hence the erection of the twelve stones in the bed of the river, to remind the twelve tribes of that which the Almighty hand had wrought for them, in fulfilment of the promise made to their fathers. The material monument would, however, be insufficient of itself to preserve this memory. The story it commemorated must be told from generation to generation. Joshua, as the representative of the people of Israel, speaks thus to the twelve men chosen to carry the twelve stones : " This shall be a sign among you, that when your children ask their fathers in time to come, saying, What mean ye by these stones ? Then ye shall answer them, That the waters of Jordan were cut off before the ark of the covenant of the Lord, when it passed over Jordan " (vers. 6, 7). After the crossing of the river the same precept is repeated, and now not only to the twelve representatives of the people, but to the entire nation. "And Joshua spake unto the children of Israel, saying, Ye shall let your children know, saying, Israel came over this Jordan on dry land." This narrative shows us the way in which the memory of the Divine story of salvation should be handed down.

I. THERE NEEDS TO BE AN INDESTRUCTIBLE MONUMENT OF THE FACTS OF RE-DEMPTION, not liable, like a mere verbal tradition, to human additions and interpolations. The twelve stones here represent this character of immutability, by which the truth of God is preserved from misrepresentation. We ourselves have more than one memorial graven by God's own hand in the rock for ever. We have a Divine Book—the Holy Scripture—which has preserved for us the great and glorious facts of revelation in their integrity and purity. We must never suffer this sacred monument either to be altered or added to.

II. The twelve stones, commemorative of the passage of the Jordan, WERE PLACED THERE BY THE HANDS OF THOSE WHO HAD THEMSELVES BEEN WITNESSES OF THE GREAT MIRACLE. The twelve men who reared this monument marched at the head of Israel when the waters of the river were driven back. So was it also with the sacred writers of the Old Testament. So was it with the Apostles—the first twelve representatives of the new people of God. Their testimony is at once irrefragable and of primary authority, for those who reared the monument of the Scriptures can say with St. John, "That which we have seen and heard declare we unto you " (1 John i. 1). Our first duty, as those who are concerned for the preservation of the truth of God, is fidelity to this original and sacred testimony. Let us carefully separate from it all which is merely fabulous—the creation of our own imagination or reason.

III. IT IS NOT ENOUGH, HOWEVER, TO PRESERVE THE LETTER OF SCRIPTURE UN-IMPAIRED, and to fence it round with our respect and veneration, as it would not have been enough for the children of Israel to have simply guarded against destructive forces the twelve stones of commemoration. It was needful, further, that the story of the great miracle should be repeated day by day, not only in the solemnities of the altar, but also at the domestic hearth. No other priesthood can be a substitute for the priesthood of every man in his own household. Let every Christian father himself tell to his children the story of salvation, taking it from the pure source of Holy Scripture ; and so let this history form part of that spiritual heritage which is the best legacy to succeeding generations. Let the altar of remembrance—the Book of God—be set up in the midst of the house ; thus will the sacred tradition be handed down in all its purity. Let the story of salvation be told by the lips of father and mother, familiar to the child from its very cradle ; and thus preserved in its purity, the gospel tradition will become an element of vital power in the heart of the rising race.—E. DE P.

Ver. 7.—*Memorial stone.* Look for a little at this cairn or Druidical circle, or whatever other shape the twelve stones combined produced. Our text reads as if two such enclosures were raised : one by Joshua in the bed of Jordan, laved at least by its waters ; and one in Gilgal, the rising ground about midway between Jordan and

Jericho. The first erection made by Israel in the promised land was this stone of remembrance. It was not casually or carelessly done. God enjoined it before they crossed, and men were told off to gather the stones fit for such a purpose during the crossing over. The first religious act they did was this memorial act; and the first bit of Canaan which they took possession of was hallowed as a memorial site. Is there anything analogous to this which we ought to do? And would there be any advantage in our doing it? Let us see what this action would suggest as our proper course.

I. WE SHOULD ALL TAKE SPECIAL MEASURES TO REMEMBER OUR MERCIES. For our own sakes memorial stones are not valueless. Our power of recollection is slight, and innumerable things make their claims upon it. Our misfortunes ask loudly to be remembered. The slights we receive, the injuries we endure, the disappointments we meet with are clamorous in their appeals to memory. While mercies of God, kindness of man, tranquil delights and satisfactions ask to be remembered with only a small still voice which is apt to be drowned in the vulgar din of the other turbulent recollections, there are some memories, as John Foster phrased it, only rows of hooks to hang grudges on. And when memory so weakly yields to clamour, or so morbidly prefers the poorer subjects of remembrance, every recollection is a depressing burden. We owe it to ourselves to remember all God's benefits, for the recollection of them is green pastures and still waters when we are weak. It is inspiration when we are depressed. It gives the joyous sense of being loved. It purifies the soul by gratitude. It binds us by the sweetest of all bonds to God's service. It brightens the future by the radiance which is at once most trustworthy and most sweet. It sends us on our way "thanking God and taking courage." And a wholesome, gracious memory being of such value, we should take pains to cherish it. We should deal with it as with a garden, not permitting anything to grow in it which intrudes itself; but we should constantly keep down the weeds, and plant, tend, and cherish the flowers of fragrance and of beauty. Keep your heart with all diligence, and especially this bit of it. And to this end special actions, stones of memory, vows of service, gifts, meditations should all be employed. There is one great stone of memory which, in obedience to the Saviour, the Church has raised. The rite of the Lord's Supper was meant to proclaim to those ignorant of it, and to recall to those acquainted with it, the great deliverance wrought on Calvary, and the infinite love which permits us to participate in it. Use that memorial; open your heart to its influence. The less in the mood a Christian man is for partaking of that rite, the more does he need to do so. It was ordained to jog the indolent memory and to warm the coldness of the heart. Use this memorial, and make it bigger by adding your own contribution to its gracious testimonies. Each tribe laid its stone on the memorial heap in Gilgal. Each man should add his stone to the memorial everywhere and always rising to the greater deliverance Christ works for us. If we should take special measures to remember our mercies in general, so most of all should we do so to remember the infinite mercy of redemption.

II. IT IS A DUTY TO REPORT TO OTHERS AS WELL, AS TO REMEMBER FOR OURSELVES, THE MERCIES OF GOD. These stones were a publication of God's dealings to all who subsequently should pass by that way: set up "for the encouragement of pilgrims," as Bunyan would say. Experience may belong to us individually, but the lessons of that experience belong to all who need them. The children of Israel must not "hide God's righteousness (i.e., mercy) within their hearts." They must tell it to the generations following. The story may be told in various ways—in a holiday like the passover, which they will keep; in a song, like Miriam's, which will linger in people's lips and hearts; or in an outward memorial like these stones. Only, Israel must tell its mercies. In a world languishing for want of a heavenly hope Israel must not be silent. So the memorial is reared—each stone a tongue telling of God's love and help. Wherever there has been mercy received, the Saviour requires that that mercy should be recorded for the good of others. He may, as a temporary precept say, "Tell no man," to those who would lose its lessons by proclaiming too eagerly their mercy. But if the prohibition of garrulous and thoughtless tattle about mercies suggests need of thought and carefulness, other precepts—as, " Go home and tell thy friends," " Show thyself to the priests," requirements of confession, the example of multitudes who have said, " Come, and I will tell you what the Lord hath done for my soul," the instincts of honour and of grace —all combine to lay on him who receives Divine mercy the duty of telling it. We have all need to beware of a guilty secrecy which thinks it a mark of refinement and modesty to be silent about its Saviour. Your neighbours are perishing, all needing, some asking for, a Saviour. Will you be guiltless if you do not say, " Here is a Saviour, Christ Jesus—He saved me"? If He has led you across the Jordan into the rest He promised you, set up your memorial, and join the rest of Israel in testifying that Jesus Christ is a great Saviour. Membership in the Church of Christ is the simplest form of testimony and is the duty of every saved man. For the sake of others set up your memorial of God's mercies in Gilgal.

III. MAKE YOUR MEMORIAL AS ENDURING AS POSSIBLE. They were to set up twelve *stones:* something that would endure, that could give testimony to many generations. As a matter of fact they did remain till, probably, some centuries after the destruction of Jerusalem.* And through all these generations that circle, or cairn, or altar, whatever it was, remained, elevating and inspiring men by its blessed memories. Let your testimony of Christ's salvation be an enduring one. Set up not a memorial of clay, which rain may soften or heat might crumble, but of stone. Keep your own memories of mercy keen and clear. Do not let them crumble away; and try to serve the generations that are to come. Inheritors should be transmitters of help. The testimony of those that have gone before us has blessed us; let our testimony bless those that follow after us. Let us not play at testifying of the grace of God, but make it seriously our work. There are men who, giving themselves to the work, have blessed many generations. Let our Saviour have from us some enduring witness which shall carry to the generations after us the record of His love. And, lastly, this lesson should be noted—

IV. THAT THE LESSONS OF THE MEMORIAL SHOULD SPECIALLY REACH OUR CHILDREN. In vers. 21 to the end it is assumed that the children will be the inquirers about the memorial, and the parents the interpreters of it, and that thus, from father to son, the story of God's grace shall be handed down, hallowing each generation. No man can complain that there is no open door set before him, when a child full of inquisitive simplicity faces him. And no one should despair of the future of a land in which parents can engage the ear of children with the story of their sacred experience. Is there not too much reticence between parents and children on the greatest of all themes? If our hearts were more devout would it be impossible for us, without undue detail, to charge our children with a sense of what we owe to our Redeemer? Might they not early learn how poor and worthless our life would have been without Him. Might they not learn something of answers to our prayers, of the blessedness of heavenly hopes, of the safety of protecting grace, of the consolations of God's love, of that "delivery from all our fears" of which the Psalmist speaks? " Ye shall let your children know, saying, Israel came over this Jordan on dry land." When we obey this precept in letter and spirit more heartily, probably we shall find our obedience will be rich in the results expected by the writer (ver. 24). " The people of the earth will know the hand of the Lord, and Israel will fear the Lord their God for ever."—G.

Ver. 14.—*Grace for beginners.* In one sense Joshua is not a beginner. For forty years he has been at work for God. As spy, as general, as servant of Moses, during all these years he has wrought in the work, and with the help of God. Yet though eighty-five years of age, this crossing Jordan is his first act of leadership. In the sovereignty of Israel he is a beginner, with a beginner's fears, difficulties, burdens. And here we see a beautiful illustration of the fact—that with a beginner's cares comes a beginner's grace as well. A marvellous miracle stamps him as the leader sent by God. The "divinity that doth hedge a king" in an unusual degree

---

* See Art. in Smith's Dictionary, ' Gilgal.'

invests him. And in his first enterprise he has such help as makes him secure of the future allegiance of all the people. Many are, and more ought to be, beginners in God's ways. Consider the testimony of this incident as it affects them, and first observe—

I. BEGINNERS NEED SPECIAL GRACE AND HELP. Evidently Joshua did. If Moses shrank, how much more might he, from this perilous enterprise, when the efforts of the people, after settlement, had no such stimulus as had been supplied by the oppression of their masters ; when he was uncommended by the signs he carried of his Divine commission ; when probably Eleazar would have been glad to have been chief ruler; when almost inevitably there would be critics who would oppose his plans and dispute the wisdom of his orders ! He had double work to do—to cross Jordan, and justify his own appointment. Nay, treble work to do—for his power of helping Israel in the future depended largely on what he would now do. Sufficient unto that day was its own troubles ; but it had to carry the justification of the past and the assurance of the future with it. Even so all beginners find their work especially arduous. "It is the first step that costs ; " the first step of the prodigal returning to his father; the leaving the nets to follow Christ; the first act of service to men. We are unaccustomed ; and that force of habit which stands us in such good stead when we have had experience of well-doing now operates the other way. All obstacles are enlarged by nervous apprehensions. In subsequent acts we may have society—the first act of right is apt to be profoundly solitary. Do not be staggered at the difficulties of beginning well. All beginners have had the same experience to contend with. But observe secondly—

II. BEGINNERS HAVE SPECIAL GRACE TO MEET THEIR SPECIAL DIFFICULTIES. As with Paul's "thorn," pity to remove which was asked, grace to endure which was granted ; so here *God does not take away the difficulty, but gives grace* to surmount it. Over and above the usual grace He gives to all His saints, there is special grace given to them. Has Moses a task imposed on him specially arduous? Not one difficulty is removed, but miraculous signs invest him with a sacred inviolable dignity, and plagues of terrific power sanction his demands. Is David indicated as future king by the whispered call of God? In the challenge of Goliath and the pouring of a "patriotic tide through his undaunted heart"—the suggested daring, and the power to achieve what he dares to undertake—the beginning of his kingly service is made possible. Does it come to Daniel as a duty to keep himself pure from defiling meats ? The beginning of his devotion is helped by a physical grace that keeps him strong and well. The beginning of Peter's consecration is helped by the miraculous draught of fishes. The beginning of the service of the seventy, by the miraculous powers so freely imparted to them. And so always there is special grace for those beginning. There is some fulness of gracious influence—clearness of light —some strengthening companionship of man—some closer presence of God—invigorating hopes—the energy which comes from the sacred calm of penitence—some clearing of the way before us—some moving of the pillar of fire and cloud, or of the Ark of God. And whenever any enterprise of Christian love is undertaken, there is always some help of a special kind. Enlargement of spirit—some power of prayer, or patience—some great strength of humility or steadfastness. As here, so always, special grace attends the beginnings of all great courses. And this is no light thing, for in all the forms of Christian life and service, "Well begun is half done." And the grace then given not merely makes the beginning possible, but all the subsequent career. "They feared Joshua as they feared Moses, all the days of his life." Always, the beginner gets special grace for the beginning of his work, and sufficient to exert an influence on all that follows after. If such is the case, consider lastly—

III. WHAT LESSONS ARE INVOLVED IN IT. There is this lesson first and foremost—

1. Shrink not from beginning the Christian life. It is difficult—nay, to naked human strength impossible. The beginning—the Jordan passage—will try you. But beginners' difficulties are more than matched by beginners' grace. You may not feel this grace : it may be "latent" grace, and not "sensible" grace ; but it will be there. omnipotent enough to carry you over every hindrance.

2. Shrink not from undertaking any duty of service with which God charges you. Do not be evilly modest, folding your pound in some napkin of seeming humility. If it be the path of duty, let no obstacles deter ; they will only prove the occasion for grander help from God than you ever dare to hope.

3. Have you just begun discipleship or service, and are you overwhelmed with difficulty ? " In your patience possess your soul," for even as a mother gives her finger to the little child just beginning to walk, so to us, who are but children of a larger growth, God lends His finger when we are beginning some great life task.—G.

Vers. 15—17.—*Prophets and priests—the order of precedence.* Here a layman commands a priest. It was not a case of royal supremacy exactly, nor did he govern them by virtue of his being the civil head of the community ; but because, though layman (he was of the tribe of Ephraim), he was a prophet. " The Lord spake to Joshua," and therefore Joshua could command even the priests of God. We have here not a question of archæological interest merely. It is a live question of to-day. Rome goes in for having an order of priests ; Protestantism for an order of prophets—*i.e.*, speakers forth of God's messages to man. *They* want a prescriptive class, elevated above their fellows, "ordained to offer gifts and sacrifices to God ;" we want, not men ordained, but men inspired, who, fresh from the vision of God and converse with Him, will be able to tell us what He is, and feels, and wants. Are they or we following the more excellent way ? Let the subordination of the priest to the prophet here help us to the answer. It may ⁿ so, for observe—

I. THE PRECEDENCE HERE is the constant precedence. Aaron was older brother and high priest. Moses was the prophet who " spake with God face to face." The order of the names invariably is " Moses and Aaron : " prophet first, priest second. In all the subsequent centuries you find prophets foremost, priests subservient. The greatest men of Israel—those who sustained their patriotism, kindled their devotion, fed the flame of hope, those who led them in the path of duty, and were the reformers of religion—were prophets, Elijah and Elisha, Isaiah, Daniel. Ezra was the only priest who, without being a prophet, can be classed with them. Jeremiah and Ezekiel were priests and prophets, but it is in the latter character they rendered their grandest service. We must not depreciate the services of the priesthood. Perhaps the tone of Dean Stanley's lecture on the Jewish Priesthood (' Jewish Church,' vol. ii. 356) is too disparaging. They tended to keep alive devotion, to familiarise men with the great idea of access to God, they guided men in the ways of gratitude and trust. Still the teachers, inspirers, leaders of souls were the prophets ; and throughout all Old Testament history down to the time of the Maccabees, it is the prophetic order that keeps alive piety in all its grand activities. And if we had applied the same terms on the Christian dispensation it might be shown that the greater of the two services has been that rendered by men of the prophetic, rather than that rendered by men of the priestly, stamp. Athanasius, Augustine, Tertullian, St. Bernard, Luther, Calvin, Knox, Wesley—those that can speak out the heart and the will of God—have, according to a law of moral gravitation, found a higher level than the most devoted and self-forgetful of ecclesiastics. Anyhow, here the prophet commands, and the priest obeys. Observe secondly—

II. THIS ORDER OF PRECEDENCE IS THE NATURAL ORDER. The rank of priest is high—an ambassador of man in the court of heaven. But the rank of prophet is higher—an ambassador of God. The priest's grandest work is supplication ; the prophet's is to mediate the promises, commands, requirements of God. For the former office the requirements were low—a certain lineage, freedom from physical defect, familiarity with ritual, rubric, and law. For the office of the prophet far higher requirements were made—purity of heart, to see God ; the open ear, that could hear His voice ; the heart of love, that could enter into His purposes ; the courage which could confront men with the Divine behest. The priest could be made by man—the prophet only by God. The former had outward and visible ordination ; the latter was ordained by the laying on of the unseen hands of the great God Himself. One reason why communities that have degenerated in faith are so emphatic in their doctrines of holy orders is that the priest is easily made, his work easily done, his claims easily asserted and enforced. But to make men prophets, or catch the inspiration of heaven, is not at all so easy. It takes a happy concurrence of grace and nature, a "bridal of the earth and sky," to make him. Naturally, therefore, because the prophet's is a higher taste demanding higher powers, the prophet ranks before the priest. Lastly, observe as the conclusion of the above—

III. PROPHETS ARE THE GREAT WANT OF THIS AND EVERY AGE. True priests are invaluable : such as by their pity and their love are spontaneous, fervent intercessors for their fellow-men. We should covet to be such : whether in or out of "orders," we may belong to " the Royal Priesthood," whose mark is not an official garb, but a compassionate heart. But the great want is prophets—not prophets of the almanack sort, dealing with the curious questions of the future ; but prophets of the Bible sort—pre-eminently engaged with "present truth " and present duty. The great want of the age is not priests at the altar, but inspired men in all the pulpits of the land—men who, walking with God, can bring to us the truth, the consolations, the requirements of God, with the authority of those who have learned from His lips what they address to our ears. Such men would speak " with authority " which all would recognise without needing demonstration of it. Their lips would feed many. Their utterances would find or make a way into all hearts. And reason approving, the heart accepting, the conscience endorsing, all their words, the people of our land would become " obedient to the heavenly vision " and " walk in the light of the Lord." Not after formal authority of the priest, but after the living inspiration of the prophet, let us all aspire.—G.

Vers. 19—24.—*Memorials.* The passage of the Jordan has been called a " priestly miracle," a natural event " turned into a miracle " by the historian for the sake of exalting the priestly office. We fail, however, to see that any such special prominence has been given to the priestly element. It is the ark that is the medium of the miracle-working power, the priests are but its servants and attendants. The ark, as the symbol and throne of the Divine presence, is the centre around which all the supernatural glory of the incident gathers. Indeed, there is rather a notable subordination of the priestly element at this period of Hebrew history. Joshua did not belong to the priestly order any more than Moses did. There was no sacerdotal rule. The twelve men who gathered these memorial stones from the bed of the river were not priests, but men chosen by the tribes for that particular work. The priestly functions were not those most brought into prominence by these incidents. There is no sign of anything like undue homage being paid to the priesthood at that period, and even as regards the religion of the people it was, as Stanley says, " a part of the mechanism of that religion rather than its animating spirit." The raising of these stones, then, to commemorate the great event that had just taken place, was the act of the whole people through their chosen representatives. Two piles of stones were raised : the one by direct Divine command, at Gilgal, where the Israelites rested for the night after the passage, and where they observed their first passover in the land of Canaan ; the other, apparently without Divine command, on the other side, at the spot where the feet of the priests first touched the brink of the flooded river. The words of Joshua present them in two lights before us : (1) As a memorial for the men of that generation, and (2) as a means of instruction for their children.

I. A MEMORIAL FOR THAT GENERATION. The wisdom of God is seen in the command to raise such a memorial. It meets that weakness in human nature by which it comes to pass that the most sacred impressions are prone to die—the lapse of time and the succeeding waves of circumstance obliterate them. Most Divine institutions have rested on this principle. God " set his bow in the cloud" as a sign and pledge of His faithfulness. The Sabbath was intended to quicken in men the sense of their Divine relations and their longing for the " rest that remaineth." The passover and other feasts were to be " for memorials ; " and when Christ said to His disciples, " Do this in remembrance of me," He asserted the same principle.

The sign was to be a stimulus to spiritual apprehension and a help to faith. The history of the olden times is full of examples of the way in which men, as by a natural instinct, have sought to create for themselves some permanent record of the most momentous experiences of their life, by the names they gave to certain scenes, or by the erection of altars, &c. (Abraham at Mount Moriah, "Jehovah Jireh," Gen. xxii. 19; Jacob at Bethel, Gen. xxviii. 18; Moses at Rephidim, Exod. xvii. 14; Samuel at Mizpeh, "Ebenezer," 1 Sam. vii. 12). All memorials of this kind have their outlook towards the past and towards the future. They serve a double purpose; they keep alive precious memories and awaken buoyant hopes, they excite gratitude and strengthen faith. We do well to set up such way-marks in the pilgrimage of our life. Their value lies not so much in the fact that they record the extraordinary—that which happened once and is not likely to happen again—but rather in the fact that they link the past with the future. They show us that through all change something abides. Our nature is the same in its needs, dangers, responsibilities; God is the same in His loving regard for us and His power to deliver. Every passing experience of His grace is a pledge that He will not fail us in emergencies yet to come. Anything is good that deepens this impression, provokes to thankfulness, and rebukes distrust. The darkest passages in our history thus leave benedictions behind them, are transformed into occasions of triumphant joy:

> "Out of our stony griefs
> Bethels we raise."

II. A MEANS OF INSTRUCTION FOR THEIR CHILDREN. "When your children shall ask their fathers," &c. A glimpse here of the simplicity and sanctity of domestic relations which was so important a feature of ancient Hebrew life. The authority of the father over his children almost absolute and unlimited. Something terrible in its despotism, if it had not been modified and softened by certain provisions defining parental duty. Instruction in the sacred traditions of the nation, its memories and hopes—an obligation continually enforced (see Exod. xii. 26, 27; xiii. 14; Deut. vi. 7—20, et seq.).

1. The beauty and worth of a spirit of inquiry in children. It is natural for the child to ask questions. A boundless realm of mystery lies all around the awakening mind, and an irresistible instinct moves it to inquire, "Why these things? What mean ye by these services?" The contact of mind with mind is needful in order to development, and of whom should the children ask, but of "their fathers," for the solution of the problems that perplex them? The most notable chapter, the only recorded chapter, in the early development of Jesus is that scene in which we behold Him in the temple, "sitting in the midst of the doctors, both hearing them and asking them questions."

2. The generous, sympathetic response this spirit of inquiry should meet with. No tender sensibility of childhood is to be suppressed, least of all any that may lead to the discovery of truth. The inquisitiveness of the child is a precious faculty that demands to be rightly directed. The indifference of many parents to the stirrings of the spirit of inquiry in their children arises from selfish indolence, and is a cruel wrong. No doubt children will often ask questions which the wisest cannot answer, but at least let the difficulty be frankly confessed; let the ground and reason of it be defined in a way adapted to the young intelligence. The very disappointment then becomes a means of Divine instruction. The higher interests of our being—the laws of God's government, the revelations of His love, the workings of His Providence and Spirit—let these especially be unfolded. What nobler office can any parent perform than to mediate between the mind of his child and the mystery of the Unseen—to lift up the veil that hides God's glory, to explain and justify His ways, to be the medium of His truth and Spirit to the young inquiring soul?

3. The practical result at which all instruction should aim. "That ye might fear the Lord your God for ever." The miracle, the memorial, the teaching, all find here their ultimate issue. All subordinate purposes must lead on to this—the

showing forth of God's glory, and the submission of His intelligent creatures to Him in reverence and godly fear. "Let us hear the conclusion of the whole matter," &c. (Eccles. xii. 13). –W.

Ver. 18.—*The passage of Jordan the symbol of death.* The passage of Jordan as the necessary way of entrance into the land of promise has always been regarded as symbolic of the death of the Christian. The same causes which allowed the children of Israel to cross the stream without being buried in its waters, operate in the case of the believing soul, to enable him also to pass through the deep water-floods without being overflowed by them. These causes may be described as threefold.

I. The passage of the Jordan was effected at the time appointed by God. It was in obedience to the command of God that Israel crossed the river, so is it also with our death. It is determined by God. To Him belong the times and seasons. Hence we can in all confidence commit our way to Him and our spirit into His hands.

II. God granted special aid to His people in this hour of trial. This He promises to us also when we are called to pass through the deep waters. " When thou passest through the waters I will be with thee." And David, full of this confidence, exclaims, " Yea, though I walk through the valley of the shadow of death, I will fear no evil, for thou art with me " (Psa. xxiii. 4).

III. Israel sees at its head a guide chosen of God, who goes before it in this dangerous passage. We also have our Divine Joshua, who has passed through the river of death before us; that mighty Saviour, who " died for our sins and rose again for our justification" (1 Cor. i. 1). He will bring us safely to Himself on that blessed shore, whither He is gone before. How heartening is the sweet song of Vinet:

" Quand le bruit des flots, l'aspect et le rivage,
　Nous diront, Ô Jourdain, nos travaux vont cesser ;
　Jésus nous recevra triomphants et lassés.
　Près de ces compagnons d'exil et d'héritage,
　Qui ne sont pas perdus, mais nous ont devancés."

" When the rush of Jordan's waters breaking on the shore
　Tells the struggling, fainting pilgrim toil is nearly o'er ;
　Jesus ready to receive him, brothers gone before,
　Welcome him with songs of triumph, ' Home for evermore ! ' "

E. DE P.

EXPOSITION.

CHAPTER V. 1—9.

THE CIRCUMCISION.—Ver. 1.—**Which were on the side of Jordan westward.** A large portion of the territory of the Amorites had, as we have seen (ch. iii. 10), been already conquered. The remaining tribes on the other side Jordan were apprehensive of the same fate. For " on the side," the original has " across." Having hitherto written of Israel as on the eastern side of Jordan, he continues the same expression after he has narrated the crossing. But writing as he did on the west side of Jordan, and for readers the vast majority of whom were on the west side of Jordan, he adds the expression " westward " (literally, *seaward*) to prevent any possibility of mis-

take. **Until we were passed over.** The Masorites, in the *Keri*, have corrected the text (*Chethibh*) into " until *they* were passed over." Kennicott states that this reading is confirmed by twenty-seven Hebrew MSS., which have probably adopted the reading from the Masoretic correction. The LXX. accepts the *Chethibh.* The probability, however, is that this is one of the many instances of a conjectural emendation of a difficult passage, it not having been seen that the historian was either quoting a document contemporary with the events described, or more probably using the word to identify himself as an Israelite with the acts of his fathers in past times. This is the opinion of Rabbi David Kimchi. Knobel refers to Psa. lxvi. 6. See also ver. 6 of this chapter, and ch. xxiv. 5, 6, 7; Judg. xi. 17; cf. 19. We must not, then, assume from this passage that the Book of Joshua was written by one who himself had a share in the events recorded, in the face of many indications we have of a later origin (see ch. iv. 9, &c.). A fuller discussion of this subject will be found in the introduction. **Their heart melted.** Confirming what Rahab had said (ch. ii. 11). Similar terror has often been struck into the hearts of peoples, especially of peoples enervated by habits of licentious indulgence, by the approach of enemies who have successfully and rapidly overcome obstacles deemed insurmountable. Such an effect was produced in Persia by Alexander's victories at the Granicus and Issus. Such an effect, again, was produced in Italy by the tidings of the approach of Alaric and Attila. If we may trust the monk of St. Gall, a similar terror fell on the degenerate Lombards at the approach of Charles the Great, after his daring passage of the Alps. In this case the miraculous element was added, and the inhabitants of Canaan, and of Jericho especially, remained for the time panicstricken, not daring to combine to strike a blow against these daring invaders, who in addition to their bravery seemed under the special protection of Heaven. When they had recovered from the consternation into which the passage of the Jordan had thrown them, the sense of an imminent danger forced them at last to make an effort at resistance (see ch. x.).

Ver. 2.—**At that time.** Ver. 1 is introduced in order to explain why Joshua ventured upon the circumcision of the children of Israel at so critical a period. Nothing could more clearly evince the spirit of confidence in Jehovah which animated not only Joshua, but all the children of Israel. We read of no murmurings, although it was well known that the performance of the rite of circumcision would unfit the Israelites for active service for some days. We may imagine, and even the silence of the sacred historian may be deemed eloquent on the point, that the marvellous passage of the Jordan had inspired the Israelites with an eager desire to renew their covenant with the God who "had done so great things for them already." And although, for religious reasons, they remained inactive for four or five days, a course of action from a military point of view highly injudicious, yet such was the terror the passage of the Jordan had struck into the hearts of the Phœnicians that no attack on them was attempted, and the inhabitants of Jericho (ch. vi. 1) remained under the protection of their strong walls. **Sharp knives,** or *knives of*

stone (צוּר; cf. צֹר Exod. iv. 25). The LXX., Vulgate, Syriac, and Arabic versions, as well as the margins of our Bibles, render thus. On the other hand, several of the Rabbis give the same translation as the text of our version. The LXX. translator, following no doubt an ancient tradition, adds after ch. xxiv. 30, that these knives were buried with Joshua (see note there). The idea which has found great favour lately of a "stone age," as anterior to an "iron age," of the world, will hardly derive support from this passage. That the use of stone preceded the use of iron scarcely admits of a doubt. But from Gen. iv. 22 we learn that the use of iron had been known hundreds of years before Joshua, and yet we find him using stone knives. And we may go further. In spite of the advance of civilisation in our own day, there are still millions of human beings who have not advanced beyond the "stone age." The idea, then, of an age in which the universal use of iron has supplanted the universal use of stone is an idea which facts compel us to reject, while admitting that the use of stone must have preceded the use of iron in the infancy of the human race. In these "knives of flint," Origen, Theodoret, and others see an allusion to Christ, the rock. **The second time.** For "circumcise again the children of Israel the second time," the literal translation is, "return (שׁוּב) to circumcise," or, "return, circumcise" them the second time. This has perplexed the commentators and translators. It has been assumed that the text involves the idea of a former general circumcision of the people, and various are the expedients which have been resorted to in order to avoid the difficulty. Some copies of the LXX. would read שֵׁב for שׁוּב (or יֵשֶׁב for וְישׁוּב Rosenmüller), and translate "sit down" (*i.e.,* halt), "and circumcise." The Vulgate leaves out the word altogether. The Syriac translates literally. The Arabic reads "to-morrow" for "again." The Rabbi Solomon Jarchi falls back on the expedient of a general circumcision ordered by Moses on the departure of the children of Israel from Egypt, on account of their neglect of that rite while they sojourned there, "Nam jam antea magna multitudo simul erat circumcisa illa nocte qua egrediebantur ex Ægypto." But this is rendered highly improbable by the fact that circumcision was an Egyptian as well as a Hebrew custom, and still more so by the improbability that such an important circumstance should have been passed over in silence. Knobel regards Abraham's circumcision with that of his household as the first time (Gen.

xvii. 23). Perhaps the best explanation is that the word שׁוּב, though it is rightly translated "again" here, and in several other places in Scripture, carries with it the idea of a *return into a former condition* (*kehre zurück*, Knobel). So Gen. xxvi. 18, xxx. 31, Hos. ii. 11 (9, in our version). In 2 Kings i. 11, 13 we have the king's *return to his former purpose* in the second and third mission to Elijah. Thus here the word is used of the *bringing back* the children of Israel to their former state, that of a people who were in the enjoyment of a visible sign and seal (Rom. iv. 11) of their being God's covenant people. The meaning therefore would seem to be, "Restore the children of Israel a second time to the position they formerly held, as visibly bound to me, and placed under my protection, by the rite of circumcision." "The person must be in favour ere the work can hope to prosper; his predecessor Moses had like to have been slain for neglect of this sacrament, when he went to call the people out of Egypt; he justly fears his own safety, if now he omit it, when they are brought into Canaan" (Bp. Hall).

Ver. 3.—**The hill of the foreskins.** The name given to the hill where the circumcision took place.

Ver. 4.—**After they came out from Egypt.** Rather "*on their journey* from Egypt." See next verse, where the same words are translated "as they came out."

Ver. 5.—**Now all the people that came out were circumcised.** The Hebrew of this passage (which runs literally thus—"Now circumcised had they been, all the people who were going forth") is sufficient to refute the idea that there was a great circumcision of the people under Moses, on account of the neglect of the rite in Egypt. For, before the exodus, Moses was not in a position to perform any general act of this kind, as the history plainly shows, while after it such a rite could not have taken place, since the Hebrew הָיוּ denotes a state of things which was completed at the time spoken of, and therefore must here be rendered (as above) by the pluperfect. **Them they had not circumcised.** Here again the Hebrew is used of the perfected action, and is therefore rightly rendered by our version, giving the idea that the Israelites who were born in the wilderness had not been circumcised up to the point which our history has now reached. See also ver. 7, where the same construction is found.

Ver. 6.—**Till all the people.** The Hebrew here is גּוֹי, not the usual word for people, but that usually applied to the Gentiles (equivalent to ἔθνος, by which word it is usually rendered in the LXX.). It is applied to the Israelites in ch. iii. 17; iv. 1; Isa. i. 4; ix. 2; xxvi. 2. See also Exod. xxxiii. 13. In the singular it means a people in the more general sense, a nation, as distinguished from a people in whom one has an interest. In the plural it always means the Gentiles. עַם (LXX., λαός), the word usually applied to the people of God, is not used here, because the people who "provoked God in the wilderness" had made themselves in a sense a rejected people. Delitzsch regards this (after Calvin) as a sign that, for the time at least, the covenant between God and Israel was annulled, permanently in the case of those who were condemned to die in the wilderness, temporarily only in their descendants, who were formally reconciled to God, and restored to their former covenant position by this solemn performance of the covenant rite of circumcision (see note on verse 2). So also Hengstenberg, 'Geschichte des Reiches Gottes,' p. 205. The difficulty about the passover may be met by supposing that those only who were circumcised—a constantly decreasing number, of course—were allowed to celebrate that feast. Knobel would understand that in consequence of the "unquiet, unsettled, uncomfortable life" the Israelites led in the wilderness, they could keep very few of the ordained feasts. He continues: "the Elohist knows nothing of any cessation." Nevertheless we read of no passover being kept after the one recorded in Num. ix. 5, so that if "the Elohist knows of no cessation," he knows as little of any continued observance of the feast. But there is no certainty on the point. Considering the loose way in which the word כֹּל is used in Scripture (see, for instance, Gen. iv. 14), we need not press the word to include *all* who were born after the departure from Egypt, but only those who were born after the rejection of the people recorded in Num. xiv. 26, *sqq.* This rejection, be it remembered, did not include all the Israelites who were born in Egypt, but only those who were over twenty years of age (Num. xiv. 29). The view of Kurz (iii. 323, Clark's translation), that circumcision was suspended on account of the continual movements of the Israelites, is refuted by Delitzsch's remark that the Israelites were *not* continually on the march, but that they often encamped in one place for a long period, a period far longer, in fact, than the time in which they abode in Gilgal. Delitzsch asks why this circumcision did not take place before, why it was not performed as soon as they crossed the brook Zered. The answer is that, until the Jordan was crossed, they had not taken formal possession of their own land. As soon as, under the Divine protection, they had crossed the Jordan, the long-delayed promise was fulfilled. God's covenant with Abraham was accomplished, and now they, in their turn, had to place themselves once more in the position of God's covenant people, bound to serve Him with their whole heart. For a fuller discussion of this question see Keil's Commentary, and Hengstenberg in the passage cited above. We may observe that God fulfils His part of the covenant first, and then it is man's duty to fulfil his. God, under the Christian dispensation, first places us in the state of salvation. Then it becomes our duty to make that salvation sure by overcoming God's enemies, by the help which He never fails to afford. **Give us.** This introduction of the first person into the middle of the sentence is unexpected. Some MSS. and editors read "to them" (see note on ver. 1, and Psa. lxvi. 6, where there is a similar change of person). **A land that floweth with milk and honey.** This, says Keil, "is a standing expression in the Pentateuch to express the great fertility of the land of Canaan. Milk and honey are produced by a land rich in grass and flowers, which were both of them plentiful in Canaan (see Isa. vii. 15, 22). Milk, not only of cows, but of sheep and goats also (Deut. xxxii. 14), and eaten sometimes sweet, at other times thick or curdled (חמאה), was a leading article of food amongst the ancient Hebrews, as it is in the present day in most Eastern countries, and Palestine was peculiarly fitted for the rearing of cattle. Honey also, especially that of wild bees, was found in large quantities (Judg. xiv. 8, *sqq.*; 1 Sam. xiv. 26; Matt. iii. 4), and is still found, notwithstanding its present desolate condition." Some have thought דְּבַשׁ to mean the newly expressed juice of grapes, which, under the Arabic name of *dibs*, is largely used at present in Palestine, and is even exported to other countries. But in Deut. xxxii. 13, Ps. lxxxi. 16, wild honey is clearly meant, which is to this day deposited by bees, in the clefts of the rock, whence it often overflows and is received into vessels placed beneath (see Prov. v. 3; Cant. iv. 11; Jahn, 'Biblical Archæology;' and Smith's Dictionary of the Bible.)

Ver. 8.—**Till they were whole.** Literally, *till they revived*, as in Gen. xx. 7; 2 Kings i. 2; viii. 8. Objections have been raised (see Keil and Delitzsch *in loc.*) to the possibility of this circumcision taking place in one day. But it has been shown by calculation that between one-third and one-fourth of the people who remained had been cir-

cumcised already, and that therefore such an operation as this could be performed with the utmost ease in a very short time. The word גוי is used here again, since the people were still Gentiles until the rite of circumcision was performed.

Ver. 9.—**The reproach of Egypt.** Either (1) the reproach which comes from the Egyptians, or (2) the reproach of having sojourned in Egypt. Keil incorrectly states that "the genitive *always* denotes the person from whom the reproach comes" (see Isa. liv. 4, "the reproach of thy widowhood," *i.e.*, the reproach which is cast upon thee for being a widow; Ezekiel xxxvi. 30, "reproach of famine," *i.e.*, the reproach which comes from being doomed to suffer famine). If we accept (1) we must refer the phrase to the reproach cast upon the Israelites by the Egyptians, that all their vainglorious boasts were worthless, and that they were never destined to occupy the land which they declared God had given to them. Hengstenberg ('Geschichte des Reiches Gottes,' p. 207) regards it strangely as the reproach the Egyptians cast upon them that they were rejected of God. If (2) it must be regarded as equivalent to the reproach that they were a nation of slaves, a reproach that was rolled away by the fact of their standing as freemen on the soil which had been promised to their fathers. But Knobel supposes (3) that it was their down-trodden miserable condition in Egypt, a condition which was only partially ameliorated during their wanderings in the wilderness, in the course of which, accustomed to a settled existence, they must have had much to endure. "With the arrival in Canaan," he adds, "all this came to an end. All those who had deserved punishment were dead, all the uncircumcised were circumcised, reproach and misery were put aside, and Israel, as the worthy community of God, entered on a new life." This interpretation, more precise and clear than (2), best satisfies all the requirements of the passage. Some have regarded their uncircumcised state as the "reproach of Egypt." But this, as Hengstenberg remarks, could hardly be, for none but the Egyptian priests were circumcised. Origen (Hom. 4, 'Lib. Jesu Nave') teaches the following lesson from this passage: "Fuimus enim nos aliquando insipientes, increduli, errantes, servientes desideriis et voluptatibus variis, in malitiam, et invidia, odibiles, odientes invicem. Non tibi videntur hæc opprobia esse, et opprobia Ægypti? Sed ex quo venit Christus, et dedit nobis secundam circumcisionem per baptismum regenerationis, et purgavit animas nostras, abjecimus hæc omnia." And again, speaking of the spiritual circumcision Christians have received, and the obligation to purity thus imposed, he adds, " Jam tibi enim non licet templo Dei uti, nisi in sanctitate, nec membra Christi ad indignum dare negotium . . . Si quando te malæ concupiscentiæ pulsat illecebra . . . dic non sum meus, enitus enim sum pretio sanguinis Christi, et membrum ipsius effectus sum." Theodoret remarks how the Israelites who had been circumcised perished in the wilderness, while their uncircumcised children were miraculously preserved and brought over Jordan. A remarkable commentary this on the words, "Now circumcision verily profiteth if thou keep the law; but if thou be a breaker of the law thy circumcision is made uncircumcision" (Rom. ii. 25. Cf. 1 Cor. vii. 19). He also remarks that " we may here learn how we, who have received spiritual circumcision, thereby laid aside the reproach of sin." Trusting by nature in the

spiritual Egypt, the house of bondage, we are slaves to sin and corruption. When we enter into fellowship with Christ, the reproach of Egypt is rolled away, and we enjoy " the glorious liberty of the children of God " (see Rom. vi. 18—22 ; Gal. v. 1 ; also John viii. 32—36). **Gilgal.** It is quite possible, since the word to roll is in Hebrew, as indeed in English, spoken of a circular motion and since גִּלְגָּל is a wheel in Hebrew, that the place, like Geliloth, *i.e.*, circles (ch. xviii. 17), originally meant a circle, and that the new signification was attached to the name from this moment. If Deut. xi. 30 be not a later insertion, the place was known by the name before this time. The root is found in the Aryan as well as in the Semitic languages (as in the Greek κυλίω, εἴλω, and the Latin *volvo*, *globus*).

HOMILETICS.

Vers. 1—9.—*The great renewal of the covenant.* Matthew Henry very felicitously quotes here and combines the two passages (Cant. viii. 5 and vi. 10), " Who is this that cometh up from the wilderness, leaning upon her beloved, who looks forth as the morning, fair as the moon, clear as the sun, and terrible as an army with banners ? " Terrible as an army in the eyes of her enemies (ver. 1); fair as the moon, clear as the sun, when the reproach of Egypt is rolled away (ver. 9).

I. ISRAEL IS A TYPE OF THE CHURCH OF GOD IN HER WARFARE AGAINST SIN. When God's Church resolutely binds herself to the conflict with the powers of evil, their heart must needs melt, neither is there spirit in them any more. " Then Satan doth fear, his citadels fall," says the hymn. For the Church comes in the strength of her Lord. The " strong man armed " must have his " armour, wherein he trusted," taken from him, and the spoils of human souls which he has so industriously acquired must be divided, because " the stronger than he " has come upon him and bound him. Satan has no weapons for a hand-to-hand conflict with the Body of Christ. His weapons are to corrupt, to deceive, to persuade to a spirit of compromise with the world. So it has ever been that he has triumphed by corrupting the Church of God. Whenever God's disciples have gone forth to battle boldly and unflinchingly against evil, they have been victorious. They first humbled impurity and licentiousness, as well as unbelief. If they did not destroy these enemies of the soul, they at least compelled them to hide their heads, to shrink into corners, to admit unwillingly the superiority of purity and faith by ceasing to parade sins of this kind openly before the world. Next came the conflict with brute violence, which was kept in awe by the sacred character of the ministers of religion. Shameless and cynical effrontery in vice among those very ministers of religion, when the Church became corrupt, was next put down, even in spite of the weapons of force and temporal authority. So in later days a good cause has ever been victorious against the most overwhelming odds, when it has been prosecuted with perseverance and faith. Witness the abolition of slavery, first here, and next in America, so that even the Portuguese themselves, once the most hardened offenders in this respect, are now offering their co-operation with the English to put it down. So, again, the voice of God's faithful ones has spoken, and men dare not now stand up to take away one another's lives in this Christian land for a few hasty words, spoken without reflection. This may embolden us when we take up our weapons of prayer and holy exhortation to denounce the sins that yet remain among us—the reproach of intemperance, the scandalous opium traffic by which the revenue of India is largely supported, our commercial dishonesty, and all the other reproaches of our age. Against these must the Church of Christ gird on her armour, and never cease to wage a conflict, until the promised day shall come, when "the earth shall be full of the knowledge of the glory of the Lord, as the waters cover the sea." But one caution must be borne in mind. When we buckle on our armour afresh to contend against our enemies, we must first cross our Jordan. We must solemnly, that is, sever ourselves from the wayward and wandering past. Like Daniel (chap. ix.), we must "speak, and pray, and confess our sin, and the sin of our people." And then we must solemnly renew our covenant, our broken covenant, with God. Then may we advance without fear to the attack, and if Jesus be our leader, the battle may be long, but we cannot fail to have victory in the end.

II. ISRAEL IS A TYPE OF THE INDIVIDUAL SOUL IN THE SAME WARFARE. Just as in the case of the Church, so in the case of the individual, must there be the moment of conversion, the settled and deliberate resolve to break with the past, and the passage, under the guidance of the ark of the covenant, the law of God, and the conscience, the sign of His presence in the heart, into the condition of fellowship with God. Then must come the solemn renewal of the covenant, the circumcision of the heart, the mortifying of the flesh, the cutting off even those innocent enjoyments which have been found dangerous in times past, through the weakness of the flesh. Then the feast by faith upon the flesh and blood of the true Paschal Lamb, the making memorial of our deliverance through Him from a cruel bondage, and then we must prepare for the assault. Nor need we fear defeat. Satan trembles when he sees us determined. His heart melts within him as he sees us advancing under the leadership of Jesus, the Captain of our salvation, and as long as we are resolute in the strife, the victory is secure. Yet it is not always won in the same manner. Some sins fall like Jericho, by the might of prayer. Some, like Ai, when evil has obtained a lodgment within, are only overcome after a shameful humiliation, repaired by a firm determination to put away the secret defilement. Others, like the rest of the cities which Joshua destroyed, will only succumb after a determined and persevering resistance. But the result is the same in the end. "No weapon that is formed against thee shall prosper," if thou art only steadfast in following wherever Jesus leads. "Terrible as an army is she who cometh up out of the wilderness, leaning on the arm of her beloved."

III. WORLDLY WISDOM MUST BE LAID ASIDE WHEN WE HAVE TO BATTLE WITH SIN. Nothing could be more foolish, humanly speaking, than for Joshua to have ordered a general circumcision of the children of Israel at this time. Simeon and Levi (Gen. xxxiv. 25) had taken advantage of this moment to overcome the Shechemites. And, leaving God out of the question, if the inhabitants of the land had descended upon the Israelites at the moment of their helplessness, they would have been sure of an easy victory. But these Israelites were under the protection of God. He could have worked another miracle to protect them from their enemies, as easily as He had brought them over Jordan. But He worked no miracle this time. He inspired terror into the minds of the inhabitants of Canaan, so that they dare not attack them. They were quite safe under His protection, as long as they obeyed His voice. This should teach us—

1. *Not to slight the means of grace.* "Circumcision is nothing and uncircumcision is nothing, but the keeping of the commandments of God." And yet it is equally true that he who refused to be circumcised as God had commanded him, "that soul" was to be "cut off from his people." So in these days, those who "forsake the assembling of themselves together," who make light of Christian baptism, who neglect the Lord's Supper, who treat with disdain the ordinances set up by lawful authority in the Church, who kick at authority and despise reproof, shall not be unpunished.

2. *Not to combat sin with worldly weapons.* Such maxims as "honesty is the best policy," and other similar ones which put the practice of virtue upon grounds of success in this life and worldly convenience, will always fail us at the critical

moment. Let the temptation be only strong enough; let it only be clearly more to our advantage at the moment when we are assailed to yield than to resist, and the " cunning bosom sin " (George Herbert) will " blow away " all that " array " of " fences" which worldly wisdom has set around our actions. Nothing but the rooted conviction, " Thou God seest me ; " nothing but the question, " How can I do this great wickedness and sin against God ? " will be powerful enough to defeat the assaults of sin in cases of secret overwhelming temptation. If that is not motive strong enough, nothing will be. Had the Israelites omitted to fence themselves with the protection of God's covenant, their prudence would not have availed them against the overwhelming numbers of their adversaries. But confidence that they were in the keeping of a higher power led them to consecrate themselves first to God, and then to go out to battle against His enemies and theirs.

3. *Not to neglect our duty for fear of consequences.* No one could have been under a greater temptation to do this than Joshua. By his obedience he was placing himself and his people in a position of the most imminent peril. Yet we hear of no hesitation. He does what he ought to do as a matter of course. Faith is weaker with the great mass of professing Christians than it was with Joshua. Both in public and private affairs men continually plead the urgency of the case as an excuse for a slight dereliction of duty. This is the case (a) in affairs of State. And this is especially the case when the duty is what is (though erroneously) called a *religious* duty. Thus in India, some years ago, our missionaries were discouraged in their efforts, because it was supposed that British authority would be endangered by their successes. The opium traffic, above referred to, is defended on the ground of the evils to India which would result from a financial deficit. We sometimes hear " British interests" put above duty. Yet without attempting to decide whether this has been so in any given case, the broad general principle must be laid down that no fear of consequences to our vast and most valuable power ought to induce us, as a nation, to take one single step that cannot be defended on the grounds of abstract justice. We may be certain that in the long run the most conscientious policy will be the most advantageous. Yet even if not, "let justice be done, though the heavens should fall." We find the same tendency at work (b) in the affairs of the Church. Those who are in high office in the Church often display over-timidity from the sense of the grave responsibility that action throws upon them. Nor should such a sense of responsibility be absent. Yet where duty is clear there is no responsibility at all. Consequences in such a case should not be weighed. They may sometimes—though not so often as is supposed—serve to help in the decision where duty lies. But they cannot be pleaded as an excuse for neglecting duty. Lastly (c), we come to the case of private persons, and we find the same tendency at work. The tradesman or professional man adopts the commercial morality of his fellows, whether it be right or wrong, and says that he shall be ruined if he does not. Let him take example by Joshua.

IV. The solemn renewal of the covenant was a renewal of its responsi-bilities and blessings. The covenant of circumcision had its spiritual mean-ing, which Moses as well as St. Paul pointed. " Circumcise therefore the foreskin of your head."

1. *It was a covenant of mortification.* It implied the restraint of the lusts of the flesh by a painful process. This is to be the Christian's daily work. In the place of comfort, luxury, and ease, we are to be the disciples of Him who "had not where to lay his head." The promptings of our lower nature are constantly to be kept in check. Strict and severe moderation in all allowed comforts is our duty. Even our leisure and our recreations must often be broken in upon by the thought of the needs of those for whom Christ died, and for whom He would have us live. " Christ suffered for us, leaving us an example that ye should follow his steps." The Christian life, therefore, is incompatible with self-indulgence.

2. *It was a covenant of warfare.* The covenant was solemnly renewed on the entrance into the promised land. But it was understood that, before the blessings of that land could be enjoyed, every nation that inhabited it must be extirpated. In like manner the Christian is pledged to an unceasing warfare with sin.

3. *The covenant, once broken, could be renewed when the Israelites were willing to renew it.* And so it is with the Christian. He may cast himself out of the favour of God by his disobedience. But God yearns after him, and, as in the parable of the prodigal son, sees him when "yet a great way off," and runs to meet him. Only there must be the willingness to endure the restraints of the covenant. The step to reconciliation is circumcision. That is, we cannot be reconciled to God until we have sincerely resolved to "mortify and kill all vices;" to live a hard and self-denying life; to be watchful against the flesh and its tyranny, and to devote ourselves heart and soul to the service of our Master, with all its grievous restraints upon self-pleasing and self-interest.

4. *The renewal of the covenant removed the reproach of Egypt.* The Scriptures of both the Old and New Testament are full of God's mercy to penitent sinners. "Is Ephraim my dear son? Is he a pleasant child? For since I spake against him I do earnestly remember him still" (Jer. xxxi. 20). "Bring forth the best robe, and put it on him: . . . for this my son was dead, and is alive again; he was lost, and is found" (Luke xv. 22—24). The past is forgotten when the sinner turns to God. "Their sins and iniquities will I remember no more." "Ye were as sheep going astray, but are now returned unto the Shepherd and Bishop of your souls" (1 Pet. ii. 25. See also 2 Cor. v. 17—21; Eph. ii. 1—6, &c.). We may approach God in all confidence as our loving Father (Eph. ii. 18; iii. 12); not from any trust in our own merits, but because we are "accepted in the beloved" (Eph. i. 6).

HOMILIES BY VARIOUS AUTHORS.

Vers. 6—11.—Circumcision and the passover were the two sacraments of the old covenant. The first set forth the truth that enrolment among the people of God must be accompanied with the putting away of evil. The second represented the past deliverance from the bondage of Egypt, and the future deliverance from all the perils of the wilderness by entrance into Canaan, and the final possession of the land of promise. On the eve of the decisive conflict, God commands His people to make a solemn renewal of these two covenants. Israel must be afresh consecrated to Him by that covenant of circumcision which symbolises holiness by the crucifixion of the flesh, and by that passover feast, which is at once the symbol of past and future deliverances. Thus also should the Christian gird himself for the conflict of the spiritual life. When he enlists under the banner of his God, he ought, as it were, to renew his baptismal vows, by what St. Peter calls "the answer of a good conscience," thus dedicating himself to God in the renunciation of all the defilements of sin, by that circumcision of the heart which was the deep truth signified by the old fleshly rite. And further, by partaking of the Christian passover feast, he should testify his entire trust in redeeming love by receiving this most sacred pledge of love, and deriving from it the needed renewal of spiritual strength. That which is true of the individual Christian is true also of the Church. It requires to be constantly baptized afresh with the Spirit of God, and to receive the pledges and seals of the grace of redemption, as a preparation for its spiritual conflicts. There is one remarkable feature in the sacred narrative. It is said that on the occasion of this first passover celebrated beyond the Jordan, the Israelites "did eat of the old corn of the land" (ch. v. 10, 11). Thus they not only had in this feast a pledge of the promised deliverance, BUT AN EARNEST OF THE GOOD THINGS TO COME. They not only had a fresh guarantee of the promise, but a beginning of its fulfilment. The same thing is true of the Christian sacrament. While it is an essentially spiritual feast, it still gives in part that which it sets forth and symbolises. Faith receives the Holy Spirit in baptism, and feeds upon the invisible Christ in the Lord's Supper. Christ is to the soul "the living bread which came down from heaven" (John vi. 31). Thus even before the Jordan is crossed, the Christian soul eats of the corn of the land of promise.—E. DE P.

Vers. 9, 10.—*Sacramental consecration of life.* We may with advantage linger over the story of this chapter. It has lessons which will never die, and appeals which will never grow old. It is a testimony against a form of evil so common and so dangerous that all branches of the Church of Christ suffer from it. *It brings before us the question of the neglect of sacraments, and the wisdom of repairing that neglect. To bring the chief points before us, observe first—*

I. WE ARE PRONE TO NEGLECT THE SACRAMENTS OF GOD. The neglect reported here strikes us as very strange. With the great miracles in recollection which had accompanied their leaving Egypt, it should, we feel, have been impossible for them to have forgotten or disobeyed their God. But here we have the statement that the entire nation had neglected the sacramental circumcision; and the narrative leaves some uncertainty as to whether there had not been some irregularity in the observance of the passover as well. It is not easy to explain such neglect. Perhaps the first sacrament was overshadowed by the law given at Sinai, the pre-occupation with the new rites leading to the neglect of the old. The more so as, excepting the precept implied in the word, "No uncircumcised person shall eat thereof," there was no precept given at Sinai concerning this rite. Probably the neglect of the one carried with it the neglect of the other. Possibly some sullenness and dissatisfaction with the length of their desert wanderings intensified this feeling. However that may be, here we have the fact that beneath the eyes of the law-giver the people neglect the observance of one or both of these rites. It is not, I think, that they are under any interdict, as some have imagined. There is no trace of a prohibition to observe them. It seems to have been simple, sheer neglect. If we feel it strange they should neglect these rites, we ought to feel it stranger still that they find so many to-day who resemble them in doing so. Like Israel, we have sacraments. As they had one for the individual confession of belonging to God, we have the rite of Baptism; as they had the social sacrament of the Passover, we have that of the Lord's Supper. But everywhere, from some reason or other, we see both neglected. Both meant to be observed by those who can make intelligently the avowals which they express, both are neglected. Sometimes, through carelessness and misconception, baptism will be neglected; but sometimes, merely because it is irksome, or because it seems not essential to salvation, or because it carries with it reproach for Christ, or involves responsibility, persons are found neglecting the rite of baptism, which the Saviour meant them to observe. And for much the same reasons the other, the social sacrament, is neglected. Around every Christian Church there is a fringe composed of persons alive to the glory of the gospel who yet shrink from the formal rites of covenant with God. How much they lose by it, none can tell. The mental clearness; the safety that lies in a well-defined position; the higher purpose; the greater ease with which the confession of Christ is made and the denial of Christ avoided; the closer and firmer fellowship with God's saints, with all its quickening influences— these are all forfeited by the dull neglect of a blessed rite. And how much the Church and the world lose by their lukewarmness, by their refusal of service, by their unintentional but serious influence in abating the spirit of religious earnestness! Of these they never think. It is more agreeable to the indolence of their natures, or the timidity of their hearts, to abstain from all avowals; and so, like Israel, they neglect the sacraments of God. Let those guilty of such action remember that the sacraments are commandments which cannot be neglected without sin on the one hand and danger on the other. Secondly observe—

II. GOD PERMITS US TO REPAIR OUR NEGLECT AND ENTER INTO COVENANT WITH HIM. It is a marvellous thing that we should be permitted to enter into covenant with God; that in rites in which all the promises made are made by Him, not by us, He should bind Himself to be our redeeming God; that in the one sacrament He should make offer of cleansing from all guilt, and in the other of the bread of immortal life. It is a matter more marvellous still that to those who have neglected those rites for stretches of years He yet extends the permission to approach them. But so it is. Here is an illustration of this willingness. He had little hope of much honour or satisfaction from Israel. They would be a rebellious and gain-saying people through all their future. Yet here He allows them again to resume their relation to Him, to "lay hold on his covenant." It is no slight mercy to us that God is willing still to enter into an "everlasting covenant with us, ordered in all things and sure." If now our neglect is regretted, let not despair prolong it. Whatever falseness to conscience we have been guilty of, He keeps the door open, and gives us what we have no title to expect—the opportunity to repair neglect. He lays it as a charge on all to observe these covenant rites, so that we cannot without being disobedient keep outside of a covenant relation to Him. Belong to the Church of the redeemed. Let the name of God and of the city of God be upon you. When God permits us to repair our neglect, let us do so. Thirdly observe—

III. ALL BEGINNING ANY NEW ENTERPRISE SHOULD BEGIN IT WITH GOD. Isreäl has a great task before it. He will do well to lay hold on God's strength to help him. The messenger of God's justice, he must himself be just. "They must be holy who bear the vessels of the Lord." Exposed to great strain and great difficulty, they act wisely to close with God, and gain Him on their side. In this we have lessons for several classes. First, for the young, and those beginning life. When life is yet all before you, and the struggle with your foes yet to come, join your redeeming God in solemn covenant. Many a life would have been saved from wreck had this been done. Save yours. You will be saved many a grief, and come safe out of every danger, if in the beginning of your career before leaving Gilgal you enter into sacramental covenant with your Saviour. Well begun is half done. And a good beginning of the better life secures its perfectest and easiest development. The earliest is always the most convenient season for the great religious decisions of life. (2) Those not young, but yet entering on some new career, some new set of experiences or duties or dangers, will always act wisely by consecrating the opening of a new career. Begin all things with God. His wisdom will preserve from error, and His power from all danger. Hallow the new undertaking, the enjoyment of the new mercy, the experience of the new trial, by getting closer to God. *Commence business life, commence married life, commence your life in a strange land, by special consecration.* Let all ponder these matters. Let those who have made, keep their sacramental vows, and those who have neglected make them; for while the Saviour is honoured by them and rejoices in them, their blessings on ourselves surpass all our conceptions.—G.

EXPOSITION.

CHAPTER V. 10—12.

THE PASSOVER AND THE CESSATION OF THE MANNA.—Ver. 10.—**And kept the passover.** In reference to the question which has been discussed above, whether the passover was kept after the rebellion at Kadesh-Barnea, Keil notices, as a remarkable fact, that not only no mention of a passover as having been kept is found in the Pentateuch, after Num. ix. 1, but there is not even any instance given of the law of sacrifice having been observed in the plains of Jericho; see above, ch. iv. 13. "Vides ergo quia nemo immundus facit pascha, nemo incircumcisus sed quicumque mundus fuerit et circumcisus, sicut et apostolus interpretatur dicens etenim pascha nostrum immolatus est Christus. Itaque diem festum celebremus non in fermento veteri, sed in azymis sinceritatis et veritatis" (Origen, Hom. 5, on Joshua). "When soldiers take the field,

they are apt to think themselves excused from religious exercises (they have not time nor thought to attend to them); yet Joshua opens the campaign with one act of devotion after another" (Matthew Henry).

Ver. 11.—**The old corn.** The *produce* of the land; literally, that which passes from off it, from עָבַר to pass over. Whether new or old we have no means of telling. The barley would be ripe (see note on ch. ii. 6), but the wheat harvest had not yet taken place. **The morrow after the sabbath.** The 15th Nisan (see Num. xxxiii. 3). The law of the wave sheaf (Levit. xxiii. 10, 11) was intended to apply to corn raised by the Israelites on their own land, after Canaan had been divided to them for an inheritance (see Exod. xxiii. 16). **And parched corn;** *i.e.,* ears roasted at the fire, and the grain afterwards rubbed out, a custom still in use among the Arabs (see Levit. ii. 14; 1 Sam.

xvii. 17; 2 Sam. xvii. 28, &c. See also for the precept here followed, Levit. xxiii. 14). This verse therefore adds some confirmation to the view that until their arrival in Palestine a full observance of the precepts of the law was impossible (see above, ver. 6).

Ver. 12.—**The manna ceased.** It ceased when the Israelites entered a cultivated region. The eastern portion of their inheritance, though well suited for pastoral purposes (see ch. i. 12), was not a land of agricultural produce. Therefore the manna did not cease until the Israelites had crossed the Jordan.

HOMILETICS.

Vers. 10—12.—*The passover and the cessation of manna.*

I. THE RENEWAL OF THE COVENANT MUST BE ATTENDED WITH THE OBSERVANCE OF ITS LAWS. When the Christian desires to return and to serve God after a period of disobedience and rebellion, he must prepare himself, by repentance and mortification, to feed on the flesh of the slain Lamb of God in the sacrament which He has ordained. Thus he makes a memorial of the death of Christ, through which alone he has obtained pardon ; he feeds on the flesh and blood of the Son of God ; he applies to himself all the blessings which come from the Sacrifice of the Cross. And he moreover calls men to witness, by thus joining his brethren in the solemn celebration, of his intention to be henceforth an obedient servant of Christ. Thus he sets his seal to the vow of obedience which he has just made, he invokes the sympathy and assistance of his brethren in his recovery from the snare of Satan ; he binds himself to them anew in his renewed participation with them in the new life of the Spirit.

II. WHEN THE PROMISED LAND IS ENTERED, ALL EXTRAORDINARY DISPENSATIONS OF GOD'S PROVIDENCE CEASE. This is the case (1) in the history of the Christian Church, (2) in that of the individual.

1. *In the history of the Church.* Nothing is more remarkable than the way in which all the miraculous gifts of God, healing, prophecy, the working of miracles, ceased when Jesus Christ had ascended into heaven. Up to His coming the world had been under tutors and governors, and the Father needed continually to intervene with revelations and portents, and interferences with the ordinary course of nature. After His coming these were gradually withdrawn. The Church passed from the region of the extraordinary dispensations of God's providence to the ordinary working of His laws. Before those laws were fully matured, there needed perpetual interferences to compensate for their imperfection. His whole counsel once made known in Christ, the laws of the spiritual, like those of the natural world move on in their regular course.

2. *In the history of the individual.* When man is wandering in the wilderness, an alien from the covenant of God, and out of His favour, he is not under the ordinary dispensations of God's grace. He is kept alive, so far as he lives at all, by unexpected manifestations of His mercy. Smitings of conscience, restraints of circumstances, checks imposed in unexpected ways to the unrestrained indulgence of his passions, prevent him from dying a miserable death in a land where no bread or water is. But when he returns to the fold of God these extraordinary manifestations are vouchsafed no longer. There are the ordinary supplies of grace to be obtained in God's Church—the treasures of God's Holy Word, the answers to daily public and private prayer, the uplifting of the heart which follows on the exercise of prayer and praise, the outpouring of Divine life which follows on the devout reception of Holy Communion. And all these have their blessed results in a steady growth in grace. The miraculous manna ceases. In its stead we eat of the old corn of the heavenly Canaan, in which we find ourselves placed by the loving-kindness of the Lord.

III. THE PASSOVER MUST NOT BE EATEN BY THE UNCIRCUMCISED. Hence we learn that no one can spiritually feed on Christ who is harbouring unrepented sin. Such an one is not fit to come to the Christian Passover, the Sacrament of Holy Communion. He may " carnally and visibly press the sacrament with his teeth, yet is he in nowise partaker of Christ." He who would feed on "Christ our Passover," who "has been sacrificed for us," must do so with the unleavened bread of purity (εἰλικρινεία) and truth. And finally, none can sit down at the marriage supper of the Lamb save he that hath on the wedding garment. Compare the rules for the passover in Exod. xii. 43—49; and Num. ix. 10—14.

HOMILIES BY VARIOUS AUTHORS.

Ver. 12.—*The special and the customary.* This verse is one of the proofs that the supply of manna was miraculous, ceasing as it did at the exact moment when it was no longer needed. Other proofs are, that a double portion fell each Friday, and none on the Sabbath; and that if kept longer than a day it became corrupt and stank, except on the day of rest, when it remained pure and wholesome. Let us look at—

I. MANNA, AS A SPECIAL PROVISION FOR A SPECIAL EXIGENCY. 1. The exigency shows us that *even under the guidance of God there is no exemption from trial.* At first all had seemed easy and comfortable. Passing through the sea as on dry ground, the Israelites soon beheld their late tyrants dead on the seashore. The bitter waters of Marah were sweetened and Elim furnished its wells and palm-trees for their refreshment. A month passed. The dough cakes were nearly finished, and provisions began to fail. The murmuring of fear and discontent was heard. Those whom the sea had not devoured quaked lest the hungry wilderness should destroy them. Forgetting the tasks and bondage of Egypt, they remembered only its flesh-pots, garlic, onions, and bread, and now they could wish rather to have died in ravenous plenty than live in noble penury. The Almighty will thus prove His people. He does not always conduct them by easy roads, for He values the discipline of their spirits more than the external comfort of their bodies. Faith is to be tested that it may come forth as " gold tried in the fire." 2. The provision assures us that *under the leadership of God all real wants will be supplied.* The glory of the Lord had appeared in the cloud. Quails—feathered fowl—were sent in the evening, and in the morning, manna—bread from heaven. God would not suffer His people to remain in absolute need. He would give them the "finest of the wheat," and "honey out of the rock." They should have the bread of angels and the meat of kings. Infinite wisdom and might sit on the throne, and these are engaged for the believer's support. The light may flicker, it shall not be extinguished; or if ordinary sources of relief fail, other springs shall be discovered. " Your heavenly Father knoweth that ye have need of all these things." The gift by God of His beloved Son to die for the world is the transcendent example of God's benevolence. Christ is the true Manna, which satisfies the hunger of the soul. Christianity, or the scheme of redemption, is the remedy which Eternal Love has devised to meet the emergency of a sin-stricken world hastening to ruin.

II. THE CESSATION OF THE MIRACULOUS SUPPLY teaches us—1. *Not to expect to be furnished directly from God with what He enables us to procure by our own exertions.* Apparently the inhabitants of the land had fled for refuge to Jericho and the neighbouring towns, abandoning to the Israelites the harvest ripening in the fields and the old stores housed in the granaries. The Almighty economises His acts. Extraordinary occurrences are for extraordinary needs. We see in the life of Christ that He would not perform wondrous works merely to gratify inordinate curiosity or to satisfy the demands of unreasonable scepticism. The lesson of realising our responsibilities is important. It will not do to indolently expect the Divine providence and power to supply the lack of human effort. Prayer and work must go together. Not only faith is necessary, but exertion, if the Divine purposes are to be accomplished. If on a specially appointed mission our Father may take care of us as He does of the birds of the air, it is ordinarily our duty to " sow and reap and gather into barns," but without anxiety or corroding care. 2. *To be thankful for a return to ordinary ways and means.* The Israelites got tired even of "angels' food;" they loathed "this light bread," with all its sweetness. As at present constituted, variety is pleasing to men. Certainly man is not yet fitted for the splendours and employments of the beatific state. Moses and Elijah spent many days on the mount with God, but probably a return to earthly scenes was essential to their continued life. When glorified, man may be able to live entirely on the manna of heaven, the life hidden with Christ in God. In seasons of affliction wondrous revelations are sometimes granted; there is a support given which raises the soul above the surrounding sorrow, causing it to exclaim, "It is good to be here!" Deprived of the usual ordinances and channels of consolation, the Spirit ministers of the things of God, illumines the sacred page, makes the promise of Christ's presence a fulfilled reality. Nevertheless, it rejoices the Christian to be permitted to resume wonted occupations and to enjoy the customary privileges. To revel for a time in the glorious scenery of the Alps does not diminish the satisfaction with which we behold again the quiet beauty of our much-loved home. As the ceremonies connected with the passover were renewed, the exchange of manna for ordinary corn was at least fitting, if not absolutely necessary. 3. *The duty of keeping in remembrance past displays of the might and compassion of God.* According to Exod. xvi. 32, a (golden) pot was to be filled with manna and deposited in the ark as a memorial of grace and favour received in the wilderness. Naught more treacherous than the memory. The picture of the past is a dissolving view that grows fainter daily until it disappears from sight. To remember what the Almighty has done is pleasing to Him and beneficial to us. It rebukes ingratitude and faithlessness. Hence the need of erecting our altars, which shall call to mind continually the blessings which have been bestowed.

III. The different form which God's interpositions assumed, varying according to the requirements of His people. The following verses narrate the appearance of Jehovah to Joshua, and the instructions given respecting the siege of Jericho. The stoppage of the manna nowise implied the withdrawal of the Divine presence. The toils of the wilderness were left behind, the dangers of Palestine commenced Help must be afforded by different means. And the Christian life calls into prominence certain principles at certain crises. To-day we want food, to-morrow weapons; to-day strength, to-morrow guidance; now hope, then charity. We are variously tested; and manifold are the aids of the Divine Spirit; thus a perfect character is cultured. The text speaks to us of the everlasting rest into which we hope to enter. It shall be a Sabbath in which we shall live on the principles which were made ours during the working week, and it shall also be a Canaan where we shall no longer need the food of the wilderness. Faith, as trustful love, shall survive for ever, whilst faith, as believing hope, shall vanish in glorious sight and full fruition. What a Passover shall that be when the Supper of the Lamb is celebrated! The intermediary dispensation shall terminate. "Then cometh the end, when he shall have delivered up the kingdom to God, even the Father." Can we anticipate with joy the renouncing of the life on earth for a life beyond the grave? "He that eateth me," said Christ, "shall live for ever." "To him that overcometh will I give to eat of the hidden manna."—A.

EXPOSITION.

CHAPTER V. 13—15.

Ver. 13.—**When Joshua was by Jericho.** The preposition בְ, the principal meaning of which is "in," signifies here "in the immediate neighbourhood of," as in 1 Sam. xxix. 1 (where, however, the LXX. read "*in Endor*"), Ezek. x. 15. Perhaps Joshua had ascended some hill in the close vicinity of the city to reconnoitre it alone, and here he

received the directions which resulted in the miraculous capture of the city (see also Gen. xiii. 18, where בְּאֵלֹנֵי cannot mean "in the oaks," nor בְּחֶבְרוֹן "in Hebron"). The LXX. translates the first by παρὰ τὴν δρῦν. The Vulgate has "juxta" (cf. Gen. xiv. 13). Origen is much hampered in his exposition here by the translation "in." He asks how Jericho can possibly be holy ground when it is still in the possession of the enemy; and answers ingeniously that wherever the captain of the Lord's host is must needs be holy ground). **He lift up his eyes.** Usually, though not always (cf. Gen. xiii. 10), used of an unexpected or marvellous sight (see Gen. xviii. 2; xxii. 13; Num. xxiv. 2; 1 Sam. vi. 13; 1 Chron. xxi. 16). **A man.** This Divine or angelic vision came, as was often the case, in human shape (cf. Gen. xviii. 1, 2; xix. 1, 2, 10; xxxii. 24; Judg. xiii. 3, 6, 11; Daniel x. 16, 18; xii. 6, 7. See note on next verse). **With his sword drawn in his hand.** As in Num. xxii. 31; 1 Chron. xxi. 16 (cf. Gen. iii. 24). **And Joshua went unto him and said.** It appears from this, says Calvin, that Joshua was alone, and was prepared to fight with the apparition, if it appeared that he had fallen in with an enemy. For at first, unexpected as the appearance was, he recognised nothing supernatural in it.

Ver. 14.—**And he said, Nay.** Many MSS. which are followed by the LXX. and Syriac versions, have לוֹ for לֹא here. The Chaldee and Vulgate read לֹא, and the Masorites do not reckon this among the 15 passages in which לוֹ is read for לֹא (Keil). But when Keil adds that a comparison of this passage with ch. xxiv. 21 decides the point, he is going too far, since כִּי often stands, like the Greek ὅτι, before a quotation, in the place of our inverted commas (see, for instance, Gen. xxix. 33; Exod. iii. 12, &c.). The various reading has no doubt arisen from the ambiguity of the passage, for it appears grammatically doubtful to which part of Joshua's question the particle of negation applies. Yet it is obvious enough practically that it is in answer to the last portion of it. **But as captain of the Lord's host am I now come.** Literally, "*for* (or *but*) *I, the captain of the Lord's host, have now come.*" As though he would say, "the struggle is now imminent; the conflict is all but begun; and now, at the critical moment when my help is needed, I, the captain of the hosts of the Lord, the leader of all that vast army of unseen confederates, who are destined to marshal the forces of nature, the elements of supernatural terror and dismay, on the side of the Israelites, am come to help you." That the Lord's host must mean the angels is clear from such passages as Gen. xxxii. 2; 1 Kings xxii. 19; Psa. ciii. 20, 21; cxlviii. 2; St. Luke ii. 13 (cf. 2 Kings vi. 17). Hengstenberg, in his 'Christology,' illustrates by Matt. xxvi. 53. Two opinions have been held by the early Church concerning this manifestation. The first regards it as the appearance of the Son of God in a visible form; the second sup-

poses it to have been a created being—an angel—through whom Jehovah was pleased to manifest Himself. The former opinion was general in the earliest ages of the Church. The appearance of the Arian heresy, however, brought this interpretation into discredit. It was felt to be dangerous to admit it, lest it should lead to the notion that the Logos, however great and glorious a being he might be, however superior to all other created beings, was nevertheless removed by an infinite interval from the Supreme God Himself. The Jewish interpreters differ on the point. Maimonides and others (see next note) do not regard the appearance as a real one. The majority seem to have supposed it to have been the Archangel Michael. We will proceed to examine the scriptural and patristic evidence on the subject. That appearances, believed to be manifestations of God Himself in a visible form, are recorded in Scripture, is a fact which cannot be denied. Thus we have the voice of God (קוֹל יְהוָֹה) walking in the garden (Gen. iii. 8). Again, in ch. xv., though first God appears to Abraham in a vision, the nature of the manifestation would seem to have changed in some respects afterwards, for we read " he brought him forth abroad " (ver. 5). Again, in ch. xviii., we find that Jehovah " appeared " to Abraham as he dwelt by the oaks of Mamre (ver. 1), and the narrative would suggest that Jehovah Himself appeared, and two attendant angels. This is further corroborated by the fact that Abraham remains in conference with Jehovah, while the two angels who arrived in the evening at Sodom do not appear to have been spoken of as Jehovah, or to have received Divine honours from Lot. The " man " who (Gen. xxxii. 24) wrestled with Jacob is described afterwards (ver. 30) as " God." The " angel of the Lord " who (Exod. iii. 2) " appeared " unto Moses " in a flame of fire, out of the midst of a bush," is immediately afterwards described as Jehovah and Elohim (ver. 4), and, as in the present passage, Moses is instructed to remove his shoe from his foot in consequence of the holiness of the place in which so great a Being appeared. And here we are led to investigate the nature of that mysterious being who is described as " the angel of the Lord," the " angel," or, as the word is sometimes translated, " messenger of the covenant." He appears to Hagar (Gen. xvi. 7), and she immediately proceeds (ver. 13) to express her belief that it is God whom she has seen. The angel who appears to Abraham at the sacrifice of Isaac (Gen. xxii. 11, 12, 18) speaks of Himself as God. The voice of the angel, again, is regarded by Leah and Rachel as the voice of God (Gen. xxxi. 11, 16), and He calls Himself so (ver. 13). Jacob speaks of the angel as having "redeemed him from all evil" (Gen. xlviii. 16), but here the term Göel, though it means a ransomer, is not necessarily connected with *moral* evil. After His appearance to Moses in the bush He becomes the special guide of the children of Israel. His divinity is again asserted in Exod. xiii. 21, for the Being there spoken of as Jehovah is described in ch. xiv. 19 as His angel. The solemn terms in which the God of Israel refers to him in Exod. xxiii. 20, 21 must not be passed over. He is the "Angel of Jehovah." He is sent to "keep" Israel "in the way." They were to take heed and not rebel against Him (so LXX.); for, adds Jehovah, "My name is in His inward parts" (not בּוֹ but בְּקִרְבּוֹ denoting close and intimate union). Cf. ver. 23 and Exod. xxxii. 34; xxxiii. 2. This angel is called the Face, or Faces, of the Lord (Exod. xxxiii. 14; cf. Isa. lxiii. 9), and is thus specially identified with the revelation of Him, like the term εἰκών in the New Testament. The angel that withstood Balaam assumes a tone of authority in harmony with this view (Num. xxii. 22—35). Whether the angel at Bochim (Judg. ii. 1) were a Divine or human messenger does not appear from the narrative, and the word is occasionally, as in Hag. i. 13, used of a prophet. But the appearance to Gideon and Manoah has a Divine character (Judg. vi. 11—22; xiii. 8—22). And the special reference to Jehovah, the angel of the covenant, in Mal. iii. 1 seems to point in a special manner to the Second Person in the Blessed Trinity. This view, as has been stated, is the view of the earlier Fathers, nor does there seem any reasonable ground for its rejection by those of later date. The idea that the Logos, always the medium of the Father's revelation and impartation of Himself, in creation as in redemption, frequently took a visible form under the old dispensation in order to communicate the Divine will to mankind, does not in the least militate against the doctrine of His consubstantiality with the Father. On the contrary, it rather emphasises the fact which the New Testament teaches us throughout, that the Logos was ever the manifestation, the ἐξήγησις (John i.) of the Father, the eternal medium whereby He communicates Himself beyond Himself. This was in the main the view of the earliest Fathers. They might use an incautious expression now and then, but they ever intended to be true to the doctrine of the Consubstantial Son of the Father, who took a visible shape to convey the Father's mind to man. Thus Justin Martyr ('Dial. cum Tryphone,' 56)

cites Gen. xviii. 1, 2 to prove that, as he says, "there is another God under (ὑπὸ) the the Creator of all things, who is called an angel because he announces (ἀγγέλειν) whatever the Creator of all things desires him to announce." This being, he adds, "was also God before the creation of the world." He was another God than the Creator of the world in number (ἀριθμῷ), not in mind (γνώμῃ). And from the expression "the Lord rained down fire and brimstone from the Lord out of heaven" (Gen. xix. 24), he deduces the belief that this Being was "Lord from beside (παρά) the Lord who is in heaven." He proceeds to cite the passages from the Old Testament which have just been mentioned, and to draw from them the conclusion which has just been drawn, that this Being was one who ministered (ὑπηρετοῦντα) to God who is above; the word, the ἀρχή whom He begat before all creation (sec. 60, 61). Similarly Theophilus ('Ad Autolycum,' ii. 22) says that the Word of God held a colloquy with Adam in the person (or representation, προσώπῳ) of God. Irenæus ('Adv. Haer.,' iv. 7, 4) speaks of the Being who spake to Abraham at Mamre and Moses in the bush as superior to all created angels, and as, in fact, the Word of God; though afterwards (ch. xx. 11) he modifies this statement into a manifestation of "claritatem et dispositiones patris," "secundum dispositionum ejus causas sive efficaciam." It is to be remembered that we unfortunately chiefly possess Irenæus in a very unsatisfactory Latin dress. Similar passages may be found in Clem., 'Alex. Pæd.,' i. 7; and Tertullian, 'Adv. Prax.,' 14. The latter says that God was "invisible as the Father, but visible as the Son," the latter being the means whereby the former was revealed. The passage from Clement is embodied and improved upon in a passage in the 'Apostolic Constitutions,' which presents the primitive doctrine on this point in clearer language than any other. "To Him (Christ) did Moses bear witness, and said, ' The Lord received fire from the Lord, and rained it down.' Him did Jacob see as a man, and said, ' I have seen God face to face, and my soul is preserved.' Him did Abraham entertain, and acknowledge to be the Judge and his Lord. Him did Moses see in the bush. Him did Joshua the son of Nun see, as captain of the Lord's host, for assistance against Jericho" ('Apost. Const.,' v. 20). One passage more will be cited on this point. "Who else," says Origen, in his Homily on this passage, "is the prince of the host of the virtues of the Lord, save our Lord Jesus Christ?" "Joshua would not have adored," he adds, "unless he had recognised God." The fact that the later Fathers (St. Augustine, for instance, and Theodoret, who holds that it was Michael the Archangel who appeared to Joshua) rejected this interpretation would not be sufficient to outweigh primitive testimony at once so explicit and so general, unless it were supported by the strongest arguments. The fact that it was rejected rather from prudential motives, and that such prudence was, in point of fact, entirely unnecessary, robs the later interpretation of much of its weight. Thus much at least is certain, that we may adopt the earlier one without fear of prejudicing thereby the doctrine of the divinity of Christ. Further information on this point will be found in Hengstenberg's 'Christology,' in Liddon's 'Bampton Lectures' (Lect. ii.), in Bull ('Defens. Fid. Nicen.,' i. 1), and in Keil's Commentaries upon the various passages of the Old Testament, cited above. "He here appeared as a soldier, with His sword drawn in His hand. To Abraham in his tent He appeared as a traveller; to Joshua in the field, as a man of war. Christ will be to His people what their faith expects and desires" (Matthew Henry). **And Joshua fell on his face.** The apparition had no doubt taken Joshua by surprise. He believed himself to be alone, when suddenly he found himself confronted by a warrior, with his sword drawn. Uncertain, in those days when Divine interposition was more common than it is now, whether what he saw was a proof that he was watched by enemies, who had resolved to cut him off by surprise, or whether God had vouchsafed to appear to him, but evidently quite prepared to expect the latter, he addresses a question to the apparition, which of itself implies at least a half-belief that what he saw was something above nature. He needs but the simple reply just recorded to lead him to prostrate himself in simple faith before the Mighty One who now stood before him, to be the defence and shield of His people from all their adversaries. Maimonides, in his 'Moreh Nevochim,' and others (as, for instance, Hengstenberg, 'Geschichte des Reiches Gottes,' p. 209) have regarded this as a vision seen by Joshua when he was alone, plunged in deep meditation on the difficult task before him. But without denying that many of the Divine interpositions

recorded in Scripture (as, for instance, that in Gen. xxii. 1) took place through the inner workings of the mind as the medium of their action, yet here, as in Gen. xxxii., and most probably in Exod. iii., we have visible appearances of God to men in deep anxiety of heart, pondering "great matters" which were "too high for them." Whether we choose to accept or reject the historical narrative as a whole, there can be no rational ground for doubting that the Hebrew historians wrote under the full persuasion that they and their forefathers lived under a dispensation of continual Divine interpositions, sometimes taking place by secret inward intimations, sometimes through the Urim and Thummim; sometimes, at a crisis in the history of the nation or of an individual, by actual external appearances of God in a visible form, and that we have here an account of one of these. The purport of the appearance is, however, obscured by our present division of chapters. The narrative proceeds without a break as far as ch. vi. 5. Ch. vi. 1 is simply parenthetical and explanatory. Thus we gather that Joshua was meditating the plan of his future campaign, and deliberating on the best mode of capturing the strong walled city close by which (ver. 13) he stood, when God appeared to him in the form of a warrior, and solved all his doubts by commanding him to prepare for a miraculous intervention of His Providence, and in the place of warlike expedients to resort to a religious ceremony, which should be the external token to all the surrounding nations that the invading host was under the protection of the Lord of heaven and earth; a fact of which they were more than half convinced by the supernatural passage of the Red Sea and the Jordan (see ch. ii. 10; vi. 1).

Ver. 15.—**Loose thy shoe from off thy feet.** Cf. Exod. iii. 6. We have here a clear proof (see also ch. vi. 2) that He who now spoke to Joshua was a Divine Person. The loosing the shoe from the feet is regarded by Origen and other patristic commentators as emblematic of the removal of worldly engagements and pollutions from the soul. **Now Jericho was straitly shut up.**

HOMILETICS.

Vers. 13—vi. 21.—*The vision and the command.* Three points demand our special attention in this passage. First, the apparition to Joshua; next, the command that was given him; and, lastly, the results of that command, the fall of the walls of Jericho, and the subsequent sack of the city. Each of these points yields important lessons.

I. HE WHO APPEARED WAS THE SON OF GOD. This seems the most probable conclusion from the foregoing notes, as also from the fact that Divine worship was paid to Him by His own command (cf. Rev. xix. 10; xxii. 8, 9). The Son of God was ever the link of communication between God and the external world. By Him God created it; through Him He has been for ever pleased to deal with it; He revealed the final dispensation of God's will to it; He shall come again to judge it. Under the patriarchs and the law He temporarily assumes a visible shape to communicate God's purposes to man; under the gospel He eternally retains the visible form of man to save the world. He was the Angel of the Old Covenant; He is no less the Angel or Messenger of the New. And by His Spirit He still reveals God's will to man, though no longer by means of a visible form. And thus the continuity of God's dealings with man is preserved. It is "one God who shall justify the circumcision by faith, and the uncircumcision through faith;" one God who has adopted the same means throughout, yet with ever-increasing efficiency, to bring man back to his obedience.

II. HE APPEARED WHEN JOSHUA HAD BEEN CAREFUL TO OBEY GOD'S COMMANDS. "To him that hath shall be given." Joshua had been careful to restore the broken covenant between Israel and Jehovah. He had then ordered a general celebration of the great Israelitish national festival. And having thus discharged his religious, he was now intent upon his worldly, duties, both of which he performed with an equal devotion to God's commands. He was, doubtless, now either reconnoitring the city, or lost in reflection how he should best capture it. Then appears the Captain of the Lord's host, and gives him full directions for his task. So to the Christian warrior against sin will the Son of God appear, and direct him in his task, when he has duly sought the Lord in the appointed ordinances of religion, and is seriously addressing himself to the task of battling with sin.

III. JOSHUA IS SURPRISED, BUT NOT DISMAYED, BY HIS APPEARANCE. He was in the way of duty, and he had been bidden (ch. i. 6, 9) to "be of good courage." Therefore he boldly questions the apparition, prepared to welcome him, if he proved to be a friend, to do battle with him if he turned out to be an enemy. God's dispensations often come to us in such doubtful guise that we are compelled to question with them. But whereas men are generally apt to be terrified when "beneath a frowning Providence" God "hides a smiling face," the boldness of Joshua should be our example. "The Lord is on my side, I will not fear what man doeth unto me" (Psa. cxviii. 6), should be the perpetual attitude of the Christian. Thus the true Joshua set His face as a flint to go up to Jerusalem (Mark x. 32; Luke ix. 51), careless of the dangers that awaited Him there. So when opposition or distress come upon us because of our religion, we should not fear. It is the Captain of the Lord's host come to aid us in our assault on some stronghold of sin. If we boldly go up to Him and question Him, He will tell us who He is.

IV. JOSHUA IS COMMANDED TO DO REVERENCE TO HIM WHO APPEARS TO HIM. The removal of the shoe from the foot, on entering a holy place, was in order that nothing that defiled should be brought in (see Rev. xxi. 27). So when Jesus appears to us to give us instructions concerning any great struggle that is impending over us, we must "lay aside every weight, and the sin which doth so easily beset us," and devote ourselves with single heart to the work that we have in hand. There must be no secondary motives, no worldly ambitions, no desire of gain or applause, cleaving to us as we buckle to our task. What these bring in their train we see in the case of Ai. In awe of the Divine Presence, and that we may duly receive the Divine commands, we must recognise the fact that we are on holy ground, and that God requires of us an absolute devotion to His will.

HOMILIES BY VARIOUS AUTHORS.

Vers. 13—15.—*The captain of the host.* As Moses, on entering on his mission, was favoured with a marvellous Divine manifestation (Exod. iii. 1—6), so with Joshua, now that he is about to make his first onslaught on the strongholds of the Canaanites. The angel of the Lord appeared to Moses in a flame of fire. God spoke to him from the midst of the bush that burned but was not consumed. The supernatural radiance was the vehicle of the Divine Presence. God clothed Himself with light as with a garment. The vision and the voice were alike wonderful. The apparition in Joshua's case was of a different kind. It was the common semblance of a man prepared for battle. There seems to have been nothing supernatural in his aspect, and nothing in Joshua's question indicates that he was startled or alarmed by what he saw, or that the Being who appeared before him was other to his view than a veritable flesh-and-blood warrior who was come to take his place on one side or the other of the conflict that was at hand. And yet as he gazed more intently upon the warrior form he must have discovered something in it that told him it was no mere "man"—some majesty of mien or look, some grandeur of the Spirit shining through the countenance. The form was that of a man, the eyes were "as a flame of fire." And it was in the consciousness that he stood in the immediate, though veiled, presence of Jehovah Himself, the Prince and Leader of His own hosts, that Joshua "fell to his face on the earth and did worship." In each of these cases the form of the manifestation was adapted to the circumstances of the time and the speciality of the Divine purpose. Moses was taught that the light of the Lord's presence should be with him and his people—a guide, a glory, a defence—and that through whatever fiery ordeal they might pass they should not be consumed. Joshua, whose heart might well quail and tremble at the prospect before him, was made to know that the Captain of a mightier host than his was with him, the sword of whose strength was drawn and ready for the fight. With such forces on his side victory must everywhere attend his steps. This "Captain of the Lord's host" we believe to be none other than the Eternal Son of God, whose function it has ever been to be the channel of communication from the infinite Father-Spirit—the "word" of His thought, the arm of His power—and whose appearances in the olden time in human and angelic forms were prophetic of His after manifestation in the flesh. This view makes the scene before us strikingly suggestive of the relation in which He stands towards His redeemed Church in its grand conflict with the evil powers of the world. Observe—

I. CHRIST'S PRESENCE WITH HIS PEOPLE. These miraculous manifestations give a tone of great solemnity to the history of the olden times, and invest the leading men of those times with an aspect of something like superhuman grandeur. But we greatly err if we fail to link those times with our own and those men with ourselves—if we look on these ancient records as relating to a condition of things altogether exceptional and foreign to our own experience. The remote and occasional miracle bears witness to the abiding, ever-present truth. God gave those signs and wonders that we might know Him to be always near in the fulness of His love and power. "The good will of him that dwelt in the bush" is the perpetual inheritance of the Church. The "Captain of the Lord's host" is ever going forth before His armies, and it is by the sharpness of His sword and the strength of His right arm they win all their victories. Distinguish between the miraculous form of the incident and the truth enshrined in it. The one belonged to that particular age, and was suited to its exigencies; the other belongs to every age, and meets the permanent necessities of all individual and social religious life. In the heightened spirituality and richer grace of our Christian times we have the substance which those mystic visions did but shadow forth. In place of startling signs and symbols we have Divine *words of promise*—appeals not to sense but to faith—awakening the intelligence, kindling the heart; words of assurance to the individual believer, "If any man love me," &c. (John xiv. 23); to the worshipping Church, "Where two or three are gathered together," &c. (Matt. xviii. 20); to all faithful heralds of gospel truth, "Lo, I am with you alway, even unto the end of the world" (Matt. xxviii. 20). No need of miraculous manifestations if our faith can grasp the full meaning of gracious words like these.

II. THE LORDSHIP OF CHRIST OVER THE HEAVENLY POWERS. "Captain of the host of the Lord"—*i.e.*, the angelic host. The profoundly interesting, and not altogether profitless, question of the relation of the angelic world to our humanity is opened up to us here. Angelic ministry in human affairs is a fact to which Old and New Testaments alike bear abundant witness. "Are they not all ministering spirits?" &c. (Heb. i. 14). Every age has had its "heirs of salvation," whose history, if we knew all its secrets, would illustrate this truth. Here, too, the supernatural wonders of the past inspire faith in the enduring reality. Why not believe that between us and the Infinite there is a glorious gradation of pure, personal spirit-life linked in kindly interest and helpful service with our own? The relation of *Christ*, however, to the angels is chiefly indicated. In what way these earlier manifestations of the Son of God, and His after assumption of our nature, may have affected the interests of their being, we know not. But their personal subjection to Him is made evident. "When he bringeth in the first-begotten into the world, he saith, And let all the angels of God worship him" (Heb. i. 6). The gospel and apostolic histories are full of proof of their subordination to his redeeming purpose. He leads the heavenly host—leads them in the great conflict with the foes of God and man. If our eyes were opened, as were the eyes of Elisha's servant, we should see that we are not so much alone as we sometimes suppose. The angels that "ascend and descend upon the Son of man" are powers that He sways by the impulse of His sovereign will and makes the instruments of His almighty love. Shall our hearts yield to fear when we know that such forces as these are fighting on our side? Shall we hesitate to follow the leading and obey the behests of the great "Captain of salvation," who has such armies as these at His command?

III. THE SANCTITY THAT BELONGS TO SCENES OF SPECIAL DIVINE MANIFESTATION. "Loose thy shoe," &c. The incarnation of Christ has consecrated all the earth and made every part of it hallowed ground. He has withdrawn again behind the veil, only to come more near to us, to fill all places with the energy of His viewless Spirit. But there are times when the veil seems to be uplifted; states of consciousness in which the Divine Presence is intensely real; manifestations that

> " Dissolve the soul in ecstasies,
> And bring all heaven before our eyes."

Shall we tread with thoughtless or irreverent feet the spots hallowed even by the memory of seasons such as these?—W.

Vers. 13—15.—*A soldier's interview with his captain.* It adds much to the general power of the Bible as an ethical handbook, that great part of its instruction is conveyed in the pleasing form of history, political and individual.

I. JOSHUA'S ANXIETY. Gilgal, where the ceremonies related in preceding verses were celebrated, was not far from Jericho, the great stronghold which protected the eastern district of Palestine and which it was necessary for the Israelites to capture before they could advance into the country with safety. The opening words of the 13th verse imply that Joshua had gone out alone to view Jericho, to survey its defences, and to form plans of assault. He was deeply concerned for the success of the siege. It was his first conflict in the promised land, and the Israelites were inexperienced in attacking fortified cities. We can well believe that this thoughtful leader was deep in meditation, pondering over the past promise of God, and praying that it might be fulfilled in his hour of need. Unworthy are those men of high places in God's Church who are not concerned for the welfare of the Divine purposes committed to their charge, who do not "watch as they that must give an account." In some sphere or other we are all masters or captains; let us endeavour to realise the responsibility resting upon us. We are informed how Joshua's *anxiety was relieved.* "He lifted up his eyes and saw," &c. In the season of exigency Jehovah (vi. 2) appeared. He could not violate His word and leave His servant alone. Here is comfort for the careworn and despairing. Said Jesus, "Lo, I am with you always." Whilst we forget not to use diligently our talents and resources, let our eyes be lifted from the earth that we may see Him who stands by us as He did by Paul in the cell at Jerusalem, saying, "Be of good cheer" (Acts

xxiii. 11). We go not to the warfare at our own cost. Let us *learn to expect His presence.* We will think of the future, but not take over-anxious thought. Not work but worry saps the strength. Let our councils wait till Christ is present to preside.

II. HIS COURAGE. Not in vain had the admonition, "Be courageous," been bestowed upon him. Nowise affrighted, Joshua went up to the man with the sword and put the inquiry, "On whose side art thou come to fight?" Ignorant of the stranger's dignity, his warlike attitude did not daunt our hero. He would know the truth, even if unpleasant and at the hazard of his life. Truly many a trouble would have its gigantic dimensions lessened if we faced it stoutly and investigated its nature. That new theory which wears such hostile aspect may after all confirm the old position. *Joshua knew but of two armies.* And to our conflict with sin there are but two sides. "He that is not with us is against us." It is well to put the query to our acquaintance, "Art thou for us?" Notice also that *God appears in the form best suited to His servant's need.* He contended as an athlete with Jacob that by wrestling the patriarch's faith and knowledge might be increased. To Moses, needing to be reminded of the indestructibility of the Church of God, there was shown a burning bush unconsumed. And now, to inspirit Joshua for the campaign, God reveals Himself as a warrior armed and as the "Prince of the Lord's host," Captain of the visible and invisible armies, the Israelites and the angels. Analogous to these varied appearances are the titles of God, framed to assure His people that He can "supply all their need." To the afflicted He is the "God of all comfort," to the depressed the "God of hope." In our loneliness He is a Friend, in orphanhood the Father of the fatherless, in the storm our refuge, amid the waves our Rock, and in battle our Captain and Shield. Thankful may we be for the chequered experience of life, if it reveals to us the many-sidedness of our God, and the satisfaction to be found in Him of every want.

III. HIS HUMILITY. The words and bearing of the speaker, even if they did not at once render Joshua conscious of His exalted character, were quite enough to indicate the need of reverence. Accordingly he bowed and worshipped, and, great general though he was, exhibited his readiness to receive commands or advice respecting the management of the siege. This is the spirit in which the approach of Christ to the heart should be met. We must say with Saul, "What wilt thou have me to do?" Men who cavil at every utterance of the Saviour are not likely to be favoured with a full disclosure of His glorious person. If the heart has been stirred by some appeal of Scripture or some religious argument, it is only right that we should display a willingness to listen further and to follow the light whither it may lead us. A lowly attitude befits the proudest intellect in the presence of messengers and messages from heaven. Let us, like Joshua, inquire, "What saith my Lord unto his servant?" *Humility prepared the way for the reception of a command that clearly revealed a present Jehovah.* Not to the disrespectful will such a revelation be granted. Therefore to the doubting we say, Bow at the feet of Christ, and there shall come a mandate which by its own inherent authority shall manifest His dignity and dismiss uncertainty. Often have the very absoluteness of the commands of Christ, and the very thoroughness of the claim He makes to men's homage, assured them of His being the Son of God. Imposture and falsehood stand not forth in such clear light, they would be instantly detected.

IV. HIS OBEDIENCE. Promptly did Joshua loose the shoes from off his feet, recalling, doubtless, the similar order issued to Moses in the desert. *The presence of God is true consecration.* He is everywhere; but where He manifests Himself, there the place is holy. As the shoe partook of the defilement of the earth, it was not fit to remain on holy ground. The New Testament does not diminish the awe inspired by the majesty of the Most High, though it brings pre-eminently into view His character of love. Not outward prostration, however, do we want so much as the bowing of the heart and bending of the will. "Rend your hearts and not your garments." *Obedience was rewarded with directions and a promise.* By instant compliance with the behest, Joshua displayed a hearty acceptance of his Prince's will, and a fitness to receive further proofs of Divine favour. For the gifts of God are conditioned by the preparedness of the recipient. And if in answer to our repeated prayers there has come a seemingly strange command, let us immediately obey. No further revelation will be ours till we have thus shown our fitness to participate in heavenly blessings. We shall find that in keeping the commandments we acquire a true knowledge of God, and that therein is eternal life. "If any man will do his will, he shall know of the doctrine."—A.

Vers. 13—15.—*The Captain of the Church.* At the very time when the battle of Israel against the idolators of the land of Canaan was about to commence, Joshua saw a mysterious warrior stand before him sword in hand. "Art thou for us or for our enemies?" he cried. "I am come," is the answer, as Captain of the Lord's host.

I. This Divine Captain has never left the army of the holy, though He may not at all times have made Himself visible. He was with the Church when it entered upon the conflict with the old world. Weak, insignificant, without power, and without prestige as it was, His sword of fire sufficed to ensure it the victory. It was He whom Luther saw in the dawn of the Reformation morning, when he sang: "The Son of God goes forth to war."

II. This Divine personage is the same with whom Jacob wrestled all the night at the Ford Jabbok. He begins by turning His sword against His own soldiers, and plunges it deep into their hearts to destroy their pride and sin. Blessed wounding, which makes them in the end more than conquerors, and Israelites indeed. We must not, then, marvel if, often in the early stages of its warfare, the Church is humbled, foiled, for a time it might seem almost crushed. Neither should we be surprised if the Christian soul is made victorious only through suffering. Soon the Divine Captain will take command of the host which He has disciplined, and will lead them on to victory. This Captain is the very same whom St. John saw in vision with a flaming sword in His mouth. He is the Word made flesh, the Redeemer (Rev. v.). He Himself was wounded before He triumphed. The conquering Head of the Church is "Jesus, who was crucified."—E. DE P.

EXPOSITION.

CHAPTER VI. 1—21.

The victory.—Vers. 1.—This verse (see above) is parenthetical. It explains why the captain of the Lord's host appeared unto Joshua. The inhabitants of Jericho, though in a state of the utmost alarm, were nevertheless fully on their guard against the children of Israel. The commencement of hostilities imposed a great responsibility on Joshua. Success at the outset was, humanly speaking, indispensable. We may see what defeat involved for him by his distress in consequence of the check at Ai. The alternative was victory or annihilation, for the Israelites had no homes or fortresses to which they could retire. Joshua was therefore encouraged by a visible proof that he was under the protection of the Most High, to be yet farther assured by the marvels that were to follow. The use of the Pual participle with its fullest intensive sense, to strengthen the affirmation of the action by the Kal, is a singular construction. Literally rendered it is "shutting and closely shut up," thus including (1) the act of closing,

and (2) the continuance of that act, συγκεκλεισμένη καὶ ὀχυρομένη (LXX.), "clausa atque munita" (Vulg.). So also the Chaldee paraphrase. The remainder of the verse strengthens still more the assertion of the state of siege. The king of Jericho, such was his alarm, regarded his city as a beleaguered one, from the mere presence of Joshua and his host in its vicinity.

Ver. 2.—**And the Lord said.** This is no new source of information for Joshua. *Jehovah* is here obviously identical, as commentators are generally agreed, with the "Captain of the Lord's host" in the last chapter (comp. Gen. xviii. 2, 13; Exod. iii. 2, 4). **Thus shalt thou do six days.** "Seven days together they walk this round; they made this therefore their Sabbath day's journey; and who knows whether the last and longest walk, which brought victory to Israel, were not on this day? Not long before, an Israelite is stoned to death for but gathering a few sticks that day; now all the host of Israel must walk about the walls of a large and populous city, and yet do not violate the day. God's precept is the rule of the justice and holiness of our actions " (Bp. Hall).

Ver. 4.—**And seven priests shall bear before the ark.** The Vulgate puts " on the seventh day " in connection with this part of the sentence ; Luther also translates thus. The LXX., which Calvin and our translators and the majority of commentators follow, regard this part of the sentence as stating what was to be done on the six days, and rightly so, as vers. 8—14 clearly show. That the historian, as has been before remarked, did not always give the full instructions Joshua received is evident from this passage. The priests are not said to have been instructed to sound the trumpet on the six days ; yet we learn from v. 13 that they did so. It is rather implied than expressed that the ark was also to be borne in procession ; but that this was done is evident from ver. 8. **Seven trumpets of rams' horns.** There is no mention of rams' horns in the original, which is שׁוֹפְרוֹת הַיּוֹבְלִים trumpets of jubilee, *i.e.*, of triumph (hardly as Gesenius, "alarm trumpets," though not necessarily, with Dr. Vaughan in his 'Heroes of Faith,' "the emblems of festival, not of warfare"). The word יוֹבֵל is derived from the same root as the Latin is in the phrase Io Triumphe (cf. Greek ἰώ), and according to Gesenius our word "yule" is also derived from this root. The שׁוֹפָר as the next verse shows, was a curved instrument, in shape like a ram's horn, though not necessarily of that material ; whereas the חֲצֹצְרָה was a straight trumpet. **Seven times.** The importance of the number seven as indicative of completeness is here strongly indicated. Seven priests were to carry seven trumpets for seven days. The word for to swear, נִשְׁבַּע literally to be *sevened*, means to have one's vow consecrated and confirmed by seven sacrifices or seven witnesses (see Gen. xxi. 28, 30). The number seven, says Bähr in his 'Symbolik des Alten Testament,' i., 187, 188, is the sign of the relation, union, communion between God and the world, as represented by the number three and four respectively, just as twelve is in another relation (see note on ch. xxi. 3). Its meaning, according to Bähr, among the heathen is somewhat different. There it means the harmony of the universe, and is signified by the seven stars, to which, and neither more nor less, was the power of influencing man's destiny ascribed. **And the priests shall blow with the trumpets.** "Fac tibi tribas ductiles, si sacerdos es, immo, *quia* sacerdos es (gens enim regalis effectus es et sacerdotium sanctum, de te

enim scriptum est), fac tibi tribas ductiles ex Scripturis sanctis" (Orig., Hom. 7 on Joshua).

Ver. 5.—**When they make a long blast with the ram's horn.** Literally, *as they draw out with the horn of jubilee, i.e.*, blow a prolonged blast (cf. Exod. xix. 13). Here the word used is *horn of jubilee*, but not necessarily of *ram's* horn, as our version, any more than the modern *horn*, though it takes the place of the more primitive instrument made of that material, must itself be a ram's horn. So Rosenmüller. The word קֶרֶן in Hebrew is used in different senses, all, however, growing out of the one original sense. Thus it is used for a *musical instrument*, for *rays of light*, for the *projections extending from the corners of the altar*, and in Isa. v. 1, for a *mountain peak* (like the German Schreckhorn, Gabelhorn, Weisshorn). Origen compares the blast of the trumpet at which the walls of Jericho fell, to the sound of the last trumpet, which shall finally destroy the kingdoms of sin. **When ye hear.** The Keri substitute here, as in many other places, כְּ for בְּ but unnecessarily. The Keri means *at the very moment when*, the Chethibh simply and less emphatically, " when " (see ver. 15). **Flat.** Literally, *underneath it, i.e.*, the walls were to give way from their very foundations. **Every man straight before him.** There was no need to *surround* the city, nor to endeavour to enter it through a "practicable breach." The walls were to give way entirely, and the warriors might advance at once, in the order of battle, and from the place in which they were at the moment when they raised the shout of triumph (יָרִיעוּ) for the inhabitants of Jericho alone were evidently no match for them in numbers (cf. chap. x. 3 ; xi. 1—3), though they might have hoped to hold out some time under the protection of their walls.

Ver. 7.—**And he said.** The text has *they said.* Our translators follow the Masoretic emendation. If we follow the original we must suppose that the priests, or, as with Keil and Knobel, the Shoterim (ch. i. 10), conveyed Joshua's command to the troops.

Ver. 8.—**He that is armed,** or rather *disencumbered, i.e.*, prepared for battle (see ch. iv. 13). Similarly, in the next verse, " the armed men," *i.e.*, the host in marching order, as we say. Kimchi and Jarchi refer this to the Reubenites and their brethren, but without sufficient authority. Keil thinks that it was impossible that the unarmed people would have gone with the procession as "the rereward" (see note on v. 13), because no command to that effect is given in ver. 3. But as he has told us in ch. iii., iv., and as we have just seen in ver. 4, the command to Joshua is *not* fully given. A short abstract of it is given, and it is to be filled up in detail from the subsequent narrative.

Ver. 10.—**Ye shall not shout.** No sign of triumph was to be raised ; but the Israelites, their priests, and the ark of their covenant were in solemn silence to encompass the city day by day, until they were commanded to raise the shout of victory. The people of Jericho knew only too well what this religious procession meant. As a military manœuvre (so Calvin) it was worse than useless, it was ridiculous. It actually invited attack ; nay, it afforded, if the interpretation in the note on ver. 8 be correct, an admirable opportunity for the slaughter of defenceless women and children by a sudden sally from the city. But the history of the Exodus was not unknown to the king and people of Jericho. The inspired law-giver, with his miraculous powers, and his claim to direct intercourse with the Most High, was a personage only too well known to them, and his mission was only too sure a token of the Divine sanction which rested on their proceedings. His supernatural qualifications had evidently descended to his successor, and now it was terribly clear that this awful silent march, with the army equipped for battle, but not attempting to engage in it, the seven priests with their seven trumpets, the visible symbol of the Presence of the God of Israel, attended by the awe-struck multitude awaiting the Divine pleasure, was but the prelude to some new interposition from on high, the mysterious foreshadowing of some hitherto unheard-of calamity which should befall the devoted city. There seems in this narrative no choice between rejecting the whole as an absurd fable, or accepting it as the record of a "notable miracle." The account is minute in its detail. The historian, if he be an historian, is distinctly impressed with the idea that he is relating a miracle. The obvious course for Joshua, if he were not relying on supernatural aid, was either to assault or to blockade the city. To perambulate it for days in the expectation of some convulsion of nature such as, we are told, frequently happened in that volcanic region, would have been the extreme of childish folly, and quite contrary to that common sense and military skill with which, as we have seen, Joshua undoubtedly was endowed. If he were possessed, seven days beforehand, with a conviction that an earthquake were imminent, such a persuasion would be of itself miraculous. *Paulus'* idea of a mine having been sprung is still less compatible with our narrative. Von Lengerke, in his ' Cana   supposes that the

astonishing success of the Israelites grew into a wonder in the hands of the narrator. But this involves the entire falsehood, not only of the command given to Joshua by Jehovah, but of the seven days' perambulation of Jericho, and the remaining incidents of the siege, a theory not easily reconcilable with the minute accuracy of detail displayed throughout the narrative. The seven days' circuit of Jericho must, therefore, either be denied altogether, in spite of the numerous evidences of genuineness which meet us in the narrative ; or, if explained, the only explanation which is consistent with the fact is, that Joshua had received an intimation that he was not to expect to effect the reduction of the city by natural means, but was to wait patiently for an interposition from on high.

Ver. 13.—**The rereward** (see v. 9). Literally, *the gathering together* and then the body of troops which collects the stragglers, the *rear-guard*, as in Num. x. 25 ; Isa. lii. 12 ; lviii. 8. Calvin renders here by *quis cogebat agmen.* But the LXX. and Vulgate render by ὁ λοιπὸς ὄχλος and *vulgus reliquum.* So Luther, *der Haufe.* The LXX., however, in ver. 9 translates the same word by οὐραγοῦντες, *i.e.,* "qui extremum agmen ducunt, et quasi caudam efficiunt" (Rosenmüller). The word is not the same as that translated *rereward* in 1 Sam. xxix. 2, the only other place where our version has "rereward," where there can be no question of the rendering being correct, since the literal meaning there is *the hindermost.*

Ver. 15.—**And it came to pass on the seventh day.** Why did God command this long pause of suspense and expectation ? Even to teach us that His ways are not as our ways, and that we had far better leave the issue in His hands, than by our impatience to anticipate, and not unfrequently frustrate, the course of His Providence.— *Calvin.* There is a time to act and a time to wait patiently. If we seek His guidance by prayer, God will tell us when to do either. And when it is our duty not to do anything ourselves, but to wait for the deliverance which He never fails to send in His own good time, let us be careful to restrain ourselves, lest by our rash intermeddling with His designs, we bring disgrace and disaster upon ourselves and His cause. Had the Israelites disobeyed His command, and instead of the solemn procession round Jericho, ventured to attack the city at once, it would have fared worse with them than at Ai, or at the wilderness of Paran (Num. xiv. 45). **About the dawning.** So the Chethibh. The Keri substitutes כְּ for בְּ, *i.e.*, as soon as it was dawn. Literally, "as the dawn went up." **After this manner.** Literally, *according to this judgment*, "sicut dispositum erat" (Vulg.). For a similar use of מִשְׁפָּט see Gen. xl. 13, and compare the proverb *mos pro lege*.

Ver. 16.—**When the priests.** There is no "when" in the original, nor is it needed (see Keil).

Ver. 17. — **Accursed.** Rather, *devotea*, ἀνάθεμα LXX. The original meaning of this word is derived from הרם to "shut up." Hence it originally means "a net." With this we may compare the well-known Eastern word *harem*, meaning the enclosed apartments reserved for the women of the family. Hence it comes to mean *under a ban, devoted*, generally to utter destruction under the pressure of a vow to God, as in Num. xxi. 2, or in consequence of His command (see Levit. xxvii. 29 ; Deut. xiii. 15 (Hebrew 16) ; 1 Kings xx. 42, "the man of my *devoting*," חֶרְמִי, &c). But in Levit. xxvii. 21 ; Num. xviii. 14, the חֵרֶם as devoted to the Lord, became the property of the priest. This ban was the most solemn and tremendous religious sentence, the absolute and final excommunication of the old law. The sin of Saul (1 Sam. xv.) was the sparing of anything whatever in the city which had been laid under the ban—a ban which Saul had been specially commanded to execute (1 Sam. xv. 3) according to the principles laid down in Deut. xiii. When Keil, however, states that the ban "could never be pronounced upon things and property alone, but only upon open idolaters, either with or without their possessions," he appears to have overlooked Levit. xxvii. 16—21, where a man may devote irredeemably to God property of *his own* (cf. ver. 28 of the same chapter). In his subsequent work, however, Keil qualifies this assertion by a consideration of this very passage. Idolatrous worship was the one thing which justified the Israelites in laying one of their own cities under the ban (see Deut. xiii. 12—18, above cited). But (Deut. vii. 2) it had been pronounced against the Canaanites. Property, however, save in the case of Jericho, seems to have been exempted from the ban (see ch. viii. 2). Even at Jericho the silver and the gold, the brass and the iron, were placed in the treasury of the Lord (v. 19, 24). "Why," says Theodoret, "was the city thus devoted? It was devoted on the same principle which offered the first fruits to God, since it was the first fruits of their conquests." **Because she hid.** See for the peculiar form of this word as though it came from a quadriliteral הבאה

Ver. 18.—**Accursed thing.** Better, "thing *devoted*," as this keeps up the idea of something solemnly set apart to God, to be dealt with as He thinks fit. **Lest ye make yourselves accursed when ye take of the accursed thing.** Rather, with Keil and Rosenmüller, *lest ye devote the city to destruction, and then take of what has been thus devoted.* **And make the camp of Israel a curse.** Literally, *and put the camp of Israel in the position of a thing devoted*, **And trouble it** (cf. ch. vii. 25, 26 ; also Gen. xxxiv. 30).

Ver. 19.—**Consecrated unto the Lord.** Literally, as margin, *holiness unto the Lord* (cf. Exod. xxviii. 36 ; xxxix. 30 ; Levit. xxvii. 14, 21 ; Jer. ii. 3). An expression used of anything specially devoted to God.

Ver. 20.—**So the people shouted when the priests blew with the trumpets, and it came to pass.** Literally, *and the people shouted, and they blew with the trumpets, and it came to pass as soon as the people heard the sound of the trumpet.* The latter part of this sentence is a more full and accurate repetition of what is stated in the former. The shouting and the blowing with the trumpets were all but simultaneous, but the latter was in reality the signal for the former—a signal which was immediately and triumphantly responded to.

Ver. 21.—**And they utterly destroyed all that was in the city.** For a discussion of the difficulties arising from this fulfilment of a stern decree, see Introduction.

HOMILETICS.

Vers. 1—21.—We come now to the command that was laid on Joshua. And here we may observe three points.

I. SUCCESS WAS CERTAIN IF GOD'S COMMANDS WERE OBEYED. God does not say, "I will give," but, "I have given" Jericho into thine hand. Not only has the fiat gone forth, but the work is done, when the soldier of the Lord has made up his mind to obey the Lord's commands. Thus, whatever be the work to which we set our hands, be it public or private, in the world or in our own hearts, so that it be for God, and it is our duty to do it, we must regard our success as assured. Moses hesitated and argued about his fitness for the task laid upon him. Jeremiah shrank from facing the children of Israel with his message of wrath. But the apostles of Christ, when sent forth to conquer the world by no other means than the proclamation of the truth, never stood appalled by the magnitude of the work, but were filled with a sublime confidence that all should be as God had said. So when we go forth to besiege some modern Jericho, let us hear beforehand the voice of God saying, " See, I have given it into thine hand." We have only to ascertain clearly that the duty is laid upon us, that we are not laying a presumptuous hand upon a task which is not meant for us. This done, we may go boldly forward on our way.

II. There are strongholds which will yield to prayer alone. Jericho was taken by no other means than by the seven days' procession. The rest of the cities of Canaan were taken by storm in the ordinary way. But Jericho was the first of them. Thus it often pleases God, when we enter first upon our warfare, to remove some temptation from us in a striking and wonderful manner in answer to prayer. This is to serve as an encouragement to us, as a proof both of His presence and of His power. Many of God's saints can tell of such encouragements, mercifully vouchsafed to them when commencing the struggle against sin, that they might know experimentally for themselves, and not by the report of others, that the Lord was indeed the Almighty. When some work is going on for God in which it is impossible for us to join, we may aid it by our prayers. And those prayers may prove mightier than the feeble efforts of those actually engaged in the work. When those in whom we have an interest are wandering far from God, and it is not our place to instruct or rebuke them, we may pray for them; and many are the souls which have been converted to God through the might of prayer alone. So when the Church of Christ suffers persecution from worldly men, she is not to use worldly weapons in her defence. Let her be steadfast and diligent in her daily offering of intercession and praise, and the walls of Jericho that frown above her shall fall down flat, and she shall divide its spoils.

III. Each has his appointed share in the attack on evil. Our attack is to be an united and orderly one. No disorderly rout encompassed Jericho, each " fighting for his own hand." There was a fixed order in the attack, in which each had his proper share. The ark of God was carried by the priest; that is, the ministers of religion are to lead the way in public and private intercession for the cause. They blow with the horns of jubilee; that is, they sound the note of war against the evil against which they are arrayed. They stir God's people up to the fight. And when the time appointed has come that the assault has to be made, their prayers, intercessions, exhortations are redoubled; the people respond to their efforts by raising their voices unanimously in the same holy cause; the bulwarks of the stronghold of evil give way; and Israel advances, every man straight before him, to raze it to the ground.

The actual fulfilment of God's commands now demands our notice. We may observe here :—

I. That God's people are secure from all danger when in the way of duty. From a military point of view, as has been already observed, these dispositions were absurd. To compass the city in this manner was to invite attack. Yet it was done because God commanded it, and no evil ensued. So a Christian is ever safe, however much worldly wisdom may condemn him, if he be in the path of duty. " No weapon that is formed against him shall prosper." We must not mind exposing ourselves to the scoffs and jeers of the profane, the grave remonstrances of the worldly-minded, the prophecies of failure on the part of the timid and time-serving. No matter how imprudent our action, according to the world's standard; so long as it be right it will certainly prosper at last. All great movements for good have been branded at the outset as enthusiastic folly. Yet faith and perseverance have succeeded in the end. The walls of many a spiritual Jericho have been brought to the ground by a steady persistence in what was known to be right, however unreasonable it may have seemed to unbelievers.

II. We must not be " weary in well doing." For seven long days did the strange procession encompass Jericho. Not the slightest effect was produced of any kind till the prescribed task was accomplished. Bishop Hall, regarding the number seven as indicative of completeness, tells us that there are many of our infirmities which we must not expect to overcome till the end of our lives. Not till then will God vouchsafe us the measure of faith to overthrow them finally. Meanwhile we must watch and pray and follow the ark and continue in our round of devotion, until the time comes for God to visit us. We must not be depressed if no signs of progress appear, if, after having encompassed the city six days, and six times on the seventh day, all appears as usual. We must patiently wait God's time, and when He announces the hour of triumph, and not till then, we may rejoice that our enemies are in our power.

III. GOD DEMANDS THE ABSOLUTE SURRENDER OF ALL CARNAL AFFECTIONS. Jericho and all it contained was to be utterly destroyed. And so, as far as we are concerned, must all the desires of this lower world be put down. No doubt it was a great temptation to the Israelites (Achan's case proves that it was so) to see so great a store of valuable things doomed to destruction. "To what purpose is this waste?" was a question which must have occurred to many there. So it is a sore temptation to the Christian to see this world's goods within his reach and he forbidden to grasp them. They were intended to be enjoyed, and why should he not enjoy them? Youth seeks after the indulgences of the flesh, after recreations and amusements. Manhood strives after the prizes of this world—power, wealth, honours, rewards. They are innocent in themselves; why should we not possess them? Because they are *devoted*. This does not refer to pleasures and blessings God has put in our hands. If He has blessed them we may safely use them. But pleasures, and honours, and emoluments for their own sake, things which to grasp at would lead us from the path of duty—these are the spoils of Jericho, devoted to God, which we may not touch. Self-denial, simple discharge of duty from conscientious motives, and the consequent absence of ambition or greed of gain, willingness to accept the lowest place, disinclination to accept riches, honours, positions of influence, and authority, unless to decline them would clearly be wrong—these are the characteristics of the true servant of God. He makes a holocaust of all vain desires and selfish motives, and is willing to give up the richest prizes earth can offer, unless God gives them to him.

HOMILIES BY VARIOUS AUTHORS.

Ver. 3.—*Siege of Jericho.*—The Red Sea; a land where there was no water; want of food; terrors of the spies; the warlike people of Bashan; Jordan impossible; a Jericho impregnable. Such are the successive strains made on the faith and resolution of Israel. God's people go from strength to strength, but also from difficulty to difficulty. Never is it the case that the difficulties are entirely done and the prospects entirely bright. On their newest difficulty let us spend a little time; for all of us have our Jerichos to face and to subdue. And I ask you to observe first,

I. THE IMPOSSIBLE TASK HERE SET THEM. I doubt not the stoutest warriors so estimated it. Kitto (Pictorial Bible on this chap.) describes, from his own experience of a siege, the confidence felt by all Asiatics when protected by walls, and the despair with which they face them, even to-day, though in some degree familiar with the use of artillery. Before that was invented a walled city was deemed almost unreducible, except by starvation, by the desultory warriors of Syria. Here they could hardly, without themselves starving, starve them out. They were unfamiliar with all the science of war. Had no theory of sapping or breaching to aid them. To leave such a fortress in their rear would be to subject themselves to attack from that side, while to carry it by assault was utterly beyond their power. *An impossible task is set them.* And such are many of the tasks assigned us. Sometimes, indeed, there are easy duties assigned to our opening powers. "The bruised reed is not broken" with a burden beyond its strength. But our duties in this world are always on a scale which assumes we have omnipotent help within our reach: Abraham's charge to leave ancestral home: that of

Moses to invade Egypt and liberate God's people: that of David to earn a right to the throne of Israel: that of Esther to save her people: that of the Apostles to "heal the sick and cast out devils," and subsequently to "go and teach all nations:" that of all the saints in all ages. Bushnell has a sermon on "Duty not measured by ability," his text being the command to feed the multitude—"Give ye them to eat"—given to men with only five barley loaves and two small fi hes. We have all tasks like the reduction of Jericho, utterly beyond our unaided strength. To enter through the strait gate; to keep the narrow way; to overcome in the conflict with principalities and powers in high places; to be steadfast unto death; to secure, by our testimony, our efforts, our prayers, the salvation of those who are perishing around us; to hope against hope; to gather meetness for the inheritance of the saints in light—oh, what impossible tasks are these? But we "can do all things through Christ, which strengtheneth us," and instead of being dismayed at the impossibilities we should rather rejoice, *for a precept of impossibility is a promise of omnipotent help.* Shrink not from the Jericho you have to assail. God will give it into your hand. Secondly observe—

II. THE METHODS OF FAITH. Prescribing their task. He prescribes the method of it as well. They are to march round Jericho once a day for six days, and on the seventh day seven times; the people silent, the priests sounding the trumpets and horns. Only once, when specially bidden, is Israel to shout. We read nothing of mounds, battering rams, slingers picking off the soldiers on the walls, nothing of mines or ladders. The method was not one of war but one of faith. The very trumpets are priestly trumpets, the sounds of which were calls to prayer and promises of help. So much they were to do, and nothing more. In subsequent engagements they would have to fight; in this God alone would work. And the method prescribed is accordingly one virtually of prayer and waiting. "Stand still and see the salvation of God:" a method in which their faith is at once (1) tried, (2) honoured, and so increased. In this respect how like many methods which Christ prescribed. In His miracles, for instance, you will observe that the faith of the recipient was invariably in some way or other tested, brought to light, and only then rewarded. "Go to the pool of Siloam and wash," seemed a precept as unlikely to bring sight as marching round Jericho was to destroy its walls. "Take thy hook and take up the first that cometh up," was an unlikely way of paying tribute. "Go show yourselves to the priests," He said to the ten lepers, and only after they had started they were cleansed. His methods are always such as *try* our faith first and then reward it. Here is a road to the conquest of Jericho which the doubters in the camp thought would prove very long indeed. "Of what use could it be to march round and round, always reconnoitring, and never doing anything more?" How they would point to the growing confidence of the besieged, who from their walls could be seen mocking the futile display of strength! But such was the method prescribed to test and elicit their faith. As the multitude fed by Christ were required to sit down on the grass, to indicate thereby their faith and expectation, so Israel was required to march round Jericho. And we sometimes are required to pursue methods of faith which seem little likely to work much result: to be meek where high spirit would seem more useful; to wait with patience where fussy enterprise would seem more effective; to meet error with argument instead of repressing it by force; to observe sacraments whose object or philosophy we can hardly understand; to obtain the things we desire by deserving rather than by greedily seeking them. Do not murmur at the methods of faith which are enjoined. In the case of Jericho the method was successful. On the seventh day, when the people shouted at Joshua's signal, the walls of Jericho fell flat. "The earth shook and trembled: the foundations of heaven moved and shook because he was wrath." And in an instant, without a stone protecting them, without their people marshalled, without any array against their foes, Israel can enter and destroy. The ways of the enemy seem short, but are long and fruitless. God's ways seem likely to be long, but are short and direct. Take His ways, and however for a while your patience may be tried, the end, bringing all you hoped for, will reward you for all suspense and all delay.—G.

Ver. 20.—*The taking of Jericho.* The taking of Jericho is the first great victory of the Israelites over the Canaanites. It is a type of the victory of the people of God over their adversaries. We learn from it the secret and the method of success in this conflict.

I. The first thing demanded of the people of Israel is A GREAT ACT OF FAITH. It was no slight exercise of faith to believe that the sounding of the sacred trumpets would suffice to overthrow those massive walls which rose like impregnable ramparts around the city. It was necessary that the besiegers should rise above all the merely material aspects of the situation, and endure, as said the writer of the Epistle to the Hebrews, "as seeing him who is invisible," and relying wholly on His word (Heb. xi. 27).

II. This faith is not a mere feeling of trust; IT INVOLVES ALSO A POSITIVE AND PERILOUS DEED. The Israelites are not to wait in inaction the working of a miracle on their behalf; they have a direct command to obey. The ark is to be triumphantly borne, sometimes to the stirring sound of trumpets, around the walls of Jericho, from the top of which the enemy might take deadly aim at the besiegers. Thus, for Israel to believe is to obey; it is to act in spite of danger. This is the faith of which it is said that it " overcomes the world " (1 John v. 4).

III. THIS FAITH FINDS A RESPONSE IN THE MIGHTY GRACE OF GOD. That grace delights in sovereign manifestations. In the exercise of His absolute freedom, God has often chosen " things that are not to bring to nought things that are," (1 Cor. i. 28), thus magnifying His grace by the very disproportion between the results and the apparent means used to effect them. What power is there in the sound of a trumpet to shake the solid foundation of a city wall? Can its shrillest blast make the massive granite tremble to its fall? God will show that the power is His alone; that Israel's confidence must be in no arm of flesh, but in Him only. Undoubtedly He does often make use of those natural means which are of His own appointment, and His grace is not in the ordinary course of things opposed to nature. Religious life is not magic, but those grand manifestations of Divine sovereignty which are called miracles bring us into immediate contact with the sovereign power of God from which all blessed influences flow. Let us not forget, moreover, that there is a distinction to be observed between what may be called the creative period of the religion of redemption, and its subsequent stage of pre-servation and development. The current of the new life must first hollow out its channel, before it can pursue its even way between the banks of a defined course. Hence with regard to miracles, there is a great difference between the age which saw the first beginnings of Christianity, and our own day, which is an era of develop-ment only.

IV. The fall of the walls of Jericho before the blast of the sacred trumpets is an apt symbol of THE TRIUMPH OF SPIRIT OVER MATERIAL FORCE. The sacred trumpets accompanied the songs of Israel, its hymns of worship raised to the true God. It was this glorious truth of the one living and true God which finally subdued the Canaanitish nations. *Mens agitat molem.* Mind moves matter; it always triumphs over material obstacles. Force can avail nothing against it, because it is itself the power of God. Primitive Christianity saw the citadel of paganism fall before it. All-powerful Rome fell prostrate when the gospel trumpet sent forth its sonorous voice into the midst of a down-trodden and decaying world. Thus, also, in a later age did the fortress of Romish superstition crumble into ruin before Luther's hymn, which embodies the whole spirit of the Reformation. The hymn on justification by faith was like Israel's trumpets to the Papal Jericho. "Believe only, and thou shalt see the glory of God " (John xi. 20).—E. DE P.

Ver. 20.—*Strongholds.* When the writer of the Epistle to the Hebrews says, " By faith the walls of Jericho fell down after they had been compassed about seven days " (Heb. xi. 30), he sets his seal to the supernatural character of this event. Not by any kind of natural force—undermining, storming, or even earth-quake—but by the faith that lays hold on the unseen power of God, was the effect produced. It was a link in the chain of marvellous Divine manifestations by which those times were signalised. The miraculous element is inseparably interwoven with the fabric of the history. It can be denied here only by those who are prepared to relegate the whole to the region of fable and romance. The fall of this fortified city of Jericho had a peculiar meaning, and stood in important relation to the events that followed. As the strongest fortress of Canaan, its conquest was the key to the possession of the whole land. As pre-eminent, probably, in its wickedness, its doom was a prophecy of the unmitigated judgments of God on the abominations of Phœnician idolatry. The solemn procession of the ark, time after time, around the city was a significant declaration of His sovereignty over it and all that it contained; and when at last it fell, it was as the first-fruits of the harvest-field, "accursed"—devoted—to show that the whole land was His. Thus were the Israelites taught that an inheritance which they had not won for themselves by their own skill and strength, but which had been given to them by the Lord (vers. 2, 16), must be held in unreserved allegiance to Him (Psa. xliv. 3). We see in this event a typical representation of the Divine conquest of the powers of error and evil in the world. It prefigures the assault of the kingdom of light upon the kingdom of darkness, and sets forth, as in acted parable, the apostolic truth, "The weapons of our warfare are not carnal, but mighty through God to the pulling down of strongholds" (2 Cor. x. 4).

I. In Jericho itself we see a type of the strongholds of iniquity in the world.—The city was "*straitly shut up;* none went out and none came in" (ver. 1). The combination of the passive and active forms here indicates how the natural strength of the fortifications was supplemented by the resistive spirit of the people. We are reminded of those conditions of the human soul in which it is impenetrable by the influence of Divine truth; resolute in its unbelief, impenitence, corrupt affection, evil habit; closely shut against the powers that would bring into it a new and nobler life. But the picture of the closed city suggests not so much the resistance of the individual soul to redeeming influence, as that of the conspicuous forms of evil existing in the world—false systems of thought, corrupt institutions, pernicious social usages; strongholds of infidelity, vice, tyranny, superstition, idolatry. We are reminded how deeply rooted they are, how strong in the radical tendencies of human nature and in the traditionary custom of ages. Like Jericho, the very hot-bed of Canaanite pollution, in the midst of its glorious palm-groves, so do these forms of evil stand as blots on the fair creation of God, and cast their deadly shadow on the otherwise glad life of man. It is against these that the kingdom of truth and righteousness wages an exterminating war, "casting down imaginations and every high thing that exalteth itself against the knowledge of God, and bringing into captivity every thought to the obedience of Christ."

II. The mode of the city's fall is suggestive of the relation existing between the human instrument and the Divine power in this spiritual conflict. Note the apparent *impotence* of the means used in view of the end to be answered. This silent procession of the ark and the armed host round and round the walls, the silence broken only by the rude music of the priests' rams' horns—what a solemn farce it must have seemed! We can imagine with what derision it was greeted by the men of the city. If *that* is all the power that can be brought against them, they have little need for fear. The spiritual analogy is plain. To men destitute of faith, incapable of discovering the resistless force that lies behind them, the instruments of the kingdom of Christ seem very feeble. The workers of iniquity, within their refuges of lies, bold in the strength of "blood and custom," laugh at weapons such as these. "The preaching of the cross is to them that perish foolishness" (1 Cor. i. 18). But outward appearances are a very false rule of judgment. The sovereign power can work through meanest, simplest instruments. Their efficacy is often in inverse ratio to their apparent feebleness. "We have the treasure in earthen vessels, that the excellency of the power may be of God, and not of us (2 Cor. iv. 7). "God hath chosen the foolish things of the world to confound the wise," &c. (1 Cor. i. 27—29).

III. The delay of the issue affords a lesson in the patience that waits on God in the path of obedience and service. The seven days' process, in addition to its symbolic meaning, was a trial of the faith and constancy of the people. "By faith the walls fell down," because it was confidence in the unseen Power that kept both priests and warriors steadfast in their seemingly meaningless and profitless round till the appointed time. All great issues in the onward progress of the kingdom of Christ—the fall of corrupt institutions, the doom of reigning iniquities —have their appointed time. This applies pre-eminently to the grand final issue : "Of that day and hour knoweth no man." But in the fulness of the time the glorious vision shall appear. The slowness of the process of destruction and restitution is strange to us. We cry, in our moments of impatience—

> "Oh, why these years of waiting here,
> These ages of delay ? "

But "he that believeth shall not make haste." He knows how to wait, "For the vision is yet for an appointed time," &c. (Hab. ii. 3, 4). Faith, on its watch-tower, sees the grand procession of events moving on to the end of the days, when " the Lord himself shall descend from heaven with a shout, with the voice of the archangel and the trump of God," to lay the last stronghold of Satan in ruins, and " create the new heavens and the new earth wherein dwelleth righteousness " (1 Thess. iv. 16 ; 2 Peter iii. 13).—W.

Ver. 20.—*Delusive trust.* "The wall fell down flat." A strong city besieged ; yet no trenches opened, no batteries erected against it, no engines of assault employed. Armed men in two divisions, separated by the ark and priests who precede it, compass the city once a day in silence, save for the sound of the horns blown by the seven priests. After six days the marching commences early in the morning, and the circuit is completed seven times, when the priests blow a long peculiar blast, the whole host upraises a loud cry, and behold the wall of Jericho, with its lofty battlements, totters and falls. The joyful soldiers, in perfect order, rush triumphantly into the city, and put to the sword the dismayed inhabitants. Many days have these inhabitants wondered at the strange method in which they are besieged. Fearing the Israelites, they have remained behind the shelter of their fortifications, and waited to receive their foes' attack, and lo ! in a moment they are laid bare to a merciless onslaught. History is instructive ; it contains lessons for all ages. Let us try and read some lessons written clearly on the prostrate walls of Jericho.

I. We are reminded of THE INSECURE DEFENCES ON WHICH MANY RELY. All men are not unmindful of the ills of life to which they are exposed ; many distinctly recognise the fact that the castle in which they dwell is, or soon may be, surrounded by foes. But against these they have made preparation, and are confident of their ability to resist the most impetuous attack. A store of wealth has been accumulated to guard against poverty ; and to be the centre of a group of friends will surely prove an adequate security against the invasion of loneliness or melancholy. Alas ! how unstable are the foundations on which rest the hopes of men. Successive losses reduce the millionaire to beggary ; and removals and deaths strip the gayest man of the company in which he delighted.

> " After summer evermore succeeds
> Barren winter, with his wrathful, nipping cold."

Lest a good man should be forgotten, we erect a tablet " in lasting memory," and ere a year has elapsed a fire consumes it to ashes.

II. THE SUDDENNESS WITH WHICH TRUSTED DEFENCES ARE CAST DOWN. Often there is little warning prior to the catastrophe, scarcely the rumbling that precedes an earthquake. Feasting amid splendour, the handwriting is seen on the wall, while the enemy is entering the city by the dry bed of the river. The head of a family labouring to provide for its wants is stricken down by disease or accident, and the strong arm which kept the foe at bay is suddenly powerless.

III. THE REASON OF THE DESTRUCTION IS SOMETIMES TO BE FOUND IN THE FACT

THAT MEN WERE FIGHTING AGAINST GOD. Hitherto we have considered the general lot without distinction of persons. All are subject to a reverse of fortune; " There is one event to the righteous and to the wicked." Yet the author of this last clause remarks, " Surely I know it shall be well with them that fear God ; but it shall not be well with the wicked, neither shall he prolong his days, which are as a shadow, because he feareth not God." The downfall of the seemingly impregnable fortifications of Jericho was due to the might of Jehovah fighting on behalf of His people. It was a strife between true religion and idolatry. And to-day, whilst " all things work together for good to them that love God," the troubles which beset the ungodly may be intended as correctives or judgments. We cannot be oblivious of modern instances where the thunderbolt of Divine wrath has fallen on guilty nations and individuals. The hand of the Almighty can be as truly traced as in the sudden overthrow of Sodom and Gomorrah. His day comes upon men " like a thief in the night," and *just when the wall of defence is most needed does it fall*, leaving the inhabitant a prey to terrible assault. If the vessel's unseaworthiness were discovered in the harbour, what mattered it ? but to find it out on the tempestuous ocean, this is misery indeed. Call to mind Voltaire's wretched lament upon his deathbed, that popular applause could then do naught to help him : " I have swallowed nothing but smoke ; I have intoxicated myself with the incense that turned my head." Happy may we count ourselves when God exerts His power, and shows us the penetrable character of our security, while yet there is time to seek a remedy. Did not Paul rejoice that the bright light from heaven revealed the darkness in which he had been travelling, and that the " knowledge of Christ " completely overcame his old self-righteous ideas ? His boasted privileges and conformity to law yielded at the first breath of the words of Christ, and Christianity, defied so arrogantly, reigned within his breast. Perhaps, O Christian, thou wast rating too highly some of the pleasures of earth, refined though they were, and in mercy thou hast been at a stroke deprived of them !

IV. THE IRRETRIEVABLE DESTRUCTION which God effects. The walls of Jericho were not rebuilt, at least by the inhabitants ; and on the man who in after-years presumptuously endeavoured to act in defiance of the threat of Joshua was seen a terrible fulfilment of prophecy. The temple of Jerusalem is another example of lasting ruin. But in the spiritual realm it is no matter for regret that a curse rests upon the reconstruction of a wicked security. The obstacle to the admission of the Saviour into the heart once surmounted should never again be built up. The hold of the world once loosened should never be allowed to environ us again. Never can the hour in which the utter defencelessness of the soul was realised be blotted out of the book of memory ; and all the after-lessons which stern experience has taught us are indelibly imprinted upon the mind. The uprooting of our affections caused by the loss of a loved one ; the failure of friendship in the time of exigency ; the sickness that dismissed the shows of life and confronted us with the realities of eternity : these events have burnt themselves into our very being, and are become part of ourselves. To bring the matter to a practical issue, ask, Where do we place our trust ? Is it not wisdom to choose as our refuge the unchanging God ; not to trust any arm of flesh, but to rest in the mercy and love of the Eternal ? Not to structures which human skill erects, but to the everlasting hills will we look for aid. " As the mountains are round about Jerusalem, so the Lord is round about his people."—A.

EXPOSITION.

CHAPTER VI. 22—27.

RAHAB'S DELIVERANCE. THE CURSE ON JERICHO.—Ver. 22.—**Had said.** Here we have an instance of the use of the perfect as a pluperfect. We can hardly suppose, as Keil observes, that Joshua gave these orders in the midst of the turmoil and confusion attendant on the sack of the city (see above, ch. i. 11 ; ii. 1). **Go into the harlot's house.** The preservation of Rahab's house must have been a part of the miracle, since it was upon the city wall (cf. Heb. xi. 30, 31).

Ver. 23.—**Brought out.** Therefore the

mediæval legends concerning Rahab's house must be classed among superstitious fables. Rahab and her family and relations were saved, but her house shared the destruction which befel the rest of the city. Origen cites in reference to the deliverance of Rahab the harlot, 1 Cor. vi. 11, and Tit. iii. 3 (cf. also Eph. ii. 1—3; v. 8; Col. iii. 7). **Without the camp of Israel.** Not *in the camp of Israel outside the city*, as some have rendered. The Hebrew distinctly connects the word מַחֲנֶה with the camp. They were as yet, as Gentiles, unclean (cf. Num. v. 2; xxxi. 19).

Ver. 25.—**Unto this day.** This may either be interpreted of herself, or, according to a common Hebrew idiom, of her family (cf. ch. xvii. 14—18; xxiv. 17). For a fuller discussion of the bearing of this passage on the date of the Book of Joshua, see Introduction. There is no mention of Rahab's marriage in the Old Testament. Lightfoot ('Hebrew and Talmudical Exercitations,' Matt. i. 5) mentions a tradition that she married *Joshua!* Dr. W. H. Mill, in his treatise on the genealogies of our Lord, defends the tradition St. Matthew has followed by showing that Salmon's age at the time gives immense probability to the statement. Some (see the Bishop of Bath and Wells' article in Smith's 'Dictionary of the Bible') suppose that Salmon was one of the spies.

Ver. 26.— **And Joshua adjured them.** Caused them to swear, *i.e.*, bound them by an oath, as the Hiphil implies here. This was the strict meaning of "adjure" at the time our version was made (cf. Matt. xxvi. 63). But it had also the less definite meaning which it now has, of solemnly warning a person to do something or to leave it undone (see 1 Kings xxii. 16; Mark v. 7; Acts xix. 13). The object of this solemn adjuration (see above) was to preserve Jericho as a spot devoted to God for ever; and for this reason a curse was pronounced upon any one who should attempt to found a city upon the devoted spot (cf. Deut. xiii. 16, "It shall not be rebuilt.") This curse actually fell on the reckless Hiel (1 Kings xvi. 34; cf. Josephus, 'Antiq.,' V. i. 8), and he saw the laying of its foundations marked by the death of his eldest son, while the death of his youngest followed its completion. It does not seem that it was forbidden to build habitations on the spot, for Jericho is frequently mentioned in the New Testament, and the house of Zacchæus (Luke xix. 5) was there. What seems to have been forbidden was the erection of a fortified city there (see Hengstenberg, 'Geschichte des Reiches Gottes,' p. 214). The mention of Jericho in ch. xviii. 21 does not imply that it was an inhabited city, but simply that the site of Jericho fell within the border of the tribe of Benjamin. For Jerusalem is also mentioned, and we know that it did not become theirs until the time of David. Whether the "city of palm-trees" (Judges iii. 13) is Jericho, may be questioned. But in 2 Sam. x. 5 and in 2 Kings ii. 5 express mention is made of Jericho, the last time as the site of the school of the prophets. Some commentators have endeavoured to restrict the sense of the word בָּנָה used here to the building of fortifications. But this is unduly to restrict its meaning, for it is constantly used also of houses and altars (see Gen. ii. 22; viii. 20; 1 Kings viii. 27). But the mention of gates clearly implies a fortified city. Commentators cite as parallel instances the curse of Agamemnon on Troy, of Crœsus on Sidene (so Grotius from Strabo, lib. 13 de Ilio), and of Scipio upon Carthage, and it is observed that when Augustus rebuilt Carthage he carefully avoided the old site. **In his first-born.** בְּ is often used of the price paid for a thing, as in Gen. xxix. 18; Isa. vii. 23. **And in his youngest son.** The commentators have remarked on the rhythmical parallelism here, and Keil and others have supposed the passage to be an extract from an old Hebrew song-book, such as that of Jasher (ch. x. 13). But this parallelism is not only a characteristic of poetry, but of all solemn and impassioned utterances in the language. (See, for instance, 2 Sam. xviii. 32; 1 Kings xvii. 14; xxi. 19). Masius, Munsterus, and others interpret the passage that the eldest son died when the foundation was laid; all the rest, but the youngest, in the interim; the youngest when the gates were set up.

HOMILETICS.

Vers. 22—27.—1. The first lesson we learn from this portion of the narrative is *salvation by faith*. Had Rahab not believed in God, she would not have saved the spies; and had she not saved the spies, she would not have been saved herself. We have St. James's authority (ch. ii. 25) for citing this passage as an illustration of the connection between faith and works.

I. Works "do spring necessarily out of a lively faith." Had Rahab not believed as she did, she would not have acted as she did. Her works were the direct result of her belief. On the other hand, had she not acted as she did, she would have proved that, whatever her profession to the spies might have been, she did not really believe what she pretended to believe about the power of Jehovah, and the ultimate success of Israel. Here we may discern a clue to the labyrinth of the controversy about the efficacy of faith and works respectively in the scheme of salvation. For (a) a man who believes is naturally inclined to act upon what he believes. If he believes that he is saved through Christ, he will act as if he were saved through Christ. And (b) it becomes important to ask, From what is he saved through Christ? And the Scripture tells us that he is not saved merely from the punishment of sin, but from sin itself. The scheme of salvation through Christ involves a belief in a "full, perfect, and sufficient sacrifice, oblation, and satisfaction, for the sins of the whole world." But it also leads us on from that reconciliation with God to the idea of an indwelling in Christ through His Spirit, which shall enable us to "put off," to "slay," to "crucify" the "flesh" or "old man," and to rise up to a renewed life of sanctity and holiness. A man who believes this must begin to do it. He must, as a matter of course, gird himself up to a conflict with all within him which is not subdued to God's will, as revealed in Christ. If he does not undertake this conflict, it is because he does not believe that he is redeemed through Christ, and that that redemption leads on to sanctification by a necessary law, that of union with Christ. Thus we learn (c) that all whose life is avowedly and systematically inconsistent with their Christian profession, who do not try to root out all evil and to practise all kinds of good, or who set up another standard before them in their actions than that set up in God's Word, are not real believers in Christ, let their profession be what it may.

II. There is no salvation for those who do not manifest their faith by their works. Had Rahab not shown her faith in God by delivering the spies, there could not have been any escape for her. Whatever her private belief might have been, she would have been involved in the general destruction that overtook the whole city. And thus St. Paul and St. James alike insist upon the necessity of our Christian conduct being the manifestation of our inward belief. If it be asked how our faith should be manifested, it may be replied that there must be (a) an abiding sense of God's goodness as displayed in the forgiveness of sins, and (b) an earnest striving after likeness to Christ in every action of life. And this last will stir us up to deeds of active loving-kindness like that of Rahab, who, as we have seen forgot herself and the dangers that beset her in the anxious desire to befriend first the messengers of God, and next those who were near and dear to herself. If we do not these things we are none of Christ's, and, despite our loud profession that we have always belonged to Him, He will have no other greeting for us at the last than, "Depart from me, ye workers of iniquity."

III. Salvation is by Christ's blood alone. Had Rahab not hung the scarlet cord in the window, she would have perished as surely, though she had saved the spies, as if she had done nothing. So our good deeds avail nothing without faith in God's mercy through Christ. They are but the deeds of the Pharisees, unless coupled with the deepest sense of our own unworthiness. We must own that when we have done all, we are unprofitable servants. "Not of works, lest any man should boast." Thus no trace of self-satisfaction must mingle with our obedience, or all will be worthless. This was the fatal mistake of the Pharisees, and this was the reason of the anger of the Lord against them. The deepest humility, combined with the most absolute reliance upon the atoning merits of the Saviour, are among the first requisites of the regenerate life. This thought alone will preserve to the greatest saint that indispensable grace of humility which is the salt that prevents his religious profession from corruption. This alone will maintain those relations with the Author of our salvation which are necessary to keep His life present within us. If we are numbered among God's saints, if we are raised to high places in Israel, if we are the means of salvation to others, it is all due to the scarlet cord in the window.

2. A second lesson taught by this part of the narrative is that *salvation works results in those who are saved.*

I. RAHAB'S FAITH WAS THE CAUSE OF THE SALVATION OF OTHERS. Had she not believed in God, her relatives would have shared the fate of Jericho. So in all other cases. Faith is an expansive principle. It is not content with doing good to its possessor ; it stirs him up to benefit others. Jesus sent forth those who believed in Him to " preach the gospel to every creature." And all faithful Christians are their successors. They must needs " show forth the praises of him who called them out of darkness into his own marvellous light." They must strive to benefit others (*a*) by trying to proclaim the gospel to the heathen abroad, or the worse than heathen at home ; (*b*) by intercessory prayer for all good works; and (*c*) by active works of love to all who are in any way within their reach.

II. RAHAB, ONCE SAVED, WAS EXALTED TO GREAT HONOUR. She became a " mother in Israel," and espoused one of its princes. She attained in ages far remote the immortal honour of being mentioned as one of the progenitors of the King of kings. Thus we learn (*a*) that the " cup of cold water " does not lose its reward. Every kind action done for the love of God and Christ shall be repaid a thousandfold. We are also taught (*b*) that no amount of previous sin shall be weighed in the balance against us when we have truly repented. Rahab's sin was thought no more of when she was saved from the slaughter of Jericho. And so God's forgiveness is full and free, through Christ, when its condition, true repentance, is attained. Though He may see fit to leave us to the discipline of the natural consequences of our sin awhile, it is for our good. He does not cast our past sins in our teeth when we have returned to Him. He will not listen to our request to be as the least and lowest of His hired servants. He puts the best robe upon us, and rings on our fingers, in token of His joy at our return. When our heart is once more whole with Him, we are as truly His dear children as if we had never left Him, and may sun ourselves as fearlessly as they in the light of His mercy. Lastly (*c*), though we may not exactly go so far as to say " the greater the sinner, the greater the saint," we may at least say that there is no reason why a great sinner may not become a great saint. We ought not to be deterred by our past sins, grievous and (but for God's mercy) unpardonable as they are, from pressing forward to the utmost heights of holiness that are within our reach. We are taught to forget those things that are behind, and reach forth unto the things that are before. The records of God's Church are full of such histories. From Mary Magdalene, and after her St. Augustine, to our own day the examples of men steeped to the lips in sin, who have repented and advanced to great heights of holiness, are before us to teach the sinner not to despair, but to trust in His loving-kindness who hath raised " the poor out of the mire, that he may set him with the princes, even with the princes of his people."

3. The third lesson this narrative contains is the *exceeding sinfulness of sin.* Jericho was a sinful city, and therefore it was a devoted city. God had plainly stated (Deut. ix. 5) that the Israelites were the ministers of His vengeance against sin ; that for no virtue of their own, but for the appalling crimes which had called down vengeance from on high upon the Phœnician nations, they had been selected to drive them out. Many interesting questions arise here, some regarding the idea of God, some regarding the true nature of sin, indicated to us in this passage.

I. IS GOD UNRIGHTEOUS THAT TAKETH VENGEANCE ? As this question is fully discussed in the Introduction to this Book, a few hints will be all that is necessary here. We may observe (*a*) that whatever difficulties attach to the command given to Joshua, apply equally to every idea of God that we can form. He, the All-wise and All-good, has at least permitted these chastisements upon men for their sin. We might go further. We might say that He has enjoined them. God has clearly made it a law of our humanity that nations wallowing in the indulgence of sensual passion, permitting themselves to enjoy unchecked the pleasures of injustice, oppression, rapine, cruelty, have in the end been punished by being made the victims of similar cruelty. The Almighty Disposer of events has allowed man again and again to inflict cruelties as severe upon other nations, for their sins, as

Joshua did upon the Canaanites. Thus whatever objections (see Butler's 'Analogy' here) may be raised to the possibility of God giving such a commission to His servant as that narrated in this Book, apply with equal force to the facts of history. Either, therefore, there is no God at all, or He is not good, or He can, consistently with truth and justice, incite man to exercise His vengeance upon those who have sinned. We may further observe (b) that physical suffering does not seem so terrible a thing in God's eyes as it does in ours. Famines, wars, pestilences, accidents, shipwrecks, with all their attendant horrors and miseries, have happened, and will still continue to happen. And God seems not to heed. But is it not because He sees the whole, while we see but a part of His doings? Were this the only world, we must come to the conclusion that God is not goodness, but cruelty; not justice, but the most gross and aggravated injustice. "If in this life only we have hope in Christ, we are of all men most miserable." But granted that there is another world, in which all that goes amiss here will be set right, and these difficulties disappear. The sorrows of this life will seem but a momentary pang as we live through the ages of eternity. And in that good land we shall smile at the doubts of God's perfections which have caused us such uneasiness here. Again (c): we may note that history now shows that the Hittites were once a great and flourishing people. Yet until lately they had been so entirely forgotten that their very names were unknown. Why this complete obliteration, as it were, from the map of humanity? Why, but because they had sinned against the Lord, and He must destroy them? Israel was not the only instrument of His vengeance. Far to the northward of the Holy Land, where their empire flourished on the banks of the Orontes and in Asia Minor, He sent the Egyptians and Assyrians against them, till their name was blotted out from among the nations of the earth. And so will it be till time shall be no more. The nation which holds not God in remembrance shall be cut away from His hand.

II. TOUCH NOT THE UNCLEAN THING. This lesson will be yet farther enforced in the next chapter. Yet here we may note that the Christian is to have no dealings whatever with ungodliness and its treasures. The good things of this life, save as things to be used for God, are to be steadfastly renounced. The desire of possessing them is not to be a motive for action. They who serve God for filthy lucre's sake are unsparingly condemned under the gospel. It is, of course, a difficult task to decide how far innocent pleasures may be enjoyed, or rewards, honours, wealth, accepted, when God seems to have put them in our way. All the cities were not devoted to God, but Jericho only. Yet it may safely be said that in these days of a widely-diffused profession of Christianity, the verdict of Christian society on these points is too lenient a one. The love of money and of the good things of this life is too freely admitted as a motive for action. The deliberate preference of a life of poverty and self-denial is too often looked down upon with disdain, though it is recommended to us by the example of Christ. Nay, it may even be doubted how far St. Paul's rule of excommunication of the covetous man (1 Cor. v. 11) is carried out by the Christian Church, even when money has been made or honours attained by unfair means. The man who, as director of a public company, gives his sanction, by carelessness or weakness, to acts which, as a private individual, he would not have committed—the man who by bribery obtains a position among the law-makers of this great empire—the man who amasses a vast fortune by indirect means—is he courted or condemned by the collective Christian conscience in these days? It may be doubted whether, among all the advances we have unquestionably made of late in Christian principle, the spirit of Achan, rather than Joshua, does not predominate among us still.

III. WHAT GOD HAS PROMISED WILL SURELY COME TO PASS. The ungodly often cry, "Tush, God hath forgotten; he hideth his face and he will never see it." But it comes to pass just the same. The wicked Hiel laughed Joshua's prophecy to scorn. Yet it came true. And so do many thoughtless persons now laugh to scorn the declarations of God's Word. They ridicule the idea of chastisement for national sins; they will not hear of days of humiliation for national misfortunes; they tell us all things are ordered by invariable law. But God punished nations of old for their sins, and He does so still. Nor does He act otherwise with individuals. He has declared that sin brings punishment in its train ; but men sin wantonly, and hope to escape its necessary consequences. But either in this world or the next these consequences arrive. What God has said will surely come to pass. And then man wishes in vain that he had never offended Him. As in Hiel's case, so now, God fulfils to the very letter the predictions He has uttered. Let us be wise in time, and so avoid the misfortunes which a presumptuous contempt of God's Word is sure to bring on us.

HOMILIES BY VARIOUS AUTHORS.

Vers. 22—24.—*A city of destruction.* If any city ever was such a "City of Destruction" as Bunyan fancied, it was Jericho. Itself and all within it were devoted to destruction, only Rahab, like another Noah, with her family escaping. It is an awful fact to contemplate the destruction of a whole city. No escape, and little warning! Old and young, one day in possession of wealth, ease, comfort, and the next day captured and destroyed. The judicial principles on which God acts and on which He here commands the destruction of Jericho, are beyond us, but some of the lessons are clear and useful. Study these :

I. THERE IS A PENALTY FOR SIN. There is nothing wanton in God's ways. Israel was God's chosen, and the nations of Canaan His rejected, because morally the former, with all its faults, infinitely surpassed the latter. You get glimpses of the evil of the primitive races with their religions in the story of Baal-Peor; in the vice and atrocity which perpetually mark every relapse of Israel into idolatry; in the nameless defilements of modern heathenism. Dr. Arnold, no narrow theologian, defends the destruction of the Canaanites as a great gain to the welfare of humanity. It is these cruelties and abominations of heathenism which required and explain the destruction of the Canaanites. For God punishes sin. There is no truth more undeniable, and none the knowledge of which is more widely spread. We suffer for every fault we commit. As root and fruit, so wrong and wretchedness, go together. However subtle the fault, God's providence operates in penalties still more subtle. The eating of any forbidden fruit always has its two penalties—loss of power, and loss of some sort of Eden. Sins of sinners have their penalties. And God's people receive " double for all their sins "—a heavier stroke for the less excusable transgression. It is not because God is wrathful that He punishes, but because He is gracious. *God is love, and therefore will not let us harm ourselves or others.* His infinite love impels Him to "stamp out" evil by penalty. It is blasphemy to think God can sit still and see, with indifferent eye, the poison of sin working its mischief in the world. For love is neither in God nor man a merely sentimental thing. It is wise, it is strong, it is stern. "Love is inexorable," says one of our greatest teachers (George Macdonald). So God's love makes Him "a consuming fire." He pardons sin, when His grace working penitence has got it out of us, but punishes it until we deplore and loathe it. The creed of Jericho was probably a very free and easy one. But as God's facts do not accommodate themselves to our creeds, it is better to adjust our creed to God's facts. Your sins will not pass unpunished. Blessed be God's name, He loves us too well for that. There will be an element of correction in all penalty, until correction becomes impossible; and then, in mercy at once to ourselves and others, God steps in to prevent the further accumulation of guilt by us, and the further infliction of mischief on others. The city of sin is a city of destruction, and your sin will receive the penalty due to it, however secure you may feel in your power to evade it.

II. PENALTY IS OFTEN LONG DEFERRED, AND IS THEN SUDDENLY INFLICTED. Jericho had, I suppose, stood long. The destruction of the cities of the plain had not extended to it. It is possible that, alike from the calamities of war as well as those of nature it had been free. And its prosperity and wealth, its abounding trade with East and West, suggested that there was really no reason to be afraid of God's judgments. Yet suddenly, like a thunderbolt out of a clear sky, destruction fell on them. There is often delay in inflicting a punishment. God prolongs opportunity. "This year also" He spares the barren fig tree, reluctant to destroy what might produce fruit. He is not willing that any should perish. He is "slow to anger." His long-suffering is salvation. He lengthens "the days of tranquillity" that we may at last repent. But when all delay is abused, and the postponement of doom only awakes presumption, at last the stroke comes," suddenly and without remedy." The flood came suddenly, and so did the destruction of Sodom, so did that of Jezebel and Nabal, and Belshazzar, and Herod, and Judas, and that of multitudes that cannot be numbered. Do not mistake postponement of penalty for pardon of sin. Of all our unrepented sin that has not yet been smitten, the punishment is only suspended. We cannot dig so deep but God will find us, nor strengthen our defence so stoutly as to defy His power. Be wise and use the days of reprieve for repentance. "Seek the Lord while he may be found," as we are here taught there is a penalty for every sin, and that, long suspended, it yet at last falls suddenly. So observe also lastly—

III. THEY WHO WOULD AVOID DESTRUCTION MUST BECOME FOLLOWERS OF THE GOD OF ISRAEL. Only one woman with her relatives seems to have done this. We do not read of any persons fleeing from the city of doom, or making any provision for capitulation or escape. The enervation of luxury and immorality is on them. They alternately sink in despair or are puffed up in the confidence of their walls. But one person, rising in repentance from the guilt of a long neglect, sees the glory of God and chooses Him as her hope and Master. When she cannot save the city with her, she saves herself, and, expecting the wonderful works of God, enlists in His service. Repent thou, and take Jesus Christ as thy Lord, ending with serious change of thought and action all the evil of your life. And then the infinite love which weeps when it can only smite will pardon the sin that you forsake, and give you "a place amongst the children," and the great salvation which you long to enjoy.—G.

EXPOSITION.

CHAPTER VII. 1—5.

THE DEFEAT BEFORE AI.—Ver. 1.—**Committed a trespass in the accursed thing.** The word מָעַל, here used, signifies originally to *cover*, whence מְעִיל a garment. Hence it comes to mean to act deceitfully, or perhaps to steal (cf. the LXX. ἐνοσφίσαντο, a translation rendered remarkable by the fact that it is the very word used by St. Luke in regard to the transgression of Ananias and Sapphira. But the LXX. is here rather a paraphrase than a translation). It is clearly used here of some *secret* act. But in Levit. v. 15 it is used of an *unwitting* trespass, committed בִּשְׁגָגָה, in error of fact, but not of intention. **Achan.** Called Achar in 1 Chron. ii. 7, no doubt from a reference to the results of his conduct. He had "troubled Israel" (עָכַר), ver. 25, and the valley which witnessed his punishment obtained the name of Achor. The copies of the LXX. vary between the two forms, the Vatican Codex having Achar; the Alexandrian, Achan. **Zabdi.** *Zimri* in 1 Chron. ii. 6. Such variations of reading are extremely common, and are increased in our version by the va-

rieties of English spelling adopted among our translators (see Shemuel for Samuel in 1 Chron. vi. 33). The LXX. has *Zambri* here. **Took of the accursed thing.** Commentators have largely discussed the question how the sin of Achan could be held to extend to the whole people. But it seems sufficient to reply by pointing out the organic unity of the Israelitish nation. They were then, as Christians are now, the Church of the living God. And if one single member of the community violated the laws which God imposed on them, the whole body was liable for his sin, until it had purged itself by a public act of restitution (see Deut. xxi. 1—8). So St. Paul regards the Corinthian Church as polluted by the presence of one single offender, until he was publicly expelled from its communion (see 1 Cor. v. 2, 6, 7). The very words "body politic" applied to a state imply the same idea—that of a connection so intimate between the members of a community that the act of one affects the whole. And if this be admitted to be the case in ordinary societies, how much more so in the people of God, who were under His special protection, and had been specially set apart to His service? In the history of Achan, moreover, we read the history of secret sin, which, though unseen by any earthly eye, does nevertheless pollute the offender, and through him the Church of God, by lowering his general standard of thought and action, enfeebling his moral sense, checking the growth of his inner and devotional life, until, by a resolute act of repentance and restitution towards God, the sin is finally acknowledged and put away. " A lewd man is a pernicious creature. That he damnes his own soule is the least part of his mischiefe; he commonly drawes vengeance upon a thousand, either by the desert of his sinne, or by the infection" (Bp. Hall).

Ver. 2.—Ai. עַי or הָעַי " the ruins " (cf. Iim and Ije-abarim, the *ruins* or heaps of Abarim, Num. xxxiii. 44, 45; and Iim, Josh. xv. 29. Probably it is the same as הָעַוִּים which we find mentioned in conjunction with Bethel in ch. xviii. 22, 23. It becomes עַיָּא in Neh. xi. 31, and the feminine form is found in Isa. x. 28. The latter, from the mention of Michmash in the route of Sennacherib immediately afterwards, is probably the same as Ai. Robinson and Keil — the former very doubtfully — place it at Turmus Aya, an eminence crowned with ruins above Deir Duwân. But Vandevelde contests this, and places it at Tell-el-Hajar, *i.e.*, the Tell or heap of ruins; and G. Williams and Capt. Wilson have independently fixed on the same spot, though they call it et-Tel, or " the heap," and suppose the " el-Hajar " to have been added in answer to the question, " what heap? " This situation seems best to suit the requirements of the narrative. For it is " on the southern brow of the Wady-el-Mutyah " (Vandevelde), near that " wild entanglement of hill and valley at the head of the Wady Harith," which " climbs into the heart of the mountains of Benjamin till it meets the central ridge of the country at Bethel " (Stanley, ' Sinai and Palestine,' p. 202). Its situation, unlike that of Turmus Aya, is calculated to give cover to an ambush of 5,000 men, and it also answers to the conditions in its nearness to Michmash, from which Turmus Aya is more than three hours' journey distant. The Tell is " covered with heaps of ruins " (Capt. Wilson, ' Palestine Exploration Fund Quarterly Statement,' iv. p. 124). Conder, however (' Handbook,' p. 254), identifies Ai with Haiyan, two miles from Bethel, in the same Wady, but why, he gives no hint. A fortress so situated was one which Joshua could not leave in his rear, and so its capture was a matter of necessity. By its position, if not from the number of its inhabitants, it was

necessarily a very strong one. Ai is mentioned as early as Gen. xii. 8, and we find that it was inhabited down to the Captivity, for the " men of Bethel and Ai " are mentioned (and, it may be observed, in close proximity to those of Rama, Geba, and Michmash—see Isa. x. 28 above cited) in Ezra ii. 28. See also Neh. xi. 31, above cited. The name Ai, or ruins, found so early, implies that the aboriginal inhabitants had built a city in that almost inaccessible situation. Lieut. Conder gives a very vivid description of the site et-Tel in ' Palestine Exploration Fund Quarterly Statement,' April, 1874. There are, he says, " huge mounds of broken stone and shingle ten feet high. The town," he adds, " must have been pounded small, and the fury of its destruction is still evidenced by its completeness." He continues: " The party for the ambush, following the ancient causeway from Bethel to Jordan (which we have recovered throughout its entire length) as far as Michmash, would then easily ascend the great wady west of Ai, and arrive within a quarter of a mile of the city without having ever come in sight of it. Here, hidden by the knoll of Burjums and the high ground near it, a force of almost any magnitude might wait unsuspected. The main body in the meanwhile, without diverging from the road, would ascend the gently sloping valley and appear before the town on the open battle-field which stretches away to its east and south. From the knoll the figure of Joshua would be plainly visible to either party, with his spear stretched against the sky " (see ch. viii. 18). But the site still eludes investigation. Lieut. Kitchener, Mr. Birch, Mr. Guest, would place it at Kh-Haiy, or the rock Rimmon. When those who have visited the country are so divided in opinion, nothing but silence remains for those who have not. **Beth-aven** (cf. 1 Sam. xiv. 23). This place has not yet been identified. It was close by Ai, and not far from Bethel, as the transference of its name to Bethel by Hosea (iv. 15; v. 8; x. 5) shows. It could not have been a place of any importance, or the historian would not have found it necessary to explain where it was. Hosea has perhaps derived his knowledge of it from this passage. Some writers have identified it with Bethel. But this is obviously incorrect, since the literal rendering of the Hebrew here places Ai " in the immediate proximity of Beth-aven, *eastward* of Bethel." The LXX. omits all reference to Beth-aven. But there are many various readings. **Bethel.** Formerly Luz (Gen. xxviii. 19; xxxv. 7; Judg. i. 23). The last-cited passage seems to prove that Bethel was not among the cities taken during Joshua's campaign;

though this is extraordinary in the face of the fact that the inhabitants of Luz gave their assistance to the men of Ai in the battle (see ch. viii. 17, where, however, it is remarkable that the LXX. omits all reference to Bethel). We may observe that there is no mention of the capture of Bethel, or the destruction of the inhabitants, and that this exactly agrees with Judg. i. 22—26. This is an undesigned coincidence well worthy of note. We may also remark on the exact conformity between the situation of Bethel as described here and in Gen. xii. 8. The city to which the name Bethel was attached was not the place of Abraham's altar, as we learn from the passage just cited, but was in its immediate neighbourhood. The ruins which now mark its site are of a later date than the events recorded in Scripture. Its modern name is Beitin. **Go up and view the country.** Rather, *spy* (or *reconnoitre*); literally, *foot the country*. Joshua does not refuse to avail himself of human expedients because he is under Divine guidance (see also ch. ii.). The reasons for this reconnoitring expedition are made clear enough by the passage quoted from Lieut. Conder's survey above.

Ver. 3.—**Make not all the people to labour thither;** or, *weary not the people* with the journey *thither*. "Good successe lifts up the heart with too much confidence" (Bp. Hall).

Ver. 5.—**Unto Shebarim.** LXX., καὶ ἕως συνέτριψαν αὐτούς, as though we had שְׁבָרִם (or, as Masius suggests, הַשְּׁבִירִים) from שָׁבַר to break in pieces. So the Syriac and Chaldee versions. But this is quite out of the question. The Israelites were not annihilated, for they only lost about 36 men. Nor is Shebarim a proper name, as the Vulgate renders it. It has the article, and must be rendered either with Keil, the stone-quarries (literally, *the crushings* or *breakings*), or with Gesenius, *the ruins*, which, however, is less probable, since Ai (see above) has a similar signification. Munsterus mentions a view that it was so called in consequence of the slaughter of the Israelites. But this is very improbable. **In the going down.** Ai stood in a strong position on the mountains. The margin "in Morad" is therefore not to be preferred. It means, as the Israelites and their antagonists descended from the gates. **The hearts of the people melted and became as water.** This was not cowardice, but awe. The people had relied upon the strong hand of the Lord, which had been so wonderfully stretched out for them. From Joshua downwards, every one felt that, for some unknown reason, that support had been withdrawn.

HOMILETICS.

Vers. 1—5.—*The sin.* One of the most valuable uses of the historical portions of the Old Testament is the valuable moral lessons they convey. "The Old Testament is not contrary to the New." Both come from God, and the offences God denounces and punishes under the old dispensation will be equally denounced and punished by Him under the new. Let no sinner flatter himself that he will escape because his doctrine is sound, or because he belongs to an orthodox body of Christians, or because he feels assured of salvation. If he sins he will be punished. And he sins when he does what God has forbidden under the law as well as under the gospel. To be a moral man will not save the soul; but not to be a moral man will assuredly ruin it. We should therefore take good heed to the lessons of morality taught in the Old Testament.

I. THE EVIL OF OVER-CONFIDENCE. Even the good Joshua errs sometimes. We hear of no counsel being taken of God here, any more than when the Gibeonite embassy arrived. The report of the spies is acted upon at once. The siege of Ai seems to have been undertaken relying upon human means alone. But the Israelites were to learn how entirely dependent they were upon Divine aid. We need the lesson as much as they. In cases of difficulty we betake ourselves to God. In ordinary affairs we trust to ourselves. Yet we need His aid as much in the one as in the other. How many of our failures in the conflict with ourselves, or with the evil around us, are due to forgetting this truth? Or we take scant pains about what we think easy work. We need not "weary" ourselves, we think, with that. And our scanty preparation is inadequate to the task, since we are compassed with infirmity.

II. The exceeding sinfulness of sin. It was ruin to the Israelites' campaign. It brought disgrace, not only to the sinner, but to the cause. So now, (1) the sin of the individual falls on the community. Religion suffers severely for the short-comings of its professors. Every religious community is cruelly injured by the faults of its members. Even the great conflict against evil itself has failed of complete success as yet, solely from the sins of those who have been carrying it on. The defeats of the army of the Lord in the great struggle against Satan are to be explained on the same principle as the defeat before Ai. There needs a humilia-tion, an awakening, a casting-out of the offending member, before any new success can be achieved. And (2) the conflict against sin within is subject to the same laws. We cannot subdue our evil passions, or tempers, or habits. It is because there is some hidden sin indulged secretly, which mars all our efforts. We have some Achan within, some master passion which hugs a secret unlawful indulgence to itself, perhaps unperceived even by ourselves. Our defeats ought to teach us to institute the inquiry, bring the offender to light, and cast him out without mercy.

III. The danger of disobedience and covetousness. God had given no *reasons* for His command about Jericho and its spoils. It is true that they were obvious enough to an inquiring mind. But some minds will not inquire, except to find reasons for disobedience. Of such a disposition was Achan. *Why* should such a command be given? "To what purpose is this waste?" What is the *good* of it all? And the promptings of self-interest are sufficient to outweigh the obvious reason that this solemn ban upon Jericho and all that was therein was to impress upon the minds of the Israelites the awful and irrevocable nature of the sentence God had pronounced against the inhabitants of the land. Such abstract considerations had little weight besides the concrete fact of a wedge of gold and a Babylonish garment. The welfare of society, the necessity to its well-being of God's moral laws, are cobwebs easily brushed aside when interest or passion impel us to break those laws. We look at the temptation and look again. We let the idea gain possession of our minds. "Where is the harm?" we cry, and then we commit the sin, and involve ourselves in its terrible, and even upon repentance, to a certain extent, irremediable consequences. Though our Joshua has redeemed us from the extremest penalty of His outraged law, yet must He bring us to detection and shame, and consequent punishment. "The valley of Achor" may be given us "for a door of hope," but the anguish must come before the peace, to which, by His mercy, it is destined to lead. One lesson from Achan's sin is that no one can disobey God's laws and come off scathless. Not for nought does He say, "Thou shalt not do this thing." He who in wilful folly transgresses His commands must bear his burden, whosoever he be.

IV. The deceitfulness of sin. It seemed a light thing to Achan when he did it. "I did but taste a little honey"—a little of the sweetness of forbidden pleasure— "and lo, I must die." So almost all sin seems light when committed. A little deceit or lying, a little indulgence in impure imaginations or actions, a little com-pliance with the customs of an evil world, a little yielding to the promptings of anger or avarice, seem slight matters when they occur. But they often bring serious consequences in their train. Repeated acts become habits, and habits are not easily broken off. We are their captives before we are aware, and then we wish, and wish in vain, that we had never made ourselves their slave.

> " 'Twas but one little sin
> We saw at morning enter in,
> And lo! at eventide the world is drowned."
> *Keble,* ' *Christian Year,*' *Septuagesima Sunday.*

HOMILIES BY VARIOUS AUTHORS.

Ver. 1.—*Sin committed.* By the narrative before us we are reminded of several characteristics of sin.

I. IT DISOBEYS A COMMANDMENT. Only two precepts had been issued at the sacking of Jericho, one to spare Rahab and her family, another to "keep from the accursed thing," and the latter precept was broken. The command was distinct, unmistakable; no difficulty in comprehending its import. Scripture defines sin as the "transgression of the law." "By the law is the knowledge of sin." A prohibition tests man's obedience perhaps even more than an injunction to perform some positive act. The tempter easily lays hold of it, keeps it before the eye, irritates man's self-will, and insinuates doubts respecting the reason of the prohibition. Christ endorsed the moral law of the old dispensation—nay, made it even more stringent; but He altered the principle of obedience, or, better still, increased the power of the motives to compliance. When we sin we still transgress a law, and sins of wilful commission are, in number, out of all proportion to sins of ignorance.

II. SIN IS OFTEN THE EFFECT OF COVETOUS DESIRES.—Achan saw, coveted, and took (ver. 21). The seeing was innocent; the dwelling on the object of sight with desire was sinful. "Coveted" is the same word as used in Gen. iii. 6. "Saw . . . a tree to be *desired.*" "When lust (desire) hath conceived it bringeth forth sin." The outward object has no power to make us fall except as it corresponds to an inward affection. If the object be gazed upon long, the affection may be inordinately excited, and desire produce sinful action. Hence the counsel of the wise man regarding "the path of the wicked :" "Avoid it, pass not by it, turn from it, and pass away." It is not mixing in the world to perform our duties that is reprobated, nor even that amount of care which shall secure us an honourable position therein; but such an intent fixing of the eye upon riches, honour, pleasure, as denotes a love of the world and the things that are in it. Our affection must be set on things above as the best preservation against the influence of unholy passions; for where the heart is occupied, there evil finds it hard to effect a lodgment.

III. SIN ROBS GOD.—All the metals were to be brought to the treasury, to be dedicated to the use of Jehovah (ch. vi. 19). But Achan wished to appropriate a portion to his own ends, thus taking what belonged to God. He set up self in opposition to his God. Sin deprives God not only of gold, but of honour, love, obedience, and the use of those talents committed to men, that they may be faithful servants and stewards, not sordid proprietors. From the sinner's heart ascends no sweet incense of faith and love; in the household of the worldling there is no family altar with its grateful offering of prayer and praise; the body of the unbeliever, instead of being a temple of God, is part of the kingdom of darkness.

IV. SIN IMPLIES A DELIGHT IN WHAT GOD ABOMINATES. The possessions of the Canaanites were placed under the ban; they were denominated "the accursed thing." The Babylonish garment was to have been burnt, and the silver and gold could only be redeemed from the curse by being set apart for sacred uses. The very fact that the Almighty had condemned the property should have been sufficient to deter any one from seeking to seize it. And so with us; regard for our Father in heaven ought at once to make us shun what He has declared hateful, and look upon it with aversion; and belief in His unerring discernment should cause us readily to acquiesce in His judgment, even if at first sight the places and practices condemned do not appear hideous or sinful. The grievous nature of sin is evinced in its betrayal of a hankering after what the laws of God denounce, and consequently its revelation of a character differing from that of God, loving what is unlovely in His sight.

V. SIN IN GOD S PEOPLE IS A VIOLATION OF A COVENANT. Achan had transgressed the "covenant" (vers. 11 and 15), or, as it is expressed in ver. 1, had "committed a trespass"—*i.e.*, a breach of trust—had acted faithlessly. Jericho, as the first city taken, was to be made an example of, and therefore none of the spoil was to accrue to the Israelites, but the plunder of other cities was to be allowed to enrich them. Yet Achan disregarded the understood agreement. Nor must it be forgotten that Israel stood in a peculiar relationship to the Almighty, who promised to bless them if they adhered to the terms of the covenant, which required them to be very obedient unto every commandment which the Lord should give by the mouth of His accredited messengers. A similar covenant is re-affirmed under the gospel dispensation, only it is pre-eminently a covenant of grace, not of works. Jesus died that they who lived should henceforth live unto Him who died for them. "Seek ye first the kingdom of God, and all other things shall be added unto you," was the stipulation of the great Teacher. To "sin wilfully" is to count the blood of the covenant wherewith we are sanctified an unholy thing (Heb. x. 29). Jesus is the Mediator of a "new covenant." The same epistle concludes with a prayer that the God who, in virtue of the blood of the everlasting covenant, raised Christ from the dead, may perfect His people in every good work, that thus on both sides the "conditions" may be observed.

VI. SECRECY IS THE USUAL ACCOMPANIMENT OF SIN. Achan did not wear the "garment" or exhibit the "gold," but hid his plunder "in the earth in the midst of his tent" (ver. 21). The attempt to cloak sin may arise either from a feeling of shame, or from the fear of detection and punishment. This last is a baser motive than the first. Shame is an evidence that the man is not wholly bad, that the voice of conscience has not been totally silenced. That after the Fall our first parents did not set their faces like a flint was a testimony that evil had not acquired complete mastery over them. Oh that men visited with these compunctions of conscience would attend to the self-attesting nature of sin! We may rejoice in the endeavour to conceal crimes, so far as it indicates that society is not yet so corrupt as unblushingly to acknowledge sin as such. Since God mentions the "dissembling" of Achan as aggravating his offence, it is probable that he was afraid of the vengeance which discovery would bring upon his head. Already sin was inflicting its punishment. There could not be open, unrestrained fruition of ill-gotten gains. Rejoicing naturally demands the presence of others to share our joy, and by participation to increase the common stock; but there can be no such gathering to greet the result of sins, for they—

> " The cloak of night being plucked from off their backs,
> Stand bare and naked, trembling at themselves."

Conclusion. Thankfulness for a Saviour, born to "save his people from their sins," the Light of the world revealing our natural dark, degraded condition, but bringing to us, if we will bask in His rays, knowledge, purity, and happiness. "God be merciful to me a sinner," the prelude to "They shall walk with me in white, for they are worthy."—A.

Ver. 1.—*The way of the transgressor.* In order to understand Achan's sin, we must bear in mind the absolute nature of the decree that everything belonging to Jericho should be devoted to the Lord—all living beings slain, and destructible materials consumed as a sacrifice to His offended Majesty; all indestructible materials—silver and gold, vessels of iron and brass—consecrated to the service of the sanctuary. The sin was, therefore, something more than an act of disobedience. It was a violation of the Divine covenant. It was sacrilege, a robbery of God, an impious seizure, for base, selfish purposes, of that which belonged to Him. And the secrecy with which the sin was committed was a defiance of the Divine Omniscience. Trifling as the offence may seem on a mere superficial view of it, it thus contained the essential elements of all transgression. The penalty was terrible; but the moral exigencies of the time demanded it. The sovereignty God was asserting so solemnly over the Canaanites could suffer no dishonour among His own people. "Judgment must begin at the house of God." The point of interest in this passage is the view it gives of the connection between Achan and all Israel in this transgression; it speaks of his deed as the deed of the whole nation, and one that brought down on it the anger of the Lord. Consider (1) the relation of Achan and his in to the people; (2) the relation of the people to Achan's sin.

I. Note the influence the sin of one man may have on the life and destiny of many others. Nothing is said about the effect of Achan's trespass on his family, except that it involved them with himself in the same miserable end. We are not told whether he had any associates in crime. Probably he had. Men are seldom able to keep dark secrets like this locked up long in their own bosoms. But however this may be, we cannot well confine our thoughts to the mere participation in punishment. We are reminded of those bearings of human conduct which are at work long before the final issues stand revealed—the near, as well as remote, effects of wrong-doing. Men cannot sin alone any more than "perish" alone (ch. xxii. 20). Consider that great law of moral action and reaction that underlies all the superficial forms of social life, and which is to it very much what the laws of chemical affinity or of attraction and gravitation are to nature. By this men are held together, linked one with another, cemented into one living and organic whole. By virtue of this we are continually giving and receiving impulses. And it is as impossible that we should act without producing effects on others, as that the smooth surface of a lake should be broken and there be no undulations spreading to the banks. This influence will be for good or ill according to a man's personal character. Our words and deeds, charged with the moral quality of our own inner life, tend thus inevitably to awaken something like them in others. Every good man diffuses a moral influence that assimilates all around him to his own goodness. Every bad man stands in the midst of human society the moral image of the deadly upas tree, blighting and withering every fair thing that comes within its shadow. "Ephraim is joined to idols: let him alone!" Go not near him. For your own sake "let him alone!" So with every single act of transgression. We may not be able to trace its moral issues; only know that it adds to the ever-accumulating sum of the world's evil. So far as its power reaches it is another contribution to the building up of Satan's kingdom among men, another blow struck at the kingdom of truth and righteousness. Moreover, sin cannot always be hid, though men seek the darkness for the doing of their dark deeds—though the memorials of their guilt be carefully concealed, like the "costly garment," &c., of Achan beneath the ground—yet God's eye "seeth in secret," and He will sooner or later "reward it openly." "For nothing is secret that shall not be made manifest," &c. (Luke viii. 17). "Be sure your sin will find you out" (Num. xxxii. 23). And as its influence spreads far beyond the place of its birth, so its penalty will fall on the innocent as well as the guilty. All this may seem out of harmony with the present dispensation of grace. But not so. Christianity does not alter the fundamental laws of moral government. These considerations clothe the sinner with guilt independently of the intrinsic quality of his deed. They deepen the shadow that rests on the path of the transgressor.

II. The relation of the people to Achan's sin. The crime of this one man is imputed to all Israel on the principle of the organic unity of the nation. As the body is said to be diseased or wounded, though the malady may lie only in one of its members, so his trespass destroyed the moral integrity of the whole nation. We are reminded of certain ways in which a community may be implicated in a wrong actually done by only one of its members. (1) When the sin does but give definite expression to a spirit prevailing more or less through all. Distinct forms of practical evil often bring to light principles that are secretly leavening a whole society. It is very possible that Achan's solitary trespass was indicative of a spirit of insubordination, or of selfish greed among the people, that would have utterly subverted the Divine purpose if it had not been thus sternly rebuked at the beginning. Upon this principle of fellowship of spirit Christ said that "all the righteous blood shed on the earth" should come on that generation (Matt. xxiii. 35); and Peter charged the multitude on the day of Pentecost with having slain "the Holy One and the Just," though many of them can have had no actual part in the transgression (Acts ii. 23; iii. 14, 15). (2) When the many connive at that sin, or share the profit of it. Men sin by proxy, and thus think to secure the end without involving themselves in the wrongful means that lead to it. But to consent to reap any part of the profit of an iniquitous transaction—to place yourself willingly in any sort of connection with it—is to share its guilt. Indeed, the moral sense of mankind declares that there is a special criminality, an added element of baseness and meanness, belonging to him who has such indirect interest in the wrong-doing of others. The question of so-called "national sins" arises here. A national sin is one committed in the name of a nation by its representatives, or on which the State sets the stamp of its authority and license. If Achan's sin had been connived at by Joshua and the elders it would have been a national sin. (3) When those who are aggrieved by the sin fail to bear faithful witness against it. The guilt of this "trespass" rested on all Israel until, by public condemnation, it was wiped out (2 Cor. vii. 11).—W.

Ver. 1.—*The accursed thing.* Immediately after the taking of Jericho, Israel found itself suddenly arrested in its career of conquest. Its advanced guard received a humiliating repulse from the inhabitants of the small town of Ai. Joshua was driven almost to despair by this defeat, because it seemed to doom the army of Israel to feebleness and failure, by the withdrawal of the presence and power of God. It seemed as if the heavens were closed against him, and he could no more reckon upon that invincible Divine aid which had been hitherto the strength of his arms. He rent his garments and called upon God, and the answer came, "Israel hath sinned . . . for they have taken of the accursed thing." This transgression of the covenant was the cause of their defeat, and this alone. And in our own day it is "the accursed thing" which is still the sole obstacle to the victories of the people of God, and to His blessing resting upon them. Let us look at this sin in its cause, in its effects, and in its reparation.

I. THE CAUSE OF THIS SIN is covetousness born of the selfishness which leads to rebellion. The unhappy Achan could not resist the desire to secure for himself a share of the booty. He sought his own selfish ends in the cause of God. That cause requires to be served with complete self-devotion, and with an eye to God alone. Achan thought first of satisfying his own avarice. A holy war must be waged holily. From the moment when the base passion of selfishness creeps in, it ceases to be a holy war. It is then even worse than any other war, for God will not suffer His name to be profaned. Whenever the so-called defenders of the Church have sought their own glory, when they have aimed at securing power or fortune for themselves, they have paved the way for defeat. This is equally true of individuals. To make use of the cause of God for one's own ends is not only to dishonour, but fatally to compromise it; for it is then no longer the cause of God, but the cause of the devil.

II. THE EFFECT of intermeddling with the accursed thing IS TO LOSE THE HELP OF GOD, and to bring down His anger. The heavenly Father is no blind and unjust parent, who has favourites whose transgressions He winks at. He chastises those whom He loves, and because He loves them; He does not allow them to harden their hearts in rebellion against Him. Hence He makes them feel the Father's chastening rod (Heb. xii. 16). It is not tolerable, moreover, that the cause of God should be confounded with that of ambition and self-seeking, or that His name should be used as a cloak for covetousness. Therefore, as soon as Israel violates the covenant of God, it is visited with condign punishment. The victory of the rebel who makes use of the name of God would be, for that very reason, worse than his defeat. Defeat will show that the honour of God cannot be sullied by the sins of His people, for He repudiates them. We must not be surprised at finding that in every age God has made His people pass through the sharpest ordeal of chastisement. The heaviest of all chastisements is the interruption of communication with God. The heavens are pitiless iron and brass so long as the accursed thing is tampered with. The sin forms a wall between God and the soul, which there is no passing through.

III. THE REPARATION OF THIS EVIL IMPLIES TWO SUCCESSIVE ACTS. 1. Its confession. Achan must acknowledge his sin before all the people. 2. The utter putting away of the accursed thing. Under the stern discipline of the old covenant, the guilty man perished with his unlawful prey. Under the new covenant, the justice of God is satisfied with that inward death which is called mortification, and which ought to be a true sacrifice of self. It is equally true now, however, that mere confession is not enough; that the idol must be consumed in the sacrificial fire. Any one who keeps in his possession the accursed thing, places himself under condemnation from which there is no escape. It does not signify whether the forbidden thing be materially of much or little value. It might have been thought that the theft of a single garment and of two hundred shekels of silver was of small account amidst all the rich booty of Jericho. It is the act itself which God condemns. The smallest forbidden thing retained is enough to shut up the heavens, and to draw down upon our Church, our home, and ourselves the severe judgment of God till it has been confessed and put away.—E. DE P.

EXPOSITION.

CHAPTER VII. 6—15.

JOSHUA'S PRAYER AND GOD'S ANSWER.—Ver. 6.—**And Joshua rent his clothes.** A token of grief usual among the Jews (see Gen. xxxvii. 29, 34; xliv. 13, &c. Knobel cites Levit. xxi. 10); and though Joshua was not the high priest, yet from his peculiar position he might be expected to adopt somewhat of the high priest's demeanour, and at least not to display this outward sign of grief without the strongest reason. The words "before the ark" are omitted in the LXX. **And put dust on their heads.** A sign of still more abject humiliation. The head, the noblest part of man, was thus placed beneath the dust of the ground from whence he was taken (see 1 Sam. iv. 12; 2 Sam. i. 2; xiii. 19; xv. 32; 1 Kings xx. 38; Job ii. 12; Lam. ii. 10). It was a common custom among the Greeks. (See Lucian, De Luctu, 12). Homer mentions the custom (Iliad, xviii). Pope's translation runs thus:—

"Cast on the ground, with furious hands he spread
The scorching ashes o'er his graceful head.
His purple garments and his golden hairs,
Those he deforms with dust, and these he tears."
                                    Lines 26—30.

Ver. 7. — **Wherefore hast thou at all brought.** The LXX. seems in some way to have read עבר for עבר; they translate "why did thy servant cross?" But their rendering is a clear grammatical blunder, for the Masorites remark that the ה is to be preserved. **Would to God we had been content.** Calvin makes some severe remarks on Joshua's folly and want of faith under this reverse. But it may be paralleled by the conduct of most Christians in adversity. How few are there who can bear even temporal calamity calmly and patiently, even though they have abundant reason to know that temporal affliction is not only no sign of the displeasure of God, but the reverse! And when, through allowing secret sin to lurk within the soul, the Christian is overcome and brought to shame by his spiritual enemies, how much more seldom it is that he has the courage to gird up the loins of his soul and renew the conflict, in full confidence that victory will be his in the end! How much more frequently does he despair of victory, wish he had never undertaken the Christian profession, give up his belief in the protecting care and guidance of God, and desist, at least for a time, from the good fight of faith, to his own serious injury and to the detriment of God's Church! "It is not," adds Calvin, "a new thing for pious minds, when they aspire to seek God with holy zeal, to obscure the light of faith by the vehemence and impetuosity of their affections. And in this way all prayers would be rendered valueless, did not the Lord in His boundless indulgence pardon them, and, wiping away all their stains, receive them as if they were pure. And yet while in thus freely expostulating they cast all their care upon God, this blunt simplicity, though it needs pardon, is yet far more acceptable than the feigned modesty and self-restraint of the hypocrites."

Ver. 8.—**What shall I say?** To encourage the people who will be downcast by this defeat, while their enemies will gather courage.

Ver 9.—**For the Canaanites and all the inhabitants of the land shall hear of it.** The invariable argument of Moses (Exod. xxxii. 12; Num. xiv. 13—16; Deut. ix. 28; xxxii. 26, 27). The disgrace which the sin of man brings upon the cause of the Lord is a real and very terrible thing (cf. 2 Sam. xii. 14; Ezek. xxxvi. 23).

Ver. 10. — **Get thee up.** Not puerile lamentation, but action, is ever the duty of the soldier of the Lord. If defeat assails either the individual or the cause, there is a reason for it, and this must be promptly searched out, and with God's aid be discovered. The sin or error once found out and put away, the combat may be renewed and brought to a successful issue.

Ver. 11.—**Israel hath sinned.** A simple but satisfactory explanation. It is not God who changes. It is we who frustrate His counsels of love and protection against our enemies. We have here another assertion of the principle that if one member suffer all the members suffer with it. Achan's sin was the sin of all Israel. So the sin of one man is still the sin of the whole Church. **And have also stolen.** The accusation is cumulative. Israel, which was all involved in the sin of one among their number, had (1) broken a solemn vow; (2) had stolen what was not theirs; (3) had acted deceitfully (בְּחַשׁ); and (4) had appropriated to themselves what belonged to God, which, as Keil remarks, was the last and gravest feature of their crime. This is strongly brought out by the fivefold repetition of גַּם in the original.

Ver. 12.—**Therefore.** This plain statement disposes of the idea that the repulse before Ai was simply the result of Joshua's rashness in sending so small a body of troops. The vivid narrative of the detection of Achan, obviously taken from contemporary records, precedes the account of the final capture of the city, although Joshua, who, as we have seen, does not neglect to employ human means, resolves to take greater precautions before making a second attack. Not a hint is dropped that the former number of men was insufficient, or that Joshua had been misled by the information brought by the reconnoitring party. In the mind of the historian the defect is entirely owing to the existence of secret sin in the Israelitish camp. **Except ye destroy the accursed from among.** Dr. Maclear, in the 'Cambridge Bible for Schools,' calls attention to the fact that 1 Cor. v. 13 is a quotation from the LXX. here, substituting, however, τὸν πονηρὸν for τὸ ἀνάθεμα.

Ver. 13.—**Sanctify the people.** See note on ch. iii. 5. **Thou canst not stand before thine enemies.** Observe the singular number here, intensifying the testimony of the whole history to the fact that Israel was one body before the Lord. And observe, moreover, how the existence of secret sin, even though unknown to and undetected by him in whom it lurks, has power to enfeeble the soul in its conflict with its enemies. Hence we learn the duties of watchfulness and careful examination of the soul by the light of God's Word.

Ver. 14.—**Taketh,** *i.e.*, by lot, as in 1 Sam. xiv. 42 (הַפִּילוּ make it *fall;* cf. 1 Sam. x. 20) (cf. Jonah i. 7; also Prov. xviii. 18). **According to the families.** The gradual centering of the suspicion upon the offender is one of the most striking features of the history. The genealogies of the children of Israel were very strictly kept, as the Books of Chronicles, Ezra, and Nehemiah show. Achan's name is carefully given in the genealogy of Judah in 1 Chron. ii. 7. The subdivision of the tribes into families (or *clans*, Keil) and households (or, as we should perhaps say, *families*) was for convenience of enumeration, military organisation, and perhaps of assessment. Oehler, 'Theologie des Alten Testaments,' Sec. 101, takes the same view as Keil. The tribes, he says, were divided into מִשְׁפָּחוֹת or אֲלָפִים *i.e.*, Geschlechter (LXX. δῆμοι, for which the best English equivalent is *clans*, as above); these into families or houses (בָּתִּים), or fathers' houses (בֵּת אָבוֹת); and these again into single heads of a house (גְּבָרִים). The principle, he adds of a Mosaic family, is as follows: Every "family" forms a distinct whole, which as far as possible must be maintained in its integrity. Each tribe, says Jahn ('Hebrew Commonwealth,' Book II.), acknowledged a prince (נָשִׂיא) as its ruler. As its numbers increased, there arose a subdivision of the tribe into collections of families. Such a collection was called a house of fathers, a מִשְׁפָּחָה or clan, or a thousand. But this explanation is not so satisfactory as that given above. Kurz remarks on the important part family life played among the Hebrews, with whom, in consequence of their descent from Abraham, and the importance they attached to it, the nation was developed out of the family. See Introduction.

Ver. 15. **He that is taken with the accursed thing;** or, according to Keil, "he on whom the ban falls. " **He and all that he hath** (cf. ver. 24). The opinion that Achan's family had in some way become participators in his sin would seem preferable to the idea that his sin had involved them in the ban (see Deut. xxiv. 16, which qualifies Levit. xxvi. 39; so Hengstenberg, 'History,' p. 218). The destruction of their possessions is due to the fact that all the family had come under the ban.

Folly נְבָלָה used of the heart as well as the head (cf. Gen. xxxiv. 7: Deut. xxii. 21; Judg. xix. 23, 24, xx. 6; 2 Sam. xiii. 12; Psa. xiv. 1). The LXX. render by ἀνόμημα, and the Vulgate by *nefas*, but Theodotion renders by ἀφροσύνη.

HOMILETICS.

Vers. 6—15.—*The humiliation.*

I.—THE BITTERNESS OF REPENTANCE.

1. *The sting of sin is sharper than its pleasure.* The uneasiness which followed on Achan's transgression far outweighed any pleasure he could have derived from it. For, first, the possession of his treasure was itself a trouble. He had to hide it in his tent, and to watch carefully lest any one should discover it. Next, he brought death upon thirty-six of his innocent fellow-countrymen. Lastly, he brought the keenest distress and humiliation upon Joshua and the whole congregation. So it always is. The sting which follows on our first deliberate disobedience of God's commands is always far keener than the pleasure that disobedience gave us. The fear of detection, the oppression of a guilty secret, far outweighs any happiness sinful indulgence can give. And the distress which our misdeeds are apt to bring on those who are bound to us by the nearest and dearest of ties is frequently altogether out of proportion to the momentary satisfaction we have derived from our wrong-doing.

2. *The reaction that follows on sin is often fatal to faith.* Thus Joshua's courage gave way. He reproached God, he made sure of defeat and destruction, he wished he had never crossed Jordan. So are we often weakened in our warfare against God's enemies by the discouragements and disasters the sins of Christians (perhaps unknown to ourselves) have brought on us. So in our own hearts, after some great failure, the consequence of hidden evil within us which we have not been careful to detect, we are overwhelmed with sorrow and confusion, we think it useless to strive, we are tempted to abandon our Christian profession, we wish we had never undertaken its responsibilities, we cry, " Would God we had been content and dwelt on the other side Jordan ! "

II.—THE REPROACH OF SIN. Achan's sin brought not only sorrow, but *disgrace*, after it. " The Canaanites and all the inhabitants of the land shall hear of it." Consequences flow from sin which we had never thought of when we committed it. Our relatives and friends have to suffer for our misdeeds. Our order in society must bear the burden of our misconduct. The cause of Christ must be beaten back because we have abandoned it. There is a never-failing connection between sin and shame. If we do not feel it for ourselves, others must feel it for us.

III.—THE PROMPT MEASURES NECESSARY TO AVERT ITS CONSEQUENCES. This may be regarded as affecting religious bodies or individuals. (1) Excommunication has fallen into disfavour, and indeed it has been shamefully abused. And yet the expulsion of the offender, at least until he gave unequivocal proofs of repentance, was one of the first principles of the Christian Church (see 1 Cor. v.). And so now, no society owning the name of Christ ought to tolerate within its borders any person whose life is a scandal to the religion he professes. " With such an one no not to eat " is a Scripture maxim. And observe the holy eagerness Joshua displayed in the matter. There was no delay. He rose up early in the morning. God left him no doubt about the course he ought to pursue. And the evil was at once and for ever put away. It were "much to be wished" that the " godly discipline " of the early ages of the Church were restored. Calvin and many other of the Reformers laboured hard to restore it; but they too often lacked judgment and mercy. Yet it were well could the congregation of the Christian faithful resolve to "put away from " them adultery, fornication, drunkenness, dishonesty, open and notorious covetousness or profaneness, and to refuse to live in friendship or intimacy with those who thus bring disgrace on the Christian name. (2) Our dealings with ourselves should be on the same principle. There should be no delay in our repentance, no dallying with sin. As soon as we are conscious of its evil presence, we should do our best to cast it out. If it be not cast out at once it will be our ruin. We must " rise up early in the morning," examine our actions one by one, bring our dispositions and habits to be tested by the unerring judgment of God, and that one which He pronounces to be guilty must be condemned and sacrificed to His just vengeance. And we may remark, moreover, how often sin lurks within us, unsuspected even by ourselves. We go out to battle like the children of Israel, against God's enemies, unconscious that there is a traitor within the camp. When we meet with disgrace and disaster in a conflict in which God is pledged to aid us, we may be sure that the fault is within ourselves. We ought at once to betake ourselves to self-examination, to detect the hidden evil, and when found we ought at once to put it away.

HOMILIES BY VARIOUS AUTHORS.

Ver. 14.—*Sin discovered.* This leads us to remark that—

I. EVERY SIN IS KNOWN TO GOD. Joshua was ignorant that Achan had secreted spoil, but the searching glances of God reached further than the most watchful oversight of the leader. As afterwards, when the disciples did not suspect the character and intents of Judas, the Lord discerned the sinister purposes of his heart. The omniscience and omnipresence of the Almighty have been strangely disregarded even by His own servants. Witness the curious flight of Jonah, as if he could really " flee from the presence of the Lord." " I know thy works " is the heading to the practical address in nearly each of the seven letters to the Churches of Asia. "Thou God seest me."

II. SIN REVEALED BY FAILURE IN AN UNDERTAKING. The overthrow of Jericho inspired the Israelites with such confidence that they disdained to employ all their forces in assaulting Ai. To their surprise, their attack was repulsed with loss. The greater the previous security, the more intense the subsequent alarm. They were unconscious of the presence of a traitor in the camp. The theft of Achan was a stronger opponent than the men of the city. Sin destroys our power. As one has quaintly observed, " In running a race, an inward pain hinders more than if a dozen men jostled you." When men have taken cold, they immediately reflect where they could have been exposed to draught, and non-success in any enterprise causes us to inquire, What have we done amiss? Trouble leads us to scrutinise our past life, conscience accuses of sins which have deserved, if they have not actually drawn upon us, this proof of Divine displeasure. Self-examination is healthful if not carried to excessive lengths; it may produce " carefulness, clearing of ourselves," &c. (2 Cor. vii. 11). *The effect of sin is not confined to the particular guilty member.* Sin taints the community, or often involves it in its suffering. As a drop of ink discolours a whole glass of water, so thousands of innocent persons may be affected by the neighbourhood of one sinner. This concerns us *individually*, for if one limb offends, the body is defiled; and *collectively*, as members of Churches, and as belonging to a nation.

III. THE OFFENCE MADE KNOWN IN ANSWER TO PRAYER. Deep was Joshua's solicitude. With the elders of Israel he rent his clothes and fell prostrate before the ark all day. To a lover of God, the belief that His favour is withdrawn is the most overwhelming sorrow. Nor is the grief merely selfish in its origin. Joshua lamented the dishonour which would be affixed to the glorious name of Jehovah when the news of Israel's defeat was bruited abroad. Prayer is the believer's unfailing resource. Receiving any woful tidings, he " spreads the letter," like Hezekiah, before the Lord. He ventures to plead, to expostulate, to argue. And the answer surely arrives though it appear long to tarry. In this narrative we find Joshua reproved for imagining that God would arbitrarily desert His people. He might have known that something was wrong in the conduct of the nation, and his inquiry should have been, Wherein have we offended? We must not at once rush to the conclusion that the events which befal us are " judgments," for when we think God's smile is absent, it may be that the clouds of our marshy land interrupt the heavenly rays. Nevertheless the advice of the preceding paragraph holds good, and the rebuke administered to Joshua may be often seasonably applied to ourselves.

IV. THE OFFENDER MANIFESTED. The drawing of a lot was the means resorted to on all important occasions for appointment to positions of honour or shame. Picture the gradual contraction of the circle of fire till it enwrapped only "the troubler of Israel," and he stood before all the people as the cause of a national disgrace. The slow and stately discovery, as well as the proceedings of the day before, *afforded time to the criminal to reveal himself*, if he would. What must have been his feelings as he saw detection drawing nearer and nearer till it pointed its finger to his breast, saying, "Thou art the man!" The method of manifestation also *afforded time for the spectators to be thoroughly aroused*, so that they might appreciate more deeply the awfulness of the sin committed, and be ready with one shout to inflict the penalty due thereto. God may advance slowly, but His step is sure. Delay is no presumption of final impunity.

V. We see lastly, THE FOLLY OF SIN. Achan "wrought folly in Israel" (ver. 15). The word means stupidity—as Abigail uncomplimentarily remarked of her husband, "Nabal is his name and folly is with him." Sin is certain of detection. Known to the Almighty, He often brings it into the light of day here, and will surely manifest it hereafter. Sin imperils real, enduring bliss for the sake of transitory gratifications. A little pleasure, and severest pain; for brief fame, lasting infamy; for temporary wealth, eternal loss.—A

EXPOSITION.

CHAPTER VII. 16—26.

THE DISCOVERY OF ACHAN'S SIN.—Ver. 16.—**The family of Judah.** The expression מִשְׁפַּחַת is remarkable. Many commentators would read מִשְׁפְּחֹת, not without some MSS. authority. Keil objects that the Chaldee and Syriac have the singular. But the LXX. has κατὰ δήμους, and the Vulgate *juxta familias*. On the whole it seems more probable that as מִשְׁפַּחַת occurs twice in this passage, it has been so pointed where the same letters occur for the third time, than that, with Poole, it means tribe (so also Gesenius and Winer); or that, as others suggest, it is used for *omnes* or *singulas gentes*. See, however, Judg. xiii. 2, where it is unquestionably used in the sense of *tribe*.

Ver. 19.—**My son.** This is no mere hypocritical affectation of tenderness. Joshua feels for the criminal, even though he is forced to put him to death. So in our own day the spectacle is not uncommon of a judge melted to tears as he passes sentence of death on the murderer. The expression seems almost to imply a belief that, though Achan must undergo the extremest penalty of the law in this world, Joshua entertained a hope that he might be forgiven in the next. It certainly proves that, stern as the law of Moses was, it was felt, at least in those early days, to be rather against the sin than the sinner that its severity was directed. In commenting upon the severity of the Mosaic covenant, whether towards offenders against its provisions or against the Canaanites, we must remember Bishop Butler's caution, that in this world we see but a very small portion of the whole counsel of God. **Give glory to the Lord God of Israel, and make confession unto Him.** Literally, *offer* (or *impute*) *glory to the Lord God of Israel*, and *give* confession (or *praise*) unto Him (cf. John ix. 24). The meaning is to give honour to God as the all-seeing God, the revealer of secrets, by an open confession before men of what is already known to Him. It may have been a common formula of adjuration, though Masius thinks otherwise.

Ver. 21.—**A goodly Babylonish garment.** Literally, "*a mantle of Shinar, one goodly one.*" Babylon was in the "land of Shinar" (see Gen. xi. 2; xiv. 1; Isa. xi. 11; Zech. v. 11). The אַדֶּרֶת derived from אדר great, glorious, was an ample cloak, sometimes of hair or fur (Gen. xxv. 25; cf. 1 Kings xix. 13, 19; 2 Kings ii. 13, 14; Jonah iii. 6, &c.). The Babylonish mantle was famed for its beauty (ποικίλη, LXX.), and was, no doubt, worked artistically with figures of men and animals. "Of all Asiatic nations, the Babylonians were the most noted for the weaving of cloth of divers colours. Into these stuffs gold threads were introduced into the woof of many hues. Amongst those who traded in 'blue clothes and embroidered work' with Tyre were the merchants of Asshur, or Assyria; and that the garments of Babylon were brought into Syria and greatly esteemed at a very early period, we learn from their being classed amongst the most precious articles of spoil, even with gold, in the time of Joshua" (Layard, 'Nineveh,' II. 413). From this, among other passages, we may infer the early date of the Book of Joshua. It marks an early stage of civilisation when an embroidered garment can be considered as in any degree equivalent to gold. The Israelites, it must be remembered, were not unaccustomed in Egypt to the highest degree of civilisation then known. "Nam Persarum, finitimarumque gentium luxum eo se ostentare solere vel ex eo constat quod captis ab Alexandro Magno Susis illic inventa fuerit 10 millia pondo, sive talenta purpuræ Hermionicæ, teste Plutarcho in Alexandro" (Corn. a Lapide). A wedge of gold. Literally, "a *tongue* of gold." Some derive our word ingot from the French *lingot*, or little tongue. But others derive it with greater probability from the Dutch *ingieten*, the same as the German *eingiessen*, to pour in. "Si ergo invenias apud philosophos perversa dogmata luculenti sermonis assertionibus decorata, *ista est lingua aurea*. Sed vide, ne te decipiat fulgor operis, ne te rapiat sermonis aurei pulchritudo: memento, quia Jesus anathema jussit esse omni aurum quod in Jericho fuerit inventum. Si poetam legeris modulatis versibus et præfulgido carmine Deos Deasque texentem, ne delecteris eloquentiæ suavitate. *Lingua aurea est*: si eam sustuleritis, et posueris in tabernaculo tuo: polluis omnem ecclesiam Domini" (Orig., Hom. 7 on Joshua).

Ver. 23.—**Laid them out before the Lord.** This shows the directly religious nature of the proceeding. God had directed the lot, the offender was discovered, and now the devoted things are solemnly laid out one by one (for so the Hebrew seems to imply, though in 2 Sam. xv. 24 it has the sense of planting firmly, as molten matter hardens and becomes fixed) before Him whose they are, as a confession of sin, and also as an act of restitution.

Ver. 24.—**Took Achan, the son of Zerah.**

Great-grandson in reality (see ver. 1; cf. 1 Kings xv. 2, 10). **And his sons and his daughters** (see note, ver. 15). **Brought** them. Hebrew, "brought them *up*." The valley of Achor was above Jericho, whether higher up the valley or on higher ground is not known. **The valley of Achor** (see ch. xv. 7; Isa. lxv. 10; Hos. ii. 15). *Achor* means trouble (see note on ch. vi. 18).

Ver. 25.—**Stoned him with stones.** The word here is not the same as in the last part of the verse. It has been suggested that the former word signifies to stone a living person, the second to heap up stones upon a dead one; and this derives confirmation from the fact that the former word has the signification of piling up, while the latter rather gives the idea of the weight of the pile. Some have gathered from the use of the singular here, that Achan only was stoned; but the use of the plural immediately afterwards implies the contrary, unless, with Knobel, we have recourse to the suggestion that "them" is a "mistake of the Deuteronomist" for "him." It is of course possible that his family were only taken there to witness the solemn judgment upon their father. But the use of the singular and plural in Hebrew is frequently very indefinite (see Judg. xi. 17, 19; Psa. lxvi. 6. See note above, on ch. vi. 25).

Ver. 26.—**And the Lord turned from the heat of His anger.** There is no contradiction between this and such passages as 1 Sam. xv. 29; James i. 17. It is not God, but we who turn. Our confession and restitution, by uniting our will with His, of necessity turn His wrath away. Yet of course it is through Jesus Christ alone that such confession and restitution is possible, and they are accepted simply because by faith they are united with His.

HOMILETICS.

Vers. 16—26.—*The detection.* Objections have been raised to the morality of the whole narrative. We will deal first with this subject, and then turn to the religious and moral questions involved.

I. WHY DID GOD NOT REVEAL THE OFFENDER WHEN HE REVEALED THE OFFENCE? The answer is, that He might still further display the hardness of Achan's heart. He did not at once come forward and confess his crime. He not only had offended against God's laws, but he persisted in his offence. His was not a tender conscience, sensitive to the least reproach. He saw what disaster he had brought upon Israel, yet he clung to his ill-gotten gains as long as he could. He was not driven, either by remorse for the injury he had done his brethren, or by the clear evidence that God had found him out, to confession and restitution. He concealed his guilt till concealment was no longer possible, and thus added as much as he could to his guilt. So do men in these days hug their sins to their bosom as long as they are not found out. They cry, "Tush, God hath forgotten. He hideth His face and He will never see it;" thus adding all possible aggravation to their guilt.

II. THE JUSTICE OF JOSHUA is worthy of remark. Even Achan's confession was not regarded as final. The wedge of gold, the garment, and the silver were brought and solemnly laid out before God and the congregation as proof of his guilt. Not till then was judgment pronounced. We have here a warning against hasty and uncharitable judgments. No man can justly be visited with censure or punishment until his guilt be fully proved.

III. We should next observe THE NATURE OF ACHAN'S SIN. 1. It was *sacrilege*, the most presumptuous of all sins. The tendency of modern thought is to ignore such sins. To steal what is devoted to God's service is not worse than to steal anything else. To break an oath is not worse than to break one's word. Do not such reasonings ignore the personality of God? And do not religious people very often unthinkingly surrender a fundamental article of their faith when they yield to such reasoning? If there be indeed a God—if He be nothing but the embodiment of the principle of humanity, as we are now taught, does it not add the most awful of all insolence to the sin in itself when we rob Him, or lie to Him? All sins are, it is true, a denial of His being; but that denial assumes a more naked and a bolder form when the offence is directed against Him. For then all disguises of self-interest are swept away, and the offender says deliberately in his heart, "There is no God." Let us take heed, therefore, how we "rob God," whether "in tithes and offerings," or in any other way. 2. The sacrilege was committed just when sacrilege was most inexcusable. The hand of God had been clearly visible in the capture of Jericho. The dedication of the spoil to Him was an acknowledgment of His awful power. Not long before God had dried up the waters of Jordan before His people. They had but just renewed their covenant with Him by a general circumcision of the people, and had sanctified that renewal by partaking of the passover. And God foreknew that Achan would persist in his sin, in disbelieving in the Almighty power of God until his offence was brought home beyond the possibility of mistake to his own door.

The lessons we learn from this event are four.

I. THE AWFULNESS OF THE SENTENCE AGAINST SIN. "The soul that sinneth it shall die." "The wages of sin is death." All unrepented sin is leading us up to this end. Achan is the type of impenitent sinners. He persists in his sin till the great moment of unveiling comes, as sinners persist in their sin until they are brought to the bar of God's judgment. Then is it too late to cry for mercy, when it is the time of judgment. We must learn to confess and forsake our sin in time.

II. THE CERTAINTY OF DETECTION. The heavens did not shake, nor the earth tremble, when Achan committed his sin. No lightning descended from above upon his head. No sign appeared in the earth or sky to betray him. The sun rose and set as usual. Nothing disturbed the ordinary routine of the camp until the reverse at Ai. Yet God saw all and meant to bring it to light in His own good time. Achan fancied himself undiscovered, but he was mistaken. And so are they mistaken who fancy that God does not see their secret sins. They may go on for years undiscovered, but God knows all, and can, and often does, in the most unexpected way bring all to light. If not before, yet on that day when the secrets of all hearts shall be revealed, shall the sin which the sinner has hugged so closely to his bosom be displayed in its native hideousness before God, angels, and men.

III. THE NECESSITY OF CONFESSION AND RESTITUTION. Repentance which does not involve these is no repentance at all. To repent of sin is to forsake it; but forsaking sin is impossible without confession and restitution. *Confession*, that is, to the person whom we have offended. If we have sinned against God, we must confess our sin to Him. If we have done wrong to man, we must acknowledge the wrong we have done to him who has suffered by it. *Restitution*, again, is a sore trial to the offender; he would fain persuade himself that it is unnecessary. But unless we restore our ill-gotten gains we are persisting in the very sin we profess to have renounced. We cannot really hate and desire to break off any sinful habits, while we retain as our own that which those sinful habits have gained for us. Achan was compelled (1) to acknowledge the sin he had committed, and (2) to acquiesce in the restoration of what he had stolen. And those who, in our days, hope that they may be held blameless because they confess to God, which means to themselves, sins the shame of which they ought to endure, and the profit of which they are bound to restore, will certainly undergo the punishment which Achan, even when confessing and restoring, did not escape. The duty of confession to the person offended is incumbent on those who have slandered, or insulted, or wounded the feelings of another. That of restitution is due from those who have wronged God or man, either by withholding from the former what was due to Him, or by taking undue advantage of the ignorance or necessity of the latter. Those who defraud the widow and the fatherless, or " oppress the hireling in his wages," or drive a corrupt or unjust bargain, who use "the bag of deceitful weights," must either disgorge their ill-gotten gains, or suffer the vengeance of a just God. So the Scriptures tell us throughout.

IV. THE GRAVITY OF SIN DEPENDS ON ITS CIRCUMSTANCES. The taking of a piece of gold or silver and a garment is not in itself an offence that deserves death, nor was it ever so regarded under the law. What constituted the gravity of Achan's offence we have already seen. We may gather hence that in estimating sin, the position of the offender, his opportunities of enlightenment, the nature and strength of the temptation, his means of resisting it, must be taken into account. A sin is infinitely worse when committed by a man who has made a high profession of religion, and must have known the gravity of the offence when committing it. A sin is infinitely worse when an utter indifference to the existence of God or His justice is ostentatiously shown. It may possibly be that one weak in faith and holy resolution, and exposed to overwhelming temptation, may plead the intensity of the temptation, as well as his own ignorance and inexperience, as some palliation of his error. " The publicans and the harlots go into the kingdom of God before you," said our Lord to the scribes and Pharisees. And so the sin-stained multitudes in our large cities may be nearer to God than many decent professors of religion who combine with their comfort and decency the coldest and most cynical selfishness.

HOMILIES BY VARIOUS AUTHORS.

Ver. 19.—*Sin confessed.* A notable scene. The people of Israel assembled in solemn conclave. In silent excitement the national offender has been detected, and waits to hear his doom from the lips of the great commander. Whilst every eye is bent upon Achan, Joshua addresses him in the language of the text. Note how guilty Joshua speaks, grieving over the offence rather than severely censuring it, calling the criminal " my son," and inviting a full disclosure from his own lips. Out of his own mouth was Achan to be condemned. Yet not with delight did Joshua await the confession. His fatherly heart was sorely pained at such a revelation of iniquity in his erring child.

I. CONFESSION IS DUE TO THE HONOUR OF GOD. All sin is committed against God, inflicts a wrong upon His Divine Majesty. To acknowledge this is the least reparation the sinner can make, is a sign of a right disposition, indicates that the basis of God's government remains firm within the sinner's bosom, though transgression had clouded it for a time. Confession magnifies the broken law and makes it honourable. Its omission from the Pharisee's prayer was a fatal defect; whilst the publican went down "justified " because of his proper attitude with reference to a holy God. The penitence of the thief upon the cross was evinced by his utterance, "We indeed justly, for we receive the due reward of our deeds." To confess is, in truth, to " give glory unto God," and hence is required, though not for His information, yet as essential to His character and law.

II. CONFESSION RELIEVES THE BURDENED BREAST. One of the clearest proofs that man was designed for companionship is to be seen in the tendency of any strong emotion to create an eager desire to communicate the same feeling unto others. In our joys we long for the congratulations of our friends, and we seek their sympathy in our sorrows. And though the consciousness of sin is naturally accompanied at first by an endeavour to screen it from the gaze of our fellows, yet very soon the desire for secrecy is overcome by the more potent wish to speak of the deed which lies so heavily upon the conscience. Otherwise, as with the Spartan boy who, in hiding a fox under his tunic, allowed it to devour his very entrails, we shall discover that our concealment of sin can only end in the destruction of our being. And if it be thus helpful to discharge our woes and our follies into the ear of a fellow-creature, how much greater must be our satisfaction when we have poured our tale into the audience of our heavenly Father. Men may view us with loathing, and shrink from future contact with us; they may fail even to make allowance for the strength of the temptation and the difficulties under which we laboured; but our Father is acquainted with all the circumstances, loves us as His children, and, whilst pained at our backsliding, is glad to witness our contrition. In Achan's confession there are several features worthy of imitation.

1. *It was a full confession.* There was no more dissembling, but an open declaration of all he had done. No attempt to extenuate his guilt; he laid it bare in all its enormity. The antithesis to confession is covering our sins, which may take place in various ways. We may try to justify them as necessary or excusable, as Saul did when he spared Agag. We may show that the matter was comparatively trifling and unimportant, as when we give names that soften vices and lessen our apprehension of them. Or we may charge other persons or things with the responsibility, shifting the blame from ourselves, pleading the requirements of business, the rules of society, the expectations of our friends, and the solicitations received, as when Adam replied, "The woman thou gavest, she gave me of the tree."

2. *It acknowledged that the chief injury had been committed against God.* "I have sinned against the Lord God of Israel." He had displayed a spirit of ingratitude and disobedience, and though he had brought evil upon the nation, and deserved their reprobation, he knew that it was the Almighty whom his conduct had especially wronged. So David cried, "Against thee, thee only have I sinned." Jesus Christ joined together the two branches of the moral law; but there are many who seem to think that if they fulfil their duty to their neighbour, their duty to God matters not. They say, "I have never done harm to any, have always paid my debts, been truthful and honest, charitable and upright; what sin, then, have I been guilty of?" We might in answer deny the accuracy of their statements, since due regard to others can hardly be observed apart from regard to God; but it is better, perhaps, to insist upon the obligation resting upon every man to "love the Lord with all his might," and to point out the numerous instances in which the worship and ordinances of God have been uncared for at the same time that selfish pleasures have been indulged in to the full. When the prodigal comes to himself, he does not merely resolve to reform, and that in future he will not join in the rioting of the world, but will live soberly before men; his one thought is to return to his Father and to confess, "Father, I have sinned against heaven and before thee."

3. *It was a confession to the people,* since they had suffered through his misconduct. Achan's avowal was made in the face of Israel, and was followed by punishment according to the law. "Confess your faults one to another."

Conclusion.—The day approaches when "God shall bring every work into judgment, with every secret thing, whether it be good or whether it be evil."—A.

Ver. 21.—*A sin of greed.* Here we have much profitable study. Some sins are peculiar to certain ages or countries. But greed is found in all lands and times. It specially thrives in periods of wealth and of prosperity. It creeps in where faults of uglier aspect are denied admission. It flourishes wherever the power of religion has decayed while its profession continues. Here is an instance of its action in all its meanness, disclosure, mischief, and retribution. Consider it.

I. Mark ACHAN'S FAULT. There was this feature peculiar in the capture of Jericho—that man had no hand in it. It was God's work throughout. No risk, no loss was entailed on Israel. The earthquake of God—if such was the mode of its destruction—threw the walls down flat. The capture, God's work; the spoil was, in a special sense, God's spoil. The first-fruits of their booty; He required the entire consecration of all the gold and silver to His service. In all their subsequent operations of war the spoil they take will be their own. In this God claims all. In such a prescription there was nothing that was unreasonable, but much that was divinely wise. Israel as a whole obeyed the Divine command, doubtless helped thereto by the solemnity which the presence and miracles of God imparted to their task. The destruction—righteously ordained—was carried out as God ordered. The whole of the wealth that was indestructible was reserved for God. But Achan is tempted. He suddenly lights on one hundred ounces of silver and twenty-five ounces of gold—a large sum in those days—probably more in purchasing power than a thousand pounds to-day. To see is to covet intensely, and to find a score of reasons rising within him for disobedience. " To take it hurts no one." " Nobody need know anything about it." " The sanctuary is quite rich enough." " There will be plenty left untouched by his more scrupulous neighbours." " It will stock a farm and build a house." So the vivid imagination of greed discovers a multitude of reasons for taking the spoil. And, somehow, the suddenness of the opportunity and the impulse stuns all his better nature and makes it speechless. There is no voice to remind him that he will despise himself, or that he imperils his nation. It is nothing to him that within an hour, and just at hand, God's omnipotence had been working a miracle. Under the very shadow of the Almighty he dares to sin. And every thought but that of his material advantage banished from his mind, he takes the forbidden treasure, and, concealing it in his clothes, hurries with it to his tent, and, with or without the connivance of his family—more probably the former— buries it in the earth. It is these sudden temptations that test a man. *A good habit is the only protection from a bad impulse.* Had he been habitually honourable, he would not so have sinned. But he was one of those who like to be deemed smart and clever, and who often imagine that self-preservation is " the fulfilling of all law." Did he enjoy his loot that night? Probably with some faintest misgiving he enjoyed it greatly, and his wife and family and himself made out a most plausible case of self-justification, and built pleasant castles in the air out of their treasures. *But—*

II. Mark how ACHAN'S SIN FINDS HIM OUT. No sin is ever entirely concealed. Every virtue puts its seal upon the brow, and every fault its mark. When concealment is perfect, the man is still embarrassed—pre-occupied. His taste, and with his taste his look, degenerates. Something of restlessness makes at least his spirit a " fugitive and a vagabond in the earth." His eye is on fence, and he alternates between a glance which, in its curiosity to know whether you suspect him, glares on you, and the averted look which shuns your eye altogether. So every fault, however secret, gives some tokens of something being wrong—so much so, that the special form of wrong can often be detected in the mere look. And in addition, how strikingly is it the case that often just one precaution has been left untaken that brings the truth to light. *God is light*, and is always illuminating by His providence our hidden deeds of darkness; sometimes by methods more, and sometimes by methods less miraculous, God does this. In this instance how swift, terrible, and certain is the discovery! The unexpected, needless failure of the attack on Ai, where success was easy, suggests something wrong. In answer to Joshua's prayer, God's oracle reveals it. The culprit is not named, but, using the lot probably, the tribe to which he belongs, then his division of the tribe, then his family, then himself, are successively indicated; and he who but a day or two before felt so secure in the absolute secrecy of his crime, stands revealed to all the people in all the meanness of his greed! Your sin and my sin will find us out. It is better for us to find it out, to own and end it. Plume not yourself on craft or subtlety. For God's light will disclose whatever God's eye discerns. If you do not wish a wrong thing to be known, keep it undone. All sin finds out the doer of it.

III. Mark THE RESULTS OF HIS WRONG. How different from what they dreamed! There was no comfort; no farm, no castle ever came of it—only shame, disappointment, death. Mark specifically its mischiefs. 1. Israel was damaged. In the two attacks on Ai rendered necessary by this sin, many lives were lost needlessly. The heart of the people was discouraged, and the success of their enterprise imperilled. 2. Then there is the probable corruption of the man's family, the digging and hiding being hardly possible without their knowledge. It is an awful penalty of a parent's sin that it tends so directly and strongly to corrupt the children. Let us see that those whom God has given us be not harmed by what they see in us. 3. It involves all his family in the penalty of death. The law of Moses was explicit that the child should not be put to death for the father's sin. But here—whether because the family had been partakers of his crime, or because that crime was one of terrible presumptuousness—the family share his fate. Whatever the reason, it reminds us of the fact that God "visits the iniquity of the fathers upon the children to the third and fourth generation of those that hate him, and shows mercy unto thousands [of generations] of them that love him and keep his commandments." Here the parent's fault involves the family in ruin. Such is too often the case. Let us guard against the possibility of it. 4. It costs him his own life : he is stoned to death. Late repentance perhaps letting him make a fairer start in the other world, but not availing to prolong his existence here. How dearly he paid for his silver and his gold ! How commonly men do this ; how much they part with to get what sometimes only hurts them when they gain it ! Let not greed be our ruin. Be generous in self-protection, if from no higher motive. Only goodness is wisdom, and they consult worst for their own advantage that seek to further it with craft or with impiety.—G.

Ver. 26.—*Sin punished.* I. A TERRIBLE PUNISHMENT. Achan is stoned to death, and his goods are then burnt with fire. He lost not only that which he had stolen, but even his own property, and above all his life. Such is the sinner's mis-reckoning !

1. *The laws of God have their sanctions annexed.* Sin is followed by its pecu-liar immediate effects, which are a punishment in themselves, and there are besides the retribution awards of the Legislator. Achan must have felt a gnawing and a fire within him as soon as the evil deed was done ; but this was only preliminary to the pain of detection and subsequent penalty of stoning. It is not well with the wicked even in this world, and we cannot forget the hints of the Bible respecting stripes to be inflicted in the world to come.

2. *This narrative is intended to impress us with a deep sense of the evil of sin.* God speaks to us solemnly respecting the deserts of sin. So swift a retribution could not but act as a warning to the Israelites, and the record of it may serve the same purpose with respect to ourselves. If Jehovah seemed stern for a season, He dealt in real kindness with the people, for surely it was expedient for one family to die, rather than that the whole nation should be disobedient and suffer extinc-tion.

3. *Seldom does the sinner suffer alone.* Achan's family lost their lives also. Perhaps they had connived at his theft. " By one man sin entered into the world, and death by sin, and so death passed upon all men." If we are reckless of our own interests, let us not cruelly blight the prospects of others.

II. THE SIDE OF THE DIVINE CHARACTER HERE REVEALED. He is shown to be a jealous God, hating sin, and taking vengeance upon those who disregard His precepts. " The fierceness of God's anger " may not be such a pleasant object of contemplation as the exceeding riches of the love of God, but it is good for us to think of it in connection with evil, and is part of our notion of a perfect character. The meek and lowly Jesus could kindle into holy indignation at the sight of the hypocrisy and oppression of the scribes and Pharisees, and a cloud of brightness that has no element of fire is not the representation given in Scripture of the appearance of God. Daniel saw " a fiery stream, which issued and came forth from before " the Ancient of days.

III. THE COMFORTING ASPECTS OF OUR THEME. 1. We are *not informed of Achan's final destiny*, and this thought may alleviate the difficulty which some minds feel. Tempted as we are to disbelieve the genuineness of forced confessions and late repentance, it may be that Achan was sincere, and God chastised the flesh that the spirit might be saved. His death was necessary for example's sake, and the burning of the bodies and the heaping them with stones all indicated the horrid nature of sin which, like a leprosy, frets inward till all be consumed. But the offender himself may have been saved "so as by fire;" and eternal life was purchased at the expense of temporal death. God grant, however, that we may live the life, and so die the death, of the righteous.

2. *The gospel offers of mercy* stand out in striking contrast to the severity of the ancient dispensation. "If we confess our sins, he is faithful and just to forgive us our sins, and to cleanse us from all unrighteousness."—A.

EXPOSITION.

CHAPTER VIII. 1—29.

THE CAPTURE OF AI.—Ver. 1.—**Fear not.** Joshua was downcast at his former failure, and well he might. "Treacherous Israelites are to be dreaded more than malicious Canaanites" (Matthew Henry). **Take all the people of war with thee.** Not, as has been before stated, because 3,000 men were too few to take the city, for the capture of Jericho was a far greater marvel than that of Ai with this number of men. The true reason is indicated by Calvin, and is indeed suggested by the words "Fear not, neither be thou dismayed." It was to reassure the people, whose hearts had "melted and become as water." Sometimes God calls upon His people for a display of faith, as when He led them through the Jordan, or commanded them to compass Jericho seven days. But in days of despondency He compassionates their weakness and permits them to rely upon visible means of support (see also below, ver. 3). Matthew Henry thinks that a tacit rebuke is here administered to Joshua for sending so few men to Ai on the former occasion. He ought to have permitted all to have shared the toil and glory. **I have given into thy hand.** The work, let man do his best, is God's after all. **The king.** For the political condition of Palestine before the Israelitish invasion see Introduction. **And his land.** As in the case of the early Germanic peoples, there was a certain portion of their land in the neigbourhood attached to each city which was used for agricultural purposes (see Introduction; also ch. xiii. 28, xiv. 4).

Ver. 2.—**Only the spoil thereof.** Ai was not solemnly devoted, like Jericho, though (see Deut. xx. 16, 17) the Canaanitish people were. **Behind it.** Joshua was advancing from the south-east. The ambush (אָרֵב literally, "a lier in wait," here a band of liers in wait, the word itself originally signifying to *plait, weave,* hence to *design*)

was therefore (ver. 12) on the opposite, or west side of the city. The question which has been raised whether God could rightly command a stratagem seems scarcely to require discussion.

Ver. 3.—**Thirty thousand.** In ver. 12 we read 5,000, and this must be the true reading. Thirty thousand men could hardly have been posted, without detection, in the ravines around Ai, whereas we are informed by travellers that there would have been no difficulty in concealing 5,000 men there. See, however, the passage cited from Lieut. Conder's Report in the note on chap. vii. 2. The confused condition of the numbers in the present text of the Old Testament is a well-known fact, and it is proved by the great discrepancies in this respect between the Books of Chronicles and those of Samuel and Kings. Some have thought (*e.g.*, Hävernick, 'Introduction to the Old Testament,' II. i. 15) that *two* bands were laid in ambush, one on the north-west and the other on the south-west. This is a possible, though not probable, solution of the difficulty (see below). Then we must suppose that the city was nearly surrounded, Joshua and the main body on the southeast, the larger detachment on the north (ver. 13), and the smaller ambush on the west (see note on ver. 13). Keil, in his earlier editions, supposed that Joshua assaulted Ai with 30,000 men, out of whom he chose 5,000 as an ambush. So also Hengstenberg's 'Geschichte des Reiches Gottes,' p. 219. But this only introduces a third contradiction, for we are told both in vers. 1 and 3 that Joshua took with him "all the men of war." Keil has, however, abandoned that supposition, which is contrary to all the ancient versions, including the present text of the LXX. The Bishop of Lincoln suggests that 5,000 men may have been detached to reinforce the former detachment of 30,000. But to say nothing of the improbability of an ambush of

35,000 men remaining undetected (and they were specially instructed—see next verse—not to station themselves far from the city), we have the plain statement in ver. 12 וַיָּשֶׂם אוֹתָם אוֹרֵב "he stationed (or *had stationed*) them as an ambush."

Ver. 5.—**We will flee before them.** A common expedient of a sagacious general when contending with undisciplined troops is a strong position. Many instances will occur to the student of history, and among others the celebrated feigned flight of William the Conqueror at Hastings. St. Augustine doubts whether this stratagem were lawful. Cajetan and the Jesuit commentators reply that it was so " quia mendacium non tam facile committitur factis, quam verbis " (Cornelius à Lapide).

Ver. 6.—**For they will come.** Literally, "*and* they will come." **We have drawn.** Literally, *caused to pluck away* (see note on ch. iv. 18). Luther translates well by *reissen*, and the LXX. by ἀποσπάσωμεν.

Ver. 8.— **According to the commandment of the Lord.** The LXX. seems to have read כִּדְבָר הַזֶּה *according to this word.*

Ver. 9.— **Between Bethel and Ai** (see above, ch. vii. 2).

Ver. 10. — **And numbered the people.** Or *reviewed*, or *mustered*. The word is frequently translated *visited* in Scripture. It then came to mean a visit for the sake of inspection. **The elders of Israel.** Joshua's council, alike of war and of peace. **Before the people.** Literally, *in their sight* (κατὰ πρόσωπον, LXX.), *i.e.*, at their head.

Ver. 11.—**And all the people, even the people of war that were with him.** Literally, *all the people, the war that were with him.* Probably the word אִישׁ has been omitted by an early copyist. Implying, no doubt, that the non-warlike portion of the community had been left under a guard at Jericho (see also ver. 1). **On the north side.** Joshua made a *detour*, and encamped on a hill on the other side of the wady. **Now there was a valley.** Literally, *and the valley was.* This valley, the Wady Mutyah (see Robinson II. sec. 10, and note on ver. 2, ch. vii.), is a remarkable feature of the country round Ai. Our version misses this sign of personal acquaintance with the locality on the part of the historian.

Ver. 12.—**And he took about five thousand men** (see above, ver. 3). We must translate *had taken*. The repetition is quite in the manner of the Hebrew writers. This passage is of course, according to the Jehovist and Elohist theory, " quite irreconcilable " with the rest of the narrative. So we are told that this is a Jehovistic interpolation (Knobel). **Of the city.** The Maso-

rites and LXX. prefer the reading *Ai* (*i.e.*, עַי for עִיר), in the margin of our Bibles, to that in the text, which is followed by the Vulgate and Luther.

Ver. 13.—**And when they had set.** This may mean the leaders of the detachment of 30,000. Joshua does not appear to have been with them, for he is not mentioned till the latter part of the verse (see note on ver. 3). **Joshua went that night.** Having made all his dispositions, he descended in the evening from his vantage-ground on the hill into the plain, so as to invite attack in the morning, a stratagem which (see next verse) was completely successful. Some MSS., however, have וַיָּלֶן "and he rested," for וַיֵּלֶךְ "and he went," here. **The valley.** The word here is עֵמֶק not גַּי as in ver. 11. Therefore the narrow waterless ravine in which the troops in ambush were to lie hid is not meant here, but a wider valley. A consideration of this fact might do something to settle the much-disputed question of the situation of Ai. The עֵמֶק though deep, as the name implies, was a valley large enough for cultivation or luxuriant vegetation (Job xxxix. 10; Psa. lxv. 14; Cant. ii. 1). Even a battle might be fought there (Job xxxix. 21). Such a valley as that of Chamonix or Lauterbrünnen would answer to the description, and so would the passes of Glencoe and Killiecrankie.

Ver. 14.—**When the king of Ai saw it.** The particle כְ here employed signifies *immediate action*. **At a time appointed.** Or, *at the signal.* Keil, following Luther, would prefer *at the place appointed*, which seems to agree best with what follows. Some copies of the LXX. have ἐπ εὐθείας. **Before the plain.** Literally, *before*, or *in sight of ; i.e.*, in the direction of *the Arabah* (see above, ch. iii. 16).

Ver. 15.—**Made as though they were beaten.** "Joshua conquered by yielding. So our Lord Jesus Christ, when He bowed His head and gave up the ghost, seemed as if death had triumphed over Him ; but in His resurrection He rallied again, and gave the powers of darkness a total defeat " (Matthew Henry). **By the way of the wilderness.** North-westward, in the direction of the wilderness of Bethel (ch. xvi. 1)

Ver. 16.—**Were called together.** So the Masorites. Perhaps it would be better to translate, *raised a cry* ("at illi vociferantes." Vulgate. "Da schrie das ganze Volk." Luther). This gives us the scene in all its picturesque detail. We hear the exultant shout of the men of Ai, as they thought the victory won. The LXX. appear to have read חָזַק for עָזַק for they translate ἐνίσχυσε. **The city.** The

Masorites correct here again into "Ai." But the LXX. and Vulgate render as the English translation.

Ver. 17.—**Or Bethel.** These words are not in the LXX., and they may possibly have been a marginal gloss, for the intervention of the people of Bethel in this battle is very unintelligible. See note on ch. vii. 2. On the other hand, it is quite possible that the difficulty involved in their retention may have caused their omission from the LXX., and it may perhaps be thought possible that, on the capture of Ai, the Bethelites returned with all speed to their city, and that Joshua postponed its capture in consequence of the formidable confederacy (ch. ix. 1, 2), which his success had called into existence, or, perhaps, by a desire to signalise at once the victory at Ai by the ceremony (vers. 30—35) at Gerizim. We read in ch. xii. 16 that Bethel was taken. In Judg. i. 22 we read that it was not (see note on ch. xii. 16).

Ver. 18.—**The spear.** כִידוֹן, a kind of long and slender lance, probably, like those of our lancers, with a flag attached. It is thus described by Kimchi. Jahn, in his 'Archæologia Biblica,' takes this view (sec. 276). But the Vulgate here, followed apparently by Grotius and Masius, suppose it to be a shield, though the LXX. render by γαῖσος. In 1 Sam. xvii. 6 the LXX. render by ἄσπις, and our version by *target*. It is to be distinguished from the lighter חנית or flexible javelin (see, for instance, 1 Sam. xiii. 22, xviii. 10, which was thrown at the adversary, whereas the כִידוֹן was used to transfix him in close combat.

Ver. 20.—**And they had no power.** Literally, *no hands*. Our version here follows the Arabic, Syriac, and Chaldee versions. The LXX. and Vulgate render no *direction* in which to fly. But in this case לָהֶם would seem preferable to בָּהֶם. The Vulgate translates the last clause of the verse, "Præsertim cum hi, qui simulaverint fugam . . . fortissime restitissent." They could not flee back to the city, for it was in flames. They could not advance northward, because the Israelites had faced about and were coming to meet them. To flee in any other direction would be to cut off the last hope of saving the city. For יָד in the sense of *side* or *direction*, however, see Exod. ii. 5; Deut. ii.

37, and especially the dual, as here, in Gen. xxxiv. 21; Isa. xxxiii. 21.

Ver. 22.—**So that they let none of them remain or escape.** Literally, *until there remained to them neither remainder nor fugitive.*

Ver. 24.—**In the wilderness.** The LXX. must have read בַּמּוֹרָד *in the going down*, or *descent*. **Returned unto Ai and smote it.** According to God's command, the defenceless inhabitants must share the fate of the army (see Deut. xx. 17).

Ver. 25.—**All the men of Ai.** Clearly all the population, as the context shows.

Ver. 26.—**Utterly destroyed.** Hebrew, הֶחֱרִים (see note on ch. vi. 17).

Ver. 27.—**Only the cattle** (see ver. 2).

Ver. 28.—**And Joshua burnt Ai.** He continued the work of destruction which the ambush had begun, until the city was entirely destroyed. The word in ver. 19 (יצת) has rather the sense of kindling a fire; the word here (שׂרף), more the sense of destruction by fire. **A heap for ever.** תֵּל־עוֹלָם a heap of eternity; *i.e.*, a heap for ever, at least up to the time of our writer. But the Ai mentioned in Ezra ii. 28 may have been a city built, not on precisely the same spot, but near enough to it to take its name. And if Ai signifies ruins, and Dean Stanley be right in regarding it as referring to ruins in the days of the Philistines, the name would be particularly suitable to this particular city. Travellers have identified the place with Tel-el-Hajar, immediately to the south of the Wady Mutyah. But see note on ch. vii. 2 for Robinson's conclusion, which is confirmed by Canon Tristram, from the belief that Tel-el-Hajar does not answer to the description of Ai in the Scripture narrative. **Hanged on a tree.** Literally, " on *the* tree." Perhaps after his death. But see Gen. xl. 22; Deut. xxi. 22. **Until eventide.** We find here a remarkable coincidence with the precept in Deut. xxi. 23. The fact that no notice is here taken of that passage is conclusive against its having been inserted with a view to that precept in later times, and this affords a strong presumption against the Elohist and Jehovist theory. **Heap.** Here גַּל, an expression usually applied to a heap of stones, a *cairn*, though not always in precisely this sense (see Jer. ix. 10).

HOMILETICS.

Vers. 1—29.—*Renewed effort after disaster.* The Christian warfare, whether from an individual or from a general point of view, is no record of invariable success. The career of each Christian, as of the Christian Church, is a chequered course. It has its periods of triumph and its moments of disaster. We learn here many valuable lessons as to our conduct under adverse circumstances.

I. WE ARE NOT TO INDULGE DESPONDENCY. (1) In consequence of evil allowed to lurk within you, you have had a grievous fall. Your duty is plain : to examine carefully into yourself, with God's help, to detect the hidden evil, and to cast it out. This done, your next duty is to renew the strife. He who is cast down by failure so much as to give up all effort, is lost. The only way to inherit the land of promise is to continue the strife ceaselessly until every one of God's enemies be destroyed. To Joshua, a catastrophe like that of Ai only occurs once. In the case of most ordinary Christians it occurs many times. But the same course is necessary, how many times soever it befalls us. Stone Achan with stones till he die ; then "Fear not, neither be dismayed:" "Arise, go up to Ai ; see, I have given it into thy hand." (2) The history of the Church is the same as that of the individual. Its conflict is more prolonged, more mysterious, and more complete. Therefore it has many Achans, its failures like those of Ai are more numerous, and its need of such encouragement as is here given far greater. Whatever the strife may be, its failures are due to the sins, sometimes unsuspected and undetected, though open, of the Achans of the flock. Many a generation of Christians has failed in their strife against evil, because they have not sought enlightenment from God, and so have called good evil and evil good, have put darkness for light, and light for darkness. After a failure they have not cast lots for the offender, and often they have given up the fight. But the fight must never be given up. Whatever is recognised as not of God must be contended against to the last. If success seems to have deserted us, let us look out for our Achan ; try and find out the reasons for our failure. Somewhere or other, if we are sincere in the search, we shall find the hidden evil that paralyses our efforts. Our first task must be to cast it out; our next to renew the conflict with greater energy and more precautions. No amount of failure ought to daunt us. If still success does not crown our efforts, let us seek for new Achans, and immolate them to the justice of God. But our duty is still to persevere, still to arise up against Ai, and never to cease our efforts until it, and the king thereof, and all the souls that are therein, are involved in one common ruin.

II. WE MUST GIVE HONOUR WHERE HONOUR IS DUE. Some successes are entirely God's doing. Man may not claim credit or in any way seek profit by them. Others are due to man's individual energy and courage—God, of course, working with him, and prospering his efforts. For these he may lawfully enjoy the credit, and be "held in reputation," provided he is careful "not to think more highly of himself than he ought to think, but to think soberly, as God has dealt to every man the measure of faith." So the spoil of Jericho, which God put into the hands of the Israelites, was devoted to Him. Achan, in seizing it for himself, was robbing God of His right. But the spoil of Ai, which God permitted the Israelites to take by their own exertions, was given into their hands. "God is not unrighteous that he should forget your works and labours of love." He or she has a right to be "beloved" who has "laboured much in the Lord."

III. YET MAN MAY NOT CLAIM UNDUE CREDIT FOR WHAT HE HAS DONE. Nothing can be done without God's help. Our greatest successes are the result of talents entrusted us by God. "What hast thou that thou hast not received?" asks the apostle. Therefore "Not unto us, but unto God's name be the praise." The greatest saint must therefore preserve the grace of humility. While he joyfully employs the influence and authority his faith and patience have won for him in God's cause, he must never forget who it was that enabled him to do what he has done ; that if he has been "working out," either his "own salvation," or any blessed works for the salvation of others, it was through God who was working in him.

Joshua could not take Ai, had not God given it into his hand.   Therefore whatever we have done, we are still unprofitable servants.   We have done no more than our duty.   " Let us not be high-minded, but fear."

IV. WE MUST ASSAIL OUR ENEMIES INDIRECTLY AS WELL AS DIRECTLY.   Joshua employs stratagem as well as force against Ai.   It is to be feared that Christian Churches need no exhortations to this course.   Many have been the stratagems and devices of various religious bodies to gain their ends, which have brought not success but disgrace upon the cause.   Yet we may remember that it is not therefore necessary to rush to the opposite extreme, and imagine that nothing but violent denunciation and open force are the methods to be employed.   There is a wisdom of the serpent which may be lawfully employed in God's cause.   The man who is not won by argument may be won by persuasion.   The mind that is repelled by vigorous denunciation may be open to satire or raillery.   We may frequently gain over antagonists by appearing to yield to them.   Sometimes it is even the best way to remove an abuse by allowing it to have full course, and work out its own evil results, and then turning round and pointing out its true character.   But stratagems of the character of pious frauds, stratagems which do violence to the Christian's character for truth and honesty, deliberate concealment of aims which should be avowed, compromises with error for the ultimate advantage of truth—these are predestined to fail.   If they gain their immediate object, they will most certainly in the end be detrimental to God's cause.

HOMILIES BY VARIOUS AUTHORS.

Vers. 1, 2.—*God's people victorious.*   Frequently does Scripture describe the Christian life as a warfare.   We are to war against the evil in ourselves and around us.   In the management of our forces for the conflict we may derive comfort and rules of action from the narrative before us.   It was not unintentionally recorded. It shows how God fulfils His word, going forth with His people conquering and to conquer ; His presence makes the feeble strong, and lends wisdom to the simple.

I. THE PREPARATIONS FOR THE BATTLE.

1. *The putting away of known sin may lead us to expect the favour of God.* Whilst Achan's theft defiled the Israelites there was no hope of winning the fight. The soldiers of the cross must not entangle themselves with the affairs of this life (2 Tim. ii. 4).   Those must be clean who are to bear the vessels of the Lord.   Sin purged, the light of God's countenance again shone upon His people, and His encouragement—" Fear not "—sounded in their ears.   We need be afraid only when doing wrong.   Without God we are " without hope," helpless and undone ; but when He is our light and salvation whom shall we fear ?   Advance to the strife courageously !

2. *All our strength must be brought to bear upon the contest.*   So confident had the Israelites been that they deemed 3,000 men sufficient to capture the place. This time no foolish security must be displayed ; a second defeat would be disastrous.   " All " the people must attack Ai ; that is to say, a fully representative force, in contrast with the few who previously made the assault.   The help of the Almighty does not release us from the necessity of " bestirring " ourselves (see 2 Sam. v. 24).   And what we do we must do with our might.   He who is always reserving his power for some future occasion will grow feeble, and when he at length essays a strenuous effort will discover his weakness.   Nor must we underrate the strength of the enemy.   " We wrestle against principalities, powers, rulers, spiritual wickedness in high places ; " wherefore let us take to ourselves " the whole armour of God."

3. *Prudence an ingredient in the Christian warfare.*   A detachment was appointed to lie in ambush. (Several reasons render it probable that vers. 9 and 12 refer to the same ambuscade, composed of 5,000 men ; the larger number in ver. 3 being a copyist's error.   The same position is assigned in each case ; in the account of the battle only one party of men ambushed is mentioned ; and 30,000 would be too

large a force to remain concealed near the city, even in a valley.) The lawfulness of stratagem in war cannot be disputed, nor does the Bible know anything of that excessive refinement which will hide nothing but requires the blunt truth to be always stated. See 1 Sam. xvi. 2, where the adoption of a fair pretext to prevent bloodshed is sanctioned—yea, proposed—by the Lord. There must be no falsehood or deception practised ; but it is allowable to be "wise as serpents," and to try to win men to the truth by innocent devices. Christian tactics are permissible without pleading the goodness of the end as sanctifying the means employed. Our Captain demands the use of our discretion as well as of our valour.

II. The battle itself.

1. *Temporary success blinds the workers of evil.* Joshua well knew that the enemy would exultingly exclaim, "They flee before us as at the first," and rush to their doom. Misplaced assurance is the bane of God's enemies. For a season they may flourish and swell with hope and pride, but consider their end ! "How are they brought into desolation as in a moment ! " What terms can set forth the delusion of those who fight against God ?

2. *Fidelity to commandment ensures the Christian's triumph.* The emphatic assertion, "See, I have commanded you," reminded the troops of their duty, and of obedience as essential to success. All orders were faithfully executed and victory crowned their arms. If we pretend to greater wisdom than our Captain, or think fragmentary adherence to precept will suffice, the battle may be the Lord's, but it will not be ours. Constant study of our war manual and a resolute determination to observe its instructions can alone secure us the victory. Our ears must be attentive to the notes of the clarion, and whither we are sent we must go. Rom. xiii. 11—13 and Eph. vi. 10—18 must be pondered and put into practice.

3. *Diversity of position not incompatible with union.* In the occupation by the two forces of Israel of separate posts an illustration is afforded of a truth sometimes overlooked. There are different regiments in the Christian army, and to a soldier in the ranks it may appear as if there was a want of connection with any other division. But there is real working unanimity perceptible to the chief, and when the signal is given the enemy shall be attacked on many sides. The end desired is one and the same, the extermination of the empire of evil.

4. *No reason for discouragement if at first the battle goes against us.* It may be part of the plan that the enemy should be demented by success prior to his over- throw. However distressed, we may, like David, encourage ourselves in the Lord our God.

III. The destruction of the enemy.

1. *Prophetic of the final overthrow of Satan and his host.* Jesus, "the Son of God, was manifested that he might destroy the works of the devil." "Death, the last enemy, is being destroyed."

2. *Indicative of the Divine hatred of sin.* The men and women of Ai were slain and their city set on fire ; their king hanged, and a heap of stones his sepulchre. Thus would the Divine wrath extirpate idolatrous abominations. All His judgments were not purifying, this sentence was penal. What a warning to the Israelites ! Dull consciences must be aroused by flashes of fire. Granite hearts must have the inscription cut with toil and pains. Inattentive or forgetful scholars must have the teaching imprinted on their minds by irresistible examples. The preceding chapter proves how needful to Israel was the ocular demonstration of the hatefulness of sin.

Conclusion. "Who is on the Lord's side ? " If this is our position, secure and blissful, diligent and courageous we may be. May we " endure hardness as good soldiers." But if numbered amongst those hostile to God, what terms can describe the dread future that awaits us, unless we repent betimes and seek forgiveness, and receive change of heart and state through Jesus Christ ?—A.

Ver. 19.—*On trying again.* A Jewish proverb says there are three men who get no pity—an unsecured creditor, a henpecked husband, and *a man that does not try again.* This faculty of trying again is one of the qualities of noble natures.

Napoleon at once blamed and praised the English for never knowing when they were beaten. Here Joshua exhibits the same kind of quality. He gathers from his defeat humility, purity, prudence, but never thinks of gathering from it despair. If they have been defeated before this once, they must try again with purer hands and in stronger force. And, trying again thus, they succeed grandly. Let me say a little on " trying again." In the spiritual as in the carnal warfare—indeed, in all parts of our manifold life—we need to learn this lesson. I therefore ask you to consider one or two reasons why we should always try again.

I. Because NO FAILURE IS ALTOGETHER LOSS, AND ESPECIALLY NO FAILURE OF FIRST EFFORTS. If you ask why a first effort is so often a failure, you will find one great reason is, that in it we are trying to learn too many things at once. If it is a first effort to make a toy for a child, how many things are to be learned while making it; the qualities of the material with which we work, the use of our tools, an eye for form and size, the way to combine effectively the various parts. Now, if in the making of it we had only to learn one thing instead of four, we might manage; but to learn simultaneously all of them is beyond our power, and so we fail. But the failure does not mean total loss of time and material; for though we have not learned all we need in order to effect our object, we may have learned half, and learning the other half the second trial we then succeed. So here; there were some things Joshua and Israel had to learn: e.g., not to despise an enemy; to conquer brave foes as well as timorous ones; not to act on the suggestion even of the wisest captains without first inquiring of God; that victory without purity was impossible. Here, elate with their success at Jericho, Joshua does not ask the counsel of God, which would have forbidden movement till the stain of Achan was removed, and sends only a " few thousands " to perform a task for which a much stronger force was requisite. And God mercifully lets him make a failure on a scale easily retrieved, and so prevents a failure through similar mistakes, which, from its magnitude might have been irretrievable. In almost every case of failure, the great cause of it is that there were some things the learning of which was essential but had not been attained. We had not the measure of the obstacles to be overcome—a knowledge of our own weakness, an acquaintance with the methods by which the result desired could be alone effected. And the art of life consists very much simply in turning such failures to good account. It is all but impossible to avoid making them. A child cannot learn to walk without some falls ; and we are but children of a larger growth, who learn through improving our failures. And the wisest man is not he who makes fewest failures, but he who turns the failures that he makes to best account, addresses himself to learn their lessons. A failure is a schoolmaster, who can teach the art of succeeding better than any one else can do it. Do not yield, then, because you fail once, or even many times. *Failures are never entirely losses.* Secondly, observe—

II. THOSE WHO USE WELL THEIR FAILURES FIND THEM FOLLOWED BY GRAND SUCCESS. Joshua, learning from the first failure to hallow the people, to consult God, to take His way, to send a larger force, when he tried again took Ai without the slightest difficulty. Moses failed on his first attempt to raise Israel against their oppressors. He was going to do it in the strength of his youthful enthusiasm, and expected to find they would hail him as a judge and a deliverer. He failed, was rejected of Israel, and had to become a fugitive from Pharaoh. But in his second effort, going at God's command, in His way and with His backing, he succeeded in the grand emancipation. Israel failed in its first attempt to enter the promised land through their fear and faithlessness ; repairing these faults, their second was successful. The disciples failed to cast out the devil from the child ; learning the need of deeper sympathy (prayer and fasting), their next efforts were crowned with complete success. Mark broke down in his first missionary effort, leaving Paul and Silas to pursue it alone. But prayer and gracious shame so retrieved the failure that he was Paul's truest comrade in the pains and dangers of his last imprisonment. Peter failed in his first effort to confess his Master among his foes ; but learning lowliness and prayer from failure, he lived to retrieve it grandly. It is so in all departments of life. Alfred the Great and Bruce, for instance, both learned the art of victory from the experience of defeat. Great inventors have rarely hit on their great secrets the first time they have attempted to achieve their purpose. The story of almost all great inventions has been *failure well improved.* The first efforts of poets do not always give the promise of their later powers. So is it in all directions of Christian life. If in your effort to confess Christ you fail, try again, and success will come with the greater earnestness and humility of your second effort. If you make a resolution and break it, try again with more of prayer, and the second effort will succeed. If you make some effort to do good, but your " 'prentice hand " bungles, and shame covers you, the next effort you make on a smaller scale, perhaps more wisely, modestly, and earnestly, will be a blessed success. And if it is not one but many efforts have failed, and life itself seems one long mishap and unsuccessful effort still, do not despair.

> " Deem not the irrevocable past
> As wholly wasted, wholly vain ;
> For, *rising on its wrecks,* at last
> To nobler greatness we attain."
>
> *Longfellow's ' Ladder of St. Augustine.'*

Therefore let us always "try again."—G.

Vers. 30—35.—*The fruits of victory.* "Then Joshua built an altar unto the Lord. . . . And he wrote there upon the stones a copy of the law of Moses. . . . And he read all the words of the law." There is always danger in the moment after victory. We remember how Hannibal lost, amid the enervating luxuries of Capua, the fruit of the battle of Cannæ. The most seductive Capua to the people of God is spiritual pride, which seeks to take to itself the glory which belongs to God alone. Woe to those who sleep upon the laurels of spiritual success, or who are intoxicated with self-complacency. " Let him that thinketh he standeth, take heed lest he fall (1 Cor. x. 12). Joshua shows us by his example how the people of God should conduct themselves after a victory.

I. He gives all the glory to God. He builds an altar to offer thereon a sacrifice of thanksgiving. Let us do the same, and render, as he did, all glory to God.

II. He summoned the people to a yet stricter obedience to the Divine law by placing it afresh before their eyes. He knows well that never are men more prone to forget the sacred obligation of obedience than in the hour of religious success. Without obedience sacrifice is but external and vain. The true sacrifice is that of the will. Let every new blessing, every fresh victory only bring our mind and heart into more complete subjection to the will of God !

EXPOSITION.

CHAPTER VIII. 30—35.

The copy of the law.—Ver. 30.—**Then Joshua built an altar unto the Lord God of Israel in Mount Ebal.** This passage has been pronounced to be an interpolation by Meyer, De Wette, Maurer, Rosenmüller, Knobel, and others. The LXX. does not introduce it here, but after ch. ix 2. For other authorities see below. It is very easy to see why its genuineness has been disputed. The Book of Joshua has many marks of having been written not so very long after the events described in it. But it has been a favourite opinion with the school which disputes the authenticity of the books of the Bible, that Deuteronomy was a late revision by Ezra of the law of Moses, though

this (see Introduction) has lately been discarded for another hypothesis. But we have, if the present passage be genuine, a distinct proof that the Book of Joshua was written after the Book of Deuteronomy. Deuteronomy is here quoted as the " book of the law of Moses " (cf. Deut. xxxi. 9, 24, 26). The grounds on which the genuineness of the passage has been denied are these : First, the passage begins with אז followed by an imperfect, or future, as does the interpolated passage in Deut. iv. 41—43. This is Maurer's theory. But in this case we must reject every passage which begins thus, and certainly we should do so on grounds which, to say the least, are very slender. Next, we are told that Joshua could not have ventured to trust himself so far in the heart of a hostile country. But why not? Gerizim was not more than twenty miles from Ai. The Canaanites, we are told, were panic-stricken at Joshua's success. The Gibeonites were not disposed to offer any hindrance to his progress; on the contrary, they hastened to form an alliance with him. And these solemn religious rites, performed by a people so clearly under the protection of the Most High, were more likely to increase than lessen the awe felt by the surrounding tribes. The only difficulty is that the women and children (v. 35) are expressly said to have gone thither also, and it seems improbable that they, whom we have supposed to have been left under a guard at Gilgal, should have been brought so far while the country was as yet unsubdued. And the difficulty is increased by finding Joshua again at Gilgal in ch. ix. 6. But there is the hypothesis that this was another Gilgal to fall back upon, and this (see note on the passage just mentioned) is an extremely probable one. The suggestion of many commentators, that the passage has been transposed, is of course possible. We can only leave the difficulty unsolved, as one which a fuller knowledge of the facts, could we obtain it, would clear up at once. But we may be sure that if the passage were an interpolation, some explanation would have been given of the circumstances which seem to us so perplexing. And on the other hand we must remember that, as has been already contended, the notion that the whole camp of Israel performed this journey at a time when stupefaction had seized upon the Canaanitish tribes, though involving some amount of impossibility, is by no means impossible. (See also note on ver. 33). A number of extraordinary interpretations of this passage have been given. A favourite Rabbinical interpretation (see note on next verse) was that this altar was erected on the very day on which the Israelites crossed the Jordan. This was of course a physical impossibility. Josephus, on the contrary, supposes that five years elapsed before its erection, while Rabbi Israel, in the Jerusalem Talmud, thinks that it was deferred until after the expiration of fourteen years, and after the land had been divided. So Masius *in loc.* **In Mount Ebal.** Between it and Gerizim stood the city of Shechem, or Sychar, as it is called in St. John iv. Gerizim was close to this city, as Judg. ix. 6, 7 and St. John iv. 20 testify, as well as Deut. xi. 30, compared with Gen. xii. 6. Dr. Maclear, in the 'Cambridge Bible for Schools,' suggests that the Israelites took this opportunity of

interring the bones of Joseph (Gen. l. 25, 26) in the piece of ground which Jacob bought of the sons of Hamor (Gen. xxxiii. 19). (See Exod. xiii. 19).

Ver. 31.—**As Moses the servant of the Lord commanded** (see Exod. xx. 25; Deut. xxvii. 4, 5). Here, and in ver. 33, we find the writer making an extract from the Book of Deuteronomy. As has been before said, the natural explanation is that the Book of Joshua was written after the Book of Deuteronomy, and that the Book of Deuteronomy was written by Moses, or how could Joshua have carried out instructions which had never been given? The Elohist, Jehovist, and Deuteronomist theory supposes the compiler of the Book of Joshua to have done his work in so perfunctory a fashion, that it is quite possible for critics living at a distance of three thousand years and more to detect the various fragments of which his mosaic is constructed. He is so void of common sense as to have inserted this narrative in a place so obviously unsuitable that it involves a palpable contradiction to probability and common sense, and this when he could have placed it in a dozen other parts of the book where no such improbability would be involved. Yet, in spite of the incredible carelessness with which he put his materials together, we are required to believe that "the Deuteronomist" had the foresight to insert the fulfilment of the command of Moses which he had invented in Deut. xi. 26—30, xxvii. 1—26; and that in so doing he abbreviated the narrative so as to leave out many details of his own invention. Now, under the supposition of a later fabrication of supplementary observances to be imposed upon the children of Israel, it is hardly probable that the account of the plaster with which the stones were to be plastered, and the enumeration of the tribes and the curses, would be omitted, since by the hypothesis the object of the Deuteronomist was to secure implicit obedience to the sacerdotal enactments he was inventing. But on the hypothesis of the genuineness of both writings everything fits in naturally enough. **An altar of whole stones, over which no man hath lift up any iron.** As though to intimate (see Exod. xx. 25) that all should be natural and spontaneous in the worship of God, and that as little of human devising should be introduced as possible. The altar must be raised by man, but the principles of the worship must not be devised by him. This interpretation, however, is rejected by Calvin, who thinks that all that was meant was to preclude the perpetual existence of the altar (though how the substitution of whole for hewn stones could effect this is not apparent); and Keil and Bähr ('Symbolik,' i. pp. 487, 488), who think that the altar ought (Exod. xx. 24) properly to be of earth, since sacrifice is rendered necessary by man's earthly or carnal nature, and that unhewn stone is the only substitute for earth which is allowed. But surely man's handiwork is the offspring of his unregenerate nature, and therefore may, from this point of view, be rightly employed in sacrifice. Hengstenberg ('Geschichte des Reiches Gottes,' p. 223) thinks that the reason of the command was that, since only one place of worship was permitted for all Israel, an altar had sometimes to be hastily thrown up. But when we consider the symbolic character of the Mosaic worship, we are compelled to reject this interpretation as unsatisfactory. Benjamin of Tudela (see Drusius *in loc.*) appears to have supposed that these stones were those which had been taken out of Jordan. Masius devotes considerable space to the refutation of this opinion (see also note on last verse). **And they offered thereon.** Delitzsch remarks on the inversion of the order here, as compared with Deut. xxvii. But this is obviously the true order. The worship would naturally precede the ceremony rather than follow it.

Ver. 32.—**And he wrote there upon the stones;** *i.e.*, upon the plaster, as we read in Deut. xxvii. 2, 4. " The wall destined to receive the picture," and it was just the same with inscriptions—was covered with a coating of lime and gypsum plaster. The outline was then sketched with red chalk, and afterwards corrected and filled in with black (Kenrick's 'Egypt,' i., p. 271). Thómson ('Land and the Book,' p. 471) says that he has seen writings in plaster which could not have been less than two thousand years old. This passage shows that our author had Deut. xxviii. 2, 3 in his mind. The stones of the altar, which alone have been mentioned, are clearly not meant here, but the erection of plastered stone on which the law was to be written. **A copy of the law of Moses,** "Deuteronomium legis," Vulgate. So also LXX. Not the whole law, nor yet the Book of Deuteronomy, for time would not permit, but the decalogue, as the word מִשְׁנֶה duplicate, from whence the word Mishna comes, signifies. It is to be observed that the word is definite, *the* copy, not *a* copy, of the law. This (Deut. v. 22) was what was written on the two tables of stone, which (Exod. xxiv. 12, xxxi. 18) God gave to Moses. Yet it is possible that, as some commentators suggest, and as ver. 34 may be held to imply, what is meant is the

curses and blessings mentioned in Deut. xxvii. and xxviii. The formal setting up of this memorial was intended to remind the Israelites, by a perpetual standing witness, of the conditions on which they held the land of Canaan. And it is to be observed that the moral, rather than the positive, precepts of the law were thus solemnly enjoined on them, since neglect of the moral law of God is the invariable source of national degradation and decay. **Which he wrote.** Namely, Joshua.

Ver. 33. — **And all Israel** (see ch. xxiii. 2; xxiv. 1, 2). The word כֹל is used very loosely in Hebrew (see Gen. iv. 14). We need not, therefore, assume as a matter of course that the whole people, men, women, and children, were taken up to Shechem to behold this ceremony. It is quite possible that during all Joshua's marches and campaigns a large number of the people remained under guard at Gilgal (see ch. ix. 6), which remained the head-quarters of the Israelites until the country was subdued. All that is here meant is that a very great number of the people were gathered together, and that every tribe, every age, and each sex were largely represented at this important ceremony. **And officers.** Shoterim (see ch. i. 10). **Half of them.** Origen's explanation of the spiritual meaning of this passage is noteworthy, even though somewhat far-fetched. He regards those of the tribes who stood on Mount Gerizim to bless, as the type of those who are led, not by fear of God's threatenings, but by a longing for God's promises and blessings; those who stood on Mount Ebal to curse, as the type of those who are driven by the fear of punishment to obey the will of God, and these finally attain salvation. The former, he adds, are the more noble of the two; but Jesus, who reads the hearts, gives each their proper station, and places some on Mount Ebal to curse, not that they themselves may receive the curse, but, by regarding the curse pronounced on sinners, may learn thereby how to escape it. **Over against.** אֶל־מוּל rather, " in the direction of." The command in Deut. xxvii. 12 is that they shall stand *upon* the two mountains. No doubt certain representatives of the tribes stood *on* the mountain, and the rest of the people at the foot of the mountain, on either side of the valley, "crowding the slopes," as Canon Tristram says. The valley is narrow here, and the voice in mountainous regions, where the air is rarer, carries far. Under special circumstances, such as frosty weather, the voices of men crying their wares have been distinctly heard across the Humber in our own country.

And in mountain passes, as any one who has travelled in them may easily ascertain, conversations may be carried on from opposite sides of a valley or ravine without the slightest difficulty. In this particular place Canon Tristram tell us ('Land of Israel,' pp. 149, 150) that when on Mount Gerizim he heard every word uttered by a man who was then driving his ass down Mount Ebal, and that afterwards two of his party recited the commandments antiphonally from the two sides of the valley without the least difficulty.

Ver. 34.—**All the words of the law, the blessings and the curses.** The form of this expression, combined with the words of the next verse, seems to include not only the special curses in Deut. xxvii., but ch. xxviii. at least, and possibly chs. xxix. and xxx. as well.

Ver. 35.—**That were conversant with them.** Literally, *who were going in the midst of them; i.e.,* the strangers who had attached themselves to them, either at their departure from Egypt, or since their conquest of Eastern Palestine.

HOMILETICS.

Vers. 30—35.—*The setting up the law.* The provision for the due observance of God's law was one of the most remarkable features of the invasion of Canaan by Joshua. Twice was the command given in Deuteronomy by Moses (Deut. xi. 29, 36, and xxvii. 2—13), and the spot fixed on beforehand, no doubt because of its central position in Palestine. We have already observed, in the notes on ch. v., on the scrupulous care to fulfil the provisions of the law with which the invasion of Canaan was commenced. The present is an event of the same character. Joshua forbears to press further his warlike operations in the land, until he has pushed his way to the central point, and anticipated the conquest he is about to make by setting up there the law which was to be observed in it, when it had become the possession of the Israelites. The following considerations suggest themselves :

I. Joshua's FAITH. As in the case of the circumcision, so here, obedience is superior to all earthly considerations. From a worldly point of view this march from Ai to Gerizim while the nations of Canaan are still unsubdued was a hazardous and foolish act. Modern philosophers would deride it ; modern public opinion would condemn it. But it is just here that modern opinion requires correction by God's Word. When a thinker of the present day, not usually regarded as superstitious or fanatical, tells us we have "forgotten God," it may be worth while to ask whether He is still a factor in the problem of life with statesmen, generals, and politicians. No doubt there is a superstitious way of carrying out the principle here indicated. So there was, as has already been pointed out, among the Israelites, when they took the ark to battle with them, fancying it could act as a talisman which could secure them from the consequences of their own sins. Yet we may venture to commend the scrupulous regard for God's commands shown by the Christian Indians in North America, who were willing voluntarily to forego the large take of fish—and they got their living by fishing—which offered itself to them on the Lord's day, rather than the conduct of the clergyman, who, seeing a glint of sunshine on a wet summer's day while he was preaching, led his flock into the harvest-field, though it was Sunday, because, as he said, it was wrong to allow God's good gifts to be wasted. There may be much to be said on both sides. Yet it were well at least to allow that faith is superior to sight, and obedience to expediency. We may be assured that in all cases a strict obedience to God's precepts, and a sublime disregard of consequences when duty is involved, is the only path a sincere Christian can possibly follow. This is true whether (1) national, (2) commercial, or (3) private interests are involved. The nation which deliberately adopts a wrong policy, or refuses to carry out a right one, because it is its interest to do so, will most assuredly reap its reward. The commercial transaction which in its efforts after profit neglects the plain command of God shall in the end bring more harm than good. The man who habitually sets aside God's commands for his own private ends shall " reap his reward, whosoever he be."

II. CIRCUMCISION VERILY PROFITETH IF THOU KEEP THE LAW. Joshua here plainly shows the children of Israel that the formal renewal of the covenant which was made as soon as Jordan was crossed was of no avail in God's sight, unless the law were set up as the necessary consequence of that covenant. So we learn that it is of no use for us to be God's covenant people unless we have the law written in our hearts. For one of the first conditions of that covenant is that God shall give us His Spirit. Woe be to us if we grieve or quench Him. He gives us power to fulfil the law of God. To neglect to carry out that law is to resist Him and fight against Him. This entails upon us the same consequences as it did to Israel, first in the wilderness, and afterwards in Canaan—rejection from the high privileges they had inherited. After our admission into covenant with God there must be (1) the engraving the law in our hearts by the study of its precepts, and (2) the earnest endeavour to walk after the law thus set up in our midst.

III. THE LAW WAS READ. This public reading of the law was a feature of Jewish public solemnities when their faith had waxed cold, and it needed revival (see 2 Kings xxiii. 2, 3; 2 Chron. xxxiv. 30, 31; Neh. viii. 1—8). It does not appear to have formed part of the ceremonies either of David or Solomon, or even of Hezekiah. Perhaps it would have been better if it had, although these ceremonies were pious and edifying. So we cannot agree with those who would remove from the Church of England Service that continual recitation of the Ten Commandments which was added to the Communion Service at the Reformation. We cannot tell how much this reading of the law has tended to keep alive in the nation an abhorrence of certain sins, has preserved among us a regard for God's holy day, for domestic purity and order, for honesty and truthfulness, which some other nations have lost. So the daily and weekly reading of the Scriptures, as a whole, is a feature of the Church system which we would not willingly see surrendered. And he who neglects the private reading of the law must expect the life of his soul to be deadened thereby.

IV. THE LAW HAS CURSES AS WELL AS BLESSINGS. The sterner features of God's law are kept out of sight by many in these days. They talk of a God of love, but they forget that a God of love must, as such, punish sin, and therefore sinners, as long as they cling to their sin. It would be no love to leave sin unpunished, for that were to encourage men to commit it. And as sin, by its very nature, is the parent of misery, the God who does not punish sin is rather a God of hate than a God of love. No preaching of the blessings of the gospel is of any avail which systematically conceals the terrors of the gospel; which tries to exalt the love of God in Christ while studiously ignoring the vengeance which is pronounced against them who " obey not the gospel of our Lord Jesus Christ." No reading of the law is of any avail, except Ebal be read from as well as Gerizim. Joshua read "all the words of the law, the blessings and the cursings, according to all that is written in the book of the law." So must the Christian minister rehearse faithfully to his flock all that is written in the book of the law of Christ.

V. THE ARK OF GOD WAS IN THE MIDST. That is, the reading of the law was no mere formal recitation. There was the altar, the offerings, and the sacrifices. It was a religious celebration. God's presence was recognised. The devotion of the heart was required. The whole celebration would have been a pretence had it not been carried on as in God's sight. So now, when God's Word is read in the congregation, it should not be a mere form. There should be the ardent desire to profit by it, the solemn reverence for the spoken word of the Most High. And when studied in private, it should not be a cold, critical, merely intellectual study. The warmth of devotion should be kindled. The reading should be distinctly a religious act. The presence of God, alike in the word He has given, and the heart He has renewed, should be recognised, and a mutual glow be derived from the contact. And this glow should be further inflamed by the simultaneous sacrifice of the thoughts and intentions of the heart to God.

HOMILIES BY VARIOUS AUTHORS.

Vers. 30—35.—*The altar on Ebal, and the reading and recording of the law.*
We come on this scene unexpectedly. War, with its stratagems, its carnage, its
inversion of ancient order, was filling our mind. But suddenly, instead of the
camp, there is the religious assembly; sacrifice instead of slaughter; instead of the
destruction of heathen cities, the erection of monumental inscriptions of the law.
The mustering of the whole people to learn and accept afresh God's great law. It
was not a casual gathering, but one prescribed by Moses in 27th chapter of
Deuteronomy; what tribes have to stand on the slopes of Gerizim, to respond to all
the benedictions of the law, and what tribes are to stand on Ebal to respond to its
curses, are all detailed. The ark in the valley between; an altar reared on one of
the heights; the law, solemnly read, and greeted with the responses not of a
congregation, but of a gathered nation; covenant sacrifices offered; the inscription
on memorial stones of the leading precepts of the law—these all constitute a scene
of utmost impressiveness. A nation accepting a solemn league and covenant,
hallowing their conquest, taking formal possession of the country for their God, in
the heart of the land hallowing a mountain for His throne—this is not an every-
day occurrence, but one full of moral meaning. Consider some of its lessons.

I. SACRED RESTS SHOULD BE MIXED WITH ALL WORLDLY WORK. Not many
would have gathered a nation at such a time for such a work. At most only the
conquest of the middle of the land had been achieved. The kings of the south and
the north were forming their leagues to crush the terrible invaders. A saint less
heroic or a hero less saintly would have postponed all such solemn assemblies till
the conquest was complete. But Joshua "sets the Lord alway before him;" an l
at the very outset he seeks to hallow their fighting and their victories. As in Gilgal,
he tarried to observe the sacraments of the law, so here in Shechem he tarries to
build an altar and rehearse the law. That time is not lost which we spend in calm
communion with God. And in the degree in, which, like the occupations of these
invaders, our daily work is absorbing and worldly, in that degree it is well to arrest
our activities, and turn ear and eye and heart to God. In Israel's case, such a halt
would tend to prevent the coarsening of their feelings in their bloody work; would
put them in the position of executors of God's judgment; would help to make them
abhor the sins of those they extirpated; would suggest that "they should be holy who
carried the " sword " of God." Our daily tasks are not so absorbing nor so rough
as theirs; but, like Israel, it will always be well that we should take time or make
time to keep in Gilgal the ordinances, and take time or make it to learn in Shechem
the law of God. "Prayer and meals stop no man's work." Israel went from
Shechem with more unity, faith, and gravity—that is, with all its elements of strength
invigorated. Keep your Sabbaths well. Have a sacred closet and enter it. Take
time regularly to get calm and to listen to the voice of God. Joshua mixes sacred rest
with worldly activity.

II. Observe secondly: WITH NEW POSSESSIONS, THEIR RESPONSIBILITIES SHOULD
BE RECOGNISED. Is the centre of the land won, it is not theirs to do with as they
like. There is a law whose blessings they should aspire to, whose curse they should
avoid. Their new possessions are not theirs to do with what they like. Masters of
the Canaanites, they are only servants before God. With all possession of
wealth, and all consciousness of strength, there is apt to rise a certain degree of
wilfulness and self-assertion. Men think that wealth is a sort of holy orders, giving
a power of absolution from every unpleasant duty. It is well whenever we have
attained what we desired, or come into the enjoyment of any sort of wealth, that we
should take the position of servants, and listen to God's law. Otherwise the
mercies that should bind us closer to our God separate us from Him, and blessings
which should leave us more free for gracious work secularise all our moods and
motives. "The desire accomplished is sweet to the soul," but it is only helpful
when in Shechem we listen to God's law. How much wiser would some have been
if gaining wealth, or power, or whatever their hearts' desire, they had hallowed

some spot like Shechem and distinctly realised their duty in connection with it—the blessings of discharging it, the curses of neglecting it; and then low at God's altar had hallowed all. Our own is not ours to do with as we please. Property has duties as well as rights, and all mercies should be hallowed by cherishing a lively sense of the responsibilities attendant on them. Have you gained a footing in any Canaan of your hopes ? Build your altar and listen to God's law.

III. Observe: JOSHUA'S FIRST BUILDING IS AN ALTAR, NOT A FORTRESS. You would not have been surprised to find him taking Shechem and fortifying it, raising thus a central fortress in the land. But he builds not a fortress, but an altar; and raises not the storied monument of his victories, but a register of God's law. It is a striking and characteristic thing, this altar-rearing in such circumstances. And yet the altar, by its inspiration, contributes more to the power of the people than any fortress could by its security. *The soul is the seat of power*, in the individual, the army, the nation; and Joshua takes the directest means to increase and perpetuate the nation's strength when he builds an altar, and links at once the old land and the new people to God. No people will lack country, safety, freedom, that rears altars to the living God. Let religion die out in any people and liberty will not very long survive. What we want for strength and joy in life is some great interest, a grave duty, a sublime hope. When Joshua raised this altar, and thereby quickened the religious life of the people, he was doing far more than if he had raised walls or gathered chariots. God is a nation's only fortress. To have Him in us is to be secure.

IV. Lastly observe: THE WISE MAN SEEKS TO MAKE RELIGION INTELLIGENT. The priestly instinct would have been satisfied with the sacraments of Gilgal; but Joshua adds instruction at Shechem. All the people, the aged, the children, warriors, and women, the true Israelite and the hangers-on, have the entire law read to them; and to increase the intelligent knowledge of God's will, the law is painted like frescoes on tablets raised on the mountain. God wants intelligent service. Ignorance is the mother of superstition, not of devotion. "God is a spirit, and they that worship him must worship him not only in spirit"—that is—in sincerity; but in truth—that is, with intelligence, understanding Him—giving Him the sort of homage which is His due. To my judgment, there is a savour of sound Protestantism in this gathering at Shechem. The people taught, the law imparted to all. This is a sort of prelude of the reign of the open Bible—a religion addressed to the minds and hearts and consciences of men. All true religion has its Shechem as well as its Gilgal, its teachings of truth and duty as well as its observance of the sacraments. We should all seek light; reverent, but still self-respectful; too serious to "make believe," too truthful to shut our eyes. The higher our reason, the heartier will be our religion. Joshua taught the people the law, and when printing was impossible, published it on the frescoes of Gerizim. We only do well when we do our best to make "all the congregation of Israel, with the women and the little ones, and the strangers that are conversant among them," familiar with the law and the gospel of the grace of God.—G.

Vers. 30—35.—*Sacrifice and law*. This religious solemnity is a fulfiment of the command given by Moses in Deut. xxvii. It is expressive of the fidelity of Joshua to the sacred traditions of the past, and his loyalty to the Divine order and the Divine authority. The time is appropriate for such public homage to be paid to the God of Israel. It is the "right hand of the Lord" that has done so valiantly in the recent victories; to Him be all the glory. The land has been taken possession of in His name; let it be consecrated henceforth to Him by this solemn act of worship. The solemnity consists of two parts—(1) the building of an altar and offering of sacrifice, (2) the inscription and proclamation of the law.

I. SACRIFICE. This was at once an acknowledgment of the sovereignty of God, and a renewal of the covenant by which the people and their inheritance were devoted to Him. There were two kinds of sacrifice, "burnt offerings" and "peace offerings." It is doubtful how far the distinction between these can, in this case, be clearly defined. But we at least discern in them a double element, (1) eucharistic, (2) propitiatory.

1. *Eucharistic.* There was thanksgiving for victories and deliverances thus far vouchsafed. Well might the hearts of the people rise to God with the smoke of their sacrifices, after such proofs as He had given them of His favour. Every fresh manifestation of Divine goodness demands a fresh ascription of praise; the providence that "redeems our life from destruction and crowns us with loving-kindness" calls for daily acknowledgment. Gratitude is a perpetual obligation, because God's love is ever assuming some new phase of benediction. Let every stage in our career, every vantage-ground gained, every difficulty surmounted, every peril passed, every victory won, be signalised by some new expression of personal devotion. To the devout spirit life will be a continual thank-offering, a ceaseless hymn of praise.

> "If oh our daily course our mind
> Be set to hallow all we find,
> New treasure still of countless price
> God will provide for sacrifice."

2. *Propitiatory.* These oft-repeated sacrifices kept the grand truth of atonement by expiation continually before the minds of the people. *We* need to keep it continually before our minds, inasmuch as we live by the mercy of God through the self-immolation of a sinless victim. Every revelation of God is fitted to awaken the sense of our own sinfulness, and so prompts a constant reference, in penitence and faith, to the "Great Propitiation." Daily life should be a perpetual presentation in spirit before the mercy-seat of the sacrifice of Him by whom we "receive the atonement." But such trust in the sacrifice of Christ is of no avail unless coupled with a personal surrender that draws its inspiration from His. The "burnt offering" and the "peace offering" must go together. "Ye are not your own, for ye are bought with a price: therefore," &c. (1 Cor. vi. 19, 20).

II. THE PROCLAMATION OF THE LAW. There was a peculiar fitness in this, inasmuch as the people had now gained a firm footing in the land which was to be the scene of their organised national life. They are made to understand the fundamental moral conditions of that life. Observe—

1. *The supremacy of the law of God over all human law.* The commonwealth of Israel was emphatically a theocracy. But every commonwealth is a theocracy in the sense that harmony with the Divine will is the secret of its order and prosperity. As righteousness alone "exalteth a nation," so the public assertion and vindication of God's law is essential to the well-being of any land and people. Human law has enduring authority in proportion as it accords with the Divine (Prov. viii. 15, 16).

2. *The breadth of the law of God as embracing all relations of life, all classes and conditions of men.* "The whole congregation of Israel" heard the law, with the "elders, officers, and judges," the "women, little ones, and strangers." All social relations, all official functions, all periods and conditions of life are amenable to this supreme authority, this impartial Judge.

3. *The weal or woe of every man depends on his relation to the law of God.* Here lies the alternative of blessing or cursing, life or death (Deut. xxx. 19). What was read may have been only that summary of the law contained in Deut. xxvii. and xxviii. But of the whole law, in its essential principles, this is true: moral and practical harmony with it is the condition of blessedness.

4. *Men are brought into their true relation to the law only by the gospel of Christ.* "Christ is the end of the law for righteousness," &c. (Rom. x. 4). Faith in Him disarms the law of its terrors. "Christ hath redeemed us from the curse of the law," &c. (Gal. iii. 13). In Him the blessing overcomes the curse, the voice of Gerizim prevails over that of Ebal, "mercy rejoiceth against judgment." Christ engraves the law not on tables of stone, but on the living hearts of men (Jer. xxxi. 31, 34; Heb. viii. 10, 12). In Him the law is not, as in Moses, literal, local, adapted to special circumstances and the moral needs of a particular people,

but spiritual and universal. Not that Christianity has less to do in shaping the relative duties of human life, or enters less minutely into its details, but rather has so much to do with everything that, like the all-pervading atmosphere and the gladdened sunshine, it is the very vital air of every social problem, and the guiding light in the determination of every question between man and man.—W.

EXPOSITION.

CHAPTER IX. 1—27.

The Gibeonites.—Ver. 1.—**And it came to pass, when all the kings.** According to the explanation given above (ch. vi. 5, 15) of the particle כְּ with the infinitive, this must mean immediately. We must therefore suppose that the distance at which they lived from the scene of the events had prevented them from comprehending their astounding character so clearly as those who lived in the immediate neighbourhood (see ch. ii. 11; v. 1; vi. 1). **The kings** (see Introduction). **In the hills.** "The land is classified under three heads: the hills (or mountain district), the plain, and the sea coast over against Lebanon" (Keil). The hills are not the Lebanon and Anti-Lebanon range, the operations against which are detailed in ch. xi., but the mountains of Ephraim and Judah. The word translated "valleys" here is neither עֲרָבָה nor כִּכָּר (see above note on ch. iii. 16), but שְׁפֵלָה or low country, i.e., the great plain from Joppa, or Carmel, to Gaza. The חוֹף or sea coast probably refers to the coast between Tyre and Joppa. **The Hittite.** The Girgashites are the only tribe omitted here from the list in ch. iii. 10.

Ver. 2.—**With one accord.** One *mouth*, according to the Hebrew, referring not merely to their opinions, but to the expression of them. "O that Israel would learn this of Canaanites, to sacrifice private interests to the public welfare, and to lay aside all animosities among themselves, that they may cordially unite against the common enemies of God's kingdom" (Matthew Henry).

Ver. 3.—**The inhabitants of Gibeon.** That is, of a confederation of cities (see ver. 17), of which Gibeon was the head. Gibeon was a city of some importance (ch. x. 2). Though it was for size and importance "as one of the royal cities," we hear nothing of a king there. Hengstenberg, in his history, describes it (p. 227) as "eine freie Stadt," with daughter cities dependent on it. In fact, the Phœnician cities (see Introduction) seem to have had as great a variety of constitution as those of ancient Greece. Its inhabitants were Hivites (ver. 7, and ch. xi. 19). Its name (compare Gibeah and גִּבְעָה a hill)

signifies hill-city, like the termination *dunum* in Latin, as Lugdunum, or Lyons; dune in Anglo-Saxon, as *Ethandune*. Compare also Dunkirk. Robinson, in his 'Biblical Researches,' ii. 135—9, identifies it with el-Jib, a village on an eminence in the midst of a fertile plain, where the remains of large buildings may still be seen. (So Vandevelde and Conder.) "Onely the Hivites are wiser than their fellowes, and will rather yeeld and live. Their intelligence was not diverse from the rest; all had equally heard of the miraculous conduct and successe of Israel; but their resolution was diverse. As Rahab saved her family in the midst of Jericho, so these foure cities preserved themselves in the midst of Canaan; and both of them by beleeving what God would do. The efficacie of God's marvellous works is not in the acts themselves, but in our apprehension" (Bp. Hall).

Ver. 4.—**They did work wilily.** Rather, *and they worked—they also—with craft.* The reference, no doubt, is to the confederacy of the other kings. The Gibeonites also acted upon what they had heard, but they preferred an accommodation to war. So Calvin and Rosenmüller; also Drusius. And they felt that they could only effect their purpose by craft. Other explanations are given, such as that a reference is made to Joshua's stratagem at Ai. Keil rejects both, and proposes an explanation of his own, which is unintelligible. Origen's interpretation here is interesting as a specimen of the theology of the third century. He regards the Gibeonites as the type of men who, though they are enrolled in the Church as believers and have faith in God, and acquiesce in all the Divine precepts, and are ready enough to take part in all the external duties of religion, are yet involved in vices and foulnesses, like the Gibeonites in their old garments and clouted shoes. They display no signs of improvement or alteration, yet Jesus our Lord concedes to them salvation, even though that salvation does not escape a certain stigma of disgrace. That there may be some persons in a condition somewhat resembling this described by Origen may be admitted, but it is difficult to see how any one in a state of salvation can display no signs of improvement whatever. There are many who do not improve as they might, whom we should yet hesitate to pronounce altogether reprobate from God. But surely the entire absence of all improvement is a manifest sign of reprobation. This passage is one of many among the voluminous works of Origen in which that holy and learned man has not sufficiently weighed what he was saying (see below, ver. 23). **Made as if they had been ambassadors.** "Sent an embassy" (Luther). If we take this reading, we must suppose, with Grotius and others, the word to be the Hithpahel of צִיר to go, to revolve. But the form is rare, and the word is elsewhere unknown, at least in Hebrew, though an Arabic form of it is found. It is therefore better to read יִצְטַיָּדוּ "they prepared themselves provisions." This is the reading of the LXX., the Vulgate, the Chaldee, the Syriac, and of most modern editors. It is rendered still more probable by the occurrence of the same word in ver. 12. **Old sacks.** Rather, *worn out*, and so throughout the passage. The usual mode of conveyance still in the East is in sackcloth bags on the backs of horses, mules, camels, and asses. Such bags are apt to meet with rough usage in a long journey. **Wine bottles.** Rather, *wine skins*, the wine then being kept in skins, not in vessels of glass. This explains how they could be burst open (מְבֻקָּעִים) and tied up. These skins were hung up frequently in the smoke (Psa. cxix. 83), which gave them a shrivelled appearance. The first bottles were made of such skins, as Herodotus tells us. The Egyptian monuments confirm his statements, displaying as they do skins of animals so used, with the legs or the neck forming what we still term the "neck" of the bottle (cf. Homer, Iliad, iv. 247, ἀσκῷ ἐν αἰγείῳ). Similar bottles are depicted on the walls of Herculaneum and Pompeii, and the like may be seen still in Italian villages. They were pitched over at the seams to prevent leakage (cf. Job xxxii. 19; Matt. ix. 17; Mark ii. 22; Luke v. 37, 38. See also Kitto's 'Cyclopædia of Biblical Literature'). **Bound up.** The usual mode of mending in the East, except when a patch is inserted, is to tie or sew up the hole.

Ver. 5.—**Shoes.** Literally, *things tied on; i.e.*, sandals, attached with straps to the sole of the foot. **Clouted,** *i.e.*, patched. The intensive Pual suggests that they were *very much* patched. The participle Kal is translated "spotted" in Gen. xxx. 32, 33, 35. **Mouldy.** נְקֻדִים literally, *marked with points, i.e.*, mildewed. *Provision* צֵידָם. "Proprie venationem" (Vatablus). "Panis enim mucidus punctis respersus est albis viridibus et nigris" (Rabbi David, *in libro Radicum*). So

the LXX., Theodotion, and Luther. This gives a better sense and more according to the derivation than the interpretation *crumbs of bread*, given by Gesenius and Keil, after Aquila, Symmachus, and the Vulgate, which has "*in frustra comminuti.*" The *cracknels* (the same word in Hebrew as here) in 1 Kings xiv. 3 were probably biscuits marked with points by a sharp-pointed instrument, in the same way as the Jewish passover cakes are at the present day.

Ver. 6.—**To the camp at Gilgal.** Many commentators, among whom we may number Vandevelde and the recent Palestine Exploration Expedition, suppose that the Gilgal mentioned here is *another* Gilgal, and certainly the supposition derives great force from the fact that there is a place the modern name of which is Jiljilia, situated near the oaks of Moreh, whose situation would be far more central, and would fall in better with the rest of the history (see notes on ch. viii. 30), than the original Gilgal. That such a second Gilgal is known to Jewish history would appear from Deut. xi. 30, where its situation is clearly pointed out as that of the modern Jiljilia, near the oaks of Moreh, and near the Arabah (*champaign*, Authorised Version), which runs in that direction. Jiljulieh, in the plain of Sharon, is supposed by Vandevelde and the Palestine explorers (see 'Quarterly Statement,' Jan., 1879) to be a *third* Gilgal, and Jerome, in his 'Onomasticon,' has identified it (see note on ch. xii. 23). The Gilgal in 1 Sam. xiii. 4—12 seems to require a central position like that of Jiljilia, rather than a place near the fords of Jordan. As Ewald reminds us, the earlier Gilgal lay out of the road from Jericho to Bethel (see also 2 Kings ii. 1—6). The only argument against such a second Gilgal is the improbability of a removal of the camp without any mention of such removal by the historian (see Hengstenberg, 'Geschichte des Reiches Gottes,' p. 207), and the improbability of there having been a second Gilgal as the place of encampment of the Israelites. It is possible, however, that the second great place of encampment received the memorable name of the first, from the keen sense that the Israelitish encampment was the abode of a people from which the "reproach of Egypt" was for ever rolled away. Another explanation is suggested by a comparison of ch. xv. 7 with ch. xviii. 17 (see note on the former passage). The second Gilgal, if it really existed, was well suited for its purpose. "It was in the centre of the country, situated upon a steep hill, with a good table land at the top, and commanded a most extensive prospect of the large plain in the west, and also towards the north and east " (Keil)—precisely the place which an able general would be likely to select. Though "in a high position" (Vandevelde), it was "lower than Gibeon," and was "an hour west of Sinjil on the Jerusalem-Shechem road." Its situation enabled Joshua to strike a decisive blow without delay (ch. x. 7, 9). It is clear that this suggestion entirely obviates the difficulty of the concluding verses of ch. viii. And as the name implies a circular form as well as motion, and early camps were usually circular, it may have been the ordinary name for an encampment among the Hebrews.

Ver. 7.—**And the men of Israel said.** The Keri here has the singular number instead of the Chethibh plural, in consequence of Israel speaking of itself collectively in the word בְּקִרְבִּי and of the singular אִישׁ. But this last with a plural verb, as a noun of multitude, occurs in the historical books in places too numerous to mention. See, for instance, 1 Sam. xiv. 22, just as עַם in many passages, e.g., 2 Sam. xviii. 7, is the nominative to a plural verb. **The Hivites** (see note on ver. 3). **Peradventure ye dwell among us, and how can we make a league with you?** This was strictly forbidden in Exod. xxiii. 32; xxxiv. 12; Deut. vii. 2, in reference to neighbouring nations, on account of the polluting influence their example had exercised (Num. xxv. 1—3), and was sure to exercise, as the subsequent history of the Israelites from Judg. ii. onwards, proves.

Ver. 8.—**We are thy servants.** This does not mean altogether, as ver. 9 shows, that the Gibeonites intended by this embassy to reduce themselves to servitude. Their object, as Grotius remarks, was rather to form an alliance on terms of something like equality. The phrase was one common in the East as a token of respect (e.g., Gen. xxxii. 4, 18; l. 18; 2 Kings x. 5; xvi. 7). But no doubt the Gibeonites (see ver. 11) expected to have a tribute laid on them. And they would willingly accept such an impost, for, as Ewald remarks ('History of Israel,' iv. 3), their object was "to secure the peace which a mercantile inland city especially requires" (see also note on ch. iii. 10). **From whence come ye?** Joshua uses the imperfect, not the perfect, tense here. Commentators are divided about its meaning. Some suppose that the perfect, "from whence have ye come?" is more direct and abrupt than "from whence may you have come?" or, "from whence were you coming?" and certainly an indirect question is in most languages considered more respectful than a direct one (see Gen. xlii. 7). But

perhaps with Ewald we may regard it simply as implying that their mission was still in progress.

Ver. 9.—**And they said unto him.** "I commend their wisdom in seeking peace; I do not commend their falsehood in the manner of seeking it. Who can looke for any better in pagans?" (Bp. Hall.) It is worthy of the craft of the Gibeonites that they evade the first question, and as it is of vital importance to the success of their mission, they throw their whole force upon the second. The course of conduct enjoined on Joshua had reached the ears of the Canaanitish peoples, as we learn from ver. 24. They also take good care to say nothing of the more recent successes of the Israelites. With consummate astuteness they confine themselves to the successes "beyond Jordan." No wonder such mastery of the arts of deceit should have imposed on the Israelites. But inasmuch as the historian lacked the stimulus of that "necessity" which is proverbially "the mother of invention," we must recognise here a sign of the genuineness of the narrative.

Ver. 10.—**Sihon, king of Heshbon, and Og, the king of Bashan** (see Num. xxi. 21, 35). **Ashtaroth** (see ch. xii. 4; xiii. 31; also Deut. i. 4). In Num. xxi. Edrei only is mentioned. This is not the Ashtaroth-Karnaim of Gen. xiv. 5, which is so called from the worship of the horned Astarte, or crescent (see below), to distinguish it from this Ashtaroth. The two cities were close together. Eusebius and Jerome state that they were only nine miles apart. The site of this city has been identified with Tel Ashtereh, in a wide plain on the east of Jordan. It appears as Astaratu in the Karnak list of cities captured by Thothmes III. The name has been identified with the Assyrian *Ishtar*, the Persian, Greek, and Latin *aster* and our star. So Gesenius, 'Thesaurus,' *s.v.* Whence Lucian seems to have been wrong in his idea that the worship of Astarte, like that of Artemis at Ephesus, was that of the moon. But Rawlinson, in his 'Ancient Monarchies,' decides against this identification. The last mention of this city in Jewish history is in the bold and successful expedition of Judas Maccabæus into Gilead, in which he penetrated as far as this city (called Karnaim), and brought the Jews residing there and in the neighbourhood to Jerusalem (1 Macc. vi.). Kuenen, in his 'History of the Religion of Israel,' makes a distinction between the worship of Ashtaroth and of Asherah. The former he regards as the worship of the moon, and a pure worship; the latter of Venus, and an impure one.

But though Asherah and Ashtaroth, or Ashtoreth, are undoubtedly distinct, yet both worships may have been impure, as the worship of Artemis of the Ephesians (the *Diana Multimamma*, or the image of fecundity) unquestionably was. "It is probable," says Mr. G. Smith, "that the first intention in the mythology was only to represent love as heaven-born, but in time a more sensual view prevailed, and the worship of Ishtar became one of the darkest features in Babylonian mythology." The Babylonian Mylitta, or Venus, was worshipped under a crescent form, as Babylonian sculptures prove. A Syrian altar with the crescent on it is now in the Fitzwilliam Museum at Cambridge. It has a female figure on one side, with the crescent, and a male figure—of Baal, no doubt—on the other. Another is mentioned in a late able article in the *Times*, as having been found in Carchemish, the Hittite capital. The Chaldæan astronomers had, no doubt, discovered the use of telescopes (though in the translucent sky of Chaldæa perhaps the crescent Venus might be seen without them), for we find Saturn represented on their monuments with a ring (see Proctor, 'Saturn and his System,' p. 197). Consequently the worship of the crescent Venus involves no anachronism. Asherah, often wrongly translated "grove" in our version (see Judg. vi. 25), is probably the goddess Fortune, derived from אֶשֶׁר, happiness. Ashtaroth is spelt, not with Aleph, but with Ain.

Ver. 11.—**Our elders.** Gibeon and its allied cities did not possess a regal government (see note on ver. 3).

Ver. 14.—**And the men took of their victuals.** Most commentators prefer this rendering to that of the margin, "and they received the men because of their victuals." The natural explanation—though several others are given, for which see Keil *in loc.*—would seem to be that the Israelites relied on the evidence of their senses, instead of upon the counsel of God. They could see the condition of the garments, sacks, and wine-skins of the Gibeonites. They tasted of their victuals to convince themselves of the truth of those statements of which the sight was insufficient to take cognisance. **And asked not counsel at the mouth of the Lord.** Even in the most obvious matter it is well not to trust too implicitly to our own judgment. Nothing could seem more clear or satisfactory than the account given of themselves by the Gibeonites—nothing more easy for the unassisted intellect to decide. And yet Joshua and the congregation were deceived. It is perhaps too much to say, with some commentators—Maurer, for instance—that Joshua disobeyed a plain command in

acting thus. The passage in which Joshua is instructed to "stand up before Eleazar the priest, who shall ask counsel for him at the judgment of Urim before the Lord (Num. xxvii. 18—23), does not require him to do so in all cases. But it was clearly "an act of gross carelessness" (Calvin). And the inference may safely be drawn that in no case whatever is it wise to trust to ourselves. However obvious our course may be, we shall do well to take counsel with God by prayer.

Ver. 15.—**The princes of the congregation.** Literally, *the exalted ones*, נְשִׂיאֵי of the congregation, "Die obersten der gemeine" (Luther); that is, the heads of the various tribes (see Num. i. 44; and note on ch. vii. 14).

Ver. 17.—**On the third day.** After the trick was discovered. Keil remarks that we need not suppose that the three days were consumed on the march. Not only did Joshua, when celerity was necessary, perform the journey in a single night, but the whole distance was not more than eighteen or twenty miles, if we accept the hypothesis of a second Gilgal. **Now their cities were.** Beeroth still exists, we are told, as el-Bireh (Robinson ii. 132. So also Vandevelde and Conder). Jerome identified it with a place only seven miles from Jerusalem, which is an obvious error. It contains nearly 700 inhabitants, and is only about twenty minutes' walk from el-Jib, or Gibeon. Kirjath-jearim (the name means *the city of forests*) is well known in the history of Israel (*e.g.*, Judg. xviii. 12). But it is chiefly remarkable for the twenty years' sojourn of the ark there (1 Sam. vii. 2). It was also known by the name of Baalah, Kirjath-Baal (ch. xv. 9, 60; 2 Sam. vi. 2). The Hivites seem to have been removed thence (probably to Gibeon), for there is no trace of any non-Jewish element in the population in the account of the reception of the ark among them (see 1 Sam. vi.). It is called Baale of Judah in 2 Sam. vi. 2 (cf. ch. xviii. 15). The Jewish population seems to be due to one of the posterity of Caleb (see 1 Chron. ii. 50—53). Modern explorers, with the exception of Lieut. Conder, have identified Kirjath-jearim with Kuriet-el-Enab, "the city of the grape," about four miles from el-Jib, or Gibeon. This is the opinion of Robinson and Vandevelde. Supposing it to be near Beth-shenesh, on the authority of Josephus, Lieut. Conder places it at 'Arma, west of Bethlehem, and identifies the waters of Nephtoah with a fountain nearly due south of the valley of giants or Rephaim (see ch. xv. 9). But this is too far from Gibeon.

He identifies Kuriet-el-Enab with Kirjath in ch. xviii. 28, and regards this as one of the cities of Benjamin within the border. But this Kirjath may be Kirjath-jearim, and may as reasonably, standing on the border, be accounted to belong to both tribes, as Zorah, Eshtaol (mentioned in the boundaries of Judah and Dan), Beth-arabah, possibly Gibeah or Gibeath (belonging to Judah and Benjamin), and even Jerusalem itself (see ch. xv. 53). The identification of Kirjath-jearim with Kuriet-el-Enab, of the waters of Nephtoah with Ain Lifta, giving a line running north-westward from the valley of Rephaim, seems more probable as the border of Judah and Benjamin, and the word " compassed," or rather deflected, adds probability to this interpretation (see ch. xv. 9, 10, and notes).

Ver. 18.—**And the children of Israel smote them not.** There is great difference of opinion among the commentators as to whether this oath were binding on the Israelites or not. This difference is to be found among Roman Catholics as well as Protestants, and Cornelius à Lapide gives the ingenious and subtle arguments used on both sides by the Jesuit commentators. Many contend that as it was obtained by fraud, and especially by a representation that the Gibeonites did not belong to the tribes which Joshua was specially commanded to destroy (see Deut. xx. 10—18, with which compare the passages cited in note on ver. 7), it was null and void, *ab initio*. But the Israelites had sworn by the sacred name of Jehovah to spare the Gibeonites. It would have been to degrade that sacred name, and possibly (ver. 20) to bring trouble on themselves, to break that oath under any pretence whatever. If they had been deceived the fault was their own. The Jehovah by whom they swore had provided them with a ready mode of detecting such deceit, had they chosen to use it. Calvin, though he thinks the princes of the congregation were unnecessarily scrupulous, remarks on the superiority of Israelitish to Roman morals. It would have been easy enough for the congregation to argue, as the Romans did after the disaster at the Caudine Forks, that the agreement was of no effect, because it was not made with the whole people. Cicero, however, had no sympathy with such morality. He writes ('De Officiis,' i. 13), "Atque etiam si quid singuli temporibus adducti, hosti promiserunt, est in eo ipso fides conservanda." And not a few instances of similar perfidy since the promulgation of Christianity may lead us to the conclusion that the example of Israel under Joshua is not yet superfluous. As instances

of such perfidy, we may adduce the battle of Varna, in 1444, in which Ladislaus, king of Hungary, was induced by the exhortations of Cardinal Julian to break the truce he had entered into with Amurath, sultan of the Turks. It is said in this case that Amurath, in his distress, invoked Jesus Christ to punish the perfidy of His disciples. Be that as it may, a signal defeat fitly rewarded their disregard of truth. Later instances may be drawn from the conflict between Spain and the Netherlands in the latter part of the sixteenth century, in which the Spaniards frequently and wantonly, in the supposed interests of religion, violated the articles of capitulation formally entered into with the insurgents. These breakers of their plighted word also found that " wrath was upon them ; " that God would not prosper the arms of those who, professedly for His sake, were false to their solemn obligations. Both the princes, in the narrative before us, in withstanding the wrath of the congregation, and the congregation in yielding to their representations, present a spectacle of moral principle which few nations have surpassed. Cornelius à Lapide, after giving the opinions of others, as we have seen, and remarking on the opinion here followed as "probabilior," sums up in the following noble and manly words : " Disce hic quam sancte fides, præsertim jurata, sit servanda hosti, etiam impio et infideli. Fide enim sublata, evertitur omnis hominum contractus et societas, quæ fidei quasi basi innititur, ut homines jam non homines, sed leones, tygrides, et feræ esse videantur." Would that his Church had always acted upon these inassailable principles of justice and morality ! In after years a terrible famine visited the Israelites as a chastisement for the infringement of this agreement (see 2 Sam. xxi. 1–9). **Murmured.** Literally, *were stubborn.*

Ver. 20.—**Lest wrath be upon us.** The original is not quite so strong : " and wrath will not be upon us (καὶ οὐκ ἔσται καθ' ἡμῶν ὀργή, LXX.).

Ver. 21.—**Said unto them,** *i.e.*, to the Israelites. **But let them be.** Rather, *and they were,* with Rosenmüller and Keil. See Keil *in loc.* for the force of the Vau conversive. The LXX. and Vulgate render as our version. **Hewers of wood and drawers of water.** Some amount of casuistry has been displayed upon this passage. But the fairness of the proceeding seems clear enough. The Gibeonites had escaped death by a fraud. For that fraud they deserved punishment. Their lives were spared by virtue of a solemn oath. But equality of rights had never been promised them. They might think themselves well off if they escaped destruction, even though they might be condemned permanently to occupy a servile condition. They appear to have assisted at the tabernacle worship, since they were condemned to serve, not individual Israelites, but the congregation. Such was the office of the נְתִינִים (*Nethinim, i.e.*, the given or devoted) in the later history of Judah (see 1 Chron. ix. 2 ; Ezra ii. 43—54, 58, 70; and viii. 20. See also Drusius and Masius *in loc.*). The latter discusses the question whether the Nethinim were really the Gibeonites, or whether David, as stated in Ezra viii. 20, instituted a new order of persons to take their place. If the latter were the case, then we have a proof that the Book of Joshua was written anterior to the time of David. It seems quite possible that Saul (2 Sam. xxi. 6) had all but exterminated the Gibeonites, and that David was compelled to institute a new order in their stead. If this suggestion be correct, and it is far from improbable, we have here an undesigned coincidence strongly supporting the credit of the narrative, in the place of Knobel's insinuation, contained in the words, that " the Elohist in Saul's time gives no hint of this, although he took the greatest interest in the persons engaged in God's service." **As the princes had promised them.** These words as they stand are unintelligible. No such promise had been given. The literal rendering is " as the princes " (see note on ver. 15) " said to them," by the mouth of Joshua, as recorded in ver. 23. The Syriac Version supplies some words here to make up for a supposed deficiency in the text. But this is not necessary. The repetition in vers. 23 and 27 is quite in the manner of the historian. Nor are the words " as the princes said to them" explicable on the supposition that the words after, " let them live," are the words of the princes (see note above).

Ver. 23.—**There shall none of you be freed from being bondmen.** Literally, as margin, *there shall not be cut off from you a servant*, as in 2 Sam. iii. 29, and 1 Kings ii. 4. The sense is, " you shall not cease to be servants." The term " bondmen " is somewhat too strong. The עֶבֶד was usually a bondman among the Hebrews, but not always (see 1 Sam. xxix. 3 ; 1 Kings xi. 26, &c.). But the Gibeonites were to be em-

ployed for ever in servile work. Hewing of wood and drawing of water was a task frequently imposed on the strangers (probably captives) dwelling among the Israelites, as we learn from Deut. xxix. 11. We are not directly told that, as Keil and others have stated, the " lowest of the people " had to perform this office. It is, however, implied that the stranger who performed it occupied the lowest social station in the community. " Si qui tales sunt in nobis, quorum fides tantummodo habet ut ad Ecclesiam veniant, et inclinent caput suum sacerdotibus, officia exhibeant, servos Dei honorent, ad ornatum quoque altaris vel Ecclesiæ aliquid conferant, non tamen adhibeant studium ut etiam mores suos excolant, actus emendent, vitia deponant, castitatem colant, iracundiam mitigent, avaritiam reprimant, rapacitatem refrenant, maleloquia et stultiloquia, vel scurrilitatem et obtrectationum venena ex ore suo non adimant, sciant sibi, qui tales sunt, qui emendare se nolunt, sed in his usque in senectutem ultimam perseverant, partem sortemque at Jesu Domino cum Gabaonitis esse tribuendam " (Orig., Hom. 10 on Joshua).

Ver. 24.—**The Lord thy God commanded** (see Exod. xxiii. 32 ; Deut. vii. 1, 2). The prophecies of Moses during their sojourn in " the plains of Jordan by Jericho " (see Num. xxii. *sqq.*). **We were sore afraid.** Prophesied in Exod. xv. 14.

Ver. 26.—**That they slew them not.** See ver. 18, which attributes the preservation of the Gibeonites to the action of the heads of tribes. Perhaps this should be rendered, *and they slew them not*.

Ver. 27.—**And for the altar** (see note on ver. 21). **In the place which he should choose.** This phrase, and especially the use of the imperfect tense, implies that Solomon's temple was not yet built. The ark of God, and the tabernacle which contained it, had several resting-places before its final deposition in the temple (see note on ch. xxiv. 1). And the grammatical construction just referred to also implies that there was more than one place. It is also clear, from the language of 2 Sam. xxi. 1—6, that this narrative was already in existence when that chapter was penned. It is equally clear that the author of this passage knew nothing of that (see Introduction).

HOMILETICS.

Vers. 1—27.—*God's people off their guard.* This chapter contains the record of a venial sin ; an act, that is, which was rather one of thoughtlessness than of deliberate intention to offend. It is one thing to forget for a moment God's superintending providence, and to act without consulting Him. It is quite another to act systematically as if there were no God. Thus we read of no very serious results flowing from this inadvertence. God is "not extreme to mark what is done amiss," and distinguishes between human infirmity and human depravity.

I. "THE CHILDREN OF THIS WORLD ARE WISER IN THEIR GENERATION THAN THE CHILDREN OF LIGHT." The Canaanitish kings see the necessity of union. They act with one accord. It is strange that God's people should find it more difficult to unite than others. It is, however, but an illustration of the old adage, "Corruptio optimi pessima." It is zeal for the truth, which, when carried to an extreme, becomes bigotry, and leads to dissension. Thus the Jews at the siege of Jerusalem were divided among themselves when Titus and his legions were at the gates. So now Christians are quarrelling among themselves when infidelity is abroad, and threatening the very foundations of the Christian faith. We are wrangling about non-essentials as though they were essentials, and men thus come to think that there can be no truth at all among those who seem unable to agree on a single point. We strive for pre-eminence, social, political, numerical, and while we strive, the enemy of souls comes and carries off too many of the prizes for which we are contending. We are united upon the fundamentals of the Christian faith, yet we fail to see it ourselves, so eagerly do we contend for the objects of our unchastened desires. The heathen rebuke us, for they could act unitedly in a moment of danger for a common cause. The very devils shame us, for they combine to thwart, were it possible, the counsels of the Most High. It is only Christians who can carry on their intestine conflicts when the foe is thundering at the doors. Could we but learn (1) what are the fundamentals of the Christian faith, and (2) that whatever lies outside these is legitimate matter for argument and amicable controversy, but not for strife and disunion, we should no longer have to deplore souls lost to Christ for this cause, and it alone.

II. WE OUGHT TO REFER ALL OUR ACTIONS TO GOD. Joshua and the princes in this narrative made a distinction which many of us make, and which is not warranted by the Word of God; the distinction, that is, between matters of import-ance, which we should never think of deciding without prayer, and comparatively unimportant matters, in which the exercise of our own judgment is sufficient. But the truth is, that no matter is unimportant. Everything, strictly speaking, should be the subject of prayer; not necessarily of formal and prolonged prayer, but of a momentary ejaculation to God for help. This may be thought impossible, but it is in truth the secret of Christian perfection. "Pray without ceasing," says the Apostle, and he only has the true key to Christian progress who has acquired the habit of continual approach to God in prayer. Prayer should be the golden thread which binds together our whole life, consecrating every act and thought of it silently and secretly to God's service. This habit is only gained by perseverance, and it must itself be sought with prayer ; but only he who has attained it can be truly said to "walk with God."

III. A PROMISE IS SACRED, AND MUST BE KEPT AT ALL RISKS. There may, of course, be exceptional cases in which a promise may not be kept. If we have promised to do what is wrong, it were clearly worse to keep our promise than to break it. But then it must be clear that it would be morally wrong to keep our promise. Israelite casuistry here decides that a positive command of God—one, that is, which is not grounded upon a moral necessity—is outweighed by the obliga-tion to keep an oath. God had commanded them to make no covenant with the people of the land, and they had unwittingly bound themselves by an oath to break that command. It was a nice point for the moralist. There was no moral necessity to put men to death. The command to exterminate the Canaanites was imposed upon them as the ministers of God's vengeance. But the duty of keeping an oath was of universal obligation. To absolve one's self from it would be to set one's self free from the elementary principles of morality. Thus the duty of keeping one's word is important enough to outweigh even a command of God, where that command is not of primary necessity. It would be wrong, for instance, to commit a murder, or a theft, because we had promised to do so. But if we had wrongly promised to neglect some one of the external duties of religion, it would seem that we were bound to keep our promise, unless it were clear that God's cause would suffer thereby. It is, however, difficult to find any precept of God's law under the Christian dispensation which we may venture to neglect; because the ceremonial law is abrogated, and there is no precept of Divine obligation left which does not involve the weightier matters of the law. Two considerations may be drawn from this history.

1. *Be very careful how you promise.* Joshua and the Israelites promised lightly, and found to their regret that they ought not to have promised at all. Many young Christians entangle themselves as lightly in engagements which they find should never have been made, and thus involve themselves in troubles and difficulties from which Christian prudence would have kept them free.

2. *Keep your promise, when made,* unless, as has been said, to keep it would be a sin. The difficulties in which it involves you are sent by God to make you more careful for the future. They will not overwhelm you if you have faith in God. But it were better to suffer some anxiety and annoyance than lose your hold on truth. Inconvenience is no sufficient reason for breaking one's word, though it may be for not giving it. It is as true, as a rule, of promises made to man, as of vows made to God; "better is it that thou shouldest not vow, than that thou shouldest vow, and not pay."

HOMILIES BY VARIOUS AUTHORS.

Ver. 14.—*The Israelites outwitted.* A story that bears on its face the evidences of authenticity. A wiliness displayed quite in keeping with our notions of Oriental duplicity. Has lessons appropriate to modern days. Whilst some incidents of this book enjoin courage, this induces discretion, and thus are we preserved from a one-sided development of our spiritual life. No study more instructive than that of history, and no history more suggestively written than that of the Israelites.

I. THE STRATAGEM OF THE GIBEONITES shows us — 1. *The different courses adopted by different men in respect of the same dangers.* The overthrow of Jericho and the destruction of Ai struck terror into the hearts of the neighbouring inhabitants of Palestine. Would not their turn come next? How should they deal with the difficulty that threatened them? The only safety seemed to lie in united opposition. So reasoned many of the kings, and they organised their forces for battle. But the Gibeonites determined to act otherwise. To contract a treaty with the foe would be a greater safeguard than to encounter him in war. This they accordingly endeavoured to secure in the subtle manner which this chapter records. This variety of sentiment is being constantly exhibited in the plans men pursue regarding the "terrors of the Lord" or the assaults of conscience. Conviction of sin and of the retribution to which it exposes the sinner does not always incline him to sue for mercy. Some brave the attack, and with incredible folly fight against God. Though others have been overcome, they hope to be successful. The fall of other cities does not deter them from vain enterprises. Some, like the Gibeonites, are teachable, and if we cannot commend the deception they practised, we can at least exhort that the impossibility of staying the spread of God's kingdom be practically recognised. " Be ye reconciled unto God."

2. *The pains taken to preserve life.* Self-preservation is accounted one of the strongest instincts of our nature. These Gibeonites spared no trouble in order to gain their end. And yet how often are the things relative to eternal life utterly neglected!

3. *The desire often entertained by the world to enter into an alliance with the Church* Simon Magus could desire the gift of the Holy Ghost for his own selfish purposes. It suits the plans of many to be considered religious; they assume the garb of piety to carry on their nefarious work unmolested. The Church of Christ is bound to exercise discipline, but prevention is better than excommunication. Guard against the intrusion of ungodly men. Seek the direction of God, who will keep His Church pure. The Gibeonites said nothing about adopting in heart the

religion of the Israelites, about renouncing idolatry and serving the true God; they only wanted the advantages which would accrue from making a league with the Israelites. If we would share the advantages we must become God's people in heart and life.

4. *The success of craft.* Mental is sometimes more powerful than physical force in overcoming a difficulty. The Midianites were able to seduce the Israelites into sin though they could not injure them in open battle. There is undoubtedly a legitimate use of craft; according to the Apostle's declarations, " I have caught you with guile," " becoming all things to all men." There must be, however, nothing inherently wrong in our procedure, no tampering with truth, as in the case of the Gibeonites. For we proceed to remark—

5. *Deceit is certain of ultimate detection.* Hypocrisy must ere long have its veil removed. Show will not always be taken for reality. God knows the actual state of the heart and often makes it manifest to others. Soon did Israel discover the trick which had been practised on them. Our subject contains a warning to mere professors of godliness. Privileges secured by appearance of conformity are only temporary.

II. THE MISTAKE OF THE ISRAELITES teaches us—1. *That the senses easily lead us astray.* The mouldy bread, the damaged bottles, the clouted shoes seemed plain proof of the truth of the strangers' words. Many persons think all their doubts would vanish if they once saw an angel or heard the voice of the Almighty; but the irrefragable testimony might be a delusion just as much as the convincing sights beheld by the Israelites. The things touched and viewed are what they are; the error is in the conclusions drawn from them. The bread was mouldy, but it did not warrant the belief that it had become so by a long journey. We must be careful in our reasonings. Earthquakes and pestilences do not necessarily prove God's anger, nor do they furnish testimony against the perfections of His character as a God of love. Prosperity is not conclusive evidence of God's favour or man's desert, nor adversity of man's ill-desert and his Maker's displeasure. In various directions the caution may be employed.

2. *The weakness of human wisdom.* All appeared so natural that the Israelites forbore to consult the Lord. Was not their path clearly indicated? They soon repented of their haste and simplicity. And has no similar error befallen us, the way seeming so evident that we have rushed into it without due deliberation and prayer? God expects us to use the sagacity He has bestowed upon us, but not to rely upon it wholly. It must form only one element in the judgment reached. " O Lord, I know that the way of man is not in himself; it is not in man that walketh to direct his steps." We are so biassed, so influenced by inclination, have such perverse feelings, that we are not fit to be guides to ourselves. Experience attests this fact, Scripture often asserts it, reason corroborates it, and history proves it. The pride of the Israelites was probably flattered by the notion of their fame having extended to such a distant nation.

3. *The importance of seeking the counsel of the Almighty.* There is the reflex influence of prayer, purifying the desires, calming the passions, revealing the mischievous nature of much that seemed desirable, and leading to a clearer perception of principles. It cleanses "the thoughts of the heart." There is the answer granted to prayer. The mind is divinely directed, the Spirit of God fastens the eyes on particular passages of Scripture, and upon certain indications of Providence in external circumstances. To God, nothing that concerns His children is of trivial import; we may submit to Him matters great or small. " Commit thy way unto the Lord."—A.

Vers. 18, 19.—*An oath observed.* Recapitulate the chief circumstances: The embassage from Gibeon. Described in chap. x. as "a great city," and "all the men thereof mighty." Not because they were inferior to the other inhabitants of the land did they seek to make a compromise with Israel. The surprise of the Israelites on discovering the nearness of Gibeon. "Those old shoes had easily held to carry them back to their home."

I. THE ANGER AND WISH OF THE PEOPLE arose from—1. *Their mortification at being outwitted.* Pride had been honoured by the arrival of such an apparently distant deputation. The evidences were incontestable. All the stronger would be the consequent revulsion when the trickery was discovered. Each man thinks himself as wise as his neighbour, and cannot endure to be triumphed over in any transaction. If we did not rate ourselves so highly, we should not be troubled with such pangs of shame.

2. *The natural hatred of deception.* One of the proofs of the existence of a moral sense, and therefore of the moral constitution and government of the world, is found in the condemnation universally pronounced upon underhanded dealing. Commerce and intercourse must cease where no bond of good faith is observed. The Gibeonites perjured themselves by words and deeds. The fiercest reproofs of our Lord were administered to the hypocritical scribes and Pharisees. He called them "whited sepulchres;" they "made clean the outside of the cup and platter, but within were full of extortion and excess."

3. *A mingled remembrance of God's commandment and their own desire for plunder.* The craft of the Gibeonites could not fail to make them regarded as enemies of God; and if this wholesome sentiment was sometimes feeble in operation, it was certainly strengthened on this occasion by the sight of the rich booty which the Israelites would have enjoyed but for the league entered into under such false pretences. Moral indignation is vastly swelled by a sense of personal injury. Interest quickens resentment and action. Not so with the Almighty. Raised far above all our petty interests, His wrath against sin is pure, a bright flame that has no base admixture to sully its awful grandeur.

II. THE DETERMINATION OF THE PRINCES. 1. *Regarded the sacredness of their word.* Like Jephthah, they had given their word, and could not go back. They were prepared to face the opposition of the populace. In this they showed themselves worthy of their position as heads of the people. On all leaders a great responsibility rests; it is sometimes necessary to check as well as to urge forward their followers. They must be ready to resist the clamours of the multitude. To think weightily of a spoken word, a promise, is an all-important matter. Words are in the truest sense deeds. "By thy words thou shalt be justified, and by thy words thou shalt be condemned." Language is not meant to conceal but to express our thoughts, and a spoken should be as binding as a written speech. Here should Christians be well to the front. In business their every utterance should be capable of being trusted, and they should risk much rather than excuse themselves from the performance of their contracts.

2. *Respected the inviolableness of an oath.* When Jesus Christ prohibited all swearing, He did but, in the paradoxical method of statement He adopted, interdict all useless, vain, needless interlarding of conversation and business and legal declarations with the introduction of holy names and things. He Himself used the most solemn formulas in His public teaching and before the high priest; the apostles invoked the witness of God to the truth of their statements; and the Lord God is said to have "sworn with an oath." An oath is therefore permissible, but ought not to be lightly taken; it implies solemnity and deliberation. Only, therefore, under exceptional circumstances can it be considered right to break an oath. Doubtless a promise made upon the strength of the promisee's false statements is not always obligatory, but the case cannot be generally determined. Few will doubt that in the instance before us the princes acted wisely. They attributed special importance to the fact that they "had sworn unto them by the Lord God of Israel," and they looked to the evil effects that would be produced if the name of Israel's God should be dishonoured. It was their own fault, their heedless hurry, that they had committed themselves to the rash oath. Note, too, that the narrative, by not condemning the resolve of the princes, seem to sanction it. And in after years the Israelites incurred the grievous displeasure of the Almighty, because Saul had, in his mad zeal, sought to slay the Gibeonites in contravention of this agreement (2 Sam. xxi. 1—11). In the result these Hivites gained their life, but were reduced to servitude. The curse pronounced upon Canaan (Gen. ix. 25)

was fulfilled; these men were "cursed" (ver. 23), and became a "servant of servants" unto the Israelites.

This incident reminds us of—

THE SAFETY OF RELIANCE UPON THE WORD OF GOD. "He is not a man that he should lie." He cannot contradict Himself. If He does seem to "repent," it is because His promise was conditional; and if we seek His favour and do His will, His "repenting" will be only for our good, it will mean the removal of some threatened punishment. On the other hand, if we observe not the terms of the covenant, we cannot complain if God withdraws His promised blessings. God has confirmed His word to His people with an oath. "The Lord hath sworn, and will not repent." This indicates that what is said is *irrevocable*. Note the argument in Heb. vi. 17—19, and the rock-grasping anchor which makes stable the Christian's hope among all the waves and winds of life's stormiest sea. He is acquainted with all the circumstances of the case; He cannot be deceived. To Him the dateless past and the endless future are an ever-present now. He bids us receive in Christ life for evermore. Who would not build on this unshakable foundation, the "word and oath" of the living God?—A.

Vers. 15—23.—*The Gibeonites.* The manner in which Joshua dealt with the Gibeonites shows how inflexible is the respect God requires for truth. That respect is exemplified in two ways in this narrative. First, in the fulfilment of the oath made to the Gibeonites, that their lives should be saved; and second, in the punishment with which they are visited for their falsehood. They deceived Joshua by their miserable subterfuge of mouldy bread and way-worn garments, and thus passed themselves off as the inhabitants of some distant region instead of a neighbouring city. Therefore, while their lives were spared, they were reduced to a state of slavery (ver. 23).

I. NOTHING IS MORE HATEFUL TO THE HOLY GOD THAN A LIE. He is in His very essence light (1 John i. 5). Falsehood and cunning pervert all the relationships of life. Lying breaks the social bond, since a man's word is the only medium of moral exchange between men; and when mutual confidence is lost, the foundations of the social edifice are undermined. Therefore St. Paul says, "Lie not one to another . . . for ye are members one of another." In the direct education which God gave to His people Israel, He has given unmistakable demonstration of His horror of all deceit. Hence the punishment of the Gibeonites.

II. THE PUNISHMENT which these unhappy men brought upon themselves rested not only upon them as individuals, but upon their whole nation. God thus showed that evil is not transformed into good by being made to subserve a public cause. There are not two codes of morality—one for private and another for national life. Politics ought to be as scrupulously governed by the law of God as the life of the individual. Although since the abolition of the theocracy, the sphere of religion and of the civil power ought to be kept altogether distinct, it is no less incumbent on the State to adhere to the plain principles of morality. In spite of all that may seem to argue the contrary, every violation of these principles brings its own punishment. History is in its essence one long judgment of God.

III. By not allowing the Israelites to break their oath to the Gibeonites, even though they had been deceived by them, GOD TEACHES US THAT WRONG DONE BY OUR NEIGHBOUR DOES NOT AT ALL VINDICATE US IN BEING GUILTY OF A LIKE WRONG. One sin never justifies another. We are to "overcome evil with good," and it is this which distinguishes the people of God from all other people. It is by not being conformed to this world we triumph over it. If the people of God were to act in the same way as the Canaanites, there would be no reason for giving them the ascendancy. When the Church becomes worldly it falls under the condemnation of the world. Let us be, then, everywhere and always men the rule of whose life is the law of God. The only retaliation we must ever allow ourselves is rendering good for evil. "Be not overcome of evil," says St. Paul, "but overcome evil with good" (Rom. xii. 21).—E. DE P.

Vers. 3, 4.—*A stolen treaty.* The Canaanite kings are at last roused to united action against Joshua and the host of Israel. But their confederation is not complete. The inhabitants of Gibeon, on the principle that "discretion is the better part of valour," endeavour, in something like selfish treachery to the common cause, to make peace with the invaders. A suggestive example of the spirit that animates the corrupt social life of the world. When men are bent on saving themselves they care little for the ties that bind them to others. Self-interest is a very insecure bond of social unity. It was natural, however, that these men should seek to save themselves, and their suit for a treaty of peace would have had no wrong in it but that it took the form of deceit.

I. THE STRATAGEM. It was cleverly devised and skilfully carried out. It was both an acted and a spoken lie. Their profession of reverent submission to the God of Israel ("Because of the name of the Lord thy God," ver. 9) was a hollow pretence. Their whole behaviour forbids our attributing to them the honesty of purpose that Rahab manifested. Base, slavish fear was their real motive (ver. 24). Observe (1) how one sin leads on to another, perhaps a greater. The path of transgression is a downward way. Every fraud needs a falsehood to cover it. When men have once placed themselves in a false position they know not in what meanness and shame it may involve tnem. (2) If half the ingenuity men show in the pursuit of their own carnal ends were spent in the service of truth and righteousness, how much better and happier the world would be. The followers of Christ may learn many a lesson in this respect from the facts of secular life around them, and even from their adversaries. "The children of this world are wiser in their generation than the children of light" (Luke xvi. 8).

II. ITS SUCCESS. They gained their end so far as this—that their lives were spared, secured to them by a treaty and a solemn oath (ver. 15). They gained it through the too easy credulity of Joshua and the princes, who supposed that things were as they seemed to be, and through the unaccountable omission of Joshua to "ask counsel of the Lord" (ver. 14). (1) Trickery often seems to prosper in this world. It trades upon the generous trustfulness of men. But its success is short-lived. It carries with it its own condemnation. Better always be the deceived than the deceiver. (2) We must expect to fall into practical error when we fail to seek Divine direction. The wisest and best need something higher than their own judgment to guide them in the serious businesses of life. "In all thy ways acknowledge him, and he will direct thy steps" (Prov. iii. 6).

III. ITS PENALTY. They saved their lives at the cost of liberty and honour (ver. 21). The servile condition to which they were reduced fulfilled the curse pronounced by Noah on the children of Ham (Gen. ix. 25). Joshua and the princes did right in regarding their oath as sacred and binding, even though it had been won by deceit. The people would have had them violate it. "All the congregation murmured against the princes." Popular impulses may as a rule be trusted; but are sometimes very blind and false. *Vox populi* not always *Vox Dei.* Happy the people whose rulers are able wisely to curb their impetuosity and present before them an example of inflexible rectitude. If the oath of Joshua and the princes had pledged them to a thing essentially wrong, they might have used the fact that they were beguiled into it by fraud as an argument for disregarding it; but not so seeing that, while it bound them to nothing absolutely unlawful, they were involved in it by their own neglect. That God approved of its observance is seen in the fact that, when the Canaanite kings sought to inflict vengeance on Gideon for the clandestine treaty, He gave Joshua a signal victory over them (ch. x. 8—12); and also in the fact that the curse of blood-guiltiness came upon the land in after days because Saul broke this covenant with the Gibeonites and slew some of them (2 Sam. xxi. 1, 2). These men, however, must pay the penalty of their deceit. The decision of Joshua respecting them is of the nature of a just and prudent compromise. It avoids the dishonour that would be done to the name of God by the violation of the oath; but saves Israel from the disgrace of a dangerous alliance with the Canaanites by reducing them to a state of absolute subjection. Learn (1) the sanctity of an oath. A righteous man is one who "sweareth to his own hurt, and changeth not" (Psa. xv. 4). He who "reverences his conscience as his king" will never treat lightly any verbal pledges he may have given, or endeavour sophistically to rid himself of their responsibility. His "word will be as good as his bond." However false others may be, let him at least be true. (2) The need of a spirit of wisdom to determine aright the practical problems of life. The path of duty is often the resultant of different moral forces. The most difficult points of casuistry are those at which impulses equally good (fear of God, self-respect, humanity, &c.) seem to be at variance. Let every right motive have due weight. "Of two evils choose the least." (3) How men sometimes disqualify themselves for any high and noble position in the Church of God by their former infatuation in the service of sin. These Gibeonites are delivered from destruction, but their perpetual servitude is a perpetual disgrace. So do saved men often bear with them, as long as life lasts (in moral disability, or social distrust, &c.), the marks of what they once have been. They may well be thankful when their past transgressions, for Christ's sake, are forgiven, and they are permitted to take any place in His kingdom, even "as slaves beneath the throne"—"hewers of wood and drawers of water unto all the congregation."—W.

Vers. 3—27.—*The submission of the Gibeonites.* According to the explicit law of Moses (in Deut. xx. 10—18), there were three courses which Israel might pursue towards the cities they besieged: 1. In the event of a city refusing to capitulate, they were, after taking it, to destroy all the males who survived, but take the women and the little ones and the spoil, and divide the same. This first course, however, was only to be pursued to such cities as were outside the boundaries of the promised land. 2. In the event of cities *within these boundaries* refusing to capitulate, then, on taking them, they were to slay all the inhabitants of either sex, lest they should "teach them to do after their abominations." 3. But, thirdly, in the event of any city, within or without these boundaries, submitting to them without resistance, then they were to make the people "tributaries to them;" but no life was to be taken. From ch. xi. 19, 20, it is obvious that every city had the opportunity of capitulating, and would have saved its inhabitants from extermination by doing so; but that the thought of capitulation did not enter the hearts of any community, but that of Gibeon only. These remarks seem necessary to enable us to understand aright the exact position of affairs. They suggest: 1. That the submission of Gibeon was a right thing wrongly done. 2. That the wrong part of their action—the lie— was needless, as they would have been saved without it; and fruitless, as they would have had probably a better lot had there been no attempt to mislead. 3. That, accordingly, we have not here the example of a profitable lie (a thing that has never been seen since the fall), but only the example of wisdom in yielding to the inevitable, and seeking peace with the earthly representatives of God. Thus understood we may gather from their action two or three lessons worth our consideration.

I. AVOID DOING GOOD THINGS IN A BAD WAY. This is a common fault. Often all the grace of kindly acts is lost by an ungracious way of doing them. We give— perhaps avowing reluctance to do so. We confess mistakes—but exhibit a churlish regret, not for the mistake, but for the necessity of acknowledging it. We take good advice—but sullenly. We act on a good impulse—but slowly. We yield our hearts to God—but only with much misgiving, and after long delay. We do the right and just part, but only after earnestly trying to avoid doing it. So these Gibeonites rightly submit, but make the submission, which is right, in a wrong way, using falsehood and pretence. taking away from Israel the grace of generosity and the friendly spirit that would have moderated their lordship over them. Do not so blame them as to forget that every fault is a mirror, looking into which each may see some likeness of his own imperfection. You and I are like the Gibeonites in this, that always some bit of evil creeps into and mixes with the good. Such mixtures, in God's mercy, may not be fatal to our welfare, but they will always mitigate it. In this case a less abject and menial form of servitude would have been the result of their submission if they had possessed the courage of their wisdom. Do your good things in a good way.

II. Prompt acceptance of the inevitable is one of the highest parts of wisdom. The other cities of Canaan were not more brave, they were only more foolish than Gibeon. They lacked the imagination of faith which could realise the fate awaiting them. They dreamed of safety without taking measures to secure it. They believed in that " chapter of accidents which is the Bible of the fool." Like some Oriental governments which we have seen, they stared destruction in the face, and did nothing to ensure success in averting it. Wisdom averts the preventible, but sets itself to work at once to accept the inevitable. And Gibeon deserves credit for its clear perception of its danger, and its sagacity in trying to make the best of what could not be avoided. Perhaps, being more republican than any of the other nationalities, we have here an instance of the superior wisdom of the popular instinct to that of the rulers'. Without dwelling, however, on the source of their wisdom, we may with advantage follow its example. One of the chiefest parts of the art of life is frankly, promptly accepting the inevitable. Whatever the pressure that you cannot avoid, proceed at once to make the best of it. If it be poverty, do not with desperate ventures attempt to win back wealth, but with contentment and industry set yourself to make the best of it. If disease affects you from which you cannot free yourself, come to terms with it. Send your ambassadors and make a covenant with it. And accepting the situation in which you find yourself, address yourself to gather the " sweet uses of adversity," and you will find weakness a great teacher and not without its compensations. If you have done wrong, and to humble yourself is a necessity of honour, do so like Gibeon, at once. If submission to your redeeming God has become a necessity of your case, do not, like the other cities of Israel, dream and defy, and then fall before the destroyer; but with timely overtures seek Him while He is near. Thus in all relations of life accept frankly the inevitable. Agree with thine adversary quickly, and with the force you cannot resist make such terms as will allow you to enjoy a less dignity, but yet some degree of happiness.

III. God crowns with His reward all good, however mixed with evil. In the action of the Gibeonites there is the good of a rudimentary faith, there is the evil of deceit. It is to be observed that, while the evil is punished, the good is not ignored. God does not require the retractation of the oath; and when, centuries later, Israel breaks the oath, He shows His disapproval of their course. God sanctions their being spared, and thus approves the good that is mixed with evil. Happily for us, God is still the same. Perfect motive He never finds, and unmixed good He never looks on. But, in His infinite compassion, whatever of good there is in our action receives a rich reward. His love holds as keen a scrutiny as His justice, and wherever in the action of men the slightest good appears, then He rewards it.

IV. Whatever opposes God's cause will either be made subservient to it, or be destroyed. The fate of Ai or Gibeon, destruction or service, are the only alternatives of Canaan. It is a great pity when the foe declines to become a friend, and when those outside lack the aspiration to be reconciled thoroughly. For unreconciled they must serve, or disappear. Philosophies that oppose the gospel will turn round and speed on the triumph of truth, or they will melt away like a cloud before the warmth of dawn. Policies that seem adverse to the prosperity of the Church will prove productive of advantage to it, or be swept into oblivion. No weapon formed against the Church of God ever prospers. Be not on the wrong side. However strong you may appear, if you do not side heartily with the cause of God, you will be made its reluctant servants, or its extinguished foes.—G.

Ver. 14.—*The oracle neglected.* Between Joshua and Eleazer, the ruler and the high priest, a noble heritage was divided. The one has the obedience of Israel, the other the secrets of God. They have at their command respectively human power and Divine wisdom. According to Num. xxvii. 21, Joshua was taught to expect to find a heavenly oracle in the Urim and the Thummim of the priest; and constantly the promised oracle was given. In this case, however, it was not sought. Joshua and the rest were flattered with the story of their fame, and too readily assumed the insignificance of the occasion. Otherwise, had they asked they would have received counsel, and have been set on the track of discovering the fraud. It probably did not materially matter to Israel then. The chief loss to that generation was the booty they would in that case have divided, and the private advantage of so many slaves divided amongst the families, instead of having a servile tribe allotted to the ministry of the tabernacle. Still the historian notes the neglected oracle as if Joshua had learned here a lesson of carrying even things that seemed little to his God. The occasion gives two or three lessons worth learning.

I. THERE IS AN ORACLE WHICH WILL WISELY GUIDE ALL WHO FEAR GOD. God has never been at a loss to guide the willing steps of men ; but to the heart that has sought He has always given guidance. In various ways He has led men. Abraham through a whispering of His great name ; Jacob and Joseph through dreams ; Moses through voice and vision and miracle alike ; Joshua through some gleaming of the high priest's breastplate ; Gideon through the angel ; Samuel through a raised state of every faculty ; the prophets by the breathings of great thoughts and feelings ; Jonah's sailors by the lot ; the wise men from the East by a star ; the Ethiopian by a page of prophecy. He seems to accommodate all and give them their guidance where they expect to find it. God still " fulfils Himself " in many ways. The African rain-maker rebuked Livingstone, by declaring his methods of getting rain were really prayers which the good God was in the habit of granting. The Moravians, who expect Divine guidance through the casting of the lot, doubtless find it there, though no one else would get it. Sometimes through the providential barring of dangerous paths ; sometimes through a restraint like that which Paul described in the words " the spirit suffered us not ; " sometimes through inward impulse of a cogent kind, a being " bound in the spirit to go " in a certain direction ; sometimes by the mere commendation of certain courses to our taste, our judgment, or our conscience. God still gives guidance to all who ask it.

> " No symbol visible
> We of Thy presence find,
> But all who would obey Thy will
> Shall know their Father's mind."

Pray for light, and in some way it will reach you. There is a living oracle for all who wish to walk according to the will of God.

II. TRUE WISDOM COMMITS SMALL THINGS AS WELL AS GREAT TO GOD'S CARE. A child tells all to the parent that it trusts ; the least discomfiture—the greatest distress. And when we have the child-like heart we commit all to God, feeling that the least is not too little for His great love. The ability is developed of rising on every occasion in thought to Him, till the mood becomes so confiding, so expectant, that it forms a " prayer without ceasing." And this habit of committing all becomes fortified by the wisdom which observes how often the issues of things are to be in the inverse ratio of their seeming importance : vast consequences flowing from what seem most trivial events, and events that seem of a stupendous character leaving no trace of influence on after history. So, little things as well as great are lifted by the devout heart to the Divine ear. Joshua here thought recourse to the oracle needless because the matter seemed unimportant. But it had more importance than he knew. *Strangely enough, this compact with Gibeon fixes the resting-place of the ark for centuries, right down to the time of David.* For Kirjath-jearim was one of the cities of Gibeon, and it was probably the residence there of the Gibeonites that determined the resting there of the ark. This, in its turn, threw the centre of the national life to the southward, helped the supremacy of Judah, the choice of Jerusalem as capital, the subordination of Ephraim and Samaria. If Joshua had seen all that hung on his decision, he would not because of the seeming insignificance of the matter have neglected the oracle. Take God into thy counsel in all matters, less and larger. Commit the little acts to His decison, surrender the little things which self-will would decide. " Faithful in least, faithful in much ; " and, even so, devout in least, devout in much. Christ raised the dead, and then said, " Give her something to eat ; " the omnipotent miracle, the homely kindness, being equally characteristic of Him.   Walk with God always.   In least things consult His oracle.

III. ALL MAKE MISTAKES, BUT GOD'S SAINTS PROFIT BY THEM.   This is the second mistake of the same kind which Joshua has made since crossing Jordan. Not consulting the oracle, he sends too few men against Ai.   Not consulting the oracle, he makes this covenant with Gibeon.   But our text *recording the mistake shows how it was discovered,* and the repetition of it avoided.   There is no mistake which is absolute mischief, it will always give us at least a lesson.   Blessed are they who can turn all their faults into schoolmasters.   For though such school-masters use the lash, they give good teaching, being skilled to teach humility, watchfulness, dependence on God.   Turn your faults to good account, and every act of folly into a spring of wisdom.   Lastly, observe, that not only did Joshua turn the fault to account, but—

IV. GOD MAKES THE BEST OF A GOOD MAN'S MISTAKES.   After all, the alliance with Gibeon gave them entrance into a position of importance, became the occasion of the great victory of Beth-horon, and has no traceable results of mischief.   Thus it ever is.   *God makes the best of us and of our work.*   When the heart is right our every failing is turned to good account.   Be not too nervous about the results of our actions.   For when the purpose is honest and devout—

> "Our indiscretions ofttimes serve us well.
> There's a Divinity that shapes our ends,
> Rough-hew them as we will."

G.

EXPOSITION.

CHAPTER X. 1—43.

THE BATTLE OF BETH-HORON, AND THE SUBJUGATION OF SOUTHERN PALESTINE.—Ver. 1.— **Adoni-zedec** (cf. Melchizedek in Gen. xiv. 18).   The *name* given to the king of Jerusalem was good enough, and no doubt was a survival of earlier and purer times.   In the days of Melchizedek the name corresponded to the character. **Jerusalem.** Hebrew, *Jerushalaim,* with the usual dual termination. It has been generally supposed to be the same with Salem, or rather Shalem, the city of which Melchizedek was king, and this is supported by the fact that the name of Salem is given to Jerusalem in Psa. lxxvi. 2.   But it is by no means certain that this is the case. The first to dispute the identity of the two places was St. Jerome, who declares that the Salem of Melchizedek was eight miles from Scythopolis, and that the ruins of the palace of Melchizedek could still be seen there (see also Gen. xxxiii. 18).   The term Salem, as indicative of the security and strength of Jerusalem, might not unnaturally be applied to it by the Psalmist; while, on the other hand, the dual form of Jerusalem seems difficult to account for on the theory of the identity of Jerusalem and Salem. This dual form has been a difficulty to critics; and Mr. Grove, in the 'Dictionary of the Bible,' conjectures that it may have arisen from an attempt to twist the archaic Phœnician form into agreement with the

more modern Hebrew idiom, just as the Greeks afterwards twisted the name into Hierosolyma, or the holy Solyma.   But a simpler explanation may be found in the fact that Jerusalem, like many other cities, consisted of two parts, the upper and the lower town (cf. Judg. i. 8 with ver. 1, 7 and 21, and 2 Sam. v. 6—8), while in earlier times the upper or lower town alone existed.   Plural names of cities were not uncommon in later ages, as Athenæ and Thebæ.   The name has been variously derived.   Some have thought that as it is also called Jebus (ch. xviii. 28 ; Judg. xix. 10), from its being the chief city of the Jebusites, it was originally Jebus-salem, and hence by a corruption Jerusalem.   But this derivation has now been abandoned, and opinions differ as to whether it is derived from יְרוּשׁ and שָׁלֵם signifying " peaceful inheritance " (Ewald, Keil), or from יָרָה and שָׁלֵם " peaceful settlement " (Gesenius, Lee).   Gesenius objects to the former derivation that it would require dagesh in the שׁ.   The fathers and mediæval divines, misled by Origen, translate it " vision of peace."   This translation is alluded to in the well-known hymns *Urbs beata Sion* and *O quanta qualia.*   Origen supposed it to come from רָאה.   Another difficult question is *when* the name was given, for there can be little doubt that the Book of Joshua was written before the time of David. It is possible that the name may have been given by the Jebusites themselves, in consequence of their secure possession of it, notwithstanding the subjugation of the surrounding country by the Israelites. And when David had seized upon it and made it his capital, he would not be likely to change so suitable a name. For the Jebusites, evidently by their invariable position last among the nations of Canaan, the most insignificant among them, were enabled to defy the Israelite power long after their more powerful neighbours had succumbed. and David no doubt chose the situation of Jerusalem for his capital not only because, unlike Hebron, it enabled him to dwell among his own people without cutting himself off from intercourse with the other tribes of Israel; but because, as a mountain fastness remote from the plains of Esdraelon and the Orontes, which were the great highways of the Egyptian and Assyrian kings on their military expeditions, it would enable him to consolidate his power, and to secure that empire which became his from the force of his genius and the favour of God. We may remark upon the antecedent probability of the fact that the king of a place situated as Jerusalem is should stand at the head of this league.

Ver. 2. — **That they feared greatly.** Joshua had certainly obtained an excellent strategic position in the heart of the country; but it was not this which apparently most alarmed the kings who constituted the confederacy, though they did not fail to observe that, as the words "and were among them" show. It was the weight and importance of Gibeon itself, and the fact that its inhabitants were now enlisted, not on the side of the Canaanites, but against them. **As one of the royal cities.** Observe the minute accuracy of the historian. No king is mentioned in the narrative in ch. ix. We now earn indirectly that they had none. The Vulgate misses the point of the historian by leaving out "as" altogether.

Ver. 3.—**Hoham king of Hebron.** It was a powerful confederacy which the Phœnician tribes in their desperation formed against Joshua. At its head stood the king of Jerusalem, which, from its central situation and its almost impregnable position (see notes on ch. xv. 63), might naturally stand at the head of such a league. Next came Hebron, which, from its importance from an early period (Gen. xxiii. 2; xxxv. 27), and the gigantic stature of its inhabitants (Num. xiii. 33; Deut. i. 28; ii. 10, 11; ix. 2), as well as its daughter cities (ver. 37), would prove a formidable addition to the strength of the confederates. Colossal blocks of stone, testifying to the presence

there of the primeval races of Palestine, are still to be found in the neighbourhood. Hebron stands in "the hill country of Judæa." Its situation has been much admired, standing as it does nearly 3,000 feet above the level of the Mediterranean, and commanding the most extensive views of the Holy Land. This is one of the most interesting in its reminiscences of all the cities in Palestine. Here Abraham pitched his tent, near the "oak of Mamre." Here was the burying-place of Abraham and Sarah, which has been kept in memory by an unwavering tradition even to this very day; and, sacred ground though it be to the Mohammedans, was opened to the Prince of Wales and his companions in 1862. This was the inheritance of Caleb, and here, where the affections of every Israelite would most closely centre, David fixed his capital until compelled to change it by reasons to which we have already referred. Hebron seems to have been successively occupied by various members of the Phœnician confederation. It was first founded, we learn, seven years before Zoan in Egypt (Num. xiii. 22). When we first hear of it, it is in the possession of Mamre the Amorite (Gen. xiii. 18; xiv. 13). In Gen. xxiii. it has clearly passed into the possession of the Hittites, and the mention of the children of Heth is too express for us to suppose that the term Hittite is used generally for the inhabitants of the land. At a much later period the Canaanites, or lowlanders, had, strangely enough, obtained possession (Judges i. 10), and here again the accurate acquaintance of the historian with the names of the tribes (see Judg. i. 4, 21, 26, 35) forbids us to suppose that he is speaking loosely. **Piram king of Jarmuth.** Jarmuth is mentioned in ch. xv. 35, and in Neh. xi. 29. It has been identified with Yarmuk (see Robinson, II. sec. 11, with whom Vandevelde and Conder agree), where there are the remains of very ancient walls and cisterns. Of its size and importance in the time of Joshua we know nothing. **Japhia king of Lachish.** Like Jarmuth, Lachish was in the Shephelah, or lowlands, of Judah, and we frequently hear of it in the later history of the Jews, as in 2 Kings xiv. 19; xviii. 14, 17; xix. 8; also 2 Chron. xi. 9. It has been identified by Von Raumer and Vandevelde, whom Keil follows, with Um Lakis, though Robinson ('Biblical Researches' II. 388) denies this on the authority of Eusebius and Jerome; "but not on any reasonable grounds" (Vandevelde). This is the more clear in that Robinson rejects the authority of the Onomasticon in the case of Eglon. Um Lakis is only an hour and a quarter's journey from Ajlân, or Eglon, and this nar rative (vers. 31—36) shows that Eglon was on the way from Lachish to Hebron. Conder, in his 'Handbook' and in 'Pal. Exploration Fund Quart. Paper,' Jan., 1878, p. 20, suggests Tell el Hesy, a name which he thinks may "be a corruption of Lachish." This is a great mound on the main road from Eleutheropolis to Gaza. It is a strong argument for Um Lakis that there are an immense number of instances where the places retain their ancient names. The strongest argument for Tell el Hesy is that Lachish was evidently a place of some strength. Joshua, we read (ver. 32), " encamped against it " (this is said only of Lachish and Eglon), and "took it on the second day," and it successfully resisted the king of Assyria. Now Tell el Hesy was a " great mound " (Conder) ; but Um Lakis is described by Vandevelde as situated on " a low mound." **Debir king of Eglon.** This, the modern Ajlân, according to the best authorities, was on the road from Eleutheropolis to Gaza, not far from Lachish. Ruins are to be found there ; but we have no means of ascertaining the size and importance of the town in the time of Joshua. The LXX., here and elsewhere in this chapter, render by 'Οδολλάμ. In ch. xii. 11 they read 'Εγλών. There is considerable similarity between Gimel and Daleth, Mem and Nun in the ancient Hebrew character. From this a various reading no doubt resulted.

Ver. 4.—**Come up unto me.** Most of these kings were in the lowlands. Hence the expression "Come up" is accurate in the mouth of the king of Jerusalem, and strengthens the claim of the narrative to be regarded as authentic. **That we may smite Gibeon.** Or, *and we will smite Gibeon.* The conjunction ן often, but not always, signifies the purpose with which a thing is done. Here there is nothing to guide us in the decision whether the passage indicates the purpose or the result. It is in keeping with the whole history, and is one of the life-like touches with which it abounds, that the king of Jerusalem does not dare to suggest an attack upon Joshua. He can only venture upon assailing Gibeon, standing in less fear of it than of the divinely-protected invaders, and hoping at least by this measure to deprive Joshua of formidable allies. " Cum anima humana Verbo Dei se sociaverit, dubitare non debet, statim se inimicos habituram, et eos, quos ante habuerit amicos, in adversarios vertendos " (Orig., Hom. 2 on Joshua. See also Ecclus. ii. 1 ; 2 Tim. iii. 12). "As Satan, so wicked men, cannot abide to lose any of their communitie. If a convert come home, the angels welcome him with songs, the Devils follow him with uprore and furie,

his old Partners with scorne and obloquie " (Bp. Hall).

Ver. 6.—**To Gilgal.** See note on ch. ix. 6. **That dwell in the mountains.** Another life-like touch. The details of the confederacy were not fully known to the Gibeonites. There had not been time for that. It was only known that the storm was to break on them from the mountain region, Jerusalem (ver. 4) being the head-quarters of the expedition. As a matter of fact, the kings who formed the confederacy principally inhabited the lowlands, as we have seen. No one could have hit upon this apparent contradiction yet real agreement but one whose narrative was compiled from authentic sources.

Ver. 7.—**Joshua ascended.** Keil insists upon the military sense here, as against the literal one, " went up." He believes in the second Gilgal, which was on higher ground than the first (see ch. ix. 6), where, however, we learn that the second Gilgal was not so elevated as Gibeon. **And all the mighty men of valour.** A selection of the bravest troops seems to be implied here, by the copulative particle. Cf. Gen. iii. 16, " Thy pain and (especially in the time of) thy pregnancy."

Ver. 8.—**Fear not.** The key-note of Joshua's career, as of the career of every soldier of God (see ch. i. 9 ; xi. 6).

Ver. 9.—**Suddenly.** By a night march, so that he might surprise the confederates at the dawn of day. One of Joshua's chief characteristics as a general was celerity (see ch. xi. 7). Masius praises Joshua for his prudence and diligence, and adds, " Qua arte Julium Cæsarem tot victoriis clarum fuisse ne ipse quidem dissimulavit." **And went up.** There is no " and " in the original. It runs thus : " All the night he went (or had gone) up from Gilgal."

Ver. 10. — **Discomfited.** The original meaning of the word is to *disturb, put in motion.* Hence, as here, to *throw into confusion, put to rout.* **Going up to Beth-horon.** Beth-horon, or the house of the hollow, consisted of two towns. The one is now called Beit Ur el Foka, or Upper Beit Ur, the other Beit Ur el Tachta, or Lower Beit Ur. To the former led a difficult pass from Gibeon, called the ascent (מַעֲלֵה) to Beth-horon. From the former to the latter ran a path so rocky and rugged that steps have been made in the rock to facilitate the descent. This is the " going down " (מוֹרַד) to Beth-horon, mentioned in the next verse. So Maccabees iii. 16–24. (Cf. Robinson, vol. iii. sec. 9). Speaking of the view from Beth-horon, he says, " The prospect included the hill country and the plain as far as the eye could reach. . . . Upon the side of the long hill that skirts the valley on the south, we could perceive a small village on the W.S.W. called Yâlo." **To Azekah.** See ch. xv. 35; cf. 1 Sam. xvii. 1. This place is known to after Jewish history, having been fortified by Rehoboam (2 Chron. xi. 9), besieged by Nebuchadnezzar (Jer. xxxiv. 7), which shows it to have been a place of some importance. It continued to be inhabited after the captivity (Neh. xi. 30), and has been identified by Vandevelde with Ahbek, a place standing upon a mountain. He supposes it to have been identical with the Aphek in Judah (1 Samuel iv. 1). But this would be better identified with Aphekah (ch. xv. 53). Lieut. Conder (' Palest. Expl. Quart. Paper,' Oct., 1875) identifies it with a place called Deir el Aashek, eight miles north of Shochoh. But apparently in the 'Handbook' he has abandoned this idea, though he makes no reference to this passage. **And unto Makkedah.** One of the lowland cities of Judah (see ch. xv. 41). Vandevelde identifies it with Summeil, a place where there are the ruins of a very ancient city (see ver. 28), built of large uncemented stones, a sign of great antiquity, and a large cave, such as that described in ver. 16. See Robinson, vol. ii. p. 368, who gives not a hint, however, that it is to be identified with Makkedah, nor does he mention a cave. Lieut. Conder (' Palest. Expl. Quart. Paper,' July, 1875) identifies it with the present El Moghar (The Caves), twenty-five miles from Gibeon along the valley of Ajalon, where several caves are found, the only ones, apparently, in the district. Summeil is a very long distance from Gibeon, and if we are to identify this with Makkedah, which there appears no ground for doing, supernatural assistance would have been required in more than one way for so protracted a pursuit during the same day.

Ver. 11.—**Great stones from heaven.** Calmet has taken great trouble to collect evidence for showers of actual stones from heaven upon the enemies of Israel. But the next sentence of the verse states that they were *hail*stones, אַבְנֵי בָרָד. And even if there were not sufficient evidence of the fall of hailstones large enough to do great destruction to man and beast, we might fall back upon the theory that this was a miraculous hailstorm, since the whole history teems with miraculous intervention. But in point of fact this is unnecessary. We need not go further back than the famous storm of August 2nd, 1879, for an account of hailstones of enormous size falling within fifty miles of London. And in tropical climates still more destructive storms are of

no infrequent occurrence. Every treatise on physical geography teems with instances. Masius refers to the well-known story of the relief afforded by a sudden shower to Marcus Aurelius and his army, which he follows, Eusebius in thinking attributable to Christian prayers, but which the emperor, in a medal struck on the occasion, attributed to Jupiter Pluvius (see Neander, ' Hist. of Christian Church,' vol. i.). He also cites the verses of Claudian on a similar victory of Theodosius :

" O nimium dilecte Deo, tibi militat æther
Et conjurati veniunt ad prælia venti."

They were more which died with hailstones. A conclusive proof, both to the Israelites and their antagonists, that the victory was owing rather to the favour of God than to the power of man, and suggesting the exclamation of the Psalmist, " Not unto us, O Lord, not unto us, but to Thy Name give glory" (Psa. cxv. 1). See also Deut. ix. 4, 5. It is, perhaps, worth while to remark that the printers have modernized this passage. For *more* the original edition has *moe;* cf. Shakspeare's 'Lover's Complaint,' line 47—" Found yet *mo* letters sadly penned in blood." " Faith and troth they would no *mo* " (Greene, ' Shepherd's Ode ').

Ver. 12.—**Then,** אָז. See ch. viii. 30. The period is here more strictly defined by the addition of the words, " on the day when the Lord delivered up the Amorites before the children of Israel." **Spake Joshua to the Lord.** The preposition לְ (literally, " to ") used here, has a variety of meanings in Hebrew. It is employed in such a phrase as " a Psalm of David " (literally, " to David "), but the sense requires " by." So in Psa. iii. 9 (8 in our version) ; Isa. xxii. 5, &c. It has the sense " on account of " in Gen. iv. 23 (where it is rendered " to " in our version) ; but the sense requires " in return for," " on account of." So also in Joshua ix. 9, where our version renders " because of." In the latter part of this verse it signifies " before " (see note there). In a passage so much disputed as this it is necessary to remember the indefiniteness of the original. Though the rendering, " to the Lord," is the natural and obvious one, the other meanings cannot be excluded. The more probable rendering is that in the text. Yet, as no address to God is afterwards recorded, the meaning may be " by," *i.e.*, by the inspiration of, or " because of," *i.e.*, on account of the great success God had vouchsafed to him, and which he earnestly desired to complete ; or " before," as though Joshua spoke with a consciousness of God's immediate presence and help. For a full discussion of this remarkable passage the reader is referred to the Introduction. **In the sight of Israel.** לְעֵינֵי, "before the eyes of." This brings the scene vividly before our eyes : the storm rolling away over the mountains, the enemy in full retreat and wild confusion, the sun bursting forth from behind the clouds, and the leader of the Israelites, in the sight of all his troops, perhaps on the crest of the eminence on which Gibeon stands, or perhaps at Upper Beth-horon (see note on ver. 10), uttering his sublime apostrophe to the "two great lights" which God had given to mankind, not to withdraw their presence until the Lord had "avenged him of his adversaries." The battle had been short, but decisive. The Israelites had no doubt (ver. 9) fallen upon the enemy unawares at the dawn of day as they were preparing for the attack on Gibeon. A few hours had sufficed to put them to the rout, but the utmost expedition would be necessary to complete their destruction before the darkness set in. Hence the ejaculation of the Jewish commander as the difficulty of the task he had imposed upon himself, namely, of utterly annihilating that vast host before light failed, flashed upon him. **Sun, stand thou still.** The poetic form of this passage is clear to every one who has the smallest acquaintance with the laws of Hebrew poetry. For the Book of Jasher, from which it is apparently a quotation (see Introduction, Sec. 2). **Stand thou still.** This is not the literal rendering of the original. In no other passage has the verb דָּמַם this sense. The sense "stand still" here would seem to be an inference from ver. 14. The literal rendering is, "be dumb." Hence in Exod. xv. 16, and in Lam. ii. 10, it signifies to be dumb with amazement or terror. In 1 Sam. xiv. 9 it seems to mean, "stay your advance" ("tarry," Authorised Version), and the word rendered "stand still" in the last part of the verse is עָמַד. See also Psa. iv. 5 (Heb.), where it is rendered "be still," i.e., "be silent ;" and Job xxx. 27, and Lam. ii. 18. The word must not therefore be pressed to mean that the sun's course was completely arrested in the heavens. All that can be assumed is that it did not set until the people were avenged of their enemies. The passage is evidently part of a triumphal song, like that recorded in Judges v., where in ver. 20 there is a very similar thought, which no one ever thinks of interpreting literally. **Upon Gibeon.** Beth-horon was north-west of Gibeon. The meaning of the phrase would perhaps be, "Sun, rest thou (i.e., cease not to shine)

in (or upon) Gibeon." **In the valley of Ajalon.** The valley of the deer, according to the Hebrew. The word for valley is Emek here (LXX. φάραγξ). See note on ch. viii. 13. Ajalon became afterwards a Levitical city (see ch. xxi. 24), and was in the inheritance of Dan (ch. xix. 42). See also 1 Sam. xiv. 31. It has been identified with the modern Yâlo (so Robinson, Vandevelde, and Conder), and was therefore four hours' journey westward from Gibeon. It was possibly near the time of full moon, and Joshua called for the light of the moon to help him when the sun had set. The very fact of his having called upon the moon to come to his assistance is an argument against the literal interpretation of the passage. The moon could have been no help to him as long as the sun was in the heavens. It is thought by some that the moon must have been already in the heavens, or why should Joshua have addressed her? This may have been the case, and he might thus have adjured the moon to give him her help after the sun had gone down, by which time he would have arrived at Ajalon, a supposition which is quite consistent with probability.

Ver. 13.—**The moon stayed.** The word עָמַד, which does mean to stand still, is used here. See also Habak. iii. 11. But if we are to apply it to the moon and not to the light of the moon, where would be the use of the moon's standing still in the valley of Ajalon, when she would be low down in the sky westward, and incapable of rendering Joshua any help? If we regard the light of the moon as meant, there is no phrase more common in poetry and poetic prose than to speak of moonbeams "resting" upon an object. **The people.** The word here is גּוֹי. See note on ch. v. 6. **The Book of Jasher.** See Introduction, Note vi. **And the sun stood still.** Here the word עָמַד is used of the sun. But, as before, it refers naturally enough to the sun's light. The declining sun continued to shine upon Gibeon, and in the neighbourhood, upon the descent from Beth-horon the Upper, and on the whole region throughout which the fugitive Canaanites were scattered. We need not suppose that all the discomfited host fled in one direction, and possibly in the neighbourhood of Gibeon itself there remained quite enough of the scattered portions of the host to need urgently the sun's light to complete their destruction. **The midst.** The Hebrew here is not the usual word for midst. It signifies literally, the half. **About a whole day.** Literally, as a perfect day. The LXX. renders οὐ προσεπορεύετο εἰς δυσμάς εἰς τέλος ἡμέρας μιᾶς, and the Vulgate, "Non festinavit occumbere spatio unius diei." What is the precise meaning of this passage it is difficult to say. The language is very obscure. It has been usually interpreted to mean that the sun remained in the heavens twelve hours longer than usual. But this, though the most natural, is by no means the only interpretation of the passage. The words, "did not hasten to go down as a perfect day," cannot be *proved* to have this meaning. In fact, it is difficult to fix a precise meaning on them. They belong rather to the domain of poetry than history, and their language is that of hyperbole rather than of exact narration of facts. Consequently, we are not entitled to build conclusions upon them, or draw arguments from them. It seems tolerably clear that twelve additional hours could hardly have been required by the Israelites for the complete extermination of their enemies.

Ver. 14.—**There was no day like that before it or after it.** Cf. for this expression 2 Kings xviii. 5; xxiii. 22, 25.

Ver. 15.—**And Joshua returned.** The historian had at first intended to complete his narrative of these transactions here. But he seems to have altered his intention, and added the execution of the five kings and the subjugation of the remaining cities of southern Palestine which had adhered to the league, as well as their immediate neighbours. He then (ver. 43) repeats what he had subjoined here. It is not contended (see Introduction) that the Book of Joshua could not have been compiled from accounts previously existing, though a different view has been taken in this commentary. But what is denied is (1) that this was an unintelligent or perfunctory compilation, and (2) that we can at this distance of time, by the simple evidence of style, disintegrate and separate into contradictory fragments the various portions of earlier histories, which we find here digested into a whole. Some copies of the LXX. leave the verse out altogether.

Ver. 16.—**In a cave.** "In *the* cave" according to the Masoretic pointing. So the LXX., τὸ σπήλαιον. Dr. Maclear remarks on the number of caves in Palestine (see Gen. xix. 30; Judg. xx. 47), as well as the well-known caves of Adullam and Engedi (1 Sam. xxii. 1, xxiv. 3), and the cave in which a hundred prophets were concealed by Obadiah (1 Kings xviii. 4). Also see note on ch. ii. 22. But Lieut. Conder believes that in this particular neighbourhood there were few caves. See note on Makkedah above, ver. 10. For "*these* five kings" the original has simply "five kings." The order of the narrative is somewhat interrupted by the introduction of Joshua's adjuration, and the account of the flight of the five kings. Compare ver. 11 with ver. 20.

Ver. 19.—**And stay ye not.** The original is stronger, *and as for you, stand not still.* The active general was not to be diverted from his purpose of annihilating the enemy by the important news that the heads of the confederacy were in his hands. He takes immediate measures to secure their persons, but for the present throws his whole strength, as well as that of his army, into the task of following up the advantage he has gained. **And smite the hindmost of them.** Literally, "and *tail* them," a verb denominative from זָנָב, tail. The LXX. renders καταλάβετε τὴν οὐραγίαν. The word is of rare occurrence in the Hebrew, but its obvious meaning is as the text. Comp. also the Vulgate, *extremos quosque fugientium cædite.*

Ver. 20.—**Until they were consumed.** An expression not necessarily involving the destruction of every individual, but the entire annihilation of them as an army. A few scattered fugitives only remained, who sought the protection of the fortified towns. "Si ea quæ per Moysen de tabernaculo vel sacrificiis, et omni illo cultu adumbrabantur, typus et umbra dicuntur esse cœlestium, sine dubio et bella quæ per Jesum geruntur, et regum et hostium strages, cœlestium rerum umbra et typus esse dicenda sunt, eorum duntaxat bellorum quæ Dominus noster Jesus cum suo exercitu et magistratibus id est credentium populis atque eorum ducibus contra diabolum et ejus angelos præliatur" (Orig., Hom. 12 on Joshua). **Fenced cities.** These were (1) walled, (2) crowned with battlements (פֻּנוֹת), and (3) defended by towers. See for further information the article in Smith's 'Dictionary of the Bible.'

Ver. 21.—**Makkedah.** Because Joshua, in his resolute pursuit of the enemy, had not forgotten the important intelligence reported to him concerning the kings. Most likely the pursuit lasted one or two days. After the return to Makkedah the execution of the kings was carried out with much ceremony (ver. 24), and their bodies hung up before all Israel, not so much as a memorial of the victory, as to impress upon the Israelites the duty of exterminating their enemies, a duty which the after history of the twelve tribes shows them to have been very prone to forget. **None moved his tongue against any of the children of Israel.** Literally, *He did not sharpen against the children of Israel, against a man, his tongue.* The Hebrew construction here is somewhat unusual. Houbigant and Maurer suppose that לְ is a mistake of the copyist, and that אִישׁ is the subject of the sentence. They would translate as the LXX., "no man muttered with his tongue against the children of Israel." But Keil and Rosenmüller prefer a rendering agreeing with that of the Authorised Version, *none moved* (or *sharpened*) *his tongue against the children of Israel, not against a single man of them.* And this is a far more forcible way of expressing the awe in which they were held. A still stronger expression is to be found in Exod. xi. 7; cf. Judith xi. 19.

Ver. 23.—**The king of Jerusalem.** The names of the kings are mentioned to emphasise the significance of the action recorded in the next verse. The LXX. has Ὀδολλάμ again here.

Ver. 24.—**Which went with him.** There is a very unusual Hebrew phrase here. Not only is the article used instead of the relative pronoun אֲשֶׁר which occasionally occurs, as in 1 Chron. xxix. 17, but the form of the verb is Arabic. None of the commentators give a satisfactory explanation of this fact, and perhaps the suggestion of Houbigant is to be adopted, that the א which follows הָלְכוּ has been accidentally doubled by the transcriber. Kennicott thinks that some Arabic transcriber has inadvertently given the verb an Arabic form, which is very improbable. Keil thinks that it is a sort of intermediate step between the more ancient termination וֹן and the more modern one in וֹ. But if so, it is strange that we should only meet with it twice in Holy Scripture. Hävernick (Introduction, § 22 B) regards it as an archaic form. **Put your feet on the necks of these kings.** This was a most common Oriental practice, as the Assyrian and Egyptian monuments prove. Calvin explains the otherwise " boundless arrogance " of the act by the Divine command. But, as Keil remarks, it was a " symbolical act, intended to inspirit the people." See also Psa. cx. 1 ; 1 Cor. xv. 25. The fact that this was done, not by Joshua, but by the captains (קָצִין from קָצָה to cut off), *i.e.*, the inferior officers of the Israelitish army, makes a wide distinction between this and the usual arrogance of Oriental conquerors, and marks the very great moral superiority of Joshua over any other leader known to history either in his own time or in subsequent ages. For whereas the act was usually an act of arrogant triumph on the part of the leader himself, here the leader modestly disclaims any such superiority, and calls upon his subordinates to assume it, as a sign that the Israelitish people, whose representatives they were, should triumph over all their enemies. The next verse explains the reason of the injunction. To the kings themselves no insolence was displayed, for

it was but the well-known and perfectly understood symbol of their undeniable condition of subjection at that moment. But, of course, we are not to look for that gentleness and humanity in so far distant an age, which would at the present day be shown by a Christian general, or even for the moderation and clemency displayed in the hour of victory by an Alexander, a Scipio, a Cæsar, trained under the maxims of Latin and Greek philosophy. See a fuller discussion of the subject in the Introduction. Origen remarks here, " Atque utinam Dominus meus Jesus filius Dei mihi istud concedat, et jubeat me pedibus meis conculcare spiritum fornicationis, et calcare super cervices spiritus iracundiæ et furoris, calcare avaritiæ dæmonem, calcare jactantiam, conterere pedibus superbiæ spiritum."

Ver. 25. — **Fear not, nor be dismayed.** As Keil remarks, these are the very words which God used to Joshua when He bade him enter upon his great task. See ch. i. 9. So now may the experience of one Christian in the warfare against the powers of evil be imparted as encouragement to another. **Ye fight.** The word " ye " is emphatic. Perhaps Joshua would convey the idea that the Israelites were not to attribute their success to their leader, or to any Divine favour resting upon him as an individual, but to believe that, as long as they served God faithfully, His presence would be as much with them as it was at that particular time and under that particular leader.

Ver. 26.—**And hanged them.** This was also a symbolical act, intended to encourage Israel in their warfare. All that day, until its close, were the bodies of the five kings visible to the whole host, to remind them of the signal victory God had vouchsafed them. The same thing had been done at Ai. See ch. viii. 29.

Ver. 27.—**At the time of the going down of the sun.** See Deut. xxi. 23. Joshua set the example to the Israelites of a strict observance of the law. And we may observe that this law is only to be found in Deuteronomy. On the " Deuteronomist " theory we have to suppose that the Deuteronomist, with a lynx eye to the chance of recommending the provisions which he had invented, and to the importance of representing Joshua as a strict observer of them, inserted this piece of detail with an obvious purpose. It is a wonder that this should be almost the only " Deuteronomist " precept thus emphasised. We find it noticed above (ch. viii. 29), and in both cases the obvious explanation is that this sign of triumph made a great impression on those who witnessed it, and that it was carried out in strict fulfilment of enactments already existing. On the other hand, as we have seen, there is no attempt in ch. viii. 30—35 to emphasise thus the obedience to the command in Deut. xxvii. 2—8. It is from minute details of this kind, which escape the superficial observer, that the authenticity of the Book of Deuteronomy is established. **Until this very day.** The form of the expression here is singularly different from the expression found elsewhere when the meaning suggested by the Authorized Version is to be conveyed. But for the word עַד we should translate "on the self-same day," as in Gen. vii. 13, &c. עַד may be a slip of the pen for עַל which is seldom, if ever, used of time (only, if at all, in Psa. xlviii. 15, and Prov. xxv. 11), though the idiom is found in Arabic, in Greek (as in ἐπ᾿ ἤματι), in German (as in *auf den Tag*.) and in English, " on that day ; " or we may, with Keil, refer back to ver. 18, and translate "they cast them into the cave where they had been hid, and where they had placed great stones unto that very day." For there may have been an interval of several days between the confinement of the kings in the cave and their death at the hands of Joshua. See note on ver. 21.

Ver. 28.—**And that day,** *i.e.*, the day of the battle of Beth-horon. Not only did Joshua smite his enemies "unto Makkedah," but the incarceration of the kings in a cave at Makkedah showed that in the headlong flight of the enemy, Makkedah, which though not mentioned by name among the cities of the confederation, was no doubt, to a certain extent, implicated in it. It is worthy of remark that while Libnah, Debir, and Makkedah are mentioned among the cities destroyed in this campaign, though they are not named among the cities of the league, Jarmuth, on the contrary, though it is one of the cities named, does not appear to have been taken with the rest. **With the edge of the sword.** Literally, "to the mouth of the sword," from its devouring character. **All the souls.** All the human beings. The ban under which everything in Jericho was laid did not apply to the other cities, though (see note on ch. viii. 26) all the inhabitants, without distinction. were to be exterminated.

Ver. 29.—**All Israel.** The expression is not to be pressed in a literal sense. " All Israel " is simply equivalent to " all his disposable troops." **Libnah.** This belonged to the lowlands of Palestine. See note on ch. ix. 1; also ch. xv. 42. It became a Levitical city. It revolted from Judah in the reign of Joram (2 Kings viii. 22). It seems to have returned to its allegiance, since we find it not included in the conquest

of Israel by Shalmaneser, while, on the other hand, it undergoes a siege among the fenced cities of Judah (2 Kings xviii. 13 ; xix. 8). The cause (see Blunt ' Undesigned Coincidences,' part ii. 27) of this return is not far to seek. The Levites cast off the authority of Joram " because he had forsaken the Lord God of his fathers " (2 Chron. xxi. 10, 11). It probably remained independent—for it was not likely to have joined itself to Israel, either from geographical position or religious principles— until the accession of Joash terminated the connection between the royal house of Judah and the descendants of the wicked Ahab. Libnah, or the white city, has been identified with Tell es Safieh, the *Blanche Garde* of the Crusaders. See Stanley, ' Sinai and Palestine,' pp. 207, 258. Lieut. Conder, however, supposes it to have been Eleutheropolis, now Beit Jibrin, and Capt. Warren believes he has found it at Ibna. Vandevelde suggests yet another site. But Lieut. Conder's description of the hill on which Tell es Safieh stands as " a white precipice of many hundred feet" ('Pal. Expl. Fund, Quart. Paper,' July, 1875), would account for the name Libnah.

Ver. 31.—**And Joshua passed.** No indication of time is given in the rest of this chapter. The campaign was probably an affair of some weeks, though none of the cities could have made a prolonged resistance.

Ver. 33.—**Then Horam king of Gezer.** It is remarkable that, as Gezer lay somewhat out of the line of march, Joshua did not capture it. Accordingly, in spite of the alleged carelessness of our compiler, who is credited with having put together shreds of the various narratives in the most perfunctory manner, he takes care to add (ch. xvi. 10) that the inhabitants of Gezer were not driven out. In like manner, with the single exception of Hebron, the people of which must have at once chosen another king, he carefully omits the mention of the king in the cities which had lost their kings in the battle before Gibeon. See also note on ver. 32. Thus a careful examination of the narrative puts the care and accuracy of the history very carefully before us. With regard to the situation of Gezer, it has been accurately determined by the Palestine Exploration Society. The Levitical boundaries, with Greek and Hebrew inscriptions, signifying the boundary of Gezer, have been discovered by M. Ganneau (see ' Quarterly Paper' for October, 1874). Tell el Jezer was first identified by M. Ganneau with Gezer. Continuing his researches, he found on a slab of rock nearly horizontal and very nearly two inches in length a bilingual inscription, in Greek and Hebrew, signifying the limit of Gezer (גזר תהם). Since the inscription is Greek and Talmudical in its character (the word תהום has not the signification of "limit" in the Hebrew Scriptures) it must, in spite of the early form of the letters, belong to a period long subsequent to the Babylonish captivity. M. Ganneau suggests the Maccabean period. (See below.) But it is, no doubt, the result of a re-measurement in accordance with the rules laid down in Num. xxxv. 5. Some have supposed the above to have been designed to fix the limit of the sabbath day's journey. But it is more probable that it served as a boundary between the Levitical and the tribal territory, the more especially as the words are so placed as to be read by one *entering* the town. It was a Levitical city (Josh. xxi. 21; 1 Chron. vi. 67), or at least assigned to the Levites; but Judg. i. 29 shows that the Canaanitish population lived on with the Levites. It may have been the nondescript character of the population that caused it to fall an easy prey to Pharaoh (1 Kings ix. 16, where note that the Canaanites had never been driven out); but when Solomon espoused his daughter he restored Gezer to Israel. Under the same name Gazara it plays a conspicuous part in the wars of the Maccabees (1 Macc. ix. 52; 2 Macc. x. 32). From the latter passage we learn that it was "a very strong hold." It retains its old name, being now known as Tell el Jezer.

Ver. 36.—**Went up.** The accuracy of the geographical details must here be noticed. Joshua "passes" from one city to another in the plain. He "goes up" to Hebron, which is situated among the hills. See note on ver. 3; cf. also ch. xi. 21; xiv. 12. **Hebron.** Commentators of the school of Maurer and De Wette regard the taking of Hebron and Debir as irreconcilable with ch. xi. 21, xiv. 12, xv. 13—17. But this is by no means certain. The operations of Joshua were sudden, and, so far as they went, decisive. But it is never pretended that his conquest of southern Palestine was complete. It is impossible to assert this in the face of such passages as ch. xvi. 10, xvii. 12, 13, and especially in the face of such a fact as the continued existence of the Philistine power. Joshua extirpated the inhabitants of the cities he took, but there were many others—some of at least equal importance —which he did not take. We may instance Gaza, Gath, and Ashdod. See ch. xi. 22. Their inhabitants came and occupied again the cities which Joshua had destroyed, first when he was engaged in operations in the north and west, and again when the Israelites had begun to repose upon their laurels, and to neglect the task God had set them, namely,

the complete extermination of the Canaanite race from Palestine. Thus Joshua returned from the north and found a large part of the country he had subdued reoccupied by the giant tribes of the south. He "cut them off from Hebron and Debir," *i.e.*, he compelled them to evacuate those cities, but there was no necessity for a second of either. Yet at a later period they still lurked in the neighbourhood (ch. xiv. 12), perhaps in the mountain fastnessess (a very common thing in the history of nations, as the history of our own country, of the Basques in the Pyrenees, and of Swiss freedom shows), and were strong enough to regain Debir (ch. xv. 17). Jerusalem itself (see note on ver. 1) had a similar fate. After the capture of Jerusalem the Israelites were unable to hold it permanently (ch. xv. 63; cf. Judg. i. 8, 21). And such expressions as "all the cities thereof" show that the south of Palestine was thickly populated. Each city was, like Gibeon, the head of a small confederacy. And as the chief cities smitten by Joshua would have been but a tithe of the confederations existing in the south, the task of reoccupying must have been an easy one. It seems to be implied in Judges i. that Caleb took Hebron and Debir after Joshua's death.

Ver. 38.—**And Joshua returned.** Rather, Joshua *turned*. Debir was not on the way *back* from Hebron to Eglon, but in a different direction. His march was now southward instead of eastward. **Debir.** A city of importance, since only Hebron and it are mentioned in the history of the campaign as having cities dependent on them. It is also called Kirjath-Sepher (Josh. xv. 15; Judg. i. 11), and Kirjath-Sannah (ch. xv. 49). The first name signifies "the city of the book," from whence it has been argued that it was the seat of what we should now call an university. Recent discoveries have rendered this supposition by no means improbable. The Hittite remains have proved that people to have been a more influential and intellectual people in early times than had ever been supposed until lately. Others have suggested that it was the abode of an oracle, which is rendered probable if Debir be connected with דָּבָר word. The meaning of Kirjath-Sannah is by no means clear. Some have derived it from the Arabic "sunna," *law*, or *doctrine* (whence the Sunnite sect among the Mohammedans), and some from סַנֶּה or סְנֶה, a palm branch, or more probably a thorn-bush. Ritter thinks that both Kirjath-Sepher and Kirjath-Sannah imply the place where the public records were kept. Perhaps what is meant is that, like Mona or Anglesea to the Druids, Debir was the home of the Canaanitish religious traditions. Debir appears as Dapur in the list of fortified cities in Canaan captured by Seti I. and Rameses II. of Egypt. They are depicted on the monumental records. See Tomkins, 'Studies of the Time of Abraham,' p. 84. Debir has lately been identified by the Palestine Survey. Lieut. Conder ('Quarterly Paper,' Jan., 1875, p. 48) fixes it at El Dhoheriyeh or Dhâheriyeh. The identification depends upon the passages ch. xv. 19, and Judg. i. 15. See note on the former. The grounds of the identification are as follows: 1. Debir (see last note) was southward of Hebron. 2. The circumstances require an arid locality, but within a moderate distance two sets of springs, or pools of water. 3. There must be signs of ancient dwellings, and, as Debir was a royal city, it must be the converging point of the various roads. All these conditions are fulfilled by El Dhâheriyeh. The rock excavations, the sign of the most ancient dwellings, are plentiful there; ancient roads are found converging in all directions. And six miles and a half north of the village fourteen springs, or pools, are found, some at the head of the valley, some lower down, and some at a lower level still. The distance of these from Debir is in exact accordance with the narrative. They are too far off to be included as a matter of course within the boundaries of Debir, and would naturally enough become the object of such a petition as Achsah is said to have preferred in the passage above cited. Wilson's 'Lands of the Bible,' i. 351, speaks of the excavations here, but does not appear to have been aware of their antiquity. He describes the inhabitants as living in them. But he remarks—and it is a singular confirmation of Lieut. Conder's subsequent discovery—that the sites of five out of the ten cities mentioned in conjunction with Debir in Josh. xv. 48—51, are to be found in the immediate neighbourhood of Dhâheriyeh (ibid. p. 353). From this passage and some others, however, Knobel has anticipated Lieut. Conder's suggestion. He describes Thaharijeh, as he calls it, as on the high road from Gaza, with ruins of great antiquity, situated in the midst of a country which, though barren in appearance and destitute of trees and arable land, is yet rich in pasture. But he says nothing of the springs, the only thing wanting to make the evidence complete. Ritter's description of the place as the "first place of importance" on arriving in Palestine from the south, and as the meeting-place of the roads from Beersheba, from Gaza and Egypt, and from Petra and Sinai, confirm Lieut. Conder's view, but Ritter does not seem to have identified it with Debir, though he regards

it as "one of a series of fortresses designed to protect the southern frontier of Judæa" (iii. 193, 288). It became a Levitical city (ch. xxi. 15; 1 Chron. vi. 58).

Ver. 40.—**So Joshua smote.** We have now before us the defined *locale* of Joshua's operations. He smote "the hills," or rather the "hill-country," a tract of country extending from Jerusalem southward. This limestone range formed the watershed between the Mediterranean and the Dead Sea. The south, now often spoken of by travellers by its Hebrew name of Negeb, was, as the name signifies, an almost waste district of limestone hills (cf. the Mount Halak, or *smooth mountain*, of ch. xi. 19). It was once more fertile than it is at present, but could never have been a very fruitful region. As Knobel says, it is midway between waste and fertile land. It possesses grass and herbs and flowers, especially in the rainy season, and is thus suitable for pasture. But there are many tracts of sand and heath, and it is not watered by brooks, characteristics it has in common with the wilderness. It was also hilly, though not so precipitous as the mountain district. Tristram ('Land of Israel,' pp. 365, 366) describes some of the mountains as rising gradually to a height of 3,200 feet. Bartlett, however, who devoted more time to the south country, describes it as treeless, but fertile as a corn-producing country, and as very distinct in its physical features from the desert, or what is known as the "Wilderness of Judæa" ('From Egypt to Palestine,' ch. xvii., xviii.). The best description of this region is found, however, in 'Scripture Lands,' by the late Rev. G. S. Drew. He says (p. 6), "For a few weeks late in spring-time a smiling aspect is thrown over the broad downs, when the ground is reddened by the anemone in contrast with the soft white of the daisy and the deep yellow of the tulip and marigold. But this flush of beauty soon passes, and the permanent aspect of the country is not wild indeed, or hideous, or frightfully desolate, but, as we may say, austerely plain; a tame, unpleasing aspect, not causing absolute discomfort while one is in it, but left without one lingering reminiscence of anything lovely, awful, or sublime." The rocks are occasionally rendered fertile by the system of terrace cultivation, more common, as almost every traveller since Maundrell has remarked, in former times than now. That keen observer remarks, that if any one were to object that Palestine could not have maintained the vast population stated in Scripture to have inhabited it, he would be confuted by the fact that the most cursory observation shows that "the very rocks were made fruitful," perhaps even to a greater extent than plains could be, " by this method." The "vale," or Shephelah (see note on ch. ix. 1), was a low strip of coast extending from the foot of Carmel to near Gaza. The אֲשֵׁדֹות, or " springs," as it is translated in our version (better, "water-courses," or "slopes," as Knobel),was a fertile country, intersected by ravines and brooks, situated between the mountains and the sea. The word only occurs in the Pentateuch and Joshua (a fact to be noted in forming an opinion on the genuineness of these books). See Num. xxi. 15 (where it is translated *stream* in our version ; Deut. iii. 17 ; iv. 49. The root, signifying *pouring forth*, is found in Chaldee and Syriac. The LXX. renders this, as well as " the south," strange to say, as a proper name. See note on ch. xv. 19. The Vulgate follows its example in the former case, but not in the latter. The Syriac also renders as a proper name. **Utterly destroyed all that breathed, as the Lord God of Israel commanded.** See for the word translated " utterly destroyed," ch. vi. 17. These words are a quotation from Deut. xx. 16, 17. It seems impossible to evade one of the alternatives, either that Deuteronomy was written before the events recorded in the book of Joshua, or that we have no historical evidence that Joshua *did* " utterly destroy all that breathed." The hypothesis that the Divine sanction for such a war of extermination was invented centuries after the Israelites had come to terms with the inhabitants and were daily utterly violating its spirit, and that they then readily allowed themselves to believe it to be of Divine origin, will scarcely bear examination. The attitude of the people toward Gentiles after their captivity is only to be explained by the hypothesis that it was the result of a belief that their misfortunes were due to a law which they had previously received and neglected to obey. Calvin observes how thoroughly these passages bear witness to the fact that the Israelites felt themselves to be the ministers of a Divine purpose in this slaughter. Origen (Hom. 15 on Joshua) says that the Apostles gave order that the Scriptures of the Old Testament were to be read in church, which, he adds, " they would not have done had not these carnal wars prefigured the spiritual warfare which we have to carry on ' against principalities, against powers, against the rulers of the darkness of this world, against spiritual wickedness in high places.' " **Gaza.** Hebrew *Azzah* (or *strong*), as in 1 Kings iv. 24. Joshua's conquests extended to, but did not comprise, Gaza (ch. xi. 22 ; xiii. 2, 3). It was to have been the uttermost limit of the Israelitish territory (see Gen. x. 19). It ac-

tually was so in the days of Solomon (1 Kings iv. 24). But until then the Israelites had not been able to subdue it, though (ch. xv. 45—47) the whole land of the Philistines was assigned to Judah. What results this failure produced upon the after history of Israel we read in the Books of Judges and Samuel. Not till the reign of David was the Philistine power entirely broken. And Gaza played a very important part in the Philistine confederation. See Judg. xvi. 1—4, 21 —23; 1 Sam. vi. 16, 17. Gaza has retained its importance even to the present day. Its situation near the sea, and, still more, its position upon the high road from Palestine to Egypt, and from the Mediterranean to Arabia Petræa, have secured it this permanence. When Robinson visited it its population was between fifteen and sixteen thousand—larger even than that of Jerusalem. And it seems to have largely increased in population since the beginning of the century. **Goshen.** Γοσομ, LXX. Not, of course, identical with the land of Goshen in Egypt, but inasmuch as it lay to the south-east of Palestine, in the direction of their former habitation, it may possibly have been so named in memory of that sojourn. A city of that name is mentioned in the mountains of Judah, together with Debir (Josh. xv. 51). It clearly (ch. xi. 16) refers to a large district in the south-east, but its precise locality is not known. **Even unto Gibeon.** The conquests of Israel did not extend further in the north-west than Gibeon, from whence Joshua had set out on his triumphant campaign.

Ver. 42.—**At one time**, *i.e.*, in one campaign, carried on without a respite. **Because the Lord God fought for Israel.** It is the peculiar feature of Old Testament history that it draws the veil from the unseen. Other historians are content to note the secondary causes. The Scriptures trace all to their original source—the will of God. And it is His will, as the page of history shows, with exceptions that do but prove the rule, that a just cause, assisted by bravery, purity, and devotion combined, will not fail, in the long run, to overcome force and fraud. Wars of independence, wars undertaken to chastise wickedness and oppression, seldom fail in their object. And when they do fail, it is generally from the presence of similar crimes among those who undertake the righteous cause, and sully it by their own vices and crimes. History furnishes us with abundant instances of this. The leaders of the struggle for the Protestant Reformation in Europe were often almost as crafty, as ambitious, as self-seeking, as immoral, as those against whom they contended. Struggles patriotic in their origin have been marred by the selfish aims of those who carried them on. Selfishness inspires distrust, and distrust produces disunion. But where "the Lord God fights for Israel," where noble objects are pursued by worthy means, there is a moral strength which triumphs over the greatest obstacles. Such an instance we have in modern history in the career of a man like William the Silent. Nearly ruined by the cowardice, obstinacy, and selfishness of his associates, his faith, courage, and perseverance carried a struggle hopeless at the outset to a triumphant conclusion. Men may cry that "Providence is on the side of the big battalions," but "the Lord's hand is not waxen short."

Ver. 43.—**Unto the camp at Gilgal.** See note, ch. ix. 6; ch. x. 15 confirms the view taken in ch. ix. 6.

HOMILETICS.

Vers. 1—43.—*The great victory and its results.* Many of the considerations which this passage suggests have been already anticipated. Thus the celerity of Joshua's march (ver. 9) suggests the same set of ideas as ch. iv. 10. The destruction of the cities teaches the same lessons as the destruction of Jericho; while the miraculous interposition in the battle of Beth-horon is hardly to be distinguished, as a source of spiritual instruction, from the destruction of Jericho. Again, the confederacy of the kings (vers. 1—5) has been already treated under ch. ix. 1, 2. Yet some few points remain to be noticed.

I. DIVINE HELP DOES NOT EXCLUDE HUMAN EXERTION. Joshua went forth to battle relying upon a special promise of God. Yet he went up "suddenly," we are told. Thus, so far from the certainty of success diminishing energy, it should rather increase it. The apostles went forth relying on a Divine promise that God's truth should permeate the world. But though this promise relieved them from the restless anxiety which too often oppresses their successors in the work, it did not relieve them from the necessity of exertion. And accordingly we find them untiring in their exertions to spread the gospel, and also to lay firmly the foundations of the Christian Church. The same untiring spirit of exertion should animate us now. Success is assured in the end, and for that very reason we should not slacken, but rather the contrary, in our efforts to propagate truth. The two opposite errors which retard the success of God's cause are (1) a needless anxiety for immediate results, which cause us to take measures which betray a want of faith, and which therefore, relying on the arm of flesh, are predestined to fail; and (2) a blind fatalism which leaves all to God, forgetting that the forces of His kingdom require to be set in motion by man before they can take effect. What is wanted is (1) a sublime carelessness about results, when the means God has directed to be employed have been employed; and (2) a continual effort to put those means in operation. Untiring in preaching the gospel, in using the means of grace, and in " good works and alms-deeds," we are yet to be content with doing what is ordained, and leaving God to prosper, as He pleases, what we have done.

II. THE ANSWER TO PRAYER IS MORE EFFECTIVE THAN OUR WORK. Had Joshua not done his best, the hailstones would not have fallen. But inasmuch as he was doing his work, God helped him, and more execution was done by God from heaven than by Joshua's troops on earth. So he who works and prays not will be rewarded with less success than he who works and prays. If we are not as successful as we could wish, we may ask whether we have asked God to work with us. It is a touching story which has been told of Sir D. Brewster's father, that he was so well known as a man of prayer that when any unexpected and almost marvellous conversion occurred in his parish, it was attributed by his people to his prayers. Perhaps one of the reasons why the Roman Catholic Church still maintains so strong a hold upon the world is because of the fervent belief still retained among her people of the power of prayer. Such prayer is often sadly misdirected, and yet, as a recognition of a power above that hears and answers prayer, it must be more acceptable in God's sight than the philosophical Protestantism which denies the existence of a Father in heaven, ridicules prayer to God, especially for temporal blessings, on the ground of the invariability of law, and thus practically abolishes the God of the Old Testament and of the New, and makes void the gospel of Jesus Christ. Surely superstition itself is better than this denial of the loving Fatherhood of God. The lesson here concerns spiritual rather than temporal blessings, but it none the less contains a protest against the sceptical spirit which would lead us to think it unnecessary to maintain by prayer an attitude of continual dependence on God.

III. HEAVENLY LIGHT SHALL NEVER FAIL HIM WHO IS FIGHTING IN GOD'S CAUSE. Joshua asked for light, that he might destroy God's enemies. So must the Christian ask for light, that he may distinguish friends from foes—truth from falsehood. He has the light of God's Word, which, coming direct from God, is symbolised by the sun ; and the light of man's preaching of that Word, which, inasmuch as it only reflects the Word itself, is not inaptly typified by the moon. We need not fear that that light will ever fail us ; and yet we do well to pray that it may continue to be afforded us. We may, in the strength of faith, pray that the sun may for us stand still upon Gibeon and the moon in the valley of Ajalon, until God be avenged on His enemies, sin and falsehood and their allies, through our means.

IV. WE SHALL " SPEAK OF HIS TESTIMONIES EVEN BEFORE KINGS, AND SHALL NOT BE ASHAMED." Joshua makes a great point of the subjugation of the *kings* to the *people* of Israel. He makes his captains set their feet upon their necks to show that none can resist the armies of the Lord. (1) So our Joshua tells us that we shall stand " before governors and kings for his sake." And so it has been in the history of His Church. " The kings of the earth stood up, and the rulers took counsel together, against the Lord and against his Anointed." First, in the case of those who first preached the gospel. It was preached for three centuries in direct defiance of the highest human authority, among Jews and Gentiles alike. Next, the defenders of true against false doctrine, of justice and mercy as against violence and cruelty, had to stand before kings and rebuke them in the name of the Lord. When the great revival of zeal and reverence for God's Word took place in the fifteenth century, the influence of the mighty was frequently exerted to crush it. And so it will ever be. " Not many mighty, not many noble," are to be found in revivals of faith and zeal. Authority frowns on them, prescription is against them, force is invoked to put them down, yet they thrive. The hand of man is powerless against the truth. The battle is long and fierce, but it is won at last. And the principles but lately despised are triumphant. Their holders put " their feet on the necks of kings," for the rulers who resisted to the utmost are forced to own the power of the truth against which they contended as long as they were able. Thus we learn the lesson of confidence taught by Joshua, " Fear not, neither be dismayed, be strong and of a good courage, for thus shall the Lord do to all your enemies against whom ye fight." Again (2) we learn the same confidence against tyrant lusts, " which war against the soul." Long and obstinate is the conflict ; but if it be waged in faith and prayer, the Lord fights for us out of heaven ; light is shed upon our onward path, the light of a right judgment and a Christian prudence, until at last we put our feet upon the necks of those " kings " that would have enslaved us, and then our Joshua slays them, that they trouble us no more.

HOMILIES BY VARIOUS AUTHORS.

Ver. 1.—*Adoni-zedek, a lesson for nations and individuals.* These Jebusites had two or three ideas at least which are worth remarking. They had a true idea of the essential condition of a nation's prosperity—for the people of Jebus had called their city " *Salem* "—that is, " peace." And the title of their king was Melchi-zedek, or Adoni-zedek—King or Lord of Righteousness. These names are amongst the earliest contributions to the science of political economy. The one name, " Salem," contains as much valuable suggestion as is found in many books on " the wealth of nations." The second condenses all principles of sovereignty into a single word. No one is a good ruler unless the title Adoni-zedek would suit him. King or Parliament, the Father in his family, the Prime Minister in his Cabinet, all should remember that the ruler of men is really an usurper unless the title, Lord of Righteousness, suit him. Let us look at this name, and observe—

I. We have here A GRAND TITLE FOR A RULER. Perhaps the people had degenerated since the days of Abraham. Then this ruler was that Melchi-zedek, who was a "Priest of the Most High God." However degenerate, they cling to this title, and as the kings of Egypt were Pharaohs ; and those of Gath, Abimelechs ; and those of Damascus, Benhadads ; so those of Jerusalem were Adoni-zedeks. There is an instinct in all people that desires the throne to be filled with righteousness. Just as in our days, the Khan of Merv has carried the same titles—King of Righteousness and King of Peace—so in the absence of constitutional checks on regal power, they gave their kings the title which was meant to be at once impulse and restraint. The lesson of this title should be learned by all of us. In a ruler of men there are many qualities requisite. Wisdom to perceive the true necessities of those under his care ; strength and energy enough to carry out the dictates of wisdom ; courage to face and provide calmly against every danger. But when the utmost value has been allowed to these supreme qualities, an accurate judgment will still allow a higher value to one other—that of EQUITY. In outside relations, equity will enable a king to maintain peace with neighbouring peoples better than any diplomacy or strength could do. In ancient days, the king was the judge of all causes, from those of our County Courts to those of the Court of Chancery. What a boon to a people when the judge was an embodiment of justice — inaccessible to bribes, ready patiently to unravel the entangled case, never misled by partiality or by antipathy, but to those liked or disliked meting out even-handed justice. This old people saw all these things, and when a Magna Charta was an impossibilty, they tried to compass its ends by giving their king this stimulative and restraining title. Righteousness is still the most essential quality of a statesman. Fairness of mind that holds the balance evenly between all conflicting claims—this has been the distinguishing quality of all the English statesmen of this century who have earned the nation's gratitude. It is the quality needed in our Legislature to-day. It is the quality needed by every employer of labour. The serving classes want no favour, nor mere amiability in a master. Fairness will ever secure their deepest attachment. A father in a family should be a "Lord of Righteousness." In short, this equity is the supreme want everywhere. People would be more charitable if they were more just. And peace in homes, in churches, in nations would be much less frequently imperilled, if only fairness of mind moderated the claims we make, and permitted us to see whatever element of right lay in the claims made upon us. If we have here a good title, observe secondly—

II. We have A GREAT TITLE BORNE BY ONE OF A POOR NATURE. Name and nature do not always correspond. And here " The Lord of Righteousness " is found acting unrighteously. Gibeon with its sister cities was probably disliked for its republican institutions by all those neighbouring states that maintained a monarchy. Now to the fault of liberty it adds the sin of wisdom. A maxim, unfortunately not obsolete to-day, was accepted then—that the making of any alliance containing a possibility of danger to us is a sufficient *casus belli* against the state that makes it. His title had not sufficiently instructed this ruler to make him see the wrong of this position. He is perhaps the more easily led to make war against Gibeon because, guarding as it did one of the great passes into the heart of the kingdom, to seize it seemed the best way of securing the safety of the country from Israelitish attack. And so unrighteously the " King of Righteousness " attacks his neighbours ; and, like so many, shows that the grandeur of a title is not always matched by greatness in him who bears it. A long way from us in time, locality, and circumstances, how near us in nature does this characteristic bring him. Sometimes we inherit great names, and forget the lesson of the poet—

> " They who on the deeds of ancestors enlarge,
>   Do but produce the debt, not the discharge."

Sometimes God gives us names, which it is our duty to illustrate and justify. "Children of Light," " Sons of God," " Heirs of God," " Chosen Generation,"

"Royal Priesthood." Is there never any discrepancy between the titles we bear and the lives we lead? We cannot help having these great names applied to us. They belong to all who have been born again by the birth which is from above. And God gives us them that they may "marshal us the way that we are going." Let us try and act up to our name, and not have the melancholy fate of being condemned by the very title that we bear. Lastly observe—

III. PROFESSION CANNOT SAVE FROM PERDITION. This man with the grand name perishes miserably—dishonoured, hanged, involving in his own ruin that of his people and that of all those confederated with him. The providence and the judgment of God are no respecters of persons. As we sow we reap. The obedience of faith is salvation. The unrighteousness of self-will is destruction. Let us see that we have more than the "name to live," lest the greater name only condemn us to the greater destruction.—G.

Ver. 4.—*Connection with the Church a source of worldly trouble.* The trouble which came upon Gibeon through her connection with Israel affords an illustration of the experience of all who associate themselves with the career and destinies of the Church.

I. THE EXISTENCE OF THIS TROUBLE. Though the true Church is an ark of safety, she is an ark upon stormy waters. He who joins the Church on earth joins the Church militant, and shares her dangers (John xv. 18). (1) So long as the *world is at enmity with God*, they who stand on the side of the people of God will be subject to the assaults of the world in (*a*) persecution, (*b*) social ostracism, (*c*) calumny, (*d*) ridicule, &c. (2) While the Church is fulfilling her *mission to conquer the world* for Christ, she will bring the hatred of the world upon all who are identified with her (2 Cor. xi. 23—27). (3) It is vain to expect to receive the *advantages of religion* and to escape from the *cost* of them (Luke xiv. 28). He who would win heaven must lose something on earth (Matt. vi. 24).

II. THE ADVANTAGES OF THIS TROUBLE. All trouble permitted by Providence is blessing in disguise. So is this: (1) It serves as a *test of genuineness.* We may join the Church (*a*) from motives of selfish pride and profit, (*b*) under the influence of superficial sentiment. Worldly trouble directly arising out of our Church relations proves the genuineness of our attachment to Christ by showing whether we are willing to risk danger and suffer loss for Him (Matt. iii. 12; xiii. 21). (2) It promotes *union among Christians.* The Gibeonites were drawn closer to the Israelites by the threatened danger. Selfish isolation, mutual jealousy, divisions, and ecclesiastical quarrels spring up in times of peace. Sympathy and charity are developed in seasons of adversity. (3) It cultivates *unworldliness.* The friendship of the world is a dangerous snare. The favour of the world brings with it the spirit of the world. In worldly prosperity the Church tends to worldly habits. The enmity of the world drives us to the sympathy of God and refuges of unworldly living.

III. THE REMEDIES FOR THIS TROUBLE. Gibeon was threatened with destruction, but on her appeal to Israel her allies fought for her, and God secured them the victory. (1) The remedy for worldly trouble arising from our religious associations will be found *in mutual help.* The Christian Church is a brotherhood. We are called to bear one another's burdens (Gal. vi. 2). The rich should help the poor, the strong the weak, the prosperous at home the persecuted abroad. (2) The remedy will also be found *in the Divine aid.* God fought with Israel in the defence of Gibeon (ver. 13). They who are brought into danger for the cause of God will find that God is on their side and will secure their deliverance. The real danger is to those who are fighting against God. It is safer to be in trouble with the people of God than in prosperity with their enemies, for God must and will triumph in the end, and then His people will share His victory (John xvi. 33).— W. F. A.

Vers. 8—11.—*The battle of Beth-horon and its lessons.* It may seem as if there was too much carnage about this account for Scripture purposes. Yet it is well to dwell on it. Dean Stanley treats this battle as the Marathon of the religious history of the world. It was the crisis in which the hosts who were, unconsciously to some extent, fighting for truth, righteousness, progress, and liberty, met with those fighting, to some extent unconsciously, for a depraved religion, licentious morals, for retrogression and decay. Like the siege of Leyden, or the defeat of the Armada, such a battle means far more than is obvious on the surface. The sacred cause of man is involved in it. And it is worth our while to linger over some of its lessons. Mark at least these.

I. GOD USES OUR EFFORT TO FULFIL HIS PROMISES. Israel was apt, perhaps, to expect the possession of the land to come too easily. Jericho was got by a miracle, Ai by stratagem, Gibeon by submission; and perhaps the ease of these successes led them to dream dreams of gaining the whole land without an effort. But all the steps of progress are not to be so easy. Miracles come only where weakness needs them. In the degree in which they develop vigour and self-reliance, the miraculous element in their experience will grow less. Always sufficient—there will never be more help of God than is needed. And so with the confidence and vigour developed by their successes, comes greater strain upon their powers. The nations of southern Canaan gather together to oppose their progress: to gain possession of that Gibeon which commands the entrance by the pass of Beth-horon to the land. And at once "foemen worthy of their steel" confront them. God will fulfil His promise to give them the land of Canaan; but He will employ their effort and their prowess to realise the fulfilment of His promise. And to some extent by their efforts is His promise fulfilled. Such is all life. It is the heir of promises which, however, require our effort for their fulfilment. (a) For instance: *Truth is a land of promise.* Only when God gives can we get it. "The Spirit of truth" alone can impart it. It is a land flowing with milk and honey—the home of God's elect. But though thus a land of God's promises, and in a special sense His gift, it comes not to the inert or the supine—to the critics that are at ease in Zion. It comes to the *fighters only.* When we face bravely all lies, strive fearlessly to see and grasp and own the truth, get lodgment for it in the heart by obeying it, strive against doubts that rise within us, and fears disabling us, then do we gain "the promised possession." (b) *Salvation is God's promise,* and a Divine gift in all its elements. Obviously it is beyond our power to compass it. *Only the God that made us can mend us.* And atonement, grace, repentance, faith, perseverance to the end, are all God's gift. But there is the battle of Beth-horon at the outset of every Christian life, and many a conflict afterwards, a strait gate to begin with, and a narrow way to follow. And if we do not make the effort and fight for the attainment of what we desire, we shall not find it. (c) *Character is another Canaan.* A thing of promise, but only reached by effort. Daily deeds of self-denial lead to it; and daily conflicts with doubts and disinclinations. (d) *Usefulness is,* perhaps, *the grandest of all God's promises.* It is that in which we most resemble God. Its joys are the likest of any to those of the everlasting home. It comes not to the dreamer, but to the fighter. The abolition of slavery was a fight. Mary Carpenter's triumph in getting a place for Ragged Schools, Industrial Schools, and Reformatories in English legislation, required thirty years of effort. When the Church faces the abounding drunkenness of the land, she will find God will help her to destroy it, but that His help will be conditioned on a tremendous effort. Do not believe in salvation made easy. It is always simple, it is never easy. The possession of every Canaan is a Divine promise, and needs Divine power; but one of the conditions of its fulfilment is the forth-putting of human effort. Take a second lesson.

II. THE HEARTIER THE EFFORT IS, THE MORE SURELY AND EASILY SUCCESS WILL COME. Joshua saw the need for action, had God's guidance in it, and then with an energy which had something Napoleonic in it, threw himself into his task. Was Gibeon threatened? within a few hours of his knowing it, Israel is on the march. Doubtless there were counsellors advising caution, consideration, and delay. Joshua had gathered the wisdom, but not the weakness, of old age, and knew the value of *energy.* That night the host is marshalled for its uphill, moonlit march over the fifteen or eighteen miles of valley intervening between them and Gilgal. And before the five kings have any thought of his approach, he rushes "like a torrent" on the foe. And such is the energy, the surprise of that charge, that, martial as are the habits of the enemy, they are obliged to yield. Apparently a long fight takes place, the enemy disputing every inch of ground so long as the gradual rising to the Upper Beth-horon gives them the advantage. But the sun stands still over Gibeon to let them finish the fight; and then a headlong flight down to Lower Beth-horon, and then to the valley of Ajalon and the plains that skirt the Mediterranean, subjects them to terrible destruction. A great hail-storm breaks on the fugitive masses, not extending far enough eastward to affect Israel. And the moon stands over the valley of Ajalon after the sun has set, to let them finish their pursuit and complete their victory. It is as fine an instance of the value of decision, of energy, of heartiness in our work as the whole Bible gives. "What thy hand finds to do, do it with thy might." The impact of any projectile is in the ratio of its *mass*, multiplied by its *velocity*. And a thing of slight mass, but of high velocity, will be more effective than one of much greater mass, whose velocity is sluggish. So is it in the world of morals. Weight multiplied by *momentum* measures the power. Most of us are inefficient, because, while weighty enough, we have little or no momentum. We languidly pursue the good, and half-heartedly oppose the evil. Unlike St. Paul, it is not one thing, but twenty-one, that we do. In everything decision and heartiness is needed, but in religion it is indispensable. Be cold or hot, not lukewarm. If the gospel be true, it is tremendously true; if a dream, ignore it altogether. Half-hearted fighting prolongs the contest, invites defeat, loses the benefits of victory. In march, attack, pursuit, we have an example of the supreme advantage of doing heartily whatever has to be done by us. Take a third lesson.

III. THE GOOD FIGHT, WHEN WELL FOUGHT, ALWAYS ENDS IN VICTORY. It might have seemed a very dubious affair, this war with the nations of Canaan. The Canaanites were the English of that period: the nation leading the world in maritime enterprise and daring, and wealthy and strong in their successful commerce. Israel had been for generations in slavery, debased and weakened by servitude. But against these odds on the side of Canaan there were some things to be set.

1. *Immorality is destructive of courage.* Paganism, with its debasements, destroyed *self-respect* and that *interest* in life, home, and liberty which is the soul of patriotism. For heroism religion is an essential element. Cromwell's Ironsides, Nelson's Methodists, Havelock's regiment of Teetotallers, the power of resistance to oppression developed by religion in Holland and in Scotland, show how immediate and direct is the influence of godliness in vitalising all the manlier virtues. Corruption of character followed corruption of creed, and was followed by deterioration of courage.

2. The enemy of the good has never Divine guidance. These nations were badly advised. Their true policy was a defensive one. Within their ramparts the labour of conquering them would have been terrific and inevitably slow. All uniting, in the open they lose the advantage of their cities "walled up to heaven," and a single disaster is a fatal one. "A good understanding have they that love God's law;" and all others unwatchful in presumption, or feverish in solicitude, lack wisdom which they need.

3. And God fights on behalf of those who fight for Him. The long day, the moonlight night, the destructive hail, are all Divine, however we may abate the miraculous significance of the poetic history. And they who aim at any form of good find a secret providence furthering their enterprise: many influences co-operating with them, strange providential openings, a Divine backing which, all uniting, make it that, however weak they may be, they are more than conquerors through Christ that loved them. "Wherefore take to yourselves the whole armour of God," and FIGHT THE GOOD FIGHT OF FAITH.—G.

Vers. 8—11.—*The victory over the five kings.* The battle against the five kings is the most remarkable episode in the conquest of the Canaanites. Israel might well have had cause to tremble in presence of such allied enemies. But Divine aid gives it a signal victory. That aid comes under two forms: 1. It consists, first, in a miraculous intervention of the Divine power, which sends down a fierce storm of hailstones upon the Canaanitish armies, and so lengthens out the day as to make the conflict decisive. No one believes now that the sun stood still. Holy Scripture speaks the popular language of the day, and makes no pretension to being scientific in its records. God reveals only that which man has no power to discover, and it was not the calling of Joshua to be a Galileo or Copernicus. Do we not still speak in common parlance of the rising and setting of the sun? All that is essential is, that we hold fast our faith in the miracle itself. Let us not marvel that such a prodigy was wrought for so small a nation ; for that nation was the depository of the promise that in it should all nations of the earth be blessed. The God of nature may surely show Himself the King and Master of nature, and it is most fitting that the heavens which declare His glory should do His command- ments. The supreme law of the universe is not the physical law, but the depen- dence of that law upon the sovereign will of the Almighty. 2. This Divine aid was manifested, in the second place, by the heroic confidence and courage infused into the hearts of his people. " Fear them not," was the message to Joshua, who might well have been dismayed at so powerful a league of enemies, " for I have delivered them into thine hands." " Therefore," as we read in the following verse, " Joshua came unto them suddenly." The Divine word alone gave him courage to go forward, and courage is in itself an irresistible power, even more formidable than the storm of hailstones from heaven. With more than redoubled force, Israel rushes on to certain victory. Thus the noble words of the Psalm xxi. are antici- pated and fulfilled : " Some trust in chariots and some in horses, but we will trust in the name of the Lord our God " (ver. 8). Did not Elisha describe Elijah as the chariot and the horsemen of Israel? Let us place unwavering trust in all our conflicts in this Divine aid, and that confidence will be the first condition of victory. —E. DE P.

Vers. 12—14.—*The sun and moon stayed.* Whatever opinions we may entertain relative to the exact nature of the incident celebrated in the poem of the Book of Jasher, there are certain general principles and religious truths which that poem brings distinctly before us.

I. GOD IS ACTIVELY CONCERNED WITH THE EVENTS OF HUMAN HISTORY. Divine powers aided Joshua in resisting the onslaught of the Canaanites. God is present, when He is not clearly so recognised, in all crises of life. (1) His overruling power so disposes of the *order of creation* that even without miracle the outward world works His will. (2) His providential control of the *minds of men and the course of their lives* determines ultimate events. Therefore note : God has not left the world to go its own course only to be judged and rectified at a future judgment day. He judges now, and intervenes now, and works on the side of right, for the pro- tection of those who submit to His rule, and to the loss of such as fight against His will (Psa. lxviii. 1, 7, 24).

II. NATURE IS SUBSERVIENT TO THE WILL OF GOD. Miracles are not rare and occasional instances of the way in which God makes His will felt in nature. They are rather abnormal manifestations of the Divine power which is equally present in the regular course of nature. God is as much working in the natural as in the miraculous event, though the miraculous serves to impress us with the conscious- ness of His power. If we believe in God at all, it is unreasonable to suppose that He would create the universe in some age of dim antiquity, and then leave it to itself like a self-acting machine, which being once wound up only needs adjusting by miracle now and again to suit special emergencies. It is much more reasonable to regard the universe as an organism of which God is at once the creating, the inspiring, the energising, and the controlling spirit. Thus the sun and moon and stars and the earth always move by His power, and at every moment express His will (Psa. civ. 2—4, 16, 21, &c. ; Rom. i. 20).

III. NATURAL EVENTS ARE LINKED WITH HUMAN DESTINIES. Like all great delusions which have exercised wide influence over men, astrology was the perversion of a deep truth. Our lives are connected with the stars. All nature is one, and we—in our earthly life—are part of nature. The processes of nature affect us; *e.g.*, possibly sun-spots acting through atmospheric phenomena have some influence over human calamities, and even over moral relations. Therefore note: (1) God touches us through nature, and we must regard nature as an instrument in His hands for our discipline. (2) Nature should be studied in its bearings upon human life for our practical instruction.

IV. NATURE FIGHTS AGAINST THOSE WHO RESIST THE WILL OF GOD. The Canaanites were resisting God's will concerning the settlement of the land, and thus they made themselves enemies to God's servant, nature. So the stars *out* of their courses fought against Sisera (Judg. v. 20). It is objected that it is unworthy of the character of God to suppose that He would intervene by means of natural agencies to assist in a work of destruction. But it should be remembered that God is always employing destructive agencies in nature, as earthquakes, storms, &c., and that physical destruction is a less evil than moral corruption.—W. F. A.

Vers. 14.—*A day of wonders.* The Canaanite kings were slow in gathering their forces together to repel the advance of Joshua, but they were ready enough to come down in vengeance upon the Gibeonites for having made peace with him. The men of Gibeon found the advantage of having a strong and generous protector, one who would be true to his pledges, even though they had been extorted from him by fraud. Joshua responds at once to the cry that comes to him from the beleaguered city, and God makes its deliverance the occasion for a signal display of His power and the furtherance of His purpose in the overthrow of the kings. The blending of the natural and supernatural in the events of this day is very remarkable. The two elements are so interlaced and interwoven that it is not for us to say where the one ends and the other begins. We only feel, in following the course of the narrative, that we are in the presence of a marvellous Divine power that carries all resistance before it. Such records as this, however, have their true effect upon us when they lead us the more clearly to recognise the supernatural force in the natural, to discern behind the common, familiar order of things the mystery and majesty of the Divine. With the vexed question as to the historic truth of the declaration that "the sun stood still in the midst of heaven," we have not now to do (see Exposition). We simply note that, if the use the historian makes of the poetic quotation from the Book of Jasher compels us to regard it as having some basis of fact, there is no need on that account to believe in any actual arrest of the order of the universe. May not natural agents and natural laws be used miraculously by Him who is the Author of them? Just as He who created the hailstones could, without injury to the Israelites, turn them as engines of destruction against their foes, so surely He who at the beginning "commanded the light to shine out of darkness" could, in ways to us unknown, prolong the day in answer to Joshua's prayer. Two broad lessons grow out of this:

I. THAT GOD'S SOVEREIGNTY OVER NATURE IS SUBSERVIENT TO THE HIGHER PURPOSES OF HIS SPIRITUAL KINGDOM. We look through these outward incidents to the Divine end which they were all helping to work out. God was "forming a people for his praise." Giving them a local habitation, that they might the better conserve His truth and show forth His glory. He drove out the heathen before them, and planted them there that they might bear rich fruits of blessing to the world, that in them and in their seed all the earth might be blessed. Everything is to be looked at in the light of that moral purpose. (1) The whole visible universe exists for spiritual ends—the revelation of the invisible Divine beauty and order; the magnifying of the law of eternal righteousness. Its activity and its rest, its discords and its harmonies, its terror and its loveliness, all have a moral meaning and intent. (2) The forces and laws of the universe are against those who are against God. You must be morally one with Him if you would have them befriend you. "The stars in their courses fight against Sisera." How terrible to think of some of the forms in which the Creator might, if He pleased, array the powers of nature against sinful men! His long-suffering beneficence is their only safeguard. "It is of the Lord's mercies that we are not consumed" (Lam. iii. 22). (3) The created universe attains its consummation only in the final spiritual triumph of the Redeemer. The groaning creation waits for the "manifestation of the sons of God." The glorious presence of the Lord will be "the restitution of all things." There will be "nothing to hurt or to destroy" in the "new heavens and the new earth wherein dwelleth righteousness."

II. THAT MAN IS AN EFFICIENT INSTRUMENT IN SERVING THE CAUSE OF RIGHT-EOUSNESS JUST SO FAR AS HE HAS FAITH TO LAY HOLD ON THE SOVEREIGN POWER OF GOD. "There was no day like that before it or after it," not because there was anything singular, unparalleled, in God's "hearkening to the voice of a man." This was simply a conspicuous and noteworthy example of a universal law. "The effectual fervent prayer of a righteous man" has always "availed much." The resources of heaven wait upon it. Such prayer is

" A breath that fleets beyond this iron world,
And touches Him that made it."

(1) Let the Church "stir itself up to lay hold on God." Its strength lies in faith and prayer. The Lord will never fail to "fight for Israel" when she is true to her high calling. The weapons of her warfare are mighty through Him. "God is in the midst of her; she shall not be moved: God shall help her, *and that* right early" (Psa. xlvi. 5). This pledge of Divine protection and deliverance is given, not to ecclesiastical systems, which may have much that is of man rather than of God in their constitution, but to that Church which Christ has redeemed and chosen out of every land and nation to represent His own cause of truth and righteousness. When the Church goes forth in the energy of faith and prayer, its enemies flee before it. (2) Let the individual Christian recognise the true source of moral power. No emergency of life need be overwhelming to one who casts himself un-reservedly on God. "If God be for us, who can be against us?" Move on steadily in the path of duty and fear not. In all conceivable times of difficulty and danger, of temptation and sorrow, Christ's answer to the cry of His faithful ones is the same—"My grace is sufficient for thee. My strength is made perfect in weak-ness."—W.

Vers. 24, 25.—*The conquered kings.* The fate of those kings has its moral analogies. We may regard them as typical of the principles and powers of spiritual evil, and their end as suggestive of the certain issue of God's conflict with those evil powers. Observe—

I. THE DECEITFULNESS OF SIN. It deludes the transgressor, and leads him blind-fold to ruin. It moves men to seek false refuges, inspires them with a vain hope. They think to hide themselves, but God's laws and retributions always find them out. Jonah would fain "flee from the presence of the Lord," but God's "strong wind" was swifter than his flight, and the sea, by which he thought to escape, only brought him face to face with his Judge. The subterfuges to which men resort in any guilty way often become the very means of their detection and punish-ment. The kings dream of safety in their cave; it turns out to be the very thing that shuts them up hopelessly to Joshua's vengeance. As Matthew Henry puts it: "That which they thought would have been their shelter, was made their prison first, and then their grave." So do sinful purposes often defeat themselves. "The wicked is snared in the work of his own hands" (Psa. ix. 16).

II. THE HUMILIATION THAT, SOONER OR LATER, BEFALLS A PROUD DEFIANCE OF DIVINE AUTHORITY. See here an illustration of high-handed rebellion against God. Its overthrow in the end is sure. "The wheel of fortune turns and lowers the proud." Kings are as helplessly subject to the Divine power by which that wheel revolves as other men (Psa. lxxvi. 12; Isa. xli. 25). Into what abject misery have they sometimes fallen, under the mighty hand of God, who once, in the career of their ambition, set all Divine and human law at defiance, and made the earth to tremble ! Let not the wicked exalt themselves ; there is a power that can easily lay them low.

III. THE VICTORY THAT REWARDS FAITHFUL AND PATIENT MORAL CONFLICT. The captains are called, in the presence of all the men of Israel, to "put their feet upon the necks" of these doomed kings. So shall it be the honour and joy of all earnest warrior souls to see their enemies at last subdued under them. "The God of peace shall bruise Satan under your feet shortly" (Rom. xvi. 20). 'Tis hard work to be continually fighting against some form of evil in the world without or the world within ; to have continually to confront some new foe, or " old foes with new faces ; " to be compelled often to drag forth some lurking iniquity from its hiding place in our own hearts that it may be slain. But let us be resolute and patient and we shall " come off more than conquerors through him who hath loved us," and at last plant our feet proudly on the necks of all our adversaries.

IV. THE FINAL GLORIOUS VICTORY OF CHRIST. It is the eternal purpose of God that every stronghold of evil should fall before Him and all His enemies be put beneath His feet, and the events of time are all helping in some way or other to bring about that issue (Psa. cx. 1 ; 1 Cor. xv. 25 ; Phil. ii. 9—11).—W.

Ver. 25.—*Courage and strength.*

I. THE DUTY TO BE BRAVE AND STRONG. This is often insisted on in the Book of Joshua (*e.g.*, i. 6). Christianity gives prominence to gentler graces of humility, mildness, and the forgiving spirit. But it does not therefore exonerate us from the more masculine duties (1 Cor. xvi. 13 ; Eph. vi. 10). (1) It is our duty to be *brave.* Cowardice is a sin in a Christian even more than in a pagan, because the Christian has higher motives for courage. The exhortation, " Fear not," is not only an encouragement to comfort ; it is an incitement to duty, because cowardice leads us to shrink from (*a*) danger, (*b*) responsibility, (*c*) pain and loss, (*d*) ridicule ; and yet all of these may come in the way of our life's work. (2) It is our duty to be *strong.* We should not simply bewail weakness as a calamity ; we should repent of it as a failing. Moral weakness comes from moral corruption. It makes us fail in our work of resisting sin and doing good. It is therefore needful that we should overcome it if we are to fulfil our mission.

II. THE CALL FOR THE EXERCISE OF THIS DUTY. (1) We are surrounded by *alarming dangers ;* (*a*) in our own sinful hearts ; (*b*) in the evil of the world, and the troubles and temptations which arise from this ; (*c*) in the mystery of life. He who is not brave with God's courage will sink before these terrors when once he realises their full proportions. (2) We are called to *difficult tasks ;* (*a*) like the Israelites, we are invited to take possession of an inheritance. The kingdom of heaven is not won without fighting (1 Cor. ix. 26) ; (*b*) like the Israelites, we have foes to resist in sin within and temptation without (1 Peter v. 8, 9) ; (*c*) like the Israelites, we have territory to conquer for God. We have not to fight for our own inheritance and safety only or chiefly, but that we may win the world for Christ (1 Tim. vi. 12 ; 2 Tim. ii. 3).

III. THE SECRET OF COURAGE AND STRENGTH. (1) They are *derived from God.* We are not to fear, because God is with us (Isa. xliii. 1, 2). We are to be strong in His strength (Psa. xxix. 11 ; Phil. iv. 13). Therefore those naturally most timid and weak can be strong and brave in God (Isa. xl. 31 ; 2 Cor. xii. 10). (2) They are *encouraged by experience.* To us it appears a brutal source of courage—those Hebrew captains planting their feet on the necks of the conquered kings in triumph. But rejoicing in the victory, it was well that they should see God's hand in it, and gain strength from it. We may seek strength and courage in the contemplation of the way in which God has helped us in the past (Psa. xxxiv. 6). (3) They are *increased by practice.* The text is an exhortation. Though strength and courage come from God, they come through our own efforts to be brave and energetic. We must exercise Divine grace in order to realise its efficiency (Phil. ii. 12). (4) They are *mutually helpful.* Courage and strength are associated. Courage without strength is rash. Strength without courage is futile. We must be strong to justify our courage and brave to use our strength. Thus the various Christian graces are

linked together in arming a soul with the whole armour of God (Eph. vi. 11).—
W. F. A.

Ver. 40.—*The extermination of the Canaanites.* The apparent cruelty of the
Israelites in the conquest of Canaan arouses moral and religious questions of great
interest, especially those which are suggested by the conduct of Joshua, the relation of God to the slaughter of the Canaanites, and the contrast between the earlier
and the later religious dispensations.
I. THE CONDUCT OF JOSHUA. This appears cruel and murderous. But note:
(1) It was in accordance with the *customs of the times.* Christian lenity was unknown. A man must be judged in the light of his age. It is wrong to "follow a
multitude to do evil" (Exod. xxiii. 2), when we know it is doing evil, because the
number of guilty persons does not mitigate the guilt of each individual. But our
own judgment of what is right and wrong is largely determined by the prevalent
ideas and unblamed conduct of our contemporaries; and if, when we have used the
best light at our command, "our hearts condemn us not" (1 John iii. 21), we cannot
be accounted guilty. (2) It was in obedience to the understood *command of God.*
A supposed command from heaven is no justification for an act which a man sincerely believes to be wrong, because in no case is he justified in violating conscience,
and because he has more reason for doubting the Divine origin of the voice without
than that of the voice within. But when the certainty of the Divine command is
so strong that it carries conviction to the conscience, it becomes right for a man to
obey. (2) It was in execution of what was believed to be a *Divine decree of
judgment.* Joshua did not consider that he was destroying the Canaanites simply
to make way for the Israelites. He believed that he was a "scourge of God," sent
to bring doom to the guilty, to rid the land of men who lived only to dishonour it,
and to introduce a better race in their stead.
II. THE RELATION OF GOD TO THE SLAUGHTER OF THE CANAANITES. Did God
really command it? and if so, how can we reconcile this with His character of
goodness? (1) If God commanded this slaughter, He was ordering *no more than
He does directly* in natural events—in tempests, earthquakes, famines, plagues, and
visitations of death generally. (2) If men deserve destruction for their sins, it is
really *no more harsh for this to be sent by human agency than for it to come from
physical causes,* as with the destruction of Sodom and Gomorrah. (3) If the
punishment of sin generally is reconcilable with the goodness of God, this particular
instance may be so. (4) The extermination of the Canaanites was a *blessing to
the world.* (5) It was *no real evil to the Canaanites.* If men are living in sin
and will not repent, the judgment which shortens their lives and prevents further
evil is rather a blessing than a curse; for any loss or suffering is better for us than
that we should be permitted to live on in sin (Luke xvii. 1, 2). It is better for *us*
that we should be punished for sin than that we should continue in sin unpunished.
III. THE CONTRAST BETWEEN THE EARLIER AND THE LATER DISPENSATIONS. (1)
Joshua brought *punishment and destruction* to sinners. Christ brings *forgiveness
and life.* (2) Joshua could only find room for his people after *exterminating their
predecessors.* Christ has *room for all* who will come to His kingdom (Luke xiv. 22).
(3) Joshua proved himself fit for the inheritance of his nation by the exercise of
destructive warfare. Christians are made meet for their inheritance by the practice of Christ-like *deeds of charity* (Matt. xxv. 34—36).—W. F. A.

Ver. 40.—*The extermination of the Canaanites.* "So Joshua smote all the
country of the hills, and of the south, and of the vale, and of the springs, and all
their kings: he left none remaining, but utterly destroyed all that breathed, as the
Lord God of Israel commanded." The attributes of God are the foundation of
religion. From the relation in which we stand to Him as His creatures some
regards are due to Him; but this relationship of inferiority could not of itself suffice
to demand that entire devotedness to His services, that complete surrender of our
affection which we denominate religion. God's requirement (as stated in Deut.
x. 12) can only be justified by reference to the perfections of His character. If

there be the least flaw, implicit trust cannot be expected of us.   Herein all heathen systems of religion are defective, presenting to us a deity whom we cannot worship, a creature maimed, liable to the same passions as ourselves.   The Christian religion bears traces of its Divine origin in the grandeur of its conceptions concerning the character of God.   There is a height that dwarfs into littleness the puny gods invented by man; there is a many-sidedness of view which could not have been the product of imagination.   Just and holy, merciful and gracious, all-knowing and Almighty, the Creator and Sustainer, a Friend and Judge, our Father and King, such He is declared to be.   Hence it is that those objections are felt to be most serious which are urged, with any show of reason, against the reality of God's perfections.   Especially when His benevolence is challenged do we fear lest the dark shadow becloud the skies and chill our hearts.   Now, in the text there is an account of a sweeping destruction executed on the south of Canaan by command of God. No quarter was given.   So dreadful the desolation that some have called it cruelty. And though it is not incumbent on us to justify all the ways of God, yet as some are led from passages like the present to entertain hard thoughts of God, it may be well for once to look the implied objection calmly in the face.

A command from God may render that action lawful and right, which done without His authority would be deserving of reprobation.   He is the Lord and owner of life.   He gave, and it is His to take away.   He commits no more injustice than when a parent redemands from his children the goods of which they are making an improper use.   The text is therefore no excuse for the unauthorized seizure of the land of one nation by another, or for those violent acts for which no direct behest of God can be alleged.

These were single detached commands against particular foes.   There was no injunction "to cultivate the principles of treachery or cruelty;" "none of these precepts are contrary to immutable morality" (Bp. Butler).   When an army was led blindly into Samaria the king said, "Shall I smite them?"   "No," answered the prophet Elisha in effect (2 Kings vi. 21, 22).   On another occasion the prophet Elijah had rebuked King Ahab because he had allowed a king to escape, whom "the Lord had appointed to utter destruction."   The reason of the case alters the nature of the action.

The extermination of the Canaanites was a punishment for wickedness.   See Lev. xviii.   "The land is defiled . . . vomiteth out her inhabitants."   The very earth stank with their practices, and yearned to be rid of its unhallowed burden. "Ye shall not walk in the manners . . . for they committed all these things, therefore I abhorred him."   Again, in Deut. xviii., "Because of their abominations the Lord doth drive them out from before thee."   So also Deut. ix. 5.   It is to be remembered that the things censured were not merely occasional acts, but abominable customs.   Indeed, the odious practices were a part of their religion, incorporated into their most solemn services.   So degraded had they become.

A considerable period of respite had been granted, but without avail.   God had said to Abraham, "The iniquity of the Amorites is not yet full."   When the cup of iniquity was filled to overflowing, then did the righteous fiat issue.   During that period warnings of the severest character were given.   Sodom and Gomorrah perished in a terrible manner, and later the kings of Og and Sihon had fallen.   Still no repentance.   It is useless to say that the warnings were not sufficiently distinct. We see the same indifference to-day.   Men destroy their health by sinful habits, grow worse and worse.   Do they need a Divine hand on their shoulder or an actual voice in their ear to warn them?   The warning is plain, if only they will attend to it.   But no! and the fearful end arrives.

The method of punishment adopted was one of which the nations of Palestine would not complain, since it was in keeping with their own conduct.   They would find no injustice done them.   They would defeat other nations and dispossess them of life and territory if they could.   They believed in the tenure or lease of the strong arm.   Granted, therefore, that God was executing righteous judgment, the prevailing code removes all charge of cruelty.   The judgments as well as the favours of God must be conditioned as to form by men's surroundings.   In legislating for the Israelites, whilst we expect and find such purity and such an anticipation of the opinions of modern times as justly entitles the "the law of Moses" to be considered a revelation from God, yet would it have been Quixotic to take no account of prevalent opinions and tendencies, to demand of the Israelites exactly what Christianity now demands after so many centuries of civilisation. There is no change, therefore, in the character of God, no advance in wisdom or love supposed, only such a difference of reputation as is necessitated by a due regard for the condition of those to whom Divine commands are given. We must not, therefore, talk of a contradiction between the spirit of the gospel maxim, "love your enemies," and the precept followed in the text as seeming to say, "act with barbarity." As a rule, God's judgments here do not distinguish degrees of guilt. Famines and pestilences of old times scourged a whole neighbourhood. So in the present instance the sword visited all with punishment. Let us not forget, however, that these judgments are not final. Nothing is determined respecting the ultimate state of those involved in the general destruction. Minute discrimination is for the other world.

Is not God's love exemplified even in the stern precept of the text?

1. *Love to surrounding nations.* This terrible example might prove beneficial. The only proof to them of superior power was prowess in war. This alone could bring them to acknowledge that the God of Israel, " he was Lord."

2. *To His own people.* The danger was lest the Israelites should be contaminated, and after events showed the wisdom of God's command. The people were so easily seduced from their allegiance to Jehovah. And God was impartial. He threatened that if the Israelites did evil, their fate should be similar.

3. *To the whole world.* Since if the chosen people had utterly lost the truth, the light would have been universally extinguished. Through Israel the promised Messiah was to come. Woe to the world if the way were blocked up, and no Saviour appeared dawning as the Sun of Righteousness on this benighted earth.

Many lessons may be drawn. We learn the authority of God, and His hatred of sin. Ours is no emasculated religion. If God were a being of kindness only, then kindness with sin would mean total misery. "Except we repent we shall all likewise perish." When we look at His anxiety for the welfare of His people, and the preparation made for the gift of His Son, we are taught "the goodness and severity of God" (Rom. xi. 22).—A.

EXPOSITION.

CHAPTER XI. 1—23.

THE PROSECUTION OF THE WAR.—Ver. 1. —**And it came to pass.** The political constitution of Palestine was, humanly speaking, the cause of its overthrow. The division of the country into a host of petty states, and the consequent want of cohesion and concert, made its conquest a comparatively easy task. Had the kings of the north rallied round the standard set up in Central Palestine by Adoni-zedek, a far more formidable opposition would have been offered to Joshua at Gibeon. Calvin takes us, however, at once to the fountain head, and remarks how God fitted the burden to those who had to bear it. In spite of the great things God had done to them, they might have been driven to despair (and every one knows how weak their faith was) by the overwhelming numbers of the enemy. But by reason of the slackness of their opponents they were able to meet and overcome them in detail, without any opposi-

tion but what their weak faith enabled them courageously to confront. **Jabin king of Hazor.** Jabin (the Hebrew meaning of this word is *intelligent*) was, like Pharaoh in Egypt, the usual name for the king that reigned in Hazor (see Judg. iv. 2, 23, 24). He was a powerful monarch, and if not before, at least after, the Israelitish invasion became the acknowledged head of the league formed among the Canaanites against the Israelites. The first mention we have of Hazor in history is before the Exodus. The temple at Karnak, in Egypt, contains an account of an expedition into Palestine by Thotmes III., in which Kedeshu, Magedi, Damesku, Khatzor or Hazara, and other places are mentioned. We may no doubt identify these with Kedesh - Naphtali, Megiddo, Damascus, and Hazor (see Palest. Expl. Quart. Paper, April, 1876). Hazor, like *fort* in French and German, *caer* in Welsh, and the termination *cester* in English (so also *chester*), signifies a castle or fortified town. Like the names above mentioned, it was by no means an uncommon name. Beside the present Hazor, which was in northern Palestine, two cities of that name are mentioned in the south (ch. xv. 23, 25). It rose from its ashes during the period of inaction which followed the death of Joshua, and though (ch. xix. 36) it was assigned to the tribe of Naphtali, became once more the centre of a strong Canaanitish organisation. It was, perhaps, the city Solomon is stated to have fortified (1 Kings ix. 15), though this is not expressly stated. This becomes more probable when we find this Hazor among the cities of northern Israel captured by Tiglath-Pileser (2 Kings xv. 29). " Yet still, in spite of the destruction by the Assyrians, the name lived on till the time of the Maccabees, and the great contest betweeen King Demetrius and Jonathan the Maccabean took place upon the plain of Hazor " (Ritter, ii. 225). Josephus also mentions the πεδίον Ἀσώρ in this connection. Robinson identifies it with Tel Khuraibeh, on the lake of Huleh, the ancient Merom. Conder regards it as represented by Jebel and Merj Hadîreh, on the borders of this lake. Dean Stanley places it above the lake, while Vandevelde finds a place called Hazûr, with extensive ruins, some distance westward. The names, however, Hazûr and Haziri, are very common. Of Madon and Shimron nothing is known. Knobel would identify Achshaph with Acco or Ptolemais. Robinson supposes it to be the modern Kesâf. But this is not certain, for Achshaph (ch. xix. 25) formed the border of Asher, while Kesâf is in the extreme north. According to Conder, it is the present el Yasîf.

Ver. 2.—**On the north of the mountains.** Rather, *to the northward, in the mountain district.* Not necessarily the Lebanon and Anti-Lebanon range, but the mountains of Galilee, which lay within the boundaries of Naphtali. The LXX. reads יַרְדֵן for צָפֹן and therefore renders κατὰ Σιδῶνα, adding τὴν μεγάλην from ver. 8. **The plains south of Chinneroth.** Rather, *the Arabah south of Chinneroth* (see note on ch. iii. 16). The word Arabah is given untranslated in ch. xviii. 18. This was, no doubt, the great Ghôr, or depression of the Jordan, or at least the northern part of it, extending for some distance south of the town of Chinneroth (ch. xix. 35 ; Deut. iii. 17). This town gave its name to the lake or inland sea now better known to the student of Scriptures as the sea of Tiberias, or lake of Gennesareth (see Num. xxxiv. 11). " As we enter upon the geological character of the basin which contains the sea of Galilee, we see at once that it is simply one element of the Jordan Valley and the Dead Sea, which extends due north and south for a distance of sixty hours. This is the Ghôr, or Sunken Valley of the Arabah " (see note on ch. iii. 16), " extending from Hasbeya to the Ælanitic gulf as a continuous cleft—the deepest one known to us " (Ritter, ii. 241). He goes on to enumerate the various signs of volcanic agency in this region ; the frequent earthquakes, the form of the basin of Gennesareth (though he denies it to be a crater), the hot springs, the frequent caves, the naphtha deposits and springs, the hot water springs to be found even *in* the Dead Sea, the lofty crystalline masses of the Sinaitic peninsula, and the porphyritic dykes found at the southern end of the Ghôr, as well as the general conformation of the country east of Jordan. The sea of Chinneroth, or Tiberias, is stated by Conder (Handbook, pp. 212, 216) to be 682·5 feet below the level of the Mediterranean. **And in the valley.** The Shephelah, or lowland district (see above ch. ix. 1). **The borders of Dor.** Rather, the *heights,* or *highlands* (נָפוֹת Vulg. *regionibus*) of Dor. This elevated position was a remarkable feature of the neighbourhood, though the various translations of the word (as "coast," ch. xii. 23 ; "region," 1 Kings iv. 11) rather obscure the prominence given to this physical characteristic in the Scripture narrative. Rosenmüller would translate it the "promontory" of Dor, for Dor (now *Tantura, Tortura,* or *Dandora*) was upon the sea coast south of Carmel, and nine Roman miles north of Cæsarea. Thus situated, its position on a hill, though the hill is not a lofty one, would strike the observer, and it accounts for the peculiar form of speech noticed above, which is so common that in the LXX. it is usually given as part of the proper name, Ναφεδδώρ (cf. Ναφαθδώρ, ch. xii. 23 ; Νεφθαδώρ, 1 Kings iv. 11). And behind it are still higher rocky ridges, to which the name also applies. Dor, with its excellent harbour, was a noted place of commerce in ancient times, especially in the *murex coccineus,* from which the far-famed Tyrian dye was obtained. These are a species of mussel, and Seetzen mentions two varieties, the *murex trunculus* of Linnæus, and the *Helix ianthina.* The latter is of a whitish green, but when taken out of the water it passes from red to purple, and after death to violet. Its use has been superseded by that of the cochineal insect, but the Tyrian purple was in great demand in early times. Its costliness may be inferred from the fact that in each insect a little pouch behind the head, not the size of a pea, contains the dye. See Ritter, iv. 280, 281 ; Pliny, ' Nat. Hist.' 9,

36 (60 in some editions); and 'Epist.' 50, 10, 26. The allusions to it by Horace, Virgil, Juvenal, and other classical authors are too numerous for quotation. We may take as instances Virgil, Georg. iii. 17 : " Illi victor ego, et Tyrio conspectus in ostro " (cf. Æn. iv. 262): and Juvenal, Sat. vii. 134 ; "Spondet enim Tyrio stlataria purpura filo." The ruins of the ancient city still crown the steeps of its site (see Vandevelde's Memoir, and Conder's Handbook. Also Keil *in loc.*). **On the west.** The LXX. renders, "And to the Amorites on the sea coast " (see last note), leaving out all mention of the Canaanites.

Ver. 3.—**To the Canaanite** (see note on ch. iii. 10). This confederacy was yet more formidable than the other (ver. 5), but was as signally defeated by Joshua's promptitude (see ver. 7). We are reminded of the swift march of our own Harold, and its results at Stamford Bridge ; with this difference, however, that the enemy, instead of being engaged in triumphant festivity, was preparing for an expedition against a much-dreaded enemy, who was believed to be far off. Napoleon had nearly achieved a similar surprise at Quatre Bras and Ligny. **The Jebusite in the mountains.** Jerusalem was not yet taken. From the neighbourhood of that as yet unconquered city, and probably from itself, Jabin drew his auxiliaries, while Joshua was as yet fully occupied in the south. **Hermon in the land of Mizpeh.** Mizpeh, or Ham-mizpah, as it is usually called (save in ver. 8 ; Judg. xi. 29 ; 1 Sam. xxii. 3 ; Hos. v. 1), *i.e.*, the watch-tower, was a common name among the Israelites. There was one in Judah (ch. xv. 38), in Benjamin (ch. xviii. 26), in Gilead (Judg. xi. 29 ; cf. Gen. xxxi. 49 ; Josh. xiii. 26), and in Moab (1 Sam. xxii. 3). Ritter (ii. 353) mentions the large number of watch-towers, of which the ruins may still be traced, along the line of the great watershed of Judæa. This one was probably far to the north, on the north-western side of Hermon, commanding a view of the plain of Cœle Syria, which extended from south-west to north-east between Lebanon and Anti-Lebanon. This vast plain is still known as the Bukei'a (see note on ch. v. 8), though Robinson denies that this Bukei'a is meant, because the Bukei'a properly so-called was not under Hermon. This makes it possible that Mizpeh might have been on the southeastern side of Hermon, where also an extensive view might be had. Ritter, however, says it can be no other than " the great plain which extends north of Lake Huleh, from its narrow western margin to Banias, that is, the plain south and south-*west* of Hermon. Some have supposed the meaning of

Mizpeh to be equivalent to Belle Vue **in** modern days. But the meaning " watch-tower " suggests ideas more in keeping with those rude times, in which our modern appreciation of scenery was a rare quality. It was not the beauty of the view which was valued, but its extent, as giving timely notice of the approach of an enemy. Mount Hermon has already been mentioned in the note on ch. i. 4. Some further particulars may here be added. We find in Deut. iii. 9 that the Amorites call the mountain Shenir, and the Sidonians Sirion. It is very remarkable, and bears on the authorship of the Song of Solomon, that the Amorite name Shenir is given to Hermon in Cant. iv. 8. Was the song addressed to a Hittite wife, or had Solomon an Amorite one? In Deut. iv. 48 Hermon is called Sion. With the former of these passages we may compare Psa. xxix. 6. But we must not confound (as even a writer so well informed as Ritter does) the Zion, or Tzion (sunny mount), of Psa. cxxxiii., where Hermon is mentioned, with the Sion, or " lofty mountain " (spelt with *Sin*, not *Tzade*), in Deut. iv. 48. Vandevelde asks why the mountain is called by so many names, and replies that it is because " it is a cluster of mountains many days' journey in circumference." A much better reason is suggested by the fact mentioned in our former note—that, as the highest ground in Palestine, it was visible from every part of it. The name Sirion, or the *coat of mail*, was no doubt given from its glittering surface. It is to be feared that the reason given above for the Sidonian name diminishes the probability of the remarkable argument in Blunt's ' Coincidences,' part ii. 2, derived from the Sidonian settlement (Judg. xviii.) at the foot of Hermon.

Ver. 4. — **And they went out.** Dean Stanley (Lectures, i. 259) compares this " last struggle " of the Canaanites with the conflict between the Saxons and the British chiefs " driven to the Land's End." The comparison is more picturesque than accurate. In the first place, it was by no means a " last struggle " (see ver. 21 ; ch. xviii. 3 ; xix. 47 ; Judg. iv. throughout). In the next, the Britons were never driven to the Land's End, but Dorsetshire, which retained its independence for 200 years, was treated by Ina as Gezer (ch. xvi. 10), was treated by the Ephraimites, while Devonshire and Cornwall came very gradually and almost peacefully under the hands of the conquerors. And thirdly, even had it been otherwise, there is a vast difference between a handful of desperate men driven to bay on a tongue of land surrounded nearly on every side by the sea, and a powerful, though defeated, nation with a vast continent in its rear. Yet there are many features common to the history of the Israelites in Canaan, and of the Teutonic tribes in Britain (see Introduction). **As the sand that is upon the sea shore.** This poetic phrase is common in the Hebrew writings (see Gen. xxii. 17; xxxii. 12; Judg. vii. 12; 1 Sam. xiii. 5; 1 Kings iv. 20, &c.). Solomon's capacious intellect is compared to the sand on the sea shore, in 1 Kings iv. 29. The word translated "shore" is "lip" in the original, a word which adds to the poetry of the passage. **And horses and chariots very many.** Literally, *many exceedingly*. The Israelites appear to have held cavalry and chariots in great awe (see Exod. xiv. 18, and the song of triumph in Exod. xv.; cf. also ch. xvii. 16, 18; Judg. i. 19; iv. 3). In later times they appear to have become more used to them. See, for instance, 1 Sam. xiii. 5, where the historian gives their number, large as it was, instead of regarding it as past all computation. This battle must have taken place on level ground, or the chariots would have been useless. Accordingly the historian fixes its scene on the banks of "the waters of Merom," where such ground is to be found—another instance of his historical accuracy (see Vandevelde, Journey ii. 413, who places the battle on the great plain southwest of the latter). The use of chariots in battle dates from an early period. Homer's heroes are described as driven to battle in them. But perhaps the scythe-chariots are here meant, which are not found on early Egyptian monuments, but which Xenophon in his Cyropædia says were introduced by Cyrus. We find them, however, in use in Britain, in the days of Julius Cæsar, and they could hardly have obtained the idea from the Persians. Potter (Antiquities, bk. iii. ch. i.) says that they were gradually abandoned when they were found more dangerous to those who used them than to the enemy. That this kind of chariot is here meant seems pretty certain from the alarm they caused. No such alarm would have been caused by chariots simply used to convey the chieftains to the fight (see Gesenius, *s.v.* ; Xenophon, Cyr. vi. 4; and 2 Macc. xiii. 2). **All their hosts.** The LXX. reads מַלְכֵיהֶם their *kings*, for מַהֲנֵיהֶם.

Ver. 5.—**The waters of Merom.** Robinson and the later travellers generally identify this with the Samochonitis (Joseph, Ant. v. 1; Bell. Jud. iii. 9. 7; iv. i. 1), now Huleh. Keil and Delitzsch deny this, but it may be regarded as established, on the authority of Ritter, Vandevelde, Tristram, in short of all who have visited Palestine during the last thirty years. But its name,

"the waters of height," would seem to answer to this, the highest of the inland lakes of Palestine. The Jordan runs through it, and it is also the reservoir for numerous other streams. "In the centre of this plain, half morass, half tarn, lies the uppermost lake of the Jordan"—the little lake Phiala excepted—"about seven miles long, and at its greatest width six miles broad, the mountains slightly compressing it at either extremity, surrounded by an almost impenetrable jungle of reeds, abounding in wild-fowl, the sloping hills near it scoured by herds of gazelles" (Stanley, 'Sinai and Palestine,' p. 382).

Ver. 6.—**And the Lord said unto Joshua.** The encouragement was not unnecessary. The task before Joshua was harder than any that had yet befallen him. The enemy was far more numerous and better equipped. And it is a well-known fact that men of tried courage are often daunted by unaccustomed dangers. Therefore all Joshua's strength of mind was required to inspirit even men who had experienced God's wonderful support at the passing of the Jordan, at the siege of Jericho, at the battle before Gibeon, now that they were face to face with the unwonted spectacle of a vast host, furnished with all the best munitions of war known to that age. The Israelites had nothing to depend upon but their own tried valour, and the reliance they felt upon God's support. "Unequal in arms and tactics," says Ewald ('Hist. Israel.,' ii. 2. C.), "they could oppose to the Canaanites only courage and confidence." **To-morrow about this time.** The promise was made on the eve of the encounter, but not, of course, as some have supposed, while Joshua was still at Gilgal. We are not told how long Joshua was on the march. Probably (as in ch. ii.) he had sent scouts forward, who brought him intelligence on the day before the battle of the vastness of the host, and the formidable nature of its equipment. The martial spirit Joshua had infused into the host, and the spirit of faith in God begotten of His recent acts of favour, contrast remarkably with the conduct of the Israelites described in Num. xiv. To each servant of God His own special gift is vouchsafed. Moses was the man to inspire the Israelites with a reverence for law. Joshua had the special aptitudes for the leader in a campaign. It is a confirmation of this view that, in the one successful engagement recorded during the forty years' wandering in the desert, Joshua, not Moses, was the leader of the troops, while the aged law-giver remained at a distance, encouraging them by his prayers (see Exod. xvii. 8—13). But while we thus regard the secondary influences of individual character, we must not forget that the Israelites were also sustained at this moment by the assurances of Divine protection given at Jericho, at Ai, at Beth-horon, which had not been vouchsafed to them while under Moses's leadership in the wilderness. **Will I deliver up.** The " I " in the original is emphatic. And the use of the present participle in the Hebrew adds vividness to the promise. **Slain.** LXX. and Vulg., *wounded.* **Thou shalt hough their horses.** To *hough* (or *hoxe*, Wiclif) is to *hamstring*, νευροκοπεῖν, LXX., to cut the sinews behind the hoofs, the *hocks*, as they are called. This rendered the horse useless, for the sinew could not reunite. The effects of the horses and chariots upon the mind of Joshua and his host, who had neither, is here traceable. " Those very horses and chariots, which seem to you so formidable, will I, the Lord of hosts, be to - morrow at this time delivering into your hand. The horses shall be for ever useless to your enemies, and the dreaded chariots shall cease to be." Why should Joshua have destroyed the horses? Perhaps (as Keil, following Calvin, suggests) in order that the Israelites should not put their trust in chariots or in horses (Psa. xx. 7; cxlvii. 10), but in God alone (cf. Deut. xvii. 16). But more obvious considerations of policy may have dictated the measure. God never (see Matt. iv. 1—7) makes use of supernatural means when natural ones are sufficient. Now the Israelites were unacquainted with the use of horses in warfare, while their enemies were not. To retain the horses while the country was as yet unsubdued would have been a double burden to them, for they would have had not only to keep them themselves, but to prevent the enemy from regaining them. On the same principle in modern warfare do we spike guns we cannot carry off, and destroy provisions we cannot convert to our own use.

Ver. 7.—**Suddenly** (see remarks in Introduction on Joshua's characteristics as a general. Also ch. x. 9). **And they fell upon them.** This phrase denotes the rapidity of the onset. While they deemed him to be leagues away, he suddenly appeared at the head of his army, no doubt debouching from one of the mountain passes of Upper Galilee ; and before they could set themselves in battle array, his troops, without giving the enemy time to rally, or themselves a moment's breathing-time, commenced the attack. The LXX. adds " in the hill country " here, an obvious blunder. The translator must have carelessly read בהר for בהם.

Ver. 8.—**And the Lord delivered them**

(see ch. x. 42). The issue of every battle is in God's hands. The natural man attributes it to human skill. The spiritual man, whether under the law or under the gospel, acknowledges the truth that " there is no restraint to the Lord, to save by many or by few " (1 Sam. xiv. 6). But if victory should ever side with numbers, if God appears not to " defend the right," it is that anxiety and sorrow may chasten the hearts of its upholders, lead them to " crucify the flesh with its affections and lusts," and so conduct them to a final victory when they are fitted to resist the intoxication of prosperity. Many a lesson in history has taught us that immediate success is by no means a blessing, even to those who are in the main fighting for a good cause. **Great Zidon.** So called, not to distinguish it from any other city, but to mark (so also ch. xix. 28) its importance as the capital of Phœnicia. This expression, " great Zidon," marks the early date of the Book of Joshua. In Homer's Iliad, Sidon is represented as the great home of the arts, though the historian Justin tells us that, even when Homer wrote, her superiority had passed to Tyre (see Il. vi. 290, xxii. 743 ; Odyssey iv. 618, xiii. 285, xv. 425. Homer speaks of it as " well peopled," famous for " much brass " and the like (see Kenrick's ' Phœnicia '). In later years, Tyre, known only to the Book of Joshua as " the strong (literally, ' fortified ') city." Tyre (ch. xix. 29) outstripped her rival, and from the time of David till that of Alexander the Great, in spite of her destruction by Nebuchadnezzar, retained her pre-eminence (see the vivid description of Tyre in Ezek. xxvi., xxvii.). Sidon, now called Saida, is still a commercial city of some importance, whereas Tyre is, or was, a few years ago, little better than a collection of huts. This is not difficult to explain. The pre-eminence of Tyre was due to her military strength in a time of warlike enterprise, that of Sidon to natural position. " This ancient city of Phœnicia, ' the eldest born of Canaan ' " (see Gen. x. 15), " stood on the north-west slope of a small promontory which runs into the sea, and its original harbour was formed by three low ridges of rocks, with narrow openings between them parallel to the shore in front of the city. On these islands there are remains of massive substructions, the work of the ancient Phœnicians. There is a spacious but unprotected bay on the south of the promontory. . . . No traces of the ancient city can be seen on the mainland, but at a short distance to the north are sepulchral grottoes, which probably mark the necropolis." The plain of Sidon is prolonged as far as Sarepta, the Zarephath of the Old Testament, eight miles to the south, which stands on a rising ground near the sea, and shows the remains of ancient walls (Kenrick, 'Phœnicia,' pp. 17, 18). **Misrephoth Maim.** Literally, *burnings of waters.* *Kimchi* conjectures that these were hot springs, whereas *Jarchi* more reasonably supposes them to have been salt-pits, in which the water was evaporated and the salt left. *Masius,* whom most modern commentators follow, thinks that glass houses, of which thᵣe were several near Sidon (" constat enim eas apud Sidonem fuisse plurimas "), are meant. But it is difficult to translate the Hebrew with him and Gesenius, " burning *near* waters," and the idea of some that water stands here for glass is absurd. Knobel regards it as equivalent to water-heights, *i.e.,* cliffs rising from the sea, and derives the word from an Arabic root, *saraph,* to be high. The LXX. renders it by a proper name. Symmachus, " from the sea," reading מִיָּם for מַיִם. The Chaldee has " fossas aquarum." Misrephoth Maim (see ch. xiii. 6) was not far from Sidon. **Valley.** The word here, Bik'a, signifies an open, wide valley between mountains (see ver. 17). Sometimes, as in Gen. xi. 2, it is equivalent to *plain.*

Ver. 10.—**Turned back.** From his march toward Sidon. **For Hazor beforetime was the head of all those kingdoms** (see note on ver. 1).

Ver. 11.—**Utterly destroying them** (see note on ch. vi. 17; so below, ver. 12). **There was not any left to breathe** (see note on ch. x. 40). **And he burnt Hazor with fire.** Comparing this verse with verses 13 and 21, there can be little doubt that Joshua had heard that the Anakim had succeeded in re-occupying the cities he had captured in the south. He resolved to prevent this in the case of Hazor, which had been the capital of the neighbourhood, though he did not think the same step necessary in the case of the inferior cities. Hazor was afterwards rebuilt and re-occupied by the Canaanites (Judg. iv. 2), though not in the time of Joshua. For the present, this destruction of the stronghold of Phœnician power in the north was a decisive measure, and would have been so permanently had the Israelites followed up the policy of Joshua.

Ver. 13.—**The cities that stood still in their strength.** This is the rendering of the Chaldee version. The LXX. has κεχωματισμένας, heaped up, *i.e.,* defended with mounds. Rather, *on their hill* ("in collibus et in tumulis sitæ," Vulg.). As many of the towns in Italy, and the castles in Germany

in the middle ages, so these Phœnician cities were placed upon hills, that they might be more easily defended. The various tribes of Palestine were no doubt continually at war, and, as regards these northern tribes at least, were not accustomed to subsist by commerce. Therefore each of these cities stood (the Hebrew עָמַד surely implies *situation* here) on its own hill, a detail possibly obtained from an eye-witness, who was probably struck by this feature of the district, a feature he had not observed before. The expression is used, however, as Masius observes, by Jeremiah (ch. xxx. 18). Knobel observes that all the early versions have no suffix here. What he calls the " free translation," however, of the LXX. (which has αὐτῶν) requires the suffix, though the Vulgate requires none. We must not adopt the very plausible explanation of Knobel and others that Joshua burnt the cities in the valleys, but spared the cities on the hills, because they could be more easily defended (see ch. xvii. 16; Judg. i. 19, 34), since we read that Hazor alone was burnt. The word here translated hill (*Tell,* Arabic) is one with which we are familiar in the modern name of places in Palestine (see note on ch. viii. 28).

Ver. 14.—**Took for a prey unto themselves** (see ch. viii. 2, 27, and notes).

Ver. 15.—**As the Lord commanded Moses** (see note on ch. x. 40). **So did Joshua.** The implicit obedience of Joshua to all the commands he had received of God, whether directly or indirectly through Moses, is a striking feature of his character. Like most great soldiers, he possessed remarkable simplicity of disposition. He reminds us, in his rapidity of conception and execution, of Napoleon, but in his single-minded eye to duty he is much more like our own Wellington. Only one instance in which he erred, that of the league with Gibeon, is recorded, and this was but an illlustration of the unsuspicious straightforwardness of his character (see notes on ch. xix. 49—51; xxiii. 2; xxiv. 15).

Ver. 16.—**All that land.** Rather, " all *this* land;" the land, that is, which has been spoken of in all the previous narrative. It must not be pressed to mean the utter destruction of all the Canaanites, and the undisturbed possession of the country. **The hills.** The mountain country of Judah, in the south. The same word is translated "mountain" immediately afterwards, to the confusion of the sense, which contrasts the mountains of Israel with the mountains of Judah (see ver. 21). This would seem at first sight to lead to the conclusion that the Book of Joshua was composed after the jealousy between Judah and the rest of

Israel had sprung up in the time of David (see 2 Sam. xix. 41—43). But Dr. Edersheim has suggested another explanation. Judah, he says (see ch. xiv. 6; xv. 1), entered upon their inheritance, while the other tribes were still in Gilgal. In the same way Mount Ephraim is so called because it was given to that tribe, and occupied by them shortly after. While as the remaining seven tribes remained without their inheritance (Reuben and Gad as well as Manasseh and Ephraim being now provided for), the rest of the mountains were known as the mountains of Israel. This explanation is ingenious, but hardly satisfactory. Ephraim (see Judg. viii. 1, 2; xii. 1) early acquired a preponderance over the other tribes. We should therefore expect a threefold division of the mountain district, the mountains of Judah, of Joseph, and of Israel, especially as Ephraim was the next after Judah to enter upon its inheritance. The internal evidence seems to prove that the Book of Joshua was written by one of the tribe of Judah, or by a Levite residing within the borders of that tribe. Perhaps this affords the best explanation, but is quite possible that the whole mountain district of Palestine is here meant. **The south.** The Negeb, or dry country (see ch. x. 40). **The valley.** The *Shephelah*, or lowlands (see note on ch. ix. 1). This must have extended from Gaza northward to Joppa, while the Shephelah of Israel mentioned immediately below must be the lowland tract from Joppa to Mount Carmel. **The plain.** The Arabah (see note on ch. iii. 16). **And the valley of the same.** Rather, *his* (*i.e.*, Israel's) *lowland*.

Ver. 17.—**The Mount Halak.** *The smooth mountain.* Literally, "monte glabro," Vulg.; λεῖον, Symmachus. This may either be interpreted " the mountain bare of foliage," as opposed to Seir, the hairy or wooded mountain, as Masius and Rosenmüller suppose, or, as the latter also suggests, it may mean the mountain which has a smooth outline, as opposed to a precipitous cliff. This falls in with the character of the hills on the south of Palestine (see note on ch. x. 40). The LXX. renders by a proper name. But this the article forbids. The Syriac interpreter renders " the *dividing* mountain." But חלק rather signifies in this sense to *assign by lot*. Keil would identify it with " the row of white cliffs which cuts the Arabah obliquely at about eight English miles to the south of the Dead Sea," and divides the great valley into two parts, the Ghor and the Arabah. He gives up the other " smooth " or " bald " mountains, because they do not " go up to Seir." Later

explorers have failed to settle its situation. **Seir.** This mountainous region was well known as the territory of Esau (see Gen. xxxii. 2). **Baal-gad in the valley of Lebanon.** For *valley* (בִּקְעָה) see note on ver.

8. Baal-gad has been by some identified with Baalbek, or Heliopolis, a Syrian city, whose vast ruins strike the beholder with astonishment even now. But Baalbek lay considerably to the north of Palestine. It has therefore with greater probability been identified by Robinson, Von Raumer, and others, with Paneas or Cæsarea Philippi. Baal-gad signifies " the lord of fortune," an aspect under which the Babylonian Baal or Bel was frequently worshipped. The word Gad, erroneously translated " troop " in our version (Gen. xxx. 11; Isa. lxv. 11), is properly " fortune," and hence the god Fortune. The worship of Pan in later times supplanted that of Baal, but traces of both cults, in inscriptions and niches, may be found in the neighbourhood to the present day (see Tristram, 'Land of Israel'). All travellers speak with enthusiasm of the situation of Banias. Josephus says that it affords a profusion of natural gifts. Seetzen corroborates him. Dean Stanley compares it to Tivoli, and Canon Tristram thinks that in its rocks, caverns, and cascades there is much to remind the visitor of what is perhaps the loveliest place in all Italy. He continues, " The situation of Banias is indeed magnificent. With tall limestone cliffs to the north and east, a rugged torrent of basalt to the south, and a gentle slope for its western front, Banias is almost hidden till the traveller is among the ruins." Banias stands at the end of a gorge of the Hermon range with the wide range of the Huleh plain opening out before it, as the Campagna and Rome in the distance are seen from the mouth of the gorge at Tivoli. Vandevelde, however, identifies Banias with Beth-rehob, on the insufficient ground that Baal-gad is said to be in, not at, the mouth of the valley or Bik'ath of Lebanon. He prefers the castles either of Bostra or of Aisafa, the one an hour and a half, the other three hours north of Banias. It should be added that an arm of the Jordan rises and rushes through the gorge here, " præceps," like the Anio at Tivoli. The valley of Lebanon is supposed by some not to be the valley between Lebanon and Anti-Lebanon, but the country on the southern declivity of Mount Hermon. But the term בִּקְעָה here unquestionably means the well-known Bukei'a or Cœle Syria, *i.e.*, the tract between Lebanon and Anti-Lebanon (see Knobel).

Ver. 18.—**A long time.** Hebrew, *many*

days. The campaign in southern Israel lasted for weeks, perhaps even months. But the campaign in northern Palestine must have lasted longer. The vast host which gathered at the waters of Merom was destroyed, but the task of capturing the innumerable cities which dotted that region must have been a protracted one. We may, with Josephus, infer from ch. xiv. 10 that it occupied five years, or perhaps, with other of the ancient Rabbis, seven years, since the wanderings in the wilderness after the rebellion of the Israelites lasted thirty-eight years.

Ver. 20.—**To harden their hearts** (cf. Exod. iv. 21 ; vii. 23). Müller, 'Christian Doctrine of Sin,' ii. 412, says that "Scripture never speaks of God's hardening men's hearts, save in connection with His revelations through Moses or Christ." This passage evidently had not occurred to him when writing. His explanation of the difficulty is hardly satisfactory. We are not to suppose that the free-will of the Canaanites was in any way interfered with. God no doubt left them to themselves as the due punishment of their iniquities. Sin in general, by God's own appointment, and especially the sensual sins in which the Canaanites were steeped, has a tendency to produce insensibility to moral or even prudential considerations, and to beget a recklessness which urges on the sinner to his ruin. Some have argued that had they all come, like the Gibeonites, as suppliants, they must all have been massacred in cold blood. But this is not likely. Rather we must imagine that God foresaw that they would not believe the signs He would give in favour of the Israelites, and that by meeting them in battle they brought a swift and speedy destruction on themselves.

Ver. 21.—**And at that time** (see ver. 18). What is meant is, during the continuance of the war in which the country above described was conquered. The destruction of the Anakim was the conclusion of the work, and was rendered necessary by their having re-occupied the places Joshua had taken (see notes on ch. x. 36—39). **The Anakims.** Literally, the *long-necked* men. Called the "children of Anak" (Num. xiii. 28, 33 ; also Josh. xv. 13, 14). Gesenius would derive the German *nacken* and the English *neck* from this root. The word is used of the chains on the necks of camels (Judg. viii. 26. So also Cant. iv. 9, of a necklace). They were men of gigantic stature (Num. xiii. 32), and were no doubt a hill tribe of the Amorites. It is worthy of remark that to the two fearless men whose faith did not fail them at the sight of the walled cities, and of the giant

forms of their inhabitants, was entrusted the task of overcoming these antagonists, and thus of proving the truth of their own words. Thus it ever is in the counsels of God. "To him that hath shall be given, and from him that hath not, even that which he hath shall be taken away." To Joshua, who had confidence in God, the whole land of Canaan was given into subjection. From the Israelites, who had not that confidence, the inheritance of their fathers was taken away (cf. also Matt. xxv. 21, 28). Many writers suppose that these Anakim (like the Rephaim of ch. xii. 4) were the aboriginal inhabitants, and of Turanian descent (see note on next verse). **Anab.** A town about ten miles south-west of Hebron (cf. ch. xv. 50). It was apparently one of the daughter cities of Debir, and there is still a place of that name in the immediate vicinity of Dhâharijeh. **Mountains of Judah.** For this and the "mountains of Israel" see note on ver. 16.

Ver. 22.—**Only in Gaza.** This statement is confirmed by what we afterwards read. In Gath especially (1 Sam. xvii. 4 ; 2 Sam. xxi. 18—22 ; 1 Chron. xx. 4—8, the last passage preserving the true text, which has become hopelessly corrupt in the second Book of Samuel) we find the race of giants remaining till David's time. But it had almost died out. Goliath and his brethren seem to have been regarded by the Philistines, as much as by the Hebrews, in the light of prodigies. It may be that the race deteriorated in size and strength, when driven from the mountain district. Gaza (Hebrew Azzah, as in Deut. ii. 23 ; 1 Kings iv. 24 ; Jer. xxv. 20) was a stronghold of the Philistines. We first find it mentioned as the border of Canaan in Gen. x. 19. It was the scene of the exploits of Samson, related in Judg. xvi. It, with Gath, Ekron, Ashdod, and Ashkelon, formed the five Philistine lordships mentioned in ch. xiii. 5. Gaza does not appear in the list of cities captured by David, although Gath does. Perhaps the strength of its position (Azzah signifies strength) may have enabled it to resist David and Solomon, whose dominions are said to have extended to, but not to have included, Azzah. We read little more of it in the Old Testament. Jeremiah says that Pharaoh smote it (ch. xlvii. 1) ; Amos and Zephaniah threatened it with punishment. It is mentioned in Acts viii. 26 as a place of some importance. And it still exists, at about an hour's journey from the sea, and is now called Ghazzeh (see also note on ver. 41). **Gath.** Also one of the five Philistine lordships. In David's time it had a king, with whom David took refuge (1 Sam. xxi. 10 ; xxvii. 2).

It was afterwards conquered by David (2 Sam. xxi. 20 ; 1 Chron. xviii. 1 ; xx. 6). We find it in Solomon's jurisdiction, though under the government of one of its own royal family (1 Kings ii. 39). Rehoboam fortified it (2 Chron. xi. 8). Hazael, the powerful king of Syria, wrested it from Jehoash, and was only bought off from assailing Jerusalem. Uzziah re-took it once more (2 Chron. xxvi. 6). Hezekiah seems to have retained it (2 Kings xviii. 8). After this we hear no more of it. Modern travellers and commentators have identified it with Beit-Jibrin (the house of the mighty—perhaps a reminiscence of Goliath and his kindred), now Eleutheropolis (so Knobel). Others suppose it to be the Blanche Garde of the Crusaders, or Tell-es-Safieh, an opinion supported, among others, by Mr. J. L. Porter and Lieut. Conder. See, however, the note on Libnah, ch. x. 29. **Ashdod.** Later Azotus, now Esdûd. Here the ark was carried after the disastrous defeat related in 1 Sam. iv. It was conquered by Uzziah (no doubt it had formerly been reduced by David), who built forts to overawe it (2 Chron. xxvi. 6), but it fell into the hands of Sargon, king of Assyria, a little later (Isa. xx. 1). It is frequently mentioned by the prophets, and we find that Jonathan, the brother of Judas Maccabæus, burnt the temple of Dagon there (1 Macc. x. 83, 84). It is mentioned as Azotus in Acts viii. 40.

Ver. 23.—Joshua took the whole land. The word must not be pressed to mean that every Canaanitish stronghold was razed or appropriated. The word בֹל, as has been before remarked, has a very loose signification in Hebrew. What is meant is simply this. Joshua had established an unquestioned military preponderance in Palestine. He had broken down all resistance ; but before he completed his conquests to their full extent, he had to provide for the peaceable settlement of the tribes in the territory he had seized. The complete extermination of the Canaanites formed no part of his commission or his plan (Deut. vii. 22 ; cf. Exod. xxiii. 29, 30). To have effected it would have been to throw the land out of cultivation, and to expose its possessors to the usual inconveniences of depopulated districts. Therefore it was Joshua's policy to leave the Canaanites to be extirpated by degrees, and to encourage the Israelites to cultivate the arts both of war and of peace ; to nourish a martial spirit by remembering that numerous and active enemies still dwelt in their midst, while yet they were not neglectful of the importance of a settled and civilised, an agricultural and pastoral life. See also Judges iii. 1, 2. This purpose was defeated, not only by the usual effects of civilisation upon hardy or savage tribes, but also by the Israelites becoming addicted to the pleasant but enfeebling vices of the races they had supplanted. We see in the Israelitish history the best exemplification of St. Paul's theory that the "law worketh wrath," although it is "holy, just, and good." The excellence of the moral precepts delivered by Moses did but serve to manifest more clearly the inherent depravity of our nature (Rom. iii. 20 ; v. 20 ; vii. 7, 8), and its need of a Saviour, who should render obedience possible by the gift of regeneration, and the infusion of His own Spirit. **According to their divisions.** Literally, *their divisions by lot*, the word being derived from the same root as the word Halak in ver. 7, because a smooth stone was usually employed in casting lots. Hence it came to mean any authoritative division or distribution, as the courses of the Levites (1 Chron. xxiii. 6), the classification for purposes of enlistment (1 Chron xxvii. 1) and the like. **And the land rested from war.** That is to say, the Canaanites were so thoroughly cowed and dispirited that they dared offer no further resistance to the Israelites in their task of portioning out the land. They were quite contented to be allowed to live in peace in such of their cities which remained, and had no disposition to court an overthrow such as took place at the battles of Gibeon and Merom, with its inevitable results of the absolute extermination, not only of every one who took up arms, but of every human being in the city to which they belonged. Thus the Israelites were able to give their whole attention to the survey and apportionment of the territory according to the relative size and importance of the tribes.

HOMILETICS.

Vers. 1—23.—*The continuation of the struggle.* The same class of thoughts is suggested by this chapter as by the former. We have, as before (1), the confederacy of evil against good, (2) the conflict, (3) the victory, (4) the utter destruction of the enemy. But the course of the narrative gives a somewhat different form to our reflections.

I. JOSHUA NEEDED SPECIAL ENCOURAGEMENT ONCE MORE, in spite of his previous signal victory. This was because he had a new class of enemies to contend against. These kings, with the king Hazor at their head, seem to have possessed a higher civilisation than the southern tribes. We read (vers. 4, 6) of their *chariots*, and these, as we have seen (see Exposition), seem to have been regarded with peculiar terror by the Israelites. So it is ever with the Christian Church. It was so at the beginning. At first she had only to contend with the obstinate jealousy and prejudice of the Jews, but as her sphere of operations enlarged she had to contend with the whole force of the civilised Roman empire. It is so still. The Church has confronted the barbarism of the middle ages, the superstition and formalism that followed it. But now she has to contend with modern civilisation, with its horses and chariots of iron—that is to say, its modern developments of physical force, as well as knowledge. These have to be attacked and brought under Christ's yoke.

II. THE PROGRESS OF CHRISTIANITY INVITES COMBINATION AMONG HER ENEMIES. This, too, was the case at the outset of Christianity. As soon as our religion was seen to be a power in the world, capable of surviving the execution of its leader, and the punishment of His followers, and of spreading nevertheless from city to city, from country to country, a widespread combination, formed of elements the most opposite, arose against it. Jew joined with Gentile to put it down. The emperor waged war against it, because it had formed a secret society, dangerous, he thought, to the stability of his throne. The lawyer and statesman opposed it, because it had taken upon itself to exist without the permission of the law. The priest opposed it, because it set up an altar against his. The philosopher opposed it, because it struck a blow at his proud exclusiveness, and combated some of his favourite dogmas. The tradesman opposed it (Acts xix. 27), because it struck at his gains. The mob opposed it, because it robbed them of their spectacles and brutalising amusements. The man of vicious life opposed it, because it put a curb upon his habits of sinful indulgence. Yet our heavenly Joshua led his forces against these enemies, and the unholy combination was utterly defeated. Nor is it altogether different now. To Christianity as a creed no such opposition is offered. But let us strive to put the practical precepts of Christianity in operation, and we still meet on many points with the combined opposition of various sections of society. The statesman is indifferent to measures which will array an interested opposition against him, or diminish his sources of revenue. The philosopher derides the movement, because success, from a human point of view, is improbable, or because it offends against the canons of his school of philosophy. The man of rank, perhaps, opposes it because it strikes a blow at his privileges ; the man of fashion because he is incapable of earnest thought, and hates everything that gives him trouble. The vicious does his utmost against it for the same reason as of old ; while it is still not impossible to array against it the clamours of an unthinking mob. Yet here, as elsewhere, perseverance is success.

III. JOSHUA NOW WAS AT WAR WITH CIVILISATION. This is one of the enemies which must be brought under the yoke of Christ. (*a*) *Civilisation increases luxury*. and luxury is a foe to Christian self-denial. Luxury leads to ease and self-pleasing, and ease and self-pleasing are the very opposite of the Christian spirit. One great work of the Christian Church will be to teach men thankfully to accept the good gifts of their heavenly Father, and yet to consecrate those gifts to His service, and not to the formation of selfish habits. (*b*) *Civilisation augments enormously the power of man for evil* as well as for good. Who can predict the tremendous results for evil which may result from modern discovery, unless, under our Joshua, we manfully confront its advance, destroy its power for evil, and convert what it might misuse into instruments of good ? Again (*c*) *Modern discovery exalts the pride of man*. And the first requirement of Christianity is that he shall lay that pride aside. Therefore it is our duty to show modern knowledge its limits, to remind him who is puffed up by it that there is a gulf which his highest efforts cannot pass. He can but tell us what is ; he cannot tell us *how* it is. He may consider himself entitled to overleap the barrier which separates us from the unknown, but the attempt involves as great an assumption as it ever did. The barrier is as wide as ever, though the ground on this side of it is undoubtedly better surveyed. Concerning God, we shall be always in need of a revelation, however much He may reveal Himself in His works. So that it is still as true as it ever was, in reference to our spiritual condition, that truth is hidden from the "wise and prudent" in their own sight, and is "revealed unto babes."

IV. JOSHUA HAD STILL TO COMBAT NATURAL STRENGTH. To the men against Jabin succeeded the campaign against the uncivilised but powerful Anakim. So civilisation does not destroy our natural passions. It may (a) give them another direction, but it rather augments them than otherwise. The refinements of civilised life are unfavourable to brutal violence, but brutal indifference is not less common, and not less cruel. Against vulgar license the civilised man sets his face, but is refined licentiousness less destructive to the soul? History has proved that civilisation, unchecked by Christianity, does but increase the natural appetite for sinful pleasure. And it is Christianity alone that keeps the temptations incidental to a life of luxury within bounds. Remove that obstacle, and Nature will assert her power, and the animal in man will once more dominate civilisation to its own cruel appetites, as in past times. But (b) it is a noteworthy fact that civilised life has everywhere a fringe of aggravated naturalism. In the element that we call "rough," which is ever found where society is most highly organised, we find the most shocking perversion of natural appetites, combined with their utmost strength. Is there any place upon earth where brutality, ferocity, recklessness, animal indulgence, rages more uncontrolled by any moral considerations, than in the "slums," as we have named them, of our greatest cities? This is the direct product of the thoughtlessness, the selfishness, the recklessness of civilisation, which thrusts out of sight all that is foul and hideous of its own creation, and leaves it to fester alone. Civilisation may be won to Christianity; but there remains a long and terrible conflict with the Anakim, those giant perverted natural forces which hang on the outskirts of civilisation.

V. JOSHUA DID NOT BURN ALL THE CITIES. That is to say, there are uses to which the discoveries of civilisation and the force of natural temperament may be put. Hazor, the centre of the combination against Joshua, was burnt. So civilisation and natural disposition, so far as they are employed for self, instead of for God and mankind, must be rooted out. But where discovery is used, not to exalt men's pride, but to increase his knowledge of God's ways; not to manufacture luxuries and enjoyments to be the exclusive privilege of the few, but to augment the happiness of all, then need we not destroy but welcome them. So natural disposition need not be destroyed, but converted to a good purpose. Thus the ardent temperament of a St. Paul, diverted from its misuse in fierce persecution, became the parent of a burning zeal for the diffusion of Christianity. A cold, critical spirit may become useful in ridding the true cause of false allies. A calm, unimpassioned judgment may make its possessor an useful guide to the passionate and impulsive. The quiet, contemplative soul may furnish abundant stores of thought for those who have no leisure to think for themselves, and a busy, active disposition may find scope for its energies in the multiplicity of good works which our complicated state of society has brought into being. And even those passions which, wrongly directed, will cause widespread misery through sensual indulgence, may burn with a restrained and steady and harmless flame in the charities of family life.

VI. THE WAR LASTED MANY DAYS. So does the struggle (1) of the Christian Church against evil, and (2) that of the Christian soul against temptation. It is not (1) until the final consummation of all things, and (2) till the close of life, that "the land" can "rest from war."

VII. GOD IS SAID TO HARDEN MEN'S HEARTS, but only in the sense in which this is done by the operation of His laws. He has so ordained, that if a man's heart is not softened by His loving-kindness, it is hardened. The man who resists the pleadings of His Spirit becomes insensible to their influence. The man who succumbs to temptation becomes incapable of resistance, indifferent to the beauty of holiness. The man who apologises for vice sees no excellence in virtue. The man who is puffed up by a sense of his own sufficiency is unable to perceive the evidence for God's truth. And this is in a sense God's doing, because He has willed that it shall be so. It is not an arbitrary law. It exists by a moral necessity. We can see that it is but an effect following a cause. "Wherefore the law is holy, and the commandment holy, just, and good." And if that which is good works evil to any, we may not blame God, but man, who has turned his meat into poison, and extracted death from God's most righteous law.

HOMILIES BY VARIOUS AUTHORS.

Ver. 1—5.—*Many adversaries.* Another league is here. One in the south destroyed; another in the north is formed. A formidable one scattered; one more so gathers. Four kings are mentioned, and probably a dozen others of those mentioned in the following chapter are associated with them. They marshal all the fighting power of the northern half of Palestine. As the land was then (as repeatedly afterwards) very populous; as war was the most familiar of all employments; as numbers of the cities—almost impregnable by nature—were fortified as well; as the army gathered was strong in chariots and horses, and had taken up a position on the great plain of Jezreel, where cavalry could operate with ease—it seemed as if the outlook for Israel were very dark indeed. A nation of fugitive slaves assailing a Phœnician people of vast wealth, enterprise, civilisation, and numbers! What chance of success was there? But they unite only for their easier destruction. Cheered by God, falling thereon suddenly, the terrific shock of Israel's charge was irresistible, and this "battle of the league" at once leads to Israel's easy conquest of the whole of this half of the kingdom. Take this story as an example of the way in which God's warriors have always "many adversaries." And observe—

I. THE NATURAL CHANCES ARE ALWAYS AGAINST GOD'S PEOPLE. The sacred history is little more than a list of conflicts of one sort and another, fought invariably against great odds, but followed invariably by victory. The chances were many against Israel getting away from Egypt, taking Jericho, winning at Beth-horon, gaining a victory here. It was not otherwise in the case of Jephthah, of Deborah, of Gideon. Who would have ventured to describe David as having a single chance in his conflict with Goliath? How pathetic is Elijah's estimate of the odds against him in his fight for truth. Baal's prophets and Astarte's prophets are numbered by hundreds, backed by the whole power of the court and the perversity of the people. But "I am left alone, and they seek my life." The odds were heavily against Daniel and his three friends—say 10,000,000 to 1. Neither Ezra nor Nehemiah felt they had anything approaching a level chance. The Babe of Bethlehem had all superstitions, vices, prejudices of the world against His cause. The Apostle of the Gentiles had all the philosophies, religions, and weaknesses of men against him and his simple gospel. The great theologian of the early centuries lamented that he stood "Athanasius against the world." Luther had Church and State throughout all Europe against him. Every missionary to a heathen land, every philanthropist seeking to remove abuses, have had the same experience. The Church to-day sometimes deems herself "hardly bested" by science, secularism, the pre-occupation of men with their necessary cares, the sluggishness of the human heart to adopt a higher principle of life. Each Christian man finds such weaknesses and perversities within him and such obstacles without that it seems often as if it would be impossible to hold his ground, much less to make advance. Be not astonished if, in the part of the field assigned to you, the odds are altogether and absolutely against you. They always are against God's people and God's children. But observe secondly, though the chances are against them—

II. THE WINNING FORCES ARE ON THEIR SIDE. *Inward forces* are on their side. The heart makes the hero. Nelson's Methodists were his best sailors. God infuses such energy of purpose, confidence, self-sacrifice, that these intensify natural force a hundredfold. [See Shakespeare's 'Cymbeline,' for illustration of effect of moral energy in war.] Good is the strongest and sturdiest thing under heaven; evil, cowardly and self-ashamed in its presence. Duty, peace, hope, gracious memories, self-respect, God's smile—these are forces which the world can never match, and which all operate in the direction of victory. Outward forces are also on their side. Divine guidance is imparted, Providence aids them, concurrently with their efforts the efforts of God are put forth. When God fights His battles of mercy there is no lukewarmness in His conflict. He uses us. The weapons of our warfare are heavenly, while the weapons of His warfare are often earthly. And so, while the world has the appearance, the Church has the reality, of a preponderant weight on her side. Is it a case of a battle of the northern league with you? Fight on, for they that are with you are far more than they that are with them.—G.

Ver. 15.—*God's commandment and man's faithfulness.* I. GOD'S COMMANDMENT IS ENDURING. The commandment to Moses is transmitted to Joshua. God's will is changeless. What is right is right eternally. We must not regard God's laws as obsolete when they are ancient. The precepts of the Bible are not the less binding upon us because they are old (Psa. cxix. 160; Isa. xl. 8). Nevertheless (*a*) what God commands relative to certain circumstances will be modified if those circumstances are changed; (*b*) a larger commandment coming later exonerates from the observance of the details of a smaller commandment when these are by their nature preparatory to the larger. Thus the larger Christian law of love frees us from the narrower preparatory law of ordinances (Rom. xiii. 10).
II. FAITHFULNESS TO GOD CONSISTS IN SERVING GOD IN OBEDIENCE TO ALL HE COMMANDS US. (1) Faithfulness is shown in *devotion to God.* Moses and Joshua regarded themselves as God's servants. The Christian is not to live for self, but for Christ (Rom. xiv. 8). (2) This devotion must be exercised in *active service.* Belief, religious feeling, and acts of worship will not satisfy God. We are called to *do* His will (Matt. vii. 24—27). (3) Faithful service is *obedient service.* We must not simply work for God, but work for God in His way, doing *His* will, and fulfilling His commandments. Self-will is fatal to the merit of the most zealous service. Much of our most devoted service is spent in serving God according to our own will instead of simply doing His will (Psa. xl. 8; John vi. 38). (4) Perfect fidelity requires *obedience in all things.* We are tempted to choose our favourite commandments for obedience, and to neglect others. Some are not obvious; we should search for them. Some are difficult; we should seek special strength to do them. Some are dangerous; we should be brave and firm before them. Some are distasteful; we should sacrifice our feelings to God's will. (5) Perfect fidelity will make us endeavour to secure the *fulfilment of God's commandments by others* when we cannot accomplish all ourselves. Moses transmitted the commandment to Joshua. We should think more of the execution of the work than of the honour of the agent. Jealousy sometimes leads us to refuse sympathy for a good work if we cannot do it ourselves. (6) The *justifying grace* of God in Christ does not free us from the obligation of perfect fidelity. No man is perfectly faithful. As Christians, we are accepted by God, not on account of our fidelity, but for the sake of Christ and through the mercy of God. But the receipt of God's forgiving grace brings upon us the greater obligation to be faithful to Him in the future (Rom. vi. 1). (7) The *liberty of the gospel* does not exonerate us from the duty of fidelity. We are freed from the bondage of the letter of the law that we may obey the spirit of it. We are delivered from the legal servitude of fear that we may serve the better in the "sweet lawlessness of love" (Rom. viii. 3, 4).—W. F. A.

Ver. 20.—*Hearts hardened by God.* I. WHEN GOD HARDENS A MAN'S HEART IT IS BECAUSE HIS CHARACTER IS SUCH AS TO TURN GOD'S RIGHTEOUS ACTION TO THIS RESULT. The same act of Providence which hardens one heart softens another. Prosperity will harden one in selfish, worldly satisfaction, and soften another to grateful devotion and active benevolence. Adversity will harden one in discontent and unbelief, while it softens another to penitence and trust. The experience of life will deaden the spiritual insights of one, and quicken that of another. The effects of God's work with us is thus largely determined by the condition of our own minds. God never hardens a man's heart except through his own abuse of providential actions and spiritual influences which are kindly and wholesome in themselves, and prove themselves so to those who receive them aright (Matt. xiii. 11—15).

II. GOD HARDENS A MAN'S HEART NOT BEFORE, BUT AFTER, HE HAS SINNED. The Canaanites had hardened their hearts in sin before God hardened them for judgment. God never predisposes a man to sin, nor does He harden a man in sin against any desire for amendment. The Divine hardening of the heart is not a cause of sin but a fruit of it.

III. GOD DOES NOT HARDEN A MAN'S HEART SO MUCH BY MAKING THE WILL STUBBORN AS BY BLINDING THE EYES TO PRESENT DANGER AND FUTURE CALAMITY. The Canaanites were not made more wicked, they were only rendered blind to their danger and doom, so that they resisted where resistance was hopeless, and attempted to make no terms with the invader. When a man will not repent in obedience to conscience, it may be best that he should not find a means of escaping punishment through the exercise of prudence. So long as conscience is blind it is better for all moral purposes that prudence also should be blind. Note, however, as a warning, while sin tends to blind us to its approaching punishment, we are not the less in danger because we feel a sense of security.

IV. WHEN THE CONSCIENCE IS DEAD TO GOD'S LAW IT MAY BE WELL THAT THE INTELLECT SHOULD BE BLIND TO HIS TRUTH. It is better not to receive the truth into the intellect than to hold it with a disobedient heart. Otherwise (1) we shall misunderstand, abuse, and misapply it; (2) we shall deceive ourselves by supposing we are the better for knowing what is good although we do not practise it; and (3) we shall be less susceptible to the influence of truth when it comes at the right moment to reveal our guilt and direct the way to redemption. Christ expressly said that He spoke in parables that they who were in a wrong condition of heart to benefit by His teaching might not receive it to their hurt and its dishonour (Matt. xiii. 13).—W. F. A.

Ver. 20.—*Doomed to destruction.* The evil men do often appears to be attributed in Scripture to the Divine will and agency (Exod. iv. 21; Judg. xiv. 4; 1 Kings xii. 15; Rom. ix. 17. 18). Reason and conscience, indeed, confirm the view St. James gives of the history of all transgression (James i. 13—15). Every man's sin is emphatically *his own*—born of his own inward impulse, nourished by influences to which he freely and wilfully yields himself, and its deadly issue is his just and natural recompense. God has nothing to do with it but to condemn and punish. How, then, can it be said of any form of evil that it is " of the Lord," or that a man does it because the Lord " has hardened his heart " ? Is it so that the wrongdoer is after all but the passive instrument of a Divine purpose, and his life the working out of a Divine decree ? The perfect solution of this difficult problem may be beyond us; but there are considerations that will shed much interpreting light upon it, and under the guidance of which we may

" assert eternal Providence,
And justify the ways of God to man."

I. THE HARDENING OF MEN'S HEARTS IN EVIL COURSES IS THE RESULT OF CERTAIN LAWS OF WHICH GOD IS THE AUTHOR. A suggestive analogy is found in the realm of material things. Nature has its stern impartial laws, its latent dangers, destructive powers, deadly poisons, &c. If a man deals wantonly and recklessly with these, he arms them all against himself; but the blame of the mischief thus done cannot be laid on Him who made or ordained them. What is man's business in this world but just to utilise for good ends—to " use and not abuse "—the laws and resources of the sphere in which the Creator has placed him ? So, morally, the circumstances of our existence upon earth work out good or evil results according as we are voluntarily disposed to use them. The very influences that in one case tend to nourish the principles of a true and noble life, in another case harden the heart in sin. God's part in this is simply to determine the conditions under which the process shall go on. The evil men do is their own; the powers they prostitute to their base purposes, the place they occupy among their fellow-men, the advantages that favour the working out of their designs, the laws that govern the development of their sin to its fatal issues, are " of the Lord."

II. WHEN MEN SHOW THAT THEY ARE RESOLUTELY BENT ON EVIL COURSES, GOD MAY SEE FIT TO LEAVE THEM TO THEMSELVES. There is in morals, as in mechanics, a law of *inertia* by virtue of which we remain in a chosen state, or continue to move in a chosen direction, unless some stronger force is brought to bear upon us. Will and habit rivet the chain of iniquity. When a man's heart is thoroughly " set in him to do evil," God sometimes abandons him to his own choice, leaves him to become the prey of his own wayward and wicked infatuation (Prov. i. 31). In such a case the law of sin is simply left to take its course. The Divine act is negative rather than positive. It lies in the withholding of restraining or delivering grace. And there is no injustice in this—nothing unrighteous in God thus allowing the heart to harden itself. Moreover, it is by the operation of a law of our nature that he who *will* not turn from his evil way shall at length come to a point at which he *cannot* (Jer. xiii. 23).

> " Sins lead to greater sins, and link so straight,
> What first was accident, at last is fate."

And God, who established that law, is often said in Scripture to do that which takes place by virtue of it, or which results from it. He has framed the whole constitution of things under which it comes to pass that the impenitent sinner gradually becomes obdurate and closes against himself the door of hope. In this sense only can it be true that " it is of the Lord to harden men's hearts."

III. GOD OFTEN WORKS OUT, THROUGH THE WORST FORMS OF HUMAN EVIL, HIS GRANDEST ISSUES OF GOOD. In tracing the course of earthly affairs, we have to draw a very distinct line of separation in our minds between the wicked will and purpose of man, and the overmastering will and purpose of God. The sovereignty of the latter is most triumphantly asserted when the former has been suffered to reach its utmost limits, and work its deadliest work. The utter destruction of these Canaanites, aggravated by their own mad resistance, was essential to a full display of the majesty of the God of Israel, and the vindication of eternal righteousness. How important a part it has played in the general progress of humanity, who shall say? The triumph of redeeming mercy was brought about through the most heinous of all human crimes. " Him being delivered by the determinate counsel and foreknowledge of God," &c. (Acts ii. 23). The " hands " were none the less " wicked " because through them God accomplished His holy and loving will. The Son of man was born into the world to be betrayed and crucified and slain; but that does not lighten the curse that falls on the betrayer and the murderer. Across the dark thunder-cloud of man's evil, God casts the bright and beautiful rainbow of hope. The darkness is man's—the hope is from Him " who is light, and in whom is no darkness at all."—W.

Ver. 20.—*The extermination of the Canaanites.* The terrible extermination of the Canaanitish nations remains a mystery too hard for us to understand. " It was of the Lord," we read (ver. 20). The history of Israel is designed to bring out in an impressive manner, by outward and visible facts, the constant intervention of God in human destinies. The history of our race is a fearful drama of blood and tears, in which ruin and devastation meet us on every hand. The Old Testament teaches us that in this history the purposes of Divine justice are carried out. It shows us the great Justiciary perpetually working. We might almost say that the veil which usually conceals His operation is lifted, so that we see that " our God is a consuming fire " (Heb. xii. 29). If we look into the causes of this extermination of the Canaanites, we see that it was brought about by the excessive corruptness of the life of these people, under the influence of their impure idolatries. The same conditions are found to-day at the root of all the woes that afflict humanity. The sin is always greater than the suffering. The just God is also the God of love. His justice paves the way for His mercy. The triumph of Israel is to be turned to the account of the human race, since the establishment of the sons of Abraham in the land of promise is a necessary condition and antecedent of the universal salvation. We do not for a moment deny that an awful mystery rests upon these dark records of the Old Testament. It is impossible to think without shuddering of these myriads of human beings, swept away in a deluge of blood. But surely we may believe that even in this there was some hidden secret of love Divine, and may cling with the early Church to the "larger hope," that redemption may have come to them in that mysterious abode of spirits in prison to which Jesus Christ went to preach (1 Peter iii. 17). We do not see why the victims of the first deluge should have been the only ones thus privileged. Alike in public and private misfortunes, let us ever recognise the justice of the Holy God. Let us bow beneath His mighty hand, remembering that it is at the same time the hand of our Father, and that " all things work together for good to them that love Him."—E. DE P.

Vers. 21, 22.—*The destruction of the giants.* These giants had been the terror of Israel. In the evil report of the unfaithful spies they are mentioned last in the ascending scale of difficulties which seemed to make the conquest of the land an impossibility. The dread of their prowess had provoked the mutiny in the wilderness which led to the forty years of homeless journeying. But here we have the account of their destruction ; the brevity of the account itself suggesting what everything subsequently stated confirms, that the most dreaded was not the most arduous part of their task, but somehow a part which was done like all the rest, without hitch or strain. There is much here that is very suggestive.

I. THERE ARE GIANTS THAT WE HAVE TO FIGHT. The spies had made a true report. Their report erred not in the measurement of the difficulty, but in the estimate of the nation's power with God's help to overcome it. It was true enough that scattered over the land were these tribes or families of great stature—Anakim, Emim, Zamzummims, Rephaim, as they are variously called. The Israelites being probably a people of less than ordinary stature found themselves thus face to face with a most stalwart and lordly race, with a people whose strength is still evinced in those marvellous remains of "the giant cities of Bashan," which impress all who behold them. And the land cannot be theirs until these giant tribes in their mountain fastnesses are destroyed. It is with them as it is with all men—all have to fight some giants in their fight of life. Our outlook should be made hopeful by faith, not by illusion. There are giants before us whom we shall have to fight if we are faithful. Difficulties, temptations, huge griefs, loneliness of spirit, impulses of wrong, cares and anxieties, still make a great tribe of the children of Anak. We shall find them scattered all over the land—in Bashan and in Hebron, and throughout all the hill country. Wherever the conquest would be hard enough without them, there are they found to make it harder still. It is well to abjure self-deception. The way of righteousness is hard, and many a battle will try all our nerve and all our endurance. Life itself is stern and full of conflict. Be not surprised if the strain on you be terrific, if the number and force of the enemy alike distress you ; there has nothing new happened to you. All have had giants to fight with in their course through life. Israel could not possess the land until the giants were conquered, and your apprehensions of the future are so far accurate that you will have to encounter them without doubt. Secondly observe—

II. WE CANNOT HELP BEING AFRAID OF THEM, BUT WE MUST KEEP THE FEAR WITHIN PROPER LIMITS. It is useless to forbid fear, and perhaps unwise. Useless, because so long as our nervous system is what it is, and the possibilities of life are so solemn and various, it is inevitable that solicitude should be awakened. It would be unwise, for the fear, kept within proper limits, is one of the most valuable of all our instinctive emotions. The eye, by a sort of fear instinctively operative in it, brings down its lid over it whenever anything approaches it. And by the physical apprehensiveness of the organ itself its delicate arrangements are protected. And what is done for that organ by its nerves of peculiar sensibility is done for our lives in all their complexity by an instinctive apprehensiveness which "scents the danger from afar." While there are giants it is desirable that there should be some fear of them. For fear, within bounds, makes men brace up their energies— take all precautions against surprise, sends them to God for guidance and for help, sets them to repair their weak point, whatever it may be. It is only in excess that fear is mischievous—that is, when it occupies the entire thought, paralyses all the energies of the life, and itself directly aids the overthrow it was meant to avert. It may perhaps be expressed accurately thus : Fear is a good servant but a bad master. So long as it does not rule us, but only suggests precautions and helps to make our protection complete, so long it is a blessing. Whenever it becomes master, and commands instead of merely advising us, then our manhood is destroyed, and the ills we fear overtake us all the faster for our alarm. Israel did not do wrong in fearing the Anakim, but only in letting their fear exceed its proper limits, and fill their souls to the exclusion of all faith in God and hope of His help. Do not needlessly blame yourself for the agitation and apprehension produced by the possibilities of the future, only limit these things by faith and prayer and watchfulness, so that, thus kept in its place, your fear may serve you well. Thirdly observe—

III. Israel has not to fight the giants till it is strong enough to conquer them. Somehow—we hardly know how—the fight with the Anakim comes last. Perhaps because they occupied the fortresses formed by Nature—the mountain fastnesses; and naturally the first attention was given to the more regular and more numerous combatants inhabiting the cities. Whatever the reason, they were five years in the land before Caleb led the first attack on them (see ch. xiv. 10). And only when they were flushed with victory, every man a conqueror— when the *prestige* of their miraculous forces conquered men's hearts before a sword was drawn—only then are they exposed to the strain of what seemed such an unequal conflict. And meeting them when they were thus grown in courage and prowess, their defeat requires no more effort than many of the lesser struggles which taxed their less developed powers. There seems something here characteristic of a universal experience. God's Israel are never unequal for a conflict, when the time has come for it. There is always such growth of force, or such heavenly aid, that when the fight comes it is found that fitness for it has come before it. You perhaps look forward with extreme solicitude to the giants that will dispute your passage. Remember, there is some distance between you and them, and much may happen before you reach them. You are gathering strength every step you take on the right road. And every lesser victory is giving you force and nerve to win a greater one. And should the giants not die before you get to them, you will find that, like Israel, you have grown fit to fight them before you are called to fight them. You will be strong enough for victory over them before you are required to enter into conflict with them. Lastly observe—

IV. They found out that the worst part of the giants was the terror they could inspire. The great power of the giants was over the imaginations of their foes. And they had no real force at all equal to the terror they excited. Israel saw in imagination the size of the men, heard with alarm of the length of their spears and the weight of their armour. They did not remember that in any match between a great soul and a big body, the big body has but little chance. And so they were overpowered by the mere imagination of their enemy's force. But when they actually face them, they find that valour avails more than muscle, energy than height, faith than armour, soul than body. By beating them they found that the chief power of the giant was his power of affecting the imagination of his opponent. So is it still. "The worst ills are those that never happen," as the French proverb says. They threaten us, alarm us, agitate us, and after all turn off in some other direction, and do not come to us. And so is it with our giants. Their worst part is something which exists only in our imagination. They kill us by frightening us, and they frighten us by the powers they borrow from our imagination. Let us be of good courage and not afraid. And if giants many and strong threaten us let us keep fear in the bounds of faith, let us remember on warfare is ordained for us except where victory is possible, and let us put a check on the too easily affected imagination which needlessly dreads a foe, whose outward bigness is no accurate measure of the dimensions of his real force.—G.

Ver. 23.—*Rest from war.* These words bring us a grateful sense of relief. We are weary of reading the long catalogue of bloody victories—how of one city after another it is said, " They smote all the souls that were therein with the edge of the sword, utterly destroying them; there was not anything left to breathe." We are ready to say with the Prophet, " O thou sword of the Lord, how long will it be ere thou be quiet?" (Jer. xlvii. 6). If it were not for our conviction that an all-wise and righteous Divine purpose determined all this (Carlyle's distinction between the " surgery" of God's judgments and " atrocious murder "), we should turn with loathing from the sickening tale of slaughter. Certain thoughts about war are suggested.

I. THE CAUSES OF WAR. The baser passions of human nature are the sources from which it always more or less directly springs. These are the root of all its practical wickednesses. " Whence come wars and fightings among you? Come they not hence, even of your lusts that war in your members?" (James iv. 1). Vain ambition, the desire for territorial aggrandizement, the thirst for power, jealousy, revenge, &c.—these are the demons that kindle its destructive fires. Other and more plausible motives are but the false veil that hides their hatefulness. There is no real exception. Self-defence is no doubt an imperious instinct of nature, and there are interests (liberties, sanctities of social life, principles of eternal righteousness) which it may often be a noble thing for a nation, even by utmost force of arms to guard. But there would be no need to defend if there were no lawless lust or cruel wrong to endanger them. These " wars of the Lord" are no exception to the rule. They were waged by the Divine command, but their *cause* lay in the moral evil that cursed the land—those foul iniquities which, to the view of Infinite Wisdom, could be wiped out only by such a baptism of blood.

II. THE MISERIES OF WAR. It is the very symbol of almost all the woes of which human nature is capable, and that can darken with their shadow the field of human life. (1) The frenzy of malignant passions, (2) physical suffering, (3) the cruel rending of natural ties, (4) the arrest of beneficent industries, (5) the imposition of oppressive burdens, (6) the increase of the means and instruments of tyranny. These are some of the calamities that follow in the track of war. Their sadness and bitterness cannot be exaggerated.

III. THE POSSIBLE BENEDICTIONS OF WAR. It is a marvellous proof of the Divine beneficence that reigns supreme over all human affairs that even this deadly evil has something like a fair side to it, and is not unmixed with good. (1) It developes certain noble qualities of character—self-reliance, self-control, resolution, fortitude, mastery of adverse circumstances, &c.; so much so that men have been led to look upon the experience of great wars as essential to the vigorous life of a nation, necessary to save it from the lethargy of moral indifference and the enervating influence of self-indulgence. We may give due weight to those heroic qualities that war calls forth, and yet feel that they in no way counterbalance the crimes and horrors that attend it. (2) It prepares the way for new and better conditions. As storms clear the air, as a great conflagration in the city destroys its dens of shameful vice and loathsome disease, so wars which dislocate the whole frame of society, and let loose lawless passions, and inflict unspeakable miseries, do, nevertheless, often bring about healthier conditions of national life, and clear the ground for the spread of truth and righteousness. God " makes the wrath of man to praise him," though in itself it " worketh not his righteousness." And when the land rests from war there often arises a benign power of restoration that soon changes the face of things—

> " softening and concealing,
> And busy with its hand in healing,"

the rents and ravages the sweep of the destroyer may have made.

IV. THE CURE FOR WAR. There is no cure but that which is supplied by the redeeming influence of the Prince of Peace. (1) It will uproot and destroy those hidden evils in the heart of man from which all war arises, substituting for them that " love which worketh no ill to his neighbour." (2) It will turn those energies of our nature to which war gives a false and fatal impetus into worthier directions, enlisting them in a purely moral conflict with the abounding evils of the world (2 Cor. x. 4, 5; Eph. vi. 12—18).—W.

Ver. 23.—*Victory and rest.* I. THE TRUE CHRISTIAN WARFARE IS DESTINED TO END IN VICTORY. (1) Victory is *promised in God's Word.* From the first promise that " the seed of the woman should bruise the head of the serpent " (Gen. iii. 15), to the latest assurance of a " crown of life " to those who are " faithful unto death " (Rev. ii. 10), success is assured to the faithful soldier of God. So the land was taken " according to all that the Lord said unto Moses." (2) Victory is *secured by God's help.* In the passage of the Jordan, the fall of the walls of Jericho, and the success of the battle-field, it is everywhere indicated that God was aiding His people. In our spiritual warfare we are victorious because God is fighting for us (Psa. cxviii. 6), and gives us strength to fight (Psa. cxviii. 14), and because Christ has first conquered our enemies (John xvi. 33; 1 Cor. xv. 57). (3) Victory is *attained through our fighting.* " Joshua took the land " after hard fighting. The Christian must fight to win (Eph. vi 10, 11; 1 John v. 4).

II. WHEN VICTORY IS ATTAINED IT WILL BE AN AMPLE COMPENSATION FOR THE HARDSHIPS OF THE CHRISTIAN WARFARE. (1) The *fact of victory* will in itself be a great reward. To have conquered sin and mastered self and to be independent of the world will be attainments full of blessing. (2) Victory will introduce us to *a great inheritance.* We have our Canaan to possess after the battle of life is over. Heaven will be a great inheritance to us, as (*a*) the home of our souls and the abode of our Father, (*b*) the " land flowing with milk and honey," wherein our souls will receive all needful nourishment and inspiration ; (*c*) the place for peaceful, honourable service. After fighting the Israelites had leisure to till the soil and tend their flocks; after our fighting will come the happy service of heaven. (3) Victory will secure to us *rest from further warfare.* " The land rested from war." War is always an evil, though sometimes a necessary evil. Happy the land that has " rest from war " ! The Christian is not to live for ever in the toils and dangers of spiritual warfare. In heaven he will be free from the assaults of evil. Note : True rest is not rest from service—idleness, but rest from war—peace.—W. F. A.

Ver. 23.—*The promise fulfilled.* It is well to note the absolute fulfilment of God's promises. That which He has done for others He will do for us, if we trust Him. All who commit the keeping of their souls and the guidance of their life to Him have a promised land—the enjoyment of which seems often so distant as to move them to despair. Here we see a great promise grandly redeemed. God promised safe deliverance from Egypt, safe conduct to the promised land, and the possession of the whole of Canaan. And now we find Joshua took (ver. 18) " all that land, the hills and all the south country, and all the land of Goshen, and the valley, and the plain, and the mountain of Israel, and the valley of the same, even from Mount Halak that goeth up by Seir, down to Baal Gad in the valley of Lebanon under Mount Hermon." It took him several years—seven at least—to make the conquest. Even when made, and the enemies subdued, they were still in various localities in sufficient force to dispute the possession and enjoyment of certain points of the country. But the land of Canaan had become the possession of Israel, and was to continue to be theirs for more than a thousand years to come. It is a bright and conspicuous instance of God's faithfulness. Consider this fulfilment of promise. Observe—

I. IT DID NOT COME AS THE YOUNG MAN HOPED. When Joshua first came from Egypt he had doubtless his roseate dreams. To him the projected conquest would seem the easiest of all things. A journey of a few weeks, a bold entrance, a vigorous blow, the strenuous efforts of a united nation, helped by the enthusiasm of grace and the assistance of Providence—such would seem to him all that was requisite for complete and grand success. Even when he had traversed the land he still believed in the perfect possibility of its conquest, and had all a hero's difficulty in believing in anything tending to prevent it. But God's promise came, not as the young man hoped or expected. Youth sails too fast, underrates the difficulties to be surmounted, does not realise its own weakness, and the weakness of coadjutors, so that five-and-forty years elapse before the promise receives its ripe fulfilment. God's promises to us will all find realisation, but not quite so swiftly, perhaps, as in our youth we dream. Perfect victory over sin within ourselves will not be achieved in one conflict, and abuses will not be destroyed by one assault. The might of God's help is greater than ever we deem it, but our own weakness and faultiness are inadequately known. Our scheme of philanthropy will meet a stouter opposition and a feebler backing than we anticipate. Be not discouraged. God's promises will all be fulfilled, though not so fast as the young expect them. Observe secondly—

II. GOD'S PROMISE WAS FULFILLED EARLIER THAN THE MIDDLE-AGED MAN DARED TO HOPE FOR. I expect Joshua felt the years of pilgrimage longer than any one else felt them. "When would the nation be fit to strike for its earthly home?" Some centuries of bondage had been required to give them unity; would a similar stretch of wandering be required to produce courage and faith? To his eye, doubtless, virtues grew far too slowly. And when he witnessed their murmurings, their readiness to decline to lower paths and viler practices, there could hardly fail to rise within him the feeling that the conquest of the land was daily becoming a more distant thing. And when he saw three of the hardiest tribes settle on the east of Jordan, and saw a great reluctance on the part of the rest to cross that river, doubtless he began to think the promise of God tarried, and to wonder whether he would ever see his people settled. But faith sufficient to cross the Jordan and courage sufficient to take the land did not require centuries to grow. God's purposes ripened faster than the faith of even His most believing servants, and accordingly, in all probability, long before Caleb and Joshua would have dreamed the people ready for the task, Canaan is won. God sees more than we see. He hastes not, but He tarries not. Our despairing thoughts are not our wise ones. More forces are working on our side than we imagine. God sleeps not. The desire of your heart will come sooner than, in your despondency, you deem either likely or possible. And when, perhaps, hope deferred has made the heart sick, then, like a morning without clouds, it comes in all its fulness. Lastly observe—

III. WHEN GOD FULFILS HIS PROMISES, HE DOES SO GRANDLY. It is not half-done, or three-quarters. All the land is given them. Nay, good measure, pressed down and shaken together and running over. On the south their territory extends to Seir; on the east it passes over Jordan and embraces almost all within the edge of the desert. It is given easily. They have war, but no defeat; difficulties, but none insuperable; much left to be done (as in a new house there always is), but still the conquest is complete. Won far more easily than any could have imagined, the land is theirs. So in God's own time—*i.e.*, the really fittest time—every promise will be fulfilled. The promise of answers to our prayers, of the heart's desire, of a blessing on our work, of growth in grace, of the abundant entrance into the inheritance of the saints in light—all will be given to us at last, more richly, more fully, more easily than we have ever dared to hope.—G.

EXPOSITION.

CHAPTER XII. 1—24.

THE EXTENT OF JOSHUA'S CONQUESTS. Ver. 1.—**Now these are the kings.** The historian now enters upon a complete description of the whole territory which had, up to this date, fallen into the hands of the Israelites. First he traces out the border of the trans-Jordanic possessions of Israel, which he describes as bounded on the south by the river Arnon, on the west by course by the Jordan, and as extending from Hermon, past the Sea of Chinneroth, to the borders of the Dead Sea. The eastern border is not clearly defined, but the boundary extended far further eastward in the north than in the south, since the territory of Og was much more extensive than that of Sihon. On the west of Jordan the territory is described as extending " from Baal-gad in the valley of Lebanon (*i.e.*, Baalbec or Cæsarea Philippi; see note on ch. xi. 17) unto the Mount Halak which goeth up to Seir, which we have seen to be a range of mountains extending southward from near the south point of the Dead Sea. The border of the Israelitish possessions is more accurately defined in the succeeding chapters, but it was, after all, a slip of territory not more than 180 miles in length by about 100 in breadth. Its influence upon the history of the world, like that of Athens and Sparta, must not be measured by its size, but by its moral energy. As the former city has attained undying fame by its intellectual power, the second by its military capacity, so Palestine has derived her title to fame from her indestructible national life — indestructible because built alone, of all the religious systems of the ancient world, upon the foundations of the unity and Fatherhood of God; indestructible, moreover, because it came by revelation from God. There is no greater argument for the Divine origin of the Mosaic law than the unique spectacle of a national life like that of the Jews, subsisting for nearly two thousand years after their expulsion from their land. **From the river Arnon** (see Num. xxi. 24). The word Arnon signifies *the swift stream* (see Gèsenius, 'Thesaur.' s.v.). It is now called by the Arabs, *El-Mujeb*. Seetzen represents the region round its mouth to be naturally most fertile, but as abandoned now to a few wild plants. **Unto Mount Hermon.** Now *Jebel-es-Sheikh*. We have a vivid description of the scenery of Hermon in Psa. xlii., with the noise of its foaming torrents, the " deep calling unto deep " from the recesses of its dark ravines, where the infant Jordan rushed along its rocky bed. The Psalmist pictures to himself his troubles as overwhelming him like the billows of the numerous streams that streaked the mountain sides. And yet again Hermon is introduced as the image of peace and plenty and brotherly love. The refreshing dews which distilled from the side of the giant mountain were the source of blessing to those who dwelt afar off, and even the dry and parched sides of Mount Zion were cooled by their delicious influence. In Psa. xlii. 6 the Psalmist speaks of Hermon in the plural. Some have regarded this (*e.g.*, Ritter) as referring to the double peak of the mountain. The phrase most probably refers

to the region, though Hermon has really three peaks (see note on ch. xi. 3). **And all the plain on the east.** The Arabah (see ch. iii. 16). The depression of the Jordan, which lay eastward, of course, of Palestine. This is much insisted on in the following verses.

Ver. 2.—**The river Jabbok.** Literally, the pouring or emptying stream. It is remarkable that, while the LXX. renders here by χείμαῤῤος, a winter torrent, it steadily renders the same Hebrew word, when referring to Arnon, by φάραγξ. This latter word indicates the rocky cleft through which the water flows; the former, the fact that, though rapid and impetuous in winter, it was usually dried up in summer. Cf. the term χείμαῤῤος, applied to the Kedron by St. John (ch. xviii. 1); a remarkable instance of accuracy, by the way, if, as we are confidently told, the author of that Gospel was an Ephesine Gentile who had never seen Jerusalem and was imperfectly acquainted with Jewish localities and customs. The Jabbok has been identified with the Wady Zerka, or *blue stream*.

Ver. 3.—**And from the plain.** There is no "from" in the original, which here ceases to describe the territories of Sihon, but continues the account of the Israelite dominions, which included the Arabah (not the *plain* as in our version) up to the sea of Chinneroth. **On the east**; *i.e.*, the east of Jordan. So also below. **The way to Beth-jeshimoth** (see Num. xxxiii. 48, 49). There was a desert tract near the Dead Sea called Jeshimon, or the waste district. It is described by travellers as the most arid portion of the whole land. In this, Beth-jeshimoth (the house of desolations) was situated. It was south of the acacia meadows (see note on ch. ii. 1), and it formed part of the territory of Reuben (ch. xiii. 20). As it lay upon Jordan, it must have been near the extreme northernmost point of the Dead Sea. We are to understand, not that Sihon's territory extended to Beth-jeshimoth, but in that direction. Possibly some of the western Canaanitish tribes here extended their territories across the Jordan. **And from the south.** The word here is not Negeb, but Teman, *i.e.*, the literal south, which lay on the right (יָמִין) to one looking eastward. **Ashdoth-pisgah.** For Ashdoth see ch. x. 40. Pisgah was the northernmost point of the Abarim range, of which the well-known Nebo was the chief peak. Thither Moses went up to view the land which he was not permitted to enter. There Balaam built his seven altars and essayed in vain to curse the children of Israel. There were the watchmen (Zophim) stationed to protect the land, in the days before the Israelitish invasion, from the incursions of the tribes on the other side of Jordan (Num. xxiii. 14). The position of Pisgah has not been precisely identified, but the range extended on the eastern side of Jordan to a point nearly opposite Jericho. See Deut. xxxiv. 1.

Ver. 4.—**The giants.** Hebrew, *Rephaim* cf. Gen. xiv. 5 ; xv. 20 ; also Josh. xvii. 15). The word, according to Ewald, is equivalent to " s'retched out." It was also applied to the dead. The Rephaim were one of the various tribes of giants, like the Anakims, Zuzims, and Emims, of whom we read in the land of Canaan. They occupied the land of Bashan and " half Gilead "—that is, its northern portion (see Deut. iii. 13). The term " remnant " would imply that they had suffered some reverses at the hands of the other tribes, though they still remained in possession of their populous territory in the north. This view is confirmed by Gen. xiv. 5. **Ashtaroth** (see note on ch. ix. 10). **Edrei.** Or "the strong city," "the city of the arm," according to Gesen., ' Thes.,' s.v. This name, together with the immense number of ruined cities which have been found of late years in a marvellous state of preservation in this region, shows that Og was a powerful monarch. The ease with which he was overcome bears witness to the enervating effects of luxury and licentiousness upon a people of strong *physique*, vast numbers, and high civilisation.

Ver. 5.—**The Geshurites.** See ch. xiii. 2, 11, 13 ; and Deut. iii. 14; also 2 Sam. xiii. 37, where we find the principality of Geshur still in possession of its independence. It was in the north-east corner of Bashan, abutting upon Syria, and is called " Geshur in Syria " (2 Sam. xv. 8). It is perhaps an instance of undesigned coincidence that Maachah, the mother of Absalom and the daughter of the king of Geshur, was so named, since she probably derived her name from the adjoining territory of Maachah (see note on ch. xiii. 2).

Ver. 6.—**Moses, the servant of the Lord, gave.** Theodoret makes the tribes which received their inheritance through Moses the types of the believing Jews, and those who received it through Jesus (Joshua) the types of the believing Gentiles. Reuben, Gad, and Manasseh were the first-born of their respective mothers, and were thus types of the Jews, who were God's first-born. As they passed over armed before their brethren, so we received the good tidings of salvation from the lips of Jews. This is a characteristic specimen of the allegorical interpretation of the early fathers. But it will be observed that the children of Bilhah, who might have been selected more

naturally than those of Zilpah, are entirely omitted.

Ver. 7.—**And these are the kings of the country.** We now proceed to the enumeration of the kings whom Joshua had overcome on the western side of Jordan. And the first thing that strikes us is their immense number, as compared to the two potentates who alone occupied the large tract of country subdued on the other side of Jordan. Such a divided territory could hardly have maintained itself in the face of the powerful monarchs Sihon and Og to the eastward of Jordan. We are thus led to the conclusion that the smaller kings must have been tributary to some more powerful monarch who was the head of the confederacy. Such *Bretwaldas,* to borrow a term from our own history, the kings of Jerusalem and Hazor appear to have been, the one the head of the northern, the other of the southern tribes of Palestine, while possibly the five Philistine cities may have constituted another league, as they appear to have successfully defied the power of the Israelites from the first. That such confederacies existed at a much earlier time, we find from Gen. xiv. 1—5, where the king of Elam, or Persia, appears as the head of such an one, though of a more extensive character. The resistance to his power organised by the kings in the neighbourhood of the Dead Sea is another case in point. Possibly in later times Persia and Babylon found their hands full in their conflict with one another, and with Egypt under Thothmes III., as afterwards under the all-conquering Rameses II., better known as Sesostris, and they had to leave the tribes of Palestine awhile to themselves. Or the rulers of the central power at Carchemish (see Introduction) may have exercised a kind of suzerainty over all. The next point to be observed is that, in the list of kings that follows, a good many are mentioned beside those enumerated in ch. x. No doubt, as in the earlier history of this island, there were not only heads of leagues, and their tributary monarchs, but under-kings also, who were actually subject to the reigning monarchs, and involved in their fall. Compare the other cities mentioned in connection with Gibeon, ch. ix. 17. **Baal-Gad, in the valley of Lebanon.** See for this whole passage note on ch. xi. 16, 17.

Ver. 8.—**The mountains.** "Which, as the mountains of Judah (ch. xv. 48), Ephraim (ch. xvi. 1), and Naphtali (ch. xix. 32), ran through the midst of the land " (Knobel). See ch. xi. 16, 21, and note.

Ver. 9.—*The list of the cities subdued.* **The king of Jericho, one.** Here follows a list of the royal cities of the Canaanites, the remainder being daughter, or dependent cities, or else, perhaps, like Gibeon, cities whose government was not regal. See ch. ix. 3, and Introduction.

Ver. 13. — **The king of Geder.** Perhaps the same as Gederah in ch. xv. 36. If so, it is the Gedor of the Onomasticon, ten miles from Beit-Jibrin, or Eleutheropolis, now Jedireh. Conder, however, with whom Vandevelde seems to agree, places Geder in the mountain region, and identifies it with Gedor (ch. xv. 58) and the modern Jedûr, in the Hebron mountain. So Keil and Delitzsch, Robinson, and others. The Gedor in 1 Chron. iv. 39 may be the same place. It is described as on the east side of the "gai," or ravine, but no clearer indication of the place is given. It is, however, unlikely that the Simeonites would have found the children of Ham undisturbed in the mountains of Hebron in the reign of Hezekiah (see vers. 40, 41). The LXX. reads Gerar, and this is very probably the true reading. There was a "Nahal," or winter torrent, there (Gen. xxvi. 17, 19), and therefore possibly a "gai." The whole passage in 1 Chron. should be consulted.

Ver. 14.—**Hormah, Arad.** Cities in the Negeb, near the border of Edom (see Num. xiv. 45; xxi. 1, 3; xxxiii. 40). Hormah was originally known as Zephath (see Judg. i. 16, 17, where the fullest description of the locality is given). It was in the wilderness of Judæa, in the arid country (Negeb) of Arad. Mr. Palmer identifies it with Sebaita, in the centre of the Negeb, in the Magrah-el-Esbaita, a mountain valley sloping down into the Wady-el-Abyadh. Other explorers prefer Sulifât, and Rowlands and G. Williams, Sepata.

Ver. 15.—**Adullam.** In the Shephelah (*valley* in our version. See ch. xv. 33—35). Canon Tristram in his 'Bible Lands,' as well as Conder in his 'Handbook,' identify this with Aîd-el-Ma, or Mieh, in the Quarterly Paper of the Palestine Exploration Fund for July, 1875 (see also Jan., 1874), Lieut. Conder details a visit to this place, previously identified by M. Clermont-Ganneau. These explorers reject the idea approved by Vandevelde and others, that this Deir Dubban is the ancient Adullam. The place he prefers fulfils all requirements. It is in the Shephelah. It is near Jarmuth and Socoh. It is an ancient site with "rock-cut tombs, good water supply, and main road, and communications from different sides, and it is moreover a strong military position. It contains no remarkable cave, but a number of small ones, now used as habitations by the peasantry." Keilah, which David saved from the Philistines (1 Sam. xxiii. 1—5), was within a reasonable distance.

The present name, Aid-el-Ma or Mieh, the feast of the hundred, may be a misapprehension of the word Adullam similar to that which converts the Welsh "yr eifel," in Carnarvonshire, into the English "the rivals," or which identifies in many English names the English *burn* (brook) with the French *borne* (boundary). One of the greatest objections to the theory is that the Hebrew so frequently speaks of the place as Cave-Adullam (Ma'arah-Adullam), as though some special cave existed there. Adullam plays a somewhat important part in Scripture history. We hear of it as early as Gen. xxxviii., where Hirah the Adullamite is spoken of as a friend of the patriarch Judah. It is well known as the refuge of David and his mighty men (1 Sam. xxii. 1; 2 Sam. xxiii. 13—17). It was the place where David composed two of his psalms, the 57th and the 142nd. Rehoboam fortified it (2 Chron. xi. 7). It seems to be regarded as a refuge in Micah i. 15. And it is mentioned among the cities re-occupied after the return from the captivity in Neh. xi. 30.

Ver. 16.—**Bethel.** This city is here mentioned as smitten by Joshua. See notes on the capture of Ai, and Judg. i. 22—25.

Ver. 17. — **Tappuah.** Literally "apple city." It is difficult say whether this was Tappuah in Judah (ch. xv. 34; *cf.* ver. 53), or in Manasseh (ch. xvi. 8; xvii. 7, 8). The mention of Aphekah in ch. xv. 53, and of Aphek here, would suggest the former, or the mention of Socoh in ch. xv. 34 (see below on Hepher). But the mention of Lasharon, the fact that there is more than one other Aphek, that Tappuah on the borders of Ephraim and Manasseh seems to have been an important city, and that the cities of the south are mentioned first, those of the north afterwards, and that Tappuah seems to lie about midway, suggest the more northern city. This is Knobel's opinion. Gesenius inclines to the southern Tappuah. Conder identifies it with Yassûf, at the head of the Wady Kanah, south-east of Shechem. Vandevelde with 'Atûf, four hours north-east by east from Shechem. Keil prefers the former site. **Hepher.** This appears, from 1 Kings iv. 10, to have been near to Socoh, but nothing more is known of it. **Aphek.** Literally, *fortress*, though some think it comes from a Syriac root kindred to the Hebrew, signifying to *hold fast*, to *embrace*, and that it has reference to the sensual worship of Ashtaroth and Thammuz. There were several towns of this name (see notes on xiii. 4; xv. 53; xix. 30). **Lasharon** is probably the same as Sharon, or Hasharon (Isa. xxxiii. 9). This is the plain between Joppa and Carmel (Vandevelde). Conder and Knobel identify with Sarona, or Saroneh, a place near the sea of Tiberias. See, however, Acts viii. 32—38. **Madon** is mentioned in ch. xi. 1, and has been conjecturally identified with Madin, near the sea of Galilee. **Shimron-meron** is also mentioned in ch. xi. 1. It appears among the cities assigned to Zebulun in ch. xix. 15. Ewald ('Hist. Israel,' ii. 2 c.) remarks on the antiquity of this list, referring as it does to cities which are never heard of again. **Achshaph** lay within the borders of Asher (ch. xix. 25). It has been supposed to be the modern Yasîf, near the shores of the Mediterranean (see note on ch. xi. 1). **Taanach and Megiddo** are frequently mentioned together (see ch. xvii. 11; Judg. i. 27; v. 19). The former became a Levitical city. The latter, being in the great plain of Jezreel, or Esdraelon, lay in the way of most Eastern conquerors. Hence we find it mentioned in the Karnak inscription by the name of Magedi in the victorious expedition of Thothmes III., in which "the whole of the Syrian, Palestinian, and Arabian nations were overcome and forced to pay tribute." (Cooper, 'Egyptian Obelisks,' p. 33; see also 'Records of the Past,' i. 30). The great battle on the slopes of Mount Tabor was carried on as far as Megiddo (Judg. v. 19). Not far from this were the Midianites pitched, who fell victims to the valour of Gideon (Judg. vii.). Another and a disastrous battle of Megiddo, against the king of Egypt, weakened Judæa, and caused it to fall an easy victory to the power of Nebuchadnezzar (2 Kings xxiii. 29, 30; 2 Chron. xxxv. 20—24. The valley of Megiddo, or Megiddon, is mentioned in Zach. xii. 11. Solomon fortified Megiddo (1 Kings ix. 15), assigned it to Baana, the son of Ahilud, with Taanach, as one of the cities required to provide food for the royal household (1 Kings iv. 12.) And the Jewish writer of the Apocalypse makes this great battle - field of his race the scene of the battle of the great day of the Almighty (Rev. xvi. 14, 16). For Armageddon is Har Mageddon, the mountain of Mageddon, or Megiddo. Megiddo and Taanach are also found in later periods of Egyptian history. The Mohar mentioned above (ch. i. 4) notices the former among the places he visited ('Records of the Past,' vol. ii.), while the latter is among the places captured by Shishak, as an inscription testifies. The latest explorers reject the identification with Legio, or Lejjun, and suggest Mejedda, at the foot of Gilboa, near Beth - shean. See Palestine Exploration Fund, Quarterly Paper, January, 1877.

Ver. 22.—**Kedesh**, *i.e.*, Kedesh-Naphtali (see ch. xix. 7). **Jokneam of Carmel.** This city is mentioned as one of the cities of purveyance to Solomon's court (1 Kings iv. 12), with Beth-shean, Taanach, and Megiddo. It has been identified by explorers, from Robinson downwards, with Tell-el-Kaimun, on the southern slopes of Mount Carmel. It is the Cammona, or Cimana, of the Onomasticon, the "Cyamon over against Esdraelon" of Judith vii. 3. It was a Levitical city (ch. xxi. 34), but in the list in Chron. vi. we miss it in its proper place, and find it taking the place of Kibzaim in Ephraim. But, as the margin of our version remarks in the latter chapter (ver. 68), the names of the cities in the two lists very frequently do not correspond.

Ver. 23.—**The nations of Gilgal.** Or *the nations* that belong *to Gilgal.* This is identified by Vandevelde and Conder with Jiljulieh in the plain of Jordan, north of Antipatris, and is therefore, if this identification be correct, a third Gilgal. The word "nations" most probably signifies a diversity of tribes of various races gathered together under the headship of the king of Gilgal, much in the same way that the kingdom of Mercia arose in England from a confused mass of various tribes, gathered together on the *marches,* or military frontiers, between Britons, Saxons and English, or in the same way that the Austrian and Turkish empires have been formed out of a congeries of various nationalities. So we read of "Tidal king of nations" in Gen. xiv. 1. But others regard the "nations" (Goim) mentioned there as equivalent to the Gutium of the Babylonian tablets—*i.e.,* Semitic tribes imperfectly organised, then dwelling in Babylonia, and prefer the LXX. reading, Θαργάλ, in Gen. xiv. 1, which Sir Henry Rawlinson considers equivalent to the Accadian Tur Gal, or "great chief." So Sayce, 'Babl. Lit.,' p. 23; Tomkins, 'Studies on the Time of Abraham.' See Introduction III.

Ver. 24.—**Tirzah** meets us as the residence of the kings of Israel for a time in the narrative in 1 Kings. Jeroboam's wife went thither after her interview with Ahijah (ch. xiv. 17). Baasha dwelt there (ch. xv. 21, 33; xvi. 6), Elah was slain there by Zimri (ch. xvi. 9, 10), and it remained the capital until Omri built Samaria (ch. xvi. 23, 24). Thenceforward we hear no more of it till the time of Menahem (2 Kings xv. 14, 16), when it disappears from history. It has been variously identified—by Robinson and Vandevelde (whom Knobel follows) with Talluza, two hours' journey north of Shechem; by Conder with Teiasû, where there are numerous rock sepulchres. It was a place of great beauty, if we may judge from Cant. vi. 4, "Thou art beautiful, O my love, as Tirzah, comely as Jerusalem."

HOMILETICS.

Vers. 1—24.—*The extent of the conquest.*   A few detached considerations occur to us here.

I. GOD WILL NOT BE WORSE THAN HIS WORD.   The reduction of the whole land had not yet been effected, but it had been rendered possible if Israel were disposed to follow up his advantage.   The list of cities captured covers nearly the whole extent of Palestine, and Canaan had been deprived of all capacity of resistance. So it is with the Christian who has entered into covenant with God.   The mastery over sin has been placed in his power.   " Sin shall have no more dominion over him," unless he pleases.   Every part of his nature is under the dominion of Jesus. Satan and his angels can but cower and submit, unless the Christian prefer accommodation to warfare, and allow himself to be led into alliance or fellowship with evil.   It is the making marriages with Canaan, entering into amicable relations with the enemies he has subdued, that betrays Israel to his ruin.   God has placed everything in his power.   If he will not destroy his enemies when he can, he has but himself to blame.

II. ISRAEL'S POSSESSION IS A VARIOUS ONE.   The land of Israel had various characteristics.   Mountains and fertile plains, strange deep depressions, declivities, desert, dry arid ground, all formed part of the land flowing with milk and honey.   So in the Christian life there are diversities of gifts, but the same Spirit.   The heights of rank and intellect, the fertile soil of usefulness and energy, the depths of poverty, ignorance, and absence of mental power, the various inequalities of fortune, the trials of sorrow and adversity, the dryness of soul in prayer, the privation of sympathy and consolation—all these are various elements of the spiritual life, regions on the map of the spiritual Canaan; but all are subject to the power of Jesus, and may, if we will, be made useful in His cause.   As the most arid or the most rocky soil in Palestine became, by man's industry, highly productive, so the oil, olive, and honey, the figs, and pomegranates, and vines of our spiritual Israel, may be raised, if we will but be fellow-workers with God, out of the most unpromising natural disposition.

III. JOSHUA'S VICTORIES WERE CAREFULLY KEPT IN REMEMBRANCE.   So may the Christian, at the end of a long career under the guidance of God's Spirit, look back to the former triumphs he has achieved by His aid, provided he does so in no spirit of Pharisaical boasting, but in gratitude to Him who " has done so great things for him."   Many a victory over his enemies without and within, many a recollection of a hard-fought field, will occur to the veteran in Christ's army when, in the evening of life, he turns his thoughts backward to review the past.   And so will the student of history as he reflects on the manifold difficulties encountered by God's Church, and the number and power of the confederacies arrayed against her, enumerate with loving pride the cities she has destroyed, and look forward with confidence to her final triumph.

HOMILIES BY VARIOUS AUTHORS.

Vers. 7—24.—*The catalogue of the vanquished.*   A melancholy document, meaning little more to us than a column in a directory, but meaning much to multitudes.   Many of these kings would be lamented in elegies as sweet as David's song over Saul and Jonathan.   Some, doubtless, were noble, perhaps some devout, but implicated in a national fate to the deserving of which they had not contributed.   Linger over these a little and observe—

I. ALL ARMIES WILL FIND THEIR PLACE IN ONE OF TWO CATALOGUES—THAT OF VICTORS, OR THAT OF VANQUISHED.   We lament that to place Israel God must displace others.   That heroism conquering a home assumes also heroism fighting in vain to keep one.   Life in its deepest action must always be a struggle, ending in victory or defeat.   Every foolish life ends in failure, and in a consciousness like that of a beaten general, of plans unwisely formed and forces unhappily employed. Those who follow God's guidance in all the affairs of life are fighters in a combat in which their success confers blessings on themselves and on society at large. All who refuse God's guidance in their general affairs are fighters in a combat in which their success, if achieved, would damage others still more than their failure would hurt themselves. Those who choose wrongly thus find life a losing game, a disastrous battle. It would be well if all realised that *not to win a victory with life is to suffer a terrible defeat*, is to be left with loss of power, and with infinite damage. In one or other list we all shall be. Crowned as victors, humiliated and discredited as failures.

II. Most of those in that list never expected to be in it. Why should they? They had theories like ours to-day of the superiority of training in arms, of fortifications, of what they called their civilisation, to any rude force which nomadic hordes could bring. But they are beaten. Pride goeth before destruction. Many reliant in their strength of purpose are destroyed by temptations they despised. Youth dreams of only bright and golden issues to its life. Too often the only issues are deplorable. Do not assume your life is going to be a grand success. Victory is desert—not drift, achievement—not accident. Even to retain requires energy. These men could not transmit to others what had been transmitted to them.

III. They were not saved by profession of sanctity. Some of the cities here had already had a long reputation for sanctity. "Jerusalem" had been Melchizedek's seat; "Bethel," the old name of the locality (though the city was Luz), means "the house of God." "Kedesh" means "a holy place." These all seem to have been spots consecrated to the service of the true God. Consecrated peoples have God's protection; consecrated places go without. "Judgment" does not spare, it "begins with the house of God." Later inhabitants of Jerusalem may say, "The temple of the Lord, the temple of the Lord are these." But the sanctity of the site increases, it does not avert the punishment of those profaning it. There is something very solemn in this removal of the candlesticks which had served the Pre-Abrahamic Church. England is to-day a great Bethel, a sublime Kedesh. May we have grace to act worthily of, and so retain, our eminence.

IV. The individual shares the fate of the community. Some of these kings and their people, doubtless, were worthy of a better fate. But implicated in the fortunes of the general community, leaguing with it for its defence, they come in for its fate. It is strange how the individual has to share the lot of the community. The accident of our birth may determine our calling, our fortune, even our creed, and our character. Advantages for which others have wrought, disabilities which others have transmitted, are inherited by us. "Other men have laboured, and we have entered into their labours." Sometimes other men have sinned, and we have entered into their penalty. There is, indeed, an inner realm whose fortunes depend only on ourselves. But we are members one of another, and must participate the general fortune. *We should therefore cherish more patriotism, more religious interest in our country's politics and action.* The welfare of those yet unborn depends on the wisdom of the generation to-day existent. Let us not leave to our successors a "heritage of woe," such as was left to these kings of Canaan. Look on them with pity, with modest humility, asking of your soul, "Who maketh thee to differ?" It may be some Canaanitish bard lamented the dead at the waters of Merom, as the Scottish bard did those who fell at Flodden, and sang tenderly of "the flowers of the forest being a' wede away." Let us be thankful that in the past we have been spared such a doom, and careful in the future to avoid it.—G

Vers. 7, 8.—*Diversity of lots.* The diversity of situation and character in the several lots of the tribes of Israel is illustrative of the similar diversity which is seen in all human experience.

I. Diversity of lots is a necessity. If we could attain uniformity we could not retain it. (1) Diversity necessarily results from the inevitable differences in the arrangement of the *physical world* and the course of external events. The world is not large enough for all men to live on the most fertile soil and in the most genial climate. (2) Diversity is also necessitated by the difference in *human capacities*. Since these sources of diversity are found in nature, they must be sanctioned by God. Therefore to complain of them is (*a*) futile, (*b*) distrustful.

II. Diversity of lots is less severe than it appears to be. (1) There is much *compensation* for inequality. We are inclined to notice only the hardships of our own lot and the favourable circumstances of our neighbour's. There are cares peculiar to riches and blessings peculiar to poverty. (2) *Custom* accommodates us to our lot. It softens the hardest lot and robs the pleasantest of its interest. The back becomes fitted to the daily burden. The daily luxury becomes insipid. (3) Happiness depends more on the character of the *inner life* than on the circumstances of the external lot. A peaceful mind is better than all riches. The cheerful poor man is more favoured by Providence than the melancholy rich man (Prov. xv. 17).

III. Diversity of lots is beneficial to us individually. Justice is not equality, but fitness. It is not fit that we should all receive equal lots. For some the highlands are most fit, for some the plains, for some the valleys. (1) Fitness depends on our *capacity*. One can serve best in one lot, and another with different faculties in a totally different lot. The talents are given " to every man according to his several ability " (Matt. xxv. 15). (2) It depends on our *disposition*. We are not all capable of appreciating the blessings which are given to others. If we chose for ourselves we could not tell what would be most agreeable to us until we had experienced all kinds of lots. We often think we should enjoy things for which we have no capacity, as weak and timid people, delighting in stories of adventure, imagine they should like to be the heroes of them. (3) It depends on our *need*. Our lots are apportioned to us for probation, discipline, and education. The lot which is most attractive may not be most beneficial. Various methods of training are needed according to our various characters. Some plants flourish best in the sunshine, others in the shade. Some souls are healthiest in prosperity, others in adversity.

IV. Diversity of lots is useful for the general welfare of mankind. Dull uniformity would leave human life at a low level. Civilisation must become complex as it advances. Diversity of lots is necessary for division of labour. " The whole family " is most prosperous when the several members quietly accept their various lots. The mountain lot serves for the shepherd and his flock, the valley for the tiller of the soil. Thus the common life of the whole nation is advanced. They who suffer most often have a special part to serve in the ministry of life for the good of their brethren.—W. F. A.

Vers. 12, 13.—*The partition of the land of Canaan.* " Now therefore divide this land for an inheritance unto the nine tribes " (ver. 7). In the partition of the land of Canaan there was nothing arbitrary. God Himself directed it, and assigned to each tribe its lot, save only to the tribe of Levi, which was to occupy an exceptional position. There was a very special reason why the inheritance of the various tribes should be marked out by God Himself, since Israel was His chosen people, destined to give to the world its Messiah and Saviour, so that nothing could be indifferent in its history. Every tribe was to feel that in tilling the soil allotted to it, it was accomplishing the task which God had given. Every tribe knew that it held its possessions directly from God, and that it was in His name its appointed work was to be done. Thus everything even in the outward life of Israel was elevated, ennobled, and consecrated. Let us apply these same principles, first to God's greater people—mankind—and then to the Church and to the family. (1) St. Paul in his sermon at Athens said that " God had made of one blood all nations to dwell on all the face of the earth, and had determined the times before appointed, and the bounds of their habitation; that they might seek the Lord " (Acts xvii. 26). Thus the natural fatherland has been determined for every nation by God Himself. This is the heritage He has assigned to each, to be received in humble recognition of His fatherly will, and with the grateful acknowledgment of all the capacities for its development.   But if God has thus given man an inheritance in this great world, He has done so not only in order that man may supply himself with food and with all that is essential to his bodily well-being ; it is not even that he may avail himself of all the appliances of a brilliant civilisation.   It is that he may fulfil here upon earth his higher destiny; that He may seek God and serve Him.   Every nationality has its mission in this great work; it has its special gifts to employ for the common cause.   Each one is to rehearse in its own tongue the wonderful works of God, and to glorify Him as it has opportunity.   (2) Every family is in like manner bound to recognise the hand of Providence in its earthly lot.   Whether it be straitened by poverty, or abounding in wealth, it is equally bound to serve God in the station wherein He has placed it.   All outward prosperity is to be received and held as a trust from Him.   It is no more ours of right than the land of Canaan belonged to the Israelites.   " The earth is the Lord's and the fulness thereof," and we are His stewards.   It is for Him we are bound to use it; and to use it for Him is to use it for the good of our fellows, since He reckons any love and service done to them as to Himself.   Nor is it only for our material possessions, but for our whole position and attitude among our fellow-men, that we are responsible to God.   Whether masters or servants, princes or peasants, our lot has been assigned us by God for one sole end, namely His service.   Thus before Him, and in view of this Divine purpose, there is no distinction of rank.   All that is done for Him acquires dignity from that fact.   The one essential is that in our earthly life, whether high or low, we do His work.   The poor are often richest towards God, like that tribe of Levi, which, though it possessed not a foot of land, was, as we shall see, the great spiritual aristocracy of Israel.—E. DE P.

EXPOSITION.

CHAPTER XIII. 1—33.

THE DIVISION OF THE TERRITORY.—Ver. 1. —**Now Joshua was old.** This is usually regarded as the second part of the Book of Joshua ; the first being devoted to the history of the conquest of Palestine, while the second is engaged with the history of its division among the conquerors.   Dean Stanley, in his ' Sinai and Palestine,' as well as in his ' Lectures on the History of the Jewish Church,' describes this portion of the Book of Judges as the 'Domesday Book' of the land of Canaan, and the remark has been constantly repeated.   There is, however, a considerable difference between the great survey of the Conqueror and this one.   The former was an accurate account, for purposes of taxation, national defence, and public order, of the exact extent of soil owned by each landowner, and it went so far as to enumerate the cattle on his estate, to the great disgust of the Saxon chronicler, who had an Englishman's dislike of inquisitorial proceedings.   There is no trace either of such completeness, or of such an inquisitorial character in this survey, neither has it quite the same object.   It assigns to each tribe the limits of its future possessions, and enumerates the cities contained in each portion of territory.   But it makes scarcely any effort to describe the pos-

sessions of particular families, still less of individual landowners.   Joshua and Caleb are the only exceptions.   Knobel observes that the most powerful tribes were first settled in their territory—those, namely, of Judah and Joseph.   He remarks that the author must have had written sources for his information, for no single Israelite could have been personally acquainted with all the details here given.   **And stricken in years.** Rather, *advanced in age.* There is no foundation for the idea of some commentators that the Jews, at the time this book was written, made any formal distinction in these words between different stages of old age.   The Hebrew language rejoiced in repetition, and this common phrase is only a means of adding emphasis to the statement already made.   **And there remaineth yet very much land to be possessed.** The Hebrew מְאֹד is stronger than our version.   Perhaps the best equivalent in modern English is, " *And the amount of land that remaineth for us to occupy is very great indeed.*" We may observe here that, as with the literal so with the spiritual Israel, whether the antitype be the Christian Church or the human heart, the work of subduing God's enemies is gradual.   One successful engagement does not conclude the war.   The enemy renews his assaults, and when force fails he tries fraud ; when direct temptations are of no avail he resorts to enticements. The only safeguard in the war is strength, alertness, courage, patience. The faint-hearted and unwatchful alike fail in the contest, which can be carried on successfully only by him who has learned to keep guard over himself, and to direct his ways by the counsels of God.

Ver. 2.—**This is the land which yet remaineth.** The powerful league of the Philistines, as well as the tribes near them, remained unsubdued. In the north, likewise, the neighbourhood of Sidon, and the territory of Cœle, Syria, which lay between Lebanon and Anti-Lebanon, was as yet in the hands of the enemy. Rabbis Kimchi and Solomon Jarchi translate by "borders." Masius suggests the French *marque* (which was the old German *mark*), and the modern German *grenze*. **All the borders of the Philistines.** Literally, all the *circles* (Geliloth) of the Philistines. The expression is found in several places in this book (see ch. xviii. 17 ; xxii. 10, 11). We may compare the expression the *circles* of Swabia, Franconia, &c., in the history of Germany. The expression here may have more affinity with what is known as the "mark system" in the history of ancient Germany, and refer to the patch of cultivated ground which extended for some distance round each city. But this is rendered improbable by the fact that one circle only retained its name (ch. xx. 7 ; xxi. 32), and is still known as Galilee (see notes on these passages). Galilee was too large a district to have been originally a clearing round a town. **Geshur** (see note on ch. xii. 5). Ewald (see also Hitzig,'Geschichte des Volkes Israel,' p. 20) conjectures that these Geshurites were the aboriginal inhabitants of the country (see 1 Sam. xxvii. 8), and were the same as the Avites or Avvites. See next verse, where the Avvites are distinguished from the five lords of the Philistines. It is worthy of remark that the name Talmai, the name of one of the "sons of Anak " (ch. xv. 14), comes in again as the name of a king of Geshur (2 Sam. iii. 3 ; xiii. 37). It occurs, however, as a Hebrew name in Bartholomew, or Bar-Tolmai, *i.e.*, the son of Talmai, or Tolmai, one of the twelve apostles. Ewald supposes that these aborigines were dispossessed by the Canaanitish tribes, and that the old name of Geshur was still applied to those regions on which this primitive race had retained its hold.

Ver. 3.—**From Sihor.** This word, which has the article in Hebrew, is literally *the black river.* This has been thought to be the Nile, known to both Greeks and Latins by that title. The Greeks called it μέλας. So Virgil says of it, "Ægyptum nigra fœcundat arena." The Vulgate has " a fluvio turbido qui irrigat Ægyptum." The LXX. translates by ἀοίκη-

τος. The phrase which is "before " (עַל־פְּנֵי) Egypt seems to exclude the idea of the Nile, since the Nile flowed through the centre of Egypt, and it is impossible to make עַל־פְּנֵ equivalent to בְּקֶרֶב. As Drusius remarks, moreover, the Nile is always called either יְאֹר or " the river of Egypt." The interpretation which has found most favour of late, therefore, refers this expression to a small river that flows into the sea at the extreme southern border of Palestine. This river was known as the " river of Egypt" (Gen. xv. 18), and is now called the *Wady-el-Arisch* (cf. also ch. xv. 4, 47, as well as Num. xxxiv. 5 ; 1 Kings viii. 65 ; Isa. xxvii. 12, where the word is *nahal*, or *winter torrent*, a word inapplicable to the Nile). For Sihor, or Shichor, see Isa. xxiii. 3 ; Jer. ii. 18, and especially 1 Chron. xiii. 5, which seems decisive against the Nile. **Which is counted to the Canaanite.** These words are connected by the Masorites with what follows : *The five lords of the Philistines are reckoned to the Canaanite.* **The five lords of the Philistines.** The Philistines (Deut. ii. 23. Cf. Gen. x. 14, and 1 Chron. i. 12) are supposed to be of Egyptian origin. Ewald (also Hitzig, ' Geschichte des Volkes Israel,' p. 20) believes Caphtor to be Crete, and supposes the Cherethites and Pelethites who formed David's body-guard (2 Sam. xv. 18) to be Cretans and Philistines (see Ezek. xxv. 16). But this opinion is disputed by many commentators of note, and is far from probable in itself. They were David's most trusted and faithful troops, and it seems hardly probable that so truly national a monarch would have assigned the post of honour around his person to the hereditary enemies of his race. Ritter, however, believes the Cherethites and Pelethites to be Philistines, and appeals to 1 Sam. xxx. 14, and still more forcibly to Zeph. ii. 4, 5. It should be remembered, too, that Ittai was a Gittite, or native of Gath (see 2 Sam. xv. 21). The term here used, translated *lords* (*satraps*, LXX.), is peculiar to the Philistines. It is to be found also in Judg. iii. 3 ; 1 Sam. v. 8, &c. In 1 Kings vii. 30 the word means an *axle*, or perhaps the outside plating of the wheel, and in the kindred languages it signifies a wheel. The expression is remarkable in connection with the phrase " *circles* of the Philistines." **The Eshkalonites.** The inhabitants of Ashkelon, as the Gittites are of Gath. **Also the Avites.** Literally, "*and the Avites.*" There is no " also " in the original, though the Avites or Avim are supposed (see Deut. ii. 23, and note on Geshuri in the last verse) to have been aborigines preceding the Canaanites, and dispossessed by the Philistines. Keil, however, disputes this view, and holds that we have no evidence that any but a Canaanitish people dwelt in south-western Palestine. This Canaanitish tribe, he thinks, was driven out by the Philistines. Some few of the Avites, or rather Avvites, continued to dwell among their conquerors. But the coincidence between Deut. ii. 22, 23, and 1 Sam. xxvii. 8, makes strongly for Ewald's view above. And Keil and Delitzsch, in their later joint work, incline to it. See Introduction III. The word Avvim, like Havoth, or Havvoth (see ver. 30), is supposed to mean villages, or inhabited enclosures.

Ver. 4.—**From the south.** The LXX. and the best modern commentators connect these words with what precedes. This gives a better sense than joining it to what follows. For the south was not " all the land of the Canaanites," but a large part of it belonged, as we have just seen, to a tribe *not* of Canaanitish origin, while the land of the Canaanites (see note on ch. iii. 10) extended far to the northward. Therefore we must understand the words " all the land of the Canaanites " to begin a fresh section, and to be descriptive of the territory extending from Philistia northward towards Sidon. So the Chaldee, Syriac, and Arabic. **Mearah.** The margin has " the cave." But there is no article in the original. The LXX. reads ἀπὸ Γάζης for Mearah, having clearly, as Masius observes, substituted Zain for Resh. But this mistaken reading compels a mistranslation of the passage. Vandevelde supposes it to be a remarkable cave still existing near Sidon, which is mentioned by William of Tyre as having been fortified by the Crusaders. He speaks of it as *municipium quoddam*, and states that it was commonly known as the " cave of Tyre." " spelunca inexpugnabilis." It was afterwards " the last retreat of the Emir Fakkred-Dîn " (Vandevelde, s.v. Mearah). There is a village now, north of Sidon, called Mogheiriyeh, or the village of the cave. So also Knobel. **Beside the Sidonians.** Rather, *near*, or *in the direction of*, or *which belongs to*, the Sidonians. **Aphek.** Or *Aphekah*. This (Knobel) was the northern Aphek (ch. xix. 30 ; Judg. i. 31), in the tribe of Asher, known later as Aphaca, and now as Afka. Not the Aphekah of ch. xv. 53, probably the Aphek of 1 Sam. iv. 1. It is the same Aphek which in later times was captured by the Syrians, and was the scene of several decisive victories of Israel (1 Kings xx. 26, 30 ; 2 Kings xiii. 17). It is doubtful which Aphek is meant in ch. xii. 18, though it is probably the southern Aphek. The situation is described as one of "rare beauty "

(Delitzsch), " on the north-west slopes of Lebanon," amid exquisite groves (Conder). Here the Syrian Astarte was worshipped, and the ruins of her temple, dedicated to her as mourning for Tammuz, or Adonis, may still be seen. See Kenrick, ' Phœnicia,' 310, 311, and Mover's ' Die Phönizier,' i. 192. Perhaps it was never actually occupied by the Asherites, but remained in the hands of Syria, and as a place of great resort was the natural point to which the attacks of Israel would be directed. Vandevelde, however, believes in four and Conder in *seven* cities of this name, and they suppose the Aphek which was the scene of the battle with the Syrians to have been on the east of Jordan, from the occurrence of the word " Mishor " in the narrative in 1 Kings xx. The term " Mishor " is, however, applied to other places beside the territory east of Jordan (see Gesenius, s.v. Mishor). The Aphek in 1 Sam. xxix. 1 cannot be identified with any that have been named. **To the borders of the Amorites.** This can hardly be anything but the northern border of the kingdom of Bashan, in the neighbourhood of Mount Hermon.

Ver. 5.—**The Giblites.** The inhabitants of Gebal, called Jebail (*i.e.*, hill-city, from *Jebel*) by the Arabs, and Byblus by the Greeks. This is Masius's idea, and other commentators have accepted it (see 1 Kings v. 32 ; Psa. lxxxiii. 7 ; and Ezek. xxvii. 9, where the LXX. translates by Byblus). In the first-named passage the word is translated " stone squarers," in our version (where it is the 18th and not the 32nd verse). All the other versions render " Giblites " as here, and no doubt the inhabitants of the Phœnician city of Jebail are meant, since in the ruins of Jebail the same kind of masonry is found as is seen in Solomon's temple. Byblus (Kenrick, ' Phœnicia,' l.c. Movers, l.c. Lenormant, ' Manual of the History of the East,' ii. 223) was the great seat of the worship of Tammuz, or Adonis. Here his father Cinyras was supposed to have been king, and the licentious worship, with its corrupting influences, was spread over the whole region of Lebanon and even Damascus. This territory was never actually occupied by the Israelites (see for this passage also ch. xi. 8, 17 ; and xii. 7). **Hamath.** The spies penetrated nearly as far as this (Num. xiii. 21), and David reduced the land into subjection as far as the borders of this territory. But the Israelites never subdued it. Toi, king of Hamath, was an ally, not a tributary of David (2 Sam. viii. 9). The border of Israel is always described as extending " to the entering in of Hamath " (1 Kings viii. 65 ; 2 Kings xiv. 25), though Jeroboam II.

is said to have "recovered" (v. 28) Hamath itself. This "entering in of Hamath" commences at the end of the region called Cœle Syria, according to Robinson, 'Later Biblical Researches,' sec. 12, at the north-east end of the Lebanon range. So Vandevelde and Porter. Vandevelde remarks that the expression refers to an "entrance formed by Nature herself," namely, the termination of the Lebanon and Anti-Lebanon ranges. The city of Hamath, which gave its name to the territory, is situated on the Orontes, and was known later as Epiphaneia, no doubt after Antiochus Epiphanes, king of Syria.

Ver. 6.—**All the Sidonians.** The word כֹּל here, as elsewhere, must be taken in a restricted sense. A large portion of the Sidonian territory was taken, but Sidon retained its independence (see Judg. i. 31, 32). It is clear, too, that the promise was conditional. Had not the Asherites been willing to tolerate the existence of the Canaanites in their midst, they need not have done so (see Judg. i. 28).

Ver. 8.—**With whom.** Literally, *with him.* The construction is defective, but the meaning is clear enough. To avoid the repetition of the words "the half-tribe of Manasseh," the historian writes עִמּוֹ meaning thereby the *other* half of the tribe.

Ver. 9.—**Aroer.** Three, or even four, cities of this name were known, and have been identified by modern travellers under names somewhat similar. 1. Aroer upon Arnon, on the north bank of that river, at the extreme south of the territory of Reuben (see Deut. ii. 36; iii. 12; iv. 48; Josh. xii. 2; xiii. 9, 16; and probably Jer. xlviii. 19). 2. Aroer in Gad (ch. xiii. 25), described there as "before," *i.e.*, on the way to "Rabbah." It was no doubt some short distance to the westward of this chief city of the Ammonites (see also Num. xxxii. 34, where the Gadites are said to have built it). These two are probably the "cities of Aroer" referred to in Isa. xvii. 2 (but see next note but one, where also 2 Sam. xxiv. 5 will be discussed). 3. A city in Judah (1 Sam. xxx. 28). To one of these cities probably belonged Shammah or Shammoth, the Hararite or Harorite (2 Sam. xxiii. 11; he is called Harodite in ver. 25, and 1 Chron. xi. 27). **The river Arnon** (see note on ch. xii. 2). **The city that is in the midst of the river.** This city (or perhaps cities) has received but little attention from commentators, probably by reason of its bearing no name. Those who have tried to identify it have failed In Deut. ii. 36, in this passage, and in 2 Sam. xxiv. 5, it is mentioned in connection with Aroer. In ch.

xii. 2, instead of "the city that is in the midst of the river," we find simply "the middle (תּוֹךְ) of the river." But as 2 Sam. xxiv. 5 stands in our version, the city referred to stood in the middle of the *river of Gad.* This would suggest the idea that the old derivation of Aroer by Wells and others from the word עִיר (city) doubled, with the signification of the *double city,* is nearer the mark than that of *wasteness,* or *desolateness,* or nakedness, as of a region bare of trees, which has found favour of late, and it is not without support in Hebrew forms. A city, moreover, in the midst of or "on the brink of" a winter torrent would be less likely to be waste or desolate than in other situations. But we are not yet at the end of our difficulties. The word Nahal, which comes before Gad in the passage of which we are now speaking, has the article. Thus the translation, "river of Gad" cannot be maintained. And besides, the enumeration of the people must have begun at the Arnon, or southern border of Israel beyond Jordan. It is possible that the text may be corrupt here, as it is in other parts of 2 Samuel, and possibly the meaning may be that the officers pitched in Aroer, passed through Reuben, and having come within the confines of Gad arrived at Jazer. This again is rendered doubtful by the close connection of Aroer and Jazer in ch. xiii. 25. It is of course, therefore, possible that the reference in 2 Sam. xxiv. is to the Jabbok, not the Arnon ravine. A question of such intricacy can only be settled, if settled at all, by an investigation on the spot. **The plain.** The word here is מִישׁוֹר. This, derived from the root יָשַׁר signifies level ground, and is applied to the region north of Moab, especially that part of it which belonged to Reuben. Flat, and almost unbroken, even by trees, it was particularly adapted for grazing land (see also note above, and on ver. 4). **Medeba.** This is mentioned in Scripture, together with Dibon, as here in Num. xxi. 30; Isa. xv. 2. It was on the level ground before mentioned (see Gesenius, s.v. מִישׁוֹר). **Dibon** (see Jer. xlviii. 18, 22, called Dimon in Isa. xv. 9; but Dibon in Isa. xv. 2; see also Num. xxxiii. 45, 46). It was one of the cities built by the children of Gad (Num. xxxii. 34). It is now called Dhibân, and is a short distance north of the Arnon. The Moabite stone, found at Dibon in 1868, mentions the occupation of Medeba by Omri, and implies that Dibon, the principal city in those parts, was also subject to him, but recovered finally by Mesha.

Ver. 11.—**Geshurites and Maachathites.**

See note on chap. xii. 5, of which this passage is little else but a repetition.

Ver. 12.—**Giants.** See note on ch. xii. 4.

Ver. 14.—**Only unto the tribe of Levi.** See Num. xviii. 20—24, where the original command is recorded. Like the clergy under the Christian dispensation, it was seen that they could not at once perform the duties of the priesthood, and act as instructors of the people, if they were burdened, like the rest, with the duty of carrying on war. Their place was supplied by the division of the tribe of Joseph into two, so that the inheritance of Israel was still divided among twelve tribes. Bähr, in his ' Symbolik des Alten Testaments,' ii. 48, 49, gives other reasons for the dispersion of the Levites throughout the land. If the Levites were to keep the Law and Word of God, to take measures for its being properly kept by the nation in general, to spread abroad a knowledge of the precepts of the religion of Israel, to stir up the tribes to a devout and religious life, it was not merely desirable, but absolutely necessary, that they should be scattered among the tribes. On the other hand, to secure a proper *esprit de corps*, a mutual sustaining influence, and a common action, too complete a dispersion would have been a mistake. Hence their collection into the Levitical cities, which, however (see note on ch. xxi. 11), were not given up wholly to them. The Divine wisdom which dictated the provisions of the Mosaic law is clearly visible here. The instinct of the Christian Church in early times devised a similar provision for the evangelisation of the people in the organisation of the ancient and mediæval cathedrals. **As he said unto them.** This quotation of Num. xviii. 20, 24 by a later writer would, under all ordinary circumstances, be regarded as a proof that the Book of Joshua was quoting one of the books of Moses. But the "Elohistic" and "Jehovistic" theory escapes this conclusion in the cumbrous fashion to which reference has been already made. Origen regards this passage as symbolical of the more spiritually earnest among the laity, who "so excel others in virtue of mind and grace of merits, as that the Lord should be called their inheritance." "How very rare," he says, "are those who devote themselves to wisdom and knowledge and preserve their mind clear and pure, and exercise their minds in all excellent virtues, who illuminate the way wherein they walk for simpler souls by the grace of learning, and thus attain to salvation. They are the true priests and Levites, whose inheritance is the Lord, who is wisdom" (Hom. 17 on Joshua). **The Sacrifices.** The word is derived from עִשָּׁה *fire*. It does not itself, as

Keil asserts, signify *fire* in any place in Holy Writ, but it is used of the shewbread in Levit. xxiv. 7, 9. It thus came to mean any sacrifice, whether offered by fire or not. And thus the tenth which (Num. xviii. 21, 23, 24) was given to the Levites, as being offered for God's service, might be reckoned as in some sense a sacrifice. With this passage we may compare various passages in the New Testament, where, in this respect at least, the Christian ministry stands on the same footing (1 Cor. ix. 11, 13 ; Gal. vi. 6, 7). Thus the maintenance of the Christian ministry is a kind of sacrifice—as we find such deeds called, in fact, in Heb. xiii. 16. And an order of men who are set apart to the ministry of souls has a right to claim a sufficient maintenance at the hands of those to whom they minister—a point which in these days of affluence and clerical destitution combined ought to be more largely recognised than it is (see Num. xviii. 20—24). " For the law is entrusted to the priests and Levites, and they devote their energies to this alone, and without any anxiety are able to give their time to the Word of God. But that they may be able to do this, they ought to depend upon the support of the laity. For if the laity do not allow the priests and Levites all the necessaries of life, they would be obliged to engage themselves in temporal occupations, and would thus have less time for the law of God. And when they had no time to spare for the study of God's law, it is thou who wouldst be in danger. For the light of knowledge that is in them would grow dim, because thou hast given no oil for the lamp, and through thy fault it would come to pass, what the Lord said, ' If the blind lead the blind, shall they not both fall into the ditch ? ' " (Orig., Hom. 17 on Joshua). These words are well worthy of attention now, when a multiplicity of worldly business and a weight of worldly cares are devolved upon God's ministers by a laity which has to too great an extent washed its hands of all co-operation in the work of God's Church.

Ver. 15.—**Reuben.** This passage is an expansion of Num. xxxii. 33—42. We learn from it that the Israelites actually took possession of this land. But in the reigns of the wicked kings Omri and Ahab the power of Israel declined, and after the battle of Ramoth-Gilead, and the defeat and death of Ahab, the Moabites succeeded in shaking off the Israelitish yoke, and in wresting from Israel moreover a considerable portion of the territory of Sihon. In the next reign an attempt was made to regain possession of the lost territory. We learn from the Moabite stone that the important towns here mentioned, Medeba, Dibon, Baal-meon, Kiriathaim (or Kirjathaim, as it is here called), Ataroth, Nebo, Aroer, had fallen into the hands of Mesha at the rebellion, and that he had erected a citadel at Dibon, which had become his capital. Hence the endeavour to invade Moab from the south, recorded in 1 Kings iii., which, however, though successful as a military promenade, was attended with no permanent results. For Isaiah (ch. xv.) and Jeremiah (ch. xlviii.) mention most of these places, as well as Elealeh and Heshbon, the former capital of Sihon, as being strongholds of the Moabite power. Jahaz, too, the place where Sihon gave battle to the Israelites, is numbered by Mesha, as well as at a later date by Isaiah and Jeremiah, among the possessions of Moab; while Horonaim, mentioned among the Moabite cities by the two prophets, is incidentally noticed by Mesha as having been captured from the Edomites. In this early extinction of the tribe of Reuben we may see the fulfilment of Jacob's prophecy (Gen. xlix.). **The plain by Medeba.** See ver. 10; so again in the next verse.

Ver. 17.—**Bamoth Baal.** The *high places* or *altars of Baal.* The frequent mention of Baal in this passage shows how common the worship of Baal was in Palestine. The Moabites worshipped him under the name of Chemosh, to whom Mesha, on the Moabite stone, attributes all his victories (cf. Num. xxi. 29; Judg. xi. 24; 1 Kings xi. 7, 33. So Beth-Peor below (cf. Num. xxv. 3).

Ver. 19.—**Sibmah** (see Num. xxxii. 38). The vine of Sibmah forms a feature in the lament of Isaiah (xvi. 8) and Jeremiah (xlviii. 32) over Moab. It was close by Heshbon, on the borders of Reuben and Gad (cf. ver. 17 with ch. xxi. 39). **Zareth-shahar,** or the *splendour of the dawn,* now *Zarar,* was on the borders of the Dead Sea. Canon Tristram, in his 'Land of Moab,' mentions the gorgeous colouring of the landscape here, more beautiful and varied, no doubt, at dawn than at any other time of the day.

Ver. 21.—**Cities of the plain.** "Mishor" once more. See above, ver. 9, not as in Gen. xix., where the word is *Ciccar.* These, therefore, were *not* Sodom and its neighbours, but cities of the Amorites. Such touches as this, which display the minute acquaintance of our author with his subject, are almost of a necessity lost in a translation. But where our version has "plain," the original has Mishor when the uplands of Gilead and Bashan are meant, Arabah when the writer is speaking of the Wadys in the neighbourhood of the Dead Sea, Shephelah when he refers to the lowlands of Western Palestine, bordering on the Mediterranean,

Bik'ah when he speaks of the great valley of Cœle Syria, Ciccar when he speaks of the territory due north of Jordan. **With the princes of Midian.** The word here used, נְשִׂיאֵי signifies *exalted persons,* persons of rank, as we should say. It would seem to imply rather civil functions than the more absolute authority which the word שַׂר also rendered "prince" in Hebrew, carries with it. With this passage compare Num. xxxi. 8. The Hebrew has no "with," so that the difficulty some have found in the passage need not have arisen. It is nowhere said that Moses smote the "princes of Midian" together with Sihon. All that is stated is that they, as well as Sihon, were smitten, as the history in Numbers tells us they were. **Dukes of Sihon.** According to Gesenius, Rosenmüller, and others, the word here translated "dukes" is derived from נָסַךְ to *pour out,* means "anointed." See Psa. ii. 6, where it is translated "set." But Keil rejects this interpretation, and says that the word never signifies to anoint. It is always used, he says, of *foreign* princes. But he has overlooked Micah v. 4 (Heb.). See Knobel, who explains it of drink offerings, and regards these "dukes" as men pledged by a solemn treaty to be Sihon's allies, though not vassals. Kimchi thinks that Sihon, before his reverses at the hand of Israel, had held some authority in Midian, and these were his prefects, or under-kings. The term is applied to Zebah and Zalmunna in Psa. lxxxiii. 12 (in the Hebrew).

Ver. 22.—**The soothsayer.** Or *diviner,* one who pretended to foretell future events. Balaam, it would seem, instead of returning to his own land, went to visit the Midianites, whose elders had joined in the invitation given by Moab (Num. xxii. 7), and persuaded them to entice the Israelites into idolatry and licentiousness (see Num. xxv.) For this crime he met with the punishment he had deserved, and was involved in the destruction which fell on the Midianites by God's express command, in consequence of their treachery (Num. xxv. 16—18. See Blunt, 'Undesigned Coincidences,' Part I. 24).

Ver. 23.—**And the border thereof.** These words have been omitted in the Vulgate, which does not understand them. The LXX. translates, "And the borders of Reuben were the Jordan-border." This seems to be the meaning of the original. The phrase often occurs, as in ch. xv. 12 and Num. xxxiv. 6. Knobel's explanation is probably the correct one, that the phrase means to refer to the natural boundary marked out by the river or sea and its banks. "The boundary of the children of Reuben was Jordan and the natural boundary thus formed." As Dean Stanley reminds us in his ' Lectures on the Jewish Church,' Reuben, as predicted by Jacob (Gen. xlix. 4), sank at once into insignificance. No ruler, no judge arose from this tribe and its territory. **Villages.** Hebrew חַצְרֵי, LXX. ἐπαύλεις, Vulgate *viculi.* The original meaning is a piece of ground enclosed by a hedge or wall. Here it would mean, either with Gesenius and Keil, *farm hamlets,* or perhaps *clearings* of cultivated ground, which in Palestine would naturally be enclosed in some way, to prevent the ravages of wild beasts. In the primitive villages of Servia, where wild beasts are not entirely extirpated, not only ᴜre all the homesteads enclosed, but a fence is placed across the road, and removed when a vehicle has to pass through. Or perhaps the primitive Jewish community was similar to the primitive Teutonic community as described by Marshall in his ' Elementary and Practical Treatise on Landed Property,' published in 1804, who described the early distribution of land in this country as follows : " Round the village lay a few small enclosures for rearing young stock. Further afield the best land for arable purposes was chosen, and divided into three parts, for the necessary rotation of fallow, wheat or rye, and spring crops. The meadows near the water-courses were set aside for the growth of fodder for the cattle or for pasturage for milch cows, &c. The irreclaimable lands were left for what we now call 'common' uses—for fuel, and the inferior pasturage." These arrangements are found to exist in India (see Sir H. Maine, ' Village Communities,' sec. iv.). But there, as in Palestine, the necessity for water was the cause of important modifications. Since the word is used to denote the court (1) of a *prison,* Jer. xxxii. 2 ; (2) of a *palace,* 1 Kings vii. 8 ; (3) of a private house, 2 Sam. xvii. 18 ; (4) of the *temple* in numberless places, and as it is used of the enclosure of a nomadic camp (Gen. xxv. 16, where our version has *towns ;* perhaps Deut. ii. 23, where our version has *Hazerim,* following the LXX.—which, however, alters the word to the more usual *Hazeroth*—and the Vulgate ; Isa. xlii. 11, with which compare the expression *tents* of Kedar, Psa. cxx. 5), the translation *villages* can hardly be the correct one here or elsewhere (see also ver. 28). Ver. 24.—**Unto the tribe of Gad.** The border of Gad extended further eastward than that of Reuben. Westward, of course, its border was the Jordan. Its northern border was nearly coincident with that of the land of Gilead, and passed by Mahanaim and Jabesh Gilead, unto the extreme

southernmost point of the sea of Galilee. Many of these places also are mentioned in Isa. xv. and Jer. xlviii. (see note above, ver. 16).

Ver. 25.—**Aroer that is before Rabbah.** A different Aroer to that mentioned in ver. 9. This was near (Hebrew, *opposite to*, the expression being equivalent to the French *en face*) Rabbah, or the great city of the children of Ammon. Keil supposes that this territory had been taken from the Ammonites by Sihon, since the Israelites were not permitted to possess themselves of the land of the Ammonites (Deut. ii. 19). For Rabbah, see 2 Sam. xi. 1 ; xii. 26. It is called Rabbath in Deut. iii. 11.

Ver. 26.—**Ramath-Mizpeh.** This is identified with Ramoth-Gilead by Vandevelde, and must have been the Mizpeh of Gilead mentioned in Judg. xi. 29. It is supposed to be identical with the place called Mizpah, Galeed, and Jegar-sahadutha by Jacob and Laban respectively (Gen. xxxi. 47—49). If it be the same as Ramoth-Gilead, it is the scene of the celebrated battle against the Syrians, in which Ahab lost his life (1 Kings xxii.), and where the fall of the dynasty of Omri was brought about by the revolt of Jehu (2 Kings ix.). Conder, however, thinks the two are distinct places, and fixes Ramoth-Mizpeh on the north border of Gad, about 25 miles west of Bozrah.

Ver. 26.—**Mahanaim.** The dual of מַחֲנֶה *two hosts* or *camps.* It received its name from Jacob, who with his own company met the angels of God, and who commemorated the meeting by this name (see Gen. xxxii. 2). Here Ishbosheth was crowned (2 Sam. ii. 8). Here David took refuge when he crossed the Jordan, to avoid falling into the hands of Absalom (2 Sam. xvii. 24). **Debir.** Not the Debir mentioned in ch. x., but another Debir in the land of Gilead, whose site is unknown.

Ver. 27.—**The valley.** The *Emek* (see ch. viii. 13). **Beth-Nimrah** (see Num. xxxii. 36). Afterwards Nimrim (Isa. xv. 6 ; Jer. xlviii. 34). Now Nimrîn. **Succoth.** I.e., *booths.* Here Jacob rested after his meeting with Esau (Gen. xxxiii. 17). Here Gideon " taught the men of Succoth," who had declined to provide food for his army (Judg. viii. 5, 7, 16). It is mentioned in connection with Zarthan, or Zaretan (cf. ch. iii. 16) as being in the tract or כִּכָּר of the Jordan, where the metal-work of the temple was cast (1 Kings vii. 46 ; 2 Chron. iv. 17). **Zaphon.** Perhaps, *and the North ; what remained of the kingdom of Sihon,* i.e., as is implied above, the part which was not assigned to Reuben. **Jordan and his**

border. Literally, Jordan *and* a border (see note on ver. 23). **The edge.** Rather, the *end* (see note on ver. 24).

Ver. 28.—**This is the inheritance of the children of Gad.** The cause of the difference between the Reubenites and the Gadites may perhaps be thus explained. While both inhabited a similar tract of country, a country from its open and pastoral character likely to develop a hardy and healthy race of men, the Reubenites were exposed to the seductions of the Moabitish worship of Chemosh, which, when combined with an ancestral temperament by no means prone to resist such influences (see Gen. xlix. 4), soon proved fatal to a tribe, itself not numerous (Deut. xxxiii. 6), and hemmed in on every side but the north by the unbelievers. The temperament inherited by the Gadites added to their more favourable situation and the nature of their pursuits, developed a hardy and warlike race ready to do battle, and fearless of their foes (1 Chron v. 18). Of this tribe came the valiant Jephthah, and of it also came the brave soldiers of David, whose qualifications stir to poetry the sober chronicler of Judah (1 Chron. xii. 8). We may see here the influence of circumstances on the character of a people. Originally (1 Chron. v. 18) the Reubenites and the Gadites were alike. But the Reubenites, as we have seen, from unfavourable surroundings, lost the character which the Gadites, more favourably situated, were enabled to preserve. And the distinctions of tribes, producing as they did a separate *esprit de corps* in each tribe, will serve to explain why one tribe did not immediately succumb to influences which proved fatal to another. In the end, as we know, all the people of Gad fell victims to the temptations which surrounded them, and, save in the case of Levi, Judah, and Benjamin, and the few faithful Israelites who went over to them, irrevocably. The same phenomenon may be observed in the history of nations generally. As long as their manners were simple and their morals pure, they have preserved their liberty, and in many cases have acquired empire. As soon as their bodies were enervated by luxury, and their minds corrupted by vice, they fell a prey to foes whom formerly they would have despised. Thus fell the Greek and Roman republics, thus the Britons became an easy prey to the Saxons, and the Saxons to the Danes. In every instance the history of a tribe and of a nation serves to illustrate the maxim that "righteousness exalteth a nation, but sin is a reproach to any people."

Ver. 29.—**The half-tribe of Manasseh.**

The word used for "tribe" in the first and second half of this verse is not the same. Some German critics have derived an argument for the hypothesis that the historical and geographical portions of the book are not by the same hand, from the supposed fact that the former of these words is used almost exclusively in the first, or historical portion, and the latter in the second, or geographical portion, of the book. The word "almost" would be *almost* sufficient to overthrow the theory, but this verse is an insuperable objection to it. Is it seriously contended that one half of this verse is taken from one author, and the other from another? Or is it possible that the writer of the book may actually have understood the language he was using, and meant to use the two words in somewhat different senses? Gesenius, it is true, would explain the words as being precisely synonymous. But his own etymological remarks are fatal to his theory. מַטֶּה the latter of the two words, is a *bough*, or *shoot* (derived from a word signifying to *grow*), capable of throwing out blossoms (Ezek. vii. 10). It refers, therefore, to the natural descent of the tribe from Manasseh their father. But שֵׁבֶט is allied to שָׁפַט to judge, and the Greek σκῆπτρον, and perhaps the English *shaft*, and signifies a rod as the emblem of authority. Thus it is used in Gen. xlix. 10, of a royal sceptre. So Psa. ii. 9, an iron sceptre, Psa. xlv. 6. Thus the latter word has reference to the tribe as an organised community, the former to it in reference to its ancestral derivation. This view would seem to be supported by ver. 24, where the מַטֶּה of Gad is further explained to mean his *sons* and *their families*, as well as by this verse, where the שֵׁבֶט is used absolutely, the מַטֶּה in connection with the family

Ver. 30.—**The towns of Jair.** Literally, *Havoth-Jair*, as in Num. xxxii. 41; Deut. iii. 14. The word חַיָּת is derived from חוה to *live*, and the word is compared by Gesenius to the names Eisleben and the like in Germany. So we use the phrase "live," as synonymous with "dwell." Why the term is confined to these particular cities is not known. Gesenius regards it as equivalent to "nomadic encampment." But the ruins of the giant cities of Bashan, recently re-discovered in our own time (by Mr. Cyril Graham, in 1857), and displaying all the signs of high civilisation, dispose of this idea. These cities are mentioned in Deut. iii. 4 as "threescore cities, all the region of Argob," and again in ver. 13, "all the region of Argob with all Bashan, which is called the land of giants." "To the east he (Abraham) would leave the barren and craggy fatnesses of the formidable Argob, still (*i.e.*, in Abraham's time, not Joshua's) the asylum of the fiercest outlaws; and would jealously avoid the heathen haunts in groves and on high places where smoke arose to the foul image, and the frantic dance swept round." (Tomkins, 'Studies on the Time of Abraham,' p. 69. See also note on 'Judah upon Jordan,' ch. xix. 34). **Threescore cities** (cf. ch. xvii. 1). It was the martial character, as well as the half-tribe of Manasseh, that qualified him to receive and subdue this important territory with its wide extent and teeming population. In the article on Manasseh in Smith's 'Dictionary of the Bible,' reference is made to the fact that, while Ephraim only sent 20,800, and Western Manasseh 18,000, Reuben, Gad, and Eastern Manasseh sent the immense number of 120,000, and this while Abner, the supporter of Ishbosheth, had his head-quarters at Mahanaim. But the numbers are suspicious, especially when Judah, always a powerful tribe, comes below the insignificant tribe of Simeon in number. And a comparison of 2 Sam. v. 1 with 1 Chron. xii. 22, 23, would lead to the idea that the coronation of David after the death of Ishbosheth is the event referred to (see also 1 Chron. xii. 38—40).

Ver. 31.—**The one half of the children of Machir.** See this question fully discussed in note on ch. xvii. 5, 6.

Ver. 32.—**Moses** (see Num. xxii. 1; xxxiv. 15). **Plains.** Hebrew, *Araboth* (see ch. iii. 16).

HOMILETICS.

Chap. XIII.—XIV. Ver. 5.—*The allotment of the inheritance.* I. THERE COMES A TIME WHEN WE MUST GIVE PLACE TO OTHERS. Joshua felt that his end was drawing nigh, and most likely, since we are not told otherwise, as in the case of Moses, his natural force was abated. So with ourselves. We cannot expect to see the end of our work. We must do what God has set before us, and leave results to Him. Yet we, unlike Joshua, need not fear the failure of our efforts. The law could not make its votaries perfect; but the bringing in of a better hope did. In this later dispensation no work shall altogether fail of its effect if done to God.

II. WE MUST " SET OUR HOUSE IN ORDER " BEFORE WE GO HENCE. Though Joshua had to leave the completion of the task to others, he did not fail to put it in train. So we, when we have begun a good work, are bound to make proper and reasonable provision for its being carried on when God warns us that our time draws nigh. We are not to expect God to work miracles where our own reason would suffice. We must leave the result to God, but not until we have done all in our power to procure the fulfilment of His will. We must leave proper directions behind us to indicate what our wishes are, and a proper organisation, so far as possible, to carry out our purposes. We find nothing left to God in the Bible but what is plainly beyond the reach of man.

III. GOD ASSIGNS TO EACH MAN HIS PORTION. In parcelling out the land of Israel, Joshua is a type of Christ, " dividing to each man severally as He will." The various powers and faculties we have, bodily, mental, spiritual, are given us by God. Each one has his own proper share, according to the work God requires of him. There must be no murmuring or disputing. The foot must not ask why he is not the hand, nor the hand why he is not the head. Each has his own proper portion of the good gifts of God, and according as he has so will it be required of them. All murmurings were hushed in Israel because Joshua committed the disposal of the inheritance to the Lord. We are equally bound to refrain from discontent because it is clear that God has portioned out the gifts of the spiritual Israel. One man has wealth, another strength, another intellect, another imagination, another wisdom, another energy, another power over others, or these various gifts are apportioned in various degrees for God's own purposes. Let none think of questioning the wisdom of the award.

IV. GOD'S MINISTERS ARE TO BE DEPENDENT UPON THEIR FLOCKS FOR SUPPORT. Such is the meaning of St. Paul when he speaks of the double honour (no doubt in a pecuniary sense, as we use the word " honorarium ") to be given to the elders who rule well. In consequence of their special aptitude for the work, they were to be relieved from the burden of their own maintenance, that they might be able to devote more time to the supervision of the flock. Not necessarily that each minister should be maintained by his *own* flock, for he might be thereby deterred from speaking faithfully to them in the name of Christ. We do not find that each individual priest and Levite was maintained by some special synagogue of the Jews. But they who ministered in holy things lived of the sacrifice nevertheless. The offerings made at the temple at Jerusalem formed a general fund out of which the tribe of Levi was maintained, as its members went up by rotation to perform the duties of their office. And beside this, a proper number of cities was provided them, with a share, most probably (see note on ch. xxi. 12), in the privileges of their fellow-citizens, of the tribe to which the land belonged. This ample provision for the ministers under the old law is in striking contrast, save in some special instances, to the provision made by Christians for their ministers now. A due maintenance for their clergy was one of the special characteristics of the Jewish religious system. According to the principles laid down by the apostles of Christ, and always acted upon, save in some special instances, it was an equally marked characteristic of the Christian Church.

V. GOD IS THE PORTION OF HIS MINISTERS. A great comfort for those who are in straitened circumstances, as many are. They may remember the words, "I have been young and now am old, yet saw I never the righteous forsaken, nor his seed begging their bread." If they abstain from murmuring, rigidly adapt their expenditure to their means, careless of appearances, careful only to do right, they will find their reward in God's love and favour. He will be in truth their portion. Having food and raiment, they will be therewith content, for they will have abundance of spiritual blessings, the reward of an approving conscience, and the respect of all right-thinking men. Nor is the promise confined only to those who lack the good things of this life, but it is given to those who, by God's disposition possessing them, know how to use them. *All* God's ministers who love and serve Him shall have Him as their portion, and they will treasure this above all earthly goods. "They that fear Him lack nothing." The Lord is the strength of their life, and their portion for ever.

HOMILIES BY VARIOUS AUTHORS.

Ver. 1.—*Life ending and the work not done.* The rest of the land from war, then (ch. xii. 23), was not that of final and completed victory. It was only a temporary truce. The whole land was not yet in the possession of Israel, but enough of it was subdued to prove God's absolute sovereignty over it. And now rest is needful to review the field and secure the ends that have been so far gained. Joshua is too old any longer to carry on the strife, but there is a work that he can do, and which must be done, before he is gathered to his fathers—the division of the land which in the Divine purpose, if not as an accomplished fact, is already Israel's inheritance. Note here—

I. THE HONOURED ENDING OF A LIFE OF NOBLE DEVOTION TO THE SERVICE OF GOD. There is no Divine approval of Joshua's fidelity actually expressed here, but the spirit of it seems plainly to breathe through these words. It is as if God said to him, "Thou art old; thy work of life is done—done faithfully and well—now rest; review thy path of service; gather up the fruits of it; set thy last seal to the truth of My word of promise, and enter into thy reward." Old age has great dignity and beauty in it when it crowns a life of earnest practical godliness. "The hoary head is a crown of glory, &c." (Prov. xvi. 31). Like the rich glow of autumn when the fields have yielded their precious store to the hand of the reaper, and the song of harvest-home is sung; like the golden sunset closing a day of mingled brightness and gloom, giving assurance of a glorious rising in the world beyond; such is the halo that surrounds the head of one of God's veterans. Think of the moral grandeur of the Apostle Paul's position when, in view of his past life-work, and in prospect of its eternal issues, he could say, "I am now ready to be offered, and the time of my departure is at hand. I have fought a good fight," &c. (2 Tim. iv. 6—8).

Such honour, in their measure, have all those who consecrate their days with whole-hearted devotion to the service of the Lord.

II. THE FAILURE OF THE LONGEST AND THE NOBLEST LIFE COMPLETELY TO FULFIL ITS OWN HIGH AIMS. "There yet remaineth very much land to be possessed." This is not said in reproach of Joshua. He had accomplished the work to which God had called him. But it reminds us that, however rich a human life may be in the fruits of practical devotion, it is after all but a *contribution towards* the full working out of the Divine purpose—small, feeble, fragmentary indeed in comparison with the grandeur of God's providential plan. Great as may be the victories it has achieved, it leaves "much land yet to be possessed." Moreover, the noblest spirit fails to reach its own ideal, the most fruitful life fails to realise its own aspirations. Human life at the best is but a tale half told, a song that dies away into silence when only a few timid notes have sounded. It is but a beginning, in which the foundation is laid of works that it is left to other hands to furnish, and purposes are born that find elsewhere their actual unfolding. How many a man in dying has had a painful sense of having fallen far short, not only of the diviner possibilities of his life, but even of the realisation of the hopes that inspired him in his earlier years. There is always a touch of sadness in the autumn gleam.

> "The clouds that gather round the setting sun
> Do take a sober colouring from an eye
> That hath kept watch o'er man's mortality;"

because they remind us of the brevity of our life-day, and reflect the vanishing glory of so many of its fairest dreams. Full as it may have been of high endeavour and grand achievement, how much remains undone! "There remaineth yet very much land to be possessed." This is capable of many applications. (1) As regards *science*. Marvellous as its progress has been, how many undiscovered secrets has Nature still locked up in her bosom! (2) As regards the *practical uses of life*. God has made man "to have dominion over the works of His hands;" but what vast resources of the material world still remain unutilised in His service! (3) As regards *personal spiritual development*. The best of us fall sadly short of the Scripture standard of character. When good men die, how far off still appears to them the goal of Divine perfection—like the horizon that seems to recede and widen and become more unapproachably glorious as we reach forth towards it. (4) As regards the *progress and consummation of the kingdom of God among men*. Its triumphs thus far have been very wonderful, but how much remains yet to be done! How far as yet are the kingdoms of this world from having become "the kingdoms of our Lord and of His Christ"! How small the circle of light as compared with the vast outlying realms of darkness! comparatively few of those who profess the faith of Christ, knowing anything of the living power of it, two-thirds of the human race being still heathen.

III.—THE STEADFASTNESS OF THE DIVINE PURPOSE, in spite of the decay, one after another, of the instruments by which it is accomplished. Much land remains to be possessed, and it *shall be possessed* though Joshua pass away from the scene of conflict. "Them *will I drive out* from before the children of Israel (ver. 6). God raises up men to take their particular part in His great work, some more prominent, some less, but He is independent alike of all. The fall of His heroes on the field of battle in no way checks the onward march of the great unseen Captain of the host to final victory. All true leaders in the holy war point us, alike in their life and in their death, to Him whose presence is never withdrawn, whose years fail not, whose eye never becomes dim, whose force is never abated. In following their faith, and considering how their "conversation" ended, let us not forget that "Jesus Christ is the same yesterday, and to-day, and for ever" (Heb. xiii. 7, 8).—W.

Ver. 1.—*Old age*. The most active servant of God may be overtaken by old age before he has completed what he believes to be the task of his life. This fact suggests various reflections.

I. THE GREATNESS OF DUTY AND THE LIMITS OF TIME TOGETHER URGE UPON US THE NEED FOR DILIGENT SERVICE. (1) We must not postpone the commencement of work. Joshua began to serve God in his youth; yet his work was not finished in his old age. (2) We must not be satisfied with any amount of work done. Joshua had accomplished great things, but much remained undone. (3) We must not be willing to work at intervals or with wastefulness of time. The work of life is too great for the longest, most earnest life. Time is short; the day of work will soon pass. "Work while it is day" (John ix. 4).

II. IN GOD'S SIGHT THAT LIFE IS FINISHED WHICH HAS ACCOMPLISHED ALL WITHIN ITS POWER. Life is long enough for all that God requires of us. We may not be able to do all we wish, all we set before ourselves, all that appears to be needed, all that we think it our duty to do. But God apportions our duty according to our opportunities. Therefore in His eyes the broken, unfinished life is really finished if all is done for which opportunities have been given.

III. GOD JUDGES US BY FAITHFULNESS, NOT BY SUCCESS. It is not they who effect much, but they who serve truly, whom God accepts. We cannot command success. The finishing of our work is not in our hands. We *can* be faithful (Luke xvi. 10).

IV. THE UNFINISHED EARTHLY LIFE IS A PROPHECY OF A FUTURE LIFE. Our aspirations exceed our capacities. It is not simply that we desire the unattainable; but we are conscious of duties which reach beyond present opportunities, and of possibilities within us which the limits of life prevent us from developing. If God is too wise to waste His gifts and too good to deceive His children, we may take the broken life, and still more the incomplete life even of old age, as mute prophecies of a larger life beyond.

V. IN THE FUTURE LIFE THERE WILL BE NO OLD AGE. The pain of declining powers, of insufficient time, and of all other limits of earthly life will be gone. Eternity will give leisure for all service. The eternal life will not grow old, but flourish in perpetual youth.

VI. IT IS A PROVIDENTIAL BLESSING THAT GREAT MEN SHOULD NOT BE ABLE TO FINISH THE WORK THEY SET BEFORE THEMSELVES. It is well that they should leave work for smaller men. The necessity thus created becomes a stimulus to others. When one falls, another is raised to continue his work (John iv. 37, 38).

VII. NO MAN FULFILS EVEN SO MUCH OF LIFE'S WORK AS COMES WITHIN HIS POWERS. At best we are unprofitable servants; but we are all also negligent and slothful. We have left undone many things which we ought to have done. None of us can say with Christ, "It is finished." Therefore we should review our lives with humility, contrition, and repentance, seeking forgiveness for the failings of the past and more grace for the duties of the future.

VIII. CHRIST'S WORK ALONE IS THE GROUND OF ACCEPTANCE BY GOD. Our work is unfinished. It is faulty for the negligence it proves. It can earn us nothing on its own merits. Christ's work is finished. On this our faith can rest. Then we may offer our own imperfect work to God through Christ, and He will transform it for us by lifting it into the light of His merits, till it will be worthy as dust shines like gold when the sunbeam passes through it.—W. F. A.

Vers. 2, 7.—*The land allotted, though not yet secured.* "There remaineth yet very much land to be possessed." "Now therefore divide this land for an inheritance"—form a somewhat strange pair of precepts. It seems as if Joshua was dividing what he had not got; and as if Israel were casting lots rather for perils than property. It is not quite so extreme as this. The point in the conquest was reached when nowhere was there a resistance needing a nation in arms to quell it. The several tribes were each strong enough to make good the conquest of their several heritages. The work of the nation as a nation was over. The work of each tribe had now to begin. Still there is some of the grandeur of a Divine method in giving us something that still needs conquering; enriching us with something for which some fighting still requires to be done. Look at it.

I. GOD'S GIFTS ARE GENERALLY HALF-HOLDING AND HALF-HOPE. All He imparts has this double character—it is always at once a possession and a responsibility His gifts resemble, say, a colonial estate needing to be cleared; a good house half built—requiring to be finished before it can be used; a mine requiring to be wrought. They are always of vast value to those who will develop their value; but of little to the indolent or timorous. For the same gift, accordingly, some will be devoutly thankful, some thankless. Hebron, given to Caleb on condition of clearing out the Anakim, seems a fee simple, unencumbered, and he rejoices at his fortune. "The wood" still harbouring the enemy seems to Ephraim for a while at least a doubtful possession. Some—the heroic—rejoiced with abounding gratitude over God's gifts; some—the indolent—deemed them so hopelessly encumbered as to be valueless. So that His gifts were great to the great-hearted, and little to the mean-spirited. God's gifts are ever of this kind. He gives daily bread, but only through the toil that wins it; saving grace, but only on condition of repentance and obedience which will use it. He gives not bags of either earthly or heavenly gold, but *chances, opportunities, potentialities.* "A little strength and an open door" gives the power of making our own blessed destinies, is God's usual gift to all as well as the Church at Philadelphia. His grace is power to win character; not a certain pulp which, without effect, shapes itself into goodness; nay, it is something which we cannot keep except on the condition of getting more of it. The land divided is, in great part, a land yet to be possessed. Observe secondly—

II. GOD'S METHOD IS THAT OF WISDOM AND OF MERCY. His gifts would not be blessings if action were needless for their improvement and enjoyment. That would then be stagnation of our powers with consequent enfeeblement. But the gift of that which requires enterprise and action, developes all qualities of strength, vigour, courage, self-denial, self-respect. Those who have no part in winning what they get generally lack power to keep it. Each tribe held with a stronger hand what it conquered for itself. The sense of possession was more secure, the enjoyment of it more perfect. If God were to give dignities instead of duties, enjoyments without responsibilities attached to them, how dull and earthly would His very gifts make us. In His mercy He gives us "high callings," "new commandments," "fights of faith to fight," and so developes all manliness and godliness. Do not murmur that your bit of the land of promise can only be got, secured, and enjoyed by fighting; it is the mercy of God that so orders it.

III. IN COUNTING OUR WEALTH WE SHOULD ALWAYS INCLUDE THE LAND NOT YET POSSESSED. God's Israel are always in this position. They have a little secure and a grip of a great deal that needs still to be secured, but easily may be. "The good I have not tasted yet" was rightly included in her list of mercies by one of the sweet singers of our own day. With others "a bird in the hand" may be worth "two in the bush;" with us, the "two in the bush"—being attainable—are to be discounted as of far greater worth. Caleb was thankful for the hill of Hebron, while yet the Anakim disputed its possession with him. Your land to be possessed is yours by title, by promise, by the power given you to win it. Be thankful for it and take it. In your gratitude remember the victories you have still to win; attainments which you yet will make; all the answers to your prayers that are on their way to you; the heavenly Canaan you yet will gain. For, though not yet "possessed," these are all yours by God's deed of gift, and we act wisely and devoutly only when we discount God's promises as being absolutely true and certain to be redeemed.—G.

Vers. 14, 33.—*The inheritance of Levi.* I. THE TRIBE OF LEVI RECEIVED NO INHERITANCE OF LAND. (1) They who devote themselves to the service of God must be prepared to make *earthly sacrifices.* We cannot serve God and mammon. If our service of God costs nothing it is worth nothing (Luke xiv. 33). Therefore count the cost (Luke xiv. 28). (2) Earthly *possessions distract our attention* from heavenly service. Therefore it is hard for the rich to enter into the kingdom of heaven (Luke xviii. 24). (3) It is right that they who have the care of souls should be *freed from the care of earthly business.*

II. THE TRIBE OF LEVI HAD ITS TEMPORAL WANTS ADEQUATELY PROVIDED FOR (see verse 14). (1) They who serve at the altar have a *right to live by the altar* (1 Cor. ix. 7). This is (*a*) just (1 Cor. ix. 11), (*b*) necessary for unhindered service, and (*c*) not injurious to true devotion so long as the servant of God does not degrade his vocation into a trade by working for money instead of receiving money that he may have means for work. (2) In contributing to the support of God's servants we are offering *sacrifices to God.* The sacrifices were the priests' and Levites' portion (Deut. xviii. 1). We cannot benefit God by our gifts, but we can give to God through His servants (Matt. xxv. 40). It is our duty to provide in temporal things for those who minister to us in spiritual things. He who starves the ministers of Christ is as guilty as if he starved their Master (Matt. xxv. 45).

III. THE TRIBE OF LEVI FOUND ITS TRUE INHERITANCE IN GOD. The sacrificial gifts of the people were not its chief inheritance, but only the small necessary earthly portion of what it was to receive. Its true heritage was spiritual. (1) The Christian minister should not regard the earthly returns which he receives for his service as his main reward. To do so is to commit the sin of simony. His real reward is *spiritual.* (2) He who makes any sacrifice for God will be amply compensated in *Divine riches* (Mark x. 29, 30). (3) It is better to have *God for our portion* than any earthly inheritance (Psa. lxxiii. 26). To have God for an inheritance is (*a*) to enjoy communion with Him; (*b*) to be protected by Him; (*c*) to live for His service. This is the best inheritance, because (*a*) it is satisfying to the soul, while the earthly inheritance is full of dissatisfaction, and can never supply our greatest wants; (*b*) it is eternal; and (*c*) it is pure and lofty.

Note: In the Christian Church, though there is diversity of orders (Rom. xii. 6—8) there is no distinction of caste. All Christians are called to the altar of sacrifice (Heb. xiii. 10), all are to serve as priests of the temple (1 Pet. ii. 9), and all should find their true inheritance in God (1 Pet. i. 4).—W. F. A.

Ver. 22.—*The fate of Balaam.* I. WHEN SPIRITUAL GIFTS ARE USED FOR UNSPIRITUAL PURPOSES THEY LOSE THEIR SPIRITUAL VALUE. In the Book of Numbers Balaam appears as a prophet inspired by God. In the Book of Joshua he is only named as a common soothsayer. All spiritual gifts, of insight, of power, of sympathy, are worthy only so long as they are well used. As they become degraded by evil uses they lose their Divine character and become mere talents of cleverness and ability.

II. THE ABUSE OF SPIRITUAL GIFTS FOR PERSONAL GAIN IS A SIN WHICH CANNOT GO UNPUNISHED. Balaam had sold his prophetic powers for money, consenting to use them on the side of evil and falsehood. Now his sin has found him out. He who receives great gifts incurs great responsibility. No spiritual power is bestowed for merely selfish uses. The greater the talents we abuse, the greater will be the judgment we shall invoke.

III. THE POSSESSION OF SPIRITUAL GIFTS IS NO GROUND FOR THE ASSURANCE OF PERSONAL SALVATION. Balaam had great gifts, yet he suffered the fate of the heathen. Our privileges are no proof of a Divine favour which will overlook our sins. Salvation comes not from the gifts of the Spirit, but from the grace of God in Christ. The least gifted has as good ground for salvation as the most highly endowed. Pulpit power, the "gift of prayer," theological insight, and religious susceptibilities may all be found in a Christless life, and if so they will be of no avail as grounds of merit in the day of judgment.

IV. THE KNOWLEDGE OF THE TRUTH ONLY INCREASES THE GUILT OF THOSE WHO WILL NOT FOLLOW IT. Balaam knew the true God and the way of right. But not living according to his knowledge, his guilt was aggravated, and his doom certain. It is worse than useless to know Christian truth unless we obey it (Jas. i. 22—24). The faith in Christ which secures to us salvation is not the bare intellectual belief in the doctrines of redemption (Jas. ii. 19), but submissive trust and loyal obedience to Christ as both Lord and Saviour (Mark ii. 14).—W. F. A.

Ver. 22.—God is patient in the exercise of His justice as well as in His compassions, for He is the Lord, with whom "a thousand years are as one day." He knows that His threatenings, like His promises, cannot fail. Of this we have a striking proof, both in the punishment which came upon Balaam, during the war for the conquest of Canaan, and in the blessing of Caleb.

I. For many years Balaam had been untrue to his own conscience, in going back to the idolatries of Canaan, after having been made for one day the organ of the most glorious oracles of the true God. He is thus an illustration of the truth that the baser passions of the heart, if not subdued, will always quench the clearest light of the intellect. Balaam chose wittingly the evil part. He plunged again into the corrupt practices of the heathen. For a long time it seemed to the eyes of men, who judge only by the appearance, that he had made the right choice. Was it not better to sit under his own vine and fig tree, and enjoy the riches heaped upon him by Balak, than to join the Israelites in their dreary desert pilgrimage, beneath a blazing sky, and over the burning sand ? Had not Balaam acted wisely ? Unquestionably he had if the rule of true philosophy be, " Let us eat and drink, for to-morrow we die ; " that is to say, if God does not reign in righteousness for ever and ever. But when the old soothsayer fell beneath the sword of those Israelites whose warfare he had not been willing to share, he understood too late that it was these despised people who had alone been wise, and that, in spite of all the light he had received, he had lived and acted like a fool. How many are there now living who recognise with their minds the truth of the gospel, but who are unwilling to give up their sinful indulgences, until there rises upon them the terrible day of the Lord. Happy those for whom this day of awakening comes before death, so that they do not go down to the grave with their hearts made gross by merely material prosperity, only to be aroused by the stroke of Divine retribution. Let us remember the punishment of Balaam, which came surely, though it seemed to tarry, when the prosperity of the wicked seems to us a stumbling-block.

II. The promises of God's love are not less faithful and sure than His threatenings, though they also may seem slow of fulfilment. This is illustrated in the history of Caleb, who courageously served his people through a long lifetime, bringing back a good report of the land garrisoned by the enemy, which Moses sent him to explore. "Therefore Moses sware on that day, saying, Surely the land whereon thy feet have trodden shall be thine inheritance and thy children's for ever, because thou hast wholly followed the Lord thy God" (ver. 9). This promise was not forgotten. Caleb received, as an inheritance, that hill of Hebron which was assured to him in the name of the God whom he served. Thus the promises of God are yea and amen.—E. DE P.

Ver. 22.—*Balaam*. A study of pathetic interest ; one of the great " might-have-beens " of the world. One capable of winning an immortal fame, but actually finding only an immortal infamy. The Judas of the Old Testament: one travelling on the right road till within sight of heaven, and then turning aside to perdition. Consider—

I. THE GREATNESS OF THE MAN. Evidently his position is one of great dignity and influence. He has raised himself to priest-kingship among the Midianitish tribes. He is considered to have such power in divination and forecast that he is brought all the way from a city in Mesopotamia to the borders of Canaan to " curse Israel." This reputation would lead you to expect to find him at least a man possessed of great spiritual insight ; able at least to guess well concerning all moral probabilities. He has, moreover, reached a clear knowledge of God ; has not become entangled by any service of the lower deities whose degrading worship was so prevalent ; showing that he was a spiritually minded man, who had gone on and on following the light which reached him, until that light exceeded that of any one else among his people. His divination is no black art—carried on by appeals to demons—but by pure sacrifices offered to the supreme God. He had evidently been accustomed to utter exactly what God imparted. Pleasant or painful, what God sent him he said. And his honesty and courage are conspicuous in his actual declarations concerning Israel. When we have put together these qualities : spirituality sufficient to discover and serve the true God ; great strength of integrity; the keen perception which can discern the essential differences and destinies of things; the fear of God to which "the secret of the Lord is always revealed"—you get a character of the first quality, one that has in it the making of a Moses or an Abraham, one who could and should have been one of the grandest of the prophets of the Lord. If only he had reached the full development of his spiritual powers, Midian might have been another Israel, for generations a source of highest good. Doubtless till middle life this course of high righteousness, consecration to and communion with God had gone on. But beginning well and running well, he falls at last into ignominy and shame. Mark—

II. THE PROCESS OF HIS FALL. It must not be dated strictly from the temptation before which he fell. There is always, or almost always, some declension before a fall. No one falls into crime by one stumble. Can we trace the process? The writer of the Apocalypse, with his power of going straight to the mark, sums up in one word: He loved the *wages* of iniquity; not iniquity, but what iniquity could give him. First the selling of his spiritual power was a declension. To seek God's light in order to get man's money was an activity damaging to his conscience. Whether it be the sale of masses, absolutions, indulgences, or oracles, the vitiation is in each case the same. A seemingly slender line divides Samuel's acceptance of an honorarium from Balaam's eager desire for it. But seeming alike, they essentially differ. In Balaam's case the greed got headway, and instead of the prophet's simple acceptance of gifts as a means of living, there was a valuing of all his spiritual powers and privileges only for their market value. [It is an awful thing when a Christian minister values his creed and his experience only as a means of making money.] Then hankering after money, he soon loses the fine edge of honour. When once God refused to give him leave to go with the messengers of Balak, there should have been no re-opening of the question. But so anxious is he for the "rewards of divination," that on their second embassy he goes to God for a second time, for the chance of finding Him permit what He had already refused. Declining to accept a *reluctant service*, God at once permits and punishes a less honourable course. Again and again he tries to get permission to curse Israel, just in order to get gold. That desire to get a different light from what God has given him is degrading and demoralising. Each dishonourable and dishonouring attempt to get God's anathemas to hurl against a righteous nation fails to hurt Israel, but terribly damages himself; until, hunting after some means of possessing himself of Balak's gold, in the pursuit he falls down, and down in degradation until, God refusing to inspire him with evil, his heart is ready to welcome and utter an inspiration from below. And his character is so disintegrated in this hankering after money, that at last he gives the most diabolical advice that man could give; viz., that instead of fighting Israel, they should endeavour to corrupt them (Num. xxxi. 16). The licentious feasts, the heathen orgies are of his counselling, and but for Phinehas might have been as disastrous to Israel as their intent was diabolical. What a fall, from the level of highest character, influence, and opportunity, down to the level of a Satanic crime. The love of money is daily making wrecks equally disastrous and irreparable. Beware of it.

III. Lastly observe THE RETRIBUTION. Likely enough he got his reward, and was for a moment as pleased as Achan. But had he satisfaction in it? (1) Israel, in whose future well-being he recognised the source of the world's best help, is crippled, degraded, weakened through his advice, and that would pain him. (2) Midian is all but completely annihilated. All the males and most of the women are slain (Num. xxxi.). (3) Balaam himself has but a short-lived enjoyment of his wealth, for he also is slain (Num. xxxi. 8). (4) The loss of life probably pained less than the everlasting infamy that made what hitherto had been an honoured name a proverb for the vilest form of treacherous wickedness. These penalties are obvious. In the world of spirits there must have been others more serious still. May we fear dishonourable gold, as that which makes the heaviest of all millstones to drown men in perdition!—G.

Ver. 31.—*The border keep.* "Machir was a 'man of war,' therefore he had

Gilead and Bashan." These cities include the group which form such a striking stronghold in the northern part of the land beyond Jordan. Mr. Porter, in his 'Giant Cities of Bashan,' has described the surprising strength of the architecture of these cities—the failure of even three thousand years of change and wear to render the houses unfit for habitation; and has also described the strange formation of the district of Argob, rendering it a natural fortress of the most formidable kind. Here, by special adaptation of place with people, this district is assigned to the family of Machir. It was wisely so assigned, for through all the succeeding generations the keeping of the frontier in this direction was well done. We may gather one or two hints not altogether valueless from this assignment. Observe—

I. MACHIR HAS FOR HIS LOT THAT WHICH BY HIS COURAGE HE HAD CONQUERED. From Num. xxxii. 39 we learn that, gigantic as were the inhabitants of Gilead, strong as was its cities, impregnable as its natural fortress seemed, the children of Machir "took it," and dispossessed the Amorite that was in it. Now they enjoy that which their unusual valour won. Like Caleb, whose daring made him ask Hebron, even when it was in the hands of the enemy, they chose a difficult spot, and conquering, inherited it. More than any other they had a right to this, for their courage had conquered it. *Your best inheritance will always be some Gilead that you conquer for yourself.* The truth you discover for yourself will do you most good. The experience you develop for yourself will be your best guide. Even the money you make for yourself will be that which you at once employ and enjoy the best. Conquer what you want to have. By courage, diligence, enduring hardness, achieve what you would like to keep.

II. "A MAN OF WAR" IS THE RIGHT MAN FOR FRONTIER DUTY. The Jacobs in the middle; the Esaus are better on the borders of the land. The bravest should be those nearest the foe. They who keep the gates of a kingdom should be those to whom conflict has no terrors. Theologians that keep the frontiers of truth should be brave. Timid Christians that think all the world is going to turn catholic or infidel are not men for warfare on the border. Against assaults there should be placed those who have been through all the fights of faith and unbelief in their own hearts, and who can bring a strenuous, cheerful energy to the task of fighting for the truth. Those strong enough to expect a perpetual victory of truth are those alone fit to deal with the assaults of error. Ministers of religion, keeping the frontier between the Church and the world, should be in a good sense men of war; on their guard against encroachment of worldliness; strong enough to brave opposition and to be above the seductions of the flattery which a compromising spirit may win from the world; strong enough to keep out the intrusions of the secular spirit in all its forms of caste-feeling, of cold-heartedness, of indifference to the perishing; strong enough to carry the war into the enemy's country, and secure by extending the kingdom of Christ. On all frontiers there is need of vigour. Wherever the enemy is near, set what is bravest and stoutest in you to watch. The pugnacious element in our nature is very valuable—if it operates in Gilead. There is deficiency of it too often; and too often where it is, it is just in some position where it quarrels with its friends instead of with the temptations and the wrongs and the difficulties which are its proper foes. For frontier-work of all kinds, courage is the prime qualification. Lastly—

III. THERE IS NO CITADEL LIKE A FORTRESS WON FROM THE ENEMY. What he won was his reward, but it was something more. It was the best stronghold he could have against the enemy. The conquered fortress makes the best defence. The vigour enough to win it grows stronger and becomes the power to keep it. A victory is always a point of strength and a stronghold conquered, a vantage-ground against the foe. The Church differs from all other communities in this, that she is never weaker by extension; each new conquest gives her a better frontier; every Gilead subdued becomes a new line of defence, making her more impregnable against attack. By God's blessing, conquer a rebellious heart and subdue it to Him, and it becomes a fortified post from which you can assail or defend more powerfully than before. Graces that are easily gained are easily lost. But those that are won with arduous difficulty are invariably much more securely held. None keep truth like those who have fought hard to get it. None are more generous than those who have fought hard with selfish tendencies within them. None keep elevation of thought and feeling more persistently than those who have reached it by crucifying the flesh. A conquered temptation is a grand fortress in which you are stronger to resist seduction than ever before. A grief conquered by faith becomes a quiet resting-place, and one secure against all assaults of despair. Keep making daily some conquest, and so you will perfectly secure all that you have won.—G.

EXPOSITION.

CHAPTER XIV. 1—15.

Ver. 1. — **Tribes.** The word here for "tribes," in connection with the word "fathers," is the one which implies genealogical descent (see note on ch. xiii. 29). **Eleazar the priest, and Joshua the son of Nun, and the heads of the fathers of the tribes.** A picture of national unity; the head of the Church, representing the religious aspect of the community; the head of the State, representing its civil aspect; the heads of the tribes, to signify the general assent of the body politic. A work so begun was likely to be satisfactorily carried out. And accordingly the distribution of the land, recognised as carried out according to the will of God, displayed no partiality, and excited no jealousies.

Ver. 2.—**By lot was their inheritance.** The commentators, following the Rabbis, have amused themselves by speculations *how* the lot was taken. The question is of no great practical importance; but no doubt the contrivance was a very primitive one, as the word גּוֹרָל a small pebble, used here, seems to imply. What is of more importance is the fact that the distribution of territory was the result of no one's caprice, or ambition, or intrigue. The whole matter was referred to God, and the leader of the Israelitish hosts and the high priest presided over the ceremony. It was a common belief among the Gentiles, as well as the Jews, that the use of the lot was to refer the matter to a Divine decision. So we read in the Proverbs, "The lot is cast into the lap, but the whole disposing thereof is of the Lord" (Prov. xvi. 33; cf. xviii. 18). It is a strong evidence for the truth of this narrative that we read of no conflicts between the various tribes respecting the division of territory. Jealousies sprung up between the tribes, as the narratives in Judg. viii., ix., xii.; 2 Sam. xix. 43, are sufficient to show. But in no one case was there any complaint of unfairness, any attempt to disturb the territorial arrangement made at the time of the original settlement in Palestine. There

can be little doubt that Keil is right in supposing this original division to have been in outline merely. It is obvious from the onward course of the narrative (especially ch. xviii.) that no very minute accuracy in detail could possibly have been arrived at. The country was roughly mapped out at first, and the complete adjustment of boundaries was a matter which would naturally be put off until the land were actually in possession.

Ver. 4.—**For the children of Joseph were two tribes** (see Gen. xlviii. 5) : **therefore they gave.** There is no "therefore" In the original. The passage is a simple repetition of what we find in ch. xiii. 14, 33, and is added here to explain how the twelve tribes who actually divided the land were composed. **Suburbs.** Rather, "pasture lands;" literally, places where the cattle were *driven out* to pasture (cf. Num. xxxv. 2; 1 Chron. xiii. 2, where the Hebrew is "cities of driving out"). We may illustrate this phrase by the similar arrangements made by the Germanic tribes in early times. "The clearing," says Professor Stubbs, in his 'Constitutional History of England,' p. 49, "is surrounded by a thick border of wood or waste. . . . In the centre of the clearing the village is placed. . . . The fully qualified freeman has a share in the land of the community. He has a right to the enjoyment of the woods, the pastures, the meadow and the arable land of the mark. . . . The use of the meadow land is definitely apportioned. . . . When the grass begins to grow the cattle are driven out, and the meadow is fenced round and divided into as many equal shares as there are mark-families in the village. For the arable land similar measures are taken, although the task is somewhat more complex" (see note on ch. xiii. 23). Some similar arrangement must have taken place in the primitive Jewish settlement of Palestine. For the rude huts of the Teutonic tribes we must substitute the more civilised "cities, walled up to heaven," of the Phœnician races; for the scanty supply of grain and pasture, provided by a northern climate, we must substitute the rich plenty of a land "flowing with milk and honey," and with all the produce of a southern sky. The area of land assigned to each of the Levitical cities was definitely marked out (see Num. xxxv. 4, 5), and subdivided, as the hints in the narrative seem to imply that all the land was, into as many sections as there were "mark-families" — that is, families of freemen exclusive of the servile classes in the town.

Ver. 6.—In Gilgal (see ch. ix. 6). **Caleb the son of Jephunneh the Kenezite.** Or, *descendant of Kenaz*, as was his kinsman Othniel. As far as we can make out from the genealogy in 1 Chron. ii, Caleb and Kenaz were family names, for the Caleb or Calubi (1 Chron. ii. 9) the son of Hezron (1 Chron. ii. 18), the Caleb the son of Hur (1 Chron. ii. 50), and Caleb the son of Jephunneh (1 Chron. iv. 15), could not have been the same persons. And Caleb was a Kenezite, or descendant of Kenaz; he had a grandson, apparently, of that name (so the LXX. and Vulgate translate, 1 Chron. iv. 15), and a brother, according to the most probable rendering of the Hebrew of both ch. xv. 17 and Judg. i. 9. See also 1 Chron. iv. 13. For Caleb was the son of Jephunneh, not of Kenaz. Hitzig, 'Geschichte des Volkes Israel,' i. 105, thinks that Caleb was a descendant of the Kenaz mentioned in Gen. xxxvi. 11; or, see 15. Some think he was a Kenizzite (see Gen. xv. 19). The Bishop of Bath and Wells, in his article in Smith's 'Dictionary of the Bible,' thinks that the view that he was not of Jewish origin agrees best with the Scripture narrative, and removes many difficulties regarding the number of the children of Israel at the Exodus. It certainly serves to explain why the tribe of Judah came with Caleb, when he preferred his request, and the statement in ch. xv. 13, which seems to imply that Caleb was not one of the tribe of Judah by birth, but one of the "mixed multitude" that went up with the Israelites (Exod. xii. 38), and acquired afterwards by circumcision the rights of Israelites. If this be the case, it is an illustration of the truth declared in Rom. ii. 28, 29; iv. 12; Gal. iii. 7. By his faithfulness to God he had well earned the reward which he now sought. **Concerning me and thee.** And yet Knobel asserts that, according to vers. 8 and 12, Joshua was not one of the spies! He accordingly sees the hand of the "Jehovist" here. So accurate is the criticism which pretends to be able to disintegrate the narratives in the Hebrew Scriptures, and to assign each part to its separate author (see Num. xiv. 24). As well might we conclude that this verse in Num. xiv. is by a different hand to vers. 30 and 38 in the same chapter, in spite of

the obvious coherence of the whole narrative.

Ver. 7.—Forty years old. The Hebrew expression is "the son of forty years." Compare the expressions "son of man," "sons of Belial," "son of the perverse rebellious woman." **As it was in my heart.** Literally, *according as with my heart, i.e.*, in agreement with what I saw and felt. The LXX. reads "according to *his* mind," *i.e.*, that of Moses. Houbigant and Le Clerc approve of this reading, but it seems quite out of keeping with the character of Caleb. He did not endeavour to accommodate his report to the wishes of any man, but gave what he himself believed to be a true and faithful account of what he had seen and heard (see Num. xiii. 30; xiv. 7—9; Deut. i. 36).

Ver. 8.—But I wholly followed. Literally, "*I fulfilled after*." That is to say, he rendered a full obedience to the precepts of the Most High. So also in the next verse.

Ver. 9.—And Moses sware on that day (cf. Num. xiv. 21—24; Deut. i. 35, 36). Keil raises the difficulty that in the above passage not Moses, but God is said to have sworn, and that no special inheritance is promised to Caleb, but only that he shall enter the promised land. But this is not the fact, as a comparison of this passage with Deut. i. 36 will show. That either passage gives the *ipsissima verba* of Moses is unlikely. The main sense of the promise is given in each. And there is no impropriety in speaking of the proclamation by Moses of God's decree as an oath pronounced by Moses himself.

Ver. 10.—Forty and five years. This marks the date of the present conversation as occurring seven years after the invasion. Caleb was forty years of age when he went to spy the land of Canaan. For thirty-eight years the Israelites wandered in the wilderness. And Caleb was now eighty-five years old. This remark has been made as far back as the time of Theodoret. Doubtless the apportionment of the land, and its occupation by the Israelites, was a long and tedious business (see also ch. xiii. 1). **Even since.** Literally, *from the time when*.

Ver. 11.—As yet am I as strong this day. A vigorous and respected old age is ordinarily, by Nature's own law, the decreed reward for a virtuous youth and a temperate manhood. Caleb's devotion to God's service had preserved him from the sins as well as from the faithlessness and murmuring of the Israelites. And thus, with a body not enfeebled by indulgence, he presents himself before Joshua with undiminished strength, at a time when most men are sinking under the weight of their infirmities, and is ready still for battle with the most formidable foes.

Ver. 12.—**This mountain.** The neighbourhood of Hebron is described by Bartlett ' Egypt to Palestine,' p. 401, as " a region of hills and valleys." In one of the hollows in this " hill country of Judæa " Hebron still nestles, but at a height which (see Stanley, ' Sinai and Palestine,' p. 102) is " only 400 feet lower than Helvellyn," the highest point but one in England. The Dean remarks on the fact that Palestine was a mountainous country, and that therefore in its history we may expect the characteristics of a mountain people. **Whereof the Lord spake in that day.** There must therefore have been a promise made to Caleb, regarding which the Pentateuch, having to deal with matters of more general interest, is silent, that he should lead the forlorn hope, as it were, of the children of Israel, and that the task of subduing the mountain fastnesses of the most powerful tribes in Palestine should be assigned to him. That the original inhabitants re-occupied the districts round Hebron, while the Israelites were otherwise engaged, we have already seen (see note on ch. xi. 21). The final work was to be carried out by Caleb. Houbigant, it is true, thinks that here the same incident is referred to as in ch. xi. 21, 22, and that Joshua is there credited with what was done by Caleb at his command. But we read that that expedition followed close upon the battle of Merom, whereas seven years elapsed before the final expulsion of the Anakim by Caleb. It is important to notice that the author of the Book of Joshua has access to sources of information beside the Pentateuch. This, though not sufficient to disprove, does at least seem inconsistent with the " Elohist " and " Jehovist " theory. **For thou heardest in that day.** The LXX. and Vulgate avoid the difficulty here by referring these words to what goes before—*i.e.*, the promise made to Caleb. In that case we must render the second בִּי " for," instead of " that," or " how." Joshua can hardly have heard for the first time that the Anakim were in Hebron if, as Num. xiii. 22 appears to assert, he, in common with the other spies, had visited the place. But it is possible, though the narrative as it stands seems to

suggest that they went together, that the spies went different ways, either separately or in pairs, and that Caleb visited Hebron, and that Joshua heard the account of it for the first time from Caleb's lips, as they brought their report to Moses, and that Caleb then asked and received the grant of Hebron. We may observe the minute agreement here in matters of detail between the Pentateuch and the Book of Joshua. The Pentateuch states that the spies visited Hebron. The Book of Joshua, without mentioning this, makes Caleb appeal to Joshua as a witness that a promise had been made to him, long before the entrance of Israel into the promised land, that this particular place should be allotted to him. The description of Hebron also in Num. xiii. agrees in every respect with what is stated here. **Fenced.** Literally, *inaccessible*, as surrounded by walls. **If so be.** Rather, *perhaps*.

Ver. 14.—**He wholly followed** (see above, ver. 8).

Ver. 15.—**And the name of Hebron before was Kirjath-arba.** Hengstenberg, according to Keil, has conclusively shown that Hebron was the original name of the city. At the time of Joshua's invasion, however, it was known as Kirjath (or " the city of ") Arba, from a giant named Arba who had conquered the city. Hebron is known as Kirjath-arba in Gen. xxiii. 2, but the way in which it is mentioned by Moses seems to bear out Hengstenberg's theory. The Rabbis translated " the city of four," and assert that the four patriarchs, Adam, Abraham, Isaac, and Jacob, were buried there. The word translated " man " here is Adam. The Vulgate follows this tradition, translating " Adam maximus ibi inter Enacim situs est." And our own Wiclif literally translates the Vulgate " Adam moost greet there in the loond of Enachym was set." Rosenmüller renders the words translated " a great man " by " the greatest man." And certainly the words have the article ; and this is also the way in which the superlative is expressed in Hebrew. It also adds to the force of Caleb's request. He desired the most important city of a warlike race. **And the land had rest from war** (see ch. xi. 23).

HOMILETICS.

Vers. 6—15. — *Caleb's faithfulness and its reward.* The history of Caleb seems to have a special fascination for the sacred historian. We read of him here, and in the next chapter, and in Judg. i. Whether this were due to his bravery, his sincerity, his hale and hearty old age, or (see note on ver. 6) his foreign extraction, coupled with his zeal for his adopted country and tribe, or from the combination of all these, it is not necessary to decide. Sufficient to remark (1) that he was beloved by the people; and (2) that he was a favourite character in the inspired Jewish history.

I. THE BRAVE MAN WINS RESPECT. This is sure to be the case in the long run. He may be accused of rashness, want of judgment, intemperance of language or of purpose; but in the end he secures the confidence and attachment of all. The lesson is especially needed in the present age. One of its most marked characteristics is moral cowardice (as even John Stuart Mill has remarked). Men are incapable, for the most part, of incurring the disapprobation of the set in which they live. Politicians vote with their party for measures of which they disapprove. People in society dare not raise their voices against what passes current in their own *coterie*; they yield to practices, admit persons to their intimacy of which and whom, in their own better judgment, they disapprove. They dare not brave the unfavourable verdict of their acquaintance. Yet if they did they would lose nothing by it. Even the careless and thoughtless respect fearlessness, and delight to honour the man who dares to say what he thinks. They may condemn at first, but in the end they come round to a sounder judgment. History continually repeats itself. The history of Caleb is the history of every man who is honest in setting himself above the prevailing opinions of the day. His report was unpopular at first. The people sympathised with the cowardly ten. But events demonstrated the correctness of his view, and he became a popular hero. His tribe came with him to support his request, and if he were not of Israelite origin this incident makes the moral still more clear.

II. WE SHOULD ALWAYS SPEAK THE TRUTH. Caleb brought word according to what his heart told him. He sought neither to say what Moses would wish, nor what would be palatable to the people. What he thought, that he said. And this is one of the results of a heart devoted to God. Caleb "wholly followed" Him, and thus he had that sincerity and integrity which is the result of single-mindedness. All Christians, and especially God's ministers, should learn to shun the fear or favour of man, but everywhere and always to "declare the whole counsel of God." As we have seen, we do not thereby lose the favour we have not sought. Because we have not asked for it (1 Kings iii. 11), we have it. But this is not to be taken into consideration. Those who "wholly follow the Lord their God" will be men who never fail to speak according to the dictates of the regenerate heart.

III. THE RIGHTEOUS SHALL NOT FAIL OF HIS REWARD. Moses had sworn to Caleb that he should have the land for his inheritance of which he had brought so true a report (no doubt, see notes, the spies went diverse ways). And now, after years of hardship and toil, he gained it. So has Christ promised a reward to them who seek Him. They must join their brethren in the toil; they must ever be foremost in the conflict, and they may be sure that their Joshua will give them an everlasting inheritance in the mount of God.

IV. THE REWARD THAT THE RIGHTEOUS SEEKS. Observe that Caleb does not seek a rich nor easy inheritance, but one full of danger. The Anakim, defeated over and over again, still lurked in the inaccessible recesses of the hill country, and their giant strength, protected as it was by the fortifications of these mountain fastnesses, made it a task of the utmost danger to dislodge them. This task the gallant old warrior asks for himself. "Let me," he says, "inherit the stronghold of the Anakim. Let me have the city of their chief" (see notes). Such a man was St. Paul. His reward was the having preached the gospel without charge (1 Cor. ix. 18). He desires no other. And so the true Christian, he who "wholly follows" Christ, will desire as his reward the privilege only of being allowed to do and dare all for Him.

V. THERE IS A REWARD FOR THE GODLY IN THIS WORLD. Even the laws of the physical universe have provided a reward for virtue. A temperate life secures a hearty old age. The spectacle of Caleb, as ready for war at eighty-five as he had been forty-five years previously, may be a rare one now with our luxurious habits. But the principle holds good that men who live hard, work hard, and abstain from all over-indulgence in their appetites, will as a rule preserve their physical vigour to an advanced age. This is a gospel which may not be very palatable to the sons of luxury, but it is true nevertheless. Common sense and Christianity are ever really allied, however much a narrow view of the former may seem to conflict with the latter. Luxury, sloth, excessive indulgence even in permitted pleasures, are fatal to the body as to the soul. Even the weakly may retain their energies to old age by care and self-restraint. The strongest man will sink into an early grave who deems such things unnecessary. So true is it that " Godliness has the promise of the life that now is " as well as of " that which is to come " (1 Tim. iv. 8).

VI. The true secret of success. Caleb (see ch. xv. 14—17) did not fail in his dangerous undertaking. But it was because he said, " if the Lord be with me." So is it always in our undertakings. He that is sure he shall resist temptation, because he is confident in himself, will find his confidence fail him in the day of trial. He who trusts in the Lord only, will emerge a conqueror from the struggle. In all things our support and trust must be in Him. If we purpose a thing in our hearts it must be " if the Lord will " (James iv. 13—15). If we have done anything by His help we must say, " Not unto us, O Lord, but unto Thy name be the praise " (Psa. cxv. 1). Had Caleb relied upon his unabated strength, or on his undaunted courage, he would have fared as Israel before Ai. But since he relied on the Lord his God, the three sons of Anak could not stand before him ; the stronghold of Debir must needs open its gates to his daughter's suitor.

HOMILIES BY VARIOUS AUTHORS.

Vers. 1—5.—*The allotment of the tribes.* This record of the division of the land among the tribes is suggestive of principles that are capable of a wider and more general application, and also of one that is narrower and more individual. Note—

I. The Divine Providence that determines the sphere and surroundings of all human life. This is indicated in the division being made by lot. Whatever the form of the lot may have been, its meaning was that the destination of each particular tribe should not be a matter of human judgment or caprice, but should be left with God. It was no mere reference of the issue to blind chance. The faith of the age was too simple and real for that. Joshua and the elders had too deep a sense of the presence and guidance of the living God. We pass from this mere tribal allocation to think how the same law holds good for *all the nations of the world.* St. Paul showed his freedom of spirit from the limitations of Jewish prejudice when he declared to the Athenians how God, having made of one blood all nations to dwell on all the face of the earth, " determined for them the times before appointed and the bounds of their habitation " (Acts xvii. 26). Christianity reveals a God who is the Father of all mankind, and not of one particular people. The true patriotism is that which acknowleges God's interest alike in all the nations, and teaches us to cherish and use the gifts He has conferred specially on our own country for the common good. Again : the Providence that determines the lot of the nations has the same control over the *individual human life.* Every man's position in the world is in some sense the fulfilment of a Divine purpose. It may seem to be the result merely of the fortuitous commingling of circumstance, or the capricious drift of man's own choice. But we do well to see through all outward appearances the sovereign hand that guides the course of circumstances and determines the issue. It is God, after all, who chooses our inheritance for us. " The lot is cast into the lap, but the whole disposing thereof is of the Lord " (Prov. xvi. 33). The recognition of the Divine Providence that is over us has many beneficial moral effects. (1) It gives the sanctity of a higher meaning to life, (2) provokes to thankfulness, (3) rebukes discontent and distrust, (4) restrains inordinate ambition, (5) teaches that respect for the rights and interests of others on which the order and well-being of society depend.

II. The human agency by which the purpose of Divine Providence is fulfilled. The land is divided according to the will of God, but the people must go in and possess it for themselves. God will drive out the Canaanites that are still there, not without them, but "*from before them*" (ch. xiii. 6). The decision of the lot seems to have had reference only to the general local situation of the tribes ; the actual extent of the territory in each case was left to be determined by the discretion of Joshua and the leaders. There was no caprice in this Divine decision. Nothing God does is arbitrary or reasonless. It was, no doubt, determined according to the peculiar characteristics of each particular tribe, and in such a way as that its geographical conditions should be best fitted to develop its latent powers. Important practical lessons are suggested. (1) However devoutly we may recognise the Divine Providence that is over us, we have to determine for ourselves the path of duty. (2) The circumstances of life place possibilities of good within our reach, which it remains for ourselves to actualise. (3) Every man's life in this world supplies the needful conditions of moral education, if he have but wisdom to discern and skill to improve them.

III. The separateness of those who are specially devoted to spiritual work in the world. This is indicated by the peculiar position of the tribe of Levi. To them was given no inheritance, " save cities to dwell in with their suburbs.' " The sacrifices of the Lord God made by fire " (as also tithes and first-fruits) " were their inheritance " (ch, xiii. 14). " The Lord God of Israel Himself was the lot of their inheritance " (ch. xiii. 33 ; Num. xviii. 20—24). Their position thus bore witness to the sanctity of the whole nation as " a kingdom of priests " unto the Lord (Exod. xix. 6). They were the representatives of its faith and the ministers of its worship. And their representative character was made the more effective by the fact of their cities being scattered throughout the tribes (ch. xxi.). This principle of separateness is illustrated—(1) In the various provisions by which the sanctity of the priesthood was maintained under the economy of the law. (2) In the New Testament institution of a certain order of men who should be set apart—not, indeed, as a hierarchy to whom mystic powers belong, but as the ministers of spiritual instruction and edification to the Church of God (Eph. iv. 11, 12, 13 ; 1 Cor. ix. 13, 14). (3) In the Apostolic teaching as to the unworldliness of spirit and life that becomes the followers of Christ (Phil. iii. 20 ; Col. iii. 1, 2, 3 ; Heb. x. 34 ; 1 Peter ii. 9).—W.

Ver. 2.—*Inheritance by lot.* While the trans-Jordanic tribes chose their own inheritance, the nine-and-a-half tribes submitted to the distribution by lot, and thus signified their desire to have their possession chosen for them by God. Submission to the lot was a sign of good qualities which we may well imitate, although altered circumstances and fuller light make it our duty to show them in other ways.

I. Belief in Providence. The Jew believed that God superintended the lot (Prov. xvi. 33). If there be Providence there can be no chance. The word " chance " describes the appearance of events to us: it is indicative of our ignorance. A perfect providential care will guide the smallest events (Matt. x. 29).

II. Submission to the will of God. These tribes resigned the choice of their possession to God, and were willing to take whatever He assigned them. We are not free to take our destinies into our own hands. We are God's servants, God's children. Dutiful obedience implies submission to God's will in the shaping of our lives (1 Sam. iii. 18).

III. Trust in the wisdom and goodness of God. The submission was fearless and trustful. We often shrink from God's will even while we bow to it. We submit sadly as to some painful necessity. We should say, " Thy will be done," not with dread and sorrow, but with confidence and hope ; making the utterance not merely a reluctant concession, but an earnest prayer, because God's will is *best for us.* It is best that He should " choose our inheritance for us," because (1) He knows all the character of the inheritance—we only its superficial aspects. (2) He knows future events—we only present appearances. (3) He knows our true needs —we our foolish desires. (4) He knows our best life's mission—we our selfish aims. Lot suffered by choosing his own inheritence (1 Gen. xiii. 11).

IV. Fairness and generosity in business arrangements. Those who submitted to the lot did not choose the best for themselves. They allowed a division which was fair for all. In business we are too selfish and grasping. The principle of competition should yield to the principle of co-operation. It is wicked for the able and clever to grow rich by taking advantage of the weakness and incapacity of those with whom they transact business (Phil. ii. 4). In the end the individual gains by the exercise of such generosity and fairness as promotes the welfare of the whole community. "We are members one of another." If one suffer all ·suffer (1 Cor. xii. 26). This is not only Christian morality, it is the highest truth of political economy. Before concluding we must look at a question suggested by this subject, viz., Are we right and wise in resorting to the lot in the present day? We have no Divine authority for the present use of it. We have other means of learning God's will. We live under a dispensation of fuller light. Decision by lot corresponds to rule by law—it is authoritative, requiring blind obedience. Christianity opens our eyes to *principles* of conduct and to *principles* of Providence. If God now guides us in other ways, we have no right to suppose that He will so direct the lot as to signify His will thereby. To resort to this is to fall back on lower means of guidance. It often implies both indolence and superstition. —W. F. A.

Vers. 6—15.—*Caleb.* I. THE CHARACTER OF CALEB. (1) *Independence.* He and Joshua had stood alone in the almost universal panic. It is difficult to discern the right and be faithful to it when all around us go wrong. The sanction of the multitude is no justification for an evil course. Truth and right are often with the minority (Matt. vii. 13, 14). (2) *Truth.* Caleb says, "I brought him word again as it was in mine heart." We are tempted to hide our convictions when they are unpopular. The true man speaks what is in "his heart," not the mere echo of the voice of the multitude (Acts iv. 19, 20). (3) *Courage.* Caleb had advocated the course which seemed to be most dangerous. He is now willing to receive for inheritance a possession from which he will have to expel the Anakims (ver. 12). Courage is a form of unselfishness and a fruit of devotion to duty. (4) *Unselfishness.* Though Caleb had shared with Joshua the honour of being faithful and brave in the day of general failure, he has lived quietly ever since, seeking no peculiar honour, and now the brave old man asks for inheritance a mountain region infested with hordes of the fiercest Canaanites, and offers to conquer it for himself. Like Lot, we commonly choose the pleasant places, and are greedy of much reward for little service. Caleb thinks himself no martyr. It is happy to have the humility and unselfishness which not only ask for little but are satisfied with little. (5) *Whole-hearted devotion to God* (ver. 8). This is the secret of Caleb's character. Devotion to God makes us independent of men, true in the light of His searching eye, brave with trust in His help, and unselfish in obedience to His will. Half-hearted devotion fails of this. We must serve God *wholly* if we would grow strong and true and brave.

II. THE REWARD OF CALEB. (1) *Long life.* He and Joshua were the sole survivors of the Jews who escaped from Egypt. The cowards perish. The brave are spared. For us the corresponding blessing is not long earthly life but eternal spiritual life. (2) *Continued strength and opportunity for service.* His strength remains (ver. 11). His inheritance makes new claims on his courage and energy (ver. 12). The lot of greatest comfort is not the lot of highest honour. The best reward is renewed ability to serve (Matt. xxv. 23). (3) *A possession, the advantages of which he had long since discerned.* Caleb and Joshua had stood alone in opposing the unbelief of the people in prospect of the promised land. Now their position is justified. The reward of solitary defenders of the truth will come in the ultimate triumph of it. Those who now best appreciate the heavenly inheritance will enjoy it best hereafter. (4) *Rest.* The land had rest, and Caleb must have shared the rest. The rest of heaven will be sweetest to those who have toiled and borne most on earth.—W. F. A.

Ver. 8.—"*I wholly followed the Lord my God.*" I. TRUE RELIGION IS BASED ON

PERSONAL RELATIONS WITH GOD. Caleb ascribes his courage and fidelity to his connection with God, and he speaks of the Lord as "my God." (1) Religion is *individual*. We must pass from " our " God to " my " God. Each soul is called to as private communion with God as if there were no other souls in existence. (2) Religion establishes *close relations* with God. In His personal dealings with the soul God comes near to it, so that He appropriates the soul and the soul lays claim to possessing God.

II. RIGHT PERSONAL RELATIONS WITH GOD WILL BE SHOWN BY OUR FOLLOWING HIM. It is not sufficient that we believe, worship, manifest affection. We must show our devotion by a consistent course of life. (1) This is to seek to be *near* to God, love and duty drawing us Godward. (2) It is to *obey* His commands, following the course of His will. (3) It is to *emulate* His example—trying to do as He does (Matt. v. 48). Christianity consists in following Christ (Mark i. 17, 18).

III. WE ONLY FOLLOW GOD ARIGHT WHEN WE FOLLOW HIM WHOLLY. We cannot serve God and mammon. We must choose whom we will serve. Half-hearted service is no true service. Following God wholly implies (1) *not desisting* from service on account of loss or trouble incurred; (2) taking no account of the opinion and conduct of *other men* when these would deflect us from fidelity to God; (3) serving God in *all the relations* of life, business, social, domestic, and private.

IV. UNDIVIDED DEVOTION TO GOD IS NECESSARY FOR SUCCESS IN HIS WORK. We see how thoroughness and singleness of aim are essential to success in secular pursuits—in business, science, art, literature. They are not less essential in spiritual things. Much of our work fails for lack of thoroughness. Hesitating belief, divided aims, mingled motives, often render religious efforts weak and futile. We need to be more perfectly devoted, giving ourselves *wholly* to God's service (1 Tim. iv. 15). —W. F. A.

Ver. 6—14.—*Caleb and his inheritance.* Caleb is one of those Scripture characters in whom we feel a personal interest not measured by the amount of historical information given us respecting him. Scanty as the materials are, they present us with a moral portrait very real and life-like and full of dignity. All that we know of him is greatly to his honour. The more so if, as some say, he was of Idumæan rather than Israelitish origin, adopted rather than born into the tribe of Judah. The courage and fidelity he displayed when, as one of the spies, he dared, with Joshua, to counsel the craven-hearted people to go in and possess the land (Num. xiii. 30 ; xiv. 6, 10 ; Deut. i. 36), are illustrated again now that almost another half-century has passed. The old man has still the same spirit in him. While some of the tribes are so slow to move that Joshua has occasion to rebuke them for their lethargy (ch. xviii. 3), he is eager to secure at once his promised inheritance, defying in the strength of God the formidable sons of Anak. In several lights Caleb appears before us here as a worthy example. We see in him—

I. AN HONEST SPIRIT, FORMING A TRUE ESTIMATE OF ITS OWN VIRTUES AND CAPACITIES. He recounts with honourable pride the doings and distinctions of the past—how he had been faithful to his own convictions in his report of the land, not following the evil example of the other spies, or fearing the anger of the people; how Moses had honoured him, and the vigour of which he was conscious even "this day " was his Divine reward. There is no vain boasting here. His grateful recognition of God disproves that. It is the frank acknowledgment of an honest mind. The true heart is conscious of its own integrity and need never shrink from avowing it. It is well that experience of the happy effects of fidelity to the path of duty should be recorded for the encouragement of others. There are times when we may properly " thank God that we are not as other men are." This may be done in the spirit of profoundest lowliness and self-distrust. Self-depreciation is often but a mock-humility. We honour ourselves and God when we duly estimate the worth of the moral qualities with which He has endowed us and the moral victories He has enabled us to win. Let no man " think more highly of himself than he ought to think," but at least let him " think soberly, according as God has dealt to him the measure of faith " (Rom. xii. 3). Recognise the Divine origin of every virtue you possess, and it will never make you vain; be true to yourself and to your noblest impulses, and you find in yourself an unfailing source of satisfaction and rejoicing (Prov. xiv. 14; Gal. vi. 3, 4).

II. A BRAVE SPIRIT GATHERING FROM THE MEMORY OF THE PAST AN INCENTIVE TO NEW ENDEAVOUR. There was a moral unity in Caleb's life. He had obeyed the voice of conscience and discharged manfully the sacred responsibility that was imposed on him forty-five years ago, and now he feels the recollection to be stimulating and strengthening to him. He has been lost to us through all the intermediate time, but we may be sure that his life in the desert, as a leader of the great tribe of Judah, had sustained the reputation of early days. And the dauntless spirit of his old age is but the result of habitual fidelity to the call of duty and of God. Such is the moral continuity of our life. So true is it that—

> " Our deeds still travel with us from afar,
> And what we have been makes us what we are."

Every victory of our better nature over the power of meaner motives lays the foundation for further and completer victories. Even the memory of it becomes an inspiration and a strength to us. The fruit of it is seen after many days. Accustom yourself to do the right and to " follow wholly " the path the Lord your God marks out, and there shall be stored up within you a fund of strength that will enable you to look calmly in the face of the most formidable difficulties—to storm the strongholds of the Anakims and "drive them out."

III. A DEVOUT SPIRIT LEANING ON GOD FOR THE FULFILMENT OF HIS OWN PROMISE. We gather from ver. 9 that God had given Caleb a distinct promise of the possession of that mountain in addition to the general promise recorded in Num. xiv. 24. To the apprehension of faith every Divine word is a living seed that must one day bring forth the fruition of its own fulfilment, and the mercies of the past are pledges of future help and benediction.—W.

Ver. 8.—*Personal influence.* Assuredly no Israelite could look without emotion upon the face and form of Caleb, the utterer of the words of the text. His very existence was a memorial of a memorable day. And when he arose and stood before Joshua, and the two engaged in the conversation recorded in this chapter, who could note them without recollecting that out of the laymen of Israel they were the only survivors of the generation to which they belonged? Like venerable towers that rear their heads above the building which is attached to them but plainly bears the marks of more recent construction, these two men stood an age above their surroundings, but with strength as unyielding as that of their latest compeers. Time and sickness had levelled their contemporaries with the dust, but they remained " with eye undimmed and natural force unabated." God had kept His threat and promise. Caleb's utterance may suggest some useful reflections.

I. THE FACILITY WITH WHICH MEN ARE DETERRED FROM NOBLE ENTERPRISES. What a lamentable incident was that to which these words refer : " My brethren that were with me made the heart of the people melt." Recall the story of the twelve men and their reconnoitring expedition. They searched the south of Palestine, and admired the fruit which grew there in such abundance; but the hearts of the majority were terrified at the sight of fenced cities and the giants who inhabited them. And so when they returned to their brethren they gave such a discouraging account that the people cried, " Would to God we had died in Egypt!" Caleb tried to still their murmuring, but in vain. The cowardly spirit prevailed. Apparently fear is more easily engendered than hope. It is easier to depress than to cheer. How many religious undertakings have failed through the excessive caution of even good men? It is noteworthy that in the account which Moses gives in Deut. i. 21 he refers to the fact that on the arrival of the Israelites at Kadesh he exhorted them to " go up and possess the land : fear not." Well would it have been if they had acted on the bold counsel of their leader. But they came near and suggested what seemed an exceedingly wise plan—to send men first to spy out the land—and dire was the ultimate effect! We do not inculcate rashness; we only say that courage is sometimes better than caution, and quick action than slow resolves. We need a holy enthusiasm that will minimise dangers and make us "strong in faith."

II. THE DANGER OF EXERTING AN EVIL INFLUENCE. Great responsibility rested on the men who were the means of damping the ardour of their countrymen. Whilst they themselves died of the plague, the rest of the people were condemned to forty years' weary traversing of the desert. So fierce was the wrath of God at the unbelief of the Israelites. This gift of influence God has bestowed on every person. We all wield this power to a greater or less extent. We may repel or attract, and in either case we are helping to mould the opinions and form the practices of our neighbours. We direct their aspirations and colour the spectacles through which they look at men and things. Is our life-report for good or for evil?

III. THE SECURITY AGAINST WIELDING AND YIELDING TO AN EVIL INFLUENCE. It is to be noted that Caleb did not seek to persuade his fellows to renounce the idea of invading the Holy Land, and also did not allow himself so to be persuaded by them. He gives us in the text the reason which swayed him and the power which sustained him in opposition to the fears of the other Israelites: "I wholly followed the Lord my God." There might be times in which the mind would be left in suspense as to the proper course to pursue, in which the chief difficulty would be in ascertaining the will of Heaven. But on this occasion there seemed to Caleb but one thing to be done. Precepts and promises clearly showed that it was the duty and privilege of the Israelites to march to the possession of their inheritance. The path was plainly marked; to hesitate was to turn aside from following the Lord. *Unswerving obedience to God's declared will is the grand security* against ill-conduct. All that we read of Caleb proves him to have been a man of strong determination. Whatever he did he did with his might. There is a deal of meaning in that word "wholly." A man whose face is partly to God and partly to the world may have his attention distracted, but he who maintains an attitude that has respect to God only will remain uninfluenced by either the hopes and fears or the blandishments and threats of men. Urge *the necessity and helpfulness* of taking a decided step, *of becoming openly connected with God's people,* of avowing an attachment to Christ. Some may raise a difficulty in the way of imitating Caleb's whole-heartedness. This man was gifted with force of character. Now an objector may say, "I by nature am weak, irresolute, easily moved. Why am I blamed if I do not manifest that firmness which others display?" This inquiry runs into a fundamental problem—the reason of the election of men to different degrees of intellectual and moral ability, and the different degrees of accountability resulting therefrom. We cannot well separate the direct gifts of God from the achievements of the individual. We are bound to honour men even for what they owe entirely to God, since the honour reaches higher than men and is laid as an offering before the Throne. But what we must remember is that we are capable of acquiring qualifications which we previously lacked, and we may to a wonderful degree strengthen and improve the powers with which we are endowed.—A.

Ver. 12.—*The Anakims.* I. WE HAVE "ANAKIMS" IN OUR INHERITANCE. Some of the highest blessings are fenced about with the greatest difficulties. 1. No earthly inheritance is without its peculiar disadvantages. Some of the "Anakims" which resist us in our efforts to fulfil our mission are (*a*), the evil in our own heart, *e.g.*, indolence, fear, earthliness; (*b*) the temptations of the world, arising from bad examples, customs, distracting pleasures; (*c*) direct hindrance in persecution and opposition growing out of the world's ignorance, prejudice, envy, &c. 2. Nevertheless it is best for us, as it was for Caleb, to have such an inheritance. Difficulties (*a*) try our faith and courage; (*b*) give scope for energy and devotion; (*c*) make the ultimate peace the more blessed. 3. Apply these truths (*a*) to private life; (*b*) to Church work and the difficulties in evangelising the world; (*c*) to public interests, and the hindrances to the work of high-principled statesmen and philanthropists which stay the progress of liberty, civilisation, and national prosperity.

II. WE HAVE MEANS FOR OVERCOMING THE "ANAKIMS." 1. *God with us.* This fact is Caleb's ground of confidence. God does not only approve of the right; He aids it. He does not merely send assistance for the battle of life; He is present as the light to guide and the power to strengthen. Caleb had faith in the real and active presence of God. 2. *Brave effort.* Caleb says, "I shall be able to drive them out." He names God's help first as indispensable; but he does not stay with this. God's grace is no excuse for man's indolence. God fights for us by fighting in us. Ours is the effort, while His is the strength. True faith in God will not paralyse our energies, but inspire them; because it will show us (*a*) that, while the victory will not be given unless we fight, when we fight in the strength of God omnipotence is on our side; (*b*) and that God then assures us of victory, and that as He is faithful we may be confident of it. Caleb is confident that with God's help he will drive out the Anakims, because this is "as the Lord said."—W. F. A.

Ver. 12.—*Caleb's inheritance.* But little comparatively is said in the sacred writings concerning Caleb. What is recorded is decidedly in his favour. He stands before us as a model of unbending integrity. Selected from among the princes of Judah to be one of the twelve appointed to search the land of Canaan, he remained stedfast in his adherence to the will of God. Neither the remembrance of the giant sons of Anak and their fortified towns, nor the passionate wailings of his brethren, could make Caleb falter and falsify the report he had to give, and the recommendation he desired to make. For this he received the praise of Jehovah, and the promise that, not only should he be preserved to enter the land of Palestine, but also that the very part of the country concerning which some had given an unfavourable report should be allotted to him as his portion. Forty-five years had passed. The wilderness was full of graves. Joshua had succeeded Moses as leader of the Israelites; had overthrown in pitched battles the chief nations of Canaan; it was time to distribute to the tribes their inheritance. The partition was made in the first instance by lot. Then the arrangements for families were made by commissioners, and, as one of these, Caleb might have seized the city he desired. But, avoiding all suspicion of unfairness, he came with the children of Judah publicly to offer his petition. The text presents us therefore with—

I. A REQUEST FOR THE FULFILMENT OF A PROMISE. "Give me this mountain whereof the Lord spake in that day." As God's representative Joshua is desired to see that the ancient oath is not made void. The declaration of God would not remain without effect, yet observe the manner in which it was to be accomplished, viz., by the petition of the man to whom the declaration was granted. Caleb *set a high value on the promise of God.* Lightly would he have treated it had he allowed it to rest uncherished in his thoughts. God loves to see His people appreciate what He has offered to bestow. He has given "exceeding great and precious promises," and yet "will be inquired of" to do it for them. Our duty is clear. To lay hold of the announcements of His Word and ground on them our requests. Surely the reason why multitudes never pray is that they think little of the blessings promised to those that ask. *We need quickened memories.* Are the Scriptures to be empty volumes or full of life and power? The Bible may be our charter; the will of our Father bequeathing rich portions in this world and the world to come; our catalogue of precious furniture that may be had to adorn the household of saints. How many things we have never asked for or claimed as our own! Graces to beautify, gifts to enrich for evermore. "All Scripture is given that the man of God may be perfect, thoroughly furnished unto all good works." *Man is expected to do his part* even in the obtaining of a privilege. Some think, "If we are to be saved we shall be." Caleb might have thought similarly, and neglected to make his request, and gone without his portion. God requires men to use their reasoning powers, to examine the evidences of religion, to repent and believe in Christ—yes, to ask for the adoption that shall make them members of His family.

II. A REWARD SOUGHT LITTLE TO BE DESIRED IN THE EYES OF SOME. Hebron was a large city, a royal city, but the surrounding hills were the fastnesses of giants, who must be attacked and driven away. Before the owner could settle down on the estate he must dislodge the former proprietors. No easy conquest was to be anticipated, yet the courageous soldier said, " Give me this mountain. Others may choose quiet resting-places, let me go to the high places of the field." Is there not here *an example worthy of imitation?* Who will be the advanced guard of the Christian army to attack the fortresses of Sin and Satan? *An infusion of Caleb's spirit would do much to reconcile us to what we mourn over as the hardships of our lot.* We should take a different view and regard them as our reward, increasing the honour put upon us by God. One man has to struggle in business against fearful odds, another is plagued by a wretched temper, a third is sorely tempted to murmur under a heavy bereavement. God intends these various trials as discipline and as honours. The troubles are the Anakim, who must be cheerfully, bravely encountered. How deep-felt will be the joy of triumph! No soldier ought to lament when placed by God in the forefront of the battle. When Jesus drew near His hour of suffering He exclaimed, " Now is the Son of man glorified." Caleb believed that *special power had been given for special work.* He appealed to facts as indicative of Jehovah's intention respecting him. Not for indolence had he been "kept alive these forty and five years," and his strength preserved, his strength "for war both to go out and to come in" (vers. 10, 11). This principle admits of wide application. The gifts of God are various. To one is granted money, that institutions may be supported and enterprises commenced. To another the power of speech, that he may "speak to the people all the words of this life." To another a persuasive manner, a winning smile, the grace of hospitality. These are so many talents of which the Master will exact an account. Nor will the question turn so much on actual accomplishment as on the ratio of abilities to results.

III. AN ACKNOWLEDGMENT OF DEPENDENCE UPON THE HELP OF GOD. His speech would sound like the utterance of self-confidence and presumption did there not run through it a tone of devout thanksgiving, which removes the charge of boastfulness and reveals the source of his assurance. The Lord had kept him alive, and if the Lord were with him he would soon drive out the giants from their strongholds. When David essayed to fight the Philistine he reasoned from past experience. "The Lord that delivered me . . . bear, will deliver me from . . . Philistine." The same succour is assured to all Christian warriors. *We want this mingled dependence and confidence.* "If God be for us, who can be against us?" The commission, "Go therefore, preach the gospel to all nations," was preceded by the announcement, "All power is given unto Me in heaven and in earth." Can we complain of tribulation and distress? "Nay, in all these things we are more than conquerors;" they do but heighten the victory we gain, "through Him that loved us."—A.

Ver. 13.—*A true man.* Consider Caleb—the companion of Joshua in early enterprise, constant faithfulness, Divine reward. From the epithet Kenazite, constantly applied to him; the fact that one of the "dukes of Edom" bears the name Kenaz; and the expression, "Unto Caleb he gave a part *among the children of Judah*" (ch. xv. 13), which suggests that though settled amongst them he was not really of them, many have, with considerable probability, concluded that Caleb was a proselyte. One of those who, like Heber the Kenite, threw in his lot with Israel—perhaps a Midianitish youth who attached himself to Moses—and by force of faith, energy, and wisdom commended himself for any service of special difficulty. Whatever his origin, he was one of the twelve prominent men chosen to survey the land and report on the best method of invasion. The result of that expedition was, unfortunately, a unanimous testimony to the excellence of the land, but an all-but unanimous testimony to the impossibility of taking it. Ten out of twelve declared its conquest impossible. Two only—Caleb and Joshua—asserted its practicability. They were too brave and too believing to yield to despair. They reckoned on more than natural probabilities, arguing, "The Lord is with us; and their defence is departed from them." But overborne by the numbers of those on the other side, and by the unbelief of the crowd, they can only grieve over what they cannot avert. And Israel turns back to the wilderness—where the carcases of all the grown men except these two fall before they next approach to Canaan. Now he re-appears after the conquest of the land to ask the fulfilment of the promise made by Moses to him. This district of Hebron was consecrated by early recollections of Abraham. The Amorites, though driven out from the city temporarily, are still in possession of the mountains about Hebron. Full of the old heroic fire, Caleb asks for a land still in the hands of enemies. Joshua grants it, and the Lord gives it him. And the land which saw his courage became his inheritance for generations. Let us consider a few features of this story in Numbers xiii. and xiv., and Joshua xiv. and xv.

I. First observe—THERE IS NEED FOR GOOD MEN IN SUBORDINATE AS WELL AS IN EXALTED STATION. Caleb is not over all Israel, not even prince of Judah. Only a spy—he is a man of eminence, but not of the highest. He fills a humbler place which some would have thought not worth while adorning. But, in addition to integrity and service in those at the head of the State, you want righteousness and courage throughout all classes of it. Had they had twelve Calebs for spies the land would have been theirs forty years before it was. As it was, the heroism of Caleb and Joshua was not wasted. Their testimony remained, inspiring wanderings ; round it the purpose of the nation crystallised. Their testimony of the possibility, of conquering Canaan, helped to create the possibility. Their faith was a leaven that took forty years to do it, but ultimately leavened the whole lump. In whatever station we be, remember, there is need for faith, energy, and service, and there is reward for the exercise of these in the lowly as well as in the lofty sphere.

II. Secondly observe — GODLINESS BEGETS MANLINESS OF THE NOBLEST KIND. What a charm there is in *manliness*, in its vigour, its honesty, in its fortitude and daring. What worth is in the manliness that dares to differ from friends, as well as to defy foes. The happy union of strength and spirit, which knows not fear nor halting. Besides the charm and worth, there is great joy in it as well. It feels no dread or dismay. It enjoys the leisure of the lofty nature, and its quickening self-respect. "Add to your faith *manliness*," says Peter. Courage to avow and to obey your faith. Most failures in conduct are preceded by failures in courage. To face duty as well as danger requires hardihood of spirit. Now observe the magnificent manliness of Caleb. It gleams through his report as a spy. It is apparent in this choice of the as yet unconquered territory. It comes out in the energy of his old age. And this simple quality in one man was of incalculable service to Israel. We all need this quality, men and women.

> " Our doubts are traitors,
> And make us lose the good we oft might win,
> By fearing to attempt."

More manliness would mean less falsehood, less failure, less wretchedness of apprehension, more enterprise and grand success. And godliness begets it. For godliness gives larger thought, greater dignity, scope for grand purposes, consciousness of help laid up in all providential law and processes. By communion with God man attains calmness, wisdom, strength, and help. Neither David nor Elijah was less manly, but more so, for being devout. If you would form a list of the kingliest men you will be surprised how many of the godliest are in it. John Knox and Luther amongst teachers, Cromwell and William the Silent among statesmen, Sir Philip Sidney and Henry Havelock among soldiers. We are short of manliness because short of godliness. If religion ever enervates a man, or withers him, it is a superstitious and not the genuine thing. Nelson said his Methodists were his best sailors. Let the young note this. Godliness does not enfeeble, it enlarges every essential element of manhood.

III. Thirdly observe—THE GREAT REWARDS OF CONSECRATION. That manliness was its own magnificent reward, as it produced an expansion of nature, which would be immortal. But there were besides, special rewards. (a) *Accurate light.* Good judgment grew from it. Knowledge of the possible, a grand self-measurement, in which no vanity exaggerated nor dismay diminished powers marked him. " A good understanding have all they that love Thy law." Walk with God and the light in which you walk will illumine common as well as sacred things. (b) *Providential mercies attend him.* With Joshua, he is only man who has length of days sufficiently given him to lead from Egypt to Canaan. Natural influences of devotion tend to preserve life, and they were in his case intensified by special providence. It may be said with all reverence and truth devotion saves numberless lives by preserving men from worry, folly, brooding, and needless quarrelling. God never fails to set His seal on goodness. " Corruption wins not more than honesty." (c) *Justice is done* him in the judgment of his fellows. When he protested against the evil report of the other spies the people " sought to stone him with stones." But now all the princes of Judah are proud to come with him to support his prayer ! He has the opportunity of justifying himself and his report, and he does it grandly. (d) THE PLACE WHERE HIS FAITH TRIUMPHED OVER FEAR BECOMES THE PLACE OF HIS INHERITANCE. He believed Hebron could be won. He has liberty to win it and permission to keep it for himself when it is won. It had fallen to his lot to survey that district especially, and although three tribes of giants were there, yet he was fearless. That fastness against which his valour would have led his brethren becomes his own possession. Not only his in title and grant, but his in possession. Is there not something typical here ? All things that threaten and oppose become *serviceable* when we face them bravely. That which threatens to destroy becomes a quiet resting-place and peaceable habitation. The enemies become the servants, the hindrances the helps, terrors change to fountains of refreshment. Let us be braver, refusing to despair, and refusing to shrink from difficulty. The same Saviour rules now as then, calls us to noble, and therefore difficult, duties. There are lots of children of Anak still ; fear them, and you doom yourself to wilderness wanderings and a dishonourable grave. Meet them, and you conquer them easily. Shame and reproach for Christ are children of Anak ; the fear of falling is another ; a corrupting taste and an indolent inclination is another. Christ has grand rewards and blessed helps for such as face these. As to Caleb, so always, He gives ultimate inheritance and present rewards. Let us not miss these, but seek to secure them with all our heart.—G.

Ver. 15.—"And the land had rest from war." *Rest from war.* I. REST FROM WAR IS ONE OF THE GREATEST EARTHLY BLESSINGS. Even if war be a necessity it is a fearful necessity. Rarely are the advantages of a successful war equal to the cost of it. Rest from war affords occasion (1) for the undisturbed enjoyment of the fruits of the earth and unbroken social and domestic life; (2) for the practice of peaceful works—the cultivation of science, art, and literature ; (3) for progress in political institutions and the development of civilisation; (4) for the extension of benevolent efforts and of the missionary work of the Church. Therefore peace should be sought for in prayer and enjoyed with gratitude.

II. UNIVERSAL REST FROM WAR WILL BE ONE OF THE CHIEF FRUITS OF THE TRIUMPH OF THE GOSPEL. Christ is the Prince of Peace. The Messianic age is prophetically described as an age of peace (Isa. xi. 6—9 ; Luke ii. 14). We must look to Christianity for the means of abolishing war, because this only can conquer (1) the injustice, (2) the ambition, and (3) the unruly passions which are the causes of most wars. War can only cease when right and justice are respected by nations and the brotherhood of all mankind is universally recognised. These are moral conditions. Education, trade conventions, political schemes will not produce them. They are the highest fruits of Christian principle.

III. SPIRITUAL REST FROM INWARD WARFARE IS SECURED TO THE CHRISTIAN BY CHRIST. (1) *The Christian must first fight* against indwelling sin, temptation, the evil of the world (1 Tim. vi. 12). Earth is our battle-field ; heaven our Canaan of rest. (2) The Christian will be *aided by Christ* fighting for him and in him. Jesus is the New Testament Joshua. He has conquered the great enemy. He is the source of His people's strength for that inward battle which all must fight. (3) By the grace of Christ the Christian will ultimately enjoy " rest from war." This is promise (a) for the individual Christian in heaven (Heb. iv. 9), (b) for the whole human family at the time of the complete triumph of Christ (Isa. ii. 4).—W. F. A.

Ver. 1.—*Peasant proprietorship.* The land of Canaan is divided not amongst nobility and gentry, but amongst the people. Each family has its little farm—probably averaging about ten acres. Divided equally amongst the people, the Mosaic law expressly forbade its alienation in perpetuity from any family. The jubilee year was ordained in order that twice in a century any too great inequalities of condition which had crept in might be redressed ; that every family which, through misfortune or even fault, had fallen out of property, might regain their land, and with it the means of maintenance for their families. In that jubilee year his freedom reverted to the slave, and his family heritage to him who had fallen into poverty. There was no injustice, for the value of the land was assessed in the case of every sale as that of a leasehold having so many years to run. Every tax and every religious charge upon the land similarly varied, according as the jubilee year was near or distant. None hurt by this system ; numerous and incalculable advantages arose from it. It prevented the rise of a feudal aristocracy, with the inevitable degradation of the poor. It put Israel in the best of all conditions for developing self-respect in the individual. Its equality was a school for liberty. It averted many of the most prolific causes of poverty. It diffused a homely comfort throughout all the land. It made the well-being of the State a matter of vital interest to every citizen, giving each able-bodied man a " stake in the country." It made Israel a model commonwealth, where the land was the home of all, and all classes without envy and without arrogance enjoyed the gifts of God in fairly even distribution.   Observe—

I. THE GROUNDS OF SUCH A PLAN OF DISTRIBUTION. The first " idea " lying at the root of this distribution of land is, that land is, unlike all other property, *not proper to be the possession in perpetuity* of any holder. The land is like the air of heaven, like the rain and the sunshine, like the fisheries of the sea, meant to be a common blessing for all, rather than the private good of any. Its productiveness is due to Nature's chemistry as much as to man's art. What man has no part in producing, he has no title to possess, and therefore no man can legitimately possess himself, to the exclusion of others, of that Divine part of the earth's fruitfulness. Accordingly, the theory of Moses is, that God is the great and only landlord ; none having more than life interests in the land. Every fifty years it all was to fall into His hands again. Under God the land belonged to the nation, and the jubilee year permitted it to be so divided that all the families of the nation would enjoy it with a rough equality. A second idea lying at the base of this legislation was, that great wealth and great poverty were both of them great evils, to be prevented at any cost. The evils of poverty are obvious. Insufficient food, physical degeneracy, the development of a servile and dependent spirit ; or of a reckless, turbulent spirit, that in its haste to relieve its hunger is apt to overthrow the State. Strife of classes inevitably springs from it. There is a poverty the result of indolence, which the law wisely would not attempt to prevent ; and one the result of accidents, which it was impossible to foresee, and so provide against. But every State should direct its first and most patient attention to poverty produced by law ; for that is generally the worst kind of all, as well as being a very general kind. And wealth corrupts equally with poverty. Wealth is full of fears, and fear begets tyranny and injustice. Too much is good for no one. The body is weakened by being pampered, the mind by want of constant occupation, the character by the softness that comes from the absence of struggle with difficulties. Ignorance of many of the ills of life begets hard-heartedness, and destroys the finer sympathies. The presence of great wealth and great poverty, side by side, intensifies the mischiefs of each, and becomes one of the greatest perils that any community has to contend with. The law of Moses, and the carrying out of it by Joshua, was thus directed to prevent the development of the two great evils of modern civilisation—

excessive wealth and excessive poverty. A third idea, lying at the foundation of this legislation, was that the equality of the citizens is the condition most favourable to the well-being of the State. All exaggerated differences of condition tend to divide and alienate classes, depriving the land in some degree of co-operation in enterprise, in defence of liberties, in practice of religion. Joshua aimed not at a stagnant communism, which would rob life of its energy, but yet of a brotherly state in which all would have a fair chance of comfort, and none an unfair chance of inordinate wealth. In the present circumstances of our country the land legislation of Moses is especially worthy of our study. We differ from Israel in one important condition—England finds the chief part of her national wealth, not in agriculture, but in manufactures and in commerce. This fact has made land laws, such as every other civilised nation has abolished, tolerable here. But even for England, and still more for Ireland, which is an agricultural land, the time has come when the needless loss and harm and waste which they produce should terminate. In these circumstances mark—

II. SOME SUGGESTIONS FOR LAND LEGISLATION AT HOME CONTAINED IN THE LAWS OF CANAAN. 1. These present us with *the ideal* at which to aim; viz., to get the land into as many hands as possible. 2. Such an ideal should, it is almost needless to say, be pursued only in a righteous and peaceful way. In a land of such wealth and resource as ours any other method would be as foolish as wicked. 3. Every facility that the law can give for the sale and transfer of lands ought to be given. Entail ought to be forbidden at once, as unjust to the younger children of a family, and injurious to the State. Settlements destroying the right of sale should be prohibited. These two alterations would at once bring much land into the market. 4. A law for division of property among his children on the death of the holder would in two or three generations effect a marvellous revolution in the present most deplorable distribution of land, and would work the same blessings here as such a law has wrought in France, Belgium, Denmark, &c. Instead of 2,000 persons (2,148 exactly) holding more than one-half of the land in the United Kingdom, it is desirable 2,000,000 of persons should share it. If by facilities for sale, the abolition of feudal laws tending to accumulate property in few hands which survive nowhere but here, the land could be by justice and peace brought again into the possession of the people, the gain to the nation would be incalculable. An enormous increase in productiveness would, judging from the experience of the other nations of Europe, at once accrue. This would be the least of the benefits. There would be less poverty, more self-respect, more energy, more patriotism, more union amongst our people; perhaps, with the extinction of so much injustice, more religion too. And we should find in this, as in other things, that modern civilisation is never so wise as when it sits at the feet of ancient inspiration. Moses and Joshua are the grandest of all political economists.—G.

Ver. 6—end.—*Caleb the son of Jephunneh.* Few characters finer than that of Caleb. If Moses was pattern of faithful leader, Caleb was of faithful follower. There are some things which suggest he was not an Israelite by birth. Kenaz the name of his father or brother, is an Edomite name, and the expression in ch. xiv. 14, "Hebron became the inheritance of Caleb . . . because that he wholly followed the God of Israel;" and that of ch. xv. 13, "Unto Caleb he gave a part *among the children* of Judah," are expressions which suggest that he was associated with that tribe rather than sprung from it. Whether or not he was an Israelite in flesh, he was earnestly so in faith. If not by birth an Israelite, he is an instance of the converting power of truth, and of the way in which identity of heart and aim supersedes all diversity of nature. He was one of the twelve spies. Had there been other ten like him, the invasion of Canaan would have begun and finished forty years earlier. There was no delusion in his mind; he saw all his colleagues saw—the stature of the men, the walls of the cities, the difficulty and all but impossibility of the conquest. But he saw what only Joshua saw besides him—the presence and the power of God. And seeing that, he believed in the possibility of what seemed to others impossible. Consider some elements of instruction here.

I. GOOD MEN ARE NEEDED FOR SECOND PLACES AS WELL AS FIRST. We cannot all be statesmen, rulers, missionaries. There are many more humble positions than exalted ones. Twelve spyships for one lordship. Good men are needed for all stations. Men who fear to do wrong, who fear to grieve God, and who have no other fear. Complain not of an obscure lot, of a slight opening for your powers; but do the duties of the lot, and avail yourself of the openings you have, and all will be well.

II. Second, observe THE PERSEVERANCE OF SAINTS. He believed in his prime, he believes in his old age. Ready to follow God's leading then, ready now. "As my strength was then, even so is my strength now for war, both to go out and to come in." There is, of course, a miraculous element in this persistence of physical strength and mental vigour at such an age. But it is only a miraculous extension of what is a blessed fact of daily experience. It is strange the *vis inertiæ* of souls. Forty years ago some were faithless, and are so now; others believing, they are so now. There is a tendency for the unjust to be unjust still, and for the righteous to be righteous still. Motion or rest alike tend to be eternal. Rise up and follow Christ, and you tend to follow Him on through countless ages. Forsake Him, and you tend to go on forsaking Him. This persistence of habit is nature; but the persistence of better habit is partly grace as well. God keeps the feet from falling, daily charms the spirit afresh, while each step of progress in a good path reveals new reasons for choosing and pursuing it. Do not despair. Of Christ's flock none is lost. "They go from strength to strength; every one of them appeareth before God in Zion." We may not, like Joshua, see eighty-five, and long before the life ends our powers may wither; but grace will not wither.

III. Observe THE USEFULNESS OF SUCH A LIFE OF PROGRESS. Eighty-five years of steady well-doing! of right aiming and right action! of the boldness of faith. Joshua and He were left alive, as a sort of leaven to leaven the whole lump of Israel, and they did it. One steady, progressive life of goodness—the same to-day as yesterday—how invaluable in a village, in a church, in any community. If you would be useful, *keep on*. Remember Abraham Lincoln's policy for the conquest of the secession—it was to "keep pegging away." Seeming hopeless, it was crowned with success.

IV. Lastly, observe, CALEB'S FAITH HAS A GRAND REWARD. A manifold reward. 1. In the contagiousness with which it spread. It infects his own family (see ch. xv. 17). It infects, as we have seen, many besides. 2. His faith has the opportunity of proving its wisdom. That city, which was impregnable, he took; and these Anakim, who seemed terrific, he mastered. Some men, some things, some forces may be stifled for want of opportunity. But God will always see that there is a candlestick for the light. An "open door" for the "little strength" which can enter it. 3. His faith gets an earthly inheritance of a noble kind. Hebron is his family's for an everlasting possession. *The shortest road to getting anything is deserving it.* While the clever, the tricky, the greedy, the saving see only what they aspire to "afar off," the deserving go straight on and reach it. His property we can trace in the possession of his descendants down to the time of David (1 Sam. xxx. 14). It is not sufficiently observed how essential to goodness the courage of faith really is. Let Caleb's example commend it to us.—G.

EXPOSITION.

CHAPTER XV. 1—63.

THE LOT OF JUDAH. Ver. 1.—**The lot of the tribe of the children of Judah.** The first twelve verses of this chapter define the boundaries of Judah. With it compare Num. xxxiv. 3—5, which gives the southern border of the Israelitish territory, corresponding closely with this account of the southern border of Judah. The word *tribe* here is, as might be expected from the context מַטֶּה and not שֵׁבֶט. **Even to the border of Edom.** The literal translation, which makes the passage clearer, is, "the border of Edom, the wilderness of Zin towards the dry region (נֶגְבָּה) from the extreme limit of the south" (תֵּימָן). The ıatter of these words, derived from יָמִין "right hand," being the position of the south' when regarded from the point of view of a man looking eastward, denotes the southward *direction* (see above, ch. xii. 2). The former word has reference to the physical conditions of the country, its heat and dryness. The LXX. does not attempt to translate the former word and has evidently מִקְדָּשׁ for מִקְצֵה. **The wilderness of Zin.** Not to be confounded with the wilderness of Sin (Exodus xvi. 1; cf. Num. xxxiv. 11, 36). This wilderness was on the border of Edom (Num. xx. i.; xxvii. 14). Thence the border of Judah (which here includes the small portion afterwards allotted to Simeon) extended to the utmost limits of the south (see ch. xix. 1, 9). A wall of mountains extends south-westward from the southern extremity of the Dead Sea, and formed the natural boundary of Judæa.

Ver. 2.—**The shore of the salt sea.** Literally, the *extremity*, *i.e.*, the *south* extremity. **From the bay.** Literally, *tongue* (so margin). The LXX. translates by λοφία, *ridge*. The whole southern portion of the sea is cut off from the rest by a peninsula near Kerak, the ancient Kir of Moab. It is called the Lisan. Whoever was the writer of the Book of Joshua, these details prove him to have had an accurate acquaintance with the geography of Palestine. He was no priestly inventor of fables attached to the temple at Jerusalem. Canon Tristram gives a vivid description of the neighbourhood in his 'Land of Israel,' ch. xv. The ridge of Jebel Usdum—one large mass of rock salt—on the west of this "tongue" of water, the salt marsh of the Sebkha on the south-west, with its treeless waste—"not a plant or a leaf could be seen save just under the hills"—and its mirage like that of Sahara, the barren outline of the Lisan itself, to the eastward rising to an elevation of from five to six hundred feet, and the fertile oasis of the Ghor-es-Safieh at the southern extremity of the Dead Sea, give an unique character to this remarkable region.

Ver. 3. **And it went out to the south side to Maaleh-acrabbim..** Or, perhaps, *and it went to the southward of Maaleh-acrabbim*, translated in Num. xxxiv. 4, "the ascent of Acrabbim." The literal meaning of Maaleh-acrabbim is Scorpion Rise (see Judg. i. 36). Keil thinks that it was a pass in the Mount Halak, or the Smooth Mountain, mentioned in ch. xi. 17, xii. 7. "De Saulcy suggests the Wady Zouara, and testifies to the scorpions found under every pebble" (Stanley, 'Sinai and Palestine,' p. 113). And Ainsworth, 'Travels in Asia Minor,' ii. 354, says that some spots are almost uninhabit-

able in consequence. Knobel supposes it to be the pass es-Sufah on the road between Petra and Hebron. But the border of Judah seems to have gone in a south-westerly direction. **To Zin.** Rather, *in the direction of* Zin. **On the south side unto Kadesh-barnea.** Or, as above, *southward of Kadesh-barnea.* The exact position of Kadesh-Barnea has not been ascertained. It was between the wilderness of Zin and that of Paran (Num. xiii. 26; xx. 1). Dean Stanley identifies it with Petra, which was about 30 miles in a north-easterly direction from the Gulf of Akaba on the Red Sea, and close to Mount Hor. A more recent traveller (see Bartlett, 'Egypt and Palestine,' pp. 366—376) identifies it with Ain Gadis, about 60 miles to the westward of Petra, and he claims Winer, Kurz, Kalisch, and Knobel as supporters of his view. The latter founds his view on the discovery of Ain Gadis. by Rowlands, and supports it by the authority of Ritter. Ritter, however, as his translator informs us, embodied the results of the investigations of Mr. Rowlands' while his work was preparing for the press, and did not give the matter that full consideration which he was accustomed to do. The chief objection to it is that (see ver. 1) Ain Gadis can hardly be described as on "the border of Edom." The general view is that it lay somewhat to the north-east of Hezron and to the north-west of Petra, at the foot of the range of mountains which form the southern boundary of Judæa. Here the spies brought their report to Moses (ch. xiv. 6, 7; Num. xiii. 26). Here Miriam was buried, and where Moses incurred the wrath of God from his mode of working the miracle which supplied the Israelites with water (Num. xx.). It was "a city in the uttermost border" of Edom (Num. xx. 16), and it was some distance from Mount Hor, for we find it described as a journey (Num. xx. 22); and by passing from Kadesh to Mount Hor, and thence by the way of the Red Sea, the Israelites "compassed the land of Edom" (Num. xxi. 4), a fact which seems to prove that Petra and Kadesh-barnea were not the same place. Kadesh is supposed by M. Chabas to be the "Qodesh of the country of the Amaor," or Amorites, in the monuments of Seti I. and Rameses II. It is depicted as "on a hillside with a stream on one side," and is thus distinguished from Qodesh of the Kheta or Hittites, which is in a flat country beside a lake (Tomkins, 'Studies of the Time of Abraham,' p. 84). **Fetched a compass to Karkaa.** Rather, *was deflected in the direction of Karkaa.* Nothing is known of the places here mentioned. Cf. Num. xxxiv. 4, where Karkaa is not mentioned, but the deflection in the neighbourhood of Asmon is.

Ver. 4.—**The river of Egypt** (see above, ch. xiii. 3). " Westward, as far as Egypt, there is a sandy, salt, barren, unfruitful, and uninhabitable waste" (Knobel). The land, he adds, is better near Gaza, but near the sea it is still pure waste. **And the goings out of that coast were at the sea.** The word coast, derived through the French from the Latin *costa*, signifies, like it, a *side*. It is now used only of the border formed by the sea, but at an earlier period it had a wider signification. The Hebrew word is translated " border" in ver. 1. The meaning is that the boundary line of Judah ran as far as the sea. **This shall be your south coast.** Or, *this shall be to you the southern boundary*. The historian here quotes the directions given to Moses in Num. xxxiv., with the evident intention of pointing out that the south border of the children of Israel coincided with that of the tribe of Judah.

Ver. 5.—**To the end of Jordan.** The spot where it emptied itself into the Dead Sea. **The bay of the sea at the uttermost part of Jordan.** As in ver. 3, the word here translated bay is *tongue* in the original. What is meant is that the northern boundary started from the point where the Jordan entered the Dead Sea.

Ver. 6.—**Beth-hogla** (see ch. xviii. 19). It is still known as *Ain Hadjla* or *Hajla*, where, says Keil, a beautiful spring of fresh and clear water is to be found. The place lies about two miles from Jordan. Beth-hogla means "the house of the partridge." " Leaving the probable site of the ancient Gilgal and advancing southward along the pilgrims' route to the Jordan, an hour and a quarter brings us to the spring Ain Hajla, in a small and well-watered grove " (Ritter). He adds, " Robinson and Wilson both recognised in the name Hajla the ancient Canaanitish city Beth-hogla." **Beth-arabah.** Or " the house of the Arabah " or desert. Its site is not known (see ver. 61 and ch. xviii. 18, 22). The Beth-arabah in ver. 61, however, must have been another place, since it was in the wilderness of Judæa, not far from the Dead Sea. **The stone of Bohan the son of Reuben.** All we know of this stone is that it was westward of Beth-arabah. The boundary of Benjamin in ch. xviii. is mentioned in precisely reverse order, and since here the stone was on the ascent from Beth-araba, and there (ver. 17) it is described as on the descent from Geliloth, it must have been on the side of the declivity. Of Bohan nothing further is known. We must understand here, as in many other places of Scripture, *descendant* by "son " (cf. ch. vii. 24).

Ver. 7.—**Toward Debir.** Not the Debir of ch. x. **The valley of Achor** (see ch. vii. 26).

This is now the Wady Kelt. **Gilgal.** Keil says that this is not the Gilgal where the Israelites first encamped. It is called Geliloth, or " circles," in ch. xviii. 17, where the same place is obviously meant as here. The question is one of some difficulty. If it be not the Gilgal mentioned in ch. iv. 19, which is described as being eastward of Jericho, still less can it be Jiljiliah (see note on ch. ix. 6) which was near Bethel, and therefore on the northern border of Benjamin. In that case the only supposition that will meet the facts in this case is that Gilgal, which signifies a wheel or circle, was the common name given to all the Israelitish encampments. But there seems no reason to doubt that the Gilgal of ch. iv. 19 is meant. This is Ewald's view in his 'History of Israel,' ii. 245. **Adummim**, or " the red (places)," has been identified with Maledomim, *i.e.* Maaleh Adummim, or Talat el Dumm (Conder), on the road from Jerusalem to Jericho. Jerome explains it as " ascensus ruforum seu rubentium propter sanguinem qui illic crebro a latronibus funditur." Every one will at once call to mind the narrative in St. Luke x., which has no doubt suggested this explanation. But at one particular point in the route from Jerusalem to Jericho a " large mass of purplish rock " is found (Stanley, ' Sinai and Palestine,' p. 424, note). It was called " terra ruffa," " the red earth," from the colour of the ground, and recent travellers state that it is called the " red field " still, from this cause. Conder tells us the name is derived from " the brick-red marks here found amid a district of red chalk (see also Mr. Tyrwhitt Drake in Pal. Expl. Fund Quart. Paper, April, 1874). So Knobel speaks, on the authority of numberless travellers of " der rothen Farbe des dortigen gesteins." And the Quarterly Paper just quoted mentions the " bright limestone and marl." **Which is on the south side of the river.** The *Nahal*, or summer torrent, in the original ; " the Wady Kelt, south of Riha " (Knobel). **The waters of En-shemesh**, or the fountain of the sun, supposed to be Ain Haud, or the " Apostles' well," near Bethany. There is an *Arak* (cave) *esh Shems*, about two miles off. All these places have been identified on or near the pilgrims' route to the Jordan. **Enrogel** (see ch. xviii. 17). It was close by Jerusalem, and was where Jonathan and Ahimaaz lingered to gain tidings for David, and where Adonijah repaired to hold the great feast when he endeavoured to obtain the kingdom. " Now Ain Um ed Deraj in the Kedron Valley " (Conder). Vandevelde supposes it to be Bîr Eyub, Joab's well, at the point where the Kedron Valley meets the Gai Hinnom. This seems most probable. **The valley of the son of Hinnom.** The word here for valley (**'ג**) signifies properly a deep cleft in the rock, through which no water flows. The valley of Hinnom has been generally taken to be the deep valley running from west to east, and lying to the west and south of Jerusalem, described by Tobler as forked at its north-western end, bending to the southward about its middle, and joining the valley of Jehoshaphat at its eastern extremity. In the Quarterly Paper of the Palestine Exploration Fund for October, 1878, however, it is contended that the now partially filled up Tyropœon Valley, running through the city, is the valley or ravine of Hinnom. The manner in which this is demonstrated reminds the reader somewhat of a proposition in Euclid, and the question arises whether Euclid's method be exactly applicable to a point of this kind. The arguments used are not without force, but no notice is taken of the peculiar position of the valley of Rephaim (see next note but one), which, we learn from the sacred historian, was so placed that its extremity coincided with the mountain which closed the ravine of Hinnom at its western side. If the Tyropœon Valley answers to this description, it may be accepted as the true valley of Hinnom, but not otherwise. Mr. Birch incorrectly cites Gesenius in favour of his theory; and the most recent discoveries appear to have thrown discredit upon it. The most weighty argument in favour of his theory is that a comparison of Josh. xv. 63 with Judg. i. 3—8, leads to the supposition that Jerusalem was partly in Benjamin and partly in Judah (see, however, Neh. xi. 30). This valley, called sometimes Tophet, and sometimes, by a corruption of the Hebrew, Gehenna, whatever its situation may have been, is conspicuous in the after history of Israel. This deep and retired spot was the seat of all the worst abominations of the idol-worship to which the Jews afterwards became addicted. Here Solomon reared high places for Moloch (1 Kings xi. 7). Here children were sacrificed at the hideous rites of that demongod (2 Kings xvi. 3; 2 Chron. xxviii. 3; Jer. vii. 31, 32; xix. 2, 4). It was defiled by Josiah (2 Kings xxiii. 10, 13, 14), and was looked upon in later times as an abomination (see Jer. xix. 13). There the carcases of animals were cast to be burned, and hence it is used by our Lord (Matt. v. 22) as the type of the utmost wrath of God. It is hardly possible to suppose that there is no allusion to Tophet and its fiery sacrifices in Isa. xxx. 33, in spite of the different form of the word, to which some scholars, *e.g.*, Gesenius, assign an Aryan rather than

a Semitic origin, and in spite of the fact that the LXX. suspects no such allusion there. St. James alone, beside the writers of the Gospels, mentions it (ch. iii. 6), "*set on fire* of hell," or *Gehenna*.

Ver. 8.—**The south side of the Jebusite.** Literally, *the shoulder of the Jebusite from* (or *on*) *the south* (see 1 Kings vi. 8; vii. 39, margin). Thus Jerusalem lay to the north of the border, in the tribe of Benjamin. **The same is Jerusalem.** Formerly called Jebus, from the Jebusites who dwelt there (Judg. xix. 11; 1 Chron. xi. 4). The city lay on the borders of Judah and Benjamin (see note on ch. x. 1). **The valley of the giants.** Hebrew, *Rephaim* (see ch. xii. 4). The word here translated valley is **עֵמֶק**. In the former part it is **'ג** (see note on last verse). The word here used signifies originally *depth*, and is applied to wide valleys embosomed among lofty hills. Such were the valley of Elah (1 Sam. xvii. 2, 19); the King's Dale (Gen. xiv. 17; 2 Sam. xviii. 18); the valley of Siddim (Gen. xiv. 3), of Jezreel (Judg. vi. 33). "The word Emek shows that this was neither a winter torrent nor a narrow, dry ravine, and it is best identified with its traditional site, the shallow basin west of the watershed south of Jerusalem, now called el Bukei'a" (Conder). We read of this valley in 2 Samuel v. 18, 22. From these passages we may gather a confirmation of the view above expressed, that the valley here meant is an open valley, since only in such a valley could the Philistine army take up a position. It gradually narrows towards the south-west. On the south it extends as far as Bethlehem. The range of mountains which lie to the west of the valley of Hinnom from the northern boundary of the plain or valley of Rephaim.

Ver. 9.—**Was drawn.** Or, *extended.* **The fountain of the waters of Nephtoah.** If these be identified with En Etam, as is done by the Rabbis (whom Conder follows), and if we suppose it to have supplied Jerusalem with water by the aqueduct which ran from a point south-west of Betlehem to Jerusalem, we must place it south of Bethlehem, and imagine that the border ran directly south here. Far more probable is the notion of Vandevelde, which places it north-west of Jerusalem, at Ain Lifta. Conder's view is dominated by the situation he has assigned to Kirjath-jearim (see note on ch. ix. 17). If the view there given in these notes is sound, the border now ran in a north-westerly direction from Jerusalem to within five miles of Gibeon (see also note on ch. xviii. 14). **Kirjath-jearim.** See ch. ix. 17. To the authorities mentioned there in favour of Kuriet el Enab we may add

Knobel, Ritter, and Tristram, in his last book, 'Bible Lands.' The view taken above corresponds to the minuteness of detail with which the boundary is given. To place Nephtoah south of Bethlehem and Kirjath-jearim at 'Arma would make the boundary far less distinct.

Ver. 10.—**Compassed.** Or, *deflected* (see ver. 4). This is in accordance with the view taken above. The border line which had run north-west from Jerusalem now bent backwards in a south-westerly direction, and followed the ridge towards Chesalon (see note on Chesalon). **Mount Seir.** Not the dwelling-place of Esau, afterwards the country of the Edomites (Gen. xxxii. 3 ; xxxvi. 8), but a range running south-westward from Kirjath-jearim, part of which is still known as Sairah, or Saris, " auf welchem *Saris* und *Mihsir* liegen " (Knobel). Since Kirjath-jearim means the " city of the forests," and Seir means "hairy," we may conjecture that the name was given to the ridge on account of its wooded character. This also is implied by " Mount Jearim." **The side of Mount Jearim.** Literally, *the shoulder* (see above, ver. 8). **Which is Chesalon.** This is identified with *Kesla*, a point on the summit of the ridge stretching south-west from Kirjath-jearim. The fact that the border passed northward of Chesalon is a confirmation of the view taken above. We learn from ch. xix. 41 (cf. ver. 33 of this chapter), that the border passed by Zorah and Eshtaol in the Shephelah, through a neighbourhood described in Conder's Handbook as " an open corn country." **Beth-shemesh.** The " house of the sun," identified with the modern Ain (or fountain of) Shems. It is called Ir-shemesh in ch. xix. 41. It was close to the border of the Philistines, and was the scene of the transactions recorded in 1 Sam. vi. The propinquity to the Philistines appears to have affected the principles of its inhabitants, and their conduct contrasts most unfavourably with that of the inhabitants of Kirjath-jearim. This was the more disgraceful, in that Beth-shemesh (ch. xxi. 16) was a priestly city, and being inhabited by those whose "lips should keep knowledge," might have been expected to set a better example. It was required to furnish Solomon's household with provisions (1 Kings iv. 9), it witnessed the defeat and capture of Amaziah (2 Kings xiv. 11—13 ; 2 Chron. xxv. 21) by Joash, king of Israel. It fell into the hands of the Philistines at the time of the decay of the Jewish power under Ahaz (2 Chron. xxviii. 18). The name, like Baal-Gad and Ashtaroth-Karnaim, is worthy of remark, as pointing to the character of the early Phœnician worship.

Timnah. Sometimes called Timnath in Scripture (see Judg. xiv. 1—6), and Timnatha in ch. xix. 43.

Ver. 11.—**Ekron.** This important Philistine city (see ch. xiii. 3) lay close to the northern border of Judah. As a matter of fact, however, the tribe of Judah never succeeded in permanently occupying this territory, which only fell under their yoke during the reigns of David and Solomon. The cities of the Philistines were, it is true, most of them captured (Judg. i. 18), but we soon find the Philistines once more in possession of them (see 1 Sam. v. 8—10). **Northward.** The border turned sharply northward until past Ekron, when it once more turned westward until it reached the sea.

Ver. 12.—**And the coast thereof.** See ch. xiii. 23.

Ver. 13.—**And unto Caleb.** This passage, at least from ver. 15, is found with the slightest possible variation in Judg. i. It has been argued from the variations that the one passage was not copied from the other, but that both were derived from a common document. No such conclusion, however, can be safely drawn from the text. For first, the present narrative deals exclusively with this portion of the history of Caleb. That in Judges, down to ver. 12, deals more generally with the subject, including the exploits of Caleb, under the general history of the progress of Judah. But from the time that the history becomes that of Caleb in particular, the agreement between the two narratives is verbal, including the very unusual word צנח, with one or two most insignificant exceptions. Thus we have הָבָה לִּי for תְּנָה לִּי, we have גִּלִית for גְּלִיות, and we have מִמֶּנּוּ interpolated in Judg. i. 13, and Othniel (or Kenaz) is spoken of as the *younger* brother of Caleb. But unless we hold that it was a sacred duty of the writer in Judges to reproduce every single word of the narrative in Joshua, there is nothing whatever that can support the conclusion that the writer in Judges was not copying the earlier narrative. The variations are such as would naturally happen where a writer was transferring a narrative to his pages with a desire to give the exact sense of the original without tying himself to every particular word. Since the use of inverted commas has been introduced we can find multitudes of instances where a writer, when professing to quote another accurately, has introduced far more variations into his quotation than are to be found here, where the writer, though quoting the Book of Joshua, and quoting it correctly, does not say that he is doing so.

No one doubts that Jeremiah in ch. xlviii. is quoting Isa. xv., although the passages are not verbally coincident. We may safely regard this quotation of the Book of Joshua in that of Judges, as under all ordinary laws of criticism an evidence that the former book was in existence when the latter was written, just as the quotations of Deuteronomy in Joshua may naturally be taken as evidence that the Book of Deuteronomy was in existence when that of Joshua was composed. **The son of Jephunneh.** (see ch. xiv. 6). **A part.** Literally, a *lot.* **Among.** Rather, *in the midst of.* Our version is obscure here. **Arba the father of Anak, which city is Hebron.** (see ch. xiv. 6—15). Keil thinks that he was the tribefather, or chief (sheikh, as the Arabs would call him), of the children of Anak.

Ver. 14.—**The three sons of Anak.** This also must not be pressed literally. Possibly these men were three chiefs of the Anakim. **The children of Anak.** יְלִידֵי *descendants,* thus supporting the view taken in the last note (see for the word Gen. xiv. 14; xvii. 12, where it is used of a slave *born in the house).*

Ver. 15.—**Kirjath-sepher** (see note on ch. x. 38).

Ver. 16.—**And Caleb said** (cf. 1 Sam. xvii. 25; 1 Chron. xi. 6).

Ver. 17.—**The brother of Caleb.** The Hebrew does not inform us whether Othniel or Kenaz were Caleb's brother. But the fact (see note on ch. xiv. 6) that Caleb was the son of Jephunneh leads to the idea that the latter is meant. Othniel was a valiant and capable commander, as we learn from Judg. iii. 9.

Ver. 18.—**As she came to him.** Whether the bridal procession of the later Jews were already in existence or not, we have no evidence to show. **A field.** The narrative in Judges has "*the* field," meaning the particular field mentioned in the passage. **Lighted off.** Or, *sank down;* spoken of gradual motion, as of the nail which, when smitten by Jael into Sisera's temples, went down into the ground. So Knobel. Our translation renders it "fastened" there, which is hardly the meaning. This word has been a difficulty to translators. The LXX. renders ἐβόησεν ἐκ τοῦ ὄνου, and the Vulgate still more strangely, "Suspiravit, ut sedebat in asino." The LXX. seems to have read צעק for צנח. The Chaldee, Syriac, and Arabic render as our version. **What wouldest thou?** Or, *what is the matter?* Literally, *What to thee?* Achsah's conduct surprised Caleb. It was probably accompanied by an imploring gesture, and occurred before she had reached the house of

Othniel, who no doubt had come to meet her; or possibly, according to the later Oriental custom, had escorted her the whole way. **A blessing** (see 2 Kings v. 15; also Gen. xxxiii. 11; 1 Sam. xxv. 27). The use of the word in the sense of "gift" comes from the fact that to *bless* is to bestow benefits upon the person blessed (see Deut. xxviii. 1—6, 11, 12).

Ver. 19. — **A southland.** Hebrew, *the* southland. The word Negeb signifies dry (see note on Negeb, ch. x. 40). It must be remembered that it became the word for south, because the south of Palestine was an arid tract. Therefore Achsah must be understood as saying, "Thou hast given me a dry country, give me also a reservoir of water." The Vulgate translates Negeb twice over," australem et arentem" (arentem only Judg. i. 15). The LXX. translates both Negeb and Gulloth as proper names. But in the parallel passage in Judges Negeb is translated "south," and Gulloth appears as λύτρωσιν, as if from גלה to remove. Nothing can more clearly show that the LXX. translation is the work of different hands. **Springs of water.** גֻּלֹּת akin to our *well* and the German *quelle,* and derived from גלל to roll, from the circular motion observable in springs, as also from the *rolling* of waves. The Chaldee renders *the house of irrigation* (בֵּית שַׁקְיָא). Knobel translates *reservoirs.* **The upper springs and the lower springs** (see note on Debir, ch. x. 38).

Ver. 20.—**This is the inheritance.** The territory of Judah is divided into four parts, in the summary which follows: the "south," the "valley," the "mountains," and the "wilderness." **Tribe.** Here מַטֶּה (see note ch. xiii. 29).

Ver. 21.—**Coast.** Rather, *border* (see note ver. 4). **Southward.** The term here used (see above, ver. 19) for "south" is the one which has the signification of dryness. It is, however, occasionally used in a less strict sense, as in ch. xix. 24. Though the south country was in the main an arid region, yet its intersection by numerous wadys, with their attendant streams, provided fertile spots at intervals, where the traveller might rest, cattle might be watered, and corn and other produce raised. The only places of any importance in Scripture history mentioned here are Beersheba (see Gen. xxi. 31), and Hormah (see Num. xiv. 45; xxi. 3; and cf. ch. xii. 14; xix. 4; and Judg. i. 17). This last passage explains why the city is mentioned among the cities of Simeon as well as Judah, and is another instance of the remarkable accuracy of our author.

Ziklag is famous as the residence of David (1 Sam. xxvii. 6). It is noteworthy that it was given to him by Achish, king of Gath, in whose possession it therefore was at that time. It was burnt by the roving bands of Amalekites (1 Sam. xxx. 1).

Ver. 22.—**Their villages** (see note ch. xiii. 28).

Ver. 22.—**Kinah.** Knobel suggests that this was the city of the Kenites, a supposition which derives some support from Judg. i. 16 and 1 Sam. xv. 6.

Ver. 24.—**Telem.** This is identified by Knobel with the Telaim mentioned in 1 Sam. xv. 4. Conder, in his ' Handbook,' supports this view, but nothing more is known of the place.

Ver. 29.—**Iim.** The Alexandrian version of LXX. has Ἀνείμ here. If this be correct, the city was named after the Avim (see note on ch. xiii. 4). If we take the reading in the text we must interpret by *ruins* (see note on Ai, ch. vii. 2).

Ver. 32.—**Ain, Rimmon** (see ch. xix. 7 ; 1 Chron. iv. 32 ; Neh. xi. 29). More likely the name of one place Ain-Rimmon, *the fountain of* the god Rimmon. For Rimmon see 2 Kings v. 18. The word signifying *eye*, or *fountain*, is written indifferently Ain or En in our version (see En-shemesh and En-rogel in this chapter). Rimmon is mentioned in Zech. xiv. 10 as " south of Jerusalem." Now Umm er - Rumâmîn (Conder).

Ver. 32. **Twenty-nine.** There is another of the very common errors of numbers here. The actual number is thirty-six. The error is as old as the LXX. version.

Ver. 33. **The valley.** בַּשְּׁפֵלָה (see note on ch. ix. 1; x. 40). This was the fertile part of Judah, and formed a part of the rich plain which has been described as extending northward as far as Carmel. It was "renowned for the beauty of its flowers" (Delitzsch). With the exception of Zorah and Eshtaol, border towns to the tribe of Dan (ch. xix. 41; Judg. xiii. 25), famous in the history of Samson (see Judg. xiii.—xvi.), and mentioned in 2 Chron. xi. 10; Neh. xi. 29, the cities remarkable in history have been noticed already. It is worthy of remark that the cities of the Philistines were included in this list. But the Philistines, save during the reigns of David and Solomon, retained their independence, and in earlier and later times alike even encroached upon the Jewish territory (see 1 Sam. xiii. 5 ; 2 Chron. xxviii. 18; and note on ver. 11).

Ver. 44.—**Mareshah.** One of Rehoboam's fortified cities (2 Chron. xi. 8). Here Asa met Zerah the Ethiopian, or Cushite, and overthrew him (2 Chron. xiv. 9). Here

lived the prophet who foretold the destruction of Jehoshaphat's navy (2 Chron. xx. 37. See also Micah i. 15). Now Marash, close to Beit-Jibrin or Eleutheropolis (Tristram, Conder). If it be the same as Moresheth-Gath in Micah i. 14, this adds additional probability to the identification of Gath with Beit-Jibrin (see note on ch. xiii. 3).

Ver. 45.—**Ekron, with her towns and her villages.** Literally, her *daughters* and her *farm-hamlets* (see note on ch. xiii. 28). These cities of the Philistines had, like Gibeon, daughter-cities dependent on them, and must therefore have been, like Gibeon, " great cities as the royal cities " (ch. x. 2). They do not appear to have come under regal government till later times (cf. 1 Sam. v. 8, 11, with 1 Sam. xxvii. 2). " Around it (Gezer) and along the sides were distributed a series of small isolated centres of agglomeration. . . . This disposition to scatter itself, of which Gezer surely does not offer us the only specimen, explains in a striking manner the Biblical phrase, ' the city and her daughters'" (Pal. Expl. Fund, Quart. Paper, Jan., 1874). This explanation, however, is doubtful (see ch. ix. 17). According to Knobel, this passage cannot have been written by the Elohist, because he confines himself to the description of the cities the Israelites actually possessed. Why a later writer, writing presumably when Israel's fortunes were at a lower ebb, should have added a description of the territory Israel did *not* possess, he does not explain.

Ver. 48.—**The mountains.** Compare the expression, " the hill country of Judæa " (τῇ ὀρεινῇ, the same as here in the LXX.), Luke i. 65. It extends northwards from near Debir to Jerusalem, attaining at Hebron a height of about 2,700 feet. The physical characteristics of the country are vividly described in Deut. viii. 7, 8. Dean Stanley (' Sinai and Palestine,' p. 100) descants on the home-like character of the scenery and vegetation to an Englishman, and remarks on the contrast between the life, activity, and industry displayed there, as contrasted with the desolation of the greater part of Palestine. A later traveller, who would not, of course, be so struck with the resemblance to English scenery, speaks of the fertility of the ground as a matter of possibility, rather than of fact. The rocky soil, when broken up by the combined influences of heat, rain, and frost, is, like the soil of other rocky districts, extremely susceptible of cultivation when laid out in terraces. He remarks how the signs of ancient cultivation in this manner are to be seen on all sides, and laments the misrule which has converted the " land flowing with milk and honey " into a wilderness (see Bartlett,

'Egypt and Palestine,' ch. xix., and note on ch. x. 40). The time has not yet come for the Jews, now asserting their ancient greatness in statesmanship, literature, and art in every country in the civilised world, to return to their own land. Not till then, it is to be feared, will the prophecy in Isaiah xxxv. be fulfilled, and " the desert rejoice, and the wilderness blossom as the rose, while waters break out in the wilderness and streams in the desert, the parched ground becoming a pool, and the thirsty land springs of water."

Ver. 51.—**Giloh.** Perhaps the city of Ahithophel.

Ver. 55.—**Maon, Carmel, and Ziph.** These, as Dean Stanley reminds us (' Sinai and Palestine,' p. 101), still retain unaltered their old names. "That long line of hills was the beginning of the 'hill country of Judæa,' and when we began to ascend it the first answer to our inquiries after the route told us that it was 'Carmel,' on which Nabal fed his flocks, and close below its long ranges was the hill and ruins of Ziph," close above the hill of Maon. Wilson also (' Lands of the Bible,' i. 380) makes the same remark. Maon is to be remembered as David's hiding - place from the enmity of Saul (1 Sam. xxiii. 24—26), and as the home of Nabal (1 Sam. xxv. 2). Carmel (not the famous mountain of that name) meets us again in the history of Saul and of David (1 Sam. xv. 12; xxv. 2, 5, 7, 40). The neighbourhood of Ziph was also one of David's hiding-places, and is described as a "wilderness" in which there was a " wood " in 1 Sam. xxiii. 15, 19; xxvi. 1, 2. See also the prologue to Psa. liv. Another Ziph is mentioned in ver. 24.

Ver. 60.—**Kirjath Baal.** Before these words the LXX. insert the names of eleven more cities, among which Tekoah and Bethlehem are included. For the former see 2 Sam. xiv. 2; 2 Chron. xi. 6; xx. 20. The prophet Amos was one of its herdsmen (Amos i. 1). We learn from 1 Maccab. ix. 33, &c., that it was near Jordan, and had a waste district in its vicinity. It has been identified with Tekn'a, two hours south of Bethlehem. Of Bethlehem itself, the home of Ruth and David, the birthplace of Jesus Christ, it is unnecessary to speak. But the incidents related concerning Bethlehem in Judg. xvii., xix. (which seem to indicate that the author of the book had special information about Bethlehem), as well as the narrative of the Book of Ruth, lead us to suppose that the verse inserted here by the LXX. is genuine, since Bethlehem was, in early times, a town of sufficient importance to be noticed in a list like this, and that its omission in the Hebrew text is due to the mistake of some transcriber.

Ver. 61.—**The wilderness.** מִדְבָּר: This was the eastern part of the territory of Judah, bordering on the Dead Sea. Here David took refuge from the pursuit of Saul (Psa. lxiii. 1), and here St. John the Baptist prepared the way of Christ. It is described by Tristram (' Land of Israel,' p. 197) as " a wilderness, but no desert." Herbage is to be found there, but no trees, no signs of the cultivation formerly bestowed upon the hill country (see above, ver. 48). And the fewness of the cities in early times is a proof that its character has not been altered by time. The hills, says Canon Tristram, are of a "peculiar desolate tameness," and are intersected by the traces of winter watercourses, seaming the sides of the monotonous round-topped hills. Other writers describe this country in less favourable terms, denying it even the scanty herbage found there by Canon Tristram.

Ver. 62.—**The city of Salt.** Probably near the valley of Salt (2 Sam. viii. 13 ; 2 Kings xiv. 7; 1 Chron. xviii. 12), which must have been near the border of Edom, and in close proximity to the Dead Sea (see note on ch. iii. 16). **En-gedi.** The "fountain of the kid." Here David took refuge from Saul (1 Sam. xxiv. 1). This place, now Ain Jidy, is situated in " a plain or slope about a mile and a half in extent from north to south " (Tristram, ' Land of Israel,' p. 281). Here the ruins of the ancient city of Hazezon Tamar, or " the felling of the palm trees " (Gen. xiv. 7), are to be found, a city perhaps " the oldest in the world," may still be seen. " The cluster of camphire " (or rather of *henna*, the plant with which Oriental women stained their nails—Cant. i. 14) may still be found there, and its perennial torrent dashes still into the Dead Sea. In later times than those of the Old Testament the Essenes planted their head-quarters here.

Ver. 63.—**As for the Jebusites.** This passage, compared with Judg. i. 8, 21, and 2 Sam. v. 6, implies that the people of Judah took and set on fire the lower city, but were compelled to leave the stronghold of Zion in the hands of the Jebusites (see note on ch. x. 1). Origen and Theodoret see in the Jebusites the type of the nominal members of Christ's Church, who are not His disciples indeed. The former refers to Matt. xiii. 25. **Unto this day.** A clear proof that this book was written before David became king.

HOMILETICS.

Vers. 1—63.—*The inheritance of Judah.* This chapter does not suggest much matter for homiletic treatment. The chief points to be noticed are (1) the fulfilment of the prophecy of the pre-eminence of Judah uttered by Jacob (Gen. xlix. 8—12), due no doubt originally to the pre-eminence of Judah for gentleness and justice above all his brethren except Joseph ; (2) the picture of filial and parental affection in the family of Caleb, as evinced by the manner in which Achsah made her request, and the readiness with which, being a reasonable one, it was granted ; (3) the valour of Othniel, fitting him for his future eminence as a deliverer and judge of Israel ; and (4) the want of faith, noticed more particularly elsewhere, which, while cities of such importance as are here enumerated had been given by God into the hand of Judah, this tribe did not appropriate to itself the promise, and the Philistine cities became the sorest thorns in their sides of all their surrounding enemies. We may add (5) that Caleb's behaviour to Achsah supplies us with an illustration of the text, " If ye, being evil, know how to give good gifts to your children, how much more shall your heavenly Father give good things to them that ask Him " (Matt. vii. 11).

HOMILIES BY VARIOUS AUTHORS.

Vers. 16—19.—*Fulness of blessing.* Achsah had something of her father's spirit in her—ambitious, vigorous, resolute, quick to seize the present opportunity. Having so lately won his own suit Caleb could scarcely deny her her's. Through the simple, Oriental form of this narrative we see the working of deep and universal principles of human life. Let us regard it as suggestive of that restless craving of our nature which can find satisfaction only in the realisation of the higher good. I. NATURE'S CRAVING. Achsah covets a prize that is as yet beyond her reach. " Give me a blessing. Thou hast given me a south (dry, barren) land ; give me also springs of water." How expressive is this of that yearning of the heart by virtue of which it cannot rest content with present possessions, but is ever reaching forth towards something more, a richer inheritance, a completer blessing, the perfect filling up of its capacity, the sense of absolute blessedness. 1. *There is an appetite in the soul of man which is not only insatiable but often becomes more intense the more it is fed with finite gratifications.* What is the meaning of life's restless toil and endeavour, and the perpetual craving for some new form of excitement in the giddy round and dance of pleasure ? It simply shows what power there is in earthly good to awaken hopes and longings that it cannot gratify, to quicken an appetite that it cannot appease. It is not enlargement of possession, the conquering of fair kingdoms either of knowledge, or wealth, or social distinction, or means of enjoyment, that can bring contentment to the soul. This will only feed its discontent unless other conditions are supplied. Man has that within him which spurns all his attempts to satisfy it thus. It is the mark of his essential greatness that he is conscious of a hunger which no earth-grown food can satisfy, a thirst which earthly streams cannot slake, " an aching void the world can never fill." Study the facts of your own consciousness. The day-dreams of your imagination and your heart have never been realised. Many a pleasant prospect has proved like the mirage of the desert. Many a fondly-cherished purpose has been like a river that loses itself in the sand. Many a stay in which you trusted has been but as a reed that breaks and wounds the hand that leans upon it. The world has not satisfied you. Your fellow-creatures have not satisfied you. You have least of all been satisfied from yourself. Amid the happiest arrangement of circumstances you dream of one that is better. Rich as your earthly inheritance may be, there are times when it seems dry and barren to you, and, like Achsah, you crave for something more, (2) *When this appetite lifts itself up consciously to the higher level, fixes itself upon the spiritual good, it is the evidence of a new Divine life in the soul.* We come here to an altogether peculiar and distinctive element of feeling. The mere experience of the unsatisfactoriness of all other kinds of good does not of itself prepare men to seek after the joys of faith. God said to His sense-bound people in the prophetic age, "Thou art wearied in the greatness of thy way, yet saidst thou not, There is no hope" (Isa. lvii. 10). Their vain carnal life disappointed them, but they did not repent of it. They were wearied in it, disgusted with it, and still they clung to it. They hoped on notwithstanding the blighting and withering of all their hopes. How true to human nature and human experience in every age! The carnal appetite will never resolve itself into the spiritual. They are essentially different things, and point to essentially different causes. The long series of life's disappointments may be gathered up at last into one sad, deep sigh of conscious emptiness and weariness—"All is vanity," &c. But does it necessarily assume the form and tone of an upward yearning for "the things that are above"? Nay, there is no saving virtue in the mere groans of a discontented heart. One dare not place much confidence even in deathbed confessions of the vanity of the world. The attraction earthwards may have ceased, but perhaps there is no attraction heaven-wards to take its place. The lights of earth may be growing dim, but there is no soul-captivating view of brightening lights that shine along the eternal shore; natural desire fails, but there is no longing for the pure satisfactions of a higher and a better sphere. So that it is a momentous revolution in the spiritual history of a man, happen when it will, when he first begins distinctly to reach forth towards the heavenly and Divine. He becomes a "new creature" when there is thus awakened within him the aspiration of a pure and holy life that he has never known before. The appetite of his being has taken a new direction, assumed an altogether new character. He hungers for the "bread of life," and thirsts for the "river of the water of life"—"hungers after righteousness," and "thirsts for the living God."

II. Its TRUE SATISFACTION. Achsah's request is immediately granted. She receives from her father a completed "blessing"—the richer land added to the poorer to supplement its deficiency. 1. *God is ever ready to respond to every pure aspiration of our nature.* He who "opens His hand and satisfies the wants of every living thing" will never disregard the cry of His suppliant children. Every true spiritual desire of which we are conscious contains in itself the pledge of its own fulfilment. 2. *Christ is God's answer to the soul's deepest craving.* In Him is the fulness of all satisfying good. "Whosoever drinketh of the water that I shall give him shall never thirst; but the water that I shall give him shall be in him a well of water springing up into everlasting life" (John iv. 14). In Him we find the rest of absolute contentment. 3. *The joy of the higher life that Christ gives deepens and purifies every natural joy.* As the "upper springs" feed the "nether," so when He has conferred on us the Diviner good we discern a richer meaning and worth in the inferior good.

> "Our heart is at the secret source
> Of every precious thing."

All that is naturally fair and pleasant upon earth becomes invested with a new charm, and in that which before seemed barren and profitless there are opened to us unexpected fountains of delight.

> "We thirst for springs of heavenly life,
> And here all day they rise."

W.

Vers. 16—19.—*The story of Achsah.* I. LOVE IS THE STRONGEST MOTIVE OF CONDUCT. As Othniel was nephew to Caleb, and therefore must have known Achsah, it is probable that he accepted the challenge to seize Kirjath-sepher from motives of real affection for the daughter of Caleb. God has providentially arranged that human love should serve as a help for the performance of difficult tasks. Christianity appropriates and consecrates the emotion of love by directing it to Christ. Love is worthless when it will not encounter danger and attempt hard tasks. The highest human affection is shown not in mere pleasing emotions, but in sacrifice and toil.

II. HUSBANDS AND WIVES SHOULD EXERCISE MUTUAL CONFIDENCE. Achsah first consults her husband and then proffers her request to her father. Though husbands and wives have separate spheres of duty, each should be interested in that of the other. There should be no secrets between them. They should learn to act as one in important questions. True sympathy will be shown in questions of conduct and choice, not merely in circumstances of trouble.

III. THE DESIRE OF EARTHLY CONVENIENCES IS NOT IN ITSELF WRONG. Achsah cannot be accused of covetousness. Her request was reasonable. If we do not put earth in the place of heaven, nor grasp for ourselves what is due to others, nor forget duty and generosity in greed and self-seeking, the attempt to improve our condition in the world is natural and right.

IV. CHILDREN SHOULD COMBINE CONFIDENCE WITH SUBMISSION IN THEIR CONDUCT TO THEIR PARENTS. Achsah is an example of this combination. She shows confidence in making her request. She shows submission in alighting off her ass and asking the favour from her father as a " blessing." Reverence and humility are always becoming, but slavish fear is a proof either of the tyrannous character of the parent, or of the mean nature of the child. Confidence joined to submission constitutes the right attitude of Christians in approaching their heavenly Father (Rom. viii. 15).

V. NO EARTHLY BLESSING IS PERFECT IN ITSELF. The southland is of little use without the springs of water. In every condition of life we feel the need of something more to give us satisfaction. Wealth generates the hunger for greater wealth. As the field is barren without the waters of heaven, so any earthly inheritance is profitless to us unless there are added the showers of spiritual blessings (1 Tim. iv. 8).—W. F. A.

Ver. 63.—*Invincible Jebusites.* The failure of the men of Judah to conquer the Jebusites is illustrative of the failures men too commonly encounter in the attempt to accomplish the aims of life.

I. NO MAN PERFECTLY SUCCEEDS IN THE TASK OF HIS LIFE. If a man is satisfied that he has accomplished all his aims, this is a proof that those aims were low. We are bound to aim at the highest though we never reach it. The most successful life is still a broken life. Like the rainbow with half the arch melted away, like the waterfall blown into mist before it reaches the ground, like the bird's song cut short by the storm, life's work ends ragged and unfinished. When failure arises from the magnitude of the task, we are free from blame if we have laboured our best at it. But it is usually aggravated by our indolence, cowardice, and culpable weakness. Only Christ has perfectly succeeded (John xvii. 4). We need a higher view of the requirements of duty, a deeper conviction of our own past failure, more trust in God's power to help us, more consecration of soul and earnest, self-sacrificing effort.

II. NO CHRISTIAN WHILE IN THIS WORLD PERFECTLY SUCCEEDS IN EXPELLING HIS SINS. The Christian life is a warfare with sin. Though God pardons sin immediately on our repentance and faith in Christ, and gives us grace with which to conquer it, He requires us to fight against it. The war is not decided by one battle. It is a life-long conflict. He who claims to have completely conquered is deceiving himself (1 John i. 8). This is a fact, but one to cause shame, for it is not a physical necessity. We ought to conquer all sin, and in Christ we have the means for this perfect victory.

III. THE CONQUEST OF THE WORLD FOR CHRIST IS SLOW. The Jebusites were not completely subdued till the days of David (2 Sam. v. 6, 7). Christian mission work proceeds slowly. Strongholds of sin, of heathenism, of unbelief, of worldliness still seem invincible. (1) This fact should not shake our faith in the truth of Christ, for it was predicted while ultimate triumph was promised (Matt. xiii. 31, 32). (2) It should convince us of our own want of faithfulness. Christ has entrusted the extension of His gospel to His Church. It is to the shame of the Church that she is so remiss in carrying out her great mission.

IV. NO EARTHLY INHERITANCE IS WITHOUT ITS DISADVANTAGES. Canaan was not paradise. The land flowing with milk and honey also brought forth thorns and briars. Jerusalem, the future capital of the land, was the last place to be subdued. So we find something amiss in the very core of life. This is owing (1) partly to our failure to make the best use of this world, and (2) partly to the fact that God has given us natures too great for any earthly satisfaction. Therefore we must expect disappointment here. The perfect inheritance is reserved for the next world.—W. F. A.

Ver. 63.—*Failure.* We have here the first hint of the incompleteness of Israel's conquest of the land. The effects of this failure fully to carry out the Divine command in the extermination of the heathen were very manifest afterwards in the moral and social life of the people. " Their whole subsequent history, down to the captivity, was coloured by the wars, by the customs, by the contagion of Phœnician and Canaanite rites, to which, for good or evil, they were henceforth exposed" (Stanley). " They *could not* take Jerusalem." The reason lay in themselves. The fault was their own. They had not enough faith, and of the courage that springs from faith. If they had had more of the spirit of their great leader in them they would not thus have quailed before their foes, or left the work half finished. The historic fact finds its analogue in the moral and spiritual life of men.

It suggests—I. THE FEEBLENESS THAT IS THE RESULT OF FAITHLESSNESS. Want of power is in various ways coupled in Scripture with want of faith. There were times when Christ could not do mighty works among the people " because of their unbelief " (Matt. xiii. 58 ; Mark vi. 5). The disciples could not cure the lunatic child " because of their unbelief" (Matt. xvii. 20). Peter could no longer walk on the water when he began to doubt (Matt. xiv. 31). As the Jews " could not enter in " to the land of promise " because of their unbelief," so may we fail to secure our inheritance in God's everlasting rest (Heb. iii. 19 ; iv. 1—14). These examples suggest that faithlessness is weakness, inasmuch as (1) it severs the soul from the Divine fountain of strength ; (2) it obscures the soul's vision of those spiritual realities which are the inspiration of all high and holy endeavour ; (3) it robs the soul of all firm standing in the hope of the eternal future. That must be a source of fatal weakness to a man which thus disconnects him from the higher interests of his being and leaves him at the mercy of things " seen and temporal." " All things are possible to him that believeth." To him that believeth not, nothing, great or good, is possible in this world.

II. THE ILL EFFECTS OF SUCH MORAL FEEBLENESS. The results of Israel's failure to exterminate the Canaanites are typical of conditions only too common in the moral life of men. The delay it involved in the settlement of the State—politically, ecclesiastically ; the perpetual unrest ; the national disgrace ; the corruption of the national life by the contagion of idolatry ; the reproach cast on the name of Jehovah among the nations—all these have their resemblance in the penalties of moral failure.

1. *Personal dishonour.* When a man has not the courag to face and combat the evils of his own heart and life, or that confront him in the world without, he generally falls into the shame of some kind of base compromise. He deals sophistically with his own conscience, suppresses the nobler impulses of his nature, belies the essential principles of his religious faith, disowns the bond of his allegiance to Christ. No greater dishonour possible to a man than this.

2. *Spiritual degeneracy.* As an enfeebled body is liable to the infection of disease, so moral laxity leaves men a prey to the destroyer. Corrupting influences readily take effect upon them. The gates are open, the sentinel is asleep, no wonder the foe enters and takes possession of the citadel. " From him that hath not shall be taken away," &c. (Matt. xiii. 12).

3. *Exaggeration of opposing difficulties.* The sense of moral weakness and falseness conjures up obstacles in the path of duty or endeavour that do not really exist. High moral excellence seems impossible to him who is content to grovel. The faithless heart always " sees a lion in the way."

" The wise and active conquer difficulties
By daring to attempt them. Sloth and folly

> Shiver and shrink at sight of toil and danger,
> And make the impossibilities they fear."

4. *Defective witness for God.* Every such case of spiritual failure is a hindrance to the progress of the kingdom of heaven among men, thwarts so far the Divine purpose in the triumph of truth and righteousness. The hostile forces of the world laugh at a half-hearted service of Christ. The strongholds of iniquity can never fall before a church enfeebled by the spirit of unbelief.—W.

EXPOSITION.

CHAPTER XVI. 1—10.

THE INHERITANCE OF EPHRAIM AND MANASSEH. Ver. 1.—**Fell.** Literally *came forth, i.e.,* out of the urn. **The water of Jericho.** "This is the present fountain of es Sultan, half an hour to the west of Riha, the only large fountain in the neighbourhood of Jericho, whose waters spread over the plain and form a small brook" (or small stream, according to Von Schubert), "which flows in the rainy season through the Wady Kelt into the Jordan" (Keil and Delitzsch). This spring, which rises amid the nebek trees and the wheat fields, "springs from the earth at the eastern base of a little knoll; the water is sweet, clear, and agreeable, neither cold nor warm" (Ritter). It flows, he adds, into a basin nine feet broad, in which many fish may be seen playing. This border coincides with the northern border of Benjamin (see ch. xviii. 11—20). Ritter mentions another spring, nearer to the Kuruntul or Quarantania range, and adds that, "under the wise management of an efficient government, and with the security of the district from the depredations of predatory savages, the oasis of Jericho might unquestionably resume the paradisaical aspect it once bore." **To the wilderness.** Or, by or *along* the wilderness. The Hebrew requires some preposition to be supplied. This wilderness is the same as that spoken of as the wilderness of Beth-aven in ch. xviii. 12. **Throughout Mount Bethel.** The Vulgate has, "*to* Mount Bethel." The LXX. renders, "unto the hill country unto Bethel." The Hebrew may be rendered, "along the hill country unto Bethel" (see ch. xviii. 12). The Syriac renders, "up to the mountain which goeth unto Bethel;" but we must understand this of a range of mountains, and then we can identify the border with the double rocky ridge which stretches from the Mons Quarantania, of which we have already heard (ch. ii.), and from the pool of Ain es Sultan, just mentioned, as far as Bethel. Ver. 2. — **From Bethel to Luz.** Like Jerusalem and Ælia Capitolina, or old and new Carthage, the new city did not

coincide precisely in its site with the old one (see ch. xviii. 13; also Gen. xxviii. 19; xxxv. 6; Judg. i. 23). Bethel was probably built, as far as could be ascertained, on the spot near the Canaanitish city where the wanderer Jacob spent the night in which the famous vision appeared to him (see Gen. xxviii. 11). Knobel, however, renders literally, Bethel-Luzah, as though the older and later names had been here conjoined. **The borders of Archi.** Rather, the borders of *the Archite* (cf. 2 Sam. xv. 32; xvi. 16; 1 Chron. xxvii. 33). This is the only clue we have to the residence or tribe of Hushai.

Ver. 3.—**Japhleti.** Rather, the *Japhlethite;* but it is unknown what this family was. **Beth-horon the nether** (see ch. x. 10). In ver. 5 we have Upper Beth-horon, but the places were close together. For *Gezer*, see ch. x. 33.

Ver. 5.—**The border of the children of Ephraim.** The Hebrew word is translated indifferently by *coast* and *border* in our translation. The border of Joseph is very slightly traced out by the historian. It is difficult to give a reason for this fact, when we remember that Joseph, consisting as it did of the preponderating tribe of Ephraim, together with half the tribe of Manasseh, constituted by far the most important portion of Jewish territory. See, however, Introduction for the bearing of this fact on the authorship of the book. It is by no means easy to define the boundaries of the tribes; but, with the utmost deference to the authority of one so long engaged in the actual survey of the Holy Land as Mr. Conder, I feel unable to accept the maps he has given us in his 'Handbook' as an accurate account of them. Sometimes, perhaps, an eager attempt at the identification of certain places may lead astray those who are most familiar with their subject. But there are certain plain statements of the Book of Joshua which cannot be lightly set aside. Thus the extremity (תֹצְאֹת) of the border of Ephraim is distinctly stated in ver. 8 to be the sea. To translate "westward" would rob the

expression תֹצְאֹת of all meaning, even if
יְמָה had not the article. Thus Dan can
only have approached towards Joppa, but
cannot have reached it. And it will be observed in ch. xix. 46, in accordance with this
view, that the outgoings of the Danite border
are *not* said to have been the sea. Next, it
would seem that the Ataroth of ver. 2
(not of ver. 7) and Ataroth - addar are
either the same place or close together, and
that the present verse gives a small portion
of the south-eastern boundary as far as
Beth-horon. Why the boundary is not
traced out further (" the author only gives
the western part of the southern border,
and leaves out the eastern," Knobel) we cannot tell, but the natural translation of ver. 6
is, " and the western border ran to Michmethah on the north " (so Knobel). There
was so small a portion of Ephraim on the
sea that the line of the Wady Kanah in a
north-easterly direction to Michmethah,
near Shechem, might be called a western,
as it certainly was a north-western, border.
Then the border deflected (נָסַב) and ran in a
south-westerly direction to Jericho. Manasseh seems to have been bounded by Asher
on the north and Issachar on the east, from
the borders of Asher to Michmethah, and
its western boundary the sea from the Wady
Kanah to the neighbourhood of Dor. It
seems impossible, with the distinct statement that Dor was in Asher (ch. xvii. 11)—
it could hardly have been in Issachar—and
that Carmel was part of its western border
(ch. xix. 26), to thrust a wedge of Zebulun
between Manasseh and Asher, as Mr. Conder has done. The invention of an Asher-
ham-Michmethah must not be allowed to
set aside the plain statement (ch. xvii. 10)
that Manasseh impinged (פָּגַע) upon Asher
in a northerly direction — that is, was
bounded on the north by that tribe. Then,
as Asher was the northern, so it would
seem from the passage just cited that
Issachar was, as has been suggested, the
eastern boundary, and that Issachar was
bounded by the Jordan eastward, Manasseh
westward, and by Ephraim to the south-
west, and some distance further south than
is usually supposed. Yet ch. xvii. 11 must
not be forgotten in fixing the boundary of
Issachar (see note on ch. xix. 17—23). Its
northern border, comprehending Jezreel,
and bounded by Tabor, was thrust in
between Zebulun and Naphtali. Tabor
was evidently the border of these three
tribes. It is with much diffidence that
I venture to offer these suggestions,
but they appear to have the sanction of
the plain statements of the sacred writer.
It would seem as though the comparative
smallness of the territory assigned to

Joseph led to the cession of some of the
towns northward of the Wady Kanah
by Manasseh to Ephraim, Manasseh receiving compensation by receiving Beth-
shean, Ibleam, Dor, Endor, Taanach, and
Megiddo from Issachar and Asher. The
possession of Beth-shean by Manasseh may
be due to the fact that the boundary of
Manasseh ran along the chain of mountains bordering the great plain of Esdraelon,
until it almost reached the Jordan. Additional reasons for entertaining these
opinions will be given in the following
notes. **On the east side was Ataroth-
addar.** It is hardly possible to avoid
the conclusion that a passage has been
omitted here by the transcriber. If so,
it must have been at a very early period,
since the LXX. shows no sign of it, save
that some copies add " and Gezer." But
this is probably added from ver. 3, and is
in no sense an *eastern* border.

**Ver. 6.—And the border went out towards
the sea.** Or, " and the western border." **On
the north side.** Or, " northward." Apparently a line is drawn from the sea, which
(ver. 3) is given as the termination of the
southern boundary to Michmethah, near
Shechem (ch. xvii. 7). Knobel thinks that
Michmethah (the signification of which is
perhaps *hiding-place*) was upon the watershed, and thus served as a dividing-point.
Went about. Rather, *deflected.* The border
ran in a north-easterly direction to Michmethah. It then bent back and ran in a
south-easterly direction to Jericho.

Ver. 7.—Ataroth. Another Ataroth, on
the *northern* border of Ephraim. The
name, which signifies *crowns*, is a common
one (see Num. xxxii. 3, 34, 35 ; 1 Chron. ii.
54). **Came to Jericho.** Or perhaps *skirted*
Jericho. The word used (see note on ver. 5)
is akin to the Latin *pango* and our *impinge.*

**Ver. 8.—The border went out from Tap-
puah westward.** This would seem to be a
more minute description of the border line
drawn from the sea to Michmethah above.
Tappuah seems to have been near Michmethah, and on the border (ch. xvii. 8) of
Manasseh. According to Knobel, Tappuah
signifies *plain,* which is a little inconsistent with his idea that Michmethah, close
by, was the water-shed. Tappuah elsewhere
signifies *apple.* **Unto the river Kanah.** The
winter-bound torrent Kanah, so named
from its reeds and canes, formed the border
between Ephraim and Manasseh. **And the
goings out** (literally, *extremities*) **thereof
were at the sea.** This is the only possible
interpretation of the passage, in spite of
the obscurity caused by the same word being
used for " sea " and " west."

Ver. 9.—And the separate cities. Literally, *and the cities divided off.* The word "were," in our version, is misplaced. It should be read thus: "And there were cities divided off and assigned to the tribe of Ephraim in the midst of the inheritance of the sons of Manasseh" (see note on ver. 5). This fact, together with the compensation given to Manasseh, may serve to explain the cohesion of the ten tribes in opposition to Judah. The boundaries of the latter tribe were more strictly defined, her attitude more exclusive. We may almost discern this in the prominence given to Judah in the present book. Ephraim, already enraged at the passing away of the pre-eminence from itself, which had not merely been predicted, but, as Judg. viii. 1—3 and xii. 1 show, had been actually enjoyed, was closely allied to Manasseh, and Manasseh to

Issachar and Zebulun, by the arrangement we are considering. It would naturally be able, by its position and these circumstances, to combine together the rest of the tribe against the somewhat overbearing attitude of the tribe of Judah (see 2 Sam. xix. 43).

10. **And they drave not out.** The Ephraimites soon grew slack in the fulfilment of the Divine command. There is a distinction, apparently, between this passage and ch. xv. 63. There the tribe of Judah was unable to drive out the Jebusites from their stronghold, and no mention is made of tribute. Here the Ephraimites seem deliberately to have preferred the easier task of reducing the Canaanites to tribute to the sterner and more difficult task of destroying them utterly.

HOMILIES BY VARIOUS AUTHORS.

Ver. 10.—*Canaanites still in the land.* I. CANAANITES STILL IN THE LAND WERE A WITNESS TO THE FAILURE OF THE JEWS TO ACCOMPLISH GOD'S WILL. They may have failed (1) from weakness and indolence, (2) from mercenary motives, thinking to make profit out of the Canaanites with their tribute. But these Canaanites were a cause of future trouble and a constant temptation to idolatry and immorality. We shall always suffer when we neglect God's will for worldly convenience.

II. CANAANITES REMAINING IN THE LAND WERE AN INSTANCE OF THE MIXED CONDITION OF HUMAN SOCIETY. Wheat and tares grow together. The Church and the world are in close contact. It is dangerous to associate with evil company when we can avoid it (Psa. i. 1). But it is also wrong for Christians to neglect their duty to the world in order to escape the contamination of the world's wickedness.

III. CANAANITES REMAINING IN THE LAND WERE AN EXAMPLE OF A COMMON CAUSE OF NATIONAL WEAKNESS. Much of the trouble of the dark age of the Judges arose from this fact. A nation to be strong must be united as one body, and it can only be so united when there are common sympathies binding the people together. The government which is effected through the forcible subjugation of unwilling peoples must always rest on an unstable basis, and can never accomplish the highest good of the subject races. Therefore it should be the aim of a government to avoid, if possible, the conquest of new, unwilling subjects, to cultivate the affections of all classes beneath it, and to weld them together by just equality of administration, and the development of common interests. Where national assimilation is impossible it is better that a common government should not be attempted.

IV. CANAANITES REMAINING IN THE LAND WERE A TYPE OF SINS REMAINING IN THE HEART OF THE CHRISTIAN. (1) *Most* of the land was conquered. The heart of the Christian is conquered by Christ. Christ sits enthroned there. Sin is dispossesse l of the citadel. (2) Canaanites still *lurked in obscure corners* of the land. Sin still lingers about the life of the Christian. It retains its old character unaltered, and must be regarded as dangerous (Rom. vii. 23). (3) These Canaanites were so far *subdued* that they served under tribute. The sin that remains in the Christian's heart no longer reigns there. It is a defeated enemy. It will be ultimately exterminated. The temptation to it may be converted into an instrument of wholesome discipline.—W. F. A.

EXPOSITION.

CHAPTER XVII. 1—18.

Ver. 1.—**There was also a lot.** The preferable translation is, "*and the lot for the tribe of Manasseh—for he was the firstborn of Joseph—was (or fell) to Machir the son of Manasseh.* That is to say, the proper possession of the tribe of Manasseh fell to Machir and his descendants only, because of their warlike spirit, and possibly on account of their numbers also. They were sufficient to occupy the land of Gilead and Bashan, extensive and powerful though it was, while the rest of the tribe had a share in the inheritance westward of Jordan (see also ch. xiii. 29—31). **For he was the firstborn of Joseph.** There has been much discussion why these words were introduced. It is probable that they are intended as an explanation of the existence of Ephraim and Manasseh as separate tribes; or possibly this is introduced to suggest the reason for mentioning the tribes in this order since Ephraim was not the firstborn (see Gen. xlviii. 5, 14). **The father of Gilead.** There seems no reason to accept Keil's *dictum,* that because Gilead here has the article, whereas in other places where it signifies Machir's son it has not, the country and not the man is meant, and " father " must be taken as equivalent to "lord." The usage is found in Arabic and Ethiopic, but not in Hebrew. The reason why Gilead as the name of the individual has the article here is most likely because he gave his name to the territory mentioned immediately afterwards. **Therefore he had.** There is no " therefore " in the original, where we find " *and* he had." We must understand this as spoken of the tribe, not personally of Machir, who had been long dead (see note on ch. vi. 25).

Ver. 2.—**There was also a lot.** Or, *and* (the lot) *was* (or *fell*). **Abiezer** (see Judg. vi. 11 ; viii. 2). Gideon, therefore, was of the tribe of Manasseh. He is called Jeezer in Num. xxvi. 30. **The male children.** Rather, the male *descendants.* None of the persons here mentioned were (Num. xxvi. 30, 31 ; 1 Chron. vii. 18) the sons of Manasseh.

Ver. 3.—**Zelophehad** (see Num. xxxvi.). The inheritance here described as being given to the daughters of Zelophehad was so given on condition of their marrying within the limits of their own tribe, a condition which was fulfilled. Thus the name of Zelophehad, and the portion of land belonging to him, was not blotted out from the memory of his descendants.

Ver. 4.—**And they came near.** In order to demand the fulfilment of the decree of Moses just referred to, to which they appeal in support of their claim (see also Num. xxvii. 1—7).

Ver. 5.—**And there fell ten portions.** Literally, *and the measured portions of Manasseh fell ten* (*in number*). It will be observed that the descendants of Manasseh, exclusive of Hepher, are five in number. These, with the five portions allotted to the family of Zelophehad, the son of Hepher, made up ten.

Ver. 6.—**The rest of Manasseh's sons.** Namely, the descendants of Machir (see ver. 1). The ambiguity is due to the indefinite way in which "son " is used in Scripture. Thus the B'ne Israel, which we translate " children of Israel," is literally, " sons of Israel," or Jacob. So the sons of Manasseh, in like manner, are Manasseh's descendants.

Ver. 7.—**Coast.** Rather, *border.* **Asher.** This has been supposed not to be the *tribe* of Asher, for this was on the north, but a city which has been identified with the modern Yasir, about five hours' distance from Nablous, or Neapolis, on the road to Beisan, or Beth-shean, where, says Delitzsch, there are " magnificent ruins " now to be seen. See, however, note ver. 10. **Michmethah** (see ch. xvi. 6). This place has not been identified. All we know is that it is opposite (עַל־פְּנֵי) Shechem. Some have thought that this is simply the denominative of Asher, to distinguish it from the tribe, and that for "Asher to Michmethah " we should read "Asher-ham-Michmethah." But this could hardly be the Yasir above, since it is opposite Shechem. **Shechem.** Now Nablous. This place is famous both in the Old and the New Testament. We first read of it, under the name of Sichem, in Gen. xii. 6. It was the abode of Shechem and Hamor his son, when Jacob abode in Canaan after his return from Padan-aram. It was situated between Gerizim and Ebal, and became an important city in the days of the Judges (Judg. ix.). It was destroyed by Abimelech (Judg. ix. 45), but it seems to have recovered. It was thither that Rehoboam went to be crowned, and there that his injudicious answer alienated for ever the ten tribes from his rule. Jeroboam made it his capital and is said to have " built " it (1 Kings xii. 25). He afterwards, however, abandoned it for Penuel, and Penuel again apparently for Tirzah (1 Kings xiv. 17), and Tirzah for Jezreel, which remained the capital until Omri built Samaria (1 Kings xvi. 24). It is no doubt the Sychar mentioned in St. John iv. Most travellers have admired the picturesque situation of Shechem. It has even extorted a tribute from Dr. Peterman, in his 'Reisen im Orient,' a work which, however full of valuable information regarding the condition and customs of the people, does not abound in description of scenery. He becomes almost poetical as he speaks of this town, resting on the slopes of Gerizim, a mountain fruitful to its summit, and having opposite the bare, stony el Ebal, its outline unrelieved by verdure, the haunt of jackals, whose howls, like the cry of wailing children in distress, disturb the silence of the night. Thomson ('Land and the Book,' p. 470) thus describes the scene: "A valley green with grass, grey with olives, gardens sloping down on each side, fresh springs rushing down in all directions; at the end a white town embosomed in all this verdure lodged between the two high mountains which extend on each side of the valley; this is the aspect of Nablous, the most beautiful, perhaps it might be said the only beautiful, spot in Central Palestine. Thirty-two springs can be traced in different parts. Here the bilbul delights to sit and sing, and thousands of other birds delight to swell the chorus."

Ver. 9.—**Southward of the brook.** It would seem as if some words had fallen away here also. The LXX. adds Jariel, translates אלה (these) by terebinth, and omits the word "cities." The cities southward of the brook belonged of course to Ephraim. But what is meant here is that Ephraim had cities *north* of the brook. That the border of Manasseh lay to the northward of the brook is asserted twice over in the latter part of this and the next verse. **These cities of Ephraim are among** (literally, *in the midst of*) **the cities of Manasseh** (see ch. xvi. 9). If exact and minute accuracy is found in this record, how is it that accusations of inaccuracy are so readily made against its author, when his narrative is clearly very much abbreviated, and where a fuller knowledge of the facts might possibly clear up what now appears obscure? Our present text has not the names of these cities.

Ver. 10.—**And they met together.** Rather, *they* (*i.e.*, the Manassites) *impinged* (this is the very same word as the Hebrew יִפְגְּעוּ), *i.e.*, "touched upon." There has been great discussion concerning this passage. The literal meaning is clearly that Manasseh was bordered by Asher on the north, and Issachar on the east. The idea of an Asher-ham-Michmethah must be given up if we take this rendering of the Hebrew. Its only justification is the fact that if Mich-

methah be at once the northern border of Ephraim and Manasseh, the territory of Manasseh is cut almost in half. And, in fact, such a supposition makes confusion worse confounded. Is it probable that in vers. 7 and 10 Asher-ham-Michmethah is meant; that the town Asher is mentioned in similar terms to the tribe Issachar in the latter verse; and that in ver. 11, without a single intimation of the change of meaning, the tribes Issachar and Asher are mentioned? Again: if Dor—considerably to the south of Mount Carmel—was within the territory of Asher (ver. 11), how can we possibly, as Conder's 'Handbook' does, place the limits of Asher at Accho, and bring Zebulun to the sea (which it never reaches, for "toward the sea," in ch. xix. 11 clearly means "westward"), interposing a large strip of territory between Manasseh and Asher, placing Dor, in spite of ver. 11, far within the limits of Manasseh, and giving this last tribe, or rather half-tribe, an extraordinarily disproportioned share of the land? (See the complaint in ver. 16). Zebulun, too, was on the eastern border of Asher (ch. xix. 27), and it is by no means certain that Shihor Libnath (see ch. xix. 26) is not the Wady Zerka, south of Dor. This is the view of Knobel, a commentator by no means void of acuteness. This contraction of Manasseh's territory explains why cities had to be given to it out of Asher and Issachar, as well as the complaint in the latter part of this chapter. Issachar, too, must have stretched considerably southward. But the vagueness of the description of Manasseh's border, especially on the north, prevents us from assigning any limits to Issachar in this direction; while it is impossible, with a writer in the Quarterly Papers of the Palestine Exploration Fund, to suppose that it extended from Jezreel and Shunem and Endor on the north as far as Jericho to the south.

Ver. 11.—**And Manasseh had in Issachar and in Asher** (see ch. xvi. 9). **Beth-shean.** Afterwards called Scythopolis, now Beisan. It was a "noble city" in the days of Eusebius and Jerome. Many travellers have remarked on its splendid situation, "in this vast area of plain and mountains, in the midst of abundant waters and exuberant fertility" (Robinson, 'Later Bibl. Res.' sec. 7). "Just beyond, and separated by a narrow ridge, is another stream, also perennial, and on the peninsular formed by these two, with a bold, steep brow overlooking the Ghor, stood the citadel of ancient Beth-shean—a sort of Gibraltar on a small scale—of remarkable natural strength, and inaccessible to horsemen. No wonder that it was long ere Israel could wrest it from the Canaanites. The eastern face rises like a steep cone, most incorrectly stated by Robinson to be ' black, and apparently volcanic;' and by Porter, 'probably a crater.' Certainly there are many blocks of basalt lying about, but the hill is simply a limestone bluff." (Tristram, 'Land of Israel,' p. 501). He goes on, " How clearly the details of the sad end of Saul were recalled as we stood on this spot " (the summit of the cone). " There was the slope of Gilboa, on which his army was encamped before the battle. Round that hill he slunk by night, conscience-stricken, to visit the witch of Endor. Hither, as being a Canaanitish fortress, the Philistines most naturally brought the trophies of the royal slain, and hung them up just by this wall. By the Yasir, and across that plain below us, the gallant men of Jabesh-Gilead hurried on their long night's march to stop the indignity offered to Israel, and to take down the bodies of their king and his sons." Jabesh-Gilead was not far off, and though in full view of the mountain, yet the men of Jabesh could creep along the Ghor by night and climb the steep face of the rock unsuspected by the warriors above ; while the roar of the brook would drown all the sounds they might make (see Thomson, 'Land and the Book,' p. 454). **And her towns.** Literally, *daughters*, κῶμαι LXX. ; *viculi*, Vulgate. Canon Tristram remarks how each hill in some parts of Palestine is crowned by a village, a number of which still cluster, as of old, round the chief city of the district. So in Italy we may see how times of unsettlement led to a similar policy. The fear of the northern pirates led to the planting the mediæval towns on hills, and the disturbed state of the country kept them there till a comparatively late period. But many of them are deserted in this more peaceful age. **Ibleam.** Only known as near the place where Jehu gave Ahaziah his death-blow. It was near Megiddo (see 2 Kings ix. 27). **Dor** (see above ch. xi. 2). Keil thinks that Dor and all the cities after it are in the accusative to " could not drive out " in the next verse. But it is more probable that אֵת was an anacolouthon. Vandevelde (' Travels,' i. 333) says that he did not wonder that the faint-hearted Manassites shrank from attacking Dor when he saw its formidable position. **Endor.** This, the abode of the famous witch, still bears the old name. It is four miles south of Mount Tabor, in a country honeycombed with caves, and it stands on the shoulder of Little Hermon. The word signifies the " fount of Dor," or " the dwelling." **Taanach.** For this and Megiddo see ch. xii. 21. **Three countries.** Rather, three

hills, or elevated spots (Napheth, see note, ch. xi. 2). Gesenius compares the name Tremont. The reference is to Endor, Taanach, and Megiddo. Keil suggests *province*, but he does not explain how a derivative of נָפַת can have this latter signification (cf. Psa. xlviii. 3. Beautiful for its height (נוֹף) is Mount Zion). The LXX. and Vulgate regard it as a proper name, and translate, " the third part of Nopheth." They are puzzled by the expression here, as in ch. xi. 2.

Ver. 12.—**Would dwell.** The LXX. and Vulgate translate, " *began* to dwell," an obvious mistake here, though the word sometimes has this signification. They *willed* to dwell there, in spite of their defeats, and their purpose was not frustrated.

Ver. 14.—**And the children of Joseph.** The attitude of the children of Joseph throughout the history of the twelve tribes is in precise accordance with the hint given here. They were proud of their numerical preponderance over the remaining tribes. Thus they, and they only, ventured to remonstrate with Joshua about the inadequacy of the portion allotted to them. Such a sensitiveness was likely to degenerate into insolence when the authority of the great leader was removed. And the history of Gideon (Judg. viii. 1—3) and of Jephthah (Judg. xii. 6) shows that this was actually the case. Here, again, we have a sign of that deep under-current of consistency which underlies our history, and is a guarantee of its authenticity. **Seeing I am a great people.** The tribe of Joseph, at the census described in Num. i., outnumbered every tribe but that of Judah. At the census in the plains of Moab (Num. xxvi.) the tribe of Joseph outnumbered them all, though the relative proportions of Ephraim and Manasseh were altered, the latter being now considerably the larger of the two tribes. The whole number of the fighting men of Israel underwent a slight diminution during the passage through the wilderness. But the demand of the tribe of Joseph seems to have been a little unbecoming, since Joseph had obtained *two* lots and *two* portions, since half the tribe of Manasseh had settled on the east of Jordan. Hence no doubt the covert sarcasm of Joshua's reply, for, as Delitzsch shows, Judah, and even Dan, considerably outnumbered Ephraim and the half-tribe of Manasseh. Part, however, of their complaint was no doubt caused by the idea that Joshua, as one of themselves, ought to have taken more care of the interests of his own tribe. Joshua, however, as a true servant of God ought to be, was above such petty considerations, though many who live under a higher dispensation find it impossible to emancipate themselves from such bondage. **Forasmuch as the Lord hath blessed me hitherto.** Or, *hath blessed me to this extent* (but see Exod. vii. 16). There is doubtless here an allusion to Jacob's blessing (Gen. xlviii. 20; xlix. 22—26), the fulfilment of which would naturally make a deep impression on the minds of the children of Joseph. Blessing was the word reiterated over and over again by the dying patriarch as he gazed upon the children of his best-beloved son. Here, again, we have one of those delicate touches, impossible to a writer of fiction, which show that we have here an authentic record of facts. No doubt the consciousness of the enthusiastic language of Jacob, reiterated upon an almost equally solemn occasion by Moses (Deut. xxxiii. 13—17), coupled with the obvious fulfilment of these predictions, led the tribe of Joseph to demand as a right the leadership in Israel, and no doubt predisposed the other tribes to concede it. The rivalry of Judah, to which reference has already been made, and which culminated in the sovereignty of David, was calculated to produce a breach which it required the utmost tact to heal. Pity it was that the Ephraimites and Manassites forgot the fact that the blessing was conditional, and neglected to lay to heart the terrible warnings in Deut. xxviii. But it is too often so with men. They expect the fulfilment of prophecies which predict their aggrandisement, and too often strive themselves to hasten the hand of God, while the warnings of God's Word, since they are less pleasant to the natural man, are permitted to pass by unheeded (see vers. 12, 13, which was the first step on the downward road).

Ver. 15.—**If thou be a great people.** As though Joshua would say, "You are ready enough to boast, but unwilling to act. If your tribe be as large as you say it is, it is capable of taking care of itself. There is the vast forest of Central Palestine before you. Do not complain to me, but go and take possession of it." **Get thee up into the wood country.** The word "country" is not in the original, which is, strictly speaking, in the *direction* of the wood. Whether this be the "wood of Ephraim" mentioned in 2 Sam. xviii. 6 has been much disputed. For not only David is related to have crossed the Jordan, but Absalom also, in hot pursuit of his father (see 2 Sam. xvii. 22, 24). Neither army is mentioned as having recrossed the river; and it is a question whether it is more probable that there happened to be a "wood of Ephraim" on the other side of Jordan, or that Joab and Absalom, with their respective armies, recrossed Jordan without a word being

said of the fact by the historian; the more especially as David (see 2 Sam. xix. 15—17, 31) remained on the other side Jordan, while yet it was possible for the Ethiopian attendant, as well as Jonathan, to run to him with tidings of the defeat and death of Absalom. For the wood country in this neighbourhood cf. Psa. cxxxii. 6. Ewald would regard the language here as figurative, and the wood as referring to the powerful Phoenician tribes in the neighbourhood. He regards this answer as a sign of Joshua's "wit." But the interpretation seems farfetched and improbable. **Cut down.** Or, *make a clearing*, just as emigrants do now in the primeval forest. This wood, or forest, has now disappeared, though sufficient wood still remains to testify to the correctness of the history. **Perizzites and of the giants.** The *Rephaim* (see notes on ch. iii. 10; xii. 4). **If Mount Ephraim be too narrow for thee.** This fastness in the heart of the land, the refuge of Ehud, the dwelling-place of Deborah, the early home of Samuel, was well adapted to purposes of secrecy and defence, but not so well suited for a place of habitation.

Ver. 16.—**And the children of Joseph said.** This reply justifies Joshua's sarcasm. The Ephraimites and Manassites blame Joshua when they ought to be blaming themselves. They excuse themselves from a task which they are too idle to execute, and wish Joshua to make arrangements for them which are wholly unnecessary. **The hill is not enough for us.** Literally, the hill *is not found* for us—that is, is not sufficient (see Num. xi. 22; Zech. x. 10). **Of the valley of Jezreel.** Rather, *in* the valley of Jezreel. The word for valley in this verse is עֵמֶק (see note on ch. viii. 13). Jezreel abutted on the great plain of Esdraelon, a name which is but a corruption of Jezreel (see note on ch. xix. 18), where the chariots of iron could be used with effect, a thing impossible in the mountain districts. Hence the fact that the hill country of Palestine was more rapidly and permanently occupied than the plains (see Ewald, 'History,' ii. 2 C., and Ritter's 'Geography of Palestine,' ii. 328. Cf. Judg. i. 19, and note on ch. xi. 6). Here, once more, we have a proof that we have real history before us, and not a collection of poetic myths.

Ver. 18.—**But the mountain shall be thine, for it is a wood.** This passage makes it clear that it was not the whole territory of Mount Ephraim, but only the portion habitable at present, that was too small for Ephraim and Manasseh. When cleared it would afford them more space. But Joshua also recommends them to extend their operations beyond its borders, as is clear from the mention of the "plain," and the "chariots of iron" (see next note). **The outgoings.** Not only the mountain itself, but the country to which the mountain passes led. **Thou shalt drive out.** Perhaps *thou mayest drive out*—i.e., it is in thy power. **Though they have iron chariots, and though they be strong.** "No weapon can prosper" against him who trusts in the Lord. Yet, in spite of the encouragement given by Joshua, the children of Joseph did not drive the Canaanites out, as vers. 11—13 show. The only reason of this was that they did not trust in God, but preferred an unworthy compromise with neighbours who, however rich in warlike material, were sunk in sensuality and sloth. Keil would render

"because" for "though," and regard the very fact of the strength of the Canaanites as the reason that the sons of Joseph would subdue them. But Exod. xiii. 17; Ps. xlix. 17 supply us with other instances of כִּ in the sense of although, which certainly is the best sense here. "Let it be remembered how long it was before the Saxons were firmly established in Britain, the Islamite Arabs in Egypt. Israel could look for no reinforcements from kindred left behind. So much the worse might afterwards be the position of the nation, left alone without hope of kindred auxiliaries to meet the repeated outbreaks of the half-subdued Canaanites" (Ewald, 'Hist. Israel,' ii. 2. c.).

HOMILETICS.

Ver. 18.—*The lot of Joseph.* I. No COMPROMISE WITH SIN. The Israelites, as we have seen, were promised the possession of Palestine on condition that they should exterminate its inhabitants. They did not do this, either (1) because they were indisposed to the exertion, as in the case of the Jebusites (ch. xv. 63), or (2) because they found the process of exacting tribute more convenient. No type of the ordinary conduct of Christians is more precisely accurate. Constantly in youth they either (1) will not give themselves the trouble to root out evil habits, but give way to them, because the task is so difficult, or (2) indulge themselves in sin because it is so pleasant. The consequences are a disastrous captivity to sinful habits which lasts half a lifetime, and leaves its mark upon the sinner for his *whole* life. Great and mighty deliverers may arise within, as they did in Israel, but there is a liability to relapse, which long asserts itself. Instances of these truths are hardly difficult to find.

II. THEY THAT TOUCH PITCH SHALL BE DEFILED THEREWITH. The command to exterminate the Israelites was not an arbitrary one. It was given because of the terrible depravity of the Phœnician people, and because of the equally terrible attractiveness of their sins. God well knew (and the narrative in Num. xxvi. is sufficient to prove it to us) that the Israelites could not resist the contamination of this evil influence if they allowed themselves to be exposed to it. But they did not, or would not, believe this. And consequently, till the Babylonish captivity, with its stern lessons, taught them better, they continued to fall lower and lower into the abominations of the abominable, revolting, and unfeeling worship of their neighbours; nor was it surprising, when we find that Solomon, with all his wisdom, could not escape the contagion. We may learn thus that neither intellect, nor prudence, nor even the sanctifying influences of a holy calling, will enable us to resist the allurements of bad company, when we voluntarily surrender ourselves to them. The only safe way for the Israelites to meet the Canaanites was in battle array, with arms in their hands. So the Christian's only safeguard against evil company is never to enter it, save on the path of duty, and never to part with his weapons of faith and prayer. "Surely," then, "in vain is the net spread in the sight of any bird" (Prov. i. 17).

III. WE MUST MAKE THE MOST OF THE OPPORTUNITIES WE HAVE. Ephraim complained of the narrowness of his lot, instead of cutting down the woods and thus finding room in what had been assigned to him. He is the type of many Christians who complain of the scantiness of their opportunities, while they are leaving one half of them unemployed. God will not vouchsafe us more opportunities if we neglect those He gives us. He did not give five more talents to the man who kept the one he had wrapped in a napkin.

IV. WE MUST NOT MAKE CIRCUMSTANCES A REASON FOR NOT DOING OUR DUTY. The Ephraimites wanted an increase of territory, no doubt at some one else's expense, while they did not make the most of their own. They not only did not cut down the wood, but they assigned as a reason for not driving out the Canaanites that they had chariots of iron, in spite of the promise God had given them that these should not be a hindrance to their success. So men assign circumstances now (1) as a reason why they succumb to temptation, (2) as a reason why they do not combat evil habits, (3) as a reason why they leave work undone which they ought to have undertaken and carried out. Let such remember Joshua's words, "Thou shalt drive out the Canaanites, though they have iron chariots, and though they be strong."

V. GOD'S BLESSINGS WILL NOT BE GIVEN TO THOSE WHO NEGLECT THE CONDITIONS UNDER WHICH THEY WERE PROMISED. Ephraim had inherited blessings, and was fully conscious of the fact. Yet he makes this a reason why God should prosper him without any effort on his own part. So Christians very often expect God to work out their salvation for them without any labour or effort of their own. They permit evil tempers to take root in their hearts, and to grow and flourish there. They make no effort to cast them out, because "God hath blessed them hitherto." They are called to inherit God's blessings, and so they think they will have them without any trouble. They are "called to be saints," and expect to be so without the self-discipline saintliness requires. God will not fulfil such expectations. He has promised " His Holy Spirit to them that ask it," but He expects them to "work out their own salvation " with His aid. Those who would appropriate the promises of Christianity without the endeavour necessary to give them effect, either become self-deceiving professors, who "have a form of godliness but deny the power thereof," or if more sincere in heart and less capable of hypocrisy, fall back into a state of indifference because their Christian calling has failed to realise all the hopes that they had formed.

HOMILIES BY VARIOUS AUTHORS.

Vers. 3, 4.—*Woman's rights.* I. WOMEN HAVE RIGHTS WHICH MEN COMMONLY DENY THEM. The justice of the Mosaic law and the just privileges accorded to women in the Jewish state stand out in favourable contrast with the almost universal injustice which marks the historic relations of men with women. In barbarous nations women are required to do the hardest manual labour. In semi-civilised nations they are kept in ignorance, idleness, and jealous seclusion. In more advanced nations they are hampered with needless social restrictions which prevent them from enjoying their fair privileges as human beings. This injustice may be traced to (1) the superior brute force of men, (2) the natural retiring nature of woman, and (3) false sentiment which dishonours true modesty. Chivalrous customs and domestic affection may soften the effects of injustice, but they do not remove the fact.

II. WOMEN SHOULD BE ALLOWED TO PROVE THEIR OWN RIGHTS AND CAPACITIES. Hitherto one half of the human race has taken upon itself to settle the position and destiny of the other half. Women have been treated as though men knew their rights and capacities better than these were known to themselves. It is at least just that women should be allowed some liberty of choice, some opportunity for proving their capacities to the world. If they then fail they take a lower position fairly. But it is most unreasonable to assert that they have not certain capacities, while men are jealously closing every channel through which they might prove the existence of those capacities by putting them into practice.

III. SCRIPTURAL PRINCIPLES REQUIRE JUSTICE TO WOMEN. This is required by the law (Num. xxvii. 8). It is still more fully required by Christianity. The spiritual privileges of the gospel are equally open to men and women. The elevation of women is one of the most beneficial fruits of the gospel (Matt. xxvi. 13; Luke x. 38—42; Phil. iv. 3).

IV. Justice to women does not imply the equality of women with men. There must ever remain essential differences between the careers of men and women in many directions, owing to the essential differences of their physical and mental natures. Justice does not demand that all should receive the same privileges, and perform the same duties, but that there should be fairness in the distribution.

V. The exercise of rights by women carries with it the obligation of corresponding duties. Duty corresponds to right. The extension of rights increases the obligation of duties. If women obtain larger privileges, in justice they will be called upon to undertake heavier responsibilities. Happily this was realised in Scripture history. The women of the Bible enjoying greater advantages than their neighbours are often distinguished by peculiarly noble conduct. Women are conspicuous for devotion and sacrifice among the early disciples of Christ (Luke viii. 2, 3). Much of the best work of Christendom has been done by good women. There is large work in the Church for women now.—W. F. A.

Ver. 6.—*Woman's rights.* This is rather a remarkable case. The family of Machir, one of the most warlike in Israel, had contributed more to the conquest of Gilead than any other, and there had been accordingly allotted to them a large share of it. It so happened that in one branch of the family there was not a single male among the children. Five women alone represented a warlike sire. They appeal to Moses, with an energy derived from their great ancestor, to prevent the passing of their property out of their hands. It is apparently the last cause which comes before Moses before his death. The great lawgiver takes occasion from it to make a general law applicable to all such cases. If there be a son left, then the son inherits; the daughter being supposed to find her provision in that of the husband she marries, and to be supported by her brother till she does so. But in the case of there being no brother, they were to inherit their father's land, and marry in their own tribe, so that the tribe might still retain its possessions intact, and all families have maintenance for their representatives, even though male issue should fail. It falls to Joshua to apply the principles Moses laid down, and accordingly he gives the five ladies " an inheritance amongst the sons" of Manasseh. We do not suggest that Moses legislated in the spirit of the advanced theorists on woman's rights; it would have been impossible for one so wise to legislate some thousands of years ahead of the general sentiments of mankind. But it is worth noting how ready Moses was to do justice by the weaker sex; and to pass a law, doubtless little to the mind of the rough men who would look enviously on women inheriting considerable estates. It raises the question how far Moses would have sanctioned the views of those who plead that men and women should stand on exactly equal platforms before the law. We can only briefly suggest the answer to this question. Every woman under the Mosaic legislation was more or less sufficiently provided for. The double portion of the firstborn was, by the usage of the East, assigned him chiefly that he might support his widowed mother and unmarried sisters. When marriage was universal, a temporary provision of this kind was all that was required. And where land was not wealth, but only the material out of which it could be gathered, we do not wonder at the law dividing the land (after the eldest son's double portion) equally among the other sons. Wherever, on the other hand, no sons were left, then the daughters divided equally the property between them, subject to the restriction that they should marry within their own tribe. We may venture to suggest that the spirit of these laws would, in the altered circumstances of our country, be altogether in favour of the equal distribution of property between sons and daughters. The patriarchal system that gave the widow and the unmarried daughters an established home in the old family house which the elder brother inherited, and made their maintenance a charge upon the double birthright, has passed away; and it is no longer the case that sisters share whatever an elder son inherits. Marriage is neither so early nor so universal now. And in the multiplicity of remunerative pursuits open to men in our land there is no longer any special reason for restricting the inheritance of the land to those able personally to work upon it. Thus woman has less protection if unprovided for, less certainty of the resource of marriage; and man less need for special provisions in his favour. In these altered circumstances it is probable that what Moses ruled for the daughters of Zelophehad he would have expanded into a larger rule, and would have required invariably the equal division of all property amongst sons and daughters alike. If we are right in urging this, a few conclusions of practical moment emerge from it.

I. Parents who, in their wills, make the shares of their sons much larger than those of their daughters, take a course which the spirit of Bible legislation forbids, and are guilty of grave injustice.

II. The laws of every country ought, with especial care, to protect the property of women, as being the weaker parties in disputes and the likeliest, therefore, to suffer.

III. A considerable improvement in the position of women would be effected by the general adoption of such rules by parents and by states. Probably, if women in all directions found equal justice yielded them with men, the equality of legislative power and influence which some seek would be found superfluous.—G.

Vers. 14, 15.—*Greed and grumbling.* Joseph—*i.e.*, Ephraim and Manasseh —wants a larger lot. He pleads his numbers, as giving him a right to more. There is, perhaps, in his discontent a modicum of justice. They were very numerous, and part of the land allotted them was that valley of Jezreel, which, though the richest part of Palestine, from its being good for cavalry, had been as yet retained by the enemy. There was, however, more of discontent than of hardship. One half of Manasseh had already had a large part of Gilead assigned them. The shares allotted to Ephraim and the other half were ample — in fact, probably double as large in proportion to their numbers as some of the adjoining tribes. But Ephraim, descended from Joseph, the saviour of Israel, the tribe of Joshua, its great captain, wanted to take the lead as the governing tribe. They feel, accordingly, that while their wants are met their dignity is not sufficiently endowed. "They are a great people," therefore Joshua should have allowed them a larger portion. It is not unusual for those conscious—legitimately or otherwise—of greatness to make somewhat loud complaints and large demands. But Joshua—the embodiment of justice—cannot be unfair, even when his own tribe solicit him. He meets their claim in a fine spirit. He admits their greatness, but argues otherwise from it. They are so many? Why, then, not clear the mountain of its forests and find thus an easy and unselfish enlargement? It is true the Canaanites hold Jezreel, and they are not yet in possession of the fertile plain. But Joshua argues that that is a reason for fighting their enemies with courage, and not for filching from their brethren, with meanness. "Thou shalt drive out the Canaanites, though they be strong," he says, with a fine, genial, bracing blending of irony and encouragement. We have thus a fine example of a question with two sides; a necessity with two ways of meeting it; a fact with two conclusions. "I am numerous. There are foes on my land," says Joseph; "therefore give me a slice off what has fallen to Judah." "Thou art numerous, and enemies are still on thy land," says Joshua; "therefore clear the mountain of its forests and the plains of thine enemies." The example of Manasseh and Ephraim here, and the reply of Joshua to them, has much in it suggestive. Observe first—

I. A LITTLE HEART SOMETIMES SPOILS GREAT POWERS. The complaint from which Ephraim was suffering was this: *his heart was too little for his body;* poor circulation of the vital elements. These tribes had plenty of power, plenty of stalwart men to clear the waste or to conquer their enemies; but they had not moral force to match. They were short of enterprise, resource, courage. What they could easily have won by work or war they prefer that others should give them. The breath they should have kept for conflict they waste in grumbling. They want to be the dominating tribe, without paying the price of lordship in daring and willingness to encounter difficulty and hardship. There are many Ephraims in the world who have it in their power to make for themselves any lot they like, who, instead of improving, merely lament their lot. Many keep troubling friends to do for them what it is quite within their power to do for themselves. Some are merely indolent—capable of work, but disinclined to do it. Some suffer from a feebleness which exists only in their imagination, but which prevents their working more than actual frailty would. Some are merely proud, and think they have a right to something more in the world than they have got. So some grumble for want of earthly comforts they are too dull to get for themselves. So some go about expecting to get by "interest" and "favour" what they would be wiser to seek by self-reliance and energy. So some in the realm of religion go to God and complain they have not larger delights and richer usefulness and more power, when, as a matter of fact, all these things are within their reach if they would only put forth the powers they already have. This is a very general ailment. Few have the energy, the earnestness, the faith to do with their powers anything like the whole of what is possible to them. We are engines, built to work up to 30 lbs. pressure on the square inch, and we only work up to seven and a half. Seek not so much greater powers as the heart to use the powers you have. Observe secondly—

II. TRUE KINDNESS OFTEN DECLINES TO DO FOR MEN WHAT THEY CAN DO FOR THEMSELVES. When Ephraim has the power to win as much land as he needs, it is better that he be set to win it for himself. Men can rarely keep well any more than they can win bravely. To give Ephraim what he wants would be only to increase his indolence, his arrogance, and his weakness. To set Ephraim to get what he wants by his own prowess, increases his enterprise, his brotherliness, his courage, his diligence, his self-respect. We learn best what we learn ourselves. We profit most by our own experience. It is no kindness to grant the requests of indolence and greed. The true kindness is Joshua's—to point out how much is within the reach of the aspiring, and set them to conquer it for themselves. Lastly observe—

III. GREATNESS SHOULD DWELL UPON ITS DUTIES RATHER THAN ON ITS CLAIMS. "I am a great people . . . give me," is the tone which a great multitude, besides Ephraim, assume. "I am a great people . . . therefore ought to work and fight," is the tone they ought to use. True greatness speaks in the latter, bastard greatness in the former tone. Sometimes it is an *aristocracy* that declares itself to be the most important class in a country, and with something of Ephraim's pitiable lament presents its claims for more consideration and influence. Sometimes a *priestly order* will, on the score of its greatness and importance, claim more authority than the people are disposed to grant it. Sometimes an ignorant class, puffed up with ambition, will desire more power than it has got. It is well to remember greatness is not given us to constitute a claim on others' services, but as a power to serve them and ourselves together. He is greatest who is servant of all, and he is chief who ministers to all. If you and Ephraim are so great and worthy, use your greatness and power for the good of yourselves and others, and none will grudge you what in this way you win.—G.

Vers. 14—18.—*Self-help.* I. IT IS FOOLISH TO COMPLAIN OF OUR LOT UNTIL WE HAVE MADE THE BEST USE OF IT. The Ephraimites had not cleared their forest, yet they complained of the narrowness of their possession. We do not know the extent of our advantages till we try them. In murmuring at the privations of life we spoil the enjoyment of its blessings. Hardships which we ascribe to the arrangements of Providence may often be traced to our own indolence. The one talent is buried because it is not five. We have no excuse for complaints before we have made the full use of what we possess. This may be applied to (1) abilities, (2) opportunities of service, (3) means of self-improvement, and (4) sources of enjoyment.

II. OUR LOT IN LIFE WILL IMPROVE AS IT IS USED WELL. Joshua showed to the complaining Ephraimites that if they cleared their forest and so recovered the waste land, their lot would thereby be doubled. The neglected inheritance runs to weeds and becomes worthless. The cultivated possession improves with cultivation. Exercise strengthens the weak. If we make a good use of what opportunities for service we now possess, these will develop new and better opportunities. If we use well what powers God has given us, these will grow more effective. The talent that is not neglected produces other talents.

III. GREAT CLAIMS SHOULD BE SUSTAINED BY GREAT ACHIEVEMENTS. The Ephraimites claim to be great, and therefore deserving of a great inheritance. Joshua replies, " If thou be a great people, then get thee up to the wood country and cut down for thyself there," &c. High rank should justify itself by high service, large wealth by large beneficence, titles of honour by deeds of sacrifice. Duty is proportionate to faculty. The more advantages we claim the more obligations shall we contract.

IV. THE BEST RIGHT TO A POSSESSION IS TO HAVE OBTAINED IT THROUGH THE EXERTION OF OUR OWN ENERGIES. Joshua bids the Ephraimites increase their lot by the exercise of their valour in exterminating the Canaanites, and of their industry in felling the forest. (1) It is unworthy to look to *personal favour* to secure us a position in the world not earned by merit or work. Joshua belonged to the tribe of Ephraim, and the Ephraimites seem to have expected favours on this account, but in vain. (2) It is weak to depend on the *paternal interference of the State* when our own industry should obtain our rights. (3) It is wrong to wait idly for a *providential interposition* on our behalf. God will give us our inheritance, but we must conquer it and cultivate it. He helps us when we do our best, but never so as to justify our indolence.—W. F. A.

Vers. 14—18.—Let us make some further observations on *the division of the land of Canaan among the tribes of Israel.* The descendants of Joseph receive but a small lot. They complain bitterly of this, saying, "*We are a great people.*" Joshua replies that, just because they are a great people, they may be contented with the share assigned them, for they will have the opportunity of perpetually extending their borders. " The mountain shall be thine; for thou shalt drive out the Canaanites, though they have iron chariots and though they be strong" (ver. 18). In this passage of their history there is a beautiful SYMBOL OF THE POSITION OF THE CHURCH IN THE WORLD. Manasseh and Ephraim have no assured possession. In order to retain what they have and to acquire sufficient territory, they must be ever fighting. Ever fresh conquests are the necessary conditions of their retaining that which they already possess. If they do not strengthen their position and enlarge their borders, they will be at once invaded by their enemies. Such is the position of the Church in the world. (1) For the Church too, conquest is the condition of security. Pressed on every hand by a hostile world, it must be ever in an attitude of active self-defence: it must ever have in its hand the sword of the Spirit. As soon as it falls asleep, in a supposed peaceful security, it finds itself assailed, and the enemy is in its midst before it is aware. Nothing is more easy, nothing of more frequent occurrence, than this intrusion of the world into the Church. Therefore the Church is bound to be ever armed with all the panoply of God, and ready for the fight. "We wrestle not," says the apostle, "against flesh and blood, but against principalities, against powers, against the rulers of the darkness of this world, against spiritual wickedness in high places" (Eph. vi. 12). This defensive warfare is also in a manner aggressive; for every new generation born within the outward precincts of the Church needs to be won afresh for Jesus Christ. No one is born a Christian, though it may be a great advantage to be born in a land of historic Christianity. It is necessary, therefore, constantly to reconquer from the world and from the merely natural life, the posterity of Christians. In this primary sense the Church cannot hold its own without ever fresh conquests. (2) Nor is this enough. Antichrist, under the form of paganism, or of simple infidelity, is still a formidable power on every hand. He who said to His disciples, "Go and teach all nations," opened before them a limitless field of conquest. The mission of the Christian Church is the fulfilment of the command of Joshua to Ephraim and Manasseh: "Thou art a great people and hast great power; get thee up to the wood country, and cut down for thyself there in the land of the giants" (ver. 15). The might which is in the Church, though invisible, is greater than that of the giants of antichrist, for it is the strength of Him who said, "Lo, I am with you alway, even unto the end of the world" (Matt. xxviii. 20).—E. DE P.

EXPOSITION.

CHAPTER XVIII. 1—28.

THE CONTINUED DIVISION OF THE LAND.—
Ver. 1—**Congregation.** The word signifies
a body of persons gathered together at a
spot before indicated. The LXX. renders
by συναγωγή. The idea is evidently that of
an assembly gathered together for some
specific acts of worship. This passage teaches
the duty of a national recognition of religion.
Whatever evils there might be in Israel at
that time, the absence of a general and
formal acknowledgment of God was not one
of them. When that public acknowledgment of Him ceased, the downfall of the
nation was at hand. It was the absence of
such acknowledgment that was the ruin of
Israel, while the hypocritical and purely
external recognition of God by Judah was
equally offensive in God's sight. **Assembled.**
Literally, *was summoned;* by whom, we are
not told. But this general gathering to set
up the tabernacle at once an act of due
homage to Him by whose power they had
done so many great deeds, and also the
establishment of a centre of national life.
As long as the worship of God was maintained in its purity, the unity of Israel
would be preserved, in spite of the twelve-
fold division into tribes, and without the
need to introduce the monarchical power.
When fidelity to the outward symbol of
Israelitish unity, the tabernacle at Shiloh,
relaxed, then dissension and weakness crept
in, and Israel became a prey to her enemies.
A remarkable instance of an opposite character meets us in the history of our own
country. The prey of various unconnected
Teutonic tribes, the island was one vast
scene of anarchy and confusion, until the
great Archbishop Theodore came over and
founded a National Church. It was this
religious unity and co-operation which
tended to harmonise the conflicting forces
in the land and steadily pioneered the way
to an union of the rival tribes under one
head. Without attempting to say whose fault
it is that this religious unity is lost, or how
it may best be re-established, it surely is
the duty of every patriot and every Christian to co-operate to the best of his ability
and knowledge, with all the forces that he
sees tending towards unity, and both pray
and labour for the coming of the day when
men may once more "with one mind and
with one mouth glorify God, even the Father
of our Lord Jesus Christ," and be willing
to meet together "with one accord in one
place." **Shiloh.** In Deut. xii. 5, 11, 14, we
find God prescribing that only in a place

chosen by Himself shall the public worship
of the congregation be paid to Him. Thither
were all the males to resort three times a
year. It is obvious how such a regulation
tended to keep alive national feeling among
the Israelites. The reason for the choice of
Shiloh (which was probably made by Urim
and Thummim, the case being important
enough for such a decision) is to be found in
its central position, five hours south of Shechem, and eight hours north of Jerusalem.
Its situation is minutely described in Judg.
xxi. 19. It is difficult to understand why;
since Shiloh must have been well-known to
all the dwellers in Israel at that time, unless
it was to explain to those who were not
acquainted with the localities in the tribe of
Benjamin the reason for the selection of
Shiloh, namely, that it lay close by the road
between Bethel and Shechem (see, however,
note on ch. xxiv. 1). The place has been
identified. It is the modern Seilûn, but
only a few ruins remain to mark the place
once so famous in the history of Israel,
where Eli abode, where Samuel spent his
early years. Rejected by God Himself, as
the Jewish Psalmist relates with patriotic
pride (Psa. lxxviii. 60, 67—69), it fell into
utter neglect, and even in the days of
Jeremiah it seems to have become a by-word
(see Jer. vii. 12, 14; xxvi. 6, 9. Also Pal.
Expl. Fund, Quart. Paper, Jan., 1873, where
an account, with a plan, is given of the
place in its present condition. There are a
few rock-hewn tombs there). Whether it
was named Shiloh on account of the word
used in Gen. xlix. 10, it is impossible to say.
The name appears to signify *rest,* and was
an appropriate name to be given to the
visible symbol of rest from warfare which
Joshua had obtained for Israel (see ch. xi.
23; xiv. 15; xxi. 44; xxii. 4). The difficult
passage in Gen. xlix. 10 is not of course
included in this interpretation of the
meaning of the word Shiloh. **Congregation.**
The word here differs slightly from the word
translated "congregation" in the first part
of the verse, but it comes from the same
root. **And the land was subdued before
them.** That is, the land in which the
tabernacle was set up. We know from the
next verse that the land as a whole was not
subdued.

Ver. 3.—**How long are ye slack?** This
"slackness" (the translation is a literal
one) in the arduous conflict against the
powers of evil is not confined to Jews. The
exhortation needs repeating to every generation, and not less to our own than any
other, since the prevalence of an external

decency and propriety blinds our eyes to the impiety and evil which still lurks amid us unsubdued.

Ver. 4.—**Give out from among you.** Calvin enlarges much upon the boldness of these twenty-one men in venturing upon the task of the survey, rightly supposing that the difficulty of the task was enhanced by the number who undertook it (see note on ch. xiv. 12). And here it is impossible to come to any other conclusion than that the twenty-one commissioners went together, for the object of their selection was to obviate complaints of a kind which, as we have already seen, the Israelites were not slow to make (see ch. xvii. 14—18). But the Israelites had inspired quite sufficient awe into the inhabitants of the land to make such a general survey by no means a difficult task. Nor is it probable that the commissioners were unprovided with an escort. **Three men for each tribe.** Literally, for *the* tribe. This selection, which was intended to secure an impartial description of the country, would render impossible all future complaints, since the boundaries would be settled according to reports sent in by the representatives of each tribe.

Ver. 6.—**Ye shall therefore describe the land into seven parts.** Literally, *ye shall write the land, seven parts.* Similarly in ver. 8. That is to say, a written report was to be brought up in seven parts, a fair and equal division of the land having previously been agreed upon among the commissioners. This report having been accepted, division was afterwards made (ver. 10) by lot. Bishop Horsley and Houbigant here, as elsewhere, would re-arrange the chapter, supposing it to have been accidentally transposed. But there seems no ground for the supposition. The repetition, with its additional particulars at each repetition, is quite in the style of the author (see ch. ii. and notes). **That I may cast lots.** Or, *and I will* cast a lot. The somewhat unusual word ירה to *throw*, is used here. The more usual word is הפיל *caused to fall,* though other expressions are also used.

Ver. 7.—**But the Levites** (see ch. xiii. 14, 33). **The priesthood of the Lord.** An equivalent expression to that in ch. xiii. Here the office of the priesthood, there, more accurately, the sacrifices which it was the privilege of that tribe to offer up, are said to be the possession of the tribe of Levi. **By cities.** It was evidently not a land survey, entering into such particulars as the physical conditions of the ground, its fitness for agriculture, for pasture and the like. The division was made *by cities.* These cities had been taken and destroyed

by Joshua, and now it was the intention of the Israelites to be guided by the ancient political system of the country, to occupy those cities, and to cultivate the adjacent land, as the Phœnicians had done before them. Thus, not so much the area of the land, as the size and importance of its cities, was to be the leading principle of the division. And not unwisely. The Israelites were about to relinquish their nomad life, and if they settled in Palestine, how, without walled cities, could they hold their own against the powerful nations round about them? **And came again to Joshua.** " The result of this examination, which was unquestionably a more careful one than that made by the spies of Moses, was that the unsubdued territory was found to be too small for the wants of seven tribes, while that apportioned to Judah was seen to be disproportionately large. To remedy this difficulty a place was found for Benjamin between Judah and Ephraim, and the portion of Simeon was taken out of the southern portion of Judah, while both Judah and Ephraim had to give up some cities to Dan " (Ritter).

Ver. 8.—**Shiloh** (see note on ver. 1 and ch. xxiv. 1). The seat of the tabernacle became, for the present at least, the head-quarters of the Israelites.

Ver. 10.—**Cast lots.** Here, and in ver. 8, yet another phrase is used to describe the casting of the lots.

Ver. 11.—**The children of Benjamin.** Lying as their inheritance did between that of Ephraim and Judah, the chief places of note on their border have been already mentioned either in ch. xv. or in ch. xvi.

Ver. 14.—**And the border was drawn thence, and compassed the border of the sea.** This is a serious mistranslation, arising from the same word being used for *sea* and *west* in Hebrew. The LXX. has πρὸς (some copies have παρὰ) θάλασσαν. The literal translation is, *and the border extended, and deflected to the western side.* What is meant is that the further portion of the border now described was the western side of Benjamin. **Southward.** The western border of course ran in a southerly direction. **Quarter.** This is the same word that is translated *border* above, in the phrase, "border of the sea." **Kirjath-jearim.** Any one who will take the trouble to examine a map will see how much more probable the site Kuriet el Enab is here, than any place " four miles from Beth-shemesh," as suggested by Lieut. Conder. The distance from nether Beth-horon to Kuriet el Enab is not great. It is improbable that the boundary should have run double that distance without any mention of locality.

Ver. 17.—**Geliloth** (see ch. xv. 7).

Ver. 23.—**Avim.** Most probably Ai (see note on ch. vii. 2).

Ver. 24.—**Ophrah.** Not the Ophrah of Gideon, who (Judg. vi. 11; viii. 2, 32) was a Manassite. **Gaba.** Some (as Knobel) think this the same as Gibeah of Saul. But see below, ver. 28. Also Isa. x. 29. Gibeah and Gaba, however, must have been near together, for Ramah is near both of them (see Ezra ii. 26).

Ver. 26.—**Ramah.** Now er-Ram. This would seem, from Jer. xxxi. 15, and from a comparison of Jer. i. 1 and xl. 1, to have been the Ramah of later history, famous as the dwelling-place of Samuel (1 Sam. i. 1, &c., for Mount Ephraim is applied to territory in Benjamin. Cf. Judg. iv. 5; 2 Sam. xx. 1, 21). It was near Gibeah (Judg. xix. 13; Isa. x. 29), and not far from Bethel (Judg. iv. 5). It was rebuilt by Baasha (1 Kings xv. 17, 21). **Mizpeh.** This is the Mizpeh, or Mizpah, of Benjamin, whither the tribes were wont to gather together, and where the tabernacle appears to have been removed (see Judg. xx. 1, 3; xxi. 1—8). If, as Lieut. Conder supposes, Nob and Mizpeh were identical, and were near Jerusalem, this would explain the presence of the tribes within the border of Benjamin on this occasion. They were near the border, and the Benjamites had retired to their mountain fastnesses. This seems almost implied in Judg. xx. 3. Similar gatherings are recorded in the Book of Samuel (1 Sam. vii. 5—7, 11, 12, 16; x. 17). Mizpeh was the seat of Gedaliah's administration, and of the tragedy of his assassination (2 Kings xxv. 23—25; Jer. xl. 10—13; xli.).

Ver. 28.—**Gibeath.** Almost certainly the same as " Gibeah of Saul " (1 Sam. xi. 4). It was Saul's home (1 Sam. x. 26; xiii. 2, 15, 16). It was near Saul's home, at the time his temporary refuge, that the Philistines encamped when Jonathan (1 Sam. xiv.) made his daring attack on them. It was the scene of the terrible outrage recorded in Judg. xix. Lieut. Conder has identified it with Jeba, not far from Michmash, situated on one of the branches of the precipitous Wady Suwaynit. The situation explains the otherwise unintelligible narrative in 1 Sam. xiii., xiv. **This is the inheritance of the children of Benjamin.** Dean Stanley (' Sinai and Palestine,' ch. iv.) reminds us how the very names suggest the "remarkable heights " which constitute the " table land " of which the inheritance of Benjamin consists. Thus Gibeon, Gibeah, Geba, or Gaba, all signify *hill.* Ramah signifies high place, and Mizpeh, watch tower, which of necessity must be situated on an eminence. Only by narrow passes along deep torrent beds could access be obtained to this mountainous region. Thus it was that the otherwise inexplicable resistance to all Israel in arms, recorded in Judg. xx., xxi., was maintained. In a country like this the skill of the Benjamites with the sling (Judg. xx. 16) and the bow (2 Sam. i. 22) could be used with terrible effect upon foes powerless to come to a hand-to-hand conflict. To Dean Stanley's vivid description of the physical geography of the country the student is referred for a detailed account.

HOMILETICS.

Vers. 1—28.—*Progress in the great work.* The tribes gathered together at Shiloh, set up the common tabernacle for worship, and then proceeded, at Joshua's instance, to complete the division of the land. Several detached considerations may be derived from this chapter.

I. THE DUTY OF A PUBLIC RECOGNITION OF GOD. The duty of public worship has been universally recognised in all religions, and is founded in a natural tendency of mankind. Philosophical sects, in which religious observances are neglected or proscribed, show by that very fact their exclusiveness. Religions, however perverted, exist for mankind as a whole ; philosophies, for the cultivated few. Christianity has provided fewer forms than perhaps any other religion for the gratification of this instinct, but the principle is clearly acknowledged. At first, the disciples met together weekly to "break bread." At the Reformation, the abuses that had crept into the doctrine and practice of the Lord's Supper led to its more infrequent reception. Yet still the precept, "not forgetting the assembling of yourselves together," has continued to be recognised, and the man who habitually neglects public worship is scarcely regarded as a Christian at all. The duty of a public *national* recognition is a matter of more difficulty in the midst of our present religious divisions. Yet it is practically not neglected. The fact that the nation as such recognises Christianity is proved by the spectacle presented by our country every

Lord's Day, a spectacle which drew from a distinguished French Roman Catholic writer the admission that England was the most religious country in the world. And in times of national rejoicing, or national distress, the various religious bodies in the country do not fail, according to their various forms, to unite in common thanksgiving, or common humiliation and intercession. A more complete external agreement in the manner of such national recognition of religion may or may not be desirable. But it would be folly to conclude that no such recognition exists because it is not externally organised into a system. Perhaps in God's eyes the agreement is greater than it seems to us : that where we discern conflicting institutions and rival denominations, He sees the tribes of Israel gathered together at Shiloh, and offering up united praises and supplications to Him for His mercy and His bounty. Be it ours to recognise more and more a real union under seeming disagreement, and to abstain from all uncharitable expressions, which are out of harmony with the voice of praise and thanksgiving, of prayer and intercession, addressed to our common Father in heaven.

II. BEHOLD HOW GOOD AND JOYFUL A THING IT IS, BRETHREN, TO DWELL TOGETHER IN UNITY. This consideration has been partially anticipated already. It was the *whole* congregation that assembled together. None stayed away, still less refused to come. And though perhaps, in view of the wide freedom allowed in the Christian Church, the minor differences of ceremonial do not prevent us from coming as one body before the throne of grace ; yet, in so far as these divisions of opinion produce jealousy, suspicion, unkindness, bitter accusations and revilings, they exclude those who are so affected by them from a part in the common worship. Such persons are unclean, and cannot enter into the congregation of the faithful ; they are unloving, and can have neither part nor lot in the worship of Him who came to call us to unity and peace. We may be sure that as there is no more certain method of checking the progress of the Church on earth than a contentious spirit, so there is nothing more sure to deprive us of the favour of God. Let the spectacle, then, of an united Israel, worshipping peacefully before God in Shiloh, lead us to beware how we promote disunion among God's people, remembering the exhortation, " Let all bitterness and wrath and anger and clamour and evil speaking be put away from you, with all malice," and "walk in love, as Christ also hath loved us, and hath given himself for us, an offering and a sacrifice to God for a sweet-smelling savour."

III. REST IN GOD. Shiloh means rest, or peace. And rest and peace is only to be found in the presence of God. "Peace on earth," cried the angels at His birth. " I will give you rest." " My peace I give unto you," said He Himself. " He is our peace," said the apostle. Through Him we possess the " peace that passeth all understanding." And, thanks be to Him, we are never far from His tabernacle. The tabernacle of God is among men, and He will dwell with them, and wherever a soul pours itself out in prayer to Him, there is His tabernacle and Shiloh, or restful dependence on Him.

IV. WHAT HAS TO BE DONE SHOULD BE DONE THOROUGHLY. Many a Christian has fallen into serious trouble by neglecting this precept. Some think that a certain profession of religion ought to excuse all shortcomings. Some even go so far as to think that the careful and punctual performance of duty is a legal work, below the attention of a redeemed and sanctified man. Such a view receives no confirmation from Scripture. Our Lord did not neglect the lighter matters of the law Himself, nor advise others to do so. St. Paul did not consider the minutest details beneath his attention. And here the survey was made with the most scrupulous exactness, and recorded in a book. Let Christians learn hence the duty of performing, accurately and punctually, whatever falls to their lot to do. Christ did not give His Spirit to men to make them slovenly, careless, indifferent to what they undertake, but the reverse. Both the Old Testament and the New combine to enforce on us the lesson, " Whatsoever ye do, do it heartily, as to the Lord, and not unto men."

HOMILIES BY VARIOUS AUTHORS.

Ver. 1.—*Shiloh, the sanctuary.* The choice of Shiloh as a resting-place for the tabernacle was not left at Joshua's discretion: it was a matter of Divine appointment (Deut. xii. 10—12). At the same time it was not without its natural reason. The situation was both central and secluded; in the midst of the land, as the tabernacle had always been "in the midst of the camp" in the wilderness (Num. ii. 17), and yet removed from the main routes of the country's traffic. Its name, dating probably from this time, while expressive of the fact that God had now given His people rest from their enemies, was also suggestive of the deeper thought of His settled dwelling among them, and was in harmony with the retired and tranquil aspect of the scene. Shiloh, the sanctuary, the place of rest. In this establishment of the tabernacle at Shiloh the Israelites were performing the highest function of their life as a people. It was a devout recognition of God; the majesty of His being, His sovereignty over them, their dependence on Him as the living root of all their social order and prosperity, that testimony for Him which it was their high calling to present before the nations. The tabernacle at Shiloh stands as a type of all places where people assemble to pay their homage to the Supreme.

I. THE SANCTITY OF THE SCENE OF WORSHIP. The tabernacle was the centre and home of all devout thought and feeling. The highest acts of worship could alone be performed there. It represented the unity of the religious life of the people, as opposed to a scattered and divided worship. It was called "the tabernacle of witness" (Num. xvii. 7; Acts vii. 44). In several ways is every scene of worship, every "house of prayer," a witness.

1. *As a symbol of the presence of God with His people.* It bears witness to the fact of His spiritual nearness and accessibility. It could have no meaning if personal and "congregational" communion with God were not a blessed reality. The fundamental idea of the tabernacle was that it is the place where man "meets with God," and finds a gracious response to his seeking. "In all places where I record my name I will come unto thee, and I will bless thee" (Exod. xx. 24). "There will I meet with thee, and I will commune with thee from above the mercy-seat" (Exod. xxv. 22). And Christ perpetuates and confirms the promise with a freer, richer grace: "Wheresoever two or three," &c. (Matt. xviii. 15). This gives sanctity to any place; makes it a true sanctuary. What other consecration can be needed than the realised presence of the living God?

2. *As a memorial of the hallowed traditions of the past.* The historic associations of the tabernacle were distinctive, wonderful, supernatural. Its origin: made "after the pattern shown to Moses in the mount" (Exod. xxvi.); the "glory-cloud" that rested upon it; its varying fortunes; the changing scenes through which it had passed—scenes of human shame, and fear, and sorrow, and scenes of joyous triumph and marvellous Divine interposition—all this invested it with extraordinary interest. Every true house of prayer has its hallowed memories. Some small chapter at least of the sacred story of the past is enshrined in it. It speaks to us of struggles for truth and liberty, purity of faith and worship, freedom of conscience, in former days. It represents the earnest thought and self-denying labour of devout men and women who have long, perhaps, been numbered with the dead. It has been the scene of many a solemn spiritual transaction: revelations of truth, searchings of heart, stirrings of sympathetic emotion, heavenly aspirations, visions of God. However lowly a place it may be, the memory of these lingering about it gives it an interest and a distinction that no outward charm can rival.

3. *As a prophecy of the better future.* The tabernacle, though it had come now to a resting-place after all its wanderings, was still only a temporary provision, a preparation for something more substantial and enduring. The time came when "Ichabod" must be pronounced on Shiloh. The ark of God was taken, the sanctuary was desecrated, and the faded glory of the sacred tent was lost at last in the greater splendour of the temple; until *that* also should pass away, to be followed by a nobler shrine. So is it with all earthly scenes of worship. They

are but temporary and provisional. They are expressive, after, all, of our human weakness—dimness of spiritual vision, imperfection of spiritual life. They remind us ever of the " vail that hangs between the saints and joys Divine." They " have no glory by reason of the glory that excelleth." They speak to us of the "more perfect tabernacle not made with hands." We see in them a prophecy of the nobler worship of the future, and learn through them to lift our longing eyes to that eternal city of God of which it is written, "I saw no temple therein, for the Lord God Almighty and the Lamb are the temple of it" (Rev. xxi. 22).

II. THE PEACEFUL ASSOCIATIONS OF THE SCENE OF WORSHIP. " Shiloh " is a name that becomes every place of prayer, every scene of Divine manifestation and communion. It ought to be a place of rest in the midst of earthly agitations, a quiet resort for the spirit from the traffic and turmoil of life, a refuge for the weak and weary, a sanctuary for those who are harassed by the contradictions and pursued by the animosities of a hostile world. Unhappily the house of God is too often connected in men's minds with far other ideas than those of tranquillity and peace. It is suggestive to them of division, and enmity, and bitter contention. The mischief done by those historic strifes about faith and worship that have raged around it, or those mean discords that have reigned within, can never be exaggerated. And yet wherever there is a place of Christian assembly there stands a testimony to the "one Lord, one faith," &c. Beneath these superficial distractions lies the bond of a true spiritual unity. Let that essential unity become manifest, then shall the "glory of the Lord " be again upon His tabernacle, and it shall attract the world to itself as a true sanctuary and place of rest.—W.

Ver. 1.—*Shiloh.* Shiloh was at once the seat of public worship and the centre of tribal union ; the symbol of established peace and the witness to that Divine law on which the maintenance of peace and prosperity depended. Christendom needs its Shilohs. It is true that our privileges of worship are not confined to consecrated buildings, holy days, priestly ministrations, and church ordinances. Anywhere, on the lonely hill-side or in the busy street, at any hour—in the silent night or at the noisy noon—every Christian can claim the privilege of one of God's priests and offer up secret worship, which God will accept and bless. There is often a depth and spirituality in such worship which is not attained in the observance of public religious services. Nevertheless there are special advantages connected with public worship.

I. PUBLIC WORSHIP AFFORDS AN OPPORTUNITY FOR SPIRITUAL REST. The tabernacle was set up when " the land was subdued." The seat of worship was named " Shiloh," the " place of peace." Our churches should be homes of spiritual peace ; our Sundays, Sabbaths of spiritual rest. The ejaculatory prayer of sudden emergencies, and the " praying without ceasing" of those who " walk with God" and enjoy constant communion with Him, are not sufficient means for withdrawing us from the spirit of the world and revealing to us the heights and depths of heavenly things. For this we want a more complete separation from common scenes, and a longer season of quiet meditation.

II. PUBLIC WORSHIP AFFORDS THE MEANS FOR THE OUTWARD EXPRESSION OF SPIRITUAL WORSHIP. All true worship must be internal and spiritual (John iv. 24). External ordinances without this are a mockery; but spiritual worship will naturally seek some external expression. The body is so connected with the soul that all emotion tends to bodily manifestations—joy to smiles, sorrow to tears, anger to frowns. So emotions of worship find their outlet in articulate prayers and songs of praise. Such expression is (1) natural, (2) helpful.

III. PUBLIC WORSHIP IS AN OCCASION FOR A PUBLIC TESTIMONY TO RELIGION. The tabernacle was set up in the sight of the people as a visible witness for God. We have our " altars of witness." It is our duty (1) to *confess our faith* (Matt. x. 32) ; (2) to *glorify God* by declaring His character to the world and thanking Him before men for the blessings we have received ; (3) to *preach Christ* by making the light of His gospel shine through the worship of His Church (Matt. v. 13—16).

IV. PUBLIC WORSHIP IS A STIMULUS TO PRIVATE DEVOTION. It counteracts the depressing influence of worldly occupations and the variations of private experience resulting from our own changing moods. It stimulates us (1) by the direct influence of the religious exercises of prayer, praise, and the reading of Scripture and preaching; (2) by mutual sympathy.

V. PUBLIC WORSHIP HELPS US TO REALISE CHRISTIAN BROTHERHOOD. The erection at Shiloh was "the tabernacle of the *congregation*." There the tribes assembled together. It was to them the centre of national unity. In our worship we should forget our differences. Rich and poor meet together first as one in sin and want and helplessness, and then as one in redemption, spiritual joy, and Christian service. No duty is more important than that of maintaining a spirit of Christian brotherhood (John iv. 20, 21). By no means is this more fully realised than by union in the deepest emotions of the spiritual life.—W. F. A.

Vers. 2, 3.—*Slackness.* I. MUCH OF THE CHRISTIAN INHERITANCE IS NOT YET POSSESSED. (1) *Multitudes of men have not yet received the advantages of the gospel which are freely offered to all.* Christ died for the whole world; God desires the redemption of all men; all are freely invited (Rev. xxii. 17). Yet some live on in sin, some in distress, some in unbelief. Let these know that the distribution of God's grace has not ceased. There is yet abundance to be given for those who seek. The festal chamber is not full. There is yet room. The door is still open (Luke xiv. 22, 23). (2) *The Church has not yet conquered the world for Christ.* He claims the whole world. So long as there are heathen nations abroad and godless men at home the work of the Church militant will be incomplete. It is foolish to be satisfied with the triumphs of the past. We should rather lament the slow progress of the gospel. (3) *Christians have much of their inheritance in Christ not yet possessed.* The half has not been told us. No one can conceive the fulness of the riches of Christ (Isa. lxiv. 4). (*a*) Christians do not enjoy on earth all the blessings which they might have ; (*b*) greater blessings are reserved for heaven (1 John iii. 2).

II. IT IS OWING TO THE SLACKNESS OF MEN, AND NOT TO THE WILL OF GOD, THAT SO MUCH OF THE CHRISTIAN INHERITANCE IS NOT YET POSSESSED. Not God's will, but man's impenitence, delays his acceptance of the blessings of the gospel. Not God's will, but the Church's tardiness, hinders the spread of Christianity through the world. Not God's will, but the Christian's weakness, prevents him from enjoying the full privileges of redemption. This slackness to take full possession of the Christian inheritance is culpable, and arises from various causes. (1) *Satisfaction with the present.* The Israelites became too well satisfied with their achievements before all the land was conquered. We are too readily tempted to "rest and be thankful" before half our work is done. Our watchword should be "Forward" (Phil. iii. 13, 14). (2) *Indolence.* Even when we know that more should be done we are slothful and unwilling to rouse our energies for continued service. This may arise (*a*) from weariness when it shows the need of the Divine help for continued exertion; or (*b*) from culpable remissness when it is a distinct proof of cooling zeal. (3) *Habits of delay.* Some seem to follow the rule of never doing to-day what can be postponed till the morrow. Every day has its task. To postpone this to the morrow will hinder the task of the morrow. All is ready on God's side; there is no excuse for delay. While we delay the opportunity may pass (Psa. xcv. 7). (4) *Unbelief—*(*a*) in the need of Christ, (*b*) in the greatness of the Christian blessings, (*c*) in the Divine power, through which they may be obtained.—W. F. A.

Ver. 3.—*An exhortation to advance.* In ch. xiii. 1 we find an address delivered to Joshua by Jehovah, in which he was reminded how much remained to be done ere his work was finished, and his age forbade the belief that many years would intervene before his death. To the assembled tribes of Israel the exhortation of the text was consequently given. The tribes of Manasseh, Reuben, and Gad had received their inheritance on the east of the Jordan, Judah occupied the south of Palestine, and Ephraim a domain in the centre, Levi was to have no special territory assigned, and seven tribes waited for the determination of their settlements.

I. THE POSITION OF THESE ISRAELITES.   After years of wandering they were permitted at last to tread the soil of the land of promise.   They might well indulge feelings of gratification at the thought of their surroundings, that the wilderness was passed, and their eyes beheld the country which their fathers had in vain desired to see.   A spot had been selected where the tabernacle should remain, being, according to the promise and prophecy of God, "in the midst of all their tribes."   Still the Israelites had only attained to a half-way position.   The rest of arrival must be succeeded by the warfare of acquisition before they could reach the rest of enjoyment.   Jehovah had granted to them the land of the enemy, had conducted them safely thither; now let them grasp the privilege placed so near.   Few of God's gifts but necessitate effort on the part of the recipients, efforts to appropriate and improve.   According to the old fable, treasures are buried in the fields, and only diligent search and cultivation will bring them to light and make us master of them.   What men pay for or have a hand in securing, they value; what they strive after, they esteem; hence the necessity laid upon us to labour in order to receive is a beneficial law.

II. WHAT THE REPROOF OF THE TEXT ARGUES UPON THE PART OF THE REPROVED. (1) *Indolence of disposition.*   It was doubtless pleasing to the Israelites to indulge for a season their love of ease.   They could live for a time on the bounty of their brethren and on the fertile produce of the land which had cost them no trouble to till.   They were "slack to go in to possess the land."   Indolence is one of the most difficult foes to overcome.   The great majority evince a decided disinclination to energetic exercise of their powers.   Indolence is not only a state of privative loss in respect both of character and happiness, it is also a dangerous state, leaving man open to any incursion of the arch enemy.   History abounds in instances of failure on the part of men to become great because they relaxed their efforts and progress ceased.   A little longer struggling and the summit of ambition and fame had been scaled.   "Idleness," says Seneca, "is the burying of a living man."   (2) *Insensibility to the privileges possible to be acquired.*   Desire of gaining an end in view is the chief incentive to exertion, and the strength of the desire depends upon the amount of appreciation of the advantages which will be thereby secured.   He who is not attracted by the pictures drawn of heaven will not manifest any resolute endeavours to get there.   That kind of exhortation is most successful which causes hearers to glow within them at the thought of the precious jewels which may be obtained by seeking.   Emotions are regulated by the keenness or dulness of our perceptions.   (3) *Forgetfulness of direct command.*   Sloth was, in fact, disobedience. The very purpose for which God had preserved the tribes was, that they might, in obedience to His behests, occupy their respective territories, and drive out the inhabitants who had defiled the land.   Many persons excuse their dilatoriness in complying with the precepts of Scripture by various pleas which discover an insufficient acknowledgment of the obligation resting upon them not merely to leave undone what ought not to be done, but to do at once what they ought to do.   In this they are verily guilty.   We must not be oblivious of the sins of omission as well as of commission.   Woe to us if we know our Lord's will and do it not!   Constantly let the inquiry be made, "Lord, what wilt thou have me to do?"

III. THE APPLICATION OF THE FOREGOING.   *To Christian attainments.*   The Christian life is described in many terms, nearly all of which represent it as a progress, a "reaching forth unto things that are before."   It is called a warfare, a race, a pilgrimage, a building, &c., denoting continuous effort, in the shape of assault or resistance to assault.   There are strongholds to be taken, plains to be seized, fountains and woods and rivers to be gained, trophies to be won.   The followers of Christ are expected to advance in faith, hope, and love, in knowledge, purity and holiness, in gifts and graces, in self-discipline and improvement, and in usefulness to others and to the Church.   *To secret discipleship.*   There was a time when you were under the servile yoke of sin, and being released entered the wilderness of doubt to be affrighted by the thunders of the law.   But you have found a High Priest, a Mediator, who has also been a Deliverer to lead you into the land of rest.   You have believed in Christ, and are rejoicing in your condition.   But you have not taken your rightful position among your brethren.   Some are engaged in tending the ground, planting and sowing, erecting houses and expelling the enemy, whilst you are content to remain by the tabernacle of the Lord. You do not enjoy the privileges of communion at the table of the Lord, and of occupying your station in the Church of Christ. To stay where you are is an injury to yourselves, it is a loss to the Church, and dishonours the Redeemer.—A.

EXPOSITION.

CHAPTER XIX.—1—51.

THE LOT OF THE REMAINING TRIBES. Ver. 1.—**And their inheritance was within the inheritance of the children of Judah.** Literally, *in the midst of*. ἀνὰ μέσον, LXX.; *in medio*, Vulgate (cf. ver. 9). Simeon, at the last census (Num. xxvi. 14), was the smallest of the tribes of Israel, a fulfilment of the prophecy of Jacob, and possibly the result of the command given in Num. xxv. 5, since the Simeonites were the chief offenders on that occasion (Num. xxv. 14; see also 1 Chron. iv. 27). The distribution of territory was in accordance with this, and it is possible that the lot only determined the priority of choice among the tribes. The territory of Judah seems to have been recognised as too large, in spite of the importance of the tribe. They therefore willingly gave up a portion of their territory to the Simeonites.

Ver. 2. — **Beersheba.** A locality well known in Scripture, from Gen. xxi. 31 onwards. **And Sheba.** Some would translate here, *or* Sheba (see below). No doubt the city, of which nothing further is known, derived its name from Beer-sheba, "the well of the oath," close by. It is true that some little difficulty is caused by the omission of this city in Chron. iv. 28, by the identification of Shebah with Beer-sheba in Gen. xxvi. 33, and by the fact that in ver. 6 we are told that there were thirteen cities in this catalogue, whereas there are fourteen. On the other hand, Keil has remarked that in ch. xv. 32 the number of names does not correspond to the whole number of cities given; and we have a Shema, probably a mistake for Sheba, in ch. xv. 26, mentioned before Moladah among the cities of Judah. And, lastly, we have very few instances in Scripture of the disjunctive use of ו, though it seems impossible to deny that it is used in this sense in 1 Kings xviii. 27.

Ver. 3.—**Hazar-shual.** The "hamlet of jackals." The word Hazar is translated "village" in our version (see note on ch. xv. 32). So also with Hazar - susah or Hazar - susim, "the hamlet of horses" (1 Chron. iv. 31) below.

Ver. 9.—**Therefore the children of Simeon had their inheritance.** Of the later history of the children of Simeon we find a little recorded in 1 Chron. iv. 39—42, and some suppose that the event recorded there is a fulfilment of the prophecy in Obadiah 19. Dr. Pusey mentions a tribe still existing in the south, professing to be of the sons of Israel, and holding no connection with the Arabs of the neighbourhood, and supposes them to be the descendants of the five hundred Simeonites who took possession of Mount Seir in the days of Hezekiah. No border seems to have been given of Simeon.

Ver. 10. — **Sarid.** This seems to have been a middle point, from which the border is traced eastward and westward, as in ch. xvi. 6, and perhaps in ver. 32. But the LXX. and other versions have a variety of readings here.

Ver. 11.—**Toward the sea.** Rather, *westward*. The original is touched or skirted (פגע). **River that is before Jokneam.** This, with the assistance of ch. xii. 22, which mentions Jokneam as near to Mount Carmel, enables us to identify this river (or rather, *winter torrent*), as "that ancient river, the river Kishon." Knobel, however, says that if the Kishon had been meant it would have been called by its name, and that we must therefore understand the Wady-el-Mil'h. But this is by no means a safe conclusion.

Ver. 12.—**Chisloth-Tabor.** The loins or flanks of Tabor. Tabor (the name signifies either quarry—see note on Shebarim, probably a kindred word, ch. vii. 5—or navel), is one of the most conspicuous mountains of Palestine. Like Soracte, above the Campagna of Rome, "the cone-shaped figure of Tabor can be seen on all sides," though it rises only 1,750 feet (French) above the level of the sea, 800 above the plain at its northeastern base, and 600 above Nazareth on the north-west (Ritter, ii. 311). Chisloth-Tabor was on the north-west side of the base of Tabor. Tabor has been supposed to have been the scene of the Transfiguration. But Ritter points out that from the time of Antiochus the Great, 200 years before Christ, to the destruction of Jerusalem, the summit of Tabor was a fortress. And he notices that while Jerome and Cyril mention this tradition, Eusebius, who lived 100 years earlier, knows nothing of it.

Ver. 13. — **Gittah - hepher.** Or, Gath-hepher (1 Kings xiv. 25) was the birthplace of the prophet Jonah. Now el-Mesh-hed, where the tomb of Jonah is still shown. The Rabbinical writers and the Onomasticon mention this tradition.

Ver. 14.—**Compasseth it.** The verb נסב is here used transitively. The meaning is that the border makes a curve round the city of Neah. Neah seems to have been the extreme eastern border. Methoar is sup-posed to be the Pual participle, and has been freely translated, "which is marked out," or, "which belongs to," Neah. But the passage is obscure. Knobel would alter the reading, in view of the grammatical difficulty. Yet this, perhaps, is not in-superable in view of ch. iii. 14 (see Gesen, 'Grammar,' sec. 108, 2. c.). **Valley.** 'נ (see note on ch. viii. 13 ; xv. 8). So in ver. 27.

Ver. 15.—**Beth-lehem.** This name, sig-nifying the "house of bread," would natu-rally enough be given to a place in a fertile situation. We are not to suppose that it was "Bethlehem - Ephratah, among the thousands of Judah" (Micah v. 2). It is now Beit-lahm, about eight miles in a westerly direction from Nazareth.

Ver. 16.—**The inheritance of the children of Zebulun.** It is strange that the beautiful and fertile land occupied by the tribe of Zebulun does not appear to have brought prosperity with it. Possibly the fact that the "lines" of this tribe had "fallen in pleasant places," had tended to induce sloth. Certain it is that we hear but little of this tribe in the after history of Israel. They were not, like Reuben, absent from the great battle of Tabor, for there we read that, like Issachar, they "jeoparded their lives unto the death" for their homes and liberties. Yet though they seem thence-forth to have slackened in their zeal, theirs was a fair portion. It bordered on the slopes of Tabor, and seems (though the fact is not mentioned here) to have extended to the Sea of Galilee, as we may gather from Isa. ix. 1.

Ver. 18.—**Jezreel.** The valley (עֵמֶק) of Jezreel, known in later Greek as the plain of Esdraela or Esdraelon (Judith i. 8 ; vii. 2 ; 2 Macc. xii. 49) was "the perennial battle-field of Palestine from that time to the present" (Cooper, 'Egyptian Obelisks,' p. 33). Lieut. Conder (' Quart. Paper, Pal. Expl. Fund,' Jan., 1873), however, takes exception to this statement. "The great battles of Joshua," he says, "were fought far to the south." We presume he would make an exception on behalf of the action by the waters of Merom, and that he does not wish us to forget that the majority of Joshua's other "battles" were sieges.

"David's wars were fought with the Philis-tines," he continues, "while the invasions of the Syrians were directed to the neigh-bourhood of Samaria." But here, again, he would seem to have forgotten 1 Sam. xxix. 1, 1 Kings xx. 26, 2 Kings xiii. 17, 25, while he expressly admits that the great battles of Gilboa and Megiddo, in which Saul and Josiah were defeated and met their deaths, were fought here. And we have already seen that twice did the Egyptians invade Syria by this plain. One of these invasions took place while Moses was in Egypt, under Thothmes III. The other was the famous expedition of Rameses II. against Syria, about the time of Deborah and Barak. If we add to these the victory of Gideon over the Midianites and the overthrow of Sisera, we shall have reason to think that the epithet " the battle-field of Palestine " applied to this plain is not altogether mis-placed, especially if, with a large number of critics, we regard the Book of Judith as founded on fact, but relating to events of some other time than that of Nebuchad-nezzar. " Well may it be fertile," exclaims Mr. Bartlett (' From Egypt to Palestine,' p. 478), " for it has drunk the blood of the Midianite, the Philistine, the Jew, the Roman, the Babylonian, the Egyptian, the Frenchman, the Englishman, the Saracen, and the Turk. It is a singular group to summon up to the imagination, Gideon, Saul, and Jonathan, Deborah, Barak, and Sisera, Ahab, Jezebel, Jehu, Josiah, Omri, and Azariah, Holofernes and Judith, Vespa-sian and Josephus, Saladin and the Knights Templar, Bonaparte and Kléber." The list is a striking one. But certain it is that the plains of Jezreel have been noted as the highway of every conqueror who wished to make the fertile fields of Palestine his own. The Israelitish invasion alone seems to have been decided elsewhere than on that plain, stretching as it does from the foot of Carmel in a south-easterly direction, and divided in the direction of Jordan by Mount Gilboa and Little Hermon into three distinct branches, in the midst of the southernmost and most extensive of which stands the famous city of Jezreel — God's acre, or sowing-ground, as the name indicates. Here Barak and Deborah fell upon the hosts of Jabin (Judg. iv. 14), descending suddenly from the heights of Tabor with 10,000 men upon the vast and evidently undisciplined host that lay in the plain. Here Gideon encountered the vast host of the Midianites (Judg. vii. 12), who, after laying waste the south country, finally encamped in this fertile plain (accurately called עֵמֶק in Judg. vi. 33), and with their leaders Oreb and Zeeb, and their princes Zebah and Zalmunna, were

swept away in one of those sudden and irrational panics so often fatal to Eastern
armies. Here Saul, hard by Jezreel, dispirited by his visit to the witch of Endor,
on the north of Gilboa, gathered his men
together as a forlorn hope, to await the
attack of the Philistines, their numbers at
first swelled by a number of Israelites
whom Saul's tyranny and oppression had
driven into exile (1 Sam. xxix.). Advancing to Jezreel, the Philistine host carried
all before them, and drove the Israelites
in headlong flight up the steeps of Gilboa,
where Saul and his sons fell fighting
bravely to the last (1 Sam. xxx.). In the
later and sadder days of the Israelitish
monarchy, when the ten tribes had been
carried into captivity by the Assyrian conqueror, Josiah courted disaster by a rash
onslaught upon the Egyptian troops as they
marched against Assyria. No details of this
fight at Megiddo are preserved, save the fatal
fire of the Egyptian archers, who marked
Josiah as their victim, and drove, no doubt,
his leaderless troops from the field (2
Kings xxiii. 29; 2 Chron. xxxv. 22). At
Jezreel, too, Ahab made his capital. Hither
Elijah, when "the hand of the Lord was
upon him " (1 Kings xviii. 46), ran after the
wondrous scene on Mount Carmel, when he
alone, in a strength not his own, withstood
the "prophets of Baal, even four hundred
and fifty men." Here Jehoram stood on the
hill, with its commanding view, watching
with an uneasy distrust the furious rush of
Jehu with his troop from the other side
Jordan, and here, in the plat of Naboth the
Jezreelite, so fatal to Ahab and his house,
did the vengeance decreed overtake the unhappy monarch (2 Kings ix. 25). The spot
may be still identified. It is the modern
Zerin. Ritter describes it (and so does
Robinson) as standing on the edge of a
precipice 100 feet high, and commanding a
fine view of the plain of Beth-shean on the
east, and of Esdraelon on the west. There
is a tower here which commands the same
view as the watchmen of Jehoram commanded, bearing witness to the accuracy of
the historian. So in 1 Kings iv. 12, the
mention of Taanach, Megiddo, and the region
of Beth-shean, as *beneath* (מִתַּחַת לְ). Jezreel
is another instance of topographical detail
which marks the correctness of the record.
Another point is that we read in the narrative above mentioned of "chariots." Wilson
(' Lands of the Bible,' ii. 303) was surprised, on leaving the rugged heights of the
hill-country, to find how easily the
civilisation of Palestine permitted, excellent
roads might be made throughout this region;
and Canon Tristram ('Land of Israel,' p. 421)
has remarked on the desolate appearance

now presented by that fertile region, the
result of the insecurity for life and property
which is so commonly remarked by all who
have travelled in the East. Here, where
under a better rule would be the abode of
peace and plenty, no cultivator of the land
dare venture to pass the night, exposed to
the depredations of the wild tribes that
infest the country. Only a mountain fastness, hard to climb and comparatively easy
to defend, affords a secure retreat for those
who would live peaceably in that once
favoured land. **Shunem.** Now Sulem: the
place of the encampment of the Philistines
before they "pitched in Aphek " (1 Sam.
xxviii. 4; xxix. 1). It was "five Roman
miles south of Mount Tabor " (Vandevelde)
and an hour and a half (*i.e.* about six miles)
north of Jezreel (Keil and Delitzsch). Here
Abishag the Shunammite lived (1 Kings i. 3;
ii. 17, 21), and here Elisha lodged, and afterwards restored the son of his entertainers
to life (2 Kings iv., viii.).

Ver. 21.—**En-gannim.** Supposed to be
the same as the "garden house" (the Beth-
gan of the LXX.) mentioned in 2 Kings ix.
27) where Ahaziah, king of Judah, met with
the wound of which he afterwards died at
Megiddo. It was one of the Levitical cities
of Issachar (ch. xxi. 29). Robinson, Vandevelde, and others identify it with the
modern Jenîn, the Ginæa of Josephus. The
meaning of the name is "fountain of the
gardens" and the present Jenîn is situated,
so Robinson tells us, in the midst of
gardens.

Ver. 22.—**The coast reacheth.** Literally,
the border skirteth, as in ver. 11. **Tabor.**
Perhaps the same as Chisloth-Tabor in ver.
12 (cf. 1 Chron. vi. 77). It would therefore
be, as Mount Tabor certainly was, on the
boundary between the tribes of Issachar and
Zebulun. **Beth-shemesh.** Not the well-
known town in the tribe of Judah (ch. xv. 10).
The repetition of this name is a proof of the
extent to which sun-worship prevailed in
Palestine before the Israelite invasion.

Ver. 23.—**This is the inheritance of the
tribe of Issachar.** Jacob, whose dying eye
pierced far into the future, discerned beforehand the situation of the tribe of Issachar,
and its results upon its conduct. Situated
in the midst of this fertile plain, accessible
alike to Egypt by the way of the Shephelah,
and to the east by way of the fords of
the Jordan, the tribe of Issachar became in
the end the prey of the various nationalities,
who made the plain of Esdraelon their
battle-field, and it was the first to "bow his
shoulder to bear" and to "become a servant
unto tribute" (Gen. xlix. 15). It seems to
have been to the east of Manasseh (see
ch. xvii. 10), and may have extended much

further south than is usually supposed. Since but small mention of the Jordan is made in the boundary of Joseph, it may have extended as far or farther south than the Jabbok (see also note, ch. xvii. 10). The general belief of explorers at present is that the inheritance of Issachar extended from Jezreel to the Jordan, and from the Sea of Tiberias southward as far as the border of Manasseh, above mentioned.

Ver. 25. — **Helkath.** A Levitical city (ch. xxi. 31; 1 Chron. vi. 75, where it is called Hukok).

Ver. 26.—**Reacheth.** Literally, *toucheth*, *i.e. skirteth*, as in vers. 11 and 22. So in the next verse, with regard to Zebulun. The term appears to be the invariable one when a district, not a particular place, is spoken of. **To Carmel westward.** The Carmel range appears to have been included in the tribe of Asher. For we read (ch. xvii. 10, 11) that Asher met Manasseh on the north, whence we conclude that it must have cut off Issachar from the sea, and that as Dor was among the towns which Manasseh held within the territory of Issachar and Asher, it must therefore have been within the boundaries of the latter. **Shihor-libnath.** For Shihor see ch. xiii. 3. Libnath, which signifies white or shining, has been supposed by some to mean *the glassy river*, from its calm, unbroken flow, though this appears improbable, since Shihor means turbid. It is far more probable that the current was rendered turbid by a quantity of chalk or limestone which it carried along in its course, and hence the name "muddy white." Keil thinks it to be the Nahr-el-Zerka, or crocodile river, of Pliny, in which Reland, Von Raumer, Knobel, and Rosenmüller agree with him. But when he proceeds to argue that this river, being blue, "might answer both to *shihor*, black, and *libnath*, white," he takes a flight in which it is impossible to follow him. Gesenius, from the glazed appearance ot burnt brick or tiles (*l'banah*), conjectures that it may be the Belus, or "glass river," so called, however, in ancient times because the fine sand on its banks enabled the manufacture of glass to be carried on here. But this, emptying itself into the sea near Acre, has been thought to be too far north. Vandevelde, however, one of the latest authorities, as well as Mr. Conder, is inclined to agree with Gesenius. The difficulty of this identification consists in the fact that *Carmel* and *Dor* (ch. xvii. 11) are said to have been in Asher (see note on ch. xvii. 10). The Nahr-el-Zerka has not been found by recent explorers to contain crocodiles, but it has been thought possible that they have hitherto eluded observation. Kenrick, however

(' Phœnicia,' p. 24), thinks that as *crocodilus* originally meant a lizard, the *lacertus Niloticus* is meant, the river being, in his opinion, too shallow in summer to be the haunt of the crocodile proper (see also Tristram, ' Land of Israel.' p. 103, who believes it possible that the crocodile may be found there, though no specimen has as yet been produced). The Zerka is described in Palestine Exploration Fund Quarterly Paper, January, 1874, as " a torpid stream flowing through fetid marshes, in which reeds, canes, and the stunted papyrus grow." When it is added, " and where alone in Palestine the crocodile is found," no evidence is given in favour of the statement. It empties itself into the sea between Dor and Cæsarea, a few miles north of the latter.

Ver. 27.—**Beth-dagon.** We learn that Dagon, the fish-god, was worshipped here as well as in the south of Palestine (see ch. xv. 41). **The Valley of Jiphthah-el.** This valley, or *gai*, is spoken above, ver. 14, as the extreme northern border of Zebulun. **Cabul.** We read of a Cabul in 1 Kings ix. 11—13, but it can hardly be this place, though clearly not far off. For we read that the name given to that territory was given then by Hiram. There is a κωμὴ Χαβωλὼ Πτολεμαίδος μεθόριον οὖσα mentioned by Josephus. There is a village four hours north-east of Acre, which still bears this name.

Ver. 28.—**Hebron.** Rather, Ebron. It is not the same word as the Hebron in Judah, but is spelt with Ain instead of Hheth. In ch. xxi. 30, 1 Chron. vi. 59, Abdon is the name of the city assigned to the Levites in Asher. Twenty MSS., says Keil, have the same reading here. But the LXX. has Ἐβρων here and Αβδων in ch. xxi. 30. The Hebrew ד and ר are so much alike that there is no doubt that the mistake has arisen earlier than the time when that translation was made. It is true that the lists of Levitical cities in Joshua xxi. and 1 Chron. vi. do not entirely correspond. But the resemblance here between the names is too striking to allow of the supposition that two different cities are meant. **Great Zidon.** This city, as well as Tyre, remained unsubdued, although assigned by Joshua to Asher. The boundary of Asher appears to have been traced first towards the west, then eastward, from a middle point on the southern border (see note on ver. 11), then to have been carried northward from the same point (the *left hand* usually means the north ; see note on Teman, ch. xv. 1), on the east side till it reached Cabul. Then the northern border is traced westward to Sidon. Then the border turned southward along the sea, which is not mentioned, because it would seem to be sufficiently defined by the mention of Ramah and Tyre. Between Hosah and Achzib there would seem to have been a greater paucity of cities, and therefore the sea is mentioned.

Ver. 29.—**The strong city Tyre.** Rather, the *fortified* city. The general impression among commentators appears to be that the island city of Tyre, afterwards so famous, had not as yet come into existence. And the word here used, מִבְצָר seems to be more in accordance with the idea of a land fortress than of one so exceptionally protected as an island fortress would be. This expression, like "great Zidon" above, implies the comparative antiquity of the Book of Joshua. The island city of Tyre, so famous in later history, was not yet founded. The city on the mainland (called Ancient Tyre by the historians) was "the chief seat of the population till the wars of the Assyrian monarchs against Phœnicia" (Kenrick, 'Phœnicia,' p. 344). He adds, "The situation of Palæ-Tyrus was one of the most fertile spots on the coast of Phœnicia. The plain is here about five miles wide; the soil is dark, and the variety of its productions excited the wonder of the Crusaders." William of Tyre, the historian of the Crusades, tells us that, although the territory was scanty in extent, "exiguitatem suam multa redimit ubertate." The position of Tyre, as a city of vast commercial importance and artistic skill in the time of David and Solomon, is clear enough from the sacred records. It appears still (2 Sam. xxiv. 6, 7) to have been on the mainland, for the successors of Rameses II., up to the time of Sheshonk, or Shishak, were unwarlike monarchs, and the Assyrian power had not yet attained its subsequent formidable dimensions. We meet with Eth-baal, or Itho-baal, in later Scripture history, remarkable as the murderer of the last of Hiram's descendants, and the father of the infamous Jezebel, from which we may conclude that a great moral and therefore political declension had taken place since the days of Hiram. The later history of Tyre may be inferred from the prophetic denunciations, intermingled with descriptive passages, found in Isa. xxiii. and Ezek. xxvi., xxvii. ; Joel (iii. 3—8) and Amos (i. 9) had previously complained of the way in which the children of Israel had become the merchandise of Tyre, and had threatened the vengeance of God. But the minute and powerful description in Ezek. xxvii. shows that Tyre was still great and prosperous. She was strong enough to resist the attacks of successive Assyrian monarchs. Shalmaneser's

victorious expedition (so Alexander tells us) was driven back from the island fortress of Tyre. Sennacherib, in his vainglorious boast of the cities he has conquered (Isa. xxxvi., xxxvii.), makes no mention of Tyre. Even Nebuchadnezzar, though he took and destroyed Palæ-Tyrus, appears to have been baffled in his attempt to reduce the island city. Shorn of much of its ancient glory, Tyre still remained powerful, and only succumbed, after a resistance of seven months, to the splendid military genius of Alexander the Great. But Alexander refounded Tyre, and its position and its commercial reputation secured for it a large part of its former importance. The city continued to flourish, even though Phœnicia was for a long period the battle-ground between the Syrian and the Egyptian monarchies. To Christian readers, the description by Eusebius of the splendid church erected at Tyre by its Bishop Paulinus will have an interest. He describes it as by far the finest in all Phœnicia, and appends the sermon he preached on the occasion. Even in the fourth century after Christ, St. Jerome ('Comm. ad Ezek.,' 26. 7.) wonders why the prophecy concerning Tyre has never been fulfilled. "Quod sequitur, 'nec ædificaberis ultra,' videtur facere quæstionem quomodo non sit ædificata, quam hodie cernimus nobilissimam et pulcherrimam civitatem." But the present state of Tyre warns us not to be too hasty in pronouncing any Scripture prophecy to have failed. Even Sidon is not the wretched collection of huts and ruined columns which is all that remains of the once proud city Tyre. **And the outgoings thereof are at the sea from the coast to Achzib.** Rather, *and the western extremity is from Hebel to Achzib.* Hebel signifies a region or possession, as in ver. 9. Here, however, it seems to be a proper name. **Achzib.** "A city of Asher, not conquered by that tribe (Judg. i. 31), now the village of Zib, two-and-a-half hours north of Akka," or Acre (Vandevelde). Keil and Delitzsch make the journey a three hours' one. But Maundrell, who also corroborates St. Jerome in the distance (nine Roman miles), states that he performed the journey hence to Acre in two hours.

Ver. 30.—**Aphek** (see ch. xiii. 4). **Twenty and two cities with their villages.** The difficulty of tracing the boundary of Asher seems to be that it was traced, not by a line plainly marking out the territory, but less accurately, by a reference to the relative position of its principal cities.

Ver. 31.—**This is the inheritance of the tribe of Asher.** Asher appears to have been allotted a long but narrow strip of territory between Naphtali and the sea.

The natural advantages of the territory must have been great. Not only was it described prophetically by Jacob (Gen. xlix. 20) and by Moses (Deut. xxxiii. 24, 25), but the prosperity of the two great maritime cities of Tyre and Sidon was due to the immense commercial advantages the neighbourhood afforded. St. Jean d'Acre, within the territory once assigned to Asher, has inherited the prosperity, so far as anything under the Turkish rule can be prosperous, once enjoyed by her two predecessors. Maundrell, the acute English chaplain at Aleppo, who visited Palestine in 1696, describes the plain of Acre in his day as about six hours' journey from north to south, and two from west to east; as being well watered, and possessing " everything else that might render it both pleasant and fruitful. But," he adds, " this delicious plain is now almost desolate, being suffered, for want of culture, to run up to rank weeds, as high as our horses' backs." Asher, however, never employed the advantages its situation offered. They never subdued the Canaanites around them, but, unquestionably at a very early date (see Judg. v. 17) preferred a life of compromise and ignoble ease to the national welfare. But it would be incorrect to suppose that because the tribe is omitted in the list of rulers given in 1 Chron. xxvii., it had ceased to be a power in Israel. For Gad is also omitted in that list, while among the warriors who came to greet David when he became undisputed king of Israel, Asher sent 40,000 trained warriors, a number exceeding the men of Ephraim, and those of Simeon, of Dan, and of the half-tribe of Manasseh (see 1 Chron. xii.), and far exceeding the numbers of Benjamin, which had never recovered the war of almost extermination waged against it, in consequence of the atrocity at Gibeah (Judg. xx.). Possibly the reason why so few are mentioned of the tribe of Judah on that occasion is because so many were already with David. There seems no ground for the idea of Dean Stanley, that the allusion to Asher in Judg. v. 17 is any more contemptuous than the allusion to any other tribe.

Ver. 33.—**From Allon to Zaanannim.** Or, *the oak which* is at Zaanannim (cf. Allonbachuth, the oak of weeping, Gen. xxxv. 8). Zaanannim is the same as the Zaanaim mentioned in Judg. iv. 11. For (1) the Keri is Zaanannim there, and the word here rightly translated " oak " is rendered there "*plain*," as in Gen. xii. 6 and elsewhere. It has been supposed to lie north-west of Lake Huleh, the ancient Merom, whence we find that the scene of that famous battle was assigned to the tribe of Naphtali. The

border of Naphtali is more lightly traced than any previous one, and is regarded as being sufficiently defined, save toward the north, by the boundaries of the other tribes.

Ver. 34.—**And then the coast turneth westward.** Here the words are literally translated without any confusion between the *west* and the *sea*, nor any misapprehension of the meaning of the word נסב. **Reacheth.** This is the same word translated *skirteth* above, ver. 11, note. We have it here clearly stated that Naphtali was bordered on the south by Zebulun, on the west by Asher, and on the east by " Judah upon Jordan." **To Judah.** These words have caused great trouble to translators and expositors for 2,000 years. The LXX. omits them altogether, rendering, "and the Jordan to the eastward." The Masorites, by inserting a disjunctive accent between them and the words that follow, would have us render, "and to Judah: Jordan towards the sunrising," or, " is towards the sunrising," a rendering which gives no reasonable sense. They unquestionably form part of the text, since no version but the LXX. omits them. A suggestion of Von Raumer's has found favour that the cities called Havoth Jair, which were on the eastern side of Jordan, opposite the inheritance of Naphtali, are meant. Jair was a descendant of Judah by the father's side, through Hezron. So Ritter, iv. 338 (see 1 Chron. ii. 21—23). It would seem that the principle of female inheritance, having once been admitted in the tribe of Manasseh, was found capable of further extension. But to the majority of the Israelites this settlement would no doubt be regarded as an offshoot of the tribe of Judah.

Ver. 35.—**And the fenced cities.** The remark is made in the 'Speaker's Commentary' that the number of fenced cities in the north were no doubt owing to a determination to protect the northern boundary of Israel by a chain of fortresses. The word fenced is the same that is rendered strong in ver. 29, " the strong city Tyre." **Chinnereth** (see ch. xi. 2).

Ver. 36.—**Hazor** (see above, ch. xi. 1—10).

Ver. 37.—**Kedesh** (see ch. xii. 22). It was the residence of Barak (Judg. iv. 6). Known to Josephus (Bell. Jud., 4. 2. 3.) as Cydoessa, to Eusebius and Jerome as Cydissus; it is now Kedes (see Robinson, ' Later Biblical Researches '). **Edrei.** Not the Edrei of Og, which was beyond Jordan.

Ver. 38.—**Migdal-el.** The Magdala of the New Testament. It lay on the lake of Gennesareth. **Beth-shemesh.** A common name, derived from the worship of the sun.

This is neither Beth-shemesh of Judah nor of Issachar (see ver. 22).

Ver. 39.—**The inheritance of the tribe of the children of Naphtali.** Of Naphtali, beyond the not too heroic leader Barak, we hear nothing in the after history of Israel, until the fulfilment of the prophecy in Isa. ix. 1, 2. Galilee, the scene of the greater part of our Lord's teaching and miracles, was divided between Issachar, Asher, Zebulon, and Naphtali. The majority of the places mentioned in the Gospels were within the borders of Zebulon. But as we learn that our Lord penetrated as far as "the coasts of Cæsarea Philippi," in the extreme north of Palestine, He must have preached also in the cities of Naphtali. Naphtali sent a goodly number of warriors to welcome David as "king over all Israel" (1 Chron. xii. 34). The inheritance of Naphtali was in the main fertile, but there was a large mountain district, known as the mountain region of Naphtali (ch. xx. 7). Some of the mountains rose to the height of more than 3,000 feet.

Ver. 41.—**Zorah and Eshtaol.** On the border between Judah and Dan, but abandoned by the tribe of Judah to the Danites (see Judg. xiii. 2, 25). "The wild and impassable wadies, the steep, hard, rocky hills, their wildernesses of mastic, clear springs, and frequent caves and precipices, are the fastnesses in which Samson was born, and from which he descended into the plain to harry the Philistines (Lieut. Conder in Pal. Expl. Fund, Quart. Paper, Jan., 1874). Robinson identifies Zorah with Surat. **Irshemesh.** Another sign of sun-worship. Ir-shemesh is "the city of the sun."

Ver. 42.—**Aijalon,** or Ajalon (see ch. x. 12). One of the Levitical cities.

Ver. 43.—**Ekron** (see ch. xiii. 3).

Ver. 44.—**Gibbethon.** A Levitical city, as was also Eltekeh (see ch. xxi. 23). It was the same city as that mentioned as "belonging to the Philistines" in 1 Kings xv. 27; xvi. 15, 17.

Ver. 45.—**Gathrimmon.** Also a Levitical city (see ch. xxi. 24; 1 Chron. vi. 69). **Mejarkon.** The waters of the Jarkon.

Ver. 46.—**Before.** Or *opposite.* **Japho.** The Joppa of the New Testament, and the modern Jaffa. It is called Joppa in 2 Chron. ii. 16, in Ezra iii. 7, and in the book of Jonah (ch. i. 3), in all which places it is mentioned as a famous seaport, a position it still maintains, being still, as it was of old, the port of Jerusalem. The LXX. and Vulgate have Joppa here, and it is unfortunate that our translators, in this instance only, should have adhered to the Hebrew form. Joppa appears to have been an important city in the time of the Mac-

cabees (see 1 Macc. x. 75, 76; and 2 Macc. iv. 21). Its mention in the New Testament as the place where St. Peter's vision occurred will be known to all. The name signifies "beauty," though Joppa does not seem to be distinguished above all other places in Palestine by the beauty of its situation. But according to Movers, Japho signifies in Phœnician, "high place." It is certainly built on a range of terraces above the sea, but the term "high place" would seem unsuitable. The soil is very productive, and it is "the only harbour in Central Palestine" (Ritter).

Ver. 47.—**Went out too little for them.** The Hebrew is, went out *from them; i.e.,* either went out beyond their own borders, or went out too small a distance to be sufficient for them. The first is the explanation of Masius ("extra se migrasse"), the second of Jarchi. Houbigant suggests for וַיֵּצֵא "and it went out" וַיֵּצֶר "and it was narrow." But the LXX. has the same reading as ourselves, and the explanation given above is quite consistent with the fact. The border of Dan did "go out" far beyond the borders originally assigned to the tribe, in fact to the extreme northern limit of Palestine. The account of the taking of Laish, or Leshem, is given more fully in Judg. xviii. The inheritance assigned to Dan was extremely small, but it was also extremely fertile.

Ver. 48.—**This is the inheritance of the children of Dan.** We read little of Dan in the after history of Israel. Samson is the only hero this tribe produced, and his exploits were limited to a very narrow area, and his influence apparently to his own tribe.

Ver. 49.—**When they had made an end.** The LXX., both here and in ver. 51, reads יָלְכוּ *they went.* The last thing Joshua thought of was himself. It was only when his work was done, and Israel had received her allotted territory, that Joshua thought it right to take his own inheritance. Calvin remarks that it was "a striking proof of the moderation of this servant of God" that he "thought not of his own interest until that of the community was secured."

Ver. 50.—**The city which he asked.** He asked for a city, certainly. But the law of the inheritance was not to be set aside for him any more than for the meanest in Israel. Timnath-serah was in his own tribe. **Timnath-serah.** Called Thamna by Josephus and the LXX., and Timnath-heres, or Timnath *of the sun* by a transposition of the letters, in Judges ii. 9. Rabbi Solomon Jarchi gives a singular reason for the latter name. It came to be so called because there was a representation of the sun upon the tomb of him who caused the sun to stand still. Timnath-serah must not be confounded with Timnah, or Timnathah, in the tribe of Dan (ver. 43). For a long time its site was unknown, but within the last 40 years it has been identified with Tibneh, seven hours north of Jerusalem, among the mountains of Ephraim. Dr. Eli Smith was the first to suggest this, and though it was doubted by Robinson, it has since been accepted by Vandevelde and other high authorities. Tibneh seems to have anciently been a considerable town. It is described in Ritter's ' Geography of Palestine ' as a gentle hill, crowned with extensive ruins. Opposite these, on the slope of a much higher eminence, are excavations like what are called the Tombs of the Kings at Jerusalem. Jewish tradition, however, points to Kefr Haris, some distance south of Shechem, as the site of Joshua's tomb, and several able writers have advocated its claims in the papers of the Palestine Exploration Fund, on the ground that on such a point Jewish tradition was not likely to be mistaken.

Ver. 51.—**At the door of the tabernacle of the congregation.** The lots were drawn under Divine sanction. The ruler of the State and the ruler of the Church combined in this sacred act, hallowed by all the rites of religion, and confirmed by the presence and approbation of the heads or representatives of all the tribes. Accordingly, as has been said above, we hear of no murmurings or disputings afterwards. However much the Israelites may have quarrelled among themselves, there is not a hint of dissatisfaction with the final distribution of terri·tory. Three points may be noticed here—1. The authenticity of the narrative is confirmed by these evidences of the internal agreement of its parts. 2. We learn the value of mutual consultation, of open and fair dealing, from this narrative. The parcelling out of the inheritance of Israel under God's command was carried out in such a manner as to preclude the slightest suspicion of partiality. 3. The duty of hallowing all important actions with the sanctions of religion, of uniting prayer and a public recognition of God's authority with every event of moment, whether in the life of the individual or of the body politic, finds an illustration here. An age which, like the present, is disposed to relegate to the closet all recognition of God's authority, which rushes into wars without God's blessing, celebrates national or local ceremonials without acknowledging Him, contracts matrimony without publicly seeking His blessing, receives children from Him without caring to dedicate them formally to His service, can hardly plead that it is acting in the spirit of the Divine Scriptures. A well-known writer in our age declares that we have "forgotten God." Though the external and formal recognition of Him may be consistent with much forgetfulness in the heart, yet the absence of such recognition is not likely to make us remember Him, nor can it be pleaded as proof that we do so.

HOMILETICS.

Vers. 1—51.—*The completion of the work.* The reflections suggested by this chapter are identical with those which have already occurred to us. They are, perhaps, emphasised by ver. 51, in which the solemn public division of the land is once more, and yet more plainly, declared to have taken place with the assent of the heads of Church and State, and to have been attended with a religious ceremony. Without pretending to say whose fault it is, or how such a desirable state of things may be once more attained, we may be allowed to lament that what was the rule with our forefathers before the Norman conquest is impossible now. No doubt the separation of ecclesiastical from civil jurisdiction which the Conqueror effected has been to a great extent the cause of this, as that measure was also the cause of an assumption of authority by ecclesiastics which was afterwards found to be intolerable. There should be no separation between the religious and civil interests of the community. Every man in the kingdom is, or ought to be, interested in its ecclesiastical arrangements. No single act of the State ought to be considered as outside the sphere of religious influence. At the same time we must remember that the present state of things is the natural result of religious freedom, a freedom which Christ Himself proclaimed (John xviii. 36), but which was unknown to His Church for many centuries, as also to the Jews before He came (Gen. xvii. 14; Exod. xii. 15; xxx. 33, 38; xxxi. 14; Levit. vii. 20, 27, &c.). As has been already intimated, an example which cannot be fulfilled in the letter may be fulfilled in the spirit. We may strive to hallow great national events with one heart and soul, though with different forms, waiting for the day when "our unhappy divisions" have ceased. We may, however, add one consideration derived from this chapter alone.

SELFISH AIMS OUGHT NOT TO INTRUDE INTO A GREAT CAUSE. This principle is illustrated (1) by the conduct of Judah, (2) by the conduct of Joshua. The rule of the world is (1) to covet power and possessions, and (2) that the successful conqueror has a right to be first considered in the division of the spoil. Observe how completely the narrative of this chapter implicitly rebukes a view of things which is assumed as a matter of course in the ordinary concerns of the world. In past history we read of the greed of individuals and nations for the annexation of territory, and of the wars and bloodshed thus caused. It has been a maxim that any ruler or any nation may, and ought to, add to its territories if it can, without much regard to the principles of justice or the general good. A man, it is still believed, may heap to himself possessions in land or money as much as he chooses, and would be a fool if he did not. The first of these doctrines has only lately begun to be questioned among us. The second is still an established principle of action. Yet Judah voluntarily surrendered its territory to Simeon for the national welfare. And Joshua takes care that every one is served before himself. It is this marvellous self-abnegation on the part of the leader of a military expedition, unparalleled until Christianity came into the world, that is the best proof of the claim of the Mosaic dispensation to have been Divine. Cases like those of Cincinnatus cannot be adduced in refutation of this argument. His position is in no way parallel to that of the leader of an expedition like Joshua's. Such utter self-abandonment as was displayed by Moses and Joshua marks them out as men fifteen or twenty—we might perhaps say thirty—centuries before their age. The invasion of Canaan has been declaimed against as cruel; but its cruelty was at least the fruit of a moral idea, a righteous indignation against an obscene and ferocious religion, which was itself the cause of infinite misery to mankind; while Joshua's cruelty was kindness itself compared to the revolting atrocities recorded at their own instance by the Eastern conquerors of old, Egyptian, Assyrian, Babylonian, Moabite. We hear *ad nauseam* of the impossibility of God's ordering the slaughter of the unoffending Canaanites (see this subject further discussed in the Introduction). We hear nothing of the high morality, the sublime disinterestedness, the devotion to a grand and sublime ideal which characterised the giver of the Law and the conqueror of Canaan. Such characters have been rare since Christ came into the world. Save the two great men whom we have just known, they were unknown before it.

HOMILIES BY VARIOUS AUTHORS.

Ver. 9.—*Brotherhood.* I. THE IDEA OF BROTHERHOOD MUST BE RECOGNISED IN ORDER THAT TRUE PRINCIPLES OF JUSTICE MAY BE ESTABLISHED. Justice does not imply equality. To deal equally with all is often unjust, since different men have different needs. It would have been unjust to have given equal portions to Judah and Simeon. In the family, justice does not require the treatment of all the children alike, but the treatment of each according to his disposition and requirements. But in order to do this there must be mutual understanding and sympathy. Therefore these are necessary for the administration of justice. Rude social equality will not regenerate society. The idea of brotherhood must come first and bring with it the thoughtfulness and sympathy, without which we cannot be just to one another. Note: Providence is often more just than it appears, because it does not aim at establishing a mechanical equality, but studies the individual condition of each man, and acts according to special requirements of special cases which may be entirely unknown to us.

II. THE IDEA OF BROTHERHOOD MUST BE REALISED IF MEN WOULD SEE THE PRACTICAL APPLICATION OF PRINCIPLES OF JUSTICE. Judah had too much. Few men are willing to admit that they have too much, and hence they often wrong others and greedily hold what they do not need. Until men feel their brotherhood with others they will not see the measure by which to judge whether or no they have more than their due share of the advantages of life. Selfishness magnifies a man's needs and deserts, and minimises the requirements and merits of others. To be just we must conquer selfishness with brotherliness.

III. The idea of brotherhood must take possession of men before they can practise that mutual accommodation which is required by justice. The children of Simeon had their inheritance within the inheritance of the children of Judah. This could only be enjoyed peaceably so long as the two tribes lived on terms of brotherly kindness. Justice will not be obtained under a system of jealous competition in a selfish race for wealth. This leads to the weak and unfortunate losing, and the strong and fortunate gaining, more than is fair. The idea of brotherhood will prevent men from taking unfair advantage of one another, will establish the principle of co-operation in place of that of competition, and will substitute the mutual benefits of the family for the selfish profits of a state of internecine warfare.

IV. The idea of brotherhood can only be fully realised under the influence of Christianity. Revolutions which have dispensed with Christianity have boasted of their power to realise this idea, but the attempt to do so has too often led through bloodshed to despotism. Christianity realises it (1) by pointing to a common fatherhood, (2) by joining to one brother, Christ, (3) by exalting brotherly charity to the first rank among the Christian graces (1 Cor. xiii. 13).— W. F. A.

Ver. 49.—*Joshua's portion.* "When they had made an end of dividing the land," Joshua gets his share. Not first, as kings usually do, but last. When all are helped, then comes his turn. Though he waits longest, yet it does come to him. And when it does come it is all the more welcome from being well earned. Observe two or three things that are thus brought before us.

I. A trait of honour. Honour is the bloom of uprightness; the finer instinctive working of it in matters too delicate to be touched by law. It is not so common as it ought to be; for our natures are often coarse, and honour is always costly. We prefer going in for cheaper virtues, especially for such of them as are loud and obvious, as well as cheap. Even those who attend to the "honest and just and true" of Paul's precept, sometimes overlook "the pure and the lovely and that which is of good report." Here Joshua comes out, as we would expect him, as a man of honour. Such faith as he had never existed in a selfish heart; such courage as marked him, naturally had emotions of similar nobility to keep it company. Doubtless, some foolish and flattering friends urged him to accept his lot first; and pleaded, perhaps, his first right to it, both as faithful spy and successful leader. Something before Shakespeare had whispered—

> "Love thyself last: let all the ends thou aim'st at
> Be thy country's, God's, and Truth's."

And the still small voice of sacred honour within him did not speak in vain. Like as in a sinking ship, a brave captain is the last to leave her and seek for safety, so Joshua elects to be the last served. All the best bits of the country others eagerly go in for. Joshua sees it disposed of by lot, but is not moved by the sight of its going to envy others, nor does he catch any greed from the contagion of their example. Quite calm, feeling rich in enriching others, at rest in giving others rest, he has rewards above any freehold, and joys above any wealth. There is here an example all ought to follow. The insistance on our rights is sometimes a duty. In the interest of others we may be obliged to resist and dispute injustice. But such insistance ought always to be practised with regret, and avoided wherever possible. The precept requiring us to give the cloak to him who covets the coat certainly inculcates the surrender of rights wherever any moral advantage can accrue from it. For our own sake, to keep the soul in proper and worthy mood, we ought to cultivate this honourableness that thinks of something sublimer than its private rights. And for the sake of others also, for honour is one of the subtlest, but the strongest, forces of good anywhere existent. It allures men to a better way, charms them to integrity, is a root of brotherliness and peace. Especially should all leaders of their fellows cultivate this honour. It is not too common amongst either sovereigns or statesmen. Men are apt to forget that selfishness is vulgar, whether it seeks to get a throne, in ambition, or to keep its halfpence in sordid avarice. All selfishness is mean; and in the great it is greatly mischievous. It breeds civil wars; it corrupts the patriotism of a people; it prevents the rise of that confidence in the justice and the patriotism and the wisdom of the rulers which gives the nations rest. In leaders in smaller circles—boroughs, churches—there is the same scope for this high principle. Israel was blessed in this, that its most unselfish man was its leader. And he who was highest in place was highest in honour. Secondly observe—

II. HONOUR HAS ITS REWARD AT LAST. He had had abundant reward all through. Rivalries and competitions which, under a selfish ruler, would have broken out, and perhaps flamed up into strife and tumult, are repressed by the silent, dignified example of one whose thoughts were above the vulgar delights of wealth. And this reward of being able to compose the conflicting claims of a great multitude was the grandest reward he could have. To win victory over his nation's foes, and keep contentment and peace in her own borders, was reward indeed. But he does not go without even the material reward. All Israel come and give him Timnath-serah. We cannot identify it now with any definiteness. But it was doubtless worthy of the nation that gave it—of the man that received it. Honour often seems, to the coarse-hearted, to go without reward. But that is only because the reward is of a sort too subtle for coarse vision to detect. It has always a grand reward in the influence with which it crowns the head of him who practises it. It has, besides, even common outward rewards. The race is not always to the swift, nor the gold to the greedy. We make our own world, and teach men how to deal with us. The world is froward to the froward; it is honourable to the honourable. The fairest treatment men ever give is given to those who treat them fairly. The best masters get the best service. The truest friends form richest friendships. Honourable men rarely meet with dishonourable treatment. And without any clamour or fighting they get a better Timnath-serah than in any other way they could have gained. "Trust in the Lord and do good: so shalt thou dwell in the land, and verily thou shalt be fed." Lastly observe—

III. THE INHERITANCE GOT BY DESERT, AND HELD WITHOUT BEING ENVIED, IS THE PERFECTION OF A LOT. Not all riches comfort us. Ill-gotten riches curse us. Riches gotten by others and passed on to us are insipid. Wealth gathered by penury is a burden. But the lot that comes as the reward of diligence, consecration, honour, has a special sweetness, and the man who gets it has a special power of enjoying it. Especially when it is ungrudged; no neighbour coveting it; no peasant thinking that by right it should be his; all men glad to see it in such worthy hands. We shall do well to resolve that we will have no fortune and no inheritance which does not in its way resemble TIMNATH-SERAH.—G.

Vers. 49, 50.—*Joshua's inheritance.* I. JOSHUA RECEIVED AN INHERITANCE AMONG HIS BRETHREN. After labour and battle come rest and recompense. Though Joshua was a man of war he was not to spend all his days in fighting. It is sometimes well that the active should have a quiet time of retirement in old age. For all God's servants there is an inheritance of rest when this world's work is done (Heb. iv. 9).

II. JOSHUA'S INHERITANCE WAS GIVEN ACCORDING TO A DIVINE PROMISE. True devotion is founded on unselfish motives. Yet the prospect of reward is added by God's grace as an encouragement. Christ looked forward to His reward (Heb. xii. 2). We are only guilty of acting from low motives when the idea of personal profit is allowed to conflict with duty, or when it is the chief motive leading us to perform any duty.

III. JOSHUA'S INHERITANCE WAS SIMILAR TO THAT OF HIS BRETHREN. He was the ruler of the people, yet he took no regal honours. He had led them to victory, yet he received no exceptional reward. Like Cincinnatus, he quietly retired to private life when he had completed his great task. This is a grand example of unselfishness, simplicity, and humility. It is noble to covet high service rather than rich rewards. Ambition is a sin of low selfishness cloaked with a false semblance of magnificence. The Christian is called to fulfil the highest service with the lowliest humility (Luke xxii. 26). Christians are all brethren under one Master (Matt. xxiii. 8). Joshua is a type of Christ in his great work and unselfish humility (John xiii. 13—16).

IV. JOSHUA RECEIVED HIS INHERITANCE FROM THE HANDS OF THE PEOPLE. He was not forward to take it for himself. He submitted to the choice and will of the people. It is a mark of true magnanimity to refuse to use influence and power to gain personal advantages. Joshua is a noble example of a man who exercised authority over others without developing a spirit of despotism which would fetter the popular choice. It is a great thing to have a strong, united government ruling over a free people.

V. JOSHUA DID NOT RECEIVE HIS INHERITANCE TILL AFTER ALL THE OTHER PEOPLE HAD RECEIVED THEIR POSSESSIONS. He was first in service, last in reward. The true Christian spirit will put self last. He who is rightly devoted to duty will not seek for his reward before his task is completed. The world is too often tardy in recognising those who have rendered it most valuable service.—W. F. A.

EXPOSITION.

CHAPTER XX. 1—9.

THE CITIES OF REFUGE.—Ver. 1.—**Cities of refuge..** The original is more definite, *the* cities of refuge. So LXX. **Whereof I spake to you.** In Exod. xxi. 13; Num. xxxv. 9; Deut. xix. 2. Here, again, Joshua is represented as aware of the existence of the Pentateuch. It must, therefore, have existed in something like its present shape when the Book of Joshua was written. The words are partly quoted from Numbers and partly from Deuteronomy; another proof that these books were regarded as constituting one law, from the "hand of Moses," when Joshua was written.

Ver. 3. — **Unawares and unwittingly.** Literally, *in error, in not knowing.* Num. xxxv. 16—18 and Deut. xix. 5, give a clear explanation of what is here meant. Knobel notices that the first of these expressions is found in Levit. iv. 2, and the second in Deut. iv. 42. The latter is "superfluous," and therefore a "filling up of the Deuteronomist." The "Deuteronomist" must have been very active in his "filling up." If he were really so lynx-eyed in a matter of style, it is a wonder that he was so careless, as we are told he is, in matters of fact. To more ordinary minds it would seem as if the author, familiar with the books of Moses, was quoting Deuteronomy for the precept, and Leviticus for the nature of the offence. **The avenger of blood.** The Hebrew word is worthy of notice. It is Göel; that is, literally, *redeemer,* one who buys back at the appointed price what has fallen into other hands, as a farm, a field, a slave, or anything con-

secrated to God. Hence, since the duty of such redemption, on the death of the owner, devolved upon the nearest relative, it came to mean "blood relation." Thus Boaz (Ruth iv. 1, 6, 8) is called the Göel of Elimelech and his widow. In the present passage, the phrase "the redeemer (LXX. ἀγχιστεύων, next of kin) of the blood" signifies the exactor of the only penalty which can satisfy justice, namely, the death of the murderer. So we are taught in Gen. ix. 6; Exod. xxi. 12, 14; Levit. xxiv. 17, 21. This duty, which in civilised society belongs to the government, in uncivilised tribes is usually left to the relatives of the murdered man. Hence the terrible blood-feuds which have raged between families for generations, and which are not only to be found among savage nations, but even in countries which lay claim to civilisation. In Ireland, for instance, it is not so long ago since one of these blood-feuds in the county Tipperary had acquired such formidable proportions that the authorities of the Roman Catholic Church there were compelled to resort to a mission in order to put an end to it. A man had been killed nearly a century before in an affray which commenced about the age of a colt. His relatives felt bound to avenge the murder, and their vengeance was again deemed to require fresh vengeance, until faction fights between the "Three-Year-Olds" and the "Four-Year-Olds" had grown almost into petty wars. A thrilling story written by the late Prosper Mérimée turns upon the Corsican *vendetta,* and so true is this story to life that in the very year (1879) in which these words were written an occurrence precisely similar, save in its termination, was reported in the daily journals to have taken place in that island. The only way in which the feud could be terminated was by summoning the representatives of the two families before the authorities and exacting an oath from them that they would cease their strife. It is no small corroboration of the Divine origin of the Mosaic law that we find here a provision for mitigating the evils of this rude code, and for at least delivering the accidental homicide from the penalty of this law of retaliation. Yet for the offence of wilful murder the penalties enjoined by the Jewish law were terribly severe. A deliberate violation of the sanctity of human life was an offence for which no palliation could be pleaded. No right of sanctuary was to be granted to him who had wantonly slain a fellow-creature. "No satisfaction" was to be taken for his life (Num. xxxv. 31). "The land cannot be cleansed of the blood that is shed therein, save by the blood of him that shed it" (ver. 33). Such provisions might be expected of a lawgiver who had laid down as the fundamental principle of humanity that man was created "in the image of God," after His likeness; that God had "breathed the breath of life" into him, and man had thus "become a living soul" (Gen. i. 27; ii. 7). Such inward harmony is there between Moses' inspired revelations concerning God's purpose in creation, and the precepts he was commanded to deliver to the children of Israel.

Ver. 4.—**And when he that doth flee unto one of those cities.** This passage is in accordance with the instructions given in Num. xxxv., but is not a quotation from it. The passage may be translated, "and he shall flee ... and shall stand." **Shall declare his cause.** Literally, shall *speak*. This was to be done at the "gate of the city," the place where all legal business was transacted (see Ruth iv. 1; 2 Sam. xv. 2).

Ver. 5.—**And if.** Or, "and *when*." **Deliver.** Literally, *cause to shut up* (συγκλείσουσι, LXX.), implying the completeness of the deliverance, from which no escape was possible. **And hated him not beforetime.** Daun, cited in Keil's Commentary here, remarks on the difference between the Jewish law of sanctuary and that of the Greeks and Romans. The former was not designed to save the criminal from the penalty he had deserved, but only the victim of an accident from consequences far exceeding the offence. The Greeks and Romans, on the contrary, provided the real criminal with a mode of escape from a punishment which he had justly merited.

Ver. 6.—**Until he stand before the congregation.** That is, until he had had a fair trial. It was no object of the Jewish law to make a man a victim to passion. **Until the death of the high priest.** The further to protect the unwitting homicide from the consequences of an unjust revenge, he was, if innocent, to return to the city of refuge, and to dwell there until there was reasonable ground to suppose that the anger of the relatives of the slain man should have abated. This is clear from Num. xxxv. 24, 25. Why the period of the death of the high priest should have been fixed upon is not easy to explain. Keil thinks it is because the death of the high priest was typical of the death of Christ, and refers to Heb. ix. 14, 15. But the reference is not to the point. The high priest's death was in no sense typical of the death of Christ. His yearly entrance into the holy place once a year, on the Day of Atonement, was so typical. It might have been supposed that this yearly atonement would have been regarded as a propitiation for all the sins committed during the year. Certainly the fact that the high priest died the common death of all men, and the inauguration of his successor to fill his place could in no way be regarded as an atonement for sin. There is more force in Bähr's suggestion in his 'Symbolik' (ii. 52). The high priest, on this view, is the head of the theocracy, the representative of the covenant. He concentrates in his person (so Bähr puts it in another place—see vol. ii. 13) the whole people of Israel in their religious aspect. His death, therefore, stands in a connection with the life of Israel which that of no other man could do. "It is," says Maimonides ('Moreh Nevochim,' 3. 40), "the death of the most honoured and beloved man in all Israel. His death plunges the whole community into such distress that private sorrow is lost in the general affliction." Thus the covenant in a way recommences with the inauguration of the new high priest. Bähr complains that Philo has carried this view to an extravagant and fanciful extent. Hengstenberg ('Geschichte des Reiches Gottes,' vol. ii. sec. 3, p. 258) takes the same view as Maimonides, that the high priest's death was "a great calamity," affecting the whole nation.

Ver. 7.— **And they appointed.** The original, which, strange to say, the LXX. and Vulgate, as well as our version, have neglected to render, is *sanctified* (*heiligten*, Luther). The selection is itself a proof that our author knew well what he was writing about. It is not likely that in the later times of Jewish history, when the law had been forgotten (2 Kings xxii. 8) and its precepts had long been in abeyance, that the institution of the city of refuge remained in full force. But we find three cities selected on each side of Jordan. Those on the west were in the tribe of Naphtali on the north, of Ephraim in the centre, and of Judah in the south. The same is the case with those on the other side Jordan. Thus every little detail of the narrative, when closely scrutinised, does but show more entirely how free this narrative is from the reproach so hastily cast upon it of being a loose and inaccurate compilation, attempted by a man who had not the slightest literary fitness for the task he had undertaken. A corroboration of this view may be found in the fact that all these cities were Levitical cities. Thus, as the crime of homicide was looked upon under the Mosaic law as a crime apart from all other crimes, inasmuch as it was an offence against the life which was God's gift, and man, who was God's image, so the offender who pleaded extenuating circumstances for his offence was placed, until his trial could be held, under the special protection of the Divine law. For " the priest's lips should keep knowledge, and men should seek the law at his mouth." It was the special privilege of the tribe of Levi to possess the " key of knowledge." It was to them that the duty of ascertaining the will of God by Urim and Thummim was assigned (Num. xxvii. 21). Thus a special acquaintance with the law (Deut. xxxiii. 8), and a special fitness for deciding the difficult questions sometimes arising out of it, would naturally be found in the elders of those cities which had been set apart as cities of refuge. **In Galilee.** Hebrew, *Hag-Galil*, the circle. Here we have the masculine, as in xiii. 2; xvii. 17; xxii. 10, 11, the feminine form. This is the first place in Scripture in which the word Galil, or Galilee, is applied to this region. Gesenius regards it as having been originally a district of twenty towns round Kedesh in Naphtali. Such a region of twenty towns is mentioned in 1 Kings ix. 11 (see also Isa. viii. 23; or, ix. 1 in our version). Kedesh has already been noticed (see also ch. xxi. 32).

Ver. 8.—**By Jericho eastward.** Or, eastward of Jericho. This, of course, only refers to Bezer. **The plain.** The Mishor, or table-land (see ch. iii. 16, ix. 1, and notes). Our version, by its renderings, obscures the beautiful precision with which our historian never fails to hit off the physical geography of the country. Thus, the plain of Bashan, Gilead, and Reuben is always the Mishor; the strip of land between the mountains and the Mediterranean is always the Shephêlah; the depression of the Jordan Valley and the country south of the Dead Sea is invariably the Arabah; wide plains shut in between ranges of hills or situated on their slopes are distinguished by the title of Emek; while narrow waterless ravines are known by the name of Ge. We may quote here the emphatic words with which Canon Tristram concludes his ' Land of Israel,' " While on matters of science the inspired writers speak in the ordinary language of their times (the only language which could have been understood), I can bear testimony to the minute truth of innumerable incidental allusions in Holy Writ to the facts of nature, of climate, of geographical position — corroborations of Scripture which, though trifling in themselves, reach to minute details that prove the writers to have lived when and where they are asserted to have lived; which attest their scrupulous accuracy in recording what they saw and observed around them; and which, therefore, must increase our confidence in their veracity, where we cannot have the like means of testing it. I can find no discrepancies between their geographical or physical statements and the evidence of present facts. I can find no standpoint here for the keenest advocate against the full inspiration of the scriptural record. The Holy Land not only elucidates but bears witness to the truth of the Holy Book." **Ramoth in Gilead.** See ch. xiii. 26, where it is called Ramoth Mizpeh; also ch. xxi. 38. All these cities of refuge were Levitical cities. It is famous as the headquarters of Jehu's rebellion, in which he clearly had the support of the priestly party (2 Kings ix.). The key to his subsequent conduct is found in this fact. His " zeal for the Lord," displayed so ostentatiously to Jonadab, who we may suppose, as being of the " family of the scribes," to have become identified with the Levites (cf. 1 Chron. ii. 55 with Judg. i. 16, and 1 Chron. xxvii. 32 with Ezra vii. 12, Jer. viii. 8), was simply a stroke of policy, to bind to his interest the sacerdotal party, to whom, with the army, he owed his throne. Just such a policy commended itself to the worldly wisdom of our own Lancastrian princes, and led to the enactment of the infamous statute *de heretico comburendo* in the fifteenth century. Jehu, we find, was contented with the one vast sacrifice of idolaters, for whom he cared nothing, and gave himself no further trouble to secure purity of worship for his people. The one great value of the geographical and political details in the book of Joshua is that when carefully studied they supply us with the key to many a mystery in the after history of Israel, which, but for their aid, we should scarcely have unravelled.

Ver. 9.—**Appointed.** Or, *of refuge or*

resort. Our version has followed the LXX. and Vulgate here. Greek, *unawares;* Hebrew, *in error* or *inadvertently*, as above. Matthew Henry's note on the cities of refuge is worthy of remark. He says, "I delight not in quibbling on names, yet am willing to take notice of these." Thus Kedesh, he reminds us, is *holy*. Shechem, a *shoulder*, reminding us of Him upon whose shoulder the government was to be. Hebron is fellowship, recalling the fellowship we have in Christ. Bezer is a *fortifi-* cation, reminding us of God our stronghold (later criticism, however, gives another derivation to this unusual word, which in Job xxii. 24, 25, means the ore of a precious metal). Ramoth is height or exaltation, and to such exaltation we are called in Jesus Christ. Lastly, Golan is exultation, so says Matthew Henry, deriving it from גִיל or גָּל. But Gesenius derives it with equal probability from גלה " to make bare," hence to lead into captivity.

HOMILETICS.

Vers. 1—9.—*The cities of refuge.* The institution of these cities was intended to put bounds to revenge, while providing for the punishment of crime. As Lange remarks, the Mosaic law found the principle of vengeance at the hand of the nearest relative of the deceased already recognised, and desired to direct and restrain it. Three considerations suggest themselves on this point.

I. THE VALUE OF HUMAN LIFE. The most serious crime one man could commit against another (offences against God or one's own parents are not included in this estimate), according to the Mosaic, and even the pre-Mosaic code, was to take his life. The sanctity of human life was ever rated high in the Old Testament. Nothing could compensate for it but the death of him who violated it. The duty had always been incumbent on the nearest blood relative, and Moses did not think it necessary to institute any other law in its place. He only placed the restriction upon the avenger of blood, that in case the murderer should reach a city of refuge, he should have a fair trial before he was given into the hands of his adversary, in case it should prove that, instead of murder, the deed was simply homicide by misadventure. It has been strongly urged that capital punishment, even for murder, is opposed to the gentler spirit of Christianity. Without presuming to decide the question, this much is clear, that God in His law has always regarded human life as a most sacred thing, and any attempt to take it away as a most awful crime. It may be observed, moreover, that in Switzerland, where the punishment was abolished, it has had in several cantons to be reimposed. It is also a curious fact, and one somewhat difficult to explain, that a higher value is set, as a rule, upon human life in Protestant than in Roman Catholic communities. There can be no doubt that the severer view is in accordance with the Old Testament Scriptures, and we may see why. The evil effect of other crimes may, in a measure, be repaired, but life once taken away can never be restored. Man, moreover, is the image of God, and life His greatest gift. To deface the Divine image, to take away finally and irrevocably, so far as the natural man can see, what God has given, is surely the highest of crimes.

II. VENGEANCE MUST BE UNDER THE DIRECTION OF THE LAW. The rule for Christians as individuals is, never to take vengeance at all, but to submit to the most grievous wrongs in silence. But there are times when a Christian is bound to regard himself as a member of a community, and in the interests of that community to punish wrong-doers. We learn a useful lesson from the chapter before us. We may not take the law into our own hands. We are not the best judges in our own cause. The punishment we inflict is likely to be disproportionate to the offence. We are bidden, if our neighbour will not listen to us (Matt. xviii. 15—17) to take others with us to support us in our complaint, and if that be in vain, to bring the matter before the assembly of the faithful, who take the place in the Christian dispensation of the elders of Israel. But in all cases the decision must not rest with ourselves. It would be well if every one, before bringing an action or prosecution at law against another, would submit the matter to some perfectly disinterested persons before doing so. It would be well if the Christian congregations exercised more frequently the power of arbitration, which was clearly committed to them by Christ. It should be the city of refuge to which the offender should betake himself, and he should be free from all penalties until the " elders of that city" declare that he has deserved them.

III. WHERE WE CANNOT ABOLISH AN EVIL CUSTOM, WE MAY AT LEAST MITIGATE ITS EVIL EFFECTS. It must often happen to the Christian to find laws and customs in existence which we feel to be opposed to the spirit of Christianity. Two courses are open to us, to denounce and resist them, or to accept them and try to reduce the amount of evil they produce. There are, of course, some customs and laws against which a Christian *must* set his face. But there are many more in which it would be fanaticism, not Christianity, to do so. Such a spirit was displayed by the Montanists of old (as in the case of Tertullian, in his celebrated treatise ' De Coronâ'), who frequently reviled and struck down the images of the gods. Such a spirit is often displayed by Christians of more zeal than discretion now. A remarkable instance of the opposite spirit is shown by the attitude of Christ's apostles towards slavery. Slavery is alien to the first principles of Christianity. And yet the Christians were not forced to manumit their slaves, but were only enjoined to treat them gently and kindly. Such was obviously the best course, so long as Christianity was a persecuted and forbidden religion. It is often our duty so to deal with customs which are undesirable in themselves, but which, as individuals, we have no power to put down. So long as we have it in our power to remove from them, in our own case, what is objectionable or sinful, it is our duty to conform to them, at the same time hoping and praying for better times.

HOMILIES BY VARIOUS AUTHORS.

Ver. 1—*Cities of refuge.* The institution of cities of refuge interests us as at once an admirable instance of the spirit of the Mosaic legislation, and as an arrangement of gracious wisdom. In the absence of courts of law and any sufficient arrangement for the administration of justice, a system has uniformly arisen in all primitive tribes, and is found in many places to-day, of charging the nearest male relative with the duty of putting to death the murderer of his kinsman. The Vendetta, as it is termed, is still practised among the Arab tribes, and even survives vigorously in the island of Corsica. By it there was always a judge and an executive wherever there was a crime. And doubtless such a custom exercised a highly deterrent influence. At the same time a rough and ready system of punishment like this was incapable of being applied with that discrimination essentially necessary to justice. In the heat of revenge, or in the excitement and danger incident to what was regarded as the discharge of a kinsman's duty, men would often not inquire whether the death was the result of accident or of intention. It might chance that none bewailed the death more than him who committed it. But the rude law left the responsible kinsman no alternative. The one who slew might be his own relative, it might be that a blow of anger, not meant to kill, or some sheer accident, took away the life of one dear to him who struck the blow, or was the unhappy cause of the accident. But where blood had been shed, blood was to be shed. And so one fault and one bereavement not infrequently involved the commission of a greater fault, and the experience of a greater bereavement. In this position of things Moses stepped in. And in the legislation he gave on the subject there is much that is worthy of notice.

I. Observe, WHAT HE DID NOT PRESCRIBE. The payment of "damages" for a death inflicted has been a form in which the severity of these rules for the punishment of a murder has been mitigated. In Saxon times in England, blood-money was continually offered and taken. In many other lands a fine has been laid on the murderer for the benefit of his family. The Koran permits such a compensation; and to-day, in some Arab tribes, a man may escape the penalty of murder if he can pay the fine which custom prescribes. But though such an alternative must have been familiar to Moses, it is not adopted by him. On the contrary, *he expressly*

forbids the relatives to condone a crime by receiving any money payment for it:
(see last chapter of Numbers). This is a very striking fact, for many would very
much have preferred a law allowing the giving and receiving of such a fine, to the
law actually given. His not adopting such a rule shows that Moses was apprehensive of the danger of conscience being dulled, and crime encouraged by any compromise effected between guilt on the one side, and greed on the other. Such a rule
would always mitigate the abhorrence of crime; would make it safer for the rich to
indulge their animosities, than for the poor to injure, by accident, a fellow-man.
Law, duty, self-respect would be lowered. Life would be held less sacred.
Instead of its being invested with a Divine sanction, and the destruction of it made
an awful crime, it would appear as something worth so many pounds sterling, and
men would indulge their taste for the murder of those they disliked, according to
their judgment of what they could afford to pay. The poor substitute of a fine
instead of the punishment of death is not only not accepted, but explicitly forbidden.
And so far the legislation of Moses suggests that whatever course our criminal
legislation may take in dealing with crime, it will do well to maintain the sanctity
of life and to guard against such a method of dealing as would increase the crime that
it should prevent. But observe, secondly, that while the sanctity of life is maintained,

II. JUSTICE IS SUBSTITUTED FOR REVENGE. The six cities of refuge were simply
six cities of assize, where an authoritative verdict could be found as to whether
the death was wilfully or unintentionally inflicted. The man who had taken a life
claimed of the elders of the city (ver. 4) protection, and received it until his case was
adjudicated on. He was tried before *the congregation*, the assembly of the adult
citizens. As these were all Levites (the six cities of refuge being all of them
Levitical cities) they were familiar with law, and had, probably, a little more moral
culture than their non-Levitical brethren. A calm unbiassed "judgment by their
peers" was thus provided for every accused person—a tribunal too large to be
moved by animus or corrupted by bribes. If on explicit evidence of two or three
witnesses it proved to be a case of wilful murder, further asylum was denied him, and
he was delivered to death. If it proved a case of either accident or manslaughter, the
asylum was lengthened, and beneath the protection of God he was safe, as long as
he kept within the precincts of the city and its suburbs. How admirable such an
arrangement! A better court of judgment in such cases, than such a jury of two
or three hundred honest men, could not be devised. It was costless; it was simple;
it involved no delay. It restrained a universally recognised right, but did it so
wisely and fairly none could complain. A provision of unconditional asylum, as it
developed later in connection with religious buildings, has proved an unmitigated
evil even in Christian lands, an encouragement to all crimes, promoting not
morality, but only the cunning which committed them within easy reach of such a
sanctuary. This gave Israel, for the most important of all cases, a court of justice
that protected innocence, that soothed revenge, that prevented blood feuds settling
and growing to large dimensions. It is a lesson for us, as individuals, always to
guard against our being carried away by passion, and to import into every quarrel
it may be our unhappiness to fall into, the calm and unbiassed judgment of others.
It may be our duty to others to prosecute or punish a criminal. But revenge is an
unholy passion which has no sanction from on high. Lastly observe:

III. A CURIOUS PROVISION IN THE LAW. If innocent of wilful murder, the man
had a right of asylum in the city. But leaving the city, he lost it, and might
lawfully be slain. The nearness of living Levites was his protection. But the
perpetual residence in the city of refuge was not enjoined. For when the high priest
died, he could go back to his proper home and dwell there. *The high priest was to
be thought of—as an intercessor who had entered within the veil—beneath the
protection of whose prayers all these refugees were sacred; and for them the
whole land became one great place of refuge.* THE DEATH OF ANOTHER HIGH
PRIEST WAS AN ENTERING WITHIN THE VEIL, WHICH BENEFITS WITH DIVINE
PROTECTION ALL WHO TAKE REFUGE IN THE DIVINELY APPOINTED PLACE. They by
innocence got the benefit of his pleading—we by repentance. Are we all under the
shadow of the heavenly Intercessor?—G.

Vers. 1—6.—*The manslayer and his refuge.*　The institution of the cities of refuge stands as a conspicuous memorial of the beneficent spirit of the Mosaic economy.　It bore a resemblance to that right of asylum, or sanctuary, which in some form or other has found a place in the usage of all nations from the earliest times, but it was not liable to the same abuse.　Every provision of the Mosaic economy enshrined some enduring principle.　Some great moral lesson was intended to be impressed by it on the minds of the people.　The institution changes or passes utterly away ; the principle, the lesson, remains.　Note here—

I. THE SANCTITY OF HUMAN LIFE.　The institution bore striking witness to this. This was its root-principle.　It was intended as a check on that form of ferocity for which Oriental tribes have ever been remarkable—the thirst for vengeance in the shedding of blood.　It threw a shield over an endangered life.　This at once commends it to a radical instinct of our nature.　God has implanted in our breasts an intuitive sense of the value of life.　Not only the instinct of self-preservation (" skin for skin," &c., Job ii. 4), but something also that prompts to respect for the life of another.　The most barbarous conditions of humanity are not altogether destitute of the traces of this.　The natural effect of religion and civilisation is to develop it.　Mainly on this instinct rests the admiration we feel for any marvellous triumph of surgical skill, for the rescue of imprisoned miners, or of a shipwrecked crew, or of a wounded comrade from the battle-field.　It is not merely satisfaction in beholding consummate skill, resolute endurance, deeds of daring and self-sacrifice—but in the fact that *life is saved.*　The " vital spark," so mysterious in itself, and so mysteriously kindled, is kept from being extinguished.　The humane spirit, the spirit in sympathy with humanity as such, feels just the same however feeble or apparently worthless and despicable the life may be.　We don't stay to consider either its actual conditions or its latent possibilities; we only know that it is good to save it.　There is no higher mark of Christian civilisation than the diffusion of a nobler sentiment as to the inherent value of human life.　" The Son of Man came not to destroy men's lives, but to save them " (Luke ix. 56). This fact has its manifest, though indirect, bearings on the question of man's immortality.　If physical life is surrounded by such sanctions and safeguards, does it not at least suggest the indestructibility of the essential being of the man ?

> " That not one life shall be destroyed,
> 　Or cast as rubbish on the void,
> 　　When God shall make the pile complete."

II. FORFEITURE OF LIFE.　This principle of sanctity bears on the slain as well as on the slayer.　If it shields the one, not less does it avenge the other.　The right of asylum was based on the foregoing right of the *Goel,* the blood-avenger (see Numb. xxxv. 19, *et seq.,* Deut. xix. 11—13).　This was the outgrowth of the ancient law given to Noah, " Whoso sheddeth man's blood, by man shall his blood be shed " (Gen. ix. 6).　And, again, to Moses at Sinai, " Life for life, eye for eye, tooth for tooth," &c. (Exod. xxi. 23, 24).　So severely was this rule to be applied, that no kind or measure of " satisfaction " could be taken for the forfeited life of the murderer (Numb. xxxv. 31).　Such was the Mosaic law.　The gentler spirit of Christianity inculcates a different rule.　As *that* softened and restrained the natural savagery of the olden times, so *this* brings in the reign of still nobler principles of moral and social life (Matt. v. 38, 39 ; Rom. xii. 19).　It is questionable whether the teaching of Christ and his Apostles does not throw such an air of sanctity over the being of every man, and make restorative love rather than retributive justice the universal law, as completely to annul the old order of " life for life."　At the same time the principle of retribution is in no way obliterated—less literal, less circumstantial, entrusted less to the hands of man, but not less real.　The avenger still tracks the steps of the transgressor.　He cannot escape " the righteous judgment of God, who will render to every man according to his deeds " (Rom. ii. 5, 6). Vengeance may suffer even " the murderer to live," but he bears the penalty and the curse within.　" Be not deceived ; God is not mocked : for whatsoever a man soweth," &c. (Gal. vi. 7, 8).

III. THE IMPORTANCE OF THE SPIRIT ABOVE THE FORM OF EVERY DEED. The city of refuge was a provision for the protection of the manslayer from lawless and indiscriminate violence, that he might be subject to judicial inquiry as to the real meaning and intent of what he had done. He must be brought before a tribunal of the people. The " congregation " must judge between the slayer and the avenger, and if it is shown that he was not the enemy of the man slain, nor " sought his harm," he shall be delivered (Numb. xxxv. 22—25). Here was a striking witness to the principle that it is the spirit, the purpose, that determines the real quality of every deed. God is the " Searcher of hearts," and He would have man, according to the measure of his insight, estimate everything by what gives birth to it there. The " Sermon on the Mount" is a Divine lesson on the importance of the spirit above the form (Matt. v. 21, *et seq.*). The law of Christ is a " discerner of the thoughts and intents of the heart." It is the motive that determines the merit or demerit of every deed. God has given us no power infallibly to trace or weigh the motives of men, but as far as they are disclosed so let us judge.

IV. THE BLENDING OF JUSTICE WITH MERCY IN THE TREATMENT OF TRANS-GRESSION. The city of refuge bore witness to the principle of equity between man and man, and equity is the qualification of law by reason and humanity. The manslayer, however innocent, must suffer for the ill that he has done, but safe-guards are provided against his being subject to any flagrant wrong. Whatever it may cost him he must flee to the city, but it is not more than six miles distant and the way is clear. He loses his liberty, home, perhaps property, but he is safe. In all this there is a remarkable blending of regard for the majesty of law and the sanctity of social order, with kindly protection of human weakness.. It is full of instruction. A true social economy is the due balance of reciprocal rights, interests, &c. We deal righteously with each other only when mercy tempers justice, when law is interpreted liberally and applied with charity.

V. AN ANALOGY IS OFTEN INSTITUTED BETWEEN THE CITY OF REFUGE AND THE GOSPEL WAY OF SALVATION. There is an essential mark of difference between the two ; the one was for the protection of the innocent, the other is God's provision for the redemption of the guilty. But they are alike in this, that they tell of shelter from the fatal stroke of the avenger. We are reminded how—

> " All the lives that are were forfeit once,
> And He who might the vantage best have took
> Found out the remedy."

When He " maketh inquisition for blood," then shall it be found that " there is no condemnation for them that are in Christ Jesus," who have " fled for refuge to lay hold on the hope set before them."—W.

Ver. 2.—*Cities of refuge.* I. THE APPOINTMENT OF CITIES OF REFUGE EXEMPLI-FIES UNIVERSAL PRINCIPLES OF JUSTICE. We do not need such cities because we can attain the end they were set apart to accomplish by simpler means, but we are called to observe the principles they were instituted to maintain. (1) *The justice which brings retribution on offenders is natural and right.* But this must be distinguished from vengeance. Justice seeks the honour of law and the maintenance of the public good. Vengeance aims only at the infliction of harm on the offender. The latter is unchristian and wicked. (2) *We should not be hasty in passing judgment.* The city of refuge afforded time for evidence to be collected and a mature judgment to be formed. First impressions are often deceptive. Anger blinds judgment. (3) *It is well to refer our quarrels to the decision of others.* The avenger of blood was required to refer his case to the congregation. Interested persons can rarely form impartial opinions. It is well to resort to Christian arbitration when differences cannot be settled amicably in private (Matt. xviii. 15—17). (4) *It is difficult to judge of the conduct of others, because of our uncertainty as to their motives.* The man-slayer may be a murderer or he may be innocently concerned in a pure accident. Thus he may be guiltless, while the person who inflicts no harm on another may be a murderer at heart. " Whosoever hateth his brother is a murderer" (1 John iii. 15). Guilt attaches to motives, not to outward acts. Therefore (*a*) do not judge others needlessly (Matt. vii. 1) ; (*b*) when it is necessary to judge do not be deceived by outward appearance, but consider differences of motive (John vii. 24).

II. The appointment of cities of refuge is an illustration of God's grace of redemption. (1) *God provides a city of refuge in Christ.* He is a refuge from the dangers that beset us, from the consequences of our own acts, from the indwelling power of sin. (2) *This refuge is for the most guilty.* The Levitical cities were for the innocent ; Christ is a refuge for the guilty. Men fled to them for justice ; they flee to Christ for mercy (Matt. ix. 12, 13). (3) *This refuge is in our midst.* The six cities of refuge were situated in convenient central positions at different points of the land, so that every Israelite might be within reach of one. Yet even this arrangement could not secure safety in all cases. Christ is in our midst. We have not to bring Him from heaven ; He dwells among us. He is near and ready to receive us at any moment. None need perish on the road to Christ. (4) *This refuge must be entered to secure safety.* It was vain for the fugitive Israelite merely to run in the direction of the city, or even to be within sight of it, if he did not enter its precincts. It is useless for a man only to have inclinations towards Christianity, to know the truth of it, to begin to turn Christward. He must seek Christ and come to Him in trust and submission. As the fugitive must enter the city to be safe, so the sinner must be " in Christ " (Rom. viii. 1). (5) *It is dangerous to delay entering this refuge.* While the fugitive stayed, the avenger of blood was upon him. "Now" is the appointed time. The opportunity may soon pass.—W. F. A.

Vers. 2, 3.—*Danger and safety.* The Book of Joshua supplements the Pentateuch. It tells us of the execution of the behests contained in the law. Hence it preaches a continual lesson of obedience. How far do our lives exhibit a conformity of practice to gospel precepts ? Surely God says to us, as to Joshua, " Be mindful of the commandment given by the hand of My servant."

I. A prevalent custom modified. The rights of kinsmen were various and strongly insisted on. The exaction of vengeance for the death of a relative was deemed among the most important of these rights. The nearest kinsman became the "avenger." To abrogate such an institution might have been impossible ; at any rate, it was wisely ordained that particular rules should regulate its operation and soften its character. Legislation must ever have regard to the prevalent opinion, must not be too far in advance of the age. This principle of directing popular thoughts to more wholesome channels was recognised by the Church of the early centuries, when it sought to lead men away from orgies and revelries to joyous Christian festivals, and missionaries of modern days have adopted this plan with success. We may alter the ship's course even if we cannot absolu'ely check her progress. The modification of Goelism introduced (1) *Acknowledged the sanctity of human life.* (2) *Distinguished between the quality and the matter of actions*— a vital distinction in ethics, which regards the intention as well as the consequence of behaviour, before it can be censured or approved of. To slay a man unwittingly was not murder. On the other hand, Jesus Christ afterwards showed that the indulgence of an angry thought towards a brother is an infraction of the sixth commandment. So also 1 John iii. 15. (3) *Placed this department of equity under the special supervision of the religious authorities.* The places of refuge were chosen from the Levitical cities, whose rulers might be trusted to carry out the law in respect both of justice and of mercy. The unintentional man-slayer was considered as the prisoner of the high priest, and on the death of the latter was released. Religion never looks more beautiful than when she wears her benign garb of mercy, protecting the helpless and friendless. It is part of her office to prevent injustice and oppression. The laws of God are deposited with the Church as a sacred trust for the benefit of mankind. How she perverts her functions when she employs her strength in bitter enmity and persecution !

II. Points of resemblance between the cities of refuge and the salva-

TION OFFERED IN THE GOSPEL. That the ordinances of the Israelites were a figure for the time to come, is in many places of the New Testament expressly affirmed (see 1 Cor. x. 6, 11 ; Heb. ix. 9 ; x. 1). And with great likelihood the words of Heb. xi. 18 have been supposed to refer to the very institution now under discussion. (1) *Easiness of access.* The cities were so selected as to be scattered throughout the land at equal distances, no part of the country being remote from one of these centres. And Jesus Christ is nigh unto every one of us, a very present help in trouble. It need not take even half a day to reach Him, the heart may be surrendered to Him at once and find rest. (2) *The way readily known.* The road to the nearest city of refuge was plainly indicated by the words "Refuge ! Refuge !" written at each turning, and the way was always kept clear of obstacles (see Deut. xix. 3). "He that runneth can read" and understand the plan of salvation. Redemption freely offered in Christ, who died for sinners. Prophets and apostles point to Him, saying, "Behold the Lamb of God." (3) *Available for every inhabitant.* Equally for the stranger or sojourner and one born in the land (ver. 9). God is no respecter of persons. He gave His Son, that "whosoever believeth in Him should not perish." "Whosoever, will let him take the water of life freely." (4) *The gates always open.* We learn this from Maimonides, as also that the rulers of the city furnished the refugee with shelter and food so long as he remained with them. Jesus "ever liveth to make intercession for those who come unto God by Him." No sinner need fear lest the door of mercy should be shut against him. There are no specially appointed days for obtaining relief. It is always, "now is the accepted time." God will not allow one of His little ones to perish. "Seek first the kingdom of God and His righteousness, and all other things shall be added unto you." Several other particulars might be mentioned, such as that even the suburbs of the city were a refuge (Num. xxxv. 26, 27), like as to touch the hem of Christ's garment heals the sick ; and the cities saved by virtue of God's appointment, not so much by reason of their natural strength, even as God hath set forth Christ to be a propitiation through faith in His blood. But let us note—

III. THE SUPERIORITY OF THE GOSPEL SALVATION. (1) *Accessible even to the guilty.* In fact, there are no innocent ones, "all have sinned." The Apostle called attention to the mercy and longsuffering of Jesus Christ, who "came into the world to save sinners ; of whom I am chief" (1 Tim. i. 15). "The blood of Jesus Christ cleanseth from all sin." Ho ! ye despairing ones, there is hope for you. And ye who are polluted with stains of deepest dye, you may be "clothed in white robes," and to you there shall be "therefore now no condemnation." (2) *The refuge no confinement, but rather enlargement of liberty.* The man-slayer was unable to follow his ordinary avocation or to resume his wonted place until the death of the high priest. Our Saviour has been already slain as the victim, and is entered as High Priest into the holiest of all ; hence there is no period of waiting for us, but instant pardon and deliverance from thraldom. The busy man goes to business with lighter heart, and the mother, troubled with domestic cares, has obtained ease and rest by casting her burden upon the Lord.

CONCLUSION. Flee to this refuge ! Delay, and the footstep of the avenger shall be heard close behind you, and fear shall paralyse your flight. "Satan hath desired to have you ; " but haste to the Saviour, let His strong arms protect you, and sheltered 'neath His smile your panting heart shall cease tumultuously to beat. And if you have won Christ and are "found in Him," not having your own righteousness, how secure and peaceful you may be. What rejoicing should be yours ! To be tormented with doubt while you are in such a stronghold is foolish, and impairs the glory of the salvation Christ hath wrought. "Neither shall any man pluck them out of My hand."—A.

Ver. 2.—*The cities of refuge.* We know how strictly the law of Moses applied the avenging law. He who had killed was himself to be killed. The nearest relation of the victim had the right, and it was his duty, to pursue the offender. He was the avenger of blood. The law, under its original form, made no distinction between a murder committed purposely and of premeditation, and an unintentional murder. It may well be said that in this respect it was the inexorable law of the letter which killeth.

I. The establishment of cities of refuge, intended to serve as a sanctuary to the murderer who had killed some one by accident, IS LIKE THE FIRST STEP TOWARDS THE NEW LEGISLATION WHICH DEALS RATHER WITH THE INTENTION THAN WITH THE ACT, and is aimed primarily at the heart. The last commandment of the Decalogue, which prohibits covetousness, carries the Divine law into the inner region of the moral life, showing that its scope is far wider than the sphere of outward action or speech. The man who has unintentionally committed murder, finds in the city of refuge a means of escaping the vengeance of the pursuer. This provision is in itself a protest against the Pharisaic spirit which based its judgment upon the outward act alone. The new covenant gives yet fuller application to the same moral principle, when it declares that hatred in the heart involves the moral guilt of murder, as lust does of adultery.

II. The establishment of cities of refuge IS AN ADMIRABLE EMBLEM OF THE CHURCH. The Church is the city set upon a hill, whose gates stand open day and night to those whom the law condemns. Only those to whom it offers shelter are not exclusively persons who have transgressed unwittingly, as was the case with the Israelitish cities ; all who have broken the law of God, even with open eyes, may there find shelter, on the one condition that they enter by the door. "I am the door," says Jesus Christ, "no man cometh unto the Father but by me " (John x. 7). This is a strait gate—so strait that none can pass through it except on bended knees and laying aside every weight. By repentance and faith everything that is of self and sin must be abjured. But so soon as these conditions are fulfilled, the door is opened. No one is too great a sinner to enter there. Publicans and harlots, all the sorrowful and sinful, let them hasten, arise and enter in. The city of refuge is open for all. The Church of the middle ages restored in a literal sense the Jewish custom of having cities of refuge. It opened its sanctuaries to murderers and spread over them the shield of its protection. This was called the privilege of sanctuary; but it became a grave abuse. Let us cleave to the one great privilege of finding refuge in the true Church built upon the great Corner-Stone. The old cities of refuge promised safety from the avenging arm of the inflexible law. We have a further pledge of our safety in the blood that was shed for our sins, in the redeeming sacrifice by which our debt was paid. Sheltered beneath this outspread wing of everlasting love, we are safe from the condemnation of the righteous law which we have broken.—E. DE P.

EXPOSITION.

CHAPTER XXI. 1—45.

THE INHERITANCE OF THE LEVITES.

Ver. 1.—**Then came near the heads of the fathers of the Levites.** We are not to suppose, with Calvin, that the Levites had been overlooked. Such a supposition is little in keeping with the devout spirit of him who now directed the affairs of the Israelites, who had been minister to Moses the Levite, and had but lately been concerned with Eleazar, the high priest, in making a public recognition of that God to whose service the Levites had been specially set apart. The delay in appointing to the Levites their cities arose from the nature of the arrangement which had to be made for the Levitical cities. The prophecy which threatened (Gen. xlix. 7) to "scatter them in Israel" was to be fulfilled for the benefit of the whole people. Instead of a portion for himself, Levi, as we have been repeatedly informed (ch. xiii. 33 ; xiv. 3 ; xviii. 7), was to have "the Lord God of Israel for his inheritance." Since, therefore, their cities were to be assigned them within the limits of the other tribes, it was impossible to apportion them until the other tribes had been provided for. **Unto Eleazar the priest.** The close connection between the military and the sacerdotal power is kept up throughout the book. Warned by his one act of neglect in the case of the Gibeonites, Joshua never again appears to have neglected to have recourse to the high priest, that he might ask counsel of God for him, as had been prescribed in Num. xxvii. 21.

Eleazar is placed first here, because, as the acknowledged head of the tribe, he was the proper person to prefer its request to the leader. But the whole history shows how entirely Joshua and Eleazar acted in concert. **And unto Joshua the son of Nun.** In a matter of ecclesiastical organisation the ecclesiastical took precedence of the civil leader. **And unto the heads.** The position of Joshua was that of a chief magistrate ruling by constitutional methods. The representatives of the tribes were invariably consulted in all matters of moment. Such appear to have been the original constitution of all early communities, whether Aryan or Semitic. We find it in existence among Homer's heroes. It meets us in the early history of Germanic peoples. It took a form precisely analogous to the Jewish in the old English Witan, where the chief men in Church and State took counsel with the monarch on all matters affecting the commonweal of the realm; and the remains of this aristocratic system still meet us in our own House of Lords.

Ver. 2.—**At Shiloh.** Another instance of exact accuracy. Shiloh was now the place of assembly in Israel (see ch. xviii. 1). **The Lord commanded.** The command is given in Num. xxxv. We have here, therefore, another quotation from the books of Moses. If we refer to it we find how exactly the precepts were carried out. First, the six cities of refuge were to be appointed, and then forty-two more were to be added to them. Calvin, not noticing this, has complained that this narrative is not in its proper place, and that it should have been inserted before the details in ch. xx. The very reverse is the fact. These cities of refuge are included, in what follows, among the number of forty-eight cities in all, assigned to the Levites. **Suburbs.** See ch. xiv. 4. And so throughout the chapter.

Ver. 3.—**Out of their inheritance.** Out of that of Israel (see note on ver. 1). **These cities.** The number are forty-eight, i.e., four times twelve. Bähr ('Symbolik des Alten Testaments,' i. 221) remarks on the symbolical meaning of this number. He compares it, first, to the twelve tribes marching in four detachments, the ark of God and its guard in the centre (see Num. ii.). Four, he says, is the number of the world, and three the sign of God, and twelve of the combination of the two. Thus we are reminded of the heavenly city which "lieth four-square," which has "twelve foundations of precious stones," "twelve gates of pearls, and at the gates twelve angels," and the names of "the twelve tribes of Israel" written thereupon, and wherein was

" the tree of life," with its "twelve manner of fruits," which were "yielded every month " (Rev. xxi. 12, 14, 16, 19, 21; xxii. 2).

Ver. 4.—**And the lot came out.** As in the distribution of the land among the tribes, so in the division of the cities among the tribes of Levi, the whole matter was referred to the judgment of God. Thus solemnly placed in His hands, the division would not afterwards become the occasion of jealousy or dispute. The division was first made between the descendants of the three sons of Levi, Gershon, Kohath, and Merari (see Exod. vi. 16—25), and then, as regards the Kohathites, between the priests, the descendants of Aaron, and the rest of the Levites. We have remarked above (ch. xix. 50) on the disinterestedness of Joshua. We have now to remark on the same characteristic as displayed by Moses. There was no attempt on the part of Moses to " found a family," the object of ambition with most men, whether kings or private persons possessed of wealth. No special privileges belonged to his descendants. They merged in the undistinguished herd of the Levites generally. In this Moses contrasts favourably with most public men in our own day; he stands out prominently before nearly all the great leaders and conquerors before or even after the Christian era. The same may be said of Joshua, his successor. Cincinnatus may be in some measure compared with them, but as a dictator simply in time of danger, his power was by no means so absolute, nor were his temptations so great as those of the two successive leaders of the Israelites. **Thirteen cities.** It has been contended by Maurer and others that this number of cities was largely in excess of what could possibly be required for the descendants of Aaron in so short a time. But we have to consider (1) that the cities were probably not, at least at first, inhabited exclusively by the priests; (2) that the Israelites multiplied rapidly, and that the number of descendants in the fourth generation would probably be nearly a thousand, and in the fifth, above five thousand ; (3) that all the cities were not, as yet, actually taken from the Canaanites at all, and so therefore were in all probability only intended as an eventual possession of the priests, and (4) that the cities themselves were probably not of any very great size. It may be worthy of remark, as a proof of the accuracy of the writers of the Old Testament, and as a means of approximately ascertaining the date of the Book of Joshua, that Nob, mentioned as a priestly city in 1 Sam. xxii. 11, 19, is not found in the list given here. For the number of priests being sure to increase, it is not surprising that in the course of time additional cities should be assigned to them. And since Nob is not mentioned here, we have good grounds for concluding that the Book of Joshua was not a compilation put together after the reign of Saul. Calvin does not fail to remark on the prescience of God here demonstrated. He had fixed upon Jerusalem as the place where he would " put His Name." He therefore directed that the lot of the priests should fall within the limits of the tribes of Judah and Benjamin, on whose borders Jerusalem stood. Simeon is also mentioned, but the territory of that tribe (ch. xix. 1, 9), was contained within the borders of Judah. **For theirs was the first lot.** Not because Kohath was the first-born, for this Gershon appears to have been, but because to Aaron and his sons had the priesthood been reserved.

Ver. 11.—**In the hill country of Judah.** The word in the original is הָר, mountain, the title which is consistently applied to the highlands of Palestine in the Bible, while our version translates indiscriminately by "mountain" and "hill."

Ver. 12.—**The fields.** The original is in the singular. We are not necessarily, therefore, to suppose that the land was mapped out into divisions analogous to our fields. Our word " land " would more accurately represent the meaning of the original, which refers to the arable and pasture land in the neighbourhood of the city, with the agricultural villages or homesteads dotted about it. Keil contends that the Levites only received as many houses within the city as they needed, and that the rest belonged to Caleb. Bähr, moreover (' Symbolik,' ii. 49), supposed that the Levites dwelt with the other inhabitants of the city, and that the pasture land within the distance of 2,000 paces from the city was reserved for them, the rest of the land belonging to the inhabitants of the tribe (see note on Gezer, ch. x. 33). This seems the most probable explanation. The land in general was owned by the descendants of Caleb. But the Levites had certain pastures reserved for them, whither they drove their cattle (see note on suburbs, ch. xiv. 4). The special information about Hebron here again is worthy of notice. It is copied by the author of 1 Chron. in ch. vi.

Ver. 13.—**Hebron with her suburbs to be a city of refuge for the slayer.** Rather, *the city of refuge for the slayer, Hebron and her cattle-drives* (see note above on ver. 2). The translation in our version obscures the meaning, which is clearly that the cities of refuge were first fixed on, and then assigned

to the Levites. Most of the cities in the following list have been noticed already.

Ver. 16.—**Ain with her suburbs.** We have " Ashan " in 1 Chron. vi. 59. If the view taken above of Ain (see note on ch. xv. 32, and ch. xix. 7) be correct, Ashan is the true reading here.

Ver. 18.—**Anathoth.** The birthplace of Jeremiah, where we find that Anathoth was still a priestly city (ch. i. 1). No doubt it was for this reason that it was chosen (1 Kings ii. 26) as the place of Abiathar's banishment. Here again we see to how close an examination the writers of the Old Testament may be submitted without in the least degree shaking their testimony. Observe, too, the geographical accuracy of Isaiah's mention of Geba and Anathoth in his description of an Assyrian invasion through the passes at Ai or Aiath and Michmash (Isa. x. 29, 30).

Ver. 21.—**To be a refuge for the slayer** (see above ver. 13). This order is observed in every case but one, which is explained in the note on ver. 36.

Ver. 25.—**Tanach.** The same as the Taanach before mentioned, ch. xii. 21. In 1 Chron. vi. 70 (56 Heb. text) we have Eth-aner, an obvious blunder, as the Hebrew shows, Resh having been read for Hheth, and Aleph having been inserted to form the Eth of the accusative case. This reading existed, however, as far back as the LXX. version. **Gath-rimmon.** There is a blunder also here, where Gath-rimmon has crept in by the mistake of a copyist from the last verse. The true reading is preserved in 1 Chron. vi. 70, where we find Ibleam (see ch. xvii. 11), or as it is there written Bileam; no doubt by mistake; the Hebrew letters (omitting the Jod, which has dropped out), being those that compose the familiar name of Balaam the prophet. The LXX. reads *Jebath* here.

Ver. 27.—**To be a city of refuge** (see above, ver. 13). **Be-eshterah.** Thus printed by the Masorites, and thus translated by the LXX., but no doubt the same as Og's city Ashtaroth (see ch. xii. 4, and 1 Chron. vi. 71).

Ver. 30.—**Abdon** (see note on ch. xix. 28).

Ver. 32.—**Galilee** (see above, ch. xx. 7).

Ver. 36.—**And out of the tribe of Reuben.** This verse and the succeeding have the Masoretic note appended that they are not found in the Masora or true tradition. Kimchi therefore rejects them. But they are found in the LXX. and the rest of the ancient versions, and they are necessary to make up the number of forty-eight cities. Dr. Kennicott, as well as Michaelis, Rosenmüller, and Maurer defended their genuineness. So does Knobel, who complains that Rabbi Jacob Ben Chajim, in his Rabbinical

Bible of 1525, has very improperly omitted these towns on the authority of the Masora, and that many editors have foolishly imitated him. They have no doubt been omitted by the mistake of a copyist, who passed on from the אַרְבַּע (four) of ver. 35 to that of ver. 37, omitting all that lay between. The LXX. adds here " the city of refuge for the slayer," words which may have possibly formed part of the original text, as they do in every other instance. **Jahazah.** It is worthy of remark that this city, with Heshbon and Jazer and Mephaath, fell into the hands of the Moabites in later times, a sad indication of religious declension (see Isa. xv., xvi.; Jer. xlviii. 21, 34).

Ver. 38. — **To be a city of refuge** (see above, ver. 13). **Mahanaim** (see ch. xiii. 26). Perhaps the unquestionable *entente cordiale* between David and the sacerdotal party may have determined him to fix on this as his refuge when fleeing from Absalom, in addition to its situation beyond Jordan, and near the fords (2 Sam. xvii. 22, 24).

Ver. 42.—**These cities.** Rather, perhaps, *these cities were*, (*i.e.*, "have been enumerated," or "were given "), *city by city, and their cattle-drives surrounding them, thus was it with all these cities.*

Ver. 43.—**And the Lord gave.** The LXX. adds before this passage : " And Joshua completed the division of the land in its boundaries, and the children gave a portion to Joshua, by the commandment of the Lord. They gave to him the city for which he asked, Thamnath Sarach gave they him in Mount Ephraim, and Joshua built the city, and dwelt in it. And Joshua took the stone knives, with which he had circumcised the children of Israel, which were in the way in the wilderness, and he placed them in Tamnath Sarach." The repetition is very much in the manner of the sacred historian, and it is possible that we have here an authentic passage, which some copyist has omitted in the Hebrew text. **All the land.** As has been before remarked, the Hebrew כֹל must not be pressed to mean literally " all." Yet, in a sense, the word is true here. The land had been put in their power. They had only to exert themselves to complete its conquest. This they failed to do, and not only so, but violated the conditions under which the land was granted them. Thus they soon fell under the dominion of those who had been their own vassals. Ritter thinks (vol. iii. 187—189) that the Asherites and Danites submitted to the inhabitants of the land in consequence of being allowed equal citizen rights with them. He draws this inference from Judges v. 17, supposing that these

tribes addicted themselves to the commercial and maritime life for which the Phœnicians were so famous.

Ver. 44.—**And the Lord gave them rest.** LXX. κατέπαυσεν. The student of Scripture will not fail to recall the passage in the Epistle to the Hebrews (ch. iv. 8) in which reference is made to this passage, and especially to the LXX. version of it. The word signifies rather rest from wandering than rest from toil, though in some passages (*e.g.* Exod. xxiii. 12 ; Deut. v. 14) it has the latter signification (cf. Deut. xii. 10). **Round about.** Or, *from* round about, *i.e.*, from the assaults of the surrounding nations. **According to all that he sware** (Exod. xxxiii. 14). **There stood not a man of all their enemies before them.** This was true, as far as the present history is concerned. We read that the Ephraimites did not, or " could not," drive out their enemies, and that the other tribes also failed to obtain complete possession of the land. But (1) we are not told that this was in the time of Joshua, and (2) it is intimated that this was their own fault. How could it be otherwise ? Had the same faith been theirs which caused the Jordan to dry up, and the towers of Jericho to fall down at their march, which discomfited one vast confederacy at Beth-horon, and annihilated another vast confederacy, even better supplied with munitions of war at Lake Merom, they could not have failed to root out the scanty remnant of their humiliated and disheartened foes. As has already been remarked (see ch. xi. 23, note), it was from no neglect on Joshua's part that this was not done at once, for it had been God's own command that it should not be done, lest the country should become a desert (Deut. vii. 22). Calvin concludes a similar argument with the words, " nothing but their own cowardice prevented them from enjoying the blessings of God in all their fulness."

Ver. 45. — **Ought of any good thing.** Literally, *a word from all the good word.* This Keil regards as the " sum " of all the gracious promises that God had made." But he should have added that דָּבָר, beside signifying, as it does, " word," is also the word for " thing " in Hebrew (see, for instance, Gen. xv. 1 ; xx. 10), and innumerable other passages, as well as the use of לֹא דָבָר for " nothing. ' The translation " thing " makes the best sense, and is more agreeable to the Hebrew idiom. **All came to pass.** The Hebrew is singular, *the whole came*, the word translated " came to pass " in our version being a different one from that usually so translated.

HOMILETICS.

Vers. 1—45.—*The ecclesiastical settlement of Canaan.* Though the ecclesiastical institutions of the Christian Church differ, in some respects materially, from those of the Jewish, yet inasmuch as the law and the gospel came from the same All-wise Hand, we may naturally expect that the main principles of each will be the same. Perhaps we have insisted too much of late on the fact that the law was "done away in Christ," and too little on the qualifying truth that Christ came "not to destroy, but to fulfil it." It may be well, therefore, to consider briefly what the duties of the priests were under the old covenant. From this we may be able to infer what their duties should be under the new. The New Testament Scriptures contain some information on the point, but not so much as to render it unnecessary to seek some enlightenment from the Old. The reaction from an obedience to powers unduly claimed and unjustly used, has rendered it all the more necessary that we should recur to first principles in the matter. The hatred of what is called "sacerdotalism" has resulted on the part of the laity in general to something like an undue impatience of the just influence of ministers of religion, and this can only lead to disorder in the Christian body. We may observe, then, (1) that the performance of the public duties of religion belonged exclusively to them, and the cases of Korah, Saul, Uzzah, and King Uzziah show how rigidly this law was to be observed. For the sacrifies of the old law we must substitute the spiritual sacrifices of prayer and praise in the congregation, the administration of the sacraments, the ordering of the services of the sanctuary. They had (2) to "bear the iniquity of the sanctuary" (Num. xviii. 1) which would seem to mean, in the case of the Christian clergy, that they are bound to take upon themselves the office of public and private intercession for God's people, just as Daniel did during the Babylonish captivity (Dan. ix. 3—20). Nor is this to be confined to their own particular flocks. Who can tell the blessing to Christian society if all the ministers of religion kept up a ceaseless intercession for the sins of Christian people in general, and especially for those of their own country and Church? Again, (3) the decision of difficult causes is referred to them as well as the judges. To claim such a right would be regarded in these days as an unbounded instance of priestly arrogance. Yet it has been claimed, not only by ecclesiastics of the Roman Church, but by Calvin and his followers, by John Knox, and by the Puritans in the reign of Elizabeth. No doubt the claims of all these parties were pushed to inordinate lengths. But, on the other hand, it does not seem extravagant to believe that in a healthy state of society, the influence of those whose studies are chiefly concerned with the word of God, should be considerable in matters relating to the application of the principles of morality. Of course nothing like an absolute authority is claimed for them. All that Scripture gives them is a consultative voice, a co-ordinate with that of the magistrate or legislator. Such was actually the position given to the clergy in Anglo-Saxon times, and though, no doubt, the increased and increasing complexity of modern society renders special study more and more necessary for the interpretation of laws, the same rule does not hold good regarding their enactment. Lastly, the priests of the old covenant, though not formally charged with it by the law, yet (see Levit. x. 11 ; Deut. xvii. 9—12) became practically (4) the interpreters of God's revealed will. We learn this from the text, "The priests' lips should keep knowledge, and they should seek the law at his mouth" (Mal. ii. 7). This office, though not formally committed to the clergy under the gospel, any more than under the law, is yet at present vested in them exclusively by common consent. They are the authorised expounders of the truths of religion. Not that the people are bound to accept implicitly whatever they say. For it is implied in the passage above cited and by many others, that the priests' lips did *not* keep knowledge, and that men sought the law at his mouth in vain. It is the duty of the laity to test the truth of what is delivered to them by the word of God. But, except in very rare instances, that of Origen for example, the task of the public exposition of the oracles of God has been reserved for those who have been called to the office of the ministry. In these four respects the ecclesiastical arrangements of a Christian country should correspond, it may fairly be urged, with the ecclesiastical arrangements of the promised land. On the other hand, it must not be forgotten that the whole history of Israel, from Moses downwards, shows that the civil magistrate had a large influence in ecclesiastical affairs. Not to go beyond the limits of the present book, we have instances of the exertion of such an influence in ch. iii. 5, 6; iv. 10, 17; v. 2, 3; vi. 6; xxi. 1. Some additional considerations are added.

I. THE LEVITES RECEIVED THEIR INHERITANCE LAST OF ALL. This self-abnegation was fitting among those who were specially appointed to the service of God. So, in like manner, should the ministers of Jesus Christ, instead of grasping eagerly at power or pelf, be desirous of being "last of all and servant of all," in imitation of Him who was among His own disciples as one that serveth. It may be added in a spirit, not of boasting, but of thankfulness, that never was there a time, since the hour of the first fervour of the gospel in the days of the Apostles, when this spirit was more abundantly displayed than in our own age and country—when there were so many ministers of God content to serve God in the sanctuary, without the prospect of earthly countenance or reward. Let them not murmur if men take these things as a matter of course, but look forward to the "recompense of the reward."

II. PROPER PROVISION WAS MADE FOR THE SERVICE OF GOD. The Levites were carefully dispersed throughout all the tribes of Israel, not, of course, for the service of the sanctuary, which was kept up at one place only, but obviously in order to diffuse among the tribes a knowledge of and attachment to the law of God. A similar provision has been made in all Christian countries. At first, bodies of men were gathered together in the chief cities of a country, from whence the rural districts were gradually evangelised. Thence, by an extension of the principle of Levitical dispersion, came our present institution of a resident minister or ministers in every village. To this institution, more than to any other, do we owe the diffusion of Christian principles throughout the whole land. It would be the sorest of all calamities were any untoward event to overthrow it.

III. PROPER PROVISION WAS MADE FOR THE MAINTENANCE OF THE CLERGY AND MINISTERS OF RELIGION. Here we may do well to quote Matthew Henry, who says, referring to the words, "The Lord commanded by the hands of Moses," and observing that the Levites based their claim, not on their own merits or services, but on the command of God: "Note, the maintenance of ministers is not an arbitrary thing, left purely to the good-will of the people, who may let them starve if they please, but a perpetual ordinance that 'those who preach the gospel should live of the gospel' (1 Cor. ix. 14), and should live comfortably." Many other passages in the New Testament enforce this truth (e.g., 1 Cor. ix. 7, 11; Gal. vi. 6). The clergy may feel a natural repugnance to enlarge upon that in which they themselves have a personal interest, and which their flocks might find in the word of God. But they should not be deterred by an over-scrupulous feeling from doing their duty. They are bound to declare the whole counsel of God. And if, by an insufficient provision for God's ministers, the cause of God is likely to suffer (and it is to be feared that such is now very often the case), if the energies which should be devoted entirely to God's cause are dissipated in worldly anxieties, in endeavours to keep the wolf from the door, in efforts to eke out a too scanty income by other labours than those of the sanctuary, it is plainly their duty to speak out. Instead of "living of the gospel," it is to be feared that there are many clergymen and their families starving of the gospel, though they have too much self-respect to let the fact be known. And while the spectacle of ecclesiastics rolling in riches and living idly and luxuriously is a hateful one, on the other hand, our present haphazard regulations, which deprive a good many estimable clergymen of the wherewithal to purchase their daily bread, and keep a good many more in anxious suspense, whether it may not one day be so with themselves, are no less an offence in the eyes of God.

HOMILIES BY VARIOUS AUTHORS.

Ver. 3.—*The cities of the Levites.* The Levites were scattered among the other tribes of Israel, and yet not individually but in clusters, in cities of their own. This arrangement must have had some object :—

I. THE LEVITES WERE SET APART FOR THE SERVICE OF GOD. They were freed from the claims and cares which fell on the other Israelites. They were maintained by the offerings of the people. Those who minister in spiritual things have temporal wants which the people who are benefited by their services should care for. They are not the less men because they are servants of God, and their home comforts should be secured that they may be free for spiritual work.

II. THE LEVITES WERE ABLE TO MINISTER TO THE PEOPLE BY LIVING AMONGST THEM. When it was not their turn to be serving at the temple, the Levites appear to have been engaged in educational work and religious ministrations among the people of their neighbourhood. Church services are useless unless the private lives of men are improved. We must carry the gospel to those who will not come to hear it in the regular place of worship. It is the duty of Christians not to live apart from the world for their own sanctification, but to live in the world for the world's redemption—to be the leaven leavening the whole mass, the light of the world shining into the dark places. Thus the world will be Christianised (1) by the gospel reaching those who are out of the way of ordinary religious influences ; (2) by example ; (3) by direct personal persuasion.

III. THE LEVITES WERE ABLE TO CULTIVATE THEIR HUMAN SYMPATHIES BY LIVING AMONG THE PEOPLE. The religion of complete separation from the world is unnatural. It destroys some of the finest qualities of human life. Godliness cannot exist without humanity. The man of God is most truly human. Sympathy for human affairs, active pity for the distress of the world, and brotherly kindness are essential to the Christian life. Therefore the best school for the saint is not the hermit's cell, but the market-place. Complete separation from the world for religious ends developes (1) morbid subjectivity, (2) spiritual selfishness, (3) pride, (4) idleness.

IV. THE LEVITES WERE ABLE TO CULTIVATE THEIR SPIRITUALITY BY MUTUAL INTERCOURSE. They lived in cities together ; though in the midst of the tribes of Israel. Christians should unite in Church fellowship. Solitary mission work is difficult and painful. Christian society secures (1) mutual sympathy, (2) wholesome emulation. The Church should be a home for the Christian. It is bad to be always in worldly society.—W. F. A.

Vers. 43—45.—*God's faithfulness.*

I. WE MAY ASSURE OURSELVES OF GOD'S FAITHFULNESS BY A CONSIDERATION OF THE GROUNDS ON WHICH IT RESTS. (1) The *unchangeableness* of God. This is seen (*a*) in nature—in changeless laws, as of light and gravitation, and in geological uniformity ; (*b*) in revelation, the development of which is like that of a tree retaining unity of life and growing according to fixed principles. (2) The *omniscience* of God. Men cannot foresee (*a*) the novel circumstances under which they will be required to redeem their word, and (*b*) the breadth of the issues to which their promises may lead them. When God promises He knows (*a*) all future circumstances to which His word may apply, and (*b*) all that is involved in the pledge He gives. (3) The *omnipotence* of God. We may promise help, and fail in the hour of need from inability to render it. This is seen in business engagements, national treaties, pledges of friendship, &c. God has all the sources of the universe at His command.

II. WE MAY ILLUSTRATE GOD'S FAITHFULNESS BY A REVIEW OF THE INSTANCES IN WHICH IT HAS BEEN PROVED TO US. (1) In *history* ; *e.g.*, the return of the seasons and the production of the fruits of the earth, according to the promise to Noah (Gen. viii. 22) ; the possession of Canaan promised from the time of Abraham (Gen. xii. 7) ; the return from the captivity promised in the law (Deut. xxx. 3) ; the advent of Christ (Isa. xi. 1), and the enjoyment of Christian blessings (Matt. xi.

28—30). (2) In *personal experience; e.g.*, deliverance from sin, comfort in sorrow, guidance in perplexity, strength for duty. Andrew Fuller says, "He that watches Providence will not lack a Providence to watch."

III. WE MAY STRENGTHEN OUR BELIEF IN GOD'S FAITHFULNESS BY AN EXAMINATION OF APPARENT EXCEPTIONS. These may often be explained by noting important circumstances. (1) *Time* of fulfilment. God does not always fulfil his promise immediately, or when we expect. He will do so in His own time, at the right time, in the fulness of time. (2) *Mode* of fulfilment. The promise is not always fulfilled in the way we expect, because (*a*) we misinterpret God's word, and (*b*) God is educating us by illusions which cover greater truths than we can at first receive. (3) *Conditions* of fulfilment. God's promises are conditional on our faith and conduct. His covenant is sure so long as we keep our side of it. He is faithful to us if we are true to Him. We often fail to receive a promised blessing because we neglect to carry out the conditions God has attached to it.

IV. WE MAY APPLY THE PRINCIPLE OF GOD'S FAITHFULNESS TO OUR OWN EXPERIENCE BY NOTING THE REGIONS OVER WHICH IT EXTENDS. (1) It extends to *all God's promises*—the threats of chastisement as well as the assurances of mercy. (2) It extends to *all time*. God's promises are as fresh now as when He first uttered them. (3) The fruits of it are *enduring*. The people "possessed the land and dwelt in it." (4) The realisation of it is *perfect*. "All came to pass." —W. F. A.

Ver. 3.—*The portion of the tribe of Levi.* There might seem at first something strange in the withholding from the tribe of Levi its share among the cities of Canaan, divided by lot among the other tribes. There were, however, as we shall see, substantial reasons why the tribe of Levi should not be treated like the other tribes in the apportionment of the land of Canaan. IT HAD ITS OWN PECULIAR WORK TO WHICH IT WAS TO BE ENTIRELY CONSECRATED. Set apart for the service of the altar, it was not to be distracted by other interests. The sacrifices of the Lord were its inheritance. On the other hand, as it must have means of subsistence, every tribe was to set apart from its own lot that which was needful for the sacrifices and service of God. These temporal conditions of the tribe of Levi in the land of Canaan give us a very fair idea of the priesthood of the old covenant, and we shall be able to derive from their consideration several principles applicable to the priesthood of the new covenant. (1) The fact that the tribe of Levi was to have no portion of its own, shows that it is *not the will of God that His service should be mixed up with temporal and material interests.* (2) *It is made incumbent on the whole nation to provide for the maintenance of the Levites.* This is a sacred duty which cannot be neglected without prejudice to the service of God. In fulfilling this duty, the people associate themselves with the priesthood. The Levites, whom they maintain, are their representatives. The eleven tribes have their delegate in the twelfth. This truth was impressed on the minds of the children of Israel by the offering by which they had to redeem the first-born of their male children. Thus even under the old covenant, the great idea of the universal priesthood was implicitly recognised. Now all Israel is a nation of priests, for, as says St. Peter, in Christ "we are made kings and priests unto God" (1 Pet. ii. 9). Still the Church has its ministers; but these are not a clerical class apart; they are but the representatives of the people; or rather, they do but devote themselves specially to that which is at the same time the duty of every Christian. In fulfilling this ministry, they are called, as was the tribe of Levi, to renounce all earthly ambition, and not to attempt in any way to make holy things the handle for securing their own material advantage. Freely they have received, freely they are to give; or they will come under the condemnation of Simon Magus. It is for the Church to maintain these her servants by voluntary gifts. This duty was urged by the apostles. "Let him who is taught communicate unto him that teacheth in all good things" (Gal. vi. 6). (3) The Church has become altogether a race of priests. *As a Church she has no right to secular dominion.* When the papacy pretended that temporal power was a condition of safety for the Catholic

Church, it ignored the laws concerning the priesthood, both under the old covenant and the new. Whenever a Church seeks to reign after the manner of temporal sovereigns, she becomes guilty of the same rebellion, and forgets the great words of her Divine Founder: "My kingdom is not of this world" (John xviii. 36).—E. DE P.

Ver. 41.—*The established Church of Israel.* These words project before us essentially the Church establishment of ancient Israel. It is quite true that the Old Testament priesthood in its functions differed in very many most essential points from the clergy of any modern Church. Their function was ritual rather than instruction. Their office came, not by fitness, choice, or ordination, but by birth and training. Throughout its history, from its earliest institution, when it was named "The Host," down to the days of the Maccabees, the priestly was one of the most warlike of all the tribes. According to Dr. Stanley ('Jewish Church,' vol. ii., Lecture on Jewish Priesthood), the employment of the Levites in the temple service was that of the butcher rather than of the theologian. And though distributed in every tribe, there was no attempt to secure that distribution of the Levites in every city, which would have been essential if their work had partaken in any great degree of the educational character marking that of the Christian ministry. Still they were a religious order. Chiefly serving in the temple at Jerusalem, they had yet some instruction work to do in their provincial homes. To them belonged the duty of "preserving, transcribing, and interpreting the law." They were the magistrates also who applied it (Deut. xvii. 9—12; xxxi. 9, 12, 26). Though only a portion of their time occupied in attendance on the temple, and thus left free to pursue other labours, yet their service was recognised by a national provision. Roughly one-twelfth of the population, Levi had as its share the tithes of the produce realised by the other eleven tribes. It had no land, excepting a little suburban pasture land, given it; but forty-eight cities situate in all the tribes were given them for their dwelling. And while the priesthood never had the glory belonging to the line of prophets, it yet rendered splendid service to the land. It was a bond of unity between the various tribes. It linked them to God, it gave persistence to the national history, was the most enduring part of the most enduring people that the earth has seen; gave some of the finest psalmists, *e.g.*, Heman and Asaph; produced grand prophets, *e.g.*, Samuel, Jeremiah, Ezekiel, and probably Isaiah, Joel, Micah, Habakkuk, and others; statesmen, like Ezra; patriots, like the Maccabees. While the Ten Tribes to-day are lost, in the frequency of the names Cohen and Levy you see the grand persistence of the tribe and the stamp of God's approval of at least much of its service. In all this ordering of the Levitical institutions, and the provision made for the support of the tribe, we have a conspicuous example of a *Church Establishment.* As such consider it—

I. As an illustration of RELIGIOUSNESS OF MAN. How strange is the universality of religious provision in the world! Egypt had its caste of priests; large provision was made in Greek and Roman societies for religious service; India has its caste of Brahmins; China has its Buddhist priests and monks; Israel has here its sacred tribe. Whatever else such a provision may import, it certainly involves a wonderful testimony to the force of the religious principle in man. *Man cannot be utterly secular.* The mystery around him, conscience within him, all aspirations of the heart, make him grope after God. However vague the creed and limited the law, every nation from the beginning has been religious. Israel's Church establishment illustrates this fact.

II. This example suggests that IN ALL THINGS A NATION OUGHT TO ACT RELIGIOUSLY. The writer questions the expediency, on grounds hereafter to be noticed, of a Church establishment in England to-day. He, at the same time, would equally protest against the opposite extreme, which would deny to a State any right to recognise the truth of God, God's claims, or the spiritual nature of man in its legislature. It is desirable that at once our national policy and law should in all points harmonise with those highest teachings of morals which we find in the word of God. If all do not agree in their views on these points, then, as in all other cases, the majority should have the power of carrying out their opinions, while the minority should have perfect freedom individually to hold and to propagate theirs. Recognising God and His claims, the policy and laws of a land would be more elevated in their tone. Is the question one of war, our English parliament should ask, What would God have us do? and should do it. On such questions as Sunday trading, the demoralising traffic in strong drink, religious education, or laws of marriage, the State could not without grave harm omit religious considerations from its grounds of action; on the contrary, it ought to place them in the forefront, and in all such questions adopt as its course that which, in its judgment, most accords with the will of God, and most furthers the spiritual as well as temporal benefit of man. If it believes God's will to be revealed in the Bible, it should appeal to and boldly follow the teaching laid down there. No desire to keep sacred things from irreverent handling should be permitted to divorce legislation from religion. No undue regard for sensibilities of a minority should keep the majority from acting according to its highest views, so long as the freedom of the minority is unimpaired. Without religion government degenerates into a thing of police and sanitation; and is apt to become mean in its tone, reckless in its principles, and adverse to the nation's real good.

III. Every patriot should seek for his country the diffusion of true religion. *In what way* this is to be done is a grave question. But if we aim at the right end, probably not much harm results from endeavouring to reach it in various ways. In Moses' time God ruled that the best way was a Church establishment. Expedient then, it seems to the writer *inexpedient* (not unlawful) now. He mentions a few out of many grounds. (1) Christianity, as being a more spiritual system, is much less dependent on external support than Judaism was. (2) There the order of precedence was Church before State; the whole nation being a theocracy, the law of Moses the statute book. While this was the order, the Church was free to carry out its mission in allegiance to God. In almost every modern union of Church and State the Church has had to purchase State support by a serious sacrifice of its spiritual self-government and freedom of action. (3) There is an absence of the harmonious, united feeling which alone makes a national Church a possibility. (4) The wealth of the nation, and its religious interest, are so great that it can easily provide for the effective maintenance of all Christian activities, without needing anything beyond the freewill offerings of the people. On such grounds it is suggested that a Church establishment is to-day inexpedient. But, if a national provision of religious ordinance is inexpedient, a provision of religious ordinance throughout the land should be made in some other way; and it behoves every lover of his God and of his country to consecrate wealth and give labour to secure in every community a house of God, and to put within reach of all the preaching of the gospel of Christ. A church of Christ in every village, training children, consecrating youth, supporting manhood, glorifying age, the home of gentle charities, a quiet resting-place, where all learn to love each other beneath the smile of God, is a provision on which God would smile, and by which man would be highly blessed; and feeling this, every true patriot will take every means and make every sacrifice to secure that something, thus answering to a tribe of Levi, shall in our land diffuse the immeasurable advantages of religious truth and united worship. Let all strive to establish, by the consecration of their gifts and labours, the Church of Christ more firmly in our native land.—G.

Ver. 45.—*The record of God's faithfulness.* A beautiful little word, recording a nation's experience, and one adopted as the correct statement of the experience of multitudes that none can number! Look at it, and observe first—

I. God speaks good things to the house of Israel. "Good things," *i.e.*, " of its future: "exceeding great and precious promises—words on which He causes us to hope." Man lives not in the present only. The past clings to him; the future presses on him. Especially this future—near and further! Our bliss comes chiefly from its hopes, our sorrows from its fears. With the present it is easy to deal; its form is fixed, and we can determine at once how to meet it. But the future is filled with "may-bes" so indefinite and changeful in their form that we cannot settle how to meet or what to do with them. In the case of Israel, God covered all this darkness with His good words of hope. He would go before them; they should be brought to a land flowing with milk and honey; no enemy should stand before them; vineyards they had not planted, cities they had not built, should be theirs. They should find an earthly dwelling-place singularly suited for their habitation: fertile for their sustenance, secure for their safety, central for the diffusion of their truth. So God speaks to all His Israel. To every one some promise is given. Even His prodigal children have some promise to cheer them. His sun of promise rises on the evil and on the good; but on the good it sheds its richest warmth. There are great words given to us. Providential mercies are promised; support of the Spirit of all grace is assured us: the Voice behind saying, "This is the way, walk ye in it:" and that temptations shall not overpower, nor inward weakness destroy us; that we shall be more than conquerors through Him that loved us; that death itself shall be a ministering angel, wrestling with us, but blessing us at "break of day;" that there will be an abundant entrance into the everlasting kingdom, a perfected likeness to our Lord, an occupation before the throne, in which all our power will find delight and all our capacities be filled with satisfaction. These are the pledges given us. It is well to realise how vast they are, how worthy of the generosity of the infinite God. Be not dismayed, there is no sorrow whose consolation is not pledged in some word of promise, and no perplexity the solution of which is not tendered in some other. Marvel not that the words seem too vast to belong to us. The dimensions of mercy are Divine. Put against every thought of fear these words of comfort and of hope. We are sad and fearful chiefly because we forget them. God speaks good things unto Israel. Observe secondly—

II. It seemed impossible that these words should not fail. When Moses brought them, the people "believed not for anguish of spirit and cruel bondage." How could such promises be redeemed? They, a nation of slaves, whose spirit was ground out of them; their oppressor having a standing army, strong in cavalry? Impossibilities multiplied as they advanced. By the route they took they found themselves hemmed in by ranges of hills on either hand, sea in front, foe behind them. How could they reach the other side? There were desert difficulties, or rather impossibilities, as to water and food. How could they possibly dispossess the Canaanitish nations, all of them stronger than themselves—these peoples of Gilead in their fortresses, impregnable by nature, and rendered still more so by consummate art and by the marvellous vigour of the inhabitants? Without artillery of any kind, how could it be deemed a possibility to reduce the fenced cities of the Canaanites? How was Jordan to be crossed, with its deep ravine and swift stream that made it one of the strongest lines of defence that any nation ever had? Ten out of the twelve spies—all of them of course chosen for their courage—declared the task an utter impossibility. And it is worth our while to mark this, for there is a sort of family likeness running through all God's promises; and almost all have this look of impossibility about them. I suppose all spies are apt to feel that the promises God has made to us cannot possibly be fulfilled. One battling with doubts deems continuance in saintly living impossible, though God promises grace sufficient. One battling with strong proneness to sin feels it impossible that a feeble seed of grace should survive and conquer forces so much stronger than itself. The promise of usefulness resulting from our labour seems impossible of fulfilment, so does the promise of answers to our prayers. The promise of some survival of death and of our fragile spirit weathering all storms, and reaching a perfect home, seems impossible to be fulfilled. It is well to mark exactly the force of the favourite promises. They are not poor probabilities. They are the grand impossibilities of life. The supernatural enters into all our hopes. They cannot be realised unless God troubles Himself about them. We must not try and eke out faith with the consideration of natural probabilities. The natural probabilities are all against any one of the grander promises being fulfilled. But thirdly observe—

III. All the promises were fulfilled. "All came to pass." There failed not ought of any good thing the Lord had spoken. The sea was crossed; the desert had its food and water; Bashan was subdued; Jordan crossed; the whole land possessed. And all this took place easily, without any hitch whatever, so long as Israel was willing simply to go on. And from then till now the experience of the Church of Christ has, on a large scale and with invariable uniformity, been, that however impossible the fulfilment of God's promises might seem, they have all been realised exceeding abundantly above all asked or thought. God is the same to-day as yesterday: not further from us in heart, not feebler in powers. His anointing is not exhausted; He is still fresh to do what He has promised. And if we faithfully follow on in the way in which He leads us, there will not fail ought of the good that God hath spoken to us.—G.

Vers. 43—45.—Last among the tribes to know the particular inheritance assigned to them came the Levites, since they were not to occupy a distinct territory, but certain selected cities in each district. By this arrangement each tribe recognised the duty of providing for the support of the service of God, and had religious instructors abiding within its borders. The sacred historian having finished his narrative of the partition of the land, deems it a fitting opportunity to bear witness to the fact that God had proved equal to His word. He had brought His people into their possession, and they were busily engaged in arranging their habitations, tilling the soil and other occupations of landed proprietors. The Israelitish dispensation was typical, foreshadowing the dispensation of the fulness of times, of which theirs was but a dim anticipation, an emblem and a shadow. As mind is superior to matter, and spiritual are preferable to bodily satisfactions, as righteousness is more important than wealth, and elevation of soul more desirable than prowess in war, so do the advantages of which believers in Christ are partakers immeasurably outweigh all that was the portion of the Israelites in their brightest period.

I. AN ENUMERATION OF PRIVILEGES. (1) Mention is made of the *inheritance*, the land which they now possessed, and wherein they dwelt. Hope was at last fruition. Buoyed up in their journeys by the thought of the " land flowing with milk and honey," they had crossed the Jordan and planted their feet on the soil that was to be theirs. When a man realises his sonship to God, the whole earth becomes his. For him the trees unfold their leaves and the birds sing. He takes fresh interest in the world of nature, it is his Father's garden. But our thoughts centre chiefly in those mercies bought for the Church by Christ at such enormous cost. Forgiveness, justification, adoption, sanctification, whole acres of fruitful soil that yield sustenance to the soul, yea, spiritual luxuries, if only we be diligent. Our inheritance is not to be enjoyed without appropriating effort. The word of God is the register of our estate. The territory expands by viewing, " 'tis a broad land of wealth unknown." The higher we ascend on the hill of meditation, the better shall we behold our property, stretching far and wide, up to heaven and away to eternity. The ground furnishes all manner of fruit ; the graces of the Spirit are many. The believer enters into the kingdom of God, an empire larger than that of Charlemagne and he is made richer than Crœsus. Angels are his attendants. (2) *Rest* is spoken of, *rest from wanderings*. There may be some of vagabondish tendencies to whom incessant travelling, with the variety it affords, is pleasing, but a nomadic life is neither desired by the majority nor healthful for them. Forty years in the wilderness did not reconcile the Israelites to the continual shifting of the camp. Perhaps no more piteous nor clamorous cry is heard to-day than the demand for rest. The rush of life is everywhere bewailed. Turmoil and bustle may delight for a season, but soon pall upon the taste and tire the faculties. A gospel intended for men must be capable of meeting the legitimate demands of every age. And the gospel of Jesus Christ claims to give rest to the weary. Not that the Christian is summoned to a position requiring no vigilance nor exercise of his talents. To superficial observers, the disciples who embraced the offer of Jesus may have appeared to lead an extremely unquiet life, now tossing on the waves at their Master's command, then journeying on foot through hamlets and towns, and finally proclaiming the truth in the midst of foes and persecutors. But rest is not idleness, carnal ease. The Israelites had still their proper work to do. But they were not tormented by the constant need to transport themselves, their wives, and children, and their baggage, to a different residence. The Christian has obtained peace of conscience, rest of soul, by reposing in Christ for security. (3) The text speaks of *victory*, or *rest from conflict*. The inhabitants of Canaan had been defeated in several pitched battles. Many were slain, and others remained scattered in small groups through the land. The period of warfare necessary to acquire possession was at an end. " There stood not a man of all their enemies before them," &c. And victory is another blessing which God grants the believer. Satan has been driven from the citadel, and the rightful king installed. Sin staggers under a mortal wound. The contest may be long and sharp. The agonised soul cries, " What must I do ? " Hopes and fears struggle for the mastery, passions fierce rend the breast, the thunders of Sinai roll, temptations darken the sky. But the radiance of the cross, the glory of the risen Saviour, the brightness of the ascension cloud, these dissipate the gloom, and the believer shouts, Victory ! Victory ! "Thanks be to God which giveth us the victory through our Lord Jesus Christ." Henceforth the character of the fight is changed. The enemy may not be completely extirpated ; he may be left to prove the Christian, who has only to be true to his Lord, and the country shall be reduced to entire subjection. All the equipment, guidance, and succour requisite are provided ; he may go from strength to strength, and if not triumphant, the blame is attributable to himself alone.

II. Some general observations upon the text. (1) *The Author of our blessings* must be held in constant remembrance. Four times in three verses is the name of the Lord repeated. Herein lies the distinction between morality and religion. We are but heathen, if we speak of warring against evil, expelling selfishness, and slaying vice without acknowledging the impulse derived from on high. We are not Christians unless we ascribe the merit of the victory to the Lord, " Thou hast redeemed us by Thy blood." (2) *Blessings are all the sweeter from contrast with previous trials.* Poverty teaches thankfulness for riches, labour enhances subsequent rest. It is the lame man healed that leaps and runs in the joy of his newfound powers. Angels can never know the delight of exclaiming, " Whereas I was blind, now I see." In this way will God recompense the afflicted. The pained in body will be overjoyed to experience ease. The desolate will understand the comfort of sympathy and association with like-minded saints. These vagrant Israelites, harassed by perpetual marching and warfare, estimated highly the privilege of a restful settlement. And to any struggling with difficulty, we say, " Hereafter it shall delight thee to remember these thy labours." The veteran soldier will talk with honest pride of his wounds, and the traveller of his fatigues. (3) Reminded of two truths that are like sunbeams in the word of God. *The Lord is mindful of His oath*, and *able to redeem it* to the very letter. " There hath not failed ought of any good thing. . . . all came to pass." How often the Israelites murmured because of the length of the way, were tempted to think the promised land a delusive mirage, that it was better to return to Egypt with its certain bondage, but also certain leeks and bread. The report of giants afield overwhelmed them with dismay. They would not look at the stars in the sky, the power of God and His covenant faithfulness. Now, in a class at school, what the teacher says to one is intended for the information of all. And what the Almighty has done to one individual or nation is for the instruction, refreshment, consolation of all. Unbelief is ever ready to lodge suspicion in our breasts. "Hath God forgotten to be gracious ? " The holiest men have known seasons of despondency. Shut up in the ark they believe they are safe, but the floods are all around, and the time of release is long in coming. If tempted to doubt the execution of God's plans, we must rise above the crowd, and from the tower behold the growth and grand proportions of the city. Withdraw a little, and try to obtain a comprehensive glance at history past and present, and your faith will be confirmed in the accomplishment of the Almighty purposes concerning mankind. Order will be educed out of fancied confusion. The building of your faith cannot fall. Seize its pillars and test their strength, the pledged word and omnipotence of God, and all your fright will vanish. (4) *It is ever seasonable to record with gratitude the fulfilment of God's promises.* If we only acted upon this statement in proportion to our consciousness of its truth, there would oftener issue from our complaining lips a burst of thanksgiving. The declaration of the text was reiterated by Joshua in his solemn charge to the people (xxiii. 14), and a similar testimony was borne by Solomon at the dedication of the temple (1 Kings viii. 56). What monuments were constructed and institutions established in order to commemorate the faithfulness of Jehovah! And we to whom "the fulness of the time" is come, ould surely tune our harps to louder, nobler anthems, by reason of the more excellent gifts poured upon us from the treasury of Infinite Love, in accordance with His prophecies. " Praise our God all ye people! " His glory and our welfare concur in demanding this tribute of gratitude.

THIS SUBJECT RAISES OUR THOUGHT TO HEAVEN, as the place to which perfect rest and enjoyment of our inheritance are reserved. We have here " the spirit of promise as the earnest of our inheritance until the redemption of our purchased possession." This is the morning twilight, that the noon; this the portico, that, the inner palace; this the foretaste, that the banquet; this the type, that the reality. Here " we groan being burdened," there we have the house eternal, the body that is the out-flashing glory of the spirit. Here we slake our thirst and appease our hunger, and soon we crave again; there "they hunger no more, neither thirst any more," for the Lamb doth feed them, and lead them to living fountains of water. Here we revive under the physician's touch, and fall ill again; there the inhabitants never have to say, "I am sick."—A.

Ver. 45.—*God's faithfulness.* This cannot mean that the Divine plan in reference to Israel's possession of the land was now in all respects completely fulfilled. The Canaanite still dwelt in certain parts of it, and was never really cast out. But in the main the work was done. The country, as a whole, was subdued, and the invaders no longer had any formidable opposition to contend with. Moreover, God's part in the work was fully accomplished. Whatever partial failure there may have been was due to Israel's faithlessness and weakness. There was no failure in God. He had been inflexibly true to His purpose. His word had not been broken. " There failed not ought," &c. The absolute fidelity of God to His purposes and promises is our theme. Let us take a broad view of it.

I, THE GENERAL CONSTITUTION AND ORDER OF THE UNIVERSE ILLUSTRATES THE DIVINE FAITHFULNESS. The universe of being is but an embodiment of the thought of God. A Divine purpose governs every part of it. His laws are not only expressions of His will, but are of the nature of pledges and promises, and no law is ever frustrated, no promise ever broken. They partake of the eternal steadfastness of His essential Being. " They stand fast for ever and ever, and are done in truth and uprightness." (1) *It is so in the material realm.* Physical laws are simply the impress of the eternal mind on matter and the method by which that Mind sees fit to mould and govern it. The " course of nature " is but a continual unfolding of the steadfast thought and purpose of God. The world passed through many structural changes before it was trodden by the foot of man, and has passed through many since, but the laws that govern it have been the same from the beginning. Ages pass before those laws are discovered, but they existed of old. Great liberty of action is given to man within the natural order, but he cannot change it in one iota. It is a rock against which the waves of his self-will and vain ambition only dash themselves in pieces—so beneficent and yet so terrible in its inflexibility; rewarding his trust, yet rebuking his presumption; inflicting on his ignorance and feebleness so severe a penalty, and yet guarding and befriending it. Our place in this great system of things is that of learners. Our highest science and skill are but a feeble answer to its truth and certainty. Life proceeds on the principle of trust in the constancy of nature, which is but another name for the faithfulness of God. (2) *It is so in the moral sphere.* The material order is but the shadow and reflection of the moral. Moral laws belong to a world not of shadows and appearances, but of substantial and enduring reality. " The things that are seen are temporal," &c. If there is fixity in the principles that govern the outer, how much more in those that govern the inner, life of man. Our earthly existence is a restless ebb and flow of circumstance and feeling. No two human histories, no two social situations, events, experiences, are alike. And yet there is " nothing new under the sun." " That which hath been is now " &c. (Eccl. iii. 15). As the kaleidoscope, out of a few simple shapes and colours, presents ever-changing forms of beauty to the eye, so does the revolution of our days and years embody in an endless variety of forms the primary principles and laws that govern our moral life. Those laws partake of the nature of the Lawgiver. They change not, " fail not," because He is " without variableness," &c. Whether as regards the threatening of evil or the promise of good, all infallibly " come to pass." Conceive it in a single case to be otherwise, and the whole moral system of things is involved in utter confusion and hopeless ruin.

II. The sphere of fulfilled prophecy illustrates it. Prophecy, as at once an inspiration and a revelation, is essentially supernatural, Divine. As regards its predictive element, it is as a passing gleam of light from the Infinite Intelligence, to which all things, past, present, and future, are alike " naked and opened." The prophet, as a seer, is one for whom God's own hand has for a moment lifted the veil of the future. Every really prophetic word is thus a Divine pledge, and its fulfilment is the redemption of that pledge. Biblical revelations from the beginning breathe the spirit of prophecy, and biblical history is rich in the verification of it. What is the whole career of Israel—its national existence, its captivities and deliverances, the advent of Messiah and His glorious kingdom, the after destiny of the Hebrew people—but the translation of prophecy into history ? Thus does age after age present some new testimony to the truth and faithfulness of God. Dispensations change, the generations come and go, but His purposes move on steadily to their accomplishment. " Not one faileth." Heaven and earth may pass away, but His word shall not pass away.

III. The covenant of grace illustrates it. In this the covenant made with Abraham found its consummation (Gen. xxii. 18). David died in the calm, glad faith of it. " Yet hath He made with me an everlasting covenant, ordered in all things and sure" &c. (2 Sam. xxiii. 5). Having its birth in the depths of a past, eternity, being no mere " after thought," it was manifested " in the fulness of time " in Him " in whom all the promises of God are yea and amen." His blood is the seal of the everlasting covenant. In Him God " performed the mercy promised to the fathers," and " the word that He spake by the mouth of His holy prophets since the world began." And as all foregoing ages foreshadowed it, so do the after ages give ever accumulating witness to its truth and certainty. Every earnest Christian life—every reward of obedient faith, every answered prayer, every new victory over death—confirms it. Our fathers trusted in it and were not put to shame. They passed peacefully away with its language on their lips, and the hope of immortality it enkindled in their hearts. We ourselves are learning more and more daily how worthy it is of our trust. And we know that when the tale of our changeful life is told, and we also shall have passed away, our children will enter into the inheritance of blessing with the " long interest " of added years: " heirs together with us of the grace " it reveals.

> " The words of God's extensive love
> From age to age endure ;
> The angel of the covenant proves
> And seals the blessing sure."

" All flesh is grass, and all the glory of man as the flower of grass. The grass withereth, and the flower thereof falleth away; but the word of the Lord endureth for ever. And this is the word which by the gospel is preached unto you " (1 Peter i. 24, 25).—W.

Vers. 43—45.—" The Lord is not a man that He should lie, or the Son of Man that He should repent." His promises are " yea and amen." This is the great truth brought home to us by the beautiful conclusion of the partition of the land of Canaan. " The Lord gave to Israel all the land which He sware to give unto their fathers. There failed not ought of any good thing which the Lord had spoken unto the house of Israel; all came to pass " (vers. 43, 45). Heaven and earth may pass away, but the word of the Lord must stand. (1) *His word cannot return to Him void; for it is always instinct with vital power.* " In the beginning was the Word ; and the Word was with God ; and the Word was God." God spoke, and a world sprang into being. Every word of prophecy has been fulfilled in the history of our race. His promises in like manner can never be empty words—they must have an answering reality. (2) He is *the God of truth,* ever faithful to Himself. (3) He is the *God of love,* and His love cannot belie itself. (4) He is *the God of eternal ages.* To Him there is no interval between the promise and its fulfilment ; it is to our apprehension only that the promise tarries. The new Israel may say, like Israel of old, " Not one good word has failed of all that He has spoken." The covenant of grace is a new land of promise. In it the Church has found a settled abiding place : it has overcome its adversaries and shall go on conquering and to conquer. So also shall it be with the third great land of promise, the heavenly Canaan. Upon this inheritance shall the redeemed at last enter singing, with a new meaning, this old song of triumph : " The Lord hath given us rest round about, according to all that He sware unto our fathers " (ver. 44).—E. DE P.

EXPOSITION.

CHAPTER XXII. 1—34.

Ver. 1.—**The Reubenites and the Gadites.** According to the Hebrew idiom, these are in the original in the singular, as in Gen. xii. 6. Thus a tribe, as has been before remarked, or even a family (ch. vi. 25), is spoken of frequently as a single individual (cf. ch. xvii. 14, 15, 17, 18). It seems probable that this chapter occurs in strict chronological order, and that the soldiers of the two tribes and a half remained under the national banner at Shiloh until the work of survey and appointment was completed. But this cannot be affirmed with certainty. The word אָז with which the chapter commences, is not the usual word for chronological sequence, though it does not preclude it (see note on ch. viii. 30). And the time during which these soldiers must in this case have remained separated from their wives and families was a very long one. Some have even supposed that it lasted fourteen years (see ver. 3). On the other hand, the words " gathered together to Shiloh," in ver. 12, implies that the tribes west of Jordan had left Shiloh. Nor did there seem to be the least need for their services after the battle of Merom. We must be content to leave the matter in uncertainty, with the remark that if the armed men of the two tribes and a half did remain during this long period away from their homes, our sense of their ready obedience must be greatly enhanced, as also of the personal influence of the leader at whose instance they did so. **The half tribe of**

Manasseh. Some cities read שֵׁבֶט here for מַטֵּה, and as the tribe is spoken of in a political and not in a genealogical point of view, the reading, as far as internal considerations go, would seem preferable. The two words, however, are not always used with complete strictness, but are sometimes regarded as synonymous (see note on ch. xiii. 29).

Ver. 3.—**Many days** (see note on ver. 1). The expression in the original implies more, a *great many* days, the usual expression for a period of considerable length. Thus the military service of these tribes must under any circumstances have been a prolonged and arduous one, and they well deserved the encomiums which Joshua here lavishes upon them. It is a remarkable and almost inexplicable fact, that while the sojourn in the wilderness is represented as one long catalogue of murmurings, not one single complaint (unless we may call the gentle expostulation of the tribe of Joseph, in ch. xvii., a complaint) disturbs the peace of the tribes while Joshua led them. This remarkable consistency of the narrative throughout, so great a contrast to what precedes and what follows, and felt to be so by the writer (ch. xxiv. 31), is of itself no small pledge of the trustworthiness of the whole. A collector at random from various narratives, themselves to a considerable extent fictitious, could hardly have managed to cull portions which would form an harmonious whole. A writer who was inventing his details would hardly have thought of making his history so great a contrast to the rest of the history of Israel, save with the idea of exalting the character of his hero. But there is no attempt to set Joshua above Moses, or any other Jewish leader. In fact, it is an argument for the early composition of the book that there is no reference, not even an allusion, to any later events in the history of Israel. Why there was this marked difference between Israel under Joshua, and Israel at any other time, is a question somewhat difficult to determine. Yet we may believe that it was the evidence of visible success. While the Israelites were wandering in the wilderness, they felt keenly, as men accustomed to a civilised and settled life, the inconveniences of a nomad existence. By their mingled impatience and cowardice they had forfeited their claim to God's protection. Even the observance of their feasts, and still further the rite of initiation into the covenant itself, were in abeyance (see notes on ch. v. 2—8). So uncertain, humanly speaking, was their future, that it was as difficult a task, and one the successful accomplishment of which was above unassisted human powers, for Moses to keep them together in the wilderness, as it was for Joshua to lead them to victory in the promised land. And it is one of the commonest of Christian experiences, both in the history of individuals and of the Christian Church, that times of prosperity are times of content and outward satisfaction. It is the times of adversity that try men's faith and patience. As long as the Israelitish Church was subduing kingdoms, winning splendid victories, experiencing the encouragement derivable from God's sensible presence and intervention, there was no discontent, discouragement, or wavering. But the trials of the long wandering, as well as those incident to the quiet, unostentatious discharge of duty, were fatal to their faith and patience. Can theirs be said to be a singular history? **Kept the charge.** The words in the original have reference to the punctual discharge of a duty entrusted to a person to fulfil. It may be rendered, "kept the observance of the commandment." This commandment, as we have before seen, was given in Num. xxxii. (see also ch. i. 12—18).

Ver. 4.—**Given rest.** LXX. κατέπαυσε, the word used in Heb. iv. 8.

Ver. 5.—**But take diligent heed.** This passage is a quotation from the Book of Deuteronomy (chs. vi. 5; x. 12; xi. 13, 22; xxx. 6, 16, 20, &c.) The expressions, as Keil well remarks, are "crowded together, so that obedience to God's commands may be the more deeply impressed on their hearts." It is worthy of remark, that while beginning with the love of God, Joshua does

not end there. The best proof of love is our conduct towards the person loved. If love be genuine, it is the practical principle which produces diligent service, punctual obedience, faithful attachment, the devotion of the heart and soul. **Commandment and law.** The first of these words, derived from a root signifying to *set up*, has rather the force of what we call a *positive* precept, referring to single acts. The word translated *law*, derived from the root to *cast*, hence to stretch out the hand, to point out, refers rather to *moral* precepts. The Greek νόμος and our *law* are used in the same sense. **Cleave unto Him.** The Hebrew is stronger, cleave *into* Him, as though regarding not so much isolated actions as principles of life. Our life was to be " rooted and grounded," to use an apostolic phrase, in His. But the full significance of these words could not be understood till One had come who enabled us by faith to " eat His flesh and drink His blood," and so be united to Him as the branch to its root.

Ver. 6.—**To their tents.** It would seem that, during the whole of these " many days," the conquered cities had remained tenantless, waiting for the return of the warriors from their long expedition. " Those that were first in the assignment of the land were last in the enjoyment of it; so ' the last shall be first and the first last,' that there may be something of equality " (Matthew Henry). The first part of the quotation is due to Bishop Hall, who also says, " If heaven be never so sweet to us, yet may wee not runne from this earthen warfare till our great Captaine shall please to discharge us."

Ver. 7.—**Now to the one half of the tribe of Manasseh.** We have here, as Keil remarks, a specimen of our author's habit of repetition. Four times do we read (chs. xiii. 14, 33; xiv. 3; xviii. 7) that the Levites were to have no share in the division of the land. Four times (in chs. xiii. 8; xiv. 3; xviii. 7, and here) does he repeat that the tribe of Manasseh was divided into two, and had its inheritance on either side Jordan. The same kind of repetition occurs in the narrative of the passing of the Jordan. It has been before remarked to be a characteristic of the style of the Old Testament generally, but nowhere is it found to a greater degree than in the Book of Joshua. Yet this, to which critics of the analytical school have objected as a sign of spuriousness, is in fact one of those peculiarities of style which mark the individuality of the writer. It is to inspired history what the Gospel and Epistles of St. John are to inspired theology. The form belongs to the author; the matter, at least as regards its general purport, belongs to God. A Hebrew writer, we are reminded in the 'Speaker's Commentary,' does not quote or refer to what has been already stated. If it is necessary to make his narrative clear, he repeats it.

Ver. 8.—**Riches.** The word here used is an uncommon one, and occurs only here and in the later Hebrew. **Divide the spoil of your enemies with your brethren.** This was the just reward for their toils. And here, as elsewhere, we may observe the strict and scrupulous integrity of Joshua. The division of the spoil by other leaders has often been the cause of heart-burnings and even of mutiny. Here each man has his due, and no room is left for reproach or dissatisfaction.

Ver. 9.—**Out of Shiloh.** See note on ver. 1. **In the land of Canaan.** To distinguish it from Gilead, the land of their possession, on the other side of Jordan. **Whereof they were possessed.** Another instance of that repetition which was according to the genius of the Hebrew language.

Ver. 10.—**The borders of Jordan.** Literally, the *circles* (cf. notes on ch. xiii. 2; xviii. 17; xx. 7; xxi. 32). Conder suggests *downs*, and it is most probable that the word refers to curved outlines, such as we frequently see in the hollows of our own chalk downs, or in any place where the strata do not yield easily to the action of water, and yet have been moulded by such action. **That are in the land of Canaan.** Again the intention is to lay stress upon the fact that the historian is still speaking of the country west of Canaan. **A great altar to see to.** Literally, *an altar great to sight, i.e.,* large and visible from a great distance. Bishop Horsley, however, would render a great altar *in appearance*, supposing that what is meant is that it only looked like an altar, and was not intended to be used as one. One of the most valuable results of the Palestine exploration movement has been the discovery of the site of this altar, which seems probable, in spite of Lieutenant Conder's abandonment of the theory in his 'Tent Work in Palestine,' ii. 53. The reasons for the identification are as follows. The altar must be near one of the fords of Jordan. It must be on this side of Jordan (see note on vers. 24, 25). It must be in a conspicuous position, as we have just seen. Now Kurn Sartabeh or Surtubeh (see note on ch. iii. 16), visible from a great distance on all sides, from Ebal, from near Gennesaret, thirty miles off, from the Dead Sea, from the eastern high lands, and from the Judæan watershed (see Quarterly Paper of the Palestine Exploration Fund, Oct. 1874), fulfils all these

conditions. Dr. Hutchinson replies (Quarterly Paper, Jan. 1876) that the altar is stated by Josephus to have been on the east side of Jordan, and that it was improbable that the two and a half tribes would have erected the altar on the cis-Jordanic territory, or so near to Shiloh, because Ephraim would have resented this. Moreover, the words, " a great altar *to be seen*," would imply that it was to be visible from a long distance, so that the two tribes and a half might see it from their side of Jordan. It must be confessed that the evidence for the identification is but slight, but so also are the arguments against it. For (1) Josephus is not infallible, and the Hebrew text seems to assert the very opposite of what he says. And (2) the other tribes *did* resent the erection of the altar. Lieutenant Conder now admits that it is possible that the words stating that the tribes crossed "by the passage of the children of Israel " (ver. 11, but see note there) leads to the idea that the ford by Jericho is meant, and not the Damieh ford by Kurn Sartabeh. See, however, the translation given below. The fact that the Arabs call the place the ascent of the father of Ayd, which has a close resemblance to the Hebrew word *Ed*, " witness," does not appear conclusive, though it lends some degree of probability to the theory. On the other hand, it might be contended that if the Reubenites and Gadites had not erected the altar on their own territory, it would not have excited the wrath of the remaining tribes. But as the best authorities are content to leave the matter uncertain, it must be left uncertain here.

Ver. 11. — **Half tribe of Manasseh.** Throughout this part of the narrative, when the body politic, rather than the descent of the tribe, is to be indicated, we have, not מַטֶּה, but שֵׁבֶט. See above, ch. xiii. 29. **An altar.** The original has *the* altar. **Over against.** אֶל־מוּל. It is difficult to fix the meaning of this expression. מוּל seems to have meant the *front* of anything, and therefore אֶל־מוּל would naturally mean *towards* the front of, or *in* front of. Thus we have had the expression in ch. viii. 33 (where see note), where it seems to mean, *in the direction of*, and in ch. ix. 1, where it seems to have the same meaning. With verbs of motion it signifies *towards*, as in Exod. xxxiv. 3, and 1 Sam. xvii. 30. Here it clearly cannot be pressed to mean *across* Jordan. See note below. **The borders of Jordan.** As above, ver. 10, the *circles* of Jordan. **At the passage of the children of Israel.** The word translated "the passage of," literally, "unto over," has originally the sense of " across,"

Here, however, it means "*towards the region opposite to the sons of Israel*," i.e., *in the direction of* the country on the other side Jordan. The country across Jordan was usually designated as בְּעֵבֶר or מֵעֵבֶר Jordan. אֶל־עֵבֶר, the phrase used here, we find in Exod. xxviii. 26, apparently in the sense of *across* (so Exod. xxxix. 19). In Deut. xxx. 13 it is used of moving in the direction of a place, "across" or "over the sea." In Ezekiel i. 9, 12, with the addition of פָּנָיו, the phrase means "straight forward." In 1 Sam. xiv. 40 לְעֵבֶר אֶחָד means "on one side." In 1 Kings vii. 20 לְעֵבֶר means "over." Thus the altar was not necessarily on the other side Jordan.

Ver. 12.—**Gathered themselves together at Shiloh.** The commentators refer here to Levit. xvii. 8, 9, and Deut. xii. 4—14. See also Levit. xvii. 4. The punishment for the sin is to be found in Deut. xiii. 12—16. We have before remarked (note on ver. 3) upon the singular obedience of the Israelites during the life of Joshua. The present incident is another exemplification of the fact. It is not Joshua who summons the children of Israel, it is they who voluntarily gather themselves together. The solemn provisions of the law have been infringed, they hasten at once, if necessary, to put the law in execution. The vivid sense of the triumphs they had enjoyed under Joshua, and the safety in which they now were enabled to dwell, filled their hearts with a strong, if short-lived, feeling of gratitude to Him who had done so great things for them, and of indignation against his foes. We may here observe two points which demonstrate the consistency of the narrative, and are evidences for its genuineness. (1) The children of Israel were not remarkable for their obedience to the law, or to heaven-sent leaders. Both their previous and subsequent history forbid us to predicate for them the quality of obedience. Whence, then, comes this new-born and ephemeral "zeal for the Lord," which displays itself in such a remarkable manner on the present occasion? Whence, but from the long catalogue of splendid victories and wonderful Divine interpositions recorded in this book, and from the sense of security arising out of them? Whence, but from the great fear of the children of Israel that had fallen upon the inhabitants of Canaan, so that, to use the striking expression of our historian in ch. x. 21, "none moved his tongue against any of the children of Israel." (2) The offence and its penalty are recorded in the book of the law, and especially in the Book of Deuteronomy.

Unless, therefore, we are to conclude that all this history, in spite of its natural and life-like character, was entirely the invention of later ages, we can scarcely avoid the conclusion that Deuteronomy, as well as the other books of the Pentateuch, was in existence when these events occurred. For if not, where was the offence of the two tribes and a half? How was its gravity to be determined? What induced the rest of Israel, including apparently the other half of the tribe of Manasseh, to prepare for war with their brethren? The only rational explanation of the history is that the tribes beyond Jordan had contravened the provisions of the law of Moses, contained in the Book of Deuteronomy, and that the rest of Israel were preparing to inflict the punishment decreed in that law against such contravention. And these provisions and that punishment we find in the five books of that law as it is at present handed down to us. Our only alternatives, then, would seem to be, to reject the history, or to accept the law *in toto*. And if we take the former, we have to explain how it is that the law and the subsequent history, though entirely fabulous, came to be arranged into so harmonious and consistent a whole. **To go up to war against them.** Calvin blames the Israelites a little unjustly here. They did not act rashly, as he asserts. Though they prepared to visit the offence with instant chastisement, they gave their brethren an opportunity of explanation. And when that explanation was given, it proved so entirely satisfactory that all hostile intentions were laid aside. "Not onely wisdom, but charitie moved them to this message. For grant they had been guilty, must they perish unwarned? Peaceab'e meanes must first be used to recall them, ere violence be sent to persecute them" (Bp. Hall). It is to be feared that Christians have not always so restrained their impetuosity when the cry that the faith was in danger has been raised, and that the zeal, so well tempered by discretion, of the Israelitish congregation at this time, is an example of both qualities which puts many Christians to shame. Even Masius cautions us here that we should not "temere moveamur suspicionibus." But he derives hence an argument, and cites St. Augustine in favour of it, for the doctrine that heretics may be proceeded against by the civil sword. Knobel's remark upon this verse is a perfect gem of the "destructive criticism." The account of all Israel gathering together to war against the two tribes and a half "is unsuitable to the circumspect and mild Elohist." Are *all* writers of history, except those who have no battles or sieges to describe, rash and savage by nature? And even the "circumspect and mild Elohist," or a member of the Peace Society itself, might venture to describe a gathering which, though at first it assumed a warlike form, ended in mutual explanations and a perfect understanding. Of a very different stamp is Bp. Hall's apostrophe, "O noble and religious zeale of Israel! Who would think these men the sonnes of them that danced around the molten calf?"

Ver. 13.—**Phinehas the son of Eleazar the priest.** Their messenger was well chosen. He was the representative of the high priest, whose duty it was to call attention to all infringements of the law. He had proved his own fiery zeal for the purity of Israelitish faith and life by his conduct at a critical moment of his country-men's history, when Balaam's miserable intrigues had brought the Israelites to the brink of destruction (Num. xxv. 7). Such an envoy, if the trans-Jordanic tribes had indeed disobeyed God's command, was well qualified to bring them to a sense of their sin. Once again we find him in his proper position, at the head of the children of Israel (Judg. xx. 28), and that was when they were once more assembled to avenge the atrocious crime of the men of Gibeah.

Ver. 14.—**And with him ten princes.** Phinehas represented the tribe of Levi, the high priest being too great to permit of his forming part of such a deputation. The actual head of each tribe accompanied him; that is, the head of the family, as we should call it, in each tribe. This seems pre-ferable to Keil's idea, that some tribes were represented by a prince, and some by heads of families, which seems inadmissible from the fact that the Hebrew states that each tribe was represented in the same manner, נָשִׂיא אֶחָד נָשִׂיא אֶחָד. What is doubtless in-tended here is to emphasize the weight and importance of the deputation sent with Phinehas, a weight and importance be-fitting an embassy which might have to announce the determination to exterminate the two and a half tribes as completely as Jericho had been exterminated. The men-tion of *ten* princes shows that the cis-Jordanic half tribe of Manasseh was repre-sented. **Tribes.** The word here, after "father's house," is the genealogical מַטֶּה not the political שֵׁבֶט. **The thousands.** Or *families* (as in Judg. vi. 15; 1 Sam. x. 19). See however Introduction, p. xxix.

Ver. 16.—**Trespass.** The Hebrew word signifies to act deceitfully or faithlessly. It was an act of ingratitude towards the God who had established them in the good land in which they now found themselves. Such

ingratitude and desertion of God was equivalent to rebellion, the term used im-mediately afterwards. The embassy clearly assumed that the fault had been committed, and that it would be necessary to proceed to extremities. Yet, deeply moved as they were, they did not refuse to listen to reason, and rejoiced that it was not necessary to inflict the fearful vengeance which other-wise would have been their duty. How great a contrast is this to the readiness, nay, even the eagerness, which many own-ing the Christian name have displayed to destroy the body, and the soul also, if that were possible, of their brethren in Christ, who have been overtaken, or have been sup-posed to be overtaken, in a similar fault!

Ver. 17.—**Is the iniquity of Peor too little for us?** How natural the illustration in the mouth of the speaker! It was Phinehas who had avenged the iniquity of Peor, and arrested the judgment for that offence as it was about to fall. How natural that the occurrence should be, as it were, branded upon his memory with a hot iron, and that the mention of it should spring at once to his lips when he saw his brethren, as he thought, upon the verge of a similar offence! Peor is, of course, a contraction for Baal-Peor (Num. xxv. 3). This god derives his name probably from Mount Peor, or "the cloven mountain" (Num. xxiii. 28). **From which we are not cleansed until this day.** Here we have the expression of the feeling which was never removed until Christ came. It was not possible that the blood of bulls and of goats could take away sin. No ceremonial lustrations could "cleanse us from its guilt and power." No destruction of the prime mover of the offence, though it may avert the wrath of of God, can remove the moral reproach which lies upon the sinner. Not even the destruction of twenty-four thousand persons (Num. xxv. 9) can purify Israel from the taint of pollution. In the eyes of a sincere servant like Phinehas, the stigma rests upon Israel still, nor could anything avail to take it away. Truly, the law was, indeed, "our schoolmaster, to bring us to Christ." What Keil says of Calvin's explanation, that "the remembrance was not yet quite buried, nor the anger of God extinct," is unsatis-factory. His own explanation, that "the heart of Israel still delighted in their sin," is even more so, since we have no evidence whatever that this was the case at the time of which we are speaking. We have here again to remark that the history in Numbers is here presupposed, and an allusion to an incident in Numbers is here placed in the mouth of one of the chief actors in it. How natural, if the history be a veracious one!

How marvellously ingenious, if it be not! The circumstance is mentioned again in Hosea, in the time of Jotham or Hezekiah, and again in Psa. cvi., which would appear to have been written during the captivity. Thus we have a chain of testimony concerning it which makes it difficult to assign a time for the invention of the story, if it be invented, since all references to it in Scripture are perfectly consistent with each other, and display none of the signs of gradual growth which we invariably find in the case of legends. **A plague.** The original is noticeable, *the* plague; a natural mode of speech for one who well remembered it.

Ver. 18.—**But that ye must turn.** The original has the imperfect, of an action not completed, " *and* ye *are* turning." There is no need to give the adversative sense to ）. The *ye* also is emphatic. " *Ye* are turning against the Lord to-day, to-morrow ye will involve the whole congregation in calamity." **That to-morrow he will be wroth with the whole congregation of Israel.** This passage also is quite consistent with the circumstances and with the position of the speaker. Not merely anger but fear is visible throughout—fear of His wrath who had manifested His power so signally of late. There was no longer any temptation to rebel against Him. The Israelites were no longer suffering the daily pressure of comparative privation and distress, such as it was impossible to avoid in the wilderness. While, on the contrary, there was every reason to remember His power Who had driven the heathen out before them and planted them in, Who had not failed to punish them when they deserved it, and Who, by the fate of their enemies, had made it clear that His hands were not waxen short. Thus the heads of the tribes, and Phinehas especially, were alarmed lest Israel should forfeit the prosperity they at present enjoyed, and exchange it for those terrible woes that God had shown He could inflict when His people rebelled against Him.

Ver. 19.—**If the land of your possession be unclean.** Rather, *be defiled*, either by the idolatrous nations around, or by being cut off from the worship of the true God at Shiloh. The only satisfactory explanation of this somewhat difficult passage which has yet been given is that of Masius, who explains it of a possible belief on the part of the two and a half tribes, that they were cut off by Jordan into another land, a land which had no title to the promises and privileges of Israel, no share in the worship of the one true God at Shiloh. If they entertained such an idea, then, however unfounded their conviction, it were better

far to abandon the land, how suited to their circumstances soever it might be, and come across the Jordan, and dwell in the midst of their brethren, and under the protection of the tabernacle of the Lord. **Beside.** That is, *separate from*, suggesting the idea of an exclusion of those who committed such an act from the worship of the Lord.

Ver. 20.—**Did not Achan the son of Zerah.** Here again the reference to the past history of Israel is suited to the speaker and the circumstances, and this appeal, therefore, strengthens our conviction that in the history of Achan we have fact and not fiction. The case of Achan is even more in point than that of Peor. In his case the Israelites had a clear proof that "one man's sin," unless completely and absolutely put away, brought God's displeasure on " all the congregation " (Num. xvi. 22). The repulse at Ai, fresh as it must have been in the memory of all, was sufficient evidence of this. How much more then would His displeasure fall upon Israel, if they condoned this act (as it seemed) of gross and open rebellion against the Lord who had brought them out of Egypt, and had put them in possession of the land He had promised them ? **Commit a trespass** (see note on ver. 16). **In the accursed thing** (see note on ch. vii. 1). **And that man perished not alone in his iniquity.** Literally, *and he*, one man, *did not expire in his iniquity*. The Vulgate has, " and he was one man, and would that he had perished alone in his iniquity." The sense is the same as in our version. Achan did not perish alone, for not only did he involve his family in his ruin, but the loss of life at the first assault of Ai lay also at his door (see ch. vii. 5).

Ver. 21.—**The thousands.** See above, ver. 14.

Ver. 22.—**The Lord God of gods.** The double repetition of this adjuration is suited to the greatness of the occasion. No words can suffice to express the horror and detestation of the two and a half tribes at the sin of which they have been supposed guilty. Nor does our version at all approach the majesty of the original form of oath. The Vulgate and Luther approach nearer to it when they render the one, " fortissimus Deus Dominus," and the other, " der starke Gott, der Herr." But no translation can do justice to the vigour of the original. The three names of God, El, Elohim, and Jehovah, are each twice repeated in their order. El representing the earliest Hebrew idea of God, strength (as that of the Aryans was splendour) comes first. Then Elohim, with its *pluralis excellentiæ*, suited to a nation whose theological horizon was expanding, and suggesting the manifold ways in which El the mighty one displayed His greatness, as the source of all power, mental, moral, and physical, in heaven and in earth. Then came the name by which He had revealed Himself to Moses, Jehovah, the Self-existent One, the author of all being, He whose supreme prerogative it was to have existed from all eternity, and from whose will all things were derived. It was impossible for any Israelite to have devised a more awful formula by which to clear themselves from the charge of rebellion against God. The same striking phrase is adopted by Asaph in the fiftieth Psalm, when he desires to give especial emphasis to the words of God which follow. Some of the Rabbis interpret Elohim here of angels, and explain, "the God of angels." Dr. Perowne, on Psa. l. i., prefers the LXX. θεὸς θεῶν. Lange, on this passage, translates feebly, "God, God Jehovah," but he abandons this in his commentary on Psa. l. for the interpretation given above. Ewald prefers the LXX. rendering. Vaihinger suggests, "the mighty God Jehovah." But the majority of recent commentators prefer the rendering given above, and it is supported by Jewish authorities of credit (cf. Jer. xxxii. 14 ; Neh. ix. 32). **He knoweth**. These words are in the strictest Hebrew form of the present tense. It is not merely implied that " God knows " as a general fact, but He is called to witness in the most emphatic manner. " He is at this moment aware that we are speaking the truth." **Save us not this day**. These words are not parenthetical, as in our version, but in their eagerness to clear themselves (another fact of vivid narration not to be lost sight of, as indicating that the information came originally from an eye-witness) they change the construction. " El Elohim Jehovah, El Elohim Jehovah, He is witness, and Israel shall know—if in rebellion, and if in transgression against the Lord, mayest Thou not save us this day—to build an altar to us, to turn from after the Lord." The whole sentence betokens the strong agitation of those who uttered it—" ex vehementissima animi perturbatione effundunt illi potiusquam pronunciant " (Masius)—and to whatever period we may attribute the composition of the Book of Joshua, there can be little doubt that he had access to authentic documents, written by eye-witnesses of the scenes that are described. Rosenmüller discusses another interpretation, which regards these words as an address to Phinehas ; but while admitting that it is a possible one, rejects it as less suitable to the context. Besides, it may be remarked that " save us " can only be addressed to

God. To man, " spare us " would have been said.

Ver. 23.—**Let the Lord himself require it.** Or, *the Lord, He shall exact, i.e.*, the penalty.

Ver. 24.—**From fear of this thing.** This translation cannot be correct. Had the Hebrew original intended to convey this meaning, we should have had מִדְּאָגַת הַדָּבָר הַזֶּה. The literal rendering is, "from anxiety, from a word." The word here translated "anxiety" (LXX. εὐλάβεια) is applied to the sea, and is translated " sorrow" in Jer. xlix. 23. It is translated " heaviness " in Prov. xii. 25. In Ezek. iv. 16 ; xii. 18, 19, it is translated " care," " carefulness," and is applied to eating food. It obviously refers to agitation or anxiety of mind, and the proper translation here is, " we did it out of anxiety, for a cause." So Masius and Rosenmüller, who render the word דְּאָגָה here by *sollicitudo*.

Ver. 24, 25.—**What have you to do with the Lord God of Israel ? For the Lord hath made Jordan a border.** Literally, *What to you and to Jehovah the God of Israel, since He hath given a border between us and between you, sons of Reuben and sons of Gad, even the Jordan.* Thus the reason for the erection of the altar was the very converse of what it had been supposed to be. So far from considering themselves as shut out from the communion of Israel by the natural boundary formed by Jordan, the two and a half tribes were resolved that no one else should ever think so. If the descendants of the remainder of the Israelites should ever venture to assert anything of the kind, there was the altar, erected in a conspicuous position on the west side of Jordan, left as a perpetual memorial of the great struggle in which Reuben, Gad, and the half tribe of Manasseh had taken part, and which had resulted in the final occupation of the land of Canaan. Keil and Delitzsch remark that there was some reason for this anxiety. The promises made to Abraham and his posterity related only to the land of Canaan. For their own advantage these tribes had chosen to remain in the trans-Jordanic territory conquered by Moses. It was quite possible that in future ages they might be regarded as outside the blessings and privileges of the Mosaic covenant. For the present, at least, they valued those blessings and privileges, and desired to have some permanent memorial of the fact that they had a right to share them. **From fearing.** It may be worth while to notice, as a sign of later, or at least of different authorship, that the Pentateuch employs a different (the feminine) form of the infinitive for the form found here.

Ver. 26.—**Let us now prepare to build us an altar.** Literally, *let us make now to build to us an altar.* **Burnt offering, nor for sacrifice.** In the " burnt offering " the whole victim was consumed. In the " sacrifice " part only was offered on the altar. The rest was eaten by the priest or the person who offered it.

Ver. 27.—**But that it may be a witness.** Rather, *for this altar is a witness before Him.* Literally, *before His face;* in the tabernacle, that is, where His special presence was enshrined.

Ver. 28.—**Behold the pattern.** Rather, *Look at* this *fac-simile.* The Hebrew is even stronger than our version. The existence of an exact reproduction of the altar in Shiloh, erected on Canaanitish ground by the two and a half tribes before their departure across Jordan, was an incontestible proof of their original connection with Israel. And the fact that they had erected it, not on their own territory, but on that of their brethren, was, though they do not use the argument, proof positive that it was not intended to be used in contravention of the precepts of the law. The nature of the *fac-simile* is explained by Exod. xx. 24, where the precise form of altar seems to have been presented as a contrast to the stone altars employed by the heathen.

Ver. 29.—**God forbid.** Literally, *profane* or accursed to us be it from Him. So Keil, Gesenius, and Knobel. **That we should rebel against the Lord.** The embassy had the effect not only of eliciting an explanation, but of showing how earnest, at that time at least, the tribes of Israel were in the service of God. And we may learn here, as Robertson remarks of St. Paul's frank and explicit vindications of himself, the value of explanations. Many a misunderstanding would be averted, many a feeling of rankling displeasure, culminating in an inexcusable explosion of anger, might be avoided, nay, many an unjust suspicion against a fellow Christian's honesty and sincerity of purpose might be dispelled, if men would but follow the example of the ten tribes on this occasion, or lay to heart the words of our Lord in St. Matt. xviii. 15, " If thy brother shall trespass against thee, go and tell him his fault between thee and him alone ; if he shall hear thee, thou hast gained thy brother."

Ver. 30.—**It pleased them.** The genuineness of their zeal for God's service is shown by their readiness to be appeased by a plain explanation. Had they been actuated by jealousy or party spirit, they would have admitted no defence, or have endeavoured out of the clearest exculpation to find some new topic for complaint. So religious party spirit has been wont to inflame men's minds in later times, so that they desired rather victory over a supposed antagonist than the discovery that no offence at all had been committed. True religious zeal is slow to anger, and easy to be appeased, when it appears that no harm has been intended. It might have been contended in this case, if controversy rather than truth had been the object, that the action had a dangerous tendency ; that though the altar was not intended for sacrifice, it might be used for that purpose ; that it was unwise to put a temptation in the way of future ages to substitute worship there for worship in the tabernacle. Such arguments are not unknown even to Christian zealots. Israel was satisfied that no harm was intended. It was not thought necessary to point out possibilities which were not likely to be realised.

Ver. 31.—**Now ye have delivered the children of Israel out of the hand of the Lord.** The word here rendered " now " is rather *then*. But the Hebrew word, like our own, is used as implying not only consecution of time, but consequence of action (see Psa. xl. 8; lxix. 5 ; Jer. xxii. 15). Thus the meaning here is, " We see, then, that instead of bringing upon us heavy chastisement, as we had feared, ye have acted in a way which secures us from the punishment of which we were afraid.

Ver. 33.—**Did not intend.** Literally, *did not speak.* That is, no one, after the explanation, was found to support the proposal which had previously been found to be necessary.

Ver. 34.—**Ed.** This word is not in the original. It is found in some late MSS. and in the Syriac and Arabic versions, but not in the LXX. or Chaldee. Even in the MSS. which have it, the word is found sometimes before and sometimes after the Hebrew word signifying " altar." This may either be because, once omitted, it was conjecturally supplied, but it is more probable that it was never there at all. The passage may be rendered, "And the sons of Reuben and the sons of Gad gave a name to the altar, ' for it is a witness between us.'" But it seems more likely that the word " Ed," though not expressed, is intended to be understood. The LXX. and Vulgate give incorrect renderings of the passage. **The Lord is God.** Rather, as in 1 Kings xviii. 39, Jehovah is the God ; that is, the one true God. Some MSS. have interpolated הוּא here from the above cited passage. Such altars, or mounds, of witness seem not to have been unusual among the Eastern nations (see Gen. xxxi. 47—52).

HOMILETICS.

Vers. 1—34.—*Reuben and Gad and the half-tribe of Manasseh at home.* Three points are especially noticeable in this chapter. First, the reward of those who have laboured on behalf of their brethren; next, the duty of claiming our privileges as Christians when severed from our brethren; and lastly, the necessity of zeal for the purity of religion.

I. SELF-DENIAL SHALL HAVE ITS REWARD. Our Lord tells us that he who gives a cup of cold water to his brother shall not lose his reward. We find a similar statement in Matt. x. 41. The reward includes this life as well as the next (Mark x. 30). Joshua blessed the two tribes and a half, and sent them to their inheritance. So does Jesus say to those who have laboured in His cause, "Well done, thou good and faithful servant, enter thou into the joy of the Lord." And as the Reubenites and their brethren were blessed with silver and gold and a multitude of earthly possessions, so the Christian enjoys riches which are far above what earth can give, even the riches of the glory of God's inheritance among the saints. If he leaves home and friends for the work of the Gospel; if he devotes himself to a long and weary warfare against sin, the time will come when the true Joshua will dismiss him to his inheritance, across the Jordan-stream of death.

II. WE MUST NOT LET ISOLATION DEPRIVE US OF THE PRIVILEGES OF THE COVENANT. Many an Englishman is in the position of the two tribes and a half. He emigrates to distant lands, and he often forgets to assert his oneness with those whom he has left behind. So did the members of the Church of England neglect in America to reproduce the organization of their native land. So continually do men (*a*) cast off all religious profession whatever, or (*b*) neglect to keep up sufficient connection with their brethren at home, and thus to keep up the solidarity and mutual brotherhood of Christian churches. Of late this evil has been much diminished. The "great altar to see to" is visible on all sides. Those who leave us for the colonies, or for foreign lands, are not left without the ministrations of their own nation and faith. Christians deprived of the superintendence of the ministers of religion assemble for prayer and reading of the Scriptures. Thus a witness is set up before God and man that they have both part and lot in the Christian brotherhood. It is the one worship of the one God. There is no desire to set up altar against altar, to break the bonds of Christian love and fellowship. The new communion has its own laws and regulations, suited to its own peculiar needs, for the gospel practically forbids us to set up one hard and fast rule for all races and regions alike. But the one faith and the one Church exists throughout, united, not in the unity of external rules and rites, and organization and tribunals, but in the holy bond of truth and peace, of faith and charity.

III. WE MUST BE ZEALOUS FOR THE CAUSE OF TRUE RELIGION. Had the Jews continued to display the same zeal for God which they showed in this instance, they would have escaped the fall which afterwards befel them. So, had Christians maintained their first zeal and purity and mutual love, the Christian Church would have been spared much of its sad history, and so large a portion of the world would not have remained heathen. But as the Jews allowed mixed marriages and intercourse with heathen tribes to undermine their attachment to God and His law, so has familiarity with the world deadened the zeal for true religion among Christians. The zeal which was displayed in early Christian times concerned faith more than morals. The zeal shown now concerns morals rather than faith. But a true Christian spirit will care for both. Faith is the salt that keeps practice from corruption, and a carelessness or tendency to compromise in matters affecting the fundamental principles of Christian truth or worship is as sinful as would have been the conduct of the Israelites had they suffered the erection of the altar of witness to pass without explanation. Such a spirit of compromise is the danger of our own day. It is our duty (*a*) to decide for ourselves what *are* the essentials of Christianity, and (*b*) when we have decided it, to declare perpetual war against those who would deny them. While we are careful not to insist upon anything as essential which is not "contained in Scripture, or may be proved thereby," we must make the maintenance of the recognised truths of Christianity a *sine qua non*. The spirit abroad which maintains that no teacher should be removed from his post for any consideration whatsoever, is as opposed to truth as that which would remove him without fair trial or sufficient cause. The task of deciding on the limits of religious freedom is a difficult one, and demands exceptional gifts. But the denial that there *are* such limits is contrary to the main principles of law and gospel alike.

IV. WE ARE BOUND TO RESTRAIN ZEAL WITHIN PROPER BOUNDS. The Israelites did not proceed to action without due inquiry. They sent a deputation to their brethren to invite them to clear themselves if they could. And the result was an honourable acquittal, though there was a strong *prima facie* case against them. Would that all religious investigations had been as fair! For though the duty of maintaining the purity of the Christian faith is most undeniable, yet the converse is equally true, that we must be sure that it is the Christian faith that is at stake. The practice on the part of the mediæval Church authorities, of treating suspicion of heresy as a crime, was a violation of the commonest laws of justice. The practice of holding a teacher responsible for every inference which could be drawn by a merciless logic from his theses, although these conclusions are energetically repudiated by himself, was not the offspring of zeal for the truth, but of prejudice and passion. The custom of declaring views heretical which, though opposed to the voice of authority and the force of numbers, did not touch the essentials of the faith, was an outrage against Christian liberty, and a violation of the great principle laid down in this chapter, of subordinating the letter to the spirit. For the Reubenites and their brethren had unquestionably broken the *letter* of the law. The erecting of such an altar as they had erected was strictly forbidden. And yet by that very violation they had been proving their sincere adhesion to the spirit of the violated law. And their defence was not only accepted, but joyously and thankfully accepted (ver. 31). If in those days the spirit was set above the letter, how much more in our own. Let us take heed then that we do not, misled by blind party zeal, fall upon those who are our allies in the great and holy work. Let us not exact too strict a conformity with the letter of Holy Scripture, but let us seek hearts purified by love to God to discern its real spirit. It is no easy task, no doubt, but it may be performed through prayer and love to God and man. With hearts so filled with the sacred fire, it may well be that we shall often gather together to Shiloh ready and burning for the conflict, yet be appeased when we learn what seemed a foul wrong to God was inspired by the deepest devotion to His cause, and may say with Phinehas, whose zeal for the truth cannot be disputed, "This day we perceive that the Lord is among us, because ye have not committed this trespass against the Lord."

V. ALWAYS BELIEVE THE BEST. "Charity hopeth all things," says the apostle. The Lord Himself bade us always, when we had a cause of complaint against our brother, to begin by talking the matter over with Him. So also says the wise man in the Apocrypha, in words which well deserve to be remembered. "Admonish a friend, it may be he hath not done it, and if he have done it, that he do it no more. Admonish thy friend, it may be he hath not said it, and if he have, that he speak it not again. Admonish a friend, for many times it is a slander, and believe not every tale." It is *never* safe to neglect this counsel. The case may look very bad against your friend, but so it did against the two tribes and a half. In fact, in their case, nothing could be worse. They were caught *in flagrante delicto*. There was the altar, erected in a most conspicuous situation—a great altar *to be seen*. The Israelites might have argued that it was useless to ask explanations when they had the fact before their eyes. But they were not so rash. And the result showed that they would have been blameable indeed if they had been so precipitate. How many a friendship has been severed, how many a life-long estrangement has been caused, how much misery has been brought about, by the want of courage to go frankly to a friend and ask for an explanation of what seems indefensible. You may have your testimony from unimpeachable witnesses, or witnesses you believe to be unimpeachable, and if in truth they are not slanderers, or mischief makers, they may yet not be in possession of certain material facts which give the case an altogether different aspect. At least the rule is clear—never condemn any one unheard. Wounded feeling or offended pride may make us averse to seek the explanation; the effort may be painful, almost intolerable, yet justice demands that it should be made. And you may afterwards have reason to "bless God" that you did not "go up against your brother to battle." Either he may repent, and then "thou hast gained thy brother," or he may never have offended, and then the bonds of Christian friendship will never be relaxed at all.

HOMILIES BY VARIOUS AUTHORS.

Ver. 30.—*A misunderstanding.* Rarely do we find such an instance of misconception as is here recounted. The two and a half tribes, whose territory lay to the west of Jordan, had acted with the highest honour. During the five or six years occupied in the conquest of their land, they had voluntarily accepted the task of fighting—and fighting in the van in all the battles of Israel. When they leave a completed task behind them, they return laden with spoil: rich in the gratitude of their brethren; solemnly blessed by Joshua. And yet within a few weeks, all their brethren—including those of their own tribes who had settled to the west of Jordan —are up in arms, ready to exterminate them. All this change is brought about by one of the most deplorable things in life—A MISUNDERSTANDING. Such things happen still, and it may illustrate and remove some of them if we observe the course of this. In the misunderstanding before us, we observe, first—
I. THE INNOCENT CAUSE. The two and a half tribes were, as they explain, solicitous to keep in unity with Israel. The possibility of their being treated as outsiders weighed on them. The erection of an altar precisely the same in pattern with that in the tabernacle struck them as a means of embodying a testimony that they had enjoyed the same access to the sanctuary with their brethren on the west of Jordan. By weighty precepts, Moses had forbidden any multiplication of altars. One God, one worship, one people, was to be the rule : Levites in every tribe, sacrifice only in the central consecrated spot. They were alive to the sin of schism, and the wickedness of seceding from their people, and the thought of it does not enter their minds. They would have acted more wisely if they had consulted the priests first, explaining their desire and purpose. But their very innocence makes them neglect to take precautions against being misunderstood. So far from desiring to break, they are solicitous to keep the unity of Israel. And the altar which their brethren think will destroy was erected by them to keep it. Yet they are misunderstood. So shall we be, and so will others be by us. There is hardly a word we can speak but can carry two meanings, or an act we can do but can carry two aspects. And if we attempt by the avoidance of speech or action to escape misunderstanding the endeavour will be in vain. At the same time, the fact that a large proportion—say 75 per cent.—of misunderstandings have an innocent cause should set us on our guard against the next thing we observe here, viz.—
II. A HASTY CONSTRUCTION PUT UPON IT. How discreditable was this haste to assume that the worst explanation was the truest! If any part of the community had proved their patriotism, brotherliness, their honour, and their faith, it was these unselfish warriors who had laboured so generously for the general well-being. But haste always leaves its fair judgment at home. It argues from its fears, its temper, its prejudice, its suspicions. Judgment being a slow-moving thing, that does not come to conclusions quick enough for its purpose. And so here, instantly there is put upon this act the construction that it evinces a purpose of secession, first, from the religion, and, next, from the people of Israel. Israel is not the only community disposed to hasty and harsh constructions. There is in all of us a vile readiness to believe the worst of men; a certain disposition to chuckle over the discovery of what seems a fault; an evil suspicion, arrogating to itself peculiar wisdom, suggests always that the worst view must be true. Observe here, the hasty construction is

not only mistaken but utterly mistaken. It has concluded the very opposite of the truth. And our hasty constructions are not more accurate. Let us be on our guard. The truth may be the very opposite of what on the first blush it appears to be. What seems presumptuous and unholy may spring from the deepest devoutness. Observe thirdly—

III. A SENSIBLE INQUIRY. Phinehas, the high priest, and the ten princes of the nine and a half tribes are sent first of all to ask, " What trespass is this that ye have committed? " Some cooler heads and calmer hearts have suggested that before civil war be entered on there should be, at least, an explanation sought. None can cavil at a suggestion so prudent and pertinent. The best men for such a task are sent, not with weapons of war, but with words of peace—words still hasty and suspicious, but yet spoken in love and with a desire for the right. Then, for the first time, the two and a half tribes learn the evil construction which might be put on their deed. And the surprise with which they receive the accusation, convince all of their innocence of the things of which they were accused. *The simple inquiry* was all that was necessary to get the most perfect satisfaction. How many misunderstandings would at once be killed if men had just the courage to ask a question! But the suspicion which hastily concludes the worst is generally wedded to the cowardice which dare not ask if its conclusions are right, and so misunderstandings endure. If in a friend there is that which pains you, ask himself why he does it. Let the inquiry be a respectful one. *Let the priestly and princely part of your nature make it.* Let it be direct and full. Let no fear of being suspected to be yourself uncharitable permit you to be uncharitable. " If thy brother sin against thee, go and tell him his fault, between thee and him alone." If there was more of the manliness that would expostulate, there would be more of the saintliness that could forgive. Lastly, observe that the inquiry leads to—

IV. A HAPPY TERMINATION. There was every probability of the misunderstanding having a most disastrous termination. What would have been the issue of such a war? To crush a third part of Israel, and that the most warlike portion, would probably have cost the lives of another third ; and the remnant surviving would at once have been at the mercy of the remnants of the Canaanite still surviving, and able to form strong alliances with Phœnician and Philistine neighbours. *The extinction of Israel neither more nor less trembled on the verge of probability through this misunderstanding.* Blessed are the peacemakers. The inquiry elicits the most satisfactory facts. The momentary doubt of their brethren's good faith passes away. Their confidence in their faith and patriotism is resumed ; for many, many centuries mutual suspicion is destroyed, and Israel on both sides of Jordan is an undivided people. A little wisdom, a little delay in speech or action until knowledge becomes certainty, a brotherly approach to those who have offended us, might bring our most hopeless misunderstandings to the same satisfactory end.—G.

Vers. 1—4.—*Service and reward.* I. THE SERVICE. This is characterised by the following points of merit : 1. *Obedience to discipline.* The two tribes and the half tribe are commended for obedience to their supreme commanders. Soldiers, servants, employés, all persons under authority, should recognise the duty of loyal obedience from the heart, and perform it (*a*) conscientiously—" not with eye-service as men-pleasers ; " (*b*) diligently—working as laboriously as if for their own pleasure ; and (*c*) cheerfully. 2. *Brotherly-kindness.* These tribes had not left their brethren. They had been foremost in conquering Canaan for them. Humanity, patriotism, and Christianity should lead us to labour unselfishly for the welfare of the world, our country, and fellow Christians. 3. *Faithfulness to God.* These tribes had " kept the charge of the commandment of the Lord their God." We have a charge from God to keep. Our duty is not confined to our relations with men ; we have duties to God (Mal. i. 6). Even our duties to men should be discharged with a supreme regard to the will of God (Col. iii. 22), and our religious devotion should guide and inspire us in human duties.

II. THE REWARD. This is marked by the following features : 1. *It is delayed till the service is complete.* The Reubenites and their associates were the earliest tribes to have an inheritance apportioned to them; but they were the latest to enter into possession of it. Thus the first are last. We must not expect the rewards of faithfulness before our work is complete. It is wrong to desire to hasten to our heavenly reward at the neglect of earthly duty. The "rest which remaineth" is secure, though the enjoyment of it is delayed. The force of God's promises is not weakened by time. 2. *It is so appointed as to satisfy the desires of those who receive it.* The two tribes and the half tribe preferred to settle on the east of Jordan, and they were permitted to do so. As they chose for themselves they must take the consequences, whether for good or for ill. God allows us much liberty in shaping our own destinies. When He does not give us what we desire, the refusal is not arbitrary but merciful. In the end He will give us our heart's desire—either the thing we desire now, or something else to which He will incline our hearts, so that we shall desire *that.* As there are varieties of dispositions among Christians, so there will be differences in the heavenly reward. 3. *It takes the form of rest and peaceful occupation.* The army is disbanded. Warfare was a temporary necessity; it was not to be regarded as a constant occupation. Home-life is most natural and most blessed by God. The spiritual warfare of Christians is only temporary. It will be followed by (*a*) rest, (*b*) reunion, (*c*) the home-life of heaven.—W. F. A.

Ver. 5.—*Loyalty to God in separation from the Church.* I. THE CIRCUMSTANCES OF TRIAL. 1. *Isolation.* The Reubenites and their associates had chosen an inheritance which would separate them from their brethren. There was danger lest the separation should injure their fidelity to God. The influence of Christian example and the sympathy of the Church are great aids to devotion. When these are lost special care is needed to prevent devotion from growing cold. This applies (*a*) to those who go from their homes to business occupations which separate them from old religious associations, (*b*) to those who leave their country for the colonies. &c. 2. *Evil surroundings.* These tribes were about to settle amongst a heathen population. In addition to the loss of the good example of their brethren's devotion, they would become liable to the injurious influence of bad associates. If duty calls us to live amongst those whose lives are unchristian we need to be watchful against the fatal influence of their example. Lot was injured by living in Sodom. 3. *The cost of religious ordinances.* Though these tribes established worship for themselves, they must have missed the good of the tabernacle services. They who live beyond the reach of such religious ordinances as they have found profitable in the past—as in lonely country places, or the backwoods of colonies—should be on their guard against the spiritual deadness which may result unless they are assiduous in private devotion. The proximity of a suitable place of worship should be a first consideration in the choice of an abode. Convenience, society, health, beauty of situation are too often considered to the neglect of this important requisite. Heads of families should know how much this affects the character and destinies of their children.

I. THE DUTY OF LOYALTY. The duty is illustrated in various phrases that it may be made clear and be well insisted on. This is no small matter. It should engage our chief attention. Several points are here included, viz., 1. *Devotion of heart.* This is the root of true loyalty. It springs (*a*) from *personal love* to God, and cleaving to Him; (*b*) from the service of *inward desire*—serving with the heart; (*c*) from *thoroughness*—serving with the whole heart. 2. *Obedience in life.* This is "to walk in all His ways." True loyalty does not confine itself to the secret desires of the heart. It comes out in the life. There is not only seen in definite acts but in the general course of conduct. We are not to be faithful only in supreme moments, but to *walk* obediently—to continue a constant course of obedience. 3. *Diligence in fulfilling God's commands.* (*a*) These tribes were to *take heed.* We need thought to consider what is God's will, and care to see that we are doing it. (*b*) They were *to keep God's commandments.* The details of duty must be observed after we have cultivated the general spirit of devotion.—W. F. A.

Vers. 1—9.—We have seen the Reubenites and Gadites generously taking their part in the war for the conquest of Canaan, though they had already come into possession themselves of their assigned share on the other side of Jordan. In this way the solidarity of the nation was vindicated. Joshua now sends back these soldiers of their country to their own inheritance, and we see in the verses before us the reward of their fidelity to duty.

I. THEIR FIRST RECOMPENSE IS A MATERIAL ONE. They carry away a goodly share of the booty which accrued to Israel from its successful warfare. The man of God cannot always count upon this temporal reward. It may never be his. And yet it is certain that, as a general rule even in this life, the fulfilment of duty is a condition of prosperity. Evil gives only deceptive and evanescent joys; it is opposed to the Divine law, which must in the end prevail. It entails also terrible consequences. Is not all sensual indulgence a deadly and ruinous thing? Does not hatred kindle with its accursed torch fire and war, only to be quenched with blood? Does not the wicked dig the pit into which he himself falls (Psa. vii. 15). Punishment may tarry. Penalty is slow-footed, as Homer says, but it is guided by the unerring hand of Divine justice. The people who fear God and work righteousness are in the end always the blessed people, and the Psalmist rightly pronounces them happy.

II. The highest recompense is not however this material prosperity, BUT THE APPROVAL OF GOD. "Ye have kept," says Joshua to the Reubenites and Gadites, "all that Moses the servant of the Lord commanded you" (ver. 2). There can be no purer joy than to hear words like these from the Master's lips: "Well done, good and faithful servant, &c." (Matt. xxv. 21). They waken in the depths of our hearts the glad echo of an approving conscience. This is not the proud satisfaction of self-righteousness; it is the joy of having rejoiced the heart of God; of having done something for the Saviour; of having in some measure responded to the love freely received.

III. OBEDIENCE LEADS TO OBEDIENCE; GOOD BEGETS GOOD. "The path of the just is as the shining light, shining more and more." So Joshua, in sending back these valiant soldiers of their country, gives them in parting some holy admonitions. We see that he judges them worthy to apprehend the law of God in its " true breadth and length," in the spirit and not in the letter. It is to be noted that he sums up the whole in that commandment which is ever new, and never to be abrogated, that which St. John calls the old and the new commandment (1 John ii. 7): " Love the Lord your God, and walk in all his ways; keep his commandments, and cleave unto him and serve him with all your heart, and with all your soul" (ver. 5). Thus does each step or word in the Divine life prepare the way for a yet further advance, and so we go from strength to strength, from grace to grace.—E. DE P.

Vers. 9—21. The feeling excited in the people of Israel by the news that the Reubenites and Gadites had set up an altar beyond Jordan is a proof that the religious condition of the nation after the great benefits received by it was very healthy, while the act of the Reubenites and Gadites is no less an evidence of their gratitude to God. The indignation of the ten tribes is aroused by their impression that the Reubenites and Gadites have committed an act of rebellion against the holy law of God, in seeking to offer sacrifices on any other than the national altar. They are filled with holy zeal for the name of God and jealousy for His glory. " Ye have turned away this day from following the Lord," say their messengers to the two tribes supposed to be thus rebellious. If we inquire into the causes of so keen a spiritual life in this people usually so stiffnecked and prone to estrangement from God, we find that it can be accounted for in two ways.

I. ISRAEL HAS VIVIDLY IN REMEMBRANCE THE CONSEQUENCES OF ANY VIOLATION OF THE LAW OF GOD. Did not Achan the son of Zerah commit a trespass in the accursed thing, and was not the anger of the Lord kindled against all Israel? It was not Achan alone who perished because of his sin; the whole congregation suffered on his account (ver. 20). In this holy fear we see the vindication of the stern judgment of God. " Whom he loveth he chasteneth, that they may be made partakers of his holiness."

II. The second explanation of this healthy moral condition is gratitude for blessings received in the signal victory over the Canaanites, which the people felt they could never have achieved in their own unaided strength. Thus we need the discipline both of adversity and of prosperity in our spiritual education. Prosperity alone does but harden ; adversity unrelieved would sink the soul in despair. God knows our proneness to wander, hence He chastises us to put us in mind of our sins and of His holiness. But He remembers that we are but dust. Hence He blends joy with sorrow in our changeful lives, and the two together work out in us the gracious purposes of eternal love.—E. DE P.

Ver. 21—34. The Reubenites and Gadites easily vindicate their conduct. They have had no intention of setting up a rival altar, for they do not mean to offer any sacrifices except in the place appointed by God. Their altar is to be simply a memorial. They have built it under a sort of apprehension that possibly, in times to come, their children might be led, in ungrateful forgetfulness of the past, to forsake the Lord and His service. The Reubenites and Gadites teach us a wholesome lesson. It is incumbent on us to strive, as they did, to keep alive the memory of the great things which God has done for us, that we may not fall under the reproach addressed by Christ to His disciples : " How is it that ye do not remember? " (Mark viii. 18). Christ knows how prone we are to forgetfulness. He has therefore given us two great aids to memory—Holy Scripture and the sacraments. Nothing can ever take the place of the Scriptures. These alone give us the full story of redemption. But it was needful that that story should be brought before us also in a symbolic form, which should appeal vividly to the heart. Baptism and the Lord's Supper supply this necessity for the Church. " As often as ye eat this bread and drink this wine, ye do show the Lord's death till he come," says the Master (1 Cor. xi. 26). The bread which we break is the communion of the body of Christ, broken for our sins. The cup which we bless is the communion of His blood, shed for our offences. Thus does the Lord's Supper recall to us the sacrifice of Calvary, as the altar of the Reubenites and Gadites brought to their remembrance the tabernacle sacrifices. But they had not, and we have not, to offer for ourselves upon this altar of remembrance, for there can be no other sacrifice than that offered once for all upon the cross. The Mass, by its pretension to be a real sacrifice, belies the true meaning of the Eucharist. The church which celebrates it commits exactly the error into which the tribes beyond Jordan would have fallen, if they had presumed to offer upon their altar sacrifices which could be legitimately presented only upon the one altar of the nation. Let us be on our guard against materialising the sacraments, and so offering to God a worship which must be abhorrent to Him, since it seeks acceptance in virtue of another than the one efficient and perfect sacrifice.—E. DE P.

Vers. 10—34. *Misunderstandings among good people.* Bitter contention often arises from simple misunderstanding. The Israelites were on the verge of a civil war as a result of a simple mistake of judgment. Much unhappiness might be avoided if the lessons of this incident were well considered by Christian people.

I. Consider the incident in relation to the trans-Jordanic tribes. They erected an altar of witness which was supposed by their brethren to be an altar of sacrifice, a rival to the altar at Shiloh, a mark of national secession and religious schism. (1) We should be careful to *avoid the appearance of evil.* These tribes had voluntarily chosen a position of isolation. They were now acting in a way which exposed their conduct to suspicion. It is our duty to prevent the misinterpretation of our conduct when possible (*a*) lest quarrels be engendered ; (*b*) lest the name of God be dishonoured ; (*c*) lest the weak be hindered. (2) We must *expect sometimes to be misunderstood.* There are persons who are always ready to give an evil interpretation to ambiguous actions. We must not refrain from doing right for fear of being misjudged. False judgment is a trial to be endured with patience and accepted as a means of discipline to humble us and drive us to the sympathy of God (1 Cor. iv. 3). (3) A refuge from the misunderstanding of men may be found in the *knowledge and sympathy of God*. The suspected tribes appeal to the " Lord God of gods," who knows everything. When men misjudge, God sees the truth. It is better to be blamed by all the world and approved by God, than to win the world's approval at the expense of God's disapproval. (4) We should *explain our conduct* when it is questioned by those in whose good opinion we are interested. The trans-Jordanic tribes made a full explanation of their motives in building the altar. The pride which disdains an explanation is (*a*) foolish, for it injures ourselves; (*b*) unjust, for it allows the world to suffer for a false impression; and (*c*) ungenerous, since our brethren have a right to expect us to justify our conduct when this is possible.

II. Consider the incident in relation to the ten tribes. These tribes were hasty in judgment, but wise in conduct. (1) *Zeal for God's honour is always commendable*. Phinehas and his friends feared dishonour to the name of God. It is well to be jealous for God's truth rather than for our private interest. (2) *We should be cautious of passing an adverse judgment on others*. Phinehas was too hasty. Many are too ready to form an unfavourable opinion of the conduct of others. Charity should incline us to view this in the best light (1 Cor. xiii. 7). (3) *Contentions often spring from mistakes*. It is so in the wars of nations, in ecclesiastical differences, in personal quarrels. (4) *It is our duty to inquire well into the grounds of a quarrel* before taking an active part on either side. The Israelites sent a deputation to their brethren. It is unjust to decide and act on the uncertain information of mere rumours. Before saying anything ill of a person we should endeavour to see the accused himself, and hear his explanation. (5) *We should frankly recognise our errors of judgment*. The Israelites admitted their mistake. It is mean and unchristian to hold to a mistaken judgment from feelings of pride. The Christian should always work for peace (Matt. v. 9).—W. F. A.

Vers. 26—28.—*The altar of witness*. I. The objects aimed at. The Israelites were proved to have been in error when they assumed that the erection of the altar was a sign of religious schism and tribal secession. On the contrary, it was intended to prevent those very evils. (1) It was erected to *preserve the unity of the nation*. National unity is always a desirable end of patriotic efforts. It secures strength, mutual help, brotherly sympathy, and the means of progress. Christians should aim at restoring the unity of the Church; or, where this is not possible, at preventing further divisions. While the external unity of the Church is broken, oneness of spirit and oneness of aim should be bonds of common sympathy between Christians. It would be well if Christians could make it evident that their points of difference are far less important than that common ground of essential faith on which all are united. Less emphasis would then be given to the internal controversies of the Church, and more weight to the great conflict with sin and unbelief and the great mission to evangelise the world. (2) The altar was erected to *maintain the religious faith* of the trans-Jordanic tribes. Religion is more important to a people than fertile lands and well-built cities. We make a poor exchange when we sacrifice privileges of worship for worldly convenience. Separation from the ordinances of religion endangers the faith of religion. It should be our first duty to see that religious wants are supplied (*a*) for ourselves, (*b*) for our families, (*c*) for destitute places, such as newly built suburbs of great towns, outlying hamlets, the colonies, &c.

II. The danger feared. The men who built the altar of witness thought that the national unity and religious faith were endangered. (1) *Separation from the other tribes* was a source of danger. It is difficult to be faithful when we stand alone. (2) *Time* would increase the danger. These men built the altar with a view to the future. The severest test of faithfulness is the trial of endurance. Christians rarely forsake Christ suddenly. Early impressions linger for a time and fade gradually; but they will fade unless they are renewed. We cannot maintain the faith of a life on the lessons of youth. For constant faith we need constant " means of grace." (3) *New generations* would be less fortified against the

danger. The altar was built chiefly for the sake of the children of the future. The
Church can only be maintained by bringing the children into the places of the
elders as these pass away. Children do not become Christians instinctively, or by
the influence of the mere atmosphere of religion about them ; they must be taught
and trained ; therefore the education of the young should be a primary object of
Christian work.

III. The means employed. An altar of witness was erected. This was not for
sacrifice and worship, to rival that of the tabernacle, like the altars attached to the
calves at Bethel and Dan (1 Kings xii. 28, 29). (1) *It was simply a visible symbol.*
(*a*) It was a *symbol*—truth is often suggested most clearly by parables and illustrations. (*b*) It was *visible*. Truth should be made clear and striking. (*c*) It was
substantial. Truth should be established by solid evidence, not melted down into
vapid sentiments. (*d*) It was *enduring*. We should not be satisfied with superficial impressions, but aim at establishing an enduring faith. (2) *The Christian
has altars of witness*, *e.g.*, (*a*) the Bible preserved to us through the dark ages,
(*b*) the institutions of the Church, baptism, the Lord's supper, and public worship ;
(*c*) inwardly to the Christian, the indwelling Christ who is first our altar of sacrifice
and then our altar of witness, bearing testimony to the fact that we are His, and
one with his true Church by the Spirit He gives to us, and the fruits of this Spirit
in our lives (Rom. viii. 9).—W. F. A.

Vers. 26, 27.—*A misunderstanding removed.* Having completed their engagement, the auxiliaries of Reuben, Gad, and half Manasseh were dismissed by Joshua
in peace and honour to their homes, now at length to settle down to the enjoyment
of their possessions on the east of the Jordan. Joshua had strictly charged them
" to love the Lord," and " to walk in all his ways," and to share with their brethren
the spoils acquired in war. One of their first acts on arriving in Gilead was to
erect an altar, conspicuous by size and position, and framed after the pattern of
the altar before the tabernacle.

I. The intention of the eastern tribes. (1) *To have a memorial of their unity
in religious faith* with their brethren across the river. Religious ceremonies were
inseparably interwoven with the national life, so that to be refused a right to participate in the former would imply a denial of their claim to kinship. The Jordan
might hereafter be regarded as a natural barrier of exclusion from the privileges of
dwellers in the land of promise. When the Reubenites, &c., had proffered their
request to be permitted to dwell on the east of the river, they had not perceived
this possible difficulty so clearly, but now, after having trodden the promised land,
and viewed the habitations of their brethren, they were seized with anxiety lest in
after years they might be regarded as " aliens from the commonwealth of Israel."
Their conduct exhibits a respect for God. Their chief care was not for horses or
trophies of war, but for the preservation of a common interest in the worship of the
true God, and all the advantages thereby secured. They feared the selfishness of
the human heart. Men so often like to reserve to themselves peculiar honours and
privileges, to be esteemed the only true people of the covenant. Brotherly love
and sympathy are forgotten in the attempt to surround ourselves with walls of
exclusiveness. And against this narrowing of the national bounds the altar was to
be a continual guard, a silent yet eloquent and forcible " witness " to the brotherhood of all the tribes. And amongst Christians of to-day some such voice is not
unneeded to remind us of our common interest in the " altar" (Heb. xiii. 10), the
cross of Christ, whereby we are made "one body." (2) *To prevent a lapse into
idolatry on the part of their descendants.* The altar would be a standing reminder
of the commandment of God, which forbade the rearing of strange altars for sacrifice. These easterns showed a right sense of the importance of preserving the
religion of their fathers, and of handing it down uncorrupted to remotest ages.
If the knowledge of the true God vanished, then farewell to all prosperity ! What
a hint to parents ! Men toil to gather wealth for their heirs, to found an estate, to
perpetuate the family name ; it is more important to perpetuate piety, to train up
the children in the nurture and admonition of the Lord. " The fear of the Lord"

(ver. 25) is the choicest treasure which children can inherit, and apart from it riches do not prove a blessing. Religion and prosperity eventually go hand in hand. Statesmen, if wise, will seek to establish the throne in righteousness. Their aim will be that religion shall flourish in the land, not necessarily by direct enactments, but by removal of all restrictions to its progress. It is not our commerce, our arts, our resources for war that constitute our strength or hope for the future, but love to God, the prevalence of honesty and integrity, peace and truth. We need not so much ascendancy over other nations as over ourselves, our own passions and prejudices, vices and errors. (3) *To secure the offerings of the proper sacrifices at the tabernacle.* Not only rights were remembered, but consequent duties. The altar would ever call these tribes to attend to the performance of their obligations, not to neglect "the service of the Lord." Some of the people would have a long distance to travel, and might grow weary of providing for ceremonies celebrated at such a distance from their dwellings. What shall be the "witness" in each household, testifying to the duty incumbent upon its members to contribute of their substance to the support of God's cause? The Bible? The missionary box? And in our churches the first day of the week is a mute appeal, seconded by the gathering now and again around the table of the Lord.

II. The INDIGNATION of the western tribes. (1) *Exhibited in a striking manner their jealousy for the Lord God.* Though these brethren had been lately endangering their lives and strength on their behalf, marching at their head and capturing their places of abode, nevertheless this kindness does not excuse an after fault. Our gratitude must not blind us to derelictions on the part of our friends. It were mistaken love that hesitated to reprove error. Nor did the westerns delay, they were prompt in action to prepare to root out evil. They knew the value of early attention to it. A little water quenches a fire which, if allowed time to spread, will surpass the power of a flood to extinguish. Let us not say of any sin, "Is it not a little one?" Attack the disease at its commencement or it will defy all treatment! Better lose a limb than the whole body. (2) *Manifested the abiding impression produced by past events.* Peor and its dreadful plague, Achan with the loss in battle and dire retribution exacted from the offender and his family, had written in letters of fire and blood the wrath of God against iniquity. The lessons were remembered. Punishment graves the commandment deep within the conscience. Well for us if the past is not forgotten, its events recorded not on the sands but on the rocks. The reasoning of the Israelites was clear. If two and a half tribes transgressed, surely it was to be feared that God would chastise the entire nation; perhaps blot it out from under heaven, since he had in previous days manifested such severe displeasure at the defection of a few of the people. We cannot allow our brother to persevere in sin and ourselves remain unharmed. The contagion spreads. "Am I my brother's keeper?" is a foolish inquiry and a groundless plea. (3) *Rested on a misunderstanding.* And so does much of the strife which prevails. It is frequently impossible for men to know all the reasons by which others are actuated, and a partial view is often unjust. We do not advocate false leniency, or a total suspension of judgment. In the sermon wherein our Lord gave the warning, "Judge not that ye be not judged," He also declared, "By their fruits ye shall know them." We are apt to be hasty in drawing our conclusions, and it is probable that concerning a brother's behaviour we are especially quick in rushing to an adverse judgment. If acquainted with all the circumstances we might praise where now we blame. Let us try to avoid putting uncharitable constructions upon each other's acts. Appearances deceive. In heaven the harmony of love will be perfect, for we shall know even as also we are known. No veil of flesh shall intercept the vision of the spirit. Every signal flashed is clearly deciphered in the pure light of the presence of God; there is no cloud, no haze, to mar the reflection of His glory.

III. The MISUNDERSTANDING REMOVED. (1) *The right method was pursued by the complainants.* Before proceeding to the arbitrament of the sword they resolved to send an influential deputation to remonstrate, and to seek to dissuade their brethren from the indulgence of idolatrous practices. They manifested their sincerity and affection by offering to provide settlements within the land of Palestine, if the eastern tribes were now repenting of having chosen an unclean possession (ver. 19). Such is the method of dealing with brethren whom we believe to be sinning against God. Inquire and expostulate! "If thy brother shall trespass against thee, go and tell him his fault; if he shall hear thee, thou hast gained thy brother." Reformation is better than excommunication. Wisdom and affection concur in urging the adoption of such a course. (2) *The apparent offenders displayed similar reasonableness of spirit.* They willingly explained what they had done; did not stand sullenly upon their rights, refusing to render reasons for their action. They did not ask what business their brethren had to interfere with them, "Who made you rulers and judges over us?" Their procedure conveys lessons for modern days. Peaceable overtures must be peaceably met, and even unjustifiable suspicion must be pardoned. (3) *The suspected altar became a pleasing object to all.* The explanation was accepted, and the deputation, gratified with the answer they received, bore home a favourable account, and the dispute was amicably terminated. The end was even better than the beginning, for the affair reflected credit upon all concerned. God grant that all misapprehensions among believers may vanish with equal celerity and happiness! that no root of bitterness be allowed to spring up and trouble them. Nothing should delight us more than to be enabled to exonerate our brethren from blame. Discovery of their freedom from guilt is a sweet proof of the presence of God in our midst (v. 31).

CONCLUSION. This narration begets the inquiry whether we have any part in the Lord. Can any secret place of prayer, or any word or deed testify that the Lord is our God? The strongest union is formed by religious ties. Where families are thus united the bands of love are indissolubly cemented. Have we a family altar, not material but spiritual, a witness to the Lord? May the lessons thus derived from an old book be indelibly stamped upon our hearts.—A.

Ver. 31.—*God's presence manifested in the faithful conduct of His people.*
I. GOD IS PRESENT IN THE MIDST OF HIS FAITHFUL PEOPLE. By the nature of things, God is present everywhere (Psa. cxxxix. 7—10). Yet there is a more intimate and revealed presence of God which is not universal, but which is the peculiar privilege of some, while to others it is denied. This consists in the outflow of sympathy; the exercise of special grace, the nearness of spiritual communion. Two persons can be locally near, and yet in thought and sympathy very distant from one another. Spiritual presence is conditioned not by space but by sympathy. When we are out of sympathy with God He is far from us. When we are one with Him in sympathy He is near. This is a real presence. God does not simply send blessings and breathe benedictions from a distance. He makes the bodies of His people a temple (1 Cor. vi. 9), and their hearts the home of His Spirit (John xiv. 23).

II. GOD'S PRESENCE IS A FACT OF GREAT INTEREST TO HIS PEOPLE. Phinehas expresses satisfaction in the recognition of God's presence. (1) God's presence should be a source of blessing, since (a) He is our father, and we are homeless without Him; (b) He is the Almighty One, and we are full of need; (c) He is the light and life of all things, and without Him we are in darkness and death, like a planet without its sun. (2) God's presence is proved by experience to be a source of blessing, bestowing (a) safety, (b) purity, (c) joy, (d) glory. The possession of all the treasures of the world without God would leave the soul poor indeed. His presence is a pearl of great price.

III. GOD'S PRESENCE CAN BE RECOGNISED BY THE CONDUCT OF HIS PEOPLE. (1) *God's presence is discernible.* It is not for ever secret and hidden. Phinehas perceives the presence of the Lord. We do not always perceive it, but there are events which make it strikingly apparent. If we know how to recognise it, we need not be always asking, "Is the Lord among us or no?" but, like Hagar (Gen. xvi. 13) and Jacob (Gen. xxviii. 16), we shall be surprised and satisfied with the manifestation of God in our midst. (2) *God's presence is manifested in the conduct of His people.* (a) It is not proved by our opinions: we may have very correct ideas about the nature and character of God while we are far from Him. (b) It is not made manifest by our feelings: emotions are deceptive, and very strong religious feelings may be found in a very godless life. (c) It is seen in conduct.

IV. THE CONDUCT WHICH PROVES THE PRESENCE OF GOD IS FAITHFULNESS IN HIS SERVICE. Phinehas perceives "that the Lord is among us, because ye have not committed this trespass against the Lord." Faithfulness in the service of God, and a consequent spirit of brotherly kindness and sympathy, such as that now manifested among the tribes of Israel, are good signs of the presence of God in a Church. (1) His presence is the cause of fidelity. Our fidelity reveals His presence, but it does not secure it. He is present first, and inspires devotion, and binds His people together in united affection through their common devotion to Him. (2) He must need depart from His people when they become unfaithful. No past enjoyment of God will secure His abiding presence. If God depart, though wealth and ease and numbers testify to apparent prosperity, we may exclaim, " Ichabod—the glory has departed."—W. F. A.

Vers. 30, 31.—*A mistake and its rectification.* When Joshua dismissed the trans-Jordanic tribes to their homes he pronounced his benediction upon them, in grateful acknowledgment of the services they had rendered to their brethren of the other tribes, and with full confidence in their loyalty to the God of Israel. It soon seemed, however, as if this confidence had been misplaced. Their building of a "great altar over against the Land of Canaan " had a suspicious appearance. What could it be intended for but as a rival to the altar at Shiloh, and therefore a wicked violation of the Divine command in reference to the one chosen place of sacrifice? (Levit. xvii. 8, 9; Deut. xii.). The issue proved this suspicion to be groundless; and what seemed likely at first to lead to a serious breach in the religious unity of the nation ended in a signal manifestation of the presence of the " one Lord" in the midst of it (ver. 31). We see here—

I. A NOBLE EXAMPLE OF ZEAL FOR GOD AND FOR THE PURITY OF HIS WORSHIP. It was a true instinct that warned the leaders of the ten tribes of the danger of a rival altar on the other side of the Jordan. They saw how easily the river might become a cause of moral and spiritual separation, the geographical boundary a dividing line of conflicting sympathies and interests. A flame of holy indignation was kindled within them at the thought of the glory of Israel being thus turned to shame. Their zeal is shown (1) in their instant resolution forcibly to arrest the evil at its very beginning (ver. 12). Though they had so lately ceased from war, they will at once take up arms again, even against their brethren and compatriots, rather than suffer this wickedness to be done. (2) In the wise measures they adopt. They will hear and judge before they strike, and the dignity of the appointed court of inquiry (Phinehas and a representative prince from each of the tribes) indicates their sense of the solemnity of the crisis. (3) In the earnestness of their remonstrance. Their words are somewhat overstrained (ver. 16). The slightest departure from the appointed order is to them an act of guilty rebellion. (4) In the sense they have of the latent propensities of the people to idolatry, in spite of all the sad lessons of the past (ver. 17). (5) In their readiness to suffer loss themselves by the narrowing of their own inheritance rather than this supposed evil should be done. All of which is greatly to their honour, inasmuch as it shows how true they were to their allegiance to the God of Israel, and how earnest their purpose to maintain the religious unity of the commonwealth.

II. A SUCCESSFUL ACT OF SELF-VINDICATION. If the suspected tribes were rash in raising the altar without having first consulted the heads of the nation, and especially the high priest from whom the will of God was to be known, and without duly considering the aspect it might bear to their brethren on the other side of the river, yet they themselves were also wronged by this too hasty judgment on the meaning and motive of their deed. The honesty of their purpose is abundantly made manifest. Note (1) the spirit in which they receive the remonstrance. This at once bespeaks the purity of their intent. It is a serious charge that is brought against them, but they meet it with no angry recrimination. There is surprise, but nothing like resentment. This, perhaps, not only quenched the arrow of rebuke, but turned it back upon the source from whence it came. "Innocence doth make false accusation blush," and the guilelessness of their bearing must have brought a feeling of shame to their accusers, for having so hastily condemned them. In nothing is the moral quality of a man indicated more than in the way in which he receives an unmerited rebuke. (2) Their desire to approve themselves to their brethren, as well as to Him who knew what was in their hearts. "The Lord God of gods, he knoweth, and Israel he shall know" (ver. 22). No right-feeling man will be indifferent to the good opinion of his fellow men. (3) Their thorough religious sympathy with the leaders of the people. The building of the altar, instead of being meant as an act of revolt, was done "*for fear of this very thing.*" We are reminded not only how possible it is to mistake men's motives, but how the same motive may prompt to actions that seem to be at variance. Formal differences and separations in the Church are not necessarily schism. They may be the outgrowth of that very loyalty to truth and conscience which is one of the main elements of its living unity. The principle that binds men in allegiance to Christ may be at the root of much that seems to separate them from one another. A truly upright spirit rejoices in spiritual uprightness that may assume forms widely different from its own; and that is the most *Christian* conscience that most respects the consciences of others. (4) Their prudent regard to the possibilities of the future. Not as a substitute for the altar at Shiloh, but as the shadow and memorial of it, did they rear this altar; that their children, looking upon it, might never fail to claim their part and lot in the fellowship of Israel. The loyalty of a godly soul will always manifest itself in the desire and practical endeavour to hand down its own inheritance of blessing unimpaired to coming generations.

III. A GREAT CALAMITY AVERTED BY A POLICY OF MUTUAL FORBEARANCE. What might have been a disastrous feud was arrested at the beginning by a few frank outspoken words. Honesty of purpose on the one side detected and appreciated honesty of purpose on the other. The "soft answer turned away wrath." "Charity covered the multitude of sins." And thus the very altar that seemed likely to break the bond of the nation's unity, rather became a witness to it and a means of strengthening it. So may it ever be. The true cure for the discords of social life and of Church life lies in fidelity to conscience, tempered by the forbearance of love. "If thy brother trespass against thee, go and tell him his fault between him and thee alone; if he shall hear thee, thou hast gained thy brother" (Matt. xviii. 15). "Let us not therefore judge one another any more; but judge this rather, that no man put a stumbling block or an occasion to fall in his brother's way" (Rom. xiv. 13).—W.

EXPOSITION.

CHAPTER XXIII. 1—16.

JOSHUA'S SOLEMN CHARGE. — Ver. 1. — **Waxed old and stricken in age.** Literally, *was old, advanced in days* (see ch. xiii. 1). But this refers to a more advanced age still, when the patriarch felt his powers failing him, and desired, as far as his influence went, to preserve the Israelites in the path in which they had walked since their entrance into Canaan. Calvin has some good remarks on the "pious solicitude" shown by the aged warrior for those whom he had led in time of war and guided in time of peace. He seems to have sent for the chief

men in Israel to his home at Timnath-Serah, where apparently he had led a retired and peaceful life, only coming forward to direct the affairs of the nation when necessity required. His address is simple and practical. He reminds them that they will soon lose the benefit of his experience and authority, and of the work that he had done, under God's direction, in settling them in the land. Then he proceeds to urge strict obedience to the law of God, reminding them that victory is assured to them, if they will but be true to themselves and their calling as the servants of God, but that as certainly as they neglect to do so, wrath and misery will be their portion. He emphasizes his words by reminding them how amply God had fulfilled his promise, and concludes with a picture of the evil which will befall them if they rebel against God.

Ver. 2.—**All Israel.** By their representatives, as subsequently mentioned. **For their officers** (see ch. i. 10). In the original the pronoun is in the singular throughout (see note on ch. vi. 25). **And said unto them.** This speech is not, as Calvin, Maurer, and others have suggested, the same as that in ch. xxiv. (see notes there). Maurer believed that he was the first to entertain this idea, but he has been anticipated by Calvin. It consists largely of quotations from Deuteronomy.

Ver. 3.—**Because of you.** Literally, *before you.*

Ver. 4.—**Divided unto you by lot.** Literally, *caused to fall,* the lot being of necessity understood. **These nations that remain.** Israel had therefore not driven them out. This, however, need not of necessity be imputed to them as a sin. For, as we have seen, the conquest was to be gradual. No doubt there was enough to be done in consolidating the conquests already made, in settling the tribes in their possessions, to occupy all the days of Joshua, and even possibly a longer period. At least we may be sure that, as long as Joshua lived, the heathen settlements were kept distinct from the Israelitish community, that intermarriages were not allowed, nor rights of citizenship granted to any but the Gibeonites. **Cut off.** Joshua's speech here exactly agrees with the statements in ch. vi. 21; viii. 26; x. 28—41; xi. 11, 14, 21. Here at least, if Joshua's speech and the history were taken from two different sources, neither of them precisely accurate, the first postulate of the destructive criticism, we might have expected some slight discrepancy. But Joshua uses a word which implies total extermination, a feature, be it observed, of the campaigns of Moses and Joshua only, and not of the later Israelitish history. **Westward.** Literally, *the going down of the sun.*

Ver. 5.—**And the Lord your God, he shall expel them.** Or, *Jehovah your God, He shall thrust them out.* Joshua here uses the unusual word found in Deut. vi. 19; ix. 4, another instance of quotation from Deuteronomy. The word occurs in the sense of *thrust* in Num. xxxv. 20, 22. **From out of your sight.** Rather, *from before you.*

Ver. 6.—**Be ye therefore very courageous.** The original is stronger, *Be ye exceedingly courageous* (see note on ch. i. 6). **That is written in the book of the law of Moses.** A yet more distinct intimation that the words of Moses had been collected into a

book at this early period, and that it was known as the Book of the Law of Moses. It seems incredible that such a book should have been invented at a time when the precepts it contained were lightly regarded, and should have been represented as the proper standard of conduct when every one knew that it could never have been anything of the kind.

Ver. 7.—**That ye come not among these nations** (see note on ver. 4). We can here perceive that the Israelites, though living among these nations, held no intercourse with them. **Neither make mention of the name of their gods.** Cf. Psa. xvi. 4, which however is not a verbal quotation of this passage. The LXX. here has, καὶ τὰ ὀνόματα τῶν θεῶν αὐτῶν οὐκ ὀνομασθήσεται ἐν ὑμῖν; the Vulgate simply, " ne jureti̇s in nomine deorum earum." The Hebrew has the signification (1) to bring to remembrance, (2) to praise or celebrate. The former is the better idea here, " let them not be named among you, as becometh saints," let them be quite forgotten, as though they had never been heard of ; and this not with a purely theological, but with an ethical purpose, since " fornication and all uncleanness and greediness" (πλεονεξία; see Ephes. v. 3) were the first principles of their rites (see Introduction). **Nor cause to swear by them.** These words are found in connection with what follows in Deut. x. 20. So with " serve" and " bow down" (see Exod. xx. 5; Deut. iv. 19; v. 9; viii. 19, &c.). Here again we have Joshua quoting Deuteronomy as the book of the Law of Moses. According to the " Deuteronomist" theory, the quotation is an audacious fiction, manufactured by the person who was at that moment forging the book from which he pretended to quote.

Ver. 8.—**But cleave unto the Lord your God.** Or, *ye shall cleave unto Jehovah* your God. The phrase denotes the intimate union between God and the soul (see above, and Gen. ii. 24).

Ver. 9.—**For the Lord your God hath driven out.** So the Masora and the LXX. The Vulgate and the margin of our version translate by the future. So Luther also. The next verse is undeniably future. An appeal to their experience, which did not fail (see ch. xxiv. 31) to be effective as long as the memory of these things was fresh in their minds. So in the Prayer Book of the Church of England we find the appeal, " O God, we have heard with our ears, and our fathers have declared unto us, the noble works that thou didst in their days, and in the old time before them." And the passage (Psa. xliv. 1—3), from which the idea of this petition is taken, is an allusion to this speech of Joshua. And we often, in times of faintheartedness or sloth, need to be thus reminded of the moral and spiritual victories of the true Israel, under the true Joshua the Saviour, over the enemies with whom we are forbidden to make a compromise.

Ver. 10.—**One man of you shall chase a thousand.** A quotation from the song of Moses (Deut. xxxii. 30).

Ver. 11.—**Take good heed to yourselves.** This is quoted from Deut. iv. 15, word for word. The Hebrew is, *take heed exceedingly to your souls;* but the meaning is either "as you value your lives" (Gesenius), or "with all your soul" (Keil). The former appears preferable. A third interpretation, however, "guard your souls diligently," is suggested by a comparison of Deut. iv. 9, 15.

Ver. 12.—**Go back.** Literally, *return.* **Cleave.** A word (see ver. 8) signifying close and intimate relationship. And the intimacy of the relationship is indicated, as in ver. 8, by the use of the preposition בְּ. **Make marriages with them.** No closer or more intimate relationship is possible than this. Nothing, therefore, would be more certain to draw the Israelites away from their allegiance to God, and to seduce them and their children into the false and corrupt worship of the nations around them. "Unde deprecor vos qui fidelis estis, ut ita vitam vestram et conversationem servetis, ne in aliquo vel ipsi scandalum patiamini vel aliis scandalum faciatis; sit in vobis summi studii, summæque cautelæ, ne quis in hanc sanctam congregationem vestram pollutus introeat" (Orig., Hom. 21 on Joshua). **Go in unto them.** Rather, *go among them.* Spoken of the familiar intercourse of friendship. It is equivalent to our words "associate with them."

Ver. 13.—**Snares and traps.** Perhaps, rather, *nets and snares.* The LXX., where our translation has snare, has παγίς, and for traps has incorrectly σκάνδαλα. The snare or *pach* was evidently (Amos iii. 5) laid upon the earth; but there is no evidence for Gesenius' idea that the *mokesh* which follows, there as here, means the stick of the trap, which when displaced involved the bird in the net. As the primary signification of this latter word, which is akin to קֶשֶׁת a bow, seems to mean something curved, it is probably a noose or springe. And the word and its cognates are used of involving, or catching, people by its use. Fürst's Lexicon confirms this view, which has been independently arrived at. **Scourges.** The Hebrew word is in the singular. It is translated ἥλους, nails, in the LXX., and *offendiculum* in the

Vulgate. **In your sides.** Rather, *on* your sides. The words here are very similar to those in Num. xxxiii. 55. Moses, however, does but use two of the similes of which here we have four. He has, moreover, a different word (שִׂכִּים) for thorns, and the word here translated thorns is there substituted for scourges; "thorns in your sides." Joshua crowds together his similes "to describe the shame, and trouble, and oppression which they would bring upon themselves by joining in the idolatry of the Canaanites" (Keil). **The Lord your God.** Here, as elsewhere in this and many other passages, we have in the original, *Jehovah your God.* It is important to remember that the sacred writer is calling the God of Israel by His own proper name, that by which He was distinguished from the gods of the nations round about.

Ver. 14.—**And not one thing hath failed thereof.** This is a good instance of the habit of repetition so common to Hebrew writers. It is to be remembered that they had no italics, no stops, and, owing to the want of copiousness in their language, a great want generally of the means possessed in more modern languages of emphasizing their words. They, therefore, had recourse to what is still a favourite rhetorical artifice, the practice of repetition.

Ver. 15.—**All good things.** Literally, *all the good word.* That is to say, the prophecies of good had been fulfilled. Joshua uses this as an argument that the evil also will not fail to follow, if Israel provoke God to inflict it. But the memory of these words, and of the great deeds of Jehovah, faded quickly from their minds. And then, like the people of the earth before the flood, like the men of Sodom before it was destroyed, and like many other people since, they turned a deaf ear to the prophecies of evil which faithful souls foresaw and foretold. The warnings of the prophets are but a variation upon the predictions of Moses in Levit. xxvi. 14—33, Deut. xxviii. 15—68, xxix. 14—28, and of Joshua, here addressed to a generation who had brought some of the predicted evil upon themselves, and would not see that by refusing to listen, they would bring upon themselves yet more. How terribly have these predictions been fulfilled! First, the Babylonish captivity; then the disorders and anarchy in a territory which the Jewish people inhabited, but which they were not strong enough to rule; then the siege of and destruction of Jerusalem under Titus with its accompanying horrors. Then the dispersion of the Jews among all the nations, the barbarous and inhuman persecutions they met with in the

Middle Ages from priest and monarch alike: the Inquisition in Spain, the contempt and hatred which continued to be felt for them among more enlightened nations, as evidenced in Marlowe's 'Jew of Malta,' and Shakespeare's 'Merchant of Venice,' in the days of our own Queen Elizabeth. Only in our own age has a brighter day begun to dawn on them, and three thousand years of oppression, relieved only by the brief glories of David and his dynasty, are beginning to be compensated by a share in the world's rewards and honours. **All evil things.**

Literally, *all the evil word;* or *thing;* every evil thing, that is, which had been foretold. Ver. 16.—**Transgressed.** The English is the precise equivalent of the Hebrew, which signifies to "pass over," with the idea of going beyond bounds which had previously been prescribed in the covenant between God and His people. **Other gods.** See ver. 7. Here again we have the usual repetition for the sake of emphasis. **Ye shall perish quickly.** A verbally accurate quotation of Deut. xi. 17. The original is even more emphatic—*with haste.*

HOMILETICS.

Ver. 1—16.—*The last words of the aged servant of God.* The influence gained by a long and successful life is immense. It was so in Joshua's case, for it outlasted his life, and continued as long as any of his former colleagues and companions in arms were alive. It was only when a fresh generation arose who knew him not, save by the report of the younger men, such as Othniel, that Israel declined from the true path. Joshua's last charge, therefore, is full of interest and profit.

I. How A LONG LIFE OF USEFULNESS MAY BEST BE CLOSED. When Joshua felt his life drawing to an end, he assembled those who had been partakers of his toils, reminded them of the great things God had done during his leadership, and warned them of the danger of departing from the course which had been marked by such signal and uninterrupted success. So may those who, by God's grace, have been the means of improvement or usefulness to others, parents to their children, pastors to their flocks, men who have won for themselves a moral influence in the religious or even the social, philosophical, or political world, when they feel their powers failing, assemble those who have worked with them, review the past, and draw a moral from it for the future. The last words of any one we deeply respect have a weight with us which no others have, and live within us when those who uttered them have long since passed away. This is even the case with the last words our Lord and Master spoke before His crucifixion, though in His case they were *not* His last, for not only did He rise from the dead, but He hath since spoken to us by His Spirit. Yet His dying command concerning the bread and wine has touched the heart more than any other; and His last speech in John xvii. has always had a peculiar interest for Christians. Perhaps His followers have too much shrunk, from Christian modesty, from the most powerful means of influence they have. Forms of belief vary. The religious earnestness of our age is replaced by a different form of religious earnestness in another. The new wine has to be put into new bottles. Thus exhortations to maintain a particular form of doctrine or organisation may fail of their effect, or when (as is very often the case) they do *not* fail, they may be undesirable. But exhortations to love, joy, peace, zeal, energy, self-restraint, indifference to the world, may derive a vast additional force when they are the farewell words of one whose life has been a life-long struggle to practise them.

II. WE MUST OBEY THE WHOLE LAW. We are not to pick and choose either in doctrines or precepts. There is an eclecticism now, as there was in the apostle's day, which rejects particular doctrines or precepts of Christianity as "unsuitable to the times." We are of course to distinguish between doctrines and development of doctrines, the last being, perhaps, the product of a particular age, and unsuitable or impossible for philosophic or scientific reasons in another. So again, the *form* of a precept (*e.g.*, those touching almsgiving) must be altered from time to time, as Christian principles are transforming society by permeating it. But the *spirit* of a precept is for ever binding. And, we may observe, excess is as bad as defect. It was said of the law, that men should "add nought to it," as well as "diminish ought from it;" and we know what Christ thought of those who "taught for doctrines the commandments of men." Yet there has been in all ages a spiritual Pharisaism which has turned aside to the right, as there has been a Sadduceeism which has turned to the left. Every age has had its teachers who added to the essentials of religion as well as those who would explain them away. And the tendency has been to magnify these positive precepts of particular religious parties, until it has been held more criminal to disobey them than to offend against the first principles of the Christian religion. For their sake the fundamental law of love has been laid aside, and transgression against a law Christ never imposed has been visited with a bitterness and a fury which He has expressly forbidden. Whether excess or defect have been more fatal to the cause of Christianity is a point which must be left undecided. But that grievous evils to the cause of religion in general and the souls of individuals have arisen from the practice among Christians of insisting upon what Christ has never enjoined cannot be denied. Let it be our case, then, to observe the whole law of Christ, neither to turn to the right nor to the left, but to keep all, and no more than all, that He has commanded. For "His commandments are not grievous." His "yoke is easy and His burden is light." There is the more reason, therefore, why we should keep it to the very letter.

III. WE ARE EXPRESSLY EXHORTED TO AVOID COMPLIANCE WITH THE WORLD. This is a more difficult precept now than ever. Once there was a broad line of demarcation between the religious and the worldly man. Now Christianity has so far externally leavened society that the conflict has been forced inward. Decency and propriety of behaviour is everywhere enforced where education has penetrated. Cursing and swearing are banished at least from general society, and open profaneness is seldom met with. Yet the conflict must be continued, and continued within. St. Paul's advice in 1 Cor. v. 10 must be kept. A Christian *must* go into society and mix with the people he finds there, though he must not choose them for his intimates. But he must be more on the watch than ever to detect the tone of his associates when it jars with the gospel precepts. Still, as ever, there are false standards of right and wrong set up, false doctrines of honour and morality inculcated, principles laid down which Christ would have abhorred, conduct tolerated which He would have emphatically condemned. The worship of rank and fashion and wealth; the polite depreciation of all enthusiasm; the utter failure to recognise the glory of self-sacrifice, except it be for tangible rewards, such as glory among men; the absence of all reverence; the veiled (or it may be *unveiled*) selfishness of a life of indolence and ease, the cynical indifference to the welfare of even the existence of others, except so far as it contributes to the pleasures of our own—these are habits of mind utterly repugnant to the spirit of Christ. They must not be tolerated, they must be steadily and openly resisted by the Christian. And yet, so insidious are they, that they frequently creep into the souls of those who imagine themselves to be uncorrupted soldiers of the Cross. They have made mention of the names "of these gods of the nations around them," have "served" them and "bowed down" to them without knowing it, though they *could* have known it, had they been on the watch. And then they become "snares and traps," "scourges in their sides and thorns in their eyes"—the causes, that is, of manifold cares and troubles and annoyances which to the Christian are unknown. And if unrepented of, they poison the Christian life at its source, till the once believer "perishes from off the good land which the Lord his God has given him."

IV. THE IMPORTANCE OF CHRISTIAN MARRIAGE. "Neither shall ye make marriages with them," says the sacred writer; and the precept has been continually repeated. It is surprising how little the New Testament says on this important point of the selection of a partner for life. It would seem as though Christ and His apostles thought it so obvious that it were superfluous to speak of it. "Only in the Lord " (1 Cor. vii. 39) is the only precept given on this important point, unless 2 Cor. vi. 14 be held indirectly to include it. But the Old Testament, which is, equally with the New, a guide of life, is full of such cautions, from Isaac, Esau, and Jacob downwards. Moses perpetually warns the children of Israel against contracting such alliances with the idolatrous Canaanites. Ahab is a standing warning of their danger, and the taint invaded the kingdom of Judah through the weakness of the otherwise pious Jehoshaphat, and ended in the ferocious treachery of Athaliah. What Nehemiah thought of it in the reviving fortunes of Israel after the captivity may be read in his own words (ch. xiii.). There is no difficulty, therefore, in gathering from Scripture a condemnation of marriage between those who are not of one mind on the most essential point of all, that of religion. The Roman Catholic Church has forbidden mixed marriages, and wisely. It were well if Churches of the Reformed faith were as outspoken in their condemnation of them. Yet unwise as are unions between those who differ in religious views, they are far worse when contracted between Christians and unbelievers, between those who are "conformed to this world" and those who hope to be "transformed by the renewing of their mind" into the image of Jesus Christ. There can be but one result to such unions. They must ever be "snares and traps," "scourges in the side and thorns in the eyes" of those who contract them, even though the end be not the destruction from out of the "good land which God has given." Those whom "God hath joined together" ought not to be "put asunder" by a discordance of opinions on all the main duties and objects of life. No temptations of beauty, of wealth or prospects, or even of personal preference, can outweigh the misery and danger of a condition like this, especially when it is considered that the results are not confined to those who are parties to such marriages, but that those whom God has sent into the world to be heirs of eternity will be considered by one, perhaps eventually by both their parents, as the creatures of a world that is passing away. The words "only in the Lord," though spoken but once, and then incidentally, ought nevertheless to be well pondered. They constitute the only ground upon which a Christian can enter into the most sacred and enduring of human ties; the only one that can ensure a blessing; the only one possible to those who are pledged to order all their actions by the inspiration of God's Holy Spirit.

HOMILIES BY VARIOUS AUTHORS.

Vers. 6—8.—*Cleaving unto the Lord.* I. THE DUTY. (1) *Personal devotion.* God seeks the devotion of our hearts. It is inward and spiritual, and not merely a fact of visible conduct. It implies drawing near to God in prayer, walking with God, delighting in Him, seeking to be like Him, aiming at pleasing Him. (2) *Active obedience.* Joshua exhorts the people to "be very courageous," "to keep and to do all that is written in the book of the law of Moses." Devotion of heart is a mockery unless it leads to obedience in conduct. We must cleave to God in action as well as in feeling. (3) *Purity.* The people are exhorted to avoid the contamination of heathen society and the sin of idolatry. Anything that takes the place of God in our heart is an idol. All sinful pleasures and worldly interests that are not consistent with pure devotion to God separate us from Him and vitiate our service. God cannot accept our sacrifices while we approach Him with sinful affections (Isa. i. 13). II. THE DANGER. Joshua saw that there was a danger that the people should cease to "cleave unto the Lord." This arose from various causes: (1) *Prosperity.* It was now "a long time after that the Lord had given rest unto Israel." In times of prosperity we are often off our guard, and become indolent, and hence are in danger. (2) *Bad example.* The Canaanites who remained in the land would be a source of temptation to idolatry and immorality. We need to be especially careful if we are surrounded by those who live worldly and unholy lives. The influence of an ever-present example is insidious and powerful. (3) *The inherent difficulty of duty.* The people were exhorted not to turn aside to the right hand or to the left. The path of duty is narrow (Matt. vii. 13, 14). There are many wrong ways, but only one right way. (4) *The loss of an old leader.* Joshua was about to die. He feared for the people after his guiding hand was removed. When trusted leaders are called away the Church is thrown back on the individual responsibility of its members to preserve its fidelity.

III. The motives for overcoming the danger and fulfilling the duty. The great source of devotion is love to God. Joshua says, "Take good heed, therefore, unto yourselves, that ye love the Lord your God." We cannot cleave to the Lord out of a mere sense of duty. We must feel attracted by the influence of His love to us, rousing our love to Him (Hosea xi. 4). This influence will be realised as we reflect upon the goodness of God in the past. Joshua appeals to the experience of the people and their memory of God's great goodness and powerful help. We have not only the providential grace of God to reflect upon, but also the wonderful love He has revealed in the sacrifice of Christ (2 Cor. v. 14). If we have been at all faithful in the past, the thought of this fact should stimulate us to maintain our fidelity. Joshua says, "Cleave unto the Lord your God as ye have done unto this day." Past devotion is no security ageinst future unfaithfulness. But it is a motive to fidelity, because, failing this, the fruits of the labour and sacrifice of the past will be lost; because the habits of the past will make it easier to be true in the future—the greater difficulties being overcome, it would be foolish to yield before the lesser; and because the experience of the blessings which accompany fidelity should make us see that our joy and peace are in "cleaving unto the Lord."—W. F. A.

Ver. 10.—*Victory assured through the help of God.* I. Victory is assured. (1) The people of God are few and weak in comparison with the host of their enemies. This was the case with the Jews. It is so in the comparison of the Church with the great godless and heathen world. It is true of our own spiritual resources and the dangers which beset our inner life. The comparison is as one to a thousand. (2) It is a Divine law that success shall not turn on questions of numbers and visible strength. God is not always "on the side of the big battalions." Even in material warfare there are possible "accidents" and "mistakes" which vitiate arguments drawn from statistics. In spiritual warfare visible superiority counts for very little. Paul the tent-maker was stronger than the Sanhedrim. The monk Luther was victorious over the Pope and the whole Roman hierarchy. Nothing could have looked feebler than Christianity when it appeared in the upper room at Jerusalem; yet in three centuries it conquered the Roman Empire, and it is now the most powerful factor in the life of the foremost races of mankind. (3) God assures victory to His people. The victory is not only possible in spite of apparent weakness; it is certain. It is promised by God. Anticipations are constantly seen, as in the successes of Israel, the triumphs of Christianity, the victory of the Christian over his old sins, &c. Therefore let us see that we are on the side of right and truth and God, and then let us be trustful and hopeful.

II. The secret of victory is the help of God. Israel must be brave and faithful, and must labour and fight. Yet victory is not secured by these means alone. Joshua points to the true ground of assurance: "The Lord your God, He it is that fighteth for you." How does God fight for us? (1) He fights for us *in His providence.* (a) God so overrules events that they shall minister to the victory of His people; His complete government of all things renders it certain that no calamities or temptations can fall upon His people against His will, and He can regulate and temper those that He permits. (b) God guides the thoughts and inner lives of men. Pharaoh the oppressor and Nebuchadnezzar were led by God to do His will, though unconsciously. Even the bitterest opponents of God's will cannot shake off this unseen control. (2) God fights for us by *inspiring us with strength* to fight. (a) He leads the mind to those thoughts which help us to resist evil and advocate truth and right with enthusiasm. (b) He is the source of direct spiritual influences which strengthen the will in the determination to brave all for the right. —W. F. A.

Ver. 11.—*Love to God.* We are called to love God. It is not enough that we discharge our duty to our neighbour; we have a distinct duty to God (Mal. i. 6). This duty is not fulfilled by the most scrupulous devotion to external service alone. God claims the affection of our hearts.

I. The NATURE OF LOVE TO GOD. (1) *It has all the qualities of genuine love.* (*a*) It is personal. We love God in loving goodness and all things Godlike; but the perfect love of God implies a personal relation between our soul and His. We love Him as our Father. (*b*) It is seen in the delight we have in God, the attraction He is to us, our desire to be in His presence, and the greater brightness of our lives as we grow nearer to Him. True love finds its greatest joy in loving. The love which is merely benevolent, which wishes well without feeling delight, is cold and faint. (*c*) It is proved by sacrifice. Love sacrifices itself to death, and prefers the person loved to its own joy. So our love to God must lead to self-devotion and willingness to suffer loss for His sake. (2) *It has special features of its own.* There are different kinds of love, determined by the different relations of men, as friends, brothers, parents and children, husbands and wives. Our relation to God is unlike any other relation, and the love which flows from this must have a peculiar character. God stands to us in the ideal of all relations, as the friend, the father, the husband of His people, and our love to God should be the perfection and ideal of all love. Still God needs no help from us; therefore the element of pity which characterises the love of the strong to the weak does not belong to this love. God is unseen and spiritual; therefore our love to Him does not naturally take the form of sensuous rapture, but rather that of calm and rational devotion. God is infinitely above us; therefore our love to Him must be inspired with reverence and humility. In its perfection it must become an all-absorbing devotion. Yet even then it will be characterised by strength and depth rather than by passion and visible emotion.

II. The SOURCES OF LOVE TO GOD. We are to " take good heed "—an admonition which implies that it rests with us to cultivate our own love to God. (1) *Consider the grounds* we have for loving God: (*a*) In His *love* to us, seeing that He has loved us before seeking for our love, and has proved His love by His goodness in creation, providence, and redemption; (*b*) in His *nature*. He attracts by the " beauty of holiness; " He is love; the more we know of God the more do we see of His goodness. (2) *Realise the presence of God.* Love is strengthened by communion. Contemplation of God with faith in His personal presence will draw the soul near to Him, and deepen the feeling of affection to Him as a real being—" our Father "—and not as the mere abstraction of perfect attributes which is all that the name of God suggests to some men. (3) *Live in His spirit.* As we love what God loves, as we grow like Him, as we approach Him in sympathy, we shall learn to love God.

III. The EFFECTS OF LOVE TO GOD. (1) *Obedience.* We shall desire to serve and please Him, and shall do this more heartily than from fear, self-interest, or a cold conviction of duty (Rom. xiii. 10). (2) *Likeness to God.* Love naturally assimilates by the influence of (*a*) admiration and (*b*) sympathy. (3) *Love to man.* This is a direct fruit of love to God, because (*a*) it pleases Him, (*b*) it is Godlike, (*c*) love to God must flow out in all forms of unselfishness and benevolence (1 John iv. 20). (4) *The highest blessedness.* Heaven consists in the enjoyment of God through love. He secures, on earth, peace and satisfaction to the deepest yearnings of the soul.—W. F. A.

Ver. 11.—*A needed caution.* Whilst the words of the youthful sometimes claim our attention, none can forbear to give earnest heed to the advice of him whose head is whitened with the snows of many winters. Respect is due to the aged, and never more so than when lessons taught them by a long and varied experience drop from their venerable lips. Let us bend our ears to listen to the counsel of Joshua, " old and stricken in age." The period at which it was delivered was one of peculiar interest. The honoured leader of the Israelites felt the time to be drawing near when he must pass away from the people whom he regarded as a father does his children. Knowing how soon they would be deprived of his presence and control, he assembled the people, as Moses had previously done, and like Samuel and David afterwards, and addressed them in words of solemn exhortation, which may be summarised in the language of the text, " Take good heed," &c. The purpose of most addresses is to strike a note of warning, to put men on the alert to guard against some danger. Our sleepy senses get so steeped in forgetfulness that there is constant need of the pealing alarm, "Take heed!"

I. THE IMPORTANCE OF THE CAUTION. (1) *It directs attention to the centre and substance of religion.* Our Saviour endorsed "Thou shalt love the Lord thy God" as "the first and great commandment." His condemnation of the Jews was expressed, "I know you that ye have not the love of God in you." The first sin consisted in a turning away from God in consequence of the tempter's insinuation that want of love was the motive of the seemingly harsh prohibition. Hence the incarnation and crucifixion were the stupendous exhibition of Divine love intended to regain the love of man. Affection alone can secure ready and earnest and constant obedience. "Keep thy heart with all diligence, for out of it are the issues of life." Love becomes "the fulfilling of the law." It is the mainspring of a godly life, the fountain whence flow streams of holy activity. Striking is it to observe how love is demanded and insisted on even under the old dispensation. The lawgiver knew that the sternest threats and severest penalties could not ensure compliance with the commands of the Almighty, unless love were enthroned in the heart as the ruling passion of the life. All the attributes of God require corresponding recognition on the part of His creatures; and love as His chief, all-embracing excellence challenges our love in response, and we are guilty if we withhold it. (2) *It is highly necessary on account of man's nature and surroundings.* He is engrossed by the senses and their gratifications, and is averse to what is spiritual. To worship God requires an effort of the mind, an abstraction from things carnal. The spirituality of the Divine nature was a source of difficulty to the Israelites. Even though they had seen the cloud, the fire, the Shechinah, they wanted to set up idols, visible images ever present. And as many of the miraculous elements had disappeared, there was the greater tendency to forgetfulness of Jehovah. To-day men urge, "How can we love a Being whom we have never seen?" His laws appear in many instances stringent, and to obey is painful. Evidences of thoughtful, loving design seem rebutted by contrary appearances of disharmony and wrath. It is acknowledged to be difficult to hush the voice of passion, and to hear the "still small voice" that betokens the presence of God. The difficulty is increased by our surroundings. If Israel had been alone upon the earth, it might have maintained intact the worship of the true God. But, encircled by idolatrous tribes and abominable practices, there was constant liability to mix with the evil and catch its infection (see vers. 7, 8). Our position is strictly analogous. We are "in the world," and daily brought into contact with those who make self their aim and treat pure religion with contempt. Easily may the contagion spread. The smoke of the city obscures the heavens, and amidst its din the tones of the angels fall but faintly on the ear. If this applies to believers who know and serve God, how mighty the barriers that interpose between Him and His "prodigal" sons! What dire need of sounding aloud the caution that they may speedily "come to themselves," and return to their Father! (3) *History confirms the necessity of attending to the caution.* Joshua well knew how frequently the Israelites had already become estranged from God. Many were the mementos of rebellion left in the wilderness, many the stones which bore the traces of their stumbling. Thus reasoning had its conclusions verified by experience. And which of us has not memorials of folly? If a pillar marked each scene where was displayed absence of regard for our Maker, how thronged with such tokens would be the route by which we have travelled. Call up the remembrance of the acts of childhood and youth and manhood. Each sin was a step upon the path of enmity against God, for it evinced a liking for that which is displeasing to Him. His mercy checked us from utter aberration. The warning of Joshua was proved necessary by the actual event. Standing on the mountain-top, he thence surveyed both the past and the future. In spite of the special covenant recorded in the following chapter, the Israelites ceased to love the Lord, and lapsed into idolatry and licentiousness. Would that no similar case could be pointed to amongst those who have been professing Christians! Of how many may it be said,

"Ye did run well"? Let history shed its beacon-light athwart the waves, reminding us of the rocks, and bidding us remain in the calm open sea of the love of God. (4) *Consider the risk incurred in neglecting the advice of the text.* Folly is in proportion to the hazard which neglect involves. Scripture wisely employs every legitimate motive to urge men to adopt its plans. Threats are mentioned as well as promises, and punishments as well as rewards. Joshua declared that the spurning of his counsel would result in the withdrawal of God's aid in battle (ver. 13), and in their visitation with all manner of evil until destruction ensued (vers. 15, 16). Who shall estimate the peril of encountering the wrath of God? Even with His smile resting upon us the trials of life are hard to bear, but what if we have departed from Him and trials partake of the nature of judgments? True, believers are "kept by the power of God." Nevertheless, declension may cause the serious inquiry whether we have been really classed with believers. Hence the hypothetical statements and warnings of Holy Writ. It is not wise to swim on the verge of a whirlpool. Nor need we try how close to the edge of the cliff we can walk, lest we fall and there be no overhanging bough of Providence to arrest our awful descent.

II. PRACTICAL METHODS OF CULTIVATING THE HOLY AFFECTION ENJOINED. A preliminary objection may be raised respecting the inoperativeness of a command relating to the affections. Give an order with regard to the physical powers and it can be obeyed; the intellect will answer a call; but love is a spontaneous product, of internal not external origin, and cannot rise at will. Such an objection overlooks the fact that affection can be influenced, if not absolutely forced, by fixing its attention upon an object, by noting the qualities in it deserving of esteem and regard. Point one man to another whom he sees casually, and no emotion is excited. But describe the man, picture him as a loving friend, generous, noble, and true, and there will be created a desire to know more of him, and acquaintance will ripen curiosity into love. Accordingly we recommend (1) *Frequent meditation upon the character of God.* He is the embodiment of every perfection. He is life, light, and love. If, when we observe traits of goodness in our fellow-creatures, our hearts go out to them in loving sympathy, what must be the fervency of affection produced by contemplating the fount of goodness as it resides in the Almighty. In men it is but a shallow stream, often dry when most we need it, subject to widest fluctuations and to all changes of temperature, but in God it is an exhaustless perennial flood of all-powerful holiness and benevolence. We cannot let our minds dwell too much on the measureless perfections of the Deity. Let us stand upon the mount with Moses while God passes by, revealing His glory in His excellent name. To shut out the world for a season, and ascend in contemplation to the glorious temple, "where dwells eternal love," will be like exchanging the murky atmosphere of the city for the pure, bracing, inspiring Alpine mountains. We shall return strengthened for work and warfare, less enchanted by the world's allurements. And yet does the Almighty seem far removed from our ken, and do we need an assurance that He is one whom doubting finite minds can think of with delight? He has provided us with a clear portrait of Himself, His only-begotten son, "the brightness of His glory," the lustre of Deity shaded, that our weak eyes may gaze uninjured, living amongst men, and displaying all the qualities that can command our highest, deepest reverence and love. (2) *A constant passing in review of favours bestowed.* Joshua reminded the people that every promise had been fulfilled (vers. 14, 15). The Lord had vanquished the enemy (ver. 3), the land was partitioned, each tribe was enjoying its inheritance. If they adhered to God, memory would be prophetic. Surely gratitude would constrain them to yield loving service unto Him who had done and would do great things for them. And each has but to survey his present position, to let the eye light on many a proof of love Divine. Temporal prosperity, true-hearted friends, the delights of honest labour and rest, health and strength, knowledge and taste, for some of these or a hundred other blessings has every one to thank the author of "every good and perfect gift." Be it noted that mercies augment love, since they teach us plainly the goodness of the Giver. They are to us the revelation of His character, and it

must needs be that when we are brought into personal contact with Him, made
personally the recipients of His bounty, then we understand Him better, appreciate
more the warmth of heavenly rays than when we hear the testimony of others, or
behold the sunlight flashing upon them from the throne of God. But what shall
we say of God, revealed to us in Jesus Christ as the Father of our spirits, the forgiving God, who by His spirit hath quickened us from the death of sin, and is
fitting us for the enjoyment of His immediate presence ? And when we call to
mind His providential care exercised over us, and the seasons in which He prevented the billows from overwhelming us in despair, and the fires of temptation
from scorching us, what joy must it be to comply with the precepts of the text, to
"arise and seek Him whom the soul loveth." (3) *Watchfulness against sin.* The
"expulsive power of a new affection" is a two-edged sword that fights both for
good and for evil. The tendency of sin is to blind the judgment, pervert the
imagination, and to deaden spiritual emotion. If it were one and uniform we
should know how to attack it, but it is insidious and wraps itself in disguises, and
encroaches on every side, hence we must be ready to act on the defensive. Joshua
cautioned the Israelites against mingling with the degraded inhabitants of the land
(vers. 12, 13). This is an entanglement to many a youthful Christian. First, on
speaking terms, then follows familiarity, and lastly, participation in the very practices condemned. Not all at once did he rush into flagrant transgression, but
gradually walked into the snare, until the love of God was stifled in his breast.
Bodily sight depends on the state of the health, and the eye of the soul is dimmed
through the indulgence of fleshly lusts. A traitor is admitted into the camp, and
the true friend is ousted from his seat of honour. Guard, then, against sin ; say
not, "it is a little one ; " cherish not a viper in your bosom, it will mar your peace,
pollute your dwelling, and leave a sting which no palliative shall be able to soothe.
But if you are now repenting of sin, be assured of God's willingness to pardon,
"believe in Him that raised up Jesus from the dead ; who was delivered for our
offences and was raised again for our justification." Then say, "I love Him because
He first loved me."—A.

Joshua before his death twice calls together the people of Israel to urge on them
one exhortation of supreme importance. On the first occasion he reminds Israel of
its great mission, which is to be a holy nation, the priesthood of the Lord for all
mankind, separated by this its high calling from all association with the pagan
nations around, and bound to abstain from all contact with idolatry. Let us notice
the command and its sanction. (1) "The Lord hath driven out from before you
great nations and strong ; no man hath been able to stand before you unto this
day." "Take good heed, therefore, unto yourselves that ye love the Lord your
God ; lest ye in any wise go back and cleave unto the remnant of these nations
that remain among you and make marriages with them (vers. 9—12). Israel is
thoroughly to understand that it has not been put in possession of the land of
Canaan, to lead the same unholy life as those whom it had expelled. There is a
priesthood to be exercised. This priesthood implies separation from the ungodly
and from idolators. This separation, however, is to be for a time only, for all the
nations of the earth are finally to be blessed in the seed of Abraham (Gen. xii. 3).
Israel is separated from the rest of mankind for the good of the whole. This
separation is not merely external, it is moral, for it is only realised by a life of
holiness. Such is still the high calling of the people of God. They are to be
priests of the most High, separated from the world by the elevation of their life and
experience, even more than by privilege of position. The elect are a priesthood.
Their election does not terminate in their own advantage, but seeks through them
the good of the whole race, for which they are to prepare the way of salvation.
Under the new dispensation, the people of God are no longer divided by material
boundaries from the world. There is, therefore, all the greater necessity that the
line of spiritual separation be bright, strong, and distinct. (2) The commandment is enforced by a solemn sanction. "If ye go in unto these nations and they to
you, know for a certainty that the Lord your God will no more drive out any of these

nations from before you; but they shall be snares and traps unto you, and scourges in your sides, and thorns in your eyes, until ye perish from off this good land which the Lord your God hath given you" (vers. 12, 13). The punishment threatened has this notable characteristic—that it is to come by means of those very nations with whom Israel shall have entered into unholy alliance. These shall be made, in the hand of God, the scourge and the goad to His rebellious people, just as Israel had been, in the first instance, the sword of Divine justice to visit the iniquity of the Canaanites. So is fulfilled the great moral law that sin brings its own punishment. "Sin, when it is finished, bringeth forth death." Every time that Israel entered into compact with the heathen nations it fell under the hand of the heathen. So whenever the Church allies itself with the world, the world entangles, corrupts, and destroys its life, though, it may be, stealthily and without violence. "Strangers have devoured his strength, and he knoweth it not" (Hosea vii. 9). The worldliness of the Church silently saps its spiritual power.—E. DE P.

Ver. 15.—*Threats as true as promises.* There are those who deny God's threats of punishment the same validity which they ascribe to His promises of blessing. Joshua here ascribes equal certainty to both.
I. GOD MUST BE TRUE TO HIS THREATS. God desires to bless, and He can only punish reluctantly, since His nature is love. Hence it might appear that He would not be so true to His threats as to His promises. But, on the other hand, note:— (1) To threaten without intending to execute would be *deceitful;* God is true and must be faithful to His word. (2) It would be *cruel;* a merciful God would not terrify us with groundless alarms. (3) It would be *ineffectual;* the emptiness of the threat would be ultimately discovered, and then the delusion would cease to be a terror and become a mockery. (4) Punishment is ordained *not to satisfy vengeance,* but to establish justice and to vindicate and restore righteousness. It is a good sent for good ends, and to refrain from it would be a mark of weakness, not of mercy.
II. THE APPARENT UNCERTAINTY OF GOD'S THREATS ADMITS OF EXPLANATION. (1) They are *conditional.* The punishment does not always come because the conditions of the threat are altered. Repentance and faith in Christ are conditions on which God exercises mercy and refrains from executing His threat. The turning from evil is declared to be an alteration of circumstances which makes the threat no longer to apply (Ezek. xxxiii. 19). The force of gravitation is not suspended when we arrest the motion of a falling body. The law is not frustrated by the counter-action of the gospel. (2) Threats are often *misunderstood.* The Church has added monstrous physical horrors to the threats of the Bible, against which men revolt. It is not our interpretation of the threat, but God's meaning, that will be fulfilled. (3) Threats apply to the *future;* because God is long-suffering, men refuse to believe that He is just. The delay of punishment is no ground for dis-believing in the reality of it. (4) Threats are *unpleasant;* many persons will not entertain unpleasant ideas. Yet a fact is not the less true because it does not please us.
III. THE APPLICATION OF GOD'S THREATS SHOULD BE SERIOUSLY CONSIDERED. (1) *It is dangerous to neglect them.* We do not improve our health by ignoring the opinion of a physician simply because this is unfavourable. If the Divine warnings are true, they are terribly true, and no soul should be at rest till it has found safety in Christ. (2) *It is foolish to despair.* Why are these threats recorded in the Bible? Surely not simply to torture us! If they were inevitable it would be most merciful to conceal our doom from us till the last moment. But they are *warnings.* The very fact that they are recorded implies that the evil they describe may be avoided. The threat is true, but it is conditional. Therefore let us flee the danger by escaping to the refuge which God has provided (Rom. viii. 1).—W. F. A.

Ver. 24.—*The old man eloquent.* With much in the detail of these chapters which is of interest, the final farewell of Joshua is worthy of our study in its entirety. The dignity and serenity of saintly ripeness, the vigour of his exhortations, and the assurance of his faith, are facts worthy of the study of every one of us. Consider a few features of this farewell, and observe—

I. HIS GRACES ENDURE TO THE END. Bodily vigour leaves even his stalwart frame. Nervous energy begins to flag even with him. The mind loses elasticity and keenness. But his graces thrive. He chose God in his youth; he clings to Him in his age. His faith expected much in his manhood; it still enthrones God as the fountain of all that blesses a man or a people. His hope was bright, and still continues bright. His love of his God and of his country warm his whole being at an age when the chill of wintry age seems as if it must lower all warmth of interest. The outward man perishes; the inward man has been renewed day by day. What a sight to animate us! No regrets lament the early choice. No declension stains the early purpose. The bitter words of the elder D'Israeli, " Youth is a mistake, manhood a struggle, old age a regret," are all of them contradicted here. They are too often true. They are so when the early choice is made by passion rather than by principle. But when we choose God, we go " from strength to strength until we appear before the Lord in Zion." The perseverance of the saints is beautifully illustrated in such a case as this. Let the faint-hearted be of good cheer. Grace, however feeble, is a " living and incorruptible seed; a living and deathless seed; " and whatever its varying fortunes, it will persist until it reaches its great reward. Connected with this, yet worthy of separate mention, observe—

II. THE LONGER THE GOOD MAN'S EXPERIENCE, THE LARGER IS HIS SATISFACTION WITH HIS CHOICE. A short experience sometimes leaves good people in doubt whether their goodness will be worth its cost. Moses, when he had to flee to Midian, was very much tempted to repent of the zeal with which he had taken up the cause of his oppressed people in Egypt. In the Slough of Despond Christian was tempted to regret his setting out on pilgrimage. Joshua was tempted, when they refused the advice of Caleb and himself and talked of stoning them, to wish he had not unsettled the minds of the people by avowing his dissent from the conclusions of the majority of those sent out to spy the land. And often we drift into a mood the reverse of that of Agrippa, and are " almost persuaded" to cease to be Christians. But a longer experience always means a stronger sense of the wisdom of our choice. The earlier doubts of a Moses or a Joshua all fade away, and the aged saint is only thankful for his early choice. This should hearten us, and keep us from attaching too much weight to temporary depression, or even failures. When we choose God we choose " the good part" which shall not be taken away from us. Observe—

III. THE GOOD MAN'S LAST SERVICE IS HIS BEST SERVICE. He had done illustrious service throughout: as the faithful spy; as the faithful helper of Moses; as the heroic warrior; as the wise and upright divider of the land. But here he conquers not the arms of enemies, but the hearts of friends: infuses the energy to win not an earthly, but a heavenly kingdom: leads them into covenant with God: secures that deepening of conscience and strengthening of faith which will give them, in the degree in which it endures, the power to keep all that they had conquered. There is something characteristic of grace here. The last service may always be—and perhaps almost always is—the best. As it was said of Samson so, in a different sense, it may be said of the Saviour Himself and of all God's saints, " The dead slew in his death were more than all they that he slew in his life." The progressive usefulness of the saintly life is a very marvellous feature of it. Rejoice and hope in it. Lastly observe—

IV. HOW FIT FOR IMMORTALITY THE OLD MAN STANDS. There may be a physical theory of another life which convinces some of the truth of the Christian doctrine of immortality; but the great argument for immortality lies in men's meetness for it. The Enochs and the Joshuas were in early ages—and such spirits are to-day—the great arguments of immortality. Such ripeness of spirit cannot be wasted by Him who gathers up the fragments even that nothing may be lost. For such power to serve and faculty for enjoyment men could not help feeling there must be some provision and some scope beyond the grave. The other world is hidden, but occasionally the entrance of a great soul brightens it. They, lifted up, draw our hearts and thoughts up after them. And when, like the men of Galilee, we stand gazing upwards after those who leave us, like them we see the angels, and receive the promise of a blessed heritage with those who have gone. The belief in immortality has existed ever since good men died; and while there are good men to love, the belief in a bright glory will survive. Joshua stood ready for heaven, proving the existence of a heaven by that readiness. Let us, like him, be fit for the other world as well as this, that, to the last, hope, purpose, and usefulness may be rich and bright.—G.

EXPOSITION.

CHAPTER XXIV. 1—28.

THE LAST RENEWAL OF THE COVENANT. —Ver. 1.—**To Shechem.** The LXX. and the Arabic version read *Shiloh* here, and as the words "they presented themselves (literally, *took up their station*) before God" follow, this would seem the natural reading. But there is not the slightest MSS. authority for the reading, and it is contrary to all sound principles of criticism to resort to arbitrary emendations of the text. Besides, the LXX. itself reads Συχέμ, in ver. 26, and adds, "before the tabernacle of the God of Israel," words implied, but not expressed in the Hebrew. We are therefore driven to the supposition that this gathering was one yet more solemn than the one described in the previous chapter. The tabernacle was no doubt removed on this great occasion to Shechem. The locality, as Poole reminds us, was well calculated to inspire the Israelites with the deepest feelings. It was the scene of God's first covenant with Abraham (Gen. xii. 6, 7), and of the formal renewal of the covenant related in Gen. xxxv. 2—4 (see note on vers. 23, 26), and in Joshua viii. 30—35, when the blessings and the curses were inscribed on Mount Gerizim and Ebal, and the place where Joseph's bones (ver. 32) were laid, possibly at this time, or if not, at the time when the blessings and curses were inscribed. And now, once again, a formal renewal of the covenant was demanded from Israel by their aged chieftain, before his voice should cease to be heard among them any more. Rosenmüller reminds us that Josephus, the Chaldee and Syriac translators, and the Aldine and Complutensian editions of the LXX. itself, have Sichem. Bishop Horsley makes the very reasonable suggestion that Shiloh was not as yet the name of a town, but possibly of the tabernacle itself, or the district in which it had been pitched. And he adds that Mizpeh and Shechem, not Shiloh, appear to have been the places fixed upon for the gathering of the tribes (see Judg. x.

17; xi. 11; xx. 1 (cf. ver. 27); 1 Sam. vii. 5). See, however, Judg. xxi. 12, as well as Josh. xxi. 2; xxii. 12. Some additional probability is given to this view by the fact noticed above, that it is thought necessary to describe the situation of Shiloh in Judg. xxi. 19, and we may also fail to notice that the words translated "house of God" in Judg. xx. 18, 26 in our version, is in reality Bethel, there being no "house of God" properly so called, but only the "tabernacle of the congregation." The tabernacle in that case would be moved from place to place within the central district assigned to it, as necessity or convenience dictated. Hengstenberg objects to the idea that the tabernacle was moved to Shechem that it would have led to an idea that God was only present in His Holy Place, to which it is sufficient to reply, (1) that this does not necessarily follow, and (2) that such a conception was entertained, though erroneously, by some minds. The Samaritan woman, for instance, supposed the Jews to believe that in Jerusalem only ought men to worship (John iv. 20). When Hengstenberg says, however, that the meeting in the last chapter had reference to Israel from a theocratic and religious, and this one from an historical point of view, he is on firmer ground. The former exhortation is ethical, this historical. He goes on to refer to the deeply interesting historical traditions centering round this place, which have been noticed above. The oak in ver. 26, Hengstenberg maintains to be the same tree that is mentioned in Gen. xii. 6 (where our version has, erroneously, "plain"), and which is referred to both in Gen. xxxv. 4 and here as *the* (*i.e.*, the well-known) terebinth in Shechem (see note on ver. 26). He has overlooked the fact that the tree in Gen. xii. 6 is not an אֵלָה but an אֵלוֹן. He goes on to contend that the terebinth was not merely "by" but "in" the sanctuary of the Lord, which he supposes to be another sanctuary beside the tabernacle, perhaps the sacred enclosure round Abraham's altar. But he is wrong, as has been shown below, (ver. 26), when he says that ‫ב‬ never signifies near (see ch. v. 25). The question is one of much difficulty, and cannot be satisfactorily settled. But we may dismiss without fear, in the light of the narrative in ch. xxii., Knobel's suggestion that an altar was erected here on this occasion. If there were any altar, it must have been the altar in the tabernacle. **Other gods.** That the family of Nahor were not exactly worshippers of the one true God in the same pure ritual as Abraham, may be gathered from the fact that Laban had teraphim (Gen. xxxi. 19, 30). But recent researches have thrown some light on the condition of Abraham's family and ancestors. If Ur Casdim be identified, as recent discoverers have supposed, with Mugeyer, which, though west of Euphrates as a whole, is yet to the eastward of one of its subordinate channels (see ' Transactions of the Society of Biblical Archæology,' iii. 229 ; Tomkins, ' Studies on the Time of Abraham,' p. 4), its ruins give us plentiful information concerning the creed of its inhabitants. We may also find some information about this primeval city in Rawlinson's ' Ancient Monarchies,' i. 15, and in Smith's ' Assyrian Discoveries,' p. 233. The principal building of this city is the temple of the moon-god Ur. One of the liturgical hymns to this moon-god is in existence, and has been translated into French by M. Lenormant. In it the moon is addressed as Father, earth-enlightening god, primeval seer, giver of life, king of kings, and the like. The sun and stars seem also to have been objects of worship, and a highly developed polytheistic system seems to have culminated in the horrible custom of human sacrifices. This was a recognised practice among the early Accadians, a Turanian race which preceded the Semitic in these regions. A fragment of an early Accadian hymn has been preserved, in which the words "his offspring for his life he gave" occur, and it seems that the Semitic people of Ur adopted it from them. A similar view is attributed to Balak in Micah vi. 5, 6, and was probably derived from documents which have since perished (see Tomkins, ' Studies on the Time of Abraham,' p. 24). Hence, no doubt the Moloch, or Molech, worship which was common in the neighbourhood of Palestine, and which the descendants of Abraham on their first entrance thither rejected with such disgust (see also Gen. xxii., where Abraham seems to have some difficulties connected with his ancestral creed). Other deities were worshipped in the Ur of the Chaldees. Sumas,

the sun-god, Nana, the equivalent of Astarte, the daughter of the moon-god, Bel and Belat, "his lady." "In truth," says Mr. Tomkins, in the work above cited, "polytheism was stamped on the earth in temples and towers, and the warlike and beneficent works of kings. Rimmon was the patron of the all-important irrigation, Sin of brickmaking and building, Nergal of war." A full account of these deities will be found in Rawlinson's ' Ancient Monarchies,' vol. i.

Ver. 2.—**All the people** (see note on ch. xxiii. 2). **The Lord God of Israel.** Rather, *Jehovah, the God of Israel* (see Exod. iii. 13). Until the vision to Moses, the God of Israel had no distinctive name. After that time Jehovah was the recognised name of the God of Israel, as Chemosh of the Moabites, Milcom of the Ammonites, Baal of the Phœnicians. Our translation, "the Lord," somewhat obscures this. **Your fathers dwelt on the other side of the flood.** Rather, *of the river.* Euphrates is meant, on the other side of which (see, however, note on last verse) lay Ur of the Chaldees. It is worthy of notice that there is no evidence of the growth of a myth in the narrative here. We have a simple abstract of the history given us in the Pentateuch, without the slightest addition, and certainly without the invention of any further miraculous details. All this goes to establish the position that we have here a simple unvarnished history of what occurred. The manufacture of prodigies, as every mythical history, down to the biographies of Dominic and Francis, tells us, is a process that cannot stand still. Each successive narrator deems it to be his duty to embellish his narrative with fresh marvels. Compare this with the historical abridgment before us, and we must at least acknowledge that we are in the presence of phenomena of a very different order. Professor Goldziher has argued, in his ' Mythology among the Hebrews,' that Abraham, Sarah, Isaac, and Jacob are solar myths, such as we find in immense abundance in Cox's ' Aryan Mythology.' Abraham (father of height) is the nightly sky. Sarah (princess) is the moon. Isaac (he shall laugh) is the smiling sunset or dawn. It would be difficult to find any history which, by an exercise of similar ingenuity, might not be resolved into myths. Napoleon Bonaparte, for instance, might be resolved into the rushing onset of the conqueror who was never defeated. The retreat from Moscow is a solar myth of the most obvious description. The battle of Bull's Run is clearly so named from the cowardice displayed there by the sons of John Bull. It is remarked by Mr. Tomkins, that Ur, the city of the moon-god, lends itself most naturally to the fabricator of myths. There is only one objection to the theory, and that is the bricks, still in existence, stamped with the words Uru, which compel us to descend from this delightful cloud-land of fancy to the more sober regions of solid and literal fact (see ' Studies on the Times of Abraham,' pp. 205—207). **In old time.** Literally, *from everlasting, i.e.,* from time immemorial. ἀπ ἄρχης. The Rabbinic tradition has great probability in it, that Abraham was driven out of his native country for refusing to worship idols. It is difficult to understand his call otherwise. No doubt his great and pure soul had learned to abhor the idolatrous and cruel worship of his countrymen. By inward struggles, perhaps by the vague survival of the simpler and truer faith which has been held to underlie every polytheistic system, he had " reached a purer air," and learned to adore the One True God. His family were led to embrace his doctrines, and they left their native land with him. But Haran, with its starworship, was no resting-place for him. So he journeyed on westward, leaving the society of men, and preserving himself from temptation by his nomad life. No wandering Bedouin, as some would have us believe (see Drew, 'Scripture Lands,' p. 18), but a prince, on equal terms with Abimelech and Pharaoh, and capable of overthrowing the mighty conqueror of Elam. Such an example might well be brought to the memory of his descendants, who were now to be sojourners in the land promised to their father. Guided by conscience alone, with every external influence against him, he had worshipped the true God in that land. No better argument could be offered to his descendants, when settled in that same land, and about to be bereft of that valuable support which they had derived from the life and influence of Joshua.

Ver. 5.—And I plagued Egypt, according to that which I did among them. This verse implies that the Israelites possessed some authentic record which rendered it unnecessary to enter into detail. Add to this the fact that this speech is ascribed to Joshua, and that the historian, as we have seen, had access to authentic sources of information, and we cannot avoid the conclusion that the hypothesis of the existence of the written law of Moses at the time of the death of Joshua has a very high degree of probability. The word rendered "plagued" is literally *smote*, but usually with the idea of a visitation from God. **And afterward I brought you out.** The absence of any mention of the plagues here is noteworthy. It cannot be accounted for on the supposition that our author was ignorant of them, for we have ample proof that the Book of Joshua was compiled subsequently to the Pentateuch. This is demonstrated by the quotations, too numerous to specify here, which have been noticed in their place. We can only, therefore, regard the omission made simply for the sake of brevity, and because they were so well known to all, as a sign of that tendency, noticed under ver. 1, to abstain from that amplification of marvels common to all mythical histories. Had Joshua desired to indulge a poetic imagination, an admirable opportunity was here afforded him.

Ver. 6.—Unto the Red Sea. There is no *unto* in the original. Perhaps the meaning here is *into the midst of,* the abruptness with which it is introduced meaning more than that the Israelites arrived at it. But though without the *He locale,* it may be no more than the accusative of motion towards a place.

Ver. 7.—And when they cried unto the Lord. This fact is taken, without addition or amplification, from Exod. xiv. 10—12. The original has *unto Jehovah,* for "unto the Lord." **He put darkness** (see Exod. xiv. 19, 20). The occurrence, which there is most striking and miraculous, is here briefly related. But the miracle is presupposed, although its precise nature is not stated. **You.** This identification of the Israel of Joshua's day with their forefathers is common in this book (see notes on ch. vi. 21, &c.). **A long season.** Literally, *many days.* Here, again, there is no discrepancy between the books of Moses and this epitome of their contents. If both this speech and the Pentateuch were a clumsy patchwork, made up of scraps of this narrative and that, flung together at random, this masterly abstract of the contents of the Pentateuch is little short of a miracle. Whatever may be said of the rest of the narrative, this speech of Joshua's must have been written subsequently to the appearance of the books of Moses in their present form. But is there any trace of the later Hebrew in this chapter more than any other ?

Ver. 8.—And I brought you into the land of the Amorites (see ch. xii. 1—6 ; Num. xxi. 21—35 ; Deut. ii. 32—36 ; iii. 1—17).

Ver. 9.—Then Balak, son of Zippor. We have here the chronological order, as well as the exact historical detail, of the events carefully preserved. **Warred against Israel.** The nature of the war is indicated by the rest of the narrative, and this tallies completely with that given in the Book of Numbers. Balak would have fought if he dared, but as he feared to employ temporal weapons he essayed to try spiritual ones in their stead. But even these were turned against him. The curse of God's prophet was miraculously turned into a blessing.

Ver. 10.—**But I would not.** The Hebrew shows that this is not simply the conditional form of the verb, but that it means *I willed not.* It was God's "determinate purpose" that Israel should not be accursed. **Blessed you still.** Rather, perhaps, *blessed you emphatically.* **And I delivered you out of his hand.** Both here and in the narrative in Numbers xxii.—xxx. it is implied that Balaam's curse had power if he were permitted by God to pronounce it. Wicked as he was, he was regarded as a prophet of the Lord. There is not the slightest shadow of difference between the view of Balaam presented to us in this short paragraph and that in which he appears to us in the more expanded narrative of Moses.

Ver. 11.—**And ye went over Jordan.** This epitome of Joshua's deals with his own narrative just as it does with that of Moses. The miraculous portions of the history are passed over, or lightly touched, but there is not the slightest discrepancy between the speech and the history, and the miraculous element is presupposed throughout the former. **The men of Jericho.** Literally, the *lords* or *possessors* of Jericho. The seven Canaanitish tribes that follow are not identical with, but supplementary to, the lords of Jericho. **Fought against you.** The word is the same as that translated "warred" in ver. 9. The people of Jericho did not fight actively. They confined themselves to defensive operations. But these, of course, constitute war.

Ver. 12.— **The hornet.** Commentators are divided as to whether this statement is to be taken literally or figuratively. The mention of hornets in the prophecies in Exod. xxiii. 28, Deut. vii. 20 is not conclusive. In the former passage the hornet seems to be connected with the fear that was to be felt at their advance. The latter passage is not conclusive on either side. The probability is — since we have no mention of hornets in the history—that what is meant is that kind of unreasonable and panic fear which seems, to persons too far off to discern the assailants, to be displayed by persons attacked by these apparently insignificant insects. The image is a lively and natural one, and it well expresses the dismay which, as we read, seized the inhabitants of the land when their foes, formidable rather from Divine protection than from their number or warlike equipments, had crossed the Jordan (see Josh. ii. 9—11; v. 1; vi. 1). Where the figure came from is not far to

seek. Joshua was quoting the prophecies of Moses mentioned above. **The two kings of the Amorites.** Sihon and Og, who were driven out, beside the tribes on the other side Jordan who have just been mentioned.

Ver. 13.—**Labour.** The word here used is expressive of the fatigue of labour, and is more equivalent to our word *toil.* The whole passage is suggested by Deut. vi. 10.

Ver. 14. — **Sincerity and truth.** These words, rendered by the LXX. ἐν εὐθύτητι καὶ ἐν δικαιοσύνη, are not the precise equivalent of those so translated in other passages in the Bible, nor is St. Paul, in 1 Cor. v. 8, quoting this passage. The word translated sincerity is rather to be rendered *perfection,* or *perfectness.* The Hebrew word signifying truth is derived from the idea of stability, as that which can stand the rude shocks of inquiry.

Ver. 15.—**Or the gods of the Amorites, in whose land ye dwell.** There is a *reductio ad absurdum* here. "Had ye served those gods ye would never have been here, nor would the Amorites have been driven out before you." The reference to the gods of their fathers seems to be intended to suggest the idea of an era long since lost in the past, and thrown into the background by the splendid deliverances and wonders which Jehovah had wrought among them. **But as for me and my house, we will serve the Lord.** Or, *Jehovah.* Here speaks the sturdy old warrior, who had led them to victory in many a battle. He invites them, as Elijah did on another even more memorable occasion, to make their choice between the false worship and the true, between the present and the future, between the indulgence of their lusts and the approval of their conscience. But as for himself, his choice is already made. No desire to stand well with the children of Israel obscures the clearness of his vision. No temptations of this lower world pervert his sense of truth. The experience of a life spent in His service has convinced him that Jehovah is the true God. And from that conviction he does not intend to swerve. In days when faith is weak and compromise has become general, when the sense of duty is slight or the definitions of duty vague, it is well that the spirit of Joshua should be displayed among the leaders in Israel, and that there should be those who will take their stand boldly upon the declaration, "But as for me and my house, we will serve the Lord."

Ver. 16.—**And the people answered and said, God forbid that we should forsake the Lord.** There could be no doubt of the sincerity of the people at that moment. The only doubt is that afterwards expressed by Joshua, whether the feeling were likely to be permanent. The best test of sincerity is not always the open hostility of foes, for this very often braces up the energies to combat, while at the same time it makes the path of duty clear. Still less is it the hour of triumph over our foes, for then there is no temptation to rebel. The real test of our faithfulness to God is in most cases our power to continue steadfastly in one course of conduct when the excitement of conflict is removed, and the enemies with which we have to contend are the insidious allurements of ease or custom amid the common-place duties of life. Thus the Israelites who, amid many murmurings and backslidings, kept faithful to the guidance of Moses in the wilderness, and who followed with unwavering fidelity the banner of Joshua in Palestine, succumbed fatally to the temptations of a life of peace and quietness after his death. So too often does the young Christian, who sets out on his heavenward path with earnest desires and high aspirations, who resists successfully the temptations of youth to unbelief or open immorality, fall a victim to the more insidious snares of compromise with a corrupt society, and instead of maintaining a perpetual warfare with the world, rejecting its principles and despising its precepts, sinks down into a life of ignoble ease and self-indulgence, in the place of a life of devotion to the service of God. He does not cast off God's service, he does not reject Him openly, but mixes up insensibly with His worship the worship of idols which He hates. Such persons halt between two opinions, they strive to serve two masters, and the end, like that of Israel, is open apostasy and ruin. For "God forbid" see ch. xxii. 29.

Ver. 17.—**For the Lord our God.** Rather, *for Jehovah our God* (see note on ver. 2). The Israelites, we may observe, were no sceptics, nor ever became such. Their sin was not open rebellion, but the attempt to engraft upon God's service conduct incompatible with it, which led in practice to the same result—a final antagonism to God. But they believed in Jehovah; they had no doubt of the miracles He had worked, nor of the fact that His protecting hand had delivered them from all their perils, and had achieved for them all their victories. Nor do we find, amid all their sins, that they ever committed themselves to a formal denial of His existence and authority. To this, in the worst times, the prophets appeal, and though Israelitish obstinacy contested their conclusions, it never disputed their premises. **Did those great signs.** Here the people, in their answer, imply the circumstances which Joshua had omitted.

This remark presupposes the miraculous passage of the Red Sea and the Jordan, and the other great miracles recorded in the books of Moses and Joshua. **And among all the people through whom we passed.** The Hebrew is stronger, "through *the midst* of whom." As the destruction of the Amorites is mentioned afterwards, this must refer to the safe passage of the Israelites, not only among the wandering bands of Ishmaelites in the wilderness, but along the borders of king Arad the Canaanite, of Edom, and of Moab (Num. xx.—xxv.). This close, yet incidental, agreement on the part of the writers of two separate books serves to establish the trustworthiness of the writers.

Ver. 18.—**Therefore will we also serve the Lord.** There is an ambiguity in our version which does not exist in the Hebrew. There is no " therefore," which only serves to obscure the sense, and which is borrowed from the Vulgate. The LXX., which has ἀλλὰ καί, gives the true sense. After the enumeration of the great things God Jehovah has done for them, the Israelites break off, and, referring to the declaration of Joshua in ver. 15, " but as for me and my house, we will serve Jehovah," reply, " we too will serve Jehovah, for He is our God."

Ver. 19.—**And Joshua said unto the people, Ye cannot serve the Lord.** Calvin thinks that Joshua said this to rouse the sluggish heart of the people to some sense of their duty. But this is quite contrary to the fact, for the heart of the people, as we have seen (ch. xxii.), was *not* sluggish. As little can we accept the explanation of Michaelis, who paraphrases, " Ye will not be able, from merely human resolutions, to serve God." Joshua was stating nothing but a plain fact, which his own higher conception of the law had taught him, that the law was too "holy, just, and good " for it to be possible that Israel should keep it. He had forebodings of coming failure, when he looked on one side at the law with its stern morality and rigorous provisions, and the undisciplined, untamed people that he saw around him. True and faithful to the last, he set before them the law in all its majesty and fulness, the nature of its requirements, and the unsuspected dangers that lay in their weak and wayward hearts. No doubt he had a dim presentiment of the truth, to teach which, to St. Paul, required a miracle and three years' wrestling in Arabia, that by the deeds of the law "shall no flesh be justified in God's sight, for by the law is the knowledge of sin " (Rom. iii. 20). As yet the Spirit of God had barely begun to unveil the figure of the Deliverer who was to declare at once God's righteousness and His forgiveness. Yet none the less did Joshua do his duty, and strove to brace up the Israelites to theirs, not by disguising the nature of the undertaking to which they were pledging themselves, but by causing them to be penetrated with a sense of its awfulness and of the solemn responsibilities which it entailed. St. Augustine thinks that Joshua detected in the Israelites already the signs of that self-righteousness which St. Paul (Rom. x. 3) blames, and that he wished to make them conscious of it. But this is hardly borne out by the narrative. **He is a holy God.** The *pluralis excellentiæ* is used here in the case of the adjective as well as the substantive. This is to enhance the idea of the holiness which is an essential attribute of God. **He is a jealous God.** The meaning is that God will not permit others to share the affections or rights which are His due alone. The word, which, as its root, " to be red," shows, was first applied to human affections, is yet transferred to God, since we can but approximate to His attributes by ideas derived from human relations. Not that God stoops to the meanness and unreasonableness of human jealousy. His vindication of His rights is no other than reasonable in Him. " His glory " He not only " will not," but cannot " give to another." And therefore, as a jealous man does, yet without his infirmity, God refuses to allow another to share in what is due to Himself alone. The word, as well as the existence of the Mosaic covenant, has no doubt led the prophets to use, as they do on innumerable occasions, the figure of a husband and wife (Jer. ii. 2 ; Ezek. xxiii. 25 ; Hos. ii. 2, 13, 16 (margin), 19, 20) in describing the relations of God to His Church, and approximate to His attitude towards His people by the illustration of an injured husband towards a faithless wife (see also Exod. xxxiv. 14 ; Deut. vi. 15). **He will not forgive your transgressions nor your sins** (see Exod. xxiii. 21). There were many words used for " forgive " in Scripture : נשׂא, כפר, and סלח (see Pearson's learned note in his 'Treatise on the Creed,' Art. X.). The one here used signifies to remove or to bear the burden of guilt, corresponding to the word αἴρω in the New Testament. The word here translated " transgressions " is not the same as in chap. vii. 15, and the cognate word to the one rendered " transgressed " in chap. vii. 11, is here rendered " sins." It signifies a " breach of covenant," while the word translated " sins " is the equivalent of the Greek ἁμαρτία.

Ver. 20.—**Then he will turn.** There is no contradiction between this passage and James i. 17, any more than our expression, the sun is in the east or in the west, conflicts with science. St. James is speaking of God as He is in Himself, sublime in His unchangeableness and bountiful purposes towards mankind. Joshua and the prophets, speaking by way of accommodation to our imperfect modes of expression, speak of Him as He is in relation to us. In reality it is not He but we who change. He has no more altered His position than the sun, which, as we say, rises in the east and sets in the west. But as He is in eternal opposition to all that is false or evil, we, when we turn aside from what is good and true, must of necessity exchange His favour for His displeasure. **Do you hurt.** Literally, *do evil to you.* **After that he hath done you good.** This implies what has been before stated, that it is not God who is inconsistent but man, not God who has changed His mind, but man who has changed his.

Ver. 22.—**Ye are witnesses against yourselves.** Joshua has not disguised from them the difficulty of the task they have undertaken. Like a true guide and father, he has placed the case fully and fairly before them, and they have made their choice. He reminds them that their own words so deliberately uttered will be for ever witnesses against them, should they afterwards refuse to keep an engagement into which they entered with their eyes open. They do not in any way shrink from the responsibility, and by accepting the situation as it is placed before them, render it impossible henceforth to plead ignorance or surprise as an excuse for their disobedience. And it is well to observe, as has been remarked above, that such an excuse never was pleaded afterwards, that the obligation, though evaded, was never disavowed.

Ver. 23.—**Now therefore put away, said he, the strange gods which are among you.** Keil and Delitzsch notice that the words translated "among you" have also the meaning, "within you," and argue that Joshua is speaking of inward tendencies to idolatry. But this is very improbable. For (1) the word is the same as we find translated in ver. 17, "through whom." And (2) the internal scrutiny which the law demanded was hardly so well understood at this early period as by diligent study it afterwards became. The plain provisions of the law demanded obedience. Comparatively little heed was given at first to inward feelings and tendencies. There can be little doubt that the meaning is precisely the same as in Gen. xxxv. 2, and that though the Israelites dare not openly worship strange gods, yet that teraphim and other images were, if not worshipped, yet preserved among them in such a way as to be likely to lead them into temptation. The history of Micah in Judg. xvii. 5 is a proof of this, and it must be remembered that this history is out of its proper place. The zealous Phinehas (Judg. xx. 28) was then still alive, and the worship at Micah's house had evidently been carried on for some time previous to the disgraceful outrage at Gibeah. The putting away the strange gods was to be the outward and visible sign, the inclining of the heart the inward and spiritual grace wrought within them by the mercy of God. For it is not denied that God desired their affections, and that those affections could scarcely be given while their heart went secretly after idols. It may be further remarked in support of this view that the Israelites are not exhorted to turn their *heart* from the false gods, but to put them away. It is a plain, positive precept, not a guide for the inner consciousness. On the other hand, the command to incline the heart to the Lord rests upon the simple ground of common gratitude. St. Augustine thinks that if any false gods were secretly in Israel at this time, they would have been met by a severer punishment than that accorded to Achan. Masius—" pace divini viri "—proceeds to argue that murders, thefts, and adulteries were worse sins than those of Achan, that it were not reasonable to suppose that Israel was free from such sins, and they were not punished like Achan's. He forgets to urge (1) that the condition of the children of Israel was very different in Achan's time to that of the death of Joshua, and (2) that Achan's was a special act of disobedience to a very special enactment, considerations which would have materially strengthened his argument.

Ver. 24. — **And the people said unto Joshua.** The triple repetition of the promise adds to the solemnity of the occasion and the binding force of the engagement.

Ver. 25.—**So Joshua made a covenant.** Literally, *cut* a covenant, a phrase common to the Hebrew, Greek, and Latin tongues, and derived from the custom of sacrifice, in which the victims were cut in pieces and offered to the deity invoked in ratification of the engagement. The word used for covenant, *berith*, is derived from another word having the same meaning. This appears more probable than the suggestion of some, that the *berith* is derived from the practice of ratifying an agreement by a social meal. **And set them a statute and ordinance.** Or, *appointed them a statute and a judgment.* The word translated " statute " is derived from the same root as our word *hack*, signifying to *cut*, and hence to engrave in indelible characters.

The practice of engraving inscriptions, proclamations, and the like, on tablets was extremely common in the East. We have instances of it in the two tables of the law, and in the copy of the law engraven in stones on Mount Ebal. The Moabite stone is another instance. And the Egyptian, Assyrian, and Babylonian monarchs seem to have written much of their history in this way (see note on ch. viii. 32). The word rendered " ordinance " is far more frequently rendered " judgment " in our version, and seems to have the original signification of a thing set upright, as a pillar on a secure foundation. **In Shechem** (see note on ver. 1).

Ver. 26.—**And Joshua wrote these words.** Or, these *things*, since the word (see note on ch. xxii. 24; xxiii. 15) has often this signification. Joshua no doubt recorded, not the whole history of his campaigns and the rest of the contents of what is now called the Book of Joshua, but the public ratification of the Mosaic covenant which had now been made. This he added to his copy of the book of the law, as a memorial to later times. The covenant had been ratified with solemn ceremonies at its first promulgation (Exod. xxiv. 3—8). At the end of Moses' ministry he once more reaffirmed its provisions, reminding them of the curses pronounced on all who should disobey its provisions, and adding, as an additional memorial of the occasion, the sublime song contained in Deut. xxxii. (see Deut. xxi. 19, 22). Joshua was present on this occasion, and the dying lawgiver charged him to undertake the conquest of the promised land, and to maintain the observance of the law among the people of God. Hitherto, however, God's promise had not been fulfilled. It seems only natural that when Israel had obtained peaceful possession of the land sworn unto their fathers, and before they were left to His unseen guidance, they should once more be publicly reminded of the conditions on which they enjoyed the inheritance. It may be remarked that, although Joshua's addendum to the book of the law has not come down to us, yet that it covers the principle of such additions, and explains how, at the death of Moses, a brief account of his death and burial should be appended by authority to the volume containing the law itself. The last chapter of Deuteronomy is, in fact, the official seal set upon the authenticity of the narrative, as the words added here were the official record of the law of Moses, having been adopted as the code of jurisprudence in the land. **And took a great stone** (see notes on ch. iv. 2, 9). **An oak.** Perhaps *the tere-*

binth. So the LXX. (see note on ver. 1). The tree, no doubt, under which Jacob had hid the teraphim of his household. This was clearly one of the reasons for which the place was chosen. **By the sanctuary.** Keil denies that בְ ever means *near.* It is difficult to understand how he can do this with so many passages against him (see ch. v. 13; 1 Sam. xxix. 1; Ezek. x. 15). He wishes to avoid the idea of the sanctuary being at Shechem.

Ver. 27.—**A witness** (see note on ch. xxii. 27). **For it hath heard.** Joshua speaks by a poetical figure of the stone, as though it had intelligence. The stone was taken from the very place where they stood, and within earshot of the words which had been spoken. Thus it became a more forcible memorial of what had occurred than if it had been brought from far. **Ye deny your God.** To deny is to say that He is not. The Hebrew implies "to deny *concerning* Him," to contest the truth of what has been revealed of His essence, and to disparage or deny the great things He had done for His people. The whole scene must have been a striking one. The aged warrior, full of years and honours, venerable from his piety and courage and implicit obedience, addresses in the measured, perhaps tremulous, accents of age the representatives of the whole people he has led so long and so well. Around him are the ancient memories of his race. Here Abraham pitched his tent in his wanderings through Canaan. Here was the first altar built to the worship of the one true God of the land. Here Jacob had buried the teraphim, and solemnly engaged his household in the worship of the true God. Here was the second foothold the children of Abraham obtained in the promised land (see ver. 32), a foretaste of their future inheritance. The bare heights of Ebal soared above them on one side, the softer outlines of Gerizim rose above them on the other; and on their sides, the plaster fresh and the letters distinct and clear, were to be seen the blessings and the curses foretold of those who kept and those who broke the law. In the midst, Shechem, in a situation, as we have seen, of rare beauty, bore witness to the fulfilment of God's promise that the land of their inheritance should be "a good land," a "land flowing with milk and honey." No other place could combine so many solemn memories; none could more adequately remind them of the fulness of blessing God had in store for those who would obey His word; none could be fitter to impress upon them the duty of worshipping God, and Him alone.

HOMILETICS.

Vers. 1—28.—*The possession of the inheritance and its responsibilities.* The difference between this address to the children of Israel and the former is that, in the former, Joshua's object was to warn them of the danger of evil-doing, whereas in this he designed to lead them, now they were in full possession of the land, to make a formal renewal of the covenant. For this purpose he briefly surveys the history of Israel from the call of Abraham down to the occasion on which he addressed them. Up to that time the covenant had been given them as one which it would be their duty to fulfil when the time arrived. Now, he reminds them, the time *had* arrived. And just as the Church calls upon those who were dedicated to God in infancy to solemnly affirm, when they are old enough, their obligation to fulfil the engagement that was then contracted for them, so Joshua, now Israel was in a position to carry out fully the terms of the covenant, chooses a place as well as a time most fitting for the ceremony, and obtains from them a full recognition of the duties to which they were bound. In this address there is no appeal to their feelings. It is no question of personal influence to guide them into the right path. They are now simply asked to affirm or deny the position in which, whether they affirm or deny it, they really stand before God.

I. THE CONTRAST BETWEEN THE PAST AND PRESENT CONDITION OF GOD'S PEOPLE. "Your fathers dwelt on the other side of the flood in old time . . . and served other gods." So St. Peter tells us, "Ye were as sheep going astray, but are now returned to the Shepherd and Bishop of your souls" (1 Peter ii. 25. Cf. i. 14, 18; ii. 10; iv. 3). So St. Paul tells us (Ephes. ii. 1—3, 11, 12; Titus iii. 3, &c.). When we entered into covenant with God we crossed the flood, and were placed in the promised land, though not yet to possess the fulness of our inheritance. But if each one of us for himself has to cross the flood and put himself in covenant with Christ, it is because our Head has Himself trodden the same path. Born in "the likeness of sinful flesh," as the representative of sinners not yet fully reconciled to His Father, "made sin," not for Himself, but for us, He dwelt " on the other side " of the river of death; but that stream once crossed, He ascended into heaven, there to win blessings which we should inherit after Him. We must ever, while rejoicing in the privileges we now enjoy, remember how they were won, and what we once were, " children of wrath even as others," but now, being "made free from sin and become servants to God, ye have your fruit unto holiness, and in the end everlasting life."

II. THE COVENANT MUST BE RENEWED BY EACH FOR HIMSELF. The promises of God are general, to all mankind. But they are also special, to each individual. They must be applied personally by each man to his own soul, by faith. For this reason the Church of God has always required a profession of faith from each person when they entered into covenant with God at baptism. But this *formal* profession is practically inoperative, unless each man makes a *personal* profession of faith, in his own heart, on which he means to act, as soon as he is conscious of his own individual responsibility to God. Thus Israel, when the time had come for the fulfilment of the covenant by reason of his possession of his inheritance, was called upon to avow his readiness so to do. And thus he was the type of all Christians, who cannot appropriate to themselves the blessings of the covenant until they have acknowledged the obligation on their part to fulfil its conditions.

III. WE DID NOT GAIN THE BLESSINGS FOR OURSELVES (see ver. 15). The Israelites were continually reminded that the good things they enjoyed were not of their own procuring (see Deut. vi. 10; ix. 5). And so the Christian is reminded that he owes all to God. The Christian covenant is one of mercy, not of works. Any merits the Christian possesses are not his own, but the gift of God. " What hast thou, that thou hast not received? " If the gift of salvation through Christ, it was not thine by merit, but by God's free gift. If thou hast any bodily or intellectual gifts, they came down " from the Father of lights." If thou possessest any moral or spiritual qualities worthy of praise, they have been the work of God's Spirit within thee. Boast not, then, of anything thou art. Be not highminded, but fear. Take heed to use the gifts that have been given you to God's glory, and to be ever thankful to Him for His mercy, to whom you owe all you have and all you are.

IV. THE COVENANT IS A HARD ONE TO OBEY. The law of Moses was singularly strict and searching. It bound men to a close and minute scrutiny of their lives, and forced them to remember every hour the obligations they lay under. Nor is the Christian covenant one whit less searching. Nay, it is far more so, for it embraces not merely every act and word, but even the " thoughts and intents of the heart." God still punishes those who, even in the least point, offend against His law, and thus forsake Him and serve strange gods. It is still true that we " cannot" in our own strength " serve the Lord." But it is also true that He will forgive us our shortcomings through Jesus Christ, and that He will furnish us with the strength we lack to fulfil the precepts of the wide-reaching law which He has set us.

HOMILIES BY VARIOUS AUTHORS.

Ver. 1.—*Public worship.* "And they presented themselves before God." Eminent servants of God were remarkable for their solicitude respecting the course of events likely to follow their decease. " When I am gone let heaven and earth come together" is a sentiment with which a good man can have no sympathy. Note the instructions given by Moses (Deut. xxxi.), David (1 Kings ii.), Paul (2 Tim. iv. 1—8), and Peter (2 Pet. i. 12—15). As Jesus Christ looked to the future (John xiv.—xvii.; Acts i. 3), so did His type Joshua. He was determined that the people should be bound to the service of the true God, if solemn meetings and declarations could bring it about. Nothing should be wanting on his part, at any rate. The gathering of the Israelites may remind us of the purposes for which we assemble every Lord's day. We come—

I. To MAKE SPECIAL PRESENTATION OF OURSELVES BEFORE GOD. Always in the presence of the Almighty, yet do we on such occasions "draw nigh" to Him. The world, with its cares and temptations, is for a season excluded. We leave it to hold more immediate intercourse with our heavenly Father. We approach to pay the homage that is His due from us. Surely those who plead that they can worship in the woods and fields as well as in God's house, in solitude as in society, forget that the honour of Jehovah demands regular, public, united recognition. We have to consider His glory, not only our individual satisfaction. "I will give Thee thanks in the great congregation." It is our privilege also to proffer our requests, to implore the blessings essential to our welfare.

II. To LISTEN TO THE WORD OF GOD. We have the "lively oracles," the revelation of God to man. It behoves us to give reverent attention thereto. In business or at home other matters may distract our attention; here we can give ourselves wholly to the "still small voice." It may instruct, inspire, rebuke, and comfort. The utterance of God's messenger claims a hearing as the message from God to our souls. "Thus saith the Lord" (ver. 2). The speaker may (1) *recall the past to our remembrance*. Joshua reviewed God's dealings with His people, speaking of their call (ver. 2), deliverance from bondage (ver. 5), guidance (ver. 7), succour in battle (vers. 9—11), and possession of a goodly land (ver. 13). Such a narrative is fruitful in suggestions; provocative of gratitude, self-abasement, and trust. (2) *State clearly the present position*. Acquainted with God and the rival heathen deities, it was for the Israelites to make deliberate choice of the banner under which they would henceforth enrol themselves. In God's house Christians are taught to regard themselves as "strangers and pilgrims," as "seeking a better country," as those who are "on the Lord's side." If they will they may turn back and desert the Master whom hitherto they have followed. There must be "great searchings of heart." (3) *Briefly sketch the future*. Religion does not confine itself to the narrow region of present circumstances; it looks far ahead, desires no man to take a leap in the dark, but rather to weigh calmly the respective issues dependent upon the actions of to-day. None who have experienced the tendency of earthly occupations to absorb, to engross the interest, will deny the advantage accruing from the quiet contemplations of the sanctuary, where it is possible to calculate correctly afar from the bustle of the city, where on wings of the spirit we rise to an altitude that dwarfs the loftiest objects of worldly ambition, and brings heaven and its glories nearer to our view.

III. To RE-CONSECRATE OURSELVES TO GOD'S SERVICE. We remain the same persons and yet are continually changing. Like the particles of the body, so our opinions, affections, &c., are in unceasing flux. To dedicate ourselves afresh is no vain employment. It brightens the inscription, "holiness unto the Lord," which time tends to efface. Are not some idols still in our dwellings? some evil propensities indulged, which an exhortation may lead us to check? To keep the feast we cast out the old leaven. Man is the better for coming into contact with a holy Being. The contrast reveals his imperfections and quickens his good desires.

CONCLUSION. If inclined to say with the men of Beth-shemesh, "Who is able to stand before this holy Lord God?" (1 Sam. vii. 20) let us think of Christ, who has entered as our Forerunner into the Holiest of all. In His name we may venture boldly to the throne of grace. Some dislike the services of the sanctuary because they speak of the need of cleansing in order to appear before the Almighty. Men would prefer to put aside gloomy thoughts and to stifle the consciousness that all is not right within. But does not prudence counsel us to make our peace with God now, to "seek Him while He may be found," clothed in the attribute of mercy, instead of waiting for the dread day when we must all appear before the judgment-seat, when it will be useless to implore rocks and mountains to hide us from the presence of Him that sits upon the throne? Behold Him now not as a Judge desirous to condemn, but as a Father who hath devised means whereby His banished ones may be recalled, who waits for the return of the prodigal—yea, will discern Him afar off, and hasten to meet him in love.—A.

Vers. 14, 15.—*A rightful choice urged.* The most solemn engagement we can make is to bind ourselves to be the servants of Jehovah. Such a bond not even death dissolves, it is entered into for eternity. There are periods, however, when it becomes us to ponder the meaning of the covenant, and to renew our protestations of fidelity. To consider the exhortation of Joshua here recorded will benefit alike the young convert and the aged believer, and may lead to a decision those "halting between two opinions."

I. AN APPEAL FOR HEARTY RE-DEDICATION TO THE SERVICE OF GOD. (1) *Its necessity* arises from the proneness of man to settle down upon his lees, neglecting the watchfulness observed on his first profession of religion. Enthusiasm cools; men sleep and tares are sown among the wheat; the Christian athlete rests content with the laurels already gained; the warrior, having defeated the enemy, allows him time to gather his forces for another battle. The temple was beautifully cleansed, but inattention has allowed it to grow filthy, and it needs a thorough renovation. (2) *Its leading motive* is gratitude for Divine goodness in the past. How skilfully Joshua, in the name of Jehovah, enumerates the chief national events wherein His mercy had been conspicuous. Brethren, review the past! Your mercies have been numberless, like the drops of the river flowing by your side. If you can tell the stars, then may you catalogue the blessings you have received. The retrospect teaches the character of your God, and may inspire you with hope for the future. Reverence the Almighty, and your highest expectations will not be disappointed but far surpassed. (3) *Its method* prescribes severance from idolatry and a sincere determination to follow the Lord fully. Self-examination will reveal many sins still cherished in the heart, like the gods which Israel had allowed to remain in the camp. It were well for us, like David, to go in and sit before the Lord (2 Sam. vii. 18). In the presence of Him who has loaded us with benefits temporal and spiritual, our vision will be clarified, and we shall be filled with an earnest desire to "cleanse ourselves from all filthiness of the flesh and spirit." All avowals of a change of heart are to be distrusted which are unaccompanied by evident renunciation of evil habits. The outward act not only affords an index of the inward feeling, but also materially contributes to its strength.

II. AN ALTERNATIVE PRESENTED. Notwithstanding all that had been done for the Israelites, some of them might deem it "evil," unpleasant, irksome, laborious to serve the Lord. Hence the option of forsaking Him, and bowing before the gods whom their fancy should select. The alternative suggests that, in the opinion of the speaker, (1) *some kind of service is inevitable.* Without acknowledging some superior powers, the Israelites could not remain. Absolutely free and independent man cannot be, though his idol may assume any form or character. In every breast there is some predominating principle or passion, be it piety, morality, intellectualism, æstheticism, or love of selfish pleasure. (2) *The freedom of the will is seen in the power of choice.* Choose man must; but he can choose what seems best to him. God has a right to demand our homage; but He is content to let us decide for ourselves the equity of His claims. He appeals to the judgment and the conscience. He makes His people "willing in the day of His power," not by enchaining their wills and constraining obedience, but by appropriate motives and inducements, leading them to consider it their glory to lay themselves at His feet "Who then is *willing* to consecrate this service this day unto the Lord?" (1 Chron xxix. 5). Freedom of choice is too frequently a beautiful and dangerous gift, which, like a sword in the hands of a child, injures its possessor. Yet we are unable to divest ourselves of the responsibility that attaches to free agency. Some plan of life is ruling us, even if it be a resolve to live aimlessly. We may deliberately weigh our decision, bringing to bear upon our comparison of conflicting claims all the strength of our moral nature and power of discernment, or we may refuse to face the points at issue, and let our judgment go by default, imagining that we shall thus escape the onus of a formal determination; but in the latter case, no less than in the former, we have made our choice, and are serving some master, though we recognise it not. The alternative indicates (3) that *neutrality and compromise are each impossible.* If God be not the object of adoration, then any occupant of the throne must be considered as God's enemy. Multitudes think that if they are not found openly opposing religion there is naught to be complained of in their attitude and conduct. Herein they are terribly at fault. "He that is not with Me is against Me." Those who advance not to the help of the Lord are treated as His foes (cf. Judg. xxi. 8 and 1 Sam. xi. 7). Nor will God accept a divided allegiance. Dagon must fall from his pedestal when the ark of God's presence enters the chamber of the heart. How could the Israelites be true at once to Jehovah and to idols ? "Ye cannot serve God and mammon." Religion modifies the character of every action, transforming it into an offering laid upon the altar to the glory of God. All that we have and are we send to the Royal Mint, and receive it back, stamped with the Sovereign's image, and fashioned according to His desire.

III. A FIXED RESOLVE. "As for me and my house, we will serve the Lord." Joshua set *a noble example*, which powerfully affected his followers. The expressed determination of a pastor, a teacher, a parent may produce widespread beneficial results upon those under their charge. Joshua showed himself fit to lead men. He did not wait to see what the majority of the people would approve before he committed himself to a particular course of action ; but boldly stated his intention to cleave with full purpose of heart unto the Lord. The Ephraimites, slow to come to the rescue in the hour of danger, but swift to claim a place of honour when a victory has been won (Judg. xii.1, 2), have found many imitators in every age. Men who wait to see in which direction the current of popular feeling is setting ere they risk their reputation or their safety by taking a decided step. We may dislike isolation, but are not alone if the Father is with us. Joshua's resolve was *never regretted*. What man has ever been sorry that he became a follower of Christ ? Even backsliders confess that they were never happier than when they attended to the commandments of the Lord. True religion furnishes its votaries with self-evidential proofs of its Divine authority in the peace of mind and satisfaction of conscience which they experience. To enjoy the favour of God is felt to be worth more than any earthly friendship or worldly gain.

CONCLUSION. This theme is suitable for the beginning of a year, when untrodden paths invite you to choose a method of travel. Or perhaps some crisis is occurring in your life, when you are entering upon a fresh sphere of employment. Use it as a time to commence a period of devotion to God's service. Young people, decide which is the more honourable, to serve God or the world. Do not spend the finest of your days in a manner which will hereafter pierce you with remorse.—A.

Vers. 1—22.—Joshua gathers all the tribes together to Shechem, and calls for the elders of Israel, and for their heads, and for their judges, and for their officers, and they presented themselves before God. "And Joshua said unto the people, Ye are witnesses against yourselves that you have chosen you the Lord to serve Him. And they said, We are witnesses. So Joshua made a covenant with the people that day." There are few more beautiful incidents in the Old Testament than this renewal of the covenant between God and His people, at the moment of their entering into possession of the promised land, and on the eve of the death of Joshua. It seems to us an admirable model of the covenant which ought to be constantly renewed between successive generations of the people of God in all ages, and the Father in heaven. (1) Let us observe, first, that the piety of the fathers does not suffice for the sons, and that while it is a great blessing to have pious parents, and gives the children a strong vantage-ground for the spiritual warfare, it does not do away with the necessity that they should for themselves ratify the holy resolves of their progenitors. God made a covenant with Abraham, but, nevertheless, both Isaac and Jacob renewed that holy covenant for themselves. And it needed, as we see, to be ratified again by their descendants when at length they entered into possession of the promised land. So is it with ourselves. Though we had in our veins the blood of the most glorious saints, their holiness would not make us the less culpable if we did not yield our own selves a living sacrifice unto God. What avails it to be children of Abraham according to the flesh, since God is able of the stones to raise up children unto Abraham ? (Matt. iii. 7.) These principles find a special application in the gospel economy, in which everything is made to depend upon the birth.   Not only should the covenant with God be concluded by each new generation of Christians, but it needs to be ratified by every individual for himself apart.   (2) " They presented themselves before God," it is said, on this solemn day. It is before Him and in His sight that the great pledge is to be taken which marks our entrance into His covenant of grace.   We have not to do with His representa-tives, the ministers of His Church, nor even with the Church itself, but with Him. Let us rise above all that is human, and let us come into the very presence of God when we yield ourselves to Him and to His service.   (3) In this solemn meeting between Israel and Israel's God, to renew their covenant, it is God who leads the way by recalling to His people the glorious manifestations of His love in choosing them, delivering them from the bondage of Egypt, bringing them through the desert, and making them victorious over the nations of Canaan.   All is of His mercy; His free grace is the basis of reconciliation.   It is the offended one who makes the first advance.   " He *first* loved us," says St. John (1 John iv. 18).   (4) Preventing grace does not nullify human freedom.   God proposes, invites, beseeches, and in His very entreaty there is a virtue which enables us to respond to Him.   But we must respond, we must decide for ourselves, it must be our free act.   The question is put in the most categorical form to the people of Israel : " If it seem evil to you to serve the Lord, choose ye this day whom ye will serve " (ver. 15).   " The people answered and said, God forbid that we should forsake the Lord to serve other gods." "And Joshua said unto the people, Ye are witnesses against yourselves, that ye have chosen you the Lord to serve Him.   And they said, We are witnesses " (ver. 22). This decisive dialogue ought to pass between every individual soul and God.   Its form may differ, but in substance it is always the same.   " Lovest thou Me ? " says Christ to Peter, on the shores of the Lake of Tiberias.   " Yea, Lord, Thou knowest that I love Thee " (John xxi. 15).   It is the interchange of this question and answer which seals the covenant between the soul and Christ.   Woe to those who forsake the good way after having once chosen it !   " If we sin wilfully after that we have received the knowledge of the truth, there remaineth no more sacrifice for sins, but a certain fearful looking-for of judgment " (Heb. x. 26, 27).—E. DE P.

Vers. 1—13.—*Review of Providence.*   I. IT IS WELL TO REVIEW THE PAST. (1) The life which is wholly occupied with the present is necessarily superficial. Recollection and anticipation broaden and deepen life.   They are essential to the consciousness of personal identity.   Memory retains possession of the past and thus enriches life.   The past is not wholly gone ; it lives in memory ; it lives in its effects ; it will be called up for judgment.   (2) A review of the past should make us (*a*) *grateful* for the goodness of God, (*b*) *humble* in the consciousness of our own failings, (*c*) *wise* from the lessons of experience, and (*d*) *diligent* to redeem the time which yet remains.

II. NO REVIEW OF THE PAST IS COMPLETE WHICH DOES NOT RECOGNISE THE DIVINE PROVIDENCE.   The chief value of biblical history is in the fact that it clearly indi-cates the action of God in human affairs.   (1) The highest historical study is that which searches for " God in history."   To do this is to trace events to their first cause, to see the connecting ideas of unity which bind all things together, and to follow out the course of all changing movements towards their destined end.   (2) We may see indications of the active presence of God in history and in private life by noting (*a*) material and spiritual good things enjoyed ; (*b*) providential deliver-ances in trouble ; (*c*) solemn acts of judgment ; (*d*) good thoughts and deeds which all have their origin in God, the source of all good, and (*e*) the general onward and upward movement of mankind.   (3) Let us practically apply the duty of noting God's action in human affairs to national history, church history, and private experience.

III. A RIGHT REVIEW OF GOD'S ACTION IN THE PAST WILL SHOW THAT THIS IS CHARACTERISED BY GOODNESS AND MERCY.   We single out striking calamities for difficulties to the doctrine of Providence.   We should remember that these are striking just because they are exceptional.   We are often tempted to fix upon the troubles and neglect the mercies of the past. A fair review of the whole will show that the blessings infinitely outnumber the distresses. (1) Such a review should stimulate *gratitude*. It is most ungrateful to be receiving innumerable blessings every day of our lives and rarely to recognise the Hand from which they come, while we complain that others are not added, or murmur if any cease. (2) Such a review should increase our *confidence and hope*. God is changeless. As He has been He will be. "Hitherto the Lord hath helped us." Threatening clouds have burst in beneficent showers. Deliverance has come when all seemed hopeless. Let us believe that the same will be in the future, and press forward to dark and uncertain days with more assurance of faith.

IV. THE GOODNESS OF GOD IN HISTORY WILL BE CHIEFLY SEEN IN THE PROMOTION OF THE HIGHEST HUMAN PROGRESS. History in the main is the story of the progress of mankind. This was the case with Joshua's review of Jewish history. It showed progress from idolatry to the worship of the true God, from slavery to liberty, from poverty to a great possession, from homeless wandering to a happy, peaceful, settled life. Thus God is always leading us upwards from darkness to light, from bondage to liberty, from ignorance, superstition, sin, and misery to the golden age of the future (Rom. viii. 19—23).—W. F. A.

Ver. 14.—*The call to God's service.* I. THE CALL. (1) It is a *direct appeal.* Religion is practical, and preaching must be practical. We must not be satisfied with the exposition of truth. We must aim at persuasion such as shall affect the conduct of men. For this purpose there is room for direct exhortation. Men are ready to admit the truth of propositions which lie outside the sphere of their own experience. The difficult matter is to translate these into principles of conduct and to apply them to individual lives. The Bible is sent for this ultimate purpose. As a message from God the Word of God is not merely a revelation of truth; it is supremely a call from the Father to His children. God is now calling directly to us by the undying voice of Scripture, by providence, by His Spirit in our consciences (Rev. xxii. 17). (2) The call is based on a *review of past experience*. After this review Joshua says, "*Now, therefore,* fear the Lord," &c. God's goodness to us in the past is a great motive to incline us to serve Him (*a*) because it lays us under a great obligation to Him (1 Cor. vi. 20), and (*b*) because it reveals His character as that of a Master worthy of devotion and delightful to serve. (3) The call is urged with the *last words of a dying man*. Joshua is old and about to die. At such a time an address would naturally be characterised by supreme earnestness. What is then urged would be felt by the speaker to be of first importance. Mere conventionalism, objects of passing political expediency, trifles and crotchets sink out of view. The dying message of the old leader must concern the highest welfare of the people. With all the force of these circumstances Joshua selects the need to fear and serve God for His one urgent exhortation. Surely this fact should lead us all to put it before ourselves as a question of first importance, taking precedence of all considerations of worldly pleasure and interest.

II. THE OBJECT OF THE CALL. (1) The *end* to be aimed at is to "fear and serve the Lord." The fear characterises the spirit of internal devotion, the service covers the obedience of active work. The fear precedes the service; because we cannot rightly serve God with our hands till we are devoted to Him in our hearts. The fear of God here required is not the abject terror which the slave feels for the tyrant, but reverence, awe, worship, the dread of displeasing, and the humble submission of our souls. This must be found in all true devotion. Yet it is most prominent in the stern Hebrew faith (Psa. ii. 11). For the Christian, love is the leading motive, though this love must be an awed and reverent affection. After the fear, then, must follow the service; for God will not be satisfied with passive veneration, He requires active obedience. (2) The essential characteristic of the fear and service here noted is *sincerity*. There is always danger of worship becoming unconsciously formal even when it is not knowingly hypocritical; because pure worship involves the highest effort of spirituality, great abstraction from sense, and a purity of thought which is very foreign to the habits of sinful beings (2 Tim. iii. 5). Yet God abhors unreal devotion (Isa. xxix. 13), and can only be worshipped at all when He is served spiritually (John iv. 24). (3) The necessary condition of this fear and service is a *departure from all things inconsistent* with it. The people must give up all lingering habits of idolatry. We must repent and forsake our old sins. We cannot retain devotion to the world and to sin whilst we devote ourselves to God. No man can serve two masters. Therefore choose.—W. F. A.

Vers. 2, 3.—*Abraham the heathen.* "Your fathers . . . served other gods," is an incidental statement of the utmost value. It throws a light on Abraham's antecedents in which we do not always see them, and enhances the significance of his abandonment of home and country, and his clear faith in a living God, in a degree which nothing else does. Observe first of all—

I. The fact that Abraham was originally a heathen. He was not merely born and bred an idolater, as we might have gathered from the story of Rachel's teraphim, but was a pagan in exactly the same condition of belief as many in India or in China are to-day. Some, in later times especially, and indeed in all times, worshipped the true God, but employed an idol to assist their imagination of Him; that is, they simply sought ritualistic and sensuous aids to religious thought and feeling. But Abraham began life far lower down in the religious scale. His fathers *served other gods;* the deified powers of nature representing little more than the forces and tendencies of life. Primitive tradition had lost any brightness it ever had. The religious sentiment had lost that reverence and habit of attention which soon begins to perceive God and to feel that the God constantly appealing to it is one and the same. The worship of several deities is always a mark of a superstitious ingredient blending with faith. Terah's family were in this condition. They were not only idolaters but polytheists—without Bible or sacrament, promise, or law. Abraham was precisely in the same sort of spiritual circumstances, and had been taught the same sort of religious ideas, and trained in the same superstitions, as are found in all pagan lands to-day. Yet with advantages so slight, he became the spiritual father of the religious nation of antiquity—type of all saintliness, of everything bright in faith and unquestioning in obedience. There is some reason to suppose that a god of vengeance was one of those deities most reverently regarded by his people; and yet he finds and worships a God of love ! He, like all of us, had Christ, the light that lighteth every man that cometh into the world. He, unlike most of us, followed the Christ-light within him. Following the Divine light, it grew ever clearer, and his vision became stronger to perceive and his heart to follow it. Amongst a multitude of silent deities, One spoke to him through his conscience, with more and more of frequency, and, in the degree in which He was obeyed, with more and more of clearness, both in the comforts He whispered and the commands He enjoined, till gradually he felt there was but one great God, who governed all, and should receive the homage of all; who was the friendly refuge as well as the omnipotent Creator of men. Gradually his life began to revolve around this unseen Centre, and the outward aspect and inward purpose of his life stood out in palpable difference from that of his fellows. Doubtless he preached his deep conviction, gathered about him some kindred spirits; perhaps had to endure persecution; till at last he got a strong impression borne in upon his conscience that his path of duty and of spiritual wisdom was to leave his native land and seek a new home for what was a new faith amongst men. His coming to Ur of the Chaldees, and then to Canaan, may be compared with the expedition of the Pilgrim Fathers. Like them he sought " freedom to worship God," and like them founded a great nation in doing so. In any view of his character, his decision, his devotion, the clearness of his faith, the promptness of his obedience, are marvellous. But they become much more so when we mark the fact that Joshua here brings out, that Abraham began his career in heathen darkness—that the father of the faithful began life as a mere pagan. Observe—

II. Some lessons of this fact. For evidently it has many. We can only suggest them. (1) *A little grace and a little light go a long way when well used.*

How little had Abraham to begin with! But, using what he had, it grew more, and was enough to do more for him than light a thousand times as clear does for some of us to-day. A man who has light upon his next step of duty has really an "abundance of revelation." Do not go in for being omniscient, postponing all obedience until you get light on all truth. Use your little light well whatever it is, and so you will get more. (2) *Obedience is the mode of self-enlightenment.* "If any man will do God's will, he shall know God's doctrine." So says Christ. Doing duty is the way of discovering truth. Since the creation of the world there has been no other. Take this. (3) *All the sacraments are means of grace, not conditions of salvation.* The Church has always been tempted to exaggerate *the helpful* into *the essential,* until it says, "Extra ecclesiam, nulla salus." Paul, in the Epistle to the Romans, arguing with those who held the sacrament of circumcision essential to salvation, quotes Abraham as reaching all his spirituality and accept-ance with God, "not in circumcision, but in uncircumcision," *i.e.,* not by sacra-ments, but without them altogether. Sacraments are aids. The mercy that gave them to be such will, in the absence of them through error or inadvertence, use some other way of enriching and enlightening the obedient heart. (4) *However sunk in superstition the heathen may be, they are capable of religion.* The difference between the Christian and the heathen in the matter of spiritual advantages is not a difference between having all and having nothing, but between having more and having less. They have the Christian inward light—movings of God's spirit, lessons of God's providence. God speaks to them, and "wakes their ear in the morning." They lack the testimony of God's saints, their examples, the revelation of God's highest law, a clear light on immortality ; above all, the light which comes from the life and death of the Son of God—"the light of the knowledge of the glory of God in the face of Jesus Christ." This fuller light would multiply vastly the number of the devout amongst them, and give a higher character to their devotion. But they may be saved, as we are taught explicitly both by Peter and by Paul, by a Saviour they feel and follow, though they do not know the story of His love. (5) *The heathen being thus capable of religon, and our higher advantages being influential to produce it, we ought to extend to them the full light of the Saviour's glory.* Our neglect of Christian missions grows from our despair of heathen men. We ought to think of the millions in heathen darkness as Abraham's brethren, and capable of appreciating and responding to all that is true and gracious. If we rightly reverence them, we should not eat our morsel of the bread of life alone, but should share it with them. Let us seek to extend the knowledge of the gospel of Christ, and we shall yet behold many an Abraham rising up in heathen lands.—G.

Vers. 14, 15.—*The great appeal.* From the trembling lips of one within a step of death comes the appeal which through all the centuries since has pierced and moved and won the hearts of men. Often urged, it is not always represented accurately. Elijah may address a more degenerate generation with a challenge to serve God or to serve Baal, insisting on this as if the chances of either alternative being adopted were even. Joshua does not say, "Choose ye this day whom ye will serve—God or another," but bids them serve God, urging His claims. In the event of their being unwilling to yield to these claims, he urges with some irony, that shows the keenness of moral energy still in Him, that in that case they should choose amongst the deities whose feebleness they had witnessed the one least helpful. There are several things here worthy of notice. Observe, first, an assumption underlying this appeal, viz.:

I. SOME PLAN OF LIFE SHOULD BE SOBERLY THOUGHT OUT AND FOLLOWED WITH DECISION. Our "miscellaneous impulses" always prove a poor guide. There can be neither progress, peace, strength, nor usefulness if life is desultory. We cannot employ anything to good advantage, much less life, unless we know its nature, what it is made for, what can be done with it, its resources and its proper ends. The first question of the ' Shorter Catechism,' " What is the chief end of man ? " stands as the first question of the catechism of life. Until we form some aim and keep to it, to-morrow will be always moving in a different direction from to-day, will lose what to-day has won. An aim permits life to be cumulative, always gathering richer force, fuller joys—always completing and rounding off its conquests. Joshua here assumes that a plan of life is essential to the proper pursuit of it, and on this assumption his appeal is based. Take note of this, for a planless is a powerless life.

Observe—

II. HE CLAIMS THEIR LIFE FOR GOD. "Now, therefore, serve Him." He does not timorously present any alternative. There is no reasonable alternative to this. One plan, and only one, of life should be entertained by a serious nature. The only wise and only rational plan of life is the service of God. A multitude of reasons concur to commend it. (1) *Conscience requires it,* as the only right course. Serving God, every law will be kept, every duty done, every claim met, every wrong avoided. Conscience points like a compass-needle to the throne of God, and its every suggestion is in one form or other a suggestion to do His bidding. It is a solemn fact that the holiest and the deepest instinct of our nature bids us serve God. (2) *Gratitude requires it.* God had delivered them, led them, helped them, enriched them; given them liberty, victory, home. In addition to these national blessings, He had to each individual given life, faculty, joys, home-loves, duties that dignified, comforts that gladdened life. The instinct of gratitude is to ask, What shall I render to the Lord for all His benefits? We have still larger benefits—a Saviour, a home above. Gratitude should constrain us to serve God. (3) *Wisdom should constrain us to serve Him.* Serve self—and server and served are both ruined. Serve God—and God is pleased, and we are safe. Service of God developes all our higher faculties; is the only state in which we are safe; is the course in which we are useful. Growth, safety, usefulness, what can compare with them? Pitiable is the state of those who do not serve. *They do not live* in any proper sense of the word. Therefore Joshua urges on them to serve their redeeming God. And the grounds which suited them 4,000 years ago are all intensely valid to-day. Consider this claim, and if disposed to dispute it, consider next—

II. THE CHALLENGE HE GIVES TO THOSE UNWILLING TO SERVE GOD. "If it seem evil unto you to serve the Lord, choose ye whom ye will serve; the gods whom your fathers served, or the gods of the Amorites in whose land ye dwell." Thus he presents them with the discredited deities around them, and bids them choose. Will they choose the gods that Abraham forsook—forsook because power-less to help, degrading in their influence? by forsaking whom he found all his grandeur, all his blessedness, all his reward? or will they take the gods of the Amorites whose powerlessness to protect their servants had been just witnessed, who betrayed those who trusted in them? With what force does the mere form in which he urges his challenge deter men from it! Would that all who reject the Saviour would realise what they are about! If it seems not good to you to serve Christ, whom will ye serve? The gods your fathers left? The gods whose power-lessness to bless men is manifest around you? Such a goddess as *Pleasure,* which fools think the best to worship, which fritters away all strength of soul, de-stroys conscience, and heart, and intellect, and body alike—would you choose that? or *Money,* coyest of all deities? whom he that seeketh rarely findeth, and he that findeth never finds so rich as he had hoped? who seems to be a god that can give everything, but it is found to be unable to give any one of the things most desired by us? Or *Power,* the deity sought by the ambitious, who never permits any one to say, "He is mine" in anything like the degree he had hoped, and even when possessed is found to be insipid as the insignificance from which men fled? Is it *Indulgence?* the deity that degrades men? or *Self-will,* the deity that destroys them? Choose which. There ought to be no trifling. We must serve some God. Who is to be the source of all you hope for if you put away the Saviour of Calvary? To use the experience of others is the part of a wise man; to buy experience dearly for yourself is the part of a foolish man. There is none amongst all the deities that clamour for your service which the wise and the good have not forsaken, or the foolish and the worldly have not repented of cleaving to. Betake not yourself to such, but serve the Lord.—G.

Vers. 14—16.—*The grand choice.* Joshua's words derive added force from the historic associations of the place in which he uttered them. Shechem was not only a scene of great natural beauty, but one around which lingered memories peculiarly in harmony with the circumstances of the time. Here Abraham first pitched his tent and raised an altar, consecrating that spot to the living God—a witness against the heathen abominations of the Canaanites who dwelt in the land. Here, probably under the same oak, Jacob buried the "strange gods"—the teraphim and the amulets that some of his family had brought from Padanaram—in token of his resolute renunciation of these sinful idolatries. What more fitting place could be found for a solemn appeal like this to the tribes to remain true to the God of their fathers? Besides which, Joshua's venerable age, the blameless integrity of his character, and the renown of his exploits as their leader, gave such weight to his appeal that they would well deserve the threatened penalties if they failed to profit by it. Certain important principles of religious life are illustrated in this appeal—

I. THE SERVICE OF GOD IS A MATTER OF FREE PERSONAL CHOICE. "Choose you this day," &c. The simple alternative they were called on to decide was, either the service of the Lord Jehovah, or the service of the false gods of Egypt and of the Amorites. No middle course was open to them. There could be no compromise. It must be one thing or the other—let them choose. And substantially the same alternative is before every man in every age. There is something to which he pays supreme homage, and it is either to the great invisible King, the only living and true God, or else to the idols, more or less base, of his own self-will or of the vain world around him. (1) *It is the glory of our nature that we can make such a choice.* God has so constituted us that this self-determining power is one of our most essential prerogatives. And in His dealings with us he always respects the nature He has given. He never violates the law of its freedom. That were to destroy it. No man is compelled to serve Him, nor yet forbidden by any imperious necessity of his being or life to do so. Human nature knows nothing either of necessary evil or irresistible grace. (2) *This freedom of choice gives worth to every religious act.* There would be no moral worth in anything we do without it. The basis of all personal responsibility, it is also the condition of all moral goodness and acceptable service. God would have nothing at our hands that is not voluntarily rendered. If we would serve Him at all, His service must be our free unfettered choice.

II. IT IS A CHOICE DETERMINED BY RATIONAL CONSIDERATIONS. "If it seem evil," &c. Joshua sets the alternative with perfect fairness before them that they may weigh the conflicting claims and judge accordingly. If these gods of the heathen are really nobler, better, more worthy of their gratitude and trust than the Lord Jehovah, then by all means let them follow them! But if the Lord be indeed God, if they owe to Him all that gives sanctity to their national character, and glory to their national history, then let them put these "strange gods" utterly and for ever from them, and cleave to Him with an undivided heart. It is a deliberate judgment between contrary and wholly irreconcilable paths to which they are called. Religion is our "reasonable service" (Rom. vii. 1). It is no blind act of self-surrender. It involves the consent of all our powers—the mind embracing divinely discovered truth, the heart yielding to gracious heavenly influence, the conscience recognising a supreme obligation, the will bowing to that higher will which is "holy and just and good." No man is called to declare for God without sufficient reason.

III. IT IS A CHOICE WHICH CERTAIN CRITICAL OCCASIONS MAKE TO BE SPECIALLY IMPERATIVE. "Choose you *this day,*" &c. "This day" above all other days—because the motives to it are stronger to-day than ever; because the matter is one that it is neither right nor safe to defer to another day. While self-consecration to the service of God is a perpetual obligation, there are seasons of life in which it is peculiarly urgent, when many voices combine with unwonted emphasis to say, "now is the accepted time," &c. (1) Youth, (2) times of adversity, (3) times of special religious privilege or awakening, (4) times when new social relations are being formed, and new paths of life are opening.

IV. It is a choice encouraged by noble personal examples. " As for me and my house," &c. Here is an example (1) of manly resolution, (2) of the strength that can dare to stand alone, (3) of family piety directed by paternal authority and influence. Such an example has an inspiring effect above that of mere persuasive words. It quickens and strengthens every germ of better thought and feeling in the breasts of men. There is no stronger incentive to religious life than the observation of the exemplary forms it assumes in others (1 Cor. iv. 15, 16; Phil. iii. 17).

V. It is a choice that must lead to appropriate practical conclusions. " Now therefore put away," &c. (ver. 23). The honesty of their purpose, the reality of their decision, could be shown in no other way. They only have living faith in God who are " careful to maintain good works " (Titus iii. 8 ; James ii. 18).—W.

Ver. 15.—*Choice and decision.* After exhorting the people to fear and serve the Lord, Joshua calls to them to consider the alternative of rejecting Him, and to make a decisive choice. It is well to be brought to a practical decision in full view of all the issues which face us. These may be clearly seen. Truth does not shun the light. Christianity can well bear comparison with all other systems of worship and modes of life.

I. The call to choose. (1) We are *free to choose.* Joshua is the leader of the people, yet he does not command submission to God, and forcibly compel it. He exhorts, but he leaves the choice open. God has left our wills free to choose or to reject Him. This liberty is essential to voluntary service—the only service which is true and spiritual. God would not value forced devotion. The worth of devotion depends on its free willingness. Yet the freedom God accords is not release from obligation, but only exemption from compulsion. It is still our duty to serve God. (2) *We cannot serve God without voluntarily choosing* Him for our Master. This is a consequence of our liberty. We shall never come to be truly Christian by accident, or by the unconscious influence of a Christian atmosphere. Religion depends on a decisive action of the will. This need not be so sudden and pronounced as to take the dramatic form it assumes in the narrative before us, and in some cases of sudden conversion. But the fact must be proved by a consequent decisive course of life. (3) *Indecision* is a fatal error. We may not choose the evil, yet we practically abandon ourselves to it while we refrain from choosing the good. In ordinary life indecision is a sure cause of failure ; so it is in religion. Though we may doubt many points of doctrine, if only we know enough for choice we must not hesitate in the region of practice. (4) There is *no reason for delay*. Joshua called for immediate decision. This is most safe, most easy, and secures the longest life of service (Heb. iii. 7).

II. The alternatives of choice. (1) Joshua anticipated the position of those to whom it might " seem evil to serve the Lord." This might arise (*a*) from misunderstanding the character of God's service, (*b*) from fear of the inevitable sacrifices and toils which it involves, or (*c*) from lingering affection for the evil things which must be abandoned on entering upon it. (2) Joshua challenged the people to choose whom they would serve if they rejected the Lord. It is well not only to defend the truth, but to show the difficulties which must be faced if this is rejected. We should look at our prospect all round. It is not fair to object to the difficulties of Christianity until we have weighed well the consequence of any other course of life. We must have some God. Israel must choose—if not for Jehovah, then for the gods of their fathers or the gods of their neighbours. There is irony in Joshua's way of setting out the alternatives. Either the people must go back to the past, deliverance from which they are now rejoicing at, or they must accept the worship of those gods whom they have defied and defeated in the overthrow of their enemies. If we have not God we must follow the world, Satan—our evil past, or the worst foes of our present welfare.

III. The example of decision for God. Joshua chooses independently of the popular choice. He is not swayed by the opinion of the multitude. Rather he would guide it by example. It is weak to refuse to choose till we see how the world will choose. Truth and right are not affected by numbers. Every man must make the great choice for himself. (1) Joshua first chose for *himself.* We must be decided before we can influence others aright. Yet let us beware lest in saving others we ourselves become castaways (1 Cor. ix. 27). (2) Joshua also chose for *his house.* We should seek to bring strangers to the right way, but our first duty is with our own household. It is a good sign when a man is able to speak for the decision of his house.—W. F. A.

Ver. 19.—*The difficulties of God's service.* I. THERE ARE DIFFICULTIES IN THE SERVICE OF GOD. All are freely invited to serve God; all may find ready access to God; there is no need for delay, all may come at once and without waiting to be worthy of Him; after coming through Christ, the yoke is easy and the burden light. Yet there are difficulties. Sin and self and the world must be sacrificed; God cannot be served with a divided heart, hence complete devotion must be attained; the service itself involves spiritual endeavours and tasks and battles, before which the strongest fail. It is impossible to serve God in our own strength. We can only serve Him aright because what is impossible with men is possible with God; *i.e.,* we can only serve Him in His strength and through the inspiration of His Spirit.

II. THE DIFFICULTIES IN THE SERVICE OF GOD ARISE FROM THE DISAGREEMENT BETWEEN OUR CHARACTER AND HIS. God does not willingly make His service hard; it would not be hard if we were not sinful. It is difficult while we have evil habits and affections lingering about us, and it is impossible so long as we cling to these voluntarily. (1) God is *holy,* therefore He cannot accept service which is tainted with cherished sin (we must distinguish between cherished sin which makes acceptable service impossible, and resisted sin which hinders, but does not utterly prevent, such service). (2) God is *jealous,* therefore He will not accept divided service. Israel must choose either the service of the Lord or the worship of the heathen gods. Both cannot be embraced. We must choose. So long as we give one-half of our heart to the world or to sin God will not accept the other half. (3) God is, in some respects, *unforgiving.* He forgives the worst sins of the worst men on repentance; but whilst the least sin is cherished God cannot forgive it. No time will soften His resentment. Hence if we come to His service with evil knowingly in our hearts, He cannot overlook it and accept us.

III. IT IS WELL TO CONSIDER THE DIFFICULTIES IN THE SERVICE OF GOD. Israel was too ready hastily to accept God's service without considering all that it involved. If difficulties exist they must be faced. It is best to count the cost before making choice (Luke xiv. 28). Those representations of the gospel which are confined to invitations and promises, and ignore the call to repentance and to sacrifice for Christ, are false and unjust. Christ would have the new disciple face the cross (Luke xiv. 27). Such considerations should not deter us from the choice of God's service. They should make us (1) careful to compare both sides of the question till we see how immensely the obligations and advantages of religion outweigh the difficulties, (2) humble and free from boasting and presumption, and (3) wholly dependent on the help of Christ to make us worthy of His service, to give us strength to serve, and to make our service acceptable (Phil. iv. 13).—W. F. A.

Vers. 21—25.—*The covenant.* I. THE TERMS OF THE COVENANT. It was to bind the people to their promise to renounce the old life of sin and idolatry, and to enter upon and remain in the true service of God. Nations are proud of protecting treaties, constitutional pledges, charters of liberty, &c. No nation ever took a more important covenant than this. The chief question for all of us is whether we will live for the world or for God. The gospel brings to us a new covenant. The promises are greater, the terms are more light. Yet we must choose and resolve and yield ourselves in submission to it if we would enjoy the advantages its offers. This covenant has two sides. God pledges His blessings, but we must pledge our devotion. His is the infinitely greater part. Yet if we fail in ours God's promises of blessing no longer apply.

II. THE OBJECTS OF THE COVENANT. (1) It was to *preserve the memory* of the pledge. Men make resolutions in moments of exaltation which they are apt to forget when the feelings which gave rise to them have subsided. Yet it is just then that they are most necessary. They are not needed when they are freely made, because the impulse to resolve would carry out the action without the resolution. Their real value is for those seasons of trial and service when the lack of a strong spontaneous impulse makes it necessary to fall back on some fixed principle. (2) It was to *secure the execution* of the pledge. It is easy to promise. The difficulty lies in the performance. God is only mocked with the devotion of the sanctuary which is not followed by the service of the daily life. Hence we need to preserve and carry the high impulses of worship into the work of the world. Many men live two lives, and the life of the Sunday has no bearing on that of the week-day. We should use all means to bring religion into life.

III. THE FORM OF THE COVENANT. (1) There was an appeal to *memory*. The people were to be witnesses against themselves. We should treasure in the memory and often call to mind the thoughts of our seasons of spiritual elevation. (2) There was *a written record*. Writing remains unchanged with the varying moods of men. It may be well to write our higher thoughts and deeper resolves for our own subsequent private meditation. The New Testament is a written covenant. (3) There was a *memorial stone*. This would be always visible. So the covenant would be often called to mind. We often need to have our memories refreshed and our thoughts called back to the great practical truths of Christianity. Hence the utility of preaching not only new ideas, but truths that all of us know, and yet that all need to be reminded of, and to have often brought before us for practical application. The stone would not lose its value as it became old and familiar. Truth does not grow feeble with age, nor is it the less important because it is the more familiar. —W. F. A.

Vers. 19—21.—*A strict master.* Great as was Joshua's anxiety that the Israelites should renew their covenant with the Almighty, he would not secure this end by concealing the rigorous nature of the service it involved. Instead of accepting immediately the people's ready response (ver. 18) to his appeal, he proceeded to speak of Jehovah in stern, almost chilling, language. True religion is honest, does not gloss over the requirements which will be insisted on, nor seek to entrap men by fair, smooth promises of an easy rule. Jesus Christ spoke of the necessity of taking up the cross, of leaving home and friends, of enduring hatred, persecution, and trouble, so that none could afterwards complain of being deceived about the requirements and difficulties of discipleship. Men who undertake an enterprise with eyes open are the more likely to persevere; they have already afforded a proof that they are not to be daunted by the prospect of labour and hardship.

I. THE CHARACTER OF GOD, AND THE KIND OF SERVICE HENCE EXPECTED. 1. He is *holy*, and consequently *demands abstinence from sin*. There is in Him entire rectitude of attribute, both in essence and in exercise. The seraphim cry, "Holy is the Lord of Hosts." His vesture is spotless, and He expects His servants to attend Him in uniform unstained (see Levit. xix. 2). Also note the incidents of Moses at the burning bush, Nadab and Abihu consumed for offering unhallowed fire, and the men of Beth-shemesh constrained to exclaim, "Who is able to stand before this holy Lord God?" The sinlessness of Jesus proclaims Him Divine, and sometimes evokes the petition, "Depart from me, for I am a sinful man, O Lord." God is of purer eyes than to behold iniquity, and condemns every act that is inconsistent with the relations in which we stand to Himself, to our fellow-creatures, and the material world. 2. He is *jealous*, and therefore *exacts whole-hearted allegiance*. Annexed to the second commandment was a statement of Jehovah's jealousy, which could not permit His glory to be paid to graven images. When the tables of the law were renewed it was expressly affirmed, "The Lord whose name is Jealous, is a jealous God." The word means, glowing with heat, hence the Almighty is compared to a "consuming fire" that subdues every work of man. Idolatry was the sin to which Israel was prone, and every prostration at the shrine of an idol was a derogation from the honour due to God, and excited His indignation. He is not content with an inferior share of affection, He must be loved and served with all our strength. "He that loveth father or mother more than Me is not worthy of Me." The true disciple is ready to forsake all and follow Christ. The will of the Lord is for him law, his only inquiry being, "Lord, what wilt Thou have me to do?" 3. He is *immutable*, and *requires unvarying fidelity*. "If ye forsake the Lord, then He will do you hurt after that He hath done you good." He rewards every man according to his doings, and visits transgression with punishment. The Israelites were fickle, moved like water by every passing breeze. God is not the son of man that He should repent. He cannot be false to His nature, and look with pleasure on offenders. Past obedience is no answer to the charge of present guilt. Each day brings its own need of sanctification. It is not possible, in God's service, to work so hard one week as to enable us to spend the next in idleness, nor can we accumulate a store of good works to cover deficiencies in a time of sin. "It had been better for them not to have known the way of righteousness than to turn from the holy commandment delivered unto them."

II. The people's determination to serve this exacting God. 1. Indicates a feeling that *only such a Master is worthy of men's service*. Conscience testified that worship should not be offered to other than a perfect Being, and that such a Being could rightly claim these high prerogatives. The rock on which the vessel of mythology has been wrecked is the evil character assigned to its deities, proving them the offspring of human imagination in a debased state. The remembrance of the past, and hopes and fears respecting the future incited the Israelites to continue in their position as the Lord's peculiar people. And have not we experienced that to be the happiest day when we have thought most of God, and most frequently lifted our hearts in prayer to Him for guidance and succour? If called to renounce ease or sinful practices, have we not been amply repaid in the consciousness that we have acted rightly, and are walking in the light of God's countenance? To set upon the throne of our hearts one who would be content with meagre devotion and occasional conformity to righteousness might please for a while, but could not durably satisfy our moral aspirations. 2. Intimates a belief that *God chiefly regards the sincere endeavours of His servants* to please Him. The Israelites could point to Joshua's own demand in ver. 14—"serve Him in sincerity and in truth." What is really displeasing to the Most High is wilful violation of His commandments, or hypocritical pretences of loyalty when the heart is estranged. These He visits with severest condemnation. Jehovah declared Himself in the same commandment both a "jealous" God, and one "showing mercy." And though the disciples of Christ had often exhibited a spirit of worldlinesss, of impatience and unbelief, yet their Master looking on His little company at the Last Supper could even after their unseemly dispute concerning precedence, recognise what was good in them and say, "Ye are they who have continued with Me in My temptations." He who knows all our works (Rev. iii. 8), appreciates the humblest effort to keep His commandments. 3. Suggests an assurance that *imperfections of service can be atoned for* by confession, sacrifice, and intercession. Joshua's assertion was quite true. Neither the Israelites nor any other nation could serve the Lord perfectly. Limitations of knowledge and frailties of temper produce at least temporary deviations from the path of obedience. But the people no doubt remembered the provision made in the law for sins of ignorance, the trespass offerings, the day of atonement "to cleanse them that they might be clean from all their sins before the Lord." Nor were they unmindful of the prayers which had been heard on their behalf when Moses pleaded for them, and the gracious forgiveness that had often followed their national repentance. And what was dimly foreshadowed in the Levitical economy now blazes brightly for our instruction and comfort under the Christian dispensation. Jesus Christ hath by one offering perfected them that are sanctified. His perpetual priesthood is a guarantee for the final salvation of those who come unto God by Him. "Christ is the end of the law for righteousness to every one that believeth." "Ye are complete in Him." 4. Leads us to *anticipate a period of perfect service*. However the goodness of God may pardon our faults and, beholding us in Christ, take note of the direction rather than of the success of our attempts, it is impossible for us to rest content with our present experience. The spirit cries out for entire emancipation from the thraldom of sin, and longs for the redemption of the body. When shall we be conformed to the image of Christ, and enjoy to the full what now we know only by brief moments of rapture and sudden hasty glimpses? This question is answered by the promise of a "manifestation of the sons of God," when, in unswerving obedience to His Father's will, they shall realise truest liberty. You who so delight in Christian work as to wish you could spend all your time and energy therein, look to the years to come! "They serve Him day and night in His temple." "His servants shall serve Him, and they shall see His face."—A.

EXPOSITION.

CHAPTER XXIV. 29—33.

JOSHUA'S DEATH AND BURIAL.—Ver. 29. —The servant of the Lord. The theory of some commentators, that this expression is evidence of a later interpolation because "the title only dates from the period when Moses, Joshua, and others were raised to the rank of national saints," need only be noticed to be rejected. It is a fair specimen of the inventive criticism which has found favour among modern critics, in which a large amount of imagination is made to supply the want of the smallest modicum of fact. What is wanting here is the slightest evidence of such a "period" having ever existed, except at the time when these saints of the old covenant closed their labours by death. All the facts before us go to prove that Moses, as well as Joshua, was held in as high, if not higher, veneration at the moment of his death as at any other period of Jewish history. Died. His was an end which any man might envy. Honoured and beloved, and full of days, he closed his life amid the regrets of a whole people, and with the full consciousness that he had discharged the duties God had imposed upon him. The best proof of the estimation in which he was held is contained in ver. 32.

Ver. 30.—In the border of his inheritance in Timnath-Serah. Rather, perhaps, within the border. For Timnath-Serah, see note on ch. xix. 50. The burial-place of Joshua has been supposed to be identified by the Palestine Exploration Committee. Lieutenant Conder describes what he saw at Tibneh. Amid a number of tombs he found one evidently, from more than 200 lamp-niches on the walls of the porch, the sepulchre of a man of distinction. The simple character of the ornamentation, he thinks, and the entire absence of it in the interior of the tomb itself, not only suggest an early date, but are in harmony with the character of the simple yet noble-minded warrior, whose tomb it is supposed to be (see Quart. Paper, Oct. 1873). In later papers, however (see Oct. 1877, and Jan. 1878), Lieutenant Conder abandons Tibneh for Kefr Haris, on the ground that Jewish tradition, usually found to be correct, is in its favour. And more mature reflection has induced him to modify his former opinion as to the early date of the tombs. Until these researches commenced, the situation of the hill Gaash was unknown, though it is mentioned in 2 Sam. xxiii. 30 ("the brooks" or "valleys of Gaash"), and 1 Chron. xi. 32. Nothing in these places serves to identify it. This passage is copied, with a few minute verbal discrepancies, into the Book of Judges (ch. ii. 6—9), a strong ground, according to all ordinary laws of literary criticism, for concluding that the latter book was written after the former. This is the chain of evidence by which the authenticity of the historical books of the Scriptures is established, not, of course, beyond the reach of cavil or dispute, but to the satisfaction of practical men. The LXX. as well as the Arabic translators have added here the following words: "There they placed with him in the sepulchre, in which they buried him there, the stone knives with which he circumcised the children of Israel in Gilgal, when he led them out from Egypt, as the Lord commanded, and they are there unto this day." This passage is not found in the Hebrew. And as the Arabic and the LXX. do not altogether agree, the probability seems to be that some apocryphal legend was inserted here at a very early date.

Ver. 31.—And Israel served the Lord (cf. Judg. ii. 10). We see here the value of personal influence. Nor is such influence altogether unnecessary among us now. The periods of great religious movements in the Christian Church are in many ways very like to the time of the Israelitish conquest of Palestine by Joshua. They are times when God visibly fights for His Church, when miracles of grace are achieved, when the enemies of God are amazed and confounded at the great things God has done. The successes, so clearly due to the interposition of a Higher Power, have a sobering rather than an intoxicating effect, and the influence of the grave, wise, earnest men at the head of the movement is great with their enthusiastic followers. But with the removal of these leaders in Israel a reaction sets in. The fervour of the movement declines, the era of slackness and compromise succeeds, and a generation arises which "knows not the Lord, nor yet the works which He had done for Israel." In our times such reactions, living as we do in the full blaze of gospel light, are far more transient and less fatal than in the days of Israel. But in our measure we continue to experience the working of that law by which intense energy is apt to be followed by ʳoldness, and every earnest movement for ood needs a continual rekindling at the altar of God of the fire which first set it at work. **That overlived Joshua.** Literally, *that lengthened out their days after* Joshua.

Ver. 32.—**And the bones of Joseph** (see Gen. l. 24, 25 ; Exod. xiii. 19). Nothing could more fully show the reverence in which the name of Joseph was held in Israel than this scrupulous fulfilment of his commands, and the careful record of it in the authentic records of the country. This passage is another link in the chain of evidence which serves to establish the authenticity and early date of the present book. For though Joseph's name was always a striking one in Israelitish history, it is unquestionable that as time went on his fame was overshadowed by that of his ancestors. It is Abraham, Isaac, and Jacob on whom the national mind was fixed. It is their names that the prophets recall, the covenant with them which is constantly brought to mind. But during the Israelites' sojourn in Egypt, and while the departure from Egypt was yet recent, the conspicuous position which Joseph occupied in Egyptian history could not fail to be remembered, and the command he gave concerning his bones, as well as his conviction that the prophecy concerning their departure would be fulfilled, was not likely to be forgotten. The emphatic way in which the fulfilment of Joseph's charge is here recorded affords a presumption for the early date of the book, as well as against the theory that it was a late compilation from early records. We are not necessarily to suppose that the interment of Joseph's remains took place at this period. The Hebrew, as we have seen, has no pluperfect tense (see for this Judg. ii. 10), and therefore it may have taken place,

and most probably did take place, as soon as Shechem was in the hands of Israel. **In a parcel of ground.** Rather, *in the portion of the field* (see Gen. xxxiii. 19). Our word *parcel* is derived from *particula*, and was originally identical with the word *particle*, a little part. So Chaucer speaks of *parcel-mele, i.e.,* by parts. Shakespere has a " *parcel*-gilt goblet," that is, a goblet partly gilt. It has now come to have a widely different meaning. **Pieces of silver.** There can be little doubt that this is the true translation. The cognate word in Arabic, signifying " justice," is apparently derived from the idea of even scales. A kindred Hebrew word signifies " truth," probably from the same original idea. Another kindred Arabic word signifies a balance. It therefore, no doubt, means a coin of a certain weight, just as the word *shekel* has the original signification of weight. The Rabbinical notion, that the word signified " lambs," rests upon no solid foundation, though supported by all the ancient versions. Some commentators, however, think that a coin is meant upon which the figure of a lamb was impressed. So Vatablus and Drusius. The LXX. has ἀμνάδων, the Vulgate " centum novellis ovibus."

Ver. 33. — **A hill that pertained to Phinehas, his son.** The LXX., Syriac, and Vulgate translate this as a proper name, Gibeath or Gabaath Phineas. But it may also mean Phinehas' hill. A city may or may not have been built there. Keil and Delitzsch believe it to be the Levitical town, Geba of Benjamin ; but of this we cannot be sure. The tomb of Eleazar is still shown near Shechem, " overshadowed by venerable terebinths," as Dean Stanley tells us. And so the history ends with the death and burial of the conqueror of Palestine, the lieutenant of Moses, the faithful and humble servant of God, and of the successor of Aaron, who had been solemnly invested with the garments of his father before that father's death. A fitting termination to so strange and marvellous a history. With the death of two such men a new era had begun for the chosen people ; a darker page had now to be opened. The LXX. adds to this passage, " In that day the children of Israel took the ark and carried it about among them, and Phinehas acted as priest, instead of Eleazar his father, until he died, and was buried in his own property at Gabaath. And the children of Israel went each one to his place and to his own city. And the children of Israel worshipped Astarte and Ashtaroth, the gods of the nations around them. And the Lord delivered them into the hand of Eglon king of the Moabites, and he had dominion over them eighteen years." The passage is an obvious compilation from the Book of Judges. It has no counterpart in the Hebrew, and the mention of Astarte and Ashtaroth as different deities is sufficient to discredit it.

HOMILETICS.

Vers. 29—33.—*The end of the work.* We now reach the conclusion of the narrative. Like every other biography, it ends with death. Well were it for us all if death came at the conclusion of a well-spent life like Joshua's.

I. A GOOD MAN'S END. We read in the Book of the Revelation, " Blessed are the dead who die in the Lord . . . their works do follow them." Few have been privileged to be "followed" by their works like Joshua. He led the Israelites into the promised land, and left them there. For many hundred years—the seventy years' captivity excepted—they dwelt there. For their rejection of Him of whom Joshua was the type they were cast out. But even now they remain a distinct people, and entertain hopes of a return to the land which, humanly speaking, Joshua gave them. If we ask the cause of this great success, whose results have lasted even to our own day, it is to be found in the unique character of the conqueror. Simple, straightforward adhesion to duty, intense moral earnestness, earnest piety, prompt and unquestioning obedience to God, the highest public spirit, the utter absence of all self-seeking and ambition, mark a character altogether without parallel in the history of conquest. Conquest generally is associated with fraud and wrong. It has its origin in the greed and ambition of the conqueror ; it is carried out amid injustice and oppression ; it leaves its evil results behind it, and is avenged by the hatred of the oppressed, and by the sure and often swift collapse of a power founded in wrong. Cruel, according to our modern ideas, Joshua was, no doubt. But he was centuries in advance of his age ; his cruelty was the result of a moral purpose. And we must remember that for our modern notions of cruelty we are indebted to Jesus Christ. It is a fact that God *did* permit (whether He *ought* to have done so is a question we cannot discuss here) men to live for thousands of years in ignorance of the true law of mercy. It is not strange, then, if Joshua was not in this respect conformed to an ideal which was not permitted to exist until Christ revealed it. In all other respects, he was the model of what a commander should be, and hence the durability of his work. We cannot hope to become so famous. Yet if we imitate Joshua's obedience, earnestness, piety, unselfishness, we, too, may achieve results as durable, though it may never be known to whom they are owing. For a good deed never dies. It associates itself with the other good influences at work in the world, each of these producing good results on others, and thus steadily working on to the great consummation of all things. What Joshua was it is shame to us if we are not, according to our opportunities. For the Spirit of God is now freely shed forth in all the world, and given to them that ask it.

II. THE MEMORY OF THE JUST IS BLESSED. Joseph's bones were interred in Shechem. Thus we learn (*a*) that patriarch's affectionate love for his brethren, in that he desired in death to be among them, and would have his memory cherished as an encouragement to serve God faithfully. And (*b*) we learn the duty of commemorating God's saints. The extravagant veneration paid to saints and martyrs by those of another communion has caused us to be somewhat too neglectful of their memory. The martyrs of the Reformation are not commemorated among us. We publish biographies of our good men, and straightway forget all about them. Yet surely we might be greatly cheered and encouraged on our way by the recollection of the triumphs of God's Spirit in our fellow-sinners. Surely the pulses of the spiritual life may lawfully be quickened by a sympathy with the great and good who have gone before. Surely all noble examples, all holy lives, are a part of the heritage of the saints designed to advance God's cause. The victories of God's Spirit over the devil, the world, and the flesh, in various ages, among various nations, under various circumstances, will surely best encourage that catholic spirit of sympathy with all that is great and good, without which no Christian perfection can exist. " Let us then praise famous men, and our fathers that begat us." Let the Josephs and Joshuas of the new covenant be held in the deepest honour among us. And thus we shall rise from the contemplation of their struggles to the vision of the Great Captain of their salvation, by whom alone they had victory in the fight.

III. The influence of a good man lives after him. As long as the memory of Joshua's personal influence was felt, so long did the children of Israel keep to the right way. Or rather, perhaps, we may better put it thus : the example and influence of Joshua gradually gathered round him a number of men like-minded, who were placed in positions of authority, and who were capable, like him, of guiding and directing others. When they died, their places were filled by men whose recollection of Joshua's conduct was less distinct, and who possessed in a less degree his power of ruling. Thus Israel fell into disobedience, and it is worthy of remark that when oppression brought them to their senses, it was Othniel, one of those on whom the example of Joshua may be supposed to have had most effect, that they looked for deliverance. We see these facts (a) repeated constantly in the history of God's Church. (1) The great leader of a religious movement trains a number of men like-minded, who guide and direct the movement in his spirit after he has passed away in the spirit, and for the ends that he intended. But (2) a time comes when the first fervour of the movement dies away, when its principles become popular, and thereby vulgarised. They are corrupted by the admixture of the worldly element, the peculiar features of the system are unduly pressed, and deprived of that balance which they possessed in its founder's mind by being kept in check by a wider sympathy and a larger grasp. From a revival of forgotten truths the movement degenerates into a sect or party; the salt has lost its savour, and there needs some other regenerator to arise, who shall give a new direction to the flagging spiritual energies of men. There is no need to give instances of this. They will occur in numbers to every student of history. Also (b) the same truth meets us in the life of individuals. Whether in a public and private position, either as a minister of Christ, or as a member of a congregation, God is pleased to raise up some one whose life of piety is at once an encouragement and an incentive to others to lead the same kind of life. He dies, and for a long time his name is a household word to those who knew him. From his grave he is a preacher of righteousness to those who live near and where he is known. His example is brought forward, his words are quoted, to those who have never seen him. And so the tradition of his excellence lives on among those who come after him. Yet it grows fainter as the years roll on, until it becomes a tradition of the past. Others come in his place who knew him not. Other influences are at work in the pulpit where he preached, the parish where he laboured, the place where he dwelt. His influence has not really died out—good influence, as we have said, never dies—for the good seed he sowed sprung up in the most unexpected quarters, and in the most unexpected ways. But his own place knows him no more. His name is now but a shadow in the distant past. It is no longer an influence full of power. Very often there is a declension in the neighbourhood when the good man is taken away. Very often the aged who remembered him have too good cause to lament a change which is not for the better. But the good work goes on. The torch of love flames more brightly, now here, and now there. But God does not fail to raise up deliverers for His people. His Spirit does not cease to work powerfully in human hearts. His faithful servants still continue to battle against sin, and shall do so until He come again.

HOMILIES BY VARIOUS AUTHORS.

Ver. 29.—*The death of Joshua.* It has been well remarked that "this Book of Joshua, which begins with triumphs, ends with funerals." All human glory ends in the grave. The longest life is soon passed. The most useful men are taken from their work on earth, leaving the unfinished task to other hands. Joshua being dead yet speaketh.

I. JOSHUA IS AN EXAMPLE FOR US. (1) His *character* is an example of (*a*) courage, (*b*) energy, (*c*) independence, (*d*) trust, (*e*) unselfishness. He is the type of the soldier of God, the pattern of active and masculine excellence. (2) His *mission* is an example. Christians are called to possess an inheritance, to conquer the earth for Christ, to fight against and overcome the evils and temptations of the world. (3) His *career* is an example. We see how Joshua was true to his character and fulfilled his mission. He served through a long life. There are some whose devotion is like morning dew. There are others who are roused for great deeds at critical moments, but are negligent in the longer intervals which are left for quiet service. It is a great thing to be long and continuously faithful. It is selfish to desire an early death. Rather, if it is God's will, should we welcome the opportunity of long service. (4) His *end* is an example. Joshua was faithful to death, and faithful in death. His last act was to bind the people to the service of God with a solemn covenant, and pledge his own devotion and that of his house. The Christian's death-bed should be a blessing to others.

II. JOSHUA IS A TYPE OF CHRIST. Jesus is our Joshua, with marks of resemblance and of contrast to the Hebrew leader. (1) Jesus Christ exemplifies in perfection all those good *characteristics* for which Joshua is famous. Though mild and gentle, our Lord was not weak and effeminate. Fidelity, firmness, courage, energy, are seen in Him to perfection. As the perfect man, he combined and harmonised the excellences of all good types of character. (2) Jesus Christ, like Joshua, lived a life of *warfare.* Joshua was a warrior. Christ is a captain of salvation. He met constant opposition from men; He was opposed by the powers of Satan, and he conquered. Yet (*a*) Joshua fought enemies of flesh and blood, Christ fought spiritual foes; and (*b*) Joshua used the sword, Christ conquered by submission and suffering and sacrifice. (3) Jesus Christ, like Joshua, is a *Saviour.* (*a*) He delivers from real present enemies. He saves not only from the future consequences of evil, but from our present sins and troubles. (*b*) He saves those who trust Him, follow Him, and fight with Him, as Joshua not only fought himself, but led the people to battle. (4) Jesus Christ, like Joshua, leads His people to an *inheritance*, but in this there are no Canaanites remaining; it is "an inheritance incorruptible and undefiled, and that fadeth not away, reserved in heaven for us" (1 Peter i. 4). (5) Jesus Christ, unlike Joshua, "*ever liveth.*" Joshua lived to old age and died in honour, and was buried, and ceased to serve his nation. Jesus Christ was cut off in early life and crucified in shame, but rose from the dead, and is now with His people, and will remain till all have entered into their inheritance (Matt. xxviii. 20).—W. F. A.

Ver. 29.—"After these things Joshua, the son of Nun, the servant of the Lord, died, being a hundred and ten years old." Having thus reached the close of the life of Joshua, it is fitting that we should form a general estimate of his character and work. He occupies an honourable place among the great leaders of the people of God. He well deserves to be called a servant of the Lord, for this was the one aim and object of his life. His brow is not crowned with the halo of glory which lighted up that of Moses when he came down from the mount, where he had talked with God as a man talketh with his friend. He is a less sublime type of man, but not, therefore, the less admirable; for in the kingdom of God there is no room for rivalry among those who have fulfilled each his appointed task. First, Joshua was a man of implicit obedience to the Divine behests. He did nothing but that which was commanded him, neither more nor less. Second, he was a very humble man. He never took to himself, in any degree, the glory which belongs to God alone. After the most glorious battles in which he acted as commander, he forgot self in the fervent recognition of the invisible power of which he was but the organ, and his song of gratitude and praise went up to God alone. Third, he was a man of unfaltering faith and courage. His heart never failed him for an instant. He never doubted God; and it was from this confidence that he derived the boldness which he communicated to the children of Israel, to march undaunted against an enemy superior in numbers. Fourth, he united true love for his nation, manifested on repeated occasions, with holy severity when there was just ground for rebuke. Fifth, he was absolutely disinterested in all his service. He never dreamed of handing down his power to his children; his one thought was to do the will of God and to finish His work. When his task was done, he spoke words of solemn warning to his people, and then was gathered to his fathers, or rather to his God. A saintly and noble life truly, and one which teaches us the secret of success in the righteous war with evil. To obey, to be wholly consecrated to God, to believe in the fulfilment of the Divine promises, to fight fearlessly with eye fixed upon the Captain of our salvation, whose strength is perfected in weakness—this is the unfailing secret of success for the Church. Joshua well deserves, not only by his name, but by his faithfulness and devotion to the cause of God, to be the type of our great Leader, "the Author and Finisher of our faith;" the true Joshua, who has conquered for us "a better country, that is an heavenly."—E. DE P.

Vers. 16—31.—*A great decision.* One of the beautiful things about Scripture is the fine endings of all courses in which God has been leader. This book is no exception. The last view we have of Israel shows them entering into a solemn covenant with God, and one which, speaking roundly, all who made it kept. They respond grandly to Joshua's challenge. "God forbid that we should serve other gods." And even when reminded of the difficulty of serving Him, their purpose remains unshaken. In this great decision there are many things worth noting.

I. HE WHO LEADS MEN RIGHTLY WILL NEVER LACK FOLLOWERS. Some say, Go, and men go not. But when they say, "Come with us," they find men responsive. Advice that costs nothing is futile, but example that costs much constrains. Joshua leads grandly, because he moves before the people. "As for me and my house, we will serve the Lord." It is strange the contagiousness of faith and goodness; the force of unconscious influence. The courage of another wakes courage; the honour of another wakes honour. The faith of others is itself "evidence of the things unseen." A man like Joshua is a pillar of cloud by day, and a pillar of fire by night, that "marshals men the way that they were going." However arduous the calling to which you summon men, if you can say, "*As for me, I will serve,*" you will always be answered by some, "*We will serve the Lord.*" Despair not of holy and saving influences. Every one marching on the Divine way of duty, mercy, faith will have more followers than he dared to hope for. It is the grandest illustration of the influence of man on man that we can guide men even to heaven itself by the constraint of a good example. Note this, the good leader has always good followers. [See a beautiful treatment of this subject in Horace Bushnell's sermon on ' Unconscious Influence.'] Secondly observe—

II. A GREAT DECISION SHOULD BE SOLEMNLY AND FORMALLY MADE. He leads them to make a formal covenant with God. He constrains them at once to give up their idols, and in the spot where Jacob had buried the idols which his family had brought with them from Padanaram he buries them; and he sets up a pillar as a memorial. These several things all tend to fortify and consolidate the resolution to which they had come. Sometimes we make a great decision, but fail to keep it through some neglect to fortify it with special solemnities. One great object of the sacraments ordained by the Saviour, unquestionably, was to give to religious decisions this solemn and formal character. They were meant to bring vague feelings to a point; to detach utterly from the world; to attach strongly to the Saviour. If we mean to serve Christ, the idols should be brought out and buried, and the covenant rites of God entered into.   There should be openness, for without confession we remain constantly amid entanglements.   There should be thoroughness, for a great change is often more easily made than a gradual one.   There should be the sacramental covenant and vows that we may have at once the strength and the constraint which come with the feeling that we belong to God.   As here the determination was avowed—carried out thoroughly—solemnised in a covenant—so ours should be.   Men do not know what they lose by a secret and uncovenanted sanctity. When we are secret disciples there is a perpetual danger of the secresy destroying the discipleship.   We lose the protection of a definite position, the power that lies in fellowship, and much of the usefulness which our goodness might carry if it were not counteracted by our reserve.   If you are deciding to serve God, let your decision be thorough, open, sacramental.   Observe lastly—

III. THE GRAND RESULTS OF THIS GREAT DECISION.   Sometimes good resolves are badly kept.   They are like " grass on the house-tops, which withereth afore it groweth up."   Whether they are well kept or not depends largely on whether they are well made.   Generally it will be found where they are broken that there was some defective part : sin not wholly left ; the surrender to God not absolutely made. Here the great decision is worthily and thoroughly made, and the grandest results flow from it.   (1) *They keep the covenant they enter into with God.*   From the 31st verse we might conclude what from Judges ii. 7, 10 we learnt explicitly, that all that generation which made the covenant kept it.   We are called to resolve on what seem impossibilities : to deny self ; to walk with God ; to follow the Saviour's leading.   But when the great resolve is well made, the very making of it ensures the keeping of it.   " Well begun is half done."   Each step well taken developes strength to take the next.   Each good deed done imparts the power to do one still better.   God supplies the grace on which men depend.   His smile heartens ; His providence helps them.   Be not afraid to enter into covenant with God.   Perhaps none ever finally fall away from a great decision, thoroughly and religiously made.   (2) *They have a period of freedom from assault in which to complete their occupation of the land.*   This period has been computed to be thirty-two years (Smith's ' Dict. Bible,' art. Chronology).   Godliness is not detrimental, but profitable for all things.   A nation devout is a nation sober, united, strong ; one left unattacked, or easily resisting an attack.   It was of great moment that they should settle down, become accustomed to possession, multiply in strength, secure whatever of the inheritance was still in the enemy's hands.   And, following God, they enjoy the favour of God, and find just the period of rest which they require.   Is there not something here to which the experiences of individual men furnish many a parallel ?   Your earthly welfare will not be wrecked by your Christian action.   Your honesty will promote, it will not prevent success.   No lie and no dishonour is necessary for getting on in life, only the weak and foolish think so.   It is not the grasping that inherit the earth, but the meek.   It is wisdom, not greed, that has " in her right hand length of days and in her left hand riches and honour."   It is one of God's " open secrets " that the shortest way to the enjoyment of anything we desire is simply deserving it.   Enter into covenant with God, and keep His covenant, and " thou shalt dwell in the land, and verily thou shalt be fed."—G.

Vers. 30, 32, 33.—*Three graves.*   Such is the story of life.   The end of it is always in some sepulchre.   " They buried Joshua."   " They buried the bones of Joseph."   " They buried Eleazer."   So the land is taken in possession.   Every grave becoming a stronger link, binding the people to each other and to the land God gave them.   Look at these graves.   And observe—

I. EVERY LIFE AT LAST FINDS A GRAVE.   However strong the frame and long the conflict, at last the priest must lay down the censer, the statesman resign command, the warrior retire from fields of strife.   Immortality is not for earthly surroundings, nor for the imperfect spirit and body we have here.   If we are to live for ever it must be somewhere where character is perfect, and a frame suited for a perfect spirit is enjoyed.   It is well that an existence so faulty is so brief.

Out of Eden it is better that we should be out of reach of any tree of life that can give earthly immortality. The average life is long enough for the average power of enjoying it. And it is well that it should be "rounded off by sleep." This destiny is too much overlooked. It may be so contemplated as only to injure us. When we anticipate it with dread, without the light of God's smile upon it or of His home beyond it, when it only shrivels up the warmth and energy of life, then its influence is harmful. But it need not have any such influence. If we remember that God is love and death a Divine institution, we shall feel that there must be some service rendered by even death ; and this feeling destroying the dread of it, we shall then be in a condition to profit by its helpful influence. Amongst many wholesome influences these may be noted : (1) *It should correct the folly that wastes life.* Some make two mistakes. They treat time as if it were eternity, and eternity as if it were time. And this mistake produces a purposeless existence that turns life to no account. The thought of death should wake those wasteful of life. It reminds us that the day of life has its task, that there is a serious account to be rendered of how we spent it. It says, " Awake thou that sleepest, and arise from the dead." It bids us live while we live, and work while it is called day. (2) *It comforts the heavy-laden.* Life has many burdens. Duty is often a heavy load. Regrets, cares, sorrows make between them a burden of huge dimensions. God's saints, though they take more peacefully what is sent them, are not insensible to its troubles. On the contrary, "many are the afflictions of the righteous." Death comes when the burden is too heavy, and whispers, "It is not for long." "The light affliction is but for a moment." The glory is eternal.

> " *Brief* life is here our portion,
> *Brief* sorrow, *shortlived* care,
> The life that knows no ending,
> The tearless life is there."

How many would have fainted utterly but for the thought that trials were only mortal. If to some death had seemed a great foe, to many others it has seemed the

> " Kind umpire of men's miseries,
> Which, with sweet enlargement, does dismiss us hence."

If it is a great consoler of the suffering, observe further (3) *it gives zest to every activity of life.* How vapid would life become if death were not the lot of men ! How dull the activity which had eternity for its work ! How poor the low delight would become if anything fixed for ever the conditions which for the moment are sufficient to produce it. But a brief life, ever changing, with no time to waste, gives keenness and zest and joy to all our existence. And lastly, *it makes us look for immortality.* It raises the eye above. The other world is lighted by those who, dying, enter it. The thought of our own impending death makes us desire some "everlasting habitation" when the stewardship here is ended. So mortality protects immortality, keeps it from being forgotten, undervalued, or endangered. And, like some schoolmaster whose harshness yet helps the learning of some lesson, so death is the great instructor and preparer for the life beyond. Lament not Joshua, or Joseph, or Eleazer. Death is mercy to all such. It is not a calamity, it is the sleep God gives His beloved. If it is well to remember that all life comes to a grave, it is still more important to remember—

II. THAT NEITHER LIFE NOR USEFULNESS END THERE. (1) *Life does not end there.* Who could imagine that that grave at Timnath-serah was the end of Joshua? When ripest and fittest for high employment, to what purpose would have been " the waste of such ointment " ? " God gathers up fragments that nothing may be lost ; " would He waste such a splendid aggregate of saintly forces ? Men could not believe it. Jacob spoke of his approaching death as a being " *gathered to his people,*" as if his great ancestors were all above waiting to welcome him. What nature has whispered to the hearts of all men the Saviour has revealed more clearly. He has " abolished death." And now we rejoice to believe life does not end, but only takes a new departure from the grave. Death in the case of all God's saints is only the fulfilment of the Saviour's promise, " I will come again and receive you unto Myself." If life does not end with the grave, observe (2) *usefulness does not end with it.* There is something touching in these earliest graves of Israel—Machpelah, Shechem, Timnath, Mount Ephraim. Such graves were thrones, on each of which a great spirit sat and ruled, teaching spirituality, truth, courage, communion with God. The very graves consecrated the land. As of the great cathedral of Florence the poet sang :

> " In Santa Croce's holy precincts lie
> Ashes which make it holier. Dust which is
> Even in itself an immortality ; "

so we feel these graves were a leavening consecration which made Palestine indeed a holy land. England is rich in graves. Its soil is rich with the dust of the great and good.

> " Half the soil has trod the rest
> In poets, heroes, martyrs, sages."

What impulses of courage, of philanthropy, and consecration have come from the graves of Bruce, of Howard, of the Wesleys, of a multitude that none can number ? If we have the Divine life within us, death cannot end our usefulness. On the contrary, its touch canonises. Death makes the neglected counsel the revered oracle ; and the neglected example the pattern on the mount ; and the despised creed the life-giving truth. " Except a corn of wheat fall into the ground and die it abides alone ; but if it die, it bringeth forth much fruit." Death robs us of ruler-ship over a few things only to give us rulership over many things. Let us live so that, like these, our graves may brighten and bless the land of our burial.—G.

Ver. 32.—*Joseph's bones.* I. THE BURIAL OF JOSEPH'S BONES WAS A JUSTIFICA-TION OF HIS FAITH. Joseph had been so sure that God would give the promised land to Israel that he had made his brethren swear to bring up his bones with them (Gen. l. 25). (1) True faith will lead to *decisive action.* It is vain to profess to believe in our heavenly inheritance unless we behave consistently with our belief. (2) Faith is concerned with the *unseen and the future.* If we could see all there would be no room for faith. (3) Faith is *justified* on earth by providence. It waits its full justification in heaven. As Joseph's faith was justified in the entrance into Canaan, so the old Messianic faith was justified in the advent of Christ, and the Christian faith will be justified at the " consummation of all things."

II. THE BURIAL OF JOSEPH'S BONES WAS AN EXAMPLE OF DEFERENCE TO THE WISHES OF THE DEAD. It is well that children should respect the wishes of departed parents. Much good may be learnt by considering the thoughts and purposes of our ancestors. The people which has no respect for its past is wanting in reverence and in depth of national life. Yet there must be a limit to the influence of antiquity. The ancients lived in the childhood of our race ; wisdom should grow with enlarged historical experience. At best they were fallible men, and cannot claim to extinguish the reason and responsibility of their descendants. New circumstances often render the rules and precedents of antiquity entirely obsolete.

III. THE BURIAL OF JOSEPH'S BONES WAS AN ILLUSTRATION OF THE ONENESS OF MANKIND. Ages had passed since the death of Joseph. Yet his bones were pre-served and buried in the very " parcel of ground which Jacob had bought." There is a family unity, a national unity, a church unity, a human solidarity. The past lives on in the present. Men are insensibly linked and welded together. We are members one of another. Therefore we should consider the good of each other, and of the whole community, and should take note of past experience and future requirements.

IV. THE BURIAL OF JOSEPH'S BONES REMINDS US OF THE DELAY WHICH PRECEDES THE ENJOYMENT OF THE HIGHEST BLESSINGS. There were centuries of delay between the promise and the possession of Canaan. Many ages passed after the first prophecy of redemption and before the coming of Christ. The second advent of Christ has often been anticipated by the Church and longed for by His people, but it is not yet accomplished. The Christian must wait on earth during years of service before receiving his heavenly inheritance. This is occasioned (1) by our unbelief—as the unbelief of Israel deferred possession of Canaan; (2) by the need of fitness—the people needed to be trained in the wilderness; the world needed preparing for Christ, who came in the "fulness of time;" Christians must be made "meet for the inheritance of the saints in light;" the world must be prepared for the full and perfect reign of Christ." Yet, note, the promise is not violated because the fulfilment is delayed. Finally, the Christian inheritance will not be the unconscious possession of a grave in the promised land, but the enjoyment of heaven with the faculties of an eternal life.—W. F. A.

HOMILETICAL INDEX

TO THE BOOK OF JOSHUA

CHAPTER I.

THEME	PAGE
Joshua's Commission	5
Consolation for Bereaved Workers	7
God's Gift to the Church	7
Joshua, the Successor of Moses	9
The Source of Joshua's Confidence	11
The Leader's Promise	12
A Renewed Covenant	12
The Study of the Bible	14
Joshua's Command to the People	18
Joshua and the Reubenites	18
Duties of Brotherhood	19
An Agreement Remembered	21
The People's Answer	23
Loyalty	24

CHAPTER II.

THEME	PAGE
Rahab and the Spies	29, 39
Forethought	32
A Brand Plucked from the Fire	33
The Harlot Rahab	35
Rahab's Faith	37
The Oath of the Spies, and their Return to Joshua	41

CHAPTER III.

THEME	PAGE
The Command to Cross Jordan	44
The Crisis of Life	46
Preparation for beholding Displays of Divine Power	49
The Entry into the Promised Land	50
God's Wonders	51
The Passage of the Jordan	56
" "	58
The Division of the Waters	60

CHAPTER IV.

THEME	PAGE
The Memorial	66
The Children's Question	68
Memorials	70
Memorial Stones	70
Grace for Beginners	72
Prophets and Priests—The Order of Precedence	74
Memorials	75
The Passage of Jordan the Symbol of Death	77

CHAPTER V.

THEME	PAGE
The Great Renewal of the Covenant	81
The Two Sacraments of the Old Covenant	84
Sacramental Consecration of Life	84
The Passover and the Cessation of the Manna	87
The Special and the Customary	88
The Vision and the Command	92, 100
The Captain of the Host	93
A Soldier's Interview with his Captain	95
The Captain of the Church	97

CHAPTER VI.

THEME	PAGE
The Siege of Jericho	102
Strongholds	104
Delusive Trust	106
Salvation : its Cause and Effects	108
A City of Destruction	112

CHAPTER VII.

THEME	PAGE
The Sin	115
Sin Committed	117

THEME	PAGE
The Way of the Transgressor	118
The Accursed Thing	120
The Humiliation	123
Sin Discovered	124
The Detection	126
Sin Confessed	128
A Sin of Greed	129
Sin Punished	131

CHAPTER VIII.

THEME	PAGE
Renewed Effort after Disaster	135
God's People Victorious	136
Trying again	137
The Fruits of Victory	139
The Setting up of the Law	142
The Altar on Ebal, and the Reading and Recording of the Law	144
Sacrifice and Law	145

CHAPTER IX.

THEME	PAGE
God's People off their Guard	152
The Israelites Outwitted	154
An Oath Observed	155
The Gibeonites	157
A Stolen Treaty	158
The Submission of the Gibeonites	159
The Oracle Neglected	160

CHAPTER X.

THEME	PAGE
The Great Victory, and its Results	173
Adonizedek: a Lesson for Nations and Individuals	174
Connection with the Church a source of Worldly Trouble	176
The Battle of Beth-horon, and its Results	176
The Victory over the Five Kings	178
The Sun and the Moon Stayed	179
A Day of Wonders	180
The Conquered Kings	181
Courage and Strength	182
The Extermination of the Canaanites	183

CHAPTER XI.

THEME	PAGE
The Continuation of the Struggle	193
Many Adversaries	196
God's Commandment and Man's Faithfulness	197

THEME	PAGE
Hearts Hardened by God	197
Doomed to Destruction	198
The Extermination of the Canaanites	199
The Destruction of the Giants	200
Rest from War	202
Victory and Rest	203
The Promise Fulfilled	203

CHAPTER XII.

THEME	PAGE
The Extent of the Conquest	209
The Catalogue of the Vanquished	209
Diversity of Lots	210
The Partition of the Land of Canaan	211
The Allotment of the Inheritance	220

CHAPTER XIII.

THEME	PAGE
Life Ending and the Work not done	221
Old Age	222
The Land Allotted, though not yet Secured	223
The Inheritance of Levi	224
The Fate of Balaam	225—227
The Border Keep	227

CHAPTER XIV.

THEME	PAGE
Caleb's Faithfulness and its Reward	231
The Allotment of the Tribes	233
Inheritance by Lot	234
Caleb	235
Caleb and his Inheritance	236
Personal Influence	237
The Anakims	238
Caleb's Inheritance	239
A True Man	240
Rest from War	242
Peasant Proprietorship	243
Caleb, the son of Jephunneh	244

CHAPTER XV.

THEME	PAGE
The Inheritance of Judah	253
Fulness of Blessing	253
The Story of Achsah	254
Invincible Jebusites	255
Failure	256

CHAPTER XVI.

THEME	PAGE
Canaanites still in the Land	259

CHAPTER XVII.

THEME	PAGE
The Lot of Joseph	264
Women's Rights	265
Greed and Grumbling	267
Self-help	268
The Division of the Land	269

CHAPTER XVIII.

Progress in the Great Work	272
Shiloh the Sanctuary	274
Shiloh	275
Slackness	276
An Exhortation to Advance	276

CHAPTER XIX.

The Completion of the Work	285
Brotherhood	286
Joshua's Portion	287
Joshua's Inheritance	288

CHAPTER XX.

The Cities of Refuge	292
Cities of Refuge	293, 296, 298
The Manslayer and his Refuge	295
Danger and Safety	297

CHAPTER XXI.

The Ecclesiastical Settlement of Canaan	303
The Cities of the Levites	305
God's Faithfulness	305
The Portion of the Tribe of Levi	306
The Established Church of Israel	307
The Record of God's Faithfulness	308
The Privileges of the Jewish Church	310
Fulfilment of God's Promises	313
God's Faithfulness	312

CHAPTER XXII.

Reuben, Gad, and the Half-tribe of Manasseh at Home	322

THEME	PAGE
A Misunderstanding	324
Service and Reward	325
Loyalty to God in Separation from the Church	326
The Cause of this Outbreak of Wrath	327
Its Vindication	328
Misunderstandings among Good People	328
The Altar of Witness	329
A Misunderstanding Removed	330
God's Presence Manifested in the Faithful Conduct of His People	332
A Mistake and its Rectification	333

CHAPTER XXIII.

The Last Words of the Aged Servant of God	337
Cleaving unto the Lord	339
Victory Assured through the Help of God	340
Love to God	340
A Needed Caution	341
The Command and its Sanction	344
Threats as True as Promises	345
The Old Man Eloquent	345

CHAPTER XXIV.

The Possession of the Inheritance and its Responsibilities	354
Public Worship	355
A Rightful Choice Urged	357
The Renewal of the Covenant	358
Review of Providence	359
Abraham the Heathen	361
The Great Appeal	362
The Grand Choice	364
Choice and Decision	365
The Difficulties of God's Service	366
The Covenant	366
A Strict Master	367
The End of the Work	371
The Death of Joshua	373
A Great Decision	374
Three Graves	375
Joseph's Bones	377

GEOGRAPHICAL INDEX

	PAGE
Achor, Valley of	247
Achshaph	208
Achzib	282
Adam	55
Adullam	207
Adummim	247
Ai	114
Ajalon (or Aijalon)	165, 166, 284
Allon	283
Amorites	54
Anakim	192
Anathoth	301
Aphek	207, 214
Arabah	55
Arad	207
Archi	257
Arnon	205
Aroer	215, 218
Ashdod	193
Ashdoth	172, 205
Ashtaroth	149
Ataroth and Ataroth-addar	258
Avim	272
Avites	213
Azekah	165
Baal-gad	191
Bamoth-baal	216
Beeroth	150
Beer-sheba	278
Beth-arabah	247
Beth-aven	114
Beth-dagon	281
Beth-el	114, 257
Beth-hogla	247
Beth-horon	164
Beth-jesimoth	205
Beth-lehem	252, 279
Beth-nimrah	218
Beth-shean	261, 280
Beth-shemesh	249, 280
Cabul	281
Canaanites	52
Carmel	252
Chesalon	249
Chinneroth	186
Chisloth-Tabor	278
City in the midst of the river	215

	PAGE
Debir	170
Dibon	215
Dor	186, 262
Ebal	140
Ed	321
Edrei	206
Eglon	164
Ekron	249
Endor	262
Engannim	280
En-gedi	252
En-shemesh	247
Eshtaol	284
Euphrates	4
Gaash	369
Galilee	291
Gath	192
Gath-rimmon	284, 301
Gaza	172, 192
Geshur	206, 213
Gezer	169
Gibbethon	284
Gibeah, Gibeath	272
Gibeon	147
Giblites	214
Gilead	217, 218
Gilgal	64, 81, 148, 208, 247
Giloh	252
Girgashites	53
Gittath-hepher	278
Halak, Mount	191
Hamath	214
Hazar-shual	278
Hazor	185
Hebron	163
Helkath	281
Hepher	207
Hermon	205
Hinnom, Valley of the son of	248
Hittites	4, 52
Hivites	53
Hormah	207
Ibleam	262
Jabbok	205

	PAGE
Jair	219
Japhleti	257
Japho (Joppa)	284
Jarmuth	163
Jearim, Mount	249
Jebusites	54
Jericho	26, 63
Jerusalem	162
Jezreel	279
Jiphthah-el	281
Jokneam	203
Jordan	3
Judah-upon-Jordan	283
Kadesh-barnea	246
Kanah	258
Karkaa	246
Kedesh	208, 283
Kirjath-Arba (Hebron)	163
Kirjath-baal	252
Kirjath-jearim	150, 249, 271
Kirjath-sepher (Debir)	170, 250
Kurn Sartabeh	55, 316
Lachish	163
Lasharon	207
Lebanon	3
Lisan	246
Maaleh-acrabbim	246
Madon	208
Magdala	283
Mahanaim	218, 302
Makkedah	165
Maon	252
Medeba	215
Megiddo	208
Me-jarkon	284
Merom	188
Mishor	214, 215
Misrephoth Maim	190
Mizpeh	272
Nephtoah, Waters of	248
Ophrah	272

	PAGE
Perizzites	53
Pisgah	205
Quarantania	40
Ramah	272
Ramath-Mizpeh	218
Ramoth-Gilead	291
Red Sea	29
Rephaim, Valley of	248
Salt, City of	252
Sarid	278
Sea of the plain	55
Seir, Mount	249
Sheba	278
Shebarim	115
Shechem	260, 354
Shephelah	147
Shihor-libnath	281
Shiloh	270, 300
Shimron-meron	208
Shittim	25
Sibmah	217
Sihor	213
Sidon	189
Succoth	218
Taanach	208
Tappuah	207, 258
Timnath-serah	285, 369
Tirzah	208
Tyre	282
Ur Casdim	348
Zaanannim	283
Zaphon	218
Zaretan	55
Zareth-shahar	217
Zidon (or Sidon)	189
Zin	246
Ziph	252
Zorah	284

JUDGES

EXPOSITION AND HOMILETICS BY

A. C. HERVEY

HOMILIES BY VARIOUS AUTHORS

A. F. MUIR   W. F. ADENEY

THE BOOK OF JUDGES

INTRODUCTION.

THE Book of Judges, called in Hebrew שופטים,[1] in the Septuagint KRITAI, and in the Vulgate LIBER JUDICUM, or JUDICES, takes its name, like the other historical books,—the five Books of Moses, the Book of Joshua, the Book of Ruth, the Books of Samuel and of the Kings, the Books of Ezra and Nehemiah, and the Book of Esther,—from its contents, viz., the history of certain transactions which took place in Israel under the judges. The judges were those extraordinary civil and military rulers who governed Israel in the interval between the death of Joshua and the foundation of the kingdom of Israel; except only that the judgeship of Samuel was a kind of connecting link between the two—Samuel himself being a judge, though of a different character from those that preceded him, and his government merging in the latter part of it into the kingdom of Saul; so that the times of Samuel occupy a middle place between the Judges and the Kings, belonging partly to both, but wholly to neither.

The age of the world in which the transactions recorded in the Book of Judges occurred was somewhere between the years B.C. 1500 and 1000. It was one marked by the same peculiar features in different parts of the earth It was the dim twilight of history ; but, as far as we can judge from those mythological accounts which precede the existence of true history, it was a time of much movement, of the birth of heroic characters, and of the incipient formation of those nations who were destined to be foremost among the nations of the earth. The mythologies of Greece tell of exploits of heroes which imply unsettled and disturbed times, the clashing of race with race, fierce struggles for the possession of lands, terrible conflicts for dominion or existence. And as far as such mythologies contain, as they doubtless do, some shreds of historical truth, and reflect something of the character of the men of the period, they are in accordance with the picture contained in the Book of Judges of the times which were more or less contemporary. Instead of a comparison of the Greek mythologies leading to the

---

[1] This is the same word as the Carthaginian *Suffetes*, as their chief magistrates are called (Liv., Hist., xxvii. 37). The Tyrians had a similar name for their magistrates, translated by Josephus (App., i. 21) δικασταί.

conclusion that the history in the Book of Judges is mythological also, it rather lends a valuable confirmation of that historical character which the internal evidence of the book so abundantly claims for it.   The features which are common to the Greek mythologies and the Hebrew history, the wars of new settlers with the old inhabitants, the recklessness of human life, the fierce cruelty under excitement, the heroic deeds and wild adventures of a few great leaders, the taste for riddles, the habit of making vows, the interference of gods and angels in human affairs, the frequent consultations of oracles, and so on, are the products of the same general condition of human society at the same epoch of the world.   The difference between the two is, that the Greek traditions have passed through the hands of countless poets and story-tellers, who in the course of generations altered, added, embellished, confused, distorted, and invented, according to their own fertile fancy and their own creative imaginations; while the Hebrew records, by the special providence of God, have been preserved some 3000 years and upwards uncorrupted and unchanged.

CHRONOLOGY.

The first thing one looks for in a scientific history is a careful and accurate chronology.   But such is entirely wanting in the Book of Judges, for the reason that it is not a scientific history, but a collection of narratives having a moral and religious purpose; illustrative, that is, of the evil of idolatry, of God's providential government of the world, and of his special rule over the chosen race of Israel.   We are obliged, therefore, to construct our chronology out of the indications which every true history contains in itself of the sequence and connection of events.   But these are necessarily inexact, and cannot always be made to determine the time within a century or more, especially when there is no accurate contemporary history.   There are also special circumstances which increase the difficulty in the case of the Judges.   The date of Joshua's death, which is the *terminus a quo* of the book, is uncertain by about 200 years.   Then the time occupied by the elders who outlived Joshua, which intervened before the action of the book commences, is indefinite; it may mean ten years, or it may mean thirty or forty years.   Again, the point of junction of the close of the book with 1 Samuel which follows it is uncertain; we do not know certainly how far the latest events in the judgeship of Samson ran into the judgeships of Eli and Samuel.   But there is another element of uncertainty which largely affects the chronology of the Book of Judges.   The history is not the history of one kingdom or commonwealth, but of several almost separate and independent tribes.   Except on great occasions, such as the national gathering at Mizpeh (and that was very soon after the death of Joshua), Gilead, *i. e.* the tribes to the east of Jordan, had little communication with Western Israel; and even on the west of Jordan, Ephraim and the northern tribes were divided from Judah and Simeon and Dan on the south. The great tribe of Judah is not so much as mentioned in the enumeration of the tribes which fought under Barak, nor in the victories of Gideon.   Hence it is apparent that it is at least very possible that some of the events narrated may be not consecutive, but synchronous ; that wars may have been going on in one part of Israel while another part was at rest ; and that we may possibly be led into as great a chronological blunder by adding together all the different servitudes and rests, as a reader of English history would be if he made the reigns of the Anglo-Saxon kings of the heptarchy consecutive instead of simultaneous.

And there is yet another cause of uncertainty as to the chronology. Long periods of eighty and forty years are named without a single event being recorded in them. Now it is notorious that numbers are peculiarly liable to be corrupted in Hebrew manuscripts, as, e. g., in the familiar example of 1 Sam. vi. 19; so that those numbers are very uncertain, and not to be depended upon.

On all these accounts an accurate and certain chronology is, in our present state of knowledge, impossible. There is, however, one source, though not in the Book of Judges itself, from which we may fairly look for some more certain help, and that is from those genealogies which span the time occupied by this history. The chief of these is the genealogy of David appended to the Book of Ruth, repeated in the First Book of Chronicles, and again reproduced in the Gospels of St. Matthew and St. Luke. This genealogy gives three generations between Salmon, who was a young man at the time of the occupation of Canaan, and David. These three are, however, about equivalent to five, when we take into account the age of Boaz at his marriage with Ruth, and the probable age of Jesse at the birth of David. They may also admit of some further extension, if Salmon, whose exact age at the entrance into Canaan we do not know, did not beget Boaz till ten or more years afterwards, and if Jesse was a younger son of Obed. Reckoning, however, the generations as *five*, and allowing thirty-three years for a generation, we get $5 \times 33 = 165$ as the approximate length of the period from the entrance into Canaan to the birth of David ; and, deducting thirty years for the time of Joshua and the elders, 135 years from the beginning of the times of the judges to the birth of David. But this is probably rather too short, because, if we turn to other genealogies covering the same period, we find that the generations between those who were grown men at the entrance into Canaan and those who were David's contemporaries were six or seven, as in the genealogy of the high priests given in 1 Chron. vi., where there are seven generations between Phinehas and Zadok the son of Ahitub. Again, the list of Edomitish kings in Gen. xxxvi. and 1 Chron. i. 43, &c., gives eight kings as having reigned before Saul was king of Israel, the last of them being Saul's contemporary, and one of them being king at the time of the exodus. If he was the first king, that would give six between the entrance into Canaan and David. The genealogy of Zabad (1 Chron. ii. 36, &c.) gives six or seven between the entrance into Canaan and David.

And it may be said on the whole, that of *nine*[1] genealogies, *eight* agree in

---

[1] The nine genealogies are those of Zadok, Heman, Ahimoth, Asaph, Ethan, Abiathar, Saul, Zabad, and the Edomitish kings.

requiring the addition of one or two generations to the *five* indicated by David's, while not one requires a larger number. The genealogy of Saul is of the same length as David's. If *six* is the true number, we have a period of 198 years between the entrance into Canaan and the birth of David. If *seven* is the true number, we get 221 years. Deducting thirty years for Joshua and the elders, and (say) ten years for the interval between the close of the times of the judges and the birth of David, we get in the first case 158 years as the time of the judges (198 — 40), and in the second 191 (231 — 40). But the consent of all the genealogies seems to preclude the possibility of such long periods as 400, 500, 600, and even 700 years, which some chronologists assign to the interval between the entrance into Canaan and the building of Solomon's temple.[1]

As regards the age in the world's history to which the events of the Book of Judges belong, we get at it by reckoning backwards from the birth of David. This may be assigned with some confidence to about the year B.C. 1083. If then we assume ten years to have elapsed between the close of the period of the judges and the birth of David, we get the year B.C. 1093 as the date of the end of the period of the judges; and if we then assume 158 years as the duration of the times of the judges, we get 1093 + 158 = 1251 as the date of the commencement of the times of the judges; and if we then add thirty years for Joshua and the elders, and forty years for the sojourning in the wilderness, we get (1251 + 30 + 40) 1321 for the date of the exodus, which is within eight years of the Jewish traditional date B.C. 1313, and brings us to the reign of Menephthah, or Menephthes, who is the most probable Pharaoh of the exodus who has been proposed. This is a considerable support to the system of chronology here advocated.

STRUCTURE AND CONTENTS OF THE BOOK.

It has already been remarked that the history is not that of one united people, but of several separate tribes. The truth of this remark will appear if we consider the great length and detail of some of the narratives, quite out of proportion to their importance relatively to the whole Israelitish nation, but quite natural when we look upon them as parts of the annals of particular tribes. The preservation of Deborah's magnificent ode, the full details of the history of Gideon, the long story of Abimelech's reign, the highly interesting narrative of the birth and adventures of Samson, the detached accounts of the expedition of the Danites, and of the fall of the tribe of Benjamin, which close the book, are probably all due to the fact of their being taken from existing records of the several tribes. These were all brought into harmony and unity of purpose by the compiler, who selected (under the guidance of the Holy Spirit) those portions which bore upon his main purpose, which was to denounce idolatry, to confirm the Israelites in the service of the Lord the God of their fathers, and to illustrate the faithfulness, the

---

[1] Keil makes 533 years from the entrance into Canaan to the building of Solomon's temple, assuming the 300 years of Judges xi. 26 to be a real date.

mercy, and the power of their covenant God. And certainly if anything could confirm a fickle people in their faith and obedience to the living and true God, the exhibition of such deliverances as those from the Canaanite and Midianite and Ammonite invasions, and of such examples of faith and constancy as those of Barak, Gideon, and Jephthah, were well calculated to do so.

And this leads us to observe a very important feature which the Book of Judges has in common with the later historical books, viz., the union of contemporary narratives and documents with late editorship. The method of the Hebrew historical writers seems to have been to incorporate into their work large portions of the ancient materials without altering them, only adding occasional remarks of their own. The method of modern historians has usually been to read for themselves all the ancient authorities, and then to give the result in their own words. The information got from a variety of authors is all welded together, the unimportant details are omitted, and a harmonious whole, reflecting the author's mind perhaps quite as much as that of the original authorities, is presented to the reader. But the Hebrew method was different. The ancient records, the Book of the wars of the Lord, the Book of Jasher, the Chronicles of the kingdom, the visions of Iddo the Seer, the Book of the Acts of Solomon, the Chronicles of the kings of Judah, and so on, were searched, and whatever was required for the author's purpose was inserted bodily in his work. Hence in the Book of Kings the lengthened episodes concerning Elijah and Elisha, the great length at which the reign of David is given in the Books of Samuel, and so on. This same method is very apparent in the Book of Judges. It seems scarcely open to doubt that the mass of the book consists of the original contemporary annals of the different tribes. The minute and graphic details of the narratives, Deborah's song, Jotham's fable, Jephthah's message to the king of Ammon, the exact description of the great Parliament at Mizpeh, and many other like portions of the book, must be contemporary documents. Then, again, the history of Samson the Danite, and that of the Danite expedition to Laish, indicate strongly the annals of the tribe of Dan as their common source ; while the importance attached to Gilead in chs. x., xi., and xii. points to annals of Gilead. But at the same time the presence of a compiler and editor of these various documents is distinctly visible in those prefatory remarks contained in ch. ii. 10—19 ; iii. 1—7, which review, as it were, the whole subsequent narrative, as well as in casual observations thrown in from time to time, as at ch. xvii. 6; xviii. 1; xix. 1; xx. 27, 28; xxi. 25, and in the general arrangement of the materials.

This sketch of the structure and contents of the Book of Judges must not be concluded without mentioning the light thrown upon the condition of the neighbouring nations, the Canaanite tribes, Mesopotamia, the Philistines, the Moabites and Ammonites, the Amalekites, the Midianites, and the Sidonians. Nor must a brief reference be omitted to the repeated angelophanies, as in ch. ii. 1 ; vi. 11—23; xiii. 3, &c. Again, we find the great institution of prophecy existing, as in ch. iv. 4 ; vi. 8, and, in a certain sense, wherever the Spirit of the Lord came upon a

judge, as ch. iii. 10 ; vi. 34 ; xi. 29, &c.   In other passages where the word of God
comes to men it is not clear whether it is through prophets, through an ephod, or
by direct operation of the Holy Ghost (see ch. ii. 20 ; vi. 25 ; x. 11 ; &c.).

It is also worthy of observation that there are in this book many direct references to the law and the books of Moses.   The inquiry of the Lord (ch. i. 1 ; xx.
27) ; the mention of the commandments " which God gave by the hand of Moses"
(ch. iii. 4) ; the allusion to the exodus, and to the very words of Exod. xx. 2 (ch. vi.
8, 13) ; the dismissal by Gideon of all that were fearful according to Deut. xx. 8
(ch. vii. 3) ; the lengthened reference to the history in Numb. and Deut. (ch. xi. 15—
26) ; the institution of Nazarites (ch. xiii. 5 ; xvi. 17); the mention of the tabernacle
and the ark (ch. xviii. 31 ; xx. 27, 28) ; the reference to the high priest and to the
Levites as the ministers of God (ch. xvii. 13 ; xix. 18 ; xx. 28), are among the
many proofs that the law of Moses was known to the writer or compiler of the
Book of Judges.

We must look, therefore, to some other cause for the singular silence in this
history concerning the services of the tabernacle, and the high priests after
Phinehas, and that change in the line of the high priests which must have taken
place in the time of the judges between Phinehas of the line of Eleazar and Eli of
the line of Ithamar.   There must have been in all probability two or three high
priests between Phinehas and Eli, whose names are not recorded, at least not as
high priests.   Josephus, however, says that Abishua (whose name is corrupted
by him into Josepus) was high priest after Phinehas, and that Eli succeeded
Josepus, being the first high priest of the house of Ithamar, and that the other
descendants of Phinehas named in the genealogy of the high priests (1 Chron. vi.
4—8) remained in private life till Zadok was made high priest by David.   However this may be, it is certainly strange that not a single allusion to a high priest
occurs in the whole book except that one in ch. xx. 28, while Phinehas was still
alive.   Perhaps the explanation is, that in the de-centralisation of Israel above
spoken of the central worship at Shiloh lost its influence (as Jerusalem did after
the ten tribes had revolted from the house of David) ; that in the troubled times
that followed each tribe or cluster of tribes set up its own worship, and had its own
priest and ephod ; and that the descendants of Phinehas were weak men who
could not make the priesthood respected, or even retain it in their own families.
Add to these considerations that the narratives are all taken from tribal annals ;
that apparently not one is taken from the annals of the tribe of Ephraim (in which
Shiloh was), seeing that in them all the great tribe of Ephraim appears to disadvantage ; and, lastly, that we have in this book not a regular history of Israel,
but a collection of narratives selected on account of their bearing on the author's
main design, and we have perhaps a sufficient explanation of what at first appears
strange, viz., the absence of all mention of the high priests in the body of the book.

The book consists of three parts : the preface, ch. i. to ch. iii. 6 ; the main
body of the narrative, from ch. iii. 7 to the end of ch. xvi. ; the appendix, containing
the separate and isolated narratives concerning the settlement of the Danites and

the civil war with Benjamin, and belonging chronologically to the very beginning of the narrative, very shortly after Joshua's death. The preface dovetails in an extraordinary manner into the Book of Joshua,—which, or the materials from which it was composed, the compiler must have had before him,—and probably also into 1 Samuel.

DATE OF COMPILATION.

There is nothing peculiar in the language (except some strange architectural terms in ch. iii. in the part relating to Ehud, and some rare words in Deborah's song, in ch. v.) from which to gather the date of compilation. But from the phrase in ch. xviii. 31, " all the time that the house of God was in Shiloh," and that in ch. xx. 27, "the ark of the covenant of God was there in those days," and from the description of the situation of Shiloh (ch. xxi. 19), it is quite certain that it was made after the removal of the ark from Shiloh. From the repeated phrase (ch. xvii. 6; xviii. 1; xix. 1; xxi. 25) that "in those days there was no king in Israel," it seems equally certain that it was made after the foundation of the kingdom by Saul; while the mention of the Jebusites in ch. i. 21 as dwelling in Jerusalem "unto this day" points to a time prior to David. On the other hand, the phrase (ch. xviii. 30) "until the day of the captivity of the land" would make it probable that it was written after the deportation of the ten tribes, when it is likely the settlement at Dan was broken up by the Assyrian conqueror. This might be in the reign of Jotham or Ahaz. There does not seem to be any other special mark of time in the book itself.

But, on the other hand, the allusions to the Book of Judges, or to events which are recorded in it, in other books of the Old Testament must be taken into account. In 1 Sam. xii. 9—11 there are not only allusions to the events which form the subject of Judges iii., iv., vi., vii., viii.; x. 7, 10; xi., but *verbal* quotations which make it morally certain that the writer of 1 Sam. had before him the very words which we now read in Judges iii. 7, 8; iv. 2; x. 10, 15, and probably the whole narratives as they are now contained in Judges. It necessarily follows that either the Book of Judges was already compiled when Samuel spake these words, or that Samuel had access to the identical documents which the compiler of Judges afterwards incorporated in his book. The same argument applies to 2 Sam. xi. 21, where the verbal quotation is exact. In Isa. ix. 4; x. 26, spoken in the reign of Ahaz, the reference is more general, though in the last passage there is the production of three words from Judges vii. 25—*upon*, or *at* (Heb. ב), *the rock Oreb*. Again, in Ps. lxxxiii. 9—11 there is a distinct reference to the narrative in Judges vii., viii.; and in Ps. lxxviii. 56, &c., and cvi. 34, 45, there is a general reference to the times of the judges, as to one the history of which was well known. Taking, however, into account the fact that all the three psalms are of uncertain date, no very distinct argument can be brought to bear from them on the date of Judges. On the whole then it would meet all the requirements of the passages in the Book of Judges (except the reference to the captivity of the ten tribes), and in the other books in which reference is made to Judges, if we were to assign the compilation to the reign of Saul, the separate contents of the book being known even earlier ; but it must be confessed that this conclusion is uncertain, and that there is much to be said in favour of a much later date.

The Book of Judges has always been contained in the canon. It is referred to in Acts xiii. 20, and Heb. xi. 32.

Note.—The chronology indicated in Judges xi. 26 has not been taken into account for the reasons given in the note on that passage ; that in 1 Kings vi. 1 because it is generally given up by critics and commentators as an interpolation, and is unsupported by the Book of Chronicles and by Josephus ; and that of the A. V. of Acts xiii. 20 because the true reading, "happily restored by Lachmann from the oldest MSS., A. B. C., and supported by the Latin, Coptic, Armenian, and Sahidic Versions, and by Chrysostom" (Bp. Wordsworth in *l. c.*), gives quite a different sense : "he divided their land to them by lot in about 450 years" —from the time, *i. e.*, when he made the promise to Abraham.

LITERATURE OF THE BOOK.

COMMENTARIES ON THE BOOK OF JUDGES, AND OTHER NOTICES.

ROSENMÜLLER'S 'Scholia,' in Latin (1835), are very useful both for the Hebrew scholar, and generally for exegesis, and historical and other illustrations. He speaks very highly of the Commentary of Sebastian Schmidt. DE WETTE'S 'Introduction to the Old Testament' (English translation, 1858) contains some valuable remarks, but must be used with caution. He refers to the commentaries of Schnurrer, Bonfrere, Le Clerc, Maurer, and others. BERTHEAU, in the 'Kurtzgefasstes Exegetisches Handbuch' (1845), is, as always, very able, very learned, and exhibits much critical acumen. The commentary of KEIL and DELITZSCH (English translation, 1865) is useful, and orthodox, but deficient in critical discernment. It frequently differs from Bertheau. It has the advantage of acquaintance with the discoveries of the most recent travellers. HENGSTENBERG ('Dissertation on the Pentateuch') may also be consulted. POOLE'S Synopsis gives the views of the earlier commentators. Of English commentators it may suffice to mention Bishop Patrick, Bishop Wordsworth, and the 'Speaker's Commentary.' Bishop Wordsworth's list of the chief commentators among the Fathers contains the names of Origen, Theodoret, Augustine. Procopius, Isidore, and Bede ; and among the Jewish commentators those of Kimchi, Aben Ezra, and Jarchi. Of other books most useful in helping to understand the scenes where the dramatic action of the Judges took place, may be mentioned especially Stanley's 'Sinai and Palestine ;' also Robinson's 'Biblical Researches,' and the geographical articles in the 'Dictionary of the Bible ; ' Van de Velde's map, and especially the new 'Great Map of Western Palestine' by the Palestine Exploration Committee, from the recent survey, on the scale of an inch to a mile. For historical purposes Josephus's 'Jewish Antiquities' should be studied throughout, though he does not throw much additional light upon the narrative. Stanley's 'Lectures on the Jewish Church' contribute much vivid and picturesque description of the persons and scenes, and give great reality and fulness to the narrative. The historical articles in the 'Dictionary of the Bible' may also be consulted with advantage. Bishop Lowth, on Hebrew poetry, has some striking remarks on the song of Deborah, and Milton's 'Samson Agonistes,' besides its beauty as a poem, is a really good commentary on the history of Samson. For the very difficult chronology of the times of the Judges the reader may consult, besides the above-named commentaries, Jackson's 'Chronological Antiquities,' and Hale's 'Analysis of Chronology ;' and, for the system adopted in this commentary, Lepsius's 'Letters on Egypt and Ethiopia,' Wilkinson's 'Manners and Customs of the Egyptians,' and the present writer's chapter on 'The Discordance between Genealogy and Chronology of Judges,' in his work on the genealogies of our Lord Jesus Christ.

THE BOOK OF JUDGES

CHAPTER I.

Ver. 1.—**After the death of Joshua.** The events narrated in chs. i. and ii. 1—9 all occurred before the death of Joshua, as appears by ch. ii. 8, 9, and by a ,comparison of Josh. xiv. 6—15 and xv. 13—20. The words, *and it came to pass after the death of Joshua,* must therefore be understood (if the text is incorrupt) as the heading of the whole book, just as the Book of Joshua has for its heading, "Now after the death of Moses the servant of the Lord it came to pass." **Asked the Lord.** The same phrase as ch. xviii. 5; xx. 18, where it is rendered *asked counsel of.* So also Numb. xxvii. 21, where a special direction is given to Joshua to make such inquiries as that mentioned in this verse before Eleazar the priest, through the judgment of Urim and Thummim (cf. 1 Sam. xxiii. 10, 12). A still more common rendering of the Hebrew phrase in the A.V. is "to inquire of God" (see, *e. g.* ch. xx. 27,

28; 1 Sam. xxii. 13, 15; xxiii. 2, 4; xxviii. 6, and many other places). Such inquiries were made (1) by Urim and Thummim, (2) by the word of the Lord through a prophet (1 Sam. ix. 9), or (3) simply by prayer, (Gen. xxv. 22), and improperly of false gods (2 Kings i. 2, 16), of teraphim, and semi-idolatrous priests (ch. xviii. 5, 14).

Ver. 5.—**Bezek.** The site of it is unknown; it is thought to be a different place from the *Bezek* of 1 Sam. xi. 8. **Adoni-bezek** means *the lord of Bezek.* He was the conqueror of seventy petty kings.

Ver. 6.—**Cut off his thumbs,** &c. These cruel mutilations, like the still more cruel one of putting out the eyes (ch. xvi. 21; Numb. xvi. 14; 1 Sam. xi. 2; 2 Kings xxv. 7), were intended to cripple the warrior in his speed, and to incapacitate him from the use of the bow, or sword, or spear, while yet sparing his life, either in mercy, or for the purpose of retaining his services for the conqueror.

HOMILETICS.

Vers. 1—7.—*Inquiry of God.* *Three* lessons stand out from the above section which we shall do well to consider in the order in which they present themselves.

I. The *first* is, THAT BEFORE TAKING IN HAND ANY IMPORTANT BUSINESS WE OUGHT TO SEEK GOD'S DIRECTION. Distrust of our own wisdom, misgivings as to our motives, and the feeling that the issues of all events are in the hands of God's unerring providence, should always prompt us to look to God for guidance. Even when we do so no little care is needed to be sure that our interpretations of God's will are not biassed by our inclinations. We read in Jer. xlii. that the captains of the forces of the remnant of the Jews went to Jeremiah after the deportation of their countrymen to Babylon, and said to him, "Pray for us unto the Lord thy God, that he may show us the way wherein we may walk, and the thing that we may do," and even bound themselves by a solemn oath to obey the voice of the Lord, and do whatsoever he should command them by the mouth of Jeremiah. But when, after ten days, God's answer came, bidding them abide in the land of Judah, and condemning in distinct terms the course on which their hearts were set, viz., to go down to Egypt, they boldly accused Jeremiah of falsehood, and went down to Egypt in spite of his prophetic message. And so it too often is. Men ask God's direction, hoping that the answer will be in accordance with their own inclinations, and do their best to twist it into such accordance. But if this is impossible they act in bold defiance of it. In seeking God's guidance, therefore, especial care should be taken so to mortify our self-will that we may be ready to act upon the answer of God, however contrary it may be to the dictates of our own hearts. This may be applied to cases where pecuniary loss, or sacrifice of worldly advantages or pleasures, or self-humiliation and self-denial, or mortification ·of enmities, resentment, jealousy, pride, vanity, love of praise, and so on, are involved in an entire obedience to the dictates of the word and Spirit of God given in answer to prayer. As regards the ways in which a Christian now can "ask the Lord" concerning the course he ought to pursue on any particular occasion, we may say, following the analogy of the inquiries to which our text refers, that—1. He may inquire or *ask counsel of Holy Scripture*. He may seek light and truth from that word which is the expression of the mind and will of God. There is no state of darkness, or perplexity as to the true path of duty, to which Holy Scripture, wisely and prayerfully interrogated, will not bring satisfactory light; no question of morality or conduct on which it will not shed the ray of truth. The old superstition of the *sortes Virgilianæ* applied to the Bible, so that the page opened at random should supply the answer required, had this much of truth in it, that the Bible has an answer for every question of an inquiring soul. But this answer must be sought in intelligent, prayerful study, and not as a matter of blind chance, or in the presumptuous expectation of a miraculous answer. The answer may be obtained either from the example of some eminent saint under similar circumstances, as of Abraham giving up his right in order to avoid strife with Lot (Gen. xiii. 8, 9), Elisha refusing Naaman's gifts, Job blessing God in the extremity of his affliction, and the numerous examples in Luke vi. 3; Heb. xi.; James v. 17, &c.; or by impregnating the mind with the teaching of the word of God, such as Deut. vi. 5, or the Sermon on the Mount, or the precepts in Rom. xii., xiii.; Gal. v. 22, 23; Ephes. iv. 22, *sqq.*, and 1 Pet. throughout. And either way the answer will be sure if it is sought faithfully. 2. A Christian may inquire of the Lord *by seeking the counsel of a wise and honest friend,* who will give him impartial advice. The prophets were distinguished for their faithful boldness in speaking unwelcome truths as much as for their inspired knowledge. Nathan speaking to David, Isaiah counselling Hezekiah, Daniel reproving Nebuchadnezzar or Belshazzar, Jeremiah advising Zedekiah, are instances of such faithfulness. Let the Christian then who is in doubt or perplexity as to the course which he ought to take seek the counsel of a wise and faithful friend, whose mind will not be biassed by passion or prejudice, and let him act according to it. 3. *God's guidance may be sought by simple prayer.* Just as Hezekiah in his great perplexity and distress spread Sennacherib's letter before the Lord, and betook himself to earnest prayer, so may a Christian man spread out before God all the particular circumstances of his case, and all the doubts and difficulties by which he is harassed, and in simple-minded earnestness ask God to direct and guide him aright. And the answer will doubtless come, either by the Holy Spirit suggesting to his mind the considerations which ought chiefly to influence him, or strengthening feeble convictions, and confirming uncertain opinions and hesitating reasonings, or clearing away the clouds which obscured his path, or in some providential interference barring, as it were, the wrong course, and throwing open the gates of the right one for him to pass through. The opportune arrival óf Rebekah at the well while Abraham's servant was in the very act of prayer (Gen. xxiv. 15); the arrival of the messengers of Cornelius while Peter was in doubt what the vision which he had seen might mean (Acts x. 17); the dream which Gideon heard the Midianite tell to his fellow, just when he was hesitating whether he ought to attack the Midianite host, are examples, to which many more might be added, how providential circumstances come in to give to the servant of God the guidance which he asks. It is obvious to add that these three modes of inquiry may be combined.

II. The *second* lesson is THE ADVANTAGE IN ALL IMPORTANT UNDERTAKINGS OF CO-OPERATION AND THE MUTUAL ASSISTANCE OF FRIENDS. The answer from God to the inquiry, Who shall go up first? had come. "Judah shall go up: behold, I have delivered the land into his hand." Yet none the less did Judah say to Simeon his brother, "Come up with me, . . . and I likewise will go with thee into thy lot." It is not enough then even to have the help of God: the laws under which humanity is placed by God require that man have also the help of man. "As iron sharpeneth iron, so a man's countenance his friend." Our Lord sent out the seventy "two and two before his face." "Separate me Barnabas and Saul for the work whereunto I have called them," was the saying of the Holy Ghost. The strength of two is greater than the strength of one. The wisdom of two is better than the wisdom of one. In co-operation one can supply what the other lacks. One has courage, another has prudence. One has knowledge, another knows how to use it. One has wealth, the other has the wit to use wealth. One has wisdom, but is "slow of speech;" the other "can speak well," but is foolish in counsel (Exod. xxxii.). No man has all the qualities which go to make up perfect action, and therefore no man should think to do without the help of his fellow-man. It is a presumptuous state of mind which makes a man seem sufficient to himself, and an uncharitable state of mind which prompts him to withhold help from his fellow. A beautiful lesson may be learnt from the co-operation of the blind with the deaf and dumb in institutions where they are trained together. What the blind learn by the ear they communicate to the eye of the deaf, and what the deaf learn by the eye they communicate to the ear of the blind. And so it should be in everything. A man should seek help from his neighbour, and should be equally ready to give help to him in return. "Come up with me into my lot, . . . and I likewise will go with thee into thy lot," should be the law of human fellowship running through all the transactions of human life. But yet not so as to weaken individual responsibility, or to destroy just independence of character; but so as to give to each the full help towards the performance of duty which God has provided for him, and to nourish man's care for his neighbour by listening to his neighbour's calls for help.

III. The *third* lesson may be briefly stated. DIFFERENT PARTS ARE ASSIGNED TO DIFFERENT PERSONS: MORE SHOWY ONES TO SOME, MORE HUMBLE ONES TO OTHERS. But the humbler part may be as really useful and as acceptable to God as the more showy one. To some the lot is assigned of merely helping others to rise to their destined eminence, and then being forgotten. And yet they really have a share in all that is well done by those whom they helped to raise, and who could not have risen without their help. Thus Simeon helped Judah to take possession of his lot, and Judah ever after took the foremost place among the tribes of Israel; but Simeon almost disappears from view. In like manner Andrew first brought his brother Simon to Jesus; but it is Simon Peter to whom were given the keys of the kingdom of heaven, and who occupies the first place among the twelve. Barnabas took Saul and brought him to the apostles, and again went to seek him at Tarsus, and brought him to Antioch; but the place filled by St. Paul in the Church of God as far transcends that of Barnabas as the place of Judah among the tribes transcends that of Simeon. This should give encouragement to those whose work is humble and out of sight. Let the servant of God do "what he can." Let him not envy the talents, the brilliant gifts, the powers, the fame, the glory of others. But let him be content if by the grace of God he can in any way help forward the work of God's Church on earth, although his name be not mentioned till he receives his reward before the judgment-seat of Christ.

HOMILIES BY VARIOUS AUTHORS.

Vers. 1, 2.—*Transfer of authority.* Periods when supreme power passes from rulers to their descendants are always of critical importance. It is then that the greatest constitutional modifications take place. Partly from the differences of disposition and view, partly from the force of new circumstances, partly from the failure or creation of peculiar official sanctions and dignities, the legislative or executive function seldom remains wholly unchanged in passing from one holder to another. In this case, as the dignity and authority of Moses did not entirely pass to Joshua, so the office the latter filled must have greatly altered with its occupancy by the numerous body, "the sons of Israel," or elders and tribesmen. More frequent deliberation, the consultation of competing interests, &c., had to precede any national action against the common enemy. The great *Lawgiver* had passed away, the *Soldier-Dictator* had also been gathered to his fathers, and now it devolved upon a simply appointed but sacredly authoritative *constitutional assembly* to carry into effect the purposes of their predecessors. Compare with this the rise of parliamentary influence in Europe, and especially in England.

I. THE MODIFICATION OF GOVERNMENT. Sometimes this is sudden, sometimes gradual. Here it does not affect the essential principle of the theocracy. There is something very pathetic in the spectacle of an orphaned nation appealing to the "God of their fathers." It was not an extraordinary outburst of reverence and religious humility, but the beginning of a habitual and necessary practice. The voice of Jehovah through his authorised representatives was the supreme law for Israel. 1. *It behoves all nations and individuals to ask God for wisdom and direction, especially at such times of transition.* The altered conditions of life; the transfer of legislative authority; the attainment of mature years; a youth's leaving home; the death of parents, guardians, rulers, &c., are reasons for a closer walk with God, and a more attentive heed to his word. 2. *Responsibility is inevitably transferred with authority.* A sacred war is the legacy of the fathers of Israel to the children. If they are disposed to lag in its carrying forward, untoward events prick them on, and discomfort and disorder increase the necessity for action. "Uneasy lies the head that wears a crown." The peasant envies the king, the child the parent, only to be in turn regarded with a greater envy by those they assume to be fortunate and happy. Authority tempers and chastens power. The assumption of the latter without regard to its obligations is a profane and wicked thing, and must in the end defeat itself. Responsibility is the moral and religious side of authority; duty of right. In no case has a ruler or government lightly to regard inherited responsibilities. Freedom is not the result of violent changes, but "broadens slowly down from precedent to precedent." That one has had no part or choice in the making of an agreement or the inauguration of a policy is no reason by itself for repudiation. What is wrong must be put right, and false steps retraced; but the practicable policy of the present is generally a modification of the former and traditional one, rather than entire departure from it. The oneness of responsibility in past and present ought to be carefully observed, and acknowledged even where changes are introduced. None of us makes his own circumstances. Most of them are inherited. Our duties are often born before ourselves, awaiting us in the appointed time. 3. *The advantages and disadvantages of a plurality of rulers are here illustrated.* (1) Where there are several or many in power there is a *representation of popular views and interests*, (2) the advantage of *collective and deliberative wisdom*, and (3) *mutual stimulus and emulation.* On the other hand, (1) they are *liable to jealousies and envies*, (2) *it is difficult to preserve a good understanding*, (3) they are *more subject to popular panics*, and (4) are *unlikely to take a bold initiative.*

II. UNCHANGEABLENESS OF THE SUPREME AUTHORITY. Under all circumstances the ideal government for Israel must ever be the theocracy. Moses, Joshua, the elders, the judges, the kings—these are but the human representatives of the absolute and Divine; they are but the stewards of a heavenly mystery, holding authority from the Supreme, and liable at his bidding to restore it again. Paul (Rom. xiii. 1—5) summarises the general aspects of this principle:—"Let every soul be subject unto the higher powers. For there is no power but of God: the powers that be are ordained of God. Whosoever therefore resisteth the power, resisteth the ordinance of God: and they that resist shall receive to themselves damnation. . . For he is the minister of God to thee for good. . . . Wherefore ye must needs be subject, not only for wrath, but also for conscience sake." 1. This must be recognised by human delegates. The elders immediately and publicly "asked Jehovah." The force of the original expression is that no time was lost. Only as he led them could they be preserved from error. 2. To make men subject to the Supreme must ever be the goal of their efforts. Their whole policy will be, therefore, in a wide sense evangelical, viz., to bring men to God, to deepen their reverence for truth, righteousness, purity, and to encourage a personal attachment to Christ as the embodiment of these.—M.

Ver. 1.—*Spiritual initiatives.* The one stern fact facing every Israelite is God's command to uproot the Canaanite. There must be at least one land wholly consecrated to Jehovah and freed from idolatry. The warfare is an inheritance, even as the land is. There is a common obligation to fulfil this task; but it is not to be done severally, at haphazard. United action being difficult on account of the loss of the great captain, representative action is the next best. Now upon one tribe, and now upon another, will the honour devolve of carrying the war into the ranks of the enemy. It is a kind of conscription of the tribes, the honour of the burden being borne in turn by one for all. In this case no lot is cast. Jehovah is the disposer of the forces of his kingdom.

I. THE LEADERSHIP IS MADE KNOWN THROUGH PRAYER AND INQUIRY. As yet no tribe had premier rank amongst its fellows. God must decide who shall go up first. He is the fountain of honour, and he must be approached by the wonted avenues. Accordingly, the priest or the prophet is called upon to exercise his functions. There is something very beautiful and pathetic in this united asking of Jehovah by the tribes. Where God is acknowledged as the Supreme Arbiter, harmony is certain to prevail. It is well for Christians to submit all their anxieties to their Divine Father. So we find the early disciples praying after their Master's ascension. And the Church at Antioch observed a like rule ere it sent its missionaries forth to the region beyond. Spiritual work must ever be prefaced by prayer; and although God may not declare the leaders of it by a special utterance, tokens will be given which will enable them to be discovered.

II. IT IS RENDERED OBLIGATORY BY A "CALL." We are not informed as to the precise manner in which the will of God was made known. Probably the Urim and Thummim were consulted. Joshua is never mentioned as doing this; like Moses, he receives the word of God directly. The leaders of Israel receive the word of God from the priest, and the response is not oracular, but clear and definite. A twofold advantage pertained to this decision. It obtained for the chosen one the recognition of his brethren, and confirmed his own faith. An articulate supernatural "call" is not always required for undertaking God's work, but we have a right to demand of those who assume the lead in spiritual things that they shall have clear and unmistakable proof of a vocation. And it stands to reason that one who feels a "necessity laid upon him" to do certain spiritual work shall be more likely to succeed in it.

III. THE DIVINE CHOICE IS JUSTIFIED BY THE CHARACTER AND PAST CAREER OF ITS SUBJECT. This is not to say that these furnish a reason for it. With regard to all Divine work it may well be asked, "Who is sufficient for these things?" But frequently human insight and experience justify Divine measures, so far as they go. It was Judah who delivered Joseph from the pit. He confessed his sins (Gen. xxxviii. 26). Jacob intrusted Benjamin to his care, and blessed him in the words—"Thy brethren praise thee; the sceptre shall not depart from Judah." His tribe became the most numerous and warlike (Numb. ii.); and of the commissioners appointed to allot the land, the representative of Judah is first mentioned (Numb. xxxiv. 19). But above all, it was Judah and Ephraim alone who furnished the spies that gave a faithful account of the land—Caleb and Joshua. The former still lived, chief of the tribe of Judah. Ephraim, the tribe of Joshua, being already settled, Judah's turn comes next. We see therefore that although human merit cannot be said to determine Divine appointments, the latter will often be found to run in the same line.—M.

Ver. 3.—*Alliances in the holy war.* The lots of Judah and Simeon were closely united. The former's prerogative of leading off is therefore shared with the weaker tribe, which in all things is carefully considered by its "brother." It was impossible completely to separate the interests of these two; the understanding was honourable to both sides.

I. IN SPIRITUAL UNDERTAKINGS THE GREATER SHOULD EVER CONSIDER THE LESS. It is in this way that our Saviour's injunction, "Let him that would be chief among you be as him that serveth," is often best interpreted. The onus of brotherly consideration and charitable construction is with the stronger because of the advantage they already possess. It is also the more to be admired in them because of the rarity of its exercise. On this occasion Judah lost nothing, and Simeon secured a powerful ally, and an opportunity of distinction. Besides this, the kindliest sentiments were encouraged on either side.

II. By commencing in this spirit it is the more likely that moral elevation, magnanimity, and brotherly affection will be preserved all through. The waiving of personal precedence is not only graceful, it has a tendency to perpetuate itself. Our future work takes its character from the first step.

III. It is an example to our brethren, and a witness before the world to the unity of God's people. Spiritual men above all others should not first ask, "What is our right?" but, "What is our obligation, and how can we best illustrate the spirit of the Master?" The tone was set to all the other tribes, and jealousy either at Judah or one another checked ere it appeared. True unity was the strength and safety of Israel. That the neighbouring nations were impressed with the spirit of brotherhood and unity in Israel there is abundant proof. They felt they were dealing not with a mere aggregate of numbers, but with a whole inspired by common sentiment and religious enthusiasm. It is this spirit which most perfectly realises the aim of Christ's kingdom, and his prayer "that they all may be one;" "that they may be made perfect in one."—M.

Ver. 7.—*Correspondence of crime and requital.* The crime of Adoni-bezek was against not any special national law, but humanity. It was one calculated to create and foster the most cruel disposition, the moral sense being rendered callous by habituation to a spectacle of abjectness and suffering dishonouring to our common nature. Frequent amongst the heathen nations of the East, it was all the more necessary that it should be punished in an emphatic and exemplary manner. "Thumbs were cut off to incapacitate the hand from using the bow; great toes to render the gait uncertain." The circumstance stands forth here as an ancient "instance" of an eternal law, which may be thus expressed:—

I. There is a close connection between every sin and its punishment. This may be taken as a conviction more universal in its influence than religion itself. Yet it is not wholly reducible to experience. It is as truly rooted in faith as any other axiom of the spiritual life. In order to reinforce it we have (1) what may be termed *pictorial illustrations* of it. The traditions and histories of the world are full of these. Neoptolemus murdered at the altar, and at the altar he was murdered ('Pausanias,' iv. 17, 3); Phaleris roasted men in a brazen bull, and in like manner was he himself punished ('Gesta Rom.,' xlviii.). Bajazet carried about by Tamerlane in an iron cage, as he intended to have done Tamerlane. Cardinal Beaton, upon whom Wishart's sufferings were avenged in a violent death, &c., &c. This affects the popular imagination more powerfully than any direct proof; and hence the crowd of real or fancied instances that have been recorded. It is in the light of this conception probably that Exod. xviii. 11 is to be interpreted. (2) *The principle reveals itself in the history of nations and individuals.* Ishmael is the grand type of this. The story of the mutineers of the Bounty is still fresh in memory. And how many family records would show the family likeness of sins and their Nemesis, and the natural connection and development of the one from the other! In Judas the betrayer it shines with tragic grandeur. (3) *The confessions of sinners themselves strengthen the belief.*

II. The justice of God is faithful and exact. "When the Olympian," says Homer, "does not speedily punish, he still does it later" ('Iliad,' iv. 160). "The Almighty may not punish this week or next, my Lord Cardinal," said Anne of Austria to Richelieu, "but at the last he punishes." In the incidents of human life we seem to see links of an almost invisible chain connecting sin with judgment, as cause with effect. And if in the few cases we know the punishment is so finely, even dramatically, adjusted, are we not justified in believing that beneath the surface there is even a finer and more inevitable equivalency observed? It is here too we have another evidence of the superior moral influence of the doctrine of providence as compared with fate. Both are inevitable, but the former rationally and rectorially so.

III. BUT BY AWAKING REFLECTION AND REPENTANCE OUR PUNISHMENT MAY BECOME OUR SALVATION. There is a gleam of something more than fatalism in Adoni-bezek's confession. It is just possible that it betrays an unfeigned repentance. The higher law of grace may step in to rescue us from the law of vengeance. Many a soul has drawn back before the hideous vision of "sin when it bringeth forth."—M.

Vers. 1, 2.—*The death of the great.* The circumstances which accompanied and followed the death of Joshua are suggestive of the common difficulties which arise on the death of great men, and the conduct of Israel is an example of the right spirit in which to face these difficulties.

I. THE MOST USEFUL MEN ARE OFTEN CALLED AWAY BEFORE THEIR WORK IS FINISHED. The measure of work which God requires of them may always be accomplished, for he sets no task for which he does not supply all needful talents and opportunities. But the work which a man aims at accomplishing, which he sees needing to be done, which men trust him to achieve for them, is commonly greater than his time and powers allow of perfect performance. 1. This fact should teach the most active workers (1) *diligence*, since at the best they can never overtake their work, and (2) *humility*, in the thought of the little that the ablest can accomplish compared with what he aims at. 2. This fact should lead all men (1) not to lean too much on any one *individual*, (2) to be ready to welcome *new* men, (3) to train *children* to take the places of their parents.

II. THE DEATH OF GREAT MEN SHOULD INSPIRE US WITH A DESIRE TO CONTINUE THEIR UNFINISHED WORK. 1. It is foolish to be content with *idle panegyrics*, as though we could live for ever on the glory of the past. Life must not be spent in a dreamy contemplation of the sunset, however brilliant this may be. While we gaze the radiance fades; night will soon fall. We must be up and preparing for shelter under the darkness, and for work in a new day. 2. It is weak to sink into mere regrets and despondency. We do not honour the dead by wasting our lives in barren grief. When the great and good are gone the future may look blank and hopeless; but God is still with us, and he will still provide for us. Therefore we should do as Israel did. Not satisfied with the glory of Joshua's victories, nor stunned by the blow of his death, the people look forward, seek for guidance for the future, and endeavour to continue his unfinished work. The richest legacy we can receive from the great is the unfinished task which drops from their dying hands. The noblest monument we can erect to their memory will be the completion of that task; the most honourable epitaph we can write for them will be the story of the good works for which their lives and examples have inspired their successors.

III. AS POSTS OF RESPONSIBILITY BECOME VACANT, IT IS WISE TO SEEK THE GUIDANCE OF GOD IN THE CHOICE OF NEW MEN TO OCCUPY THEM. After the death of Joshua Israel consulted "the Eternal." It is a blessing that the loss of our most trusted earthly friends should drive us to the refuge of the great heavenly Friend. In the present case new leaders do not now arise by selfish ambition, nor are they chosen by popular election. The selection of them is referred to God. Israel thus recognises its constitution as a theocracy. Every nation should consider itself under a supreme theocracy. Political leaders should be chosen by a Christian nation only after prayer for Divine guidance. Much more evident is it that the selection of men for service in spiritual things, as ministers, as missionaries, &c., should not be left to the mere inclination of the individual or the unaided human judgment of others, but determined after the most earnest prayer for Divine light (Acts i. 24). Note—such a method of election implies a willingness that the chosen leaders should be called to do God's will, not merely to humour the popular caprice.

IV. WHEN GREAT MEN ARE TAKEN AWAY IT IS OFTEN THE CASE THAT NO MEN OF EQUAL ABILITY ARE FOUND TO SUCCEED THEM. Joshua was not equal to Moses, but he was still well able to take the staff of leadership from his master's hand. But Joshua left no successor. Nothing but anarchy faced the nation "after the death of Joshua"—it seemed as though there could be no "after." There are advantages in the absence of great men. The multitude may become indolent, trusting too much to the work of the few. When these are removed men are thrown back on their own resources; thus the courage and energy of the whole people is put on trial. Yet on the whole we must feel that it is better to have the great among us. The death of Joshua is the signal for the decadence of the nation from its ancient heroic glory. Therefore let us pray that God will continue the race of good and great men, and seek to educate and discover such among the young. Let us be thankful that our Joshua—Christ—will never be taken from his people (Matt. xxviii. 20).—A.

Ver. 3.—*Mutual help.* I. IN THE ABSENCE OF UNITY OF AUTHORITY WE SHOULD SEEK FOR UNION OF SYMPATHY. After the death of Joshua the loss of leadership endangers the national unity of Israel. In the text we see how two tribes, no longer united by a common government, draw together for mutual help. The union of free attraction is nobler than that of external compulsion. The highest unity of Christendom is to be found not in the Roman Catholic organisation of a central authority and uniformity of creed and worship, but in the spiritual conception of common sympathies and common aims.

II. BROTHERLY KINDNESS IS A PECULIARLY CHRISTIAN GRACE. Love of the brethren is a proof of regeneration (1 John iii. 14). The law of Christ as contrasted with the barren Levitical law of ordinances is characteristically summed up in the obligation to "bear one another's burdens" (Gal. vi. 2). 1. This implies *active help.* Simeon and Judah went to battle for an inheritance. Mere feelings of sympathy are wasted sentiments unless they lead to active and fruitful service. 2. This implies *sacrifice.* The Simeonites and men of Judah risked their lives for the benefit of one another. Cheap charity is worthless charity. Our brotherly kindness is of little value till it costs us something—involves pain, loss, sacrifice. Christ is the great example of this. It is our mission to follow Christ here if we would be his true disciples (Phil. ii. 4—8). 3. This implies *mutual* help. Judah helps Simeon; Simeon in turn helps Judah. Charity is often too one-sided. The poor and needy can often make more return than appears possible if invention is quickened by gratitude. A miserable penitent could wash the feet of Christ with her tears (Luke vii. 38).

III. THE WORK OF LIFE IS BEST DONE BY UNION AND CO-OPERATION OF WORKERS. Judah and Simeon conquer their two possessions by union. Both might have failed had they acted singly. "Union is strength." The advantage of mutual help is seen in trade, in manufactures, in education, in the advance of civilisation generally. The spirit of Cain is fatal to all progress (Gen. iv. 9). The same applies to Christian work. Therefore Christ founded the Church. Though Christianity is based on individualism, it works through social agencies. The society of Christians, the Christian family, find means of useful effort which private Christians could never attain, *e. g.* in the Sunday school, foreign and home missions, the work of Bible and tract societies. Simeon and Judah united to conquer their several lots successively. So it is sometimes wisest for us to unite and do together one work well at one time, rather than to spread our divided energies over a wide field of weak agencies. The river which runs out over a broad plain may be swallowed up in the sands of the desert, while that which flows in a narrow channel is strong and deep.—A.

Vers. 6, 7.—*Retribution.* I. THERE IS A LAW OF RETRIBUTION. 1. *The desire for retribution is instinctive.* It is one of the elementary ideas of justice. To those who have no vision of a higher law, the execution of this is not a cruel crime of vengeance, but a righteous exercise of justice. 2. *The fitness of retribution is not affected by the motive of those who accomplish it.* It is possible that the Israelites were ignorant of the old crimes of Adoni-bezek, and may have been guilty of wanton cruelty in treating him as they did. If so, his wickedness was no excuse for their barbarity. But then their harsh intentions did not affect the justice of the king's sufferings. God often uses the crime of one man as a means of punishing the crime of another. He does not originate or sanction the retributive crime, but he overrules it, and so turns the wrath of man to the praise of his righteous government. Thus Nebuchadnezzar was no better than an ambitious tyrant in his conquest of Jerusalem; yet he was the unconscious agent of a Divine decree of justice. 3. *Sin will surely bring retribution.* (1) No rank will secure us against this. The sufferer in this case was a king. (2) No time will wear out guilt. It is likely that Adoni-bezek had committed his crimes in bygone years, as he referred to them in a way which suggests that the memory of them was suddenly aroused by his own experience. 4. *Retribution often bears a resemblance to the crimes it follows.* The *lex talionis* seems to be mysteriously embedded in the very constitution of nature. The intemperate slave of bodily pleasures brings on himself bodily disease; cruelty provokes cruelty; suspicion arouses distrust. As a man sows so will he reap (Gal. vi. 7, 8). 5. *One of the most fearful elements of future retribution will be found in an evil memory.* Men bury their old sins out of sight. They will be exhumed in all their corruption. The justice of the retribution will then increase the sting of it (Luke xvi. 25).

II. THE HIGHER CHRISTIAN LAW OF LOVE. Christianity does not abolish the terrible natural laws of retributive justice, but it reveals higher principles which can counteract the disastrous effects of those stern laws, and a more excellent way than that of zealously advocating the execution of them. 1. *The Christian is bound not to desire vengeance.* He is called to forgive his enemies (Matt. v. 38, 39). If retribution must fall, let us leave it to the supreme Judge (Rom. xii. 19). 2. *The highest purpose of punishment is seen to consist in the preservation and the restoration of righteousness*—not in the mere balancing of sin with pain. Punishment is not an end in itself. The vengeance which seeks satisfaction to outraged honour in the humiliation of its victim is as unworthy of the character of God as it is foreign to the principles of Christian duty. Punishment is a means to an end, and that end is not mere revenge, but the deterring of others from evil, and, where possible, the restoration of the fallen (Heb. xii. 5, 6, 11). 3. *In the gospel forgiveness is offered for all sin.* The law is not evaded; it is honoured in the sacrifice of Christ. Now he has borne the sin of the world he can also release the world from its fatal effects. Therefore, though the thunder-cloud of retribution may seem as dark as ever, if we only look high enough we shall see the rainbow of God's mercy above it promising peace and forgiveness to all who repent and trust in his grace (Acts xiii. 38, 39).—A.

EXPOSITION.

Ver. 8.—Read *Fought against Jerusalem, and took it, and smote it.* It is the continuation of the narrative of the exploits of Judah and Simeon in conquering their respective lots.

Ver. 9.—**The valley,** *i. e.* the *Shephelah*, or lowlands, between the mountains and the coast of the Mediterranean, occupied by the Philistines.

Ver. 10.—**Hebron.** See Numb. xiii. 22; Josh. xiv. 13—15; xv. 13—19. Hebron was the burial-place of Abraham and Sarah (Gen. xxiii. 2, &c.; xxv. 9), of Isaac and Rebekah, and of Jacob and Leah (Gen. xxxv. 27—29; xlix. 31; l. 13), and the mosque, within whose massive walls the tombs of Abraham and the other four above mentioned are still preserved with the utmost reverence, is the most remarkable object in the modern city, which is called *El-Khalil* (the friend), after Abraham, *the friend of God.* A very interesting account of the Prince of Wales's visit to the Mosque of Hebron in 1862 is given in Dean Stanley's 'Sermons in the East.' David reigned in Hebron seven years and six months before he transferred the seat of power to Jerusalem (see 2 Sam. ii. 1, &c.; v. 1—5).

Ver. 13.—**Caleb's younger brother.** See note on ch. iii. 9.

Ver. 14.—**She moved him,** &c. There is some obscurity in this verse, which seems to tell us that Achsah, on her wedding-day, when she was going to her husband's house, persuaded him to ask of her father *the field,* viz. that in which the springs of water were, and which were not included in her original dower; and then goes on to tell us that Achsah herself made the request. The Septuagint reads, "Othniel urged her to ask the field of her father," and the Vulgate has, "Her husband told her to ask her father," and then it follows naturally, "and she lighted from off her ass," &c. But the Hebrew reading may be right, and it may be that when her husband, brave in storming a city, but timid in asking a favour, hung back, she, with the tenacious will of a woman, sprang off the ass herself, and successfully preferred her request. Dean Stanley identifies (though not with absolute certainty) the "field" thus obtained by Achsah with an unusually green valley amidst the dry, barren hills of the south country, lying south or west of Hebron, called Wady Nunkur, through which Caleb and Achsah must have ridden on their way from Hebron to Debir, or Kirjath-sepher. This valley breaks into a precipitous and still greener ravine, and both the upper and lower pastures are watered by a clear, bubbling rivulet, which rises in the upper meadow, and flows to the bottom of the ravine below. The name of a village, *Dewir*, seems to represent the ancient *Debir*.

Ver. 16.—**The children of the Kenite, &c.** It appears from this verse that the invitation given by Moses to his "father-in-law," or rather "brother-in-law," Hobab, to accompany him and the Israelites to the land of promise, though at first rejected (Numb. x. 29, 30), was eventually accepted. Hobab and his tribe, a branch of the Midianites, called Kenites, from an unknown ancestor, *Kain*, at first settled in the city of palm trees, *i. e.* Jericho (Deut. xxxiv. 3) ; but it seems that when Judah started on his expedition with Simeon to conquer the south land, the Kenites went with him. A subsequent migration of a portion of this nomadic tribe is mentioned (ch. iv. 11). **Dwelt among the people,** *i. e.* the people of Judah. For *Arad* see Numb. xxi. 1.

Ver. 17.—**Judah went with Simeon.** In ver. 3 *Simeon went with Judah,* because the places which follow were all in Judah's lot ; but now we read, *Judah went with Simeon,* because *Zephath* or *Hormah* was in Simeon's lot (Josh. xix. 4). For Hormah, identified by Robinson (ii. 181) with *Es-sufeh,* see Numb. xxi. 3. The Hebrew verb for "they utterly destroyed" is the root of the name *Hormah,* i. e. *utter destruction.*

Ver. 18.—**Gaza, &c.** Gaza, Askelon, and Ekron, were all cities of the Philistines. But though Judah took these cities, it seems he was not able permanently to expel the inhabitants.

Ver. 19.—**Chariots of iron.** The chariots of the Canaanites were very formidable to the Israelites, who had no means of coping with them. Thus we are told of Jabin, king of Canaan, who reigned in Hazor, that he had 900 chariots of iron, and mightily oppressed the children of Israel. They were later an important part of King Solomon's army (1 Kings x. 26). See too Josh. xvii. 16.

Ver. 20.—**They gave Hebron, &c.** Caleb, the son of Jephunneh, the Kenezite, an Edomitish tribe, was one of the spies sent up to spy the land, and in doing so he came to Hebron, and there saw the giants, the sons of Anak (Numb. xiii. 22). When all the spies brought up an evil report of the land, and by doing so raised a rebellion against Moses and Aaron, Caleb the Kenezite, alone with Joshua, stood firm, and, as a reward of his faithfulness, received the promise that he and his seed should possess the land on which his feet had trodden. Accordingly Hebron became the inheritance of Caleb the Kenezite (see Numb. xiii., xiv.; Deut. i. 36 ; Josh. xiv. 6—15; xv. 13, 14).

HOMILETICS.

Vers. 8—20.—*Faith.* The principal incident in this section is the conquest of Hebron by Caleb (see note, ver. 20), and in it we have a most striking illustration (1) of the nature of faith, (2) of the triumph of faith, (3) of the faithfulness of God's promises, and (4) of the extension of God's covenant to men of every nation and kindred.

I. THE NATURE OF FAITH. When the Israelites were in Kadesh Barnea, near the borders of Canaan, in the second year of the exodus, it was determined on their own suggestion, with the full approval of Moses, to send spies to search out the land, and to bring back word what road they ought to take, and into what cities they would come. Thus far there had been only a due exercise of human wisdom and caution. But when the spies returned after forty days they brought back a mixed report. On the one hand they reported that it was indeed a goodly land. Its fertile soil, its genial climate, its beauty and its richness, were attested by its abundant produce. As they held up the heavy bunch of the grapes of Eshcol, a burden for two men to carry upon a staff, as they showed them the luscious figs and the juicy pomegranates, who could doubt that it was a land worth possessing ? It was rich too in its pastures and in its cattle, and its wild-flowers were as good as the thyme of Hymettus for the bees that swarmed amongst them. It was a land flowing with milk and honey. But here their good report stopped. This good land was guarded, they said, by a mighty people. It was a gigantic race that possessed it, and they dwelt in fenced cities with Cyclopean walls rising up to heaven. How could the children of Israel hope to wrest their land from them ? It would be a vain enterprise, and could only end in their own discomfiture and death. Those men of great stature would crush them like grasshoppers under their feet. At these unbelieving words the hearts of the whole congregation melted within them, and anger against Moses filled every breast. The suggestion ran from mouth to mouth to choose a captain and return to Egypt. The promises of God were all forgotten. The mighty wonders at the Red Sea, at

Sinai, in the wilderness, were lost sight of, and their hearts sunk through unbelief. Then Caleb's faith shone out, and spoke out before the people. " Let us go up at once and possess the land, for we are well able to overcome it." " Fear not the people of the land ; for they are bread for us: their defence is departed from them, and the Lord is with us: fear them not." " If the Lord delight in us, then he will bring us into this land and give it us." That was faith, laying hold of God's promises and God's almighty power, and making no account of apparent difficulties, or of human weakness. Just such was Abraham's faith, who " staggered not at the promise of God through unbelief, but was strong in faith, giving glory to God, and fully persuaded that what he had promised he was able also to perform " (Rom. iv. 20, 21). Such has been the faith of saints at all times, piercing through the mists and clouds of the present, and seeing the bright sun of the future ; despising the visible because, like Elisha in Dothan, it sees the invisible (2 Kings vi. 13—17) ; calculating truly, because it takes into account the power and faithfulness of God which are left out of the calculations of the unbelieving.

II. The triumph of faith. And we see here the triumph of faith. The whole congregation of the unbelieving, of those who in their hearts turned back to Egypt, and dared not face the sons of Anak, had all perished in the wilderness. They died and were buried, and never saw the land of promise. But Caleb was alive, and in the full vigour of his strength he marched against the stronghold of the Anakim, and took it, and slew the sons of Anak in spite of their great stature, and took possession of their city in spite of its lofty walls, and it became his possession for ever. That was the triumph of faith, that faith which disappoints not, and maketh not ashamed.

III. The faithful promises. We have here too an eminent illustration of the faithfulness of God's promises. Caleb's triumphant possession of Hebron chimes in in exact harmony with all the records of God's *performances* as compared with his *promises.* " He hath holpen his servant Israel as he promised to our forefathers " (Luke i. 54). " He hath remembered his mercy and truth toward the house of Israel " (Ps. xcviii. 3). " He hath visited and redeemed his people, as he spake by the mouth of his holy prophets, . . . to perform the mercy promised to our fathers, and to remember his holy covenant; to perform the oath which he sware to our forefather Abraham " (Luke i. 68—73, Pr. B. Version). " He is faithful that promised ' (Heb. x. 23). " Blessed is she that believed: for there shall be a performance of those things which were told her from the Lord " (Luke i. 45). " There failed not aught of any good thing which the Lord had spoken unto the house of Israel; all came to pass " (Josh. xxi. 45). A thorough appreciation of faithfulness to his Word as one of the prominent attributes of God is the inevitable result of a full knowledge of the Scriptures, as it is most conducive to the stability of the Christian character. " For ever, O Lord, thy word is settled in heaven ; thy faithfulness is unto all generations " (Ps. cxix. 89, 90).

IV. A glimpse of the mystery. But we must also notice the illustration here given of God's purpose to extend his covenant to men of all nations. Caleb was not an Israelite by birth. He was a Kenezite, *i. e.* a descendant of Kenaz, whose name is a clear proof of Edomite origin (Gen. xxxvi. 15, 42). And accordingly we are told, " Unto Caleb the son of Jephunneh he gave a part *among the children of Judah* " (Josh. xv. 13) ; and again, " Hebron became the inheritance of Caleb the son of Jephunneh *the Kenezite,* because that he wholly followed the Lord *God of Israel* " (Josh. xiv. 14), language clearly pointing to Caleb's foreign origin. We have here then the breadth of God's grace and love breaking out in the narrowness of the Jewish dispensation ; we have a glimpse of the mystery, which St. Paul spoke of so rapturously, that it was God's good pleasure in the dispensation of the fulness of times to gather together into one all things in Christ, and that the Gentiles should be fellow-heirs, and of the same body, and partakers of his promise in Christ by the gospel (Ephes. i. 9, 10; iii. 6). Caleb, possessing his inheritance in the midst of Judah because he wholly followed the Lord the God of Israel, was the forerunner of that great multitude of all nations and kindreds and peoples and tongues who shall stand before the Lamb clothed in white robes and palms in their hands, and shall sit down with Abraham, Isaac, and Jacob, in the kingdom of God.

HOMILIES BY VARIOUS AUTHORS.

Vers. 11—15.—*The public spirit of Caleb.* He offered his daughter to the soldier who should be successful in destroying the inhabitants of Debir. It was of supreme importance that this stronghold should be taken, if the rest of the district was to be peaceably held. But some reward was required in order to stimulate the heroism of his followers to face the hazard and danger of the enterprise. We have here then—

I. AN IDENTIFICATION OF HIMSELF WITH THE INTERESTS OF HIS TRIBE. Caleb was an Edomite, and might have enjoyed his own lot without such special effort or sacrifice. He is evidently deeply interested in the welfare and honour of his adopted tribe. This might be called a signal illustration of public spirit. And yet it is probable that Caleb himself was quite unconscious that there was anything singular in his action. As the greatest blessings to a nation arise from the public spirit of its citizens, so the greatest curses are frequently entailed by the want of it. As in warfare every soldier, however insignificant, is an influence that tells upon the success or failure of the campaign, so in a government, with representative institutions whose action binds the nation and measures its progress, it is requisite that every citizen should actively interest himself in electing and supporting the legislative authority. The free play of an intelligent, generous, and enthusiastic public criticism will tend to the health of the whole body politic, and *vice versa.* Even more cogent is the need for public spirit in the church. Its honour and dishonour are ours, its success or failure. And it represents interests of the most tremendous importance. " England expects every man to do his duty " is a sentence of historic importance. Although not called upon to preach, or even to pray in public, the private member of the church ought to regard the affairs of Christ's kingdom with enthusiasm, and be prepared to make great sacrifices for its advancement :

II. HIS PROOF OF THIS IN BESTOWING ONE OF HIS MOST PRECIOUS POSSESSIONS. We do not know much about Achsah, but probably she was very beautiful. Her forethought and carefulness are described in the fourteenth and fifteenth verses. She was his only daughter, born to him in later life (1 Chron. ii. 49). That she was dear to her father we may take for granted. How much a daughter may be to a father history has frequently and strikingly shown. The grief of Jephthah for the consequences of his rash vow is recorded in this very book. Apart from the personal attractions of Achsah, the influence which might be obtained by intermarriage with the family of Caleb is not to be ignored.

III. IT WAS A SACRIFICE WHICH HAD IN IT THE SECURITY FOR ITS OWN REWARD. An offer like this was an appeal to the chivalry of the tribe. It suggested vividly that on account of which the bravery of the warrior is so necessary. The soldier who stormed such a fortress was sure to possess the noble and manly qualities and the religious zeal calculated to make a good husband. So in political and spiritual matters, generous offers and challenges appeal to what is noblest in the nature of men, and secure a loftier and more heroic response.—M.

Vers. 14, 15.—*Compensations.* Of the wisdom and carefulness of Achsah we have here abundant proof. They were nobly and honourably exercised. She is the daughter of a rich man, and becomes the bride of a brave soldier who had evidently little but his sword and his reputation to boast of. She is jealous lest he should be rewarded with a mere titular distinction. He has been nobly oblivious of material rewards, *she* shall be proportionally watchful over his interests. She therefore urges her husband as he passes in triumph to Hebron to ask for the field through which they march. The thoughts of the hero are not to be directed into any such sordid channel. But she, taking advantage of the occasion as she lights from off her ass, asks her father in symbolic language to compensate her for the poverty to which he had consigned her. " Thou hast given me a south land (*i. e.* married me to a poor younger son); give me also springs of water." To this reasonable request Caleb makes generous response. " She slides from her ass, suddenly, as if she fell, so that her father asks, ' What is the matter with thee ? ' Her answer has a double sense, ' Thou gavest me away into a dry land ; give me also springs ' " (Cassel).

I. A BLESSING WITH A DRAWBACK. Of the bravery of Othniel there could be no question ; of his poverty there could be as little. It might be honourable for her to be his wife, but she would have to suffer many sacrifices in leaving the wealthy home of her father, and her husband would have an additional burden to sustain. Are not the dispensations of providence, even when we judge them on the whole to be best for us, frequently as mysteriously qualified and limited ? No man would probably care to exchange his life for another's, but "there's a crook in every lot." Material blessings generally contain within them elements of discipline, and sometimes even of punishment. But they are alike the gift of a loving father, and are to be accepted in the spirit of trust and affection.

II. COMPENSATIONS. Is the gift of Achsah's father open to grave drawbacks ? It is not therefore unalterable. Something may be done to lessen its inconveniences, if not entirely to remove them. Her father is reasonable, and she at once makes appeal to his sense of what is fit and proper. Her request is granted. So with ourselves. Our heavenly Father who apportioned our lot is surely as reasonable and affectionate as any earthly one. It is for us to exercise the same wisdom as Achsah, and request that God will give us such alleviations to our portion in life, or reveal to us those that already exist. Sometimes there are compensations latent in the very circum-stances of which we complain: springs of water to moisten a sun-parched soil. In any case God is able to bestow upon us exceeding abundantly above all that we can ask or think.—M.

Ver. 19.—*Divine help* versus *material obstacles.* The statement of this verse is perplexing ; hardly softened if we render "there was no driving out," &c. On the one hand, apparently, infinite power is on the side of Judah ; on the other, there are sharply-defined limits to his success, and singular reasons for his failure. (Describe inhabitants of mountain and valley.) One would suppose that if God had really been with Judah, the chariots of iron would be neither here nor there in the question. "If God be for us, who can be against us ?" But the difficulty arises from looking at the problem wholly from the Divine side. The same difficulty faces us to-day. "But this temptation was so great !" "But was not the Lord with you ?" *Infinite power may be on our side, but we may be debarred by failure of faith from making full use of it.*

I. UNREALISED SPIRITUAL POWER. Many of the brutes have power greater than man, but they cannot bring it to bear. Is man never similarly unfortunate ? In what sense can the power of God in the saint be unrealised ? It is not power *wasted* or *lying idle*, but simply like a cheque unused. Our spiritual nature is not developed enough.

II. INSUFFICIENT REASONS FOR FAILURE OR SUCCESS. These arise from the same cause as the preceding. The tool in hands of tyro and master. The true panoply of a Church is spiritual ; and its material advantages may sometimes be as Goliath's armour to David ; and so may the spiritual advantages, if we do not realise them, keep ourselves in continual communion with them, and test their virtue by continual exercises of faith.

III. WAYS IN WHICH MAN LIMITS GOD. By failure of faith. By neglect of the means of grace. By personal unholiness. "*God's* arm is not shortened," &c., "but ye are straitened in your own selves."—M.

Vers. 19—21.—*A title to be made good.* Each of these—Judah, Caleb (of the same tribe), and Benjamin—had received their portion at the hands of the Lord ; but they had to conquer it. Judah partially succeeded, Caleb wholly succeeded, and Benjamin had a grievous drawback to his success. *This is suggestive of the blessed-ness to be attained by Christians.*

I. THE PROMISE IS COMPLETE AND ABSOLUTE TO EVERY CHRISTIAN. "This is the victory that overcometh the world even your faith." The least Christian is assured of this splendid triumph.

II. ITS REALISATION WILL DEPEND UPON THE MEASURE OF HIS FAITH, &c. The estate with a mortgage. Judah had already "fought against Jerusalem" and subdued it, at least the southern portion abutting upon, or included in, their boundary. But they did not subdue the citadel, which was in Benjamin's lot. The latter, on the other hand, are too careless, unwarlike, or indisposed to make good their possession.—M.

Ver. 19.—*The presence of God in the battle of life.* The most remarkable circumstance connected with the wars of ancient Israel is the religious faith which guided and inspired the people for battle. In this respect the conduct of those wars is typical of the Christian method of spiritual warfare.

I. GOD IS WITH HIS PEOPLE IN THE BATTLE OF LIFE. God is not only the Refuge in distress and the Father of peaceful mercies; he is the Source of strength and of courage, and the Inspirer of the masculine virtues of the Church militant—he is with us in *battle.* God does not grant his aid from a distance, through messengers, &c.; he is *present* in the active exercise of his power. 1. *When God calls people to any task, he will follow and help them in it.* God had chosen Judah for the work of conquering the Canaanites. He also followed Judah to battle. Divine election was followed by Divine power. God never expects us to undertake any work in which he will not aid us. If he calls us to any difficult task, he will go first, and prepare the way for us, and then will accompany us in it, as our Guide and Protector. 2. *They who are united in the service of God have peculiar reason for expecting the presence of God.* Judah and Simeon were united, and God aided them in their common task. God does not desert the solitary: *e. g.* Hagar (Gen. xvi. 13), Jacob (Gen. xxviii. 16), Elijah (1 Kings xix. 9). But we have a special right to expect his presence when we co-operate in brotherly sympathy. Christ is present where two or three are met together in his name. The Holy Ghost came on the day of Pentecost, when the whole Church was assembled together (Acts ii. 1).

II. THE PRESENCE OF GOD IS THE CHIEF SOURCE OF SUCCESS IN THE BATTLE OF LIFE. God was with Judah, *therefore* he obtained possession of the mountains. If God is with his people in their time of toil and difficulty, his presence is a security of active aid. He is with us not merely to approve, but to help. The victory comes from him. It is not all who have faith and spiritual insight to discern this truth. God does not come with a visible host and with " chariots of iron ; " but his presence and aid are felt in the providential control of events ; in the inspiration of strength and courage ; in the enlightenment of Divine wisdom. The best human securities for success will not justify us in neglecting the help of God. Simeon and Judah were united, and were the stronger for their union ; yet it was not the human strength thus obtained, but God's presence, which brought victory. There is a danger lest we should trust too much to imposing human arrangements, large societies, elaborate organisations, &c. The most splendid Christian army will be miserably defeated if it ventures to enter the field without the leadership of the " Captain of salvation."

III. THE PRESENCE OF GOD WILL NOT ALONE SECURE PERFECT AND IMMEDIATE SUCCESS. Though God was with Judah, still Judah could not drive out the inhabitants of the valley. 1. *God's presence and aid do not dispense with human effort.* It is Judah, not God, who fails. We may fail on our side of the work while God is not wanting on his. 2. *God's presence does not make us entirely independent of earthly circumstances.* God did not annihilate the chariots of iron. We must not expect God to work such violent miracles as shall liberate us from all the inconveniences of life. 3. *Human weakness may still linger about us after we have been blessed with the aid of God's presence.* The Israelites were too weak to overcome the inhabitants of the valley. Possibly they feared to face the chariots of iron. The measure of help we have from God is not limited in itself, but it is limited by our faith. If we had perfect faith we should have perfect success. But when we look away from God to the iron chariots of our foes, or, like Peter, from Christ to the threatening waves, we may fail from fear and human weakness, and God's almighty power will not then save us from defeat.—A.

EXPOSITION.

Ver. 21.—This verse is identical with Josh. xv. 63, except that there we read "the children of Judah" instead of "the children of Benjamin," as in this verse. The boundary line between Judah and Jerusalem passed through JEBUS or JEBUSI, as Jerusalem was anciently called (see Josh. xv. 8 ; xviii. 28 ; Judges xix. 10, 11 ; 1 Chron. xi. 4, 5). Jebus was not finally held by the Israelites till the time of David (see ch. xix. 10, note.)

Ver. 22. — **The house of Joseph,** *i. e.* Ephraim, but probably here spoken of as "the house of Joseph" because in the original document, from which both this chapter and Josh. xv. 63, and xvi., xvii. are taken, the mention of "the lot of the children of Joseph" occurs, embracing both Ephraim and Manasseh. See Josh. xvi. 1 and xv. 23, with which the twenty-first and twenty-second verses of this chapter are manifestly identical.

Ver. 23.—**Bethel,** now Beitin. The name (house of God) had been given by Jacob (Gen. xxviii. 19), but obviously would not be likely to be adopted by the Canaanitish inhabitants, by whom it was called Luz. As soon, however, as the Ephraimites conquered it, they reimposed the name, in memory of their father Jacob. The Saxon charters exhibit an analogous change in such transitions of name, as that from *Bedericksworth* to *Bury St. Edmunds,* which took place after the transfer of St. Edmund's body to the church there, the old name continuing for a time along with the new one, but at last disappearing.

Ver. 24.—**We will show thee mercy.** Compare the saving of Rahab alive, with all her house, at the taking of Jericho (Josh. vi. 23). This history is not preserved in the parallel place in Josh. xvi.

Ver. 28.—**Put the Canaanites to tribute,** or made them tributaries, as in vers. 30, 33, *i.e.* imposed forced labour upon them, as the Gibeonites were made hewers of wood and drawers of water (Josh. ix. 21, 27 ; see 1 Kings ix. 21).

Ver. 32.—**The Asherites dwelt among the Canaanites.** In verses 29 and 30 it was said that the Canaanites dwelt among the Israelites ; but here we read that the Asherites, and in ver. 33 that Naphtali, *dwelt among the Canaanites,* which seems to imply that the Canaanites were the more numerous people of the two, yet the Israelites were able to keep them in subjection.

Ver. 36.—**The going up to Akrabbim.** See Josh. xv. 3, *Maaleh-acrabbim.* In Numb. xxxiv. 4 "the ascent of Akrabbim." The whole name, put into English, is "the ascent, or going up, of Scorpions," a mountain pass so called from the abundance of scorpions found in the whole region. The exact locality is uncertain, but it is thought to be the pass *El-Safeh,* immediately to the south of the Dead Sea. The neighbourhood to Mount Hor and Petra is indicated by its connection here with "the rock," in Hebrew *has-selah,* which is the distinctive name of the rocks or cliffs on which Petra is built, and the name of *Petra* (the rock) itself. Speaking roughly, a line drawn westward from El-Safeh to the Mediterranean Sea, near the "river of Egypt," formed the southern boundary of Judah, and of the Amorites whom they displaced. The battle with the Amorites (Deut. i. 44), in which the Israelites were discomfited and pursued, is thought to have been at El-Safeh.

HOMILETICS.

Vers. 21—36.—*Weak faith producing weak action.* This section, contrasted with the preceding, gives us an instructive picture of a weak faith—not of absolute unbelief forfeiting the whole promise of God, but of a weak faith—coming short of the fulness of the blessing of the gospel of Christ. Caleb's faith, we have seen, was strong, and so his success was full. The faith of the tribes here enumerated was weak, and so their success was only partial. In the career of those who are of weak or little faith we may notice the following features which usually belong to them :—

I. THE WANT OF A HIGH AIM. These tribes did not rise to the full purpose of God to give them the land for their possession. They were content with a partial possession. So many Christians do not aim at perfect obedience to the law of God, or a perfect conformity to the mind of Christ, but are content with a conventional standard of Christian morality, very far below the measure of the stature of the fulness of Christ. They do not aim high enough in knowledge, or in character, or in works, or in godliness, or in the victory over sin, or in self-control, or in heavenly-mindedness.

II. THE OVER-ESTIMATE OF DIFFICULTIES. These tribes thought the iron chariots invincible, shrunk from encountering them in the valleys, and slunk away into the hills and fastnesses out of their way. So to those of little faith the difficulties in the way of a thoroughly godly life seem insuperable. The fashions and customs of the world, the adverse opinions of men, the possible losses in trade or worldly advantage, or in useful friendships, the sacrifice of inclinations or interests, cannot be got over. Their hearts quail before difficulties and obstacles, and they are ever of a fearful and doubtful mind.

III. THE DISPOSITION TO COMPROMISE. These tribes could not or would not drive the Canaanites out, but they would make them tributaries. That was something done, if not all that ought to be done. So the weak in faith compromise in respect to their Christian duties. They do not yield a bold, whole-hearted obedience at any cost, but they will go half-way, and stop. They will curb the flesh, but not crucify it; they will check, but not destroy, the body of sin; they will follow Christ's directions up to a certain point, and then, like the young ruler, go away sorrowful. And this want of thoroughness is as fatal to the peace and comfort of a Christian's walk with God as was the compromise of the Israelites to their enjoyment of the promised land. In their case the enemies whom they failed to destroy were constant thorns in their sides—rising against them whenever they were weak, always ready to join their enemies, taking advantage of every opportunity to harass and distress them. And so in the case of these Christians of little faith: the sins which they spare, the affections with which they compromise, the habits which they will not utterly break off, and the unfinished victories at which they stop short are continually marring their peace, and even threatening their hold on the kingdom of God. And the result is seen in the general condition of the Church of God: one of compromise instead of mastery, of hollow truce instead of decisive victory.

IV. AN UNDERRATING OF THE POWER AND GRACE OF GOD. This is the cause of all the evil, and is of the very essence of a weak faith. When God's power and goodness and grace are underrated, all goes wrong. Low aims, fear of difficulties, base compromises are sure to prevail. But with the due sense of all-sufficient grace all goes well. "My grace is sufficient for thee," saith the Lord to his believing servant. "I can do all things through Christ which strengtheneth me" is the servant's answer. Let us make a due estimate of the glorious grace of God in Christ Jesus our Lord; so shall we be "strong in the Lord, and in the power of his might."

HOMILIES BY VARIOUS AUTHORS.

Vers. 22—26.—*An unwilling helper of the cause of God.* Into the motives that actuated him we need not pry. Chief of all was the great one of self-preservation. Was it honourable? Was it right for the soldiers of God to make use of such an instrument? There may have been other considerations that had weight with him. It might have been virtuous to resist the offer: was it necessarily vicious to yield to it?

I. THERE ARE MANY WHO HELP THE TRUTH FROM LOWER MOTIVES WHO MIGHT DO SO FROM HIGHER. Expediency; public benefits of religion; ties of relationship; reputation. How great the blessing to Christ's cause if the *same things* were done from higher motives!

II. THEY ARE BLESSED, BUT NOT AS THEY MIGHT OTHERWISE HAVE BEEN. A better service would have secured a higher reward.

III. THEY CANNOT BE RELIED UPON, AND THEREFORE MAY NOT BECOME PART OF GOD'S PEOPLE. The conquering host could not trust the traitor whose help had won them the city. He must go forth with his reproach. Many churches contain the elements of weakness and ruin because they have failed to exercise a wise censorship over those admitted to their communion. The true Church is composed of those who serve God from the purest motives.—M.

Ver. 28.—*Human wisdom versus Divine.* No option was left to the Israelites as to the mode in which they were to deal with the Canaanites. Even if they were unable to subdue the Canaanites because of their own weakness, it would not be without fault; for had they not to sustain and direct them? But the sin of Israel was the greater that, when they were able to obey God's direction, they set it aside in favour of a policy of their own. This was direct disobedience, however it might be disguised by the name of prudence or expediency. In the end they had to rue their own folly.

I. PEOPLE IN PROSPEROUS CIRCUMSTANCES ARE FREQUENTLY TEMPTED TO FOLLOW A WORLDLY INSTEAD OF A HEAVENLY LINE OF CONDUCT, AND TO QUALIFY THE DICTATES OF OBVIOUS DUTY BY CONSIDERATIONS THAT ARE PURELY SELFISH AND PRESUMPTUOUS IN THEIR NATURE.

II. WHEN MEN THUS SHIRK OBVIOUS DUTY, THEY DO IT FROM A TWOFOLD MISCONCEPTION—(1) of their own power and wisdom, and (2) of the true character of that with which they tamper.

III. IN THE END THEIR FOLLY WILL MANIFEST ITSELF IN DISASTER AND RUIN.—M.

Vers. 34, 35.—*The failure of duty of one an occasion of inconvenience to another.* Joseph, strong enough to have destroyed the Amorites, made them tributaries. The same people a little further away were thereby enabled to afflict and annoy a companion tribe. " The Amorites forced the children of Dan into the mountain," &c. The cause of Dan ought to have been the cause of Joseph. The latter was therefore guilty of intense selfishness.

I. IT IS A SIN FOR CHRISTIANS TO REAP ADVANTAGE AT THE EXPENSE OF LOSS OR INCONVENIENCE TO THEIR BRETHREN.

II. GOD OFTEN MAKES THE UNWORTHINESS OR FAULT OF ONE OF HIS CHILDREN A DISCIPLINE TO ANOTHER.

III. BUT THIS DOES NOT FREE THE LATTER FROM THE RESPONSIBILITY OF DOING HIS BEST. Dan might be annoyed, and justly, at the indirect help given to his oppressors, but all the same he ought to have invoked the aid of Jehovah and gone forth to do battle against them. He might have delivered himself from the inconvenience to which he was subject. And so with all the indirectly produced ills of life ; a heroic faith is certain to overcome them, or render them comparatively innoxious.—M.

EXPOSITION

CHAPTER II.

It is often extremely difficult to make out the *sequence* of a Hebrew narrative, the narrator going back and travelling over the same ground in *respect of time* which he had already traversed, in order to introduce some circumstances which had been omitted. (see ch. vii. 25, note, and viii. 4, note). This appears to be the case with this section. The mention of Gilgal in ver. 1 seems to point distinctly to the early time of the entrance into Canaan under Joshua, because it was quite in the beginning of the Israelite occupation that the camp was at Gilgal, and it was there that the angel of the Lord spake to Joshua (Josh. v. 9, 10, 13—15). We find the camp still at Gilgal in Josh. x. 9, 43, and it was from the camp at Gilgal that Caleb went forth to his conquest (ch. xiv. 6), and also that Ephraim and Manasseh went forth to take their inheritance (chs. xvi., xvii.); but in ch. xviii. 1, 9, 10 we find Shiloh, in the hill country

of Ephraim, the place of the national gathering of " the host," and the tabernacle pitched there ; and the same in ch. xix. 51 ; xxi. 2 ; xxii. 9, 12. Josephus tells us that Joshua moved his camp from Gilgal to Shiloh in the hill country at the close of the fifth year (' J. A.' v. i. 19). This ascent of the angel from Gilgal in the plains of Jericho to Bochim in the hill country would seem, therefore, to have been about the beginning of the sixth year of the occupation of Canaan, and the rebuke in it to apply chiefly to Ephraim and Manasseh, though in part to Judah also. The place of this section chronologically would be between ver. 29 and ver. 30 of ch. i. It should be noticed also that this section is very closely connected with Josh. xxiv. ; for, first, Judges ii. 6 is identical with Josh. xxiv. 28, and the verses that follow Judges ii. 6 are also identical with those that follow Josh xxiv. 28. It is likely, therefore, that what immediately precedes Judges ii. 6 should be very closely connected with what immediately precedes Josh. xxiv. 28, and should relate to the same time. Now the discourse of Joshua (xxiv. 1—15) is only an expansion of the brief address of the angel in Judges ii. 1—3. The expostulation about the strange gods in Josh. xxiv. 14, 23, is in exact accordance with the complaint of the angel in Judges ii. 2; and the warm protestation of the people, "We will serve the Lord," in Josh. xxiv. 18, 21, 24, is in full accordance with what is said Judges ii. 4: "The people lifted up their voice, and wept." Again, the mention in Josh. xxiv. 1 of the people presenting themselves "before God," and of "the sanctuary of the Lord" (ver. 26), agrees with what is said Judges ii. 5: "They sacrificed there unto the Lord." And lastly, the somewhat mysterious words in Josh. xxiv. 27, "This stone . . . hath heard all the words of the Lord which he hath spoken to us," would have an easy solution if the message of the angel (Judges ii. 1—3) had been spoken before it. The inference is that Joshua's address in Josh. xxiv. was delivered immediately after the transaction recorded in this section.

Ver. 1.—**An angel of the Lord.** Rather, *the angel of the Lord,* i. e. the angel of his presence, whose message consequently is delivered as if the Lord himself were speaking (see Gen. xvi. 7, 9, 11, &c.). A good example of the difference between a message delivered by a prophet and one delivered by the angel of the Lord may be seen by comparing ch. vi. 8 with ch. vi. 11—16. **Bochim,** i. e. weepers (vers. 4, 5). The site is unknown, but it was probably near Shiloh. The phrase "came up" denotes that it was in the hill country.

Ver. 3.—**I said,** i. e. I now declare to you my resolve. It was this that made the people weep. **Thorns in your sides.** This is not a translation of the Hebrew text, which only has "for sides," but a partial adaptation of Josh. xxiii. 13, where the phrase is "scourges in your sides and thorns in your eyes." Either the words for "scourges in" have fallen out of the text, or the word here rendered "sides" should be rendered, as some think, "enemies." **A snare.** See ch. viii. 27, note.

Ver. 5.—**They sacrificed.** A clear intimation that they were near Shiloh, where the tabernacle was.

Ver. 6.—**And when Joshua,** &c. The same words as Josh. xxii. 6, marking the identity of time.

HOMILETICS.

Vers. 1—6.—*The expostulation.* We have here an extraordinary messenger, the angel of the Lord, but the message is one which in its spirit might be addressed to men at any time, and at any place. For it speaks of God's flowing mercy arrested by man's stubbornness. "I made you to go up out of Egypt—I have brought you into the promised land. I have faithfully kept my covenant, but you have altogether failed to do your part. Ye have not obeyed my voice." The one requirement of God that, when they took possession of the land, they should make no league with its inhabitants, but should throw down their abominable altars, they had neglected to fulfil. They had thought of their own interest and convenience, and not of the honour of God. They had taken God's earthly gifts, but had rejected his word. They had shown themselves to be self-seekers, greedy, carnal, and forgetful of him from whom they had all. It was the old story of self slipping into the place of God —self as the supposed giver, and self as the person for whose glory the gift was to be used. "My power and the might of mine hand hath gotten me this wealth," and therefore I will use it to my own ends. "Is not this great Babylon that I have built for the house of the kingdom, by the might of *my power,* and for the honour of *my majesty?*" This is the spirit that is constantly slipping in, in a greater or less degree, even in the Church of God, and frustrating the purposes of his unbounded grace. For it is just as in the case of Israel. When they used the gift of Canaan not for God's purposes but for their own, which were quite contrary to God's—for God's purpose was the extirpation of idolatry; their purpose was the enjoyment of vineyards which they had not planted, and wells which they had not digged—they at once closed up the fountain of God's grace. "I will not drive them out from before you; they shall be as thorns in your side, and their gods shall be a snare unto you." And their future history was the history of the fulfilment of this threat. So it was in the history of the Church. The grace of God bestowed in such rich abundance upon the early Church at Pentecost and afterwards, that those who named the name of Christ might be patterns to an evil world of love and purity and unselfish service, was soon stayed and checked by strife and discord, by worldly ambitions, by compromises with sin, and by fellowship with the corruptions of heathenism. So too it is with individual Christians. We check God's grace by not using it to the full; we hinder his mercy by not appropriating it, and not valuing it; we stop the flow of his good-will to us by setting up the objects of our own carnal desires and pursuing them, while we neglect the things which make for the glory of God. And just as the entire conquest of the Canaanites was not stopped by any deficiency of power in Almighty God, nor by any failure in love or faithfulness on his part, but simply by the sin of Israel, so now we may be quite sure that there is an infinite fulness of grace in Christ Jesus for all the Church's needs, and all the spiritual wants of each individual disciple, if only the hindrances of man's selfish disobedience are taken away, and an open channel is kept for God's free mercy to flow unimpeded in its gracious course. But, be it ever remembered, the disobedience to God's word, whatever it be, must be taken away. It is not enough to lift up the voice and weep over the consequences of sin past; it is not enough to sacrifice unto the Lord in hopes of averting his threatened punishments ; there must be an entire return to the path of obedience, to walk with a whole heart in the way of God's commandments, and to obey his voice. For that is the end for which God bestows his grace "Elect unto obedience and sprinkling of the blood of Jesus Christ." Let the Church, let the individual disciple, throw themselves unreservedly into this path of obedience, and God will fulfil in them all the good pleasure of his goodness, and their peace shall flow like a river.

HOMILIES BY VARIOUS AUTHORS.

Vers. 1—5.—*Bochim*. Who this "angel of the Lord" was we do not, probably were not meant to, know. He might have been Phinehas, the same who, according to Rabbinical interpreters, was the mouth-piece of Jehovah after the death of Joshua (ver. 1). But the probabilities are decidedly against such a supposition. It is " an angel," or messenger. At any rate the personality of the messenger (surely no celestial visitant, else why the journey and apparently public discourse ?) is kept in the background. He is nothing, a mere "voice," but a voice giving utterance to Israel's consciousness of offending, and addressing and rousing it. The mere circumstance that he came from Gilgal, the first spot touched by Israel in Canaan, gave significance to his message. Bochim was probably at Shiloh, the appointed meeting-place of the tribes.

I. A PLACE OF SOLEMN RECOLLECTION AND RE-STATEMENT. Shiloh, the place of Israel's worship and sacrifice, is also the place of Israel's repentance. A name, Bochim, is given to it. "They named the place from their tears." So the house of God becomes the monument and memorial of our deepest religious experiences. No new revelation is here made. The simple facts of the Divine deliverance of the people, their perfidy and faithlessness, are recited ; in contrast with which God's steadfastness is mentioned. The foundation article of the covenant is rehearsed, and the question asked, "Why have ye done this ? " And then the connection of their punishment with their sin is set forth.

II. A PLACE OF INQUIRY, REMONSTRANCE, AND SORROWFUL APPEAL. The tone of this address is sympathetic and yet severe. The question, "Why have ye done this ? " suggests to the people how foolish and profitless their conduct has been. How fitting would such a question be to many sinners of to-day. We too have broken plain precepts and sinned against the light of truth. What reason has there been in the conduct of God, in the nature of the duties neglected, or in the advantages we supposed we should secure ? An appeal to conscience like this is of infinitely more value than a speculative disquisition. He is a true angel who bears such a message.

III. A PLACE OF REPENTANCE. Israel is invited to change its mind. God is solicitous for its repentance. He has sent " an angel " to produce this result. The tears that flow so freely are precious in his sight, and may avail, if followed up, to recover his favour and to reinstate them in their lost possessions. How great a privilege was this ; not that it was a place of tears only, but that it might become a place of repentance, a turning-point in Israel's history. This Esau found not, though he sought it carefully with tears. Let it therefore be seized as a blissful augury that God wills not the death of a sinner, but that all men may turn to him and live. Such experiences are not to be artificially produced. A faithful recalling of God's real dealings with us in the past ought to make tears flow from the most hardened of sinners. But let the next step be taken, and beyond the tears, even beyond the ostentatious sacrifice, let reformation commence at once with his help and blessing. Then shall we have reason to recall our tears with gratitude when we discover that our repentance is not to be repented of.—M.

Vers. 1—5.—*The preaching of repentance.* I. THE MISSION. 1. A *special messenger* is sent to preach repentance. There are men whose peculiar gifts and position mark them out as called to this difficult work, *e. g.* Elijah, John the Baptist, Savonarola, John Knox. 2. This man was *sent by God.* It needs a Divine call and inspiration to speak rightly to men of their sins as well as to preach the gospel of peace. He who is thus called must not shrink from fear or false kindness to men. 3. The preacher is simply commissioned to convey a *message from God.* The voice is a man's, but the words are God's. The true preacher must always regard himself as the messenger of God, not at liberty to indulge in his own speculations, or to claim authority for his own judgment, but simply to declare, and interpret, and apply, the truth which God has entrusted to him (1 Tim. i. 11). 4. The preacher *carries the message* to the people. He does not wait for an audience to assemble about him; he does not wait for a spontaneous repentance. He journeys from Gilgal to Bochim. They who most need the preacher are least likely to come to hear him. Therefore he must go after them. The visitor, the city missionary, &c., have here a special work to reach those who will never enter the church, but all preachers of repentance must learn to seek their hearers.

II. THE MESSAGE. 1. This commences with a review of *God's goodness and faithfulness.* If we have been sinful he has still been merciful to us. He has kept his side of the great covenant, so that if we miss the good fruits of it this must be because we fail on our side. It is well to call attention to these facts before pointing out the sin of men, (1) that this may be felt more deeply in contrast with the goodness of God, (2) that the purpose of God in calling to repentance may be recognised as gracious, not vindictive (Rom. ii. 4). 2. The message contains a *definite charge of sin.* This must be definite to be effective. All admit they are imperfect. The difficult and delicate task of rebuking consists in making men see their special guilt in regard to particular sins. (1) In the present case the sin consists in guilty tolerance of evil. Religion should be aggressive. The Church is called to separate herself from the world (1 Cor. v. 11). (2) The root of the sin is disobedience. All sin is disobedience to the written law, or the law in our hearts; it is the setting up of our will against God's will. 3. The message closes with a *warning of punishment.* This punishment was to be a direct consequence of their tolerance of evil. Punishment is a natural fruit of sin.

III. THE RESULTS. We see the preaching of repentance producing the most varied results. Some turn a deaf ear; some hear and resent it; some hear and approve, but apply the message to others; some hear and admit the truth of the rebuke, but have no feeling of the sting of it; some feel sorrow under the rebuke, but do not rise to the active repentance of *will.* In the present instance the people heard meekly, humbly, and penitently, and the word bore fruit in genuine repentance and reformation. 1. They *wept.* Sorrow for past sin is natural and helpful towards future amendment, though if left to itself it will be a barren sentiment. 2. They *sacrificed.* Thus they acknowledged guilt, sought forgiveness in the mercy of God, and reconsecrated themselves to his service. It is not repentance, but faith in Christ, the sacrifice for sin, following this, that secures to us God's forgiving mercy. 3. They *served the Lord.* This is the final outcome, and certain proof of genuine repentance. The depth of our repentance must be measured not by the number of tears we shed, but by the thoroughness of our amendment of life, and the faithfulness of our subsequent service of God (Luke iii. 11).—A.

EXPOSITION.

Ver. 7.—**And the people served,** &c. This verse is the epitome of the religious history of Israel from the time of the expostulation of the angel till the dying off of all those who had been elders in the time of Joshua. It probably includes some forty or fifty years from the entrance into Canaan, viz., about thirty years of Joshua's lifetime, and ten, fifteen, or twenty years after Joshua's death. The record of the people's continuance in the service of the Lord connects itself with the promise made by them in Josh. xxiv. 21, 24. **All the great works,** &c. Scarcely those prior to the crossing of the Jordan, though some might remember some of the events in the wilderness when they were mere children (Numb. xiv. 31), but the victories in Canaan.

Vers. 7—9.—These three verses are identical with Josh. xxiv. 29—31, except that the order is slightly varied.

Ver. 8.—**An hundred and ten years old.** Caleb was eighty-five years old, he tells us (Josh. xiv. 10), when he went to take possession of Hebron, forty-five years after the spies had searched Canaan from Kadesh-Barnea, and consequently some time in the seventh year of the entrance into Canaan. Joshua was probably within a year or two his contemporary.

Ver. 9.—**Timnath-heres.** Probably, though not certainly, the modern *Tibneh*, six miles from Jifna. It is called in Josh. xix. 50 and xxiv. 30 '*Timnath-serah*, the letters of which are identical, but the order is inverted. *Timnath-heres* is probably the right form. It means "The portion of the Sun." We have *Mount Heres* in ch. i. 35, near Ajalon. *Ir-shemesh* (city of the sun) and *Beth-shemesh* (house of the sun) are other instances of places called from the sun. Some have supposed some connection between the name *Timnath-heres*, as Joshua's inheritance, and the miracle of the sun standing still upon

Gibeon at the word of Joshua (Josh. x. 12, 13). The neighbourhood of Timnath-heres to Ajalon (ch. i. 35) may give some countenance to this. The **hill Gaash** is only elsewhere mentioned as the birthplace of Hiddai or Hurai (2 Sam. xxiii. 30 ; 1 Chron. xi. 32), but the exact site is unknown.

Ver. 10.—**Which knew not the Lord,** &c. The memory of God's great works gradually faded away, and with this memory their influence upon the hearts of the people. The seductions of idolatry and the influence of heathen example were ever fresh and powerful. Had the people obeyed the voice of the Lord, the idolatry and the idolaters would have been out of the way. We may notice by the way the value to the Church of the sacrament of the Lord's Supper in keeping alive a perpetual memory of Christ's precious death until his coming again.

Ver. 12.—**They forsook the Lord,** &c. Here again there is a manifest allusion to Josh. xxiv. 16, 17.

Ver. 13.—**Baal and Ashtaroth.** *Ashtaroth* is the plural of *Ashtoreth*, the goddess of the Zidonians (1 Kings xi. 5, 33), just as *Baalim* (ver. 11) is the plural of Baal. The many images of Baal and Ashtoreth are, in the opinion of some, indicated by the plural ; but others think that different modifications or impersonations of the god and goddess are indicated. Thus we read of *Baal-berith*, the god who presides over covenants ; *Baal-zebul*, or *Zebub*, the god who presides over flies, who could either send or remove a plague of flies, and so on. " Baal (lord or master) was the supreme male divinity of the Phœnician and Canaanitish nations, as Ashtoreth (perhaps *the star*, the planet Venus) was their supreme female divinity. Baal and Ashtoreth are frequently coupled together. Many Phœnician names—Hannibal, Asdrubal, Adherbal, Belus, &c.—are derived from Baal."

HOMILETICS.

Vers. 7—13.—*Influence.* Joshua holds a distinguished place among the worthies of the Old Testament. As the faithful minister of Moses, as the servant of God, as the bold and believing spy, as the successor of Moses, as the captain of the hosts of Israel, as the conqueror of Canaan, as the type of the Lord Jesus, whose name he bore, he stands in at least the second rank of the great men of the sacred history. But in nothing is he more conspicuously great than in the INFLUENCE which he exercised upon others by his authority and example. We learn in this section that his weight and influence with the Israelitish nation was such that for a period of not much less than half a century it sufficed to keep the fickle people steadfast in their allegiance to the God of their fathers. By his own influence while he lived, and after his death by the influence of those whom he had trained during his lifetime, the contagion of idolatry was checked, and the service of God maintained. It is not all great men who have this faculty of influencing others, but it is a most invaluable one.

I. THE QUALITIES WHICH SEEM NECESSARY TO GIVE IT ARE—(1) Force of character. There must be a firm and steady will, moving always in the orbit of duty, and propelled by inflexible principle, in those who are to influence others. (2) There must be also a quick discernment, a sound judgment which makes few or no mistakes, and a high range of morals and of intellect. (3) There must be a lofty courage to cope with difficulties without flinching, to inspire confidence, and to break down obstacles. (4) There must be unselfishness, and a noble, generous purpose soaring high above petty worldly objects, so as to provoke no rivalries and to excite no suspicions. (5) There must be the qualities which attach men—kindness, geniality of disposition, fairness, considerateness, love; and the qualities which excite admiration, and make it a pleasure and an honour to *follow* him that has them. (6) There must be an absence of vanity and self-conceit and love of praise, and a genuine simplicity of aim. (7) And above all, to make a man's influence strong and lasting, there must be in him the true fear and love of God, and the conscious endeavour to promote his glory in everything. Joshua seems to have possessed all these in a high degree, and his influence was in proportion. That he not only possessed but actively exerted this influence for good we see by his address to the people recorded in Josh. xxiv. And this perhaps should make us add, (8) as one more quality necessary in those who are to influence others largely, that moral courage which makes a man speak out boldly what he knows to be true for the express purpose of persuading and guiding others.

II. While, however, *influence* on the scale in which Joshua exercised it can be possessed by few, EVERY CHRISTIAN MAN OR WOMAN, whatever may be their station, CAN AND OUGHT TO BE EXERCISING A HEALTHY INFLUENCE IN THEIR OWN IMMEDIATE CIRCLE. The light of a genuine Christian life is a light which will make itself seen wherever it shines. In the home, be it palace or cottage, in the village street, in the town court, in the shop, in the factory, in the camp, in the ship, in the social circle, be it humble or be it exalted, be it rude or be it refined, be it unlettered or be it literary and scientific, the influence of a pure, humble, vigorous, devout Christian life must be felt. It must be a power wherever it is. The object of these remarks is to stimulate the reader to desire and to endeavour to exercise such an influence for good, and to supply a motive for checking any action, or course of action, which may weaken or impede such influence. An outbreak of temper, a single grasping or unscrupulous action, a single step in the path of selfishness, or uncharitable disregard of another's feelings or interests, may undo the effect of many good words and good works. A conscientious desire to influence others for their good and for God's glory will supply a strong motive for watchful care to give offence in nothing.

III. But this section supplies an important caution to those who are influenced. When Joshua and the elders were dead, the children of Israel did evil in the sight of the Lord. THEY HAD NO *selbständigkeit*, NO INDEPENDENT STRENGTH, NO POWER TO STAND FIRM BY THEMSELVES. Their religion, their good conduct, depended upon another. He was the buttress that supported them; when the buttress was taken away they fell. Hence the caution not to trust in mere influence, but to look well to the foundations of our own faith. The influence of another man is no substitute for a converted heart, and for soundness in faith and love. St. Paul well knew the difference in some of his followers when he was present and when he was absent, and so would have their faith stand not in the wisdom of men, but in the power of God. It behoves us all to take care of our real principles of action, to examine ourselves, to prove our own selves, whether we be in the faith, whether Christ be really formed in us, whether we are seeking only to please those who have influence over us, or to please God. Else that may happen to us which happened to the Israelites, our upright Christian walk will last as long as we have the support of the good and strong, and no longer. We shall serve the Lord for a while only, and end by serving Baalim and Ashtaroth. The sober Christian life will be exchanged for folly and dissipation, and the pure creed degenerate into superstition or unbelief.

HOMILIES BY VARIOUS AUTHORS.

Vers. 6—13.—*The force of personal testimony and influence.* These verses are an explanation of how the evils came about which Israel deplored at Bochim. They explain, too, the fact that idolatry had not yet made much way amongst the people. "They described the whole period in which the people were submissive to the word of God, although removed from under the direct guidance of Joshua. The people were faithful when left to themselves by Joshua, faithful after his death, faithful still in the days of the elders who outlived Joshua. That whole generation which had seen the mighty deeds which attended the conquest of Canaan stood firm. Our passage says, 'for they had *seen*,' whereas Josh. xxiv. 31 says, 'they had *known*.' 'To see' is more definite than 'to know.' The facts of history may be known as the acts of God without being witnessed and experienced. But this generation had stood in the midst of events; the movements of the conflict and its results were still present in their memories" (Cassel). A new generation arises which "knows not Jehovah, nor yet the works which he had done." The "elders"—Joshua and his contemporaries— did this service; not only were they themselves faithful to God, but they kept alive the recollection of his mighty deeds and the national piety of Israel.

I. TESTIMONY IS OF GREATEST EFFECT WHEN IT IS THAT OF THOSE WHO HAVE SEEN AND KNOWN. St. John makes this claim for himself and his fellow apostles (1 John i. 1), and even St. Paul declares that Christ was manifested to him also as unto one that was born out of due time. It is a law of our nature upon which this proceeds. The nearer we are to our own personal experience, other things being equal, the more are we impressed with the reality of events. It was as if the people themselves had seen the miracles of the exodus when they had still amongst them Joshua and the elders. This advantage may be realised by Christians to-day. The gospel facts must become a real experience in the heart of him who would seek to influence others. By faith it may be so. We too may see our Saviour face to face. The preacher's vivid realisation of the supernatural and the Divine often exercises an overwhelming effect upon the hearer; whereas, on the other hand, to speak of our Saviour and his works as if we were telling an idle tale is to expose ourselves to certain failure. A Church that could *relive* the heroisms of the cross would be irresistible.

II. IT RECEIVES FRESH CONFIRMATION IN THE BEHAVIOUR OF THE WITNESSES. They were holy men. They lived in the constant remembrance of those awe-inspiring scenes. This was the most effective way of conveying to others their own impression and enthusiasm. Witness like this is within reach of all, and does not require scholarship to make it possible.

III. DEATH AND TIME ARE THE GREAT IMPAIRERS OF THIS INFLUENCE. With each good man who dies a witness disappears. The further we get in years from the actual scenes of miraculous power, the less effect are they calculated to produce. But the word of God liveth and endureth for ever, and God repeats spiritually the signs and mighty acts of his salvation in the experience of every true believer.—M.

Vers. 11—13.—*Israel's apostasy.* The repeated apostasy of Israel and the consequences of it furnish the ever-recurring theme of the darker pages of the Book of Judges. It may be well, therefore, to look at the subject generally, apart from special instances.

I. THE NATURE OF THE APOSTASY. 1. It consisted in *forsaking God.* All sin begins here, because while we live near to him it is impossible for us to love and follow evil. If we *cannot* serve God and mammon, so long as we are faithful to God we shall be safe from the idolatry of worldliness. The guilt of forsaking God is great because it involves (1) disobedience to our Father, (2) ingratitude to our Benefactor, (3) the fall from devotion to the Highest to lower pursuits. 2. This apostasy consisted in *the worship of other gods.* The shrine of the heart cannot long be empty. Man is a religious being, and he will have some religion; if not the highest and purest, then some lower form of worship. We must have a master, a God. 3. There was nothing *inventive* in the apostasy of Israel. The people only worshipped the old deities of the native population. They who give up Christianity for supposed novel forms of religion generally find themselves landed in some old-world superstition. 4. The guilt of the apostasy was aggravated by the *character* of the worship into which the people fell. This was (1) false—the worship of supposed gods which possessed no Divine power; (2) materialistic—the worship of idols in place of the unseen spiritual God; and (3) immoral—the worship of impure deities with impure rites.

II. The causes of the apostasy. 1. *Defective education.* So long as Joshua and his contemporary elders lived the people remained faithful. Apostasy arose in a new "generation which knew not the Lord, nor yet the works which he had done for Israel." But if the former generation had trained its children aright they would not have been thus ignorant. The Church should feel the supreme importance of the religious education of the young. Her continued existence depends on this. Children do not inherit their father's religion by natural succession. They must be trained in it. 2. *Circumstances of ease.* While the people were surrounded with the perils of the wilderness they displayed a moral heroism which melted beneath the sun of peaceful prosperity. Worldly comfort brings a great inducement to religious negligence. 3. *Tolerance of evil.* The earlier generation had failed to extirpate the idolatry of Canaan, and now this becomes a snare to the later generation. Indifference and indolence in regard to the wickedness which is around us is certain to open the door of temptation to our children, if not to ourselves. 4. *The worldly attractions of the lower life.* The service of God involves high spiritual efforts, purity of life, self-sacrifice, and difficult tasks (Josh. xxiv. 19). The service of the world is more agreeable to the pleasures of sense and selfishness. Regarded from the low ground of sense and with the short sight of worldly wisdom, it is easier to worship Baal than to worship the Eternal.—A.

EXPOSITION.

Vers. 14, 15.—**The anger of the Lord**, &c. These verses contain an awful view of the wrath of God excited by wilful sin, and are a practical illustration of Exod. xx. 5 : "*I am a jealous God.*" Compare Ps. lxxix. 5, which shows how closely allied the notions of *anger* and *jealousy* are in Hebrew. **He sold them.** A forcible expression, implying the handing over of the people into the hands of their enemies, as if God had no more any property in them or concern about them ; as if he said, "Ye are not my people, and I am not your God;" as if he said to the heathen, "Take them, and do as you will with them ; they are yours, not mine" (see Levit. xxvi. and Deut. xxviii.). **As the Lord had sworn,** &c., showing that God fulfilled his threatenings as well as his promises.

Ver. 16.—**Raised up judges.** Hence the name of this book, which recites the names and exploits of those whom God raised up to deliver them out of the hand of their enemies. The title *Judges* (Hebrew, *shophe-* *tim*) is, as is well known, identical with the Carthagenian *suffetes.* Mark the riches of God's mercy.

Ver. 22.—**To walk therein.** The Hebrew has *in them.* Probably for *way* we should read *ways*, as Deut. viii. 6 ; x. 12, &c. This verse does not seem to be part of what the Lord said, but to be the comment of the writer. The A. V.—**that through them I may prove**—inserts an *I* which is not in the original. Ver. 22 depends upon ver. 23. The literal rendering is, *For the sake of proving Israel*, &c., . . . *the Lord left those nations.* The writer, after rehearsing the Lord's reason for not completing the extirpation of the nations after the death of Joshua, adds the further information why they had not been delivered into Joshua's hand in his lifetime (cf. ch. iii. 1, 4). In Exod. xxiii. 29, 30 ; Deut. vii. 22, an additional reason is given for the gradual extirpation of the Canaanites—"*lest the beasts of the field increase upon thee.*"

HOMILETICS.

Vers. 14—23.—*The goodness and severity of God.* To know God as he is relatively to man—not as the absolute, which is impossible to be known, but such as he is relatively to man—is the highest of all knowledge which man can attain, and the most important for him to possess. Accordingly, one main purpose of revelation is to give us such knowledge. And this is given in two ways. One is by descriptions of God's character, as, *e. g.*, that in Exod. xxxiv. 6, 7: "The Lord God, merciful and gracious, long-suffering, and abundant in goodness and truth, keeping mercy for thousands, forgiving iniquity and transgression and sin, and that will by no means clear the guilty; visiting the iniquity of the fathers upon the children," &c. The other is by the authentic record of God's acts, specially in the gift of his only be-gotten Son to be the Saviour of the world, and in the Saviour's work as related in the Gospels, and also generally in his providential dealings with his people Israel, as set forth in the Old Testament. Of the latter method the Book of Judges, of which this section is an epitome, is a striking and instructive specimen. In it we have represented to us in vivid colours two characteristic features of the mind of God.

I. GOD'S HATRED OF SIN. With the usual anthropomorphism of Holy Scripture, we are told that when the children of Israel did evil in the sight of the Lord, they "provoked the Lord to anger." "The anger of the Lord was hot against them," it is twice repeated, and "his hand was against them for evil." Here, then, we see God's hatred of sin. And if God is infinitely good and holy, and if he knows the full misery that sin has brought into his creation, with what other sentiment can he regard sin but with that of hatred and indignation? Sin excites a holy anger in his mind, and his hand must be stretched out to punish and to check. If we reflect calmly, we must see that both of these are inevitable. God must look upon sin with displeasure, and he must ACT upon that displeasure. Evil must excite displeasure in one that is perfectly good ; and in the moral Governor of the universe such displeasure cannot be quiescent and impotent, it must be active and effective. Reason teaches us so, and revelation sanctions, enlarges, and enforces the lesson.

II. GOD'S EXCEEDING AND TENDER MERCY. To use the same anthropomorphism as before, we see God ever relenting, ever yearning over the miseries of his people, ever repenting of the evil that he had brought upon them, when he heard their groanings, ever forgetting their provocations and offences, and stepping forward to deliver them. It is impossible to have mercy, forgiveness, benevolence, and love, depicted in more vivid colours. Anything more remote from the idea of a vindictive, hard, unfor-giving nature it is impossible to conceive. And when we go on to inquire what are the conditions in man which, so to speak, draw out these not opposite, but different sides of the Divine character, we find that it is against persistent sin that the wrath of God burns, and upon which his heavy hand falls to smite ; and that it is to the contrite and penitent who forsake their sins that his quick and willing mercy is extended. And then a little further reflection seems to show that just as in nature different forces are found ultimately to resolve themselves into one common force, so these two attributes of God, hatred of sin, and mercy, may really be expressed by one term—goodness, or love. Goodness or love relatively to persistent sin is right-eous punishment; relatively to penitent sorrow it is mercy and forgiveness. And the reason of this is plain. Sin involves the misery of all who are subject to it, and of all God's creation, if it is suffered to continue and grow in it. It must therefore be the part of a good and loving God to extirpate sin, and that doubtless is the purpose of punishment, which is only another way of saying that punishment is remedial: remedial, if possible, to the being punished, that is, if it brings him to repentance ; but anyhow remedial to creation, which in the continued punishment of the impenitent sees the evil of sin, and avoids .it. The further doctrine of the ATONEMENT does not arise here, but it may just be observed how entirely it agrees with what we see here of God's character, since in it, as made by the death of the only begotten Son upon the cross, the two attributes of hatred of sin, and ineffable mercy, stand out with marvellous force and brightness. We conclude then that while mercy is goodness acting towards those who are not beyond the reach of goodness, severity is goodness acting with a view as far as possible to the happiness of the whole creation. And we see in the atonement a provision of infinite wisdom, by which the risk of injury to the many by mercy to the few is removed and done away with, and by which the severity and the mercy infinitely enhance and magnify each other. *Sin when it is finished bringeth forth death.* Other important lessons of the DEADLY FRUIT OF SIN, and of the INVETERATE PERVERSENESS OF MAN, recurring to sin again and again, in spite of bitter experience, like a moth flying into the candle, and of the BARRIERS which man's stubborn disobedience sets up against the coming in of all the good things which God's love had prepared for him, flow spontaneously from the narrative in this section. So also does the lesson of the use of trouble as THE TRIAL OF FAITH (1 Pet. i. 7) and the test of obedience. In fact it opens a large and comprehensive chapter on the providential government of the Church and of the world.

HOMILIES BY VARIOUS AUTHORS.

Vers. 14—18.—*Mercy in the midst of judgment.* As the sin of Israel continues and multiplies, the anger of the Lord waxes hot. As the misery of his people deepens, his compassions fail not. There is no contradiction in this. The mercy of God is not a weakness, it is the minister and honourer of his law. The judges, who represented the mercy of God, by whom they were raised up in faithless times, were also witnesses of his righteousness, and living embodiments of his kingdom amongst men.

I. THE MERCY OF GOD DOES NOT CONSIST IN ALTERING THE LAWS OF HIS KINGDOM, BUT IN LEADING MEN TO CONFORM MORE PERFECTLY TO THEM. The covenant is still felt as a living power even when it is ignored. The evils foretold come to pass, and in ever-increasing force. But God pursues a plan of restoration. This plan is never one of destruction or reversal. Not one jot or tittle of the law has to pass in order that the gospel may have effect. God seeks to change the hearts of his erring children, and by the punitive operation of the laws of his kingdom to make them loyal subjects. The law that curses will also, when obeyed, be found to bless. The judges were a continuous witness to righteousness and protest against sin, and by the prestige of their mighty acts and the constant influence of their lives they led men back again to God and goodness. They were the embodiments of his mercy.

II. THE VICTORIES OF SIN ARE NEVER CONSIDERED BY HIM AS IRREVERSIBLE. It was said in praise of English soldiers that they did not know when they were beaten. How much truer is this of God and his people! The most appalling apostasy has not daunted our Heavenly Father, or driven him utterly away from his world. "Where sin abounded, there did grace much more abound." Some of the best of men and most comforting of doctrines were born in ages of spiritual darkness. He has never left himself without a witness. The course of revelation is never stopped. The succession of prophets, apostles, and martyrs is never interrupted. The servants of God in Old Testament times might be driven away or destroyed, but they, being dead, yet speak, and in the fulness of time he sends his Son; he, too, may be crucified, but nevertheless the Father will send the Comforter in his name. And so in the individual life this law will be found to operate. The darkest conscience has not been without its light.

III. ON THE WHOLE THE SPIRITUAL GAINS OVER THE CARNAL IN THE PROGRESS OF THE KINGDOM OF GOD AMONGST MEN. One judge passes away and another rises. The apostasies which they have to correct may become darker and more terrible; but greater deeds are forthcoming. The testimony is more and more emphatic. The principles of God's kingdom are illustrated and honoured, and Israel gradually emancipated from its ignorance and inexperience.—M.

Vers. 21, 22.—*Tested by temptation.* The pagan nations of Canaan were a constant source of temptation to idolatry and immorality. If they were left in the land, the fidelity of Israel would be tried by the way in which this temptation was met.

I. TEMPTATION IS NOT IMMEDIATELY SENT BY GOD. Israel had been commanded to expel the Canaanites; it was owing to the indolence and weakness of the invaders that their work was not completed. Having failed on their side, they now find that God will no longer secure them victory over their enemies. The temptation which thus resulted from the presence of the heathen in their midst grew out of their own conduct. God never tempts us (James i. 13). Temptation often arises out of negligence, indolence, needless pleasure, wilful presumption. It is vain to pray, "Lead us not into temptation," while we are creating temptations for ourselves.

II. TEMPTATION MUST OFTEN BE REGARDED IN THE LIGHT OF A PUNISHMENT.   1. It frequently comes as the *consequence* of former sin.   The memory of sin, the contracted habit of sin, the associations of sin, and the weakness resulting from sin are all sources of new temptation.   2. Temptation is one of the most *painful* consequences of sin.   If we have any love for goodness, one of the saddest results of our sin must be the consciousness of new temptations to which it renders us liable. For a good man to suffer temptation is to suffer pain.   3. We must therefore conclude that all the temptations we meet with are *not unavoidable and necessary*.   We bring them on ourselves ; we might have escaped them ; they are dangerous calamities which we must deplore.   We need not wish to be tried.   If temptation is often a punishment, it is better to rest humbly ignorant of our own weakness than to court trial which will reveal the extent of it.

III. TEMPTATION IS USED BY GOD AS A TEST OF FIDELITY.   The people of Israel would be proved by the temptation arising out of the presence of immoral idolaters in the midst of them.   1. Fidelity consists (1) in *care and firmness,*—"to *keep* the way of the Lord,"—and (2) in *diligence and progressive activity*—"to *walk* therein." 2. This fidelity is tested by the *attractions of evil ways*.   We cannot be said to keep the way simply because we are found in it.   But when the way is contested, or a more pleasing path opens out near to it, the strength of our fidelity will be put to the test. Some men need the test of temptation more than others.   If they have already shown weakness, the punishment which comes in the form of a temptation may be a useful means of self-revelation.   This need of proof, however, is a humiliation.   It is better to be so clearly true as neither to invoke the punishment of temptation nor require the test it affords.—A.

EXPOSITION.

CHAPTER III.

Ver. 1.—**Now these are the nations**, &c. We are now told in detail what was stated in general in ch. ii. 22, 23, after the common method of Hebrew narrative.   **To prove Israel**.   This word *to prove* is used here in a somewhat different sense from that which it bears in ver. 4 and in ch. ii. 22.   In those passages it is used of their moral probation, of proving or testing their faith and obedience ; but here it is rather in the sense of "to exercise," or "to accustom them," to train them to war.   A considerable period of *rest* had followed Joshua's conquest, during which the younger Israelites had no experience of war ; but if they were to keep their hold of Canaan, it was needful that the warlike spirit should be kept up in their breasts.

Ver. 3.—**The five lords**, &c.   The title *seren*, here rendered "lord," is one exclusively applied to the lords of the five Philistine cities enumerated in Josh. xiii. 3 ; 1 Sam. vi. 17, 18, viz., Gaza, Ashdod, Ashkelon, Gath, and Ekron.   It occurs repeatedly in ch. xvi. ; 1 Sam. v., vi., xxix., &c.   The word means an *axle-tree*.   **The entering in of Hamath**.   There are two theories in regard to Hamath.   Some, as Professor Rawlinson in the ' Dictionary of the Bible,' identify it with *Hamah*, a large and important city on the Orontes in Upper Syria, and consider that the kingdom of Hamath, which was overthrown by the king of Assyria (2 Kings xviii. 34 ; xix. 13), and of which Hamath was the capital, was for the most part an independent Hamitic or Canaanite kingdom (Gen. x. 18), but occasionally, as in the days of Solomon and Jeroboam (1 Kings viii. 65 ; 2 Kings xiv. 28 ; 2 Chron. viii. 4), subject to Israel.   Others, however, justly considering the great improbability of the Israelite dominion having ever extended so far north as the valley of the Orontes, and observing how it is spoken of as an integral part of Israel (1 Kings viii. 65), look for Hamath much further south, in the neighbourhood of Beth-rehob (see ch. xviii. 28, note).   As regards the phrase "the entering in of Hamath," the identical Hebrew words occur seven times, viz., Numb. xiii. 21 ; xxxiv. 8 ; Josh. xiii. 5 ; in this passage ; 1 Kings viii. 65 ; 2 Kings xiv. 25 ; 2 Chron. vii. 8, and are variously rendered in the A.V. : "as men come to Hamath;" "unto the entrance of Hamath;" "the entering into Hamath;" "the entering in of Hamath" (three times); and "the entering of Hamath."   The exact meaning of the phrase seems to be "the approach to Hamath," some particular spot in the valley from whence the direct road to Hamath begins ; very much like the railway term for certain stations which are the nearest to, though at some little distance from, the place from which they are named, as, *e. g.*, Shapwick Road, Mildenhall Road, &c.   The latter words of the verse describe the territory of the Hivites, which reached from Mount Baal-hermon in the Lebanon range as far as the point where the road leads to Hamath.

Ver. 5.—**The Canaanites**, &c. The same enumeration of the tribes of the Canaanites as in Exod. xxxiv. 11.

Ver. 6.—**They took their daughters**, &c. Here is a further downward step in the disobedience of the Israelites. Intermarriage with the Canaanite nations had been expressly forbidden (Exod. xxxiv. 15, 16; Deut. vii. 3; Josh. xxiii. 12), and the reason of the prohibition clearly stated, and for some time after Joshua's death no such marriages appear to have been contracted. But now the fatal step was taken, and the predicted consequence immediately ensued: "they served their gods; . . . they forgat the Lord their God, and served the Baalim and the Asheroth."

HOMILETICS

Vers. 1—6.—*Ungodly marriages.* The distinctive lesson of this section seems to be the fatal influence of an ungodly marriage. And this lesson is one of such daily importance to Christians in every station in life, that we shall do well to concentrate our attention upon it. On entering upon the history of that troublous and calamitous time for the tribes of Israel which intervened between the triumphant governments of Moses and Joshua and the glorious reigns of David and Solomon,—the time of the Judges,—we find it initiated by the intermarriage of the Israelites with the idolatrous Canaanites. No sooner was that shameful alliance contracted than the national apostasy followed instantly. "They forgat the Lord their God, and served Baalim and Ashtaroth." And the connection between this religious apostasy and the first servitude by which they lost their national independence was no less close. "The children of Israel served Chushan-rishathaim." If then we read Scripture with a view to our own admonition, our attention must be arrested by this striking example of the danger of ungodly unions. And the example does not stand alone. The marriage of Esau with the daughters of Heth, in connection with the loss of his birthright and his blessing; the degradation and death of Samson in spite of his splendid gifts and powers; the tarnished fame of Solomon's old age, and the break-up of his kingdom after his death; the dynastic ruin and destruction of Ahab and all his house from his marriage with Jezebel,—these and many other examples in Holy Scripture convey a solemn warning against the peril of ungodly marriages. And it must be so in the nature of things. The marriage union is so close and intimate, it gives the opportunity for such constant influence, it makes continual resistance to that influence so irksome and tedious, it gives such advantage to the working of influence through the affections, that no man with a due regard for his own soul's salvation would expose himself to such peril. Moreover, the true notion of the partnership of marriage is a fellowship in heart, in thought, in affection, in interest; an identity of aim and purpose in life, each helping the other, each contributing a portion to the common aim; a joint action in all that relates to God and man; united counsels in fulfilling the various duties of the home, of the human society, of the Church of God. How could the Israelite, seeking the glory of Jehovah, wrapped up in the triumphs of his own favoured race and pure creed, and hating the detestable abominations of heathenism, so insulting to God, and so injurious to man, have such fellowship with the daughter of an Amorite or Canaanite? And how can any true servant of the Lord Jesus Christ have such fellowship with one whose heart is wholly given up to the world, and has no concern for the kingdom of heaven. "Marriage is not to be taken in hand unadvisedly, lightly, or wantonly by any Christian man or woman, but reverently, discreetly, advisedly, soberly, and in the fear of God." And it is the object of these remarks to induce young men and young women, in deciding upon marriage, to take into consideration the probable influence of their partner upon their moral and religious life, and the aid or the hindrance they are likely to have in the fulfilment of their Christian duties. The life-long loss of domestic happiness, the blighting of affections, and a heavy crop of trouble and vexation, the sure fruit of an ill-assorted union, is a heavy price to pay for the momentary gratification of a mere fancy; but the permanent loss of moral tone, and forfeiture of one's place in the kingdom of God, is an unspeakably heavier one.

HOMILIES BY VARIOUS AUTHORS.

Vers. 1—4.—*The proving of Israel.* The general lesson of the Book of Judges is here repeated. There is shown to have been a Divine providence prevailing through and above the defections of Israel. God uses the consequences of their neglect as a means of grace. The nations that had not been rooted out became in turn their tempters and their tyrants; and thus they outlive their minority, and are prepared for the great place they have to take in the history of the kingdom of God.

I. IT WAS A RESULT OF PARENTAL NEGLECT. The fathers had left much of their task undone. A determined attitude on their part, and vigorous measures, would have rid the land of the nuisance. One generation may do much good or evil to its successors. We never reap all the results of our own misdoing; a great portion is left for the children of after generations. The neglect of the laws of health, of the canons of a moral life, of educational institutions, social and political progress, may entail grievous disadvantage upon those who come after us; as much that comes in this way, comes in this way alone, and cannot be produced suddenly. And so it is with the growth of theological truth, and the habits and usages of the spiritual life.

II. BUT THE CHILDREN TOO WERE TO BLAME. The oracle of God at Shiloh could have been consulted still. God's will could easily have been ascertained. Thorough and absolute trust in Jehovah, and devotion to his service, would have rid them of their enemies. They were therefore the children of their fathers in this also, viz., that they were not wholly given to God's service and the desire after righteousness. How much of human guilt consists in *mere letting alone*, or in supinely submitting to evils as if they were inevitable or incurable!

III. IT WAS AN INSTANCE OF EVIL DIVINELY UTILISED. A probation. To call forth the courage and faith of the new generation. To prevent them accepting the situation as a final one, or calmly submitting to and acquiescing in the wicked customs and idolatries of their neighbours. Some natures find the way of transgression harder than others. They are finer, more susceptible, have more deeply-set longings after goodness. They feel the inherent contradictions of evil more acutely; its penalties press more heavily upon them. This is not an injustice on the part of their Maker; it is a mark of his goodness and mercy. He would have them fenced in by the sanctions of righteousness; driven back into his fold. He has meant them for a better life. So it was with his elect people then. They and their heathen neighbours were upon a different footing. It was the destiny of Israel not to be let alone. A later experience in order to the comprehension of an earlier experience. One of the most valuable uses of experience—to throw light backward. It reveals the true value of an inheritance, and renders precious things more precious. Otherwise the younger Israelites who entered into the conquests of the first warriors would not have known the severity of their toils, or the mighty hand of God which wrought their deliverance. There are some lessons every man must learn for himself. A true appreciation of God's saving grace is a personal and, for the most part, an incommunicable thing. "*To teach them war,*" i. e. to inure them to it as a necessary discipline, and as the preliminary work that had to be done ere the kingdom of God could be brought in; and, as above, to show them how much spiritual privileges cost, and how difficult and yet how honourable it was to defend and secure them. Still it was—

IV. AN INSTANCE OF A PROVISIONAL ALLOWANCE OF COMPARATIVE IMMORALITY. The world was not ripe for the morality of Jesus. The self-contradiction of a continual state of warfare was to be their schoolmaster to bring them to Christ. The *state* of peace is not of itself more moral than that of war. It is "the things that make for peace," the spirit of brotherhood and Christian charity, that are the aim of the righteous mind. The world must first be righteous ere it can be peaceful.—M.

Vers. 5—7.—*The forbidden covenant.* When Israel entered the land it was on the express condition that no terms of marriage or intercommunion should be entered into with the aboriginal tribes of Canaan (Deut. vii. 1—3). This seems either to have been forgotten or deliberately ignored. The consequences predicted came to pass, and the hearts of the people were led away from the worship of the true God.

I. THE LIMITS OF COMMUNION BETWEEN THE CHILDREN OF GOD AND THE WORLD.

The law of extermination prescribed to Israel made the path of duty very clear. It was God's purpose to disentangle the national and individual life of his people from the perversions, corruptions, and self-contradictions of idolatrous worship. He desired to separate them entirely to himself. Severe and uncharitable as this rule might at first appear, it was true mercy to the world as yet unborn, and to the future that was to be redeemed to God. Some comforts and conveniences, a few really valuable fruits of pseudo-civilisation and the contact with the currents of thought and life in the great world of men, had to be sacrificed, but the advantage was more than worth them all. The same problem presents itself to-day to the Christian. How far is it allowable for the life of a child of God and a child of this world to intermingle? What relations of this life are to be kept apart from the world, and to subsist only between Christians, and what relations may be shared with the world? The letter of the ancient prescript is of course obsolete, but the spirit must still be binding. Evidently, however, the relations of what are strictly religious communions can only be sustained between true Christians. And many of the higher relations of our natural life, as, for instance, marriage, can only be worthily sustained by Christians. The spirit of the old law was, immediately, severe, but, ultimately and more largely, merciful. So ought the disposition of the Christian to be. Of course the extent and direction in which we observe this law of heavenly prudence must be left to every man's conscience in the sight of God. It ought to be remembered that often when it seems to act against others it is really for their good.

II. How intimate association with the world affects the tone and quality of the spiritual life. 1. Habit blunts the conscience to unlawful customs. 2. Personal attachments and friendships lend attraction to social and religious observances which are really unrighteous. 3. The relations of civil life create entanglement and perplexity. 4. The peculiar, intimate, and profound relations of marriage add to the force of all influences that affect the religious nature and the spiritual life.—M.

EXPOSITION.

This section introduces us into the actual narrative of the Book of Judges, the prefatory matter being now concluded. The whole book proceeds on the same model as this section does. The apostasy of Israel; their servitude under the oppressor sent to chastise them; their cry of distress and penitence; their deliverance by the judge raised up to save them; the rest which follows their deliverance. There is infinite variety in the details of the successive narratives, but they are all formed on the same plan.

Ver. 7.—**The groves.** The *Asheroth*, here and elsewhere (ch. vi. 25, 26; Deut. xvi. 21, &c.) wrongly rendered *groves*, were large wooden images or pillars in honour of Ashtoreth, and so are properly coupled with *Baalim*. This verse is in fact identical in meaning with ch. ii. 13, of which it is a repetition (see note to ch. ii. 13, and ch. viii. 23).

Ver. 8.—**Chushan-rishathaim**, *i. e.*, as usually explained, Chushan the victorious, or the wicked. His name, Chushan, or Cushan, points to Cush, the father of Nimrod (Gen. x. 6—8), and the seat of his kingdom in Aram-naharaim, or Mesopotamia, agrees with Nimrod's kingdom in "Babel

. . . in the land of Shinar" (*ibid.* ver. 10). An earlier invasion of Palestine by conquerors from Mesopotamia is mentioned Gen. xiv. 2, where Amraphel, king of Shinar, is one of the five kings who invaded Sodom. Bela, son of Beor, king of Edom, seems by his name to have been clearly from Mesopotamia, as Balaam the son of Beor was (Numb. xxii. 5; xxiii. 7); and in the time of Job we read of bands of Chaldeans looting in the land of Uz (Job i. 17). *Chushan*, as the name of a people, is coupled with Midian in Hab. iii. 7; but we have no accounts of the state of Mesopotamia at the time of Chushan-rishathaim.

Ver. 9.—**A deliverer.** Hebrew, *Saviour*, as ver. 15 (see Neh. ix. 27). **Othniel**, &c. Mentioned ch. i. 13; Josh. xv. 17, and 1 Chron. iv. 13, where he is placed under "the sons of Kenaz," and seems to be the father of Hathath and Meonothai. According to Judith vi. 15, he had a descendant, *Chabris*, living in the time of Holofernes. The Hebrew, though grammatically it favours the view that Othniel was the brother of Caleb, does not absolutely exclude the rendering that Kenaz was his brother, and so Othniel his nephew. Compare Jer. xxxii. 7, where the words "thine uncle" apply to Shallum, not to Hanameel, as is clear from ver. 8.

And as the chronology seems to make it impossible that Othniel should be Caleb's brother, since Caleb was eighty-five years old at the time of Othniel's marriage, and Othniel therefore could not be less than fifty-five, an improbable age for his marriage ; and since, again, Othniel could not well have been less than eighty at Joshua's death, which, allowing only ten years for the elders, and reckoning the eight years for Chushan's dominion, would make him ninety-eight when he was raised up to deliver Israel, it is a lesser difficulty to take Othniel as the nephew of Caleb, by understanding the words, *Caleb's younger brother*, to apply to Kenaz. But perhaps the least objectionable escape from the difficulty is to take the phrase in its most natural grammatical sense, but to understand the word *brother* in its wider and very common sense of *kinsman* or *fellow-tribesman*. They were both sons of Kenaz, or Kenizzites. Caleb was the head of the

tribe, and Othniel was next to him in tribal dignity, and his junior in age, but probably succeeded to the chieftainship on Caleb's death. This would leave the exact relationship between Caleb and Othniel uncertain.

Ver. 10.—**And the Spirit,** &c. This marks Othniel as one of the extraordinary *Shophetim*, or judges, Divinely commissioned to save Israel (see ch. vi. 34 ; xi. 29 ; xiii. 25 ; xiv. 6, 19).

Ver. 11.—**And Othniel,** &c. The arrangement of this verse suggests that Othniel lived through the whole forty years of rest, but this is highly improbable. The first part of the verse only belongs to the preceding section, which it closes quite naturally. The result of Othniel's victories was a rest of forty years (cf. ver. 30 ; v. 31 ; viii. 28, &c.). The latter half of the verse—**And Othniel the son of Kenaz died**—begins a new section, and is introductory to the first apostasy, which followed after his death.

HOMILETICS.

Vers. 7—11.—*God's scourge.* In a remarkable passage (Deut. xxxii. 8) Moses tells us that when the Most High divided to the nations their inheritance, he set the bounds of the people according to the number of the children of Israel. In like manner the sacred history teaches us how the movements of the nations and the restless invasions and conquests of heathen kings and warriors had a special relation to the chosen race. They indeed did not mean so. They were actuated merely by ambition, by the lust of conquest, by the appetite for plunder and dominion. But in the wonderful providence of God they were made instruments for chastening and correcting, or for saving and delivering, his people, as the case might be. Here we find the unsettled state of the Mesopotamian tribes, which led them beyond the borders of their own land, bringing them to Palestine at the very time when the Israelites in the wantonness of their fickle hearts had fallen away from the service of the living and true God to that of the idols of Canaan. There they were living at ease, having partly extirpated the Canaanites, and partly entered into league and amity with them. Seduced by their vices, captivated by their sensuous religion, they had forgotten all the works of God, and no longer trembled at his word, and did not feel their need of his favour. Yet a little while and their apostasy would have been complete, and the very end of their election would have failed. But this was not to be. So Chushan-rishathaim, who had perhaps never heard of their names, and knew nothing of their religion or of their apostasy, mustered his hosts, marched his army, and at the critical moment fell like a rod upon the peccant people. We are left to imagine the misery of those eight years of servitude under a heathen tyrant : the injuries and indignities, the terror and unrest, the grinding servitude, the hard bondage, the bitterness of soul, the wasting and oppression of spirit. The crops for which they toiled eaten by another ; their goodly houses tenanted by their foes, and themselves turned into the street ; their wives and daughters bondwomen, and their sons made slaves ; their national glory turned to shame, their cherished hopes withered into despair. And we are left to imagine how that misery bent the iron sinew of their neck, and brought them back to God. No doubt their self-confidence was broken down. Their illusive dreams of pleasure had ended in an awakening to their self-inflicted pain ; sin appeared in its true colours as an enemy and betrayer ; the false gods were found to be no helpers. Why not turn to God ? He had been very good to them. Why had they ever forsaken him ? He and he alone could save them, as he had saved their fathers from the hands of Pharaoh. But would he ? They would try. They would turn to him in penitence and prayer ; they would confess their

sins; they would humble themselves in his sight; they would call upon his blessed
name; they would plead his covenant, his promises, the glory of his own great
name. And they did so. Nor did they call in vain. Their cry of distress entered
into the ears of the Lord of hosts. His wrath turned to pity; he who chastened
when they sinned, now comforted when they prayed. He had sent a scourge; he
now sends a deliverer. Chushan was invincible when his mission was to strike; but
when his mission was ended his arm fell broken at his side. Othniel the deliverer
went forth in the might of God's Spirit, and Chushan's power was gone. The waters
of the Euphrates which had overflowed their banks were dried up again, and the land
of Israel had rest for forty years. And so has it ever been. The obscurer movements
of Philistines, and Ammonites, and Midianites, as well as the grand historic drama of
Assyria, and Egypt, and Babylon, and Persia, and Greece, and Rome, have always
had one special design in the correction or deliverance of God's people. And though
we have no inspired interpreter to expound to us the later movements of the peoples,
yet may we be sure that the great events of modern history have been appointed to
work out the purposes of God with reference to his Church, either for correction or
deliverance, and that the rise and fall of empires, the ambition of kings and statesmen, the conquests of warriors, and the revolutions of peoples, will in the end be
found to have been overruled for the glory of God, and for the extension of the
kingdom of Jesus our Lord. And in this confidence the Church may rest and be at
ease in her integrity, while she is careful not to provoke God's anger by turning
aside from his truth, or growing weary of his blessed service.

HOMILIES BY VARIOUS AUTHORS.

Ver. 8.—*Idolatry and its Nemesis.* The effects of this communion with idolatrous
peoples speedily appear. It was no accident that Israel became the subject of a
heathen power, nor are we to suppose it an arbitrary exercise of the right of Divine
providence.

I. AS FAITH STRENGTHENS, SUPERSTITION DESTROYS, MORAL POWER. In all these
punishments the external and physical disadvantage appears to be the first perceived.
But the real loss was sustained beforehand, when faith in the one God was lost. The
whole moral life which this dogma encouraged and sustained was thereby undermined. Monotheism was the foundation of the moral life, correcting and purifying
it; idolatry pandered to the worst passions, and chained the spirit of man to the
outward and sensuous.

II. MORAL ENTHUSIASM IS THE ESSENCE AND INSPIRATION OF HEROISM AND THE RUL-
ING QUALITIES. The reverence of Israel in the worship of Jehovah was called forth
towards qualities that were truly noble and admirable. The sustaining force of an
Israelite's piety was absolutely righteous and super-sensuous; and it had appeared
superior to all that the arm of flesh could bring against it. The Israelite was taught,
therefore, to despise the material, the outward, and the merely human. His faith,
therefore, became heroic. And as the influence of the Divine Being repressed the
passions and developed the spiritual power, it enabled him to restrain himself, to
pursue after distant and vast aims; and, in making him heedless of the attractions
of sense and penalties which only affected the outward man, it made him influential
over others. Hence the religion of Israel marked it out for political superiority and
power.

III. THE "SERVICE" THAT IS WASTED ON WORTHLESS OBJECTS IS AVENGED BY A
"SERVICE" THAT IS SEVERE AND INVOLUNTARY. This was the result of a special appointment, and also of a Divine law. The people that had become effeminate by
idolatrous indulgence were an easy prey to any military and ambitious power; and
so that which had been a weak yielding, or a choice, became binding and imperative.
National liberty was lost; the purest and noblest traits of national character were
repressed. What a special political power did in this instance evil habit itself may do;
and there are other influences whose yoke waits upon the loss of moral power.—M.

Vers. 9, 10.—*True deliverance must ever come from God.* It is a curious fact in
the history of Israel that it is never until they have acknowledged God as the source

of salvation that they achieve any permanent success.   It is as if this people were to learn that only by supernatural means is it ever to fulfil its destiny.

I. HE INSPIRES TRUE HEROISM. Of Othniel we have already heard ; he stands as a representative of early Israelitish chivalry. But on the occasion on which he distinguished himself formerly, the inspiration was hardly so lofty as to mark him out as especially the servant of God.   He is, however, on the threshold of the great life of self-denial and generous self-sacrifice which characterised the judge of Israel. He is a vessel chosen of God for better service.   Of the particular influences which marked him out for the high office to which he was called we are not informed.   All that we know is, that the Spirit of the Lord came upon him.   That he was well qualified otherwise for warlike exploits we know ; but the merely human traits of character which he has displayed are nothing without this distinctive inspiration. God finds the man for the hour.

II. THE MORAL AUTHORITY IS DIVINELY CREATED.   Israel gravitates towards Othniel as its moral centre.   By a kind of moral necessity he becomes its judge, and there is no one to dispute his ascendancy.   The prestige which he gains in his magistracy is not injured by military failures.   We are to look upon all this as proof that God was with him, preserving and increasing his reputation, and developing the powers which he possessed.   When it is said (ch. ii. 18), "And when the Lord raised them up judges, then the Lord was with the judge, and delivered them out of the hand of their enemies all the days of the judge," we are invited to behold no series of merely human successes, but that which is directly due to his presence and help.   And so with all whom he inspires for special service ; he will make their moral influence his care, sustain their strength, and secure uninterrupted success if they put their trust in him.—M.

Natural advantages and endowments perfected and crowned by consecration. I. THE BEST CHANNEL FOR OTHNIEL'S ABILITIES WAS THAT INDICATED BY THE DIVINE CALL.
II. IN OBEDIENCE OF GOD'S SPIRIT HE SECURED THE MOST COMMANDING INFLUENCE.
III. AS SERVANT OF JEHOVAH HE ATTAINED ENDURING RENOWN.—M.

Vers. 10, 11.—*The secret of individual and national greatness.* It was as a judge of Israel that Othniel first attained influence.   This necessitated a righteous life and a consistent character.   In this way he obtained command over his people, and was able to transfer their attachment and respect to the battle-field.   So it was, as Israel learned to obey the servant of Jehovah in civil affairs, and learned to respect the law of righteousness, that it was able to face its enemies with an irresistible front. It is righteousness that exalteth a nation and a man.

I. TO MAINTAIN AND ADVANCE A RIGHTEOUS CAUSE WE MUST BEGIN AT HOME.
II. THE VICTORY OVER OUR ENEMIES CONSISTS MORE THAN HALF IN THE VICTORY OVER OURSELVES.
III. HABITUAL RECTITUDE AND A GOOD CONSCIENCE PREPARE FOR SUDDEN AND ABIDING SUCCESS.—M.

Ver. 11. — "*And the land had rest*"—*the true peace.* I. IT IS A REWARD OF CONSECRATED EFFORT AND SELF-DENIAL.
II. A PREPARATION FOR HIGHER CONCEPTIONS AND REALISATIONS OF RIGHTEOUSNESS.
III. A SABBATH OF CONSECRATED TIME AND SERVICE TO THE HIGHEST.—M.

Vers. 9, 10.—*Great men.* The Book of Judges brings before us the heroic age of Israel.   The multitude of the people are in a condition of moral and political degradation, but great men appear from time to time whose individual heroism secures the salvation of their nation.   Othniel, the first of the judges, may serve as a type of the rest.   The characters and mission of these men may throw some light upon the function of great men in the economy of Providence.

I. GREAT MEN OWE THEIR GREATNESS TO GOD.   Many of the judges sprang from obscure families ; they were not hereditary rulers, but men sent of God with individual vocations.   Othniel belonged to the honourable family of Caleb, and shared in the fame of that family, perhaps, partly in virtue of hereditary qualities. But even he is described as owing his greatness to God. 1. Great men are *sent* by God. When the people "cried unto the Lord, the Lord raised up a deliverer." There are men who are born heroes—men whose great qualities are owing to their nature, not to their culture or their conduct. He who believes in providence will recognise that such men are "raised up" by God. 2. Great men *derive their highest powers directly* from God. "The Spirit of the Lord came upon Othniel." The military and political ability of Othniel as warrior and judge are ascribed to a Divine inspiration. All truly great men are inspired by God. Not only are they originally formed and sent by God, but they owe their powers to the constant influence of God within them. Bad men of genius receive their genius from God, and are therefore guilty of prostituting the noblest Divine gift to evil purposes. Such men attain to no more than an earthly greatness. In the sight of God their low aims destroy the character of heroism which their abilities rendered possible. On the other hand, all Christians may attain to a measure of greatness in proportion as they receive the Spirit of God ; yet we must distinguish between the graces of the Spirit, which are for all Christians, and the gifts of the Spirit, which are special, and bestowed on individual men.

II. GREAT MEN HAVE A MISSION TO THEIR FELLOW-MEN. 1. *Great men are intrusted with great talents for the benefit of others.* To devote these to selfish ends of ambition or pleasure is a mark of gross unfaithfulness. We are members one of another ; and that member which has the highest capacities will produce the largest amount of harm if it refuses to perform its functions in promoting the welfare of the whole body. 2. *Great men are needed by the world.* The heroic age has passed, and there is now more power in the general thought and life of men than in primitive times. The work of individual men has often been overrated when compared with the deep, silent strength of public opinion, and the slow, steady movement of national progress. Yet it is real and large. Christianity would have lived if Paul had never been converted ; the Reformation would have come without Luther. But these movements would have taken a different form, and probably would have made much slower progress without the help of their leading spirits. Great inventors, legislators, reformers have left a distinct individual stamp on the history of our race. Christianity is not a product of the spirit of its age ; it owes its origin to the life of the greatest of men.

III. THE MISSION OF GREAT MEN VARIES ACCORDING TO THE NEEDS OF THEIR AGE. In the heroic age of Israel the great men are warriors who deliver the people from the yoke of invaders ; later they appear as kings who lay the foundations of constitutional government, *e. g.* David and Solomon ; later as prophets, &c. Perhaps the gifts for all varieties of excellence exist in every age, but a natural selection brings to light only those which are suitable for each particular age. But possibly there is a providential economy which shapes the great man according to the needs of his age. In either case it is clear that there is a breadth and variety of Divine inspiration, so that we cannot limit it to any one form of manifestation, nor deny that it may be found in some novel and startling shape as the requirements of the world assume new features.—A.

EXPOSITION.

Ver. 13.—**The children of Ammon**. The technical name of the Ammonite people (see Gen. xix. 38 ; Deut. ii. 19, 37 ; Judges x. 6, 11, 17, &c.). Sometimes, however, they are called *Ammon*, or *Ammonites* (see Deut. xxiii. 3 ; 1 Sam. xi. 11, &c.). *Amalek*, or the *Amalekites*, were the hereditary enemies of Israel (see Exod. xvii. 8—16 ; Judges v. 14 ; vi. 3, 33 ; vii. 12 ; 1 Sam. xv. 2, &c.). The Amalekites appear, from Gen. xxxvi. 12, to have been a branch of the Edomites, and the latest mention of them in the Bible finds a remnant of them in the neighbourhood of Mount Seir in the days of Hezekiah (1 Chron. iv. 41—43). **The city of palm trees,** *i. e.* Jericho, as Deut. xxxiv. 3 ; Judges i. 16. Jericho was the first city in Canaan which any one crossing the fords of the Jordan would come to (see Josh. ii. 1 ; vi. 1, &c.). Though no longer a fenced city, it was important from the fertility of the plain, and from its commanding the fords.

Ver. 15.—**Left-handed**. It was a peculiarity of the warriors of the tribe of Benjamin to be left-handed (see ch. xx. 16; 1 Chron. xii. 2). A left-handed man wearing no sword or dagger on his left side, and using his right hand for other purposes, would naturally throw a man off his guard. Thus Joab took Amasa by the beard with his right hand to kiss him, and then smote him with the sword in his left hand (2 Sam. xx. 10). **A deliverer.** Hebrew, a *saviour* (ver. 9). **A present**, *i. e.* their tribute.

Ver. 19.—**The quarries.** It is uncertain whether this is the meaning of the Hebrew word. Its common meaning is *images*, as Deut. vii. 25, and elsewhere.

Ver. 20.—**For himself alone.** It seems to have been Eglon's habit to sit quite alone in this summer parlour for coolness sake, his attendants waiting in the adjoining ante-chamber. On this occasion he appears to have dismissed them from the antechamber, for greater privacy, while Ehud spake to him.

Ver. 22.—**The haft**, &c. Ehud, feeling the necessity of killing Eglon at one blow, plunged the dagger into his body with such force that the handle went in with the blade, and he was unable to draw it out. Leaving it, therefore, buried in his fat, he *went out* at once into the *parshedon*, or antechamber, for so it is best to render the last words of the verse, and thence into the *misederon*, the outer porch, having first locked the door of the summer chamber. The words *parshedon* and *misederon* occur only here, and the former is very variously rendered.

Ver. 24.—**Covereth his feet**, *i. e.* is asleep (see 1 Sam. xxiv. 3). The servants, finding the door locked, and all quiet within, con-

cluded that he was taking his *siesta* in the heat of the day.

Ver. 26.—**The quarries.** See above, ver. 19. *Seirath*, or rather *has-seirah*, is not known as the name of a place. It seems to mean the *rough* or woody district, the forest in the hill country of Ephraim, where there was good shelter to hide in.

Ver. 27.—**He blew a trumpet.** Like Alfred in the marshes of Somerset, he gather-ed a host around him in the shelter of the forest; and then, full of faith in his Divine mission, "strong in the Lord, and in the power of his might," dashed down boldly into the plain, and, seizing the fords, cut off all communication between the Moabites at Jericho and their countrymen east of the Jordan. They could neither escape into Moab nor get help from Moab. Thrown into confusion by the death of their king and the suddenness of the attack, the Moab-ites fell to the number of 10,000 men; and so ended the second servitude, to be followed by a rest (if the numeral in the text is sound) of eighty years.

Ver. 31.—**Of the Philistines.** This is an isolated movement of the Philistines, alluded to in ch. x. 11, but of which we have no further details. In ch. x. 6 we read of Israel worshipping the gods of the Philis-tines, and of an alliance between the Am-monites and Philistines to vex Israel; but the precise connection between the events of the two chapters, or the exact time when either occurred, cannot be determined with certainty. Nothing more is known of Sham-gar, except the mention of him in Deborah's song (ch. v. 6).

HOMILETICS.

Vers. 12—31.—*Miscellaneous Thoughts.* Sin and punishment, repentance and ready mercy, prayer and answer to prayer, and the providential government of God, ordering all things after the counsel of his own will, are the general subjects which the course of the narrative still sets before us. But other questions of considerable difficulty arise from the history of Ehud to which we shall do well to direct our attention. To avoid repetition the analogous case of Jael recorded in ch. iv. may be considered at the same time.

I. MORAL PROBLEMS. Ehud and Jael are both represented to us as signal deliverers raised up by God to save Israel from his oppressors. Ehud holds a con-spicuous place among the judges, and Jael is declared in the song of Deborah to be "blessed among women." But if we try this hero and this heroine by the standard of morality set up by Christianity and by modern Christian civilisation, we find that they were both guilty of acts of assassination coupled with deceit and treachery. Ehud deceived Eglon into his confidence by pretending to have a message to deliver to him from God, and then stabbed him; and Jael enticed Sisera into her tent with the offer of hospitality that she might murder him in his sleep. Some commentators on this history have justified both these actions on the dangerous ground that they were done by God's special command, and that what would in themselves have been crimes became virtues under the dispensing power of God's sovereign will. But such an explanation is neither warranted by Scripture nor satisfactory in itself. The true explanation is to be found in deeper views of God's providential government of the world, by which man's free will is reconciled with the sovereignty of God. It is manifest that, given the existence of evil in the world, and given the truth that the Most High doeth according to his will in the army of heaven and among the inhabitants of the earth, it must be that bad actions as well as good ones subserve and bring about the purposes of God. That Jacob's deceit obtained his father's blessing, or that the malice of the Jews brought about the great sacrifice of the death of Christ, are no proofs that God approves either deceit or malice, but are merely instances how man's free-will, whether choosing good or evil, brings about the will of God—a truth which, however unfathomable to our reason, we can see to be necessary to the existence of the government of the world. This view, too, while it does not disturb our trust in the perfect righteousness of God, confirms our trust in the absolute sovereignty of his power. It leaves to the righteous a sense of perfect security amidst the perplexing spectacles of wrong and wickedness triumphing for a time.

II. GOOD AND EVIL IN THE SAME HUMAN WILL. But are we then to set down Ehud and Jael among the wicked of the earth? By no means. But we must turn to another difficult problem, the co-existence of good and evil in the same human will. It is a simple fact, borne witness to by profane as well as sacred history, that in individuals the main bent of whose character is towards good, a great amount of evil may remain, when such evil is countenanced by the public opinion of their day, and by the practice of their contemporaries. Just as even wise men retain many gross popular errors in science till they are refuted and exploded by the light of new discoveries, so even good men remain unconsciously under the dominion of special evils till some new light has shined upon them and exposed their real nature. The cruelty of our penal laws down to the present century, the existence of the slave-trade and of slavery within our own memory, persecution unto cruel deaths for religious opinions, the severities of arbitrary governments till exploded in the light of freedom, are familiar examples how things evil in themselves may be approved by good and humane men when they are sanctioned by prevalent custom and by public opinion. And the observation of these and numerous analogous facts teaches us the folly as well as the injustice of judging men of one age by the standard of another. Turning then to Ehud and Jael, we know that in their days human life was not more valued than it is in Afghanistan to the present hour. We know that the life of an enemy was looked upon as a lawful and desirable prey to be seized whenever possible. We know that, in times when the weak have no protection from the strong by the action of law, the only weapon of defence that remains to them, that of cunning and deceit, becomes sharpened by constant use, and is habitually worn at their side. Guile in communities where there is no justice is not the exception but the rule, and feigned blandishments have a tendency to increase the fierceness which they were intended to conceal, when the time for concealment is past. When, therefore, Ehud and Jael in their respective times saw the people of God whom they loved trampled underfoot by cruel tyrants and oppressors; when they saw the glory of God in whom they believed profaned by the triumphs of idolatry; when they heard the cries and groans of those who were reduced to bondage and were plundered of their lands; when indignation burnt in their hearts, and the blush of shame rose to their cheek, for the indignities which the people suffered at heathen hands—can we wonder that their generous hearts planned vengeance and deliverance, and that they accomplished their purpose by such weapons as came to hand. Violence was no crime, deceit was no sin in their eyes. They had not, it is true, the grace to wait in patient faith, and to say, "How long, O Lord?" but they had the fervent zeal and the heroic courage to take their lives in their hands and risk it freely for their country and their God. They had the noble spirit of self-sacrifice, seeking nothing for themselves, ready to give all they had on the altar of religion and patriotism. They had the faith in God which marks the saint, and the disdain of danger which marks the hero. And so he who in his compassionate estimate of human conduct accepts a man according to what he hath and not according to what he hath not, accepted their virtues and covered their sin, even as we hope he will accept us when we act up to the light given to us, even though our best deeds are mixed up with sin, and our holiest works fall immeasurably short of the purity and holiness of God.

III. The CONCLUSION WHICH WE THUS ARRIVE AT IS, THAT GOD'S PURPOSE OF DELIVER-

ANCE TO HIS CHURCH MAY BE ACCOMPLISHED BY BAD MEN AS WELL AS BY GOOD, and by bad as well as good actions; that the degree in which good men fall short of the glory of God varies widely according to their opportunities; and that God graciously accepts the thoughts and intents of loving and faithful hearts in spite of sin committed in ignorance of his will, dealing with men's souls through the infinite merits of the death of his dear Son, and with respect to the full satisfaction of his atoning blood—to whom be glory and praise for ever and ever! We learn also to take a juster view of the great figures which are set before us in Holy Scripture. They are not ideal figures or perfect characters. They are faithful delineations of the real lives of men and women who lived two or three thousand years ago; who stood up head and shoulders above their contemporaries in certain great gifts and qualities, but who necessarily partook of the character of the age they lived in. While we try to emulate their faith, we must judge of their actions by the light of the perfect law of God.

HOMILIES BY VARIOUS AUTHORS.

Vers. 12—14.—*Continued and repeated offence entails more signal punishment.* Jehovah is spoken of here as if he had become the God of heathen nations. He takes the side of the enemies of Israel, and strengthens them for the subjugation of his own people.

I. THE INSTRUMENT OF CHASTISEMENT IS SPECIALLY PREPARED BY GOD.

II. A VISIBLE SIGN OF DISGRACE EXISTED IN THE CONQUEST OF JERICHO.

III. THE PERIOD OF OPPRESSION WAS MORE THAN DOUBLED.—M.

Vers. 15—26.—*Ehud.* There is no grandeur of character about Ehud, nor can he boast of an illustrious descent; yet he is sufficient for the purpose of delivering Israel. The defectiveness of the instrument makes the Divine agent the more conspicuous. We see here:—

I. GOD'S USE OF OBSCURE AGENTS AND INSTRUMENTALITIES. He was of the less important tribe; personally obscure; physically defective. So God uses the weak things of this world to confound the mighty, &c., that the praise may be given to the true source of power and wisdom. On the present occasion the choice was singularly felicitous, as it emphasised both subjection and deliverance as Divine. The left-handedness of Ehud also becomes curiously and instructively prominent. His very defect proved his fitness for the special task he had to accomplish. Is his power but a one-sided one, and hardly available for regular service? If he be in earnest an opportunity will be given for its effective use. It is exacted by God's servants that they do what they can; the rest is to be left with himself.

II. DEFECTIVE POWERS AND CHARACTER RESTRICTED TO THEIR PROPER SPHERE. We can see from the history that the moral character of Ehud is not high. His success, humanly speaking, depended on duplicity, boldness, sleight of hand. He has decision enough to improve upon the advantage which he has thus obtained, and to weaken the enemy by a terrible blow. But there is no sign of the judicial faculty, nor even of great military skill. He rendered a signal service, and then apparently retired into obscurity. He held no high office, or great public responsibility.—M.

Ver. 31.—*Shamgar.* A long interval has elapsed. The moral effect of Ehud's feat is beginning to lessen. Another warning is required. It is given from the opposite side of Israel in the incursion of six hundred Philistines. These are not many, but they may be spies, pickets, the vanguard of great armies. If any effect is to be produced upon those who are behind them it must be by a sudden and decisive blow. The example of Ehud is a precedent. Another hero rises to deliver Israel at a stroke. And by a rude and apparently ill-adapted weapon. Shamgar illustrates:—

I. THE INFLUENCE OF EXAMPLE. "After him"—an Ehud inspires a Shamgar.

II. OF THE GREAT EFFECTS WHICH MAY BE PRODUCED BY IMPERFECT MEANS WHEN ZEALOUSLY AND SEASONABLY USED. The slaying of the six hundred deterred perhaps a whole series of invasions. It lent itself easily to poetic treatment, and appealed to popular imagination. The inspiration of the deed was unmistakable. A common man, a rude implement used by Jehovah at a set time for the deliverance of his people.

III. OF THE SIGNIFICANCE AND VALUE OF A SINGLE GREAT DEED. We hear nothing of Shamgar before or after. 1. *Its greatness lay in the agent rather than the means.* Previous preparation of character was required. 2. *The moral effect was sudden, wide-spread, and decisive.* God used it for a greater purpose than was immediately contemplated. 3. *But it did not qualify for permanent official usefulness.* It was followed up by no spiritual witness, or succession of services. It might be that Shamgar outlived his fame, or obscured it by unworthy life, &c. The constant service ought to supplement the individual exploit.—M.

Ver. 15.—*A man left-handed.* The left-handed man may be regarded as a type of the abnormal, the eccentric. The existence and position of such people deserves notice.

I. THE PROVIDENTIAL GOODNESS OF GOD PERMITS PECULIAR VARIATIONS FROM THE NORMAL TYPE OF HUMANITY. God does not form all men according to one exact pattern. There is great variety in the nature, capacity, position, and vocation of men. While most are more or less near to the central type, some are far removed from it. 1. Such people should be *treated with delicacy and consideration.* In the present instance the variation is too slight to be an affliction, but in more severe cases the sufferers are likely to be painfully conscious of their peculiarity. Christian courtesy will devise means of making this as little apparent as possible. 2. The *common human likeness* which belongs to all men should be recognised beneath the few discrepancies which strike us forcibly just because they contrast with the multitudinous points of agreement. The peculiarities are superficial. The deeper nature is true to the normal type of the great human family. The left-handed man has the same heart as the right-handed man. If we had more breadth of sympathy, more care for real and deep human qualities, and less regard for superficial and trivial points, we should recognise more genuine humanity in the most eccentric people. 3. Peculiarities of constitution should be borne with *calm faith* in the wisdom and goodness of God. They may be severe enough to constitute a heavy cross. Yet they come from the hand of our Father who will not willingly afflict. It is well therefore to proceed to see how they may be turned to good account, or how the evil of them may be ameliorated.

II. DIRECT ADVANTAGES MAY BE DERIVED FROM THE PECULIARITIES OF ABNORMAL CONSTITUTIONS. Ehud is able to effect his terrible purpose the more securely through the surprise occasioned by his unexpected action (ver. 21). It is foolish to aim at eccentricity, because such an aim would result in abnormal habits without abnormal capacities. But where the peculiarity is natural it must be regarded as providential, and we should then cast about to see if it may not be turned to some advantage, so that the thing which appears at first as nothing but a hindrance may be found a source of some special aptitude. If the peculiarity be a positive affliction, it may enable those who suffer from it to sympathise with and help their companions in similar affliction. Thus the blind may have a mission to the blind. If the peculiarity compel an unusual manner of acting it may be the means of accomplishing some special but much-needed work.

III. PECULIAR DISADVANTAGES IN ONE DIRECTION ARE OFTEN COMPENSATED FOR BY PECULIAR ADVANTAGES IN ANOTHER. The man who is weak in the right hand, is left-handed, *i. e.* he has special strength and skill with his left hand. The blind often have a rare skill in music. Muscular weakness is often accompanied by intellectual strength, deficient health by fine spiritual powers. Therefore instead of complaining of the peculiarity with which he is tried it would be well if the person who suffered under it were to be thankful for the special advantages with which he may be favoured. No peculiarity which may seem to exclude from the advantages of human society will sever from the love of God or from the sympathy of Christ the Good Physician.—A.

EXPOSITION.

CHAPTER IV.

Ver. 2.—Sold them. See ch. ii. 14, note. **Jabin king of Hazor.** The exact site of *Hazor* has not been identified with certainty, but it is conjectured by Robinson, with great probability, to have stood on the Tell now called *Khuraibeh*, overlooking the waters of Merom (now called Lake Hûleh), where are remains of a sepulchre, Cyclopean walls, and other buildings. In Josh. xi. 1—14 we read of the total destruction by fire of Hazor, and of the slaughter of Jabin, the king thereof, with all the inhabitants of the city, and of the slaughter of all the confederate kings, and the capture of their cities ; Hazor, however, "the head of all those kingdoms," being the only one which was "burnt with fire." It is a little surprising, therefore, to read here of another Jabin reigning in Hazor, with confederate kings under him (ch. v. 19), having, like his predecessor, a vast number of chariots (cf. ch. iv. 3, 13 with Josh. xi. 4, 9), and attacking Israel at the head of a great force (cf. ch. iv. 7, 13, 16 with Josh. xi. 4). It is impossible not to suspect that these are two accounts of the same event. If, however, the two events are distinct, we must suppose that the Canaanite kingdoms had been revived under a descendant of the former king, that Hazor had been rebuilt, and that Jabin was the hereditary name of its king. **Gentiles,** or *nations*, or *Goim*, as Josh. xii. 23, and Gen. xiv. 1. Whether *Goim* was the proper name of a particular people, or denoted a collection of different tribes, their seat was in Galilee, called in Isa. ix. 1 ; Matt. iv. 15, *Galilee, of the nations*, or *Gentiles*, in Hebrew *Goim*.

Ver. 5.—The palm tree of Deborah. The tree, which was probably still standing in the writer's time, was known as " the palm tree of Deborah," just as a certain oak tree in the forest of Hoxne, in Suffolk, was known for many hundred years as King Edmund's oak.

Ver. 6. — Kedesh-naphtali, *i. e.* Kedesh in the tribe of Naphtali (Josh. xix. 37), as distinguished from Kedesh in the south of Judah (Josh. xv. 23), and others. It still keeps the name of *Kades*, and lies four miles north-west of Lake Hûleh. There are numerous ancient remains. **Hath not the Lord,** &c. She speaks as "a prophetess," announcing God's commands, not her own opinions ; declaring God's promises, not merely her own hopes or wishes.

Ver. 10.—Called, or rather *gathered together,* as the same word is rendered in ver. 13. **Went up,** viz., to Mount Tabor, as in

vers. 6 and 12. Translate the verse. *There went up ten thousand men at his feet,* i, e. following him.

Ver. 11.—Translate, *Now Heber the Kenite had severed himself from the Kenites,* viz., *from the sons of Hobab,* &c. The Kenites, as we read in ch. i. 16, had settled in the wilderness of Judah, south of Arad, in the time of Joshua. Heber, with a portion of the tribe, had migrated later to Naphtali, probably at the time when the Philistines were pressing hard upon Judah, in the days of Shamgar and Jael (ch. iii. 31 and v. 5).

Ver. 13.—Unto the river (or brook) **of Kishon,** now the Nahr Mukûtta. In the plain of Esdraelon, through which the Kishon flowed into the Mediterranean, there would be room for all his chariots to come into action.

Ver. 14.—And Deborah, &c. Observe how throughout Deborah takes the lead as the inspired prophetess.

Ver. 15. — The Lord discomfited, &c. Deborah had announced that the Lord was gone out before the host of Barak, and so the victory was not man's, but the Lord's. "Not by might nor by power, but by my Spirit, saith the Lord of hosts." "The Lord is a man of war, the Lord of hosts is his name." **Sisera lighted down off his chariot,** &c., and—

Ver. 16. — Barak pursued after the chariots. Barak, supposing Sisera still to be with the chariots, pursued after them, and seems to have overtaken them, as they were embarrassed in the rotten, boggy ground which had been suddenly overflowed by the swollen waters of Kishon. Many were swept away by the flood and drowned, the rest put to the sword while their horses were floundering in the bog (ch. v. 21, 22). But Sisera had meanwhile escaped on foot unnoticed, and fled to the tents of the friendly Kenites.

Ver. 18.—With a mantle. Rather, "*with the coverlet,*" such as was always at hand in the nomad tent.

Ver. 19.—A little water. Faint and thirsty as he was, he did not ask for strong drink, but only water.

Ver. 21.—Then Jael, &c. Sisera, having taken every precaution, had lain him down to rest ; not, like David, trusting to the Lord to make him dwell in safety, but confiding in Jael's friendship and his own crafty directions. But no sooner had he fallen into a deep sleep, than the crafty and courageous woman, into whose hands Sisera was to be sold, took a tent pin and the heavy hammer with which they drove the pin into the ground, and with a desperate blow forced it through his temples, and pinned him to the ground. Without a struggle, he swooned and died. Instead of **and fastened it into the ground**, it is better to translate, *that it* (the pin) *came down to the ground.* It is the same word as is translated *lighted* Josh. xv. 18. In the last clause put the full-stop after *asleep*, and read, *So he swooned*

and died. It is impossible for us to view Jael's act in the same light as her contemporaries did, on account of its treachery and cruelty; but we can admire her faith in the God of Israel, her love for the people of God, and her marvellous courage and strength of mind in carrying out her purpose, and make allowance for the age in which she lived.

HOMILETICS.

Vers. 1—22.—*The variety of God's instruments. The weakness of God's instruments.* Nothing is more remarkable in the history of God's providential dealings with his people, whether under the Old or New Testament dispensations, than the great variety of instruments by which he carries out his designs. And amidst this variety a marked feature often is the weakness in themselves of those instruments by which the greatest results are accomplished. "God," says St. Paul to the Corinthians, "hath chosen the foolish things of the world to confound the wise, and God hath chosen the weak things of the world to confound the things which are mighty, . . . that no flesh should glory in his presence" (1 Cor. i. 27—29). "We have this treasure," he says again, "in earthen vessels, that the excellency of the power may be of God, and not of us" (2 Cor. iv. 7). THESE TWO FEATURES OF VARIETY IN THE CHOICE OF INSTRUMENTS, AND OF THE WEAKNESS OFTTIMES OF THE INSTRUMENTS THEMSELVES, RUN THROUGH THE BIBLE. To look only at the deliverances in the Book of Judges,—Othniel the Kenite, a stranger and a foreigner; Ehud, the left-handed Benjamite; Shamgar, the son of Anath, armed with an ox-goad; Barak, the timid, hesitating Naphtalite; Gideon, one of the least of a poor family of Manasseh, threshing his wheat secretly for fear of the Midianites, and then rushing upon the Midianite camp with his 300 followers, armed with lamps and pitchers and trumpets; Jephthah, the wild outcast Gileadite; and Samson, the man of supernatural strength, with his impulsive actions and his unrestrained passions,—what an infinite variety do they display of character, of circumstance, and of resource. And so the manna in the wilderness, the drying up of the waters of the Red Sea, the flight of quails, the falling of the walls of Jericho at the blast of the trumpet, the ministry of Samuel, the character and kingdom of David, the grand episode of Elijah the Tishbite, the deliverance of Hezekiah from the army of Sennacherib, the succession of the prophets, the great figure of Daniel, and the countless other incidents and personages which stand out in the pages of Holy Scripture, how largely do they exemplify the manifold resources of the power of God, working out his ends with unerring wisdom and unfailing certainty. The present chapter supplies another striking example. Here we see the Israelites in extreme distress: their independence gone; a great heathen power overshadowing and oppressing them by military violence; all means of resistance at an end; their princes slaves; their warriors cowed; their leaders dispersed. But their time of deliverance was come. And who were they that should break that iron yoke, and let the oppressed go free? who were they before whose might the heathen hosts should melt away, the iron chariots be burnt with fire, and the invincible chieftain be laid low in death? Two women! One known only for her prophetic speech and her skill in civil judgment; the other an alien, belonging to a weak and broken tribe of foreigners. The one, filled with the spirit of God, awakens the sleeping spirit of a captain and 10,000 of her countrymen, and urges them to battle and to victory; the other, alone and unaided, with her single hand slays the leader of unnumbered hosts. The people are set free from their oppressors, and have rest for forty years. The lesson then which this chapter impresses upon us, in addition to those which it teaches in common with the preceding, is the variety and the strangeness of the methods of God's deliverances, and especially THAT GOD'S STRENGTH IS MADE PERFECT IN HUMAN WEAKNESS. He ordains strength in the hands of weak women, as well as out of the mouths of babes and sucklings. "Fear not, thou worm Jacob; I will help thee, saith the Lord," is an exhortation which under every possible circumstance is made easy to comply with by the recollection of these wonderful acts of God.

HOMILIES BY VARIOUS AUTHORS.

Vers. 1—11.—*Temporary influences and a permanent tendency.* In this section are presented several influences, such as affect the life of man in every age—the personal influence of Ehud, the material or physical influence of Sisera, and the spiritual influence of Deborah. In judging of conduct we must take into account all the circumstances that are brought to bear upon a person or a nation. The penalties inflicted will then appear reasonable or otherwise.

I. THE PERMANENT TENDENCY TO EVIL. "*When* Ehud was dead" should be "*for* Ehud was dead." The eighty years of "rest" which the land enjoyed, and during the whole or most of which Ehud had ruled, now came to an end. But not causelessly. The "children of Israel again did (continued to do) evil in the sight of the Lord." The interval of comparative piety is over, and the under-current of distrust and idolatry again resumes its influence. The spiritual fidelity of Israel is an occasional thing; the apostasy is the result of a permanent tendency, often checked, but ever recovering its sway. "The imagination of man's heart is evil from his youth" (Gen. viii. 21). "And God saw that . . . every imagination of the thoughts of his heart was only evil continually" (*ibid.* vi. 5). Israel is described as "a people that provoketh me to anger continually" (Isa. lxv. 3), &c. The best of men have been the first to confess their inherent depravity. At a religious meeting held in Florence, when the lowest and vilest of the city were present, the question was asked, "Is there one here who is not a sinner?" Only one man dared to say in bravado, "I am not!" but he was speedily silenced by the jeers and condemnation of the audience. The duty and wisdom of all is, therefore, not to question the existence of this tendency, but to guard against it. *Unbelief* is "the sin that doth so easily beset us" (Heb. xii. 1). Nor are we only the passive subjects of improving influences in the providence of God and the order of the world. We are to be "fellow-workers with God," "to work out our own salvation with fear and trembling, for (or because) it is God that worketh in us," &c. (Phil. ii. 12). In dealing with our fellow-men or ourselves we must ever reckon upon this, the force of inborn corruption.

II. TEMPORARY MORAL INFLUENCES. That these have such weight at one time or another is a strong proof that salvation is not from within, neither, on the other hand, can it be wholly from without. We see here—1. *How much is involved sometimes in a personal influence.* Ehud, by the moral ascendancy he had acquired, is for the time the bulwark of his people's faith. Such power is a precious gift. In measure like this it is the possession of the few. But every one has some moral influence, either for good or evil. "None of us liveth to himself, and no man dieth to himself" (Rom. xiv. 7). It ought to be our care so to behave that our influence shall be increasingly for righteousness. But there are limits and imperfections in this. Although "the memory of the just smells sweet, and blossoms in the dust," it is present influence with most of us that is most vividly impressive and practically effective. Still we can never gauge the extent of our influence. In God's hands it may be multiplied indefinitely. In Christ we see the most glorious instance of personal, spiritual ascendancy. And his power shall never fail. 2. *The moral effect of a material advantage.* The presence of Sisera in "Harosheth of the Gentiles"—'probably *Harethieh*, a hill or mound at the south-eastern corner of the plain of Acca, close behind the hills that divide this plain from that of Jezreel, on the north side of the Kishon, yet so near the foot of Carmel as only to leave a passage for the river' (Thomson, 'The Land and the Book,' ch. xxix.)—with "nine hundred chariots of iron" overawed the Israelites (cf. ch. i. 19); and "twenty years he mightily oppressed" them. This force powerfully affected their imagination, and rendered them all but helpless. They forgot that God is able to break the chariots in pieces, and to make all their massive strength a disadvantage and a difficulty, as when the Egyptians laboured heavily in the Red Sea sand and waves; that the spirit that animates an army is greater than weapons or fortifications. But this cowardice of Israel just corresponds with the fear that so often unmans Christians of to-day, when confronted with great names, popular prejudices, and the shows and forces of the world. Nothing is easier than to over-estimate opposition of this sort. We have to learn in strenuous contest that "greater is he that is in us than he that is in the world" (1 John iv. 4). 3. *Spiritual power vindicating itself amid external weakness.* Amidst the universal decay of religion there are ever a few who "have not bowed the knee unto Baal." God never entirely deserts even his unfaithful ones. Some are left from whom the new era may take a beginning. (1) *Jehovah does not leave his people without a witness.* As at other times of national misfortune a judge is raised up, "Deborah, a prophetess, the wife of Lapidoth, she judged Israel at that time." Her authority is recognised, for "the children of Israel came up to her for judgment." A certain negative and secular respect is accorded to her. Divine ideas have no active power over the lives of the people; but Divine officials and institutions are still acknowledged in the general government and social life of Israel. She herself, however, is evidently full of the Spirit of Jehovah, and magnifies her office. The singularity of a woman exercising judicial functions has a powerful effect upon the national mind. Even the leading men and mighty soldiers obey her. (2) *This witness is an instance of strength in weakness.* The witness is only a woman. A sign this of the decay of the heroic spirit. But she initiates a bold and warlike policy. Evidently rising above the weakness of her sex, like Joan of Arc, she is determined to break the spell of the "nine hundred chariots of iron." The moral power she has obtained is seen in the obedience of Barak to her call and her instructions, the general answer of the nation to her summons, and the refusal of Barak to go against the enemy unless she accompanied them. So in the Messenian war ('Paus.' iv. 16) "the soldiers fought bravely because their seers were present." We are not to understand Barak's insistency as cowardliness or perversity, but as a further tribute to the presence of God in his servant. The Ironsides fought bravely when they went into battle from praise and prayer. As the exigency is great, so the instrument of restoration is most insignificant and humiliating.—M.

Vers. 12—17.—*The battle of the brook Kishon, or material force* versus *spiritual.* The armies are a contrast in respect of resources, numbers, strategic position, prestige, and skilled leadership. In all these respects the army of Sisera had the advantage of that of Israel. But the Canaanite force was a mercenary one, probably of mixed nationality (hence term "Gentiles"), and enervated with luxury and dominance; whereas Israel was represented by men desperate through long suffering, familiar with the strategic possibilities of their country, and fired with new-found repentance, patriotism, and Divine inspiration. Instances of the impotence of inequalities like these when so compensated for on the spiritual side, to decide results, have been frequent in the history of the world, especially so in that of Israel. Here we see that—

I. HE WHO DEPENDS UPON MATERIAL RESOURCES WILL BE SUBJECT—1. *To sudden alarms.* It reads like a surprise. They were at ease, relying upon military strength and prestige, when the news of Barak's march upon Mount Tabor came to their ears. But how disproportionate the force Sisera so suddenly summons to arms! It is ignorance trying to cope with experience and skill; scanty equipment confronting all that a great and powerful nation could invent and provide for military defence and offence. Yet already it was a point in favour of Israel that it had aroused such apprehension for so slight a cause. The conscience of the wicked is never easy. The least sign of danger is sufficient to rouse it, and to occasion the most disproportionate exertions. 2. *To rash exposure of his resources.* "All the chariots of iron," the military power and glory of the oppressor, are at once called into exercise. This was unwise. A little more consideration would have suggested a better and more prudent disposal of his forces. It is evidently feeling, and not far-seeing military prescience, that dictates the pompous demonstration. How often do the oppressors of God's "little ones" drive their tyranny too far, and defeat their own end by overeagerness and domineering imperiousness! The heart that God has inspired will look upon such things—the threats, &c.—as of little moment. 3. *To utter collapse.* The suddenness of the levy was adverse to its efficiency. Subject as Eastern troops are to panics, and difficult as it must have been for such cumbrous vehicles to deploy upon such varying levels, it was only necessary for the handful of Israelites to be led by a skilful general for them to produce confusion and dismay in the unwieldy host. And when once the huge army began to yield, its own size and bulk would make its defeat the more disastrous. And *all* was risked at once. There was nothing more upon which, quickly enough, to fall back. So in the hour of the Church's peril and extremity God has found his opportunity. The Pope's bull is burnt, and the Reformation commences boldly and decidedly. "Fear not, I am with thee," has been the voice that has made the turning-point in many a career. All the pomp and show of the world is brought to bear upon the saint; he sees through it; a step, a stroke, and it melts like the "airy vision of a dream," and he is free !

II. HE WHO DEPENDS UPON GOD will—1. *See opportunity and hope against overwhelming odds.* "Up, for this is the day in which the Lord hath delivered Sisera into thine hand.' So David—"The Lord that delivered me out of the paw of the lion, and out of the paw of the bear, he will deliver me out of the hand of this Philistine" (1 Sam. xvii. 37). So Gideon. This is the insight of faith. 2. *Make careful preparation.* "Trust in God, and keep your powder dry." The means, however inadequate, the best means at our disposal, must be employed. "God doesn't require my knowledge." "No more does he require your ignorance." It is a sign of respect to God, and a mark of thorough-going faith in him, that we make scrupulous use of the means he dictates. Often the "means of grace" are despised, to a Church's loss, to a Christian's loss, and sometimes destruction. "They that wait upon the Lord shall renew their strength," &c. 3. *Confide in the Divine presence and promises.* Abraham is sure that "God will provide himself a lamb; " David sings, " Though I walk through the valley of the shadow of death, yet will I fear no evil ; " and the Hebrew children were confident that the "God whom they served was able to deliver them.", Faith as a grain of mustard seed "will remove mountains."—M.

Vers. 17—22.—*Vide* ch. v. 24—27.—M.

Vers. 8, 9.—*Deborah and Barak.* I. THEY WHO UNDERTAKE TO ADVOCATE DIFFICULT TASKS SHOULD BE WILLING TO SHARE THE RESPONSIBILITY OF THE EXECUTION OF THEM. Deborah urges Barak to fight ; Barak will raise the standard only on condition that the prophetess will accompany him. There are prophets who sit with Deborah under the palm tree and advise noble deeds while they excuse themselves from facing the danger of achieving them. In the spiritual warfare of the Church we find critics who can see the defects of the work others are doing, and advise great improvements, yet who will never encounter the perils of the mission-field or the drudgery of more homely work. It is well to devise good measures, but it is better, like Deborah, to help in the execution of them.

II. IN THE BATTLE OF LIFE A GREAT VARIETY OF SERVICE IS REQUISITE FOR FINAL SUCCESS. Deborah cannot lead the army, but she can inspire it. Barak cannot prophesy, but he can fight. Thus Deborah cannot secure victory without Barak, nor Barak without Deborah. We are members one of another, and all the members have not the same office. There is work for the seer and work for the warrior. The world always needs its prophets and its heroes. The worker without the thinker will blunder into confusion ; the thinker without the worker will fail for want of power to execute his designs. Brain work is at least as important as mechanical work. It is therefore foolish for practical men to despise the men of thought as mere theorists, and foolish for the thinkers to treat the active men of business with philosophical contempt. It is peculiarly woman's work to cheer and encourage those who are called to the dangerous tasks of life. Wives and mothers who dissuade their husbands and sons from their duty because it appears to be dangerous are indulging in a weak and foolish affection. The highest love will seek to encourage those who are loved in all that is great and noble.

III. IN THE SERVICE OF GOD THE FIRST REQUISITE FOR SUCCESS IS THE INSPIRING AID OF THE SPIRIT OF GOD. Deborah is a prophetess. She is gifted with the wisdom and enthusiasm of direct inspiration, and thus becomes the inspirer of Barak and his troops. Barak feels that if Deborah goes with him God's counsel and encouragement will be given him. Do we not trust too much to the mere machinery of our Church organisations in the execution of our work ? One prophet in our midst is worth a thousand dull, earthly-minded men The great need of the Church in her battle with the evil of the world is the presence of the Spirit of God in light and power, to guide and to energise her dark and weak efforts. It is foolish to go up to our spiritual warfare without seeking the presence of God to accompany us (Exod. xxxiii. 15). If God go with us we shall need no special order of prophets, for then every soldier of Christ will be a prophet (Joel ii. 28).—A.

Ver. 21.—*Patriotic treachery.* I. OPPRESSION ROUSES THE DARKEST PASSIONS OF THE OPPRESSED. Jael's treacherous murder of Sisera did not occur in an age of peace and comfort, but after her nation had been terribly crushed by the Canaanite power. The worst evil of tyranny is not found in the mere distress which it brings on those who suffer from it, but in the bad passions which it provokes. The oppressed are degraded *morally;* they grow revengeful; unequal to open resistance, they become treacherous; misery blinds them to the claims of humanity Slaves are too often cruel and treacherous. This fact, instead of excusing slavery, is its heaviest condemnation.

II. CRUELTY MAY EXPECT TO BE REWARDED WITH TREACHERY. Sisera was no innocent soldier falling in the discharge of loyal service to his country. He had "mightily oppressed the children of Israel." Harshness may appear to silence all opposition, but it really provokes the most dangerous enmity—secret and treacherous enmity. Sisera meets with a just doom. There is something cowardly in brutal oppression; it is fitting that the man who descended to practise it should not fall in honourable warfare, but meet his miserable fate at the hands of a deceitful woman.

III. THE GUILT OF A CRIME MUST BE MEASURED BY THE MOTIVE WHICH INSTIGATED IT. A cold-blooded crime committed for low ends of personal profit is far more wicked than the same deed done in the heat of provoked passion. The act which is committed for the good of others is *less* wicked than that which is entirely selfish in its motives. The motive of Jael was patriotic. She anticipated no danger to herself from Sisera, but she thought to rid her country of a great and cruel enemy. So far she was brave and noble.

IV. THE UTILITY OF THE END WILL NEVER EXCUSE THE WICKEDNESS OF THE MEANS EMPLOYED TO SECURE IT. Jael was no vulgar murderess. Her patriotic motive mitigated the guilt of her crime, but it did not destroy that guilt. She was guilty of a breach of the sacred rights of hospitality. Did she meditate murder when she welcomed Sisera into her tent ? Possibly not. It may be that the sight of the sleeping man suggested the temptation to an easy way of delivering her nation from a great enemy. If so, her treachery was so much the less guilty. But the very warmth of her ostentatious hospitality offered to such a man as Sisera suggests only too forcibly that she·meant treachery from the first. That grim scene—the weary soldier trusting himself in the hands of the murderous woman, while she lavishes her hospitality on him with fearful schemes working in her brain—is surely no picture of womanly glory, in whatever age we set it, with whatever provocations we mitigate its dark horror. Jael is plainly guilty of a gross breach of trust. We must not shut our eyes to her criminality because she did a deed on the side of the Jews which we should have condemned with loathing if it had been committed by a less enlightened, heathen, Canaanite woman. Reverence for the teaching of Scripture does not require us to excuse the faults of the Jews.—(Jael the Kenite was practically a Jewess.) It is most degrading to the conscience to read the dark pages of Hebrew histor with the understanding that we must condemn nothing done by an Israelite. It is also false to the intentions of Scripture. In the Bible we see the failings of good men and the personal wickedness of some who took their stand on the right side. The merit of their cause does not destroy the guilt of their individual conduct. Deceit and cruelty have sometimes been practised in the interests of Christianity, of liberty, of humanity ; but the only service God will accept must be fair, and true, and pure.—A.

EXPOSITION.

CHAPTER V.

Ver. 1.—Then sang Deborah, &c. The ode which follows was doubtless the composition of Deborah the prophetess, and was sung by her (as the gender of the Hebrew verb indicates), assisted by Barak, who perhaps sang the antistrophe (cf. Exod. xv. 1, 21). It is a song of wonderful beauty and lyric power, somewhat difficult, as all Hebrew poetry is.

Ver. 2.—Her first feeling was one of patriotic joy that her countrymen had been roused to the venture of war, and of gratitude to God that it was so. "For the bold leading of the leaders of Israel, for the willing following of the people, praise ye the Lord."

Ver. 3.—Her song was worthy to be listened to by kings and princes. She calls their attention to the tale she had to tell of the great acts of the Lord.

Vers. 4, 5.—The recent victory recalled the glories of those days when God brought up Israel from Egypt into Canaan. She specifies the march from Seir or Hor, and the day when Mount Sinai was altogether on a smoke, and the whole mount quaked greatly.

Ver. 6.—From what misery God had saved the people! In the days of her predecessor Shamgar, when the Philistines overran the country, when Heber the Kenite still dwelt in the south of Judah, all traffic ceased in the land. The caravans were stopped, and travellers slunk into the by-ways.

Ver. 7.—Instead of **The inhabitants of the villages ceased**, some render *the leaders ceased*. Till Deborah arose and stirred up Barak, there was no one to put himself at the head of the people.

Ver. 8.—The cause of this misery was not far to seek; it was the idolatry of the people which provoked God to anger. Then their enemies were let loose upon them, and they dared make no resistance.

Ver. 9.—What a contrast with that faint-hearted submission was the recent triumphant rising! Exultation and thanksgiving for the devotion of the people break out again, as in ver. 2.

Ver. 10.—She appeals to the nobles who ride on white (or roan) asses, and sit on rich saddle-cloths (not *sit in judgment*), and to the people who walk by the way, alike to speak of the great deliverance.

Ver. 11.—A very difficult verse, and very variously rendered. For *archers* some give the interpretation *dividers*, i. e. MEN SHARING THE BOOTY THEY HAVE TAKEN; or, SINGING IN ALTERNATE VERSES. For *they that are delivered* from, some render *far away* from. Others again take the preposition *from* in the not uncommon sense of *more than*, meaning here *louder than*. The chief different senses which emerge are—(1) that of the A. V.: "Those that can now draw water from the wells without being molested by the hostile archers shall sing praises to God in the very spots where they were wont to be attacked." (2) "Far from the noise and tumult of those that divide the spoil among the water-troughs, there shall they sing," &c. (3) "With a louder voice than that of the *shepherds* who sing among the water-troughs (while they are watering their flocks), there shall they rehearse," &c. Or, (4) combining (2) and (3), "With a voice louder (and more exultant) than that of those who divide the spoil, there shall they rehearse," &c. **The inhabitants of his villages.** Render *his leaders*, as in ver. 7. **Then shall the people . . go down to the gates** of the cities for judgment, or to the bazaars, as in old times, without fear of their enemies.

Ver. 12.—Awake, &c. She seems to go back in thought to the moment when she received the Divine call to her mission of deliverance, and executed it by the voice of her stirring prophecies. Then she lashed her soul into action, and roused Barak from his lethargy by the promise of spoil and victory.

Ver. 13.—Then he gave dominion to a mere remnant of Israel over the powerful among the people of Canaan, the Lord gave me dominion over the mighty men of Jabin.

Ver. 14.—They who spring (whose root is) from Ephraim *went* against Amalek, following thee, O Benjamin, with thy people; from Manasseh (Machir, son of Manasseh, Gen. l. 23) came down governors (literally, *lawgivers:* cf. ver. 9), and out of Zebulun they that handle the bâton of the commander, i. e. the military chiefs.

Ver. 15.—He was sent on foot into the valley. It was a mark of extraordinary valour that he rushed down from Mount Tabor on foot against the 900 iron chariots in the plain (ch. iv. 14). **For the divisions,** &c. Or, *among the water-brooks*, i. e. the Reubenites, dwelling amidst their flocks among the water-brooks, were much perplexed with doubts whether they should stay still or join their countrymen.

Ver. 17.—In ships. The celebrated harbour of Joppa (Jonah i. 3), now Jaffa, was in the tribe of Dan. **His breaches.** The creeks and bays where they kept their fishing-boats.

Ver. 19.—The kings came and fought (cf. Josh. xi. 1, 2, 5). **They took no gain of money.** These words may mean, (1) they did not stop to plunder, they were intent only upon slaughter ; or, (2) they took no ransom for their enemies' lives ; or, (3) they got nothing by their fighting, for they were all killed themselves.

Ver. 20.—According to Josephus, a great storm in the face of the Canaanites led to their utter discomfiture, and also swelled the Kishon to overflow its banks.

Ver. 21.—**Ancient**. The word so rendered is only found here. *The brook of ancient* days, or things, probably means the brook celebrated from of old by the warlike deeds done on its banks.

Ver. 22.—**Their mighty ones**. Applied to bulls, Ps. xxii. 12, &c. ; and to horses (A. V., *his strong ones*), Jer. viii. 16 ; *his strong* horses, Jer. xlvii. 3.

Ver. 23.—**Meroz**, in the time of Jerome *Merrus*, a village otherwise unknown, twelve miles from Samaria. **The mighty**. Not the same word as that so rendered in ver. 22, but that usually rendered *a mighty man*, or *a man of war*.

Ver. 24. — **Blessed above women**, &c. With the selfish indifference of the men of Meroz she contrasts the valorous enthusiasm of Jael the Kenite, and blesses her for it as emphatically as she curses the inhabitants of Meroz.

Ver. 25.—**A lordly dish**. A dish fit for princes ; perhaps one reserved for the most illustrious guests.

Ver. 26.—**With the hammer**. These words are not in the Hebrew, and should be omitted. *She smote* (not *smote off*), yea, she wounded (Psalm lxviii. 21); *she pierced through his temples*.

Ver. 30.—**Sped**, *i. e.* come across some booty. **For the necks of them that take the spoil**. Literally, *for the necks of spoil*. It is a difficult and obscure expression. *The spoil* may mean the camels, horses, or mules taken from the enemy, and the articles described may mean the housings and trappings for their necks. Or *the necks of spoil* might mean the necks of the beasts of burden laden with spoil.

Ver. 31.—A fine application of the whole subject ! Each such victory was a foretaste of the final victory over sin and death, and of the glory of the redeemed Church.

HOMILETICS.

This splendid ode, so full of poetic fire and vivid dramatic effect, with its startling contrasts, its picturesque descriptions, its glowing eulogiums, its burning patriotism, its striking characters thrown into high relief by the stroke or two of genius, its passion and its pathos, is not deficient in ethos. We will single out two or three ethical lessons from their surroundings.

I. SELF-SACRIFICE FOR THE GOOD OF OTHERS. The ninth verse is an awakening call to voluntary sacrifice on the altar of the public good. While men in general are hanging back from exertion and danger in sloth or timidity, unwilling to run any risk, or to make any effort, there are those who, with high-minded zeal for their country's or their Church's weal, burst asunder the restraining bonds of selfishness, and, with their life in their hands, offer themselves willingly for the common cause. Deborah's burst of generous admiration toward those who did so in her time is a stirring call to us to imitate their example. But let us not imagine that such self sacrifice is confined to extraordinary occasions, or can be executed only on the platform of great emergencies. Unselfish efforts for the good of others find room for their exercise in the common round of every-day life. He who works when he is weary, who overcomes his natural shyness or timidity, who lays aside his own schemes or tastes and takes up work which is distasteful to him, who risks losses in money, in consideration, in convenience, in comfort, in ease, in leisure, that he may do something which he believes will be useful to others, is treading in the steps of these "willing governors," and deserves like them the warm approval of all generous hearts.

II. WORLDLY HINDRANCES. But we may see in the examples of Reuben and Gad what are the hindrances to such self-sacrificing work. There is a counter-call to the call of duty and of love, and that call is too a louder and a more persuasive one— the call of gain and worldly interest. When Deborah's message came to the Reubenites and Gileadites, and the blast of Barak's trumpet sounded in their ears, calling them to the help of the Lord against the mighty, the bleatings of their flocks and the lowing of their herds among the rich pastures of Jazer and Gilead seemed to tell them a different tale (see Numb. xxxii.). How could they leave those peaceful pastures, and exchange them for the battle-field ? Jabin's iron chariots were nothing to them. What would become of their flocks and herds while they were far away? As their eyes ran through the sheep-folds, and they reckoned up in thought the wealth which they contained; as they thought of the lambing, and the sheep-shearing, and the sheep-market, and told the increase which they might expect, they seemed tied to those sheep-folds by bonds which could not be broken, and by a spell which could not be loosed. After a few doubts and hesitations they abode among the folds, and left their brothers across the Jordan to fight by themselves. And so it was with Dan and Asher. The movements of Sisera had not interfered with the trade of Joppa, or the fishing-boats of the sea-coast. The ships of Tarshish were coming and going as of old, laden with merchandise from all parts of the world; some touching there on their way to Tyre, others supplying the markets of Palestine with wrought iron, and cassia, and sweet calamus. Already perhaps the silver and iron, the tin and the lead, brought by the ships of Tarshish from the Cassiterides, found their way to the fairs of Joppa; and the wheat of Minnith, and the oil and honey and pastry (Hebrew, *pannag*) of Judah, went out through its harbour to Tyre and Sidon (Ezek. xxvii. 12, 17, 19). And the men of Dan were all busy by that sea-side. Lading and unlading the ships, carrying the bales of merchandise on their strong backs, giving and receiving orders, piloting the foreign ships into harbour, plying to and fro as they handled the oar, stopping the leaks or mending the sails of ships that had come out of rough waters—there was no end of business to be done, and of money to be made. Why leave these peaceful gains and rush inland to perish by the sword? Surely they might be excused if they remained in ships, and continued on the sea-shore, enriching their country by their industry, while they left it to others to jeopard their lives in the high places of the field. And they did so; and in doing so have left us an instructive warning as to the hindrances which the world continually places in the way of high-minded action and generous self-sacrifice. "Love not the world, neither the things that are in the world," if you would be free to serve either God or man, is the precept that settles upon the thoughts as we consider the gaps in the muster-roll of Israel at the battle by the waters of Megiddo.

III. THE ENMITY OF NEUTRALITY. But ver. 23 reads us a yet sterner lesson. There are occasions when not to act for God is to act against God. There are occasions when a man cannot be neutral. When the Lord calls for help against the mighty, he that withholds that help is cursed. By so doing he is helping the enemies of God, and among the enemies of God he will fall. Here was Meroz in the very thick of the fight. Ephraim and Benjamin, Issachar and Manasseh, Zebulun and Naphtali, were pouring out their thousands to defend their altars and their homes. The honour of God, the freedom of God's people, the cause of truth against heathen error, the kingdom of God against the tyranny of Satan, were trembling in the balance. A few hundreds more or less might turn the scale. All Israel was awake and alive to the noble task before them. There was music in the tramp of the thousands of devoted men marching to the war which might have aroused the dullest soul and kindled the faintest spirit. It did not move the men of Meroz; they hung back in sullen indifference; they skulked behind their walls. No zeal for the glory of God, no sympathy with their brethren, could pierce through their heartless selfishness. As the angel of the Lord looked out from the windows of heaven, he saw their cowardice, he marked their back-drawing, he pronounced them cursed. There are times, our own times are such, when the enemies of the cross of Christ are unusually active against the truth. At such times Satan musters all his forces, and would fain overthrow the Church of God. Infidelity stalks through the land. The leaders of sceptical opinion join hand in hand. Science and literature, wit and intellect, the press and the platform, fashion and numbers, are pressed into the service, to cast discredit upon the everlasting gospel of the grace of God. At such a time to be neutral and indifferent is to be a traitor to the Lord Jesus Christ. At such a time he calls to his help against the mighty all who believe in him, who love him, and who hope in his salvation. "Who is on the Lord's side, who?" is his appeal to his redeemed. Let no believer hold back from giving what help is in his power: the help of word and deed; the help of bold confession and of unflinching countenance; the help of tongue and pen; the help, if need be, of suffering and of martyrdom; the help of a devoted life, and of a holy

Christian walk, in all humility, and purity, and faith, knowing whom he has believed, and fully assured that faith will be crowned with victory.

IV. THE END OF THE UNGODLY (ver. 31). All the enemies of the Lord will surely perish. The day is not far off which will mark the difference between the righteous and the wicked, between him that serveth God and him that serveth him not. The Lord Jesus shall be revealed from heaven with his mighty angels, in flaming fire taking vengeance on them that know not God, and that obey not the gospel of our Lord Jesus Christ; and then they that love him shall be as the sun when he goeth forth in his might. The righteous will shine forth as the sun in the kingdom of their Father, and they who confessed Christ before men will be confessed of him before the angels of God. Such are the fuller prophecies of the New Testament, confirming the obscurer prophecies of the Old, and encouraging us to hold on our faith without wavering, in the certainty of the great reward.

HOMILIES BY VARIOUS AUTHORS.

Ver. 2.—*Self-sacrifice and its Inspirer.* There are two other renderings of this verse, viz., "That in Israel wildly waved the hair in the people's self-devotion,—praise God" (Cassel); and, "For the leading of the leaders in Israel, for the free self-offering of the people, praise Jehovah" (Stanley, after LXX.). It is immaterial which of these we prefer; the chief thought is evidently that which appears in all. It is the key-note of this heroic song, as it is the essence of heroism and true religion always—self-sacrifice to God.

I. THE SPIRIT IN WHICH GREAT DEEDS ARE WROUGHT. The outburst has its source in Divine patriotism or religious enthusiasm. A consciousness of a representative character and destiny animates the Israelites. Religious devotion binds them into complete communion. Private aims and interests are forgotten. 1. *It is this spirit which rescues the war of deliverance from objections to war simply as such.* As an act of self-devotion it was a truly devout, and therefore religiously legitimate, war. No hope of personal gain animates the host of Israel. It is patriotism in its noblest form. These soldiers are all volunteers; they obey a Divine voice. How many wars would cease were such feelings consulted! The saints' contest with evil should be conducted from a like principle. We should know what "manner of spirit" we are of. 2. *It was this spirit which made so effectual the struggle in which they were engaged.* They were desperate, devoted men. No half-measure would be tolerated. Having counted the cost, they were willing to carry it on à outrance. God's battle with error and wickedness has suffered because of the half-heartedness of those who wage it. 3. *It was this spirit which conferred upon the deed its æsthetic beauty and epic grandeur.* It is a fine question to determine what that is that gives the essential character to the noble, chivalrous, and religious enthusiasms of men. A careful survey of any considerable number of them will show that not only *unselfishness,* but *self-sacrifice,* is their fundamental principle. Selfish aims, or the impulse of self-aggrandisement, vitiates the deed, however externally magnificent; and *vice versâ,* the magnanimous forgetfulness of self, the conscious foregoing of personal ends and aims, will give nobility and piety even to works externally indifferent or apparently ignoble. The sentiment of a deed is its true character. Here it assumes a dignity and glory that command the admiration of the poet and the artist. It is part of the excellence of noble deeds to inspire. There is nothing so inspiring as self-devotion. But this is the vital breath of all true religion. Religious enthusiasm is contagious. The pious hero cannot long remain alone. True worship is the praise of the cross, where the power of darkness sustained its signal, final defeat. "By the obedience of one shall many be made righteous." If we are truly religious our lives also will blossom forth in acts that poets might sing and orators extol.

II. THE INSPIRER OF GREAT DEEDS. That they are not a spontaneous outgrowth of our nature is the general confession of those who have wrought them. The object of Israel's admiration and obedience was Jehovah. It was in the inspiration derived from him the deliverance was wrought. God in Christ, as embodying the highest excellency in sympathetic relation with ourselves, is an even more powerful stimulus to heroism and piety. "For Christ's sake" is a formula that covers a vast proportion of " whatsoever things are true, whatsoever things are honest, whatsoever things are just, and pure, and lovely, and of good report," in the world's history.—M.

Vers. 6, 7.—*National ruin and the true deliverer.* The mighty deed of Shamgar did not avail to reduce the interior of Israel to a state of order and security. Whoever Jael (the Helper) may have been, whether Ehud, Shamgar, or some other hero, even he was unable to restore confidence to the dwellers in the country, or to render communication between the towns and villages easy and secure. The description here reminds one of Germany in the tenth century, or Sicily and Greece in our own times. A strong hand and a central government are required in order to inspire confidence and to render the conditions of life uniform and reliable. A country may be great in military strength, and yet, socially and politically, at a standstill because of the absence of due internal administration, of public institutions, and zeal for the public welfare. We have here—

I. A VIVID PICTURE OF NATIONAL DECAY. 1. *The means of inter-communication were rendered useless.* " The highways were deserted." Main thoroughfares have ever been requisite for the proper inter-communication of the different parts and towns in a country. They are therefore one of the first means employed for opening up internal resources and developing commerce and civilisation. All really great governments have distinguished themselves in road-making; as, for instance, the Incas of Peru, the Chinese, and the Romans. It was the boast of the Roman writer that the circuit of the empire could be made through Europe, Asia, and Africa, without risk to life or property, by a private traveller. The sight of deserted highways suggests the collapse of commerce and social intercourse. It is more striking than the complete absence of roads would be. And highways that continued in disuse would soon get out of repair and be rendered impassable. In the present day a similar state of things prevails over a large part of Palestine and Asia Minor. Travellers make their journeys by night, and avoid the villages and public roads. The wandering Arab brings the desert with him wherever he goes. 2. *The country districts depopulated.* This would rapidly reduce the country to barrenness, and render the support of the nation more precarious. A mere tithe of the population could then be supported, and the nation would be kept in a state of weakness.

II. THE SECRET OF NATIONAL REGENERATION. Deborah was a mother in Israel. The military hero played his part, but failed of highest success. It was for her, by wise and statesmanlike measures, internal administration, and a strong central government, to bring to the people's doors the fruits of military success. She fostered a national spirit, encouraged a respect for law, and rendered it as safe to dwell in the country as within the walled city. The continuous policy of Deborah achieved the reconstitution of the land and its freedom from internal lawlessness.—M.

Ver. 8.—*The peril of national irreligion.* The conscience of Israel is here addressed. The coincidence of new idolatries with " war in the gates " was strikingly suggestive. It could not be accidental. There was nothing in which Israel had had more continued experience than in the connection of idolatry with national weakness and misery.

I. DECLINE COMMENCES WITH THE FIRST DEPARTURE FROM THE WORSHIP OF JEHOVAH. It was as they trusted in Jehovah and acquainted themselves with him that they were able to drive out their enemies. The weakening of this religious principle undermined the moral character and strengthened the force of sensuous influences. It is only as the soul anchors itself on the Eternal that it is able rightly to regard the outward and temporary affairs of life.

II. THE ADOPTION OF OTHER GODS IS PUNISHED AS A CULMINATING AFFRONT. In this we see not so much the indirect results of idolatrous practice as the immediate chastisement of Jehovah's own hand. The apostasy is deliberate; punishment must be proportionately stern and extreme. Those who have known his character and will, and yet deliberately despise them, deserve the more condign punishment. We see this principle at work in many a life. There are sins which seem to invite a terrible vengeance. Do *we* provoke God's anger? Let us remember that he can be a consuming fire. Deliberate rejection of God is a direct invitation and challenge to his wrath.

III. The final result of idolatry is effeminacy and abject helplessness. This is proved by an appeal to history. The Israelites had an instance of it in their own experience. There may have been weapons in Israel, but the idol worshipper had lost the courage to wield them. Idolatry, as a degraded conception of God, degrades its votaries. It has ever been linked with licentiousness and vice. The conscience is gradually destroyed, and with it all moral strength disappears.—M.

Vers. 10, 11.—*Testimony and thanksgiving the duty of the redeemed.* The classes here addressed are representative of the entire nation—nobles, judges or elders, and common people. The deliverance affected all, and those specially benefited are called out. The hand of God is to be publicly acknowledged and celebrated in song; and this was seemly and right. So it is the duty of the redeemed of Christ to rehearse his marvellous works and ways with them.

I. This ought to be done severally and in particular. In the case of each there is some peculiarity. It will illustrate afresh God's manifold mercy. "This poor man cried, and the Lord heard him, and saved him out of all his troubles."

II. It ought to be done publicly and collectively. The national recognition of God is a most impressive and instructive spectacle. It becomes the more so if spontaneous, and not the result of legislative enactment or meaningless tradition.

III. The reasons for this are manifold. 1. *It is due to him.* The work of Christ is very great, involving vast effort and suffering. It is full of love and wisdom, adapted to our special need. And in all the work of redemption no credit is to be taken to ourselves; the merit is wholly his. "By the grace of God I am what I am." To withhold the praise is therefore worse than theft. 2. *It is the highest and most blessed exercise of the religious nature.* Man was born " to glorify God, and to enjoy him for ever." In so doing his nature attains its highest end and complete spiritual development. The harmony of praise and prayer has its reflex influence upon the utterer, and as God in Christ is the most glorious object of adoration, the heart is expanded, uplifted, strengthened, and purified. There is nothing we are so liable to as forgetting God's mercies, and our dependence upon them; and therefore it is well to rehearse them. 3. *It is a benefit to others.* The world is full of misconceptions and low thoughts of God, and indifference towards the Divine. By such rehearsals the true character of God is vindicated. Men are taught to trace all blessings to their real Author. Doubters, &c. are counselled and directed towards clear, healthy, and health-giving ideas of God. Thus the gospel of the grace of God is preached most effectively. Others catch the contagion. Are we silent? What is the cause? Ingratitude; or it may be we are strangers to the grace of God. Let us yield ourselves to it now. Perhaps we too shall sing in a higher realm "unto him that loved us, and washed us from our sins in his own blood."—M.

Vers. 14—23.—*National defence a common responsibility.* We have here an interesting glimpse of the behaviour of the various tribes in the war of freedom. Not all were summoned to battle; but of these only two answered to the call.

I. Who are summoned to the great war? All the tribes whose interests were threatened in the first place; but the others might have come from a feeling of brotherhood. Through Christ the solidarity of the race is revealed. We have nearer and further claims, a more and a less imperative call, yet the interest of each is involved in that of the whole. The debt we all owe to Christ binds us henceforth " not to live to ourselves." "Am I my brother's keeper?"

II. Who respond? Two tribes and a friendly alien. This showed a lack of public spirit, and of a true national conception. The Captain of our salvation calls. Who are willing? "Will ye also go away?" A few, all over. In every Church one or two have to bear the burden and heat of the day. Is this right?

III. The excuses and occupations of those who hold back. Very picturesque is the description—not a little satirical. How sorry the figure cut by those who tarry at home when the battle rages! the excuses of those who were asked to follow Christ!

IV. Strict account will be taken of the conduct of each, and the reward will be given accordingly. The sharp eye of the prophetess scanned the host she accompanied. To each is apportioned the praise or blame. *God* sees the heart.—M.

Ver. 20.—*The hopelessness of opposition to God.* This verse is variously interpreted as an astrological allusion—as descriptive of a thunder-storm, accompanied by wind, hail, and floods, producing confusion (Josephus); or as suggestive of the delay which lost Sisera the opportunity. The explanation of Berthau, referring it to the *Divine intervention,* appears more reasonable and spiritually sufficient. All through the mind of the prophetess dwells upon God as the Helper and Avenger. But there is room for an intermediate idea. The stars are symbols of an unvarying law and universal destiny. Generalise upon the great contest between right and wrong. The combatants are not only men; the whole universe is involved. Angels join in the fray. God himself is against the sinner. The latter must be vanquished.

I. The ultimate character of the contest of the wicked with the righteous. An accidental circumstance may excuse it; a temporary character may be assumed by it. We may not divine the whole scope and drift of the quarrel. Truth may not be wholly on one side or the other. Sometimes a prophetic insight assures us that we are with God, or against him. Ultimately the question is one of right and wrong.

II. The combatants involved. Not human opponents merely; the question too large for this. The laws of the universe; the angels of God; destiny; God himself —visibly contending in the person of his Son, invisibly in the councils of eternity.

III. The certainty of the issue.—M.

Ver. 23.—*The curse of Meroz.* The site of this city or district not verified. A singularity about the people's conduct. Others had withheld as well as they; but they had either (1) special reasons for fidelity, or (2) aggravating circumstances connected with their inaction. The consequence was that they inherited the primacy of the curse. Was it that the ban destroyed the very name and memory of the place from the face of the earth? It became a *"locus classicus* in Talmudic expositions of the ban against persons and things" (Cassel).

I. There are circumstances in which indifference and inaction with respect to the cause of God in the world constitute a fearful crime. The nation they belonged to represented for them the kingdom of God. It was suffering from grievous servitude. When the short, desperate struggle for freedom took place, everything might depend upon the faithfulness of those situated as they were. They hung back, or co-operated with the enemy. This was a sin against the Divine brotherhood and the cause of God. Indifference at any time is wicked; but the habit may some time or other suddenly reveal itself in tremendous heinousness. Special efforts to promote the kingdom of Christ, to prevent the dying out of religious institutions or movements, critical periods in individual lives, ought to call forth our most generous and self-denying aid. It might just be *our* help that was needed in order to success; our indifference that sealed the fate of a soul turning towards God, or a religious movement upon which depended important results.

II. Greater responsibilities and privileges entail a greater curse upon unfaithfulness. Terrible vengeance was taken upon the erring city. Of how much greater punishment shall Christian apostasy be thought worthy? (Heb. x. 28—30). We sin against greater light. How great is our debt to grace! What issues depend upon our being found faithful! Remember Christ's warnings (Matt. xi. 23; xviii. 6; xxiii. 37).—M.

Ver. 24.—*The conduct of Jael.* A moral perplexity to modern times. This arises from the advance, amounting almost to a revolution, in the spiritual sentiment of the world. It is from the higher platform of the New Testament that we see the deed in its true relations and proportions.

I. Its justification. There are several grounds, upon any or all of which the deed may be defended. 1. *That of a relative and imperfect morality.* Morality in that age was not perfectly revealed or realised. With increasing light of revelation and spiritual experience come new moral levels and tests. A thing may be comparatively or relatively right which is not absolutely so. The fact that we condemn the action is not due to our superior natural light, but simply to the teachings of Christianity, the outgrowth and perfecting of the crude morality of the Old Testament. 2. *On the principle that the obligation to tell the truth depends upon the existence of a normal and friendly relation between men; the permission to kill carrying with it that of dissimulation* (Mozley). 3. *Because Jael followed as a mere instrument the impulse of the Absolute.* Is it not credible that persons may be moved by a superior reason to do things justifiable from the standpoint of that superior reason, but which, if they fully realised what they were doing, would be utterly unlawful for them to do?

II. ITS BEARINGS UPON INSPIRATION, &c. OF HOLY SCRIPTURE. The inspiration of Scripture cannot be affected by the inspired sanction of such a deed. Inspiration does not necessarily involve a knowledge of the "whole counsel of God." It has its degrees, and is reliable so far as it goes. A merely human production would have avoided such apparent self-contradictions. That there are moral mysteries and difficulties in the Bible, which are nevertheless seen to have possible solutions beyond the immediate knowledge of man, is a strong presumption in favour of its being Divine.

III. HOW FAR IS JAEL AN EXAMPLE TO BE IMITATED? In no wise. This is an exceptional case, all of whose circumstances must be taken into account. She is, like many whom a special destiny seems to isolate from their fellows, almost to be pitied, save for the thought that she acted as the servant of God. The instincts by which we condemn her deed are evidently of God, and must therefore be followed.—M.

Ver. 31.—*The sunlike life.* Cf. Prov. iv. 18. A beautiful simile. Many points of resemblance between the course and nature of the sun and the character and life of the Christian.

I. PROGRESS. *Steady.* By gradual, regularly increasing advance. The hours and days and years can be measured by it. We can calculate upon it. *Continual.* Not by fits and starts. Ever forward, even when not seen. *Culminating.* Noon is splendour and strength; sunset is fulfilment.

II. ILLUMINATION. In the Christian life nothing need be concealed. We are "children of the light, and of the day." Openness, honesty, actions of simplicity and good report. Knowledge is light, and it is by knowing the Eternal that we live. The spiritual are the light of the world. Christ is so *par excellence;* but all Christians shine with his brightness, and exhibit his character. We are so to live as that others can take knowledge of us that we have been with Jesus, and that they may follow us as we follow him. The figure also suggests that Christians may become clear, and bright, and free from darkness as light itself is. Spiritual illumination is not ever a borrowing from without. We may have light and life in ourselves. The sun is independent of circumstances, and shines on even when half the world is dark. It is also a figure for vindication and triumph. The day shall declare how much! The glory and beauty of the spiritual man shall then be revealed.—M.

Ver. 7.—*A mother in Israel.* The position and character of Deborah and her mission to Israel are suggestive of the Scriptural teaching concerning women and their work.

I. GOD RAISED UP A WOMAN FOR THE DELIVERANCE OF HIS PEOPLE. Deborah appears in the line of deliverers. The others are all fighting men. In the present instance a warrior, Barak, is associated with the prophetess; yet it is not he, but the woman, Deborah, who secured victory, for she tells us that the hamlets were deserted *until* she arose. The Bible assigns great honour and high privileges to women. In Jewish history they are often prominent and famous for noble services. Women were among the most honoured of the disciples of Christ. In spite of the narrow views regarding the rightful position of women with which St. Paul is credited, that great apostle was ready to recognise the valuable work of women in the Church (Phil. iv. 3). Women have peculiar powers for such work as requires sympathy and the gentleness which is at the root of true greatness (Ps. xviii. 35). And many women who are not called to imitate the heroic career of Deborah may take example from the compassion of Pharaoh's daughter, the hospitality of Abigail, and the charity of Dorcas.

II. THE WOMAN CHOSEN FOR THE DELIVERANCE OF ISRAEL WAS A MOTHER. The peculiar virtue of celibacy is a late invention which finds no basis in the Bible. There marriage is honourable (Heb. xiii. 4), and to mothers a peculiar honour is given (1 Tim. ii. 15). The joys and cares of maternity deepen the nature of women and develop the noblest and most Divine of all affections—a mother's strong, tender, devoted love. A true mother will not have the less affection for others because her first duty is to her own children. She is no perfect mother, even, whose whole affection and care is confined to her family. With her maternal affection is little more than a form of selfishness, the offspring being regarded as an enlargement of the personality of the parent. The true mother is motherly in her nature, and shows her motherliness in all relations of life; so that to her friends, her nation, and the needy, her thought and care partake of the mother's fond, self-sacrificing devotion. Therefore patriotism is not antagonistic to maternal affection, but offers a field for its noblest efforts.

III. THOUGH A MOTHER IS CHOSEN FOR THE WORK OF DELIVERING ISRAEL, SHE IS NOT CALLED TO SACRIFICE ANY WOMANLY GRACE IN PERFORMING THE TASK. Deborah was no Amazon. Hers was not the fierce fighting of Barak. She was a prophetess. 1. Her mission was to *inspire and encourage*. This is one of woman's noblest works. Women are unfaithful when they check their sons or husbands in the performance of dangerous duties. 2. Her mission was also to *utter God's praises* after victory had been secured. Women, more sensitive than men, should be able to arouse songs of thanksgiving, while men may be slower to awake to the full feeling of gratitude. In leading the praises of the Church women have a truly womanly mission.—A.

Ver. 9.—*Self-dedication.* Deborah's heart turns in motherly affection to those rulers of Israel who have willingly offered themselves to the service of their God and their country. It should be the aim of the Christian to emulate such self-devotion in the cause of Christ and of humanity.

I. THE OFFERING WAS TO GOD AND THE COUNTRY. 1. *It was to God.* Though this fact is not expressly named here, as in the case of Jehoshaphat's captain, Amasiah (2 Chron. xvii. 16), it is plainly implied, inasmuch as the people had been incited by a Divine messenger and were living under a theocracy. God was the King, and the soldier's fidelity to his king was fidelity to God. Men devote themselves to business, pleasure, art, literature, science. The highest object of devotion is to live to God. This may be pursued through the necessary earthly occupations, elevating and consecrating them by making them part of God's service. 2. *The devotion was also to the country.* Patriotism is a Christian duty. But the Christian is called to care for the large human world. We are called upon to live for the good of others, to aim at increasing their happiness and spiritual welfare. This aim is not divergent from that of serving God. We render him service by working for the good of others according to his will, and so as to render him honour.

II. THE OFFERING OF THE GOVERNORS WAS OF THEMSELVES. God is not satisfied with our gifts; he asks for our hearts (Prov. xxiii. 26). The true preachers of God's will will say, " We seek not yours, but you " (2 Cor. xii. 14). No gifts will be acceptable to God until we have first given our own selves to him (2 Cor. viii. 5). The sacrifice of self-dedication, which was symbolised to the Jew in the whole burnt offering, is a sacrifice still looked for under the Christian dispensation, not as a propitiation for sin, but as a thank offering. This, and no less, constitutes our reasonable service (Rom. xii. 1). We offer ourselves to God when we render him the homage of our hearts in love, when we sacrifice our wills to his will in submission and obedience, when we make it the object of our life to please and serve and honour him. We cannot compensate for lack of personal devotion by payment, as in some countries the conscript can do in regard to military service. Our gifts will not take the place of our work. We cannot serve God by proxy. The work of the missionary or of any professional agent of the Church must not be regarded as a substitute for the work of the private Christian. God claims the personal service of all of us.

III. The offering was voluntary. Deborah rejoices in the fact that the governors offered themselves willingly. 1. *The only acceptable service of God must be willing service.* God leaves us free to accept or reject his service, he uses no violent compulsion to drive us into it. There is no conscription for recruiting the regiments of the kingdom of heaven; all soldiers in that glorious army are volunteers. This is important, because (1) only voluntary service can come from the heart,—God values devotion of the heart more than work of the hands,—and (2) only voluntary service will be vigorous and enthusiastic and inspired with the devotion which insures success. 2. *We have every motive to render this willing service.* We are free from compulsion, but we are not free from obligation. We are to blame if we do not freely offer ourselves, and if we persist in refusing it will go ill with us at the last. (1) *Duty* requires the service. The people were summoned by a Divine messenger. We are summoned by the preaching of the kingdom. They were living under the rule of God; God is our King and Lord. They were bound to defend their country in its need; we are bound by nature and Christianity to help our fellow-men in their distress and sin. (2) *Gratitude* makes the service one of love. The Jews had seen mighty Divine deliverances; we have the sacrifice of Christ for us and his love constraining us (2 Cor. v. 15).

In application of these truths it may be noticed that some are waiting to be called into the Church or for service. Such waiting is a mistake. Christ is waiting for us. He has called us; he expects our free self-dedication. Let us not wait to be sought or asked, but freely offer ourselves to his service.—A.

Ver. 14. — *Literary occupations.* Whether these men of Zebulun were poets, chroniclers, or only merchants' clerks, their occupation was distinctly different from that of their brethren, and the peculiar duties attaching to it may serve to illustrate those which belong to a corresponding class of men in our own day.

I. Literature is a field of honourable industry. It is a foolish misnomer which characterises handicraftsmen as the only "working men." Men can and do work at least as hard with their brains as with their hands; and such work is not the most unworthy of honourable effort. We cannot make a greater mistake than to confine the epithet "manly" to the exercise of brute force, an exercise in which a Hercules would be out-matched by a gorilla. True manliness is the right development of all the noblest powers of a man, among which the intellectual must take a high place.

II. Literature may be made a source of the highest good to mankind. Writing is a means of expressing, preserving, and disseminating ideas. This means has been chosen by God for the promotion of religion, viz., in the Bible. Therefore it is foolish to despise literature as unpractical; it may be the most useful instrument for benefiting mankind. This should be remembered by those who have literary power, and should prevent them from wasting their talents on the selfish enjoyment of intellectual luxury. Literary ability is, like the gift of tongues, a Divine gift bestowed on men for the good of the whole world.

III. In order that literature may effect the greatest good, it must be enlisted in the service of God. They who " handle the pen of the writer " must be among those who " willingly offer themselves " to the service of the Lord. God claims our best for his work. Men who have literary gifts should understand that they are not at liberty to write simply for occupation, for amusement, for money, or for fame, but for the honour of God and the good of men. Such considerations should secure more conscientiousness in writing; the observance of the great literary duties of truthfulness, fairness, purity, and charity; and the pursuit of elevating themes.

IV. They who are called to literary duties must not feel themselves exonerated from more general obligations. The literary man must sometimes lay down the pen and draw the sword. The danger of sedentary and literary occupations is that they should lead to indolence and an unpractical habit of life. It will not do for any of us to live in the delicious seclusion of dream-land. There are stern tasks and serious burdens which all true men will have to encounter if the terrible realities of the world's wickedness and misery are to be faced as the claims of God and humanity demand of us. While the trumpet sounds to war it is treason for the men of Zebulun to linger behind in learned leisure; and while God calls his people to do battle for him against the ignorance and sin of the world, there is no excuse for the most gifted, the most fastidious, or the most occupied to shirk their share of the dangers and toils of hard warfare.—A.

Ver. 16.—*Indolent indecision.* The men of Reuben who refused to obey the call to arms appear to have indulged at once in questioning criticism and in selfish inactivity, and thus they illustrate the close association of indolence and indecision. Indolence encourages indecision by checking the energy requisite for choice, and indecision encourages indolence by closing all doors of action. The situation of indolent indecision may be considered from the point of view of indolence and from that of indecision.
I. THE SITUATION REGARDED ON THE SIDE OF INDOLENCE. 1. *Private business* was one excuse for negligence of public duty. People often make their business an excuse for not undertaking the work Christ calls them to (Matt. xxii. 5). But this results either (1) from idleness, since more energy would make time for Christ's service, or (2) from selfishness, inasmuch as we have no right to devote our whole time to our private interests. 2. *Love of ease* led to negligence of public duty. It was less arduous to tend the flocks than to assemble for war. 3. Love of *peace* may have had the same effect. The Reubenites may have been peculiarly men of peace, while the Ephraimites were men of war. There are times, however, when the peaceful habit is sinful, and when we are only hiding our indolence under the cloak of peace, and when it is our duty to take up the cross, which is involved in facing the confusion and harshness of conflict. It is wrong to refuse to maintain the right and to rebuke falsehood and wickedness out of the love of peace. 4. *Pleasure* may have inclined to indolence. That was no time for dreaming pastoral idyls when the nation was in jeopardy and a Deborah was sounding the war-trumpet. Music and poetry, and the love of nature and art have their place among the innocent amenities of life ; but when æstheticism becomes a religion, and the graces of life take the places of its duties, the harmless pleasures which allure us from stern tasks become positive sins. The wretchedness, the vice, the crime which darken the very atmosphere of Christendom leave none of us free to luxuriate in soft dreams of imaginary bliss, instead of doing our utmost to conquer these hideous monsters.
II. THE SITUATION REGARDED ON THE SIDE OF INDECISION. 1. Indecision is often the effect of directing intellectual energy to *negative criticism* rather than to practical contrivance. Criticism is most valuable in its place ; but when it is carried to the point of fastidiousness it becomes nothing less than a fatal, paralysing influence. Reuben was divided in counsel, uncertain as to the best course to pursue, and therefore did nothing. So there are people who waste their energies in exposing the defects of all plans of action, and yet have not the inventiveness and strength to discover and pursue better plans. But it is better to work in an imperfect method than not to work at all. 2. Indecision can only be conquered by cultivating *strength of will and convictions of duty* It is the will that decides. When the intellect is cultivated at the expense of the will, moral paralysis is the result. Strength of will can be best attained in its right form by the exercise of what will we already have under convictions of duty. We should remember that our chief mission in the world is not criticism, but work. God calls us to action, and even if we work imperfectly and often fail, he will be better pleased at our well-meant, though perhaps mistaken, efforts to do what we believe to be right than at the inactivity which refuses to do anything from fear of committing the smallest error.—A.

Ver. 23.—*The curse of Meroz.* I. THE CURSE WAS FOR INACTIVITY. Meroz had committed no offence, but is solely to blame for failing in action. Innocence of positive guilt is not enough to secure us from condemnation in the judgment of God. We shall be judged by what we have left undone as well as by what we have done. In Christ's vision of judgment, those who are made to stand on the left of the throne and are then condemned to outer darkness are not offenders against the moral law, but simply persons who have neglected the active duties of charity (Matt. xxv. 45). It is a very common error for people to suppose that they are blameless so long as they keep themselves unspotted from the world, forgetting that the first duty of religion is the energetic exercise of charity (James i. 27). Better to have some faults and much useful service than to be faultless and useless. The soldier who returns from war with scarred face and stained garments is nobler than he who fears to enter the battle lest he shall soil his raiment or mar his countenance.

II. THE CURSE WAS FOR INACTIVITY IN REGARD TO PUBLIC DUTY. Meroz was unpatriotic. Possibly the men on whom the curse fell were diligent farmers and kind and careful parents. But they neglected their duty to their country. We must beware of the narrowness of the parochial mind. The congregation which studies its own edification alone, and has no care for the evangelising of the nation and for mission work among the heathen, brings itself under the curse of Meroz. In the faithful payment of taxes, in the conscientious use of the franchise, in the right use of influence in public matters men have a constant call to patriotic duty. But we have all larger duties to men as men, and so long as misery, ignorance, and wickedness prevail none of us can escape condemnation until we have done our part to remove those evils.

III. THE CURSE WAS FOR INACTIVITY IN A TIME OF WAR. 1. It was the time of the nation's *greatest need and danger* when Meroz was discovered to be indolently unpatriotic. Great emergencies reveal the evil which has existed unobserved in quieter times. If we are not faithful in that which is least we shall be proved unfaithful in that which is greatest. The evil which may be fatal to our nation in times of danger may be lurking among us unseen in these more quiet times. Therefore the shameful failings of those who are held up to the reprobation of history may be no worse than the mean selfishness which pervades the lives of multitudes who meet with no blame, simply because the day of trial has not yet made their character apparent to the world. 2. The danger in which the unfaithfulness of Meroz was revealed brought a call to *aggressive action*. Meroz was found wanting in a time of war. We are called to resist evil. If we permit others to be oppressed by injustice and cruelty when we might deliver them by any sacrifice and toil of our own, we bring ourselves under the curse of Meroz. Christianity is aggressive. It is the duty of Christians not merely to promote purity, and charity, and truth, &c., but to expose and attack the vices and wrongs of the world.—A.

Ver. 31.—*The triumph of the Church.* The triumph of Israel after the overthrow of the Canaanites is an illustration of the ultimate triumph of the Church.

I. THE FACT OF THIS TRIUMPH. We have encouragements to think that the Church will not only be saved, but will be saved with honour—will triumph. 1. This implies the *destruction of her enemies.* We need not look for that in violence, after the manners of the Crusades or of the Inquisition. (1) *Spiritual* foes, such as sin, temptation, death, will cease to exist. (2) *Human* foes will cease to be foes by the turning of enmity into submission to Christ. 2. It implies the bestowal of *honour* on the Church. She shall shine like the sun, no longer despised. 3. It implies the enjoyment of *great happiness.* Darkness represents sorrow; sunlight represents joy. 4. It implies the gift of *power.* No influence on earth is so powerful as that of the sun. The people of God will have opportunity for noble service and for the exercise of large faculties. 5. It implies the exercise of *benevolence.* The sun scatters light, warmth, life. He brings new life out of the death of winter, and spreads beauty and glory over the face of the earth. The triumph of the Church will not be like that of old tyrannies, marked by bloodshed and misery, but a source of life and joy and glory to all within its reach. There is *healing* in the wings of the Sun of righteousness.

II. THE SOURCE OF THIS TRIUMPH. 1. It is accorded by *God.* Deborah speaks of it in prayer. It was not the courage of the warrior, but the unseen help of God that secured the victory to Israel. We grow fearful as we see the raging might of evil, and compare this with the trembling weakness of our own hearts. But God is with us; he makes the cause of the Church his own. Christ has already conquered, and now he calls us only to meet defeated foes. 2. It is secured through *devotion to God.* The enemies of God perish. These are not men whom God treats as enemies, but such as set themselves in enmity against him. They who triumph are the lovers of God. The essence of religion is love to God, and this is here the ground of the assurance of victory given by him. 3. It is attained by *silent and gradual* means.

The sun does not burst out suddenly, he makes no noise to announce the coming day. So the triumph of the Church is gradual as the growing dawn, silent as the spreading light. Yet, like the light, it will be recognised by its visible presence and its bountiful fruits.—A.

EXPOSITION.

CHAPTER VI.

Ver. 1.—**Midian.** In Numb. xxii. 7 we read of the Midianites as allied with the Moabites in their hostility to the children of Israel, and we find them willing agents of Balaam's iniquitous counsels (Numb. xxv. 6, 17, 18 ; xxxi. 7, 8), and suffering a terrible chastisement from the Israelites in consequence. An abiding national feud was the natural consequence ; and this, added to their love of plunder, no doubt led to the present invasion in company with the Amalekites (ch. iii. 13, note). Observe the contrast between the victory described in Numb. xxxi. and the defeat narrated in this chapter.

Ver. 2.—**The dens . . . and caves.** In the writer's time certain hiding-places called by the above names were traditionally known as the places where the Israelites took refuge during the terrible Midianite invasion. The limestone hills of Palestine abounded in such caves.

Ver. 3.—**Children of the east.** We first find this term in Gen. xxix. 1, where it is applied to the people of Haran. Comparing the analogous phrases, "the east country" (Gen. xxv. 6), "the mountains of the east" (Numb. xxiii. 7), "the men of the east" (Job i. 3), "the east" (Isa. ii. 3 ; Matt. ii. 1),

we gather that the country lying to the east of Palestine as far as the river Euphrates was called the east country, and that the various tribes of Arabs and others who peopled that desert were called "the children of the east" (see ver. 33 and ch. vii. 12 ; viii. 10).

Ver. 4.—**Left no sustenance,** &c., *i. e.* neither grass, nor corn, nor fruit. It is added, **neither sheep, nor ox, nor ass.** These all either died for want of food or were seized by the Midianites. The next verse explains that the enormous multitudes of their cattle and camels consumed the whole produce of the ground.

Ver. 5.—**As grasshoppers.** See the striking description of the destruction caused by locusts in Joel iii. I have heard travellers in India describe the sudden darkening of the sky by a flight of locusts.

Ver. 8.—**A prophet.** Literally, *a man, a prophet,* just as Deborah was described as *a woman, a prophetess* (ch. iv. 4). It is interesting to observe the flow of the spirit of prophecy in those early days between Moses and Samuel, before the dispensation of the prophets had risen to its height. **I brought you up from Egypt.** Note the constant reference to the exodus as a fixed point in their national and religious life (see ver. 13 ; ch. ii. 1).

HOMILETICS.

Vers. 1—10.—*The fruit of ingratitude.* What a condemnation of Israel there was in the simple statement of facts by the mouth of the prophet, without exaggeration and without comment. God had brought them up from the land of Egypt with a mighty hand and a stretched-out arm ; when they were in bondage he had broken their yoke ; when they were oppressed he had set them free ; when the multitudes of Moabites, and Ammonites, and Midianites, and Canaanites, had opposed their entrance into the land of promise, God had brushed them all away and given their land to the Israelites. He had accompanied these acts of grace and power with a simple command not to worship the idols of Canaan, but to remember that Jehovah was their God, but they had not obeyed his voice. They had forsaken God, to whom they owed all they had, and they had turned to heathen vanities. What need to say any more? They were now reaping what they had sown. They were helpless because they had cast off him who had helped them so wondrously, and who would have been their help in every time of need if they had not so wantonly forsaken him. And in like manner how often will a bare statement of facts be enough to overwhelm us with guilt and shame! Let any man be his own prophet, and with unflinching truth record the incidents of a year or a day of his own life. "God in his abounding grace and love redeemed me by the blood of his dear Son ; he freely forgave me my trespasses and sins ; he received me into the adoption of children, by Jesus Christ, unto himself ; he sealed me with the Holy Spirit of promise ; he crowned me with loving-kindness and tender mercy; he showed me the kingdom of heaven, and bid me enter into it; he showed me the deadly evil of sin; he showed me the beauty and loveliness of goodness; he said to me, Abhor that which is evil, and cleave to that which is good. But I have not hearkened to his voice; I have forgotten his love, and despised his grace; I have disbelieved his word, and have believed the lying promises of sin; I have loved the world; I have been the slave of my own lusts, and the subject of my own passions; I have turned aside with the multitude of evil-doers, and I am now eating the fruit of my own doings; I have forsaken God, and so God has forsaken me."

HOMILIES BY VARIOUS AUTHORS.

Vers. 1—6.—*Israel's extremity.* With repeated defection a severer punishment is needed and inflicted. Midian is not only a neighbour, but one who encircles Israel on south, south-east, and east. It was a name given to the great Arab tribes living east of the Red Sea, and south and east of Canaan. Unlike a comparatively civilised nation, they are not satisfied with receiving tribute; they render husbandry and the arts of civilised life impossible by lawless raids, ceaseless devastation, and wanton destruction. It is a new terror. Israel may be overwhelmed and stamped out if this curse of the wilderness be not restrained.

I. ISRAEL'S ABANDONMENT OF JEHOVAH IS PUNISHED BY AN APPARENT ABANDONMENT OF ISRAEL BY JEHOVAH. It seems a light punishment; really there could scarcely be a harder one. Let the sinner and the backslider consider what their condition would be were God *just to treat them as they treat him.* Even the mildest phase of such discipline could not be long bearable. Simply to be left to oneself—let alone —what tragic possibilities does that suggest! But when enemies of the most ruthless description overrun our land, and have us at their mercy, how much does abandonment mean! It is in such times we learn how much we owe to Divine interposition hour by hour. The *moral* consciousness of Israel was consequently lowered. So of all in like cases.

II. THE MANNER AND EXTENT OF THEIR DISCIPLINE ARE SUGGESTIVE OF THE HEINOUSNESS OF THEIR OFFENCE. Things had come to such a pass that only a full experience of the worst of their heathenish and idolatrous neighbours would avail. There is little or no love of God left; let the consequences of their unbelief teach them a bitter hatred of evil; in time it will drive them back to the doctrine and practice of truth for very life. By and by they will learn to love it again. We have but to think of God's loving nature and infinite tenderness to see how desperate such a measure is. If forbearance failed, no other remedy would suffice but this. All unbelief is this potentially. It was a glimpse of the horror of a godless world.

III. IT WAS A SALUTARY DISCIPLINE, BECAUSE IT LED THEM TO REPENTANCE AND PRAYER. God had no pleasure in this long agony; but neither, on the other hand, would he shorten it until due cause appeared. The result justified the severity. Saints often regard their calamities amongst their greatest mercies. How roughly handled have been some of God's dearest ones! But the worst is not ours to bear, since Christ died. There is no calamity we cannot take to him. He will distil sweetness from wormwood itself, and give us help in time of sorest need. "Whom the Lord loveth he chasteneth, and scourgeth every son whom he receiveth." He may be nearer to us in the affliction than in the prosperity.—M.

Vers. 7, 8, 11, 34.—*Divine mercy: its adaptation and sufficiency.* The cry of distress is heard instantly by Jehovah, and the answer begins to come at once. But only as is best for the sinning nation. As there was discipline in the misery to which Israel was reduced, so there is still discipline in the succession and several instalments of the mercy of God. The aim is not merely nor so much to deliver from the material evil to which they were subject, but to root out the unbelief and develop the spiritual life and moral heroism of the people.

I. THE IMMEDIACY OF GOD'S MERCY. "*It came to pass, when the children of Israel cried, . . . that the Lord sent a prophet.*" There appears to be no interval. God begins to readjust his relations with Israel at once. But the material boon is not granted then. The sting must rankle until true repentance is forthcoming. Deliverance would have been a very questionable blessing under the circumstances. Freedom and independence are responsibilities as well as birthrights. So God hears the cry of the sinner always. "Not what we wish, but what we want," that in the end what we wish may be rendered spiritually advisable and blessed. The measure of comfort here was that God was not silent, prayer was not unavailing. There is hope in the opening of mercy's door, even though it be in reproof.

II. THE SUCCESSIONS OF GOD'S MERCY. First the cry of desperation and repentance, then the outward reproof, then the direction, encouragement, and training of a deliverer, then the recovery of national freedom, prosperity, and prestige. Flowerlike. So God adapts his blessings to the moral and spiritual capacity of his people. The Divine view of our misery and its requirements is the reverse of the human ; we think of the material suffering, God of the moral defect and sin. These mercies as they come in train are manifestly education, that the work of grace may be effectual. "Grace for grace" is a law of his kingdom. And the dignity of God is never lost.

III. MERCY IN ITS CULMINATION. God did not stop short of ultimate deliverance, although it was not achieved at once. So "he crowneth us with his loving-kindness and tender mercy." It is no mere secular and vulgar deliverance. It is national re-creation. The chivalry of Israel is called forth. It is even more a religious than a military triumph. So the salvation of the soul has its splendours and glories. It is absolute, complete, and magnificent, crowning the life of the faithful. "An *abundant entrance* will be ministered" into the kingdom of his Son. "We are more than conquerors" through him.—M.

Vers. 7—10.—*Merciful reproof.* The answer to prayer begins in reproof. An anonymous messenger is sent, a prophet probably from amongst the Israelites themselves. In such a season of distress and seclusion they would become strangers even to themselves. No biography is given of the prophet. He is raised for the occasion. His message is simple. But it is the utterance of the people's own national and individual conscience. He is a "voice crying in the wilderness," and saying, "Repent!"

I. THERE IS ENCOURAGEMENT EVEN IN GOD'S CHIDINGS. For—1. *They are better than absolute and final silence.* 2. *They are meant to bring us back to him, and not to drive us away.* 3. *His severity is to prepare us for his gentleness.*

II. IT IS OFTEN AS NECESSARY AND PROFITABLE TO BE IMPRESSED WITH WHAT WE ALREADY KNOW AS TO RECEIVE NEW TRUTH. Revelation is not primarily intended to satisfy intellectual cravings, but to stimulate and enrich the moral nature. A sermon may be a mere exhortation, an impressive *resumè* of acknowledged truth, and yet more valuable than if it were full of theological discoveries. Knowledge of God becomes religious and living when it is *realised* and acted upon. In this connection notice—1. *How impressive the personality of the prophet.* 2. *The heightening of the conscience of sin by contrast with remembered and recited mercies.* 3. *The tone and style of the discourse.* It was short, direct, spoken to the conscience. Its chief message and its sting is in the conclusion. No word of comfort is uttered. The people are left with their consciousness of sin. But this in itself is a gracious work, and preparatory for everything that is good. Thorough repentance is the condition of deep and lasting piety.—M.

Vers. 7—10.—*God sought and found in times of trouble.* I. TROUBLE DRIVES MEN TO GOD. The people forsook God in their prosperity, and neglected his service so long as they enjoyed their comfortable homes in peace. But now they are miserable fugitives hiding in wild mountain caves, they remember his goodness and cry to him for help. This is a common experience. It is to our shame that it must be confessed. We ought to seek God for his own sake, to worship him in the beauty of holiness, not merely to obtain blessings for ourselves. In prosperity we should recognise tokens of his love, and so lift up our thoughts to him in grateful recognition of his goodness. To turn to God only in the hour of our need is a sign of base selfishness. Nevertheless it is better to seek him then than not at all. And if it is disgraceful in us that trouble should be needed to drive us to God, it is merciful in him to send the trouble for that object. The calamity which leads to this result is the greatest blessing. Herein we may see the end of many of the most severe forms of adversity. They are sent to us in our indifference to rouse us to our need of God, and lead us to seek him. Hence we may conclude that if we sought God aright in happy circumstances we might be spared some of the troubles which our spiritual negligence renders necessary to our soul's welfare (Hosea v. 15).

II. IF GOD IS TRULY SOUGHT IN TROUBLE HE WILL CERTAINLY BE FOUND. As soon as the people cried God heard them, and sent them first a prophet and then the deliverer Gideon. If we forsook God in our prosperity it would be reasonable that God should forsake us in our need. But he does not deal with us according to our sins. Our claim does not lie in our merit, in our obedience and fidelity, in anything of ours, but in his nature, and character, and conduct. Because God is our Father he hears us not out of consideration for our rights, but out of pity for our distresses. Therefore we need not fear that he will not respond to our call. To doubt is not to show our humility, but our distrust in the mercy of God and influence of Christ's sacrifice and intercession (Jer. xxix. 11—13).

III. WHEN GOD IS FOUND IN TROUBLE HE DOES NOT ALWAYS BRING IMMEDIATE DELIVERANCE. Israel called for help in need. God did not send the help at once. The people expected a deliverer, God sent a prophet. No word of promise is given by the prophet that relief will be accorded to the temporal distress of the nation. He speaks only of sin, and shows the ingratitude of the people, that they may feel how richly they deserve the calamities which have fallen upon them. They think most of their distresses, God of their sins. They cry for deliverance from the yoke of the Midianites, God wishes first to deliver them from the yoke of iniquity. Therefore the prophet of repentance comes before Gideon the deliverer. So we must expect that when God visits us in our sins he will deal with us so as to save us from spiritual evil before relieving us of physical distress. Christ bore the sicknesses and infirmities of his people, but his great work was to save them from their sins (Matt. i. 21).

IV. THE CONSCIOUSNESS OF SIN WHICH MUST PRECEDE DELIVERANCE IS PRODUCED BY A PROPHET'S MESSAGE IN THE MIDST OF TROUBLE. The trouble is necessary to soften the hearts of the people, and make them willing to listen to the prophet. Yet the trouble does not produce repentance. For this a prophet is needed. The prophet does not make any prediction, nor does he give any revelation of God; he simply reveals his hearers to themselves. We need prophets to show to us our own true character. Much of the Bible is a revelation of human nature which would not have been possible without the aid of prophetic inspiration. The call to repentance consists (1) in recounting the ancient mercy of God, for it is in the light of God's goodness that we see most clearly our own wickedness; and (2) in directly charging Israel with ingratitude and apostasy. All sin includes the sin of ingratitude. Till we feel this it is not well that God should show us more mercy. Therefore the stern John the Baptist must precede the saviour Christ; but as Gideon followed the prophet, full salvation will follow repentance and submission.—A.

EXPOSITION.

Ver. 11.—**An angel**, &c. Rather, *the angel of the Lord*, otherwise called "the angel of his presence" (Isa. lxiii. 9). In vers. 14, 16, 23, for *the angel of the Lord* we have simply *the Lord* (see ch. ii. 1, note). **An oak.** Rather *the oak*, or *terebinth*, as it should be rendered. It was doubtless a well-known tree still standing in the writer's time (see ver. 19). Compare the mention of *the oak* (terebinth) at Shechem (Gen. xxxv. 4); *the great oak* (terebinth) in which Absalom was caught (2 Sam. xviii. 9); *Deborah's palm tree* (ch. iv. 5, where see note). Observe the simple way in which the ministration of the angel is introduced, as if it were a matter of course in the eyes of him who is the Lord of the millions of the heavenly host, those ministers of his who do his pleasure. Human scepticism, the twin sister of human selfishness, would blot out all creation except itself. **To hide it,** &c. These graphic touches give a lively picture of the straits to which the Israelites were reduced by the Midianite occupation.

Ver. 12.—**Appeared.** Angels were not always visible when present (see Numb. xxii. 31; 2 Sam. xxiv. 17; 2 Kings vi. 19, &c.).

Ver. 13.—**If the Lord be with us,** &c.

The utter dejection caused by the Midianite oppression breathes in every word spoken by Gideon. But how reassuring the angel's words were. **Which our fathers told us of.** This is a distinct reference to the national traditions, which are elsewhere alluded to (cf. Exod. xii. 26, 27 ; Ps. xliv. 1 ; lxxviii. 3—5 ; Jer. xvi. 14).

Ver. 15.—**Wherewith shall I save Israel?** &c. Compare the unwillingness of Moses (Exod. iii. 11 ; iv. 10, 13), of Saul (1 Sam. x. 21, 22), of Jeremiah (Jer. i. 6), of Amos (Amos vii. 14, 15), and of St. Peter (Luke v. 8). Also in ecclesiastical history that of Ambrose, Gregory the Great, and others. The least fit are usually the most forward, the most fit the most backward, to undertake great offices (ch. ix. 8 — 15). True humility is the usual companion of true greatness (see 2 Cor. ii. 16 ; iii. 5).

Ver. 17.—**A sign that thou talkest with me**—that it is indeed thou thyself that speakest to me, even God, and that there is no illusion.

Ver. 18.—**My present.** *Minchah* means sometimes a *present* made to man, as in ch. iii. 18 ; but it more commonly means a sacrificial offering (Gen. iv. 3 — 5), which seems to be its meaning here, as explained vers. 19, 20. When coupled with *zevach*, the animal sacrifice, *minchah* means the meat and drink offering.

Ver. 19.—**Unleavened cakes** (Gen. xix. 3 ; 1 Sam. xxviii. 24). The necessary haste gave no time for the use of leaven, which is one explanation of the unleavened bread at the passover (Exod. xii. 33, 34, 39). **Presented it.** A word specially used of sacrifices and offerings (Amos v. 25).

Ver. 20.—**Lay them upon this rock,** as upon an altar, **and pour out the broth,** as a drink offering or a libation (see ch. xiii. 19).

Ver. 21.—**There rose up fire,** &c. The consuming of the sacrifice by fire from heaven was the token of its being accepted (cf. ch. xiii. 20, 23 ; also 1 Kings xviii. 23, 33, 38 ; 1 Chron. xxi. 26). **The angel of the Lord departed,** &c. In the very similar case of the angel who appeared to Mánoah (ch. xiii. 15—20), the angel ascended in the flame of the altar. It is probable that he did so in the present instance, though it is not expressly stated how he disappeared (cf. Acts viii. 39).

Ver. 22.—**Gideon perceived,** &c. Gideon's suspicions were now turned into a certainty. It was indeed God that had spoken to him by his angel (ver. 17). **Alas,** &c. Gideon speaks thus in terror of the death which he thought must be the penalty of seeing the angel of the Lord (see ch. xiii. 22, and note). **Because.** Rather, *therefore*, or *to this end*, viz., that I should die.

Ver. 23.—**Peace,** &c. Cf. Dan. x. 19, and John xx. 21, 26 ; Luke xxiv. 36 - - 39. Hence the name of the altar, Jehovah-shalom—"The Lord is peace," is at peace with me.

Ver. 24.—For naming altars built in commemoration of particular events see Gen. xxii. 14 ; xxxi. 47—49 ; xxxiii. 20 ; Josh. xxii. 34, &c.

Ver. 25.—**The grove.** See ch. iii. 7. The size of the *asherah* is indicated by the order in ver. 26 to use it for the altar fire.

HOMILETICS.

Vers. 11—24.—*The preparation.* God's agents, whether kings, or judges, or prophets, or apostles, are reasonable agents. They are not inanimate machines or blind instruments ; they are living, thinking, feeling, reasonable, men. When they are called to great and heroic works they must be endued with great and heroic thoughts. A high sense of justice (2 Sam. xxiii. 3), a noble contempt of gain (1 Sam. xiii. 3), wisdom with lofty courage (Ezek. ii. 6, 7), the enthusiasm of love with the moderation of prudence (2 Cor. vi. 3—10), are the qualities that must be found in them respectively. The sword which is to pierce must first be sharpened ; the intelligence which is to guide must first be enlightened ; the arm which is to prevail must be strengthened ; the spirit which is to triumph over difficulties and obstacles must be awakened, and fed, and sustained. The work to which Gideon was called was no common work. A nation to be upheaved from the lowest vassalage of spiritless slaves and dejected helots into victory and freedom ; another nation to be dragged down from power, and possession, and supremacy, and dominion, with no apparent instruments with which to effect it. And who was Gideon ? The least considered member of a poor family, of a divided tribe, of which no name was famous in the annals of his country ; a man unknown and unheard of, whose occupation was to thresh corn stealthily, lest the Midianites should take it ; a man thought nothing of by his own countrymen, and contemptuously overlooked by his foreign masters. But he was the chosen instrument for delivering Israel. HE MUST THEN BE PREPARED. And two things were necessary in the first place : one *to awaken in him a thorough trust in God ;* the other *to inspire him with a proper trust in himself,* springing from his trust in God. And so the angel began at once with the startling words, "The Lord is with thee." And the answer of doubt and despair from the lips of Gideon was met by a look of God—a turning of God's face upon him, a lifting up of the light of God's countenance upon him, with a power of unutterable grace, and a word of further encouragement: "Go in this thy might ; . . . have not I sent thee?" and again he said, "Surely I will be with thee !" And the scene that followed— the tarrying of the angel till his return with the kid and the unleavened cakes ; the solemn sacrifice on the altar of rock ; the outstretched staff in the angel's hand touching the flesh and the cakes ; the bursting forth of the fire from the rock ; the word of comfort, Peace be unto thee ! and the disappearance of the angel as mysteriously as he came—was all directed to the same end, to work in Gideon's mind the deepest possible conviction that God was with him, and that the whole love and power of the Almighty was on his side.

But it was also necessary to inspire him with a proper trust in himself. As long as he thought of himself only as the drudge of the family, a thresher of wheat, a skulker by the wine-press ; as long as he felt himself one of a degraded caste, as long as he had no hope, no spirit, no sense of having a mission, he would and could do nothing great. The man, the warrior, the captain, the deliverer, the hero, the martyr, must be aroused within him. And so the voice of God addresses him, "The Lord is with thee, thou mighty man of valour. Go in thy might, and thou shalt save Israel from the hand of the Midianites. Surely I will be with thee, and thou shalt smite Midian as one man." And if these words fell, as no doubt they did, upon a spirit already chafed with a sense of his country's degradation ; if burning thoughts of shame and humiliation were smouldering in his mind as he threshed his wheat in secret, trembling at every sound, and casting suspicious glances on every side, for fear some Midianite should be near, how would these words of homage and respect from the mysterious stranger awaken his soul to a new estimate of his place in the world. It was no longer a time to hide, and despair, and complain, and whine, and use the weapons of the weak, guile and subtlety, it was a time to rise, and act, and dare, and risk, and he was the man to be at the head of this new movement. This was Gideon's preparation.

HOMILIES BY VARIOUS AUTHORS.

Vers. 11—15.—*The call of Gideon.* Unexpected by himself and undreamt of by the nation. The whole land is given over to idolatry and wretchedness, but God is at no loss to find his servant. A strong man—a hero, ignominiously concealed, he is a symbol of Israel's helplessness.

I. THE PERSONALITY AND RELATIONS OF GIDEON ARE A REBUKE TO ISRAEL, A VINDICATION OF THE SOVEREIGN WILL OF GOD, AND A REVELATION OF THE SOURCE OF ALL TRUE POWER. He is the youngest scion of an insignificant family in a secondary tribe. Not only has he had no special religious or political training, he is an idolater, or at any rate belongs to an idolatrous family. And he is addressed whilst acting in a manner of which he must have felt ashamed. Hidden, helpless, a sceptic regarding Divine existence or intervention. The culture and religion of Israel are ignored. So God always chooses whom he will to act, to preach, to suffer. There was no danger that Gideon would be credited with the work of deliverance as an achievement of his own originality and innate power.

II. THE OCCASION WAS SIGNIFICANT OF THE HELP GOD INTENDED TO GIVE. He comes when things are at the worst. It was a sign that he would work out a radical deliverance. Not partial help, but complete salvation would be due to him.

III. GIDEON IS AN INSTANCE OF THE POWER OF RELIGIOUS KNOWLEDGE. He has heard in some way or another of God's works in his nation's history. Evidently his thoughts have been occupied with them. A rough interpretation has been arrived at, helping him to grasp the meaning of the situation. His was not total ignorance, but a knowledge preparing for higher revelations and corresponding achievements. Truth smoulders in the mind until it bursts into flame. Inward impressions and realisations of sacred knowledge prepare for the Divinely-arranged circumstances of life, critical moments, and heavenly visitations.

IV. GOD'S MANNER OF DEALING WITH THE DIFFICULTIES AND OBJECTIONS OF HIS INTENDED SERVANT IS VERY INSTRUCTIVE. He accommodates himself to the thoughts passing through Gideon's mind. By his words he drives the brooding mind into distressful paradox. The past achievements of Gideon are remembered, and a corresponding respect shown him. The revelation of himself is gradual. He is considerate, gracious, and painstaking with the heart he intends to make his own. "Have not I sent thee" is sufficient guarantee for God's servant. There ought to be no misgiving when that assurance has been given.—M.

Vers. 12, 13.—*The paradox of the Divine presence.* It has ever been the case that spiritual blessing is hard to be realised in the absence of material prosperity. There is something almost ironical in the contrast between the assertion "Jehovah is with thee," and the actual condition of the person addressed. It was the more inconceivable because of the external nature of the religious sanctions and rewards of the age. Mosaicism abounds in material and temporal blessings. A natural question, then, for Gideon was, "Where are these?" There are many who think very similarly to-day. Are they right or are they wrong? If God be with a man ought he not to prosper? Notice first—

I. THE DIFFICULTY OF GIDEON. It was to reconcile the assurance of God's presence with the signs of actual weakness and distress all around him. There is something very ingenuous in the identification of himself with his people. "Thee" is altered by him to "us." It is full of promise for the future of the hero. He knows of no blessing in which his country does not share. And that is the right temper in which to face all such problems. The glorious past of Israel rose up before his mind's eye. How different from the days in which his lot had fallen! Had God any favour to his people? Why, then, this utter inaction? this absence of all miraculous intervention? If the old records were to be credited God had delivered his people with a "high hand and an outstretched arm;" now to all appearance the heavens had "withdrawn, and become astronomical." And yet how great and immediate the need for God's help! Day by day deeds were wrought under the sun that could not be spoken of. So there are times in these days when crimes are committed, nascent movements of religious and secular moment are withered, and the dial of civilisation is set back. The great calamities of war, pestilence, earthquake, &c., seem to call to heaven, but it is silent. Is it indifferent? Has the hope of man been a dream?

II. HOW IT MAY BE ANSWERED. *Other things being equal,* the blessing of God ought to make rich, and happy, and prosperous. But that is not its chief end in the present. It is first to make right. And God is in the seed as much as in the plant. He has many ways of fulfilling his promises. The blessing of Gideon was a *potential* one. It began even then in him, but it was to be communicated to others. It was as really a blessing for Israel as if the oppressor had been driven from her borders, &c. Spiritual influences begin deeply, secretly, and mysteriously; but they are ere long known by their fruits. God was with Israel repentant in the moment of her repentance. And yet the external evils of her condition were as yet unchecked. God can be with a man in fulness of blessing and help, even when he is poor, and wretched, and helpless; but he will not continue so if he be obedient to the heavenly will. Spiritual blessing then should be expected to show itself, at least first, spiritually and inwardly; and an individual may be the holder of it vicariously for a nation or the race.—M.

Ver. 14.—*The assuring thought of God's servant.* "Have not I sent thee?" This is one of those words by which the saint has often been "strengthened with all might in the inner man." It lifted the heroes of Israel, the reformers, the men of the commonwealth of England, above the common weaknesses of their age and race. "A man, a woman, with a mission"—why not? Some careers are wholly explained by it; some simple achievement critical in history; and many unostentatious, secret services rendered in the Master's name, under the influence of overpowering impulses, more or less transient or permanent.

I. THE LIFE IS THEREBY CONSECRATED AND DIRECTED. A man is not at liberty to follow his own private aims when the heavenly voice speaks thus within him. A higher plane of life and action is thereby created. An unseen influence isolates and consecrates him. This usually imparts greater definiteness to his conduct. He does not " beat the air."

II. THE MOST DIFFICULT DUTIES ARE IN THIS FAITH RENDERED PRACTICABLE. " If God be for us, who can be against us ? " " All things are possible to them that believe." The fatalists of history—Cæsars and Napoleons—have left their mark and proved the strength of a ruling idea. But this conviction is reasonable and of infinite power. The greatest changes the world has seen have been wrought under its influence—apostolic mission, reformation, missionary enterprise at home and abroad, Sunday school origin and extension. And so in the things of the individual life and private sphere.

III. THROUGH ITS INFLUENCE A PRESENT CONSOLATION AND AN ETERNAL REWARD ARE SECURED. Has God sent us ? Then he will take note of our behaviour, and sustain our flagging strength. Has God sent us ? our service cannot be for earthly gain. He is our Master; and as he sends no man " a warfare at his own charges," so the saint is sustained by the hope of the " crown of glory that fadeth not away."—M.

Ver. 17.—*Asking for a sign.* The stranger said, Have not I sent thee ? I will be with thee. Gideon wanted a proof that he was one who had authority, &c., to use such words. That he was a supernatural visitor he suspected; he wanted to be sure. But it was rather to ascertain the reality of his own heavenly calling, which at first he could hardly believe. There was no other evidence open to him; and he asked the evidence peculiar to his epoch. He was altogether different therefore from the Jews of Christ's time, who required a sign, but no sign would be given them, save the sign of the prophet Jonas. They had signs enough already, but had no spiritual perception.

I. THIS REQUEST AROSE NOT FROM WANT OF FAITH, BUT FROM SELF-DISTRUST. Might not this all be a dream ? And who was he himself ? It is the doubt of a mind suspicious of its own sanity, &c. All this argues a deep humility than which nothing could fit him better for the work he has to do. God forgives a desire like this, and answers it; but doubts as to himself and his character, &c., are of another sort.

II. GOD ENCOURAGES ALL TRUE SERVANTS BY SOME TOKEN OF HIS PRESENCE AND HELP. Moses at Horeb; Paul in the temple in his trance—"Depart: for I will send thee far hence unto the Gentiles" (Acts xxii. 21). Many holy men have had such inward urgings and impulses. And all earnest service is accompanied by tokens of the Divine blessing. We are encouraged, therefore, to look for these signs. Their absence ought to cause no concern. Their nature will depend upon the kind of work we are doing.—M.

Vers. 18—21.—*The sign—the present turned into a sacrifice.* The narrative speaks for itself; it is a picture of Eastern hospitality. Gideon's sense of the extraordinary nature of the visit expresses itself in his taking upon himself the duties of servant as well as host, to keep it secret. As the angel said to Manoah, " I will not eat of thy bread" (ch. xiii. 16), so the visitor betrays his true character as an angel of Jehovah in abstaining from the food. Of the phrase " and they did eat" in Gen. xviii. 8, the Targum gives the gloss, " they seemed to him to eat." Angels, not having a corporeal nature, do not require mortal sustenance. But the most striking incident in the narrative is the touching of the flesh and cakes with the angel's staff, and their being consumed by fire from the rock. This circumstance betokened not rejection of the gift, but its acceptance in a higher sense; the present becomes a sacrifice.

I. ALL BEST GIFTS ARE SACRIFICIAL. That which is given in order to a return; from gratification of self-love, ostentation, vanity; from custom; or without any real sense of loss, sacrifice, &c., is not accounted great by generous minds, however intrinsically precious it may be. As the sentiment enhances the value of the gift, even trifling in our eyes, so that which has cost pain, effort, loss of loving hearts, is "above rubies." Personality often thwarts the purpose of a well-intended gift; therefore it has often to be effaced ere the true end is attained.

II. HOW GOD OFTEN DEALS THUS WITH THE GIFTS OF HIS SERVANTS. It is not in a few isolated miracles that this has taken place. The mode of procedure is a principle of his kingdom, and is seen in every true life. 1. In carrying on a spiritual work to unforeseen developments, and so that demands are made the agent did not at first contemplate. Some kinds of spiritual effort are like sinking a shaft for a mine, the ultimate expenditure of labour and means is not ascertainable. That which was almost a pastime becomes a serious task. Consequences are evolved that call for heroism and generous self-devotion. 2. Results which were aimed at in the first instance are withheld, and the labourer has to continue steadfast amidst apparent want of success. 3. The labour itself becomes dear, and enthusiasm makes the greatest efforts easy, and the heaviest burdens light. At first it is "our" work; by-and-bye it is "God's" work. We lose ourselves in the presence of the "not ourselves that maketh for righteousness," who accepts our feeble labours and turns them towards infinite and inconceivable purposes.

III. WHAT IS SUBSERVED BY THIS CONVERSION. 1. It is educative. The subject of it is being taught a nobler life. He is wooed gradually out of the narrow shell of self into the larger atmosphere and arena of Divine love. At first God provokes us to the disinterested passion for himself, then he surprises us into fitting expression of it. The bridges of retreat are cut. 2. Our vague intention is interpreted to our spirits, and is set free. The alchemy of Divine love turns our dross into gold, our water into wine. 3. The permanent utility of man's work is thereby secured. Like the devotion of Christ, it receives an absolute worth in perfected sacrifice.—M.

Vers. 22—24.—*Jehovah Shalom, or spiritual forebodings stilled.* The religious experience of one is often of help to others. At all times has the commerce of man with the unseen taken place; it is a necessary element in his spiritual life. The test of true religion is the sentiment thus awakened.

I. THE NATURAL FEAR OF GOD, AND ITS CAUSE. The sentiment expressed by Gideon a general one, but peculiar to Israelites. The Greek knew not this fear, because his conception of the nature of the gods was different. They were but as men, only more glorious and powerful. To the Israelite God was the Supreme in holiness and authority. Reverence for the character of God deepened into fear, because of the tradition that a visitation such as he now received meant death, either immediate or near at hand, and because of the sense of sin. No man could see God and live. We have the remnant and echoes of this belief still among us, in the fear of supernatural appearances and intimations. It is the dread of the simple, absolute holiness and goodness of God, deepened by our sense of sinfulness. The culprit trembles in presence of the judge. Had Israel rightly served God, this dread would have disappeared. Were men's hearts right with him, they would welcome his presence and prize his visitations.

II. THE WHISPER OF PEACE. It is a token of good-will. The terror which overcame the strong man is allayed. Christ gives a deeper tranquillity. He fills the breast with the sense of spiritual reconciliation—"the peace of God which passeth all understanding." And this is felt in the trial hours of life, and in the agony of dying. It steadies and evens the spirit amidst the most afflicting circumstances. In conversion the fear of the sinner under conviction is often intense. But who shall tell the rapture when peace is found?

III. THE MEMORIAL. How fitting that it should be commemorated, and by such a symbol! The altar is the meeting-place of man and God. The monument. The church. It told to others of an individual, secret transaction and experience. Here was won a victory over self, a triumph of duty more signal than Marathon, Bannockburn, or Morgarten. It is well to tell men of God's mercies to us; and this intimation was an eloquent appeal to men to draw near and receive a like blessing.—M.

Vers. 11—14.—*Diffidence.* Gideon was a great and gifted man who distrusted his own powers, and was in danger of failing to follow his true vocation through modest diffidence. When the angel accosted him as a "mighty man of valour," the expression overwhelmed him with astonishment. It came upon him as a new revelation. While there are conceited persons who value themselves too highly, and are over-ready to undertake rash enterprises for which they are quite incompetent, there are also good and able men like Gideon who are not aware of their own powers, and are in danger of neglecting the high trusts God has committed to them from self-distrust and modesty.

I. THE GROUNDS OF DIFFIDENCE. 1. *Adversity.* Gideon could not believe in the presence of God and the possibility of relief for his country, because the troubles of the time seemed to preclude all hope. We are tempted to distrust while the prospect is dark. Yet God is often nearest to us when the distress is deepest. 2. *The absence of any sign of God's presence.* Gideon saw no miracle, and he could not discern the presence of God in less striking events. As sensationalism in religion is a dissipation which unfits the soul for quiet, natural modes of worship, so the habit of depending on marvels and prodigies for faith in Divine truth weakens the sense of the Divine in the calm and orderly movements of nature and providence. 3. *Lowly circumstances.* Gideon considered himself the least important member of a poor and obscure family (ver. 15). Possibly he was despised in the household for his retiring habits. Men are often taken at their own estimate of themselves until their true character is put to the test. A man's own relatives are sometimes the last to recognise his merits. We are all more or less influenced by surrounding circumstances, and given too much to judge by appearances.

II. THE MEANS FOR OVERCOMING DIFFIDENCE. 1. *God knows his servants' true nature and powers.* He takes no note of outward appearances. Rank, riches or poverty, family honour, count for little with him. He seeks out the right man wherever he is to be found—at the threshing-floor, by the sheep-fold, in the fishing-boat. God never calls any man to any task for which the man does not possess the requisite talents. 2. *God is with his servants when they are obeying his voice.* He never calls a man to a special task without giving him special grace to perform it. If he commands his servant to undertake a difficult mission, he is certain to go with him and stand by him in the time of need. Diffidence comes from regarding self; true confidence from looking away to God. So Moses was diffident as he thought of his own weakness, but made brave to face Pharaoh by the assurance of God's presence (Exod. iii. 11, 12); and Paul dared to stand alone before Cæsar with confidence because "the Lord stood with" him (2 Tim. iv. 17). 3. *God sometimes uses special means to confirm the faith of his servants.* Gideon asked for a sign, and it was given him. To some no sign can be granted (Matt. xii. 39). If no special signs are granted us now, we should remember (1) we are not called to Gideon's work, and (2) we are not left in the religious obscurity of Gideon's age, but have the revelation of God in Christ, the greatest of "signs."—A.

EXPOSITION.

Ver. 25.—**The same night,** &c. The iron was hot; it was time to strike. As regards what follows, there are two ways of understanding the verse. One, that of the A. V., supposes that only one bullock is spoken of, and that "the young bullock" belonging to Joash is further described as "even the second bullock of seven years old;" to which it is objected that a bullock of seven years old is not "a young bullock," "the bullock of an ox," as the Hebrew phrase is, and that there is no explanation of the meaning of "the second bullock;" and that the Hebrew manifestly describes two bullocks: (1) Joash's young bullock, and (2) the bullock of seven years old. The other supposes two bullocks, and instead of *even* has the more natural rendering *and.* The

only objection to this, by far the most natural rendering, is that Gideon is not told what to do with the first bullock. But it is a simple explanation that the two bullocks were used in the laborious work of demolishing the altar of Baal, and removing the earth and the stone to build the altar of the Lord, and that when the work was finished one of the bullocks—the seven-year-old—was sacrificed. For **the grove** see ch. iii. 7, note.

Ver. 26.—**This rock.** Rather, *the keep* or *stronghold* of Ophrah, where also the high place was; just as the temple was in the stronghold of Zion, and the hold of the house of Baal-Berith at Shechem was in the citadel of the place (ch. ix. 46). **In the ordered place.** The meaning of this phrase is uncertain. It may either be rendered as in the A.V., meaning on the levelled ground ordered and prepared for the building of the altar ; or it may more probably be rendered *with the arranged material,* i. e. the stones which were laid in order at the bottom, and the wood which was laid in order upon the top of the altar (cf. Gen. xxii. 9). *The material* may either refer to that taken from the altar of Baal, which had been thrown down, and which was then ordered to be used in building the altar of the Lord, or to its own *arranged material* or *superstructure,* the wood of the *asherah.*

Ver. 27.—**Then,** *i. e.* the next night. He would have done it the next day; but even his father's household, as well as the men of Ophrah generally, were so infected with the idolatry of the times, that he was afraid of being interrupted by violence.

Ver. 28.—**The grove.** See ver. 25. **The second bullock.** There must be some special meaning in this description, *the second.* Can it refer to his place in the team, the young

bullock being the leader, *the first,* and the seven-year-old the wheeler, *the second ?*

Ver. 29.—**They said, Gideon hath,** &c. No doubt one of the ten servants (ver. 27) employed by him had spoken about it.

Ver. 31.—**Stood against him.** The words describe their hostile, menacing, attitude, clamouring to have Gideon brought out that they might kill him. **Will ye plead,** &c. The emphasis is on the *ye.* Joash met and silenced their pleading by threatening death to any that should plead for Baal. Baal shall plead for himself. Joash's courage was rising under the influence of his son's brave deed.

Ver. 32.—**Jerubbaal,** i. e. *Jarov Baal,* let Baal plead. In ch. vii. 1 ; viii. 29, 35 ; ix. 1, &c., *Jerubbaal* is used as the synonym of *Gideon,* just as in English history Cœur de Lion is used as a synonym for Richard. The name *Jerubbaal* appears as *Jerubbesheth ; besheth* or *bosheth,* meaning *shame,* i. e. a shameful idol, being substituted for *Baal,* as in the name *Ishbosheth,* for *Eshbaal* (see 2 Sam. ii. 8 ; 1 Chron. viii. 33).

HOMILETICS.

Vers. 25—32.—*The action commenced.* Idolatry was the evil which Israel had done in the sight of the Lord. Idolatry was the sin which had brought upon Israel the terrible Midianite servitude. The hour of deliverance had come, but it must be the hour of repentance too. And repentance must be in deed, not in word. Baal must be cast off before the Lord would go forth with their armies. The first blow in the great contest that was coming on must be a blow struck against Baal-worship, and then the Lord would strike a blow against Midian. And so we see the mighty man of valour, who had been prepared for his work by his interview with the angel of the Lord, and who was to sweep the Midianite locusts from off the soil of his beloved country, commence his work as a bold religious reformer. How could he fight the battles of Israel while the altar of Baal crowned the heights of his native city? how could he call upon the Lord to help him while the shameful abomination stood up to testify against his own flesh and blood? And so his action began with a deed as bold as that of Luther when he burnt the Papal bull in the sight of all the people. While men were asleep, little dreaming of what was about to happen, he rose from his bed, called ten of his servants to him, and, marching straight up to the altar of Baal, surrounded as it was with awe and superstition, he threw it down. He cut down the statue or pillar of Ashtoreth, and before the morning light shone upon Ophrah, the altar of Jehovah was smoking with its whole burnt offering as openly and as conspicuously as the altar of Baal had done. It was with amazement that the men of the city saw the great altar of their god levelled to the ground, and a new altar standing in the sacred inclosure. But Gideon nearly paid for his holy boldness with his life, and his great work was well-nigh nipped in the bud ; for when it transpired that he had thrown down the altar, there arose a cry for his blood. The angry idolaters surrounded the house of Joash, and demanded that Gideon should be brought out to them, that they might slay him and avenge the insult done to their god. It was a critical moment, and Gideon's life hung upon a thread. But God had a work for him to do, just as he had for Peter when Herod put him in prison and sought to kill him. and so he was not suffered to fall into their hands. His father's happy word, Let Baal plead for himself, was caught up by the people, and all thoughts of punishing Gideon seem to have gone out like a candle before a puff of wind. He was now free to pursue his great enterprise. But here we may pause for a moment to read some great lessons to ourselves. *We dare not enter upon any*

work for God while any known sin is casting its deadly shade upon us. Are you
seeking to do something for God ? begin by plucking out the right eye that offends,
by throwing down the altar of the false god within you.   Lay the axe to the root of
the tree, and at any risk or cost clear yourself of complicity with sin.   Then you
may begin your work.   Again, *be bold in a right cause ;* do not quail before risk
and danger, because no great work was ever done without it ; and if our work is of
God, dangers will fade away before his Almighty help.   God can brush away the
difficulties and hindrances that threaten us, like cobwebs.   Again, remember that
nothing creates enthusiasm and attracts companions so much as courage and daring.
The timid may work single-handed all their lives ; but a leader "bold and brave"
never lacks followers.   There is excitement in bold action, and courage commands
confidence.   Beyond a doubt "the boldness of Peter and John" (Acts iv. 13) was
one of the things that helped to build up the Church in those days of danger and
persecution.   St. Paul's unflinching courage in the face of Jews and Gentiles was a
great power in his missionary work.   The fearless attitude of Luther and of the
English Reformers before all the power of Pope and priests and the civil sword
breathed a spirit of untameable resolution into the hearts of their followers.   And so it
always has been, and always will be.   Boldness of action springing from deep conviction of truth is the surest presage of success.   Let us learn to be courageous
in every good thing ; not flinching from dangers, or shirking consequences, or hanging back in cowardly delay, when once our judgment is clear of what is right to be
done.   Then may we hope to lead others and to stir up many to help in the good
cause of truth and righteousness.   Enthusiasm, decision, and courage, coupled with
a sound mind, are among the great wants of our day.

HOMILIES BY VARIOUS AUTHORS.

Vers. 25—30. — *The first work.*   The training of Gideon has now fairly commenced, and it is not allowed to lag.   There is no interval between command and
execution.   The growth of Gideon's spiritual character is gradual, and there is a
beautiful fitness in each step ; but it is also rapid and decisive.

I. IT IS A RELIGIOUS WORK OF INDIVIDUAL AND NATIONAL CONSEQUENCE.   An idolatrous altar to be razed, an altar to the true God to be reared.   The plan of the altar
of Baal was different from that of the altar of Jehovah, and could not be mistaken
for it.   The whole neighbourhood knew.   How many such substitutions are taking
place every day—the symbol of wickedness and unbelief giving place to that of
faith.   Our works are our true words to men.   Much of the Christian religion consists in witnessing.   There cannot be too marked a contrast, if it be real.   A
religious revolution of the most radical description took place.   The whole question
of religion was once more raised, and settled otherwise.

II. IT WAS A COMPLETE WORK.   Not only destruction, but construction ; negative
and positive.   All true witnessing should be such.   Negative criticism merely is
mischievous.   It is not enough to declare ourselves by abstention and inaction, or
by rebuke and captious judgment ; we must do the works of God.   We must build
as well as destroy.

III. IT WAS A TEST OF HIS SINCERITY.   1. *It committed Gideon.*   There could
be no drawing back.   It was a challenge to the whole people.   The hill-top was
seen from afar.   2. *It required energy.*   No slight task even as a manual labour.
Organisation, leadership, vigorous and timely effort were necessary.   3. *Courage
was demanded.*   A new beginning, a great reform, had to be made.   Difficult to
take the initiative.   Many reasons could have been found for conformity to established usages.   The most rancorous hatred would be at once aroused.   Only high
faith and clear, Heaven-informed purpose could have secured his success.

III. IT WAS A PERSONAL, IMMEDIATE, AND DOMESTIC WORK.   Joash, infirm as his
faith in Baal was, was responsible for the erection and maintenance of the altar of
Baal.   The worship was popular, and he patronised it.   That had to be publicly
retracted.   How near at hand was the field of Gideon's first work !   His own life had to
be openly changed ; his home had to witness his zeal for God.   There are many
who profess to be at a loss for something by which to testify their love for God and

righteousness. Let them do righteously, love mercy, and walk humbly before God, and there will soon be disturbance and persecution. Our own homes are to be the scenes of our first obedience. What have we done there? And although, apparently, a day intervened between the vision and the work of demolition, yet no time was lost. The first fitting opportunity is sought and utilised, and the interval is occupied with the necessary preparations. So God expects prompt obedience from all his children. The smoke of that new altar—how much it signified! Are we yet his? Let us lose no time in giving our hearts to him. What is our record? Let our deeds speak for us. Time is short.—M.

Vers. 29, 30.—*Who hath done this thing?* A frequent inquiry. A natural curiosity—to trace up to causes; a religious rancour—to visit punishment upon the author.

I. THE WORLD TAKES NOTE OF THE ACTIONS AND LIVES OF THE RIGHTEOUS. The effects of religion are ever an astonishment, a delight or a vexation. There is something in them that piques curiosity and rouses interest. Men tried to explain Christ. Religious questions ever the most keenly discussed.

II. THE REASON OF THIS IS IN THE VITAL IMPORTANCE OF THE QUESTIONS INVOLVED. Temporal convenience and interests are compromised. The craftsmen of Ephesus. Life and death eternal depend upon our conduct here. Christians are a reproof to the unfruitful works of darkness.

III. IT IS WELL WHEN OUR DEEDS ARE INQUIRED ABOUT THAT THEY SHOULD BE GOOD, AND NOT EVIL. The detective usually tracks the criminal. How much better so to act that we shall not fear when men discover our works. So act that when revelation comes " they may be ashamed who falsely accuse our good conversation in Christ." To our own Master we stand or fall. In that day we shall not heed the judgments of men.—M.

Vers. 31, 32.—*Jerubbaal, or, Is an idol anything?* How mighty the work was Gideon had wrought at once appeared from its effects. His father is won over, and so argues for him that the Abi-ezrites are first silenced, and then converted. The nickname of Gideon showed the process of the change.

I. THE GRAND ARGUMENT AGAINST IDOLATRY. Isaiah (ch. xliv.) expresses the contempt of the true Israelite for idols. But no one has formulated the argument better than Joash. It is as forcible to-day in India and Africa as in the days of Gideon. The same is true of the world-powers and principles idols represent.

II. THE LIVING WITNESS TO THE FORCE OF THIS ARGUMENT. No monument could equal himself. It was an instance of a man against a god—yea, against all the gods of heathenism. A heathen convert is such a witness. And the heroes of faith are the grand arguments against the evil principles and influences they overthrew and survived. The gospel reveals an extended view of the same question, beyond death and the grave ; " Fear not them which kill the body," &c.—M.

Vers. 25, 26.—*Gideon the iconoclast.* I. REFORMATION MUST PRECEDE DELIVER-ANCE. As the prophet of repentance appeared before Gideon the deliverer, so even Gideon did not undertake the work of fighting the Midianites until he had first effected a religious reformation among his own people. It is vain to treat symptoms when the radical seat of a disease is untouched. Spiritual apostasy had brought on Israel national humiliation. The distress could not be safely relieved till the sin was destroyed. God will not deliver us from the trouble into which sin has brought us before we begin to turn from the wicked course which made the trouble a necessary chastisement. It is true that under the gospel we are not made to wait for the return of Divine favour until all sin is destroyed. On the contrary, it is one great characteristic of this new dispensation of mercy that restoration to the favour of God does not wait for, but precedes, and is the chief cause of, a perfect reformation of life. Nevertheless, (1) this is only possible after *repentance,* which is the turn-ing from sin in desire, and (2) when accompanied by *faith in Christ* as both Master and Saviour, which implies submission to his will, and carries the prophecy of a new life inseparably connected with the spiritual fruits of faith (Acts iii. 26).

II. REFORMATION BEGINS WITH THE DESTRUCTION OF EVIL. Gideon's first work is to destroy the altar and idol of false worship. To wrench out the stones of the massive altar of Baal and tear up the "Asherah" was no easy work; yet it was necessary. It is pleasant to prophesy smooth things, and we should prefer to trust entirely to the power of light to dispel the darkness, of life to overcome death, of the gospel of peace to supplant all forms of evil. But it is not possible to succeed by this means alone. Evil must be exposed, challenged, resisted, overthrown. Sin must be rebuked ; wrong practices must be directly thwarted and frustrated. This implies aggressive action on the part of the Church, and long, arduous, united efforts to throw down the great structures of sinful institutions, and uproot inveterate habits of vice and crime. Intemperance, commercial dishonesty, religious hypocrisy, &c., must be directly met and fought by practical agencies suited to cope with the strength and size of great national sins.

III. REFORMATION IS NOT COMPLETE WITHOUT THE SUCCESSFUL ESTABLISHMENT OF A NEW AND BETTER ORDER. Gideon's reforming work is not complete when he has thrown down the emblems and instruments of idolatry. This is but half his work. He must next erect an altar to the true God and sacrifice thereon. The danger of every attempted reformation is lest it should stay with the work of destruction—lest the iconoclast should not be also a *re*former. It is more easy to throw down than to rebuild. The passions of the destroyer are not always joined to the patient, calm wisdom and energy of the renovator. Yet it is vain to cast out the evil spirit unless we fill the place of it with a better spirit (Matt. xii. 43—45). Mere negative Protestantism, negative temperance, negative anti-war movements are likely to lead to abortive issues unless they are supplemented by influences which promote and establish positive good. Conviction of sin must be followed by the creation of a new heart if the future life is to be pure (Ps. li. 10).—A.

EXPOSITION.

Ver. 33.—**The Midianites**, &c. See ver. 3, note. **The valley of Jezreel.** Rather, *the plain,* "the great plain of Esdraelon," as the Book of Judith styles it (Judith i. 8 ; see ch. iv. 13, note). The great plain of Jezreel, or Esdraelon (which is the Greek form of the name), through which the Kishon flows, is eight hours in length from east to west, and five hours (twelve miles) in breadth from north to south. It is described as "a very extensive and fertile plain shut in between the mountain ranges of Samaria and Mount Carmel on the south, and of Galilee on the north," and extending from the Mediterranean at the Gulf of *Caipha,* or *Haipha,* to the valley of the Jordan. The access to it from the fords of Jordan in the neighbourhood of Bethshan (or *Beishan,* called by the Greeks *Scythopolis*) made it the natural place for invasion by the wild tribes east of Jordan, as it is to this day. Particular parts of this great plain are called "the valley of Megiddo" and "the plain of Samaria." For a full account of the plain of Esdraelon see Stanley, 'Sinai and Palestine,' ch. ix. **Went over,** *i. e.* crossed the Jordan. It appears from vers. 3—5 that these invasions were repeated at certain seasons. When they had plundered all they could get, and eaten up all the produce of the land, they would go back for a while to their own country east of Jordan, and then return again. So they did

now, but they met with a different reception this time.

Ver. 34.—**The Spirit of the Lord,** &c. See ch. iii. 10 ; xi. 29 ; xiii. 25 ; xiv. 6, 19 ; cf. Isa. xi. 2 ; lxi. 1 ; John xx. 22 ; Acts xiii. 2 ; xx. 28 ; and 1 Cor. xii. 4. **Abi-ezer.** His own family (ver. 11 ; see Josh. xvii. 2). In Numb. xxvi. 30 the name appears as *Jeezer,* by a very defective transliteration— *Aiezer* represents the Hebrew letters. The *b* has probably fallen out by accident. Here we have the immediate fruit of Gideon's daring in the cause of God. The whole family of Abi-ezer, numbering probably thousands, sprang to his side.

Ver. 35.—**He sent messengers,** &c. Manasseh, Asher, Zebulun, and Naphtali were the adjacent tribes—Manasseh (*i. e.* the half tribe of Manasseh, west of Jordan) on the south, Asher on the west, and Zebulun and Naphtali on the north. Three of these were the very tribes who had fought under Barak, and it is pleasing to see Asher now joined with them instead of abiding in his breaches. This ready compliance with the call was the consequence of the Spirit of the Lord being upon Gideon. **Came up.** No doubt Gideon was encamped upon one of the southern hills that overlooked the plain, probably Gilboa, just as Barak was on Mount Tabor (see ch. viii. 8—12). **To meet them,** *i. e.* Gideon and the Abi-ezrites.

Ver. 36.—**If thou wilt save**, &c. There is something touching in Gideon's diffidence of himself, even now that he found himself at the head of a large force. The thought that he was "the least in his father's house" seems still to possess him, and he can hardly believe it possible that he is to save Israel. In his humility he craves a sign that he is indeed chosen and called.

Vers. 37—40.—It is difficult to guess what led to this somewhat quaint sign which Gideon asked. Possibly the dews were usually heavy upon the hill of Gilead (ch. vii. 3, note) where Gideon was encamped, as they seem to have been on Mount Gilboa (2 Sam. i. 21) and on Hermon (Ps. cxxxiii. 3), and sheep-skins may have been a common protection against the cold nights, as in Afghanistan; and he may have noticed how often in the morning both the skin that covered him, and the ground around, was wet with the heavy dew. And this may have suggested the double test, by which his faith was, through God's condescending mercy, confirmed and established.

HOMILETICS.

Vers. 33—40.—*The Divine side of human history.* This section reveals an extraordinary change in the whole aspect of things in Israel. At the beginning of the chapter we see the people utterly cowed before their enemies, skulking in caves and dens and hiding-places, while their insolent masters take possession of their land, their food, their substance, and all that they had. For seven years had this state of things endured. It had become a matter of course that, when the season came, the Midianites and their allies should swarm across the Jordan, cover the land, devour everything, stay as long as they pleased, and then return unresisted to their own country. But at the close of the chapter a change, like the sudden melting of the snow in the spring, has taken place. There are indeed the same Midianite hosts, "like grasshoppers for multitude, and their camels without number, as the sand by the sea side for multitude" (ch. vii. 12); there are the same kings in all their pride of power, and the same princes as greedy as ravens for their prey, and as hungry as wolves in pursuit of the spoil (ch. vii. 25, note). But when they have reached the well-known plain of Jezreel, instead of tame submission, instead of the frightened people running like rabbits to their holes, they find a nation in arms. Manasseh was up and in the field; Naphtali and Zebulun had flocked armed to the national standard; Asher had answered the call of the trumpet; and 32,000 men were at the feet of their leader. Instead of running, hiding, and yielding, there was arming, and combining, and defiance throughout the land. Now what was the cause of this great change? The respective numbers of the Midianites and Israelites were the same, the respective qualities of the nations were the same, the shape of the ground was the same, the resources of the two peoples were the same; whence the difference? The difference lay in the motive power of the will of God. Before, his will was to give Israel up into the hands of Midian to punish their idolatry; now, his will was to deliver them on their true repentance. It is just the lesson taught by the prophet Isaiah in the sublime message which he delivered to Sennacherib: "Hast thou not heard long ago, how I have done it; and of ancient times, that I have formed it? now have I brought it to pass that thou shouldest be to lay waste fenced cities into ruinous heaps. Therefore their inhabitants were of small power, they were dismayed and confounded: they were as the grass of the field, and as the green herb, as the grass on the house-tops, and as corn blasted before it be grown up." What regulates the world is the motive power of the will of God acting upon and through the wills and the capacities of men. There are in the men virtue, courage, sagacity, ability, prudence, wisdom, counsel, on the one hand; or meanness, cowardice, blindness, weakness, rashness, folly, inconsequence, on the other; and these qualities have each their own proper force and momentum; but it is the will of God which gives to them their direction and their results. It is to be noted too that God in his providence raises the instruments and gives the qualities which are to accomplish his will. As was observed before, God's agents are reasonable men, and it is by their great qualities that they accomplish the work committed to them. But who gives them those great qualities? How came Abraham, and Joseph, and Moses, and Samuel, and David, and Judas Maccabeus to appear on the world's stage just when they did? It is very true that Abraham's faith, and

Joseph's prudence, and the wisdom of Moses, and the integrity of Samuel, and the heroism of David and Judas accomplished those great results at critical moments in their country's history which have made their names famous for ever. And if we are looking at events on their human side, it is quite true to say that Abraham founded the Hebrew race, and that David founded the Jewish monarchy, and Judas rescued his country from destruction. But it is of supreme importance, if we would see God in history, and in the history of our own times in particular, to recognise in the sages, and heroes, and reformers, and also in the philosophers, and discoverers, and inventors, whose several labours have changed the aspect of the world at particular epochs, God's special instruments sent for that very thing ; and to recognise in the changes brought about, not merely the action of those instruments, but the results of the will of God. As long as God is pleased to preserve a nation in greatness and power, he continues to raise up among them warriors, divines, men of genius, and statesmen. When the set time of decadence is come there arise no great men among them ; their mighty men become as women (Jer. li. 30), and counsel perishes from the wise (*ibid.* xviii. 18). In applying these truths to our own Church and country it behoves us to remember that we owe all our own national prosperity, both in spiritual and temporal things, to the undeserved mercy of God ; that the continuance of that prosperity depends upon the continuance of his favour ; and that the only way by which to preserve that favour is to walk in righteousness and godliness. Unless God wills to maintain our power and greatness among the nations, all the courage and policy in the world will not suffice to do so ; and even courage and policy may cease to grow among us. The example of Gideon further teaches us that boldness on God's side is the prelude of triumph over foes, and that what makes leaders of the right stamp is their investiture by the Holy Spirit of God.

HOMILIES BY VARIOUS AUTHORS.

Vers. 33—40.—*The crisis and the confirmation.* Gideon's first task demanded moral rather than physical courage. It was restricted in its sphere. It witnessed to the principle that sin must be removed ere national or individual calamities can be permanently cured, or God's help vouchsafed. The stage now clears for the larger life and wider influence. I. THE ENEMY PRESENTS HIMSELF IN SUDDEN, OVERWHELMING FORCE. A remarkable juncture. Esdraelon, the battle-field of Canaan. Here thrones and kingdoms had been lost and won. To the heart of flesh it would have been the death-knell of hope. There was no proportion between the extent of his possible preparation and the magnitude of the crisis. Many would have advised a policy of temporizing inaction. To the sent of God the circumstances pointed all the other way. Elijah at Horeb. Paul at Athens. The Son of man longing for his "hour." Are you in a minority ; the only Christian in your office ; with everything to discourage and tempt you ? "Let not your heart be troubled." Outward difficulties are balanced and overpowered by spiritual reinforcements. "The Spirit of the Lord came upon him." II. GIDEON'S SUMMONS TO ARMS MEETS WITH UNEXPECTED SUCCESS. "He blew a trumpet," *i. e.* he used the means. But probably he did not expect anything like the result. He was touching chords that vibrated in unforeseen directions. He didn't know the moral power he had acquired by his first work. We never can gauge the extent of our moral influence. Jerubbaal is the magnet. Strong in God, in himself, at home, throughout the nation. We are all guilty herein ; we think God's people fewer and worse than they are. How much one steadfast, heroic soul can effect ; how many others he can fire with enthusiasm and endue with courage by his example and actions ! III. SUDDEN SUCCESS OCCASIONS HUMILITY AND DOUBT. Clearly this man is not as others. He becomes strong against odds and vast oppositions, weak and hesitating when all goes well. Adversity and difficulty are plainer in their problems to the spiritual man than prosperity. But perhaps it was the quality of his soldiery he mistrusted. They did not seem of the right stuff for a duel *à outrance.* Perhaps the very suddenness of his power terrified him. IV. HE SEEKS FOR WISDOM AND CONFIRMATION OF THE HEAVENLY GRACE. 1. *Pro-*

bably the very scene of his first vision. Association helps an imaginative spirit. Spiritual associations are mightiest. 2. *He proposes a sign that shall reveal his duty.* Under ordinary circumstances this is dangerous and misleading. But the whole background of Gideon's career is miraculous, and he had a warrant to expect miracles. We have a complete revelation and a Divine example. The dew abundant in Canaan; the wetting of the fleece a rustic idea. The doubt is then suggested, What if all this be natural? Therefore—3. *The proof is reversed.* As in experimental science the test of variations is employed, so here in spiritual divination. God accommodates himself to our weakness that he may vanquish it. Henceforth the path is clear and his mind is made up. Have we done all that conscience and revelation have made plain and obligatory? Have we gone to the Divine footstool for the wisdom and strength we required?—M.

EXPOSITION.

CHAPTER VII.

Ver. 1.—**Jerubbaal.** The mention of this name seems intended to keep before our minds that it is emphatically the servant of the Lord who is going forth to victory. **The well of Harod,** i. e. of *trembling,* so called, no doubt, from the incident recorded in ver. 3, that every one who was *afraid* (Hebrew, *hared*) departed from Mount Gilead. The well of *Harod* is not mentioned elsewhere; though two of David's mighty men are called Harodites (2 Sam. xxiii. 25); but it is thought to be identical with "the fountain which is in Jezreel" (1 Sam. xxix. 1), on the slope of Mount Gilboa, and now called *Ain Jahlood,* the spring of Goliath. **On the north side,** &c. Gideon and his Abi-ezrites were naturally on the south side of the plain, on the hill, apparently Mount Gilboa, which there shuts in the plain. The Midianite host was encamped to the north of him (so it is in the Hebrew), in the valley, i. e. the plain of Jezreel (ch. vi. 33, note). **By the hill of Moreh.** Nowhere else mentioned; probably only a hillock, of which there are many in that part of the plain.

Ver. 2.—**And the Lord said,** &c. It must be remembered that this whole movement was essentially a religious one. It began with prayer (ch. vi. 6, 7), it was followed up by repentance (ch. vi. 27, 28), and the great purpose of it was to turn the hearts of the nation back to the God of their fathers. The Lord himself, therefore, graciously forwarded this end by making it plain that the deliverance from their oppression was his work, and his only. For the general sentiment compare Deut. viii. 10—18; Ps. xliv. 3—8; Zech. iii. 6, &c.

Ver. 3. — **Depart early.** The Hebrew word so rendered only occurs here. Its exact meaning is uncertain, but the old versions generally give the meaning of "depart," "go back." Some, with much probability, connect the word with the Hebrew for a sparrow, and give the sense of "fly-

ing," i. e. returning in haste. The sense of "early" expressed in the A. V. does not seem to be any part of the meaning of the word. See Deut. xx. 8 for the form of the proclamation. **From Mount Gilead.** These words cannot be explained with certainty. The conjectures are—1. That there may have been a Mount Gilead on the western side of Jordan, on which Gideon's army was encamped, though it is not elsewhere mentioned. 2. That *Gilead* is a transcriber's error for *Gilboa,* which only differs by one letter in Hebrew. It is pretty certain that Gideon was encamped on Mount Gilboa. 3. That the phrase was the *formula* used by the whole tribe of Manasseh, on the west as well as on the east of Jordan, although properly applying only to those on the east. 4. Some (reading *maher,* in haste, for *mehar,* from the mount) render "let him return in haste to Gilead," i. e. to his home.

Vers. 5, 6.—**The water,** viz., of the well or spring of Harod. **That lappeth,** &c. It showed a much more soldierly and self-controlled spirit just to quench the thirst by lapping the water out of the palm of the hand, than to kneel down and drink without stint out of the spring itself. The Lord saw the difference of character indicated by the two actions, and chose his instruments accordingly.

Ver. 7. — **By the three hundred,** &c. Compare the saying of Jonathan, "There is no restraint to the Lord to save by many or by few" (1 Sam. xiv. 6). The same principles which run through the choice of God's instruments on other occasions appear here. The instruments are to be such in quality or in quantity as to make it quite manifest that the excellency of the power is God's, not man's; and yet the instruments themselves are to be conspicuous for their rare excellence. The shepherd boy who sat on the throne of Israel was manifestly made to sit on that throne by the appointment of God; but what a ruler, what a noble character David was! It has always been deemed one of the proofs of the Divine origin of Christianity that its ʃapostles were men of such humble station, and yet were able to change the whole religion and morality of the world; and yet what noble stuff Peter and John and Paul were made of! And so here the overthrow of the hosts of Midian by three hundred Israelites was manifestly the effect of the power of God fighting on their behalf. But yet what marvellous heroism was there in those three hundred! what strength of purpose, what iron-firmness of nerve, to see above thirty thousand of their comrades leave them in the face of the myriads of their foes; to remain quietly at their post, and, when the time came, to leave their camp and pour down into the plain. Their self-possession and self-restraint and absence of

self-indulgence in the matter of the water was a true index of the unequalled qualities which they displayed in the sequel.

Ver 8.—**So the people took,** &c. It is almost certain that the passage ought to be rendered, " And they took the victuals of the people in their hands, and their trumpets," *i. e.* the three hundred took or borrowed what provisions they needed for a few days, and the trumpets, which were to play an important part in the stratagem, from the people who were about to return to their homes. **And the host of Midian,** &c. The writer repeats this to give a perfect picture of the situation. The whole army returned to their homes; the three hundred alone with Gideon in the camp; the Midianite host in the plain beneath.

HOMILETICS.

Vers. 1—8.—*The sifting.* When we consider the extraordinary reduction of Gideon's army from 32,000 to 300 by a process of winnowing, not merely as an isolated fact, but as a portion of the instruction of God's word, we are at once struck with its analogy, in principle, to other broad teachings of the same Scriptures. Let us first consider the case before us, and then compare with it the analogies to which we allude.

I. In a great emergency, at the call of Gideon, 32,000 men with much apparent devotion flocked to his standard. Leaving their homes and their families and their substance, they came forward willingly to meet danger and to endure hardship. To all outward appearance they were all animated by the same spirit, and might alike be credited with a resolution to die for their country and for their faith. But by and by a test was proposed: " Whoever is fearful and afraid, let him return and depart;" and forthwith more than two-thirds of that band shrank from the undertaking. Their hearts failed them; they thought of their homes left unprotected, they thought of the dreadful Midianites and Amalekites and children of the East, so numerous, so fierce, and so irresistible; their faith in God was a dead letter; the shame of deserting their comrades was not sufficient to restrain them; they left the camp and returned, 22,000 in number, to their own homes. But 10,000 remained true to the cause. These faced the danger and stood firm. Another test was then proposed, which should go much deeper, and sift the very choicest spirits from those of more ordinary mould. Of the 10,000 that remained, only 300 were found whose rigid self-denial, and stern self-discipline, and self-possessed presence of mind, showed them to be of that stamp which was necessary for a hazardous undertaking requiring boldness, endurance, watchfulness, and perseverance to insure success. And these 300 elect were accordingly retained to do the work alone; and they did it.

II. Now this is in accordance with THE ANALOGIES both of nature and of Holy Scripture. Take the creation of mankind viewed as intended to glorify God by the proper exercise of the splendid gifts bestowed upon them. Sift them first through a coarse sieve which will only separate the grossly wicked and ungodly, and yet what a large number will thus be found to come short of the purpose for which they were created. If all the irreligious, all the evil livers, all the impure and violent and unjust among mankind, stand separate, what a comparatively small number will remain who seem true to the end of their being, even in outward appearance and in the rough! But if we go on further to sift with a finer sieve, so as to separate the careless, and the selfish, and the worldly, and the hypocrites, and the lukewarm, and so on, and so as to isolate the true saints of God, the little flock, the faithful followers of the Lamb, those who shall shine as the sun in the kingdom of their Father, and be to him for a name and a praise, alas, how will the number be reduced! Apply the same method to Israel. The seed of Abraham were separated from the rest of mankind to be God's peculiar people, to fulfil a special purpose in the world as witnesses for God's unity and truth. But, as St. Paul teaches us, "they are not all Israel, which are of Israel: neither, because they are the seed of Abraham, are they all children: but, In Isaac shall thy seed be called." There be many called but few chosen. There were the multitude, a disobedient and gainsaying people; and there was the remnant according to the election of grace, who believed the gospel, and who trusted in the promised Messiah and obeyed his voice. Or take the parable of the sower. One lot of seed falls by the wayside, and the fowls of the air devour it; another lot falls on the rock, and is soon burnt up by the scorching sun; a third is choked by the thorns, and brings no fruit to perfection; it is only one quarter of the seed sown that falls on good ground, and brings forth fruit with patience. Any one looking at the whole sample would have thought it all destined to be fruitful; but lo! only one fourth part comes to anything.

Now it is important to note this:—1. *With a view to ourselves, that we may sift ourselves before any winnowing of God comes unawares upon us.* There are states of the world, or states of society, or conditions of outward circumstances, when the grain and the chaff, the wheat and the tares, the good fish and the bad, all pass muster, and there is no marked difference between them. Gideon's 32,000 all pass for good men and true. There come changes of circumstances, there comes a winnowing of God, events and situations which try men, which test their character, which put their faith, their integrity, their sincerity, their conscientiousness, their principles, to the proof, and presently of the 32,000 only 300 stand firm. Now it is a matter of infinite moment that we should examine our own selves and prove our own selves before such a sifting takes place. Just as workmen try the strength of the iron which is to support a certain weight, and do not leave it to chance whether it shall be found strong enough or not, so ought we carefully to try our own religious principles, whether they are of a kind that will stand the day of temptation, or of the kind that will break down. It is not enough to come to the front like Gideon's thousands for a moment; are we prepared to stick to our post like Gideon's 300 in the day of conflict and danger? It is not enough to be on the Christian side with the world's multitude for a time; we want that strength and perseverance which will secure our standing with the few when the multitudes fall away. It is important— 2. *To notice this lesson of sifting with a view to forming a correct estimate of the probable issues of events.* Look at any number of men engaged in any work, secular or religious, that requires steadfastness, tenacity of purpose, fixedness of principle, fortitude to brave danger and meet difficulties, and the probability is that only a small proportion of them will go through with what they have begun. Faint-heartedness, weariness, fickleness, inconstancy, and clashing considerations, will stop the many midway, and the work, if accomplished at all, will be the work of the few. Especially in work done for our Lord Jesus Christ, for the advancement of his kingdom and for the good of his Church, we must look to the few. The men of prayer, the men of earnest faith, the cross-bearing men, the men whose conversation is in heaven, and who are waiting for Christ, are the handful; but they are the men who will fight the real battle, and who, by grace, will win the real victory.

HOMILIES BY VARIOUS AUTHORS.

Vers. 1—8.—*Divinely-ordained tests.* What a contrast the present position of Gideon as Israel's leader, within a few hundred yards of the dreaded foe, from that in which we first find him, threshing wheat in the wine-press secretly! Thus far has the Lord brought him, but much has to be done ere the soldiery he has shall be rendered efficient. Both leader and men have to pass through an ordeal such as must try them to the utmost. Not yet is the onset to be made that shall definitively retrieve the fortunes of Israel. Truly God's thoughts are not as men's thoughts. Everything is in apparent readiness, but delay is observed, and two mysterious tests are enjoined.

I. THE DESIGN OF THESE TESTS. Although they must have seemed arbitrary, if not capricious, to many concerned, there is evidently "method in the madness." A partial explanation is given in the words, "The people that are with thee are too many for me to give the Midianites into their hands, lest Israel vaunt themselves against me, saying, *Mine own hand hath saved me.*" The tests are meant, there-fore—1. *To check the unbelief and self-conceit of men.* The vast multitude is reduced to a few that men may give the praise to God, and his power be manifest. It is easy to suppose that such a tendency would show itself amongst the miscellaneous crowd. God could do the work by "many or by few," and it was well for them all to know it. 2. *To secure efficiency.* This would consist, first, in the tried courage and discipline of those who remained ; and, secondly, in their faith and inspiration.

II. THEIR ADAPTATION TO THIS DESIGN. By the adoption of the first expedient we are not to suppose that so many as left were lacking in ordinary courage. But they were not all heroes, and it was the heroic spirit that was needed. The anxious, irre-solute, and timid were got rid of, and those who remained were men in earnest. The second test revealed the presence or absence of rarer qualities. This seems to be its rationale : the Israelites were close to the camp of the Midianites, who must have been watching the singular manœuvres of their foes. The water where they drank must have been within easy reach for a demonstration, but they remained inactive. This created carelessness, a spirit of bravado in most. When they came to the water, therefore, they thought only of their thirst, and either forgot or despised the enemy. Flinging themselves down, they abandoned themselves to the luxury of quenching their thirst, and by their attitude exposed themselves to surprise and panic. But the three hundred stood up whilst drinking, and so had to lap. In this way they kept themselves alert, and showed that duty, not self-indulgence, was upper-most in their minds. It is the combination of prudence and self-denial with courage which is the most valuable thing in a soldier. The soldiers so tried are kept for the special effort, and the others who had not gone away are held in reserve to follow up the first blow struck. But over and above the special aim of each test, there was a discipline in the compulsory waiting and observing all that they involved—the loss of time, the trial of temper by apparent folly and arbitrariness, and the insignificant handful surviving the tests. So were Israel and its leader prepared. Is not all this like the discipline of life ? God is so dealing with his children. The revelation and guardianship of great truths are committed only to the tried few ; the signal move-ments and heroic duties of his kingdom are the care of elect souls, who when tested have been found true. The qualities requisite for a critical movement in a campaign are just those most valuable in life—faith in the leader, dauntless courage, superiority to self-indulgence, and constant prudence. We are to endure hardness as good soldiers of Jesus Christ. We know not what faults have to be corrected, what high service lies before us.—M.

Ver. 2.—"*Mine own hand hath saved me.*" Nothing more impressive than the secrecy observed by God in bringing on his kingdom. He is not lavish of signs and wonders. Sufficient for the occasion, and no more. Not always asserting himself. So unobtrusive, that vain and empty minds are ready to conclude him non-existent or inoperative. "Verily thou art a God that hidest thyself, O God of Israel, the Saviour." The place of God at the beginnings of things—the springs and roots ; and the spiritual nature of God accounts for much of this. He loves to work by despised instruments and obscure agencies. "Thy *gentleness* hath made me great."

I. HOW PRONE THE NATURAL MIND IS TO THIS IMPRESSION. Israel, as here stated, was constantly imagining it. The moral systems, ancient and modern, social and political nostrums and panaceas, of men show this. The glorification of courage, intellectual gifts, material resources.

II. ITS MISCHIEVOUS EFFECTS. Egotism ; materialism ; intellectual and moral pride. "For they being ignorant of God's righteousness, and going about to establish their own righteousness, have not submitted themselves unto the righteousness of God" (Rom. x. 3). "Ye will not come to me, that ye might have life" (John v. 40).

III. PROOFS THAT MAN CANNOT BE HIS OWN SAVIOUR. 1. The miraculous deliver-ances of Israel. The weakness of luxurious and materially enriched times. The providences of life. The soul's inner experiences. 2. *The true conception of salva-tion.* A spiritual more than a material fact. Our relation to the law of God. "Not by works of righteousness which we have done," &c. (Titus iii. 5). "And be found in him, not having mine own righteousness," &c. (Phil. iii. 9). Inward witness— " By the grace of God I am what I am " (1 Cor. xv. 10).—M.

Ver. 2.—*Success not dependent on numbers.* One of the first objects of a general's anxiety is to see that he has a sufficient number of men under his command. But Gideon is made to understand that he has too many, and must reduce his hosts before going to battle with the sanction and assistance of God. In Christian work the tendency is to rely on external appearances of strength manifested by a great array of workers rather than on the inconspicuous spiritual sources of real power. While remembering the need of more labourers of the right kind for God's field (Matt. ix. 37, 38), we must also understand that the work may be suffering through excess in numbers of those labourers, whose character and method of work are not of the highest order.

I. THE POWER OF GOD IS FAR MORE IMPORTANT THAN ANY HUMAN AGENCY. In all Divine work the real energy is centred in God. We are but the instruments in his hands. The temptation is to forget that the true power and blessing come wholly from him (Deut. viii. 17), and to think so much of our labour in planting and watering as to ignore the one most important thing, God giving the increase (1 Cor. iii. 7). A gardener can only minister to the spontaneous life of nature ; and if he becomes so infatuated with his skill as to attempt to manufacture a plant, his total reliance on his own resources will, of course, only reveal folly. So anything which leads us to magnify human agencies at the expense of Divine power will as surely produce failure. 1. *The imposing appearance of too great numbers may lead us to neglect the aid of God.* When we are few we feel our helplessness, and so learn to turn to God for strength ; when we are many we imagine ourselves strong, and thus while we are (apparently) strong in ourselves we are really most weak. Presumption takes the place of faith, and human agency is relied on instead of Divine energy. The numbers of the Church, the elaborate organisation of her societies, the gifts and genius of individual men are all snares if they tempt us to neglect the one supreme source of success. The danger of the Church in the present day is to rely too much on the machinery of her institutions, instead of seeking the vital power which can alone inspire the energy of spiritual work. 2. *The character of too great numbers may be such as to hinder the bestowal of the help of God.* God cannot bestow his spiritual gifts on a people who are not spiritually-minded. If we gain numbers at the expense of spirituality, we do this also at the expense of Divine aid. Better be few, and constituting such a worthy temple that the Holy Ghost can dwell and work in us, than numerous, but possessed by a worldly spirit which degrades the temple into a house of merchandise.

II. THE QUALITY OF ANY HUMAN AGENCY IS MORE IMPORTANT THAN THE SIZE OF IT. It has been well said that it would be better for the cause of Christianity in the world " if there were fewer Christians and better ones." Xerxes found the vast numbers of his Asiatic hordes a hindrance to effective warfare with the disciplined Greeks. The great want of the Church is not more labourers, but better ones— better ministers, missionaries, teachers ; not more sermons, but more able preaching ; not a more ponderous library of Christian literature to meet the attacks of unbelief, but a few more powerful works (one book, ' Butler's Analogy,' was probably more effective in counteracting the influence of Deism than all the rest of the voluminous apologetic writing of the eighteenth century). It would be well if Church discipline were a reality, and Christian workers selected with conscientious care. The workers should be sifted by tests applied to their character and abilities. 1. Tests of *courage* and *zeal* are useful ; so Gideon dismissed the timid, and only willing men were retained. The only valuable soldiers in Christ's army are the volunteers who delight in his service. 2. *Slight incidents* will often reveal character, and serve as tests of the quality of God's servants (ver. 7).—A.

EXPOSITION.

Ver. 9.—**Get thee down,** &c., *i. e.* attack the camp at once with thy 300 men. But if thou art afraid to do so, go down first alone with Phurah thy servant, and hear what they are saying in the camp.

Ver. 11.—**The armed men.** The exact meaning of the word here rendered *armed men* (*chamushim*), and which occurs Exod. xiii. 18 ; Josh. i. 14 ; iv. 12, is a little uncertain, but it is generally thought to be synonymous with another word (*chalutsim*), also rendered *armed* (Numb. xxxii. 32 ; Deut. iii. 18), and to mean literally *girded*, i. e. prepared to fight. These fighting men, as distinguished from the numbers of the nomads who were with their camels and cattle scattered all along the plain, were all collected in the camp, to the edge of which Gideon and Phurah crept stealthily in the dark.

Ver. 13.—**A cake.** The Hebrew word occurs nowhere else. **Of barley bread.** The commonest kind of bread, the food of only the poorer classes, indicating, therefore, the humble origin and station of Gideon. **A tent.** Rather, *the tent ;* what in a Roman camp would be the *pretorium,* the general's tent. The words at the end of the verse are heaped up to indicate the total and entire upsetting and overthrow of the tent, symbolic of the rout and destruction of the Midianite host.

Ver. 14.—**This is nothing else,** &c. The dream and the interpretation are striking evidences of the terror which Gideon's name had already inspired among the Midianites. Because, although both the dream and the interpretation were of God, for the encouragement of Gideon in his great undertaking, yet they followed the course of nature and the laws of psychology. The presentiment that God had delivered Midian into Gideon's hand is exactly like the terror in the minds of the Canaanites which preceded the arrival of Joshua (Exod. xxiii. 27 ; Deut. ii. 25; xi. 25 ; Josh. ii. 9—11).

Ver. 15.—**It was so,** &c. The effect upon Gideon was like magic. He not only learnt the state of panic in which the Midianites were, but he had a further certainty that God was with him. His simple piety and adoring gratitude threw him at once upon his knees to thank God, and to cast himself anew upon his strength with undoubting trust. His hands were indeed strengthened, and he lost not a moment in returning to his 300, relating in a few words the incident of the dream, and bidding them follow him. **The Lord hath delivered,** &c. Cf. 1 Sam. xiv. 20.

Ver. 16.—**Trumpets,** which had been collected from the whole army (ver. 8, note).

Lamps. Rather, as in the margin, *torches,* within the pitchers, so as not to be seen till the pitchers were broken, when the torches would flare with a sudden blaze. The *pitchers* were vessels for drawing water, as appears from Gen. xxiv. 14, 16, 18, 20. They were doubtless of earthenware, as they were so easily broken.

Ver. 18.—**The sword of the Lord,** &c. The word *sword* is not in the original here, though it is in ver. 20. It has either dropped out of the text accidentally, or what we have here is the shorter form of the war-cry. It is observable how careful Gideon is to put the name of Jehovah first. It was his cause against Baal, and the battle was to be fought in his strength, and the glory of the victory was to be his. The cry, "The sword of Gideon," would be peculiarly terrible to the many who had heard of the dream, of which the fulfilment was come so quickly.

Ver. 19.—**The middle watch.** The ancient Israelites divided the night into three watches of four hours each, from sunset to sunrise, *i. e.* from six p.m. to six a.m. The first watch, from six to ten, is not mentioned in the Old Testament ; but we have the *middle watch* mentioned here (from ten to two), and the *morning watch* (from two till six) : Exod. xiv. 24 and 1 Sam. xi. 11. According to this, Gideon's attack would have taken place soon after ten p.m., or towards eleven, the time when the sleep would be the deepest, the watchmen of the first watch having lately fallen into their first sleep. The later Israelites adopted the Roman division of the night into four watches (Matt. xiv. 25 ; Mark vi. 48; cf. Luke xii. 38 ; Mark xiii. 35).

Ver. 21.—**They stood,** &c. Gideon's men did not advance, but stood, each company in the place assigned to them, at different sides of the camp. This had the effect of awakening the whole camp simultaneously, and they started to their feet and ran hither and thither in confusion, shouting as they went. Undisciplined troops, especially excitable Orientals, are very liable to be thus thrown into a panic. **Fled.** The Cethib has, *caused to fly,* i. e. either "put to flight," or "carried away," as in ch. vi. 9 ; Exod. ix. 20. In the former case the nominative must be *the Israelites ;* in the latter, *their tents, herds, stuff,* &c., must be understood. Both are very awkward. The Keri, *fled,* is probably right, unless *caused to fly* has the sense of "bid them fly," in which case the preceding word, *cried,* might be taken in its common sense of *they sounded an alarm.* The whole clause would then run thus : *And all the camp ran ; and they sounded a retreat, and bid them flee.*

Ver. 22.—**Blew the trumpets,** &c. Hearing the confusion, the three companies blew their trumpets, probably more loudly than before, to give the impression of a hot pursuit being at hand. The Midianites, thinking the enemy were upon them, and not being able in the dark to distinguish friend from foe, mistook their flying comrades for pursuing Israelites, and fell upon and slew one another. In like manner the Philistines had done when attacked by Jonathan and his armour-bearer (1 Sam. xiv. 20), and the Ammonites, Moabites, and Edomites when attacked by Jehoshaphat (2 Chron. xx. 23). **Beth-shittah.** House of acacias. The exact situation of it, and of Zererath and Tabbath, is unknown. They must have been villages lying on the route from the plain of Esdraelon to the banks of Jordan, probably between Little Hermon on the north and Mount Gilboa on the south, where there was a very ancient high road from Jezreel to the Jordan by Beth-shan. Indeed it is highly probable that *Shutta*, a village mentioned by Robinson, marks the site, as it retains the name of Beth-shittah. For **Zererath** some read, with some of the old versions and manuscripts, *Zeredath* (*r* and *d* being scarcely distinguishable in Hebrew), and identify it with *Zarthan* near Succoth, mentioned Josh. iii. 16 and 1 Kings iv. 12 ; vii. 46. **Abel-meholah** (the meadow of the dance) was the birthplace of Elisha (1 Kings xix.16), and is mentioned in conjunction with Beth-shan, Jezreel, and Zartana in 1 Kings iv. 12. Eusebius tells us that in his time Abel-meholah was called Beth-maiela, and situated ten miles below Beth-shan, or Scythopolis. There was also, he says, close by an *Abel-maiela*.

Ver. 23.—**The men of Israel,** &c. Gideon's disbanded army got together again very quickly when they heard of the flight of the Midianites. Zebulun is not mentioned.

Ver. 24.—**Mount Ephraim.** Rather, *the hill country of Ephraim.* For some reason Gideon had not invited the Ephraimites to join in the war before (ch. viii. 1); but now, seeing the extreme importance of seizing the fords of Jordan, so as to stop the escape of the Midianites, he sent messengers in all haste to the men of Ephraim, who accordingly "took the *waters* unto *Beth-barah* and Jordan." The *waters* seem to mean a number of streams running from the hill country of Ephraim into the Jordan, and which had to be crossed by the Midianites before they could reach the Jordan fords. The site of *Beth-barah* is unknown. It is not thought to be the same as *Bethabara beyond Jordan,* where John was baptising (John i. 28). *Beth-barah* must have been on the west of Jordan.

Ver. 25.—**Oreb,** a raven, and **Zeeb,** a wolf. The rock known afterwards as the *rock of Oreb* (Isa. x. 26), and the wine-press (see ch. **vi.** 11) known as the *wine-press of Zeeb,* were so called from being the places where these two princes were taken and slain by the Ephraimites. In like manner the *well of Harod* is called by the name it afterwards received (ver. 1), and the *palm tree of Deborah* in like manner (ch. ii. 5), and *Lehi* (ch. xv. 9). These are valuable indications (to which many more might be added) of a living tradition older than the written history. The capture of Oreb and Zeeb is celebrated in Ps. lxxxiii. 11 and Isa. x. 26. **On the other side Jordan,** *i. e.* the east side of the river, which Gideon had now crossed, as is related in ch. viii. 4. The narrative runs on here to complete the history of the doings of the men of Ephraim, and goes back at ch. viii. 4 to take up the thread of the history of Gideon (see ch. ii. 1—6, note).

HOMILETICS.

Vers. 9—25.—*Faith.* The whole Book of Judges is so full of lessons of faith, as the author of the Epistle to the Hebrews teaches us when he refers to "Gideon, and Barak, and Samson, and Jephthah " (Heb. xi. 32), that we cannot help recurring to the subject of faith if we would honestly draw the instruction which each portion of Scripture is intended to convey. But though the same general lessons of faith— its nature, its triumphs, its sure rewards—recur in the successive histories, yet each has some proper lesson peculiar to itself. Referring then to the remarks on ch. i. 8—21 for such general lessons, we will notice some peculiar trials to which the faith of Gideon was subjected.

I. THE SACRIFICES OF FAITH. Let us put ourselves in Gideon's place. Suddenly called out of insignificance and obscurity, he had played the part of a statesman, a leader, and a general. As the result of his well-concerted measures, he found himself at the head of 32,000 men. As he reviewed this great force, so unexpectedly got together, how must his heart have swelled with pride and hope ! No doubt that great army was the instrument by which he was to deliver Israel, and he could but feel some self-gratulation at the success of his plans. To a man of an eager spirit as he must have been, no greater disappointment could have occurred than to be told to dismiss that army without striking a blow.   Just when he was about to acquire immortal fame to himself, and to save his country, and establish the great religious reformation which he had begun, by their means, to see them, and all his own prospects with them, melt away like a heap of snow before the sun, and that by his own act, must have been a trial indeed.   But Gideon's faith stood the trial.   Before God's clear command all his natural feelings and wishes gave way at once.   He might have said with St. Paul, " What things were gain to me, those I counted loss for Christ ; " for he acted in that self-same spirit.   His faith prompted him to obey, at whatever sacrifice of inclination and natural desire.   That places him on a very high pedestal among believers.   But let us look again at the extraordinary singleness of eye with which Gideon's faith led him to act.   The loss of the first 22,000 men was indeed a heavy one, but still they went away of their own free will.   But the 10,000 who remained had given proof of a brave and constant spirit, and how could he put upon them the affront of sending them away, after a test of an arbitrary kind, as men unfit to face the enemy?   It was now not Gideon's ambition only, not his *amour-propre*, which would rise in rebellion against a hard command, but his feelings as a soldier, as a comrade, as one who desired to retain the good opinion of his countrymen, and who wished to be popular amongst them.   Dismiss the 9700 men who had left home, and were come to share the danger with him, and who had refused to leave him when they might have done so !   Expose himself to the charge of fickleness and folly—to be thought like a man who builds a house and then plucks it down with his own hands ; to be liable all his life to the hatred and resentment of those whom he had so affronted !   (See 2 Chron. xxv. 10.)   How could he obey such a hard command ?   But if Gideon's natural man spake thus, the voice of his faith spake in contradiction to such thoughts, and spake with authority.   His faith still prompted him to obey, and he did obey, because he looked with a single eye to the will of God, and took no count of consequences to himself or others.   Here again then his faith was of a very high quality.

II. THE RISKS OF FAITH.   But we may look at Gideon's faith in a little different light, and mark the immense risks that he ran, having all human probabilities against him, and only the promise of God for him.   Here was a vast host of 135,000 men within less than an hour's march of him.   His position was anyhow one of the utmost danger.   To weaken his force even by 1000 men must seem an act of great imprudence.   To denude himself of his whole force except a handful of 300 men was like courting destruction, like putting his head in the lion's mouth.   Humanly speaking, Gideon and his 300 would be crushed like insects under the feet of the Midianite host.   And yet he deliberately reduced his force to 300 men, and then marched down from his stronghold into the enemy's camp.   He set the word and promise of God on one side, and all the fearful risks and dangers on the other, and these last were in his eyes as nothing in comparison with the former.   He went down with his 300 in full confidence of the victory which he won.   In this too his faith was worthy of all praise and imitation.

III. VERIFICATION OF THE WORD OF GOD.   But here perhaps a caution is necessary, lest we mistake what faith is.   Faith is such an entire trust in the word of God that it produces obedience to that word, whatever it requires of us.   But we must not mistake our own fancy, or our own wishes, or our own opinion, for the word of God.   Had Gideon rushed down upon the Midianite host upon the impulse of his own courage, or in reliance on his own stratagem, or under an unfounded belief that God had sent him, instead of admiring his faith, we should have had perhaps to blame him for foolhardiness, or to accuse him of foolish vanity, or to pity him for his fanaticism.   It was because his course was founded upon the clear and distinct word of God that it is held up to us as an object of admiration and imitation.   And it is worth observing in this connection what abundant assurance was given to Gideon that the very word of God was his warrant for what he did, and how cautious Gideon was to obtain such assurance.   The distinct appearance and words of the angel at first, his tarrying by the terebinth tree at Gideon's request, the fire which consumed the sacrifice at the touch of the angel's staff, the vanishing of the angel out of his sight, his reappearance that same night, the sign, twice repeated, of the fleece of wool, the reiterated communications by the word of the Lord, and the dream that he heard in the Midianite camp are so many proofs upon proofs, like our Lord's appearances after his resurrection, given by God to make his revelation certain, and so many evidences of Gideon's wise caution in ascertaining beyond a doubt that it was the word of God which was directing him in this terrible enterprise. In trying to take Gideon's faith as a model of our own, we must first imitate his care in ascertaining what the word of God really does require of us. The sad mistakes that have been made by misguided men in all ages, confounding the passions of their own hearts, or the hallucinations of their own brains, with the requirements of the 'written word of God, and even in their heated fanaticism imagining that special revelations were made to them by the Holy Ghost, confirms the lesson, given us by Gideon, of not accepting anything as the word of God upon light or insufficient evidence. To accept as the word of God without sufficient evidence any impression, or impulse, or vision, or dream, or interpretation of Scripture, is not a proof of a strong faith, but an evidence of a weak, and rash, and credulous mind. We may place, therefore, as first in order of importance, as well as the first that rises to the surface from the history of Gideon, the lesson of taking all due care and caution in verifying the word of God. This implies, circumstanced as we are, diligent and prayerful study of Holy Scripture, so as to be imbued with its true spirit, and to know thoroughly what it requires of us under the various circumstances of life. But when once the requirements and meaning of the word of God are plain, then a true faith will obey it, in spite of any sacrifice of worldly interest or self-pleasing which such obedience may incur, and in spite of any risks of worldly evil which may ensue. And the reason is obvious. Faith rests upon the perfect goodness and infinite power of God. If once, therefore, we know that God commands us to do such or such a thing, or to leave such a thing undone, we are certain that it is really for our good to do it, however much appearances may be the other way. We are certain too that the power of God is sufficient to bear us harmless through all dangers, however insuperable they may seem to us. It is of the very essence of faith, therefore, to give more weight to the unseen power and love of God than to the visible losses and dangers which threaten to be the result of obedience to God's word, and to make light of sacrifice of worldly advantages, or of selfish interests, in view of that closer communion with God which comes of obedience to his commandments. So Gideon acted, so Abraham acted, and so Moses acted, and thus must we act if we would be reckoned with them. The sacrifices we are called to make and the risks we are called to run by a conscientious obedience to the word of God in all its breadth will probably be much smaller than theirs were; perhaps only the sacrifice of some gratification to our vanity, or some addition to our self-esteem, the risk of some loss to our gains, or some check to our haste to get rich; but every such sacrifice made in the spirit of a true faith, and every such risk run in simple trust to the promises of the word of God, will be accepted of God in his Fatherly love, and will help to make us rich in faith, and to secure our place among the heirs of that kingdom which God hath promised to them that love him.

HOMILIES BY VARIOUS AUTHORS.

Vers. 9—15.—*The crowning sign.* All through this drama the spirit of Gideon was being trained for a decisive service. His faith had been tried to the utmost. Alone of all that host had he borne the responsibility of reducing it to 300 men. God's influence upon Gideon was from beginning to end moral and spiritual.

I. GOD JUSTIFIES HIS WAYS TO THOSE WHO PUT THEIR TRUST IN HIM. It was a grace that this additional sign should be given. The patience and faith of the servant of God are recognised by a spiritual reward. The deep harmony, hitherto unsuspected, of the steps he had taken at the Divine instance with the process going on and assisted by God's influence in the minds of his enemies must have, when combined with the circumstances,—the still night, the darkness, the vast host in whose dangerous neighbourhood he lay,—produced a profound impression upon his mind. In such a revelation there is communion and spiritual rapture. It was a reward for all he had passed through. The wisdom of everything was plain. There are times like this in every true life. They come unexpectedly, as a grace from our heavenly Father. He leads us into his counsels, and confirms us. Obedience leads on to knowledge,

II. SUGGESTION IS GIVEN HOW TO PERFECT OUR SERVICE. In every saint's life there is something wanting—an indefinite incompleteness and crudity. Such revelations and providences remove this. Their practical utility is evident. Here were several matters made known to Gideon he had not probably dreamt of. 1. The carelessness of the watch, arising probably from the notion that Israel had disagreed and dispersed. 2. The liability of an army so composed, &c., to panic. 3. The influence of his own name (the use he made of this we know by the cry). 4. The secret fear in the hearts of his adversaries.

III. IT IS BY THE MORAL INFLUENCE OF GOD'S PEOPLE THE WORLD IS OVERCOME. Christians are too much afraid of the world. *Fear not*, says the Master, *for I have overcome the world.* Vivid realisations of this are sometimes afforded us. The whole stress of attention ought therefore to be laid upon character, obedience to God's will, and submission to his leadership. Though few and weak, the "little flock" will receive the kingdom. It is Christ in us of whom the wicked and the demons are afraid. Of what consequence all their multitude and array? Secretly the world respects and fears the self-denial and faith of Christians.

IV. A GRACIOUS REVELATION LIKE THIS HAS TO BE RECOGNISED ADORINGLY AND BY IMMEDIATE PRACTICAL OBEDIENCE. Gideon "worshipped" Jehovah. It was a time when every obstacle had been removed, and his way was clearly revealed. He could now sympathise with God and admire his consummate wisdom. For himself too he must have felt grateful. God was better to him than he had hoped. Victory was potentially his. No wonder that his heart poured itself forth in such unrestrained and adoring emotion. But the lesson of the sign was not lost. Practical advantage was at once taken of it. He "returned unto the host of Israel, and said, Arise," &c. Do not allow God's gracious revelations in our lives to be a dead letter. Act upon them, that our lives may be brought into subjection and harmony with his will.—M.

Vers. 15—22.—*Inspired tactics.* The strategy of Gideon is one of the military marvels of antiquity. It seems simple and well adapted to its end; but that did not appear at first. In truth he was taught of God, inspiring his mind and illuminating his common sense, his experience, and his spiritual faculties. From the "lamps, pitchers, and trumpets," we learn—

I. HOW THE ENEMIES OF GOD ARE TO BE DEALT WITH. 1. *The means to be employed are of Divine appointment.* Not what human wisdom would devise, nor as appealing to material aid. "Gideon overcame Midian with unarmed soldiers, bearing only trumpets, torches, and pitchers. So Christ overcame the world by unarmed apostles, bearing the trumpet of preaching and the torch of miracles" (Theodoret). 2. *Prompt and intelligent advantage is to be taken of the opportunities presented.* What served at this juncture would have been entirely useless at another time. Knowledge of men is of immense advantage to the Christian worker; tact, and perception of the capabilities of the several means of grace. The power of Christian truth can never be overrated, but it may be misapplied. 3. *Unity and co-operation should be shown by God's servants.* Nothing could be finer than the device, save the manner in which it was carried out. Greater works than these shall be done when all Christ's servants are of one heart and one mind.

II. IN WHAT LIGHT THEIR POWER IS TO BE REGARDED. Gideon began his enterprise with the conviction, which he communicated to his followers, "The Lord hath delivered into your hand the host of Midian." The victory is already potentially ours if we use the right means in the right spirit. All the pomp and influence of sin ought not to daunt us. It is a house divided against itself, and subject to a thousand alarms. The least saint, in God's strength, may put an "army of aliens" to flight.

III. UPON WHOM THE SOLDIER OF THE TRUTH OUGHT TO DEPEND. Gideon is filled throughout with a profound trust in Jehovah. It is that which gives the moral character to his plans. Although he saw how potent his own name was amongst the Midianites, he did not content himself with the war-cry, "The sword of Gideon," but preferred "The sword of the Lord (Jehovah) and of Gideon." Christians can rely implicitly upon spiritual means and methods, because they believe in God, who informs and directs all earnest effort. The Israelites stood still and the Lord fought for them.—M.

Ver. 22—ch. viii. 4, 10—13.—*Following up advantage.* A model of diplomatic skill, judicial sternness, and soldier-like hardihood and resolution. Far from home, amid hardship in strange regions, he tracks the enemy even into the inaccessible Hauran. There is a Syrian proverb, *He fled into the Wa'r of the Sâfa,* i. e. into an unassailable refuge.

I. THE CO-OPERATION IS SOUGHT OF ALL ISRAELITES WHO CAN BE OF HELP. He had reasons for keeping the glory to his own trusty band. But there is no selfishness in his disposition. The advantage of his nation and the glory of Jehovah is uppermost in his mind. He finds work, therefore, for all. All are engaged, that it may be a national victory. Some have to lay the foundations, begin the work, sow the seed ; others can then carry out. The least Christian has something he can do. It is a duty of leaders to make and indicate fitting work for all. "The harvest truly is great, but the labourers are few." Ephraim can do one part of the work best ; he another. And having hitherto abstained, they were quite fresh now.

II. A SAGACIOUS AND KINDLY FORBEARANCE IS SHOWN TO THE JEALOUSIES OF BRETHREN. No word of rebuke is spoken to the tribes that held back. Persuasion is used, opportunity for usefulness is presented, the patriotism of the tribes is relied upon. It was no time for questions and wranglings. Well would it be for the different branches of Christ's Church did they follow a similar policy. Would that we were all so busy that we had no time for doctrinal disputes and questions of precedence and apostolic authority !

III. NO PAUSE OR REST IS OBSERVED UNTIL THE TASK IS COMPLETED. The deserted Midianite camp with all its riches does not tempt. Hunger and thirst and weariness are endured rather than lose the advantage. Only a determination to follow up the surprise with thorough and exemplary vengeance could have sustained him. So the conflict with sin and the world is to be conducted. Better to wear out than to rust out. Evil habits, unholy practices, false principles have to be tracked out to their last refuges and finally disposed of. It is harder work to live out Christianity than to be converted to it ; harder work to follow out in detail, and into the practice and life of every day, the great doctrines of righteousness than to understand and explain them intellectually. There is a loud call for vigour, thoroughness, patient continuance in well-doing. The day is Christ's ; let us make it wholly his.—M.

Vers. 16—18.—*Gideon's ruse.* I. THE ASSURANCE OF SUCCESS IS A HELP TOWARDS ATTAINING IT. Gideon had feared to attack the hosts of Midianites and Amalekites till he had discovered that they feared him ; then he took courage and energy to devise the plan of victory. Too much diffidence is dangerous. Hope inspires with ingenuity as well as with courage ; it is a brightness, an influence that enlivens thought. Therefore hope has its place in the first rank of Christian graces (1 Cor. xiii. 13). The promises of the Bible are not only comforting, they are inspiring. Our great encouragement should be that the powers of evil fear Christ and his army.

II. THOUGHT IS SOMETIMES MORE NEEDFUL THAN FORCE. Gideon's victory was a triumph of thought, of contrivance. The right disposition of our energies is more important than the mere sum of them. It would be well if Christians practised on behalf of the cause of Christ the same wisdom which men of the world display in business, in politics, &c., so far as this is not inconsistent with perfect honour (Luke xvi. 8). Christ requires us to be wise and harmless (Matt. x. 16). Dulness is not holiness. Intellectual gifts should be consecrated to God, not despised as unfit for his service. The diplomatist and the tactitian may find work in the service of Christ. In mission work organisation, economy of strength, ingenious adaptation of means to ends should be carefully studied, and the gift of wisdom sought in addition to that of zeal.

III. MORAL INFLUENCE IS BETTER THAN PHYSICAL FORCE. Gideon had conquered before he had struck a blow. The dismay he created and the confusion this produced in the hostile camp secured him victory. Though we cannot be justified in descending to deception, we may aim at influencing others by thought and feeling rather than by direct physical means. Christianity is a triumph of ideas. It is a sign of intellectual and spiritual failure when the Church desires to effect by the aid of the law what she should have done by the influence of moral suasion, as in restraining immorality, &c.

IV. IGNORANCE IS WEAKNESS. The Midianites and Amalekites were ignorant of the number of Gideon's army, or they would not have been deceived. They were too self-confident to inquire, as Gideon had done, concerning their condition. Ignorance and superstition create imaginary foes. An evil conscience is quick to imagine danger (Prov. xxviii. 1). The terrors which surround us are worse in imagination than in reality. Darkness and ignorance make men their own worst enemies (ver. 22).—A.

EXPOSITION.

CHAPTER VIII.

Ver. 1.—**The men of Ephraim.** It is possible that the transfer of the birthright from Manasseh to Ephraim (Gen. xlviii. 13—19) may have produced some estrangement between the tribes. It is also possible that Ephraim, in view of their great tribal power, and the distinction conferred upon them by the judgeship of Joshua the son of Nun (Numb. xiii. 8), and the possession of his grave (Josh. xxiv. 30), may have grown haughty and domineering, and perhaps more disposed to rest upon their former glories than to embark in fresh undertakings. Anyhow Gideon did not consult them, nor ask their aid, in the first instance. Now that the war had been so successful, the men of Ephraim were much displeased at not having been consulted.

Ver. 2.—**What have I done,** &c. Gideon's character comes out splendidly in this answer. Humble and unassuming (ch. vi. 15, 36, note),

and indisposed to glory, he was willing to give the Ephraimites full credit for their share in the great victory; prudent, and a lover of his country, he saw the immense importance of union among themselves, and the danger of intestine divisions and discord, and so at once met Ephraim's taunts by the soft answer which turneth away wrath (Prov. xv. 1). **The grapes.** The insertion of the word *grapes*, which is not in the Hebrew, rather spoils the proverb. It would run better, The gleaning of Ephraim is better than the vintage of Abi-ezer. The word *vintage* sufficiently shows that the *gleaning* meant was a gleaning of grapes. Ephraim, who came in at the end of the fight, like the gleaner when the vintage is finished, had got more glory by the capture of Oreb and Zeeb than the Manassites, who had gone through the whole campaign. The passage above referred to in Isaiah (ch. x. 25) implies that a great slaughter of the Midianites took place at the rock of Oreb.

HOMILETICS.

Vers. 1—3.—*The blindness of self-love.* Nobody admires pride, envy, jealousy, and petulance, when they see them pictured in the character and conduct of other men. Everybody, on the contrary, recognises the beauty of humility, gentleness, and forbearance, and admires self-control and patience under provocation, and the postponement of private feelings to the public good. How is it that we so often yield to the passions which we condemn in others, and so seldom and so imperfectly practise those graces of which we see the beauty and excellence? Lord, help us to put off the old man, which is corrupt according to the deceitful lusts, and to put on the new man, which after thee is created in righteousness and true holiness. Help us to be what we approve, and to leave off in ourselves what we disapprove in others.

HOMILIES BY VARIOUS AUTHORS.

Vers. 1—9, 13—17.—*Dealing with obstructives.* Ephraim, Succoth, and Penuel. I. THEY OUGHT NOT TO BE SUFFERED TO INTERFERE WITH THE CHIEF ENDS AND PRESSING CLAIMS OF DIVINE SERVICE. Gideon hastens after the routed and retreating foe. The sullen apathy of Ephraim, the refusal of Succoth and Penuel to meet the demands of patriotism and humanity, do not turn him aside. When the last blow has been struck and the power of Midian is laid low he will return and mete out to each according to their deserts. This is an illustration of how side issues may often arise, and of the manner in which they are to be dealt with. It is seldom that the difficulties and oppositions of life, however annoying and restraining they may be, can utterly prevent the graver duties or excuse dilatoriness. Frequently the petty nature of the opposition is revealed by steadfast continuance in the path of duty, and solitary resolution. We must do what we can, leaving with others the responsibility for their own conduct. The greatest workers in Christ's vineyard have had to labour and live on amidst misunderstanding, obloquy, and hindrance; but their work has been achieved nevertheless, and its moral effect has been all the greater.

II. WHEN THE PROPER TIME ARRIVES THEY MUST BE DEALT WITH ACCORDING TO THE NATURE AND DEGREE OF THE OPPOSITION. A wise discrimination is needed. Where gentleness will avail, harsh measures are to be avoided. Gideon knew the haughty character of Ephraim, the wound their ambitious spirit had sustained when the leadership was wrested from their hands, and so he exercised forbearance, and was gentle and pacific. Civil war was averted when it might have involved national ruin, and the generous side of Ephraim was appealed to. "A soft answer turneth away wrath." After all, Ephraim had atoned for past misbehaviour by the timely and effective service rendered even in the face of an unexplained misunderstanding. It is wise to credit our opponents with the best motives, and to speak gently and reasonably, abstaining from self-glorification. But where the hindrance had been a national crime and a violation of the first principles of humanity a different course was pursued. Here the functions of the judge were called into exercise. The punishment was stern and exemplary, but carefully meted out. Succoth and Penuel are visited with prompt and terrible recompense. But the princes and elders are punished, as being the chief culprits; the common people, who were helpless, were spared. All heresy and schism, unholiness of life, spiritual opposition, &c., is not to be regarded in the same light. Gentleness may win a brother. A little blame may rest with ourselves. Allowance is to be made for the failings of human nature. But we are to have no fellowship with the profane, the blasphemer, the unbeliever, &c. Difference of opinion may co-exist with real co-operation and fellowship.—M.

EXPOSITION.

Ver. 4.—**Came to Jordan.** The narrative goes back to ch. vii. 24, to follow up the personal history of Gideon, from which the writer had been diverted to relate the result of Gideon's message to the Ephraimites, which is told in vers. 24 and 25, and ch. viii. 1—3 (see ch. vii. 25, note; ii. 1—6, note).

Ver. 5. — **Succoth.** On the east side of Jordan, as appears plainly from the narrative in Gen. xxxiii. 17, 18; for we read there that Jacob journeyed from Mount Gilead to Mahanaim, thence to Penuel, and from Penuel to Succoth, so called from the *booths* or tabernacles which he made for his cattle; and that after leaving Succoth he came to the city of Shechem (called Shalem), "in the land of Canaan," showing that Succoth was not in the land of Canaan. In Josh. xiii. 27 we are also distinctly told that Succoth was in the trans-Jordanic tribe of Gad (which lay south of the Jabbok), in the valley of the Jordan, where its proximity to *Mahanaim* (vers. 26, 30) shows it to be the same place as Jacob's *Succoth*, which was also near the Jabbok (Gen. xxxii. 22). The identification of Succoth with any modern representative is very uncertain. Jerome mentions a trans-Jordanic place named *Sochoth*, in the region of Beth-shan, or Scythopolis; and Burkhardt also mentions a place described by him as "the ruins of Sukkot," two hours from Bysan (Beth-shan), and on the east of Jordan. But this, as well as the

Sakût of Robinson and Van de Velde, on the west of Jordan, about ten miles south of Beth-shan, is too far north for the Succoth of Jacob, which is shown to be the same as the Succoth of Gideon by the connection of the latter with Penuel (ver. 8), and which, as above noticed, is shown to be the same as the Succoth of Josh. xiii. by its proximity to Mahanaim. We must await some further light before we can decide the exact position of Succoth.

Ver. 6.—**And the princes of Succoth, &c.** Nothing could be more selfish, cowardly, and unpatriotic, than the conduct of the chief men of Succoth. Instead of aiding Gideon in his gallant enterprise for the deliverance of his country, they refused even food to his weary followers, for fear of the possibility of incurring the anger of the Midianites in case Gideon should fail. Their conduct and that of the men of Penuel is perhaps one among many indications how little real union there was between the tribes on the opposite sides of the Jordan (see ch. v. 16, 17).

Ver. 7.—**I will tear your flesh, &c.** These words breathe a fierce and vindictive spirit; such, however, as cannot surprise us in the age and country of which we are reading (cf. vers. 9 and 21). The provocation, it must be allowed, was very great, but still the spirit was very different from that which dictated the prayer under far greater provocation, "Father, forgive them, for they know not what they do." **Thorns of the wilderness.** The nature of the punishment here threatened, and the execution of which is related in ver. 16, is uncertain. The word here rendered *tear* means literally *to thresh*. Hence some suppose that the punishment here spoken of was a severe kind of capital punishment inflicted by threshing instruments with sharp iron points, called here "thorns of the wilderness," and "briers" (though some again understand literally *thorns* and *briers*); and they compare 2 Sam. xii. 31, where the word rendered *harrows* means *threshing instruments*, as also Isa. xxviii. 27; xli. 15. But others, as Bertheau, Keil, and Delitzsch, do not think it was a capital punishment at all, and take the word *thresh* figuratively in the sense of *punishing severely*, and think that literal thorns and thistles were the implements of punishment.

Ver. 8.—**He went up thence to Penuel.** When Jacob was returning from Padan-aram to Canaan he reached Penuel first, and Succoth afterwards (Gen. xxxii. 30; xxxiii. 17). Gideon, travelling in the opposite direction from Canaan, naturally reaches Succoth first, and Penuel afterwards. Going from Succoth to Penuel too, he *went up* out of the Jordan valley towards the mountains on the east. Penuel appears to have been a place of importance, since Jeroboam repaired its fortifications with a view of retaining his hold on trans-Jordanic Israel (1 Kings xii. 25). The *tower* here mentioned shows it was a strong place, but its exact situation is unknown.

Ver. 10.—**Karkor.** Or, rather, *the Karkor*. We are still on unknown ground. The situation assigned to it by Eusebius and Jerome, as being the same as a castle called Carcaria, near Petra, is quite out of the question, as being greatly too far south. As an appellative it suggests the idea of a walled-in space (*kir* = a wall; *kir-kir* = a space walled all round; cf. the Latin *carcer*, a prison); possibly an enclosed sheep or cattle fold on a large scale (see Numb. xxxii. 36: "built . . . folds for sheep"), affording some protection to the Midianite soldiers.

Ver. 11.—**Gideon went up.** See ver. 8, note. Implying that his direction was eastward away from the Jordan valley. **Nobah** was in the half-tribe of Manasseh. Nobah, who gave his name to the city, which was before called *Kenath*, seems to have been of the family of Machir (Numb. xxxii. 42). **Jogbehah** was in the tribe of Gad (Numb. xxxii. 35). These two cities appear to have been on the eastern frontier of their respective tribes, but the exact site of them is utterly unknown. It is a conjecture that possibly *Kunawat* may be *Nobah*, retaining its ancient name of *Kenath*. East of these cities was the desert, inhabited by nomads dwelling in tents, where Karkor was, and where Zebah and Zalmunna had encamped out of reach, as they thought, of their pursuers. But Gideon, falling suddenly upon them, routed the host, and took the two kings prisoners (see Ps. lxxxiii. 11).

Ver. 12.—**He discomfited.** Rather, as in the margin, *he terrified*. Those who were not killed in the first onslaught, when "he smote the host," were so terrified that they fled without further resistance, and many probably escaped, as all Gideon's efforts were directed to the capture of the two kings.

HOMILETICS.

Vers. 4—12.—"*Faint, yet pursuing.*" We do wrong in looking to the Scriptures only for spiritual lessons; they teach us also lessons of conduct in the affairs of this life. And it is a matter of great moment that we should conduct ourselves well and wisely in all the business of life. That lessons of worldly wisdom are not beneath the scope of Holy Scripture the whole Book of Proverbs teaches us, as does Solomon's prayer (2 Chron. i. 10) for wisdom to rule well and judge rightly, and the whole body of the law of Moses. The biographies of remarkable men given in the historical books teach us the same thing if we would use them rightly. But the exaggerated habit of allegorising and spiritualising the Old Testament has somewhat interfered with their usefulness in this respect.

I. The lesson which this portion of Gideon's history seems to teach us is THE VALUE OF PERSEVERANCE; of doing thoroughly whatever we take in hand, of going through with it to the end, and not leaving off till it is completed. Joash king of Israel was rebuked by Elisha the prophet on his death-bed because he only smote upon the ground thrice, and then stayed, satisfied with an imperfect result. The example of Gideon shows us one who was not satisfied with imperfect results, who had formed a complete conception of what he had to do, and did it. He was not stopped in his career by either successes or difficulties. True, he had driven the children of the east across the Jordan. There had been a great slaughter at the rock Oreb, the kings were fugitives, the power of Midian was broken. Some might think enough had been done. But Gideon no doubt had the future as well as the present moment in view. The wrongs and misery of his country during the Midianite oppression, seven long years of grinding, cruel servitude, were fresh in his memory. He would not have the plain of Jezreel again the prey to those locusts from the east. And so Midian must be crushed. But could his strength and the strength of his 300 hold out any longer? The long and hurried march, the hand-to-hand fights, the heat, their hunger and thirst, the weight of their arms, which they had doubtless taken in lieu of the pitchers and trumpets, had nearly exhausted their powers; even their own countrymen would not help them; they were weary and faint; might they not now stop and rest? No, their work was not complete; so, though faint, they must still pursue. Methinks that as we read this stirring tale of energy and perseverance we must feel ashamed of our own faint-heartedness; we must feel rebuked at our own readiness to succumb to hindrances, or to be content with half successes; we must resolve that we will put a little more energy into our own daily work, or extraordinary tasks, and that, in spite of weariness and discouragement, in the face of hindrances and opposition, we will persevere and carry through to the end whatever work we have in hand, of which we are convinced that it is right to do it. This is the first lesson given to us by Gideon—faint, yet pursuing.

II. But we may no doubt also spiritualise the lesson, AND APPLY IT TO OUR SPIRITUAL WARFARE, AND TO THE STRUGGLES OF THE SOUL FOR THE MASTERY OVER SIN. Here the importance of doing our work thoroughly, and persevering, in spite of successes and hindrances alike, till our task is complete, is certainly not less than in the affairs of this life. In resisting temptations, in resolutely subduing fleshly lusts and unruly appetites which war against the soul, in determined self-conquests, in perfecting holiness in the fear of God, in encountering the opposition of the world, and the contradictions of sinners, and the wiles and assaults of the devil, we must expect to be often faint. It is so easy to give up the struggle, to be content with imperfect results, to seek for rest and ease in giving up the close pursuit which we had begun. But this is not the spirit of Gideon. If we would be in our spiritual warfare such as he was in his conflict against his earthly foes, even when we are faint and weary we must be still pursuing; we must persevere to the end, and never slack our hands nor rest our feet till we have gained a complete and final victory through the grace of our Lord Jesus Christ. To him be glory for ever.

HOMILIES BY VARIOUS AUTHORS.

Ver. 4.—" *Faint, yet pursuing.*" A splendid and really *forced* march. Humanly speaking, it was the real battle. The grandest qualities were called forth, and the greatest results secured. A picture of the Christian life.

I. GOD OFTEN SUFFERS HIS SERVANTS TO ENDURE HARDSHIP IN DOING HIS WILL.

II. THOSE WHO ARE DOING IMPORTANT SERVICE UNDER CIRCUMSTANCES OF HARDSHIP OUGHT TO BE ENCOURAGED AND SUPPORTED.

III. DUTY AND THE HIGH CALLING OF CHRISTIANS OUGHT TO TRIUMPH OVER WEAKNESS, HARDSHIP, AND OPPOSITION.

IV. THE GREATEST RESULTS OFTEN DEPEND UPON PERSISTENCY EVEN AMIDST DISADVANTAGES.—M.

Ver. 4.—" *Faint, yet pursuing.*" The faintness of Gideon's troops may illustrate the spiritual faintness of Christians, and the influence of this on their conduct in life.

I. FAINTNESS MAY OVERTAKE US WHILE PURSUING THE CHRISTIAN COURSE. 1. Note the *characteristics* of this faintness. It is (1) loss of strength, so that we are not able to attain so much nor to progress so fast as we should otherwise do; (2) a sense of distress, making every movement a pain, and robbing the Christian life of its bright hopefulness and cheerful enthusiasm. 2. Note the *existence* of this faintness in the pursuit of the Christian course. Though still pursuing the right way, we may experience faintness. It is not the deviation to bye-path meadow alone which brings distress. We may grow weary *in* well doing (Gal. vi. 9). Therefore (1) let us not be over confident because we are in the right, and (2) let us not be dismayed at the experience of faintness, as though this were a sign of spiritual defection.

3. Note the *causes* of this faintness. (1) These may be observed in the *circumstances* of life:—in the length of the course; the great difficulty being not to nerve ourselves for a few heroic actions, but to continue pressing on through the long hot day, through the long weary night:—in the speed of the pursuit; life is a race swift and stern, and the difficulty often is to overtake the duties which accumulate so fast that those who, so to say, " take things easily " must always find themselves behindhand:— in the impediments of the way, leading through tangled thickets of prejudice and error, and up craggy heights of noble attainments. (2) The causes of faintness may also be traced to our own *habit* and *condition:* such as want of nourishment—the soul which is always working, and does not seek renewed strength in spiritual feeding upon the bread of life, in prayer, in the reading of Scripture, in meditation, in communion with Christ, will surely grow faint; want of rest—there is a spiritual insomnia, a habit of restless activity, which invariably results in faintness. Christ required rest, and called his disciples apart to rest (Mark vi. 31).

II. FAINTNESS NEED NOT STAY US IN THE PURSUIT OF THE CHRISTIAN COURSE. Though the troops of Gideon were faint, they still pursued. 1. *Faintness is not death.* If our strength is slight, this is a good reason for making the best use of it. If faintness reduce our talents to one, we have no excuse to bury that one. 2. God expects our *attainments to be no more than proportionate to our strength.* He knows our weakness (Ps. ciii. 14). He is no hard task-master, expecting us to make bricks without straw; so we need not despair of pleasing God because our faintness permits of but slight service. 3. The real source of victory is *not our strength, but God's might.* When we are most faint, God's strength made perfect in our weakness may be most effective (2 Cor. xii. 9). The little one may chase a thousand, because God is with him. When we are most faint we are least self-confident, and in our humility and helplessness driven to the mighty for strength, so that our faintness may be the means of leading us to the real strength which alone can accomplish great things. 4. *Faintness can be overcome.* Faintness is not necessarily the precursor of death. It may be but temporary. We may find in God a sure remedy for spiritual faintness, because " they that wait on the Lord shall renew their strength " (Isa. xl. 31). 5. If we are faithfully pressing on in spite of present faintness, we shall be rewarded with *future rest and triumph.* Gideon's troops were well recompensed for their brave pursuit. The short race of life will end in a haven of rest, in a home of honour. Let us then be brave and true, remembering that in proportion to the weariness of present toil will be the sweetness of future rest (2 Cor. iv. 16—18).—A.

EXPOSITION.

Ver. 13.—**Before the sun was up.** There is a wonderful diversity in the renderings of this verse. Some of the old versions and Jewish Rabbis interpret it *before sunset.* Many of the best Jewish commentators, however, understand the phrase as the A. V. does—" Before the going up of the sun," *i. e.* before sunrise; supposing Gideon's attack on the Midianitish camp to have been a night attack, and Succoth to have been so near to Karkor that he was able to reach it by sunrise. But others say that the word here rendered *sun* (*heres*) is only used in poetry, and that the word rendered *up* is never used of sunrise, but, as in the phrase " the going up of Akrabbim " (ch. i. 36), of an ascent up a hill. They therefore take *heres* as a proper name, and translate " from the going up of Heres." Others again, by an almost imperceptible change in the last letter, read " the mountains " instead of *Heres.* But the A. V. may be well defended, and

gives an excellent sense. In ch. xiv. 18 the same word for the *sun* is used in the very similar phrase, " before the sun went down." In Gen. xix. 15 the phrase, " the morning arose," has the verb from which the word here rendered *up* is derived; and a note of time here exactly suits the context. It marks the celerity of Gideon's movements that he was actually on his way back to Succoth at sunrise, after having reached the Midianites and taken their two kings prisoners.

Ver. 14.—**He described.** Rather, *he wrote down,* i. e. gave him a list of the princes and elders.

Ver. 15.—**The men of Succoth.** Meaning the princes and elders.

Ver. 16. — **He taught,** *i. e.* corrected, punished. It is, however, very probable that the true reading is *he threshed* or *tore* (*yadash* for *yadah,* the final letters ע and ה being very similar). We have then the fulfilment of Gideon's threat in ver. 7 recorded in the same words with regard to Succoth, just as the *breaking down* of the tower of Penuel in ver. 17 is in verbal agreement with ver. 9. The Septuagint and Vulgate both seem to have found *he threshed* in their copies.

Ver. 17.—**He slew the men of the city.** This makes it probable that the *threshing* of the men of Succoth was a capital punishment, as there is no reason why the men of Penuel should be more severely punished than the men of Succoth.

Ver. 18. — **What manner of men,** &c. An incident not before related is here brought to light, viz., that on some unknown occasion, possibly as soon as the rising of the Israelites under Gideon became known, or when, as related in ch. vi. 2, they had sought to hide themselves in Mount Tabor, but had been caught, Zebah and Zalmunna had put to death Gideon's brothers. We may observe in passing how characteristic this is of a true narrative in which everything that happened cannot possibly be related (see ch. x. 11, 12, note). The word here rendered *what manner of*, i. e. *of what sort*, means, in every other place in which it occurs, *where?* and the sense *of what sort* is only inferred from the answer, *As thou art, so were they.* But it is not safe thus to change the universal meaning of a common word. It is better to take the words of Gideon, *Where are the men whom ye slew at Tabor?* as an upbraiding of them for the murder of his brethren, and a threat that where they were their murderers would soon

be. The answer of Zebah and Zalmunna, which is not given in its entirety, was no doubt intended to be soothing and deprecatory of Gideon's wrath. They pleaded the necessity they were under in self-defence to slay them ; they were men of such royal stature and prowess that their own lives would have been in danger had they spared them. But Gideon turned a deaf ear to their plea. He must avenge the death of his own brothers, his own mother's sons. He would have spared them as prisoners of war (2 Kings vi. 22), but he must do his part as *goel* or *avenger* (Numb. xxxv. 12). Observe the stress laid on their being not merely his father's sons by another wife, but his own mother's sons, a much more tender relation (cf. Ps. l. 20).

Ver. 20.—**He said unto Jether,** &c. These marks of savage life are painful to contemplate in such a man as Gideon. But it is well for us to be made aware how the best and greatest men cannot rise above the manners and received maxims of their age ; and it teaches us to make due allowance for the faults of uncivilised men with whom we have to do, whether Afghans, or Zulus, or others.

Ver. 21.—**The ornaments.** Literally, *little moons*, crescent-shaped ornaments of gold and silver, which as well as " chains " (ver. 26) were hung as ornaments on their camels' necks (cf. ch. v. 30). It would seem from ver. 26 that the kings themselves also wore these ornaments; and in Isa. iii. 18 they are enumerated among the articles of female attire—*round tires like the moon*, A. V.

HOMILETICS.

Vers. 13—21.—*The complete revenge.* If any man ever stood on the very apex of success and triumph, it was Gideon on his return from the pursuit of the Midianites. He had saved his country ; he had set a whole people free from a foreign yoke ; he had restored the worship of the true and living God in his native land, and uprooted a vile and debasing idolatry ; he was the conqueror of a vast host with most inadequate means ; he had subdued and taken prisoners two powerful kings ; he had avenged the death of his own brothers upon those who, in pride and wantonness, had slain them ; and he had chastised the insolent, cowardly, and unpatriotic conduct of his own countrymen who, at his time of greatest need, had insulted instead of helping him ; and he stood in the proud position of having undertaken an almost impossible task, and having succeeded beyond his utmost expectation. But in the very height of this success we seem to see an overbalancing towards a fall. It is very slight ; there was still a wonderful moderation of mind (as seen in vers. 22, 23) ; but the weak human heart had a stronger draught of success than it could bear. As long, indeed, as his eye was quite single, and it was only the glory of God that he sought, and the welfare of his country, all went well (see ver. 2). But Gideon was not perfect. Had he been without the pride of fallen humanity, he would not have slain the captive kings, he would not have put to death the insolent men of Succoth and Penuel, richly as they deserved punishment. But it is here that we seem to see the first clouding of the singular brightness of Gideon's disinterested zeal. When we have made every allowance for the customs and opinions of the age, we cannot help feeling that something different from zeal and love for God was at work within him when he took away those lives. Zebah and Zalmunna had slain *his* brothers, and so had done an injury to *him*, and put a slight upon *him ;* the men of Succoth and Penuel had taunted and affronted *him*, they had undervalued his power, they had taken advantage of his momentary weakness to put him to shame. He must have his revenge. In his hour of more than human greatness the littleness of humanity started into birth. It was no doubt true that the law of the avenger of blood justified the slaughter of the kings, and the base conduct of the Succothites and Penuelites would secure a universal acquiescence in the justice of their punishment. But still we cannot help seeing that the pride of self, albeit unperceived by Gideon, had a hand in these actions, which cast a distinct shade upon Gideon's shining path, and which we cannot read of even at this distance of time without a pang of regret. How glad we should be if that noble spirit, in the very flush of victory, had risen sufficiently above the spirit of his age and above his own anger to spare his prostrate foes ; and if in the height of his glory he had despised the meanness of the men of Succoth, and left them to the punishment of their own shame, and the contempt of their fellow-men ! (see 2 Sam. xix. 23). But it could not be. And perhaps the lesson of human weakness is more valuable to us as it is ; for it leaves us a warning not to seek *a complete revenge* for ourselves under any circumstances, but to be content to commit our cause to God : and that it is better for man to be thwarted and humiliated than to have everything his own way. He cannot bear it.

EXPOSITION.

Vers. 22, 23.—Rule thou, &c. The gratitude of Israel to their great deliverer, added to a sense that it would be for their own security, and to a desire, already perhaps beginning to be felt, to be like the nations around them (1 Sam. viii. 5), naturally led to the offer, "Rule thou over us." But the time predicted by Moses (Deut. xvii. 14, 15) was not yet come. And so Gideon returned an answer replete with moderation and piety : "I will not rule over you, neither shall my son rule over you: the Lord shall rule over you" (cf. 1 Sam. viii. 7 ; x. 19 ; xii. 12).

Ver. 24.—I would desire a request of you. Again human weakness breaks out in this great man, and we seem to see the effect of great prosperity in stirring up selfish desires in his heart. It was perhaps not without significance that mention was made in ver. 21 of his taking the ornaments that were on the camels' necks in connection with the slaughter of the kings. Anyhow we have now a second instance of a love of spoil. It seems to have been a national custom with the Ishmaelites, among whom the Midianites are reckoned (see Gen. xxxvii. 25—28), to wear golden rings ; hence when they came to strip the slain there was a vast booty of gold rings. These Gideon asked for as his share, and the people readily agreed to the request. **Ear-rings.** The word is singular in Hebrew, which agrees with its more proper signification of *nose-ring*, an ornament often worn by both men and women in the East. Gesenius mentions having seen at Leipsic some Indian dancing women with nose-rings.

It is distinctly marked as a nose-ring in Gen. xxiv. 22, 30, 47, because in the last verse Abraham's servant says that he "*put the ring (han-nezem) upon her nose*" (*face*, A.V.). Again, in Ezek. xvi. 12 the Hebrew is, "*I placed a ring upon thy nose*" (I put a jewel upon thy forehead, A.V.). So also Job xlii. 11, "*one ring of gold*," implies that it was a nose-ring, and not an ear-ring. In other passages, however, as Gen. xxxv. 4 ; Exod. xxxii. 2, it is expressly said that these rings were worn in the ears ; while in others, again, there is nothing to mark whether they were worn in the ears or in the nose, as Prov. xxv. 12 ; Hosea ii. 13, except that in the latter passage the singular number in the Hebrew is more favourable to the *nose-ring* than to the *ear-rings*, as the A.V. translates it. It is thought by many, with some probability, that the nose-ring did not pierce the gristle of the nose, but hung down upon the nose from a fillet round the forehead. In every case they were of gold.

Ver. 25.—A garment. Rather, *the cloak*. Probably Gideon's military cloak (see Isa. ix. 5), which lay in his tent ready for use as a cloak by day or a coverlet by night (Deut. xxii. 17).

Ver. 26.—A thousand and seven hundred shekels—equal to about fifty pounds weight, and probably to above £3000 worth of our money, reckoning a shekel of gold at £1 16s. 6d. If the rings, like that given to Rebekah (Gen. xxiv. 22), weighed each half a shekel, they would be the spoil of 3400 dead bodies. If they each weighed less it would of course imply a larger number of slain. **The ornaments,** as in ver. 21, *the collars.* The word so rendered seems rather to mean *drops* or *pendants.* When worn by women (Isa. iii. 19, *chains,* A.V.) they were often of single pearls. The **purple raiment,** the famous Tyrian purple, made from the juice of a shellfish which is found in the Mediterranean, which was the distinctive colour of royal and imperial raiment. **Chains.** Perhaps the *ornaments* mentioned in ver. 21 as on the camels' necks were suspended to these chains. In Cant. iv. 9 the *chain* is mentioned as an ornament of a woman's neck; in Prov. i. 9 of a man's neck. Many interpreters understand these last-mentioned articles as not being part of Gideon's spoil, but being the people's portion. But it seems much more probable that the spoil of the kings should be Gideon's portion, as indeed ver. 21 implies. It is best, therefore, to take all these articles as being the property of the kings, and to understand the writer to tell us that Gideon had the rings, which were the people's spoil, in addition to all the spoil which naturally fell to his own share.

Ver. 27.—**Gideon made an ephod thereof.** There is great difference of opinion among commentators as to the significance of this statement. The ephod (Exod. xxviii. 4, 6—30) was that part of the high priest's dress (1 Sam. xiv. 3; xxi. 9) which covered the breast in front, and the upper part of the back behind, the two parts being clasped together by two large onyx stones, one on each shoulder, and kept together by the curious girdle, just above which was fastened the breastplate of judgment. In a modified form the "linen ephod" was worn by all priests; but it was especially worn by the high priest when he inquired of God by Urim and Thummim (1 Sam. xxiii. 9; xxx. 7). Hence it was also connected with idolatrous worship, as we see by ch. xvii. 5, and Hosea iii. 4, being probably used for purposes of divination, as we know that idolatrous kings of Israel, instead of inquiring of the Lord, inquired of the false gods (2 Kings i. 2, 3). What, then, was Gideon's purpose in making this costly ephod? We may infer from his proved piety that at all events his intention was to do honour to the Lord, who had given him the victory. Then, as he was now at the head of the State, though he had declined the regal office, and as it was the special prerogative of the head of the State to "inquire of the Lord" (Numb. xxvii. 21; 1 Sam. xxii. 13; xxiii. 2, 4, &c.; xxviii. 6, &c.), he may have thought it his right, as well as a matter of great importance to the people, that he should have the means ready at hand of inquiring of God. His relations with the great tribe of Ephraim may have made it inconvenient to go to Shiloh to consult the

high priest there, and therefore he would have the ephod at his own city of Ophrah, just as Jephthah made Mizpeh his religious centre (ch. xi. 11). Whether he sent for the high priest to come to Ophrah, or whether he made use of the ministry of some other priest, we have no means of deciding. The people, however, always prone to idolatry, made an idol of the ephod, and Gideon, either because it was a source of gain or of dignity to his house, or thinking it was a means of keeping the people from Baal-worship (ver. 33), seems to have connived at it. This seems to be the explanation best supported by the little we know of the circumstances of the case. **A snare,** *i. e.* as in ch. ii. 3, that which leads a person to eventual destruction. See Exod. x. 7, where Pharaoh's servants say of Moses, *How long shall this man be a snare unto us?* See also Exod. xxiii. 33; xxxiv. 12; Deut. vii. 16; 1 Sam. xviii. 21, &c. Observe in this verse how the narrative runs on far beyond the present time, to return again at ver. 28 (see note to ch. ii. 1—6; vii. 25; viii. 4).

Ver. 28.—**Lifted up their heads no more.** Thus showing the wisdom of Gideon's perseverance in pushing on his victory to completeness (see Homiletics on ch. viii. 4—12). The narrative goes back to ver. 26, or perhaps rather to ver. 21.

Vers. 30—32.—**Gideon had threescore and ten sons,** &c. This notice helps us to fill up the picture of Gideon's state after the Midianitish victory. He had indeed nobly refused the kingdom, as a Pericles would have refused to be tyrant of Athens. But he did not return to poverty and obscurity, as L. Q. Cincinnatus, in the Roman legend, returned to his plough after his victory over the Volscians. He was judge over Israel for forty years, with a household and a harem like a great prince, living in his paternal city, with the ephod set up there, himself the centre round which the powers of Church and State gathered; directing the affairs of his country, both civil and ecclesiastical, with eminent success, so that the country was at peace for forty years (a peace as long as that which followed the battle of Waterloo), and the detestable Baal-worship was effectually suppressed. And having lived in wealth and honour, he died in peace, and was buried in the sepulchre of his father at Ophrah in a good old age. He remains to us as one of the most remarkable characters of the Old Testament, not indeed without faults and blemishes, and not wholly unspoiled by prosperity, but still a great man, and an eminent servant of God.

Ver. 31.—**Whose name he called.** This is badly translated; it should be, *he gave him the name of Abimelech*—literally, *he set his name Abimelech.* There are two phrases in

Hebrew. The one, *he called his name* Seth, Noah, Ishmael, Isaac, Esau, Jacob, &c., as the case may be. And this is the phrase always, though not exclusively (see, *e. g.*, Gen. xxxv. 10; ch. vi. 32), used of the name given to a child at its birth or circumcision. The other is, *he gave* or *set him the name*, or, *he gave* or *set his name* so-and-so, and this phrase is only used of additional names, or surnames given later in life. The examples are ch. xiii. 31; 2 Kings xvii. 34; Neh. ix. 7; Dan. i. 7; v. 12. The inference is that the name of *Abimelech*, which means *father of a king*, and was the name of the royal family of Gerar, was given to Abimelech as a significant surname, and was

perhaps one of the causes which induced him to seize the kingdom. A third phrase is found in 2 Kings xxiii. 34; xxiv. 17; 2 Chron. xxxvi. 4: *he turned his name to Jehoiakim; changed his name to Zedekiah.* The Hebrew is the same in all these passages. Ver. 33.—**And it came to pass,** &c. Cf. ch. ii. 11, 12, 19; iii. 7; iv. 1; v. 1; x. 6; xiii. 1. **Baal-berith.** See ch. ii. 13, note. He was like the Ζευς Ὅρκιος of the Greeks, the god of covenants. Ver. 35.—**Neither showed they kindness,** &c. Forgetfulness of God is often the parent of ingratitude to men. The heart of stone which is not touched by the love of Christ is also insensible to the kindness of man.

HOMILETICS.

Vers. 22—35.—*Prosperity.* God has two ways of trying men: one in the furnace of affliction, that the trial of their faith, being much more precious than of gold that perisheth, may be found unto praise and honour and glory at the appearing of Jesus Christ; the other in the fining-pot of prosperity, and this is much the harder trial of the two. Affliction tends to humble and soften and subdue; but in prosperity, self-esteem, self-reliance, self-satisfaction, self-will, pride, and security, are prone to spring up with a rank luxuriance. Disregard for the rights and feelings of others strengthens with the inordinate estimate of the regard due to a man's self. The Scripture lessons as to the dangers of prosperity, and the snare which the possession of unbounded power is to men in general, are very many and very striking, culminating in our Saviour's saying, "A rich man shall hardly enter into the kingdom of heaven" (Matt. xix. 23). The latter part of David's reign compared with the first part of his life, the latter part of Solomon's contrasted with the beginning, Uzziah (2 Chron. xxvi. 16), Joash king of Judah (2 Chron. xxiv. 22), Amaziah after his successful campaign in Edom (2 Chron. xxv. 14—16), even good Hezekiah (2 Chron. xxxii. 27—31), all teach us the danger of prosperity, and the inability of the human heart to drink a full cup of success without intoxication. If we turn to secular history it is still the same story. Men of diverse characters and temperaments have all alike deteriorated under the influence of too much success in life, and shown themselves unfit to be trusted with unlimited power. Nebuchadnezzar, Alexander the Great, Nero, Constantine, Charlemagne, Louis Quatorze, Napoleon Buonaparte, men of the most different characters, may all be cited as having shown in different ways and degrees how hard it is for man to pass through the fining-pot of prosperity without bringing to light more or less the dross of a corrupt heart. It is an interesting and instructive inquiry how far Gideon passed through this fining-pot uninjured, and with his religious character undimmed. We have already glanced (Homiletics, ch. viii. 13—21) at the brilliancy of Gideon's success, and at the great qualities by which, under God, he obtained it. We had occasion too (Homiletics, ch. vii. 9—25) to notice the singular strength and perfectness of Gideon's faith, and the excellent fruits which it bore in practice. The humility and simplicity of purpose displayed by him, the docility and trustful obedience, the entire surrender of himself into the hands of God, without a thought for himself or a fear of the result, which marked his course, were of the highest calibre of human excellence guided and informed by the Holy Spirit of God. It is not, as we have already seen (Homiletics, ch. viii. 13—21), till his wonderful victory was consummated by the capture of the two kings that we can see any flaw in his character at all. The fining-pot had not yet begun to do its work. But when we come to the incident of the severe punishment of the men of Succoth and Penuel, to the slaughter in cold blood of the captive kings, and the plunder of their spoils, even when we have made every allowance for the manners and opinions of the times, and given due weight to the circumstances of the case, it is impossible not to feel that certain dormant passions of pride, and resentment of injuries, and "insolent joy," born of overmuch prosperity, had been aroused by his successes. His request for the gold rings which formed a portion of the people's prey, and the making therewith a costly ephod, without any direction from God or knowledge that he was doing what would be acceptable to him, showed a presumption far removed from the trustful docility which had been so beautiful a feature in his previous conduct; and we see a departure from the simplicity of his early life in his many wives and concubines, and in his connivance at the irregular concourse of the Israelites to Ophrah for a semi-idolatrous worship before the ephod, which conduced to his own worldly dignity, and was perhaps a source of emolument to him. These things are undoubtedly blots in Gideon's fame. On the other hand, his pious moderation in refusing the hereditary kingdom offered to him, the persistent "goodness which he showed to Israel" to his life's end, as we may safely conclude from the last verse of the chapter, the good government by which he gave rest to the land for forty years, and the continued repression of Baal-worship as long as he lived, are all evidences that he maintained his integrity before God, and never forfeited his claim to be a servant of God; and it is in entire agreement with this view that we read that he "died in a good old age, and was buried in the sepulchre of Joash his father," words by which the sacred historian evidently means to set before us the picture of one who, under God's favour, was happy in his death, as he had been in his life. Nor can we doubt for a moment what it was which held him up in the slippery path of worldly greatness. If God left him, as he did Hezekiah, "to try him, that he might know all that was in his heart," he did not leave or forsake him wholly. The faith in God which had carried him down to the Midianite camp, though it may have been dimmed, was never extinct. The communion with God, if less fresh and less constant, was never wholly interrupted. His belief that God is, and that he is a rewarder of them that seek him, once so deeply graven upon his heart and confirmed by his experience, never, we may be sure, departed from him. "Faint, yet pursuing," may probably describe the warfare of his soul at the most unfavourable times of his life. For ourselves, let us rise from the contemplation of Gideon's career with the firm determination to shake off those things which may be a snare to us, and not to slacken our pace in the pursuit of those things which are above. It is by constant prayer that our faith must be kept alive; it is by resolute resistance to those manifold lusts which war against the soul that our spirit must be kept free for holy obedience, and the eye of our mind kept clear to discern between the precious and the vile. We must keep a close watch against the first buds of those sinful dispositions in our hearts which are stimulated into growth by objects of carnal desire, or by wrongs or insults or taunting words, and we must nip them in the bud by crucifying the flesh with its affections and lusts. And if we find ourselves prosperous in this world, if riches increase, if friends multiply, if all goes well with us, if the world smiles upon us, if we are rising in consequence, in power, in the estimation of men, if new sources of gratification are opened to us, and life puts on its gayest, gaudiest colours for us, then above all it behoves us to be on our guard, and to maintain the supremacy of the love of God within us. Then let us humble ourselves before the cross of Christ; then let us bring the glories of the kingdom in full view, till the glories of earth pale before them; then let us strive more earnestly than ever to feel how immeasurably the pleasure of doing the will of God rises above the pleasure of pleasing ourselves, and how far the happiness of obedience to God's law transcends the happiness of yielding to our own desires. Such a victory over ourselves will be far more glorious than the conquest of ten thousand Midianites, and ours will be a richer booty than the richest spoils of kings.

HOMILIES BY VARIOUS AUTHORS.

Vers. 22—27.—*Noble self-abnegation.* The whole situation naturally described. In the flush of victory the impulse is to honour Gideon, and secure a permanent connection with the glory of his name by establishing a hereditary monarchy in his family. This honour he refuses. We have here—

I. GENEROUS BUT MISTAKEN GRATITUDE. It was a natural impulse in the soldiers.

But their mistake was twofold—(1) in exalting man instead of God, and (2) in seeking to put an end to the theocracy. The natural mind acts always thus, in the face of the plainest signs of Divine intervention and authority ; building itself out from the Unseen by human authorities and institutions. The chain of connection with God is weakened by lengthening it. The plainest commands of God are disobeyed in mistaken self-interest. The human agent is depended upon because the perception of the Divine is weak. Exalting one of themselves was but a species of self-glorification. The motive of Gideon too is misunderstood.

II. DISINTERESTED SERVICE. The honour is refused. If prudence aided the decision, it was chiefly due to unaffected faith and reverence for Jehovah. He may have felt that his " might " and success were solely individual, and due to direct inspiration ; and the incapacity and disagreements of his children may have already betrayed themselves. He thereby vindicates his own patriotism and disinterestedness. His humility and magnanimous loyalty to God as only Sovereign for Israel outshine all his exploits. 1. How hard it is for men to believe in the disinterestedness of benefactors ! 2. God, who imparts might and inspiration, can also purify the heart from worldly ambitions and weaknesses.

III. DEVOUT RECOGNITION OF DIVINE AID AND AUTHORITY. The ephod is explained and described in Exod. xxviii. It is the priestly garment, with breastplate attached to it, worn in the sanctuary. The Urim and Thummim were also used in connection with it for oracular consultation. It meant, therefore, a tabernacle and its service wherever it was placed. 1. So far as this was to the honour of God and commemoration of his mercy, it was a pious act. 2. By using the spoils of the people for its construction, a national sacrifice was effected. 3. But by placing it in Ophrah he encouraged schism, gave his own family undue importance, and tempted his countrymen to superstitious practices.—M.

Vers. 24—27.—*The mistake of a good man.* I. ORIGINATING IN MOTIVES FOR THE MOST PART NOBLE AND HONOURABLE. (1) Desirous of a national testimony to God's gracious deliverance, and a commemoration of it to future ages, he (2) persuades the Israelites to make a national offering, and (3) increases the means of grace in his own district.

II. REFLECTING THE DEFECTS OF HIS CHARACTER AND BETRAYING ITS LATENT VICE. In his zeal for the religious reformation of Israel he did not sufficiently consider the bearings of the step he had taken. It was a hasty and crude expedient, from which greater experience or sage advice, or, above all, God's Spirit, would have saved him. And therein lay the root of the mischief. He relied on his own wisdom, and forgot to ask God's guidance. In getting to look upon himself as in a special sense the re-introducer of the Jehovah-worship, and the exponent of the mind of Jehovah, he forgot that it was only as he was taught of God that he could be preserved from error. Of all inventions, religious ones are to be most carefully scrutinised. And in the background of this assumption there lay a secret tendency to self-esteem because of his spiritual endowments and character, and the great achievements of the past. Pride because of his own humility—is it not a failing that many have shared ? By this mistake he sowed the seeds of grave evils : schism, superstition, hero-worship. But—

III. THE SUBSTANTIAL GOOD DONE WAS NOT WHOLLY DESTROYED. Whilst he lived— a quiet, steadfast, righteous life—the people observed the true worship of Jehovah. His own example was a guide and a deterrent. And when at his death superstition ran riot, and the old licentious idolatry flowed back in an obliterating wave over the land and the institutions of Jehovah's worship, there were some things that could not be destroyed, remaining as germ ideas in the spiritual consciousness of Israel— the immediate obligation of the moral law upon every one, the direct responsibility of every one to God, and faith in the personal help of Jehovah. (1) God superintends the development of his truth, and (2) restrains the evil that mingles with the good in men's works.—M.

Vers. 29—32.—*The after life.* It is interesting to watch the after life of great men. In some it is a continual progress, in others a growing weakness of character and faculty. Gideon's was—

I. A REWARD AND CONSEQUENCE OF FAITHFUL SERVICE TO JEHOVAH. Long life, quietness, prosperity, honour.
II. KEPT ON THE WHOLE RIGHT, AND MADE A BLESSING BY THE GRACE OF GOD. He had begun well. His youth was a consecrated one ; his old age was its true outcome. And yet not by natural virtue, but by the blessing of God.
III. CONTAINING THE GERMS OF NATIONAL EVILS. He was not ever on the heights of spiritual excitement. Perhaps his was a nature that required great difficulties to be surmounted in order to keep it right. At any rate he fails to rise above the laxities of his age, and he enters into connection with the Canaanites. How much too of his after-life could be explained as a living on the memory of a glorious past, and a growing estimation of the part he himself had played. The ephod, the natural son by the Canaanitish woman, the conflicting interests of the many heirs to his influence and renown—these were the occasions of untold evil.—M.

Vers. 33—35.—*The consequence of the imperfect recognition of Jehovah.* I. AN IMPURE, DEFECTIVE WORSHIP OF THE TRUE GOD PREPARED FOR THE WORSHIP OF FALSE GODS. "False worships make way for false deities."
II. UNDUE MAGNIFYING OF HUMAN IMPORTANCE AT THE EXPENSE OF THE HONOUR DUE TO GOD ALONE, DIVERTED FROM THE WORSHIP OF JEHOVAH, AND SO CUT THE ROOTS OF THE PERSONAL RESPECT IN WHICH HIS SERVANT WAS HELD. True religion is the foundation and safeguard of all the esteem and respect due from one to another. The heavenly Father is the key-stone of the whole house of life.—M.

Vers. 22, 23.—*Gideon and the theocracy.* This incident may be regarded in relation to the conduct of the men of Israel, to that of Gideon, and to the historical fact of the theocracy.
I. THE INCIDENT REGARDED IN RELATION TO THE CONDUCT OF THE MEN OF ISRAEL. 1. These men *assumed a power* which they did not rightfully possess. They had no authority to revise the constitution, no right to elect a king. The election of Gideon was an act of rebellion against "the Eternal." 2. These men were so dazzled by the splendour of human achievements that they *ignored the Divine influence* which was the source of them. Gideon's campaign was especially designed to avoid the danger of the people attributing to men what was really the work of God (ch. vii. 4). Yet they regarded Gideon as the sole hero, and forgot to glorify God. We are all too ready to recognise the human instrument only, and ignore the Divine power which is the source of all that is good and great. The very richness with which God has endowed a man of genius may tempt us to make this mistake. Yet the more gifted a man is, the more reason have we to attribute his greatness to the Giver of every good and perfect gift. 3. These men were drawn aside from trust in the Unseen to a *desire for earthly greatness.* The glory of Israel was its government by the unseen King. This implied faith. But the temptation often was to lose this faith and the holy life and simple state it required, and desire a human kingship and the pomp of an earthly court, such as that of the heathen nations. There is always great difficulty in living in the power of the spiritual. Tangible force and visible display tend to allure us from the serene spirituality of life in the unseen.
II. THE INCIDENT REGARDED IN RELATION TO THE CONDUCT OF GIDEON. 1. Gideon proved himself to be an *unselfish patriot.* True patriotism is incompatible with personal ambition. A nation has no greater enemies than its ambitious men of genius. The worthy statesman is he who aims at his country's good to the neglect of his own aggrandisement. 2. Gideon showed himself strong in *resisting the popular wish* when he knew this was unwise. We must not mould our character simply in obedience to the dictates of public opinion. The wish of the people is no excuse for doing wrong. There is no more difficult feat than to resist successfully the mistaken kindness of those who are seeking to promote a man's own honour and greatness, though in a way which he believes to be wrong. 3. Gideon proved himself *firm in fidelity to God.* Here lay the secret of his resistance. He had been called from the threshing-floor by God. He held himself throughout to be the servant of God. It is better to be a servant and faithful to God than a king and in rebellion against him. 4. Gideon showed his discernment at once (1) of the existence and

power of the theocracy which his contemporaries appear to have ignored, and (2) of its suitability for the happy government of his nation.

III. THE INCIDENT REGARDED IN RELATION TO THE THEOCRACY. 1. It is *not wise to propose a revolution* of government except for great and necessary ends. It is easy to overthrow the present order; it is not so easy to be sure that what we substitute will be better. We cannot calculate on the possible uses to which the new power we create may be appropriated. 2. The best method of government is that which is *best suited to the condition* of a nation. There came a time when a human kingship was necessary for Israel. The attempt to force this on before the country was ripe for it only ended in disaster (ch. ix. 5). 3. No government can be better than a *true theocracy*. This must be distinguished from the rule of priests and prophets which is sometimes falsely named a theocracy, although it is as much a human government as the rule of kings and soldiers. Nothing can be better than for a people to be guided by the thought of God to do the will of God. The government of the Church is a theocracy. The Papal assumption is therefore treason to Christ. " One is our Master " (Matt. xxiii. 8). To substitute any human authority for the direct guidance of Christ is to fall back to a lower state, like the conduct of Israel when the people were willing to abandon their Divine King for a human monarch.—A.

Vers. 34, 35.—*Forgetfulness and ingratitude.* As we pass through the historical records of the Bible we must often be struck with the stern faithfulness with which Jewish chroniclers describe the wicked and shameful deeds of their own nation. This fact is not only valuable as a proof of the unvarnished truthfulness of the narratives; it gives to the history of the Bible a universal character by making it a mirror of human nature. Thus the forgetfulness and ingratitude here recorded are unhappily typical of the too common conduct of mankind generally.

I. THE PREVALENCE OF THIS CONDUCT. Unnatural and monstrous as it appears in the narrative, it is so common in experience as to be scarcely noticed. It was constantly repeated in the history of Israel (Ps. lxxviii. 11, 42). It is prevalent in Christian communities. 1. It is not limited to *atheism*. The atheist denies the existence of God. The godless man believes that God exists, yet ignores his existence. The atheist is rare. But is there not something pharisaical and hypocritical in the horror with which he is regarded, as though the great multitude of men were far better than he, though so many of them forget the God of whose existence they are champions, and never render him worship or obedience. 2. It is not limited to *open irreligion*. We must not suppose that all people who do not go to church are utterly godless; but neither can we believe that all who do engage in public acts of worship really acknowledge God in their hearts. It is possible to forget God in the house of God, and to be guilty of base ingratitude while singing his praises. 3. It is not limited to *total godlessness*. There are those who, like the Jews, have known God, but have since forgotten and neglected him, and those who live nearer to him for a season, but are tempted at times to forsake him.

II. THE CAUSES OF THIS CONDUCT. 1. *Sin.* The people of Israel went after Baalim, and the result was that they forgat the Lord. We cannot have two supreme gods. Immorality is fatal to religion. 2. *Worldly distraction.* When no special fall into great sin has been experienced the mind may be drawn aside from Divine things, and so engrossed in business, politics, or the cares and pleasures of life, that no time or energy is left for spiritual thoughts (Matt. xiii. 22). 3. *Unspirituality.* Even when there is no great worldly distraction we may sink into a low, unspiritual habit of life, in which the thought of God becomes faint and feeble. It does require some spiritual effort to preserve the memory of God fresh and bright, because (1) he is invisible, and can only be apprehended in the inner life, and (2) his action is gentle, and does not rouse our attention by sensational methods (Hab. iii. 4). 4. *Loss of love to God.* We remember what we love. Indifference of heart creates negligence of thought. 5. *Selfishness.* Israel remembered God in the time of need and forgot him in the season of prosperity. Selfishness inclines us to remember God only when we want his aid.

III. THE GUILT OF THIS CONDUCT. 2. It implies *disloyalty to the rightful authority of God.* If we forget God we forget his will and neglect his service. We are not free to do this, for we are naturally subjects of his supreme sovereignty. 2. It implies *indifference to his Fatherly nature.* He is our Father, and we are bound to him by ties of nature (Deut. xxxii. 18). 3. It implies *an unworthy return for his goodness.* Thankfulness is closely associated with thoughtfulness. The unthankful forget; those who do not take the trouble to think fall into gross ingratitude. Ingratitude to God is joined to ingratitude to his servants. The same spirit is seen in both sins. We are not likely to be true to man until we are first true to God.—A.

EXPOSITION.

CHAPTER IX.

Ver. 1.—The son of Jerubbaal. Throughout this chapter Gideon is spoken of by the name of Jerubbaal. There must be some cause for this. The simplest and most probable cause is that this whole history of Abimelech is taken from some other source than the preceding chapters. And a considerable difference in the style of the narrative, which is feebler and more obscure, seems to bear out this inference. **Went to Shechem.** This revolt from the house of Gideon in favour of Abimelech seems to partake of the nature of an Ephraimite rising against the supremacy of Manasseh. It was doubtless galling to the pride of the great tribe of Ephraim (ch. viii. 1, 2 ; xii. 1—6) that Ophrah of the Abi-ezrites should be the seat of government, and Gideon's ephod the centre of religion for the tribes of Israel. And so they seem to have taken advantage of Gideon's death, and of Abimelech's connection with Shechem, to make a league with the Hivite inhabitants of Shechem (see vers. 27, 28) to set up Abimelech as king, and to restore the worship of Baal, under the title of Baal-berith (ch. viii. 33 ; ix. 4, 27, 46), at Shechem for all Israel to resort to.

Ver. 2. — All the sons, . . . which are threescore and ten persons. Mark the evils of polygamy—producing family discord, extinguishing natural affection, causing civil strife, multiplying pretenders, and producing an ignoble and contemptible herd of helpless princes.

Ver. 3. — His mother's brethren. Presumably the Hivite population of Shechem.

Ver. 4.—Threescore and ten of silver, *i. e.* shekels, which is always understood. Equal in value to about seven pounds ; quite enough with which to hire a band of "vain and light persons," who would afterwards maintain themselves by plunder. **Out of the house of Baal-berith.** The custom of collecting treasures at the temple, both that of the true God and of idols, whether they were offerings and gifts for the service of the temple, or treasures deposited there for safety, was very general (see Josh. vi. 19 ; 1 Kings xv. 18 ; 1 Chron. xxix. 8 ; Dan. i. 2, &c.). The treasures belonging to the

temple of Apollo at Delphi were very great, and excited the cupidity of Xerxes, who sent an army to plunder the temple, but was foiled in the attempt. The Phocians are related to have seized 10,000 talents from the treasury of Delphi, nearly two and a half millions sterling. The temple of Diana at Ephesus had considerable treasures in money, as well as other valuable articles. Many other notices of the riches of temple treasures occur in classical writers. **Vain and light persons.** Cf. Judges xi. 3 ; 1 Sam. xxii. 2 ; 2 Sam. xv. 1 ; 2 Chron. xiii. 7. *Vain,* literally, *empty ; light,* literally, *boiling over.* Applied to the false prophets (Zeph. iii. 4). In German, *sprudel-kopf* is a hot-headed, hasty man.

Ver. 5. — Upon one stone. Used as a block, on which the victims were executed one after another. Compare the similar wholesale murders of the seventy sons of Ahab by order of Jehu (2 Kings x. 7), of the seed royal of Judah by Athaliah (2 Kings xi. 1), of the whole house of Jeroboam by Baasha (1 Kings xv. 29), of the whole house of Baasha by Zimri (1 Kings xvi. 11, 12). Timour, on his conquest of Persia, is said to have destroyed the whole male family of the king. At the conquest of Bagdad he is said to have made a pyramid of 90,000 human heads. In Persia and Turkey in modern times it has been a common practice for the sovereign to slay or put out the eyes of all his brothers and cousins. So destructive of natural affection is polygamy, and so cruel is power.

Ver. 6.—The house of Millo. Millo must have been some strongly fortified post in the neighbourhood of Shechem, and no doubt the place where the tower was, mentioned in vers. 46, 47. At Jerusalem we read of *Millo* as a part of the city of David in 2 Sam. v. 9, apparently so called by the Jebusites, and the strengthening of it was one of Solomon's great works (1 Kings ix. 15, 24). It is called *the house of Millo* in 2 Kings xii. 20, where it is mentioned as the scene of the murder of King Joash. Here, therefore, *the house of Millo* probably means the citadel or keep of Shechem, a fortress analogous to the Bala-hissar in relation to Cabul, though possibly at a distance of a mile or two (ver. 46,

JUDGES.

note). The phrase, *all the house of Millo,* means all the men who dwelt in the house of Millo, probably all men of war. **Made Abimelech king.** We seem to see the hand of the Canaanite population in this term *king,* which was proper to the Canaanites (Josh. xi., xii.), but was not yet domesticated in Israel. **The plain of the pillar.** This translation is clearly wrong. The word translated *plain* means an *oak* or *terebinth tree.* The word translated *pillar* is thought to mean a *garrison,* or *military post,* in Isa. xxix. 3 (A. V. *mound*) ; but, according to its etymology and the meaning of other forms of the same root, may equally well mean a monument, or stone set up and this is probably the meaning here. The translation will then be *the oak of the monument,* a sense supported by the modern names of the mosque there, of which one is "the Oak of Moreh," and another "the Saint of the Pillar" (see Stanley's 'Sermons in the East,' p. 182). And we are very strongly led to this conclusion by the further fact that there was a famous oak at Shechem, mentioned Gen. xxxv. 4 as the place where Jacob hid the idols of his household ; and that Joshua took a great stone and "set it up under the oak that was by the sanctuary of the Lord" at Shechem (Josh. xxiv. 1, 25, 26). It marks a sad declension in the condition of Israel at this time, as compared with the days of Joshua, that the Shechemite Abimelech should be made king with a view to the restoration of Baal-worship on the very spot where their fathers had made a solemn covenant to serve the Lord. It is remarkable that the narrative in this chapter gives us no clue as to the relations of the rest of Israel with Abimelech.

HOMILETICS.

Vers. 1—6.—*Self-aggrandisement.* If we study the characters of men famous either in profane or sacred history with a view not merely to their capacity, but to their moral worth, we shall observe one very marked distinction between them. Some, the few, evidently used their great powers and their great opportunities with entire disinterestedness, with singleness of purpose to promote God's glory and the happiness and welfare of their country, and not in any wise for self-aggrandisement. Such men, for example, as Moses, and Joshua, and Samuel, though they wielded all the power of the state, were entirely above the littleness of self-seeking. They had each a great mission, and they fulfilled it to the utmost of their ability with unswerving fidelity ; they had each a weighty task intrusted to them, and they executed it with unflagging perseverance ; but the idea of enriching themselves, or exalting their own families, seems never to have entered into their heads, or, at all events, never to have influenced their conduct. We can say the same of a few great names in profane history. It was true to a certain extent of Charlemagne ; it was true pre-eminently of Alfred the Great ; it was true of some of the early patriots of Rome, like Scipio Africanus, or Cincinnatus ; of Washington, of Pitt, and of the Duke of Wellington. But in the bulk of the great men of history we cannot help seeing that the motive force which called forth their energies and stimulated their powers was ambition, the lust of conquest, the desire of wealth and greatness—in a word, self-aggrandisement. The career of such men of might as Alexander the Great, Julius Cæsar, Louis Quatorze, Napoleon Buonaparte, whatever eminent qualities of head or heart they may have displayed, gave unmistakable signs that they were really pursuing their own greatness as the end of their performances in the cabinet or in the field. We may trace the same distinction between men who have filled much less important places in the world. Compare, for example, Dunstan with Wolsey. The first, though we may think him mistaken, pursued a disinterested purpose with concentrated energy ; the second had constantly in view the royal favour or the Papal throne. A comparison of Gideon and Abimelech presents the same sharp contrast. Gideon was roused by the call of God to seek his country's deliverance from a galling yoke, and to restore the worship of the true God in his native land. With the self-devotion of a Hofer, and the unflinching enthusiasm of a Luther, he gave himself to his double task, and accomplished it at the risk of his life without a thought of himself or any selfish ends. Abimelech, seeking power for himself, pretended to have in view the people's interest, and, to secure their favour, restored an abominable idolatry. His kingdom, founded in bloodshed, abetted by falsehood, and fostered by a base and cruel policy, had no end or motive but self-aggrandisement. There is exactly the same difference in the characters and conduct of men in the commonest affairs of every-day life. Some men have high aims, and pursue them by righteous paths. Others have selfish ends, and pursue them in unscrupulous ways. Be it ours to aim at doing the will of God in the commonest as well as in the greatest actions of our lives. Let us steadily set before us the thing that is right as the end which we are to seek. Let us consider that our powers, be they great or small, are given to us that in the exercise of them we may give God glory and do good to man. Without calculation of selfish interests let us follow God's call, devote ourselves to do his good pleasure, seek our neighbour's welfare, and trust to God's loving-kindness to order for us what seems best to his godly wisdom. In so doing we shall be meet for the kingdom of God.

HOMILIES BY VARIOUS AUTHORS.

Vers. 1—6.—*Ambitious usurpation.* Nothing shows the extent and significance of Gideon's influence so much as the anarchy that followed his death. The presence of *one* may check, restrain, direct, &c. in a degree wholly inexplicable until its removal. The retrogression of peoples—how difficult to comprehend! Sometimes a single individual (at most a few) concentrates in himself all the highest tendencies of his time, the only original of what appears a common possession. The weakness—mental, spiritual, political, and religious—of the nation now reveals itself. A time like that following upon Gideon's judgeship tries men and declares their real motives. Of the usurpation now attempted, notice—

I. THE AIM. Worthy men seek to emulate the moral and intellectual excellence of the great deceased; unworthy, merely to succeed to their office and to enjoy their honours. It was a splendid opportunity which now presented itself to carry on, and to higher issues, the work initiated by Gideon. Instead of this, personal aggrandisement is the all-absorbing aim. Unscrupulous advantage is taken of the interregnum in the judgeship. And the more utterly base appears the project, inasmuch as it is not only what Gideon enjoyed that is sought, but what he rejected, as considering himself unworthy.

II. THE SPIRIT. 1. *Irreligious.* No betaking of himself to the oracle; no recognition of God as Supreme Arbiter and Judge-maker. 2. *Immodest.* Personal fitness is not questioned, nor is the superior qualification of others considered. 3. *Selfish.* The rights of others are trampled upon, human blood is spilled like water, and the nation is regarded only as a *corpus vile* for political experiments and ambitious aims.

III. THE MEANS AND METHODS. *Arguments.* Falsehood and sophistry. The alternatives presented—" Whether is better for you, either that all the sons of Jerubbaal, which are threescore and ten persons, reign over you, or that one reign over you ? "—are not real. Charging others with the same aims as his own. Appeals not to the nation's sense of right, but to expediency, and kinship, &c.- Its *occasion* is the misfortune and weakness of others. Its *instrumentality,* unhallowed gold and a mercenary soldiery. Its *method,* a series of wrongs culminating in murder.

IV. THE SUCCESS. Apparently sudden, complete, absolute; really hollow, involving constant distrust and fear, and ever new outrages, and having in itself the elements of ultimate judgment.—M.

Vers. 2, 3.—*Unrighteous claims of kindred.* A great force in the arrangements and promotions of human life. The unrighteousness of it often felt when it cannot be explained. As much to be deprecated in the endeavour to secure the ordinary advantages of life as in the competition for its great prizes and honours. Let us look closely at this plea, " He is our brother."

I. IT IS THE EXAGGERATION AND PROSTITUTION OF A NATURAL AND PROPER AFFECTION. Of the true claims of " our brother" how much might be said ! A basis for moral obligations, and rights, and duties seldom fairly acknowledged. But to the desirable things of the world and " out in the open" there are many claimants whose title has to be weighed. The fond mother, desirous of such things for her son, may be asked, " Why *your* son, and not another's ? "

II. IT IGNORES AND TRAMPLES UPON GENERAL INTERESTS FOR THE SAKE OF INDIVIDUAL ADVANCEMENT. Next to the absolute appointment by God, and often indicative of it, is the "greatest good of the greatest number." The king or other public officer is *for the people*, not *vice versâ*. Although absolute right may be sometimes waived because of general advantage, when both are wanting the claim is weak.

III. THE TRUE TITLE-DEEDS TO ADVANCEMENT ARE NOT RECOGNISED OR APPEALED TO. Divine appointment; unique capacity; desire for the good of others rather than the advantage of self; service rather than office; duty than right.—M.

Ver. 5.— *Shortcomings of unscrupulous schemes.* That there are instances of seemingly complete and permanent success cannot be denied. But the cases in which the act just falls short of success are too frequent and dramatically striking not to be pondered.

I. A MORAL GOVERNMENT OF THE WORLD IS WITNESSED TO.

II. IF EVIDENT IN SOME CASES, MAY NOT THE SAME LAW EXIST WHERE NOT CLEARLY VISIBLE ?

III. IN THIS IS ILLUSTRATED THE ESSENTIALLY MORAL CHARACTER OF HIGHEST REASON. The wicked always leave something unconsidered or unprovided for. The lives and schemes of the wicked are based on fallacies. Truth and righteousness coincide.—M.

Ver. 6.—*Abimelech.* The character and life of Abimelech furnish us with a terrible picture of ambition in its bad origin, wicked character, temporary triumph, and fatal issues.

I. THE BAD ORIGIN OF AMBITION. This is illustrated in the circumstances which were associated with the early days of Abimelech. 1. *Irregular social habits.* The parentage of Abimelech would (1) stir in him a sense of injustice, and (2) incline him to lawless conduct (ch. viii. 30). Loose morals undermine the peace of society. Whatever desecrates the sanctity of the home tends to derange the order of the state. 2. *Parental vanity.* The high-sounding name of Abimelech is significant as an index to the character of his mother, and the thoughts she would instil into his mind. The vanity of the parent may be the curse of the child.

II. THE WICKED CHARACTER OF AMBITION. Abimelech displays some of the worst features of ambition. 1. *Selfishness.* The ambitious upstart has no thought of his nation's prosperity, his sole aim is his own aggrandisement. 2. *Deceit.* Abimelech deceives his brothers and the men of Shechem. True greatness is simple and frank ; the bastard greatness of ambition is mean, false, treacherous. 3. *Cruelty.* The new king soon abuses the confidence of his brethren, and develops into a murderous tyrant. Ambition inclines to cruelty (1) because it isolates the ambitious man, and destroys the safeguard of the sympathy and influence of equals, and (2) because it creates dangers from which there seems no escape but by violence.

III. THE TEMPORARY TRIUMPH OF AMBITION. Abimelech reaches the throne at which he aims. 1. We must not be surprised at the temporary success of wickedness. It is easier for the unscrupulous to obtain a low worldly triumph than for the conscientious to reach their more noble goal. The irony of providence is apparent in the fact that these men "have their reward" (Matt. vi. 2). 2. We must not judge of conduct by worldly success. Success is no vindication of character. Bad conduct is not to be justified because it proves to have been expedient. The sycophancy which flatters triumphant ambition, while it execrates the ambition which fails, is one of the meanest characteristics of popular opinion.

IV. THE FATAL RESULTS OF AMBITION. 1. To the people who shamefully countenance it it brings disaster. Israel was the worse for tolerating Abimelech, and Shechem, which accepted and encouraged him, suffered the heaviest calamities at his hand. Instead of securing strength and peace, the new throne only flung disorder and misery into the nation. 2. To the ambitious man his conduct brought ultimate defeat, shame, and death. Greed of power is punished by a triumph of weakness. Pride and vanity meet with humiliation and ridicule.—A.

EXPOSITION.

Ver. 7.—On the top of Mount Gerizim.
Mount Gerizim rises on the south-west side
of Samaria or Shechem as a sheer rock about
800 feet in height, facing Mount Ebal,
which is separated from it by the narrow
valley, "some 500 yards wide," in which
Samaria, now Nablûs, is built. It was
from Mount Gerizim that Joshua, in accordance with the directions given by Moses in
Deut. xi. 29, caused the blessings of the
law to be proclaimed, after the capture of
Ai, while the curses were proclaimed from
Mount Ebal (Josh. viii. 33, 35). Some
explain the name to mean "the mount of
the Gerizzites," or Gerzites (1 Sam. xxvii.
8); but the absence of the article makes
this doubtful. **Lifted up his voice.** Implying that a considerable effort was necessary
to be heard by the people below. The
narrowness of the valley, however, and the
rocky nature of the cliffs there largely increase the sound. I have myself heard the
human voice utter an articulate word at a
measured distance of one mile one furlong
and seventeen yards; but it was in a peculiar state of the atmosphere. The experiment has been made in recent years, and it
has been proved that a man's voice can be
distinctly heard in Nablûs, and also upon
Ebal, from Gerizim. It is thought that
Jotham, having emerged from one of the vast
caverns, overhung with luxuriant creepers,
which are in the mountain's side, "stood
upon a huge projecting crag of Gerizim"
just above the ancient site of Shechem, and
thence addressed the people who were assembled beneath him. The rich vegetation
of that well-watered spot, "unparalleled in
Palestine," supplied the materials of his
fable; for the olive, the fig, the vine all
grow in that rich valley; while the bramble,
which creeps up the barren side of the
mountain, and which is still used to kindle
the fire to roast the lamb at the Samaritan
Passover, was to be seen there in abundance.

Ver. 8.—The trees, &c. This is the earliest example of a *fable* in Scripture; indeed
the only one except that in 2 Kings xiv. 9.
It is remarked that in the Indian and Greek
fables the animals are the *dramatis personæ*,
the fox, the lion, the ass, &c.; whereas in
the only two specimens of Hebrew fable remaining to us, the members of the vegetable
kingdom, the olive, the fig, the vine, the
bramble, the cedar, the thistle, are the actors
and speakers. The *parable*, of which Isa. v.
1—7 is a beautiful example, is quite different
in its structure. Like the inimitable parables
of our Saviour in the New Testament, it sets
forth Divine truth under an image, but the

image and all its parts are in strict accordance with nature. In the Scripture *allegory*
real persons and their actions prefigure the
actions and the persons which they are intended to represent (see Matt. xii. 39, 40;
Gal. iv. 21—31; Heb. xi. 19). Allegorical
personages may, however, be fictitious, as in
the 'Pilgrim's Progress.' The general meaning of this fable is clear. The trees worthy
to reign for their intrinsic excellence refused
the proffered kingdom one after another.
The vilest and most unworthy accepted it.
The result would be that a fire would burst
out from the despicable bramble, and set fire
to the lofty cedar tree. Thus Gideon refused
the kingdom, and his sons had virtually
refused it likewise. The base-born Abimelech had accepted it, and the result would
be a deadly strife, which would destroy both
the ungrateful subjects and the unworthy
ruler.

Ver. 9.—They honour God and man: God,
by the frequent offerings of oil with the
meat offerings (Levit. ii. 1—16, &c.); and
man, *e. g.*, by the solemn anointing with oil
of kings, priests, and prophets (1 Sam. xvi.
12, 13; 1 Kings xix. 16; Ps. lxxxix. 21).
To be promoted, literally, to *wave*, or *move,
over,* i. e. to rule, in the case of a tree.

Ver. 13.—Which cheereth God and man.
The wine is said to cheer, or make to rejoice,
God because the drink offering which accompanied the meat offering consisted of
wine (Numb. xv. 7, 10), and God was well
pleased with the offerings of his people (cf.
Gen. viii. 21; Phil. iv. 18; Heb. xiii. 16).
The idea in this verse, as in vers. 9 and 11,
is, that while the olive, the fig, and the vine
were occupied in *waving* their branches over
the other trees, in token of their superiority,
they would necessarily be neglecting their
own proper gift and office, which was to
produce oil, and figs, and grapes.

Ver. 14.—The bramble. A prickly shrub;
in Greek ῥάμνος, Rhamnus, "the southern
buckthorn" (Gesenius). The same plant as
is mentioned in Ps. lviii. 9 (thorns, A.
V.) as used to make fires with (see note to
ver. 7).

Ver. 15.—If in truth, i. e. *truly,* as the
same phrase is rendered in vers. 16, 19, with
integrity of purpose and sincerity of heart.
The English would be less ambiguous if it
ran, "If ye anoint me king over you in
truth." The speech of the bramble indicates
the grounds for suspicion already existing
between Abimelech and the men of Shechem.
Let fire come out, &c.—keeping up the propriety of the image, as the natural function
of the bramble was to kindle a fire, and as it
had no other use; showing, too, how a base

bramble could destroy a noble cedar, and the base-born Abimelech could bring ruin upon the lords of Shechem.

Vers. 16—20.—**Now therefore, &c.** The fable being ended, now comes the forcible and bitter application. The simple reference to Gideon's great actions, and the juxtaposition of the base and bloody deed in which the Shechemites and the men of the house of Millo had made themselves accomplices by choosing Abimelech for their king, formed an indictment which could not be answered. With lofty scorn and irony he wishes well to them if they had acted honourably; but if not, he predicts the inevitable Nemesis of an alliance founded in bloodshed and treachery and wrong, viz., the mutual hatred and destruction of the contracting parties. Observe how "the house of Millo" is consistently spoken of as a separate community from "the men of Shechem."

Ver. 21.—**Jotham ran away.** Being close to the top of Gerizim, Jotham had the open country before him. It would take the men of Shechem twenty minutes to ascend the hill, by which time Jotham would be out of sight, and two or three miles on his way. **Beer,** to which he fled, is thought to be either the same as *Beeroth,* among the heights of the tribe of Benjamin (Josh. ix. 17), now *El-Bireh,* "the first halting-place for caravans on the northern road from Jerusalem" ('Sinai and Palestine,' p. 210); or a place called by Eusebius *Bera,* now *El-Bireh,* eight Roman miles from Eleutheropolis (now *Beit Jibrin),* and possibly the same as the place of the same name described by Maundrell as four hours from Jerusalem, and two hours west of Bethel; or, as Ewald thinks, *Beer* beyond Jordan (Num.b. xxi. 16). It is impossible to decide which, or whether any, of these is the place designated as Jotham's place of refuge.

HOMILETICS.

Vers. 7—21.—*The handwriting on the wall.* Among the many dramatic scenes which invest the pages of Holy Scripture with such singular interest, and give them such a hold upon the minds of all who read them with intelligence, perhaps none is more striking than that depicted in the fifth chapter of the prophet Daniel. A gorgeous spectacle is there presented to our view. The monarch of one of those mighty Oriental monarchies, which were a fearful embodiment of irresponsible human power over the lives and destinies of millions, was sitting in high estate in the palace of his kingdom; around him were a thousand of the highest nobles of his empire; the walls of the banqueting hall were adorned with the symbols of his royal power, and the emblematic images of the Babylonian and Assyrian gods. Upon the king's table were placed the golden and silver vessels which had once been used in the temple of the Lord at Jerusalem—trophies of past victory to feed his own pride with; trophies of the triumph of Bel and Nebo over the God of the Jews, with which to do homage to the gods of gold and silver, of brass and iron, of wood and stone. The wine sparkled in the goblets; the halls rang with hymns of blasphemous praise; insolent mirth, and voluptuous luxury, and security of power, and pride of dominion kept their high revel with audacious pomp. All faces were flushed with wine, all hearts beat high with self-confidence and arrogant success. One would have thought they held a lease of their power and pleasure for the term of eternity. The revel was at his height, when suddenly but noiselessly there came forth the fingers of a man's hand, and upon the wall just opposite the king's throne, on which the lamps were throwing the full glare of light, wrote the fatal words, Mene, Mene, Tekel, Upharsin. The agony that passed over the king's face, the tumultuous terror of his heart, the smiting of his trembling knees, the frightened cry for the astrologers and magicians, the impotent honours to the servant of the living God, the breaking up of the festival, the consternation of the company, were but the prelude to what the sacred writer records with such pithy brevity. "In that night was Belshazzar the king of the Chaldeans slain, and Darius the Median took the kingdom." Not very different in its spirit, though dressed in such a different garb, is the moral of the history in the verses which form the subject of our present meditation. By treachery, by wholesale fratricide, and by the help of the vainest and lightest in the land, the worthless Abimelech had risen to that place of kingly power which his great and patriotic father had refused to occupy. He had sought and obtained the co-operation of the idolatrous party among the people, he had appealed to the selfishness of the Shechemites, he had freely scattered bribes, and by such means he had obtained the desire of his heart. All seemed safe and prosperous, when from the heights of Gerizim a voice of ill omen—it might seem a prophetic voice, certainly a voice big with unwelcome truth—rang in the streets of Shechem. The passers-by, the throng in the market-place, the base adherents and flatterers of the new-made king, were startled by the sound, and looking up to the rock which overhung their town, saw Jotham, the youngest son of their great benefactor and deliverer Jerubbaal, of him who had saved their country from slavery, and their people from Baal-worship, and the one member of his family who had escaped from the murderer's hand, standing upon the rocky ledge. With ready eloquence he caught their ear and fixed their attention, while he uttered his cutting rebuke, and poured out his prophetic curse. Surely the sweet morsel in the mouths of the successful conspirators must have turned to gall and wormwood as their own base ingratitude and treachery and the vileness of their worthless king were thus gibbeted before their eyes. Surely their guilty hearts must have sunk within them as the sure consequence of their misdeeds was held before their eyes with such marvellous power of conviction. It is this inevitable Nemesis, this certainty that men will reap what they have sown, this exposition of the naked hideousness of wrong-doing, this vileness of sin, breaking through all the glitter of success and all the glare of present prosperity, wealth, or power, in a word, the just judgment of God written by the finger of God upon the wall, or declared by the voice of God from the pulpits of his truth, that men so obstinately close their ears and shut their eyes to, but which the word of God so resolutely declares. It is the teacher's office to proclaim it, to enforce it, to urge it, to insist upon it, whether men hear or whether they forbear. But there are certain bye-truths connected with this central one of the ultimate bursting of ungodly prosperity which we shall do well also to consider. One is the absence of cohesion in the various elements of evil. There can be no real lasting friendship between bad men; they are incapable of love. The bonds of interest and of some common evil purpose may bind them together for a time, but the shifting of these interests bursts those bonds asunder, and real hatred succeeds to seeming love. Unscrupulous ambition may coalesce with base ingratitude, but it is only for a moment. The only real and lasting union is that of love in Jesus Christ; and here is the security of the Church of God. The divers instruments of the powers of darkness may combine against her, and harm her for a moment, but they have no principle of cohesion in them. But the love which unites the saints to one another and to Christ is indissoluble and eternal. Thus, for example, infidelity and superstition may combine to destroy the faith, but they will soon turn against each other with deadly hatred as exasperated foes. They that are Christ's will be one in Christ for ever and ever. The fable has also some striking touches of character which are very instructive. The forwardness and levity of empty self-conceit, the love of power just in proportion to a person's unfitness to wield it, the utter unscrupulousness of a selfish ambition, the meanness of personal pride, the fickleness of men who have not the ballast of integrity to steady them; and, on the other hand, the humility of true greatness, the true dignity of being useful to others rather than of being exalted ourselves, the propriety of mind which enables a man to discern his right place and to perform his proper duty—these and many other traits of character which it is most profitable to discern come out spontaneously from the sharp imagery of the fable. It is no mean part of personal religion to perfect a man's character in these and such like respects. The neglect of the lessons of Scripture in such practical details has sadly lessened the influence of religious men in the society in which they live. It has diminished their usefulness and lowered their happiness, while it has deprived the world of the full evidence which it might have had that God was in them of a truth.

HOMILIES BY VARIOUS AUTHORS.

Vers. 7—20. — *Jotham's fable; or, popular election, its dangers and abuses.* The earliest instance in Scripture of this literary form. Proneness of the Eastern mind to apologue. Advantage of vivid, picturesque personification of principles and of natural objects. Cryptic teaching and political suggestion may be thus embodied. Christ's parables instances of noblest use of this vehicle of thought. The following principles are taught by Jotham:—

I. NATIONS MAY BE ACTUATED BY CAPRICE AND FALSE CRAVINGS, AS WELL AS BY MORAL OBLIGATION.

II. GOOD AND WORTHY MEN WILL REFUSE TO BE THE PLAYTHINGS AND VENAL INSTRUMENTS OF OTHERS.

III. THERE ARE SACRIFICES FOR WHICH POLITICAL ADVANCEMENT DOES NOT COMPENSATE, AND WHICH IT DOES NOT JUSTIFY ONE'S MAKING.

IV. THE CHARACTER OF A PEOPLE IS REFLECTED IN THEIR POLITICAL REPRESENTATIVES.

V. HIGH POSITION MAGNIFIES POWERS OF MISCHIEF AS OF BLESSING.

VI. THE TRUST THAT HAS BEEN WON BY UNWORTHY ACTS WILL BE AS BASELY BETRAYED.—M.

Ver. 21.—*Strength in weakness.* How ridiculous does it sound: "*Jotham ran away!*" The bodily presence and outward achievements of really great men are often contemptible. But Jotham, like many another, is not to be estimated from without.

I. THE CONSCIENCE OF THE NATION WAS APPEALED TO THROUGH ITS IMAGINATION. He had shown himself to the whole people. The literary simplicity and charm of his fable would rivet the attention of men upon the essential wrong committed, and the folly.

II. THE MORAL FORCES OF THE WORLD ARE ITS STRONGEST, AND WILL IN THE END PREVAIL. The "case" had been portrayed by a stroke of genius, so that no craft or sophistry could ever justify it. The claim of Abimelech, &c. was stripped of all its pretensions. To leave a matter with the conscience of men and with God is often harder than to contest it by force of arms. Christ yielded to the physical force and perverted authority of the Jews, but by his bearing at the judgment and by the matchless clearness of his statements he put his persecutors for ever in the wrong, and became the mightiest Ruler the world has known.—M.

Vers. 8—15.—*Jotham's parable.* By casting his ideas in the form of a parable, Jotham not only makes them graphic and striking, he exalts them into the light of general principles, and thus teaches lessons which are applicable in all ages.

I. MEN ARE TOO READY TO SHELTER THEMSELVES UNDER THE INFLUENCE AND RESPONSIBILITY OF LEADERS OF THEIR OWN CHOOSING. The trees combined to elect a king; but this was contrary to their natural functions. They fulfilled their vocation perfectly in their individual life and fruit-bearing. So Israel resolved to have a king, though in opposition to the simple form of government which a realisation of the idea of the theocracy would have shown to be the noblest and happiest. Men trust too much to organisation; but organisation is injurious without wisdom and strength to use it aright. There is a common temptation to throw upon others the responsibility which should be borne in common. Thus in the kingdom of Christ the Church is inclined to leave to ministers and official persons the work which belongs to all her members. Men generally fear to be independent, though they are proud of their boasted liberty. The usual habit is to repose under the leadership of others. Such conduct implies unfaithfulness to our supreme King and the neglect of our own responsibility.

II. POSITIONS OF HONOUR DEMAND SACRIFICE FROM THOSE WHO CAN RIGHTLY OCCUPY THEM. Each of the fruit trees sees that it must sacrifice its own peculiar advantages in undertaking to rule over the forest. Rank and power involve loss of opportunities for private usefulness, anxiety, danger, responsibility. The quieter life is the happier. Nevertheless, it will be wrong to press these personal considerations to the neglect of public duty. For the good of others we should be willing to suffer personal inconvenience. It might have been better if one of the fruit trees had accepted the crown instead of letting it fall on the bramble. The selfishness which allows public offices to come into the hands of inferior men is a sin on the part of the more capable.

III. USEFULNESS IS BETTER THAN RANK. The olive, the fig, and the vine are fruitful. Unless they were absolutely needed as kings, the world would be the poorer by their forsaking their useful vocations for the glory of royalty. It is better to feel that we are doing good, however obscurely, than that we are reaping barren honours. God is glorified not by our fame or rank, but by our fruitfulness (John xv. 8). To bear good fruit we must be rooted like the tree—be content, patient, willing to fill a small space if God be glorified. There is nothing so fatal to Christian fruitfulness as ambition.

IV. THE LOWEST NATURES ARE THE MOST AMBITIOUS. The bramble alone covets the crown. Ambition aims at greatness, but it arises out of littleness. The ambition of great men is their weakness, the smallest, meanest thing in them. True greatness will perceive the hollowness of the rewards of ambition, and the true glory of honest, faithful work in whatever sphere it is done. We must not therefore be deceived into judging of the fitness of a man for any post by the eagerness with which he seeks it. For ourselves we should learn that self-seeking in all its branches is a low and despicable habit of life.

V. THE EXALTATION OF THE MEAN WILL END IN DISASTER. Weakness is better than ill-lodged power. Better have no king than a bad king. As a good government is the first blessing of a nation, so a bad government is its greatest curse. They who enter blindly into needless obligations will have their eyes opened when these begin to work them harm. It is easier to confer power than to withdraw it. There is one King under whose shadow all can rest secure (Isa. xi. 1—5).—A.

EXPOSITION.

Ver. 22.—**Had reigned.** The Hebrew word here used is quite a different one from that in vers. 8, 10, 12, 14, and elsewhere, where the reign of a king is designated. It means to exercise dominion, to be a chief or captain over a people. The use of it here suggests that though, as we read in ver. 6, the Canaanite men of Shechem and the house of Millo had made him their king, yet he was not made king by the tribes in general, only he exercised a kind of dominion over them, or over a sufficiently large portion of them to warrant their being called *Israel.*

Vers. 23, 24.—These two verses contain the summary of what is related in detail in the rest of the chapter, and we are told that it all happened providentially, *that the violence done to the sons of Jerubbaal, and their blood, might come to be laid* (literally, *for some one to lay*) *upon Abimelech,* &c. **Which aided him**—literally, *strengthened his hands,* by giving him money, and encouraging him to make way to the throne by killing his brothers.

Ver. 25.—**The men of Shechem,** &c. The narrative now gives the details of that "treacherous dealing" on the part of the Shechemites which was spoken of in the gross in ver. 23. Their disaffection first showed itself in acts of brigandage "against the peace of their lord the king," to use the language of our own mediæval lawyers. The road to Shechem was no longer safe; lawless freebooters, in defiance of Abimelech's authority, stopped and robbed all travellers that passed that way, probably including Abimelech's own officers and servants. **For him.** It may have been their intention even to lay violent hands upon Abimelech himself should he come to Shechem.

Ver. 26.—**Gaal the son of Ebed.** Who he was, or of what tribe or race he and his brethren were, we have no means of knowing; he seems to have been an adventurer who sought to turn the growing disaffection of the Shechemites to his own advantage by offering himself as a leader of the malcontents. Several MSS. and editions and versions read *Eber* for *Ebed.*

Ver. 27.—**And they went out,** &c. The next step forward in the rebellion was taken at the time of the vintage, probably when they were inflamed with wine; for, after they had gathered in and trodden the grapes, they kept high festival in the temple of Baal-berith, on occasion of offering to their god the solemn thank offering for the vintage. And then, speaking freely under the influence of wine, they cursed Abimelech. The whole talk of the company was of his misdeeds, and seditious and rebellious words were freely uttered on all sides. **Made merry.** Rather, *offered their thank offerings.* The same word is used in Levit. xix. 24: "In the fourth year all the fruit thereof (*i. e.* of the vineyard) shall be holy *to praise the Lord withal*"—literally, *praise offerings to the Lord.* These offerings were made by the Shechemites to Baal instead of to God.

Ver. 28.—**And Gaal,** &c. Gaal now saw his opportunity, and encouraged the revolt. **Who is Abimelech, and who is Shechem, that we should serve him?** The meaning of these words, though somewhat obscure at first, becomes plain if we compare the two similar passages, 1 Sam. xxv. 10; 1 Kings xii. 16. In the first we have the contemptuous question, "Who is David?" and in the second the analogous one, "What portion have we in David?" but in both we have the same person described by different terms:

"Who is David? and who is the son of Jesse?" and, "What portion have we in David? neither have we inheritance in the son of Jesse." Here, therefore, it is clear that *Shechem* is merely another name for *Abimelech;* and it is easy to see why. Abimelech's mother was a Canaanite bond-woman, a Shechemite; and the plea for making Abimelech king was, "for he is our brother" (vers. 2, 3). *Shechem,* or *the son of Shechem,* was therefore a natural description of Abimelech. But, adds Gaal, **is not he the son of Jerubbaal? and** (is not) **Zebul his officer?** *i. e.* he is not a real Shechemite; he is the son of Jerubbaal; and what right has he to reign over you Shechemites? And why should Zebul lord it over you? He is only Abimelech's officer. No; **serve the men of Hamor the father of Shechem.** Fling off the yoke of the Abi-ezrite stranger, and set up a real Canaanite government from the old race of Hamor, the true founder and head of Shechem (cf. 1 Chron. ii. 50—52).

Ver. 29.—**And would to God,** &c., *i. e.* "If you will only trust me as your leader, I will soon remove Abimelech, and then you can have a national government." It seems that the people at once closed with his offer, and, thus emboldened, he sent a challenge to Abimelech to come out and fight him.

Vers. 30, 31.—**And when Zebul,** &c. Zebul, it appears, was governor of the city under Abimelech, and when the words of Gaal were reported to him, he privately sent off messengers to the king to tell him the state of affairs at Shechem, and urge him to come in person. Zebul meanwhile temporised, not being strong enough to resist Gaal openly. **Privily.** The word only occurs here. It probably means a little more than *privily,* —viz., *with subtlety* or *deceit,*—because he pretended all the while to be a friend of Gaal. Some make it a proper name, "In Rumah," taking it for the same place as Arumah (ver. 41)

Ver. 35.—**And Gaal,** &c. It does not appear certain whether Gaal, who, as is clear from ver. 36, was accompanied by Zebul, went out of the city gate with his men in consequence of any intelligence of Abimelech's movements, or any alarm or suspicion of danger, or merely upon some other enterprise. But whatever the cause was, as soon as he was there, Abimelech, according to Zebul's advice in ver. 33, had begun to descend from the mountains into the valley to "set upon the city." Gaal's quick eye detected them in the morning light.

Ver. 36.—**Saw the people,** *i. e.* Abimelech's followers. **He said to Zebul,** whom he looked upon as a friend and confederate. **Zebul said to him,** &c. Partly to give Abimelech time, and partly to conceal his own complicity in Abimelech's movements,

Zebul affected not to see the men, and explained the appearance as being merely the shadows of the mountains cast before the rising sun.

Ver. 37.—**Gaal spake again,** &c. Of course, as the men got nearer, it was impossible to mistake them for anything but men. Gaal could see two bands distinctly, one coming down the hill-side, the other marching by the road of the soothsayers' oak. **The middle of the land.** The word rendered *middle* only occurs again in Ezek. xxxviii. 12, "the midst of the land," A. V. It is so rendered from the notion of the old interpreters that it was connected with a word meaning "*the navel.*" It is usually explained now to mean *the height.* There may have been some particular height in the ridge called *Tabbur ha-aretz.* **The plain of Meonenim.** Rather, *the oak* (or terebinth tree) *of the soothsayers,* some large terebinth or turpentine tree under which the soothsayers used to take their auguries. Dean Stanley would identify it with the *oak of the pillar* in ver. 6, where see note.

Ver. 38.—**Then said Zebul,** &c. Zebul now throws off the mask, and dares Gaal to carry out his boast in ver. 28.

Ver. 39.—**Before the men of Shechem,** *i. e.* at their head, as their leader, as the phrase not uncommonly means (Gen. xxxiii. 3; Exod. xiii. 21).

Ver. 40.—**Were overthrown and wounded.** The simple translation of the Hebrew is, *and there fell many slain even unto the entering of the gate,* showing that Abimelech's men pursued them to the very gate of the city.

Ver. 41.—**Arumah.** A place not otherwise known, but apparently (ver. 42) very near Shechem, and possibly the same place as *Rumah,* the birthplace of Queen Zebudah (2 Kings xxiii. 36), and, from its name, apparently among the mountains. **Zebul thrust out,** &c. Gaal was so much weakened by his defeat that Zebul was now strong enough to expel him and the remainder of "his brethren" from the city.

Vers. 42, 43.—**And it came to pass,** &c. The Shechemites, believing Abimelech to have retired, and hoping that he would be satisfied with the chastisement inflicted upon them in the battle of the day before, left the protection of their walls next morning to pursue their usual avocations in the field. Abimelech's spies in the city being aware of their intention immediately reported it to him. Upon which he hastily took his army, divided them as before into three companies, lay in ambush in the field till the Shechemites were well out in the country, then attacked the Shechemites in the field with two of the companies, and himself at the head of the third rushed to the city gate to intercept their retreat.

Ver. 44.—**The company.** The Hebrew has *companies*, but the sense requires the singular.

Ver. 45.—**Abimelech fought against the city**, &c. When all the Shechemites in the field were smitten or dispersed, Abimelech stormed the city, weakened as it was by the previous loss of so many of its defenders. The city made an obstinate defence notwithstanding, but was taken before night, and all the inhabitants were put to the sword. The walls were then razed to the ground, and the site was sown with salt to express the wish that it might be barren and uninhabited for ever (cf. Ps. cvii. 34, marg.; Jer. xvii. 6). This action of sowing with salt is not elsewhere mentioned ; but it is well known that salt destroys vegetation, and is used by gardeners for this very purpose. Pliny (quoted by Rosenmüller) says, *Omnis locus in quo reperitur sal sterilis est.*

Ver. 46. — **The men of the tower of Shechem.** The tower of Shechem is no doubt the same fortified building as was spoken of in vers. 6 and 20 by the name of the house of Millo (see note to ver. 6). **An,** or rather *the*, **hold.** The word so rendered occurs elsewhere only in 1 Sam. xiii. 6, where it is rendered *high places*, and is coupled with *caves, thickets, rocks*, and *pits*, as one of the hiding-places of the Israelites from the Philistines. It was probably some kind of keep built on an eminence, and the place where the treasure of the temple was kept (ver. 4). It appears from the narrative that the tower of Shechem, or house of Millo, was not actually part of Shechem, nor immediately contiguous, since the report of the capture of Shechem had to be carried thither. **The god Berith.** It should rather be *El-berith*, the same as *Baal-berith* in ver. 4— *El*, i. e. *god*, being substituted for *Baal*.

Ver. 48.—**Mount Zalmon**, *i. e.* the *shady* mount, so called from the thick wood which grows upon it. It was in the neighbourhood of Shechem, and is perhaps the same as that mentioned in Ps. lxviii. 14 as famous for its snow-storms. **An axe.** The Hebrew has *axes*. If this is right, the phrase **in his hand** must be rendered *with him*, as 1 Sam. xiv. 34 : Each one his ox *in his hand*, i. e. *with him;* Jer. xxxviii. 10 : Take thirty men *in thy hand*, i. e. with thee ; and elsewhere.

Ver. 49.— **Set the hold on fire** — thus literally fulfilling Jotham's curse in vers. 15 and 20. It is thought by many that those who thus perished miserably by suffocation and fire in the hold of the temple of Baal-berith had taken sanctuary there, not occupied it for the purposes of defence.

Ver. 50.—**Thebez.** A place so called still existed in the time of Eusebius between Neapolis (*i. e.* Shechem) and Scythopolis (*i. e.* Beth-shean), about thirteen miles from Shechem. It still survives in the large and beautiful village of *Tubas*, which, Robinson tells us, is on the Roman road between Nabulus and Beishan. Thebez had evidently joined the rebellion against Abimelech.

Ver. 51.—**They of the city.** In Hebrew (*baaley*) *the men of the city*, i. e. the owners or citizens, the same phrase as is used throughout the chapter of *the men of Shechem* (cf. Josh. xxiv. 11 ; 1 Sam. xxiii. 11, 12). The English phrase *master*, or *my masters*, is very similar. The A.V. has here paraphrased it *they of the city*, to avoid the repetition of the word *men*. **The top**—the flat roof or *house-top*.

Ver. 52. — **To burn it with fire** — encouraged by his success at the tower of Shechem.

Ver. 53.—**A millstone.** The word here used means the *upper millstone*, which *rides* as it were, or moves, over the fixed nether stone. **All to brake his skull.** This obsolete English phrase has been the subject of a recent controversy. In the older English of Chaucer and his immediate successors such compounds as *to-break, to-burst*, &c. were very common, and were frequently preceded by the adverb *all*. Hence, some English scholars would read the phrase here, *and all to-brake his skull*. It is, however, certain that before the time when the A. V. was made the compounds *to-break, to-burst*, &c. had become entirely obsolete, and the compound *all-to* had come into use. The right way, therefore, in which to read the present phrase is, *and all-to brake his skull*, i. e. smashed it, dashed it in pieces. The prefix *all-to* gives intensity to the verb.

Ver. 54.—**His armour-bearer**—an office of trust, entailing much intimacy. Saul loved David greatly, and he became his armour-bearer (1 Sam. xvi. 21). Compare the similar incident of Saul and his armour-bearer in 1 Sam. xxxi. 4—6.

Ver. 55.—**The men of Israel**—Abimelech's followers (see ver. 22).

Ver. 56.—**Which he did unto his father.** It is remarkable that the sacred writer, in calling attention to the righteous vengeance which fell upon the head of Abimelech, marks especially the conduct of Abimelech as undutiful to his father (see Exod. xxi. 17 ; Matt. xv. 4 ; cf. also Gen. ix. 24—26).

Ver. 57.—**The men of Shechem.** Not here *baaley*, but simply *men*. Each such evidence of the righteous judgment of God is a presage of the judgment to come, and encourages the reflection of the Psalmist : "Verily there is a reward for the righteous ; doubtless there is a God that judgeth the earth" (Ps. lviii. 10, Pr. B. vers.).

HOMILETICS.

Vers. 22—57.—*Be sure your sin will find you out.* We are living under the government of God, and though many things happen in the world which seem strange and inexplicable to us upon the theory of God's righteous rule over mankind, yet we have but to be patient, and to observe impartially the end of things, in order to see by many infallible proofs that God is good to those who are of a clean heart, and that the end of the ungodly is that they shall perish. Nor can we afford to lose the evidences of God's righteous judgment. The immediate present fills such a large space in our view; ungodly mirth, successful wickedness, prosperous iniquity, bold blasphemy, the triumphs of sin, the rewards of selfishness, the impunity of evil livers, parade themselves so ostentatiously in the world, that the steps of our faith in God might easily slip if we did not keep steadily in mind the lessons taught us by the providence as well as by the word of God. Now it may be safely affirmed that the whole course of this world presents to the impartial observer continuous evidence that "the way of transgressors is hard," and that "there is no peace to the wicked;" while, on the contrary, the "way of the just is as the shining light, which shineth more and more unto the perfect day." It is quite true that this evidence is from time to time, as it were, crossed and checked in its flow by puzzling phenomena of a different character. But just as the ebbing or flowing tide is apparently interrupted by single waves which exceed or fall short of their expected place, and yet for all that is steadily receding or advancing; or as the temperature of the advancing spring for a time declines, or that of the advancing autumn increases, and yet a sure advance is being made towards summer heat or winter cold, so it is with the righteous judgment of God. Under it, in spite of apparant exceptions and temporary diversions, the righteous are advancing in the way of peace, and the ungodly are bringing upon themselves a righteous retribution. Fasten the eyes of your mind then upon these truths; observe them working themselves out in the daily lives of men before your eyes, and in the career of nations as delineated in the page of history. See how the sins of a man are continually finding him out in the most unexpected ways, and at the most unexpected times. Mark how evil deeds, unpunished at the time, nay, apparently successful, forgotten by the doer, and thought by him to be for ever passed away, yet come back to him, stand in his way, become thorns in his sides, frustrate his hopes, mar all his purposes, break out into deadly consequences, cast a dark shadow upon his life. Look at the life of nations. The barbarians of the North avenging the abominations of imperial Rome; the Turkish empire withering away because of its bloody deeds, its cruel oppressions, its detestable sensualities; the expulsion of the Jews; the wrongs of the Indians; the butcheries of the Inquisition, still wasting away the life and power of Spain; the French nation, receiving in bloody revolutions and still more bloody wars the just reward of the adulteries and unblushing vices of her monarchs and nobles: and, most striking of all, the Jewish race, suffering through eighteen centuries of slaughter and pillage and persecution and wandering, without a home and without a country, the vengeance which they called down upon themselves for the blood of the Son of God, whom they crucified and slew. Or learn the same lesson in another way. Observe how in the very nature of things the tendency of wickedness is to defeat its own ends, and to bring sorrow upon them that work wickedness. The successful lie when found out works distrust and suspicion in all with whom a man has to do. The deed of violence and blood arouses hatred and abhorrence in the breasts of those cognisant of it. The act of unscrupulous power awakens fear and jealousy and resentment in the beholders. The wrongs of women raise up avengers among men. The avarice which plunders and wrings treasures from their possessors leaves a sting of resentment behind it; and when a man has surrounded himself with distrust and suspicion, and hatred and abhorrence, with envies and jealousies, and resentment and fierce revenge, what room is there left for happy enjoyment or quiet possessions? His sin finds him out in the very midst of his success, and he reaps according to what he has sown; so that in the very operation of the natural laws which attach to right and wrong we see the just judgment of God. In the marvellous pages of Holy Scripture these natural lessons are illustrated, exemplified, and enforced with a clearness and a vigour unequalled and unapproached in any writings of man. They culminate in the declaration of the coming of the day of judgment, when God will reward every man according to his works. The observed tendencies of good and evil will then be fully confirmed. Every work will then have its proper recompense of reward: all inequalities will be redressed, the temporary exceptions will disappear, the just procedure will be vindicated to the utmost. In the full court of heaven and earth God will show himself a righteous judge, when all men shall stand before the judgment seat of Christ. The flood which drowned the world of the ungodly, the fire which burnt up the cities of the plain, the miserable end of the tyrant Abimelech, the dogs which licked the blood of Ahab by the vineyard of Naboth, the flames which devoured the temple at Jerusalem, and the instances which every day brings before us of shame and sorrow springing out of sin, are but prophetic voices, to which we shall do well to take heed, confirming the announcement in the word of God of that great and terrible day when God will judge the secrets of men by Jesus Christ, and will reward every man according to his works

HOMILIES BY VARIOUS AUTHORS.

Vers. 22—57.—*The Nemesis of usurpation.* The quick succession of events shows that the political situation is one of unstable equilibrium. The movement of affairs is rapid, as if the stage were being cleared for the real and important action that is to follow.

I. A NATURAL ELEMENT. The instruments of usurpation soon display their untrustworthy and turbulent character. Their help to Abimelech was chiefly in the interests of disorder. When the hard rule of the tyrant (force of word "reigned") was felt they became restive. The accession to their ranks of Gaal the marauding chieftain gives them the requisite stimulus toward open rebellion. So in time the drunken revels, the highway robberies of Shechem move irresistibly onward toward open revolt, and its consequence, overwhelming destruction. In this way the perpetrators of the *coup d'etat* are made the agents of the Divine vengeance upon each other. In punishing the rebels a seeming accident made Abimelech the victim of a woman's hand. Blood for blood. " Without shedding of blood there is no remission." The tragic element in human history.

II. A DIVINE ORDERING OF EVENTS. So natural does the development of events appear, that there is danger of overlooking the overruling providence of God. What may be termed the " poetic justice " of the political movements of the time and their results renders it impossible to credit the sublimely neutral forces of nature with the working out of the issues. God wrought through the natural forces and the complications of the political sphere. His people have to be led onward in the pathway of national progress and religious illumination, therefore such obstacles must be swept out of the way. Yet all this is consistent with the moral freedom of those whose actions and end are so promotive of the Divine purpose. What was done in one development of events might equally have been secured by another. This principle that "maketh for righteousness" is evident to every careful and devout student of history. It may be detected in the individual private life, and in the history of a nation. How far the evolution of events which we esteem secular and blind is so informed by the Divine purpose we shall not discover in this life. But enough is laid bare to encourage the holy and righteous, and to awaken in the breast of the wicked "a fearful looking for of judgment and of fiery indignation, which shall devour the adversaries."—M.

Vers. 30—33, 36—38.—*A worthy servant of a worthless master.* Zebul served Abimelech faithfully according to his lights. His devotion appears strangely misplaced.

I. GOD RELATES THE LIVES OF THE GOOD AND THE BAD FOR WISE ENDS. " Never any man was so ill as not to have some favourers : Abimelech hath a Zebul in the midst of Shechem" (Bp. Hall). Every situation has its moral complications.

II. THE WORTHLESSNESS AND IMMORALITY OF A SUPERIOR DO NOT EXONERATE FROM EXTERNAL RESPECT AND FAITHFUL DUTY, UNLESS HIS AUTHORITY IMPOSES UNRIGHTEOUS

TASKS. Much of the routine of life is neutral from a moral point of view, otherwise it would be impossible for the righteous to live amongst men. We must fulfil our bond until the conduct of our employer renders it impossible for us to serve God in serving him. So with natural duties, as of a child to a parent.

III. ON THE OTHER HAND, FAITHFULNESS IN DETAILS WILL NOT ATONE FOR NEGLECTING TO STUDY THE MORAL DRIFT OF THE WHOLE SITUATION OF WHICH THESE DETAILS ARE A PART. The judgment of Abimelech involves Zebul. There comes a time when we share the guilt of the master in continuing to serve him. An honourable quittance should be sought at once in such a case. "The Lord will provide." Otherwise we shall be involved in the same judgment.—M.

Ver. 55.—*Without a leader.* Nothing is more striking than the contrast between the conduct of mercenary or coerced soldiers in such circumstances and that of men inspired by noble enthusiasm and great principles.

I. THERE ARE TIMES WHEN THE DEATH OF SOVEREIGNS, &C. APPEAR AS NATIONAL JUDGMENTS, OVERAWING MEN'S HEARTS AND SEARCHING THEIR CONSCIENCES. Did not Israel feel now what a fool's errand it had been going? What better could it do in its irresolution and dismay than retire into privacy, and there in penitence and prayer await the new unfoldings of God's purpose?

II. ONLY A GREAT CAUSE CAN KEEP TOGETHER THOSE WHO HAVE LOST THEIR NATURAL BOND AND AUTHORITY. Self-interest, fear, absence of common enthusiasm, scattered the army of the dead Abimelech. So shall misfortune and Divine judgments break up the confederacies of the wicked. "The stars in their courses fought against Sisera." But the Church of Christ can never be leaderless. "Lo, I am with you alway, even unto the end of the world."

III. THE INFLUENCE OF THE WICKED SOON PERISHES. There is no talisman in the name of the son of Shechem now that he is dead. His body is left to the wolves and vultures. Only "the memory of the just smells sweet, and blossoms in the dust." The saintly departed rule us from their graves. The name of the Crucified an eternal, infinite power.—M.

Vers. 53, 54.—*Reputation.* In the moment of his death Abimelech is anxious to save his reputation, which he thinks would be dishonoured if it could be said that a woman slew him.

I. REPUTATION AMONGST MEN IS SOMETIMES VALUED MORE HIGHLY THAN INNOCENCE IN THE SIGHT OF GOD. Abimelech is anxious about the opinion of the world, he cares nothing for the judgment of God. He is concerned with what will be said of him, he is not troubled about what he really is. He is dying after a most wicked life, yet he has no thought about his evil nature and his vile misdeeds, but only anxiety about his fame. So we constantly see people much more occupied in securing a fair appearance than in living a true life. Yet how hollow is this pursuit! After our death it matters nothing to us what men may say, but everything turns on what God will do. A man's future state will depend not on the splendour of the fame which he leaves behind in this world, but on the character of the revelation which will be made of his life in the other world. An epitaph is no passport to heaven.

II. REPUTATION AMONGST MEN IS OFTEN DETERMINED BY A FALSE STANDARD OF CHARACTER. Abimelech knows that his misdeeds have been blazed through the country, yet he has no concern for the judgment of men on these, but very much concern for their opinion of the accident of his death. He sees no dishonour in cruelty and treachery, but great dishonour in death from a woman's hand. The code of honour differs from the code of God's law. Public opinion is too much formed on artificial points of merit and superficial appearances. Thus cowardice is commonly felt to be more disgraceful than cruelty; yet it is at least as bad not to be just and generous as not to be brave. Men commonly think more of masculine excellences than of saintly graces. Both are good, but the first obligation lies on the more Christian. Among the Christian duties which a consideration of merely worldly reputation leads men to neglect in comparison with lower obligations, are—(1) purity on the part of men, (2) humility, (3) forgiveness of injuries, (4) charity.

III. THE INFLUENCE OF REPUTATION SHOWS THE IMPORTANCE OF CULTIVATING A

HEALTHY PUBLIC SENTIMENT. Whilst so many are governed by the opinion of the world, it is imperative that this should be purified as far as possible. There is something natural in respect for reputation. The bad man who has lost this proves himself to be utterly abandoned. Next to the fear of God, shame before men is the strongest safeguard for conscience. A healthy social atmosphere is an immense aid to goodness. The society of the Church is helpful for the preservation of the faithfulness of the Christian. A pure Christian home is a most valuable security for the character of its members. It is dangerous to stand alone ; therefore, while regarding right and God's will first, and rising above the fear of man which bringeth a snare, let us reverence Christian public sentiment, and seek to keep it pure.—A.

EXPOSITION.

CHAPTER X.

Ver. 1.—**Tola the son of Puah, the son of Dodo.** Nothing more is known of Tola than what is here told us, viz., his name, his parentage, his dwelling-place, his office, the length of time which he held it, and the place of his burial. Who were the enemies from whom Tola was raised up to save Israel we are not told. There was probably no great invasion or grievous servitude, but perhaps frequent border wars requiring an able and watchful chief to maintain the independence of Israel. Tola and Puah (otherwise written Puvah) were both names of families in Issachar (Gen. xlvi. 13 ; Numb. xxvi. 23). **Shamir in mount Ephraim,** to distinguish it from *Shamir* in the hill country of Judah (Josh. xv. 48). Both are otherwise unknown.

Ver. 3.—**Jair.** We read of Jair the son of Segub, the son of Machir's daughter by Hezron, in 1 Chron. ii. 21—23, and are there told that he had twenty-three cities in the land of Gilead (called Havoth-jair), which were included in the territory of the sons of Machir. The same information is given in Numb. xxxii. 40—42, and in Deut. iii. 14, 15, in both which passages Jair is styled the son of Manasseh, and is stated to have called the cities after his own name, Havoth-jair. In the present verse we are also told that Jair the judge was a Gileadite, and that he had thirty sons who had thirty cities in Gilead called Havoth-jair. The question arises, Can these two be the same person ? If they are, Deut. iii. 14 must be a later parenthetical insertion, as it has very much the appearance of being. The notice in Numb. xxxii. 41 must also refer to later times than those of Moses, and we must understand the state-

ment in 1 Chron. ii. 22, that " Segub begat Jair," as meaning that he was his lineal ancestor, just as in Matt. i. 8 we read that " Joram begat Ozias," though three generations intervened between them. If, on the other hand, they are not the same, we must suppose that Jair in our text was a descendant of the other Jair, and may compare the double explanation of the name Havoth-jair with the double explanation of *Beer-sheba* given Gen. xxi. 31 ; Gen. xxvi. 31—33 ; the threefold explanation of the name *Isaac*, Gen. xvii. 17 ; xviii. 12 ; xxi. 6 ; and the double explanation of the proverb, " Is Saul among the prophets ? " given in 1 Sam. x. 11, 12 ; xix. 23, 24. The Hebrew name *Jair* is preserved in the New Testament under the Greek form of *Jairus* (Mark v. 22).

Ver. 4.—**Thirty ass colts.** The number and dignity of these knightly sons of Jair shows that Jair himself, like Gideon (ch. viii. 30), assumed the state of a prince. The word in Hebrew for *ass colts* is identical with that for *cities*, as here pointed, and this play upon the words belongs to the same turn of mind as produced Jotham's fable and Samson's riddle (ch. xiv. 14).

Ver. 5.—**Jair . . . was buried in Camon.** A city of Gilead according to Josephus, and probability. Polybius mentions a *Camoun* among other trans-Jordanic places, but its site has not been verified by modern research. Eusebius and Jerome place it in the plain of Esdraelon, but without probability. The careful mention of the place of sepulture of the judges and kings is remarkable, beginning with Gideon (ch. viii. 32 ; x. 2, 5 ; xii. 9, 10, 12, 15 ; xvi. 31 ; 1 Sam. xxxi. 12 ; 2 Sam. ii. 10, &c.).

HOMILETICS.

Vers. 1—5.—*The lull.* In the affairs of nations, as in the lives of men, there are occasional periods of uneventful quietness, when the storms and winds of stirring interests and aggressive actions are lulled, and a monotonous rest succeeds to exciting change. At such times no great characters stand out from the historic canvas, no activity of mind producing a clashing of opinion agitates the surface of society, no great measures are called for, no striking incidents of a prosperous or of an adverse kind diversify the scene. It is so likewise sometimes in the Church. Heresy is still; persecution is still; aggressive movements of parties are still; controversy is hushed; Christianity folds her wings and takes no flight into distant lands; there are no reformers at work. Fanaticism is asleep; the uniformity of slumber supersedes the diversities of energetic religious life. Such periods of stillness may have their uses in Church and State, but they have their evils likewise. And they are only temporary; often only the lull before the storm. Such were the forty-five years of the judgeships of Tola and Jair. In their days we read of no invasions of their foes. No Gideon comes to the front with the strong life of unquenchable faith and indomitable courage. The only events chronicled are the peaceful ridings of Jair's sons upon their asses' colts amidst their ancestral cities. But troublous times were at hand. It was the lull before the storm. Would the storm find the people prepared? The sequel will show. Meanwhile the reflection arises, Be it our aim in quiet times not to fall asleep; in times of excitement not to lose the balance of a sober mind and the calmness of a deep-rooted faith.

HOMILIES BY VARIOUS AUTHORS.

Vers. 1—5.—*The calm after the storm.* Partly exhaustion, partly consciousness of Divine judgment, restrains the spirit of Israel. The punishment of its unfaithfulness had come from within itself, and was the more felt. The pendulum now swings slowly back.

I. IT WAS A "PEACE OF GOD." The hand of Jehovah was seen. The consciences even of the wicked had been touched. So in the lives of individuals and nations there are times given of God after judgments in which to repent and amend; and these are not of their own creation, but a result of a gracious Providence. But as they are each a calm after a storm, so, being unimproved, they may be but the portentous lulls before greater judgments. The enemy from without is restrained, as if to say that the real danger could only arise from within.

II. ITS CHARACTER. Undistinguished by great individual exploits; but showing a general advance in civilisation, the arts of peace, and external respect for government and religion. The solid monuments of the people's industry and foresight (the cities of the circle of Jair, &c.) remained. A happier generation lived and throve over the ashes of the guilty past; and some steps were taken towards the more settled and permanent type of government, the monarchy.

III. ITS IMPORT. God's punishments and judgments are intended to prepare for peace. The sinner can never say he has had "no room for repentance." But this was only external and temporary peace—a truce with an unreconciled Heaven. It is precious, therefore, only as making for and typifying the kingdom of Christ, and the peace of believers, which follow upon storm and overturning and Divine chastisements, but confer unspeakable blessings and make happy.—M.

Vers. 1—5.—*Quiet times.* I. THE BEST MEN ARE NOT ALWAYS BEST KNOWN. We know nothing of Tola and Jair in comparison with what we know of Abimelech. Yet the very fact that little is said of them is a proof that they were good and honest men. We are too ready to mistake notoriety for fame and both for signs of greatness. They are not the greatest men who make the most noise in the world. It is something if this censorious world can say no ill of us. Aim at doing well rather than at striking attention.

II. QUIET TIMES ARE HAPPY TIMES. Israel was now experiencing the happiness of the people whose annals are dull. It is generally a miserable thing to be the subject of an interesting story; the more full of incident the story is, the more full of distress will be the person to whom it relates. Happiness generally visits private lives in their obscurity, and forsakes those which are protruded into the glare of vulgar curiosity. David's happiest days were spent with the sheep on the hills of Bethlehem. Christ found more happiness at Capernaum than in Jerusalem.

III. QUIET TIMES ARE OFTEN HEALTHFUL TIMES. There is a quietness which betokens the stagnation of death, and there is a condition of ease which favours indolence luxury, and vice. But there is also a quietness of healthy life (Isa. xxx. 15). The flowers grow, not in the noisy storm, but in soft showers and in quiet sunshine. In times of quiet a nation is able to effect legislative improvements, to open up its internal resources, to develop commerce, to cultivate science, art, and literature, and to turn its attention to the promotion of the highest welfare of all within its borders. In times of quiet the Church is able to study Divine truth more deeply and to carry out missionary enterprises with more energy. In times of quiet rightly used the soul enjoys the contemplation of God and grows under the peaceful influences of his Spirit (Ps. lxxii. 6).

IV. QUIET TIMES ARE MORE FREQUENT THAN WE COMMONLY SUPPOSE. History directs inordinate attention to scenes of tumult, and necessarily so. Hence we are likely to magnify the range of these. In times of war there are vast areas of peace. The terrible seasons which attract our attention are separated by long intervals of quiet which pass unnoticed. Thus it was (1) in the history of Israel, which is really not so dark as it appears because so many generations were spent in peaceful obscurity; (2) in the history of our own country, of the Church, and of the world; and (3) in our own lives, since we commonly recollect the troublesome times (which are striking partly just because they are abnormal), and ungratefully ignore the long, quiet seasons of unbroken blessings.—A.

EXPOSITION.

Ver. 6.—**Did evil again.** We may conclude that Tola and Jair had used their influence to maintain the worship of Jehovah; but at their death idolatry broke out with more virulence than ever. Not only were the many altars of Baal and Ashtoreth honoured, as in former times, but new forms of idol-worship, according to the rites of all the neighbouring nations, were introduced among them. The gods of Syria, i. e. Aram, who are not usually named, but whose worship is spoken of (2 Chron. xxviii. 23), and whose altar attracted the attention of Ahaz (2 Kings xvi. 10), and one of whom was Rimmon (2 Kings v. 18); the gods of the Zidonians, Baal and Ashtoreth, probably with rites somewhat differing from those of Canaan; Chemosh, the god of the Moabites; Milcom or Moloch, the god of the children of Ammon; and Dagon, the god of the Philistines—all were worshipped, while the service of Jehovah was thrust aside (see 1 Kings xi. 5—7).

Ver. 7.—**The anger of the Lord**, &c. See ch. ii. 13, 14. **Into the hands of the Philistines.** Probably the same Philistine domination as is described more fully in the history of the judgeship of Samson (chs. xiii.—xvi.). But now the writer confines his attention first to the oppression of the Ammonites.

Ver. 8.—**That year.** It does not appear clearly what particular year is meant. Jarchi explains it as the year in which Jair died. It may mean the very year in which the idolatries spoken of in ver. 6 were set up, so as to mark how closely God's chastisement followed the apostasy from him. **They,** i. e. the children of Ammon. **Eighteen years.** The same length as that of the Moabite servitude (ch. iii. 18). **The land of the**

Amorites, i. e. the territory of Sihon king of the Amorites, and Og the king of Bashan (Numb. xxxii. 33). **In Gilead**—in its widest acceptation, including, as in Deut. xxxiv. 1; Josh. xxii. 9, 13, 15; Judges xx. 1, the whole country held by the Amorites on the east of Jordan, and given to Reuben, Gad, and the half-tribe of Manasseh. But in its narrower and stricter sense Gilead was bounded on the north by Bashan proper, and on the south by the *Mishor*, or plain of Medeba, which lay between the valley of Heshbon and the river Arnon, thus excluding that part of the territory of Reuben from Gilead (see Josh. xiii. 9—11). Originally, as we learn from ch. xi. 13—22, the territory bounded by the Arnon on the south, by the Jabbok on the north, by the wilderness on the east, and by the Jordan on the west, had belonged to Moab, but the Amorites had taken it from them before the conquest of Sihon by the Israelites.

Ver. 9.—**The children of Ammon**, &c. It would seem that at this time the king of the children of Ammon was also king of the Moabites, since he laid claim (ch. xi. 13, 24) to the land which had once belonged to Moab. If we may trust the king of the Ammonites' statement, the object of the war was to recover that land, and he carried the war across the Jordan into the territory of Judah and Ephraim in order to compel the Israelites to give it up.

Ver. 11.—**Did not I deliver you,** &c. These references to former deliverances are of great historical value, and not the least so as they allude to events of which the existing records give no account, or a very imperfect one. They show the existence of a real history in the background of that which has been preserved in the Bible (see ch. viii. 13, note). **From the Egyptians,** as related at large in the Book of Exodus ; **from the Amorites,** as related in Numb. xxi. 21—35 ; **from the children of Ammon,** who were confederate with the Moabites under Ehud, as we learn from ch. iii. 13 ; **from the Philistines,** as is briefly recorded in ch. iii. 31. Ver. 12.—**The Zidonians also.** This allusion is not clear ; it may mean the subjects of Jabin king of Canaan, as the northern Canaanites are called *Zidonians* in ch. xviii. 7 ; and this agrees with the order in which the deliverance from the Zidonians is here mentioned, next to that from the Philistines, and would be strengthened by the conjecture that has been made, that Harosheth (ch. iv. 2) was the great workshop in which the tributary Israelites wrought in cutting down timber, &c. for the Phœnician ships ; or it may allude to some unrecorded oppression. **The Amalekites,** who were in alliance with the Midianites (ch. vi. 3, 33), as previously with the Moabites (ch. iii. 13) and with the Canaanites (ch. iv. 14), and whose signal defeat seems to have given the name to the mount of the Amalekites (ch. xii. 15). **The Maonites.** It is thought by many that the true reading is that preserved in the Septuagint, viz., *the Midianites,* which, being the greatest of all the foes of Israel, could scarcely be omitted here (see chs. vi., vii., viii.). If *Maonites* or *Maon* is the true reading, they would be the same people as the *Mehunim,* mentioned 2 Chron. xxvi. 7 (*Maon,* sing., and *Meunim,* plur.).

Ver. 16.—**And they put away the strange gods.** Here at length were " the fruits meet for repentance," and " the returning to the Lord their God ;" the intended result of the severe but loving correction (see Homiletics, ch. vi. 25—32). Cf. Gen. xxxv. 2 ; 1 Sam. vii. 3, in which passages, as here, the phrase *the strange gods* is the correct rendering ; not, as in the margin, *gods of strangers.* The Hebrew phrase here rendered **his soul was grieved** occurs Numb. xxi. 4 ; Judges xvi. 16 ; Zech. xi. 2 ; it means *was impatient* —literally, *was shortened,* i. e. he could bear it no longer. A somewhat similar description of the Divine relenting is contained in the beautiful passage Hosea xi. 7—9.

Ver. 17.—This verse ought to begin the new chapter. The preliminary matter of Israel's sin, of their oppression by the Ammonites, of their repentance and return to the God of their fathers, and of God's merciful acceptance of their penitence and prayer, was concluded in the last verse. The history of their deliverance by Jephthah begins here. **And the children of Ammon, &c.,** *i. e.* they encamped, as they had done during the previous seventeen years, in Gilead, either to carry off the crops or to wring tribute from the people, or in some other way to oppress them, expecting no doubt to meet with tame submission as before. But a new spirit was aroused among the Israelites. By whatever channel the bitter reproach in vers. 11—14 had been conveyed to them, probably by the same channel, whether angel, or prophet, or high priest, had an answer of peace come to them on their repentance, and so they were roused and encouraged to resistance. As a first step, they **encamped in Mizpeh** (see ch. xi. 11, 29, 34). Mizpeh, or Mizpah of Gilead, is probably the same as Mizpah in Gilead where Laban and Jacob parted (Gen. xxxi. 25, 49) ; as Ramoth-Mizpeh (Josh. xiii. 26), called simply *Ramoth in Gilead* (Josh. xx. 8 ; 1 Chron. vi. 80) ; and as the place well known in later Israelite history as *Ramoth-Gilead* (1 Kings iv. 13 ; xxii. 3, 6), situated in the tribe of Gad, and a strong place of much importance. It was the place of national meeting for the whole of Gilead. *Mizpah* means *the watch-tower,* and would of course be upon a height, as the name *Ramoth-Mizpeh,* the heights of Mizpeh, also shows. It almost always preserves its meaning as an appellative, having the article prefixed, *ham-mizpah,* which is its usual form ; only once *ham-mizpeh* (Josh. xv. 38), and *Mizpeh* (Josh. xi. 18 ; Judges xi. 29 ; 1 Sam. xxii. 3), and once *Mizpah* (Hosea v. 1). Whether Mizpeh in ch. xx. 1—3 is the same will be considered in the note to that passage. The modern site is not identified with certainty ; it is thought to be es-Salt.

Ver. 18.—**Gilead.** See note to ver. 8. **The people and princes.** There is no *and* in the Hebrew. It is perhaps better, therefore, to take the words in apposition, as meaning, *And the assembly of the chiefs of Gilead.* The first step was to find a competent leader, and they agreed to appoint such an one, if he could be found, as their permanent head and captain.

HOMILETICS.

Vers. 6—18.—*The Ethiopian's unchanged skin.* Among the invaluable lessons of Holy Scripture, not the least valuable is the insight given by its histories into the true nature of the human heart. "The heart is deceitful above all things, and desperately wicked," is the prophet's description of the heart of man, and the history of the Israelites is a signal illustration of its truth. We are apt to think that if we had passed through the waters of the Red Sea, and seen Mount Sinai on a blaze, and eaten the manna from heaven, and drank the water out of the stony rock, and been led to victory by a Joshua, a Barak, a Deborah, or a Gideon, we never could have forgotten such signal mercies, could never have been unfaithful to the gracious Author of them, could never have preferred the vain idols of the heathen to the living God. Still more do we think that if we had seen the only begotten of the Father, full of grace and truth, had heard his wondrous words and seen his mighty works, or had been witnesses of his cross and passion, and talked with him after his resurrection, we should not be the worldly, lukewarm disciples we now are   But we are wrong in thinking so.   The image of the human heart reflected in the history of the Israelite people is a more true and faithful one than that portrayed by our own self-love.   And that image is one of the depraved human will constantly deflecting from rectitude, constantly drawn aside from truth and godliness by the power of selfish affections and corrupt lusts ; occasionally, as it were, turned back toward God, either by strong influences from without, as stirring events, heavy chastisements, striking deliverances, powerful examples, faithful warnings ; or by strong emotions from within, as fear, or gratitude, or hope ; but as soon as these influences begin to cool, regularly returning to their old habit of thinking and acting, and falling back into their own evil ways.   The particular kind of sins to which the heart is most prone varies indeed in different ages of the world, and with the different conditions of the human society.   With the Israelites it was idolatry.   The fascination of the heathen idols was incredibly strong.   In spite of reason, in spite of experience, often of the most bitter kind, they were attracted to the rites of heathenism by the strongest sympathies of their own perverse hearts.   While they shrunk from the lofty obligations of the holy service of God, they abandoned themselves with willingness of mind to the base servitude of the idols, consenting to their shameful requirements, and gloating in their abominable rites.   The desire to be like the nations, the influence of example all around them, the mysterious power of superstition, the agreement between their sensual hearts and the sensual rites of idolatry, were forces steadily turning them away from God, and constantly prevailing over the temporary influences which from time to time had moved them to repentance. But it is just the same with other kinds of sin which strike their roots deep into the hearts of men, and find a ready consent in the diseased moral conditions of those hearts.   For a moment perhaps their power may be weakened by some opposite force, but, unless the fountain of the will is really renewed and sweetened by the indwelling Spirit of God, the same spectacle will be exhibited, as in the case of the Israelites, of the character which had been forced back returning surely and steadily to its natural bent ; of the old influences of pride, selfishness, and lust resuming their former sway ; and of the previous tastes, and manners, and ways of life being restored to their old supremacy.   And it will be found that neither reason, nor experience, nor common sense, nor even self-interest, are able to prevent this.   The Ethiopian cannot change his skin, nor the leopard his spots.   No more can they do good that are accustomed to do evil (Jer. xiii. 23).   The evil bent of a corrupt nature will ever be towards evil.   It is the knowledge of the evil that is in us, and the consequent distrust of ourselves, which is the first real step towards a lasting change. Not till this evil is experimentally felt do the two great doctrines of the gospel, atonement for sin by the sacrifice of Jesus Christ, and regeneration by the Holy Spirit of God, assume real significance and value in our eyes.   When it is known and felt, the inestimable blessing of forgiveness of sin is known and valued too.   So is the all-sufficient grace of the Holy Ghost.   Then too comes watchfulness against the deceit and treachery of the heart ; then a steady striving against sin ; then a firm resolution not to open the heart to the subtle influences of sin, but rather to crucify the flesh with its affections and lusts ; and so what was impossible to unassisted nature becomes an actuality through God's all-sufficient grace.   The Ethiopian skin is transformed to a holy whiteness, the leopard's spots are done away, the corrupt heart is renewed in holiness after the image of God, and the old man becomes a new creature in Christ Jesus the Lord.

HOMILIES BY VARIOUS AUTHORS.

Ver. 6.—*Recurring habits of evil.* The external peace and order do not break the entail of evil habit—"*they continued to do evil.*"

I. OBSERVANCE OF EXTERNAL DECENCIES OF LIFE IS NO SAFEGUARD AGAINST INBRED DEPRAVITY. Only the hearty love and service of God. Probably the "whoring after other gods" began beneath the cloak of an orthodox worship. For a certain time material prosperity may consist with religious laxity.

II. BESETTING SINS, UNREPENTED OF, ASSUME MORE AGGRAVATED PHASES. Like the man out of whom the devil had been cast, which, returning from the "dry places," and finding his heart "empty, swept, and garnished," "bringeth seven other devils," &c. It was an idolatrous confusion; there could be no rationale of these systems, harmonising them with the conscience, or even with one another. All sense of niceness has deserted Israel. It plunges heedlessly into a sea of obscurity and filth.—M.

Vers. 7—10.—*Immediate and effectual retribution.* I. IN THE PUNISHMENT IN-FLICTED THE CALAMITY WAS CLEARLY CONNECTED WITH THE SIN. 1. *The sin committed is at once followed by penalty.* 2. *The punishment lasts whilst the transgression is unrepented of.* 3. *The seducers become the instruments of punishment.*

II. THE UNHELPFULNESS OF IDOLATRY WAS EXPOSED. The Ammonites, whose unholy practices they had copied, take advantage of their weakness, and pitilessly despoil and harass them. The tender mercies of the wicked are cruel. Of all the gods they had served, Baal, Molech, Astarte, &c., not one could deliver them. Only Jehovah can hear, and to him they are at last driven. Even Gilead—the heroic land—is rendered helpless before the despised Ammon, as if to show that real bravery is a moral quality. And the old "fear of Israel" which kept the heathen nations back was gone. The Ammonites wax bold, and cross the Jordan even into Judah.—M.

Vers. 10—14.—*God answering hardened transgressors.* He seems to deny the petition. Is this capricious? There is surely not only cause for it, but a purpose working through it.

I. THE AIM OF THE SEVERITY IS TO AWAKEN TRUE REPENTANCE. Inconvenience, dis-comfort, distress, humiliation may all be felt without true repentance. The latter arises from sorrow for and hatred of sin as sin.

II. THIS IS SECURED by—1. *An appeal to memory of manifold deliverances and mercies.* 2. *Holding the sinner under the yoke of his own choosing when he no longer chooses it.* 3. *The temporary horror and despair of rejection.* "I will deliver you no more."—M.

Vers. 15, 16.—"*Works meet for repentance.*" A wonderful summary; an evan-gelical anticipation.

I. IN WHAT THESE CONSIST. 1. *Heartfelt sorrow and confession of sin.* 2. *Abso-lute yielding of oneself into the hands of God.* 3. *Forsaking the sins that have deceived and destroyed.* 4. *Serving Jehovah with new obedience and zeal.*

II. HOW THESE APPEAL TO THE MIND OF GOD. "His soul was grieved for (literally, endured no longer) the misery of Israel." The alternate hardening and melting of God's soul an accommodation to man's conceptions and feelings; yet with a reality corresponding to them in the Divine nature. They have a disciplinary effect, and their succession is impressive. So God "repents." To our heavenly Father the proofs of our sincerity are an irresistible petition. He welcomes the first signs of true repentance, and leads it forth into saving faith. The truly repentant were never yet rejected. In working this repentance in their minds he began to answer their prayer even whilst rejecting it.—M.

Vers. 17, 18.—*Faith restoring courage and might.* I. BY PROMOTING THE UNITY OF GOD'S PEOPLE. The worship of Jehovah is the uniting and inspiring principle. All other worship disunites and weakens. The very site of their camp was instinct with solemn, Divine associations.

II. ENABLING THEM TO FACE RESOLUTELY THE GREATEST TROUBLES OF LIFE. Israel is in the field against Ammon, a circumstance full of meaning. When the Spirit of

God enters a man he looks upon difficulties with a new resolution. It enables him "to take arms against a sea of troubles, and by opposing, end them."

III. RENDERING THEM WILLING TO ACCEPT THE LEADER GOD SHALL INDICATE. It is no lusting after a king now. The only King is Jehovah. But a leader and judge is sought. So the true Christian will reverence and follow all who are inspired and appointed by God.—M.

Ver. 10.—*From God to Baal.* I. MAN MUST HAVE SOME RELIGION. If God is forsaken, Baal is followed. The soul cannot endure a void. This temple must always have some deity in it. If the higher religion is rejected, a lower superstition will take the place of it. The decay of the national religion of old Rome was accompanied by the adoption of strange Oriental cults, and by the spread of a religion of magic. Modern scepticism gives birth to extraordinary forms of superstition—religions of nature, of humanity, of spiritualism. Accordingly, the effort to attain freedom by escaping from the restraints of Christianity is a delusion, and ends only in the bondage of some lower influence. The soul must have some master, and if it rebels against God it will serve Baal, mammon, the world, the flesh, or the devil. True liberty is only found in willing obedience, in the submission of love, in sympathy with the mind of God, in delighting in his law. Perfect freedom of will arises from perfect harmony between our will and God's will, so that we gladly desire what he requires (Ps. xl. 8).

II. SIN HAS TWO LEADING FEATURES, A POSITIVE AND A NEGATIVE. It is forsaking God and serving Baalim ; omission and commission. The tendency is to regard one of these two much to the neglect of the other. Over-scrupulous people are very sensitive about the minutest act of positive wrong, but sometimes indifferent in regard to the neglect of duty. Energetic people often make the opposite mistake, and show great anxiety to do good service, while they are not sufficiently careful to avoid hasty acts of a questionable character. These two sides of sin are closely connected. Devotion to God is the great safeguard to purity ; when this grows cold the soul is open to the attack of temptation, leading to direct transgression. On the other hand, positive sin is poison to religious faith. The commission of evil deeds inclines us to the omission of duties. Impurity paralyses zeal. We cannot serve God while we are serving Baalim.

III. CONDUCT ALWAYS TENDS TO RUN INTO EXTREMES. We serve God or Baalim, light or darkness, good or evil. There is no middle course. There appears to be more variety, gradation, and mixed character in life than is allowed for in Scripture (*e. g.* 1 John iii. 8—10). But life is only yet beginning to develop, its true nature will be seen in eternity. Two seeds may look much alike, and the first sprouts from them may not be very dissimilar, yet the gardener who knows the natural history of the plants, judging by their whole growth, may pronounce them to be very different. In this early growth of the soul's life on earth, the great question is, What tendencies does it show? The twilight of sunrise looks very like the twilight of sunset, yet the one is the prophecy of day and the other the portent of night. Two streams which flow from one watershed are at first near together, yet if one is running east and the other west, they may come at last to be divided by a whole continent, and to end in two separate oceans. We must be moving in one or other of two directions. The question is, Are we going to the light or from the light, to God or from God ? The tendency determines the character of the life, and this must be justly estimated by the full issues involved in the tendency, not by the present early stages of it. Thus we are all children of the light or children of the darkness, ripening into saintly servants of God or corrupting into wretched slaves of sin.—A.

Vers. 13, 14.—*The test of trouble.* I. WE ALL NEED A REFUGE FOR TROUBLE. Life is so mixed that even to the happiest it is full of disappointments and anxieties. Though it may be smooth at present, we know that it cannot continue so for ever. The storm must fall at some time on every soul that is making the voyage of life. "Man is born to trouble" (Job v. 7). The self-assurance that suffices us in prosperity will not be enough when the tribulation comes. Some refuge every soul must then seek.

II. THE GREAT REFUGE FOR TROUBLE IS IN RELIGION. This is not the sole function of religion. It is also a light, an inspiration, an authority. But all men who have a religion turn to it as their supreme haven when the storms drive. We are naturally religious. Instinctively we look up—if not to the light, then to the darkness, the mystery, the unknown above us.

III. THE VALUE OF RELIGION IS TESTED BY ITS EFFICACY AS A REFUGE IN TROUBLE. The breakwater is tested by the storm; the armour is tried by the combat; the medicine is proved by the disease; the consolation is revealed by the distress. If the lamp of our religion will only burn while the sun of prosperity shines, and goes out when the night of adversity closes in, it is worthless. Men make gods of their pleasures, their business, their science. What can the husk of old pleasures do in the "winter of discontent," when no new pleasure can be evoked? What will the idols money, fame, knowledge avail in the agony of the wreck of a life's hopes, in the mystery of death and eternity? How foolish to be engrossed in pursuits which will leave us destitute in the hour of our greatest need!

IV. IF WE HAVE NOT SUBMITTED TO THE TRUE RELIGION IN PROSPERITY WE HAVE NO RIGHT TO EXPECT TO ENJOY THE REFUGE OF IT IN ADVERSITY. There are men who postpone attention to the claims of Christ till the time of trouble, and find no way to him when they most need him. They will "make their peace with God" on their death-bed. But this is not so easy as they suppose. Apart from the wickedness and insult to God which such conduct implies, it is also the height of folly, and is based on a complete misconception of the first elements of true religion. It is true that God is willing to receive us whenever we honestly return to him in repentance; but (1) the selfish terror of approaching calamity is not repentance; (2) genuine repentance, involving a change of desire, is not easily created by selfish fear; (3) it is not well that men should too readily escape from all the consequences of their sins.—A.

Vers. 15, 16.—*Repentance.* I. REPENTANCE INVOLVES CONFESSION OF SIN. The people admit their guilt to themselves and declare it frankly to God. 1. *We must confess sin.* We cannot turn from sin till we are conscious of sin. God will not forgive our sin till we confess our guilt. These two things, the self-knowledge and the self-revelation before God, which are implied in confession, must be found in true repentance. Pride would simply forget the past, but this cannot be forgotten till it is forgiven, nor forgiven till it is confessed (1 John i. 9). 2. *The confession must be to God;* because (1) it is against God that sin is committed; (2) he alone can forgive sin; (3) we have no warrant for believing that he delegates this Divine prerogative to any human deputy.

II. REPENTANCE INVOLVES SUBMISSION TO GOD. No repentance is complete which does not involve self-renunciation. This is necessary, (1) because, since sin arises from self-will and rebellion against the will of God, the return from sin must be marked by a return to obedience; (2) because the penitent is conscious of his utter ill desert, and of his absolute dependence on the mercy of God, so that he dares claim nothing but what God may think fit to give him, and knows that at the worst this can be no harder than what he merits; and (3) because repentance involves the admission that while we were sinful and foolish in forsaking God, he was always good to us, and will never do for us anything short of what is best. Repentance thus recognises again the despised fatherhood of God, and willingly trusts to his grace.

III. REPENTANCE INVOLVES PRACTICAL AMENDMENT. The children of Israel put away the strange gods from among them, and served the Lord. If repentance is genuine it will show itself in conduct—it will bring forth fruits (Matt. iii. 8). This does not imply—1. That we must complete the reformation of our own lives before God will forgive us, because (1) that is impossible (Jer. xiii. 23); and (2) the very object of the gospel is to do this—*i. e.* to save us from our sins (Acts iii. 26). 2. Neither does it imply that any measure of reformation will be regarded as penance, as sacrifice, as a meritorious work securing forgiveness, since the essence of forgiveness lies in its freeness. But it implies that the genuineness of repentance must be tested by its effects. Repentance is not a mere feeling of grief; it is not seated in the emotions, but in the will. It is a change of desire, and the wish to do better.

This is active, and must manifest itself in conduct. The conduct will be twofold: (1) the giving up of old evil ways, and (2) the commencement of the service of God.

IV. REPENTANCE IS FOLLOWED BY TOKENS OF GOD'S MERCY. When the people repented God could no longer endure their misery. He never willingly afflicts (Lam. iii. 33). He only waits for our repentance to show his compassion. It is possible then because (1) there is no longer the necessity for continued chastisement; (2) the justice and righteousness of God no longer require him to look upon us in wrath; and (3) we shall not be injured by the kindness which falls upon us in our humiliation, but rather healed and strengthened for a better life by the influence of God's love.—A.

EXPOSITION.

CHAPTER XI.

Vers. 1—11.—The narrative here goes back probably some years, to explain the antecedents of Jephthah, who was about to play so prominent a part in the ensuing history. Jephthah we learn was a bastard son of Gilead by a foreign harlot, an Aramitess, if there is any connection between this verse and 1 Chron. vii. 14; and when the sons of Gilead's wife were grown up, they expelled Jephthah, and refused to let him have any share in the inheritance of their father, because he was the son of a foreigner; Jephthah therefore fled from Gilead, and took up his residence in the land of Tob, apparently an Aramean settlement (2 Sam. x. 6, 8), and presumably the land of his mother's birth, where he gathered round him "vain men" (ch. ix. 4), and became a famous freebooter. There he was at the time of the Ammonite invasion mentioned in ch. x. 17, and thither the Gileadites sent for him to come and be their captain, after the consultation in ch. x. 18, with the promise that if he came he should be the head or prince of all the inhabitants of Gilead. After some demur he agreed, and came, and was installed as head of the State at the Gileadite metropolis of Mizpah (ch. x. 17, note).

Ver. 1.—**Jephthah the Gileadite.** Gilead has two meanings: it is the name of the country so called (ch. x. 8, note), and it is the name of the son or descendant of Machir the son of Manasseh (1 Chron. vii. 14, 17; Numb. xxvi. 29, 30). *Gileadite* also may be explained in two ways: it may mean an inhabitant of Gilead (ch. x. 18), or it may mean a member of the family of the Gileadites, either an actual son or a more remote descendant of Gilead (Numb. xxvi. 29)—two meanings which would usually coincide. **Gilead begat Jephthah.** Here *Gilead* must mean

the person so called, *i. e.* the son or descendant of Machir, from whom the family, including Jephthah, were called Gileadites; but whether son or descendant cannot positively be affirmed. All that is certain is that he was that one of Machir's descendants who was the head of that division of the Manassites who were called *Gileadites*. Again, when it is said *Gilead begat Jephthah*, we cannot be certain whether it is meant that Gilead was Jephthah's father, or merely his ancestor (see ch. x. 3, note).

Ver. 2.—**And Gilead's wife.** Whenever Gilead lived, besides the son by the foreign harlot, whom Jephthah represented, he had sons and descendants by his legitimate wife, who claimed to be his sole heirs, and who therefore drove Jephthah from the inheritance of their father's house. They might, as far as the language used is concerned, have been Gilead's own sons, or they may have been his grandsons or great-grandsons, and so either the brothers or the cousins and fellow-tribesmen of Jephthah.

Ver. 3.—**The land of Tob.** This is certainly the same country as is spoken of in Ish-tob, *i. e.* the men of Tob, of whom 12,000 were hired by the children of Ammon to fight against David. They are thus named side by side with the men of Beth-Rehob, and Zoba, and Maacah, other small Aramean or Syrian states (2 Sam. x. 6, 8). Tob is again mentioned in all probability in 1 Macc. v. 13; 2 Macc. xii. 17, and the *Thauba* of Ptolemy agrees in situation as well as in name with Tob, but no identification with any existing place has been hitherto effected. **Vain men,** as in ch. ix. 4.

Ver. 4.—This verse brings us back to ch. x. 17, and reunites the two streams of narrative.

Ver. 5.—**The elders of Gilead.** The same as the princes in ch. x. 18.

Ver. 6.—**Our captain.** A military term, as in Josh. x. 24. It is also used in Isa. i. 10 for the *rulers* of Sodom.

Ver. 7.—**Did not ye hate me, &c.** Jephthah's reproach to the "elders of Gilead" strongly favours the idea that "his brethren" in ver. 3, and the "father's house" in ver. 2, are to be taken in the wider sense of fellow-tribesmen and "house of fathers," and that his expulsion was not the private act of his own brothers turning him out of the house they lived in, but a tribal act (taking *tribe* in the sense of *house of fathers*), in which the elders of Gilead had taken a part. If this is so, it removes a great difficulty about Jephthah being Gilead's son, which it is very hard to reconcile with chronology.

Ver. 9.—**Shall I be**, &c. There is no interrogative in the Hebrew. The words may be taken as the laying down of the condition by Jephthah, to which in the following verse the elders express their assent.

Ver. 11.—**Head and captain.** Both civil ruler or judge, and military chief. **Uttered all his words before the Lord.** The expression "before the Lord" is used in Exod. xxxiv. 34 ; Levit. i. 3 ; Judges xxi. 2 (*before God*), and elsewhere, to signify the special presence of the Lord which was to be found in the tabernacle, or with the ark, or where there was the priest with an ephod. And this must be the meaning of the expression here. Jephthah was installed at the national place of gathering and consultation for Gilead, viz., at Mizpah in Gilead, into his office as head of the State, and there, as in the capital, he performed all his duties under the sanctions of religion. Whether, however, the ark was brought there, or the altar, or a priest with an ephod, or whether some substitute was devised which the unsettled times might justify, it is impossible to say from want of information. There seems to be some reference in the words to Jephthah's vow, in ver. 31, as one of such utterances.

Ver. 12.—**And Jephthah sent**, &c. His first attempt was to make an honourable peace by showing that there was no just cause of quarrel. **What hast thou to do with me ?** or, rather, *What business*, what cause of quarrel, *is there between you and me?* (he speaks in the name of Israel, as head of the State) what is it all about ?

Ver. 13.—**And the king**, &c. The Ammonite king stated his ground of quarrel very distinctly. He claimed the land between the Arnon and the Jabbok as Ammonitish or Moabitish territory, and demanded its surrender as the only condition of peace. It appears from Josh. xiii. 25 that part of the land of the tribe of Gad, that, namely, " on the western side of the upper Jabbok," had once belonged to the Ammonites, but had been conquered by the Amorites, from whom Israel took it, together with that which had formerly belonged to the Moabites.

Ver. 16.—**When Israel came up**, &c. In this and the following verses there is a distinct reference to the history in Numbers

and Deuteronomy, and in some instances verbal quotations. Thus in this verse the words below which are put in italics are found in Numb. xiii. 26 ; xiv. 25 : *Israel . . walked* **through** *the wilderness* **unto** *the* **Red** *Sea*, **and came** *to Kadesh.*

Ver. 17.— *Then* **Israel** *sent messengers unto the king of Edom*, **saying**, *Let me*, *I pray thee, pass through thy land* (*country* in A. V. Numb. xx. 17). The words in italics are found in Numb. xx. 14, 17. **And Israel abode in Kadesh.** These words are in Numb. xx. 1 ; see also Deut. i. 46. **The king of Edom would not hearken.** This is related in substance in Numb. xx. 18—21. **And in like manner they sent unto the king of Moab.** There is no mention of this in the Mosaic narrative. The knowledge of it must have been preserved either by tradition or in some other now lost writings ; perhaps in the Book of the Wars of the Lord (Numb. xxi. 14). It is in itself very probable that such a message should have been sent to the king of Moab, whose territories Israel was forbidden to meddle with (Deut. ii 9, 19).

Ver. 18.— **Then they went along**, &c. The narrative here follows Deut. ii. 1. For **they compassed the land of Edom.** Deut. ii. 1 has, " *we compassed Mount Seir;*" but Numb. xxi. 4 has, " *to compass the land of Edom.*" **By the east side**—literally, *by the sun-rising side*, as in Numb. xxi. 11. **They pitched on the other side of Arnon.** The identical words occur in Numb. xxi. 13. **For Arnon was the border of Moab.** The identical words of Numb. xxi. 13, where it is added, "*between Moab and the Amorites.*" South of the Arnon belonged to Moab, and north to the Amorites. The route taken by the Israelites is carefully traced (Numb. xxi. 11—20).

Ver. 19.—**And Israel**, &c. The text here follows Numb. xxi. 21—24 almost verbatim ; but the expression, " *the king of Heshbon*," is from Deut. ii. 24, 26, 30.

Ver. 20.—**In Jahaz.** Otherwise *Jahazah* (Numb. xxi. 23 ; Deut. ii. 32 ; Isa. xv. 4 ; Jer. xlviii. 21, 34). It seems to have lain immediately to the north of the Arnon.

Vers. 21, 22.—These verses are an epitome of Numb. xxi. 24—32. Cf. also Deut. ii. 33—36. **The wilderness** is the country lying east of Moab up to the hill country (see ch. x. 8, note). From the Arnon to the Jabbok is the measurement from south to north ; from the wilderness to the Jordan, from east to west.

Ver. 24.—**Chemosh.** The national god of the Moabites (cf. Numb. xxi. 29 ; 1 Kings xi. 7, 33 ; Jer. xlviii. 7, 13, 46, &c.). **Thy god.** The phrase indicates a very close connection between Moab and Ammon at the present time, both possibly being under one king. Chemosh, rather than Moloch, is mentioned because the territory had belonged to the Moabites, but Chemosh had not been able to save it from the Amorites. **The Lord our God.** Jehovah was the God of Israel as truly as Chemosh was the god of Moab, in one sense. Possibly Jephthah had not risen to the conception of Jehovah as the God of the whole earth.

Ver. 25.—**Art thou anything better, &c.** Jephthah now advances another argument to prove the justice of his cause and the unreasonableness of the Ammonite claim. If the territory in question was Mòabite property, how came it that Balak laid no claim to it? He was an enemy of the Israelites, and yet when Israel took possession of the land, and dwelt in Heshbon, its capital, and the daughter cities or villages thereof, and in Aroer and her daughter cities or villages, and in all the cities on the banks of the Arnon, Balak never strove about them with Israel, or went to war to recover them—a plain proof that he did not look upon them as his property. If they were his, that was the time to claim and recover them, but he had not done so.

Ver. 26.—The occupation of the cities and villages referred to is related in Numb. xxi. 23 and following verses, and in Deut. ii. 36; see too Josh. xii. 2. **Aroer** is not mentioned among the cities of Moab taken by the Amorites in the ancient book quoted in Numb. xxi. 27—30, and it has been conjectured that it may have been built by the Amorites to secure their new frontier. It is described by Eusebius and Jerome in the 'Onomasticon' as built on a hill overhanging the bank of the Arnon, and a ruin called Araïr has been found on the very spot so described. The Aroer mentioned in ver. 33 (where see note) is probably a different place. **By the coasts of Arnon,** i. e. on the banks. The Septuagint for *Arnon* reads *Jordan*, which was the western boundary, as Arnon was the southern (ver. 22). The corresponding description in Deut. ii. 36 is, *From Aroer, which is by the brink of the river of Arnon, and from the city that is by the river, even unto Gilead, there was not one city too strong for us: the Lord our God delivered all unto us.* **Three hundred years.** These words seem quite unintelligible and out of place. They are also chronologically impracticable. One expects the number of the cities, as in ver. 33, rather than the number of years; and it is remarkable that the whole number of cities taken by the Israelites on the east of Jordan must have been just about 300, since the half-tribe of Manasseh had sixty. If Gad and Reuben had the same proportion, it would be exactly 300 (5 × 60). **Within that time.** The Hebrew phrase, which occurs about seventy times, invariably means *at that time*, and here can only refer to the time of the first settlement in the days of Balak, of which he had been speaking—another proof that the enumeration *three hundred years* is out of place here. If the reading *years* is not, as above suggested, an error for *cities*, the whole sentence, *three hundred years*, may very probably be an interpolation by a professed chronologist. The adding up of all the numbers of the servitudes and rests given in the book gives 301 years from the commencement of the oppression by Chushan-rishathaim to the death of Jair. But this method of reckoning gives the impossible period of 600 years from the exodus to the building of the temple.

Ver. 27.—Jephthah now asserts his own entire blamelessness, and appeals to the justice of God to decide between him and the Ammonites.

HOMILETICS.

Vers. 1—28.—*The controversy.* The first element of peace, whether in private or in national controversies, whether in civil or religious disputes, is the genuine desire to be fair. When men have that spirit of justice that they do not desire to claim anything which is not really theirs, or to withhold from their opponents anything that is their due; when their aim is to ascertain what is true, and not to overbear truth by force; when they strive for truth, and not merely for victory—there is a fair chance of both sides arriving at the same result, and so being at peace. The first step in any dispute, therefore, should be a calm and careful examination of the facts of the case. It should not be taken for granted that the views which self-interest, or personal predilection, or party prejudice, incline us to are the right ones, but we should remember that our opponents have equal rights with ourselves, and that it is at least possible that their predilections and prejudices may rest upon as good grounds as our own. A fair and impartial examination of the facts of the case is therefore the first step in every controversy; and that the examination may be fair, we should patiently allow our opponent to state his own case in his own way. The same fact may wear a different aspect according to the mode of stating it, and according to the side of it which is brought prominently into view. Thus Jephthah acted fairly when he asked the king of the sons of Ammon to state the grounds on which he invaded Israel, and when on his side he refuted that statement by an historical retrospect of the transactions in question. Though, however, the spirit of fairness gives the best chance of an amicable settlement of controversies, it does not always lead to such a settlement. Often fairness on one side is met by prejudice and unfairness on the other. But even when both parties are actuated by the like desire of getting at the rights of a question, it may happen that there is that measure of doubt in some matter on which the controversy hinges, that honest minds may differ about it, and that it is inevitable that men's different interests, prepossessions, and prejudices, should incline them different ways. Thus in Jephthah's controversy with the Ammonites there was room for doubt how far the defeat and dispossession of the children of Ammon by the Amorites had for ever extinguished the claim of the former to the ownership of the land. That Israel had not taken the land from the children of Ammon, or displayed any hostility towards them, was undoubtedly true. But it did not necessarily follow that the Ammonite claim was wholly unrighteous. The question how long a time it takes to establish or to invalidate ownership is obviously a debateable one, in the decision of which personal feelings will carry much weight. In the Franco-German war of 1870 the Germans no doubt felt about Alsace and Lorraine that even 200 years possession by France had not wholly abrogated the German rights. And so it may have been with the king of the children of Ammon. He may have thought that he was justified in claiming the land which had once belonged to his people ; and the matter could only be decided by the arbitrament of war. The practical lesson, however, to be learnt is, in all the business of life, whether in politics, or commerce, or in social intercourse, or in religion, to cultivate a spirit of fairness. In religious controversies especially the value of fairness, with a view to truth, and to the peace of the Church, cannot be overrated. It is as humiliating to our Christian character as it is prejudicial to the real interests of religion, when men approach religious questions in a spirit of heated partisanship, seeking only to crush their opponents by ridicule, or abuse, or vehemence, and treating them with insult and indignity. It is no less painful to see falsehood, and suppression of truth, and pious frauds, imported into controversies, the professed object of which is to vindicate the glory of God and the truth of his holy word. If religious controversialists would approach all subjects of difference in a spirit of thorough fairness, would look at their adversaries' arguments with a sincere desire to understand and appreciate them, would give due weight to them, and would believe it possible that they may have reason and justice on their side, there would be a good chance of agreement on many points which now keep Christians hopelessly asunder. And if there should remain some points on which temperament, or education, or habits of thought, in different men, were too diverse to admit of unanimity on doubtful points, then heavenly charity would step forward and maintain that agreement in love which could not be attained in opinion. The unity of the spirit would not be broken, the peace of the Church would not be violated, and the enemies of the gospel would not find their way to victory through the divisions and hatreds of the servants of one Lord. May the Spirit of God come as a Spirit of fairness upon all that name the name of Jesus Christ!

HOMILIES BY VARIOUS AUTHORS.

Vers. 1—3.—*The shaping influences of life.* These different in their nature from that of which the poet speaks—"There's a divinity that shapes our ends, rough-hew them how we will" (*Hamlet*, V. ii.). It is an anticipative part they play. In many lives the manner in which they are thus influenced is apparent; but even when otherwise the effect is none the less powerful and lasting. It has been questioned whether this be not the most important part of the work of creation. Of these influences, notice—

I. How STRONG AND VARIED THEY ARE. 1. *In Jephthah's birth.* He was a child of shame, the fruit of an age of licentiousness and idolatry. He receives the title Gileadite, yet it is said Gilead was his father ; he must therefore either have had a father with such a name, a member of the tribe of Manasseh, living in Gilead, or, having no clear proof of his paternity, have received the tribal name in that relation. A foundling, with a shameful mystery lying behind his life. 2. *In the behaviour of men towards him.* Those who were his brethren according to the flesh acted a most unbrotherly part. Either from selfishness or a false feeling of shame, they expelled him from his father's house, closing the door of peaceful, honourable toil, and compelling him to resort to a career of bloodshed and irregularity. The very men who might, any of them, have committed a like sin to that of Jephthah's father are forward to rid themselves of its results. The world judges of men rather from their misfortunes than from their personal misdeeds. And where nature has been unkind, "man's inhumanity to man" is only the more signal. A social stigma is worse to bear up against than many of the greatest calamities which do not involve it. 3. *In the force of his circumstances as they arose.* He is compelled to take up his abode in a far off border town, near to Ammon, the hereditary enemy of Israel, and surrounded by the conditions of a desert life, where he had to be "a law unto himself." A life of guerilla warfare, with its comparatively loose *morale,* is thrust upon him. Men of like misfortune and disposition, all more or less compromised with their tribes or nations, gather about him, and look to him for direction and initiative. But—

II. NEVERTHELESS, THEY DO NOT DETERMINE DESTINY. He has somehow managed to preserve a measure of morality and religious observance, even in that wilderness stronghold. The worship of Jehovah is maintained, and the heart of the chieftain beats true to all the traditions of Israel. His personal influence and warlike prowess are at its service. His greatest exploits are not those of the private marauder, but of the patriot. It is character alone that determines destiny, and character is in our own keeping. One is continually meeting with such people—people who in difficult circumstances are yet kept on the whole pure and faithful. Such were "they of Cæsar's household." And—

III. IF RIGHTLY ENCOUNTERED THEY MAY REDOUND TO ADVANTAGE AND HONOUR. In the hour of Israel's need, repentant and humble, its elders approach the outlaw whom they had expelled. The man himself is not prepared for the singular conversion. He questions them suspiciously, nay, with all his magnanimity, reminds them of their different behaviour in years gone by. They admit all ; but they are too humbled to make evasion and to conceal their real motive. He is master of the situation. His whole previous training and reputation now stand him in good stead, and he understands a little of God's dealings with him. The Bible is full of instances of men who have gained power and fame through the overcoming of difficulties. Time and God are on the side of them who, notwithstanding temptation, are found faithful. And is there not One who outshines all others in this ? "The stone which the builders rejected is become the head stone of the corner." His career is our incentive and example (Phil. ii. 5—11). Have not all rejected Christ ? In our need let us go to him, a nobler than Jephthah.—M.

Vers. 4—11.—*Magnanimity of patriotism.* In the behaviour of Jephthah on this occasion we have a noble illustration of the blending of the religious and the patriotic spirit.

I. PERSONAL WRONGS ARE FORGIVEN. He might have brooded over them, sulked, and rejoiced over the elders in their trouble. But he felt that his country's distress was not a time or occasion for revenging the contumely and wrong that were past. This is the true spirit of the patriot. The individual is lost in the commonwealth.

II. HIS COUNTRY'S NEED IS GENEROUSLY RESPONDED TO. What an opportunity for an unprincipled, irreligious man ! He might have turned Israel's loss to his own gain.

III. HIS OWN FORTUNES ARE LOST SIGHT OF IN THE GREATER AMBITION OF BEING THE SAVIOUR OF HIS COUNTRY. Rank he does not value. He refuses leadership until it is shown that he is the Divinely revealed leader. He gives all the honour to Jehovah. From that moment he was at the service of his people, and the unselfish "servant of Jehovah." Men are found who will behave thus for earthly fatherlands and temporal attachments. Often the human tie and the Divine conflict. Jephthah was serving God and country at once. The Christian will serve his friends and his country best by serving God first. How dear should the Church and kingdom of God on earth be to us! All other considerations should be lost sight of in the zeal for our Master's glory.—M.

Ver. 11.—*Recognition of God in positions of honour and responsibility.* How many would have at once swollen with self-conceit! &c. It is a test of the inner life of Jephthah. We may all be more or less tested in this way.

I. HE ENTERED UPON HIS GREAT TASK WITH A SENSE OF SOLEMN RESPONSIBILITY TO GOD. Mizpah was the reminder of an ancient covenant, and its associations are honoured.

II. HE MADE PUBLIC CONFESSION OF JEHOVAH.

III. HE LOOKED TO JEHOVAH FOR GUIDANCE AND HELP.—M.

Vers. 12—28.—*The model diplomatist.* I. THE PROFOUND SAGACITY AND SENSE OF INTERNATIONAL COURTESIES AND OBLIGATIONS DISPLAYED BY JEPHTHAH. An historical site is chosen, which had significance to all the nations neighbouring upon it. At Mizpah had Jacob and Laban made solemn covenant. To their descendant nations the place could not but possess a religious interest. It was a distinct advantage, therefore, to take up his head-quarters there. All his soul is possessed by the old associations of the place. It appears even in his language (vers. 10, 11). This persistent reference to the place was a guarantee of good faith and brotherly feeling. He speaks of the gods of Ammon and Israel from a neutral point of view.

II. HIS APPEAL TO HISTORY. It is sacred history, with the seal of God upon it. He recounts the details of the conquest by Israel, so far as they are relevant; shows that their own land is held by that title, and asks why for 300 years Israel's occupancy of the disputed territory had not been contested. The example of Balak, who saw that it would be destruction for him to contend with Israel, and forbore, is quoted aptly. The geographical limits are carefully indicated.

III. ALL THIS WAS WORTH WHILE, *even with a heathen adversary.* It stated the case upon broad, intelligible grounds; it raised no irrelevant questions, but was conciliatory; and there was no attempt at compromise. It is a moral gain when a point in dispute is thus clearly and dispassionately argued. It did not avert war, but it justified it. *And Israel were strengthened and encouraged.* The people could grasp the outlines of this great claim. They could go forward with confidence that their cause was righteous, and therefore the cause of God. Disputes between individuals and nations should be settled—(1) upon common grounds and associations; (2) courteously and kindly; (3) with careful regard to facts; and (4) God should be the great Witness.—M.

Ver. 7.—*The friend in need.* I. THE VALUE OF A TRUE FRIEND IS SEEN IN THE TIME OF ADVERSITY. Jephthah was hated by the elders of Israel in prosperous times, but when trouble came he was discovered to be their best friend. The wise man will endeavour to cultivate the friendship of the good and great. It is foolish to let valued friends pass away from us through negligence or slight offence. There are few forms of earthly riches more valuable than that of a treasury of friendships. We may be careless of this in circumstances of ease; but if so, trouble will reveal our mistake. Christ is a Friend who sticketh closer than a brother, too often neglected in prosperity, but found to be the one needed Helper in the hour of darkness (Isa. xxxii. 2).

II. THE BEST FRIEND IS NOT ALWAYS THE MOST POPULAR. He may be poor, unpretending, eccentric, or dull. It is foolish to choose our friends by the superficial attractions of social amusement. The boon companion may prove a shallow friend. Sterling qualities of fidelity, self-denying devotion, &c. are not always accompanied by brilliant conversational gifts and such other pleasing characteristics as shine in festive scenes. Christ, the best of friends, was despised and rejected of men. It may be that the very excellency of the friend is the cause of his unpopularity. He will not lend himself to low pursuits, and so is considered morose; he refuses to flatter our weakness,—perhaps bravely and disinterestedly rebukes our faults,—and is therefore thought censorious and offensive; he aims at raising us to what is worthy of our efforts, and is voted "a bore." The time of trouble will destroy this unjust estimate, but it would be more wise and generous in us to value our friends at all times for their best qualities, even though the sobriety of them may appear dull.

III. THE TRUE FRIEND WILL NOT REFUSE HELP IN NEED, ALTHOUGH HE MAY HAVE RECEIVED UNWORTHY TREATMENT IN PROSPEROUS TIMES. Jephthah naturally reproaches the elders of Israel, but he is too noble to refuse to come to their help. True friendship is generous, unselfish, and forgiving. It does not stand "on its rights," "on its dignity." It is more concerned with the welfare of those in whom it is interested than with their deserts. The patriot will not let his country suffer because he is personally piqued at the conduct of its leaders. The Christian should learn not to injure the cause of Christ through the pride and offence which the wrong conduct of responsible persons in the Church may excite. Israel is larger than the elders of Israel. The Church is greater than her doctors and ministers. Jephthah is a type of Christ, who does not refuse to help us though we have rejected him in the past.—A.

EXPOSITION.

Ver. 29.—**Then the Spirit of the Lord came upon Jephthah**, as upon Othniel, upon Gideon, and upon Samson (ch. iii. 16 ; vi. 34 ; xiii. 25 ; xiv. 19 ; xv. 14). **He passed over**, i. e. he went all through, **Gilead, and Manasseh**,—for the purpose, no doubt, of collecting forces,—**and passed over Mizpeh**. It should be *to Mizpeh*. Mizpeh was the capital and mustering place of his army, and his base of operations (ch. x. 17 ; xi. 11, note). Having organised his forces at Mizpeh of Gilead, **he passed over to the children of Ammon**, i. e. commenced his attack upon the invaders, as it is stated in ver. 32, which takes up the thread of the narrative.

Vers. 30, 31.—**And Jephthah vowed a vow**. This verse and the following go back to relate something which preceded his passing over to the children of Ammon, viz., his rash and unhappy vow. This is related, as so many things in Scripture are, without note or comment, and the reader must pass his own sentence upon the deed. That sentence can only be one of unreserved condemnation on the part of any one acquainted with the spirit and letter of the word of God. Many attempts have been made to show that Jephthah only contemplated the offering of an animal in sacrifice ; but the natural and indeed necessary interpretation of the words shows that he had a human victim in mind. He could not expect any but a human being to come forth from the doors of his house, nor could any but a human being come forth "to meet him"—a common phrase always spoken of men (Gen. xiv. 17 ; xxiv. 65 ; Exod. iv. 14 ; xviii. 7 ; Numb. xx. 20 ; 1 Sam. xxv. 34, &c., and below in ver. 34). Obviously, in the greatness of his danger and the extreme hazard of his undertaking (ch. xii. 3), he thought to propitiate God's favour by a terrible and extraordinary vow. But if we ask how Jephthah came to have such erroneous notions of the character of God, the answer is not far to seek. Jephthah

was "the son of a strange woman," probably, as we have seen, a Syrian (ch. xi. 1—11, note), and had passed many years of his life as an exile in Syria. Now it is well known that human sacrifices were frequently practised in Syria, as they were also by the Ammonites, who made their children pass through the fire to Moloch, and it cannot surprise us that a man brought up as Jephthah was, and leading the life of a freebooter at the head of a band of Syrian outlaws, should have the common Syrian notion of the efficacy of human sacrifices in great emergencies. His language, indeed, about Jehovah and Chemosh in ver. 24 savoured of semi-heathenism. Nor is it any valid objection that we are told in ver. 29 that "the Spirit of the Lord came upon Jephthah." The phrase does not mean that thenceforth he was altogether under the guidance of the Holy Spirit, so that all that he did was inspired by the Spirit of truth and wisdom, but that the Spirit of the Lord inspired him with extraordinary strength and power for the great task of leading Israel to battle against the Ammonites. **And I will offer.** The rendering suggested by some, *or I will offer*, meaning, if the first-comer is a human being he shall be the Lord's, or if it is an animal I will offer it as a burnt offering, is wholly inadmissible.

Ver. 32.— **So Jephthah.** The narrator takes up again the thread of the narrative, which was interrupted at ver. 29, the words *he passed over unto the children of Ammon* being repeated.

Ver. 33.—**From Aroer . . . to Minnith.** The *Aroer* here mentioned seems to be that in the tribe of Gad (Numb. xxxii. 34 ; Josh. xiii. 25), now *Nahr Ammân. Minnith* is thought to have been situated four Roman miles from Heshbon, on the road to Rabbah of the children of Ammon, afterwards called Philadelphia. It was called *Manith* in the time of Eusebius. **The plain of the vine-**

yards, better taken as a proper name, *Abel-ceramim*. The site is not certainly known. Eusebius speaks of two *Abels*, both fertile in vineyards, one seven Roman miles from Rabbah, which is probably the one here meant.

Ver. 34.—**To his house.** See ver. 11. **His only child** (*Je'hid*)—the same term as is applied to Isaac (Gen. xxii. 2). Eusebius says that Cronus sacrificed his only son, who on that account was called Jeoud, which in the Phœnician tongue means an *only son* ('Prep. Evang.,' iv. 17).

Ver. 35.—**Thou hast brought me very low**—literally, *thou hast thoroughly bowed me down*, i. e. with sorrow. **I cannot go back.** A forcible illustration of the evil of rash vows. He who makes them is so placed that he must sin. If he breaks his vow, he has taken God's name in vain; if he keeps it, he breaks one of God's commandments. So it was with Saul (1 Sam. xiv. 24, 39—45), with Herod (Mark vi. 23); so it has often been since with those who have made unauthorised vows, and who in attempting to keep them have fallen into deadly sin.

Ver. 36. — **My father**, &c. See Numb. xxxii. 2. The touching submission of Jephthah's daughter to her unnatural and terrible fate, while it reveals a most lovable character, seems also to show that the idea of a human sacrifice was not so strange to her mind as it is to ours. The sacrifice of his eldest son as a burnt offering by the king of Moab, some 300 years later, as related 2 Kings iii. 27; the intended sacrifices of Iphigenia and of Phrixus in Greek mythology; the sacrifices of children to Moloch, so often spoken of in Scripture; the question in Micah vi. 7, " Shall I give my first-born for my transgression, the fruit of my body for the sin of my soul?" the Phœnician

custom mentioned by Sanchoniatho (quoted by Porphyry), of sacrificing to Saturn one of those most dear to them in times of war, pestilence, or drought; the yearly sacrifice at Carthage of a boy chosen by lot (' Sil. Italicus,' 4, 765), and many other examples, prove the prevalence of human sacrifices in early times, and in heathen lands. This must be borne in mind in reading the history of Jephthah.

Ver. 37.—**And bewail my virginity.** It is a striking evidence of the strong desire among Hebrew women to be mothers, as seen in Sarah, Rachel, Hannah, and others, that it was the prospect of dying unmarried which seemed to Jephthah's daughter the saddest part of her fate. So in Ps. lxxviii. 63, *their maidens were not given to marriage* is one of the items of the misery of Israel (see too ver. 39).

Ver. 39.—**Who did with her according to his vow.** Nothing can be more express than this statement. In fact, except the natural horror we feel at a human sacrifice, there is nothing to cast the least shade of doubt upon the fact that Jephthah's daughter was offered up as a burnt offering, in accordance with heathen notions, but, as Josephus says, neither " conformably to the law, nor acceptably to God." Most of the early Jewish commentators and all the Christian Fathers for ten or eleven centuries (Origen, Chrysostom, Theodoret, Jerome, Augustine, &c.) held this view. Luther's comment is, " Some affirm that he did not sacrifice her, but the text is clear enough." **She knew.** Rather, *she had known.*

Ver. 40.—**The daughters of Israel**, &c. No other trace of this custom, which was probably confined to Gilead, remains. **To lament.** The word rather means *to praise*, or *celebrate*, as in ch. v. 11 (*rehearse*).

HOMILETICS.

Vers. 29—40.—*Human perverseness embittering the sweet cup.* The tragic history of Jephthah and his daughter is one of the saddest in the Bible. It forms a drama full of pathos, and with terrible contrasts of joy and sorrow. Indeed the whole life of Jephthah was one of startling incident. Driven from his home in youth to become a fugitive and an exile; leading the wild and exciting life of a captain of freebooters till middle age; then recalled to his father's house to take his place as head of the State with all the pomp and power of a great prince, a great warrior, a conqueror, and a judge; in the height of his joy and triumph struck to the ground by a sorrow of the intensest bitterness, which must have blighted the few remaining years of his life—his whole life was one of strange vicissitudes and sensational events. The stain of his birth was not, of course, any fault of his; but it led to that irregular course of lawlessness and violence which must have laid the seeds of many faults of character—recklessness, impulsiveness, and indifference to human rights and human sufferings—which were mingled with many great and heroic qualities. Especially we see how the habit of fighting for plunder, and for the purely selfish ends of a livelihood for himself and his followers, produced that lower type of greatness which bartered his own energies and prowess for place and power, instead of the generous self-sacrifice for the good of his country which marked the career of Ehud and Gideon. What, however, is here especially to be remarked and treasured up in our minds is, that the cup of prosperity and joy which God's goodness had mixed for Jephthah was turned into a cup of bitterness by his own perverse folly and rashness and ignorance of God's grace. See what great things God had done for him. He had delivered him from his life of lawlessness; he had placed him in a high and honourable estate; he had brought him from banishment to the land and house of his fathers; he had filled him with his Spirit, and mightily strengthened him for his great task; he had gone forth with his army, and driven his enemies before his face, and crowned him with victory. Jephthah returned to his home as the deliverer of his country, the restorer of peace to the homesteads of Gilead, all glittering with success and glory. Nor was he wanting in sources of a softer and tenderer happiness. A bright and loving spirit, full of affection and joyous sympathy, overflowing with dutiful pride and beaming sympathy, was awaiting his return. His daughter, the light of his home, the solace of his cares, was there to welcome him and to double his happiness by sharing it. And as he looked forward to the future, he might hope to see her the mother of children who would perpetuate his name and his race. Such was his lot as God had prepared it for him. His own rash and perverse act, springing from a culpable ignorance of the character of God, and directed by heathen superstition and cruelty instead of by trust in the love and mercy of Jehovah, poured an ingredient of extreme bitterness into this cup of joy and poisoned his whole life. The hour of triumph was turned into desolation, the bright home was made a house of mourning, what should have been years of peace and honour were turned into years of trouble and despair, and Jephthah had no one but himself to blame for this lamentable reverse. Alas, how often we can match this scene by similar instances of human perverseness embittering the sweet cup of life! A nation's career is checked by crime, or cruelty, or treachery; an individual's life is marred by some act of ungodliness which entails a life-long harvest of bitter fruits; domestic enjoyment is destroyed by the sins of selfishness and self-willed folly. Bountiful gifts of a gracious Providence, wealth and abundance, splendid opportunities for good, intellectual endowments, rare talents, or, in humbler life, openings for advancement and usefulness which might have led to distinction, are through the perverse folly of their possessors worse than wasted, and dark shadows are thrown across what should have been the brightness of a happy life. And then men speak of their bad luck, and murmur against the providence of God; as if one could sow the wind and not reap the whirlwind, or cut off the shadow of sin, remorse and shame and death.

HOMILIES BY VARIOUS AUTHORS.

Vers. 29—33.—*The spirit of sacred warfare.* There is much at which the modern reader stumbles in the stories of Old Testament warfare. The pitilessness, the assumption that all the right of the question between the belligerents is on one side, the carnage even to extermination, are all repugnant to modern feeling. It is well to look at the Divine background and relation of these wars: therein, and therein alone, will be found their apology, if apology be forthcoming. In the Ammonite war of Jephthah—

I. JUSTIFICATION IS FOUND IN THAT, ON THE LOWEST GROUND, IT WAS A WAR OF SELF-PRESERVATION; AND, ON THE HIGHEST, ISRAEL WAS DEFINITELY AND AUTHORITATIVELY IDENTIFIED WITH THE CAUSE OF GOD'S TRUTH AND RIGHTEOUSNESS, AND APPOINTED THE INSTRUMENT OF HIS JUDGMENTS. In a sense there was "no quarter" in these wars. The claims of the foes of God's people were of the most extreme and exacting character. The barbarians had no pity. It would have been of small moment to them to have "utterly cut off" every man, woman, and child. The greatest crimes were perpetrated by them on the smallest provocation; and they could not be trusted. There was one argument, and one alone, that could be understood—the sword. But there were also weighty interests represented by Israel, for the sake of which it was pre-eminently important that it should continue to exist, and that under conditions of freedom and religion. It was its mission to reveal the will of God to men, not only as a verbal communication, but as a law illustrated in life and conduct. These interests were the highest interests of the world, and Israel was custodian of them for all future ages. There is a humanitarianism that discounts truth, and would reduce all duty to the nearer and more external utilities of life. The Bible, whilst not ignoring the brotherhood of men (no book guards this so jealously), is careful to ground it upon a Divine fatherhood, and to secure its true observance by enforcement of morality and righteousness. Israel, too, was not at liberty to exercise forbearance. " The iniquity" of these nations "was full." They were guilty of unnameable crimes, rejecters of Divine revelation, and cumberers of the ground yet to be occupied by God's gracious purposes.

II. ALL THROUGH JEHOVAH WAS RECOGNISED AS THE TRUE ARBITER. Nothing could be more impressive than the attitude of Jephthah. He is anxious to obtain a just settlement without recourse to arms. He sets forth his statement of the case with the utmost courtesy, exactitude, and forbearance. Every opportunity is given for peaceful understanding; but Ammon turns a deaf ear. Solemnly then, under the peculiar dispensation in which they lived, they put the question in the hands of God. Jehovah is to witness between the disputants, and the war is no longer a confused strife, but a punitive judgment. Israel, under such circumstances, was not at liberty to waive its moral claims, and to grant a truce ere the enemy had yielded the point at issue. Israel is the instrument of Divine vengeance upon a wicked and obstinate nation. It is an anachronism of the gravest consequence to judge of the wars of the ancient world by the ameliorated conditions of modern life.

III. THE LEADER OF ISRAEL RECEIVED HIS COMMISSION DIRECTLY FROM THE HANDS OF GOD. Nothing else can be meant by " then the Spirit of Jehovah came upon Jephthah." Divine impulse, Divine wisdom, Divine obligation are all implied. It is no longer a war whose main issues and movements are subject to fallible human conditions ; it is really in God's hands. He bears the blame, so far as his commands are observed. If the mode of warfare, &c. appear inhuman, it will be because our minds fail to grasp the tremendous importance of that righteousness of which they were the slow precursors and rude witnesses.

IV. THE WAR IS CARRIED ON IN THE SPIRIT OF SELF-SACRIFICE AND IMPLICIT DEVOTION. The vow of Jephthah shows this. He anticipates his return in victory, and the people's enthusiastic welcome to him as their deliverer. Like Gideon, he will not accept this ; it is Jehovah's alone. To Jehovah, therefore, he vows of his own " whatsoever cometh forth (out) of the doors of my house to meet me." No gratification of self, therefore, could be the motive of such a campaign. If, on the other hand, there is not that repugnance to bloodshed displayed by Jephthah that might be looked for in a Christian leader, we must remember that the religious nature developed slowly in human history, and God chose his instruments not because they were perfect, but, such as they were, to bring on higher possibilities and a better time.—M.

Vers. 30, 31, 34—40.—*Jephthah's vow.* What it involved has been much disputed. But the wording of the vow certainly admits of an interpretation consistent with the highest humanity. The object is expressed neutrally, as being more comprehensive; but there is a distinction introduced into the consequent member of the sentence which shows that regard is had to a dual possibility, viz., of the object being either personal or otherwise. If the former, he or she was to be " Jehovah's," an expression unnecessary if it was to be made a burnt offering, and which could only mean " dedicated to perpetual virginity or priesthood." If the latter, he would " offer it for a burnt offering." It bears out this that his daughter asks for two months " to bewail her virginity." The inference is imperative. It was not death, but perpetual virginity, to which she was devoted. In this vow we observe—

I. THE SPIRIT OF CONSECRATION IT EVINCED. Its meaning was evident. Jehovah was the true Judge and Deliverer of Israel. His, therefore, should be the glory when Israel returned in victory. There was to be no diverting of honour from him to Jephthah. A sacrifice, therefore, should be made before all men to acknowledge this. But as Jephthah is the person most in danger of being tempted to forget God's claim, he himself gives anticipatively of his own, and of his own, especially, which might be considered as specially for his honour. It was a " blank form " to be filled up by Providence as it would.

II. THE UNEXPECTED FORM THE SACRIFICE ASSUMED. How it astonishes men when God takes them at their word ! Not that they do not mean what they say, but they do not realise all it implies. God ever does this that he may educate the heart in loving sacrifice, and reveal the grandeur and absoluteness of his own claim upon us.

III. THE GRACE THAT INVESTED IT from—1. *The mutual love of parent and child.* They both sorrow because she is an only child, and they are all in all to one another. It was a keen, real sacrifice. 2. *The unquestioning and cheerful obedience of the child.* Like Isaac and Christ. 3. *The unwavering fidelity of Jephthah to his vow.* It was the wisest course, and the one that proved best the fidelity and infinite love of God. There was sorrow, but who will say that there was not a compensating blessedness in the act, and a " more exceeding weight of glory " in the ages to come ? This is what God expects. Have we ever vowed to him ? If so, have we paid our vows ? Negligence in this matter will explain much that distresses and perplexes us. Honesty towards God—how few practise it! Yet this is the true proof of him (Mal. iii. 10).

IV. HOW AN ABSOLUTE PERSONAL SACRIFICE MAY BECOME A NATIONAL IDEAL AND ATONEMENT. The circumstances were such that all Israel sympathised with the act of self-devotion. It fell in with the national mood and carried it to heroic pitch. The " custom in Israel " shows how profoundly the spirit of the people had been touched. The maiden offered to Jehovah is adopted as the offering of her people, a vicarious sacrifice of their repentance and faith. So does the Lord Jesus, the Son of God, become the world's atonement (2 Cor. v. 14, 15).—M.

Ver. 29.—*The Spirit of the Lord.* I. THE SPIRIT OF THE LORD IS NOT A MERE INFLUENCE, BUT A LIVING PRESENCE. It is taught throughout Scripture that God does not only bestow graces, but also comes personally into our souls (John xiv. 16, 17). This Divine presence may not be perceived by the senses, as in the visions of the dove (Matt. iii. 16) and of the cloven tongues of fire (Acts ii. 3). It need not give rise to any ecstasy or visible excitement, as in the case of the Corinthian Church (1 Cor. xiv. 2). It may be without the immediate consciousness of the subject. But it will be proved by its effects.

II. THE SPIRIT OF THE LORD COMES UPON A MAN TO INSPIRE HIM FOR SERVICE. God does not simply inhabit a man as a temple; he infuses his life into the very being of the man ; transforms, elevates, enlightens, strengthens. Thus Jephthah found the Spirit to be the source of his power for battle. God's Spirit is always the spring of the Christian's highest energies. It is foolish to attempt to do any good work without the aid that is given by the indwelling power of God.

III. THE SPECIAL FORM OF THE INFLUENCE OF THE SPIRIT OF GOD WILL BE DETERMINED BY THE CAPACITIES OF THE RECIPIENT AND THE REQUIREMENTS OF HIS WORK. There is a variety of gifts. 1. God's Spirit affects us differently, according to our *natural differences.* To the thoughtful man he is a spirit of understanding. To him who hungers and thirsts after righteousness he is a spirit of holiness. To the sympathiser, the comforting friend, he is a spirit of love. To the active worker he is a spirit of power. 2. God's Spirit also affects us differently according to the *needs of the times.* God does not waste his influence ; he adapts it to requirements. Therefore we must not think that his Spirit is less with us than with men of old because the manifestation is different, nor that he is less with those who have not the form of spiritual influence which we esteem most than with those who possess it (1 Cor. xii. 6).

IV. THE SPIRIT OF THE LORD DOES NOT ANNIHILATE THE INDIVIDUAL CHARACTERS OF MEN. Jephthah retains his natural characteristics, and still shows them. 1. God's Spirit does not supersede natural talent, but enlightens, purifies, and strengthens. 2. God's Spirit does not destroy human weakness. Jephthah has the Spirit of the Lord, yet he may be rash and may err. The spirit of wisdom does not necessarily accompany the spirit of strength. We may have the presence of the Spirit, and yet not be filled with the Spirit, so that human weakness may linger by the side of Divine power.—A.

Vers. 30—40.—*Jephthah's vow.* Jephthah's conduct should be viewed in the light of his age and of his own conscientious convictions, and not judged by the clearer light and changed convictions of Christendom. Measured by modern standards, it may appear superstitious, cruel, insane ; but measured by the only standards to which Jephthah could bring it, his conduct was noble beyond expression. From the incident generally we may gather the following lessons :—

I. THE HAND OF GOD SHOULD BE RECOGNISED IN OUR GOOD AND FRUITFUL WORKS. The elders had called upon Jephthah to deliver them from the Ammonites. Yet the warrior saw that his own right hand could not secure the victory ; if this came, it must be from God. Such conduct shows *humility*—a difficult grace for a popular hero to practise in the midst of his triumph ; and *faith* in discerning the secret of success in the presence of God, and trusting to this before entering the battle.

II. IT IS RIGHT THAT WE SHOULD RECOGNISE GOD'S CLAIMS IN RETURN FOR THE RECEPTION OF HIS GRACE. The thank offering belongs not to the Levitical law alone, but to all religion (Rom. xii. 1). It is foolish to think to buy the help of God by promising him devotion in return (Gen. xxviii. 20—22). But it may be helpful to our fulfilment of the duties of gratitude if we recognise the obligation of thankfulness even before we receive the special blessing of God, as we are more likely to realise it fully then than after we are relieved and satisfied. It should always be remembered that we have already received such great bounties from God that we are under constant obligations to him, that he claims our hearts, our possessions, our all, and that our true blessedness is only found in perfect surrender to him.

III. IT IS GENERALLY FOOLISH AND WRONG TO MAKE A VOW THE CONSEQUENCES OF WHICH WE DO NOT FORESEE. There may be an occasional advantage in the vow to bind the soul by a solemn recognition of its obligations ; but we are equally required to give God our all whether we make a vow or no. Nothing is more weak than to vow at a time when we are not called to make a sacrifice, and then to prove unequal to the sacrifice when this is required. It is better to count the cost and refrain from making the vow if necessary (Luke xiv. 28). The vow is often only a sign of presumption. It would be well for us to turn our vows into prayers, and instead of promising that we will do some great thing, to ask God to give us grace to do it. Still, viewed from the standpoint of devotion, there is something noble in the perfect surrendering of self, and the brave trustfulness of Jephthah's vow.

IV. WE SHOULD CONSIDER OURSELVES BOUND TO KEEP THOSE VOWS WHICH WE MAKE TO OUR OWN HURT SO LONG AS WE DO NOT FEEL THIS TO BE WRONG. Our own inconvenience is no excuse for declining to fulfil an obligation, just because we did not anticipate the trouble in entering into the obligation (Ps. xv. 4). But our conviction of wrong is a reason for not keeping our promise. A promise to do evil is void from the first. It is wrong to make such a promise ; to fulfil it is to add a second wrong. We can never bind ourselves by vow to do that which it would not be right for us to do without the vow. Therefore for us, with our Christian light, it would be sinful to fulfil such a vow as Jephthah's. Nevertheless, the great Hebrew hero clearly felt that it was his duty to fulfil it, and therefore to him the vow was binding. If we blame him, it must be (1) for the rashness which allowed him to contract himself into an obligation which he would never have entered with his eyes opened, and (2) for the ignorance of the character of God which is shown in his supposition that God could be pleased with the sacrifice of his daughter. Even the imperfect revelation of God then vouchsafed should have prevented such a frightful misconception if it had been rightly used (Gen. xxii. 12). But we may find more of good example than of warning in the whole incident. Pathetic as is the error of Jephthah, his magnificent fidelity is a model of religious heroism.—A.

EXPOSITION.

CHAPTER XII.

Ver. 1. — **Northward**, or, otherwise rendered, *to Zaphon*, a city of the Gadites mentioned in Josh. xiii. 27 together with Succoth, and thought to be the modern *Amateh* on the Wady Rajib (see Vanderveld's map). It is difficult to say with certainty which rendering is right, but on the whole the latter seems most probable. Although Gilead does lie north-east of Ephraim, it hardly seems a natural description of the Ephraimite movement to say they "went northwards;" whereas if they marched to Zaphon the phrase would be precise. The previous phrase, **gathered themselves together**, means *mustered for battle*, as in ch. vii. 23, 24. **We will burn thine house**, &c.—the same savage threat as the Philistine youths made use of to induce Samson's wife to discover and reveal his riddle (ch. xiv. 15), and as the Philistines actually put in practice upon her and her father in revenge for the destruction of their corn (ch. xv. 6). **Passedst thou over**, as in ch. xi. 29, 32; xii. 3.

Ver. 2.—**When I called you.** This incident is not mentioned in the previous narrative. Probably Jephthah asked the help of Ephraim when he was first made chief of the Gileadites, and they refused partly because they thought the attempt desperate, and partly because they were offended at Jephthah's leadership.

Vers. 4, 5.—The English version of these somewhat obscure verses is obviously wrong, and devoid of sense. The obscurity arises partly from verses 5 and 6 being merely an amplification, *i. e.* a narrative in detail of what is more briefly related in ver. 4; and from the insertion of the explanatory words, "*Gilead* lies in the midst of Ephraim and in the midst of Manasseh," in ver. 4. The literal translation of the two verses is as follows: — *And the men of Gilead smote Ephraim* (at the fords of Jordan), *for, said they, ye are fugitives of Ephraim. (Gilead lies in the midst of Ephraim and in the midst of Manasseh*, i. e. between Manasseh and Ephraim, so that in coming from Manasseh, where they had taken refuge, to return to Ephraim they were obliged to pass through Gilead, *and the Gileadites had taken the passages of Jordan before the Ephraimites; and it was so, that when the fugitives of Ephraim said, Let me pass over, that the men of Gilead said, Art thou an Ephraimite? If he said, Nay, then said they unto him, Say now Shibboleth*, &c., *i. e.* they put him to the test of pronunciation; and if they found by his pronunciation of the word Shibboleth, viz., Sibboleth, that he was an Ephraimite, in spite of his denial, *then they took him and slew him* (killed him in cold blood) *at the passages of Jordan.) And there fell at that time*, &c. The direct narrative goes on here from ver. 4.

Omitting the long explanatory parenthesis from the latter part of ver. 4 to the latter part of ver. 6, the narrative runs (ver. 4), *And the men of Gilead smote Ephraim, for, said they, ye are fugitives of Ephraim; and there fell at that time of the Ephraimites forty and two thousand.* The parenthesis explains why the Ephraimites had to pass through Gilead, and how the Gileadites ascertained in each case whether a man was an Ephraimite or not.

Ver. 6. — **Say now Shibboleth**, &c. We have thus, as it were, accidentally preserved to us a curious dialectical difference between the Ephraimites and the inhabitants of Gilead. A similar difference exists at the present day between the pronunciation of the inhabitants of different parts of Germany. What the Hanoverians call *stein*, a stone, the other Germans call *shtein*. *Shibboleth* means both *an ear of corn* and *a stream*. **Forty and two thousand.** It is possible that the war between Jephthah and the Ephraimites may have lasted a considerable time, though only the single incident of the slaughter at the fords of Jordan is mentioned, so that the large number of 42,000 men may be less improbable than it seems at first sight. There is, however, always some doubt as to the correctness of numbers (see 1 Sam. vi. 19).

Ver. 7.—**Six years.** Perhaps his sorrow for his daughter shortened his life. **Then died Jephthah the Gileadite.** Better, *And Jephthah the Gileadite died*. **In one of the cities.** His exact burial-place was perhaps unknown, and therefore the general phrase *in the cities of Judah* was used, as in Gen. xiii. 12. Lot is said to have dwelt *in the cities of the plain*, and in Neh. vi. 2 Sanballat asked Nehemiah to meet him *in the villages of the plain*. Still the phrase is not what you would expect here, and it seems unlikely that Jephthah's burial-place should be unknown. The Septuagint, Vulgate, Syriac, and Arabic versions read, "in his city Gilead," as if Gilead had been the name of Jephthah's paternal city. Another conjecture is that there might have been an *Ar of Gilead* as well as the well-known Ar of Moab, or there might have been a collection of towns called Arey - Gilead (the towns of Gilead), after the analogy of Havoth-jair (ch. x. 4), but there is no evidence in support of these conjectures.

HOMILETICS.

Vers. 1—7.—*The envy of the small great at the great deeds of the small.* The detection of faults of character is useful to those who wish to correct and perfect their own, and for this reason the observation of the tendency of particular positions to produce particular faults is very valuable. The particular vice of the human mind which the shameful and unpatriotic arrogance of the Ephraimites towards the deliverer of their country brings to light, is the tendency on the part of those in high places to resent and envy the great deeds and successes of those whom they look upon as very inferior to themselves. Ephraim was the largest and most powerful of the tribes of Israel. The great leader, Joshua, was of that tribe, and they seem to have thought that they had an hereditary primacy among the tribes. We have already seen this spirit breaking out fiercely in their strife with Gideon (ch. viii. 1—3), and now again in their hostile attack upon Jephthah. Nay, even in Joshua's time something of the same arrogance drew down upon them the rebuke of their great captain (Josh. xvii. 14—16). They seem to have thought that, being the chief tribe, they were entitled to be considered first in everything; that their advice was always to be sought, their wishes always to be consulted; and that the maintenance of their dignity ought to be the first consideration of all the other tribes. And yet we do not find them maintaining their claims by pre-eminent zeal for the public service, by a spirit of self-sacrifice for the public good, nor by furnishing the most eminent men to take the lead in civil or military affairs. They were not the first to risk life and limb against the Midianite hosts; they were not the first to repel the invasion of the children of Ammon. Their own dignity, and not their country's good, was their chief concern. Hence, when an unknown Gideon, of one of the inferior houses of Manasseh, or a half-caste Jephthah on the other side Jordan, rose to the first rank as saviours of their country, the envy of Ephraim burst out into a flame. What business had such as they to do great things? It was an invasion of the prerogative of the "great people." It was presumption; it was a slight put upon Ephraim. No punishment was too bad for such insolence. "We will burn thine house upon thee with fire." This history then illustrates the pride of caste. It shows us men, having a great opinion of themselves, not influenced by that good opinion to do as much as possible for others, but only to exact as much as possible for themselves. It shows us how an overweening estimate of themselves induces men to envy others, whom they think inferior, if they distinguish themselves, and rise superior to them in public estimation. It was very much the same spirit which showed itself in the Pharisees when our Lord's fame as a teacher drew such multitudes to hear him. They thought they had the monopoly of teaching, that no doctrine which did not emanate from their schools ought to be listened to, that knowledge could proceed from no mouth but that of a Rabbi. And so when the carpenter's Son opened his mouth and poured forth his lessons of exquisite wisdom and power, and enchained the attention of the multitudes, and was acknowledged as a prophet, their envy was excited. Instead of rejoicing that God had sent them a teacher mighty in word and deed, they only plotted how they might silence the eloquent tongue. Instead of sitting at his feet and learning at his mouth the true will of God and the way of life, they were only roused to hatred, and persuaded the multitude to say, Let him be crucified. The same spirit is common in our own days in every profession. The small great envy the great deeds of the small. But God's gifts are not confined to any caste or class; and they only are truly great who rejoice in great qualities wherever they are found, and view without envy the career of those who outstrip them in the race of doing good and advancing the glory of God.

HOMILIES BY VARIOUS AUTHORS.

Vers. 1—3.—*Ingratitude the frequent reward of benefactors.* The triumph of Jephthah is marred by another incident. Ephraim, the most powerful tribe west of the Jordan, confronts him in hostile array. His experience must have been bitter and hard to comprehend. But he is not alone in the results which his good deeds brought upon him. Benefactors in every age have met with a like reception.

I. THEIR GOOD DEEDS ARE THEMSELVES AN OFFENCE. This has its root and ground in the incapacity of the natural mind to perceive and appreciate spiritual motives; but it seldom takes the form of direct, simple objection to the good deed. Other forms of excuse for opposition are easily discovered. 1. *The spirit in which they are wrought is misunderstood or misinterpreted.* The key to our judgments of others is in ourselves. If then we are evil, our judgments will be perverted. All through the history of God's Church this influence is apparent, from the old ill-natured query, " Does Job serve God for nought?" to the culminating wickedness described in the gospel: "The light shineth in darkness, and the darkness comprehended it not. . . . He was in the world, and the world was made by him, and the world knew him not. He came unto his own, and his own received him not" (John i. 5, 10, 11). "To the pure, all things are pure," and *vice versâ*. 2. *They present an unwelcome contrast to the conduct of others.* Every good deed is as a light which brings to view things of like kind, and inspires similar behaviour; but also reveals the hideousness and hatefulness of the ordinary life of man. This is an offence against the *amour propre* of the sinner, and therefore unpardonable; it is also an exposure of hypocrisy, and sadly inconvenient. It makes the heart of good men ache to see this, and to cry, "When will goodness not be the exception, but the rule?" 3. *The honour they acquire for their authors is coveted.* To minds not actuated by the spirit of goodness, the only thing that can be desired in good works is the outward fame and advantage they bring. The exclusion from this is keenly resented. Hundreds are eager to share the crown of the righteous who are far from breathing his spirit or emulating his example.

II. How HARD IS IT FOR EVEN GOOD MEN TO UNDERSTAND THIS! Jephthah argues his case, and asks, "Wherefore are ye come up unto me this day, to fight against me?" The law of Moses promised temporal advantages to those who fulfilled it. Occasionally these were not enjoyed, and there was a consequent perplexity. But we are not to suppose that this wonder and mental trouble were confined to that dispensation; they are deeply human characteristics. Our Saviour himself experienced them when he asked, "Many good works have I showed you from my Father; for which of those works do ye stone me?" (John x. 32); and again, "Are ye come out as against a thief with swords and staves for to take me? I sat daily with you teaching in the temple, and ye laid no hold on me" (Matt. xxvi. 55). The key to this mystery is furnished by the beatitude of the persecuted for righteousness' sake (Matt. v. 11, 12), and realised in the spirit of Christ's sacrifice.—M.

Ver. 4.—*The reproach of the righteous.* "Ye Gileadites are fugitives of Ephraim among the Ephraimites, and among the Manassites."

I. THOSE WHO ARE OPPOSED TO TRUTH AND GOODNESS OFTEN OBJECT TO THE CIRCUMSTANCES IN LIFE AND THE CHARACTER OF THOSE WHO ARE REPUTED TO DO GREAT WORKS IN GOD'S SERVICE. "Fugitives" is a term of social reproach. It suggests vile reasons which made it convenient for them to leave their own home. So it was said, "Is not this Joseph, the carpenter's son?" and, "Can any good thing come out of Nazareth?" So John ix. 24, 29.

II. THIS OBJECTION IS INCONSEQUENT. It ignores the real authorship of goodness, and the method of his working, and character of his instrumentalities in all time. It is *self-contradictory* (John ix. 31).—M.

Vers. 5, 6.—*Shibboleth:—The importance of little defects, faults.* &c. This not absolute, but relative.

I. WHEREIN THIS IMPORTANCE CONSISTS. 1. *In what they suggest or reveal.* A slip in accidence, or a blunder in the statement of matter of fact, may discredit the pretended scholar. A difference in tone or manner may mean indifference or enmity or hypocrisy. Temporary neglect of a child may prove want of real parental affection. Neglect of private or public prayer may be little in itself, but it may spring from the alienation of the soul from God. The glib utterance of a "white lie" may make us doubt the whole moral character of the speaker. Grave diseases often declare themselves by comparatively slight symptoms, as leprosy, paralytic *ataxia*, &c. 2. *We see it in the order of life as a whole.* In the vegetable and animal world the law of the "survival of the fittest" often works through comparatively slight organic adaptations. In human life the advantage and ultimate success of men often depends upon their slight superiority to other competitors. A little ignorance, extravagance, carelessness, &c. may work ruin. "A stitch in time saves nine." "Ready, aye ready," is a noble motto. Great discoveries have been made by men who were just a little in advance of their fellows. 3. *A critical occasion may give a trifle an unlooked-for importance.* The cackling of geese saved Rome, according to the myth. Peter's uncouth accent occasioned the observation of the maid, and his emphatic denial of Christ. Vessels have been wrecked because of a little carelessness in taking observations when mists have suddenly arisen, or rocks were in the course. Souls have been lost through impressions produced by the inconsistencies of professing Christians.

II. OUR DUTY WITH RESPECT TO THEM. "Of course it is to correct them, to get rid of them," you say. Yes; but how? Sometimes they are so related to us that we cannot remove them. It is necessary then that we should do all in our power to compensate for them by cultivating other qualities, &c., or to neutralise their influence by timely explanations and clear proofs of our real intention, spirit, character, &c. Mere punctilio, or the scrupulosity of the martinet will not do. We must beware of the folly of those who "strain at a gnat and swallow a camel." Let the whole life be emphatic in contradiction, and let the spirit of Christ so shine through us that men will learn to know us in spite of those failings and defects which give us the lie. "Not far from the kingdom of heaven" may be worse than entire alienation from it.

Tests: their good and evil. As a means of discovering the Ephraimite, the device was highly natural and ingenious. In the main and roughly it was successful. Some such method was evidently required. There was no time to enter into minute detail or examination. But, on the other hand, it was quite possible that some who were not Ephraimites were slain by mistake. So in determining fitness for Church membership, office, or spiritual responsibility—

I. TESTS MAY BE NECESSARY. There are times when it is of the utmost importance for us to know who are God's people and who are not. We are to "have no fellowship with the unfruitful works of darkness, but rather reprove them." From the unholy, disorderly, unbelieving we are commanded to withdraw ourselves. But this injunction were impossible of fulfilment were the distinction between saints and sinners not capable of being made. Christ has happily supplied a test—"By their fruits ye shall know them." The confession of the lips is another element, but it must not be dissociated from the former. So in the life of every day we require to know men, and accordingly have to form our opinions and judgments of them. This is so vital and necessary to safety and happiness, that we do it almost automatically, unconsciously. The honest and the dishonest, the true and the false, the friend and the enemy, we learn to distinguish by actions and words, and the course of their conduct. It is foolish, therefore, for persons to object to tests—they are necessary throughout the whole range of life, temporal and spiritual. But—

II. THEY MAY MISLEAD. In the nature of things they must be superficial, local, accidental, &c. They are observed and interpreted by fallible men. Trifling differences may acquire factitious importance. A man is not to be condemned for a word; a careful study should be made of the whole conduct and character of the man. The Christian life has many "notes," and where one is not forthcoming another may be present. The Epistles have, therefore, a variety of points upon which Christians may test themselves and others. God alone knoweth the heart, and in Christ he will judge the world by infallible judgment. It is better to err on the side of leniency to offenders than on that of severity. It matters not how we may commend ourselves to men, our condition in the sight of God is of chief account.—M.

Vers. 1—6.—"*Vaulting ambition,*" which "*o'erleaps itself.*" This was not the first time of such offence on the part of Ephraim. Gideon had to bear with their unreasonableness, and was gracious enough to permit their co-operation in securing the results of his victory. But now the "cup of their iniquity is full." Not for Ammon's destruction alone is Jephthah raised up; he has a punishment to mete out to Ephraim. They knew it not, but this pride of theirs was on the verge of its fall. They presumed on former exemption from evil consequences, and blindly rushed upon their chastisement. We see here—

I. PRIDE IN ITS DEVELOPMENT AND CAREER. Past kindness and consideration only hardened and strengthened it. Past achievements and the prestige acquired through them are relied upon instead of present obedience to God, &c. Ephraim cared more for its own position and advantage than to serve the commonwealth. By its inaction in the past and its hostile attitude to Jephthah on the present occasion it plays the traitor. It despised its brethren, and refused to recognise the leader God had chosen, and now it threatened to overthrow the advantage acquired by the Ammonite victory. It became a public nuisance and a political danger.

II. PRIDE IN ITS DIVINE CHASTISEMENT. In the various details of its punishment it is hard to repress a certain measure of sympathy for it. There is something always in the humiliation of a proud nature that commands our sympathy. And yet it was necessary and right that Ephraim should be taught a terrible lesson. 1. *That very tribe, membership with which had been their boast, they would now fain deny.* 2. *The taunt of being "fugitives," which they had used against the Gileadites, is now turned against themselves.* 3. *The martial strength upon which they had relied is now effectually and suddenly reduced.* So will it be with all who set themselves against Christ and his kingdom. "Upon whomsoever this stone shall fall, it will grind him to powder." If God is against us, or, what is the same thing, we are against God, we may expect patient forbearance, and at first gentle chidings ; but, if we persist, a terrible retribution. Sin is pride ; it refuses to bow to God's will, or to accept the methods of his salvation.—M.

Ver. 1.—*Jealousy.* The men of Ephraim are angry with Jephthah because he has repulsed the Ammonites without their aid.

I. GREAT MEN ARE COMMONLY ASSAILED BY THE JEALOUSY OF THEIR RIVALS. 1. This is no proof of any *failing* on the part of those who are thus attacked. While some of the noblest of men have brought trouble upon their own heads through want of consideration for the petty weaknesses of their inferiors, the best and most conciliatory of men have not been able to avoid the envy and misjudgment of meaner natures. It is impossible to please all classes in doing a work of any magnitude and value. They are not always the worthiest men who have the fewest enemies. Christ had more foes than friends. 2. This is no proof of the *claims* of the rivals of great men. People who cannot improve a work can criticise it.

II. THEY WHO ARE BACKWARD IN ENCOUNTERING THE DANGER OF BATTLE ARE EAGER IN COVETING THE HONOUR OF VICTORY. There is no reason to believe that the men of Ephraim showed any willingness to join with Jephthah till after his great success. Weak and selfish people who will not enter into any enterprise until they see it has succeeded are plentiful enough, but they are worthless. The true men are they who will advocate the right cause when it is at a low ebb, when it is unpopular, when it seems doomed to failure, when the service of it involves risk and loss.

III. THE TASK FROM WHICH MEN SHRINK BEFOREHAND LOOKS EASY AFTER IT HAS BEEN SUCCESSFULLY PERFORMED. Now that Jephthah has defeated the Ammonites, the men of Ephraim think his work was only a safe road to honour in which they would gladly have accompanied him. When we see the master of some art working with deft skill and unerring accuracy, nothing looks more easy than to do as he does. His very triumph destroys the appearance of the difficulties which lie in its way. Thus the honours of the artist and the orator, and, in religious matters, of the martyr and the missionary, inspire jealousy in men who think they are cheaply won just on account of that very excellency which conceals the necessary sacrifice, suffering, or toil by the perfect conquest of it.

IV. SELFISH PEOPLE ARE MORE CONCERNED ABOUT THEIR OWN SHARE IN THE HONOUR OF A GREAT ENTERPRISE THAN ABOUT THE SUCCESS OF IT. The men of Ephraim do nothing to encourage Jephthah ; they are only anxious to share his honour. We see in public life personal ambition overcoming public spirit, in Christian work the honour of the agent exalted above the success of the work. But the patriot should be supremely anxious for the welfare of his country, no matter by whom this is secured, and the Christian should be simply desirous of the triumph of Christ and the extension of Christianity, though he may not share the honours of victory. The jealousy which would hinder the good work of others because we have no share in it is treason to Christ. It is unworthy for the Christian to covet or to hold a post which he knows another will occupy better than himself.—A.

Ver. 6.—*Shibboleth.* I. IF A MAN'S PROFESSION IS FALSE TO HIS CHARACTER, THIS WILL BE MADE MANIFEST BY THE HABITS OF HIS LIFE. The Ephraimite who denied his tribal relation was betrayed by his dialectic pronunciation. Thus Peter was convicted of falsehood (Matt. xxvi. 73). It matters little what we say if our conduct belies our words. No man can ultimately conceal his character; it will come out in his countenance, it will colour his speech, it will shape his action. If a man would completely suppress his character, he must destroy it, because while it exists it must obey its nature, which is to be the source of all conduct. You cannot quench a volcano by building over its crater, nor stay the flow of a stream by walling it in. Our true nature, whether it be good or bad, must reveal itself (1) in great critical epochs, when it can endure no restraint; or (2) in casual accidents, when we are off our guard and do not consider the occasion sufficiently important to demand much concern; or (3) in the general course and colour of our life (Matt. vii. 16). II. SMALL SUPERFICIAL SIGNS MAY INDICATE GREAT FUNDAMENTAL DISTINCTIONS. The test of the "Shibboleth" has been much misunderstood, as though it were an instance of the importance which is sometimes unduly given to mere trivial distinctions. The test was simply a means of discovering the tribal relations of men. The Gileadites cared nothing for the difference of pronunciation in itself. They simply used it as a means for determining a really important point—the truth or falsehood of the profession of those who said they were not men of Ephraim. The same mistake was involved in Gibbon's famous sneer about the great division of Christendom on the question of a diphthong. It was not a diphthong, but the fundamental truth of the perfect Divinity of Christ that Athanasius and his friends were contending with the Arians about, and the use of the diphthong was simply a convenient form in which to bring the question to a definite point. So the recent controversies about vestments have been ridiculed as though they were questions of "ecclesiastical millinery," while both parties know quite well that these outside and apparently trivial differences are the signs of fundamental questions concerning priestly authority and sacramental grace. 1. We must beware of judging of the magnitude of a question by the comparative insignificance of its external indications. 2. We must, nevertheless, be careful not to assume that trivial external distinctions are signs of deep and important differences until we have proved the fact. We may erect the test of a "Shibboleth" to separate people who have no such fundamental distinctions as those of the men who had been true to Jephthah and the men who had enviously opposed him. The danger is that we should thus magnify the importance of the "Shibboleth" itself, and so become narrow and sectarian.—A.

EXPOSITION.

Ver. 8.—**Ibzan of Bethlehem.** It is uncertain whether Bethlehem of Judah is meant, or Bethlehem in the tribe of Zebulun, mentioned in Josh. xix. 15. Josephus says that Ibzan was of the tribe of Judah, and of the city of Bethlehem, and some have supposed a connection between the names of Boaz and Ibzan. But as Bethlehem of the tribe of Judah is generally called Bethlehem of Judah, or Bethlehem-Ephratah, and as Elon and Abdon were judges in North-East Israel, it is perhaps more probable that Bethlehem of Zebulun is meant. Dr. Robinson has identified it with a village—a "very miserable one"—called *Beit Lahm*, six miles west of Nazareth.

Ver. 9.—**He had thirty sons,** &c. From no record of Ibzan's judgeship being preserved, except this domestic incident, we may infer, as in the case of Jair, that no important events took place in his time.

Ver. 10.—**Then died,** &c. Render, *And Ibzan died.*

Ver. 12.—**In Aijalon.** Not Aijalon in the tribe of Dan, mentioned Josh. x. 12; xix. 42, but another city, only spoken of here, whose name is probably preserved in the ruins of *Jalûn,* four hours east of Akka. It is remarkable that the two names *Elon* and *Aijalon* are identical in Hebrew as far as the consonants are concerned. It looks as if Aijalon, which is not mentioned among the Zebulonite cities in Josh. xix. 10—16, was named from Elon, its possessor.

Ver. 13.—**A Pirathonite,** *i. e.* an inhabitant of Pirathon in the tribe of Ephraim, in the mount of the Amalekites (ver. 15), afterwards famous as the birthplace of Benaiah, one of David's mighty men (2 Sam. xxiii. 30). The *Pharathon* which is mentioned in 1 Macc. ix. 50, and by Josephus, following its authority, as fortified by Jonathan the brother of Judas may have been the same, though its collocation between Timna and Tekoah rather suggests a more southern position; and the *Ferata* found by Robinson between two and three hours from Samaria, south-south-west, on the way to Jerusalem, seems certainly to represent *Pirathon*.

Ver. 14.—**Nephews.** Rather, *grandsons*. Hebrew, *son's sons*. The number of his family, and their being all mounted on asses, are indications of his wealth and state (see above, ch. viii. 30 ; x. 4), and perhaps also of peaceful and prosperous times.

Ver. 15.—**The mount of the Amalekites.** This name points to some incident of which the memory is lost, though, with the usual tenacity of names, the name which once recorded it survives. It may have been some ancient settlement of the Amalekites, who were a very wandering, wide-spread race, which gave the name ; or it may have been some great defeat and slaughter which they suffered from the Israelites, whose land they invaded (ch. vi. 3, 33), just as the rock Oreb and the wine-press of Zeeb (ch. vii. 25) commemorated the victory over those princes.

HOMILETICS.

Vers. 8—15.—*The calm after the storm.* Jephthah's day of life had been a stormy one indeed. The strife with his own brethren; the strife with the children of Ammon ; the strife between nature and superstition, and the throbbings of a distracted heart ; the strife with the tribe of Ephraim, and the strife with a premature death under which he sunk, marked him as a "man of strife" (Ver. 2 in the Hebrew, and Jer. xv. 10) all his days, both him and "his people." But now there came quiet, uneventful days both for Israel and his rulers. There is no mention of foreign foe or of domestic discord. Scenes of family life take the place of the martial muster and the bloody fight. There is nothing to record save how long the judges judged, when they died, and where they were buried. We infer, indeed, from the fact that there were judges the continual care of God for his people, and from the absence of invasion and servitude we infer that the people did not forsake God. But more than this we do not know, nor over how great a part of Israel these judgeships did extend. But the reflection cannot but arise that it is not good for a people to be in continual strife. Struggles for supremacy over enemies without, and conflict for the settlement of government at home, should have their term, and give way to enjoyment of prosperity and peace. The happiest times in a nation's life are not always those that shine the brightest on the page of history. And so in the life of the individual. Though the surface of his life be not ruffled, nor its tenor varied by any startling changes, there may be a hidden work of God going on in the soul more momentous than the gain or loss of fortunes, or any vicissitudes of sickness and of health. Faith may be waxing stronger, and love may be burning brighter ; patience may be perfecting her work, and the spirit of meekness may be steadily gaining ground over the spirit of wrath and intolerance ; the knowledge of Jesus Christ may be filling the field of the soul's vision, and the kingdom of heaven may be drawing nearer to the soul's embrace, and yet the outward life may be monotonous and uneventful. Anyhow let us use the calm and untempestuous moments of our life to make undisturbed progress in the great business of our salvation ; and in the assurance of God's unwearied love let us pursue our own quiet round of meditation, and prayer, and praise. Great events and mighty deeds figure on the page of history, but the soul's progress in holiness is worthy to be recorded by an angel's pen.

Vers. 8—15.—Cf. on ch. x. 1—5.—M.

EXPOSITION.

CHAPTER XIII.

Ver. 1.—**Did evil again.** It by no means follows from this phrase that this chapter is in direct chronological sequence to the preceding. The scene is shifted to the tribe of Dan, and to the Philistines on the west, and there is nothing to guide us as to the exact time when the things narrated occurred. But the end of the **forty years** probably coincided with the judgeship of Samuel ; for there was no complete deliverance in the time of Samson, only occasional checks to the Philistine domination (see ver. 5). It was not till the days of Samuel that the Philistines were really smitten (see 1 Sam.

vii. 3—14). We may suppose the date of the ensuing narrative to be somewhere in the first decade of the Philistine oppression.

Ver. 2.—**Zorah.** Enumerated among the cities in the tribe of Dan in Josh. xix. 41, but ascribed to Judah, *ibid.* xv. 33 (there transliterated *Zoreah*) and in 2 Chron. xi. 10. Probably the boundary passed through the city, as that of Judah and Benjamin did through Jerusalem. In Neh. xi. 29 it is transliterated *Zareah,* and also ascribed to Judah. It is almost always coupled with Eshtaol, as in ver. 25 of this chapter. It was situated in the Shephelah, or plain country, and was fortified by Rehoboam (2 Chron. xi. 10). It is supposed to be represented by the modern *Surah,* at the entrance of the Wady Ghurab. **The family of the Danites.** It appears from Numb. xxvi. 42, 43 that there was only one *family* in the *tribe* of Dan, so that in this case tribe and family were co-extensive.

Ver. 3.—**Thou shalt . . . bear a son.** It is obvious to compare the promise to Abraham and Sarah (Gen. xvii. 19 ; xviii. 10, 14), to Hannah (1 Sam. i. 17), to Elizabeth (Luke i. 13), and to the blessed Virgin (Luke i. 31).

Ver. 5.—**The child shall be a Nazarite,** &c. So it was said, though not in the same words, concerning Samuel (1 Sam. i. 11) and concerning John the Baptist (Luke i. 15). A Nazarite (or, more correctly, a *Nazirite*) means *one separated,* and specially dedicated to God. The law of the Nazarites is contained in Numb. vi., where, however, only *Nazarites of days,* i. e. Nazarites for a definite time, are spoken of. Samson, Samuel, and John the Baptist were *perpetual Nazarites,* Nazarites of *for ever,* as the Mishna classifies them. Abstinence from strong drink, and from anything made of the grape ; letting the locks of the head grow unchecked by the razor ; and keeping quite clear of any pollution from a dead body, even in case of the death of his nearest relations, were the chief articles of a Nazarite's vow. St. Paul took the vow of a Nazarite of days, and offered the prescribed sacrifices, together with "the hair of the head of his separation," as we read in Acts xviii. 18 ; xxi. 23—26. **He shall begin,** &c. This is an exact description of what Samson did. He did not "deliver Israel" as the other judges did ; but he began to shake the Philistine power, and prepared the way for the deliverance of Israel in the time of his worthier successor Samuel.

Ver. 6.—**A man of God,** *i. e.* a prophet, applied to Moses, Samuel, David, Shemaiah, Elijah, Elisha, and other prophets, and to Timothy in the New Testament. Manoah's wife applies it to the angel, not being sure that he was not human. It would not be

improper to apply to an angel, seeing that *Gabriel* means *man of God.* **I asked him not,** &c. No doubt from awe. Jacob, on the contrary, asked the angel with whom he had wrestled, "Tell me, I pray thee, thy name" (Gen. xxxii. 29). See vers. 17, 18. In the Septuagint (Cod. Alex.) and Vulgate the *not* is omitted. "I asked him, but he did not tell me."

Ver. 10.—**And the woman . . . ran,** &c. Acting in the true spirit of a loving and trustful wife, and showing that she felt that neither angel nor man of God stood before her own husband in the claim to her confidence and obedience.

Ver. 12.—**Let thy words come,** &c. The verb is singular in the Hebrew here and in ver. 17. Possibly the true reading is *word,* as in the Septuagint. If the text is correct, *words* must be taken collectively, as making one promise. The saying marks Manoah's earnest desire for a son. Some, however, construe it, *If thy words come.* **How shall we order,** &c.—literally, *What will be the manner of the child,* and what will be his doing ? i. e. either, *What will be his manner* (cf. 1 Sam. viii. 11, and following verses), *and what will be his action or work ?* or, *What will be his proper treatment, and what shall be done to him ?* The former is the most natural rendering of the words, and though the latter seems at first more suitable to the angel's reply, yet if we take the angel's reply as referring Manoah to what he had said before in vers. 4 and 5, we have a distinct answer to the questions. His *manner* will be to live as a Nazarite, and his action or work will be to begin to deliver Israel (cf. Gen. xvi. 12, where both the *manner* and the *actions* of Ishmael are foretold). In fact, Manoah's question refers directly to vers. 4 and 5, and is a request to have a confirmation of what was then said ; just as David asked again and again, *What shall be done to the man that killeth this Philistine ?* (1 Sam. xvii. 26, 30).

Ver. 14.—**She may not eat of anything,** &c. Nearly the identical words of Numb. vi. 4.

Ver. 15.—**Let us detain thee,** &c. He wishes to detain him as a guest till he has had time to cook a kid for him (cf. Gen. xviii. 7). **For thee.** The Hebrew is *before thee.* The phrase is elliptical. The full sentence would be, *until we have dressed a kid* and set it *before thee,* as in Gen. xviii. 8.

Ver. 16.—**I will not eat of thy bread,** &c. The angel refuses to eat of his meat, but suggests that if he would offer the kid as a burnt offering, he must **offer it to the Lord.** The angel, perhaps perceiving that Manoah was in doubt as to who he might be, had a holy dread lest he might offer the kid to him, just as the angel whom St. John was about to worship said, "See thou do it not" (Rev. xxii. 9); and Barnabas and Paul ran in among the people of Lycaonia to restrain them from offering sacrifice to them (Acts xiv. 14—18). The order of the words, which is rightly given in the A. V., makes it a clear direction to offer the sacrifice to no one but the Lord.

Ver. 17.—**What is thy name?** See note to ver. 6. The phrase is very peculiar, literally, *Who is thy name?* as if he had been going to say, *Who art thou?* and then changed the form to *is thy name.* The Hebrews seem to have attached great importance to names, a circumstance due, in part, to every name being significant in the spoken language (see Gen. iv. 1, 25 ; v. 29 ; xvi. 5, &c.; xvii. 19; xxv. 25, 26 ; xxix. and xxx. ; 1 Sam. i., xx.; Isa. ix. 6; lxii. 4; Jer. xxiii. 6 ; Ephes. i. 21; Phil. ii. 9, 10 ; Rev. xix. 16, &c., and many other passages). Compare also the phrase, *the name of the Lord* (Isa. xxx. 27 ; Exod. xxiii. 21 ; xxxiii. 19 ; xxxiv. 5, 6, 7). Manoah had certainly some suspicions as to the mysterious character of his visitor, and expected the name to reveal his true nature. **We may do thee honour.** Manoah seems throughout to use ambiguous language, suitable either to a man, if he was speaking to a man, or to a celestial visitant, should he be angel or God.

Ver. 18.—**It is secret.** The Hebrew word does not mean *secret,* but *wonderful,* as it is rendered in Isa. ix. 6, and elsewhere. His name was one which, as St. Paul expresses it, it is not lawful, or possible, for a man to utter (2 Cor. xii. 4), it was so transcendently wonderful. The feeling of the Hebrews in abstaining from uttering the name יהוה was akin to this. Some take the angel to say that WONDERFUL is his name, but the A. V. is right in prefixing *seeing—seeing it is wonderful.*

Ver. 19. — **Offered it,** &c. He had the angel's sanction for doing so in ver. 16. But we must not look for strict compliance with the Levitical law in the lawless days of the Judges, though we find many of its prescribed ordinances in use, as, for instance, the institution of Nazarites, and here the offering of the meat offering with the burnt offering (Levit. ii. 1, &c.). **And the angel.** These words are rightly inserted, to give the sense of the original, as more fully explained in the following verse. **Did wonderously**—literally, *was wondrous in his doing.* The verb here is the same root as the substantive or adjective *wonder,* or *wonderful,* in ver. 18. Compare the similar account in ch. vi. 21.

Ver. 20. — **Looked on** *it.* There is no occasion for the italic *it,* the phrase is identical with that at the close of ver. 19; but the rendering would be better, *And when Manoah and his wife saw it, they fell,* &c.

Ver. 21.—**But.** It is better rendered *and,* in close sequence to the preceding words. It follows, **Then,** *i. e.* when they saw him go up, **they knew that he was an angel.**

Ver. 22.—**We shall surely die,** &c. Similarly Gideon (ch. vi. 22, 23) expressed his alarm because he had "seen an angel of the Lord face to face," but was assured, "Thou shalt not die." And so Isaiah said, "Woe is me! for mine eyes have seen the King, the Lord of hosts" (Isa. vi. 5). So again the Lord said to Moses, "There shall no man see me and live" (Exod. xxxiii. 20). The name of the well, Beer-lahai-roi, is also thought to mean the well of him that is alive after seeing God (Gen. xvi. 14). And Jacob called the name of the place where he wrestled with the angel Peniel, "for I have seen God face to face, and my life is preserved" (Gen. xxxii. 30). See too Exod. xx. 19. The same belief also prevailed amongst the heathen, that seeing a god without his special permission was visited by death or some grave calamity, as Callimachus, quoted by Grotius, says—

> "The laws of Saturn thus decree,
> Who dares immortal gods to see
> Shall suffer loss, whoe'er he be."

Ver. 23.—**But his wife said,** &c. The woman's faith saw more clearly than the man's fear. With the acceptance of the sacrifice the conscience was cleared from guilt. The ascent of the angel in the flame of the altar was to her the same evidence of an accepted sacrifice as the resurrection and ascension of the Lord Jesus are to us.

Ver. 24.—**Called his name Samson.** No doubt the name was significant of what the child should be (see note to ver. 17), but the etymology and meaning of the name are doubtful. Josephus ('Antiq.,' V. viii. 4) says the name means "a strong one," but he does not say in what language, and it does not appear to have such a meaning in any Semitic dialect. It is commonly interpreted to mean *like the sun,* from *shemesh,* the common word for the sun; and so Jerome in his 'Onomasticon' expounds it as *the sun's strength,* possibly with an allusion to ch. v. 31. Others make it equal *shim-shom,* from the Pilpel conjugation of *shamem, to devastate.* Another possible derivation is from the Chaldee *shemash, to minister,* specially in sacred things, a root from which the Nestorian, Syriac, and Arabic names for a deacon are derived. If this were the derivation, it would be a reference to his dedication to God as a Nazarite from his mother's womb, the only thing his mother knew about him when she gave him the name.

Ver. 25. — **The Spirit of the Lord,** &c. See ch. iii. 10, note. **To move him**—to urge and impel him to strange actions by fits and starts. It is an uncommon expression. In Gen. xli. 8 the passive of the verb means to be *troubled* or *agitated*, and the substantive is the common word for *a time* in the phrases *time after time, twice, thrice* (according to the number specified), *other times*, &c. ; also *a footstep;* and its derivatives mean *an anvil, a bell.* The idea is that of sudden, single impulses, such as are described in the following chapters. **In the camp of Dan,**

or, as in ch. xviii. 12, *Mahaneh-Dan*, where the reason of the name is explained. For **Zorah** see ver. 2, note. **Eshtaol** has not hitherto been identified with any existing place, but it ought to lie east or north of Mahaneh-Dan, since this last was between Zorah and Eshtaol (see note on ch. xviii. 12). *Kustul*, a conical hill one hour west of Jerusalem, has been suggested.

HOMILETICS.

Vers. 1—25.—*Married life.* Many deep and valuable teachings may be gathered out of this chapter. The ministry of angels to the heirs of salvation, and, connected with it, the sublime conception of the countless hosts of heaven ; for the presence of one angel upon earth brings tidings, as it were, from distant spheres of principalities and powers, of thrones and dominions, of angels and authorities, of cherubim and seraphim, peopling the realms of space, filling the heavens with intelligence and praise, and having a community with mankind in the grace and love of God ; and one converse of an angel with men suggests a future intercourse of inconceivable wealth of enjoyment, and unbounded variety of interchange of thought, and a fellowship in adoration and praise with unnumbered worlds of holy and mighty intelligences. The mysterious nature of the angel of the Lord, baffling all human attempts to explain it—at one moment seeming quite separate from the Godhead itself, and next moment seeming to be one with it, as if a kind of anticipation of the incarnation were taking place, and God himself were speaking by the angel's mouth. And then there is the predestinating grace of God, calling into being whom he will, assigning to his creature his proper work, and marking out his future course before he was born ; endowing him with great and singular gifts, pouring freely and fully upon him his Holy Spirit, and yet leaving his free will unshackled, and his responsibility unimpaired. And there is the doctrine of sacrifice, and of answers to prayer ; and there is the question of temperance, and total abstinence from the fruit of the vine ; and the duty of hospitality, and of gratitude for kindness received ; and that of giving honour to whom honour, and worship to whom worship is due, and other lessons besides. But the one lesson which stands out above the others and runs through the whole chapter is that of the conjugal relation of man and wife, which is set forth with inimitable simplicity and force, and which we shall do well to study for a few minutes as one that bears with singular influence upon the happiness and well-being of mankind. It is obvious to notice in the first place that Manoah was the husband of one wife, according to the institution of marriage in paradise. Such mutual confidence and help as we here see could not have been found in Gideon's harem, or in the households of Ibzan and Abdon. The real conjugal union of interests, and oneness of aim, and transparent openness of intercourse springing from having nothing to conceal, can have no existence where polygamy exists. Nor is it in the nature of things that a woman's entire love and trust should be given to the man who has only a fraction of affection to give in return. If Christianity had done nothing else for mankind than restore the primitive law of marriage, and guard it with the highest sanctions of religion, it would have conferred upon our race an inestimable boon. The holiness and happiness, the peace and union, of countless homes, is due to the marriage law of the gospel of Christ. But then this law must be kept in the spirit as well as in the letter. The conduct of Manoah's wife after her first interview with the angel is a beautiful exemplification of this spirit in the wife : "Then the woman came and told her husband." Many things might have moved her to secrecy. The fear of exciting her husband's suspicions, the risk of being disbelieved, the possibility that the stranger had deceived her with false hopes ; or, on the other hand, a feeling of pride and self-sufficiency at the marvellous apparition and revelation made to herself, not to her husband, and a spirit of independence engendered by such a distinction—such feelings as these, had they existed, or had they ruled her conduct, might have led her to conceal the mysterious interview. But the wife's instinct led her straight to the mark : "she came and told her husband." He was her husband, her natural, legitimate, only counsellor and adviser. His was the ear into which to pour her strange confidence. What she knew, he ought to know, and her conduct must be guided by his counsels. So she came at once and told her husband. But the lesson has peculiar force from the supposed office of the stranger. She took him for "a man of God," and his very announcement of what was to happen hereafter invested him with a sacred and awful character, which was likely to affect powerfully the sensibilities of a woman. But not for one instant was "the man of God" allowed to stand between her and her husband. She had no secrets for the "man of God" which were to be hidden from her husband, nor had the angel any counsel to give which her husband was not to know of. It was on the second time of his appearing as on the first: "she made haste, and ran, and showed her husband, and said unto him, Behold, the man hath appeared unto me." It is a very forcible lesson to the effect that no pretence of spiritual authority can justify interference with the laws of nature, which are the laws of God. If the mutual love and mutual confidence between man and wife in the holy estate of matrimony is the ordinance of God for the happiness of man, the secret influence of another man which is to override the influence of the husband is not, and cannot be, according to the will of God. If the wife is to obey her husband, no other man can of right exact a higher obedience ; if she is to trust her husband, she may not keep secret from him what she reveals to others ; she may not receive counsel from others which is to be hid from him. The function of a confessor and spiritual director is incompatible with the Christian law of marriage, as it is with the "first commandment with promise," when it stands between children and their parents. Nor is Manoah's trust in his wife less conspicuous than her trust in him. Not a shadow of doubt as to the truth of her statement crossed his mind, not a shade of jealousy that the message came to her rather than to him. In the desire for further information his wisdom suggested prayer that the Lord would send again the man of God ; but the language of his prayer was beautifully expressive of the union that was betwixt them two. "Let the man of God come again unto *us*, and teach *us* what we shall do unto the child." And when the second time the angel appeared to the woman alone, he took it as the answer to his prayer. As she came quickly to him, so he quickly followed her. With manly courage he asked the questions which her feminine modesty had not dared to put, and appeared at once in his proper place, ordering and directing what was to be done with regard to the rites of hospitality and piety ; and yet when his own fears were excited by having seen the angel of God, he sought counsel from his wife, and readily acquiesced in her pious trust in the mercy and loving-kindness of the Lord. And exactly the same perfect union between them appears many years afterwards, when Samson was grown up (ch. xiv. 2—5), so that the whole passage is a beautiful idyll of conjugal love and concord. They both fulfil their proper parts with the utmost simplicity and propriety ; they both contribute to the common stock of wedded happiness what each had to contribute ; neither of them had one word of reproach or bitterness to the other ; neither of them attempted to usurp the other's place, or shrunk from occupying their own. And they have left for our study and imitation as beautiful an example of the mutual help and harmony of married life as is to be found in the whole range of Scripture. May it find its counterpart in every Christian family in the land !

HOMILIES BY VARIOUS AUTHORS.

Vers. 2—5.—*A natural desire and its gracious fulfilment.* In the East it is a reproach to be childless, and the greatest anxiety is displayed by married people to have a son. In ancient times the possibility of becoming the mother of the promised Messiah was a hope which greatly influenced this, but it had its root in the natural longing to continue one's name and influence after death. This " will to live," which is so strong in the natural man, God sanctified by religious sanctions. It is ever a healthful and lawful desire when the " chief end " of man is respected.

> " Ill fares the land, to hastening ills a prey,
> Where wealth accumulates and men decay."

The natural life of man or woman is incomplete apart from the married state, and children are the blessing and crown of marriage. But they may also be its curse. It is only as God shapes their destiny and moulds their character, only as he "builds the house," that happiness and prosperity can be insured. Improvident marriages and parental neglect have been amongst the greatest causes of misery and vice in all ages. As in later ages we have learnt that there is no virtue in being a mother, so we have discovered that the single life is not the only possible one for the saint.

I. GOD DELIGHTS IN GRATIFYING OUR LEGITIMATE NATURAL DESIRES. It is but fitting that he who made us as we are constituted should supply, or place within our reach, that which shall satisfy our natural cravings. To do otherwise would be a refined and terrible cruelty. But our sin has forfeited for us this claim upon his providence. It would be perfectly lawful for him to withdraw natural supplies, and leave a rebellious world to perish, because of a broken covenant. But it has been far otherwise. The providence of God has been extolled by the heathen as by the Christian, by the sinner and the saint. He makes his sun to rise and his rain to fall upon the just and the unjust. Save his grace, there is no more pathetic and wonderful thing in the doings of God than this persistent and impartial providence. And in visitations like this to Manoah's wife we have glimpses of the feeling which inspires it. A real pleasure is felt by our Father in helping and gratifying his children. The mother has no more pleasure in giving suck to her infant than God has in making it possible for her to do so. Care and interest like this prepare us for the grander exhibitions of his grace in the gift of his only begotten Son. It could only be sustained in the breast of one who "so loved the world." A part of this Divine love is due, doubtless, to the possibility of some of those he fosters becoming his spiritual children and heirs of his kingdom.

II. HE DOES IT IN SUCH A MANNER AS TO IMPRESS UPON THE SUBJECT OF THE BLESSING THE SACREDNESS OF THE GOD-GIVEN LIFE, AND THE TRUE GLORY OF MOTHERHOOD. The child promised is to be devoted to God from his birth. His whole life is to be a Divine service. A special commission is to be given him for the deliverance of God's people. To this end a life of self-denial—a Nazarite life—is to be his. This conception of Samson's future is typical and representative. Every first-born in Israel was so regarded. And every child should be so regarded, and taught so to regard himself or herself. There is nothing so beautiful under the sun as a life wholly and from beginning to end devoted to God. And this, though it may seem a hard and difficult thing to realise, is the shortest and truest way to happiness. The mother of such a child—every mother—is therefore called upon to sanctify herself, that her offspring shall receive from her no evil tendencies or desires. Hereditary influence is everywhere recognised throughout Scripture.

III. THE OFFSPRING THUS GRANTED IS MADE THE INSTRUMENT OF BLESSING AND DELIVERANCE TO HIS PEOPLE. There are always considerations for and against granting a boon outside and independently of the ordinary course of nature. Consecration of the gift thus bestowed is the surest way of avoiding injustice to others, and justifying our own super-abounding good. What a thought this for every mother to ponder! In lesser proportion and degree hers may be the wonder and forethought of Mary, the mother of our Lord, when "she hid these things in her heart."—M.

Ver. 5.—*The difficulty of salvation.* "And he shall begin to deliver Israel." There is a parsimony of expression here that is highly expressive. It is not said, "he shall deliver," as of a complete work, but only "he shall begin" to do so. How many reasons were there for this! Do they not also hold good for the grander work of human salvation?

I. HINDRANCES TO THE COMPLETE SALVATION OF ISRAEL. 1. *It was a work which required to be, in the first place, and mainly, spiritual in order to its being thorough.* 2. *In order to this the penalty of past transgression had in greater measure to be felt.* The transgression had been great, repeated, and habitual. A stern lesson had to be read to the guilty. It was an evil inflicted in order to induce repentance. The moral depths of human nature were being sounded and discovered to itself, that in the fulness of time a Divine Saviour might be sought. 3. *Meanwhile the nature and*

character of the deliverer did not admit of such a work being completed. He was but a man: his consecration was merely or chiefly external; the faults of his character were glaring. His deeds, accordingly, are those of physical heroism and strength. Only once or twice do any hints of more than human wisdom occur.
II. CONSOLATIONS ATTACHED TO THIS INCOMPLETE SALVATION. 1. *It was actually begun.* 2. *God had undertaken it, and provided the instrument.* 3. *As being a professedly partial undertaking, it showed a far-reaching and thorough scheme.* 4. *The conditions of its ultimate accomplishment were with themselves.*—M.

Vers. 2—5.—*God's use of unlikely means for gracious ends.* The crisis was grave, relief being, humanly speaking, impossible. The family chosen for the experiment an ordinary one, of no social standing. The mother of the promised child barren. The sustenance enjoined of the most meagre description, not likely to produce strength or furnish artificial stimulus. No inward holiness is shown by Samson.
I. IT SHOWS A PURPOSE OF ENGAGING THE SINNER, EITHER PERSONALLY OR REPRESENTATIVELY, IN THE TASK OF HIS OWN SALVATION. The humblest transgressor cannot be saved without his own self-surrender and willing co-operation.
II. THE HIGHER SPIRITUAL PRINCIPLES, FAITH, HOPE, &C., ARE EVOKED IN THOSE WHO ARE THUS SAVED. The human agent is thus put in his right place. He secures the sympathies of his fellow-countrymen. Their hopes rise or fall as he prospers or is hindered in his task. The blessing of God must therefore be invoked, and the promise of God implicitly believed.
III. ALL THE GIFTS OF OUR NATURE ARE SHOWN TO BE DIVINE IN THEIR ORIGIN, AND THEIR CONSECRATION IS ENCOURAGED.
IV. THE SAVING GRACE OF GOD IS THUS VINDICATED AS HIS OWN, AND HE HIMSELF DECLARED THE ONLY SAVIOUR.—M.

Vers. 1—5.—*Divine punishment and preparation of deliverance simultaneous.* The heaviest judgments in human history have been secretly charged with such merciful provisions. This circumstance alters the character of the infliction; it ceases to be mere vengeance, and becomes discipline.
I. INSTANCES OF THIS IN SACRED HISTORY. The Fall and promise of the Seed. In Joseph's sale and slavery we see the *anticipation* of an evil not yet experienced. Esther is raised up in the Persian captivity. The age of the destruction of Jerusalem was the age of the gospel.
II. WHAT THIS PROVES. 1. *God does not "afflict willingly" and for the sake of afflicting, but for ultimate good.* 2. *The wrath of God exists at the same time as his love, and is penetrated and overruled by it.* 3. *The mercy of God is far-seeing, wise, and painstaking.*—M.

Vers. 8—11.—*Repetition of Divine favours.* There are visitations of God and signs of his favour that are not fully comprehended the first time, and their repetition alone can satisfy the cravings of the heart and the wonder of the spiritual understanding. And God is considerate of our human weakness. "In the mouth of *two or three* witnesses shall every word be established." The blessing is then realised in absolute certainty, and a communion of faith.
I. GOD'S PROMISES ARE SO PRECIOUS THAT WE WISH TO BE ASSURED OF THEM. His words, so mysterious and far-sent, are like clouds full of rain for the thirsty soil, if we can only secure the blessing. When he condescends to visit thus the home of men it is for good, and not evil. And the blessings which he promises are not such as the world can give. The spiritual understanding can alone discern their true worth, and alone yearns for their fulfilment. The mere repetition of the terms and words is soothing and confirming. And to the faithful they will be spoken again as a token of favour, and the signs will be repeated; but to a "faithless generation shall no sign be given," save that which plunges in deeper wonder or increases the certainty of doom.
II. HOW ARE GOD'S PROMISES TO BE REALISED? 1. *By interested attention to them.* Manoah's mind is full of the message received by his wife. He does not

dismiss it from mind and memory as a trifling thing. It is this pondering and waiting and searching spirit that is blessed. "How shall we escape if we neglect so great salvation?" 2. *By implicit faith.* He does not question the reality of the Divine message. He is eager to hear it, so that all its significance may be understood. He speaks even at first of "the child that shall be born." 3. *By believing prayer.* How earnest is this man ! "Manoah *entreated* Jehovah." There is no unnecessary delay : "God hearkened to the voice of Manoah." He loves to hear the voice of praying men. He loves to be "inquired of," and "entreated," and "wrestled" with. "The effectual, fervent prayer of a righteous man availeth much." 4. *By expectation, and diligent watching for the answer.* The reality of our prayer is thus shown. How often is prayer but an idle word uttered thoughtlessly when in a devout frame ! Let us look for what we ask, and God will not weary our patience or betray our confidence. Ask, seek, knock (2 Tim. iv. 8 ; Titus ii. 13).—M.

Vers. 12—14.—*Parental anxiety and its satisfying.* Questions of great importance, which every parent ought to study. Circumstances may occur that render the responsibility of the parent peculiarly heavy.

I. ALL PARENTS, OR THOSE ABOUT TO BE PARENTS, SHOULD BRING THEIR PARENTAL CARES TO GOD. 1. *It will relieve anxiety.* 2. *The sense of moral responsibility will be deepened and confirmed.* 3. *Direction will be given for duty and usefulness.*

II. THE BEST SAFEGUARD OF THE CHILD IS THE CONSECRATION OF THE PARENT. To regard the child-blessing as a trust. To seek the benefit of others through that which is a joy and gratification to oneself. To keep oneself pure and temperate, that no taint or evil tendency may pass to one's posterity, and that in oneself, as in one's children, God may be glorified.—M.

Vers. 15—21.—Cf. on ch. vi. 17—21.—M.

Vers. 17, 18.—*The wonderful name.* The balance of critical authority is in favour of the rendering "wonderful," or wonder-working, and not that of "secret." It is to be taken as expressive not only of the general character of God as mysterious, glorious, and ineffable, but as doing wonders, *i. e.* mighty deeds of manifestation and salvation. This characteristic of God is to be studied as—

I. PROVOCATIVE OF CURIOSITY. The Divine element has ever maintained its presence in human life, has kept the horizons of human consciousness wide apart and constantly extending, and has exercised the counteractive and saving influence required by the action of the world-spirit upon the nature of man. God has never left man alone. Ere a single page of inspiration was penned he dwelt "in the conscious breast," and drew reverent eyes and feet after his marvels in the physical world. Man is, perforce of his moral constitution being linked and blended with his physical, a being "between two worlds." The gate is ajar, and no mortal can ever effectually close it. Led by this "presence of the threshold," the fathers of faith began that religious movement that received its loftiest impulse and satisfaction in Christ. There were partial and progressive revelations, each new "wonder" laying firmer hold upon the imagination and the heart. Jacob at Bethel and at Penuel (Gen. xxxii. 24—30), Moses at Horeb, Elijah in the cave of the desert, and David at the threshing-floor of Araunah, are grand typical figures, milestones in this spiritual pilgrimage. And there is no individual life, even of this secularised modern world, that is not the theatre of "even greater works than these," speaking in it of a heavenly Father, and keeping it within sound of his voice. If we are true to our own inner selves and to our spiritual history we must be worshippers of him whose name is Wonderful.

II. IN PROCESS OF REVELATION THROUGH MIRACLES. "And the angel did wondrously," *i. e.* true to his name, he acted miraculously. Creation, providence, the unfolding work of the world's salvation, are so many series of revelations in act and work. The general impression produced upon the mind by the scheme of the universe is enhanced and led up into religious fervour by these miracles, of which our latest physical science does not well know how to dispose. The moral and spiritual lessons they teach, and the impression they produce upon the human heart, run parallel with, but indefinitely above, the ordinary lines of (so-called) "natural religion," and constitute a distinct revelation, of which the core is reached in the miracles of Jesus Christ. As this moral or Divine side of miracle is increasingly studied, the riches of the Word made flesh will grow upon us, fascinate and convert the soul. At the tribunal of Jerusalem the old, old question is asked anew, and again in effect is the answer returned, "My name is Wonderful."

III. ASSERTIVE OF JEHOVAH AS THE SUPERNATURAL CAUSE OF THE DELIVERANCE OF ISRAEL. It is not Moses, or any judge, or David even, who is able to save. Jehovah is the great Deliverer, and he works above nature in a realm in which he can have no co-worker. Samson even is a "child of the promise," and no product of the influences of his time. His strength is to be from above, and its great exercises and feats are distinctly miraculous.

IV. PREPARING MEN FOR THE MESSIAH, IN WHOM IT WAS MOST PERFECTLY MANI-FESTED. The depths of the world's consciousness, in seer and saint, are ceaselessly stirred until the look of the ages fastens itself on him whose name is "Wonderful, Counsellor, mighty God, everlasting Father, Prince of Peace" (Isa. ix. 6). And as we look back on the brief episode of his life, ever new wonders declare themselves, and we feel that his example, his sufferings, his sacrifice, his resurrection, and ascension are potent to save and to sanctify, &c. Truly "his name is Wonderful."—M.

Vers. 22, 23.—*Reassurance of Divine favour.* Manoah is now uncertain whether to consider himself blessed or miserable. He has the deep-rooted superstition of a fleshly age strong within him, and is alarmed. But this arises from a defective spiritual education. He does not consider sufficiently the method and the manner of God's approaches to him. I. FEAR REGARDING GOD'S VISITATIONS IS A NATURAL FEELING. The consciousness of sin is easily roused to alarm, and the unknown is ever awe-inspiring. Our own littleness too is made the more manifest: "What is man, that thou art mindful of him? and the son of man, that thou visitest him?" (Ps. viii. 4). II. HOW IT MAY BE OVERCOME. *Considering,* 1. *The character of God;* 2. *His continuous scheme of redemption;* 3. *The blessings he has already bestowed;* 4. *The voice of Christ* ("Fear not"), *and the witness of the Spirit* ("Abba, Father"). III. GOD WILL NOT LEAVE HIS CHILD IN UNCERTAINTY OF HIS MEANING. "Two are better than one." How often in life is the husband, wife, parent, child, brother, sister, or friend, close beside us, the witness of God and the spiritual help-meet! The simple soul teaches the more complex and experienced, being itself taught of God. And so, somewhere or other, he is never without a witness.—M.

Vers. 24, 25.—*Fulfilment of promise.* The history of this promise to the worthy pair reads like an unbroken tale. Outwardly it was with them only as it was with numberless others of their neighbours. The circumstance is woven into the web of contemporary village life. The birth is as any other, the child as any other, up to a certain point; and then the true character and destiny begin to declare themselves. I. THE ORDINARY ASPECT OF DIVINE FULFILMENTS IN THEIR BEGINNINGS. II. PRIVATE JOY AND SATISFACTION ACCOMPANYING THE GIFT OF A PUBLIC BENE-FACTOR AND FULFILLER OF THE DIVINE PURPOSE. "The Lord blessed him." III. THE GRADUAL DIFFERENTIATION OF THE DIVINE AGENT FROM THE MERELY HUMAN RELATION. It soon appears that the lad is not meant for the mere solace of his parents' age and light of their home. "The Spirit of the Lord began to move him at times." Like Christ, the time comes when he "must be about his Father's business."—M.

Ver. 5.—*Samson the Nazarite.* I. THERE ARE MEN WHOM GOD CALLS TO HIS SERVICE FROM THEIR BIRTH. This is seen in the fact that the earliest events of their lives are made to train them for their subsequent mission in the world. Parents should consecrate their children to God in infancy, and not wait for later years before using those means which will fit them for the work of life in God's service. Manoah . and his wife are taught these lessons with special reference to the condition of a · Nazarite. Other vocations may require external varieties of training, but the essen-

tial characteristics which fit us for the service of God are the same in all cases, so
that it is not necessary to know the exact form of service to which God will call a
child, in order to lay the foundations of his character in the main principles which
devotion to God's service in any form involves.

II. ABSTEMIOUSNESS IS FAVOURABLE TO THE DEVELOPMENT OF VIGOUR. Self-indulgence is enervating. Self-restraint both husbands and enlarges strength. That
which is apparently most helpful to us may prove in reality to be a hindrance.
Appetite and desire are neither to be regarded as masters nor as enemies, but as
servants. As wine excites rather than strengthens, so there are influences of a mental
character which add nothing to our power for work, although they appear to do so by
rousing excitement. The soul will not grow strong on the heating, but not nourishing,
diet of religious sensationalism.

III. DEVOTION TO GOD REQUIRES PURITY OF LIFE. The Nazarite was to touch no
unclean thing. Unhappily Samson was satisfied with this ceremonial purity, and did
not cultivate purity of soul, as the spirit of the Nazarite's vow plainly required him
to do; hence his moral weakness and failure to attain perfect success. Samson
"began to deliver Israel," he was not able to finish. Only the spotless One could
say, "It is finished." In proportion to our holiness will be our spiritual strength.
Religious devotion without moral purity cannot be accepted by God (Isa. i.
11—15).

IV. FULNESS OF LIFE BELONGS TO THOSE WHO LIVE TO GOD. No razor, no iron
(the symbol of death), was to come upon the Nazarite. Consecration to God involves
self-denial, but it brings a deeper joy and a fuller life than a self-seeking course will
secure. 1. Religion does not require the destruction of any part of our true human
nature, not even to the injuring of one hair of the head. 2. Religion requires the
consecration of our whole being unmaimed, even to the not severing of one hair of the
head from the perfect sacrifice.

V. CONSECRATION TO GOD IS A SOURCE OF USEFULNESS TO MEN. Samson was a
Nazarite; he was also a deliverer of his people. God calls us not to the hermit's
life of useless devotion, but to the servant's life of devotion practised in active good
works. The religiousness which forbids useful work in commerce, in politics, in
literature is a false sentiment. The Christian can best serve God by labouring for
the good of his fellow-men.—A.

Ver. 8.—*The training of children.* I. CHILDREN NEED TRAINING. 1. Children do
not attain to the best character and conduct *spontaneously*, by natural growth and
development. Left to themselves they would make little progress and many errors.
But they cannot be thus left. If good influences are not brought to bear upon them,
they cannot be entirely shielded from evil influences which will prove fatal unless
they are counteracted. Training is necessary (1) to assist and promote the natural
development of the good which is already in children, (2) to check and eradicate
hereditary tendencies to sin derived from parents, *e. g.* the inclinations to intemperance
likely to be felt by the children of the intemperate, and (3) to counteract the effect
of the temptations of the world. 2. Children do not attain to the best character and
conduct *without care and effort*. They need specific training. Example does much;
the atmosphere of a Christian society is also effective. Yet these general and vague,
though real and powerful, influences are not sufficient without definite teaching and
personal discipline. Christianity must be taught, and it cannot be learnt from any
spirit of Christianity in the air.

II. THE TRAINING OF CHILDREN SHOULD BEGIN EARLY. The danger accompanying
the process of intellectual forcing which results in unnatural precocity is not so great
in moral training. The intellect need not be taxed with complex dogmas, nor the
feelings stirred with unhealthy emotions, and yet children may be trained in integrity
and unselfishness, in love to God and man—the great fundamental principles of the
highest moral character. It is foolish to postpone this training. It is most easy
when the mind is plastic. A natural economy would teach us that it is better that
the whole life should be right from the first, than that there should be an early time
of mistakes and faults and a subsequent conversion to better things.

III. THE SUPREME END OF THE TRAINING OF CHILDREN SHOULD BE TO FIT THEM

FOR THE SERVICE OF GOD. Samson is to be trained for God. Parents are too negligent of the highest ends of their children's lives. Careful to preserve their health and develop their natural powers of body and mind, anxious to instruct them in useful and liberalising secular knowledge, energetic in securing them a prosperous career in the world, parents often forget the real purpose of life, and fail to fit their children for the great mission of serving God. Children should be regarded as God's from their birth, and as only lent by him. The significance of baptism, as implying God's claim on the children and their dedication to him, should be remembered in all the subsequent training of them.

IV. THE CHIEF RESPONSIBILITY OF THE TRAINING OF CHILDREN RESTS ON THEIR PARENTS. This cannot be delegated to teachers. Though the work may be largely done by special teachers, the responsibility still remains on the father and mother, and can never be shifted. They too have the most influence by the constant intercourse of home, the force of parental example, authority, and affection, their knowledge of their children and interest in them.

V. GUIDANCE FOR THE TRAINING OF CHILDREN SHOULD BE SOUGHT FROM GOD. Manoah and his wife show their humility, their faith, and their devotion in praying for guidance. This is necessary for many reasons. The issues of the work are supremely important; error may lead to fearful disaster. The execution of the work is exceedingly difficult. The ideal to be aimed at is great and high. There is mystery in the character of every soul, mystery in the will of God as to its destiny, mystery in the innumerable subtle influences which play upon it. He who realises these things will seek light as to the end of the training of the children and the method of pursuing it.—A.

Vers. 17, 18.—*The mystery of a name.* Names denote persons and describe characters. The nameless one wraps both his individuality and his nature in mystery. Naturally Manoah, like Jacob, desires to solve such a mystery (Gen. xxxii. 29), and in response to this wish, unlike " the traveller unknown," the angel reveals a name, though one of partial mystery.

I. MANOAH'S QUESTION (see ver. 17). 1. *Manoah does not know that his visitor is an angel of the Lord* (ver. 16). Divine visitations are not always recognised. The true nature of Christ was unknown to most of his contemporaries. We cannot always trace the hand of God in his providential action. Heaven is about us unnoticed; unseen ministries attend our lives; God is nearer to us than we suspect. 2. *Manoah desires to know the name of his mysterious visitor*—(1) from natural curiosity, (2) from a desire to strengthen his faith in the message of the unknown, (3) from a wish to give him thanks when his promise should be fulfilled. The thirst to solve the strange questions which surround our spiritual life is natural, and not inconsistent with humility nor with faith. It would be better if we were more anxious to inquire for indications of God and of his character in the experience of life.

II. THE ANGEL'S REPLY (see ver. 18). 1. *He begins his reply with a question.* We should not assail heaven with unjustifiable prayers, but should be ready to give a reason for our petitions. Revelation is not intended to quench human thought, but to stimulate it. Every new voice from heaven, while it answers some questions, starts new questions. 2. *The angel implies that Manoah's request was needless,* either (1) because he ought to have recognised the nature of his visitant from the character of his message and conduct, or (2) because it was more important to consider the meaning of the message than to inquire into the nature of the messenger. We sometimes pray for more light when we only need better eyes to use the light we have; not a fresh revelation, but discernment, reflection, spiritual feeling to appreciate the revelation already received. God's truth is more important than the person of the prophet, apostle, or angel who brings it to us. 3. *The angel gives Manoah a name.* He is "Wonderful." This was a partial answer to Manoah's question. (1) It carried his thought to God, who is the supreme mystery, and suggested the greatness, the wonder, the awe of all that pertained to him. Thus it was a revelation of the Divine. (2) Nevertheless the name was but a partial explanation, as its very meaning suggested the unknown. The deepest questions cannot be solved on earth. But it matters little that the rays of revelation seem to melt into the darkness of the Infinite if only they shine bright and clear on our path of duty.—A.

Vers. 22, 23.—*The fear of the vision of God.* The Divine vision was connected with a blessing to Manoah and his wife. The vision of God by the soul is itself the highest blessing; yet, as in the case of Manoah, it fills men with fear.

I. THE CAUSE OF THE FEAR. 1. *Mystery.* We naturally dread the unknown. Darkness hides possibilities of danger. Superstition peoples the unseen with horrors. 2. *Guilt.* "Conscience makes cowards of us *all.*" So Adam and Eve hid themselves from God in the garden (Gen. iii. 8). Because we are all sinners before God we have a natural shrinking from him (1) who knows our secret hearts, (2) against whom we have offended, (3) who is holy to hate sin and (4) just to punish it. 3. *Unbelief.* We do not sufficiently understand the character of God nor trust his grace. If we did, we should feel safer with all our guilt in his hands than we are when left to ourselves and to the world. Men fear God because they do not know him.

II. THE REMEDIES OF THE FEAR. Manoah's wife encourages her husband. Though men may be brave before physical danger, women sometimes show more courage in spiritual difficulties. This moral courage is nobler than the brute courage which man shares with the lower animals. It has its source in true excellences of character. 1. *Self-possession.* Manoah is confused and dismayed by terror beyond the power of reflection; but his wife is calm and collected, and thus able to see indications of mercy in the vision. 2. *Reflection* on the character of the vision. God has given to us powers of observation, discernment, reasoning. Superstitious terrors more commonly haunt the minds of those people who have neglected to use those powers, while weakly yielding to foolish emotions. Religion to be healthy must be thoughtful. God has given us sufficient indications of his character in the Bible, in Christ, in life, to deliver us from slavish fear, if only we consider and reflect on these. The more we know of God, the less shall we be afraid of him. May not the most fearful learn to reason with Manoah's wife—"If God had meant harm to us, would he have blessed us as he has done hitherto?" The Christian may go further, and be sure that after the great gift of his Son, God must wish well to us in all lesser things (Rom. v. 10). 3. *Faith.* We cannot see perfect evidence that God is blessing us in every mystery; but if we know his character we ought to trust his actions, even when they seem most alarming, as they cannot be contrary to his nature. 4. *The acceptance of sacrifice.* God had accepted Manoah's sacrifice, therefore he could not regard him with disfavour. He has accepted the sacrifice of Christ, and accordingly our guilt need not make us fear God if we rely on the atonement Christ has effected.—A.

Vers. 24, 25.—*The young Samson.* I. HIS NAME. Samson—the sun. This was a great name, full of inspiring significance. It is well to have a good name, one which is a constant appeal to a man to be worthy of it, and to live up to its meaning.

II. HIS GROWTH. Samson the hero was first a child at the mercy of the weakest. The grandest river springs from a little streamlet. The noblest man enters life, as the meanest does, in helpless infancy. So the spiritual life of the saint, the martyr, the apostle is seen first in him as in a babe in Christ. It is therefore no dishonour to have a small beginning, but it is a dishonour to remain small. The one question is, Do we grow mentally, spiritually, in knowledge, in holiness, in power? There is more to be expected of the minute growing seed than of the dead stump, which is at first vastly larger. Better be a growing child of the Lord than a dwarf adult Christian man.

III. HIS BLESSING. "The Lord blessed him." We are not told how; this matters not. Perhaps he did not recognise the blessing. God blesses us silently, with no formal benediction, and perhaps in ways which to us seem hard and injurious. Still better than health, riches, pleasure is the fact God does give a man the thing that is for his highest good, which is what we mean by "a blessing."

IV. HIS INSPIRATION. "The Spirit of the Lord began to move him." 1. Samson's heroic strength was an inspiration of God, not a mere brute muscular force. We see how in great crises men are nerved to do what is beyond their power in ordinary life. The abnormal strength of insanity is an instance of the same principle, applied in circumstances of disease. 2. Inspiration assumes various forms. To Samson it brought neither the grace of purity nor the gift of prophecy; but it gave him the special gifts which he needed for his special work. He would have been a nobler man if he had sought the Spirit of God also to help him in more spiritual ways. Samson had a supernatural gift of the Spirit with little of its ordinary grace of holiness. It is better to have this grace first, though, if God will, we may receive the gift also.

V. HIS IMPERFECT POSSESSION BY THE SPIRIT. He was moved at times. 1. God's special gifts are *limited to occasion*. There is an economy of Divine power. When we need extraordinary grace he will give this, but only then. 2. The receipt of spiritual gifts depends on the *condition of our spirit*. Samson was only rightly disposed to receive the Spirit at intervals. Our spiritual life fluctuates; we are not long at our best. 3. We are only moved when we *respond*. God may have visited Samson more often than Samson profited by his visit. We can resist the Sp'rit. We are helped only when we willingly yield to it.—A.

EXPOSITION.

CHAPTER XIV.

Ver. 1. — **Timnath**, or, more correctly, *Thimnathah*, as in Josh. xix. 43, a town in the tribe of Dan, the name of which survives in the modern *Tibneh*, about three miles south-west of Zorah (ch. xiii. 2, note). It may or may not be identical with Timnath in Gen. xxxviii. 12—14, and with *Timnah* in Josh. xv. 10. It appears to have been in the possession of the Philistines at this time.

Ver. 2.—**Get her**, &c. Rather, *take her*. It is the technical phrase (1) for a man *taking* a wife for himself, as Gen. iv. 19; vi. 2; 1 Sam. xxv. 39, 43, and vers. 3, 8 of this chapter; (2) for a man's parents *taking* a wife for him, as Exod. xxxiv. 16; Neh. x. 30. The parents of the bridegroom paid the dowry agreed upon (see Gen. xxxiv. 12; 1 Sam. xviii. 25).

Ver. 3.—**Uncircumcised**. Cf. Gen. xxxiv. 14. A term of reproach here added to deter Samson from the marriage. It is particularly applied to the Philistines (see ch. xv. 18; 1 Sam. xvii. 26, 36; xviii. 29; xxxi. 4; 2 Sam. i. 20, &c.).

Ver. 4.—**It was of** or *from* **the Lord**. It was the method decreed by God's providence for bringing about a rupture with the Philistines. **That he sought**. Rather, *because he sought*. The writer explains the purpose of the providence. It is doubtful whether "he" refers to Samson or to the Lord. Most commentators refer it to Samson; but it is contrary to the whole tenor of Samson's impetuous course, and to all probability, that he should have asked for the Timnathite damsel merely for the sake of quarrelling with the Philistines; whereas the statement that Samson's obstinate determination to take a Philistine wife was the means which God's secret purpose had fixed upon for bringing about the

eventual overthrow of the Philistine dominion is in exact accordance with other declarations of Holy Scripture (cf. *e. g.* Exod. vii. 3, 4; Josh. xi. 20; 1 Sam. ii. 25; 1 Kings xii. 15; 2 Chron. x. 15; xxii. 7; xxv. 20). **An occasion**. The noun only occurs here; but the verb, in its several conjugations, means, *to happen at the right time; to bring a person or thing at the right time* (Exod. xxi. 13, *deliver*, A. V.); *to be brought at the right time* (Prov. xii. 21, *happen*, A. V.); *to seek the right time for injuring any one* (2 Kings v. 7, *seeketh a quarrel*, A. V.).

Ver. 5.—**Went down**, showing that Timnath was on lower ground than Zorah; it was in fact in the *Shephelah*. **The vineyards of Timnath**. The valley of Sorek (ch. xvi. 4), so famous for its vines (Isa. v. 2; Jer. ii. 21), from which it derived its name (*Sorek*, translated in the above passages *the choicest vine*, and *a noble vine*), is thought to have been in the immediate neighbourhood. Probably the whole district under the hills was a succession of vineyards, like the country round Bordeaux. Samson had left the road along which his father and mother were walking, at a pace, perhaps, too slow for his youthful energy, and had plunged into the vineyards. Of a sudden a young lion,—a term designating a lion between the age of a cub and a full-grown lion,—brought there, perhaps, in pursuit of the foxes or jackals, which often had their holes in vineyards (Cant. ii. 15), roared against him.

Ver. 6.—**The Spirit of the Lord**, &c.—as a spirit of dauntless courage and irresistible strength of body. **Came mightily**. Hebrew, *fell upon him*, or *passed over upon him*, as in ver. 19; xv. 14; 1 Sam. x. 6, 10; xviii. 10, &c. **He rent him**, &c. He "had nothing in his hand," no weapon or knife, nor even a stick; but he rent him with as much ease as the kid is rent. The Hebrew has *the kid*, with the definite article, which is not prefixed unless some particular kid is meant, as in Gen. xxxviii. 23. Perhaps *the* kid means the one about to be served, which the cook rends open either before or after it is cooked. Unless some such operation is alluded to, it is not easy to understand what the rending of the kid means. **He told not his father,** &c. This is mentioned to explain ver. 16; but it shows that Samson had wandered some distance from his parents among the vineyards (see note to ver. 5).

Ver. 7.—**Went down**, as in ver. 1, where see note.

Ver. 8.—**He returned to take her.** All the preliminaries being settled between the parents, he returned to Timnath to take his bride by the same road which he and his parents had travelled by before, and, remembering his feat in killing the lion, very naturally turned aside to see what had become of the carcase. **And, behold, there was a swarm of bees,** &c. This has been objected to as improbable, because bees are very dainty, and would not approach a putrefying body. But as a considerable time had elapsed, it is very possible that either the mere skeleton was left, or that the heat of the sun had dried up the body and reduced it to the state of a mummy without decomposition, as is said to happen often in the desert of Arabia.

Ver. 9.—**And . . . he went on eating,** &c. Compare the account of Jonathan finding and eating the wild honey (1 Sam. xiv. 25, and following verses).

HOMILETICS.

Vers. 1—9.—*The link of the chain.* A swarm of bees light one day in the carcase of a lion which had been killed in the vineyards of Thimnathah. They construct their hive there, and make their honey. It was no doubt an unusual circumstance that the bees should form their hive in such a place rather than in a hollow tree, or the cleft of a rock, but beyond its interest as a fact in natural history nobody would have attached any importance to it. But this action of the bees was linked to curious antecedents, and to peculiar consequences. The lion had been slain by Samson, that mysterious person of gigantic strength, whose life is such a remarkable episode in the history of Israel; and Samson had been led to the spot where the lion was by his ill-regulated love for a daughter of the Philistines, who were the masters and oppressors of his country. And as to what happened after the swarming of these bees, the marriage of Samson to his Philistine bride took place after an interval just sufficient for the bees to have filled their hive with honey, and Samson on his way to the wedding, impelled by a natural curiosity to see the lion which he had killed, had turned aside from his path, and had eaten the honey which was strangely found there. It was the custom of the time and of those people to beguile the long hours of the idle wedding-feasts with curious questions and strange riddles. In the gambling spirit which is such a frequent accompaniment of insufficient occupation, whether among the lazaronis of Naples or the wealthy nobles of modern society, such riddles were made the occasion of wagers, and such wagers often led to deadly quarrels. In the present instance Samson's double adventure with the lion suggested to him the riddle, "Out of the eater came forth meat, and out of the strong came forth sweetness." Baffled in their attempts to guess the riddle by fair means, they set on Samson's wife to worm the secret out of him and divulge it to them. Samson at once perceived the treachery, broke with his wife, slew thirty Philistines, and took their spoil wherewith to pay the lost wager, and followed up the feud by successive slaughters of his enemies, thus preparing the way for the eventual overthrow of the Philistine domination. The point for our special remark is that a swarm of bees lighting on a particular spot was an important link in the chain of providence by which the destinies of a great people were guided to independence; and the observation is not only a curious one, but has an important bearing upon the difficult subject (see Homiletics, ch. iii. 12—21) of the use made of men, and of men's actions, in the providential government of the world. Samson in slaying the lion, and the bees in swarming in its carcase, did things which were links in the chain of events which God foresaw, or fore-ordained, as he did also the effects of Samson's marriage with the Philistine. But just as the bees only followed their instinct in building their hive, so Samson, in fixing his affections on the Timnathite, and in attacking the lion, and in eating the honey, and in propounding the riddle, and in avenging himself for his wife's treachery, was merely following the bent of his own inclinations and the leading of his own will, though in so doing he was bringing about God's purpose for the deliverance of Israel. What, however, we have here to notice is the wonderful way in which God brings about his own purpose, and also the infinite foreknowledge of God. We look back, and we can trace the successive steps of causation, as one follows the other, like wave upon wave. But God looks forward from the beginning, foresees the effect of each cause in endless succession, and so orders them as to accomplish his own will. The most trivial events may be necessary links in the great chain; and while men are blindly following their own inclinations, with little thought and no knowledge of what will come of them, God is making use of them with unerring wisdom to work out his own eternal purposes, for the good of his people and for the glory of his own great name.

HOMILIES BY VARIOUS AUTHORS.

Vers. 1—4.—*Human desire overruled for Divine ends.* This incident in the life of Samson has a universal human interest. He no sooner comes to manhood than his destiny begins to determine itself. He sees a woman of the Philistines, and at once his fancy is captivated, and the strong natural desires of the young man over-leap all the traditional restraints of God's people. He manufactures a law for him-self; "she pleaseth me well" may mean, "it is pleasing, or right, in my own eyes." The perplexity and distress of the parents, unaware of the meaning of this strange freak, so opposed to the future they had been led to imagine for their son. Notice—

I. THE FATALITY OF DESIRE. A sudden, unreasoning, and unreasonable passion is scarcely the augury one would expect for the career of a promised deliverer. A crisis in his moral history, a pivot upon which his whole subsequent life must turn. Sexual attachments are amongst the determining factors of human character and life, and the bases of society. Yet there are no circumstances of our life so independent of mere reason, and the power of the subjects of them. Still as a rule the outward realisation of such attachments is within the control of the individual. Recognition should be made of God's share in producing them, and the matter should be laid before him. He has been blamed for "heavily loading the dice" in this matter for his own universal ends, and for wantonly subjecting the subject of passion to misery and disadvantage. Moral and intellectual progress are thus, it is said, indefinitely hindered. If it could be written, how full of light upon the moral and intellectual history of the race would be an account of the intermarriages of nations, the *mésalliances* of individuals! &c.

II. THE ENTANGLEMENT AND PERPLEXITY IT OCCASIONS. Here it meant connection with the idolatrous and sensual life of the Philistines. The relatives on both sides could not be cordial. A relaxation of moral principles must ensue. Children would bring a fresh discord. How could a man so related lift up his hand against the Philistines? An instance like this throws strong light upon the traditional objection of God's chosen people to intermarriage with neighbouring tribes and nations. It is not for nothing that it is written of Noah, and of one and another beside, "*And he was perfect in his generation.*" "The daughters of Heth" are ineligible in the eyes of the patriarch's wife for other than mere social reasons. There can be no doubt but that the same caution ought to characterise Christian parents in the alliances they encourage their children to make.

III. THE FURTHER AND HIGHER MINISTRY OF DESIRE. Behind and beyond all this sinister appearance was the Divine purpose,—"*For he (Jehovah) sought an occasion from the Philistines.*" God's will is fulfilled in many ways, and by alternatives. When sin refuses to be put under then it can be utilised; and the end more com-pletely served, albeit not to the immediate happiness or advantage of the guilty agent. How often "by a way they knew not" have the sons of men been led by an unseen providence to gracious ends. An ill-assorted marriage is a great calamity, but it may be the determining cause of important spiritual results, and by arranging a new relationship and set of conditions, prepare for a higher and nobler, though less immediately happy, development, of inward character. Thus the whole question of the determining force of sexual desire, which has been a matter of grief and despair to the pessimist, is capable of another interpretation. The past history of our race shows that "where sin abounded, there did grace much more abound." Let us not therefore despair before these mysterious fatalities and complications, but commit the way of ourselves and children into the hands of him "who seeth the end from the beginning," and who makes "all things work together for good" to them that love him.—M.

Vers. 5, 6.—*The lion in the way.* Very natural is this description. The wild beast in the vineyards, the weaponlessness of the hero, &c., are all in keeping with the character of the times. Local names still extant prove the former existence of lions in Palestine; the particular district was a border one between militant nations, and therefore likely to be less thoroughly brought under; and Israel as temporarily subdued had been deprived of arms. The young lover, full of his mistress, and not on the best terms with his parents, prefers to keep by himself, a little apart. All this is highly suggestive of parallel circumstances in the spiritual life: *e. g.*—

I. Youth is often subjected to great and sudden temptations. Our streets, the social circle, sexual relations, &c., all abound with concealed perils. These threaten the destruction of the soul.

II. These are, from their nature, generally encountered alone and in secret. Bulwer Lytton says somewhere, that boys learn many things at school of great value to them through life, that were never bargained for by their parents, or represented in the school-bill. The youthful sense of growing power, and assertion of independence, creates a little world of which guardians are but dimly conscious. There is, too, the inability of age to sympathise with youth; and the natural reticence concerning matters of affection, &c. Every youth is centre of a number of invisible but potent influences that may make or mar him for life; and he ought therefore to be frequently commended to the care of his heavenly Father, and to be treated with gentleness and consideration by those in authority.

III. The Spirit of the Lord can render timely and effectual help. The phrase, "came suddenly upon him," expresses opportuneness.

The fearlessness and modesty of the spiritual hero are here strikingly illustrated.

I. If earthly affection will make men brave great dangers and inconveniences, how much more ought the love of God!

II. With the Spirit of God nothing is impossible, and he makes all things easy and simple to them that believe.

III. Humility is the characteristic of the spiritual hero.—M.

Ver. 6.—*The mystery of spiritual might.* "And he had nothing in his hand." This is typical of the Christian. Christ's injunctions to the seventy. In Samson's case it was probably due to the regulation imposed by the Philistines upon a conquered people. Christians are commanded not to put their trust in earthly equipment or the arm of flesh.

I. That our conflicts with Satan may be true spiritual exercises and not merely outward triumphs.

II. The influx and withdrawal of the Holy Spirit limit the authority and secure the humility of the agent. How helpless even a Samson but for the Spirit! Temptations of our own seeking may be left to our own resources. No enterprise ought to be undertaken without the aid of the Holy Spirit, and the Divine blessing. What God brings upon us he will help us to overcome.

III. The faith of the Christian soldier and worker must be wholly in God.—M.

Vers. 8, 9.—*Recalling past deliverances.* In this case Samson is led to do so either by curiosity or the impulse of God's Spirit. He revisits the scene of the exploit, and meets with welcome but unexpected refreshment. There are various ways of recalling spiritual experiences of God's saving power in the past. Sometimes an accident (?) may bring up vividly some forgotten circumstance of Divine grace, and we are overwhelmed with the recollections that crowd upon the mind. Soldiers who have fought side by side in famous battles have their anniversaries of fellowship and celebration. Are there no circumstances that justify these amongst Christians? It is a spiritual education and confirmation to recall circumstances and revisit scenes of God's saving mercies.

I. THE DUTY OF THANKFUL RECOLLECTION OF DIVINE INTERPOSITIONS.

II. THE SECRET AND UNSHARED COMMUNION OF THE SUBJECT OF GRACE WITH HIS SAVIOUR.

III. ITS ADVANTAGE AND BLESSING.—M.

Vers. 5, 6.—*Samson and the lion.* I. THE DANGER. 1. It came *unsought.* It is foolish for the bravest to court danger. We have only ground for meeting it bravely when we have not rashly provoked it. 2. It was *unexpected.* Had Samson expected to encounter the lion he would probably have chosen another path, or have armed himself against it. One of the worst features of the great dangers of life is that we can rarely foresee and provide against them. 3. It was when Samson was on a *pleasurable journey.* He went to seek a wife, and met a lion! The greatest trouble may spring upon us at the moment of highest elation. Earthly joy is no safeguard. 4. It was when Samson was acting in a *questionable* manner. He was seeking a wife among the Philistines. His parents disapproved of this course though their affection sought an excuse for it (ver. 3). His conduct was contrary to the law of God (Exod. xxxiv. 16). We may meet with trouble in the path of duty, but we must expect to meet with it in the way of transgression (Jonah i. 4).

II. THE TRIUMPH. 1. It was effected in the might of the *Spirit of the Lord.* Herein is the distinction between Samson and Hercules. The Jewish hero does not trust to his own muscular strength. Strong man as he is he can only do great things in God's strength. This is the redeeming feature of his character. It shows him as one, though amongst the lowest, of the heroes of faith. If Samson needed the strength of inspiration, how much more do we weaker men need to be clothed in the panoply of God's might before we can face the dangers of life! 2. The Spirit of God came upon Samson in *especial force in his greatest need.* God gives us strength according to our requirements. In our hour of weakness it seems impossible to face the future difficulty, but when this comes how wonderfully is the new strength bestowed to meet it (Deut. xxxiii. 25). We must not, however, abuse this truth and neglect natural expedients. Samson would have been wrong in going unarmed if he had expected to meet the lion. We have only a right to believe that God will help us in sudden emergencies when we are not rashly and negligently increasing the danger of them. 3. The Spirit of God helped Samson by inspiring him to an extraording exercise of his *natural powers.* It was to Samson the strong, a spirit of strength. God works in us through our natural faculties and helps us differently according to our various gifts. Though the might is God's, the daring, the will, the effort must be ours. God gave him strength, yet Samson slew the lion with his own hands. 4. After victory, Samson modestly concealed his triumph. It is better to be more than we seem than to seem more than we are. If the source of our victory is God's strength we have no ground for boasting.—A.

EXPOSITION.

Ver. 10.—**So his father went down.** It is not clear what is meant by this mention of his father alone; but it was probably some part of the wedding etiquette that the father should go to the bride first alone; perhaps, as Kimchi says, to give her notice of the bridegroom's approach, that she might get ready. Among the preparations may have been the selection of the thirty young men to be "the children of the bride-chamber" (Matt. ix. 15). As these were all Philistines, the inference is that they were selected by the bride, just as with us the bride has the privilege of choosing the minister who is to officiate at the marriage.

Ver. 11. — **When they saw him,** *i. e.* when the father and mother and friends of the bride saw him approaching, they went to meet him with the thirty companions who had been selected. We still see a strong resemblance to the wedding arrangements referred to in Matt. ix. 15, and xxv. 1—12; only in this case they were young men instead of young women who went out to meet the bridegroom. We may observe, by the way, that the scale of the wedding feast, as regards numbers and duration, indicates that Samson's family was one of wealth and position.

Ver. 12. — **Riddle.** The Hebrew word is the same as that which is rendered *hard questions* in 1 Kings x. 1, and *dark questions,* Numb. xii. 8, and occurs also in Ezek. xvii. 2, where the phrase is the same as here and in ver. 16, as if we should say in English, *I will riddle you a riddle.* In English, however, *to riddle,* as a verb active, means *to solve a riddle,* not, as in Hebrew, *to propound* one. The derivation of the Hebrew word and of the English is the same as regards the sense—something *intricate* and *twisted.* **Thirty sheets,** or rather, as in the margin, *shirts,* a linen garment worn next the skin. In Isa. iii. 23 spoken of the women's garment, "*the fine linen,*" A.V., as also Prov. xxxi. 24. The word (*sadin,* Sanscrit *sindu*) means Indian linen. **Change of garments**— the outward garment of the Orientalist, which was part of the wealth of the rich and great, and was, and is to the present day, one of the most frequent presents on all state occasions (see Gen. xlv. 22 ; 2 Kings v. 5, 22 ; Isa. iii. 6, 7 ; Matt. vi. 19, &c.).

Ver. 15.—**On the seventh day.** There is some apparent difficulty in understanding how to reconcile this statement with what was said in ver. 14, that they could not in *three days* expound the riddle ; and also with what is said in vers. 16 and 17, that Samson's wife *wept before him the seven days of the feast.* And several different readings have arisen from this difficulty : viz., in this verse, the reading of the *fourth* day for the *seventh,* and the omission of the words, *And it came to pass on the seventh day ;* and, in the latter part of ver. 14, *seven* days for *three* days. But all difficulty will disapppear if we bear in mind the peculiarity of Hebrew narrative noticed in note to section vers. 1—6 of ch. ii., when we come to consider ver. 16. **Entice thy husband.** Cf. ch. xvi. 5. **That he may declare unto us.** If the text is sound, they must mean to say, *declare it unto you, that you may declare it unto us,* i. e. declare it unto us through you. But it is simpler either to read with the Septuagint, *that he may declare unto you,* &c., or to read, *and declare unto us,* in the imperative mood. **Burn with fire.** See ch. xii. 1, and xv. 6. **Have ye called us,** &c., *i.e.* Did you invite us to this feast in order to impoverish us, to plunder us of our property ? We shall conclude that you did so if you do not disclose to us the riddle.

Ver. 16.—**And Samson's wife,** &c. This statement does not follow ver. 15, but is a *parallel* narrative to that beginning in ver. 14, "*And they could not in three days,*" &c., down to the end of ver. 15, bringing the story down to the same point of time, viz.,

the seventh day. One stream of the narrative tells us what the young men did when Samson had propounded his riddle ; the other tells us what Samson's wife did. From the very first, no doubt, she had wished to be in the secret, not perhaps from treacherous motives, but from curiosity, and the natural desire to be in her husband's confidence, and she pressed her request with cajolery and petulance. The young men at the same time had tried to find out the riddle by fair means. But on the seventh day they threatened to burn her and her father unless she found out the riddle for them, and under the terror of this threat she extracted the secret from Samson and divulged it to the Philistine young men. The only difficulty is to explain why a gap of four days occurs in the account between vers. 14 and 15. The most likely thing is, that after three days' vain attempt to find out the riddle, they began to tamper with Samson's wife, offering her money, as the Philistine lords did to Delilah (ch. xvi. 5), though the narrative does not mention it ; but that on the seventh day, becoming desperate, and thinking that the woman was not doing her best, they resorted to the dreadful threat of burning her.

Ver. 17.—**She lay sore upon him.** In ch. xvi. 16 the same word is rendered *pressed him.* **It came to pass on the seventh day.** This is the confluence of the two streams of narrative.

Ver. 18.—**The men of the city**—the same as were spoken of in ver. 11 as Samson's companions. **Before the sun went down**— just in time, therefore, to save the wager, as defined in ver. 12. This is the uncommon word for *the sun* used also in ch. viii. 13, where see note. **What is sweeter,** &c. They put their answer in a form to make it seem as if they had guessed the riddle ; but Samson instantly perceived his wife's treachery, and showed that he did so by quoting the proverb of plowing with another person's heifer. They had not used their own wit to find out the riddle, but had learnt the secret at Samson's cost, through his wife. He insinuates that had they acted fairly he would have won the wager.

Ver. 19.—**The Spirit of the Lord,** &c.—as in ver. 6 and ch. xiii. 25, where see notes. The verb here, *came upon him,* is the same as in ver. 6. **Thirty men**—the number of the companions to whom he felt bound to pay the thirty changes of garment. **Ashkelon** (ch. i. 18)—one of the five Philistine cities, but the least often mentioned, owing, it is thought, to its remote situation "on the extreme edge of the shore of the Mediterranean, far down in the south." It still preserves its ancient name, and was famous in the time of the Crusaders. "Within the walls and towers now standing Richard

(Cœur de Lion) held his court." The onion called eschalot, or shallot, is named from Eshkalon, or Ashkalon. **Their spoil**—that which was stripped from them. **His anger was kindled** — against the Philistines in general, and his wife in particular, so that he went back to his father's house without her.

Ver. 20.—**His companion**—no doubt his "best man," the "friend of the bridegroom."

The parents of the Thimnathite, having no doubt obtained Samson's dower, and supposing him to have finally broken with his treacherous wife, proceeded to give her in marriage to the Philistine young man who had been Samson's friend—perhaps the man to whom she had told the riddle. The sad end of this unhappy alliance fully justified the opposition of Samson's parents to it in ver. 3.

HOMILETICS.

Vers. 10—20.—*Another view of married life.* The lessons which we drew from the married life of Manoah and his wife seem to receive a striking confirmation, by contrast, from the unhappy union of their son with the daughter of the Philistines. Here everything was against a reasonable prospect of happiness. Their religion was different, one might say opposite. Samson had been brought up in the faith of the LORD God of Israel. He was in covenant with him by circumcision. His creed was that there was one true and living God, the Lord of heaven and earth, and that all the gods of the heathen were but vain idols. His religious duty was to love the Lord his God with all his heart, and with all his soul, and with all his might, and to serve him alone. His wife did not believe in the Lord, nor love him, nor fear him, but was a worshipper of Dagon, whose temples were at Gaza (ch. xvi. 21—30) and at Ashdod (1 Sam. v. 1—5). There could therefore be no union for them in that great bond of union which is the living God. Righteousness can have no fellowship with unrighteousness, nor light with darkness, nor the believer with an infidel, nor the temple of God with idols. Then again the interests of their respective peoples were opposite. To break off the Philistine yoke from the neck of Israel ; to set his people free from a shameful bondage ; to rescue his native towns, and fields, and vineyards, from the usurped possession of the uncircumcised invader ; to drive out the foreigner from the land which God gave to his forefathers ; was Samson's natural aim, and the use which he must needs make of his supernatural strength. But his wife's sympathies were all with the children of her people. Her heart would swell with pride as she thought of their conquests over Israel, of Dagon's conquests over the people of Jehovah. She would look with scorn upon the subject race, and be proud of her kindred with the conquerors. Every movement of either people must at once put them on opposite sides. What was joy to him would be grief to her ; and what made her glad would make him sorry. Their language was different, their tastes were different, their habits of thought and life were different. They had nothing in common to cement their hearts and interests together, and to bind their life into one. He was pleased with her beauty, and she was gratified by his admiration. That was all. And how long would that last? What strong temptation, what powerful motive of action, what great provocation, would those influences be able to withstand ? What promise did they give of unity of sentiment, and harmony of conduct, amidst the difficulties of troublous times, and the intricacies of conflicting duties ? One week in their case was sufficient to supply the answer to these questions. A betrayed husband, a deserted wife, discord, strife, bloodshed, were the fruit of seven days of this ill-assorted union. The wife married to another husband is cut off by murderous hands in the prime of her youth and beauty. The husband married to another wife is again betrayed and given up to his enemies to be mocked, and blinded, and to die. The man of splendid gifts, but irregular passions, lives a stormy life, and dies a violent death. He has no gentle, clear-sighted woman to restrain and guide him ; no sympathising wife to share his sorrows, and by sharing to lighten them. He only knows what is bad in woman, because he only seeks them on the bad side. And that one week of disappointed love in an unhappy and unholy wedlock casts its shade upon a whole life which might have been a most happy and glorious one. We seem, therefore, to be taught by the ill-starred marriage of Samson with the Thimnathite, as forcibly as by the blessed union of his father and mother, what to seek and what to avoid in choosing a partner for life. The union of two souls in the love of God and in the faith of the Lord Jesus Christ; the union of two minds in all rational and sober pursuits, whether intellectual, political, or social; the identity of interests; the community of purpose to make the most of what God has given to each for the common stock of happiness; the care of each for the other as the first human duty, and the faithfulness of each to the other in the whole series of actions, from the least to the greatest—this is the ideal of Christian wedlock to which we are led by the failures of the one as well as by the virtues of the other. It is sad to think how frequently happy married life is an idea only, and not a reality, from the entire failure on both sides to carry out the conditions upon which happiness depends. A foolish choice at first, based only upon beauty and vanity, upon wealth and position, upon whim and fancy, without consulting religion, or reason, or true affection, is followed up by independent and selfish action, by each crossing the other's wishes, by mutual neglect, by mutual reproach, by mutual violation of the spirit of the marriage contract. There follow in different cases various degrees of unhappiness and disorder according to the various measures of temper, and violence, and self-will, and disregard of solemn vows, and contempt of God's word, of the parties concerned. In one home it is the constant jarring of antagonistic wills, and unloving tempers; in another it is the coldness of distant and reproachful spirits; the constant sense of injury from unfulfilled duties; in others, the man having failed to find in his wife the kindness, the solace, the help, which he expected, seeks to indemnify himself in the flatteries and cajoleries of other women; and the wife, wounded in her pride, and hurt in her affections, looks for balm and for revenge in the attentions of the profligate, and the admiration of the licentious. In both cases true manhood and womanhood are marred and crushed, and the whole life is distorted, and like a building in ruins. Public duties in the cabinet and in the field may indeed be performed by men of gifted minds and transcendent powers, in spite of their aberrations from moral rectitude; but the delicate organisation of affections and faculties which were given to make up the charm and beauty of private and domestic life cannot live in an atmosphere of vice; and when there is a breakdown of the love and obedience due to God, there is a breakdown also of the dignity and happiness of man. The careful study by married people, in a spirit of true Christian philosophy, of what is necessary to make wedlock the blessing God intended it to be when he "made the woman and brought her unto the man," and the careful daily endeavour, in the spirit of saintly obedience, to perform each his or her part in the mutual contract, in spite of difficulties and hindrances, would be a large contribution to human happiness, and to the beauty of the Church of God.

HOMILIES BY VARIOUS AUTHORS.

Ver. 14.—*Samson's riddle.* A strong impression had been produced by the circumstance upon the mind of Samson. This was one of the means used by God to penetrate and awaken the moral nature of his servant. A certain Divine wisdom is given for its interpretation, and for its suitable statement to the world, the heathen of his day. The form which the circumstance assumes when declared to the Philistines is a favourite one to this day amongst Eastern and primitive peoples. It constituted a distinct portion of God's great revelation of himself to man, but for many and weighty reasons it was not a plain declaration, but the "wisdom of God in a mystery."

I. The phenomena of the natural world link themselves with, and become symbols of, spiritual experience. Thus the deepest things of the spiritual universe may be uttered by those who are but dimly conscious of their meaning. And no man is wholly destitute of spiritual teaching. The teachings of revelation thus become indefinitely enriched and extended.

II. To the awakened spirit of man the Divine meanings of life and the world are alone important. How vast is the relationship of the truth thus generalised! For many days will such food sustain the soul. *Trials may become the sources of spiritual consolation if overcome in God's strength. Death is the gate of Life.*

III. To the unbelieving is the truth of God spoken in parables, that seeing, they may not perceive, and hearing, they may not understand. This might be called the "gospel of the Philistines." It is a mighty revelation. How near were these heathen, if they had known it, to the wisdom and kingdom of God! So is it to-day with the preaching of the gospel to unbelievers. The moral character, and not the mere intellectual power, of men is tested in this way. What the Spirit of the Lord inspires the same Spirit can interpret. God will bestow illumination upon those who seek it. How often has God spoken through striking incidents to those who would not care to hear the preaching of his word, or to whom it has not been granted! Do not let any one hastily say, "I never heard." Do not let Christians despair of those who have not heard, and who will not hear the preaching of men. God has his own way to every heart.—M.

Vers. 15—20.—*Unlawful methods of interpreting Divine mysteries.* Samson is betrayed into revealing his riddle. It was a mean subterfuge, and the fraud is promptly avenged.

I. THERE ARE ILLEGITIMATE WAYS OF GETTING AT DIVINE TRUTH. False prophets, Unwilling prophets, as Balaam. Mercenary attempts at obtaining a peculiar knowledge, as of Simon Magus (cf. Acts viii. 9—24; xix. 13; Col. ii. 17, 18).

II. THE ESSENTIAL MEANING OF THE TRUTH CANNOT BE THUS DISCOVERED. The Philistines only learnt the historic circumstance; they were still in outer darkness as to the evangelic significance of the parable or riddle. So it is with those who "intrude into those things which they have not seen or heard, vainly puffed up in their fleshly minds." God will deliver them over to strong delusion, and the belief of a lie.

III. THIS IS FULL OF DANGER, AND WILL BE PROMPTLY AVENGED. Partly in the apparent illumination, but real ignorance, of such men; and partly in the consequences attending an incomplete or garbled gospel. Here the vengeance was both spiritual and physical. How sorry the gain that involved their fellow-countrymen in such a death!—M.

Ver. 18.—*Ploughing with another's heifer.* The saying derives itself from the occasional discovery of hidden treasure by the plough, and the superstitious belief that the homebred heifer knew where the furrow ought to be drawn, because it has been shown the way before, when the treasure was hid.

I. SO SATAN AND HIS SERVANTS BETRAY MEN THROUGH THEIR HABITUAL TEMPERAMENT OR BIAS—THE WEAKNESS PECULIAR TO THEM. The weak place in Samson was his sensuality. His enemies speedily discovered this, and were unscrupulous enough to take advantage of it.

II. SAINTS SHOULD BE DISTRUSTFUL OF UNHOLY CONFIDENCES, AND SHOULD LEAVE "NO UNGUARDED PLACE" IN THEIR SPIRITUAL CHARACTER OR RELATIONS. All habitual relations or companionships with worldly persons are dangerous. Our sin will find us out, to our confusion. Safety can alone be found in perfect consecration—putting on the whole armour of God. Relations in life which, when both parties are holy, are full of comfort and help, when they involve us in close fellowship with the wicked may be our destruction.—M.

Ver. 20.—*How confidence in wicked men is rewarded.* The world is full of such instances of misplaced trust. The fable of the viper and the husbandman. It is hard to persuade men of the utter folly of worldly friendships and alliances. Only the most severe warnings and painful consequences will suffice to disabuse the mind. At the same time that the carnal nature of God's servant draws him towards the enemies of his country and his faith, God's providential dispensations are working out an effectual divorce, and preparing Samson for deadly hostility to his quondam friends.

I. THE CONFIDENCE WE PLACE IN THE WICKED WILL CERTAINLY BETRAY US.

II. GOD SEEKS BY STERN LESSONS TO SEPARATE HIS PEOPLE FROM THE WORLD.

III. NONE ARE SO OPPOSED TO THE CHARACTERS AND PRACTICES OF THE WICKED AS THOSE WHO HAVE BEEN BETRAYED BY THEM.—M.

Ver. 14.—*Samson's riddle.* The first intention of Samson's riddle is plainly, as he shows in the interpretation, to wrap up in mystery a simple event of his own experience. But, with the Eastern instinct for imagery, Samson may well be supposed to intend also to set forth general principles which he sees illustrated in that event. The words seem to suggest the beautiful truth that things harsh and destructive may be found to contain within them sources of happiness and life.

I. SOURCES OF LIFE MAY BE FOUND IN POWERS OF DESTRUCTION. Out of the destroyer came forth food. 1. The *destroying agencies of nature* prepare the way for fresh life. Geological catastrophes renew the face of the old earth with virgin fields of fertility. The products of decay are the food of new life ; the rotting leaves of autumn nourishing the blooming flowers of spring. 2. *National revolutions* sometimes introduce a better order. Out of the corruption and disintegration of the Roman empire the separate nationalities of modern Europe sprang into being. 3. *Religious destructive agencies* prepare the way for new religious institutions. The work of the Hebrew prophets, of Christ and his apostles,—especially St. Paul,—of the leaders of the Reformation, was largely destructive, and only after a certain amount of ruthless breaking up of old revered habits and doctrines was it possible to introduce the good things they were ultimately destined to establish. We may be too fearful of needful but painful destroying agencies, and by joining the new cloth to the old garment may only increase the final rent. 4. Destructive influences in *private life* are overruled by God's providence to produce fruitful issues. Our cherished hope is dashed to the ground ; for the moment we are in despair. But in time out of the grave of the past God makes a purer, nobler hope to spring. 5. *The death of Christ is the source of the Christian's life.* In his broken body we see our bread of life (1 Cor. xi. 24).

II. SOURCES OF QUIET BLESSEDNESS MAY BE FOUND IN MOVEMENTS OF VIOLENT STRENGTH. Out of the strong comes forth sweetness. 1. It is only *in strength that we can find true gentleness.* While gentleness makes us great, greatness is necessary to the perfection of gentleness. Soft weakness is not gentleness. Self-control, forbearance, quiet work in the midst of difficulty are signs of gentleness, and they all imply great strength of soul. Christ's shadow shelters us because he is a great rock (Isa. xxxii. 2). 2. *Violent exercises of strength are sometimes required to remove an unsettled, restless condition of things*, to establish an equilibrium, and so secure more peace. Storms clear the air and bring about a more stable calm than that which preceded them. The troubles of life subdue our passions, rebuke our wilfulness, chasten our affections, and thus prepare us to receive the peace of God. 3. A healthy exercise of strength is the means of bringing *happiness to others*. Sentimental sympathy is of little use. If we wish to sweeten the lot of the most miserable classes of men, we must be prepared for active measures of improvement. 4. In proportion to the violence of earthly trials will be the *sweetness of the heavenly rest.*—A.

EXPOSITION.

CHAPTER XV.

Ver. 1.—**Within a while**—the same expression as that in ch. xiv. 8, rendered "after a time," and in ch. xi. 4, rendered "in process of time." **In the time of wheat harvest**—about the month of May. The harvest, as appears from ver. 5, had begun, some corn being already cut, and in shocks ; the rest still standing, and, being ready to be cut, of course extremely dry and inflammable. **With a kid**, as a present, intended no doubt to make peace (Gen. xxxviii. 17). His anger (ch. xiv. 19) had now passed away, and his love for his wife had returned. He was little prepared to find her married again to his friend.

Ver. 2.—**Is not her younger sister**, &c.

Samson's father-in-law might well have thought that Samson had forsaken his wife, and would never forgive her treachery. Possibly too he was a covetous man, and glad to get a second dower. Anyhow, his answer was conciliatory ; but Samson was not in a mood to accept excuses, or be softened by conciliation.

Ver. 3.—**I shall be more blameless than the Philistines.** The phrase rather means, *I shall be blameless* (or guiltless) *before the Philistines*, i. e. in relation to the Philistines, —they will have nothing to lay to my charge ; my revenge will be a just one,—as in Numb. xxxii. 22 : *Then shall ye be guiltless before the Lord, and before Israel.* He means that so grievous an injury as he had received in having his wife taken from him and given to a Philistine will justify any requitals on his part.

Ver. 4.—**Foxes.** The word here rendered *fox* (*shu'al*, in Persian *shagal*, which is etymologically the same word as *jackal*) includes the jackal, which is as common in Palestine as the fox. Here, and in Ps. lxiii. 10, the gregarious jackals, the *canis aureus*, are undoubtedly meant. **Caught.** The Hebrew word means especially *caught in nets* or *snares*. See Amos iii. 5 (have *taken* nothing at all); Ps. xxxv. 8 (let his net *catch* himself); Jer. xviii. 22; Isa. viii. 14 (*taken*), &c. And it is in this sense that the A. V. uses the word *caught*. A clever sportsman, as no doubt Samson was, would have no difficulty whatever in netting or snaring 300 jackals, which always move in packs, and would be attracted by the vineyards of Thimnathah, for which their partiality is well known (see ch. xiv. 5, note). The writer of the additional article *Fox* in Smith's 'Dictionary of the Bible,' states that he had tried the experiment of throwing grapes to the foxes, jackals, and wolves in the Zoological Gardens. The wolves would not touch them, the others ate them with avidity. **Took firebrands,** &c. Many cavils have been directed against the truth of this account, but without the slightest reason. The terrified animals, with the burning torches and the blazing straw behind them, would necessarily run forwards. Samson would, of course, start the couples at numerous different points, and no doubt have a number of Hebrews to assist him. To the present day the corn-fields in that part of the *Shephelah* extend continuously for twenty or thirty miles.

Ver. 5.—**The shocks and the standing corn.** See ver. 1, note. **With the vineyards and olives.** The Hebrew text has *the orchards of olive trees*—the word *cherem*, usually translated *vineyard*, meaning also any *orchard;* but the Septuagint in both codices supplies *and*, as does the A. V., which gives the more probable sense, *vineyards and olives.* It is unlikely that the vineyards should not be mentioned, in a district abounding in them.

Ver. 6.—**And the Philistines . . . burnt**

her and her father with fire. See ch. xiv. 15. It appears from Gen. xxxviii. 24; Levit. xx. 14; xxi. 9; Josh. vii. 15, 25, that burning with fire was a judicial punishment among the Hebrews. Possibly the Philistines, in their fear of Samson, and perhaps also from a rude sense of justice, inflicted this punishment upon the Thimnathite and her father as the real authors of the destruction of their corn-fields, by giving Samson so unheard-of provocation. Note the fact of the identical fate overtaking Samson's wife which she had sought to escape by base treachery (cf. John xi. 48 with what actually happened).

Ver. 7.—**And Samson said,** &c. There are two ways of understanding Samson's speech: one, with the A. V., as meaning to say that *though* the Philistines had taken his part, and repudiated all fellowship in the shameful deed of the Thimnathite and her father, yet he would have his full revenge upon them; the other, translating the particle in its more common sense of *if*, makes him say, "If this is the way you treat me, be sure I will not cease till I have had my full revenge." This is perhaps on the whole the most probable meaning. It still leaves it uncertain whether the Philistines meant to do Samson justice, or to do him an additional injury, by putting his wife and her father to death.

Ver. 8.—**He smote them hip and thigh,** &c. A proverbial expression, the origin of which is uncertain; it means, he smote them with a great and complete slaughter. It is reasonable to suppose that he had gathered a few Hebrews round him to help him. **He went down,** &c. This shows that *Etam* must have been situated lower than Timnath, and seems to preclude its identification with *Urtas*, in the hill country of Judah, between Bethlehem and Tekoah, which apparently represents the *Etam* of 2 Chron. xi. 6. But there is another Etam in the tribe of Simeon (1 Chron. iv. 32), which may possibly be the Etam of our text. **In the top of the rock.** Rather, the *cleft* or *fissure* of the rock — some narrow and inaccessible ravine. The site has not been identified.

HOMILETICS.

Vers. 1—8.—*The progress of the feud.* In tracing the steps of any quarrel which has gone on to the bitter end, we can usually see that there were moments when reconciliation was very near, but was hindered by the hasty action of one party, and that after such failure the enmity becomes more fierce and bitter than ever. Thus in the quarrel between Samson and the Philistines. After the first burst of anger at his rwie's treachery, Samson's impatient nature had cooled down, his love for his wife had fevived, and he returned to her house with a present intended as a peace offering, hoping no doubt to find her penitent and to receive a warm welcome from her. Had

it been so, his breach with the Philistines might have been healed, and his whole
future career would have been changed. But this was prevented by the intemperate
haste of Samson's father-in-law. Instead of waiting to see whether Samson's just
anger would subside, and keeping the door of reconciliation open, he gave Samson's
wife to his friend. When Samson returned in a spirit of generous forgiveness, he
found the false woman on whom he threw away his love already wedded to another,
and the door closed against him. His fury knew no bounds. Everything Philistine
was hateful in his eyes. The former wrong was lost in the glare of the far greater
wrong which succeeded it. The Philistines were made to pay dearly for the insult
and injury they had done him. And then, as so often happens in embittered resentments, even the attempt to pacify him only added fuel to the flame. His wife's
adultery had been a cruel blow; the punishment of that adultery by a horrible death
was a still deadlier one. The burning of corn-fields had been a sufficient revenge
for the one; the slaughter of the Philistines was the only expiation for the other.
And so the quarrel went on from bad to worse; the enmity became more deadly, the
strife more embittered. It went on through bloodshed and captivity, till Samson and
his enemies perished together under the ruins of the temple of Dagon. If quarrels
are to be healed, there must be patience on both sides. Neither side must credit the
other with an unappeasable hatred or with an inextinguishable wrath. Hasty insults
and hasty overtures of peace must alike be avoided. Time must be given for resentment to cool and for the sting of the wrong to be forgotten. Otherwise things will
grow from bad to worse; the petty insult or annoyance will be succeeded by the
mortal wrong, and the melancholy spectacle will follow of two human beings, who
ought to love one another as children of the same heavenly Father, using all their
powers and opportunities to wound each other's feelings, and to inflict injuries upon
one another. But the only real remedy for enmities is to be found in the true spirit
of Christian love: "Be ye kind one to another, tender-hearted, forgiving one another,
even as God for Christ's sake hath forgiven you." In the presence of the cross
enmities and hatreds are crucified. The bitterest offence given and wrong suffered
will only provoke the prayer, "Father, forgive them, for they know not what they do."

HOMILIES BY VARIOUS AUTHORS.

Vers. 1—3.—*Atonements of the unrighteous.* A great wrong had been done. An
act of warfare against the country of Samson's wife is punished by domestic treachery
and wrong. For fear of the Philistines, Samson's wife is given to another. The fear
of Samson takes the place of the fear which inspired the unrighteousness. Suggested
atonement does not allay the wrath of the wronged, but magnanimously he turns his
wrong into an occasion of renewed hostility to the Philistines. A national calamity
thus springs from a private offence.

I. GREAT WRONGS ARE COMMITTED UNDER THE INFLUENCE OF FEAR.
II. THE ATONEMENTS AND EXCUSES OF THE UNRIGHTEOUS BUT ENHANCE THEIR GUILT.
III. THE CONSEQUENCES OF EVIL ACTIONS CANNOT BE FORESEEN OR ADEQUATELY
WARDED OFF BY THE OFFENDER (*vide* ver. 6).
IV. PRIVATE WRONG MAY BE PUNISHED BY NATIONAL DISASTER.—M.

Vers. 1—5.—*God's servant set free by the providences of life.* The entanglements
into which Samson fell were brought upon himself. God by painful circumstances
destroys these. Samson then felt that he was at liberty to carry on war against the
enemies of his country.

I. GOD'S SERVANTS ARE FREQUENTLY HAMPERED BY THEIR OWN IMPRUDENCES AND
FOLLIES.
II. THE PURPOSE OF THE DISCIPLINE OF LIFE IS TO REMOVE THESE ENTANGLEMENTS
AND TURN THEM INTO A STRONGER INCENTIVE TOWARDS HIS SERVICE. Entanglement
and re-entanglement, deliverance beyond deliverance, is the history of Samson's
career.—M.

Vers. 4, 5.—*Foxes and firebrands.* This circumstance has become classic. It
vividly illustrates—

I. THE INGENUITY OF INSPIRED VENGEANCE.

II. LITTLE CAUSES OF MISCHIEF AND GREAT CONSEQUENCES.

III. THE MISCHIEF GOD'S ENEMIES ENTAIL UPON THEMSELVES. It is *unexpected*, *overwhelming*, and *vital*. The year's produce, upon which the life of the people depended, was swept away at a single stroke. No one knows how to punish the rebel against his kingdom as God himself does.—M.

Vers. 6—8.—*Those who have occasioned evil punished for those who caused it.* Of this policy amongst individuals and nations the world is full.

I. WICKED MEN ARE OFTEN WISER THAN THEIR ACTIONS WOULD INDICATE. It was well to inquire, "Who hath done this?" but when the agent was discovered, they were too afraid of him to punish him, so they wreaked their vengeance upon those who could not defend themselves. Greater care is shown by men in removing occasions of evil than in curing the source of it.

II. HUMAN INJUSTICE MAY UNCONSCIOUSLY EFFECT THE ENDS OF DIVINE JUSTICE. The father-in-law and wife of Samson deserved punishment, but hardly from those through dread of whom they had done Samson wrong.

III. BY ACTING AS THEY DID THE PHILISTINES ONLY BROUGHT UPON THEMSELVES GREATER DISASTERS.

IV. ONE WRONG LEADS TO ANOTHER.—M.

Vers. 8—16.—*Requiting evil for good, and good for evil.* It was truly unhandsome conduct on the part of the men of Judah. They had received aid and service from Samson, and their enemies had been put to shame; and now, when they are threatened with consequences for harbouring him from their foes, they are ready to betray him.

I. THOSE WHO HAVE RECEIVED THE GREATEST BENEFITS OFTEN BETRAY THEIR BENEFACTORS. Wallace was betrayed by a Scotchman; Christ by Judas, and rejected by the Jews. This arises partly from failure to comprehend the work done by great men; partly from ignoble nature, that fails to attain the level of heroic action.

II. A MAGNANIMOUS MIND WILL RATHER SUFFER EVIL THAN BE THE OCCASION OF IT TO OTHERS.

III. MEN INJURE THEMSELVES WHEN THEY EVADE DUTY IN COMPROMISE. These 3000 men of Judah might have driven the Philistines before them, and delivered their land, had they been inspired by a heroic spirit. They afterwards discover that the work is done in spite of them which might have been done by them, and thus lose the credit and blessing that might have been theirs. Samson is thus completely detached from the nation he was raised up to deliver. *So Christ stands alone as the Saviour of the world.*

IV. GOD MAY OVERRULE MEN'S MISDOINGS TO THEIR ULTIMATE ADVANTAGE. Grace can extract a blessing even from sin. But atonement has been made, and the spirit purged from its mean and unholy disposition. The crucifixion of Christ, the work of men, is the means of the salvation of men.

V. EXTERNAL BONDS CANNOT EFFECTUALLY BIND THE SERVANT OF GOD.

"Stone walls do not a prison make,
    Nor iron bars a cage."

Persecutions tend to further the influence of truth. God breaks the bands with which men confine his servants and his word.—M.

Vers. 4, 5.—*Ingenuity and originality.* I. INGENUITY IS OFTEN AS EFFECTIVE AS STRENGTH. Samson is not merely the hero of brute force; he shows wit, intelligence, inventiveness. We constantly see how effective these faculties are in business, in war, in politics. The Christian needs the wisdom of the serpent (Matt. x. 16). In many of our Christian enterprises the requisite for greater success is not more money, more workers, nor even more zeal, but wiser methods. Samson's ingenuity was wholly on the side of destruction. Would that the soldiers of Christ's army of salvation showed as much intelligence and wisdom in conducting the campaigns of the

Church militant for the saving of men as the soldiers of the armies of ambitious monarchs display in their warfare, which brings little else than death and misery! Ingenuity is quickened by interest. If we had a more practical sense of the end of the Christian battle with the evil of the world, more earnest desire to effect real results, more heart in the whole work, we should be more wise and thoughtful. It is the half-hearted who are dull and sleepy soldiers of Christ.

II. ORIGINALITY OF METHOD IS OFTEN ONE GROUND OF SUCCESS. Samson showed great originality; consequently his enemies were not provided against the novel attack he made upon their land and its produce. Mere novelty is little recommendation. But we are all too much wedded to old habits of life. Novel methods in the work of the Church are sometimes advisable, (1) because the old may be effete, (2) because the old may have lost their interest or be well provided against by opponents, (3) because there is room for variety of work even when the old ways of working are successful, (4) because, though the old style may be good, we should always be seeking for improvements till we attain to perfection, and (5) because new circumstances require new treatment. We need no new gospel, no new Christ; but we do need fresh applications of the gospel, new adaptations to the wants of the times. There is room for the richest originality in those who have the most loyal attachment to the ancient truths of Christianity.—A.

EXPOSITION.

Ver. 9.—**Went up,** *i. e.* from their own country in the Shephelah to the hill country of Judah. As Samson had avenged his wrongs on the whole Philistine people, so they now came up to Judah to take vengeance for Samson's injuries. **In Lehi,** or, rather, *hal-Lehi, the Lehi,* the place afterwards so called, as related in vers. 17 and 20 (see ch. vii. 25, note). Lehi has been identified by some with *Tell-el-Lekhiyeh,* four miles above Beer-sheba; and by others with *Beit-Likîyeh,* in the Wady Suleiman, two miles below the upper Beth-horon, and so within easy distance of Timnath and other places mentioned in the history of Samson. But no certainty can at present be arrived at.

Ver. 11.—**Men of Judah.** It is rather *three thousand men went down from Judah,* showing that the rock Etam was below. **The top.** It should be the *cleft,* as in ver. 8. **Knowest thou not,** &c. The language of these cowardly men shows how completely the Philistine yoke was fastened upon the necks of Judah. The history gives no account of the Philistine conquest, except the brief allusion in ch. x. 6, 7; but Samson's story brings to light the existence of it. The abject state to which they were reduced is shown by their complaint of Samson, "What is this that thou hast done unto us?" instead of hailing him as a deliverer. **As they did unto me,** &c. It is instructive to read Samson's defence of himself in the very words used by the Philistines in ver. 10. "An eye for an eye, and a tooth for a tooth." There is no end to rendering "evil for evil."

Vers. 12, 13.—**We are come down to bind thee.** There is something very base in this deliberate agreement with their Philistine masters to deliver up Samson bound into their hands. But it is not very unlike the spirit in which the Hebrews looked upon Moses when he first began to work to rescue them from their Egyptian bondage (Exod. ii. 14; Acts vii. 25—28). Samson's forbearance towards his own countrymen is commendable. **Brought him up**—from the deep ravine or cleft in which he was hid. His place of concealment was probably unknown to the Philistines, or may be they had quite a superstitious fear of Samson from their experience of his prowess.

Ver. 14.—**When he came,** *i. e.* as soon as he was come to Lehi, where the Philistine camp was (ver. 9). **Shouted against him.** Rather, *shouted* as they ran out *to meet him.* It expresses concisely the double action of their all going out to meet him, and shouting with joy when they saw him bound and, as they thought, in their power.

Ver. 15.—A most vivid and stirring description! The Spirit of the Lord (ch. xiv. 19), with that suddenness which marks his extraordinary movements (1 Kings xviii. 12; 2 Kings ii. 16; Acts ii. 2; viii. 39, &c.), came upon Samson, and mightily strengthened him in his outer man. The strong new cords snapped asunder in an instant; and before the Philistines could recover from their terror at seeing their great enemy free, he had snatched up the heavy jawbone of an ass recently dead, and with it smote the flying Philistines till a thousand of them had fallen under his blows.

Ver. 16.—**And Samson said,** &c. The exploit gave birth to one of Samson's punning, enigmatical, sayings: "*With the jawbone of the ass, one heap, two heaps of slain.*" '*Hamôr,* ah ass, means also *an heap*. If one were to imitate the passage in English, supposing that the jaw of a sheep had been the implement, it might run something like this—*By the jaw of a sheep they fell heap upon heap*. A Latin imitation is, *Maxilla cervi, acervum acervos* (Bochart). He adds, as if in explanation, *With the jaw of an ass have I slain a thousand men*. So the women sang, *Saul hath slain his thousands, and David his ten thousands* (1 Sam. xviii. 7). And a Latin song is quoted, in which Aurelian is made to say after the Sarmatic war—"Mille Sarmatas, mille Francos, Semel et semel occidimus, Mille Persas quærimus" (Bp. Patrick on Judges xv.).

Ver. 17.—**Made an end of speaking**, *i. e.* of reciting the song about the heaps of slain. It is singular that the word rendered *speaking* might also be rendered *destroying*, as in 2 Chron. xxii. 10. **Called that place Ramath-lechi**, i. e. *the height of Lechi*, or *of the jawbone*, or, rather, *the throwing away of the jawbone*. He commemorated the exact spot where the slaughter ceased and the weapon was thrown away by giving it the name of *Ramath-Lechi*, or, as it was called for shortness, *Lechi* (or hal-Lechi).

Ver. 18.—**He was sore athirst**. The incredible exertions which he had made in pursuing and slaying the Philistines put him in danger of his life from thirst. He thought he should die, and be found and abused by his uncircumcised foes. His only resource was prayer to God, who had helped him hitherto. We may note by the way that the more God gives, the more he encourages us to ask.

Ver. 19.—**But** (or, *and*) **God clave**, &c. Cf. Exod. xvii. 6; Numb. xx. 8, 11. The A. V. (as the Septuagint and Vulgate seem to have done, and Luther and others) has quite misconceived the statement in the text, as if God had cloven a hollow place in the jawbone, and brought out the water

thence; whereas the statement is quite clear that *God clave the hollow place which is in Lehi* (*hal-Lehi*, ver. 9, note), and that a spring of water came out, to which Samson gave the name *En-hakkoreh*, the spring of him that called upon God, which name continued till the time of the writer. The spring apparently continued till the time of St. Jerome, and of other later writers, in the seventh, twelfth, and fourteenth centuries; but Robinson was unable to identify it with any certainty ('B. R.,' ii. 64). The word translated *the* (not *a*) *hollow place* (*hammaktesh*) means *a mortar*; also the *cavity in the jaw* from which the molar teeth grow. The hollow ground from which the spring rose, with which Samson quenched his thirst, from its shape and from the connection with *hal-Lechi* (the jawbone) was called *hammaktesh*. In Zeph. i. 11 it is also a proper name, apparently of some spot near Jerusalem. **The name thereof**, *i. e.* of the fountain, with which *thereof*, which is in the feminine gender, agrees. **Which is in Lehi unto this day**. This punctuation does not agree with the Hebrew accents, which put a strong stop after *Lehi*. The Hebrew accents rather convey the sense that the name *En-hakkoreh* continued to be the name of the well unto the day of the writer.

Ver. 20. —**And he judged Israel**, &c. See ch. xvi. 31. It looks as if it had been the intention to close the history of Samson with these words, but that ch. xvi. was subsequently added, possibly from other sources. Compare the close of chs. xx. and xxi. of the Gospel of St. John. A possible explanation, however, of this verse being placed here is that it results from the statement in ver. 19, that Samson's spirit came again, and he revived, or came to life again, after being on the very point of death; and, adds the writer, he judged Israel after this for twenty years.

HOMILETICS.

Vers. 9—20.—*Man without God, and man with God.* These 3000 men of Judah of whom we read in ver. 11 present us with a pitiable view of man's spirit crushed by misfortune, when it is not upheld by trust in Almighty God. These men of Judah were among those who did evil in the sight of the Lord, and were in consequence delivered into the hand of the Philistines. But this chastisement, instead of leading them to repent of their sin and folly in forsaking God and putting their trust in false gods, only led to a kind of sullen despair. They said in their hearts, "There is no hope: no; for I have loved strangers, and after them will I go" (Jer. ii. 25). Utterly unmindful of their high privileges and vocation as the people of God, they acquiesce in their own degradation: "The Philistines are rulers over us." They had rather not be disturbed. Let us alone, they said. Let us be as we are, fallen, sunken, degraded. All good within them was blunted and quenched. Self-respect was gone; love of country was gone; aspiration after all that is good and high was gone; courage, honour, enterprise, love of freedom, pride in their own matchless institutions, remembrance of a glorious past, hope for a glorious future, all was crushed within them because they had no trust in God. The elevating, ennobling, sustaining feeling that they were God's chosen people, and that the unchanging love and power of God were on their side to sustain them in every virtuous effort, and give effect to every good and holy desire, was extinct within them. Their calamities and injuries, not being mixed with confidence in God, and prayer to him for deliverance, had only trodden out their manhood. It was the sorrow of the world working death. Now such a state of mind as this is a very common effect of unsanctified misfortunes. Sorrows, brought on perhaps by misconduct, which do not send men to God in penitence and prayer only harden and depress. They produce sullenness, and they destroy the spring of hope. Men sink on to a lower platform even in regard to their fellow-men. They are not humbled, only lowered. They take a lower, darker view of human life and human responsibilities. Virtue, truth, love of neighbours, kindness, generosity, and the charities of life burn very low and dim within them, if they are not wholly extinct. A cold, hard selfishness, and even that not an aspiring selfishness, wraps itself around the centre of their being. Every appeal to the higher qualities of human nature is resented or scoffed at. " Leave me alone," is the silent language of their attitude towards humanity. " Trouble me not," is their answer to every call upon them for virtuous effort. And as to the still higher and nobler calls of religion, every invitation to rise toward God, to act in the spirit of his holy word, to follow the leading of his Holy Spirit, to walk in the steps of the Lord Jesus Christ, is received with a cynical sneer; and even those who, in better days, seemed to be actuated by religious hopes and feelings, under the pressure of such unsanctified cares and sorrows fall into a thoroughly low region both of religion and of morals. Now contrast with those men of Judah the feelings and the conduct of Samson. Conscious of Divine aid, and of having unfailing strength in God, his courage never drooped in the darkest days of the Philistine oppression. Conscious of his own high calling, and of the election of Israel to be the people of God, he could not brook the notion of being ruled over by the uncircumcised, nor did he lose the hope of some great deliverance. He was ready for the service of God and of his country. And even the feeling that he stood alone did not quench his spirit. He did not lose sight of hope, because he did not lose sight of God. The weight of the great national calamity, in which he also was involved, did not utterly depress and crush him, because he believed in the mighty hand of God, which could lift up that weight in a moment, whenever it seemed good to him to do so. And so all the natural resources of his mind were kept alive and ready for action, as well as his great supernatural strength, whenever the opportunity should arise. And Samson's supernatural strength is only a type to us of that invincible spiritual strength which they have who are the faithful servants of the Lord Jesus Christ. " I can do all things through Christ which strengtheneth me," is the truth embodied in Samson's exploits. In the Christian's steady, unwearied, resistance to evil, in his patient continuance in well doing, in the quiet, hopeful endurance of sufferings and afflictions, in the undaunted spirit which quails under no dangers, and faints under no adversities, and in the faith which eventually triumphs over all the powers of the world, we have the spiritual counterpart of Samson's great bodily strength. The brave, hopeful struggle of such, ending in victory, is in striking contrast with the desperate succumbing to evil of which we have spoken. And we may see it on a large scale in the Church herself. Often has the Church of God seemed weak and helpless before the powers of darkness, even while she had in herself the secret of an invincible strength. Often would her professed friends bind her in the fetters of worldly compliances, and hand her over to be shaped according to the fashion of this world, lest she should overthrow the accustomed sway, and break down the traditionary rules. But as often has the Spirit of the Lord come mightily upon her, and she has awakened as a giant refreshed with wine, and gone forth with irresistible might. The most trivial instruments have been in her hands weapons of supernatural power; her fiercest foes have sunk before her victorious progress; God has raised up refreshments to her in her hours of need; when she called upon God for help she was helped; and many a monument of God's saving grace and helping hand has deserved to be inscribed as *En-hakkoreh*—the supply granted to the cry of faithful prayer. O Lord, let thy Spirit come upon us now, in this our day of trial; hear thy Church's prayer, and let her cry come unto thee !

HOMILIES BY VARIOUS AUTHORS.

Vers. 14—16.—*Imperfect means made effectual by Divine inspiration.* It was but the jawbone of an ass, yet it slew as many as might have fallen in a battle.

I. IN THE CONFLICTS OF TRUTH IT IS OF CHIEF CONSEQUENCE THAT WE BE ON THE SIDE OF TRUTH, AND ANIMATED BY THE SPIRIT OF GOD.

II. THROUGH GOD'S BLESSING THE GRANDEST RESULTS HAVE BEEN PRODUCED BY THE RUDEST AND SIMPLEST MEANS. The preaching of the gospel by unlettered fishermen. " The solitary monk that shook the world " with the disused weapon in God's armoury. The "simple gospel" and the evils of our age.

III. NOTWITHSTANDING OUTWARD ADVANTAGES, THE ENEMIES OF GOD ARE CERTAIN IN THE END TO BE DISCOMFITED.

IV. THE ABSOLUTENESS AND SPLENDOUR OF SPIRITUAL ACHIEVEMENTS. Pentecost; missionary triumphs; the song of Moses and of the Lamb.—M.

Vers. 17—19.—*The self-refreshment of Divine service.* After his great exploit Samson was exhausted and athirst. The zeal for the glory of Jehovah is upon him, and he cannot brook the tarnishing of his glorious victory by a base surrender to the Philistines. He immediately calls upon God, and is answered in the very scene of his warfare.

I. IN MOMENTS OF GREATEST EXALTATION AND POWER THE SAINT IS REMINDED OF HIS WEAKNESS AND DEPENDENCE UPON GOD. Paul and the "thorn in the flesh." The great deed and heroic uplifting of soul accompanying it are a Divine gift—a treasure in an earthen vessel. "By the grace of God I am what I am."

II. THE TRUE SAINT WILL FRANKLY ACKNOWLEDGE THIS, AND BETAKE HIMSELF TO PRAYER FOR DIVINE HELP. The faith that made Samson irresistible in battle now makes him prevail with God. A sense of spiritual fitness forbids the notion that God will suffer such an anti-climax. The victories that spring from acknowledged weakness are more glorious than those which proceed upon our fancied independence and self-sufficiency. "When I am weak, then am I strong."

III. THE CONDITIONS OF AN EFFECTUAL PRAYER. 1. *Sincerity and faith.* God had helped him already; he is convinced, therefore, that he will still help. 2. *Because of wants and hardships necessitated by Divine service.* He is immediately answered, and in the very scene of it. No earthly hand is suffered to help. 3. *Zeal for the glory of God.* The idea of neutralising his triumph by yielding through physical distress is obnoxious to him. He asks God to preserve the splendour of the exploit which brought such glory to his name.—M.

Ver. 15.—*The jawbone of an ass.* I. IT WAS A NOVEL WEAPON. Samson again shows his inventiveness and originality (see ver. 4). To succeed in sudden emergencies we must have presence of mind to choose and act rapidly and freshly. The slave of routine is helpless in every critical moment of life.

II. IT WAS THE MOST CONVENIENT WEAPON AVAILABLE. If Samson could have laid his hand on a sword he would not have picked up the bone. It would be foolish, rash, and presumptuous to reject the better means in order to make a display of strength or originality in the use of inferior means. But when the only thing available is a comparatively poor expedient, it is better to use this than nothing. While we are waiting for the perfect weapons to be forged the opportunity for victory passes. Thus inferior men and inferior methods must often be used for want of better ones. It is wrong for us to refuse to do any work for Christ because we have not the best possible natural powers or cultivation. It is better to serve as we are than not at all.

III. IT WAS A SIMPLE WEAPON. Many would have despaired with such a prospect as Samson's. But difficulty is the inspiration of genius. In spiritual warfare God sometimes blesses the poorest means when faith and zeal are making the best use of them. God's strength is thus most perfect in our weakness, because then we most need it, are most likely to seek it trustfully, and will be most inclined to use it obediently.

IV. IT WAS A RIDICULOUS WEAPON. The hero would seem to be humiliated as he condescended to use such a weapon. But he was great enough to despise ridicule. It is weak and wrong to decline to use the only available means of rendering God good service because we fear they are undignified. True dignity is found not in pedantry and pomp, but in simple, brave independence. Great needs conquer foolish v nity. When the Philistines are on us we are in no mood to ask or to care whether our conduct will excite the laughter of the idle. If Christians realised more fully the awful depth of the world's sin and misery, they would be less sensitive to the trivial ridicule with which men may regard their work. How many promising lives have been poisoned by the narcotic of a false respectability !

V. IT WAS A SUCCESSFUL WEAPON. This is the one matter of consequence. Success refutes all objections. Ridicule is now turned into admiration. The very simplicity and folly of the means increases the glory of the result. So the great question in the Christian warfare against evil is that this is effective. If so, all the world's foolish criticism will be drowned in the triumph of victory.—A.

Vers. 18, 19. — *Distress after triumph.* I. ONE GREAT DELIVERANCE IS NO SECURITY AGAINST ALL FUTURE TROUBLE. Samson is surprised and vexed that a new trouble should fall upon him after his great victory. There is a danger lest we should rest contented with past triumphs. The Christian warfare can only end with the final victory over death. Till then we are in the enemy's land, and must expect that one battle will only be succeeded by another. Though we may have a season of calm, an oasis in the desert, a quiet resting-place, "*this* is not our rest." Let us beware of the confident self-elation which often follows the conquest of a temptation ; it may be an introduction to a new and more dangerous one.

II. SLIGHT EVILS MAY PROVE MORE DANGEROUS THAN GREAT ONES. Samson feels it humiliating to be in danger of dying of thirst after his victory over a much more imposing enemy ; but he had means to meet the greater foe, and none with which to face the smaller one. Evils are injurious not so much in proportion to their simple magnitude as in proportion to our susceptibility to them. The force of a particular temptation depends on a man's special disposition and peculiarity of character, not simply on its inherent alarming or alluring qualities. It should humble us to learn that after escaping the greatest dangers by the help of God we may succumb to very small dangers if left to ourselves.

III. SEASONS OF TRIUMPH ARE OFTEN FOLLOWED BY SEASONS OF DEPRESSION. Samson is despondent and querulous after his victory. So was Elijah (1 Kings xix. 4). No doubt this common experience is partly the result of nervous reaction. Excitable people oscillate between the extremes of ecstasy and despair. It has also moral grounds. We grow over-confident, we expect too much, we forget that life cannot always be pitched in the heroic mood. The career of the loftiest souls is not one unbroken epic ; even this has its seamy side, its stale and unprofitable moments. There is a Divine purpose of discipline in this painful experience to keep us humble and in trustful submission.

IV. GOD HELPS US IN OUR DEPRESSION AS WELL AS IN OUR ELATION. God came to the rescue of Samson. Though he murmured, God had compassion on him. God understands our weakness, and, understanding, pities it. He does not treat his servants as heroes, but as children (Ps. ciii. 13). The depression of feeling which destroys our consciousness of assurance does not destroy God's grace. It is important to observe that the faith which is the condition of God's help is not our confidence in our own salvation, but the simple trusting of ourselves to God's care, so that when we least expect his help this may come upon us and surprise us, if only we thus cast ourselves upon his mercy.—A.

EXPOSITION.

CHAPTER XVI.

Ver. 1.—**Then.** It should be *and*. There is nothing to show when the incident occurred.

It may have been many years after his victory at hal-Lechi, towards the latter part of his twenty years' judgeship. **Gaza,** now *Ghuzzeh,* one of the five chief cities of the Philistines, once a strong place, but now a large open town. It was the last town in South-West Palestine on the road from Jerusalem to Egypt (Acts viii. 26, 27). It played an important part in history in all ages—in the times of the Pharaohs, the Seleucidæ, the Maccabees, the Romans, the Khalifs, and the Crusaders. It was within the limits of the tribe of Judah (Josh. xv. 47). It is first mentioned in Gen. x. 19, as the south-west border of the Canaanites. Its real transliteration from the Hebrew is 'Azzah, as it is actually expressed in the A. V. of Deut. ii. 23, and 1 Kings iv. 24. *Gaza* is the Greek form.

Ver. 2.—**And it was told.** These words have no doubt accidentally fallen out of the Hebrew text, but they are necessary to the sense, and are expressed in all the ancient versions. We have no clue as to the motive of Samson's visit to Gaza, whether he was meditating its conquest, or an assault upon its inhabitants, or whether he came merely in the wild spirit of adventure, or upon civil business. We only know that he came there, that, with his usual weakness, he fell into the snare of female blandishments, that the Philistines thought to have caught him and killed him, but that he escaped by his supernatural strength. Gaza is about thirteen hours' march from Thimnathah. **They compassed him in.** The Hebrew does not express this idea, nor is it what the Gazites did. It should be rendered, *They went about and lay in wait for him.* Instead of attacking him directly, they took a round-about course, and set an ambush for him in the city gates, probably in the guard-room by the side of the gate, intending when he came forth unsuspectingly in the morning, at the hour of opening the gates, to rush upon him and kill him.

Ver. 3.—**Samson arose at midnight.** Possibly the woman had learnt the plot, and gave Samson warning, after the manner of Rahab ; or she may have been his betrayer, and reckoned upon retaining him till the morning ; anyhow he arose at midnight, when the liers in wait were sleeping securely, and tearing up the two gate-posts, with the gates and the cross-bar attached to them, walked off with them "as far as the top of the hill that is before Hebron." **Took the doors,** &c. Rather, *laid hold of.* For **went away with them,** translate *plucked them up.* It is the technical word for plucking up the tent pins. **Bar and all,** or, *with the bar.* The bar was probably a strong iron or wooden crossbar, which was attached to the posts by a lock, and could only be removed by one that had the key. Samson tore up the posts with the barred gates attached to them, and, putting the whole mass upon his back, walked off with it. **The hill that is before Hebron.**

Hebron "was about nine geographical, or between ten and eleven English, miles from Gaza, situated in a deep, narrow valley, with high hills on either side." It is approached from Gaza over a high ridge, from the top of which Hebron becomes visible, lying in the valley below at fifty minutes' distance. This spot would suit very well the description, "the hill that is before Hebron." Some, however, think that the hill called *el Montar,* about three-quarters of an hour from Gaza, on the road to Hebron, is here meant, and that the plain *before Hebron* merely means *towards,* as in Gen. xviii. 16 ; Deut. xxxii. 49.

Ver. 4.—**Sorek.** See ch. xiv. 5, note. The name has not yet been discovered as applied to any existing spot; but Eusebius in the 'Onomasticon' speaks of a village *Caphar-sorek* as still existing near Zorah. The term *valley* (*nachal*) describes a *wady,* i. e. a narrow valley with a stream.

Ver. 5.—**Lords.** See ch. iii. 3, note. **His great strength lieth**—literally, *wherein* (or *by what means*) *his strength is great.* They guessed that it was through some charm or secret amulet that his Herculean might was nourished. **Eleven hundred pieces,** or shekels, **of silver.** The whole sum promised by the five lords would be no less than 5500 shekels, equal to about £620 of our money. The curious notation, *eleven hundred pieces,* occurs again ch. xvii. 2. The reason of it is unknown.

Ver. 7.—**As another man**—literally, *as one of men,* i. e. of mankind, not different from other men. As regards the word rendered *withs,* it is not certain whether strings of catgut are not meant. In Ps. xi. 2 the same word is used of a bow-string. The word rendered *green* means *fresh* or *new,* and might be equally applied to catgut strings or withs.

Ver. 9.—**There were men lying in wait**—literally, *and the liers in wait were abiding for her in the chamber.* She had hid some three or four men in the chamber unknown to Samson, that they might be ready to fall upon him should his strength really have departed from him. The word for *liers in wait* is in the singular number, but is to be taken collectively, as in ch. xx. 33, 36—38. In ch. xx. 37 it is joined to a plural verb. It is to be presumed that through some concerted signal the liers in wait did not discover themselves.

Ver. 10.—**Wherewith,** or rather, as in ver. 8, *by what means.*

Ver. 11.—**Ropes**—literally, *twisted things ;* hence *cords* or *ropes,* as Ps. ii. 3 ; Isa. v. 18. **Occupied**—an old obsolete phrase, for which we should now say *used.*

Ver. 12.—**Took new ropes.** She had them by her, apparently, or could easily procure them, as it is not said that the lords brought them to her. **And there were liers.** Rather, as before, *and the liers in wait were abiding*, &c. Each time she had persuaded the lords that Samson had divulged his secret, and that she would deliver him into the hands of the men whom they sent.

Ver. 13.—**The seven locks,** by which we learn that his mass of hair as a Nazarite was arranged in seven locks or plaits. His resistance was becoming weaker, and he now approached the dangerous ground of his unshorn hair. **With the web.** This must mean the *warp*, which was already fastened in the loom, and across which Samson's locks were to be woven as the woof.

Ver. 14.—**And she fastened it with the pin.** The Septuagint and many commentators understand that she used the pin (it is the common word for a tent pin) to fasten the loom or frame to the ground, or to the wall. But a good sense comes out if we understand the phrase to mean, *So she struck with the shuttle*, i. e. she did what Samson told her to do, viz., wove his locks into the warp which was already prepared. This was done by successive strokes of the shuttle, to which the hair was fastened. *To strike with the peg or shuttle* may have been the technical phrase for throwing the shuttle with the woof into the warp ; and it is a strong argument in favour of this interpretation that it makes her action the simple fulfilment of his directions. He said, "Weave my locks into the warp. So she struck with the shuttle." **With the pin of the beam, and with the web.** The Hebrew word '*ereg* cannot mean *the beam*, as it is here translated ; it is the substantive of the verb *to weave* in ver. 13. Its obvious meaning, therefore, is *the woof*. The pin of the woof, therefore, is the shuttle with the woof attached to it, i. e. Samson's hair, which was firmly woven into the *warp*. **He went away with.** This is the same word as was applied in ver. 3 to his *plucking up* the gate-posts. Now, with the strength of his neck, he tore up the shuttle which fastened his hair to the warp, and so dragged the whole solid frame along with it. However, as we do not know the technical term of the art of the weaving among the Hebrews and Philistines, nor the precise construction of their looms, some obscurity necessarily attaches to this description.

Ver. 15.—**Thy great strength lieth**—as before, ver. 6, *thy strength is great.*

Ver. 16.—**So that.** Omit *so.* The meaning is, that in consequence of her daily solicitation his soul was vexed (ch. x. 16) to death—literally, was so short, so impatient, as to be at the point to die.

Ver. 17.—**That he told her.** This begins a new sentence. Read, *And he told her.* **Any other man.** Rather, *like all men. Man*, though singular in the Hebrew, is collective as in ver. 7, and as *the lier in wait* in vers. 9 and 12, and is properly rendered *men* in English.

Ver. 18.—**He hath showed me.** So the Keri ; but the written text has *her* instead of *me*, which is favoured by the tense of the verb *came up*. If *her* is the true reading, these words would be the addition of the messenger, explaining why she told them to come up once more, or of the narrator, for the same purpose. **Brought money.** It should be *the money*, the stipulated bribe (ver. 5).

Ver. 19.—**She called for a man.** It is *she called to the man*—the man whom she had secreted in the chamber before she put Samson to sleep, that he might cut off the locks. **She caused him to shave.** In the Hebrew it is *she shaved*, but it probably means that she did so by his instrumentality. **She began to afflict,** or humble, **him.** His strength began to wane immediately his locks began to be shorn, and it was all gone by the time his hair was all cut off.

Ver. 20.—**And shake myself,** *i. e.* shake off the Philistines who encompass me ; but when he said so he knew not that the Lord had departed from him, and that he was indeed become weak like other men (see a fine sermon of Robert Hall's from this text).

Ver. 21.—**Put out his eyes.** One of the cruel punishments of those times (see Numb. xvi. 14 ; 2 Kings xxv. 7), and still, or till quite lately, practised by Oriental despots to make their rivals incapable of reigning. So King John, in Shakespeare, ordered Arthur's eyes to be put out with a hot iron (*King John*, Act IV. scene i.). Herodotus (Melp. iv. 2) says that the Scythians used to put out the eyes of all their slaves. **He did grind**—the most degrading form of labour, the punishment of slaves among the Greeks and Romans (see too Isa. xlvii. 2).

HOMILETICS.

Vers. 1—22.—*Presumption leading to a fall.* One of the most instructive observations we can make with a view to our own guidance is that of the extreme danger of self-confidence. Humility is of the very essence of the Christian character, and the moment that presumption takes the place of humility the danger to the soul commences. Now humility is not necessarily an underrating of our own powers or our own gifts. Our powers are just what they are, and our gifts are of a certain value, neither more nor less, and there is no reason why we should not appraise them at their true value. Samson did not overrate his strength when he submitted to be bound by the men of Judah, nor when he put the gates of Gath upon his shoulders, and carried them to the hill over against Hebron. But the transition to presumption commences as soon as we forget that we have nothing which we have not received, and begin to use what we have for our own purposes, and not for God's glory, and reckon upon its continuance, whatever use we make of it. When a gift or power generates self-conceit, as if it originated with ourselves, presumption has begun; the use of it for our own glorification is the next step; security in its continuance, however much we abuse it, is the third stage of presumption. We seem to see this in the history of Samson. He was the child of prayer, and of great expectations. From his mother's womb he was consecrated to God in the bonds of a special covenant. From his birth he had the special blessing of God resting upon him. From his youth he was moved in an extraordinary manner by the Spirit of the Lord. Before his birth he was announced as the deliverer of Israel. To enable him to fulfil his grand destiny, he was endowed with supernatural strength; and to mark how entirely that strength was God's gift, it was tied to the outward sign of his Nazarite vow, his unshorn locks. But very early he began to show a certain unfitness for his great task. His marriage with the Timnathite was a distinct downward step from the platform of heroic self-consecration to the service of God. That God designed to make use of that act in forwarding his own purposes does not in the least affect its nature as a subordination of high spiritual resolves to self-will and carnal lusts. Again, in his assaults upon the Philistines we see much more of a wayward resentment of personal injuries than of enlightened patriotic efforts to deliver his country from a degrading foreign yoke. His wife betrays his secret, so the Philistines of Ashkelon are slaughtered and plundered; his wife is given to another man by her father, so the whole country is wasted with fire to avenge the wrong; she is put to death, and he avenges her death by a great slaughter of her countrymen. His visit to Gaza, and the extraordinary feat of carrying away the gates upon his shoulders, savoured more of the wanton display of great powers for self-glorification than of a sanctified use of them for God's glory. But it is in the painful transaction with Delilah that we chiefly see that presumptuous abuse of great gifts which precedes a great fall. Unwarned by the previous treachery of Philistine women, unmindful of previous deliverances from imminent peril by the mercy of God, he gave himself up to the wantonness of self-confidence. Either not seeing or despising her designs for his destruction, he went on step by step toward his ruin, as an ox goeth to the slaughter; he tampered with his solemn vow as a Nazarite, which hitherto he had respected, and placed it at the mercy of a heathen harlot, and never woke from his delusion and presumption till he found himself a helpless captive in the hands of his enemies, deprived of his eyesight and of his liberty, an object of scorn, and, still worse, an occasion of blasphemy against God. The lesson is a striking one in every way, and it is one much needed; for nothing is more common, or more fruitful in falls and failures, than a selfish misuse of God's gifts, and a presumptuous confidence in the possession of them. We see it in men like Napoleon Buonaparte. A giant in abilities, but those abilities were used only for self-exaltation. Success led him on to blind self-confidence. He thought his power was his own, and could never be taken from him. He fell at last into the wantonness and fatuity of presumption, acting with incredible folly, and bringing upon himself an utter ruin. But we see the same thing with regard to spiritual gifts. The possession of spiritual discernment, or of eloquence in expounding the word of God, or of influence over men, begets conceit. The sense of having only what God has given us, and of being tenants at will of his mercies, becomes weakened, and spiritual pride is permitted to grow. Then men begin to use their gifts unfaithfully, i. e. not with a single eye to the glory of God and the good of men's souls, but for themselves. They use them and display them to feed their own vanity, to increase their own consequence and importance. They use them to gather parties around themselves of which they may be the heads and leaders. Sometimes they use them for gain, for filthy lucre, seeking the advancement of their own worldly interests, while they are ostensibly working for God. Every kind and degree of such a spirit needs to be carefully guarded against and nipped in the very bud. That simplicity of aim and purpose which was so sublimely apparent in the words and works of the Lord Jesus should be the mark which his disciples should constantly strive to attain. The work which is done partly for a man's self is only half done. The work which is done entirely for God is done wholly. The thorough practical feeling that all our gifts and powers, be they great or small, are given to us by God for his service is a great help towards such pure and righteous use of them. But we must not forget that there is a further stage of this abuse of spiritual gifts which can only end in a grievous fall. God is very patient and long-suffering, and puts up, maybe, with our lesser offences in this respect, only gently rebuking us, and giving us significant warnings of our danger. But if these warnings are neglected, the state of presumption may grow till there is no remedy. In this state of mind men rush into temptation as if there could be no danger for them. They repudiate or neglect prayer, as if prayer was not needful for them. They lose all the marks of a gracious soul, and yet they are not frightened at their absence. And then comes a fall, maybe into the gross darkness of unbelief, maybe into the abyss of sensual sin, which to the world seems sudden, but which had really been steadily advancing through the successive stages of presumption and self-confidence. The Spirit of the Lord departs from them, and Satan enters into them. *Gifts without grace unprofitable.* But we cannot dismiss the sad history of Samson without the reflection that gifts, however splendid, and powers, however eminent, are useless without the grace to use them aright. What might not Samson have effected for his country and his generation if his extraordinary strength had been used humbly, wisely, and consistently in the service of God and for the good of Israel! If his own passions of lust, and anger, and revenge had been under the control of that Holy Spirit which so wondrously strengthened his body, and his single aim had been to walk with God and do good to man, what a career his would have been! But as it was all went to waste. Desultory actions leading to no lasting result, mighty efforts followed by shameful weakness, and heroic courage defeated by his own imbecility of purpose, made a life all marred and blotted, aimless and purposeless—a brilliant disappointment, a splendid failure, a glorious shame. But it has left this further lesson to be weighed and pondered by us all, and especially by those who are most richly endowed with intellectual or spiritual gifts, that while God can accomplish his own designs through our abuse as well as our use of his good gifts, and through our failures as well as through our successes, it rests with ourselves to improve each talent committed to us, and so to use them that they may be found unto our own honour and praise and glory at the appearing of Jesus Christ.

HOMILIES BY VARIOUS AUTHORS.

Vers. 1—3.—*God redeeming the error of his servant.* The visit to the "harlot" is not to be explained away. The character of Samson explains its nature. This was the side where he was weak, the love of women. His sensuality betrays him into a great danger. God shows his affection for his servant, and for Israel whom he had delivered, by granting strength for a signal and unexpected escape, which was marked by trophies covering his enemies with shame.

I. WE OUGHT TO BEWARE OF A ONE-SIDED MORALITY. External morality, like Samson the Nazarite's, is almost certain to be of this kind. The saint should leave no unguarded place. Only the indwelling of the Holy Ghost can deliver from besetting sins. The blood of Jesus Christ, God's Son, cleanseth from *all* sin.

II. A SINGLE SIN MAY UNDO THE FAME AND SUCCESS OF A LIFETIME.

III. WHEN SAINTS FALL INTO SIN THE WICKED TRIUMPH AND ARE CONFIDENT OF THEIR RUIN. The conception which the world has of sainthood is one of perfect external blamelessness, the least infraction of which is hailed as utter failure. When one failing like this is discovered, many more are imagined. How sure are these cowards of the capture of their foe! Or do they only seem to be so, using words of confidence and procrastination to conceal their inward fear? Is there not an unsounded mystery, &c., that cannot be calculated upon, in the defections of God's people? What and if Peter be restored again? The awaking of him whom God rouses from fleshly slumbers will ever take the wicked by surprise. The evil is that the Church too often shares the world's view about the irrecoverableness of backsliders. How often have God's saints been able to shout, "Rejoice not over me, O mine enemy!"

IV. The grace of God sometimes delivers his servants from the consequences of their own folly and sin. Sometimes, but not always. Frequently enough for hope, but not for presumption. But the victory will be wholly his own. The trophy of deliverance will reflect no credit upon the delivered one. He would rather deliver us from our sin itself. He has promised that he will heal our backslidings.

V. The temporary triumphs of sin are swallowed up in the eternal redemptions of God. The gates of Gaza, the chief city of Philistia, are lifted off and carried to the top of the hill beside Hebron, the chief city of Judah. Every Israelite could see them in their exalted place of exhibition. So shall it be with the victories of the Lamb. He in whom was no sin, but who was made sin for us, shall deliver from all sin, and make us "more than conquerors." The seed of Abraham was to "possess the gate of its enemies" (Gen. xxii. 17; cf. xxiv. 60). The gates of hell shall not prevail against the kingdom of Christ.—M.

Vers. 4—21.—*Samson's betrayal and fall.* The long-suffering of God, which the saints are exhorted (2 Pet. iii. 15) to account salvation, is in Samson's case presumed upon, and the besetting sin at last finds him out. The sin is single, but it is not the first of its kind, nor is it isolated. The years of self-indulgence were preparing for this—a mad revel of voluptuousness and a deliberate denial of Jehovah. The scenes of this tragedy have a typical interest, and they are sketched lightly but indelibly by a master hand. In the gradual but deliberate breaking of his vow we have a parallel to Peter's threefold denial of his Lord.

I. Sensuality lulls the soul into a fatal slumber, and destroys its sense of duty and its capacity for usefulness.

II. Companions in guilt may do us more harm than our worst enemies. Here the serviceableness of Delilah is at once perceived by her fellow-countrymen, and they hasten to make use of her. The bribe offered, not necessarily ever paid, not only shows the importance of Samson in their eyes, but the value they set upon the influence of this lustful woman. How much mischief can a single transgressor do, not only directly, but through influence! Here it was not only a man betrayed to his enemies, but a soul undone. "What shall a man give," &c. "He knoweth not that the dead are there, and that her guests are in the depths of hell" (Prov. ix. 13—18). The harlot's house, and what it introduces to.

III. The ungodly misapprehend the secret and nature of spiritual strength. The Philistines evidently thought Samson's power lay in the efficacy of some charm. It is this they seek to obtain. They are incapable of thinking of a higher influence. Samson accordingly plays with this superstitious fancy, giving at the same time in each of his answers a parabolic or riddle-like shadowing forth of the true secret. So Satan and his servants tempt the Christian by altering the outward circumstances of life, associations, habits, &c., through which the life works, but of which it is independent. Until the saint yields it up, the secret of his life with God is safe.

IV. Even in the moment and crisis of spiritual downfall there are Divine interpositions, retardations, and occasions for repentance. The Spirit of God was evidently working through the mind of Samson, and suggesting the evasive riddles, parables, &c., that "seeing they might not see," &c. The question of his downfall is thereby brought several times before himself ere it actually takes place. So Peter and the cock-crow. In how many lives is this providential method illustrated! Temptation is played with until, constrictor-like, it springs upon its prey. Recollections of childhood's lessons, early scenes, &c. are very potent at such times.

V. When the saint's vow to God is broken, all is lost. The secret is out, and the charmed life is helpless. A wreck of a man. Nothing left but the memory of an irreparable past and the burden of self-wrought helplessness. There are no ruins so pitiful as those of men who once were saints and Christian workers, Sunday-school teachers, ministers, &c. How dark is the world and life when the soul's light has gone out! *With* God the weakest is strong, *without* him the strongest is weak. "His eyes, blinded by sensuality, saw not the treason; soon, blinded by the enemy, he should see neither sun, nor men, but only God. That done, he turned back, and God came back to him" (Lange).—M.

Ver. 20.—"*And he wist not that the Lord (Jehovah) was departed from him.*" A common state with many in Christ's Church. They are useless, helpless, and miserable, and they do not realise its significance. They try the customary methods, duties, &c., but fail to produce the looked-for results. They "go out as at other times before," but still is the spirit bound. Hitherto the Philistines knew not the secret of his strength, now he does not realise the secret of his weakness.

I. SPIRITUAL IGNORANCE RESULTS FROM SPIRITUAL DOWNFALL. This is a partial converse of "he that doeth the word shall know of the doctrine." A mark of those in whom the truth is not, is that they deceive themselves; they fancy they are still the same as formerly. How subtle yet infinite is this distinction—with God, without God!

II. THE LOSS SUSTAINED BY THE FALLEN SOUL IS GREATER THAN IT REALISES. Only gradually does the experience work itself out, in a Judas's remorse or a Peter's repentance. Samson thought his strength merely had gone—it was *God*, the Giver of his strength. "Whoever has God knows it; whomsoever he has left knows it not" (Lange).—M.

Vers. 15—17.—*Samson's weakness.* Samson's weakness is twofold. Through lack of moral strength he reveals the secret of his physical strength, and is thus betrayed into the loss of this also.

I. SAMSON'S MORAL WEAKNESS. This is the man's great failing, apparent throughout his history, but reaching a climax in the present incident. Physical endowments are no guarantees for spiritual graces. Must not some of our young athletic barbarians of the aristocracy, adored by the multitude for chest and muscle, be condemned by true standards of judgment for contemptible weakness of character? Such weakness is far more deplorable than the bodily weakness of palsy and paralysis. St. Paul was considered miserably deficient in physical power and presence (2 Cor. x. 10), yet his strength of soul exalts the apostle immeasurably above Samson. The moral weakness of Samson is illustrated by the circumstances of his great defeat. 1. *Sin.* Samson was neglecting his duty and degrading himself with those evil communications which corrupt good manners. There is nothing so enervating as the conscious pursuit of a guilty course. 2. *Pleasure.* Instead of toiling, fighting, and sacrificing himself for his country, Samson was wasting his hours in pleasure. Apart from the wrongness of this conduct, the lax, self-indulgent spirit it engendered was weakening. In seasons of pleasure we are off our guard. 3. *The allurements of false affection.* Samson can resist a host of Philistine warriors, but he cannot resist one Philistine woman. Strong against rude violence, he is weak before soft persuasion. Pure love is the loftiest inspiration for self-sacrificing devotion; but love degraded and corrupted is the deadliest poison to purity of character and vigour and independence of action. How many saints and heroes have found their humiliation in the same snares which caught the strong Samson and the famous St. Antony! 4. *The self-confidence of strength.* Samson plays with the curiosity of Delilah, sure of the power which will come to his aid in the moment of danger, till by degrees he is persuaded to betray the secret of that very power. Had he been less strong, he would have been less rash. Presumption is more dangerous than conscious weakness (1 Cor. x. 12).

II. SAMSON'S PHYSICAL WEAKNESS. This resulted from his moral weakness. In the end the faults of the inner life will bear fruit in trouble to the outer life. 1. Samson's strength was a *Divine gift.* He had not attained it by self-discipline nor merited it by service. It was a talent intrusted to his care to be used for God. What God gives God can withhold. 2. Samson's strength was derived from *spiritual sources.* Samson was not a mere prodigy of brute force. He was one of God's heroes, and the glory of his strength lay in this fact, that it was the outcome of an inspiration. The most exalted powers we have for earthly work are derived from spiritual sources. If these sources are cut off, the energies which issue from them will be exhausted. Samson grows weak through the departure of the Spirit of the Lord. 3. Samson's strength depended on his *observance of the Nazarite's vow*. When the vow was broken the strength fled. God has a covenant with his people. He is always true to his side, but if we fail on ours the covenant is void and the blessings dependent on it cease. (1) The vow of the Nazarite implied consecration to God. God bestows graces on us so long as we live to him, but our departure from him necessitates the just withholding of those graces. (2) The vow required obedience to certain regulations. These were trivial in themselves; but the obliga- tion of obedience is determined not by the importance of the commands given, but by the authority of the person giving them. Disobedience is shown not to the law, but to the authority. A small test may be sufficient to reveal this. Disobedience to God is the fundamental element of all sin, and, as in Samson's case, it will be the sure cause of our ruin.—A.

Ver. 20.—*God's departure from the soul unrecognised.* " He wist not that the Lord was departed from him."

I. THE FACT. 1. There are men whom *God has forsaken*. No man is utterly for- saken by God; our continued existence is an evidence of the continued presence of him in whom we live and move and have our being. But the fuller presence of God, that which secures strength and blessing, may depart. 2. His departure is the *greatest curse* which can fall upon a man. The consequences of it are weakness, shame, ruin. The conscious realisation of it is hell. 3. The cause of this departure of God is in *the conduct of men*, not in the will of God. Samson forsook God before God forsook him. God does not visit his people casually, and only for seasons ; he abides, and will never leave them (Isa. xli. 17) till they wilfully depart from him. 4. A *past enjoyment* of God's presence is no guarantee against his future departure. God is not only absent from those who never knew him, he departs from some in whose hearts he has once dwelt. If the Christian has left his first love, he will find that all his previous experience of God's blessings will not secure him against the dreary night of a godless life.

II. THE IGNORANCE OF THE FACT. Samson was unconscious of the fearful loss he had sustained. So there are men who retain their honoured position in Christian society and in the Church while, even unknown to themselves, the source of the life which gave it them is ebbing away. The causes of this ignorance should be traced. 1. The presence of God is *spiritual*, inward, silent, secret, and his departure makes no outward sign. 2. *Old habits* continue for a season after the impetus behind them has ceased, as the train runs for a while after the steam has been shut off. 3. God may leave us *gradually* as we forsake him by degrees. The fall is not sudden and violent, rather it is a quiet gliding back ; and the loss of Divine grace is not often (as in the case of Samson) sudden, but little by little it leaves us. 4. One of the worst effects of God's departure is that it leaves us in a state of *spiritual indifference*. As with the death which follows extreme cold, the very fatality lies in the fact that the more dangerous our condition is, the more numbed are our faculties to any feeling of distress. The man from whom God has departed has neither the keenness of con- science to discern the fact, nor the feeling of concern to take any notice of it. 5. The tests of God's absence are not always *immediately applied*. The rotten tree stands till the storm strikes it ; the corpse mocks sleep till corruption ensues ; Samson does not know of God's departure till the Philistines are on him. But though post- poned for a season, the revelation must come in the end. How much better to discover the evil first by self-examination ! (2 Cor. xiii. 5).—A.

EXPOSITION.

Ver. 23.—**Gathered them,** *i. e.* themselves. **To rejoice.** The Hebrew is *for a festivity*, or *merry-making*, or *feast*. There was to be a great feast upon the sacrifices offered to Dagon their God. **Dagon** (from *dag*, a fish in Hebrew), the national male god of the Philistines, as *Atergatis*, or *Derceto*, was their goddess. Both the male and female divinities seem to have had the head and breast and hands human, and the rest of the body fish-shaped (see 1 Sam. v. 5). The fish was a natural emblem of fertility and productiveness, especially to a maritime people. The fish-shaped idol is found upon old Phœnician coins, and also on the monuments of Khorsabad, and on some Assyrian gems in the British Museum. One of the chief temples of Dagon was at Gaza. Several towns bore the name of Dagon, as *Beth-dagon* in Judah (Josh. xv. 41) and in Asher (Josh. xix. 27), *Caphar-dagon* near Diospolis, &c., showing that the worship of Dagon was widespread.

Ver. 24.—**And when the people,** &c. The *people*, as distinguished from the *lords* in the preceding verse, to show how universally the capture of Samson was ascribed to Dagon. Rulers and people alike praised Dagon. **Saw him.** Not on the occasion of his being brought into the temple as mentioned in ver. 25, but after his capture, and whenever they saw him grinding or elsewhere. It was this universal ascription of praise to Dagon that led to the celebration of this great feast. This praise of Dagon is also dwelt upon to show that God, in what happened, vindicated the glory of his own great name, which was blasphemed by the servants of Dagon when they thus made him superior to Jehovah. So Milton makes Samson say, " All the contest is now 'Twixt God and Dagon. . . . He, be sure, will not connive or linger, thus provoked, but will arise, and his great name assert." Generally, the ' Samson Agonistes ' is an excellent commentary on the history of Samson.

Ver. 25.—**When their hearts were merry.** They would not have acted so imprudently as to bring Samson out of his prison had not their judgment been clouded with drink. **That he may make us sport. And he made them sport.** The two verbs are not the same in Hebrew, but they have much the same meaning. It is not certain whether the idea conveyed is that of the A. V., that Samson was brought there to be as it were baited by the populace, jeered and jested at, reviled and reproached, perhaps struck or pelted ; or whether the words do not simply mean *to dance with music*, which is certainly the meaning of the latter verb (*he made sport before them*, A. V. and margin) in 1 Sam xviii. 7 (*played*, A. V.; see ver. 6); 2 Sam. vi. 5, 21 ; 1 Chron. xiii. 8 ; xv. 29. **They set him between the pillars,** *i. e.* when he had done dancing ; because he must have been dancing outside the house for the people on the roof to see him.

Ver. 26.—**Suffer me,** or it may be rendered, *Let me rest.* He pretended to be tired, and asked to be allowed to rest a few minutes and lean against the pillars. **That I may**

feel, or, literally, *and make me feel*. He adds his motive for making the request— **that I may lean upon them**—to rest himself after the severe exercise of dancing.

Ver. 27.—**Now the house was full,** &c. We do not know what was the construction of Philistine temples or houses of amusement ; but from the description here given it seems that the interior was ranged like an amphitheatre, with seats for the lords and principal people, and with an open front, so as to command a view of the stage just outside, and that front supported by pillars on which the beams of the roof, both the transverse beam and the longitudinal ones running into it, rested. The roof itself was flat, and had the weight of 3000 people upon it, throwing a great strain upon the beams which rested upon the pillars. The sudden removal of the pillars would bring the roof down at that end, crowded as it was with the people, and would inevitably drag the whole mass in the same direction one over another, while the swaying of the people would bring the whole roof down upon the heads of those beneath, who would be crushed by the heavy timbers and stones and bodies of men falling upon them.

Ver. 28.—**And Samson called unto the Lord.** This is the first mention we have of Samson praying since the memorable occasion when he gave the fountain the name of *En-hakkoreh* (ch. xv. 19, note). Perhaps we may see in this an evidence that his affliction and shame had not been without their effect in bringing him back to God humbled and penitent. The language is very earnest. " O Lord, Jehovah, remember me, . . . strengthen me only this once, O God ! " The threefold name by which he addresses the Almighty implies great tension of spirit. **That I may be at once avenged.** Meaning *at one stroke* —he would take one vengeance so terrible that it would be sufficient for his two eyes, which makes very good sense if the Hebrew will bear it. The literal translation would be, *that I may be avenged with a vengeance of one stroke.* Others take it, *that I may be avenged with a vengeance for one of my two eyes*, which it is not easy to understand the meaning of.

Ver. 29.—**The two middle pillars.** There may have been, say, four pillars in the front ; the two middle ones standing near together, and the other two nearer the sides.

Ver. 30.—**Let me die,** or, *my life shall perish with* the Philistines. He knew it was certain death to himself, but he did not shrink from it. His last act should be to destroy the oppressors of his country. **So the dead which he slew,** &c. The words sound like the snatch of some song or proverb in which Samson's death was described.

Ver. 31.—**His brethren,** &c. Some infer

from this that Samson's mother bare other children after the birth of Samson. But the Hebrew use of the word *brethren* is so wide, applied to cousins, or members of the same house of fathers, or of the same tribe, that it is by no means a certain inference. Here *his brethren* might mean the Danites generally, and *all the house of his father* those who were more nearly related, as belonging to the house of his father. His father was probably dead, and indeed the mention of his father's *burying-place*, or rather *sepulchre*, makes it certain that he was, so that Milton was in error in making him alive. **Zorah and Eshtaol.** See above, ch. xiii. 2, 25, note. **And he judged Israel.** See ch. xv. 20. The parallel between Samson and Hercules is in many respects very remarkable, and has been drawn out by Serdrius and others. The supernatural strength of each, the slavery to women ("Quem non mille fer, quem non Sthenellius hostis, Non potuit Mavors vincere, vicit amor." Ovid), the tearing asunder of the lion, the violent death of each, partly voluntary and partly forced, are all points of strong general resemblance. But one of the most remarkable is the connection of Hercules with two pillars. The "pillars of Hercules" on each side the straits of Gibraltar, Mount Abila and Mount Calpe, were said to have been rent asunder by the strength of Hercules' arms. And Herodotus relates that in the temple of Hercules at Tyre were two remarkable pillars, one of refined gold, the other of smaragdus, some green stone like an emerald (ii. 44). But the account given of a visit of Hercules to Egypt is still more remarkable, as compared with the history of the binding of Samson and the slaughter of the Philistines, as related in ch. xv. The following are the words of Herodotus :—"The Greeks say that when Hercules went down to Egypt, the Egyptians surrounded him, and led him in a procession to sacrifice him to Jupiter ; that he kept quite still for a time, but that when they were commencing the sacrifice at the altar" (the first act of which was cutting off the hair) "he turned in self-defence, and by his prowess slew them all." On which Herodotus remarks, "How was it possible for him, being but one, and being only a man, to slay many myriads ?" The prevalence of the worship of Hercules among the Phœnicians, as, *e. g.*, at Tyre and Thasos, a Phœnician colony, and the close connection of Egypt with Gaza, where the prowess of Samson was so well known, are points not to be omitted in considering the probability of some of the legends of Hercules being drawn from the history of Samson. So also is the title of the Phœnician Hercules, the saviour or deliverer, as compared with ch. ii. 16, 18 ; xiii. 5.

HOMILETICS.

Vers. 23—31.—*The short-lived triumph.* One of the severest trials to which the faith of the people of God is exposed, is that triumph of evil over good, and of the enemies of Christ over his Church, which from time to time is permitted by God, and which in truth is one of the features of this disjointed age. The most signal and most awful triumph of the powers of darkness over the kingdom of light was when the only-begotten Son of God, Jesus our Lord, in the midst of his life of perfect goodness, and his service of perfect obedience to the will of his Father, was betrayed into the hands of sinners, and given up to suffer death upon the cross. When he hung in shame upon the cross, helpless and forsaken ; when he bowed his head and gave up the ghost ; when he was laid in the silent tomb, and the light of the righteous One was quenched in the darkness of the grave, then indeed the triumph of sin was at its height, and the hope of the servants of God was brought very low. But when on the third day the doors of that grave were burst open, and the prisoner of hope came forth in the power of an endless life, and he that was crucified ascended up to heaven, and sat down on the right hand of the majesty on high, from thenceforth expecting till his enemies be made his footstool, that brief triumph of the powers of darkness was turned into the far greater triumph of the kingdom of light ; the enemies of Christ were put to shame, the servants of Christ were enabled to rejoice, and the joyful hope was exceedingly revived and established, that in due time there will be a final deliverance from evil, and that the kingdom is God's, and the power and the glory for ever. In the light of the resurrection the Church looks forward with unmoved confidence to the time when the Son of man shall come in the clouds of heaven with power and great glory, and shall take to himself his everlasting kingdom of righteousness, and reign with his ancients gloriously. But meanwhile the Church must expect many short-lived triumphs of evil over good, and of darkness over light.

There will be many occasions on which the world will say, Let us rejoice, for our god hath delivered our enemy into our hand. We may expect that many an isolated affair, or even a connected chain of events, will take that turn that the servants of Christ will be put to shame, and ungodliness and irreligion will seem to have it all their own way. It may even come to pass that the champions of the gospel shall seem fit only to make sport for an unbelieving and self-sufficient age. Nor is it the least part of the trial that some of these discomfitures are brought on by the errors and failures of the servants of God. The presumption and self-confidence, the blindness and moral weakness, of some like Samson; the intemperate, fiery spirit of others like the Boanerges; the fear of man in others like Peter, and so on, provoke defeat by putting religion in a false light in the eyes of those who are always looking out for occasions to bring it into contempt. But in the midst of these trials of faith, whether they take the form of private discouragements, or of public checks to the progress of religion, and public triumphs of the spirit of ungodliness, it is the Church's unfailing comfort to know that the triumphs of evil are short-lived, and the triumph of truth is eternal. *Magna est veritas et prævalet.* We should never forget for one moment that behind the passing cloud there is shining the unchanging sun. The faith and patience of the saints are indeed required, sometimes more, sometimes less, but are always required in this present age. The depression of the truth, the insolent aggressions of the various forms of evil, the discomfiture for a time of the champions of the cause of Christ, and the temporary victories of Antichrist, are very painful episodes in the history of the world and of the Church. But the pages of Holy Scripture, and even the pages of the experience of centuries, continually testify that the triumphs of falsehood and evil are but for a moment, the victory of truth and righteousness will be for ever.

HOMILIES BY VARIOUS AUTHORS.

Vers. 21—31.—*A hero's exodus.* The blind captive, led by a boy, and degraded to the office of a buffoon in the idolatrous services of the Philistines, is a sad spectacle. But inwardly he was nobler than when carrying the gates of Gaza. His soul's eye has opened, and he repents. The locks that had been shorn grow again, and with them, gradually and, apparently, unconsciously, his strength returns. The Divinely-offered opportunity. The last act an atonement.

I. GOD OFTEN SUFFERS HIS ENEMIES TO OVERLEAP THEMSELVES. Here they are exultant. They rejoice as over a foe utterly vanquished. They do not know that their festival, blasphemy against God, is to be the occasion of their destruction. "The green bay tree" may be nearer to the axe than insignificant fruit tree.

II. THERE IS AN "UNKNOWN QUANTITY," NOT TO BE CALCULATED UPON, IN THE REPENTANCE OF THE BACKSLIDER. Even the ruin of a believer may be the temple of the Holy Ghost. A short time with God's blessing may suffice to retrieve the errors of a lifetime. "Faith as a grain of mustard seed" can "remove mountains." How often has Satan been disappointed of his prey! Some of the greatest of God's servants have been won back from backsliding. Let the wicked beware then of their companion and laughing-stock, and let the believing Church work on; the poor useless wreck over which we despairingly weep may yet become a man again, a blessing and a comfort to many souls.

III. THE PRAYER OF REPENTANCE AND FAITH MAY RETRIEVE A SOUL'S RUIN. Can God give ear to this heart-touching cry, and shall he not listen to his captive children in the dungeons of sinful habit or the temples of superstition? "This once," "only this once." One prayer, one look at the Crucified, one grand effort in God's strength, how much it may do!

IV. EVEN THE WEAK ONES OF GOD ARE MIGHTIER THAN THE GREAT ONES OF THE WORLD.—M.

Vers. 28—30.—*Samson's heroic death.* The death of Samson was more honourable to the man and more useful to his nation than any event in his previous career. The heroism of his death followed the return of God's strength.

I. THE RETURN OF STRENGTH. 1. It followed *a great fall.* We may learn lessons from our own failures. Through our very weakness we may discern the secret of strength. The humility which should accompany failure is one of the first steps towards wiser conduct. 2. It came in a season of *distress*. Samson was a prisoner, defeated, insulted, mutilated. Sorrow is one road to God's grace, (1) as it teaches us the folly of the evil conduct that produced it, (2) as it leads us into a mood of serious and heart-searching reflection in which true wisdom is found, and (3) as it teaches us our helplessness, and compels us to turn to God for deliverance. 3. The return of strength followed a *return to obedience*. This was suggested by the growing of Samson's hair and the return to fidelity to his vow. It was gradual. We are received into God's favour immediately we return in penitent faith; but we only conquer evil consequences of sin and regain lost powers and position by degrees. 4. The return of strength was realised through *prayer*. Samson now knows his weakness. In his own soul he is weak. Strength must come from above. There is no prayer which God will more certainly hear than that which invokes his aid in our performance of some great self-sacrificing duty.

II. THE HEROIC DEATH. 1. Samson uses his new strength for the *deliverance of his nation*. It is not given him merely for the amusement of the Philistines. If God gives us any special powers, he does so for some high purpose. We must not waste these in idle amusements, but put them to practical service. 2. Samson can only accomplish the greatest feat of his life by means that *bring death to himself*. (1) This was partly a result of his sinful weakness, which had betrayed him into the hands of his enemies, and brought him to such a position of bondage that his own death must be involved in that of the Philistines. Thus sin leaves consequences which produce suffering even after repentance and a return to a better life. (2) It was also an instance of that strange law which makes the greatest good to men depend on the *sacrifice of the benefactor*. It has thus something in common with the death of Christ, though with many points of difference, Samson's death involving the destruction of his enemies, while Christ's death is expressly designed to give salvation to *his* enemies.—A.

EXPOSITION.

CHAPTER XVII.

Ver. 1.—We here light upon quite a different kind of history from that which has preceded. We no longer have to do with judges and their mighty deeds in delivering Israel from his oppressors, but with two detached histories, which fill up the rest of the book, relating to the internal affairs of Israel. There is no note of time, except that they happened before the time of Saul the king (ch. xvii. 6; xviii. 1), and that Phinehas the son of Eleazar was alive at the time of the occurrence of the second (ch. xx. 28). Both, no doubt, are long prior to Samson. The only apparent connection of the history of Micah with that of Samson is that both relate to the tribe of Dan, and it may be presumed were contained in the annals of that tribe. Compare the opening of the Books of Samuel (1 Sam. i. 1). **Mount Ephraim**, *i. e.* the hill country of Ephraim, as in ch. iii. 27; vii. 24, &c.

Ver. 2.—**The eleven hundred**. See ch. xvi. 5, note. **Thou cursedst**. The Cethib and the Alexandrian Codex of the Septuagint read, *Thou cursedst*, i. e. adjuredst *me*, which is a better reading. There is a direct and verbal reference to the law contained in

Levit. v. 1. The word *thou cursedst* here and the voice of *swearing* in Leviticus are the same root. It was in consequence of this *adjuration* that Micah confessed his guilt. Compare Matt. xxvi. 63, when our Lord, on the adjuration of the high priest, broke his silence and confessed that he was Christ, the Son of God. In Achan's confession (Josh. vii. 19, 20) there is no distinct reference to Levit. v. 1, though this may have been the ground of it.

Ver. 3.—**I had wholly dedicated**. It is not clear whether the words are to be rendered as in the A. V., *had dedicated*, expressing the dedication of them before they were stolen, or whether they merely express her present purpose so to dedicate them. But the A. V. makes very good sense. Her former purpose had been that the money should be given for her son's benefit to make his house an house of gods. Now that he had confessed, she resumed her purpose. **Now therefore I restore it unto thee—** that is, in the shape of the graven and molten images, as it follows in the next verse. The narrative gives a curious example of the semi-idolatry of the times. **A graven image and a molten image**. There is a good deal of difficulty in assigning the exact meaning of the two words here used, and their relation to one another in the worship to which they belong. *The molten image (massechah)*, however, seems to be pretty certainly the *metal*, here the *silver*, image of a calf, the form which the corrupt worship of Jehovah took from the time when Aaron made the molten calf (Exod. xxxii. 4, called there *'egel massechah*, a molten calf) to the time when Jeroboam set up the golden calves at Dan and Bethel (1 Kings xii. 28, 29). And that *massechah* means something *molten* is certain both from its etymology (*nasach*, to pour) and from what Aaron said in Exod. xxxii. 24: "I cast it into the fire, and there came out this calf." Here too Micah's mother gives the silver to the *founder*, i. e. to the fuser of metals. The *pesel*, or *graven image*, on the other hand, is something hewn or graven, whether in wood or stone, and sometimes overlaid with gold and silver (Deut. vii. 25). One might have thought, from the language of ver. 4, and from the mention of the *pesel* alone in ch. xviii. 30, 31, that only one image is here intended, which was graven with the chisel after it was cast, as Aaron's calf seems to have been. But in ch. xviii. 17, 18 they are mentioned separately, with the ephod and teraphim named between them, so that they must be distinct. From the above passages the *pesel* or *graven image* would seem to have been the most important object, and the difficulty is to assign the true relation of the *massechah* or *molten image* to it. Hengstenberg thinks the *massechah* was a pedestal on which the *pesel* stood, and that the ephod was the robe with which the *pesel* was clothed, and that the teraphim were certain tokens or emblems attached to the ephod which gave oracular answers. But this is not much more than guess-work. Bertheau considers the ephod, here as elsewhere, to be the priest's garment, put on when performing the most solemn services, and specially when seeking an answer from God. And he thinks that the *massechah* formed a part of the ornament of the ephod, because in ch. xviii. 18 the Hebrew has "the *pesel* of the ephod." The teraphim he thinks are idols, a kind of *Dii minores* associated with the worship of Jehovah in this impure worship. But there does not seem to be any means at present of arriving at any certainty. The *massechah* might be a rich gold or silver overlaying of the wooden image, possibly movable, or it might be the separate image of a calf supposed to belong, as it were, to the *pesel*, and to symbolise the attributes of the Godhead.

Ver. 4.—**Yet he restored.** Rather, *So he restored*, repeating what was said in ver. 3, and adding the consequence, that his mother

took two hundred shekels and gave them to the founder. It is a great puzzle to explain why *two hundred* shekels only are here spoken of, and what became of the other *nine hundred*. Bertheau thinks the *two hundred* were different from the eleven hundred, and were the fifth part of the whole value stolen, which the thief, according to Levit. vi. 5, was bound to give in addition to the principal. He therefore translates ver. 4 thus: "So he restored the money to his mother (and his mother took two hundred shekels), and she gave it (the money = 1100 shekels) to the founder," &c. Others understand that two hundred only were actually made into the graven and molten image, and the other nine hundred were devoted to other expenses of the worship. **In the house of Micah.** This explains, *Now I will restore it unto thee*, and, *for my son to make*, &c., in ver. 3.

Ver. 5.—**And the man Micah,** &c. It is impossible to say for certain whether the state of things here described in respect of Micah preceded the events narrated in the preceding verses, or was consequent upon them. If it preceded, then we have the reason of his mother's vow: she wished to make her son's "house of God" complete by the addition of a graven and molten image. If it was consequent upon his mother's vow, then we have in the opening verses of this chapter a history of the circumstances of the foundation of Micah's "house of God," which was to play an important part in the colony of Danites, whose proceedings are related in the following chapter, and for the sake of which this domestic history of Micah is introduced. **House of gods.** Rather, *of God* (Elohim); for the worship was of Jehovah, only with a corrupt and semi-idolatrous ceremonial. **An ephod.** See ch. viii. 26, 27, note. **Teraphim.** See Gen. xxxi. 19 (images, A. V.; teraphim, Heb.); 1 Sam. xv. 23 (idolatry, A. V.; teraphim, Heb.); xix. 13 (an image, A. V.; teraphim, Heb.); Hosea iii. 4, &c. They seem to have been a kind of Penates, or household gods, and were used for divination (Ezek. xxi. 21; Zech. x. 2). **Became his priest.** One function of the priest, and for which it is likely he was much resorted to, was to inquire of God by the ephod (ch. xviii. 5, 6). What his other duties might be does not appear.

Ver. 6.—**There was no king.** This must have been written in the days of the kings of Israel and Judah, and perhaps with reference to the efforts of such kings as Asa (1 Kings xv. 13) and Jehoshaphat (1 Kings xxii. 43) to put down idolatry.

Ver. 7.—**Of the family of Judah.** These words are difficult to explain. If the man was a Levite he could not be of the family or tribe of Judah. Some explain the words to be merely a more accurate definition of Bethlehem-judah, as if he would say, *I mean Bethlehem in the tribe of Judah.* Others explain them to mean that he was one of a family of Levites who had settled in Bethlehem, and so came to be reckoned in civil matters as belonging to Judah. Others, that he was of the family of Judah on his mother's side, which might be the cause of his settling at Bethlehem. But many commentators think them spurious, as they are not found in the Septuagint (Cod. Vat.), nor in the Peschito, nor in No. 440 of De Rossi's MSS. The Septuagint has *Bethlehem of the family of Judah.*

Ver. 8.—**From Bethlehem-judah.** Rather, *out of.* The whole phrase means, *out of the city,* viz., *out of Bethlehem.* **Mount Ephraim**—the hill country of Ephraim, as ver. 1, where see note.

Vers. 10, 11.—**A father.** This is not a common application of the word *father* in the Old Testament. The prominent idea seems to be one of honour, combined with authority to teach and advise. It is applied to prophets (2 Kings ii. 12; vi. 21; xiii. 14), and to Joseph (Gen. xlv. 8). The idea is implied in the converse phrase of *son,* applied to those to whom the prophets stood in the relation of spiritual fathers (see 2 Kings viii. 9; Prov. iv. 10, 20, and frequently elsewhere). The abuse of the feeling which dictates the term as applied to human teachers is reproved by our Lord (Matt. xxiii. 9). It has been freely used in the Christian Church, as in the titles *papa* or *pope* applied to bishops, *abbot* and *abbas, father in God, fathers of the Church,* &c. Here there is perhaps a special reference to the function of Micah's priest to ask counsel of God, and then give

that counsel to those who came to inquire (see note to ver. 5). It may be added that the idea of *counsellor* seems to be inherent in the word *cohen* or *priest,* as in 2 Sam. viii. 18; 1 Kings iv. 5, &c. **Ten shekels**—a little over a pound of our money, but probably equivalent to £20, when considered relatively to articles of consumption. **A suit of apparel.** There is great doubt as to the exact meaning of the word rendered *suit* in this connection. The word means anything *arranged,* i. e. put in a *rank,* or *row,* or *order.* In Exod. xl. 23 it is applied to the shewbread: "He ordered the bread in order." Thence it came to mean the *estimation* or *worth* of a person or thing—somewhat as we use the word *rank.* From this last sense some interpret the word here to mean the *worth* or *price* of his clothes. Others, including St. Jerome and the Septuagint, interpret it *a pair* of vestments, meaning summer and winter clothing. But perhaps the A. V., *suit,* meaning the whole set of under and upper garments, is after all the best interpretation. **The Levite went in.** The Hebrew is *went,* i. e. according to the common use of the word, *went his way.* And such is probably the meaning here. He went his way to consider the proposal made to him. The result is given in the next verse: *And the Levite was content,* &c.

Ver. 13.— **Then said Micah,** &c. We may notice this incidental proof that the Levites in the time of Micah held the religious position which is ascribed to them in the Pentateuch. **I have a Levite.** Rather, *the Levite,* meaning the particular Levite of whom it is the question. *A Levite* would be without the article, as in ver. 7, or would be expressed as in ch. xix. 1 (Heb.), *a man a Levite.*

HOMILETICS.

Vers. 1—13.—*The superstitious worship of the true God.* The natural history of religion is a very curious one. There is first the broad division between worship given to false gods and that which is given to the one true and living God, Creator of heaven and earth. The heathen of old, like the heathen of to-day, worshipped those that were no gods. Either they had no existence at all, and were the creatures of man's imagination, divinities supposed to preside over the various powers of nature and the affections of the human heart; gods of the weather, of the earth, and sea, and sky; malignant spirits supposed to influence human destiny, and requiring gifts to propitiate them; personifications of light, or death, or even of criminal human passions; or else they were beings who had indeed a real existence,—sun, moon, stars, stones, animals, angels, demons, or the spirits of dead men,—but who were not God. This worship of false gods we know from Holy Scripture, and from the annals of all nations, was prevalent over the whole ancient world, and we know that it exists in heathen lands to the present day. But that is not the form of corrupt religion to which this chapter calls our attention, nor is it that into which there is any probability of Christians falling in this nineteenth century. We turn, therefore, to the varieties of the worship offered to the one true God. And first to look at the particular case before us. The mother of Micah seems to have been in her way a devout woman. The scraping together 1100 shekels was probably not effected without considerable effort and self-denial, for it was a large sum (more than £110), eleven times the yearly wages of the Levite. She meant to consecrate it to Jehovah, the God of Israel. She seems too to have been a good mother, for she intended this consecration to be for her son's benefit, and her language and conduct, when her son confessed his guilt, were pious and forgiving. And yet we find her disobeying the express command of God, and making a graven and a molten image to be used in his worship and service. In like manner we find Micah giving signs of a tender conscience and of the fear of God in confessing his sin when adjured according to the law; we find him anxious for the favour of God, and looking to him to do him good; we find him liberal and large-hearted in providing at his own expense for the worship of God; and yet, with a strange inconsistency, we find him doing the very things which God's word forbad, and setting up images, and teraphim, and a superstitious ephod in a "house of God" of his own devising, and under a priest of his own consecration. In like manner again we find even Aaron making a golden calf for the people to worship, and saying (Septuagint), or encouraging the people to say, "This is thy God, O Israel, which brought thee up out of the land of Egypt," and building an altar before it, and keeping a feast in its honour. We read of the golden calves of Jeroboam, and we read too of the high places and the sacrifices upon them even under the pious kings. These then are distinct examples of the superstitious worship of the true God, and lead us to the anxious question, how we are to worship God. Under the Old Testament this was not left to chance or human choice. In the nonage of the Church, before the coming of Christ, all the ordinances of Divine service were prescribed with minuteness and exactness. The sanctuary itself, the Aaronic priesthood, the Levitical ministrations, the feasts of the Lord, the gifts and offerings and devotions of the people, were all ordered by the authority of the word of God. But under the New Testament, when the fulness of the time is come, and the Church has entered into the full possession of the privileges of adopted sons, it is so no longer. Besides a few general principles and broad rules, and the institution of the two sacraments, and the Lord's Prayer, the Church has received from Holy Scripture no form of Divine service. She has to frame her rules and canons of Divine worship according to the light and wisdom vouchsafed to her by the Holy Spirit of God. In doing this she must have regard to two things. 1. The character and mind of God, so that the worship may be of a kind that will be pleasing and acceptable to him. 2. The nature and character of man, so that the worship may be of a kind to assist the worshipper to raise his heart to God, and impress him with a sense of the majesty, and holiness, and goodness of God. With regard to the *first*, the general intimations of him who alone knows the things of God, even the Holy Spirit of God, are very clear. "God is a spirit, and they that worship him must worship him in spirit and in truth." "The sacrifices of God are a broken spirit; a broken and contrite heart, O God, thou wilt not despise." "Let us offer the sacrifice of praise to God continually, that is, the fruit of our lips giving thanks to his name." "To do good and to communicate forget not: for with such sacrifices God is well pleased" (see too Micah vi. 6—8). Every attempt to substitute costly gifts, or gorgeous ceremonies, or showy processions, or lights, or music, or gestures, or anything bodily and sensuous, for the ritual of repentance, faith, fear, love, and self-consecration—consecration of the will and affections—to the service of Almighty God can only be made in ignorance of his character and mind as revealed to us in Holy Scripture. It is as truly superstitious as were Micah's images, and teraphim, and ephod, and house of God. With regard to the *second*, the outward accessories of worship must be of a kind to assist the worshipper in his endeavour to draw near to God and worship him with all the powers of his soul. Under the pretence of purely spiritual worship, it is very easy so to get rid of all outward acts and circumstances as to get rid of worship itself. The light of religion in the soul cannot burn unless in an atmosphere which feeds the flame. Reverence and awe, prayer and praise, forgetfulness of the world, and thoughts of heaven need to be quickened and encouraged by the posture of the body, by the words of the lips, by sights and sounds expressive of those invisible things which the soul seeks to handle in its approaches to the throne of God. It is therefore a legitimate subject of consideration what forms of worship are most calculated to increase and heighten the devotion of the worshippers. Forms which tend merely to please the senses are worthless; forms which tend to soothe the conscience of the impenitent, and to stifle its questionings by creating a feeling of duty performed and of satisfaction made to God, are pernicious; and forms which so fill the thoughts as to the manner of performing them as to leave no room for thoughts of God are injuries rather than benefits to the soul. Forms, again, which leave the soul self-satisfied, which convey a false impression of God's favour and grace being given when he is really displeased and offended, and which comfort and encourage those who ought to be horribly afraid and trembling for fear of God's judgments, are manifestly destructive of the souls of those for whose benefit they purport to exist. A faithful Church will root up all such as dishonouring to God and as very hurtful to man. One other characteristic of superstitious worship must be noted. It is compatible with vice, and with the dominion of sin in the heart. Superstition has no tendency to correct the principles of action, or to purify the thoughts and affections of the inner man. The sequel of Micah's history supplies a notable instance of this. The Danites, in their superstitious desire to possess the images of Micah's chapel, and the religious services of Micah's priest, scrupled not to break the commandments of God by stealing, and, if need were, by committing murder. Stealing sacred relics and transporting them by guile or violence from one religious house to another is a well-known form of mediæval superstition. The brigands in the mountains of Italy have been often known to kneel before an image of the Virgin, and ask the blessing of the priest or bishop, and then return to their work of plunder or murder. Superstition is no check upon the passions, and no bar to the reckless pursuit of what men deem to be their interests or know to be their desires. There is no gulf between superstitious worship and immoral conduct. The man who mistakes the aspect of God towards superstitious vanities is prone to mistake also his aspect towards moral disorder and sin. But he who really enters into the tabernacle of God, and communes with God in spirit, comes forth with his face shining with inward righteousness, the reflection of God's glory in the face of Jesus Christ. His life is a continuation of his prayers, his praise culminates in good works. In the interests of moral goodness, as well as for the honour of God, it is of supreme importance that the worship of the Almighty be free from superstition.

HOMILIES BY VARIOUS AUTHORS.

Vers. 1—13.—*The history of a man-made ministry:*—1. *Its genesis.* It belongs to the main design of the book to show how the various disruptive tendencies of a religious and social nature increased unchecked when "there was no king in Israel." The book begins with a note of unity—"the children of Israel asked Jehovah." Repeated idolatrous defections are chronicled, and mention made of the setting up of an ephod in Ophrah, the city of Gideon, and its evil consequences. In one respect the schisms from the national religion were even more dangerous than complete departure from it. The unity of Israel was thus destroyed in its chief sanction and sign, the universal sacrifice and confession at Shiloh. Another of these schismatic points of departure is here related. The description is full of realistic force, and is governed by the dogmatic purpose of exposing the immoral motives of it, and thus discrediting it in the eyes of every true Israelite. It is exposed as the private and selfish appropriation of a national blessing. As the political unity of Israel depended upon maintaining a central religious authority and a uniform ritual and priesthood, the setting up of a house of gods was in itself, irrespectively of its motives, a crime of the first magnitude. The New Testament idea of Church and ministry is different. There the unity of the Spirit is the prevailing aim. But whenever separation originates in similar motives to those here depicted, the sin of schism equally exists.

I. THE CHARACTER OF ITS AUTHORS. Avaricious mother, dishonest son. Both superstitious. Not honesty, but fear of a curse, actuates Micah to restore the " eleven hundred shekels." The getting back of the money is the chief concern of the mother, and so she straightway blesses whom she had cursed (cf. James iii. 10). Only 200 shekels are actually appropriated to the end proposed.

II. ITS MOTIVES. Apparently the warding off of the curse is the first concern with both. But an equally powerful motive was the securing of the gain resulting from fees and gifts. In this way they would become rich. Where the aim is selfish and impure, the character of the worship becomes of secondary consequence, and the latent tendency towards idolatry begins to show itself. It is the motive that is of chief concern in questions of religion. Everything else will be dominated by this: "Is it for self, or is the glory of God my chief aim?" Founders of churches and religious institutions, and candidates for the ministry, should examine themselves ere they are committed to the work upon which they have set their hearts.

III. THE COMPLEXION OF THE WORSHIP. It is a "house of gods," containing a "graven image and a molten image," an ephod, and teraphim, which is the outcome of their religious or superstitious zeal. In its nature eclectic, in the crudest sense of the word, this system of religious worship is on the face of it a sacred means to a vulgar, secular end. The house became a place of irregular worship, of sooth-saying and divination.

IV. THE INSTRUMENT OF THEIR DESIGNS. A son is the first expedient in the direction of a priesthood; but this is not considered sufficiently authoritative. Accident throws in the way a young Levite of Bethlehem-judah, who appears to have taken to a wandering life through discontent, curiosity, idleness, or restlessness. A shiftless, unscrupulous, easily impressible character, in a needy condition, and with the Levitical status, just the fitting occupant of such an office. The undue influence of Micah is thus secured permanently. Promising that he should be a "father and a priest," and receive clothing, board, and "ten shekels" wages, to the needy adventurer "making his way" he thus becomes patron; and the promised standing of the priest relatively to Micah is soon reversed—he "was unto him as one of his sons." The consecration too is from Micah. The good and the evil of patronage, private and otherwise, in religion; the dependence of the ministry—"like people like priest;" the question of "consecration" and "orders."

V. THE SUPERSTITIOUS PRESUMPTION OF FALSE RELIGION. There is the more care as to the external ritual, the priestly "succession," &c. in proportion to the earthliness of the underlying motive. 1. *Where the heart is wrong undue reliance is placed upon externals in religion.* The priest's advantage of descent was vitiated by his becoming a mercenary and a schismatic. Rites and ceremonies are multiplied in default of the "Presence" at Shiloh and its simple service. The error is in placing the virtue in the external observances instead of the reality of worship, purity of life and motive, and the presence of the Spirit of God. Romanism has been defined as "a system of position and imposition, or of posture and imposture." 2. *Jehovah is supposed to countenance a religion which is essentially opposed to him.* God cannot take rank or be associated with other gods. His glory must be the chief object of the worshipper, the priest, and the patron. Selfish aims, disobedience to his clearly-revealed will concerning his service and Church, can never receive his blessing. Yet observe the self-deception of Micah. He does not see all this, or the evils soon to come upon him. On the other hand, "the *pure in heart*" shall see God. His presence is independent of the external completeness, &c. of ritual. True priesthood is a Divine unction, and not a human monopoly.—M.

Vers. 1—4.—*Avarice and superstition.* The story of Micah and his mother illustrates the strange blending of avarice and superstition which may be observed in those people who have lowered themselves to a worldly habit of life without entirely losing the influence of religion.

I. WHEN RELIGION SINKS INTO SUPERSTITION, ITS UNWORLDLY SPIRIT IS QUENCHED AND AVARICE IS UNRESTRAINED. The religion of Israel is now most degraded, and one result of its degradation is seen in a correspondnig lowering of morality. Great devotion to a superstitious religious system is not incompatible with a very low tone of moral life. 1. This is seen in the *avarice of Micah's mother*, (1) Tempting to deception, if not complete dishonesty, on the part of the son, (2) giving rise to unseemly temper and blind cursing on her own side, and (3) to a mean and unworthy attempt at restoring family peace by a compromise between selfish greed and religious devotion—200 shekels only are devoted to the image, and, though Micah had intended all to go to this object, the remaining 900 shekels are retained by the mother. 2. The same degradation of morality is seen in the *unworthy conduct of the young man*. He shows no confidence in his mother. He thinks he can honour God with the proceeds of deception. It is only under a dark religion of superstition that we can suppose the end to justify the means—a sacrificial object to excuse domestic fraud.

II. WHEN, UNDER THE INFLUENCE OF A WORLDLY SPIRIT, AVARICE IS UNRESTRAINED, RELIGION TENDS TO SINK INTO SUPERSTITION. Covetousness is idolatry (Col. iii. 5). The habit of setting the affections on earthly things blinds the soul to the perception of pure spiritual truth. This is seen in the story of Micah and his mother. 1. Micah displays a *dread of his mother's curse*, but no consciousness of guilt. His confession and restitution are not the result of repentance, but of superstitious fear. 2. His mother shows *no grief* at the revelation of his conduct, but only delight at seeing the money, and a desire to remove the effect of her curse by pronouncing a blessing on her son. 3. Subsequently the young man *dreads to touch the money* which is affected with his mother's curse, though she offers it to him, and she feels bound to use it, or part of it, in the service of God. 4. Religious feelings do not seem to affect the moral conduct of either person, but only to *incline them to image-making*. Thus worldly greed drags down religion till this becomes merely a worldly habit of gross idolatry and magic spells. We may see in the present day religions of mere ritual and superstitious practices attracting the most worldly people, and not restraining, but rather shaping themselves into the mould of their low and earthly affections.—A.

Ver. 6.—*No king*. The writer of the Book of Judges more than once attributes the social disorders of Israel to the want of a king. This idea has its bearings on national interests and on private conduct.

I. THE NEED OF A KING IN CONNECTION WITH NATIONAL INTERESTS. 1. *A centre of authority is essential to the peace and prosperity of a nation*. As the first duty of a government is to maintain order, so the need of authority and organisation for the maintenance of order makes the establishment of a government essential to a nation. This is necessary, (1) to punish violence and crime, (2) to restrain the unjust encroachment of one man upon the rights of another, (3) to arbitrate between the conflicting claims of individual men and of great classes of the community, (4) to promote national objects which are too large for private enterprise, and (5) to cement the unity of the nation and organise this for defence against foreign invasion. 2. *When a nation is not prepared for self-government it is best for it to be ruled by one strong hand*. Apart from political requisites, certain moral conditions must be fulfilled before a people can practise self-government. There must be unity of sympathy and self-control. Neither of these conditions was fulfilled by the tribes of Israel in the days of the Judges. Mutual jealousy and antagonism prevailed among them, and violent measures were too common for the minority to submit peaceably to the will of the majority. The spiritual vision of the Divine King which had maintained the unity of the nation in the days of Moses was fading away, and now that sublime and unearthly government was nearly lost, there was no hope for the people but in the establishment of a human monarchy. It is foolish to maintain in words an ideal which is too high for practice. Better confess our degeneracy and shape our conduct according to the means within reach.

II. THE NEED OF A KING IN CONNECTION WITH PRIVATE CONDUCT. The soul needs a king. We are born to obey. We need some authority above us to keep us right. 1. It is not *safe* for every man to do what is right in his own eyes, because (1) we are swayed by passion and selfish greed, and (2) in our best moments we are liable to prejudice, and are too short-sighted to see what is best. The anarchy of universal self-seeking without restraint would bring the world to ruin. For the good of all it is necessary that each should not be at liberty simply to please himself. 2. It is not *right* for every man to do that which is right in his own eyes. We are members one of another, and are morally bound to respect the rights, and needs, and wishes of our neighbours. We are children of the great King, and under a supreme obligation to respect his law. The Church is not a republic; it is a kingdom. The Christian is not free to follow his fancy; he is required to submit to and to obey the mind and will of Christ. Christian liberty is not found in the license of self-will, but in the willingness of obedience and the love which delights to fulfil the will of God and to do to others as we would that they should do to us.—A.

Ver. 13.—*Faith in the priest.* I. FAITH IN THE PRIEST IMPLIES A DESIRE FOR GOD'S BLESSING. The priest is trusted for his influence with God. He is sought after because God's blessing is desired. So far the faith in the priest indicates good qualities. It is a sign of religious ideas, though these are vague and perverted. There is something pathetic in Micah's utterance. Now at last he may expect blessing. His mother's graven image did not secure this; his temple and its elaborate worship left him dissatisfied; but he can have no rest till he is assured that God is blessing him. He is wealthy, but wealth will not satisfy him without the blessing of God. So he presses on to find this one source of true peace. How many men are ready to mock at Micah's superstition who have no gleam of his true faith! It is better to be seeking the blessing of God, though in mistaken ways, than, while discerning the folly of these ways by the light of a cold rationalism, to be dead to any yearnings for the supreme good.

II. FAITH IN THE PRIEST IMPLIES A CONSCIOUS NEED OF AN INTERCESSOR. All priestly religions spring out of a true instinct of conscience. They are not simply the fabrications of a tyrannical priestcraft. Religion requires a priest. It is right to feel, like Micah, unworthy and unable to obtain God's blessings for ourselves, and, like him, to look for an intercessor. Christianity is based on these ideas; it is the religion of a mediator, a priest. Christ satisfies this desire to seek God's blessing through the help of another, through the work of a priest (Heb. vi. 20).

III. FAITH IN THE PRIEST IMPLIES SUPERSTITIOUS TRUST IN RELIGIOUS OFFICIALISM. The error is to be found, (1) in choosing a merely human priest, and (2) in placing a wrong kind of trust in him, and not simply in believing in the idea of priesthood. 1. This priestly superstition expects blessings *irrespective of the character of the priest.* Micah has had a priest before—his own son. He has no reason to believe that the Levite is a better man. He only knows that he belongs to the sacred tribe of temple officials. This is characteristic of the superstition of priestliness. It supposes that the office sanctifies the man, not the man the office. It looks for good from the priest simply through his official functions. Christ is a priest not by reason of birth or anointing (he was not of the tribe of Levi), but by reason of nature, and character, and work. 2. This priestly superstition expects blessings *apart from the religious character of the recipient.* Micah believes that the mere presence of the Levite in his house will benefit him. He does not think of the Levite influencing his character for good. So there are people who imagine the priest can do them good apart from their own character and conduct. But Christ, the true Priest, only brings to us the blessings secured by his sacrifice and intercession when we submit to him so as to receive a new birth to a holy life.—A.

EXPOSITION.

CHAPTER XVIII.

Ver. 1.—**In those days**, &c. See ch. xvii. 6. **The tribe of the Danites sought them an inheritance**, &c. This does not mean that the whole tribe of Dan were still seeking their inheritance. The bulk of the tribe, as we read in Josh. xix. 40—48, did receive their inheritance by lot before the death of Joshua (*ibid.* ver. 49) and Eleazar (*ibid.* ver. 51). But as long as any part of the tribe was not settled, the tribe as such, in its unity, was still seeking a settlement. The land

for their inheritance had not yet fallen to the tribe in its integrity. This is in part accounted for by what we read ch. i. 34, that the Amorites would not suffer the children of Dan to come down to the valley, so that those who could not get possession of their land there would be crowded into other parts of the tribal territory. These Danites, of whom we are here reading, were dwelling in Zorah and Eshtaol (ch. xiii. 1, 25), as we see by vers. 2, 11. **Unto that day**, &c. Translate this clause, *For unto that day* the land (meaning *the whole land*) *had not fallen unto them in the midst of the tribes of Israel for an inheritance.* The words *the land* must be supplied after the analogy of Numb. xxxiv. 2. What follows in this chapter is a more detailed account of what was briefly mentioned in Josh. xix. 47, where, however, the A. V. *went out too little for them* is not a translation of the Hebrew text, which is very difficult to explain. Houbigant, by an ingenious conjecture, gives the sense *was too narrow for them.* From the mention of this migration in the Book of Joshua, it is probable that it took place not many years after Joshua's death.

Ver. 2.—**They came to Mount Ephraim** (ch. xvii. 1, 8). The hill country of Ephraim would be on their way to the north from Eshtaol. They would naturally avoid the plain where the Amorites and Philistines were strong.

Ver. 3.—**When.** Rather, *while.* **By the house.** Rather, *in* or *at* the house. **They knew the voice,** having, as some think, known him before he left Bethlehem, or perceiving a southern accent. But it may merely mean that they discerned his voice as he was singing or reciting prayers in the house of God. Micah's house seems to have been a collection of houses (vers. 14, 22), approached by one gateway (ver. 16), in one of which the Levite dwelt. **They turned in thither.** This seems to have been next morning, when they were starting on their journey. Hearing the Levite's voice, they turned aside into his house. **What makest thou,** &c. Rather, *What doest thou in this place? and what is thy business here?*

Ver. 4.—**And I am his priest,** or, *to be his priest.*

Ver. 5.—**Ask counsel of God,** or simply *Ask God,* as the identical phrase is rendered in ch. i. 2, where see note.

Ver. 6.—**And the priest said,** &c., having first, it is to be presumed, put on the ephod (see ch. viii. 26, 27, note ; xvii. 5). **Before the Lord is your way,** *i. e.* he looks upon it with favour, has respect unto it, and will make it successful, as it is said in Ps. xxxiv. 15 : "The eyes of the Lord are upon the righteous." "Whether," says Bishop Patrick, "he had any answer from the teraphim, or feigned it out of his own head, is uncertain."

Ver. 7.—**To Laish.** Called in Josh. xix. 47 *Leshem,* which is perhaps a corruption caused by the statement that they called it after the name (*Ke-shem*) of Dan, or it may be only another form. The name is strangely corrupted in the Septuagint of ver. 29 of this chapter into *Oulamais,* and in Josh. xix. 47 into *Lasen-dan.* St. Jerome, misled by the Septuagint, has *Lesem Dan.* Laish was situated four Roman miles from Banias, on the road to. Tyre, on one of the sources

of the Jordan. Robinson identifies it unhesitatingly with *Tell-el-Kady,* "the mount of the judge" (where *Kady* has the same meaning as *Dan*), close to the great fountain, "one of the largest fountains in the world," called *el-Leddan,* which is the source of the lesser Jordan (Josephus), and which may very possibly be the ultimate form of ed-Dan, corrupted into Eddan, el-Eddan, Leddan, el-Leddan, by successive incorporations of the article *el* into the word itself, of which there are other examples. The remainder of this verse is exceedingly obscure ; a probable translation is as follows : "And they saw the people that was in the midst of it dwelling in security after the manner of the Zidonians, '*quiet and secure, and none doing any injury to any one in the land, possessing wealth ;*' and they were far from the Zidonians, and had no business with any man." The words in italics are probably a poetical quotation, descriptive of the people of Laish, which would account for the peculiar diction and the grammatical changes ; for whereas the word *dwelling* is in the feminine gender, agreeing with *people,* the words *quiet* and *secure* and *possessing* are in the masculine, which can be readily accounted for if they are a quotation. This would also account for the tautology, "dwelling in security," "quiet and secure," and for the poetical character of the phrase "*possessing wealth,*" and for the unusual form of the word here rendered *wealth* ('*etzer* with an ain, instead of the usual *otzar* with an aleph), in accordance with the Septuagint and Vulgate and Gesenius, who derive the meaning of *wealth* from *collecting,* from which the common word *atzereth* derives its meaning of a *collection* or *congregation* of people.

Ver. 9.—**To go, and to enter.** The exact meaning is, Be not slothful to go (*i. e.* to go on your way from hence), so as to enter in and possess the land. This would be expressed by leaving out *to* before *enter—to go and enter.*

Ver. 10.—Translate, "When ye come, ye shall come unto a people secure ; and the land is very large (for God hath given it into your hands), a place where there is no want," &c. The Hebrew of *very large* is, literally, *wide on both hands.* The parenthetic *for God hath given it into your hands,* merely explains why they speak so confidently about it (cf. Deut. viii. 9).

Ver. 11.—**The family**—meaning the *tribe* (see ch. xiii. 2, note, and cf. Josh. vii. 17). Possibly a reason for the use of the word *family* here and in ver. 2, as applied to Dan, may be that there was only one family in the tribe of Dan, that of the Shuhamites (Numb. xxvi. 42). **Six hundred men.** With their wives and sisters and children (see ver. 21), the whole company' must have amounted to two or three thousand souls.

Ver. 12.—**Kirjath-jearim** (city of forests), otherwise called *Kirjath-Baal* and *Baalah,* in the hill country of Judah (Josh. xv. 60). It lay on the border of Benjamin (Josh. xviii. 14, 15). Its modern representative in all probability is *Kurit-el-enab,* nine miles from Jerusalem, on the road to Joppa. The district is still very woody. **Mahaneh-dan,** *i. e.* the camp of Dan (see ch. xiii. 25). **Behind,** *i. e.* to the west of. The exact site of *Mahaneh-dan* has not been identified with certainty. Mr. Williams was shown a site called *Beit-Mahanem* in the Wady Is-mail which answers well in position, but it has not been noticed by any other traveller (' Dictionary of Bible').

Ver. 14.—**In these houses,** showing that Beth-Micah, the house of Micah, was in fact a small village (see ver. 22).

Ver. 15. — **Even unto the house,** &c. Rather, *at Beth-Micah.*

Ver. 17.—**Went up,** viz., into the upper chamber, where it appears the chapel was. So we read in 2 Kings xxiii. 12 that there were altars *on the roof of the upper chamber of Ahaz* (cf. Jer. xix. 13). *And* came up, *and* took. There is no *and* in the Hebrew, and the tense of the verb is changed. A fuller stop must be put after *went up.* And then the account proceeds, with a certain solemn-ity of diction, *They came in thither; they took the graven image, and the ephod, and the teraphim, and the molten image* (full stop). The narrative goes on, *Now the priest was standing in the entering of the gate,* &c. *But these five went into Micah's house,* &c., as just related, and of course brought them out to the gate where the priest was standing with the 600 Danites.

Ver. 18.—**The carved image.** It should be the *graven image,* as elsewhere. The Hebrew text here has *the graven image of the ephod,* as was noticed in ch. xvii. 3, note. But it is very possible that the *vav, and,* has fallen out of the text by accident, and it does not seem likely that a different phrase should be adopted in this one place from that followed throughout in the enumeration of the articles in Micah's chapel, so that the A. V. is probably right. **Then said the priest,** &c. When he saw the idols and teraphim in the hands of the five men he cried out in alarm. It is remarkable that here and in the preceding verse he is styled *the priest.*

Ver. 19.—**Lay thine hand upon thy mouth.** Cf. Job xxi. 5; xxix. 9; xl. 4. **A father and a priest.** See ch. xvii. 10, note.

Ver. 20.—**The priest's heart was glad,** &c. The prospect of greater dignity and greater emolument stifled all sentiments of grati-tude and loyalty to Micah, and made him

cheerfully connive at an act of theft and sacrilege.

Ver. 21.—**They turned,** *i. e.* turned their backs upon Beth-Micah, and went on their way to the north. **The little ones.** The term necessarily includes the women of the emigrant party. Compare Jacob's care for his wives and children (Gen. xxxiii. 1—5); only Jacob expected an attack from Esau in front, the Danites an attack from Micah from behind. **The carriage.** It is the same word as is translated in Gen. xxxi. 1 *glory;* it might be rendered *valuables.* It would no doubt include the precious images and ephod which they had just stolen.

Ver. 22.—**The houses near to Micah's house.** See ver. 14, note. *Near to,* the same Hebrew word as is rendered *by* in ver. 3, where see note.

Ver. 23.—**That thou comest,** &c.—liter-ally, *that thou art gathered together,* the same word as in ver. 22. It is the idea of the clan, or family, or tribe which causes the phrase. Just as *Israel* or *Judah* desig-nates the whole nation, or the whole tribe, under the name of their patriarch, so here Micah would include all the clan who dwelt in Micah's house; and hence the Danites speak of Micah being gathered together.

Ver. 24.—**My gods,** or, as some render it, *my god.* But the plural is probably right, as Micah was thinking of the molten and graven images, and the teraphim, and called them *gods,* without perhaps meaning to im-ply that there was any God but Jehovah.

Ver. 25.—**Run upon thee.** Rather, *run, or fall, upon you;* it is the plural pronoun, comprehending the whole party. The argu-ment of the Danites was the argument of the stronger.

Ver. 26.—The verse tells us what the two parties did, but not in the order in which an English writer would express it; for no doubt the Danites, encumbered with their women, and children, and baggage, did not *go on their way* till Micah and his party had turned back, though in English the contrary order is rather implied. The He-brew merely puts the actions side by side, and leaves the order to be inferred.

Ver. 27.—**And they.** In the Hebrew the *they* is emphatic. It would be better ex-pressed in English by repeating *The children of Dan.* The repetition of the epithets *quiet and secure,* as applied to the people of Laish, rather seems to indicate the writer's reproba-tion of the deed as cruel, like that of Simeon and Levi in slaying Hamor and Shechem. **They smote them with the edge of the sword**—a phrase denoting an exterminating slaughter (Exod. xxxiv. 26; Josh. xix. 47; 1 Sam. xv. 8, &c.). **And they burnt the city,** &c. Perhaps they had made the people and city a *cherem,* a devoted thing, and therefore slew the one and burnt the other (cf. Numb. xxi. 3 ; Josh. viii. 19 ; xi. 11, &c.) ; or the burning of the city may have been one of the means by which they destroyed the people.

Ver. 28.—**Because it was far,** &c. He reverts again to the description given in ver. 7. **That lieth by Beth-Rehob.** It is literally, *which belongeth to Beth-Rehob,* i. e. the valley here spoken of was part of the territory of the Syrians of Beth-Rehob in the time of David (and very likely earlier), as we read in 2 Sam. x. 6. It seems to have taken its name, *House of Rehob,* from Rehob the father of Hadadezer, king of Zobah (2 Sam. viii. 12), and to have been called *Beth-Rehob* very much as Micah's settlement was called *Beth-Micah.* It was also called for shortness *Rehob,* as Numb. xiii. 21 ; Judg. i. 31 ; 2 Sam. x. 8. It was situated, as we learn from ch. i. 31, in the bounds of the tribe of Asher, in the extreme north of the Holy Land, near the entering in of Hamath, the site of which, however, is unknown (see Numb. xiii. 21). The valley is that through which the Leddan fountain flows (ver. 7, note), and is the upper part of the plain called *el-Hulleh,* which is the northern continuation of the Jordan valley. **They built a city.** Rather, *they rebuilt the city.*

Ver. 29.—**Howbeit Laish was the name,** &c. The strange form here given in the Septuagint, *Oulamais,* arises from their having taken the Hebrew word for *howbeit* (*oulam*) as part of the name, and left out the L of Laish (see ver. 7, note).

Vers. 30, 31.—**And the children of Dan,** &c. It was probably the long existence of this semi-idolatrous worship of the graven image at Dan that induced King Jeroboam to set up one of his golden calves at Dan, as we read 1 Kings xii. 28—30. **And Jonathan, the son of Gershom, the son of Manasseh.** The Hebrew text really has *the son of Moses.* But a little *n* is written above the line between the M and the S of Moses (Mosheh),

so as to be read *Manasseh,* as thus : MSH ; so that they avoided the pain of reading aloud that the grandson or descendant of Moses was an idolatrous priest, without actually altering the written text. It is indeed most sad that it should have been so, though like examples are not wanting, as, *e. g.,* the sons of Eli and of Samuel. For Gershom the son of Moses see Exod. ii. 22 ; xviii. 3 ; 1 Chron. xxiii. 14—16. It does not follow that Jonathan, the priest of the Danites, was literally the son of Gershom. It may merely mean that he was of the family of which Gershom was the head. **Until the day of the captivity of the land.** There is great diversity of opinion as to the meaning of this phrase. Many understand

it, as is the obvious meaning of the words, of the Assyrian captivity (2 Kings xv. 29 ; xvii. 6). But some of the best commentators, as Kimchi among the Jews, and many moderns, think it refers to the taking captive of the ark by the Philistines in the days of Eli, because this is the time indicated in the next verse by the mention of the house of God in Shiloh. The ark of God never returned to Shiloh after it was taken thence (1 Sam. iv. 3, 4) and captured by the Philistines (*ibid.* ver. 11). It is also noticed that the expression, *The ark of God is gone into captivity* (is *taken,* A. V.), occurs in 1 Sam. iv. 21, 22. It certainly would be strange that one verse (30) should speak of the worship of the graven image lasting till the Assyrian conquest of the land, and the next verse (31) limit it to the time that the house of God was in Shiloh, some 300 years earlier. At the same time it should be noticed that ver. 30 speaks of the time that Jonathan's sons were priests to the tribe of Dan, and ver. 31 of the worship of Micah's image. It is quite possible that the descendants of Jonathan may have been appointed priests at Dan to Jeroboam's golden-calf worship, though the original graven image of Micah may have been destroyed by Saul or David ; and in the interval between such destruction of Micah's image and the setting up of Jeroboam's calves they may have been the priests of an irregular worship on a high place at Tell-el-Kady. And this would enable us to give what is certainly its natural meaning to the words, "the captivity of the land." But no certainty can be arrived at without more actual knowledge. Many commentators adopt Houbigant's conjecture to read *ark* for *land* at the end of ver. 30 (*arôn* for *aretz*). Others think that some deportation of the Danites by the Syrians or other neighbouring people not recorded in history is here spoken of. **All the time the house of God,** &c. This must have been written not earlier than the time of Samuel, and possibly much later. The house of God, *i. e.* the tabernacle, was in Shiloh from the days of Joshua (Josh. xviii. 1) till the days of Eli (1 Sam. i. 3), after which we have no account of where the house of God was till the ark was brought up to Jerusalem by King David from the house of Obed-edom the Gittite (2 Sam. vi. 12), and placed in the tabernacle that David had pitched for it (2 Sam. vi. 17) ; but whether this was the tabernacle that had been pitched at Shiloh or a new one does not appear. It is not improbable that Samuel may have moved the tabernacle from Shiloh to Ramah (1 Sam. vii. 17). The ark had rested in the house of Abinadab at Baaleh or Kirjath-jearim for twenty years (1 Sam. vii. 2) previous to its removal by David.

HOMILETICS.

Vers. 1—31.—*Society without a head ceasing to be society.* The writer of the five last chapters of the Book of Judges had a painful task to perform. Writing the history of his people, and they the people of God, he had to tell a tale of violence, plunder, bloodshed, brutality, civil war, and extermination, on the secular side, and of superstition, schism, and idolatry, on the religious side of his story. And we may observe, by the way, that we have a striking evidence of the truthfulness and impar-tiality of the narrator in this merciless exposure of the sins and misdeeds of his countrymen. Nor are we at a loss to draw the lesson which he intended us to draw from the account which he has given; for no fewer than four times in the course of his brief narrative does he impress upon the mind of his readers the fact that in the days when these shameful deeds were done "there was no king in Israel, but every man did that which was right in his own eyes" (ch. xvii. 6 ; xviii. 1 ; xix. 1 ; xxi. 25). No doubt the writer referred particularly to that government with which he was acquainted, the government of kings properly so called, of whom Saul was the first, and David and his long line were the successors. But when we remember that in its best days the Israelitish nation had no king but God, and was governed under him by such rulers as Moses, Joshua, Gideon, Samuel, and the other judges, we shall perceive that the lesson to be learnt is not so much that of the superiority of monarchy over other forms of government (how-ever true this may be), as of the absolute necessity, for the religious and civil welfare of a people, that a firm government should exist, to control by the force of law the excesses of individual will, and to compel within certain limits the action of individuals for the sake of the public good. Looking at their several influences upon the body of the Israelite people, how pernicious was the theft by Micah of his mother's hoarded treasure ; how injurious to the community was the idolatrous worship set up by Micah, and that for generation upon generation ; how disastrous to the commonwealth of Israel was the brutal outrage of the men of Gibeah ; how intolerable was the marauding expedition of the Danites, both to the quiet dwellers in the land and to peaceful neighbours beyond its border ; and what a complete loosen-ing of all the joints of social life do the several transactions display ! Nowhere do we see any common aim for the common good, but each man's covetousness, super-stition, lust, anger, cruelty, pursuing private objects at the expense of public interests. The ideas of a society, a commonwealth, a Church, a nation, were lost in individual selfishness. Now this was in a great measure due to the want of a central supreme authority to repress, to direct, and to overrule. Just as material nature, if the power of gravitation were removed, would fall to pieces, and all cohesion would be gone, so, without a common authority wielding the power of law, human society would fall to pieces, and be reduced to chaos. Men are blinded by their own passions ; par-ticular sections of society can see nothing but their own fancied interests ; lawless violence would plunder here ; impulsive zeal would rush onwards there ; a fanatical superstition would set up its altars where it ought not ; fierce rivalry would rise upon the ruins of its antagonist ; revenge would glut itself with destruction ; one trade would seek the suppression of all that stood in its way ; one interest would devour another, one class supplant another, one rank tread down another. It is the business of law wielded by sovereign power to look with an equal eye upon all the different interests of the State, to favour all by favouring none at the expense of others, to repress all individual action which would hurt the whole, and to regulate all the separate forces which would be injurious to the whole. Law, like the eye of God, is impartial in its look-out ; its end is to produce order, harmony, and peace. Under the even reign of law eccentric violence is unknown, and its steady but irresistible pressure gives consistency and strength to the whole fabric of society. Under its reign full scope is given to every energy for good, and all the scattered forces of the separate parts are concentrated for the benefit of the whole. Under its wholesome restraints the selfish passions of man are not allowed to injure themselves or others, and the folly of the foolish and the wickedness of the wicked are checked in their injurious courses. Not that which is right in his own eyes, and which self-will desires, but that which the law, the reflection of God's mind, commands, is the rule by which every man's actions must be squared. The perfection of a human polity is one in which wise laws govern the whole social movement as surely as the laws of nature govern the material world. It is the interest of all classes of the community to bow to this supremacy of law, and to unite in a firm compact to support the central authority in repressing every act of lawlessness, whether committed by an individual or by a company. It is only thus that social chaos can be avoided, and that civil cosmos, which alone is civilisation, can be maintained for the true liberty and welfare of mankind. It is just the same with the Church of God, which is the commonwealth of his saints. In it the word of God must reign supreme. In it individual opinions, sentiments, wishes, and feelings must all be subordinated to the Divine law. In it selfish eccentricities, ambitions, activities must all be restrained by a wise and even rule if the Church is to be the abode of order, peace, and love. In the surrender of individual will to the discipline of the supreme authority the sacred commonwealth finds its perfect balance, and each member is enabled to yield that service which indeed is perfect freedom; because the unchecked power to do that which is right in his own eyes is not a man's liberty, but his bondage. Self-will is set in motion by sin; but law is the fruit of wisdom and justice moving for the happiness of all, securing right, and stopping up the gangways of wrong. From the spirit of lawlessness deliver thy Church, O Lord!

HOMILIES BY VARIOUS AUTHORS.

Vers. 1—13.—*The history of a man-made ministry:*—2. *Its abuse.* A special instance of the manner in which it wrought mischief afforded in the migration of the Danites. The proximity of Micah's house to the great northern highway made it a natural resting-place for travellers, and so the spies find their way there. By them the young priest, who turns out to be a previous acquaintance, is recognised. The existence of the "house of gods" is thus made known, and they desire him to consult the oracle concerning their fortunes. Although their adventure was a wicked and unscrupulous one, they are told, "Go in peace: before the Lord is your way wherein ye go." The visit of the spies to Laish, their report to their brethren, and the setting out of the 600 Danites, who arrive in the first stage of their march once more at Micah's house, are then narrated. We see, therefore—

I. How A MERCENARY PRIESTHOOD AND SHRINE MAY BE PROSTITUTED TO BASE USES. The oracle at Shiloh was symbol and seal of the national· unity, and its priesthood represented the national conscience. It would have been impossible for them to sanction such a crime. But it was otherwise with Micah's priest and "house of gods." The latter was a mercantile speculation, a private enterprise, and was therefore obnoxious to any temptation like this. A striking parallel to this is afforded by the Church of Rome, with its sale of indulgences, &c.

II. How EAGER UNHOLY MEN ARE FOR RELIGIOUS SANCTIONS IN THEIR FRAUDULENT AND MURDEROUS DEEDS. When religion becomes a matter of money, and its advantages are sold to the highest bidder, it ceases to be the judge of right and wrong. The contradiction between the errand upon which they were sent and the spirit of God's revelation ought to have struck them. Yet this is but one instance of an all but universal error. They imagine that true religion can call evil good and good evil.

III. How THEREBY A TURBULENT TRIBE IS ENCOURAGED IN ITS DESIGNS UPON A PEACEFUL DISTRICT, AND A PERMANENT WRONG IS INFLICTED. The moral latent in the incident is thereby sharply pointed. It must appear to all how mischievous, how subversive of human society and of religion, such an institution must be. The only safeguard against such evils is in the central authority at Shiloh being recognised, and that authority being enforced by a duly elected king.—M.

Vers. 14—31.—3. *Its transfer and establishment in a lawless community.* The spies had evidently taken counsel with the 600, for the theft of the gods is done in a cool, business-like way; and they have evidently a settled design concerning them. Everything that would encumber or be detrimental to them is sent on in front. The real or feigned remonstrance of the priest, and his willing compliance with their desire, and the pursuit by Micah, are realistic touches that add greatly to the interest and naturalness of the narrative. That the slaughter, &c. at Laish was of the most horrible description is suggested—" There was no helper."

I. THOSE WHO SUBVERT THE PRINCIPLES OF MORALITY SHOULD NOT EXPECT TO BE TREATED ACCORDING TO THOSE PRINCIPLES.

II. HOWEVER APPARENTLY RELIGIOUS WRONG-DOERS ARE, THEIR CONDUCT DOES NOT LOSE ITS ESSENTIAL CHARACTER, AND WILL BE JUDGED. The record of the occurrence has preserved it for all time, and it is condemned before the bar of the righteous conscience.

III. THE GREATEST CARE SHOULD BE TAKEN AT THE FIRST INDICATION OF SCHISM OR ERROR, AS SUCH THINGS TEND TO PERPETUATE THEMSELVES. A regular priesthood is instituted, with its hereditary privileges and duties.

IV. THE REAL EFFECT OF SUCH RELIGIOUS MOVEMENTS IS TO THE DETRIMENT OF TRUE RELIGION. The "house of gods" at Laish is a rival to the "house of God" at Shiloh. During those early days of Hebrew nationalisation and religious training, the mischief and hindrance occasioned by it must have been enormous. True religion is ever opposed in the world. Its worst foes are those who most nearly resemble it in outward ceremony, but whose motives are impure.—M.

Vers. 23, 24.—4. *The idolater's distress.* Micah has at one fell swoop lost gods and ephod and priest. As his chief gains and his fancied importance were derived from this source, he was desolate.

I. THOSE WHOSE TRUST IS IN OUTWARD THINGS, AND WHOSE HEART IS BOUND UP IN THEM, ARE EXPOSED TO GRAVE DANGERS AND DISADVANTAGES. The losses of life; the anxieties and dreads; bereavement. The religion of external details, how easily disarranged! The whole "establishment" may be swept away!

II. THE SPIRITUALLY-MINDED ARE FREED FROM THESE CARES, AND ALTHOUGH SUF-FERING SIMILAR DEPRIVATIONS AND LOSSES, ARE NOT WITHOUT COMFORT. "God is a spirit, and they that worship him," &c. The heart that rests on Christ is secure against all outward perils. Forms, externals, &c. are not essential to true religion. The "means of grace" are not to become an end in themselves, and where the end is reached otherwise they can be dispensed with.—M.

Ver. 5.—*The religion of convenience.* I. MEN WHO ARE UNWILLING TO DO THE WILL OF GOD ARE SOMETIMES ANXIOUS TO SECURE HIS HELP. These Danites are little better than freebooters; they are determined to go their own way; they have no wish to be guided by God; they simply wish to be assured of success. So there are many who have sufficient religious faith to desire the blessing of God on their life, but not sufficient to submit to his guidance and authority. True loyalty to God will make us not merely consult him as to the success of our work, but as to its rightness, and not merely inquire whether the way in which we are determined to go shall prosper, but ask what way God would have us take.

II. THE PRAYER FOR PROSPERITY UNACCOMPANIED BY SUBMISSION TO GOD'S WILL DOES NOT JUSTIFY THE COURSE OF ACTION TO WHICH IT RELATES. We have superstitions about prayer. We are too ready to imagine that all is well if we have sought God's blessing upon our work. But we have only a right to ask for this when we are doing right. Prayer cannot sanctify a bad action. The Danites were not justified in their marauding expedition because they first consulted a supposed Divine oracle. Men seek God's blessing on their business while they conduct it dishonestly, on their country while they favour aggressive wars and national injustice, on their private lives while they pursue a worldly, perhaps even an immoral, course. Such conduct rather aggravates than mitigates guilt, because it betrays blindness of conscience in the searching light of God's presence.

III. AN ASSURANCE OF SUCCESS IS NO PROOF OF THE FAVOUR OF GOD. We are too ready to worship success as though it were a justification of the means by which it was attained. In this world, viewed from a human standpoint, goodness often fails and wickedness often succeeds. Our own feeling of assurance is no ground of reasonable confidence. They who are on the best of terms with themselves are not therefore on the best of terms with God. The timid, diffident, despondent soul may be really regarded with favour by God, while the vain, self-elated soul may be living under his frown. The faith which saves is not self-confidence nor the assurance of success, but submissive and obedient trust in a Lord and Saviour.

IV. THEY WHO MAKE A CONVENIENCE OF RELIGION WILL FIND IN THE END THAT IT WILL BE THEIR CONDEMNING JUDGE. The priest told the Danites that their way was before the Lord. God would watch them. They had invoked his name. They would see ultimately what his presence involved. The recognition of God which is involved in seeking his blessing will increase our condemnation if we disregard his will.—A.

Vers. 19, 20 —*The mercenary priest.* Greed and ambition are the besetting sins of depraved priests. Both of these evil characteristics are apparent in Micah's Levite.

I. THE PRIESTLY OFFICE IS DEGRADED BY MERCENARY GREED. Micah had adopted the Levite when he was homeless and destitute, and had treated him with the kindness of a father to his son ; yet as soon as he discovers a chance of better pay, the miserable man deserts and robs his patron. No man can serve God truly if the money wages of his service are the chief consideration with him. Though he may take such just payment as is given to him if he is God's faithful servant, he will, like the faithful Levites, feel that his real portion is the Eternal (Josh. xiii. 33). Such a man should also consider himself bound by ties of affection and friendly obligation to the people among whom he ministers. If he seeks promotion simply for the sake of pecuniary advantage, and irrespective of the loss which may be sustained in his present sphere, and of his possible unfitness for a larger sphere, he is guilty of gross worldliness and wicked selfishness.

II. THE PRIESTLY OFFICE IS DEGRADED BY SELFISH AMBITION. The Levite is tempted by the prospect of exercising his functions in a larger way as the priest of a tribe. Such an offer would only be possible in Israel under circumstances of religious decline and social disorder. Even then the Levite must have known that he was no priest at all according to the law of God, for he did not belong to the family of Aaron. But ambition tramples on law for its own advancement. Of course there are occasions when a man may naturally endeavour to rise in the world, and if he can be sure that he will extend his usefulness, it is his duty to do so. But— 1. The opportunity of enlarged service elsewhere is no justification for unfaithfulness to our present service. Plainly the Levite was treating his benefactor with unpardonable ingratitude and treachery in deserting him for the service of the Danites. 2. It is only a culpable ambition which will lead a man to seek a higher position simply for his own honour and profit, and not for the good of those who are intrusted to his care. The priest exists for the people, not the people for the priest. But the latter condition has been only too apparent in the course of the corruptions of Christendom. Office has been sought solely for the satisfaction of the greed and ambition of the aspirant. How contrary to the teaching of Christ, who said, " Whosoever will be great among you, let him be your servant " ! (Matt. xx. 27).—A.

Ver. 24.—*The lost gods.* Micah's distress at the loss of his gods and priest may be regarded on two sides—on the side of superstition and on that of genuine devotion.

I. THE SUPERSTITIOUS SIDE OF MICAH'S DISTRESS. 1. The god that can be stolen must be no true God. Micah should have seen the folly of his idolatry in the catastrophe which had befallen him. If the idols could not protect their own shrine, what could they do for their owner's home ? 2. The man whose character is corrupt is worthless as a priest. Yet after the Levite had behaved in the vilest way Micah still felt the loss of him bitterly. This distress came from his superstitious belief in the efficacy of the residence of an official priest in his house, no matter what was the baseness of the man's character or the emptiness of his services. 3. A religion which depends on any material things or human offices for its efficacy is foreign to the character of the spiritual worship of the true God. It was a mistake for Micah to suppose that he would lose the presence of God by losing the images which he had made, or the blessing of God by losing his priest. Nothing that is done to a man's outside life can affect his religious blessings. God dwells in the shrine of the heart. No persecution can rob us of his presence. The Waldenses in their mountain cave had lost every earthly comfort, but they had not lost God. God's blessings are not dependent on external ordinances, though these are the usual channels through which they flow. If we have no visible temple, altar, priest, or service, God can still bless us fully.

II. THE NATURAL SIDE OF MICAH'S DISTRESS. There is much in it which speaks well for Micah. Micah is a religious man. To him the loss of what he believes to be the source of religious blessings is a great trouble. Are not they who can lose the real presence of God in their hearts without any feeling of compunction far more astray than this man with all his idolatry and superstition? God is the light and life of the soul. How strange then that any should live without him and yet not know that anything "aileth" them! But whatever a man makes into a god for himself will interest him deeply. If he makes a god of his money, his art, his child, the loss of his god will plunge him into the darkness of despair. 1. Since we are thus deeply affected by the object of our supreme devotion, let us see that this is no earthly thing which can be stolen or destroyed, but the true, eternal God who will never leave us. 2. God sometimes takes from us the earthly treasures of which we have made gods that we may see the mistake of our idolatry, and so learn to lift up our hearts to the ever-abiding presence.—A.

EXPOSITION.

CHAPTER XIX.

Ver. 1.—**When there was no king** (ch. xvii. 6; xviii. 1; xxi. 25). It appears from ch. xx. 27, 28 that the events narrated in these three last chapters of the Book of Judges happened in the lifetime of Phinehas, and while the ark was at Shiloh (see ch. xx. 27, note). Phinehas evidently outlived Joshua (Josh. xxiv. 29, 33), though there is no evidence to show how long. The events in these chapters must have occurred in the interval between the death of Joshua and the death of Phinehas. **A certain Levite,** &c. It is a curious coincidence that both the Levite whose sad story is here told, and the Levite the son of Gershom of whom we read in the preceding chapters, were sojourners in the hill country of Ephraim, and also closely connected with Bethlehem-judah. Perhaps the legitimate inference (see ver. 18, and ch. xx. 26, 27) is that in both cases the Levites were drawn to Ephraim by the ark being at Shiloh, and also that there was a colony of Levites at Bethlehem-judah. Whether there was any connection between the presence of Levites at Bethlehem and the annual sacrifice at Bethlehem which existed in David's time, and which argues the existence of a high place there, can only be a matter of conjecture (see 1 Sam. ix. 13, and xx. 29). All we can say is that there was the universal prevalence of high-place worship during the time of the judges, and that the services of Levites were sought after in connection with it (ch. xvii. 13). **On the side.** Hebrew, *sides*. In the masculine form the word means the hip and upper part of the thigh; in the feminine, as here, it is applied only to inanimate objects, as a house,

the temple, a cave, the north, a pit, a country, &c., and is used in the dual number (see 1 Sam. xxiv. 4; 1 Kings vi. 16; Ps. xlviii. 3; cxxviii. 3; Isa. xxxvii. 24; Ezek. xxxii. 23, &c.). It means the innermost, hindmost, furthermost parts. Its application here to the northern side of Ephraim seems to imply that the writer wrote in the south, probably in Judah. **A concubine.** An inferior wife, who had not the same right for herself or for her children as the *wife* had (see Gen. xxv. 6).

Ver. 2.—**Played the whore,** &c. Perhaps the phrase only means that she revolted from him and left him. Her returning to her father's house, and his anxiety to make up the quarrel, both discourage taking the phrase in its worst sense. **Four whole months.** Literally, *days, four months;* meaning either *a year* and *four months,* as in 1 Sam. xxvii. 7, where, however, the *and* is expressed; or *days* (i. e. many days), viz., *four months.* For the use of *days* for *a year* see Exod. xiii. 10; Judges xvii. 10, &c.

Ver. 3.—**To bring her again.** So the Keri. But the Cethib has *to bring* him, *i. e.* it, *again,* viz., her heart. But the phrase *to speak to her heart* is such a common one for *to speak friendly* or *kindly* to any one that it is not likely that it should here be used otherwise, so that the pronoun should refer to *heart.* If the masculine is here the right reading, it may be an archaism making the suffix of the common gender like the plural suffix in ver. 24, which is masculine, though applied to women, and like the masculine pronoun itself, which is so used throughout the Pentateuch and elsewhere (see also ch. xxi. 12; Exod. i. 21). **A couple of asses.** One for himself and one for her. **He rejoiced.** No doubt, in part at least, because the expense of his daughter's maintenance would be transferred from himself to his daughter's husband.

Ver. 4.—**Retained him.** See the same phrase 2 Kings iv. 8, where it is rendered *she constrained him.* The full phrase is in Gen. xxi. 18, *hold him in thy hand.*

Ver. 5.—**Comfort thine heart, &c.** Compare Gen. xviii. 5.

Ver. 6. — **For the damsel's father had said,** &c., or rather, *And the damsel's father said.* He had not at first intended to stay on, but to go on his way after he had eaten and drunk (ver. 5). But when they had prolonged their carousal, the father of the damsel persuaded him to stay on another night.

Ver. 7.—**He lodged there again.** Literally, *he returned and lodged there.* The Septuagint and one Hebrew MS. read, *And he tarried and lodged there.*

Ver. 8. — **And they tarried.** It should rather be rendered in the imperative mood : *And tarry ye until the afternoon.* **So they did eat both of them.** The imperative *comfort thine heart* is in the singular because only the man and the father-in-law are represented throughout as *eating and drinking both of them together.* The imperative *tarry ye* is in the plural because it applies to the wife as well as the man.

Ver. 9.—**Draweth toward evening.** The Hebrew phrase, which is uncommon, is, *The day is slackening to become evening,* i. e. the heat and the light of the day are becoming slack and weak, and evening is coming on. **The day groweth to an end.** Another unusual phrase ; literally, *Behold the declining of the day,* or, as some render it, *the encamping of the day,* as if the sun after his day's journey was now pitching his tent for the night. **Go home.** Literally, *to thy tent,* as in ch. xx. 8. So the phrase, *To your tents, O Israel,* means, Go home (see 1 Kings xii. 16, &c.).

Ver. 10.—**Jebus.** See ch. i. 21, note. Jerusalem is numbered among Joshua's conquests at Josh. x. 23 ; xii. 10. But from this verse it would appear that the Israelite population had withdrawn and left the city to be entirely occupied by the Jebusites, who held it till the time of David (2 Sam. v. 6). Jerusalem is only about two hours from Bethlehem.

Ver. 12.—**Gibeah** (or ha-Gibeah, the hill). In the tribe of Benjamin (Josh. xviii. 28) ; Saul's birthplace. Its modern name is *Jeba.* It would be about two and a half hours' further journey from Jerusalem.

Ver. 13.—**Ramah** (ha-Ramah, the height). Now er-Râm, less than an hour's journey from Gibeah, both being about equi-distant from Jerusalem.

Ver. 15.—**A street of the city.** Rather, the broad space or place near the gate, such as is usual in an Oriental city (cf. Ruth iv. 1). **There was no man that took them into his house.** This absence of the common rites of hospitality toward strangers was a sign of the degraded character of the men of Gibeah (see Gen. xviii. 3—8 ; xix. 2, 3 ; Rom. xii. 13 ; Heb. xiii. 2 ; 1 Pet. iv. 9.

Ver. 16. — **Which was also of mount Ephraim.** The Hebrew is, *And the man was from the hill country of Ephraim.* It does not mean that he also, as well as the Levite, was from Ephraim.

Ver. 18.—**The side of mount Ephraim.** See ver. 1, note. **I am going to the house of the Lord,** *i. e.* to the tabernacle at Shiloh. But some translate the words I *frequent,* am *conversant with, walk* in, the house of the Lord, *i. e.* am a Levite. But the former seems the best rendering on the whole.

Ver. 19.—**Yet there is both straw, &c.,** *i. e.* he only wanted shelter, he had all his provisions with him, it was but little that he asked for, and yet no man would take him in.

Ver. 20.—**They washed their feet.** See Gen. xviii. 4 ; xix. 2 ; Luke vii. 34 ; 1 Tim. v. 10, &c.

Ver. 22.—**Making their hearts merry—** as in vers. 6, 9, and in ch. xvi. 25 ; Ruth iii. 7. But there is nothing in the expression implying any excess in drinking. **Bring forth the man.** The abandoned character of the men appears in this, that not only did they offer no hospitality to the stranger themselves, but were ready to violate the sanctity of the hospitality of the old man's house by their brutal violence. There must have been a fearful absence of all law and order and government when such deeds could be done without any interference on the part of magistrate or elder or ruler of any kind. The singular resemblance of the whole narrative to that in Gen. xix. suggests that the Israelites by their contact with the accursed Canaanites had reduced themselves to the level of Sodom and Gomorrah. Surely this shows the wisdom of the command to destroy utterly the workers of abomination. **Sons of Belial.** See ch. xx. 13, where the same Hebrew phrase is rendered *children of Belial.* Belial in this common phrase is not a proper name, but a noun meaning *worthlessness.* Sons or men of Belial means worthless fellows.

Ver. 23.—**He pleads the sanctity of hospitality.**

Ver. 25.—**The man took his concubine, &c.** One's blood boils at such selfish baseness and such cowardly cruelty. It is not quite clear whether *the man* means the Levite or the old Ephraimite.

Ver. 26.—**Till it was light,** or, as the words may mean, *at daylight.*

Ver. 27.—**The woman was fallen down at the door**, &c. Poor thing! with her last breath she turned to the house where he was who should have been her protector, but who had deserted her in her hour of need.

Ver. 29.—Compare 1 Sam. xi. 8.

Ver. 30.—**And it was so**, &c. Some translate this verse quite differently. They understand the whole verse as what the Levite said when he sent the twelve pieces of the murdered woman to the twelve tribes,

as thus: "*He sent her into all the coasts of Israel* (ver. 29), saying, *It shall come to pass that all who see it will say, There hath been nothing done and nothing seen like this from the day*, &c. But the A. V. makes very good sense, and the Hebrew will bear it. **Consider of it**, &c. The general sense of the whole nation was to call a national council to decide what to do. The Levite had succeeded in arousing the indignation of the twelve tribes to avenge his terrible wrong.

HOMILETICS.

Vers. 1—30.—*The downward progress.* It is certainly not without a purpose that we have in Holy Scripture from time to time exhibitions of sin in its most repulsive and revolting forms. The general rule which tells us that "it is a shame even to speak of those things which are done of them in secret" is, as it were, violated on these occasions, because it is more important that the depravity of which human nature is capable at its worst should be revealed, than that the blush of shame should be prevented by its concealment. Sin, in some of its forms, is so disguised, and toned down, and softened, that the natural mind of man does not shrink from it with abhorrence, or perceive its deadly nature, or its fatal consequences. But it is essential that sin should be known to be what it is, and especially that it should be made clear by what *gradual descents* a man may glide from one stage of wickedness to another, till, under favouring circumstances, he reaches a depth of vileness which at one time would have seemed impossible. The process by which this descent is reached is not difficult to trace. There is in every man a certain moral sense which restrains him from the commission of certain acts, whether of falsehood, dishonesty, cruelty, injustice, sensuality, or any other form of sin. And while that moral sense is maintained in its vigour, such acts may appear to him impossible for him to commit. But this moral sense is weakened, and more or less broken down, by every action done in contradiction to its authority. At each successive stage of descent there is a less shock to the weakened moral sense by the aspect of such or such sins than there was at the preceding stage. The sin appears less odious, and the resisting power is less strong. It is very true that in many instances, even after the moral sense is broken down, the force of public opinion, the sense of a man's own interests, habit, the authority of the law, and other causes external to a man's self, operate to keep him within certain bounds, and to restrain him from certain excesses of unrighteousness. But, on the other hand, it may and often does happen that these counteracting causes are not in operation. A man is placed in a society where public opinion countenances vice, where he does not seem to be in danger of any loss in reputation or in fortune by the basest acts of villainy, where the authority of law is in abeyance, and, in a word, where there is no barrier but the fear of God and his own moral sense to restrain him from the lowest depths of wickedness. Then the melancholy transition from light to darkness takes place without let or hindrance. Self-respect, honour, decency, kind feeling towards others, reverence for mankind, justice, shame, burn gradually with a dimmer and a dimmer light within, and finally the last spark of the light of humanity goes out, and leaves nothing but the horror of a great darkness, in which no crime or wickedness shocks, and no struggle of the conscience is kept up. The men of Gibeah had reached this fearful depth. Not suddenly, we may be sure, for *nemo repente fiet turpissimus;* but by a gradual downward progress. There must have been for them a time when God's mighty acts by the Red Sea, in the wilderness, in the wars of Canaan, were fresh in their thoughts, or in their, or their parents', memories. The great name of Joshua, the living example of Phinehas, the traditions of the surviving elders, must have set before them a standard of righteousness, and impressed them with a sense of being the people of God. But they had not acted up to their high calling. Doubtless they had mingled with the heathen and learnt their works. Their hearts had declined from God, from his fear and service. Idolatry had eaten as a canker into their moral principle. Its shameful licentiousness had enticed and overcome them. The Spirit of God was vexed within them. The light of his word was quenched in the darkness of a gross materialism. Utter callousness of conscience came on. They began to sneer at virtue, and to scoff at the fear of God. When the fear of God was gone, the honour due to man and due to themselves would soon go too. And thus it came to pass at the time of this history that the whole community was sunk to the level of the vilest heathenism. Hospitality to strangers, though those strangers were their own flesh and blood, there was none; pity for the homeless and weary, though one of them was a woman, there was none either; respect for neighbours and fellow-townsmen, common decency and humanity, and every feeling which distinguishes a man from a wild beast or a devil, had wholly left their vile breasts, and, people of God as they were by privilege and covenant, they were in their abandonedness wholly the children of the devil. The example thus recorded with unflinching truth is needed for our generation. The Israelites were separated from God by abominable idolatries. The attempt of our age is to separate men from God by a blasphemous denial of his Being. The result is the same, however it may be arrived at. Let the fear of God be once extinct in the human breast, and reverence for man and for a man's own nature will inevitably perish too. Virtue cannot survive godliness. The spirit of man is fed by the Spirit of God. Extinguish the spiritual, and nothing of man remains but the corrupt flesh. And man without spirit is no man at all. It is in the cultivation of spiritual affections, in the constant strengthening of the moral sense, in steady resistance to the first beginnings of sin, and in steadfast cleaving to God, that man's safety lies. It is in the maintenance of religion that the safety of society consists. Without the fear of God man would soon become a devil, and earth would become a hell.

HOMILIES BY VARIOUS AUTHORS.

Ver. 1.—Cf. on ch. xviii. 1—13.—M.

Vers. 4—10.—*Troublesome hospitality.* There is no more vivid picture of this extravagance. The Levite is delayed beyond all his reckoning, and perhaps through this is exposed to the evils subsequently narrated. There is a latent purpose betrayed by the anxiety of his host, which robs the offer of its simplicity and true hospitality. Like all who simulate a virtue for other than the mere love of it, he oversteps the bounds of modesty and decorum, and becomes an inconvenience instead of a help.

I. True hospitality should be for the sake of the guest, and not the host.

II. Excess of hospitality may entail inconvenience and wrong upon our guest.

III. Where hospitality is offered for some extrinsic purpose, it loses its true character.

IV. Christ the grand example of the host. His moderation; careful calculation as to needs of his guests; fulness of human sympathy; impartation of spiritual grace to the humbler viands.—M.

Vers. 14—21.—*Exceptional hospitality.* How *welcome!* Few of us but have at some time or other been belated in a strange place. We know nobody, and perhaps the people are reserved and suspicious. In such a case one friend, the only one, and, like this man, depending upon daily work for daily bread, becomes of inestimable service. The feeling of homelessness would be deepened in the case of the Levite when he recalled the good cheer from which he had come.

I. Those who have been strangers themselves are best able to sympathise with strangers. "He *sojourned* in Gibeah."

II. The poor are often more hospitable than the rich. Their occupation often introduces them to persons in distress. "What would the poor do if it were not for the poor?" Simplicity of life tends to cultivate true sympathy.

III. There is no place so wicked and unloving as to be without some witness to truth and goodness. What a hell this Gibeah! Yet in it was one "like unto the Son of man." What judgments he may have averted from its guilty inhabitants! Exceptional piety like this is no accidental thing; still less can it be the product of surrounding social influences. There are many ways in which we may serve our fellows, if the love of God be in our hearts. Perhaps the people thought him eccentric; many would despise him as poor and a stranger; but he was the one man who did God's work at a time when it sorely needed to be done. Shall not such hospitality be remembered in the kingdom? "I was an hungred, and ye gave me meat; I was thirsty, and ye gave me drink; I was a stranger, and ye took me in," &c. (Matt. xxv. 35, 40).—M.

Ver. 30.—*Unparalleled crime: the spirit and method in which its problems are to be met*   The narrative of the book has been gradually deepening in tragic interest and moral importance; it now reaches its climax. The sentence which the people themselves passed upon this crime is repeated, that public inquiry may be directed to the significance of it, to the causes of its production, and the means for preventing the recurrence of similar enormities. To the author the unity of the nation, publicly represented in the tabernacle at Shiloh and the throne of the new kingdom, as the outward symbols of theocratic government, is the grand specific, and the proof of this may be said to be the dogmatic purpose of his work. Studying the same problem in its modern illustrations, we are carried onward to a deeper and more radical cause, and, consequently, to the need of a more potent and inward influence of restraint and salvation. But do we study sufficiently, from the higher philosophic and religious standpoint, the great crimes that startle us from day to day? Would it not be a "means of grace" by no means to be despised were we to grapple with the spiritual and practical bearings of such occurrences? There could not well be a more judicious course in such events than that advised by the writer. It is terse, natural, philosophic.

I. PERSONAL MEDITATION. "*Consider it.*" In all its relations; our own as well as others. Let it show us the measure of public declension in morals and religion. Ask what neglect in the matter of education, social fellowship, or religious teaching and influence will account for it. How far am I as an individual in sympathy with the ideas, customs, and whole cast of public life in my time? How far am I my brother's keeper? Can anything be done to rouse the public conscience to a keener and more influential activity? How easy or how difficult would a similar crime be to myself? Prayers that I may be kept from such a thing, and may lead others into a better way.

II. CONSULTATION. Not at random, but of persons qualified to advise. The deliberations of the "Prisoners' Aid Society" would furnish a model for practical discussion. But "statistics" will never solve the problem. It is a question of human depravity, and a general repentance and alarmed attention is needed.

III. JUDGMENT. A careful, mature, well-informed and advised opinion; but, *as being the opinion of the nation, it must be carried into effect.* Something must be *done*, as well as thought. How valuable and influential such a judgment! It carries within itself the seeds of reformation and the conditions of recovery.—M.

Vers. 16—21.—*Hospitality.* I. THOUGH MEN WHO ARE ABANDONED TO SINFUL PLEASURES MAY DELIGHT IN THE SOCIETY OF BOON COMPANIONS, THEY WILL SHOW THEMSELVES WANTING IN THE GENEROSITY OF TRUE HOSPITALITY. The men of Gibeah would unite in seeming friendliness for riotous wickedness; but they were wanting in the almost universal Eastern kindness to the stranger. The intemperate and vicious may appear to be more generous in their boisterous freedom than persons of more strict habits; but they are too selfish for real generosity. Self-indulgence is essentially selfish; vice is naturally morose.

II. WE SHOULD ENDEAVOUR TO DO RIGHT, THOUGH THIS MAY BE CONTRARY TO THE EXAMPLE OF OUR NEIGHBOURS. The old man was shocked at the inhospitality of the men of Gibeah. He was not a native of the place, and though he may have lived there long, he retained the kinder habits of his native home. When at Rome we are not to do as Rome does if this is clearly wrong. Englishmen abroad may find it difficult to resist the bad social influences of foreign towns; but if they are Christians they will feel that the universal prevalence of a bad custom is no justification for their adoption of it. Yet how difficult it is to see our duty when this is contrary to the habits of the society in which we live, and how much more difficult to be independent and firm in performing it!

III. KINDNESS TO STRANGERS IS A DUTY OBLIGATORY UPON ALL OF US. The graphic picture of the old man returning from his work in the fields at even and taking note of the houseless strangers is the one relieving feature in the terrible story of that night's doings. Modern and Western habits may modify the form of our hospitality, but they cannot exonerate us from the duty to show similar kindness under similar circumstances. From the mythical gentleman who excused himself for not saving a drowning man because he had not been introduced to him, to the Yorkshire native, who, seeing a strange face in his hamlet, cried, "Let's heave a brick at him!" how common it is for people to limit their kindness to persons of their acquaintance! The parable of the good Samaritan teaches us that any one who needs our help is our neighbour (Luke x. 29—37).

IV. KINDNESS TO STRANGERS MAY BE REWARDED BY THE DISCOVERY OF UNKNOWN TIES OF FRIENDSHIP. The old man finds that the Levite comes from his own part of the country. Doubtless he was thus able to hear tidings of old acquaintances. The world is not so large as it appears. The stranger is often nearer to us than we suspect. Though true hospitality expects no return (Luke xiv. 12—14), it may find unlooked-for reward in newly-discovered friendly associations.—A.

Vers. 22—28.—*Monstrous wickedness.* Now and again the world is horrified by the news of some frightful atrocity before which ordinary sin looks almost virtuous. How is such wickedness possible?

I. MONSTROUS WICKEDNESS IS A FRUIT OF SELFISHNESS. The men of Gibeah were abandoned to gross self-indulgence till they utterly ignored the rights and sufferings of others. Nothing is so cruelly selfish as the degradation of that most unselfish affection love. When selfish pleasure is the one motive of conduct, men are blinded in conscience more than by any other influence.

II. MONSTROUS WICKEDNESS IS ATTAINED THROUGH SUCCESSIVE DEGREES OF DEPRAVITY. No man suddenly falls from innocence to gross licentiousness and heartless cruelty. The first step is slight; each following step seems but a small increase of sin, till the bottom of the very pit of iniquity is reached almost unconsciously. If the wicked man could have foreseen the depth of his fall from the first he would not have believed it possible. Men should beware of the first step downward.

III. MONSTROUS WICKEDNESS IS MOST ADVANCED IN THE SOCIETY OF MANY BAD MEN. As fire burns most when drawn together, vice is most inflamed when men are companions in wickedness. Each tempts the rest by his example. Guilt appears to be lessened by being shared. Men excuse their conduct by comparing it with that of their neighbours. Thus the greatest depravity is most often seen in cities—in the concourse of many men. In the excitement of a mob men will commit excesses from which they would shrink in solitary action. Yet responsibility is still individual, and each man must ultimately answer for his own sins.

IV. MONSTROUS WICKEDNESS IS MADE POSSIBLE BY THE VERY GREATNESS OF MAN'S NATURE. Human nature has a wide range of capacities. Man can rise infinitely above the brute, and he can fall infinitely below the brute. He can rise to the angelic, he can fall to the devilish. His originality of imagination, power of inventiveness, and freedom of will open to him avenues of evil as well as pathways of good which are closed to the more dull life of the animal world. The greater the capacity of the instrument, the more horrible is the discord which results from its getting out of tune. Those men who have the highest genius have the faculty for the worst sin. So tremendous is the capacity of the soul both for good and for evil, that the wise and humble man, fearing to trust it alone to the temptations of life, will learn to "commit it to the keeping of a faithful Creator" (1 Pet. iv. 19).—A.

Ver. 30.—*The duty of considering painful subjects.* I. IT IS WRONG FOR THE CHURCH TO IGNORE THE WICKEDNESS OF THE WORLD. The Church is not at liberty to enjoy the flowers and fruits of her "little garden walled around" to the neglect of the waste howling wilderness outside. She has no right to shut her eyes to the world's sin while she dreams fair dreams of the ultimate perfection of mankind. A good deal of foolish optimism is talked by people who will not take the trouble to inquire into the real state of society. That is a false fastidiousness which refuses to take note of dark subjects because they are revolting and contaminating. True purity will be shocked not simply at the knowledge of evil, but more at the existence of it, and will find expression not merely in shunning the sight of it, but in actively overcoming it. Such action, however, can only be taken after the evil has been recognised. It is, therefore, the work of the Church to consider seriously the fearful evils of profligacy, intemperance, and social corruption generally. The duty of contemplating heavenly things is no excuse for ignoring the evil of the world, which it is our express duty to enlighten and purify by means of the gospel of Christ.

II. Monstrous wickedness should excite deep and serious consideration. It is easy to be indignant. But the hasty passion of indignation may do more harm than good. It may strike in the wrong place; it may only touch superficial symptoms and leave the root of the evil; and it is likely to die down as quickly as it springs up. Great sins should be visited not with the rage of vindictiveness, but with grave, severe justice. We should " consider and take advice," reflect, consult, discuss the cause and the remedy. Undisciplined human nature will express horror and seek revenge at the revelation of a great crime. It wants Christian thoughtfulness and a deep, sad conviction of duty to practise self-restraint in the moment of indignation, and to investigate the painful subject with care after the interest of a temporary excitement has flagged.

III. It is our duty to speak out and take action in relation to painful subjects when anything can be done to effect an improvement. Evils are allowed to go unchecked because a false modesty dreads to speak of them. The men and women who overcome this and bravely advocate unpopular questions should be treated with all honour by the Christian Church. If the Christian does nothing to check the vicious practices and corrupt institutions which surround him, he becomes responsible for their continued existence.—A.

EXPOSITION.

CHAPTER XX.

Ver. 1. Went out, *i. e.* from their several homes to the place of meeting. **The congregation.** The technical term (not, however, found in Samuel and Kings, except in 1 Kings xii. 20) for the whole Israelitish people (Exod. xii. 3; xvi. 1, 2, 9; Levit. iv. 15; Josh. xviii. 1, &c.). **From Dan to Beersheba.** Dan, or Laish (ch. xviii. 29), being the northernmost point, and Beersheba (now *Bir-es-saba*, the springs so called) in the south of Judah the southernmost. It cannot be inferred with certainty from this expression that the Danite occupation of Laish had taken place at this time, though it may have done so, because we do not know when this narrative was written, and the phrase is only used as a proverbial expression familiar in the writer's time. **The land of Gilead.** In its widest sense, meaning the whole of trans-Jordanic Israel (see ch. x. 8; xi. 1, &c.). **Mizpeh,** or, as it is always written in Hebrew, *ham-Mizpeh*, with the article (see ch. xxi. 1). The Mizpeh here mentioned is not the same as the Mizpeh of ch. x. 17; xi. 11, 29, 34, which was in Gilead, but was situated in the tribe of Benjamin (Josh. xviii. 26). That it

was a national place of meeting in the time of Samuel is clear from 1 Sam. vii. 5—12, and we learn from ver. 16 of that same chapter that it was one of the places to which Samuel went on circuit. We find it a place of national meeting also in 1 Sam. x. 17, and even so late as 2 Kings xxv. 23, and in the time of the Maccabees (1 Macc. iii. 46). Its vicinity to Shiloh, where the tabernacle was, was probably one reason why it was made a centre to the whole congregation (see especially 1 Sam. x. 17, 22, 25). Its exact site is not known with certainty, but it is thought to be that of *Nebi Samuil*, from which Jerusalem is seen at about two hours' distance to the south-east. **Unto the Lord,** *i. e.* in the presence of the tabernacle, which was doubtless brought there, on so solemn an occasion, from Shiloh (cf. Exod. xxxiv. 34; Levit. i. 3; Judges xi. 11; xxi. 2, and ver. 26 of this chapter).

Ver. 2.—**The chief.** The word here used means the *corner-stones* of a building. Hence it is applied to the chief men, who, as it were, bind and keep together the whole people. Their presence at this great meeting is mentioned to show that it was a regularly constituted assembly of all Israel. The same phrase occurs 1 Sam. xiv. 38, and Isa. xix. 13 (*the stay of the tribes*, A. V.). The numbers (400,000) are of course those of the whole congregation. **The assembly of the people of God.** So, Numb. xvi. 3 ; xx. 4, Israel is called *the congregation of the Lord;* and Neh. xiii. 1, *the congregation of God.* Not dissimilar was the first great council of the Church, consisting of the Church (ἡ ἐκκλη- σια, *i. e.* the assembly of disciples) and the apostles and elders (who were the corner- stones, the *lapides angulares*, thereof). See Acts xv. 4, 6, 12. **Four hundred thousand.** See ver. 17. The enumeration in the wil- derness gave 603,550 (Numb. ii. 32 ; xi. 21), and at the second numbering 601,730 (Numb. xxvi. 51). In 1 Sam. xi. 8 a general assembly of the whole people, summoned by sending a piece of the flesh of a yoke of oxen "throughout all the coasts of Israel," amounted to 330,000. David's numbering gave of Israel 800,000, and of Judah 500,000, in all 1,300,000 ; but these were not as- sembled together, but numbered at their own homes. Jehoshaphat's men of war amounted to 1,160,000 according to 2 Chron. xvii. 14— 18. In the time of Amaziah there were of Judah alone 300,000 men able to go forth to war (2 Chron. xxiv. 6).

Ver. 3.—**The children of Benjamin heard,** &c. This seems to be mentioned to show that the absence of the Benjamites from the national council was not from ignorance, but from contumacy. **Tell us,** &c. This was addressed to all whom it might concern. The Levite answered.

Ver. 5.—**And thought to have slain me.** This was so far true that it is likely he was in fear of his life ; but he doubtless shaped his narrative so as to conceal his own coward- ice in the transaction. We have a similar example of an unfaithful narration of facts in the letter of Claudius Lysias to Felix (Acts xxiii. 27). **The men of Gibeah.** The *masters*, as in ch. ix. 2, meaning the citizens.

Ver. 7.—**Ye are all children of Israel.** He appeals to them as men bound to wipe away the shame and disgrace of their common country. He speaks with force and dignity under the sense of a grievous wrong and a crushing sorrow.

Ver. 8.—**The people**—with the emphatic meaning of *the whole people of Israel*, the *assembly of the people of God*, as in ver. 2. **As one man.** There was but one resolve, and one sentiment, and one expression of opinion, in that vast multitude. Not one would go home till due punishment had been inflicted upon Gibeah of Benjamin. **To his tent,** *i. e. home*, as in ch. xix. 9.

Ver. 9.—**We will go up by lot against it.** The words *we will go up* are not in the Hebrew, but are supplied by the Septuagint, who very likely found in their Hebrew copy

the word *na'aleh*, we will go up, which has since (perchance) fallen out of the Hebrew text from its resemblance to the following word *'aleha* against it. The sense will then be, Not one of us will shrink from the dangers of the war ; but we will cast lots who shall go up against Gibeah, and who shall be employed in collecting victuals for the army, 40,000 having to be told off for the latter service. And exactly in the same spirit (if indeed the answer was not actually given by lot) they inquired of the Lord who should go up first (in ver. 18), and, we may presume also, who should follow in the subsequent attacks, though this is omitted for brevity. Others, however, think the words *against it by lot* are purposely abrupt, and that the meaning is that Israel would deal with Gibeah as they had done with the Canaanites, viz., destroy their city, and divide its terri- tory by lot among the other tribes, after the analogy of Josh. xviii. 8—10. But this interpretation is not borne out by what actually happened, nor is the phrase a likely one to have been used.

Ver. 12.—**Tribe of Benjamin.** The Hebrew has *tribes*, meaning probably *families*, as the word is used Numb. iv. 18. *Vice versâ, family* is used for *tribe*, ch. xvii. 7 ; xviii. 11. **What wickedness,** &c. The message was perhaps too sharp and peremptory to be successful. It roused the pride and tribal independence of the Benjamites to resist. We must suppose the message to have pre- ceded in point of time the hostile gathering recorded in ver. 11. It was probably sent before the council broke up (see above, ch. vii. 25 ; viii. 4, and note).

Ver. 13.—**Children of Belial.** See ch. xix. 22, note. There seems to be a reference here to Deut. xiii. 12—15.

Ver. 14.—**But the children of Benjamin.** It should be *And the children*, &c. It is not dependent upon the preceding verse, but begins a new head of the narrative. **From the cities,** *i. e.* the different cities of the tribe of Benjamin, enumerated in Josh. xviii. 21— 28, twenty-six in number.

Ver. 15.—**Twenty and six thousand.** The numbers of Benjamin in the wilderness were at the first numbering 35,400, and at the second 45,600 (Numb. i. 36 ; ii. 23 ; xxvi. 41). It is impossible to account with cer- tainty for the falling off in the numbers by so many as near 20,000 ; but perhaps many were slain in the wars of Canaan, and the unsettled times were unfavourable to early marriages. For the whole of Israel there was, as appeared by ver. 2, note, a falling off of nearly 200,000 men, or, to speak exactly (601,730—400,000 +26,700), of 175,030. **Which were num- bered.** There is some obscurity in this latter clause ; but, in spite of the accents being opposed to it, the A. V. seems certainly right.

The rendering according to the accents, "they (the Benjamites) were numbered, besides the inhabitants of Gibeah, seven hundred chosen men," makes no sense, and does not explain who the 700 were. The population of Gibeah would be about 5 × 700, *i. e.* 3500, according to this statement.

Ver. 16.—**Seven hundred . . men left-handed.** It is curious that the tribe of Benjamin, which means *son of the right hand*, should have this peculiar institution of a corps of left-handed men. Ehud the Ben-

jamite was *a man left-handed* (ch. iii. 15 ; see also 1 Chron. xii. 2). The Roman name *Scævola* means *left-handed*. For the use of the sling see 1 Sam. xvii. 40, 49. Diodorus Siculus (quoted by Rosenmüller) mentions the remarkable skill of the inhabitants of the Balearic Islands in the use of the sling, adding, in terms very similar to those of the text, that they seldom miss their aim.

Ver. 17.—A repetition of the statement in ver. 2.

HOMILETICS.

Vers. 1—17.—*Temper.* It is impossible to suppose that the whole tribe of Benjamin really sympathised with the foul deed of the men of Gibeah, or could have felt otherwise than that such a deed deserved the severest punishment that could be inflicted. We must seek the cause, therefore, of their desperate resistance to the just decree of the nation in some other motive than that of consent to their brethren's "lewdness and folly." Nor is such motive far to seek. We find it in that unreasonable movement of human pride and selfishness which we commonly call *temper ;* a movement which sets up a man's own dignity, self-importance, self-will, self-esteem, above the laws of God, above righteousness, justice, truth, and the law of kindness, and yet so blinds him, that in vindication of his own dignity he does the most foolish and degrading actions, lowering himself where he sought to raise himself, making himself ridiculous where he thought to be an object of superior respect. Let us analyse the case of the Benjamites. Had the men of Gibeah belonged to the tribe of Ephraim or Judah, they would no doubt have been forward to join in their punishment. Their natural perceptions of right and wrong, their right feelings of the dishonour done to the whole congregation of Israel, the congregation of God, and of the profanation of the holy name of Jehovah, would have led them to wipe out the stain by the punishment of the offenders. But because the offenders were Benjamites, immediately all these right feelings were stifled, and in their stead the one selfish feeling that Benjamin would be dishonoured among the tribes, and that they themselves would be degraded in their fellow-tribesmen's shame, was allowed to prevail. Their pride was wounded and their temper was up. Possibly they had not been properly consulted in the first instance ; possibly the message sent to them was too peremptory and haughty ; possibly the other tribes, in their just indignation, had scarcely treated them with the deference due to brethren ; and if so, this was fresh fuel added to the flame of temper. But the result was that they were incapable of right feeling or of right judgment ; that they were blind to what duty and self-interest alike required of them ; and that, under the guidance of temper and stubborn pride, they rushed on to their own destruction, braving the wrath of a body nearly sixteen times as powerful as themselves, and withal tarnishing their own reputation by identifying themselves with the basest villainy. We see exactly the same results of temper on a smaller scale every day around us. Men will not do the right thing, or the just thing, or the wise thing, not because they are wicked and unjust and destitute of good sense under ordinary circumstances, but because their tempers are up. Their false pride blinds and enslaves them. They see a personal humiliation in the way of acting rightly ; their resentment against individuals for insult or wrong done to them stiffens their necks and hardens their will. If doing right will please them, or promote their interests, they had rather do wrong. They will not do anything they ask, or submit to any of their demands, however just they may be in themselves. And as for their own interests, and even their own good name, they are ready to sacrifice them at the imperious bidding of temper. Much of human unhappiness is caused by temper, which is as injurious to the peace of those who yield to its dictates as to those who are exposed to its outbreaks. It ought not to exist, certainly not to have dominion, in any Christian breast. Fellowship with the cross of Christ is the great help in subduing human pride. As real humility grows, as the mind which was in Christ Jesus is more perfectly formed within, as the old man is crucified with Christ, and the desire to do the perfect will of God displaces more and more the self-will, and the glory of God becomes more entirely the aim sought, in lieu of self-glorification, the dominion of temper becomes enfeebled, till, like a flickering flame, it goes out, and is still before the rising power of the Holy Spirit of God.

HOMILIES BY VARIOUS AUTHORS.

Ver. 1.—*National atonement.* There are times when a nation is stirred to its depths. Its consciousness is then a religious one. A solemn unity of sentiment pervades it, and prevails over all lesser differences. It is then ready and effective as the servant of the Lord. Observe—

I. THE UNIFYING INFLUENCES. 1. *A common detestation of the crime.* 2. *A common danger.* 3. *The Spirit of Jehovah.*

II. THE MEASURE DETERMINED ON. *By the council of the nation.* 1. *Immediate punishment of the criminals.* 2. *Failing their delivery, the punishment of those who protected them and condoned their wickedness.*—M.

Ver. 11.—*Union.* I. THE NATURE OF UNION. 1. This implies *conjunction.* The individuality of the parts is not destroyed when these are united. Each of the separate stones retains its shape after it is built into the common structure, and the union is formed by cementing all close together. So union amongst men does not destroy the personality and character of each man, but, instead of acting separately, men in union act in common. 2. This implies *harmony.* Conjunction without harmony brings not union, but confusion, and the nearer the conjunction, the fiercer is the internal conflict. Thus civil war is more cruel than war with a foreign nation, family feuds more bitter than quarrels with strangers. Harmony implies diversity, but agreement, as the several stones in a building, though each may be different in shape and size from others, fit in together, and fit the better because they are not all alike. 3. This implies the *subordination of the individual to the whole.* So far there may be a partial suppression of individuality; but in the end this develops a higher individuality. The several organs of the body are made not to exercise their functions for their own sakes, but for the good of the whole body. Yet this differentiation of parts allows of the more full development of each organ, and so leads to a more complete individuality in its form and character. When men are working under a social system, each is able to contribute his part to the good of the whole by a more free exercise of his own special talents than would be possible in a condition of isolation.

II. THE ADVANTAGES OF UNION. 1. Union increases *strength.* There is not only the gross force resulting from the addition of the units of force; there is a multiplication of strength, an economy of power. The nation can do as a whole what all its citizens could not do if acting separately. The Church can accomplish work for Christ which private Christians would fail to do. 2. Union promotes *peace.* When men are knit together as one they forget their private differences. Though we cannot attain the peace of uniformity, we should aim at securing the peace of harmony. 3. Union favours *growth and development.* Israel suffered from her disintegration. Her national unification was requisite for any solid advance of civilisation. This development of harmonised and organised union distinguishes civilised nations from savage tribes. As the Church learns to think more of common Christian charity than of narrow sectarian differences, she will advance in likeness to the mind of Christ and in the enjoyment of the graces and blessings of the gospel.

III. THE GROUNDS OF UNION. Men need some cause to draw them together—some common ground of union. 1. This may be found in a great wrong to be removed. A fearful crime stirred the hearts of all Israel. In presence of this the tribes forgot their minor grievances. Should not the great sin of the world be a call to Christians to sink their ceaseless quarrels in one united effort to destroy it with the power of Christ's truth? 2. This may be found in the attack of a common enemy. When the invader is on our coast, Tories and Radicals fight side by side, moved by a common instinct of patriotism. When the truth of Christianity is assailed by infidelity and her life by worldliness and vice, should we not all rally round the standard of our one Captain for a united crusade against the power of our common enemy the devil? 3. This may be found in a good cause of universally recognised merit. Fidelity to truth, love to mankind, devotion to Christ should unite all Christians.—A.

EXPOSITION.

Ver. 18.—**The house of God.** In this rendering the A. V. follows the Vulgate, which has *in domum Dei, hoc est, in Silo.* But the Septuagint has Βαιθήλ, and all the ancient authorities, as well as modern commentators, generally agree in rendering it *Bethel.* The reason, which seems a conclusive one, for so doing is that the Hebrew בית אל invariably means *Bethel,* and that *the house of God* is always expressed in Hebrew by בית האלהים (*beth-ha-elohim*). The conclusion is that at this time the ark of God, with the tabernacle, was at Bethel, which was only seven or eight miles from Shiloh. Bethel would be eight or ten miles from Gibeah, *i. e.* about half way between Shiloh and Gibeah. **Asked counsel.** The same phrase as ch. i. 1, where it is rendered simply *asked* (see note to ch. i. 1, and vers. 23, 47). In following this precedent the Israelites put the men of Gibeah on the footing of the Canaanite inhabitants of the land. With reference to ver. 9, it is worth considering whether this is not the fulfilment of the purpose there expressed by the Israelites, to go up against Gibeah *by lot;* either by understanding that the answer asked was given by a Divinely-directed *lot,* according to which Judah's turn came first (see Josh. vii. 14—18 ; 1 Sam. xiv. 41 ; Acts i. 24—26 ; &c.), or by taking the expression *by lot* in a wider sense, as meaning generally Divine direction.

Ver. 20.—**The men of Israel**—meaning here of course *the men of Judah.*

Ver. 21.—**Came forth out of Gibeah, &c.** Gibeah (sometimes called *Geba,* literally, *the hill*) was doubtless very difficult to assault, and the steep approach greatly favoured the defenders. The men of Judah probably came up carelessly, and with an overweening confidence, and so met with a terrible disaster. The word *destroyed* here used is the same as is applied to the destroying angel (Exod. xii. 23 ; 2 Sam. xxiv. 16 ; see also 2 Chron. xxiv. 23).

Ver. 23.—**And the children of Israel went up and wept, &c.** This verse must precede chronologically ver. 22, and explains the circumstances under which the battle referred to in ver. 22 took place. The unexpected repulse they had met with had begun to produce its intended effect. There was a humbling of themselves before God, a broken-

ness of spirit, a deepened sense of dependence upon God, and a softening of their feelings towards their *brother* Benjamin. All this was shown as they again went to the tabernacle at Bethel *to ask the Lord* (ver. 18).

Ver. 24.—**And,** or *so,* repeating what had been said in ver. 22, but giving it this time as the result of God's answer recorded in ver. 23. **The second day.** Not necessarily, or probably, the next day, but the day of the second battle.

Ver. 25.—**Of the children of Israel.** We are not told upon which tribe the lot fell, or the answer was given, that they should go up the second day.

Ver. 26.—**Then all the children of Israel, and all the people, &c.** Observe the word *all,* twice repeated, as showing how the whole congregation was roused and stirred to a man by this second reverse. *The people,* as distinguished from *the men of Israel,* the army, probably means the non-fighting people, the aged, the infirm, women, &c. **The house of God.** Render, as in ver. 18 (see note), *Bethel.* **Sat there.** Sitting with the Jews, especially on the ground, was the attitude of grief and mourning (Job ii. 13 ; Isa. xlvii. 1, 5 ; Lam. ii. 10, &c.). The Jews at the present day often sit on the ground at the place of wailing in Jerusalem. **Before the Lord,** *i. e.* before the tabernacle (see ch. xi. 11, note). **Fasted until evening.** The usual time for terminating a fast among the Jews, as at the present day among Mahomedans. For similar fasts on solemn occasions of national guilt or grief, see 1 Sam. vii. 6 ; 2 Sam. i. 12 ; Jer. xxxvi. 9 ; Neh. ix. 1 ; Joel i. 14, &c. **Peace offerings.** Usually thank offerings (Levit. iii. ; vii. 11, 12), but applicable to any voluntary sacrifice of which the flesh might be eaten the same day, or the day following, by the offerer (Levit. vii. 15, 16). Doubtless the people at the close of their fast ate the flesh of these peace offerings.

Ver. 27.—**Enquired of the Lord.** In the Hebrew, *Asked the Lord,* as in vers. 18, 23. **For the ark of the covenant, &c.** A most important statement, defining the time of these occurrences, within the lifetime of Phinehas, and also giving a strong intimation that the writer of these words lived after the tabernacle had been removed from Shiloh and its neighbourhood to Jerusalem. **Was there.**

Where? The natural answer to be given is, At Bethel; for Bethel is the only place that has been named. But it is not in accordance with the other intimations given us concerning the tabernacle, that Bethel should be its resting-place under the high priesthood of Phinehas. In Josh. xviii. 1 we have the formal pitching of the tabernacle of the congregation at Shiloh; in Josh. xxii. 12 we find it there, and Phinehas the son of Eleazar the priest before it; in 1 Sam. i. 3; ii. 14; iii. 21; iv. 3, we find it settled there till taken by the Philistines; and in Ps. lxxviii. 60 we find Shiloh described as the abode of the tabernacle till its capture by the Philistines, and there is no hint anywhere of Bethel or any other place having been the resting-place of the ark before it fell into the hands of the Philistines. Neither, again, is the explanation of some commentators, that the words *the ark . . . was there in those days* implies "that the ark of the covenant was only temporarily at Bethel," at all satisfactory. *In those days* has naturally a much wider and broader application, like the expression (ch. xvii. 6; xviii. 1), *In those days there was no king in Israel*, and contrasts the time of Phinehas and the judges with the times of the monarchy, when the ark and the high priest were at Jerusalem. Unless, therefore, we understand Bethel in vers. 18, 26, 31 to mean the house of God, which seems quite impossible, we must interpret the word *there* to mean Shiloh, and suppose that the writer took no count of the temporary removal to Bethel for the convenience of consultation, but considered that it was at Shiloh in one sense, though momentarily it was a few miles off. Possibly too in the fuller narrative, of which we have here the abridgment, the name of Shiloh was mentioned as that to which *there* referred.

Ver. 29.—**Set liers in wait.** Made wiser by misfortune, they now act cautiously.

Ver. 30.—**As at other times**, or, *this time as the other times* (see the same phrase, ver. 31, ch. xvi. 20; Numb. xxiv. 20).

Ver. 31.—**The house of God.** Here manifestly *Bethel*, as in the margin. **Gibeah in the field.** The A. V. is the natural rendering of the Hebrew words, which imply a *Gibeah in the field* different from *Gibeah*, as the Septuagint seems to have understood them (Γαβαὰ ἐν ἀγρῷ). It is a happy conjecture, borne out by the existing roads, that this Gibeah-in-the-field is the same as *Geba*, now *Jeba*. Indeed it is almost impossible to conceive how the pursuers, coming out of Gibeah, could be described as coming to two highways, of which one led to Bethel and the other to the very place they had come from. The latest explorers of the district fully concur in this identification of Gibeah-in-the-field with Jeba.

Ver. 32.—**And the children of Benjamin**, &c. This verse is parenthetical, being explanatory of the conduct of both parties. The Benjamites pursued recklessly, because they thought the fight was going as on the two previous days; the Israelites fled in order to draw them to the highways, and so to enable the ambushment to get between the Benjamite army and the city.

Ver. 33.—**Rose up out of their place.** The narrative is singularly obscure and broken, and difficult to follow. But the meaning seems to be, that when the Israelite army had reached Baal-tamar in their flight, they suddenly stopped and formed to give battle to the pursuing Benjamites. And at the same time the liers in wait came out from their ambushment and placed themselves in the rear of the Benjamites on the direct road to Gibeah. **Baal-tamar**, a place of palm trees. The site has not been identified, but may possibly, or probably, be the same as the palm tree of Deborah, between Ramah and Bethel (ch. iv. 5). **The meadows of Gibeah**, Hebrew, *Maareh-Geba*, may very likely have been, as the Septuagint takes it, a proper name, denoting some locality outside Gibeah (here called Geba) where the ambush was concealed. The meaning of the word *maareh* is thought to be a bare tract of ground without trees—something like a heath or common. It may have had pits, or deep depressions, where the ambush would be hid both from the city itself and from the high road, or other facilities for concealment.

Ver. 34.—**Against Gibeah**, *i. e.* against the army of Gibeah. The sense seems to be that the 10,000 Israelites who had been fleeing before Benjamin, and drawing them away from the city, now faced them, and commenced a resolute attack upon them, which at first the Benjamites, not knowing of the ambushment in their rear met with equal resolution, so that "the battle was sore." But the result, the details of which are given at length in vers. 36—46, was that 25,100 Benjamites fell that day (see ver. 46).

Vers. 36—41.—**The children of Benjamin saw that they were smitten.** Not of course after 25,000 of them had been smitten, but at that period of the battle more fully described in vers. 40, 41, when the Benjamites, looking behind them, saw Gibeah in flames, and immediately broke and fled towards the wilderness. In the latter half of this verse and in the following verses to ver. 41 the writer recapitulates all the preceding circumstances, some of which have been already mentioned, which led to the particular incident mentioned in the beginning of the verse, that "Benjamin saw that they were smitten;" viz., the feigned flight of the Israelites, the seizing and burning of Gibeah by the liers in wait, the signal of a great smoke, and the turning again of the flying Israelites. It was then that "the men of Benjamin saw that evil was come upon them," and turned their backs and fled. Thus vers. 36 (latter half)—41 bring us back through the details to the identical point already reached at the beginning of ver. 36. In vers. 39, 40 there is another retrograde movement in the narrative, in which the statement of vers. 31, 32 is repeated in order to bring into close juxtaposition Benjamin's keen pursuit of the enemy with his terror when he saw the smoke rising in his rear. **Hasted** (ver. 37). This is an amplification with further particulars of ver. 33. The liers in wait not only came forth out of their place, but they made a dash to get into Gibeah before the men of Gibeah, who were pursuing the flying Israelites, could be aware of their intention. **Rushed upon.** Perhaps better rendered *fell upon*. It is exactly the same phrase as 2 Sam. xxvii. 8, there rather tamely rendered *invaded* and in ver. 10 *made a road*. **Drew themselves along.** Some take the word in the common sense of *blowing the trumpet*, but it rather means *spread themselves out* (ἐξεχύθη, LXX.) through the defenceless city, so as to slay and burn in all parts simultaneously. **That they should make a great flame with smoke,** &c. (ver. 38). The Hebrew of this verse is difficult to construe, but the A. V. gives substantially the right sense. They seem to be the very orders given to the leader of the ambush. "Make them (the ambush) multiply to send up (*i. e.* send up in great quantities) the column of smoke from the city." It seems that the appearance of the smoke was the signal for the Israelites to turn (ver. 41). **The flame,** &c. (ver. 40). Rather, *the column began to go up in* (or *as*) *a pillar of smoke*. **The flame of the city.** Literally, *the whole of the city*, meaning of course the whole city in flames.

Ver. 42. — **Therefore they turned their backs,** &c. The narrative now at length advances one step. The result of the Benjamites finding themselves between the ambushment and the army of Israel was that they took to flight in an easterly direction (ver. 43) toward the wilderness, *i. e.* the wilderness described in Josh. xvi. 1 as "the wilderness that goeth up from Jericho throughout Mount Bethel," where the direction of the wilderness relative to Ephraim is also described as being "on the east." In like manner Zedekiah fled towards the *plain* (*arabah*) or plains of Jericho—a term nearly synonymous with *wilderness* (2 Kings xxv. 4, 5). **Them which came out of the cities,** &c. This is a very obscure passage, and is very variously explained. *Those which came out of the cities* must be the same as are so de-

scribed in ver. 15, and designates the Benjamites who were not inhabitants of Gibeah. The simplest way, therefore, to understand the passage is to render it without reference to the accents: "And the battle overtook him and those that were from the cities (*i. e.* the men of Gibeah and the rest of the Benjamites), destroying him (the whole Benjamite army) in the midst of him," *i. e.* going right into the midst of them, and destroying right and left. Some, however, render it *in the midst of it*, i. e. of the wilderness. The plural participle *destroying* agrees with the singular noun of multitude, *the battle* or *war*, meaning, *all the men of war*.

Ver. 43.—**Thus they inclosed,** &c. Another difficult passage, having all the appearance of being a quotation from some poetical description of the battle. The tenses of the verbs and the absence of any conjunctions in the Hebrew makes the diction like that of ch. v. 19. The italic words *thus* and the two *ands* ought to be omitted, to give the stately march of the original. "They inclosed, &c.; they chased them; they trod them down," &c. *They inclosed* seems to refer to the stratagem by which the Benjamites were *surrounded* by the ambush in their rear and the Israelites in front. Then came the pursuit—"they chased them;" then the massacre—"they trod them down." The three verbs describe the three stages of the battle. **With ease.** It does not seem possible that the Hebrew word *menuchah* can have this meaning. It means sometimes *a place of rest*, and sometimes *a state of rest*. Taking the latter meaning, the words *they trod them into rest* may mean *they quieted them by crushing them to death under their feet*, or *in rest* may mean *unresisting*. Some render it *unto Menuchah*, as if *Menuchah* was the name of a place, or *from Nochah*, as the Septuagint does. Others, *at the place of rest*, *i. e.* at every place where they halted to rest the enemy was upon them.

Vers. 44—46.—**And there fell,** &c. The account in ver. 35, anticipating the details of the battle, had already given the gross number of casualties in the Benjamite army on this disastrous day as 25,100. We now have the items of the account, viz., 18,000 in the pursuit, in the open plain ; 5000 in the highways, *i. e.* either the highways mentioned in ver. 31, or, as the expression *gleaning* rather intimates, the highways by which straggling bodies tried to reach any neighbouring cities after the great slaughter had taken place ; and 2000 more who were making for Gidom ; in all 25,000, which is only 100 men short of the reckoning in ver. 35. **The rock of Rimmon.** See ver. 47, note. **Gidom.** Not elsewhere mentioned, nor identified with any modern name.

Ver. 47.—**But six hundred men turned.**

If these 600 survivors are added to the 25,000, or 25,100, enumerated as slain (vers. 35, 44), it gives a total of 25,700. But the total number of Benjamites, as given in ver. 15, was 26,700. There remain, therefore, 1000 men unaccounted for. These may have been killed partly in the two first days' successful battles (vers. 21, 25), and partly in the different cities into which they had escaped, when the general massacre recorded in ver. 48 took place. **The rock Rimmon.** There are two proposed identifications of this place. One makes it the same as *Rummon*, "a village perched on the summit of a conical chalky hill," "rising on the south side to a height of several hundred feet from the Wady Muti-yâh," and defended on the west side "by a cross valley of great depth," which lies three miles east of Bethel, and seven miles north-east of Gibeah (Tuleil el-Ful), and is situated in the wilderness between the highlands of Benjamin and the Jordan. This is advocated by Robinson ('Biblical Researches,' i. 440), by Mr. Grove in the 'Dictionary of the Bible,' and by Lt. Conder ('Quart. State. for July 1880,' P. 173). The other is advocated by Mr. W. F. Birch ('Pal. Expl., Quart. State. for April 1880'). This identifies it with the *Wady er-Rummon*, discovered by Mr. Rawnsley, where there is a vast cave, *Mugharet el Jai*, about a mile and a half from Geba, capable, according to the local tradition, of holding 600 men, and used to the present day by the villagers as a place of refuge from the government persecutions According to this view, the statement that they abode *in* the rock Rimmon is strictly correct.

Ver. 48.—**Turned again**, not the same word as the *turned* of vers. 45, 47, but *turned back*, came again by the way by which they had gone in pursuit of the Benjamites, and on their return towards Bethel (ch. xxi. 2) entered into all the Benjamite cities, which lay thick together east and north of Gibeah, and ruthlessly put all the remaining population to the sword ; burning all the cities, and treating the whole tribe of Benjamin, with all that belonged to them, as a *'herem*, a thing devoted to utter destruction, like Jericho.

HOMILETICS.

Vers. 18—48.— *Pure and impure zeal.* That the indignation of Israel was justly excited by the wickedness of the men of Gibeah who can doubt ? That they had a just cause of quarrel with the men of Benjamin for refusing to join them in the punishment of the offenders is no less certain. But that the merciless destruction of the whole tribe by fire and sword was a ferocious and cruel deed equally admits of no contradiction. A state of mind, therefore, was generated between the first rising of their wrath on account of the foul crime of their countrymen, and the final execution of the fierce vengeance, which calls for our notice and our reprobation. That state of mind was what the Greeks called ζῆλος, a burning, unreasoning passion or heat, which hurries men on to words or actions of which in their cooler moments they repent and are ashamed. Under the influence of such passion, whether it be anger, or jealousy, or envy, or any other intemperate emotion of the mind, men are no longer their own masters. As in the case of that state of feeling which we lately considered under the name of *temper* (Homiletics on ch. xx. 1—17), reason ceases to guide and control the actions, and the voice of conscience cannot make itself heard. The man is like a ship without a rudder, driven by the storm whither he would not. Now when we consider that under the influence of passion we are liable to say and do things that are wrong, and that are very contrary to our own real feelings and opinions, and, maybe, very hurtful to our neighbours, it is obvious how watchful every Christian man should be to keep such passion under strict control, and to set a watch upon the various movements of his heart. This is doubly necessary, because, as we have seen in the history before us, what in its beginning is right is apt in its course to become wrong. It is not merely a question of degree. But for the most part the *nature* of the passion changes in its onward flow. Thus, in the case of the Israelites, the first feeling of indignation at a great wrong, the shame at the pollution of the name of Israel, their common inheritance, and their grief at the dishonour done to the name of God, were righteous and commendable feelings. There was no need to water them down or to reason them away. It would have been base and wrong not to follow them out to their legitimate consequences in action. But in the course of doing so the pure stream became fouled by far baser passion. Anger at the contradiction and opposition offered to themselves, wounded pride at the success of their adversaries in the first days' battles, the fierce determination to quell and destroy their enemies, and the heat and blood-thirstiness which are the natural result of war and strife, lashed them into madness. And so it is with ourselves. In war, in politics, in private quarrels, though we may begin by being in the right, yet the original cause is often lost sight of in the progress of the strife, and new jealousies, personal enmities, selfish resentments, and unwarrantable violence of feeling, which spring up, as it were, by the way, are allowed to get possession of us, and hurry us on to injustice and wrong. But especially does this painful narrative suggest a caution to those who take upon themselves to be the champions of right as against wrong to be very careful that no mere passions mix themselves up with their championship. We would say to every Christian brother, Be very zealous for right against wrong. Be very zealous for truth against falsehood. HAVE NO RESPECT OF PERSONS; and be as firm in rebuking wrong when it is found in those nearest and dearest to you as when it is found in strangers or enemies; and when it is found in the great and honourable, as when it is found in the meanest and lowest of mankind. But be very careful to keep your zeal pure. Let it be a simple zeal for God's honour and glory, and for his law and his truth. It will then never betray you into wrong speaking or wrong doing; and, moreover, it will effect its purpose among men. It will be a real witness for God, and it will make itself felt. While mere anger and passion are utterly feeble and worthless, and usually injure the cause they are meant to serve, the calm, steadfast opposition to wrong, by word or deed, will always have its weight. Such was the testimony of the words and life of the Lord Jesus upon earth. His zeal for his Father's honour was as a consuming fire; but it went hand in hand with an inexhaustible patience and gentleness towards men. We always feel in reading the Gospels that his severest rebukes sprang from his hatred for sin, and were combined with infinite love for the sinner. His whole life was a protest against wrong, but as gentle as it was firm, as winning as it was decided. Such should be the rebukes of his disciples—springing from principle, not from passion; severe, yet tender; unflinching, but never given without necessity; not unmixed with sympathy for the pain they cause, and anxiety to add the balm of love and forgiveness so soon as they have wrought repentance; never aggravated by personal feelings or heat of anger; never uttered in scorn, or with a sense of the rebuker's own superiority; but the outcome of an upright mind hating evil and zealous for God's honour, yet at the same time clothed with humility and tempered with heavenly charity.

HOMILIES BY VARIOUS AUTHORS.

Ver. 18.—Cf. on ch. i. ver. 1.—M.

Vers. 26—28.—*The difficulty of punishing evil-doers.* It is a desperate strife. The avengers are at first punished more than the guilty. Yet they continue steadfast, and humiliate themselves before God.

I. PRIVATE WRONGS ARE PUBLIC MISFORTUNES AND DANGERS. It was a peril to all peace-loving citizens that one of their number should suffer outrage. Yet also was it a further trouble and loss to punish such transgressors. How many will rather suffer wrong than take the trouble to bring it to justice! This is treason to the commonwealth.

II. HOW HARD IT IS TO ROOT OUT AN INDIVIDUAL OR NATIONAL SIN. How many are found to sympathise with or condone the deed, and to shield the transgressor! What ties connect the transgressor with ourselves!

III. THE SIN OF ONE IS OFTEN DUE TO THE GENERAL SPIRIT AND CONDITION OF THOSE AROUND HIM; THEY ALSO ARE GUILTY WITH HIM. Benjamin is but an exaggeration of the prevalent tone and manners of the time. Many crimes and sins of individuals may be traced up to wider influences. The sin or the righteousness of our brother is, in a measure, our own. Vicarious suffering and atonement.

IV. THE DUTY OF RIGHTING WRONG MUST BE CARRIED OUT AT WHATEVER EXPENSE OF TROUBLE AND LOSS. The humiliation of Israel. Defeat only nerves them to a higher and more heroic struggle. Religious principle and feeling are more influentially present. The absolute claim of God's righteousness. Like Israel the Church has to right a great wrong; but in a different way. Frequent discomfiture. The difficulty of evangelising one's own neighbourhood; far less the world! Yet it *has to be done*, and it can be done; but not in our own strength. Only as we submit ourselves wholly to God and his Son can we fulfil the mighty task. Let us too wait upon God, and pluck wisdom and heroism from defeat. The Spirit of God is with us, and the promise of Christ is ours.—M.

Ver. 34.—" *They knew not that evil was near them.*" How descriptive this of all men! Our misfortunes often overtake us unawares. There is no earthly security. The sinner especially should not encourage himself in fancied immunity. The Son of man cometh as a thief in the night, for judgment and for reward.

I. THE UNCERTAIN NATURE OF THE FUTURE.

II. THE IGNORANCE AND HEEDLESSNESS OF SINNERS RESPECTING GOD'S JUDGMENTS.

III. HOW TO BE DELIVERED FROM FEAR AND THE REAL EVILS OF THIS IGNORANCE. A righteous life the great safeguard. But how attained? Christ's the only authoritative " Fear not." External evils will through him minister to our eternal welfare and well-being. This trust in him should be implicit, and an active force in every life.—M.

Ver. 23.—*Lessons of defeat.* The Christian sometimes encounters defeat in the enterprises of spiritual warfare—in the battle of the inner life, in efforts to destroy the wickedness and misery of the world, in missionary campaigns.

I. DEFEAT SHOULD AROUSE REFLECTION. The Israelites had acted hastily under the impulse of sudden indignation. In defeat they were thrown back to think of the object and methods of their war. This war against a brother tribe was a terrible undertaking. Was it necessary? No war should be undertaken till it is absolutely necessary. It may be our duty to oppose our own brethren; but this should be done only after serious reflection. We are sometimes allowed to fail that we may consider more deeply all that is involved in actions attended with serious consequences.

II. DEFEAT SHOULD INDUCE HUMILITY AND REPENTANCE. The Israelites had been too self-confident. Enraged at the wickedness of one town, they had not realised their own sin, nor how this wickedness was but one act of national depravity. They were now the champions of justice. The position thus assumed by them would blind them to their own failings and stimulate pride. When Christian men do battle against some monstrous evil, they too are in danger of falling into similar failings of pride and self-righteousness. Defeat is then a wholesome humiliation leading to repentance. If we are to testify against the sin of others, we too must not forget that we also are sinners.

III. DEFEAT SHOULD LEAD US TO SEEK COUNSEL OF GOD. 1. The Israelites had consulted some oracle, some " gods," before going to war. After defeat they turned to the true God, the Eternal. We often need to fail before we will learn to pray. Then we see that our wisdom is to follow God's will. 2. The Israelites did not simply ask for success. They asked whether or no they should go up to war. We should not pray for God's blessing on the enterprise which we are obstinately pursuing irrespective of his will, but should first ask for light to teach us whether we should pursue it. 3. The Israelites did not ask for God's strength, but only for his guidance. Perhaps if they had invoked his aid they would not have failed a second time. We need trust in God and reliance on his help for perfect success.

IV. DEFEAT SHOULD LEAD TO RENEWED AND IMPROVED EFFORT. Through repeated defeats Israel persevered on to victory. So it is with the Christian. " Though he fall, he shall not be utterly cast down " (Ps. xxxvii. 24).—A.

Ver. 47.—" *An escaped remnant.*" I. THERE IS USUALLY AN ESCAPED REMNANT FROM THE MOST SEVERE PROVIDENTIAL ACT OF JUDGMENT. So it was in the flood, in the destruction of the cities of the plain, in the captivity, in the conquest of Jerusalem by the Romans. God does not totally destroy. Mercy is mingled with judgment. Though this is some mitigation of the calamity, it is no reason for rash indifference to danger, because (1) the remnant may be but a small minority, (2) none can tell whether they will be included in it, and (3) the remnant, though escaping the worst fate, suffers great hardships.

II. THE REMNANT DOES NOT NECESSARILY CONSIST OF BETTER MEN THAN THOSE WHO ARE DESTROYED. If one is taken and another left, this diversity of treatment is no proof of difference of character. As they who are subject to signal calamities are not to be regarded as especially wicked (e. g. Job, the men on whom the tower of Siloam fell, &c.), so those who are favoured by remarkable deliverances have no right to be considered especially virtuous. Their position is one to excite special gratitude, but not to encourage pride. Sometimes, indeed, it is dishonourable to them. It may be a result of cowardice, indolence, or falsehood. The traitor may escape while the true man falls. Barabbas escaped while Christ was crucified. In times of persecution the unfaithful are saved and the faithful suffer martyrdom.

III. THERE IS A PROVIDENTIAL END TO BE SECURED BY THE PRESERVATION OF A REMNANT. The idea of "the remnant" is familiar to the reader of Scripture (e. g. Isa. i. 9). There must be some Divine purpose in it. Can we discover that purpose? Possibly it is this—every nation, every tribe, every community of men which has special characteristics of its own has also a special mission to the world dependent on those characteristics. If, therefore, it is entirely blotted out of existence, the fruits of that mission will be lost to the world. A remnant is spared that the special gifts may be transmitted through a small hereditary line, and thus be preserved and turned to the continued service of the world. Israel had a mission to the world dependent on her peculiar endowments. If the remnant of Israel had not been delivered from Babylon, this mission would have been destroyed, and the human side of the origin of Christianity, such as we now see it, made impossible. Benjamin had a mission. From this tribe sprang the first king of Israel and the chief of Christ's apostles. If the 600 Benjamites had not been spared St. Paul would never have appeared.—A.

EXPOSITION.

CHAPTER XXI.

Ver. 1.—**Now the men of Israel**, &c. A circumstance not mentioned before is now brought forward, as is another in ver. 5, on which the events about to be narrated in this chapter depend, viz., that the men of Israel had taken two solemn oaths at Mizpeh (ch. xx. 1)—the one that no Israelite would give his daughter in marriage to a Benjamite; the other that whosoever did not come up to the national assembly there should be put to death.

Ver. 2.—**And the people**, &c. The narrative now proceeds. After *the people*, i. e. the Israelite army, so described ch. xx. 3, 8, 22, &c., had finished the work of destruction in the cities of Benjamin, they returned to Bethel (**the house of God**, A. V., here and in ch. xx. 18, 26, 31, where see notes), and, their rage having now subsided, gave way to violent grief on account of the destruction of Benjamin their brother. With passionate Oriental feelings they passed the whole day weeping, and probably fasting (see ch. xx. 26), before the tabernacle. **Wept sore**. Hebrew, *wept a great weeping*. The expression **lifted up their voices** shows that it was a loud wailing and lamentation.

Ver. 3. — **And said.** Better, *And they said.* **One tribe lacking.** The existence of the twelve tribes was an essential part of their covenant existence as the people of God

(Gen. xxxv. 22; xlix. 28; Exod. xxiv. 4; Numb. i. 5—15; Josh. iv. 3, 4, &c.; Matt. xix. 28; James i. 1; Rev. vii. 4, &c.). With one tribe missing Israel would be no longer Israel.

Ver. 4.—**Offered burnt offerings and peace offerings.** See ch. xx. 26, note.

Ver. 5.—**And the children of Israel said.** The idea evidently occurred to them that they might supply wives to the 600 Benjamites in the way that actually came to pass, and they asked the question, *Who is there among all the tribes*, &c., with this view.

Vers. 6—9.—**And the children of Israel**, &c. This verse goes back a little to explain why the children of Israel asked the question, viz., because they repented them for Benjamin, and wished to repair the mischief resulting from their rash oath not to give their daughters to a Benjamite; therefore they said (repeating ver. 5), What one is there that came not up to Mizpeh? (ver. 8) and on numbering the people it was found that no one had come up from **Jabesh-gilead**. This is the first time that Jabesh-gilead is mentioned in Scripture. It comes up twice afterwards. First in 1 Sam. xi., on occasion of its being besieged by the Ammonites and rescued by Saul; and secondly in 1 Sam. xxxi. 11—13, when the inhabitants of Jabesh-gilead took down the bodies of Saul and his sons from the wall of Beth-shan, and buried them at Jabesh, for which **brave and pious** act David thanked them (2 Sam. ii. 5). The name of *Jabesh* is only preserved in the Wady *Yabis*, which debouches on the eastern bank of the Jordan about lat. 32·24. Robinson thinks the ruins called ed Deir in this valley are the remains of Jabesh, which agrees exactly with the situation assigned to it by Eusebius in the ' Onomasticon.'

Vers. 10, 11.—**Ye shall utterly destroy,** &c. Devote to destruction, as a '*herem*, an accursed thing. They followed in the severity of the punishment the precedent of the destruction of the Midianites (see Numb. xxxi. 17), and even in the numbers sent to destroy them—a thousand from every tribe (Numb. xxxi. 5). Revolting to our feelings as such wholesale massacres are, including women and children, it must be remembered in mitigation that the '*herem* was the solemn devotion of a thing or person to destruction under the sanction of an oath. **Of the valiantest.** *The sons of valour* simply means *valiant men* (2 Sam. xiii. 28 ; xvii. 10).

Ver. 12.—**To Shiloh,** whither it should seem they had now taken the tabernacle back, the war with Benjamin no longer requiring its presence at Bethel. **Them.** It is masculine in the Hebrew, though it refers to the women. So again in ver. 22, *their fathers and their brothers* in the masculine (see above, ch. xix. 23, and vers. 21, 22). It is perhaps an archaism. **In the land of Canaan.** This is inserted to contrast it with Jabesh in Gilead (Gen. xxxiii. 17, 18, and ch. viii. 5, note).

Ver. 13.—Translate the whole verse thus : *And the whole congregation sent and spake to the children of Benjamin, &c., and proclaimed peace to them* (see Deut. xx. 10). They sent ambassadors or heralds to them as it were with a flag of truce.

Ver. 14.—**Benjamin came again,** i. e. *returned* to their own homes in the tribe of Benjamin, as in ver. 23. **Yet so they sufficed them not** — or, *Yet so they* (the Israelites) *did not provide enough for them* (the Benjamites) ; or, *Yet so they* (the Benjamites) *had not enough for themselves.*

Ver. 16.—**Seeing the women.** It is rather more in accordance with the Hebrew style to take the words as the narrator's explanation of the question, *What shall we do?* They said this because all the women of Benjamin had been destroyed.

Ver. 17.—**There must be an inheritance for them that be escaped of Benjamin.** The passage is difficult to construe and to explain. If the words *There must be* are properly supplied in the A. V., the sense will come out more clearly if we take the word *inheritance* to mean rather *succession*, which is the idea contained in the root. *There must be a succession for the escaped of Benjamin,* i. e. there

must be heirs to succeed, and therefore we must find wives for them. The word *peleytah* without the article can hardly mean *the remnant*, as has been proposed, but must be defined by being taken with *Benjamin*.

Ver. 18.—**We are not able.** Note again the evil of rash vows, and how often chicanery is necessary in order to evade their evil consequences.

Ver. 19.—**There is a feast of the Lord in Shiloh yearly.** Compare the exactly similar description, 1 Sam. i. 3, 7. There is a great difference of opinion among commentators as to what feast is here meant. Hengstenberg, Keil, Delitzsch, and others think it was the passover ; Bishop Patrick and others think it was the feast of tabernacles, a more joyous feast; Rosenmüller and others think it was a festival peculiar to Shiloh, after the analogy of the yearly sacrifice of the family of Jesse at Bethlehem (1 Sam. xx. 29), and more or less in accordance with Deut. xii. 10—12. It is not easy to say which view is right, but the last seems not improbable. **In a place which is on the north side,** &c. The words *in a place* are not in the Hebrew, and do not seem to be implied by the context. But the description is that of the situation of Shiloh itself, which is very exact (see ' Palestine Exploration Fund,' Map of West Palestine). **Lebonah** survives in el - Lubbun, about two miles north-west of Seilûn, and to the west of the road to Shechem or Nablûs. It seems strange that so particular a description of the situation of Shiloh should be given ; but it may probably indicate that the writer lived after the tabernacle had been moved to Jerusalem, and Shiloh had relapsed into an obscure village (see ch. xx. 27, note). The situation of the descriptive words in the Hebrew, with the pronoun *which*, separated from *Shiloh* by the word *yearly*, indicates that they are an explanation added by the narrator.

Ver. 21.—**Come out.** The verb is in the masculine gender, though *the daughters of Shiloh* is the subject (see above, ver. 12, note). **To dance in dances.** Bishop Patrick says that the feast of tabernacles was the only feast at which Jewish maidens were permitted to dance. **Go to the land of Benjamin.** The close vicinity of the high road leading from Shechem to Bethel on the border of Benjamin would facilitate their flight.

Ver. 22.—**Be favourable unto them for our sakes.** Rather, *Grant us them as a favour*, the masculine *them* referring to *the daughters of Shiloh*, as in ver. 12, and the verb *grant a favour* being followed by a double accusative. **We reserved not to each man his wife,** &c. These words are somewhat difficult. If we may insert the word *to*, as the A. V. does, before *each man* (for it is wanting in the Hebrew), the sense is good. The Israelites acknowledge their own fault in not reserving women enough to be wives to the Benjamites, and ask the fathers and brothers of the daughters of Shiloh to do them a favour by enabling them to repair their fault. But it is rather a strain upon the words. The omission of the *to* is not natural in such a phrase (Numb. xxvi. 54 is hardly to the point, nor is Gen. xli. 12, where the *to* had been expressed before the *us*), and *reserved* is a forced interpretation of the verb. If the words were spoken by the Benjamites, all would be plain and easy: "We receive not each man his wife in the war." Hence some put the speech into the mouth of Benjamin, as though the Israelites meant, We will say in your names, in your persons, as your attorneys, so to speak, "Grant them to us," &c. But this is rather forced. Others, therefore, follow the Peschito, and read, "*because* THEY received not each man his wife," &c., which makes very good sense, but has not MS. authority. **Ye did not give,** &c., *i. e.* you need not fear the guilt of the broken oath, because you did not *give* your daughters, so as to violate the oath (ver. 7), but they were taken from you by force. The A. V. gives the probable meaning of the passage, though it is somewhat obscure.

Ver. 23.—**According to their number,** *i. e.* so as to provide the 200 with wives. **The cities,** as in ch. xx. 15, 42.

Ver. 24.—**Every man to his inheritance.** Compare the breaking up of the national assembly in the days of Joshua (Josh. xxiv. 28; Judges ii. 6).

Ver. 25.—**In those days,** &c. See ch. xvii. 6; xviii. 1, &c.

HOMILETICS.

Vers. 1—25.—*War.* Who can think of the flourishing tribe of Benjamin reduced to a handful of 600 men, clinging for life to an inaccessible rock, but having to mourn the loss of wives and daughters, and sisters and children, all ruthlessly slaughtered with the edge of the sword, and not shudder at the horrors of war? It is a distressing picture to bring before the mind, but the picture must be looked at in its details if we would form a right judgment on the subject. Well, then, in war there is first the snapping asunder of the bonds of neighbourhood and friendship which once existed between the parties. There is the exchange of hatred, and ill-will, and the desire to injure and destroy, for amity and kindness and benevolence. The word "the enemy" takes the place of that of "friend," and the change of conduct corresponds to the change of name; for there soon follow the acts of destruction and vengeance. Precious life, that mysterious gift of God, is spilt like water on the ground. The bleeding wounds, the mangled limbs, the lifeless corpse, take the place of the buoyant spirits, the active frame, and the healthful vigour, of youth and manhood. The happy home where affection and social mirth and bright hopes and schemes made happiness and light, becomes the house of mourning where all hope is put out. The husband, the betrothed, the brother, the darling son, is laid low in dust and blood; and what is life any longer to the wife, to the expecting bride, to the sister, to the bereaved mother? And in such a war as this with Benjamin there are still more revolting images to be contemplated. The ground strewed with innocent babes and little children unconscious of wrong, and unsuspicious of harm. Merry youths and laughing maidens cut down in the spring-time of their life. Homesteads, orchards, gardens, whole streets, whole cities, reduced to heaps of rubbish and ashes. All the works of men's hands, the fruit of their labours, the product of their skill, the ornament, the comfort, the very shelter and food needful for human life, spoiled, wasted, and destroyed; human progress thrown back for a century, and seeds of hatred sown to bring forth a crop of bitterness in times to come. Thank God, war has been shorn in our days of its savage cruelty. Soldiers no longer slaughter women and children and defenceless men, nor destroy in the mere wantonness of power. Most true also is it that in war some of the noblest qualities of men are developed, and that kindness, mercy, and generosity, are the frequent companions of daring courage, resolute endurance, and inflexible will. The brave leader of men is deserving of all the gratitude and all the enthusiasm of his fellow-men; and as long as war is a necessity, he who conducts it to a successful end for his country's good will always merit his country's praise. But for all that, it must be acknowledged that war, even in its mitigated form, is a blight upon humanity, and that its continuance is a blot upon civilisation, and still more upon the national profession of

Christianity. He would indeed be a benefactor of the human race who could discover and establish the machinery by which national quarrels and disagreements could be settled by some other arbitrament than that of the sword. Viewed even in an economic point of view, how great would the gain be to nations if the half million or the million of men in the prime of life who are now supported in industrial idleness at the expense of their countrymen were, instead, contributing their own quota to the production and to the wealth of the country! And if the vast sums of money now spent on a single war were devoted to useful works and to great social improvements, how greatly would the world be benefited, instead of being, as now, impoverished and made desolate! How to get rid of war, and at the same time maintain the national dignity and not compromise the national safety, is indeed a problem difficult to solve. The existence of force may be necessary for the maintenance of right. But for all that, the discovery of the means by which bloody wars might be exchanged for some binding code of national law, to which the strongest as well as the weakest should be subject, would be a signal blessing to mankind. The subject is well worth the consideration of every Christian philanthropist. Surely, too, we are encouraged to hope for success by the glowing words of prophecy. A day will come, we know, when "nation shall not lift up sword against nation, neither shall they learn war any more" (Isa. ii. 4). The Psalmist saw a blessed vision of a time when there shall be "abundance of peace so long as the moon endureth" (Ps. lxxii. 7). The Holy Ghost speaks of a time when "they shall not hurt nor destroy in all my holy mountain: for the earth shall be full of the knowledge of the Lord, as the waters cover the sea" (Isa. xi. 9). And, even if in no other way we can hope to succeed, let us, at least, use our utmost endeavour to spread that knowledge of the Prince of peace at home and abroad which is the surest guarantee of peace. We know not when or how the kingdom of righteousness and peace shall be established. But we know that in proportion as the gospel of peace influences men's hearts, controls their passions, and incites them to brotherly love, the motives to war will be diminished, the motives to harmony and union will be strengthened. May the time come quickly when in the love of Christ, whether present in glory, or still dwelling in the heavens, the love of man to man shall so abound that in the family, in the nation, and in the world, there may be only PEACE!

HOMILIES BY VARIOUS AUTHORS.

Ver. 1.—" *There shall not any of us give his daughter unto Benjamin to wife.*" A rule of justice, morality, and prudence. Benjamin represents the libertine, a character too common in our own day. Here is a method of dealing with such men that ought to commend itself to every parent.

I. PARENTAL RESPONSIBILITY IN SANCTIONING MARRIAGE.

II. THE CONSIDERATIONS THAT OUGHT TO GOVERN IT. The welfare of the child; the possibility of greater happiness and usefulness; and provision for the future. Moral soundness ought therefore to be a *sine quâ non* in all aspirants to the hand of a Christian man's daughter. What security can there be for the wife of a licentious man, even if he be as wealthy as Croesus? Righteousness of life and a Christian character should be the first and indispensable qualifications of a son-in-law.

III. ADVANTAGES OF SUCH A COURSE AS THIS. If parents would exclude from their homes, their drawing-rooms, and the society of their children persons known to be licentious, it would exert great influence—1. *In checking such conduct.* 2. *In preventing society from thinking lightly of it.*—M.

Ver. 25.—" *In those days there was no king in Israel: every man did that which was right in his own eyes.*" This is the key-note, as it is the refrain, of the whole book. The point raised is one of great significance in dealing with the foundations of Society and the State.

I. THE EVILS ARISING FROM AN EXCESS OF INDIVIDUALISM AMONGST MEN.

II. THE NECESSITY FOR SOME COMMON EXTERNAL BOND AND SANCTION FOR CONDUCT AND LIFE.—M.

Vers. 2—4.—*Sorrow for others.* I. IT IS NATURAL TO BE DISTRESSED AT THE TROUBLES OF OTHERS. 1. It is natural on *personal* grounds. We are members one of another, so that if one member suffer, all suffer. The Israelites felt that it would be a common calamity to the whole nation for one tribe to be blotted out. It would not only be a judgment on that tribe, it would be "a breach in the tribes of Israel." England suffers through the wars and famines and storms which devastate even remote countries. If adversity falls upon one great town, one trade, one class, the whole community feels the effect of it. It is foolish, on selfish considerations alone, for the rich and happy to ignore the distresses of the poor and wretched. 2. But it is natural to be distressed at the troubles of others on *unselfish* grounds. When we are not hardened by sin we must naturally feel sympathy. The law of Christ requires us to bear one another's burdens (Gal. vi. 2). If Jews of old felt for their brethren in their trouble, how can Christians, who owe all their best blessings to the compassion and suffering of Christ for them, harden their hearts against the cries of the world's misery, when they in turn are expected to show the spirit of Christ in sympathy and vicarious sacrifice?

II. IF WE ARE CALLED TO PUNISH MEN FOR THEIR SIN, WE SHOULD ALSO PITY THEM FOR THEIR DISTRESS. Israel had punished the tribe of Benjamin, but the sight of the ruin thus wrought filled all the people with grief. It is right and necessary to be firm in repressing wickedness; yet this should not be done in hot hatred, in callous sternness, nor in complacent self-satisfaction, but with grief, mourning for the distress, and more for the sin occasioning it. So does God chastise, in grief, like a father loving his child, and therefore the more hating the iniquity which produces all the trouble.

III. DISTRESS FOR THE TROUBLES OF OTHERS SHOULD LEAD US TO GOD ON THEIR BEHALF. The people came to the house of God, and wept there before God. We should bring all our trouble before God, and, when we know not what to ask for, confide in him and relieve our souls by leaving the burden with him. If we are really and deeply grieved for others, we shall be constrained to do the same with the sorrow of sympathy. All Christians are called to be priests, intercessors for others. We should pray most earnestly for those who will not pray for themselves. We should humble ourselves for their sin, since the oneness of the human family brings shame upon all when any go astray. Such sorrow before God will incline us to fresh acts of self-sacrifice and dedication. As the Israelites offered burnt offerings, we shall consecrate ourselves to God, that we may be more capable of relieving those for whom we grieve.—A.

Ver. 5.—*The penalty of desertion.* It was quite in accordance with the rude and cruel age of the judges that a whole town should be visited with the death-penalty for deserting the tribes in the assembly of war. The punishment was not so unreasonable as it might appear at first sight, though there are circumstances in the whole transaction which reflect discredit on the Israelites.

I. DESERTION IS A GREAT CRIME. In war-time, even among civilised nations, desertion is punished with death. 1. Negative wickedness may be as bad as positive sin. If we know that an equally injurious result will follow inaction, this is equally guilty with an active offence. Thus the refusal of a ship's master to save a drowning man is morally equal to the guilt of murdering him. 2. We must not measure the value of our actions by their individual effects, but by the effects of the principles they express. One act of desertion may have no perceptible effect. But if one is justifiable, many are, and thus the principle of freedom to desert allows of total desertion resulting in total ruin. Desertion from the cause of Christ is a great sin. To refrain from obeying his call to action is as guilty as to actively disobey him. 3. The crime which is heinous when committed by one man is equally bad when committed by a whole community. We should not think of destroying a town for the crime for which we should execute an individual; but this is because of our horror of wholesale slaughter, &c., and not because evil desert is lessened when it is shared by a number.

II. CHARITY IS NO EXCUSE FOR THE NEGLECT OF DUTY. That was a terrible work to which the tribes were summoned—the slaughter of the Benjamites. Yet if they felt it to be a necessary act of justice sanctioned by God, as they evidently did feel it to be, they had no right to shrink from it out of feelings of kindliness. It is terrible to be called to such a duty; but it is brave and noble to accept the odium when the necessity is felt, and weak and selfish to avoid it. Charity is not honoured by the sacrifice of justice. It is more charitable to punish wickedness than to let it work its evil unchecked. Charity to the criminal often means cruelty to the victim. There is a danger lest we should become so mild that we should virtually punish the innocent in order to spare the guilty.

III. The purity of justice is violated when punishment is administerd with interested motives. It appears that the great motive of the Israelites in executing the threat of their oath on the people of Jabesh-Gilead was not a regard for strict justice, but a desire to secure wives for the escaped Benjamites. This motive vitiated the character of their action. The difficulty of executing punitive justice lies in the danger of other motives than a simple regard for right entering into our conduct. We desecrate the temple of justice when we convert it into a house of merchandise.—A.

Ver. 24.—*The return of peaceful prosperity.* I. Men find their most happy condition in the pursuit of peaceful occupations and the enjoyment of home life. It is pleasing to see this concourse of war break up, and the Israelites return home to their farms and their families. War is unnatural, and should be treated as a monstrous evil. The nation which regards military exploits as the chief occupation for its energies is forsaking solid happiness for empty glory. 1. *Politically* a nation is prosperous when industry flourishes, trade is unchecked, literature finds patrons, science and art are pursued, and general education, morality, and religion are sedulously promoted by the leading men of the age. 2. *Religiously* a people is prosperous when angry controversy gives place to the peaceful cultivation of holiness, and practical efforts to conquer the sin of the world and spread the blessings of Christianity. 3. *Personally* men are prosperous when they are at liberty to work in peace and enjoy the fruits of their labours without molestation. In proportion as war, controversy, jealousy, and competition give place to quiet home life and simple endeavours to do our daily duties will happiness be enjoyed as a solid, lasting human treasure.

II. It is sometimes not possible to enjoy solid peace till after the faithful performance of the duties of warfare. The peace which the Israelites now enjoyed was the reward which followed the faithful performance of painful acts of justice. The cry of "peace at any price" may be the ignominious utterance of blindness, indolence, cowardice, or selfishness. We can have no worthy peace while the wrongs of any who have claims upon us call for our active interference. 1. *National peace* must follow the establishment of order and justice. Better all the horrors of civil war than unchecked tyranny, unpunished violence, or outraged innocence. 2. *Religious peace* must follow the righteous maintenance of truth and right. We must not let false religions go unchallenged, or unholy conduct unrebuked, for the sake of preserving peace. Christ came to send a sword (Matt. x. 34), and his peace comes after the valiant overthrow of the lies and sins which oppose his rule. 3. *Personal peace* must follow the battle of the soul with its sins and doubts. That is a hollow peace which comes from stifling doubt. We must fight it down. No true peace is possible while sinful habits are unopposed; these must be "resisted unto blood." True peace follows victory over evil.

III. A peaceful life is secured and maintained through the effort of each man to take his own place and do his own work. Trouble too often arises from our forsaking our post and interfering with other people. 1. *Industry* is favourable to peaceful prosperity. The children of Israel went home immediately after settling affairs in the disturbed district. They went straight from war to work, and wasted no time in idle self-indulgence as a reward for victory. 2. *Orderly* arrangements promote peace. Every man went to his tribe. Let each of us find his own place in the world, and seek quietly to occupy *that*, and nothing else. 3. *Domestic* life inclines to peace. Every man went to his family. The home is the foundation of the most solid blessings of the State. If we desire happiness and peaceful prosperity, let us cherish the sanctities of the hearth. 4. *Property* favours peace. The men went to their several inheritances. When a man has possessions he is reluctant to create a social disturbance. Therefore lovers of peace should promote thrift and efforts to facilitate the acquisition of property by the people generally—of course as the fruits of honest industry. 5. *Religious convictions* form the most solid foundations for peaceful prosperity. The Israelites accepted their inheritances quietly in obedience to a Divine distribution. We shall enjoy a peaceful life best if we believe that God chooses our inheritance, and accept our lot in contentment and trustfulness from him, endeavouring to use it as his stewards, and hoping for the perfect inheritance of the everlasting home which he will give to his faithful people.—A.

HOMILETICAL INDEX

TO

THE BOOK OF JUDGES

CHAPTER I.

THEME	PAGE
Inquiry of God	1
Transfer of Authority	3
Spiritual Initiatives	5
Alliances in the Holy War	5
Correspondence of Crime and Requital	6
The Death of the Great	7
Mutual Help	8
Retribution	8
Faith	10
The Public Spirit of Caleb	12
Compensations	12
Divine Help versus Material Obstacles	13
A Title to be made Good	13
The Presence of God in the Battle of Life	14
Weak Faith producing Weak Action	15
An Unwilling Helper of the Cause of God	16
Human Wisdom versus Divine	16
The Failure of Duty of One an Occasion of Inconvenience to Another	17

CHAPTER II.

THEME	PAGE
The Expostulation	18
Bochim	19
The Preaching of Repentance	20
Influence	21
The Force of Personal Testimony and Influence	23
Israel's Apostasy	23
The Goodness and Severity of God	24
Mercy in the midst of Judgment	26
Tested by Temptation	26

CHAPTER III.

THEME	PAGE
Ungodly Marriages	28
The Proving of Israel	29
The Forbidden Covenant	29
God's Scourge	31
Idolatry and its Nemesis	32
True Deliverance must ever come from God	32
Natural Advantages and Endowments Perfected and Crowned by Consecration	33
The Secret of Individual and National Greatness	33
"And the land had rest"—the True Peace	33
Great Men	33
Miscellaneous Thoughts	35
Continued and Repeated Offence entails more Signal Punishment	37
Ehud	37
Shamgar	37
A Man Left-handed	38

CHAPTER IV.

THEME	PAGE
The Variety of God's Instruments. The Weakness of God's Instruments	40
Temporary Influences and a Permanent Tendency	41
The Battle of the Brook Kishon, or Material Force versus Spiritual	42
Deborah and Barak	43
Patriotic Treachery	44

CHAPTER V.

THEME	PAGE
Self-Sacrifice and its Inspirer ...	48
National Ruin and the True Deliverer	49
The Peril of National Irreligion ...	49
Testimony and Thanksgiving the Duty of the Redeemed	50
National Defence a Common Responsibility	50
The Hopelessness of Opposition to God	51
The Curse of Meroz	51
The Conduct of Jael	51
The Sunlike Life	52
A Mother in Israel	52
Self-Dedication	53
Literary Occupations	54
Indolent Indecision	55
The Curse of Meroz	55
The Triumph of the Church ...	56

CHAPTER VI.

The Fruit of Ingratitude	57
Israel's Extremity	58
Divine Mercy: its Adaptation and Sufficiency	58
Merciful Reproof	59
God Sought and Found in Times of Trouble	59
The Preparation	61
The Call of Gideon	62
The Paradox of the Divine Presence ...	63
The Assuring Thought of God's Servant	63
Asking for a Sign	64
The Sign—the Present turned into a Sacrifice	64
Jehovah Shalom, or Spiritual Forebodings stilled	65
Diffidence	65
The Action commenced	67
The First Work	68
Who hath done this Thing? ...	69
Jerubbaal, or, Is an Idol Anything?	69
Gideon the Iconoclast	69
The Divine Side of Human History ...	71
The Crisis and the Confirmation ...	72

CHAPTER VII.

The Sifting	74
Divinely-ordained Tests	75
"Mine own hand hath saved me" ...	76
Success not Dependent on Numbers ...	77
Faith	79
The Crowning Sign	81
Inspired Tactics	82

THEME	PAGE
Following up Advantage	83
Gideon's Ruse	83

CHAPTER VIII.

The Blindness of Self-Love	84
Dealing with Obstructives	84
"Faint, yet pursuing" ...	86, 87
The Complete Revenge	89
Prosperity	92
Noble Self-Abnegation	93
The Mistake of a Good Man ...	94
The After Life	94
The Consequence of the Imperfect Recognition of Jehovah ...	95
Gideon and the Theocracy ...	95
Forgetfulness and Ingratitude ...	96

CHAPTER IX.

Self-Aggrandisement	98
Ambitious Usurpation	99
Unrighteous Claims of Kindred ...	99
Shortcomings of Unscrupulous Schemes	100
Abimelech	100
The Handwriting on the Wall ...	102
Jotham's Fable; or, Popular Election, its Dangers and Abuses	103
Strength in Weakness	104
Jotham's Parable	104
Be sure your sin will find you out ...	108
The Nemesis of Usurpation	109
A Worthy Servant of a Worthless Master	109
Without a Leader	110
Reputation	110

CHAPTER X.

The Lull	111
The Calm after the Storm	112
Quiet Times	112
The Ethiopian's Unchanged Skin ...	114
Recurring Habits of Evil	116
Immediate and Effectual Retribution	116
God answering Hardened Transgressors	116
"Works meet for repentance" ...	116
Faith restoring Courage and Might ...	116
From God to Baal	117
The Test of Trouble	117
Repentance	118

CHAPTER XI.

The Controversy	121
The Shaping Influences of Life ...	122

THEME	PAGE
Magnanimity of Patriotism	123
Recognition of God in Positions of Honour and Responsibility ...	124
The Model Diplomatist	124
The Friend in Need	124
Human Perverseness embittering the Sweet Cup	126
The Spirit of Sacred Warfare ...	127
Jephthah's Vow	128
The Spirit of the Lord	129
Jephthah's Vow	130

CHAPTER XII.

THEME	PAGE
The Envy of the Small Great at the Great Deeds of the Small ...	131
Ingratitude the Frequent Reward of Benefactors	132
The Reproach of the Righteous ...	133
Shibboleth :—The Importance of Little Defects, Faults, &c.	133
Tests : their Good and Evil ...,	134
"Vaulting Ambition," which "o'er-leaps itself"	134
Jealousy	135
Shibboleth	136
The Calm after the Storm	137

CHAPTER XIII.

THEME	PAGE
Married Life	140
A Natural Desire and its Gracious Fulfilment	141
The Difficulty of Salvation ...	142
God's Use of Unlikely Means for Gracious Ends	143
Divine Punishment and Preparation of Deliverance Simultaneous ...	143
Repetition of Divine Favours ...	143
Parental Anxiety and its Satisfying ...	144
The Wonderful Name	144
Reassurance of Divine Favour ...	145
Fulfilment of Promise	145
Samson the Nazarite	145
The Training of Children	146
The Mystery of a Name	147
The Fear of the Vision of God ...	148
The Young Samson	148

CHAPTER XIV.

THEME	PAGE
The Link of the Chain	150
Human Desire overruled for Divine Ends	151
The Lion in the Way	152

THEME	PAGE
The Fearlessness and Modesty of the Spiritual Hero	152
The Mystery of Spiritual Might ...	152
Recalling Past Deliverances ...	152
Samson and the Lion	153
Another View of Married Life ...	155
Samson's Riddle	156
Unlawful Methods of interpreting Divine Mysteries	157
Ploughing with Another's Heifer ...	157
How Confidence in Wicked Men is Rewarded	157
Samson's Riddle	157

CHAPTER XV.

THEME	PAGE
The Progress of the Feud	159
Atonements of the Unrighteous ...	160
God's Servant set Free by the Providences of Life	160
Foxes and Firebrands	160
Those who have Occasioned Evil punished for those who Caused it ...	161
Requiting Evil for Good, and Good for Evil	161
Ingenuity and Originality	161
Man without God, and Man with God	163
Imperfect Means made Effectual by Divine Inspiration	165
The Self-Refreshment of Divine Service	165
The Jawbone of an Ass	165
Distress after Triumph	166

CHAPTER XVI.

THEME	PAGE
Presumption leading to a Fall ...	168
God redeeming the Error of His Servant	170
Samson's Betrayal and Fall ...	171
"And he wist not that the Lord (Jehovah) was departed from him" ...	172
Samson's Weakness	172
God's Departure from the Soul unrecognised	173
The Short-lived Triumph	175
A Hero's Exodus	176
Samson's Heroic Death	176

CHAPTER XVII.

THEME	PAGE
The Superstitious Worship of the True God	179
The History of a Man-made Ministry : 1. Its Genesis	181
Avarice and Superstition	182

THEME	PAGE
No King	183
Faith in the Priest	184

CHAPTER XVIII.

THEME	PAGE
Society without a Head ceasing to be Society	188
The History of a Man-made Ministry: 2. Its Abuse	189
Its Transfer and Establishment in a Lawless Community	189
The Idolater's Distress	190
The Religion of Convenience ...	190
The Mercenary Priest	191
The Lost Gods	191

CHAPTER XIX.

THEME	PAGE
The Downward Progress	194
Troublesome Hospitality	195
Exceptional Hospitality	195
Unparalleled Crime: the Spirit and Method in which its Problems are to be met	196
Hospitality	196
Monstrous Wickedness	197

THEME	PAGE
The Duty of considering Painful Subjects	197

CHAPTER XX.

THEME	PAGE
Temper	200
National Atonement	201
Union	201
Pure and Impure Zeal	205
The Difficulty of punishing Evil-Doers	206
"They knew not that evil was near them"	207
Lessons of Defeat	207
"An Escaped Remnant"	207

CHAPTER XXI.

THEME	PAGE
War	210
"There shall not any of us give his daughter unto Benjamin to wife" ...	211
"In those days there was no king in Israel: every man did that which was right in his own eyes" ...	211
Sorrow for others	212
The Penalty of Desertion	212
The Return of Peaceful Prosperity ...	213